Oxford Dictionary of National Biography

Volume 25

Oxford Dictionary of National Biography

IN ASSOCIATION WITH

The British Academy

From the earliest times to the year 2000

Edited by

H. C. G. Matthew

and

Brian Harrison

Volume 25

Hanbury–Hay

OXFORD

UNIVERSITY PRESS

OXFORD
UNIVERSITY PRESS

Great Clarendon Street, Oxford OX2 6DP

Oxford University Press is a department of the University of Oxford.
It furthers the University's objective of excellence in research, scholarship,
and education by publishing worldwide in

Oxford New York

Auckland Bangkok Buenos Aires Cape Town
Chennai Dar es Salaam Delhi Hong Kong Istanbul Karachi
Kolkata Kuala Lumpur Madrid Melbourne Mexico City Mumbai Nairobi
São Paulo Shanghai Taipei Tokyo Toronto

Oxford is a registered trade mark of Oxford University Press
in the UK and in certain other countries

Published in the United States
by Oxford University Press Inc., New York

British Library Cataloguing in Publication Data
Data available

Library of Congress Cataloging in Publication Data
Data available: for details see volume 1, p. iv

ISBN 0-19-861375-X (this volume)
ISBN 0-19-861411-X (set of sixty volumes)

Text captured by Alliance Phototypesetters, Pondicherry
Illustrations reproduced and archived by
Alliance Graphics Ltd, UK
Typeset in OUP Swift by Interactive Sciences Limited, Gloucester
Printed in Great Britain on acid-free paper by
Butler and Tanner Ltd,
Frome, Somerset

LIST OF ABBREVIATIONS

1 General abbreviations

AB	bachelor of arts	BCnL	bachelor of canon law
ABC	Australian Broadcasting Corporation	BCom	bachelor of commerce
ABC TV	ABC Television	BD	bachelor of divinity
act.	active	BEd	bachelor of education
A$	Australian dollar	BEng	bachelor of engineering
AD	*anno domini*	bk *pl.* bks	book(s)
AFC	Air Force Cross	BL	bachelor of law / letters / literature
AIDS	acquired immune deficiency syndrome	BLitt	bachelor of letters
AK	Alaska	BM	bachelor of medicine
AL	Alabama	BMus	bachelor of music
A level	advanced level [examination]	BP	before present
ALS	associate of the Linnean Society	BP	British Petroleum
AM	master of arts	Bros.	Brothers
AMICE	associate member of the Institution of Civil Engineers	BS	(1) bachelor of science; (2) bachelor of surgery; (3) British standard
ANZAC	Australian and New Zealand Army Corps	BSc	bachelor of science
appx *pl.* appxs	appendix(es)	BSc (Econ.)	bachelor of science (economics)
AR	Arkansas	BSc (Eng.)	bachelor of science (engineering)
ARA	associate of the Royal Academy	bt	baronet
ARCA	associate of the Royal College of Art	BTh	bachelor of theology
ARCM	associate of the Royal College of Music	*bur.*	buried
ARCO	associate of the Royal College of Organists	C.	command [identifier for published parliamentary papers]
ARIBA	associate of the Royal Institute of British Architects	*c.*	*circa*
ARP	air-raid precautions	c.	*capitulum pl. capitula*: chapter(s)
ARRC	associate of the Royal Red Cross	CA	California
ARSA	associate of the Royal Scottish Academy	Cantab.	Cantabrigiensis
art.	article / item	cap.	*capitulum pl. capitula*: chapter(s)
ASC	Army Service Corps	CB	companion of the Bath
Asch	Austrian Schilling	CBE	commander of the Order of the British Empire
ASDIC	Antisubmarine Detection Investigation Committee	CBS	Columbia Broadcasting System
ATS	Auxiliary Territorial Service	cc	cubic centimetres
ATV	Associated Television	C$	Canadian dollar
Aug	August	CD	compact disc
AZ	Arizona	Cd	command [identifier for published parliamentary papers]
b.	born	CE	Common (*or* Christian) Era
BA	bachelor of arts	cent.	century
BA (Admin.)	bachelor of arts (administration)	cf.	compare
BAFTA	British Academy of Film and Television Arts	CH	Companion of Honour
BAO	bachelor of arts in obstetrics	chap.	chapter
bap.	baptized	ChB	bachelor of surgery
BBC	British Broadcasting Corporation / Company	CI	Imperial Order of the Crown of India
BC	before Christ	CIA	Central Intelligence Agency
BCE	before the common (*or* Christian) era	CID	Criminal Investigation Department
BCE	bachelor of civil engineering	CIE	companion of the Order of the Indian Empire
BCG	bacillus of Calmette and Guérin [inoculation against tuberculosis]	Cie	Compagnie
		CLit	companion of literature
BCh	bachelor of surgery	CM	master of surgery
BChir	bachelor of surgery	cm	centimetre(s)
BCL	bachelor of civil law		

Cmd	command [identifier for published parliamentary papers]	edn	edition
CMG	companion of the Order of St Michael and St George	EEC	European Economic Community
		EFTA	European Free Trade Association
Cmnd	command [identifier for published parliamentary papers]	EICS	East India Company Service
		EMI	Electrical and Musical Industries (Ltd)
CO	Colorado	Eng.	English
Co.	company	enl.	enlarged
co.	county	ENSA	Entertainments National Service Association
col. *pl.* cols.	column(s)	ep. *pl.* epp.	*epistola*(*e*)
Corp.	corporation	ESP	extra-sensory perception
CSE	certificate of secondary education	esp.	especially
CSI	companion of the Order of the Star of India	esq.	esquire
CT	Connecticut	est.	estimate / estimated
CVO	commander of the Royal Victorian Order	EU	European Union
cwt	hundredweight	ex	sold by (*lit.* out of)
$	(American) dollar	excl.	excludes / excluding
d.	(1) penny (pence); (2) died	exh.	exhibited
DBE	dame commander of the Order of the British Empire	exh. cat.	exhibition catalogue
		f. *pl.* ff.	following [pages]
DCH	diploma in child health	FA	Football Association
DCh	doctor of surgery	FACP	fellow of the American College of Physicians
DCL	doctor of civil law	facs.	facsimile
DCnL	doctor of canon law	FANY	First Aid Nursing Yeomanry
DCVO	dame commander of the Royal Victorian Order	FBA	fellow of the British Academy
DD	doctor of divinity	FBI	Federation of British Industries
DE	Delaware	FCS	fellow of the Chemical Society
Dec	December	Feb	February
dem.	demolished	FEng	fellow of the Fellowship of Engineering
DEng	doctor of engineering	FFCM	fellow of the Faculty of Community Medicine
des.	destroyed	FGS	fellow of the Geological Society
DFC	Distinguished Flying Cross	fig.	figure
DipEd	diploma in education	FIMechE	fellow of the Institution of Mechanical Engineers
DipPsych	diploma in psychiatry		
diss.	dissertation	FL	Florida
DL	deputy lieutenant	*fl.*	*floruit*
DLitt	doctor of letters	FLS	fellow of the Linnean Society
DLittCelt	doctor of Celtic letters	FM	frequency modulation
DM	(1) Deutschmark; (2) doctor of medicine; (3) doctor of musical arts	fol. *pl.* fols.	folio(s)
		Fr	French francs
DMus	doctor of music	Fr.	French
DNA	dioxyribonucleic acid	FRAeS	fellow of the Royal Aeronautical Society
doc.	document	FRAI	fellow of the Royal Anthropological Institute
DOL	doctor of oriental learning	FRAM	fellow of the Royal Academy of Music
DPH	diploma in public health	FRAS	(1) fellow of the Royal Asiatic Society; (2) fellow of the Royal Astronomical Society
DPhil	doctor of philosophy		
DPM	diploma in psychological medicine	FRCM	fellow of the Royal College of Music
DSC	Distinguished Service Cross	FRCO	fellow of the Royal College of Organists
DSc	doctor of science	FRCOG	fellow of the Royal College of Obstetricians and Gynaecologists
DSc (Econ.)	doctor of science (economics)		
DSc (Eng.)	doctor of science (engineering)	FRCP(C)	fellow of the Royal College of Physicians of Canada
DSM	Distinguished Service Medal		
DSO	companion of the Distinguished Service Order	FRCP (Edin.)	fellow of the Royal College of Physicians of Edinburgh
DSocSc	doctor of social science	FRCP (Lond.)	fellow of the Royal College of Physicians of London
DTech	doctor of technology		
DTh	doctor of theology	FRCPath	fellow of the Royal College of Pathologists
DTM	diploma in tropical medicine	FRCPsych	fellow of the Royal College of Psychiatrists
DTMH	diploma in tropical medicine and hygiene	FRCS	fellow of the Royal College of Surgeons
DU	doctor of the university	FRGS	fellow of the Royal Geographical Society
DUniv	doctor of the university	FRIBA	fellow of the Royal Institute of British Architects
dwt	pennyweight	FRICS	fellow of the Royal Institute of Chartered Surveyors
EC	European Community		
ed. *pl.* eds.	edited / edited by / editor(s)	FRS	fellow of the Royal Society
Edin.	Edinburgh	FRSA	fellow of the Royal Society of Arts

FRSCM	fellow of the Royal School of Church Music	ISO	companion of the Imperial Service Order
FRSE	fellow of the Royal Society of Edinburgh	It.	Italian
FRSL	fellow of the Royal Society of Literature	ITA	Independent Television Authority
FSA	fellow of the Society of Antiquaries	ITV	Independent Television
ft	foot *pl.* feet	Jan	January
FTCL	fellow of Trinity College of Music, London	JP	justice of the peace
ft-lb per min.	foot-pounds per minute [unit of horsepower]	jun.	junior
FZS	fellow of the Zoological Society	KB	knight of the Order of the Bath
GA	Georgia	KBE	knight commander of the Order of the British Empire
GBE	knight or dame grand cross of the Order of the British Empire	KC	king's counsel
GCB	knight grand cross of the Order of the Bath	kcal	kilocalorie
GCE	general certificate of education	KCB	knight commander of the Order of the Bath
GCH	knight grand cross of the Royal Guelphic Order	KCH	knight commander of the Royal Guelphic Order
GCHQ	government communications headquarters	KCIE	knight commander of the Order of the Indian Empire
GCIE	knight grand commander of the Order of the Indian Empire	KCMG	knight commander of the Order of St Michael and St George
GCMG	knight or dame grand cross of the Order of St Michael and St George	KCSI	knight commander of the Order of the Star of India
GCSE	general certificate of secondary education	KCVO	knight commander of the Royal Victorian Order
GCSI	knight grand commander of the Order of the Star of India	keV	kilo-electron-volt
GCStJ	bailiff or dame grand cross of the order of St John of Jerusalem	KG	knight of the Order of the Garter
		KGB	[Soviet committee of state security]
GCVO	knight or dame grand cross of the Royal Victorian Order	KH	knight of the Royal Guelphic Order
		KLM	Koninklijke Luchtvaart Maatschappij (Royal Dutch Air Lines)
GEC	General Electric Company		
Ger.	German	km	kilometre(s)
GI	government (*or* general) issue	KP	knight of the Order of St Patrick
GMT	Greenwich mean time	KS	Kansas
GP	general practitioner	KT	knight of the Order of the Thistle
GPU	[Soviet special police unit]	kt	knight
GSO	general staff officer	KY	Kentucky
Heb.	Hebrew	£	pound(s) sterling
HEICS	Honourable East India Company Service	£E	Egyptian pound
HI	Hawaii	L	lira *pl.* lire
HIV	human immunodeficiency virus	l. *pl.* ll.	line(s)
HK$	Hong Kong dollar	LA	Lousiana
HM	his / her majesty('s)	LAA	light anti-aircraft
HMAS	his / her majesty's Australian ship	LAH	licentiate of the Apothecaries' Hall, Dublin
HMNZS	his / her majesty's New Zealand ship	Lat.	Latin
HMS	his / her majesty's ship	lb	pound(s), unit of weight
HMSO	His / Her Majesty's Stationery Office	LDS	licence in dental surgery
HMV	His Master's Voice	*lit.*	literally
Hon.	Honourable	LittB	bachelor of letters
hp	horsepower	LittD	doctor of letters
hr	hour(s)	LKQCPI	licentiate of the King and Queen's College of Physicians, Ireland
HRH	his / her royal highness		
HTV	Harlech Television	LLA	lady literate in arts
IA	Iowa	LLB	bachelor of laws
ibid.	*ibidem*: in the same place	LLD	doctor of laws
ICI	Imperial Chemical Industries (Ltd)	LLM	master of laws
ID	Idaho	LM	licentiate in midwifery
IL	Illinois	LP	long-playing record
illus.	illustration	LRAM	licentiate of the Royal Academy of Music
illustr.	illustrated	LRCP	licentiate of the Royal College of Physicians
IN	Indiana	LRCPS (Glasgow)	licentiate of the Royal College of Physicians and Surgeons of Glasgow
in.	inch(es)		
Inc.	Incorporated	LRCS	licentiate of the Royal College of Surgeons
incl.	includes / including	LSA	licentiate of the Society of Apothecaries
IOU	I owe you	LSD	lysergic acid diethylamide
IQ	intelligence quotient	LVO	lieutenant of the Royal Victorian Order
Ir£	Irish pound	M. *pl.* MM.	Monsieur *pl.* Messieurs
IRA	Irish Republican Army	m	metre(s)

m. *pl.* mm.	membrane(s)	ND	North Dakota
MA	(1) Massachusetts; (2) master of arts	n.d.	no date
MAI	master of engineering	NE	Nebraska
MB	bachelor of medicine	*nem. con.*	*nemine contradicente*: unanimously
MBA	master of business administration	new ser.	new series
MBE	member of the Order of the British Empire	NH	New Hampshire
MC	Military Cross	NHS	National Health Service
MCC	Marylebone Cricket Club	NJ	New Jersey
MCh	master of surgery	NKVD	[Soviet people's commissariat for internal affairs]
MChir	master of surgery		
MCom	master of commerce	NM	New Mexico
MD	(1) doctor of medicine; (2) Maryland	nm	nanometre(s)
MDMA	methylenedioxymethamphetamine	no. *pl.* nos.	number(s)
ME	Maine	Nov	November
MEd	master of education	n.p.	no place [of publication]
MEng	master of engineering	NS	new style
MEP	member of the European parliament	NV	Nevada
MG	Morris Garages	NY	New York
MGM	Metro-Goldwyn-Mayer	NZBS	New Zealand Broadcasting Service
Mgr	Monsignor	OBE	officer of the Order of the British Empire
MI	(1) Michigan; (2) military intelligence	obit.	obituary
MI1c	[secret intelligence department]	Oct	October
MI5	[military intelligence department]	OCTU	officer cadets training unit
MI6	[secret intelligence department]	OECD	Organization for Economic Co-operation and Development
MI9	[secret escape service]		
MICE	member of the Institution of Civil Engineers	OEEC	Organization for European Economic Co-operation
MIEE	member of the Institution of Electrical Engineers		
		OFM	order of Friars Minor [Franciscans]
min.	minute(s)	OFMCap	Ordine Frati Minori Cappucini: member of the Capuchin order
Mk	mark		
ML	(1) licentiate of medicine; (2) master of laws	OH	Ohio
MLitt	master of letters	OK	Oklahoma
Mlle	Mademoiselle	O level	ordinary level [examination]
mm	millimetre(s)	OM	Order of Merit
Mme	Madame	OP	order of Preachers [Dominicans]
MN	Minnesota	op. *pl.* opp.	opus *pl.* opera
MO	Missouri	OPEC	Organization of Petroleum Exporting Countries
MOH	medical officer of health	OR	Oregon
MP	member of parliament	orig.	original
m.p.h.	miles per hour	OS	old style
MPhil	master of philosophy	OSB	Order of St Benedict
MRCP	member of the Royal College of Physicians	OTC	Officers' Training Corps
MRCS	member of the Royal College of Surgeons	OWS	Old Watercolour Society
MRCVS	member of the Royal College of Veterinary Surgeons	Oxon.	Oxoniensis
		p. *pl.* pp.	page(s)
MRIA	member of the Royal Irish Academy	PA	Pennsylvania
MS	(1) master of science; (2) Mississippi	p.a.	per annum
MS *pl.* MSS	manuscript(s)	para.	paragraph
MSc	master of science	PAYE	pay as you earn
MSc (Econ.)	master of science (economics)	pbk *pl.* pbks	paperback(s)
MT	Montana	*per.*	[during the] period
MusB	bachelor of music	PhD	doctor of philosophy
MusBac	bachelor of music	pl.	(1) plate(s); (2) plural
MusD	doctor of music	priv. coll.	private collection
MV	motor vessel	pt *pl.* pts	part(s)
MVO	member of the Royal Victorian Order	pubd	published
n. *pl.* nn.	note(s)	PVC	polyvinyl chloride
NAAFI	Navy, Army, and Air Force Institutes	q. *pl.* qq.	(1) question(s); (2) quire(s)
NASA	National Aeronautics and Space Administration	QC	queen's counsel
NATO	North Atlantic Treaty Organization	R	rand
NBC	National Broadcasting Corporation	R.	Rex / Regina
NC	North Carolina	*r*	recto
NCO	non-commissioned officer	*r.*	reigned / ruled
		RA	Royal Academy / Royal Academician

RAC	Royal Automobile Club
RAF	Royal Air Force
RAFVR	Royal Air Force Volunteer Reserve
RAM	[member of the] Royal Academy of Music
RAMC	Royal Army Medical Corps
RCA	Royal College of Art
RCNC	Royal Corps of Naval Constructors
RCOG	Royal College of Obstetricians and Gynaecologists
RDI	royal designer for industry
RE	Royal Engineers
repr. *pl.* reprs.	reprint(s) / reprinted
repro.	reproduced
rev.	revised / revised by / reviser / revision
Revd	Reverend
RHA	Royal Hibernian Academy
RI	(1) Rhode Island; (2) Royal Institute of Painters in Water-Colours
RIBA	Royal Institute of British Architects
RIN	Royal Indian Navy
RM	Reichsmark
RMS	Royal Mail steamer
RN	Royal Navy
RNA	ribonucleic acid
RNAS	Royal Naval Air Service
RNR	Royal Naval Reserve
RNVR	Royal Naval Volunteer Reserve
RO	Record Office
r.p.m.	revolutions per minute
RRS	royal research ship
Rs	rupees
RSA	(1) Royal Scottish Academician; (2) Royal Society of Arts
RSPCA	Royal Society for the Prevention of Cruelty to Animals
Rt Hon.	Right Honourable
Rt Revd	Right Reverend
RUC	Royal Ulster Constabulary
Russ.	Russian
RWS	Royal Watercolour Society
S4C	Sianel Pedwar Cymru
s.	shilling(s)
s.a.	*sub anno*: under the year
SABC	South African Broadcasting Corporation
SAS	Special Air Service
SC	South Carolina
ScD	doctor of science
S$	Singapore dollar
SD	South Dakota
sec.	second(s)
sel.	selected
sen.	senior
Sept	September
ser.	series
SHAPE	supreme headquarters allied powers, Europe
SIDRO	Société Internationale d'Énergie Hydro-Électrique
sig. *pl.* sigs.	signature(s)
sing.	singular
SIS	Secret Intelligence Service
SJ	Society of Jesus
Skr	Swedish krona
Span.	Spanish
SPCK	Society for Promoting Christian Knowledge
SS	(1) Santissimi; (2) Schutzstaffel; (3) steam ship
STB	bachelor of theology
STD	doctor of theology
STM	master of theology
STP	doctor of theology
supp.	supposedly
suppl. *pl.* suppls.	supplement(s)
s.v.	*sub verbo* / *sub voce*: under the word / heading
SY	steam yacht
TA	Territorial Army
TASS	[Soviet news agency]
TB	tuberculosis (*lit.* tubercle bacillus)
TD	(1) *teachtaí dála* (member of the Dáil); (2) territorial decoration
TN	Tennessee
TNT	trinitrotoluene
trans.	translated / translated by / translation / translator
TT	tourist trophy
TUC	Trades Union Congress
TX	Texas
U-boat	*Unterseeboot*: submarine
Ufa	Universum-Film AG
UMIST	University of Manchester Institute of Science and Technology
UN	United Nations
UNESCO	United Nations Educational, Scientific, and Cultural Organization
UNICEF	United Nations International Children's Emergency Fund
unpubd	unpublished
USS	United States ship
UT	Utah
v	verso
v.	versus
VA	Virginia
VAD	Voluntary Aid Detachment
VC	Victoria Cross
VE-day	victory in Europe day
Ven.	Venerable
VJ-day	victory over Japan day
vol. *pl.* vols.	volume(s)
VT	Vermont
WA	Washington [state]
WAAC	Women's Auxiliary Army Corps
WAAF	Women's Auxiliary Air Force
WEA	Workers' Educational Association
WHO	World Health Organization
WI	Wisconsin
WRAF	Women's Royal Air Force
WRNS	Women's Royal Naval Service
WV	West Virginia
WVS	Women's Voluntary Service
WY	Wyoming
¥	yen
YMCA	Young Men's Christian Association
YWCA	Young Women's Christian Association

2 Institution abbreviations

All Souls Oxf.	All Souls College, Oxford
AM Oxf.	Ashmolean Museum, Oxford
Balliol Oxf.	Balliol College, Oxford
BBC WAC	BBC Written Archives Centre, Reading
Beds. & Luton ARS	Bedfordshire and Luton Archives and Record Service, Bedford
Berks. RO	Berkshire Record Office, Reading
BFI	British Film Institute, London
BFI NFTVA	British Film Institute, London, National Film and Television Archive
BGS	British Geological Survey, Keyworth, Nottingham
Birm. CA	Birmingham Central Library, Birmingham City Archives
Birm. CL	Birmingham Central Library
BL	British Library, London
BL NSA	British Library, London, National Sound Archive
BL OIOC	British Library, London, Oriental and India Office Collections
BLPES	London School of Economics and Political Science, British Library of Political and Economic Science
BM	British Museum, London
Bodl. Oxf.	Bodleian Library, Oxford
Bodl. RH	Bodleian Library of Commonwealth and African Studies at Rhodes House, Oxford
Borth. Inst.	Borthwick Institute of Historical Research, University of York
Boston PL	Boston Public Library, Massachusetts
Bristol RO	Bristol Record Office
Bucks. RLSS	Buckinghamshire Records and Local Studies Service, Aylesbury
CAC Cam.	Churchill College, Cambridge, Churchill Archives Centre
Cambs. AS	Cambridgeshire Archive Service
CCC Cam.	Corpus Christi College, Cambridge
CCC Oxf.	Corpus Christi College, Oxford
Ches. & Chester ALSS	Cheshire and Chester Archives and Local Studies Service
Christ Church Oxf.	Christ Church, Oxford
Christies	Christies, London
City Westm. AC	City of Westminster Archives Centre, London
CKS	Centre for Kentish Studies, Maidstone
CLRO	Corporation of London Records Office
Coll. Arms	College of Arms, London
Col. U.	Columbia University, New York
Cornwall RO	Cornwall Record Office, Truro
Courtauld Inst.	Courtauld Institute of Art, London
CUL	Cambridge University Library
Cumbria AS	Cumbria Archive Service
Derbys. RO	Derbyshire Record Office, Matlock
Devon RO	Devon Record Office, Exeter
Dorset RO	Dorset Record Office, Dorchester
Duke U.	Duke University, Durham, North Carolina
Duke U., Perkins L.	Duke University, Durham, North Carolina, William R. Perkins Library
Durham Cath. CL	Durham Cathedral, chapter library
Durham RO	Durham Record Office
DWL	Dr Williams's Library, London
Essex RO	Essex Record Office
E. Sussex RO	East Sussex Record Office, Lewes
Eton	Eton College, Berkshire
FM Cam.	Fitzwilliam Museum, Cambridge
Folger	Folger Shakespeare Library, Washington, DC
Garr. Club	Garrick Club, London
Girton Cam.	Girton College, Cambridge
GL	Guildhall Library, London
Glos. RO	Gloucestershire Record Office, Gloucester
Gon. & Caius Cam.	Gonville and Caius College, Cambridge
Gov. Art Coll.	Government Art Collection
GS Lond.	Geological Society of London
Hants. RO	Hampshire Record Office, Winchester
Harris Man. Oxf.	Harris Manchester College, Oxford
Harvard TC	Harvard Theatre Collection, Harvard University, Cambridge, Massachusetts, Nathan Marsh Pusey Library
Harvard U.	Harvard University, Cambridge, Massachusetts
Harvard U., Houghton L.	Harvard University, Cambridge, Massachusetts, Houghton Library
Herefs. RO	Herefordshire Record Office, Hereford
Herts. ALS	Hertfordshire Archives and Local Studies, Hertford
Hist. Soc. Penn.	Historical Society of Pennsylvania, Philadelphia
HLRO	House of Lords Record Office, London
Hult. Arch.	Hulton Archive, London and New York
Hunt. L.	Huntington Library, San Marino, California
ICL	Imperial College, London
Inst. CE	Institution of Civil Engineers, London
Inst. EE	Institution of Electrical Engineers, London
IWM	Imperial War Museum, London
IWM FVA	Imperial War Museum, London, Film and Video Archive
IWM SA	Imperial War Museum, London, Sound Archive
JRL	John Rylands University Library of Manchester
King's AC Cam.	King's College Archives Centre, Cambridge
King's Cam.	King's College, Cambridge
King's Lond.	King's College, London
King's Lond., Liddell Hart C.	King's College, London, Liddell Hart Centre for Military Archives
Lancs. RO	Lancashire Record Office, Preston
L. Cong.	Library of Congress, Washington, DC
Leics. RO	Leicestershire, Leicester, and Rutland Record Office, Leicester
Lincs. Arch.	Lincolnshire Archives, Lincoln
Linn. Soc.	Linnean Society of London
LMA	London Metropolitan Archives
LPL	Lambeth Palace, London
Lpool RO	Liverpool Record Office and Local Studies Service
LUL	London University Library
Magd. Cam.	Magdalene College, Cambridge
Magd. Oxf.	Magdalen College, Oxford
Man. City Gall.	Manchester City Galleries
Man. CL	Manchester Central Library
Mass. Hist. Soc.	Massachusetts Historical Society, Boston
Merton Oxf.	Merton College, Oxford
MHS Oxf.	Museum of the History of Science, Oxford
Mitchell L., Glas.	Mitchell Library, Glasgow
Mitchell L., NSW	State Library of New South Wales, Sydney, Mitchell Library
Morgan L.	Pierpont Morgan Library, New York
NA Canada	National Archives of Canada, Ottawa
NA Ire.	National Archives of Ireland, Dublin
NAM	National Army Museum, London
NA Scot.	National Archives of Scotland, Edinburgh
News Int. RO	News International Record Office, London
NG Ire.	National Gallery of Ireland, Dublin

NG Scot.	National Gallery of Scotland, Edinburgh
NHM	Natural History Museum, London
NL Aus.	National Library of Australia, Canberra
NL Ire.	National Library of Ireland, Dublin
NL NZ	National Library of New Zealand, Wellington
NL NZ, Turnbull L.	National Library of New Zealand, Wellington, Alexander Turnbull Library
NL Scot.	National Library of Scotland, Edinburgh
NL Wales	National Library of Wales, Aberystwyth
NMG Wales	National Museum and Gallery of Wales, Cardiff
NMM	National Maritime Museum, London
Norfolk RO	Norfolk Record Office, Norwich
Northants. RO	Northamptonshire Record Office, Northampton
Northumbd RO	Northumberland Record Office
Notts. Arch.	Nottinghamshire Archives, Nottingham
NPG	National Portrait Gallery, London
NRA	National Archives, London, Historical Manuscripts Commission, National Register of Archives
Nuffield Oxf.	Nuffield College, Oxford
N. Yorks. CRO	North Yorkshire County Record Office, Northallerton
NYPL	New York Public Library
Oxf. UA	Oxford University Archives
Oxf. U. Mus. NH	Oxford University Museum of Natural History
Oxon. RO	Oxfordshire Record Office, Oxford
Pembroke Cam.	Pembroke College, Cambridge
PRO	National Archives, London, Public Record Office
PRO NIre.	Public Record Office for Northern Ireland, Belfast
Pusey Oxf.	Pusey House, Oxford
RA	Royal Academy of Arts, London
Ransom HRC	Harry Ransom Humanities Research Center, University of Texas, Austin
RAS	Royal Astronomical Society, London
RBG Kew	Royal Botanic Gardens, Kew, London
RCP Lond.	Royal College of Physicians of London
RCS Eng.	Royal College of Surgeons of England, London
RGS	Royal Geographical Society, London
RIBA	Royal Institute of British Architects, London
RIBA BAL	Royal Institute of British Architects, London, British Architectural Library
Royal Arch.	Royal Archives, Windsor Castle, Berkshire [by gracious permission of her majesty the queen]
Royal Irish Acad.	Royal Irish Academy, Dublin
Royal Scot. Acad.	Royal Scottish Academy, Edinburgh
RS	Royal Society, London
RSA	Royal Society of Arts, London
RS Friends, Lond.	Religious Society of Friends, London
St Ant. Oxf.	St Antony's College, Oxford
St John Cam.	St John's College, Cambridge
S. Antiquaries, Lond.	Society of Antiquaries of London
Sci. Mus.	Science Museum, London
Scot. NPG	Scottish National Portrait Gallery, Edinburgh
Scott Polar RI	University of Cambridge, Scott Polar Research Institute
Sheff. Arch.	Sheffield Archives
Shrops. RRC	Shropshire Records and Research Centre, Shrewsbury
SOAS	School of Oriental and African Studies, London
Som. ARS	Somerset Archive and Record Service, Taunton
Staffs. RO	Staffordshire Record Office, Stafford

Suffolk RO	Suffolk Record Office
Surrey HC	Surrey History Centre, Woking
TCD	Trinity College, Dublin
Trinity Cam.	Trinity College, Cambridge
U. Aberdeen	University of Aberdeen
U. Birm.	University of Birmingham
U. Birm. L.	University of Birmingham Library
U. Cal.	University of California
U. Cam.	University of Cambridge
UCL	University College, London
U. Durham	University of Durham
U. Durham L.	University of Durham Library
U. Edin.	University of Edinburgh
U. Edin., New Coll.	University of Edinburgh, New College
U. Edin., New Coll. L.	University of Edinburgh, New College Library
U. Edin. L.	University of Edinburgh Library
U. Glas.	University of Glasgow
U. Glas. L.	University of Glasgow Library
U. Hull	University of Hull
U. Hull, Brynmor Jones L.	University of Hull, Brynmor Jones Library
U. Leeds	University of Leeds
U. Leeds, Brotherton L.	University of Leeds, Brotherton Library
U. Lond.	University of London
U. Lpool	University of Liverpool
U. Lpool L.	University of Liverpool Library
U. Mich.	University of Michigan, Ann Arbor
U. Mich., Clements L.	University of Michigan, Ann Arbor, William L. Clements Library
U. Newcastle	University of Newcastle upon Tyne
U. Newcastle, Robinson L.	University of Newcastle upon Tyne, Robinson Library
U. Nott.	University of Nottingham
U. Nott. L.	University of Nottingham Library
U. Oxf.	University of Oxford
U. Reading	University of Reading
U. Reading L.	University of Reading Library
U. St Andr.	University of St Andrews
U. St Andr. L.	University of St Andrews Library
U. Southampton	University of Southampton
U. Southampton L.	University of Southampton Library
U. Sussex	University of Sussex, Brighton
U. Texas	University of Texas, Austin
U. Wales	University of Wales
U. Warwick Mod. RC	University of Warwick, Coventry, Modern Records Centre
V&A	Victoria and Albert Museum, London
V&A NAL	Victoria and Albert Museum, London, National Art Library
Warks. CRO	Warwickshire County Record Office, Warwick
Wellcome L.	Wellcome Library for the History and Understanding of Medicine, London
Westm. DA	Westminster Diocesan Archives, London
Wilts. & Swindon RO	Wiltshire and Swindon Record Office, Trowbridge
Worcs. RO	Worcestershire Record Office, Worcester
W. Sussex RO	West Sussex Record Office, Chichester
W. Yorks. AS	West Yorkshire Archive Service
Yale U.	Yale University, New Haven, Connecticut
Yale U., Beinecke L.	Yale University, New Haven, Connecticut, Beinecke Rare Book and Manuscript Library
Yale U. CBA	Yale University, New Haven, Connecticut, Yale Center for British Art

3 Bibliographic abbreviations

Adams, *Drama* — W. D. Adams, *A dictionary of the drama*, 1: *A–G* (1904); 2: *H–Z* (1956) [vol. 2 microfilm only]

AFM — J O'Donovan, ed. and trans., *Annala rioghachta Eireann / Annals of the kingdom of Ireland by the four masters*, 7 vols. (1848–51); 2nd edn (1856); 3rd edn (1990)

Allibone, *Dict.* — S. A. Allibone, *A critical dictionary of English literature and British and American authors*, 3 vols. (1859–71); suppl. by J. F. Kirk, 2 vols. (1891)

ANB — J. A. Garraty and M. C. Carnes, eds., *American national biography*, 24 vols. (1999)

Anderson, *Scot. nat.* — W. Anderson, *The Scottish nation, or, The surnames, families, literature, honours, and biographical history of the people of Scotland*, 3 vols. (1859–63)

Ann. mon. — H. R. Luard, ed., *Annales monastici*, 5 vols., Rolls Series, 36 (1864–9)

Ann. Ulster — S. Mac Airt and G. Mac Niocaill, eds., *Annals of Ulster (to AD 1131)* (1983)

APC — *Acts of the privy council of England*, new ser., 46 vols. (1890–1964)

APS — *The acts of the parliaments of Scotland*, 12 vols. in 13 (1814–75)

Arber, *Regs. Stationers* — F. Arber, ed., *A transcript of the registers of the Company of Stationers of London, 1554–1640 AD*, 5 vols. (1875–94)

ArchR — *Architectural Review*

ASC — D. Whitelock, D. C. Douglas, and S. I. Tucker, ed. and trans., *The Anglo-Saxon Chronicle: a revised translation* (1961)

AS chart. — P. H. Sawyer, *Anglo-Saxon charters: an annotated list and bibliography*, Royal Historical Society Guides and Handbooks (1968)

AusDB — D. Pike and others, eds., *Australian dictionary of biography*, 16 vols. (1966–2002)

Baker, *Serjeants* — J. H. Baker, *The order of serjeants at law*, SeldS, suppl. ser., 5 (1984)

Bale, *Cat.* — J. Bale, *Scriptorum illustrium Maioris Brytannie, quam nunc Angliam et Scotiam vocant: catalogus*, 2 vols. in 1 (Basel, 1557–9); facs. edn (1971)

Bale, *Index* — J. Bale, *Index Britanniae scriptorum*, ed. R. L. Poole and M. Bateson (1902); facs. edn (1990)

BBCS — *Bulletin of the Board of Celtic Studies*

BDMBR — J. O. Baylen and N. J. Gossman, eds., *Biographical dictionary of modern British radicals*, 3 vols. in 4 (1979–88)

Bede, *Hist. eccl.* — *Bede's Ecclesiastical history of the English people*, ed. and trans. B. Colgrave and R. A. B. Mynors, OMT (1969); repr. (1991)

Bénézit, *Dict.* — E. Bénézit, *Dictionnaire critique et documentaire des peintres, sculpteurs, dessinateurs et graveurs*, 3 vols. (Paris, 1911–23); new edn, 8 vols. (1948–66), repr. (1966); 3rd edn, rev. and enl., 10 vols. (1976); 4th edn, 14 vols. (1999)

BIHR — *Bulletin of the Institute of Historical Research*

Birch, *Seals* — W. de Birch, *Catalogue of seals in the department of manuscripts in the British Museum*, 6 vols. (1887–1900)

Bishop Burnet's History — *Bishop Burnet's History of his own time*, ed. M. J. Routh, 2nd edn, 6 vols. (1833)

Blackwood — *Blackwood's [Edinburgh] Magazine*, 328 vols. (1817–1980)

Blain, Clements & Grundy, *Feminist comp.* — V. Blain, P. Clements, and I. Grundy, eds., *The feminist companion to literature in English* (1990)

BL cat. — *The British Library general catalogue of printed books* [in 360 vols. with suppls., also CD-ROM and online]

BMJ — *British Medical Journal*

Boase & Courtney, *Bibl. Corn.* — G. C. Boase and W. P. Courtney, *Bibliotheca Cornubiensis: a catalogue of the writings … of Cornishmen*, 3 vols. (1874–82)

Boase, *Mod. Eng. biog.* — F. Boase, *Modern English biography: containing many thousand concise memoirs of persons who have died since the year 1850*, 6 vols. (privately printed, Truro, 1892–1921); repr. (1965)

Boswell, *Life* — *Boswell's Life of Johnson: together with Journal of a tour to the Hebrides and Johnson's Diary of a journey into north Wales*, ed. G. B. Hill, enl. edn, rev. L. F. Powell, 6 vols. (1934–50); 2nd edn (1964); repr. (1971)

Brown & Stratton, *Brit. mus.* — J. D. Brown and S. S. Stratton, *British musical biography* (1897)

Bryan, *Painters* — M. Bryan, *A biographical and critical dictionary of painters and engravers*, 2 vols. (1816); new edn, ed. G. Stanley (1849); new edn, ed. R. E. Graves and W. Armstrong, 2 vols. (1886–9); [4th edn], ed. G. C. Williamson, 5 vols. (1903–5) [various reprs.]

Burke, *Gen. GB* — J. Burke, *A genealogical and heraldic history of the commoners of Great Britain and Ireland*, 4 vols. (1833–8); new edn as *A genealogical and heraldic dictionary of the landed gentry of Great Britain and Ireland*, 3 vols. (1843–9) [many later edns]

Burke, *Gen. Ire.* — J. B. Burke, *A genealogical and heraldic history of the landed gentry of Ireland* (1899); 2nd edn (1904); 3rd edn (1912); 4th edn (1958); 5th edn as *Burke's Irish family records* (1976)

Burke, *Peerage* — J. Burke, *A general [later edns A genealogical] and heraldic dictionary of the peerage and baronetage of the United Kingdom [later edns the British empire]* (1829–)

Burney, *Hist. mus.* — C. Burney, *A general history of music, from the earliest ages to the present period*, 4 vols. (1776–89)

Burtchaell & Sadleir, *Alum. Dubl.* — G. D. Burtchaell and T. U. Sadleir, *Alumni Dublinenses: a register of the students, graduates, and provosts of Trinity College* (1924); [2nd edn], with suppl., in 2 pts (1935)

Calamy rev. — A. G. Matthews, *Calamy revised* (1934); repr. (1988)

CCI — *Calendar of confirmations and inventories granted and given up in the several commissariots of Scotland* (1876–)

CClR — *Calendar of the close rolls preserved in the Public Record Office*, 47 vols. (1892–1963)

CDS — J. Bain, ed., *Calendar of documents relating to Scotland*, 4 vols., PRO (1881–8); suppl. vol. 5, ed. G. G. Simpson and J. D. Galbraith [1986]

CEPR letters — W. H. Bliss, C. Johnson, and J. Twemlow, eds., *Calendar of entries in the papal registers relating to Great Britain and Ireland: papal letters* (1893–)

CGPLA — *Calendars of the grants of probate and letters of administration [in 4 ser.: England & Wales, Northern Ireland, Ireland, and Éire]*

Chambers, *Scots.* — R. Chambers, ed., *A biographical dictionary of eminent Scotsmen*, 4 vols. (1832–5)

Chancery records — chancery records pubd by the PRO

Chancery records (RC) — chancery records pubd by the Record Commissions

CIPM	*Calendar of inquisitions post mortem*, [20 vols.], PRO (1904–); also *Henry VII*, 3 vols. (1898–1955)
Clarendon, *Hist. rebellion*	E. Hyde, earl of Clarendon, *The history of the rebellion and civil wars in England*, 6 vols. (1888); repr. (1958) and (1992)
Cobbett, *Parl. hist.*	W. Cobbett and J. Wright, eds., *Cobbett's Parliamentary history of England*, 36 vols. (1806–1820)
Colvin, *Archs.*	H. Colvin, *A biographical dictionary of British architects, 1600–1840*, 3rd edn (1995)
Cooper, *Ath. Cantab.*	C. H. Cooper and T. Cooper, *Athenae Cantabrigienses*, 3 vols. (1858–1913); repr. (1967)
CPR	*Calendar of the patent rolls preserved in the Public Record Office* (1891–)
Crockford	*Crockford's Clerical Directory*
CS	Camden Society
CSP	*Calendar of state papers* [in 11 ser.: domestic, Scotland, Scottish series, Ireland, colonial, Commonwealth, foreign, Spain [at Simancas], Rome, Milan, and Venice]
CYS	Canterbury and York Society
DAB	*Dictionary of American biography*, 21 vols. (1928–36), repr. in 11 vols. (1964); 10 suppls. (1944–96)
DBB	D. J. Jeremy, ed., *Dictionary of business biography*, 5 vols. (1984–6)
DCB	G. W. Brown and others, *Dictionary of Canadian biography*, [14 vols.] (1966–)
Debrett's Peerage	*Debrett's Peerage* (1803–) [sometimes *Debrett's Illustrated peerage*]
Desmond, *Botanists*	R. Desmond, *Dictionary of British and Irish botanists and horticulturists* (1977); rev. edn (1994)
Dir. Brit. archs.	A. Felstead, J. Franklin, and L. Pinfield, eds., *Directory of British architects, 1834–1900* (1993); 2nd edn, ed. A. Brodie and others, 2 vols. (2001)
DLB	J. M. Bellamy and J. Saville, eds., *Dictionary of labour biography*, [10 vols.] (1972–)
DLitB	Dictionary of Literary Biography
DNB	*Dictionary of national biography*, 63 vols. (1885–1900), suppl., 3 vols. (1901); repr. in 22 vols. (1908–9); 10 further suppls. (1912–96); *Missing persons* (1993)
DNZB	W. H. Oliver and C. Orange, eds., *The dictionary of New Zealand biography*, 5 vols. (1990–2000)
DSAB	W. J. de Kock and others, eds., *Dictionary of South African biography*, 5 vols. (1968–87)
DSB	C. C. Gillispie and F. L. Holmes, eds., *Dictionary of scientific biography*, 16 vols. (1970–80); repr. in 8 vols. (1981); 2 vol. suppl. (1990)
DSBB	A. Slaven and S. Checkland, eds., *Dictionary of Scottish business biography, 1860–1960*, 2 vols. (1986–90)
DSCHT	N. M. de S. Cameron and others, eds., *Dictionary of Scottish church history and theology* (1993)
Dugdale, *Monasticon*	W. Dugdale, *Monasticon Anglicanum*, 3 vols. (1655–72); 2nd edn, 3 vols. (1661–82); new edn, ed. J. Caley, J. Ellis, and B. Bandinel, 6 vols. in 8 pts (1817–30); repr. (1846) and (1970)
DWB	J. E. Lloyd and others, eds., *Dictionary of Welsh biography down to 1940* (1959) [Eng. trans. of *Y bywgraffiadur Cymreig hyd 1940*, 2nd edn (1954)]
EdinR	*Edinburgh Review, or, Critical Journal*
EETS	Early English Text Society
Emden, *Cam.*	A. B. Emden, *A biographical register of the University of Cambridge to 1500* (1963)
Emden, *Oxf.*	A. B. Emden, *A biographical register of the University of Oxford to AD 1500*, 3 vols. (1957–9); also *A biographical register of the University of Oxford, AD 1501 to 1540* (1974)
EngHR	*English Historical Review*
Engraved Brit. ports.	F. M. O'Donoghue and H. M. Hake, *Catalogue of engraved British portraits preserved in the department of prints and drawings in the British Museum*, 6 vols. (1908–25)
ER	The English Reports, 178 vols. (1900–32)
ESTC	*English short title catalogue, 1475–1800* [CD-ROM and online]
Evelyn, *Diary*	*The diary of John Evelyn*, ed. E. S. De Beer, 6 vols. (1955); repr. (2000)
Farington, *Diary*	*The diary of Joseph Farington*, ed. K. Garlick and others, 17 vols. (1978–98)
Fasti Angl. (Hardy)	J. Le Neve, *Fasti ecclesiae Anglicanae*, ed. T. D. Hardy, 3 vols. (1854)
Fasti Angl., 1066–1300	[J. Le Neve], *Fasti ecclesiae Anglicanae, 1066–1300*, ed. D. E. Greenway and J. S. Barrow, [8 vols.] (1968–)
Fasti Angl., 1300–1541	[J. Le Neve], *Fasti ecclesiae Anglicanae, 1300–1541*, 12 vols. (1962–7)
Fasti Angl., 1541–1857	[J. Le Neve], *Fasti ecclesiae Anglicanae, 1541–1857*, ed. J. M. Horn, D. M. Smith, and D. S. Bailey, [9 vols.] (1969–)
Fasti Scot.	H. Scott, *Fasti ecclesiae Scoticanae*, 3 vols. in 6 (1871); new edn, [11 vols.] (1915–)
FO List	*Foreign Office List*
Fortescue, *Brit. army*	J. W. Fortescue, *A history of the British army*, 13 vols. (1899–1930)
Foss, *Judges*	E. Foss, *The judges of England*, 9 vols. (1848–64); repr. (1966)
Foster, *Alum. Oxon.*	J. Foster, ed., *Alumni Oxonienses: the members of the University of Oxford, 1715–1886*, 4 vols. (1887–8); later edn (1891); also *Alumni Oxonienses … 1500–1714*, 4 vols. (1891–2); 8 vol. repr. (1968) and (2000)
Fuller, *Worthies*	T. Fuller, *The history of the worthies of England*, 4 pts (1662); new edn, 2 vols., ed. J. Nichols (1811); new edn, 3 vols., ed. P. A. Nuttall (1840); repr. (1965)
GEC, *Baronetage*	G. E. Cokayne, *Complete baronetage*, 6 vols. (1900–09); repr. (1983) [microprint]
GEC, *Peerage*	G. E. C. [G. E. Cokayne], *The complete peerage of England, Scotland, Ireland, Great Britain, and the United Kingdom*, 8 vols. (1887–98); new edn, ed. V. Gibbs and others, 14 vols. in 15 (1910–98); microprint repr. (1982) and (1987)
Genest, *Eng. stage*	J. Genest, *Some account of the English stage from the Restoration in 1660 to 1830*, 10 vols. (1832); repr. [New York, 1965]
Gillow, *Lit. biog. hist.*	J. Gillow, *A literary and biographical history or bibliographical dictionary of the English Catholics, from the breach with Rome, in 1534, to the present time*, 5 vols. [1885–1902]; repr. (1961); repr. with preface by C. Gillow (1999)
Gir. Camb. opera	*Giraldi Cambrensis opera*, ed. J. S. Brewer, J. F. Dimock, and G. F. Warner, 8 vols., Rolls Series, 21 (1861–91)
GJ	*Geographical Journal*

Gladstone, *Diaries* — *The Gladstone diaries: with cabinet minutes and prime-ministerial correspondence*, ed. M. R. D. Foot and H. C. G. Matthew, 14 vols. (1968–94)

GM — *Gentleman's Magazine*

Graves, *Artists* — A. Graves, ed., *A dictionary of artists who have exhibited works in the principal London exhibitions of oil paintings from 1760 to 1880* (1884); new edn (1895); 3rd edn (1901); facs. edn (1969); repr. [1970], (1973), and (1984)

Graves, *Brit. Inst.* — A. Graves, *The British Institution, 1806–1867: a complete dictionary of contributors and their work from the foundation of the institution* (1875); facs. edn (1908); repr. (1969)

Graves, *RA exhibitors* — A. Graves, *The Royal Academy of Arts: a complete dictionary of contributors and their work from its foundation in 1769 to 1904*, 8 vols. (1905–6); repr. in 4 vols. (1970) and (1972)

Graves, *Soc. Artists* — A. Graves, *The Society of Artists of Great Britain, 1760–1791, the Free Society of Artists, 1761–1783: a complete dictionary* (1907); facs. edn (1969)

Greaves & Zaller, *BDBR* — R. L. Greaves and R. Zaller, eds., *Biographical dictionary of British radicals in the seventeenth century*, 3 vols. (1982–4)

Grove, *Dict. mus.* — G. Grove, ed., *A dictionary of music and musicians*, 5 vols. (1878–90); 2nd edn, ed. J. A. Fuller Maitland (1904–10); 3rd edn, ed. H. C. Colles (1927); 4th edn with suppl. (1940); 5th edn, ed. E. Blom, 9 vols. (1954); suppl. (1961) [see also *New Grove*]

Hall, *Dramatic ports.* — L. A. Hall, *Catalogue of dramatic portraits in the theatre collection of the Harvard College library*, 4 vols. (1930–34)

Hansard — *Hansard's parliamentary debates*, ser. 1–5 (1803–)

Highfill, Burnim & Langhans, *BDA* — P. H. Highfill, K. A. Burnim, and E. A. Langhans, *A biographical dictionary of actors, actresses, musicians, dancers, managers, and other stage personnel in London, 1660–1800*, 16 vols. (1973–93)

Hist. U. Oxf. — T. H. Aston, ed., *The history of the University of Oxford*, 8 vols. (1984–2000) [1: *The early Oxford schools*, ed. J. I. Catto (1984); 2: *Late medieval Oxford*, ed. J. I. Catto and R. Evans (1992); 3: *The collegiate university*, ed. J. McConica (1986); 4: *Seventeenth-century Oxford*, ed. N. Tyacke (1997); 5: *The eighteenth century*, ed. L. S. Sutherland and L. G. Mitchell (1986); 6–7: *Nineteenth-century Oxford*, ed. M. G. Brock and M. C. Curthoys (1997–2000); 8: *The twentieth century*, ed. B. Harrison (2000)]

HJ — *Historical Journal*

HMC — Historical Manuscripts Commission

Holdsworth, *Eng. law* — W. S. Holdsworth, *A history of English law*, ed. A. L. Goodhart and H. L. Hanbury, 17 vols. (1903–72)

HoP, *Commons* — *The history of parliament: the House of Commons* [1386–1421, ed. J. S. Roskell, L. Clark, and C. Rawcliffe, 4 vols. (1992); 1509–1558, ed. S. T. Bindoff, 3 vols. (1982); 1558–1603, ed. P. W. Hasler, 3 vols. (1981); 1660–1690, ed. B. D. Henning, 3 vols. (1983); 1690–1715, ed. D. W. Hayton, E. Cruickshanks, and S. Handley, 5 vols. (2002); 1715–1754, ed. R. Sedgwick, 2 vols. (1970); 1754–1790, ed. L. Namier and J. Brooke, 3 vols. (1964), repr. (1985); 1790–1820, ed. R. G. Thorne, 5 vols. (1986); in draft (used with permission): 1422–1504, 1604–1629, 1640–1660, and 1820–1832]

IGI — *International Genealogical Index*, Church of Jesus Christ of the Latterday Saints

ILN — *Illustrated London News*

IMC — Irish Manuscripts Commission

Irving, *Scots.* — J. Irving, ed., *The book of Scotsmen eminent for achievements in arms and arts, church and state, law, legislation and literature, commerce, science, travel and philanthropy* (1881)

JCS — *Journal of the Chemical Society*

JHC — *Journals of the House of Commons*

JHL — *Journals of the House of Lords*

John of Worcester, *Chron.* — *The chronicle of John of Worcester*, ed. R. R. Darlington and P. McGurk, trans. J. Bray and P. McGurk, 3 vols., OMT (1995–) [vol. 1 forthcoming]

Keeler, *Long Parliament* — M. F. Keeler, *The Long Parliament, 1640–1641: a biographical study of its members* (1954)

Kelly, *Handbk* — *The upper ten thousand: an alphabetical list of all members of noble families*, 3 vols. (1875–7); continued as *Kelly's handbook of the upper ten thousand for 1878* [1879], 2 vols. (1878–9); continued as *Kelly's handbook to the titled, landed and official classes*, 94 vols. (1880–1973)

LondG — *London Gazette*

LP Henry VIII — J. S. Brewer, J. Gairdner, and R. H. Brodie, eds., *Letters and papers, foreign and domestic, of the reign of Henry VIII*, 23 vols. in 38 (1862–1932); repr. (1965)

Mallalieu, *Watercolour artists* — H. L. Mallalieu, *The dictionary of British watercolour artists up to 1820*, 3 vols. (1976–90); vol. 1, 2nd edn (1986)

Memoirs FRS — *Biographical Memoirs of Fellows of the Royal Society*

MGH — Monumenta Germaniae Historica

MT — *Musical Times*

Munk, *Roll* — W. Munk, *The roll of the Royal College of Physicians of London*, 2 vols. (1861); 2nd edn, 3 vols. (1878)

N&Q — *Notes and Queries*

New Grove — S. Sadie, ed., *The new Grove dictionary of music and musicians*, 20 vols. (1980); 2nd edn, 29 vols. (2001) [also online edn; see also Grove, *Dict. mus.*]

Nichols, *Illustrations* — J. Nichols and J. B. Nichols, *Illustrations of the literary history of the eighteenth century*, 8 vols. (1817–58)

Nichols, *Lit. anecdotes* — J. Nichols, *Literary anecdotes of the eighteenth century*, 9 vols. (1812–16); facs. edn (1966)

Obits. FRS — *Obituary Notices of Fellows of the Royal Society*

O'Byrne, *Naval biog. dict.* — W. R. O'Byrne, *A naval biographical dictionary* (1849); repr. (1990); [2nd edn], 2 vols. (1861)

OHS — Oxford Historical Society

Old Westminsters — *The record of Old Westminsters*, 1–2, ed. G. F. R. Barker and A. H. Stenning (1928); suppl. 1, ed. J. B. Whitmore and G. R. Y. Radcliffe [1938]; 3, ed. J. B. Whitmore, G. R. Y. Radcliffe, and D. C. Simpson (1963); suppl. 2, ed. F. E. Pagan (1978); 4, ed. F. E. Pagan and H. E. Pagan (1992)

OMT — Oxford Medieval Texts

Ordericus Vitalis, *Eccl. hist.* — *The ecclesiastical history of Orderic Vitalis*, ed. and trans. M. Chibnall, 6 vols., OMT (1969–80); repr. (1990)

Paris, *Chron.* — *Matthaei Parisiensis, monachi sancti Albani, chronica majora*, ed. H. R. Luard, Rolls Series, 7 vols. (1872–83)

Parl. papers — *Parliamentary papers* (1801–)

PBA — *Proceedings of the British Academy*

Pepys, *Diary*	*The diary of Samuel Pepys*, ed. R. Latham and W. Matthews, 11 vols. (1970–83); repr. (1995) and (2000)
Pevsner	N. Pevsner and others, Buildings of England series
PICE	*Proceedings of the Institution of Civil Engineers*
Pipe rolls	*The great roll of the pipe for . . .*, PRSoc. (1884–)
PRO	Public Record Office
PRS	*Proceedings of the Royal Society of London*
PRSoc.	Pipe Roll Society
PTRS	*Philosophical Transactions of the Royal Society*
QR	*Quarterly Review*
RC	Record Commissions
Redgrave, *Artists*	S. Redgrave, *A dictionary of artists of the English school* (1874); rev. edn (1878); repr. (1970)
Reg. Oxf.	C. W. Boase and A. Clark, eds., *Register of the University of Oxford*, 5 vols., OHS, 1, 10–12, 14 (1885–9)
Reg. PCS	J. H. Burton and others, eds., *The register of the privy council of Scotland*, 1st ser., 14 vols. (1877–98); 2nd ser., 8 vols. (1899–1908); 3rd ser., [16 vols.] (1908–70)
Reg. RAN	H. W. C. Davis and others, eds., *Regesta regum Anglo-Normannorum, 1066–1154*, 4 vols. (1913–69)
RIBA Journal	*Journal of the Royal Institute of British Architects* [later *RIBA Journal*]
RotP	J. Strachey, ed., *Rotuli parliamentorum ut et petitiones, et placita in parliamento*, 6 vols. (1767–77)
RotS	D. Macpherson, J. Caley, and W. Illingworth, eds., *Rotuli Scotiae in Turri Londinensi et in domo capitulari Westmonasteriensi asservati*, 2 vols., RC, 14 (1814–19)
RS	Record(s) Society
Rymer, *Foedera*	T. Rymer and R. Sanderson, eds., *Foedera, conventiones, literae et cuiuscunque generis acta publica inter reges Angliae et alios quosvis imperatores, reges, pontifices, principes, vel communitates*, 20 vols. (1704–35); 2nd edn, 20 vols. (1726–35); 3rd edn, 10 vols. (1739–45), facs. edn (1967); new edn, ed. A. Clarke, J. Caley, and F. Holbrooke, 4 vols., RC, 50 (1816–30)
Sainty, *Judges*	J. Sainty, ed., *The judges of England, 1272–1990*, SeldS, suppl. ser., 10 (1993)
Sainty, *King's counsel*	J. Sainty, ed., *A list of English law officers and king's counsel*, SeldS, suppl. ser., 7 (1987)
SCH	Studies in Church History
Scots peerage	J. B. Paul, ed. *The Scots peerage, founded on Wood's edition of Sir Robert Douglas's Peerage of Scotland, containing an historical and genealogical account of the nobility of that kingdom*, 9 vols. (1904–14)
SeldS	Selden Society
SHR	*Scottish Historical Review*
State trials	T. B. Howell and T. J. Howell, eds., *Cobbett's Complete collection of state trials*, 34 vols. (1809–28)
STC, 1475–1640	A. W. Pollard, G. R. Redgrave, and others, eds., *A short-title catalogue of . . . English books . . . 1475–1640* (1926); 2nd edn, ed. W. A. Jackson, F. S. Ferguson, and K. F. Pantzer, 3 vols. (1976–91) [see also Wing, *STC*]
STS	Scottish Text Society
SurtS	Surtees Society

Symeon of Durham, *Opera*	*Symeonis monachi opera omnia*, ed. T. Arnold, 2 vols., Rolls Series, 75 (1882–5); repr. (1965)
Tanner, *Bibl. Brit.-Hib.*	T. Tanner, *Bibliotheca Britannico-Hibernica*, ed. D. Wilkins (1748); repr. (1963)
Thieme & Becker, *Allgemeines Lexikon*	U. Thieme, F. Becker, and H. Vollmer, eds., *Allgemeines Lexikon der bildenden Künstler von der Antike bis zur Gegenwart*, 37 vols. (Leipzig, 1907–50); repr. (1961–5), (1983), and (1992)
Thurloe, *State papers*	*A collection of the state papers of John Thurloe*, ed. T. Birch, 7 vols. (1742)
TLS	*Times Literary Supplement*
Tout, *Admin. hist.*	T. F. Tout, *Chapters in the administrative history of mediaeval England: the wardrobe, the chamber, and the small seals*, 6 vols. (1920–33); repr. (1967)
TRHS	*Transactions of the Royal Historical Society*
VCH	H. A. Doubleday and others, eds., *The Victoria history of the counties of England*, [88 vols.] (1900–)
Venn, *Alum. Cant.*	J. Venn and J. A. Venn, *Alumni Cantabrigienses: a biographical list of all known students, graduates, and holders of office at the University of Cambridge, from the earliest times to 1900*, 10 vols. (1922–54); repr. in 2 vols. (1974–8)
Vertue, *Note books*	[G. Vertue], *Note books*, ed. K. Esdaile, earl of Ilchester, and H. M. Hake, 6 vols., Walpole Society, 18, 20, 22, 24, 26, 30 (1930–55)
VF	*Vanity Fair*
Walford, *County families*	E. Walford, *The county families of the United Kingdom, or, Royal manual of the titled and untitled aristocracy of Great Britain and Ireland* (1860)
Walker rev.	A. G. Matthews, *Walker revised: being a revision of John Walker's Sufferings of the clergy during the grand rebellion, 1642–60* (1948); repr. (1988)
Walpole, *Corr.*	*The Yale edition of Horace Walpole's correspondence*, ed. W. S. Lewis, 48 vols. (1937–83)
Ward, *Men of the reign*	T. H. Ward, ed., *Men of the reign: a biographical dictionary of eminent persons of British and colonial birth who have died during the reign of Queen Victoria* (1885); repr. (Graz, 1968)
Waterhouse, *18c painters*	E. Waterhouse, *The dictionary of 18th century painters in oils and crayons* (1981); repr. as *British 18th century painters in oils and crayons* (1991), vol. 2 of *Dictionary of British art*
Watt, *Bibl. Brit.*	R. Watt, *Bibliotheca Britannica, or, A general index to British and foreign literature*, 4 vols. (1824) [many reprs.]
Wellesley index	W. E. Houghton, ed., *The Wellesley index to Victorian periodicals, 1824–1900*, 5 vols. (1966–89); new edn (1999) [CD-ROM]
Wing, *STC*	D. Wing, ed., *Short-title catalogue of . . . English books . . . 1641–1700*, 3 vols. (1945–51); 2nd edn (1972–88); rev. and enl. edn, ed. J. J. Morrison, C. W. Nelson, and M. Seccombe, 4 vols. (1994–8) [see also *STC, 1475–1640*]
Wisden	*John Wisden's Cricketer's Almanack*
Wood, *Ath. Oxon.*	A. Wood, *Athenae Oxonienses . . . to which are added the Fasti*, 2 vols. (1691–2); 2nd edn (1721); new edn, 4 vols., ed. P. Bliss (1813–20); repr. (1967) and (1969)
Wood, *Vic. painters*	C. Wood, *Dictionary of Victorian painters* (1971); 2nd edn (1978); 3rd edn as *Victorian painters*, 2 vols. (1995), vol. 4 of *Dictionary of British art*
WW	*Who's who* (1849–)
WWBMP	M. Stenton and S. Lees, eds., *Who's who of British members of parliament*, 4 vols. (1976–81)
WWW	*Who was who* (1929–)

Hanbury, Benjamin (1778–1864), historian, was born at Wolverhampton on 13 May 1778. He was a great-grandson of Joseph Williams of Kidderminster, whose diary (much commended by Hannah More) he edited in 1815. Most of his education was received from his uncle, the Revd Dr Humphrys, pastor of the Union Street congregation, Southwark, London, and afterwards principal of Mill Hill School. For a time Hanbury was engaged in a retail business for which he had no taste. On 18 September 1801 he married Phoebe Lea of Kidderminster, who was a relative of his. They had a son and a daughter.

In June 1803, through the influence of Ebenezer Maitland, Hanbury obtained a situation in the Bank of England, and remained there until 1859. He became one of the deacons at Union Street in May 1819, and held that office until 1857, when he removed to Clapham and from there to Brixton. He published a monograph on the origin of the Union Street congregation entitled *An Historical Research Concerning the most Ancient Congregational Church in England … Union Street, Southwark* (1820). Hanbury was a strong nonconformist; for more than thirty years he was one of the 'dissenting deputies', who were the guardians of the political rights of the associated nonconformist bodies; and he entered, as an advocate of the voluntary principle, into the controversy on establishments which followed the repeal of the Test and Corporation Acts in 1828. He was a member of a 'society for promoting ecclesiastical knowledge', instituted for the publication of works bearing on nonconformist theories. He edited Richard Hooker's *Ecclesiastical Politie* in 1830, the edition including Walton's *Life*. For the Library of Ecclesiastical Knowledge, he wrote a short life of Calvin (1831). In the same year, on the formation of the Congregational Union of England and Wales, he became its treasurer and held that post until his death. His most important literary service to his denomination was his *Historical Memorials Relating to the Independents … from their Rise to the Restoration* (1839–44), a rich and accurate collection of documents illustrating the rise of nonconformity. Hanbury died on 12 January 1864 at his residence, 16 Gloucester Villas, Loughborough Road, Brixton, and was buried on the 19th in the Norwood cemetery. His wife and son had predeceased him in 1824 and 1836 respectively, but his daughter, Mary Ann Hanbury, survived him.

ALEXANDER GORDON, *rev.* NILANJANA BANERJI

Sources *The Nonconformist* (20 Jan 1864) · J. Bennett, *The history of the dissenters, 1808–1838* (1839), 226 · *Evangelical Magazine and Missionary Chronicle*, [3rd ser.], 6 (1864), 166–7 · *CGPLA Eng. & Wales* (1864) · R. W. Dale, *History of English congregationalism*, ed. A. W. W. Dale (1907), 634, 689, 724
Wealth at death under £1500: probate, 6 Feb 1864, *CGPLA Eng. & Wales*

Hanbury, Charlotte (1830–1900). *See under* Hanbury, Elizabeth (1793–1901).

Hanbury, Daniel (1825–1875), pharmacologist, was born on 11 September 1825 at Bedford Lane, Clapham, Surrey, the elder son of Daniel Bell Hanbury (1784–1882), and his wife, Rachel, *née* Chrisby. His father was a partner in Allen and Hanbury's, an old-established Quaker chemist and

Daniel Hanbury (1825–1875), by Charles Henry Jeens, 1876

druggist, situated at Plough Court in the City of London. Educated at a private school and, from 1833, at Clapham grammar school, Daniel joined the family business in 1841. He followed the family's traditional route into pharmacy, by qualifying as a pharmaceutical chemist at the Pharmaceutical Society in 1857.

Although groomed for a career at Plough Court (he eventually became a partner with his cousin, Cornelius Hanbury, in 1868), Hanbury's career took a different direction. At the Pharmaceutical Society he was influenced by some of the leading pharmacists and botanists of the day, such as Jonathan Pereira, Jacob Bell, and Theophilus Redwood, who awakened his interest in science. Botany became a passion with him, as it was for other Hanburys. (Daniel's younger brother, Sir Thomas Hanbury, laid out a famous botanic garden—La Mortola—at Ventimiglia in Italy.) Daniel became devoted to the study of pharmacognosy, or the knowledge of drugs, which at that time meant a close study of their botanical and geographical origins. While continuing with his work at Plough Court, he began writing to botanists, pharmacists, travellers, government officials, and anyone who could supply him with information and materials. He familiarized himself with classical and contemporary literature, and foreign languages, and, when he could, he travelled abroad extensively to collect specimens. He was particularly interested in Chinese materia medica and the origins of storax.

Hanbury retired from the family business in 1870, after what he described as 'a great deal of weary but not too disagreeable occupation' (Tweedale, 64), so that he could concentrate on research. In 1874 he published *Pharmacographia*, a joint work with Professor F. A. Flückiger, a teacher of pharmacognosy at Bern. The aim of this book was to investigate anew the field of vegetable materia medica in order, as far as was possible, to remove some of the uncertainties which surrounded the subject. Within a few decades, the development of the pharmaceutical industry was to make such researches seem dated. Nevertheless, Hanbury's investigations into the minutiae of plants and drugs were highly influential among his contemporaries, and were collected and published posthumously in a series of over eighty articles in his *Science Papers* (1876).

Hanbury became a member of several professional societies—the Linnean Society (1855), the Chemical Society (1858), and the Royal Microscopical Society (1867)—and was elected a fellow of the Royal Society in 1867. He was also active as an examiner in the Pharmaceutical Society, which later commemorated his life with the biennial Hanbury memorial medal. However, his lifestyle was that of a shy and reclusive scholar, and he disliked social occasions. This may have reflected his strict Quaker upbringing (though his scholarship seems to have left little time for religious works). He disliked tobacco and alcohol, avoided meat, and never married. His abstemious eating and drinking was said to have contributed to his early death; he died aged forty-nine from typhoid fever at Hollywood, Clapham Common, on 24 March 1875 and was buried at the Quaker burial-ground, Wandsworth, London.

GEOFFREY TWEEDALE

Sources G. Tweedale, *At the sign of the plough: 275 years of Allen & Hanburys and the British pharmaceutical industry, 1715–1990* (1990) • A. A. Locke and A. Esdaile, *Plough Court: the story of a notable pharmacy, 1715–1927*, rev. E. C. Cripps (1927) • D. Chapman-Huston and E. C. Cripps, *Through a City archway: the story of Allen and Hanburys, 1715–1954* (1954) • E. J. Shellard, 'Daniel Hanbury, one of the founders of pharmacognosy', *Pharmaceutical Journal*, 214 (10 May 1975) • J. Ince, 'Memoir', in D. Hanbury, *Science papers* (1876)
Archives GlaxoSmithKline, Greenford, Middlesex, letter-books relating to writing of *Pharmacographia* • NRA, priv. coll., family corresp. • Royal Pharmaceutical Society of Great Britain, London, corresp., notes, and papers • Wellcome L., letter-book | RBG Kew, letters to Sir William Hooker
Likenesses C. H. Jeens, stipple, 1876, BM, NPG [*see illus.*] • oils, Royal Pharmaceutical Society of Great Britain, London
Wealth at death under £14,000: probate, 8 April 1875, *CGPLA Eng. & Wales*

Hanbury [*née* Sanderson], **Elizabeth** (1793–1901), philanthropist and centenarian, was born in Leadenhall Street in the City of London on 9 June 1793. She was the younger daughter of John Sanderson (1750–1816), a tea merchant, formerly of Armthorp, Yorkshire, and his second wife, Margaret, *née* Shillitoe (c.1749–1795). Possibly because of the early loss of their mother, Elizabeth and her sister, Mary (later married to Sylvanus Fox of Wellington), were soon actively engaged in the life of the Quaker circle in which they were raised, working in the anti-slavery movement and visiting Newgate prison with Elizabeth Fry. Elizabeth Sanderson was especially concerned with improving the conditions of women sentenced to transportation, and also campaigned against capital punishment for minor offences. On 21 November 1826 she married Cornelius Hanbury (1796–1869), a chemist of Plough Court, Lombard Street, who was a partner with his first wife's father, William Allen, in the pharmaceutical firm of Allen, Hanburys, and Barry. As both her parents were no longer living, Elizabeth was married in Bristol, presumably from the home of an uncle.

Although in the 1830s many evangelical Friends left the society, Cornelius and Elizabeth Hanbury continued as active members, and Elizabeth was acknowledged as a minister in the society in 1833. Their home was at Stoke Newington, Middlesex, though they often spent some winter months in their other London house at Plough Court. They also had a summer 'retreat' at Bonchurch on the Isle of Wight. In 1858, when her husband retired from business, they moved to Wellington, Somerset, the home of their relatives in the Fox family, and seven years later they went to live at The Firs on the Blackdown hills, Somerset, where in 1869 Cornelius Hanbury died. Even in her eighties Elizabeth Hanbury was said by a local observer to 'go dappin' along the road like a maid of sixteen', and she retained a lively interest in the work of her descendants, who maintained the family's tradition of Christian philanthropy. She was in full sympathy with the projects of her daughter, Charlotte [*see below*], and in the missionary work of her granddaughters: Elizabeth Wilson with the China Inland Mission, and Charlotte Hanbury in India with the Zenana Missionary Society. In 1887 she moved with Charlotte to the home of her son Cornelius at Richmond, Surrey. In May 1900, her 108th year, she sent a message to the Friends' yearly meeting in London and another greeting to Queen Victoria from 'her oldest subject'. She retained her sight until her 105th year, and up to her death could hear with the aid of an ear-trumpet. She died at Dynevor House, Richmond, on 31 October 1901, aged 108 years, 4 months, and 3 weeks, and was buried in the Quaker burial-ground at Wellington on 5 November.

Her daughter, **Charlotte Hanbury** (1830–1900), philanthropist, was born at Paradise Row, Stoke Newington, Middlesex, on 10 April 1830. She worked as a girl in local ragged schools in Bonchurch and Stoke Newington. She did not entirely sever her connections with the Quakers, but her Christian activities are better described as evangelical and interdenominational. She was greatly concerned for the welfare of the rural inhabitants of the Somerset and Devon uplands, and her active support of George Brealey's mission and day school work on the Blackdown hills reflects her appreciation of the ministry of the Open Brethren, with whom he was associated. She travelled widely on the European continent, more especially spending time in Germany with the family of Count Adelbert von der Recke Volmerstein, whose daughter had married Elizabeth's half-brother William in 1862. Further afield, from 1889 she began to visit Tangier and Morocco where she became concerned about the conditions of Moorish prisoners. In this connection she established a refuge in Tangier with a reading room from which unobtrusive mission work was conducted. When, in 1900, she learned that she had not long to live, she entrusted the care of the Tangier mission to her cousin Henry Gurney and dictated her autobiography which was edited by her niece Caroline Head in 1901. She died at Dynevor House, Richmond, on 22 October 1900, and was buried in Highgate cemetery, Middlesex, three days later.

TIMOTHY C. F. STUNT

Sources A. A. Locke and A. Esdaile, *Plough Court: the story of a notable pharmacy, 1715–1927*, rev. E. C. Cripps (1927) · D. Chapman-Huston and E. C. Cripps, *Through a City archway: the story of Allen and Hanburys, 1715–1954* (1954) · 'Dictionary of Quaker biography', RS Friends, Lond. [card index] · *The life of William Allen, with selections from his diary and correspondence*, 3 vols. (1846) · A. A. Locke, *The Hanbury family*, 2 vols. (1916) · C. Hanbury, *Charlotte Hanbury: an autobiography*, ed. Mrs A. Head (1901) · C. Hanbury jnr, *Life of Mrs Albert Head by her sister* (1905) · R. H. White, *Strength of the hills: the story of the Blackdown hills mission* (1964)

Likenesses P. Bigland, portrait, 1893; formerly in possession of Lady Hanbury, La Mortola, Ventimiglia, in 1910 · photograph, 1893, repro. in Locke, *Hanbury family*, vol. 2, facing p. 304 · photograph, repro. in Chapman-Huston and Cripps, *Through a City archway*, facing p. 150

Wealth at death £1613 19s. 11d.: probate, 2 Sept 1902, *CGPLA Eng. & Wales*

Hanbury, Harold Greville (1898–1993), jurist, was born on 19 June 1898 at Compton Verney, Wellesbourne, Warwickshire, the only child of Basil Hanbury (1862–1933), gentleman of independent means, and his wife, Patience, *née* Verney (1873/4–1965), younger daughter of Henry Verney, eighteenth Baron Willoughby de Broke. He was educated at Warren Hall, Eastbourne, and Charterhouse School, before going up to Brasenose College, Oxford, on a classical scholarship in 1915. During the First World War his father served as a major in the Warwickshire yeomanry, and was made honorary lieutenant-colonel. Hanbury himself enlisted in 1916, serving first in the Artists' Rifles and then (as a lieutenant) in his father's regiment. In 1939, on the outbreak of the Second World War, he re-enlisted, and served as a staff captain until 1942 when he was discharged to run courses for allied troops. It was not surprising that patriotism was an important element in his life.

After the First World War Hanbury returned to Oxford, and took his degree in jurisprudence in 1920, being awarded the Vinerian scholarship. He then came top in the examination for bachelor of civil law in 1921. In that same year he was elected a fellow of Lincoln College. He remained there as a fellow for twenty-eight years, and was an honorary fellow thereafter. On 21 July 1927 he married Anna Margaret Geelmuyden Dreyer (d. 1980), daughter of Hannibal Dreyer of Copenhagen, and niece of Georges Dreyer, professor of pathology at Oxford.

At the time of Hanbury's election Lincoln College was less distinguished than it later became, and its poverty was renowned. Hanbury, however, became the archetypal Lincoln man, serving as dean, senior tutor, and sub-rector. His style fitted in well with the Oxford of the 'Brideshead' generation, with rather limited academic expectations of undergraduate commoners at a typical college. Expectations of college tutors were also modest, but this did not prevent Hanbury from publishing *Essays in Equity* (1934), *Modern Equity* (1935)—a textbook which ran to thirteen editions by 1989—and a brief history, *English Courts of Law* (1944; fifth edn, 1979).

Hanbury was immensely popular with his undergraduates. He and his wife entertained warmly and generously. Having no children of his own he took an especially keen interest in the lives and successes of his former pupils. He loved cricket, and also liked cats and was vice-president of the Oxford Cat Club. He was the model of a college man of that era. He was active in university affairs, and served as senior proctor twice, in 1933–4 and 1944–5.

Hanbury was a disciple (and literary executor) of Sir William Holdsworth, the leading academic lawyer of the inter-war years, at a time when academic law in England was in the doldrums. He and A. L. Goodhart edited the last four volumes of Holdsworth's *History of English Law* (1952–66); the final volume was put together from boxes of notes found after Holdsworth's death. The newly created readership in equity was offered to Hanbury in 1948 and it seemed an appropriate reward for college and university service. When in the following year Hanbury was elected Vinerian professor and thus fellow of All Souls, there was considerable surprise, his success owing more to the dislike of more obvious candidates than to Hanbury's academic distinction. He held the chair until 1964 without producing any significant research, though he published the engaging *Vinerian Chair and Legal Education* in 1958. He remained a popular figure: his rather discursive style of lecturing and writing was appreciated by a core of admirers. His tall, ambling, spare figure was a familiar Oxford sight.

Hanbury served on a number of government committees inquiring into industrial disputes (such as the committee of inquiry into the provincial omnibus industry, 1954) and as chairman of inquiries in the West Indies (board of inquiry into West Indian Airways, 1958) and Gibraltar (tribunal for industrials, 1960). He was an honorary bencher of the Inner Temple, London, and was made an honorary QC in 1960. In 1962–3 he served as visiting professor and acting dean of the law faculty at the new University of Ife, Nigeria; and, following his retirement as Vinerian professor, he was dean of the law faculty at the University of Nigeria from 1964 to 1966. He was subsequently an advocate of the Biafran cause, publishing *Biafra: a Challenge to the Conscience of Britain* in 1968.

Following the death of his wife in 1980, Hanbury was consumed with grief and went to live with a god-daughter in South Africa, whence he bombarded friends and acquaintances with letters. He died in a nursing home in Pinetown, Natal, South Africa, on 12 March 1993.

ROBERT STEVENS

Sources *The Times* (18 March 1993) · *The Independent* (30 March 1993) · *WWW, 1991–5* · Burke, *Peerage* · Burke, *Gen. GB* · personal knowledge (2004) · private information (2004) · b. cert.

Archives Bodl. RH, corresp. relating to Nigeria, Trinidad, Gibraltar, Biafra · Bodl. RH, corresp. with Margery Perham relating to Nigeria

Likenesses photograph, repro. in *The Independent*

Wealth at death £116,169: probate, 30 Dec 1994, *CGPLA Eng. & Wales*

Hanbury, Sir James Arthur (1832–1908), military surgeon, was born on 13 January 1832 at Somerstoun House, parish of Laracor, near Trim, co. Meath, Ireland, one of the fourteen children of Samuel Hanbury, a large landowner, and his wife, Louisa, daughter of Charles Ingham, rector of Kilmessan and Kilcool, co. Meath.

Hanbury studied at Trinity College, Dublin, and graduated MB in 1853. In September of that year he entered the Army Medical Service as an assistant surgeon. A brother, William, also in the Army Medical Service, was with the 24th regiment when it was annihilated at Chilianwala in 1849, and assisted Florence Nightingale in establishing the hospital at Scutari. He was in charge of Netley Hospital until his death. Another brother, Fleet Surgeon Ingham Hanbury RN, distinguished himself at Tell al-Kebir, was mentioned in dispatches, and received the bronze decoration and CB.

Hanbury steadily rose through the military ranks. He was promoted surgeon on 20 February 1863; surgeon-major on 1 March 1873; brigade surgeon on 27 November 1879; deputy surgeon-general on 5 May 1881; surgeon major-general on 14 June 1887. He retired from the service on 13 January 1892. He was elected an honorary FRCS Ireland on 19 July 1883, and FRCS England on 14 April 1887 (his diploma of membership being dated 23 February 1859).

Hanbury was quartered for some years at Halifax, Nova Scotia, before being sent to China and then to India. He served with the Bazar valley expedition in the Anglo-Afghan War of 1878–80, and was present during the march from Kabul to the relief of Kandahar. He was under fire in the battle of 1 September in that campaign, and besides being mentioned in dispatches in 1881, he received the CB, and the medal with clasp and the bronze decoration. As principal medical officer under Lord Wolseley during the Egyptian campaign of 1882, he was present at the battle of Tell al-Kebir, where he was instrumental in causing wounds to be dressed for the first time on the battlefield. Twice mentioned in dispatches, he was appointed KCB, the medal with clasp, the second class of the Mejidiye, and the khedive's star, in 1882. He served as principal medical officer at the Horse Guards and at Gibraltar (1887–8), and was surgeon-general of the forces in Madras (1888–92). In 1905 he received the distinguished service reward.

In 1876 Hanbury married Hannah Emily, daughter of James Anderson of Coxlodge Hall, Northumberland, and widow of Colonel Carter. Tall, alert, and handsome, of great independence and energy, Hanbury was a popular master of hounds at Ootacamund, India. He died at his home, Frondjern, Manor Road, Bournemouth, on 2 June 1908, and was buried on 7 June in Bournemouth. His wife survived him.   D'A. POWER, *rev.* CLAIRE E. J. HERRICK

Sources V. G. Plarr, *Plarr's Lives of the fellows of the Royal College of Surgeons of England*, rev. D'A. Power, 1 (1930), 495–6 · *The Lancet* (13 June 1908) · *BMJ* (13 June 1908), 1463 · private information (1912) **Wealth at death** £1702 4s. 1d.: probate, 10 July 1908, CGPLA Eng. & Wales

Hanbury, John (1664?–1734), landowner and ironmaster, was born at Gloucester, where he was probably baptized at St Nicholas's Church; he was the eldest son of Capel

Hanbury (*d.* 1704) and his first wife, Elizabeth, the daughter of William Capel of Barnwood, Gloucestershire. Capel Hanbury's elder brother Richard died in 1660, leaving him sole heir to the family's estate in Worcestershire and Gloucestershire, and also to property (mostly leasehold) in Monmouthshire, on which the family had operated several ironworks since the 1570s.

Hanbury matriculated at Pembroke College, Oxford, on 26 March 1681 and enrolled at the Middle Temple in 1683. But he soon abandoned the law in favour of the family's iron-making interests, of which he seems to have assumed control about 1685, as soon as he was twenty-one. In his own words:

> I read Coke upon Littleton, as far as tenant in dower; but on the suggestion of a friend that I should gain more advantage from the iron works at Pontypool than from the profits of the bar, I laid aside tenant and dower, and turned my attention to mines and forges.   (HoP, *Commons*, 105)

He settled at Pontypool, where in the early 1680s his father had built a mansion and created a park close to the ironworks. By 1685 his father had remarried and was living at Hoarstone, Gloucestershire, leaving the family's south Wales interests entirely to John, who became known as Major Hanbury from a commission in the militia.

Capel Hanbury's death in 1704 prompted John to take stock of the ironworks: he decided to concentrate operations closer to Pontypool by giving up outlying sites, and also began using the profits of the business to buy land in adjacent parishes, thus laying the foundations of the Pontypool Park estate of later generations.

Hanbury's ironworks were the scene of two major technical advances, although how far the credit for these should be assigned to him and how far to his managers, notably Thomas Cooke and Edward Allgood, is unclear. Between 1695 and 1697 Hanbury introduced a water-powered rolling mill, with adjustable rolls, at Pontypool, which made it possible to roll iron into thin sheets ('blackplate') of a uniform gauge, thus overcoming one of the major obstacles to the establishment of a tin-plate industry in Britain. Some years later, apparently in the early 1720s (although the date remains uncertain), tin plate itself was produced on a commercial scale for the first time in Britain at Pontypool, after those in charge of the works had overcome the problem of cleaning the blackplate prior to tinning. These two innovations paved the way to the establishment of an industry which remained concentrated in south Wales (although principally further west, around Swansea) until modern times.

In 1701 Hanbury married Albinia, daughter of Major-General William Selwyn of Matson, Gloucestershire, and in the same year, under the patronage of her family, entered parliament as one of the members for Gloucester, a seat which he held as a whig until he was defeated in the general election of 1708. Albinia died in 1702, possibly in childbirth, and on 3 July 1703 Hanbury married Bridget (*d.* 1741), the daughter of Sir Edward Ayscough of South Kelsey, Lincolnshire. She was a friend of Sarah, duchess of

Marlborough, and was probably introduced to Hanbury by his first wife's elder brother John Selwyn, who was for a time aide-de-camp to the duke. The Hanburys remained friends of both the duke and duchess for the rest of their lives; Hanbury was one of Marlborough's executors in 1722. In 1704 Hanbury leased 24 Golden Square, London, as a town house; and he retained this until he built a much larger house on a plot in the old privy garden of Whitehall Palace under a lease of 1721.

In 1720, five years after unsuccessfully contesting another election at Gloucester, Hanbury was chosen as an independent member of parliament for Monmouthshire, a seat which he retained until his death. He was no speaker but proved a competent man of business and chaired several committees. Hanbury died at Pontypool Park, Trevethin, on 14 June 1734 and was buried in Trevethin church, where a monument describes him as one 'who by his great understanding and humanity made the people of this place and neighbourhood rich and happy; and they will tell their children to latest posterity that he was a wise and honest man'. He and Bridget had eight sons who survived infancy, of whom the third, Capel, was his eventual heir. The fourth son, Charles, inherited a fortune from his godfather, Charles Williams, and (as Sir Charles Hanbury *Williams) had a successful career as a diplomat.   PHILIP RIDEN

Sources R. H. Tenison, *The Hanburys of Monmouthshire* (privately printed, Pontypool, 1995) • A. A. Locke, *The Hanbury family*, 2 vols. (1916), vol. 1 • W. Coxe, *An historical tour in Monmouthshire*, 2 (1801) • J. A. Bradney, *A history of Monmouthshire*, 1/2 (1906); facs. edn (1992) • F. W. Gibbs, 'The rise of the tinplate industry, pt 3: John Hanbury (1664–1734)', *Annals of Science*, 7 (1951), 43–61 • W. E. Minchinton, *The British tinplate industry: a history* (1957) • HoP, *Commons*
Archives Gwent RO, Cwmbrân | Glos. RO, Ducie MS, D340 • Pontypool Park estate office, estate and family MSS • Yale U., Farmington, Lewis Walpole Library, Hanbury Williams MSS
Likenesses G. Kneller, oils, priv. coll. • attrib. J. Richardson, oils, NMG Wales • marble bust (on his monument), Trevethin church, Monmouthshire • marble bust, Clytha Park, Abergavenny, Monmouthshire • portrait (as a young man), Clytha Park, Abergavenny, Monmouthshire • portrait (in middle age), Clytha Park, Abergavenny, Monmouthshire
Wealth at death see will, PRO, PROB 11/666, sig. 159, summarized Locke, *Hanbury family*, vol. 1, p. 161

Hanbury, John (1700–1758), merchant, was born at Llanfihangel, Monmouthshire, on 15 August 1700, the son of Charles Hanbury (1677–1735) of Pant-teg, and his wife, Grace (d. 1710), widow of Jenkinson Beadles. The Hanbury family had been active in the Society of Friends from his grandfather's time. Although John's active career was spent almost entirely in London, there are no surviving records of an apprenticeship there or of his admission to a livery company. He first appears as an independent trader in London about 1724, suggesting that he had spent the immediately preceding years away from London, most likely as a factor in the Chesapeake for an English merchant. He soon became conspicuously active in the London tobacco import trade, ranking second in 1729–31, and first by 1747. His Virginia business was primarily that of a

commission merchant, receiving from planters consignments of tobacco for sale, and returning cargoes of manufactures and other goods as ordered. His Maryland business, by contrast, involved substantial dealings with local independent merchants. In both trades he reduced costs and risks by sending out relatively few vessels of his own, depending instead on chartering as needed. To superintend the frequent adjustments needed, he employed a principal agent in each colony with broad powers to charter shipping.

Hanbury's Virginia and Maryland correspondents included planters from the most prominent local families. To attract such a clientele he was expected to provide political as well as the usual commercial services. By the 1740s he was a key player in the competition to influence appointments to desirable public positions in both colonies. In Maryland he was very close to Lord Baltimore, whom he served as 'banker', and in Virginia to Lieutenant-Governor Gooch, whose executor he became. He was also reportedly on excellent terms with all the major figures in the Pelham and Newcastle ministries. Through his access to Lord Granville, lord president of the council, he was able to deflect British legislation requiring loyalty oaths that would have excluded Pennsylvania Quakers from public office. When the issue became pressing at the start of the Seven Years' War, Hanbury negotiated the compromise under which Quakers withdrew from the Pennsylvania legislature during the war but retained their rights to future membership.

In 1747 Hanbury took in as partner his cousin Capel Hanbury (d. 1769), son of a Bristol soap maker. Both partners had numerous acquaintances in Bristol and were able to cultivate a political interest there. John Hanbury particularly pleased the duke of Newcastle by soliciting votes and guaranteeing funds for the election in 1754 of Robert Nugent as member for Bristol. Hanbury's closeness to the ministry became controversial at the time of Braddock's expedition the next year. In 1747 the local planters and merchants organizing the Ohio Company of Virginia had asked Hanbury to take a share in the company and act as its London agent. As such, he was consulted by both Henry Pelham and the duke of Newcastle on the French military challenge in North America. He also contracted to pay and victual Braddock's troops; in this work his agents and the warehouses of the Ohio Company were utilized. When the expedition ended in disaster, Dr John Shebbeare and other anti-ministerial publicists tried to depict John Hanbury as the hypocritical and self-serving Quaker mastermind behind the ill-fated strategy. In fact, from 1726 Hanbury had been the member of the Quakers' meeting for sufferings, responsible for correspondence with Virginia and Maryland. Even so, he attracted unfavourable comment from more strictly pacifist Friends for arming his ships in wartime and for investing in privateers in the 1740s.

This John Hanbury, usually termed of Tower Street, must be distinguished from several namesakes, including Major John Hanbury of Pontypool (1664?–1734), ironmaster and MP, and John Hanbury (1671–1732), governor of the

Hamburg Company and subgovernor of the South Sea Company. In 1728 John Hanbury of Tower Street married Anna Osgood (d. 1754) from a prominent Quaker family originally from Bristol. When he died intestate on 22 June 1758 at Holfield Grange, Coggeshall, Essex, his real estate (primarily in Essex) passed to his only son, **Osgood Hanbury** (1731–1784), and his personal estate was divided equally between Osgood and his sister, Anna, wife of Thomas Barnard of Kingston, Surrey. She had no children so that, at her death, her share of her father's fortune also went to Osgood's children, including the brewer Sampson Hanbury.

Osgood Hanbury at first continued his father's North American firm in partnership with Capel Hanbury. After the latter's death in 1769, Osgood began to disengage from the now politically exposed Chesapeake trade and thus reduced his ultimate losses from the American War of Independence. In 1757 he married Mary, daughter of Sampson *Lloyd (1699–1779) of Birmingham, Quaker iron dealer and banker. During the American War of Independence he compensated in part for the loss of his Chesapeake trade by expanding his West Indies business through the firm of Hanbury and Gosling. In 1770 he had also joined in founding the London bank of Hanbury, Taylor, Lloyd, and Bowman in partnership with his father-in-law. This firm, continued by his descendants for four generations, served as the London correspondents of Taylors and Lloyds, the family's bank in Birmingham, until absorbed in 1884 into what ultimately became the modern Lloyds Bank. Through the marriage of his daughter Anna to Sir Thomas Fowell Buxton, bt, brewer and antislavery activist, Osgood Hanbury was also the progenitor of the numerous Buxtons and Hanburys who over many generations managed the Truman, Hanbury, and Buxton brewery. He died in 1784.   JACOB M. PRICE

Sources A. A. Locke, *The Hanbury family*, 2 vols. (1916) · J. M. Price, 'The great Quaker business families of eighteenth century London', *The world of William Penn*, ed. R. S. Dunn and M. M. Dunn (1986), 363–99, esp. 363–9 · J. M. Price, *Overseas trade and traders: essays on some commercial, financial, and political challenges facing British Atlantic merchants, 1660–1775* (1996) · J. M. Price, *Capital and credit in British overseas trade: the view from the Chesapeake, 1700–1776* (1980) · 'Correspondence of Governor Horatio Sharpe, 1753–1757', ed. W. H. Browne, *Archives of Maryland*, 6, 9, 14, 31 (1888–95) · J. M. Hemphill, 'Freight rates in the Maryland tobacco trade, 1705–1762', *Maryland Historical Magazine*, 54 (1959), 36–58, appx 153–87 · CUL, Cholmondely (Houghton) MSS, 29/12, 29/29, 29/13 · L. Cong., manuscript division, Curtis family MSS · M. Tinling, ed., *The correspondence of the three William Byrds of Westover, Virginia, 1684–1776*, 2 vols. (1977), vol. 2, pp. 463, 494–6, 550–52 · *Lloyd's Register of Shipping* · [J. Banning], *Log and will of Jeremiah Banning (1773–1798)* (1932) · D. M. Owings, *His lordship's patronage: offices of profit in colonial Maryland* (1953) · *Joshua Johnson's letterbook, 1771–1774: letters from a merchant in London to his partners in Maryland*, ed. J. M. Price, London RS, 15 (1979) · [J. Shebbeare], *A letter to the people of England upon the militia, continental connections, neutralities, and secret expeditions* (1757) · [J. Shebbeare], *A fourth letter to the people of England*, 2nd and 6th edns (1756) · *Chain of friendship: selected letters of Dr. John Fothergill of London, 1735–1780*, ed. B. C. Corner and C. C. Booth (1971) · marriage settlement, 9 Sept 1728, Essex RO, acc. 6268 box 5 · will, PRO, PROB 11/1113, sig. 79 [Osgood Hanbury]
Archives Essex RO | LMA, Truman, Hanbury, and Buxton MSS · RS Friends, Lond., Lloyd MSS

Hanbury, Sir John (1782–1863), army officer, second son of William Hanbury (d. 16 Nov 1800) of Kelmarsh, Northamptonshire, and his wife, Charlotte, the daughter of Charles James Parke, was born at Kelmarsh and educated at Eton College. He was appointed ensign of the 58th regiment on 20 July 1799, his subsequent military commissions being lieutenant (26 September 1799), captain (3 June 1802), lieutenant-colonel (20 December 1812), colonel (25 July 1821), major-general (22 July 1830), and lieutenant-general (23 November 1841). Hanbury saw much service with the 58th in Egypt in 1801, where he was present at Abu Qir Bay and Alexandria in March, and received the sultan's gold medal given to the British officers present at these actions.

After a period on half pay Hanbury transferred to the 1st foot guards and served as aide-de-camp to General Warde in Portugal and Spain in 1808–9, being present in the retreat to and subsequent battle of Corunna. He also served with the 1st foot guards at Walcheren, in the retreat from Burgos, and in the campaigns in the south of France in 1813–14. He commanded the 1st battalion of the 1st foot guards, in the expeditionary force under Sir Henry Clinton, which was sent to the aid of the princess regent in Portugal in December 1826. The guards brigade under Major-General H. Bouverie was stationed initially in the area of Santarem, and the 1st foot guards were warmly praised for their high morale and discipline during arduous marches over bad roads in poor weather. In spring 1827 the guards were sent to Lisbon to quell rioting, which was done with great effectiveness. Stationed in Lisbon until 1828, Hanbury returned with his battalion to London in April that year. He was made a knight-bachelor in 1830, and colonel of the 99th regiment in October 1851. He was also a KB (1832), KCH (1832), and KCB (1862). Hanbury married on 17 May 1842 Charlotte, the eldest daughter of Sir Nelson Rycroft, second baronet; she survived him. Hanbury died at his residence, 15 Charles Street, Berkeley Square, London, on 7 June 1863. Hanbury's elder brother, William (1780–1845), was raised to the peerage as Lord Bateman in 1837.

H. M. CHICHESTER, *rev.* JAMES FALKNER

Sources *Army List* · *GM*, 3rd ser., 15 (1863), 113 · *Hart's Army List* · F. W. Hamilton, *The origin and history of the first or grenadier guards*, 3 vols. (1874) · *Colburn's United Service Magazine*, 3 (1849), 140 · GEC, *Peerage* · *Dod's Peerage* · Boase, *Mod. Eng. biog.* · Burke, *Peerage*
Likenesses Kneller, portrait (as a young man), priv. coll. · Richardson, portrait (in old age), priv. coll.
Wealth at death under £20,000: probate, 18 July 1863, CGPLA Eng. & Wales

Hanbury, Osgood (1731–1784). *See under* Hanbury, John (1700–1758).

Hanbury, Richard (c.1535–1608), goldsmith and ironmaster, was born at Elmley Lovett, Worcestershire, the only son of John Hanbury of Elmley Lovett and his first wife, Elizabeth, daughter of John Brode of Dunclent, Worcestershire. He came of a long line of small landowners in Worcestershire. He married Alice (1538–1593), heir of Jasper Fisher, royal goldsmith to Queen Mary, on 28 April

1560. They had two daughters and lived first in Goldsmiths' Row, in the City of London, and later at Riding Court, near Datchet in Buckinghamshire.

Sworn in as a freeman of the Goldsmiths' Company in 1555, Hanbury progressed through the various offices to prime warden in 1591. Meanwhile in 1570 he had been introduced to the Company of Mineral and Battery Works (founded in 1565) and thereafter concerned himself mainly with developing an iron industry in south Wales. The older iron industry in Sussex and the weald of Kent was by then in decline, at a time when the demand for iron goods was rising fast.

Hanbury's first efforts as an ironmaster were devoted to making a success of the company's wireworks at Tintern and to supplying the necessary high-grade (osmund) iron from his own forges. As time went by, however, he saw better prospects in disengaging from the wireworks and, in effect, holding them to ransom by securing as many as possible of the local sources of ore and most of the nearby woods suitable for charcoal making. As a spokesman for the company put it in 1593, 'the works have no provision of good osmond iron but from him [Hanbury] both that for all the best mines in Monmouthshire be his and almost all the woods within ten miles compas thereof be his also' (Sir Richard Martyn to Lord Burghley, BL, Lansdowne MS, 75/90). However, osmund iron was expensive to produce and there was more profit in producing merchant iron for a wider market. When Hanbury began sending cheaper iron to the wireworks, the company appealed to the privy council, making much play of the hardship caused to the workers and their families when the poor quality of the wire made it difficult to sell. Despite continued pressure on him, Hanbury continued to send inferior iron to Tintern until in 1598 the privy council ordered his arrest, together with his son-in-law Edmund Wheeler, and they were committed to the Fleet prison. Three months later they made their submission and were released. The supply thereafter of reasonable quantities of osmund iron to the wireworks, at a price Hanbury still claimed was uneconomic, does not seem seriously to have reduced his profits.

Another contentious issue at times had been the cutting of timber for charcoal, which had culminated in two or three clashes between Hanbury's woodcutters and armed parties of those who felt that their ancient rights to cut what they needed were being put at risk. For whatever reason, these disputes died down after 1580 and it is now possible to see that the extra value given to Monmouthshire woods by the demand for charcoal did much to ensure their survival.

Richard Hanbury was the most enterprising and successful ironmaster of the sixteenth century in Wales, not least because he had the deviousness and lack of scruple needed to overcome entrenched opposition. His works were principally concentrated around what later became the town of Pontypool, but he also had forges in Brecknockshire and Glamorgan, as well as depots in Bristol and London. His workforce, probably never more than 200

strong, would spend the summer months in the woods producing charcoal, and the winter, when the rivers were better able to turn the water-wheels that worked the bellows, making iron. Hanbury sat for Minehead in the parliament of 1593; Minehead was probably one of the ports to which he shipped his iron.

Richard Hanbury died on 20 May 1608 and was laid beside his wife in Datchet church. His total bequests, besides land in Buckinghamshire, Worcestershire, and south Wales, amounted to £17,850, together with £5000 invested in the ironworks. These last, and his land in south Wales and Worcestershire, passed to his nephew and executor, John Hanbury.

RICHARD HANBURY-TENISON

Sources A. A. Locke, *The Hanbury family*, 2 vols. (1916) · M. B. Donald, *Elizabethan monopolies: the history of the Company of Mineral and Battery Works from 1565 to 1604* (1961) · R. H. Tenison, *The Hanburys of Monmouthshire* (privately printed, Pontypool, 1995) · HoP, *Commons, 1558–1603*, 2.245–6
Likenesses engraving on memorial plaque, 1593, Datchet church, Buckinghamshire
Wealth at death over £25,000: will

Hanbury, Robert William (1845–1903), politician, born on 24 February 1845 at Bodehall House, Tamworth, was the only son of Robert Hanbury of Bodehall, a country gentleman of moderate landed estate but of ample means derived chiefly from collieries, and his wife, Mary, daughter of Major T. B. Bamford of Wilnecote Hall, Warwickshire. Left an orphan in early childhood, Hanbury was educated at Rugby School and at Corpus Christi College, Oxford, where he was well known as an 'oar'. He graduated BA in 1868 with a second class in *literae humaniores*. At the age of twenty-seven he became in 1872 one of the two Conservative members for the safe Tamworth seat. In 1878 he resigned it to move to North Staffordshire at a by-election when he was unopposed. But in 1880 he came third in that two-member constituency. For the next five years he threw himself energetically into the work of Conservative organization. He contested Preston unsuccessfully in 1882, but won the seat in 1885, retaining it with increasing majorities until his death.

A vigilant and unsparing critic of the estimates even in the Conservative parliament of 1886–92, Hanbury was regarded at first as something of a freelance; but when the Liberals returned to power in 1892, he and his allies, Thomas Gibson Bowles and George Christopher Trout Bartley, kept up a ceaseless warfare in the committee of supply upon the policy of the government in every department. He was particularly energetic in attacking from the financial side Gladstone's Home Rule Bill of 1893, and it was largely due to him that the question of the national store of cordite assumed the importance that inspired the motion of June 1895, on which the Rosebery ministry was defeated and resigned.

In Salisbury's subsequent government, Hanbury was made a privy councillor and financial secretary of the Treasury. That post he held until 1900. The Unionist ministry was then reconstructed after the general election of that year, and Hanbury succeeded Walter Long as president of the Board of Agriculture, with a seat in the cabinet. The change was regarded with some suspicion by the agricultural community; but Hanbury went among the farmers on all available occasions, delivered speeches at agricultural gatherings, and won general confidence.

Hanbury was twice married (but had no children): first, in 1869 to Ismena Tindal (d. 1871), daughter of Thomas Morgan Gepp of Chelmsford; second, in 1884 to Ellen (d. 1931), only child of Colonel Knott Hamilton, who survived Hanbury, marrying shortly after Victor Bowring, and taking the name of Bowring-Hanbury. Hanbury was known for his exceptionally fine physique. He died suddenly at his London home, Herbert House, Belgrave Square, on 28 April 1903, from pneumonia; he was buried in the churchyard at his country house, Ilam, near Ashbourne. There was an unpleasant family lawsuit about the terms of Hanbury's will and his substantial fortune; it was eventually resolved in a compromise by the law lords (*Times Law Reports*, 21.252).

ERNEST CLARKE, rev. H. C. G. MATTHEW

Sources *The Times* (29 April 1903) · *The Times* (7 May 1903) · *Annual Register* (1903), 130 · D. Brown, 'Business enterprise and social mobility: a study of the Hanburys of Norton Canes', *Staffordshire Studies*, 6 (1994), 45–71
Likenesses S. P. Hall, pencil sketch, NPG · Spy [L. Ward], caricature, chromolithograph, NPG; repro. in *VF* (28 May 1896) · B. Stone, two photographs, NPG
Wealth at death £204,260 19s. 11d.: probate, 20 June 1903, *CGPLA Eng. & Wales*

William Hanbury (1725–1778), by Richard Earlom (after Edward Penny)

Hanbury, William (1725–1778), Church of England clergyman and horticulturist, was born at Bedworth, Warwickshire, on 26 September 1725 and baptized there on 10 October, the son of William Hanbury (d. 1750) of that parish and later of Foleshill and his wife, Ann, *née* Ward. He matriculated at Magdalen Hall, Oxford, on 17 January 1745 and graduated BA from St Edmund Hall in 1748. The degree of MA was subsequently conferred on him by St Andrews University on 11 November 1769 in recognition of his achievements in planting.

Hanbury's keen interest in gardening was nurtured at Oxford, after which he sought entry into the established church. He was ordained deacon on 25 September 1748 and priest the next year. A living, latterly acquired by his father, was already awaiting him: the prosperous rectory of Church Langton, Leicestershire, comprising five hamlets and three churches. Hanbury was instituted on his own petition. He married Sarah (*bap*. 1735, d. 1813), daughter of Benjamin and Sarah Ellis of Arthingworth, Northamptonshire, on 18 April 1754. Three years earlier he had commenced extensive planting and gardening schemes in Church Langton with a view to raising money for charity from plant and tree sales. By spring 1753 'the seed-beds smiled with their numerous progeny' (Nichols, 2.686) and Hanbury wanted to expand his plantation onto adjacent land. The roots of his ultimate failure lay in the haste with which he pursued these plans before endearing himself sufficiently to influential parishioners—particularly necessary for an outsider of relatively humble origins in

mid-Georgian England. He fatally lacked both the charm and diplomatic qualities necessary to win over the two major landowners in the parish, the widowed sisters of West Langton Hall, Dorothy Pickering and Frances Byrd. They judged his expansionist schemes both hurried and unwarranted, and advised against using glebe land for plantations where there existed a right of common after the hay harvest. By 1757 a mortified and frustrated Hanbury would brook no further delay and instead concentrated on his nursery at Tur Langton and his plantation at Gumley, procuring for this purpose seeds and plants from many sources, including North America.

Hanbury's plantations in 1758 were generating sufficient income from the sale of plants, trees, and shrubs for him to vest his enterprise in trustees drawn predominantly from the local gentry; they were annually to dispose of the produce and devote the profits to the creation of a fund. Hanbury's ambitious hopes of growth were set out in his *Essay on planting, and a scheme for making it conducive to the glory of God and the advantage of society* (1758), which he dedicated to Oxford University in the hope of attracting wider notice. He insisted that planting was a patriotic duty as well as suited 'to the preserving of Health, and the prolonging of Life' (Hanbury, *Essay on Planting*, 17). According to this scheme, when the fund reached £1500 the interest was to be applied to the decoration of the church at Langton, providing it with an organ, an organist, and a schoolmaster; when it reached £4000 a village hospital would be founded. Advowsons were to be purchased, by which the trustees could reward deserving clergymen. In 1760 Hanbury published *A Plan for a Public Library at Church Langton in Leicestershire*, which added a further dimension to his plans for the village: a vast academic library. Though he donated books worth £100 and appealed to the learned world to send him manuscripts the trustees were not impressed and the scheme was stillborn. They were more supportive of fund-raising by means of annual choral festivals for the performance of Handel's oratorios, which began in 1759 at Langton, then moved to Leicester in 1762 and Nottingham in 1763. These festivals were well attended—for the concert on 26 September 1759 'more than two hundred coaches, chariots, landaus, and post-chaises' were seen at Church Langton (Hanbury, *History*, 81)—but failed to bring in the quick profit that Hanbury sought. They were further soured when disputes occurred with the conductor, William Hayes, professor of music at Oxford University, who defended himself in *An Account of the Five Music Meetings* against 'this GOLIAH, who, armed *cap a pie* in his self-sufficiency, bids defiance to all the world' (p. 3). The quarrel and inadequate returns persuaded Hanbury to abandon music as a fund-raiser. His side of the disputes with the trustees and with Hayes was given *inter alia* in his *History of the Rise and Progress of the Charitable Foundations at Church Langton* (1767).

Hanbury's relations with the trustees were not easing by that date; they queried his increasingly unfeasible schemes, he suspected them of suppressing orders for trees. He accordingly established a fresh deed of trust in 1767, which provided for only ten trustees, mostly from non-gentry backgrounds. It coincided with the issue of more ambitious plans. Hanbury proposed that funds should be allowed to accumulate from the annual proceeds of his plantations until the income reached £10,000 or £12,000 p.a. and then (1867 was reckoned an attainable starting date) he prescribed the creation of a minster church 660 ft long and lavishly decorated, comparable with St Peter's, Rome. It would have a major choral establishment, a public library (1000 of his own volumes were set aside for such a purpose in his lifetime), a college with six associated professorships, including one in antiquities (Richard Gough praises it in his *British Topography*), a picture gallery, a hospital for poor women, schools, a printing office, and an annual dole of beef. A further scheme of 1773 provided for the foundation of a major choral college in Oxford with 100 choral scholars for the celebration of divine worship, a convent for women, almshouses for men, a physic garden, and a massive library in the Italianate style. Hanbury's grandiose charitable plans would, his obituary in the *Leicester Journal* suggested, have taken a millennium to be effected. After heavy sales of trees in 1761 income fell far short of expectation, with trust capital in 1778 standing at just £4823. Moneys were regularly invested until in 1863 the whole basis of Hanbury's charity was reordered. A sum of £5000 was raised under a scheme established by chancery court order of January 1864, to be laid out mainly on the churches of Church Langton, Tur Langton, and Thorpe Langton. Educational

provision has also been made from the trust for the Langtons at intervals since that date.

The wrangling and the failure to generate income quickly was exacerbated by personal tragedy when Hanbury's son John (Jackey) died, aged ten, in February 1774. Hanbury himself died on 1 March 1778 and was buried at Church Langton in a mausoleum in the churchyard, according to his instructions. His other publications were *The Gardener's New Calendar* (1758) and *A Complete Body of Planting and Gardening* (2 vols., 1770–71), one of the earliest encyclopaedias on forestry and gardening, which was the distillation of his life's work and learning and shows his familiarity with the Linnaean system. A projected translation of Virgil came to nothing through the premature deaths of his friends and collaborators, Charles Churchill and Robert Lloyd. His belief that a programme of controlled tree-planting would accrue large profits was misplaced but never ceased to exercise the imagination of this well-meaning parochial autocrat. Hanbury always proclaimed his good intentions: 'As the amusement of gardening is innocent and the profits arising from it are intended for the glory of God and the good of mankind, I think I cannot be censured for pursuing this bent' (Wilshere, 1). Despite the fact that he never employed a curate he did not allow his passion for planting to sideline his duties as incumbent, although services in the outlying chapelries of Thorpe Langton and Tur Langton were kept to a minimum. Charges for dereliction of duty brought against him by a churchwarden in the archdeaconry court were withdrawn when the official involved recanted on 31 March 1766. His widow died on 17 November 1813, aged seventy-eight.   NIGEL ASTON

Sources Foster, *Alum. Oxon.* · J. Nichols, *The history and antiquities of the county of Leicester*, 2/2 (1798), 685–92 · R. G. [R. Gough], *British topography*, [new edn], 1 (1780) · papers relating to a history of William Hanbury and the Hanbury Trust, Church Langton, Leics. RO, DE4211 · J. H. Hill, *The history of the parish of Langton* (1867) · H. St George Cramp, 'The life of William Hanbury', Leics. RO · T. H. Ross, *Hanbury and Handel* (1936) · J. E. O. Wilshere, *The Reverend William Hanbury (1725–1778) of Church Langton, Leicestershire* (1978) · J. Prophet, *Church Langton and William Hanbury* (1982) · W. Hanbury, *Essay on planting, and a scheme for making it conducive to the glory of God and the advantage of society* (1758) · W. Hanbury, *History of the rise and progress of the charitable foundations at Church Langton* (1767) · parish register, Bedworth, Warks. CRO, 10 Oct 1725 [baptism] · parish register, Foleshill, Warks. CRO, 27 Dec 1750 [burial; William Hanbury, father]
Likenesses E. Penny, oils, 1763, Church Langton School, Leicestershire · R. Earlom, mezzotint (after E. Penny), NPG [*see illus.*] · sculpture, relief bust, St Peter's Church, Church Langton, Leicestershire

Hance, Henry Fletcher (1827–1886), diplomatist and botanist, was born on 4 August 1827 at Gloucester Terrace, Old Brompton, London. His early childhood was spent mainly with his maternal grandfather, Colonel Fletcher RN, at Plymouth, but he was educated in London and on the continent, mainly in Belgium, where he learned French, German, and Latin. At the age of seventeen (1844), already a self-taught botanist, he entered the civil service of Hong Kong. On 27 May 1852 he married (Anne) Edith, the daughter of William Baylis, an accountant; they had one son, Alfred Charles.

In 1854 Hance transferred to the superintendency of trade in China, and shortly afterwards to the British consulate at Canton (Guangzhou). During the riots there caused by the *Arrow* affair, he lost valuable collections of books and botanical specimens when the foreign factories were burnt. War followed, and Hance left for Hong Kong. In 1856–7 he visited Amoy (Xiamen) to collect plants. After the conclusion of the treaties he returned to the consulate at Canton. In 1861 he was appointed vice-consul at nearby Whampoa (Huangpu), but he returned to Canton in 1878 to act as consul. In 1866 he made a botanical excursion up the North River with Theodore Sampson, travelling some 125 miles from Canton. They also visited the island of Hainan; Hance went to Saigon in 1875. His first wife, Edith, died in 1872. Hance remarried in September 1875, and had three further children.

In 1881 and in 1883 Hance again acted as consul at Canton; in September 1883 there were serious riots and the foreign settlement was attacked. Hance sent his wife and children to safety and returned alone to his post, showing courage and good sense. In May 1886 he was appointed acting consul at Amoy.

Despite his capacity to acquit himself well and his forty-two years' experience as a consular official, together with his aptitude for languages, Hance declined to study Cantonese or Mandarin, and so did not rise in his profession as a diplomat. He devoted all his leisure and energy to botanical studies, collecting specimens from travellers and missionaries and encouraging the study of botany throughout China. Both his wives and his son Alfred Charles took an interest and collected for him. Hance's work added significantly to contemporary knowledge of the flora of China. He contributed many papers to Hooker's *Journal of Botany*, and he added a supplement to Bentham's *Flora Hongkongensis* containing seventy-five new species of plants. He was a frequent contributor to the *Journal of Botany*, the *Proceedings of the Linnean Society*, the *Annales des Sciences Naturelles*, and other scientific journals, and his work won respect from eminent botanists of the day. Sir Joseph Hooker, for example, declared that Hance displayed 'rare ability in mastering the technicalities of structural and descriptive botany'; and Theodore Sampson, while feeling that Hance was 'rather too fond of making new species', nevertheless admitted that his contributions to the science of botany were extensive. Hance was awarded an honorary PhD from Giessen University in 1849, and in 1877 was elected a member of the Deutsche Akademie der Naturforscher Leopoldina, one of the oldest scientific institutions in Germany; he was also made a fellow of leading botanical societies in England and abroad. He left his herbarium, consisting of more than 22,000 different species or varieties, to the British Museum, where it was placed in the natural history section. He died of fever on 22 June 1886 at Kulangsu, Amoy, and four days later was buried at Happy Valley, Hong Kong.

R. K. DOUGLAS, rev. LYNN MILNE

Sources F. B. Forbes, 'Henry Fletcher Hance', *Journal of Botany, British and Foreign*, 25 (1887), 1–11 · Desmond, *Botanists* · E. Bretschneider, *History of European botanical discoveries in China*, 2 vols. (1898) · *House and Garden* (March 1975) · FO List (1885) · m. cert., 1852 · d. cert.
Archives NHM · RBG Kew, corresp. | Harvard U., Arnold Arboretum, letters to Asa Gray · Royal Pharmaceutical Society of Great Britain, London, corresp. with Daniel Hanbury
Likenesses photograph, repro. in *House and Garden* · photograph, repro. in *Journal of Botany*, frontispiece · portrait, News Library

Hanckwitz, Ambrose Godfrey, the elder. *See* Godfrey, Ambrose, the elder (1660–1741).

Hanckwitz, Ambrose Godfrey, the younger. *See* Godfrey, Ambrose, the younger (c.1685–1756), *under* Godfrey, Ambrose, the elder (1660–1741).

Hanckwitz, Boyle Godfrey. *See* Godfrey, Boyle (1682/3–1753), *under* Godfrey, Ambrose, the elder (1660–1741).

Hanckwitz, John Godfrey. *See* Godfrey, John (d. 1766?), *under* Godfrey, Ambrose, the elder (1660–1741).

Hancock, Albany (1806–1873), zoologist, was born at Bridge End, Newcastle upon Tyne, on 26 December 1806, the third of the six children of John Hancock (d. 1812), a saddler and ironmonger, and his wife, Jane Baker, daughter of Albany Baker of Chester-le-Street. His father had made collections of plants, insects, and especially of shells, and, although he died when Albany was six years old, four of the six children, none of whom married, took up the study of natural history. Of these Thomas studied geology, Mary devoted herself to drawing natural history objects, and John and Albany are best-known as zoologists.

Hancock was educated in Newcastle upon Tyne and, at nineteen, was articled to Thomas Chater, a local solicitor. After a time spent in London he took an office over the shop of his friend the conchologist Joshua Alder in 1830 but did not remain long in the law. He had already in the previous year become one of the original members of the Natural History Society of Northumberland, Durham, and Newcastle upon Tyne, and communicated some notes to Alder's *Catalogue of Land and Freshwater Shells* (1830). He associated with a number of Newcastle naturalists, including Thomas Bewick, William Robertson, an able botanist, and his neighbour Alder. At this time he corresponded with W. J. Hooker, then professor at Glasgow, and Dr Johnston, the marine zoologist of Berwick, with reference to a proposed quarto work on British birds, some of the plates for which his brother John had already executed. Though this work was never carried out, it bore fruit in the magnificent John Hancock collection of birds now in the Hancock Museum at the University of Newcastle. Clever with his fingers from boyhood, Hancock from 1835 to 1840 devoted his time very largely to modelling in clay and plaster.

The first of the long list of Hancock's scientific papers, of which over seventy appear in the Royal Society's catalogue, is dated 1836. These are short notes on birds in Jardine's *Magazine of Zoology and Botany*. The great work of his life began in his association about 1842 with Alder in the study of the Mollusca. The main result of this partnership was the *Monograph of British Nudibranchiate Mollusca*, published by the Ray Society between 1845 and 1855. In this work many of the descriptions and most of the drawings for the eighty-three coloured plates, including all those that are anatomical, are the work of Hancock. The plates are remarkable, alike for beauty of drawing and for delicacy of colour. The type specimens and original drawings are preserved in the Hancock Museum. Having described many new species, in 1844 Hancock began, in conjunction with Dr Embleton, lecturer on anatomy at the Newcastle school of medicine, an exhaustive inquiry into the structure of *Aeolis*, the sea slug. This joint research extended to 1849, and was followed between 1850 and 1852 by a similar investigation of the genus *Doris*, the 'sea-lemon'. Meanwhile Hancock had taken an active part in promoting polytechnic exhibitions at Newcastle in 1840 and 1848, and in founding the Tyneside Naturalists' Field Club in 1846. To the *Transactions* of this club he contributed a series of papers on the boring apparatus of sponges, molluscs, and barnacles, a subject on which he corresponded extensively with Charles Darwin. In 1857 he published in the *Philosophical Transactions* one of his most valuable contributions to anatomy, 'The organisation of Brachiopoda' (lampshells), and in the following year, partly on Darwin's recommendation, he was awarded the royal medal of the Royal Society; but he was too modest to become a candidate for fellowship, or even to accept the presidency of any of the local societies. In 1862 he became a fellow of the Linnean Society, and in 1868 there appeared in the journal of that society his paper 'On the anatomy and physiology of the Tunicata', which was the preliminary to a proposed monograph of the British representatives of the group which he was never able to complete. In 1863, on the occasion of the meeting of the British Association, in conjunction with his brother John, he got together a magnificent collection of scientific and artistic treasures in the Newcastle Central Exchange; and for many years he was an active member of the Literary and Philosophical Society of Newcastle upon Tyne.

Although a modest man, Hancock was very active in the social and scientific life of Newcastle and allowed himself insufficient rest or exercise, ruining his health. Unable for three years to work at his microscope, with characteristic energy he turned his attention to the fossil fish and reptiles of the permian and carboniferous series, and produced, in conjunction with Thomas Atthey, and afterwards with Richard Howse, no fewer than fifteen papers on them. Hancock died at his home in St Mary's Terrace, Newcastle, on 24 October 1873, and was buried in Jesmond cemetery in Newcastle four days later. He was unmarried. The Hancock Museum was proposed by his brother John as a memorial to his work, but was eventually opened as a memorial to both brothers after John's death in 1890.

G. S. BOULGER, *rev.* E. A. REES

Sources T. R. Goddard, *History of the Natural History Society of Northumberland, Durham and Newcastle upon Tyne, 1829–1929* [1929] • R. Welford, *Men of mark 'twixt Tyne and Tweed*, 2 (1895) • D. Embleton, *Transactions of the Northumberland Natural History Society*, 5 (1875), 118 • H. B. Brady, *Nature*, 9 (1873–4), 43–4 • R. S. Watson, *The history of the Literary and Philosophical Society of Newcastle-upon-Tyne, 1793–1896* (1897) • *The correspondence of Charles Darwin*, ed. F. Burkhardt and S. Smith, 1–9 (1985–94) • J. Hancock, 'Letters from C. Darwin Esq. to A. Hancock Esq.', 8 (1880–89) • parish register, St Nicholas, Newcastle upon Tyne [baptism] • parish register, St Nicholas, Newcastle upon Tyne [burial] • *Newcastle Daily Journal* (28 Oct 1873)

Archives U. Newcastle, Hancock Museum, corresp. and papers | ICL, letters to Thomas Huxley • NHM, letters to Joshua Alder and Alfred Merle Norman

Likenesses photograph, repro. in Goddard, *History*

Hancock, Anthony John [Tony] (1924–1968), comedian, was born at Small Heath, Birmingham, on 12 May 1924, the second of the three sons of John Hancock, hotelier, and his wife, Lilian Thomas. He was educated at Durlston Court, Swanage, and Bradfield College, Reading. He spent much of his youth in Bournemouth, where his father, himself a semi-professional entertainer, kept a small hotel which was often frequented by those appearing in the seaside resort's shows (including Elsie and Doris Walters) from whom Hancock gained an interest in show business.

Hancock found it difficult to settle into employment (he worked briefly for the civil service, and more briefly for a tailor in Birmingham), and made his stage début in Bournemouth in 1940. After joining the RAF in 1942 he graduated naturally to Entertainments National Service Association tours and to the Ralph Reader gang shows, which at that time had a military rather than a scouting membership. On demobilization he struggled to find his feet in variety, and, like many other former service comics, appeared at the Windmill Theatre ('We never closed'), a foil to the stationary nudes and scantily clad showgirls who gave it its reputation. He was never as celebrated for his stage performances as he was for those on radio and television—his regular fare of 'cod' impersonations was a trifle banal. He had some success, especially in a revue in the 1950s at London's Adelphi Theatre, and his presentation as a caged budgerigar in the royal command variety show of 1958 is widely regarded as a classic harmonization of the demands of stage and television screen.

But it was the domestic privacy of radio and television that best suited Hancock's genius for personally button-holing his audience. He took part in radio programmes such as *Workers' Playtime* and *Variety Bandbox*, and then in 1951 appeared in the popular series *Educating Archie* as tutor to Peter Brough's ventriloquial doll, Archie Andrews, and his irritated catch-phrase, 'Flippin' kids', drew national attention. On 2 November 1954 his own show, *Hancock's Half Hour* was broadcast for the first time. His character, Anthony Aloysius St John Hancock, and his faded address, 23 Railway Cuttings, East Cheam, became famed throughout the land exactly at the moment that television aerials sprouted from the rooftops; the show translated to television in 1956. With Ray Galton and Alan Simpson as his sympathetic and alert writers (he had previously worked with them on *Happy Go Lucky*), and with

Anthony John [Tony] **Hancock** (1924–1968), by Bob Collins, 1958–9

highly capable support from Sid James (playing the crafty Sancho Panza to Hancock's pretentious Don Quixote), Bill Kerr, and Kenneth Williams, Hancock was hailed by critics and public as an immense comic talent. He was incapable of writing his own material and Galton and Simpson were crucial to his success; reworkings of their material in the 1990s with Paul Merton in Hancock's part indicate how much was owed relatively to performance and script.

The tedious Sunday afternoon, with its pre-Pinteresque pauses and hesitations and its quizzical side-glance at John Osborne's *Look Back in Anger*; the burlesque of Henry Fonda's *Twelve Angry Men* jury film (in which Magna Carta was hailed as 'that brave Hungarian peasant girl'); and the single-handed cameos, such as 'The Blood Donor' and 'The Radio Ham', all contributed richly to a pronounced Hancockian cult: quoting from Hancock was widespread among the same sorts of audience who would later regale each other with recitations of Monty Python's 'Dead Parrot' sketch. Whatever the role, Hancock was always the same picture of injured dignity, outwardly brazen, inwardly uncertain, as he suffered the buffets of life's enduring difficulties, forever sustaining the wordy stream of the semi-cultivated man. In 'The Blood Donor', for instance, possibly the most fondly recalled of the episodes, he was at once boastful of the precious fluid he deigned to offer and scared witless that a pint, rather than a pinprick, was the standard measure.

By eschewing the tinselly showbiz trappings associated with most radio and television comedy at this time, and by committing himself to uninterrupted dialogue and monologue, Hancock at once defined radio and television comedy in his own terms and made it difficult for stand-up stage comics to transfer successfully to the screen (Morecambe and Wise were, by conscious, exaggerated application, the rule-proving exception). This was to be Hancock's lasting professional heritage: he helped to make television safe, not for the conventional comedian, but for the comic actor, such as Ronnie Barker, Leonard Rossiter, and David Jason. Hancock's own comic models included Sid Field, of the versatile gallery of genial characterizations, and, ironically, tragic private life, and Jacques Tati, the popular French comedian of angular frame and optimistic mien.

Hancock's heavily jowled features, all pouches and creases, were moved occasionally to smug conceit, but more often to ruminative melancholy, while the unmistakable voice swooped from complacency to introspection. Together with the Homburg hat, the shabby fur-collared overcoat, the clodhopping feet, and the slightly clumsy, stooping posture, they formed a veritable picture of vanished grandeur, unrealized ambition, and irked resentment, which clearly resonated loudly in the Britain of the 1950s.

However, Hancock became bored with his routines; the radio *Half Hour* ended in 1959, the television series lasted until 1961. As Arthur Marshall observed, 'Seldom has such a dazzling career disintegrated so quickly' (*DNB*). Hancock parted company with Galton and Simpson and Sid James, having already jettisoned much of his talented supporting cast (Kenneth Williams's immensely popular 'snide' character, with his catch-phrase, 'Oooh, stop messing about', was sidelined and he left the show in 1959) and, with grandiose plans for establishing himself as an international star, came uncomfortably close to realizing in reality his comic persona. He made five poor films, starring in two, *The Rebel* (1961) and *The Punch and Judy Man* (1962), and an unsuccessful series for ITV. He sought psychological truth in comedy—he had tactlessly told Kenneth Williams that he did not want to do 'those funny voice "cardboard" characters of yours'—but comedy based on truth' (*Kenneth Williams Diaries*, 287)—but without the support of first-rate scriptwriters Hancock stopped being funny. There was nothing humorous about his private life, either. His first marriage, to Cicely Janet Elizabeth Romanis (1930–1969), a model, began on 18 September 1950 and ended in divorce on 6 July 1965, and his second, to his publicity agent, Freda (Freddie) Ross (b. 1930), on 2 December 1965, which also ended in divorce, a week before his death in 1968, were both marred by heavy drinking and domestic violence. A tense and neurotic performer, driven by a tortured ambition to evolve and perfect his art, and a most troublesome and discourteous colleague to boot, Tony Hancock drank heavily from 1952, significantly at the very onset of his years of success. As he lurched from occasional generosity to frequent and obstreperous aggression his private life lacked any sign of the ordinary or normal. Many British comedians have been self-confident, self-made, publicly anarchic, and privately conservative: Hancock was not of that ilk. It all added up to a tragic downward spiral, both personal and professional. While visiting Australia with a view to making a television series about a disgruntled 'pommy' immigrant, Tony Hancock committed suicide in his flat at Bellevue Hill, Sydney; his body was discovered there on 25 June 1968. He was cremated in Sydney, but his ashes were returned to Britain.

Hancock the man left a bitter personal memory, especially among those whom he had slighted: Kenneth Williams's animosity was not alleviated by Hancock's death, and there was certainly truth in his summing up: 'It seems a futile end, but the man was incredibly destructive all his life—never did anyone *waste* people & opportunities, as he did' (*Kenneth Williams Diaries*, 329). Tony Hancock the comedian's legacy was happier: *Hancock's Half Hour* set the standard and the style for British television comedy, and continues to find new audiences whenever it is revived.

ERIC MIDWINTER

Sources *DNB* · R. Wilmot, *Tony Hancock: artiste* (1978) · E. C. Midwinter, *Make 'em laugh: famous comedians and their worlds* (1979) · J. Fisher, *Funny way to be a hero* (1973) · F. Hancock and D. Nathan, *Hancock* (1969) · *The Times* (26 June 1968) · *The Kenneth Williams diaries*, ed. R. Davies (1993) · *CGPLA Eng. & Wales* (1968)
Archives FILM BFI NFTVA, *Heroes of comedy*, Channel 4, 2 Feb 1998 · BFI NFTVA, advertising film footage · BFI NFTVA, performance footage | SOUND BBC WAC · BL NSA, 'Briers on Hancock: an echo of remembered laughter', H3248/02 · BL NSA, documentary recordings · BL NSA, performance recordings
Likenesses B. Collins, photograph, 1958–9, NPG [*see illus.*] · H. Cartier-Bresson, bromide print, 1962, NPG · photographs, Theatre Museum, London · photographs, Mander and Mitchenson Theatre Collection, London · photographs, Hult. Arch.
Wealth at death £32,559: probate, 10 Dec 1968, *CGPLA Eng. & Wales*

Hancock [*married name* Donovan], **Dame Florence May** (1893–1974), trade union leader, was born on 25 February 1893 in Factory Lane, Chippenham, Wiltshire, one of fourteen children of Jacob Hancock, cloth weaver, and his second wife, Mary Pepler, *née* Harding, who had also been married before. Between them her parents already had ten children from their earlier marriages. Florence was the eldest child of this marriage and had two younger brothers and a sister whom she had to care for when both her parents died before she was eighteen. She was educated at the local elementary school, but left at the age of twelve to start work as a washer-up in a café. Two years later she took employment in a factory, the Nestlé Condensed Milk Company, where she was employed for 55 hours a week for a wage of under 6s. The factory was nonunionized, but in January 1913 the Workers' Union, a general union which sought to organize less skilled workers, including women, sent its woman organizer, Julia Varley, to hold a recruitment meeting at the factory.

Florence Hancock was the only woman who attended the meeting and this proved to be the beginning of her lifetime's involvement in the trade union movement. Two of the men who had called the meeting were dismissed, and in the strike which resulted Florence became a member of the strike committee. After the establishment of a union branch at the factory she took on the role of dues

Dame Florence May Hancock (1893–1974), by Elliott & Fry, 1956

collector and then secretary of the branch. In 1917 she was appointed full-time organizer for the Workers' Union and was district officer for Wiltshire. She later recalled that she was given a great deal of support by Julia Varley, who 'gave me all the help that a good colleague could … I always knew that I could go to her for advice and help which she gave willingly' (Hancock).

Hancock always believed that trade unions needed to take part in politics. Her own interest in political events was awakened at an early age through the influence of her father, a radical, who encouraged his daughter to read to him from *Reynold's News* and to discuss current affairs. She later recalled that her mother, a member of the local co-operative society, had also been willing to heckle speakers at political meetings. Although Florence supported the suffragette movement, the emphasis of her politics for most of her life was on the achievement of gradual progress. In 1915 she joined the Independent Labour Party (ILP), and in the 1920s was chair and then secretary of the Gloucester ILP as well as being active in the Labour Party in the south-west. She also went to Clay Cross during general elections to help Charles Duncan, general secretary of the Workers' Union, to defend his parliamentary seat. Despite her political interests, however, she increasingly concentrated her energies on the trade union movement, and when the Workers' Union merged with the Transport and General Workers' Union (TGWU) in 1929 she was made women's officer in Bristol, a post she held until 1942.

Between the wars Florence Hancock worked hard to organize women in the newly expanding light engineering and consumer industries, where it was difficult for unions to retain female members. With her soft west-country voice and neat appearance, usually wearing a tailored suit and blouse, she cut a respectable figure whose effectiveness as a trade union leader was increasingly recognized by her contemporaries. Women working within mixed-sex trade unions, however, found that their male colleagues often had little interest in organizing women or taking account of their needs, and they therefore sought ways to ensure that women's voices would be heard. Along with others, including Ellen Wilkinson MP and Anne Loughlin of the Tailors' and Garment Workers' Union, Hancock pressed the Trades Union Congress (TUC) to set up a women's advisory committee whose members would all be women. This was finally agreed in 1931 at the Conference of Unions Enrolling Women, which she attended as a delegate from the TGWU, and she soon became a member of the committee. She also took part in numerous movements to improve conditions for women workers, such as the campaign in 1937 against legislation which allowed women and young people to work excessive overtime, and on behalf of the TUC she joined in agitation for the establishment of a national maternity service. From 1935 to 1958 she was a member of the general council of the TUC and began to take a prominent part in a range of TUC activities. She took a particular interest in the international trade union movement and visited numerous countries in her role as TUC nominee on the International Labour Organization (ILO).

During and immediately after the Second World War Florence Hancock developed new areas of activity. She was promoted to be chief woman officer in the TGWU in 1942 and was chair of the women's advisory committee between 1941 and 1944, and then again between 1948 and 1952. Her long years of service and her abilities were recognized when she was made chair of the general council of the TUC in 1947–8. Throughout this period she continued to press for improvements in the work conditions of women and children. At the request of Ernest Bevin, minister of labour, she prepared a report, published in 1945, with Violet Markham on the post-war organization of private domestic workers which called for them to be included within unemployment insurance and to receive training. She was also a member of the committee on the Juvenile Employment Service which reported in 1945.

Florence Hancock was one of the first generation of women trade union leaders, along with others including Anne Loughlin and Anne Godwin, who made a career within the trade union movement and became influential both within their own unions and within the TUC. They faced conflicts of loyalty, however, in pursuing women's interests as workers while at the same time seeking to support trade union and Labour Party leaders. Over time Florence Hancock lost her early militancy and was less inclined to push male officials towards an understanding of the needs of rank-and-file women. Instead she developed a strong loyalty towards trade union leaders such as Citrine and Bevin and towards the leadership of the Labour Party, becoming identified after 1945 with the right wing of the TGWU and the TUC. Her presidential address to the annual conference of the TUC in 1948, for example, emphasized how important it was for workers to act responsibly to enable the Labour government to carry out its policies and was critical of all those who tried to incite industrial unrest.

Hancock's aim to support the Labour Party while also pursuing the interests of low-paid women workers did, however, lead to some ambivalence in her attitudes, in particular towards the campaign for equal pay. In her evidence to the royal commission on equal pay in 1944 she criticized employers who refused to pay women the same rate for the job as men, and in 1949 she played an influential role in the ILO conference in Geneva which drafted convention 100 calling for equal pay for work of equal value. On the other hand, when the Labour government refused to accept immediate implementation of all the recommendations of the royal commission on equal pay in 1946 on the grounds that this would lead to wage inflation and hamper economic recovery, she supported its position and emphasized the national interest. As chair she ensured that the women's advisory committee also supported the stand of the government, which meant that she had to face considerable criticism from a younger generation of trade union women who believed that they were being ignored by the TUC. With her strong sense of duty and fierce loyalty to the labour movement she weathered these criticisms and remained 'brisk, cheerful and good natured' (The Times, 16 April 1974). Her close colleague Dame Anne Godwin claimed that she made an enemy of anyone—whether communists, non-unionists, or bad employers—who sought to undermine the trade union movement, and that this 'may have made her a little narrow in her outlook at times'. None the less, she also claimed that Florence was 'a wonderfully loyal friend and a trustworthy colleague, incapable of any dirty tricks' (letter from Anne Godwin, quoted in Soldon, 126). Florence Hancock was honoured for her public service when in 1942 and 1947 she was appointed OBE and CBE respectively, and in 1951 was made a dame of the British empire.

Hancock's knowledge and experience of industrial organization meant that she was frequently in demand to sit on public bodies and to give evidence to investigations. She sat on numerous committees of inquiry, including the royal commission on capital punishment (1949–53), the Piercy committee on provision for the disabled, and the Franks committee (1955), which reviewed the operation of administrative tribunals. She was a governor of the BBC between 1956 and 1962, a director of the Daily Herald (1955–7), a director of Remploy Ltd (1958–66), a JP, and president of Hillcroft College. Many of these activities continued after her retirement from the TGWU and the general council of the TUC in 1958, when she was sixty-five.

Late in life, on 3 September 1964, Hancock married John Donovan (1891–1971), the son of John Donovan, a stevedore, whom she had known for thirty years as a colleague in the TGWU. A widower with six grown-up children, he became a member of the docks and inland waterways executive of the British Transport Commission after his retirement from the TGWU in 1947. They lived in Bristol. Hancock died on 14 April 1974, while visiting her sister's home in Chippenham.   JUNE HANNAM

Sources N. C. Soldon, 'Hancock, Dame Florence (May)', *DLB*, vol. 9 · *DNB* · E. Bywater, 'Rank and file personalities no. 7: Florence Hancock', *Socialist Review*, new ser. (1 Oct 1926), 37–8 · *The Times* (16 April 1974) · S. Lewenhak, *Women and trade unions* (1977) · R. Hyman, *The Workers' Union* (1971) · F. Hancock, 'Julia Varley: an appreciation', U. Hull, Brynmor Jones L., Varley papers · b. cert. · m. cert.
Archives University of Warwick, TUC papers · University of Warwick, Transport and General Union papers · University of Warwick, Workers' Union papers | FILM BFI NFTVA, 'Women in our time ', 1948
Likenesses photograph, 1939–40, Dictionary of Labour Biography collection · Elliott & Fry, photograph, 1956, NPG [*see illus.*] · photograph, repro. in Lewenhak, *Women and trade unions* · photographs, Trades Union Congress, London
Wealth at death £13,995—gross: Soldon, 'Hancock, Dame Florence (May)'

Hancock, Sir Henry Drummond (1895–1965),

civil servant, was born in Sheffield on 17 September 1895, the only child of Percy Griffen Hancock, manufacturer of electroplate, and his wife, Margaret Drummond. His father died three years later, the business passed out of the family, and his mother moved to Portsmouth. After periods at school in France and Germany, Hancock was educated at Haileybury College and as a scholar of Exeter College, Oxford. In the First World War he served in the Sherwood Foresters and the intelligence corps, and was mentioned in dispatches. In 1920 he entered the administrative class of the civil service, and was appointed to the Ministry of Labour. He early became secretary of a committee of inquiry into the working of the Trade Board Acts. Then followed a period, which included the general strike, when he was private secretary to Sir Horace Wilson, the permanent secretary. On 1 September 1926 he married Mary Elizabeth, elder daughter of Engineer-Captain Henry Toop RN, of Portsmouth; they had one son and one daughter.

During the ten years from 1928 Hancock was deeply involved in the problems created by unemployment. He first helped to administer various schemes for the transfer of unemployed workers to places where industry was expanding. In 1929 Labour took office, and J. H. Thomas was made lord privy seal to head a team to stimulate and co-ordinate schemes for the relief of unemployment. Hancock was appointed to be his private secretary, a post in which he showed his quality, although the financial orthodoxy of Philip Snowden as chancellor of the exchequer left Thomas without the resources to make any impact on the problem. When Labour went out of office in 1931, Hancock returned to the Ministry of Labour to deal with the problem of assisting those who had exhausted their right to unemployment benefit. He helped to frame the legislation which set up the Unemployment Assistance Board, and in its early years was a member of its staff,

helping to build the first nationwide organization to take over responsibilities hitherto left to the poor law.

In 1938 Hancock was transferred to the Home Office to take charge of a division concerned with the expenditure of local authorities, who had been called on to administer a system of air raid precautions. There he put the arrangements for financing civil defence on a sound footing. In 1941 he was sent to the United States as secretary-general of the British Purchasing Commission and the British Raw Material Commission. For his work there he was appointed CMG (1942). He returned to Britain in 1942 to be deputy secretary of the Ministry of Supply, where he had three strenuous years at the hub of war production.

With the return of peace in 1945 and a Labour government in power, the centre of gravity moved back to the social services, and Hancock moved with it, becoming deputy secretary, under Sir Thomas Phillips, of the new Ministry of National Insurance. This was established to frame and administer the comprehensive scheme, based on the Beveridge plan, which replaced and extended the former separate and partial schemes of health and unemployment insurance, old-age and widows' pensions, and workmen's compensation. Hancock was appointed KBE in 1947 and this, and his appointment to succeed Phillips as permanent secretary in 1949, showed how his work was regarded. He was appointed KCB in 1950. By 1951 the national insurance scheme was established and Hancock was moved to a new field of activity, as permanent secretary to the Ministry of Food. The end of rationing could now be foreseen, and it became Hancock's business to dismantle the system of wartime controls and state purchase, so that the remaining functions of the Ministry of Food could be absorbed into what thus became the Ministry of Agriculture, Fisheries and Food. In 1955 this work was done, and Hancock was appointed chairman of the Board of Inland Revenue, a post which he filled with distinction until he retired in 1958.

All through his career in the civil service, Hancock had shown remarkable versatility, and was moved from one critical point to another as the need arose, particularly when some new organization was to be created or some major development of policy had to be steered. In the last ten years he had been permanent head of three major departments, and the principal adviser of three Labour and five Conservative ministers. For him retirement simply meant a change of occupation, and he continued to work as hard as ever. Of his new activities, the most onerous were the chairmanship of the Local Government Commission for England, appointed under the act of 1958 to review the boundaries of county and county borough areas, and membership of the boards of two large companies, Booker Bros., McConnell & Co. and the Yorkshire Insurance Company. To all these he was deeply committed and never spared himself, winning affection by his kindness as well as respect for his thoroughness, clear thinking, and wisdom. No business problem was too much trouble; and, even more important, he was always ready to listen sympathetically and helpfully to the working and personal problems of his colleagues, young and old. In 1962 he was promoted GCB. But he had taken on too much. On 24 July 1965 he died suddenly at Bacita, Nigeria, while on business. His wife survived him.

Hancock's dedication to work left him little time for outside activities, but he read widely, was fluent in French and German, and had a considerable knowledge of antiques and architecture. In his younger days he was a great walker, and knew many country churches and country houses. But London was his home throughout his working life except in the war; he never owned either a house or a car.   EDWARD HALE, *rev.*

Sources *The Times* (26 July 1965) · *The Times* (29 July 1965) · *The Times* (30 July 1965) · personal knowledge (1981) · private information (1981) · *CGPLA Eng. & Wales* (1965)
Likenesses W. Stoneman, photograph, 1950, NPG
Wealth at death £24,604: probate, 16 Nov 1965, *CGPLA Eng. & Wales*

Hancock, John (1737–1793), merchant and revolutionary politician in America, was born on 12 January 1737 in Braintree, Massachusetts, the son of John Hancock (1702–1744), a Congregational minister, and Mary Thaxter Hawke, who later married Daniel Perkin, and who outlived her son. Upon the death of his father his mother sent him to live in Boston with his childless aunt Lydia Hancock (1714–1776) and his uncle, Thomas *Hancock (1703–1764), perhaps the richest merchant in New England. After attending the Boston Latin school, John went to Harvard College in 1750 and graduated AB in 1754. Upon Thomas's death in 1764 he inherited a fortune of about £70,000. Aged thirty-eight, Hancock surprised his acquaintances by marrying, on 28 June 1775, Dorothy (Dolly) Quincy (1747–1830), who was living as the ward of his aunt Lydia. Dolly was probably his mistress before they married, for they had travelled to the continental congress together. They had two children, Dorothy, who died in infancy (1776–1777), and John George Washington Hancock, who lived to be eight (1778–1787).

Hancock was no businessman: he left most of his commercial affairs in the capable hands of his secretary Ezekiel Price, who managed to keep Hancock's wealth from shrinking despite his extraordinary largesse. (Price also doubled as secretary of the Boston Sons of Liberty.) Hancock turned his attention to politics, forging an alliance with Samuel Adams and the opponents of British policy in the Boston town meeting around the time the Stamp Act was passed in 1765. He spent money lavishly: he gave £1000 to the Congregational Brattle Street Church which he attended, bought the town of Boston a new fire engine, and hosted innumerable parties and patriotic celebrations. He ingratiated himself with the people in a time of economic depression by treating them familiarly, in contrast to most members of the élite, and hiring workers to extend Hancock's Wharf and build the first house on Beacon Hill. (This beautiful mansion later fell into disrepair and was torn down in 1863 after a futile campaign to persuade the state legislature to purchase it.)

Such generosity, along with the £39,000 Hancock and his aunt had out on loan and seldom sued to collect, assured his rise in resistance circles, although he was not a

John Hancock (1737–1793), by John Singleton Copley, 1765

writer, a speechmaker, or an organizer of the calibre of John and Samuel Adams. Hancock was first elected a representative to the Massachusetts assembly from Boston in 1765, a post in which he served until he was elected to the continental congress in 1774. Elected to the provincial council in 1768, he was criticized by the governor, Francis Bernard, for his resistance activity, although he did serve as a councillor in 1772 during a brief rapprochement with Governor Thomas Hutchinson.

Like his uncle and many Boston merchants, Hancock earned much of his fortune in illegal trade, notably the importation of rum and wine. In June 1768, the newly arrived American board of customs commissioners seized one of his ships, symbolically named *Liberty*, for failing to declare a cargo of Madeira wine. The Boston crowd rose on Hancock's behalf, if not at his request, dragged the customs house boat in front of Hancock's house, burned it, roughed up the commissioners, and chased them out of town. They responded by informing their superiors of their mistreatment, which caused British soldiers to be sent to Boston. After a complicated case characterized by intimidation of the witnesses against Hancock, the customs officers dropped the prosecution the following March.

Although he flirted with the loyalist faction headed by Hutchinson during the early 1770s, Hancock irrevocably committed himself to the resistance in May 1773. He announced that the Massachusetts house of representatives had come into possession of some (stolen) letters of governors Bernard and Hutchinson which convinced the house that they had intended to overthrow Massachusetts's representative government and establish arbitrary power. Hancock next moderated the town meetings which protested against the shipment of East India Company tea and plotted the famous Boston tea party of 16 December 1773. According to some witnesses he joined the festivities himself, poorly disguised as a Mohawk Indian.

Hancock's influence in Boston was such that the Impartial Administration of Justice Act, which parliament passed in 1774 to respond to the tea party, singled him out, along with Samuel Adams, as the two individuals to be brought to Britain for trial, possibly for treason. Hancock thereupon fled with Adams to Concord, a farming town 17 miles north-west of Boston. The American War of Independence was sparked on 18 April 1775, when British troops were sent to seize these two men along with illegally stockpiled munitions in Concord.

Having been unanimously elected president of the first continental congress in 1774, Hancock foolishly hoped that body would select him, despite his total lack of military experience, to lead the revolutionary army. Although disappointed in this hope, Hancock at first performed the largely ceremonial functions of his office well, for he craved personal popularity, enjoyed pomp and ceremony, and conciliated many delegates because he had no strong political ideas. His florid signature beneath the Declaration of Independence—which according to folklore he inscribed so large that King George could read it without his spectacles—is so famous in the United States that 'John Hancock' has become a synonym for 'signature'. As he continued to preside over congress, Hancock found himself increasingly attracted to the lavish-spending delegates of the southern and middle states and alienated from his moralistic and parsimonious fellow New Englanders. He grew increasingly lackadaisical in the performance of his duties. When in October 1777 he asked to be restored to office following a two-month leave of absence, only two delegates supported him. His own state of Massachusetts joined a majority of six (to four) which refused even to thank him for his services.

Hancock returned to Massachusetts, and made sure that his popularity with the people remained undiminished. He continued to spend great sums of money, reimbursing Massachusetts troops in silver out of his own pocket in exchange for their paper money, accepting inflated continental paper money at par in his business dealings, donating firewood to the Boston poor, and riding about town in a beautiful coach escorted by fifty horsemen since he commanded the Massachusetts militia. He continued to bridge the gap between classes by treating lower-class people as equals, welcoming them into his mansion and finding employment for them. On 25 October 1780 he became the first governor of the state of Massachusetts under its new constitution.

Hancock was annually re-elected governor, with little opposition, for the rest of his life, except for the years 1785 and 1786, during the tumultuous period of Shays's rebellion, when he decided not to run. Although many of the élite deplored his familiar relations with the people, and the ministers condemned his extravagance and irreligiosity, Hancock retained power by continuing to spend money and avoiding offensive political positions. Following the suppression of Shays's rebellion by his successor Governor James Bowdoin, he benignly pardoned almost all the protesters and conciliated their followers.

Although he personally favoured a strong central government, Hancock hedged his support of the proposed United States constitution, coming down with the gout which he made sure habitually incapacitated him when he had to make a controversial decision. When his supporters persuaded him that he would be a logical choice as president or vice-president, however, his influence narrowly carried the constitution in the Massachusetts ratifying convention by 187 to 168. Disappointed that he was elected to neither national office, he pleaded gout when President George Washington visited New England. He had fancied that Washington would call upon him first and thus acknowledge the precedence of state governors. When Washington refused, Hancock had himself swathed in bandages to emphasize his discomfort and ceremoniously carried to meet the president. In the early 1790s Hancock was reconciled with his old friend Samuel Adams—they had been estranged throughout most of the 1780s. Adams became his lieutenant-governor and then governor upon his death; they won repeatedly despite their anti-federalism in an otherwise staunchly federalist state.

Hancock's opponents, first loyalists and then élite federalists who despised his personality and lack of strong principles, criticized him as superficial and a mere seeker of popularity. They were right about his weaknesses, but they were blind to his virtues. He deserves credit for keeping the resistance movement in Boston alive for much of the decade 1765 to 1775. Unlike many revolutionaries who used public office to enrich themselves, Hancock spent his seemingly bottomless fortune on the people of Massachusetts. He also served invaluably as a genial and impartial symbol of nationalism around which the continental congress in the mid-1770s and the people of Massachusetts in the 1780s could rally. If he did not become president, as he wished, he fulfilled a role similar to that of George Washington by being a figure around whom people of different opinions could rally.

Hancock died in Boston after a protracted illness on 8 October 1793, and was buried at Boston's Park Street churchyard. He left a fortune approximately equal to the one he inherited and his wife, who later married the retired captain of one of his ships, inherited over £12,000, enough to live in comfort for the rest of her days. One of Hancock's extra-political roles was that of treasurer of Harvard College: he lost the books, which were recovered in his stables and elsewhere, some as late as 1936. That he had taken them to Philadelphia when he went to serve in congress and forgotten about them symbolizes the paradoxical mixture of indifference to money, self-centredness, and disinterested patriotism which characterized this fascinating historical figure.

WILLIAM PENCAK

Sources W. T. Baxter, *The house of Hancock: business in Boston, 1724–1775* (1945) · W. M. Fowler, *The baron of Beacon Hill: a biography of John Hancock* (1980) · H. S. Allen, *John Hancock, patriot in purple* (1953) · J. Tyler, *Patriots and smugglers* (1986) · W. Pencak, *War, politics and revolution in provincial Massachusetts* (1981) · L. Sears, *John Hancock: the picturesque patriot* (1913) · W. M. Fowler, 'Hancock, John', *ANB* · C. K. Shipton, 'John Hancock', *Sibley's Harvard graduates: biographical sketches of those who attended Harvard College*, 13 (1965), 416–46 · J. T. Adams, 'Hancock, John', *DAB* · A. E. Brown, ed., *John Hancock: his book* (1898) · Boston tax list, 1771, Massachusetts archives, Old Court House, Boston, vol. 132 · grave, Park Street churchyard, Boston
Archives New England Historic Genealogical Society, Boston, papers
Likenesses J. S. Copley, oils, 1765, Museum of Fine Arts, Boston [*see illus.*] · J. S. Copley, portrait, repro. in F. W. Bayley, *Five colonial artists* (1929) · C. W. Peale, miniature, priv. coll. · E. Savage, portrait, Library of Corcoran Gallery, Washington; repro. in *Art in America* (autumn 1952) · J. Trumbull, oils, Yale U. Art Gallery
Wealth at death £70,000: Allen, *John Hancock*

Hancock, John (1825/6–1869), sculptor, was born in Fulham, Middlesex, the son of John Hancock (1788–1835), an inventor and rubber manufacturer, and his wife, Fanny Maria Francis (*bap.* 1794). After his father's death John and his eight brothers and sisters lived in Stoke Newington, Middlesex, with their uncle, Thomas *Hancock, a noted manufacturer who discovered the process of the vulcanization of rubber. He was also related to the inventor Walter *Hancock (1799–1852) and to the animal painter and inventor Charles Hancock (1800–1877).

On 16 December 1842 Hancock was admitted to the Royal Academy Schools at the age of seventeen; however, he probably attended for only a short period and it was about this time that he came into contact with Dante Gabriel Rossetti and other artists of the emergent Pre-Raphaelite Brotherhood. He was a member of the Cyclographic Society, a sketching club active until 1848 which included John Everett Millais and William Holman Hunt, and from 1849–50 his appearance at Pre-Raphaelite gatherings is recorded in William Michael Rossetti's diary, the *P. R. B. Journal*. These associations, and his interest in literary themes in his work, have led to Hancock's being identified as a 'Pre-Raphaelite' sculptor—the *Journal* records that he asked in 1849 whether he might put 'PRB' to his works—although, unlike the sculptor Thomas Woolner, he never became a member of the group. In 1849 he was involved in setting up their magazine *Monthly Thoughts*, which later became *The Germ*, but afterwards withdrew his financial support. In the same year his portrait was painted by Millais.

Outside the Pre-Raphaelite circle Hancock achieved notable early success as a sculptor. His design for a bas-relief representing *Christ's Journey to Jerusalem* (exh. RA, 1849) won the premium in a competition organized by the Art Union of London in 1849, and at the Great Exhibition of 1851 in London his plaster statue of *Beatrice* (1850, V&A), his finest surviving work, gained wide praise. He was appointed a local commissioner to the Great Exhibition, and he later sent works to the international exhibitions in Paris (1855) and London (1862). He contributed frequently to the Royal Academy exhibitions between 1843 and 1864.

On 30 August 1851 he married Eliza Ann Ferneley at St Pancras Old Church, Pancras Road, London.

Most of Hancock's recorded works represented 'ideal' subjects—those few which survive show that he was a sensitive modeller of form, with an eye for both classical and Renaissance sculptural precedents. He treated subjects from Shakespeare (*Ariel* and *Ophelia*, both exh. RA, 1858), Milton (*Comus*, exh. RA, 1845), Spenser (*Una and the Lion*, exh. RA, 1848), and Baron de la Motte Fouqué (*Undine*, exh. RA, 1851), as well as religious and allegorical subjects. His statue of *Penserosa* (1862), based on Milton's poem, was placed in the Egyptian Hall of Mansion House, London, and he designed a series of allegorical relief panels (1864–5; still *in situ*) on the former National Provincial Bank in Bishopsgate, London. His only known church monument is that to Edward Colston (*c.*1859) at St James the Great, Devizes, Wiltshire.

Hancock produced few portraits—a staple of the income of most Victorian sculptors—and it has been suggested that the wealth of his uncle Thomas allowed him a relatively carefree career as a sculptor. His last years though remain something of a mystery. In its obituary *The Athenaeum* stated that, after initial success, 'the anticipated progress of the sculptor was somewhat suddenly stayed and not renewed' (23 Oct 1869, 535). Ill health was given as a possible cause, though, despite the assistance from his uncle, Hancock seems to have run into financial difficulties: at his death his assets amounted to under £20. William Michael Rossetti, who harboured some animosity towards Hancock, referred to certain 'unfortunate circumstances into which it is not my affair to enter' (*Reminiscences*, 1.150). He described him as 'an ungainly little man, wizened, with a long thin nose and squeaky voice' (the latter immortalized in 1851 in Dante Gabriel Rossetti's comic poem 'St Wagnes' Eve'; ibid.). Hancock died at 35 Grafton Street East, Tottenham Court Road, London, on 17 October 1869 at the age of forty-three, of gastric irritation and exhaustion.   MARTIN GREENWOOD

Sources T. B. James, 'John Hancock: Pre-Raphaelite sculptor?', *Pre-Raphaelite sculpture*, ed. B. Read and J. Barnes (1991), 71–6 · R. Gunnis, *Dictionary of British sculptors, 1660–1851* (1953); new edn (1968) · Graves, *RA exhibitors* · *DNB* · B. Read, *Victorian sculpture* (1982) · B. Read, 'Was there Pre-Raphaelite sculpture?', *Pre-Raphaelite papers*, ed. L. Parris (1984), 97–110 · *The P. R. B. Journal: William Michael Rossetti's diary of the Pre-Raphaelite Brotherhood, 1849–1853, together with other Pre-Raphaelite documents*, ed. W. E. Fredeman (1975) · W. M. Rossetti, *Some reminiscences*, 1 (1906), 149–50 · *The Athenaeum* (23 Oct 1869), 535 · P. Atterbury, ed., *The Parian phenomenon* (1989), figs. 591, 882 · private information (2004) [T. B. James] · *CGPLA Eng. & Wales* (1869) · *IGI* · d. cert. · m. cert.
Archives NRA, priv. coll., family archive
Likenesses J. E. Millais, oils?, 1849 · group portrait, photograph, repro. in James, 'John Hancock', 71, fig. 42
Wealth at death under £20: probate, 28 Dec 1869, *CGPLA Eng. & Wales*

Hancock, Sir (William) Keith (1898–1988), historian, was born in Melbourne, Australia, on 26 June 1898, the youngest in the family of three sons and two daughters of the Revd William Hancock, incumbent of St Mark's, Fitzroy, and later archdeacon of Gippsland, Australia, and his

Sir (William) Keith Hancock (1898–1988), by unknown photographer

wife, Elizabeth Katharine McCrae. He was educated at Melbourne grammar school, the University of Melbourne, and, after a short spell lecturing at the University of Western Australia, as a Rhodes scholar at Balliol College, Oxford, where in 1923 he gained first-class honours in modern history and became the first Australian to be elected to a fellowship of All Souls College (1923–30). From that base he wrote *Ricasoli and the Risorgimento in Tuscany* (1926). Like much of his later work, the book was about the complexities of nationalism. Already the prose was fluent, supple, and elegant. From 1924 to 1933 he held the chair of modern history at the University of Adelaide. There he wrote *Australia* (1930), which remained the most professional and profound single volume about the country. The young professor had mixed feelings about his native land. Having been accepted at the heart of empire and now returned to a province, he would never be completely at home in either place. His speaking voice was neither quite English nor quite Australian. An account of his life to 1954, entitled *Country and Calling*, signalled the tension.

Birmingham University called Hancock to the chair of modern history in 1934 and Oxford to the Chichele chair of economic history in 1944. He was again a fellow of All Souls from 1944 to 1949. Dearly though he loved Oxford, he was not wholly comfortable in that chair, and left it for the University of London in 1949. Here he directed (until 1956) the new Institute of Commonwealth Studies, which was a monument to his own work. Hancock's *Survey of British Commonwealth Affairs* (3 vols., 1937–42), blending general perspectives with brilliant case histories and exhibiting what he often declared to be the historian's three cardinal virtues of attachment, justice, and span, had transformed the study of empire. The British Commonwealth was in his vision the most benign of modern polities, able, if wisely led and liberally inspired, to deliver democracy and welfare not only to Australians and Canadians but also to Indians and Africans. Jan Smuts, the subject of his two-volume biography *Smuts: the Sanguine Years*

(1962) and *Smuts: the Fields of Force* (1968), appealed to Hancock as avatar of the new Commonwealth: a former enemy who freely chose imperial loyalty.

In the First World War Hancock was too young to join up without permission, which his bereaved parents refused, his brother Jim having been named among the missing on the Somme. Like many young British men of his generation who missed the war, he lived after 1918 with a sense of shame and a high appreciation of bravery. In London during the Second World War he threw himself into the most active service he could find, by day directing (1941–6) the production of a thirty-volume civil series of official war histories, by night watching for fires from German bombs. Margaret Gowing, his co-author of the official volume *British War Economy* (1949), thought that by 1945, though not yet fifty, he looked venerable, with 'white hair and end-of-war exhaustion'.

Theaden, daughter of John George Brocklebank, farmer, was even more exhausted. Like Jan Smuts, Keith Hancock had fallen in love with a fellow student of great ability who had had to settle for country school-teaching and then, in 1925, married a man needing (Hancock's words on Sybella Smuts) unfaltering support and heroic constancy. Theaden had been the wife of a busy, prolific, and preoccupied professor ever since their marriage in 1925. In *Country and Calling* he convicts himself of 'barbarous insensitiveness' to her. She found rewarding employment in wartime London as a producer of talks for the Overseas Service of the BBC, but collapsed into depression under the burdens of life and work. Her ill health was among reasons why Hancock did not accept until 1957 an invitation first extended some years earlier to go to Canberra as professor of history (until 1965) and director of the Research School of Social Sciences (until 1961) at the new Australian National University. In Canberra, country and calling were now as nearly reconciled as they would ever be.

Colleagues and postgraduate students in awe of a legend discovered that Hancock was short, slight, charming, and playful; he was also intellectually exacting, and tough and wily (some called him Sir Fox) in his determination to win resources for his school and distribute them according to his own judgement of quality. He had an undisguised sense of his own achievement, no envy, and a humble curiosity. He was good at coaxing underproducers to get on, as he would say, with their scribbling. He encouraged interdisciplinary and intercultural studies before they were fashionable in his world. He had blind spots, among them an Anglophile disdain for many things American and a patrician distaste for trade. He became a kind of archbishop among Australian historians, at a time when most of the bishops, the professors of history in state universities, were Balliol men. The earliest and most enduring project of archiepiscopal inspiration was the *Australian Dictionary of Biography* modelled on the British *Dictionary of National Biography*, which he had served in Oxford as a member of the central committee; eleven gratifying volumes appeared during his lifetime.

Hancock and his wife lived happily in Canberra, enjoying both bush and society, until Theaden was stricken by cancer; she died in 1960. In the following year, as she had counselled, Hancock married Marjorie Eyre (daughter of William Henry Eyre, of Enfield, Middlesex), who had worked for him on every project since the civil war histories, and who gave him support and constancy for the next quarter of a century; she died in 1995. There were no children from either marriage.

After retirement in 1965, country and calling led Hancock to the region south of Canberra, on which he wrote a pioneering study in environmental history, *Discovering Monaro* (1972). He became an activist in the cause of conservation, a member of an alliance which tried in vain to prevent a telecommunications tower from being installed on the forested peak he loved just behind the university, and he served as the group's war historian in *The Battle of Black Mountain* (1974). In a post-imperial epoch, and in his own eighties, he was attracted by the idea of armed neutrality for Australia, and campaigned against the presence of American communication bases on his country's soil. He went on writing, and talking in seminars and on the radio, almost to the end. 'Beyond all else', wrote his close colleague and friend Anthony Low, 'he was the academic animateur'.

Hancock was knighted in 1953 in recognition of a successful mission to Uganda as a negotiator, and appointed KBE in 1965. He was a fellow of the British Academy (1950) and universities and academies in four continents conferred honours on him. When asked to list his achievements, he might leave some out but he included a medal of the Royal Humane Society won at the age of nine for rescuing another child from drowning. He died on 13 August 1988 in Canberra. K. S. INGLIS, *rev.*

Sources W. K. Hancock, *Country and calling* (1954) · W. K. Hancock, *Professing history* (1976) · D. A. Low, 'William Keith Hancock, 1898–1988', *PBA*, 82 (1993), 399–414 · personal knowledge (1996)
Archives Bodl. Oxf., corresp. with L. G. Curtis · NL Aus., corresp. and papers relating to Smuts · TCD, corresp. with Thomas Bodkin · U. Lond., Institute of Commonwealth Studies, Smuts and Buganda papers and corresp.
Likenesses J. Mendoza, portrait, Australian National University · photograph, British Academy [*see illus.*]

Hancock, Robert (*bap.* 1731, *d.* 1817), engraver, the son of John Hancock, was born in Badsey, Worcestershire, and was baptized there in St James's Church on 7 April 1731. It is generally accepted that he was apprenticed to the Birmingham engraver George Anderton on 28 January 1746. He was mainly active as an engraver of plates used in the transfer-printing of porcelain and enamels, besides producing book illustrations, mezzotints, and pencil and chalk portraits. He has traditionally been associated, as a key designer and engraver, with Stephen Theodore Janssen's York House enamel works at Battersea before his entry about 1756 as an engraver in the Worcester porcelain works run by John Wall, William Davis, and the Holdship brothers. However, more recent scholarship suggests that it is unlikely that his engravings were used at York

House, even though he may have spent some time in London in the early 1750s. Instead of working at Battersea, it is now believed that he and Louis Philippe Boitard were largely responsible for the production of transfers on Birmingham enamels. The so-called swan group of *galant* subjects—which incorporates a pair of swans painted in the foreground of the compositions and dates from about 1751–6—can be seen as a representative example of the Hancock–Boitard co-operation.

Less certain is Hancock's involvement with Bow: according to his biographer Cook, he worked there for some months after the termination of his (now refuted) employment at Battersea. A transfer-printed Bow version of about 1755 of the widely disseminated rococo motif of *L'amour*, designed by Charles Nicolas Cochin, may well have been engraved by Hancock. As was customary in the case of eighteenth-century porcelain designs, only very few examples of transfer-printed pottery bear Hancock's signature or his rebus (a gamecock perched on a hand). This was partly because so few porcelain designs could be described as original compositions: Hancock, for instance, generally adapted motifs from engravings by or after a range of the most popular *genre pittoresque* and rococo artists, including François Boucher, Antoine Watteau, Jacopo Amigoni, Jean Pillement, Nicolas Lancret, Boitard, Francis Hayman, and Francis Barlow. He also used engravings of portraits after Allan Ramsay and Thomas Worlidge.

Hancock remained with the Worcester works until 1774 (by 1772 as one of a new group of partners), when an acrimonious dispute resulted in the buyout of his share by his partners and in his retirement from the manufactury. At Worcester, Hancock had lost considerable savings in a bank failure about 1757, but was able to retain two properties adjoining the porcelain works. One of these houses was relinquished in 1798, the other remained in his property until November 1804. In Cook's evaluation, Hancock's contribution to the manufacture for almost two decades marked the 'heyday of transfer-printing at Worcester' resulting in many sought-after collectors' pieces. In addition to his long-term involvement with the manufactury at Worcester, Hancock was active as a freelance designer for the Caughley porcelain works near Broseley, Shropshire, and for the enamel trade in south Staffordshire. The Victoria and Albert Museum holds a rare example of a signed Hancock piece, a south Staffordshire snuff-box of about 1765, transfer-printed with *The Tea Party*, a motif which was one of the most popular in eighteenth-century ceramics.

A study of Hancock's transfer-printed subject matter provides interesting insights into aspects of English mid-eighteenth-century decorative taste. French influence is very evident in the earlier period, with the production of a range of *galant* and mythological subjects after the artists mentioned above. Another group could be described as nationalist and commemorative, celebrating British achievements in the Seven Years' War. A Birmingham enamel made before 1753 bears an aggressively nationalist motif, probably adapted by Hancock after a design by

Boitard: The *Free British Fishery Society Plaque* has been described by S. Benjamin as probably 'the most famous English enamel' (Benjamin, 68).

Hancock exploited grand tour nostalgia in transfer-printed Worcester pieces featuring scenes of Roman ruins derived from engravings after Gianpaolo Pannini. Another distinct group, of decoratively disposed 'naturalistic' fauna, was, like the French *galanteries*, often derived from contemporary drawing and model books such as Robert Sayer's *The Ladies Amusement* (2nd edn, 1762) and *The Artist's Vade Mecum* (1762). Hancock himself contributed to such publications, including some seven subjects for the 1762 edition of *The Ladies Amusement*. His engravings for model books were not only applied to enamel or porcelain, but, as in the case of the print *The Waterfall* from *The Ladies Amusement*, could also serve as a design resource for textiles. *The Waterfall*, for instance, supplied part of the design of a well-known Bromley Hall calico print of about 1770 entitled *The Country Village*.

After his departure from Worcester in 1775, Hancock allegedly worked as an agent or partner at Caughley, the pottery works by then part owned by his former apprentice at Worcester, Thomas Turner. From 1780 onwards the artist seems to have worked primarily on mezzotint and stipple portraits and engraved book illustrations. In 1780 he was recorded at Oldbury, a year later in Tividale, near Dudley, and in 1784 probably in Birmingham. There he produced a number of book illustrations for the publishers Pearson and Rollason, including some plates for a family Bible and illustrations to the surgeon William Meyrick's *The New Family Herbal*. Among his mezzotints, small portraits in oval of Lady Chambers and of the governor of Fort William, William Kingsley, after Joshua Reynolds, are among the most accomplished. Somewhat more schematic are a number of mezzotints after a Joseph Wright, including the short, stout figure of *William Hopley, Verger of the Cathedral Church of Worcester*, the large portrait of the seated astronomer *R. Lovett, of the Cathedral Church of Worcester, Author of Philosophical Essays in Three Parts*, and another large print of the dwarf *Edward Scofield, Clerk of St Chads, Shrewsbury*. Hancock also engraved a mezzotint of his own portrait, probably by Joseph Wright of Derby, of which an unfinished proof in the British Museum appears to be the only known impression. The marked difference in quality between some of his often mediocre mezzotints and stipples, especially when compared with his delicate, elegant book illustrations, may have contributed to the suggestion (since refuted) that there were two Robert Hancocks at work in the period.

Between 1796 and 1798 Hancock was in Bristol, where he produced some highly regarded pencil and chalk portraits of Robert Southey (1796), Samuel Taylor Coleridge (1796), William Wordsworth (1798), and Charles Lamb (1798), all of which are now in the National Portrait Gallery in London. These drawings were later reproduced in stipple by R. Woodman in illustration of J. Cottle's *Recollections* (1850), while the portrait of Southey was additionally engraved in stipple as a plate to C. C. Southey's *Life of Robert Southey* (1850). Hancock's last recorded works appear to be the two pictures *Portrait of a Gentleman* and *Children and a Donkey*, exhibited at the Royal Academy in 1805 while he was based in Pall Mall. Nothing is known of the last years before his death on 14 October 1817, in Brislington, near Bristol. He was buried in Brislington churchyard on 21 October. His wife, Martha (*b.* 1744), whom he married in Worcester about 1769, survived him for about twelve years. Hancock left all the prints, drawings, and paintings in his possession to one of their seven children, Robert, probably the contemporary miniature painter and drawing-master of that name in Bristol. Another son, Thomas, was active as an engraver in Birmingham. From the later nineteenth century, in spite of the gaps in the artist's biography and the uncertainties of attribution in the field of ceramics, Hancock has received a considerable, and increasing, amount of attention and has been widely recognized as one of the most important and talented contributors to the transfer-printing of porcelain and enamels.   ANNE PUETZ

Sources C. Cook, *The life and work of Robert Hancock* (1948) • N. Stretton, 'Hancock, Robert', *The dictionary of art*, ed. J. Turner (1996) • J. M. Handley, *18th century English transfer-printed porcelain and enamels: the Joseph M. Handley collection* (Carmel, CA, 1991) • S. Benjamin, *English enamel boxes from the eighteenth to the twentieth centuries* (1978) • S. F. Parkinson, 'Robert Hancock of Worcester and of Tividale: one property, one leaseholder', *Transactions of the English Ceramic Circle*, 15 (1993–5), 258–64 • E. Benton, 'Robert Hancock of Tividale', *Transactions of the English Ceramic Circle*, 12 (1984–6), 57 • M. Snodin and E. Moncrieff, eds., *Rococo: art and design in Hogarth's England* (1984) [exhibition catalogue, V&A, 16 May – 30 Sept 1984] • J. M. Handley, 'Robert Hancock and G. P. Pannini', *Transactions of the English Ceramic Circle*, 11 (1981–3), 99–101 • T. Clayton, *The English print, 1688–1802* (1997) • N. E. A. Torrant, 'A Hancock print', *Textile History*, 16 (1985), 103–5 • Graves, *RA exhibitors* • *Engraved Brit. ports.* • N. Stretton, 'Robert Hancock's birthplace', *Transactions of the English Ceramic Circle*, 14 (1990–92), 125 • S. Jervis, *The Penguin dictionary of design and designers* (1984)

Likenesses R. Hancock, self-portrait, mezzotint (after J. Wright), BM

Wealth at death see will, Cook, *Life and work*, 11

Hancock, Thomas (1703–1764), merchant and politician in America, was born on 17 July 1703 in Cambridge Farms, Massachusetts, the son of John Hancock (1671–1752), the local pastor, and Elizabeth Clark (*c.*1681–1760). Having been apprenticed to Boston bookseller Samuel Gerrish between the ages of fourteen and twenty-one, Hancock opened his own bookshop in the North End, and quickly expanded into publishing and a general trade that soon involved the entire British empire. Some of his leading endeavours were the export of rum, whale oil, and fish to England, the West Indies, Spain, and Portugal; the building of ships; and the importation of books and luxuries from Europe. In 1730 he married Lydia (1714–1776), the daughter of Daniel Henchman, a prominent Boston bookseller and his partner in making paper. He then built a mansion, the first house on Beacon Hill, which in 1856 the Massachusetts legislature refused to save in the interest of urban development.

After his marriage Hancock went into partnership with Charles Apthorp and rose to be one of the leading merchants in Boston. During the War of Jenkins's Ear (1740–44),

King George's War (1744–8), and the French and Indian War (1754–63), Hancock made an even larger fortune supplying British soldiers and sailors in the West Indies, Nova Scotia, and Canada. He held no political office, but remained in close touch with leading figures both in Boston and London such as province agent Christopher Kilby, who facilitated his lucrative military contracts. In 1755 seventeen sloops engaged by Hancock and Apthorp were used to transport the Acadians from Nova Scotia to Louisiana. Other ships served as privateers. Despite this royal bounty Hancock also smuggled tea, paper, and sailcloth from the Netherlands and foreign molasses from the West Indies into New England, though this universal practice among American merchants was legitimate, if not legal, in colonial eyes.

In his later years Hancock suffered from gout and a nervous disorder, which led him to turn more and more of his business over to his nephew, John *Hancock, a future signer of the Declaration of Independence. The Hancocks were childless, and in effect adopted the son of Thomas's brother John, who had died in 1744. Thomas entered politics formally in only 1758, as a member of the Massachusetts council, but was not among its more active members. On 1 August 1764 he died of a stroke while entering the council chamber.

Hancock's fortune has been estimated at upwards of £70,000, one of the largest, if not the largest, in colonial New England. His widow and nephew combined had £21,000 in Massachusetts money (approximately £15,000 sterling) on loan at interest in 1771. John Hancock took less and less interest in business after his uncle's death, leaving it to Ezekiel Price, also the secretary of the Boston Sons of Liberty. Ironically, he spent much of his inherited fortune funding the Bostonian's resistance to British authority, thereby undermining the imperial connection that had been its source. WILLIAM PENCAK

Sources W. T. Baxter, *The house of Hancock: business in Boston, 1724–1775* (1945) · W. M. Fowler, *The baron of Beacon Hill: a biography of John Hancock* (1980) · W. Fowler, 'Hancock, Thomas', *ANB* · E. Edelman, 'Hancock, Thomas', *DAB*
Archives Harvard U., Baker Library | Massachusetts Archives, Boston, Massachusetts
Likenesses portrait, Harvard U., Fogg Art Museum; repro. in Baxter, *House of Hancock*, frontispiece
Wealth at death over £70,000—of Massachusetts money: Baxter, *The house of Hancock*

Hancock, Thomas (1783–1849), physician, was born on 26 March 1783 in Lisburn, co. Antrim, the son of Quaker parents, Jacob Hancock and his wife, Elizabeth, *née* Phelps. He was sent to the Quaker school in Ackworth, Yorkshire, after which his medical education began with an apprenticeship to a surgeon-apothecary in Waterford. Hancock graduated MD from Edinburgh in 1806 with a thesis entitled 'De morbis epidemicis', which was dedicated to Dugald Stewart and Alexander Crawford. Following his graduation he moved to London, and in 1809 he became a licentiate of the Royal College of Physicians. From his home in Finsbury Square he developed a considerable practice, and he was elected physician to the City and Finsbury dispensaries. In 1810 he married Hannah Strangman

(d. 1828), of Waterford. They had eight children: Thomas (b. 1813), Emma (b. 1814), Elizabeth (b. 1816), Mary (b. 1818), George (b. 1820), John (b. 1822), Jacob (b. 1824), and Hannah (b. 1828). A deeply religious man, Hancock wrote a number of works promoting his Quaker faith and attacking those who criticized it. He was made an elder of his meeting in 1817.

The subject of epidemic disease was one in which Hancock was interested throughout his life. In 1820 he addressed the Medical Society of London on the subject. At their request he published a book on the subject of his address in 1821 entitled *Researches into the laws and phenomena of pestilence, including a medical sketch and review of the plague of London in 1665 and remarks on quarantine*. He returned to this subject in 1831 when he published a work entitled *On the Laws and Progress of Epidemic Cholera*. In 1824 he also published *An Essay on Instinct and its Physical and Moral Relations*, in which he criticized the remarks of a surgeon named Lawrence on the creation. His book *The principles of peace exemplified in the conduct of the Society of Friends in Ireland during the rebellion of the year 1798* (1825), contains eye-witness accounts of the rebellion from a number of Irish Quakers and provides an interesting perspective on that conflict.

Following the death of his wife on 13 October 1828 Hancock left London and moved to Liverpool. There in 1835 he wrote a work defending the Quaker doctrines of immediate revelation and universal and saving light which had been attacked in a work by Isaac Credson entitled *A Beacon to the Society of Friends*. An admirer of John Locke, Hancock translated a number of essays on the philosopher written by Pierre Nicole, a French theologian. He also possessed a small manuscript by Locke. Hancock was an earnest advocate of the abolition of capital punishment, and took a deep interest in many philanthropic movements. In 1840 he addressed the question of Britain's Caribbean colonies in *Are the West India colonies to be preserved? A few plain facts; showing the necessity of immigration into British Guiana and the West Indies, and the utter futility of all efforts towards the abolition of slavery and the slave trade which do not include this*, a work which expanded the views he expressed in a letter to the *Morning Post* in the same year. In 1838 he left Liverpool and returned to Lisburn, where he died from heart disease on 6 or 16 April 1849, aged sixty-six. KARL MAGEE

Sources 'Dictionary of Quaker biography', RS Friends, Lond. [card index] · *DNB* · Munk, *Roll* · R. J. Hayes, ed., *Manuscript sources for the history of Irish civilisation*, 11 vols. (1965)
Archives RS Friends, Lond., letters · U. Edin., MD thesis | NL Ire., Genealogical Office, confirmation of family arms

Hancock, Thomas (1786–1865), rubber manufacturer and inventor, was born at Marlborough, Wiltshire, on 8 May 1786, the second son in the family of twelve children raised by James Hancock, a timber merchant and cabinetmaker at Marlborough, and his wife, Elizabeth, *née* Longman. Walter *Hancock was a younger brother. Thomas was educated at a private school in his native town, and after spending his 'earlier days in mechanical pursuits', according to his *Personal Narrative*, he moved to London

Thomas Hancock (1786–1865), by unknown artist

and by 1815 was in partnership with his younger brother John as a coach-builder, with a factory in Pulteney Street and a shop in St James's Street.

About 1819 Hancock became interested in the uses of rubber, hitherto little used because of the problems of importing and working raw natural latex. His experiments to dissolve and manipulate solid rubber began in 1819 and his first patent, of 1820, covered the application of rubber to various articles of dress, to make them more elastic. He eventually made use of thin strips of Pará rubber and produced numerous articles including braces, waistbands and straps at his new factory in Goswell Road. Observing that two freshly cut surfaces of rubber readily adhered by simple pressure, he was led to the invention of the 'masticator', as it was afterwards called, in which a roller set with teeth chewed up pieces of rubber and worked them into a plastic and homogeneous mass. The rubber that emerged from the masticator was then pressed into blocks, or rolled into sheets. The masticating process was never patented, but remained a secret in the factory until about 1832, when it was divulged by a workman. Experiments showed that masticated rubber was much more easily acted upon by solvents than ordinary rubber, and this discovery brought Hancock into communication with Macintosh, the well-known manufacturer of waterproof garments, who carried on business in Manchester. In February 1826 Hancock obtained a licence from Macintosh for the use of the patent to produce double-layer fabrics sealed with rubber. Hancock's masticated rubber was better able to dissolve as a strong solution than that of Macintosh, and in 1830 they agreed that Hancock would supply Macintosh with his masticated rubber. Eventually Hancock became a partner in the firm of Charles Macintosh & Co., though he still carried on his own business in London.

Rubber articles still possessed serious defects due to the material itself; they became sticky, and at low temperatures lost their elasticity. In 1842 specimens of 'cured' rubber, prepared in America by Charles Goodyear according to a secret process, were exhibited in England. Hancock investigated the matter, suspected that sulphur was involved, and filed a provisional patent on 21 November 1843. His experiments were successful: he discovered that when rubber was immersed in molten sulphur a change took place, yielding 'vulcanized' rubber, which was capable of resisting extremes of heat and cold, and was very durable. He was thus able to submit his specification during the six months allowed by the Patent Office. Goodyear had not applied for a British patent. Hancock also discovered inadvertently that if the vulcanizing process was continued, and a higher temperature employed, a hard substance, known as vulcanite or ebonite, was produced. This material was found to be impervious to chemicals and to be electrically insulating, which made it of considerable value to industry.

Hancock took out sixteen patents in all relating to rubber between 1820 and 1847. He displayed remarkable ingenuity in suggesting uses for what was practically a new material, and the specifications of his patents cover the entire field of rubber manufactures, though many of his ideas were not carried out at the time. His brothers Charles, John, Walter, and William were also associated with him, and were concerned in patents for developing various branches of the trade.

Hancock never married. He retired between 1842 and 1845, handing over his business interests to his nephew James Lyne Hancock, and the factory continued in production until 1939, having been taken over by the British Tyre and Rubber Company Ltd. He died of heart and kidney disease on 26 March 1865, at Marlborough Cottage, Green Lanes, Stoke Newington, where he had lived for fifty years.   R. B. PROSSER, rev. ANITA MCCONNELL

Sources T. Hancock, *Personal narrative of the origin and progress of the caoutchouc or India-rubber manufacture in England* (1857); repr. (1920) • F. Duerden, 'Thomas Hancock, an appreciation', *Plastic and Rubber International*, 11 (3 June 1986), 22–6 • patents, 1820–47 • d. cert. • census, 1857

Likenesses Dalziel, woodcut, BM • medallion, Sci. Mus. [*see illus.*] • photograph, Sci. Mus. • portrait, repro. in Hancock, *Personal narrative*

Wealth at death under £60,000: probate, 2 June 1865, *CGPLA Eng. & Wales*

Hancock, Walter (1799–1852), engineer and inventor of steam carriages, was born on 16 June 1799, the sixth son of James Hancock, a timber merchant and cabinet-maker at Marlborough, Wiltshire. Thomas *Hancock (1786–1865), who developed the manufacture of rubber, was his brother. After serving an apprenticeship to a watchmaker and jeweller in London, he turned his attention to engineering, and in 1824 invented a steam engine in which the ordinary cylinder and piston were replaced by two flexible bags, consisting of several layers of canvas bonded with a rubber solution, and alternately filled with steam. The engine having worked satisfactorily at Hancock's factory at Stratford, east London, it occurred to him that its lightness and simplicity of construction made it particularly

Walter Hancock (1799–1852), by R. Roffe, pubd 1836 (after Charles Hancock)

suitable for powering road vehicles—a use for steam traction to which much attention was then being directed.

Hancock's experiments with vehicles using the new engine were not successful; but he continued to work at the subject, carrying out many trials on the roads in and around London, before introducing an experimental steam carriage, the Infant, into passenger-carrying service between Stratford and the City of London in February 1831. In the following year he built another vehicle, the Era, for the London and Brighton Steam Carriage Company, one of many similar commercial concerns which came into existence about that time, when the success of the Liverpool and Manchester Railway had raised the hopes of speculators. The Era was followed by the Enterprise, which was operated by the London and Paddington Steam Carriage Company from April 1833. In October of the same year the Autopsy ran for a short time between Finsbury Square in the City and Pentonville in north London. It ran again in October 1834, alternately with the Erin, between the City and Paddington. Hancock appears to have continued his efforts until about 1840, by which time he had built ten carriages, making many trips through various parts of the country. After that year the success and rapid expansion of the railways led to a decline in public interest in steam-powered road transport, and all the steam carriage companies which had been formed ultimately failed.

Of all the projectors of steam locomotion on the roads, Hancock was the most successful; his vehicles were ingenious and well built, and often performed very well. He afterwards turned his attention to the manufacture and processing of rubber, working with his brother Thomas, and in 1843 he obtained a patent for cutting rubber into sheets, and for a method of preparing rubber solutions. He died on 14 May 1852, at West Ham, Essex.

R. B. PROSSER, *rev.* RALPH HARRINGTON

Sources W. Hancock, *A narrative of twelve years' experiments* (1824–1836) *demonstrative of the practicability and advantage of employing steam carriages on common roads* (1838) · *Mechanics' Magazine*, 10–28 (1831–40)
Likenesses R. Roffe, stipple (after C. Hancock), BM, NPG; repro. in *Mechanic's Magazine* (1836) [*see illus.*]

Hancock, William Neilson (1820–1888), lawyer and economist, was born on 22 April 1820, at Lisburn, co. Antrim, the second son of William John Hancock, land agent and later a poor-law commissioner, and his wife, Mary, daughter of Samuel *Neilson of Belfast, who took part in the 1798 rebellion. He was educated at the Royal Belfast Academical Institution from 1830 to 1834 and at the Royal School, Dungannon, co. Tyrone, from 1834 to 1838. From there he entered the University of Dublin, Trinity College; he graduated BA in 1843 with a senior moderatorship and gold medal in mathematics. Called to the Irish bar in 1844, Hancock took the degrees of LLB in 1846 and LLD in 1849. In 1846 he entered for the quinquennial examination by which the Whately chair of political economy in the University of Dublin was then filled, and was the successful candidate. In some of his published lectures Hancock showed considerable potential as an economic theorist; but since the magnitude of the calamity which the potato blight had brought upon Ireland was becoming evident, Archbishop Whately suggested to him that he give first priority to considering the relevance of economic doctrine to the case of Ireland, and from that time onwards all Hancock's economic work was applied and policy-oriented.

In 1847 Hancock was the prime mover in founding the Dublin Statistical Society (later renamed the Statistical and Social Inquiry Society of Ireland) and he went on to play a major role in the society's development. When the new Queen's College at Belfast opened in 1849, Hancock became its first professor of jurisprudence and political economy, and for the next two years he discharged the duties of both the Dublin and Belfast chairs. In 1851 he took up residence in Belfast, but in the same year he was appointed secretary to the royal commission inquiring into the affairs of Dublin University. He resigned from the Queen's College post in 1853 and thereafter used his economic and legal expertise in a series of public appointments while continuing his legal practice in Dublin.

Hancock once described himself as a 'liberal unionist' and when Liberal governments were in power he was frequently asked for advice or reports on economic and social questions, as well as being appointed to a number of mainly legal offices. He acted as secretary to four other royal commissions between 1854 and 1867 and was clerk of the custody of papers in matters of idiots and lunatics in the court of chancery from 1855 until 1858, and again from 1859 to 1866. From 1863 until 1873 he was responsible for judicial, criminal, and local taxation statistics for

Ireland and gained a high reputation for accuracy and fairness in collecting and compiling them. He became a QC in 1880, but gave up his practice at the bar in 1881 on being appointed keeper of the records of the Irish land commission; his last public appointment brought him back to the Irish court of chancery, as clerk of the crown and hanaper, from which office he resigned in 1885 because of ill health. In 1858 Hancock married Mary Anne (Nannie), daughter of James *Haughton of Dublin. He died, as the result of a heart attack, at Craigpeatton Cove, the Dunbartonshire home of his brother-in-law James Thomson on 10 July 1888. Survived by his wife, he was buried a week later at Mount Jerome cemetery, Harold's Cross, Dublin.

Hancock was an energetic, compassionate, and fair-minded man, eager for economic and political reform, who strove to reconcile the principles of political economy as he knew them with the needs and problems of the Ireland of his time. His initial conviction was that 'the true business of government' was to establish a framework of just laws within which private enterprise could, and would, ensure progress to prosperity. In later life, however, he came to recognize that more positive action by government was necessary and inevitable, particularly on the question of land tenure in Ireland; the advice on which Gladstone acted in framing his Irish Land Bill in 1869–70, the first measure to recognize the tenants' right to compensation for improvements and damages for eviction, came largely from Hancock.

R. D. COLLISON BLACK

Sources J. K. Ingram, 'Memoir of the late William Neilson Hancock', *Journal of the Statistical Society of Ireland*, 9 (1889), 384–93 · W. H. Dodd, 'W. Neilson Hancock', *Belfast Literary Society, 1801–1901: historical sketch* (1902), 105–8 · R. D. C. Black, 'William Neilson Hancock', *The Statistical and Social Inquiry Society of Ireland centenary volume, 1847–1947* (1947), 57–61 · J. McEldowney, 'William Neilson Hancock, 1820–1888', *Irish Jurist*, new ser., 20 (1985), 378–402 · *Irish Times* (13 July 1888) · *Belfast News-Letter* (14 July 1888) · W. N. Hancock, *Impediments to the prosperity of Ireland* (1850) · W. N. Hancock, 'Ireland', *Fortnightly Review*, 33 (1880), 1–25 · d. cert.
Archives NA Ire., papers · NL Ire., papers relating to land question | BL, memoranda and corresp. with W. E. Gladstone, Add. MS 44421 · NA Ire., Official MSS, papers relating to academic appointments, 1848, no. 144; 1853, 9673 · NL Ire., Larcom MSS · PRO NIre., Abercorn MSS, statistical returns signed by Hancock
Likenesses photograph, c.1880, repro. in Black, *Statistical Society of Ireland*, facing p. 2
Wealth at death £9471 17s. 2d.: probate, 3 Aug 1888, CGPLA Ire.

Hand, Thomas (d. 1804), painter, was a follower and assistant of George Morland, and one of his closest companions. His life is shadowy but he exhibited a small landscape with the Society of Artists in 1790, and between 1792 and 1804 was an occasional exhibitor at the Royal Academy. His pictures were painted in Morland's style and are sometimes misattributed to Morland. Hand may even have assisted Morland in the completion of some of his later paintings. He died in London in September 1804. The Tate collection holds a signed *Cottage and Hilly Landscape* by Hand dated 1797.

L. H. CUST, rev. MATTHEW HARGRAVES

Sources Redgrave, *Artists* · Graves, *RA exhibitors* · F. P. Seguier, *A critical and commercial dictionary of the works of painters* (1870) · M. H.

Grant, *A chronological history of the old English landscape painters*, rev. edn, 4 (1959), 354–5 · Waterhouse, *18c painters*

Handasyde, Charles (*fl.* **1751–1776**), miniature painter, is first heard of in an advertisement dated 1 October 1751, which stated that Handasyde had:

> returned from Tunbridge Wells and now lodges at Mr. Brooksby's, Milliner, in Pall Mall; where he continues to draw likenesses in India ink on vellum at 1 guinea apiece and in black lead at ½ a guinea. One hour's sitting only required. (Foskett, 555)

He exhibited two miniatures in enamel and two in watercolour at the Incorporated Society of Artists in 1761, and three miniatures in enamel and one in watercolour at the Free Society of Artists in 1762. In 1765 he received a premium from the Society of Arts for a historic painting in enamel. In 1776, from 3 Hatton Street, London, he exhibited a portrait miniature in enamel at the Royal Academy. He mezzotinted two or three small portraits of himself. On the back of an impression of one of these he is described as 'Mr. Handiside of Cambridge' (BM).

L. H. CUST, rev. EMMA RUTHERFORD

Sources B. S. Long, *British miniaturists* (1929) · D. Foskett, *A dictionary of British miniature painters*, 2 vols. (1972) · L. R. Schidlof, *The miniature in Europe in the 16th, 17th, 18th, and 19th centuries*, 4 vols. (1964) · E. Lemberger, *Meisterminiaturen aus fünf Jahrhunderten* (1911) · J. J. Foster, *Dictionary of painters of miniatures* (1926) · H. Clouzot, *Dictionnaire des miniaturistes sur émail* (Paris, [1924])
Likenesses C. Handasyde, self-portrait, etching, BM · C. Handasyde, self-portraits, mezzotint, BM · C. Sharp, mezzotint, BM

Handel, George Frideric (1685–1759), composer, was born on 23 February 1685 at his family's home on the corner of Kleine Ulrichstrasse and Grosser Schlamm (now Grosse Nikolaistrasse) in Halle-an-der-Saale, then recently transferred from Saxony to Brandenburg. He was the second son of Georg Händel (1622–1697), surgeon, and his second wife, Dorothea Elisabeth (1651–1730), daughter of Georg Taust, pastor of Giebichenstein. The English form of Handel's name is found consistently in signatures on documents that he signed with the full form, the earliest surviving example being on a letter dated 29 June 1716 concerning payment of a dividend on South Sea stock. The register of his baptism at the Lutheran Liebfrauenkirche (also Marienkirche or Marktkirche) in Halle on 24 February 1685 gives his name as Georg Friederich Händel, but Friedrich is the form of his second name found on the signature in the matriculation register of the University of Halle (1702) and on his surviving letters in German. In Italy he mainly used the form G. F. Hendel. The date of his birth is given authoritatively in the funeral sermon for his mother, printed in 1731.

Family and education Handel's grandfather Valentin Händel (1582–1636) was a coppersmith from Breslau who had settled in Halle early in the seventeenth century. His father, Georg Händel, was the sixth son of Valentin, on whose death the coppersmith's business passed to Georg's elder brothers; Georg himself took up the career of surgeon and barber, and was apprenticed to Andreas Beger (a son-in-law of the musician William Brade) and

George Frideric Handel (1685–1759), by Philip Mercier, *c.*1730

Christoph Oettinger. When the latter died Georg married his widow and took over Oettinger's medical practice. From 1645 he was also surgeon for Halle's northern suburb of Giebichenstein. His career must have prospered, for in 1666 he bought a substantial house in the centre of Halle, at which he also renewed the licence for selling wines. By then he had the title *Geheimer Cammerdiener und Leib-Chirurgo* ('chamber servant and personal surgeon') at the court of Duke August of Saxony, who reigned from Halle as administrator of the former episcopal principality of Magdeburg; his appointment was continued (as chamber servant and honorary surgeon) by the administration of the elector of Brandenburg in Halle from 1680, and he later received promotions. In 1682 his first wife (and his eldest son) died during an epidemic, and on 23 April he married Dorothea Elisabeth Taust at Giebichenstein.

The first child of this second marriage, a son, died soon after his birth in 1684; the second son, Georg Friedrich, born early the next year, fared better, as did his sisters Dorothea Sophie (1687–1718) and Johanne Christianne (1690–1709). Of the children from Georg senior's first marriage, two daughters (who probably lived in the family home) died in 1687 and 1690, the other daughter had married in 1668, and the surviving son, Karl (1649–1711), had followed in his father's profession and become surgeon to Duke Johann Adolf I of Saxe-Weissenfels.

For information on Handel's youth and the early part of his career the principal source is John Mainwaring's biography of the composer, published anonymously in 1760. More than half of the biographical text describes Handel's

life before he went to London: most of the material probably came, directly or indirectly, from the composer himself during his last years, and, while the chronology of some events is in doubt, the substance of the narrative is convincing. From this source come the stories of his father's opposition to Handel's early enthusiasm for music, the smuggling of a clavichord into the attic of the family home so that secret practice could be undertaken, and the young child's determination to accompany his father on a visit to his half-brother at Weissenfels, as a result of which the duke heard Handel playing the organ and persuaded his father to provide the child with a proper musical education. About 1692–3 Handel became a student of Friedrich Wilhelm Zachow (1663–1712), organist of the Liebfrauenkirche in Halle's market place, where Handel had been baptized: the training he received was probably in keyboard music and composition, and according to Mainwaring he found himself deputizing at the church for his master, who had a 'love of company, and a chearful glass' (Mainwaring, 15). During the following years he also became proficient in playing the violin (and possibly the oboe), though the organ, harpsichord, and clavichord received his principal attention.

On 14 February 1697 Handel's father died, and young Georg contributed to a collection of memorial poems. In the following years he presumably continued his studies under Zachow and received a good general education at the *Gymnasium*: his letters and business dealings in later life suggest that he never had problems with literacy or numeracy and that he took an interest in languages, literature, and fine art as well as music. On 10 February 1702, just before his seventeenth birthday, he enrolled at the University of Halle; it is not known which faculty he attended, but he may have contemplated an eventual career as a lawyer, as his father had apparently wished.

Professional experience in Halle and Hamburg On 13 March 1702 Handel was appointed organist of the Domkirche in Halle, for a probationary year in the first instance. This helped relieve his mother of financial obligation for supporting him during his time as a student: the post carried a salary of 50 thalers a year and the right to a free lodging in the Moritzburg Castle. The Dom, as part of the former property of the archbishop of Magdeburg, was now administered by the Prussian court (as that of Brandenburg had become in 1701), who paid his salary. His musical duties were not as extensive as those at the Liebfrauenkirche because the liturgical practices were Calvinist: the Dom had been granted to Halle's Huguenot community, who had settled in the city with official encouragement in 1686. The organist's attendance was required on 'Sundays, Thanksgiving Days and other Feast Days, to play the organ fittingly at Divine Service, and for this purpose to pre-intone the prescribed Psalms and Spiritual Songs' (Burrows, *Handel*, 10).

At this time Handel seems also to have formed a friendship with Georg Philipp Telemann (1681–1767), then a student in Leipzig, about 20 miles from Halle and the closest comparable city. Telemann, while formally studying law, was active in his pursuit of music, in which he currently enjoyed a more diverse career than Handel: in 1702 he founded a student *collegium musicum* (concert society) and became conductor at the opera house. His friend's activity may have stimulated Handel to look for a career beyond the opportunities offered by his native city. From Halle it would have been natural to investigate the possibilities for patronage from the Prussian court at Berlin, which also received distinguished foreign visitors. According to Mainwaring, Handel and his family declined an offer of support (including an offer of musical training in Italy) from Berlin because it would eventually have tied him to court service there, but apparently the effect of the visit was that, on his return to Halle, Handel became 'conscious of his own superiority' as a musician (Mainwaring, 26).

Handel initially directed his ambitions to the city state of Hamburg. He must have travelled there soon after completing his contractual year at the Dom, where a replacement organist was appointed in September 1703. Hamburg's principal attraction was the opera house, supported by the city and founded in 1678, though the city also had a flourishing tradition in church music and there were opportunities for private music teaching among the international diplomatic and mercantile community. The opera house's leading manager and composer, Reinhard Keiser, had connections in Weissenfels and Leipzig which may have been useful in Handel's transition to his new environment, and he formed a new friendship soon after his arrival with the composer and tenor singer Johann Mattheson (1681–1764). Mattheson subsequently wrote several books on musical subjects and recorded various stories about the exploits of the two young musicians, though his narrative was coloured by the deterioration of his relationship with Handel. In the summer of 1703 they travelled together to Lübeck to investigate the prospects for an appointment as organist of the Marienkirche, from which Dietrich Buxtehude was on the point of retiring, but nothing came of this, partly because the successor was expected to marry Buxtehude's daughter.

Handel's first job at the opera house was, according to Mattheson, as a back-desk violinist in the orchestra, but in about a year he advanced to a place at the harpsichord (from which the operas were directed) and as a composer. This was not achieved without some professional jealousy: Mattheson relates that, after a dispute about the occupancy of the harpsichord seat at a performance of Mattheson's opera *Cleopatra* on 5 December 1704, he and Handel fought a duel outside the opera house, the bad consequences of which were prevented when Mattheson's sword hit a metal button on Handel's coat. By then Handel had one, and possibly two, operas of his own ready for performance: his first, *Almira*, opened in Hamburg on 8 January 1705, and the second, *Nero*, followed on 25 February. He wrote at least one more opera for Hamburg which, according to the librettist Heinrich Hinsch, was so extensive that it had to be divided into two works, and these (*Florindo* and *Daphne*) had to wait for performance until January 1708. By that time Handel was no longer based in Hamburg, though he possibly returned briefly for the performances. Of his Hamburg opera

scores, only *Almira* survives in anything like a complete state, and it must be regarded as his earliest surviving major work. (There are some church cantatas and trio sonatas that have been ascribed to Handel's earlier years, but their origins are uncertain and their musical features make the attribution to Handel unlikely.) *Almira* is a colourful, rather prolix, opera well suited to the spectacle-seeking Hamburg audiences of the time.

The other principal surviving music that can be attributed to Handel's Hamburg years is for keyboard, some of it having perhaps been composed for concerts at the home of John Wych, the British resident, or as material for teaching his son. The Hamburg music suggests that Handel had a solid musical technique but a tendency to heaviness in his vocal writing, and the critical period in his development as a composer may well have been his period in Italy about the years 1707–9, which gave fluency and breadth to his style. According to Mainwaring, Handel had been offered a passage to Italy by a member of the Medici family who was on a visit to Hamburg, but he preferred to go 'on his own bottom' (Mainwaring, 41).

Italy, 1707–1709 Handel travelled to Italy during the second half of 1706, perhaps overland to Florence (as Mainwaring's account suggests) or perhaps directly by boat to Venice. He was probably the 'Saxon' who was reported as playing the organ at the church of St John Lateran in Rome on 14 January 1707; his cantata *Il delirio amoroso* is noted in the financial accounts of Cardinal Pamphili for 12 February. The manuscript of *Dixit dominus*, endorsed as having been composed at Rome in April 1707, is Handel's earliest surviving dated musical autograph, although other surviving undated manuscripts may predate it. It shows Handel as a master of exuberant concerted music for voices and orchestra, suggesting previous experience in the composition of church music for which there is now no relevant musical documentation.

Rome was one of Handel's principal centres during his Italian years. It did not provide direct opportunities for extending his operatic career since public opera was currently under a papal ban, though fine singers were employed by the musical patrons, as also were some internationally famous instrumentalists including Arcangelo Corelli. Handel's Roman repertory therefore principally comprises church music and secular cantatas: he composed outstanding works in both genres, and the cantatas in considerable quantity. His Roman patrons included Cardinal Colonna for church music, particularly relating to celebrations of the Carmelite festival, Marchese (subsequently Prince) Ruspoli for cantatas and church music, and Cardinal Pamphili for cantatas; he may also have been supported by Cardinal Ottoboni. Handel's music received essentially private performances at the palaces and estate churches of these patrons, and he was probably an honoured resident at their palaces. It was to Handel's Roman patrons that his first oratorios too owed their existence: Cardinal Pamphili was responsible for initiating the composition of *Il trionfo del Tempo e del Disinganno* (1707), and Prince Ruspoli for *La resurrezione* (1708), both works being performed in the patrons' palaces. *La resurrezione* enjoyed elaborate resources in the way of performers and a scenic setting: in spite of its private venue, the first performance (on Easter Sunday) received a papal rebuke for the employment of a woman to sing the role of Mary Magdalene, and a castrato was hastily engaged to take over the role for the repeat performance next day.

The cantatas and oratorios gave Handel the opportunity to develop his skills in the operatic forms of recitative and aria, and his first full Italian opera, *Vincer se stesso è la maggior vittoria*, now known as *Rodrigo*, written for performance in Florence towards the end of 1707, was probably mainly composed in Rome. Taken as a whole *Rodrigo* is competent opera, but *Agrippina*, written for Venice two years later, marks a considerable step forward, with its lively treatment of a racy plot involving dynastic jealousies, and with arias that are musically memorable as well as workmanlike. *Agrippina* was given as the first opera of the carnival season in December 1709, and Handel may also have been to Venice for the carnival in one or both of the previous years, when (according to Mainwaring) he met 'Scarlatti' (probably Alessandro): Mainwaring also relates a friendly competition between Handel and Domenico Scarlatti in Rome, at which Scarlatti was judged the better player on the harpsichord and Handel on the organ. In the year between his two operas Handel had an expedition to Naples in June–July 1708, when he composed an extended dramatic cantata, *Aci, Galatea e Polifemo*, for the wedding celebrations of the duke of Alvito, a continuo-accompanied Italian trio, and perhaps a couple of cantatas.

During his time in Italy, spanning just over three years, Handel thus managed to work and to gain experience in four major musical centres, but travel between them necessitated journeying through the Italian theatre of the War of the Spanish Succession. Handel's patrons were divided in their allegiances. The duke of Alvito supported the emperor, and Naples had passed from Spanish to Austrian control in 1707: on the other side, Ruspoli led a mercenary expedition from Rome against the Habsburgs in 1708. Rome's 'Arcadian' literary world, which is reflected in the pastoral texts of many cantatas, may have been partly a reaction to the harsh realities of contemporary politics, and Handel must have steered his way skilfully around the political and military hazards as he moved from one patron to another. The texts of a couple of Italian cantatas written for Ruspoli seem to make specific political reference to Ruspoli and to the pope as 'protectors' of Rome, and it was in Rome that Handel wrote his French and Spanish cantatas, one in each of the languages of the principal nations that were in friendly alliance with Rome.

Hanover and London, 1710–1715 Handel's time in Italy was successful professionally and artistically, but he did not decide to make a permanent career there. Mainwaring attributes this partly to Handel's discomfort with the prospect of living in a Roman Catholic culture, but it seems equally likely that he judged that a more satisfactory and permanent career might be found elsewhere in Europe, where there were plenty of Italian opera houses and courts that offered diverse musical opportunities. According to Mainwaring, Handel had received a warm invitation to visit London from Charles Montagu, fourth earl of Manchester, British ambassador in Venice, and there he also probably made contact with two dignitaries from the court of Hanover: Prince Ernst, the elector's brother, and Johann Adolf, Baron Kielmansegg, deputy master of the horse. Handel departed from Venice early in 1710, travelling north via Innsbruck (which he had left by 9 March). At some stage during the year he visited his mother in Halle. He arrived at Hanover early in June and was appointed kapellmeister to the court there on 16 June, with an annual salary of 1000 thalers. Letters from the dowager electress Sophia to her daughter Sophia Charlotte, queen of Prussia, speak enthusiastically of Handel's keyboard playing, which gave particular pleasure to Electoral Prince George Augustus and Princess Caroline. She also reported that he was 'quite a handsome man' (Burrows, *Handel*, 30), and that it was rumoured that he had been the lover of Vittoria Tarquini, a singer whom Handel had encountered in Italy and who was married to Jean-Baptiste Farinel, now the Hanover konzertmeister. This story is also mentioned by Mainwaring, and is the only documented hint of any sexual liaison during the composer's lifetime.

Hanover had supported a flourishing court opera company during the 1690s under Agostino Steffani's leadership, but changing financial circumstances had brought this to an end in 1698. It is possible that Handel's appointment was made with a view to a revival of the court opera or in anticipation of the prospective dynastic inheritance of the British crown. The kapellmeister apparently did not have much work to do at Hanover in 1710: from Handel's period of service there the only compositions that can be identified are a few Italian duets (a genre that Princess Caroline seems to have favoured), a few cantatas, and possibly some instrumental music. Handel's underemployment was apparently sympathetically considered at court: according to Mainwaring, when the post was offered at Hanover, Handel indicated that he had promised to visit the elector palatine and that he also intended to visit London, but was assured that 'neither his promise nor his resolution should be superseded by his acceptance of the pension proposed. He had leave to be absent for a twelve-month or more, and to go withersoever he pleased' (Mainwaring, 72). Mainwaring also said that Handel did visit the court at Düsseldorf, where the elector palatine was disappointed to learn that he was engaged elsewhere but nevertheless presented him with 'a fine set of wrought plate for a desert' (ibid., 74). The composer's more ambitious destination was London, however, where he must have arrived in November or December 1710.

Handel had probably learned in Venice that an opera company had been formed in London and was just achieving some measure of stability. From January 1708 the opera performers were based at the Queen's Theatre in the Haymarket, managed by Owen Swiny, and in March 1710 for the first time an opera performance was given entirely in Italian. Wordbooks of the operas were sold at the theatres, with the Italian text and English translation on facing pages. The War of the Spanish Succession had also had the effect of driving a number of excellent instrumental musicians to London, and others came to join them, with the result that there was the foundation for a fine permanent orchestra. Handel, as the composer, fitted exactly the opera company's need of the moment.

His first London opera, *Rinaldo*, to a libretto that was the joint work of Aaron Hill (effectively the opera manager for the 1710–11 season) and Giacomo Rossi, opened at the Queen's Theatre on 24 February 1711. The plot, a crusader story taken from Torquato Tasso's *La Gerusalemme liberata*, was given a colourful treatment that resembled the traditions of the Hamburg theatre (and to some extent also the English masque dramas from preceding decades), and made good use of the theatre's scenic effects: as *The Spectator* described it on 6 March 1711, the opera was 'filled with Thunder and Lightening, Illuminations and Fireworks'. Handel directed the performances from the harpsichord, as was customary, and the final aria in act II incorporated a harpsichord solo: the opera thus introduced him to the London public as performer, director, and composer. Equally significant for his reception in London was a private performance, presumably of arias and keyboard music, in which he took part with other opera performers before Queen Anne on her birthday (6 February) at St James's Palace: this seems to have replaced the performance of the court ode which was traditionally provided by the poet laureate and set to music by the master of the queen's music. The opera season ended in June 1711, and Handel returned to Hanover, via Düsseldorf.

By October 1712 he was back in London, completing his score of a second opera for London, *Il pastor fido*, on 24 October. This received its first performance at the Queen's Theatre on 22 November, and was soon followed by another opera, *Teseo* (completed 19 December 1712, first performance 10 January 1713). *Teseo* marked Handel's first collaboration with the librettist Nicola Haym, who was also a cellist in the opera orchestra and a composer. By the time *Teseo* received its first performance Handel was also engaged in the composition of settings of the English texts of the Te Deum and the Jubilate in anticipation of London's forthcoming celebrations for the peace of Utrecht. In a letter from Hanover, probably written in the summer of 1711, Handel was reported to be learning the English language seriously, and his first English anthem, 'As pants the hart', for the Chapel Royal choir, was probably composed towards the end of 1712. Handel's Utrecht music, and the related ode for the queen's birthday, *Eternal Source of Light Divine*, together reflect a conscious decision by Handel to make his mark in English-language musical genres that were normally the domain of the leading English court composers. The Utrecht thanksgiving service in St Paul's Cathedral on 7 July, and the preceding musical rehearsals, attracted attention from the public and from the newspapers. Towards the end of the opera season Handel had also contributed another Italian opera, *Silla*, the wordbook for which is dated 2 June 1713 but whose performance history is uncertain.

Handel's Utrecht music marked a turning point, not only because it was the composer's first major work in the English language and related to musical settings for the Anglican liturgy in a tradition that derived from Henry Purcell's orchestrally accompanied setting of the Te Deum and Jubilate of 1694, but also because it indicated a conscious attachment to the British court, at the expense of his position at Hanover. In June and July 1713 Handel became the subject of diplomatic correspondence between London and Hanover, as representatives of the Hanover court in London tried to mediate on his behalf following the elector's decision to dismiss his kapellmeister. His dismissal had taken place before the Utrecht service was performed, and the correspondence mentions Handel's wish to 'enter the Queen's service' (Burrows, *Handel*, 72). Handel was rewarded with an annual pension of £200 granted by the queen on 28 December 1713, but his status as a foreigner prevented him from receiving any office under the crown. The originality of Handel's music, and the influence that he seems to have established quickly at court, apparently enabled his music to be accepted for a national and Anglican celebration without any evidence of protest. The web of political interests that affected Handel at this time was complex: the elector of Hanover, while dismissing Handel, must have been aware that his own succession to the British throne would not be far distant and he would soon have dealings with the composer on another basis. When the elector succeeded as George I following the death of Queen Anne in August 1714, William Croft provided the new music for the coronation, but Handel's music was performed at the Chapel Royal for the services which marked the arrivals of members of the Hanoverian family in London. As king, the new ruler had no grounds for difficulty in his relations with Handel, and he continued the pension begun by Queen Anne: as elector, he finally tidied up the situation with the payment of some arrears of the Hanover salary to Handel in October 1715, possibly after a royal water party on the River Thames at which Handel's music was played, though the best-documented account of a performance of Handel's 'Water Music' comes from 17 July 1717.

London and Cannons, 1715–1720 Having established himself in London in 1713, Handel nevertheless did not contribute any new operas to the 1713–14 opera season, though he apparently had a good working relationship with the new manager, John Jacob Heidegger. His next opera, *Amadigi*, received its first performance at the King's Theatre (as it was now called) on 25 May 1715. Heidegger's dedication in the wordbook of the opera to Richard Boyle, third earl of Burlington, said that the opera had been 'composed in your own Family' (Deutsch, 67), and this has been taken to mean that Handel lived for some time at Burlington House. Mainwaring also mentioned that in his early years in London, Handel lived with a Mr Andrews of Barn-Elms (now Barnes), but there is very little firm evidence about Handel's residences or his lifestyle for the first twelve years of his career in London.

From both musical and dramatic aspects, *Amadigi* is arguably the best of Handel's early London operas, though it lacked the spectacular stage effects that had characterized *Rinaldo* and ensured its better survival in the theatre repertory. *Rinaldo* and *Amadigi* were performed again early in 1717, but by then Heidegger's opera company was near to financial collapse: the company's final performance was given on 29 June. Prospects for subsequent revival of the fortunes of the King's Theatre were set back as a result of a dispute within the royal family which resulted in the prince and princess of Wales being excluded from the court, with wider consequences in the division of the patronage base on which the opera house depended. Handel's response to this difficult situation was to find another outlet for his music with the musical establishment supported by James Brydges, earl of Carnarvon and (from 1719) duke of Chandos. For Carnarvon he composed eleven anthems and a Te Deum that were performed in the recently renovated church of St Lawrence adjoining Carnarvon's estate at Cannons in Edgware during 1717–18. His first extended English dramatic works, *Acis and Galatea* and *Esther*, were also composed at this time. *Acis and Galatea* was certainly performed at Cannons, and *Esther*, his first English oratorio, probably was too. Both works in their Cannons forms seem to have been written as a single succession of scenes without an interval, and they used the full performing resources that Carnarvon was able to employ. It is uncertain whether either work was presented in fully staged form or as a concert work in a scenic setting. The Cannons anthems followed up Handel's experience in English church music from the Utrecht music, but in a different musical context, since the anthems were written for chamber-scale performance: one of them, indeed, was an adaptation of the Utrecht Jubilate. Handel apparently lived at Cannons at least occasionally in 1717–18.

Handel's association with Cannons is important not only for the music composed there, but also as an indication that he had decided that his professional future lay in England: he did not, as the opera company broke up, seek an alternative career by returning to the continent. While the court did not patronize theatre companies or musical performances in the official manner that was normal in other European centres, nevertheless Handel probably recognized that the Hanoverian dynasty would probably provide support to him in the longer term: his own early achievements in English church music, on the other hand, gave his reputation a certain independence in London when he was in danger of being identified unfavourably with Hanoverian interests. Effectively, therefore, his time at Cannons was a waiting period while the personal and political disputes at court were settled and until a new opera company could be formed. He may have returned briefly to Germany in 1716, and he certainly planned to do so towards the end of 1718. In a letter written to his brother-in-law in Halle on 20 February 1719 he apologized that he had been unable to depart for his planned visit because of 'unavoidable business on which my future depends' (Burrows, *Handel*, 102). This 'business' was the plan for the foundation of a new opera company, the Royal Academy of Music—a title clearly making reference

to the French court opera, but planned as a joint-stock company with an impressive list of subscribers from the nobility and gentry. In May 1719 the king granted the company £1000, and it received its royal charter on 27 July. By then Handel had left London, travelling via Halle to Dresden, where he attended a lavish opera season at the Saxon court and negotiated with the singers to secure their future services in London. The main target of his attention was the castrato Francesco Bernardi, known as Senesino. At a meeting of the directors of the academy on 30 November Handel was appointed 'Master of the Orchestra with a Sallary' (Deutsch, 97), and he probably returned to London about the turn of the year 1719–20; in his absence preparations for the employment of the orchestral players had proceeded and intricate negotiations were under way to complete the cast of singers. Handel composed a new opera, *Radamisto*, for the academy's first season, but it was not performed on the academy's opening night, 2 April. Instead, Handel's opera was apparently held back until a diplomatic reconciliation between the king and the prince of Wales (and their respective political supporters) had been effected. The first night of *Radamisto*, on 27 April, was also the first public event that the king and the prince attended together: the printed libretto bore a dedication in English, over Handel's name, to the king.

The following November Handel published, apparently on his own account, a set of eight keyboard suites under the title *Suites de pieces pour le clavecin*, many of the movements of which he had probably composed or revised while at Cannons. One movement includes the set of variations on a theme that later became known as the 'Harmonious Blacksmith', associated in sentimental fiction with the local Cannons smithy. The set also included a prefatory note over Handel's name, concluding: 'I will still proceed to publish more reckoning it my duty … to serve a nation from which I have receiv'd so generous a protection' (Deutsch, 117–18). In preparation for the publication, Handel had secured a royal privilege (dated 14 June 1720) for the 'sole printing and publishing' of his music 'for the Term of Fourteen years' (ibid., 105).

The Royal Academy of Music, 1720–1727 The London opera seasons normally ran from late autumn through to the following spring or early summer, so the opening of the academy in April 1720 left only a short performing span for the first season. Senesino was not available at this time, and *Radamisto* in effect received a relaunch in December 1720 with a revised score incorporating him into the title role. *Radamisto* set the tone for the academy operas with plots involving dynastic jealousies and themes of love and duty, and it was also typical in that its libretto was based on an earlier one that had seen performance (with music by another composer) in Italy. Working principally with Haym and with Paolo Rolli, who adapted the Italian texts to forms suitable for London performers and London conditions, Handel produced a succession of impressive operas in the following years. Apart from *Radamisto*, his only contribution to the 1720–21 season was act III of *Muzio Scevola*, an opera composed jointly with Filippo Amadei (act I) and Giovanni Bononcini (act II). His subsequent operas (with dates of first performance) were: *Floridante* (9 December 1721), *Ottone* (12 January 1723), *Flavio* (14 May 1723), *Giulio Cesare in Egitto* (20 February 1724), *Tamerlano* (31 October 1724), *Rodelinda* (13 February 1725), *Scipione* (12 March 1726), *Alessandro* (5 May 1726), and *Admeto* (31 January 1727). He reached a peak about 1724–5 with *Giulio Cesare*, *Tamerlano*, and *Rodelinda*, which have scores of sustained musical quality, conveying credible characters through dramas with convoluted plots. These are also some of Handel's longest operas: *Giulio Cesare*, for example, has nearly four hours of music, and the leading characters (Cesare and Cleopatra) have eight arias each. Although there are some similarities in the themes that the plots develop, the academy operas received clearly distinguished scenic settings, and the singers' roles developed individual characterization beyond generic operatic stereotypes.

Most of Handel's academy operas were given at least a dozen performances in the seasons of their first introduction, and the seasons as a whole ran to more than fifty performances each, for which Handel presumably had overall responsibility as 'Master of the Orchestra'. The varied contributions to the score of *Muzio Scevola* provide a reminder that, in the early years at least, Handel was not the only house composer for the academy. In the early years of the academy Handel and Bononcini were perceived to be in rivalry, and this is reflected in John Byron's epigram which concludes:

> Strange all this difference should be
> 'Twixt Tweedle-dum and Tweedle-dee.
> (Deutsch, 180)

In fact, the musical styles of the composers were clearly distinct. In practice, the opera-goers were more interested in the company's singers than in the composers, and public attention focused on Senesino and the successive leading ladies—Margherita Durastanti in the early years and then Francesca Cuzzoni from her arrival at the end of 1722. A new situation arose when Faustina Bordoni joined the company in 1726: the scores of *Alessandro* and *Admeto* reflect the need to provide leading female roles for both Cuzzoni and Faustina. The coincidence of the South Sea Bubble with the foundation of the academy provoked satirical comment, but the first seasons were successful financially as well as artistically: following the 1721–2 season the academy even declared a dividend. Bononcini was dismissed from the academy in October 1722, leaving Handel as the principal composer.

Handel's other principal activity was in the area of church music. In 1724 and 1726 he composed anthems and Te Deums for services at the Chapel Royal marking George I's return from his visits to Hanover, and in 1722 he probably contributed similarly to a Chapel Royal service marking the king's return to St James's Palace from Kensington at the time of the Atterbury plot. On 25 February 1723 he was granted a second annual pension of £200 as 'Composer of Musick for the Chapel Royal'. In July of that year he also moved into the new house in Brook Street, Westminster, which became his home for the remainder of his life. By 1723–4 Handel had also become music teacher to

the prince of Wales's elder daughters, thereby adding yet another £200 annually to his income. The eldest, Princess Anne, seems to have been Handel's favourite student, and she became one of the composer's firmest supporters.

The Naturalization Act to which George I gave his assent on 20 February 1727 included Handel's name as an addition to the original text. It allowed the petitioners all property and legal rights, but excluded them from holding civil or military office or from being members of parliament or of the privy council. Following the deaths of George I in June and William Croft in August, George II—according to an annotation in one copy of Mainwaring's biography—insisted that Handel, rather than Croft's obvious successor, Maurice Greene, should compose the music for the forthcoming coronation. Handel took full advantage of the opportunity, producing in his coronation anthems (and particularly in 'Zadok the priest') works that formed a memorable and powerful adornment to the ceremony: the 'grand style' of the Utrecht music was presented once again before a glittering and influential audience. The coronation took place at Westminster Abbey on 11 October, preceded by two public rehearsals of the music. The influence of the anthems reappeared a few years later when Handel turned to theatre oratorio in English.

Extending the academy, 1727–1734 In 1727 the new academy season began early, on 30 September, in order to take advantage of the presence of the opera patrons in London for the coronation. A revival of *Admeto* was followed by a new opera, *Riccardo primo* (first performance 11 November), which, since its subject was Richard I, was apposite for the coronation season, though Handel had drafted the score in May, while George I was still alive. Two new operas from Handel followed in the new year, *Siroe* (17 February 1728) and *Tolomeo* (30 April). On 1 June the ninth and last academy season closed. There had been institutional and personal tensions within the venture for some time. More seriously, the academy had called in all its available capital, and the patrons who had provided their support in 1719–20 were now less enthusiastic. Handel and Heidegger nevertheless tried to raise a subscription for a further season, and on 18 January 1729 they came to an agreement with the academy managers. They were granted use of the theatre and the academy's capital assets (including costumes and scenery) for five seasons—that is, until the summer of 1734—and Handel set off for Italy and Germany soon afterwards to secure a cast of singers for the autumn. He returned to London on 29 June; on 10 October he performed with the opera soloists before the king and queen at Kensington Palace, and the opera season opened, with Handel's new opera *Lotario*, on 2 December. On 11 August Handel had lost an important professional colleague with the death of Haym, and this probably emphasized further the extent to which he had now to rely on his own resources.

Together, Handel and Heidegger managed to sustain five performing seasons at the King's Theatre, presumably raising a subscription for each season separately, and Senesino returned as the leading man in the autumn of 1730.

Handel's new operas for the period were *Partenope* (24 February 1730), *Poro* (2 February 1731), *Ezio* (15 January 1732), *Sosarme* (15 February 1732), *Orlando* (20 November 1732), and *Arianna* (26 January 1734); the serenata *Parnasso in festa* (13 March 1734), although less conventionally dramatic, followed the same conventions as the operas. For these opera seasons also Handel presented pasticcio operas of music by other composers in which he had a substantial part in the creative assembly of the components. In general Handel's new operas sustained the musical and dramatic quality of the preceding academy operas, and they were also rather more diverse in character: settings of the more formal librettos by Pietro Metastasio (*Poro*, *Ezio*) were complemented by the more racy *Partenope* (by Silvio Stampiglia) and the Ariosto-derived *Orlando*, featuring spectacular transformations and supernatural visitations at the behest of the magician Zoroastro.

An event that was to have historic consequences for Handel's career was his introduction of an English work for the first time towards the end of his Italian opera season of 1731–2. The work concerned was *Esther* (2 May 1732), a substantially expanded version of his Cannons-period oratorio. This followed a staged performance of the original version by the choristers of the Chapel Royal at the Crown and Anchor tavern on 23 February, which may have been preceded by a private performance at the house of Bernard Gates, a singer in the Chapel Royal choir and master of the children. The version that Handel presented at the King's Theatre used the current opera orchestra and soloists, strengthened by additional singers, some of whom were probably from the major London choirs including the Chapel Royal. The advertisements for the performance said that there would be 'no Action on the Stage' and that the 'Musick' (performers) would be 'disposed after the Manner of the Coronation Service' (Deutsch, 289), and indeed Handel slipped music from his 1727 coronation anthems into the score. A contemporary description suggests that Handel and the leading singers performed from a gallery constructed on the stage. *Esther* apparently proved a popular novelty, and Handel followed it with a similar revival of his other dramatic Cannons piece, *Acis and Galatea* (10 June), this time performed in Italian as a serenata, against a pastoral scenic background, but once again without stage action. With both *Esther* and *Acis and Galatea* Handel had to rearrange and expand the score considerably in order to create a full-length three-act evening as expected by his opera audiences.

In 1732–3 Handel also came before the London public as an instrumental composer, through the publication of sets of sonatas for solo instruments (later sometimes referred to as 'op. 1'), trio sonatas (op. 2), orchestral concertos (op. 3), and a second set of keyboard suites. The music included in these publications was collected from much earlier works, though some of the sonatas and one of the suites had been composed in the 1720s, and the editions themselves were pirated by John Walsh, who apparently produced them on his own initiative before the expiry of the fourteen-year royal privilege that had been granted to

Handel in 1720. In an effort to disguise their origins, Walsh initially put out some copies of the sonatas with spurious title-pages bearing the name of Roger (of Amsterdam) as publisher. Walsh's sources were variable in quality (and included some spurious violin sonatas), but the publications constituted substantial collected editions of Handel's music: indeed, they were almost comprehensive in some areas, for Handel wrote very few new solo sonatas or keyboard pieces after 1734. A collection of fugues, mainly dating back to the Cannons period, followed from Walsh in 1735, under his own imprint and also rather confusingly designated as 'Troisieme Ovarage', since a set of concertos had already appeared as 'Opera Terza'.

Rivalries in London, 1733–1741 In 1732 Handel was apparently successful in his continued management of London's Italian opera, and there were strong hints of the potentially broader appeal of his work through instrumental music and English oratorio. However, there were also undercurrents that threatened the security of his career. Although the musical programme of the opera company remained sound, personal relationships were becoming strained, particularly between Handel and Senesino, and a new generation of opera patrons was emerging for whom Handel and Heidegger represented an old-fashioned taste. A new rival opera company, the Opera of the Nobility, was founded, and this venture coincided with the emergence of the next generation of problems within the royal family. The Opera of the Nobility was to some extent associated with the political dissent that centred around Frederick, prince of Wales, though the prince himself apparently attempted at least a degree of even-handedness in his support of both companies.

The creation of the new opera company was probably under discussion by 1732, but did not come about until 1733. The end of the 1732–3 season was a difficult period for Handel. He introduced a new English oratorio, *Deborah* (17 March 1733), in the latter part of the opera season, but this was accompanied by a controversy over higher ticket prices; moreover, at the last opera performance of the season on 9 June Senesino announced that he would not be returning to Handel's company and, followed by most of Handel's singers, joined the Opera of the Nobility. At the end of the season Handel prepared for a visit to Oxford, where, at the time of the university's celebrations for the commemoration of benefactors, he gave six performances of four English oratorio-style works within a week, including the first performance of a new oratorio, *Athalia* (10 July). His main venue was the Sheldonian Theatre, but he also gave *Acis and Galatea* in the hall at Christ Church and performed various pieces during a service at the university church. It was said at the time that Handel had gone to Oxford to receive a doctoral degree, but there is no formal record that this was offered: for Handel, it was probably sufficient that his visit was well received and (as seems likely) quite profitable. There he may also have met the librettist Charles Jennens for the first time.

On his return to London, Handel assembled a new opera company for the following season at the King's Theatre. In 1733–4 the Opera of the Nobility performed its first season at the Lincoln's Inn Fields theatre, while Handel's agreement for the use of the premier opera theatre in the Haymarket still had one more year to run. Not surprisingly, his rivals had greater ambitions, and from the next season onwards they secured the King's Theatre. In response Handel successfully negotiated with John Rich for the use of his new theatre at Covent Garden, which had opened in December 1732. His new operas for Covent Garden were *Ariodante* (8 January 1735), *Alcina* (16 April 1735), *Atalanta* (12 May 1736), *Arminio* (12 January 1737), *Giustino* (16 February 1737), and *Berenice* (18 May 1737), plus the pasticcio *Didone* (1737). Covent Garden was not exclusively devoted to musical performances, and Handel gained the use of some of Rich's theatrical resources. Among these in the first season was a dance troupe led by Madame Sallé, for whom Handel incorporated important music into performances of *Alcina* and *Ariodante* and composed *Terpsicore* (9 November 1734), a balletic prologue to a revival of *Il pastor fido*.

With *Alcina* and *Ariodante* (and *Arianna*, first performed in the last King's Theatre season), Handel's operas reached a new peak of attractiveness and musical quality comparable to the remarkable works of the mid-1720s, but in a more expansive musical style and taking full advantage of the vocal talents of his new leading castrato, Giovanni Carestini. In 1735 Handel also gave his first substantial run of oratorios (fourteen performances) in the midst of a London opera season, using the Lenten period that would later become his regular oratorio season. He relied on his accumulated repertory (including the first London performances of *Athalia*) rather than writing new works, and he provided Carestini with some Italian arias in the context of otherwise English performances. An important innovation was his introduction of organ concertos, played between the parts of the oratorios or as overtures to the parts: with these he introduced an important new instrumental genre and also re-established himself as a soloist. At the end of the season he lost Carestini, and he had to delay the start of his next season, eventually beginning early in 1736 with a fine new setting of Dryden's *Alexander's Feast* (19 February) and then a succession of works to English texts. With the arrival of a new castrato (Gioacchino Conti) he returned to opera at the end of the season in May–June 1736, and his following season of 1736–7 had a heavy programme, principally of Italian operas but including a new version of his early Italian oratorio as *Il trionfo del Tempo e della Verità* (3 March 1737).

Handel mounted some diverse and attractive programmes during the years when he had to perform in rivalry with the Opera of the Nobility, though it was difficult to maintain an audience against a company that had Farinelli as well as Senesino for its leading roles. In addition, he may have had to steer a careful path through professional rivalries that affected English as well as Italian musicians. A dispute over the attribution of a madrigal in 1732, which hastened the conclusion of Bononcini's public career in London, may reflect local jealousies which involved Bernard Gates and Maurice Greene, and it seems likely that relations between Handel and Greene were by now rather cool. The situation would not have been improved by a contretemps over the music for Princess Anne's wedding: an anthem for the occasion by Greene was announced and publicly rehearsed, but in the end Handel was given charge of the musical programme for the ceremony on 14 March 1734, which featured his concertos and the anthem 'This is the day'. Handel also provided 'Sing unto God', the anthem for the prince of Wales's wedding on 27 April 1736, and a conflation of the two anthems for the betrothal ceremony for Princess Mary in May 1740.

By the summer of 1737 it was apparent that the Opera of the Nobility was experiencing financial and artistic problems and was not likely to continue in its original form. Handel was indisposed during the last weeks of his own opera season with a 'paraletick disorder' that prevented him from directing his performances from the harpsichord, and in September he went for a health cure to Aix-la-Chapelle, where he reputedly made an astonishingly speedy recovery. At the King's Theatre a subscription season had been arranged for 1737–8, probably managed by Heidegger in association with the remnant of the managers from the Opera of the Nobility and using such performers as were willing to return to London, but not including Farinelli or Senesino. Soon after his return to London (probably at about the time when the opera season began, on 29 October) Handel was approached by the opera company and agreed to write for it, but apparently in circumstances which did not involve him in the management of the company beyond the practical matters concerning his own works. The results were *Faramondo* (3 January 1738) and *Serse* (15 April 1738), and also *Alessandro Severo*, a pasticcio using his own music. As part of the agreement Handel was also given a benefit night at the King's Theatre, at which he performed a miscellany of his own music under the title 'An Oratorio' (28 March 1738) and which may have brought him £1000. The composition of *Faramondo* had been interrupted following the death of Queen Caroline on 20 November 1737, whereupon Handel composed an extended choral anthem, 'The ways of Zion do mourn', for her funeral on 17 December in King Henry VII's chapel, Westminster Abbey. Both this and the revision of the anthem 'As pants the hart' for the benefit performance in March 1738 include movements incorporating themes derived from German chorales, which suggests that Handel may have also visited Germany (or at least obtained a copy of a German hymnbook) during his continental visit in 1737.

The King's Theatre venture failed to raise a subscription for the season of 1738–9, and it seems very likely that his experiences in the preceding season had persuaded Handel that he could not work with the younger generation of aristocratic opera managers led by Charles Sackville, earl of Middlesex, for he seems to have repeatedly turned down requests for further commissions from them in the 1740s. Since the King's Theatre was available, Handel occupied it on his own account for the early months of 1739 and gave a programme beginning with mainly English works including two new oratorios, *Saul* (16 January) and *Israel in Egypt* (4 April). *Saul* marked a significant step into more ambitious dramatic English oratorio, while *Israel in Egypt* was a short-lived experiment in oratorio mainly presented through choral movements. *Saul* was important also as Handel's first substantial collaboration with Charles Jennens as librettist. The nearest to an opera that Handel gave in this season was *Jupiter in Argos*, a 'Dramatical Composition' in Italian that may have been semi-staged and was mostly constructed from Handel's pre-existing music. In September 1738 he had also drafted an opera score, *Imeneo*, which did not come to completion at once. A significant event during the season was a performance of *Alexander's Feast* on 20 March in support of the 'Fund for Decay'd Musicians'. Handel was one of the original members of the charity concerned, the Society of Musicians, which was founded in April 1738 and formalized by a declaration of trust in August 1739. He gave a further benefit night for the fund in 1740.

Although Handel's 1739 season was apparently well received, he probably felt that, unless he could present operas with recognizably first-rate soloists, the King's Theatre was an extravagant venue, and in the two following seasons he gave performances at the neglected theatre at Lincoln's Inn Fields. For the 1739–40 season he presented his first 'all-English' programme in London, beginning on St Cecilia's day (22 November 1739) with *Alexander's Feast* and his new setting of Dryden's shorter *Song [Ode] for St Cecilia's Day*. The major new work of the season was *L'Allegro, il Penseroso ed il Moderato* (27 February 1740), an engaging work based on the alternation of passages from Milton's poems *L'Allegro* and *Il Penseroso*. The libretto was first drafted by James Harris, a Salisbury gentleman whose family were supporters of Handel and who had entertained the composer at his house in 1739: Jennens then collaborated with Handel in revising Harris's text and adding a new part (*Il Moderato*) as a resolution between the moods of the two characters represented in the poems. Also featured in the season were performances of orchestral concertos, which Handel had composed as a set of twelve in September–October 1739: these were published as his op. 6 in April 1740. Subscriptions to the concertos and sales of the first copies were administered from Handel's house, but the publication was the work of John Walsh junior, who had taken over the family business following the death of his father in 1736. Walsh junior seems to have quickly established himself as Handel's approved publisher, for a succession of printed editions appeared which (unlike those of 1732–4) clearly carried the full authority of the composer: a handsome complete score of *Alexander's Feast* in 1737, then the sets of organ concertos op. 4 in 1738, and trio sonatas op. 5 in 1739. The score of *Alexander's Feast* was complemented by an engraved frontispiece with a portrait of Handel; yet more remarkable was the full-size statue of the composer which was commissioned from Louis Roubiliac and set up in the pleasure gardens at Vauxhall in 1738 by its owner, Jonathan Tyers.

In the summer of 1740 Handel travelled to the continent, visiting Haarlem and possibly travelling on to Hanover, Berlin, and Halle: he was back in London by early October. For his second season at Lincoln's Inn Fields in 1740–41 his programme swung back to Italian opera. His two new operas were *Imeneo* (22 November 1740) and *Deidamia* (10 January 1741), and the season included adapted revivals of oratorio-style works in a mixture of Italian and English. With the three performances of *Deidamia* in January–February 1741 Handel gave his last Italian operas in London: the final performance on 10 February was given at the Little Theatre, Haymarket, though the remainder of Handel's programme then continued at Lincoln's Inn Fields.

Dublin, 1741–1742 In July 1741 Handel composed a couple of Italian duets, presumably for singers currently in London, and then between 22 August and 29 October he drafted two major oratorio scores, *Messiah* and *Samson*, which may have been envisaged for a forthcoming London season. *Messiah* was brought near to completion, but *Samson* was left as an unfinished draft, probably because the work was on too ambitious a scale to meet his needs. By the end of October Handel knew that his immediate future lay with a season of performances in Dublin, at the recently inaugurated concert hall in Fishamble Street. The process by which Handel had arranged his Irish visit is not known, but soon after attending the first performance given by the revived opera company of Lord Middlesex at the King's Theatre on 31 October he left London, and he arrived in Dublin on 18 November. As with his sojourn at Cannons in 1717–18, he may have seen the change of venue as both a new opportunity and a timely excuse for absence from London, so that he would be beyond the reach of the politics of the new opera company.

Handel settled quickly in a house in Abbey Street and made contact with the performers in Dublin whom he would need for his concerts, probably including the singers from the choirs of Christ Church and St Patrick's cathedrals, and the instrumentalists associated with the music room, many of whom probably also held appointments as musicians at Dublin Castle, where the violinist Matthew Dubourg was master of the music. It seems that the only principal performer brought by Handel from London was the soprano Christina Avoglio, though he was also accompanied by his music copyist-cum-secretary John Christopher Smith and at least one other copyist.

Handel's initial scheme was a subscription series of six concerts beginning on 23 December 1741. In a letter written to Jennens six days later Handel recounted his satisfaction: the performers were good, the hall was pleasant, he felt inspired in his performances on the organ (presumably in the concertos), and the audience was large, full of eminent people and 'quality', and enthusiastic. The programme consisted of well-tried English works, adapted to local performing conditions, and Handel advertised for a second subscription series of six concerts, to begin on 17 February 1742. A practical problem arose early in 1742 when Jonathan Swift, dean of St Patrick's, banned his singers from taking part with a 'club of fiddlers', and Handel had to look for some new soloists: these included a tenor named Calloghan and Susannah Cibber, the sister of

Thomas Augustine Arne, who was acting in Dublin at Aungier Street Theatre. In his second series Handel included two performances of *Imeneo*, given in concert format as a serenata: these were the last performances of an Italian opera score that Handel directed.

Before the completion of the second subscription series, Handel advertised his new work, *Messiah*, to be given as an additional performance 'For Relief of the Prisoners in the several Gaols' and for the support of Mercers' Hospital and the Charitable Infirmary. It seems that in view of the charitable nature of the event (which began at noon, in contrast to the evening performances of the subscription series), the cathedral choirs were permitted to take part. Both the rehearsal on 9 April and the first performance on 13 April were well attended and well received. Handel gave two further performances in Dublin, presenting *Saul* on 25 May and *Messiah* again on 3 June, both of them apparently on his own account. Mrs Cibber and her sister-in-law Cecilia Arne also sang some of Handel's music at Mrs Arne's benefit concert at Aungier Street Theatre on 21 July. Handel left Dublin for London on 13 August. He settled down to completing the score of *Samson* and to writing a couple more Italian duets. He talked of returning to Dublin for another subscription season in 1744–5, and had clearly enjoyed his year there, but in the event he never returned.

Although probably not originally composed with Dublin in mind, *Messiah* turned out to be an exactly appropriate work to crown Handel's season there, and its success may have been partly attributable to the fact that, probably by intention, Handel presented it as an additional charity performance and not as part of his regular subscription series. For *Messiah* was not like most of his oratorios: his only precedent for a narrative oratorio with texts taken directly from scripture was *Israel in Egypt*, which had not achieved the recognition of works like *Esther*. Furthermore the subject matter of *Messiah*, which dealt directly with the interpretation of events from Christ's life, was potentially sensitive, as Handel found when he introduced the oratorio into his London theatre seasons. Handel's avoidance of directly dramatic characters in *Messiah* is uncharacteristic, as also is the relatively austere scoring. If it is the best of Handel's oratorios of its type, it is also the only one: in the context of Handel's career, it is matched in quality by other excellent works in different types of oratorio, in opera, and in instrumental music. However, it is the character of *Messiah* as well as its quality that has established the oratorio's place as Handel's best-regarded vocal work in the longer history of musical reception.

The oratorio composer, 1743–1749 For some time after his return to London, Handel was cautious about revealing his future plans. However, he must soon have entered into negotiations with Rich for the use of Covent Garden: he sent the libretto of *Samson* to the inspector of plays on 10 January 1743 with a statement of his intention to perform the work there. Between 18 February and 31 March he gave two six-performance subscription series in which *Samson* accounted for nine of the presentations: Horace Walpole

commented on 24 February that 'Handel has set up an Oratorio against the Operas, and succeeds' (Deutsch, 560). The season, fitting into the Lenten period with performances mainly on Wednesdays and Fridays when the regular use of the theatre for plays was restricted, followed a new pattern for Handel but one that would become the foundation of his subsequent career, though not immediately. The season also included the first London performances of *Messiah*, which encountered some controversy concerning the performance of its subject matter in a public theatre. Genuine concerns about its suitability may also have been inflamed in an attempt to undermine Mrs Cibber's return to a successful theatre career in London: she had been involved in a memorable matrimonial court case.

At the end of the season Handel apparently had a return of his health problems, perhaps exacerbated by pressures over *Messiah*. Nevertheless, he had recovered sufficiently by 3 June to begin the composition of two major oratorio-style works for his next season, and also a Te Deum and an anthem in celebration of the successes in the War of the Austrian Succession which were eventually performed in the Chapel Royal (27 November) after George II's return from his participation in the battle of Dettingen. During the summer Handel also had to fend off a very pressing approach from Lord Middlesex's opera company, to which he seemingly acceded initially before changing his mind. His perceived stubbornness on the matter seems to have made him unpopular with the 'opera party' in London and to have given him some trouble for the next couple of seasons, when card parties and alternative entertainments were apparently deliberately promoted on his performing nights. Nevertheless he ran a successful subscription series of twelve performances at Covent Garden during Lent 1744, with the two new major works *Semele* (10 February 1744) and *Joseph and his Brethren* (2 March 1744). The combination of a biblical oratorio with a musical drama (given 'after the manner of an oratorio') on a subject from classical sources was one that he would repeat again the next year.

By the end of the 1743–4 season Lord Middlesex's company had again become unviable, and Handel took advantage of its weakness by planning an ambitious season at the King's Theatre. He announced a subscription series of twenty-four performances, comparable in length to a conventional opera season, beginning on 3 November, initially with performances on Saturday nights only. The season soon ran into difficulties, partly on account of organized opposition from the 'opera party', but mainly because the plan was apparently overambitious in itself: no previous attempt had ever been made to run a similar concert series in a major London theatre over a period of six months. Planned performances in the early part of the season were cancelled as a result of small audiences. Handel had more regular success once the season moved into the familiar Lenten period, but by the time he closed the series on 23 April he had managed to present only sixteen of the promised twenty-four performances. The programme had included the new works *Hercules* (3 January 1745) and *Belshazzar* (27 March 1745).

Not surprisingly, the stresses of the situation brought about a return of Handel's medical problem, and in the summer he travelled to Scarborough to restore his health, visiting on the way the earl of Gainsborough's family at Exton, Rutland (in early June), where he contributed some music to a family production of *Comus*. Soon after his return to London the life of the nation was disrupted by the Jacobite rising under Prince Charles Edward Stuart. Handel contributed a patriotic song to raise the spirits of theatregoers at Drury Lane on 14 November in the face of the Jacobite threat; another song followed the defeat of the Jacobites at Culloden in April 1746. Despite the political insecurity, in February 1746 Handel managed to give three performances at Covent Garden of a new work, the *Occasional Oratorio* (14 February), offering double tickets in order to pay off his obligation for the six performances by which the previous season had fallen short. The oratorio was a morale-boosting piece based on texts (from the Old Testament, Milton, and elsewhere) asserting the ultimate victory of the righteous: as Jennens commented at the time, 'Tis a triumph for a Victory not yet gained' (Burrows, *Handel*, 289).

In the following year Handel fell back into the routine from 1743 and 1744 that served his career for the remainder of his life, presenting oratorio-type works at Covent Garden during the Lenten season. However, there was a radical change in that he abandoned the subscription system, and for the first time relied on the paying audience for each performance. He usually gave about a dozen performances each season, with a repertory of about five works: tickets followed the general level of opera prices, which were rather higher than the normal ticket prices for plays at Covent Garden or Drury Lane. For the 1747 season Handel composed *Judas Maccabaeus* (1 April 1747), an oratorio with a storyline celebrating military victories and with a libretto that was dedicated to William, duke of Cumberland, the victor of Culloden. Two new oratorios rather similar in tone, but rather more subtle in their subject matter and dramatic characters, followed for the 1748 season: *Joshua* (9 March 1748) and *Alexander Balus* (23 March). Between the parts of his oratorios this season Handel presented large-scale orchestral concertos involving complementary groups of wind instruments. This trend reached an impressive climax in 1749 with the 'Music for the Royal Fireworks', performed in Green Park on 27 April as an introduction to the firework display that was part of the official celebrations for the treaty of Aix-la-Chapelle. With this event and the preceding rehearsal at Vauxhall on 21 April, Handel's music enjoyed the largest audience of his lifetime. Handel also contributed some music for the royal thanksgiving service for the peace in the Chapel Royal on 25 April.

The fireworks music followed soon after the completion of Handel's normal oratorio season at Covent Garden, which had included two fine new oratorios, *Susanna* (10 February 1749) and *Solomon* (17 March 1749). After the fireworks, Handel undertook yet another exceptional project by contributing a charity concert in aid of the completion of the chapel of the Foundling Hospital on 27 May 1749: in addition to repeat performances of some of his recent music, the programme included an anthem specially composed for the occasion, now known as the Foundling Hospital anthem. The concert marked an association that remained significant for the rest of the composer's life: the London children's charity may have been related in his mind to the Franckesche Stiftung, the combination of schools and orphanage built in Halle during his youth. The concert itself was a significant social event, attended by the prince and princess of Wales: the Foundling Hospital anthem, and the concert as a whole, concluded with the 'Hallelujah' chorus transferred from *Messiah*, a work that by then Handel had performed only six times in London.

The final decade, 1749–1759 With his oratorio season, the fireworks, and the Foundling Hospital concert, the 64-year-old composer had been on peak form during the summer of 1749; by contrast, the following years saw an abrupt reduction in his activity. In June–July 1749 he drafted one new oratorio for the next season, and he then went to Bath in mid-August. The significance of this need not be exaggerated: by now his stock of oratorios was such that he did not necessarily need to produce two new ones each year, and his visit to Bath may have been for relaxation as much as for attention to a pressing health problem. When he returned to London in September he wrote to Jennens, suggesting the specification for an organ for the chapel in Jennens's Leicestershire home. Just after Christmas he composed music for a planned production of Tobias Smollett's play *Alceste* at Covent Garden. Then, having written a new organ concerto as well, he presented his usual Lenten oratorio season at Covent Garden, introducing his new oratorio *Theodora* (16 March 1750). These works did not receive the attention they deserved, partly because Londoners were disturbed by earthquake tremors. Nevertheless a new castrato singer, Gaetano Guadagni, contributed a welcome musical stimulus to the performances.

Handel had presented the Foundling Hospital with an organ, and the hospital asked him to give a performance to mark its inauguration. He chose to give *Messiah* in the chapel on 1 May 1750, and the event proved so popular that another performance had to be given a fortnight later for the members of the audience who had been turned away the first time. These performances became the start of a tradition whereby Handel gave *Messiah* as the last performance of his Covent Garden season and then presented another performance or two after Easter at the hospital. *Messiah* raised more than £6000 for the charity during Handel's lifetime: the Foundling Hospital performances also played a large part in establishing the reputation of the oratorio. As one member of the audience wrote in 1750 of the first performance at the hospital, 'two or three of the Bishops were there; so that I hope, in a little while, the hearing of oratorios will be held as orthodox' (Burrows and Dunhill). Following the success of the *Messiah* performances, Handel was elected a governor of the hospital on 9 May 1750, without having to pay the conventional £50 donation; unlike Hogarth, however, he never took any active role in the administration of the charity, preferring (as he said) to 'serve the charity in his way' (Burrows, *Handel*, 299). The 1750 performances of *Messiah* at the Foundling Hospital were important musically for the new settings of some movements that Handel composed for Guadagni, including the version of 'But who may abide the day of his coming?' that is most frequently performed today. By the summer of 1749 the *Alceste* project had apparently been abandoned by Covent Garden, and Handel reused most of the music in the course of a one-act 'musical interlude', *The Choice of Hercules*, that he composed in June and July 1750.

In August 1750 Handel travelled to the continent, and he was reported as having been hurt in a coach accident between The Hague and Haarlem. He was in Haarlem on 27 August and 20 September, and in Deventer on 10 September, when he played the organ to the prince and princess of Orange; he played to them again at The Hague at the beginning of December. It is likely that during October and November he had travelled to Germany, and probably made contact with some of his relations. In London on 1 June he had made his will, in which he had named ten of his relations as beneficiaries and his niece (then living in Copenhagen) as executor.

Although Handel had been active in 1750, the only work that he had composed for the next oratorio season had been the single-act 'musical interlude', and on 21 January 1751, only a month before the next oratorio season was due to commence, he began to make good the deficiency by composing a new oratorio, *Jephtha*, to a libretto by Thomas Morell, a collaborator and personal friend at least since 1746. On 13 February, when his draft had reached the last chorus of part II, he had to abandon composition because of problems with the sight in his left eye. He took up the score again and completed part II on 23 February, but by then the oratorio season had already begun, and it seemed unlikely that he would have the opportunity to finish the score. *The Choice of Hercules* received its first performance on 1 March, complementing *Alexander's Feast*; the evening also probably saw the first performance of the organ concerto subsequently published as op. 7 no. 3, which he had composed in the early days of January. This lively concerto, one of the best of the series, was Handel's last written instrumental composition: the autographs for it are clear and fluent, suggesting that Handel's incapacity came upon him quite suddenly during the following month. The theatres were closed following the sudden death of the prince of Wales on 20 March, when Handel was two-thirds of the way through his season, so the London audiences were never aware that he did not have a new complete full-length oratorio for this year.

The organ that Handel had donated to the chapel of the Foundling Hospital was not completed in time for the 1750 performances which should have marked its inauguration, so the 1751 performances of *Messiah* were the first at which it was heard, and Handel was reported as playing a 'voluntary'; it is possible that he was not able to manage a concerto. Certainly the crisis with his health continued: on 14 March he was reported as having lost the sight of one eye. John Christopher Smith junior (a composer, a former pupil of Handel's, and son of his music copyist) was summoned from the continent to assist Handel in the future management of the oratorios, and in the first half of June Handel went to Bath and Cheltenham in the hope of improving his health. On his return to London he managed, with a considerable struggle, to finish the score of *Jephtha*. About this time he also revised the Foundling Hospital anthem, adding some new solo movements: this may have been in anticipation of the opening of the hospital chapel for public worship, which in the end did not take place until April 1753.

With the assistance of Smith junior, Handel performed the usual oratorio season in 1752, *Jephtha* receiving its first performance on 26 February. A revision to an aria for a revival of *Joshua* in this year is probably Handel's last page of musical autograph. According to a newspaper report on 17 August, a return of his 'paraletick disorder' robbed him of the remainder of his sight, and it seems that any residual vision thereafter was sufficient only for him to be able to sign his name on the codicils to his will. In spite of the attendance of William Bromfield and John 'Chevalier' Taylor, Handel was effectively blind for the last seven years of his life. With the assistance of the two Smiths, however, the routines of the oratorio season and the Foundling Hospital performances continued every year: Handel was probably present at most of the performances and even occasionally played a voluntary or a concerto, in the latter improvising solo passages between the orchestral ritornellos of his existing works. Managerial decisions were probably referred to him from time to time, and Handel may have also had some influence on the annual programme. Most of the adaptations needed for revivals of the oratorios were straightforward, such as transpositions of keys of arias, and required no creative input. Some uncertainty surrounds the responsibility for more major changes that were made in 1756 and 1757, when a new pasticcio was created from Handel's previous music to serve as part I for *Israel in Egypt*, and *Il trionfo del Tempo* emerged in an expanded and English form as *The Triumph of Time and Truth*; furthermore, according to Charles Burney, Handel composed the chorus 'Sion now her head shall raise', which was inserted in 1757 oratorio performances. It may be that all these developments were attributable to musical ideas that originated from Handel, and that he was more active at this time, but the musical execution of the new composition is in a style which does not match Handel's work. On one occasion in May 1756 Handel attended a dinner party given by Charles Jennens, but it seems that he did not leave his home much during his last years except for his professional appearances at the oratorio performances, though he went to Tunbridge Wells in August 1758. On 6 April 1759 Handel attended the last oratorio performance of the season (*Messiah*) and intended to travel to Bath soon afterwards; however, he was too ill to do so, and he died at his home in Brook Street, Hanover Square, Westminster, about 8 a.m. on 14 April (Easter Saturday). While the precise cause of his death is still unknown there is no hint of any tragic circumstance. As provided for in his will, he was buried in Westminster Abbey on 20 April 1759, and his monument, for which he had left £600, incorporating a statue of the composer by Roubiliac, was revealed to the public on 10 July 1762.

Personality and achievements Twenty-five years after Handel's death, Charles Burney described him thus:

> The figure of Handel was large, and he was somewhat corpulent, and unwieldy in his motions; but his countenance, which I remember as perfectly as that of any man I saw but yesterday, was full of fire and dignity; and such as inspired ideas of superiority and genius. He was impetuous, rough, and peremptory in his manners and conversation, but totally devoid of ill-nature or malevolence: indeed, there was an original humour and pleasantry in his most lively sallies of anger or impatience, which, with his broken English, were extremely risible. His natural propensity to wit and humour, and happy manner of relating common occurrences, in an uncommon way, enabled him to throw persons and things into very ridiculous attitudes. (Burney, *Account*, 'Sketch', 31–2)

Burney would first have known the composer in his mid-fifties, and there are no comparable descriptions relating to the early part of his career; furthermore, many of the anecdotes that might be considered revealing of his character are known only from sources dating from between 1780 and 1857, and it is impossible to distinguish authentic matter from sentimental invention. The tone of the recollections found in Mainwaring, Burney, and Hawkins, and reflected in some of the later anecdotes, indicates the presence of a forceful personality which had a strong influence on those who encountered him. His surviving letters are generally unrevealing: some are rather business-like and those to his brother-in-law are rather formal, but in the letters to Jennens from 1741–4 we can hear something of his 'voice', with a lively (and commanding) use of the English language.

Letters from Handel survive in English, French, and German; according to a source quoted by Burney, in conversation with Handel 'it was requisite for the hearer to have competent knowledge of at least four languages: English, French, Italian and German; for in his narratives he made use of them all' (Burney, *Hist. mus.*, 2.1007). He was also probably fluent in Latin, and at Rome in 1707 he set a cantata text in Spanish. It is difficult to know how seriously to take Burney's reference to his 'broken English', for his English letters show no serious deficiency in vocabulary or syntax in the context of the language as it was used in the first half of the eighteenth century. There are occasional infelicities in his setting of the English language in the oratorios: some of these may be errors, but others may be regarded as legitimate and original creative treatments of the texts. It is difficult to believe that his English was seriously 'broken' after fifty years of social contacts with English speakers living in the capital. He may, however, have retained traces of German inflections in his speech.

There is surprisingly little information about Handel's personal life, and he may have made deliberate efforts to protect his privacy. Although entertaining in company, he seems to have preferred a degree of isolation and independence. We can assume that he had friends from the musical profession, though we probably know more about the difficult relationships—with Mattheson, Senesino, or Greene, for example—than about the positive ones. There are hints that his other friendships were often with members of professional classes of the types represented in his own parentage—doctors such as John Arbuthnot, clergymen such as Thomas Morell, and lawyers such as Thomas Harris. His will suggests further friendships with successful tradesmen such as James Hunter the scarlet dyer and James Smyth the perfumer, at least in his later years. The final codicil to Handel's will includes bequests to two ladies (Mrs Mayne and Mrs Donellan) whose connection to the composer is uncertain, but who may well have been in his circle of personal friends. His sexual orientation has been the subject of some speculation, but convincing evidence on the subject is lacking, nor is it possible to know what weight to give to the rumour of his possible youthful relationship with Vittoria. Personal prudence and the effects of his early religious education probably combined to influence Handel towards caution in his personal life, and John Hawkins was probably correct when he described Handel as 'a man of blameless morals, and throughout his life he manifested a deep sense of religion' (Hawkins, 2.910). Nevertheless, descriptions of the composer are fairly unanimous in relating his short temper, his rather uninhibited language, and his enthusiasm for good food and good drink in profusion. Letters among his acquaintants from the period after his first 'disorder' express specific concern over his eating and drinking habits, and Handel's relationship with the artist Joseph Goupy is reputed to have been severed after Goupy produced a caricature ('The Charming Brute') which was taken to represent the gluttonous Handel.

Handel's London home was a relatively modest house in a prosperous area. Hawkins remarked that Handel did not keep a carriage (though an incidental reference in a letter from 1737 mentions Handel riding a horse after his recovery from illness), but he apparently maintained a lifestyle that was comparable to that of his neighbours, who included MPs, members of the professional classes, and representatives of the lesser branches of landed families. It seems that, for most of his life in London, Handel enjoyed the financial security provided by his pensions and that, while he was to some extent affected by the fluctuating success of his theatrical ventures from 1729 onwards, in the end his relatively restrained lifestyle and the overall security of his later oratorio seasons enabled him to accumulate considerable wealth. His final credit at the Bank of England was more than £17,000, and the specified bequests in his will amounted to more than £9000.

The largest bequest (nominally £1000, but in practice worth more) went to the Society of Musicians, and another provision was for a score of *Messiah* and a full set of performing material to the Foundling Hospital in order to facilitate the continuation of the performances there. Immediately after the composer's death James Smyth described him as 'the great and good Mr Handel' (Deutsch, 818): the extent of Handel's generosity to these two charities, through his efforts during his last twenty years as well as through the bequests, reflects one of the most positive aspects of his character. Handel was exceptional in that he gained considerable prosperity through his activities as a composer, performer, and impresario: apart from the extravagantly paid opera stars, most professional musicians in London were relatively poorly paid and socially insignificant. One of Handel's achievements was to combine a musical career with a social career in which he achieved both recognition and independence. While he accepted patronage from the élite classes in society, he avoided situations in which he could have been classified as a servant; this seems to account for his refusal to follow a career at Berlin early in life, and also for the absence of his name from the records of the establishments maintained by Ruspoli and Carnarvon, with whom he probably stayed as a guest rather than as a paid official. Early in his career he must have discovered how to gain direct access to situations of wealth and influence: in Rome he was quickly taken up by the leading patrons, and in London his presence was almost immediately acknowledged by Queen Anne's court, where indeed he was given preference over the resident English composers. The social recognition which he demanded for himself is perhaps best symbolized by the dinner party given by John Montagu, second duke of Montagu, on 4 May 1747, at which the duke and duchess of Montagu were joined by the earl and countess of Cardigan, Lord Edgcumbe, Lord Baltimore, and 'Mr Handell'. For his audiences at the theatre Handel relied on the upper classes in London society, though the audience for the oratorios probably included few of the most élite, and financially he relied on his royal pensions. He was able to make use of this patronage while at the same time maintaining his creative independence when faced with unacceptable situations. He led the London audience with the music that he wanted to write, preferring to ride out periods of poor support or indifference but remaining committed to a career in London.

Handel's music forms one of the peaks of the 'high baroque' style. He brought one form of Italian opera to its highest development, created the genres of the English oratorio and the organ concerto, and introduced a new style into English church music which he subsequently transferred to the development of the choral elements in his oratorios. Stylistically he forged his own musical manner against a background of a number of different German, Italian, French, and English models and influences. His use of musical ideas from other composers, which seems to have featured throughout most of his career, was formerly regarded as a moral deficiency, but the careful examination of his use of 'borrowed' material has revealed the subtlety of his compositional technique and the quality of his skill. Because of his flowing command of harmonic movement and his genius for broad effects, this skill has sometimes been taken for granted: he often shows astonishing versatility in his musical constructions, even when employing limited resources, and he

was capable of contrapuntal ingenuity when he found it appropriate. His musical autographs reflect a technical fluency which enabled him to compose at great speed and in a concentrated manner; they often also display alterations which belie the notion that he was careless or negligent on matters of detail.

Commemoration and influence The grandeur of the monument at Westminster Abbey and the publication of Mainwaring's biography indicated Handel's continuing status almost immediately after his death. It was reported that 3000 people attended his funeral, and his direct influence lived on through performances of his oratorios at the London theatres. A rather complex interrelationship gradually evolved between the performance of Handel's music and the English taste for 'antient' music that had already developed an institutional base during Handel's lifetime: in the thirty years following his death, Handel was gradually adopted in London (with the encouragement of George III) as the most revered past composer, and with this came a growing tension between supporters of 'antient' and contemporary music. The tension is readily apparent in the writings of Charles Burney, who has a well-informed admiration for Handel's music and an understanding of his historical significance, yet is impatient of 'Handel-worship' and is an enthusiast for the newer styles of music of the 1770s and 1780s (and ultimately the music of Joseph Haydn). The Concert of Antient Music, founded in 1776, devoted a large proportion of its programmes to items from Handel's music, but it was the commemoration of Handel in 1784 that both symbolized and promoted the continuing cultural authority of Handel's music in Britain.

The commemoration, marking the twenty-fifth anniversary year of Handel's death, was almost certainly the first such public celebration of the music of a particular composer, alive or dead. The programme consisted of five performances given between 26 May and 5 June 1784: two mixed programmes (mainly of church music and movements from the oratorios) and two performances of *Messiah* at Westminster Abbey, and a mixed programme including airs from the operas at the Pantheon in Oxford Street. It was managed by noble directors with royal encouragement, but another significant element was its charitable object of raising money for the Society of Musicians. Because of this charitable aspect, the commemoration was able to call on the services of a vast pool of professional musicians, drawn from the provinces as well as London, and the event became important not only for confirming Handel's canonical status, but also for instituting a new manner of performing his music. More than 500 performers, approximately equally divided between players and singers, were listed as taking part. Handel's choral movements could be performed effectively by this gargantuan assembly, though with rather different effect from anything that the composer had experienced.

An equally important form of commemoration was the attempt to publish a collected edition of Handel's music. During the 1760s and 1770s John Walsh's successors had published full scores of several of Handel's oratorios, but in 1787 a more systematic subscription edition was inaugurated, with Samuel Arnold as editor. Not surprisingly, given the sheer size of Handel's creative achievement, this never became a 'complete' edition of Handel's music, but in ten years a substantial repertory of the oratorios, church music, and instrumental works appeared, and even a few operas.

The 1784 Handel commemoration was followed by others running into the 1790s: Haydn was moved by his attendance at one of them. Within the eighteenth century Handel's music had also spread into continental Europe: in the 1770s his oratorios were performed in Hamburg and in Berlin, where the Austrian envoy Gottfried van Swieten acquired a taste for Handel's music that was to result in his promoting a series of performances in Vienna during 1788–90, for which Mozart arranged the scores. Subsequently Beethoven came to know, and to admire, Handel's music through Arnold's edition, and there is even evidence that Handel's music influenced Schubert's. However, it was in England that his music continued to be principally revered and performed, through oratorio performances and also through performances of favourite items from the church music that were given at provincial festivals. Handel's oratorios had, in any case, achieved an established place in the programmes of the Three Choirs festival and in connection with the commemoration of benefactors at Oxford, even during his own lifetime. A Handel commemoration was held at Westminster Abbey in 1834, but on the whole Handel's music received only rather dutiful attention in the first part of the nineteenth century. All this was changed, however, by the development of the Crystal Palace as a venue for choral music in the late 1850s, and by developments in musical education (principally through the sol-fa system) that brought Handel's choruses within the scope of a large number of amateur singers. Active involvement in Handel's music became available to less affluent sections of British society, for whom cheaper vocal scores of the oratorios were published on the initiative of Novello & Co. Novello published a range of Handel's oratorios, but in practice there was a trend towards the narrowing of the repertory, in which *Messiah* and *Israel in Egypt* became the dominant works performed.

The nineteenth century saw further attempts to produce a complete edition of Handel's music. The first, initiated by the English Handel Society, resulted in the publication of twelve major works and two other volumes between 1843 and 1858; the second was the complete edition inaugurated by the Deutsche Händel-Gesellschaft in 1856 and brought to completion nearly half a century later through the efforts of Friedrich Chrysander. Among Handel's devotees in this period was the Frenchman Victor Schoelcher, who ensured that Handel's 'performing scores' (or 'conducting scores') passed into responsible ownership, eventually at the Staats- und Universitätsbibliothek, Hamburg. Handel's own autographs had been designated in his will for Smith senior, from whom they passed to his son, then to the Royal Music Library, and then, by donation of Elizabeth II, to the British Museum and eventually the British Library. Among creative musicians, however, the attitude to Handel was more ambivalent by the later nineteenth century: his shadow was sometimes felt to have inhibited innovation, particularly in choral music. This often accompanied a recognition that in his oratorio-type works Handel had provided a repertory of good quality and eminently practical major works in the English language that was difficult to challenge. While Handel's operatic style to some extent survived through the arias in his oratorios, the age of the castrati had passed, public expectations of the genre had changed, and the operas as entities were no longer performed. However, some individual movements from Handel's operas were taken up on account of their melodic attractiveness: in this way the larghetto movement 'Ombra mai fù' had even achieved popular fame in instrumental guises by the 1870s as 'Handel's celebrated largo'.

Twentieth-century reputation and interpretation In Britain the nineteenth-century pattern continued into the first half of the twentieth century among groups of enthusiasts for and scholars of Handel's music, and a broader reception tradition was maintained through a small repertory of popular pieces and the established tradition of *Messiah* performances by choral institutions. A significant event was a performance of *Rodelinda* at Göttingen in 1920, which marked the first attempt for a century and a half to stage a Handel opera: other productions followed at Göttingen, but the lead was not taken up elsewhere in a substantial way until after the Second World War. The German Democratic Republic supported Halle's promotion of Handel's music during the 1950s with the establishment of an annual festival and the foundation of a new collected edition of Handel's works; both ventures continued to flourish following the unification of Germany in 1991. A third centre for the performance of Handel's works in Germany emerged in the 1980s with the foundation of the Händel-Akademie in Karlsruhe. All three German centres have played a role in the encouragement of Handelian scholarship as well as performance, though Halle retains a special position on account of the presence there of the editorial office of the Hallische Händel-Ausgabe.

The 1950s saw the publication of two books that initiated a new stage in Handel scholarship, Otto Erich Deutsch's *Handel: a Documentary Biography* (1955) and Winton Dean's *Handel's Dramatic Oratorios and Masques* (1959). The latter, in addition to being a masterly exposition of the textual history of the oratorios, provided a liberal–humanist perspective on the works, concentrating on their dramatic qualities and providing a timely reminder that they were conceived for performance in theatres rather than churches. In the same year as Dean's book appeared, which was also the bicentenary of Handel's death, a performance of *Deidamia* led to the foundation of the Handel Opera Society in London and the more systematic revival of Handel's operas in theatrical presentation. In parallel to the Handel Opera Society, an initiative at a small theatre in Abingdon, Berkshire, led to a series of opera performances by Unicorn Opera; within twenty years the combined activities of the two societies had resulted in the revival of most of Handel's operas for the first time in England since the composer's lifetime. A few of Handel's operas were also gradually taken up as repertory pieces by established opera companies, some of whom included them in their circuits of performances in provincial cities.

The movement for 'authentic' performance practices that developed momentum in the 1970s brought a revolution in the instrumental sound, and in the approach of singers, to the repertories of eighteenth-century music, and some of the most successful applications of the new techniques and ensembles were found in performances and recordings of Handel's music. The process was accelerated by developments in the recording industry. Already in the 1950s some fairly complete performances of Handel's operas and oratorios had been attempted, and this process continued sporadically in the following two decades. *Messiah* scholarship had meanwhile made a significant advance through the work of Watkins Shaw, and followed an earlier attempt by John Tobin to produce an 'authentic' performance of the work in 1950. (This was in a succession of such ventures that stretched back to the 1890s when Arthur Henry Mann conducted a well-researched performance in Cambridge, using performing forces comparable in numbers to those used by Handel.) With the advent of the compact disc, recordings of Handel's works gained yet more momentum, and by the end of the twentieth century recordings of Handel's operas and oratorios were available on a scale that would have been unimaginable half a century earlier.

The development of a broader public for opera also enabled Handel's works to reach a wider audience. Handel's operas had by the end of the twentieth century secured a regular, if not yet major, place in the repertories performed throughout Europe, and the same was to a lesser extent true of the wider repertory of his oratorios. Authenticity of staging for the operas did not keep pace with the changes in the orchestral and vocal sounds, but some performances carried the unity of purpose into areas such as scenic and costume design, dance, and gesture. Meanwhile, Handel scholarship in Britain, Germany, and the USA developed a new impetus: the period around the tercentenary of Handel's birth in 1985 saw the foundation of both the Handel Institute in Britain and the American Handel Society. In the last decade of the century plans for the institution of a museum in Handel's London house (a scheme that had been briefly contemplated seventy years earlier) promised to come to fruition, largely through individual initiative and without the municipal support that had successfully sustained the development of Handel's birth-house in Halle. In 1998 the British government announced that the Gerald Coke Handel collection, the most substantial private collection of materials relating to Handel, had been accepted for the nation, though without any matching obligation for its display, conservation, and access.   DONALD BURROWS

Sources D. Burrows, *Handel* (1994); 2nd edn (1996); 3rd edn (2001) • O. E. Deutsch, *Handel: a documentary biography* (1955) • W. Eisen and M. Eisen, eds., *Händel-Handbuch*, 4 vols. (1978–85) [incl. vols. 1–3: *Thematisch-systematisches Verzeichnis*, ed. B. Baselt; vol. 4: *Dokumente zu Leben und Schaffen*, Ger. trans. with revisions of O. E. Deutsch, *Handel: a documentary biography* (1955)] • J. Simon, ed., *Handel: a celebration of his life and times, 1685–1759* (1985) • C. Burney, *An account of the musical performances … in commemoration of Handel* (1785) • W. Coxe, *Anecdotes of George Frederick Handel and John Christopher Smith* (1799); repr. (1979) • [J. Mainwaring], *Memoirs of the life of the late George Frederic Handel* (1760); facs. edn (1964); repr. (1975) • A. Hicks, 'Handel, George Frideric', *New Grove*, 2nd edn, vol. 10, pp. 747–78 • B. Baselt, 'Handel and his central German background', *Handel tercentenary collection*, ed. S. Sadie and A. Hicks (1987), 43–60 • G. Beeks, 'Handel and music for the earl of Carnarvon', *Bach, Handel, Scarlatti: tercentenary essays*, ed. P. Williams (1985), 1–20 • G. Beeks, '"A club of composers": Handel, Pepusch and Arbuthnot at Cannons', *Handel tercentenary collection*, ed. S. Sadie and A. Hicks (1987), 209–21 • D. Burrows, 'Handel and the Foundling Hospital', *Music and Letters*, 58 (1977), 269–84 • D. Burrows, 'Handel and the 1727 coronation', *MT*, 118 (1977), 469–73 • D. Burrows, 'Handel and Hanover', *Bach, Handel, Scarlatti: tercentenary essays*, ed. P. Williams (1985), 35–59 • D. Burrows, 'Handel's 1738 oratorio: a benefit pasticcio', *Georg Friedrich Händel, ein Lebensinhalt: Gedenkschrift für Bernd Baselt (1934–1993)*, ed. K. Hortschansky and K. Musketa (1995), 11–38 • *Music and theatre in Handel's world: the family papers of James Harris, 1732–1780*, ed. D. Burrows and R. Dunhill (2002) • Burney, *Hist. mus.*, new edn • W. Dean, *Handel's dramatic oratorios and masques* (1959); 2nd edn (1995) • W. Dean, *Handel and the opera seria* (1970) • W. Dean, 'Charles Jennens's marginalia to Mainwaring's life of Handel', *Music and Letters*, 53 (1972), 160–64 • W. Dean and J. M. Knapp, *Handel's operas, 1704–1726* (1987); rev. edn (1995) • W. A. Frosch, 'The "case" of George Frideric Handel', *New England Journal of Medicine*, 321/11 (1989), 765–9 • J. Greenacombe, 'Handel's house: a history of no 25 Brook Street, Mayfair', *London Topographical Record*, 25 (1985), 111–30 • J. Hawkins, *A general history of the science and practice of music*, new edn, 3 vols. (1853); repr. in 2 vols. (1963) • R. D. Hume, 'Handel and opera management in London in the 1730s', *Music and Letters*, 67 (1986), 347–62 • R. G. King, 'Handel's travels in the Netherlands', *Music and Letters*, 72 (1991), 372–86 • U. Kirkendale, 'The Ruspoli documents on Handel', *Journal of the American Musicological Society*, 20 (1967), 222–73, 517 • L. Lindgren, 'The achievements of the learned and ingenious Nicola Francesco Haym (1678–1729)', *Studi musicali*, 16 (1987), 247–380 • J. Milhous and R. D. Hume, 'New light on Handel and the Royal Academy of Music in 1720', *Theatre Journal*, 35 (1983), 149–67 • T. Murdoch, ed., *Boughton House: the English Versailles* (1992) • J. H. Roberts, 'Kaiser and Handel at the Hamburg opera', *Händel-Jahrbuch*, 36 (1990), 63–87 • J. H. Roberts, 'A new Handel aria, or, Hamburg revisited', *Georg Friedrich Händel, ein Lebensinhalt: Gedenkschrift für Bernd Baselt (1934–1993)*, ed. K. Hortschansky and K. Musketa (1995), 113–30 • W. Siegmund-Schultze, ed., *Georg Friedrich Händel: Beiträge zu seiner Biographie aus dem 18. Jahrhundert* (1979) • R. Smith, *Handel's oratorios and eighteenth-century thought* (1995) • C. Taylor, 'Handel and Frederick, prince of Wales', *MT*, 125 (1984), 89–92 • E. Werner, *The Handel house in Halle* (1987)

Archives Handel House Trust, London, Byrne collection of MSS and memorabilia • Hants. RO, Gerald Coke Handel collection • V&A, Gerald Coke Handel collection

Likenesses attrib. B. Denner, oils, 1726–8, NPG • B. Denner, oils, *c*.1727, NPG • P. Mercier, oils, *c*.1730, priv. coll. [*see illus.*] • G. A. Wolfgang, miniature on ivory, *c*.1737, Royal Collection • L. F. Roubiliac, marble statue, 1738, V&A; model, FM Cam. • L. F. Roubiliac, marble bust, 1739, Royal Collection; terracotta variant, Thomas Coram Foundation/Foundling Museum • oils, *c*.1739–1742, NPG; version, Royal Society of Musicians, London • J. Goupy, pastel drawing, *c*.1742, FM Cam. • F. Kyte, oils, 1742, NPG • T. Hudson, oils, 1747–9, Staats- und Universitätsbibliothek Carl von Ossietzky, Hamburg; copy, Bodl. Oxf. • J. Faber junior, mezzotint, 1748 (after T. Hudson), BM • T. Hudson, oils, 1756, NPG • T. Hudson, oils, 1756 ('Gopsall' portrait), NPG • L. F. Roubiliac, marble monument, 1759–

62, Westminster Abbey; terracotta models at AM Oxf. and Coke Handel collection · H. F. Gravelot, engraving (after J. Houbraken, c.1737), repro. in G. F. Handel, *Alexander's feast* (1738) · attrib. L. F. Roubiliac, sculpture, plaster roundel, Sir John Soane's Museum, London · attrib. L. F. Roubiliac, sculpture, terracotta roundel, V&A · terracotta bust, NPG

Wealth at death over £17,500

Handl, Irene (1901–1987), actress and novelist, was born on 28 December 1901 at 13 Leith Mansions, Paddington, London, the second daughter of Frederick Handl, a bank clerk originally from Vienna, and his French wife, Maria Schiepp. She grew up in nearby St John's Wood, and later characterized herself as a fiercely affectionate and rather naïve child who, until she was 'quite old', actually believed that her name was Dolly (television interview, 18 June 1985), because that is what her family had dubbed her in reference to the popular Second South African War song 'Goodbye, Dolly Gray'. An ardent bookworm in later childhood, she was educated locally, and left the Maida Vale High School for Girls at fourteen. For the next twenty years she helped to run her father's household until, at his instigation, she decided in her mid-thirties to embark on an acting career.

Handl promptly enrolled on a short course at the Embassy School of Acting. During her audition for the school she managed to reduce the panel of interviewers to helpless laughter with what was intended to be a serious Shakespearian set piece, and it thus became apparent from the very first that her talent lay in comedy. Having completed her training, Handl made a show-stopping West End début at Wyndham's Theatre, as the maid in Gerald Savory's drawing-room comedy *George and Margaret*: she played her comical 'below stairs' role with relish for the duration of the play's two-year run, and in doing so established a reputation for outstanding character acting which dominated her entire career.

For the next fifty years Irene Handl, who had come to her vocation so relatively late in life, was never out of work. She made her first screen appearance in 1937, playing a chambermaid in the film *Missing, Believed Married*, and this led to a seemingly endless succession of cinematic roles which she undertook in tandem with her theatrical work. From rather modest beginnings (she notched up many cameo appearances in the films of the 1940s, and actually appeared uncredited as an organist in the 1946 cinema classic *Brief Encounter*), Handl went on to become a familiar figure in popular British comedies of the 1950s, 1960s, and 1970s. She featured in almost every well-known film series from *St Trinian's* to *Carry On*, and also gave notable performances as Peter Sellers's wife in *I'm All Right, Jack* (1959) and Tony Hancock's *The Rebel* (1961). Through the increasing popularity of television she became better known to an even wider audience, starring in a number of sitcoms, including *Hancock's Half Hour* (1956), *The Rag Trade* (1961), *For the Love of Ada* (1972), *Maggie and her* (1978), and *In Sickness and in Health* (1985), and in 1980 she endeared herself to yet another generation of viewers when she played the grandmother figure in the hit children's television series *Metal Mickey*. On both stage

Irene Handl (1901–1987), by unknown photographer

and screen Handl was best known for what she herself diffidently termed 'the usual old girl in the crossover apron'. Pleasantly plump and always with a twinkle in her eye, she made colourful cockney chambermaids, charladies, housewives, and matrons her dramatic forte and, as she advanced in years, eccentric old ladies of all kinds became an additional speciality. Many of her characters were based on the servants around whom she had grown up in her father's house, but Handl had what can only be described as a great comic presence, which transformed what could so easily have been workmanlike, two-dimensional character performances into something far more memorable. A fan of music-hall humour from an early age, she had an impeccable sense of comic timing, but at her very best she could bring something more to the roles she played: a curious and almost tragicomic blend of mettlesomeness, personal warmth, and childlike innocence that was uniquely hers.

Ever the late developer, Irene Handl astonished the literary scene when, at the age of sixty-four, she published her first novel, *The Sioux* (1965), a work which she had first envisaged in her teens and had, out of boredom, taken up again in the 1960s during an exceptionally long stage run as the eponymous heroine in Arthur Lovegrove's *Goodnight, Mrs Puffin*. A frenetic present-tense account of the neurosis-laden and increasingly tribalistic behaviour of a family of French aristocrats, *The Sioux* not only reflected Handl's own affluent and exclusively continental roots; it also made obvious an eloquence, an acuity of intellect, and a depth of intuition on her part which were generally masked by the kind of characters she played. She came to view the book as one of her finest and most enduring achievements and published a sequel, *The Gold Tip Pfitzer*, in 1973.

Apart from acting and writing, Handl's interests were many and eclectic. She had a passion for fishing, and was a fellow of the National Geographical Society, as well as a staunch member of the Elvis Presley Club. She was also a devoted animal lover and was for some years president of the British Chihuahua Club, a role which reflected the great affection she always felt for her own pets. She never married and her only full-time companion during the later years of her life was her dog, Rosie. During 1987 Handl was as busy as ever, and completed work on a Channel 4 sitcom entitled *Never Say Die*, in which she played an elderly medium. Towards the end of that year, however, she became unwell, and although she remained confident that 'Dr Theatre' (*The Guardian*, 30 Nov 1987) offered the best available cure, and continued to honour all her previous work commitments, her condition deteriorated.

After a short illness, Irene Handl died in her sleep on 29 November 1987 at her home, 31 Viscount Court, 1 Pembridge Villas, Kensington, London. When asked in an interview by Mavis Nicholson two years before whether she felt she would like 'to be remembered', Handl had chucklingly and with typical self-effacement replied that indeed she would 'because I am an ass' (television interview, 18 June 1985). Her considerable achievements both within and outside the sphere of British stage and screen comedy ensured, of course, that she was and will continue to be remembered as anything but.　　　GILLIAN EVANS

Sources *The Guardian* (30 Nov 1987) · *The Guardian* (6 Dec 1987) · *The Times* (30 Nov 1987) · M. Nicholson, *The time of our lives: in my experience*, Channel 4 television interview, 18 June 1985, BFI · *Tears, laughter, fears, and rage*, Channel 4 television interview, 19 Sept, 10 Oct 1987, BFI · www.uk.imdb.com [filmography] · J. Walker, ed., *Halliwell's film and video guide*, 12th edn (1997) · I. Handl, *The Sioux* (1965) · I. Handl, *The gold tip Pfitzer* (1973) · b. cert. · d. cert.
Likenesses photograph, BFI [*see illus.*] · photographs, Hult. Arch.
Wealth at death £376,134: probate, 19 Jan 1989, *CGPLA Eng. & Wales*

Handley, Thomas Reginald [Tommy] **(1892–1949)**, comedian, was born on 17 January 1892 at 13 Threlfall Street, Toxteth Park, Liverpool, the son of John Handley, a cow keeper, and his wife, Sarah Ann Pearson. Tommy Handley's father, who probably ran a dairy business, died while Tommy was still a baby. On leaving school—there is no record of his academic achievements—Handley worked as a salesman but enjoyed local prestige as a singer with local choirs and concert parties. He became a professional singer in 1916 in a touring company of the operetta *The Maid of the Mountains*. In 1917 he was called up and he served in the Royal Naval Air Service, where his talents were seized upon and he joined a concert party.

After the war Handley undertook a series of short-term touring engagements, including a number for which Jack Hylton (who became a lifelong friend), was the musical director. He eventually devised and starred in a music-hall sketch, *The Disorderly Room*, a skit on army life. This proved to be a great success and remained in his repertory from 1921 to 1941. Ted Kavanagh [*see* Kavanagh, Henry Edward

Thomas Reginald [Tommy] **Handley** (1892–1949), by unknown photographer

(1892–1958)] later recalled that it must have been played on every music-hall stage in the country. Part of its charm lay in the way that its words were fitted to popular songs. While playing at the London Coliseum in 1924 the sketch was chosen to appear in the royal command performance of that year. Soon afterwards Handley's broadcasting career began and he was a regular performer on the wireless from 1924 onwards, becoming a mainstay of BBC variety programmes, both as a solo entertainer and an actor in sketches.

Much of Handley's material in those days, and subsequently in the wartime success *ITMA*, was written by the New Zealander Ted Kavanagh. 'ITMA' (the acronym for 'It's that man again') was a saying of the 1930s relating to the aggressive policies of Adolf Hitler, but it was actually coined in the USA and was used by members of the Republican Party whenever President Franklin D. Roosevelt inaugurated some new policy in his 'new deal' approach to the depression. At first, in pre-war 1939, *ITMA* was set on a cruise ship and was not a success with listeners, but later, set more firmly on land, its mixture of quickfire patter, easily remembered catchphrases, and topical references made it the most successful BBC radio show of wartime Britain. Early in 1942 a special edition of the show was performed at Windsor Castle for Princess Elizabeth's birthday. It was the first royal command performance of a radio programme.

The poet P. J. Kavanagh, son of Ted Kavanagh, has aptly characterized Britain in 1939, at the outbreak of war, as a time of officialdom and officiousness [with] that curious strain of self importance that a crisis brings out … and … was ripe for deflation. Tommy Handley, with the voice of a disaster-prone con-man, more bent than a six pound note and cheery with it, was the ideal man to do the deflating. (Kavanagh, *People and Places*, 105)

ITMA was indeed a radio cartoon of daily life in the war years and, week by week, it relieved the tension of the times by the fun that it poked at the common hazards and endurances of the British public. In the office of twerps wartime bureaucrats were ridiculed for their pomposity and mismanagement. As the strain of war increased Handley, in a much-needed holiday mood, became mayor of the seaside resort Foaming-at-the-Mouth, with its famous charlady, Mrs Mopp, played by Dorothy Summers, whose catchphrase, 'Can I do you now, sir?', regularly brought the house down. Another very popular figure was Funf, the German spy. Handley later turned his attention to factory work, then to post-war planning, and after the war, taking a fresh leaf from the book of traditional satire, *ITMA* put on the map the island of Tantopia, where the austerities and vanished hopes of a brave new world were genially depicted.

Patrick Kavanagh sums up Tommy Handley's broadcasting style as 'so cheeky, so friendly, and so unpompous' (Kavanagh, *People and Places*, 10), and it is hard to disagree. Handley's style was that of an opportunist, quick-thinking man of affairs, surrounded by a gallery of odd and eccentric characters: there was Joan Harben as Mona Lott, whose lugubrious diatribes usually ended with 'It's being so cheerful as keeps me going'; Jack Train contributed, among other characters, Colonel Chinstrap, a confirmed boozer to whom every remark, however innocent, was an invitation to a drink, receiving the reply 'I don't mind if I do'. Credit for the brilliance of *ITMA* must also go to scriptwriter Ted Kavanagh, and to the BBC producer Francis Worsley. There were also many other regulars in a large and constantly changing cast, but Tommy Handley was the benign master of ceremonies whose crisp delivery and immaculate timing kept the show at the peak of professional excellence. Another facet of Handley's skill was demonstrated by a number of radio appearances he made with old Etonian entertainer Ronald Frankau. They called themselves Murgatroyd and Winterbottom and they jointly wrote and performed a sophisticated crosstalk of quickfire word and idea association, which was very popular on BBC variety programmes of the late 1940s.

Despite his vital and quicksilver personality, Handley remained a very private person. He was quite different from the gregarious and clubbable scriptwriter Kavanagh, whose son has depicted a professional relationship: 'they were friendly—very—but it would be difficult to call them friends. Outside working hours they hardly met.' Tommy Handley liked to go home and read: 'He was either on-stage in the public eye or invisible, gone' (P. J. Kavanagh, 105). On 19 February 1929 Handley married a singer, Rosalind Jean (d. 1958), daughter of Robert Allistone, a jeweller, and formerly wife of William Henshall. There were

no children. Tommy Handley died suddenly at 29 Cleveland Gardens, Paddington, London, on 9 January 1949; he was much missed by millions of adoring listeners. He was so much the keystone and embodiment of the actual performance that *ITMA* died with him. Undoubtedly the greatest British radio comedian of his generation, Tommy Handley was as unique in radio comedy as Charlie Chaplin was in silent film. BARRY TOOK

Sources DNB · B. Took, *Laughter in the air: an informal history of British radio comedy* (1976) · P. J. Kavanagh, *People and places: a selection, 1975–1987* (1988) · T. Kavanagh, *Tommy Handley* (1949) · CGPLA *Eng. & Wales* (1949) · b. cert. · m. cert. · d. cert. · personal knowledge (2004)

Archives BBC WAC · Lpool RO, photographs and documents | FILM BFI NFTVA, documentary footage · BFI NFTVA, news footage · BFI NFTVA, performance footage | SOUND BBC WAC · BL NSA

Likenesses E. Whitney Smith, bronze bust, 1945, BBC WAC · H. L. Oakley, silhouette, NPG · photographs, repro. in Kavanagh, *Tommy Handley* [*see illus.*] · photographs, BBC Picture Archive, London

Wealth at death £63,181 11s. 6d.: probate, 11 Feb 1949, CGPLA *Eng. & Wales*

Handlo, Robert (*fl.* 1326), music theorist, may have taken his name from Hadlow in Kent. He was the author of a treatise on music notation, the *Regule*, whose completion is dated in a colophon to 1326. No further details of Handlo's life are known, unless he is to be identified with the Robertus Haudlo or Handlo who is traceable c.1315–22 in the service of the Despensers. The treatise was not known to the earlier sixteenth-century antiquarians and literary historians; the first reference to it is a listing in the 1556 manuscript catalogue of the library of John Dee, and its first mention in print occurs in Thomas Morley's *A Plaine and Easie Introduction to Practicall Musicke* (1597).

The *Regule* is an expansion upon one version of a widely circulated brief guide to the notational practices (c.1280) of Franco of Cologne that begins in most sources with the words 'Gaudent brevitate moderni'. Handlo's additions amount to about twice the size of the core text itself; not only do they represent new material, they also appear to draw upon an earlier text of his own, and furthermore draw by name upon the work of a number of other late thirteenth- and early fourteenth-century continental music theorists, some of whom are otherwise unrecorded. The treatise is noteworthy for being one of the most comprehensive accounts of late *ars antiqua* music theory, as well as for its refinements of language and conceptualization. An English provenance is demonstrable through its discussion of certain insular notational peculiarities, its citation of known English pieces, and details of subject matter, which it shares with another British treatise, the *Summa de speculacione musice* (c.1300) of Walter Odington. The *Regule* was later taken as the point of departure for the *Summa* (c.1375) of the English music theorist John Hanboys. PETER M. LEFFERTS

Sources Robertus de Handlo and Johannes Hanboys, *Regule / The rules, and Summa / The summa*, ed. and trans. P. M. Lefferts (1991)

Hands [*née* Herbert], **Elizabeth** (*bap.* 1746, *d.* 1815), poet, was baptized in Harbury, Warwickshire, on 5 June 1746, the daughter of Henry and Ann Herbert, who at that time were resident in Harbury. Nothing further is known of the circumstances of her parents. Within a couple of years the family had moved to Rowington, where Elizabeth grew up. A sister, Mary, baptized there on 6 September 1748, was buried on 9 April 1749. A brother, Thomas, was baptized on 17 April 1750.

From a letter, dated 4 November 1788, from Henry Sacheverell Homer (1719–1791), rector of Birdingbury, to the Revd Richard Bisse Riland of Sutton Coldfield, seeking support for the publication of her poems, Elizabeth is known to have worked as a servant in the household of the Huddesford family of Allesley, near Coventry (Bedford, 113). It was in Allesley that on 6 September 1784 Elizabeth married William Hands (1746/7–1825) of Bourton-on-Dunsmore. William was then the blacksmith in Bourton, a position which had previously been held by other members of the Hands family. William and Elizabeth had two daughters: Elizabeth, baptized on 29 August 1785, and Ann, baptized on 8 August 1787. The birth of the former is referred to in the poem 'On the Author's Lying In'.

Elizabeth Hands had had no formal education. In the advertisement for the subscription for her poems it was noted that she had acquired her knowledge of poetry from the reading available to her in the households where she served. Even so, there is evidence of the breadth of her reading both in the range and skill of her handling of poetic forms, and more directly in the subject matter of some of the poems, particularly 'On Reading Pope's "Eloisa to Abelard"' and 'Critical Fragments'.

Hands's single published work, entitled *The Death of Amnon: a Poem with an Appendix, Containing Pastorals and Other Poetical Pieces*, was published by subscription in 1789. At least four of her poems had previously appeared in the Birmingham and Coventry newspapers under the pseudonym Daphne. Henry Homer's letter asserts that her poems would not have been published but for the interest taken in them by his son Philip Bracebridge Homer (1765–1838), who was an assistant master at Rugby School, and was able to enlist the support of the head of that school, Dr Thomas James, and other masters, who all agreed the poems were worthy of publication. The volume was dedicated to Bertie Greatheed of Guy's Cliff near Warwick, with thanks to him and other friends for their support. Its publication by subscription was advertised in *Jopson's Coventry Mercury* of 24 November 1788, and, having attracted some 1200 signatures, its publication was announced in the same paper on 21 September 1789. The reviewer George Ogle, writing in the *Monthly Review*, noted 'the uncommonly numerous list of subscribers' as testament to the poetic achievement of the writer (3 Nov 1790, 346). The list included local notables, literary figures such as Anna Seward and the poet laureate, the Revd Thomas Warton, and also members and friends of the Herbert and Hands families.

Richard Gough, reviewing the poems in the *Gentleman's Magazine* of June 1790, commended the title poem especially (p. 540). He noted the originality of its subject and urged readers to be tolerant of any 'unequal line' which might be found in the five blank verse cantos. The story on which this poem is based is to be found in 2 Samuel 13. Amnon, the son of David, falls in love with his sister Tamar, and with the help of a scheming friend, Jonadab, rapes her. The injury is avenged by her brother Absalom, who orders his servants to kill Amnon. While Elizabeth herself anticipated some opposition to a woman tackling the subject of a rape, she retells the story with sensitivity and control, and provides insights into character which are developed beyond the original material, through the use of dialogue and internal monologue. Hands successfully exploits the potential of blank verse to create a lively narrative which, following the model of earlier eighteenth-century writers, appropriately incorporates heroic similes and moralizing comments from the narrator. Thirty-nine miscellaneous poems complete the collection, providing a variety of poetic form: song, pastoral, ode, pastoral dialogue, epistle, elegy, and occasional poems. A number of common themes run through the collection, most prominently love and friendship. The occasional poems range in subject from the rampage of a mad cow through the village, to a visit of the king and queen to Kew.

Elizabeth Hands's consciousness of the novelty of her situation as a working-class woman poet provides the basis for two comic poems, which anticipate the criticisms her 'superiors' were likely to make: 'On the Supposition of an Advertisement in a Morning Paper on the Publication of a Volume of Poems by a Servant Maid' and 'On the Supposition of the Book having been Published and Read'.

Elizabeth Hands died in June 1815 aged sixty-nine, and was buried in Bourton-on-Dunsmore on 28 June. Her husband, William, lived another ten years, and was buried beside his wife. Hands's poetry was rediscovered in the late twentieth century through the work of Roger Lonsdale, Donna Landry, and Janet Todd, and was republished with an introduction by Caroline Franklin in 1996.

CYNTHIA DERELI

Sources D. Landry, *The muses of resistance: laboring-class women's poetry in Britain, 1739–1796* (1990), 187–209 · R. Lonsdale, ed., *Eighteenth-century women poets: an Oxford anthology* (1989); pbk edn (1990), 422 · J. Todd, ed., *A dictionary of British and American women writers, 1660–1800* (1984) · C. Franklin, 'Introduction', '*The death of Amnon: a poem' by Elizabeth Hands and 'The rural lyre: a volume of poems'* by Ann Yearsley (1996), v–xiii · W. K. R. Bedford, *Three hundred years of a family living, being a history of the Rilands of Sutton Coldfield* (1889), 112–14 · G. Ogle, review of the *The death of Amnon, Monthly Review*, new ser., 3 (1790), 345–6 · R. Gough, review of 'The death of Amnon', *GM*, 1st ser., 60 (1790), 540 · parish registers, Rowington, Harbury, Allesley, and Bourton, Warks. CRO

Handyside, Andrew (1805–1887), iron founder and engineer, was born on 25 July 1805 in Edinburgh, the son of Hugh Handyside, ironmonger, and Margaret Baird. As a young man he followed the example of his brother William *Handyside (1793–1850) by going to work with his uncle Charles Baird at his iron foundry and engineering works in St Petersburg. The Baird manufactory was known for an immensely wide range of products, from steam engines to constructional ironwork, and through his experience there Handyside became ideally qualified to manage a similar enterprise back in England. In 1839 while still in St Petersburg, he married his Polish-born wife, Anastasia Henley: they had no children.

Handyside returned from Russia about 1846 and took over the Britannia ironworks in Duke Street, Derby. This works had been established over thirty years earlier by Weatherhead and Glover and had a wide reputation for its ornamental cast ironwork known as 'Derby castings'. Under Handyside, the scope of its output was considerably extended, and the firm became a leader in the manufacture of iron products for export. During the continued development of the English railway system in the mid-nineteenth century, Handysides supplied bridges, railway equipment, and the ironwork of station buildings, including the roofs of Broad Street, London (1864–5), Liverpool Central (1872–3), and Manchester Central (1876–80) stations. The same range of products was exported for railways throughout the world, notably bridges for India and Australia and the 120 foot span roof of the main station in Amsterdam. Prefabricated buildings were also part of its export trade, supplied ready for erection complete with doors, windows, and fittings. Despite such diversification, the firm still maintained its reputation for traditional castings such as for lamp-posts, pillar boxes, and other ornamental objects, plus the manufacture of steam engines, pumps, and mining machinery.

The more important commissions that Handysides received were based on designs by consultant architects or engineers, for instance the Albert suspension bridge, London (1871–3) by R. M. Ordish, and a winter garden at Leeds Infirmary (1868) by G. G. Scott. However, under Handyside the firm developed the expertise to design as well as manufacture new structures of every kind. This accomplishment was publicized through a promotional book *Works in Iron* (1868 and subsequent editions), which helped demonstrate that less complex structures could be completed without the need for an independent designer. Handyside ran the works on a tight rein and did his best to eliminate traditional customs such as the observance of Mondays as an unofficial holiday. By 1873 he had a workforce of about 360 and decided to open a second site for the firm in Fox Street, Derby. Probably to help finance that extension, the company was incorporated with a capital of £120,000.

Handyside played a modest role in Derby public life. He was a town councillor (1855–8), and was a director of both the Derby water works and the Derby and Derbyshire Banking Company. However dour he may have seemed to his workers, he and his wife maintained Russian customs of hospitality at home, complete with a samovar on the sideboard. He died on 9 June 1887 at 16 Ashbourne Road, Derby, and was buried in the Nottingham Road cemetery. Handyside was survived by his wife. The firm which carried his name continued to flourish and was employing about 1000 people in the 1890s, but from that height of success it plunged to failure and was wound up in 1910.

ROBERT THORNE

Sources *Derby Mercury* (15 June 1887) · *Works in iron*, Andrew Handyside and Company (1868) · F. Nixon, *The industrial archaeology of Derbyshire* (1969) · M. Higgs, 'The exported iron buildings of Andrew Handyside and Co. of Derby', *Journal of the Society of Architectural Historians*, 29 (1970), 175–80 · R. Christian, 'The Handyside story', *Derbyshire Advertiser* (7 April 1961) · d. cert. · *CGPLA Eng. & Wales* (1887)

Archives PRO, J13, Nr. 00314 (1910)

Likenesses chalk drawing, Scot. NPG · charcoal drawing, Scot. NPG

Wealth at death £6622 16s. 6d.: probate, 27 July 1887, *CGPLA Eng. & Wales*

Handyside, William (1793–1850), engineer, was born on 25 July 1793, in Edinburgh, the eldest child of Hugh Handyside, ironmonger, and Margaret Baird. At the age of fifteen he became a pupil of a Mr White, a local architect, but did not complete his training. In 1810 his uncle, Charles Baird (1766–1843), invited him to join him in St Petersburg, where he had been working since 1786 and had established himself as one of the leading manufacturers of the Baird works. Handyside rapidly demonstrated his ability as an engineer, and played an important role in many of the most important contracts of the Baird works.

After working on the installation of machinery at the imperial arsenal and the imperial glassworks, in 1815 Handyside helped build *Elizabeth*, the first Russian steamship. Over the next ten years he built ten more, improving the design. He was particularly concerned with steam-engine manufacture and installation of associated machinery but displayed his genius in many other fields. For Baird he developed a sugar refining process, a gasworks for lighting the factory, and machinery for production of all kinds of military equipment.

Handyside was involved in building the first Russian suspension bridges, designed by Pierre Bazaine and Wilhelm von Traitteur for St Petersburg, and devised a testing machine for proving the chains. His most famous works were associated with the architect A. R. de Montferrand with whom he worked for many years on St Isaac's Cathedral. This included a colonnade of forty-eight granite pillars, each of 8 feet diameter and 56 feet high, and a circle of thirty-six monolithic pillars (each 42 feet high), raised 200 feet off the ground, and surmounted by an iron dome 130 feet in diameter. He developed machinery to assist in its construction and helped with the design of the iron dome, its gilding, and with casting its decorative bronze work. Handyside and Montferrand worked together on the column erected in memory of Tsar Alexander, Handyside casting the reliefs as well as arranging its erection.

Handyside initially lived with Baird. In 1829 he married Sophia Gordon Busch, a member of the British émigré community in Russia. They had four children. Following the death of Charles Baird, Handyside returned to Britain. Although he became more active in the affairs of the Institution of Civil Engineers, which he had first joined in 1822, he retired from business. Handyside's brothers had followed him to St Petersburg in the 1820s. While some remained, his younger brother Andrew *Handyside (1805–1887) returned with him to Britain and took over the Britannia ironworks, Derby. William Handyside died in Edinburgh on 26 May 1850, exhausted by a lifetime in heavy industry.

MIKE CHRIMES

Sources PICE, 10 (1850–51), 85–7 • T. Tower, *Memoir of the late Charles Baird … and of his son, the late Francis Baird* (1867) • J. G. James, *The application of iron to bridges and other works in Russia to about 1850* [1982]; abridged as 'Russian iron bridges to 1850', *Transactions* [Newcomen Society], 54 (1982–3), 79–104 • A. R. de Montferrand, *Église cathédrale de Saint Isaac* (1845) • A. R. de Montferrand, *Plans et détails du monument consacré à la mémoire de l'Empereur Alexandre* (1836) • S. G. Fedorov, *Der badische Ingenieur: Wilhelm von Traitteur als Architekt russischer Eisenkonstruktionen* (1992)

Archives Inst. CE • St Petersburg State Archives, Russia

Hanff, Helene (1916–1997), writer and Anglophile in the USA, was born in Philadelphia, Pennsylvania, USA, on 15 April 1916, the third child and only daughter of Arthur Hanff and his wife, Miriam, *née* Levy. In his youth, her father had a short-lived career 'as a song-and-dance man', but later settled down with her mother and became a shirt salesman. His love of the theatre persisted, however, and Hanff recalled with affection his depression-era activity of 'swapping shirts for passes with all the box-office men in Philadelphia' (Hanff, *Underfoot in Show Business*, 5, 6). In pursuit of a university scholarship, Hanff was educated at a special academic high school, and was awarded funding for a liberal arts programme at Temple University. After only a year there, however, the money for the scholarship ran out, and she was forced to leave. She felt 'a secret relief' at this, and began a stringent course of self-education, based on the writings of Sir Arthur Quiller-Couch:

> when all my friends were going back to college I was happily mapping out a daily course of study with Q: two hours of Q, two hours of Milton, two hours of Shakespeare, one hour of English essays (dessert). I began reading industriously all day long, unaware that my Depression-ridden parents were anxiously waiting for me to go out and get a job. (Hanff, *Q's Legacy*, 3, 6)

She was regretfully brought to this realization, went to business school, and began working in secretarial jobs, while also becoming involved in amateur theatre.

In 1936 Helene Hanff won a fellowship from the Bureau of New Plays as a result of a nationwide competition. She moved to Manhattan, and under the guidance of Theresa Helburn, a co-producer of the Theatre Guild, she began to write in earnest. She wrote twenty plays in the 1940s, but failed to have a single one produced. Her account of her life in New York at this time, *Underfoot in Show Business* (1961; 1980), is both funny and uncompromising about the hard truths of the business, reflected in chapter titles such as 'If they take you to lunch they don't want your play'. Hanff continued to write (training films for the Women's Army Corps, articles on American history for a children's encyclopaedia, children's bedtime stories) and, in the early 1950s, scripts for television, in particular for *The Adventures of Ellery Queen*. She also supported herself with work as an 'outside reader' for a film studio, reading novels, plays, and short stories, and giving her opinion on their suitability for adaptation (Hanff, *Q's Legacy*, 17). That Hanff was not entirely ahead of her time in this regard is seen in her assessment of:

> J. R. R. Tolkien (I hope I'm spelling his name wrong). I remember opening one volume to a first line which read *Mr. Bilbo Baggins of Bag End announced that he would shortly be*

celebrating his eleventy-first birthday … and phoning several friends to say good-bye because suicide seems so obviously preferable to five hundred more pages of that. (Hanff, *Underfoot in Show Business*, 116)

Hanff was never one for prose fiction, though, as she stated in her most famous book: '"The reader will not credit that such things could be," Walton says somewhere or other, "but I was there and I saw it." that's for me, I'm a great lover of i-was-there books' (Hanff, *84 Charing Cross Road*, 83). And it is the immediacy of the letters making up *84 Charing Cross Road* (1970) that turned it from a successful 'cult book' into a volume that has gone into numerous editions, and has remained in print for thirty years. The book collates the twenty-year correspondence that Helene, as an impoverished New York bibliophile, shared with Frank Doel, the manager of an antiquarian bookshop in London. Its charm persists, with Helene's requests for books becoming increasingly informal and erratically punctuated:

> Frank Doel, what are you DOING over there, you are not doing ANYthing, you are just sitting AROUND. Where is Leigh Hunt? Where is the *Oxford Verse*? Where is the Vulgate and dear goofy John Henry, I thought they'd be such nice uplifting reading for Lent and NOTHING do you send me. you leave me sitting here writing long margin notes in library books … some day they'll find out i did it and take my library card away. (ibid., 14)

Doel's own replies demonstrate a shift from a formal British reserve to a real warmth and friendship. In response to her needling signature of a 1952 letter, 'MISS Hanff to you (I'm Helene only to my FRIENDS)', Doel responds:

> I quite agree it is time we dropped the 'Miss' when writing to you. I am not really so stand-offish as you may have been led to believe, but as copies of letters I have written to you go into the office files, the formal address seemed more appropriate. (ibid., 46)

But it wasn't just about books. As Hanff put it:

> Most of the books I bought from Marks & Co were probably available in New York. For years, friends had advised me to 'try O'Malley's', 'try Dauber & Pine'. I'd never done it. I'd wanted a link with London and I'd managed it. (Hanff, *The Duchess of Bloomsbury Street*, 111)

And the link was a strong one. In addition to her persistent and teasing letters, Helene sent gifts of food parcels to the shop's staff during post-war rationing, and received back letters including recipes, photos, gift books, and even an Irish embroidered tablecloth as a Christmas present. The correspondence established a deep and lasting network of international relationships and, in its published form, helped its readers towards a greater transatlantic understanding.

Lack of money thwarted Hanff's desperate wish to visit England and in particular her friends at the bookshop. It was not until she was sent a letter conveying news of Frank's death that she collected the correspondence into a volume published to critical acclaim in America. Ironically, this generated enough interest for André Deutsch to publish it in Britain, and to bring Hanff to London for the launch. Her diary of her first visit to England was published as *The Duchess of Bloomsbury Street* (1974), and despite her own misgivings ('Garrulous Gertie comes home from London and has to tell everyone about her trip. Who the hell cares about my trip?'; Hanff, *Q's Legacy*, 37), received critical and popular acclaim.

Helene Hanff went on to write a personalized and idiosyncratic guide to New York, *Apple of my Eye* (1977), overcoming the initial disadvantage that, although a passionate New Yorker, she had 'never been to any of the tourist attractions' (Hanff, *Apple of my Eye*, 9). Her ties to London were continued and reinforced by her broadcasting work for the BBC's *Woman's Hour* from 1978 to 1984, for which she produced monthly segments on life in New York; these were later collected and published as *Letter from New York* (1992). An autobiographical tribute to Quiller-Couch, *Q's Legacy*, appeared in 1985.

84 Charing Cross Road was adapted for the stage by James Roose-Evans, and was staged successfully in Britain, though less successfully in New York. The American actress Anne Bancroft, however, was a fan of the book, and her husband, the director Mel Brooks, bought her the film rights to it as a twenty-first anniversary present. He acted as executive producer of a film version (1986) starring Bancroft as Helene. Hardly in Brooks's usual vein of slapstick and broad satire, *84 Charing Cross Road* was true to the spirit of the book. It was brilliantly cast: in addition to Bancroft, Anthony Hopkins played Frank Doel, and Judi Dench appeared as his wife, Nora. The film version was a great success, despite Helene's own reservations: 'Who could have imagined a film about a business correspondence?' (*Daily Telegraph*).

Helene Hanff never married, though Leo Marks, the son of the bookshop owner, said that 'she had a relationship with a very famous American, whom she had to share with two other ladies, and she was never sure whether she was the senior or the junior' (*The Guardian*). Hanff suffered from diabetes later in life, but continued to smoke and drink. In her last years she was 'broke', by her own account, living on royalties and social security, and accepting a $5000 grant from the Authors' League fund to help with hospital bills. In an interview she gave in 1988, expressing her dislike for electric typewriters, she joked: 'If my 1964 model breaks down before I do, I guess I'll replace it, but it looks as though we'll both go roughly at the same time' (Fox and Hanff). Both lasted another nine years; Helen Hanff died on 9 April 1997 at the De Witt Nursing Home in Manhattan, New York City. As she had always wished, she was buried in Brooklyn in memory of the Dodgers. 84 Charing Cross Road is no longer the site of a bookshop, but a plaque has been placed on the wall, stating: '84 Charing Cross Road, The Booksellers Marks & Co. were on this site which became world-renowned through the book by Helene Hanff.'

M. CLARE LOUGHLIN-CHOW

Sources H. Hanff, *Underfoot in show business* (1961); repr. (1980) · H. Hanff, *84 Charing Cross Road* (1970); repr. (1976) · H. Hanff, *The duchess of Bloomsbury Street* (1974); repr. (1976) · H. Hanff, *Q's legacy* (1985) · H. Hanff, *Apple of my eye* (1977); repr. (1978) · *Daily Telegraph* (11 April 1997) · *The Independent* (14 April 1997) · *The Times* (11 April 1997) · *The Guardian* (11 April 1997) · *New York Times* (11 April 1997) · S. Fox and H. Hanff, interview, *Sunday Times* (29 May 1988) · A. Garry, 'Helene Hanff, 1916–1997', freespace.virgin.net/angela.garry/hanffl~2.html · S. Pastore, *The library of Helene Hanff* (1998)
Archives SOUND BL NSA, documentary recordings
Likenesses E. Gaussen, oils, 1971

Hanger, George, fourth Baron Coleraine (1751–1824), army officer and writer, was born on 13 October 1751 at the family seat, Driffield Hall, Gloucestershire, the third and youngest son of Gabriel Hanger, first Baron Coleraine (1697–1773), MP, and his wife, Elizabeth Bond (1715–1780), daughter of Richard Bond, of Cowbury, Herefordshire. Educated at Reading School, Eton College, where he enjoyed affairs with local females, and the University of Göttingen, he briefly served in the Prussian army before entering the British army as an ensign in the 1st foot guards on 31 January 1771. He purchased a lieutenant's commission (which in the footguards then conferred the rank of captain in the army) on 20 February 1776. Long-nosed but reportedly considered handsome when young, he was irascible, violent, dissipated, extravagant, and individualistic sometimes to eccentricity. He fought three duels before he was twenty-one. While a guards officer he married, by Gypsy rites, a Gypsy whom he called 'the lovely Egyptea of Norwood' (Bass, 86), but she ran off with a bandy-legged tinker. He 'retired' on 25 March 1776, allegedly in disgust after a more junior officer purchased promotion over him. An extravagantly and expensively dressed 'macaroni', he claimed to have worn the first satin coat in England.

Hanger was still determined on a military career, and on returning to Germany became a captain in the Hessian Jägers and sailed with them to North America. Commanding a detachment assigned to the expedition against Charleston, South Carolina, in 1780, he was appointed aide-de-camp to the commander-in-chief, Sir Henry Clinton; but when Clinton returned to New York soon afterwards, Hanger remained in North Carolina to assist Major Patrick Fergusson organize the loyalist militia there. This soon proved uncongenial and he transferred to Banastre Tarleton's British legion on 6 August 1780, as commander of its light dragoons with the provincial rank of major, and became Tarleton's lasting friend. His début as a cavalry commander was far from auspicious. He and his men were surprised by the Americans at Wahab's Plantation, North Carolina, on 21 September 1780 and five days later performed badly in another encounter at Charlotte, North Carolina. He missed the disasters of Cowpens and Yorktown through yellow fever. In 1782 Tarleton's dragoons were taken onto the regular establishment, at which time Hanger was confirmed in the substantive rank of major on 25 December 1782. This was merely a paper transaction, however, for the regiment had surrendered at Yorktown in October 1781 and Hanger was placed on half pay when it was formally disbanded in 1783. This ended his active military career, though he was promoted brevet lieutenant-colonel on 12 October 1793.

A beau and clubman—in both senses—who affected the manners of the French court, Hanger assisted Tarleton with his faro bank at Daubigney's Tavern, London, lounging at the entrance with a huge rattan he called 'the

George Hanger, fourth Baron Coleraine (1751–1824), by unknown artist

the popular caricature of an Irish gentleman. His publications were mainly on military and sporting subjects. These ranged from the contentious *An Address to the Army, in Reply to Strictures by Roderick McKenzie (Late Lieutenant in the 71st Regiment) on Tarleton's History of the Campaigns of 1780 and 1781* (1789) to the opportunistic *Anticipation of the Freedom of Brabant, with the Expulsion of the Austrian Troops from that Country* (1792), and two treatises on the defence of London: *Military Reflections on the Attack and Defence of the City of London* (1795) and *Reflections on the Menaced Invasion …* (1804). In both the latter works he drew on his experience of hunting and shooting in the area, and his best-known work was *Colonel George Hanger to All Sportsmen, and Particularly to Farmers and Gamekeepers* (1814), with proposals for an elaborate rat trap and an anti-poacher tower with a gun firing clay balls. He also wrote his *Life, Adventures and Opinions* (2 vols., 1801). He married, before January 1823, at Wapping, London, his cook or housekeeper, Mary Anne Katherine, possibly *née* Greenwood (c.1776–1846), an ill-educated woman: the John Greenwood Hanger to whom she left her money was possibly her illegitimate son by Hanger. Opinionated, he advocated public urinals with the state profiting from the sale of the urine as fertilizer, and taxes on cutlery and 'absentee Scotchmen' who failed to reside six months a year in Scotland. On the death of his elder brother William, on 11 December 1814, he succeeded to the barony of Coleraine, but preferred to be addressed as Colonel (or General) Hanger. He died 'of a convulsive fit' (*GM*, 457) at his house near Regent's Park, London, on 31 March 1824, and was buried at Driffield, Gloucestershire. At his death the barony became extinct.

STUART REID

Sources G. Hanger, *The life, adventures, and opinions of Colonel George Hanger*, 2 vols. (1801) · R. D. Bass, *The green dragoon* (1973) · *The correspondence of George, prince of Wales, 1770–1812*, ed. A. Aspinall, 8 vols. (1963–71) · *GM*, 1st ser., 94/1 (1824), 457–8 · *Army List* · GEC, *Peerage* · *DNB* · C. Kennedy, *Eccentric soldiers* (1975)
Likenesses J. Gillray, caricature, coloured etching, pubd 1800 (*Georgey in the coal-hole*), NPG · S. Springsguth, stipple, pubd 1816 (after R. R. Reinagle), NPG · G. Cruikshank, caricature, repro. in *The Scourge* (2 Nov 1812) · J. Gillray, caricature, repro. in T. Wright and R. H. Evans, *Historical and descriptive account of the caricatures of James Gillray* (1851) · etching (after R. R. Reinagle), repro. in G. Hanger, *General George Hanger to all sportsmen*, 8 vols. (1816) · miniature; Sothebys, 28 July 1980, lot 337 [*see illus.*] · portrait, repro. in Hanger, *Life*, vol. 1, p. 2
Wealth at death no value specified in will, but references to funds and houses: will, PRO, PROB 11/1689

Infant'. He became one of the dissipated companions of the prince of Wales, indulging in gambling, racing, and pugilism. In 1787 he and Tarleton organized 'bludgeon men' for the whigs at the Westminster by-election. In November 1791 he was appointed equerry to the prince of Wales. In August 1797, in litigation against his elder brother William, third Baron Coleraine, he wrote to the prince begging a loan of £100. His critics considered him among the dregs of society. He was much mentioned in contemporary memoirs and was caricatured by Gillray, Rowlandson, Dighton, and Cruikshank.

Still on major's half pay, Hanger was in increasing financial difficulties, sold out in 1796, and obtained an ensign's commission in the 70th foot on 29 September 1796. As this commission was obtained without purchase he obtained by the exchange a small capital sum with which to pay off his more pressing creditors and at the same time secured a very modest, but assured, income. It did not, however, save him from being imprisoned for debt in the king's bench prison, Southwark, between June 1798 and April 1799. He lived for some time in Paris to avoid his creditors. In 1800, having forfeited his ensigncy, he even set up as a coal merchant. His last connection with the army came on 7 July 1806, when he was appointed captain commissary of the corps of Royal Artillery drivers. This was merely blatant jobbery: his 1808 retirement on full pay was a scandal, and was criticized by the commissioners of military inquiry in their seventeenth report.

Hanger continued to call himself Colonel Hanger and in 1816 'promoted' himself General Hanger. Throughout his life he appears to have deliberately set out to conform to

Hankeford [Hankford], **Sir William** (c.1350–1423), justice, came of a gentry family with property in and around the hamlet of Hankford, near Bulkworthy in north Devon, but his precise parentage is uncertain. He was educated at the Middle Temple and called to the degree of serjeant-at-law in Michaelmas term 1388, by which time, of course, he had been for years an active lawyer: since 1384 he had been retained as counsel by the earl of Devon. He was appointed king's serjeant in 1389 and, as well as pleading in the courts, where his contributions were frequently reported in the year-books, and acting on assize and other commissions in south-east and south-west England, he was active in royal service. He accompanied Richard II to

Ireland in 1394, and in parliament in February 1398 was one of those whose opinion was sought on the responses made by the judges in 1387 to Richard's questions on the nature of treason for which they had been condemned by the Merciless Parliament; Hankeford declared that the responses were good and loyal and that he would have given the same. On 6 May following he was promoted to succeed his friend and associate, John Wadham, who had resigned from his position as justice of the common pleas. Henry IV reappointed him to the bench in October 1399 and created him KB at his coronation a few days later. Hankeford was very active as a justice and commissioner during the following years and his reputation was clearly high, as on the accession of Henry V in 1413 he was appointed to replace William Gascoigne as chief justice of the king's bench. Most of his service was in and around London, though he continued to sit on commissions in his native Devon, and in 1414 he took the king's bench to Shropshire to deal with the endemic disorder there against which he inveighed in his charge to the jury. He seems to have attended parliament regularly, was frequently a trier of petitions, and was sometimes called in to report to the council and parliament. His appointment was renewed by the council after Henry V's death in 1422: he thus enjoyed the unusual distinction of serving as a justice under four monarchs.

Hankeford died on 12 December 1423, not in 1422, as earlier writers state. The extraordinary story of his seeking his own death, by ordering his parker to shoot anyone wandering in his park at night and then deliberately going into the park to be shot, seems first to have been related by Holinshed (who dates it to 1471), and is also told of Sir Robert Danby (d. 1474); but it is followed by Thomas Fuller and later Devon historians, who recount that it was still a strong tradition locally, and that the stump of the oak under which the incident occurred was still known as 'Hankford's oak' in the seventeenth century. It is not very plausible, but if he did die in this way it must have been suicide, for he had made his long and complex testament only two days earlier. It is likely enough that he died in Devon, to which he may have returned after the end of the Michaelmas term. Hankeford's testament is dominated by his home county—he made substantial bequests to churches, charities, and religious houses in north Devon, and asked to be buried in Monkleigh church which he had largely rebuilt; his tomb survives there. Among his executors was his successor as chief justice, Sir William Cheyne (d. 1443).

Hankeford had one younger brother, John, who died between 1420 and 1423. The parentage of his wife, Cristina (who predeceased him), is unknown, but she was certainly a minor heiress in Devon, and William also added substantially to his family lands, especially in north Devon, by purchase. They were married by 1380 and seem to have had only one son, Richard, who himself married an heiress and was twice knight of the shire for Devon, but died in his father's lifetime. William's lands were inherited by his grandson, another Richard, who was aged twenty-seven on his grandfather's death, married twice into aristocratic families, and died in 1431, leaving two daughters who eventually took the Hankeford property to Sir William Bourgchier, later Lord Fitzwarine, and Thomas, seventh earl of Ormond.

ROGER VIRGOE

Sources Chancery records · RotP, vols. 3–4 · N. H. Nicolas, ed., *Proceedings and ordinances of the privy council of England*, 7 vols., RC, 26 (1834–7), vols. 2–3 · Baker, *Serjeants* · Sainty, *Judges* · M. Hemmant, ed., *Select cases in the exchequer chamber*, [1], SeldS, 51 (1933) · T. F. T. Plucknett, ed., *Year books of Richard II: 13 Richard II* (1929) · John, Lord Campbell, *The lives of the chief justices of England*, 3 vols. (1849–57) · Foss, *Judges* · Fuller, *Worthies* (1840) · E. Lega-Weekes, 'An Account of the Hospitium de le Egle', *Report and Transactions of the Devonshire Association*, 44 (1912), 480–511, esp. 494–9 · HoP, *Commons, 1386–1421* · PRO, C 139/12/32 · E. F. Jacob, ed., *The register of Henry Chichele, archbishop of Canterbury, 1414–1443*, 3, CYS, 46 (1945), 290–93

Hankey, Beatrice [*called* Help] (1858–1933), evangelist, was born on 17 December 1858 at Bohun Lodge, Barnet, the ninth of ten children of George Hankey (d. 1893), a wealthy merchant banker of an old Cheshire family, and his wife, Caroline Donovan (d. 1878), whose family originally came from co. Carlow. Her mother's influence endowed Beatrice Hankey with deep religious faith and shaped her highly individual character. As a child she was fun-loving, fearless, and energetic, and in appearance, then and later, 'blue-eyed and fair-haired with irregular features' (Raven and Heath, 14). She was especially close to her sister Eva, five years her senior: Eva's chronic ill health required constant nursing, which Beatrice willingly gave, and they lived all their lives together in mutual dependence.

Shortly after 1871 the Hankeys moved to Henley House, Frant, in Sussex, where one of the girls, Mary, began a Bible-reading class for men on the estate. When Mary married, in 1879, Beatrice took it over and showed 'a particular gift for dealing with men'. One of the older members of the class recalled: 'You had to do what she said. She was our Queen she was, her word was law' (Raven and Heath, 20). Total abstinence from alcohol was one of her rules and if she relaxed this in later life, when the social consequences of drunkenness were less in evidence, she never abandoned the principle.

In 1888 Beatrice Hankey spent six months at St John's Hospital, Lewisham, working as a nurse, the only training that she ever had. It helped her to care for Eva and their father, whose health was failing. After his death, in 1893, the household at Frant dispersed and the sisters moved to Walmer, in Kent, where they began evangelical work with the local fishing community. They used a family legacy to build a mission hall on the seafront; by 1904 there were about 700–800 'members' of the 'Cheriton Club', which housed a sizeable branch of the British Women's Temperance Association, as well as Bible classes for men and women. Children were rigidly excluded from these, as indeed they were from all meetings over which Beatrice presided.

A turning point came in September 1902, when the Hankey sisters invited a few of their younger women relatives to a four-day retreat at the house of the bishop of Dover, William Walsh, in Canterbury, which had been lent for the occasion. There were poetry readings as well as religious discussion, and those present addressed one another by the name of the room in which they were staying—for example, Hope, Charity, and Rest, the last of which attached to Eva. At a later meeting Eva pinned on her sister's door 'One called Help', from *Pilgrim's Progress*, and it was by the name of Help that Beatrice was thereafter known. The gatherings continued annually and grew in size; those invited were exclusively young women but not necessarily family members. From 1905 they met at St Augustine's Missionary College, Canterbury. By now Help was a confident speaker, and readings from Tennyson's *Idylls of the King* formed a central part of her teaching; the fellowship became a 'knighthood' and its meetings 'camelots', while the early knights took their names from those of the round table. Though Hankey remained a member of the Church of England all of her life she disliked formal organization, and the Tennysonian imagery provided a coherence to the fellowship that was otherwise lacking.

The growth of the knighthood eventually led Help and Rest away from their calling at Walmer. In 1910 they settled in The Chantry, Sevenoaks, a large house that was a home to the knighthood as much as to themselves. It was Rest, the more conventional and less demanding of the two, who kept house, leaving Help to be the evangelical driving force. When in 1912 she learned of the extreme hardship experienced by striking miners she travelled, without any real plan, to the heart of the strike area, arriving at Hednesford, in Cannock Chase. Within days she had set up a mission in a disused drill hall, where she dispensed cocoa and buns and held religious services.

Hankey now demanded of her knights similar action. It marked a parting of the ways for some—perhaps most—of the fellowship but the following summer the remnants were at work among the colliers in Castleford, as well as Hednesford. Temperance was a central tenet of her missionary work, and both at Hednesford and Castleford she ran 'catch-my-pal' movements, devoted to total abstinence. She proved utterly determined in this cause, however unpopular it might prove with the hard-living miners and, later, soldiers among whom she worked. The knighthood was thus already mobilized when war came in 1914 and could quickly provide, to regiments accepting them, 'home huts', where soldiers could find nourishment, recreation, and religion. Help probably financed the first huts herself but later they were run on the profits from the canteens, and about thirty opened in all. During the Second South African War the mission at Walmer had been bedecked in red, white, and blue, and Help showed similar uncomplicated patriotism towards the 1914–18 conflict. She 'spiritualized the struggle as she did the rest of life' (Raven and Heath, 173), and because she interpreted it as part of God's plan for man's spiritual evolution it did not trouble her as it troubled others.

In 1915 the Mothers' Union conceived the idea of a pilgrimage of prayer to more remote villages, an initiative that developed into the 'Women Messengers' movement.

Hearing of the idea Hankey made contact and simultaneously carried out a pilgrimage in Kent, in August, with the blessing of the bishop of Rochester, John Reginald Harmer. The participating knights wore blue veils and stoles and it was thus that the Blue Pilgrims were born. They developed alongside the Women Messengers, 'but on characteristic and independent lines' (Raven and Heath, 184). In 1916 'Pilgrim Help' wrote a short pamphlet explaining their work; over the next five years other pamphlets, pilgrimages, and even 'crusades' followed.

The admission of men—'knights-chivalrous'—to the movement in the summer of 1917 signalled fundamental change. The fellowship no longer consisted of leisured young women but embraced a diverse membership, many of whom were wage-earners. The Tennysonian symbolism was mostly set aside. What remained was the atmosphere of love and friendship. In 1921 the *Dragon Fly*, the newssheet of the knighthood, made the first of its irregular appearances, later to be superseded by *The Signaller*. The four years of war, followed by three years spent nursing Rest, who died in November 1921, undermined Help's health to the extent that she took no part in the pilgrimages of the early 1920s. She nevertheless returned to Hednesford during the general strike of 1926 and again the next year. In 1928 she went to south Wales, answering her final call.

In February 1928 two knights investigated the need for relief work in the Rhondda valley. Finding the Society of Friends already active they moved to Blaenau, on the Monmouthshire coalfield, an area of 90 per cent unemployment and 'the saddest place in S. Wales' (Raven and Heath, 270). Shortly before leaving for south Wales, Hankey preached at a late-evening Sunday service in Liverpool Cathedral, under the auspices of Charles Raven, a residentiary canon there and a member of the knighthood. It was a remarkable moment for her and her movement, and a clear statement of Raven's belief in the ordination of women.

At Blaenau the Blue Pilgrims opened a clothing depot and a soup kitchen; revived the allotments association, giving out seeds and gardening implements; and found slate with which to mend roofs. But along with this practical work went an understanding of the spiritual needs of the people. Hankey insisted that respect should go hand in hand with charity, a point which she emphasized in a letter to *The Times* of 14 January 1929. During 1929, with the opening of the Mansion House fund, major relief work began operating in south Wales; the Blue Pilgrims' soup kitchen was no longer needed and the allotments organization was taken over by the Society of Friends. Instead the pilgrims concentrated their efforts on establishing a home camp at Blaenau, in a disused working men's club. It became the base for nearly a hundred men and women, the men repairing boots out of old tyres and making doormats and toys, and the women quilts. The project attracted national attention when the duke and duchess of York visited the camp in March 1932; they showed interest in the camp garden, a converted rubbish tip. Help was unable to welcome them; she was increasingly frail and at the end of June suffered a stroke, from which she never properly recovered. She died at The Chantry, Sevenoaks, on 5 February 1933 and was buried in the garden, in a grave by the chantry wall, alongside her sister.

Active membership of the Blue Pilgrims was never large—probably in the low hundreds—and there were obvious limits to what they could achieve. In south Wales the amateurism of the movement clearly frustrated more established aid organizations. Help accepted this but she disliked committees and red tape and believed that 'it was not a part of friendship to be a perpetual prop'. This was a somewhat harsh message for those who came to rely on her aid and who, by her own definition, were most in need of it. Her genius, however, lay not in her social work but in her ability to create a sense of Christian community. Charles Raven first encountered the knighthood when he spoke at its Heathfield camelot in July 1921 (Raven and Heath, 235). For him Beatrice Hankey symbolized 'the utter absurdity of excluding women from full recognition and ministry in the life of the Church'; she was, he said, 'to me and to very many others, both men and women, far more a bishop, a mother in God, than any ordained or consecrated Churchman' (Dillistone, 270).

MARK POTTLE

Sources C. E. Raven and R. F. Heath, *One called Help: the life and work of Beatrice Hankey* (1937) · F. W. Dillistone, *Charles Raven* (1975) · *DNB* · *The Times* (14 Jan 1929) · *The Times* (10 Feb 1932) · *The Times* (18 March 1932) · *The Times* (21 March 1932) · *The Times* (24 March 1932) · *The Times* (18 May 1932) · *The Times* (11 May 1933) · B. Heeney, *The women's movement in the Church of England, 1850–1930* (1988)
Likenesses photograph, repro. in Raven and Heath, *One called Help*, facing p. 316
Wealth at death £76,623 13s. 11d.: resworn probate, 6 May 1933, CGPLA Eng. & Wales

Hankey, Maurice Pascal Alers, first Baron Hankey (1877–1963), civil servant, was born on 1 April 1877 at Biarritz, where his family was wintering. He was the third son and fifth child of Robert Alers Hankey (1838–1906), and his wife, Helen Bakewell (1845–1900), the daughter of a prominent member of the Adelaide bar. His father had been educated at Rugby School and Trinity College, Cambridge; for reasons of health he later established himself as a sheep farmer in South Australia. His health proved a recurrent problem, and the family twice returned to England, finally settling in Brighton. Maurice attended a private day school at Brighton, and was then educated at Rugby School (1890–95). Driven by an ambition to go to sea, he overcame family resistance and was commissioned a probationary second lieutenant in the Royal Marine Artillery, and in 1897 passed out first with the sword of honour from the Royal Naval College. After specialized instruction at Eastney barracks, Portsmouth, he came first in all his examinations. In late 1898 he secured a choice subaltern appointment on the *Ramillies*, the flagship of the Mediterranean station, to which he soon added unofficial and unpaid intelligence work, an activity which he would maintain to the end of his public life and beyond. His performance of duties in the fleet caught the attention of several prominent figures, including that of

Maurice Pascal Alers Hankey, first Baron Hankey (1877–1963), by Sir William Orpen, 1919

the reform-minded Admiral Sir John Fisher, the Mediterranean commander and soon to be first sea lord. In April 1902 Hankey joined the staff of the naval intelligence department, his first Whitehall appointment. With a brief exception five years later, when he served as an intelligence officer upon the *Queen*, another ship of the Mediterranean Fleet, he remained in Whitehall for his entire career; his eventual mastery of its 'corridors of power' prevailed over his earlier love of the sea.

The Whitehall years Hankey's initial responsibilities at the naval intelligence department involved him with coastal defences in home waters and in the empire; on numerous occasions he represented the department at meetings of the colonial defence committee, at that time the only permanent subcommittee of the committee of imperial defence (CID), which had been established in late 1902. As his attention increasingly gravitated towards the empire's far-flung bases he was appointed to a joint Admiralty–CID committee in 1906. His capacious memory for technical details about naval matters from the Atlantic to the Pacific eventually won him 'a high reputation as a walking encyclopaedia of defence matters' (Roskill, 1.79). His travels served him well in reinforcing his facility in languages, which already included French, Italian, German, and modern Greek. Before his return to sea in 1907 he also served as secretary of an Admiralty committee which worked on naval war plans in the event of a war with Germany. On 15 September 1903 he married Adeline Hermine Gertrude Ernestine de Smidt (1882–1979), daughter of Abraham de Smidt, formerly surveyor-general of Cape Colony, who had settled in England in 1890.

Writing to his wife in 1906 Hankey hoped that his career would unfold 'not as a fighting man but as a sound peace administrator' (Roskill, 1.71). On the best of terms with his last chief at the naval intelligence department, Rear-Admiral C. L. Ottley, Hankey had been promised the post of naval assistant secretary to the CID, should Ottley secure the secretary's position. What both men hoped for came to pass, and in January 1908 Hankey returned to Whitehall. The CID, lodged in Whitehall Gardens, which was to be Hankey's base for thirty years, functioned in theory as a prime minister's department to oversee defence planning. In practice, however, it only advised on technical questions and could not contribute to the formulation of defence policies largely because of the rampant departmentalism in the fighting services. The CID advice did not force the military leaders to plan accordingly. Yet its potential role had been enlarged in 1904 by the creation of a secretariat charged with keeping a record of its proceedings, which was the task of its secretary and a permanent staff.

In later years Hankey himself made rather too much of the role of the pre-war CID, but in one significant way its planning did advance Britain's war readiness: between 1911 and 1913 the CID prepared a war book, in effect a timetable which outlined departmental responsibilities both in a 'precautionary stage' and in the first weeks of war. Hankey, with the support of Ottley and Fisher—and buoyed by a successful interview with R. B. Haldane, the war secretary—became CID secretary in 1912 and carried on with the war book, which he considered his greatest achievement. Curiously the war book did not go beyond the very first stages of the war and offered no advice about the direction of the war effort. Although his own organization was no war directorate-in-waiting, Hankey was able to place the CID secretariat at the service of the war council, which the Asquith government in November 1914 established at the sub-cabinet level to function as a 'supreme command' of the war effort. Neither this flawed body—partly advisory, partly executive—nor its two successors, the Dardanelles committee (June–October 1915), and the war committee (November 1915 – November 1916)—enabled the Asquith coalition to prevail over the military authorities in planning what remained an ineffective war effort. While wheels spun and mud was liberally applied to the reputations of 'frocks' and 'brass hats', Hankey moved freely between the British combatants, establishing himself as a key intermediary in the rancorous dialogue, and was widely perceived as a non-partisan figure and a skilled listener, enjoying considerable standing among the military figures.

Divided authority took its own particular toll on Britain's military performance. In the harsh light of the débâcle at the Somme, Hankey registered his deep dissatisfaction with civilian and military leadership alike in late 1916. Fear of 'catastrophe', which brought down Asquith in December 1916, led his successor, Lloyd George, to establish a war cabinet of five, so as to avoid any repetition of divided governmental authority. Lloyd George also moved decisively to establish what he described as 'virtually a new system of government in this country' (Naylor, 26). To organize and administer that entity the secretariat of the defunct war committee was expanded by the addition of a civil side, and Hankey headed the operation—the secretary himself drew up the procedural rules—with these responsibilities, among others:

> (1) to record the proceedings of the War Cabinet; (2) to transmit relevant extracts from the minutes to departments concerned with implementing them or otherwise interested; (3) to prepare the agenda paper, and to arrange the attendance of ministers not in the War Cabinet and others required to be present for discussion of particular items on the agenda; (4) to receive papers from departments and circulate them to the War Cabinet or others as necessary. (Naylor, 27)

Thus Hankey established the precepts for a co-ordinating and record-keeping organization which the cabinet secretariat and its seamless successor, the Cabinet Office (from 1920), subsequently followed. The creation of the cabinet secretariat was his greatest achievement.

The cabinet secretariat was a work in progress, and the precedents of CID record keeping could not settle the questions of the form and content of war cabinet minutes, nor determine the degree of access given to ministers outside the inner circle. The secretary consistently opposed a verbatim account: 'I aim not at an accurate account of what everyone said, but a general synopsis of the expert evidence upon which the Conclusion was based, and a general summary of the arguments for and against the decision taken' (Naylor, 36). Although there is occasional variation over the years Hankey's record keeping for several decades kept closely to this approach. Distribution of complete cabinet minutes (cabinet conclusions, from 1919) was deliberately limited but went to a wider circle of ministers than the war cabinet proper, while the circulation of certain extracts to other ministers involved constant *ad hoc* decisions by secretariat personnel. The circulation of cabinet papers—essentially memoranda—which served to bridge what a later generation would call an information gap between the war cabinet and the departments, also defied a definitive settlement, but by the end of the war Hankey had come to prefer a wide distribution. The reform of cabinet government significantly reduced the morass of indecision and inefficiency which had hampered the British war effort.

After the German collapse of 1918 Lloyd George extended the war cabinet's mandate for the duration of the Paris peace conference, but by October 1919 political pressures led to a governmental reorganization and a peacetime cabinet of about twenty ministers. Hankey's operation was unquestioned, and he easily adapted the secretariat's role to the new pattern, although his own responsibility for note taking—a task sometimes shared with his senior staff—had become more complex. The greater numbers at the cabinet table earned the scribes the pithy compliment from Walter Long: 'I don't know how you make any sort of record with all that talk going on' (Naylor, 65). The new cabinet also agreed to record keeping for the deliberations of cabinet committees, tying sub-cabinet proceedings into the network administered from Whitehall Gardens. Hankey's innovations were perpetuated into the post-war years, but Lloyd George's presence was key to their survival.

The appointment in 1919 of a new and able permanent secretary to the Treasury, Warren Fisher, who was also named head of the civil service, gave Hankey cause for concern about the future of his own office. However, for the most part, Fisher and Hankey, whose military responsibilities had been underscored by his appointment as secretary of a revived CID, sought to demarcate their respective positions. Yet another concern for Hankey was the constant public confusion and occasional disputes between his operation and that of the prime minister's secretariat, the so-called 'garden suburb' resident at 10 Downing Street. He probably over-involved himself in the post-war years as a prominent member of Lloyd George's travelling entourage, although the choice was not so much his as the prime minister's. Resentment was particularly keen in Foreign Office circles. In the autumn of 1922 Hankey's prospects and those of his office hinged upon the desires of the new premier, Bonar Law—once a member of the war cabinet—and his Conservative associates, a number of whom were well acquainted with the new ways of cabinet government. With Warren Fisher involved in discussions as a hardly disinterested player, and more ominously with Bonar Law sending mixed messages, Hankey fought a skilled and effective bureaucratic battle to preserve his office and himself. He successfully resisted absorption into the Treasury, and assured the autonomy and effective independence of the Cabinet Office while yielding on some technicalities to Fisher, whose take-over bid was frustrated. Indeed, Hankey's secretarial empire was enlarged in 1923 by his appointment, at Fisher's instigation, as clerk of the privy council, which Hankey regarded as a virtual sinecure but accepted as an embellishment of his office's prestige and his own standing. He retained his two secretaryships and his historic clerkship until retirement, calculating in July 1938 that he had taken the minutes of some 1700 meetings of the war cabinet and its peacetime successors.

Hankey was determined to protect the secrecy of the cabinet's proceedings. Since the cabinet accepted collective responsibility for its decisions—whatever individual ministers may have thought about particular policies prior to a cabinet decision or, for that matter, thereafter—Hankey assumed that the records of discussions and decisions would be inviolable, at least for any foreseeable future, and secured the requisite support for this policy from successive cabinets. In the early post-war period his Cabinet Office could not lay claim to the actual custody of cabinet minutes and papers, which were generally retained by ministers, contrary to Hankey's secretarial wishes. But he proved as patient as he was committed to the cause of recovering those documents, and breaches of cabinet secrecy by the press enabled him in 1934 to secure custody of 'official materials' from all but a handful of former cabinet ministers, and to establish the Cabinet Office as their repository. All ministers retained the right of access but were subject to regulation in the way those documents might in future be used. Although these guidelines would be breached in a massive way by Winston Churchill in his memoirs of the Second World War, by and large they prevailed until the altering political and legal climate of the 1960s mandated extensive reform, including public access to most cabinet documents after a stated period of time.

From early on Hankey had also undertaken the censorship—he preferred the term 'vetting'—of ministerial memoirs, acting in the name of the prime minister of the day. His tactful hand can be seen in alterations accepted in such partisan accounts of the First World War as those of Lloyd George and Churchill. By a curious turn of fate Hankey sought to publish his own diary-based account of that war as early as 1943: he asked his successor, Sir Edward Bridges to 'vet' his memoirs and was shocked to encounter strong resistance to an account which, Bridges informed him, revealed too much about his dealings with ministers. When Hankey countered, correctly, that the war period had always been treated *sui generis*, Bridges retorted that Hankey's unique perspective would compromise his own role and that of other civil servants, because any depiction of their influence could undermine the doctrine of ministerial responsibility. Despite Hankey's anguished protest Churchill's war cabinet denied him permission to publish, a situation which lasted nearly twenty years until Harold Macmillan in effect turned a blind eye to the publication of an abridged and expurgated *The Supreme Command, 1914–1918* (2 vols., 1961). Alas, the insightful and often acerbic Hankey diary had been reduced to a near anodyne form, and its full impact would not be known until the publication in 1970 of Stephen Roskill's first volume of his authoritative Hankey biography.

Military adviser and diplomatic confidant Although his secretarial work for the war cabinet after 1916 limited the time available to advisory tasks, Hankey continued to devote some time and his acknowledged tact to dealing with Britain's military leaders, including Haig, Robertson, and Henry Wilson. Inevitably he did not consistently prevail: he was a convinced 'Easterner', but his own standing seemed not to be compromised by the collapse of the Dardanelles venture in 1915. In positive terms he was involved with the initial planning of a 'land battleship' (the tank), and his contribution in overcoming Admiralty opposition to the convoy system was even more highly valued by his associates. With the revival of the CID in 1919, Hankey was well placed to influence the direction of post-war military planning. He advocated causes which were common to his generation and military training: sceptical for the future of the League of Nations, he remarked revealingly that 'the British Empire is worth a thousand Leagues of Nations' (Naylor, 58). In sum he was an unreconstructed 'traditionalist' through those years in which they and the 'collectivists' stared at each other across a great strategic divide. Hankey's support for such doctrines as 'freedom of the seas' and 'belligerent rights' underscored his commitment to the maintenance of Britain's naval strengths and his suspicions about American designs upon her empire. Though his expression of forceful opinions impresses as ministerial rather than secretarial, his holding such views was known to and accepted by such figures as Baldwin and MacDonald.

As the skies darkened upon the Versailles settlement Hankey mounted a systematic campaign against the 'ten year rule' (the assumption that no war would be fought in the next ten years) which met with some success in 1932, although its constraints upon military expenditures prevailed until late 1933. From that time Hankey chaired a defence requirements subcommittee of the CID—his old rival Warren Fisher contributed to its efforts to repair the 'worst deficiencies' in Britain's armed forces. However, Hankey could not preserve the parent CID as the sole agency for the co-ordination of Britain's defence planning, and the creation of a number of *ad hoc* committees in the defence sector blurs any precise measure of Hankey's personal achievement in securing even the degree of war readiness which Britain possessed in 1939. While he did not challenge the dominant view that the Treasury functioned as a 'fourth arm of defence', dictating a 'rationing' of the overall expenditures needed to sustain any rearmament programme, no one laboured longer, harder, or more consistently than he to move the rearmament programme forward.

During the First World War, Hankey's daily attendance upon Lloyd George led inexorably to his role as a diplomatic confidant; though his role in these matters was unofficial, he was quite willing to offer advice on virtually any aspect of war policy. Since the foreign secretary was excluded from Lloyd George's war cabinet, the prime minister's preference for private rather than official advice added further to Hankey's standing. His activities at allied conferences grew: he acted as adviser as well as functionary at the Rapallo conference of November 1917, which established the inter-allied supreme war council. At the Paris peace conference, initially serving as secretary to the British empire delegation, he soon came to preside over the secretarial apparatus of the council of ten and then the more important council of four (Lloyd George, Clemenceau, Orlando, and Woodrow Wilson). Although the foreign secretary sat in the peacetime cabinet, Hankey continued his close association with Lloyd George in world meetings, serving as secretary of the British delegation to the Washington naval conference (1921–2) and the Genoa conference (1922); the latter meeting witnessed Lloyd George's last exclusion of the foreign secretary from its councils.

When the Lloyd George coalition fell in 1922 Hankey moved quickly to improve his office's relations with the Foreign Office as a key element in his contraction of Cabinet Office responsibilities. Yet within a few weeks Hankey was 'astonished' and 'tickled' to learn from Bonar Law that as the Foreign Office was overstretched in its initial secretarial tasks, he would once more undertake secretarial arrangements for some international meetings. Thus he served as secretary-general to conferences dealing with German reparations, in London (1924) and Lausanne (1932), at the Hague conferences (1929, 1930), and at the London naval conference (1930). Already in the war years he had personally kept the minutes of the imperial war cabinet, meeting in London, and remained as secretary to the imperial conferences of 1921, 1923, 1926, 1930, and 1937. Doubtless his primary focus lay in managing these diverse proceedings, but it may fairly be added that he continued to advise in the affairs of Europe and the empire.

For a quarter-century Hankey's standing was reinforced by his growing expertise in defence matters and, if he was by no means neutral in his assessments of the roles of the three services, his experience and vast knowledge incorporated a broader overall view than individual military advisers could develop. His own recommendations were argued judiciously, and he consistently demonstrated an essential tact in dealing with ministers and their other advisers. In particular Hankey adjusted to the different temperaments of the five premiers he served, from the mercurial Lloyd George to the laconic Baldwin; yet it is the adroit courtship of MacDonald in 1924 that best illustrates his ability to transcend unwelcome political and strategic views. Though not close to Neville Chamberlain, Hankey strongly supported his policy of appeasement, albeit for reasons of military weakness rather than the premier's sense of mission. His dealings with cabinet ministers were a model of gentlemanly manners and moderation, although on occasion pent-up frustration spilled over into critical diary entries, which served in part as a release of his own convictions and emotions. He was driven to breaking point only once, in 1937 privately exchanging recriminations with Winston Churchill—'the most difficult man I ever had to work with' (Roskill, 3.656). Hankey's choice of foe would prove a fateful one, but the incident was part of a pattern, and by 1937 Hankey showed other signs of exhaustion and a shortening temper, as the burden of responsibility in an increasingly ominous European situation grew. Within the Cabinet Office Hankey's tact was less in evidence, and the atmosphere became cool.

Twilight years In July 1938 Hankey retired as clerk of the privy council office, secretary to the cabinet, and secretary to the CID. Created a peer in February 1939, he emerged from a year's retirement in September 1939, when he accepted the position of minister without portfolio and membership in Chamberlain's war cabinet. He was sworn of the privy council in that month. An ill portent for this new career may be found in his remark that 'as far as I can make out my main job is to keep an eye on Winston!' (Roskill, 3.419). In fact he assumed a range of responsibilities, including the monitoring of intelligence activities and the application of science and technology to the war effort. He chaired the cabinet's scientific advisory committee, which played a key role in the development of the atomic bomb programme in 1940–41. The leading scientists with whom he worked valued his administrative contributions sufficiently to elect him a fellow of the Royal Society in 1942. Hankey took great satisfaction from his chairing of the cabinet's committee on preventing oil from reaching Germany (the POG committee) between October 1939 and August 1940.

Predictably Hankey showed a strong interest in the maritime war, offering suggestions about convoy logistics to the new first lord, Churchill, who in May 1940 succeeded Chamberlain as premier; Hankey remained a Chamberlain loyalist to the bitter end, and he showed little sensitivity to the domestic political dynamics of the transfer of power. He was not a member of Churchill's war cabinet, though he was given the position of chancellor of the duchy of Lancaster, which enabled him to carry on his committee work and the 'special duties' which had been entrusted to him. To these functions Hankey added the chair of the technical personnel committee, which mediated between governmental needs and developing technology, including the training of required personnel. Churchill relegated Hankey to the post of paymaster-general in the ministerial reshuffle of July 1941. Hankey had read the signs of his loss of standing in the ministry, but he persisted in his criticism of Churchill's conduct of the war especially during its darkest hours in the winter of 1941–2. His criticisms ranged from Churchill's war organization and 'dictatorial' methods to a number of strategic issues. The issue about which Hankey felt most strongly was the imperative to divert converted long-range bombers away from strategic mainland bombing, and to use them to protect the lifeline of Atlantic convoys. His criticisms were not without merit, but he shared the particulars with a number of the prime minister's political opponents. Since his dissenting views were openly argued within the government he could not be accused of covert disloyalty, but predictably the breach widened. When Churchill finally dismissed him in March 1942 Hankey returned fire: 'For some time I have felt profoundly dissatisfied with the conduct of the war' (Roskill, 3.544). Thus he had no ministerial part in 'the turn of the tide'.

Hankey's years of ministerial office exposed several weaknesses, the most telling of which was an insensitivity to political nuance, apparent both in his failure to comprehend the necessity for Chamberlain to yield power to Churchill in 1940 and in his disparaging views of the capacity of Labour leaders to contribute to the reorganized government. He placed too much stock in his experiences in the First World War, often using them as a virtual template for the events of the second. Nor could he bring himself to trust Churchill's judgement—whatever his other qualities—and so was ill-placed to succeed under his domineering leadership.

After leaving office Hankey continued to chair the technical personnel committee until 1952, when he withdrew from all official committee responsibilities. He also resumed his role as a director of the Suez Canal Company. In 1938, faced with retirement and an expressed need to secure the financial security of his family, he had negotiated with Neville Chamberlain his appointment as a British government director of the company, with an annual fee of £5000. He had to give up the lucrative position while serving as a minister, but he regained it in 1945 and from 1948 served as a commercial director, consistently defending the company's role and the British military presence in Egypt, until events—and Colonel Nasser—led to the nationalization of the company in 1956. His own financial situation was adversely affected, but he felt even more acutely the diminution of Britain's world standing; nor was he any more reconciled to the predominance of the United States upon that stage than he had been with its emergence three decades earlier. He served on several company boards during his post-ministerial years and undertook some journalism. In addition to his long-suppressed war memoirs, he saw through to publication *Diplomacy by Conference* (1946), a collection of earlier papers and lectures; *The Supreme Command at the Paris Peace Conference, 1919* (1963); and *Politics, Trials and Errors* (1949). The last encapsulated his controversial campaign against the war crimes trials of German and Japanese military leaders. His plea for a general amnesty for war criminals won him little popularity generally, although he drew some strength from a like-minded group of nearly a dozen prominent figures.

Hankey's memoirs were grounded in his full and sometimes caustic diary, subsequently housed with correspondence and other materials at Churchill College, Cambridge. Their availability—thoroughly exploited in Roskill's biography—renders superfluous Hankey's own cautious use of them, essential to secure publication in his own lifetime. Hankey is revealed as a man whose public persona of tact and moderation was matched by a private and often critical perspective on individual ministerial foibles and collective failures. The diary is hubristic and sometimes self-serving, but Hankey utilized such licence to maintain his public neutrality. His own causes and beliefs reflect the certainties of a late Victorian imperialist, whose policies sought to maintain British domination abroad and to avoid as far as possible British entanglement within Europe. His patriotism stands inviolable, but his sensitivity to processes of historical change proved limited. Hankey did not altogether grasp the virulence of fascism, most apparent in Hitler's variant, except as a military threat to Britain; nor did he ever quite comprehend the changing face of domestic politics which Labour's emergence as a party of government entailed, particularly after the party's break with MacDonald and the National Government in 1931. In these shortcomings Hankey was typical of his generation and background; that his responsibility was greater lay in the fact that he was better informed than nearly any of his contemporaries.

Hankey was appointed CB (1912), KCB (1916), GCB (1919), GCMG (1929), and GCVO (1934). He held honorary degrees from Oxford, Cambridge, Edinburgh, and Birmingham. A grant of £25,000 was given to him for his services in the First World War. Although on occasion he found his family finances worrisome—he would die well off, but not wealthy—his family life was otherwise estimable, anchored not only in a happy marriage but also in a close and confidential relationship with his wife, which can be measured in his frequent and full letters while abroad.

The family—three sons and a daughter—was close knit, and Hankey's own hand, while often absent, was exercised supportively if paternalistically. Deeply felt Anglican religious values and a love of music infused the household. While the private Hankey was not on view in the office, George Mallaby offered an insider's perspective on his traits:

> He was busy always, and his moods of relaxation were known only to his family … His religion was of the type known as 'muscular Christianity'. He took a cold bath every morning, he was an advocate of alfresco meals in unwelcoming weather, he was persistent in physical exercise, and his favourite method of locomotion was on his feet. He was a man of temperate habits. He preferred a diet of whole-wheat bread, raw vegetables, fresh fruit, eggs, and nuts, and this sustained him in full vigour until he was nearly eighty-six. (*DNB*)

Mallaby described his appearance as unimpressive: he was no more than 5 feet 5 inches in height, had an inelegant figure, and was bald from an early age.

In 1958 Hankey was diagnosed with prostate cancer, which was controlled with hormones but took its toll upon his vigour; partially deaf and with diminished vision, he last attended the House of Lords in 1960. In early 1963 he underwent emergency surgery for a strangulated hernia in Redhill General Hospital, Limpsfield, Surrey, and died there in his sleep two nights later, on 26 January 1963. Hankey was buried in Limpsfield parish churchyard. A memorial service was held in Westminster Abbey on 20 February. He was succeeded in the peerage by his son, Robert (Robin) Maurice Alers Hankey (1905–1996), a member of the foreign service and at the time of his father's death the permanent United Kingdom representative to the international Organization for Economic Co-operation and Development.   JOHN F. NAYLOR

Sources S. W. Roskill, *Hankey, man of secrets*, 3 vols. (1970–74) • J. F. Naylor, *A man and an institution: Sir Maurice Hankey, the cabinet secretariat and the custody of cabinet secrecy* (1984) • S. S. Wilson, *The cabinet office to 1945* (1975) • *DNB* • *The Times* (28 Jan 1963)
Archives CAC Cam., MSS • PRO, corresp. and MSS, CAB 63 | BL, corresp. with Arthur James Balfour, Add. MSS 49703–49705 • BL, corresp. with Lord Cecil, Add. MS 51088 • BL, corresp. with Lord D'Abernon, Add. MS 48927b • Bodl. Oxf., corresp. with Herbert Asquith; letters to Lewis Harcourt; corresp. with Lord Selborne; corresp. with Lord Simon • Bodl. RH, corresp. with C. Walker relating to east Africa and India • CAC Cam., corresp. with Monty Belgion; corresp. with Lord Fisher; corresp. with Sir E. L. Spears; corresp. with Lord Weir • CUL, corresp. with Sir Samuel Hoare • HLRO, corresp. with Viscount Davidson and Andrew Bonar Law; corresp. mainly with David Lloyd George; letters to Lord Samuel • IWM, corresp. with Sir Henry Tizard; corresp. with Sir Henry Wilson • King's Lond., Liddell Hart C., corresp. with Sir J. E. Edmonds • King's Lond., Liddell Hart C., corresp. with Sir B. H. Liddell Hart • Lpool RO, corresp. with seventeenth earl of Derby • NA Scot., corresp. with A. J. Balfour; corresp. with Lord Lothian • NL Scot., corresp. with Lord Haldane • NL Wales, corresp. with Thomas Jones • Nuffield Oxf., corresp. with Lord Cherwell; corresp. with Lord Mottistone • PRO, corresp. with Sir Henry Dale, CAB 127/10 • PRO, corresp. with James Ramsay MacDonald • PRO NIre., corresp. with Edward Carson • U. Birm. L., corresp. with Lord Avon • U. Newcastle, Robinson L., corresp. with Walter Runciman
Likenesses W. Stoneman, three photographs, 1917–47, NPG • H. Olivier, oils, 1919, Gov. Art Coll. • W. Orpen, oils, 1919, NPG [*see illus.*] • F. Topolski, portrait, NPG • photograph, repro. in Wilson, *Cabinet office to 1945*, 104–5
Wealth at death £35,782 15s.: probate, 31 May 1963, *CGPLA Eng. & Wales*

Hankey, Thomson (1805–1893), politician and political economist, born at Dalston, Middlesex, on 5 June 1805, was the eldest son of the eight children of Thomson Hankey (d. 1857) and his wife, Martha, daughter of Benjamin Harrison. He was descended from Sir John Barnard; in 1855 he reprinted for private circulation, with a preface by himself, the *Memoirs* of Barnard, which had first appeared in 1820. He married, on 4 February 1831, Appoline Agatha (d. 1888), daughter of William Alexander and half-sister of Sir William Alexander, the chief baron.

Hankey joined his father's firm of Thomson Hankey & Co., plantation owners and West Indies merchants, and became its long-serving senior partner. He was elected a director of the Bank of England in 1835, and later served as deputy governor (1849–51) and as governor (1851–3). In 1853 he was elected as Liberal MP for Peterborough, a seat he held until 1868 and again between 1874 and 1880. In the House of Commons he spoke frequently, and with independence of thought, on economic issues. He also published several tracts, mostly on finance, the most important of which was *The principles of banking, its utility and economy, with remarks on the working and management of the Bank of England* (4th edn, 1887), first delivered as a lecture to the Peterborough Mechanics' Institute in 1858. Hankey held obdurately to the view, encouraged by the Bank Charter Act of 1844, that 'at all times and under almost any conceivable case, the actions of the Bank ought to be governed by the same rules as would govern the proceedings of most well-regulated private Banking Establishments' (Bank of England archives, 'Remarks and opinions on the banking acts of 1844 and 1845', 5 Nov 1856). After the commercial crisis of 1866, this view became less tenable within the bank and outside it, especially as Bagehot in *The Economist* and *Lombard Street* elaborated against Hankey the responsibilities of the bank as lender of last resort.

From April 1855 to July 1877 Hankey was a member of the Political Economy Club. He collected a special library of tracts on financial topics, and at the close of his life gave many to the library of the City Liberal Club, and others to the library of the Bank of England. He studied the works of the leading French and American writers on political economy, and corresponded regularly with them, especially on monetary questions and free trade. He also gave written evidence to the French *Enquête sur les principes … qui régissent la circulation monétaire et fiduciaire*, 1865–6. In 1878 he led a subscription for a memorial to Lord John Russell.

Hankey died at his London home, 59 Portland Place, on 13 January 1893, and was buried in the churchyard of Shipbourne, near Tonbridge, Kent; a tablet was placed in the church in his memory. He had no children, but his great-nephew Ernest Harvey entered the Bank of England in 1885 and was deputy governor, 1929–36.

W. P. COURTNEY, *rev.* A. C. HOWE

Sources *The Times* (16 Jan 1893) · archives, Bank of England · J. Clapham, *The Bank of England: a history*, 2 (1944) · F. W. Fetter, *Development of British monetary orthodoxy, 1797–1875* (1965) · *Peterborough Advertiser* (21 Jan 1893) · *Tonbridge Free Press* (21 Jan 1893) · *Debrett's Illustrated House of Commons and the Judicial Bench* (1872) · Burke, *Gen. GB* · Boase, *Mod. Eng. biog.*

Archives Bank of England archives, London · BL, corresp. with W. E. Gladstone, Add. MSS 44374–44514, *passim* · Bodl. Oxf., letters to Disraeli · Bucks. RLSS, corresp. with first Baron Cottesloe · NYPL, D. A. Wells MSS · PRO, letters to Odo Russell, FO 918 · U. Durham, letters to Henry George, third Earl Grey

Likenesses J. H. Lynch, lithograph, Bank of England, London; repro. in *ILN* (4 Feb 1854), 100 · lithograph, Bank of England archives, London, no. 242 collection case 3 · photograph, Bank of England archives, London, album m1. B671, B385 · portrait, repro. in *Daily Graphic* (18 Jan 1893), 9 · tablet, St Giles's Church, Shipbourne, Kent · wood-engraving, NPG; repro. in *ILN* (4 Feb 1854)

Wealth at death £133,482 0s. 8d.: resworn probate, Aug 1894, *CGPLA Eng. & Wales* (1893)

Hankin, Edward (1747–1835), writer, is said to have been an MD, but of what university does not appear. From 1800 to 1805 he was a curate at Mersham, Kent, and was then, on the appointment of Lord Abergavenny, rector of West Chiltington, Sussex, from 1807 until 1819. During his tenure, he was largely non-resident. Hankin's *Perpetual War, the Only Ground of Perpetual Safety and Prosperity* (1805) argued that peace would only allow France time to build ships. He published various pamphlets on ecclesiastical affairs, including *The Causes and Consequences of the Neglect of the Clergy* (1803), he frequently denounced Sir Francis Burdett, and he opposed Catholic emancipation. His *Adresse* to the European sovereigns, published in 1817, records his life as a persecutor of politicians for their supposed lack of patriotism. Hankin died at Hull on 14 July 1835.

J. M. RIGG, *rev.* H. C. G. MATTHEW

Sources *GM*, 2nd ser., 4 (1835), 329 · [J. Watkins and F. Shoberl], *A biographical dictionary of the living authors of Great Britain and Ireland* (1816) · E. Hankin, *Adresse* (1817)

Archives BL, letters to earl of Liverpool, Add. MSS 38251–38256, 38285, 38289, 38379, *passim*

Hankin, St John Emile Clavering (1869–1909), playwright, born on 25 September 1869 at Southampton, was the third son of the four children of Charles Wright Hankin, headmaster of King Edward VI School, Southampton. His mother was Mary Louisa (*d.* 1909), daughter of Edmund Thomas Wigley Perrot, who inherited estates at Craycombe, Worcestershire. In January 1883 Hankin entered Malvern College as house and foundation scholar, and at the age of seventeen he won an open postmastership at Merton College, Oxford, as well as a close Ackroyd scholarship, for which he was qualified by descent, through his mother. He took a second-class degree in classics in 1890.

Hankin next worked as a journalist in London. From 1890 he contributed to the *Saturday Review*. In 1894 he joined the staff of the *India Daily News* at Calcutta. After a year in India an attack of malaria drove him home. For a time Hankin worked on *The Times*, and contributed to *Punch*. His keen wit and shrewd common sense were seen to advantage in two series of papers which appeared in *Punch* and were afterwards published independently. *Mr*

Punch's Dramatic Sequels (1901) added supplementary acts to the great classics of the English drama, and *Lost Masterpieces* (1904) subtly parodied eminent authors in both prose and verse. In 1901 Hankin married Florence, the daughter of George Routledge, the publisher. They had no children.

Playwriting of a realistic frankness was Hankin's main ambition. The first of his plays to be acted was *The Two Mr Wetherbys*, which was privately performed in London by the Stage Society in February 1903 and later by William Hawtrey in Australia and New Zealand. When in 1905 the strain of a journalist's life in London encouraged Hankin to retire to Chipping Campden in Gloucestershire, he mainly devoted himself to writing for the stage. His translation of Eugène Brieux's *Les trois filles de Monsieur Dupont*, introduced by George Bernard Shaw, was produced, again privately, by the Stage Society in 1905, and its boldness caused controversy. Hankin achieved genuine success in the pungently ironical comedy *The Return of the Prodigal*, which was publicly produced on 26 September 1905 by Vedrenne and Barker at the Court Theatre, and was revived on 29 April 1907. His best-known play, it went through five editions after his death. *The Charity that Began at Home* and *The Cassilis Engagement*, which was perhaps the most popular of his plays among contemporary audiences, proved less incisive; both were first performed privately by the Stage Society in London in 1906 and 1907 respectively, and were afterwards successfully repeated at repertory theatres in Manchester, Liverpool, and Glasgow. Hankin published the three last-named plays in 1907 under the ironic title of *Three Plays with Happy Endings*, with a preface responding to adverse criticism in the press. In *The Last of the De Mullins*, produced by the Stage Society in December 1908 and published in 1909, Hankin's merciless realism went even further than before in telling the story of a 'new woman' opposed by her family because she chooses to earn her own living. He also wrote two one-act pieces, *The Burglar who Failed*, which had a successful run at the Criterion Theatre in November 1908, and *The Constant Lover*, which was produced at the Royalty Theatre in February 1912.

Hankin's dramatic work, in so far as it satirized middle-class conventional morality, bore traces of Bernard Shaw's influence. He cannot, however, be classified simply as a Shavian, as is clear from his preface to *Three Plays with Happy Endings*, in which he stated: 'It is the dramatist's business to represent life, not to argue about it.' His impatience with popular late-nineteenth-century sentimental theatre meant that he chiefly aimed at a coldly acute analysis of character. His finely pointed wit failed to reconcile the public at large or the critics in the press to his cynicism. He was criticized for attacking abuses but failing to suggest remedies: *The Times* described his plays as 'making even Ibsen look cheerful'. His *Collected Plays* in two volumes, edited by John Drinkwater, were published posthumously in 1912 and 1923.

Never robust in health, Hankin suffered much since 1907 from neurasthenia. In a fit of depression he drowned himself in the River Ithon, at Llandrindod Wells, Radnorshire, on 15 June 1909. His ashes were buried, after cremation at Golders Green on 22 June. His wife survived him.

G. S. WOODS, *rev.* KATHERINE MULLIN

Sources *WWW, 1897–1915* · J. Parker, ed., *The green room book, or, Who's who on the stage* (1907) · J. Foster, *Oxford men, 1880–1892: with a record of their schools, honours, and degrees* (1893) · P. Hartnoll, ed., *The Oxford companion to the theatre*, 2nd edn (1957) · *The Times* (21 June 1909) · T. F. Evans, 'A note on Hankin', *The Shavian*, 4 (1970), 52–3 · *The Athenaeum* (26 June 1909), 768 · Malvern College register, 1904 · M. Beerbohm, *A book of caricatures* (1907) · D. MacCarthy, *The Court Theatre, 1904–1907: a commentary and criticism* (1907)

Archives Bodl. Oxf., Walpole MSS

Likenesses M. Beerbohm, caricature, repro. in Beerbohm, *Book of caricatures*, no. xix

Wealth at death £2181 2*s.*: probate, 31 July 1909, *CGPLA Eng. & Wales*

Hankinson, Thomas Edwards (1805–1843), Church of England clergyman and poet, was born at King's Lynn on 19 June 1805, the third son of Revd Robert Hankinson (1770/71–1863) and his wife, Ann Edwards. He was educated at Wonersh School, near Guildford, and Corpus Christi College, Cambridge, where he graduated BA in 1828 and proceeded MA in 1831. He was ordained deacon in 1828 and priest in 1829. After serving as curate at Castle Rising, Norfolk (1828–9), and St Nicholas Chapel, King's Lynn (1829–35), he became incumbent of St Matthew's Chapel, Denmark Hill (1835–43). On 4 June 1831 he married Caroline Peacock. He published various sermons, hymns, and lectures; his theological opinions were strictly orthodox, and in a sermon published at King's Lynn in 1834 he denounced unitarians as 'blasphemers'.

Hankinson spent much of his leisure time in writing for the Seatonian prize at Cambridge for English verse, of which he was nine times the winner between 1831 and 1842; for each of his poems in 1831 and 1838 he was awarded an extra prize of £100. He died at Stainley Hall, Ripon, on 7 October 1843, and was buried at Danby Wiske. His prize poems, which contemporaries appreciated, were published severally during his lifetime, and collectively after his death with some other fugitive pieces in a small volume, *Poems* (1844), edited by his brothers. They also edited a volume of his sermons which appeared the same year.

J. M. RIGG, *rev.* MARI G. ELLIS

Sources [T. E. Hankinson], *A sketch of the life of T. E. Hankinson*, 2 vols. (1861) · Venn, *Alum. Cant.* · *GM*, 2nd ser., 20 (1843), 661 · J. Julian, ed., *A dictionary of hymnology* (1892) · d. cert.

Hanlan [Hanlon], **Edward** (1855–1908), oarsman, was born of Irish parents in Toronto, Ontario, Canada, on 12 July 1855, one of two sons and two daughters of John Hanlon, hotel proprietor, and his wife, Mary Gibbs. He married on 19 December 1877 Margaret Gordon Sutherland of Picton, Nova Scotia; they had two sons and six daughters.

Educated at George Street public school, Toronto, Hanlan developed an early taste for rowing, and he gained his first important success at the age of eighteen, when he became amateur champion of Toronto Bay. Soon after turning professional he beat all comers at the Centennial International Exhibition at Philadelphia in 1876, the year in which he unsuccessfully became a hotel proprietor in Toronto. He became champion sculler of Canada in 1877 and of the United States in 1878, beating among others Charles Courtney, the best-known of the American professionals. Further successes in America led him in 1879 to test his powers in England. On 16 June 1879 he defeated the English champion, W. Elliott of Blyth, rowing the course from the Mansion House in Newcastle to the Scotswood suspension bridge on the Tyne in the record time of 21 minutes 2 seconds. On Hanlan's return to Toronto a public subscription of £4000 was raised for his benefit. Hanlan revisited England in 1880, defeating Edward Trickett of Australia on 15 November on the Thames from Putney to Mortlake for the world championship. He beat four subsequent challengers for the title between 1881 and 1884, twice on the Thames, once on the Tyne, and then in Australia, where he contested the championship over the next four years. He was beaten by the Australian William Beach on three occasions between 1884 and 1887 and twice by another Australian, Peter Kemp, during 1888. Hanlan continued to compete well into the 1890s, mainly in North America, but by then professional rowing was losing its appeal because of charges of cheating and match rigging.

During his career Hanlan, who was 5 feet 8¾ inches in height and weighed 11 stone, won over 150 races, and as an oarsman was unsurpassed for finish and style. Unlike his English professional rivals, he used the slide simultaneously with the swing, kept his body well back, and held his arms straight long past the perpendicular before bending them, added strength being given by the skilful use of his great leg power. Hanlan died on 4 January 1908 at Toronto, where he was buried with civic honours; his wife survived him.

W. S. JACKSON, *rev.* ERIC HALLADAY

Sources *The Globe* [Toronto] (4 Jan 1908) · *The Globe* [Toronto] (6 Jan 1908) · *The Globe* [Toronto] (7 Jan 1908) · *The Times* (17 June 1879) · *The Times* (6 Jan 1908) · T. C. Mendenhall, *A short history of American rowing* (Boston, 1980), chap. 3 · S. Crowther and A. Ruhl, *Rowing and track athletics* (1905), chap. 9 · W. B. Woodgate, *Boating* (1888), 296–7

Likenesses H. H. Emmerson, portrait; known to be in family possession, 1912 · lithograph, NPG

Hanley, James (1901–1985), novelist and playwright, was born in Jervis Street, Dublin, on 3 September 1901, the son of Edward Hanley (d. 1937), a ship's stoker. The Hanleys had ten children, three of whom died in infancy; another of their sons was Gerald Hanley (1916–1992), also a novelist. The father took to the sea after moving his family to Liverpool in 1908 and they lived in Othello Street (now gone) in Kirkdale, near Bootle. The only school Hanley attended was St Alexandra's Roman Catholic primary school, near his home. At the age of twelve he left school and joined the merchant navy, serving in a submarine during the First World War; the reason for his enlisting while under age has never been made clear, except that the family was poor and needed him to start bringing in a wage. Three years later he jumped ship at New Brunswick to enlist in the Canadian Black Watch and eventually saw action in France. Invalided out of the army suffering from the effects of gas, he returned to the sea, working as a stoker on troop carriers, which he featured in some of his novels. He continued to educate himself, mainly by reading Russian literature, and having come ashore in the late 1920s earned a precarious living in a variety of jobs in docks, on the railway, and for a while at Aintree racecourse. Many of his early stories were published in the *Liverpool Echo*, the editor of which, E. Hope Prince, became his mentor.

Hanley's first novel, *Drift* (1930), and his first volume of stories, *The German Prisoner* (1930), were published shortly before his move to Wales, where he settled first at Glan Ceirw, Tŷ-nant, near Corwen in Merioneth, and then, in the autumn of 1941, at Bodynfoel Lodge and Tan-y-ffridd in the village of Llanfechain, Montgomeryshire. He lived from about this time with Dorothy Enid Thomas, *née* Heathcote (1902/3–1980), the woman whom he later married at Hampstead register office in London on 6 October 1947; their son, Liam Powys Hanley, had been born at Corwen in 1933. His second novel, *Boy* (1932), an appalling story of sexual violence on board ship, was originally published in an edition of 145 copies for subscribers only. An expurgated trade edition followed, but when in 1934 it was issued in a cheap edition, copies were seized by the police and the book was successfully prosecuted for obscenity. The publisher was fined £400 and copies of the book were burnt. At the International Congress of Writers held in Paris in 1935, which was devoted to 'the defence of culture', E. M. Forster (accompanied by Hanley) delivered a speech entitled 'Liberty in England' which criticized the workings of the obscene publications laws with reference to the trial; the speech is included in Forster's collection of essays, *Abinger Harvest* (1936). Hanley forbade republication of the novel during his lifetime and it was not reissued until 1990.

The first of Hanley's novels about the Furys, a Liverpool Irish family, appeared in 1935 and a volume of autobiography, *Broken Water*, in 1937. On the outbreak of the Second World War he found work with the BBC and later with the Ministry of Information, but his home remained in Llanfechain until 1963, when he and his wife moved to London. During the war he wrote three novels of the sea which are among his best work: *Hollow Sea* (1938), *The Ocean* (1941), and *Sailor's Song* (1943); it was to these that the novelist Henry Green referred in describing Hanley as 'far and away the best writer of the sea and seafaring men since Conrad'. He also wrote the autobiographical *No Directions* (1943), an evocation of London during the blitz. Many of his stories and radio plays were broadcast on the BBC Third Programme during the 1940s. During his long residence in Wales, Hanley wrote four books with Welsh settings: a collection of essays, *Don Quixote Drowned* (1953), and the novels *The Welsh Sonata* (1954), *Another World* (1971), and *A Kingdom* (1978). His *Selected Stories* appeared in 1947 and *Collected Stories* in 1953. His most memorable achievement is the series of novels about the Furys, which continued with *The Secret Journey* (1936), *Our Time is Gone* (1940), *Winter Journey* (1950), and *An End and a Beginning* (1958), all of which are imbued with a sense of the dignity of suffering.

Hanley was a prolific and accomplished writer but, despite the admiration of C. P. Snow, Herbert Read, Edwin Muir, and others, his work has been oddly neglected by literary critics. His output, though uneven, was prodigious: some thirty novels, sixteen volumes of short stories, six plays, numerous scripts for radio and television, and seven volumes of miscellaneous writings, including *Grey Children* (1937), a study of conditions in the distressed mining valleys of south Wales during the depression, and books about John Cowper Powys (a neighbour of his at Corwen) and Herman Melville. The reasons for his neglect may have to do with his subject matter: the brutality of life at sea, the wretchedness of his proletarian characters, and the unglamourized portrait of men at war. There is, too, a recurrent theme of violence which some readers have found repugnant. But Hanley, 'the well-known proletarian novelist', as he was described by the poet and editor John Lehmann when his work appeared in the periodical *New Writing* during the 1930s, had no interest in idealizing working-class life. Although once a member of the Bootle branch of the Independent Labour Party, he had no time for communism, and in later life was hostile to all political parties. His vision of man as essentially solitary, unable to communicate, and inhabiting a bleak and nightmarish world—though unrelenting to the point of obsession—is sometimes relieved by the quality of his writing, which can border on the poetic, and in his best fiction it is redeemed by the author's charity, humility, and courage. It is a mistake to consider Hanley as only a realist writer: there are touches of surrealism in some of his shorter novels and his main interest is always what is going on in the minds of his characters, especially in their dreams, fantasies, and fears. Some of his characters, such as the indomitable Fanny Fury, are among the most vividly drawn in modern English fiction of the first half of the twentieth century.

James Hanley died of bronchial pneumonia at his home, 11 Clevedon Mansions, Lissenden Gardens, Highgate Road, London, on 11 November 1985 and was buried in the churchyard at Llanfechain, the village which he considered his home.   MEIC STEPHENS

Sources M. Stephens, ed., *The Oxford companion to the literature of Wales* (1986) · J. Vinson, ed., *Contemporary novelists* (1972) · R. Welch, ed., *The Oxford companion to Irish literature* (1996) · m. cert. · d. cert. · private information (2004) · J. Fordham, *James Hanley, modernism and the working class* (2002)

Archives Bryn Mawr College, Pennsylvania, corresp. and papers · Lpool RO, corresp. and papers · LUL, corresp. and literary MSS · NL Wales, letters, mainly to son | Ransom HRC, corresp. with John Lane

Wealth at death under £40,000: administration, 3 Feb 1986, *CGPLA Eng. & Wales*

Hanlin, Thomas [Tom] (1907–1953), novelist, was born in Armadale, Linlithgowshire, on 28 August 1907, the son of Francis Hanlin, labourer, and his wife, Hannah, *née* McInulty. He did well at school and won prizes in his final year but his family could not afford higher education for him and he left school at the age of fourteen. After a year spent working on a farm he started work in the local coalmines, and was a miner for over twenty years.

From an early age Hanlin spent his spare time writing, making a little money by contributing stories to popular boys' papers. After an accident at work he spent three months in Edinburgh Royal Infirmary and there had leisure to write five short stories, which he was able to sell. An essay, 'Sunday in the Village', which he also reworked as a story, won Sheffield University's annual Arthur Markham prize, open to writers who were 'manual workers in or about a coal mine, or have been injured when so employed'.

In 1944 Hanlin submitted the manuscript of his first novel, *Once in every Lifetime*, as an entry in a competition run by the London publishers Wells Gardner Darton for their Big Ben Books, a ninepenny series otherwise consisting largely of thrillers. Hanlin's short novel set in a mining community won first prize. Since the publishers' telegram arrived after he had left for his day's work at the pit his sister chalked the news on a blackboard—'Big Ben Competition. First Prize. £500'—and left it for him to see when he came home at night. Hanlin thought at first that it must be a mistake or a hoax.

Once in every Lifetime was published in 1945 and was described by a reviewer as 'unforgettable in its starkness and simplicity' (*TLS*). Hanlin left the mines for full-time writing in August 1945, found an agent through the *Writers' and Artists' Yearbook*, and moved to London to concentrate on his new career.

In 1946 he received, through his American agent, an offer to work as a scriptwriter in Hollywood. He declined, after long consideration, preferring to maintain his independence as a writer, and continued to work single-mindedly at his vocation. He published two more novels, *Yesterday will Return* (1946) and *The Miracle at Cardenrigg* (1949). His short stories (many, like his novels, drawing on his mining experiences) were published in British and American magazines and he had two radio plays broadcast. However, by the late 1940s he had developed heart problems and shortness of breath, and he died at his home, 148 Mayfield Drive, in Armadale, on 7 April 1953.

Hanlin's work attracted comparatively little critical attention on publication, possibly because newspaper space was still limited at the end of the Second World War (Blake, 38). All three novels soon went out of print. *Once in every Lifetime* was included in a BBC radio series of adaptations of outstanding Scottish novels (*Annals of Scotland, 1895–1955*, broadcast in the winter of 1956–7) but his work was otherwise overlooked by historians of Scottish literature. In 1992 the critic Manfred Malzahn praised *Once in every Lifetime* as a 'proletarian novel' that had deserved more recognition in its time and ought to be rediscovered. MOIRA BURGESS

Sources H. Macpherson, 'Tom Hanlin', *Scottish Book Collector* (Feb 1989), 19–20 • G. Blake, *Annals of Scotland, 1895–1955* [1956] • J. Wilson, 'A story of humble Scottish folk', *Radio Times* (25 Jan 1957) • [E. J. Royde-Smith], 'Novels of the week', *TLS* (8 Sept 1945) [incl. review of *Once in every lifetime*] • M. Malzahn, 'Pithead metaphysics: Tom Hanlin's *Once in every lifetime*', *ScotLit*, 8 (1992), 3–4 • b. cert. • d. cert.

Likenesses photograph, repro. in Blake, *Annals of Scotland*
Wealth at death £1088 1*s.* 1*d.*: confirmation, 30 July 1953, *CCI*

Hanmer, John (1575/6–1629), bishop of St Asaph, was born at Pentrepant in the parish of Selatyn, Shropshire, one of the sons of Thomas Hanmer, a distant cousin of the Hanmers of Flintshire. He was educated at Shrewsbury School before matriculating on 2 June 1592, aged sixteen, from Oriel College, Oxford. Elected a fellow of All Souls in 1595, he graduated BA on 14 July 1596 and proceeded MA on 5 April 1600. In 1603 he became rector of Stoke Lacy, Herefordshire, but he seems to have remained mainly at college, acting as proctor in 1605; he contributed towards £100 given for the 're-edifying' of the college chapel.

Hanmer's career outside Oxford became more fully established in the mid-1610s. Appointed a canon of Worcester and a chaplain to James I in 1614, he was licensed to preach on 23 January 1615, proceeded BD and DD on 1 December, and the same year was instituted rector of Bingham, Nottinghamshire. Elected bishop of St Asaph on 20 January 1624, he was confirmed on 11 February and consecrated on 15 February. To supplement his meagre revenues he was allowed to retain the prebend at Worcester and to acquire the archdeaconry of St Asaph and other benefices, including in 1627 the rectory of Llanfyllin, valued at £150. Compared with his predecessor, Richard Parry, and his successor, John Owen, Hanmer kept a low profile, but he revealed puritan tendencies and his short episcopate showed his concern for the welfare of his clergy and of the diocese in general. He acted as guardian of his kinsman Sir Thomas Hanmer of Hanmer, Flint, who was the father of Sir John Hanmer, first baronet (1591/2–1624) and MP for Flint in 1624. In an effort to improve the quality of religious life in his diocese he persuaded Robert Llwyd, vicar of Chirk, to translate into Welsh *The Plaine Man's Pathway to Heaven*, the devotional work by Arthur Dent, the puritan vicar of Shoebury, Essex. Entitled *Llwybr hyffordd yn cyfarwyddo yr anghfarwydd i'r nefoedd*, it was couched in plain language and cast in dialogue form; it was published in 1630, soon after Hanmer's death, and dedicated to his successor, Bishop Owen. Commissioning this work was Hanmer's lasting achievement but, in addition to corresponding with the antiquary William Camden, he was also a patron of professional bards like Rhisiart Cynwal who, in an ode of praise (preserved in NL Wales, Brogyntyn MS 3241), urged him to preach in Welsh.

Hanmer's will, drawn up on 30 November 1628, contained a strong statement of his Calvinist faith, acknowledging 'the eternall glorie which [Jesus Christ] hath deerely purchased for all the Elect children of God, of which number I assure myself one' (PRO, PROB 11/156, sig. 83). Lands in Shropshire and Denbighshire were left during her lifetime to his wife and executor, Mary, daughter of Arthur Kempe of Hampshire: the date of their marriage is unknown, but the will indicated that they either had, or might expect to have, children. Other bequests went to the poor of Selatyn, Oswestry, and St Asaph, and to Hanmer's three sisters, brother Robert, uncle John Kingston, and servant and nephew Thomas Jones; his manuscripts and papers went to his chaplain, Robert Foulkes. Hanmer died at Pentrepant on 23 June 1629, probably in his fifty-fifth year, and was buried that night in Selatyn parish church. J. GWYNFOR JONES

Sources BL, Lansdowne MS 984, fol. 75 · NL Wales, Brogyntyn MS 3241 · Foster, *Alum. Oxon.* · Wood, *Ath. Oxon.*, new edn, 2.879 · *CSP dom.*, 1623–5, 158 · *Fasti Angl.*, 1541–1857, [St Paul's, London], 75–6 · *Fasti Angl.*, 1541–1857, [Canterbury], 80, 491 · P. Roberts, *Y Cwtta Cyfarwydd* (1883), 127 · B. Willis, *A survey of the cathedral church of St Asaph* (1720), 84–5 · D. R. Thomas, *Esgobaeth Llanelwy: the history of the diocese of St Asaph*, rev. edn, 1 (1908), vol. 1, pp. 227–8 · *DWB* · J. Steegman, *A survey of portraits in Welsh houses* (1957), vol. 1, p. 5 · will, PRO, PROB 11/156, sig. 83
Likenesses portrait, Carreg Wryd, Anglesey
Wealth at death see will, PRO, PROB 11/156, sig. 83

Hanmer, John (*bap.* 1642, *d.* 1707). *See under* Hanmer, Jonathan (1606–1687).

Hanmer, John, Baron Hanmer (1809–1881), poet and politician, was born on 22 December 1809 at Hanmer; he was the son of Thomas Hanmer, colonel of the Royal Flintshire militia, who died in 1818, and Arabella Charlotte, daughter of Thomas Skip Dyot Bucknell MP of Hampton Court. He was eighteenth in descent from Sir John de Hanmere, constable of Caernarfon Castle in the time of Edward I. He was educated first at Eton College and afterwards at Christ Church, Oxford, where he matriculated on 3 December 1827, but did not proceed to a degree. He was there a contemporary and friend of Gladstone.

Hanmer succeeded his grandfather, Sir Thomas Hanmer, as third baronet in 1828. He was MP, initially in the Conservative interest, for Shrewsbury from 1832 to 1837, for Kingston upon Hull from 1841 to 1847, and for the Flint boroughs in six parliaments from 1847 to 1872. He was a Peelite and then a Liberal. On 24 September 1872 Gladstone ennobled his Flintshire neighbour as Baron Hanmer of Hanmer and Flint, both in the county of Flint. Though initially a protectionist, Hanmer came to support free trade and religious liberty, voted for the total repeal of the corn laws (though his views in this respect were afterwards modified), and advocated the adoption in their place of a 'moderate fixed duty'. He sought to abolish bribery at elections, and declined to stand for Kingston upon Hull in 1847 on the failure of full assurance that 'his election should be made in obedience to and in conformity with the law'.

In 1836 Hanmer privately printed *Poems on Various Subjects* and in 1839 published *Fra Cipolla and other Poems*, containing, besides new matter, many of the shorter pieces previously printed. The title-poem is a translation of the tale of 'Friar Onion', from the *Decameron*, and the story of the 'Friar and the Ass' is founded on an old Italian novel; both indicate a keen perception of beauty, and some power of describing it. In 1840 appeared *Sonnets*, dealing mostly with Italian subjects and scenes, and nearly all of a high level of excellence. In 1872 he printed *Notes and Papers to Serve for a Memorial of the Parish of Hanmer*, subsequently enlarged for private issue in 1877 as *Memorial of the Family and Parish of Hanmer*. It contains some quaint and interesting information, and in an appendix are added 'Sonnets

and Epigrams, with other Rhymes, Written Long since by John, Lord Hanmer', many reprinted from the *Sonnets* of 1840.

Hanmer married, on 3 September 1833, Georgiana, youngest daughter of Sir George Chetwynd of Grendon Hall, Warwickshire; she died on 21 March 1880, aged sixty-six. Hanmer died on 8 March 1881 at Knotley Hall, Leigh, in Kent, and was buried on the 15th at Bettisfield, near Whitchurch; his peerage became extinct on his death. Though his political migration exactly mirrored Gladstone's, he made little impact on Victorian politics.

BERTHA PORTER, *rev.* H. C. G. MATTHEW

Sources GEC, *Peerage* · *The Times* (11 March 1881) · *The Times* (15 March 1881) · Gladstone, *Diaries*
Archives NL Wales, corresp. and papers | BL, corresp. with W. E. Gladstone, Add. MSS 44357–44783, *passim* · NL Wales, letters to P. Ellis Eyton · Trinity Cam., letters to Lord Houghton
Likenesses F. Sargent, pencil, 1870–80, NPG · G. Hayter, group portrait, oils (*The House of Commons, 1833*), NPG · wood-engraving (after photograph by Maull & Co.), NPG; repro. in *ILN* (12 Oct 1872)
Wealth at death under £35,000: probate, 13 May 1881, *CGPLA Eng. & Wales*

Hanmer, Jonathan (1606–1687), clergyman and ejected minister, was born and baptized on 3 October 1606, the youngest of the three sons and two daughters of John Hanmer or Davie (*d.* 1629), merchant of Barnstaple, Devon, and Sybil (*b.* 1566), daughter of Henry Downe of Barnstaple. From Barnstaple grammar school he was admitted in 1624 to Emmanuel College, Cambridge, from where he graduated BA in 1628 and proceeded MA in 1631. He was ordained by Bishop Theophilus Field at St Margaret's, Westminster, on 23 November 1632, and immediately instituted to the living of Instow, Devon, vacant through the death of his uncle John Downe. On 10 May 1637 he married at Bideford, Katherine (*d.* 1660), daughter of John Strange, a merchant of the town.

Hanmer's relationship with Martin Blake, vicar of Barnstaple, had a considerable influence on his career; Blake's wife was his first cousin. Blake suggested that Hanmer should preach at the archdeacon's visitation in 1635 with a view to Bishop Joseph Hall's asking him to preach at his visitation in 1636, but he asked to be excused, pleading that his years and abilities made him unworthy. When Blake was suspended as vicar in 1646, owing to his involvement in the surrender of Barnstaple to Prince Maurice three years previously, Hanmer agreed to lecture in the town every Wednesday, saying that he came out of love for Blake but would not take services as that duty belonged to the minister. In October 1647 Blake made a formal agreement with Hanmer that, when he was restored, he would preach in St Peter's every Sunday morning and Hanmer would preach every Sunday afternoon as well as giving a weekday lecture: thus both Anglicans and puritans would be satisfied.

Hanmer did not sign *The Joint Testimonie of Ministers of Devon* drawn up in 1648 in support of the solemn league and covenant but he joined the association of presbyterian ministers of Devon which founded the Exeter assembly in 1655. He continued as vicar of Instow and became vicar of Bishops Tawton in 1652. He also lectured at Barnstaple but evidently not as frequently as agreed in 1647 as Blake was accused, in 1656, of preventing Hanmer from preaching on many Sundays. Hanmer stated that, on the contrary, he had often refused to come as it was unreasonable to expect him to travel from Instow every Sunday unless Barnstaple made some provision for his subsistence.

Hanmer was evidently a presbyterian of a moderate tenor. A controversy over qualification for church membership led him to write *Teleiosis* (1657), a treatise advocating the restitution of confirmation 'to its primitive use and end'; a letter from Richard Baxter prefaced this 'Learned, Judicious, Pious Exercitation'. A second edition appeared the following year. Hanmer left many manuscript works including discourses against papists and against Quakers and a life of St Paul. Letters to him revealed his support for missionary work among the American Indians of New England.

In 1660 Hanmer's wife died, and two years later, on 7 November, he was ejected from his livings because he could not accept the revised prayer book enforced by the Act of Uniformity. He continued to preach when possible in Devon and also in Bristol and London. In Barnstaple he gathered together a congregation which met privately in a malthouse for fear of informers. Although he is said to have been forced frequently to leave them for fear of arrest, an official report certified that he lived quietly in Barnstaple without disturbing the peace of the church or state. Bishop Seth Ward's letter to secure payment of tithes due from his former parish of Bishops Tawton suggests that Hanmer had reasonable relations with the established church. When the declaration of indulgence allowed nonconformists to meet openly Hanmer was licensed, on 2 April 1672, as a presbyterian minister, his congregation built a meeting-house, and Hanmer drew up a confession of faith and rules of conduct for them. After the declaration was withdrawn in 1673 he and the congregation risked the persecution which restarted immediately in Devon. Hanmer continued with his studies, and was almost certainly the author of *Archaioskopia, or, A View of Antiquity* (1677), an account of the early fathers aimed at the improvement of the faithful. He died on 18 December 1687 in Barnstaple and was buried on 21 December at St Peter's churchyard there. He and his wife had at least six children. A daughter Katherine was the mother of the poet, John *Gay (1685–1732).

John Hanmer (*bap.* 1642, *d.* 1707), Presbyterian minister, the eldest son of Jonathan and Katherine, was baptized in Bideford on 18 October 1642. He was educated at Barnstaple grammar school and went to St John's College, Cambridge, in 1659, graduating BA in 1662. He served in two gentry households before returning to Barnstaple where he was licensed as a presbyterian minister on 11 April 1672. He was ordained privately in 1682 and became assistant to Oliver Peard, pastor of the Barnstaple congregation, whom he succeeded in 1696. The following year he preached before the assembly of united ministers at Exeter. By 1700 Hanmer's congregation was so large

that he needed an assistant and in 1705 two congregations were formed. He married Jane (*d.* 1736), daughter of Richard Parminster, a merchant of Barnstaple and had one daughter. He died on 19 July 1707 from a stroke and at his funeral in Barnstaple on 23 July was described as a talented preacher, an ardent scholar, and broad-minded enough to value a good Christian, regardless of his particular persuasion.   MARY WOLFFE

Sources Calamy rev. · J. F. Chanter, *The life and times of Martin Blake BD* (1910) · H. W. Gardiner, *Lives of Rev. Jonathan Hanmer AM and the Rev. John Hanmer AM* (1828) · E. Calamy, ed., *An abridgement of Mr. Baxter's history of his life and times, with an account of the ministers, &c., who were ejected after the Restauration of King Charles II*, 2nd edn, 2 vols. (1713) · E. Calamy, *A continuation of the account of the ministers … who were ejected and silenced after the Restoration in 1660*, 2 vols. (1727) · *Calendar of the correspondence of Richard Baxter*, ed. N. H. Keeble and G. F. Nuttall, 2 vols. (1991) · Venn, *Alum. Cant.* · parish register, Barnstaple, North Devon Record Office, Barnstaple [baptism, burial] · parish register, Bideford, Devon RO [John Hanmer, baptism] · *CSP dom., 1671–2* · P. W. Jackson, 'Nonconformists and society in Devon, 1660–1689', PhD diss., Exeter University, 1986 · R. N. Worth, 'Puritanism in Devon and the Exeter assembly', *Report and Transactions of the Devonshire Association*, 9 (1877), 250–91 · J. I. Dredge, 'A few sheaves of Devon bibliographies, pt 2', *Report and Transactions of the Devonshire Association*, 22 (1890), 324–56 · J. R. Chanter, *Sketches of the literary history of Barnstaple* [1866] · J. R. Chanter and T. Wainwright, *Barnstaple records*, 1 · J. B. Gribble, *Memorials of Barnstaple* (1830) · *ESTC* · I. Gowers, 'The clergy in Devon, 1641–62', *Tudor and Stuart Devon … essays presented to Joyce Youings*, ed. T. Gray, M. Rowe, and A. Erskine (1992), 200–26 · O. Murray, transcripts of Devon wills, extracts of wills of John Hanmer (1629), Henry Down (1614), and John Strange (1642), West Country Studies Library, Exeter

Archives Westminster and Cheshunt College, Cambridge, papers

Hanmer, Meredith (1543–1604), Church of England and Church of Ireland clergyman and historian, was born at Porkington, Shropshire, the son of Thomas, commonly called Ginta, Hanmer and his wife. He was educated at Corpus Christi College, Oxford, where he obtained a chaplaincy in 1567, and graduated BA in 1568, MA in 1572, BTh in 1581 (as a nobleman's chaplain), and DTh in 1582.

Hanmer held a number of benefices: he was rector of Long Ditton, Surrey, in 1571, and of Astbury, Cheshire, in 1572; vicar of Hanmer, Flintshire, 1574–84; vicar of St Leonard, Shoreditch, 1581–92; and vicar of Islington, 1583–90. He first came to public notice as a writer, producing in 1581 two semi-official responses to Edmund Campion's famous challenge. But his most lasting scholarly contribution was as a historian of the early church and, later, of Ireland. In 1577 he published *The Ancient Ecclesiastical Histories*, which sought to provide a detailed account of the first six centuries of Christian history by translating near contemporary sources, most notably Eusebius's *Ecclesiastical History*. Frequently republished, even down to the eighteenth century, Hanmer's work provided an essential source for those protestants who wanted to show how rapidly the church had declined from its early purity.

Hanmer married Mary Austin at Shoreditch on 21 June 1581. They had four daughters. Despite his undoubted scholarly achievements, his reputation was dogged by allegations about his personal conduct. As vicar of St Leonard's it was alleged that he had converted the brass of several ancient monuments to coin for his own use. In 1584 Hanmer was examined about the circulation of a libel that George Talbot, sixth earl of Shrewsbury, had got Elizabeth I pregnant. William Fleetwood, recorder of London, doubted the veracity of his evidence and drew the conclusion: 'surely he is a very bad man' (Wood, *Ath. Oxon.*, 3rd edn, 1.748). Hanmer was also charged between 1588 and 1590 with having celebrated a marriage 'without banns or license' (ibid.). According to an anonymous Roman Catholic opponent he was a 'filthy sodomite' who had been forced to leave his benefice because of the 'lewdness of his life' (Holmes, 56). Whatever the truth of individual accusations, there does appear to be a consistent pattern, and, like many English clergy of dubious reputation, Hanmer sought to rebuild his career in the Church of Ireland, whose desperation for protestant clergy made its standards less rigorous.

Hanmer crossed over to Ireland in or before 1591, and there acquired patronage from Thomas Butler, tenth earl of Ormond, and Thomas, or John, Norris, whom he served as chaplain. He received numerous benefices, including: the archdeaconry of Ross and the vicarage of Timoleague in 1591; appointment as treasurer of Waterford Cathedral on 4 December 1593; the vicarages of Kilbeacon and Killaghy, Muckully, and Rathpatrick in the diocese of Ossory in June 1598; and appointment as chancellor of Ossory, along with the vicarages of Fiddown and St John's, and the rectory of Aglish-Martin, in June 1603. In 1600 he was proposed for the episcopate by Ormond, who suggested to Sir Robert Cecil, principal secretary, that Hanmer be made bishop of Down, together with the remote and impecunious sees of Dromore, Kilmore, and Clogher.

But Hanmer devoted himself to more than pluralism. He developed his historical interests and applied them to Ireland, following in the footsteps of his erstwhile opponent, Campion, who had also come to Ireland and written a history of the country. In 1594 he wrote to William Cecil, Baron Burghley, lord treasurer, telling him of his intention of collecting the country's antiquities and preserving them for posterity: the results, a miscellaneous but interesting collection of contemporary and ancient sources including, significantly, some material in Gaelic, remain in manuscript in the Irish state papers. He also wrote *A Chronicle of Ireland*, which was edited by Daniel Molyneux, Ulster king of arms, and published posthumously by James Ware in 1633. It tackled that difficult period, the early history of Ireland, gathering together materials and tentatively beginning the lengthy task of separating myth, fiction, and fact.

Hanmer was commended to Sir Francis Walsingham, principal secretary, by Captain Christopher Carleill as keeping a good house, and being a diligent preacher. The 'Journal' of Sir William Russell, later first Baron Russell of Thornhough, noted him preaching before the lord deputy several times, and on one occasion his sermon is described as 'very bitter' (Brewer and Bullen, 3.235). He left some revealing and, again, somewhat bitter notes, which made

sweeping allegations about the persistence of puritanism in high places in Dublin in the later sixteenth century. Hanmer died in 1604, probably from the plague, and was buried in St Michan's Church, Dublin. ALAN FORD

Sources J. Morrin, ed., *Calendar of the patent and close rolls of chancery in Ireland*, 3 vols. (1861–3) • J. B. Leslie, *Ossory clergy and parishes* (1933) • H. Ellis, *The history and antiquities of the parish of St Leonard, Shoreditch, and liberty of Norton Folgate* (1798) • J. Weever, *Ancient funerall monuments* (1631) • R. Newcourt, *Repertorium ecclesiasticum parochiale Londinense*, 2 (1710) • W. M. Brady, *Clerical and parochial records of Cork, Cloyne, and Ross*, 3 vols. (1863–4) • J. Strype, *Annals of the Reformation and establishment of religion … during Queen Elizabeth's happy reign*, new edn, 4 vols. (1824) • *The Irish fiants of the Tudor sovereigns*, 4 vols. (1994) • P. Holmes, *Resistance and compromise: the political thought of Elizabethan Catholics* (1982) • *The whole works of … James Ussher*, ed. C. R. Elrington and J. H. Todd, 17 vols. (1847–64), vol. 15 • J. S. Brewer and W. Bullen, eds., *Calendar of the Carew manuscripts*, 6 vols., PRO (1867–73) • *CSP Ire.* • Wood, *Ath. Oxon.*, new edn • Foster, *Alum. Oxon.*

Archives PRO, SP Ireland 63/214

Hanmer, Sir Thomas, second baronet (1612–1678), gardener and writer, was born on 4 May 1612, the son of Sir John Hanmer, first baronet (*d.* 1624), of Hanmer, Flintshire, and his wife, Dorothy, daughter of Sir Richard Trevor of Trefalun, Denbighshire. Following the premature death of his father in 1624, Hanmer inherited the baronetcy the former had gained in 1620. He was a page at the court of Charles I from 1625 until 1627, when in the Easter term he matriculated from King's College, Cambridge.

At some point between 1630 and 20 February 1632 Sir Thomas married Elizabeth (*d.* 1645), daughter of Sir Thomas Baker of Whittingham, Suffolk, a lady-in-waiting to the queen. Their children included John (*d.* 1701), Thomas, and a daughter, Trevor. From 1638 to 1640, following the fashion, Sir Thomas embarked on a tour of the continent, but was home in time to be returned as MP for Flint in April 1640.

In or before 1642 Sir Thomas was serving as a cup-bearer to the king, and on the outbreak of civil war he was appointed a commissioner of array for his county, with responsibility for raising a band of archers and a dragoon regiment. Early in 1644 Prince Rupert appointed him, with Dudley Wyatt, his representative in north Wales; meeting with the county commissioners, they agreed new local taxes. His property was raided more than once by parliamentarian soldiers, and on 15 May 1644 he obtained leave to go to France with his family. He was fined for delinquency by parliament at the minimum rate.

In July 1645 Lady Hanmer died in Paris, and it seems to have been from there in 1646 that Sir Thomas supplied information to parliament about the king's negotiations with the French and Scots. Leaving his daughter in the care of a Huguenot group and dispatching his son Thomas to a Lisbon seminary, he secretly visited Hengrave Hall, Suffolk, and before February 1646 married Susan Hervey, daughter of Sir William Hervey of Ilkworth. Returning to France, the couple lived first at Nantes and then at Angers. During this period Sir Thomas compiled 'A description of France in 1648', which remained unpublished. His sons William and Thomas (*d.* 1683) were born there about 1648 and 1650 respectively.

After payment of a £1500 fine, Sir Thomas was discharged from sequestration in 1650 in the light of his 'signal service to the commonwealth' (as he was subsequently also from the 1655 decimation tax) and allowed to return to England. Initially he lived with his mother in her dower house at Halghton, before moving back to his ancestral home at Bettisfield. From then onwards Sir Thomas lived the life of a leisured gentleman, preoccupied with his family from his second marriage. He corresponded with and was closely associated with influential horticulturists including John Evelyn, John Rea, and John Rose, keeper of St James's gardens for Charles II. He was a copious note-taker and compiled a manuscript which, although completed in 1659, was not formally published until 1933 under the title *The Garden Book of Sir Thomas Hanmer*. This contained descriptive and cultural notes dealing with herbaceous plants, trees, and fruit. His text gave a perceptive and rare insight into a gentleman's garden of the time and the use of the winter house or room, which was an early form of conservatory used for the unseasonal cultivation of tender plants. Sir Thomas is credited with being the first English author to mention the cedar of Lebanon, predicting its future importance. He also contributed a chapter to John Evelyn's unpublished text 'Elysium Britannicum'.

Like many horticulturists of his time, Sir Thomas favoured tulips, but was interested in anemones, primroses, and cowslips, which he cultivated in his garden. His most outstanding tulip was one that he imported and named Agate Hanmer, which was characterized by having colours in parallel stripes. He was widely regarded as one of the most significant and influential gardeners of the Cromwellian and Restoration eras, being in the vanguard of those who sought to escape from the constriction and formalism of earlier garden design.

Having been returned for Flintshire at a by-election in 1669, Hanmer was a moderately active MP. He was listed on several occasions as a government supporter and speaker, endorsing both the suppression of conventicles and the land tax proposed in 1670, and was claimed to be receiving a £500 p.a. pension. He died on 6 October 1678 at Bettisfield, and was buried at Hanmer. His eldest son from his first marriage, John, an esquire of the body to Charles II, succeeded not only to his baronetcy but also, in 1681, to the Flintshire parliamentary seat.   JOHN MARTIN

Sources J. Robinson, 'New light on Sir Thomas Hanmer', *Garden History*, 16 (1988), 1–7 · HoP, *Commons, 1660–90* · *DWB* · J. Burke and J. B. Burke, *A genealogical and heraldic history of the extinct and dormant baronetcies of England, Ireland, and Scotland* (1838) · M. Hadfield, R. Harling, and L. Highton, *British gardeners: a biographical dictionary* (1980) · M. Hadfield, *A history of British gardening*, rev. edn (1969) · R. Duthie, 'The planting plans of some seventeenth-century gardens', *Garden History*, 18/2 (1990), 77–102, esp. 83–7 · B. Henrey, *British botanical and horticultural literature before 1800*, 3 vols. (1975) · J. Hanmer, *A memorial of the parish and family of Hanmer in Flintshire* (1877) · E. Cecil, *History of gardening in England* (1910), 164, 171–4 · J. Evelyn, 'Elysium Britannicum', Christ Church Oxf. · R. Hutton, *The royalist war effort, 1642–1646* (1982), 23, 38, 133

Archives NL Wales, corresp. and papers · Suffolk RO, Bury St Edmunds, description of France, E/18/600/3

Likenesses Van Dyck, oils, *c.*1638, Weston under Lizard, Staffordshire; repro. in Hadfield, Harling, and Highton, *British gardeners*, 144 · portrait, Hunt. L. · portrait, repro. in I. Elstob, ed., *The garden book of Sir Thomas Hanmer* (1933)

Wealth at death Bettisfield estate inherited by son

Hanmer, Sir Thomas, fourth baronet (1677–1746), politician, was born on 24 September 1677 at Bettisfield Park, Hanmer, Flintshire, the only son of William Hanmer (*d.* 1695) and his wife, Peregrina North, and the grandson of Sir Thomas Hanmer, second baronet, of Bettisfield Park. He was also heir through his mother to the estates of the North family of Mildenhall in Suffolk. He was educated at Bury St Edmunds grammar school, at Westminster School, and, from 1693, at Christ Church, Oxford, where his tutors were Robert Freind and George Smalridge. Christ Church enjoyed a reputation for nurturing tory principles and polishing a veneer of polite learning. Hanmer was no exception to this rule: although possessed of a less incisive intellect than some of his contemporaries, he was an elegant orator and literary dilettante and, to the end of his days, a committed high-church tory. Having succeeded his maternal grandfather to the Suffolk estates he left Oxford without taking his degree, and in October 1698 married Isabella, *suo jure* countess of Arlington and dowager duchess of Grafton (1667/8–1723). Not only was Isabella ten years his senior, but temperamentally they were grossly mismatched: the somewhat vulgar duchess had been one of the 'Windsor beauties', and the refined Hanmer, though 'tall and handsome', was reputedly impotent. This disparity in age, intellectual attainments, and sexual experience provoked ridicule. It was said that the marriage remained unconsummated, Hanmer preserving his legendary fastidiousness (manifested in a fetish for wearing white gloves) even in the marital bed.

Hanmer's natural progression to a seat in the House of Commons came in the first parliament in 1701. Although he might have contemplated standing for a county, he put up instead at the venal borough of Thetford, on the Grafton interest. Soon afterwards he succeeded an uncle to the Hanmer baronetcy and estates in Flintshire. Elections in that county were the preserve of a cartel of greater gentry, who rotated among themselves the representation in county and borough constituencies. As one of the principals, Hanmer could be sure of a seat in every other election, and, with a considerable proprietorial interest in Suffolk, was left with an embarrassment of possibilities whenever a new parliament was summoned. He sat for Flintshire from 1702 to 1705, for Thetford again from 1705 to 1708, and for Suffolk from 1708 until leaving parliament for good at the accession of George II in 1727.

Early in his political career Hanmer gravitated to the veteran tory Lord Nottingham, whose emphatically protestant churchmanship and stern devotion to principle he emulated. In the parliamentary session of 1703–4 he defended Nottingham over the 'Scotch plot'. He soon became one of the leading spokesmen for the tories in the lower house, and in November 1704 he took part in the campaign to 'tack' the Occasional Conformity Bill to

Sir Thomas Hanmer, fourth baronet (1677–1746), by Sir
Godfrey Kneller, c.1715

supply. His reversion to the rotten borough of Thetford in
the 1705 election did not represent a retreat from the political storm over the tack; it was his turn to step down in
Flintshire, and he did not wish to intrude on the tory candidates for Suffolk. In any case, there was something
about his character and deportment that earned him
respect even from political enemies and kept him
immune from partisan reprisals. The ministry may have
entertained hopes of him, for he was the only tory upon
whom an honorary degree was conferred during the
queen's visit to Cambridge University in 1705, in a public
blessing of the whig candidates in the university constituency.

Such a tentative advance had no effect on Hanmer's
intransigence. When parliament met he seconded the
nomination of the tory William Bromley as speaker,
against the court nominee, and then brought forward the
so-called Hanover motion, to invite over to England the
heir presumptive to the throne—a blatantly opportunist
manoeuvre designed to embarrass the ministry. Nevertheless, the secretary of state, Robert Harley, canvassed
his support for successive schemes of ministerial reconstruction, designed to free the queen from dependence on

the parties by creating a coalition of moderates and ambitious politicians of the second rank. Hanmer's parliamentary conduct betrayed little evidence of moderation, but
his self-regard was enough to afford hope that he might be
detached from the tory party chieftains by flattery. This
hope survived several disappointments: on one occasion,
although 'engaged' by a 'great manager' to make a motion
for a generous public settlement on the duke of Marlborough, Hanmer developed cold feet, excused himself, and
sat silent during the debate (Joseph Addison to George
Stepney, 7 Jan 1707, MS sold at Sothebys, 21 July 1980). Matters came to a head during the winter of 1707–8, when
Hanmer and other angry tories joined with discontented
whigs to keep up a murderous cross-fire on the court. In
January 1708 he seems to have accepted a secret offer from
Harley to become chancellor of the exchequer in a new
administration, although he did not abandon opposition,
and indeed made one of the most important speeches of
his career in the debate on the war in Spain, on the dis-
crepancy between the number of troops paid for by parliament and the number present at the battle of Almanza.
For once his measured style was suited to the occasion,
and he was credited with convincing the house to accept a
motion of censure. The collapse of Harley's intrigues
induced feelings of intense disappointment. Hanmer was
initially reluctant to continue in parliament in 1708, but
eventually rallied and was able to recover his position as a
key figure in the tory opposition.

Hanmer's response to the ministerial changes of 1710
was unenthusiastic. Beyond taking pleasure in the
removal of the whig ministry he affected indifference,
and spurned offers of a Treasury place. His name was
again mentioned in connection with the speaker's chair,
but instead he successfully proposed his old friend Bromley. He then made the motion for the loyal address, and
was said to have undertaken the drafting entirely by himself, a responsibility that implied a close association with
the court. His sentiments at this point are hard to fathom.
He shared many of the prejudices of the hotter tories and
joined the October Club, but was also inspired by a sincere
desire to see the end of the war, which he hoped the ministry would bring about. Thus he consorted openly with
ministers, and in May 1711 he found himself expelled from
the October Club. Soon afterwards Harley pressed him
again to 'consider … coming into her Majesty's service'
(Correspondence, 128–9). The response, that 'his private
affairs lie so distorted and dispersed that he cannot at
present undertake anything else without very great
inconvenience to them' (William Bromley to Lord Oxford,
June 1711, BL, Add. MS 70214), was little more than an
excuse to cover concern with safeguarding his virtue, or at
least his reputation. At the same time he was happy to
recommend several dependants to Harley (now Lord
Treasurer Oxford), including his amanuensis, the Irish soldier and playwright William Philips, who was given a
secret pension on the Irish establishment.

During the next session Hanmer inched even nearer the
court, expressing a willingness 'to come into the Queen's
service' when the session was over, in an employment

which should be 'useful' if not necessarily 'profitable' (*Portland MSS*, 5.133). But at the same time he indulged in flourishes of self-assertion. Interpreted cynically, this recovery of reputation with tory extremists may appear as a prerequisite for the work he was to undertake for the ministry in this session, preparing the way for the announcement of the peace preliminaries by his chairmanship of the committee to draft the Commons' 'representation' on the war (in which he enjoyed the unofficial assistance of Jonathan Swift). His parliamentary activity was curtailed in April 1712, when he accompanied the duke of Ormond (his wife's cousin) to Flanders. Speculation was rife that Hanmer had a secret commission on behalf of the ministry. More likely, he was anxious to be out of the way when the peace terms came before parliament. In September he made a private visit to Paris, where the French, believing him destined for high office, gave him a splendid reception. An intriguing aspect of his stay was the tentative contact established with Jacobite agents, not by Hanmer himself but through Captain Philips, who proclaimed his own allegiance to the Pretender and repeatedly hinted that something might be hoped from 'the knight'.

Even though he was disinclined to return to England, Hanmer yielded to entreaties to give his assistance to the government in the next parliamentary session. His political career was now approaching a crisis, and in the summer of 1713 he broke with the ministry in a very public fashion, though, as things turned out, not finally. Concern for the succession and resentment at Oxford's continuing 'moderation' are among the reasons that have been adduced by historians. Some contemporaries alleged disappointed ambition, which does not square with Hanmer's repeated refusal of office. A more likely explanation is concern for the maintenance of his political virtue. Whatever the cause, he made his decisive move on 18 June, in speaking against at the third reading of the bill to implement the French commercial treaty. Hanmer's motives for selecting this issue are equally problematic: he may have been alarmed at the general unpopularity of the treaty or feared for the particular consequences for his constituents. The loss of the bill prompted Oxford to swift action, with the result that five days later Hanmer was to be found proposing an address of thanks over the peace and requesting the renegotiation of the commercial treaty. Whigs accused him of having been bought off. Certainly, before he left for Suffolk he waited on Oxford to receive his 'commands' (Hanmer to Oxford, 1 Aug 1713, BL, Add. MS 70230), and in the ministerial reorganization of the summer he was offered the speakership, the only place he could accept while claiming he had preserved his liberty.

In the 1714 parliament, in which he was elected unopposed as speaker, Hanmer stood at the head of a group of Hanoverian tories, variously estimated at between thirty and eighty, some his personal followers, and others looking to him as the ablest spokesman for their point of view. His own devotion to the protestant succession is unquestionable, reinforced as it was by an attachment to the Church of England and to notions of political liberty. At first he was prepared to trust Oxford, even after his own proposal to revive the Hanover motion had been rejected out of hand at a presessional management meeting. But in April his position changed, possibly because of the shift in the centre of gravity of the ministry, where Lord Bolingbroke was becoming more assertive. Hanmer attended a meeting with Nottingham and other Hanoverian tories at which it was decided 'to live in friendship with the Whigs and concert with them measures to secure the Protestant succession' (Macpherson, 2.586–9), and on 15 April, in a debate in committee of the whole on the state of the nation, he nailed his colours to the mast in proclaiming that the protestant succession was indeed in danger under the present administration.

When Queen Anne died Hanmer had to be recalled from Flintshire to preside over the Commons. The arrival of King George was the occasion for more expressions of maidenly modesty in refusing office. Along with other Hanoverian tories he was urged to take his part in a mixed ministry, albeit in a subordinate position to the whigs. Once he was observed talking to the prince of Wales, who 'seemed to argue very closely, and had a world of action, and Sir Thomas's answers were obliging smiles' (*Wentworth Papers*, 423). Privately he confided that:

> he could not in prudence accept places which did not admit him into his Majesty's scheme of government, but when conferred on him would lose him the dependence of his friends, and then leave him at the mercy of his enemies. (BL, Add. MS 47027, fol. 179)

In 1715 Hanmer resumed his position as one of the leaders of the tory party in the Commons, making a notable speech, for example, against the Septennial Bill in 1716. At the same time he remained a committed Hanoverian, and in 1717 he attached himself to the Leicester House faction, clustered around the reversionary interest of the prince of Wales. By 1719 he had supposedly become 'the greatest man in England with the Prince' and 'the mouth of that interest' (John Menzies to the Old Pretender, 7 April 1721, Royal Archives, Stuart MS 53/13). But with the reconciliation in the royal family came the demise of Leicester House. Hanmer's political importance rapidly declined, though he was tipped for office in a putative ministerial reconstruction in 1725. He seems to have become estranged from the prince, whose decision to continue with Robert Walpole as prime minister in 1727 effectively ended any prospects of advancement.

During Hanmer's lengthy retirement from political life he combined the cultivation of his estate with some insipid literary efforts. Two anonymous works have been ascribed to him, *A Review of the Text of … 'Paradise Lost'* (1733) and *Some Remarks on the Tragedy of Hamlet, Prince of Denmark* (1736), and in 1743–4 he published an utterly unremarkable edition of Shakespeare. He also devoted considerable time to the weeding of his private papers, to preserve for posterity only the letters which showed his character in a favourable light, and in particular those beseeching him in vain to honour government with his talents. This tranquil rustication was marred by an unhappy second marriage in 1725 (the duchess of Grafton having died two years earlier), this time to a much younger woman, Elizabeth Folkes (d. 1741), who ran off with the son of one of his friends and again made him appear ridiculous. He died at Mildenhall on 7 May 1746 and was buried at Hanmer. He had no children: the baronetcy became extinct, and the estates were divided between his sister's family, who received the Suffolk property, and a cousin, who inherited in Wales. 'A sensible, impracticable, honest, formal, disagreeable man', according to Lord Hervey (Hervey, 1.78), he passed away 'without having much obliged or disobliged any person or party, and rather pitied than either hated or beloved' (Coxe, 2.48–9). D. W. HAYTON

Sources 'Hanmer', HoP, Commons, 1690–1715 [draft] • The correspondence of Sir Thomas Hanmer, … with a memoir of his life, ed. H. Bunbury (1838) • R. R. Sedgwick, 'Hanmer, Sir Thomas', HoP, Commons, 1715–54 • DNB • NL Wales, Bettisfield papers • Lord Hanmer [J. Hanmer], Memorial of the parish and family of Hanmer (1877) • J. Macpherson, ed., Original papers: containing the secret history of Great Britain, 2 vols. (1775) • BL, Add. MSS 70001–70371 • Royal Arch., Stuart papers • The Wentworth papers, 1705–1739, ed. J. J. Cartwright (1883) • Cobbett, Parl. hist. • H. Horwitz, Revolution politicks: the career of Daniel Finch, second earl of Nottingham, 1647–1730 (1968) • The manuscripts of his grace the duke of Portland, 10 vols., HMC, 29 (1891–1931) • John, Lord Hervey, Some materials towards memoirs of the reign of King George II, ed. R. Sedgwick, 3 vols. (1931) • W. Coxe, Memoirs of the life and administration of Sir Robert Walpole, earl of Orford, 3 vols. (1798) • GEC, Peerage

Archives NL Wales, corresp. and papers; papers, letters and drafts, travel journal (account of travels in France) • Suffolk RO, Bury St Edmunds, accounts, papers, incl. papers as trustee of Mary Baron's estate | BL, letters to William Warburton, Egerton MS 1957

Likenesses G. Kneller, oils, c.1715, Euston Hall, Suffolk [see illus.] • W. Bond, stipple, 1798 (after G. Kneller), BM, NPG; repro. in P. Yorke, The royal tribes of Wales (1799) • studio of G. Kneller, oils, Palace of Westminster, London

Wealth at death estates in Suffolk and Flintshire; house in Grosvenor Street, London: Hanmer, Memorial, 179

Hann, James (1799–1856), mechanical engineer and mathematician, was born at Lane House, Washington, near Gateshead, co. Durham, eldest of the seven children of James Hann (bap. 1777), colliery smith, and his wife, Elizabeth, née Smith. Hann's rudimentary formal education at school in Hebburn ceased when he began in childhood to work as a stoker for his father, superintendent of a pumping engine at Hebburn colliery. Until the age of twenty-one he was employed there as brakesman, overseeing the colliery winding engines. He married Isabella Burrell (c.1801–1854) from Gateshead, at Heworth on 14 November 1819 and the first of their eight children was born the same year.

During his twenties Hann was fireman and engineer on a succession of Tyne paddle-steamers including the Industry, which belonged to friend and Gateshead mechanical engineer Isaac Dodds, and the XL. He continued to work as enginewright in and around collieries at Backworth, Hetton, and North Shields, even as he devoured the texts of mathematical practitioners and pedagogues William

Emerson and Olinthus Gregory. From 1823 Hann was an increasingly prominent contributor to the extended mathematical section of the vivacious annual forum for provincial savants of both sexes, the Ladies' Diary (which Gregory edited), and its companion almanac, the Gentleman's Diary.

When Hann joined the Newcastle Literary, Scientific, and Mechanical Institution in its second session of 1825–6 it was as an enginewright; however, soon afterwards he was supporting a growing family by other means, working as Dodds's accountant and teaching at Friar's Goose, an industrial centre east of Gateshead. Although never a member of the venerable Newcastle Literary and Philosophical Society, in 1832 he cemented his social and philosophical ascent by reading before the organization's members a paper on the differential calculus. Soon afterwards his local and private publishing venture with Dodds, Mechanics for Practical Men (1833), met with an enthusiastic reception, enhancing substantially his standing in the worlds of letters and engineering mechanics.

Hann travelled with his family to London and the recently reformed nautical almanac office (NAO) in Somerset House, where patronage from his friend and fellow Diary contributor, the North Shields mathematical prodigy and NAO deputy superintendent (1830–37) W. S. B. Woolhouse, secured him a post as 'calculator'. He worked closely with Olinthus Gregory in the production of astronomical and other scientific computations. Hann had been brought up a Roman Catholic but had changed his allegiance to the Church of England some time before 1837, when he moved along the Strand to become a master at King's College School, a post which required conformity to the doctrines of the established church. There he replaced the writing and arithmetical master, Frederick Ribbans (who had resigned amid scandal concerning the misappropriation of stationery), and from 1841 served permanently as mathematical master, preparing pupils from the middle classes for the professions, for King's College, and for Cambridge. Infirmity and personal neglect led him to resign in the year of his wife's death (1854), though he continued to attract private pupils from the merchant classes and clergy of London.

Hann pursued a productive and remunerative career of technical authorship drawing upon earlier practical and vocational experiences. He collaborated with Woolhouse in revising Tredgold's Steam Engine and with Woolhouse and Gregory on a practical supplement to the Nautical Almanac (1841). On 13 June 1843, when Hann became an associate of the Institution of Civil Engineers, sponsorship came from Northumbrian coal-viewers and mining entrepreneurs such as John Buddle, not for practical engineering endeavours but for literary and scientific attainments. Hann's theoretical study of bridges (1843, with King's College professor William Hosking), and his short treatises on the steam engine (1847) and mechanics (1848) were produced under the auspices of John Weale, the London-based technical publisher and architectural writer. For Weale, Hann oversaw a 'rudimentary series' of cheap, accessible mathematical textbooks, writing volumes on the integral calculus, plane and spherical trigonometry, analytical geometry, and conic sections. By 1847 Hann's works had won him honorary membership of the Philosophical Society of Newcastle, Durham, and Northumberland. Like his *Mechanics*, many of them were directed, appropriately, towards large overlapping readerships of autodidacts and 'practical men'. Hann died at the age of fifty-seven on 17 August 1856 at King's College Hospital. BEN MARSDEN

Sources GM, 3rd ser., 1 (1856), 513–15, 521 · J. Latimer, *Local records, or, Historical register of remarkable events which have occurred in Northumberland and Durham … 1832–57* (1857), 384 · D. T. Hann, 'The self-taught mathematical genius', 1993, King's Lond. [also deposited in North Shields Library, and King's College School] · *Gateshead Observer* (23 Aug 1856) · candidate circular, Inst. CE · *Annual Report* [Literary, Scientific, and Mechanical Institution, Newcastle upon Tyne], 2 (1826), 15 · *Fortieth year's report of the Literary and Philosophical Society of Newcastle upon Tyne* (1833), 5 · private information (2004) · *Ladies' Diary* (1824–8) · *Gentleman's Diary* (1832) · *PICE*, 75 (1883–4), 308–14 [obit. of Isaac Dodds] · F. J. C. Hearnshaw, *The centenary history of King's College, London, 1828–1928* (1929), 263 · *Lady's and Gentleman's Diary* (1857), 69 · *The Times* (19 Aug 1856) · *Annual Register* (1856), 266
Archives King's Lond., letters

Hanna, Hugh (1821–1892), minister of the Presbyterian Church in Ireland, was born in Derry, Dromara, co. Down, on 21 February 1821, the son of Peter Hanna, a tenant farmer and former soldier, and Ellen Finiston, daughter of a soldier in the Black Watch. His parents moved to Belfast and he remained in Dromara with his grandparents until his grandmother's death. He rejoined his parents in Belfast where he completed his education at Bullick's Academy before entering the drapery trade. Influenced by the preaching of the Revd Josias Wilson of Townsend Street congregation, he became an active member of that congregation, teaching in Sunday school and, later, as a teacher in the national school associated with the congregation. This necessitated further study which he undertook in the Belfast Academical Institution, with the encouragement of his employer. His success as a teacher led to his nomination for a post as inspector of schools but he decided that he should enter the ministry, beginning his theological studies in Belfast in 1847. Licensed by the Belfast presbytery in May 1851 he was ordained for missionary work among the unchurched of north Belfast and formed a congregation in a redundant Presbyterian meeting-house in Berry Street. On 25 August 1852 he married Fanny Spence (d. 1913), daughter of James Rankin of Belfast. So rapidly did the Berry Street congregation grow that an enlarged building was necessary in 1857 and, when that proved inadequate, a church with accommodation for 2000 worshippers, St Enoch's, was built in Carlisle Circus in 1872.

Hanna was a prominent figure in the great religious revival of 1859 and was one of the speakers at a rally in the Belfast Botanic Gardens in August 1859 attended by 20,000 people. He was not only an effective preacher but a successful educationist, organizing Sunday schools for as many as 2000 children and young people and presiding over flourishing national schools—Linfield, Riversdale, Finiston, Hillman, and North Thomas Street, as well as a school attached to St Enoch's congregation. For his services to education he was made a commissioner of national education in 1880.

But it was as an alleged contributor to sectarian division and disturbance in Belfast that Hanna achieved his greatest fame or notoriety. Like many evangelical ministers, he was a regular open-air preacher. Such preaching was primarily evangelistic but was occasionally perceived as anti-Catholic. In summer 1857 sectarian tensions in Belfast were so explosive that the magistrates asked the Church of Ireland clergy of the Belfast Parochial Mission to abandon a proposed series of open-air addresses. Hanna, encouraged by Dr Henry Cooke, regarded this as a denial of liberty to preach the gospel and insisted on preaching. Riots followed and the commission of inquiry into the origins and character of the riots specified provocative open-air preaching as a major cause of the violence. Again in 1886, when tensions over the first Home Rule Bill erupted into violence, Hanna's pulpit attacks on Gladstone's government and his allegations that Roman Catholic policemen from other parts of Ireland had been brought to Belfast to crush resistance to home rule were regarded as having contributed to the explosive situation. On 26 September 1857 *Punch* lampooned Hanna in a series of verses, one of which ran:

> What's faction's flame or hatred's gall,
> What's riot, bloodshed, row or brawl,
> Roaring Hanna,
> To one who boasts an inward call,
> Roaring Hanna.

Liberal opinion may have condemned Hanna but in December 1857 he was presented with a watch and 100 sovereigns 'in testimony of his able and successful maintenance of the right of open-air preaching' and the historian of the Berry Street Presbyterian Church, writing in 1969, quoting *Punch*, commented 'Hugh Hanna was undaunted: he *had* the inward call. And out of doors as well as within the sanctuary he fearlessly wielded the sword of the Spirit … a soldier of The Cross in truth' (Combe, 15). Son and grandson of Black Watch soldiers, Hanna had a special concern for troops stationed in Belfast and was garrison chaplain from 1867, the upper gallery of St Enoch's Church being reserved for them at Sunday morning worship.

Hanna was never called to the moderatorial chair of the general assembly but he was given an honorary DD by the Irish Presbyterian Theological Faculty in 1885 and an honorary LLD by Galesville College, Wisconsin, USA, in 1888. He died suddenly of a heart attack on 3 February 1892 at 1 Clifton Terrace, Belfast, and was buried in Balmoral cemetery on 5 February. His grave is marked by an impressive pillar. In 1894 his political friends unveiled a large bronze statue in his honour in Carlisle Circus; it was destroyed by explosives in 1970. FINLAY HOLMES

Sources records of Hugh Hanna, Presbyterian Historical Society, Belfast · *In memoriam Hugh Hanna D.D., LL.D.* (1892) · J. M. Barkley, *St Enoch's congregation, 1872–1972* (1972) · *Irish Presbyterian*, 9/9, 130ff. · *Irish Presbyterian*, 30 (July 1924), 102 · J. M. Barkley, ed., *Fasti of the*

general assembly of the Presbyterian Church in Ireland, 1: 1840–1870 (1986), 42 • A. Boyd, Holy war in Belfast (1969) • H. T. Combe, The dowry of the past: the story of Berry Street Presbyterian Church (1969) • The Witness [see also other contemporary Belfast newspapers]

Likenesses photograph, repro. in Barkley, St Enoch's congregation

Wealth at death £814 1s. 0d.: probate, 4 April 1892, CGPLA Ire.

Hanna, Samuel (1771–1852), minister of the Presbyterian Church in Ireland, was born at Kellswater, near Ballymena, co. Antrim, the fifth son of Robert Hanna, a merchant. He was educated locally and at Glasgow University, graduating MA in 1789. In 1790 he was licensed by Ballymena presbytery. He was ordained as minister of the Presbyterian congregation of Drumbo, co. Down, on 4 August 1795. His reputation as a preacher grew rapidly. On 11 December 1799 he was installed as minister of Rosemary Street, Belfast. The following year he married Martha Gemmil (d. 1860), daughter of Robert Gemmil, a Belfast muslin manufacturer. They had seven children, four daughters and three sons, one of whom, the Revd Dr William *Hanna, was the son-in-law and biographer of Thomas Chalmers, the Scottish church leader.

The Rosemary Street congregation revived under Hanna's ministry and the meeting-house was handsomely rebuilt. A warm advocate of Sunday schools, Bible distribution, and missionary enterprise, Hanna was moderator of the General Synod of Ulster in 1809. In 1816 the synod resolved to provide a theological training for its students in the recently founded Belfast Academical Institution, instead of sending them to the Scottish universities. Hanna, in June 1817, was unanimously elected professor of divinity and church history, while remaining minister of the Rosemary Street congregation. In the following year he was made DD of Glasgow. In 1835 he was joined in the institution by Samuel Davidson as professor of biblical criticism, and in 1837 by James Seaton Reid as professor of ecclesiastical history and pastoral theology. In 1840 Hanna was freed from active pastoral duties by the election of William Gibson (later professor of Christian ethics in the Presbyterian college, Belfast) as his assistant and successor at Rosemary Street.

On 10 July 1840 Hanna was chosen first moderator of the general assembly, formed at that time by the union of the General and Secession synods. This was an indication of the high esteem in which he was held by Irish Presbyterians, but he was never a distinguished scholar, publishing only a few sermons and pamphlets. His appointment as professor in 1817 had signalled the growing strength of the evangelical party in the synod, and during his long tenure of the chair he exercised an evangelical influence on successive generations of students for the ministry. He held the chair until his death on 23 April 1852, at the home of his son-in-law, the Revd James Denham, minister of the Great James Street congregation in Londonderry. He was buried on 30 April in the new burying-ground in Clifton Street, Belfast. His wife survived him.

ALEXANDER GORDON, rev. FINLAY HOLMES

Sources Archives of the Presbyterian Historical Society of Ireland [S. Hanna] • R. Allen, The Presbyterian College, Belfast, 1853–1953 (1954) • J. Macnaughton, A sermon preached in Rosemary Street church, Belfast, on May 2, 1852, being the sabbath immediately after the funeral of the Rev. Dr Hanna (1852) [incl. funeral address by W. Gibson] • C. J. Reid, A history of Drumbo Presbyterian Church (1991) • J. W. Kernohan, Rosemary Street Presbyterian Church, 1723–1923 (1923) • W. D. Killen, Reminiscences of a long life (1901); repr. (1995) • The autobiography of Thomas Witherow, 1824–1890, ed. G. Mawhinney and others (1990) • R. S. J. Clarke, ed., Old Belfast families and the new burying ground: from gravestone inscriptions, with wills and biographical notes (1991) • J. S. Reid and W. D. Killen, History of the Presbyterian church in Ireland, new edn, 3 (1867), 415ff.

Archives U. Edin., New Coll. L., letters to Thomas Chalmers

Likenesses portrait, Union Theological College, Belfast; repro. in Allen, Presbyterian College, 152

Hanna, William (1808–1882), Free Church of Scotland minister and writer, was born at Belfast on 26 November 1808, the son of the Revd Samuel *Hanna (1771–1852), Irish Presbyterian minister and professor of divinity, and his wife, Martha Gemmil (d. 1860). He was educated at the University of Glasgow, where he excelled in mathematics and natural philosophy. From Glasgow he went on to study divinity in the University of Edinburgh under Thomas Chalmers; here his debating abilities became apparent.

In June 1834 Hanna was licensed as a probationer of the Church of Scotland, and he was ordained to East Kilbride, a parish near Glasgow, on 17 September 1835. He married Agnes, Chalmers's eldest daughter, on 30 March 1836; they had three sons, two of whom died young, and one daughter. In 1837 he was translated to the parish of Skirling, Peeblesshire. In the controversies preceding the Disruption, he was an active ally of Chalmers, and in 1843 he left the established church, taking his whole congregation with him. On Chalmers's death in 1847 Hanna was entrusted with writing his biography. To secure time for this work, he arranged a temporary exchange with a clergyman, and lived for a time in Edinburgh. The Memoirs of the Life and Writings of Thomas Chalmers came out in four successive volumes between 1849 and 1852, and A Selection from the Correspondence of the Late Thomas Chalmers followed in 1853. Hanna also edited the Posthumous Works of Dr Chalmers in nine volumes. The Life met with contemporary approval, and Hanna was awarded the degree of LLD by the University of Glasgow in 1852. The Life became, and remained, the standard biography of Chalmers for over a hundred years. Although an eloquent work which contains much material from Chalmers's papers and letters, it was necessarily partisan: Hanna suppressed and altered quotations which were likely to place his father-in-law in an unfavourable light.

In 1847 Hanna was appointed editor of the North British Review, a journal started in 1844 by David Welsh (1793–1845). It was designed to contrast with the Quarterly Review, which was seen as too conservative, and the Edinburgh Review, which excluded religious topics (it had neglected, for example, to detail the circumstances of the Disruption). During his editorship the North British Review enjoyed a good circulation, but failed to attract other than Scottish contributors. Having resigned his charge at Skirling, Hanna moved permanently to Edinburgh, where in 1850 he was called to be colleague to Thomas Guthrie, as minister of St John's Free Church. Here Hanna's quieter and

William Hanna (1808–1882), by Thomas Rodger

more thoughtful style of preaching acted as a foil to the flamboyant approach of his colleague.

Hanna's later publications included *Wycliffe and the Huguenots* (1860), *Last Day of Our Lord's Passion* (1862), which sold 50,000 copies, *The Earlier Years of Our Lord* (1864), *The Close of Our Lord's Ministry* (1869), and *The Resurrection of the Dead* (1872). He also edited a volume entitled *Essays by Ministers of the Free Church of Scotland* (1858) and *Letters of Thomas Erskine of Linlathen* (1877), a work which reflected his liberal theological views. Brief memoirs of a personal friend, Sir Alexander Gibson Carmichael of Skirling, and Alexander Keith Johnson were written for private circulation. Hanna was also a frequent contributor to the *Sunday Magazine* and other periodicals. In 1864 Hanna was made DD by the University of Edinburgh, and in 1866 he retired from the ministry. He died in London on 24 May 1882 and was survived by his wife. On the day of his funeral the general assembly of the established church suspended its sittings, and a tribute to his consistency and independence of mind was entered on the minutes of the Free Church assembly on 30 May 1882.   ROSEMARY MITCHELL

Sources *Fasti Scot.* · *The Scotsman* (25 May 1882) · S. J. Brown, *Thomas Chalmers and the godly commonwealth in Scotland* (1982), xiv · *Wellesley index* · *DNB*
Archives U. Edin., New Coll. L., papers | NL Scot., letters to Alexander Campbell Fraser
Likenesses C. B. Birch, statue, *c.*1894, St Enoch's Church, Belfast · T. Rodger, carte-de-visite, NPG [*see illus.*]

Wealth at death £15,177 2*s.* 10*d.*: confirmation, 19 July 1882, *CCI* · £1464: eik additional estate, 30 Sept 1905, *CCI*

Hannah, John (1792–1867), Wesleyan Methodist minister, born at Lincoln on 3 November 1792, was the third son of a corn merchant. His parents were Wesleyan Methodists in the Lincoln society. He received his early education from various local teachers, but chiefly from the Revd W. Gray of the cathedral. He obtained a respectable knowledge of the classics, and studied French, mathematics, and Hebrew with enthusiasm and success. From his earliest years his thirst for knowledge was insatiable, and his powers of acquisition remarkable. In the intervals of his studies he helped his father in his trade. In his late teens he was converted and became a Wesleyan preacher in the villages around Lincoln, preaching his first sermon at Waddington. When in 1813 Dr Thomas Coke was about to start overseas mission work to India with seven young men, Hannah accepted an offer to fill a vacancy which was anticipated, but did not occur. Nevertheless he retained a strong interest in overseas missions work throughout his life. In 1814 Hannah was received into the Wesleyan ministry, and was speedily recognized as a preacher of unusual eloquence and ability as he served in circuits in Yorkshire and Lincolnshire. He married Jane Capavor on 12 August 1817; they had eight children.

When only thirty-two Hannah came to the attention of Jabez Bunting and Richard Watson, and he was sent out to America with Richard Reece as a representative of the Wesleyan conference of Great Britain to the general conference of the Methodist Episcopal church in the United States. On his return he served in circuits in Leeds, Manchester, Huddersfield, and Liverpool. In 1834 he was appointed theological tutor of the Wesleyan Theological Institution for training candidates for the ministry. Hannah had played an important part in its establishment, despite initial opposition to the scheme. He filled the post with marked success, first at Hoxton and afterwards at Stoke Newington. In 1842 he was appointed to the theological tutorship of the northern branch of the institution, at Didsbury in Lancashire, which he held until a few months of his death. His lectures, later published with a memoir of his life, were delivered with an enthusiasm which awoke a corresponding response in his pupils. More than 400 students trained under him as tutor.

Hannah served the wider connexion as secretary of the conference from 1840 to 1842, and again from 1854 to 1858. He was twice president, in 1842 and 1851. In addition, he was secretary of the Wesleyan Methodist Missionary Society and much sought after as a public orator speaking on behalf of missions and Christian education. In 1856 Hannah crossed the Atlantic a second time, accompanied by F. J. Jobson, later his biographer, as the representative of English Methodism to the Methodists of the United States. For twenty years he was chairman of the Manchester and Bolton district. His calm judgement brought many threatened disputes to a happy conclusion. He died at Didsbury on Sunday 29 December 1867, shortly after resigning his tutorship. Hannah was an impressive preacher and a ready public speaker. Though no latitudinarian, and clinging tenaciously to the doctrines and practices of Methodism, he was devoid of bigotry or narrowness, and, while regarded with respect by the whole Methodist body, enjoyed friendly relations with the Church of England, into which church his only surviving son, John *Hannah, was ordained in 1841.

EDMUND VENABLES, rev. TIM MACQUIBAN

Sources W. Hill, *An alphabetical arrangement of all the Wesleyan-Methodist ministers, missionaries, and preachers*, rev. J. P. Haswell, 9th edn (1862) · *Minutes of the Methodist conference* · N. B. Harmon, ed., *The encyclopedia of world Methodism*, 2 vols. (1974) · F. J. Jobson, *The beloved disciple* (1868) · *Wesleyan Methodist Magazine*, 90 (1867)
Archives JRL, Methodist Archives and Research Centre, sermon registers, etc. · Wesley College, Bristol, corresp. · Wesley's Chapel, London, letters
Likenesses Armitage & Ibbetson, lithograph, BM · J. Thompson, stipple, NPG
Wealth at death under £1000: probate, 8 Jan 1868, *CGPLA Eng. & Wales*

Hannah, John (1818–1888), Church of England clergyman and schoolmaster, son of John *Hannah (1792–1867) and his wife, Jane Caparn (d. 1870), was born at Lincoln on 16 July 1818. His father was a Wesleyan minister, who was twice president of the Wesleyan conference. John was the eldest of eight children, the rest of whom died in infancy or early youth. He received his early education from his father until the latter was appointed theological tutor at the Wesleyan Theological Institution at Hoxton, when he was sent to St Saviour's School, Southwark, under the Revd Lancelot Sharpe. In March 1837 he matriculated at Brasenose College, Oxford, and in May of the same year was elected to a Lincolnshire scholarship at Corpus Christi College, Oxford. In 1840 he graduated with first-class honours in classics, and in the same year was elected to a Lincolnshire fellowship at Lincoln College, where he was a contemporary of Mark Pattison.

Hannah was attracted by the Tractarian movement, but never became an adherent of Newman; he was later described as 'an excellent churchman of the old High-Church type' (Overton, 80). In 1841 he was ordained and became a private tutor in the university. On 5 July 1843 he married Anne Sophia (d. 1876), sister of his college friend Robert Gregory, now at St Paul's. He was chaplain of the college living of Combe Longa, near Woodstock, from 1843 to 1845, dividing his time between parochial work and private tuition. In 1845 he returned to Oxford, and for the next two years was the leading private tutor in logic and moral science. He became rector of the Edinburgh Academy in 1847, and held that post with marked success for seven years. Although still only in his twenties, he proved a capable manager of the school, and an effective disciplinarian, memorably putting to flight a large gathering of boys, assembled to watch a fight, by brandishing his umbrella at them. In 1853 he took the degree of DCL at Edinburgh University in order to be dignified with the title of doctor, expected of headmasters in Scotland. Although successful as rector of the academy, he disliked having to take boarders in his house, and felt restricted in the presbyterian climate of the academy from giving Anglican religious instruction. In 1854 he accepted the wardenship of Trinity College, Glenalmond, Perthshire, which had been founded in connection with the Scottish Episcopal church. He immediately raised pupil numbers, placed the college on a sound financial footing, and acquired a cricket field for the boys. At Glenalmond he became a friend of Gladstone, who admired his business capacity, and it was to Hannah that Gladstone addressed his public letter on Irish church disestablishment in June 1865.

Hannah resigned from Glenalmond in 1870, following the death of his only daughter. He was nominated by the Gladstone government a member of the royal commission on the Contagious Diseases Acts. Later in 1870 he was presented by Richard Durnford, bishop of Chichester, to the important vicarage of Brighton. He divided the parish of Brighton into ecclesiastical districts, making each district church free and unappropriated for ever, and transferred the parochial rights of the parish of Brighton from the old church of St Nicholas to that of St Peter. A staunch defender of church schools, he was twice elected to the Brighton school board. He was appointed to the archdeaconry of Lewes in 1876. In 1887 he resigned the living of Brighton, but retained the archdeaconry until his death on 1 June 1888 at Brighton vicarage, to which his only son had succeeded him. He was buried in his wife's grave in Brighton parochial cemetery.

Hannah was not only conspicuously successful as tutor, schoolmaster, and parish priest, but achieved considerable reputation as a man of letters. In his early years he showed much literary promise. His early anonymous pieces include an amusing brochure, *Old Mother Hubbard*, written while he was a schoolboy, and a long and thoughtful article, 'Elizabethan sacred poetry', published in the *British Critic* for April 1842. The first work in his own name was an edition of *Poems and Psalms by Henry King, DD, Sometime Lord Bishop of Chichester* (1843); his next was *Poems by Sir Henry Wotton, Sir Walter Raleigh, and Others* (1845). On this work Hannah bestowed very great pains, recovering many poems from manuscript sources. A second edition appeared in 1875. In 1857 he published a volume of sermons entitled *Discourses on the Fall and its Results*; in 1862 he was appointed Bampton lecturer at Oxford, and in 1863 published the lectures under the title *The Relation between the Divine and Human Elements in Holy Scripture*. In 1870 he published *Courtly Poets from Raleigh to Montrose*, and at various times a vast number of single sermons, archidiaconal charges, and popular lectures on subjects of literary, historical, antiquarian, and practical interest. Hannah was a small man, 'slender and delicately built' with long raven-black hair in his young manhood, 'fine features, an aquiline nose, bright eyes and alert movements' (Magnusson, 140).

J. H. OVERTON, rev. M. C. CURTHOYS

Sources J. H. Overton, *John Hannah: a clerical study* (1890) · Boase, *Mod. Eng. biog.* · *Wellesley index* · M. Magnusson, *The clacken and the slate: the story of the Edinburgh Academy, 1824–1974* (1974) · V. Green, *The commonwealth of Lincoln College, 1427–1977* (1979) · G. St Quintin, *The history of Glenalmond* (1956)

Archives BL, Gladstone MSS · NL Scot., A. C. Fraser MSS · Shakespeare Birthplace Trust RO, Stratford upon Avon, notes and letters on Elizabethan poets
Likenesses photograph, repro. in Overton, *John Hannah*, frontispiece
Wealth at death £7913 7s. 7d.: probate, 28 June 1888, *CGPLA Eng. & Wales*

Hannam, Richard (*d.* 1656), thief, is an obscure figure whose life is largely to be seen through four pamphlets rushed out to capitalize on his execution in 1656. These accounts indicate he was the son of a shoemaker, also Richard Hannam, of Shaftesbury in Dorset. At school he acquired some knowledge of Latin, but was unhappy and ran away to London. He was apprenticed to a silk weaver in Shoreditch, but soon fell into the company of thieves. However, the pamphlets should be treated sceptically; even their claims as to his parentage and education may have been invented to lend plausibility to the narrative. These works all conform to the genre of the cautionary tale. Hannam appears as an apprentice who went to the bad, a thief and conman who inveigled his way into the houses of the grand, including that of the earl of Pembroke, by adopting the airs of a gentleman. He was skilled at breaking out of gaol. In his 'Europian Rambles' he reportedly robbed most of the crowned heads of Europe (including 'the Prince of Turks'; *Speech and Confession*, 5). One pamphlet hinted at a royalist Hannam who denied on the gallows that he had robbed the king of Scots—the exiled Charles II. The pamphlets all suggest that Hannam was active on the continent. Their tales of breathtaking escapes and daring thefts and frauds certainly romanticize the reality of Hannam's life, and seek to embellish his image as a glamorous rogue. One entry in the state papers hints that Hannam could indeed aim high in his targets: in December 1655 the council of state issued a warrant to pay Edward Flowers in reward 'for his services in discovering Hanham's designs upon the Exchequer' (*CSP dom., 1655–6*, 585).

Nevertheless, it was an entirely mundane robbery that brought Hannam to the gallows. In 1656 he and his father-in-law, Rudd, robbed an alehouse; caught in the act, Hannam escaped across the roof. When Rudd was accused by the publican and arrested Hannam is reported to have returned to the scene and stabbed the man, the only occasion on which he is said to have caused a victim serious physical harm. He was tried and found guilty on 16 June 1656 and was conveyed to Newgate to await execution the next day.

Later that evening Hannam was visited in the dungeon, where he lay in chains, by Edward Tuke. Hannam did not immediately welcome his visitor: 'I see not what good a minister can do for me, for the matter lies upon myself; If I pray not myself, and repent of my sins', no other man could help or comfort him (Tuke, 2–3). Tuke left a record of the prisoner's remarks on religious and other matters, which are highly abbreviated compared with his own speeches and may not properly represent Hannam's outlook. Nevertheless, however filtered through the preoccupations of an orthodox godly minister concerned with questions of sin and redemption Hannam's remarks are intriguing. He had by no means rejected belief in God: 'I do confesse, that I am a great sinner, and yet I hope there is mercy for me, for I do trust in God's mercy' (ibid., 36). But he had awkward questions on predestination, asking whether a thief sentenced to death was fore-ordained by God to die; on hearing that those who died unregenerate in such a manner were eternally damned, he responded 'that is ready to drive me or make me to despair' (ibid., 121). He rejected his earthly punishment as unjust: '[B]y the scripture thieves were not to be put to death, or men were not to be hanged for stealing; we do not read any where in the scripture that God appointed it' (ibid., 97). And he had evolved or learned some even more unorthodox ideas, which may perhaps reflect contact with London radical circles: 'I cannot think there is any hell, after this life, except that of the conscience'; 'I acknowledge one God but not three persons'; 'I cannot think I should pray unto Christ; to God I should pray but not Christ' (ibid., 25, 7, 11). Hannam also found some extenuation for his crimes: 'In the way that I have followed, I have not shed blood, or have not killed any person, and in taking away from men, I had always respect for the poor … I took from the rich and such as could spare it' (ibid., 48). Hannam thought this made him a better candidate for God's mercy, asking 'is there not difference in sins, some greater some lesser?' (ibid., 49).

On the following day, 17 June 1656, Tuke and Mr Clarke, the ordinary of Newgate, attended Hannam at the scaffold in the rounds of Smithfield. In his speech Hannam admitted his guilt but was at pains to protest the innocence of the couple from whom he rented his room. His Socinian-style rejection of the Trinity seems to have survived the hostile analysis of Tuke: 'he denied the Messias, and said he ought to pray only to the father and not to the Son, as not believing he was yet come, but that he would come' (*Witty Rogue*, 47). When he had finished speaking Hannam donned a white cap and mounted the ladder. 'When the executioner touched him on the shoulder, he turned himself off the ladder. After his body had hung about half an hour, it was cut down and carried to the Three Tuns in Smithfield, and thence in the evening to St [Se]pulchre's Churchyard and there buried' (*Hannam's Last Farewell*, 14).

STEPHEN WRIGHT

Sources *The witty rogue arraigned, condemned and executed, or, The history of that incomparable thief Richard Hainam* (1656) [Thomason tract] · *Hannam's last farewell to the world, being a full and true account and relation of the notorious life and shamefull death of Mr Richard Hannam, the great robber of England* [Thomason tract] · E. Tuke, *The soul's turnkey, or, A spiritual file for any prisoner lockt up in the dungeon and chains of sinne and Satan. Designed to open the dore, take off his fetters, and set him at liberty. Prepared for the hand of Master Hannam, prisoner in Newgate, the night and morning before he suffered* (1657) [Thomason tract] · *The speech and confession of Mr Richard Hannam* [Thomason tract] · *CSP dom., 1655–6* · *The English villain, or, The grand thief* [Thomason tract]

Hannan, William (1725–1772), painter, was born on 23 June 1725 in Kelso, Roxburghshire, and baptized there on 25 June, the son of George Hannan and Hanna Pringle. He was apprenticed in 1741 to Thomas Landall, a cabinet-maker in London. According to a contemporary, however, he had a 'great inclination to painting' (Edwards, 49). Between 1751 and 1754 he painted his best-known works: four views of West Wycombe Park, Buckinghamshire, for Sir Francis Dashwood (Lord le Despencer from 1763). Two of Hannan's drawings of the park are in the British Museum and many variations of the scenes, painted by Hannan or followers, are in collections all over the world.

The paintings were engraved in 1757, and the views appear in unexpected places, such as in *The Ladies Amusement, or, Whole Art of Japanning Made Easy* (2nd edn, *c*.1762); on a Meissen cream jug; and on Catherine the Great's celebrated 'Green Frog' service made by Wedgwood in 1773–4. Hannan was involved in the decoration of the inside of West Wycombe house, painting ceilings following ancient Roman models, probably in the 1760s. He also contributed to his patron's pioneering interest in Greek revival architecture. For the west portico, copied from the temple of Bacchus at Teos, Turkey, he painted three mythological scenes (said to be signed and dated 25 October 1770).

The market for works of art was changing, and artists began to seek a broader clientele. Ian Pears, quoting Edwards, mentions Hannan as an example of an artist dissatisfied with his dependence on one patron and unable to take advantage of an offer to go to Italy (Pears, 144). His *View of Lowther-Hall in Westmoreland* was exhibited at the Society of Artists in 1770, but Sir James Lowther still owed money to Hannan's estate in 1779. Hannan exhibited drawings and paintings, mostly views of the Lake District, with the society from 1769 to 1772, becoming a fellow in 1770. Many of his works seem to be after engravings by other artists, for example, an oil painting in Plymouth Art Gallery after George Lambert's *View of Hamoze and Plymouth Dock*. The catalogue illustrating his *Osterley Park at Dusk* (exh. Roy Miles, London, 1975; Gov. Art Coll.) refers to his 'gentle use of colour and rather serene composition'. Though his works lack originality, they continue to please, possessing 'Little power but much charm' (Grant, 86).

'A man of excellent character' (Edwards, 49), Hannan was buried in the parish church in High Wycombe, the town in which he had died, on 29 July 1772; his wife, Mary, *née* Cockburn, had been buried there on 10 December 1771. Although he left property in trust for his daughter Mary, a sad postscript describes her as a 'poor dear little Orphan … in very indigent circumstances' (Robert Wilson to Lord le Despencer, 20 May 1779, Bodl. Oxf., MSS DD Dashwood B11/13/24). Continuing interest in English eighteenth-century landscape gardens and country houses means that Hannan's topographical views are also valued as historical documents, providing evidence for research at, for example, West Wycombe and Painshill Park, Surrey.

M. J. P. EVANS

Sources 'The apprentices of Great Britain, 1710–1762, extracted from the inland revenue books at the Public Record Office, for the Society of Genealogists' (Society of Genealogists, London, 1921–8) · www.gac.culture.gov.uk [government art collection] · L. Binyon, *Catalogue of drawings by British artists and artists of foreign origin working in Great Britain*, 4 vols. (1898–1907), vol. 2 · E. Croft-Murray, *Decorative painting in England, 1537–1837*, 2 (1970) · F. Dashwood, *The Dashwoods of West Wycombe* (1987) · E. Edwards, *Anecdotes of painters* (1808); facs. edn (1970) · E. Einberg, *George Lambert* (1970) [exhibition catalogue, Iveagh Bequest, Kenwood, London] · L. A. Fagan, *A catalogue raisonné of the engraved works of William Woollett* (1885) · M. H. Grant, *A dictionary of British landscape painters, from the 16th century to the early 20th century* (1952) · Graves, *Artists* · J. Harris, *The artist and the country house: a history of country house and garden view painting in Britain, 1540–1870* (1979) · T. Knox, ed., *West Wycombe Park, Buckinghamshire* (2001) · *DNB* · *A guide to Painshill*, Painshill Park Trust (1998) · I. Pears, *The discovery of painting: the growth of interest in the arts in England, 1680–1768* (1988); repr. (1991), 144 · J. Pillement, *The ladies amusement, or, Whole art of japanning made easy*, 2nd edn (1762); facs. edn (1966) · M. Raeburn, L. Voronikhina, and A. Nurnberg, eds., *The green frog service* (1995) · *People and places: an exhibition of English and European paintings* (1975) [Exhibition catalogue, Roy Miles Fine Paintings, 9 April – 9 May 1975] · B. M. Watney, 'Sir Francis's cascade: a short paper read … at the Linnean Society Rooms on 11th December 1993', *English Ceramic Circle Transactions*, 15/3 (1995), 344–5 · will, 1772, Bucks. RLSS, D/A/WE97 · parish register, Buckinghamshire, PR 249/1/35 [burial]

Archives Bodl. Oxf., Dashwood MSS, B11/12/23, B11/13/24, B12/6/1 · Royal Bank of Scotland, London, Child & Co. customer account ledger, CH/194/16, fols. 260–62 · Society of Artists of Great Britain, London, Royal Academy archives, SA/3

Wealth at death two tenements; Frogmore, Chipping (High) Wycombe; gold mourning ring; lands and tenements, Duns near Berwick upon Tweed: will, 1772, Bucks. RLSS, D/A/WE97, proved 18 Aug 1772

Hannay, Doris Fergusson. *See* Leslie, Doris (1891–1982).

Hannay, James (1827–1873), writer, was born on 17 February 1827 at Dumfries, the son of David Hannay (1794–1864), a businessman, and Elizabeth Affleck (*d.* 1833). As a student David Hannay had been a member of the Speculative Society at Edinburgh University; in later life he was the author of an unsuccessful novel, *Ned Allen, or, The Past Age* (1849). His son's literary endeavours and his abiding interest in heraldry and family history can be traced to this source. 'Pitchforked into the world as a boy' (Gross, 93), as one modern commentator has put it, James Hannay joined the navy a few days after his thirteenth birthday, after attending schools in Westmorland and Surrey. For the next five years he combined naval duties, mostly in the Mediterranean—he served on the *Cambridge* during the blockade of Alexandria in the Syrian War—with strenuous efforts to improve his mind, even going so far as to take Latin lessons from a priest in Malta. This urge for self-improvement was a feature of his career: at late as his mid-thirties he made an attempt to learn Greek.

Although the evidence of his fiction suggests that Hannay enjoyed the confraternity of life at sea, he found naval routines irksome. This resentment extended to his superior officers, and his first excursion into journalism seems to have been a comic paper got up to ridicule the admirals and captains on the Mediterranean station. His naval service ended ingloriously in 1845, when he and two fellow officers were court-martialled for insubordination and riotous behaviour and dismissed from the service. Although the court's finding was generally thought to have been vindictive, and was eventually quashed, he did not seriously seek re-employment and instead pursued a literary life in London.

Hannay's early employments were painfully obscure. His first job was as a reporter on the tory *Morning Chronicle*. (Hannay remained an arch-Conservative throughout his life.) Subsequently he worked on the short-lived satirical papers *Pasquin* (1847) and *Puppet Show* (1848–9). A lively volume of naval sketches, *Biscuits and Grog*, appeared in 1848, but even at this early stage his chief literary enthusiasms are apparent, in particular his idolization of William Thackeray and Thomas Carlyle. The influence of both these mentors can be seen in his first novel, *King Dobbs* (1849), which attacked middle-class ostentation and features an imaginary Pacific island whose inhabitants include a 'philosophical novelist' strongly reminiscent of Thackeray and a prophet named Tomasso, transparently Carlyle.

In the 1850s Hannay's prospects began to improve. Taken up by Thackeray, whom he had met early in 1848 and to whom *King Dobbs* is dedicated, he was invited to supply the notes to the printed version of the latter's lectures on English humorists while their author was in the United States. Later he delivered his own moderately successful lecture series, 'Satire and satirists', appropriately enough at the Edwards Street Institute, London, where Carlyle had lectured on hero-worship fifteen years earlier. Two more books that made use of his naval experiences, the novel *Singleton Fontenoy RN* (1850) and *Sketches in Ultramarine* (1853), were followed by a third novel, *Eustace Conyers* (1857). On 24 February 1853 he married Margaret Anne Thompson (1833–1865), daughter of Joseph Thompson, a bank cashier; they had six children. Thackeray introduced him about this time to Whitwell Elwin, editor of *The Quarterly Review*—'a worthy and clever fellow … who loves reading and letters and is trying his best in the world-struggle' (*Letters and Private Papers*, 3.465)—and electioneering work for the tories in Scotland (he had stood unsuccessfully at Dumfries in 1857) procured him the editorship of the highly partisan *Edinburgh Courant* (1860–64).

Hannay's last years were a decline, compounded by alcoholism and waning influence. In August 1868 he married Jean Hannay (*d.* 1870)—apparently no relation; they had one child. Also in 1868 his political friends got him appointed British consul at Brest in France, a position he contrived to exchange for a similar role at Barcelona, where he skimped his duties, ran into debt, and on the night of 8–9 January 1873, in the suburb of Putchet, finally drank himself to death. His later books include an excellent *Course of English Literature* (1866), previously published in George Augustus Sala's short-lived penny magazine *The Welcome Guest: Studies on Thackeray* (1869), perhaps the best account in Victorian times of the novelist's work; and *Three Hundred Years of a Norman House* (1866), a part history of the Gurney family.　　　　　　　　D. J. TAYLOR

Sources G. J. Worth, *James Hannay: his life and works* (1964) · *The letters and private papers of William Makepeace Thackeray*, ed. G. N. Ray, 3 (1946) · *The letters and private papers of William Makepeace Thackeray*, ed. E. F. Harden, 2 vols. (1994) · J. Sutherland, *The Longman companion to Victorian fiction* (1988) · J. Gross, *The rise and fall of the man of letters: aspects of English literary life since 1800* (1969) · m. cert., 1853
Archives UCL, diaries
Likenesses photograph, *c.*1866–1869, repro. in Worth, *James Hannay*

Hannay, James Owen [*pseud.* George A. Birmingham] (1865–1950), novelist, was born at 75 University Road, Belfast, on 16 July 1865, the son of the Revd Robert Hannay, a clergyman who became rector of the parish church of St Anne's, Belfast, and his wife, Emily, daughter of the Revd William Wynne. He was educated at Haileybury School, Hertfordshire, and Trinity College, Dublin, where he graduated in 1886 as a junior moderator in modern literature. He was ordained deacon in 1888 (obtaining a curacy at Delgany, co. Wicklow) and priest the following year. In 1889 he married Adelaide Susan Wynne (1865–1933), daughter of his mother's second cousin, Canon Frederick Richards Wynne. The couple had two sons and two daughters. In 1892 he was appointed to the rectory of Westport, co. Mayo, where he remained until 1913.

Hannay had been writing under his own name since 1890: magazine stories, newspaper articles, and scholarly works such as *The Spirit and Origin of Christian Monasticism* (1903) and *The Wisdom of the Desert* (1904). It was at Westport that his first novels, beginning with *The Seething Pot* (1905) and *Hyacinth* (1906), involved him in disputes with the local commercial and ecclesiastical establishment who saw their characters impugned in his *romans-à-clef*. In 1908 he struck a vein of humour which he worked, in response to the demands of a faithful public, to the end of his life. *Spanish Gold*, published in that year, had for its central character the Revd J. J. Meldon, a red-haired curate of undaunted audacity and loquacity, and it concerned itself with mystery, treasure, and the inscrutability of the Irish character, as did many of his subsequent novels. His interest in Irish affairs led him to assist Douglas Hyde in the early years of the Gaelic League and his books dealing with Irish issues, such as *The Lighter Side of Irish Life* (1911) and *An Irishman Looks at his World* (1919), and Irish landscape, such as *The Northern Iron* (1907), are among his most characteristic productions. Similar stock characters, such as the doctor in *Send for Dr O'Grady* (1923), enlivened many later novels.

At Westport, Hannay began his career as a playwright. A visit to the rectory in 1911 from Constance Markiewicz and members of the Independent Theatre Company led to his play *Eleanor's Enterprise* opening at Dublin's Gaiety Theatre that same year, and in 1913 his play *General John Regan*, which concerns the erection in a small Irish town of a statue to a totally imaginary Irish hero, opened in London and ran for 275 performances and was later produced in the United States. Many of the novels of George A. Birmingham (the pseudonym he now used) are set around Westport—or 'Ballymoy', as he called it—and among the many islands of Clew Bay. When *General John Regan* was produced in Westport in 1914, there was a riot—ostensibly because Canon Hannay had portrayed a Roman Catholic priest on the stage.

Hannay and his wife left Westport in 1913, going on a lecture tour to the United States and returning first to England and then to a living at Mount Mappas in Killiney, co. Dublin. He returned from a second American tour in 1915 and spent the rest of the war years as an army chaplain in France. These experiences he recounted in *From Connaught to Chicago* (1914) and *A Padre in France* (1918). He was appointed rector of Carnalway in co. Kildare in 1918 and after four years became chaplain to the English legation in Budapest. It was during his time in Hungary, detailed in *A Wayfarer in Hungary* (1925), that the unexpected offer of the living in the Somerset village of Mells was made to him. He accepted and settled there in 1924. In 1929 the rectory was burnt down and in 1933 his wife died. He finally moved to London, to the church of the Holy Trinity in Kensington.

Although known to the general public as a prolific novelist—hardly a year went by without another 'Birmingham novel' being published—Hannay always thought of himself as a priest first and a novelist second. In 1946 Trinity College, Dublin, conferred upon him the honorary degree of LittD. Hannay died on 2 February 1950 at his home, 187 Queen's Gate, Kensington, London, and was buried in St Andrew's churchyard, Mells, Somerset.

M. R. BELLASIS, *rev.* BRIAN TAYLOR

Sources *The Times* (3 Feb 1950) · Burke, *Gen. Ire.* (1912) · B. Taylor, *The life and writings of James Owen Hannay (George A. Birmingham) 1865–1950* (1995) · private information (2004) · d. cert. · *CGPLA Eng. & Wales* (1950)
Archives NL Ire., corresp. · TCD, corresp. and literary papers; diaries | BL, letters to George Bernard Shaw, Add. MS 50538
Likenesses bust, St Andrew's Church, Mells, Somerset · portrait, TCD
Wealth at death £5523 4s. 10d.: probate, 22 March 1950, *CGPLA Eng. & Wales*

Hannay [*née* Wilson], **Jane Ewing** (1868–1938), schoolteacher and women's welfare campaigner, was born on 8 February 1868 at the manse, New Abbey, near Dumfries, the daughter of the Revd James Stewart Wilson, a Church of Scotland minister, and his wife, Jane Ewing, *née* Brown. At the age of fourteen she went to St Leonards School, St Andrews, where she was captain of games for two years and head of school from 1884 to 1886. She passed the London matriculation examination, division one, and subsequently entered Girton as a Girton entrance scholar (bracketed second), where she read classics. In 1889 she obtained third-class honours in the classical tripos.

In 1890 Jane Wilson returned to her former school, St Leonards, as assistant mistress in classics and German. From 1895 to 1899 she was also a housemistress. She was to retain her connection with St Leonards throughout her life; following her election to the council of St Leonards and St Katherine schools she was an active member for more than twenty years, until her death. In 1899 she resigned her teaching post to marry (19 September 1899) Robert Kerr *Hannay (1867–1940), the historian. Their only child, Robert Stewart Erskine Hannay, was born the following year. From 1901 to 1911 she lived in St Andrews

and thereafter in Edinburgh, where Robert Hannay became professor of Scottish history.

Jane Hannay became publicly prominent during the First World War, when she was active in organizing and promoting voluntary women's patrols, the forerunners of women police, which concentrated on preventive work, initially near military camps. Despite the doubts of the authorities about the scheme, a Scottish training school for policewomen and patrols was established in Glasgow with Hannay as honorary secretary. In 1918 she was elected to the first executive committee of the Edinburgh Women Citizens Association, which she used to press further for the introduction of women police.

She was a vice-president of the National Union of Women Workers (1911–12), and became a member of the Edinburgh local employment committee, set up in 1916 to assist the Home Office and the Board of Trade extend employment to women, and chair of the women's subcommittee. She was also a member of the central committee on training and employment of women until 1932, and at her death she was still vice-chair of the Scottish committee. In 1920 Hannay was appointed a member of the Scottish savings committee established by the Treasury. The post involved much public speaking, for which she was eminently suited. In 1923 she was a member of a nonparliamentary committee appointed by the Ministry of Labour to inquire into the supply of female domestic servants and the effect of the unemployment insurance scheme. She was a member of two trade boards, and in 1920 became a JP for the county of the City of Edinburgh. She was appointed OBE in 1918 and CBE in 1933.

Hannay was an active member of the Church of Scotland and on one occasion addressed the general assembly from the floor of the house. She was a member of the Church of Scotland Women's Association for Foreign Missions from 1915 and was elected to the influential General Assembly Home Mission Committee in 1930, the first year women were admitted.

Hannay died on 14 April 1938 at her home, 5 Royal Terrace, Edinburgh, after a three-week illness and was buried at New Abbey, Kirkcudbrightshire. A memorial service held on 18 April 1938 in the Moray Aisle, St Giles's Cathedral, Edinburgh, included many prominent representatives from the Scottish women's movement.

Although she might now be criticized for imposing middle-class values and assumptions on working-class women, Hannay was seen by contemporaries as someone tirelessly concerned about all spheres of women's welfare. The *Edinburgh Evening News* (15 April 1938) referred to her as a 'Scots woman pioneer' for her campaign for women police. A hard worker, she was described as having a genius for friendship, great intellectual gifts, a capacity for fun, and a sense of humour.   LINDY MOORE

Sources 'In memoriam: Jane Ewing Hannay, C.B.E., J.P., 1868–1938', *St Leonards School Gazette* (June 1938), 2 · *The Scotsman* (15 April 1938) · *Edinburgh Evening News* (15 April 1938) · 'The late Mrs Hannay', *The Scotsman* (19 April 1938) · *Scottish biographies* (1938) · private information (2004) · Church of Scotland, *Reports to the*

General Assembly, with the legislative acts (1930) • Church of Scotland, *Reports on the schemes of the Church of Scotland, with the legislative acts passed by the General Assembly* (1920) • 'Work of women police', *The Scotsman* (27 Aug 1919) • NA Scot., Edinburgh Women Citizens Association, GD 333/6/1, 333/7/21, 333/7/1 • NA Scot., Scottish Council of Women Citizens Associations minute book, GD 1/1076/5 • *The Post Office Edinburgh and Leith directory* • b. cert. • m. cert. • d. cert. **Likenesses** group portrait, photograph, *c.*1920, St Leonards School, St Andrews **Wealth at death** £3478 17*s.* 6*d.*: confirmation, 2 June 1938, *CCI*

Hannay, Patrick (*fl.* 1616–1630), poet, was the grandson of Donald Hannay, sprung of the Hannays of Sorbie and 'known / To the English by his sword', according to the complimentary poem by John Marshall prefixed to the collection of 1622. But no Donald appears in the Sorbie family tree in *Wigtownshire Charters* (p. 167). Patrick Hannay placed the Sorbie coat of arms with 'a mullet in the collar point' to signify a third son above his portrait in the frontispiece to the 1622 collection (*Poetical Works*, 49). It is, however, impossible from the evidence to advance any solid conjecture about his parentage. According to the title-pages of his two works published in 1619, he was master of arts, but he is not recorded on any of the surviving lists of the British universities. John Dunbar's complimentary verses in *Epigrammaton … centuriae sex* (6.xii) of 1616 show that Hannay had made a name for himself as a poet by that date. In London, Hannay published *A Happy Husband* (1618/1619?) and *Two Elegies on the Death of our Soveraigne Queene Anne* (1619), a piece that may indicate some attachment to the entourage of James's queen. Hannay served under Colonel Sir Andrew Gray, who raised 1500 foot and set sail in 1620 from Leith to fight for James's daughter, 'that rare Paragon', Elizabeth, queen of Bohemia, at the opening of the Thirty Years' War (*Poetical Works*, 35). Hannay was presumably in England in 1622 when he brought out *The Nightingale; Sheretine and Mariana; A Happy Husband; Elegies on the Death of Queene Anne; Songs and Sonnets*, a collection comprising his former publications and new ones. One panel of its frontispiece consists of an engraving of him, barbered, bearded, and ruffed as a Jacobean courtier should be. Possibly he ingratiated himself at the court of Charles I. On 31 July 1624 Charles granted a Patrick Hannay a patent in reversion to the clerkship of the privy council of Ireland; his tenure was disputed by the incumbent, but confirmed on 28 May 1625 because he had done James 'good and acceptable service beyond the seas, with great charge and danger of his life' and was also recommended particularly by Queen Anne. The case dragged on until October 1630. Hannay seems never to have gained occupancy, but meanwhile presumably the same man was appointed one of the masters of chancery in Ireland in 1627. Records of this Patrick Hannay continue until 1630, though an entry of March 1636 in 'The commisariat of confirmed testaments' (NA Scot., CC 8/8/57, fol. 41) speaks of his death by drowning in 1629.

Hannay's raptures and complaints as a love poet have nothing new. As a moralist of love, his concern is with 'married friendship'. 'Philomela' and 'Sheretine and Mariana' treat its breaches and *A Happy Husband* sets out its conditions, but his sententiousness is not enlivened with wit. What he does best is mythical imagining, as in the metamorphosis of Daphne depicted on Philomela's dress, the ghost of Mariana waiting passage to the underworld that opens 'Sheretine and Mariana', and the delightful Spenserian water fantasy in the second elegy on Queen Anne. Even the awfulness of living in Croydon is got up as a scene from the infernal pit with charcoal burners engaged in destructive work about its fires (song 8 in 'Songs and Sonnets'). Some Scottish linguistic forms survive his London printers. DAVID REID

Sources J. Morrin, ed., *Calendar of the patent and close rolls of chancery in Ireland, of the reign of Charles I* (1863) • *CSP Ire.*, 1625–32 • 'The commisariat of confirmed testaments', NA Scot., CC8/8/57, 41 • *Poetical works*, ed. D. Laing, Hunterian Club, 4 (1875) • R. C. Reid, ed., *Wigtownshire charters*, Scottish History Society, 3rd ser., 51 (1960) • J. Dunbar, *Epigrammaton Ioannis Dunbari megalo-Britanni centuriae sex decades totidem* (1616), 6.xii **Likenesses** T. Berry, line engraving, BM, NPG; repro. in P. Hannay, *The nightingale* (1622)

Hannay, Robert Kerr (1867–1940), historian of Scotland, was born at Glasgow on 31 December 1867, the eldest son of Thomas Hannay, ironmaster, of that city, and his wife, Elizabeth McDowall. He was educated at Albany Academy, Glasgow, the University of Glasgow (MA 1895), and University College, Oxford, where he obtained a second class in classical moderations (1891) and in *literae humaniores* (1893). In 1894 he was appointed lecturer in classics and ancient history at University College, Dundee, and in 1901 lecturer in ancient history at St Andrews University. There he began those studies in Scottish history which were to constitute his life's work. *The College of St. Leonard* (1905) was followed by *The Archbishops of St. Andrews* (5 vols., 1907–15), both written in collaboration with John Herkless; for these Hannay furnished the fresh material from manuscript sources. The reputation thereby gained led to his appointment in 1911 as curator of the historical department of the Register House, Edinburgh. In 1919 he became Sir William Fraser professor of ancient (Scottish) history and palaeography at Edinburgh University, and in 1930 historiographer-royal for Scotland. His other distinctions included the fellowship of the Royal Society of Edinburgh (1922), the honorary degree of LLD of St Andrews University (1923), and honorary membership of the Royal Scottish Academy (1933). In 1899 he married Jane Ewing (1868–1938) [*see* Hannay, Jane Ewing], second daughter of James Stewart Wilson DD, minister of New Abbey, Kirkcudbrightshire, and they had one son. Jane Hannay was appointed OBE (1918) and CBE (1933) for her social services. Hannay died in Edinburgh on 19 March 1940, where his home was 5 Royal Terrace.

Hannay was an unconventional and stimulating teacher of senior students, encouraging them, as fellow workers, to use original sources. No general history of Scotland came from his pen. In his view more research was necessary, especially in his own field of the later middle ages, before the rewriting of the existing narratives could be justified. But by his numerous contributions to the *Scottish Historical Review*, the *Juridical Review*, the publications of the Scottish History Society, the Stair Society, and the Old Edinburgh Club, and in his introductions to volumes 9 to 14 (1684–89) of the third series of *The Register of the Privy Council of Scotland* (1924–33) and *The Acts of the Lords of Council in Public Affairs, 1501–1554* (1932), as well as in such typical works as the *Rentale Dunkeldense* (1915) and *The College of Justice* (1933), he successfully challenged many accepted views on the educational, ecclesiastical, and institutional history of his country. His *Letters of James the Fourth* (1953) was edited with a biographical memoir by R. L. Mackie, and his *Letters of James V* (1954) was edited by Denys Hay. His complicated style was partly due to a supersensitive dread of inaccuracy in general statements. The style, however, was not the man. Tall and handsome, he was generous in communicating knowledge, genial and sociable, a born raconteur, an excellent golfer, and a musician of considerable gifts. H. W. MEIKLE, *rev.* H. C. G. MATTHEW

Sources *The Scotsman* (20 March 1940) · *Proceedings of the Royal Society of Edinburgh*, 60 (1939–40) · *The letters of James the fourth, 1505–13*, ed. R. K. Hannay and R. L. Mackie, Scottish History Society, 3rd ser., 45 (1953) [with biographical memoir (of R. K. Hannay)] · *University of Edinburgh Journal*, 10 (1939–40), 193–5 · personal knowledge (1949) · *CCI* (1940)
Archives NA Scot., papers, incl. collected MSS · U. Edin. L., special collections division, notebooks, lecture notes, and papers | U. Glas. L., special collections department, letters to George Neilson
Wealth at death £10,614 16s. 4d.: confirmation, 7 June 1940, *CCI*

Hanneman, Adriaen (*c*.1604–1671), portrait painter, was born in The Hague, Netherlands, into a family of Catholic government officials. He trained under the portrait painter Anthony van Ravesteyn (1580–1669), brother of Jan van Ravesteyn. There is no evidence that he worked as an assistant to Daniel Mytens, and his only known early work, *Portrait of a Woman* (1625; formerly St Lucas Gallery, Vienna), is much indebted to the style of the van Ravesteyn brothers. About 1626 he moved to London, where in 1630 he married Elizabeth Wilson, having unsuccessfully first courted the daughter of the goldsmith Nicasius Russell. Only a few works survive from this period, and all are heavily influenced by Van Dyck, indicating as well that he was probably involved primarily as an assistant in that master's studio in Blackfriars during his English period. Hanneman's best-known early portrait is *Cornelius Johnson with his Wife and Son* (*c*.1637; Rijksmuseum, Amsterdam). He also painted a portrait of the miniature painter Peter Oliver (*c*.1632; Royal Collection). In the lord mayor's survey of foreigners resident in London in 1635 Hanneman is listed as living in the parish of St Andrew, Holborn. He is recorded with one Dutch servant and no mention of an English wife is made; it is possible that Elizabeth was dead by that date.

Between 1638 and 1640, before the civil war broke out in Britain, Hanneman returned to The Hague, where his elegant, accomplished portrait style did much to spread the influence of Van Dyck throughout the Netherlands. Certainly by 1640 he was a member of the painters' guild in

Adriaen Hanneman (*c*.1604–1671), self-portrait, 1656

The Hague, the year in which he also married for the second time, on this occasion securing the hand of his master's niece, Maria van Ravesteyn. It was also in this year that Hanneman executed one of his best-known portraits, *Constantijn Huygens and his Children* (Mauritshuis, The Hague). Huygens was a learned humanist who had served the Dutch embassies in Venice and London and now acted as art adviser to Prince Frederick Henry. This accomplished work owes a compositional debt to Jacob van Campen in the placing of the figures in separate medallions. The central portrait of Huygens himself owes much to Van Dyck, but the work has a distinctive character of its own. It was a significant commission to have secured and heralded the beginning of a successful period in Hanneman's career. Although his reputation was made painting portraits, in 1644 he was commissioned to paint for the town council of The Hague the *Allegory of Justice* (Oude Stadhuis, The Hague). In 1643 he had become a governor of the painters' guild, and in 1645 he took on the role of dean. His successful portrait practice enabled him to live in some style, and he owned an imposing town house in the Nobelstraat, a smart area of The Hague. His large studio often produced numerous copies of portraits.

Hanneman found his English connections particularly useful when from the late 1640s onwards large numbers of exiled royalists began to settle in the Netherlands. He painted the portraits of some of the key figures of the period, including Charles II when prince of Wales (1648–9; original lost, known only in copies), his brother Henry, duke of Gloucester (1643; National Gallery of Art, Washington, DC), and courtiers such as Edward Hyde, first earl of Clarendon (1649; priv. coll.; of three further versions, one is in the NPG). That of the duke of Gloucester is one of Hanneman's finest works. The portrait of Clarendon, secretary of state to Charles II from 1653 to 1657, who was recorded as having patronized Hanneman, was almost certainly executed in 1648 but may conceivably have been painted in 1654, when the sitter returned to The Hague. It is a masterful characterization of the royalist historian, who went on to be lord high chancellor of England in exile in 1658 and Charles II's leading minister at the Restoration in 1660. Hanneman also found favour at the Dutch court in the 1650s, painting the young William of Orange, later the stadholder king, holding an orange and with a small dog (Rijksmuseum, Amsterdam). In addition he painted William's mother, Mary, princess of Orange, on a number of occasions. The earliest portrait of 1646 (known only from an engraving by Henry Donckerts) does not survive. Hanneman painted her again in 1659 (signed version, priv. coll.) and in the same year produced another variant (Scot. NPG), which has a curtain rather than a tree in the background, and again in 1660, the year of her death (Royal Collection, signed). In 1664 he painted a posthumous portrait of Mary wearing a feathered cloak and turban, with a black servant placing a pearl bracelet on her wrist (Mauritshuis, The Hague), for which he was paid 400 guilders. Mary was evidently an important patron of Hanneman; the painter's fluency in English made him popular with the princess, who did not speak Dutch.

The close family ties between Dutch and English royal families continued to produce commissions for Hanneman even after the royalists had all returned home. In 1664 he executed two copies of a portrait of William of Orange (both Royal Collection), for which he was paid 500 guilders. He also found patrons among wealthy residents of The Hague, including Cornelia van Wouw, whose portrait he painted in 1662 (Van Wouw almshouse, The Hague). For these sitters he combined the glamorous style of Van Dyck with the more sober Dutch tradition of portrait painting. His Roman Catholicism does not appear to have inhibited patronage: in 1661 he painted the Jesuit priest Father Roeland de Pottere (priv. coll.). Hanneman was a successful teacher, training such artists in his studio as Jan Janszoon Westerbaen the younger (1631–c.1672) and Reinier de la Haye (1640?–1695). He also received a late commission for the states of Holland, the *Allegory of Peace* (Binnenhof, The Hague).

Hanneman's success began to fade towards the end of his long career. He appears to have ceased painting in 1668, perhaps on account of illness. He married as his third wife Alida Besemer in 1670 and died in The Hague the following year, with little of his former fortune intact. He was buried in The Hague on 11 July 1671. A number of his self-portraits survive, of which the finest is in the Rijksmuseum, Amsterdam.   ANN SUMNER

Sources M. Toynbee, 'Adriaen Hanneman and the English court in exile', *Burlington Magazine*, 92 (1950), 73–80; 100 (1958), 249–50 • O. Millar, *The age of Charles I* (1972), 52 [exhibition catalogue, Tate Gallery, London] • A. Sumner, *Death, passion and politics* (1955), 85–6 [exhibition catalogue, Dulwich Gallery, London] • O. ter Kuile, *Adriaen Hanneman, 1694–1671* (Alphen aan den Rijn, 1976) • R. E. O. Ekkart, 'Hanneman, Adriaen', *The dictionary of art*, ed. J. Turner (1997) • H. J. S. Taylor, 'A. Hanneman's 1661 portrait of Father Roeland de Pottere (1584–1675)', MA diss., U. Leeds, 1998 [incl. biographical account of Hanneman]
Likenesses A. Hanneman, self-portrait, oils, 1647, Koninklijke Academie, The Hague • A. Hanneman, self-portrait, oils, 1656, Rijksmuseum, Amsterdam [*see illus.*] • A. Bannerman, line engraving (after A. Hanneman), BM, NPG; repro. in H. Walpole, *Anecdotes of painting in England*, 1 (1762) • R. van Voerst, line engraving (after A. Van Dyck), BM, NPG

Hannen, James, Baron Hannen (1821–1894), judge, was born in Peckham, Surrey, on 19 March 1821, the eldest son of James Hannen (1788/9–1857), of Kingswood Lodge, Dulwich, a London wine merchant, and his wife, Susan, daughter of William Lee of Nayland, Suffolk. He attended St Paul's School from 1831 to 1839 and then went to the University of Heidelberg, which made him a lifelong Germanophile with a taste for philosophy.

Hannen became a student of the Middle Temple on 30 October 1841, first in Samuel Warren's chambers and then, probably more to his taste, in Thomas Chitty's. He was called to the bar on 14 January 1848 and joined the home circuit. A commendation from Lord Chief Justice Campbell in *Hochster v. De la Tour* (1853) secured him a part in the *Shrewsbury peerage case* (1857–8). Thereafter his rise was rapid both in London and on circuit and he consolidated his reputation by his performance as adjudicator on the Anglo-American mixed arbitral commission of 1853–5. As an advocate he was described by a contemporary as a 'clear, but frigid and passionless speaker, accurate, precise, and painstaking, well endowed with practical good sense' (*The Times*). He also wrote for the press and reported cases for the *Morning Chronicle*.

On 4 February 1847 Hannen married his cousin Mary Elizabeth, second daughter of Nicholas Winsland; she died on 1 December 1872. He attempted to enter political life in July 1865, when he stood as a Liberal for Shoreham and Bramber, but was defeated; he never tried again. At that time he was reckoned an advanced Liberal, but he later spoke against the Home Rule Bill of 1892 in the Lords. He would have found it difficult to combine a serious political career with the demands of what had become a huge practice, particularly in mercantile and insurance law, which left him little time for his illustrious pupils, Charles Bowen, Farrer Herschell, and A. L. Smith. As junior Treasury counsel from 1863, he took part in the prosecution of the Fenians in 1867, after a policeman died in Manchester in the course of a prisoner rescue, and of Muller for a notorious railway murder in 1868.

Hannen was made a judge of the queen's bench on 25 February 1868, was sworn as a serjeant the next day, and knighted on 14 May. In queen's bench, he was not regarded as a success, the court being dominated by Cockburn and Blackburn, and on 20 November 1872 he accepted the offer to be judge of the court of probate and the divorce court, which John Coleridge had refused. He was sworn of the privy council on 27 November 1872 and in 1875 became, through the Judicature Acts, president of the new Probate, Divorce, and Admiralty Division of the High Court.

Hannen's performance in his new role was almost universally held to be masterful in manner and masterly in law. In probate, where he had already had to grapple with the case of Lord St Leonards's lost will, he gave some valuable rulings on the always vexed question of mental capacity, especially *Boughton* v. *Knight* (1873) and *Smee* v. *Smee* (1879) and on undue influence (for example, *Wingrove* v. *Wingrove*, 1885), 'models of lucid exposition and unequalled as clear statements of the law' (Holdsworth, *Eng. law*). But it was in the divorce court that he left the deepest imprint on the administration of the law.

Hannen built on the body of law created by his predecessors Cresswell and Lord Penzance, but the atmosphere of the divorce court was his own unique contribution. The 'Rhadamantine solemnity' (E. Manson, *Builders of our Law during the Reign of Queen Victoria*, 1904, 336) of his demeanour effectively discouraged any tendencies to levity or prurience; he imposed his notions of rules and practice with unarguable decisiveness and maintained an evenness of temper (the product of self-discipline rather than a natural gift) which made him, for many, the embodiment of the judicial ideal. His judgments matched his manner: concise, polished, and graceful. When Sir Robert Phillimore resigned as Admiralty judge in 1883 Hannen's initial idea as president was to have alternate Admiralty sittings with C. P. Butt, Phillimore's replacement, but this upset the practitioners accustomed to a single judge. Hannen gave way, and took little part on the Admiralty side.

Hannen's reputation for strict impartiality and integrity made him an obvious choice to head the judicial tribunal appointed in 1888 to examine the accusations in *The Times* against Parnell and the Irish nationalists. It was a novel and rather unsuccessful expedient, largely because the tribunal (Sir Archibald Smith and Sir John Day were the other members), at Hannen's instance, chose to adopt the passive (and largely silent) role with which they were familiar, patiently sifting whatever evidence was brought on behalf of the parties rather than actively seeking it out. The length of the hearings (129 days) drained public interest after Sir Charles Russell's sensational exposure of the 'Parnell letters' as forgeries. The final report—mostly Hannen's work and very ably written—was excessively cautious in its conclusions, which hardly vindicated the methods of the tribunal, or justified the length of its labours. In 1888 he also sat on a royal commission into university education in London and in the same year he was made a DCL of Oxford University. A bencher of the Middle Temple since 27 June 1878, he was a reader in 1889.

Hannen was seen as a possible successor to Sir George Jessel as master of the rolls in 1883 but Gladstone preferred Brett (Lord Esher). On 21 January 1891 he was made a law lord, taking the title of Baron Hannen of Burdock, Sussex, and in the following year was chosen as the British arbitrator in the Paris arbitration on the serious Anglo-American dispute over seal fishing in the Bering Sea. His able discharge of this heavy task added further to his reputation but his health, which had been poor for some time,

failed him during the arbitration and on 15 August 1893 he retired from his judicial duties. He died at his house, 49 Lancaster Gate, London, on 29 March 1894 and was buried at Norwood cemetery. In private life Hannen was very different from the stern figure on the bench: cultivated, well read, and fonder of rural life than society. His son James, a barrister, later served as a divorce commissioner.

The effusive tributes of contemporaries such as his successor as president, Sir Francis Jeune, and Lord Chief Justice Coleridge, who said that there had been no greater English judge than Hannen during his seventy-three years, are perhaps exaggerated, but if his best work had not been done mostly in the backwaters of the Probate, Divorce, and Admiralty Division, his enduring contribution to English law would have been greater.

PATRICK POLDEN

Sources *The Times* (30 March 1894) · *Law Journal* (7 April 1894), 225–6 · GEC, *Peerage*, new edn, vol. 6 · Holdsworth, *Eng. law*, vol. 16 · A. W. B. Simpson, ed., *Biographical dictionary of the common law* (1984) · V. V. Veeder, 'A century of English judicature', *Select essays in Anglo-American legal history*, 1 (1907), 730–836 · F. L. Wiswall, *The development of admiralty jurisdiction and practice since 1800* (1970) · *The diary of Sir Edward Walter Hamilton, 1880–1885*, ed. D. W. R. Bahlman, 2 vols. (1972) · Boase, *Mod. Eng. biog.* · J. Foster, *Men-at-the-bar: a biographical hand-list of the members of the various inns of court*, 2nd edn (1885) · E. Harrison, *Officials of royal commissions of inquiry* (1996) · H. A. C. Sturgess, ed., *Register of admissions to the Honourable Society of the Middle Temple, from the fifteenth century to the year 1944*, 2 (1949) · *Recollections of Sir Henry Dickens* (1934) · W. H. Hunt, ed., *The registers of St Paul's Church, Covent Garden, London*, 1–4, Harleian Society, register section, 33–6 (1906–8) · *directories*
Likenesses T. B. Wirgman, oils, 1890, Middle Temple, London · S. P. Hall, pencil sketches, NPG · Spy [L. Ward], chromolithograph caricature, NPG; repro. in *VF* (21 April 1888) · etching (after T. B. Wirgman), BM
Wealth at death £58,042 8s. 2d.: probate, 16 June 1894, CGPLA Eng. & Wales

Hannes, Sir Edward (1663/4–1710), physician and poet, was the son of Edward Hannes of Devizes, Wiltshire. His father's occupation was variously described; Peter le Neve said that he kept a herb shop in Bloomsbury market (*Pedigrees of Knights*, 1873). Hearne suggested that in later life Hannes was reluctant to admit his humble origins. In 1678 he was admitted as a king's scholar to Westminster School, to which he later gave a silver *poculum* or goblet, and in 1682, aged eighteen, was elected to a Westminster studentship at Christ Church, Oxford. Having graduated BA in 1686 and MA in 1689 he was given one of the five faculty studentships—in law, although his studies were now in medicine—which permitted him to retain his position at Christ Church without entering holy orders.

While at Christ Church, Hannes contributed to the collections of poems published on the death of Charles II and on the return of William III from Ireland; the latter was reprinted in *Musarum Anglicanarum analecta* (1692), the same volume which included a Latin ode by Joseph Addison in praise of Hannes. Hannes was one of a group of 'medical' poets at Oxford—including James Gibbs, William Wigan, and Robert Freind—which influenced the young Anthony Alsop. Although he was to censure Hannes's treatment of his wives, and to describe him as haughty and proud, Thomas Hearne asserted that Hannes was the greatest writer of Sapphic verse of the age. Hannes also assisted William King, a contemporary at both Westminster and Christ Church, in writing his refutation (1688) of the first volume of Antoine Varillas's history of heresy (*Histoire des révolutions*, 1686–9).

Hannes lectured in chemistry at Oxford and was appointed reader in chemistry, succeeding Robert Plot, in 1690. That same year, on 17 July, he gave an eloquent speech to Elias Ashmole at an entertainment in Ashmole's honour held in the Ashmolean museum. He received his BM degree in 1692 and his DM in 1695.

In 1699 Hannes left Oxford to set up medical practice in London. Not licensed with, even actively rejected by, the Royal College of Physicians, he found that, even for a man relying on his Oxford degrees, it was difficult to compete with established practitioners like John Radcliffe. In some desperation, and in order to make his name known in the city, he reportedly sent his footman out on to the streets of London to stop every carriage and make enquiries for the doctor. The servant continued the campaign into the coffee houses and, at Garraway's, encountered Dr Radcliffe who, in response to the servant's enquiry after the whereabouts of a nobleman who allegedly had called for Hannes, quipped that it was not the lords who needed Hannes but 'the doctor wants those lords' (Pettis, 37). Eventually the strategy paid off; his practice grew, and he was appointed principal physician at court.

Hannes resigned his studentship at Christ Church in 1699, probably because of his marriage to Anne Packer, daughter of John, lord of the manor of Shillingford, Berkshire, on 1 October 1698. Hearne suggests that Hannes was a barbarous husband who, through his inhumanity, hastened his wife's death, which must have occurred at the time of, or shortly after, the birth of their only child, Temperance, during 1699 or 1700.

In July 1700 Hannes attended William, duke of Gloucester, son of Princess Anne, on his deathbed. On 31 July he conducted a post-mortem on the duke, whose death effectively ended the Stuart succession. Rival doctors suggested that he had misdiagnosed the duke's illness; what Hannes had stated to be smallpox was, according to Radcliffe, only a heat rash brought on by excessive dancing. His prescribed remedies were, Radcliffe alleged, the cause of the duke's death, and it would have been better for the nation if the doctor had followed his father as a basketmaker. Hannes's report was ridiculed in a satirical poem called *Doctor Hannes Dissected in a Familiar Epistle by way of 'nosce teipsum'*. In spite of this, the princess appointed him her physician when she became queen in 1702. He was knighted in 1705; Hearne, rather acidly, drew attention to the liberality of the queen in her distribution of honours at this time, as did Thomas Clark, vicar of Sparsholt, Berkshire, in a pamphlet published that year.

Hannes married his second wife, Anne Bull, the widow of Dr Henry Bull, of Oxford, and the daughter of John Luffe, regius professor of medicine, on 15 June 1701. Anne was said by Hearne to have been a great beauty—although it was alleged that Hannes married her for her wealth—

and possessed of considerable and continued virtue in spite of her husband's persistent cruelty. She appears to have predeceased him. He died on 22 July 1710 of the palsy, having apparently been insane for two years, and was buried, on 12 August, in Shillingford church next to his first wife. In his will, which records him as a resident of St Anne's parish in Westminster, he left sufficient money for a memorial with a marble bust above (on the north wall of the nave of Shillingford church). He was generous in death, leaving £1000 to Westminster School for a new dormitory for the king's scholars, another £1000 to Christ Church to complete the building of Peckwater quadrangle, £2000 to Greenwich Hospital, a further £1000 to the Greycoat Hospital in Westminster, and £1000 for distribution by the governors of Queen Anne's Bounty.

J. H. CURTHOYS

Sources W. Pettis, *Some memoirs of the life of John Radcliffe* (1715) · *Old Westminsters*, vol. 1 · *Remarks and collections of Thomas Hearne*, ed. C. E. Doble and others, 11 vols., OHS, 2, 7, 13, 34, 42–3, 48, 50, 65, 67, 72 (1885–1921), vols. 1, 3 · *VCH Berkshire*, vol. 4 · D. K. Money, *The English Horace: Anthony Alsop and the tradition of British Latin verse* (1998) · Christ Church Oxf., Christ Church archives, DP ix.b.1 · PRO, PROB 11/516, sig. 160 · *The Latin prose and poetry of Joseph Addison*, eee.uci.edu/~papyri/Addison, 9 Jan 2002 · annals, RCP Lond., 7.145–6

Hanneya [Hanney], **Thomas** (*fl.* 1313), grammarian, wrote a treatise, *De quatuor partibus grammaticae* ('On the four parts of grammar'), generally known as the *Memoriale juniorum*. This work, which discusses all four parts of Latin grammar in 160 pages, is extant in complete form in six medieval manuscripts, and incompletely or fragmentarily in three. A note at the end of the table of contents states that Thomas de Hanneya compiled the treatise, beginning it at Toulouse on 20 April 1313, and completing it on 28 November of the same year at Lewes, presumably in the priory there. It was finished 'at the instance of Master John Chertsey, rector of the schools in that place' (Bodl. Oxf., MS Auct. F.3.9, p. 189). Despite the largely groundless elaborations of his career by the bibliographers John Bale (1495–1563) and Thomas Tanner (1674–1735), there appears to be no evidence that the author was an Englishman beyond his presence at Lewes. If he was English he may be assumed to have taken his name from Hanney, Berkshire. In his notebook, the *Index Britanniae scriptorum*, Bale mistakenly gives the date of the *Memoriale juniorum* as 1363.

MARIOS COSTAMBEYS

Sources R. Sharpe, *A handlist of the Latin writers of Great Britain and Ireland before 1540* (1997) · N. Orme, *English schools in the middle ages* (1973) · Bodl. Oxf., MS Auct. F.3.9
Archives Bodl. Oxf., MS Auct. F.3.9, p. 189

Hannibal, Thomas (*d.* in or before **1530**), diplomat, is of unknown origins. He studied civil law at Bologna, then at Cambridge (1495–6) where he was admitted DCL and DCnL (1502–4; incorporated DCL at Oxford, 1513). He took holy orders (subdeacon and deacon in 1503–4, priest in 1515) and in addition to a canonry and prebend of York (1504) held other benefices mainly in the diocese of Worcester, of which he was appointed vicar-general by Bishop Silvestro Gigli in 1511. He signed a letter at Bruges on 1

October 1515, together with Thomas More and others, informing Wolsey about inconclusive negotiations with Hanseatic merchants, but the major events of his career came in 1522–3. His initial commission (9 March 1522) was to negotiate in Spain an alliance against France with Emperor Charles V and King John of Portugal, but his letter to Wolsey from Plymouth (28 March 1522) suggests that instead the main purpose was to meet the recently elected pope, Adrian VI. At Saragossa in early May, Hannibal impressed Adrian with an oration affirming Henry VIII's devotion, and urged the extension of Wolsey's legatine faculties. He followed Adrian to Rome and on 8 and 12 September wrote to Wolsey describing the honour paid him at the papal coronation and his warm reception from Cardinal Campeggi (who provided lodging for him and his servants until his own house was ready) and Cardinal Giulio de' Medici. He also reported on the state of the English hospice of St Thomas and advised Wolsey to claim revenues from his title church of Santa Cecilia.

For nine months Hannibal remained sole English ambassador and proctor at Rome, repeatedly assuring Wolsey of the pope's eagerness for an Anglo-imperial offensive against France and willingness to extend Wolsey's faculties, if given financial aid; he also attended to English and Welsh provisions to benefices. On 3 June 1523, however, John Clerk arrived in Rome as ambassador, and although Hannibal and he signed letters jointly, including detailed reports of the conclave and its prospects, assuring Wolsey that if he were there in person he would be elected pope (letters from 14 September to 2 December 1523), it appears that Wolsey had lost confidence in Hannibal as his special agent in the curia. Already, on 9 October 1523, he had been appointed master of the rolls, but after the election of Cardinal Giulio de' Medici as Pope Clement VII his recall to England was still delayed. The new pope wrote to Wolsey in Hannibal's praise on 13 January 1524 ('egit fide, egit prudentia, egit industria', 'he has acted faithfully, wisely, and industriously'), and insisted that on account of age and ill health he should not travel in winter (*State Papers, Henry VIII*, 6.232; *LP Henry VIII*, 4(1), no. 23).

Hannibal finally left Rome on 3 June 1524, entrusted with the papal honour of the Golden Rose for Henry VIII and papal bulls for Wolsey's college at Oxford, but not the enlarged legatine faculties *pro non familiaribus* over which he had expended much effort in vain. He landed at Dover on 1 September and had an honourable escort into London 'to his house at St John's'. Thereafter he is recorded acting in various capacities as master of the rolls, for example, signing on 5 May 1526 the grants of possessions for Wolsey's foundation at Oxford, but he was replaced by John Taylor in June 1527. His death probably occurred before Wolsey's fall in 1530 and not in 1531 as stated in the *Dictionary of National Biography*: the only evidence cited for 1531 is a letter to Thomas Cromwell of 30 August 1531 recording that Hannibal's executor had been Dr Taylor and that Wolsey had claimed a debt (*LP Henry VIII*, 5, no. 386). The inventory of Wolsey's goods in January 1530 included some andirons and carpets 'late dr Hanyballes' (*LP Henry VIII*, 4(3), no. 6184, p. 2767). He may have been the author of an incomplete fragment (subscribed 'hanybal') recording opinions on three abstruse legal questions, whether a king's mother might act as regent, and concerning the rights of captives (BL, Cotton MS Caligula D.IX, fols. 128r–131r). D. S. CHAMBERS

Sources BL, Cotton MSS BV, BVI · Emden, *Oxf.*, 1.4 · *LP Henry VIII*, vols. 2–5 · D. S. Chambers, 'Cardinal Wolsey and the papal tiara', *BIHR*, 38 (1965), 20–30 · *State papers published under … Henry VIII*, 11 vols. (1830–52), vol. 6 · *DNB*
Archives BL, legal disquisition, Cotton MS Caligula D.IX fols. 128r–131r · BL, MSS and autograph letters, Cotton MSS BV, BVI · PRO, state papers Henry VIII, autograph letters

Hannington, James (1847–1885), Church of England bishop in east Africa, was born on 3 September 1847 at St George's in the village of Hurstpierpoint, 8 miles from Brighton, the third son of Charles Smith Hannington (*d.* 7 June 1881) and his wife Elizabeth Clark Gardner (*d.* February 1872). C. S. Hannington was a successful fabric merchant ('warehouseman') with a warehouse at Brighton, who purchased his Hurstpierpoint mansion, St George's, shortly before James's birth, and in 1873 became a JP and colonel of the 1st Sussex artillery volunteers. Hannington was educated at home, and travelled and yachted with his parents. He wanted to enter the navy but his parents refused. In 1859, by a gunpowder explosion with a homemade firework, he so injured his left thumb that it was amputated. At thirteen he was sent to the Temple School, Brighton. At fifteen he entered his father's business, which he disliked and in which he remained six years. He continued to yacht and to travel on the continent. In 1864 he was commissioned second lieutenant in the 1st Sussex artillery volunteers; he became captain in 1865, and major in 1866. His family were Independents, and his father built an Independent chapel in the grounds of St George's. In 1867 the family became Anglican, a change not unusual among wealthy dissenters and not always unconnected with social aspiration. Its minister pensioned off, the chapel too became Anglican, as St George's. In 1868 Hannington decided to become an Anglican clergyman, and so in October entered St Mary Hall, Oxford, reading classics. High-spirited—for a bet he wheeled Captain Way up the High Street in a wheelbarrow—energetic and popular, he became captain of the St Mary Hall boat club and president of the Red Club. In 1870 he was coached by the Revd C. Scriven, rector of Martinhoe, north Devon. In June 1873, after some difficulty, he took his BA degree (MA 1875, DD 31 October 1884). In September 1873 he was rejected at the bishop of Exeter's examination, but in spring 1874 he succeeded, and was ordained deacon at Exeter. He was curate of Martinhoe and Trentishoe, Devon, then on 29 September 1875 became curate in charge, without emolument, of St George's, Hurstpierpoint, the chapel his father had built. He threw himself zealously into evangelistic and temperance work, becoming a popular mission preacher throughout the British Isles. On 11 September 1876 he was ordained priest.

Hannington married on 10 February 1877 a member of his congregation, Blanche, second daughter of Captain James Michael Hankin-Turvin, formerly of Terlings Park,

James Hannington (1847–1885), by George J. Stodart, pubd 1887

Gilston, Hertfordshire; they had three children in four years, and she survived her husband. Hannington was tall, well proportioned, with clear grey eyes and a voice with 'a certain plaintive quaver' (Dawson, 46). He was an amateur naturalist, in the faunicidal fashion of his day, and became an FLS and FRGS.

In 1882 Hannington offered himself to the Church Missionary Society (CMS) for a period of not more than five years, for the Victoria Nyanza mission, offering £100 per annum to its funds provided that the CMS paid for a replacement clergyman at St George's during his absence. He was accepted, and appointed leader of a group of six missionaries for Buganda. On 7 March 1882 he broke the news to his wife, 'who was more than brave about it, and gave me to the Lord' (Dawson, 193). Believing that missionaries' wives should not be exposed to danger and disease in Africa—he wrote 'it is little short of homicide to permit them to go beyond the neighbourhood of the coast' (Dawson, 319)—he always left his wife and children in England. The party sailed from London. They reached Zanzibar on 19 June, then travelled inland to Rubaga. After many hardships they reached Msalala, but Hannington's health had so suffered from fever and dysentery that he could not continue. Leaving some of his companions to finish the journey to Rubaga he returned, carried in a hammock, to the coast, reached Zanzibar on 9 May 1883, and on 10 June was back in England. He returned to his work at Hurstpierpoint, but on recovery of his health again placed himself at the disposal of the CMS. Its committee decided that the mission churches of eastern equatorial Africa should have their own bishop. The post was offered to Hannington. He accepted, and on 24 June 1884 was consecrated at Lambeth. On 5 November he sailed for Africa, *en route* visiting Palestine, where he was commissioned by the archbishop of Canterbury to do confirmation and other duty. He reached Mombasa on 24 January 1885, and entered on the charge of his enormous new diocese. From headquarters at Frere Town—where he disliked 'the dissenterish kind of Services' (Dawson, 362)—he moved continually about it. On 31 May 1885 he ordained two Africans deacon. Impressed with the advisability of opening up a new shorter route to Lake Victoria through Maasai country, he decided to lead an expedition and on 23 July 1885 set out with a caravan 226 strong. When Alexander Mackay, the CMS missionary in Buganda, heard of Hannington's intention, he wrote warning him not to come via Busoga because of an old prophecy that strangers advancing through Busoga would conquer Buganda, but his letter reached Mombasa after Hannington had left. At Kwa Sundu, Hannington left the larger portion of the party and went on with fifty porters. In a week he walked 170 miles. By 17 October he was at Lake Victoria. Hannington and his party had anticipated possible danger from the Maasai, but thought they would be safe under Ganda rule. Meanwhile the fears of Mwanga—the young, vicious, and sodomitic kabaka (king) of Buganda, who had already martyred Christian converts—and of his chiefs had been aroused by the report of the approach of this white man by the unusual north-eastern route. Dreading conquest because of recent German annexations at the east African coast, and fearing that Hannington might be the precursor of a hostile British force, Mwanga ordered that he be seized and killed. (A plan to persuade him to retrace his steps and enter Buganda by the customary southern route across Lake Victoria aborted when he missed the boat at Kavirondo.) After eight days' confinement, on 21 October 1885 he and most of his porters were murdered at Lubya's, Busoga, Uganda, by retainers of Luba of Bunia, one of Mwanga's tributary chiefs in Busoga. Reportedly Hannington was shot with his own gun. Before he died he reportedly said: 'I am about to die for the Ba-ganda, and have purchased the road to them with my life' (Dawson, 447). His last journal, written in a Letts pocket diary, survived and was brought back to England. In Britain and later in Uganda he was seen as a martyr. His 'illustrated letters to the youngsters at home', *Peril and Adventure in Central Africa*, was published posthumously in 1886. Two books by the Revd E. C. Dawson, *James Hannington … First Bishop of Eastern Equatorial Africa* (1887) and *The Last Journals of Bishop Hannington* (1888) became best-sellers in Britain. Hannington's remains were initially buried in October 1885 at Lubya's. Later they were taken to Mumia's in Kavirondo by Basoga, who feared recent troubles had resulted from the murder. The location was divulged to Bishop Tucker in 1892 and on 31 December 1892, with a great service attended by Mwanga, Hannington's remains were reburied at Namirembe. He is commemorated by the Hannington memorial chapel in Namirembe Cathedral, Kampala, Uganda.

THOMAS HAMILTON, *rev.* MICHAEL TWADDLE

Sources E. C. Dawson, *James Hannington D. D., F. L. S., F. R. G. S. first bishop of eastern equatorial Africa: a history of his life and work, 1847–1885* (1887) · R. P. Ashe, *Two kings of Uganda, or, Life by the shores of Victoria Nyanza, being an account of a residence of six years in eastern equatorial Africa* (1889), esp. chaps. 15 and 16 · H. B. Thomas, 'The last days of Bishop Hannington', *Uganda Journal*, 8 (1940–41), 19–27 · M. Wright, *Buganda in the heroic age* (1971), 16–19 · L. Pirouet, ed., *A dictionary of Christianity in Uganda* (1969) · Boase, *Mod. Eng. biog.* · R. Oliver and G. Mathew, *History of East Africa*, 1 (1963) · b. cert.

Archives U. Birm. L., Church Missionary Society archives **Likenesses** G. J. Stodart, engraving, repro. in Dawson, *James Hannington*, frontispiece [*see illus.*] · wood-engraving (after photograph by Fradelle), NPG; repro. in *ILN* (20 Feb 1886) **Wealth at death** £1580 12*s*. 0*d*.: probate, 11 June 1886, *CGPLA Eng. & Wales*

Hannington, Walter [Wal] (1896–1966), trade union official and political activist, was born on 17 June 1896 at 22 Randolph Street, Kentish Town, London, the youngest of four sons and sixth of seven surviving children of Henry William Hannington, foreman bricklayer of Kentish Town, and his wife, Eliza Smith. Born and reared in lodgings in the basement of a three-storey house in a working-class district of north London, Wal Hannington attended the local elementary school from the age of five.

Hannington left school at fourteen and after several jobs became apprenticed to a toolmaker, joining the Amalgamated Society of Toolmakers in March 1916. Largely self-taught in Marxist literature, he joined the Marxist British Socialist Party (BSP), where he came into contact with Russian Marxist exiles such as Maksim Litvinov and Georgy Chicherin. By 1917, aged twenty-one, he was a foreman in the Beta Engineering works in Camden Town and president of the Kentish Town branch of the Toolmakers' Society. The First World War, which the BSP opposed, and the Bolshevik revolution in Russia reinforced his commitment to militant activity as part of the shop stewards' movement in the engineering trades.

After a period of unemployment in 1919 Hannington found work at the government-run Slough Transport Depot where he became chairman of the shop stewards' committee, organizing strikes and demonstrations against its eventual closure in April 1920. In July of that year he followed the Toolmakers' Society into the merger which created the Amalgamated Engineering Union (AEU) and in the same month became a founder member of the Communist Party of Great Britain (CPGB) in which the BSP was absorbed. Both the AEU and the CPGB were to retain his allegiance throughout his life.

But it was as a leader of the unemployed that Hannington rose to national prominence. Already established as a meticulous organizer, a good platform speaker, and an activist with a flair for publicity, he was instrumental in October 1920 in bringing together representatives of unemployed groups in the capital into a London district council of unemployed with himself as organizer. Demonstrations were staged outside poor-law offices with the slogan 'Work or full maintenance at trade-union rates.' In April 1921 fifty delegates from England and Wales set up a national organization, the National Unemployed Workers' Committee Movement (NUWCM), with Hannington as national organizer. In 1922 it planned the first of a series of national hunger marches which were to become the NUWCM's principal contribution to the inter-war years. Seen as a subversive organization by the government, the NUWCM was quickly penetrated by police informers and its activities were harried at local and national level.

In 1922 Hannington received his first term of a month's imprisonment for uttering seditious words. Unabashed, he made a clandestine visit to Moscow in 1923 as a delegate to the Red International of Labour Unions. In late 1925 he was one of twelve leading communists arrested and tried on charges of sedition and incitement to mutiny, for which he received twelve months' imprisonment. Released in September 1926, following the defeat of the general strike, he organized national hunger marches in 1929, 1932, and 1934, which were largely ostracized by the labour movement and were harassed by the police, sometimes leading to violence. As a result of the 1932 hunger march Hannington served another three months in prison for offences against the 1931 Incitement to Disaffection Act.

The later 1930s saw small triumphs amid a larger failure. Although led by communists, Hannington's movement was criticized by the Communist Party for failing to politicize the unemployed, large numbers of whom joined the movement only to leave it quickly once work was obtained. By the mid-1930s it was past its peak, but it played a prominent part in the agitation which led to the suspension of the National Government's Unemployment Assistance Board scheme early in 1935. The now renamed National Unemployed Workers Movement (NUWM) mounted a last national march in 1936 which obtained C. R. Attlee and Aneurin Bevan as platform speakers for its rally in London, but even this success was overshadowed by the publicity attracted by the apolitical Jarrow crusade at the same time, the one hunger march in which the NUWM was not involved. With the outbreak of war, the activities of the NUWM were suspended, and finally wound up in 1943. Hannington returned to work as a lathe turner and while serving as convener of shop stewards was elected a national organizer of the AEU in November 1941. Taking up the post in February 1942, he held it until defeated in an election in 1951. In 1952 he was elected assistant divisional organizer for division no. 25, retiring in June 1961. Ebullient, sociable, and respected even by those who disagreed with his political views, Hannington saw his work in the AEU rewarded in 1938 with the Tolpuddle award, the top award of Britain's trade union movement, and the AEU's special award of merit in 1962.

Hannington unsuccessfully contested parliamentary seats in 1929, 1931, 1934, and 1950. Among a large number of writings, *Unemployed Struggles, 1919–1936* (1936), *The Problem of the Distressed Areas* (1937), *Ten Lean Years* (1940), and his unfinished autobiography, *Never on our Knees* (1967), were important polemical documents of the inter-war years. In 1917 he married Polly Winifred, daughter of Edwin Stanley, a railway labourer. There was one daughter of the marriage.

Hannington died of a heart attack on 17 November 1966 at Hammersmith Hospital shortly after attending for a medical examination. He was survived by his wife.

JOHN STEVENSON, rev.

Sources *The Times* (19 Nov 1966) · *The Guardian* (19 Nov 1966) · J. Stevenson and C. P. Cook, *The slump: society and politics during the depression* (1977) · W. Hannington, *Unemployed struggles, 1919–1936* (1936) · W. Hannington, *The problem of the distressed areas* (1937) · W. Hannington, *Ten lean years* (1940) · W. Hannington, *Never on our knees* (1967) · *CGPLA Eng. & Wales* (1967) · C. Croucher, *We refuse to starve in silence: a history of the National Unemployed Workers' Movement* (1987)

Archives Labour History Archive and Study Centre, Manchester, corresp., reports, etc., relating to NUWM and AEU, articles, cuttings, notes for speeches · Marx Memorial Library, London, papers relating to National Unemployed Workers' Movement · People's History Museum, Manchester, communist party library

Likenesses photographs, 1922–6, Hult. Arch.

Wealth at death £1232: probate, 13 Jan 1967, *CGPLA Eng. & Wales*

Hanratty, James Francis (1936–1962), petty criminal and convicted murderer, was born on 4 October 1936 in the County Hospital, Farnborough, near Orpington, Kent, the eldest of four sons of James Hanratty (1907–1978), labourer and dustman, and his wife, Mary Wilson.

He attended St James's Roman Catholic school in Burnt Oak (1945–51) but remained illiterate. In the absence of steady or gainful employment James Hanratty spent most of his adolescent and young adult life engaged in crime—indeed, his last seven years were spent in penal institutions. In September 1954 he was put on probation for a year for taking and driving away a motor car without consent and while uninsured. Hardly had he finished his period on probation than he was before the courts and imprisoned for housebreaking and theft (1955). On this occasion he attempted suicide while in custody. Another prison sentence followed in 1957 in consequence of stealing another car. Almost immediately on release from prison he was reconvicted, in March 1958, to three years' corrective training; he left Strangeways prison, Manchester, on 24 March 1961. Overall Hanratty spent 58 of the 66 months after his nineteenth birthday in prison. Up to this time Hanratty had displayed himself as little more than a small-time hoodlum, always aspiring, ambitiously, to greater notoriety.

On 22 August 1961, however, Michael Gregsten and Valerie Storie were abducted from a Morris Minor car parked in a cornfield at Dorney Reach, Buckinghamshire. Their abductor subsequently shot Gregsten dead and raped and gravely wounded Storie at Deadman's Hill, Bedfordshire. Hanratty was charged with the murder on 14 October 1961.

Hanratty's trial (22 January–17 February 1962) was of unprecedented length for a murder trial against one defendant. It was notable for its conspicuous fairness. The trial judge, Mr Justice Gorman, even refused to allow the crown to adduce fresh evidence about some missing black nylon gloves at a boarding-house where Hanratty had contemporaneously lodged. (Valerie Storie had given firm evidence of the assailant's wearing such gloves—a telling pointer to identification.) The jury's verdict, delayed by a further direction on the meaning of 'reasonable doubt', was surprisingly against Hanratty. Junior counsel for the crown, Geoffrey Lane (later lord chief justice of England), had his pen poised to endorse his brief with the words 'not guilty'. The campaign against the verdict was launched,

with some justifiable optimism. Its supporters were convinced that they had established an alibi for Hanratty, and attached great importance to the confession to the Deadman's Hill killing by Peter Louis Alphon. A leading legal magazine in an editorial argued that sustaining James Hanratty's conviction in order to avoid embarrassment was carrying factional solidarity to unacceptable extremes. That comment followed an independent inquiry in 1975, conducted in private and largely on the documentation, by Lewis Hawser QC, a much respected practitioner and later an official referee in the High Court. His conclusion was that the case remained overwhelming, and that there was little reason to doubt the jury's verdict. Dispirited, but not dissuaded, the campaigners renewed their efforts to upset the verdict.

On 4 April 1962 Hanratty was executed at Bedford prison, in the precincts of which, on the same day, he was buried initially. He was reinterred at Carpenders Park, Watford, Hertfordshire, on 22 February 1966.

Attempts to declare Hanratty innocent of the crime focused mainly on two aspects of the forensic process: the paucity of direct evidence of complicity and the functioning of an alibi. The identification of Hanratty by the murdered victim's companion, Valerie Storie, was always imperfect, even by the less stringent tests of those days. Hanratty's defence that on the day of the crime he was a couple of hundred miles away, in the north-west of the country, was hotly contested. At the time there was no legal requirement on the defence, pre-trial, to notify the prosecution of an alibi, but, problematically, defence counsel at the committal proceedings before the magistrates at Bedford disclosed his client's case pre-emptively. The jury at Bedford assizes must have been influenced by the prosecution's previous ability to break the alibi. The lack of any scientific evidence proved unavailing.

Of all the perceived miscarriages of justice since the Second World War which scarred the face of English criminal justice, the case of James Hanratty was undoubtedly one of the few most enduring: the campaigners for quashing the 1962 conviction ceaselessly maintained a campaign of literary and other verbal output until the Court of Appeal (criminal division) pronounced finality of the judicial process in late 2001 on a referral under the Criminal Appeal Act 1995. The Court of Appeal's final verdict (the title of the most substantial study of the case by Bob Woffinden in 1997) was that the 1962 criminal investigation and trial were unsafe, but that the facts ultimately revealed that Hanratty was far from innocent of the crime. Unfortunately, this disconcerted a bewildered public about the 'wrongful conviction'. The application of a DNA test on Hanratty's exhumed body in March 2001, on order of the lord chief justice, helped to bolster the soundness of the original guilty verdict, but other aspects of that trial meant that the verdict was nevertheless unsatisfactory, and dictated a quashing of the conviction.

Hanratty's case epitomized the perennial problem of whether the quashing of a conviction was sufficient to demonstrate the individual's innocence of the crime. The public became alive to the fact that the presumption of innocence (original or revived on a successful appeal) is merely a rule of evidence and not a declaration of non-complicity in crime. As the first commentator on the Hanratty case wrote in 1963: 'Research into the causes of crime—it seems a blindingly obvious statement—should find its most fruitful material from the administration of criminal justice. Sad to relate, in England, it finds little or no assistance from the legal process' (Blom-Cooper, 133). Broadly speaking, that remains true today.

LOUIS BLOM-COOPER

Sources L. J. Blom-Cooper, *The A6 murder: Regina v. James Hanratty: the semblance of truth* (1963) · P. Foot, *Who killed Hanratty?* (1988) · 'The case of James Hanratty: report of Mr C. Lewis Hawser QC', *Parl. papers* (1974–5), vol. 15, Cmnd 6021 · E. F. L. Russell, Baron Russell of Liverpool, *Deadman's Hill: was Hanratty guilty?* (1965) · R. Woffinden, *Hanratty: the final verdict* (1997) · J. Justice, *Murder vs. Murder* (1964) · K. Simpson, *Forty years of murder* (1978) · J. Justice, *Le crime de la route A6* (Paris, 1968) · b. cert. · d. cert.
Archives FILM BFI NFTVA, *True stories*, Channel 4, 10 Aug 1995
Likenesses photographs, Hult. Arch.

Hansard, Luke (1752–1828), printer to the House of Commons, was born in the parish of St Mary, Norwich, on 5 July 1752, the eldest son of Thomas Hansard (1727–1769), an unsuccessful manufacturer, and his wife, Sarah (1717–1797), daughter of the Revd William Norfolke of Spilsbury, Lincolnshire. He was educated at the free grammar school, Kirton in Holland, Lincolnshire (1759–65). From 1 June 1765 he served seven years, though neither formally indentured nor freed, with Stephen White, printer of Cocky Lane, Norwich. He wrote in his *Auto-biography*: 'My Master was but rarely in the office … [but] i increased my diligence to serve my Master, because i loved him, and i delighted in my business … [so that] in a short space of time i became expert; I was proud in being compositor & pressman, corrector and manager, copperplate printer and shopman, book keeper and accountant to this chequered business' (L. Hansard, 9).

Hansard left Norwich for London in the summer of 1772 and soon found work as a compositor with Henry Hughes of Great Turnstile, Lincoln's Inn Fields, who had inherited a prosperous parliamentary, book, and general printing house. His master found him 'handy at jobbing and ready for anything' (L. Hansard, 31). Hughes printed for most of the leading publishing booksellers, and Hansard extended his general education through the works he was given to set and proof-read: Orme's *History of Indostan* printed for Nourse (1763) gave him 'a competent knowledge of Indian affairs, which afterwards became highly useful to himself and to the public' (*GM*, 560) when it came to printing the parliamentary investigations into the operation of the East India Company (1772–8). He was promoted to printing manager in 1793, taken into partnership in 1794 (trading as Hughes and Hansard), and in 1799 he took over the business. The same year he was admitted to the livery of the Stationers' Company. He subsequently gave £2500 for two charitable bequests, one for 'needy printers over the age of 65', the other for a 'neatly bound Church of England prayer book' to be given to every youth bound at the hall (L. Hansard, xv).

On 21 July 1775 Hansard married a Norfolk woman,

Luke Hansard (1752–1828), by Samuel Lane

Elizabeth Curson (1754–1834); they had six children, five of whom outlived their parents. Hansard bound his three sons to Hughes and freed them at Stationers' Hall. The eldest, Thomas Curson *Hansard, left his father's employ, but the younger two, James and Luke Graves (*d.* 1828), were taken into partnership, the name changing to Hansard & Sons. They eventually succeeded to the business. Hansard worked until the end of his life, but in his latter years delegated much to his youngest son and permitted himself some holidays in his native Norfolk, where he stayed with hitherto unknown relatives.

The printer to the house came under the authority of the speaker and executed all Commons printing except the *Votes* or agenda papers which were printed by John Nichols. Hansard printed the *Journal* or daily record of the decisions of the Commons and the select committee reports; he worked closely with the speaker in preparing them for publication. He served under seven speakers, but had a special rapport with the meticulous Charles Abbot, speaker from 1802 to 1816 and chairman of several major committees, including that on the public records (1800). Hansard also worked for various government departments, and acquired a virtual monopoly of private parliamentary agency work. Before the house had a library, he undertook a librarian's duties, keeping a complete run of sessional papers, which he and his son Luke Graves indexed (*Catalogue and Breviate of Parliamentary Papers, 1696–1834*). It is a lasting monument to their industry and knowledge of parliamentary procedure, and is still consulted alongside more recent indexes.

The recession of the 1790s curtailed book printing at a

time when parliamentary printing increased vastly, changing the bent of Hansard's business. He invested in more machinery and, in 1800, built a second printing house in Parker Street, which his sons managed. The secret of his success lay in his managerial skill in a rapidly expanding business, combined with meticulous attention to detail. He had a sure eye for type and consummate skill in page design when it came to reducing the complex, cumbersome matter of debates and committee reports to legible, intelligible pages. He told the select committee on public printing in 1822 that whereas in other printing offices the men were left to use their own judgement:

> As soon as the manuscript comes to me, I sit down and draw that scheme out upon paper, the very size the men are to work it to, the quantity they are to take into a page, and the various widths of each; how far they are to go, and what quantity of pages that particular paper is to make. (House of Commons select committee report on public printing, 1822)

Hansard's was the largest printing house in London, employing some 200 men. From the mid-1780s there were constant labour troubles, and at the beginning of the century Hansard combined with the other major master printers to settle disputes and control wage demands. He was a hard taskmaster, and took tough measures to ensure that Commons printing was not disrupted and costs kept down. As parliamentary printer he was caught in the crossfire of a workforce demanding higher wages in a period of inflation and political unrest and a public clamouring for parliamentary reform and a curbing of alleged privilege and exorbitant rewards. In his lifetime were held the first select committee inquiries into printing for parliament (1810, 1822, and 1828). He was called to give evidence at each, and emerged with his and his firm's reputation untarnished. The evidence of John Rickman, clerk assistant to the speaker, at the 1828 committee was a personal eulogy, reprinted as an obituary notice in the *Gentleman's Magazine*; but the committee's attitude and its recommendations, which the Hansards considered were based on ignorance of printing and trade conditions, seem to have broken his spirit and caused a rapid physical decline. He died in Southampton Street, London, on 29 October 1828 and was buried on 6 November in the parish church of St Giles-in-the-Fields. He left a widow, three sons, and two daughters. He dedicated his life to printing for parliament, was a devout Christian, a staunch tory, and a devoted family man. He wrote a memoir for his younger sons, published in 1817.   ROBIN MYERS

Sources L. Hansard, *The auto-biography of Luke Hansard, written in 1817*, ed. R. Myers (1991) · [J. Hansard and L. G. Hansard], *Biographical memoir of Luke Hansard, esq., many years printer to the House of Commons* (1829) · 'Select committee on … public expenditure: ninth report', *Parl. papers* (1810), 2.551, no. 373 [printing and stationery] · 'Select committee on printing and stationery supplied to the houses of Lords and Commons, and to the public departments', *Parl. papers* (1822), 4.401, no. 607 · 'Select committee on the expense of printing the votes and papers ordered by the house', *Parl. papers* (1828), 4.481, no. 520 · *Luke Graves Hansard, his diary, 1814–1841*, ed. P. Ford and G. Ford (1962) · *Catalogue of parliamentary reports, and a breviate of their contents* (1834); facs. edn with an introduction by P. Ford and G. Ford (1953) · T. C. Hansard, *Typographia: an historical sketch of the origin and progress of the art of printing* (1825), 329–30 · J. C. Trewin and E. M. King, *Printer to the House: the story of Hansard* (1952) · *GM*, 1st ser., 98/2 (1828), 559–66 · Nichols, *Illustrations*, 8.462, 502 · E. C. Bigmore and C. W. H. Wyman, *A bibliography of printing*, 1 (1880), 229–30 · E. Howe, 'The Hansard Family', *Signature*, 6 (1949) · *DNB*

Archives U. Southampton L., family papers, MSS autobiography; letters to his granddaughter, Eliza | Bodl. Oxf., letters to John Nichols and others · priv. coll., master printers' minute book · Stationers' Company, archives

Likenesses S. Lane, oils, 1828, Stationers' Company, Stationers' Hall, London · charcoal drawing, 1828 (after S. Lane), repro. in Hansard and Hansard, *Biographical memoir* · S. Lane, oils, House of Commons [*see illus.*] · watercolour sketch (as a baby), U. Southampton

Wealth at death approx. £80,000—£800 Stationers' Company English Stock share; plus £1404 yield of annuity and shares; printing offices, type, plant, and stock; house at Lambeth: will, PRO 11/1748

Hansard, Thomas Curson (1776–1833), printer and publisher, was born on 6 November 1776 in the Spa Fields district of Clerkenwell, London, the eldest of the four children of Luke *Hansard (1752–1828), printer, and his wife, Elizabeth (1754–1834), the only surviving daughter of John Curson of Swanton Morley, Norfolk. Thomas Hansard was apprenticed to Henry Hughes, the parliamentary printer and his father's partner, on 2 November 1790; he was admitted to the Stationers' Company (after a seven-year apprenticeship) and made a freeman of the City of London on 7 November 1797. He married Anne (or Ann) Palmby (1770–1811), the daughter of Thomas Palmby of Swaffham Prior, Cambridgeshire, at St John's, Clerkenwell, on 12 November 1797.

Through his work as a parliamentary printer, Thomas Hansard met leading politicians and government officials; he developed radical views that differed from his father's conservative opinions. Luke Hansard was also disappointed with his son's progress in the business. In 1803 Thomas Hansard left Hughes and Hansard and purchased, in 1805, the printing house of Thomas Rickaby, in Peterborough Court, Fleet Street, from the latter's executors. An admirer of William Cobbett, he undertook, from the beginning of 1809, the printing of *Cobbett's Political Register* after Cobbett fell out with Cox and Baylis, his previous printers. An article on the flogging of militiamen at Ely, written by Cobbett for the 1 July 1809 issue, led to a charge of seditious libel against Cobbett, Hansard, and the distributors of the periodical. Only Cobbett contested the charge when the trial began at the court of king's bench on 15 June 1810; all the defendants were found guilty, and Thomas Hansard was sentenced to three months in the king's bench prison, with the further obligation to enter into a recognizance to keep the peace for three months with a bond of £200 from himself and two sureties.

Hansard had printed three major publications initiated by Cobbett: *Parliamentary Debates*, *Parliamentary History*, and *State Trials*. Cobbett was persuaded to sell his interest in these titles by financial difficulties arising from his imprisonment, and after protracted and ill-natured negotiations Hansard purchased them in early 1812. While Cobbett had the foresight to initiate these important publications, Hansard had the determination and industry to continue their production on a regular basis. John Wright, who worked for both Cobbett and Hansard on the parliamentary series, was noted for his indolence, and the main burden of the work fell on Hansard, whose *Parliamentary Debates* was soon recognized as the standard record. This remains his greatest achievement.

Anne Hansard died on 21 July 1811; their two daughters had predeceased her. Hansard married secondly his sister-in-law, Mary Palmby (c.1776–1849), by licence at Swaffham Prior on 1 February 1812. He moved in 1823 to Paternoster Row, where he established the Paternoster Press. A lively interest in his craft led Hansard to publish *Typographia* (1825); this fine manual, written in a clear style, is an outstanding guide to the printer's craft and an important source for historians of printing. He included a warm tribute to his father's skills, which betokened an improvement in relations between them since the time of his brief imprisonment. Hansard also described with pride an apparatus which he invented and patented for the improvement of the hand-press. He was, however, quick to adopt the machine presses, which superseded his ingenuity. Hansard was elected one of the common councilmen for the radical ward of Farringdon Without (South Side), 1821–4, and he served on the improvement committee, 1822–4.

Thomas Curson Hansard died in Chatham Place, Blackfriars, on 14 May 1833; he was buried at St Bride's, Fleet Street, London, on 20 May. Mary Hansard, his widow, was buried at St Bride's on 4 August 1849. Hansard was succeeded in his firm by Thomas Curson Hansard (1813–1891), the eldest of his five children with his second wife. He published the parliamentary debates until the rights were sold in 1889 to the Hansard Publishing Union run by Horatio Bottomley. The use of the word 'Hansard' as a colloquial term for the written record of the parliamentary debates was common soon after 1833. When the two houses established, in 1909, their own official reports of the debates, the name disappeared from their titles. The House of Commons ordered, in 1943, that the name should be restored to the title-page of its official report, and it is now used in many Commonwealth parliaments.

DAVID LEWIS JONES

Sources E. C. Bigmore and C. W. H. Wyman, *A bibliography of printing*, 3 vols. (1880–86) • *GM*, 1st ser., 103/1 (1833), 569 • L. Hansard, *The auto-biography of Luke Hansard, printer to the house, 1752–1828*, ed. R. Myers (1991) • J. C. Trewin and E. M. King, *Printer to the House: the story of Hansard* (1952) • Hansard family genealogies, U. Southampton L., MS 59/105–106 • D. F. McKenzie, ed., *Stationers' Company apprentices*, [3]: *1701–1800* (1978) • G. Spater, *William Cobbett: the poor man's friend*, 2 vols. (1982) • *The Times* (6 July 1810) • *The Times* (10 July 1810) • parish register, Swaffham Prior, Cambridgeshire, Cambs. AS, 1 Feb 1812 [marriage] • parish register (burial), St Bride's, London, 4 Aug 1849 [M. Hansard] • parish register (burial), St Bride's, London, 20 May 1833 • apprenticeship indenture, Corporation of London, CF1/1211 • annual pocket books, 1822/3 and 1824/5, Corporation of London

Archives HLRO, corresp. and papers • U. Southampton, family MSS, MS 59

Likenesses J. Lee, woodcut (after drawing by A. Todd), repro. in T. C. Hansard, *Typographia* (1825)

Wealth at death see will, PRO, proved 19 June 1833

Hansbie, Morgan Joseph (1673–1750), Dominican friar, was the younger son of Ralph Hansbie of Tickhill Castle, Yorkshire, and his wife, Winifred, daughter of Sir John Cansfield. He was professed in the Dominican convent at Bornhem, near Antwerp, in 1696, and was ordained priest in 1698. After holding several monastic offices in that convent he was appointed in 1708 chaplain to the Dominican nuns at Brussels, and in 1711 he came on the English mission. He returned, however, to Bornhem in 1712, and in the same year was appointed vice-rector of the Dominican college at Louvain, of which he became fourth rector in 1717. In 1721 he was made provincial of his order and created DD. He was then sent to the mission at Tickhill Castle in England, his family home. In 1728 he was installed prior of Bornhem, and in 1731 appointed vicar provincial for Belgium. In the latter year he was re-elected prior of Bornhem, and a second time provincial in 1734, when he was stationed in London.

From 1738 to 1742 Hansbie was vicar provincial in England, and in 1743 he went to Lower Cheam, Surrey, the residence of the Dowager Lady Petre. Hansbie was an ardent Jacobite, and on 22 December 1745 the house was searched for arms. Only two pairs of pistols were found, but Hansbie was taken before the magistrates at Croydon. He was apparently liberated on bail, for he continued to reside at Cheam until his return to London in 1747, when he was attached to the Sardinian chapel in Lincoln's Inn Fields. In that year he was instituted vicar-general of England, and again provincial in 1748. He died in London on 5 June 1750.

Hansbie published a number of works while at Louvain in Latin, including *Philosophia universa* (1715); other theological treatises were *Theses theologicae ex prima parte (summae D. T. A.) de Deo ejusque attributis* (1716), *Theses theologicae de jure et justitia* (1717), *Theses theologicae de trinitate, homine, et legibus* (1720), and also *Theses theologicae de virtutibus in communi tribus theologicis in specie, cum locis eo praecipue spectantibus* (1721).

THOMPSON COOPER, *rev.* ROBERT BROWN

Sources Gillow, *Lit. biog. hist.* • G. Oliver, *Collections illustrating the history of the Catholic religion in the counties of Cornwall, Devon, Dorset, Somerset, Wilts, and Gloucester* (1857) • E. E. Estcourt and J. O. Payne, eds., *The English Catholic nonjurors of 1715* (1885); repr. (1969) • J. Kirk, *Biographies of English Catholics in the eighteenth century*, ed. J. H. Pollen and E. Burton (1909) • W. Gumbley, *Obituary notices of the English Dominicans from 1555 to 1952* (1955)

Hansell, Edward Halifax (1814–1884), Church of England clergyman, was born at St Mary-in-the-Marsh, Norwich, on 6 November 1814, the fourth son of Peter Hansell (1764–1841), BA of Magdalen College, Oxford, vicar of Worstead, Norfolk, and minor canon and precentor of Norwich from 1811 to his death. Edward was educated at Norwich School under the Revd Edward Valpy (1764–1832). He matriculated at Balliol College, Oxford, on 9 June 1832 but became a demy of Magdalen College in the same year, and in 1847 he was elected fellow of Magdalen. In 1835 he was placed in the first class in mathematics and in the second in *literae humaniores*. He graduated BA on 28 January 1836, MA on 6 December 1838, and BD on 21 October 1847.

Hansell was ordained deacon in 1839 and priest in 1843. He was tutor of his college and mathematical lecturer in 1842, and vice-president in 1852. He gained the Denyer theological prize in 1840; was tutor of Merton College from 1845 to 1849; Grinfield lecturer in 1861–2; master of the schools in 1841; public examiner in *literae humaniores* in 1842–3 and 1858–9; public examiner in mathematics from 1851 to 1853; and public examiner in law and modern history in 1855–6. He was also one of the classical moderators and select preacher to the university in 1846–7. In August 1853 he vacated his fellowship at Magdalen on his marriage to Mary Elizabeth, fifth daughter of David Williams (1786–1860), warden of New College. He remained divinity lecturer of his college until December 1865, when he accepted the college living of East Ilsley, on the Berkshire downs. He devoted himself to his parish duties until his death, at East Ilsley, on 8 May 1884, from the effects of an accident.

Besides the Denyer theological prize essay (1840) Hansell published some other theological works. His chief scholarly effort was on the Greek of the New Testament (3 vols., 1864); he also contributed the articles on the manuscripts of the Greek Testament to Cassell's *Bible Cyclopaedia*. A modest and retiring man, he left three sons and a daughter, his wife having predeceased him.

RICHARD HOOPER, rev. H. C. G. MATTHEW

Sources Foster, *Alum. Oxon.* · Crockford (1880) · private information (1890)

Wealth at death £38,315 16s. 5d.: resworn probate, Oct 1885, *CGPLA Eng. & Wales* (1884)

Hansom, Charles Francis (1817–1888), architect, was born on 26 July 1817 at 63 Micklegate, York, the eighth of the nine children of Henry Joseph Francis Hansom (*bap.* 1778, *d.* 1854), builder and joiner, and his wife, Sarah Simpson (*bap.* 1779, *d.* 1856). Coming from a steadfast Roman Catholic family, he was baptized the following day in the chapel of the Bar Convent. He received his professional training in the offices of his brother Joseph Aloysius *Hansom in Birmingham and Hinckley. In 1841 he married Elizabeth Muston (1817/18–1902) of Hinckley with whom he had a son, Edward Joseph Hansom (1842–1900). About the same time he sketched and measured old churches, mastering thereby the character of Gothic architecture. A turning point was the commission for the church of the Holy Sacrament and St Osburg in Coventry (1843–5) for Father William Bernard Ullathorne. By about 1845 he had moved to Clifton, Bristol, where he obtained numerous commissions through the continuing patronage of Ullathorne. In a short time churches at Edgehill (1847), Woodchester (1849), and Erdington (1850) in Warwickshire had established his reputation. Thenceforward Decorated Gothic churches and chapels to the number of about sixty dominated his output, among them examples at Rugeley (1851), Wolverhampton (1855), Selby (1856), Cheltenham (1857), and Bath (1863). His churches are distinguished by their consistent adherence to correct medieval details. Following Pugin's death, Hansom's designs shunned the wayward, experimental paths widely explored by other church architects.

From Hansom's Clifton premises, initially at 1 Richmond Hill, then from Rock House, Bellevue, and from 1866 St Nicholas's Chambers, there issued besides church designs a steady stream of other works, including colleges at Clifton (1861) and Malvern (1865) bearing both Decorated and Perpendicular details. There were also convents at Clifton (1848), Taunton (1849), Loughborough (1850), and Stone (1853) and Stoke (1857) in Staffordshire, besides numerous presbyteries realized in late Gothic domestic terms. In 1854 Hansom was joined by his brother Joseph in partnership. The arrangement was initiated by Joseph, who had more work than he could handle alone from his previous office in Preston, Lancashire. Following an illness late in 1853 Joseph summoned his brother to superintend a church at Minster Acres, Northumberland, which had to be completed by Christmas, and from this crisis the partnership arose and Joseph moved from Preston to join Charles at Clifton. As was customary, each partner carried out his own commissions, but all works issuing from the firm were publicly attributed to J. and C. Hansom. The partnership was terminated amicably in 1859.

From 1867 to 1871 Hansom had his only son, Edward, as his partner in the Clifton office, the style of the firm being C. F. Hansom & Son. From these years date the Franciscan convent at Woodchester, Gloucestershire (1869), and the conversion in 1871 of the Bristol Irvingite Church (built in 1840 from designs of R. S. Pope) to the uses of a Catholic church renamed St Mary on the Quay. Edward Hansom had trained in his father's office and in 1864 was elected a student member of the Bristol Society of Architects. In 1871 he left Clifton to join in partnership Archibald Mathias Dunn (1832–1917), who had also trained in Charles Hansom's office, and had by this time built up a flourishing practice in Newcastle upon Tyne. Numerous Catholic churches in the north-east as well as convents, colleges, and schools emanated from the partnership. Edward Hansom was elected FRIBA in 1881. Meanwhile A. M. Dunn was president of the Northern Architectural Association in 1870, and a justice of the peace for co. Durham. He published *Notes and Sketches of an Architect* (1886) and retired in 1893. By this time the partnership's secular designs had broadened into the terracotta and red brick of late Victorian secular architecture. From 1901 A. M. Dunn resided mainly at Bournemouth, where he died in 1917. While still in practice Edward Hansom died in 1900 from self-inflicted bullet wounds, having suffered from insomnia and depression for about eighteen months.

After his son's departure in 1871, Charles Hansom continued alone at Clifton, taking his former pupil Frederick Bligh Bond (1861–1945) into partnership in 1886, two years before his death. Notable works of these years are: St Joseph's Home, Bristol; Kelly College, Tavistock, Devon; University College, Tyndalls Park, Bristol; and extensive work on Clifton College. He was elected FRIBA in 1865 and was a founder member of both the Bristol Society of Architects and the Bristol and Clifton Junior Architects' Society. The aim of the latter was to revive the moribund Bristol Society of Architects (founded originally in 1850) by involving young members through meetings, drawing competitions, lectures, and publications. The society flourished between 1881 and 1884 with Charles Hansom as its president. He died at his home, 1 Claremont Place, Clifton, on 30 November 1888 and was buried on 3 December in Perrymead cemetery, Bath. *The Tablet* obituary of Charles Hansom pronounced him 'not only an able architect but a generous and most honourable man' (*The Tablet*, 909).

DENIS EVINSON

Sources *The Tablet* (8 Dec 1888), 909–10 · *Building News* (7 Dec 1888), 763 · *The Architect* (7 Dec 1888), 323 · *The Builder*, 40 (1881), 432 · *The Builder*, 41 (1881), 464 · *The Builder*, 42 (1882), 145 · *The Builder*, 44 (1883), 860 · *The Builder*, 46 (1884), 79 · *The Builder*, 54 (1888), 423 · *The Builder*, 112 (1917), 288 [obit. of A. M. Dunn] · *Building News* (7 Dec 1888), 763 · *Building News*, 78 (1900), 787 · d. cert. [Elizabeth Hansom] · J. S. Hansom, ed., 'The Catholic registers of York Bar Convent chapel … 1771–1826', *Miscellanea, IV*, Catholic RS, 4 (1907), 374–410, 383, 406 · *Miscellanea VI*, Catholic RS, 7 (1909), 269–70 · J. Hansom, *A statement of facts relative to Birmingham town hall* (1834) **Archives** Birm. CL, Hardman letters | FILM *Charles Hansom, Clifton College* (Budek Films and Slides Inc., 1969) [audiovisual slides, in series *The architecture of England, Victorian architecture, 1825–1890*; 27] **Likenesses** engraving, repro. in *The Architect* (12 Sept 1874) **Wealth at death** £554 13s. 9d.: administration, 3 June 1889, CGPLA Eng. & Wales

Hansom, Joseph Aloysius (1803–1882), architect and inventor of the safety cab, was born at 63 Micklegate, York, on 26 October 1803, the second of the nine children of Henry Joseph Francis Hansom (*bap.* 1778, *d.* 1854), joiner and builder, and his wife, Sarah Simpson (*bap.* 1779, *d.* 1856). He was descended of a staunch Roman Catholic family long settled in York. In 1816 he was apprenticed to his father, but in the following year, having shown an aptitude for designing and construction, his articles were allowed to lapse, and new ones were taken out with Matthew Phillips, an architect of York. Following his apprenticeship he, in 1820, became a clerk to Phillips, doing also some work on his own account, and teaching at a night school, where he improved his scant education. On 14 April 1825 he married Hannah Glover (1809–1880), and after settling in Halifax became assistant to John Oates, architect, where for the first time he studied the Gothic style. In 1828 he entered into partnership with Edward Welch, and with him built churches in Liverpool, Hull, and the Isle of Man. Their public and domestic buildings include Beaumaris gaol, Anglesey (1828–9), a suspension bridge at Middleham, Yorkshire (1829), the Gothic King William's College, Isle of Man (1830–33; gutted by fire 1844), and Bodelwyddan Hall, Flintshire (*c.*1830–1840), a Gothic castellated house for Sir John Williams, bt. Following its later use as a girls' school the latter was lavishly refurbished in the 1980s to create an appropriate setting for Victorian portraits from the National Portrait Gallery, including G. F. Watts's famous series of twenty-six portraits of eminent Victorians and a collection of the work of the north Wales sculptor John Gibson. In its importance to scholars of the Victorian period the status of Bodelwyddan Hall has increased since its inception as a private country house.

In 1831 Hansom and Welch won the important competition for the town hall at Birmingham. The classical design was Hansom's, and the building was erected and completed in 1833 with some modifications by Welch. The two young architects unwisely stood surety for the builders, and having underestimated the cost of transporting the hard stone from Anglesey with which the building was to be faced, went bankrupt in 1834. This disaster led to the breakup of their partnership and Hansom took up business management before resuming architectural practice.

On 23 December 1834 Hansom registered his idea of the 'patent safety cab' (no. 6733), the vehicle which was named after him. The principle of the 'safety' consisted in the suspended or cranked axle; the driver's back seat was not in the original patent, and the modern so-called Hansom cabs retain but few of the original ideas. One of the great advantages of Hansom's cab was that, the wheels being much larger than usual, and the body of the vehicle nearer the ground, it could be worked with less wear and tear, and with a diminished risk of accidents. Hansom disposed of his rights to a company for the sum of £10,000, but no portion of this money was ever paid to him. The company got into difficulties, and in 1839 Hansom took the temporary management, and again put matters in working order. For this service he was presented with £300, the only money he ever received in connection with his vehicle.

In December 1842 Hansom brought out the first number of *The Builder*. Want of capital obliged him to retire from this undertaking, and he had to content himself with a small payment from the publishers. He then resumed architectural practice, principally ecclesiastical and domestic architecture for the Roman Catholic church. From 1854 to 1859 he worked in partnership with his younger brother Charles Francis *Hansom, from 1859 to 1861 with his eldest son, Henry John Hansom, and from 1862 to 1863 with Edward Welby Pugin, with whom he then had a disagreement. At the beginning of 1869 he took his second son, Joseph Stanislaus Hansom, who had previously been articled to him, into a partnership which lasted until 1879, when he retired from the firm, retaining a life interest in the business.

Hansom's major achievement was his churches, whose stylistic character followed the trends of the age. The early, Anglican churches of Hansom and Welch at Acomb, Yorkshire, and in the Isle of Man were unscholarly essays in ill-digested Gothic terms. The authoritative teaching, however, of A. W. Pugin's books and actual buildings changed this, and from 1846, when he designed the church of the Immaculate Conception, Spinkhill, Derbyshire, his work incorporated authentic Early English or Decorated Gothic terms. Following Pugin's death, however, architects experimented with wayward details, and at St Walburge's, Preston, Lancashire (1854), Hansom introduced a controversial hammerbeam roof and a spectacular tall spire 306 feet high. His best church work appeared in the 1870s with the Holy Name, Manchester, St Philip Neri, Arundel, Sussex, and the Servite church in

London, all planned in the French Gothic manner, with tall compact outlines and apsidal east ends. Other works of his are to be found all over the United Kingdom, and further designs were carried out in France, Australia, and South America.

On 14 April 1875 Hansom celebrated his golden wedding, surrounded by his children and grandchildren. His wife died in 1880, and he himself died at his home, 399 Fulham Road, Chelsea, London, on 29 June 1882, and was buried in the cemetery of St Thomas's Church, Rylston Road, Fulham, on 3 July. Of Hansom, Gillow wrote that 'his character was one of much power, mingled with still greater gentleness' (Gillow, *Lit. biog. hist.*, 119).

G. C. BOASE, *rev.* DENIS EVINSON

Sources *The Builder*, 43 (1882), 43–4 · Gillow, *Lit. biog. hist.* · *Architectural Magazine*, 1–3 (1834–6) · J. A. Hansom, *Statement of facts relative to Birmingham town hall* (1834) · *Catholic Record Society*, 4 · *Catholic Record Society*, 7 · D. Evinson, 'Joseph Hansom', MA diss., U. Lond., 1966 · biography file, RIBA BAL · Colvin, *Archs.* · S. Foister and others, *The National Portrait Gallery collection* (1988), 239–46 · IGI · CGPLA Eng. & Wales (1882) · d. cert. · *English Heritage Magazine* (June–July 1997)
Archives Birm. CL, Hardman letters · church commissioners, Westminster, Toxteth Park and Myton letters · Co-operative Union, Holyoake, Manchester, Robert Owen letters
Likenesses oils, 1830–39, Building office, 40 Marsh Walls, London · R. & E. Taylor, wood-engraving (aged about seventy-five), NPG; repro. in *ILN* (15 July 1882)
Wealth at death £1105 3s. 3d.: probate, 2 Aug 1882, *CGPLA Eng. & Wales*

Hanson, (Emmeline) Jean (1919–1973), biophysicist and zoologist, was born on 14 November 1919 in Newhall, Derbyshire, the only child of Thomas Hanson and his wife, Emma Jane Badger, daughter of a Derbyshire police superintendent. Both her parents were schoolteachers. Her father died only a few months after her birth, and she was brought up entirely by her mother, who became headmistress of a primary school. Mrs Hanson was said to be a woman of character and wide interests, and from her Jean developed a love of music and the arts. She was educated at the High School for Girls, Burton upon Trent (1930–38), where she became interested in biology. Scholarships enabled her to attend Bedford College, London, and she graduated in 1941 with first-class honours in zoology.

As a research student Jean Hanson began a very substantial body of research on the vascular system of annelids (segmented worms). However, this work was interrupted by the evacuation of Bedford College to Cambridge during the war, where she worked on the histogenesis of the mammalian epidermis in tissue culture, at the Strangeways Research Laboratory. From 1944 until 1948 she was a demonstrator in zoology, and her PhD thesis was not finally submitted until 1951, three years after she left Bedford College. Meanwhile, in 1947, the Medical Research Council had established a biophysics research unit at King's College, London, intended to apply the powerful new physical methods that were becoming available to structural problems in biology. Jean Hanson joined the unit as a founder member in 1948 and was responsible for building up the biological side of the laboratory. At the

unit her interests in muscle began to develop and she initiated the use of isolated myofibrils (prepared from glycerol-extracted rabbit skeletal muscle) which could be caused to contract in physiological salt solutions. These were one of the first examples of the many model systems subsequently used in molecular and cell biology to study the structural and biochemical properties of assemblies of molecules under controllable conditions. Jean Hanson's experience as a microscopist enabled her to realize that myofibrils provided ideal experimental material for examination in the phase contrast light microscope, then just coming into use. After several important initial observations she realized the research would also require use of the electron microscope, an instrument of much greater resolving power, which was then coming into use in the United States. Therefore, in 1953–4, she went to the biology department of the Massachusetts Institute of Technology, which under Professor Francis O. Schmitt had already become a centre for research into biological fine structure. It was there, with H. E. Huxley, also at MIT to learn electron microscopy, that she carried out the experiments which established the structural basis of the sliding filament mechanism of muscular contraction, a theory which long dominated muscle research. Hanson and Huxley discovered the overlapping arrays of actin and myosin filaments which are responsible for the characteristic appearance of striated muscle and which slide past each other by an active process during contraction. They suggested that the sliding force might be produced by moving myosin crossbridges.

Jean Hanson returned to the biophysics research unit in 1954 and continued her studies of muscle structure by light and electron microscopy. She joined forces with a physiologist, Dr Jack Lowy, and was able to demonstrate unequivocally the existence of the double filament mechanism in a wide variety of muscle types, including several smooth muscles from invertebrates.

Jean Hanson's work then turned towards molecular aspects of the contraction mechanism, and together with Lowy she used electron microscopy to elucidate the internal structure of the actin filaments in muscle and the location of the regulatory protein tropomyosin. Her scientific contributions were by now widely appreciated and she received the title of professor of biology in the University of London in 1966 and was elected a fellow of the Royal Society in 1967.

Jean Hanson's abilities as an administrator and teacher contributed to the success of the school of biological sciences at King's College, London; and her qualities of common sense, understanding, and tenacity earned her several offers of important non-scientific office in the academic world. However, she decided to continue with her scientific work and, in 1970, became director of a muscle biophysics unit at King's College, London. Her life was cut short in 1973 when she contracted a rare brain infection and died within a few hours, at her home, 50 Southwood Park, Southwood Lawn Road, London, on 10 August 1973.

Jean Hanson was unmarried and lived alone, but her interests in music and the arts, as well as science, brought her a wide circle of appreciative friends. Her outstanding qualities in research lay in her ability to pick the right experiment, her capacity for hard work, and her enjoyment of a good scientific discovery for its own sake.

H. E. HUXLEY, rev.

Sources J. Randall, Memoirs FRS, 21 (1975), 313–44 · personal knowledge (1986) · S. Page, '(Emmeline) Jean Hanson FRS (1919–1973)', Women physiologists: an anniversary celebration of their contributions to British physiology, ed. L. Birdman, A. Brading, and T. Tansey (1993), 97–104 · CGPLA Eng. & Wales (1973)
Archives King's Lond., corresp. and papers | Bodl. Oxf., corresp. with J. W. S. Pringle
Wealth at death £46,510: probate, 15 Nov 1973, CGPLA Eng. & Wales

Hanson, John (*fl.* 1604), poet, was perhaps the scholar of Peterhouse, Cambridge, whose residence is documented from 1599 to 1603, and who graduated BA in 1604. The poet's only known work, *Time is a Turne-Coate, or, Englands Three-Fold Metamorphosis* (1604), is prefaced by an 'Epistle Dedicatorie' (addressed to Thomas Bennet, lord mayor, and to William Rowley and Thomas Middleton, sheriffs of London), dated 26 March 1604, in which Hanson claims to 'have long expected … men of greater experience and graver judgement' to have praised their governance. Its references to the currently 'requisite lawes for the supplanting and depopulating of vice', and to 'the *Anthropophagi* or *Canibals*; who … gormandize on other mens flesh', seem relevant to the dating of Shakespeare's *Measure for Measure* (I. ii) and *Othello* (I. iii). Hanson's poem is a minor contribution to the literary flood prompted by the events of 1603: Queen Elizabeth's death, King James's accession, and the visitation of plague that delayed his triumphal entry into London. Hanson accordingly appends 'A Panegyricall Pageant-speech or Idylion pronounced to the Citie of London, upon the entrance of her long expected Comfort', and three acrostic 'Pastorall Panegyricks' to the new royal family. Despite its ostentatious ambition, however, Hanson's 'Epilogomena, to Londons late lamentable Heroicall Comi-Tragedie' remains strained and inert, its heroic couplets 'turgid and inflated' (Corser, 7.148).

Another **John Hanson** (*b.* 1610/11), son of Richard Hanson (rector of Himley, Staffordshire), matriculated at Pembroke College, Oxford, on 25 June 1630, aged nineteen, and has been linked (Wood, *Ath. Oxon.*, 3rd edn, 3.473) with John Hanson of Abingdon, Berkshire, the author of a rare tract, *A Short Treatise Shewing the Sabbatharians Confuted by the New Covenant* (1658). According to its title-page, copies were 'left at Captain *Hansons* … at the West end of *Paul's*'.

NICK DE SOMOGYI

Sources T. A. Walker, A biographical register of Peterhouse men, 2 (1930) · T. Corser, Collectanea Anglo-poetica, or, A … catalogue of a … collection of early English poetry, 7, Chetham Society, 101 (1877) · Wood, Ath. Oxon., new edn · Venn, Alum. Cant., 1/2 · Foster, Alum. Oxon., 1500–1714 · Cooper, Ath. Cantab., vol. 2 · Wing, STC

Hanson, John (*b.* 1610/11). *See under* Hanson, John (*fl.* 1604).

Hanson, Sir Levett (1754–1814), traveller, was born on 31 December 1754 at Melton, Yorkshire. He was the only son

of Robert Hanson of Normanton in Yorkshire and his wife, Elizabeth, daughter of Edward Isaack Jackson, a substantial apothecary and corporation member of Bury St Edmunds. His father was the son of Benjamin Hanson and Elizabeth, daughter of Robert Levett of Normanton. Hanson went in 1766 to a school at Bury St Edmunds, and in 1769 to one at North Walsham, Norfolk, where Nelson was for two years his schoolfellow. In 1771 he studied with Thomas Zouch, sometime fellow of Trinity College, Cambridge, and then rector of Wycliffe in the North Riding of Yorkshire. In 1774 he matriculated from Trinity College, Cambridge. Owing to some brawl he migrated in July 1774 to Emmanuel College as a fellow-commoner, but did not take a degree. In autumn 1776 he made, in company with the antiquary Michael Lort, his first tour on the continent, and acquired a taste for continental life and society, which led him to live out of England. Between 1776 and his death he paid only four brief visits to England (in 1780, 1785, 1786, and 1790).

After long sojourns at many foreign courts, Hanson made the acquaintance, in 1780, of Prince Philip of Limbourg, duke of Holstein, who created him his councillor and knight of his order of St Philip. Later on Hanson was made vice-chancellor and knight grand cross of the order, and resided for several years at Ghent. In 1787 he spent some time at the court of Ferdinand, duke of Parma; in 1789 he visited Naples and saw Sir William and Lady Hamilton, and in 1791 he took up his residence at the court of Ercole III Rinaldo d'Este, duke of Modena, with the rank of brigadier-general and chamberlain. He had previously become a member of the academy of Parma. In 1794 he incurred the suspicion of the Austrian government, and was compelled to leave the court of Modena, though he retained his office and the friendship of the duke until the latter's death in 1803. On arriving at Innsbruck he was arrested, kept eleven months in confinement, and finally tried at Vienna.

On his release Hanson travelled in Germany, finding favour at various courts, notably at Saxe-Hildburghausen, where he was presented with the family order of the duke, and settled in 1797 at Erlangen. In 1800 he was created knight vice-chancellor of the order of St Joachim, an order he was afterwards instrumental in conferring on Nelson, with whom he remained in contact throughout his life. He then devoted himself to the compilation of *An Accurate Historical Account of All the Orders of Knighthood at Present Existing in Europe* (1802), which was dedicated to Nelson. In 1807 he moved to Stockholm, where he was presented to Gustav IV Adolf by the British minister. In 1811 Hanson moved for the last time, to Copenhagen, where he published in the same year his *Miscellaneous Compositions in Verse*, dedicated to his friend Warren Hastings. He died at Copenhagen on 22 April 1814. He was unmarried, and his property passed to his only sister, Mary (1745–1830), wife of Sir Thomas Gery Cullum, bt, of Hardwick House, Bury St Edmunds.

L. H. CUST, *rev.* ELIZABETH BAIGENT

Sources MSS, priv. coll. [formerly at Hardwick House, Bury St Edmunds, dem. 1927] · Venn, Alum. Cant. · J. Brown, The northern

courts: containing original memoirs of the sovereigns of Sweden and Denmark since 1766, 2 (1818), 321–6 • L. Hanson, preface, *Miscellaneous compositions in verse* (1811)
Archives Bodl. Oxf., corresp. with John Charles Brooke
Likenesses three oil portraits, Bury St Edmunds Athenaeum, Suffolk

Hanson, Sir Richard Davies (1805–1876), lawyer and politician in Australia, was born in St Botolph's Lane, London, on 6 December 1805, the second son of Benjamin Hanson, fruit merchant. Having been educated at a nonconformist school in Melbourn, Cambridgeshire, he was articled in 1822 to John Wilks, solicitor, of 18 Finsbury Place, London, and after his admission as an attorney in 1828 practised for a short time in London. He actively supported Edward Gibbon Wakefield's system of colonization, in 1830 became associated with the attempt to found the colony of South Australia, and during the thirties wrote for the *Morning Chronicle* and, after 1837, for *The Globe*. In 1838 he accompanied Lord Durham to Canada as assistant commissioner to inquire into crown lands and immigration. Here he worked with Dominick Daly, and his conclusions were published as an appendix to the main Durham report.

Hanson was subsequently employed by the Wakefieldians in the New Zealand Company; he migrated to Wellington in January 1840, but soon fell out with the company, and helped settlers who were aggrieved by its claims. In 1841 he was appointed crown prosecutor and in 1844 commissioner of the court of requests, but, opposing Governor George Grey's anti-Maori policy, in 1846 he went to South Australia; here he was admitted to the bar. He was active in court and as a journalist opposing Governor Robe. On 29 March 1851 he married his housekeeper, Ann Scanlon, *née* Hopgood (*b.* 1827), with whom he had two sons and four daughters, all born in wedlock, despite later assertions to the contrary. When Governor Sir Henry Young appointed Hanson advocate-general, he became an *ex officio* member of the legislature and the government's legal adviser. He helped to stop state aid to religion, in the next year introduced the first Education Act and the District Councils' Act, and subsequently took a prominent conservative part in the drawing up of the colony's constitution, which the imperial parliament enacted in 1856.

Hanson was immediately appointed attorney-general and from 30 September 1857 to 9 May 1860 was premier as well in a thrice reconstructed administration during which the Real Property Act (which established the Torrens system of land registration) was passed. In November 1861 he was appointed chief justice of South Australia, where he steadily opposed the pretensions of Mr Justice Boothby. On 9 July 1869, when on leave in England, he was knighted at Windsor Castle.

A voracious reader, Hanson was keenly interested in science and theology, publishing several important theological works and shocking conservative churchmen by his sympathy with Ernest Renan, Bishop Colenso, Charles Darwin, and others. He enthusiastically supported the foundation of the University of Adelaide in 1874 and was elected its first chancellor; but he died on 4 March 1876, in his garden at Woodhouse on Mount Lofty from a sudden heart attack, before he could give the inaugural address. He was buried on 8 March at West Terrace cemetery, Adelaide. He was survived by his wife, one son, and four daughters, and left an estate of £5000.   A. G. L. SHAW

Sources *AusDB* • D. Jaensch, ed., *The Flinders history of South Australia*, 2: *Political history* (1986) • D. Pike, *Paradise of dissent: South Australia, 1829–1857*, 2nd edn [1967] • C. H. Spence, 'Sir Richard Hanson', *Melbourne Review*, 1 (July 1876) • *South Australian Register* (7 March 1876)
Archives Mitchell L., NSW, Musgrave MSS • NL NZ, Turnbull L., Chapman, Revans MSS • South Australian Archives, Adelaide, governor's confidential dispatches
Likenesses photograph, Old Parliament House, Adelaide, Australia • wood-engraving (after photograph by J. Watkins), NPG; repro. in *ILN* (31 July 1869), 117
Wealth at death £5000—in Australia: *AusDB*

Hanumant Rao (*fl.* 1781–1782). *See under* Indian visitors (*act. c.*1720–*c.*1810).

Hanway, Jonas (*bap.* 1712, *d.* 1786), merchant and philanthropist, was baptized on 2 August 1712 at the parish church of St Thomas, Portsmouth, the second of four children of Thomas Hanway (*bap.* 1671, *d.* 1714), the navy's agent victualler in Portsmouth, and his wife, Mary Hoghen (*c.*1679–1755), widow of Stephen Worlidge, with whom she had had two children. According to the College of Arms, Hanway had no gentle pedigree, but his father's family since the late seventeenth century had advanced in government service, chiefly through careers in the royal and merchant marines.

Early years and foreign travels Thomas Hanway died in 1714 after falling from his horse. His widow was left with six children and slender means. No evidence exists for Hanway's earliest years except a few autobiographical references in his later writings. These suggest that the family settled in rural Hampshire where the children received the rudiments of schooling. In later years they lived in London and followed careers in the navy and in trade.

Young Jonas was sent to London in 1728, most probably to the house of his uncle John in Oxford Street. Major John Hanway, after whom Hanway Street was named, was comfortably off and familiar with the Iberian peninsula, where his nephew was sent in the spring of 1729 as a merchant apprentice to the English factory in Lisbon. He spent the next twelve years in the Portuguese capital, imbibing the patriotic, religious, and economic views of the English factory. Some of his later eccentricities in dress, as well as his philanthropy, can be traced to these formative years. John Pugh, Hanway's amanuensis and contemporary biographer, mentions that Hanway experienced an unhappy love affair in Lisbon, the only reference to a romantic interest in Hanway's life. Hanway confessed later in his life to tipping pretty servant girls well, and Pugh reports he used to entertain reformed prostitutes in his home, providing them with small gifts. However, there is no hint of contemporary scandal or indiscretion. According to Pugh, 'he loved the society of women' (p. 229).

Petitions bearing Hanway's signature suggest that he was one of several merchants to suffer losses to Spanish

Jonas Hanway (*bap.* 1712, *d.* 1786), by James Northcote, 1785

privateers during the War of Jenkins's Ear (PRO, SP foreign). He returned to London in 1741, and cast about for another opportunity in trade. On 18 February 1743 he joined the Russia Company as junior partner with Charles Dingley and Henry Klencke, and took ship for Riga in April, and thence travelled overland to St Petersburg, where he was soon engaged in fitting out an expedition to Persia by way of the Caspian Sea. Hanway's mission was to sell English broadcloth for Persian silk and to evaluate the potential of trade with Persia, then ruled by the last great steppe conqueror, Shah Nadir Kuli Khan (1688–1747). A trans-Caspian trade had been pioneered by the Muscovy Company in 1566, but it was a tenuous link, dependent on political stability in central Asia and the co-operation of rulers in both Persia and Russia—both of which were distant hopes in Hanway's time.

With only an English clerk, a Russian menial servant, a Tartar boy, and a Russian soldier, Hanway travelled to Moscow and thence to Astrakhan, where he boarded a British ship, the *Empress of Russia*, which conveyed him across the Caspian to Langarud. His destination was Mashhad, but his caravan was captured on the way by rebellious Khyars, allied to Turkomans from the steppes to the north. Robbed of his goods, and forced to flee in disguise along the bleak southern shores of the Caspian, he was rescued by merchant colleagues. He was later partially compensated by Nadir Shah, who desired cordial relations with the British in order to enlist British artisans to construct a Persian navy for the Caspian. However, Hanway, and those who sent him, had underestimated the insecurity of the route while exaggerating the potential of the trade. In

retrospect he concluded that the trade held no great promise, for Persia was too poor and Russia was wholly disinclined to see the expansion of Persian power on its southern frontier. From these adventures he derived his motto in later life, 'Never Despair'. Hanway spent the next five years in St Petersburg, trying to revive his trade and reputation, before he returned to Britain via Germany and the Netherlands, in October 1750. Apart from two brief trips to the continent in later years, the remainder of his life was spent in England.

London merchant and writer Hanway took lodgings in the Strand with his half-sister Ann and her husband, Richard Townshend, a prosperous woollen draper. Thence he regularly walked to John's Coffee House in the City, just east of the Royal Exchange. There he pursued Russia Company business until 1764. He was a good looking and well-dressed man, but his habit of carrying both a sword and an umbrella must have attracted attention, for swords, as articles of attire, were by the 1750s unfashionable, and umbrellas in the hands of a gentleman unheard-of; indeed, Pugh claims Hanway was the first gentleman to walk the streets of London with one. Through precautions such as flannel underwear, and multiple pairs of stockings, Hanway hoped to ward off ill health, a subject on which he dilated throughout his long life.

Hanway emerged from obscurity through the publication of his adventures in Russia and Persia in *An Historical Account of the British Trade over the Caspian Sea* (4 vols., 1753). This was the most original and entertaining of all his books and its success prompted him to continue writing for the remainder of his life on all manner of subjects, prompting Charles Wilson to call him 'one of the most indefatigable and splendid bores of English history' (C. Wilson, 'The other side of mercantilism', *TRHS*, 1959, 92).

In 1753 Hanway wrote *A Review of the Proposed Naturalization of the Jews* and several additional pamphlets on the same subject, all opposing a bill to permit Jews to be naturalized by private acts of parliament. The bill failed, but raised partisan passions out of all proportion to so limited a concession. Hanway claimed that the bill, if enacted, would harm British foreign interests and compromise the inseparability of church and state: his views reflected his Christian mercantilism, but also the antisemitic sentiments he had imbibed in English factories abroad. He next wrote *A Letter to Mr. John Spranger* (1754) in which he argued forcefully for the paving, cleansing, and lighting of the streets of Westminster and Middlesex.

His mother's death in 1755 prompted Hanway to return to Portsmouth where she was buried, according to her wishes. His brief trip was the inspiration for Hanway's second book, *A Journal of Eight Days' Journey from Portsmouth to Kingston upon Thames* (1756), to which he appended *An Essay on Tea*. These works led to a literary skirmish with Oliver Goldsmith and Samuel Johnson, both of whom found Hanway trite and prolix, and his opposition to tea intemperate. Johnson claimed that Hanway had 'acquired some reputation by traveling abroad, but lost it all by traveling at home' (Boswell, *Life*, 1934, 2.122), but Hanway was largely right about the adulterated beverage that passed for tea in the mid-eighteenth century.

Philanthropy Hanway in mid-life was on the fringe of a very profitable trade, for the Russia Company enjoyed golden hours in the eighteenth century. Russia Company merchants were noted for philanthropy, and it was natural for Hanway to follow suit, but he did so with a zeal and an attention to detail that would make his name a byword for philanthropy. His first venture was his election as a governor of the Foundling Hospital on 12 May 1756 on a £50 donation (the largest single donation he was ever to make to any charity). The same year he wrote *Thoughts on the Duty of a Good Citizen, with Regard to War and Invasion*. The connecting thread was his effort to increase the population of Britain at the inception of the Seven Years' War. His timing coincided with the House of Commons decision to subsidize the Foundling Hospital for its care of all infants brought to its doors. Hanway plunged into the details of this bold experiment with open admissions, concerning himself with everything from smallpox inoculations to the weight of coal buckets. The experiment with the 'parliamentary children' ended in 1770.

On 25 June 1756 Hanway called a meeting of London merchants to recruit men for the Royal Navy by providing them with clothing kits. The resulting Marine Society was not an entirely new initiative (John Fielding had been clothing boys for sea service since February of that year), but the new charity proved the most sustained and successful of its kind, and received particular support from Russia Company merchants such as John Thornton and William Wilberforce (uncle to the philanthropist). Hanway's younger brother Thomas, a navy captain, also helped in placing men on ships, and the society soon extended its charge to include boys. By the end of the war, the society had recruited 4787 boys and 5452 men volunteers for the navy.

Hanway also supported the Stepney Society, which was designed to apprentice poor boys to marine trades, and the Troop Society, to provide clothing and shoes to British soldiers in Germany and North America. Robert Dingley, another Russia merchant, proposed a charity to help girls abandoned to prostitution, and Hanway gave enthusiastic support to the subsequent Magdalen Hospital for Penitent Prostitutes, which opened its doors in rented premises in Prescot Street in 1758. For each charity he supported, Hanway wrote pamphlets laying down rules for the charity, advising potential recipients and appealing to prospective donors. He was especially prolific in his writings for the Marine Society and the Magdalen Hospital.

Yet Hanway's Russia trade did not prosper and he sought government service to supplement his income. After vainly petitioning the duke of Newcastle, the only results being Hanway's pamphlets attacking the custom of vails-giving, prompted by the duke's over-zealous servants, Hanway finally received a place on 24 June 1762 as one of the navy's victualling commissioners at an annual salary of £400 with a £65 housing subsidy. (He left the Russia Company court of assistants in 1764.) He may have owed his new office to the patronage of Lord Bute, who received favourable mention in several of Hanway's subsequent publications. No sinecure, his commission involved supervision of the bakehouse and mills, and led to writings on diet, particularly on improving the quality of bread, and to the first major dietary experiment in the British navy: the provision of sauerkraut to seamen on the North American station during the American War of Independence, in an effort to reduce the incidence of scurvy.

It is impossible to know to what extent Hanway's philanthropy was motivated by humane or religious concerns (he was a devout member of the Church of England) and to what extent by practical considerations, such as his concern for the 'deep designs' of the French (*A Letter from a Member of the Marine Society*, 1757, 4), and his conviction that '*Increase* alone can make our natural Strength in *Men* correspond with our *artificial* Power in Riches, and both with the Grandeur and Extent of the *British Empire*' (*Serious Considerations on the Salutary Design of the Act of Parliament for a Regular Uniform Register of the Parish Poor*, 1762, 26). Such arguments prevailed in his writings, and even led him to partial agreement with Bernard Mandeville that '*private vices*, in some instances may be deemed *public benefits*, particularly by increasing the number of people' through illegitimate births (*Letters to the Guardians of the Infant Poor*, 1767, 53–4). In all this Hanway found it difficult to separate his private life from his public work. He was especially prone to defend his bachelorhood, but only on the grounds that his philanthropy should be considered as an extenuating circumstance. 'Poor man', Mrs Montagu wrote, 'he never knows when to have done when he is talking of himself' (letter to her sister, 27 July 1770, *Mrs. Montagu, 'Queen of the Blues'*, ed. R. Blunt, 1923, 1.237).

Hanway's acts Hanway praised London on repeated occasions but saw it as a death-trap for infant children in workhouses or in the homes of parish nurses. In 1762 he sought support for a bill, known as the Registers Bill, to require parishes to record the fate of these children. As the expensive experience of open admissions at the Foundling Hospital was coming to an end, parliament was looking for an alternative means of helping poor children, and the bill received the royal assent on 2 June of that year (2 Geo. III c. 22, 1762). This act required parishes to keep records of children in their care and thus provided groundwork for further reform. It became known as Hanway's Act. In 1766 there appeared perhaps the most effective pamphlet he ever wrote, *An Earnest Appeal for Mercy to the Children of the Poor*, which contained accounts of specific cases of gross abuse. Hanway's intense lobbying and further pamphleteering led to the passage of an act in 1767 requiring parishes to remove infants from London to the care of rural nurses (7 Geo. III c. 39, 1767). Dorothy George called the act, which also became known as Hanway's Act, 'the only piece of eighteenth-century legislation dealing with the poor which was an unqualified success' (*London Life in the Eighteenth Century*, 1964, 47). While there were abuses that would degenerate into the baby farms of Charles Dickens's day, Hanway's own estimate that the act in his lifetime saved 1500 lives a year may not be far from the truth (PRO, TI/630, no. 395, 9 May 1786).

Hanway's least successful effort was on behalf of chimney sweeps' young apprentices. While abuses were obvious, there seemed no alternative for the cleaning of narrow, twisted flues, and the number of blighted lives was insufficient to rouse national attention. His new hospital for the treatment of venereal disease, to supplement the work of the Lock Hospital, was similarly a failure. The Misericordia, as it was called, opened in 1774, but closed about 1780. But such failures were inevitable given that there was scarcely a good cause which Hanway did not actively support. He even raised funds to relieve victims of foreign fires: one in Montreal in 1765 and another in Bridgetown, Barbados, in 1766. He was active in the SPCK, using that society to distribute improving pamphlets. However, he was most active with his pen. *Virtue in Humble Life* (1774) was a compendious two-volume work designed to improve the morals of servants. *Defects of Police* (1775) focused on the need for better order in the metropolis. In *Common Sense* (1775) he advised American colonists to submit dutifully, using arguments exactly opposite to those in Thomas Paine's pamphlet of the same name published eleven months later. *Solitude in Imprisonment* (1776) concerned prison reform, and *The Commemorative Sacrifice of Our Lord's Supper* (1777) reflected the growing interest in religious and moral renewal that characterized his later years. Indeed, his last book was *A Comprehensive View of Sunday Schools* (1786). In all, he published eighty-five known works, six of them multi-volumed; five had two or more editions. He often wrote anonymously and pirated his earlier writings to augment the later. A third of his known work was book length, the remainder in pamphlet form, and virtually all of it was exhortative. He was at his best when he wrote to advocate just one cause and supported his case with detail. Unfortunately, most of his work lacked singleness of purpose, economy of words, and telling example.

Last years Authenticated portraits, bust and prints date from his later years; the most flattering is James Northcote's oil painting (1785) in the National Portrait Gallery, but the most representative is Edward Edwards's oil painting (1779) which hangs in the Marine Society offices in Lambeth. The face suggests impatience and determination. Hanway claimed that his somewhat sour look reflected his dislike in posing.

The American War of Independence kept Hanway occupied at the victualling board and at the Marine Society, the society contributing 7955 men and 4271 boys to that war. He still found time for pamphleteering, and for opening the Maritime School in 1777. The war's end greatly reduced activity in naval victualling and Marine Society recruiting, while the Maritime School closed in 1783. The school's closing was precipitated by a small incident in which Hanway offended the governors. It was insignificant in itself, but suggestive of errors of judgement on Hanway's part. That same year he retired from the victualling board, after another dispute, this time involving a contract. His last years were spent in writing, renewed involvement with the Foundling Hospital, support of the Sunday school movement begun by Robert Raikes in 1780,

and new initiatives for the Marine Society. In March 1783 he completed a *Proposal for County Naval Free Schools to be Built on Waste Lands*, a lavish production, funded by the society, but whose cost prompted the other governors to fine Hanway for his extravagance. The event reflected the maturation of the society, which was no longer willing to accept all the founder's initiatives. His scheme to set up naval free schools was transmuted by the governors to the more modest initiative of establishing a training ship, a plan Hanway initially opposed. The ship was anchored at Greenwich, staffed and ready to receive a first contingent of boys shortly before Hanway died at his home, 23 Red Lion Square, in the early hours of 5 September 1786. Contemporary opinion ascribed his death to complications arising from an enlarged prostate and modern medical opinion suggests that the enlargement may have resulted in uremia, a condition which in turn may account for his failing judgement in his last years. Pugh claims he left an estate of less than £2000 (Pugh, 250), but his will suggests that even that amount may be an exaggeration. Hanway was buried on 13 September in the crypt of St Mary's Church, Hanwell, after an elaborate funeral designed to advertise the Marine Society's ship school as well as to honour the founder. In 1788 an impressive memorial was placed in Westminster Abbey, the first to commemorate a philanthropist. By the Victorian era he was little known, although Samuel Smiles used Hanway's career to exemplify 'Energy and Courage' (*Self-Help*, new edn, 1880, 245–50). His writings were too dreary and too closely tied to issues of the day to endure. Most of his charities did not survive his century, although the Magdalen Hospital lasted in modified form until 1958, and the Foundling Hospital, renamed the Thomas Coram Foundation and now known as the Coram Family, is still a charity but no longer a hospital. The Marine Society played a significant role in naval recruiting in the nineteenth century, and thrives at the end of the twentieth century, although with altered mission. Less tangible were his various contributions to the quantity of lives and the quality of life in London, and his example to the generation that followed of how philanthropy could lay the foundation for legislative reforms.

JAMES STEPHEN TAYLOR

Sources J. Pugh, *Remarkable occurrences in the life of Jonas Hanway*, 2nd edn (1788) · J. Hanway, *An historical account of the British trade over the Caspian sea*, 4 vols. (1753) · J. S. Taylor, *Jonas Hanway, founder of the Marine Society* (1985) [incl. comprehensive bibliography] · J. Hutchins, *Jonas Hanway* (1940) · R. E. Jayne, *Hanway* (1929) · Marine Society, record of proceedings, NMM, MSY/A/1–5, B/1–4 · admiralty, victualling board, NMM, ADM/D/33–5, ADM/C/565–652 · victualling department minutes, PRO, ADM 111/53–108 · PRO, SP foreign, Portugal, SP/89–35–41 · PRO, SP foreign, Russia, SP 91/35–53 · Foundling Hospital, general court minutes, Coram Family, London, vols. 1–3 · Foundling Hospital, general committee minutes, Coram Family, London, vols. 5–18 · D. Andrew, *Philanthropy and police: London charity in the eighteenth century* (1989) · R. K. McClure, *Coram's children: the London Foundling Hospital in the eighteenth century* (1981) · H. F. B. Compston, *The Magdalen Hospital* (1917) · PRO, PROB 11/1145/478 · PRO, TI/630, no. 395, 9 May 1786

Archives Marine Society, London, corresp. | GL, Russia Company, court minute books · NMM, Marine Society MSS, admiralty victualling records · PRO, admiralty victualling records · Thomas

Coram Foundation, London, general court and general committee minutes

Likenesses J. Dickson, marble bust, c.1775 (after wax by P. Wright), Marine Society, London · E. Edwards, oils, 1779, Marine Society, London · Wedgwood medallion, 1780/81 (after T. Orde), Wedgwood Museum, Barlaston, Staffordshire · T. Orde, engraving, 1780–89, BL · J. Northcote, oils, 1785, priv. coll. [*see illus.*] · J. Northcote, oils, second version, c.1785, NPG · T. Holloway, line engraving, 1786, BM, NPG; repro. in *European Magazine* · I. F. and J. Moore, effigy on monument, c.1788, Westminster Abbey · J. Bretherton, etching (after T. Orde), BM, NPG

Wealth at death over £400: will, PRO, PROB 11/1145/478 · under £2000: Pugh, *Remarkable occurrences*, 250

Hanworth. For this title name *see* Pollock, Ernest Murray, first Viscount Hanworth (1861–1936).

Hapgood, Edris Albert [Eddie] (1908–1973), footballer, was born on 24 September 1908 at 4 Clark's Buildings, Union Road, Bristol, the ninth of the ten children of Henry Charles Hapgood (1869–1939) and his wife, Emily Clark (1870–1945). Both parents were from humble west country families. For some fifteen years Henry Hapgood had worked in Wales as a miner, before returning to Bristol shortly before the birth of Edris Albert.

Eddie Hapgood was educated at the Emmanuel and (later) Hannah More schools in Bristol. From the age of fourteen he worked as a milkman at his brother-in-law's dairy, playing football in local leagues. Rejected by Bristol Rovers, in 1926 he joined Kettering Town of the southern league, at that time a 'nursery' club for Arsenal Football Club. The following season he signed for Arsenal, a club which, under the managership of Herbert Chapman, was emerging as a leading force in English football. Arsenal's success in the 1930s, which brought five league championships and three cup final appearances, was based on Chapman's strategy of sound defence and rapid counter-attack. Hapgood, as left full-back, played a key role in this system. Of average height and medium build, a non-smoker and teetotaller, he relied upon exceptional speed, precision in the tackle, excellent positional sense, and, despite his height, outstanding heading ability. He always strove for a high level of physical fitness, encouraged by Arsenal's advanced training methods. In the Arsenal defensive formation the full-backs provided cover for the 'stopper' centre half, and in this role Hapgood shaped a new style of full-back play which contrasted with the crude physical methods employed by many full-backs of his day. His technique was to manoeuvre his opponent away from dangerous positions, dispossess with a well-timed tackle or interception, and set up an attack with a shrewdly placed, often short, pass. He rarely used the shoulder charge. His method was acknowledged by his most redoubtable opponent, the Stoke City and England right-winger Stanley Matthews, whose threat Hapgood contained more effectively than most: '[Hapgood] could give and take a pass; a classic player, one of the first footballing full-backs' (Miller, 35). His method became the benchmark by which future generations of full-backs set their standard.

Hapgood possessed a strong self-belief which shaped both his domestic and professional life. On 16 November 1929 he married the twenty-year-old Margaret Ada (Mig),

Edris Albert [Eddie] Hapgood (1908–1973), by Fred Daniels, 1939

daughter of William Henry Althorpe, a works foreman, whom he had met in Kettering. They established a comfortable middle-class home in Finchley, where they brought up four children, to whom Hapgood was devoted. Encouraged by Mig's concern for financial security, he capitalized on his fame, supplementing his footballer's maximum wage by advertising chocolate bars and gentlemen's fashions. Socially he rarely mixed with fellow footballers. Chapman had perceived leadership qualities in him from an early stage, and made him captain of Arsenal in 1930, the season in which the club won its first league championship. He retained the post after Chapman's death in 1934, despite cool relations with the new manager, George Allison.

In 1933 Hapgood was selected for England and in November 1934 the Football Association (FA) appointed him captain of the national team. In his sportsmanship, moral probity, and dignified demeanour he exhibited much of the old amateur ethos still favoured by the FA. His first game as captain was the 'battle of Highbury', an ill-tempered match against the world champions, Italy, which tested his strength of character. A broken nose forced his temporary withdrawal from the field but, in the era before substitutions, he returned to lead his team to victory. He remained England's captain throughout the 1930s, and played thirty times. Stanley Rous, the secretary of the FA, wrote:

When talking to those who join the ranks of the professionals—an honourable calling—I always stress that they should strive to behave on and off the field as a model on which young players can mould their play and conduct. That Eddie Hapgood has done. (Hapgood, 8)

None the less, he was a man of principle, not given to subservience. In the politically sensitive match against Germany in Munich in 1938, when the FA was prevailed upon by the Foreign Office to require the England players, as a mark of goodwill to Germany, to give the Nazi salute before the kick-off, Hapgood expressed his opposition on the grounds that English teams should not be expected to participate in local political customs. Overruled, he consoled himself with his team's crushing 6–3 win.

Though Hapgood continued to play in club, international, and services football during the war, when the league resumed in 1946–7 he felt he had reached retirement age. In any event, Arsenal's failure to pay the full long-service benefit he considered was owed to him led to his leaving the club. At a time of limited career prospects for professional footballers he moved into club management, first with Blackburn Rovers, then (after a brief resumption as a player with Shrewsbury Town) with Watford and Bath City. Each club enjoyed some success under his leadership but his achievements as a manager fell far below his success as a player. He refused to comply with some of the established practices at his clubs and he made enemies, especially among directors. His leaving of Bath City in 1956, amid acrimony and litigation, marked the end of his managerial career.

In 1944 Hapgood published his memoirs, *Football Ambassador*, which sold well and went into a second edition in 1951. However, without independent means or a job in middle age he took employment as warden of a YMCA hostel for apprentices at the atomic energy research establishment, Harwell. He was deeply grateful to the organization for this post, but nevertheless considered it less than his due, and resented being unable to continue in football. He enjoyed excellent health throughout his life but at the age of sixty developed heart trouble which forced an early retirement to Leamington Spa. He suffered a fatal heart attack while attending a sports forum at Honiley Hall, Warwickshire, on 20 April 1973.

JEFFREY HILL

Sources private information (2004) · E. A. Hapgood, *Football ambassador* (1944) · J. Arlott, 'A truly great back', *The Guardian* (23 April 1973) · S. Studd, *Herbert Chapman, football emperor: a study in the origins of modern soccer* (1981) · T. Say, 'Herbert Chapman: football revolutionary?', *Sports Historian*, 16 (1996), 81–98 · D. Miller, *Stanley Matthews: the authorized biography* (1989) · C. Bastin and B. Glanville, *Cliff Bastin remembers: an autobiography* (1950) · C. Buchan, *A lifetime in football* (1955) · P. J. Beck, 'England v. Germany, 1938', *History Today*, 32/6 (1982), 29–34 · *The Times* (23 April 1973) · b. cert. · m. cert. · d. cert.
Likenesses photographs, 1932–40, Hult. Arch. · F. W. Daniels, photograph, 1939, NPG [*see illus.*] · photographs, repro. in Bastin and Glanville, *Cliff Bastin remembers*, 96–7
Wealth at death £1105: administration, 29 May 1973, *CGPLA Eng. & Wales*

Happold, Sir Edmund Frank Ley (1930–1996), civil engineer, was born on 8 November 1930 at 86 Francis Street, Leeds, the son of Professor Frank Charles Happold (1902–1991), professor of biochemistry, and his wife, Annie Margaret Maud, *née* Smith, housing economist and Labour Party politician. His parents were Fabian socialists and members of the Religious Society of Friends, committed pacifists, and involved in the Youth Hostel Association. These formative influences exerted a lifelong influence on Happold and his sister, Margaret Elfrieda.

At Leeds grammar school Happold refused to join the school's cadet force because of his pacifist beliefs. It was wartime, and to end the consequent unpleasantness in 1944 Happold went to Bootham, York, a Quaker public school. From 1949 to 1951 he attended Leeds University, where he read geology. Late in 1951 Happold was called up for national service. As a Quaker he registered as a conscientious objector and was posted to the government's experimental horticultural station at Stockbridge House, Cawood. This gave him practical experience of building a large movable greenhouse and stimulated an interest in construction. He became a junior site engineer for Sir Robert McAlpine & Sons at an office block in Leeds (1953–4) before deciding to read civil engineering at the University of Leeds (1954–7), continuing to work for McAlpines in the vacations. With the encouragement of the architect Basil Spence, who did some teaching at Leeds, he obtained a travel scholarship to study modern architecture and engineering in Scandinavia.

Early work in civil engineering design On his return to Britain, Happold began working for Ove Arup & Partners as an assistant engineer in October 1957. With a multidisciplinary approach to building and civil engineering design within one practice, Arup's ethos, and his work with leading architects of the modern movement, attracted some of the leading young engineers of the time, and Happold found the rapidly growing practice an exciting place. He worked on the design of the Sydney Opera House, a project which established Arup's international reputation, and he helped to design Basil Spence's Coventry Cathedral. He also attended evening classes in architecture at Regent Street Polytechnic. Between April 1959 and October 1960 Happold visited the United States to work with Severus, Elsted, and Krueger. He became acquainted with the cable roof or tensile structures that Severus had helped design in the 1950s.

Happold returned to Arups in November 1960 and was successively promoted until in 1968 he became executive partner of the group known as 'Structures 3'. Early projects included Ankobra Bridge, Ghana; the science buildings at Exeter University; Knightsbridge Household Cavalry barracks in London; and the British embassy in Rome. With Poul Beckmann he established a training scheme for new graduate recruits. He was also becoming more involved in the construction industry generally, organizing a conference on education in building at Cambridge and chairing a conference at Brighton on the image of the construction industry.

Happold's early upbringing informed some of his most important work of the time. He developed a long-standing relationship involving more than thirty projects with the London borough of Lambeth and their architect, Ted Hollanby, creating the Central Hill housing project (1965–73), and West Norwood Library (1964–9), where he held his wedding reception following his marriage to Evelyn Claire (Eve) Matthews (b. 1941/2), a hospital nurse, on 21 December 1967. Happold's marriage gave his energies an alternative focus to his professional work, and a long relationship which brought stability to his life. With Eve and their children, Thomas (Tom) and Matthew, he was able to pursue, in his own words 'his favourite pastime … to travel with his family experiencing together new and interesting locations' (quoted in Walker and Addis, 13).

In 1963 Arups became involved in the design of a new assembly hall at Bootham School and Happold took over this project. His personal satisfaction was enhanced by the understanding he developed with the architect Trevor Dannatt. They collaborated on the Quaker meeting-house, Blackheath (1970–72), and more importantly on several projects in Saudi Arabia. This was at a time when few Western firms had worked in Saudi Arabia, and success there brought further prestige work.

When Happold and Dannatt went out to the Middle East in January 1967 they met Rolf Gutbrod and Frei Otto, the prize-winners for the conference centre at Mecca. After discussion it was agreed that Arups would co-operate as engineers on the Mecca scheme as well. Otto was the leading pioneer of lightweight tensile structures, a structural form which Happold had encountered while with Severus in the United States. He had already seen and admired Otto's work. He seized on Otto's radical structural ideas, and tensile structures became a characteristic of much of his later work. In the meantime, further projects followed with Arups in the Middle East. Happold developed a strong working relationship with leading Saudi engineers and architects which continued throughout his life.

While Happold's work in Saudi Arabia was arguably the most significant for his later career, his best-known work with Arups is probably the Beaubourg or Pompidou cultural centre in Paris. Happold persuaded the young architects Richard and Su Rogers and Renzo Piano to enter the design competition and created one of the landmark buildings of the twentieth century. To his intense regret, after two years at the helm in Paris, Happold was called back to London full-time following the completion of the foundation work. As work on the Beaubourg proceeded (1971–5), Happold was involved with a number of other significant projects such as Kensington town hall (1970–77), again with Spence; the St Katharine's Dock, London, redevelopment (1972–3) with the architects Renton Howard Wood; and the City Club, Milton Keynes, with Derek Walker Associates.

Happold's work is generally associated with tent, canopy, and freeform tension, and pneumatic structures. Much of this work was with Otto and Gutbrod. In the early 1970s collaboration included the unexecuted design for a pneumatic supported roof to create accommodation for 40,000 people in Antarctica (1971), and a temporary humped tent for the opening ceremony at Dyce near Aberdeen of the BP Forties Field in 1975. Perhaps the most remarkable collaboration was the Mannheim Bundesgartenschau (1973–5) exhibition hall and restaurant, a timber lattice-grid shell supporting a free form PVC membrane, with Otto, and Carlfried Mutschler & Partners.

Professor at Bath University   By this time it was clear Happold was unlikely to rise to the top within the Arup organization. His multidisciplinary interests in education and the construction process, and academic background, and no doubt the prospect of a new challenge, led him to accept an offer in 1976 of the position of professor of building engineering at the school of architecture and engineering at Bath University. There he was able to address audiences combining students of architecture and engineering in a curriculum designed to preclude the compartmentalization of the design professions which often created problems within the construction industry of the time.

Happold's interest in research, already in evidence at Arups, was now capable of further development. With the support of the Wolfson Foundation, Happold established a research group to study the performance of air-supported structures, and later the Centre for Window Cladding and Technology. The research was fed into building design partly through the work of Buro Happold, the firm he established in Bath on 1 May 1976. He envisaged the practice on a Quaker model, with all participating in discussions and consensus rather than majority voting as the basis for decision making. Happold was able to attract some distinguished colleagues from Arups, such as Michael Dickson and Ian Liddell. His view, as expressed in a speech to the Institution of Structural Engineers in 1992 (*Structural Engineer*, 20 October 1992), was that 'what I know about engineering is that it has to be a group activity. The best work is done by the most diverse group of talents who can still live together.' Happold had a great ability as a team builder, and by encouraging the realization of bold ideas from young talent, he was able to attract brilliant collaborators and colleagues.

Even after Happold had left Arups, Rolf Gutbrod insisted on his involvement alongside them on the Kocummas project for the Saudi Arabian government in Riyadh. He also continued to be involved with the development with Qatar University, a project on which he had begun working while with Arups (1975–85). From 1976 for twenty years Happold was involved in a succession of exciting projects all over the world, including the Munich Aviary (1978–82); Sainsbury's extension, Worcester College, Oxford (1980–82); the sports complex at King Abdul Aziz University, Jiddah; the British embassy, Riyadh (1981–6); the Crucible Theatre, Sheffield, and Globe Theatre, Southwark (1989–96); the Diplomatic Club, Riyadh; the Royal Armoury Museum, Leeds (1993–96); and the Tsim Sha Tsui Cultural Centre, Ocean Park Aviary, and Kowloon Park—all in Hong Kong—to name but a few. Some of these, such as the Munich Aviary and structures for the Atlanta Olympics, were developments of earlier work on tensile structures, but there were important works in timber such as the West Totton and Bishopstoke schools in Hampshire (1987–90), and the development of joints for green timber at Hooke Park, Dorset (1985–91). Happold became increasingly interested in developing energy-efficient sustainable buildings; some notable projects such as the pneumatic structure in Alberta (58°N, 1981) and the Commercial Bank competition entry for Frankfurt were not realized, but the design experience informed Happold's work generally, as later exemplified by the energy-efficient Millennium Dome, North Greenwich, London.

Construction industry politics Happold's engineering practice and teaching were paralleled by significant contributions to construction industry politics. These culminated in his work as founder of the Building Industry Council in 1988, acting as its first chairman. In 1990 it became the Construction Industry Council, an inter-institution multidisciplinary body reflecting his own co-operative approach. This strategy was endorsed as an alternative to the confrontation between clients, designers, and contractors which had bedevilled the British construction industry in the second half of the twentieth century by two influential government-funded reports in the 1990s: those of Sir Michael Latham (*Constructing the team: final report of the government / industry review of procurement and contractual arrangements in the UK construction industry*, 1994) and John Egan (*Rethinking construction: the report of the construction task force … on the scope for improving the quality and efficiency of UK construction*, 1998).

From the late 1960s Happold's reputation won him national and international awards, in part in response to his own determination to enter design competitions, but largely reflecting his numerous contributions to engineering and design. These included the Institution of Structural Engineers gold medal in 1992, and the Murray Leslie medal of the Chartered Institution of Building in 1982. Actively involved in the governance of the Institution of Structural Engineers from 1974, he was elected president in 1986–7. He was also vice-president of the Royal Society of Arts (1991). Honorary fellowships and honorary doctorates abounded. Happold served on numerous government and other technical committees, including the Building Regulations Advisory Committee (from 1988) and the Design Council (1988–94). His many talents were reflected in his appointment as master of the faculty of royal designers for industry (1991–3). He was knighted for his services to the construction industry in 1994.

Sir Ted Happold died at the Royal United Hospital, Bath, on 12 January 1996, survived by his wife and sons. A memorial service was held at Friends' Meeting-House, Euston Road, London, on 31 January 1996. Personally involved in the design of some of the most exciting buildings of the late twentieth century, his work as an educator, researcher, and a driving force for change in the construction process marks Happold as an engineer in the polymath tradition of the eighteenth-century founder of the British civil engineering profession, John Smeaton, whom he much admired.　　　　　　　　MIKE CHRIMES

Sources *The Times* (23 Jan 1996) · D. Walker and W. A. Addis, *Happold: the confidence to build* (1997) [contains detailed list of publications and projects] · B. Happold, 'On being an engineer: Sir Ted Happold, 1930–1996', *Patterns*, 12 (1997) · E. Happold, 'A journey in Saudi Arabia', *Patterns*, 11 (1993) · G. Watts, 'Ted Happold', *New Civil Engineer* (18 Jan 1996) · J. D. Allen, 'Professor Sir Edmund Happold, RDI, FEng: entrepreneur, visionary, teacher', *Structural Engineer*, 74/3 (6 Feb 1996) · D. Sharp, *The Guardian* (18 Jan 1996) · *WW* · membership records, Inst. CE · b. cert. · m. cert. · d. cert. · *CGPLA Eng. & Wales* (1996)

Archives priv. coll., family archive | Arup, London, Ove Arup and Partners archives · Buro Happold, Bath, Buro Happold archives

Likenesses photograph, Institute of Structural Engineers; repro. in Walker and Addis, *Happold*

Wealth at death £1,204,250: probate, 10 April 1996, *CGPLA Eng. & Wales*

Harald Hardrada [Haraldr inn Harðráði, Haraldr Sigurðarson] (1015–1066), king of Norway, was the son of the Norwegian petty king Sigurd Sýr (Sigurd the Sow) and Ásta Guthbrandsdóttir, who had earlier been the wife of Harald Grenski 'from Grenland' (west of Oslo Fjord), with whom she had had a son, Óláf Haraldsson (St Olaf). In 1030 at the age of fifteen Harald fought in the battle of Stiklestad, in which his step-brother was killed and Harald himself was wounded. After the battle he fled east to Sweden and thence went to Russia (Novgorod-Kiev) where he stayed for three or four years at the court of King Yaroslav (*d.* 1054).

Probably in 1034–5 Harald arrived in Constantinople where he entered the service of the Byzantine emperor. This service is described in a Byzantine source, from which it seems that Harald was a gifted soldier. He rose to command the emperor's special guard of Russians and Scandinavians (Varangians). Norse sources also describe Harald's contribution to the emperor's service, but much of the description of his battles in Asia, Africa, and Sicily is reminiscent of fables and sagas. None the less, the content is partly based in fact. Harald was at one point caught up in the conflict over the Byzantine imperial succession and he amassed a huge fortune in booty. His personal wealth in the end brought him into conflict with the emperor. In 1043 he was forced to flee Constantinople after first securing his riches.

In 1043 Harald was again in Russia at the court of Yaroslav, whose daughter Elizabeth (Ellisif) he married in 1044. They had two daughters. In 1045 Harald made his way back to Scandinavia. His undisguised aim was to become the king of Norway, if necessary by waging war against the then king, Magnús Óláfsson (*r.* 1035–47), Harald's own nephew and the son of Óláf Haraldsson. In preparation for such a war Harald began negotiations with Magnús's Danish enemy, Swein Estrithson, and the Swedish king who was Swein's ally. In the face of this threat Magnús tried to reach an understanding with Harald and in 1046 they agreed to share Norwegian royal power. The following year Magnús died and Harald became sole ruler of Norway.

Harald's reign was of the greatest significance for the consolidation of a Norwegian kingdom, a development already under way but as yet incomplete. Among other things the inland areas to the east were more firmly annexed to the rest of the kingdom. Harald crushed all opposition to royal power and in general favoured the use of force to solve problems. He arranged for a parley with his chief domestic political opponents where, without provocation, he had them assassinated. If he thought it necessary he ravaged and burnt in Norway just as ruthlessly as he had done earlier during campaigns in the Mediterranean. He also had an autocratic, 'Byzantine' attitude towards the church. He came into conflict with the archbishop in Hamburg–Bremen, who had responsibility for the church in Scandinavia, because he refused to acknowledge his authority. When the archbishop protested by sending envoys, Harald is said to have replied that he knew no archbishop nor lord in Norway other than the king himself.

Harald founded the dynasty of the later Norwegian kings through his son Óláf Haraldsson the Quiet (*b. c.*1050), who was king from 1066 to 1093. Óláf's mother was Thóra Thórbergsdóttir, from one of Norway's most prominent families. They had a second son, Magnús (*c.*1049–1069), who ruled jointly with Óláf in the years immediately following their father's death (1066–9).

As the successor to the throne of Magnús Óláfsson, Harald pursued the claim to the kingdom of Denmark that Magnús had made since 1041–2. The claim was disputed by Swein Estrithson. Almost every summer Harald waged war in Denmark, but in 1064 he and Swein began peace negotiations, which resulted in each recognizing the other's kingdom. Similarly Harald claimed that, as the successor to the Danish kings, he had a legitimate claim to the English throne. The dispute over the succession in England in 1066 gave him the opportunity to try to fulfil his claim through an expedition—the last really great viking raid.

At the beginning of September 1066 the Norwegian fleet sailed for England via Shetland and Orkney, where they gathered significant reinforcements. They reached the mouth of the Tyne on about 10 September. The Anglo-Saxon Chronicle puts the number of ships at 300. It seems that contact had been made well in advance between Harald and the exiled Tostig Godwineson, although it is unlikely that Tostig had gone to Norway to seek Harald, as both the Norman chronicles and the Norse sagas suggest. It seems more likely that communication had been established via emissaries, since Tostig returned to England in April 1066. When Harald landed at the Tyne, Tostig joined him and became his earl.

The two allies' initial aim was to conquer Northumbria, but they were met by Harold Godwineson's earls Edwin and Morcar and on 20 September the two armies clashed at Fulford just outside York. Harald and Tostig won and Edwin and Morcar fled. A few days later on 24 September the citizens of York surrendered the town to Harald and Tostig. Harald began to load ships to continue his conquest further south. Meanwhile the Yorkshire thegns agreed that Harald would take hostages from the whole of Yorkshire. He awaited them with a large part of his army at Stamford Bridge, east of York, on 25 September. The choice of location could have been due to the fact that Harald had fortified the place or that he controlled the Derwent with his fleet. However, in the meantime Harold Godwineson had advanced from the south in a forced march with far stronger forces than Harald's and had the previous day arrived in Tadcaster. He attacked Harald and Tostig, taking them completely by surprise. Harold Godwineson won after a short but hard-fought battle, and both Harald and Tostig were killed. Later Óláf Haraldsson, who had remained with the ships during the battle, was allowed to take his father's body home to Norway. Among those that followed Óláf was the Englishman Skúli, head of a powerful Norwegian family, who in Norway was regarded as the son of Tostig.   CLAUS KRAG

Sources H. Koht, 'Harald Hardraade', *Norsk biografisk leksikon* (1923–83), 5.463–9 · Snorri Sturluson and B. Aðalbjarnarson, *Heimskringla*, 3 (Reykjavík, 1951) · S. Blöndal, 'The last exploits of Harald Sigurdsson in Greek service', *Classica et Mediaevalia*, 2 (1939), 1–26 · P. A. Munch, *Det norske folks historie*, 5 vols. (1852–63), vol. 2 · E. A. Freeman, *The history of the Norman conquest of England*, 6 vols. (1867–79), vol. 3 · F. M. Stenton, *Anglo-Saxon England*, 3rd edn (1971)

Harald Maddadson [Haraldr Maddaðarson], **earl of Caithness and earl of Orkney** (1133/4–1206), magnate, was the first earl of Orkney to be born of a native Scottish comital line: his father, Maddad, earl of Atholl (central highlands), married Margaret, daughter of Earl Hákon Paulsson of Orkney, so that their son Harald unusually claimed the earldoms of Orkney and Caithness through his mother. The Countess Margaret is implicated, in *Orkneyinga Saga*, in arranging for the removal of her brother, Earl Paul the Silent, and securing the succession of her son Harald to the joint earldoms at the age of five in 1139. It is probable that there were also weighty political considerations behind this activity, as there is evidence of strong Scottish interest in events in the northern earldoms at this time, particularly with a view to extending royal authority over Caithness.

Earl Rögnvald and his pilgrimage Harald had to contend with the rivalry of his half-cousin **Rögnvald Kali Kolsson** [Rögnvaldr Kali Kolsson] (*c.*1103–1158), who claimed the two earldoms through his mother, Gunnhild, the daughter of Earl Erlend (*d.* 1099), and who conquered Orkney in 1136. Two years later Rögnvald agreed to allow Harald to hold half the earldom, perhaps in return for recognition of his own rights in Caithness. That an agreement was reached by 'all the best men of Orkney and Scotland' (*Orkneyinga Saga*, 72), shows the extent of the pressure from the south on behalf of the young Harald, whose grant of the title of earl at such an age was unprecedented. Moreover, it was done without any apparent reference to the kings of Norway, although some thirteen years later Rögnvald did take Harald to visit King Inge, one of the three rival sons of Harald Gilli. Scottish interest is clearly seen in a charter issued probably between about 1140 and 1145 by King David I to Earl Rögnvald and another, unnamed, earl and the 'good men' of Caithness and Orkney, ordering them to protect the monks—probably from Dunfermline—established at Dornoch in Sutherland.

The political situation changed markedly in 1151 when Earl Rögnvald departed for Palestine on his pilgrimage. This celebrated enterprise takes up five complete chapters of *Orkneyinga Saga*, which provide a unique account of such a journey by a northern magnate from this period. An entry (sub anno 1151) in the Icelandic annals records only 'The journey to Jerusalem of Earl Rognvald Kali of the Orkneys: and of Erling Skakki' (Anderson, 2.213). The impetus for the expedition was personal piety rather than the call to join a crusade, and it may have been undertaken in emulation of King Sigurd Jorsalafarer's ('Jerusalemfarer's') famous journey in 1108. The earl, with Bishop William and other well-born companions, including Erling Skakki, left Orkney in the late summer of 1151 in fifteen ships. The fleet sailed through the Strait of Gibraltar, after which Eindrid Ungi went straight to Jerusalem with six ships while Rögnvald tarried in Narbonne. During his stay there he composed several verses—included in the saga—in honour of the lovely lady Ermingard, verses which show strong influence from courtly love poetry, possibly the first such examples in skaldic verse. Further verses, many of them Rögnvald's own composition, record events which occurred during the rest of the journey, such as his swim across the River Jordan. Having visited Jerusalem, the party made its way back north via Constantinople, where they were received by the emperor and his Varangian guard, then sailed to Apulia where they took horses for the journey to Rome, arriving back in Orkney for Christmas 1153. This is most impressive evidence for the wide-ranging role of the earls of Orkney as players on the world scene of twelfth-century Europe. They were now fully participating in the cultural and religious activities of Christian Europe rather than threatening them from the periphery.

Rögnvald's return and death Harald was left as sole ruler of the earldoms during Rögnvald's absence. The opportunity was seized by Eystein, joint king of Norway and rival to his brother Inge, to impose his authority on the young earl by a military expedition to the west (the first since that of Magnus Barelegs in 1098). Finding Harald was in Thurso in Caithness, the king sailed with only three skiffs from his fleet over the Pentland Firth to take Harald by surprise. In his submission Harald redeemed himself with 3 gold marks, a payment which has been interpreted as a feudal 'relief', although the relationship between earls and kings was as yet scarcely so formalized. In Rögnvald's absence another claimant, Erlend, son of Harald Smooth-Tongue and cousin to Harald Maddadson, rose to the fore and was given Rögnvald's half of Caithness by the Scottish king, Malcolm IV. Erlend then went to Norway and obtained a grant of Harald's half of Orkney from King Eystein. Behind him lay the support of many powerful kinsmen, including that of the unscrupulous Swein Asleifsson. The safe return of Rögnvald in 1153 from his pilgrimage led to the so-called 'war of the three earls', the events of which are graphically described in the saga narrative. It ended with the death of Erlend on the island of Damsay and the settlement of Harald and Rögnvald as co-earls.

Continuing tensions in this still-violent society led to the murder of Rögnvald on 20 August 1158 by Thorbjorn Clerk at Forsie in Caithness. One of the most talented and best-loved of all the Orkney earls, he was described as 'very popular there in the Isles and far and wide elsewhere. He had been a friend in need to many a man, liberal in money matters, equable of temper, steadfast in friendship, skilful in feats of strength and a good skald' (*Orkneyinga Saga*, chap. 104). He was buried in St Magnus's Cathedral in Kirkwall, the finest surviving Romanesque cathedral in Scotland, which was built in fulfilment of the vow which he took on his attempt to win the earldom in 1136. The expense of the building programme was partly borne by the earl's generosity, although an agreement was made with the Orkney farmers, according to which they contributed funds in return for the abandonment of the threat to impose an inheritance fee on their family estates. In this pious age, the violent death of the popular earl led to his rapid sanctification. His relics are said in *Orkneyinga Saga* to have been taken up by Bishop Bjarne in the 1190s, with leave of the pope, and he became the second Orkney saint.

Harald Maddadson and the kingdom of Scots By contrast with Rögnvald, Harald was less highly regarded, it being said of him only that he was 'a great chief, the tallest and strongest of men, obstinate and hard-hearted' (*Orkneyinga Saga*, chap. 105). Now unrivalled within his own power base, Harald's ambitions seem to have extended in the next phase of his life beyond Orkney and Caithness and southwards to Ross, which had come under the influence of previous earls of Orkney. He became involved in the complex and dangerous situation created by the pretensions of the rebel Macheth dynasty in Moray and Ross, which caused the kings of Scots problems intermittently throughout the twelfth century. That Harald associated himself with the Macheth cause is clear from his bigamous second marriage (in the 1170s probably) to Hvarflod *Macheth, daughter of Malcolm *Macheth [*see under* Macheth family], who was earl of Ross for at least six years until his death in 1168. Harald was probably also strengthening Orkney earldom claims to lands in Ross by this marriage. The military significance of this frontier zone was fully recognized by King William, who built and fortified two castles in 1179 at strategic points in Easter Ross just before the MacWilliam rebellion of 1181, in which, however, Earl Harald played no part. Not until 1196 did he show signs of acting rebelliously, which then gave the king good reason to send one, if not two, expeditions north, one of which actually reached Thurso on the northern coast of the Caithness earldom, the first time royal Scottish forces had penetrated into earldom territory. The explanation given in the later chronicle of John Fordun was that Harald had been goaded into rebelling by his wife's ambitions, and certainly one of the peace conditions demanded by King William subsequently was that Harald put Hvarflod away and take back his first wife, Affreca, daughter of Duncan, earl of Fife (*d.* 1154) (which he refused to do).

There are a remarkable number of contemporary accounts of the royal expeditions north to contain Harald, apart from *Orkneyinga Saga* itself (which is not very coherent or informative about this stage of Harald's life). Some of these accounts suggest that Harald's son Thorfinn had reacted to the presence of the Scottish king's feudal vassals on the southern frontier of earldom influence by leading an attack into Moray, thereby inviting retaliatory action by the royal Scottish forces. Fordun says that the king's expedition of 1196 subdued both the provinces of the Caithness men (Caithness and Sutherland), and also that the earl's son and heir, Thorfinn, was taken hostage. Roger of Howden says that the earldom of Caithness was first divided and then taken away from Harald altogether. Half of it was given to Harald Ungi ('the younger'), the grandson of Earl Rögnvald, who was later killed in battle near Wick. There was also, according to the saga, an attempt to replace Harald with Rognvald Godredson, king of the Hebrides. At some point Harald was forced to go south to King William's presence, accompanied by the bishops of St Andrews and Rosemarkie, in order to beg for his earldom back, but whether in 1197 or after a later incident in 1202 is not clear. There is, however, no doubt either that Harald had to pay a large fine, or that his son Thorfinn died in prison after having been blinded.

Harald compounded his own problems by making the grave mistake of antagonizing the church, which was to the forefront of Scottish policies regarding Caithness. He was considered responsible for leading the attack on the residence of the bishop of Caithness at Scrabster in 1201, when Bishop John had his tongue cut out and was partially blinded. This was the culmination of problems between the bishop and earl which had been developing in the 1190s, provoked by the bishop's ban on the payment of a church tax instituted by the earl—the ban probably represented an attempt to impose Scottish order in a part of the earl's dominion which had hitherto been under the Orkney bishop's authority. Reports about the ban on the earl's grant of the tax had reached the ears of Innocent III, as, indeed, did information about the attack on the bishop, for which a heavy penance was laid on the chief perpetrator. The mutilation of the bishop provided the earl's Scottish overlord with the perfect opportunity for an avenging expedition north, and for the attempted appointment of more rival earls. Yet the evidence also suggests that Harald was a pious and generous benefactor to the church, giving an annual gift of 1 mark of silver to the canons of Scone, as well as the above-mentioned annual tax of 1d. from every house in Caithness for the papacy (modelled on the payment of Peter's Pence which had been recently instituted in Scandinavia, including Orkney). Earl Harald is also named in a lost charter as taking the monastery of 'Benkoren' (probably Bangor, in Down) under his protection, another indication of the range of his seaborne activities.

Defeat and recovery   In his Scandinavian earldom Earl Harald also played the dangerous game of being implicated in rebellion against the established king and of having to suffer the consequences. He gave support to the *Eyjaskeggjar* rebels ('Island beardies'), who planned to restore the illegitimate son of King Magnús Erlingsson to the throne against the impostor Sverre. Two years after the defeat of the rebels at the battle of Floruvoe in 1193, Earl Harald was forced to go to Bergen and submit to King Sverre, with his close friend and relative Bishop Bjarne to plead his case. The peace terms were harsh and included the loss of the Shetland Islands and half of the revenues of Orkney, along with the imposition of a royal steward (*sysselman*) in his earldom to collect moneys and administer newly acquired royal estates. The permanent representatives of encroaching royal authority were tolerated only as long as their position was protected by their royal masters, and both the Caithness steward and the Orkney *sysselman* were eventually murdered on the earl's orders.

Harald Maddadson had the misfortune to live at a time when royal power was increasing markedly, making it inevitable that restrictions should be imposed on independent warlords of his class. He was also unlucky to be faced with determined and powerful kings in both Scotland and Norway who would not tolerate any signs of disaffection by the rulers of dangerously independent earldom dynasties, and who were able to reach out to the remoter parts of their kingdoms in their drive to extend their authority. Military expeditions into his territory, confiscations of his hereditary lands, and impositions of heavy fines for his failure to fulfil conditions and abide by restrictions imposed on him after his submission at humiliating peace meetings, all are symbols of the changed world of the late twelfth century in the most northerly kingdoms of Europe. Remarkably, when Earl Harald died in 1206, after a violent life in which he had been earl for nearly seventy years, he held the whole of Caithness once more and had also reacquired Shetland, a notable survival achievement by the last representative of the old-style free-ranging viking earl, whose authority had been challenged by new-style royal overlords.

BARBARA E. CRAWFORD

Sources A. B. Taylor, ed. and trans., *The Orkneyinga saga* (1938) · H. Pálsson and P. Edwards, eds. and trans., *The Orkneyinga saga: the history of the earls of Orkney* (1978) · P. Topping, 'Harald Maddadson, earl of Orkney and Caithness, 1139–1206', *SHR*, 62 (1983), 105–20 · B. E. Crawford, 'Peter's Pence in Scotland', *The Scottish tradition*, ed. G. W. S. Barrow (1974), 14–22 · B. E. Crawford, 'The earldom of Caithness and the kingdom of Scotland, 1150–1266', *Essays on the nobility of medieval Scotland*, ed. K. J. Stringer (1984), 25–43 · W. P. L. Thomson, *History of Orkney* (1987) · B. E. Crawford, 'An unrecognised statue of Earl Rognvald?', *Northern Isles connections*, ed. B. E. Crawford (1995), 29–46 · P. Bibire, 'The poetry of Earl Rognvald's court', *St Magnus Cathedral and Orkney's twelfth-century renaissance*, ed. B. E. Crawford (1988), 208–40 · A. O. Anderson, ed. and trans., *Early sources of Scottish history, AD 500 to 1286*, 2 vols. (1922) · A. A. M. Duncan, 'Roger of Howden and Scotland', *Church, chronicle and learning in medieval and early Renaissance Scotland*, ed. B. E. Crawford (1999), 135–60

Harald Smooth-Tongue [Haraldr inn Sléttmáli], **earl of Orkney** (d. 1131). See under Magnús Erlendsson, earl of Orkney (1075/6–1116?).

Harari [*née* Benenson], **Manya** (1905–1969), publisher and translator, was born at Baku, Russia, on 8 April 1905, the fourth child and youngest daughter of Grigory Benenson, a Jewish financier, and his wife, Sophie Goldberg. While Benenson amassed an enormous fortune Manya's childhood was spent amid the opulence of a rented top floor of

Volkonsky's St Petersburg house, and at Redkino, a splendid country estate. In 1914 the family migrated to London from Germany, where they had been visiting. Manya was educated at Malvern Girls' College and Bedford College, London, graduating with second-class honours in history in 1924. Her father refused to establish a new permanent domicile and, while he was building up another financial empire which later crumbled in the Wall Street crash, the family home was usually a luxury hotel.

In 1925, having become interested in the Jewish question, both from a religious and from a political point of view, Manya Benenson visited Palestine, where she met Ralph Andrew *Harari (1893–1969). They were married in that year. Bored by the social round in Cairo, she began to study, and was shocked by, social conditions in Egypt. Visits to Palestine, where she worked in a kibbutz in 1926, and welfare work in Cairo failed to quell a growing restlessness of spirit. In 1932 she reached a long-pondered decision and became a Roman Catholic; she remained emphatic, however, that this in no way detracted from her Jewish identification. Later, frequently visiting London, she was associated with the inauguration of the Sword of the Spirit movement by Cardinal Hinsley in 1940; she worked on the *Dublin Review* and then edited her own periodical, the *Changing World*; when publication ceased in 1942 she anticipated her husband in joining the political warfare department as a translator.

In 1946, with Marjorie Villiers as her partner, Manya Harari founded the Harvill Press, a small publishing house specializing in books on religion, metaphysics, the arts, and psychology. In 1954 Harvill became a subsidiary of Collins, with Manya and her partner continuing to direct the enterprise. It was as the publisher of *Dr Zhivago* (1958), the novel by Boris Pasternak which she translated with Max Hayward, that Manya Harari became widely known. She also helped to introduce to British and American readers Konstantin Paustovsky, Aleksandr Solzhenitsyn, Andrey Sinyavsky, Ilya Ehrenburg, and Yevgeny Yevtushenko, thus providing expression for what might be regarded as the free voice of Russia. Her discernment as a publisher was matched by her outstanding gifts as a translator.

Working from an attic room in her London home, 32 Catherine Place, Westminster, poised between typewriter and telephone, with manuscripts, authors, intermediaries, their friends, and friends of their friends all jostling for priority, clutching a huge box of cigarettes and for ever smoking, Manya Harari never lost her softness of voice and gentleness of manner; physically she was so slender that her whole presence seemed contained in the intensity and pallor of exquisitely drawn features. Totally without vanity and oblivious of her material surroundings, she pursued her diverse causes with passionate resolution. However busy, she never could bear to be tied to one environment. In 1948 she went to Palestine as a reporter. In 1955 she made her first return journey to Russia, visiting Moscow, Leningrad, and Redkino. She was to return in the spring of 1956 and again in the winter of 1961.

When her husband became seriously ill in 1968 Manya Harari already knew that she herself had only months to live. Characteristically she kept the knowledge to herself until he died in May 1969 and continued to work on an autobiography until a few days before her own death in London on 24 September 1969, having found an almost total serenity in her all-embracing religious faith.

P. J. V. ROLO, *rev.*

Sources *The Times* (25 Sept 1969) · *The Times* (1 Oct 1969) · personal knowledge (1981) · private information (1981) · *CGPLA Eng. & Wales* (1970)

Wealth at death £40,630: probate, 24 April 1970, *CGPLA Eng. & Wales*

Harari, Ralph Andrew (1893–1969), merchant banker and art scholar and collector, was born on 28 October 1893 in Cairo, the third child and elder son of Sir Victor Harari Pasha, civil servant, financier, and leading member of Egypt's Anglo-Jewish community, and his wife, Emma Aghion. The hospitality of their Cairo home during the early decades of the twentieth century provided a valued meeting point for British administrators, resident diplomats, visiting notabilities, and the Turco-Egyptian establishment. Harari was educated at Lausanne and Pembroke College, Cambridge, where he obtained first classes in both parts of the economics tripos (1912–13) and a boxing blue. Back in Egypt in 1914 he participated, as a junior officer, in the Palestine campaign of Sir Edmund Allenby, later serving as finance officer to his father's old friend Ronald Storrs, then military governor of Jerusalem. In 1920 he was appointed director of trade and commerce in the new mandate under Sir Herbert Samuel, also an old family friend. In 1925 he returned to Egypt to help his father's business enterprises. In the same year, in Paris, he married Manya (1905–1969) [*see* Harari, Manya], daughter of Grigori and Sophie Benenson, who later became a publisher and translator.

In 1939 Harari was imaginatively appointed economic adviser to general headquarters Middle East, with the rank of full colonel but no visible signs of any supporting establishment. His duties were unspecified, his services ubiquitous. His advice, modestly conveyed in oracular pronouncements, was widely sought; he became, in effect, a one-man 'think-tank'. Recalled to London for consultation with Lord Keynes after the end of the desert campaign, he was recruited, on the basis of his Cairo reputation, by Peter Ritchie-Calder, then director of plans in the department of political warfare; colleagues were impressed by his shrewdness and practical humanity. Harari was appointed OBE for his services. After the war he remained in London as managing director of the merchant banking firm of S. Japhet & Co., later taken over by the Charterhouse group of companies, whose board he then joined.

Alongside a career moulded by family tradition Harari made his own way as an art scholar and collector. Having become interested in Islamic metalwork in the twenties he emerged as its leading expert and collector, contributing the authoritative chapter 'Metalwork after the early Islamic period' in the *Survey of Persian Art* (6 vols., 1938–9); he donated his own collection to the Cairo Museum. In the early thirties he began to collect Beardsley drawings, then out of fashion. He added to these after the war and eventually formed the largest private collection, which notably enriched exhibitions in London (1966) and New York and Los Angeles (1967), and has now been acquired by the Victoria and Albert Museum. His Beardsleys were complemented by paintings and drawings of Rouault, Lautrec, Segonzac, Sickert, John, Gavarni, and Keene. It was said of Harari that 'he was essentially sensitive to style taken to the point of mannerism'; perhaps inevitably his attention turned to Japan. Before 1958 he had collected one important album of Hokusai (1760–1849) sketches, and from then onwards he became increasingly fascinated; while concentrating on Hokusai, he acquired a representative range of Japanese paintings and drawings. An exhibition organized after his death by the Arts Council at the Victoria and Albert Museum was the first public glimpse of this unique collection which, amassed without the aid of any vast financial resources, had already inspired and delighted Japanese art scholars.

Harari was also a collector of people; he believed in good food, good wine, and civilizing communication. He and his wife made an art of hospitality at their London home. Both believed passionately in the healing power of reason and persuasion, and their influence, so diverse in its impact, was probably more pervasive than they knew. Both were good listeners as well as very undemanding in their friendship. They had one son, Michael Harari, born in England in 1928, who became a psychiatrist. Ralph Harari became seriously ill in 1968, and died at his home, 32 Catherine Place, Westminster, London, on 26 May 1969.   P. J. V. ROLO, rev.

Sources *The Times* (18 June 1969), 10h · M. Harari, *Memoirs* (1972) · personal knowledge (1981) · private information (1981) · J. Hillier, ed., *The Harari collection of Japanese paintings and drawings*, 3 vols. (1970–73), introduction · d. cert.

Harben, Sir Henry (1823–1911), insurance company manager, was born on 24 August 1823 in Bloomsbury, London, the eldest of four surviving children of Henry Harben (1793–1868), wholesale cheesemonger of Bloomsbury, and Sarah (1798–1870), daughter of Benjamin da Costa Andrade, a Whitechapel merchant of Portuguese Jewish descent. The family claimed ancestry from one Thomas Harben of Seaford in Sussex, a clockmaker who became rich through the purchase of salvage in 1747 and commenced banking at Lewes. Henry Harben's grandfather, however, left banking to become a partner in the wholesale provision stores of Harben and Larkin, Whitechapel. Harben's father in turn established his own business about 1820.

Little is known of Harben's education and formative years. He was seven years old when his father left the family to live with Mary Anne Roberts, with whom he had two more children; he went bankrupt in 1835. Harben worked for his uncle in the Whitechapel stores for several years, after which he was articled to a surveyor. On 1 August 1846 he married Ann (d. 1883), daughter of James Such; his two surviving children, Mary Woodgate Harben (married name Wharrie), and Henry Andrade Harben, director and

chairman of the Prudential, and author of *A Dictionary of London* (1917), were born in 1847 and 1849 respectively.

In 1851 Harben joined the Prudential Mutual Assurance, Investment and Loan Association, founded three years earlier with a modest £2500 of capital paid-up. It had little success until Harben persuaded the directors to act on the recommendation of the 1853 select committee on assurance associations regarding the desirability of assurance for the working classes. Hitherto this had only been offered by friendly societies and the so-called 'burial clubs', which were loosely regulated and frequently unsound. Harben was instrumental in guiding the Prudential into the relatively new field of 'industrial' assurance, by which policies were sold for amounts as low as 1d. a week by agents who collected premiums weekly from working-class households. Initially the Prudential found the expense of house-to-house collection almost ruinous, but Harben's economies brought gradual improvement. In 1860 he negotiated an advantageous amalgamation with a rival company, the British Industry. His dispute with Gladstone about the benefits for working-class customers at the time of the government assurance bill in 1864 brought vindication and helpful publicity for the Prudential. Aided by the increasing public acceptance of assurance, its industrial branch grew so rapidly that during the 1870s it sometimes engaged over 1000 agents a year.

An honorary fellow of the Institute of Actuaries from 1864, Harben insisted on the detailed analysis of mortality figures and the regular valuation of liabilities; these, together with meticulous attention to economy, were the principles underlying the Prudential's success. He published the findings of his statistical department as *The Mortality Experience of the Prudential Assurance Company in the Industrial Branch 1867–1870* in 1871 and *A History of the Prudential Assurance Company* in 1880. As secretary, then as resident director from 1874 and deputy chairman from 1878, he presided over the company's phenomenal expansion: by 1891 it was insuring one person in four in the United Kingdom. Harben fostered the careers of several subordinates—in particular Thomas Dewey—and hence had a lasting influence. He was also largely responsible for commissioning the architect Alfred Waterhouse to build, between 1877 and 1905, the Prudential's London office at Holborn Bars, and twenty-one provincial offices. An Anglican with strong evangelical leanings, and a prominent freemason, Harben created a corporate ethos of self-help and moral improvement, which fuelled a wide range of Prudential cultural and sporting activities.

Harben was exceptionally energetic and hard-working; he could be autocratic, but he had considerable presence, and inspired great loyalty; he was a powerful speaker, and strikingly handsome. His Prudential colleagues encouraged him to enter politics, and he stood (though unsuccessfully) on two occasions as Conservative candidate, at Norwich in 1880 and Cardiff in 1885. He was first cousin to Joseph Chamberlain.

As a major shareholder in the Prudential, Harben became wealthy, and contributed to numerous causes. He joined the Carpenters' Company in 1878 and served as master in 1893. His most outstanding donation to its educational and charitable work was the Rustington Convalescent Home for Working Men (1897), built and endowed at a cost of over £100,000. An endowment to the British Institute of Public Health, for an annual lecture series and the award of a gold medal, reflected a lifelong interest. Being similarly interested in technical education, he supported King's College, London, in its technical education programmes.

Harben lived in Hampstead from 1865, serving first as a member of the Hampstead vestry, then representing the area on the Metropolitan Board of Works from 1880 to 1889, and the London county council until 1894. He was the first mayor of Hampstead in 1900. He funded the building of the central public library, a wing of the Hampstead General Hospital, a Hampstead hall for the London City Mission, and, with his daughter Mary Wharrie, the headquarters of the 1st cadet battalion City of London yeomanry, Royal Fusiliers, of which he was honorary colonel. He participated in the campaigns to add Parliament Hill Fields and the Golders Hill estate to Hampstead Heath.

Harben's second marriage, on 8 November 1890, to Mary Jane Bulman Cole (d. 1914), daughter of another Prudential director, Thomas Bulman Cole, coincided with his purchase of Warnham Lodge, a 90 acre estate near Horsham in his ancestral county of Sussex. As a passionate supporter of cricket, he built a fine private ground and encouraged the sport in the district. He served as a JP and as deputy lieutenant for Sussex, and was high sheriff in 1898. He was knighted in June 1897, on the occasion of Queen Victoria's diamond jubilee.

On the death of Edgar Horne in 1905, Harben became chairman of the Prudential, but he resigned in 1907 in declining health. He held the office of president until his death, of natural causes, at the age of eighty-eight, on 2 December 1911 at Warnham Lodge. He was buried on 6 December at Kensal Green cemetery, the burial-place of his mother.   LAURIE DENNETT

Sources Sussex Daily News (4 Dec 1911) · Insurance Record (8 Dec 1911) · The Times (4 Dec 1911) · Hampstead and Highgate Express (9 Dec 1911) · 'Mr Henry Harben, metropolitan board of works', Biographical Magazine (May 1888), 331–6 · H. Cockerell, 'Harben, Sir Henry', DBB · parish register (birth and baptism), St Giles-in-the-Fields, Bloomsbury, 29 Sept 1823 · Prudential Corporation plc, 142 Holborn Bars, London, Prudential Archives · d. cert.

Archives Prudential Corporation plc, 142 Holborn Bars, London, archives, boxfiles · W. Sussex RO, Sussex estate papers and papers relating to his daughter's bequests | U. Birm., Chamberlain MSS, Carpenters' Company

Likenesses photographs, 1854–1911, Prudential Corporation plc · N. Macbeth, oils, 1872, Prudential Mutual Life Assurance Association, London · T. Brock, bronze bust, 1888, Prudential Corporation plc · J. Collier, oils, 1889, Hampstead town hall, London · marble effigy on monument, St Margaret's Church, Warnham, Sussex · miniature (after bronze bust by T. Brock, 1888), Prudential Corporation plc · oils, Rustington Home, Littlehampton

Wealth at death £398,334 12s. 1d.: probate, 20 Feb 1912, CGPLA Eng. & Wales

Harben, Philip Hubert Kendal Jerrold (1906–1970), television chef and cookery writer, was born on 17 October 1906 at 40 Perham Road, Fulham, the son of Leonard Hubert Storey Harben (1878–1941) and his wife, Mary Jerrold Allen (1877–1955). His parents were both actors, known as Hubert Harben and Mary Jerrold. His sister, Joan Harben, often appeared on the West End stage and was best-known for her role in the BBC radio series *It's that Man Again*, where she played the part of the lugubrious Mona Lott, famous for her catch-phrase, 'It's being so cheerful that keeps me going.' Educated at Highgate School, Harben then went on the stage himself, and later worked with John Grierson on the documentary film *Drifters* (1929), and with Egidio Scaioni doing studio and fashion photography. On 19 July 1930 he married Katharine Joyce Kenyon (b. 1906/7), and they had a son and a daughter.

Far from being a chef, Harben never had a formal cookery lesson, but learned to cook because his parents were so often absent while on tour, leaving him to fend for himself in the kitchen. He developed a curiosity about the processes of cooking, and was technically so proficient that his friend Raymond Postgate, the author of the original *Good Food Guide*, referred to him for answers to most technical questions. A member of the avant-garde intellectual left, in 1937 Harben was cooking and running the kitchen at The Isobar, in the basement of the Isokon building, Wells Coates's architecturally advanced block of flats in Lawn Road, Hampstead.

Harben and Postgate founded the Half Hundred Dining Club, 'a poor man's food and wine society'. The club had twenty-five members each of whom could bring one guest, hence the half-hundred. The club's aim was to combine 'good dining with economy'. Members, who included Julian Huxley, Walter Gropius, Marcel Breuer, Ernst Freud, and Francis Meynell, took it in turn to 'direct' the dinner, which could involve anything from planning the menu and getting someone else to cook it, to doing the whole task—buying the ingredients and wine and cooking and serving the meal. A 'blurb' was required from the director, and could be anything from a simple menu to a full-blown mission statement. As each member and guest paid a strictly budgeted total of only 10s. (2s. 6d. for food, 5s. for wine, and 2s. 6d. for service), anything over had to come from the director's own pocket. Harben and Postgate laid down serious criteria for membership: election had to be unanimous and candidates had to profess that they were seriously interested in food and drink with 'no religious or other taboos or unsociable characteristics which may impede conversation' (www.lib.uea.ac.uk/libinfo/archives/pritchard/pp39ch.htm). The club ceased in 1940, though there was a failed attempt to revive it after the Second World War. When the war was over he was canteen manager for British Overseas Airways Corporation, where he came to the attention of the BBC. His first broadcasting work was radio cookery demonstrations after the eight o'clock news.

When BBC television resumed in June 1946 Harben was chosen to front a cookery programme. He was not the first cook on British television (that distinction went to Marcel Boulestin in 1937), but he was generally thought of as the first of the British breed of that hybrid creature—part entertainer, part teacher. Plump, bearded, and genial, with a racy delivery, his initial BBC television series, *Cookery*, ran from 1946 to 1951. The most bizarre turn required of him was on a programme celebrating Boulestin, when a 1939 sound recording was played of the Frenchman preparing his speciality, the Boulestin omelette. Harben, 'the new culinary star, mimed in vision, with split-second timing', as the eggs were whisked and the butter sizzled in the pan. This was followed by 'verbal homage from a master of the Science of cookery to the master of its Art', wrote Mary Adams, in a postscript to Harben's obituary in *The Times* (*The Times*, 29 April 1970).

In 1950 Harben presented *Cookery Lesson* for the BBC. There were several one-off cookery shows in 1952–3, including one late in 1953 called *An Evening's Diversion of Elizabethan TV*, in which, instead of wearing his usual stout butcher's apron, he cooked in a costume that featured a white ruff, doublets, and hose. In 1956 he had another series, *What's Cooking?* Rationing ended in 1954; before that, it had been difficult even for television cooks to provision their programmes, and it was said that he had sometimes used his own rations to make the programme. Audiences were drawn by his professional-looking skill, his assurance, and his evident pleasure in preparing good food, as well by his clubbable personality.

Harben was not a fraud, like Fanny Cradock, who soon followed him on the television screen, or a mere entertainer, like so many later television cooks; but he had his own lighter moments. Television shows were, of course, live in these years. One well-attested story has him going to the oven to retrieve a dish and saying, 'Well, they're not quite ready yet. Goodbye everybody.' Asked why he'd finished the programme when there were still several minutes to go, he explained, 'It wouldn't have done any good. I forgot to switch on the oven' (bbc.co.uk/thenandnow/wac_snippets).

As a journalist Harben achieved an unusual stature for a writer of recipes. Along with Correlli Barnett and Katharine Whitehorn he wrote in the post-war *Women's Own*. According to Harry Diamond, the sub-editor who handled his copy, his recipes were 'eagerly awaited each week by countless breathless housewives'. Once Diamond had to cut 'three or four completely superfluous words' from a Harben recipe to make the copy fit the layout, and 'an irate Mr. Harben phoned to speak to the "stupid fucking idiot" who had ruthlessly reduced his recipe to unintelligible rubbish'. The editor consequently relieved Diamond of responsibility for the recipe column (www.geocities.com/henry_diamond).

In 1955 Harben was appointed 'cookery ambassador extraordinary' to the government, and even sent to America to praise British cooking. (This was an era before Britain had got its bad reputation for food and cooking, a time when an American publisher could still sell copies of Samuel Chamberlain's nearly 600-page 1963 gastronomic vade-mecum, *British Bouquet*.) His Penguin book, *Cooking* (1960), explained the subject from what was then thought to be a scientific angle. In his last years he lived at 81 Albion Gate, on the Bayswater Road in west London.

Harben died on 27 April 1970 at St Mary's Hospital, Harrow Road, Paddington, from cerebral softening due to cerebral atherosclerosis. His wife survived him. He was buried in Highgate cemetery.   PAUL LEVY

Sources *The Times* (29 April 1970); (25 May 1970) · *Daily Telegraph* (28 April 1970) · A. Barr and P. Levy, *The official foodie handbook* (1984) · C. Driver, *The British at table, 1940–1980* (1983) · www.lib.uea.ac.uk/lib/libinf/find/archives/pritchard/ppframe.htm, Dec 2001 · www.bbctv_ap.freeserve.co.uk/liztv, Dec 2001 · www.andmas.co.uk.television/television_5.htm, Dec 2001 · www.bbc.co.uk/thenandnow/wac_snippets, Dec 2001 · www.geocities.com/henry_diamond, Dec 2001 · M. Bateman, *Cooking people* (1966) · b. cert. · m. cert. · d. cert. · *CGPLA Eng. & Wales* (1970)
Likenesses B. Hardy, two photographs, 1753, Hult. Arch.
Wealth at death £1607: probate, 20 Aug 1970, *CGPLA Eng. & Wales*

Harberton. For this title name *see* Pomeroy, Florence Wallace, Viscountess Harberton (1843/4–1911).

Harbin, George (*c.*1665–1744), nonjuror and historical writer, was the only surviving son of John Harbin, merchant (*d.* 1673), of St Helen, Bishopsgate, London, and his wife, Mary. The family claimed descent from the Harbins of Newton Surmaville, near Yeovil, and George's three sisters all married Somerset gentry. Harbin entered Emmanuel College, Cambridge, in 1683, graduated BA in 1687, and migrated to Jesus College in 1688. He was ordained as chaplain to Francis Turner, bishop of Ely. On 10 June 1719 Harbin married Elizabeth (*bap.* 19 April 1685), the daughter of Edward Copley of Batley, Yorkshire. Nothing more is known of her, and neither she, nor any child, is mentioned in Harbin's will.

Harbin became a nonjuror at the revolution of 1688, and lived first at Newbottle in Northamptonshire, as chaplain to Colonel Sackville Tufton. In 1699 he entered the service of Thomas Thynne, first Viscount Weymouth, at the suggestion of Bishop Thomas Ken, on Bishop Turner's recommendation. His connection with the Thynne family continued until his death, though the act of 1702 for imposing the oath of abjuration disqualified him from acting as chaplain.

Harbin read widely during these years in English history and genealogy, on which he came to be reckoned among the foremost authorities of his day. He made voluminous copies of manuscripts held at Longleat House (where he lived for many years) and in the libraries of other gentlemen of his acquaintance. In 1710 he used this learning in *The English Constitution Fully Stated*, which attacked the near equation of *de facto* and *de jure* possession argued for in William Higden's *View of the English Constitution* (1709). A second work, *The Hereditary Right of the Crown of England Asserted*, appeared anonymously in 1713; Hilkiah Bedford was prosecuted and imprisoned for it, and Harbin's authorship was not generally known until many years later.

Harbin was a nonjuror of similar stamp to his friend Bishop Ken; he would not transfer allegiance from James II, but had no enthusiasm for the nonjurors' ecclesiastical separation, or the 'Cyprianic' theology of Henry Dodwell which underpinned it. He attended the parish church in

Newbottle after the revolution, and had no recorded contact with nonjurors' meetings in London during his later years, when he lived in the parish of St James's, Westminster. His will gives no hint of any nonjuring connection. Harbin died on 20 September 1744 at his house in King Street, Westminster, and was buried at St James's, Westminster, on 23 September.   JOHN FINDON

Sources Som. ARS, Harbin MSS, DD/HN [uncatalogued] · 'Letters of Rev. George Harbin to John and Margaret Bamfylde, 1719–44', ed. S. W. Rawlins, *Notes and Queries for Somerset and Dorset*, 25 (1948–50), 149–51, 175–8, 199–200, 216; 26 (1951), 225–6, 265–8, 285–7 · BL, Add. MSS 25945, fols. 1–3; 25946, fols. 109–11 · Nichols, *Lit. anecdotes*, 1.167–8, 202 · W. B. Bannerman, ed., *The registers of St Helen's, Bishopsgate, London*, Harleian Society, register section, 31 (1904), 41, 43–5, 319 · will, PRO, PROB 11/736, sig. 256 · *N&Q*, 8th ser., 1 (1892), 214 · BL, Add. MS 32096, fols. 11–38 · *Fifth report*, HMC, 4 (1876), ix, 309, 312–13, 319, 320 · E. H. Plumptre, *The life of Thomas Ken*, 2 (1889), 54, 107–8 · J. H. Overton, *The nonjurors: their lives, principles, and writings* (1902), 203–5 · parish register, Somerset, St Mary, 10 June 1719, GL [marriage] · parish register, Featherstone, Yorkshire, 19 April 1685, W. Yorks. AS, Wakefield [baptism] · Venn, *Alum. Cant.* · *London Evening-Post* (20 Sept 1744)
Archives BL, corresp., ecclesiastical and historical collections and papers, Add. MSS 29545–29547, 47192, 47893; St MS 769 · BL, state papers collected by Harbin, together with corresp. and papers, and later additions, Add. MSS 32091–32096, *passim* · Bodl. Oxf., notebooks of extracts from John Amstis's antiquarian and genealogical MSS; transcripts and papers · Som. ARS, extracts from the lost cartulary of Athelney Abbey; notebooks and papers | BL, letters to second earl of Oxford, loan 29 · BL, letters to Lord Oxford and others, Add. MS 70423 · Som. ARS, letters to Thomas Carew
Likenesses M. Dahl, oils, Longleat, Wiltshire · portrait, Harbin seat, Newton Surmaville, near Yeovil, Somerset; repro. in *Somerset and Dorset N&Q*, XXV (1950), facing p. 224
Wealth at death £400; plus books, plate, some jewellery, and chattels: will, PRO, PROB 11/736, sig. 256

Harbord, Edward, third Baron Suffield (1781–1835), politician, born on 10 November 1781, in Albemarle Street, London, was the third and youngest son of Harbord Harbord, first Baron Suffield, and his wife, Mary, daughter and coheir of Sir Ralph Assheton, bt, of Middleton, Lancashire. He was educated at Eton College and at Christ Church, Oxford, taking his MA on 23 June 1802. In dress as a young man he was a 'little recherché and fantastic, giving a false impression of effeminacy' (HoP, *Commons*). He was a cricketer, wrestler, and boxer, and was known for running a mile in five minutes comfortably. He sometimes raced for money against professionals. He was wont to bend a poker round his neck, on one occasion nearly throttling himself.

Harbord sat in the House of Commons as MP for Great Yarmouth from 1806 to 1812, and as MP for Shaftesbury in 1820–21. He usually supported the government. Castlereagh sent him to Portugal in 1808 on diplomatic business and invited him to become his private secretary; the offer was lost through delays. He was defeated as an independent candidate for Norwich in 1818, and in 1819, to the disgust of his family, he declared himself a Liberal at a public meeting held at Norwich to petition for an inquiry into the Peterloo massacre. In 1821 Harbord succeeded on his brother's death as third Baron Suffield, and in the House

of Lords supported liberal measures with much earnestness. He framed a bill for the better discipline of prisons, the chief clauses of which were adopted in the new law on the subject passed in 1824 (4 Geo. IV, c. 64); and he secured a relaxation of the game laws, and the abolition of spring guns. From 1822 onwards Suffield persistently, and almost single-handedly, advocated in the House of Lords the total abolition of the slave trade, and sat on numerous committees of inquiry appointed by the house.

On 19 September 1809 Harbord married Georgiana Venables-Vernon, daughter of George, second Baron Vernon; she brought him £90,000, Vernon House, and her family's jewels; they had two sons and a daughter; she died on 30 September 1824. He then married, on 12 September 1826, Emily (1799–1881), daughter of Evelyn Shirley of Eatington Hall, Warwickshire, with whom he had six sons and a daughter. Suffield lived much on his estates in Norfolk, where he was an active chairman of quarter sessions; the family seat was Gunton Park, near Norwich. He was a good landlord and allotted land to his cottagers. His love of athletics made him generally popular, and he established the Norfolk cricket club. He died at his London home, Vernon House in Park Place, on 6 July 1835, after falling from his horse on Constitution Hill; the accident occurred exactly at the place where Peel fell in 1850. He was buried at Gunton Park.

[ANON.], *rev.* H. C. G. MATTHEW

Sources R. M. Bacon, *Memoir of Baron Suffield* (1838) · GEC, *Peerage* · Lord Suffield, *My memories 1830–1913 by Lord Suffield* (1913?) · W. W. Vernon, *Recollections of seventy-two years* (1917) · *GM*, 2nd ser., 4 (1835), 317–20 · HoP, *Commons*
Archives Norfolk RO, corresp. and papers | W. Sussex RO, letters to duke of Richmond
Likenesses stipple, pubd 1823 (after A. Wivell), BM, NPG · F. Grant, group portrait, oils (*The Melton hunt going to draw the Ram's Head cover*), Stratfield Saye, Hampshire · S. W. Reynolds, mezzotint (after H. Edridge), BM · portrait, repro. in Lord Suffield, *My memories 1830–1913*, 28

Harbord, William (1635–1692), politician and diplomat, was born on 25 April 1635, the second son of Sir Charles Harbord (1596–1679), second baronet, of Charing Cross and Stanninghall, Norfolk, and his second wife, Mary (*d.* 1666), daughter of Jan van Aelst of Sandwich, Kent. On 24 June 1651 Harbord was given a pass to travel to the Netherlands with his mother and sister, and on 14 October 1651 he enrolled at the University of Leiden. On 4 May 1655 entered the Middle Temple, London, but he did not stay long, for on 29 May 1656 he received a pass to travel abroad. This time he visited the Levant. Harbord had returned to England by August 1660 when he was appointed to minor local office. In February 1661 Harbord succeeded the deceased Thomas Gewen as auditor of the duchy of Cornwall, and at the general election held in April he entered parliament for Dartmouth. On 26 July 1661 he was licensed to marry Mary (*b.* 1638/9, *d.* in or before 1678), daughter and coheir of Arthur Duck DCL, of North Cadbury, Somerset. They had three daughters, one of whom, Margaret (*d.* 1698), married Robert *King, second Baron Kingston. In June 1662 Harbord secured the reversion of his father's office of surveyor-general of crown lands.

The early part of Harbord's parliamentary career saw him in the shadow of his father, who was a very active member of the Cavalier Parliament (1661–79). Harbord was seen as a court supporter in 1664, and in 1670 he was described as 'under-surveyor, and a court contriver to cheat the king of his lands' (Cruickshanks). The latter may have been a reference to Harbord's estate at Grafton Park, Northamptonshire, where he was resident. Anti-popery was always a significant theme in Harbord's parliamentary career. He was a teller on 14 February 1673 in favour of a joint address of Lords and Commons against the suspending power, and spoke on 28 February 1673 in favour of removing papists from military office. On 27 October 1673 he attacked Edward Seymour as 'an unfit person to be Speaker' (Grey, 2.188). Despite making enemies of Seymour and the lord treasurer, Thomas Osborne, Viscount Latimer (soon to be earl of Danby), in December 1673 he was appointed 'principal' secretary to the lord lieutenant of Ireland, Arthur Capel, first earl of Essex. Consequently on 20 December he was ordered to be sworn an Irish privy councillor. He seems to have owed his advancement in part to Henry Bennet, first earl of Arlington, and on 20 January 1674 was a teller against a motion for an address to the king requesting Arlington's dismissal from office. Harbord was to spend much of his time in England watching Essex's back at court in case Richard Jones, earl of Ranelagh, or James Butler, first duke of Ormond, should attempt to undermine his position. Despite Danby's enmity, on 3 May 1675 Harbord declined to support the fifth article of impeachment against the lord treasurer which related to the management of Irish affairs. However, he acted as a teller on 6 May 1675 in favour of further proceedings against John Maitland, duke of Lauderdale. Although nominally a courtier, at this juncture he was described by Danby's supporter Sir Richard Wiseman as a man who 'disserves the king' (Cruickshanks).

Harbord lost his Irish post upon the recall of Essex in May 1677. The tenor of Harbord's parliamentary speeches was now critical of France and in favour of an alliance with the Dutch. Thus on 25 May 1677 he opined that 'England is not safe but by alliance with the Dutch' (Cruickshanks). His opposition to the court saw Anthony Ashley Cooper, first earl of Shaftesbury, account him 'worthy' in his parliamentary assessment in 1677. His first wife having died, Harbord's links to the opposition to the court were enhanced on 21 February 1678 by his marriage to Catherine (d. 1702), daughter of Edward Russell and niece of William Russell, fifth earl of Bedford. Her brother was Edward *Russell, earl of Orford. They had one daughter. Marriage certainly did not temper his criticism of the government and the king's advisers. On 18 June 1678 he supported a test against corruption, suggesting that 'whoever attempts the enslaving and making the legislative power subservient to any particular subject is [guilty of] the greatest crime that can be' (Grey, 6.104–5).

Harbord was able to assist in the return to the Commons of Ralph Montagu, in a by-election for Northampton on 10 November 1678. Montagu was thus able to shelter under parliamentary privilege when he sought to destroy Danby's political career by revealing his negotiations with the French. Harbord served as the chair of the committee put in charge of Montagu's papers before they were revealed to the Commons and, as Barillon later put it, he 'contributed greatly to the ruin of the earl of Danby' (Dalrymple, 1.382). Harbord was rewarded with 500 guineas for assisting Barillon.

Harbord appears to have taken fright following the prorogation of parliament in December 1678, reportedly 'endeavouring to have gone beyond sea, so afraid he is of being taken' (*Sixth Report*, HMC, 389), and failing that taking refuge with his brother John at Gunton in Norfolk. However, he seems to have recovered his nerve with the dissolution of the Cavalier Parliament, and he was returned on 24 February 1679 for Thetford. In the new parliament he was very active, promoting the investigation of the Popish Plot and measures against popery, particularly the banishment of papists from London. However, he voted against the Exclusion Bill. Harbord chaired the committee inquiring into the navy, and was especially severe on Anthony Deane and Samuel Pepys, who were sent to the Tower. He may have had designs on Pepys's job as his old political associate, Sir Henry Capel (brother of Essex), was appointed first lord of the Admiralty in May 1679.

In June 1679 Harbord told Henry Sidney, a confidant of William, prince of Orange (afterwards William III of England), that for the good of the nation the prince should be declared 'protector, in case the succession fell into the hands of a Roman catholic prince' (*Diary of … Sidney*, 1.8). Following the dissolution of parliament Harbord was again returned for Thetford on 15 August 1679, aided by a generous bequest to the town from his father who had died in May. In July 1680 Barillon included Harbord in a list of the most considerable MPs, and by the time the parliament met in October 1680 Harbord had been converted to exclusion. Indeed, on 2 November 1680 Harbord moved for leave to bring in an exclusion bill, and in the debate on 18 December following the king's speech in which he insisted on the legal descent of the crown, Harbord responded by saying that 'without the bill, and a power to assert that bill, all will signify nothing' (*Beaufort MSS*, 99), before proposing limitations on royal power in addition to exclusion. In January 1681 he was at the forefront of attacks on George Savile, earl of Halifax, the leading exponent of limitations as an alternative policy to exclusion.

In the 1681 election Harbord was chosen for both Thetford and Launceston, choosing to sit for Thetford. After the dissolution of the Oxford parliament in March 1681, Harbord appears to have considered moving his family to Holland 'for a year or two' (*Diary of … Sidney*, 2.23–4). After the Rye House plot he was accused by a member of Thetford corporation of threatening to seize the king in 1681, and on 17 July 1683 the Northamptonshire grand jury presented him among those they felt to be 'dissatisfied and dangerous' to the government (Cruickshanks). In August Harbord complained to Sir Leoline Jenkins, secretary of state, about the grand jury's presentation and the two searches which had been made for arms at his home. He explained that he needed the few arms he had to undertake his duties as surveyor-general, and Jenkins duly ordered them to be restored to him.

After the accession of James II, Harbord fled to the Netherlands. He was ordered to return in January 1686, and in February the government took steps to try to remove him from the auditor's office in Cornwall. In the summer he was noted as attending the siege of Buda, and in July he received the thanks of Halifax for rendering his son George assistance after he had been wounded during that campaign. In October 1686 Harbord was reported to have returned to England, but 'not finding a reception to his mind' (*Seventh Report*, HMC, 500) he returned to Holland. Another summons ordering Harbord to 'set aside all excuses' and return (*CSP dom.*, *1687–9*, 192) was issued on 30 April 1688, but his only response was to offer to give up his office of surveyor-general in return for the withdrawal of the warrant.

Harbord did not return to England until he landed as part of William of Orange's invasion fleet. In November 1688 he was named one of three commissioners for collecting crown revenues in the west of England. On 7 December Henry Hyde, second earl of Clarendon, remarked upon Harbord's animosity to James II, noting that Harbord had said 'he had drawn his sword against the king; that he had no need of his pardon; but they would bring the king to ask pardon of them, for the wrongs he had done' (*Correspondence*, 2.219). When William's supporters met on 8 December at The Bear inn to decide how to answer James II's commissioners, Harbord argued for the cancellation of the writs issued by the king for calling a parliament, presumably because he felt unsure of his own election. Harbord should not have worried as he was returned to the Convention for Launceston, Thetford, and Scarborough, choosing to sit for the Cornish seat.

In the Convention, Harbord was a supporter of William's claims to the throne, telling on 5 February 1689 against the Commons accepting an amendment from the Lords which would have denied that the throne was 'vacant'. He was also an exponent of settling the government as quickly as possible, giving priority to this over the promulgation of a bill of rights. Security for the kingdom lay with voting supply and organizing an army; the government could be held to account through control of the purse, rather than legislating on the constitution, which could be very time-consuming. He was also keen to secure the exception from the Indemnity Bill of those deemed responsible for advising James II, such as Robert Spencer, second earl of Sunderland. Harbord was named a privy councillor on 8 March 1689 and that month was also appointed paymaster of the forces in Ireland. Halifax later remarked that 'at first the K[ing] took Mr Harbord for an extraordinary man of business, but a few months after his being in England, he was undeceived' (Foxcroft, 2.226). The disillusionment of William III had much to do with the travails of the Irish campaign, and the subsequent accusations that Harbord feathered his own nest while

failing in his duty to supply the troops with money. Frederick Schomberg, first duke of Schomberg, in command in Ireland, was particularly critical of Harbord's conduct, though Harbord survived a critical vote against him in the Commons in July 1689. Perhaps in response to this criticism, Harbord went to Ireland in September 1689, and stayed until December. Following his departure Schomberg was still complaining of a shortage of funds and of Harbord's non-existent volunteer company.

Harbord was re-elected for Launceston in 1690. In March he was removed as Irish paymaster. In the Commons he continued a firm supporter of the government, even to the extent that in May 1690 he defended the marquess of Carmarthen (formerly Danby), who had become a leading minister to William III. On 16 July 1690 Harbord left England *en route* for the United Provinces as ambassador, a mission of some delicacy given the naval defeat at Beachy Head and the need to gain further naval assistance from the Dutch. He returned about 26 August 1690.

In November 1691 Harbord was made vice-treasurer of Ireland, no doubt as a sweetener for his other important appointment as ambassador to Turkey. He was instructed to travel by way of Vienna (he was there in February 1692) to consult the holy Roman emperor, Leopold I, about mediating in the war with Turkey. He never reached his destination, dying at Belgrade on 31 July 1692. In his will of 20 November 1691 he referred to his wife's 'worthy behaviour to me in my many troubles', and asked her to 'keep my house and gardens at Grafton Park in reasonable good repair' (PRO, PROB 11/232r–235r). He gave his daughter from his second marriage, Letitia, a portion of £6000. Most of his personal estate he left to be divided among his four daughters, in such a manner as to protect it from the use of their respective husbands.   STUART HANDLEY

Sources E. Cruickshanks, 'Harbord, William', HoP, *Commons, 1660–90* • S. N. Handley, 'Harbord, William', HoP, *Commons, 1690–1715* • A. Grey, ed., *Debates of the House of Commons, from the year 1667 to the year 1694*, 10 vols. (1763), vols. 2–10 • will, PRO, PROB 11/412, fols. 232r–235r • H. Horwitz, *Parliament, policy and politics in the reign of William III* (1977), 6–86 • O. Airy, ed., *Essex papers*, CS, new ser., 47 (1890), 141–323 • D. B. Horn, ed., *British diplomatic representatives, 1689–1789*, CS, 3rd ser., 46 (1932), 151, 155 • J. Dalrymple, *Memoirs of Great Britain and Ireland*, new edn, 3 vols. (1790), 1.338, 358, 381–2; 2.177–80 • G. Baker, *The history and antiquities of the county of Northampton*, 2 (1836–41), 171–2 • M. J. Knights, *Politics and opinion in crisis, 1678–81* (1994), 26–138 • A. Browning, *Thomas Osborne, earl of Danby and duke of Leeds, 1632–1712*, 3 vols. (1944–51), vol. 1, pp. 303–6; vol. 2, pp. 54–6, 174; vol. 3, pp. 43–178 • R. Beddard, ed., *A kingdom without a king: the journal of the provisional government in the revolution of 1688* (1988), 21–7 • *The manuscripts of the duke of Beaufort ... the earl of Donoughmore*, HMC, 27 (1891), 99 • *Sixth report*, HMC, 5 (1877–8), 389 • *Seventh report*, HMC, 6 (1879), 500 [Verney MSS] • W. Scott, ed., *A collection of scarce and valuable tracts ... Lord Somers*, 2nd edn, 13 vols. (1809–15), 8.409 • *The correspondence of Henry Hyde, earl of Clarendon, and of his brother Lawrence Hyde, earl of Rochester*, ed. S. W. Singer, 2 (1828), 219–39 • *Diary of the times of Charles the Second by the Hon. Henry Sidney*, 2 vols. (1843), 1.8, 18, 28, 75–81; 2.23–4 • *The life and letters of Sir George Savile ... first marquis of Halifax*, ed. H. C. Foxcroft, 2 vols. (1898), 1.471; 2.226 • *CSP dom.*, *1687–9*, 192

Archives BL, letters to Lord Essex, Stowe MSS 204–212, *passim* • SOAS, corresp. with Lord Paget

Harborne, William (*c*.1542–1617), merchant and diplomat, was probably born at Great Yarmouth, Norfolk, the second son of William Harborne (*d.* 1588), administrator, of Great Yarmouth, and his wife, Joan Piers, or Pearce (*fl.* 1520–1590). Harborne senior, originally from Shrewsbury, Shropshire, became a leading citizen of Great Yarmouth, was elected bailiff in 1557 and 1572, and was initially chosen as MP for the borough in 1575 but the election was contested and another candidate got the seat. He probably had trading interests and may have invested heavily in one of his second son's commercial ventures in the Ottoman empire, the failure of which reduced him to penury in 1582 (Skilliter, 34–5, 169–70). William Harborne's elder brother, Thomas Harborne, travelled with him on at least one journey, returning from Constantinople in 1579 as courier of the first official letter from Murad III to Elizabeth I. His younger brother Piers Harborne may also have been a merchant, and was in Portugal about 1579 in contact with Dom Antonio, unsuccessful claimant to the Portuguese throne after the death of Sebastian.

Early career, 1559–1581 Harborne himself probably entered the service of the London merchant Edward Osborne about 1559 and travelled abroad first as the latter's factor and later on his own account. In 1577 he was listed as one of the sixty principal members of the newly incorporated Spanish Company. English traders who met him on the island of Chios in 1581 considered him a rich London merchant and gentleman; his personal prosperity was maintained by involvement in trade throughout his life, despite the unusual expenses of his several years' residence in Constantinople.

English commercial interest during the 1570s in establishing regular trade in the Ottoman empire was complemented by the desire of Sir Francis Walsingham, principal secretary, to explore the diplomatic advantages of having an official, potentially anti-Spanish, presence there. On Osborne's recommendation Harborne was sent as agent to Constantinople to seek from the sultan, Murad III, a guarantee of safe conduct for English traders, to enable them to sail under their own flag rather than that of France, the only other Western nation with appropriate trading privileges. Leaving London in July 1578, he took the overland route via Hamburg, Poland, and the Danubian principalities and arrived in Constantinople on 28 October. This was Harborne's preferred route for subsequent journeys (and for those of his individual couriers and agents), since it helped maintain good Anglo-Polish relations and also avoided the suspicions and hostility of the Venetians and Spanish which would inevitably have been raised by a sea voyage through the Mediterranean. As the principal English trading commodities of tin, lead, woollen cloth, and other military-related items were particularly welcome to the Ottomans after the outbreak of war with Iran in the summer of 1578, Harborne was immediately successful in negotiating individual trade concessions for Osborne, Richard Staper, and himself, confirmed in Murad's grant of privileges in March 1579, and in the opening of friendly diplomatic correspondence between the sultan and Elizabeth. The subsequent 'unilateral charter of privileges to the English nation' granted by Murad in May 1580 formed the basis of Anglo-Ottoman relations and trade capitulations for the next 300 years. English merchants generally were guaranteed freedom of passage for themselves, their servants, and their goods, by land or by sea, through territories held or controlled by the Ottomans, on condition that they 'mind their own business and be occupied with their ordinary duties'. Englishmen were not to be taken prisoner or enslaved; English ships in distress at sea should be assisted. The English trading colonies would be subject to their own regulations as decreed by the ambassador, so long as no disorder ensued; on all matters of trade or other relations with Muslims, the English would be subject to the authority of the kadi's court acting in all fairness. Englishmen would not be subject to the Ottoman poll tax and were entitled to appoint their own interpreters; none would be held responsible for the debts of other Englishmen and their goods would not be seized after death (Skilliter, 86–9). In July 1581 Harborne departed for London, his mission apparently accomplished.

Ambassador in Turkey, 1581–1583 On 11 September 1581 Elizabeth granted the first charter for the newly formed Turkey Company. Although this venture was possible only as a result of Harborne's negotiations in Constantinople, he himself is not listed as one of the twelve London merchants granted a seven-year monopoly of the Turkish trade, possibly because he was absent from London when the company was being formed, possibly because of the *Bark Roe* incident. He was, however, too prominent a figure to be ignored for long. Osborne, as head of the new company, petitioned the queen early in 1582 to send a permanent representative to Constantinople to secure the sultan's recognition of the Turkey Company and to look after the interests of the increased numbers of English traders expected there. On 20 November 1582, after considerable debate over the propriety of establishing such a resident in a non-Christian state and more particularly over who to appoint (the queen or the company was to support him financially), Harborne was named ambassador, at the company's expense. Departing from London almost immediately and this time travelling openly by the Mediterranean sea route in the company's ship *Susan*, he reached Constantinople on 29 March 1583 and was received in audience by the sultan on 24 April.

For the next five years Harborne played a dual role as Elizabeth's 'Orator, Messenger, Deputie and Agent' to the sultan and as representative of the Turkey Company. His immediate commission was to appoint consuls in the main Ottoman trading ports to oversee English interests. On 25 April he appointed Harvie Millers as consul in Alexandria and Cairo, and on 30 June Richard Forster as consul in Syria, to be based on the coast at Tripoli. His organization of the company's local agents was extended by the appointment on 30 March 1585 of John Tipton as consul at Algiers, Tunis, and Tripoli (in north Africa). Consulates may also have been established on Chios and at Patras in the Morea. Harborne was also charged with 'enact[ing] lawes and statutes' for regulation of traders' behaviour *vis-à-vis* the Ottoman authorities and fellow trading nations, and for disciplining those who failed to observe these rules and thus jeopardized the English privileges generally (Hakluyt, 5.223–4). This point was particularly important since the harm that could be done to English interests by undisciplined traders had already been seen in the *Bark Roe* incident in 1581. Having traded her cargo of cloths and metals in Livorno, Malta, and Chios (and by chance meeting Harborne there), this London-based ship engaged in a series of piratical acts which culminated in the seizure of two Greek ships, belonging to subjects of the sultan and flying Christian flags. Fearing punishment in England for piracy and for disturbing diplomatic negotiations with the Ottomans, the crew of the *Bark Roe* took refuge on Malta, where the knights of St John used the ship for carrying grain and its crew variously as mariners and soldiers before submitting several of them to the Maltese inquisition in July and August 1581. Added to the anti-Christian act of piracy were accusations of English spying in preparation for a joint Anglo-Ottoman attack on Malta, a not unreasonable fear given the long-standing enmity between the Ottomans and the knights and the unsuccessful Ottoman siege of Malta in 1565. The depositions made to the Maltese inquisition by the crew of the *Bark Roe* were read to implicate Harborne, and through him Elizabeth. Murad also had grounds to doubt English sincerity in the light of the attack on his Greek subjects, who had appealed to Constantinople for redress. The fact that the *Bark Roe* had been able to sail from Chios in March 1581 only after Harborne's personal intervention with the Jewish customs farmer detaining the ship, in which he used the new English capitulations to prove the ship's right to sail in Ottoman waters under its own flag, appeared to confirm these doubts. Harborne thus found himself suspect on all sides. He was arrested by the Ottoman authorities and held responsible for reimbursement of the debt owed the Greek shipowners. This ran counter to the stipulations about responsibility for the debts of others in the trade capitulations of May 1580, but the Ottomans argued that as Harborne remained only an 'agent', and the capitulations were still to be ratified by the accrediting of a full ambassador, the agreement was not yet in force. Ironically, Harborne had no option but to seek the protection of the rival French ambassador, whose capitulations were fully ratified, in order to secure his own release. He then wrote an abject letter of explanation and exoneration to Lord Burghley describing 'the intollerable griefe of minde which thees pirattes have caused in me' and pleading for Burghley's favourable intercession with the queen (Skilliter, 154–8).

The *Bark Roe* incident exemplifies the difficulties and pitfalls facing Harborne in his isolated role. It is testimony to his professional competence, wide experience, and strength of character that despite this set-back he was able to return to Constantinople as full ambassador in 1583, ratify the capitulations, organize the consular system, and maintain good standing in the Ottoman capital in the years following. This was achieved despite continuing French, Venetian, and Spanish attempts to discredit him in Constantinople and despite the recurrent problems of English ships falling foul of Ottoman authorities, particularly on the north African coast. Ransoming prisoners was a regular task.

Life in Turkey and writings, 1583–1617 A further complication was Harborne's dual role as servant of both queen and company. Although the company had eventually agreed to support him financially with a salary of £200 per annum, this was primarily in his capacity as their representative and they were loath to underwrite the extra present giving necessitated by his diplomatic role. Harborne complained regularly of insufficient support and irregular payment, asserting that of the £1200 due to him for his service in Constantinople, only £400 had actually been paid while he was there. The shortfall was presumably met from his own resources, as he continued to participate in trading ventures. However, other figures from a balance drawn up in August 1589 after his return from Constantinople itemize Harborne's expenditure during his embassy and suggest that the company did cover £13,246 of the total of £15,341 incurred, the remaining £2095 being met by an allowance from the sultan. One-third of these expenses appear directly connected with his attendance at court in an ambassadorial capacity; ransoming captives cost a further £1203, interpreter's wages £1028, food and housekeeping £4496 (Rawlinson, 15). Harborne's successor as ambassador, Edward Barton, also complained vehemently about insufficient financial support.

On his return to Constantinople in spring 1583 Harborne took up residence at a house he called Rapamat (a corruption of Ahmet) on the Bosphorus in the Findikli area near the arsenal at Tophane. Known to the Ottomans as 'the Lutheran ambassador', he was clearly happy to keep a discreet distance from the other Catholic European communities up the hill in Pera. Harborne's household included his secretary Barton, who accompanied him to Constantinople in 1583, his assistant John Sanderson who arrived in 1585, a locally recruited interpreter, several domestic servants, and a guard escort of at least two janizaries.

After departing from Constantinople in August 1588, leaving Barton as agent in his stead, Harborne advised the Turkey Company and the queen on the need to maintain unbroken diplomatic representation in the Ottoman capital and pressed for Barton to be given full ambassadorial status. He favoured amalgamating the Turkey and Venice Companies into the Levant Company in January 1592, and is named in the letters patent as one of the new company's principal merchants. Meanwhile he had settled at Mundham, Norfolk, and became a freeman of Great Yarmouth in 1591. He wrote an account of his time in Constantinople that was published by Richard Hakluyt in his *Principall Navigations, Voyages and Discoveries of the English Nation* (1589). An unpublished account of these years, 'The relation of my tenn yeares forraine travelle', is preserved among the Lansdowne and Tanner manuscripts. On 16

September 1589 he married Elizabeth, daughter of Anthony Drury of Besthorpe, Norfolk, and his wife. They had several children. He died on 6 November 1617 at Mundham and was buried there.

CHRISTINE WOODHEAD

Sources S. A. Skilliter, *William Harborne and the trade with Turkey, 1578–1582: a documentary study of the first Anglo-Ottoman relations* (1977) · R. Hakluyt, *The principal navigations, voyages, traffiques and discoveries of the English nation*, 2nd edn, 3 vols. (1598–1600); repr. 12 vols., Hakluyt Society, extra ser., 1–12 (1903–5), vols. 5–6 · state papers, Turkey, PRO, SP 97/1 · H. G. Rawlinson, 'The embassy of William Harborne to Constantinople, 1583–8', *TRHS*, 4th ser., 5 (1922), 1–27 · A. C. Wood, *A history of the Levant Company* (1935); repr. (1964) · E. S. de Beer, 'William Harborne', *BIHR*, 19 (1941–3), 160–62 · *DNB*

Archives Bodl. Oxf., corresp. and papers | BL, Lansdowne MSS · Bodl. Oxf., Tanner MSS

Harbottle, Michael Neale (1917–1997), army officer and peace campaigner, was born on 7 February 1917 at 57 Beach Road, Littlehampton, Sussex, the son of Captain Thomas Cecil Benfield Harbottle, Royal Navy officer, and his wife, Kathleen Millicent Kent. He was educated at Marlborough College (1930–35) and the Royal Military College, Sandhurst (1935–7), and commissioned into the Oxfordshire and Buckinghamshire light infantry in 1937. On 1 August 1940 (by then a captain) he married Alison Jean (*b.* 1917/18), daughter of Harold Thomas Humfress, chief engineer in the Air Ministry. They had a son and a daughter.

Harbottle saw war service as a company commander in Italy, where he received a mention in dispatches and was wounded, losing two fingers. Despite this he played cricket for the army until 1959, captaining the team that year. During the 1950s he served in the UK and was appointed OBE in 1959 for his work as GSO1, south-west district. He commanded the 1st battalion, Royal Green Jackets, as demonstration battalion at Warminster from 1959 to 1962. From 1962 to 1964 he was garrison commander in Aden, responsible for security at a time when British rule was continuously under challenge from local dissidents, and he was promoted brigadier. He commanded 129th infantry brigade (TA) at Oxford from 1964 to 1966.

From 1966 to 1968 Harbottle was chief of staff to General Martola, commander of the United Nations peacekeeping force in Cyprus (UNFICYP). The republic of Cyprus had become an independent state in 1960. At the end of 1963 tension between the Greek and Turkish communities turned to violence. In March 1964, at the request of the British and Cypriot authorities, UNFICYP was set up with a mandate to 'use its best efforts to avoid a recurrence of the fighting' and contribute to 'a return to normal conditions'. This type of operation had not been provided for in the United Nations (UN) charter, so the rules had to be improvised. The main features later became well known: the consent of parties to the conflict; impartiality; and use of weapons by the UN only in self-defence. These were the ingredients of classical peacekeeping later found effective in Cambodia, Namibia, and Mozambique. Harbottle was among the first to see this type of operation in a positive light. When his tour of duty expired in 1968 the

secretary-general of the UN, U Thant, asked for it to be extended. The Ministry of Defence declined, and Harbottle retired at the early age of fifty-one. He took the post of chief security officer for the British-owned mining subsidiary of the Consolidated African Selection Trust in Sierra Leone. Carrying a consignment of diamonds, he was set upon by armed bandits at Freetown airport and robbed of £1.5 million worth of stones. Acting under the implausible pretext that the company had set up its own hijack, the Sierra Leonean government expelled Harbottle and two other British employees.

His first marriage having ended in divorce, on 5 August 1972 Harbottle married Eirwen Helen Simonds (who had already changed her name to Harbottle), secretary, and daughter of Hugh Llewellyn Jones, banker. Harbottle acquired two stepdaughters to join the two children of his first marriage. He spent the 1970s writing and lecturing about United Nations peacekeeping. He was not the first in this field; Rosalyn Higgins had brought out a book in 1969, and in 1970 the International Peace Academy had been set up in New York under General Indar Jit Rikhye, former military adviser to the UN secretary-general. But Harbottle's work came as a revelation, particularly to the military. *The Impartial Soldier* (1970) dealt with his tour in UNFICYP and *The Blue Berets* (1971) assessed the five main operations going on at that time. He had worked with General Rikhye over Cyprus and was a vice-president of the International Peace Academy from 1971 to 1973. From 1974 to 1979 he was a visiting lecturer at the School of Peace Studies, Bradford University. During this period he brought out *The Thin Blue Line: International Peacekeeping and its Future* (1974) and *The Knaves of Diamonds* (1976), the latter describing his experiences in Sierra Leone. In 1978 he acted as collator of *The Peacekeeper's Handbook*, a definitive work which the UN issued to more than seventy countries as an instruction manual.

During the 1980s Harbottle's work took a disconcerting turn. From 1980 to 1982 he was general secretary of the World Disarmament Campaign, founded by Lord Noel-Baker and Lord Brockway. In 1981 he was involved in setting up Generals for Peace and Disarmament, a mixed group of retired admirals and generals, four from Greece, two from Portugal, two from West Germany (one of whom, Gerd Bastian, later shot himself and his lover, Petra Kelly, the Green Party leader, in apparent disillusionment), and one each from France, Italy, the Netherlands, and Norway. No British general joined. This group protested at NATO's deploying cruise missiles in Britain and Pershing II missiles in Germany. In conjunction with some Warsaw pact retired generals they held a conference in Vienna in 1984, of which the results were published that year as *The Arms Race to Armageddon*. Lords Chalfont and Blaker produced evidence of 'a series of direct links running from the Generals for Peace at the bottom to the Politburo at the top' (*Daily Telegraph*), and the book did indeed follow the Soviet line closely in places. In 1983 Michael and Eirwen Harbottle set up their own organization, the Centre for International Peacebuilding, based in their home in Chipping Norton, Oxfordshire, and after the collapse of the Soviet Union the generals' group became the Worldwide Consultative Association of Retired Generals and Admirals. Harbottle's 1991 monograph *What is Proper Soldiering?* became required reading at staff colleges. More international meetings followed, and in 1996 a statement was issued through the centre signed by some sixty-two officers, including three former supreme allied commanders in Europe, calling for the elimination of nuclear weapons.

Harbottle was tall, handsome, athletic, brave, and an excellent staff officer. He wrote well and his great achievement was to make United Nations peacekeeping recognized as a valuable military role in its own right. Later he and his wife became tireless warriors for peace, but in this endeavour their efforts were regarded by many as sometimes misdirected. He died on 30 April 1997 at the John Radcliffe Hospital, Oxford, of an intracerebral haemorrhage. He was survived by his second wife, Eirwen, his two stepdaughters, and the two children of his first marriage.

HUGH BEACH

Sources *The Times* (7 May 1997) · *The Independent* (14 May 1997); (28 May 1997) · *The Royal Green Jackets Chronicle* (1997) · Major-General J. Lunt, memorial address at St James's Piccadilly, 8 July 1997 [extract pubd in *The Royal Green Jackets Chronicle* (1997), 218–19] · *Daily Telegraph* (25 Sept 1984) · R. Higgins, *Middle East* (1969), vol. 1 of *UN peacekeeping documents and commentary* · www.un.org/Depts/dpko/missions/unficyp/facts.html [UNFICYP facts and figures] · *WW* (1989) · b. cert. · two m. certs. · d. cert.

Archives Bodl. Oxf., papers relating to peace-keeping duties with the UN in Cyprus · King's Lond., Liddell Hart C., corresp. and papers | SOUND BL NSA, current affairs recording

Likenesses photograph, 1966, repro. in *The Independent* (14 May 1997) · photograph, 1968, repro. in *The Times*

Wealth at death £185,000: probate, 12 Aug 1997, *CGPLA Eng. & Wales*

Harbutt, William (1844–1921), inventor of Plasticine and art teacher, was born on 13 February 1844 in North Shields,

Northumberland, the seventh of the eight children of Thomas Harbutt (*b.* 1803), a galvanizer, and his wife, Elizabeth Whitehouse Jefcoate (*b.* 1804). Details of his early education are unknown, but later he studied at the National Art Training School, South Kensington, London, where he obtained a medal and several diplomas and became an associate of the Royal College of Art.

In 1874 Harbutt became head of the Bath School of Art, but he left in 1877 after a dispute with the ruling committee. He then worked as a peripatetic art teacher and opened his own school, the Paragon Art Studio, at 15 Bladud Buildings, The Paragon, Bath, where he taught painting and modelling. His wife, Elizabeth (Bessie; 1846–1930), daughter of Owen Cambridge, bailiff, of Wimpole, Cambridgeshire, whom he married on 8 August 1876, was also an artist and teacher at the school. Of their seven children, one died in infancy, but the surviving three sons and three daughters all later worked in the family business. After leaving Bladud Buildings the Harbutts moved to Hartley House, Belvedere, Lansdown, Bath, where Harbutt, who had found that the clay used for students' sculptures was messy and dried out too quickly, first experimented with his modelling material. He then rented 15 Alfred Street, where in 1897 he began small-scale manufacture of the material, which he named Plasticine, in the basement. After experiments with mixing various ingredients he discovered a more suitable material, which consisted of calcium salts, petroleum jelly, and long-chain aliphatic acids, combined with whiting and perfume. After mixing, the material was rolled out with a garden roller and allowed to mature. It was then cut up and packed into boxes at his new studio and annex at 22 Milsom Street. At first all Plasticine was grey, but pigments were added later to produce a range of bright colours. In 1900 a box sold at 2*s*. 6*d*. and contained Plasticine in four colours, a tool, and

William Harbutt (1844–1921), by unknown photographer [with his wife, Elizabeth (Bessie) Cambridge, and their family]

a modelling frame. To promote the product Harbutt wrote *Harbutt's Plastic Method, and the Use of Plasticine …* (1897), and later he produced further publications on the subject.

'Plasticine' was registered as a trade mark in 1899 and won various awards, including gold medals at exhibitions in Birmingham and Weston-super-Mare (both 1899) and Bath (1900). As it was clean, pliable, and easy to use, it quickly became successful, and Harbutt purchased an old house and adjoining flour mill in the High Street of Bathampton, Wiltshire, where large-scale commercial production commenced on 1 May 1900. In 1912 Harbutt's Plasticine became a limited company and the product eventually achieved worldwide distribution. The company also marketed Playwax and other inventions by Harbutt. Many schools used Plasticine for sculpture, nature study, geometrical modelling, and map making; and architects and engineers liked it as well. During the First World War Plasticine modelling provided excellent therapy for convalescing soldiers.

Harbutt was a kind and generous man and a good employer, sometimes extending factory lunch hours for summer cricket matches or winter ice-skating. He was a non-smoker and teetotaller, and strongly against vaccination and vivisection. An early accident had made him lame, but he coped well with this minor disability. As a regular churchgoer he joined the Bath New Church Society in 1880, becoming president in 1905. He served as a councillor on the Bath rural district council and board of guardians, was chairman of the Bathampton parish council for many years, and supported several local societies.

Harbutt was passionately enthusiastic about his product. Indeed he constantly promoted Plasticine, and while on a business trip to the USA he caught a chill, and died of pneumonia in New York on 1 June 1921. His body was returned to England and buried in the churchyard of St Nicholas, Bathampton. He was survived by his wife. Harbutt's Plasticine has given pleasure to generations of children, and its use for the Wallace and Gromit characters in Nick Park's award-winning animated films is now well known.   CHRISTOPHER F. LINDSEY

Sources *Bath Herald* (2 June 1921) · *Bath and Wilts Chronicle* (2 June 1921) · *New Church Herald* (2 July 1921) · *The Plasticine people, 1897 to 1972: an account of the first seventy-five years*, Harbutt's Plasticine, Ltd. (privately printed, York, 1972) · 'Plasticine', *GM*, 20 (1900), 5042–4 · T. Harbutt and D. Dooley, 'What is Plasticine? When and by whom was it invented?', *N&Q*, 236 (1991), 157 · W. Harbutt, *Harbutt's plastic method, and the use of plasticine in the arts of writing, drawing, and modelling in educational work* (1897) · Glenavon, 'Art in the home', *Bath and County Graphic* (Nov 1900), 75–6 · private information (2004) · trade mark registry (Cardiff) · *Appendix to the minutes of the one hundred and fourteenth conference [of the New Church]* (1921), 67 [obit.] · C. A. Bell-Knight, *Harbutt's Plasticine, 1897–1983: a survey* (1983) · 'Health resorts, Bath', *GM*, 12 (1896), 1709 · A. Franks, 'Fame in slow motion', *Times Magazine* (2 April 1994) · m. cert. · b. cert.
Archives NRA, priv. coll., MSS | Bell-Knight Trust, MSS · Museum of Advertising and Packaging, Gloucester, Robert Opie collection, example of packaging
Likenesses E. W. Smith, bronze bust, 1911, Victoria Art Gallery, Bath · E. Cambridge-Harbutt, miniature, 1923, Victoria Art Gallery, Bath · photograph, repro. in *Gentleman's Journal*, 20 (1 Oct 1900) · photograph, repro. in Glenavon, 'Art in the home' · photographs, repro. in *Plasticine people*, frontispiece · photographs, priv. coll. [*see illus.*]
Wealth at death £31,662 11s. 8d.: probate, 9 Nov 1921, *CGPLA Eng. & Wales*

Harcarse. For this title name *see* Hog, Sir Roger, of Harcarse, Lord Harcarse (1634/5–1700).

Harclay [Harcla], **Andrew**, **earl of Carlisle** (*c.*1270–1323), soldier, was probably the eldest son of Sir Michael Harclay (*d.* before 1309), a tenant and servant of the Cliffords who later entered the service of the crown, acting as sheriff of Cumberland (1285–98), and of Joan, daughter of William Fitzjohn, a Yorkshire landowner, and brother of the theologian Henry *Harclay. The family name derived from Hartley in Westmorland. First recorded at the Westmorland eyre of 1292, which suggests that he was then at least twenty-one, Andrew Harclay campaigned in Scotland in 1304 and 1310, and in 1309 was ordered to assist Robert Clifford (*d.* 1314) in defending the English west march against Scottish attack. He was appointed sheriff of Cumberland in 1311, was chosen knight of the shire for that county in 1312, and in December 1313 gave energetic leadership against Scots then ravaging the county. Two years later, in July and August 1315, he directed the successful defence of Carlisle against a full-scale Scottish siege, led by King Robert in person—his role is given visual form in the initial letter for the royal charter that Carlisle received in 1316, in which Harclay, identifiable by his armorial bearings, hurls a spear through a Scottish soldier below the walls. Harclay himself was rewarded by a gift of 1000 marks (£666 13s. 4d.). His rise to prominence in the northwest aroused antagonism, however, and when he was captured by the Scots late in 1315 or in 1316, his temporary absence from the region gave his enemies opportunities to undermine his standing with Edward II.

Harclay had to pay at least 2000 marks (£1333 6s. 8d.) to recover his freedom. He had royal assistance in raising his ransom, notwithstanding 'malicious charges made by some persons against him at Court' (*CDS*, 3, no. 515/3). But although the king took steps to ensure that the crown's debts to Harclay were paid, only in 1319 does he appear to have been fully restored to Edward II's favour, when he became sheriff of Cumberland, keeper of Carlisle and Cockermouth castles, and warden of the west march. In the following year he was paid 1000 marks by indenture for keeping Carlisle and its march, while in 1321 he received a personal summons to parliament. The apogee of his career came in 1322, when he commanded the loyalist army that defeated Thomas of Lancaster at Boroughbridge on 16–17 March, skilfully deploying his men 'in schiltrom, after the Scottish fashion' (*Chronicle of Lanercost*, 231) to hold the crossing of the Ure against the rebels. On 25 March Harclay was munificently rewarded for his services, being created earl of Carlisle, with the promise of lands worth 1000 marks yearly (and the same amount in cash until the lands were forthcoming) to maintain him in his new dignity. The king himself girded Harclay with the comital belt. Along with his new rank, Harclay now disposed of an impressive degree of military strength. For the Scottish campaign of August 1322 he mustered 113 men-at-arms, 1435 hobelars (lightly armed cavalry), and 2069 foot soldiers, and after the campaign he was paid to retain a force of 240 men-at-arms and 500 hobelars for the defence of the English west march.

Harclay was unable to bring his men to Edward II's aid before the king's forces were routed at Byland in Yorkshire on 14 October 1322. The extent of the disaster, and Edward's inability to defend his realm against the Scots, led the earl of Carlisle to conclude that the war to conquer Scotland could not be won, and to enter into negotiations with the Scots to end it. When those negotiations began is unknown, but they were concluded on 3 January 1323, when Harclay himself went to Lochmaben to meet King Robert and Thomas Randolph, earl of Moray. Their treaty survives in two forms, clearly meant to circulate in England and Scotland respectively. They have much in common, above all the acceptance that each kingdom should be free of the other. They concur, moreover, that in return for Edward II's consent to the treaty, King Robert would found a monastery to pray for the souls of those killed in the Anglo-Scottish wars, pay the English king 40,000 marks (£26,666 13s. 4d.) over ten years, and even allow Edward to choose a wife from among his own kin for Robert's male heir. But whereas the English version lays stress on a consensual resolution of remaining difficulties, in the context of 'everything that has to be done for the common profit of both realms' (Stones, 309), the Scottish version speaks of the use of force by the negotiating parties to compel acceptance of its terms. It is certainly this version that represents most fully the intentions of the negotiators, and its terms suggest that the treaty was intended to create a military alliance between English earl and Scottish king, which would culminate in the dictation of peace to Edward II by them. Significantly, the occupants of Carlisle Castle in the following month included Sir Philip Meldrum, an important Scottish knight who can only have been there as King Robert's agent.

Edward knew that Harclay was in negotiation with the Scots within a week of the treaty's being concluded. Halfhearted attempts to secure the earl's arrest alternated with the dispatch of messengers to Carlisle, until on 28 January 1323 the dismissal there of a force of soldiers loyal to the king, followed by the sending out of agents to take oaths in support of himself, indicated that Harclay had resolved to persist in treasonable courses. But his plans were betrayed to the king, and the earl was progressively stripped of his offices, while the castles nearest to northwest England were fortified. Only on 25 February, however, was Harclay overthrown, when a small force led by Sir Anthony Lucy, who had remained at or near Carlisle and was clearly trusted by the earl, took him by surprise in Carlisle Castle and arrested him. On 3 March 1323 Harclay was arraigned for treason on the king's record before royal justices appointed for the purpose. Denied a hearing, he was degraded from his earldom by being ungirded of his sword and having his spurs cut from his heels, and was then sentenced to be hanged, drawn, and quartered as

a traitor—a fate he endured with dignity and resolution, publicly declaring at the foot of the gallows the good intentions behind his treaty with the Scots. Following his execution on Harraby Hill, Carlisle, his head was taken to Knaresborough for the king's inspection, then placed on London Bridge, while his quarters were set up at Carlisle, Newcastle, Bristol, and Shrewsbury. Only in 1328 were his remains allowed Christian burial.

The known number of Harclay's followers in his treason is very small, and nearly all of them were able to return to the king's peace after the execution of their leader, who was treated as having been solely responsible for the conspiracy to secure peace with the Scots. There seems no reason to doubt the Lanercost chronicle's claim that it was the destructiveness of the war, and Edward II's unwillingness to end it, that lay behind Harclay's action in opening negotiations. The material weakness of Carlisle may also have prompted Harclay to reflect that if peace was not made soon, the war might be ended by military defeat anyway. His conspiracy was a desperate measure, though given Edward II's refusal to renounce his claim to Scottish overlordship, it is hard to see how else the fighting and associated havoc could have been stopped. As it was, Edward II was compelled to agree to a thirteen-year truce less than three months after the earl's execution. Harclay was hardly realistic, however, if he supposed that he could be reconciled to his king once he had forced him to recognize Scottish independence, and in fact there is evidence for precautions against the failure of the conspiracy—for instance, Harclay's secretary, William Blount, later fled to Scotland and was given lands there, while there were even rumours that the earl planned to marry a sister of the Scottish king—which suggest that Harclay appreciated this difficulty himself. But on the whole there is little evidence that he possessed political as well as military skills. On the contrary, he further antagonized men in the northwest who must have been already alarmed by his dramatic rise—men like Sir Anthony Lucy, whose lands he seized in 1322 on a spurious charge of Lancastrian allegiance—and also made dangerous enemies at court, above all the king's favourite, the younger Hugh Despenser. It may be, therefore, that he failed to appreciate how far his regional pre-eminence depended on royal office and favour, and how vulnerable he might be to local hostility if the king turned against him. Even posthumously, that favour was never restored. A petition by his nephew Henry, early in Edward III's reign, that the verdict on Harclay be annulled as not made by due form of law, went unanswered. Local tradition may have remembered him kindly, on the evidence of a long passage in the mid-fifteenth-century chronicle of the Northumbrian John Hardyng, acknowledging that the earl 'wel dyd mene in takyng of that pese' (BL, Lansdowne MS 204, fol. 183). But in the records of central government Andrew Harclay was always 'lately the king's enemy and rebel'. HENRY SUMMERSON

Sources H. Summerson, *Medieval Carlisle: the city and the borders from the late eleventh to the mid-sixteenth century*, 2 vols., Cumberland and Westmorland Antiquarian and Archaeological Society, extra ser., 25 (1993) · H. Maxwell, ed. and trans., *The chronicle of Lanercost,*

1272–1346 (1913) · BL, Stowe MS 553 · Assize rolls, eyre rolls, etc., PRO, JUST/1/142 · BL, Lansdowne MS 204 · *CDS*, vol. 3 · E. L. G. Stones, ed. and trans., *Anglo-Scottish relations, 1174–1328: some selected documents*, OMT (1965) · P. A. Munch, 'Concordia facta inter Anglicos et Scotos, 3 January 1322/3', *Proceedings of the Society of Antiquaries of Scotland*, 3 (1857–60), 454–62 · Court of common pleas, plea rolls, PRO, CP40/244 m 32d

Likenesses miniature portrait, initial letter of Carlisle's royal charter, 1316, repro. in M. Prestwich, *The three Edwards* (1980)

Harclay [Herkeley], **Henry** (*c.*1270–1317), theologian, was the son of Sir Michael Harclay, a long-serving sheriff of Cumberland, who died before 1309, and brother of Andrew *Harclay, first earl of Carlisle (*d.* 1323). The family name was derived from Hartley in Westmorland. By 25 December 1296, when John Halton, bishop of Carlisle (*d.* 1324), appointed him to the rectorship of the church of Dacre, Henry Harclay was already master of arts and subdeacon. In 1297, probably on 21 December, he was ordained to the priesthood. Harclay studied theology at the University of Paris, commenting on the *Sentences* of Peter Lombard about 1300, when John Duns Scotus (*d.* 1308) was teaching there. Harclay's still unedited commentary on the first book of the *Sentences* is extant in two codices, one found in the Vatican City, Biblioteca Apostolica Vaticana, MS Vat. lat. 13687, fols. 13r–97v, and another, in a much more legible form, in Casale Monferrato, Biblioteca del Seminario Vescovile, cod. b 2, fols. 1r–84r. Scotus exercised a strong influence on Harclay at this time. In his commentary Harclay takes solutions verbatim from Scotus, frequently uses Scotus's arguments, and adopts many of his positions; but he was not a slavish disciple, rather, as an acute commentator, he offered independent criticisms which may have influenced Scotus's final edition of his own commentary, the *Ordinatio*.

Harclay returned to England, and attended the University of Oxford, becoming master of theology some time before 1312. He became embroiled in bitter controversies between the university and the Dominicans over a number of privileges claimed by the latter, and he threw himself into the battle on the side of the university, being among those who drew up new regulations that restricted those privileges. In these academic battles Harclay was not above using every means at his disposal. After the Dominican Hugh Sutton had scheduled a public disputation for 17 February 1312, Harclay, against all custom, scheduled his own public disputation for the same day, embarrassing Sutton with the meagre audience he drew. Later that year, on 11 December, Harclay was confirmed by the bishop of Lincoln as chancellor of the University of Oxford, and travelled to the papal court at Avignon on the university's behalf in pursuit of a settlement to the controversy.

Harclay was a particularly active chancellor, solicitous in maintaining the good order of the university. He saw the need for organizing the numerous university statutes, and very probably commissioned a register in book-form, *Registrum A*, that succeeded in bringing some order to the mass of statutes. On 7 July 1313, under Harclay's leadership, the university passed a statute forbidding the carrying of weapons by students and the constant quarrelling among the northern (north of England and Scotland) and southern (south of England, Wales, and Ireland) 'nations' of students. It also issued a statute requiring every master, before taking up his teaching duties, to take an oath not to endanger the peace of the university. In order to reduce the high price of food in Oxford, Harclay obtained a royal writ fixing the price of the most important commodities. On 20 May 1315, moreover, Harclay received from the king a confirmation of a number of important privileges that Henry III had granted to the university.

Harclay was vigilant for the faith, as well as the good order, of the university. On 14 February 1314 he was chairman of the assembly of masters who condemned as heretical eight opinions, held by a group of Oxford theologians, regarding the relation of the Trinity to creation. In addition, he fulfilled his duties as university preacher on feast days, as shown by a surviving sermon (LPL, cod. 61, fol. 143r a) for 29 December 1314 on the feast of St Thomas of Canterbury. During his years at Oxford he disputed a number of questions. In his twenty-nine *Quaestiones ordinariae* Harclay exhibits more independence and maturity than in his early Parisian commentary on the *Sentences*. He is familiar with, and sharply critical of, many of the positions and arguments of his contemporaries on a wide variety of theological and philosophical issues, including predestination and divine foreknowledge, the ontological status of divine ideas, universals and relations, the univocal concept of being, the eternity of the world, the plurality of substantial forms in humans, the formal distinction, whether anyone can calculate the end of the world, the immortality of the soul, and various moral questions.

Harclay was not interested in constructing a system. He was a widely read and independent critical thinker, quite anti-Thomist, whose great strength lay in questioning opinions and propositions to others self-evident. Two examples must suffice. Most, if not all, scholastics before Harclay had argued that though creatures are really related to God, he is not really related to them, for this would entail change in him. But in his long and involved question on relations, Harclay developed his own novel position, to argue that God is as really related to creatures as they are to him. Second, Harclay held rather nontraditional views concerning infinity and the 'continuous'. He argued in his own way that not all infinites are equal, that they can be added to and subtracted from without affecting their infinity, and that certain forms of an actual infinite are possible. A number of fourteenth-century thinkers, including William Alnwick (*d.* 1333), Adam Wodeham (*d.* 1358), and Thomas Wylton, attacked him, along with Walter Chatton (*d.* 1344), for being 'atomists', that is, for their non-traditional view that continua, whether of lines, distances, time, or motions of any kind, are composed of indivisibles. Harclay had a tough and creative mind with views and arguments well known and respected by his contemporaries, even when attacked, as he was for example by William Ockham (*d.* 1349), who quoted verbatim from Harclay's anti-Scotist question on universals and very likely was influenced by Harclay's question on relations. In addition to the early *Sentences* commentary and later *Quaestiones ordinariae*, there is extant his still unedited axioms dealing with relations, *Fundamenta Arcelini* (Assisi, Biblioteca Comunale, cod. 172, fols. 116v–117v).

Toward the end of his life the controversy between the university and the Dominicans rekindled, and Harclay travelled once again to the papal court at Avignon, where he died on 25 June 1317.   MARK G. HENNINGER

Sources H. Harclay, *Quaestiones ordinariae*, Auctores Britannici Medii Aevi [forthcoming] · F. Pelster, 'Heinrich von Harclay, Kanzler von Oxford, und seine Quästionen', *Miscellanea Francesco Ehrle*, 1 (Rome, 1924), 307–56 · C. Balic, 'Henricus de Harclay et Ioannes Duns Scotus', *Mélanges offerts à Étienne Gilson* (1959), 93–121, 701–2 · M. Henninger, 'Relation as condition: Henry of Harclay', *Relations: medieval theories, 1250–1325* (1989), 98–118 · R. Dales, 'Henry of Harclay on the infinite', *Journal of the History of Ideas*, 45 (1984), 295–301 · J. Murdoch, 'Henry of Harclay and the infinite', *Studi sul XIV secolo in memoria di Anneliese Maier*, ed. A. Maierù and A. Paravicini Bagliani, Studi e testi, 151 (1981), 219–61 · F. Pelster, 'Theologisch und philosophisch bedeutsame Quästionen des W. von Macclesfield O.P., H. von Harclay und anonymer Auctoren der englischen Hochscholastik in cod. 501 Troyes', *Scholastik*, 28 (1953), 222–40 · G. Gál, 'Henricus de Harclay: quaestio de significato conceptus universalis', *Franciscan Studies*, new ser., 31 (1971), 173–234 · Emden, *Oxf.* · *Hist. U. Oxf.* 1: *Early Oxf. schools* · F. Pelster, 'Die Quaestio Heinrichs von Harclay über die zweite Ankunft Christs und die Erwartung des baldigen Weltendes zu Anfang des XIV Jahrhunderts', *Archivio italiano per la storia della pietà*, 1 (1951), 25–82

Archives Biblioteca Apostolica Vaticana, Vatican City, MS Vat. lat. 13687, fols. 13r–97v · Biblioteca Apostolica Vaticana, Vatican City, cod. Borghese 171, fols. 1–32v · Biblioteca Cathedrale, Tortosa, cod. 88, fols. 82–94v · Biblioteca Comunale, Assisi, cod. 172 · Biblioteca del Seminario Vescovile, Casale Monferrato, cod. b2, fols. 1r–84r · Biblioteca Nazionale Centrale, Florence, cod. II.II.281, fols. 94–101v · LPL, cod. 61, fol. 143r a · Worcester Cathedral, cod. F.3, fols. 181v–215v

Harcourt. For this title name *see* individual entries under Harcourt; *see also* Waller, Anne, Lady Waller [Anne Harcourt, Lady Harcourt] (d. 1661).

Harcourt [de Harcourt] **family** (*per. c.*1050–1330), gentry, a family of major importance in the central midlands, was first to be found in Normandy before 1066 where sources deriving from the abbey of Bec-Hellouin identify one Anschetil as lord of Harcourt (Eure) and as a close cousin of the magnate family known as the Beaumonts, lords of Beaumont-le-Roger and Pont-Audemer. His son **Robert fitz Anschetil** (d. in or before 1118) held a large barony from the Beaumonts. The creation of the earldom of Warwick for Henry de *Beaumont in 1088 brought Robert an estate of seven fees in Leicestershire and Warwickshire formerly held in chief by Robert de Vescy but subordinated to the earldom. The Harcourts secured a number of other estates in the same counties when Henry I created the earldom of Leicester for Robert de Beaumont, count of Meulan (d. 1118), in 1107, including Market Bosworth, Leicestershire, which became the Harcourt centre in England in the twelfth century. Robert fitz Anschetil had died by 1118 to be succeeded by numerous sons, at least four of

whom took shares of his cross-channel estates. The son who founded the chief English branch of the family was **Ivo de Harcourt** (d. in or after 1166) who acquired most of the Harcourt lands in England perhaps in succession (at least in the earldom of Warwick) to his elder, childless brother, Anschetil fitz Robert, who died soon after 1130. Ivo was a major follower of Robert (II), earl of Leicester. He is found frequently in the Leicester household, and accompanied his lord to Normandy in 1154. Perhaps to simplify the problems posed by the split allegiance, Roger, earl of Warwick, transferred to Earl Robert three and a half Harcourt fees in exchange for an equal number of Leicester fees in Warwickshire, in a singular arrangement transacted before 1153. Ivo was still alive in 1166, but probably died not long afterwards.

Ivo was succeeded by his son **Robert de Harcourt** (d. c.1205). Robert attested a late charter of Robert (II) of Leicester, and although he acted as a pledge for Earl Robert (III) in a debt to Aaron the Jew before 1179, he seems largely to have separated himself from the Leicester family after 1168. He was an independent figure in the midlands, his concerns centred on estate improvement and enlargement. He promoted the status of his house at Market Bosworth by the building of a substantial private chapel, which involved him in litigation with Bertram de Verdon, patron of the parish church of the place. In the reign of Henry II, before 1184, he made a profitable marriage to Isabel, daughter of Richard (I) de Camville, obtaining in 1192 the substantial marriage portion of Stanton Harcourt, Oxfordshire, and Norton and Stratton in the soke of Rothley, valued at £56 rent p.a. Between 1198 and 1202 he was sheriff of Leicestershire and Warwickshire, and left a debt of £127 3s. 0d. which was still outstanding on his death c.1205.

Robert left several sons, but the bulk of his estates came to his eldest, **Sir William** [i] **de Harcourt** (d. c.1223), who was active in King Richard's wars in France, doing service for his father for the fee of Stanton Harcourt in 1197. He was also active on King John's behalf in the campaigns of 1215 and campaigned in 1220–21 for the regents of Henry III against the count of Aumale's rebellion and John's former sheriffs. The exchequer memoranda have him alive in the year Easter 1222–3 but there is reference to the executors of his testament in a fine of April 1223. His son answered for his considerable debts (over £400) in 1224. As with his father, William seems not to have had any magnate links, but rather to have formed a connection with the king direct and entered the group of minor curial magnates: the scale of his debts indicates that his finances may not have equalled his aspirations.

William was succeeded by his son **Sir Richard** [i] **de Harcourt** (d. 1258). Richard made a third substantial acquisition for his family in the Staffordshire manor of Ellenhall, which came to him through marriage to Orabilia, daughter of Thomas Noel. He made careful arrangements for the succession to his lands, enfeoffing his younger son, Saher, with two Leicestershire manors, Kibworth and Newton Harcourt, in his own lifetime. He died

early in 1258 leaving his brother, William, rector of Aylestone, as his executor, as appears from a later fine. His eldest son, **Sir William** [ii] **de Harcourt** (*d.* 1270), succeeded
to the bulk of his estate, doing homage to the king for his
manor of Stanton in April 1258. William [ii] made two
marriages, the first (before 1253) to Alice, sister of Alan de
la *Zouche, which brought him the manor of Tong, Shropshire, and Braunstone, Leicestershire, from his father. The
second marriage was to a certain Hilaria. This William
became involved with the Montfortian cause in 1264–5,
although there is little evidence to link him with the
Montfort affinity in the midlands before then. His brother
Sir Saher was, however, a long-term associate of Earl
Simon, and was ruined by his involvement with the baronial cause. William [ii] was burdened with fines of 500
marks, but in 1267 found a group of neighbours and relatives able to guarantee and clear 400 marks, which the
king had granted to Sir Philip Basset, and in 1269 negotiated the clearing of a further 100 marks owed to William
de Valence. William died in 1270, leaving his only son, **Sir
Richard** [ii] **de Harcourt** (1256–1293), a minor, as heir.
Richard had proof of age in 1277, when his date of birth
was agreed as having been 9 December 1256 in Oxfordshire (presumably at Stanton), which would have made
him the son of William's first marriage. Richard was
already married at that time to Margery Bek of Eresby. Sir
Richard died early in 1293 leaving as heir his son **Sir John
Harcourt** (1274–1330).

The successive heads of the Harcourt family after the
1160s were men of national significance, and although
they clearly found their minor magnate status a financial
burden, did not enter into any alliance with the greater
magnates. The Harcourts successfully maintained and
augmented their already substantial demesne interests in
three midland counties throughout the thirteenth century, largely by advantageous marriages, which must be a
tribute to their court connections and lineage. Their arms
were two bars (seal of Richard [i], *c.*1223) and later or, two
bars gules (William [ii], *c.*1285, St George's roll).

DAVID CROUCH

Sources register of Leicester Abbey, Bodl. Oxf., MS Laud misc.
625 · Bodl. Oxf., MS Ashmole 833 · Bodl. Oxf., MS Dugdale 15 · L. C.
Loyd and D. M. Stenton, eds., *Sir Christopher Hatton's book of seals*
(1950) · PRO, E159; JUST 1/734; KO26/148; E13/1E; CP
25(1)/122/24/430 · muniments, Merton Oxf., nos. 2780, 2872 ·
D. Crouch, *The Beaumont twins: the roots and branches of power in the
twelfth century*, Cambridge Studies in Medieval Life and Thought,
4th ser., 1 (1986) · *CIPM* · *Rotuli de finibus excerptis e rotulis* · *Pipe rolls*

Harcourt, Anne. *See* Waller, Anne, Lady Waller (*d.* 1661).

Harcourt, Augustus George Vernon (1834–1919), chemist, was born in London on 24 December 1834, the elder
son of Admiral Frederick E. Vernon Harcourt (1790–1883)
and his wife, Marcia (*d.* 1868), sister of the first Lord Tollemache. His grandfather was Edward *Harcourt (1757–
1847), archbishop of York. Augustus—who used Vernon
Harcourt as his surname—was educated on the old classical lines at Cheam and at Harrow, and in 1854 entered
Balliol College, Oxford. In the following year Benjamin
Collins Brodie arrived at Oxford as professor of chemistry

Augustus George Vernon Harcourt (1834–1919), by Jabez
Hughes

and the Balliol laboratory was placed at his disposal. Harcourt soon became his assistant. In 1858 Brodie moved to
the chemistry department of the new museum of the university, and took Harcourt—still an undergraduate—with
him as lecture assistant. Under Brodie at the new museum
Harcourt began his researches on the exact determination
of the oxygen absorbed by the metals potassium and
sodium. In 1859 he assisted Brodie in tutoring the prince
of Wales, and in the same year was elected Dr Lee's reader
in chemistry and a senior student at Christ Church, holding those positions until 1902. He became a close friend of
Charles Dodgson (Lewis Carroll) and was, at least in part,
the model for the White Knight in *Through the Looking-
Glass*. He also tutored a number of men who later distinguished themselves in chemistry, notably H. B. Dixon
(1852–1930), D. L. Chapman (1869–1958), and N. V. Sidgwick (1873–1952).

In the early 1860s Harcourt embarked on a programme
of research on the rates of chemical reactions. He settled
on two reactions for which the amount of chemical
change during definite periods of time could be measured
accurately. For help with the interpretation of these reactions he enlisted the collaboration of William Esson,
mathematical fellow and tutor of Merton College, and
beginning in 1865 the two published articles which for the
first time gave detailed treatments of the kinetics of different types of reactions. In 1912, when they were well in

their seventies, they again collaborated, this time on the effect of temperature on the rates of chemical reactions. Here they were not so successful, since the alternative treatment earlier given by J. H. van't Hoff and S. Arrhenius in the end proved more satisfactory. An interesting outcome of this work of Harcourt and Esson is that they predicted a 'kinetic absolute zero' at which all reaction ceases; their value of -272.6 °C is in remarkable agreement with the modern value of -273.15 °C.

In applied chemistry Harcourt was chiefly drawn to questions concerning the purification and analysis of coal gas, as he was appointed in 1872 one of the three metropolitan gas referees. One of the problems with which he was concerned was the purification of coal gas from sulphur compounds, and he devised a sulphur test which came into wide use and later led to the large-scale purification of coal gas. Perhaps his most signal improvement in the testing of gas was the introduction of the pentane lamp as the official standard of light in place of the variable spermaceti candle. Another useful investigation which occupied much of his time between 1899 and 1911 related to the administration of chloroform as an anaesthetic. After much patient labour he devised an inhaler, which his medical colleagues recommended to the British Medical Association as 'possessing the advantages of simplicity, exactness, and portability'.

Harcourt was elected a fellow of the Royal Society in 1868, and served on its council from 1878 to 1880. Admitted to the Chemical Society in 1859, he served as one of its secretaries for eight years in 1865–73, and was elected president in 1895. As became the nephew of one of the founders of the British Association—the Revd William Venables Vernon *Harcourt—he early took an interest in its meetings and made many contributions to the chemical section, of which he was president in 1875. A few years later he was elected one of the general secretaries of the association, an office which he held for fourteen years with conspicuous tact.

In 1872 Harcourt married the Hon. Rachel Mary Bruce (1848–1927), daughter of Henry Austin *Bruce, afterwards first Baron Aberdare. The couple had two sons and eight daughters, one of whom was Janet Vernon Harcourt. In 1878 Christ Church leased to Harcourt some land on the banks of the River Cherwell, and on it he built a house, named Cowley Grange (later part of St Hilda's College, named the South Building). Harcourt and his family lived there until his retirement in 1902, when they moved to the Isle of Wight. He died at his house, St Clare, near Ryde, on 23 August 1919.   H. B. DIXON, *rev.* KEITH J. LAIDLER

Sources *The Times* (25 Aug 1919) · personal knowledge (1927) · H. B. D. [H. B. Dixon], *PRS*, 97A (1920), vii–xi · C. King, 'Chemistry's White Knight: Augustus Vernon Harcourt', *New Scientist* (28 June 1979), 1110–11 · J. Shorter, 'A. G. Vernon Harcourt: founder of chemical kinetics and a friend of "Lewis Carroll"', *Journal of Chemical Education*, 57 (1980), 411–16 · M. C. King, 'Experiments with time: progress and problems in the development of chemical kinetics [pt 1]', *Ambix*, 28 (1981), 70–82 · M. C. King, 'Experiments with time: progress and problems in the development of chemical kinetics [pt 2]', *Ambix*, 29 (1982), 49–61 · M. C. King, 'The chemist in allegory:

Vernon Harcourt and the White Knight', *Journal of Chemical Education*, 60 (1983), 177–80 · M. C. King, 'The course of chemical change: the life and times of Augustus G. Vernon Harcourt, 1834–1919', *Ambix*, 31 (1984), 16–31 · K. J. Laidler, 'Chemical kinetics and the Oxford college laboratories', *Archive for History of Exact Sciences*, 38 (1988), 197–283

Archives Balliol Oxf., letters to Sir John Conroy · CUL, letters to Sir George Stokes

Likenesses J. Hughes, photograph, Royal Society of Chemistry, London [*see illus.*] · photograph, repro. in *Transactions of the Chemical Society*, 1626 (1920) · photograph, repro. in *PRS*, 97A (1920), vii · photographs, RS · photographs, Christ Church Oxf.

Wealth at death £17,168 19s. 7d.: probate, 5 Dec 1919, *CGPLA Eng. & Wales*

Harcourt, Sir **Cecil Halliday Jepson** (1892–1959), naval officer, was born on 11 April 1892 at Maitland Lodge, London Road, Bromley, Kent, the son of Halliday Harcourt, solicitor, and his wife, Grace Lilian, daughter of Dr Jepson. He was educated at Fonthill, East Grinstead, and from 1904 to 1909 at the Royal Naval College at Osborne and Dartmouth. On passing out from Dartmouth, as midshipman in 1909, he was awarded the term first prize in mathematics. By 1913 he was a lieutenant. He might have considered an alternative career as he was on the retired list in 1915, but in May 1916 he returned to the active list. He served on the battleship *Centurion* in the Grand Fleet and was present at the battle of Jutland.

Between the wars Harcourt served with the Atlantic, home, Mediterranean, and reserve fleets in destroyers and mine-sweepers. He was promoted commander in 1926 and captain in 1933. Following staff courses Harcourt was seconded to the Royal Australian Navy as captain (D) in 1935–7. These seagoing and command experiences provided a sound professional background to his appointment in 1938 as deputy director of the Admiralty's operations division. He remained with the operations division until 1941, becoming director in 1939. Thus he was in a crucial staff post at the start of the Second World War, and his contribution to the effective operational use of the navy was recognized by appointment as a CBE in 1940 and command of the modern battleship *Duke of York*. Winston Churchill was his passenger in December 1941 and January 1942 for two transatlantic journeys to meet President Roosevelt.

On promotion to rear-admiral in July 1942 Harcourt began a two-year period of service in the Mediterranean as flag officer of force Q, which comprised a cruiser squadron, destroyers, and other attached ships, such as monitors, as needed. While its main task was to give naval gunfire support to allied landings, it also carried out attacks on axis supply convoys. Force Q was part of the supporting force for the operation Torch landings in Morocco and Algeria. Harcourt's personal command contribution was recognized by the Americans by appointment to the Legion of Merit in November 1942. The citation for the award stated that 'His unfaltering support in the face of heavy odds did much to make possible the success of that operation' (*The Times*, 24 Dec 1959). After operation Torch, force Q operated from the vulnerable Algerian port of Bône, harassing axis supply convoys between December

1942 and spring 1943. Harcourt's immediate superior, Admiral Sir Andrew Cunningham, recognized the risks to Harcourt and force Q but knew that their role was critical and signalled Harcourt that he must 'stick it out' as allied support was coming to the area. For these services Harcourt was appointed CB in 1943. From June to September force Q was in regular action in support of the allied landings at Pantelleria, Lampedusa, and Limosa; in June operation Husky supported the Sicily landings and in September 1943 operation Avalanche, the Salerno landings. Harcourt was mentioned in dispatches for his contribution to the Salerno landings.

Harcourt returned to the Admiralty from February 1944 to summer 1945 as naval secretary to Cunningham, now first sea lord. He was then appointed to the Pacific Fleet as flag officer 11th aircraft-carrier squadron and then, with his carriers plus three cruisers, four destroyers, a submarine, and mine-sweeping flotillas, he commanded task group 111.2 for the reoccupation of Hong Kong in September 1945. A small number of Japanese suicide motor boats were observed near Hong Kong and Harcourt ordered his carriers' planes to destroy them. Pressure from Chaing Kai-shek meant that Harcourt had to receive the surrender of Major-General Okada and Vice-Admiral Fujita on behalf of both the British and Chinese governments. From September 1945 to June 1946 Harcourt was the *de facto* governor of Hong Kong as commander-in-chief and head of the military administration. He was a sensitive administrator, and was called by the Chinese name Ha Kok, a reference to a distinguished fourth-century Chinese nobleman Chung Kok. He was knighted in 1945 (KCB), was promoted vice-admiral in 1946, and awarded the grand cordon of the Chinese order of the Cloud and Banner.

After Hong Kong, Harcourt was appointed flag officer (Air) and second in command of the Mediterranean Fleet. In March 1948 he returned to the Admiralty as second sea lord with responsibility for all personnel and manpower issues. This was an onerous post because government economies required overall manpower reductions in the navy from 178,000 to 147,000 and maintaining even the reduced level by re-engagements was difficult because of the attractions of civilian occupations. The rate of re-engagements had fallen from 61 per cent in 1938 to 22 per cent in 1948. Harcourt was to warn in 1949 of a 'first class breakdown' (Grove, 45) in two years if the shortage of key ratings was not rectified. While second sea lord Harcourt received his final promotion to admiral in June 1949. From 1950 to 1952, when he retired, he was commander-in-chief, Nore command, and he was advanced to GBE in 1953. He was also admitted to the Norwegian order of St Olav in 1951 and the Danish order of Dannebrog in 1952.

In retirement, living in Eaton Place, London, Harcourt played leading roles in the London and Greater London Playing Fields Association, the Royal Commonwealth Society, and the Victoria League. He had married first, in 1920, the noted concert pianist Evelyn Suart, daughter of Brigadier-General W. H. Suart CMG and widow of Gerald Gould. After her death in 1950 he married Stella Janet Waghorn, the widow of Air Commodore D. J. Waghorn; she survived him. There were no children of either marriage. Harcourt died *en route* for St Stephen's Hospital, Chelsea, London, on 19 December 1959, aged sixty-seven. A memorial service was held in January 1960 at St Martin-in-the-Fields.   F. E. C. GREGORY

Sources *The Times* (21 Dec 1959) · *The Times* (9 Jan 1960) · *WW* (1947) · *WW* (1953) · J. Rohwer and G. Hummelehen, *Chronology of the war at sea, 1939–45* (1992) · S. W. C. Park, *Cunningham the commander* (1974) · E. J. Grove, *Vanguard to Trident: British naval policy since World War II* (1987) · E. Gray, *Operation Pacific* (1990) · J. Cresswell, *Sea warfare, 1939–45* (1950) · T. Dorling, *Western Mediterranean, 1942–45* (1947) · S. W. Roskill, *The war at sea, 1939–1945*, 2 (1956) · H. I. Land, *Hong Kong* (1952) · G. B. Endacott, *A history of Hong Kong* (1958) · *CGPLA Eng. & Wales* (1960) · b. cert. · d. cert.
Archives IWM, diaries and papers · Public Records Office of Hong Kong, papers | FILM BFI NFTVA, news footage · IWM FVA, actuality footage · IWM FVA, news footage
Likenesses W. Stoneman, photograph, 1942, NPG · photograph, repro. in *The Times* (21 Dec 1959)
Wealth at death £25,115 11s. 10d.: probate, 26 Feb 1960, *CGPLA Eng. & Wales*

Harcourt, Charles [*real name* Charles Parker Hillier] (1838–1880), actor, was born on 23 June 1838, at 80 Charlotte Street, Marylebone, the son of John Hillier, a servant, and Sarah Ann, *née* Parker. After obtaining some experience by acting with amateurs, he made his first public appearance at the St James's Theatre, London, on 30 March 1863, as Robert Audley in George Roberts's dramatic version of Miss Braddon's novel *Lady Audley's Secret*. Between 1866 and 1868 he was seen at Drury Lane, notably in the parts of Captain Thornton in an adaptation of *Rob Roy* and Count Henry de Villetaneuve in the first performance of A. B. Richards's *The Prisoner of Toulon*. By 1873 he had fulfilled engagements at the Royalty, the Strand, the Charing Cross, and the Globe theatres. From Easter 1871 to Easter 1872 he was the lessee of the Marylebone Theatre. Some of the most important parts he played were Captain Absolute in *The Rivals* at the Charing Cross (November 1872); Claude Melnotte in *The Lady of Lyons* at the Haymarket (May 1876); Pygmalion in the revival of W. S. Gilbert's *Pygmalion and Galatea* at the same house (January 1877); and Count d'Aubeterre in F. C. Burnard's *Proof* at the Adelphi (1878). He afterwards appeared as Mercutio in *Romeo and Juliet*, a part which he acted with spirit and discretion, and of which after the death of George Vining he was the best exponent. His last role was the outcast Bashford in Paul Meritt's *The World* at Drury Lane (1880).

Harcourt was an able, vigorous, and conscientious actor. From January 1880 he was the secretary of the National Dramatic Academy. On 18 October 1880, while rehearsing the character of Horatio at the Haymarket Theatre, he fell into the scene dock at the back of the stage, which had inadvertently been left open. The resulting scalp wound was found at an inquest to have led to erysipelas and to his death, on 27 October, at the Charing Cross Hospital. He was buried at Highgate cemetery on 2 November, leaving a widow and daughter.

G. C. BOASE, *rev.* NILANJANA BANERJI

Sources *The Times* (29 Oct 1880) · *The Times* (2 Nov 1880) · *The Era* (31 Oct 1880) · *The Era* (7 Nov 1880) · C. E. Pascoe, ed., *The dramatic list*

(1879) • C. E. Pascoe, ed., *The dramatic list*, 2nd edn (1880) • *The Graphic* (6 Nov 1880) • *Illustrated Sporting and Dramatic News* (6 Nov 1880) • b. cert. • d. cert.

Likenesses portrait, repro. in *The Graphic* • portrait, repro. in *Illustrated Sporting and Dramatic News* • woodburytype photograph, NPG

Harcourt [*formerly* Venables-Vernon]**, Edward** (1757–1847), archbishop of York, was born at Sudbury Hall, Derbyshire, on 10 October 1757, the second and younger son of George Venables-Vernon, first Baron Vernon of Kinderton (1710–1780), and his third wife, Martha (1715–1794), third daughter of Simon *Harcourt [*see under* Harcourt, Simon, first Viscount Harcourt] and sister of Simon *Harcourt, first Earl Harcourt. He was educated at Westminster School, which he entered on 5 April 1769, and matriculated at Christ Church, Oxford, on 2 July 1774. He was a fellow of All Souls from 1778 to 1783, and graduated BCL on 27 April 1780 and DCL on 4 May 1786. After ordination he was instituted in 1782 to the family living of Sudbury. On 5 February 1784, at St Martin-in-the-Fields, London, he married Lady Anne Leveson-Gower (1761–1832), daughter of Granville Leveson-*Gower, second Earl Gower, and from 1786 first marquess of Stafford. He was installed a canon of Christ Church, Oxford, on 13 October 1785 and a canon of Gloucester Cathedral on 10 November of the same year. He resigned the latter stall in 1791 but held all his other preferments until 1807, to supplement the income of his see.

Earl Gower was lord privy seal in the government of William Pitt the younger. Venables-Vernon was thus a prime candidate for a bishopric, and obtained one aged only thirty-four. This was the see of Carlisle, for which he was consecrated on 6 November 1791; he held it for sixteen years. There he began to establish his reputation as a moderate church reformer with close connections to Pitt's government. His sermons before the House of Lords in 1793–4 were published. He spent more than the whole income of the see upon the wants of the diocese as a whole. Rose Castle became a family home (ten of his sixteen children were born there) and he made many repairs and alterations to both the fabric and the gardens. This pastoral care made him a particularly suitable candidate to replace William Markham as northern primate, and he was nominated on 26 November 1807 and confirmed archbishop of York on 19 January 1808. He was also gazetted a privy councillor on 20 January 1805, and on 23 January was made lord high almoner to George III, an office that he retained for the rest of his life. He was a member of the council of eight who advised Queen Charlotte as custodian of the person of George III between 1811 and 1818, and was frequently at Windsor during those years.

Venables-Vernon was scrupulously attentive to the duties of the primacy. He conducted a primary visitation of the archdiocese in 1809, the first for almost a century, and another in 1841; there were ordinary visitations in 1817 and 1825. He also held frequent ordinations and confirmation tours. When York Minster was damaged by fire in 1829 and again in 1840 he contributed generously to both restorations, and made another gift of £2000 and

Edward Harcourt (1757–1847), by Sir Thomas Lawrence, 1823

communion plate to the minster. He was a strong supporter of the Society for the Propagation of the Gospel in York, a generous benefactor of new churches, and promoted the new institute at York for the training of schoolmasters. Bishopthorpe, like Rose Castle before it, became a family home, and a nursery was built for the children above the chapel.

In politics Venables-Vernon was a moderate Pittite, from his family connection with the Gowers. However, from his undergraduate days he was the close friend of Thomas Grenville, another future octogenarian, and voted for the election of Grenville's brother William, Lord Grenville, as chancellor of Oxford University in 1809, despite differing from him on the issue of Catholic relief. He retained his connections with the court, and preached the sermon at the coronation of George IV, in 1821, as he did at that of William IV, in 1831, and for Queen Victoria in 1838.

Venables-Vernon loved sacred music and was a director of the concerts of the Society for Ancient Music from 1811. On 23 February 1821 he entertained his fellow directors, George IV and his brothers Ernest, duke of Cumberland, and Adolphus, duke of Cambridge, and the duke of Wellington, at his house on Grosvenor Square the same night that in the adjoining house the Cato Street conspirators planned to murder the cabinet. George Canning jestingly said that the party—three members of the royal family and a war hero—were in danger of being assassinated in mistake for the ministers.

1830 brought two changes to Venables-Vernon's existence that would shape the rest of his career. In June 1830 his cousin William *Harcourt, third Earl Harcourt, died, leaving him his extensive estates, and in November a whig government under Earl Grey was formed, excluding Venables-Vernon's traditional political allies from power. The first led Venables-Vernon to change his name, when by sign manual he took the surname of Harcourt only. He made the Harcourt seat of Nuneham Courtenay, Oxfordshire, his main family residence and spent considerable sums on restoring the house and park. He was anxious for the Harcourt peerage to be recreated for his family—'not for my own sake certainly', he told Sir Robert Peel on 21 September 1841 (BL, Add. MS 40489, fol. 287)—but he reportedly rejected the offer of a peerage from the whigs, feeling that his vote would be compromised, and in the 1840s Peel refused to be bound by any previous assurances.

Grey's new administration gave him the role of a constructive conservative, helping the Church of England to come to terms with the extensive changes of the 1830s and 1840s; Lord Melbourne often consulted him when making senior church appointments. Harcourt set an example by surrendering land and income from the archdiocese of York to establish the new diocese of Ripon in 1836, and by facilitating the transfer of the archdeaconry of Nottingham to the diocese of Lincoln. He preached a valedictory sermon at York Minster on 13 November 1838 and subsequently relied heavily on his son Egerton Harcourt, while carrying out his ecclesiastical duties whenever possible. Harcourt abstained in the vote of 8 October 1831, when the Lords rejected the Reform Bill. He became increasingly detached from politics as he grew older and, though an eloquent speaker, usually reserved his interventions in the upper house for ecclesiastical issues. He was appointed one of the first members of the Ecclesiastical Commission in 1835 and attended its meetings regularly. The archbishop's vistation of the minster in 1841, when the fabric fund was found in deficit, caused particular controversy, coming only a year after the Dean and Chapters Act had reformed the administration and finance of English cathedrals. Dean Cockburn was found guilty of simony by the archbishop's commissary, although the court of queen's bench, on appeal, declared that the archbishop had no power to deprive the dean of his office without due process of law. The affair was deeply divisive and tarnished the last years of Harcourt's ministry.

Harcourt kept fit and active by riding until the age of eighty, and maintained a lifelong interest in country sports. Like his fellow archbishop, Charles Manners Sutton, he was a tall man; by temperament he was patient (though sometimes touchy) and always took his duties most seriously, despite the immense increase in his private fortune after 1831. He entertained Princess Victoria and her mother for a week when they attended the York Music Festival in 1835, and did the same for the young queen and Prince Albert, at Nuneham in 1840.

Following a fall from a bridge into a pond Harcourt died, of a chill, at Bishopthorpe Palace on 5 November 1847, and was buried at the parish church of Stanton Harcourt, Oxfordshire. His will speaks of his 'long and happy life' (Borth. Inst., vol. 218, fol. 12), whose foundation was that of an immensely stable and satisfying family life. Lady Anne Harcourt predeceased him, dying at Bishopthorpe on 16 November 1832, of peritonitis; her body and that of their daughter Caroline were moved from Bishopthorpe to Stanton Harcourt following the archbishop's death. Lady Anne had been a shy, unassuming person devoted to her family.

Harcourt's eldest son, George, succeeded to the Harcourt family estates. The second son, **Leveson Vernon Harcourt** [formerly Venables-Vernon] (bap. 1788, d. 1860), was born at Sudbury and baptized on 9 June 1788. Like his father he attended Westminster School, where he was elected king's scholar in 1801. He matriculated at Christ Church, Oxford, on 17 May 1806, having been elected head of the list of king's scholars from Westminster. He graduated BA in 1810 and MA in 1813, having been ordained priest in 1812. On 19 August 1815 he married Caroline Mary (bap. 1790, d. 1871), daughter of John Peachey, second Baron Selsey; they had no children.

Leveson Venables-Vernon was chancellor of York (installed 4 August 1827) and held one of the last prebends in the minster under the unreformed constitution, though he lived in London and seldom went to York. He too took the surname Harcourt in 1831 but retained the name Vernon. He was rector of Beckenham, Kent, from 1835 to 1838. He was the author of The doctrine of the deluge: vindicating the scriptural account from the doubts which have recently been cast upon it by geological speculations (1837), which insisted that geologists should be ready to revise their conclusion, for 'if geological speculations are at variance with scriptural history, they are not less at variance with the united testimony of all nations from the remotest time to which history or tradition extends' (preface). He also published Lectures on the Four Gospels Harmonized (1851) and A Remonstrance to the Bishop of Exeter on his Recent Letter to the Archbishop of Canterbury (1850). He died on 26 July 1860.

Edward Harcourt's other children included William Venables Vernon *Harcourt and Octavius Henry Cyril Vernon *Harcourt; many other members of the family were prominent in public life in the nineteenth and twentieth centuries.   Nigel Aston

Sources E. W. Harcourt, ed., The Harcourt papers, 14 vols. (privately printed, London, [1880–1905]) • GEC, Peerage, new edn, 12/2.260–61 • Foster, Alum. Oxon., 1.602–3 • GM, 1st ser., 100/2 (1830), 178 • GM, 2nd ser., 29 (1848), 82–4 • Fasti Angl., 1541–1857, [Bristol], 62, 96 • Fasti Angl. (Hardy), 3.245 • C. M. L. Bouch, Prelates and people of the lake counties: a history of the diocese of Carlisle, 1133–1933 (1948) • J. Wilson, Rose Castle (1912) • Fasti Angl., 1541–1857, [York], 5, 9 • G. Aylmer and R. Cant, eds., York Minster (1977), 283–7 • I. F. Dibdin, Bibliographical, antiquarian and picturesque tour in the northern counties of England, 2 vols. (1838), 1.233–30 • The Times (8 Nov 1847), 5 • The Times (15 Nov 1847), 3 • E. Churton, The remembrance of a departed primate: a sermon preached on 14 November 1847 (1847) • O. Chadwick, The Victorian church, pt. 1, 3rd edn (1971) • Old Westminsters • A. Burns, The diocesan *revival in the Church of England, c.1800–1870* (1999) • Burke, *Peerage* (1999) • IGI • d. cert. [Leveson Harcourt]

Archives Borth. Inst., official corresp. and papers • Borth. Inst., visitation and ordination records, Bp. C & P.IX • York Minster Library, letter-books, COLL 1964/3 • York Minster Library, sermon, Add. MS 117 • York Minster Library, visitation record, M1 (7)11 | BL, corresp. with W. E. Gladstone, Add. MSS 44355, fol. 243; 44358, fol. 239 • BL, corresp. with Lord Grenville, Add. MS 59003 • BL, corresp. with T. Grenville, Add. MSS 41857, fols. 156, 158, 216, 222, 224, 270; 41858, fols. 102, 154; 42058, fol. 206 • BL, corresp. with second Earl Liverpool, Add. MSS 38248, fol. 83; 38269, fol. 290; 38272, fol. 127; 38279, fol. 357; 38280, fols. 17, 47; 38284, fol. 386 • BL, corresp. with R. Peel, Add. MSS 18204, fol. 46; 37966, fol. 234; 40348, fol. 228; 40349, fol. 115; 40393, fol. 22; 40396, fol. 96; 40411, fols. 234, 299; 40419, fols. 178, 294; 40426, fols. 117–18; 40489, fols. 286, 288; 40547, fols. 361–3; 40553, fols. 256, 256b; 40557, fols. 244–5; 40582, fol. 331; 40589, fol. 383 • Carlisle Diocesan Archive, diocesan register, DRC 1/8 • Castle Howard, North Yorkshire, corresp. with fifth and sixth earls of Carlisle • Cumbria AS, Carlisle, corresp. with Lord Lonsdale, D/Lons/ L1/2/3, L1/2/6 • U. Durham L., corresp. with Earl Grey

Likenesses J. Hoppner, oils, exh. RA 1803, Christ Church Oxf. • W. Owen, oils, 1807, Bishopthorpe Palace, York • H. Meyer, mezzotint, pubd 1815 (after J. Jackson), BM, NPG • T. Phillips, oils, 1819, All Souls Oxf. • T. Lawrence, oils, 1823, Sudbury Hall, Derbyshire [*see illus.*] • M. Noble, recumbent effigy, 1855, York Minster • M. Noble, recumbent effigy on tomb chest, 1858, St Michael's Church, Stanton Harcourt, Oxfordshire • G. Brown, stipple (aged eighty-nine; after G. Richmond), BM • G. Hayter, group portrait, oils (*The trial of Queen Caroline*, 1820), NPG

Wealth at death £66,000: will, 25 Sept 1847, PRO, PROB 11/2068, sig. 81 • under £40,000—Leveson Harcourt: probate, 3 Sept 1860, CGPLA Eng. & Wales

Harcourt, Henry. *See* Beaumont, Henry (c.1611–1673).

Harcourt, Ivo de (*d.* in or after 1166). *See under* Harcourt family (*per.* c.1050–1330).

Harcourt, Sir John (1274–1330). *See under* Harcourt family (*per.* c.1050–1330).

Harcourt, Leveson Francis Vernon- (1839–1907), civil engineer, was born in London on 25 January 1839, the second son of Admiral Frederick Edward Vernon-Harcourt (1790–1883) and Marcia (1803/4–1868), daughter of Admiral John Richard Delap Tollemache. He was the grandson of Edward *Harcourt, archbishop of York, and cousin of Sir William *Harcourt, the Liberal cabinet minister. Educated at Harrow School and at Balliol College, Oxford, he obtained a first class in mathematics in 1861, and graduated with a first class in natural science in 1862.

From 1862 to 1865 Vernon-Harcourt was a pupil of the civil engineer John Hawkshaw, and was employed on the Penarth and Hull docks. After serving as an assistant, he was appointed in November 1866 as resident engineer on the new works at the East and West India docks in London, continuing in the position until their completion in January 1870. From an open competition he was elected to the post of county surveyor of Westmeath in Ireland but resigned in August 1870, at which time he married, on 2 August 1870, Alice (1843/4–1919), younger daughter of Lieutenant-Colonel Henry Rowland Brandreth RE, with whom he had a son and two daughters. During the same month he took a position as resident engineer at Alderney

harbour in Ireland, and his article on this subject (*Proceedings of the Institution of Civil Engineers*, 37, 1874, 60–83) was the first of his many papers to gain distinction from the Institution of Civil Engineers. From 1872 to 1874 Vernon-Harcourt was based in Ireland and was resident engineer on the Rosslare harbour works and the railway to Wexford. He returned to London, and between 1875 and 1878 carried out a number of surveys for Hawkshaw, investigating the disposal of sewage into the River Clyde, and surveying the River Witham and the upper reaches of the River Thames in order to analyse and report on measures to reduce flooding.

In 1882 Vernon-Harcourt began work as a consulting engineer in Westminster, and in the same year was elected professor of civil engineering at University College, London. He mainly devoted himself to the engineering of harbours and docks, rivers and canals, and water supply, and in this branch of engineering he became an acknowledged authority. During his career he reported on the rivers Usk, Ribble, Orwell, and Dee, the Aire and Calder navigation, the Ouse navigation, and the harbours of Poole, Newport, and Sligo. In the numerous books and articles that he wrote, as well as in the many parliamentary inquiries to which he was often called to contribute, he displayed his practical training as well as his natural scientific aptitude. Vernon-Harcourt's main books were *Rivers and Canals* (2 vols., 1882; rev. 2nd edn, 1896); *Harbours and Docks* (2 vols., 1885); *Civil Engineering as Applied in Construction* (1902); *Sanitary Engineering* (1907); and a popular work, *Achievements in Engineering during the Last Half Century* (1891). He also contributed eighteen articles to the *Proceedings of the Institution of Civil Engineers*, having been initially elected an associate of the body on 5 December 1865, gaining full membership on 19 December 1871. For these he was awarded the Telford and George Stephenson medals, six Telford premiums, and a Manby premium. The articles covered all aspects of his field and included 'Harbours and estuaries on sandy coasts' (*Proceedings of the Institution of Civil Engineers*, 70, 1882, 1–32), 'The River Seine' (ibid., 84, 1886, 210–57), and 'The training of rivers' (ibid., 118, 1894, 1–46). He also contributed articles to the Royal Society, the Society of Arts, and the British Association, as well as to the *Encyclopaedia Britannica* (9th edn) and other publications. Although he retired in 1905, being elected emeritus professor in 1906, he continued working in the field until his death.

Vernon-Harcourt, who was fluent in French, regularly contributed to the proceedings and organization of navigation congresses. He represented the Institution of Civil Engineers at the navigation congresses held at Brussels in 1898, at Paris in 1900, and at Dusseldorf in 1902, and was a delegate of the British government at the Milan Congress in 1905. He was the British member of the jury for the Paris Exhibition of 1900, and again at the St Louis Exhibition of 1904, during which year he also served on an international jury in Vienna to consider schemes for large canal-lifts, and for this work was created a commander of the imperial Franz-Josef order of Austria–Hungary. In 1906 he was appointed a member of the international commission of the Suez Maritime Canal, by which time his expertise had often been required outside his own country. In 1896, for example, he had gone to India to inspect the River Hooghly, reporting to the Calcutta port commissioners on a project for the improvement of the river (*Proceedings of the Institution of Civil Engineers*, 160, 1905, 100–43). Held in high regard throughout his profession, he was, at his death, the oldest member of the council of the Permanent International Association of Navigation Congresses.

Vernon-Harcourt died, after several weeks' illness, at Swanage, Dorset, on 14 September 1907, and was buried at Brookwood cemetery on 21 September. He bequeathed £1000 to the Institution of Civil Engineers for the provision of biennial lectures in his special subjects and a further £1000 to be donated to the University of Oxford after the death of his widow to fund the teaching of engineering.   W. F. SPEAR, *rev.* PHILIP N. GROVER

Sources *Engineering* (20 Sept 1907), 404–5 · *PICE*, 171 (1907–8), 421–3 · *WWW*, 1897–1915 · A. T. C. Pratt, ed., *People of the period: being a collection of the biographies of upwards of six thousand living celebrities*, 2 vols. (1897) · Burke, *Peerage* (1959) · *The Times* (17 Sept 1907) · *The Times* (19 Sept 1907) · *The Times* (21 Sept 1907) · *The Times* (30 Oct 1907) · *CGPLA Eng. & Wales* (1907) · d. cert. [Marcia Vernon-Harcourt] · d. cert. [Alice Vernon-Harcourt] · m. cert.
Likenesses Elliott & Fry, photograph, repro. in 'The late Leveson Francis Vernon-Harcourt'
Wealth at death £56,535 12s. 4d.: probate, 26 Oct 1907, *CGPLA Eng. & Wales*

Harcourt, Leveson Vernon (*bap.* 1788, *d.* 1860). *See under* Harcourt, Edward (1757–1847).

Harcourt, Lewis Vernon, first Viscount Harcourt (1863–1922), politician, was born in Pont Street, London, on 31 January 1863, the younger and only surviving son of Sir William *Harcourt (1827–1904) and his first wife, Marie Therese (1835–1863), daughter of the novelist and playwright Thomas Henry *Lister of Armytage Park, Staffordshire. Lewis Harcourt's mother died when he was born, and this resulted in an exceptionally close and protective relationship between father and son. Behind his exuberant manner Sir William Harcourt was a deeply emotional man to whom the precocious and delicate boy (known to everyone throughout his life as Loulou) was 'both a trust and a consoler' (Gardiner, 1.292). The two were constant companions throughout Loulou's childhood, and even Sir William Harcourt's second marriage in December 1876 did not significantly affect the relationship. The thirteen-year-old boy acted as best man at the ceremony in Westminster Abbey, and he was included as a matter of course on the Paris honeymoon. Loulou got on well with his young American stepmother, and in due course became very fond of his half-brother Bobby.

Early life: political partnership with his father Harcourt went to a private school in Eastbourne and then, after some hesitation on his father's part, to Eton College where, in spite of recurrent ill health, he was popular and happy. But in 1881 it was decided that he was not robust enough to go to Cambridge, and he gradually settled into

Lewis Vernon Harcourt, first Viscount Harcourt (1863–1922), by Campbell-Gray, *c.*1906–8

the position of confidential private secretary to his father, who was then home secretary in Gladstone's second government. This was to remain Lewis Harcourt's career for over twenty years, until his father's death in 1904. His surviving journals convey a fascinating picture of the unique working relationship, and also of the social and political world of the 1880s and 1890s. The Harcourts were wealthy and well connected, and Loulou knew everyone who mattered in society, and was able to claim universal entrée to London drawing-rooms and country house parties. One might have expected the father's over-indulgent upbringing to produce an intolerably self-important son, but Loulou seems generally to have been a welcome guest, especially to older women (like Mrs Gladstone) who mothered him. He was interested in everybody's affairs, was a good listener, and loved gossip. The journals also describe some of Harcourt's enthusiastic leisure pursuits—photography (he captured many of his political contemporaries on film), rare books, theatre-going, and grouse shooting.

The political partnership between father and son grew closer over the years, and in spite of the emotional intensity of the relationship, and Sir William Harcourt's fiery temper, there seem to have been no quarrels or estrangements. The physical contrast between the Falstaffian proportions of the father and those of his tall, thin son was matched by corresponding differences in temperament. Whereas Sir William Harcourt was impulsive and sometimes insensitive to his colleagues' feelings, Loulou grew up to be self-controlled and quietly determined. Although totally dedicated to his father's political interests he was not uncritical: every speech was shrewdly and expertly assessed, and gradually the father came to rely on his son's judgement.

Occasionally Lewis Harcourt realized that his career might suffer from being so closely linked to that of his father: in October 1884 he was briefly tempted by the prospect of succeeding his friend Reginald Brett as private secretary to Lord Hartington. But Sir William Harcourt was reluctant to allow his son to launch himself into the tough world of politics, and in 1892 he declined Gladstone's offer to appoint Loulou as one of the junior whips in his fourth government. Although over the years Lewis Harcourt received invitations from several constituencies to stand for parliament, he preferred to work behind the scenes as long as his father needed him. However, he acted as secretary to the Home Counties Liberal Federation from its foundation in 1887, and was a founder committee member of the National Liberal Club. In September 1893 Sir William Harcourt, then chancellor of the exchequer, asked Gladstone to consider his son for appointment as commissioner of woods and forests ('the first thing I ever asked for in my life' (BL, Add. MS 44203, fol. 96). But Loulou felt that he could not desert his father, and he later declined posts at the Royal Mint and the National Debt Office.

In 1894 Lewis Harcourt played a controversial role at the climax of his father's political career. When Gladstone retired in March 1894, the chief rival candidates for the premiership were Sir William Harcourt and Lord Rosebery. It was widely believed that the queen would send for Rosebery, and many of Sir William Harcourt's colleagues, bruised by his insensitivity over the years, would have endorsed this choice if they had been consulted. But Lewis Harcourt was determined to fight every inch of the way to secure the succession. He first tried to induce Gladstone to stay on, by seeking to persuade Lord Spencer to moderate the bid for increased naval expenditure which had caused the cabinet crisis. He also tried unsuccessfully to persuade his father to make Rosebery's premiership impossible by refusing to serve under him as leader of the House of Commons. When these attempts failed he sought to undermine the preference of John Morley for Rosebery, and to stimulate back-bench radical objections to the prospect of a party leader in the House of Lords.

The only result of all this frantic activity was to increase Sir William Harcourt's ultimate humiliation, and to sour relations between the rival candidates. They were barely on speaking terms during Rosebery's brief premiership, and during the following years in opposition the ill feeling persisted. The highly sensitive Rosebery never forgave Lewis Harcourt for the part he had played in 1894, and the dislike was mutual. When Sir William Harcourt resigned the leadership in 1898, with carefully orchestrated press publicity designed to embarrass Rosebery's supporters, he assured his son that he owed the success of this 'torpedo' to 'your devotion and capacity' (Gardiner, 2.478). However, Campbell-Bannerman and Asquith, left to pick up the pieces, were not impressed by conduct which they considered more appropriate to the nursery (Bodl. Oxf.,

MSS Asquith, vol. 9, fol. 139). Like his father Lewis Harcourt strongly opposed the Second South African War, which divided the Liberal Party, and in 1903 he helped to set up the Free Trade Union in opposition to Joseph Chamberlain's tariff reform proposals.

In parliament and cabinet, 1905–1917 In March 1904, shortly before his death, Sir William Harcourt proudly introduced his son to the House of Commons, following Loulou's unopposed return at a by-election in Rossendale, Lord Hartington's old Lancashire constituency. After spending nearly twenty-five years in partnership with his father Lewis Harcourt now embarked on a political career of his own. It lasted only twelve years, but for nearly all this time the Liberal Party was in power and Harcourt was in office. This suited him very well. He was not by temperament a back-bencher or a public speaker, but someone at home in the corridors of power: he waited two years, until he was a minister, before making his maiden speech. When Campbell-Bannerman formed his government in December 1905 Harcourt became first commissioner of works, and a privy councillor. He was promoted to the cabinet, while remaining in the same post, in March 1907.

In January 1907 Harcourt declined an offer of the education department: he was in his element at the office of works, with responsibility for the royal parks and palaces and for the facilities in the houses of parliament. Remembering his long years as a political adviser he arranged for the officials' box to be moved to a more convenient position near the government front bench in the House of Commons, and he devised improved procedures for parliamentary divisions.

When Asquith became prime minister in April 1908 Harcourt was retained in his existing post, but in November 1910 he unexpectedly succeeded Lord Crewe as colonial secretary. He was particularly interested in economic development, and during his period of office important new railway links were established in Nigeria (where Port Harcourt was named after him) and east Africa. In addition to his departmental duties Harcourt was responsible for steering several bills through the House of Commons: in 1906 a bill, subsequently rejected by the House of Lords, designed to end the abuse of plural voting by electors with property in different constituencies; in 1907 a Small Holdings and Allotments Bill; and in 1909 a London Elections Bill.

Not all of Harcourt's colleagues found his love of manipulative intrigue congenial. Charles Hobhouse, for instance, described him as 'subtle, secretive, adroit, and not very reliable or *au fond* courageous' (*Inside Asquith's Cabinet*, 229). In cabinet he sat next to Asquith and liked to chat to him in undertones rather than intervening openly in the discussion. The pair got on well: Asquith respected Harcourt's administrative competence and shared many of his social interests, and with his wife was a regular guest at Harcourt's country house at Nuneham Courtenay. The two men also shared the hostility aroused by their opposition to women's suffrage, a reform supported by several members of the cabinet. Harcourt played a leading role in the anti-suffrage campaign, and in January 1910 he was unsuccessfully opposed in the general election at Rossendale by an independent Labour candidate who campaigned on a platform of votes for women. In January 1912 a *Punch* cartoon showed Lloyd George and Harcourt as the two main government spokesmen arguing respectively for and against women's suffrage. Harcourt voted against both the Parliamentary Franchise (Women) Bill in March 1912 and the Representation of the People (Women) Bill in May 1913. His stance made him a *bête noire* for the militant suffragists, and in 1912 his home became a target for them, when an attempt was made to set fire to the children's quarters at Nuneham.

On other issues Harcourt remained a traditional nineteenth-century radical. He distrusted Lloyd George, who described him as the most implacable of the cabinet critics of the 1909 budget (Stevenson, 322). He regarded some of the budget proposals as extravagant, and blamed Lloyd George's speeches for the Liberal losses in southern England in the general election of January 1910 (Bodl. Oxf., MSS Asquith, vol. 12, fol. 77). But Harcourt strongly supported Asquith's determination to restrict the veto powers of the House of Lords (MSS Asquith, vol. 12, fol. 114; vol. 23, fols. 79 and 96), and during the 1913 home rule crisis he made bluntly clear to the king the consequences for the monarchy of not accepting the decisions of parliament (*Journals and Letters of … Esher*, 3.131). Above all Harcourt remained totally opposed, as his father had been, to the inexorable rise in naval and military expenditure, and to the assumption of diplomatic obligations in mainland Europe. In February 1908 he was deputed by the cabinet, together with Lloyd George and Reginald McKenna, to negotiate with Sir John Fisher a reduction in the naval estimates. He took an uncharacteristically blunt line, but the attempt failed. Again in 1909 Harcourt was one of a group of cabinet ministers who tried unsuccessfully to resist the increase in the naval estimates.

It was only in 1911 that Harcourt, together with most of his cabinet colleagues, learned of the military and naval conversations with the French which had begun early in 1906. Harcourt resisted any suggestion that there was either a legal or a moral obligation to support France in the event of war, and he co-operated with Haldane in his attempts to reassure Germany and to negotiate peaceful solutions to outstanding sources of disagreement, particularly those involving the African colonies. When the crux came at the end of July 1914 Harcourt was one of the group of cabinet ministers who initially argued the case for neutrality, but unlike John Morley he was persuaded to remain in office by the German invasion of Belgium and by Asquith's appeal to his colleagues to save the country from the alternative of a Conservative or coalition government.

At the beginning of the war Harcourt shared a widespread inability to grasp its likely extent and character, particularly since he was concerned mainly with the colonial aspects of the conflict. In a speech to the Victoria League on 26 January 1915 he referred to 'the thrills and the romance of thinly defended frontiers … [and] gallantly captured posts' (Hazelhurst, 167). As always Harcourt worked hard behind the scenes on the administration of the war effort, and began to show signs of exhaustion and overstrain. During 1915 he was one of the cabinet ministers most strongly opposed to conscription, having in 1913 resisted compulsory territorial training, and he became a target, together with Haldane, Simon, and McKenna, for press criticisms of the government's conduct of the war. In May 1915 Asquith yielded to the pressure to form a coalition government. Haldane was dropped, but Harcourt survived the reshuffle, being moved back to the office of works to make way for Bonar Law, whose rough manners contrasted strikingly with Harcourt's social smoothness: as Lord Esher commented, in any other country 'Loulou would be the Tory and Bonar Law the democrat' (*Journals and Letters of … Esher*, 3.137). In the summer of 1916 Harcourt was placed temporarily in charge of the Board of Trade, but his health was failing and at the end of the year he left office when Asquith resigned.

House of Lords: last years Harcourt was pleased when the king agreed in January 1917 to revive for him the old family viscountcy which had been held by Queen Anne's lord chancellor. At the age of only fifty-four his active political career was almost over, although he became chairman of the army agricultural committee, which dealt with food supplies in England, France, and Mesopotamia, and of the empire oil resources committee. He was also associated with the Imperial Institute. During 1917 Harcourt made an attempt, with Margot Asquith's enthusiastic encouragement (Bodl. Oxf., MSS Harcourt, dep. 421, fols. 212–17), to improve the efficiency of the party organization of the Asquith Liberals, and he was active in the House of Lords in January 1918, during the consideration of the Representation of the People Bill. He had finally become reconciled to women's suffrage, although he remained critical of newfangled notions such as proportional representation, which he described as 'the apotheosis of the crank, the *frondeur*, and the mugwump' (*Hansard 5L*, 27, 21 Jan 1918, 845).

In subsequent sessions Viscount Harcourt rarely appeared in the House of Lords, although he maintained his personal links with Asquith, who consulted him on party management (Bodl. Oxf., MSS Harcourt, dep. 421, fol. 218). In February 1920 Harcourt congratulated Asquith on the 'glorious news' of his victory in the Paisley by-election (Bodl. Oxf., MSS Asquith, vol. 33, fol. 194), and only a few weeks before his death Harcourt was urged by Asquith to lend his support to a Liberal demonstration in Central Hall, Westminster, on 21 January 1922 (Bodl. Oxf., MSS Harcourt, dep. 421, fol. 223).

Harcourt had many interests outside politics. On 1 July 1899 he had married Mary Ethel, the wealthy daughter of an American banker, Walter Hayes Burns, and they had a son and three daughters. The Harcourts entertained extensively at their town house at 69 Brook Street (later the Savile Club) and at the family seat Nuneham Courtenay, where Harcourt devoted much time and effort to the improvement of the estate and the gardens. He enjoyed country life, especially shooting and fishing, and he was conscientious in his many public appointments. With Lord Esher he had helped to found the London Museum in 1911, and he was a member of the advisory committee of the Victoria and Albert Museum, and of the council and executive of the British School at Rome. He was also an honorary fellow of the Royal Institute of British Architects, and a trustee of the Wallace Collection, the National Portrait Gallery, and the British Museum. The latter gave him great pleasure: he told Asquith in February 1913, when he accepted the appointment, that it was 'the only ambition which I have ever permitted myself in life' (Bodl. Oxf., MSS Harcourt, dep. 421, fol. 193). He was a competent photographer and a number of his photographs of politicians are held by the National Portrait Gallery.

On 24 February 1922 Harcourt was found dead in his bedroom at 69 Brook Street, Mayfair. He had taken an overdose of a sleeping draught, and there were widespread rumours of suicide, following accusations of sexual impropriety by Edward James, a young Etonian (Lees-Milne, 337). Similar allegations had been made before, but at the inquest a verdict of misadventure was returned, on the basis of post-mortem medical evidence that the heart was extensively diseased and that the overdose would not have been harmful in other circumstances. The coroner rejected as 'grotesque' the idea of suicide, for which there was 'not the slightest motive' (*The Times*, 1 March 1922). It is perhaps significant that Harcourt spent the last evening of his life checking draft chapters of the biography of Sir William Harcourt which he had commissioned from A. G. Gardiner. He was due to meet Gardiner on the following day to discuss the book and it seems hard to believe that Harcourt would not have wished to see through to completion an enterprise over which he had exercised tight control, and which recalled for him the glorious days of political partnership with his father. Harcourt was buried on 1 March 1922 at the old church, Nuneham Park. He was succeeded as the second and last viscount by his son, William Edward *Harcourt (1908–1979).

PATRICK JACKSON

Sources A. G. Gardiner, *The life of Sir William Harcourt*, 2 vols. (1923) · *Hansard* · *Journals and letters of Reginald, Viscount Esher*, ed. M. V. Brett and Oliver, Viscount Esher, 4 vols. (1934–8) · J. A. Spender and C. Asquith, *Life of Herbert Henry Asquith, Lord Oxford and Asquith*, 2 vols. [1932] · P. Stansky, *Ambitions and strategies* (1964) · *Inside Asquith's cabinet: from the diaries of Charles Hobhouse*, ed. E. David (1977) · M. Pugh, *Electoral reform in war and peace, 1906–18* (1978) · C. Hazlehurst, *Politicians at war, July 1914 to May 1915* (1971) · F. Stevenson, *Lloyd George: a diary*, ed. A. J. P. Taylor (1971) · Lord Ullswater, *A speaker's commentaries* (1925) · J. Lees-Milne, *The enigmatic Edwardian: the life of Reginald, 2nd Viscount Esher* (1986) · A. Birrell, *Things past redress* (1937) · d. cert. · BL, Add. MS 44203, fol. 96 · Bodl. Oxf., MSS Asquith · Bodl. Oxf., MS Harcourt dep. 421

Archives Bodl. Oxf., corresp. and papers; corresp. relating to women's suffrage; MSS, incl. journals · U. Birm. L., corresp. | BL, corresp. with Arthur James Balfour, Add. MS 49716, *passim* · BL, letters to Sir Henry Campbell-Bannerman, Add. MSS 41214–41220 · BL, letters to Sir Charles Dilke, Add. MSS 43910–43911, 43916–43920 · BL, corresp. with Viscount Gladstone, Add. MSS 45997–46002 · BL, corresp. with Lord Ripon, Add. MSS 43636–43640 · BLPES, letters to A. G. Gardiner · Bodl. Oxf., corresp. with Herbert Asquith · Bodl. RH, corresp. with Lord Lugard · Glos. RO, corresp. with Sir Michael Hicks-Brady · HLRO, letters to H. Samuel · King's AC Cam., letters to Oscar Browning · NL Aus., corresp. with Viscount Novar · Nuffield Oxf., corresp. with Lord Emmott · Nuffield Oxf., corresp. with J. E. B. Seeley · PRO, corresp. with Lord Kitchener, PRO 30/57, WO 159 · Surrey HC, corresp. with Lord Onslow · U. Leeds, Brotherton L., letters to Edmund Gosse · U. Newcastle, Robinson L., corresp. with Walter Runciman

Likenesses Campbell-Gray, photograph, c.1906–1908, NPG [*see illus.*] · W. Stoneman, three photographs, c.1917, NPG · S. J. Solomon, oils, 1922–3, London Museum · B. Partridge, ink caricature, NPG; repro. in *Punch*, 134 (1908), 291 · Spy [L. Ward], cartoon, repro. in *VF* (8 Sept 1895) · photograph (after L. Dicksee), NPG

Wealth at death £199,290 12s. 11d.: probate, 1 April 1922, *CGPLA Eng. & Wales*

Harcourt, Octavius Henry Cyril Vernon (1793–1863), naval officer, eighth son of Dr Edward Vernon *Harcourt (1757–1847), archbishop of York, and his wife, Anne, *née* Leveson-Gower (d. 1832), third daughter of Granville Leveson-Gower, first marquess of Stafford, was born at Rose Castle, Cumberland, on 25 December 1793. The family assumed the additional surname Harcourt on 15 January 1831. Octavius entered the navy in August 1806 as midshipman on the *Tigre* (74 guns), and in her the following year witnessed the surrender of Alexandria; he was also employed in boat service up the Nile. After assisting at the siege of Toulon, he was transferred into the *Malta* (80 guns); he co-operated with the troops on the south-east coast of Spain, and served in the batteries at the siege of Tarragona. Promoted lieutenant on 11 January 1814, he joined the *Mulgrave* (74 guns), and was the commanding officer of a party of seamen and marines which landed near Piombo, captured a martello tower, and brought out a convoy anchored under its protection. Later that year, in the *Amelia* (38 guns), he served at the blockade of Elba. He was on half pay from 1816 until 2 February 1818, when he was appointed to the *Sir Francis Drake*, the flagship at Newfoundland, where on 3 February 1820 he obtained the command of the sloop *Drake* and for a short time in the same year of the *Carnation* (18 guns). From 1824 to 1827 he served in the West Indies. He was promoted captain on 7 July 1827. His last appointment was to the *North Star* (28 guns), in which he surveyed the coast of Central America and California in 1834–6, returning home with a large freight.

On 22 February 1838 Harcourt married Anne Holwell, second daughter of William Gater and widow of William Danby of Swinton Park, Masham, Yorkshire: 'in her right he became lord of Masham and Mashamshire, and entered into the possession of a very handsome rent-roll' (*GM*). He resided principally at Swinton Park, and was an active magistrate. He was gazetted sheriff of Yorkshire in 1848, and was promoted vice-admiral on half pay on 4 June 1861. He was a generous benefactor of local schools, charities, and the Masham Mechanics' Institute; he built and endowed a church at Healey, near Masham, and another church at Brent Tor, Devon, as well as restoring the parish church of Masham. In 1858 he erected in Masham six almshouses, which he endowed with £1775 three per cent consols. He died at Swinton Park on 14

August 1863; his widow died on 26 June 1879, devising her Yorkshire estates to George, fifth son of Sir Robert Affleck, bt.   G. C. BOASE, rev. ROGER MORRISS

Sources O'Byrne, *Naval biog. dict.* · *GM*, 3rd ser., 15 (1863), 507–8 · *Leeds Mercury* (17 Aug 1863), 3 · P. Mackesy, *The war in the Mediterranean, 1803–1810* (1957) · R. Muir, *Britain and the defeat of Napoleon, 1807–1815* (1996) · Boase, *Mod. Eng. biog.*

Wealth at death under £250,000: resworn probate, Jan 1864, *CGPLA Eng. & Wales*

Harcourt, Sir Richard de (d. 1258). *See under* Harcourt family (*per. c.*1050–1330).

Harcourt, Sir Richard de (1256–1293). *See under* Harcourt family (*per. c.*1050–1330).

Harcourt, Robert de (d. *c.*1205). *See under* Harcourt family (*per. c.*1050–1330).

Harcourt, Robert (1574/5–1631), colonial adventurer and author, was born at Ellenhall, Staffordshire, the eldest of the five children of Walter (later Sir Walter) Harcourt (*c.*1553–1639) of Ellenhall and of Stanton Harcourt, Oxfordshire, and his wife and stepsister, Dorothy, daughter of William Robinson of Drayton Basset, Staffordshire, and his wife, Grace, daughter of Humphrey Fitzherbert of Upsall, Hertfordshire. Both the Harcourt and Fitzherbert families retained Catholic sympathies, although Sir Walter sat as an MP in the 1580s and 1590s. Robert matriculated as a gentleman commoner from St Alban Hall, Oxford, on 10 April 1590, at the age of fifteen. He remained at Oxford for three years, his studies leaving him, as his later writings on Guiana demonstrate, with a taste for scholarship as well as adventure, and the ability to express himself clearly with his pen. On 10 March 1593 he was admitted to the Middle Temple, but little is known about his activities over the next fifteen years. At an unknown date Harcourt married Elizabeth, daughter of John Fitzherbert of Norbury, Derbyshire; they had no children. Following her death he married Frances, daughter of Geoffrey Vere, the third son of John de *Vere, fifteenth earl of Oxford (1482–1540) [*see under* Vere, John de]. They had three sons, Simon *Harcourt, probably baptized on 20 May 1601, Frances (*bap.* 1605), and Vere (*bap.* 1606), and three daughters, Jane, Dorothy, and Margaret who died shortly after her birth in 1607. Harcourt's father's estates were encumbered with debt and the Oxfordshire landholdings were temporarily seized for non-payment of loans in 1595. Sir Walter conveyed the manor of Stanton Harcourt to his eldest son in 1602, presumably to avoid losing it to his creditors. Sir Walter and Robert Harcourt jointly sold off the South Leigh portion of the estate in 1604. By 1609 Robert Harcourt was receiving income from ironworks developed on the manor of Chebsey, Staffordshire.

On 13 February 1609, through the patronage of Prince Henry, Robert Harcourt and his 'freinds and Associats' received a commission to undertake 'many and sundrie longe journeys by Sea and Shippping unto the South parte of America … knowne by the name of Guiana' (PRO, C66/1986). Although he courteously attributed his venture to Guiana to a desire to 'repaire the decay' (R. Harcourt,

61), of Ralegh's enterprise, Harcourt's sense of connection to the region probably came through the Guiana enterprises of his kinsman, Sir Robert Dudley, and his approach to the prince through Sir Thomas Challoner, who had been Dudley's tutor and was now in the prince's household. Harcourt also had contact with the late Charles Leigh's associates. When he sailed for Guiana in April 1609 he took two Guiana natives with him, one 'who was a christian, and had lived in England fourteen years', and the other, who had been brought back from the Wiapoco (Oyapok) four years previously by Leigh's men (ibid., 71, 73).

Harcourt arrived in the Wiapoco on 17 May 1609 with 'one and thirtie land men, two Indians, and three and twentie mariners and Saylers' (R. Harcourt, 5). He was well received by the natives and allowed to settle his men in the villages at the river mouth. In July, once the rains had ceased, he made contact with an inland chief who had 'been heretofore in England with Sr. Walter Raleigh, to whom hee beareth great affection' (ibid., 80) and began to 'travaell abroad in search of those Golden Mountaines, promised unto us before the beginning of our voyage' (ibid., 107). When no goldmines were discovered Harcourt quelled incipient mutiny among his company by sending them out to search for other profitable commodities. His own stay on the Wiapoco was cut short by the news that his ships' drink casks were rapidly deteriorating. He set sail for home in early August leaving his brother Michael and one Captain Edward Harvey to command approximately thirty men left behind on the river. *En route* he reconnoitred the lower reaches of the Caiane (Cayenne) and Marrawini (Maroni), engaged in contraband trade for tobacco with the Spanish settlers at Port of Spain, Trinidad, and tried the hot spring on Meves (Nevis), 'one of the best and most soveraigne in the world' (ibid., 123). Driven by gales into Crookhaven, Ireland, Harcourt became separated from his company and took passage from Youghall to Bristol, arriving on 17 December 1609.

Harcourt returned home to financial troubles, as well as charges of recusancy. His attempt, at about this time, to lay claim to the manor of Norbury in Derbyshire, at the expense of his brother-in-law Anthony Fitzherbert, probably reflects his desperation to increase his income. John Smith reports that he was never subsequently able to supply his settlement, except by sending over a few colonists with Zeeland merchants who left factors on the river from 1612 onwards. In 1611 he settled the manor house of Stanton Harcourt and its demesne on his wife Frances in jointure. Michael Harcourt returned to England in 1612 with stories of rich goldmines and precious stones to be found in the interior, and of the commercial possibilities on the coast, moving his older brother to ask Prince Henry to advance his suit to the king for an exclusive administrative and commercial monopoly of the region 'betweene the Ryver of Amazones [Amazon] and the Ryver of Dessequebe [Essequibo]' (PRO, C66/1986). This was duly granted to Robert Harcourt, with his kinsman John Robinson and Sir Thomas Challoner, on 28 August

1613. In September Harcourt published his *Relation of a Voyage to Guiana*, accompanied by a prospectus setting out conditions for those who chose to adventure with him in either purse or person. Few appear to have been willing to do so. In the previous year Harcourt had sold the manor of Stanton Harcourt in order to raise funds. He may have been able to make contact through traders in late 1613 and again in 1616. One of his associates, Captain Edward Harvey, seems to have tried to carry out some men through the Dutch in 1617.

Although his colony had failed, Harcourt strongly resisted Roger North's efforts to form the Amazon Company in 1619, seeing it as an intrusion of his monopoly. The privy council settled the dispute by allocating the territory south of the Wiapoco to the short-lived Amazon Company while leaving the Wiapoco to Harcourt. However, in 1625, when Roger North saw the opportunity to revive his Amazon ventures, Harcourt showed himself willing to join with him in the formation of the Guiana Company. Samuel Purchas included the text of the first edition of Harcourt's *Relation* in volume 4 of *Purchas his Pilgrimes* in 1625, together with a brief account of explorations of the River Maroni carried out by Harcourt's men in 1610. As part of the effort to raise investors, a second edition of Harcourt's *Relation*, revised to include North's Amazon ventures, was published in 1626. In November 1628 the *Little Hopewell* left Gravesend for the Amazon, carrying out some 100 men for the company's first colony under Robert Harcourt as governor. Harcourt, however, ignored his directives to go to the Amazon, returning instead to his former haunts on the Wiapoco. Arriving in February 1629 he immediately began to undertake fortifications and parcel out land for plantation, with a view to sugar production. The second body of colonists, sent out by the company in summer 1629, settled in the Amazon, leaving Harcourt without any supply. English traders who visited the Wiapoco in late March 1630 found his settlers short of provisions, sick with fevers and dysentery, and harassed by hostile Caribs. Harcourt died on 20 May 1631, almost certainly on the Wiapoco, and was probably buried there the same day. Spanish reports indicate that some of his colonists may still have been on the river in 1637.

JOYCE LORIMER

Sources R. Harcourt, *A relation of a voyage to Guiana, 1613, 1626*, ed. C. A. Harris, Hakluyt Society, 2nd ser., 60 (1928) · S. Purchas, *Hakluytus posthumus, or, Purchas his pilgrimes*, 4 (1625); repr. Hakluyt Society, extra ser., 16 (1906), 358–412 · E. W. Harcourt, ed., *The Harcourt papers*, 14 vols. (privately printed, London, [1880–1905]), vol. 1, pp. 80–81, 102–8, 247–8 · J. Lorimer, ed., *English and Irish settlement on the River Amazon, 1550–1646*, Hakluyt Society, 2nd ser., 171 (1989), 39, 50, 149–232, 275–99, 318–97 · Wood, *Ath. Oxon.*, new edn, 2.143–4 · R. C. Anderson, ed., *The book of examinations and depositions, 1622–44*, 2, Southampton RS, 31 (1931), 65–9 · PRO, PROB 11/179, fol. 76v; PROB 6/17, fol. 27 · PRO, SP14/45, no. 63; SP14/48, no.82; SP14/95, no.22; SP16/24, no.20; SP84/81, fols. 117, 124 · PRO, PC2/27, 15 July 1613; PC2/30, pp.124, 131, 133, 218 · PRO, C66/1986, 2411 · PRO, CO1/4, fols. 17–18v · PRO, HCA13/49, fols. 217–19, 230, 245–8; HCA24/88, no. 5; HCA30/865, no. 7, schedules 1, 4 · Bodl. Oxf., MS Harcourt c. 40/8–12 · N. W. Tildesley, ed., *Ellenhall 1539–1812 with index*, Staffordshire Parish Registers Society (1944–5) · 'Transcript, Stanton Harcourt parish register', Society of Genealogists, OX/R263 · J. Smith, *True travels*, ed. P. Barbour (1630), chap. 24; in *The works of Captain John Smith*, 3 vols. (Chapel Hill and London, 1986), vol. 3, pp. 224–7 · BL, Sloane MS 750 · Foster, *Alum. Oxon.* · *VCH Oxfordshire*, 12.267–96 · J. E. Mousley, 'Harcourt, Sir Walter', HoP, *Commons, 1558–1603* · *DNB* · H. A. C. Sturgess, ed., *Register of admissions to the Honourable Society of the Middle Temple, from the fifteenth century to the year 1944*, 1 (1949), 64

Likenesses M. Gerard, portrait, repro. in Harcourt, *Relation*; formerly at Nuneham Park, Oxford

Harcourt, Sir Simon (*bap.* 1601?, *d.* 1642), army officer, was probably baptized at Leckhampstead, Buckinghamshire, on 20 May 1601, the eldest child of Robert *Harcourt (1574/5–1631), of Stanton Harcourt, Oxfordshire, and his second wife, Frances, daughter of Geoffrey Vere, the third son of John de *Vere, fifteenth earl of Oxford (1482–1540) [*see under* Vere, John de, sixteenth earl of Oxford]. A younger brother, Vere Harcourt, became a Church of England clergyman.

The Harcourt estates were already encumbered when Simon was born, a situation which his father's colonial ventures to Guiana did absolutely nothing to remedy; in 1611 Robert Harcourt settled the manor house of Stanton Harcourt and its demesne on his wife in jointure and the following year he sold the manor of Stanton Harcourt. Consequently in his late teens Harcourt went to the United Provinces to serve under the English commander, his mother's brother Sir Horace *Vere (later first Baron Vere of Tilbury), with whom he fought in the campaigns against Spain in the Netherlands. Charles I knighted him at Whitehall on 26 June 1627. In April 1629 Harcourt was in Vere's foot at the prince of Orange's campaign against 's-Hertogenbosch (Bois-le-Duc), and he served in the trenches until the city fell on 17 September. From June to August 1632 he served at the siege of Maastricht, where he was wounded by a bullet in both cheeks and by a grenade in the thigh during an assault on the city early in August. In November 1633 he returned to England on family business; his father had died in South America in May 1631, leaving an entangled and encumbered inheritance. On 14 April 1635 Simon sued Nicholas Roberts for possession of Stanton Harcourt; the latter claimed to have legitimately purchased it from one Ailworth, who had bought it for £8000. The suit went to the court of wards. Back on campaign, in mid-September 1635 he was shot in the mouth.

Harcourt gained the patronage of Elizabeth of Bohemia, who called him 'so worthy a deserving man' (*CSP dom.*, 1635–6, 266). He returned to England in March 1636 to secure his estates with the support of both Elizabeth and Archbishop Laud. The matter was to drag on through the courts for the rest of his life, eventually to be resolved in his family's favour after his death. In July 1637 he acted as a diplomatic courier for the English foreign service in the Netherlands. By late 1638 he had risen to the rank of sergeant major/major-general in the prince of Orange's army. During these years spent crossing between England and the Netherlands, Harcourt married Lady Anne Paget (*d.* 1661), daughter of William, Lord Paget; their eldest son, Philip, was baptized on 15 December 1638.

The outbreak of war in Britain led to a change of Harcourt's sphere of activities. He received command of an infantry regiment in the marquess of Hamilton's expedition against the covenanters in the first bishops' war. On 18 April 1639 his regiment, numbering 1700 men, rendezvoused at Yarmouth. Although disgusted by the quality of the men's arms, armour, and training he embarked them for the voyage to the Firth of Forth. Following Hamilton's orders, his men landed on the island of Inchcolm on 4–5 May. When Charles I recognized his field army's weakness compared with the covenanters he recalled Sir Simon's and another regiment in late May. In 1640 Harcourt again served as colonel of foot against the covenanters. His rather pedestrian campaign diary survives (*Harcourt Papers*, 1.129). On 3 November 1640 he received a parliamentary grant of Irish lands (subsequently confirmed to his widow on 26 June 1657, but lost by her in spring 1661 to Lady Margaret Boulton, widow of an Irish insurgent).

As part of the effort to crush the Irish rising of October 1641 Harcourt received a commission as colonel of 1100 foot on 26 November. By 16 December he had levied the regiment and began moving towards Ireland. The king, envisaging the continued use of his services, wrote to the prince of Orange four days later asking that Sir Simon might retain his Dutch offices during his absence.

On 31 December Harcourt landed in Ireland with his men. Although he had a royal commission as governor of Dublin the incumbent, Sir Charles Coote, would not relinquish the post. Harcourt also had difficulties in working with the lords justices, but he readily co-operated with the earl of Ormond in fighting the rebels. Near Swords, 6 miles from Dublin, he and Coote with 2000 men beat a force of 8000 insurgents while losing only three men. Late in March 1642 he led an expedition from Dublin against Carrickmain Castle, co. Wicklow. He was wounded on the second day of the attack, and died in a cottage in Merrion, Dublin, on 27 March. 'He lived while laste daye … a saintt' (*Tanner Letters*, 155). Following his death his men took the castle and butchered the 250 men, women, and children inside. Beneath his portrait at Nuneham an illuminated manuscript summarizes his career as follows: 'Holland first prov'd his valour; Scotland stood His trembling foe, and Ireland drank his blood' (*DNB*).

Harcourt's widow's puritanism is vividly witnessed by the spiritual journal which she kept: reflecting in 1649 on the mercies that God had granted her, she was thankful 'if God made me att all usefull to the good of my husbands soul' and regarded it as a providence 'that my husband dyed in an unquestionable quarrell, a usefull and much desired man' (*Harcourt Papers*, 1.170). She later married the parliamentarian general Sir William *Waller. Harcourt's son and heir Philip (*bap.* 1638, *d.* 1688) was knighted on 5 June 1660. He married first his stepsister Anne Waller, daughter of Sir William Waller and his second wife, Lady Anne Finch, and second Elizabeth Lee, daughter and heir of John Lee, merchant, of Anderwyke, Buckinghamshire. He sat in the Cavalier Parliament from 1666 as MP for Boston, Lincolnshire, and, as a whig, in the third Exclusion Parliament of 1681. He died on 20 March 1688. Coincidentally Sir Simon's descendant Sir William Vernon Harcourt married a daughter of John L. Motley, the nineteenth-century historian of the Dutch revolt.

EDWARD M. FURGOL

Sources CSP dom., 1633–43 · CSP Ire., 1633–47 · R. Bagwell, *Ireland under the Stuarts*, 3 vols. (1909–16) · C. McNeill, ed., *The Tanner letters*, IMC (1943) · C. R. Markham, *The fighting Veres* (1888) · Burke, *Gen. GB* (1886) · E. W. Harcourt, ed., *The Harcourt papers*, 14 vols. (privately printed, London, [1880–1905]), vol. 1 · IGI · L. Naylor and J. Jagger, 'Harcourt, Sir Philip', HoP, *Commons, 1660–90*
Archives Bodl. Oxf., Carte collection · Bodl. Oxf., Tanner letters · PRO, state papers domestic, state papers Ireland
Likenesses line engraving, NPG · oils, Nuneham Courtenay, Oxfordshire

Harcourt, Simon, first Viscount Harcourt (1661?–1727), lawyer and politician, was born probably in December 1661, the only son of Sir Philip Harcourt (*bap.* 1638, *d.* 1688), a landowner and politician of Stanton Harcourt, Oxfordshire, and his first wife, Anne (*d.* 1664), the daughter of Sir William Waller of Osterley Park, Middlesex.

Early years Harcourt's father was a presbyterian who conformed to the Church of England while retaining nonconformists as domestic chaplains. He sent his son to be educated at Shilton School, a nonconformist establishment run by Samuel Birch. Harcourt then entered the Inner Temple on 16 April 1676 and Pembroke College, Oxford, on 30 March 1677, aged fifteen. Although he graduated BA on 21 January 1679 he chose the law as his career, and was called to the bar on 25 November 1683.

To some extent a career was a necessity, as on 18 October 1680 Harcourt had married Rebecca, the daughter of Thomas Clarke, his father's chaplain. This match was opposed by his father, and some contemporaries attributed Harcourt's hard work as a reaction to the financial difficulties of his early married life. The couple set up home in Chipping Norton, Oxfordshire, and had three sons (two of whom died young) and two daughters before Rebecca died (she was buried on 16 May 1687). Harcourt succeeded his father on 30 March 1688, but this availed him little in financial terms, as his stepmother retained control of Stanton Harcourt until her death in 1713. Harcourt seems to have practised on the western circuit, and he became recorder of Abingdon in June 1687 and again in October 1689. His attitude to the revolution is not known, but he did not contest the elections to the Convention Parliament of 1688. He was returned for Abingdon at the 1690 election on the church or tory interest.

The House of Commons Harcourt quickly made his mark as a parliamentary speaker and soon gave evidence of that rhetorical ability which Arthur Onslow judged to be 'the greatest skill and power of speech of any man I ever knew in a public assembly' (Burnet, 5.441). He made his maiden recorded speech on 2 April 1690, and spoke regularly on matters such as the perennial bills for the reform of treason trials and also in defence of habeas corpus. In his first decade in the Commons he usually allied himself with the country tories to attack ministerial measures. He also acted frequently as a manager of legislation through the

Simon Harcourt, first Viscount Harcourt (1661?–1727), by Sir Godfrey Kneller, c.1710–15

house. Harcourt's parliamentary career in many ways complemented his legal practice, and it no doubt helped him to extend his clientele. Like many barristers, he often obtained leave of the Commons in the spring to go on circuit. He attended the trials of the Jacobite conspirators at Manchester in 1694, and was subsequently at the forefront of attempts to prosecute some of the prosecution witnesses for perjury.

Following his re-election in 1695 Harcourt was at the centre of resistance to the association of 1696 (to defend William III), being named one of the 'ringleaders' of the 'non-associators' (Kenyon MSS, 405) in the Commons, and signing the Association in Oxfordshire only after it had been made compulsory. He was a notable opponent of the bill of attainder against the Jacobite Sir John Fenwick in November 1696, speaking frequently against that method of proceeding. At some point after 1695 he married Elizabeth (1657/8–1724), the daughter and coheir of Richard Spencer, a vintner, of Aldgate, London, and Newington, Surrey, and the widow of Richard Anderson (d. 1695), of Pendley, Hertfordshire. They had no children. Such was Harcourt's reputation that he was seen as a potential speaker of the Commons after the election of 1698. In the event he faced a challenge for his seat at Abingdon, which he successfully fought off. His legal reputation continued to grow, as in June 1699 he defended Charles Duncombe from charges of falsely endorsing exchequer bills and in November he made the first of many appearances as counsel before the House of Lords.

Harcourt was one of the tories who led the attack on the whig ministers in 1700, and following the dismissal of

Lord Chancellor Somers in April of that year he was seen by some as a possible solicitor-general. Robert Harley, in some ways Harcourt's political mentor, was known to be concerned that lack of recognition might propel him into an alliance with the more rigid tories under the duke of Leeds. Harcourt remained out of office, but the admission of some tories into power saw him more amenable to court influence during 1701. However, he never wavered on party causes such as the impeachment of the leading whigs in the previous ministry, and it was Harcourt who seconded the impeachment of Lord Somers and who played a major role in producing the articles against him. In December 1701 he again secured re-election for Abingdon, despite attempts to smear him as a Jacobite.

The death of William III gave Harcourt the chance of office, and on 30 May 1702 he was named as solicitor-general. He was knighted on 1 June and received a DCL on 27 August. The next few parliamentary sessions saw Harcourt resolve the contradictions between being a country tory and a spokesman for the court in favour of the latter. Although he continued to favour tories in election disputes, and found no difficulty in adopting a tory position when it coincided with the defence of the rights of the Commons, as in the Ashby v. White case, he was also forced to ensure that nothing prevented the ministry's key policy, support for the war, from being obstructed. Most noticeably this meant that a policy he had hitherto supported, a bill against occasional conformity, had to be opposed when his erstwhile tory friends attempted to tack the bill to the Land Tax Bill in November 1704.

Harcourt lost his seat at Abingdon at the election of 1705 to a more forceful opponent of the tack. However, Harcourt was deemed sufficiently useful to the government as an ally of Robert Harley to ensure that a seat was found for him, at Bossiney in Cornwall. He was also appointed steward of the duke of Marlborough's newly acquired estate at Woodstock, Oxfordshire. Harcourt repaid Harley's support by voting for the court candidate as speaker in November 1705, and also in solid work for the court over such matters as the Regency Bill in 1706 and the Union with Scotland in 1706–7. His reward came in April 1707, when he was promoted attorney-general. However, Harcourt resigned his office on 12 February 1708, the day after the dismissal of Robert Harley, following the defeat of his plan to include more tories in a moderate mixed ministry, and thus curb the growing whig power. Although Harcourt was returned for Abingdon at the 1708 election, he was unseated on petition on 20 January 1709 in what was seen as a blatant abuse of the whigs' parliamentary majority. Harcourt, however, rose to the occasion in a speech in which he deployed all his eloquence to denounce the proceedings and which was later printed so as to be available to a wider audience.

One result of Harcourt's ejection from the legislature was that he was available to act as counsel for Henry Sacheverell in March 1710, when that rather intemperate clergyman was impeached by the Commons for a sermon he had preached in London. Harcourt's main contribution came on 3 March, when he defended Sacheverell against the first article of the impeachment. His tactic was to suggest that Sacheverell was merely reiterating the Church of England's doctrine of non-resistance to duly constituted authority in the shape of the crown in parliament and had not dealt with exceptions to this general rule such as the revolution of 1688. Many acknowledged the brilliance of the speech, including the future bishop of Bristol, George Smalridge, who thought Harcourt's 'reputation for a speaker is fixed for ever' (Nichols, *Illustrations*, 3.280–81). It was Harcourt's last contribution to the trial, because in February he had been returned at a by-election for Cardigan boroughs, and the return of the writ precluded his further participation.

Lord keeper and lord chancellor When Harcourt went on circuit following Sacheverell's trial he was fêted in each town and showered with local honours. However, the most important political effect of the case was that it paved the way for a new ministry under Harcourt's old ally, Robert Harley. Harcourt was sure to be offered office, but he was in a quandary: to accept office as Lord Cowper's replacement as either lord keeper or lord chancellor would preclude a return to lucrative private practice should the balance of power shift against the tories. Harcourt preferred a return to the attorney-general's post, which was not incompatible with, but rather enhanced, private practice. In any event he avoided the public in August while recuperating from an eye operation for cataracts. On 16 September 1710 he was named attorney-general, but within a week Lord Cowper had resigned the lord chancellorship, and after further pressure from Harley (soon afterwards the earl of Oxford) Harcourt was named lord keeper on 16 October.

On 3 September the following year Harcourt was raised to the peerage as Baron Harcourt, and on 7 April 1713 he became lord chancellor. In the battle for supremacy of the Oxford ministry, Harcourt sided with Viscount Bolingbroke. However, in August 1714 he was vital in ensuring that the dying Queen Anne appointed the duke of Shrewsbury rather than Bolingbroke as lord treasurer. Harcourt lost the lord chancellorship on 21 September 1714 following the Hanoverian succession and was removed from the privy council in October. He had made over £8000 per annum from his tenure of the lord keepership and lord chancellorship, so the loss of office was no financial hardship. In 1710 Harcourt had purchased nearby Nuneham Courtenay, which was to become the family residence, but he retired to Cokethorpe, his residence near to Stanton Harcourt, which, although now his property, was in a poor state of repair. At Cokethorpe he entertained a rich array of literary figures, such as John Gay, Alexander Pope, Matthew Prior, and Jonathan Swift.

After 1715 Harcourt resumed his political career in earnest in 1717, when he helped to organize the defence of Lord Oxford against articles of impeachment. He was in constant contact with Oxford, who was still in the Tower, providing him with information. In a 'handsome and learned speech' (Jones, 72–3) Harcourt persuaded the Lords to insist on prosecuting the charge of high treason first, thereby helping to sow dissension between the houses. He duly voted for Oxford's acquittal on 1 July 1717, and then found himself excluded by the ministry from the Act of Grace passed later that month. However, the turmoil within whig ranks in the years 1717–21 provided Harcourt with a route back into ministerial favour, and the earl of Sunderland's need of parliamentary support saw him rewarded on 24 July 1721, when he was created Viscount Harcourt. The rise of Robert Walpole did not prevent his rehabilitation, as Walpole had assisted Harcourt's efforts on Oxford's behalf. On 25 August 1722 Harcourt was readmitted to the privy council. He was able to assist Bolingbroke in his attempts to return from exile, and he was sufficiently trusted by the Walpole regime to be named a lord justice in 1723, 1725, and 1727 during George I's absence from the realm.

Following the death of his second wife on 16 June 1724, Harcourt married, on 30 September 1724, Elizabeth (*c*.1678–1748), the daughter of Sir Thomas Vernon, of Twickenham Park, and the widow of Sir John Walter (*d.* 1722), third baronet, of Sarsden, Oxfordshire. It was while calling on Walpole on 23 July 1727 that Harcourt was struck down with 'an apoplexy and dead palsy' (*Leyborne-Popham MSS*, 288). He died at 2 a.m. on 29 July at Harcourt House in Cavendish Square and was buried in the family vault in the chancel of Stanton Harcourt. He was succeeded by his grandson Simon *Harcourt, first Earl Harcourt, the child of his second son, **Simon Harcourt** (*bap.* 1684, *d.* 1720), lawyer and Jacobite sympathizer, who was baptized at Chipping Norton, Oxfordshire, on 9 October 1684. After entering Eton College in 1698 he proceeded to the Inner Temple on 28 November 1701 and Christ Church, Oxford, on 3 November 1702. He then travelled abroad, visiting Italy and attending the University of Padua in 1706, and engaging in youthful indiscretions such as drinking the health of the Pretender. On 21 July 1709 he married Elizabeth (*d.* 1760), the daughter of John Evelyn of Wootton, Surrey, the tory divine Francis Atterbury performing the ceremony. Apart from their son, they had four daughters, two of whom died young. Harcourt was returned as a tory to the House of Commons for Wallingford at the 1710 election and on 12 November was called to the bar. This honour, like the bestowal of an MA at Oxford on 13 December 1712, was due to the influence of his father. In the summer of 1713 he was in France, probably for reasons of health, but again he behaved indiscreetly while dining with the duke of Berwick. In the election of 1713 he was returned for Abingdon, but he was defeated in 1715. During the years following the Hanoverian succession he was plagued with ill health, and he died on 1 July 1720 while on another trip to Paris. His host, Viscount Bolingbroke, attributed his demise to a 'bloody flux' (*Portland MSS*, 7.278), but the ultimate cause was drink, a post-mortem examination revealing that his liver had perished. His body was returned to England and was duly interred on 1 September 1720 at Stanton Harcourt.

STUART HANDLEY

Sources DNB · S. Handley, 'Harcourt, Simon', HoP, *Commons, 1690–1715* [draft] · GEC, *Peerage* · E. W. Harcourt, ed., *The Harcourt* *papers*, 14 vols. (privately printed, London, [1880–1905]), vols. 1, 2 · *VCH Oxfordshire*, 13.274–7 · H. Horwitz, *Parliament, policy and politics in the reign of William III* (1977), 238–98 · G. S. Holmes, *British politics in the age of Anne*, rev. edn (1987) · L. K. J. Glassey, *Politics and the appointment of justices of the peace, 1675–1720* (1979), 200, 233–4 · G. Holmes, *The trial of Doctor Sacheverell* (1973), 143, 150, 179–93, 236 · A. Grey, ed., *Debates of the House of Commons, from the year 1667 to the year 1694*, new edn, 10 vols. (1769), vol. 10 · *The parliamentary diary of Narcissus Luttrell, 1691–1693*, ed. H. Horwitz (1972) · *The parliamentary diary of Sir Richard Cocks, 1698–1702*, ed. D. W. Hayton (1996) · *Remarks and collections of Thomas Hearne*, ed. C. E. Doble and others, 2, OHS, 7 (1886), pp. 164–5 · *Bishop Burnet's History*, 5.441 · Cobbett, *Parl. hist.*, 5.1016–70; 6.264–7 · *State trials*, 13.1061–106 · C. Jones, 'The impeachment of the earl of Oxford and the whig schism of 1717: four new lists', *BIHR*, 55 (1982), 66–87, esp. 68–73, 82 · W. A. Speck, 'The whig schism under George I', *Huntington Library Quarterly*, 40 (1976–7), 175–9 · *The manuscripts of the House of Lords*, new ser., 12 vols. (1900–77), vol. 4, p. 2 · Nichols, *Illustrations*, 3.280–81 · *The manuscripts of his grace the duke of Portland*, 10 vols., HMC, 29 (1891–1931) · *The manuscripts of Lord Kenyon*, HMC, 35 (1894) · *Report on the manuscripts of F. W. Leyborne-Popham*, HMC, 51 (1899)

Archives BL, corresp. | BL, letters to Robert Harley, loan MS 29
Likenesses G. Kneller, oils, *c.*1710–1715, priv. coll. [*see illus.*] · G. Kneller, oils, second version, *c.*1710–1715, Inner Temple, London · G. Kneller, oils, Nuneham Park, Oxfordshire · G. Kneller, oils, Pembroke College, Oxford · J. Simon, mezzotint (after G. Kneller), BM, NPG · mezzotint, NPG

Harcourt, Simon (*bap.* 1684, *d.* 1720). See under Harcourt, Simon, first Viscount Harcourt (1661?–1727).

Harcourt, Simon, first Earl Harcourt (1714–1777), politician and administrator in Ireland, was the only son of the Hon. Simon *Harcourt (*bap.* 1684, *d.* 1720), barrister and MP [*see under* Harcourt, Simon, first Viscount Harcourt], and his wife, Elizabeth, daughter of John Evelyn of Wotton, Surrey. He was educated at Westminster School before travelling abroad with a tutor for four years and then returning to England in 1734. On the death of his grandfather Simon, Viscount Harcourt, in 1727, he succeeded to the family titles and estates. On 16 October 1735 he married Rebecca (*d.* 1765), only daughter and heir of Charles Sambourne Le Bas, of Pipewell Abbey, Northamptonshire, and Mary Moyer. She brought a dowry of £60,000 to the marriage, and they had four children. On 9 May 1735 Harcourt was appointed a lord of the bedchamber to George II, and he was present with the king at the battle of Dettingen. During the Jacobite rising of 1745 he raised a regiment and was awarded the rank of colonel; he became a general in 1772. On 1 December 1749 he was created Viscount Nuneham of Nuneham Courtenay and Earl Harcourt of Stanton Harcourt.

In April 1751 Harcourt was appointed governor to the prince of Wales, the future George III. He did not seem ideally suited to the task. Walpole said that Harcourt was 'minute and strict in trifles', and was convinced that he had done his duty 'if on no account he neglected to make the Prince turn out his toes' (Brooke, 66). He described Harcourt as unable to teach the prince 'other arts than what he knew himself, hunting and drinking' (Walpole, *Memoirs*, 1.60). His tenure was short-lived, as in 1752 a scandal erupted over the education of the young prince. Harcourt and the bishop of Norwich accused their immediate subordinates of indoctrinating the prince with Jacobite

Simon Harcourt, first Earl Harcourt (1714–1777), by Sir Joshua Reynolds, 1754–5

principles and notions of arbitrary rule. Their allegations were unsubstantiated, and came close to treason, but they provided ammunition in later years for those who wished to point to George III's autocratic tendencies. George II was not convinced by the allegations, and he accepted Harcourt's resignation. Harcourt emerged from the episode relatively unscathed, and in July 1761 he was appointed ambassador to Mecklenburg, with responsibility for requesting the hand of princess Charlotte on behalf of the king. He was appointed her master of the horse on 10 September, and then in 1763 lord chamberlain to the queen.

A supporter of Bute and Grenville, Harcourt advised George III against repealing the Stamp Act. The king acknowledged his own reluctance to back repeal but 'said he would never influence people in their parliamentary opinions, and that he had promised to support his ministers'. In response 'Lord Harcourt threw in doubts of their being able to support themselves' and 'named Mr. Grenville as the only man in the House of Commons capable of carrying on the business there' (Smith, 3.353–5). Harcourt temporarily deserted the ministry and voted with the Bedfords against Rockingham, but he was quick to return to the government fold; ultimately he was a court man.

In 1768 Harcourt was appointed British ambassador to Paris. He clearly did not have the experience requisite for such an important post during a time of international crisis. Moreover his own commitment to the job was less than wholehearted, as between 1769 and 1772 his absences from this post added up to over a year. In June

1772 he became Irish viceroy, replacing Lord Townshend, who in reforming the Dublin Castle government had left behind a disaffected parliament and an unsettled populace. Harcourt largely succeeded in pacifying Ireland, for the most part by making judicious concessions. One of these was to be an absentee tax, regarded by Harcourt 'as an expedient likely, in its commencement, to conciliate the body of the nation' (Harcourt, 9.93). However, when an all-party group of British peers, led by Rockingham, made trouble for the prime minister, Lord North, Harcourt successfully had the tax proposals quashed. Despite patriot opposition, Harcourt was able to secure Irish parliamentary support for the American War of Independence, and he gained permission to send 4000 troops for service abroad. His costly acquisition of Henry Flood's support was a less successful move, and his financial reforms brought mixed fortunes. He reunited the revenue boards, reduced the corn bounty, and gained trade concessions. But at the same time he mortgaged a sizeable portion of Irish patronage through the distribution of peerages, offices, and pensions. Harcourt's resignation, in January 1777, resulted from his conflict with the commander-in-chief over control of military affairs. After his sojourn in Ireland he retired to Nuneham.

Walpole described Harcourt as 'an empty man, devoted to the Court but diffident and complaisant' (*Last Journals of Horace Walpole*, 1.251). He certainly had urbane manners, but his time in Ireland hinted at real political ability, and it is clear that he was more than just 'civil and sheepish' (Walpole, *Memoirs*, 1.60). Lady Harcourt died suddenly on 16 January 1765. Harcourt also suffered a precipitate death when on 16 September 1777 he fell into a well at Nuneham Park while rescuing a favourite dog and drowned. He was buried at Stanton Harcourt on 24 September. He was succeeded by his son George Simon. 　　MARTYN J. POWELL

Sources DNB · E. W. Harcourt, ed., *The Harcourt papers*, 14 vols. (privately printed, London, [1880–1905]) · J. Brooke, *King George III* (1972) · L. G. W. Legg, ed., *British diplomatic instructions, 1699–1789*, 7/4, CS, 3rd ser., 38 (1934) · Gilbert Library, Dublin, Gilbert (Harcourt) MSS 93–94 · BL, Add. MSS 38207–38208 (Liverpool papers) · NL Ire., Harcourt MS 5161 · H. Walpole, *Memoirs of King George II*, ed. J. Brooke, 1 (1985) · *The last journals of Horace Walpole*, ed. Dr Doran, rev. A. F. Steuart, 1 (1910) · *The Grenville papers: being the correspondence of Richard Grenville … and … George Grenville*, ed. W. J. Smith, 3 (1853) · D. B. Horn, *The British diplomatic service, 1689–1789* (1961) · J. Black, *Natural and necessary enemies: Anglo-French relations in the eighteenth century* (1986) · T. F. Moriarty, 'The Harcourt viceroyalty in Ireland, 1772–1777', PhD diss., University of Notre Dame, Indiana, 1964
Archives NL Ire., corresp. and papers | BL, corresp. with Charles Jenkinson, loan 72 · BL, corresp. with earl of Liverpool, Add. MSS 38197–38209, 38306, 38457–38469, *passim* · BL, corresp. with duke of Newcastle, etc., Add. MSS 32692–32974, *passim* · Gilbert Library, Dublin, Gilbert (Harcourt) MSS · U. Nott. L., corresp. with duke of Newcastle, etc.
Likenesses B. Wilson, oils, 1750, Gov. Art Coll. · J. Reynolds, portrait, 1754–5, priv. coll. [*see illus.*] · E. Fisher, mezzotint, pubd 1775 (after R. Hunter), NG Ire. · W. Doughty, portrait; known to be in possession of Edward William Harcourt, Nuneham Park, in 1890 · R. Hunter, oils, NG Ire., Ulster Museum, Belfast · J. Macardell, mezzotint (after B. Wilson), BM, NPG · D. Pariset, stipple (aged fifty-four; after P. Falconet), BM · line engraving, BM

Harcourt, Thomas. *See* Whitbread, Thomas (*c.*1618–1679).

Harcourt, Sir William de (*d. c.*1223). *See under* Harcourt family (*per. c.*1050–1330).

Harcourt, Sir William de (*d.* 1270). *See under* Harcourt family (*per. c.*1050–1330).

Harcourt, William. *See* Aylworth, William (1623–1679).

Harcourt, William, third Earl Harcourt (1743–1830), army officer and courtier, was born on 20 March 1743, the younger son of Simon *Harcourt, first Earl Harcourt (1714–1777), and his wife, Rebecca (*d.* 1765), the only daughter and heir of Charles Samborne Le Bas of Pipewell Abbey, Northamptonshire. He was commissioned ensign in the 1st guards in August 1759 and promoted captain in the 16th light dragoons on 27 October the same year, the unit, called Harcourt's black horse, having been raised at his father's expense. His father's wealth and influence rapidly advanced his military career. Harcourt transferred as a captain to the 3rd dragoons on 30 June 1760, and he held the appointment of equerry to the queen consort between 1760 and 1767 after accompanying his father to Mecklenberg Strelitz in order to conduct the future Queen Charlotte to England.

In 1762 Harcourt served as aide-de-camp to the earl of Albemarle at the capture of Havana. He was promoted lieutenant-colonel in the 31st foot on 28 November 1764, and transferred to the 4th light dragoons on 19 April 1765 and to the 16th light dragoons on 24 June 1768. In 1766 he was appointed an extra groom of the bedchamber. From 1768 to 1774 he was a tory MP for the city of Oxford, having been returned by the corporation, which then controlled representation. There is no record of his speaking in the house, and he apparently showed little interest in politics. In 1774 a corporation faction put forward the earl of Abingdon's brother, Peregrine Bertie, and, rather than face a contest, Harcourt retired.

After accompanying his regiment to America in 1775, Harcourt captured the American Major-General Charles Lee at Basking Ridge in a daring 70 mile raid on 13 December 1776. This act was rewarded by his appointment as aide-de-camp to the king and his promotion to colonel on 29 August 1777.

Having then returned to England, on 3 September 1778, at Kensington, Harcourt married Mary (1749/50–1833), the widow of Thomas Lockhart of Craighouse; she and Harcourt had no children. She was the eldest daughter of the Revd William Danby of Farnley, Yorkshire, and had married her first husband in 1772. Described as 'a woman of warm temper and small reserve' (GEC, *Peerage*), she gained a reputation for meddling in court politics. In 1795 she accompanied the first earl of Malmesbury on his voyage to take Caroline of Brunswick to England for her marriage to George, prince of Wales, but fell out of favour with the king and queen for offering Caroline some 'bad advice'. Domineering, interfering, sometimes malicious, she repeatedly quarrelled with her sister-in-law over the disposal of properties to the French Harcourts, her 'special protégés'.

When the colonelcy of the 16th light dragoons became vacant in 1779, Harcourt succeeded to this appointment on 20 October, and held it until his death. He was promoted major-general on 20 November 1782, and the same year he purchased the estate of St Leonard's Hill, near Windsor, Berkshire, from the duke of Gloucester and was appointed deputy ranger of Windsor Great Park by the king. In 1787 Pitt suggested him to the king as a possible candidate for New Windsor, but a dispute he had with the corporation made him unsuitable. About 1788 he suffered a mild paralytic stroke, and the king did not want him to again go on active service.

From May 1793 Harcourt commanded the 1st brigade of cavalry in the duke of York's army in Flanders, and on 12 October 1793 he was promoted lieutenant-general. For his leadership of the cavalry at the battle of Willems on 10 May 1794 the duke of York presented him with his own sword. He was appointed governor of Fort William on 21 March 1794. Harcourt was the senior British general officer of cavalry by August 1794, and succeeded to the command of the British troops after the departure of the duke of York the following December, whereas the command of the Hanoverians devolved upon General Wallmoden.

This was a particularly difficult period to assume such a responsibility, since the winter campaign had reduced the combat effectiveness of the allied forces considerably, as had the allies' divergent war aims. All Harcourt could do was to conduct a successful withdrawal through the Netherlands in the face of substantial French forces while trying his best to limit the alarming incidence of sickness among his troops. The army eventually halted on the line of the River Ems on 3 March 1795, soon after which the British government decided to evacuate the majority of its forces from the continent.

Harcourt was appointed governor of Hull in 1795, and continued in the post until 1801. Promoted general on 1 January 1798, on the establishment of the Royal Military College at Marlow in 1802 he was appointed its first governor. His inattention to his duties ensured an uneasy relationship with his lieutenant-governor and erstwhile protégé, Gaspard Le Marchant, but he continued in post until 18 July 1811, when he was appointed governor of Portsmouth. He also briefly held the appointment of master of the robes (1808–9).

When his brother, George Simon Harcourt, second Earl Harcourt, died on 20 April 1809, Harcourt succeeded to his titles and estates, as well as his appointment of master of the horse to the queen, which he held until her death in 1818. Two years later he walked as one of the assistants to the chief mourner, the duke of York, at George III's funeral. He was invested with the GCB on 20 May 1820. On 19 July 1821 Harcourt bore the union standard at the coronation of George IV and was promoted field marshal. His last official appointment was as governor of Plymouth, on 1 January 1827. The final act of Harcourt's long connection with the royal family occurred a few days later, on 20 January, when he bore the duke of York's baton at his funeral.

A tory member of the House of Lords, in 1829 he followed Wellington on Roman Catholic emancipation.

A tall, angular man, with a prominent nose and a stoop, in his latter years Harcourt was obstinate, dilatory, unbusinesslike, and infirm. He died on 17 June 1830 at his residence, St Leonard's Hill, and was buried at Stanton Harcourt, Oxfordshire. He left no children and his peerages died with him. His estates were left to his cousin Edward Venables-Vernon (afterwards Edward Harcourt), archbishop of York. Statues of Harcourt by Robert William Sievier were erected in 1832 in St George's Chapel, Windsor, and St Michael's Church, Stanton Harcourt.

R. N. W. Thomas

Sources GEC, *Peerage* · *GM*, 1st ser., 100/2 (1830), 177–8; 102/2 (1832), 658–9 · E. W. Harcourt, ed., *The Harcourt papers*, 14 vols. (privately printed, London, [1880–1905]), vols. 4, 11 · Fortescue, *Brit. army*, vol. 4 · *Army List* (1759–1821) · PRO, WO 1/66–172 · HoP, *Commons, 1754–90* · R. H. Thoumine, *Scientific soldier: a life of General Le Marchant, 1766–1812* (1968)

Archives BL, corresp., Add. MSS 46702–46706 · U. Mich., Harlan Hatcher Graduate Library, Harcourt collection, Mod. MSS | Bucks. RLSS, letters to Sir William Lee · PRO, papers as commander-in-chief of the British army on the continent, WO 1/166–172 · Royal Military College, Sandhurst, corresp. with J. G. Le Marchant

Likenesses R. W. Sievier, marble bust, 1828, Royal Collection · R. W. Sievier, statue, 1832, St George's Chapel, Windsor · R. W. Sievier, statue, 1832, St Michael's Church, Stanton Harcourt, Oxfordshire · R. Collins, miniature, NPG · G. Hayter, group portrait, oils (*The trial of Queen Caroline, 1820*), NPG · S. W. Reynolds, mezzotint (after H. Edridge, 1818), BM, NPG · C. A. Tomkins, group portrait, mezzotint (after J. Reynolds), BM, NPG

Wealth at death £180,000: *GM*, 1st ser., 100/2

Harcourt, William Edward, second Viscount Harcourt (1908–1979), merchant banker and public servant, was born on 5 October 1908 at 14 Berkeley Square, London, the fourth child and only son of Lewis *Harcourt, first Viscount Harcourt (1863–1922), MP and cabinet minister, and his wife, Mary Ethel (d. 1961), only daughter of Walter Hayes Burns, American investment banker, of New York and North Mimms Park, Hatfield. Known universally as Bill, he was brought up at Nuneham Park, near Oxford, and educated at West Downs School, Eton College until 1927, and Christ Church, Oxford, where he took a third in jurisprudence in 1930. From 1917 he had been known by the courtesy title of Baron Nuneham, and while still at Eton he succeeded as second Viscount Harcourt, following the suicide of his father in 1922.

The great-grandson of J. S. Morgan and the great-nephew of J. P. Morgan, both of the Anglo-American investment bank, in 1931 Harcourt joined the related English merchant bank, Morgan Grenfell; he was the last member of the founding families to work in the bank. He worked his way round the various departments in the time-honoured manner of those destined to become managing directors, after which he spent two months in New York city working at J. P. Morgan & Co. and Morgan, Stanley & Co. before settling down in London. His primary duty during the inter-war years was to support the older managing directors in their work for clients, often sitting in on

William Edward Harcourt, second Viscount Harcourt (1908–1979), by Elliott & Fry, 1959

the discussions with companies or governments, helping and learning. On 1 January 1939, at the age of thirty, he was appointed managing director, an office which he retained until 1968. He acted as chairman from 1968 to 1973, with interludes for public service. As with many merchant bankers, he sat on the boards of a number of insurance companies, serving as chairman of four of them over his working life, most notably the Legal and General Assurance Society.

Harcourt went off to war in 1939 with the 63rd Oxford yeomanry auxiliary territorial regiment, Royal Artillery; he later served at General Alexander's sometime headquarters in Bari, Italy, at the control end of the supplies and aid for the partisans in Yugoslavia. He ended his war service with the rank of captain (and the honorary rank of lieutenant-colonel), and was appointed MBE (1943) and OBE (1945). Harcourt then returned to private life. His family home, Nuneham Park, had been taken over by the army during the war, at the end of which it was sold to Oxford University. Harcourt thereafter made his home at the other family property at Stanton Harcourt and at 23 Culross Street, London W1.

Harcourt rejoined Morgan Grenfell as its youngest director and spent some years rejuvenating a bank which was prestigious, profitable, and sleepy. He brought in staff who developed the bank's overseas interests and he oversaw the birth of its corporate finance department in the 1960s, which by the 1980s had become the most powerful in the City of London. Indeed, Morgan Grenfell's aggressive backing of American Tobacco in its bid to take over the UK tobacco manufacturer Gallaher, in 1968, led it to receive the first public warning issued by the new Takeover Panel—an incident which left Harcourt in a towering fury. He was a pioneer in another area as well: when the Heath government came to an agreement with the French government for the construction of a channel tunnel, Harcourt, whose interest in the project was long-standing (he had been chairman of the Anglo-American-French channel tunnel study group since 1957), became chairman of the British Channel Tunnel Company Ltd. The project, to his disappointment, was cancelled by the Labour government in January 1975 through fear of the rapidly rising costs.

From 1954 to 1964 Harcourt devoted much of his time to public service and was absent from Morgan Grenfell. From 1954 to 1957 he served as minister (economics) at the British embassy in Washington and as head of the UK Treasury delegation in the USA; this included the position of UK executive director both at the International Bank for Reconstruction and Development (the World Bank) and at the International Monetary Fund. He developed a good personal relationship with George Humphrey, the US secretary of the treasury, which stood him in good stead during the Suez crisis in 1956, since they were able to speak plainly to each other but remain on good terms. Harcourt was realistic about the help which the UK could expect from the USA during the associated sterling crisis, and he ensured that the Bank of England and the Treasury had no illusions. When Lord Cobbold was due to retire as governor of the Bank of England in 1961, the Treasury and the bank supported Harcourt to replace him; the then economic adviser to the government, Robert Hall, wrote of him that:

> although he is primarily a business man and spends his time cultivating the right people and on negotiations—which after all is the primary requisite if you are an operator—he seems to me to have a great gift for arriving at the essence of the situation analytically, so that he is very rarely wrong on his economics even if he could not demonstrate them. (Hall, 176–7)

Though Lord Cromer was eventually chosen to replace Cobbold, Harcourt's analytical powers were put to further governmental use by his membership of the Radcliffe committee on the working of monetary and credit policy (1957–9) and of the Plowden committee on overseas representational services (1962–4).

The above activities were centred in London, as was his chairmanship from 1965 of the governors of the Museum of London, but Harcourt increasingly served a number of interests in Oxfordshire. He was from 1963 vice-lieutenant of Oxfordshire, and was sometime chairman of the Oxford Preservation Trust, but increasing amounts of time were spent in university-related activities. He was an honorary fellow of St Antony's College, and was chairman of the Rhodes Trust. With regard to the latter it was Harcourt's proud boast that under his leadership the trust, by establishing the post-doctoral Rhodes fellowships which were tenable by women at the women's Oxford colleges, had broken Cecil Rhodes's will; the Rhodes scholarships were thereby opened to women as well as to men. In 1978 he was made an honorary DCL of Oxford University, which greatly pleased him, and a DLitt by the City University.

Harcourt was twice married: first, in 1931, to the Hon. Maude Elizabeth (Betty) Grosvenor (b. 1909), daughter of Francis Egerton Grosvenor, fourth Baron Ebury; they were divorced in 1942. Then in 1946 he married Elizabeth Sonia Gibbs, daughter of Sir Harold Edward Snagge, a director of Barclays Bank, and the widow of Captain Lionel Cyril Gibbs; his second wife died in 1959. Harcourt and his first wife had three daughters, the youngest of whom, Virginia, drowned in Nigeria in 1972; he had two stepsons through his second marriage.

Harcourt was a man of intelligence and charm, jovial and without side. He had strong ties to the country, and his main weekend preoccupation was the creation of his walled garden of several acres at Stanton Harcourt.

> The house was always full of people at weekends, when hard work in the garden was a notable feature of the entertainment afforded to the guests. Harcourt was never happier than when surrounded by the debris and clutter of reclaiming his garden or bespattered with mud from cleaning out his ponds.   (DNB)

Harcourt was prominent in the City, liked and respected in Oxford, and a man of substance within the government. He had no heir, and upon his death from cancer at the Royal Marsden Hospital, London, on 3 January 1979, the viscountcy became extinct.   KATHLEEN BURK

Sources Morgan Grenfell Group archives, City of London · Bank of England archives, City of London · PRO, Treasury MSS · K. Burk, *Morgan Grenfell, 1838–1988: the biography of a merchant bank* (1989) · *The Robert Hall diaries, 1954–61*, ed. A. Cairncross, 2 (1991) · J. Fforde, *The Bank of England and public policy, 1941–1958* (1992) · DNB · Burke, *Peerage* · CGPLA Eng. & Wales (1979) · d. cert.
Archives Bank of England, London, Morgan Grenfell MSS · Bank of England, London · PRO, Treasury MSS
Likenesses Elliott & Fry, photograph, 1959, NPG [see illus.] · newspaper photographs · portrait, Morgan Grenfell Group plc, London
Wealth at death £2,642,074: probate, 9 Aug 1979, CGPLA Eng. & Wales

Harcourt, Sir **William George Granville Venables Vernon** (1827–1904)

Harcourt, Sir William George Granville Venables Vernon (1827–1904), politician, was born on 14 October 1827. It is unclear whether he was born at the rectory at Wheldrake in Yorkshire or in the Old Residence at York, where his father was a canon. It was probably at the latter location.

Family, education, and early career William came from a distinguished patrician and ecclesiastical background. His father, William Venables Vernon *Harcourt (1789–1871), was a clergyman of the Church of England, after having had a short career in the navy. He had a concurrent and greater interest in chemistry and was a founder of the British Association. He was both rector of Wheldrake and canon at York where his father, Edward Venables Vernon *Harcourt, was archbishop from 1807 until he died in his ninety-first year in 1847. The family seat was Nuneham

Sir William George Granville Venables Vernon Harcourt (1827–1904), by Sir Arthur Stockdale Cope, 1904

Park, Oxfordshire, which William's elder brother, Edward William Harcourt (1825–1891), eventually inherited. Edward was a tory MP for Oxfordshire from 1878 to 1886 and though inactive deeply resented William's being a Liberal member for Oxford. Allegedly he told his brother so from the terrace of the house at Nuneham, from which the spires of Oxford could be seen in the distance. He certainly wrote to him in 1868 deprecating his candidacy for Oxford. Sir Thomas Gladstone, Gladstone's elder brother, is said to have remarked to Edward Harcourt at the Carlton Club: 'Mr. Harcourt, you and I have two very troublesome brothers.' William had five sisters. His mother was Matilda Mary Gooch (1804–1876), a daughter of Colonel William Gooch, who was the son of Sir Thomas Gooch, in succession bishop of Bristol, Norwich, and Ely. His paternal grandfather, born in 1757, was the son of Lord Vernon; his third wife was sister of Earl Harcourt. So the future Sir William was born into the heart of the English establishment, a world which in many ways he would exemplify at the same time as being dedicated to challenging it. In 1830, when he was three, Harcourt was added to the family name when the archbishop inherited the family estates, accumulated over seven centuries, on the death of his cousin, the third Earl Harcourt.

William Harcourt had an austere childhood. He was educated at first by a Swiss governess, and then at the age of eight went to a small private school at Southwell, near Nottingham, where his uncle was a canon. His father did not wish him to attend a public school—would Harcourt have got on better with his contemporaries if he had?—but sent him instead to be educated by John Owen Parr, vicar of Durnford, from whom he received a good training in classics. In 1840 Parr and his small group of pupils moved to Preston, where Harcourt witnessed the bread riots of 1842. After leaving Preston he studied at home for two years before entering Trinity College, Cambridge, in 1846. His brother had gone to Oxford, but Harcourt's interest in mathematics led his father to choose Cambridge for him. He was tall—6 feet 3 inches—and, in contrast to his later life, thin. At Cambridge he became a member of the famous secret discussion society the Apostles; among his fellow members were Henry Maine (his tutor) and James Fitzjames Stephen, with whom he debated frequently in the union, Stephen taking the more conservative side. While at Cambridge he moved away from the traditional toryism of his family. In mathematics, which he did not actually enjoy, he was named senior optime, and also received a first in classics. While still an undergraduate he began to write for the Peelite newspaper the *Morning Chronicle*. His future possibilities were a fellowship at Cambridge, which his father preferred, or to enter politics. Choosing neither, he decided instead to pursue the law and journalism, and enrolled at Lincoln's Inn in 1852 and on 1 May 1854 was called to the bar at the Inner Temple, becoming particularly interested in international law. He did not run for political office for eight years and would not enter parliament until 1868. Harcourt's uncle, George Granville Harcourt, was married to the famous political hostess Frances, Lady Waldegrave, and they helped to launch him into London political society. When the *Morning Chronicle* closed Harcourt wrote from 1855 until 1859 for the *Saturday Review*, famed for the high quality of its contributors, among them his Cambridge friends Maine and Stephen as well as Walter Bagehot and the future marquess of Salisbury. He took an increasingly Liberal line in his admiration of W. E. Gladstone and his dislike of Lord Palmerston's foreign policy. In 1859 he stood for parliament for the first time in the Kirkcaldy burghs as an independent Liberal against the long-sitting local magnate, a Liberal, Robert Ferguson; Harcourt argued that the seat needed to be wrested from local 'hereditary rights', and he came within eighteen votes of winning in a poll of 606, much enjoying his first foray into electoral politics.

Marriage, the law, and early political career Shortly thereafter, on 5 November 1859, Harcourt married Maria Thérèse Lister, daughter of Lady Maria Theresa Lewis (formerly Lister), stepdaughter of the politician Sir George Cornewall Lewis and a niece of Lord Clarendon. Her father was Thomas Henry *Lister of Armytage Park, Staffordshire. The marriage was to be tragically brief: she died on 31 January 1863, the day on which she gave birth to her second child. The Harcourts had two sons, the first of whom died in infancy; the other, Lewis Vernon *Harcourt, became his father's devoted assistant—the intensity of their relationship owing something to the circumstances of his birth—and a prominent political figure in his own right.

The following years were devoted to Harcourt's legal practice, in which he specialized in railway law, and commentary, chiefly in *The Times*, on political matters, particularly on topics that had implications for international law. He was not yet fully committed to either political party, and, in fact, in 1866 Disraeli, whom he liked personally and disliked politically, offered him a safe Conservative seat in Wales, which he declined. He became better known through a series of letters to *The Times*, signed Historicus, arguing in favour of a strict neutrality in the civil war in the United States and a refusal to recognize the South. In this he was going against much 'informed' opinion in Britain, which tended to favour the Confederacy. He participated in the controversies over the *Trent* and the *Alabama*, taking the British side. In 1863 he published *Letters by Historicus on some Questions of International Law* and in 1865 a further collection entitled *American Neutrality*. He was thanked in 1868 by Lord John Russell for helping to maintain neutrality between the United States and Britain.

In these years Harcourt's greatest attention was devoted to his legal career; in 1866 he was made a queen's counsel, and in 1869 he became the Whewell professor of international law at his old university, which he remained until 1887, though he devoted increasingly less time to his academic duties. As he became more deeply involved in politics he had less time for the bar as well, making a considerable financial sacrifice (perhaps a loss of £10,000 p.a.). In 1868 he campaigned for the disestablishment of the Church of England in Ireland and he also pleaded for pardons for Fenians. He was also looking for a seat. Liverpool was anxious to have him, but he decided in favour of running for Oxford City, perhaps to exploit the family's connection with the area. He entered parliament in December 1868 as one of the two Liberal MPs for Oxford City (Edward Cardwell being the other) at the age of forty, comparatively late for someone of his background. Yet he rapidly became a leading figure there, largely through his skill in debate. Thanks to his frequent commentaries in *The Times*, he was already well known in the political world. He began his new career as something of an independent and moderate radical: anti-imperialist, anti-military, violently anti-ritualist, and critical of Gladstone's government over what he regarded as concessions to clerical interests in the Education Bill of 1870. He advocated the limitation of religion in schools to the reading of scripture and the repeal of the remaining religious tests at Oxford and Cambridge. His style was forceful; he was regarded as arrogant, and tact was not his strongest characteristic. He favoured reform in land law, in voting procedures, and in the judiciary. He attempted to help trade unions on the basis of the principle of equality before the law. He fought an effort by the Liberal government to limit the right of public speech in the royal parks. He was in favour of freedom and openness, which resulted in what some might regard as inconsistencies with a radical position: he was opposed to the secret ballot in 1872 and against increased regulation of drinking habits, though when he was home secretary in Gladstone's next ministry he did support local option liquor control, having become convinced of the role that drink played in causing crime. Despite Harcourt's criticisms of the government, Gladstone recognized his qualities and the high standing he had achieved both as a debater in the Commons and as a prominent speaker on behalf of the Liberal Party in the country. In November 1873 Gladstone offered him the post of solicitor-general and insisted, contrary to Harcourt's wishes, that he accept the traditional knighthood. He was only briefly in office, as the government resigned in February 1874.

Harcourt was re-elected for Oxford City in 1874, and for the next six years was a vigorous figure in parliament and a relentless critic of Disraeli's government, with some exceptions—as when, in open disagreement with Gladstone, he, as a devoted 'protestant', supported the government's Public Worship Regulation Bill of 1874. He was quite discontented with Gladstone's position as officially retired yet politically active. Harcourt thought that Lord Hartington should lead the party in fact as well as in name. On 2 December 1876 Harcourt remarried; his second wife was an American, Elizabeth Cabot Ives, widow of J. P. Ives and the daughter of the historian John Lothrop Motley. Two years later they had a son, Robert Vernon. In 1883 Harcourt built Malwood in the New Forest, an area that he had come to love. In 1876 he threw himself into the agitation over the 'Bulgarian atrocities' and attacked Turkey; yet he did not see the campaign as a way for Gladstone to return to his position of leadership.

Home secretary When the Liberals defeated Disraeli and the tories in 1880 there was no alternative to Gladstone as prime minister. Harcourt was appointed home secretary but, having been narrowly returned at the general election, was then defeated by fifty-four votes in Oxford City in the mandatory requirement that a minister be re-elected. The election was challenged by petition and his opponent unseated on the charge of corruption, but in the meantime Samuel Plimsoll had resigned his seat in Derby in order for Harcourt to return to parliament; he was elected at Derby in May 1880.

Harcourt continued his somewhat radical way in parliament, leading the fight for a game bill to give farmers the power to protect their land against hares and rabbits, and to curtail the rights of the hunting squires. He played a crucial role, as home secretary, in the growing dominance of the problem of Ireland in the deliberations of parliament, and he moved forward the government bills for the maintenance of order there, particularly as problems increased in Ireland after the murder of Lord Frederick Cavendish and Thomas Henry Burke in Phoenix Park in Dublin in May 1882 and subsequent 'outrages', including dynamiting in London itself. Despite his doubts about whether Gladstone should have returned to the leadership, he felt himself closer to him during the ministry, both politically and personally. Earlier in the session he had passed a bill through the House of Commons to improve and make more independent the governance of Scotland, only to see the bill defeated in the House of Lords. Similarly, he fought for a bill to consolidate the administration of London, which was later realized in the

London county council, but that effort had to be abandoned in the House of Commons in July 1884 (in 1883 a previous bill had involved a sharp row with Gladstone over democratic control of the police, which Harcourt wished to avoid). He was a spirited defender of the government when it was vehemently attacked over the fall of Khartoum and the death of Charles George Gordon in January 1885. Then the government's majority was reduced to fourteen, and in May it was defeated by an alliance of the Irish and tory members over an amendment to the budget.

Chancellor of the exchequer and the Liberal split Harcourt resigned with the government in May 1885 and Lord Salisbury became prime minister with the support of the Irish members. After the general election in November 1885, when Harcourt held his Derby seat, the tory government was defeated when parliament assembled in January 1886. The Irish members reverted to supporting the Liberals, as the tories had recommitted themselves to employing coercion in Ireland. In February 1886 Gladstone formed his third ministry and asked Harcourt to be the chancellor of the exchequer; he accepted even though he was quite pessimistic about the possibility of carrying home rule. Even so he delivered a strong speech in parliament in its favour when it was debated in May 1886. As chancellor he was the second in command, and along with the position went the implication that he might well be Gladstone's successor as leader of the party. He threw himself with enthusiasm into the traditional role of the chancellor: to curtail the expenses of his colleagues' departments. His first budget, introduced on 15 April 1886, was unexciting; existing taxes were to cover a deficit of £2.5 million. On 7 June 1886 the government was defeated over home rule and at the ensuing general election was greatly diminished in numbers, though Harcourt retained his seat at Derby with difficulty. The government resigned after the election, Harcourt leaving office as chancellor of the exchequer in July 1886.

Harcourt was a figure somewhat to the left of the centre of his party. He was the only one of the opponents of home rule in the cabinet—Hartington, Chamberlain, Bright, Selborne, and James—who changed his mind. He had come to the conclusion that it was preferable to coercion. His position as a compromiser was, however, made more difficult by his abrasive personality, which did not ease relations with his colleagues. In an attempt to reunite the party he held a series of talks in early 1887—the so-called 'round-table conference'—with himself, John Morley, and Lord Herschell representing the Gladstonians, and Chamberlain and Sir George Trevelyan the Liberal Unionists; the talks were unsuccessful, though Trevelyan returned to the party that year. For the next six years Harcourt was, second to Gladstone, the most important Liberal speaker in parliament, attacking the government particularly on its policy of coercion in Ireland, and working for the social programme of his party. He was also a prominent figure 'out of doors', speaking on behalf of the party. In 1889 and 1890 he was deeply involved with Parnell, initially on his side on the matter of the letters forged by Richard Pigott and defending him against the onslaught of *The Times*, in which the letters had been published in 1887. Exposure of the forgeries created a revulsion in favour of Parnell, which was then rapidly reversed when he was cited in a divorce case in November 1890. Those 'in the know' had been aware for a long time of his liaison with Mrs O'Shea; in fact Harcourt may have been the first important politician to be so, as the Home Office had had Parnell under surveillance. But once the scandal became public Harcourt was one of the Liberal leaders who advised Gladstone that the party would have to sever its relations with Parnell.

Chancellor of the exchequer again The Liberals returned to power in 1892 and Harcourt entered into the most important phase of his career. He had lost the slimness of his youth and he was now a jovial, indeed a rather Falstaffian, figure, known as Jumbo, with a formidable temper which made him many enemies, particularly among his immediate colleagues. Forming his government in 1892, Gladstone noted 'the addition of another Harcourt would have gone far to make my task impossible' (Gladstone, *Diaries*, 14 Aug 1892). He appeared to be a convinced radical, but some of his contemporaries chose to believe that he had become one because it provided the most numerous opportunities for conflict—he enjoyed, some felt, personal vendettas more than battles for principles, and seemed to pick a position for its combative possibilities. As Winston Churchill remarked about him in *Great Contemporaries* in 1937, Harcourt had 'an eye fixed earnestly, but by no means unerringly, upon the main chance'. Yet he was a vehement defender of quite a few of the more radical planks of Liberalism. Both in parliament and around the country he spoke on behalf of the Newcastle programme of October 1891, adopted by the National Liberal Federation, favouring a somewhat miscellaneous platform: home rule, disestablishment in Wales and Scotland, local veto, abolition of plural franchises, triennial parliaments, taxation of land values, abolition of entail, extension of small-holdings, the building of rural cottages, district and parish councils, and employers' liability. Parliament was dissolved in June 1892 and the Liberals won the election with a modest majority of forty. In Gladstone's last government Harcourt was again chancellor of the exchequer.

Considering Gladstone's age—he was now in his eighties—Harcourt's responsibilities in the House of Commons were considerable. The other most important members of the government were Lord Rosebery, who had joined the government reluctantly as foreign secretary, and John Morley as chief secretary for Ireland. All three men were highly ambitious, in their different ways, and extremely sensitive. It was apparent to most that Gladstone was unlikely to continue as prime minister very much longer. One of the favourite British pastimes is a leadership intrigue, and the stage was set for one of particular intensity. In theory Harcourt was in the best position to inherit the mantle, but despite the recognition of his skills his personal unpopularity and overbearing manner meant that the issue would be especially complicated. John Morley was likely to be the pivotal figure. Of the three he had the least claim for the position himself, but it would make a considerable difference where he gave his support. In terms of politics Harcourt was his natural ally, but it was far from clear that Morley would actually back him. In temperament they were very different and they disagreed on domestic policy, Morley being a far more fervent believer in home rule than Harcourt. He also supported women's suffrage and opposed an eight-hour working day; Harcourt took the opposite position on these issues. On the other hand they largely agreed on foreign policy, and shared a dislike for Rosebery's far more imperial policies.

The struggle for the Liberal leadership In the meantime ordinary politics continued with Harcourt playing a major role, presenting his budget on 24 April 1893, which raised the income tax a penny—from 6*d.* to 7*d.* A Home Rule Bill passed the House of Commons but was defeated overwhelmingly in the House of Lords in September 1893. Harcourt joined the general Liberal denunciation of the House of Lords for its destruction of legislation enacted by the popularly elected house. But undoubtedly the greatest drama of this second session was Gladstone's decision to resign, and the conflicting emotions that it aroused in his followers. They were losing the long-time leader of the party who had so much greater stature than any of his possible successors. But they were unwilling to take his advice that they should dissolve and leave office. Gladstone resigned in March 1894 because of his opposition to increased estimates for the navy, but the public reason given was the state of his eyes. The queen did not ask his recommendation for his successor. In the struggle for the succession Harcourt's abrasiveness was partially balanced by the suavity of his son, Lewis, known as Loulou, who worked tirelessly on his behalf. Harcourt had a claim upon the post by the right of position and succession. But Rosebery was a more popular figure and seemed to be a 'natural' prime minister, likely to be favoured by the queen. A significant number of the members of the cabinet were more sympathetic to Harcourt's political ideas than to Rosebery's. So the uphill task for Harcourt and his son was to persuade them to decline to serve under Rosebery, likely to be the first Liberal leader the queen would ask to form a government. It was probably true that Harcourt's views were nearer to those of the majority of the Liberal Party. Gladstone's last cabinet was on 1 March (at which Harcourt embarrassed his colleagues by reading out a lengthy encomium which Gladstone had in fact already seen); two days later Rosebery accepted the queen's invitation to attempt to form a cabinet. There had been talk of Harcourt's refusing to serve under him, but when it came to the point he remained as chancellor of the exchequer. It was a bitter blow to be denied the greatest position in the state; on the other hand with Rosebery, the prime minister, in the House of Lords, and in any case inevitably lacking Gladstone's authority, Harcourt had an even more powerful role to play. The next sixteen months of the Liberal government were the most important period in Harcourt's life.

Harcourt and the death duties The outstanding accomplishment in the time remaining to the Liberal government was Harcourt's: his budget of 16 April 1894 contained the introduction of death duties (the idea was the brainchild of Sir Alfred Milner, chairman of the Board of Inland Revenue). They and other measures in the budget were designed to pay for the increased naval estimates that had played such a large part in precipitating Gladstone's resignation: the estimated deficit was £4.5 million. The sum to be collected was not necessarily greater than the total of the various previous miscellaneous taxes already in existence. But a new principle was introduced—expanded greatly in the years to come—of a single estate duty that could be charged on all property, real and personal. While estates had paid inheritance taxes before, the new death duties were easily expandable, unlike the old fees, and introduced a novel, potentially confiscatory, attitude towards inheritance. It also meant that the state took capital and spent it as income. The proposal was very controversial, and it and other provisions of the budget were debated over three months, during which Harcourt was at his most talented in guiding the debate and belied his reputation for abrasiveness. The budget's passing, on 17 July 1894, was the greatest triumph of his career. In cabinet he was less conciliatory and battled continually with Rosebery over questions of foreign policy. They fought too over the budget, Rosebery being concerned over the loss of the support of the propertied classes. Harcourt almost welcomed such a development. On 8 April he introduced his Local Liquor Control Bill, which passed its first reading but was eventually lost. The government staggered on with difficulty, devoting a fair amount of effort to the pursuit of Welsh disestablishment, as a result of which Gladstone threatened to come out of retirement in order to oppose the issue. Harcourt's fourth and last budget was introduced on 2 May 1895 and passed with little difficulty on 10 May. It was not surprising that the cabinet almost welcomed a chance defeat on 21 June 1895 over a military issue and used it as a reason to resign.

In opposition In the general election campaign of June–July 1895 each leader went much his own way: Rosebery attacking the House of Lords, Morley emphasizing home rule, and Harcourt concentrating on local option as the best means of liquor control. The Liberals were badly defeated, the tories and the Liberal Unionists having a majority of 152. Harcourt himself lost his seat at Derby, particularly harmed by the beer interests. In this case he might have done better to follow his leader and concentrate on the House of Lords which could serve, as Gladstone envisioned when he made it the subject of his last speech in the House of Commons, as an umbrella issue covering the failures of the tories to follow the wishes of the electorate. Harcourt felt, however, that bad trade in Derby was the cause of his losing his seat. He then stood for West Monmouth in Wales and was elected there. The

shock of defeat was not sufficient to unite the leadership. Indeed, there was a semi-official separation between Rosebery and Harcourt. Rosebery was titular head of the party, Harcourt the leader in the House of Commons, but they declined to meet each other. They both continued to be active political figures, Harcourt being particularly effective in the House of Commons where, despite their great majority, he forced the tories to abandon their Education Bill. In October 1896 Rosebery resigned his position as leader of the party, using as his excuse his disagreement with Gladstone who, in his last public speech, had called for action on behalf of the Armenians against the Turks, a stand which Harcourt supported.

Rosebery's resignation strengthened Harcourt as the most important Liberal leader, but he received comparatively little support from his colleagues or from the party itself. For the next three years he played a central role inside and, to a lesser degree, outside parliament, though Rosebery was ever present as a potential threat to his position. There was no action by the party to appoint a new leader. Harcourt differentiated himself from Rosebery in his continued support of home rule and on imperial issues. He opposed British advances in the Sudan and moved for a committee of inquiry into the Jameson raid of 1895. He became a member of the committee which was appointed in July 1896 and signed the report in July 1897 blaming Cecil Rhodes, but some felt that the committee, consisting of members of both parties, had chosen to cover up the role that Joseph Chamberlain, the colonial secretary, had played in the event. Chamberlain himself undercut the significance of the report by declaring in the discussion of it in the House of Commons that Rhodes had done nothing contrary to personal honour. Indeed, Harcourt's rather inept handling of the Jameson matter, and particularly his unwillingness to pursue the question of Chamberlain's role, weakened him as party leader. In 1898 he showed signs of his old combativeness, throwing himself into a battle against ritualism in the Church of England, writing a long series of letters to *The Times* on the subject, collected in book form as *The Crisis in the Church*. Although he appeared in public less and less, it was nevertheless a considerable surprise when he resigned his position as leader in the House of Commons on 8 December 1898. His action may have been caused by some Liberal organizations showing signs of restlessness and lack of support. His son became engaged in November 1898 to a wealthy American, much to his father's delight, but without Loulou constantly at hand the impetus to remain in power might have noticeably slackened. In his private letters to colleagues he blamed Rosebery's refusal to work with him as the real cause for his resignation. He now regarded the party as hopelessly split on all major questions, particularly in the area of foreign policy and imperialism but on domestic issues as well: home rule, temperance, disestablishment, eight hours legislation, old-age pensions. On questions of imperialism, intensified by the Fashoda incident in 1898, Rosebery had the following of the bright young men in the party, sympathetic to a more aggressive stance than Harcourt was willing to take. On 6

February 1899 the Liberal members of the House of Commons elected Sir Henry Campbell-Bannerman as their leader at a meeting at the Reform Club.

Final years, death, and reputation Harcourt continued to be a prominent member of his party, though no longer on the front bench. He wished to keep to the fore the traditional domestic concerns of Liberalism, particularly as they were likely to become submerged as politics became increasingly dominated by the Second South African War. He attacked the war because of its expense, but also as a further example of the mistakes of imperialism. As some tories and their allies, most notably Chamberlain, became interested in eroding the policy of free trade, Harcourt was strong in its defence, particularly attacking Michael Hicks Beach's budget proposal in 1902 to impose a tax on imported corn. That spring Edward VII offered to make him a viscount in the coronation honours, but Harcourt declined on the ground that he was unwilling to leave the House of Commons, where he had served for thirty-four years.

Harcourt's health was becoming weaker, and in February 1904 he announced his decision not to stand for office at the next general election. In March he had a happy sense of continuity in that his son became a member of the House of Commons. Indeed, the last months of his life were dominated by family. His elder brother Edward had died in 1891. Edward's only son, Aubrey, died unmarried in March 1904 and the family estates, Nuneham Park and Stanton Harcourt (including Pope's Tower, where the poet had translated part of the *Iliad*), reverted to Harcourt, but in an impoverished state. In the discussion of death duties ten years before Rosebery had urged Harcourt to make allowances for deaths comparatively close to one another but Harcourt had declined, his decision emblematic of his willingness to go against his class interests. His own death a few months later made his family pay a high price for this determination. He still found time to attend the House of Commons and cross swords with Chamberlain over the issue of protection. His last important speech was on 17 May 1904, in which he attacked the burden of taxes, particularly those caused by war, and principally upon those less able to pay. He was now living mainly at his beloved Malwood in the New Forest, which he had no desire to leave, and less frequently at Nuneham; and it was at the latter house that he died unexpectedly on 1 October 1904, survived by his wife. He was buried in the family vault in the church in the grounds of Nuneham Park.

Harcourt was one of the more important politicians of the nineteenth century and came close to the highest office in the land. It might have been his if he had been more tactful; his allegiance to Liberalism's older ideas may also have harmed him. He shared in many worlds, having a distinguished birth, allied with the aristocracy and the church. Yet he was hard to label, moving leftwards from his political heritage, becoming something of a radical without a radical background. He became a member of the professional classes, and his training as a lawyer stood him in good stead in the House of Commons, where he revelled and was highly successful in the cut and thrust

of debate. But while he could argue a case with great effect, he did not quite have the moral stature that convinced others that particular beliefs were the essence of his being.   PETER STANSKY

Sources A. G. Gardiner, *The life of Sir William Harcourt*, 2 vols. (1923) · *DNB* · P. Stansky, *Ambitions and strategies* (1964) · Gladstone, *Diaries* · J. Butler, *The liberal party and the Jameson raid* (1968) **Archives** Bodl. Oxf., corresp. and papers | Bishopsgate Institute, London, letters to George Howell · BL, corresp. with Arthur James Balfour, Add. MS 49696, *passim* · BL, corresp. with Henry Campbell-Bannerman, Add. MSS 41219–41220 · BL, letters to John Bright, Add. MS 43388 · BL, corresp. with Sir Charles Dilke, Add. MS 43890 · BL, corresp. with Lord Gladstone, Add. MS 45992 · BL, corresp. with W. E. Gladstone, Add. MSS 44196–44203 · BL, corresp. with Sir Edward Walter Hamilton, Add. MS 48615 · BL, corresp. with Lord Ripon, Add. MS 43532 · BLPES, letters to Henry Broadhurst · Bodl. Oxf., letters to Herbert Asquith · Bodl. Oxf., letters to Benjamin Disraeli · Bodl. Oxf., letters to Lord Kimberley · CAC Cam., corresp. with Lord Randolph Churchill · CAC Cam., corresp. with Lord Esher · Chatsworth House, Derbyshire, letters to Lord Hartington · CKS, letters to Edward Stanhope · Glos. RO, corresp. with Sir Michael Hicks Beach · Herts. ALS, corresp. with Julian Fane · ICL, corresp. with Thomas Huxley · LPL, letters to Lord Selborn · LPL, corresp. with A. C. Tait · NA Scot., corresp. with A. J. Balfour · NL Scot., letters to Lord Kimberley · NL Scot., corresp., incl. with Lord Rosebery and Sir Patrick Geddes · NL Wales, letters to T. E. Ellis · NL Wales, corresp. with Lord Rendel · PRO, corresp. with Lord Granville, PRO 30/29 · Trinity Cam., letters to Lord Houghton · U. Birm., corresp. with Joseph Chamberlain **Likenesses** G. F. Watts, group portrait, fresco, *c*.1860 (*The school of legislation*), Lincoln's Inn, London · Lock & Whitfield, woodbury-type photograph, 1877, NPG · Barraud, photograph, 1890, NPG · W. Story, plaster bust, 1899, NPG · A. S. Cope, oils, 1904, NPG [see illus.] · M. Beerbohm, 1926, Sheffield City Art Galleries · *Aτη* [A. Thompson], chromolithograph caricature, NPG; repro. in *VF* (4 June 1870) · Barraud, cabinet photograph, NPG · L. Calkin, oils (after A. S. Cope), National Liberal Club, London · H. Furniss, drawings, NPG · F. C. Gould, drawing, NPG; repro. in *Westminster Gazette* (5 March 1904) · S. P. Hall, pencil sketches, NPG · Palmer, carte-de-visite, NPG · Spy [L. Ward], chromolithograph caricature, NPG; repro. in *VF* (3 Dec 1892) · B. Stone, photographs, NPG · W. Story, statue, House of Commons, members' lobby · H. J. Whitlock, carte-de-visite, NPG · possibly by H. C. S. Wright, chromolithograph, NPG; repro. in *VF* (11 May 1899) · possibly by H. C. S. Wright, chromolithograph caricature, NPG; repro. in *VF* (25 Nov 1897) · portrait, repro. in *VF* (27 Nov 1883) · portrait, repro. in *VF* (30 Nov 1886) · portrait, repro. in *VF* (30 Nov 1893) · portrait, repro. in *VF* (1 Feb 1898) · prints, BM, NPG **Wealth at death** £190,264 19s. 3d.: resworn probate, 4 Nov 1904, CGPLA Eng. & Wales

Harcourt, William Venables Vernon (1789–1871), founder of the British Association for the Advancement of Science, was born on 1 June 1789 at Sudbury, Derbyshire, the fourth son in a family of eleven boys and five girls of Edward Vernon *Harcourt (1757–1847), and his wife, Anne, third daughter of Granville Leveson-*Gower, first marquess of Stafford. His father was bishop of Carlisle (1791–1807) and archbishop of York (1807–47). Harcourt was adopted as the family surname in 1831 after Archbishop Vernon inherited the Harcourt estates at the death of the third and last earl, William *Harcourt (1743–1830). William Venables Vernon thus became William Venables Vernon Harcourt. Educated at home by his father, he imbibed a taste for chemistry from Isaac Milner, dean of Carlisle. From 1801 to 1806 he served in the navy. Intent on

William Venables Vernon Harcourt (1789–1871), by John & Charles Watkins, in or before 1866

a clerical career, in 1807 he went to Christ Church, Oxford, where he graduated in classics in 1811 and was befriended by Cyril Jackson, the dean.

At Oxford Vernon developed an interest in geology, attending Buckland's lectures and making the acquaintance of the Conybeare brothers, John Josias and William Daniel; his commitment to chemistry was strengthened by attending the lectures of John Kidd. After leaving Oxford he received private instruction from two celebrated chemists, William Wollaston and Humphry Davy. In 1814 his ordination launched him on a comfortable clerical career as the incumbent of three livings near York, at Bishopthorpe (1814–24 and 1835–8), Wheldrake (1824–34), and Bolton Percy (1838–61), all presented to him by his father, who was by then archbishop of York. In 1824 he was appointed canon residentiary of York Minster where he was active in ecclesiastical politics until he resigned in 1863. After the minster fire in 1829 Vernon took a leading part in the choir screen squabble which raged for two years. From the late twenties and especially after the minster fire of 1840, he abominated the unbusinesslike nonchalance of William Cockburn, the dean, whose adherence to scriptural geology he despised. As the leading critic of Cockburn in the York chapter, he not only persuaded his father to take the extraordinary step of holding a visitatorial court in 1841 to investigate Cockburn's

behaviour but also gave evidence against the dean. Cockburn was deprived of office, a verdict quickly quashed by the court of queen's bench. As the senior canon Harcourt published a reformist hymn-book, *Symmetrical Psalmody*, and concerned himself with diocesan training schools.

In 1824 Vernon met and quickly married Matilda Mary Gooch (1804–1876), fifteen years his junior. They had five daughters and two sons, Edward William Vernon Harcourt (1825–1891) and William George Granville Venables Vernon *Harcourt (1827–1904). Happy in his marriage and favoured with extensive and powerful family connections, Vernon interested himself in local philanthropic and scientific affairs. He laboured and lobbied hard on behalf of the Yorkshire School for the Blind, the Yorkshire County Hospital, the York Sanitary Committee, the Castle Howard Reformatory, and St Peter's School, York.

Vernon was above all a masterly developer and consolidator of organizational initiatives or suggestions made by others. In 1822 three York worthies formed a philosophical society to run a museum in the city on the basis of their collections of fossil bones from the famous cave at Kirkdale in north-east Yorkshire. Vernon transformed their plan into one for a county philosophical society which would tap local opportunity and pride by concerning itself primarily with Yorkshire geology and York antiquities. As first president of the Yorkshire Philosophical Society (1823–31), he nursed and promoted it, engaging the young John Phillips (1800–1874) as keeper in 1826 and providing for it, in the grounds of St Mary's Abbey, a Yorkshire Museum (designed by William Wilkins and opened in 1830).

When David Brewster suggested early in 1831 that a meeting of British men of science be held at York later that year, Harcourt remained in the shadow of Phillips, his lieutenant, until late summer when he sketched his ideas to various confidants about a British Association for the Advancement of Science which would give systematic direction to research, and lobby government effectively. At its first meeting, held in York in September 1831, Harcourt produced a title for the new body, proposed for it aims and a constitution which were broadly accepted, and suggested enduring mechanisms such as reports on the state of science. As the general secretary of the association from 1832 to 1837, Harcourt managed it with consummate skill. Typically he helped it in an emergency by assuming its presidency at the meeting held in Birmingham in 1839. In his address he characteristically claimed for science freedom of enquiry, but at the same time rashly pressed the claims of Henry Cavendish against those of James Watt as the discoverer of the composition of water.

Harcourt, who was elected FRS in 1824, deprecated his own scientific work, referring to himself as only a humble worshipper in the porch of the temple of science. Yet in the 1820s he was a practising and respected field geologist and in the 1840s taken seriously as a scientist by the great German chemist Liebig. His main distinction, however, lay in his launching and managing two new scientific organizations, the Yorkshire Philosophical Society and the British Association, the former becoming the mother of the latter through his efforts. As an organizer and administrator he was distinguished by a fine command of English, an intellectual vision developed in part by his reading of Francis Bacon, a tenacious dedication to the task in hand, and, in his public behaviour, by a persuasive combination of dignity, gentleness, and firmness. In 1861, on the death of his elder brother, George Granville Harcourt, he succeeded to the Harcourt estates in Oxfordshire where he continued the experiments with furnaces he had conducted for forty years. Though most of the results were inconclusive, he studied the effect of long-continued heat on minerals and, encouraged from 1862 by G. G. Stokes, the preparation and optical properties of glasses of a great variety of chemical composition. He died of bronchitis on 1 April 1871 at Nuneham Park, near Abingdon, and was buried on 6 April at Nuneham Courtenay.

JACK MORRELL

Sources E. W. Harcourt, ed., *The Harcourt papers*, 14 vols. (privately printed, London, [1880–1905]), vols. 13–14 · *PRS*, 20 (1871–2), xiii–xvii · J. Morrell and A. Thackray, *Gentlemen of science: early years of the British Association for the Advancement of Science* (1981) · J. Morrell and A. Thackray, eds., *Gentlemen of science: early correspondence of the British Association for the Advancement of Science*, CS, 4th ser., 30 (1984) · A. D. Orange, *Philosophers and provincials: the Yorkshire Philosophical Society from 1822 to 1844* (1973) · G. E. Aylmer and R. Cant, eds., *A history of York Minster* (1977) · *Report of the proceedings of the visitatorial court of the archbishop of York …* (1841) · G. G. Stokes, 'The late Reverend W. V. Harcourt's researches on glass', *Nature*, 4 (1871), 351–2 · J. B. Morrell, 'The legacy of William Smith: the case of John Phillips in the 1820s', *Archives of Natural History*, 16 (1989), 319–35 · *Jackson's Oxford Journal* (8 April 1871) · *Jackson's Oxford Journal* (15 April 1871) · Burke, *Gen. GB*

Archives Bodl. Oxf., family corresp. · priv. coll. · U. Cam., scientific periodicals library, notebook | BL, corresp. with Charles Babbage, Add. MSS 37186–37200, *passim* · BL, corresp. with Sir Robert Peel, Add. MSS 40494, 40530–40531 · CUL, corresp. with Sir George Stokes · GS Lond., letters to Roderick Impey Murchison · U. St Andr. L., corresp. with James David Forbes and his son

Likenesses F. Chantrey, marble bust, c.1833, Yorkshire Museum Archives, York · J. & C. Watkins, carte-de-visite, in or before 1866, NPG [*see illus.*] · M. Noble, plaster bust, 1872?, NPG · F. Chantrey, bust, AM Oxf. · lantern slide, Yorkshire Museum Archives, York

Wealth at death under £30,000: probate, 12 May 1871, *CGPLA Eng. & Wales*

Hardcastle, Ephraim. *See* Pyne, William Henry (1770–1843).

Hardcastle, Frances (1866–1941), mathematician, was born at Writtle, Essex, on 13 August 1866, the eldest of eight children of Henry Hardcastle (1840–1922), graduate of Trinity College, Cambridge, a barrister, and director of a brewery. Her mother was Maria Sophia Herschel (1839–1929), seventh child (fourth daughter) of Sir John Frederick William Herschel, so Frances was a great-grandchild of Sir William Herschel, inheriting a notable astronomical tradition. Two of her brothers also graduated from Trinity College; the elder, Joseph Alfred (1868–1917), later became an astronomer.

Frances Hardcastle was educated privately before entering Girton College, Cambridge, in 1888; her aunt Constance Anne Herschel (1855–1939) had previously been resident lecturer in natural sciences and mathematics there. In 1891 Frances Hardcastle passed second class in the mathematical tripos part one examinations, and went on in 1892, somewhat unusually, to sit the tripos part two, in which she gained class 2 (3). Cambridge did not then permit women to graduate but Bryn Mawr College, Pennsylvania, USA, accepted her as a graduate student, and she worked under Professor C. A. Scott, also a Girtonian. She was appointed an honorary fellow in mathematics at Chicago University for 1893/4 and held a fellowship in mathematics at Bryn Mawr during the academic year 1894/5. Her sole publication while in the United States was a translation from the German of Felix Klein's 1881 lectures on algebraic functions. However, it was probably during this time that she began her research into point groups—nowadays called 'divisors' and much studied in algebraic geometry.

Hardcastle returned to Britain in 1895 to become a graduate student at Girton. There her research matured and in papers in the *Proceedings of the London Mathematical Society* (1897–8) and the *Bulletin of the American Mathematical Society* (1898) she set out an extension of the theory of point groups which was said to display great insight. She further synthesized the topic by four articles on the theory of point groups in the *Reports of the British Association* for the years 1900 and 1902–4, which included a historical survey. She deviated only once from single-minded pursuit of this subject—appropriately, to assist Arthur Berry with the publication in 1898 of his *Short History of Astronomy* by verifying the calculations, proof-reading, and drawing many diagrams.

It seems that an accident, possibly in conjunction with ill health, caused Hardcastle to leave Cambridge in 1904 and abandon her mathematical research. She was able to live in adequate comfort on money settled on her by her father, increased later by inheritance. She and her sister Mira Francisca were named joint executors of her father's will, despite the availability of several brothers. She lived in London for a period, and worked for a year as a joint secretary, with Frances Sterling, for the National Union of Women's Suffrage Societies (the suffragist organization), before moving to Newcastle where she served as secretary of the North-Eastern Federation of Women's Suffrage Societies. She spent her eventual retirement beside the Northumberland moors at Stocksfield, in a house she had built with Dr Ethel Williams, a former Newcastle GP. She died on 26 December 1941 while visiting Cambridge, and was buried in Girton churchyard.

A. E. L. DAVIS

Sources K. T. Butler and H. I. McMorran, eds., *Girton College register, 1869–1946* (1948) · *Girton Review*, Easter term (1942), 19 · Venn, *Alum. Cant.* · private information (2004)

Wealth at death £4400: probate, 16 May 1942, *CGPLA Eng. & Wales*

Hardcastle, Thomas (bap. 1637, d. 1678), clergyman and ejected minister, was born at Barwick in Elmet, the son of John Hardcastle (d. c.1643), yeoman, and was baptized there on 24 February 1637. After attending nearby Sherburn School, Hardcastle matriculated at St John's College, Cambridge, in 1652 and graduated BA in 1656. He married Anne Gerard, daughter of the Cromwellian army officer and protectorate governor of Chester Castle, Colonel Gilbert Gerard of Crewood, Cheshire. They had two children, Prisona, alias Mary, and Joshua (b. 1678).

Hardcastle became vicar of Bramham, near Leeds, and was ejected under the 1662 Act of Uniformity. He shared the convictions of those ejected that the faith and order of the Church of England should not be subordinate to state control but to scripture; that the historic episcopate was not an essential mark of the visible church nor necessary for its effective ministry; and that the orderly public worship of God was not exclusively contained within the liturgy of a particular book. After 1662 he was employed by:

> Lady Barwick, of Toulsten in Yorkshire, to whom I had the happiness to be chaplain for several years, and must own myself to be much obliged; and no less to the right honourable the Lord Henry Fairfax, her son-in-law, and my constant and my faithful friend in my sufferings for Christ. (Palmer, 3.426–7)

(Henry Fairfax, the cousin and heir of Lord Fairfax, the civil war general, was regarded as a leading patron of the godly in Yorkshire.)

Between 1666 and 1670 Hardcastle was frequently imprisoned for his nonconformity in Leeds, Chester, Wakefield, York, and London. During 1669–70 he moved to London, where he became a member of Henry Jessey's congregation, the Swan Alley Baptist Church. In 1670, while imprisoned in London under the Conventicle Act, he was invited to consider becoming pastor at Swan Alley, and at the same time he was approached by Broadmead Baptist Church, Bristol. An account of what followed may be found from Broadmead's records, supplemented by *The Records of the Church of Christ* (1847), edited by E. B. Underhill, which contains a transcript of additional correspondence between Broadmead, Swan Alley, Edward Terrill, Vavasor Powell, and Hardcastle. When Terrill, the Broadmead elder, contacted Powell about his brother-in-law's becoming their new pastor, he was told Hardcastle was a member at Swan Alley, though presently in prison, and '*upon trial* to be their pastor' (Underhill, 108). Nevertheless, Broadmead invited him to be their pastor, despite Hardcastle's indicating that Swan Alley were 'altogether unwilling to hearken to it, or to part with their interest in me' (ibid., 111). At first Hardcastle hoped this would end the discussions, but it did not. Eventually Swan Alley asked him to visit Bristol during May 1671 to explain the situation; before he returned to London the Broadmead congregation had confirmed their invitation. His visit to Bristol completely changed Hardcastle's perception and he returned to London hoping the call to Bristol could be agreed amicably. Hardcastle wrote to Terrill, 'how little inclination I found in myself to come to Bristol, till I saw you and understood your call', but now convinced that his future lay with Broadmead, he continued 'that so far as I see at present, my call is to Bristol ... I intend to desire my dismission shortly, and if I cannot have it, I must take it' (ibid., 141, 144f.). Swan Alley wrote deprecating that Broadmead had felt 'constrained to take him by force' (ibid., 154), but Hardcastle went to Bristol on 28 July 1671, and after three years on trial was appointed pastor on 19

May 1674; his wife became a member on 12 November 1676. At that time some London Baptist ministers, who were engaged in settling a dispute in Wiltshire, were asked to ordain Hardcastle, but declined. As late as May 1678 three Swan Alley members came and tried to claim Hardcastle as their pastor.

On 5 September 1672 Broadmead secured a licence for Hardcastle to preach lawfully in their licensed Bristol meeting-house. Between October 1671 and October 1672 Hardcastle gave 'Thirty-five catechetical lectures addressed to the young', based on the Westminster catechism. These detailed expositions (which survive in manuscript in the Bristol Baptist College Library) of the Christian faith illustrate Hardcastle's ability to provide a good foundation for the congregation in the years of persecution which followed. In 1674 he published a set of sermons which he had preached, aptly titled for a congregation in the second port of the kingdom, *Christian geography and arithmetick, or, A true survey of the world: together with the right art of numbring our dayes therein*. When the licences to preach were made void by the government in February 1675 Hardcastle was immediately arrested, sent to London for trial on 15 May, and returned to Bristol on 4 June before being released on 2 August 1675. He preached at Broadmead the Sunday following his release, was rearrested under the Five Mile Act, and was imprisoned for a further six months in Newgate, Bristol.

Hardcastle issued from prison between August 1675 and February 1676 a remarkable series of twenty-two letters which were read to the church as it worshipped each week. He discusses the meaning of 'true faith' in a time of persecution and affirmed persecution by the authorities was 'a season of grace' in which:

> Ministers ... must meet with the waters of affliction and stand in them and see to the safety of the whole, with hazard to themselves, ... and ... when God calls for it, take up the cross of imprisonment when it directly lies in our way. (Underhill, 259, 265)

Christian faith in times of persecution would deepen patience, purify the heart, be a shield in danger, and bring deep and lasting joy. Christians must heed the warnings which God's judgments provide and develop an appropriate lifestyle. Hardcastle was not a controversialist and constantly sought to reconcile differences, as evidenced by his patient handling of his call to be minister at Broadmead and his broad view of believers' baptism. He believed that 'dipping or plunging into water' was 'the right sense of the word baptize, it sutes with the ends and uses of Baptisme that is to signify our being buried with Christ' (Hayden, 52). However, he was not for its imposition upon everyone, being an open-communion Baptist who refused to make believers' baptism a requirement for attendance at the Lord's supper.

Writing of Hardcastle's unexpected death at 3 a.m. on Sunday 29 September 1678, after his return from an arduous journey to Chester, Terrill calls him 'a Champion for the Lord, very courageous in his work and sufferings ... [whose] zeal provoked many' (Hayden, 203). Hardcastle was buried in St James's, Bristol, on 30 September 1678 and Terrill noted:

> Att the funeral of said Br. Hardcastle wee gave no Wyne, but some bread to the poore. Gloves and Hatt-bands to the 6 ministers that went by the Hearse; yet it amounted well towards thirty pounds, all charge paid, with putting his widdow and children in Mourning Apparel, and putting a Tombstone over his Grave. All which Cost the Church was att. (ibid., 205)

Thirty-eight Broadmead church members collected £150 for Hardcastle's widow and children, which was given to her on 12 November 1678.   ROGER HAYDEN

Sources Broadmead Baptist Church, Bristol, record book, 1640–1784, Broadmead Baptist Church, 1 Whippington Court, Bristol · T. Hardcastle, expositions of Westminster shorter catechism, Bristol Baptist College · T. Hardcastle, sermons on Colossians I and Ecclesiastes 12:1, Bristol Baptist College · T. Hardcastle, letters from prison, Bristol Baptist College [transcripts] · E. B. Underhill, ed., *The records of the Church of Christ, meeting in Broadmead, Bristol, 1640–1687*, Hanserd Knollys Society (1847), 257–354 · R. Hayden, ed., *The records of a church in Christ in Bristol, 1640–1687*, Bristol RS, 27 (1974) · *Calamy rev.*, 247 · *DNB* · *The nonconformist's memorial ... originally written by ... Edmund Calamy*, ed. S. Palmer, [3rd edn], 3 (1803), 426–7
Archives Bristol Baptist College, MSS · Broadmead Baptist Church, Bristol, MSS
Wealth at death church paid for burial and tombstone in St James's, Bristol: Broadmead Baptist Church, Bristol, record book, 1640–1784

Hardcastle, William [Bill] (1918–1975), journalist and radio broadcaster, was born on 26 March 1918 at 5 Sydenham Terrace, Newcastle upon Tyne, last of the four children of William Hardcastle (1873–1924), medical officer at Newcastle prison, and his wife, Mary Constance Wardroper (1883–1967). William (Bill) Hardcastle's education at Durham School was cut short when, aged sixteen, he contracted osteomyelitis, and was in and out of hospital for the next four years. Nevertheless he read voraciously in the intervals between repeated painful operations which left his arms and legs deeply scarred. Though he had to abandon long-standing plans to become the fourth successive Hardcastle in the medical profession, he was able, in 1938, to start work with a Newcastle house agent. He hated the job and soon left to become a cub reporter on the *South Shields Gazette* and later the *North Shields Evening News*. His three years on Tyneside during the depression of the late thirties were to leave a lasting mark.

Unfit for military service in the Second World War, Hardcastle moved to Yorkshire to become a sub-editor on the *Sheffield Telegraph* and then on to London to work briefly for Kemsley Newspapers. In 1943 he joined Reuters news agency on the editorial desk and early in 1945, after a brief spell at SHAEF (Supreme Headquarters, Allied Expeditionary Force), was sent to New York and later to Washington as Reuters junior correspondent. His first big break was a casually distributed White House handout on what had seemed a slow day for news, with President Truman on the way home from the Potsdam conference. Dull the handout was not: in a state of shock he rushed to the phone to dictate his copy to London: 'The first atomic

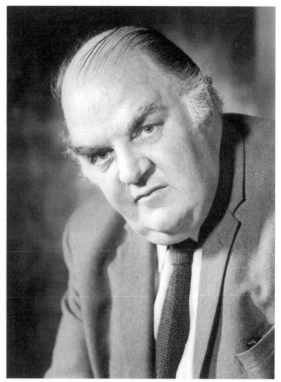

William Hardcastle (1918–1975), by Godfrey Argent, 1970

bomb, most powerful bomb in the world, was dropped sixteen hours ago on Hiroshima' (Hardcastle, 'Time of my life').

Long afterwards, Hardcastle remembered those early post-war years in the USA as 'a newspaperman's dream', and indeed it was the ideal place for an ambitious young journalist to learn his trade. He was in his element, making many friends and greatly enjoying the whole lively Washington scene with his wife and young family. He had in 1945 married the widow of a Royal Air Force pilot, Constance May Turton, *née* Ashmore (1923–1987); they had four children. The marriage was dissolved in 1960.

Hardcastle's eight years in America were briefly interrupted when, in May 1949, Reuters made him their chief of bureau in Rome—a promotion; yet after only three months in the job he resigned. Early in 1950 he was again in Washington, this time correspondent for the *Daily Mail*. In December 1952 he returned to London to become news editor and later deputy editor on the *Daily Mail*. By then Hardcastle had become every inch the tough, American-style newsman—shirt-sleeved, cigarette-smoking, hard-drinking, insatiable in the pursuit of news. So successful did he prove that in October 1959 the proprietor of Associated Newspapers, the second Lord Rothermere, appointed him as editor of the *Sunday Dispatch*, and his revitalization of that ailing journal prompted Rothermere after only two months to sack Arthur Wareham, the 'quiet man' who had edited the *Daily Mail* for eight years, and install Hardcastle in his place.

Circulation had been falling, the paper needed a face-lift, and this tough newsman seemed the man for the job. Yet, although he tried to widen the appeal of a dyed-in-the-wool Conservative journal by bringing in writers with a wider, more radical outlook and recruiting lively columnists and gossip writers, readers gradually fell away despite over a million inherited from the *News Chronicle* when it was taken over by the *Mail* in October 1960.

In fact, Hardcastle was not entirely at home in the editorial chair: for one of his temperament it provided too little action and too much administration, which he did not enjoy and for which he proved unsuited. One of his columnists, Alan Brien, recalled how his in-tray piled up with urgent decisions he seemed unable to face, and how he gradually sank into a deep depression when 'nothing seemed of any importance'. After three years Rothermere too had had enough: Hardcastle was dispatched on a fact-finding trip to the USA early in 1963, only to find himself out of a job on his return.

Without salaried employment for the first time in his working life, Hardcastle launched into freelancing for radio and television; and when, in 1965, the BBC planned an innovatory lunchtime radio news programme, *The World at One*, its editor, Andrew Boyle, chose Hardcastle as presenter. So began a second career which was not only to make his a household name in radio journalism but to give the 'wireless', as he liked to call it, a much-needed shot in the arm at a time when television seemed to be taking over.

Boyle and Hardcastle between them injected a new immediacy into the BBC's carefully correct current affairs output. Not only was the latter's urgent, breathless presentation—so alien to the hitherto customary staid and measured delivery—a somewhat startling innovation, but *The World at One* itself set out to be provocative. Stimulating new commentators were brought in; hot news was relentlessly pursued wherever it might be happening; and, basically serious though the programme remained, it took a not always reverent look at the passing scene.

Hardcastle quickly adapted to the new medium, bringing with him as presenter and interviewer an encyclopaedic knowledge of home and foreign affairs from his years in print journalism, as well as an instinctive ability to know what questions to ask, whether interviewing some quaking newcomer to the microphone or an evasive politician. With the latter his questioning was relentlessly persistent; but seldom rude and abrasive.

For Hardcastle the great attraction of radio was the speed, immediacy, and flexibility with which it could tackle the news: planned items or even a whole programme could be abandoned if some important story broke at the last moment. No wonder, then, that for him *The World at One* marked 'a real adventure in journalism', and its later Sunday edition, *The World this Weekend*, 'a further stride down the same exciting road'.

'It was journalism of the highest order,' wrote Asa Briggs, author of the official history of British broadcasting, but he continued: 'none the less, the programme did not escape criticism from politicians, including the Prime Minister' (Briggs, 578). The prime minister in question, Harold Wilson, had complained to the BBC's governors, who, while agreeing that 'occasional lapses of judgment' were unacceptable, added that they were 'loath to sacrifice the real achievements of these programmes in the field of popular news presentation' (ibid.). Yet Wilson and his Conservative successor, Edward Heath, were always ready to face yet another of Hardcastle's tough, searching grillings: according to Heath, 'an interview with him was always an important matter' (*Daily Mail*, 11 Nov 1975).

As Hardcastle wrote in *The Listener* shortly before his death, 'it would be wrong to assume that we were greatly loved. We were brash and cheeky and unappreciative of the many excellences of the BBC' (Hardcastle, 'Ten years'). For their part too, top people in the BBC hierarchy were themselves sometimes unappreciative of these often provocative programmes: indeed, when in 1974 Hardcastle's appearances as presenter were cut from four to three days a week, there were those who believed that the BBC management had yielded to political pressure on the grounds of his alleged left-wing bias, though he was always careful not to let his personal opinions obtrude.

Yet audiences for *The World at One*, *The World this Weekend*, and the afternoon edition, *P.M. Reports*, multiplied, and within a decade similar programmes had become a commonplace in both radio and television.

Hardcastle was a large, untidy person, never happier than when working under pressure in shirt-sleeves in a kind of creative chaos. He was stimulating though not always easy to work with: his professionalism made him impatient with those who did not match his high standards, though his often searing strictures were tempered by an unfailing sense of humour and ready support for inexperienced young journalists.

Always a workaholic, he drove himself too hard, with weekly columns in *Punch* and *The Listener* and other journalism, as well as the relentless pressure of twice-daily radio programmes. He paid the price: on a Friday evening after a heavy day at the BBC and on the eve of a fortnight's holiday, he had a massive stroke and died three days later, on 10 November 1975, in Epsom Hospital. He was buried at St Mary's churchyard at Headley in Surrey, across the fields from Webb's Farm Cottage, which had been his home for the past fifteen years. ELEANOR RANSOME

Sources personal knowledge (2004) · private information (2004) [family, friends, colleagues] · *The Times* (11 Nov 1975) · *The Guardian* (11 Nov 1975) · A. Boyle, 'Bill Hardcastle: portrait of a friend', *The Listener* (20 Nov 1975), 671 · W. Hardcastle, 'Ten years of *The world at one*', *The Listener* (2 Oct 1975), 426 · G. Nicholson, 'William Hardcastle', *Radio Times* (25 Sept 1969), 53 · A. Hamilton, 'Ten years hard', *The Guardian* (4 Oct 1975), 9 · A. Briggs, *The history of broadcasting in the United Kingdom*, rev. edn, 5 vols. (1995), vol. 5 · S. J. Taylor, *The reluctant press lord: Esmond Rothermere at the 'Daily Mail'* (1998), 135–8 · M. Randall, *The funny side of the street* (1988) · Q. Crisp, *Well, I forget the rest* (1991) · Reuters, 85 Fleet Street, London, Reuters Archives · *CGPLA Eng. & Wales* (1976) · *Daily Mail* (11 Nov 1975) · W. Hardcastle, 'The time of my life', BBC Radio 4, 14 Aug 1966
Archives SOUND BBC WAC · BL NSA, 'The time of my life', BBC Radio 4, 14 Aug 1966 · BL NSA, *Radio lives: William Hardcastle*, BBC Radio 4, 20 June 1991

Likenesses G. Argent, photograph, 1970, NPG [see illus.] · F. Martin, photograph, repro. in *The Guardian* (4 Oct 1975), 9 · K. McMillan, photograph, repro. in *The Listener* (20 Nov 1975), 426 · photograph, repro. in *The Times*

Wealth at death £77,687: administration, 11 May 1976, CGPLA Eng. & Wales

Hardeby, Geoffrey (*c*.1320–*c*.1385), Augustinian friar and theologian, was born in Harby, Leicestershire, and entered the order at the friary in Leicester. There he studied philosophy and theology, and was then assigned to the *studium generale* in Oxford, where he attained the degree of doctor in theology. He probably lectured on the *Sentences* of Peter Lombard in 1353–4 and incepted as master of theology in 1357. From 1357 to 1359 he acted as regent master in the university, and therefore as head of the Augustinian *studium* in Oxford, and by 23 September 1359 he was *sacre pagine professor*. In this capacity he became closely involved in the mendicant debates provoked by Richard Fitzralph (d. 1360), challenged the latter's views on dominion, and prepared the first version of his major surviving work, a defence of the mendicant orders known as the *Liber de vita evangelica* (Bodl. Oxf., MS Digby 113), which, however, he did not publish until 1385.

Hardeby received a papal dispensation from the canonical consequences of his illegitimate birth, in order to allow him to assume all offices in his order except that of prior provincial. It was presumably granted so that he could represent the English province as diffinitor at the Augustinian general chapter that opened at Padua on 28 August 1359. He collected information from a 'certain doctor' in Italy which he used in his defence of his order shortly afterwards. When the juridical status of the Friars Hermit of St Augustine was challenged at Oxford in 1360—possibly by the Benedictine Uthred Boldon (d. 1396)—Hardeby defended their position in several *quaestiones*, intended to prove that Augustine had lived as a hermit. He subsequently incorporated these into the *Liber de vita evangelica*.

On 15 May 1360 Hardeby received a further papal dispensation, clearing the way for his election as provincial of the English Augustinians, and he held the office from 1360–61 until 1366. On 23 March 1363 Hardeby once again petitioned the pope, and received permission to accept any dignity in his order short of that of prior-general. His term as provincial coincided with a period of expansion of the English province, thereby supporting the tradition that he was influential at the court of Edward III. In 1369 he again held the office of provincial, but had relinquished this by January 1372. Hardeby was granted on 8 April 1377 an annual pension of 50 marks for life; this was cut by half two years later, on 13 March 1379.

Earlier sources often refer to Hardeby as having been counsellor to Edward III. According to the fifteenth-century chronicler John Capgrave, Hardeby was 'Confessoure to the Prince', a statement which has been usually interpreted as meaning the future king, Richard II, who became prince of Wales on 20 November 1376, but is more likely to mean the latter's father, Edward, the Black Prince (d. 8 June 1376). On two separate occasions,

after 12 September 1375 and by 2 July 1376, he was proposed for the bishopric of Bangor in Wales. He revised the *Liber de vita evangelica* in the light of Wyclif's denunciation of all religious orders in 1381.

Apart from the *Liber de vita evangelica*, and his inaugural sermon preached in the church of St Mary the Virgin in Oxford, probably on 27 November 1356, few of Hardeby's writings have survived. The sermon shows Hardeby's interest in the scientific investigations current in fourteenth-century Oxford. Some *quaestiones* from his commentary on the *Sentences* have recently been discovered in a manuscript in Palermo (Biblioteca Comunale, MS 2. Qq. D. 142), and his *quaestiones quodlibeta* are known to have circulated at least in England. From contemporary reactions to his theological writings among the Dominicans in Prague, and following these some fifteenth-century German theologians, it is clear that in his commentary on the *Sentences* Hardeby adopted a critical stance with regard to indulgences. The exact date of his death is unknown, but it is likely to have been about 1385.

KATHERINE WALSH

Sources *Chancery records* · *CEPR letters*, 4.42–3 · J. G. Edwards, *Calendar of ancient correspondence concerning Wales* (1935), 194 · *Johannis Capgrave Liber de illustribus Henricis*, ed. F. C. Hingeston, Rolls Series, 7 (1858), 218 · Bale, *Cat.*, 1.458–59 · Bale, *Index*, 79 · A. Gwynn, *The English Austin friars in the time of Wyclif* (1940) · Emden, *Oxf.*, 2.869 · *Hist. U. Oxf.* 2: *Late med. Oxf.*, 6, 32–4, 179, 182, 251 · K. Walsh, 'The *De vita evangelica* of Geoffrey Hardeby O.E.S.A. (*c*.1320–*c*.1385): a study in the mendicant controversies of the fourteenth century [pt 1]', *Analecta Augustiniana*, 33 (1970), 151–261 · K. Walsh, 'The *De vita evangelica* of Geoffrey Hardeby O.E.S.A. (*c*.1320–*c*.1385): a study in the mendicant controversies of the fourteenth century [pt 2]', *Analecta Augustiniana*, 34 (1971), 5–83 · M. B. Hackett, 'The spiritual life of the English Austin friars in the fourteenth century', *Sanctus Augustinus vitae spiritualis magister*, 2 vols. (1959), 2.421–92, esp. 2.443–50 · M. B. Hackett, 'Geoffrey Hardeby's *Quaestio* on S. Augustine as founder of the order of the Friars Hermits', *Traditio augustiniana: Studien über Augustinus und seine Rezeption, Festgabe für Willigis Eckermann OSA zum 60. Geburtstag*, ed. A. Zumkeller and A. Krümmel (Würzburg, 1994), 525–56

Archives Österreichische Nationalbibliothek, Vienna, CVP 4127 · Biblioteca Comunale, Palermo, MS 2. Qq. D. 142 · Bibliothèque Mazarine, Paris, MS 986 · Bodl. Oxf., MSS Digby 113, 161 · Universitätsbibliothek, Basel, A.X.3

Hardecanute. *See* Harthacnut (*c*.1018–1042).

Hardel, William (d. *c*.1248). *See under* Moneyers (act. *c*.1180–*c*.1500).

Harden, Sir Arthur (1865–1940), chemist, was born in Manchester on 12 October 1865, the third of the nine children of Albert Tyas Harden, a Manchester manufacturer, and his wife, Eliza, daughter of John MacAlister, of Paisley. He was educated at Victoria Park School, Manchester, and later at Tettenhall College, Staffordshire. When he was sixteen years old he entered Owens College, Manchester, and studied chemistry under H. E. Roscoe. He graduated with first-class honours in chemistry in 1885 and embarked on an investigation of the action of silicon tetrachloride on aromatic amide-compounds under the guidance of Julius Berend Cohen. The results of this research were published by the Chemical Society and on its merits he was awarded the Dalton scholarship by the

University of Manchester in 1886. The next two years were spent in Germany at the University of Erlangen where, under Otto Fischer, he prepared a nitrosonaphthylamine and investigated its properties. For his thesis on this subject he was awarded a PhD there.

In 1888 Harden was appointed a lecturer in chemistry at the University of Manchester. He took his responsibilities very seriously and for the next few years was preoccupied with teaching. He published a few papers on chemical topics and in 1896, with Roscoe, an interesting piece of historical research on the genesis of the atomic theory of John Dalton. From the study of Dalton's notebooks they concluded that it was his observations on the diffusion of gases which led him to formulate his atomic theory.

In 1897 Harden became chemist to the British Institute of Preventive Medicine (later known as the Jenner Institute) in London. He became head of the new department of biochemistry in 1907 and held this position until his retirement in 1930. In 1900 he married Georgina Sydney (d. 1928), elder daughter of Cyprian Wynard Bridge, of Christchurch, New Zealand; they had no children.

In 1912 Harden was appointed professor of biochemistry at the University of London. His first venture in biochemistry was to investigate the fermentation of sugar by various bacteria. The observations were necessarily limited to a quantitative study of the products, and what happened in the intermediate stages could be only imperfectly deduced from their nature and amounts. This research laid some of the foundations of bacterial chemistry. Shortly after Harden began work on bacterial metabolism, the German chemist Eduard Büchner (1860–1917) published experiments that concluded that living yeast was not, as maintained by Pasteur, essential for alcoholic fermentation, which could be induced by an expressed juice free from cells. Appreciating that if Büchner's contention were true, his yeast juice would provide material for the study of the conversion of sugar to alcohol step by step, Harden repeated his experiments and confirmed his results. Büchner thought that yeast juice contained an enzyme zymase, which broke up the sugar, but the chemical transactions involved in the conversion of one molecule of glucose into two each of alcohol and carbonic acid were mysterious.

For the next thirty years, Harden's principal researches were directed to the solution of the mystery. In this he was supported by able pupils and collaborators and notably by William John Young and Robert Robison. He discovered that in the transformation of sugars to alcohol and carbonic acid a complex series of reactions was involved and he made two fundamental discoveries. The first was that before any breakdown of the sugar molecules occurred, combination with phosphoric acid was necessary and that it was only after this preliminary phosphorylation that they became susceptible to disruption by the zymase in yeast. The second was that yeast juice contained not one but several enzymes which catalysed different reactions during the progress of conversion of sugar into alcohol and carbonic acid. One of these he presumed to activate the preliminary phosphorylation of the sugar molecules;

another, a phosphatase, produced the separation of the phosphoric acid from the first products of the split sugar molecule, allowing it to combine with further sugar molecules. The essential part played by phosphorylation and dephosphorylation in the breakdown of sugars by yeast was soon found to apply to fermentation by other microorganisms and provided a clue to the understanding of the conversion of glycogen into lactic acid in muscle during activity. Recognition of the significance of Harden's discovery constituted a turning point in the history of muscle chemistry.

During the First World War Harden suspended his work on alcoholic fermentation to study the chemistry of the two known water-soluble vitamins. Although he did not succeed in isolating these active principles, some of his observations on their properties became useful in the solution of nutritional problems confronting the armies, and they were a valuable contribution to the early knowledge of these accessory food factors.

Harden wrote two textbooks for students on chemistry while he was at Manchester. He also revised and edited the *Treatise on Chemistry* (1894) by Roscoe and Carl Schorlemmer. His most important monograph was *Alcoholic Fermentation* (1911). He contributed the article on this subject to *Thorpe's Dictionary of Applied Chemistry*, and one entitled 'Bacterial metabolism in the system of bacteriology' published by the Medical Research Council in 1930. For twenty-five years he was joint editor of the *Biochemical Journal*.

The importance of Harden's contributions to biochemistry was recognized by his election in 1909 as a fellow of the Royal Society, and by the award in 1929 of the Nobel prize for chemistry, which he shared with Hans von Euler-Chelpin. Honorary degrees were conferred on him by the universities of Manchester (1931), Liverpool (1935), and Athens (1937). In 1935 he was awarded the Davy medal of the Royal Society and he was knighted in 1936. Harden died at his home, Sunnyholme, Bourne End, Buckinghamshire, on 17 June 1940.

C. J. MARTIN, *rev.* RACHEL E. DAVIES

Sources *The Times* (18 June 1940) • I. Smedley-Maclean, *Biochemical Journal*, 35 (1941), 1071–81 • F. G. Hopkins and C. J. Martin, *Obits. FRS*, 4 (1942–4), 3–14 • *Journal of the Institute of Brewing* (Sept 1940) • R. Kohler, 'The background to Arthur Harden's discovery of cozymase', *Bulletin of the History of Medicine*, 48 (1974), 22–40 • *CGPLA Eng. & Wales* (1940)
Likenesses photograph, repro. in *Biochemical Journal* (Nov 1941)
Wealth at death £7634 18s. 5d.: probate, 5 Sept 1940, *CGPLA Eng. & Wales*

Hardham, John [*pseud.* Abel Drugger] (d. **1772**), tobacconist, was born at Chichester, the son of a wholesale provision merchant. He is believed to have trained as a lapidary, or diamond cutter, although one source suggests he began life as a servant. He moved to London, where he was a constant frequenter of Drury Lane Theatre. He attracted the attention of David Garrick, who made him 'numberer' (counter of the pit) and under-treasurer. At one time Garrick was his security for £100. About 1744 Hardham set up as a tobacconist and snuff-merchant at the Red Lion, 106

Fleet Street. On several occasions Garrick is said to have alluded when on the stage to Hardham's No. 37 (a mixture of Dutch and rapee, or rough snuff, probably named after the number of the shop drawer in which it was kept). The snuff became fashionable among celebrities, including Sir Joshua Reynolds, and Hardham's modest trade was transformed into a prosperous business.

Under the pseudonym Abel Drugger, Hardham wrote one unsuccessful play. He taught acting in the back parlour of his shop and is said to have dissuaded the Chichester poet William Collins (1721–1759) from taking holy orders. His wide circle of friends included many entertainers and actors. Noted for his honesty, Hardham was often called upon by his wealthy patrons to act as trustee for their charitable funds. Sometimes, when the donor died, he continued to pay the annuities.

Hardham was predeceased by his wife. There were no children. He died in September 1772. In his will he set aside £10 for his funeral because, he said, 'only vain fools spent more on such pageants' (Thornbury and Walford, 1.69). Apart from minor bequests, including £10 to Garrick and £5 to each of his four nieces, he left the interest on his capital to his housekeeper, Mary Binmore, for the duration of her life, and then to John Condell, boxkeeper at Covent Garden Theatre. After the latter's death, the estate of £22,289 passed to the city of Chichester so that Hardham might benefit the city for ever. The will was unsuccessfully contested by his relatives, and from 1786 Hardham's trust was used to subsidize the city's poor rates. W. W. WROTH, *rev.* CHRISTINE CLARK

Sources G. W. Thornbury and E. Walford, *Old and new London: a narrative of its history, its people, and its places*, 6 vols. (1873–8), vol. 1 · *N&Q*, 6th ser., 11 (1885), 328, 398, 462 · *N&Q*, 6th ser., 12 (1885), 184, 311 · A. Hay, *The Chichester guide*, new edn [1804] · C. Colton, *Hypocrisy* (1812) · J. Dallaway, *A history of the western division of the county of Sussex*, 1 (1815) · private information (1890)
Wealth at death approx. £22,300: Dallaway, *History*, 6

Hardie [*née* Pettigrew], **Agnes Agnew** (1874–1951), politician, was born on 6 September 1874 at Barnhill in the Springburn district of Glasgow, the daughter of John Pettigrew, the assistant governor of the Barony poorhouse, Barnhill, and his wife, Margaret (*née* Drummond). Nothing is known of her early life and education, beyond her later recollection of a sternly religious elementary schoolmaster and her regret that she never had the opportunity of an academic education (*Hansard 5C*, 391, 21 July 1943, 965). In her teens she was working as a shop assistant, and it was during this period that she was drawn into the labour movement. About 1893 she helped to organize Scottish shoemakers, which eventually led to an appointment as the first woman full-time organizer with the National Union of Shop Assistants. She was a lifelong campaigner to improve shopworkers' conditions, citing her own experience of working twelve hours a day, six days a week: 'I never had a half holiday or a Saturday afternoon until I was married' (*Hansard 5C*, 344, 24 Feb 1939, 814; 376, 10 Dec 1941, 1564).

Hardie was active in the Independent Labour Party and in 1907 she became a platform speaker whose ability, it was said, lay in 'unfolding practical Socialism to women taking up politics for the first time' (Haddow, 63). Speaking in public was highly unusual for women at this time, but perhaps because of this Hardie was selected as the Independent Labour Party candidate in the 1909 Glasgow school board elections. She was successful and served on the board for three years. This made her the first female member of the Independent Labour Party in Glasgow to sit on a public authority board. She also became the first female member of the Glasgow Trades Council, on whose behalf she helped to organize mill girls in the sewing trade of Bridgeton, Glasgow. In 1909 she married George Downie Blyth Crookston Hardie (1873–1937), half-brother of Keir Hardie and later Labour MP for Glasgow Springburn (1922–31, 1935–7). They had one son, born in December of that year. He predeceased his parents.

During the First World War Hardie was associated with the anti-war movement as a member of the Women's Peace Crusade, which also included Helen Crawfurd and Agnes Dollan. At the end of the war she was appointed women's organizer for the Labour Party in Scotland, a position she held until her resignation in 1923, following her husband's election as MP for Springburn. The Hardies moved to London, where Agnes was active at various times in the Ealing and Finchley branches of the Labour Party.

On the death of her husband in a London hospital on 26 July 1937 Hardie herself was elected to Westminster for Glasgow Springburn, easily defeating her Conservative rival in the by-election. She represented the constituency until 1945 when she decided not to seek re-election. In the House of Commons she concentrated on social issues, particularly maternity and child welfare, school meals, and hygiene facilities in the poorer areas of Scotland. She also championed the cause of higher pensions for old people. She was strongly against conscription. In opposing the Military Training Bill of 1939 she claimed to be a pacifist, and declared: 'I have taken no part in recruiting: I could never ask anyone to go and face the horrors of a war' (*Hansard 5C*, 346, 4 May 1939, 2169). Her pacifism was reinforced by what she had seen of the effects of the First World War; for example, meeting a young woman travelling on the night train to Glasgow in trepidation at the prospect of seeing for the first time her husband in his blinded and disfigured state (ibid.). When in December 1941 conscription was extended to women Hardie again spoke in opposition, believing that the conditions of military service were inappropriate to women (*Hansard 5C*, 376, 10 Dec 1941, 1565), and she also opposed the lowering of the age at which young men could be called up: 'My little Glasgow undersized, underfed boys are to be pushed into all these horrors' (*Hansard 5C*, 385, 8 Dec 1942, 1494).

As an advocate of greater sexual equality Hardie was an outspoken critic of discrimination against women. She campaigned for more nursery schools to be built; she argued for earlier old age pensions for women; in 1942 she served on a Commons select committee that recommended payment of equal compensation for war injuries to both sexes (at that time men received 7s. a week more than women) and this was accepted by the Ministry of Pensions in 1943; as a member of a number of consultative committees set up by the Ministry of Health in 1941 she did much to improve maternity services for women.

Although progressive in the pursuit of women's rights, Hardie was old-fashioned and puritanical in other areas of social life. She was a strong temperance advocate and while serving as a member of the royal commission on licensing (Scotland) in 1930–31, chaired by Alexander Morrice Mackay, she opposed the findings of the majority report, which sought to regularize drinking in Scotland, and joined Louise Forrester-Paton, Robert Stewart, and Peter Chalmers in signing a minority report that advocated the 'complete emancipation from the tyranny of drink' (*Parl. papers*, 1930–31, 15.90, Cmd 3894). Hardie was convinced that alcohol was a major cause of vice among young people and urged that they be prevented from entering public houses. In the early 1940s she blamed the increase in the incidence of venereal disease cases in Britain upon the demoralization brought about by war, parental neglect, the lack of supervision of school leavers, the availability of alcohol, and the presence of foreign seamen (*Hansard 5C*, 385, 15 Dec 1942, 1813–18).

Hardie's views were in many ways representative of the early socialist pioneers, with her stress on the moral and social uplifting of the working class. Her pacifism was nurtured by her marriage into the Hardie family, but her idealism was tempered by an equal emphasis on the practical methods of social advance. She died in London on 24 March 1951 and was cremated at Golders Green crematorium on 2 April.   W. W. J. KNOX

Sources W. Knox, ed., *Scottish labour leaders, 1918–39: a biographical dictionary* (1984) · W. M. Haddow, *Socialism in Scotland: its rise and progress* (1922) · *Glasgow Herald* (31 March 1951) · P. Brookes, *Women at Westminster: an account of women in the British parliament, 1918–1966* (1967) · *Hansard 5C* (1937–45) · *WWBMP*, vol. 3 · b. cert. · m. cert.
Wealth at death £1695: NA Scot.

Hardie [*married name* Hughes], **Agnes Paterson** [Nan] (**1885–1947**), socialist and political activist, was born in the Scottish mining town of Cumnock, Ayrshire, on 5 October 1885, the eldest daughter of James Keir *Hardie (1856–1915), socialist and politician, and his wife, Lillias (Lillie) Wilson. Keir Hardie had two sons, James and Duncan, but it was Agnes—or Nan as she was later to be more commonly known—whom he treated as his political heir. She consequently developed an unusual political awareness and insight into labour politics and socialism, augmented by contact with many of her father's associates—such as Bruce Glasier.

On 8 August 1924 Nan married Emrys Hughes (1894–1969), acting editor of *Forward* and a well-known journalist. He was active in the labour movement and an advocate of Keir Hardie's attitudes towards pacifism and socialism. Nan placed herself mainly at his disposal, acting as housewife in Cumnock and supporting her husband's ambitions in the Labour Party. She was involved in Hughes's successful attempt to become provost of Cumnock.

In the 1930s, however, Nan became more active in municipal politics, with a particular interest in housing and welfare provision. In 1933 she was elected as a Labour candidate to Cumnock town council, and she became convenor of Cumnock public health committee in the following year. In 1935 she succeeded her husband as provost and the two of them initiated a major programme of slum clearance and council-house building. Opposition from the chief landlord in the area, Lord Bute, was eventually overcome, with the result that by the start of the Second World War three-quarters of Cumnock's population had been rehoused in low-rent, partially furnished accommodation.

Nan's campaigning led to further improvements in the leisure and welfare facilities in Cumnock. These included an open-air swimming-pool and park. As a magistrate of the juvenile court in the late 1930s, she was able to put her own liberal imprint on the treatment of offenders, preferring to encourage the participation of youth within the community through sports activities rather than imposing draconian sentences. A measure of her popularity in the area was her appointment during the war as joint chairman of the Cumnock Red Cross and war work party. This enabled her to officiate at all public meetings and to help to alleviate the wartime exigencies imposed on the inhabitants. Nan's contribution to the war effort suggests that by 1939 she had modified her earlier attachment to her father's pacifist principles, though she tended to explain her stance in terms of supporting individuals' needs rather than endorsing the country's mobilization.

In 1946 Emrys Hughes was elected as Labour MP for South Ayrshire, with Nan having relinquished her council duties during the campaign tour. When he became ill soon afterwards Nan again absented herself from duties, only then to fall seriously ill also. This compounded ailments from which she had suffered since childhood and ended her public career. She had served unopposed on Cumnock town council for more than eleven years, playing a part in the transformation of the area's welfare and housing facilities. She regarded herself as a firm supporter of the Labour Party and socialism but displayed only limited personal ambition. With both her father and her husband, her assumed role was that of a helpmate, working behind the scenes for the cause instead of acting as its crusading proponent. Her modesty and retiring nature were accompanied by a striking appearance very similar to that of her father: 'She had a distinctive and well-defined bone structure and her face had a forthright and warm expression'. In later years her white, wavy hair was offset by broad, dark eyebrows (Corr, 139).

Nan Hardie Hughes died in Ballochmyle Hospital, Mauchline, Ayrshire, on 27 June 1947, and her funeral took place in Cumnock, attended by many prominent members of various local government bodies in Ayrshire; she was buried at the new cemetery, Cumnock. Emrys Hughes continued his career as a journalist and an MP. They had no children.   HELEN CORR

Sources H. Corr, 'Hardie, Agnes Paterson', *Scottish labour leaders, 1918–39: a biographical dictionary*, ed. W. Knox (1984) · W. Stewart, *J. Keir Hardie: a biography* (1921) · E. Hughes, *Keir Hardie* (1956) · K. O.

Morgan, *Keir Hardie: radical and socialist* (1975) • I. McLean, *Keir Hardie* (1975) • m. cert. • d. cert.
Wealth at death £3713 14s. 11d.: confirmation, 12 Sept 1947, *CCI*

Hardie, Andrew (1792–1820). *See under* Baird, John (1788–1820).

Hardie, Colin Graham (1906–1998). *See under* Hardie, William Ross (1862–1916).

Hardie, (James) Keir [*formerly* James Kerr] (1856–1915), founder of the Labour Party, was born in Legbrannock, Lanarkshire, on 15 August 1856. He was the illegitimate son of a farm servant, Mary Kerr, and was named James Kerr. The probable father was William Aitken, a Holytown miner. On 21 April 1859 Mary Kerr married David Hardie, a ship's carpenter from Falkirk, in Holytown kirk. From that time onwards, their child was known as James Keir Hardie.

Mining, self-education, and marriage The family moved to Glasgow, where David Hardie found work in the Govan shipyards, but he was laid off in 1866 during a lengthy shipyard strike. The Hardies then moved back to the coalfield and settled first at Newarthill, then at Quarter in Lanarkshire. Hardie had no formal education. From the age of eleven he worked down the mine as a 'trapper', ventilating the mine through releasing the air shaft trap. It was a dangerous occupation for a young boy. Later on, he was to use the pen-name Trapper in his newspaper columns. He remained a working collier for the next eleven years in no. 4 pit, Quarter, and became a skilled hewer. He witnessed sombre events, notably the pit disaster at Blantyre in October 1877, which cost the lives of over 200 miners.

Hardie was already a worker out of the ordinary. He read widely in history and literature, and was particularly impressed by Thomas Carlyle's *Sartor Resartus*. He attended night school and taught himself Pitman's shorthand in the darkness of the mine, using the wick miners used to adjust their lamps. He also became very active in the Scottish temperance movement (partly perhaps because of his father's frequent drunkenness) and simultaneously became converted to Christianity. He joined the Evangelical Union, or 'Morisonians', in 1877, a radical offshoot of the United Secession church, and was active as a lay preacher and crusader for temperance. At this time he met Lillias (Lillie) Balfour Wilson, daughter of a Hamilton publican. They married on 3 August 1879 and were to have two sons, Jamie and Duncan, and two daughters, Agnes *Hardie (1885–1947) and Sarah (who died in childhood).

Trade unionism and socialism In 1878–9 Hardie gave up being a working miner to become involved in trade unionism. He opened a small shop and started journalistic work for a Glasgow paper. In 1879 he became corresponding secretary for the Hamilton miners; later that year, he became miners' county agent for Lanarkshire. The local coal manager promptly dismissed him: 'We'll hae nae damned Hardies in this pit' (Stewart, 8). A crucial test came in the summer of 1880, when the Hamilton miners defied their union and went on strike against a wage reduction. This so-called 'tattie strike' (the miners eked out a living by picking potatoes during the strike) was inevitably

(James) Keir Hardie (1856–1915), by George Charles Beresford, 1905

crushed, but Hardie then accepted an invitation from the Ayrshire miners to become their secretary instead. He moved to Old Cumnock in Ayrshire, where he and his family were eventually to be based for the rest of his life. The next few years were precarious as he strove to build up the organization of the Ayrshire miners. He made a living partly through working for the Evangelical Union, partly as a local insurance agent, partly as weekly correspondent for the *Ardrossan and Saltcoats Herald*. He met many leading radicals at this time, including the American land taxer Henry George when he visited Scotland. A key moment came in 1884, when Hardie left the Evangelical Union in support of a dissentient minister of radical outlook, the Revd Andrew Scott, though Hardie still considered himself a Christian in broad terms thereafter. In 1886 the Ayrshire Miners' Union came into being on a stable basis with Hardie as its full-time secretary.

Hardie was now increasingly moving on from the world of mining trade unionism and into politics. He had hitherto been a staunch Gladstonian Liberal and often spoke at Liberal meetings. But the realities of class conflict in the western Scottish coalfield pushed him into more advanced positions. He founded a monthly journal, *The Miner*, which advocated a Scottish miners' federation. Soon after, there was a bloody suppression of the Lanarkshire miners when they went on strike, with violent clashes with the police at Blantyre. Hardie had an angry political confrontation at the Swansea Trades Union Congress (TUC) with the leading Lib–Lab Henry Broadhurst.

Hardie also met the Romantic radical–nationalist, R. B. Cunninghame-Graham, who introduced him to Tom Mann in London and, through him, to Marx's colleague Friedrich Engels. By the end of 1887 Hardie's political outlook had clearly changed from orthodox Liberalism to a kind of socialism. He called openly for the overthrow of the capitalist order. Historians have differed on the precise significance of this conversion. Some regard him as an ideological socialist from then on. Most, however, see his socialism as an undoctrinaire outgrowth of advanced Liberalism, and as ethical rather than economic in its basis. He was never a Marxist. But from 1887 he was clearly an apostle of the gospel of socialism and the political independence of labour.

As an MP This emerged dramatically at the Mid-Lanark by-election of April 1888. Rebuffed by the local Liberal association in favour of a wealthy London barrister, Hardie decided to stand as an independent 'labour' candidate. He resisted financial inducements and promises of a safe Liberal seat at the next election. His campaign suffered from religious controversies with Catholic voters, and he attracted only 617 votes, coming far down at the bottom of the poll. But 'the noble 600' were a major landmark in Labour's rise as a distinct political force. Soon after, a short-lived Scottish Labour Party was founded in Glasgow, with Hardie as its secretary. Another important development was that he launched his own monthly newspaper, the *Labour Leader*. He also attended the inaugural Socialist International meetings in Paris, shrewdly attending both the Marxist and the non-Marxist congresses there. He resisted Liberal blandishments to offer him a Scottish seat. Instead, he accepted the offer of a candidacy by the Liberals of West Ham South in London, a constituency much affected by the 'new unionism' among unskilled workers. He moved to London in 1891, and resigned as secretary of the Ayrshire Miners. Thus, he largely moved from his Scottish base and into a wider world of national politics.

In the 1892 general election Hardie was returned for West Ham South as 'independent Labour' candidate, along with John Burns in Battersea. He lived at first in the Chelsea house of Frank Smith, a Salvationist and spiritualist attracted to socialism. Much later, in 1902, he was to buy a small flat in Nevill's Court, just off Fleet Street. After his election he was triumphantly driven to take his seat at Westminster by his working-class supporters. He was hailed as 'the man in the cloth cap' although in fact he wore something like a deerstalker, then and later. In the House of Commons he eloquently promoted the cause of London's unemployed. But he was not a great success as an MP and attracted much notoriety for his attack on the royal family at the time of the Albion colliery disaster in south Wales in 1894. In the general election of the next year he lost his seat at West Ham South at the hands of a Conservative, when the local Liberals withdrew their support.

The *Labour Leader*, the ILP, and the LRC However, Hardie had already developed his career in other important directions. In 1894, as editor–publisher, he started up the *Labour Leader* on a weekly basis, an important platform for his views. More crucial still, he promoted a famous meeting in Bradford in January 1893 that saw the birth of the Independent Labour Party (ILP). Its evangelistic, populist style made it appropriate for Hardie's own flexible brand of radical socialism: his lieutenants included his fellow Scot J. Bruce Glasier and his wife, Katharine. Even though its

candidates were all defeated in the 1895 election, the ILP was a rising force, not least in mining areas in the West Riding, Lancashire, and, later, south Wales. Meanwhile, Hardie established himself as an internationalist with a tour of the United States, which he was to visit on two further occasions. In later years he also travelled to Canada, Australia, New Zealand, South Africa, Japan, and India. His main strategic objective now was to create a 'labour alliance' between the trade unions and the socialist societies. In the 1899 TUC, the unions narrowly voted in favour of such a proposal. The Labour Representation Committee (LRC) subsequently came into being in February 1900, with Hardie as its first chairman. Its executive consisted of seven trade unionists and five socialists—two ILP, two from the Marxist Social Democrats (who left shortly), and one from the Fabian Society. From 1906 it was to be known as the Labour Party, a new working-class third force in politics.

MP again, and chairman of the Labour Party Hardie was now anxious for a parliamentary seat. He was heavily defeated in a by-election for East Bradford in 1896. In the 1900 'khaki' election, during the Second South African War (which he bitterly opposed), Hardie was defeated again in Preston. However, he had received an unexpected invitation from the miners and others in the two-member constituency of Merthyr Tudful. He was already known in south Wales for his speeches during the six-month lock-out of the Welsh miners in 1898. He was duly elected for Merthyr, in large measure because of a split vote among the local Liberals, and this was to remain his political base for the rest of his life.

The next few years were largely occupied in enlisting trade union support for the fledgeling LRC. The Taff Vale rail dispute and the law lords' eventual verdict, which threatened the right to strike by imposing financial penalties on trade unions, led rapidly to large unions such as the engineers and the cotton spinners affiliating, followed eventually by the miners in 1908. In political terms, Hardie's aim was to create a viable partnership with the Liberal Party, but in a way that did not compromise Labour's independence. The outcome was the secret 'entente' negotiated with the Liberals in 1903 by Ramsay *MacDonald, the secretary of the LRC and a fellow Scot, with whom Hardie had a complex relationship. This guaranteed Labour a free run in about fifty seats at the general election of January 1906. Twenty-nine of them were returned, including Hardie at Merthyr. By a one-vote majority he was then elected first chairman of the Parliamentary Labour Party.

Hardie's time as leader was not a happy one—'a trial and a torment'. He did not enjoy parliamentary politics, and felt more at home on the platform or the street-corner soapbox. His Labour members, consisting variously of trade unionists and socialists, were fractious and Hardie gave up his chairmanship at the end of 1907. His reputation as a radical figure had, however, been much reinforced in this period. His visit to India in the autumn of

1907 and a subsequent stormy visit to South Africa confirmed the Liberal government's view of him as an irresponsible agitator. At home, he became deeply involved in promoting the cause of women's suffrage. This was partly the result of his friendship with the Pankhurst family. The younger daughter, Sylvia Pankhurst, was a very close friend, and probably his mistress. Some complained that Hardie's feminism was taking over his socialism. He now combined a role as Labour's elder statesman with endorsement of a wide range of left-wing causes, though he, Glasier, and MacDonald were agreed in fighting off the grass-roots challenge within the ILP from an unstable young orator, Victor Grayson. It was, indeed, a time of frequent personal conflict for Hardie, not only with past allies such as John Burns (now a Liberal minister) and Robert Blatchford, editor of *The Clarion*, but also with many in the ILP itself. Hardie took a leading part in upholding the rights of British workers during the 'labour unrest' of 1910–14, notably the disturbances in Tonypandy, when he bitterly condemned police brutality. On the other hand, he urged the workers to adopt constitutionalism and to steer clear of ideas of class war or direct industrial action.

As an internationalist Hardie continued to build up his international role as chairman of the British section of the Socialist International, and in campaigning with German comrades against the Anglo-German naval arms race. In addition, with the French socialist Edouard Vaillant, he strove in vain to get the International to commit itself to the principle of a worldwide workers' strike against war. He remained a supremely active propagandist at home, too. He had sold the *Labour Leader*, amid much argument over the financial settlement, back in 1904, but found a new platform in the Merthyr *Pioneer* in his own constituency. He also wrote many influential pamphlets such as *Killing No Murder* (1911), after striking railwaymen were shot and killed at Llanelli. His socialism led to Merthyr Liberals proposing to run a Liberal against him, and his parliamentary base was never wholly secure. But he remained a figure of unique charisma in the world of Labour. An emotional episode came at Bradford in April 1914, when he presided over a memorable 'coming of age' annual conference for the ILP, of which he had been founder and inspiration.

War, ill health, and death Hardie's career came to a watershed on 4 August 1914, when Britain declared war on Germany. He led anti-war demonstrations in London and in his own constituency, but workers in Britain, as in Germany and France, seemed caught up in war fever. A peace meeting in Aberdâr was broken up by local workers. His health suffered from the strain of being attacked as an anti-war traitor, and his attendances in parliament became fewer. He also encountered left-wing criticism when he appeared to justify enlistment in the army. In the summer of 1915 he suffered a second breakdown and he died in a Glasgow hospital, at the age of fifty-nine, on 26 September 1915. The cause was given as pneumonia. His funeral took place at Maryhill crematorium on 29 September. His daughter Agnes (Nan) was to marry the Welsh

socialist Emrys Hughes, who lived on in the house, Lochnorris, in Old Cumnock. Hughes served as Labour member for South Ayrshire from 1946 to 1969, the last custodian of Hardie's socialism.

Reputation and character Keir Hardie was perhaps the best-hated and best-loved man in British politics. His opponents found him dour and intractable, as well as impractical. A. G. Gardiner called him 'the one man in the parliamentary Labour Party who was unqualified to lead it' (*Prophets, Priests and Kings*, 1917, 86). John Burns (in his diary) jeered at 'the leader who never won a strike, organised a union, governed a parish or passed a bill, Barren Cumnock in the Duchy of Doctrinaire' (26 Sept 1915, BL, Add. MS 46337). For them, Hardie was an extremist, a politician of protest, happiest in the doctrinal purity of the wilderness. Certainly, he was never a major theorist, political or economic. His one general book, *From Serfdom to Socialism* (1907), is a rambling historical survey, though full of shrewd insights on practical matters. He had little understanding of economics or finance, and his judgements on international issues were too often predictable and secondhand.

Yet it is difficult to escape the conclusion that without Hardie the British Labour Party would never have come into existence, at least not in the way it did. He was its leading strategist, the major architect of the working alliance of the trade unions and the socialists, devoted only to the defence of Labour in the political arena. Here he proved himself subtle and pragmatic. It was ironic that it was during the First World War, which Hardie abominated, that the opportunity arose, partly through the split in the Liberal Party, for Labour to emerge as a national party, ready for government. Again, Hardie was its supreme prophet and evangelist. More than any other politician of his time, he spoke directly from Westminster to the industrial workers of the late Victorian and Edwardian eras. His oratory, rhetorical and often sentimental, but powerful and passionate, was deeply stirring, not least to nonconformist workers in mining and textile areas alienated by the capitalist ethic of chapel congregations. Hardie's influence as a journalist in the *Labour Leader* and elsewhere, and as a pamphleteer, should also not be underestimated. In personal affairs, there were often complications on financial matters, as with the sale of the *Labour Leader* or the donations from the Kippen sisters. The latter were given to causes he favoured, rather than to Hardie personally, a distinction not always easy to draw. Yet his evident incorruptibility stood out like a beacon: he died a relatively poor man. His almost mystical strength of character gave him a kind of Christ-like simplicity. In August 1914 he observed that he now knew the sufferings of his saviour at Gethsemane.

In personal appearance Hardie was a man of average height, strong in the shoulder, broad of brow. His flowing beard and an early air of *gravitas* made him seem older than his years. Although he died at only fifty-nine, he had long been known as 'labour's grand old man'. His marriage to Lillie was not an easy one; she did not share in his political activities and was tied to family and home. There were frequent quarrels. With his daughter Agnes, however, his bonds were strong. A passionate and impressionable man, Hardie developed close attachments to several young socialist women at times, though only with Sylvia Pankhurst, perhaps, was the relationship physical. Young socialist men such as Fenner Brockway became warm disciples. The view of him as 'the man in the cloth cap', a typical Scottish miner, was misleading. In fact, his style and dress were bohemian. Cartoonists depicted him as 'Queer Hardie'. He belonged in some ways to the *fin de siècle* ethos of the 1890s. His extensive travels gave him a cosmopolitan outlook and a following in Australia, Canada, and India hardly less devoted than in Britain. He identified Labour with Indian independence and the black majority in South Africa even at this early time. At home, he could be very much the Scot, a cheerful story-teller with a love of ballads and of highland dancing. With all his limitations, Hardie's ability to project his socialist gospel against the realities of British working-class society, and to convey it in direct human terms, was unique. Sylvia Pankhurst described him emotionally as 'the greatest human being of our time' (*Woman's Dreadnought*, 2 Oct 1915). It was a view that later generations of socialists were to echo.

KENNETH O. MORGAN

Sources W. Stewart, *J. Keir Hardie: a biography* (1921) · D. Lowe, *From pit to parliament: the story of the early life of Keir Hardie* (1923) · E. Hughes, *Keir Hardie* (1956) · K. O. Morgan, *Keir Hardie: radical and socialist* (1975) · I. McLean, *Keir Hardie* (1975) · F. Reid, *Keir Hardie: the making of a socialist* (1978) · C. Benn, *Keir Hardie* (1992) · H. Pelling, *The origins of the labour party, 1880–1900* (1954) · L. Thompson, *The enthusiasts: a biography of John and Katharine Bruce Glasier* (1971) · D. Marquand, *Ramsay MacDonald* (1977) · D. Howell, *British workers and the independent labour party, 1888–1906* (1983)

Archives Baird Institute History Centre and Museum, Cumnock, corresp. and papers · Labour History Archive and Study Centre, Manchester, corresp., diary, and papers · NL Scot., corresp. and papers, incl. Indian travel notes | BL, corresp. with John Burns, Add. MS 46287 · BL, letters to Sir Charles Dilke, Add. MS 43915 · BL, corresp. with Lord Gladstone, Add. MSS 46062–46068 · BL, letters to George Bernard Shaw, Add. MS 50538 · BLPES, letters to the Fabian Society · BLPES, independent labour party National Administrative Council MSS · Glamorgan RO, Cardiff, Rose Davies MSS · Internationaal Instituut voor Sociale Geschiedenis, Amsterdam, corresp. with Sylvia Pankhurst · NA Scot., corresp. with G. W. Balfour · Newham Archive and Local Studies Library, London, letters to George Saunders Jacobs · NL Scot., deposits · NL Scot., Emrys Hughes MSS · NRA, priv. coll., letters to niece Agnes · priv. coll., Hedley Dennis MSS · State Library of Victoria, Melbourne, corresp. with John Jones · U. Lpool L., Bruce and Katherine Glasier MSS | FILM BFI NFTVA, news footage

Likenesses H. J. Dobson, oils, 1892, Palace of Westminster, London · H. J. Dobson, oils, 1893, Scot. NPG · G. C. Beresford, photograph, 1905, NPG [*see illus.*] · C. Rowe, pencil drawing, 1905 (after photograph by G. C. Beresford), NPG · C. Rowe, postcard, *c.*1906, People's History Museum, Manchester · S. Pankhurst, drawings, *c.*1910, NPG · H. Furniss, pen-and-ink sketch, NPG · F. C. Gould, pen-and-ink, NPG · B. Schotz, bust, High Street, Cumnock, Ayrshire; replica, Palace of Westminster, London · Spy [L. Ward], cartoon, watercolour, NPG; repro. in *VF* (8 Feb 1906) · B. Stone, photographs, NPG · A. Weston, cabinet photograph, NPG · photographs, NPG

Wealth at death £426 10s. 11d.: confirmation, 1915, *CCI*

Hardie, Martin (1875–1952), art historian and art administrator, was born at 1 Clifton Villas, Pancras, London, on 15

Martin Hardie (1875–1952), by James McBey

December 1875, the son of James Hardie of East Linton, near Dunbar, and his wife, Marion Pettie. Two of his uncles, John *Pettie (1839–1893) and Charles Martin Hardie, were professional artists. Hardie was educated at Linton House, a preparatory school in London, where his father was headmaster; he later attended St Paul's School, London, and there won prizes for drawing. In 1895 he went as an exhibitioner to Trinity College, Cambridge, where he took his degree in the classical tripos in 1898. Having graduated, Hardie found work in the library of the Victoria and Albert Museum; he was to stay with the museum for thirty-seven years. On 11 June 1903 he married Agnes Madeline (*b.* 1876/7), the daughter of Rear-Admiral John Robert Ebenezer Pattisson; they had three sons. The Hardies' address from 1908 to 1920 was 7 Baldwyn Gardens, Acton, and from 1920 to 1936 they lived at 82 Ladbroke Road, London.

Hardie spent his spare time studying under Sir Frank Short, professor of etching at the Royal College of Art, which at that time shared premises with the museum. Short was also president of the Royal Society of Painter-Etchers and Engravers (RE), to which Hardie was elected in 1907. After war service, in which he reached the rank of captain, Hardie was appointed, in 1921, keeper of the combined departments of painting, and of engraving, illustration, and design, at the Victoria and Albert Museum; by the time he retired, in 1935, the museum's collections of prints and drawings were among the finest in the world. Hardie was particularly conscious of his responsibility towards contemporary artists, an obligation fostered by the museum's creative relationship with the Royal College of Art. 'His study and studio were one', Dudley Snelgrove commented, Hardie's desk and the table where he drew and etched being side by side (Snelgrove, 1.3). Hardie later claimed that in a time when important acquisitions could be made for little money many of his purchases for his own considerable collection were paid for with pennies saved from his lunch money. Perhaps Hardie's most exceptional achievement was his celebrated exhibition of 1926, which reinstated Samuel Palmer as a major artist; Palmer's work was to have an immediate influence on artists such as Graham Sutherland and Paul Drury.

Hardie's many publications include catalogues of the Victoria and Albert's prints in the National Art Library (1903) and of its modern wood-engravers (1919), as well as individual works: *English Coloured Books* (1906), on John Pettie (1908), *The British School of Etchers* (1921), and on Charles Meryon (1931); he also published catalogues of the work of Short, W. Lee-Hankey, and James McBey, as well as *A Sketch-Book of Thomas Girtin* (1939) for the Walpole Society. Hardie's greatest work, his *Water-colour Painting in Britain*, in three volumes, was written in his retirement and partly as a relief from the stresses of wartime. It was published between 1966 and 1968 and remains a classic text on the subject, combining his experiences both as practitioner and as scholar.

'A man of delightful modesty', Hardie was also highly regarded as an administrator (Snelgrove, 1.3). He served as honorary secretary both to the RE and to its associate body, the Print Collectors' Club; he was also vice-president of the Royal Institute of Painters in Water Colours and a member of the Royal Scottish Society of Painters in Water-colour: in 1943 he was made an honorary member of the Royal Watercolour Society. Hardie continued to be active as an artist in his own right; as well as exhibiting regularly at the Royal Academy from 1908 he held several one-man shows. The Victoria and Albert has thirteen of his water-colour drawings, signed Martin Hardie; the Ashmolean Museum, Oxford, possesses most of his 189 prints and some twenty-five sketchbooks. In 1918 he published *Boulogne: 32 Drawings by Captain Martin Hardie*. Although Hardie painted in western Europe and Morocco his best work was done in the watery landscapes of East Anglia. His subject matter and methods were, however, derivative.

> Like Short's landscapes, Hardie's are reticent and contemplative, and humans play only a subordinate part. They vary in quality and some of the emptiest views are the most attractive. Perhaps Hardie was so familiar with the work of other men that his own efforts were unconsciously hampered, reducing him to the commonplace. (Guichard, 42)

Hardie was appointed CBE on his retirement from the Victoria and Albert. During the Second World War he served as an air raid warden; after his retirement he was active in the local affairs of Tonbridge, Kent, where he then lived. He was also an officer of the Artists' General Benevolent Institution and a vice-president of the Imperial Arts League. Aberdeen Art Gallery possesses two etchings of Hardie by James McBey, and another of his wife, made between 1914 and 1919. Of the former, one shows Hardie in his etching studio; his small face has wide-set eyes, a moustache, and a receding hairline. Hardie died at his home, Rodbourne, Yardley Park Road, Tonbridge, on 20 January 1952. SIMON FENWICK

Sources DNB · K. M. Guichard, *British etchers, 1850–1940* (1977), 24 · M. Hardie, *Water-colour painting in Britain*, ed. D. Snelgrove, J. Mayne, and B. Taylor, 1: *The eighteenth century* (1966), 3–6 · Royal Society of Painter-Etchers and Engravers · A. Bury, 'Martin Hardie', *Old Water-Colour Society's Club*, 30 (1952–3), 20 · A. Griffiths, ed., *Landmarks in print collecting: connoisseurs and donors at the British Museum since 1753* (British Museum Press, 1996) [exhibition catalogue, Museum of Fine Arts, Houston, TX, 1996, and elsewhere] ·

The Times (22 Jan 1952) · b. cert. · m. cert. · d. cert. · *CGPLA Eng. & Wales* (1952) · RE catalogues, 1908–52
Archives U. Glas. L., letters to D. S. MacColl · V&A NAL, corresp. with John Henderson
Likenesses J. McBey, drypoint, 1915, NPG · J. McBey, etching, 1916–19, Aberdeen Art Gallery · M. Beerbohm, watercolour caricature, 1924, V&A · J. McBey, etching, Aberdeen Art Gallery; repro. in *Martin Hardie in his etching studio* (1916) · J. McBey, oils, Aberdeen Art Gallery [*see illus.*]
Wealth at death £29,319 0s. 10d.: probate, 4 March 1952, CGPLA Eng. & Wales

Hardie, Matthew (1754–1826), violin maker, was born in Jedburgh, Roxburghshire, on 23 November 1754, a son of the clockmaker Stephen Hardie. He was apprenticed to a joiner, and on 19 May 1778 became a member of the south fencibles, a volunteer regiment set up by Henry Scott, third duke of Buccleuch. He obtained a discharge in 1782 by presenting another man as substitute. On 12 February 1779 he married Juliet, daughter of Alexander Baillie, from Ross-shire, in the College Kirk, Edinburgh.

Although the Hill family of violin dealers thought that Hardie may have studied with the London violin maker John Betts, no proof is available. A more likely influence is thought to be his Edinburgh contemporary John Blair (*fl.* 1790–1822), whose work is charming and beautifully varnished. Between 1784 and 1788 Hardie occasionally repaired stringed instruments for the Edinburgh Musical Society. In 1790 he was trading as a maker in Edinburgh's Old Town, in the Lawnmarket; in 1794, as a 'Fiddle Maker' (*Williamson's Edinburgh Directory*, 1794–6, 23) in Carrubber's Close; in 1795–6, at Baxter's Close; and in 1799, 'opposite the Fountain Well north side' (Hill archive, fol. 131). He and Juliet had at least two children, William (*b.* 1796) and Charles (1801–1802). By 1801 Hardie was in financial difficulties, perhaps because the Edinburgh Musical Society had disbanded in 1798, although in 1797 a cello had been commissioned for Nathaniel Gow, a 'very good Stradivari copy' (private information (C. Beare)). The quality of his work earned him the title 'the Scottish Stradivari'.

The duchess of Buccleuch sponsored benefit concerts for Hardie. One advertisement read:

> Since the conclusion of the American War, when the South Fencibles were discharged in which corp Matthew Hardie had the honour of serving, he has applied himself to making violins, etc, but on account of his numerous family, has never been able to acquire a sufficient stock to carry on trade to advantage. (Glen, 1.xxii)

The concerts may have brought him an order from an army captain for a violin, completed in 1801, which featured in an exhibition of British makers in London in 1998; the catalogue states that his best work is 'very fine, and although firmly based on classical principles and often modelled on the long pattern of Stradivari, is full of idiosyncratic touches'.

Juliet died on 17 September 1801, and on 29 May 1802, at Canongate Kirk, Edinburgh, Hardie married Hannah McLaren, with whom he had three children, Thomas (1803–1858), who succeeded him in the business, Hannah (*b.* 1804), and Henrietta (*b.* 1806). His second wife must have died by 26 May 1806, when he married Jean McBain at

Canongate Kirk. They had a more settled life 'by the Fountain Well' (*Edinburgh and Leith Post Office Directory*, 1810–11, 110) until 1811. In 1812 he moved to Baillie Fyfe's Close, and in 1814 to Low Calton. He married for the fourth time in Edinburgh on 27 July 1817; his new wife was Marion Gilles. He was living at 10 Paul's Work in 1822; and at 15 Shakespear Square in 1824, by which time he was trading as Matthew Hardie & Son with Thomas, who had probably started working with his father when he was about ten years old. Hardie had another able assistant, David Stirrat, and also may have employed Alexander Youle and George Ferguson, among others.

Hardie and his son were both reputed to be alcoholics, but if so, Hardie's condition was not so severe as to inhibit his friendships with Edinburgh's best musicians, and some of his humorous and witty stories have been recorded by various authors. In 1826 he was imprisoned for debt and sent to St Cuthbert's poorhouse, where he died on 30 August 1826. He was buried in Greyfriars' kirkyard, Edinburgh, in an unmarked grave. Many of his instruments, mostly violins and cellos, remain in use in the twenty-first century; illustrations of them may be found in various books about British violin makers.

MARY ANNE ALBURGER

Sources M. A. Alburger, *Scottish fiddlers and their music*, repr. (1996) · M. A. Alburger, 'Scottish violin making: myth and reality', *The British violin: historical aspects of violin and bow making in the British Isles* (1999), 22–33 · M. A. Alburger, *The violin makers* (1978) · *Edinburgh and Leith Post Office directory*, 1810–11; 1813–14; 1814–15; 1816–17; 1824–5; 1825–6 · A. Myers, ed., *The Glen account book, 1838–1853* (1985) · J. Glen, *The Glen collection of Scottish dance music*, 2 vols. (1891–5) · W. Henley, *Universal dictionary of violin and bow makers*, 5 vols. (1959) · W. C. Honeyman, *Scottish violin makers: past and present*, 2nd edn (1910) · W. M. Morris, *British violin makers*, 2nd edn (1920) · A. G. Murdoch, *The fiddle in Scotland* (1888) · F. J. Grant, ed., *Register of marriages of the city of Edinburgh, 1751–1800* (1922) · *Williamson's Edinburgh directory*, 1790–92, 1794–6 · Edinburgh Musical Society minute books, 4 vols., 1728–98, Edinburgh Public Library, W/Y/ML/28/MS · U. Edin., Collection of Historic Musical Instruments, Glen MSS · AM Oxf., Hill Archive · bap. reg. Scot. · *IGI* · T. Baker and others, *The British violin*, ed. J. Milnes (2000) [exhibition catalogue, Royal Academy of Music, London, 31 March – 11 April 1988]
Likenesses W. Allan, oils, Scot. NPG
Wealth at death destitute; died in poorhouse: Honeyman, *Scottish violin makers*, 55

Hardie, William Francis Ross (1902–1990). *See under* Hardie, William Ross (1862–1916).

Hardie, William Ross (1862–1916), classical scholar, was born in Edinburgh on 6 January 1862, the elder son of William Purves Hardie, tailor, of Edinburgh, and his wife, Agnes Ross. He entered Edinburgh University at fourteen and learned high ideals of scholarship from William Young Sellar. Graduating MA he went in 1880 to Oxford as a scholar of Balliol. He was the most brilliant undergraduate classicist of his generation and won an unusual number of university distinctions, including in 1882 alone the Hertford and the Ireland scholarships, and both the Gaisford prizes. Elected to a fellowship at Balliol in 1884, he spent a year abroad, mostly in Greece and Italy, and returned to his college as tutor, remaining there until his appointment as professor of humanity at Edinburgh in

1895. He held the Edinburgh chair until his death. In 1901 he married Isabella Watt, third daughter of the Revd William Stevenson, of the Madras Christian College; they had three sons and one daughter.

At Balliol, Hardie established a new tradition in the teaching of classical scholarship. He had the whole field of classical literature at his command, and in lectures and private classes discussed general literary questions in a strikingly simple manner with a wealth of illustration: some specimens of his method were published later in his *Lectures on Classical Subjects* (1903). He was a most brilliant composer with an unrivalled memory and a remarkable sense of idiom: several of his most felicitous versions were included in *Anthologia Oxoniensis* (1899). The stimulus of his teaching was perhaps accentuated by his peculiarly shy manner.

The tradition of the chair of humanity at Edinburgh concentrated Hardie's work on Latin, though at Balliol he had been regarded as an even greater Greek scholar. On large classes of pass students his fine scholarship and conscientious methods were to some extent lost, but to the honour students who could appreciate these qualities he gave himself with a rare devotion, and with the help of his assistants he developed at Edinburgh a system of individual teaching on Oxford lines. He published two characteristic volumes, *Latin Prose Composition* (1908), the introduction to which expounds the art—for such it was to Hardie—in its more advanced form, and *Silvulae academicae* (1911), a collection of experiments in Latin and Greek verse, including the *Panegyricus* composed for the 500th anniversary of the University of St Andrews. *Res metrica* (1920), published after his death, is a penetrating analysis of some problems of Latin verse-rhythms, written with his usual sanity and caution.

That Hardie's literary production was not large was due to his complete absorption in his teaching: indeed, his devotion to the work of his professorship was the chief cause of his early death on 3 May 1916. His lasting memorial, apart from his few books, was the large number of his pupils who attained distinction in academic life, in the civil service, and in other professions. Naturally taciturn, he would often sit silent even among close friends—but amused and sympathetic. He had a fine eye for colour and was a naturally gifted painter in watercolours; he was also a keen and skilled fisherman and an enthusiastic golfer.

Hardie's eldest son, **William Francis Ross [Frank] Hardie** (1902–1990), classical scholar and philosopher, was born in Edinburgh on 25 April 1902 and educated at Edinburgh Academy and at Balliol College, Oxford, where he won all the major undergraduate prizes in both classics and philosophy, and gained firsts in classical moderations (1922) and *literae humaniores* (1924). He spent a year as a fellow by examination at Magdalen College, Oxford, before being appointed in 1926 to a tutorial fellowship at Corpus Christi College, Oxford. He remained there—except for war service in the Treasury from 1940 to 1945—until his retirement in 1969. In 1938 he married Isobel St Maur Macaulay, third of the six daughters of the Revd Professor Alexander Beith Macaulay, theologian; they had two sons.

He published two books, *A Study in Plato* (1936) and *Aristotle's Ethical Theory* (1968), and numerous articles in philosophical journals; he was also credited with inventing the term 'psephology', when asked by his friend Ronald Buchanan McCallum for a word to describe the study of elections. He served as president of Corpus Christi College from 1950 to 1969 (a period when the fellowship more than doubled in size, and a new residential building was built), and in 1962 chaired the committee which investigated Oxford's admissions system, whose recommendations were subsequently implemented. He remained in close touch with his college in retirement, and died in Oxford on 30 September 1990. He was survived by his wife and one son; the other son predeceased him.

Hardie's youngest son, **Colin Graham Hardie** (1906–1998), classical scholar, was born in Edinburgh on 16 February 1906 and educated at Edinburgh Academy and Balliol College, Oxford, where (like his brother) he won all the major undergraduate prizes in classics, and gained firsts in classical moderations (1926) and *literae humaniores* (1928). He was a junior research fellow (1928–9), then fellow and classical tutor (1930–33) at Balliol, before spending three years as director of the British School at Rome. In 1936 he was appointed fellow and tutor in classics at Magdalen College, Oxford, where he remained—except for war service in the War Office (1941–3) and the admiralty (1943–5)—until his retirement in 1973. In 1940 he married Christian Viola Mary Lucas (*b.* 1910), daughter of Percival Lucas; she had graduated with a first in *literae humaniores* from St Hugh's in 1932. They had two sons. A member of the Inklings, and a friend of C. S. Lewis and J. R. R. Tolkien, he converted to Roman Catholicism in 1945. His scholarly work was devoted largely to Virgil and Dante, and for the 700th anniversary of Dante's birth he gave the Waynflete lectures on him. He was public orator in Oxford from 1967 to 1973, and was renowned for his Latin style. In retirement he lived at Rackham Cottage, Greatham, near Pulborough, Sussex, where he indulged his love of gardening. He died in Chichester on 17 October 1998, and was survived by his wife and two sons.

CYRIL BAILEY, rev. MARK POTTLE

Sources I. Elliott, ed., *The Balliol College register, 1833–1933*, 2nd edn (privately printed, Oxford, 1934) · *Edinburgh University Magazine* (1916) · personal knowledge (1927) · *Oxford Magazine* (19 May 1916), 314 · *CCI* (1916) · *WWW* · *Daily Telegraph* (3 Oct 1990) · *The Independent* (3 Oct 1990) · *The Times* (5 Oct 1990) · *The Times* (10 Oct 1990) · *The Times* (20 Oct 1998) · *The Independent* (5 Nov 1998) · *The Scotsman* (11 Nov 1998) · d. cert. [William Francis Ross Hardie] · *WW* (1993) · E. Lemon, ed., *The Balliol College register, 1916–1967*, 4th edn (privately printed, Oxford, 1969) · private information (2004) [Librarian and Archivist, St Hugh's College, Oxford]
Archives Balliol Oxf., markbooks and academic papers · U. Edin. L., special collections division, lecture notes; papers | Bodl. Oxf., letters to Gilbert Murray
Wealth at death £162 7s. 8d.: confirmation, 22 June 1916, *CCI*

Hardiman, Alfred Frank (1891–1949), sculptor, was born at 17 Orde Hall Street, Holborn, London, on 21 May 1891, the son of Alfred William Hardiman, master silversmith of Holborn, London, and his wife, Ada Myhill. On leaving school Hardiman trained as a draughtsman and entered the Central School of Arts and Crafts. In 1912 he won a London county council scholarship to the Royal College of Art. Fellow students included Charles Wheeler, Gilbert Ledward, and William McMillan, all of whom, with Hardiman, contributed to the sculptural transformation of London in the inter-war period. In 1915 Hardiman received his diploma and showed his first works at the Royal Academy summer exhibition: a bust, *My Lord of S*, and a plaque, *Madeline*. With a special talent scholarship and a British Institute scholarship he entered the Royal Academy Schools in July 1915. He enlisted in the Royal Flying Corps later that year, and served as an engineer's draughtsman when the school was closed to male students from 1916 until the armistice. Hardiman resumed his studies after the war, winning the Landseer scholarship and, in December 1920, the Rome prize with his group *Sacrifice*.

On 21 December 1918 Hardiman married Violet (1897–1977), daughter of Herbert Clifton White of London. During the years they spent in Rome Hardiman developed his style, a blend of naturalism and stylized classicism greatly influenced by Roman and Etruscan art and early fifth-century Greek sculpture. Ancient forms imbued with a strong decorative sense reflected an archaic modernism widespread in sculpture of the 1920s in the work of artists such as Paul Manship, Adolfo Wildt, and Carl Milles. Clarity of design, formal simplification, and precise craftsmanship pervaded Hardiman's career.

On his return to London in 1924 Hardiman's works such as *The Boxer* (bronze; exh. RA, 1924) and *Portrait of an Athlete* (bronze; exh. RA, 1926) displayed these influences. Fine portraits include *Cecil Rhodes*, commissioned by Sir Herbert Baker for Rhodes House, Oxford (bronze; exh. RA, 1930; *in situ*), but monumental and architectural sculpture were to dominate Hardiman's career. His stone carvings for the eastern half of County Hall, London (*c.*1925) completed the sculptural decorations begun by Ernest Cole. Hardiman's elegant classicized bronze niche figure of St George (1930) for Stephen Courtauld, originally sited in Carlos Place, London, was moved in 1936 to the Courtaulds' new residence, Eltham Palace, where it remains. Among the sculpture executed for Norwich city hall, the lions epitomize Hardiman's style (bronze, exh. RA, 1937); similar figures flanked the entrance to the British pavilion at the 1939 world fair. His other works include heraldic figures (models exh. RA, 1941) for St John's College, Cambridge (architect Edward Maufe), and the Viscount Southwood memorial, St James's Church, Piccadilly, for the architect Professor A. E. Richardson (fountain model exh. RA, 1947; two figures exh. RA, 1948; two groups exh. RA, 1949).

However, it is for the controversial equestrian statue of Earl Haig in Whitehall that Hardiman is chiefly known. A first model was commissioned in 1929 by a committee with a £10,000 grant of parliamentary funds at its disposal. Immediately criticized by Lady Haig for the absence of accurate portraiture, Hardiman's generalized artistic treatment underwent modification. A second model, revealed in the press in 1931, precipitated furious reaction to the stylized portrait of Haig and the stance and configuration of the horse. Military and civilian equestrians became art critics; equine anatomy, artistic stylization versus accurate portraiture, and the affront to protocol of the hatless earl were hotly debated in lengthy exchanges in the press. The monument's admirers praised it as a modern work in the tradition of equestrian sculpture, whose vitality was artistic, not that of flesh and blood. When the statue was finally unveiled in 1937 Hardiman's enforced compromises were evident, the newly detailed portrait resting somewhat uneasily on the simplified bodies of rider and mount. Lady Haig refused to attend the ceremony protesting that her husband would never have ridden such a horse. Hardiman's friend Charles Wheeler noted, 'through the storm Hardiman stood firm and silent; he allowed his work to speak for itself … its nobility of design … has sculpturesque qualities which are missing in many other equestrian statues in London' (*DNB*). But papers in the archives of the British School at Rome reveal that the public furore had detrimental effects on Hardiman's finances, legal affairs, and health.

Elected associate of the Royal Society of British Sculptors in 1918 and a fellow in 1938, Hardiman was awarded the society's silver medal in 1939 for the Haig memorial, and a gold medal for his bronze fountain figure (exh. RA, 1947; statue never erected) for the New Council House, Bristol (1946; architect E. Vincent Harris RA). He was elected an associate of the Royal Academy in 1936, and Royal Academician in 1944. He often lunched with friends at the sculptors' table of the Chelsea Arts Club. When the house and one of the studios at 37 Greville Road received a direct hit in 1941, Hardiman moved his family to Farthing Green, Church Lane, Stoke Poges, Buckinghamshire. He re-opened the remaining London studio after the war. He was an expert fisherman and a fine gardener. Alfred Hardiman died of cancer at his home on 17 April 1949, aged fifty-seven, and was cremated at Golders Green crematorium on 21 April 1949. His ashes lie in the garden of remembrance at Stoke Poges.   SARAH CRELLIN

Sources *DNB* · Tate collection, press cuttings collection · S. Casson, 'The statue of Marshal Haig', *Art in England*, ed. R. S. Lambert (1938) · Graves, *RA exhibitors* · corresp., archives of British School at Rome · b. cert. · private information (2004)
Archives British School at Rome, corresp. · Henry Moore Institute, Leeds | Tate collection, press cuttings collection
Likenesses W. Stoneman, photograph, 1946, NPG
Wealth at death £7707 4s. 7d.: probate, 27 Jan 1950, *CGPLA Eng. & Wales*

Hardiman, James (1782–1855), historian and lawyer, was born in Westport, co. Mayo, in February 1782. He came of a family known in Irish as O'Hartigan. His father, who owned a small estate in Mayo, hoped that his son would become a priest. Hardiman was drawn to the priesthood, but changed his mind. He went to Dublin, where he studied law and about 1814 he became a solicitor. He successfully revived the dormant peerage claim of Lord Netterville.

In 1811 Hardiman was appointed a sub-commissioner by the public records commission, where he worked on calendaring legal documents. In 1825 he wrote a report on the grants and conveyances passed under the Irish Act of Settlement, and the sales under the forfeitures of 1688. When the commission ceased work in 1830, Hardiman became solicitor to the Galway town commissioners. In 1848 he was appointed librarian and legal adviser by the new Queen's College, Galway.

Hardiman became an active member of the Royal Irish Academy and of the Iberno-Celtic Society. In 1820 he published *A History of the County and the Town of Galway*, one of the few good Irish county histories then in print. Irish was his mother tongue, and in 1831 he published *Irish Minstrelsy, or, Bardic Remains of Ireland, with English Poetical Translations*. The collection was an interesting one, but its value was diminished by the lack of attributions. The majority of the songs were probably taken from manuscript collections.

Hardiman died in Galway on 13 November 1855. He donated a thousand books from his library to the Galway Royal Institute and was a major benefactor of the Franciscan monastery of Errew, co. Mayo.

         MARIE-LOUISE LEGG

Sources 'Memoir of James Hardiman', *Journal of the Galway Archaeological and Historical Society*, 6 (1909–10), 180–81 · 'Librarians at UGC: James Hardiman, 1782–1855', *James Hardiman Library Newsletter*, 1 (1995)
Archives Royal Irish Acad. | NL Ire., Synott MSS
Likenesses oils, repro. in 'Librarians at UGC'

Hardimé, Simon (1664/1672–1737), painter, was born at Antwerp, of Walloon parentage. In 1685 he became a pupil of Jan Baptist Crepu, the flower painter, and, after remaining with him for four years, was admitted a master of the Guild of St Luke in 1689. He painted from nature both flowers and fruit, which were excellent in colour, but he was far surpassed by his younger brother and pupil, Pieter Hardimé. He received commissions from the earl of Scarbrough, from several wealthy merchants of Antwerp and Brussels, and in particular from two brothers who were canons of St Jacques at Antwerp. He was described by his contemporary Campo Weyerman as having been a droll little fellow, who spent the greater part of his time at the church or the tavern, and at length became so embarrassed that he had to leave Antwerp and go to his brother at The Hague, where he was not particularly welcome. While there, however, he did decorate rooms in a number of town houses. He then moved to London in 1700, where he died in 1737. He painted a flower piece for the palace at Breda, reconstructed by William III of England, and now a military school. There are two works by him in the museum at Bordeaux. His brother, Pieter Hardimé, was born at Antwerp in 1677, and died at The Hague in 1758.

      R. E. GRAVES, *rev.* SARAH HERRING

Sources P. Mitchell, *European flower painters* (1973), 126–7 · J. C. Weyerman, *De levens-beschryvingen der Nederlandsche konst-schilders en konst-schilderessen*, 4 vols. (The Hague, 1729–69), vol. 3, pp. 245–8 · C. Kramm, *De levens en werken der Hollandsche en vlaamsche kunstschilders, beeldhouwers, graveurs en bouwmeesters*, 3 (1859), 642–3 · J. van Gool, *De nieuwe schouburg der Nederlantsche kunstschilders en schilderessen*, 2 vols. (The Hague, 1750–51), vol. 1, pp. 418–20 · J. van den Branden, *Geschiedenis der Antwerpsche, Antwerp schilderschool*

(1883), 1149 · P. Rombouts and T. Van Lerius, *De liggeren en andere historische archieven der Antwerpsche Sint Lucasgilde*, 2 (The Hague, 1876); repr. (Amsterdam, 1961), 532 · A. von Wursbach, *Nederländisches Künstler-Lexikon*, 1 (1906), 648 · Bénézit, *Dict.*, 4th edn · C. Immerzeel, *De levens en werken der hollandsche en vlaamsche kunstschilders, beeldhouwers, graveurs en bouwmeesters ... Amsterdam* (1842–3), 16 · Thieme & Becker, *Allgemeines Lexikon*, 16.28 · A. Bredius, 'Nederlandsche kunst in Provinciale Musea von Frankrijk', *Oud Holland*, 22 (1904), 109 · M. Pilkington, *A general dictionary of painters: containing memoirs of the lives and works*, 1 (1829), 1.445

Harding [*née* Orchard], **Anne Raikes** (1781–1858), writer, was born on 5 March 1781 at Bath. She married Thomas Harding, a merchant of Bristol, who died young and intestate in 1805 and left her with three children (one of them a disabled daughter) to bring up on a few hundred pounds. Her son, Thomas Harding, became a solicitor at Birmingham, and her other daughter married the Revd William Kynaston Groves. She kept a school and worked as a governess for thirty-five years, meanwhile writing a series of novels under direct and imposing titles: *Correction* (1818), *Decision* (1819), *The Refugees* (1822), *Perseverance* (1824), *Realities, not a Novel* (1825), *Dissipation* (1827), and *Experience* (1828). All these have strong moral overtones and quote Hannah More extensively, though they are not without humour. They take for their subject matter female conduct in high and low life, in a wide variety of settings from India to Scotland. In the preface to *Realities*, Harding claims to point out 'the necessity of subduing our own passions and feelings, and of placing a firm reliance on Divine Providence, however adverse its dispensations may appear' (p. vii). She also claims that the 'incidents are all gleaned from memoranda, made during a life whose "varied hues" has offered abundant opportunity for observation, and are all strict to the letter' (ibid.). This combination of naturalism with moralism was popular with reviewers, the *European Magazine* commenting on *Correction*, for example, 'We heartily recommend this novel to the perusal of mothers' (July 1818, 55). Harding's later work, apart from *Sketches of the Highlands* (1832), became still more openly didactic or instructional (*Little Sermons*, 1840; *An Epitome of Universal History*, 1848). She was also credited with 'a number of other instructive and popular volumes; besides which Mrs. Harding was a large contributor to the reviews and different periodicals of the day' (*Morning Chronicle*, 3 May 1858).

According to her desperate application to the Royal Literary Fund, dated 18 November 1851, Harding had been retired for two years when her banker decamped after losing her hard-won savings in ruinous speculation, and she was left to manage 'a superior style of Boarding House' (at 28 Cumberland Street near Hyde Park) with great difficulty and little profit. Her son-in-law and others (including her publisher and her brother) added their support and she received £30. On 16 June 1853 she appealed again from a boarding-house in Boulogne, having retired there (possibly to avoid creditors), and received £20. A small annual subscription was made by friends. Even with assistance from her married daughter and her husband, her income was something below £50 per year; she appealed again to the Royal Literary Fund on 2 October 1855, and for a final

time on 17 November 1857, each time receiving £10. She died on 28 April 1858 at her son-in-law's house, possibly in Boulogne.   PAUL BAINES

Sources Blain, Clements & Grundy, *Feminist comp.* · BL, Royal Literary Fund file 1281, microfilm M1077 (47) · *Morning Chronicle* (3 May 1858)
Archives BL, letters and applications for relief and letters in support, Royal Literary Fund file 1281, microfilm M1077 (47)
Wealth at death received aid from Royal Literary Fund, 1851–8

Harding, Edward (1755–1840). *See under* Harding, Silvester (1745×51–1809).

Harding, Edward Archibald Fraser (1903–1953), radio producer, was born on 1 October 1903 at Palmyra, Lermot Road, Southsea, Hampshire, the elder son of Colonel Edward West Harding, of the Royal Marine Artillery, and his wife, Maria Maud Ryves. Educated at Cheltenham College (1915–22) and Keble College, Oxford (1923–6), Harding became an Oxford intellectual Marxist. His upbringing, D. G. Bridson later noted, 'was impeccably Upper Class. It was just this background which Oxford and intellectual restiveness had taught him first to challenge, then finally reject' (Bridson, 29).

A year after he entered the newly established British Broadcasting Corporation (BBC) as announcer for London Station in June 1927, Harding became a member of a special research section within the drama department, a privileged group whose sole task was to experiment with new programmes and which laid the foundation of what was ultimately to become the features department. Along with his colleagues Lance Sieveking, Mary Hope Allen and E. J. King-Bull, Harding explored the largely uncharted seas of studio-production technique. By weaving together sound, words, and music to make an aural picture, they evolved the 'feature'. It was in this spirit of adventure that Harding produced a broad range of programmes, including a memorable feature on the sixteenth-century French poet François Villon, written in collaboration with Ezra Pound, and the first British example of radio reportage, *Crisis in Spain*, broadcast in June 1931, recapturing the recent events of the Spanish revolution. In 1932 Harding produced the first Christmas day programme linking speakers from various Commonwealth countries and ending with a message from King George V. The programme was an instant success and he was immediately asked to compile a similar programme linking the countries of Europe.

New Year over Europe on the last day of 1932 was Harding's final fling in London. The new year's feature was usually a bland medley of events from the year that was passing, but Harding's more overtly political programme, which introduced the Poles with a line about how much they spent on armaments, led to a diplomatic storm in a teacup. The Polish ambassador in London protested to the Foreign Office and the BBC; there were questions in the House of Commons and letters to *The Times*. Harding was summoned before the BBC's director-general, John Reith, and banished to Manchester. He was always very proud of the fact that Reith had said to him: 'You're a very dangerous man, Harding. I think you'd be better up North where you can't do so much damage' (Bridson, 22).

Harding treated what might have been regarded as exile to the north as an opportunity to challenge London and over the course of three years as programme director, north region, he completely invigorated broadcasting. He set about collecting around him a group of talented young producers and writers who, like him, were committed to giving voice to ordinary people. Within a few months the offices in Piccadilly, Manchester, became the spearhead of new advances in technique, in programme ideas, and in microphone performance.

No one was safe from Harding's all-conquering, all-embracing enthusiasm and he effected a revolution in broadcasting by acting as a flame to set all kinds of people alight. He raided the *Manchester Guardian*—from which he captured four journalists, Kenneth Adam, Donald Boyd, Robert Kemp, and E. R. Thompson. He persuaded Edgar Lustgarten to leave the bar, he recruited Geoffrey Bridson, a budding poet and civil servant who was to go on to have a very distinguished career at the BBC, and he encouraged Francis (Jack) Dillon, then working as a tax collector, to turn to writing and production. He also nurtured the acting talents of Wilfred Pickles, Ewan MacColl, and Joan Littlewood (whom he spotted at the Royal Academy of Dramatic Art). Bridson later wrote: 'His whole attitude to the medium was stimulating and somehow exciting. To him, the microphone had been an invention no less revolutionary than the printing-press' (Bridson, 30).

In 1936 Harding returned to London to join the BBC's newly formed staff training department (known as St Beadle's, after Gerald Beadle, director of staff training, 1936–7), first as chief instructor and then as director. On 2 May 1940 he married Joan Clara Monkhouse (*b.* 1903/4), daughter of the Manchester political journalist George Leach. They had no children and lived at Byron Cottage, Highgate village, Middlesex. In 1948 Harding moved to the drama department as deputy to its director, Val Gielgud, where his most notable productions included Hardy's *The Dynasts* and Goethe's *Faust* in Louis MacNeice's translation. Indeed, Harding had recruited MacNeice to the BBC and was immortalized as Harrap in MacNeice's autobiographical poem *Autumn Sequel*.

Archie Harding, as he was known, remained throughout his life committed to radio as an art form that tested the boundaries and to the belief that broadcasting should offer listeners 'the best that the medium could provide'. He was perhaps the leading figure in the early evolution of the feature programme and the motivating force behind the long battle to get the voices of 'ordinary people' heard on BBC radio. He died on 25 January 1953 at his home in Highgate after succumbing to cancer of the pancreas.

JEANETTE THOMAS

Sources D. G. Bridson, *Prospero and Ariel: the rise and fall of radio* (1971) · P. Scannell and D. Cardiff, *A social history of British broadcasting*, [1] (1991) · I. Rodger, *Radio drama* (1982) · V. Gielgud, *Years in a mirror* (1965) · E. MacColl, *Journeyman: an autobiography* (1990) · A. Briggs, *The history of broadcasting in the United Kingdom*, 1–2 (1961–

5) · staff files, programme files, and press cuttings, BBC WAC · private information (2004) · b. cert. · m. cert. · d. cert. · O. Shapley, *Broadcasting a life: the autobiography of Olive Shapley* (1996) · J. Stallworthy, *Louis MacNeice* (1995) · *CGPLA Eng. & Wales* (1953)
Archives BBC WAC | SOUND BBC WAC
Likenesses photographs, BBC WAC
Wealth at death £17,681 3*s.* 7*d.*: probate, 5 June 1953, *CGPLA Eng. & Wales*

Harding, Sir Edward John (1880–1954), civil servant, was born on 22 March 1880 in St Osyth, Clacton-on-Sea, Essex, the only son of Revd John Harding (1841–1926) and his wife, Laura Catherine Hewlett. He had two sisters: Eleanor Laura (Nellie), who married Harry Batterbee, a friend from his university days and future civil service colleague, and Evelyn (Eva), who remained unmarried and to whom he seems to have been particularly close. He himself remained single until 15 January 1929, when at the age of forty-eight he married Marjorie (1891/2–1950), daughter of Henry Huxley, physician. There were no children.

Harding was educated at a preparatory school in Beckenham, then at Dulwich College (1893–9, with a short break in 1894–5 at Osborne House School, Margate), and finally as a scholar at Hertford College, Oxford (1899–1903). After winning a first in classical moderations in 1901 and a second in *literae humaniores* in his finals in 1903, he took his MA in 1907. He was called to the bar at Lincoln's Inn in 1912. He later became a governor of Dulwich College, and in February 1940 he was elected as an honorary fellow of Hertford College, to which on his death he left a considerable bequest.

Not only was Harding's father an Anglican clergyman, but on his paternal side so were three uncles, two great-uncles, and his grandfather. However, his great-grandfather William Harding (1766–1851) had a notable career at the Admiralty, and Edward entered the civil service by competitive examination in November 1903, when he was placed twelfth. He elected for a post as second-class clerk in the marine department at the Board of Trade, but transferred on 31 May 1904 to the Colonial Office, where he worked initially in the crown colonies division. Formal promotion was not rapid, but his abilities were noted and on 14 October 1912 Harding was appointed as assistant private secretary to Lewis Harcourt, secretary of state for the colonies. His next role as secretary of the dominions royal commission secured recognition of his abilities and defined his area of expertise. The commission was appointed following a recommendation of the Imperial Conference of 1911 that representatives of the United Kingdom, Canada, Australia, New Zealand, South Africa, and Newfoundland should report on ways of developing the natural resources and trade of the white settler societies of the British empire. Harding was not its first secretary, but it was he who in December 1912 took over the job, and with it the responsibility for arranging and accompanying the overseas tours of the commission in 1913, 1914, and 1916 and for drafting reports. In their final report (1917) the commissioners paid more than formal compliments to their secretary. He was promoted to first-class clerk on 4 June 1916, and was made CMG in 1917.

Although Harding had enlisted in the Royal Garrison

Artillery (second lieutenant, 1915; lieutenant, 1918), his abilities were put to better use during the war as junior assistant secretary at the imperial war conferences in 1917 and 1918. His personal knowledge of the dominions and of their political and business leaders ensured that after the war his expertise would be employed within the dominions division of the Colonial Office. His professional advance was thereafter rapid. He was reclassified as a principal on 1 April 1920 and promoted as one of the Colonial Office's ten assistant secretaries in 1921, in which capacity he helped to service the Imperial Conference in 1923 as deputy secretary. When the dominions division became the Dominions Office and a separate government department in 1925, Harding was a natural choice as the office's sole assistant under-secretary. The dominions commissioners in 1917 favoured centralizing the empire for the purposes of economic development and security. However, the post-war trend was towards self-government, which the British government sought to reconcile with the continued unity of the white Commonwealth through conceding dominion status. Given the sensitivity and suspicions of political leaders from the Irish Free State, South Africa, and Canada, striking the balance was tricky, but until the 1950s it was largely achieved.

Harding endorsed and increasingly guided these adjustments. Certain as to aims and flexible as to methods, he tried over two difficult decades to maintain the co-operation of the dominions with the United Kingdom. His advisory role was much appreciated by L. S. Amery, secretary of state for the dominions, at the Imperial Conference in 1926 which led to the famous Balfour declaration on dominion status. His expertise brought its rewards, a CB in 1926, a KCMG in 1928, as well as appointment on 24 January 1930 as permanent under-secretary at the Dominions Office. He was heavily involved in the passage of the Statute of Westminster in 1931 and in managing the imperial conferences in 1930, 1932, and 1937. He thus helped secure the united reaction of most of the Commonwealth when war eventually broke out in Europe and the Far East. He was promoted to KCB in 1935 and to GCMG in 1939.

Harding had one more political role to play. In September 1939 he was appointed high commissioner to the protectorates of Bechuanaland, Basutoland, and Swaziland and also to the Union of South Africa, taking up his post in January 1940. The immediate task was to secure the assistance in the war effort of the protectorates and, in a largely diplomatic role, of South Africa, in the face of some Afrikaner opposition to the allied cause. Harding helped by establishing adequate, though not warm, relations with the prime minister, J. C. Smuts, and his colleagues. Sadly, he had a heart attack late in 1940 and retired on grounds of ill health in February 1941. However, he had recovered sufficiently by 1942 to represent in Cape Town the new high commissioner (based in Pretoria) until his final retirement in 1944.

Harding's education accounts for the allusions to classical literature in his private letters and perhaps for his scrupulous concern for accuracy and clarity in official correspondence. A former junior colleague at the Dominions Office described him as a man of 'the utmost integrity' but 'a perfectionist … congenitally incapable of accepting a draft without making some amendment' (Garner, 20–21). To the same observer he appeared 'cold, even distant', with steel grey eyes, no sense of humour, no warmth, no social graces, not good at public speaking (ibid., 182). But the amused tone of his private letters leaves a different impression, and another colleague recorded a generous side to his character and 'many acts of personal kindness' (*DNB*). He also retained an interest in music and the arts and served, for example, on the council of the Royal College of Music.

Since their marriage in 1929, Marjorie had been Harding's close companion, and her death in 1950 was a terrible blow which accelerated his own decline. He died at the Royal Surrey County Hospital, Guildford, on 4 October 1954 and was cremated at Woking three days later.

STEPHEN CONSTANTINE

Sources *The Times* (5 Oct 1954) • S. Constantine, *Dominions diary: the letters of E. J. Harding, 1913–1916* (1992) • J. Garner, *The commonwealth office, 1925–1968* (1978) • *DNB* • L. S. Amery, *My political life*, 2: *War and peace* (1954) • *Colonial Office List* (1940) • b. cert. • m. cert. • d. cert. • *CGPLA Eng. & Wales* (1954) • private information (2004) • *WWW* • *The Times* (8 Oct 1954)

Archives CUL, diary letters while secretary of the dominions royal commission | BLPES, corresp. with W. H. Clark • Bodl. RH, corresp. with Sir Harry Batterbee • PRO, Colonial Office and Dominions Office papers

Likenesses group portrait, photograph (with members of the Dominions Royal Commission), repro. in *South Africa* (14 Feb 1914) • photograph (as high commissioner to Basutoland, Bechuanaland, and Swaziland), repro. in *The Times* (24 Jan 1940) • photograph (as high commissioner to Basutoland, Bechuanaland, and Swaziland), repro. in *The Times* (4 March 1940)

Wealth at death £26,639 2s. 3d.: probate, 10 Nov 1954, *CGPLA Eng. & Wales*

Harding, George Perfect (1779/80–1853), miniature painter, was born in Town Malling, Kent, the son of the miniature painter Silvester *Harding (1745x51–1809) and his wife, Sarah, daughter of William Perfect MD, also of Malling. The family came from Staffordshire where his father was born at Newcastle under Lyme and his uncle the engraver Edward Harding (1755–1840) was baptized on 1 April 1755 at St Mary's, Stafford. Harding's brother Edward, who engraved some plates for his father, died of putrid fever on 11 September 1791, aged twenty. Probably taught by his father, Harding began work as a miniature painter, exhibiting in 1802 at the Royal Academy from his parents' home, 127 Pall Mall, London. In 1804 he painted a miniature self-portrait (National Portrait Gallery, London), for which he wore the uniform of the Royal York Marylebone volunteers. He exhibited eighteen portraits at the Royal Academy up to 1840, one in 1812 of a Mrs G. P. Harding (presumably his first wife, Mary Ann). He sent to the academy two other pictures: in 1823 *The Dean of Westminster Holding the Crown at the Coronation of His Majesty King George IV*, and in 1839 *The Library at Strawberry Hill, Seat of the Earl of Waldegrave*. He also exhibited twice at the Society of British Artists.

Harding devoted himself to producing minute copies in watercolour of works of historical and antiquarian interest. In 1822–3 he published eighteen portraits of the deans of Westminster, engraved by J. Stow, R. Grave, and others, intended to illustrate E. W. Brayley's *The History and Antiquities of the Abbey Church of St Peter, Westminster* (2 vols., 1818–23), illustrated by J. P. Neale, followed by his own *Antiquities in Westminster Abbey: ancient oil paintings and sepulchral brasses, engraved from drawings by G. P. Harding, with an historical, biographical and heraldic description, by T. Moule* (1825). He produced in 1828 an elaborately illustrated manuscript account, 'The princes of Wales'; with this he issued a privately printed description. These are now in the Royal Library at Windsor. Among many other historical works to which he supplied plates was J. H. Jesse's *Memoirs of the Court of England during the Reign of the Stuarts, Including the Protectorate* (1840).

Harding moved from 38 Strand about 1822 to Hercules Buildings, Lambeth, London. He married on 25 January 1834 his second wife, Charlotte Brown (*b. c.*1800, at Mildenhall, Suffolk) at St James's, Westminster. They had two daughters, Georgina (*b. c.*1837) and Catherine (*b. c.*1839). (Harding's eldest daughter from his first marriage, Eleanor Jane, was baptized on 23 November 1815 at St Martin-in-the-Fields, London.)

In 1839 Harding was elected a fellow of the Society of Antiquaries, but withdrew in 1847. In 1840 he took a leading part in establishing the Granger Society, whose object was to publish previously unengraved historical portraits. Through mismanagement the society ended in 1843. Harding continued publication by subscription for five years, and during this period he issued a series of fifteen plates, engraved by Joseph Brown and W. Greatbach with biographical notices by Thomas Moule. With his means much reduced, his chief resource was the disposal of his accumulated works, which were sold by auction. Harding died on 23 December 1853 at his home in St Mary Newington, Surrey, aged seventy-three. Examples of his work are in the National Portrait Gallery and the British Museum, London; the Scottish National Portrait Gallery, Edinburgh; the National Museum and Gallery of Wales, Cardiff; Newport Art Gallery; and Bath City Art Gallery.

F. M. O'DONOGHUE, rev. MERVYN CUTTEN

Sources D. Foskett, *A dictionary of British miniature painters*, 2 vols. (1972) · B. S. Long, *British miniaturists* (1929) · Graves, *Artists* · Redgrave, *Artists* · B. Stewart and M. Cutten, *The dictionary of portrait painters in Britain up to 1920* (1997) · R. Walker, *National Portrait Gallery: Regency portraits*, 2 vols. (1985) · d. cert. · IGI · Graves, *RA exhibitors* · census returns, 1851

Archives Warks. CRO, letters to David Pennant

Likenesses G. P. Harding, self-portrait, miniature, watercolour, 1804, NPG · J. Brown, stipple (after G. P. Harding), BM · G. P. Harding, self-portrait, miniature, BM

Harding, Gilbert Charles (1907–1960), radio and television broadcaster, was born at Hereford on 5 June 1907. His parents, Gilbert Harding and May King, were workhouse officials, and he used to boast that he was born in a workhouse. He was educated at the Royal Orphanage, Wolverhampton, and Queens' College, Cambridge, where he obtained third classes in both parts of the historical tripos

Gilbert Charles Harding (1907–1960), by Cornel Lucas, 1960

(1927–8). A man of very deep religious feeling, he became a strong Anglo-Catholic at Cambridge and went to Mirfield to train for the Anglican priesthood with the Community of the Resurrection. He left when in 1929 he became a convert to, and a devoted member of, the Roman Catholic church, but he remained sympathetic to Anglicanism from the emotional point of view and never spoke of Mirfield with anything but the warmest affection and admiration. After some years as a schoolmaster, and as a professor of English at St Francis Xavier University, Antigonish, in Nova Scotia, he joined the Bradford city police. An accident forced his retirement and he returned to teaching in Cyprus, where he also acted as correspondent for *The Times*. He took a very strong dislike to British rule in Cyprus and was regarded with a great deal of hostility by the administration. He returned to London and read for the bar at Gray's Inn, but when war broke out in 1939 he joined the BBC monitoring service. His health prevented him from serving actively in a war to which he was very much dedicated because of his detestation of Fascism. After two years in the outside broadcasting department he was sent in 1944 to Canada where he carried out extremely useful propaganda work. Back once more in London in 1947 he got his first personal show in broadcasting as quizmaster in *Round Britain Quiz*.

From that point on, in radio programmes such as *The Brains Trust* and *Twenty Questions*, and on television in *What's my Line?*, Harding became a great popular figure, especially of television in which he was probably the best-known performer in the country. He was a man under great emotional pressure, something of which was revealed in his *Face to Face* interview with John Freeman on

BBC television in September 1960. He disliked 'the Establishment' and continually involved himself in rows with authority. He was often the victim of alleged martyrs, many of whom were bogus. The apparent rudeness which brought him much notoriety was not an act, as was widely believed; he never suffered fools gladly, and he 'loved justice and hated iniquity' in no uncertain terms (*The Guardian*, 18 Nov 1960). 'I just behave as I am and talk as I think, which for some reason appears to be remarkably novel', was his comment (private information, 1971). It was for this refreshing novelty and his genuine humanity that the public loved him; yet he thought it quite absurd that he should be so highly paid for being himself and, being fully aware of his difficulties of character and temperament, wanted desperately to be somebody different and better. His public performances often concealed the fact that he was in many ways a learned man. He had a wonderful memory for English poetry, which he loved. He was frustrated, among other things, by what he felt to be the waste of his talents, and looked upon himself as a don manqué. In this he was almost certainly deceived but quite sincere. Despite the frustrations, he was candidly enough capable of enjoying, somewhat to excess, the luxuries that his large income made possible. He had known very hard times and did not pretend not to enjoy the easier times. He was lavishly generous of time and money, and the people who knew him best liked him most. His political views were always very much to the left, and he continued in his prosperity to believe in the Labour Party and in the need for more equal distribution of wealth.

For most of his adult life Harding was in bad health, above all from asthma. He expected death to come at any moment and in fact dropped dead at 1 Portland Place on 16 November 1960, as he was leaving the studio after a performance in *Round Britain Quiz*. 'But I do wish that the future were over' (Harding, 224) had been the concluding words of his autobiography *Along my Line* (1953), a book that does not do justice to his remarkable intelligence and warmth of character. A later autobiographical volume was called *Master of None* (1958). He never married. The requiem mass in Westminster Cathedral, at which Cardinal Godfrey presided, was crowded.

D. W. BROGAN, *rev.*

Sources *The Times* (17 Nov 1960) · *The Guardian* (18 Nov 1960) · personal knowledge (1971) · A. Briggs, *The history of broadcasting in the United Kingdom*, 4 vols. (1961–79) · WWW · G. Harding, *Along my line* (1953) · CGPLA Eng. & Wales (1961)
Archives FILM BFI NFTVA, documentary footage · BFI NFTVA, performance footage |SOUND BL NSA, current affairs recording · BL NSA, oral history interview · BL NSA, performance recording
Likenesses photographs, 1953, Hult. Arch. · C. Lucas, photograph, 1960, NPG [*see illus.*] · F. Topolski, pencil, c.1960, NPG · M. Noakes, portrait, Hereford Art Gallery
Wealth at death £27,615 2s. 10d.: probate, 17 March 1961, CGPLA Eng. & Wales

Harding, Sir **Harold John Boyer** (1900–1986), civil engineer, was born in Wandsworth, London, on 6 January 1900, the younger son and younger child of Arthur Boyer Harding, who was employed by an insurance company, and his wife Helen Clinton, daughter of the Revd William Lowe. With the loss of his father in 1902, support through school, Christ's Hospital, and university depended on his mother's sister's husband, Jack Robinson. Harding entered the City and Guilds College (part of Imperial College) in 1917, serving through 1918 as a full-time Officers' Training Corps cadet. He resumed his studies in 1919, struggling in mathematics and excelling in geology. He received a BSc (Eng.) in 1922.

In 1922 Harding joined the 'old, respected and feudal firm' of John Mowlem & Co., engineering contractors, where he was to become the outstanding engineer in soft ground tunnelling and shaft construction in Britain. His early work concerned underground railway development in and around London, including the reconstruction of Piccadilly Circus Station (1926–9). The sheer complexity of this project spurred him to build, with his future wife Sophie, then a student at the Slade School of Art, a model of the underground works, subsequently displayed at the Science Museum and later at the London Transport Museum. Sophie Helen Blair, whom he married in 1927, was the daughter of Edmund Blair Leighton RI, artist. They had two sons and a daughter.

Harding's particular skills were soon exercised in overcoming major foundation problems encountered at Dagenham for the powerhouse for the Ford motor works, unwittingly placed exactly where Sir Cornelius Vermuyden had closed a breach in the Thames 300 years before. This experience led to Harding's special interest in expedients for ground treatment, with pioneering work in Britain on the Joosten and Guttman processes of chemical consolidation. From 1936 to 1939 he directed construction of the Central Line of London Underground from Bow Road to Leytonstone.

During the Second World War, Harding was responsible for defence works and emergency repairs to underground damage in London. In 1943–4 he organized the construction of precast concrete petrol barges and eight of the concrete floating monoliths of Mulberry harbour for the Normandy landings. During a night of air raids in 1941 he had a discussion with a distinguished colleague, which was to lead to a significant geotechnical advance in Britain, the foundation of Soil Mechanics Ltd in 1942. From this date he was increasingly involved in the management of the firm, being a director from 1949 to 1955; from 1950 to 1956 he was also a director of the parent company, Mowlem. Subsequently, until 1978, he worked as a consultant and arbitrator. From 1958 to 1970 he was joint consultant, with René Malcor, to the channel tunnel study group. In 1966–7 he was a member of the Aberfan disaster tribunal, chaired by Lord Justice Edmund Davies, following a flow slide of mining waste, which engulfed part of a mining village in south Wales.

Harding was an active and loyal fellow of the Institution of Civil Engineers through a period of radical reform; he served as president in 1963–4. He was first chairman of the British Tunnelling Society (1971–3) and set the pattern for its instructive informal discussions, encouraging participation by young engineers, thus recreating an original objective of the parent institution. He gave great encouragement to others to undertake research to explain phenomena he had observed, for research often lagged behind their practical manifestation. He was a governor of Westminster Technical College (1948–53), Northampton Engineering College (1950–53), and Imperial College (1955–75). In 1952 he was elected a fellow of the City and Guilds Institute. He was knighted in 1968 and received an honorary DSc from City University in 1970. In 1976 he was elected a founder fellow of the Fellowship of Engineering (later the Royal Academy of Engineering), and he became a fellow of Imperial College in 1968.

Harding was a man of great energy and application, an imposing figure with a high forehead, slightly aquiline nose and a severe expression which readily dissolved into a smile, and a penetrating eye which could be seen by the discerning to twinkle. His portrait, painted by his wife, hangs in the Institution of Civil Engineers. To his schooldays at Christ's Hospital, in the 'engineering side' taught by T. S. Usherwood, he attributed much of his command of English, interest in history, and facility for the apt quotation, learned with enthusiasm in association with science and technology. He was a witty and captivating speaker, dismissive of pomp and arrogance. He recognized that successful geotechnical projects depended on the early identification of unexpected change and the consequent need for modification of the scheme. This, he emphasized, required moral courage in those concerned to admit the errors in their original perceptions. Harding died in Topsham, Devon, on 27 March 1986.

ALAN MUIR WOOD, rev.

Sources H. J. B. Harding, *Tunnelling history and my own involvement* (1981) · Inst. CE · personal knowledge (1996) · private information (1996) · *CGPLA Eng. & Wales* (1986)
Archives Inst. CE
Likenesses Lady Harding, portrait, Inst. CE
Wealth at death £37,907: probate, 3 June 1986, *CGPLA Eng. & Wales*

Harding, James Duffield (1797–1863), landscape painter and lithographer, was born at Deptford, Kent, the son of John Harding (*c.*1777–1846), an engraver and drawing-master who had been one of the few professional pupils of Paul Sandby. His father gave him a good artistic education and a grounding in perspective, before sending him to Samuel Prout for a course of lessons in watercolour. When his father complained of the boy's lack of ideas, Prout told him, 'Let him draw till they come' (Roget, 1.509). He found trees, later his great strength, particularly difficult. Nevertheless he exhibited drawings at the Royal Academy from 1811 when he was thirteen. He was articled to the engraver Charles Pye and then worked in the office of the architect Peter Frederick Robinson, further educating himself by absorbing Turner's *Liber Studiorum* (1807–19) and James Malton's *The Young Painter's Maulstick* (1800). In 1816 he was awarded a silver medal by the Society of Arts, and two years later he exhibited for the first time with the Society of Painters in Water Colours. He was elected an associate of the society in 1820 and a member in the following year.

He resigned in 1847, in hopes of election to the Royal Academy as an oil painter, but meeting no success there returned to the watercolourists in 1856. Although he is said not to have taken to engraving during his apprenticeship, he was an early and prolific practitioner of lithography, at first working rather tentatively from drawings by others, but in time mastering the art as a means of reproducing his own work and reaching a wide public. On 29 June 1818, at St Alfege, Greenwich, Kent, he married Ann Roberts, with whom he had a son, Arthur Raymond Harding, who was baptized on 14 August 1836 in the Old Church, St Pancras, London.

As a boy in London, Harding had shyly approached an artist in Greenwich Park and been rudely rebuffed, and this had made him vow that, should he succeed as an artist, he would teach everybody. Through his numerous drawing books, as well as a successful practice as a drawing-master, he fulfilled his pledge. He also promoted schemes for training art teachers, in which he interested Sir Robert Peel and Dr Arnold of Rugby. He was something of an innovator, in materials at least. In 1830 he exhibited Italian views sketched on papers of various tints and textures. This led to the popular range of 'Harding papers' manufactured by Whatman. Then in 1841 he published *The Park and the Forest*, in which the sketches were drawn on the lithographic stone with a brush rather than a crayon. These prints he called 'lithotints'. Among his best publications were *A Series of Subjects from the Works of R. P. Bonington* (1829–30), *Sketches at Home and Abroad* (1836), which won him a Sèvres breakfast service and a diamond ring from King Louis-Philippe, and *Picturesque Selections* (1861), his last and finest achievement. He was awarded two gold medals by the French Académie des Beaux-Arts for lithographic drawings exhibited at the Louvre, and when exhibiting in Paris during the 1820s he used the address of the publisher Ostervald. According to H. Ottley in the supplement to M. Bryan's *Biographical and Critical Dictionary of Painters and Engravers* (1903, 1.626), his reputation was high among foreign artists, in particular because of his teaching books: 'In the schools of Paris especially, which he often visited, he had always an enthusiastic reception from professors and students'. In 1824 he was in Italy, probably for the first time, with the lithographer Charles Hullmandel, and he made frequent tours of France, Germany, Switzerland, and Italy. He also continued to work up views by others of places which he had not himself visited. He shared Turner's penchant for river and lake views, often on a large scale, but despite his pupil Ruskin's warm championship—'unquestionably the greatest master of foliage in Europe'—he stands high in the second rank of the English school rather than in the first (J. Ruskin, *Modern Painters*, 1843–60). On the other hand his obituarist in *The Athenaeum* was unduly dismissive on his death: 'he will be missed by Amateurs', and was a 'Society drawing master whose work would well embellish ladies' albums' (12 Dec 1863, 804). His closest colleagues were in two minds about him, as a letter from William Collingwood Smith to Joseph John Jenkins indicates: 'Although unpopular with many of our body the Society has lost a distinguished Artist and old member and the only one of our body who has gone into authorship to advance a knowledge of art in this country' (letter, W. C. Smith to J. Jenkins, Royal Watercolour Society archives J. 43/13). William Evans of Eton, himself a very difficult character, attacked him as 'a vain disappointed, jealous man … however he has not brains enough to do real mischief' (letter, W. Evans to J. Jenkins, ibid., J. 30/18). Between 1848 and 1860 Harding lived at 3 Abercorn Place, St John's Wood, London, and thereafter at 15 Lonsdale Terrace, Barnes, Surrey, where he died of granular induration of the liver, jaundice, and internal haemorrhaging, on 4 December 1863; he was survived by his wife. He was buried at the West London cemetery, Brompton. His will was proved at under £14,000, and his remaining works, together with a few drawings by colleagues from his collection, were sold at Christies on 19–20 May 1864, realizing £4000. Examples of his work are in many British public collections including the British Museum, the Victoria and Albert Museum, the Ashmolean Museum, Oxford, and the Fitzwilliam Museum, Cambridge.

F. M. O'DONOGHUE, rev. HUON MALLALIEU

Sources J. L. Roget, *A history of the 'Old Water-Colour' Society*, 2 vols. (1891); repr. (1972) · *Art Journal*, 12 (1850) · *Art Journal*, 26 (1864), 39ff. · C. Skilton, 'James Duffield Harding … a centenary memoir', *Old Water-Colour Society's Club*, 38 (1963), 37–53 · Royal Water Colour Society archives [MSS, obituaries] · d. cert. · *The Times* (21 May 1864) · *CGPLA Eng. & Wales* (1864) · M. Hardie, *Water-colour painting in Britain*, ed. D. Snelgrove, J. Mayne, and B. Taylor, 3: *The Victorian period* (1968), 32–4 · *IGI* · Bryan, *Painters* (1903–5)
Archives Courtauld Inst., account books, diaries, and notebooks | Hants. RO, letters to third earl of Malmesbury · V&A NAL, letters to W. H. Winsor
Likenesses L. Theweneti, pencil and watercolour drawing, 1825, NPG · H. P. Briggs, oils, *c*.1840, NPG · Cundall & Downes, carte-de-visite, NPG · J. P. Knight, oils, Castle Museum, Nottingham · portrait, repro. in *Art Journal* (1 June 1850)
Wealth at death under £14,000: resworn will, March 1866, *CGPLA Eng. & Wales* (1864)

Harding, John (*bap.* 1601, *d.* 1665), alchemist and translator, was baptized on 8 November 1601 at Great Haseley, Oxfordshire, eldest of the three sons and four daughters of John Harding (*c*.1562–1610), rector of Great Haseley, and his wife, Isabel, whose former married name was Clarke. As regius professor of Hebrew at Oxford University, Harding's father was one of the appointed translators of the Bible, and was president of Magdalen College in 1607–8. Harding matriculated at Magdalen on 25 October 1616; he graduated BA in 1620, held a fellowship in 1622–8, and proceeded MA in 1623. He held the offices of bursar in 1625 and of vice-president in 1626. In or after 1628 Harding married Martha (*d.* 1682); they raised at least two sons, John (*d.* 1690), who graduated at Magdalen in 1650, and Edward (*d.* 1679), who graduated at Christ Church, Oxford, in 1653 and practised medicine at Northampton.

From 1642 Harding was rector of Brinkworth, Wiltshire. In pursuit of his interest in science he had become an avid follower of Paracelsus, and while at Brinkworth he became a significant translator and disseminator of Paracelsian works. His first collection, issued in 1659, was entitled *Paracelsus his Aurora & treasures of the philosophers, as*

also the water-stone of the wise men (the third text taken from Johann Siebmacher's *Der Wasserstein der Weisen*). The second and more important collection, *Paracelsus his Archidoxes*, together with many smaller treatises, was published in 1661 and reissued in 1663 as *Paracelsus his Archidoxes, or Chief Teachings, Comprised in Ten Books*. Harding had drawn mainly on Huser's German edition, but incorporated material from other German sources. A third work, *The Triumphant Chariot of Antimony* (1660), was supposedly translated from the fictional Basil Valentine. All Harding's publications were identified simply as 'by J. H. Oxon'.

In the *Archidoxes* Harding alludes to the frustration he was experiencing with his self-imposed task of translating and publishing Paracelsian and other medical texts which formed the canon of a more empirically orientated school than the traditional one of medical practice. Its innovative element was the wedding of chemistry with medicine, wherein the body was seen as an extension of the chemical cosmos. Harding's prefaces show him to be an advocate of empirical studies. Alchemy was a tradition dominated by the search for gold and the elixir of life. With his translation of *Archidoxes*, Harding indicated his broad knowledge of Paracelsian works as well as his own wish to guide English alchemical and medical practice away from Galenic traditionalism and towards specific cures, founded on chemical substances and knowledge. In publishing these works, Harding had more than personal and academic difficulties to surmount; in the preface to *Archidoxes* he mentions his pleasure at publishing the tenth book of the work, its having previously been suppressed. Paracelsians were not popular figures in established medical or academic circles because they accused medical practitioners of ossification, callousness, and downright charlatanism.

Harding's declared intention to publish a complete translation of Paracelsus's *Paramirum* came to nought when in 1662 he was ejected from his living 'as a most violent presbyterian'. He retired to Northampton where his nephew Edward, son of Edward Reynolds, bishop of Norwich and Harding's sister Mary, held the rectory of St Peter's. He died in April 1665 and was buried at St Peter's on 19 April.

PETER K. BENBOW

Sources W. D. Macray, *A register of the members of St Mary Magdalen College, Oxford*, 8 vols. (1894–1915), vol. 3 · Foster, *Alum. Oxon.* · C. Webster, *The great instauration: science, medicine and reform, 1626–1660* (1975), 229, 281 · parish register, burial (19 April 1665), Northampton, St Peter · *Calamy rev.*, 247

Harding, John (1805–1874), bishop of Bombay, was born in Queen Square, Bloomsbury, London, on 7 January 1805, the third son of William Harding, chief clerk in the transport office, and his wife, Mary Harrison Ackland. The Revd Thomas Harding, vicar of Bexley from 1833 until 1874, was his twin brother. John was educated with Thomas at Westminster School (1818–21) and at Worcester College, Oxford, where he graduated BA (third class in *literae humaniores*) in 1826 and MA in 1829. In the latter year he was ordained priest by the bishop of Ely and became curate of Wendy in Cambridgeshire.

In 1834 Harding was appointed in London to Park

Chapel, Chelsea, and in 1836 to the rectorship of St Andrew by the Wardrobe with St Anne Blackfriars, a united parish which counted the celebrated evangelicals William Romaine (1714–1795) and William Goode (1762–1816) among its previous incumbents. Harding himself was staunchly opposed to high-church ritualism and greatly enhanced the parish's reputation as an evangelical powerhouse during his fifteen years there. He was for some years secretary of the Pastoral Aid Society and also a member of the Church Missionary Society, preaching the latter's anniversary sermon at St Bride's, Fleet Street, in 1849.

In 1851 Archbishop Sumner selected Harding as the second bishop of Bombay. He proceeded to the degrees of BD and DD at Oxford and was consecrated at Lambeth Palace in London on 10 August 1851. With only thirty chaplains, Bombay was the poor sister of the two larger and more active Indian sees, Calcutta and Madras, and Harding appears to have lacked the imagination or spirit that might have galvanized the East India Company and the Church Missionary Society into contributing more resources for pastoral and evangelical work there. Moreover, his horror of Tractarianism led him to look coldly on 'brotherhoods' and other proposed agencies of the high church for supplementing missionary work in the diocese. He presided over a period of increased church building, especially in the late 1850s and the 1860s, and in 1864 he helped to establish Bishop's High School at Poona, a future standard-bearer of European education in western India. He also articulated in a precise form the state's obligation (and hence that of the Indian people) to pay for the religious needs of the state's Christian servants. Generally, however, scholars of the Indian church have struggled to find anything outstanding about Harding's ecclesiastical administration, one concluding in the absence of evidence to the contrary that 'he appears to have been competent, devoted and sensible' (Gibbs, 170).

In 1867 poor health compelled Harding to take furlough and in 1869 he resigned the see. With his wife, Mary, third daughter of W. Tebbs, proctor in Doctors' Commons, he settled at Ore, near Hastings in Sussex. In old age his religious opinions mellowed and the clerical meetings at his house brought together clergy of widely differing views— a broadening of sympathies which was reflected in his late publication *Texts and Thoughts for Christian Ministers* (1874). He was a frequent preacher at St Mary's-in-the-Castle, Hastings, of which his friend the Revd T. Vores was incumbent. Harding died at his residence, St Helen's Lodge, Ore, on 18 June 1874, and was survived by his wife, but not by any children.

EDMUND VENABLES, *rev.* KATHERINE PRIOR

Sources W. Ashley-Brown, *On the Bombay coast and Deccan* (1937) · M. E. Gibbs, *The Anglican church in India, 1600–1970* (1972) · *The Times* (20 June 1874), 1 · *The Times* (22 June 1874), 11 · *Old Westminsters*, 1.423 · Crockford (1874) · Foster, *Alum. Oxon.* · *The Times* (14 Nov 1874), 10 · *CGPLA Eng. & Wales* (1874)
Likenesses J. Bridges, oils, 1851, Worcester College, Oxford · photograph, 1865, repro. in Ashley-Brown, *On the Bombay coast*, facing p. 162 · R. J. Lane, lithograph (after F. Talfourd), BM, NPG

Wealth at death under £3000: probate, 8 July 1874, *CGPLA Eng. & Wales*

Harding, John [Allan Francis], **first Baron Harding of Petherton** (1896–1989), army officer, was born on 10 February 1896 at Rock House, South Petherton, Somerset, the second child and only son in the family of four children of Francis Ebenezer Harding, solicitor's clerk and local rating officer, and his wife, Elizabeth Ellen, daughter of Jethro Anstice, draper, of South Petherton. At the age of ten he was sent as a weekly boarder to Ilminster grammar school. His headmaster, Robert Davidson, was a sound scholar; in later years, when already a lieutenant-general, Harding would attribute his capacity for hard work to Davidson's example and his gift of logical thinking to hours spent construing Ovid with him. The family had not enough money to finance a career either in farming, his own preference, or the law, which Davidson recommended; he became at the age of fifteen a boy clerk in the Post Office Savings Bank. After attending night classes at King's College, London, he was promoted and in his new posting he was influenced by his superior in the office to apply for a commission in the Territorial Army. Two regular officers interviewed him and, although he was only eighteen and from a station in life different from that of most regular officers, they showed discernment and lack of prejudice in recognizing his quality. He was gazetted as second lieutenant in the 1st battalion 11th London regiment (the Finsbury Rifles) in May 1914.

Harding first saw action on 10 August 1915 in the Dardanelles campaign, where he was wounded after only five days. When Gallipoli was abandoned his battalion went to Egypt. Here he decided to apply for and in March 1917 was granted a regular commission as a lieutenant in his county regiment, the Somerset light infantry. By now he was specializing in machine-guns. In the third battle of Gaza he was divisional machine-gun officer, as acting major at the age of twenty-one, and was awarded the MC (1917). In 1918 he was made corps machine-gun officer at 21st corps headquarters. From experience on the staff he learned, among other things, the value of strategic deception, which was practised with great success in both wars by British commanders in the Middle East.

Between the wars Harding served in India from 1919 to 1927, first with the machine-gun corps and then with his regiment. In 1927 he married Mary Gertrude Mabel (d. 1983), daughter of Joseph Wilson Rooke, solicitor and JP, of Knutsford, Cheshire, and sister of an officer in his regiment. They had one son. From 1928 to 1930 Harding attended the Staff College, Camberley. In May 1933 he was appointed brigade-major of the 13th infantry brigade, which was chosen as the British contingent in the international force which supervised the Saarland plebiscite. It was a good preparation for the tasks of collaborating with forces of different nationalities which were to fall to him later in the Mediterranean theatre; he also made a special study of the Italian contingent, whose light tanks were to prove so ineffective in the desert. In July 1939, at the age of forty-three, he was given command of the 1st battalion of

John Harding, first Baron Harding of Petherton (1896–1989), by Elliott & Fry, 1952

his regiment, again in India. He earned a mention in dispatches for frontier operations, but his reputation ensured that he would soon be required for more serious service; in the autumn of 1940 he was posted to Egypt, where staff officers were required.

Harding's first task was to plan Compass, the offensive against the Italian Tenth Army organized by Sir A. P. Wavell; he went on to become brigadier general staff to Richard O'Connor, commanding the western desert force, later 13th corps. Compass was brilliantly successful, expelling all Italian formations from Cyrenaica and capturing 125,000 prisoners, at little cost in British casualties. Harding's services were rewarded with a CBE (1940) and a second mention in dispatches. When the counter-attack led by Field Marshal Erwin Rommel overwhelmed the British in Cyrenaica, and both O'Connor and his successor, Philip Neame, were taken prisoner, it was Harding who took temporary charge, organized the defence of Tobruk, and persuaded Wavell that it could be held. After the first two misdirected German attacks on the fortress had been repulsed, he was transferred to be brigadier general staff of a revived western desert force at Matruh and appointed to the DSO (1941).

For Crusader, the operation which saw Rommel's army defeated in the field and the siege of Tobruk relieved, Harding was brigadier general staff to A. R. Godwin-Austen, a robustly competent commander whose qualities were harmoniously supplemented by Harding's

intellectual grasp of the often perplexing problems created by Rommel's ineffectual precipitancy. He received a bar to his DSO for this victory. In January 1942 he supported Godwin-Austen's correct appreciation of the capabilities of the German counter-offensive and found himself organizing for the second time a hurried withdrawal through western Cyrenaica. The differences between the army and the corps commanders being irreconcilable, Godwin-Austen was replaced. Harding considered he was also honour bound to ask for a transfer; he went to general headquarters as director of military training. He was promoted brigadier and then major-general in 1942.

In Cairo, Harding found himself frequently at variance, in practical matters of organization, with the chief of staff and his deputy. It was a relief to be given command, in September, of 7th armoured division, the original desert armoured formation. In the second battle of Alamein his division was originally employed on the southern flank, its purpose mainly to deceive General Stumme into maintaining the original faulty disposition of his armour; but, with the return of Rommel and the intensification of the struggle in the northern sector, 7th armoured was transferred there. In the pursuit that followed the successful change of plan, Harding fretted at the constraints imposed on him, but drove hard, always up with the forward troops. In January 1943, when approaching Tripoli, he was severely wounded by a nearby shell burst. He received a second bar to his DSO but was not graded fit to return to duty until ten months had passed.

In November 1943 Harding took command of 8th corps, having been promoted lieutenant-general, but six weeks later, by the personal decision of Sir Alan Brooke, chief of the Imperial General Staff, he was transferred to be chief of staff to Sir Harold Alexander, commander-in-chief, allied armies in Italy. This was an inspired appointment. Harding and Alexander not only got on well together but admirably complemented each other. Alexander was both an intellectual and a fighting soldier, combining a tactical grasp of the battlefield with the talent of an imaginative and fertile strategist. In Harding he had someone who could be relied on without reservation to implement his ideas.

After the capture of Rome, Harding was appointed KCB (1944). He chose to be known as Sir John Harding, that being the name he had used in the regiment and the family since 1919. After fifteen months as chief of staff he was at last, in March 1945, given the chance to command a corps in action; he took over 13th corps, with which he had served in the desert nearly five years earlier. The last battle in Italy was as hard-fought as the first. Harding's corps, originally on the British left, changed direction in the closing stages and pursued the retreating enemy up to and across the Po with a speed and effectiveness greater than he had been allowed to achieve after Alamein. That headlong pursuit brought him to Trieste on 2 May, just after the Yugoslavs, and to the centre of a long-lasting dispute with Britain's former ally. The acute stage of the confrontation with the Yugoslavs was overcome when they backed down in June, the first victory, it has been called, in the cold war. For two years Harding ruled with popular acclaim over what became the free city of Trieste in reasonable tranquillity.

In the summer of 1947 Harding was appointed to southern command and two years later became commander-in-chief, Far East. He arrived just as what was euphemistically called 'the emergency' was beginning in Malaya; it was destined to last for twelve years. The foundations of the system by which this formidable Chinese communist insurrection was eventually suppressed were laid by Harding. Malcolm MacDonald, the special commissioner for the Far East, paid a firm tribute to the sagacity and tenacity of purpose with which Harding dominated the defence co-ordinating committee.

Promoted general in 1949 and appointed GCB at the beginning of 1951, Harding was transferred in August 1951 to command the British army of the Rhine. After the Russian take-over in Czechoslovakia and the Berlin blockade, Britain had begun rearming and NATO set up the Supreme Headquarters, Allied Powers in Europe (SHAPE), commanded by Dwight Eisenhower. The British army was being transformed. New defence plans were studied. Harding had to display prodigies of inter-allied tact, organizational flair, and determination. By contrast his period as chief of the Imperial General Staff, three years from 1952 to 1955, passed off with little more excitement than the Mau Mau uprising in Kenya and the beginning of the dissolution of the British base in Egypt. In November 1953 he was promoted field marshal and presented with his baton by the young queen.

As the end of the three-year term approached and Harding was making plans for his retirement, a proposal was made to him by the new prime minister, Sir Anthony Eden, that he should become governor of Cyprus. Eden considered that his experience in Malaya and Kenya would help him to control the demand for union with Greece, which was supported by the majority of Greek Cypriots. Harding accepted reluctantly, from a sense of duty. He realized at once that the only favourable prospect lay in negotiating with Archbishop Makarios for some acceptable form of self-government. The two men were well matched in quickness of intelligence; Makarios later declared that Harding was both the cleverest and the most straightforward of the governors he had known. Though circumstances denied them the pleasure of a successful agreement, Harding's measures brought greatly improved security in the island, with the Greek Cypriot insurgent leader, George Grivas, reduced to impotent clandestinity. After the two years' term for which he had originally stipulated, Harding was able to hand over in October 1957 to his successor, Sir Hugh Foot, a sound basis for the eventual achievement of Cypriot independence.

In January 1958 Harding was raised to the peerage in acknowledgement of his service in Cyprus. In retirement he accepted several directorships, including one on the board of Plesseys, a major supplier of telecommunication equipment of which he became chairman in 1967. In 1961 he was invited to become the first chairman of the Horserace Betting Levy Board. He was colonel of three regiments, the Somerset light infantry (from 1960 the Somerset and Cornwall light infantry), the 6th Gurkha rifles, and the lifeguards. He was awarded the honorary degree of DCL of Durham University (1958).

Harding was slight in build with a frank and courteous expression, clear blue eyes, and a trim moustache. His manner was open and friendly; throughout a career that could have excited jealousy no one spoke badly of him. Apart from a notable skill in personal relationships, his leading characteristic was a lucidity of intellectual apprehension and strength of reasoning that enabled him to grasp the essence of every problem. Those who served with him were exhilarated by the speed and certainty with which he arrived at the right solution. Lady Harding died in 1983. Harding died on 20 January 1989 at his home, The Barton, Nether Compton, Dorset. His son John Charles (*b.* 1928) succeeded to the title.

DAVID HUNT, *rev.*

Sources M. Carver, *Harding of Petherton* (1978) · D. Hunt, *A don at war*, rev. edn (1990) · I. S. O. Playfair and others, *The Mediterranean and Middle East*, 6 vols. in 8 (1954–88) · *CGPLA Eng. & Wales* (1989) · personal knowledge (1996)
Archives IWM, corresp., diary, and papers · NAM, corresp. and papers
Likenesses Elliott & Fry, photograph, 1952, NPG [*see illus.*]
Wealth at death £34,111: probate, 28 June 1989, *CGPLA Eng. & Wales*

Harding, Sir Robert Palmer (1821–1893), accountant, was born on 18 February 1821, the son of Robert Harding (*d.* 1862), an auctioneer and house agent. It is thought that he had originally operated a fashionable West End hatters, a business which ran into difficulties, and according to legend a court official advised him to embark on a career in accountancy. He established a practice in July 1847, entered a partnership with Edward Pullein in August 1848, and by 1850 the firm operated from 16 Gresham Street in the City of London. In November 1857 Frederick Whinney, who joined Harding and Pullein as a clerk in December 1849, was admitted as a partner. In December 1858 James Boatwright Gibbons joined the partnership, which continued as Harding, Pullein, Whinney, and Gibbons from January 1859. Harding remained the senior partner until October 1883, when he retired from the firm, which by then was named Harding, Whinney & Co.

As a specialist in liquidations and bankruptcy work, Harding was in 1864 appointed a commissioner to inquire into the working of the Bankruptcy Acts. In 1866 he was appointed (in conjunction with William Turquand) liquidator of Overend, Gurney & Co., a long-term bank liquidation which was finalized only weeks before Harding's death. He also liquidated other large concerns, including Marylebone Bank (from 1853), Royal British Bank (1856), Mexican and South American Co. (1857), Professional Life, Life Assurance Treasury, National Assurance (Bank of Deposit) (all in 1861), Unity General Assurance (1864), and East India and London Shipping (1866). In 1866 the select committee on the limited liability acts revealed that Harding, Whinney, and Gibbons was handling the winding up of sixty-one of the 259 companies then in liquidation. Such commitments appear to have presented Harding with limited scope for audit engagements. Nevertheless, he was the auditor of the Central Argentine Railway, and he secured Morgan Bros., the Battersea iron founders, as a client of the firm.

Harding was a founding father of professional accountancy in Britain. He was among the thirty-seven accountants to sign the draft rules of the Institute of Accountants in London, founded in 1870. Later, he became a founder of the Institute of Chartered Accountants in England and Wales (ICAEW), and was its vice-president when the charter of incorporation was granted to the body on 11 May 1880. Both Harding and the institute's first president, Turquand, actually received the charter. Together with Turquand, Whinney, Arthur Cooper, and Charles Kemp, Harding was delegated to negotiate with the Board of Trade on matters which might affect the accounting profession. Harding succeeded Turquand as the institute's president and served in this role during 1882–3.

In 1883, on retiring from Harding, Whinney & Co. and the ICAEW, where he simultaneously resigned his seat on the council and also his membership, Harding accepted appointment as chief official receiver in the bankruptcy department of the Board of Trade. Appointed because of his 'large experience in the administration of estates' (*The Accountant*, 9, 1883, 4), he served in the role of chief official receiver until his retirement in 1890, when he received a knighthood—the first awarded to a professional accountant—in recognition of his contribution to the department.

An obituary in a professional journal described Harding as 'a conspicuously able man, although, unlike his talented partner [Frederick Whinney], not showing to great advantage in public. But his powers of organisation and control were superb; but this will be apparent from the long list of large concerns he was engaged in' (*The Accountant*, 19, 1893, 1093). The firm which Harding co-founded became Whinney, Smith and Whinney in 1894.

In 1845 Harding married Marion Martha, the daughter of Joseph Ryle; they had six daughters and two sons. He died of a cranial tumour at 20 Wetherby Gardens, his residence in South Kensington, on 22 December 1893, and was buried on 27 December in Stanstead Old Church, St Margaret's, Hertfordshire, the burial place of his ancestors.

GARRY D. CARNEGIE

Sources *The Accountant* (7 Jan 1883), 4 · *The Accountant*, 16 (1890) · *The Accountant* (30 Dec 1893), 1093 · E. Jones, *Accountancy and the British economy, 1840–1980: the evolution of Ernst & Whinney* (1981) · P. Magnus, 'The history of the Institute of Chartered Accountants in England and Wales, 1880–1958', Institute of Chartered Accountants of England and Wales · R. H. Parker, ed., *British accountants: a biographical sourcebook* (1980) · H. Howitt and others, eds., *The history of the Institute of Chartered Accountants in England and Wales, 1880–1965, and of its founder accountancy bodies, 1870–1880* (1966) · 'Select committee on the Operations of Companies Acts', *Parl. papers* (1877), 8.419, no. 365 · 'Select committee on the limited liability acts', *Parl. papers* (1867), 10.393, no. 329 · CGPLA Eng. & Wales (1894) · d. cert. · private information · m. cert.

Likenesses E. Boehm, bust, Institute of Chartered Accountants in England and Wales, London
Wealth at death £54,530 12s. 7d.: probate, 31 Jan 1894, *CGPLA Eng. & Wales*

Harding, Samuel (1615/16–*c*.1643/1699), playwright, was born in Ipswich, Suffolk, the son of Robert Harding. He was educated at Exeter College, Oxford, having matriculated on 17 April 1635 aged nineteen as a sojourner; he graduated BA on 29 May 1638. In 1640 his tragedy *Sicily and Naples, or, The Fatal Union* was published at Oxford by a friend signing himself P. P., reputedly without Harding's approval. He took holy orders and became chaplain to a nobleman.

There is ambiguity about Harding's subsequent career. He may have died 'about the beginning or in the heat of the Civil War' (Wood, *Ath. Oxon.*, new edn, 3.32) or he may have been the Samuel Harding who was vicar of Norwich St Stephens from 1642 to 1662, and rector of Barford in Norfolk, from 1662 to 1699, also taking responsibility for Colney, Norfolk, from 1670 to 1694. On 30 April 1670 this Samuel Harding gained a licence to marry Rebecca Burwell, widow, of Codicote, Norfolk.

F. D. A. BURNS

Sources DNB · Foster, *Alum. Oxon.*, *1500–1714*, 2.648 · Wood, *Ath. Oxon.*, new edn, 3.31–2

Harding, Sidnie Milana. *See* Manton, Sidnie Milana (1902–1979).

Harding, Silvester [Sylvester] (1745×51–1809), artist and publisher, was born at Newcastle under Lyme, Staffordshire, on 5 August 1745, the son of Sylvester and Mary Harding who married there on 11 August 1745. He was looked after by an uncle in London, but at the age of fourteen ran away and joined a company of strolling actors, with whom he played under an assumed name for some years. In 1775 he returned to London and married on 17 October 1775 at St Matthew's, Bethnal Green, Sarah, daughter of Dr William *Perfect of Town Malling, Kent. Harding took up miniature painting, exhibiting at the Royal Academy in 1776 and subsequent years. On 25 November 1776 he entered the Royal Academy Schools, when his age was given as twenty-five on '5 Augst last' (Hutchison). In 1786 he joined his younger brother Edward [see below] in setting up a book and printseller's shop in Fleet Street, where they published many prints designed by him and engraved by Bartolozzi, Delatre, Gardiner, and others. He was chiefly employed in drawing portraits of theatrical celebrities, and in copying ancient portraits in watercolours. The latter, executed with care and skill, illustrated various historical works issued by him and his brother. Their first publication of this kind was *Shakespeare illustrated by an assemblage of portraits and views appropriated to the whole suite of our author's historical dramas* (1789–93), consisting of 150 plates, issued in thirty numbers. In 1792 they moved to 102 Pall Mall, where they maintained a successful business. Here they produced Anthony Hamilton's *Memoirs of Count Grammont* (1793); *The Economy of Human Life* (1795), with plates by W. N. Gardiner from designs by Harding; G. A. Bürger's *Leonora*, translated by W. R. Spencer (1796); and John Dryden's *Fables* (1797), both illustrated with plates from drawings by Lady Diana Beauclerk. The first volume of their extensive series of historical portraits, known as *The Biographical Mirrour*, with text by F. G. Waldron, appeared in 1795. Before 1798 the brothers dissolved partnership. Silvester moved to 127 and Edward to 98 Pall Mall; the former continued *The Biographical Mirrour*, of which he issued the second volume in 1798, and the third was ready for publication at the time of his death in 1809. Among other original works by Harding were a portrait of Sir Busick Harwood MD, engraved on a large scale in mezzotint by John Jones, and a set of six illustrations to Thomas Lodge's *Rosalynde, Euphues Golden Legacie* (the source of Shakespeare's *As You Like It*), with notes by F. G. Waldron, which were engraved and published by his brother Edward in 1802. The largest of his watercolour copies, *Charles II receiving the first pine-apple cultivated in England from Rose, the gardener at Dawney Court, Bucks, the seat of the duchess of Cleveland, from a picture at Strawberry Hill*, was engraved by R. Grave in 1823. He was well known to and much esteemed by the collectors of his time. Silvester Harding died in London on 12 August 1809; his obituary in the *Gentleman's Magazine* gives his age at death as 'about 64'. Of his children, George Perfect *Harding is noticed separately. His son Edward engraved some good plates for his father's publications, but died at the age of twenty in 1796. The print room of the British Museum possesses many copies of portraits by Silvester Harding.

Edward Harding (1755–1840), engraver and publisher, was the younger brother of Silvester Harding. He was born on 29 March 1755 at Stafford and baptized on 1 April at St Mary's, Stafford, the son of Sylvester Harding and his wife, Mary. He was apprenticed to a hairdresser, and after pursuing this occupation for a few years in London he abandoned it, and set up with his brother as an engraver and bookseller. After the dissolution of their partnership he carried on business alone, for a few years, employing W. N. Gardiner as his copier of portraits, and publishing, among other works, John Adolphus's *British Cabinet* (2 vols., 1799–1800); but in 1803 he was appointed librarian to Queen Charlotte, and resided first at Frogmore, and afterwards at Buckingham Palace. He became a great favourite with the queen, and grangerized many historical works for her amusement. In 1806 he published *Portraits of the Whole Royal Family*, engraved by Cheesman and others from pictures by Gainsborough and Beechey. After Queen Charlotte's death in 1818 Harding became librarian to the duke of Cumberland, afterwards king of Hanover, and held that post until his death, which took place at Pimlico, London, on 1 November 1840.

F. M. O'DONOGHUE, *rev.* J. DESMARAIS

Sources Redgrave, *Artists* · *GM*, 2nd ser., 14 (1840), 668 · Bryan, *Painters* · Graves, *RA exhibitors* · *Checklist of British artists in the Witt Library*, Courtauld Institute, Witt Library (1991) · R. N. James, *Painters and their works*, 3 vols. (1896–7) · G. Watson, ed., *The shorter new Cambridge bibliography of English literature* (1981) · Allibone, *Dict.* · IGI · will, PRO, PROB 11/1504, sig. 757 · Mallalieu, *Watercolour artists* · S. C. Hutchison, 'The Royal Academy Schools, 1768–1830', *Walpole Society*, 38 (1960–62), 123–91, esp. 142

Likenesses group portrait, line engraving, pubd 1798 (*Sketches taken at print sales*; after P. Sandby), BM · E. Harding junior, stipple and etching with crayon and canvas (after S. Harding), BM · lithograph, BM

Harding, Thomas (1516–1572), theologian and religious controversialist, was born at Bickington in Devon. By a curious coincidence he attended Barnstaple grammar school, where John Jewel, later his chief literary opponent, was also to study. He won a scholarship at Winchester College, aged twelve, and in 1534 went to New College, Oxford, where he graduated BA in 1535 and took the degree of MA in 1542; he was admitted BTh in 1552 and inceptual DTh in 1554. He was a scholar of Hebrew, and in 1542 was elected the second regius professor of Hebrew by Henry VIII. At this point in his life Harding seems to have held at least some protestant opinions, becoming chaplain to Henry Grey, marquess of Dorset, and lending Frith's book attacking purgatory to one of his students, John Lowthe, subsequently a confirmed protestant. Harding admitted later in life, 'In certaine pointes I was deceived (I confess) by Calvine, Melanchthon, and a few others' (Harding, *A Rejoindre*, sig. CCC ir), but maintained he was never a true protestant, despite the attempts of Pietro Martire Vermigli (known as Peter Martyr) to persuade him by inviting him to the private sermons he gave in Italian at home. Harding also asked of Jewel in 1566:

> if I were so ernest and so vehement a Gospeller, as now to discredite me you say I was, why did I freely and without al compulsion geve over the Kinges Hebrew lesson, which was so good and so quiet a living, that I might not depart from that Catholike Colledge, in which I was brought up, unto Christes church in Oxford, where the freshest Gospellers were then placed? (ibid., sig. CCC iiv)

This referred to the relocation of the regius chair to Christ Church when Henry VIII refounded the college in 1546, but since Harding resigned his chair in 1547 to become chaplain to Henry Grey, it seems doubtful that the avoidance of protestantism was his chief motive. Harding also claimed that the two Paul's Cross sermons he delivered during Edward VI's time were 'very much misliked' because they praised charity and good works, deplored the marriage of priests, and warned against the misuse of God's word (ibid., sig. CCC iiir). Yet the evidence suggests that his reformed opinions were clear, if perhaps moderate, and he was certainly considered a protestant by contemporaries. He wrote an affectionate letter to Bullinger dated 19 October 1551 in which he records staying with the reformer on his way to study in Italy three years earlier. Furthermore, in 1552 Edward VI sent letters encouraging the fellows of New College to appoint Harding as the next warden, although he was not in the end elected.

Within a year of Mary's succession, however, Harding had returned to Catholicism and had been ordained priest, publicly recanting his more reformed opinions in Oxford. When this became known Lady Jane Grey wrote to him from prison, declaring:

I cannot but marvel at thee, and lament thy case, which seemed sometime to be the lively member of Christ, but now the deformed imp of the devil; sometime the beautiful temple of God, but now the stinking and filthy kennel of Satan; sometime the unspotted spouse of Christ, but now the unshameful paramour of Antichrist. (*Acts and Monuments*, 6.418)

Yet Harding's new allegiance stood firm: he became chaplain to John White, bishop of Lincoln, and chaplain and confessor to Stephen Gardiner, bishop of Winchester, both in 1555. He was made canon of Winchester in July 1554, and on 17 July 1555, Gardiner secured his appointment as treasurer of Salisbury diocese, where he was made canon on 8 October 1558. Gardiner also appointed him as one of the eight executors of his will in 1555.

On Elizabeth's accession Harding was identified as a favourer of the old religion, and his movements were limited by the ecclesiastical commissioners. He soon moved to Louvain, matriculating in the university there in 1563, and later became a professor at Douai. In exile he began to write the polemical works for which he is famous. The so-called 'Jewel–Harding controversy' arose from the 'challenge sermon', which John Jewel, bishop of Salisbury delivered at Paul's Cross in 1559, and from Jewel's *Apologia Ecclesiae Anglicanae* of 1562. Harding became Jewel's most important opponent, publishing seven vernacular works in the 1560s. *An Answere to Maister Juelles Chalenge* (Louvain, 1564) appeared first, with an augmented version published in Antwerp a year later. A further Paul's Cross sermon by Jewel prompted *A Breife Answere of Thomas Harding Touching Certaine Untruthes* (Antwerp, 1565). Jewel's work of 1565, *A Replie unto M. Hardinges Answeare*, resulted in the publication of two rejoinders, *A Rejoindre to M. Jewels Replie* (Antwerp, 1566), concentrating on the issue of 'private mass', and *A Rejoindre to M. Jewels Replie Against the Sacrifice of the Masse* (Louvain, 1567), giving a broader defence of sacramental doctrine. A second strand of debate arose over Jewel's *Apologia*, prompting Harding's work, *A Confutation of a Booke Intituled 'An Apologie of the Church of England'* (Antwerp, 1565), and after Jewel's reply in 1567 Harding published *A Detection of Sundrie Foule Errours* (Louvain, 1568).

Harding's books revealed great erudition, and quoted extensively from scripture and the early church fathers and councils. He was supported in the debate with Jewel by his fellow exiles Thomas Stapleton, John Rastell, Thomas Dorman, Nicholas Sander, and John Martiall, all of them former members of New College. The personal and academic flavour of the debate was further enhanced by the fact that Jewel was also an old Oxford contemporary. Harding suggested that he had never been much of a theologian, urging him to:

remember, that your tyme hath ben most bestowed in the studie of humanities and of the latine tonge, and concerning divinitie, your most labour hath ben imployed to fynde matter against the churche, rather then about seriouse and exacte discussing of the truth. (Harding, *An Answere*, fols. 20v–21r)

Initially Harding dealt politely with his opponent, claiming in his work of 1564 that 'my hart served me not to deal

with M. Juell myne old acquainted, felow and countreyman other wise, then swetly, gentilly and courteouslye' (ibid., fol. 6r). The debate soon became vicious, however, in part in reaction to the anti-Catholic rioting in the Low Countries in 1566, which seems to have shaken Harding. Yet he was also willing to admit the past abuses within the church, and could be broad-minded about reform. He maintained his humanist outlook, and grounded his opinions on scripture and the practice of the primitive church. He petitioned Rome, with Nicholas Sander, urging that English Catholics be given special permission to read books in the vernacular, and asking that an English translation of the Bible be produced. He was a leading member of the exile community, and seems to have been granted quasi-episcopal jurisdiction over the English community to absolve repentant heretics and arbitrate irregularities, which grant led to a publication by Thomas Norton in 1570, entitled *A bull graunted by the pope to Doctor Harding and other, by reconcilement and assoyling of English papistes, to undermyne faith and allegeance to the quene*.

Harding died at Louvain in 1572. His assets, even without his property in England, were valued at 1766 florins, and he left a range of bequests to English priests and nuns in exile, to his friends at Louvain, and £10 to New College in the event of a Catholic restoration. He was buried in the church of St Gertrude, Louvain, before the altar of the Holy Trinity, and his tomb bore a depiction of a man propping up a tottering church with his right hand.

L. E. C. WOODING

Sources T. Harding, *An answere to Maister Juelles chalenge* (1564) • T Harding, *A rejoindre to M. Jewels replie* (Antwerp, 1566) • H. Robinson, ed. and trans., *Original letters relative to the English Reformation*, 1, Parker Society, [26] (1846), 309–11 • H. de Vocht, 'Thomas Harding', *EngHR*, 35 (1920), 233–44 • Emden, *Oxf.*, 4.265–6 • BL, Lansdowne MS 981, fol. 118r • J. Strype, *Annals of the Reformation and establishment of religion … during Queen Elizabeth's happy reign*, 1 (1709), 241; appx 57–9 • *The acts and monuments of John Foxe*, ed. S. R. Cattley, 8 vols. (1837–41) • J. G. Nichols and J. Bruce, eds., *Wills from Doctors' Commons*, CS, old ser., 83 (1863), 46 • N. Orme, *Education in the west of England, 1066–1548* (1976), 94, 100, 102, 112–13 • T. F. Kirby, *Winchester scholars: a list of the wardens, fellows, and scholars of … Winchester College* (1888), 116 • S. L. Greenslade, 'The faculty of theology', *Hist. U. Oxf. 3: Colleg. univ.*, 295–334, esp. 316 • J. G. Nichols, ed., *Narratives of the days of the Reformation*, CS, old ser., 77 (1859), 55 • A. Walsham, *Church papists* (1993), 23 n. 6 • A. O. Meyer, *England and the Catholic church under Queen Elizabeth*, trans. J. R. McKee (1916); repr. with introduction by J. Bossy (1967), 475–8
Archives BL, Lansdowne MS 981, fol. 118r
Wealth at death 1766 florins, excl. property in England: de Vocht, 'Thomas Harding'

Harding, Thomas (*d.* 1648), church historian, is of obscure origins. He attended St John's College, Cambridge, where he graduated BA early in 1605, and proceeded MA in 1608 (incorporated at Oxford in 1611) and BD in 1629. He was appointed second master of Westminster School in 1610, and served until in 1622 he became rector of Souldern, Oxfordshire, a position under the patronage of his Cambridge college from 1623. In 1625 he married, by licence dated 14 May, Joyce Neile, *née* Stapleton (*c.*1600–1650), widow of William Neile (*d.* 1624), chapter clerk of Westminster Abbey, and daughter of William Stapleton of Littywood, Staffordshire. The couple were praised in their epitaphs for their piety, charity, and hospitality; the parsonage at Souldern was rebuilt during their incumbency. Harding was renowned for his command of the Greek language, but chiefly for his unpublished history of church and state affairs, 'Annals of church affairs', which relates especially to England for the eight hundred years prior to 1626 (CUL, MS 2609). A committee of the House of Commons licensed and recommended it for publication in 1641, yet this, as with several efforts made after Harding's death, did not come to fruition. About 1645 Harding was said to have been sequestered from his living. He died on 10 October 1648 and was buried at Souldern, as his epitaph put it, 'in the tyme of the great Revolution and change of Church and State … a true sonne of the church and professor of the auncient Catholique faith'. His widow died at Hart Hall, Oxford, on 28 May 1650 and was buried in the chancel of the university church, St Mary's.

E. T. BRADLEY, *rev.* PETER SHERLOCK

Sources *Historical and descriptive notices of the parish of Souldern, Oxfordshire* (1887), 16, 28 • A. Wood, *Survey of the antiquities of the city of Oxford*, ed. A. Clark, 3, OHS, 37 (1899), 112 • J. L. Chester, ed., *The marriage, baptismal, and burial registers of the collegiate church or abbey of St Peter, Westminster*, Harleian Society, 10 (1876), 122–3 • Foster, *Alum. Oxon.* • Venn, *Alum. Cant.* • F. Peck, ed., *Desiderata curiosa*, new edn, 2 vols. in 1 (1779), 503 • *Walker rev.*, 297 • funeral monument, Souldern church

Archives CUL, 'Annals of church affairs', Add. MS 2609

Harding, William (1792–1886), antiquary and army officer, third son of Robert Harding (*d.* 1804) of Upcott, Pilton, Barnstaple, Devon, and his wife, Dionisia, daughter of Sir Bourchier Wrey, bt, of Tawstock, was born on 16 August 1792. He was educated at Blundell's School, Tiverton, from 1801 to 1807, and became an ensign in the North Devon militia. He became an ensign in the 5th foot in 1812, and a lieutenant in the 95th rifles in 1813. He served in the Peninsular War from August 1812 to the end of the campaign, including the siege of Burgos, capture of Madrid, and battles of Vitoria, Pyrenees, Nivelle, Nive, Orthez, and Toulouse. He subsequently received the Peninsular medal and clasps. He became captain of the 58th foot in 1823, major unattached in 1826, and retired as lieutenant-colonel by the sale of his commissions, having first exchanged to full pay in the 2nd foot in 1841.

After his retirement from the service, Harding lived for some years at Tiverton and then at Exeter. He wrote an excellent *History of Tiverton* (2 vols., 1847), which appears to have been his only published work. He was a magistrate, a fellow of the Geological Society, and a member of some local societies. He died at his home, Upcott, on 13 January 1886. His extensive manuscript compilations on Devon and Cornwall were deposited in the North Devon Athenaeum Library, Barnstaple.

H. M. CHICHESTER, *rev.* IAN MAXTED

Sources Burke, *Gen. GB* • *Army List* • *Annual Register* (1886) • J. R. Chanter, 'Report on the Harding collection of manuscripts … relating to Devon and Cornwall', *Report and Transactions of the Devonshire Association*, 20 (1888), 49–68 • A. Fisher, ed., *The register of Blundell's School* (privately printed, Exeter, 1904) • Boase, *Mod. Eng. biog.* • *CGPLA Eng. & Wales* (1886)

Archives Devon Athenaeum, Barnstaple | Bodl. Oxf., Phillipps-Robinson MSS

Wealth at death £11,968 6s. 10d.: probate, 12 Feb 1886, *CGPLA Eng. & Wales*

Hardinge, Alexander Henry Louis, second Baron Hardinge of Penshurst (1894–1960), private secretary to Edward VIII and George VI, was born on 17 May 1894 at the British embassy, Paris, the younger son of Charles *Hardinge, later first Baron Hardinge of Penshurst (1858–1944), diplomatist, and his wife, Winifred Celina Sturt (1868–1914). He was educated at Harrow School (1907–11) and Trinity College, Cambridge, where he was recalled by a contemporary as 'perhaps the wildest of our set' (Rhodes-James, 129). His early wish to be an architect was not fulfilled. Instead he followed his father into the diplomatic service. His mother died in 1914, the same year as that in which his elder brother was killed in the First World War. Hardinge himself served in France and Belgium with the Grenadier Guards from 1916 to 1918, was badly wounded, won the MC, and became adjutant of the 4th battalion. Afterwards his health was never robust. He formally retired from the army in 1935. On 8 February 1921 he married Helen Mary (1901–1979), the only daughter of Lord Edward Herbert Gascoyne-*Cecil (1867–1918); they had two daughters and one son, George Edward Charles Hardinge (1921–1997), who succeeded him as third baron.

In 1920 Hardinge was appointed assistant private secretary to George V, serving under Arthur Bigge, Lord Stamfordham. Under the latter's tutelage he was trained in the unchanging, if reassuring, ways of George V's court, whose routine was inflexible, and he became 'the most correct of courtiers' (Rhodes-James, 129). Stamfordham believed that the king's private secretary worked directly with the sovereign, and the other private secretaries were not always taken into his confidence. Hardinge followed in this tradition. After the death of Stamfordham in 1931, Lord (Clive) Wigram became private secretary and Hardinge moved into quarters at St James's Palace in London, and in the Winchester Tower in Windsor Castle. He was appointed MVO (1925), CVO (1931), and CB (1934), and served George V until the king's death in January 1936.

In May 1936 Edward VIII appointed him private secretary in succession to the retiring Wigram after the new king's first choice, Godfrey Thomas—his private secretary as prince of Wales—had turned down the post. The elevation of Hardinge, who was sworn of the privy council in October, surprised those who thought that the new king would sweep away the more traditional of his father's courtiers. Unsurprisingly, Hardinge found the new monarch's informality uncongenial; particularly distressing for him was the king's lack of attention to official papers and relaxed attitude to their security, along with his failure to keep regular hours. The great matter of contention, however, was Edward VIII's friendship with Mrs Simpson; Hardinge later wrote of his concern in the early months of 1936 about her 'overwhelming and inexorable' influence (Donaldson, 184). When her intention to divorce Ernest

Simpson, and the king's determination to marry her, became plain, he attempted (initially, with little success) to galvanize Stanley Baldwin, the prime minister, into taking action. In October he wrote independently to Lord Tweedsmuir, the governor-general of Canada, to ascertain opinion there. When, in the same month, the anonymous 'Britannicus' letter was written to the editor of *The Times* by a British subject resident in New York, accusing the king of being 'an incalculable liability' to Britain's image abroad (Hardinge, *Loyal to Three Kings*, 121), Hardinge saw at once that it was his duty to warn him directly. He wrote to King Edward on 13 November, telling him that the silence of the British press on his relationship with Mrs Simpson was not going to be maintained; that the prime minister was meeting senior members of the government to discuss the matter; and that the resignation of the government would lead to a general election in which the sovereign's private life would be the main issue. To avoid damage to the crown, he urged the king to persuade Mrs Simpson 'to go abroad *without further delay*' (Rhodes-James, 133).

The king did not reply, but acknowledged the letter by telephone and asked to see the prime minister and others. Soon afterwards negotiations began which culminated in his abdication on 11 December. Hardinge, though still in charge of the king's normal business, was not asked for his advice, nor did the king take him into his confidence. The king channelled all his dealings with the government over the abdication through his confidant Walter Monckton, with whom Hardinge was also in touch. Hardinge, for his part, found the conduct of the king—especially in regard to the distress caused to his mother, Queen Mary— to be excusable only on the grounds of temporary derangement, a view wholly supported by Queen Mary herself.

Hardinge's prime duty during the abdication crisis was to place the interests of the crown as an institution before the wishes of an individual monarch—once Edward VIII's position as king had become untenable—and eventually to facilitate the smooth succession of the king's brother. Following the publication of memoirs by the duke and duchess of Windsor in the 1950s that showed his conduct in an unfavourable light, Hardinge went into print with his version of events in *The Times* (29 Nov 1958); after his death, his wife published a longer apologia, *Loyal to Three Kings* (1967). Both rebutted the charge that he had been a tool of Baldwin, of Geoffrey Dawson (the editor of *The Times*), and of Cosmo Lang (the archbishop of Canterbury) in a plot to remove the king; it was admitted that Hardinge had shown his November letter to the king to Dawson, but it was also asserted that its conception and wording were his alone.

Hardinge was retained in his post by George VI, and resumed his duties after taking a three-month recuperative break in India early in 1937. He was appointed GCVO and KCB that year. He had known the new king for many years, while Queen Elizabeth had been an intimate friend of both his wife and his sister, Diamond. It was he who had first warned the then duke of York about the possibility of his brother's abdication. Yet their relationship was not easy. Hardinge was astonished to discover the extent of the king's ignorance about public affairs, the business of the sovereign, and the constitutional limitations of crown authority. Hardinge's advice to the king was crucial, especially in the early years of the reign. In the first few years almost every public action, message, or statement from the king originated with Hardinge. But—once more—he found it difficult to adapt to a new king's working practices; George VI's failure to give him briefings after important meetings (as his father had invariably done) being a particular source of frustration. There were also political differences: the king supported the appeasement policy of the Chamberlain ministry, Hardinge did not. These differences led the king to turn to others for advice on political and constitutional matters, though after the German invasion of Bohemia and Moravia in March 1939 he paid more heed to his private secretary's view of international events. Hardinge's advice may have been crucial in the fortunate decision not to honour Chamberlain—as had been mooted—in the wake of the Munich agreement. How far he steered the king towards accepting Churchill as prime minister is a matter of dispute; he certainly acted as a bridge to anti-appeasement opinion, and perhaps herein lay his greatest achievement.

By the time of the king's morale-boosting visit to the troops in north Africa in June 1943, on which Hardinge accompanied him, he was already tired. The king and Queen Elizabeth were now more confident, and in a sense Hardinge had to go. Immediately on his return from north Africa, Hardinge was met at Northolt airport by Lascelles, who presented him with a letter of resignation. Lascelles was angry because he had felt unable to conduct the business of the private secretaries' office in Hardinge's absence. Hardinge maintained that he was with the king and thus still in control. But though Hardinge questioned Lascelles's resigning in the middle of a war, he realized that he could not work without Lascelles, and that, in any event, he would soon retire, his health being poor. A lengthy and acrimonious exchange of letters took place between the two private secretaries, with the eventual result that Hardinge resigned. George VI welcomed the opportunity of replacing him, noting in his diary: 'I know I shall miss him in many ways, but I feel happier now it is over' (Rhodes-James, 248).

Hardinge succeeded to his father's peerage in 1944. In retirement he was an active governor of St Bartholomew's Hospital in London and of the King's School, Canterbury, and he played a prominent role at the coronation of Elizabeth II. He died of liver cancer at his home, Oakfield, Penshurst, Kent, on 29 May 1960, and was buried at nearby Fordcombe church on 2 June.

Hardinge perceived his role as a lonely one: as the only person solely concerned with the interests of the sovereign, the private secretary must 'plough a lonely furrow', he once wrote (Bogdanor, 210). He was certainly hardworking, persevering, and fastidious, if at times inflexible. It might be argued that it was precisely this moral rectitude, as applied to the great issues of the time, that made him of greatest service to the institution of monarchy in the long term. Historians have tended to judge him harshly, giving insufficient credit to his undoubted integrity or to his achievements in difficult circumstances.

HUGO VICKERS

Sources H. Vickers, unpublished document on Alexander Hardinge, Royal Arch. · private information (2004) [Lady Murray, Sir John Johnston, Lady Johnston, George Edward Charles Hardinge, son] · papers of Alexander Hardinge, priv. coll. · A. H. L. Hardinge, correspondence, Royal Arch., Hardinge papers · H. Hardinge, *Loyal to three kings* (1967) · Harrow register · F. Donaldson, *Edward VIII* (1974) · P. Ziegler, *King Edward VIII: the official biography* (1990) · V. Bogdanor, *The monarchy and the constitution* (1995) · R. Rhodes-James, *A spirit undaunted: the political role of George VI* (1998) · S. Bradford, *George VI*, 2nd edn (1991)
Archives CUL, corresp. with his father · NRA, priv. coll., corresp. (some as royal private secretary), notes on Edward VIII's abdication, and papers · priv. colls., private papers · Royal Arch. | Bodl. Oxf., corresp. with Lord Monckton · NL Aus., corresp. with first earl of Gowrie · Nuffield Oxf., corresp. with Lord Mottistone · PRO, corresp. with Lord Ismay | FILM BFI NFTVA, news footage
Likenesses W. Stoneman, photograph, 1937, NPG · photographs, repro. in Hardinge, *Loyal to three kings*
Wealth at death £35,316 15s. 8d.: probate, 28 Feb 1961, CGPLA Eng. & Wales

Hardinge, Sir Arthur Edward (1828–1892), army officer, born on 2 March 1828, was the second son of Henry *Hardinge, first Viscount Hardinge (1785–1856), and Lady Emily Jane (1789–1865), seventh daughter of Robert *Stewart, first marquess of Londonderry, and widow of John James. Charles Stewart *Hardinge, second Viscount Hardinge, was his elder brother. Arthur was educated at Eton College, and commissioned as ensign in the 41st regiment on 7 June 1844. He exchanged to the 53rd regiment on 28 June, and in July went to India as aide-de-camp to his father, appointed governor-general. Hardinge served in the First Anglo-Sikh War, and was present at the battles of Mudki, Ferozeshahr, and Sobraon. He was mentioned in dispatches, and obtained a lieutenancy in the 80th regiment on 22 December 1845 and a company in the 16th regiment on 1 June 1849. On 22 June he exchanged to the Coldstream Guards as lieutenant and captain. He passed through the senior department at Sandhurst, and obtained a certificate.

Hardinge served on the quartermaster-general's staff in the Crimea from 8 March 1854 to 25 June 1856. He was present at the Alma with the 1st division as deputy assistant quartermaster-general, and was mentioned in dispatches. He was also at Balaklava and Inkerman and the fall of Sevastopol. After receiving a brevet majority on 12 December 1854, he became captain and lieutenant-colonel in his regiment on 20 February 1855. He was awarded the Légion d'honneur (fifth class) and the Mejidiye (fifth class), and was made CB on 2 January 1857. On 25 May 1858 he became brevet colonel. On 30 December 1858 Hardinge married Mary Georgiana Frances, eldest daughter of Lieutenant-Colonel Augustus Frederick Ellis, second son of the first Lord Seaford. They had three daughters and a son, Arthur Henry *Hardinge (1859–1933), Foreign Office official and ambassador.

Hardinge was assistant quartermaster-general at Shorncliffe and Dublin from 1 October 1856 to 29 July 1858, when he was appointed equerry to Prince Albert, on whose death in 1861 he became equerry to the queen. His subsequent military career lacked any active service or notable achievement. Following various promotions, appointments in the United Kingdom and India, and honours, he was promoted general in 1883. He commanded the Bombay army from 1881 to 1885, and was governor of Gibraltar from 1886 to 1890.

Hardinge died at 10 Belvedere, in Weymouth, on 15 July 1892 from injuries he had received in a carriage accident there nine days before. He was buried at Fordcombe church, near Penshurst, Kent.

E. M. LLOYD, rev. JAMES FALKNER

Sources *The Times* (16 July 1892) · *The Times* (21 July 1892) · *Army List* · E. Lodge, *Peerage, baronetage, knightage and companionage of the British empire*, 81st edn, 3 vols. (1912) · *Hart's Army List* · *LondG* (23 Feb 1846) · *LondG* (1 April 1846) · *LondG* (10 Oct 1854) · CGPLA Eng. & Wales (1892)
Archives Balliol Oxf., corresp. with Sir Robert Morier · BL OIOC, letters to Sir James Fergusson, MS Eur. E 214 · Bodl. Oxf., corresp. with Lord Kimberley
Likenesses Hanhart, lithograph, repro. in *Household Brigade Journal* (1877) · Morris & Co., lithograph, The Convent, Gibraltar · photogravure photograph, BM
Wealth at death £4582 4s. 9d.: administration, 1 Sept 1892, CGPLA Eng. & Wales

Hardinge, Sir Arthur Henry (1859–1933), diplomatist, was born on 12 October 1859 at 10 Chester Square, London, the only son of General Sir Arthur Edward *Hardinge (1828–1892) and his wife, Lady Mary Georgiana Frances Ellis (1837–1917). As a boy he served as a page to Queen Victoria, to whom his father was an equerry. He re-established links with the court through his marriage on 4 November 1899 to Alexandra Mina (b. 1870/71), goddaughter of the princess of Wales, and daughter of Major-General Sir Arthur Ellis, a member of the household of Edward VII, who became godfather to their second son. The couple also had a daughter.

At Eton College, where he was known as Hoppy for his peculiar gait, Hardinge was remembered for the elegance of his Latin verse. At Balliol College, which he entered in 1876, he took a second class in classical moderations, but followed with a first in modern history and, in 1881, a fellowship at All Souls. Renowned for his sparkling wit, he had a lasting affection for Oxford, timing home leaves wherever possible to attend college meetings and gaudies at All Souls, and corresponding on college business with Warden Anson until he reluctantly relinquished his fellowship in 1894.

Hardinge entered the Foreign Office in July 1880, before he had taken his degree, with a nomination from Lord Salisbury, who remained a patron. As an undergraduate he had travelled widely. He subsequently seized every opportunity to travel in remote places and was privately commended by Salisbury for his political reporting. Fluent in French from an early age, his success in Foreign Office language examinations provided welcome additions to his salary.

After spells in the Turkish and German departments of the Foreign Office, Hardinge's first overseas appointment in 1883 was to Madrid, under Sir Robert Morier. In 1885, following a short period in England as a précis writer to Lord Salisbury, Hardinge followed Morier to St Petersburg as his private secretary and subsequently travelled extensively in Russia and central Asia. There followed a series of appointments to Constantinople, under Sir William White, in 1887; to Bucharest in 1890; as a companion to the tsarevich (the future Nicholas II) to India, where he crossed swords with the redoubtable Lord Harris, governor of Bombay, for which he was commended by Lord Salisbury; and to Cairo in 1891 under Sir Evelyn Baring. Of these, Constantinople made such an impression that it became his ambition to become ambassador to the Porte. When the post went to another (Gerald Lowther) in 1906 his disappointment was such that he nearly resigned, but was dissuaded by Curzon, an old Balliol friend.

Before this, however, in 1894, Hardinge had been appointed to Zanzibar, as political agent and consul-general, a post which he had accepted with delight. To this was added in 1895 the position of commissioner for the new East Africa Protectorate. The administration of the little known territory between Mombasa and Lake Victoria, acquired for the strategic purpose of building a railway to Uganda, was a challenge to which Hardinge rose with enthusiasm. Whether defeating an Arab rebellion at the coast—and then championing the cause of dispossessed Arab slave owners—or demonstrating the efficacy of a maxim gun to potentially hostile 'chiefs', Hardinge revelled in his independence and freedom from protocol. The railway having passed through the protectorate, and rudimentary administration having been established, Hardinge left Mombasa in October 1900 amid general acclamation. The demands of more traditional diplomacy returned when he took up his next appointment, as minister to Persia, later that year. This gave him further opportunities for travel, including a visit to the gulf with Curzon, now viceroy of India, but this period also saw the early death of his first son.

Summoned to Balmoral when on leave in 1905, Hardinge recounted in his memoirs that, on the urgings of his father-in-law 'anxious for the sake of our two children and his daughter's health', he was invited by Edward VII to become minister at Brussels. His heart 'was and remained for long afterwards in the Mohammedan East' but 'domestic considerations overcame my personal preferences' and 'I decided to accept the King's offer' (Hardinge, *Diplomatist in the East* 350). From that time, it seems (to quote from a contemporary) 'he was not quite in the same bright spirit we had known', and it became clear that he was not to reach the highest positions in the service that had earlier been predicted (*The Times*, 29 Dec 1933). Hardinge's European posts after he left Brussels in 1911—minister at Lisbon from 1911 to 1913 and ambassador at Madrid from 1913 to 1920—seem to have become increasingly onerous. He retired in 1920, having been knighted in 1897 and made KCB in 1904 and GCMG in 1910.

The deaths of his two sons, in separate and tragic accidents, and his own failing health marred Hardinge's later years. His *Life of Lord Carnarvon* is thought by some to have been altered by another hand before publication in 1925. His own memoirs, *A Diplomatist in Europe* (1927) and *A Diplomatist in the East* (1928), gave excellent individual portraits of his colleagues, and flashes of his old humour. He died at his home, 31 York Avenue, Mortlake, Surrey, on 27 December 1933 and was buried in the churchyard of Fordcombe church, near Penshurst, Kent.

G. H. MUNGEAM

Sources A. H. Hardinge, *A diplomatist in Europe* (1927) · A. H. Hardinge, *A diplomatist in the East* (1928) · G. H. Mungeam, *British rule in Kenya, 1895–1912: the establishment of administration in the East Africa Protectorate* (1966) · *The Times* (29 Dec 1933) · CAC Cam., Cecil Spring-Rice MSS · All Souls Oxf., Anson MSS · King's AC Cam., Oscar Browning MSS · Hatfield House, Hertfordshire, third marquess of Salisbury MSS · CUL, Charles Hardinge, first Baron Hardinge of Penshurst MSS · Balliol Oxf., Sir Robert Morier MSS · letters to J. A. L. Riley, LPL · letters to Sir William White, PRO, FO 364/1–11 · *CGPLA Eng. & Wales* (1934) · Boase, *Mod. Eng. biog.* · m. cert. · d. cert.

Archives CUL, corresp. and papers | All Souls Oxf., letters to Sir William Anson · Balliol Oxf., corresp. with Sir Robert Morier · BL, literary papers relating to Lord Carnarvon, Add. MSS 61096–61100 · CAC Cam., corresp. with Sir Cecil Spring-Rice · CUL, first Baron Hardinge MSS · Hatfield House, Hertfordshire, Salisbury MSS · King's AC Cam., letters to Oscar Browning · LPL, letters to Athelstan Riley · Lpool RO, corresp. with seventeenth earl of Derby · PRO, letters to Sir William White, FO 364/1–11

Likenesses portrait, repro. in G. H. Mungeam, *British rule in Kenya*; formerly in possession of the Ministry of Public Buildings and Works, London

Wealth at death £2009 18s. 4d.: probate, 31 Jan 1934, *CGPLA Eng. & Wales*

Hardinge, Charles, first Baron Hardinge of Penshurst (1858–1944), diplomatist and viceroy of India, was born at Dufferin Lodge, Highgate, Middlesex, on 20 June 1858, the second son of Charles Stewart *Hardinge, second Viscount Hardinge (1822–1894) of South Park, Penshurst, Kent, and his wife, Lady Lavinia (d. 1864), daughter of George Charles Bingham, third earl of Lucan, one of the field marshals tainted by the 'Valley of Death' disaster of the Crimean War. Hardinge's other grandfather, Henry *Hardinge, first Viscount Hardinge, had also been a field marshal and from 1844 to 1848 was governor-general of India, a post to which his grandson aspired from an early age. It was not an unnatural ambition. The family had little wealth or land and knew only the professional route to acquiring honours; service to the nation was bred into the Hardinge boys.

Education, early career, and marriage Charles Hardinge, only six when his mother died, was raised by his father in a well-meaning if austere fashion at South Park before being sent, at age ten, to Cheam School, and in 1873 to Harrow, where he played cricket for the school at Lord's. A childhood hernia having disqualified him from the navy, he entered Trinity College, Cambridge, in 1876. He graduated with third class honours in the mathematical tripos in 1880. In the same year he joined the Foreign Office, attached initially to the German department. He served as attaché at Constantinople under George Joachim (later

Charles Hardinge, first Baron Hardinge of Penshurst (1858–1944), by Sir William Orpen, 1919

Viscount) Goschen and subsequently under Lord Dufferin (1881–4), as third secretary at Berlin (1885), and as second secretary at Washington (1885–6), from which last post he returned after a prolonged bout of malaria. After six months in Whitehall in the Eastern department, he went as secretary to Sofia (1887–9), and from there to Constantinople again, as senior second secretary under Sir William Arthur White.

Throughout these years he had been courting his first cousin Winifred Selina, nicknamed Bena (1868–1914), daughter of Henry Gerard Sturt, first Baron Alington, of Crichel, Dorset, a racing magnate and close friend of Edward, prince of Wales. Family opposition to the match was high on account of their cousinhood and Hardinge's relative indigence, but on 17 April 1890 they were married, and when Hardinge returned to Constantinople, Winifred went with him. It was a successful partnership. Hardinge quickly came to rely on his wife's loyal affection, and Winifred's beauty and good humour softened the impact of Hardinge's physical stiffness and off-putting regard for dignity and show. Moreover, her personal friendship with the princess of Wales (the future Queen Alexandra), whose intervention with Lord Alington had expedited their marriage, thrust Hardinge into an exceptionally well-connected circle. Winifred joked about her contacts, but there was some truth in her playful assessment of her husband's subsequent success:

> My family knows Lord Salisbury well and, as everyone knows, Lord Salisbury cannot remember names. So each time there's a new post to be filled, Lord Salisbury says to one of his staff: 'What's the name of that diplomat Winifred

Sturt married?'—and it's still Charlie Hardinge, so then he gets the post. (Hardinge, *Loyal to Three Kings*, 18)

In September 1892 Hardinge was transferred to Bucharest as chargé d'affaires (1892–3), where he negotiated the marriage of Ferdinand, crown prince of Romania, with the seventeen-year-old Princess Marie of Saxe-Coburg and Gotha, granddaughter of Queen Victoria. It was an advantageous match in more ways than one, for when the lonely princess asked for Winifred as her companion, the princess of Wales rescued the couple from permanent Romanian exile by claiming Winifred as her own lady-in-waiting. From Bucharest, Hardinge also negotiated an extradition treaty between Britain and Romania and procured the entry of British cotton goods, previously banned, into Romania. The trading agreement was not an isolated achievement; throughout his career Hardinge was considerably ahead of his colleagues in ranking British commercial needs high in his understanding of a diplomatist's duties.

In 1893, at the request of his old chief Lord Dufferin, Hardinge was appointed head of the chancery in the Paris embassy. In 1895 Lord Rosebery obtained a CB for him and in 1896, encouraged by this early recognition, he swapped Parisian elegance for promotion and became the first secretary to the legation at Tehran, a post which schooled him in Britain's long-running rivalry in Asia with Russia. He had by now earned a reputation as a sound, hardworking career diplomat. Something of his professionalism can be seen in the delight of J. R. Preece, British consul at Esfahan, at having Hardinge for his boss. To Lord Curzon at the Foreign Office, Preece enthused:

> Hardinge is without exception the very best chief I've yet served under … for the first time, I know where I am and what I can do and how far I may expect to be backed. Questions are answered and business is not allowed to take care of itself. It is a real pleasure to work under such a man. (BL OIOC, Curzon MSS, MS Eur. F111/64, fol. 26)

While Hardinge expected to enjoy every privilege due to seniority in the Foreign Office, he had few qualms about trampling on the like claims of others, and in 1898 he accepted Lord Salisbury's offer of the secretaryship of the embassy in St Petersburg, even though it meant leapfrogging over seventeen senior colleagues. Anglo-Russian relations were poor, exacerbated by competition over Persia and Afghanistan and by the Russian press's delight at Britain's early discomfiture in the Second South African War, but the Hardinges were popular at the imperial court, and Hardinge was already sufficiently worried about German expansion, and Russian fears of the same, to press slowly for Russian recognition of their common, anti-German interests.

The Foreign Office and Edward VII In 1903 Hardinge accepted nomination as one of the four under-secretaries at the Foreign Office. It was an unlikely appointment which had been pressed upon the foreign secretary, Lord Lansdowne, by *Edward VII and was also supported by Hardinge's predecessor in the job, Sir Francis Bertie, who was a close friend and shared with him an ambition to transform the Foreign Office servants from their traditional position of clerks and copyists into policy advisers of real weight. The king further favoured Hardinge by appointing him his adviser on his first major diplomatic initiative, a state visit to Portugal. Again, it was an unusual choice, as a roving sovereign was usually accompanied by a cabinet minister, not a civil servant, and Hardinge embarked on the tour in March 1903 knowing that Lansdowne was offended by his unexpected elevation. The tour was a grand success, not least for Edward's impromptu decision to visit France and attempt a *rapprochement* in Anglo-French relations. Much to the surprise of the cabinet, the king's genial courting of the French laid the diplomatic ground for the Anglo-French agreement of 1904, and, crucially, tipped the balance in favour of a British pursuit of a Franco-Russian alliance to keep the growing German threat at bay. The king and Hardinge were as one on this policy and Edward ever after treated Hardinge as one of his confidential advisers, letting it be understood that he was not to be posted beyond the continent. For Hardinge honours flowed from the royal tour. In 1904 he was sworn of the privy council and appointed KCMG and KCVO, and in May of that year, only fifteen months after his departure as first secretary, he returned to St Petersburg as ambassador. He arrived in the midst of the war with Japan, with Russian belligerence towards Britain high, especially in the navy which was using the hostilities as an excuse to attack British merchant ships. In October 1904 the crisis deepened when reports were received that Russia's Baltic fleet had fired upon British fishing trawlers off the Dogger Bank in the North Sea, killing several Britons, on the grounds that the fishing vessels had been shielding Japanese torpedo boats. Hardinge's task was a delicate one. He knew that Britain would demand appropriate reparation, but also that pro-war ministers in Russia believed that Britain was secretly aiding her Japanese treaty partner and itched for an excuse to declare outright war on her. Relying heavily on his good relations with Count Lamsdorff, the foreign minister and one of Tsar Nicholas's more peaceable advisers, Hardinge nudged both Russia and Britain towards a mutually face-saving appeal to the Hague tribunal. In this he was ably supported at home by Lansdowne and the king, and was additionally rewarded by the latter, who appointed him GCMG. By early 1905, like most independent observers, he thought that Russian defeat was inevitable, but believed that although this would weaken the value of the Franco-Russian counterweight to Germany it would also make war with Russia over Afghanistan unlikely. With this in mind, Hardinge urged Lansdowne to get the Anglo-Japanese alliance extended (which was done in August 1905), so that at the war's end Britain could face Russia with a stern but friendly offer of alliance, safe in the knowledge that Russia no longer posed much threat in the east.

Permanent under-secretary Hardinge left St Petersburg in January 1906 to become permanent under-secretary of the Foreign Office. The ambassadorship was possibly the high point of his diplomatic career; he had won widespread acclaim as Capability Hardinge and was subsequently judged to have set up the conditions for the Anglo-Russian agreement of 1907. His new post necessitated a huge cut in salary (from £8000 to £2800), but it was mitigated by another mark of honour from the king, who made him GCVO. Moreover, it was an office of real weight. The Foreign Office was now at the peak of its powers and it was accepted that the permanent under-secretary should have a say in policy making, a situation brought about partly by the relative inexperience of the Liberals' foreign secretary, Sir Edward Grey, and also by the king's great respect for Hardinge which had effectively turned him into Britain's ambassador at large. Tours with the King to Spain, Italy, and Russia were accounted political successes, but to Germany less so. Diplomatic niceties aside, Hardinge rarely saw anything of merit in nationalities other than his own, and at the Foreign Office he became the leading exponent of anti-German sentiment.

Viceroy of India In 1910 Hardinge was appointed viceroy of India and raised to the peerage as Baron Hardinge of Penshurst, and was also made GCB, GCSI, and GCIE. The appointment was widely acclaimed, and Lord Curzon, his predecessor-but-one in the post, was especially cheered by the choice, seeing in Hardinge a man to carry on his own thwarted policies. India, however, posed an unfamiliar challenge to Hardinge. His customary approach to problem-solving of relentless, conscientious application was insufficient to see him through the morass of emerging nationalism, sporadic terrorism, and, subsequently, the peculiar circumstances of war. He began well. Although a conservative by temperament, he regretted the aggravation caused by unwinnable sedition trials and pressured the Bengal government to reduce its reliance on repressive legislation. Attempts to foster technical education, to increase the Indianization of the subordinate civil service, and to defend the rights of Indians in South Africa also won him admirers, as did his support for new universities at Aligarh and Benares, Muslim and Hindu institutions respectively. He was wary, however, of addressing the most contentious issue of the day: Curzon's 1905 partition of Bengal which had turned Bengali Hindus against the government and triggered a ferocious campaign of anti-British bombings and assassinations. The new king-emperor, George V, was less cautious. He proposed visiting his Indian empire in December 1911 and wanted a reconciliation with Bengal to feature in the package of boons that he would announce at a durbar in Delhi. Hardinge held out against a reversal of the partition until, in June 1911, his home member, Sir John Jenkins, suggested that the durbar be used to announce the transfer of the imperial capital from Calcutta to Delhi. Hardinge leapt at the idea, for, by taking the capital away from Calcutta, Bengal could be reunified without seeming to reward the Hindus of Bengal for their terrorist agitation. There was a chance too that the Muslims, who by the reunification would lose the majority they had been given in the new province of East Bengal, might be placated by the recognition of the old Mughal capital of Delhi as modern India's premier city. Each idea had been mooted before, but as a package the reunification of Bengal and the transfer of the capital became Hardinge's own scheme, and he now addressed the exhausting arrangements for the durbar with new enthusiasm. Remarkably, news of the scheme was not leaked before George V proclaimed it in regal splendour at the Red Fort on 12 December 1911. Even Curzon was not told of the scheme beforehand, and while the British community in Calcutta expressed predictable outrage at their city's downgrading, this was as nothing to his howls of betrayal over the reversal of the partition. Henceforth, in public and private, Curzon sniped at Hardinge's viceroyalty, destroying their friendship and embittering their future together at the Foreign Office.

The building of Delhi, and the viceroy's near escape Whatever the criticism, Hardinge was determined that the new capital would succeed, deftly heading off London's not unreasonable worries about the cost of the move. He chose the exact location for the city, 3 miles to the south of old Delhi, and he kept a close, sometimes overbearing, watch on the principal architects—Edwin Lutyens and Herbert Baker—neither of whom was his own choice. By December 1912 the government was ready to make the formal move, and on the 23rd of that month Hardinge arrived in state at Delhi railway station and, with Winifred, mounted a caparisoned elephant to process to the Red Fort. The atmosphere was celebratory and, by Hardinge's own request, security was light. Suddenly, from the rooftop of a bank in Chandni Chauk, a member of a Bengali terrorist cell lobbed a devastating needle bomb into the viceroy's howdah, killing instantly one of his servants and ripping an 8 inch gash in the viceroy's back and neck, exposing the shoulder blade beneath the shredded muscles. Fading in and out of consciousness, Hardinge handed his blood-stained speech to an aide and ordered the ceremonies to go ahead as planned, before being rushed to the new viceregal lodge for surgery.

Remarkably, within two months, and driven almost purely by will, Hardinge was back at work. But his spirit never recovered; years of Machiavellian politicking in the courts of Europe had perhaps blinded him to the fact that peasants too could dissemble, and his bewilderment at the ingratitude of India corroded his confidence. Worse was to come. In July 1914 Winifred died suddenly in London, after an operation to remove a malignant tumour, and in the following December his elder son, Edd, succumbed to wounds received in early fighting in France. (A nephew and seven of his aides-de-camp were also to be sacrificed to the war.) Hardinge's daughter Diamond, a sparkling, good-humoured teenager, stepped into her mother's shoes as vicereine. She lifted the gloom of the viceregal residence with delightfully irreverent practical jokes, including the making of a floured apple-pie bed for the maharaja of Gwalior, but Hardinge was inconsolable. For years no-one dared mention Winifred's name in his presence and it was only his iron sense of duty that kept him at his post for a year after the expiry of his term.

The First World War and Mesopotamia It is against this background that Hardinge's failure of judgment over Mesopotamia needs to be seen. From the beginning of his viceroyalty Hardinge's military policy suffered from inconsistencies. The European diplomat in him warned that war with Germany, and probably Turkey also, was inevitable and that Indian soldiers would eventually have to be committed to the Middle East, but in matters of military reform he acted with the government of India's traditional concern for economy and concentrated his efforts on trimming what he saw as the bloated inefficiency of the Indian army. When war broke out in August 1914 he pressed for Indian soldiers to be sent to France to fight alongside Europeans, arguing with prescience that the rejection of the military colour bar would boost India's contribution to the war effort more than any other act. He was initially doubtful about the move to commit Indian troops to the Middle East, but after the first successes of the Mesopotamian expeditionary force in 1914–15, he became convinced of the 'prestige value' of a big victory such as the taking of Baghdad. His own pre-war knowledge of the Indian army's deficiencies should have led him to query the optimistic projections of the commander-in-chief of 'force D', General Sir John Nixon, but Hardinge admired Nixon as 'a great thruster' (Goold, 'Lord Hardinge and the Mesopotamia expedition', 933), and in October 1915 the representations of Nixon and Hardinge together overcame the cabinet's reservations about authorizing a further advance up the Tigris to Baghdad. One month later, at the disastrous battle of Ctesiphon on 22–4 November 1915, General Charles Townshend lost 4600 of his 14,000 men and was forced to retreat to Kut-al-Amara. There the remnants of force D's 6th (Indian) division, desperately weakened by disease and exhaustion, remained in a state of siege until they finally surrendered to the Turks in April 1916. The hopes of a great victory had been turned into humiliation at the hands of 'Orientals'.

Return from India and final years Hardinge had left India just weeks before the awful climax of the Mesopotamian campaign and, after chairing the royal commission into the causes of the Irish uprising of Easter 1916, returned to his old post of permanent under-secretary of the Foreign Office. He was unhappy and frustrated in the job; under the premiership of Lloyd George it was an office in which civil servants no longer had the power they had enjoyed before the war. Increasingly shrill and authoritarian, he regarded the official commission of inquiry into the Mesopotamian disaster as a Labour plot to destabilize the government. The commission's report, published in June 1917, was critical of Hardinge's role in the affair and Hardinge duly offered his resignation, but he bitterly resented what he saw as unjust and vindictive criticism. His resignation was not accepted (although Curzon let it be known that he thought he should have gone anyway), and it did not ultimately prevent him from being appointed, in November 1920, as ambassador to Paris. This final posting, a long-cherished goal of Hardinge's, allowed his talents for diplomacy to shine again, effecting some repair to his damaged reputation. In prickly, occasionally farcical, encounters with Curzon, he managed to soften the Foreign Office's policy towards France, but in December 1922, faced with a climate of deteriorating Anglo-French relations, he decided to retire. For all their personal animosity, Curzon had respected Hardinge as ambassador and was unexpectedly fulsome in bidding him farewell from the job.

After Paris, Hardinge settled at Oakfield, a house he had purchased near South Park. He had few interests outside his work and his retirement activities were semi-political and diplomatic ones. He represented India at the League of Nations in Geneva in 1923–4, was sometime chairman of the Kent Conservative Association, and enrolled himself as a special constable during the general strike. He revisited India in 1931–2 at the invitation of the viceroy, Lord Irwin, a trip which prompted him to publish a book of Indian hunting reminiscences, *On Hill and Plain* (1933). Always reserved, he had only a few close friends, and the picture of his latter years is one of increasing loneliness, especially following the death in 1927 of his beloved daughter Diamond. The two memoirs which, after much revision, he authorized for posthumous publication, *Old Diplomacy* (1947) and *My Indian Years, 1910–16* (1948), proved to be chiefly catalogues of achievement and self-justification, and confirmed what many of his former colleagues saw in him as an unbecoming degree of self-regard. The books stand today as testimony to the totality of the transformation of diplomacy effected by the First World War. Even at the time of their publication they appeared to refer to a bygone age.

Hardinge died at Oakfield, aged eighty-six, on 2 August 1944, and was buried in the grave of his wife at Fordcombe churchyard, Kent, on 5 August. The peerage descended to the only one of his three children to survive him, his younger son Alec, Sir Alexander Henry Louis *Hardinge (1894–1960), who achieved the unusual distinction of serving as private secretary to three kings in succession: George V, Edward VIII, and George VI.

KATHERINE PRIOR

Sources B. C. Busch, *Hardinge of Penshurst: a study in the old diplomacy* (1980) · J. D. Goold, '"Old diplomacy": the diplomatic career of Lord Hardinge, 1910–1922', PhD diss., U. Cam., 1976 · D. Goold, 'Lord Hardinge and the Mesopotamia expedition and inquiry, 1914–1917', *HJ*, 19 (1976), 919–45 · H. Hardinge, *Loyal to three kings* (1967) · Z. S. Steiner, *The foreign office and foreign policy, 1898–1914* (1969) · D. Gilmour, *Curzon* (1994) · *The Times* (3 Aug 1944), 8 · *The Times* (7 Aug 1944), 6 · G. Plumtree, *Edward VII* (1995) · BL OIOC, Curzon MSS, MS Eur. F111/64 · *DNB* · C. Hardinge, *Old diplomacy* (1947)

Archives BL OIOC, papers and memorabilia as viceroy, MS Eur. E 389 · CUL, department of manuscripts and university archives, corresp. and papers · PRO, corresp. and papers, FO 800/192 | BL, corresp. with A. J. Balfour · BL, Bertie MSS · BL, corresp. with Lord Gladstone, Add. MSS 46075–46077 · BL, corresp. with Sir Ralph Paget, Add. MS 51253 · BL OIOC, Butler MSS · BL OIOC, corresp. with Sir Harcourt Butler, MS Eur. F 116 · BL OIOC, corresp. with Lord Curzon, MSS Eur. F 111–112 · BL OIOC, corresp. with Sir William Lawrence, MS Eur. F 143 · BL OIOC, letters to Lord Morley, MS Eur. D 573 · BL OIOC, corresp. with Sir G. Fleetwood Wilson, MS Eur. E 224 · Bodl. Oxf., corresp. with Herbert Asquith · Bodl. Oxf., letters to James Bryce · Bodl. Oxf., corresp. with Lord Rumbold · CAC Cam., corresp. with Sir Cecil Spring-Rice · Cumbria AS, Carlisle, letters to Lord Howard of Penrith · HLRO, corresp. with David Lloyd George · IWM, corresp. with Sir Henry Wilson · Lpool RO, corresp. with Lord Derby · NA Scot., corresp. with A. J. Balfour · NA Scot., corresp. with Philip Kerr · NRA, priv. coll., corresp. with Sir John Ewart · U. Birm. L., special collections department, corresp. with Austen Chamberlain | FILM BFI NFTVA, documentary footage; news footage

Likenesses W. Orpen, oils, 1919, NPG [*see illus.*] · photogravure, 1920 (after portrait by P. A. de Laszlo), BL OIOC · W. Stoneman, photograph, 1939, NPG · photograph, repro. in Hardinge, *Loyal to three kings*, 17 · photographs, BL OIOC

Wealth at death £71,087 15s. 2d.: probate, 13 Dec 1944, *CGPLA Eng. & Wales*

Hardinge, Charles Stewart, second Viscount Hardinge of Lahore (1822–1894), politician, was the eldest son of Henry *Hardinge, first viscount (1785–1856), and Lady Emily Jane (1789–1865), seventh daughter of Robert Stewart, first marquess of Londonderry, and widow of John James. He was the elder brother of Sir Arthur Edward *Hardinge; he was born in London on 12 September 1822. He was educated at Eton College and destined for the army, but while a boy suffered a severe accident which compelled him to use an artificial leg for the rest of his life. In 1840 he matriculated at Christ Church, Oxford, and graduated BA in 1844. Within a month after taking his degree he accompanied his father to India as private secretary, and was with him during all the period of his governor-generalship. From 8 August 1851 to 1856 he was Conservative MP for Downpatrick, and after his succession to the peerage (in 1856) he was under-secretary for war in Lord Derby's second administration (March 1858 to March 1859). He never held office again, but always remained a supporter of the Conservative Party. In 1868 he was appointed a trustee of the National Portrait Gallery, and in 1876 chairman of the trustees, an office which he actively filled until his death. He was also a trustee of the National Gallery from 1874. Owing to his father's friendship with Sir Francis Grant (1803–1878) and Sir Edwin Henry Landseer, Hardinge was brought up among artistic influences, and was himself no mean painter in watercolours. In 1847 his friends in England published a folio volume entitled *Recollections of India*, consisting of twenty lithographs from his drawings made in India, particularly interesting for its portraits of Sikh chieftains and views of scenery in Kashmir, then an almost unknown country, which he visited in company with John Nicholson (1821–1857). In 1891 he wrote a brief memoir of his father for the Rulers of India series (Oxford, Clarendon Press).

Hardinge married, on 10 April 1856, Lavinia, third daughter of George Charles Bingham, third earl of Lucan, with whom he had a family of five sons, including Charles *Hardinge, who became viceroy of India, and three daughters; she died on 15 September 1864. Hardinge died at his home, South Park, near Penshurst, on 28 July 1894, and was buried in the churchyard of Fordcombe, Kent.

J. S. COTTON, *rev.* H. C. G. MATTHEW

Sources *The letters of the first Viscount Hardinge of Lahore … 1844–1847*, ed. B. S. Singh, CS, 4th ser., 32 (1986) • GEC, *Peerage* • personal knowledge (1901)
Archives CUL, corresp. • priv. coll., papers | BL, letters to Lord Carnarvon, Add. MS 60774 • CKS, corresp. with Lord Romney relating to Maidstone quarter sessions • NAM, corresp. with Arthur Cunynghame • W. Sussex RO, letters to duke of Richmond
Wealth at death £91,516 1s. 6d.: probate, 25 Sept 1894, *CGPLA Eng. & Wales*

Hardinge, George (1743–1816), judge and writer, was born on 22 June 1743 at Canbury Manor, near Kingston, Surrey, the eldest surviving of nine sons and three daughters of Nicholas *Hardinge (1699–1758), barrister, Latin scholar, and politician, and Jane (1708–1807), daughter of Sir John Pratt of Wildernesse in Kent and sister of Charles *Pratt, first Earl Camden. Hardinge was educated at home from an early age before moving to Kingston grammar school under Richard Woodesdon. He attended Eton College between 1753 and 1760, under the instruction of Dr Edward Barnard, where he 'took up, in the boarding-house, a rage for acting plays' (Nichols, *Illustrations*, 3.9). Two years before he graduated from Eton, Hardinge's father died, bequeathing to his fifteen-year-old son the whole of the Canbury estate. On 14 January 1761 Hardinge was admitted at Trinity College, Cambridge. Despite his taste for literature, Hardinge aspired to follow in his father's footsteps and was accordingly admitted at the Middle Temple on 15 May 1764 and called to the bar on 9 June 1769. That year, he also obtained an MA from Cambridge by royal mandate, and in November was elected a fellow of the Society of Antiquaries. By 1770 he had served for four years as secretary of commissions to his uncle, Lord Chancellor Camden, and the following year became commissioner of bankruptcy, a post he held until 1782. He had also become a friend and correspondent of Horace Walpole, with whom he shared his literary and antiquarian enthusiasms. In 1776 Hardinge visited France and Switzerland and the following year, on 20 October, he married Lucy Long (d. 1820), daughter of Richard Long of Hinxton, Cambridgeshire. The couple reputedly separated in later life and although they had no children of their own, Hardinge did adopt George Nicholas *Hardinge, son of his brother Henry Hardinge. Soon after his marriage, Hardinge moved to Ragman's Castle at Twickenham, close to his friends Walpole and the poet Richard Owen Cambridge.

In his literary pursuits Hardinge 'had a rare humility for an author, being ready at all times to adopt his friends' suggestions in preference to his own expressions' (GM, 1st ser., 86/1, 1816, 563). His major works include *Rowley and Chatterton in the Shades* (1782); *A series of letters to the Right Hon. E. Burke as to the constitutional existence of an impeachment against Mr Hastings* (1791), which was printed in three editions; *The essence of Malone, or, The beauties of the fascinating writer extracted from his immortal work … 'Some account of the life and writings of John Dryden'* (1800), published in two editions; and *Another Essence of Malone* (1801). Besides several other minor works like *The Russian Chiefs: an Ode* (1813; reprinted 1814), Hardinge also edited his father's Latin verses in one volume in 1780, published *The Filial Tribute*

George Hardinge (1743–1816), by Nathaniel Dance, exh. RA 1769

(1807) in honour of his mother, and made a profound contribution to John Nichols's *Literary Anecdotes* and *Literary Illustrations*, including extensive biographies of Daniel Wray and Sneyd Davies. Hardinge also wrote several unpublished works, including memoirs of Sir John Pratt, Lord Camden, and Richard III, and his various speeches, prose, and poetry were collected together in three volumes by Nichols and published posthumously as *Miscellaneous Works* (1818). In April 1788 he was elected a fellow of the Royal Society.

Literature provided Hardinge with a diversion from his professional endeavours. In April 1782, the year he produced his first major prose, Hardinge was appointed solicitor-general to Queen Charlotte and in early 1794 was promoted to the post of attorney-general to the queen, a position he held until his death. Although he had several unrealized ambitions during his career, including aspirations for the lord chancellorship of Ireland in 1789, a futile attempt to gain auditorship at Greenwich Hospital in 1791, and a desire to replace Henry Beaufay at the Board of Control in 1795, Hardinge nevertheless managed to distinguish himself within his profession. His vindication of Sir Thomas Rumbold as counsel in the House of Commons and his speech at the bar of the House of Lords as counsel for the directors of the East India Company in 1783 were considered 'patterns of elegance and ingenuity' (GM, 1st ser., 86/1, 1816, 470), and Lord Camden, having heard the latter speech, declared: 'I … am able to pronounce upon my judgement that in language, wit and voice he has no superior at the bar' (Namier). Some years later, in April 1792, Hardinge was counsel for those charged for damages by Joseph Priestley after the riots at Birmingham and his speech on this occasion was later described as 'a masterpiece of legal ingenuity' (GM, 1st ser., 86/1, 1816, 470). For nearly thirty years, between 1787 and 1816, he served as chief justice of the counties of Brecknockshire, Glamorgan, and Radnorshire, duties he fulfilled with 'the truest sentiments of humanity and legal discrimination' (ibid.). Hardinge was, in fact, a man of great humanity and benevolence in other aspects of his life, having collected more than £10,000 for charitable purposes over the years and serving as vice-president of the Philanthropic Society.

Despite the burdens of his professional duties, Hardinge sought political office, and unsuccessfully asked for Walpole's help in 1782. He finally secured his political ambitions in 1784 when he was returned as MP for Old Sarum by the patronage of Thomas Pitt, first Baron Camelford. He delivered his first speech on 8 June 1784 in a debate on a Westminster petition and he was subsequently returned to parliament in 1787, 1790, 1796, and 1801. In parliament Hardinge was a regular though surprisingly inconsistent orator, described in June 1786 by Daniel Pulteney as an able speaker, 'better indeed than I could have ever imagined, as I have heard him very indifferent two or three times before' (Namier). He voted in favour of William Pitt's motions for reform in the mid-1780s and was prominent in his support of Pitt's resolution on the Regency Bill on 16 December 1788. In subsequent years he often sided with the government, on issues such as the impeachment of Warren Hastings in 1790, the Aliens Bill in 1793, and the suspension of habeas corpus in 1795. Hardinge's political career came to an abortive end in 1802 when Old Sarum was sold. Forced into retirement, Hardinge spent his final years conducting his duties as a Welsh judge and devoting time to his literary interests.

Hardinge was dubiously notorious for borrowing books without promptly returning them, but this was considered by some to be his 'worst crime' (DNB). His pride in his connections to the powerful irritated Walpole, who on 12 September 1795 called him an 'out-pensioner of Bedlam' (Walpole, Corr., 35.636.). Others could find cause for great praise for Hardinge: 'so various were his powers that he was a judge, a Member of Parliament, a poet, a prose writer, and a writer of sermons. ... no one had a finer choice of words and few a more graceful delivery' (Annual Biography and Obituary, 1817, 299). He died of pleurisy on 26 April 1816 at Presteigne in Radnorshire and was buried in the family vault at Kingston, Surrey. He was survived by his wife, Lucy, although, allegedly as a consequence of Hardinge's 'very irregular' (Thorne) behaviour, she had parted from him by 1805.　　　MICHAEL T. DAVIS

Sources Nichols, Illustrations, vol. 3 · L. B. Namier, 'Hardinge, George', HoP, Commons, 1754–90 · R. G. Thorne, 'Hardinge, George', HoP, Commons, 1790–1820 · Venn, Alum. Cant. · GM, 1st ser., 86/1 (1816), 469–70, 563 · DNB · Walpole, Corr., 35.549–649

Archives PRO Ire., journal of Irish tours, D3531/J/1/3–4 · Wilts. & Swindon RO, letters, WRO 9/35/156 | BL, letters to Lord and Lady Camelford, Add. MSS 69301–69302 · BL, letters to Lord Grenville, Add. MS 58986 · BL, letters to Lord Hardwicke, Add. MSS 35647–35766 · Bodl. Oxf., corresp. with Francis Douce · DWL, corresp. with Dr and Mrs Moody, ref. 24.51

Likenesses N. Dance, portrait, oils, exh. RA 1769, LPL [see illus.]

Hardinge, George Nicholas (1781–1808), naval officer, was born on 11 April 1781, the second son of the Revd Henry Hardinge (1754–1820), rector of Stanhope, co. Durham, and his wife, Frances, daughter of James Best of Wrotham, Kent. He was the grandson of Nicholas *Hardinge and elder brother of Henry *Hardinge, first Viscount Hardinge of Lahore. He was early adopted by his uncle, George *Hardinge, attorney-general to the queen, and was sent to Eton College, where he was in the lowest form. In 1793 he entered the navy; he was midshipman of the Meleager (32 guns, Captain Charles Tyler) at Toulon and the capture of Corsica, and served under the same captain in the prize-frigate San Fiorenzo (40 guns). He was also present in the Diomede (60 guns) in Hotham's action off Hyères and in various operations on the coast of Italy, and afterwards in the Aigle (38 guns), in which he was wrecked on the Isle of Planes, near Tunis, on 18 July 1798. He was in the Foudroyant (80 guns, Captain Sir Edward Berry) at the capture of the Guillaume Tell on 30 March 1800, and obtained his lieutenancy on board the Tiger (Commodore Sir Sidney Smith) off Alexandria, during the Egyptian campaign of 1801 (in which he obtained the Turkish gold medal).

In 1802 Hardinge became a master and commander, and in 1803 commanded the bomb (that is, mortar) vessel Terror off Boulogne. Early in 1804 he was appointed to the sloop Scorpion (18 guns), in which he distinguished himself by the cutting out of the Dutch brig-corvette Atalante in Vlie Roads, Texel, on 31 March 1804. For this action he received post rank, and was presented by the committee of Lloyd's with a sword of 300 guineas' value. In August he was posted to the Proselyte (20 guns), an old collier, and ordered to the West Indies with convoy; but his friends, fearing the effects of the West Indian climate on his health, obtained his transfer to the Valorous, which proved unfit for sea. Hardinge next accepted the offer of the frigate Salsette, said to be just off the stocks at Bombay. On his way out he served on shore at the capture of the Cape of Good Hope, but on arrival at Bombay found the Salsette only just laid down. He was promised command of the frigate Pitt (late Salsette), and in the meantime was appointed to the frigate San Fiorenzo in which he made several short and uneventful cruises. The San Fiorenzo left Colombo to return to Bombay; but on 6 March 1808, off the south of Ceylon, they sighted the notorious French cruiser Piedmontaise—'which had long been the terror of the Indian Seas' (GM)—in pursuit of some Indiamen. A three days' fight followed, in which both ships were handled with bravery and skill. Hardinge was killed by a grape-shot on the third day, 9 March, during a well-contested action of 1 hour 20 minutes, which ended when the French ship surrendered. The captures of the Atalante and Piedmontaise were among the actions for which the war medal was granted to survivors some forty years later.

Hardinge, who died unmarried, was buried at Colombo with military honours, and was voted a public monument in St Paul's Cathedral, London.

H. M. CHICHESTER, *rev.* ROGER MORRISS

Sources 'Biographical memoir of George Nicholas Hardinge', *Naval Chronicle*, 20 (1808), 257–87 · 'Addenda to the biographical memoir of George Nicholas Hardinge', *Naval Chronicle*, 20 (1808), 430–35 · *GM*, 1st ser., 78 (1808), 748 · Nichols, *Illustrations*, 3.49–147 · *European Magazine and London Review*, 57 (1810), 3–8 · E. Lodge, *Peerage, baronetage, knightage and companionage of the British empire*, 81st edn, 3 vols. (1912) [under Hardinge and Hardinge of Lahore] · H. E. C. Stapylton, *The Eton School lists, from 1791 to 1850* (1863) · W. James, *The naval history of Great Britain, from the declaration of war by France in 1793, to the accession of George IV*, [4th edn], 6 vols. (1847), vol. 3, pp. 264–6; vol. 4, pp. 307–11 · Burke, *Peerage*
Likenesses H. R. Cook, stipple (after W. S. Lethbridge), BM, NPG; repro. in *European Magazine*

Hardinge, Henry, first Viscount Hardinge of Lahore (1785–1856), army officer and governor-general of India, was born at Wrotham, Kent, on 30 March 1785, the third son of Henry Hardinge (1754–1820), rector of Stanhope, co. Durham (a living then worth £5000 a year), and his wife, Frances, daughter of James Best of Park House, Boxley, Kent. Captain George Nicholas *Hardinge (1781–1808) was his brother. His grandfather was Nicholas *Hardinge (1699–1758).

Early life Hardinge passed much of his childhood at The Grove near Sevenoaks amid a deeply religious tradition and in the care of two maiden aunts, and went to school at Durham. In July 1799 he joined as ensign the Queen's rangers in Upper Canada. On returning to Britain in 1802, in March he purchased a lieutenancy in the 4th foot, went on half pay, and became a captain by purchase in the 57th foot in April 1804.

A formative military career From February 1806 to November 1807 Hardinge attended the senior department of the Royal Military College, High Wycombe, and passed his examination. He became deputy assistant quartermaster-general in Sir Brent Spencer's force which was sent, in December 1807, to join troops in Portugal under Sir Arthur Wellesley (later duke of Wellington). Hardinge took part in the battles of Roliça and Vimeiro (where he was badly wounded); and he was present at Corunna (16 January 1809) when Sir John Moore was killed, and had by then established a sound reputation in which his 'conduct and courage' (Hardinge, 14) were admired.

After a brief return home Hardinge was promoted major and took up an appointment as deputy quartermaster-general of the Portuguese forces in April 1809. Wellington soon noted his qualities; he asked General Beresford to send him 'Hardinge or some other staff officer who has intelligence, to whom I can talk about the concerns of the Portuguese army' (*DNB*). Promoted lieutenant-colonel in 1811, Hardinge saw many of the key engagements of the Peninsular War, most notably the hard-fought action at Albuera (22 May 1811) where he urged General Cole to ignore Beresford's caution and advance with the 4th division to seize the day, and at Vitoria (21 June 1813) where he was again badly wounded. The precise circumstance of Hardinge's intervention at

Henry Hardinge, first Viscount Hardinge of Lahore (1785–1856), by Sir Francis Grant, 1849 [replica]

Albuera has been debated but his actions further reinforced his reputation as a key and intrepid staff officer; he was awarded the Portuguese order of the Tower and the Sword. Despite the discomfort of his wounds from Vitoria he continued at the front and, in 1814, commanded the Portuguese brigade at the battles of Orthez and Toulouse. He was promoted, without purchase, to a lieutenant-colonelcy in the 40th foot in April 1814 and transferred to the 1st foot (later the Grenadier Guards) the following July; he was made KCB in January 1815, and received foreign orders.

After the defeat of France in 1814 Hardinge attended the Congress of Vienna, but once Napoleon's escape from Elba was known Wellington dispatched him to observe the emperor's movements. Hardinge was next attached to Marshal Blucher's staff, as brigadier-general, to liaise with the Prussians; at the battle of Quatre-Bras (16 June 1815) Hardinge's left hand was shattered, and it was later amputated at the wrist. The wound, which was initially poorly treated, prevented him serving at Waterloo (18 June) but he was again with Blucher in Paris two weeks later. In February 1816 Hardinge became assistant quartermaster-general to the British forces while retaining a liaison role with the Prussians; he remained in Paris until the withdrawal of allied forces in November 1818. Hardinge's efforts won him the Prussian order of Military Merit and Wellington's gift of Napoleon's captured sword.

Soldier turned politician Hardinge returned to the Grenadier Guards in 1818 and was elected a tory MP for the city of Durham at the 1820 general election. On 10 December 1821 he married Lady Emily Jane (1789–1865), seventh daughter of Robert Stewart, first marquess of Londonderry, sister of the second Viscount Castlereagh and widow of John James, former British minister in the Netherlands. Theirs was a loving and happy marriage; Hardinge gladly accepted Walter, Emily's son by her first husband, and they had four more children, including Sir Arthur Edward *Hardinge and Charles Stewart *Hardinge, second Viscount Hardinge.

From 1823 to 1827 Hardinge was clerk of the ordnance and worked to improve military administration. In April 1827 he retired from the army and in July 1828, once Wellington was prime minister, he became secretary at war in succession to Lord Palmerston, though without a seat in the cabinet. He held this post until July 1830; he found the office in 'a state of great efficiency' (Bourne, 132) but still proposed to reduce its staff by a seventh. Overhauling the system of military pensions to reward longer service, he established basic principles that endured for decades. He voted in favour of Catholic emancipation. In 1830 he supported Lord Ellenborough during the debate on the latter's celebrated divorce from Jane Digby; Lady Hardinge was sister to Ellenborough's first wife, Lady Octavia Stewart.

Between July and November 1830 Hardinge briefly became chief secretary for Ireland. He was initially unsure about taking on such a difficult post, but Wellington had no doubts of his ability: 'Hardinge will do; he always understands what he undertakes, and undertakes nothing but what he understands' (Hardinge, 31). In the House of Commons Hardinge had to respond to Daniel O'Connell's attacks.

Hardinge was re-elected as MP for Durham four times. At the 1830 dissolution he was considered as a candidate for Northumberland but was adopted by Newport in Cornwall, where he was returned in the 1830 and 1831 elections. In 1830 he was promoted major-general. Newport lost its member under the 1832 Reform Act, but Hardinge was next adopted by neighbouring Launceston, which he represented until he left for India in 1844. He was a leading opponent of the 1832 Reform Act. In one heated debate he told ministers: 'the next time you hear those guns they will be shotted and take off some of your heads' (Brock, 192).

Hardinge returned as chief secretary for Ireland in Peel's 1834–5 administration, and successfully introduced a settlement of the Irish tithe question. He was again secretary at war in Peel's government from 1841 to 1844, and influenced Peel over British policy in Afghanistan; he also supported the annexation of Sind. He was promoted lieutenant-general in 1841.

Hardinge had by now supplemented a distinguished military record with a solid political career. He had earned the reputation of a competent, generally popular, and indefatigable political administrator and was described as plain, straightforward, and a just if somewhat partisan politician. He had also become a close confidant of several key figures: he acted as Wellington's second in the duke's duel with Lord Winchilsea and, although of a fundamentally tory outlook, he maintained a close relationship with Peel and saw in him the only future for the Conservatives after the Reform Act.

Appointment as governor-general of India Early in 1844 the East India Company's court of directors recalled governor-general Lord Ellenborough in opposition to Peel's wishes. In a calculated move of compromise it offered the governor-generalship to Hardinge, although it seems that he was also the most generally accepted candidate. In addition, the court was attracted by Hardinge's background. As a senior officer of considerable experience he was no warlike adventurer and was more conscious of the limitations of military power than civilians such as Ellenborough. Peel agreed; Hardinge would work hard for peace despite the pressures on the ground. Peel concluded that 'I think he is by far the best man that could be named' (Letters, 4).

Hardinge himself was not so sure, having already declined going to India as commander-in-chief. His reservations were based on his age (at fifty-nine he would be the oldest governor-general to date), worries over his wife's health and children's welfare (she and the children would almost certainly have to remain at home), and an absorbing interest in redeveloping his house at South Park, near Penshurst, Kent, for retirement. Peel eventually persuaded Hardinge to accept. No doubt Hardinge was also swayed by the awareness that the governor-generalship would crown his career with one of the most important posts within the British empire and provide a lucrative addition to his family's fortune. On hearing of Hardinge's decision Lord Ripon, president of the Board of Control, wrote: 'You have made a noble sacrifice in accepting what has been offered to you. The country is deeply indebted to you' (Letters, 4).

Arrival in India Hardinge characteristically set about familiarizing himself thoroughly with Indian affairs and read much 'with profit' (Letters, 28). He arrived in Calcutta on 22 July 1844, having travelled by way of Egypt, accompanied only by his son Charles and his wife's nephew Robert Wood (as private secretary and military aide-de-camp respectively). Having adjusted to the climate Hardinge established a rigorous pattern of work. He rose at 5 a.m. and retired at 10 p.m.; official business occupied ten or twelve hours a day, usually preceded by a short ride at daybreak. Generally Hardinge found his head 'clearer' and that he could 'work longer than in England' (Letters, 32). He did, however, stop the practice of government work on Sundays. Hardinge established regular discussions with his council and normally divided his time between the governor-general's residences in Calcutta and Barrackpore. By December 1844 he was noting that 'I never knew what it was really to work until I came here' (Letters, 6); he hoped that he was working 'to good purpose' (ibid., 39), and disclosed that 'I relieve my mind by the reflection that I am doing my duty both to the public and my family' (ibid., 95). Once under way Hardinge took the work in his stride.

Apart from an insurrection in Kolhapur in western India, the first sixteen months of Hardinge's incumbency were peaceful, and he concentrated on the question of education. Hardinge was impressed by the calibre of Indians attending government colleges who could quote 'Shakespeare fluently—aye and [explain] accurately all the most difficult passages' (*Letters*, 7). He resolved that 'in every possible case a preference shall be given in the selection of candidates for public employment to those who have been educated in the institutions thus established' by government, individuals, and societies (Hardinge, 63). This was an important stimulus to education in both English and the vernaculars.

Other issues, such as law reform, continued misgovernment in Oudh, the overhaul of the Bengal salt tax, the initial steps towards railway construction, the cultivation of American cotton, the suppression of human sacrifice, the powers of the governor-general *vis-à-vis* his council, and the state of the military establishment also took up time. Hardinge oversaw the settlement of Sind with the flamboyant governor Sir Charles Napier as well. Ripon wrote approving of all that Hardinge had done in acting in accordance with his instructions which, the governor-general noted, 'I have never received' (*Letters*, 47). Turmoil was, however, growing beyond the company's borders in the Punjab. Hardinge studied events there carefully and cautiously augmented the frontier garrisons so that, by November 1845, they were doubled in strength. He recorded how he wrote 'all the most important letters myself, leaving the originals in my handwriting in the office so that the extent of my interference can be traced at any future time' (*Letters*, 52).

Crisis in the Punjab and the First Anglo-Sikh War After Ranjit Singh's death in 1839 the Sikh military leadership was riven with dissensions. In 1843 power passed to those antagonistic to British influence, while their opponents reckoned a clash with the company might destroy their rivals. By November 1845, therefore, most observers held that conflict was inevitable although Hardinge still hoped to preserve both the peace and the buffer policy on the north-west frontier. It was his firm view that 'with such an overgrown empire we want consolidation and not extension of territory' (*Letters*, 110).

On 11 December 1845, without warning, the Sikhs crossed the Sutlej, thereby initiating a war that became the pivot of Hardinge's tenure in India. They clashed with British forces at an inconclusive encounter at Mudki (18 December) and the bloody battle of Ferozeshahr (21-2 December) which the company won but at considerable cost. At Aliwal (28 January 1846) and Sobraon (10 February) British forces regained the initiative but the Sikhs had proved to be far more formidable than the British expected.

Hardinge moved up to Ambala for the conflict and, somewhat unusually, insisted on serving in the field as second-in-command to Sir Hugh Gough, the commander-in-chief, about whose rashness he had doubts. On 13 December 1845 a proclamation was issued declaring all Sikh possessions east of the Sutlej forfeit. The campaign forced a re-examination of Hardinge's frontier policy. Casualties among European troops were high, and he lacked confidence in the sepoys and doubted that sufficient force was available to prolong the war. Continued fighting might allow Afghan incursions towards Peshawar and stir unrest within the company's existing territories. Hardinge was also reluctant, following the Afghanistan débâcle of 1841-2, to share a frontier with Muslim power to the north-west:

> We shall keep what we have confiscated on this side [of the Sutlej], make them pay the expenses of the war, clip their wings and lessen their power, but I have always been averse to annex the territory [and] I still hope to keep up a Sikh nation that is a Hindoo people as contradistinguished from a Mohamedan. (*Letters*, 9-10)

Hardinge was equally reluctant to endorse a client state 'which by British bayonets enables a native govt. to grind the people to dust' and it seemed that annexation was unsound on financial grounds. Another concern was Hardinge's worry about reactions at home to the annexation of the Punjab (*Letters*, 142).

Hardinge had to make some difficult choices without access to officers versed in the ways of the Punjab in whom he had real trust. Major Broadfoot and Lieutenant Nicholson, political agents, had been killed at Ferozeshahr and his secretary Frederick Curry, whom he held in considerable respect, was a civilian while the governor-general conceived the problem mainly in military terms. Hardinge opted for a weakened but independent Punjab, and a consolidated and defended frontier. The war was ended by treaties on 9 and 16 March 1846. The Sikh army was reduced, the Cis-Sutlej states, Jullundur Doab, and Kashmir (granted in turn to Gulab Singh) were surrendered to the company, and an indemnity of £500,000 exacted. Hardinge wrote 'a diminution of strength of such a war-like nation on our weakest frontier, seems to me imperatively required' (Yapp, 543).

In practice, however, the settlement seemed unlikely to endure. Sikh military power remained beyond company control, and the presence in Lahore of a British agent and troops to support the young maharaja (Dulip Singh) provided a focus for friction. Hardinge himself recognized inconsistencies in the policy; he told Ripon that the settlement would allow easy annexation if required. By December 1846 an additional treaty (of Bhairowal) was needed. British troops would remain until 1854 and the agent, Henry Lawrence, took on supervision of the Sikh government through a regency council. Hardinge accepted these changes with great reluctance but the only alternative seemed annexation. He noted: 'It is in reality annexation brought about by the supplication of the Sikhs without entailing upon us the present expense and future inconvenience of a doubtful acquisition' (Yapp, 548). Hardinge later argued he had secured the best possible military frontier for British India in response to criticism that his Punjab policy had been too moderate.

Hardinge visited Lahore in February 1846 and was cordially received by the Sikh leadership. He next travelled to Simla, where he found it difficult to settle back 'to red boxes and the humdrum business of the state' (*Letters*, 156) because, despite the strains, the campaign had been an invigorating experience. In May 1846 Hardinge learned that he had been created a viscount in recognition for his services in India; Ripon told him that, at home, 'Everybody of whatever party, admires every part of your conduct' (Yapp, 556), although, in fact, the initial reactions to Mudki and Ferozeshahr had been horror at the scale of British losses.

Closing months in India Hardinge was by now increasingly concerned by political events at home; he always regarded Peel's motives to be both 'praiseworthy and high minded' (*Letters*, 91). On 29 June 1846 Peel resigned as prime minister in the wake of the corn law crisis. Hardinge was not attracted by the prospect of serving a whig government under Lord John Russell likely to contain old political adversaries such as Auckland; he offered his resignation but Russell refused it, urging him to remain to see the Punjab settled. Others, including Peel, also pressed him to stay. Hardinge relented and continued working hard ('I must omit nothing under Whig masters'; *Letters*, 11–12), giving particular attention to budgetary and military policy. He continued, however, to plan for a return home as soon as practicable and was unsettled by news of his wife's illness.

In January and February 1847 Hardinge again visited the Punjab and the Cis-Sutlej states before viewing progress on one of his favourite projects, the Ganges Canal. He hoped the canal would 'be some redemption of our character, for we have hitherto done very little for the people'. At this time the governor-general conducted an angry exchange with Gough over the conduct of the battle at Ferozeshahr and, although relations were restored, Hardinge's feelings were hurt. Renewed attention was given to civil administration such as the introduction of tea culture, measures against infanticide, and improved financial management in the wake of Anglo-Sikh War expenses. On 5 April he wrote home reporting his task in India was nearly complete, and saying that he intended to leave by the end of 1847. Hardinge stuck to this decision despite renewed requests for him to stay, especially as he had concluded that both Sir John Hobhouse (president of the Board of Control) and Lord Palmerston (foreign secretary) were against his Punjab policy (*Letters*, 13–14).

Hardinge left Simla for Calcutta on 26 October 1847. Overall he believed he had made a constructive contribution to Indian government: 'Every part of the country is quiet—the harvest most abundant and the crops for the spring most promising, the river [Ganges] crowded with boats and trade increasing' (*Letters*, 15). On 12 January 1848 he relinquished the government of India to his successor, the earl of Dalhousie, returning home with a tiger for Queen Victoria which had allegedly eaten thirteen people and certainly gave Lady Dalhousie fleas.

After India Notwithstanding his desire to retire Hardinge was asked by Russell's government to use his political and military experience in Ireland amid the Smith O'Brien riots of 1848. In July 1850 he attended Peel in his dying hours. From March to September 1852 he was master-general of the ordnance. Concerned at the possible French invasion threat he initiated an inquiry into the effectiveness of existing coastal batteries against steam vessels. He resisted military conservatives' demands for a return to smooth-bore muskets and—influenced by his Anglo-Sikh War experience to a belief in large-calibre field guns—he augmented and improved the artillery. In 1852 he also wrote a series of memoranda on military policy, one of which has been described as possibly the most comprehensive and important survey of the requirements of a full army produced between 1815 and 1854 (Strachan, 104–6).

After Wellington's death, in March 1852 Hardinge, allegedly because a royal favourite, succeeded him as general commanding-in-chief, and became field marshal in October 1855. Encouraged by Prince Albert, he carried out much needed reforms—including introducing Enfield rifles, improving army training with the establishment of a permanent camp at Aldershot and the School of Musketry at Hythe, and introducing heavier coastal artillery—but, overall, his new responsibilities proved onerous. Hardinge's age had begun to tell and he proved somewhat reluctant to interfere with the arrangements of his illustrious predecessor. He shared, therefore, some of the blame for army shortcomings in the Crimean War. He contributed to the 1855 committee of inquiry, accepting that he had responsibility for the equipment, stores, transport, and medical arrangements. The army did, however, also depend on its field commander (Lord Raglan) and commissariat, of whose precise arrangements Hardinge was unaware. It was Hardinge's view that no force had ever left Britain as well equipped, and he drew supporting analogies from experience in the Napoleonic wars although he also accepted that Wellington's troops were in a better state of overall efficiency. Although the inquiry laid most of the blame on the cabinet, Hardinge suffered some public criticism and could not be expected to accept the report without mixed feelings; when at Aldershot to present its conclusions to the queen, on 8 July 1856 he suffered a paralytic stroke. He never fully recovered, and on 15 July 1856 he resigned and was succeeded by George, duke of Cambridge, as general commanding-in-chief. He died on 24 September 1856 at his residence, South Park, and was buried on 1 October at Fordcombe church, near Penshurst. His wife survived him. In a general order to the army issued on 2 October 1856 Queen Victoria paid a fitting tribute to Lord Hardinge's long and varied career when she wrote of his 'valuable and unremitting services' (Hardinge, 196).

DAVID J. HOWLETT

Sources C. Hardinge, *Viscount Hardinge* (1891) · *The letters of the first Viscount Hardinge of Lahore … 1844–1847*, ed. B. S. Singh, CS, 4th ser., 32 (1986) · M. E. Yapp, *Strategies of British India: Britain, Iran and Afghanistan, 1798–1850* (1980) · *DNB* · M. Brock, *The Great Reform Act* (1973) · H. T. Lambrick, *Sir Charles Napier and Sind* (1952) · J. A. Norris, *The First Afghan War, 1838–1842* (1967) · M. F. Schmidt, *Passion's child: the extraordinary life of Jane Digby* (1976) · K. Bourne, *Palmerston: the early years, 1784–1841* (1982) · H. Small, *Florence Nightingale: avenging angel* (1998) · GEC, *Peerage* · J. A. B. Ramsay, marquess of Dalhousie, *Private letters*, ed. J. G. A. Baird (1910) · J. Sweetman, *War and administration: the significance of the Crimean War for the British army* (1984) ·

H. Strachan, *From Waterloo to Balaclava: tactics, technology and the British army, 1815–1854* (1985)

Archives CKS, family corresp., ref. U840/C51–53, 529–34 · McGill University, Montreal, McLennan Library, corresp. and MSS | BL, corresp. with Lord Aberdeen, Add. MSS 43239–43254 · BL, corresp. with J. C. Herries, Add. MS 57410 · BL, letters to Sir Robert Peel, Add. MSS 40313–40314, 40474–40475 · BL, corresp. with Lord Ripon, Add. MSS 40869–40877 · BL OIOC, corresp. with Sir George Russell Clerk, MS Eur. D 538 · BL OIOC, letters to Sir J. W. Hogg, MS Eur. E 342 · BL OIOC, letters to Henry Lawrence, MS Eur. F 85 · BL OIOC, letters to marquess of Tweeddale, MS Eur. F 96 · Borth. Inst., letters to Sir Charles Wood · CUL, letters to Sir Richard Airey · Durham RO, letters to Lord Londonderry · Herefs. RO, letters to Lord Airey, E47G · Lpool RO, letters to fourteenth earl of Derby · NA Scot., corresp. with Andrew Leith-Hay; letters to second Lord Panmure · NAM, letters to Sir Benjamin D'Urban · NAM, corresp. with Lord Raglan, 6807/279–305 · NL Scot., corresp. with Sir George Brown, MSS 1848–1859, 2845–2856, *passim* · NL Scot., corresp. with marquess of Tweeddale · NRA, priv. coll., corresp. with Sir George Cathcart · NRA, priv. coll., letters to Sir Walter James · NRA, priv. coll., letters to Lord Seaton · PRO, corresp. with Lord Ellenborough, PRO 30/12 · PRO NIre., letters to Lord Castlereagh, D3030 · Surrey HC, letters to Henry Goulburn · U. Nott. L., corresp. with duke of Newcastle · U. Southampton L., corresp. with Lord Palmerston, MS 62 · U. Southampton L., letters to duke of Wellington, MS 61

Likenesses J. Lucas, oils, 1844, Victoria Memorial Hall, Calcutta · G. G. Adams, plaster medallion, 1845, NPG · F. Grant, portrait, 1849, priv. coll.; study, NPG · J. H. Foley, equestrian statue, *c.*1853, Government House, Calcutta · J. Barrett, oils, 1856, NPG · statue, *c.*1865, BL OIOC · J. H. Foley, marble bust, Royal Collection · F. Grant, oils (after his portrait, 1849), NPG [*see illus.*] · G. Hayter, group portrait, oils (*The house of Commons, 1833*), NPG · S. W. Reynolds, engraving (after F. Grant), BL OIOC · W. Salter, group portrait, oils (*Waterloo banquet at Apsley House*), Wellington Museum, Apsley House, London; oil study, *c.*1834–40, NPG · lithograph (after W. C. Ross), BL OIOC

Hardinge, Nicholas (1699–1758), Latin poet and politician, was born at Kingston, Surrey, on 7 February 1699, the eldest son of Gideon Hardinge (*d.* 1712), vicar of Kingston, and his wife, Mary Westbrooke. He was educated at Eton College (1711–18) and King's College, Cambridge (BA 1722, MA 1726), and, with a reputation as a fine classical scholar, became a fellow of the college in 1722. While at Cambridge his analysis of a college dispute led him to take up the study of law. He was called to the bar in 1725, and in 1731 accepted the post of chief clerk to the House of Commons. He was the first person to receive a regular salary for his services and was responsible for reporting on and modernizing the parliamentary journals. In the following year he was appointed law reader for William, duke of Cumberland, for whom he wrote his *Essay on Regency*, and later he became the duke's attorney-general.

On 19 December 1738 Hardinge married Jane, the daughter of Sir John *Pratt, the lord chief justice; they had nine sons and three daughters. Hardinge was MP for the borough of Eye, Suffolk, between 1748 and 1758, during which time (17 April 1752) he resigned as chief clerk to become joint secretary of the Treasury. Alongside his political career he maintained his academic interest in the classics. He wrote Latin verses throughout his life, though no collection was published until after his death, on 9 April 1758. His eldest son, the politician and barrister George *Hardinge, published a volume entitled *Latin*

Verses by the Late Nicholas Hardinge, Esq (1780), which was later expanded to incorporate Hardinge's English verse and other writings, and published as *Poems, Latin, Greek, and English* (1818).

PHILIP CARTER

Sources R. R. Sedgwick, 'Hardinge, Nicholas', HoP, *Commons* · DNB

Archives BL, law reports, Add. MS 35997 · Essex RO, Chelmsford, corresp. with Thomas Barrett Lennard

Likenesses H. Meyer, stipple (after A. Ramsay), BM, NPG

Hardisty, Roger Michael (1922–1997), haematologist, was born on 19 September 1922 in Finchley, Middlesex, the only child of William Henry Hardisty (1878–1938), insurance assessor, and his wife, Ada Winifred, *née* Woodcock (1882–1972). Educated at Oundle School and at St Thomas's Hospital medical school, London, he qualified in 1944. After house appointments he did his national service, mostly in Germany and Denmark, as medical officer to the Welsh Guards and the British mission in Denmark. While stationed in Hamburg he met his future wife Jytte Jarnum (*b.* 1924), of Copenhagen. They married on 24 March 1947 and had two children, Jan Botli, later a photographer, and Jocelyn Sandra, later a music teacher. Following the completion of his national service Hardisty returned to work as a junior clinical pathologist at St Thomas's. He became MRCP in 1949 and proceeded MD in 1950. In 1950–51 he held a University of London travelling scholarship to Arhus, Denmark.

From 1956 to 1958 Hardisty was senior lecturer in clinical pathology at the Welsh National Medical School in Cardiff. In 1958, despite having had no formal training in paediatrics, he was appointed consultant haematologist at the Hospital for Sick Children, Great Ormond Street, London. Over the next thirty years he built up the first paediatric haematology department in Britain. This rapidly acquired an international reputation, and Hardisty trained many young paediatric haematologists from Britain and overseas. His own interests were in platelets, both in haemostasis and in initiating the processes that lead to the formation of a blood clot. In addition he ran a major centre for the treatment of haemophilia and similar disorders, and he also became involved in the management of childhood leukaemia.

By the time Hardisty was appointed to Great Ormond Street it was known that leukaemia might respond to treatment with drugs such as steroids or antimetabolites. Nevertheless, the disease inevitably recurred within a short period. The suggestion was then made that a positive response might be prolonged if more than one drug was administered at a time, and even that carefully controlled schedules might eventually produce cures. Hardisty became one of the prime movers in the development of clinical trials to determine the best combination of agents, serving first as secretary and then as chairman of the Medical Research Council's working party on childhood leukaemia. The initial difficulties were formidable: the toxic effects of the drugs added to the miseries of the disease, which might anyway recur a few months later in another guise—as a lump in the testicle or ovary, for instance, or as leukaemic meningitis (which Hardisty was the first to describe). As a result both the parents and the medical carers of the children involved were sometimes reluctant to have them treated with the new agents. Nevertheless, Hardisty showed the same attributes as his pioneering colleagues in transplantation surgery, termed 'the courage to fail'. His humane but obsessive persistence was rewarded when a trial disclosed that 70 per cent of patients with acute lymphoblastic leukaemia had survived long term. Another reward came at his retirement in 1987: a secretly organized tea party held in the Great Ormond Street boardroom attended by many survivors from leukaemia.

Hardisty was also highly influential in the development of the wider aspects of the emerging new specialism of clinical haematology. He was a founder member and later president of two societies in the field, as well as vice-president of the International Society on Thrombosis and Haemostasis. The co-author of two notable books, *Bleeding Disorders: Investigation and Management* (1965) and *Blood and its Disorders* (1974), he was an outstanding editor of the *British Journal of Haematology*. He loved pellucid prose, and would spend hours revising his own and his juniors' drafts (and shunned the reprehensible but common practice of gift authorship—the mere addition of the chief of department's name to papers with which he had not been directly concerned). He could also conduct seminars in Danish and French (for example, during his sabbatical as visiting professor at the University of Paris in 1978–9), and the French government made him a *chevalier* of the national Order of Merit in 1988.

Hardisty was quintessentially a Thomas's intellectual—irreverent, disdaining the then division between juniors and consultants, wearing bright clothes, and respecting the primacy of the National Health Service. Above all, throughout his life he saw research, followed by more research, as the priority. His outside interests were in photography, the theatre and music (Sir Thomas Beecham being a lifelong hero), travel, and food and wine. Although he continued some research into platelets as emeritus professor at the Royal Free Hospital, London, after retirement, he also devoted much time to bookbinding, which he took up with the same obsession that he had formerly devoted to his department. He died of stomach cancer at his home, 4 Ruskin Close, Hampstead, London, on 18 September 1997, and was cremated seven days later. He was survived by his wife, two children, and four grandchildren.   STEPHEN LOCK

Sources *The Independent* (24 Sept 1997) · *The Times* (9 Oct 1997) · D. Weatherall and S. Lock, 'Roger Hardisty', *BMJ* (11 Oct 1997), 955 · personal knowledge (2004) · private information (2004)
Likenesses photograph, repro. in *The Independent* · photograph, repro. in *The Times*
Wealth at death £263,046: probate, 24 April 1998, *CGPLA Eng. & Wales*

Hardman family (*per. c.*1820–1935), manufacturers of ecclesiastical furnishings, came to prominence via the family firm's association with the architect, designer, and pioneer of the Gothic revival, Augustus Welby Northmore *Pugin (1812–1852), for whom it executed designs for metalwork, stained glass, and decorative painting. The firm's founder was **John Hardman** (1811–1867), who was baptized on 9 August 1811 at St Peter's Roman Catholic Church in Birmingham, the third of the four surviving children of **John Hardman** (1767–1844), button maker and medallist, and his second wife, Lydia Wareing (*d.* 1816). His father, who later became known as John Hardman senior in order to differentiate him from his son, was a stalwart of the Roman Catholic community in Birmingham. He made significant contributions to the building of St Chad's Cathedral and founded the Convent of Mercy in Handsworth, Birmingham (three of his daughters entered the religious life), as well as a number of Catholic charitable organizations. Educated at Stonyhurst College (1824–7) John Hardman became a partner in his father's thriving button making business (Hardman and Lewis, later Hardman and Iliffe) at Paradise Street, Birmingham. The Hardmans probably met Pugin when he later was working at St Mary's, Oscott: according to Pugin's diary he was invited to dine with the Hardmans on 29 May 1837 (V&A, L 5158–1969). While there is no doubt that he admired the elder Hardman it was with the younger man that Pugin formed a close and lasting friendship. Pugin, who always experienced difficulty in finding manufacturers who met his exacting standards of craftsmanship, was evidently delighted to make the acquaintance of someone with expertise in metalwork who in addition shared his deep religious and moral convictions and interest in the Roman Catholic revival. This shared commitment to the revival of their religion and its practice evolved into a new manufacturing venture to provide furnishings mainly for churches but also for domestic use. Describing themselves as the first of the medieval metalworkers, Pugin and Hardman were supplying a modest range of articles from June 1838, including book clasps, silver mounted cruets, and ciboria designed by Pugin and manufactured by Hardman. In 1841 production was expanded to include monumental brasses. The two men were guided by Pugin's belief that the Gothic was the only appropriate Christian style. They benefited from the increasing demand for truly Gothic products from newly constructed Catholic churches as well as from new Anglican churches and those undergoing restoration. Turnover of the firm was £1000 in 1841.

Hardman had married Anne (*c.*1809–1880), daughter of George Gibson of Manchester, probably on 23 August 1832 in Manchester, and on 5 May 1843 their first son, John Bernard Hardman, was born at the family home, St John's, Hunter's Lane, Handsworth. They had two surviving sons and five daughters in all.

In 1845 Hardman's increasingly diverse enterprise moved from the premises of the button making firm into its own workshops at Great Charles Street (the button business continued to thrive and won a prize medal at the Great Exhibition of 1851.) At the new premises Hardman had a number of workshops, but he continued to employ outworkers and also used subcontractors, often local firms. The business expanded from producing church furnishings, such as candlesticks, chalices, pyxes, and thuribles in precious and base metal, to producing stained glass (from 1845) and undertaking decorative painting in addition. To the growing ecclesiastical orders from Great Britain, Europe, and Australia were added numerous and valuable requests for fitting out the Palace of Westminster, the largest secular commission that Hardmans undertook. It accounted for the rapid rise in business which saw turnover exceed £12,000 in 1848.

Pugin provided the inspiration for the astonishing quantity and range of individual designs, but without the manufacturing acumen, organizational skills, and commitment of Hardman the project could not have succeeded. From the surviving ledgers, letters, and workbooks it is clear that Hardman's role involved liaison with clients and designer, interpreting Pugin's designs for the workmen, overseeing production, and managing the accounts.

Pugin claimed to be reviving traditional working methods, and Hardman was credited with having done so, but an examination of the surviving objects reveals a more pragmatic approach. Most of the Hardman production in Pugin's lifetime was in base metal and nearly all was machine made, using the most sophisticated modern methods available in a nineteenth-century metal foundry. Objects were cast or die-stamped, bowls of chalices spun, and full use was made of electroforming. More emphasis was placed on traditional silversmithing skills in the manufacture of items in precious metal, although raising and chasing were often used in conjunction with more industrial practices. It would appear from correspondence between Pugin and Hardman that both were satisfied with an impressive finish rather than the exclusive use of medieval methods of manufacture.

The enormous orders for the Palace of Westminster (for which it supplied all the metalwork and all the stained glass except for one set of windows in the Lords' chamber), continuing important commissions, and the preparations for the Great Exhibition of 1851 must have stretched the capacity of the business to its limit. The firm's work for Pugin's medieval court at the Great Exhibition won the highest accolade, a council medal, in the general hardware class and a prize medal for church articles. Every aspect of church furnishings was shown, with the Hardmans' exhibits covering an impressive area, 560 square feet of floor space and 1360 square feet of wall space. From the unlikely formula of the strongest of religious, moral, and artistic convictions Pugin and Hardman had found a market for the products that they wanted to supply and had succeeded in making a profitable business from it. John Hardman had sacrificed his health for the business, financial strain, hard work, and anxiety all contributing to his decline. He retired from an active role in the firm in 1857 and retired completely in the summer of 1863, when he moved with his wife to Pemberton Villa, 3 Clifton Park, Bristol. He died there on 29 May 1867, his body being brought back to Birmingham for burial on 18 June in the crypt of St Chad's Cathedral in a chantry that

had been presented to his father as a gift in recognition of his benefactions. Hardman himself had been instrumental in founding a choir at St Chad's for the performance of Gregorian chant and had personally managed the choir until his departure from Birmingham. He had performed as a baritone in the choir, as had a number of his exclusively Catholic workforce. In appearance he was the archetypal middle-class Victorian gentleman, complete with goatee beard and spectacles. He was a leading figure in the establishment of a Catholic reformatory for boys at Mount St Bernard's in Charnwood Forest, Leicestershire, in 1855. For a short time he served on Birmingham town council and on one of the committees of the Great Exhibition. Above all though, as his obituary in *The Builder* (25, 1867, 408) claimed, he gave Birmingham a new industry. Hardman was succeeded as senior partner in Hardmans by his elder son, John Bernard Hardman (1843–1903); his younger son, Mary George Edward Hardman (1844–1904), was also involved in the firm.

Following Pugin's death in 1852 Hardman's nephew **John Hardman Powell** (1827–1895) became his chief designer. Powell was born in Birmingham on 4 March 1827, the seventh of the twelve children of William Powell (1789–1861), brass-founder, and his wife, Lucy (1793–1863), embroiderer, daughter of John Hardman senior and his first wife, Juliana Weetman. Lucy Powell's textile business was closely allied to her half-brother's metalworks, and she undertook commissions for vestments and other textiles for Pugin. Her firm continued in existence throughout the nineteenth century under the successive titles Mistress Powell & Daughters, Powell and Browns, and finally (after her death) the Misses Brown.

John Hardman Powell (also known as John Powell) showed early evidence of his artistic abilities and was placed under George Elkington (of Elkington & Co., Birmingham) to learn modelling. He also spent some time as a pupil at the Birmingham School of Art. However, the association of his uncle John Hardman with Pugin, and the latter's need for an assistant, led to his being dispatched in December 1844 to Ramsgate to take up residence in Pugin's home, The Grange, and to be trained by him. Powell and Pugin's own son, Edward, were his only pupils. Initially Pugin complained to John Hardman about the injury done to Powell by Elkington's style (as well as Powell's propensity for somnambulism), but soon even the perfectionist Pugin found his work satisfactory. There is evidence that even before Pugin's death Powell was drawing a significant number of cartoons for Hardman windows, as well as designing many pieces of metalwork. With the exception of the first half of 1848 Powell remained in Ramsgate until Pugin's death. Thus it was in Ramsgate on 21 October 1850 that he married Anne (1832–1897), Pugin's eldest daughter by his first wife, Anne Garnet.

Following Pugin's death Powell returned permanently to Birmingham, living in the same street as his uncle, Hunter's Lane, Handsworth, and assumed Pugin's mantle as chief designer for Hardmans. He was instrumental in the relocation of the firm's premises to New Hall Hill, where it remained until 1970. Powell was also taken into partnership by his uncle, joining his two elder brothers, William Powell (1820–1895) and James Powell (1825–1865). From the early 1850s the firm was known as John Hardman & Co. Two younger brothers, Edward (1833–1876) and Henry (1835–1882), worked for the firm in Ireland.

John Hardman Powell was concerned with all aspects of design as artistic director of both glass and metal departments until the business was divided in 1883, whereupon his activities were confined to the glass making. Although he adhered faithfully to the Gothic principles of his master, and never strayed too far from the basic premise of most of Pugin's designs, he nevertheless had his own distinct style which gave his creations a somewhat softer appearance than Pugin's. While opinion of his inventiveness varies he was without doubt an extremely talented designer who worked effectively in the diverse fields of Hardman production and was a major contributor to the firm's continued success throughout the nineteenth century, some of his windows being particularly fine. Although energetic and hard-working he was of a retiring disposition and, unlike his Hardman relatives, took no part in public life beyond a small amount of lecturing, notably to the Birmingham School of Art, and rare excursions into print. During the mid-1880s he left Birmingham and settled at 12 Lee Road, Blackheath, Kent, in order to be able to superintend the firm's London office. He died at his home of pneumonia on 2 March 1895 and was buried in the chantry of The Grange, Ramsgate. His obituary in the *Birmingham Weekly Post* (9 March) described him as modest, amiable, and charming, and surviving likenesses show him as a slightly diminutive, dark-haired, and moustachioed figure. His second and eldest surviving son, Dunstan John Powell (1861–1932), succeeded him as a partner and principal designer for the firm.

John Hardman Powell's brother William Powell appears to have been involved in the business from its earliest days, always on the metalwork side. He effectively took over control of that arm when it was divided from the glassworks in 1883 to form a distinct firm under the name Hardman, Powell & Co. and moved to separate premises in King Edward's Road, Birmingham. The declining demand by the early twentieth century for the type of metalware the firm produced led to its reabsorption into John Hardman & Co. in 1914, and, following family disagreements, to the eventual shedding of this aspect of the firm's business.

At its zenith in the third quarter of the nineteenth century John Hardman & Co. could boast that it had supplied windows or church plate or other metal furniture to the majority of the Roman Catholic and Anglican parish churches of England and Wales besides a number in Ireland. It also exported to Australia, the USA, South Africa, and other destinations abroad. The firm's popularity declined in the twentieth century, and the last family member to be involved in the business, John Tarleton Hardman (1872–1959), son of John Bernard Hardman, retired in 1935. The firm continues in existence, however, under different ownership and the slightly altered title of the John Hardman Studios, specializing in glasswork.

Ann Eatwell and Ruth Gosling

Sources Birm. CA, Hardman collection · P. Atterbury and C. Wainwright, eds., *Pugin: a Gothic passion* (1994) · J. H. Powell, 'Pugin in his home: a memoir', ed. A. Wedgwood, *Architectural History*, 31 (1998), 171–205 · IGI · D. Meara, *A. W. N. Pugin and the revival of memorial brasses* (1991) · D. Meara, *Victorian memorial brasses* (1983) · 'Councillor John B. Hardman', *Birmingham Faces and Places*, 2 (1889–90), 185–8 · *Birmingham Daily Post* (1 June 1867) · *Birmingham Daily Post* (5 June 1867) · *Birmingham Weekly Post* (9 March 1895) · *The Builder*, 25 (1867), 408 · *The Builder*, 68 (1895), 190 · Roman Catholic parish registers, St Chad's Cathedral, Birmingham Archdiocesan Archives · Index of Wills, 1867, PRO [John Hardman] · Index of Wills, 1895, PRO [John Hardman Powell] · memorials, St Chad's Cathedral, Birmingham · A. Wedgwood, *A. W. N. Pugin and the Pugin family* (1985) · Birmingham and London local directories, 1831–92, Birm. CL, local studies and history dept. · private information (2004) · *Art Journal*, 29 (1867), 172 · S. Bury, 'In search of Pugin's church plate', pt 1, *The Connoisseur*, 165 (1967), 29–35 · S. Bury, 'Pugin and the Tractarians', *The Connoisseur*, 179 (1972), 15–20 · *Birmingham gold and silver, 1773–1973*, Birmingham City Museum and Art Gallery (1973) · K. Crisp-Jones, ed., *The silversmiths of Birmingham* (1981) · J. Tallis, *Tallis's history and description of the Crystal Palace, and the exhibition of the world's industry in 1851*, ed. J. G. Strutt (1852) · P. Atterbury, ed., *A. W. N. Pugin: master of Gothic revival* (1995) · M. Harrison, *Victorian stained glass* (1980) · J. H. Powell, *Stray notes on art* (1888) · Pugin's diary, V&A NAL, L 5158–1969 · CGPLA Eng. & Wales (1867) · CGPLA Eng. & Wales (1895) · d. cert. [John Hardman]
Archives Birmingham City Archives, John Hardman & Co. business records · Birmingham Museums and Art Gallery, artefacts; designs and papers · HLRO, corresp., historical collection 304 · St Chad's Cathedral, Birmingham Archdiocesan Archives · St Mary's Convent, Hunter's Road, Handsworth, Birmingham · priv. coll.
Likenesses J. R. Herbert?, oils, c.1843 (John Hardman senior), Convent of Mercy, Handsworth, Birmingham; repro. in *Pugin*, ed. Atterbury and Wainwright, 175 · J. H. Powell, memorial brass, c.1867 (John Hardman), repro. in Meara, *A. W. N. Pugin and the revival of memorial brasses*, 74 · J. H. Powell, stained-glass window, c.1867 (of the Immaculate Conception, depicting John Hardman in bottom left-hand corner), St Chad's Cathedral, Birmingham · photograph (John Hardman), John Hardman Studios, Lightwoods House, Lightwoods Park, Hagley Road, Birmingham; repro. in Meara, *A. W. N. Pugin and the revival of memorial brasses*, 37
Wealth at death under £35,000—John Hardman: probate, 22 Aug 1867, CGPLA Eng. & Wales · £12,306 5s. 1d.—John Hardman Powell: probate, 7 Aug 1895, CGPLA Eng. & Wales

Hardman, Edward Townley (1845–1887), geologist, was born on 6 April 1845 at Drogheda, co. Louth, Ireland, of an old and respected family from that neighbourhood. He was educated at Drogheda and in 1867 won an exhibition to the Royal College of Science in Dublin. He graduated with a diploma in mining, receiving many prizes, and in 1870 joined the staff of the Geological Survey of Ireland. He was elected as a fellow of the Royal Geological Society of Ireland in 1871 and the Chemical Society of London in 1874. His early work largely involved geological mapping, mineralogy, coal geology, and the study of bone-bearing caves.

In 1883 Hardman was chosen by the Colonial Office for the temporary position of government geologist in Western Australia, primarily to report on the geology and gold prospects of the Kimberley district. He accompanied expeditions to that area in 1883 and 1884. During the second expedition, Hardman found strong traces of gold near what subsequently became known as Halls Creek in east Kimberley. The colony's first commercial goldfield was found in that area in 1885 by prospectors who were guided by Hardman's report. Although he had hoped that his appointment in the colony would be made permanent, the legislative council demurred at the cost and Hardman returned to his duties with the Geological Survey of Ireland in October 1885. The permanent appointment of a government geologist in Western Australia was finally approved in 1887, and Hardman was sent an offer of appointment. However, it arrived after he had died, at Adelaide Hospital in Dublin, from typhoid, on 30 April 1887. He left a widow, Louisa (whose maiden name was Gilholy), and two children. At the time of his death he was an applicant for the reward of £5000 that had been offered for the first discovery of payable gold in Western Australia. In 1888 the colonial government decided that the full conditions for the reward had not been met, but they made an *ex gratia* payment to Hardman's widow of £500.

Hardman was the author of many important maps and publications dealing with the geology of Ireland, but he is principally remembered for his pioneering work in Western Australia, leading to the first discovery of gold and the beginnings of the state's major mining industry. His name has been commemorated through the naming of three geographic features in the Kimberley district: Hardman range, Mount Hardman, and Hardman Point. His premature death was a tragic loss to Western Australian geology. PHILLIP PLAYFORD

Sources A. B. Wynne, *Geological Magazine*, new ser., 3rd decade, 4 (1887), 334–6 · P. E. Playford, 'Hardman, Edward Townley', *AusDB*, vol. 4 · P. E. Playford and I. Ruddock, 'Discovery of the Kimberley goldfield', *Early Days*, 9/3 (1985), 76–106 · 'Reward for discovery of Kimberley goldfields', Battye Library, Perth, Australia, Western Australia department of mines, 1286/07 (3049/70) · G. L. Herries Davies, *Sheets of many colours: the mapping of Ireland's rocks, 1750–1890* (1983), 202–25 · G. L. Herries Davies, *North from the Hook: 150 years of the Geological Survey of Ireland* (1995), 75–296 · *CGPLA Ire.* (1887)
Archives University of Western Australia, Perth, fieldbooks and watercolour paintings
Likenesses etching (after photograph by J. Forrest), Parliamentary Library, Perth, Australia; repro. in Playford and Ruddock, 'Discovery', figure 4
Wealth at death £857 18s. 2d.: administration, 8 June 1887, *CGPLA Eng. & Wales*

Hardman, Frederick (1814–1874), journalist and novelist, was the son of Joseph Hardman, a London merchant of Manchester extraction, and his wife, Frances Anna Rougemont. Joseph Hardman was a friend of Coleridge, and a contributor to *Blackwood's Edinburgh Magazine*. On leaving Whitehead's School at Ramsgate, Frederick worked briefly as a clerk in the office of his maternal uncle, but disliking the sedentary life he volunteered in 1834 for the British Legion. He was recruited by Sir George de Lacy Evans to assist the Spanish government forces against the Carlist rebels, serving as a lieutenant in the second lancers. Severely wounded in one of the last engagements with the Carlists, he spent a period of convalescence at Toulouse before returning to England, where he became a

regular contributor to *Blackwood's Magazine*. His first article (1840) was an account of an expedition with the guerrilla chief Zurbano, reprinted with other pieces based on his Spanish experiences in *Peninsular Scenes and Sketches* (1846). He published a novel of the Carlist war, *The Student of Salamanca*, in 1847. Between 1840 and 1868 he contributed almost two hundred articles and stories to *Blackwood's*, besides writing for *Bentley's Magazine*, the *Foreign and Quarterly Review*, the *New Monthly Magazine*, *Ainsworth's Magazine*, and the *Monthly Chronicle*.

A critique of the Paris salon which Hardman forwarded to *The Times* led to his engagement about 1850 as one of its roving foreign correspondents. He was stationed at Madrid in 1854, before proceeding the following year to Constantinople, where he acted as political correspondent and administered the *Times* fund for the relief of soldiers wounded in the Crimea. His exposure of the drunkenness which demoralized the British army after the suspension of hostilities led to vigorous counter-measures. After a Balkan tour he proceeded in 1857 to Turin, where he won the confidence of Cavour. In 1859 he was a war correspondent with the Spanish expeditionary force in Morocco, vividly described in his *The Spanish Campaign in Morocco* (1860), and he also reported the campaigns in Lombardy and Schleswig-Holstein. He was denied a permanent posting until March 1873, when he was finally appointed as chief correspondent of *The Times* at Paris, a post he had long coveted, but his short tenure was marred by an uneasy relationship with his assistant, Henri de Blowitz. He died unmarried at his residence, 6 rue de Solférino, Paris, on 6 November 1874.
J. G. ALGER, *rev.* G. MARTIN MURPHY

Sources [S. Morison and others], *The history of The Times*, 2 (1939) · *The Times* (13 Nov 1874) · *Blackwood*, 125 (1879), 235–6 · *The Graphic* (28 Nov 1874), 512 · R. Carr, *Spain, 1808–1939* (1966), 261, n. 1
Archives News Int. RO, papers | BL, letter to Florence Nightingale · NL Scot., letters to Blackwoods
Likenesses portrait, repro. in *The Graphic*
Wealth at death under £20,000: probate, 16 Dec 1874, *CGPLA Eng. & Wales*

Hardman, John (1767–1844). See under Hardman family (*per. c.*1820–1935).

Hardman, John (1811–1867). See under Hardman family (*per. c.*1820–1935).

Hardoon, Silas Aaron (1851–1931), merchant and property owner, was born in Baghdad, one of the six children of Aaron Hardoon. He moved with his family to Bombay about 1856. His family was poor and he received only an elementary education, possibly supported by the local Baghdadi Jewish community.

Hardoon's career was made within the trading diaspora of Baghdadi Jews in India and in east Asia. Employed while still in his teens by David Sassoon & Co., the major Baghdadi Jewish merchant house in Asia, he was transferred to its Hong Kong office about 1868, and then to its Shanghai branch in 1874. In its early years the firm competed with Jardine Matheson & Co. in exporting opium from India to China. About 1882 Hardoon left David Sassoon & Co. and after a brief engagement as cotton broker, he joined E. D. Sassoon & Co. (a firm established by one of the sons of David Sassoon) either in 1886 or 1887. In the later nineteenth century E. D. Sassoon & Co. was advancing into cotton mills, brewing, paper mills, shipping, tramways, and banking. Hardoon acted as manager and, after 1893, as partner, and mainly handled opium imports and purchase of properties. He severed his association with this enterprise in 1911.

Meanwhile, in 1901 Hardoon had founded the Hardoon Company, which also dealt in opium and real estate. It remains difficult to assess the degree of his involvement in the opium trade, but it was probably not the focus of his operations. The key to his commercial success was his continuous and far-sighted purchase of properties in the central district of the Shanghai international settlement, where the value of land rose dramatically after the beginning of the century. In 1916 he became the major owner of properties along Nanking Road, which was the main commercial thoroughfare. He served as councillor of the Conseil Municipal Français of the Shanghai Concession Française from 1892 until 1903. He was also elected, from 1900 until 1904, to the same position in the British-dominated Shanghai municipal council, where he represented the interests of E. D. Sassoon & Co.

Apart from his economic achievements, Hardoon is mostly remembered for his strong ties with Chinese society. His marriage on 26 September 1886 to Liza Roos (1864–1941), more commonly known as Luo Jialing, a Eurasian Buddhist who identified almost exclusively with her Chinese background, reinforced these links. They married according to Chinese rites, but in 1928 they also entered into a British civil marriage in the Shanghai British consulate-general. Although Hardoon and his wife did not have any offspring, they jointly adopted eleven foreign children who were brought up as Jews. Luo Jialing also adopted numerous Chinese children under her Chinese surname Luo.

Hardoon sponsored the reprinting of the canon of sacred Buddhist texts (accomplished about 1913), and also funded other Buddhist enterprises, such as the construction of the Pingshe retreat house. Such projects were conceived under the influence of his wife. After the foundation of the Chinese republic in 1911, Hardoon also financed educational and cultural activities within the most conservative Chinese intellectual circles, and he became well respected as a philanthropist. The Peking government duly bestowed on him at least twelve decorations in the seven years following 1917, including, in 1924, the first-class decoration of the Zhaowu order with Big Belt, possibly the highest honour ever conferred on a foreigner.

Hardoon remained a regular contributor to the religious and philanthropic activities of the Shanghai Jewish community. In 1925 he donated the funds to build the Beth Aharon Synagogue. His participation in community affairs was, however, considered lukewarm compared with his more enthusiastic support for Chinese causes and attracted censure from the Jewish community.

When Hardoon died, on 19 June 1931 at his private residence in Bubbling Well Road, Shanghai, his assets were estimated to be worth $35 million. He was buried on 21 June in his private garden in Shanghai, and Buddhist monks and Daoist priests attended his Jewish Orthodox funeral. An obituary in the *Shanghai Evening Post and Mercury* (3 July 1931) described him as a 'unique local character': 'He was a blend of all faiths and hopes, a talented man who lived his life in an exotic setting as he thought best' (*Israel's Messenger*, 3 July 1931). Above all, however, he was during the last quarter of his life the pre-eminent property owner in the international settlement and one of the richest foreigners in east Asia. CHIARA BETTA

Sources C. Betta, 'The rise of Silas Aaron Hardoon (1851–1931) as Shanghai's major individual landowner', *Sino-Judaica*, 2 (1995), 1–40 · C. Betta, 'Silas Aaron Hardoon and cross-cultural adaptation in Shanghai', *The Jews of China*, ed. J. Goldstein and E. Sharpe (1998), 216–29 · C. Betta, 'Silas Aaron Hardoon (1851–1931): marginality and adaptation in Shanghai', PhD diss., SOAS, 1997 · *Hatong xiansheng rongailu*, 16 vols. in 12 (Shanghai, 1932) [in Chinese; in commemoration of S. A. Hardoon] · *China Weekly Review* (27 June 1931) · *Israel's Messenger* (3 July 1931) · C. Roth, *The Sassoon dynasty* (1941) · S. D. Chapman, *Merchant enterprise in Britain: from the industrial revolution to World War I* (1992) · m. cert. · PRO, FO 671/545 · *North China Herald* (20 June 1931) · *Shanghai Times* (22 June 1931)
Archives Hardoon Company, Shanghai, Shanghai House Property Administration Bureau archives
Likenesses photographs, repro. in *Hatong xiansheng rongailu*
Wealth at death $35,000,000 [150 million Chinese dollars]: *China Weekly Review*

Hardres, Sir Thomas (1609/10–1681), lawyer and politician, was the fourth son of Sir Thomas Hardres (1575–1628) of Upper Hardres, Kent, and Eleanor, sole surviving daughter and heir of Henry Thoresby of Thoresby, a master in chancery. He was descended from a family which owned the manor of Broad Oak at Hardres near Canterbury. Shortly after his father's death Hardres entered Gray's Inn, on 15 June 1629 (as late of Staple Inn), and was called to the bar on 29 May 1636. On 21 September 1639 he was licensed to marry Dorcas (*c*.1617–1643), daughter and heir of George Bargrave of Bridge, Kent. They had one son and one daughter. Although his brother was an active member of the Kentish county committee until the second civil war, when he joined the king, Hardres was fined £15 for delinquency, and was held in suspicion by the protectorate authorities. In 1649 he became steward of Lambeth and by 1651 was married again, this time to Philadelphia (*d*. 1690), daughter of James Francklyn of Maidstone and widow of Peter Manwood of Sandwich. They had five sons and a daughter. After the Restoration Hardres was made first a freeman of Canterbury (1661), then a common councilman (1662), and eventually recorder (1664). He then succeeded the deceased recorder as MP for the borough in April 1664.

Hardres was not an active MP, but his legal career continued to progress. In November 1669 he was made a serjeant-at-law, and in 1675 survived an attempt by his political enemies in Canterbury to have him removed from the recordership after the mayor of Canterbury and several aldermen had been taken into custody by the House of Commons. Possibly with a view to winning his support in parliament the king appointed him a king's serjeant on 11 May 1676 and knighted him six days later. By this date Hardres was a court supporter, hence his appointment about 1679 to the place of steward of the chancery court of the Cinque Ports. His support for the court may explain the loss of his parliamentary seat in the first election of 1679. He won it back at the election of October 1679. He chaired the Kentish quarter sessions in January 1680, refusing to countenance a petition calling for the meeting of parliament. Hardres died on 18 December 1681, aged seventy-one, his corpse being carried from Serjeants' Inn to Upper Hardres for burial. His widow was buried on 15 April 1690. Hardres's *Reports of Cases in the Exchequer, 1655–1670* was published in 1693. STUART HANDLEY

Sources HoP, *Commons, 1660–90*, 1.276, 2.490–91 · Sainty, *King's counsel*, 20 · Baker, *Serjeants*, 516 · J. Foster, *The register of admissions to Gray's Inn, 1521–1889, together with the register of marriages in Gray's Inn chapel, 1695–1754* (privately printed, London, 1889), 188 · H. W. Woolrych, *Lives of eminent serjeants-at-law of the English bar*, 2 vols. (1869), 1.400–01 · will, PRO, PROB 11/368, sig. 182 · N. Luttrell, *A brief historical relation of state affairs from September 1678 to April 1714*, 1 (1857), 153 · R. J. Fletcher, ed., *The pension book of Gray's Inn*, 1 (1901), 327 · J. M. Cowper, ed., *The register booke of the parish of St George the Martyr* (1891), 38–9, 188 · R. Hovenden, ed., *The register booke of christeninges, marriages, and burialls within the precinct of the cathedrall and metropoliticall church of Christe of Canterburie*, Harleian Society, register section, 2 (1878), 128 · J. M. Cowper, ed., *Canterbury marriage licences*, 6 vols. (1892–1906), vol. 2, p. 454

Hardwick, Charles (1817–1889), antiquary, was born at Preston, Lancashire, on 10 September 1817, the son of William Hardwick, a coachman, and his wife, Mary Taylor. He was apprenticed to a printer, but subsequently practised as a portrait painter in the Preston area: he was, however, a 'minor talent'. Having joined the Odd Fellows friendly society, he took an important share in the reform of the Manchester Unity, and was elected grand master of the order. He was also a vice-president of the Manchester Literary Club, of which he was a founder.

Hardwick was an enthusiastic amateur historian and archaeologist. He was primarily responsible for the discovery, and first tentative investigation, of the important Roman site at Walton-le-Dale and of the motte and bailey at Penwortham. He wrote a number of local history books, of which the most important was *A History of the Borough of Preston* (1857). He died at Manchester on 8 July 1889. ALAN G. CROSBY

Sources H. W. Clemestra, *A bibliography of the history of Preston in Amounderness* (1923), 5 · private information (2004) · A. Crosby, *Penwortham in the past* (1988) · parish register, Preston, St John, Lancs. RO · C. W. Sutton, *A list of Lancashire authors* (1876), 48 · W. E. A. Axon, *The Academy* (20 July 1889), 39 · DNB · CGPLA Eng. & Wales (1889)
Wealth at death £1077 8s.: probate, 13 Aug 1889, CGPLA Eng. & Wales

Hardwick, Charles (1821–1859), ecclesiastical historian and Church of England clergyman, was born at Slingsby, near Malton, in the North Riding of Yorkshire, on 22 September 1821, one of the sons of a farmer and joiner, Charles Hardwick, and his wife, Sarah. After receiving some education at Slingsby, Malton, and Sheffield, he acted briefly as usher in schools at Thornton and Malton,

and as assistant to the Revd Henry Barlow at Shirland rectory in Derbyshire. In October 1840 he unsuccessfully competed for a sizarship at St John's College, Cambridge. He became instead a pensioner, and afterwards a minor scholar, of St Catharine's College. The influence of his tutor George Elwes Corrie in forming his taste for antiquarian scholarship and churchmanship was most marked.

Hardwick graduated BA in 1844, and became tutor in the family of Sir Joseph Radcliffe, a Yorkshire baronet, at Brussels. He returned to St Catharine's in 1845, when he was elected Skerne fellow there. He was ordained deacon in 1846 and priest in 1847, in which year he also proceeded MA. During 1846 he edited Sir Roger Twysden's *Historical Vindication of the Church of England*, and edited as a supplement Francis Fullwood's *Roma ruit* in 1847. He then edited *A Poem on the Times of Edward II* (1849) and an *Anglo-Saxon Passion of St George*, with a translation (1850). He was editor-in-chief of the *Catalogue of the Manuscripts Preserved in the Library of the University of Cambridge*, contributing descriptions of early English literature to the first three volumes (1856–8). In 1849 he read before the Cambridge Antiquarian Society 'An historical inquiry touching Saint Catherine of Alexandria', and in 1850 he helped to edit the Book of Homilies under Corrie's supervision. He was select preacher at Cambridge for that year, and in March 1851 became preacher at the Chapel Royal, Whitehall. His *History of the Articles of Religion* first appeared in 1851, 'a very remarkable work for so young a man' (*Annual Register*, 1859, 431), and a second edition, mostly rewritten, was published in 1859.

From March to September 1853 Hardwick was professor of divinity in Queen's College, Birmingham, the ill repute of which caused his speedy resignation. In the same year he printed *Twenty Sermons for Town Congregations*, a selection from his Whitehall sermons, and *A History of the Christian Church, Middle Age*. In 1855 he was appointed lecturer in divinity at King's College, Cambridge, and Christian advocate in the university. In the latter capacity he published *Christ and other masters: an historical inquiry into some of the chief parallelisms and contrasts between Christianity and the religious systems of the ancient world* (1855–9). In 1856 he was elected a member of the newly established council of the senate, being re-elected in 1858. Early in 1856 he published the second volume of his *History of the Christian Church*, embracing the Reformation period, and in 1858 completed an edition of the Anglo-Saxon and Northumbrian versions of St Matthew's gospel, begun by J. M. Kemble. For many years he was secretary of the university branch association of the Society for the Propagation of the Gospel, and enthusiastically promoted the proposed Oxford and Cambridge mission to central Africa. He also served as college praelector and chaplain, and was known for 'his pleasant courtesy, not the less acceptable to young men because rather prim' (Browne, *St Catharine's*, 225).

In 1859 Hardwick became archdeacon of Ely, and commenced BD. On 18 or 19 August of that year, during his annual energetic travels abroad, he was killed by falling down rocks in the Pyrenees. A monument was erected on the spot. He was buried on the 21st in the cemetery at Luchon, France, and memorial windows were later placed at Cambridge, Great St Mary's, and Slingsby.

JOHN D. PICKLES

Sources F. Procter, 'Memoir', in C. Hardwick, *Christ and other masters*, 2nd edn (1863) • *GM*, 3rd ser., 7 (1859), 419–21 • *Annual Register* (1859), 431–2 • *Cambridge Chronicle* (27 Aug 1859), 4 • *Cambridge Chronicle* (3 Sept 1859), 4 • G. F. Browne, *St Catharine's College* (1902), 224–6 • G. F. Browne, *Recollections of a bishop* (1915), 45 • A. St C. Brooke, *Slingsby and Slingsby Castle* (1904), 184–7 • Corrie MSS, St Catharine's College, Cambridge • unpublished biographical notes, St John Cam. • *CGPLA Eng. & Wales* (1859)
Archives St Catharine's College, Cambridge, Corrie MSS
Likenesses photograph, 1850?–1859, CUL, Collection of Cambridge Antiquarian Society Photographs
Wealth at death under £2000: administration, 6 Dec 1859, *CGPLA Eng. & Wales*

Hardwick, Elizabeth. *See* Talbot, Elizabeth, countess of Shrewsbury (1527?–1608).

Hardwick, John (1790–1875). *See under* Hardwick, Thomas (1752–1829).

Hardwick, Philip (1792–1870), architect, the youngest son and fifth child of Thomas *Hardwick (1752–1829), architect, and his wife, Elizabeth, *née* Hardwick (1763–1804), of St Marylebone, Middlesex, was born on 15 June 1792 at 9 Rathbone Place, London. 'His life,' wrote an obituarist, 'was singularly uneventful' (*The Times*, 31 Dec 1870). Having been educated at Dr Barrow's school in Soho Square he became a pupil in his father's office and entered the Royal Academy Schools in 1808; he exhibited seven drawings at the academy between 1807 and 1814. He matured at that period when it was possible to unite the skills of architect and engineer. Visiting Paris in 1815 he concentrated on French work in iron, 'as they are many years before us in this branch of building' (letter to his father, 5 Sept 1815; Hobhouse, 139, n.5). In 1818–19 he spent a year in Italy (his drawing of the Paestum temples he exhibited at the Royal Academy in 1820). On his return from France he had joined his father and subsequently took over the whole practice, paying his father an annuity. On 18 October he married Julia Tufnell (1801–1881), daughter of John Shaw (1776–1832), architect, at St James's, Westminster; the elder of their two sons died while at Eton College.

Hardwick soon collected a pocketful of surveyorships that provided a regular income: he worked for the Bridewell and Bethlem hospitals (1816–36), St Katharine's Dock Company (from 1825), St Bartholomew's Hospital, in succession to his father (1826–56), the Goldsmiths' Company (1828–68), the Westminster Bridge estates (from 1829), Lord Salisbury's London estate (1829–35), and the London and Birmingham Railway Company (from 1839). He was also surveyor to the Portman London estate, to the first duke of Wellington (from 1842), and to Greenwich Hospital. A member of the Institution of Civil Engineers from 1824, he was a founder member of the Institute of British Architects (1834), vice-president in 1839 and 1841, and gold medallist in 1854. He was elected ARA in 1840 and almost immediately promoted RA (1841; retired 1868); he was treasurer from 1850 to 1861. He was also elected FSA in 1824, FRS in 1831, and FGS in 1837. At the Paris Exposition of 1855 he exhibited drawings of Lincoln's Inn and Goldsmiths' Hall, and was awarded a gold medal (second class).

Early commissions Philip Hardwick assisted his father, Thomas, in at least one of his commissions for the Church Building Commissioners—Christ Church, Cosway Street, St Marylebone (1822–4; secularized), of which he exhibited an interior view in the Royal Academy in 1828—and probably also in Holy Trinity, Bolton, Lancashire (1823–5; Perpendicular). He himself was employed by the commissioners to design Stretton church, in Cheshire, (1826–7; dem. 1907), in a plain, Gothic, style but his subsequent church work, apart from St David's, Rhymni, Monmouthshire (1840–43), was limited to repairs and reinstatements, as at St Anne's, Limehouse, London (1850–51), after a fire.

Employed by the St Katharine's Dock Company in the complex compensation cases consequent upon the compulsory acquisition of the site (1824–5) Hardwick was then commissioned to design the dock-house (Doric, 1827) and six stacks of warehouses (1827–9; Eastern three bombed, 1940; all but one of the western ones demolished *c.*1970), 'more grand than useful' (*Dockland*, 16). He overcame the constrictions of the site by erecting these vast structures on impressive quay-edge arcades of hollow cast-iron Tuscan Doric columns, founded via inverted arches onto strip footings of brick, and carrying a Portland-stone entablature with concealed cast-iron beams; above these rose cliffs of brickwork with wide cast-iron framed windows and pilaster strips, finishing in semicircular arches. This introduced to warehouse façades the giant, blind arcade familiar in domestic architecture. Hardwick's warehouses established a lasting pattern (notably copied in Liverpool docks, where he himself contributed the Albert Dock traffic office, 1846–7).

Major commissions Far from utilitarian, however, was the work that established Hardwick's reputation as a classical architect: in the van of Sir Charles Barry's and Sir John Soane's Renaissance revival came Goldsmiths' Hall, Foster Lane (1829–35), ceremonial seat of one of the grandest City livery companies, its florid Roman façade screening Hardwick's own stair and livery hall of overwhelming grandeur, as well as a reconstruction of Edward Jerman's 1669 courtroom. His success brought the commission for the City of London Club (Old Broad Street, London, 1833–4), but again with an idiosyncratic flavour: Palladian with Doric pilasters to the upper storey, in contrast to Barry's astylar West End club-houses. He further used Doric for the Globe Insurance office, Cheapside (1837), but Sefton House, Belgrave Square (1842), and 10 Kensington Palace Gardens (1846–9; altered 1896 and 1903–4) were Italianate *palazzi* more in Barry's mould.

Hardwick employed his liking for the masculinity of Doric brilliantly in creating the greatest monument of the railway age: the propylaeum fronting the London and Birmingham Railway terminus at Euston—the so-called

'Doric arch' (1836–8, £35,000; dem. 1961–2). This was modelled on the entrance to the Acropolis at Athens, only the noblest gateway of antiquity being symbolically appropriate for such an overwhelming achievement as the world's first long-distance railway. Additional buildings at Euston, including flanking hotels, were completed in 1839, 'the last work executed by [Philip] Hardwick without the assistance of his son' (*DNB*). Major additions approved in 1846, redesigned and carried out by his son, are considered below. Hardwick's corresponding gateway for the railway's Birmingham terminus was in the Ionic order.

Predominantly working in the public eye as an institutional architect in the classical style, Hardwick had only a small country-house output, where he early adopted the fashionable 'Old English' or 'Jacobethan' style. Babraham House, Cambridgeshire (*c*.1829–37), is somewhat coarse, resembling—but more robust than—houses by his contemporary Edward Blore. Similar were his additions to Kneller Hall, Middlesex (*c*.1830), the bishop's palace at Hereford (*c*.1833–41), and Westwood Park, Worcestershire (*c*.1840), and the new house at Hall, near Barnstaple, Devon (1844–7). Tudor Gothic was also favoured for schools and hospitals, including the Bethlem Hospital's schools at Lambeth (1829–30; dem. *c*.1932) and Wainfleet St Mary, Lincolnshire (1830–32); the Goldsmiths' Company's grammar school at Stockport, Cheshire (1830–32; dem. 1923); and the naval asylum at Penge, Kent (1847–9). However, in his several additions and restorations at St Bartholomew's Hospital, London (new gateway, medical theatre, and museum, 1834–5; new ward block, 1842; recasing, 1851), he adhered to the character of James Gibbs's work.

Hardwick's important commission for a new hall, council room, and library for the great legal focus, Lincoln's Inn, London, proved innovative and was much admired—the first conspicuous metropolitan building 'in which the piquant possibilities of articulated Gothic composition were made strikingly evident' (Hitchcock, 1.315). Having criticized an inadequate plan by John White submitted for his advice in 1839 Hardwick was then himself asked to design a larger complex; he proposed a new, insulated site overlooking Lincoln's Inn Fields. His carefully researched plans were approved in 1842. Despite his classical antecedents he recommended the late fifteenth-century 'Collegiate style of Architecture … before the admixture of Italian architecture' as 'most appropriate' for the site (Lincoln's Inn, black books, xxiv, 164), isolated from the inn's Palladian Stone Buildings. Of red brick (a remarkable choice at that date but practical in the smoky atmosphere), diapered in dark brick, with crisply modelled Anston-stone trim to the windows and buttresses, the range stands out impressively, its skyline embellished with ornamented chimneys, turrets, spires, and heraldic beasts—an outstanding work of Perpendicular revival and a daring discord with the inn's earlier buildings. Also marching with the avant-garde were Hardwick's asymmetrical touches to his symmetrical T-plan, masked by the picturesque outline of the clearly articulated, functionally distinct masses of the hall and library, their high but distinct roofs at right angles and linked by the benchers' block with its crowning octagonal lantern (the hidden symmetry was subsequently distorted by Scott's eastward extension of the library in 1871–2). The contract figure of £55,000 was, however, greatly exceeded.

Contract drawings at Lincoln's Inn, dated November 1842, specify extensive use of wrought and cast iron in the construction and call for preliminary models of the remarkable hammerbeam roofs of hall and library—the former based on Westminster Hall, with pendants borrowed from Hampton Court (where Hardwick's father had been clerk of the works); the latter, resembling the roof of the great hall at Eltham Palace (though partially ceiled), with hints from that of the Middle Temple, may also be interpreted as a unique transmutation into wood and iron of the structure of the vault of Henry VII's chapel in Westminster Abbey, as represented in Professor Willis's paper to the Royal Institute of British Architects published in 1842, its giant pendants dividing the upper space of the library into nave and aisles. But as building began Hardwick, about May 1843, fell ill, followed by his son, who had been assisting him. Supervision fell to Hardwick's current assistant, John Loughborough Pearson (1817–1897); the younger Hardwick returned about January 1844 to arrange 'the crowning features and all the fittings' (Pearson, 291–2). In 1844–5 Philip Hardwick also completed Lincoln's Inn Stone Buildings to the original Palladian design of 1774.

Later years Hardwick was admired for his unswerving probity and notable business efficiency—qualities marked by his election as vice-president of the Institute of British Architects, an invitation to join a limited competition for the Carlton Club, in Pall Mall, in 1844; selection as a judge in the important Royal Exchange (1839) and Oxford Museum (1854) competitions; and appointment as an examiner of candidates for district surveyorships under the Metropolitan Buildings Act (1843). Lord Mahon in 1842 found him 'an architect of very agreeable manners and intelligent conversation' (Stanhope, 218); Thomas Henry Wyatt (1807–1880) was a pupil. From about 1845 a spinal complaint confined his practice to such 'as could be followed in his own room' (*The Builder*, 14 Jan 1871) although he was able to drag himself to committees, only gradually surrendering his offices and surveyorships before retiring from business in 1861. In the 1850s the Hardwicks had moved from bourgeois Russell Square to aristocratic 21 Cavendish Square, where they enjoyed the services of a butler, footman, lady's maid, cook, and two housemaids. Suffering from heart disease Hardwick retreated about 1865 to Westcombe Lodge, Wandsworth, where, 'helpless in body and infirm in mind' (ibid.) he died on 28 December 1870. He was buried at Kensal Green cemetery on 3 January 1871. Apart from an £800 annuity to his widow, and lesser legacies, he bequeathed his estate, sworn at £120,000, to his surviving son, **Philip Charles Hardwick** (1822–1892), architect. Born on 12 September 1822, he trained first in Edward Blore's office (when he visited Belgium and Germany) and then in that of his father. He subsequently travelled in Germany in the 1840s.

He took over on the collapse of the elder Hardwick's health, in the 1840s, eventually succeeding to many of his surveyorships, including those of St Bartholomew's Hospital (1856–71), Greenwich Hospital, and the Charterhouse. The practices of father and son form a seamless web and have left confusion about who designed what. Philip Charles Hardwick was elected fellow of the Royal Institute of British Architects in 1850 and of the Society of Antiquaries in 1860.

Philip Charles Hardwick Philip Charles Hardwick, a 'careful and industrious student of mediaeval art' and 'an extremely able and prolific sketcher and a very good draughtsman' (*Journal of Proceedings of the RIBA*, new ser., 8), nevertheless stands in the second rank of Gothic revival architects, although his work—in general cold and dry, if stylistically correct and fashionable—has occasional brilliant flashes. But apparently it suited his aristocratic patrons. For the fourth Earl Spencer, for whom he subsequently built a billiard room on the north front of Althorp (1851; dem. *c.*1891), he designed the church at Little Brington, Northamptonshire (1850; with school) and for the fourth Earl Beauchamp that at Newland, Worcestershire (1862–4; with quadrangle of almshouses, 320 ft by 170 ft, £60,000). He designed St Edmund's Clergy Orphan School and its chapel, at Canterbury, in 1854. Other churches of his design include St John's, Deptford, London (1855); St Mark's, Surbiton, Surrey (1855; bombed, rebuilt 1960); All Saints', Haggerston, London (1855–6; enlarged); St Thomas, Portman Square, London (with school, 1858; dem.); All Saints', Aldershot, Hampshire (1863); and St Barnabas, Mayland, Essex (1867). In Ireland he designed St John's Roman Catholic Cathedral in Limerick (*c.*1860). He rebuilt the churches of St Margaret, Collier Wood, Kent (1847–9); St Mary, Lambeth, London (1851–2); and St Nicholas, Elstree, Hertfordshire (1853), and was also extensively employed on restorations, both in London and small country churches.

Like his father, Philip Charles Hardwick was much employed in the City of London, where he became the leading architect of grandiose banking offices, mainly in an Italianate manner, setting the pattern for suburban and provincial designs for almost three decades. In the City he executed the Bank of Australasia (1854; dem.), Jones, Loyd & Co., Lothbury (*c.*1857; dem. 1949), Robarts, Curtis, and Lubbock, Lombard Street (1863), Barclay and Bevan, Lombard Street (1864), the Union Bank of London (Poultry, eclectic; 1865), and, at Charing Cross, Drummond's (1877–9). As architect to the Bank of England he had little to do at Threadneedle Street but altered Uxbridge House, London (1855), and designed branch offices at Hull (1856) and Leeds (1862–5). He also designed a number of large schools. The Royal Freemasons' School, Wandsworth, London (1851; dem. 1933), was his first major contribution (with the symmetrical façade characteristic of his father), in red brick with dark diapering, a central tower, and an exuberant skyline. His most important school, Charterhouse, at Godalming in Surrey (1865–72),

was in collegiate Gothic, its buildings separate yet forming an architectural group, a brilliantly asymmetric assemblage of gabled dormers, chimney shafts, oriels, and towers 'far above Hardwick's usual level', comprising 'probably the most picturesque of the C19 public schools' (*Surrey*, 143–4). He also designed several public buildings, including Durham town hall (Perpendicular; 1849–51) and markets.

The younger Hardwick's public prominence came, however, with his work for the railway companies that were establishing metropolitan termini. He continued his father's work at Euston, enlarging the station block (1846–9; £150,000), notably by introducing a great hall into station design. Roman Renaissance in style and grandiose in concept, it was executed in inferior materials, its plaster walls and columns painted to imitate granite. As surveyor to the Great Western Railway he designed the terminus hotel for Paddington Station (1851–3), 'really the first grandiose and monumental hotel in Britain' (Hitchcock, 1.211), vying with the new American and continental hotels. The *Illustrated London News* (21, 1852, 538) described its style as 'French of Louis XIV or later'; Hitchcock suggests that its plastic massing suggests 'Second Empire *avant la lettre*' (Hitchcock, 1.211). But the convex-concave roofs of the towers derive from the gatehouses at Westwood Park, Worcestershire, that Hardwick had reorganized in 1840.

Country-house commissions Unlike his father the younger Hardwick enjoyed an extensive country-house practice, partly for City contacts. Despite his reputation as a classical architect he designed his houses almost entirely in asymmetrical versions of Gothic. Hall, near Barnstaple, Devon (1844–9), often ascribed to his father, was probably his first; certainly he himself completed it. It is distinguished by its virtually free-standing, quasi-medieval great hall. At Aldermaston Court, Berkshire (1848–51; £20,000), he replaced a Carolean house destroyed by fire with a vast, restless, towered, and chimneyed Tudor-Gothic house in the diapered red brick and cream stone of Lincoln's Inn. Gilston Park, Hertfordshire (1852), is similar in character but executed in random stone rubble. In the same style he added a new wing to Adare Manor, Ireland (1850–62), begun by James Pain and A. W. N. Pugin for the third earl of Dunraven (for whom he also rebuilt two churches at Adare), though his 'Wyndham Tower' strikes a discordant, foreign note. Also with French Renaissance elements was the Jacobethan Addington Park, Buckinghamshire (1856), for the governor of the Bank of England, where Hardwick introduced plate-glass sash windows, an extensively followed innovation for Gothic houses. At Sompting Abbots, Sussex (1856), he employed the local flint in a superficially picturesque but meanly detailed Tudor (with a French tower), inconveniently planned. More satisfactory—and probably his best house—was the centrally planned Rendcomb, Gloucestershire (1865–7; over £40,000), for the bullion broker Sir Francis Goldsmid QC, superbly constructed by Thomas Cubitt in Charles Barry's Italianate style; Hardwick's dominating tower, however, is less well integrated in his composition than usual. A huge service wing is cleverly masked, and the separate stable block, of a French character, is architecturally impressive. Hardwick also designed seven blocks of semi-detached estate cottages. For Hassobury, Farnham, Essex (1868), he returned to Tudor. He found an unusually light touch in his prolonged restoration of Madresfield Court, Worcestershire (1863–85), for the fifth and sixth earls Beauchamp. Confronted with a crumbling medieval house, he considered it 'necessary to substitute reconstruction for repair' (Beauchamp, 104–10). 'The restricted site, bounded by the moat, brought out the best in Hardwick … the effect is magical', and the reconstructed inner courtyard produced 'an evocation of the world of old Nuremberg' (Aslet, 'Madresfield Court', 1460–61). Ante-room, billiard room, and library on the ground floor, with the long gallery above, are part of his work, as is the dining-room, of great-hall type, with a hammerbeam roof resembling that at Lincoln's Inn.

Hardwick exhibited regularly at the Royal Academy between 1848 and 1854, and occasionally thereafter. He was regarded by contemporaries as 'an able architect and an honest man' (The Builder, 13 Feb 1892, 120) and his 'sound common sense, combined with his artistic and literary attainments' (The Athenaeum, 6 Feb 1892), assured his professional prominence. He was selected as a participant in the competition for a memorial to Prince Albert in 1863; his huge, gilded statue of the prince, raised on a sculptured podium above a curved double staircase, initially was Queen Victoria's choice but was merely commended by the advisory committee. Much in demand as a referee, he declined to serve as a judge in the competition for a new national gallery or to compete for the new law courts (1866–7) but acted as adviser in the new War Office and Admiralty competition of 1884. Arthur William Blomfield was his pupil in 1852–5.

Personal charm and kindliness and his wide range of interests secured Hardwick many friends. Having gradually withdrawn from practice he was active in good works, particularly as treasurer of the Artists' Benevolent Institution. He married Helen (b. 1849), eldest daughter of Robert Eaton, of Bryn-y-Mor, Swansea, and Claverton Manor, Bath, on 15 August 1872; they had at least three sons and two daughters. Having for two years suffered from cancer of the rectum, Hardwick died at his home—2 Hereford Gardens, Park Lane, London—on 27 January 1892, survived by his wife and leaving an estate of nearly £211,000. Like his father he was buried in Kensal Green cemetery, on 1 February.   M. H. PORT

Sources H. Hobhouse, 'Philip and Philip Charles Hardwick', Seven Victorian architects, ed. J. Fawcett (1976), 32–49, 139–41, 151–2 · Transactions of the Institute of British Architects of London (1871–2), 4–5 · Journal of Proceedings of the Royal Institute of British Architects, new ser., 8 (1891–2), 174–5 · The Builder (1843), 39 · The Builder (1845), 521–2, 526 · The Builder (1864), 758–9 · The Builder (1865), 412–13, 607, 609 · The Builder (1870), 906 · The Builder (14 Jan 1871), 24 · The Times (31 Dec 1870), 3d · The Times (30 Jan 1892), 7b · will, 1871, probate department of the Principal Registry of the Family Division · will, 1892, probate department of the Principal Registry of the Family Division [Philip Charles Hardwick] · Colvin, Archs. · IGI · parish register, London, St Marylebone, LMA [microfilm; baptism] · census returns, 1851, 1861, 1871, 1881, 1891 · W. P. Baildon, ed., The records of the Honorable Society of Lincoln's Inn: the black books, 4 (1902); 5, ed. R. Roxburgh (1968) · Graves, RA exhibitors · The Athenaeum (1871), 23 · The Athenaeum (6 Feb 1892), 188 · contract and working drawings, Lincoln's Inn, London · DNB · London Directory (1820–92) · gravestone, Kensal Green cemetery, London, 11638/31 · London: the City of London, Pevsner (1997), 97–8, 203–4, 308–9, 331–4, 374, 389–92, 574 · J. Booker, Temples of Mammon: the architecture of banking (1990), 84, 129, 131, 147, 169, 170, 285, 318–20, 322 · C. Aslet, 'Madresfield Court', Country Life, 168/2 (Oct 1980), 1338, 1458–61, 1551–5 · C. Aslet, 'Adare Manor', Country life (1969), pt. 1, 1230–32, 1366–9 · Associated Architectural Societies' Reports, 16 (1881), 104–7 · J. Franklin, The gentleman's country house and its plan, 1835–1914 (1981), 8, 68, 122, 155–7, 261–2 · H. R. Hitchcock, Early Victorian architecture in Britain, 1 (1954), 211, 315 · G. D. M. Block, 'London's oldest rail terminus', Country Life (17 March 1960), 554–8 · Lord Stanhope, Conversations with the duke of Wellington (1998), 218 · South Lancashire, Pevsner (1969), 31, 80, 146, 166 · Dockland, North-East London Polytechnic and Greater London Council (1986), 16, 26, 33–4, 37–9 · J. Lever, ed., Catalogue of the drawings collection of the Royal Institute of British Architects: G–K (1973), vol. G–K · Survey of London, 37 (1973), 165 · WWW, 1941–50 · J. L. Pearson, Journal of Proceedings of the Royal Institute of British Architects, new ser., 8 (1891–2), 291–2 · Surrey, Pevsner (1971), 143–4 · Lord Beauchamp, 'Madresfield Court', Associated Architectural Societies Reports, 16 (1881), 104–10 · CGPLA Eng. & Wales (1871) · CGPLA Eng. & Wales (1892) · d. certs. · papers, RIBA BAL
Archives Adare Manor, Ireland, MSS and designs · Althorp, Northamptonshire, MSS and designs · Bethlem Royal Hospital, Beckenham, Kent, Archives and Museum, MSS and designs · Durham RO, MSS and designs · Gloucestershire County RO, Gloucester, MSS and designs · Goldsmiths' Company, London, MSS and designs · Lincoln's Inn, London, MSS and designs · PRO, British Transport Records, MSS and designs · RIBA, architectural drawings and MSS; architectural sketchbooks and drawings
Likenesses engraving, repro. in The Builder (1870), 906 · portrait, RIBA · portrait (Philip Charles Hardwick), RIBA
Wealth at death under £120,000: probate, 1871, CGPLA Eng. & Wales · £210,965 14s. 3d.—Philip Charles Hardwick: probate, resworn, April 1894, CGPLA Eng. & Wales (1892)

Hardwick, Philip Charles (1822–1892). See under Hardwick, Philip (1792–1870).

Hardwick, Thomas (1752–1829), architect, was born on 22 May 1752 in the parish of St Laurence, New Brentford, Middlesex, the only child of Thomas Hardwick (1725–1798), a prosperous master mason and architect, and his wife, Sarah Witham (bap. 1728, d. 1787). In 1767 he became a pupil of William Chambers, and he entered the Royal Academy Schools in 1769, in which year he won the silver medal. He exhibited at the academy almost continuously from 1772 to 1805. In October 1776 he travelled at his own expense via Paris and Lyons to Italy in company with the artist Thomas Jones, and on 27 November he arrived in Rome. He remained there, except for an excursion to Naples, until 26 May 1779, when he left for home via Venice, diligently measuring antique buildings and ruins, particularly the baths of ancient Rome, and compiling a portfolio with which to impress prospective patrons and to serve as a basis for his own designs. To hasten this work he co-operated with John Soane for a short period, and subsequently purchased reconstructive drawings by James Byers that he enlarged for his own portfolio. Hardwick was an accomplished artist, and added illusionistic landscape to his architectural drawings with skill learned from Chambers.

Soon after returning to England, Hardwick won a competition for a model female prison under the Penitentiary Act 1779, but the government turned from imprisoning to transporting criminals and his plans were never realized. He subsequently established a reputation in and around London as a church architect in a conservative neo-Palladian style. Hardwick's father had rebuilt Hanwell church, Middlesex, in 1781–2; when Hanwell's rector moved to Wanstead, Essex, in 1786 and determined to rebuild St Mary's Church, he commissioned the son (1787–90). Hardwick's design, strongly influenced by James Gibbs's St Martin-in-the-Fields (1722–6), was much admired by contemporaries, and one of only four English churches illustrated in C. L. Steiglitz's important survey of contemporary architecture (1800). Hardwick followed this success by renovating Inigo Jones's St Paul's, Covent Garden, including a thin cladding in Portland stone (1788–9; £11,700), repairing St James's, Piccadilly (1789; with a drastic refitting in 1803–4), and constructing a daughter church, St James's, Hampstead Road (1790–2; dem. c.1965), and judiciously repairing St Bartholomew-the-Great, West Smithfield, his mother's natal parish (1791; with further work in 1808), so saving it from demolition. A serious fire at St Paul's, Covent Garden, necessitated a new bell-turret and roof of improved construction and a new but Jonesian interior, where Hardwick's important architectural furniture has largely survived (1796–8; £13,300; altered 1871, 1887). Similarly conservative was his addition in 1792–4 and 1800–04 of a second quadrangle to almshouses at Bromley College, Kent, originally built in 1670–72. The shire hall, Dorchester, Dorset (1796–7; £7162), is austerely Palladian, and the St Pancras parish workhouse (1807–9; £30,000; dem.) utilitarian.

Elected FSA in 1781, Hardwick in 1785 contributed a paper on Vespasian's Colosseum (*Archaeologia*, 7, 1786, 369–73), where he had made excavations in 1777, and a model constructed to his own exact direction (later presented to the British Museum, but now lost). An original member of the Architects' Club (1791), Hardwick was regarded by his fellows as a 'very respectable man' (Farington, *Diary*, 4.1271, 6.2407), but he failed to secure election as an associate of the Royal Academy, partly through a failure to canvass academicians. Unlike his acquaintance John Soane, Hardwick, bred in comfortable circumstances, lacked not only genius but also the passion for self-advancement. Although in 1784–9 he rebuilt the interior of Ruperra Castle, Glamorgan (1784–9; gutted 1941), after a fire (a commission probably resulting from his paternal connection with the Welsh borders), he designed only one new country house, Quex Park, Birchington, Kent (1806–13). His practice was grounded in surveyorships: St James's parish (from 1789; St Paul's, Covent Garden, parish from 1795); Lord Salisbury's London estate (from 1804); and St Bartholomew's Hospital (from 1809). He was clerk of works at the office of works at Hampton Court (1810)—where he failed to reside constantly in his

official house—with Kew added in 1815; he retained all the above positions until death. His church work was also a key part of his practice, and was resumed in 1813 with a design for a chapel of ease for his home parish of St Marylebone, Middlesex, that was then aggrandized to replace the parish church (1813–17; altered 1883). St John's Chapel, St John's Wood, also in St Marylebone, followed in 1814, and then several churches for the church building commissioners under the act of 1818: St Barnabas, King Square (1822–6); Christ Church, St Marylebone (1822–4; now secularized); St John's, Workington, Cumberland (1822–4); and two small Gothic churches in Lancashire—Holy Trinity, Bolton (1823–5), and St John's, Farnworth (1824–5). He also extended the east end of Kew church, Surrey, in 1822 and rebuilt George Dance's St Bartholomew-the-Less, West Smithfield, with an iron roof (1823–5; altered 1862; restored 1950).

Having revived his early study of prison architecture to design Galway county gaol, Ireland (1802–3), Hardwick conducted preliminary works for the 7 acre, marsh-sited Millbank penitentiary, London (1812–13), but resigned after the failure of the foundations. Voting in Middlesex as a Brentford freeholder in the 1802 election, and as a householder in the 1818 Westminster election, Hardwick plumped for ministerialists. He visited Flanders in 1816 and returned to Paris in 1822. His memoir of his master, Sir William Chambers, printed in Gwilt's 1825 edition of Chambers's *Civil Architecture*, was republished in 1860 and 1862. Among Hardwick's pupils were J. M. W. Turner (whom he advised to abandon architecture for painting), Samuel Angell, John Foulston, and his younger son Philip, who became his partner and to whom about 1825 he made over his practice in return for a pension.

Hardwick married Elizabeth Hardwick (*bap.* 1763, *d.* 1804) of Credenhill, Herefordshire, on 1 December 1783. They had three sons and two daughters, of whom the youngest son, Philip *Hardwick, is noticed separately. Hardwick died at his house, 55 Berners Street, St Marylebone, on 16 January 1829, and was buried on 23 January in the family vault in the now derelict churchyard of St Laurence, New Brentford (rebuilt by his father). His elder surviving son, **John Hardwick** (1790–1875), magistrate, was born on 3 December 1790 in the parish of St Marylebone, Middlesex. An excellent linguist, he was educated privately and at Balliol College, Oxford, from 1808, where he proceeded BCL in 1815 and DCL in 1830. He practised as a barrister after being called to the bar at Lincoln's Inn, on 28 June 1816, until appointed stipendiary magistrate at Lambeth in 1821, and later transferred to Great Marlborough Street in 1841. He retired in 1856, when *The Times* commented on the 'inflexible uprightness of his judgments' and his 'extreme urbanity and courtesy of manner' (*The Times*, 3 June 1875, 12f). He was elected FRS on 5 April 1838, and was a deputy lieutenant for Tower Hamlets. He married Charlotte Aurora, daughter of colonel Thomas de Béton of the Swedish artillery, with whom he had an only son. After several years of failing health he died on 31 May 1875 at his residence at 101 Lansdowne Place, Hove. His wife survived him.   M. H. PORT

Sources Colvin, *Archs.* · will of Thomas Hardwick sen., PRO, PROB 11/1312 · will of Thomas Hardwick, jun., PRO, PROB 11/1753 · parish registers, New Brentford, St Laurence [LMA microfilm] · parish register, baptism, London, St Marylebone [LMA microfilm] · P. de la Ruffinière du Prey, 'Soane and Hardwick in Rome; a neo-classical partnership', *Architectural History*, 15 (1972), 51–67 · J. Harris, ed., *Catalogue of the drawings collection of the Royal Institute of British Architects: Colen Campbell* (1973), 89–95 · Graves, *RA exhibitors* · T. Friedman, 'Thomas Hardwick Jr's early churches', *Georgian Group Journal*, 8 (1998), 43–55 · A. P. Oppé, ed., 'Memoirs of Thomas Jones, Penkerrig, Radnorshire', *Walpole Society*, 32 (1946–8) [whole issue], esp. 40–89 · IGI · GM, 1st ser., 99/1 (1829), 92 · Farington, *Diary*, 4.1141, 1271, 1279; 6.2407 · *The parish of St Paul, Covent Garden*, Survey of London, 36 (1970), chap. 5 · *The parish of St James, Westminster*, 1/1, Survey of London, 29 (1960), 37–43 · W. E. Brown, *The St Pancras poor* (1905) · *Middlesex Poll Book* (1802) · will of Philip Charles Hardwick, 1892, 36/17 · Foster, *Alum. Oxon.* · *The Times* (3 June 1875), 12f · *CGPLA Eng. & Wales* (1875) [John Hardwick]

Archives RIBA BAL, notebooks, sketchbooks, journal, and attributed album | Baltimore, Fowler collection, Italian sketchbook

Likenesses W. Daniell, etching, pubd 1814 (after pencil portrait by G. Dance junior), BM, NPG, V&A; repro. in *A collection of portraits sketched from the life since the year 1793*, 2 vols. (1808–14)

Wealth at death life interest in father's estate; also leasehold land (house in Berners Street): will, PRO, PROB 11/1753 · under £1000—John Hardwick: will, PRO, PROB 11/1312; probate 9 July 1875, *CGPLA Eng. & Wales*

Hardwicke. For this title name *see* Yorke, Philip, first earl of Hardwicke (1690–1764); Yorke, Philip, second earl of Hardwicke (1720–1790); Yorke, Philip, third earl of Hardwicke (1757–1834); Yorke, Charles Philip, fourth earl of Hardwicke (1799–1873); Yorke, Charles Philip, fifth earl of Hardwicke (1836–1897); Yorke, Albert Edward Philip Henry, sixth earl of Hardwicke (1867–1904).

Hardwicke, Sir Cedric Webster (1893–1964), actor, was born on 19 February 1893 at Lye in Worcestershire, the eldest of three children and the only son of Edwin Webster Hardwicke, medical practitioner, and his wife, Jessie Masterston. He was educated at King Edward VI Grammar School, Stourbridge, and at Bridgnorth School. At first intended to follow his father's profession he failed in a preliminary examination and was then allowed to follow his own desire. He joined the Academy of Dramatic Art and in 1912 had some small part and understudying experience at the Lyceum, His Majesty's, and the Garrick theatres. In 1913 he joined the Shakespeare Company of Frank Benson, which gave him experience in the provinces, South Africa, and Rhodesia, and in 1914 he was in the Old Vic Company, still struggling for recognition. Up to this point he had not shown any remarkable acting talent, nor did it seem that he was taking his stage career very seriously, for when he joined the army at the end of 1914 he remained a soldier for no less than seven years, becoming in 1921 the last British officer officially to leave the war zone, having served in France in the Royal Army Service Corps horse transport and in the Northumberland Fusiliers. Hardwicke felt himself a misfit in civil life in postwar England. According to his own account in his autobiography *A Victorian in Orbit* (1961) it was a chance visit to the Birmingham repertoire theatre, at that time under the direction of Barry Jackson, that gave him 'for the first time' the desire to do something worth while as an actor.

Hardwicke joined Jackson's company in January 1922, starting his career again virtually from scratch, and for two years he remained in Birmingham playing a wide variety of increasingly important parts. In February 1924 Jackson took over the Court Theatre in London and he gave Hardwicke the chance of repeating there the three parts in Shaw's play cycle *Back to Methuselah* that he had already created. This production was followed in March by Eden Philpotts's *The Farmer's Wife*, in which Hardwicke's share was a quite extraordinary performance in a 'character' part as Churdles Ash, a bent and sharp-tongued old farm labourer. The piece did not at once find popular favour in London, but Jackson's faith in it held steady and he nursed it to success. In the end, largely owing to the growing fame of Hardwicke's performance, it had a run of 1324 performances, then one of the longest in theatrical history. After this triumph Hardwicke found himself in constant demand for important parts over a wide range of contrasted styles: in 1926 he was a crusty old misogynist in Philpotts's *Yellow Sands*; in 1928 Captain Andy in the musical *Show Boat* by Oscar Hammerstein and Jerome Kern; in 1929 the highly sophisticated King Magnus in Shaw's *The Apple Cart*; in 1930–31 the sinister Edward Moulton-Barrett in Rudolf Besier's *The Barretts of Wimpole Street*. In 1932 at the Malvern Festival he played Abel Drugger in Ben Jonson's *The Alchemist*, and he gave contemporary audiences a chance to understand why David Garrick in his day had been inspired to make this comparatively minor part into a *tour de force* of comic acting. In 1933 as the doctor in Emlyn Williams's *The Late Christopher Bean* he was a great success and was rewarded with a knighthood in 1934. His run of good fortune did not end there, for his next two plays, *Tovarich* (1935) and *The Amazing Doctor Clitterhouse* (1937), both lasted over a year. In 1936 he gave at Cambridge the Rede lecture, 'The drama tomorrow'.

The year 1938 brought Hardwicke to an altogether new phase in his career. He went to America and made his first appearance on the New York stage as Canon Skerritt in *Shadow and Substance*. After a good run in this play, followed by a tour, he went on to Hollywood, where he was destined to spend almost the whole period of the Second World War making films, such as *Stanley and Livingstone* (1939), *Tom Brown's Schooldays* (1940), and *The Moon is Down* (1943), designed in general to keep up the morale of an embattled Britain. Hardwicke had made films since 1911, and his many credits included *Nelson* (1926), *Nell Gwyn* (1934, with Anna Neagle), *The Winslow Boy* (1948), and Cecil B. de Mille's biblical blockbuster, *The Ten Commandments* (1956). But his acting on film was not of the same high quality as his stage work and, like other leading stage actors, he had a dislike of the scrappy way in which film acting has to be done. But he was one of a group of fine British players above military age whose contribution to the war effort lay in this field.

Hardwicke returned to London in 1944 and for four rather unsettled years he shuttled back and forth between London and New York, sometimes to act, sometimes to direct, but without finding anything very rewarding. In

1948 he joined the Old Vic Company at the New Theatre to play Sir Toby Belch in *Twelfth Night*, Doctor Faustus, and Gaev in Chekhov's *The Cherry Orchard*, but it was about this time that he confessed to a friend that he was finding the competition in London too hot for him. He returned to New York and spent the rest of his career there, making himself invaluable either to play the lead in, or to direct, the more important plays brought over from London.

Hardwicke was twice married: first, in 1927, to an English actress, Helena Pickard (1899–1959); second, in 1950, to an American actress, Mary Scott. Both wives divorced him; he had a son with each. Sir Cedric Hardwicke died in University Hospital, New York, on 6 August 1964.

W. A. DARLINGTON, *rev.* K. D. REYNOLDS

Sources C. Hardwicke, *Let's pretend* (1932) · C. Hardwicke, *A Victorian in orbit* (1961) · *The Times* (7 Aug 1964) · *Daily Telegraph* (7 Aug 1964) · private information (1981) · personal knowledge (1981) · *WWW* · J. Walker, ed., *Halliwell's film and video guide*, 12th edn (1997)
Likenesses H. Leslie, silhouette, 1925, NPG · W. Stoneman, photograph, 1945, NPG · photographs, Theatre Museum, London · photographs, V&A · photographs, Hult. Arch.

Hardwicke, Robert (1822–1875), publisher, was born on 2 October 1822 at Dyke, near Bourne, Lincolnshire, the third son of William Hardwicke, farmer (or butcher) and his wife, Mary. Nothing is known of his early education, but by 1897 he had obtained his articles as a printer. In that year he became a partner in the firm of Salisbury and Bateman, printers, of 4 Clement Court, near Lincoln's Inn in London. By 1850 the firm had moved and become Bateman and Hardwicke, printers, publishers, stationers, and booksellers, and in 1852 Hardwicke set up on his own at 192 Piccadilly.

Initially Hardwicke published general titles, but he had a lifelong interest in natural history, especially botany. His older brother William, a surgeon in private practice, introduced him to Edwin Lankester (1814–1874). Lankester was very active in the contemporary movement for the popularization of science and Hardwicke subsequently published a number of works by him, and by his botanist wife, Phebe. Lankester introduced Hardwicke to the Ray Society (established in 1844 for the publication of works concerning natural history), for which he eventually published thirty-six titles. Lankester also introduced Hardwicke to M. C. Cooke, then about to start his remarkable mycological career. Hardwicke subsequently commissioned Cooke's first book on fungi, an example of his 'judgement [to which] many valuable and popular books owe their existence' (*Journal of the Quekett Microscopical Club*). However, he had a hard head for business too, and both Cooke and T. H. Huxley complained of his treatment of them on occasion. Most of Hardwicke's publications were in the popular field, but his medical list was almost entirely professional and technical, the authors doubtless having been recommended to him by his brother.

In 1861 Hardwicke started a quarterly journal, the *Popular Science Review*, and three years later Cooke proposed an even more popular magazine, the monthly *Hardwicke's Science Gossip* which flourished for many years. Hardwicke's growing contribution to biological science was recognized in 1863 when he was elected a fellow of the Linnean Society for his interest in 'the progress of natural history, especially botany'.

A number of Hardwicke's authors had been meeting regularly on his premises for several years for informal discussions and in 1865 Cooke, Hardwicke, and his manager, Thomas Ketteringham, formalized this arrangement by setting up the Quekett Microscopical Club with Lankester as president and Hardwicke as treasurer. Membership rose rapidly, excursions were organized, and a journal published, and the club still flourishes.

Hardwicke was reported to be a warm and attractive character, portly, but with a pleasant face. His genial temperament allowed him to make friends easily. He had a wife, Harriet Martha; no details are known about her, and the couple had no children. Hardwicke died suddenly on 8 March 1875 at the age of fifty-two, following a stroke suffered while travelling to work from his home at 1 Versailles Villas, Upper Norwood. He died at 24 Queen Square, Bloomsbury.

In 1863 Hardwicke had made an error of judgement, undertaking the publication of Smith and Sowerby's multi-volume *English Botany* which, with its numerous hand-coloured illustrations, was extremely expensive for so small a firm to produce; indeed, it almost bankrupted it, so that on his death Hardwicke left under £1500 and leaseholds. The combination in Hardwicke of a sound knowledge of biology, encouragement of promising new authors, and an enthusiasm for popularizing natural history make his contribution to the science of his time a unique one.

MARY P. ENGLISH

Sources M. P. English, 'Robert Hardwicke (1822–1875), publisher of biological and medical books', *Archives of Natural History*, 13 (1986), 25–37 · M. P. English, 'Robert Hardwicke and T. H. Huxley', *Archives of Natural History*, 16 (1989), 245 · Quekett Microscopical Club report of proceedings, April 3, 1875, *Journal of the Quekett Microscopical Club*, 4 (1874–8), 77–8 · *Publishers' Circular* (16 March 1875) · will
Likenesses photograph, NHM, Quekett Microscopical Club
Wealth at death under £1500: probate, 19 March 1875, *CGPLA Eng. & Wales*

Hardy, Sir Alister Clavering (1896–1985), zoologist and investigator of religious experience, was born in Nottingham on 10 February 1896, the youngest of the three sons (there were no daughters) of Richard Hardy (d. 1895), architect, and his wife, Elizabeth Hannah Clavering. He attended Oundle School and entered Exeter College, Oxford, in 1914. His studies were interrupted by the First World War, during which he served as lieutenant and captain in the northern cyclist battalion, and as a camouflage officer on the staff of 13 army corps. In 1920, having returned to Oxford the previous year, he was awarded the Christopher Welsh scholarship and graduated with distinction in zoology. He also spent six months in Naples as Oxford biological scholar at Stazione Zoologica.

In 1921 Hardy was appointed assistant naturalist at the Ministry of Agriculture and Fisheries laboratory in Lowestoft; in 1924 he became chief zoologist to the Colonial

Sir Alister
Clavering Hardy
(1896–1985), by
Walter Bird, 1966

Office *Discovery* expedition, to study the biology of the Antarctic whales. He returned in 1927, the year in which he married Sylvia Lucy (*d.* 1985), second daughter of Walter Garstang, professor of zoology at Leeds. He and his wife had been fellow students, and she was behind all he did. They had a son and a daughter.

In 1928 Hardy was appointed professor of zoology (extended in 1931 to include oceanography) in the newly founded University College of Hull. In 1942 he became regius professor of natural history at Aberdeen, and in 1945 Linacre professor of zoology at Oxford. In 1961 he became professor of field studies at Oxford, retiring in 1963. He then immediately founded and became director of the religious experience research unit at Manchester College, Oxford (later renamed the Alister Hardy Research Centre, subsequently established in Oxford and Princeton, New Jersey, USA).

Hardy's professional career ranged through zoology, with special emphasis on plankton, insects, and evolution. On the *Discovery* expedition he invented the continuous plankton recorder, which for many years formed the basis of the broadest and most regular ecological monitoring system in the world. In his teaching and research Hardy stimulated innumerable students and colleagues, many of whom, especially his continuous plankton recorder team, have paid tribute to his influence. At Oxford he is said to have revitalized and integrated the work of the department.

Having had a sense of the numinous from youth onwards, in 1963 Hardy set out to lay the foundations of what he termed 'a future science of natural theology', by investigating religious experience. In this he aimed to remove the barriers between science and religion, and to reconcile current theories of evolution (he was a neo-Darwinian) with his view that religious experience is a biological fact which can be studied by scientific methods.

Hardy sketched and painted in watercolour, and wrote easily and extensively. In addition to his *Discovery Reports* (1928–1935), and many other scientific papers, he wrote three fascinating books, *The Open Sea*: part 1, *The World of Plankton* (1956), and part 2, *Fish and Fisheries* (1959); and *Great Waters* (1967). The transition to religion is developed in his Gifford lectures, *The Living Stream* (1965) and *The Divine Flame* (1966), followed by *The Biology of God* (1975) and *Darwin and the Spirit of Man* (1984), among many other books and essays.

Hardy was a tall man of enormous energy, a great walker and cyclist, and fascinated by flying. He was loyal, as demonstrated by his annual meetings with the pitmen members of his wartime cyclist company, and by the famous Christmas cards, illustrated by him with his wife's help, sent annually to countless friends.

Hardy received many distinctions and honours, from his Oxford DSc in 1938 and scientific medal of the Zoological Society in 1939, to his election as FRS in 1940 and his knighthood in 1957. He became emeritus professor on retirement in 1961 and fellow and then honorary fellow of Merton and Exeter colleges, receiving the honorary degrees of DSc of Southampton and Hull and the LLD of Aberdeen. Finally, just before being incapacitated by a stroke which shortly killed him, he was awarded the Templeton prize for progress in religion ($185,000), which he planned to spend on his new institute. He died in Oxford on 23 May 1985.   CYRIL LUCAS, *rev.*

Sources N. B. Marshall, *Memoirs FRS*, 32 (1986), 221–73 · *The Times* (24 May 1985) · *WWW* · personal knowledge (1981) · private information (1981)

Archives Bodl. Oxf., corresp. and papers | ICL, corresp. with J. W. Munro · NL Scot., corresp. with Sir James M. Wordie · Rice University, Houston, Texas, Woodson Research Center, corresp. with Sir Julian Huxley · Wolfson College, Oxford, corresp. with H. B. D. Kettlewell

Likenesses W. Bird, photograph, 1966, NPG [*see illus.*]

Wealth at death £78,071: probate, 31 July 1985, *CGPLA Eng. & Wales*

Hardy, Sir Charles, the elder (*c.*1680–1744), naval officer and politician, was a son of Philip Le Hardy (1651–1705), commissioner of garrisons in Guernsey, where Charles was born, and his wife, Marie Le Filleul. He was therefore a grandson of John Le Hardy (1606–1667), solicitor-general of Jersey, and a first cousin of Admiral Sir Thomas *Hardy (1666–1732). He entered the navy on 30 September 1695 as a volunteer on the *Pendennis*, under the command of his cousin Thomas. He afterwards served in the *Portsmouth* and *Sheerness*, and on 28 February 1701 was promoted third lieutenant of the *Resolution*, with Captain Basil Beaumont; in December 1702 he was appointed to the *Weymouth* (48 guns), and two years later to the guardship *Royal Ann*, before becoming commander of the sloop *Weasel* on 27 November 1705.

In September 1706 Hardy was moved by Sir John Leake into the *Swift*, which he commanded initially in the Mediterranean and then in the North Sea. He was appointed to the *Dunwich* on 14 January 1709, advancing to post rank in her on 28 June and commanding her on convoy duty on the east coast of England. In 1711 he commanded the *Nonsuch* and in 1713 the *Weymouth*, but neither was employed actively. About 1715 Hardy married Elizabeth (*d.* in or before 1744), only daughter of Josiah *Burchett, for many years secretary of the Admiralty. The couple had three daughters and three sons.

In 1718 Hardy was captain of the *Guernsey* in the Baltic under Sir John Norris, and in 1719–20 of the *Defiance* on similar service. In January 1726 he was appointed to the *Grafton*, but in May he was moved into the *Kent*, which he commanded in the fleet under Sir Charles Wager in the Baltic, and afterwards in support of Gibraltar. In November 1727 he was moved by Wager into the *Stirling Castle*, and in the following April he returned to England. On 9 February 1730 he was appointed to the command of the yacht *Carolina*, a position he held until promoted rear-admiral on 6 April 1742.

Hardy had been knighted on 26 September 1732, and on 14 December 1743 he was elected MP for Portsmouth on the Admiralty interest. On 7 December 1743 he was advanced to the rank of vice-admiral; a few days later he was appointed one of the lords-commissioners of the Admiralty, and early in the following year he took command of the squadron ordered to convoy a fleet of victuallers and storeships to Lisbon. Having performed this duty he returned to England by the end of May, without accident, except the loss of the *Northumberland* (70 guns), which, having parted company from the squadron, was captured by the French on 8 May. Shortly afterwards, Hardy resumed his seat at the Admiralty, where he died on 27 November 1744.

Hardy's three daughters were Elizabeth, Margaret, and Charlotte; his three sons were Josiah *Hardy, royal governor of New Jersey; Sir Charles *Hardy the younger, naval officer and governor of Greenwich Hospital; and John (*d.* 1796), a naval officer and the compiler of a *List of the Captains of his Majesty's Navy from 1673 to 1783* (1784).

J. D. DAVIES

Sources PRO, ADM 6/424, ADM 8 · will, PRO, PROB 11/736, fol. 287 · P. Watson, 'Hardy, Charles', HoP, *Commons, 1715–54* · G. R. Balleine, *A biographical dictionary of Jersey*, [1] [1948], 395–6 · *Manuscripts of the earl of Egmont: diary of Viscount Percival, afterwards first earl of Egmont*, 3 vols., HMC, 63 (1920–23) · J. Charnock, ed., *Biographia navalis*, 4 (1796), 9
Archives PRO, Admiralty MSS, ADM 6/424, ADM 8
Wealth at death £3000 bequeathed to eldest son; £2000 to eldest daughter; smaller bequests to other children: will, PRO, PROB 11/736, fol. 287

Hardy, Sir Charles, the younger (*bap.* 1717, *d.* 1780), naval officer and politician, was baptized on 7 March 1717 at St Martin-in-the-Fields, Westminster, the second son of Vice-Admiral Sir Charles *Hardy (*c.*1680–1744) and his wife, Elizabeth, *née* Burchett (*d.* in or before 1744). His elder brother, Josiah *Hardy (*bap.* 1716, *d.* 1790), later became proprietary governor of New Jersey at Charles's instigation. The younger Hardy entered the navy on 4 February 1731 as a volunteer on the *Salisbury*. On 26 March 1737 Sir John Norris appointed him third lieutenant of the *Swallow*. After serving as lieutenant of the *Augusta* and *Kent* he was promoted to command the *Rupert's Prize* on 9 June 1741, and gained post rank on 10 August 1741 when he became captain of the *Rye*, which he commanded for the next two years on the coasts of Carolina and Georgia. On 30 April 1744 he became captain of the *Jersey* and commander of

Sir Charles Hardy the younger (*bap.* 1717, *d.* 1780), by George Romney, 1780

the Newfoundland convoy, but he was unable to reach his station because of sixty-three days of adverse winds, a defence accepted by the court martial held to investigate his alleged neglect of duty. As captain of the *Torrington* in 1745 he convoyed troops from Gibraltar to Louisbourg on Cape Breton Island. In summer 1745 he commanded the *Jersey* off the Portuguese coast, fighting a fierce but inconclusive action in July against the French *Saint Esprit* (74 guns).

Hardy was unemployed from the peace of 1748 to January 1755, when he was appointed governor of New York. He arrived in the colony on 6 September 1755, having been knighted on 20 April. He was involved in the ongoing disputes over finance with the colonial assembly, and in developing New York as the main arsenal for the British forces in North America at the start of the Seven Years' War. Hardy was promoted rear-admiral in 1756 and in May 1757 hoisted his flag in the *Sutherland* as second-in-command to Vice-Admiral Francis Holburne. In June he convoyed from New York to Halifax the ships intended to support an attack on Louisbourg. The attack was abandoned, partly as a result of Hardy's urging, on the grounds that the French squadron at Louisbourg was too strong and that the weather was too bad for the British fleet to keep its station. Hardy gave up his governorship of New York on 3 June 1757, returned to England in November on the *Windsor*, and in July 1758 acted as Boscawen's second-in-command during the successful siege of Louisbourg, flying his flag successively in the *Captain* and the *Royal William*. In 1759 Hardy was second-in-command of Sir Edward Hawke's fleet, flying his flag in the *Union* during the battle of Quiberon Bay, and he helped to maintain the Brest blockade under the successive commands of Hawke and Boscawen until October 1762, when he was promoted vice-admiral. Hardy effectively retired at the peace, acquiring an estate at Rawlins, Oxfordshire, and serving as MP for Rochester from 1764 to 1768 (he subsequently served for Plymouth from 1771 until his death). In September 1767 he was one of the eight admirals who supported the canopy over the body of the duke of York during the duke's funeral at Westminster Abbey. On 28 October 1770 he was promoted admiral of the blue, and on 16 August 1771 he succeeded Holburne as governor of Greenwich Hospital, with a salary of £1000 per annum.

In March 1779 the navy was riven with faction-fighting as a result of the court martial of Admiral Augustus Keppel. Hardy was keen to take command of the Channel Fleet, and received the appointment on March 19. His seniority placed him above the squabbling of the younger admirals, but Hardy was quickly perceived as a 'political' appointment by the first lord, the fourth earl of Sandwich; the king had doubts about his ability, and others, such as the duke of Richmond, commented caustically on the facts that he had been dragged out of a comfortable retirement at Greenwich, had not been to sea in almost twenty years, and had never been more than a second-in-command. Nevertheless Hardy's natural good nature won over some of the doubters among his officers. Benjamin Thompson, who was on Hardy's flagship, *Victory*, at first thought that 'Sir Charles Hardy is not a fit person to command this great fleet at this time', but later came:

> to think that our Admiral has acted a very prudent, if not a spirited part ... he is a worthy good man, and I respect and love him from my heart ... he is good natured to a fault, and it would make you die with laughing to see him kick my hat about the deck.   ('Channel fleet in 1779', 3.136, 143)

The position Hardy faced was dire, with invasion by the combined Franco-Spanish fleet expected imminently. On 12 June 1779 he received intelligence that the French were at sea, and he sailed from Spithead with twenty-eight ships of the line. Off Ushant on 23 June he learned that the Spanish were also approaching the channel. Wind drove Hardy back to Torbay, where he arrived on 5 July. A division over strategy was now apparent among both Hardy's political advisers and his officers: some argued that he should attack even a greatly superior enemy force, while others believed that he should adopt a cautious 'fleet in being' strategy, avoiding direct action but retreating before the enemy, thereby menacing any potential invasion. Hardy sailed again on 14 July and was off Plymouth by 25 July, where he was ordered to take station west of the Lizard, regarded as the best station for guarding both England and Ireland. Adverse winds meant that he did not reach this station until 12 August, three days before the Franco-Spanish fleet of forty-five ships entered the channel. It was before Plymouth from 16 to 19 August, and Hardy tried to work eastwards towards it, but the winds meant that he reached Land's End only on 29 August. The two fleets were in sight of each other on 31 August, but the combined fleet withdrew and avoided an engagement.

Hardy then ordered his fleet to Spithead, ostensibly to replenish his water but also hoping that he could draw the enemy into more confined waters; he arrived there on 3 September 1779.

Hardy's withdrawal to Spithead prompted a torrent of criticism, for it was believed that the combined fleet was still an active threat, rather than a sickly and dispirited force which was already withdrawing towards Brest. The criticisms have often shaped the perception of Hardy as an over-cautious, incompetent commander, but many such remarks were motivated by blatant factionalism—notably those of his captain of the fleet, Richard Kempenfelt, who sought to advance himself, and of the likes of Thompson and Captain Walsingham of the *Thunderer*, who were trying to ingratiate themselves with Sandwich's rival, Lord George Germain. Indeed Hardy himself was so much a part of the political arena that he wrote to Sandwich on 12 August, 'it is my utmost wish to do everything in my power to satisfy the public and to defeat the evil designs of your Lordships' enemies and mine' (*Private Papers of ... Sandwich*, 3.56).

Modern historians take a more sympathetic view, pointing out how few options were open to Hardy, how calmly he coped with almost intolerable pressures from both above and below—though at the time his subordinates interpreted the latter as an unwillingness to take advice—and how he regularly stated his determination to fight if he got the chance. In the event Hardy remained in command of the fleet for its autumn cruise, beginning on 22 October 1779, defended his conduct in parliament on 1 December, and on 17 May 1780 hoisted his flag on the *Victory* in order to resume command once more. However, he died of a seizure caused by inflammation of the bowels at 3 a.m. on 19 May. By his will he left the estate at Rawlins to his eldest son; £1000 and an annuity of £400 to his wife; £3000 to each of his three sons; and £4000 to each of his two daughters. In July 1749 he had married Mary Tate of Delapre, Northamptonshire; she died before 4 January 1759 when he married Catherine, daughter of the historian Temple Stanyan. Catherine died on 21 February 1801 when she fell asleep in front of a fire which ignited her headdress.   J. D. DAVIES

Sources DNB · PRO, ADM MSS 1/578, 51/1036, 1/95, 6/247, 1/480, 1882–6, 5284 · *The private papers of John, earl of Sandwich*, ed. G. R. Barnes and J. H. Owen, 4 vols., Navy RS, 69, 71, 75, 78 (1932–8) · *The private papers of John, earl of Sandwich*, ed. G. R. Barnes and J. H. Owen, 2, Navy RS, 71 (1933) · *The private papers of John, earl of Sandwich*, ed. G. R. Barnes and J. H. Owen, 3, Navy RS, 75 (1936) · N. A. M. Rodger, *The insatiable earl: a life of John Montagu, fourth earl of Sandwich* (1993) · D. Syrett, *The Royal Navy in European waters during the American revolutionary war* (1998) · M. M. Drummond, 'Hardy, Charles', HoP, *Commons, 1754–90* · J. Gwyn, 'Hardy, Sir Charles', DCB, vol. 4 · will, PRO, PROB 11/1066, fol. 241 · *Naval Chronicle*, 5 (1801), 188 · *Naval Chronicle*, 20 (1808), 89–108 · 'The channel fleet in 1779: letters of Benjamin Thompson to Lord George Germain', *The naval miscellany*, ed. W. G. Perrin, 3, Navy RS, 63 (1928) · *The Barrington papers*, ed. D. Bonner-Smith, 1, Navy RS, 77 (1937), vol. 1 · *Despatches of Rear-Admiral Sir Charles Hardy, 1757–8, and Vice-Admiral Francis Holburne, 1757*, ed. C. H. Little (Halifax, Nova Scotia, 1958) · *Ninth report*, 2, HMC, 8 (1884), 382 · Hardy to Grenville, 26 July 1769, BL, Add. MS 57827, fol. 69

Archives New York Historical Society, bills and papers | Hunt. L., letters to George Pocock · NMM, corresp. with Lord Sandwich · PRO, Admiralty MSS

Likenesses R. Dawe, mezzotint, pubd 1779 (after T. Hudson), BM, NPG · R. Stewart, mezzotint, pubd 1779, BM · G. Romney, oils, 1780, NMM [*see illus.*] · J. Wollaston, oils, Brooklyn Museum, New York

Wealth at death £1000; £400 annuity bequeathed to wife; £3000 to each of three sons; estate at Rawlins, Oxfordshire, to eldest son; £4000 to each of two daughters: will, PRO, PROB 11/1066, fol. 241

Hardy, Elizabeth (1793/4–1854), novelist, was born in Ireland but nothing else is known of her personal life apart from the fact that she never married. In 1845 she published *Michael Cassidy, or, The Cottage Gardener*, which advocated small allotments, green crops, crop rotation, and hard work as a remedy for the economic misery of the Irish peasant. *Owen Glendower, or, The Prince in Wales*, a historical novel in two volumes, appeared in 1849. *The Confessor*, 'a Jesuit tale of the times based on fact' with a preface by the Revd C. B. Tayler MA, was published in 1854. Since Elizabeth Hardy published her novels anonymously, it is possible that she wrote more works than those novels attributed to her, but by the time of her death it was known that she was the author of *The Confessor*. Her novels reflected her zealous protestantism.

Elizabeth Hardy died suddenly on 9 May 1854, aged sixty, in the queen's bench prison (probably in London) where she had been imprisoned 'for about eighteen month for a small debt' (*GM*, 670). It appears that she was not able to repay the debt, nor did she have influential friends to assist her. Her death was unnoticed by both the Irish and English press, and by literary journals, suggesting that she had already sunk into obscurity during her lifetime.   BRIGITTE ANTON

Sources *DNB* · *GM*, 2nd ser., 41 (1854), 670 · S. Halkett and J. Laing, *Dictionary of anonymous and pseudonymous English literature*, ed. J. Kennedy and others, new edn, 7 (1934), 124 · S. J. Brown, *Ireland in fiction*, 2nd edn, 1 (1969), 130 · A. M. Brady and B. Cleeve, eds., *A biographical dictionary of Irish writers*, rev. edn (1985), 101 · B. Cleeve, *Dictionary of Irish writers* (1967) · Boase, *Mod. Eng. biog.*

Wealth at death in debt: *DNB*; *GM*

Hardy, Francis (1751–1812), politician and biographer, the son of Harry Hardy, was born in Dublin. He entered Trinity College, Dublin, on 8 July 1766 and graduated BA in 1771. He attended the Middle Temple and was called to the Irish bar in 1777. 'In person he was short, with penetrating eyes, and a strong voice of much compass' (*DNB*).

Through the interest of the earl of Granard, Hardy was returned as a member for the manor of Mullingar, co. Westmeath, in the Irish parliament in 1783. He represented that constituency until the parliamentary union with Great Britain in 1800. He was a political associate of Henry Grattan and other 'patriot' parliamentarians, who wished to preserve and build on the legislative independence gained in 1782. Hardy was a regular attender and speaker in the Irish House of Commons, particularly in the 1780s. In 1783 he made his first major speech, on the subject of parliamentary reform, which he favoured. His next significant speech was delivered in 1785, when he opposed Thomas Orde's motion for introducing a bill to establish

the commercial propositions. In 1789 he voted for an address calling upon the prince of Wales to assume the regency of Ireland, and supported a number of popular measures of reform. Also, in June of that year, he became one of the original members of the Whig Club formed in Dublin.

During the 1790s Hardy continued to vote with the parliamentary opposition. He supported the enfranchisement of the Roman Catholics in 1793, and favoured gradual progress towards emancipation. In 1798 he was one of the minority of nineteen who supported Sir Laurence Parsons's motion for a committee to inquire into the state of the country and to suggest conciliatory measures. Over the next two years Hardy, although in straitened circumstances, declined government overtures, by which it was sought to induce him to vote for the legislative union. Hardy's service to his country was eventually rewarded, to some degree, when he was appointed one of the commissioners of appeals in 1806—a post worth £500 per annum, out of which he had to pay £200 in expenses.

Beyond the political arena, Hardy was an active intellectual. He acquired an intimate knowledge of Latin and Greek authors, as well as of continental literature. In 1785 he co-operated with Lord Charlemont in the establishment of a society for the purpose of promoting science, literature, and antiquities, which became known as the Royal Irish Academy. In 1788 he contributed to its publications a dissertation on some passages in the *Agamemnon* of Aeschylus. His literary skills were rested during the 1790s as he focused his attention on the political scene. However, his lifelong friend, Grattan, felt that there were other reasons for his inactivity. In a letter of 25 October 1792 to the Revd Edward Berwick, Grattan described Hardy as 'that fat, lazy, studious, postponing fellow'.

Hardy planned to publish some of the writings of his friend and political ally Lord Charlemont, who died in 1799. In the end he undertook to write a biography of that peer, at the suggestion of Richard Lovell Edgeworth. For this work he received assistance from the Charlemont family, as well as from Grattan and others, and it appeared at London in 1810 entitled *Memoirs of the political and private life of James Caulfield, earl of Charlemont, knight of St Patrick, &c.* The memoirs contain much interesting matter, but are rather diffuse, and not free from inaccuracies. Hardy is most commonly remembered as the biographer of Lord Charlemont and, certainly, the memoirs are his best-known literary work. He died just weeks after the publication of its second edition, on 26 July 1812, and was interred at Kilcommon, co. Wicklow.   DAVID LAMMEY

Sources H. Cavendish, 'Notes on the debates of the Irish House of Commons, 1776–89', PRO NIre., T 3435 and MIC 12 [transcript and microfilm of the Cavendish MSS, L. Cong.] · J. Porter, P. Byrne, and W. Porter, eds., *The parliamentary register, or, History of the proceedings and debates of the House of Commons of Ireland, 1781–1797*, 17 vols. (1784–1801) · constituency history, manor of Mullingar, Westmeath, PRO NIre., ENV 5/HP/30/5PRO · T. J. Kiernan, ed., 'Forbes letters', *Analecta Hibernica*, 8 (1938), 313–71 · H. Grattan, *Memoirs of the life and times of the Rt Hon. Henry Grattan*, 5 vols. (1839–46) · M. J. Craig, *The volunteer earl: being the life and times of James Caulfeild, first earl of Charlemont* (1948) · L. Hale, *John Philpot Curran: his life and times*

(1958) • *The whole of the debates in both houses of parliament on a bill to prevent tumultuous risings and assemblies, and for the more effectual punishment of persons guilty of outrage, riot, and illegal combination* (1787) • Hobart list of commons and lords, 1788, PRO NIre., T 2627/1/1 • E. M. Johnston, 'Members of the Irish parliament, 1784–7', *Proceedings of the Royal Irish Academy*, 71C (1971), 139–246 • E. M. Johnston, 'The state of the Irish House of Commons in 1791', *Proceedings of the Royal Irish Academy*, 59C (1957–9), 1–56 • J. L. J. Hughes, ed., *Patentee officers in Ireland, 1173–1826, including high sheriffs, 1661–1684 and 1761–1816*, IMC (1960) • *DNB* • E. Keane, P. Beryl Phair, and T. U. Sadleir, eds., *King's Inns admission papers, 1607–1867*, IMC (1982), 213
Archives L. Cong., Cavendish MSS • PRO NIre., constituency papers, ENV/5/HP/30/5 • TCD, letters to Joseph Cooper Walker • U. Nott. L., letters to Countess of Charleville
Likenesses H. D. Hamilton, portrait, priv. coll. • J. Heath, stipple (after drawing by J. R. Maguire, 1811), BM, NPG; repro. in J. Barrington, *Historic memoirs of Ireland*, 2nd edn, 2 vols. (1833), vol. 1, p. 162

Hardy, Frederick Daniel (1826–1911), genre painter, was born on 13 February 1826 at Windsor, the son of George Hardy, a musician in the private band of music in the royal household at Windsor. He studied at the Royal Academy of Music in Hanover Square, London, but in 1846 devoted himself to painting under the influence of his elder brother George Hardy (1822–1909), also a painter of domestic subjects, and the painter Thomas Webster, a family friend and also the son of a royal musician.

Hardy's work strongly depended in style and subject on the early work of Webster, and on other contemporary imitators of Dutch and Flemish seventeenth-century genre painting. His earliest paintings, of the 1850s and 1860s, are small, highly finished cottage interiors with figures, combining careful detail with delicacy of tonality, lighting, and subject. They accurately depict the vernacular architecture, costume, and lives of the villagers of Buckinghamshire and Kent. From the late 1860s the social class of his subjects rose, the anecdotal content of his pictures dominated, and his handling of paint coarsened.

Hardy's work rapidly achieved critical and commercial success. In 1865 *The Leaky Roof* was described as 'preeminent for knowledge, character and objective truth' (*Art Journal*, 1865, 170); *The Sweep* (1862; replica at Wolverhampton Art Gallery) sold for £200 in 1862 and resold for £640 in 1874, at the height of his career. He exhibited ninety-three pictures at the Royal Academy between 1851 and 1898, and five at the British Institution between 1851 and 1856. His work is well represented in British public collections, most notably by the nineteen paintings at the Wolverhampton Art Gallery, including *The Clergyman's Visit* and *Preparing for Dinner*, both *c*.1852; *The Dismayed Artist*, 1866; *The Chimney Sweep*, 1866; *Baby's Birthday*, 1867; and *Sorrowful News*, 1872. Among his other better works are *The Volunteers* (1860; York); *The Young Photographers* (1862; Tunbridge Wells); *Children Playing at Doctors* (1863; V&A); and *The Wedding Breakfast* (1871; Atkinson Art Gallery, Southport).

Hardy lived in Windsor until 1852 when he married, on 11 March, Rebecca Sophia Dorrofield (*c*.1828–1906), the daughter of a farmer from Chorley Wood. They had five sons and a daughter. After a few years at Snell's Wood, near Amersham, Buckinghamshire, Hardy settled in Cranbrook, Kent, in 1854. A group of artists and friends soon gathered around him: Hardy's brother George, Thomas Webster, John Calcott Horsley, George Bernard O'Neill (1828–1917), and briefly Augustus Edwin Mulready. However, the 'Cranbrook colony' was held together more by ties of family and friendship than by artistic kinship. Hardy lived at 2 Waterloo Place, Cranbrook, from 1854 until about 1875, and had a studio in Thomas Webster's house in High Street, Cranbrook, until at least 1894. He also kept a house in Brunswick Gardens, Kensington, London, from about 1875 to 1890. He died at 1 Waterloo Place, Cranbrook, on 1 April 1911 and was buried at St Dunstan's Church, Cranbrook. His daughter (Amelia) Gertrude, the sole beneficiary of his will, continued to live and paint in Cranbrook until the 1930s.

B. S. Long, *rev.* Andrew Greg

Sources A. Greg, *The Cranbrook colony: F. D. Hardy, G. Hardy, J. C. Horsley, A. E. Mulready, G. B. O'Neil, T. Webster* (1977) [exhibition catalogue, Central Art Gallery, Wolverhampton, 22 Jan – 12 March 1977; Laing Art Gallery, Newcastle upon Tyne, 26 March – 17 April 1977] • Graves, *RA exhibitors* • Graves, *Brit. Inst.* • J. Dafforne, 'The works of Frederick Daniel Hardy', *Art Journal*, 14 (1875), 73–6 • R. Parkinson, ed., *Catalogue of British oil paintings, 1820–1860* (1990), 118–19 [catalogue of V&A] • m. cert. • d. cert. • will
Archives Wolverhampton Art Gallery
Wealth at death £326 19s. 0d.: probate, 23 May 1911, CGPLA Eng. & Wales

Hardy, Gathorne Gathorne-, first earl of Cranbrook (1814–1906), politician, was born on 1 October 1814 at the Manor House, Bradford, the third son in the family of twelve children of John Hardy (1773–1855) and his wife, Isabel, eldest daughter of Richard Gathorne of Kirkby Lonsdale, Westmorland. The basis of the Hardy family's wealth was ownership of the Low Moor ironworks. John Hardy was also a barrister, recorder of Leeds, and MP for Bradford from 1832 to 1837 and again from 1841 to 1847, beginning as a reformer but adopting Conservative colours from 1835 mainly from anxiety at challenges to the position of the established church in Ireland and England. He was of evangelical tendencies, and was friendly with William Wilberforce. Of Gathorne's two brothers, Sir John Hardy (1809–1888) also became a Conservative MP and was created a baronet, while Charles (1813–1867) managed Low Moor.

Education, early career, and home life Hardy attended preparatory schools at Bishopton, near Studley, at Hammersmith, and at Haslewood, near Birmingham, before going to Shrewsbury School in 1827 and Oriel College, Oxford, in 1833. He joined J. H. Newman's congregations. He remained staunchly opposed to Romanism, but became a devout, uncomplicated high-churchman, deeply respectful of Church of England traditions and tolerant of men of differing views within it. He graduated BA in 1836 with (to his disappointment) a second-class degree. He then studied for the bar, to which he was called in 1840, joining the northern circuit. His abilities, industry, and local connections attracted many clients and earned him substantial financial rewards. By 1855 he had obtained a complete lead on sessions, and marked success at the parliamentary bar and in the *nisi prius* courts, and he was earning around

Gathorne Gathorne-Hardy, first earl of Cranbrook (1814–1906), by Henry John Whitlock

£5000 per year. In 1854, 1855, and 1856 he applied for silk, but was refused. This upset him greatly. His father died in 1855, a rich man, and with his legacy Hardy was able to retire from the bar and devote himself to politics and to family life. On 29 March 1838, in Ireland, he had married Jane (d. 1897), third daughter of James Orr of co. Down; she was the sister of a close college friend. Their marriage was long, close, and fecund; eleven children were born in all, of whom eight survived to adulthood, and Hardy derived enormous pleasure from his role as paterfamilias, which indeed in later years distracted him from Commons attendance and other duties and detracted somewhat from his political success. From 1858 they had two homes, 12 Grosvenor Crescent, London, and Hemsted Park, near Cranbrook in Kent. Hardy aimed to spend weekends at Hemsted throughout the parliamentary session. In the 1860s he extended the estate and carried out many improvements. He paid for the restoration of the parish church and the construction of a nonconformist chapel, became lord of the manor at Benenden, and was chairman of the Kent quarter sessions from 1859 to 1867. He loved the life of a country gentleman and was an active sportsman; almost every autumn he shot, hunted, and fished in Scotland.

In office and opposition, 1856–1866 As an upwardly mobile and resolute admirer of the church and the lifestyle of the landed classes, and a warm defender of property rights and law and order, Hardy was naturally drawn to the Conservative side in politics. He had contested Bradford on his father's retirement in 1847, but had refused to give the pledges against state support for Roman Catholic schools which extreme protestants demanded, and lost. From 1856 to 1865 he was MP for Leominster, a small constituency which did not fetter his independence. On the recommendation of Spencer Walpole he became undersecretary for the Home Office during the minority Conservative government of 1858–9, headed by Lord Derby. At one point during this ministry, Hardy, a rather impetuous man who struggled with some success to control a fiery temper, offered to resign: the government had not supported the course which he had taken over a compensation case, and at the same time the whip had sent him a mild rebuke concerning his parliamentary attendance record.

In opposition between 1859 and 1866, Hardy strengthened his political reputation. This was based on his vigorous and telling parliamentary performances. He was a plausible and fluent speaker who pleased back-benchers by articulating straightforward party views effectively, trenchantly, and combatively. He was no political philosopher; nor did he care for subtlety or casuistry. He was a man in whom the Conservative squires could have confidence. Moreover, especially after 1867, he bolstered his position by making similarly reassuring speeches to audiences of propertied provincial Conservatives, defending crown, church, law, and empire with warmth. His attacks on John Bright and Lord John Russell contributed to the withdrawal of the parliamentary reform bill of 1860, while in 1862 he was active in the successful opposition to the proposal to relieve nonconformists from liability to church rate. Having proceeded to his MA degree at Oxford in 1861 in order to vote against W. E. Gladstone, the sitting MP for the university, who had moved to the Liberal camp, he was chosen by the Oxford Conservatives in 1865 to defend their interests. He won a safe victory over Gladstone at the election of that year (and was made DCL at Oxford in 1866).

At the poor-law board and the Home Office, 1866–1868 When Derby formed a minority Conservative government in July 1866, Hardy joined the cabinet as president of the poor-law board, and was made privy councillor. His major legislative responsibility in this post was the act of 1867 reforming the administration of poor relief in London. It made two changes of principle which had long-term significance for social policy: it spread the burden of the poor rate more equitably across the metropolis, rather than confining it to individual parishes of widely differing social composition; and it transferred the care of the sick poor and lunatics away from penny-pinching guardians and into specialist hospitals, recognizing that their needs were different from those of the able-bodied. These reforms owed most to pressure from lobby groups and civil servants, and reflected something of a consensus.

Hardy was at no time a pioneering social reformer, nor was he keen to extend state influence in education at the expense of the established church. However, he had never been an extreme advocate of *laissez-faire* principles, and some of the interventionist toryism prevalent in Yorkshire in the 1840s rubbed off on him. He appreciated the need for the party to introduce social legislation, approved of the idea of self-funded old age insurance in the 1870s, supported the rhetoric of his future leader Benjamin Disraeli, and, as home secretary in 1868, set up the royal commission on sanitary laws which led to the major public health legislation of 1871–5.

As a staunch opponent of radicalism, Hardy disliked the prospect of a far-reaching extension of the franchise. However, unlike three of his colleagues, he did not resign from the cabinet in early 1867 in the dispute over the major parliamentary reform bill which Derby and Disraeli had planned. His continued presence apparently reassured some back-benchers who were unhappy at the drift of events. It also benefited him. In May 1867 Spencer Walpole resigned as home secretary, after much criticism of the weakness of his policy. He had indicated the government's displeasure at the demonstration which the Reform League planned in Hyde Park, but did not use the powers which he possessed to close the area (a royal park). The demonstration took place successfully, humiliating the government in many eyes. Hardy was promoted to home secretary in Walpole's place. Given his tough reputation, this move satisfied the party, especially since it appeared to give a further security against the drift towards radical reform. In practice, it tied Hardy even more closely to the shifting reform policy being pursued by the leadership. He introduced a bill declaring illegal the use of the royal parks for meetings on political objects, but was forced to withdraw it by the Liberals.

As home secretary, Hardy had charge of the government response to the Fenian outrages at Manchester and at Clerkenwell in late 1867. He refused to commute the capital sentences passed on those convicted for the murder of a policeman during the rescue of prisoners at Manchester, despite some public sympathy for the romantic spirit in which the affair had been conducted. The explosion outside Clerkenwell Prison, which killed several bystanders, was especially embarrassing to the government since the Dublin authorities had received good advance intelligence of it, but the London police had failed to act accordingly. Hardy found the Metropolitan Police commissioner, Sir Richard Mayne, too set in his ways; his pressure resulted in an increase in the number of policemen, and the employment of a few detectives of foreign origin. He also set up a new intelligence bureau in the Home Office, reporting directly to him, headed by Captain Feilding. This, however, was only a temporary affair to meet the Fenian emergency, though one Home Office servant continued to be employed on surveillance work thereafter.

In opposition and government, 1868–1876 In opposition again after the election of 1868, Hardy attacked vigorously the Irish Church Bill of 1869, and was a forceful critic of the government on many other occasions; he was especially effective in condemning its malpractice in appointments concerning Sir Robert Collier and the Ewelme rectory. He became secretary of state for war when the Conservatives returned to office in February 1874. He continued the implementation of the reforms instituted by his predecessor Viscount Cardwell. He disliked the lack of adequate arrangements for promotion within the army, and set up a commission to address the issue, but took no major initiatives to tackle the recruiting problem. In general, during his tenure of office, the influence of the military over War Office policy increased. He supported Disraeli rather than the fifteenth earl of Derby in the cabinet debates of 1877–8 on the Eastern question, and in early 1878 was active in preparing the dispatch of an expeditionary force to the Mediterranean, in case of war. In March 1878 he became secretary of state for India. He enjoyed good relations with the viceroy, Lord Lytton, whose anxieties about Russian intentions in central Asia he shared. He upheld the policy of coercing the amir of Afghanistan into accepting British influence. The murder of the British party in Kabul in September 1879 was an embarrassment to ministers, and though Lord Roberts's victories restored the position, the situation in Afghanistan remained unsettled when the government fell from office in April 1880. Hardy was made GCSI in that year.

In the sessions of 1871 and 1872, Hardy had stood in for the ailing Disraeli on a number of occasions, and seemed a strong contender for the leadership in the Commons should it be vacated. However he was passed over in favour of Stafford Northcote when Disraeli finally departed to the Lords in 1876. He had not improved his chances by his opposition to the Public Worship Regulation Act of 1874, a measure aimed at safeguarding the church against ritualistic practices, which aggressively protestant Conservatives applauded but which he considered wrong-headed and unworkable. The main reason for the reverse of 1876, however, was the preference of Disraeli, Derby, and the whips for Northcote, whose temper and attendance seemed more reliable and whose emphasis on financial issues and especially low taxes seemed attractive and uncontroversial in the new electoral climate. Hardy was never very interested in economic questions, and it may have been thought that his image on issues of public order and strikes was too combative.

In the Lords The decision naturally upset Hardy, and proved the turning point in his career. He accepted it loyally, as he did all requests of the leadership, but indicated that in due course he wished to go to the Lords rather than to compete with Northcote. This change was effected in 1878. Hardy took the title Viscount Cranbrook of Hemsted (4 May 1878) and assumed the additional surname of Gathorne, apparently at the desire of his family. His departure from the Commons was widely regretted in the party; 150 MPs signed a memorial urging him to reconsider. Perhaps pique entered into the decision. Perhaps, had he remained in the Commons, he would have been the beneficiary of the later campaign in the party against Northcote's weak leadership. Perhaps, again, he foresaw that possibility and acted to forestall it.

In the Lords, Cranbrook lost much of his political utility and influence as a lightning conductor for back-bench sentiment. He knew that he was serving out time, and his interest in the political battle became less intense. However, he was still the most vigorous survivor among Disraeli's rather complaisant band of cabinet ministers. As such, he played an important part in the process which led to Salisbury becoming recognized as the overall leader of the party in the years after Disraeli's death in 1881. He was a respected elder statesman, sitting in the cabinets of 1885–6 and 1886–92 as lord president of the council. (He would have preferred the Colonial Office. In 1886, at a tricky time for the party, he was offered the viceroyalty of Ireland and later the foreign secretaryship, but did not consider either offer seriously, regarding the latter as out of the question on account of his poor grasp of foreign languages.) Salisbury consulted him on tactical matters, and on church appointments. The creation of a separate department for agriculture removed significant powers from the president of the council, and Cranbrook was in effect in charge merely of education, in which he saw little scope for initiative. Though friendly with Salisbury, he was never as close as to Disraeli, and relations were not helped by Cranbrook's unwillingness to assert himself against his officials in the education department, whose policy of steadily increasing the standards expected of schools in return for government grants was alienating the voluntary Church of England schools. In order to secure their position, Salisbury demanded the withdrawal and revision of an education code. He then took up the idea of 'free education', replacing parental fees for all elementary schools by government grants, but without the increased local control over denominational schools which Liberal advocates of free education desired. Cranbrook found free education a rather distastefully radical proposal, but consented to it; it became law in 1891. On the fall of the government in August 1892 he was promoted earl of Cranbrook, signalling the end of his political career near his seventy-eighth birthday.

Final years, death, and assessment Cranbrook lived another fourteen years, dying on 30 October 1906 at Hemsted Park. He was buried in Benenden parish churchyard. Almost to the end, he remained physically and mentally vigorous. He sat in the house of laymen in convocation, was a member of a number of London clubs, a governor of several schools, and a trustee of Keble College, Oxford, and in 1894 was elected an honorary fellow of Oriel. He liked visiting the theatre and art galleries, and had firm views about what he saw. He was happy in his family, his surroundings, his sport, and his religion. His political career was remarkable more for its longevity than for its achievement. He brought to parliament his barrister's facility of speaking, but was neither a legislator nor an intellectual. His guiding principle was loyalty to his party and his leaders, who naturally found this attractive. By this loyalty he

aimed to serve his country, his church, his class, his empire, and his queen; his attachment to all was very strong, and few things in politics gave him more satisfaction than his long association with Queen Victoria, who treated him as a trusty servant.   JONATHAN PARRY

Sources *Gathorne Hardy, first earl of Cranbrook: a memoir, with extracts from his diary and correspondence*, ed. A. E. Gathorne-Hardy, 2 vols. (1910) • *The diary of Gathorne Hardy, later Lord Cranbrook, 1866–1892: political selections*, ed. N. E. Johnson (1981) • P. Smith, *Disraelian Conservatism and social reform* (1967) • B. Porter, *Plots and paranoia: a history of political espionage in Britain, 1790–1988* (1989) • P. Marsh, *The discipline of popular government: Lord Salisbury's domestic statecraft, 1881–1902* (1978) • M. Cowling, *1867: Disraeli, Gladstone and revolution* (1967) • E. M. Spiers, *The late Victorian army, 1868–1902* (1992) • G. Sutherland, *Policy-making in elementary education, 1870–1895* (1973)

Archives BL, corresp., Add. MS 62537 • Suffolk RO, Ipswich, corresp. and papers | Balliol Oxf., letters to Sir Louis Mallet • BL, corresp. with duke of Buckingham, Add. MS 43742 • BL, corresp. with Lord Carnarvon, Add. MS 60768 • BL, corresp. with Lord Cross, Add. MS 51267 • BL, corresp. with Florence Nightingale, Add. MS 45787 • BL OIOC, letters to Sir Owen Tudor Burne, MS Eur. D 951 • BL OIOC, corresp. with Sir Richard Temple, MS Eur. F 86 • BL OIOC, letters to Sir H. G. Walpole, MS Eur. D 781 • Bodl. Oxf., corresp. with Benjamin Disraeli • CKS, letters to Edward Stanhope • Duke U., Perkins L., letters • Glos. RO, letters to Sir Michael Hicks Beach • Herts. ALS, letters to Lord Bulwer-Lytton • Hunt. L., letters to Grenville family • LPL, corresp. with Edward White Benson • LPL, letters to A. C. Tait • Lpool RO, letters to fourteenth and fifteenth earls of Derby • PRO, letters to Lord Cairns, PRO 30/51 • Som. ARS, letters to Sir William Jolliffe • St Deiniol's Library, Hawarden, letters to Sir Thomas Gladstone • Staffs. RO, letters from Sir Henry Green • U. Durham L., archives and special collections, corresp. with General Charles Grey • UCL, corresp. with Sir Edwin Chadwick • W. H. Smith Archive, Swindon, letters from W. H. Smith

Likenesses G. Richmond, pencil drawing, 1857, NPG • W. E. Miller, chalk drawing, 1877, Hushenden Manor, Buckinghamshire • lithograph, 1877, BM; repro. in *Civil Service Review* (1877) • Lock & Whitfield, woodburytype photograph, 1881, NPG; repro. in T. Cooper, *Men of mark: a gallery of contemporary portraits*, 5 (1881), 25 • S. Evans, pencil drawing, 1883, NPG • F. Holl, oils, 1883, Carlton Club, London; repro. in Gathorne-Hardy, ed., *Gathorne Hardy* • W. & D. Downey, woodburytype photograph, 1891, NPG; repro. in W. Downey and D. Downey, *The cabinet portrait gallery*, 2 (1891), 92 • Elliott & Fry, photograph, 1904, repro. in Gathorne-Hardy, ed., *Gathorne Hardy* • T. G. Appleton, mezzotint (after F. Holt), BM • H. Furniss, pen-and-ink sketch, NPG • H. Gales, group portrait, watercolour (*The Derby cabinet of 1867*), NPG • E. Stodart, stipple and line engraving (after photograph by W. & D. Downey), NPG • H. J. Whitlock, photograph, NPG [*see illus.*] • photograph, repro. in Johnson, ed., *Diary of Gathorne Hardy* • portrait, repro. in *Harper's Weekly*, 11 (1867), 169 • portrait, repro. in *ILN*, 64 (1874), 364 • portrait, repro. in *ILN*, 86 (1885), 650 • portrait, repro. in *VF* (24 April 1872) • prints, NPG

Wealth at death £274,098 11s. 10d.: probate, 28 Dec 1906, CGPLA Eng. & Wales

Hardy, Godfrey Harold (1877–1947), mathematician, was born on 7 February 1877, at Cranleigh, Surrey, the elder of two children of Isaac Hardy (1842–1901), a master at Cranleigh School, and his wife, Sophia Hall (b. 1846). His mathematical talent was evident early: by the time he was two he could write down numbers up to millions, and later in church he amused himself by factorizing the numbers of the hymns. Throughout his life he frequently played about with numbers of taxicabs, railway carriages, and

Godfrey Harold Hardy (1877–1947), by unknown photographer

the like. In 1890, after Cranleigh School, he went to Winchester College, where he was never taught mathematics in a class: Dr George Richardson, head of College, always coached him privately. Hardy strongly disliked public-school life; Winchester at that time was a rough place and not to his taste. Although he was grateful to the school for the excellent education it gave him, once having left it he never again visited it.

Fellowship at Trinity As a Wykehamist Hardy was expected to go to New College, Oxford. However, when he was about fifteen, he read a highly coloured novel of Cambridge life and set his heart on becoming, like its hero, a fellow of Trinity. He went up to Trinity College, Cambridge, as an entrance scholar in 1896, his tutor being Dr A. W. Verral. Even in Trinity, he thought of mathematics as an essentially 'competitive' subject. His eyes were opened by A. E. H. Love, who not only gave him his first serious conception of analysis, but also introduced him to Camille Jordan's *Cours d'analyse de l'école polytechnique*. Hardy was fourth wrangler in 1898 and in 1900 he achieved his childhood ambition when, on the basis of a dissertation, he was elected into a prize fellowship at Trinity. Hardy and J. H. Jeans, in that order, were awarded Smith's prizes in 1901.

Having secured a fellowship in Trinity, Hardy could spend all his time on mathematical research and in 1900 he published the first of his more than 350 research papers. In 1906 when his fellowship was to expire, he was made a college lecturer in mathematics, a position he held until 1919. His success in research was soon recognized: he became a fellow of the Royal Society in 1910, and in 1914

the University of Cambridge gave him the honorary title of Cayley lecturer. His book *A Course in Pure Mathematics* (1908; 9th edn, 1948) determined the outlook of English analysts for the next fifty years.

Although Hardy's earlier work had been good enough to earn his election as FRS his research really took off the following year, in 1911, when he began a collaboration with J. E. Littlewood (1885–1977), a colleague in Trinity. The Hardy–Littlewood partnership is the most famous in the history of mathematics: together they wrote a hundred papers, the first published in 1912 and the last in 1948, after Hardy's death.

Hardy and Littlewood made fundamental contributions to many branches of number theory and analysis: the summation of divergent series; the theory of Fourier series; the theory of the Riemann zeta-function and the distribution of prime numbers; the solution of Waring's problem; and the theory of Diophantine approximation. Their series of eight papers, Partitio Numerorum, on Waring's problem and the Goldbach conjecture, was especially influential. Later they worked on inequalities: with George Pólya they wrote *Inequalities* (1934), which became an instant best-seller, and a set of twenty-four papers on the theory of series.

In 1914 Hardy embarked on another successful collaboration, this time with the Indian genius Srinivasa Ramanujan, whom Hardy considered, rightly, to be his own 'discovery'. Ramanujan had no formal university education, and worked unaided in India until he was twenty-five. In 1913 he sent some of his results in a letter to Hardy in Trinity College, and Hardy and Littlewood soon decided that he was a mathematician of the highest calibre. Hardy arranged a scholarship for Ramanujan, who arrived in Cambridge in April 1914. Hardy and Ramanujan wrote five papers together, but the collaboration was cut short by Ramanujan's return to Madras in 1919, and his early death in April 1920.

In his political views and in his interest in mathematical philosophy, Hardy was a disciple of Bertrand Russell. Before 1914 Russell, Hardy, and Littlewood spent several summer holidays together, discussing mathematics, physics, philosophy, and politics. Like Russell, Hardy was strongly opposed to the First World War, although he did not go to the lengths which resulted in Russell's gaol sentence. He tried to prevent the rift between Trinity College and Russell, and was instrumental in the later reconciliation. He described the affair in a little book entitled *Bertrand Russell and Trinity*, which he had printed for private circulation in 1942 (reissued by Cambridge University in 1970).

Life at Oxford The tragedy of the war and the fight in Trinity over the Russell affair depressed Hardy, and he was relieved when, in 1919, he was elected to the Savilian chair of geometry at Oxford, and could migrate to New College. This was the happiest period of his life: his collaboration with Littlewood rose to new heights. The Oxford–Cambridge distance caused no difficulty since most of the collaboration was done by mail. According to their unwritten 'axioms', it was completely immaterial whether what they wrote was right or wrong; the recipient of a letter was under no obligation to open it, let alone read it and work on it; it was preferable that they should not both think about the same detail; and it was quite irrelevant if one of them made no contribution to the contents of a joint paper.

The informality and friendliness of New College suited Hardy—he was more at home in Oxford than he had ever been in Cambridge. He lectured on numerous subjects, including geometry (to fulfil the conditions of his chair) and mathematics for philosophers. He was an admirable research supervisor, always willing to help and always full of ideas, and many an Oxford DPhil dissertation owes much to him. He made many visits to American universities, and loved the country, but the only time he spent an extended period abroad was in 1928–9, when he visited Princeton and the California Institute of Technology.

Hardy liked all forms of ball games, and was obsessed with cricket: he would not miss a test match at Lord's and spent some of his happiest hours in Cambridge at Fenners, watching university cricket. He was an excellent batsman and, had he had any coaching at Winchester, could have come close to being first-class. His highest term of praise of a human achievement was 'in the Bradman class': thus Archimedes, Newton, and Gauss were in the Bradman class. Even in his sixties Hardy was a good real tennis player, and excelled at bowls.

Sadleirian professorship In 1931 Hardy succeeded E. W. Hobson in the Sadleirian chair at Cambridge, and became again a fellow of Trinity. As the most influential British mathematician Hardy secured jobs for many young people, and from 1933 he was deeply concerned with the fate of his fellow mathematicians on the continent, and directed attempts to find places for those whom persecution had driven out. He also took up his pen to ridicule the view that there is a strong link between mathematical creative style and race. The highlight of Hardy's later years was the Hardy–Littlewood 'conversation class', in which mathematicians of all ages lectured on a great variety of topics.

Throughout his life Hardy took a great interest in education. He was an implacable enemy of the mathematical tripos at Cambridge which he blamed for the dearth of great English mathematicians and so wished to abolish. He worked much for the success of the London Mathematical Society; he was president twice and left the royalties from his books to the society. He held honorary degrees from many universities, and was an *associé étranger* of the Paris Académie des Sciences. The Royal Society awarded him a royal medal in 1920 and its Sylvester medal in 1940; the Copley medal, its highest award, was to be presented to him on the day he died.

As an editor, Hardy was 'in the Bradman class'. It was largely due to him that the *Quarterly Journal* was started in Oxford, and as an editor of the Cambridge Tracts in Mathematics and Mathematical Physics from 1914 to 1946, he was instrumental in establishing it as a major series. He contributed four volumes to the Tracts: *Integration of Functions of a Single Variable* (no. 2, 1905); *Orders of Infinity* (no. 12,

1910); *The General Theory of Dirichlet's Series* (with M. Riesz, no. 18, 1915); and *Fourier Series* (with W. W. Rogosinski, no. 38, 1944). His last textbook, *Divergent Series*, was published posthumously, in 1949.

From the second half of the thirties Hardy's mathematical output greatly diminished, due partly to the onset of Littlewood's depression, and this reinforced his belief that mathematics was a young person's game. Nevertheless, he wrote two masterpieces: *An Introduction to the Theory of Numbers* (1938), with E. M. Wright, and *A Mathematician's Apology* (1940), the most poetic writing about being a mathematician.

Character and philosophy Writing at the outbreak of the Second World War, in his *Apology* Hardy was preoccupied with war and the role of the sciences: 'There is one comforting conclusion which is easy for a real mathematician. Real mathematics has no effect on war' (Hardy, *Apology*, 140). On a personal note, he claimed, 'I have never done anything "useful". No discovery of mine has made, or is likely to make, directly or indirectly, for good or ill, the least difference to the amenity of the world' (ibid., 150). Later there came at least two major exceptions to this claim: in 1908, in a letter to *Science* entitled 'Mendelian proportions in a mixed population', he made an important contribution to population genetics, which is now in every textbook as the Hardy–Weinberg law. Another example is modern 'control theory', in which a number of problems are best formulated in terms of the Hardy space, H_∞, of the right half-plane and require, both theoretically and computationally, a fair amount of deep theory, whose origin is in Hardy's work.

Hardy had many peculiarities. He strongly disliked mechanical gadgets, in particular the telephone, and never used a watch or a fountain pen. He was unashamedly heliotropic and loathed the English climate. He loved conversation, odd little word games, walking, and gentle climbing; he liked cats and was meticulously orderly in everything but dress. He delighted in good literature but did not appreciate music. He hated war, cruelty of all kinds, dogs, hot roast mutton (memories of Winchester!), politicians, and any kind of sham. He preferred the downtrodden and those handicapped by race to the people he called 'large bottomed'. He was indifferent to noise, even when doing creative work, and his best time of work was the long vacation, with tennis or cricket in the early afternoon. Hardy was violently opposed to religion, although he had many clerical friends: he considered God his personal enemy, and went to great lengths to foil him.

Until he was about thirty, Hardy looked incredibly young; later everyone thought him striking. According to Russell, he had the bright eyes that only very clever men have. Nevertheless, he hated mirrors: the first thing he did on entering a hotel room was to cover up the mirror. He disliked having his photograph taken—there are hardly a dozen snapshots of him. Hardy had no women friends: according to Littlewood, he was a 'non-practicing homosexual' (private information) and P. A. M. Dirac found him 'uncomfortably unusual'. He was shy throughout his life, but in his remarks he could be merciless. He was wont to pass people in the street without any sign of recognition. The Second World War and the deterioration of his creative powers and health drove Hardy into depression. After a suicide attempt and a long illness, he died at the Evelyn Nursing Home, Cambridge, on 1 December 1947, with his devoted sister, Gertrude, at his bedside.

Mathematics books age notoriously quickly; nevertheless, three of Hardy's books are not only classics, but are constantly reprinted and remain best-sellers more than fifty years after their first appearances. Hardy described himself as a problem solver rather than a theory builder, but he had a profound influence on modern mathematics and ranks as one of the greatest English mathematicians of the twentieth century. Together with Littlewood, he brought pure mathematics in England to the highest level, and was instrumental in improving the teaching of mathematics throughout the world. He was fiercely proud of pure mathematics; as he wrote in A Mathematician's Apology:

> If intellectual curiosity, professional pride, and ambition are the dominant incentives to research, then assuredly no one has a fairer chance of gratifying them than a mathematician … as history proves abundantly, mathematical achievement, whatever its intrinsic value, is the most enduring of all. (Hardy, Apology, 80)

BÉLA BOLLOBÁS

Sources E. C. Titchmarsh, *Obits. FRS*, 6 (1948–9), 47–61 • E. C. Titchmarsh, *Journal of the London Mathematical Society*, 25 (1950), 81–101 • G. H. Hardy, *A mathematician's apology* (1940) • B. Bollobás, ed., *Littlewood's miscellany* (1986) • Trinity Cam., Hardy MSS • private information (2004) • *Collected papers of G. H. Hardy: including joint papers with J. E. Littlewood and others*, ed. London Mathematical Society, 7 vols. (1966–79) • J. Todd, 'G. H. Hardy as an editor', *Mathematical Intelligencer*, 16 (1994), 32–7 • I. Grattan-Guinness, 'Russell and G. H. Hardy: a study of their relationship', *Russell*, n. s., 11 (1991–2), 165–79 • G. H. Hardy, 'The case against the mathematical tripos', *Mathematical Gazette*, 13 (1926–7), 61–71 • G. H. Hardy, 'The J-Type and the S-type among mathematicians', *Nature*, 134 (1934), 250 • d. cert.
Archives Bodl. Oxf., corresp. with British Association mathematical tables committee • CUL, asymptotic formulae and papers on Waring's problem • Trinity Cam., notebooks and papers | BL, corresp. with Albert Mansbridge, Add. MS 65258 • CUL, letters to G. E. Moore • L. Cong., O. Veblen MSS • McMaster University, Hamilton, Ontario, corresp. with Bertrand Russell • New College, Oxford, letters to E. C. Titchmarsh • Trinity Cam., corresp. with Harold Davenport • Trinity Cam., corresp. with A. E. Ingham
Likenesses G. Bollobás, bronze bust, 1989, priv. coll. • photograph, repro. in D. C. Russell, *Bulletin of the London Mathematical Society*, 18 (1986), 403–20 • photograph, repro. in D. J. Albers, G. L. Alexanderson, and C. Reid, eds., *More mathematical people* (1990) • photograph, repro. in *Obits. FRS*, 6 (1948–9) [*see illus.*] • six photographs, repro. in London Mathematical Society, ed., *Collected papers* • two photographs, repro. in Todd, 'G. H. Hardy'
Wealth at death £18,187 11s. 10d.: probate, 12 Feb 1948, CGPLA Eng. & Wales

Hardy, Henry Ernest [*name in religion* Andrew] (1869–1946), Anglican friar and Church of England clergyman, was born on 7 January 1869 at Kasauli, India, the fourth son of Colonel Edmund Armitage Hardy, Indian army officer (d. 1903), and his wife, Grace Maxwell (1838–1911), daughter of Peter Aiken of Clifton, banker. He spent his childhood in India and, after his father's retirement from the army, attended Clifton College briefly before persuading his parents to send him to an art school in Bristol. After two years there he went in 1888 to Keble College, Oxford, graduating in 1891 with a fourth in theology (he was handicapped by ill health).

His motive in forsaking art for theology had been to 'get a theory to live by and a quest to follow' (*Green Quarterly*), but he passed his Oxford days without any set religious convictions and thought only vaguely in terms of ordination. The spur to deeper involvement came from the future bishop of London A. F. Winnington-Ingram, then head of Oxford House, Bethnal Green, who was visiting the university to appeal for volunteers to serve the underprivileged in London's East End. Hardy responded to the challenge and took up residence at Oxford House in October 1891, his duties combining administration with practical welfare work. His thoughts now turned to the religious life, but his problem was to find a way of combining a vocation to such a life with a parallel vocation to work among the impoverished masses of east London.

The answer came in the form of a fateful meeting with Winnington-Ingram's predecessor at Oxford House, James Adderley, whose ideals resembled Hardy's. They were joined by a third enthusiast, Henry Chappel, and following a retreat at Pusey House, Oxford, the three pledged themselves on 20 January 1894 to a rule of life and to the religious vows of poverty, chastity, and obedience. Hardy then completed his training for the priesthood at Ely Theological College before joining his companions at Plaistow, in east London, where they took charge of the mission church of St Philip. The new community was christened the Society of the Divine Compassion (SDC), its rule and way of life resembling those of the original followers of St Francis of Assisi; it was built on the twin foundations of faith and good works.

After Adderley's departure in 1897 and Chappel's death in 1915 Father Andrew—as Hardy was now universally known—became the dominant character in the community, acting as its superior from 1912 to 1916 and again from 1924 to 1935. From 1916 until his death (apart from a year in 1932–3 at the SDC mission in Southern Rhodesia) he was priest-in-charge of St Philip's, where his influence and reputation became immense. He was also famed for his skills as a confessor and retreat conductor; he wrote endless letters to correspondents struggling with personal problems of faith and conduct; and he was a prolific author, publishing during his lifetime eight books of poems and sixteen works in prose which established him as one of the leading devotional writers of the day. He made full use of his talents and early training as a painter; he shone as a watercolourist and would sell his sketches in aid of charity. And he put his passion for the theatre to good use by writing religious plays for his parishioners to perform.

His parish suffered badly in the blitz, the church being wrecked twice, and his wartime ordeal took its toll on his health. Cancer was diagnosed in August 1945, and he died in Bushey Heath District Hospital, unmarried, on 31 March 1946. After his funeral in St Andrew's, Plaistow, on

4 April his body was borne in procession through the streets of the parish for burial in the East London cemetery.

He was a man of tall, dignified presence, a regular Friar Tuck in build, with rugged features which acquired a striking spiritual beauty over the years. Throughout his ministry he radiated holiness. 'He somehow took us up into the supernatural', one friend observed (Burne, 81). And a bishop remarked after his death: 'He was a great man, such as God sends us—only one or two—in a generation' (ibid., 86).

BERNARD PALMER

Sources K. E. Burne, ed., *The life and letters of Father Andrew, SDC* (1948) · Father Andrew, *The adventure of faith* (1933) · Father Andrew, *My year in Rhodesia* (1933) · P. F. Anson, *The call of the cloister: religious communities and kindred bodies in the Anglican communion*, 4th edn (1964) · G. Curtis CR, *William of Glasshampton: friar, monk, solitary* (1947) · P. Dunstan, *This poor sort: a history of the European province of the Society of St Francis* (1997) · A. C. Kelway, ed., *A Franciscan revival: the story of the Society of the Divine Compassion* (1908) · S. Leslie, *The film of memory* (1938) · T. P. Stephens, *Father Adderley* (1943) · B. Palmer, 'Franciscan pioneer', *Men of habit* (1994), 3–34 · B. Williams, *The Franciscan revival in the Anglican communion* (1982) · Father Andrew, *Green Quarterly*, [n.d.], LPL, records of the Society of the Divine Compassion, 1, 2 · *CGPLA Eng. & Wales* (1946)

Archives LPL, records of Society of the Divine Compassion

Likenesses photographs, repro. in Burne, ed., *Life and letters of Father Andrew*

Wealth at death £9517 4s. 2d.: probate, 5 Sept 1946, *CGPLA Eng. & Wales*

Hardy, Herbert Hardy Cozens-, first Baron Cozens-Hardy

(1838–1920), judge, was born on 22 November 1838 at Letheringsett Hall, Dereham, Norfolk, the second son of William Hardy Cozens-Hardy (1806–1895), a Congregationalist solicitor with a large practice at Norwich, and his wife, Sarah (d. 1891), daughter of Thomas Theobald, of the same city. His father had assumed by royal licence in 1842 the additional name and arms of Hardy. Educated at Amersham Hall School and at University College, London, Cozens-Hardy graduated at London University in 1858. He took the degree of LLB in 1863, and afterwards became a member of the senate of London University and a fellow of University College, London. In 1862 he was called to the bar at Lincoln's Inn after obtaining a studentship and a certificate of honour. He read in the chambers of Thomas Lewin and James Dickinson, both eminent as equity draftsmen. On 26 July 1866 he married Maria (d. 1886), the daughter of Thomas Hepburn, of Clapham Common; they had two sons and two daughters. Between 1871 and 1876 he was an examiner for London University in equity and real property law.

Cozens-Hardy soon acquired practice as a Chancery junior, his nonconformist and Liberal connections being considerable assets. After twenty busy years he took silk in 1882. Attaching himself at first to the court of Mr Justice Fry, he took his seat before Mr Justice North when Fry went to the Court of Appeal in 1883. He proved so successful as a leader that in 1893 he joined the small band of 'specials' of which John Rigby and Horace Davey were also members. In this distinguished company he held his own, and was constantly employed in heavy cases both in the Chancery Division and before the appellate tribunals.

Herbert Hardy Cozens-Hardy, first Baron Cozens-Hardy (1838–1920), by Reginald Grenville Eves

A layman 'would have been puzzled to understand' Cozens-Hardy's success as an advocate (*The Times*). Although he was of unimpressive appearance, and without the vigour of Rigby or the subtlety of Davey, he had industry, knowledge, and lucidity of speech, and judges listened to him with respect. He was kindly and courteous, and his popularity with the practising members of the profession was shown by his election as chairman of the general council of the bar. Among the important cases in which he appeared as counsel were *Sheffield v. London Joint Stock Bank* (1888, the right of a bank to sell securities deposited by a borrower with limited authority), *Bradford Corporation v. Pickles* (1895, the effect of a malicious motive on the lawful use of property), *Trego v. Hunt* (1896, the right of the seller of a business to canvass his old customers), and *Attorney-General v. Beech* (1899, the liability of a remainderman who has bought a life interest to pay estate duty).

At the general election of 1885 Cozens-Hardy was elected Liberal member of parliament for North Norfolk, and he continued to sit for the constituency until elevated to the bench in 1899. In the House of Commons, although never a prominent figure, he was a not infrequent speaker. As a rule he confined himself to matters of which he had professional or local knowledge, such as married women's property, the winding-up of companies, bankruptcy, and the law relating to trustees. His most notable achievement was the passing of an act relating to the law of mortmain, which was known among Chancery lawyers as Cozens-Hardy's Act. In 1886, when the Liberal Party split on the subject of home rule for Ireland, Cozens-Hardy remained faithful to Gladstone, having in May 1886 been wavering towards Joseph Chamberlain and the Liberal Unionist defectors. He was never a violent partisan in the politically disruptive period which followed.

In February 1899 the death of Lord Justice Chitty and the promotion to his place of Sir Robert Romer created a vacancy in the Chancery Division. Lord Halsbury, who was not ordinarily predisposed towards political opponents, disregarded Cozens-Hardy's Liberalism, and with the full approval of the profession raised him to the bench. He received the customary knighthood. Halsbury offered the post in a letter of 21 February 1899 beginning: 'My dear Cozens-Hardy. Notwithstanding your abominable politics I think you are the fittest person to succeed Romer …' (Heuston, 59). The incident inspired Theo Mathew to produce a cartoon entitled 'Kiss me—Hardy' (Mathew, 70). As a judge Cozens-Hardy showed the industry and care that had marked his work at the bar. His findings of fact were more often criticized than his decisions on points of law. In November 1901, on the resignation of Lord Justice Rigby, he became a lord justice of appeal and was sworn of the privy council.

In March 1907 Cozens-Hardy succeeded Sir Richard Henn Collins as master of the rolls. In this onerous office he performed his duties with ability and dignity. Appeals under the Workmen's Compensation Act of 1906 were numerous, and Cozens-Hardy, although unversed in this branch of the law, dealt with them satisfactorily. His familiarity with equity law and practice made him a strong president of the court when Chancery appeals were being heard. Many of his judgments as master of the rolls stood the test of appeal, and afterwards proved of value to his successors. They were marked 'by clarity of reasoning and succinctness of expression' (*The Times*). In 1913 he was one of the three commissioners of the great seal during the absence in Canada of the lord chancellor, Lord Haldane, and in July 1914 he was raised to the peerage with the title Baron Cozens-Hardy. For some years he chaired the Council of Legal Education; he was also a chairman of quarter sessions in Norfolk. His chief interests outside law were gardening and religion, and he was a frequent speaker at the Whitfield Tabernacle while his son-in-law the Revd C. Sylvester Horne was the minister there. His health had been failing for many months before his retirement in April 1918. He died at Letheringsett Hall on 18 June 1920, and was buried at Kensal Green. He was succeeded as second baron by his eldest son, William Hepburn Cozens-Hardy KC (1868–1924), who sat as Liberal coalitionist MP for South Norfolk (1918–20).

THEOBALD MATHEW, *rev.* MARK POTTLE

Sources *The Times* (19 June 1920), 10 e–f · *Law Journal*, 55 (26 June 1920), 250, 252 · Burke, *Peerage* · R. F. V. Heuston, *Lives of the lord chancellors, 1940–1970* (1987) · T. Mathew, *For lawyers and others* (1937) · W. C. Lubenow, *Parliamentary politics and the home rule crisis* (1988) · personal knowledge (1927) · Sainty, *Judges*
Archives Norfolk RO, autobiography [copy]
Likenesses R. G. Eves, oils, Lincoln's Inn, London [*see illus.*] · R. G. Eves, portrait; known to be in possession of family, in 1927 · Spy [L. Ward], chromolithograph caricature, NPG; repro. in *VF* (24 Jan 1901) · Spy [L. Ward], chromolithograph caricature, NPG; repro. in *VF* (13 April 1893)
Wealth at death £123,228 9s.: probate, 19 Aug 1920, *CGPLA Eng. & Wales*

Hardy, John (1679/80–1740), Presbyterian minister and Church of England clergyman, was born at Garstang, Lancashire, the son of the Revd Richard Hardy of Kirkland. He was educated at Mr Firbank's school at Kirkby Lonsdale before being admitted a pensioner at Christ's College, Cambridge, aged seventeen, in February 1697. After two years he left without a degree, having quarrelled with his father. 'At length they fell out to that degree, that the father turned the son out of doors, leaving him to shift for himself in the wide world, with but three shillings and sixpence in his pocket' (Calamy, 501). Being destitute, Hardy approached the dissenters of Liverpool; they sent him to finish his ministerial education at James Owen's academy in Oswestry, where he was supported by a grant of £8 a year from the Presbyterian Fund between 1699 and 1702. After he had completed his studies he went to London. Edmund Calamy discovered him starving in a garret because he was too 'modest and shy of making the particulars of his case known' (ibid., 502). Calamy paid his debts and took him into his house until he found him a place with Lady Caroline Clinton, a member of his congregation. After Hardy was ordained, she sent him to preach in the church at Sempringham near Folkingham with an allowance of £60 a year, where he 'was much resorted to by persons that came from the neighbouring parishes' (ibid., 502). William Wake noticed him during his primary visitation of the diocese of Lincoln in the summer of 1706 following complaints that Hardy acted as a minister of the Church of England though not ordained. Following opposition from Wake, Lady Clinton fitted up an old Catholic chapel on her estate and placed Hardy there with a handsome allowance. 'Now he pretends to be a Dissenter, & keeps a meeting in a chapell-house. What he really is nobody knows, but he is a ready man & a good scholar' (Sykes, 199). On 12 January 1708 Hardy married Mary (*bap.* 1686), the daughter of John Greene of Dunsby Hall, as his second wife. They had one son, Richard, and two daughters, Philippiana and Mary.

In 1714, with Calamy's encouragement, Hardy accepted an invitation from the Presbyterian congregation at High Pavement, Nottingham, to become John Whitlock's colleague following the death of John Barret the previous year. From 1714, and perhaps earlier, Hardy kept an academy preparing students for the nonconformist ministry. Caleb Fleming (1698–1779) studied theology, logic, ethics, natural philosophy, astronomy, geometry, and trigonometry with him. The names of only two other students are known, John Brekell (1697–1769), minister of Kay Street Chapel, Liverpool, and John Johnson, who later conformed and became librarian of Lambeth Palace. Hardy was a considerable scholar and antiquarian. Philip Doddridge noted that he was 'universally allowed to be an excellent critic, especially in the Sciptures', and he considered Hardy had 'few equals in learning' (*Correspondence and Diary*, 1.68, 2.361). Hardy corresponded with Ralph Thoresby of Leeds and was friendly with William Stukeley, who dedicated a plate to his erudite and dear friend in his *Itinerarium curiosum* (1724). He was also closely associated with Maurice Johnson, the founder of the Spalding Gentlemen's Society, and a considerable benefactor of the society's library, his outstanding gift being Caxton's edition of John Gower's *Confessio amantis* (1483). He was elected a member of the Society of Antiquaries on 26 August 1718 and of the Spalding Gentlemen's Society on 24 December 1724. Hardy, like his friend Thoresby, had a collection of coins and curiosities which he called his museum. After his death he left his son two-thirds of his books, as well as 'my Mathematical Instruments Natural Curiosities and other things strictly belonging to my Library and all my Medals and other parts of Antiquity' (will).

In 1727, without warning, Hardy conformed to the Church of England, to the great consternation of his congregation and of dissenters generally. He claimed that it was the result of two years of deliberation, but was presumed by the dissenters to have been influenced by the expectation of some preferment from his wife's uncle. His conformity occurred at a time when a number of younger ministers also conformed. It is 'the most considerable conquest which the Establishment has made upon us for several years; … as he was a very celebrated scholar and at the head of the dissenting interest in this neighbourhood' (*Correspondence and Diary*, 2.361). Hardy was vicar of Kinoulton, Nottinghamshire, a peculiar of the archbishop of York, from 1729 until 1735, when his son, Richard, succeeded him, and vicar of Melton Mowbray from September 1731 until his death. He died on 28 June 1740 at Melton Mowbray, and was buried in St Mary's Church. He was survived by his wife.   DAVID L. WYKES

Sources E. Calamy, *An historical account of my own life, with some reflections on the times I have lived in, 1671–1731*, ed. J. T. Rutt, 2nd edn, 2 (1830), 500–04 · *The correspondence and diary of Philip Doddridge*, ed. J. D. Humphreys, 5 vols. (1829–31), vol. 1, p. 68; vol. 2, pp. 62, 360–65 · Nichols, *Lit. anecdotes*, 6.1, 87n. · J. Peile, *Biographical register of Christ's College, 1505–1905, and of the earlier foundation, God's House, 1448–1505*, ed. [J. A. Venn], 2 (1913), 138, 224 · B. Carpenter, *Some account of the original introduction of Presbyterianism in Nottingham and the neighbourhood*, ed. [J. J. Tayler] (1862?), 126–33 · N. Sykes, ed., 'Bishop William Wake's primary visitation of the diocese of Lincoln, 1706', *Journal of Ecclesiastical History*, 2 (1951), 190–206, esp. 199 · A. R. Maddison, ed., *Lincolnshire pedigrees*, 4, Harleian Society, 55 (1906), 1242–3 · will, proved, Leicester, 14 Oct 1740, Leics. RO · J. Nichols, *The history and antiquities of the county of Leicester*, 3/1 (1800), 382 n. 5 · H. McLachlan, *English education under the Test Acts: being the history of the nonconformist academies, 1662–1820* (1931), 12 · 'Biography: memoir of the life of the Rev. Caleb Fleming', *Monthly Repository*, 13 (1818), 409 · *The autobiography of William Stout of Lancaster, 1665–1752*, ed. J. D. Marshall, Chetham Society, 3rd ser., 14 (1967), 112–13 · parish register, Melton Mowbray, St Mary's, Leics. RO, DG 36/4 [burial]

Hardy, John James (1854–1932), manufacturer of fishing tackle, was born at Grosvenor Terrace, Alnwick, Northumberland, on 4 April 1854, the second son of John James Hardy (*b.* 1831), coroner for north Northumberland, and his wife, Jane Newton. After attending Duke's School, Alnwick, in 1862–8 he was intended for a career in marine engineering but instead joined a firm making guns and fishing rods, which was founded in Alnwick in 1872 by his elder brother, William Hardy [*see below*].

The first of its type in the town, the business grew steadily. Traditional handicraft skills were combined with detailed engineering innovation to produce rods made from bamboo segments (some, especially the Palakona range, built round a steel core) and aluminium reels such as the Model Perfect, much sought after by collectors. The gunmaking was soon supplanted by angling goods, shown in increasingly comprehensive catalogues; the 1905 issue had 400 pages, mostly of items made in house. By the time it moved to a substantial new factory, Alnwick's North British Works, in 1890, the firm had acquired a reputation as the manufacturer of some of the world's finest, and most expensive, fishing tackle, with retail branches in Edinburgh, Manchester, and London, as well as extensive overseas outlets.

Although its employees grew rapidly in number, from thirty to, eventually, several hundreds, it remained a paternalistic family business, with annual works' outings paid for out of the profits; when it was made into a private limited liability company in 1907 many of the employees, including women fly tyers, bought shares. The firm's success lured competitors to Alnwick but they never matched its achievements. John James Hardy served as managing director until his seventies. He developed considerable skills as a publicist and Hardys became a major exhibitor at international exhibitions, winning fifty-two gold medals and other awards for the quality of its products. William held royal warrants from George V and from the kings of Italy and Spain.

A dedicated fisherman from childhood, John James used his prowess as a pleasure angler to win international casting competitions, using ordinary Hardy production rods as another form of advertising. After his first victory in Edinburgh in 1892, and a good placing in Scarborough two years later, he established his reputation at the Crystal Palace in 1904 by winning four separate events in the trout and salmon sections, the first person ever to do so, and then triumphed at the Franco-British exhibition in 1908, together with his nephews as back-up. After further victories in France, in competitions sponsored by the Casting Club de France, his last appearance was in London's South Norwood at the age of seventy-eight, when he demonstrated various casting techniques. He was also a prolific and highly regarded angling journalist, which led *Country Life* to commission his major standard work, *Salmon Fishing*, in 1907. In that book he demonstrated his deep understanding of riparian ecology and his passion for inventing new fishing lures.

A solid Conservative and Anglican, Hardy never married. An inveterate traveller in Britain and Europe in search of business, fishing, and shooting, he remained firmly attached to Northumberland, settling eventually in Alnmouth. He died in his house there, Alnbrae, on 24 June 1932, from the after-effects of a seizure brought on by fishing the River Coquet a month earlier; his funeral in

Alnwick parish church on 28 June was packed by Hardys employees. Apart from bequests to servants and local churches, he endowed a university entrance scholarship for boys from his old school, Duke's.

His elder brother, **William Hardy** (1852–1928), was born at Clayport Street, Alnwick, on 29 October 1852 and attended Duke's School from 1861 to 1867. Apart from founding the gun and fishing tackle business, he also had interests in the Alnwick Brewery and the *Alnwick and County Gazette*, being a director of both companies. William married, on 19 October 1882, Barbara Mary, the daughter of Robert Leighton of Felton, Northumberland; they had five sons and a daughter. Two of the sons, Lawrence Robert and Harold John, were also casting champions and all the family held posts in the firm; at incorporation seven of the family were directors. William died at his house, Oaklands, Alnwick, on 7 February 1928. He was survived by his wife.

J. R. LOWERSON

Sources *Alnwick and County Gazette* (2 July 1932) · *Fishing Gazette* (2 July 1932) · J. M. Graham, ed., *The best of Hardy's anglers' guides* (1982) · J. J. Hardy, *Salmon fishing* (1907) · *The Times* (27 June 1932) · *The Times* (14 July 1932) · *The Times* (11 Aug 1932) · *Hardy's Anglers' Guide* (1917) · J. Jamieson, *Northumberland at the opening of the twentieth century: contemporary biographies*, ed. W. T. Pike (1905), 242 · J. Lowerson, *Sport and the English middle classes, 1870–1914* (1993) · W. R. Finch and W. R. Fairclough, *A register of admissions to the Duke of Northumberland's school, Alnwick, 1811–1911* (1911), 34, 36 · *CGPLA Eng. & Wales* (1932) · *CGPLA Eng. & Wales* (1928) [William Hardy] · b. cert. · d. cert. · b. cert. [William Hardy] · m. cert. [William Hardy]
Likenesses E. Hodgsonsmart, portrait, repro. in Hardy, *Salmon fishing* · photograph, repro. in *Alnwick and County Gazette* · photograph, repro. in *Fishing Gazette* · photograph (William Hardy), repro. in Pike, *Contemporary biographies*
Wealth at death £148,270 7s. 6d.: probate, 5 Aug 1932, *CGPLA Eng. & Wales* · £44,359 19s. 10d.—William Hardy: probate, 10 March 1928, *CGPLA Eng. & Wales*

Hardy, John Stockdale (1793–1849), antiquary, was born at Leicester on 7 October 1793, the only child of William Hardy, a manufacturer of that town, and his wife, Jane Harrison. He was educated in a private school in Leicester until the age of fourteen, when he was taken into the office of his maternal uncle, William Harrison, to serve a clerkship. Harrison was a proctor, and registrar of the archdeaconry court of Leicester, a post in which he succeeded his own maternal uncle, John Stockdale, after whom Hardy was named. In due course Hardy was admitted as a proctor and notary public, and thereby qualified to practise in the ecclesiastical courts.

In addition to his practice Hardy succeeded his uncle, on the latter's death in 1826, to a number of ecclesiastical offices: he became registrar of the archdeaconry court of Leicester, registrar of the court of the commissary of the bishop of Lincoln, and registrar of the court of the peculiar and exempt jurisdiction of the manor and soke of Rothley. He also succeeded Beaumont Burnaby as registrar of the court of the peculiar of Evington, and registrar of the prebendal court of St Margaret, Leicester. He was elected a fellow of the Society of Antiquaries in 1826.

Hardy was a staunch conservative in politics and in the 1820s was a firm opponent of Catholic emancipation; he corresponded frequently with Lord Eldon on the subject and published in 1820 *A Series of Letters Addressed to a Friend, upon the Roman Catholic Question* under the pseudonym Britannicus. Hardy was a frequent correspondent of the *Gentleman's Magazine* and in 1845 he also brought out a collection of poems entitled *The Palace of Fantasy, or, The Bard's Imagery*. In pursuance of his will his *Literary Remains* were collected and published in 1852 by John Gough Nichols FSA.

Hardy married Elizabeth, daughter of Thomas Leach of Leicester, in 1827; she died childless in 1838. Hardy died on 19 July 1849 at his residence, in Friar Lane, Leicester. His funeral at St Mary's Church, Leicester (where he was buried), was attended by a large congregation of frameworkknitters, whose interests he had promoted.

MICHAEL LOBBAN

Sources *GM*, 2nd ser., 32 (1849), 433 · *GM*, 2nd ser., 37 (1852), 385
Archives BL, drafts for article on St Mary's Church, Leicester, Add. MS 63652 · Bodl. Oxf., commonplace books · York Minster Library, archives, treatise on breeding of horses
Likenesses J. Brown, stipple (after drawing by J. T. Mitchell), BM, NPG; repro. in *The literary remains of John Stockdale Hardy*, ed. J. G. Nichols (1852)

Hardy, Josiah (*bap.* 1716, *d.* 1790), colonial official, was born in Westminster, London, and was baptized there at St Martin-in-the-Fields on 7 May 1716. He was the eldest child of Sir Charles *Hardy (*c.*1680–1744), commissioner of the Admiralty, and Elizabeth Burchett (*d.* in or before 1744), daughter of Josiah *Burchett (*c.*1666–1746), MP for Sandwich, 1705–41. His brother Sir Charles *Hardy (*bap.* 1717, *d.* 1780) was the governor of New York (1755–7), and MP for Rochester (1764–8) and for Plymouth (1771–80). Hardy's early life is obscure. He was baptized in the Church of England and raised at Greenwich, Kent. His father and two brothers became admirals, but the sea did not beckon him. He held no important office until 14 April 1761, when the king appointed him New Jersey's governor—undoubtedly through his brother Charles's intercession.

The new governor crossed the Atlantic accompanied by William Alexander, a member of his council (the legislature's appointed upper house). A wealthy, sophisticated, and ingratiating country squire, Alexander spent the interval convincing the callow Hardy that his best strategy for a successful administration lay in allying himself with Alexander's political confederates, the East Jersey proprietors, who were the heirs to the individuals given private possession of that province by Charles II until it was absorbed by New Jersey in 1702. With proprietary backing, Hardy would be buttressed by his colony's wealthiest and most politically influential families—from whose ranks had come most councillors and assembly leaders since 1720—and he readily embraced their support.

Hardy established excellent relations with the legislature, in which the assembly's speaker and most councillors were eastern proprietors, and he therefore enjoyed notable success in getting his initiatives enacted. In return, he often acquiesced to proprietors' suggestions while making executive decisions and reserved the cream of the positions subject to his patronage for them or their clients.

This deference to provincial opinion became Hardy's undoing shortly after he took office. Hardy did not fully realize that British colonial policy was undergoing a fundamental change, by which Whitehall intended to reverse the colonies' drift towards *de facto* local autonomy by vigorously asserting crown prerogatives. The chief justice and two associate justices, all of the proprietary party, had applied to renew their commissions on the grounds of 'good behaviour'. Hardy had been instructed by the privy council, however, that all judges were now to serve at 'the king's pleasure'. Although the previous governor had rejected the applications, Hardy accepted them after the council unanimously resolved that the petition be granted. The privy council had previously winked at many similar indiscretions by governors, but the current administration was determined to curb the independence enjoyed by colonial judges through good behaviour appointments. Hardy hastily persuaded the three justices to accept new commissions at royal pleasure, but still could not placate his superiors. His dismissal came in August 1762.

Hardy's stoic acceptance of his fate helped his appointment as consul at Cadiz on 12 November 1764. He retired there in old age, then returned to Kent. Leaving a widow, Harriet, and at least one daughter, he died about April 1790 at Greenwich.   THOMAS L. PURVIS

Sources J. K. Martin, 'Josiah Hardy', *The governors of New Jersey, 1664–1974*, ed. P. A. Stellhorn and M. J. Birkner (1982), 69–72 · J. J. Nadelhaft, 'Politics and the judicial tenure fight in colonial New Jersey', *William and Mary Quarterly*, 28 (1971), 46–63 · W. A. Whitehead and others, eds., *Documents relating to the colonial, revolutionary and post-revolutionary history of the state of New Jersey*, 9 (1885) · *DNB* · administration, PRO, PROB 6/182 · parish register, Westminster, St Martin-in-the-Fields [baptism], 7 May 1716
Archives PRO, Colonial Office papers, board of trade and secretaries of state: America and West Indies, original corresp.
Wealth at death £1500: administration, PRO, PROB 6/182

Hardy [*née* Raven], **Mary** (1733–1809), diarist, was born on 12 November 1733 at Whissonsett, near Fakenham, Norfolk, the second daughter of Robert Raven (1707–1778), farmer, and his wife, Mary Fox (d. 1751). She was probably educated at a school in Fakenham, where she later sent her daughter. In 1765 aged thirty-two she married William Hardy (1732–1811), tenant farmer in East Dereham, from a farming family in Scotton, near Knaresborough, Yorkshire. Two sons were born in East Dereham: Raven (1767–1786) and William (1770–1842). In 1770 William Hardy took over the lease of a brewery and farm in Coltishall, near Norwich.

The diary begins on 28 November 1773 at Coltishall, when Mary Hardy was forty, and three weeks after the birth of her daughter and last child, Mary Ann (1773–1864). The first week records the first time she went to church after her lying-in, and preparing for and holding a baptism party. Mrs Hardy records almost daily her husband's activities, his travels, and his business dealings, a mixture of farming, brewing, and trading. There are frequent mentions of his negotiations for public houses to lease or buy as outlets for his beer, with prices often noted. She records tax problems, excise payments, dealings with the justices over licences, and financial transactions with the banker Gurney of Norwich. The canalization of the 'new River' Bure to Aylsham, mentioned in the diary in 1773, allowed river trade to Yarmouth. Mr Hardy acquired a staithe, and in 1776 he built his own wherry boat, the *William and Mary*. He imported cargoes of hops, coal, cinders, muck, and bricks, exporting grain and malt. He began looking for a brewery to buy, and at auction on 11 November 1780 he bought Hagon's brewery with 50 acres of land and a substantial house in the centre of the village of Letheringsett, near Holt and 4 miles from the seaport of Cley. On 1 April 1781 the family moved in. In 1799, at the age of sixty-seven, Mr Hardy retired, signing over his leases and business to his son William, then aged twenty-nine. Throughout the diary Mr Hardy was active in the town vestry.

Every day Mary Hardy described the weather and main activities of the household, its visitors and those visited. There are occasional entries by her husband and children. They walk and ride and take tea, some of the frequent social evenings lasting late into the evening. She notes births, marriages, illnesses, accidents, bankruptcies, and deaths among her Raven relatives, her servants, her friends, and neighbours. In 1777 her brother Robert spends a period in the Norwich Bethel Hospital, but recovers. She records that private care cost 100 guineas a year, the Bethel 4s. 6d. a week. She notes labourers' gatherings, boxing and wrestling matches, tithe and other frolics, election and coming-of-age dinners. The diary includes 'news from the paper': at first 'marvellous' crimes and events, and then increasingly serious entries, with notes about national events, parliament, victories in the war in America and against France, and the effects of war taxes. She was against the wars, and records several local meetings to prepare for French invasion. The family have their portraits painted by a French refugee, Mr Hugnier, in 1785.

The other preoccupation of Mary Hardy was religion. The diary regularly records sermons, with occasional adverse comments. As well as attending their parish church, the Hardy family also attended Quaker services. Mary was active in the parish Sunday school founded in 1787, but in 1790 felt excluded by Mr Burrell the rector. In 1790 there was a quarrel over access to the churchyard and Mr Hardy stayed away from the parish church for over two years. The new rector may have been upset by the family's increasing involvement with the Methodists, especially the dissenters of the Countess of Huntingdon's Connexion, who had a meeting at Briston nearby. The Hardys attended her funeral sermon there in 1791. In London in 1800 Mr and Mrs Hardy and Mary Ann went to twenty-two different chapels, tabernacles, and meetings, and also visited the Jewish synagogue. However, there was nothing puritanical about the Hardys—their main business was beer, and they enjoyed in moderation plays and dancing, dinners, fairs, travelling players, and cards.

Mary Hardy died at Letheringsett Hall on 23 March 1809,

and was buried on 29 March in the family vault in Lethersingett churchyard. The last entry in the diary was made two days before she died. The significance of the diary lies not only in its illustration of the everyday life of neighbourhood and family in rural Norfolk, but in its woman's view of a male world of business, religion, politics, and local administration. It is an impersonal diary: it records events, news, and activities with little comment or explanation; the only emotional entry is on the death of Raven Hardy at the age of nineteen. It has a wider range and is less domestic than that of Mary Hardy's contemporary, Parson James Woodforde of Weston Longville, only 20 miles away. It was edited by a descendant, Basil Cozens-Hardy, for the Norfolk Record Society in 1968.

F. ASHBURNER

Sources *Mary Hardy's diary*, ed. B. Cozens-Hardy (1968) · B. Cozens-Hardy, *The history of Letheringsett* (1957) · J. Hooten, *The Glaven ports: a maritime history of Blakeney, Cley and Wiveton in north Norfolk* (1996) · R. W. Ketton-Cremer, *Norfolk portraits* (1944) · R. W. Ketton-Cremer, *A Norfolk gallery* (1948) · R. W. Ketton-Cremer, *Norfolk assembly* (1957) · A. Young, *The farmers kalendar* (1771)
Archives priv. coll., diary | Norfolk RO, B. Cozens-Hardy MSS
Likenesses Hugnier, group portrait, pastel, 1785 · Emmanuel, group portrait, oils, 1798

Hardy [*née* MacDowell], **Mary Anne**, **Lady Hardy** (1824–1891), novelist and travel writer, born on 19 February 1824 at Fitzroy Square, London, was the only child of T. Charles MacDowell (*d.* 1823) and Eliza, his second wife. Her father, a timber merchant, had died five months before, and she was educated at home by her mother. In 1848 she became the second wife of Sir Thomas Duffus *Hardy (1804–1878), archivist. They had one daughter, Iza Duffus Hardy (1850–1922), who also became a novelist. Lady Hardy received a civil-list pension of £100 a year (later increased by £55) in recognition of her husband's services.

Hardy did not begin to publish her writings until after her marriage. In 1853 her first novel, *Savile House: an Historical Romance*, appeared, under the pseudonym Addlestone Hill, followed in 1855 by *War Notes from the Crimea*, a collection of travel writings. Other novels followed, including *The Artist's Family* (1857) and *The Two Catherines* (1862), but she enjoyed little success until 1868, when her novel *A Hero's Work* appeared, which drew upon her experiences of the Crimean War, and which was popular in Britain and the United States. She continued this success with *Paul Wynter's Sacrifice* (1869), *Daisy Nichol* (1870), *Lizzie* (1875), and *Madge* (1878). All four novels were light romances which enjoyed a wide readership on both sides of the Atlantic and which were translated into French, but they failed to find favour with contemporary literary critics. As a reviewer in the *Saturday Review* noted:

> a single personage, even when the leading one, no more makes a good novel than a single swallow makes a summer. Paul Wynter, we freely confess, is excellent; a lofty conception consistently worked out. The others are all more or less weak and forced. (*Saturday Review*, 852)

After the death of her husband Hardy toured the United States with her daughter, Iza, promoting her fiction and gathering material for two volumes of travel writings, *Through Cities and Prairie Lands: Sketches of an American Tour*

(1881) and *Down South* (1883). Towards the end of her life she wrote several essays on moral issues, and she also published many short stories in the high-class women's magazines *The Gentlewoman* and *Queen*. Hardy died on 19 May 1891 at her home, 124 Portsdown Road, Maida Vale, London, and was buried at Willesden.

ELIZABETH LEE, *rev.* KATHERINE MULLIN

Sources Blain, Clements & Grundy, *Feminist comp.* · F. Hays, *Women of the day: a biographical dictionary of notable contemporaries* (1885) · Boase, *Mod. Eng. biog.* · A. T. C. Pratt, ed., *People of the period: being a collection of the biographies of upwards of six thousand living celebrities*, 2 vols. (1897) · Allibone, *Dict.* · H. C. Black, *Notable women authors of the day* (1893), 198–204 · *The Times* (21 May 1891) · J. C. Jeaffreson, *A book of recollections*, 2 vols. (1894), vol. 2, p. 345 · *Saturday Review*, 27 (1869), 852–3 · review of *Daisy Nichol* by Lady Hardy, *The Athenaeum* (26 Nov 1870), 686–7 · *DNB* · *CGPLA Eng. & Wales* (1891) · m. cert. · b. cert. [Iza Duffus Hardy] · d. cert. [Iza Duffus Hardy]
Archives BL, Add. MS 46694
Likenesses photograph, repro. in Black, *Notable women authors*, 198
Wealth at death £135 7s. 9d.: probate, 13 June 1891, *CGPLA Eng. & Wales*

Hardy, Nathaniel (1619–1670), dean of Rochester, son of Anthony Hardy of St Martin Ludgate, London, and his wife, Ann, was born in Old Bailey in 1619, probably on 14 September, and baptized in the parish church of St Martin on 3 October. His father appears to have been a respectable well-to-do tradesman with a house valued at £15 in 1638 for its moderated rent (implying a full rental of £20 per annum) and sat on a parish committee for the election of a lecturer in early 1641. Hardy was admitted at the age of fourteen a commoner at Magdalen Hall, Oxford, on 11 October 1633. He graduated BA from Magdalen Hall on 20 October 1635 and proceeded MA from Hart Hall, Oxford, on 27 June 1638 (incorporated at Cambridge in 1639).

Having entered holy orders Hardy returned to London in the early 1640s and soon proved to be a popular preacher in the City. On 3 April 1643 the vestry of St Mary-at-Hill chose him lecturer, but later in the year, on 20 October, upon the sequestration of George Hume, the House of Commons appointed him to the ministry of St Dionis Backchurch, where he may have preached since the previous year. At this time Hardy's religious beliefs were probably puritan. However, early in 1645, while attending the treaty of Uxbridge between the commissioners of the king and those of the parliament, Hardy was won over, according to Anthony Wood, to the doctrines and worship of the Church of England by the persuasive arguments of Henry Hammond, and upon his return to the City he preached a sermon of recantation. Indeed, in the subsequent years of the revolutionary era Hardy was one of the few unsequestered ministers in puritan London whom we know to have remained loyal both to the church and to the crown. Although he took part in the proceedings of the fourth classis of the presbyterian church government in London, it is also unmistakably clear that after 1645 he declined to preach on the officially appointed fast days. During the constitutional crisis of 1648–9, as he himself later stated, he was one of 'the small number of those who did in their Pulpits earnestly deprecate, and vehemently declaim against' the army's design to put the king on trial, and after the death of Charles I, 'at the yearly Returne, either upon or near the day, I adventured to become a remembrancer' (Hardy, *Loud Call*, 'The epistle dedicatory'). He was said to have also kept a 'loyal lecture', at which monthly collections were made for poor sequestered clergymen or their widows.

Hardy occupied, therefore, a rather unusual position in civil war London. His ministry at St Dionis Backchurch had the sanction of an order from the House of Commons, and he had the firm and steadfast patronage of such prominent civic leaders as Sir John Gayre and Sir Thomas Adams. In spite of complaints about his thinly veiled denunciations of religious radicalism and rebellion he was neither molested nor silenced. Early in November 1646, when Gayre was lord mayor, Hardy was invited to preach the anniversary sermon of the Gunpowder Plot, and he turned it into a condemnation of the civil war. Using the gunpowder plotters as the foil, Hardy told the London magistrates that wicked men were always ready 'to defend slaughter with conscience, cover mischief with Necessity, patronize Rebellion with Religion'. And with rather uncommon perception he observed: 'It is the worst madness *insanire cum ratione*, nay *religione* …: men are never more violent, then when they think God is of their party' (Hardy, *Justice Triumphing*, 23). When he preached before the House of Lords on 24 February 1647 he spoke of the groans of the nation under the irregular practices of the parliamentary committees, the quartering of an army in the country, the burden of new taxations and the general decay of trade. During the Commonwealth and the protectorate Hardy became a favourite preacher of the royalists or neo-royalists. He preached at the funerals of Sir John Gayre in 1649 and Richard Goddard in 1653. In 1654 he preached on the Act Sunday at the University of Oxford. In 1653 and 1658 he delivered farewell sermons respectively for the voyages of Sir Thomas Bendish, the English resident at Constantinople, and Nathaniel Wych, president of the East India Company. On 27 May 1658 he preached at the yearly feast of native London citizens, and on 13 June, five days after the execution of Dr John Hewit for royalist conspiracy, he preached what was generally thought to be Hewit's funeral sermon at St Gregory by Paul. Perhaps more interestingly Hardy was invited to preach on 9 June 1659 at the funeral of the earl of Warwick, during whose illness, Hardy said, 'I had the Honour to wait upon and administer to him in holy things, which my conscience beareth me witnesse, I dealt with him freely and faithfully and I trust not without good success' (Hardy, *Man's Last Journey*, 27).

On the eve of the Restoration, 30 April 1660, Hardy was invited to preach before the House of Lords. As preachers at the parliamentary pulpits had played the role of 'the Trumpetters of war' in the previous twenty years, Hardy said, 'it is high time we should be now the Heralds of peace, perswading a blessed accomodation' (Hardy, *Choicest Fruit*, 29). And he made a moderate plea for future settlement: 'order in the State by a fit subordination of the Subjects Liberty to the Soveraigns authority' and 'order in

the Church by a sweet attemperation of paternall presidency with fraternall presbytery' (ibid.). In the following month he was chosen one of the ministers to attend the City commissioners to meet Charles II at The Hague, where, in a sermon on 20 May, 'he applied his discourse to the then present Estate of affairs in England so pathetically and learnedly, that there was not any one present, but admired his elegancy and learning' (Wood, *Ath. Oxon.*, 2.336–7).

Upon the return of Charles II to England Hardy was made one of the royal chaplains-in-ordinary and was created DD of Hart Hall on 2 August 1660. A week later, on 10 August, he was instituted as rector of St Dionis Backchurch. On 6 December he preached at the consecration of seven bishops in Westminster Abbey, and on 10 December was made dean of Rochester. On 6 April 1661 the king presented him to the vicarage of St Martin-in-the-Fields. He also held briefly the rectory of Henley-on-Thames, Oxfordshire. On 30 January 1662 he was invited to preach before the House of Commons in commemoration of the death of Charles I. He was installed archdeacon of Lewes in the diocese of Chichester on 6 April 1667. Hardy continued to maintain his London connections and cherished his memories as a native son of the City. In 1666 he lamented over the great fire of London in a sermon on 9 September. The sermon, delivered on the Sunday after the fire had destroyed perhaps four-fifths of the buildings in the City, was poorly received by Samuel Pepys, who had earlier heard and admired Hardy's preaching: 'a bad poor sermon, though proper for the time—nor eloquent, in saying at this time that the City is reduced from a large Folio to a Decimo tertio' (Pepys, 7.283). When the sermon was published Hardy dedicated it to Sir Thomas Adams, 'a singular Friend, as well as a prime Parishioner', from whom, Hardy gratefully acknowledged, he had received 'not only that liberal bounty, those free entertainments, but those sage advices, and forward encouragements … in the late perilous times' (Hardy, *Lamentation*, 'The epistle dedicatory'). Two years later he also preached Adams's funeral sermon.

Hardy died at Croydon, Surrey, on 1 or 2 June 1670 and was buried on 9 June in the chancel of St Martin-in-the-Fields. He was survived by his wife, Elizabeth Hardy, who, a few months later, married Sir Francis Clarke of Ulcombe, Kent. His funeral sermon was preached by Richard Meggott. In the later years of his life Hardy appears to have possessed considerable wealth, and he contributed generously to the rebuilding of St Dionis Backchurch, the embellishment of St Martin-in-the-Fields, and the repair of Rochester Cathedral.   TAI LIU

Sources Pepys, *Diary*, vols. 1, 7 · *Fasti Angl.*, 1541–1857, [Chichester] · *Fasti Angl.*, 1541–1857, [Canterbury] · N. Hardy, *Justice triumphing, or, The spoylers spoyled … preached at St. Pauls, November the 5th, 1646* (1656) · N. Hardy, *The arraignment of licentious libertie, and oppressing tyranny in a sermon preached … Feb 24, 1646* (1647) · N. Hardy, *A divine prospective: representing the just mans end … July 20, 1649* (1660) · N. Hardy, *Man's last journey to his long home … June the 9th 1659* (1659) · N. Hardy, *Lamentation, mourning, and woe* (1666) · N. Hardy, *The choicest fruit of peace … April 30, 1660* (1660) · N. Hardy, *A loud call to great mourning … preached on the 30th of January 1661*[2]

(1662) · Wood, *Ath. Oxon.*, 2nd edn · Foster, *Alum. Oxon.* · St Martin Ludgate vestry minute book, GL, MS 1311/1 · St Mary-at-Hill vestry minute book, GL, MS 1240/1 · St Dionis Backchurch churchwardens' accounts, GL, MS 4215/1 · St Dionis Backchurch vestry minute book, GL, MS 4216/1 · *DNB* · C. E. Surman, ed., *The register-booke of the fourth classis in the province of London, 1646–59*, 2 vols. in 1, Harleian Society, 82–3 (1953) · J. Spurr, *The Restoration Church of England, 1646–1689* (1991) · P. S. Seaver, *The puritan lectureships: the politics of religious dissent, 1560–1662* (1970) · Tai Liu, *Puritan London: a study of religion and society in the City parishes* (1986) · *IGI* · grant of administration, PRO, PROB 6/45, fol. 98r

Hardy, Sam (1882–1966), footballer, was born at Back Lane, Newbold, in Derbyshire, on 26 August 1882, the younger son (he had three elder brothers and three sisters) of Thomas Hardy, a coalminer, and his wife, Hannah Fidler. He went to the Newbold church school and became an enthusiastic footballer, so much so that he left his first job in a Chesterfield drapery store because it did not allow him Saturday afternoons off. He played centre forward at first and only went into goal when the selected incumbent failed to turn up. While playing for Newbold White Star he caught the attention of Chesterfield of the second division, who signed him in April 1903 at a wage of 5*s*. (25p!) a week. When Liverpool won the second division title in 1904–5 they scored six goals against Chesterfield but were so impressed by Hardy that they paid £500 for his transfer. They went on to win the championship of the first division in the following season and he made thirty appearances in the side.

Hardy's international career began in 1907 and, although it was interrupted by the war, included twenty-one appearances for England between 1907 and 1920; he also played in the three 'victory' internationals in 1919–20. With Bob Crompton and J. Pennington he formed a celebrated defence, and in 1908–9 England defeated Ireland, Scotland, and Wales without conceding a goal, with Hardy saving a penalty against the Scots. This feat had not been accomplished before and was not repeated until 1982.

In May 1912 Hardy moved to Aston Villa together with centre half J. Harrop for a combined fee of £1250. In his first season Aston Villa won the FA cup and finished second in the league. He was also in the team which won the first cup final after the First World War. In August 1921, at the age of thirty-eight, Hardy moved to Nottingham Forest, helping them to become champions of the second division in that season. He retired in 1925 after a career of 552 league appearances.

It used to be thought axiomatic that goalkeepers had a screw loose. Before 1893–4 they could be charged whether they had the ball or not. Even when the laws of the game were changed to provide them with more protection, the fact could not be hidden that if a goalkeeper made a mistake, unlike the other ten players, it was usually irretrievable. This psychological pressure helps account for their reputation for eccentricity. If that was a rule, then Samuel Hardy appears to have been a clear exception to it. He was known in the game as Silent Sam, a name which epitomized his unobtrusive style. Goalkeepers in his time did not come out and seek to dominate the penalty area in the modern fashion. Mostly they stayed on their line and

relied on accurate handling, instinctive positioning, and anticipation. Judgement was the master quality and Hardy's anticipation was such that he seemed to magnetize the ball into his arms, and only an unforeseeable deflection would oblige him to go full length to save it. In 1908 he wrote an article for the *Liverpool Echo* entitled 'Aspects of a difficult art', in which he placed anticipation as the highest of the goalkeeper's gifts. He also said that he watched the striker's foot as a clue to the likely power and direction of the shot.

Poker-faced and phlegmatic he may have been, but Hardy also showed distinct signs of an independence of character not always welcomed by the football authorities. He supported the players' union, and took part in a benefit match to raise funds in 1919. He also insisted throughout his playing career on living and training in his Derbyshire home. He married Maria Cannon of Newbold on 7 October 1908 at Chesterfield register office; they had three sons.

After retirement from football Hardy worked on the administrative side for Nottingham Forest and later acted as a scout for Aston Villa. But for many years he was the licensee of the Gardeners' Arms in Chesterfield; the magistrate who granted the licence remarked that if he kept the public house as well as he kept goal there would be nothing to complain of. He was also proprietor of several billiard halls. He died at his home, 4 West View Road, Chesterfield, on 24 October 1966. His wife survived him.

Tony Mason

Sources *Derbyshire Times* (28 Oct 1966) · *Derbyshire Times* (4 Nov 1966) · *Liverpool Echo* (25 Oct 1966) · *Liverpool Echo* (27 Oct 1966) · *Birmingham Post* (25 Oct 1966) · C. Buchan, *A lifetime in football* (1955) · M. Farror and D. Lamming, *A century of English international football, 1872–1972* (1972) · J. Harding, *For the good of the game* (1991) · b. cert. · d. cert. · *CGPLA Eng. & Wales* (1967) · Chesterfield Library, Local Studies Department

Wealth at death £4384: administration, 2 Jan 1967, *CGPLA Eng. & Wales*

Hardy, Samuel (1636/7–1691), nonconformist minister, was born at Frampton, Dorset, of unknown parents. He matriculated from Wadham College, Oxford, on 1 April 1656. After graduating BA on 14 October 1659 he returned to Dorset and became chaplain to the Trenchard family of Wolfeton House, Charminster, a peculiar to which they owned the right of presentation. Here he remained after the Act of Uniformity of 1662, refusing institution by the bishops. Exempt from harassment by the church courts, he was protected against local justices through the influence of his patron, Thomas Trenchard (1640–1671). Hardy gestured towards conformity by 'reading the scripture sentences, the creed, commandments, lessons, prayer for the king and some few other things' (*DNB*). During his time at Charminster he exerted great influence over Thomas Trenchard and his brother John, the future whig politician. He was married at least twice, first to Joyce (*d.* 1673), who gave birth to a son, Samuel (*bap.* 1672), and was perhaps the daughter of Richard Fowler, the ejected curate of Westerleigh, Gloucestershire. His second wife,

Elizabeth (*d.* in or after 1691), may have been the mother of three other sons, Peter, Nathaniel, and Eden.

In 1667, on the invitation of the parishioners, Hardy took up the ministry at the chapelry of St James in Poole, Dorset, an impropriate rectory appended to Canford Magna, a royal peculiar. Here too he could shelter from the bishop and his officers, who could not remove him. In 1668 the corporation of Poole agreed to pay Hardy £15 a quarter during the time of his curacy, and from this position of relative security he appears to have acquired great influence. During his time at Poole it is reported that he collected nearly £500 for ransoming captives from slavery. He became involved in the by-election of November 1670 on behalf of Thomas Trenchard, and seems to have been important in securing his victory over Sir Anthony Ashley Cooper's son, Anthony. Incensed, Cooper 'wrote a very angry letter to Mr Hardy. When he was in London, he was advised to wait upon the chancellor, and make his peace' which counsel Hardy found it prudent to accept (Hutchins, 1.56). After Trenchard's death Cooper was able to ensure the acceptance by the town of his nomination for the vacant seat. However, Trenchard's will left £100 to Hardy, who clung on to his ministry at Poole for more than another decade.

However, by 1681, at the Dorset assizes, the grand jury requested that the king be informed of many

> opposers of his majesties government, influenced by the [seditious] preaching of one Samuel Hardy, an hired Nonconformist preacher, who … hath made use of the church of [Poole], reading little or none of the liturgy of the church of England. (Densham and Ogle, 187)

Residents too now complained of his dissent from Anglican rites.

Given the status of the peculiar, a royal commission was appointed, headed by the bishops of Bristol and Salisbury. Hardy was initially deprived, but upon a successful petition to the lord chancellor he resumed his preaching. Later his commission of appeal was deemed irregular, however, because as a royal peculiar the church could be visited only by the king's commissioners and the only appeal from them was to the king himself. Accordingly, on 23 August 1682 Hardy was (once again) deprived for 'his manifest and incorrigible offences and disobedience, neglect of office, and not executing the same, contrary to the ecclesiastical laws of England, and canons required in his oath' (Hutchins, 1.56). He moved to Baddesley, Hampshire, but was again in trouble for nonconformity in 1683 and appears to have abandoned the public ministry shortly afterwards. In 1685–7 he was chaplain to the Heal family at Aldborough Hatch, Essex, but moved to Newbury, Berkshire, in 1688. In early 1690 it was reported that 'Att Newbury [Mr Hardy] has 1000 people as some say, has £50 per annum' (Gordon, 6). He died at Newbury, aged fifty-four, on 6 March 1691 and was buried there on 9 March. He left property in Gutter Lane, off Cheapside in London, and in the Isle of Purbeck, Dorset, to his widow and sons Samuel, Peter, Nathaniel, and Eden, who all survived him.

STEPHEN WRIGHT

Sources J. Hutchins, *The history and antiquities of the county of Dorset*, ed. W. Shipp and J. W. Hodson, 3rd edn, 4 vols. (1861–70) • *Calamy rev.* • J. P. Ferris, 'Cooper, Sir Anthony Ashley', HoP, *Commons, 1660–90*, 2.121–4 • W. Densham and J. Ogle, *The story of the Congregational churches of Dorset* (1899) • A. Gordon, ed., *Freedom after ejection: a review (1690–1692) of presbyterian and congregational nonconformity in England and Wales* (1917) • will, PRO, PROB 11/407, fol. 177 • J. T. Cliffe, *The puritan gentry besieged, 1650–1700* (1993) • *CSP dom.*, 1682 • R. B. Gardiner, ed., *The registers of Wadham College, Oxford*, 1 (1889) • Foster, *Alum. Oxon.*
Wealth at death left property in London and Dorset: will, PRO, PROB 11/407, fol. 177

Hardy, Theodore Bayley (1863–1918), army chaplain, was born on 20 October 1863 in the Southernhay district of Exeter. He was the son of George Hardy, a commercial traveller, and his wife, Sarah Richardson; George was her second husband, her first having died. George himself died in 1866 and Sarah supported her large family (several boys from the first marriage and two, including Theodore, from the second) by running a preparatory school.

Theodore was educated at home until he was nine and then went as a boarder to the City of London School, from where he went on to London University. On 13 September 1888 he married Florence Elizabeth Hastings, the third daughter of William Hastings, a Belfast civil engineer. Hardy graduated BA in 1889 and then taught for two years in London before moving to teach at Nottingham high school, where he remained for sixteen years. During this period he was ordained deacon (1898) and then priest (1899) and was licensed as a curate for Burton Joyce.

In 1907 Hardy became headmaster of a small establishment, Bentham grammar school, which had the advantage of being situated in Hardy's beloved countryside, as well as providing closer access to his wife's family in Northern Ireland. In 1913 Florence was diagnosed terminally ill, and so Hardy resigned from the school and took the living of Hutton Roof (in the diocese of Carlisle), which gave him time to nurse her. In June 1914 his wife died; their two children had left home—William studying to be a doctor in Belfast, and Elizabeth at London University. After the war broke out Hardy tried numerous times to enlist as a chaplain, and even considered alternatives, such as going as a volunteer stretcher bearer, to which end he attended an ambulance class.

Eventually Hardy was accepted as a chaplain, being commissioned as a temporary chaplain of the fourth class on 16 September 1916, despite his advanced years (he was almost fifty-three), and proceeded to France. He was attached to the infantry base depots at Étaples but pressed insistently to be sent up to the line and in December 1916 joined the 8th Lincolnshire regiment (and later was also attached to the 8th Somerset light infantry), part of 63rd brigade of the 37th division. He saw service in the Loos, Arras, Ypres salient, Somme, and Cambrai sectors.

Hardy soon became renowned for his devotion to the men under his pastoral charge. He insisted on staying in the front-line trenches, anxious to be of as much use as possible to those who were most threatened. His willingness to risk his life in looking after the wounded, or trying to ensure that men were tended, or buried, or brought in

Theodore Bayley Hardy (1863–1918), by unknown
photographer, 1918

from no man's land endeared him to those who could be
cynical about their chaplains.

The only still photographs of Hardy in the field show
him in typical mode, working at the advanced dressing
station at Feuchy chapel, near Arras. He refused all
attempts to move him back from the line, even if only to
give him a rest; he frequently said that he was a dreadful
coward, but that his place was at the front, and in any case,
with his wife dead and his children grown up, the prospect of death did not perturb him. He told his senior
chaplain, the Revd Geoffrey Vallings DSO, that he 'loved
his children intensely but that he believed that he could
do no better, if God so willed, than join his beloved wife in
the presence of the Lord' (Raw, 44).

In the opening days of third Ypres (his division was in
action to the east of Wytschaete) Hardy was made DSO
(gazetted 18 October 1917). It was awarded for his concern
for the wounded, in particular for staying out with a
wounded man, trapped in mud, in no man's land for many
hours and under constant fire, and despite the fact that his
own wrist was broken. He remained with this man until
he died. Hardy collapsed with exhaustion shortly afterwards. He was to win the MC in October 1917 for his
bravery near Hill 60 (Ypres salient) when he assisted with
the evacuation of the wounded from a heavy battery position while it was under a severe bombardment.

During the dismal winter of 1917–18 the division
remained in the salient; Hardy invariably accompanied
the ration parties to the front and then stayed on and

visited the outpost positions, bringing cigarettes, sweets,
and conversation. His arrival was frequently accompanied
by the sentence with which he is most popularly identified: 'It's only me, boys' (Raw, 61).

In a series of incidents in April 1918 the bravery that
Hardy displayed was recognized by the award of the Victoria Cross, gazetted on 11 July 1918. Among other things
he stayed with and tended a wounded officer some 10
yards from a German machine-gun position and then
sought help to bring him back to the British lines; he rescued a man buried by a shell and endeavoured to save
another, all the time under heavy shell fire; and he saved
the life of an officer by tending his wounds, received out
in no man's land while on a patrol.

Theodore Hardy was now the most highly decorated
chaplain in the army; he was presented with the VC by
George V at Frohen-le-Grand on 9 August, the event being
briefly captured on film. He was wounded on 10 October
1918 while returning from a visit to forward troops who
had recently crossed the River Selle. He died of his wounds
and pneumonia at the no. 2 base (Red Cross) hospital at
Rouen on 18 October two days short of his fifty-fifth birthday, and was buried in the vast Commonwealth war
graves cemetery, the St Sever cemetery extension in
Rouen, on October 20. A memorial was erected in Carlisle
Cathedral.   N. T. A. CAVE

Sources D. Raw, *It's only me: a life of the Reverend Theodore Bayley
Hardy, VC, DSO, MC, 1863–1918, vicar of Hutton Roof, Westmorland*
(1988) · NAM, Lummis collection (Military Historical Society), H.25
HARDY TB · M. Hardy, *Hardy VC: an appreciation* (1919) · O'M. Creagh
and E. M. Humphris, *The V.C. and D.S.O.*, 1 [1920] · *CGPLA Eng. & Wales*
(1919)
Archives Royal Army Chaplains' Department, Upavon, Wilt-
shire, medals | NAM, Lummis collection | FILM IWM, 677B
22/8/18 · IWM FVA, news footage
Likenesses group photograph, 1908, repro. in R. E. Huddleston
and J. S. Warbrick, *The history of Bentham grammar school, 1726–1976*
(1976) · two photographs, 1917, IWM · group photograph, 1918,
NAM, Lummis collection · photograph, 1918, IWM [*see illus.*] ·
T. Cuneo, oils, Army Chaplains' Department Museum · portrait
(after photograph), IWM
Wealth at death £739 16*s*. 0*d*.: probate, 14 Nov 1919, *CGPLA Eng. &
Wales*

Hardy, Sir Thomas (1666–1732), naval officer, was born in
Jersey on 13 September 1666, the son of John le Hardy (*d*.
1682), solicitor-general of Jersey, and first cousin of the
naval officer Sir Charles *Hardy the elder. Thomas was a
captain's clerk in the navy by 1688 and later became purser to Captain George Churchill, who subsequently promoted Hardy's career, and with whom he served as first
lieutenant of the *St Andrew* at the battle of Barfleur. Early
in 1693 he was promoted to the command of the *Charles*
fireship, from which he was soon afterwards transferred
to the *Swallow Prize*, stationed in the Channel Islands for
the protection of trade.

In September 1695 Hardy was appointed to the *Pendennis*
(48 guns), which he commanded until the peace in September 1697. In May 1698 he was appointed to the *Deal
Castle*, in April 1701 to the *Coventry*, and in January 1702 to
the *Pembroke*, the last forming part of the fleet on the coast
of Spain under the command of Sir George Rooke. During

Sir Thomas Hardy (1666–1732), by John Faber junior, 1722 (after Michael Dahl, 1714)

the failed attack on Cadiz the *Pembroke* ran aground because she had gone too far inshore. Subsequently she was one of a small squadron under Captain James Wishart in the *Eagle*, which put into Lagos for water. There the chaplain of the *Pembroke*, also a native of Jersey, who was assumed on shore to be a Frenchman, learned that the combined Franco-Spanish fleet from the West Indies had put into Vigo. The news was taken to Hardy, who at once sent it to Wishart, and on to Sir George Rooke. Acting on this intelligence Rooke sailed to Vigo, and there, on 12 October 1702, captured or destroyed the whole of the enemy's fleet. Hardy was sent home with the news, and, as a reward for his services, was knighted by the queen (31 October) and presented with £1,000. In January 1703 he was appointed to the *Bedford* (70 guns), in which he served under Sir Cloudesley Shovell in the Mediterranean during 1703, and with Sir George Rooke in 1704, taking part in the battle of Malaga, where the *Bedford* had a loss of seventy-four men, killed or wounded.

On 13 December 1704, soon after his return to England, Hardy was appointed to the *Kent*, and during the summer of 1705 he was again in the Mediterranean with Shovell and Sir John Leake. In the summer of 1706 he was attached to the squadron under Sir Stafford Fairborne in the Bay of Biscay and at the capture of Ostend. In November 1706 Hardy was appointed to command a small squadron cruising in the Soundings for the protection of trade, a service which extended well into the summer of 1707. In July he was ordered to escort the outward-bound trade for Lisbon, about 200 sail, clear of the channel. Meeting with contrary winds, they were only 93 leagues from the Lizard on 27 August when they saw a squadron of six French ships directly to windwards. Finding it useless to chase these, and fearing that the French might savage the convoy if he pursued them and they avoided him, Hardy contented himself with keeping his convoy well together. He escorted it to the prescribed distance of 120 leagues, after which the merchantmen proceeded safely on their way to Lisbon. On his return to England Hardy was charged with neglect of duty in not having chased the French squadron: he was tried by court martial at Portsmouth on 10 October and fully acquitted, the court finding that he had 'complied fully with his orders'. Nevertheless Hardy found himself also facing an examination before a committee of the House of Lords, his having become a 'test case' for the perceived failures of trade defence over several years. His treatment was attributed to merchants' pressure on the government and part of a broader political attack on the incumbent ministry; moreover, being 'tried' again after an acquittal at a court martial was widely denounced as 'un-English'.

Sir John Leake, who was president of this court martial, further showed his complete approval of Hardy's conduct by selecting him as first captain of the *Albemarle*, and going out to the Mediterranean as his flagship despite the fact that even some of Leake's circle thought Hardy unpopular, a coward, and an incompetent seaman, 'and of that unhappy, proud, malicious disposition, that it was impossible to live a day with him, without observing some ill-natured act' (Leake, 2.168). He returned to England in October 1708, and in December was appointed to the *Royal Sovereign*, from which in the following May he was transferred to the *Russell*, in home waters. On 27 January 1711 he was promoted rear-admiral of the blue, and during the following summer, with his flag in the *Canterbury* (60 guns), commanded the small squadron off Dunkirk and in the North Sea. In April 1711 he had been returned to parliament as tory member for Weymouth, and on 6 October he was appointed to the command-in-chief at the Nore and in the Thames and Medway, which he held during the winter. In the summer of 1712 he again commanded in the North Sea, and afterwards off Ushant, where in August he captured a convoy of five ships, which the government thought it advisable to release, owing to uncertainty over the legal status of prizes taken during the temporary armistice which prevailed while peace negotiations proceeded.

In the summer of 1715, with his flag in the *Norfolk*, Hardy was second in command of the fleet sent to the Baltic under Sir John Norris. This voyage marked the end of his active service. Like a number of other officers with secondary political careers, he found it difficult to flourish in the circumstances which prevailed after the Hanoverian succession, and he was dismissed after his return from the Baltic. At some time before 1710 Hardy had married Constance (*d*. 1720), daughter of Henry Hook, lieutenant-governor of Plymouth; they had one son, Thomas, and two daughters. Hardy was elected master of Trinity House on 2 June 1729 and again on 25 May 1730. He died on 16 August 1732, and was buried next to his wife in Westminster Abbey.   J. K. LAUGHTON, *rev.* J. D. DAVIES

Sources HoP, *Commons, 1690–1715* [draft] • S. Martin-Leake, *The life of Sir John Leake*, ed. G. Callender, 2, Navy RS, 53 (1920), 155–9, 168–9, 355–8, 393 • J. Charnock, ed., *Biographia navalis*, 3 (1795), 17–33 • *The manuscripts of the House of Lords*, new ser., 12 vols. (1900–77), vol. 7, pp. 221–6 • D. Syrett and R. L. DiNardo, *The commissioned sea officers of the Royal Navy, 1660–1815*, rev. edn, Occasional Publications of the Navy RS, 1 (1994) • W. L. Clowes, *The Royal Navy: a history from the earliest times to the present*, 7 vols. (1897–1903); repr. (1996–7), vol. 2, pp. 382, 399, 531; vol. 3, p. 26 • *The Sergison papers*, ed. R. D. Merriman, Navy RS, 89 (1950), 248 • NMM, Sergison MSS, SER/136 • PRO, ADM MSS/6/424 [list of services] • J. H. Owen, *War at sea under Queen Anne, 1702–1708* (1938)

Archives NMM • PRO | BL, letters to Lord Hatton, Add. MSS 29565–29566

Likenesses M. Dahl, oils, 1714, NMM • J. Faber junior, mezzotint, 1722 (after M. Dahl, 1714), BM, NPG [*see illus.*] • H. Cheere, statue on monument, Westminster Abbey, London • attrib. Hogarth, portrait; known to be in possession of W. J. Hardy in 1890 • portrait; thought to be in possession of J. Jervoise Le V. Collas in 1890

Hardy, Thomas (1748–1798), Church of Scotland minister and ecclesiastical historian, was born on 22 April 1748 in Culross, Perthshire, the third of five children of the Revd Henry Hardy (1717–1752) and his wife, Ann (1719–1805), daughter of John Halkerston, the town clerk of Culross. He was educated at the University of Edinburgh and was licensed to preach on 16 February 1772. He was ordained minister of the parish of Ballingry, Fife, on 16 June 1774, and married Agnes (1755–1812), the daughter of the Revd William Young, minister of Hutton, Dumfriesshire, on 28 June 1780. They had five sons and four daughters.

In 1782 Hardy published a widely read pamphlet defending the position of the moderate party in the Church of Scotland concerning the law of patronage, entitled *The Principles of Moderation* (which was reprinted in 1842 just before the disruption). He attacked the preference of the evangelical party for popular elections, and he invited them instead to join the moderates in seeking a mutually satisfactory change in the law, suggesting that a minister should be chosen by a combination of the patron and a delegate each from the heritors and the kirk session.

He was called to St Giles, the high church in Edinburgh, in 1784, and was translated there on 25 November. This large charge, although collegiate, proved too much for his weak health, and he transferred on 3 December 1786 to the New North Parish (West St Giles, or 'Haddo's Hole'). On 31 July 1788 he took up the chair of ecclesiastical history at the University of Edinburgh in conjunction with his parish. He was awarded the degree of DD on 4 October 1788. Four weeks later he was one of the ministers required to attend the notorious Deacon William Brodie at his execution. Hardy became one of the founding members of the Church of Scotland's Society for the Benefit of the Sons of the Clergy; in 1793 he was moderator of the general assembly, and was appointed a chaplain to the king and a dean of the Chapel Royal.

He was an acclaimed preacher and an exceptional lecturer. A bookseller offered to print his highly regarded

Thomas Hardy (1748–1798), by John Kay, 1793 [*The Rev'd Patriot*]

exposition of John's gospel, but Hardy had spoken only from short notes and had to decline. Similarly, he did not permit his students to take notes from his lectures, prompting the suggestion that he meant to publish them at a later date, but this did not materialize either. He presented his opinions boldly (for instance, his opposition to the slave trade), mixed with dry humour, and his classes were reputedly the best attended in the university. Besides *The Principles of Moderation* Hardy also published *The Patriot* (1793), which refuted the views of Thomas Paine and for which he received a government pension, a *Plan for the Augmentation of Stipends* (1793), and six single sermons (1775–94). He died, probably from tuberculosis, on 21 November 1798 in Edinburgh.

EMMA VINCENT MACLEOD

Sources *Fasti Scot.*, new edn, 1.142–3, 147; 2.206; 5.17 • J. Kay, *A series of original portraits and caricature etchings … with biographical sketches and illustrative anecdotes*, ed. [H. Paton and others], new edn [3rd edn], 2 vols. in 4 (1877) • A. Bower, *The history of the University of Edinburgh*, 3 (1830) • H. W. Meikle, *Scotland and the French Revolution* (1912); repr. (1969) • I. D. L. Clark, 'From protest to reaction: the moderate regime in the Church of Scotland, 1752–1805', *Scotland in the age of improvement*, ed. N. T. Phillipson and R. Mitchison (1970), 200–24 • R. B. Sher, *Church and university in the Scottish Enlightenment: the moderate literati of Edinburgh* (1985) • A. Grant, *The story of the University of Edinburgh during its first three hundred years*, 2 (1884) • J. Cunningham, *The church history of Scotland: from the commencement of the Christian era to the present century*, 2 (1859)

Likenesses J. Kay, engraving, 1793, NPG [*see illus.*]

Hardy, Thomas (1752–1832), radical and a founder of the London Corresponding Society, was born in Larbert, Stirlingshire, on 3 March 1752, the son of a merchant seaman. By his own account he was originally intended for 'the clerical profession', but his father died in 1760 returning from the Americas and the estate was mismanaged, leaving insufficient money to pay for an appropriate education. Thomas was sent to school by his maternal grandfather, Thomas Walker, and then brought up in the latter's trade as a shoemaker. He followed this trade as well as working for a short period as a bricklayer in the

Thomas Hardy (1752–1832), by unknown engraver, pubd 1794

Carron iron works. During the spring of 1774 he travelled to London, where he settled.

In London Hardy attended the dissenting congregation which met in Crown Court, Russell Street, Covent Garden. He also joined the semi-masonic order of Gregorians, and it appears to have been from them that he learned a system of organization subsequently employed by the *London Corresponding Society (LCS). In 1781 he married the youngest daughter of a carpenter and builder named Priest from Chesham, Buckinghamshire. They had six children, all of whom died in infancy. Ten years after his marriage he opened his own boot and shoe shop at 9 Piccadilly.

Shortly after Hardy's arrival in London the friction between the American colonists and the British government developed into war. Hardy subsequently maintained in his *Memoir* that his initial sympathies were with the government, but that, at the time, he also felt himself to be ill informed on political matters. In an attempt to remedy this he set about reading political and constitutional tracts; among these tracts was Richard Price's *Observations on the Nature of Civil Liberty* and this had a profound effect on his thinking. It is unclear precisely what occasioned the beginning of his public role in radical politics; towards the end of 1791 his new shop was nearly ruined when business associates let him down, and Hardy claimed that, at the same time, a re-reading of some old political pamphlets convinced him that distress in the country was the fault of a corrupt parliament whose members were interested in self-aggrandizement rather than the common good. Two tracts in particular helped

shape his ideas for reform: Major John Cartwright's celebrated *Give us our Rights* (1782), with its call for universal suffrage and annual parliaments; and the duke of Richmond's letter to Lieutenant-Colonel Sharman of the Irish Volunteers (1783), which proposed to foster reform by establishing a society to correspond with like-minded individuals and groups. In January 1792 Hardy and a group of friends founded the London Corresponding Society.

Hardy had originally intended that this new society should be made up exclusively of the unenfranchised, but he soon came round to the belief that this would make it too restricted. The LCS announced from the outset that its membership was to be unlimited, and the weekly subscription of 1*d*. ensured that it was open to all. At the inaugural meeting on 25 January 1792 at The Bell inn, off the Strand, Hardy was appointed secretary and treasurer. He was confirmed in these posts in May, when nine elected delegates from nine separate divisions met to form the first general committee. From the early summer the LCS began publishing addresses and other material calling for universal manhood suffrage and parliamentary reform. It corresponded with similar popular radical societies which had emerged elsewhere, most notably in Norwich and Sheffield. It also developed links with more genteel reformers and groups such as the Society for Constitutional Information, originally established as one of the more radical elements of the Association Movement of 1780, but revived during the excitement generated by the centenary of the revolution of 1688 and the French Revolution; indeed, Hardy acknowledged that the LCS received considerable assistance from educated gentlemen, such as the Revd John Horne Tooke, who were committed to reform. By the end of 1792 membership of the LCS ran into hundreds, but the society was also beginning to face a backlash organized principally by the Associations for the Preservation of Liberty and Property against Republicans and Levellers under the slogan 'Church and King'. There were further difficulties generated in January 1793, when the French National Convention, which the LCS had warmly congratulated the previous September, executed Louis XVI and in February declared war on Britain.

In spite of the setbacks the LCS continued to campaign throughout 1793. In May it sent a petition to parliament to coincide with Charles Grey's motion for reform. In October it sent two delegates to the Edinburgh convention organized by Scottish reformers. When this body was dispersed, and its leaders, including the two LCS delegates, were tried for sedition and sentenced to fourteen years' transportation, the society began discussing with its correspondents the possibility of a new convention to be held in England. In the event the government pre-empted such a move. On 12 May 1794 Hardy was arrested by Bow Street runners and king's messengers. Other arrests followed. The prisoners were interrogated before the privy council, and on 29 May Hardy and six of the others who had been arrested were moved from the houses of the king's messengers where they had been lodged since their arrests, and committed to the Tower of London charged with high treason. Less than two weeks after this committal, crowds celebrating Lord Howe's naval success over the French at the battle of the Glorious First of June attacked Hardy's house, even though it was appropriately illuminated in honour of the victory. Mrs Hardy, pregnant with her sixth child, escaped with the help of neighbours, but on 27 August she died in childbirth and her child was stillborn.

On 6 October the grand jury of Middlesex returned a true bill for high treason against Hardy and eleven others. Those held in the Tower were removed to Newgate on 24 October, and the accused were formally arraigned at the Old Bailey the following day. They all pleaded not guilty; at the request of their defence counsel Thomas Erskine and Vicary Gibbs, the crown agreed to try the accused separately, beginning with Hardy. Sir John Scott (later Lord Eldon), the attorney-general, who led for the crown, considered separate trials as the best move, believing that he could prove Hardy to have been actively concerned in the plans to call the English convention and that Hardy would be compromised by correspondence between the LCS and societies in Sheffield and Norwich on the subject of arming. However, the prosecution case was by no means simple. Scott argued that Hardy, and by implication the others, were guilty not of direct treason but of constructive treason; essentially he maintained that their attempt to summon a popular convention, if carried out, would have subverted both the legislature and the executive, leading ultimately to the deposition and death of the king. His introductory speech lasted nine hours. Erskine's deft summing up for the defence denied that Hardy and the others were crypto-republicans, and also insisted that the law demanded an assessment of intentions, not speculation upon possible consequences. It was Erskine's interpretation that the jury accepted and in the afternoon of 5 November, after deliberating for three hours, the jury brought in a verdict of 'not guilty'. That evening Hardy was drawn through London in a coach by crowds of exultant supporters; they paused for a few minutes' silence outside his house and shop in Piccadilly, before taking him on to the house of his brother-in-law in Lancaster Court, where he intended to lodge. Two other trials followed (those of the Revd John Horne Tooke and John Thelwall) with similar verdicts, before the government released all of the remaining prisoners.

Hardy had lost everything. He contemplated emigrating to the United States, but was dissuaded by friends and given sufficient financial assistance to open a new shoe shop in Tavistock Street, Covent Garden. Initially business boomed, not least because he was a celebrity; but soon he found himself having to lay staff off and in September 1797 he moved to a smaller establishment in Fleet Street. The month following his house was attacked by loyalists during the celebrations of Admiral Duncan's victory at Camperdown; Hardy had refused to illuminate his windows on the grounds that this had done his wife no good. Friends and members of the LCS fought with the loyalists until troops arrived and the combatants dispersed.

While he ceased to have a high profile in radical politics, Hardy maintained links with leading radicals such as Sir Francis Burdett and Major Cartwright. He does not appear ever to have argued or worked for a radical insurrection, yet he seems to have been ambivalent on the issue. He became an ardent admirer of Napoleon from the first descriptions of him in the British press, and he continued as such even after the first consul had elevated himself into an emperor, possibly with some vague ideas of French assistance for bringing about reform in Britain. The government believed that Hardy was aware of Colonel Despard's conspiracy, but that he would have nothing to do with it. He corresponded with Tom Paine in America, though he regarded the latter's *The Age of Reason* as injudicious, and he was critical of Richard Carlile's subsequent republication of the pamphlet; Hardy considered that God's word could withstand deist speculation, but he feared that the circulation of such ideas provided ammunition for those who opposed the advance of civil liberty. In the first two decades of the new century he was active in the radical cause during parliamentary campaigns in Westminster. He also became involved in City of London politics first as a freeman of the Cordwainers' Company and subsequently as a liveryman of the Needlemakers' Company. In 1798, at the request of Francis Place, he had acted as treasurer of a fund collected for those radicals arrested under a new suspension of the Habeas Corpus Act, and, twelve years later, when Maurice Margarot returned from his sentence of transportation for his part in the Edinburgh convention, Hardy took an active role in organizing financial assistance for him. He wrote numerous letters to the press under his own name and a variety of pseudonyms—Omega, Crispin, A Shoemaker—on a variety of subjects from shaking hands to leather, but his notions of liberty and justice were rarely far in the background. During 1815 to 1816, for example, he focused his attention and reformist zeal on the plight of chimney-sweep boys.

In the summer of 1815 Hardy retired from business, and at some point shortly thereafter he moved to Queen's Row, Pimlico. He had £700 saved, which he believed would support him and his widowed sister, who kept house for him, for the rest of their lives. However, by the beginning of 1823 this money was all but expended and Hardy appealed to Sir Francis Burdett for assistance. Burdett arranged for £100 a year to be available for Hardy and his sister; it was to be drawn, as needed, from William Frend and, after 1827, from Francis Place. In his last years Hardy was keen to leave a record of the political struggles in which he had been involved. He collected his personal letters, together with the first minute book of the LCS, and drafted a history of the society; all of these papers were handed over to Francis Place. Hardy lived just long enough to see the Great Reform Act of 1832. He died in Queen's Row, on 11 October 1832, and was buried in Bunhill Fields. His *Memoir of Thomas Hardy*, which he had begun towards the end of the 1790s, was published shortly after his death.

CLIVE EMSLEY

Sources T. Hardy, *Memoir of Thomas Hardy* (1832) · M. Thale, ed., *Selections from the papers of the London Corresponding Society, 1792–1799* (1983) · J. A. Hone, *For the cause of truth: radicalism in London, 1796–*

1821 (1982) • A. Goodwin, *The friends of liberty: the English democratic movement in the age of the French Revolution* (1979) • *State trials*
Archives BL, corresp., history and memoirs of London Corresponding Society, Add. MSS 22814, 27818, 65453 • BL, draft memoir, Add. MSS 65153A–B
Likenesses line engraving, pubd 1794 (after A. Jameson), BM, NPG • stipple, pubd 1794, BM, NPG [*see illus.*] • Miss McCreevy, oils, National Liberal Club, London • line engraving, NPG • medal, NPG • portrait, repro. in J. Kay, *Original portraits*, 2 (1877), 482–3

Hardy, Thomas (1840–1928), novelist and poet, was born on 2 June 1840 in the Dorset hamlet of Higher Bockhampton, the first of the four children of Thomas Hardy (1811–1892), stonemason and jobbing builder, and his wife, Jemima (1813–1904), daughter of George and Betty Hand of Melbury Osmond, Dorset. At birth—slightly more than six months after his parents' marriage (22 December 1839)—he is said to have been at first given up for dead and saved only by the watchfulness of the midwife.

Early life The family's cottage, built of 'mudwall' and thatch by Hardy's great-grandfather at the turn of the century and held on 'lifehold' tenure from the nearby Kingston Maurward estate, stood alone on the edge of open heathland. As a sickly child, not confidently expected to survive into adulthood and kept mostly at home, Hardy gained an intimate knowledge of the surrounding countryside, the hard and sometimes violent lives of neighbouring rural families, and the songs, stories, superstitions, seasonal rituals, and day-to-day gossip of a still predominantly oral culture. He had young cousins nearby but depended chiefly on the always sympathetic company of his sister Mary, just a year his junior; his brother, Henry, was born later, in 1851, his second sister, Katharine (Kate), in 1856. Their easy-going father was in only a small and sometimes unprofitable way of business, but their mother, tough-minded and managerial, held the family determinedly together and ingrained in her eldest child habits of prudence, economy, and limited expectation that became lifelong.

Hardy learned to read early and developed a love of church ritual and music. He was taught to play the violin by his father—once a member, like Hardy's uncle and grandfather, of the little group of Stinsford church musicians subsequently memorialized in the novel *Under the Greenwood Tree* (1872)—and they sometimes performed together at local parties and dances. Hardy may have attended a local dame-school and was certainly 'taken up' by Julia Augusta Martin of Kingston Maurward House, but he received no regular schooling until, at the age of eight, he entered the (Anglican) national school just opened in Bockhampton village under Mrs Martin's patronage. In September 1850 his mother—responding in part to Mrs Martin's perceived possessiveness—sent him to the (nonconformist) British School in Dorchester, the county town, some 3 miles off, a distance Hardy walked twice daily for several years, even though he remained weak and slow to develop until well into his teens. Eventually he grew more robust but remained, at around 5 feet 6 inches, rather below the average in height.

Thomas Hardy (1840–1928), by William Strang, 1893

At the British School Hardy flourished under the teaching of the headmaster, Isaac Glandfield Last, and in 1853 he followed Last to the latter's newly established 'commercial academy'—Jemima Hardy, ambitious as always for her son's advancement, finding the money for him to take Latin as an additional subject. Later on he attempted to learn Greek without formal teaching and dreamed of eventually attending Cambridge, taking orders, and becoming the incumbent of a rural parish—a position evidently envisaged as offering ample leisure for the writing of poetry. In 1856, however, his parents took the more practical step of apprenticing him to a local ecclesiastical architect named John Hicks. Hardy remained in Hicks's office for six years, and while he learned to regret his participation, then and later, in church 'restorations' that involved the destruction of ancient structures and associations, he never despised the excellent professional training Hicks had given him. The period was also marked by sustained private study of Latin and Greek, by fluctuating religious enthusiasms, and by a hesitant emotional development that was perhaps confused by the homosexuality of his much admired friend Horace Moule, the brilliantly literary but disastrously unstable son of the Revd Henry Moule, evangelical vicar of one of the Dorchester churches.

The move to London In April 1862, two months before his twenty-second birthday, Hardy left Dorchester for London, where he quickly found work as a draughtsman in the busy office of Arthur William Blomfield, a leading

Gothic architect of the day. He went to plays, operas, museums, and galleries, and seems thoroughly to have relished the vitality and density of a still 'Dickensian' London. He admired Blomfield, liked his colleagues, was elected to the Architectural Association, and won in 1863 the silver medal of the Royal Institute of British Architects for an essay (since vanished) entitled 'On the application of coloured bricks and terra cotta to modern architecture'—a success somewhat marred by the judges' withholding the cash segment of the award. He kept up his private studies, worked at shorthand, French, and art history as possible avenues to a journalistic career, and in 1865 embarked with intensity and ambition on the study and writing of poetry—as witnessed by the exercises contained in his 'Studies, specimens &c.' notebook (1865–8, published 1994) and by the survival (Dorset County Museum) of dictionaries and poetry volumes purchased in the mid-1860s and often bearing the address, 16 Westbourne Park Villas, at which he lived for most of this London period. No poems appeared in print at the time, but he did publish a humorous sketch, 'How I built myself a house', in *Chambers's Journal* for 18 March 1865.

Early writings Hardy's religious faith significantly eroded during his London years—partly, perhaps, in response to the publication in 1859 of Darwin's *On the Origin of Species*—and by the time ill health brought him back to Higher Bockhampton in the summer of 1867 he had abandoned his old aspirations to a university education and a country ministry. He now wanted to write and, if at all possible, to live by writing. In Dorset, living mostly with his parents, he resumed work as an architect—for Hicks again and then, after Hicks's death, for his successor, the Weymouth architect G. R. Crickmay—but undertook at the same time a long first-person novel called *The Poor Man and the Lady*. The central story of the socially transgressive love and marriage of an impecunious young architect and the daughter of the nearby 'great house' was once described by Hardy himself as 'socialistic, not to say revolutionary' in character (*Life and Work*, 63), and while the manuscript's readers—remarkably, they included Alexander Macmillan, John Morley, and George Meredith—recognized its narrative strengths, they advised against publication of so outspoken an attack on the attitudes and pretensions of the upper classes. Meredith in particular urged Hardy 'not to "nail his colours to the mast" so definitely in a first book' but to attempt instead 'a novel with a purely artistic purpose' and a more complicated plot (ibid., 62, 64).

The Poor Man and the Lady remained unpublished but not entirely unused, in that Hardy incorporated portions of its manuscript into later works. What did appear, in 1871, was his perhaps somewhat cynical response to Meredith's advice, a 'sensation' novel entitled *Desperate Remedies* and published in three volumes by Tinsley Brothers, partly at the unnamed author's expense. Although the few reviews were extremely mixed, Tinsleys in 1872 brought out, unsubsidized but still anonymously, a second, two-volume novel called *Under the Greenwood Tree*. The crucial moment in Hardy's career came, however, in July 1872

when Tinsleys commissioned the writing of *A Pair of Blue Eyes* as a serial for *Tinsleys' Magazine*, to be followed in 1873 by publication in three volumes with Hardy's name on a title-page for the first time. Because serial writing was the prime source of income for Victorian novelists, Tinsleys' invitation gave Hardy, just turned thirty-two, the confidence to devote himself to literature full-time.

Courtship and marriage Hardy's early fascination with Horace Moule, whose suicide in September 1873 affected him profoundly, coexisted with the series of youthful infatuations reflected in such poems as 'To Lizbie Browne' and 'To Louisa in the Lane'. While in London between 1862 and 1867 he was involved with, perhaps temporarily engaged to, the religiously-minded Eliza Bright Nicholls, who had formerly lived with her coastguard father at Kimmeridge, on the south Dorset coast. By the late 1860s that relationship—its termination probably reflected in the poem 'Neutral Tones'—had been succeeded by attachments, of uncertain depth and duration, to his young schoolteacher cousin Tryphena Sparks, later remembered in the poem 'Thoughts of Phena', and to Catherine ('Cassie') Pole, the daughter of the butler at West Stafford rectory.

Of far greater importance was Hardy's meeting in March 1870 with Emma Lavinia Gifford (1840–1912), daughter of a Plymouth solicitor and sister-in-law of the rector of the lonely and dilapidated Cornish church of St Juliot, which Crickmay had sent Hardy to inspect. Beguiled by the romantic location, entranced by Emma Gifford's social pretensions, literary enthusiasms, and vivid personality—perhaps entrapped to some degree by her eagerness (at twenty-nine) to seize a chance of marriage—Hardy entered into an engagement that distressed both families by its challenge to class barriers and assumptions. Emma Gifford gave her fiancé material assistance during the writing of *A Pair of Blue Eyes*, which drew heavily on the circumstances of their Cornish courtship, and loyally supported his exchanging the relative security of architecture for the riskier prospects of literature, but Hardy seems nevertheless to have had serious qualms about his engagement during its four-year course. The wedding itself—conducted by the bride's uncle the Revd Edwin Hamilton Gifford (1820–1905), later archdeacon of London, but otherwise witnessed only by Emma's brother and the daughter of Hardy's London landlady—took place in London on 17 September 1874, and after a short honeymoon in Rouen and Paris the couple returned to rent a share of a house in Surbiton in order that Hardy might have ready access to London and its literary market place.

Early novels Though Hardy's first three published novels are not generally considered central to his achievement, each is in its way remarkable. *Desperate Remedies* (1871), though somewhat hectically plotted, treats sensitively and even disturbingly of the physical and sexual threats encountered by its heroine, while the 'idyllic' and deeply personal *Under the Greenwood Tree* (1872) possesses a deceptively simple elegance unmatched by any of Hardy's later fiction. *A Pair of Blue Eyes* (1873) may betray signs of Hardy's having padded some instalments of this first serial, but its romantic setting, the interplay of class and gender issues within its tragicomic plot, and the vitality of its heroine (closely based on Emma Gifford) served to make it a favourite novel of many Victorians, Tennyson and Coventry Patmore among them.

Far from the Madding Crowd, however, was the first of Hardy's major novels, and the one that made him famous. Serialized in the prestigious pages of the *Cornhill Magazine* between January and December 1874, published in two volumes by Smith, Elder in November 1874, it established precisely the kind of richly specific rural and agricultural setting that was to characterize his most widely admired work. It also introduced, as integral to that setting, the fictional region of Wessex, closely based on the topography of Dorset and the adjacent counties, that became increasingly the central organizing feature of his fiction. And through the often melodramatic, sometimes humorous story of the beautiful but headstrong Bathsheba Everdene and her diverse suitors it enacted an effective variation on the kind of marriage plot Hardy had already invoked in *A Pair of Blue Eyes*.

The next novel, *The Hand of Ethelberta*, was also serialized in the *Cornhill* (July 1875 – May 1876) and published by Smith, Elder (3 vols., 1876), but its settings are more often urban or suburban than rural, its central characters either servants or their middle- and upper-class employers, and its romantic elements subordinated to the central story (perhaps remotely suggested by Hardy's having been waited on at table by Catherine Pole's father) of how, at what cost, and with what ironic implications, a butler's daughter, Ethelberta Petherwin, wins her way to social and financial power as the wife of the wealthy but dissolute Lord Mountclere. Hardy doubtless intended to demonstrate that his professional range extended beyond rural settings, but the novel was poorly received and he was never again invited to write a *Cornhill* serial.

It was only after some difficulty, indeed, that Hardy placed his next book, *The Return of the Native*, in the January to December 1878 issues of *Belgravia*, a magazine best known as an outlet for 'sensation' fiction. A renewed preoccupation with regional materials and topography is immediately signalled in the three-volume first edition (Smith, Elder, 1878) by the presence, as frontispiece, of Hardy's own 'Sketch map of the scene of the story', identifiably based on the heathland of his childhood. Also quickly apparent is the ambitiousness of the novel's conception. Its principal characters may ultimately lack grandeur—the reformist Clym Yeobright emerging as an arid idealist, the romantic Eustacia Vye as a woman of very ordinary imagination and desires—but structure, imagery, and allusions persistently evoke both a native primitivism and the conventions of classical theatre. From the very first chapter Egdon Heath, the novel's bleak setting, is powerfully established as (to quote a later Hardy novel) one of

those sequestered spots outside the gates of the world …
where, from time to time, dramas of a grandeur and unity

truly Sophoclean are enacted in the real, by virtue of the concentrated passions and closely-knit interdependence of the lives therein.   (*The Woodlanders*, chap. 1)

The Return of the Native, even so, was not enthusiastically reviewed, and Hardy, perhaps in search of more 'popular' audiences, next wrote three novels of somewhat lighter weight: *The Trumpet-Major* (3 vols., 1880), a primarily comic but sometimes poignant Wessex story of sexual rivalry and fraternal loyalty during the period of the Napoleonic wars; *A Laodicean* (3 vols., 1881), contrastively 'modern' in period and theme and drawing extensively on Hardy's experience as an architect; and *Two on a Tower* (3 vols., 1882), glancing towards contemporary science in juxtaposing a young astronomer's rapt contemplation of the stars with his inattentiveness towards the older woman who loves and assists him. During the novel's serialization in the *Atlantic Monthly* some readers objected to the spurned heroine's marrying an unsuspecting bishop in order to provide a father for her unborn child, and the magazine's editor complained that he had been promised a family story but supplied instead with a story in the family way.

Return to Dorchester The Hardys left Surbiton for a more central London lodging in March 1875 and moved again, four months later, to the Dorset seaside resort of Swanage, where *The Hand of Ethelberta* was written and partly set. In the spring of 1876, following a brief stay in Yeovil and a holiday visit to the Rhine valley and Belgium (including the Waterloo battlefield), they took a house overlooking the River Stour in the little Dorset market town of Sturminster Newton. There Hardy wrote *The Return of the Native*, responded with eager interest to local events and festivals, and enjoyed with his wife what—despite the continuing childlessness of the marriage—he later called 'Our happiest time' (*Life and Work*, 122). Their next move, to the London suburb of Tooting in March 1878, was motivated by a renewed sense of Hardy's needs as a professional novelist and by Emma Hardy's dissatisfaction with Sturminster's rural isolation. But while Hardy made good use of his professional opportunities, forming important friendships with editors, illustrators, and fellow writers, his marriage fared less well: it was at 1 Arundel Terrace, Upper Tooting, so he enigmatically remarked, 'that their troubles began' (ibid., 128). It was there also, in the autumn of 1880, that he fell seriously ill, apparently with complications from a bladder infection, just as the serialization of *A Laodicean* had begun. Bedridden throughout the ensuing winter, Hardy kept up with the printer's schedule only by invoking his wife's assistance as amanuensis.

Hardy's illness, reinforced by his growing sense that city living 'tended to force mechanical and ordinary productions from his pen, concerning ordinary society-life and habits' (*Life and Work*, 154), prompted a move back to Dorset. In June 1881 the Hardys rented a house in Wimborne, formed new friendships, and took an active part in local life—including a Shakespeare reading group. They spent several weeks in Paris in the autumn of 1882, and in the spring and early summer of 1883 initiated what became for many years a regular pattern of renting accommodation in London for up to two months of the 'season', visiting galleries and theatres, hearing music, and meeting and entertaining friends. Though not elected to the Athenaeum until 1891, Hardy was already a familiar figure at the Savile Club, took an active interest in copyright and other issues addressed by the recently founded Society of Authors, and dined occasionally with the Rabelais Club and other such convivial coteries.

That same summer of 1883 the Hardys moved finally to Dorchester itself, so central to the territory Hardy was claiming as a novelist yet rendered problematic by its associations with his humbler upbringing and by the fears—soon realized—of continued hostility between his wife and the family still living at Higher Bockhampton. A house in the town was rented for two years while Hardy's father and brother built a new house, to Hardy's own design, just outside Dorchester, on a plot of open downland purchased from the duchy of Cornwall. Called Max Gate (after a nearby toll-gate long kept by one Henry Mack) and often criticized for the villa-style eclecticism of its architecture, the red-brick building was much enlarged, if little modernized, over the years and became increasingly secluded by the Austrian pines Hardy had planted in December 1883. Though still exposed in June 1885, when the Hardys first moved in, it was a comfortable and compact house that stood solidly in its own grounds and asserted—together with Hardy's early appointment as a local magistrate—a claim to middle-class status that seems at first to have gained only grudging local acceptance.

Later fiction The move to Dorchester was reflected in Hardy's work by a renewed attentiveness to Wessex scenes and subjects. In *The Mayor of Casterbridge*—serialized (in a bowdlerized form) in the weekly *Graphic* between 2 January and 5 May 1886, then published in two volumes by Smith, Elder (1886)—Casterbridge itself is a busy market town modelled on the Dorchester of four decades earlier, economically vibrant as the nodal point of the rich surrounding countryside but riven by internal class-based conflicts. The central opposition, at once commercial and profoundly personal, between Michael Henchard, the rooted traditionalist, and Donald Farfrae, the modernizing newcomer, dramatizes the processes of historical change in the countryside even as it draws on classical and biblical analogies reminiscent of *The Return of the Native*.

The Woodlanders (serialized in *Macmillan's Magazine* from May 1886 to April 1887, published in three volumes by Macmillan in March 1887) is set in the part of north-west Dorset in which Hardy's mother's family had lived. Although it lacks the structural assurance of its predecessor, its plot again depends on the intermeshing of emotional and economic issues. The characters live among the trees on which their livelihoods depend, and when Giles Winterbourne suffers financial losses he loses also his promised bride, educated to higher levels of class expectation, and eventually his own life. In the late 1880s Hardy also began to collect the short stories he had long been

publishing in magazines. *Wessex Tales* (2 vols., 1888) comprised just five stories, among them 'The Three Strangers', 'The Withered Arm', and 'The Distracted Preacher'. *A Group of Noble Dames* followed, somewhat less impressively, in 1891, and in 1894 came *Life's Little Ironies*, containing such notable stories as 'On the Western Circuit', 'A Tragedy of Two Ambitions', and 'The Fiddler of the Reels'. A somewhat miscellaneous supplementary volume, *A Changed Man and other Tales*, appeared in 1914 and a scholarly edition of *The Excluded and Collaborative Stories* in 1992.

The final phase of Hardy's career as a novelist is curiously framed by the short and enigmatically personal fable of sexual and artistic obsession that was serialized as 'The Pursuit of the Well-Beloved' in 1891 and heavily revised for volume publication, as *The Well-Beloved*, only in 1897. Although published by the same firm—the London-based but American-owned house of Osgood, McIlvaine—as *Tess of the d'Urbervilles* (3 vols., 1891) and *Jude the Obscure* (1895, but dated 1896), *The Well-Beloved* had little in common with them beyond the hostility its sexual frankness aroused in a significant number of its reviewers. With both *Tess* and *Jude*, as on a number of earlier occasions, editorial concern at Hardy's handling of sexual matters led to his making to the serializations cuts and adjustments that were for the most part restored in the volumes.

The occasional negative reviews of *Tess*, though hurtful to Hardy himself, were overwhelmed by the popular response to the novel's deeply imagined portrayal of a heroine moving through hopes and betrayals, surmounted difficulties and deceptive idylls, to a tragic conclusion whose 'justice' the author's passionate advocacy profoundly challenges. *Tess* is also the most eloquently written of the novels, and the one in which the natural world and the topography itself—the landscapes Tess so doggedly traverses—are most continuously and richly represented. *Jude*, in contrast, is more sparely written, and its haunted characters, trapped within an intricately disastrous plot, move restlessly from one unfriendly town to another, loving without fulfilment, striving without achievement. By representing Jude Fawley as encountering persistent persecution in his attempts to gain admission to a Christminster (that is, Oxford) college and share with Sue Bridehead a life outside wedlock, Hardy was deliberately attacking the existing educational system and marriage laws. The novel's sexual directness fuelled the hostility of its reception in some quarters, and while Hardy affected to laugh off a bishop's claim to have consigned the book to the flames he could not easily remain indifferent to reviews with headings such as 'Jude the Obscene' and 'Hardy the Degenerate'.

Middle life Emma Hardy took personal offence not only at *Jude*'s attack on marriage but also at what she saw as its dark pessimism and irreligiousness. Max Gate provided Hardy himself with a congenial working environment, but it had not proved fortunate for his marriage. As a professional novelist writing to deadlines, peremptory as to his priorities and impatient of interruptions, he was not easy to live with, and he had failed—had perhaps not sufficiently tried—to resolve the antagonism between his wife and the family he now regularly visited. Emma Hardy, temperamentally restless and impulsive, lacking satisfying occupations and sympathetic friends, grew ever more deeply resentful—and publicly critical—of her husband's self-sufficiency and fame. The marriage was kept up to the end as a more or less functioning day-to-day arrangement. The Hardys shared a devotion to the Max Gate cats (subsequently buried in the pets' cemetery there) and a hatred of all forms of cruelty to animals. They continued to go to London together almost every spring and even to share occasional holidays, including an extended Italian trip in 1887. But Emma Hardy led an increasingly separate life, eventually withdrawing into the two attic rooms created at the time of the construction of Hardy's final study. And in London the literary and social worlds which welcomed and lionized her husband increasingly saw—and shunned—her as plain, ill-dressed, and dull.

It was in those same worlds, especially following the publication of *Tess*, that Hardy received flattering attentions from numerous women handsomer and more stylish than his wife and often better educated. In the late 1880s he was sexually fascinated by the poet Rosamund Tomson (who published as Graham R. Tomson), only to be deterred by a lack of genuine responsiveness on her part and perhaps by the freedom of her lifestyle. She subsequently published a description of him at that time as 'slightly below the middle height, but strongly built, with rugged, aquiline features, pallid complexion, a crisp, closely trimmed brown beard, and mustache short enough to disclose an infrequent smile of remarkable sweetness' (New York *Independent*, 22 Nov 1894, 2). His 'bright, deep-set eyes' (ibid.) and greying, slightly receding hair were also noted, but not the slightly crooked nose evident in some of the portraits and busts. The beard was evidently shaved off in the early 1890s and, to judge from contemporary photographs, that was by far Hardy's smartest decade, his appearance on social occasions attaining almost to dapperness.

In the mid-1890s Hardy was strongly attracted to another acknowledged beauty, Agnes Grove (later Lady Grove), the daughter of General Pitt-Rivers, but it was only with Florence Henniker, daughter of Richard Monckton Milnes (Lord Houghton), that he seems to have fallen seriously in love. At their first meeting in 1893 she struck him immediately as a 'charming, *intuitive* woman' (*Life and Work*, 270), and she, for her part, valued his friendship and literary eminence and was happy, as a novelist herself, to collaborate with him in a short story called 'The spectre of the real'. But she never wavered in her loyalty to her husband, a distinguished soldier, or to the religious views that Hardy so deeply deplored. The limits of the relationship are suggested by the poem 'A Thunderstorm in Town' when, trapped together inside a London cab by a sudden downpour, 'I should have kissed her if the rain / Had lasted a minute more'.

By 1900, the year of his sixtieth birthday, Hardy's melancholic temperament found much in his personal life on which to brood. Professionally, however, his position was strong. New United States copyright legislation had enabled him to profit from the American as well as the British popularity of *Tess*; the notoriety of *Jude* was further reviving interest in his earlier titles; a first collected edition of his fiction had been brought out by Osgood, McIlvaine in 1895–6; and with the general shift in publishing to a royalty system of remuneration he could expect to benefit indefinitely from future sales of what (with silent nods to Scott and Trollope) he now consistently referred to as 'the Wessex novels'.

Return to poetry It was Hardy's improved and stabilized economic situation, rather than his anger at reviewers, that chiefly determined the timing of his long contemplated return to poetry. His first collection, *Wessex Poems*, published in 1898 by Harper & Brothers (successors to Osgood, McIlvaine), brought together newly written poems, poems composed during the novel-writing years, and still others revised from originals drafted in London during the 1860s. Because a similar mix occurs in all of his volumes, individual poems are often hard to date and the volumes themselves elusive of characterization. *Wessex Poems*, however, uniquely included thirty-one of Hardy's own idiosyncratic drawings. Some reviewers saw the naïvety of the drawings as symptomatic of weaknesses in the poems themselves; others were troubled by the number of ballads in the volume; one marvelled that Hardy 'did not himself burn the verse, lest it should fall into the hands of the indiscreet literary executor, and mar his fame when he was dead' (*Saturday Review*, 7 Jan 1899, 19). Even the more favourable commentators tended to suggest that Hardy's range as a poet was narrow, his technique clumsy, and his vocabulary often perversely provincial, even dialectal. Hardy had in fact no intention of following the example of William Barnes, the Dorset dialect poet, whom he had known and admired and whose poems he selected and edited a few years later. But he declined to limit his use of distinctively English words, however unfamiliar or 'unpoetic', and remained determined to challenge what he saw as the current fashion of subordinating content to form and 'saying nothing with mellifluous preciosity' (*Collected Letters*, 2.208).

Poems of the Past and the Present, published by Harper in 1901 (but dated 1902), contained fewer ballads than its predecessor but more poems overall, varying in subject from the Second South African War (such as 'Drummer Hodge' and 'The Souls of the Slain') and the bleakness of the universal scheme of things ('The Subalterns', 'The Lacking Sense') to such intense introspections as '*In Tenebris*'. It also demonstrated—what all the succeeding poetry volumes would amply confirm—the exceptional number of different stanza forms and metres, whether inherited or invented, that Hardy was able to deploy. A third, equally various, collection, *Time's Laughingstocks* (Macmillan, 1909), reinstated the ballad as a central Hardyan verse form, notably in the shape of 'A Trampwoman's Tragedy', which Hardy himself is said to have considered, 'upon the whole, his most successful poem' (*Life and Work*, 517). It has been argued that many of the nearly one thousand poems Hardy published are too weak or trivial to have been preserved, that such proliferation was and is damaging to his reputation, and that he is best approached through selections. But for Hardy the extraordinary and the everyday were equally matter for poetry: the technical range of his verse is matched by the exceptional diversity of subjects, moods, and emotions of which it treats, and even little regarded poems are likely to seem indispensable once attentively addressed.

Hardy had long been dissatisfied that Harper & Brothers' absorption of Osgood, McIlvaine should have resulted in his having a New York publisher for his British as well as his American editions, and when his agreements with Harper expired in 1902 he transferred all British rights in his works to the house of Macmillan. Frederick Macmillan was delighted to reissue the 1895–7 collected edition of the novels as a Macmillan imprint and, in due course, to bring out the handsome and extensively revised Wessex Edition of 1912–31 and the signed Mellstock Edition of 1919–20—both containing the verse as well as the prose. He was perhaps less delighted to receive, in September 1903, the manuscript of Part First of *The Dynasts*, Hardy's long-contemplated epic drama of Britain's struggle with Napoleonic France. The initial reception of the three parts in 1904, 1906, and 1908 was generally lukewarm, but when, early in the First World War, Harley Granville-Barker adapted for the London stage what Hardy had always intended as a 'closet' drama, to be read and not performed, *The Dynasts* achieved a wider, specifically patriotic, resonance that fed into the high reputation it enjoyed between the wars.

It did not, however, share in the late twentieth-century rise in critical estimation of Hardy's poetry that led to his being recognized, uniquely, as both a great nineteenth-century novelist and a great twentieth-century poet. The verse of *The Dynasts* has come to seem flaccid, its structure ponderous, and the cosmic apparatus of the Spirits perhaps a little absurd. At the same time, it remains highly readable, impressive in its historical scope, and innovative in its visual perspectives, and the Spirits clearly offered Hardy a technique, beyond the scope of the pre-Joycean novel, for giving voice and form to his own shifting and often self-contradictory musings about human experience. It is characteristic of Hardy, whose temperamental pessimism was tempered by belief in what he himself called 'evolutionary meliorism' ('Apology' to *Late Lyrics and Earlier*), that even the central idea of *The Dynasts*—that of the universe as controlled by a blind and unconscious Immanent Will—is not rigidly sustained throughout. He always disclaimed possession of a consistent philosophy, and in the preface to *Poems of the Past and the Present* described his poems as 'a series of feelings and fancies written down in widely differing moods and circumstances'—adding, perhaps with *The Dynasts* already in mind, 'Unadjusted impressions have their value, and the road to a true philosophy of life seems to lie in humbly recording diverse readings of its phenomena as they are forced upon us by chance and change.'

Years of fame Completion of *The Dynasts* in 1908 did much to enhance Hardy's emerging status as a uniquely 'national' writer. In 1909 he was appointed to the Order of Merit and succeeded George Meredith as president of the Incorporated Society of Authors, and during his remaining two decades he was unquestionably the most famous living writer in Britain and, indeed, in the Western world. In the years preceding the First World War he was often on his own in London and elsewhere—Emma Hardy now preferring to avoid the annual dislocation of taking a London lodging—and able to pursue his friendship with a young schoolteacher and aspiring writer named Florence Emily Dugdale (1879–1937). They first met, as author and admirer, in 1905, and by the end of 1906 she was visiting the reading room of the British Museum to look up references he needed—or pretended to need—in completing *The Dynasts*. As time passed, Hardy became emotionally more dependent on her as well as increasingly exploitative of her typing skills, and she sometimes accompanied him to the gatherings, at once intellectual and congenial, hosted in Aldeburgh by his rationalist friend Edward Clodd.

In 1910, after meeting Emma Hardy at a women's literary club in London, Florence Dugdale spent several weeks at Max Gate typing and editing the poems, stories, and religious meditations which Emma was then trying to write, and although the quarrels between husband and wife deterred her from returning to Max Gate she kept up her separate friendships with both. Whether her relationship with Hardy became actively sexual cannot be known: opportunities, clearly, were ample, but Florence Dugdale was thirty-eight years Hardy's junior, her lower middle-class background was rigidly conventional, and when writing privately to Clodd she spoke freely of the comic aspects of 'the Max Gate ménage' (*Letters of Emma and Florence Hardy*, 66).

Second marriage In November 1912 Emma Hardy died, aged seventy-two. Her health had for some time been in decline—her death-certificate refers to 'impacted gallstones'—but the suddenness of her actual departure precluded any last-minute marital reconciliation and left Hardy with only the bitter comments on himself discovered in the private diaries she proved to have been keeping for many years. He soon destroyed the diaries themselves—apart from the pages (published as *Some Recollections* in 1961) devoted to his wife's early memories—but their contents contributed indelibly to the mood of remorseful retrospection that revived and glorified his early memories of Emma, impelled him to revisit St Juliot with his brother early in 1913, and inspired the astonishing sequence of elegiac love poems ('The Voice', 'I found her out there', 'After a Journey', 'Beeny Cliff', and so on) later published as 'Poems of 1912–13' and widely regarded as his finest work in verse.

Florence Dugdale, supported by Hardy's sisters, took over the running of Max Gate after Emma Hardy's death, although fear of local gossip kept her effectively housebound. The logic of the situation seemed to override the age difference and impel her towards an eventual marriage, but she hesitated over the decision and laid down a number of conditions before finally giving her consent. The wedding itself, an intensely private occasion, took place in Enfield parish church, near the Dugdale home, early in the morning of 10 February 1914, the bride and groom immediately rushing back to Max Gate in order to avoid newspaper reporters and the especially dreaded risk of a civic reception at the Dorchester railway station.

Although she was already well attuned to the rhythms of life at Max Gate, Florence Hardy's altered status brought with it a new and sometimes burdensome sense of responsibility that was soon tested by the emotional and practical pressures of the First World War, by her husband's celebration of his first wife's virtues in the 'Poems of 1912–13', published in *Satires of Circumstance* in November 1914, and by certain aspects of Hardy's behaviour in old age. Despite his achieved affluence Hardy lost neither his sensitivity to public opinion, however voiced, nor the frugal habits of his childhood. Servants and tradespeople found him mean and hard to please and were delighted, years later, to exaggerate his foibles and failings for the delectation of eager interviewers. Though genial to visitors, he could be temperamental in private; the hypochondria that coexisted with his generally excellent health was the source of frequent alarms and despondencies; and although he himself spent so much of every day working alone in his study, he would object to his wife's going away for even a single night.

Florence Hardy took over ever-increasing amounts of the voluminous Max Gate correspondence, often typing up and signing letters that Hardy had drafted in pencil. During the years 1917–20 she also made, as typist, an indispensable contribution to Hardy's secret generation of the third-person 'Life and work'—published, as always intended, after his death as an official biography authored by Florence Emily Hardy. Hardy necessarily left his life's narrative incomplete, and because his widow made alterations to the first volume, *The Early Life of Thomas Hardy* (1928), and had to write the conclusion of the second, *The Later Years of Thomas Hardy* (1930), its status as autobiography is somewhat open to question. That status was speculatively reclaimed by the re-edited *The Life and Work of Thomas Hardy* (1984), but the destruction of notebooks and other original source materials, before and after Hardy's death, had in any case bequeathed to prospective biographers a record selected, compiled, and angled by the subject himself.

Final phase Hardy in his later years depended heavily on the advice and practical assistance of Sydney (later Sir Sydney) Cockerell, the forceful director of the Fitzwilliam Museum, who had originally assisted in the distribution of his manuscripts to various libraries and subsequently facilitated Florence Hardy's publication of limited edition pamphlets of her husband's writings. But for guidance in professional matters Hardy relied on the continuation of his congenial relationship with (now) Sir Frederick Macmillan and with the Macmillan firm, publishers of all his later books. These included the four collections of poetry subsequent to *Satires of Circumstance*—*Moments of Vision* (1917), *Late Lyrics and Earlier* (1922), *Human Shows* (1925), and the posthumous *Winter Words* (1928)—as well as an important *Selected Poems* (1916) and the short verse-drama

called *The Famous Tragedy of the Queen of Cornwall* (1923), later set to music by Rutland Boughton. Even *Winter Words* contains important poems evidently written or at least drafted many years earlier, but it remains none the less extraordinary that volumes issued by a poet in his middle and late eighties should show neither a decline in quality nor any significant shift in emotions, attitudes, or beliefs. Long characterized and chastised as a 'pessimist', Hardy continued to contest any such categorization—publicly in the important 'Apology' prefixed to *Late Lyrics*, privately when noting on the page proofs of *Human Shows* (Dorset County Museum) that only two-fifths of the poems were expressive of 'tragedy, sorrow or grimness' as against three-fifths that dealt with 'reflection, love, or comedy'.

Hardy lost his beloved sister Mary in 1915 and was deeply shaken by the First World War—in which a favourite cousin, Frank George, was killed. He was apprehensive as to the long-term consequences of the Versailles treaty, and in contemplating the troubled social scene of the 1920s he was torn, as always, between an intellectual progressivism and an instinctual conservatism. He rarely ventured outside Dorchester now, but went to Oxford in February 1920 to see an Oxford University Dramatic Society production of *The Dynasts* and add an honorary degree to those already received from Aberdeen and Cambridge, and made in May 1920 a final visit to London to attend the wedding of Harold Macmillan. At the same time he remained alert to events in Dorchester itself, visiting recent archaeological excavations, making a few speeches on local occasions, and taking a particular interest in the dramatizations of his novels written, produced, and performed by the group of local amateurs who came to call themselves the Hardy Players. In 1923 he gave them the *Queen of Cornwall* to perform and in 1924 his own stage version of *Tess*, deeply distressing his wife on the latter occasion by becoming so obviously infatuated with Gertrude Bugler, the young and beautiful Dorset actress who took the part of Tess.

Max Gate was now a place of pilgrimage, and it became a regular afternoon routine for Hardy, after several hours' solitary work in his study, to come downstairs to greet the day's contingent of tea-time visitors—typically ranging from the rich, aristocratic, and powerful to Dorset relatives, acquaintances, and clergymen, old friends such as Cockerell, Edmund Gosse, Sir James Barrie, and the Harley Granville-Barkers, poets such as Walter de la Mare, Siegfried Sassoon, and Edmund Blunden, and those enthusiasts, academics, and tourists who had politely written ahead or simply refused to be turned away by the watchful Max Gate servants or even the ever-threatening presence of Wessex, the unmannerly Max Gate dog. The prince of Wales paid a much publicized call in July 1923: 'My Mother', he reportedly said, 'tells me you have written a book called *Tess of the d'Urbervilles*. I must try it some time.' A more frequent, and especially valued, visitor was T. E. Lawrence ('of Arabia'), then serving, incognito, as a private in the tank corps at nearby Bovington camp.

Although Florence Hardy underwent two operations in the 1920s Hardy himself had only occasional colds and mild recurrences of the bladder troubles he had suffered since 1881. He rode his bicycle until he was well into his eighties and Gosse, writing on 25 June 1927, could describe him as being 'in his 88th. year, exactly where he was in his 36th., when I knew him first' (letter to T. J. Wise, BL). But in December 1927 Hardy became suddenly tired and took increasingly to his bed; doctors were called, anxieties voiced, and a summons was sent out to his wife's sister Eva Dugdale, a trained nurse. He was able to contribute a final poem to *The Times* for publication on Christmas eve but grew progressively weaker as the days passed. On 11 January 1928 he rallied sufficiently to joke a little with his doctor and dictate bitter epitaphs on two *bêtes noires* of long standing, G. K. Chesterton and George Moore, only to have a sudden heart attack that evening, call out 'Eva, what is this?', and die within a few minutes.

Afterwards Hardy's family had always assumed that he would be buried at Stinsford, along with his parents, grandparents, first wife, and sister, and Hardy himself had left instructions to the same effect. Cockerell, however, appointed co-literary executor with Florence Hardy and present at Max Gate at the time of Hardy's death, insisted that the instructions were less than absolute and that Hardy, although a well-known agnostic, was too important a national figure to be buried anywhere other than in Westminster Abbey. Barrie, in London, enlisted the support of Stanley Baldwin, the prime minister, and Geoffrey Dawson, editor of *The Times*, and permission for an abbey interment was quickly obtained from an only mildly reluctant dean. Dorset opinion, however, was outraged at the thought of Hardy's lying anywhere other than in his 'own' county, and Florence Hardy, grieving and distressed, was persuaded to accept the suggestion, apparently emanating from the Stinsford vicar, that since only Hardy's ashes were to be placed in the abbey his heart might be removed before cremation and given a separate Stinsford burial. On 16 January 1928, therefore, two events took place simultaneously, the national funeral in the abbey, in the presence of Hardy's widow and sister, and the heart burial at Stinsford, attended by Hardy's brother.

Some public disapproval was prompted by the perceived grotesquerie of the duplicated obsequies and renewed, a month later, when it became known that Hardy's will, probated at the very substantial sum of £95,418 3s. 1d., included no significant bequests, public or personal, outside his own family. Partly because of negative reaction to the will, the appeal for funds for a national memorial attracted only meagre support, and the resulting Eric Kennington statue in Dorchester was, in the event, largely funded by the subject's own bequests to his wife and sister. Disagreement over the form the memorial should take proved to be only the first of many issues over which the two literary executors differed and quarrelled, and Florence Hardy's relationship with Cockerell, which had once seemed so close, collapsed in bitterness and mutual recrimination long before she died of cancer in October 1937. The contents of Max Gate, including the bulk of Hardy's library, were then dispersed at auction.

Max Gate itself was also auctioned but purchased by Hardy's sister Kate, who subsequently bequeathed it to the National Trust. And in 1948 the trust acquired, by purchase, the Higher Bockhampton birthplace.

MICHAEL MILLGATE

Sources M. Millgate, *Thomas Hardy: a biography* (1982) • F. E. Hardy, *The early life of Thomas Hardy, 1840–1891* (1928) • F. E. Hardy, *The later years of Thomas Hardy, 1892–1928* (1930) • *The life and work of Thomas Hardy*, ed. M. Millgate (1985) • *The collected letters of Thomas Hardy*, ed. R. L. Purdy and M. Millgate, 7 vols. (1978–88) • b. cert. • m. certs. • d. cert. • R. L. Purdy, *Thomas Hardy: a bibliographical study* (1968) • *The personal notebooks of Thomas Hardy*, ed. R. H. Taylor (1978) • *The literary notebooks of Thomas Hardy*, ed. L. Björk, 2 vols. (1985) • *Thomas Hardy's 'Studies, specimens &c.' notebook*, ed. P. Dalziel and M. Millgate (1994) • R. Gittings, *Young Thomas Hardy* (1975) • S. Gatrell, *Hardy the creator: a textual biography* (1988) • P. Beal and others, *Index of English literary manuscripts*, ed. P. J. Croft and others, [4 vols. in 11 pts] (1980–), vol. 4, pt 2, pp. 3–224 • R. Gittings, *The older Hardy* (1978) • *The architectural notebook of Thomas Hardy*, ed. C. J. P. Beatty (1966) • *The letters of Emma and Florence Hardy*, ed. M. Millgate (1996) • E. L. Hardy, *Some recollections*, ed. E. Hardy and R. Gittings (1961) • R. Gittings and J. Manton, *The second Mrs. Hardy* (1979) • T. Hands, *Thomas Hardy: distracted preacher?* (1989) • K. Wilson, *Thomas Hardy on stage* (1995) • M. Millgate, *Testamentary acts: Browning, Tennyson, James, Hardy* (1992), 110–74 • C. J. P. Beatty, *Thomas Hardy: conservation architect* (1995) • E. Gosse, letter to T. J. Wise, 25 June 1927, BL • *Thomas Hardy's public voice: the essays, speeches, and miscellaneous prose*, ed. M. Millgate (2002)

Archives Dorset County Museum, Dorchester, corresp., drawings, books from library, MSS of *Under the greenwood tree*, *The mayor of Casterbridge*, *The woodlanders*, *Satires of circumstance*, *Late lyrics and earlier* • Yale U., Beinecke L., R. L. Purdy collection, corresp., books from library, MS of *The hand of Ethelberta* | Birmingham Museums and Art Gallery, MS of *Wessex poems* • BL, corresp., MSS of *Tess of the d'Urbervilles*, *The dynasts* • Bodl. Oxf., corresp., MS of *Poems of the past and the present* • Colby College, Waterville, Maine, corresp., books from library • Dorset County Museum, Dorchester, Lock collection, corresp., family documents • Eton, corresp., books from library, MSS • FM Cam., MSS of *Jude the obscure*, *Time's laughingstocks* • Harvard U., Houghton L., corresp., MS of *Two on a tower* • L. Cong., corresp., MS of *A group of noble dames* • Magd. Cam., MS of *Moments of vision* • New York University, Fales Library, corresp., books from library • NL Scot., corresp. • NYPL, Berg collection, corresp., drawings, MS of *A pair of blue eyes* • Princeton University, New Jersey, corresp., books from library, MSS • Queen's College, Oxford, MS of *Winter words* • Ransom HRC, corresp., drawings, books from library, MSS • Royal Library, Windsor Castle, MS of *The trumpet-major* • U. Cal., Berkeley, Bancroft Library, corresp., MSS • U. Leeds, Brotherton L., corresp. • University College, Dublin, MS of *The return of the native* • Yale U., Beinecke L., corresp., MSS of *Far from the madding crowd*, *Human shows*

Likenesses photograph, *c.*1857, Dorset County Museum, Dorchester • Schnadhorst and Heilbronn, photograph, *c.*1863, Yale U., Beinecke L. • photograph, *c.*1883, Dorset County Museum, Dorchester • Barraud, photograph, 1889, NPG; repro. in *Men and Women of the Day*, 2 (1889) • W. Strang, etching, 1893, Glasgow Art Gallery • W. Strang, oils, 1893, NPG [*see illus.*] • W. H. Thomson, oils, 1895, Dorchester grammar school • W. Rothenstein, lithograph, 1897, NPG • C. Holland, photographs, *c.*1898, Dorset County Museum, Dorchester • W. Rothenstein, chalk drawing, 1903, Dorset County Museum, Dorchester • J.-E. Blanche, oils, 1906, Tate collection • J.-E. Blanche, oils, 1906, Man. City Gall. • H. von Herkomer, oils, *c.*1906, Dorset County Museum, Dorchester • B. Stone, photograph, 1908, NPG • W. Strang, drawings, 1910, Royal Collection • W. Strang, drawings, 1910, FM Cam. • W. Strang, drawings, 1910, Dorset County Museum, Dorchester • A. L. Coburn, photogravure, 1913, NPG; repro. in A. L. Coburn, *More men of mark* (1922) • E. O. Hoppé, photograph, *c.*1913–1914, NPG • O. Edis, autochrome photographs, 1914, NPG · double portrait, photograph, 1914 (with Florence Hardy), Colby College, Waterville, Maine · W. Rothenstein, pencil drawings, 1916, Man. City Gall. · W. Rothenstein, pencil drawings, 1916, Athenaeum, London · W. H. Thornycroft, bronze head, 1917, NPG · W. Strang, pencil drawing, 1919, NPG · W. Strang, engravings, c.1919–1920, BM · W. Strang, engravings, c.1919–1920, NPG · W. Strang, engravings, c.1919–1920, NG Scot. · W. Strang, engravings, c.1919–1920, FM Cam. · W. Strang, engravings, c.1919–1920, Glasgow Art Gallery · W. Strang, engravings, c.1919–1920, U. Glas. · W. Strang, oils, 1920, Glasgow Art Gallery · W. W. Ouless, oils, 1922, NPG · T. Spicer-Simson, medallion, c.1922, NPG · R. G. Eves, oils, 1923, NPG · R. G. Eves, oils, 1923, Dorset County Museum, Dorchester · R. G. Eves, oils, 1923, U. Texas · A. John, oils, 1923, FM Cam. · M. R. Mitchell, bronze bust, 1923, Dorset County Museum, Dorchester · R. G. Eves, oils, 1924, Tate collection · R. G. Eves, portrait, 1924, Princeton University, New Jersey · R. G. Eves, portrait, 1924, Yale U. · E. Kennington, statue, c.1931, Top o' Town, Dorchester · M. Beerbohm, caricature, Charterhouse School, Surrey · W. Bellows, photograph (with Edmund Gosse), NPG · W. & D. Downey, woodburytype, NPG; repro. in W. Downey and D. Downey, *The cabinet portrait gallery*, 5 (1894) · R. G. Eves, oils, Birmingham Museums and Art Gallery · R. E. Fuller Maitland, oils, Magd. Cam. · H. Furniss, pen-and-ink caricatures, NPG · C. Holland, photographs, NPG · F. Hollyer, photograph, U. Texas, Gernsheim collection · London Stereoscopic Co., photograph, NPG · Russell & Sons, photograph, NPG · Spy [L. Ward], chromolithograph caricature, NPG; repro. in *VF* (4 June 1892) · W. H. Thornycroft, marble head, Dorset County Museum, Dorchester

Wealth at death £95,428 3s. 1d.: resworn probate, 1928, *CGPLA Eng. & Wales*

Hardy, Sir Thomas Duffus (1804–1878), historian and archivist, was born at Port Royal, Jamaica, on 22 May 1804, the third son of Thomas Bartholomew Price Hardy (d. 1813), then a captain-lieutenant of the Royal Artillery, and his second wife, Frances Duffus (b. 1776), of Kingston, Jamaica. His family was from Jersey, and three of his forebears were admirals: Sir Thomas Hardy (1666–1732), Sir Charles Hardy (1680–1744), and Sir Charles Hardy (bap. 1717, d. 1780). Hardy moved to England at the age of seven, with his younger brother William *Hardy (1807–1887). On 1 January 1819 he was appointed a junior clerk in the record office in the Tower of London, of which his uncle Samuel Lysons (1763–1819) was then keeper. Like his brother William, Hardy owed his archival training to Lysons's successor Henry Petrie.

Hardy's post and Petrie's tuition gave him a wide acquaintance with medieval records, and during his clerkship he published editions of five categories of the early chancery rolls (charter, patent, close, Norman, and fine) in the Tower. He also in those years worked with, and came deeply to dislike, Sir Francis Palgrave. On Petrie's retirement in 1840, Hardy became a senior assistant keeper of the Public Record Office, but he remained at the Tower in charge of the records there until he moved to Chancery Lane in 1856. When Petrie died in 1842 Hardy took over the materials for the first and only volume of the *Monumenta historica britannica*, on which Petrie had laboured since 1823, and published it with a general introduction in 1848.

In 1830 Hardy married Frances Offley, younger daughter of Captain Charles Savery Andrews. She died on 2 August 1841 and he married again in 1850. His second wife was

Mary Ann MacDowell (1824–1891), who later published fourteen novels and a number of travel books, at first under her pseudonym of Addleston Hill, but later in her own name as Mary Anne, Lady *Hardy. Their elder daughter, Iza Duffus Hardy (d. 1922), was also a novelist.

Although Hardy had resented Palgrave's appointment to the deputy keepership of the public records, and was himself an adequately competent administrator, he was temperamentally more inclined to scholarly work than to management. When he became deputy keeper, on 15 July 1861, he was anxious to promote the publication of records, but his energies were increasingly directed to material outside the Public Record Office. In 1857 he had taken a substantial part in establishing Chronicles and Memorials of Great Britain and Ireland during the Middle Ages, known as the Rolls Series because its volumes, funded by the Treasury, were published under the direction of the master of the rolls. When he took over the *Monumenta* he acquired Petrie's other working papers, and he ordered and augmented them to make his *Descriptive catalogue of materials relating to the history of Great Britain and Ireland, to 1327*, which appeared in three volumes in the Rolls Series between 1862 and 1871. The notes for a fourth volume, to 1485, were bound after Hardy's death and preserved in the Public Record Office. A century's work since then, much of it stimulated by Hardy himself, has modified or superseded some of his judgements on manuscripts and individual writers, but he showed a remarkable knowledge of the medieval narrative sources, and a keen eye for their interrelationships.

Hardy published only one other work in the Rolls Series, the episcopal register from 1311 to 1316 of Richard Kellaw of Durham, under the title of *Registrum palatinum Dunelmense* in 1873–8, but Gaimar's *Lestorie des Engles*, on which he was working at the time of his death, was finished by his colleague Charles Trice Martin, and published in 1888–9. He played a considerable part in setting up the Royal Commission on Historical Manuscripts, which under its warrant is concerned with all records other than public records. In 1869, when he was knighted, he was appointed to the commission, and remained a force in its affairs until the end of his life. John Cordy Jeaffreson, for whom Hardy secured a post in the Public Record Office, has left a characteristically breezy but interesting account of the way in which his friend trained him for the commission's inspectorate.

There were several substantial developments in the Public Record Office in Hardy's time. The round reading room in the new wing was opened in 1866, and the block towards Fetter Lane was completed in 1869. The additional accommodation enabled the office to house the records of the palatinate of Durham, transferred under warrant in 1868, and the much richer records of the duchy of Lancaster, which the queen deposited as a gift to the nation in 1870. The duchy records brought Hardy's brother William, their keeper, into the office with them.

Hardy also procured, in 1866, the abolition of fees for legal searches in the records, a reform which he had long advocated. In the last years of his life he oversaw the making of the second Public Record Office Act of 1877, which sought to relieve pressures on the office by authorizing the destruction of modern records deemed to be redundant.

Hardy's administration of the office was generally characterized by common sense and humanity rather than by any strong professional purpose. His direction was criticized throughout the 1870s by the cantankerous John Pym Yeatman and some other users who wished to see more intensive work on sorting and listing the records. Whether or not Hardy used his resources to the best advantage, he certainly neglected to shape the senior management of the office, and made no effective provision for a successor. He died on 15 June 1878 at his home, 126 Portsdown Road, Maida Vale, London, and was buried at Paddington old cemetery.   G. H. MARTIN

Sources DNB · J. B. Payne, *Armorial of Jersey*, 2 vols. (1859–65) · J. D. Cantwell, *The Public Record Office, 1838–1958* (1991) · J. C. Jeaffreson, *A book of recollections*, 2 vols. (1894)
Archives PRO | Bodl. Oxf., corresp. with Sir Thomas Phillipps
Likenesses photograph (after original, probably PRO), repro. in Cantwell, *Public Record Office*, illus. no. 8 · woodcut, NPG
Wealth at death under £800: probate, 12 July 1878, *CGPLA Eng. & Wales*

Hardy, Sir Thomas Masterman, baronet (1769–1839), naval officer, second son of Joseph Hardy of Portesham, Dorset, and his wife, Nanny, daughter of Thomas Masterman of Kingston, Dorset, was born at Martin's Town, near Dorchester, on 5 April 1769. In 1781 he entered the navy on the brig *Helena*, but he left her in April 1782 and for the next three years was at school, though on the books of the guardships *Seaford* and *Carnatic*. He was afterwards a few years in the merchant service, but in February 1790 he was appointed to the *Hebe*. From her he was moved to the sloop *Tisiphone* with Captain Anthony Hunt, whom he followed to the frigate *Amphitrite* in May 1793, and in her went to the Mediterranean. On 10 November 1793 he was promoted lieutenant of the frigate *Meleager* (Captain Charles Tyler), attached during the following years to the squadron off Genoa under the immediate orders of Horatio Nelson, whose acquaintance Hardy reportedly then first made. In June 1794 Captain George Cockburn succeeded to the command of the *Meleager*, and in August 1796, on being transferred to the *Minerve*, took Hardy with him. Hardy was still there in December 1796, when Nelson hoisted his broad pennant on her, and was with her in her encounter with the *Sabina*. When the *Sabina* surrendered, lieutenants Culverhouse and Hardy were sent to her with the prize crew; and the gallant way in which they afterwards drew the Spanish squadron away from the *Minerve*, defending the prize until dismasted, earned the praise of Nelson. Culverhouse and Hardy became prisoners of war, but they were exchanged, rejoining the *Minerve* at Gibraltar. On 10 February 1797, as the frigate was passing through the straits with the Spanish fleet in chase, Hardy jumped into the jolly boat to save a drowning man. The boat was carried by the current towards the leading Spanish ship. 'By

Sir Thomas Masterman Hardy, baronet (1769–1839), by Richard Evans, 1833–4

God,' said Nelson, 'I'll not lose Hardy! Back the mizen topsail!' This bold measure caused the Spanish ship to hesitate and shorten sail, enabling the boat to reach the frigate in safety. The *Minerve* rejoined the fleet three days later and served at the battle of Cape St Vincent on the 14th.

In May 1797 the *Lively* and *Minerve*, looking into the Bay of Santa Cruz, discovered there a French brig of war, the *Mutine*, which was cut out on the 29th by the boats of the frigates under the command of Hardy, who was at once promoted by Lord St Vincent to command the prize. On 5 June 1798 Hardy, in the *Mutine*, joined Nelson near Elba, announcing the approach of reinforcement under Captain Thomas Troubridge; and he was present at the battle of Abu Qir Bay, immediately after which he was promoted to the *Vanguard*, Nelson's flagship. In the *Vanguard*, and afterwards in the *Foudroyant*, Hardy continued with Nelson at Naples and Palermo until October 1799, when he was appointed to the frigate *Princess Charlotte*, in which he returned to England. In 1801 he was again with Nelson as flag captain in the *San Josef*, and afterwards in the Baltic in the *St George*; and although the size of the *St George* prevented her taking part in the battle of Copenhagen, Hardy the night before sounded close up to and around the enemy's ships. His soundings were correct, and it was by deviating from his route, on the pilots' advice, that some of the ships grounded. On Nelson being relieved by Vice-Admiral Charles Morice Pole, Hardy remained in the *St George* and returned in her to England. He was then appointed to the *Isis*, and in the following spring to the *Amphion*, in which, in May 1803, he took Nelson out to the

Mediterranean, moved with him to the *Victory* in July, and continued as flag captain during the long blockade of Toulon and the pursuit of the combined fleet to the West Indies. He was still in command of the *Victory* when Nelson again embarked on her on 14 September 1805, and in the absence of a captain of the fleet acted virtually as such before and at the battle of Trafalgar. With Captain Henry Blackwood he witnessed Nelson's last will, was with Nelson when the latter was shot, and was frequently with him during his dying hours. It was to him that Nelson's dying words, 'Kiss me, Hardy', were addressed (R. Southey, *Life of Nelson*, 1813, ch. 9). Nelson's body was sent home in the *Victory*, and at the funeral on 9 January 1806 Hardy carried the 'banner of emblems'.

On 4 February Hardy was created a baronet, and in the spring was appointed to the *Triumph*, which he commanded for three years on the North American station under Sir George Cranfield Berkeley, whose daughter, Anne Louisa Emily, he married at Halifax, Nova Scotia, in 1807. They subsequently had three daughters: Louisa-Georgina, Emily-Georgina, and Mary-Charlotte. In May 1809 he was appointed to the *Barfleur*, in which Berkeley hoisted his flag as commander-in-chief at Lisbon, and he continued in that post until September 1812. In August 1812 he was appointed to the *Ramillies*, in which he was again sent to the North American station. On 25 June 1813, while in command of a squadron off New London, blockading an American squadron under Captain Stephen Decatur, he captured a schooner, apparently laden with provisions. Hardy, possibly remembering an attempt made thirty-seven years before, ordered her to be secured alongside another prize, and while this was being done she blew up, killing a lieutenant and ten seamen: she was an explosion vessel.

In January 1815 Hardy was nominated a KCB; he returned to England in June, and from 1816 to 1819 commanded the yacht *Princess Augusta*. On 12 August 1819 he was appointed commodore and commander-in-chief in South America, with his broad pennant in the *Superb*. The wars of independence and the different interests involved made the command one of difficulty and delicacy, and Hardy's tact won the approval of the Admiralty and the public. He returned to England at the beginning of 1824. On 27 May 1825 he became a rear-admiral, and in December 1826, with his flag in the *Wellesley*, he escorted the expeditionary force to Lisbon. On his return he commanded an experimental squadron from the *Sibylle* and later the *Pyramus*. On 21 October 1827 he struck his flag and was not employed again at sea.

In November 1830 Hardy joined the Admiralty board as first sea lord under Sir James Graham, and on 13 September 1831 he was appointed a GCB. Hardy refused to enter parliament and adopted a purely professional view of his duties; his absence from the House of Commons was a source of whig complaint. He favoured larger and more powerfully armed vessels of all classes, and the introduction of steam warships. Working with the surveyor of the navy, Sir William Symonds, he increased the sailing performance and fighting strength of the battle fleet, which

his experience convinced him was the key to naval superiority. He left office in April 1834, when the post of governor of the Royal Naval Hospital at Greenwich fell vacant, in disgust at the excessive economies pursued by Graham. He was appointed governor of the hospital, the king agreeing on the understanding that in a war before would return to active service. The rest of his life was devoted to the pensioners under his care, improving their treatment and abolishing the yellow coat with red sleeves, worn as a punishment for drunkenness on a Sunday. He became a vice-admiral on 10 January 1837. He died on 20 September 1839 at the hospital and was buried on the 28th in its old cemetery. His widow and daughters survived him, but without male issue the baronetcy became extinct. An imposing memorial pillar was erected to his memory on Black Down, above Portesham, in Dorset. Hardy's enduring fame rests on his connection with Nelson, but his subsequent service afloat and at the Admiralty revealed a man of outstanding good sense and judgement, and this was reflected in his refusal to adopt a party political line on naval expenditure.

J. K. LAUGHTON, *rev.* ANDREW LAMBERT

Sources A. M. Broadley and R. G. Bartelot, *Nelson's Hardy: his life, letters and friends* (1909) · A. D. Lambert, *The last sailing battlefleet: maintaining naval mastery, 1815–1850* (1991) · C. J. Bartlett, *Great Britain and sea power, 1815–1853* (1963) · C. K. Webster, *Britain and the independence of Latin America* (1938) · G. S. Graham and R. A. Humphreys, eds., *The navy and South America, 1807–1823*, Navy RS, 104 (1962) · W. James, *The naval history of Great Britain, from the declaration of war by France, in February 1793, to the accession of George IV, in January 1820*, [2nd edn], 6 vols. (1826) · J. H. Briggs, *Naval administrations, 1827 to 1892: the experience of 65 years*, ed. Lady Briggs (1898) · J. De Kay, *The battle of Stonington* (1990) · *GM*, 2nd ser., 12 (1839), 434, 650–52 · *United Service Journal*, 3 (1839), 383 · *The dispatches and letters of Vice-Admiral Lord Viscount Nelson*, ed. N. H. Nicolas, 7 vols. (1844–6) · J. Marshall, *Royal naval biography*, 2/1 (1824), 153

Archives NA Scot., corresp. with Sir Alexander Cochrane; corresp. with Thomas, Lord Cochrane · NMM, letters; letters to J. C. Manfield; letters to Sir William Parker · Portsmouth Museums and Records Service, letters to Edward Thorne · Royal Naval Museum, Portsmouth, letters to Henry Chamberlain and Lady Chamberlain

Likenesses oils, *c*.1801, NMM · A. W. Devis, oils, 1805–7, NMM · D. Pelligrini, portrait, 1809, NMM · R. Evans, oils, 1833–4, NMM [*see illus.*] · W. Behnes, marble bust, 1836, Royal Collection · W. Behnes, bust, 1843, Greenwich Palace Chapel · L. F. Abbott, oils, Gov. Art Coll. · I. Hill, group portrait, oils (Nelson's funeral procession from Greenwich to Whitehall; after C. A. Pugin), NMM · engraving (after Hill), NMM

Wealth at death under £25,000: *GM*

Hardy, William (*d.* 1832), horologist, was apparently Scottish, but nothing is known of his place and date of birth nor of his early life and training. Yet by 1805 he was sufficiently renowned to be one of the fifteen eminent watchmakers recruited by the board of longitude to assess the merits of the rival chronometric claims of John Arnold (*d.* 1799) and Thomas Earnshaw (1749–1829), and in the following years he regularly received awards from the Society of Arts for ingenious inventions in horology. None ever saw general adoption, due largely to trade conservatism, but the best must be recorded here.

Hardy was the first practical horologist in England, and

probably anywhere, to make comparatively accurate cyc-loidal cutters for wheels and pinions. His patterns were supplied to the famous Thomas Leyland (1790–1861) of Prescot, Lancashire, who, according to D. S. Torrens, pro-duced without doubt the finest horological gearings that have ever been known. At the time of the 1862 Inter-national Exhibition in London the great Victorian horolo-gist Charles Frodsham wrote: 'the train of wheel-work in Hardy's regulators is among the best in England, and the shape of the wheels and pinions makes the most perfect gearing I have ever witnessed' (Frodsham, 10). Hardy's car-eer reached its apogee in 1811 thanks to the truly remark-able performance of an astronomical regulator clock with a very delicate detached spring-pallet escapement made for the Royal Observatory, Greenwich. The astronomer royal, Nevil Maskelyne, had in 1807 tested its prototype at Greenwich with most promising results. Unfortunately, he died before the new regulator and a new mural circle by Edward Troughton could be used together. His succes-sor, John Pond, was at first satisfied with Hardy's clock even though its escapement needed frequent cleaning by its maker.

Good reports reached the ears of astronomers and scien-tists everywhere. Among the first was Ferdinand Hassler, a distinguished Swiss geodesist who had emigrated to America in 1805 and who in 1812 was in London seeking equipment for a survey of the east coast of the United States. He ordered from Hardy two regulators of the Greenwich type, together with box chronometers and special timers. Hardy's reputation was established. He received orders for regulators and chronometers from both observatories and amateur astronomers. In 1820 out-standingly good clock rates were recorded at Greenwich, Sandhurst, and Vilna. The celebrated astronomer William Pearson acquired a Hardy regulator in 1816 and published an illustrated description of the type in 1829. Hassler had done the same in 1824.

In 1823 Pond moved Hardy's regulator to the transit room, thus making it the most important clock in the world. In 1830, however, his records show that it had 'accelerated on its mean by nearly 4s per day'. Hardy, per-haps ill, ignored two notices to attend. Had he then simply cleaned the escapement, events would almost certainly have turned out differently. In his absence his detached escapement was removed by the envious E. J. Dent and replaced by a conventional deadbeat one. Hardy's regula-tor at the Cape observatory soon suffered the same indig-nity. Pearson's clock and those at Vilna, Cambridge, and Fyvie continued to perform well although, one by one (and in one case as late as c.1990), their fragile escape-ments were broken by inexpert handling. Hardy died at his home, 5 Wood Street, Cold Bath Square, Clerkenwell, London, on 12 November 1832. CHARLES R. P. ALLIX

Sources N. Maskelyne, *Account of the going of Mr William Hardy's clock with detatched escapement at the Royal Observatory*, 1807, CUL, RGO 14 • W. Hardy, Letters to G. Gilpin, Secretary of the Board of Longitude, CUL, RGO 14, 8 Jan 1807; 12 May 1807; 31 May 1808 • Royal Greenwich Observatory, *Public trials and improvements of clocks and chronometers*, 1779–1826, Royal Greenwich Observatory Arch-ives, 14/1, 200; 14/23, 239–42 • W. Hardy, *Communications of Inventions to the Society of Arts*, 38 (1821), 165–85 [see also vols. 1804–20] • C. Frodsham, *Catalogue of the International Exhibition: class 15, horo-logical instruments* (1862), 10 • 'To form a templet, or pattern-tooth, to facilitate the application of the cycloid and epicycloid to the teeth of racks, wheels, pinions &c', T. Gill, *Gill's machinery improved ...* (1839), 12–19 • *GM*, 1st ser., 102/2 (1832), 580 • C. R. P. Allix, 'Wil-liam Hardy and his spring-pallet regulators ... how Hardy's regu-lators inhibited sales of similar clocks by Thomas Reid', *Antiquar-ian Horology and the Proceedings of the Antiquarian Horological Society*, 18 (1989–90), 607–29 [see also 19 (1990–91), 92, for author's letter correcting certain factual misprints] • F. R. Hassler, 'Papers on vari-ous subjects connected with the survey of the coast of the United States', *Transactions of the American Philosophical Society*, new ser., 2 (1825) • W. Pearson, *An introduction to practical astronomy*, 2 (1829), 304–15 • A. J. Turner, 'Documents illustrative of the history of Eng-lish horology, II: the cost of William Hardy's regulator clock for Greenwich Observatory, 1811', *Antiquarian Horology and the Proceed-ings of the Antiquarian Horological Society*, 11 (1978–9), 615–17 • C. Wood, 'What's wrong with Hardy's escapement?', *Antiquarian Horology and the Proceedings of the Antiquarian Horological Society*, 9 (1974–6), 882–95 • C. Wood, 'What's wrong with Hardy's escape-ment? A reappraisal', *Antiquarian Horology and the Proceedings of the Antiquarian Horological Society*, 20 (1992–3), 315–23 • T. Reid, letters to B. L. Vulliamy, 1805–26, Inst. CE • D. S. Torrens, personal letter to J. E. Coleman, USA, priv. coll. • T. Gill, 'To apply the epicycloid to the teeth of wheels and watch-work', *Tech-nical Repository*, 1 (1822), 450–60 • T. Gill, 'On the successful applica-tion of the epicycloidal curves to the teeth of wheels and pinions of the time-pieces. By Mr William Hardy', *Technical Repository*, 5 (1824), 257–8 • C. R. P. Allix, 'The astronomical regulator clocks made by William Hardy', unpublished typescript, 1949, priv. coll. • W. J. Pinks, *The history of Clerkenwell*, ed. E. J. Wood, 2nd edn (1881) • D. S. Torrens, 'Rule of thumb', *Horological Journal*, 80/958 (1938), 20, 30 • J. Pond, *Astronomical observations made at the Royal Observatory, Greenwich, in the years 1811–1813*, 1 (1815) • D. Howse, *Greenwich obser-vatory, 3: The buildings and instruments (1675–1975)* (1975)

Archives BL, communications to scientific journals • CUL • NMM, Royal Observatory, Greenwich • RSA, communications to the Royal Society of Arts | Inst. CE, Thomas Reid, letters to B. L. Vulliamy

Hardy, Sir William (1807–1887), archivist, was born in Jamaica on 6 July 1807, the fourth son of Captain Thomas Bartholomew Price Hardy (*d*. 1813), of the 1st battalion, Royal Artillery, and his second wife, Frances Duffus (*b*. 1776), of Kingston, Jamaica. He moved to England in 1811 with his brother Thomas Duffus *Hardy, and was edu-cated at Fotheringhay, Northamptonshire, and later at Boulogne. In February 1823 he obtained a clerkship in the record office in the Tower of London, and like his brother Thomas, who had held a similar post since 1819, he was trained in the care and uses of archives by the keeper of the records there, Henry Petrie (1772–1842). The brothers subsequently ran a record agency in partnership. They also worked as transcribers for Francis Palgrave (1788–1861), with whom they quarrelled, and nursed a lasting animus against him.

In 1832 Hardy was appointed clerk of the records of the duchy of Lancaster, a rich archive kept mainly at the Savoy. His stipend was small, but his duties were corres-pondingly unexacting, and he was left free to continue his practice as a record agent. Robert Somerville remarked that over almost forty years of service Hardy 'left singu-larly little trace of his activities' ('The duchy of Lancaster records', *TRHS*, 4th ser., 29, 1947, B) at the Savoy. He did nevertheless spend some time in arranging and listing the records, and published *Charters of the Duchy of Lancaster* in 1845. His only other substantial publication was an edition of the historical collections of Jean de Waurin, which appeared in the Rolls Series as *Recueil des croniques et anchiennes istories de la Grant Bretagne par Jehan de Waurin, seigneur du Forestal*, and in translation as *Collection of Chronicles by John de Waurin*, between 1864 and 1891. In his time at the Savoy, however, he built up a substantial and profitable consultancy, specializing in peerage cases, and in foreshore and common rights. On 31 December 1840 Hardy married Eliza Caroline Seymour Lee, of Cholderton, Wiltshire. There were two sons of the marriage, one of whom, William John Hardy (d. 1922), an antiquary and editor, wrote the lives of his father and uncle in the *Dictionary of National Biography*.

In 1870, after some fifteen years of intermittent negotiation, the Public Record Office was able to take in the duchy records, which the queen released as a gift to the nation. Hardy then joined the staff of the office as an assistant keeper. In 1878, on his brother's death, he was made deputy keeper, and was appointed to the Historical Manuscripts Commission in the same year.

It fell to Hardy to implement the act passed in 1877 to allow the selective destruction of governmental records which were held to be of no historical value. A committee of inspecting officers was set up, of whom one was Hardy himself and another an assistant keeper who was required to be a barrister of at least seven years' standing. The office was already reviewing the records of the courts of common law, and the first schedule was submitted for parliamentary approval early in 1882, together with a description of the categories of records reviewed, and a lucid account of the processes of the court of queen's bench. Over the next decade the exercise was extended to more than thirty departments. There was at the time some public criticism of the principle of destruction, and in the course of a century opinions on the criteria of historical interest have naturally changed, but there is no doubt that some measure of control was needed.

Hardy, who was knighted in 1883, secured more generous scales of pay for all grades in the office, though at the cost of some reduction of the establishment, and he also persuaded the Treasury of the uniquely demanding nature of the department's work. He was, however, a less energetic man than his brother, and in his last years was in poor health. He left many matters of policy haphazardly to his subordinates, and added no impress of his own. After consulting the master of the rolls, Sir William Baliol Brett (later Viscount Esher), he approached Henry Maxwell Lyte (1848–1940), and asked him whether he would accept the deputy keepership. When Lyte agreed to act, Hardy resigned his post in January 1886. He died on 17 March 1887 at his home, Milton Cottage, St German's Road, Forest Hill, London.   G. H. MARTIN

Sources *DNB* · J. B. Payne, *Armorial of Jersey*, 2 vols. (1859–65) · J. D. Cantwell, *The Public Record Office, 1838–1958* (1991) · m. cert. · R. Somerville, 'The duchy of Lancaster records', *TRHS*, 4th ser., 29 (1947), 1–17, 13

Archives Herts. ALS, professional papers | Bodl. Oxf., corresp. with Sir Thomas Phillipps
Likenesses photograph, repro. in Cantwell, *Public Record Office*, figure 8
Wealth at death £4574 13s. 2d.: probate, 17 June 1887, *CGPLA Eng. & Wales*

Hardy, William (1852–1928). *See under* Hardy, John James (1854–1932).

Hardy, Sir William Bate (1864–1934), biologist and food scientist, was born at Erdington, Warwickshire, on 6 April 1864, the only child of William Hardy, of Llangollen, Denbighshire, and his wife, Sarah, eldest daughter of William Bate. As a boy Hardy was sent to sea with the Brixham fishermen—he retained a love of the sea throughout his life. He was educated at Framlingham College and entered Gonville and Caius College, Cambridge, in 1884. He was elected scholar in 1885 and was awarded a first class in the natural sciences tripos (zoology) in 1888. He was elected a fellow of the college in 1892, and was a tutor from 1900 to 1918. In 1898 he married Alice Mary, eldest daughter of Gerrard Brown Finch, barrister; they had a son and two daughters.

Hardy was a lecturer in histology within the department of physiology at Cambridge from 1898 to 1929. Sceptical of the significance of much that was seen, after fixing and staining, under the microscope, he began studying the effect of such treatment on colloidal systems. His important discoveries included the stability of colloid sols in relation to their electric charge, the theory of flocculation, the nature and importance of the iso-electric point, the theory of protein ampholytes, and the electric charges of the positive and negative colloid ions. According to Sir Ernest Rutherford, 'The modern theory of protein solutions … is very largely due to his pioneer work in that field' (E. Rutherford, Presidential address to Royal Society on awarding the royal medal to Hardy, 1926).

Hardy went on to study the molecular physics of films, surfaces, and boundary conditions, passing on to static friction and so to the action of lubricants. 'For the first time … the dependence of friction and lubrication on the structure and molecular orientation of surface films and the force-fields of molecules in relation to their structure and polarity have been elucidated' (ibid.). He had been elected FRS in 1902 and was the society's biological secretary from 1915 to 1925; he gave the Croonian lecture in 1905, 'On globulins'. In 1925–6 he became the first biologist to give the Bakerian lecture and to be awarded the royal medal.

In 1915, when Britain was dangerously short of food, Hardy organized the food (war) committee of the Royal Society, which did very important work in advising the government. He seemed a strange choice to those in the food industry, for he knew little of food and its deterioration. However, he believed strongly in scientific method and recognized how little was known about the changes occurring when food was preserved. After the formation of the Department of Scientific and Industrial Research he instigated the Food Investigation Board, becoming its first chairman (1917–28) and director of food investigation

(1917–34). He was also responsible for creating the Low Temperature Research Station at Cambridge of which he became superintendent (1922–34), the Torry Research Station, and the Ditton Laboratory. From 1919 to 1931 he was chairman of the advisory committee on fisheries of the Development Commission which issued a very valuable series of confidential reports on fisheries (including freshwater fisheries) whereby the fishery departments were strengthened and great progress made.

The organizations which Hardy founded bear the stamp of his conviction that the science of food is not simply physics, chemistry, and engineering, as previously considered, but that of living material, stating, 'one thing has been, I think, forgotten, … namely that the storage of food is primarily a biological problem and the function of the engineer is merely to express in practice biological facts' (W. B. Hardy, *Physics in the Food Industry*, 1927). Hardy 'never wavered in his conviction that no solution of a practical problem was worth while unless it was based on an adequate knowledge of the fundamental science that lay behind it'; to him biology and molecular physics were equally fundamental. His *Collected Scientific Papers* covering the years 1891 to 1934, edited by Rideal, was published in 1936.

Hardy was later disappointed by the reluctance of the British food industry to adopt his scientific results, but the colonies proved much more receptive. Hardy placed the growing resources of his group at the disposal of the various colonial administrations and trained and encouraged their research students. He was knighted in 1925. He received honorary degrees from the universities of Oxford, Aberdeen, Birmingham, and Edinburgh. In 1931 Hardy was Abraham Flexner lecturer at Vanderbilt University, USA. At the time of his death, at his home, 5 Grange Road, Cambridge, on 23 January 1934, he was president of the British Association, and had been a trustee of the National Portrait Gallery since 1922.

All his life Hardy was an adventurer in new fields, finding joy in fresh discovery, content not to interfere with others if they wished to exploit and profit by what he had found. He was large and energetic, believing strongly in self-reliance and initiative. One of the finest yachtsmen of his time, he combined with perfect seamanship a capacity for instant decision in emergency. His first yacht, *Cockatoo*, was equipped as a floating laboratory for marine biology: his last, *Estrella*, served as a houseboat on the Helford River in his later years. He became a master mariner and is supposed to have been the model for the hero of Erskine Childers's novel *The Riddle of the Sands*. He was survived by his wife.   A. V. Hill, *rev.* Isobel Falconer

Sources F. G. H. and F. E. S., *Obits. FRS*, 1 (1932–5), 327–33 · E. C. Bate-Smith, ed., *Sir W. B. Hardy, biologist, physicist and food scientist: centenary tributes* [1964] · *The Times* (24 Jan 1934) · *The Times* (25 Jan 1934) · private information (1949) · personal knowledge (1949) · *CGPLA Eng. & Wales* (1934)
Archives BL, corresp. with Sir William Ashley, Add. MS 42244 · CAC Cam., corresp. with A. V. Hill
Likenesses W. Stoneman, photograph, 1917, NPG · F. Dodd, charcoal, 1941 (after photograph by A. V. Hill), Gon. & Caius Cam. · A. V. Hill, photograph, Low Temperature Research Station, Cambridge; repro. in Bate-Smith, ed., *Sir W. B. Hardy*
Wealth at death £7271 17s. 6d.: probate, 1 March 1934, *CGPLA Eng. & Wales*

Hardyman, Lucius Ferdinand (1771–1834), naval officer, was the son of Thomas Hardyman (1736–1814) of Portsmouth, a captain in the army. His six brothers were all in the army, and three attained the rank of general. He entered the navy in 1781 on board the *Repulse*, with Captain Dumaresque, and in her was present at the battle of Dominica on 12 April 1782. In June he followed Dumaresque to the *Alfred*, and in 1783 returned to England. From 1791 to 1794 he served on the *Siren*, with captains Manley and Graham Moore. On 5 March 1795 he was promoted lieutenant, and appointed to the *Sibylle* under Captain Edward Cooke. He was first lieutenant of the *Sibylle* when, on the night of 28 February to 1 March 1799, she engaged the French frigate *Forte*, and he succeeded to the command when Cooke was mortally wounded. He won the action and was immediately promoted by Vice-Admiral Rainier to command the prize. From the East India Company, and from the insurance companies of Calcutta and Madras, he received three swords of honour.

On 27 January 1800 Hardyman was advanced to post rank, and continued to command the *Forte* on the East India station until, on 29 January 1801, she struck an uncharted rock going into the harbour of Jiddah, and became a total wreck. Hardyman was acquitted of all blame, but the master of the flagship, who was piloting her in, was sentenced to lose twelve months' seniority. In 1803 Hardyman commissioned the frigate *Unicorn*, which he commanded in 1805 on the West India station, in 1807 in the expedition against Montevideo under Sir Charles Stirling, and in 1809 in the Bay of Biscay under Lord Gambier. He was also present at the destruction of the French ships in Basque Roads on 11 April, when the *Unicorn* was one of the few ships actively engaged. He was afterwards transferred to the frigate *Armide*, which he commanded on the coast of France until the peace.

In 1815 Hardyman was made a CB; he commanded the *Ocean* from 1823 to 1825 as flag-captain to Lord Amelius Beauclerk, and became a rear-admiral on 22 July 1830. He married, on 29 December 1810, Charlotte, youngest daughter of John Travers of Bedford Place, London, a director of the East India Company; they had three daughters and one son, Lucius Heywood Hardyman, lieutenant 5th Bengal cavalry, who was killed on the retreat from Kabul in January 1842. Hardyman died on 17 April 1834 at his home, Cornwall Terrace, Regent's Park, London. His widow died, in her ninety-third year, in 1872.

J. K. Laughton, *rev.* Roger Morriss

Sources J. Marshall, *Royal naval biography*, 3/2 (1832), 245 · *United Service Journal*, 2 (1834), 218 · *GM*, 2nd ser., 1 (1834), 211 · private information (1890) · C. N. Parkinson, *War in the eastern seas, 1793–1815* (1954) · R. Muir, *Britain and the defeat of Napoleon, 1807–1815* (1996)

Hardyng, John (*b.* 1377/8, *d.* in or after 1464), chronicler and forger, is of unknown parentage, but was probably

John Hardyng (*b.* 1377/8, *d.* in or after 1464), manuscript painting

born in Northumberland. Almost all the details of his life are derived from his own writings. He says that he entered the household of Henry Percy (Hotspur) at the age of twelve, and remained there for the next thirteen years. His position in the employment of the Percys is unknown, but may have been of some consequence, since he was able to hear (or at least overhear) the first earl of Northumberland discussing the circumstances of Richard II's deposition, and he fought for the Percys in numerous border campaigns, including that of 1402 which culminated in the battle of Homildon Hill and siege of Cocklaws. Present when Hotspur was defeated and killed at Shrewsbury in 1403, Hardyng (who was then twenty-five) passed into the service of Sir Robert Umfraville, whom he greatly admired, and whose death in 1437 he lamented in the finest passage in his chronicle. He became constable of Warkworth Castle under Umfraville, with whom he served in France in 1415 and 1416. While in France, Hardyng attracted—or drew himself to—the attention of Henry V. Perhaps in response to Scottish raids into northern England in 1417, Henry wished to reassert English claims to suzerainty over Scotland, and accordingly sent

Hardyng there to find evidence in support of them. Hardyng spent three and a half years north of the border:

> On lyfes peryle, maymed, in grete distresse,
> With costages grete as was necessite.
> (BL, Lansdowne MS 204, fol. 3)

On one occasion he was pursued from Lanark to Ayr, and he claimed that his searches cost him 450 marks of his own money.

Back in England in the summer of 1421, Hardyng waited upon Henry V at the Bois de Vincennes in May 1422 with three documents, at least two of which—recording competitors to the Scottish throne submitting themselves to Edward I in 1291—he appears to have abstracted from the English treasury. As a reward for his efforts, Henry promised Hardyng the Northamptonshire manor of Geddington, but the king's death prevented this, greatly to Hardyng's disappointment. However, hoping for generosity from the government of Henry VI, Hardyng produced more documents in support of the English king's claims over Scotland, handing over six at Easthampstead in 1440, and a further six at Westminster in 1457. He may have returned to Scotland during these years, since he also produced a patent purporting to have been issued in March 1435 by James I, giving Hardyng a safe conduct to come to Scotland, and offering him 1000 gold marks for 'the thynges whiche we spake to yow of at Coldyngham' (Palgrave, *Documents and Records*, 376). However, it is just as likely that Hardyng, who by 1429 was living in Lincolnshire, and in 1434 was described as 'of Kyme' (the principal Umfraville manor in that county), had not in fact crossed the border again, for James's patent is certainly a forgery, and so are all the other documents produced in 1440 and 1457 (which were stored in the exchequer, in a box labelled 'Scocia Hardyng'). A principal motive for this campaign of falsehood was Hardyng's determination to secure his proper reward for his dubious services. Recorded in 1440 as living in the Augustinian priory at Kyme, maintained by a corrody, he continued to hanker after Geddington, even though in that same year, following the delivery of his second tranche of documents, he received a grant of £10 yearly from the Lincolnshire manor of Willoughton, specifically as the sum promised by Henry V 'for acquiring from the Scots evidences of the king's overlordship of Scotland' (*CPR, 1436–41*, 484–5). In 1451, so he claimed, he even received a writ of privy seal granting Geddington to him, but the chancellor, Cardinal John Kemp, refused to pass it. The handing over of his last six documents brought him a grant of £20 p.a. from Lincolnshire, but nothing further. His creative impulses may have been subdued by disappointment, for although he gave two documents to Edward IV at Leicester, probably in May 1462, these were copies of texts he had handed in earlier. By now a very old man, Hardyng must have lived into 1464, since his chronicle refers to Edward IV's queen, but he clearly stopped writing, and probably died, at about this time.

The work in which he referred to Queen Elizabeth Woodville was the second of two versions of a lengthy verse chronicle, relating the history of England from Brutus down to Hardyng's own time. The earlier, which contains nearly 2700 stanzas in rhyme-royal metre, is dedicated to Henry VI, and was doubtless handed over in 1457 with the last batch of forged documents. It survives in a manuscript (BL, Lansdowne MS 204) which shows every sign of being prepared for presentation to royalty, with capital letters picked out in gold, and a fine, if stylistically old-fashioned, illuminated 'pe de gre', representing the kings whose ancestry lay behind Edward III's claim to the throne of France. The second, which Hardyng must have begun soon after the completion of the first, and which contains just under 1800 stanzas, is for most of its length addressed to Richard, duke of York, but was plainly not finished before the duke's death in December 1460, for its closing verses appeal to Edward IV. The heavy stress laid in this revised version on Richard's and Edward's hereditary claim to the English throne may indicate that it was intended to serve as Yorkist propaganda. In fact the second version was never entirely completed; it survives in several texts, all of which contain metrical loose ends, indicating that Hardyng—who in one of them refers to himself as 'through age distillid in to debilite' (Riddy, 'John Hardyng in search of the grail', 428)—died before he finished work.

The two versions differ in more than length, dedications, and chronological range—the earlier concludes in 1436, the second in 1463. Thus the second version contains a more detailed account of Henry V's French wars, and of Sir Robert Umfraville's campaigns on the Anglo-Scottish borders in the years around 1420, but abbreviates the first version's recital of the virtues of Henry V, and lacks its moving eulogy of Umfraville altogether. And most notably they differ in their accounts of the deposition of Richard II and the usurpation of Henry IV. The first version describes Richard's overthrow as the result of a straightforward invasion by Henry of Lancaster, soon assisted by the Percys and others, as a result of which the king was arrested, deposed in parliament, and replaced. But the second version tells how on his return from exile Henry swore that he had only returned for his duchy, and thereby deceived the Percys, who subsequently rebelled in disgust. Yet the differences between the versions should not be overstated. Though understandably holding back from denouncing the grandfather of its dedicatee as a perjured usurper, the first version of Hardyng's chronicle does in fact contain a good deal of implicit criticism of Henry IV. And, in a series of comments, comparisons, and apostrophes, it is no less critical of the rule of Henry VI.

These interjections often appear in passages about mythical kings of early Britain, presented in distinctly anachronistic terms. And although they are technically skilled, showing that he was able to write in at least three different hands, and that he could falsify seals as well as documents, Hardyng's forgeries, too, are demonstrably lacking in historical perspective; his charter attributed to Malcolm Canmore, for instance, endows that eleventh-century king with a seal and a parliament. Yet his patent concern with the affairs of his own time sheds much light on Hardyng's outlook and personality. Taken as a whole, his work shows him to have been interested in heraldry, coins, and topography—the map of Scotland in the first version of his chronicle is the earliest separate map of that country to survive. In matters of religion he was conservative and hostile to Lollards, though himself occasionally given to speculation on such issues as predestination and divine foreknowledge. Though generally an undistinguished poet, Hardyng was a man of wide, if hardly deep, reading. He sometimes refers deferentially to authors in terms that make it clear that he had not in fact read them, but still seems to have used, among others, Nennius (referred to as Gildas), Bede, Geoffrey of Monmouth, John of Worcester, Henry of Huntingdon, Ranulf Higden, Peter Langtoft, John Gower, the *Gesta Henrici quinti*, legendary accounts of such figures as Joseph of Arimathea and St Helena, and at least one version of the *Brut*. He quotes the Latin Vulgate Bible, and appears to have known the poems of Chaucer and Lydgate. He probably also drew on northern tradition, as in his recurring references to the fortunes of the Umfravilles, and his sympathetic account of Andrew Harclay's fall.

Hardyng used this material in ways that illustrate his interests, and, indeed, his obsessions. These were interrelated. He wanted a reward for his services. He wanted the English king to conquer Scotland, which was the latter's rightful possession—as Hardyng's chronicle and forgeries set out to prove. And he wanted good government in England, both for its own sake (he was very much afraid of social disruption), and because stability at home would allow campaigns abroad, and above all in Scotland, which he believed could be conquered in three years, so recreating 'Great Britayne enclosed with a sea' (*Chronicle*, ed. Ellis, 179). And he would earn gratitude, and so his reward, by showing how this could be done, both in immediately practical terms—hence his production of a map—and through just and effective administration at home. To this end he used his chronicle to explain to Henry VI (rather less so to Richard of York and Edward IV, who presumably stood less in need of such advice) the distinguishing features of good kingship—co-operation with the barons, military success, low taxation (coupled with a willingness to live off his own, though with a display of splendour when necessary), and a constant readiness to do justice and maintain order. Arthur, and later Edward I and Henry V, were held up for admiration as models of kingship after Hardyng's heart. However pedestrian its verse, Hardyng's chronicle was evidently popular in its second version, and at least twelve manuscript texts survive. It was used by Malory, and later by Spenser, while Richard Grafton issued two printed versions in 1543, with a continuation by himself bringing the history of England down to his own time. Sir Henry Ellis published an edition of the second version of Hardyng's chronicle, based upon Grafton's edition with some additional material collated to it, in 1812. The first version, which gives the fullest access to Hardyng's idiosyncratic personality, remains unpublished.

HENRY SUMMERSON

Sources BL, Lansdowne MS 204 · *The chronicle of John Hardyng*, ed. H. Ellis (1812) · *Chancery records* · F. Palgrave, ed., *The antient kalendars and inventories of the treasury of his majesty's exchequer*, RC, 2 (1836) · F. Palgrave, ed., *Documents and records illustrating the history of Scotland* (1837) · E. L. G. Stones and G. G. Simpson, eds., *Edward I and the throne of Scotland, 1290–1296*, 2 (1978), 385–7 · C. L. Kingsford, 'The first version of Hardyng's chronicle', *EngHR*, 27 (1912), 462–82, 740–53 · C. L. Kingsford, *English historical literature in the fifteenth century* (1913) · A. Gransden, *Historical writing in England*, 2 (1982) · E. D. Kennedy, *A manual of the writings in Middle English, 1050–1500*, 8: *Chronicles and other historical writings*, ed. A. E. Hartung (1967) · F. Riddy, 'John Hardyng in search of the grail', *Arturus rex II*, ed. W. van Hoecke, G. Tourney, and W. Verbeke (1991), 419–29 · A. S. G. Edwards, 'The manuscripts and texts of the second version of John Hardyng's Chronicle', *England in the fifteenth century* [Harlaxton 1986], ed. D. Williams (1987), 75–84 · F. Riddy, 'John Hardyng's chronicle and the Wars of the Roses', *Arthurian Literature*, 12 (1993), 91–108 · *CPR, 1452–61; 1436–41*, 484–5 · *CEPR letters*, vol. 8 · BL, Harl. 661, fols. 152, 152v

Archives BL, Egerton MS 1992

Likenesses manuscript painting, Bodl. Oxf., MS Ashmole 34, facing p. 1 [*see illus.*]

Wealth at death £20 p.a. from crown estates in Lincolnshire (?): *CPR, 1452–61*, 393

Hare, Alan Victor (1919–1995), army intelligence officer and businessman, was born at 14 Bryanston Square, London, on 14 March 1919, the fourth of the four sons and six children of Richard Granville Hare, Viscount Ennismore and later fourth earl of Listowel (1866–1931), who listed his occupation as 'big game hunter', and his wife, Freda, daughter of Francis Vanden-Bempde-Johnstone, second Baron Derwent.

After education at Eton College and New College, Oxford, Hare was commissioned into the Irish Guards in March 1940. He transferred to the Household Cavalry in 1941 and served in Cyprus, the Levant, and the western desert. In 1943 he volunteered for the Special Operations Executive (SOE), Britain's secret sabotage organization. Earmarked as staff captain in Brigadier E. F. ('Trotsky') Davies's mission to help the Albanian partisans, he parachuted into occupied Albania in October 1943. After being chased by Germans and Albanian quislings through the snowbound mountains for much of the winter, Davies and many of his headquarters mission were finally caught in January 1944. Hare and another officer, Lieutenant-Colonel Arthur Nicholls, together managed to evade their hunters, but at a terrible cost. Nicholls succumbed to his frost-bitten wounds and was awarded a posthumous George Cross. Hare received an immediate Military Cross for his 'magnificent example of coolness and courage' during the ambush of Davies's party and his efforts to treat Nicholls (private information).

Hare remained in Albania until the autumn of 1944. Recovered from his own frost-bitten injuries, he worked through the spring and summer with both communist-led partisans and nationalist guerrillas, becoming one of the few SOE officers to spend extended periods with both groups. Interestingly, in view of his later activities, he was convinced of the superior dynamism and fighting ability of the partisans over the nationalists.

After leaving Albania, Hare was sent by the SOE to the east, where he served in Ceylon, and finished his military service in Thailand as a lieutenant-colonel in charge of the far eastern publicity mission and working as press attaché. In 1945 he married Jill Pegotty North. They had one son and one daughter.

After a brief spell in freelance journalism, in 1947 Hare joined the Secret Intelligence Service (SIS), where his wartime knowledge of Albania was much in demand. During his early years with the service, when he was based mostly in London and Greece, he was involved in the ill-fated efforts of the SIS and the Central Intelligence Agency (CIA) to undermine Enver Hoxha's communist regime in Albania: the first cold war attempt at 'rolling back' communism through covert force. Later his SIS career took him to Tehran, where he worked for the return to power of the shah of Iran. Other postings included Geneva in 1953 and Athens, where he was head of station, for three years from 1957. In 1960 he returned to London and was appointed head of the political intelligence section of the SIS. In the following year, although seemingly well set for a long and successful career in the service, he applied for voluntary retirement.

From 1961 to 1963 Alan Hare worked for Industrial and Trade Fairs, a subsidiary of the Pearson Group, before embarking on a rapid rise through the management ranks of the *Financial Times* (FT), also owned by Pearson. Michael John Hare (b. 1938), grandson of the second Viscount Cowdray and later the second Viscount Blakenham, was the head of the Pearson family and one-time chairman and chief executive of the group. He was also Hare's son-in-law and nephew, being the son of Hare's brother John Hugh *Hare, first Viscount Blakenham (1911–1982) and husband of Hare's daughter, Marcia, from 1965. Alan Hare was managing director of the FT from 1971 to 1978, chief executive from 1975 to 1983, and chairman from 1978 to 1984. He also held directorships at Pearson Longman Ltd from 1975 to 1983, and Industrial and Trade Fairs from 1977 to 1983, being chairman of the latter from 1979 to 1983. Unkind remarks were made in some quarters that Alan Hare owed his appointments to family connections. It was not denied that he was 'family'; what is certain is that Hare brought to his new career the same integrity, determination, and professionalism that made him such an asset in his earlier secret work.

With the retirement of Lord Drogheda in 1975, Hare inherited control of a newspaper confronted by union militancy and almost crippled by overstaffing, restrictive practices, obsolete machinery, and the general stagnation of the British press industry. One of Hare's proposed solutions was to internationalize the paper, and in 1979, despite some scepticism by the FT board, he launched its European edition in Frankfurt. After early losses and other teething problems the European edition became the cornerstone of the FT's subsequent recovery and growth. But when striking printworkers forced the paper off the stands for ten weeks in the summer of 1983, Hare faced problems he was less able to circumvent. His response, particularly his proposed deal with a rival print union to exclude the *FT*'s printworkers and instead print in continental Europe, and his idea of using a non-union plant in Nottingham, drew much criticism. Eventually Pearson gave in. The strike cost the group £6 million and Hare retired shortly afterwards.

Hare then took a job that gave him enormous pleasure and to which he was ideally suited: president of Château-Latour, at that time another of Pearson's concerns. He held the post from 1983 until 1990, living with his wife in a small château on the Gironde. Until 1989 he still maintained an active interest in the press, holding a directorship at *The Economist* from 1975 and acting as chairman of the journal from 1985. He was also a director of the English National Opera (1982–8) and from 1985 served as a trustee of Reuters.

Bespectacled since childhood and of slight, slim build, Alan Hare was a gentle, cultured man of great natural charm and kindness. Never wholly comfortable in the public eye, he loathed making speeches and perhaps lacked the aggressiveness that the world of commerce could demand. But his substantial intellect and reserves of physical and mental stamina were proven time and again, and he faced cancer in later life with typical courage and a steady faith. He died of the disease at his London home, 53 Rutland Gate, on 10 April 1995.   RODERICK BAILEY

Sources *Financial Times* (12 April 1995) · *The Independent* (13 April 1995) · *The Times* (15 April 1995) · E. F. Davies, *Illyrian venture: the story of the British military mission to enemy-occupied Albania, 1943–44* (1952) · private information (2004) [SOE adviser] · b. cert. · d. cert. · *CGPLA Eng. & Wales* (1995) · WWW
Wealth at death £113,419: probate, 24 July 1995, *CGPLA Eng. & Wales*

Hare, Augustus John Cuthbert (1834–1903), author, born on 13 March 1834, at the Villa Strozzi, Rome, was the youngest child in a family of three sons and two daughters born to Francis George Hare (1786–1842) of Herstmonceaux, Sussex, and his wife, Anne Frances, daughter of Sir John Dean Paul of Rodborough and sister of Sir John Dean *Paul (1802–1868). Augustus William *Hare and Julius Charles *Hare were his uncles. In August 1835 he was adopted by his godmother, Maria, daughter of Oswald Leycester, rector of Stoke upon Tern, Shropshire, and widow of his uncle, Augustus Hare. His godmother made her home in Herstmonceaux parish and his parents renounced all further claim on him. The account he gives of his childhood in his autobiography has unwisely been taken at face value by some authors, and his account of its grimness sits ill with his obvious devotion to his adoptive mother and his wish to be buried beside her. Hare was educated at Harnish rectory from 1843 to 1846 and was sent in 1847 to Harrow School, but ill health compelled him to leave the following year. He then studied under private tutors until in 1853 he matriculated at University College, Oxford, graduating BA in 1857. After living abroad, mostly in Italy, from June 1857 until November 1858, he returned to England and in the following year undertook for John Murray a handbook of *Berks, Bucks and Oxfordshire* (1860). A

Handbook to Durham, in the same series, followed in 1863. His adoptive mother's failing health then made residence in a warm climate necessary, and, except for occasional visits to England, he remained abroad, mostly in Italy and the Riviera, from 1863 until June 1870. In November of that year Maria died, and Hare sought to perpetuate her memory in *Memorials of a Quiet Life* (3 vols., 1872–6). The book ran into eighteen editions, and inaugurated a series of biographies written by him in the same mildly deferential key and which found an audience despite criticisms of their prolixity.

Hare's biographies were outnumbered by his guidebooks, for which with his autobiography he is now chiefly remembered. They combined his own lively and often witty observations with extracts from other books, often more copious than was justifiable. Freeman charged Hare with appropriating in *Cities of Northern and Central Italy* (3 vols., 1876) articles of his in the *Saturday Review*. He was accused, too, of copying Murray's *Handbook to Northern Italy*, and was involved in consequence in legal proceedings. But despite these complaints Hare's practice remained unaltered. His writings earned him considerable wealth: he left more than £22,000 in his will, having spent very considerable sums enlarging his home at Holmhurst, St Leonards, Sussex, and on his library and collection of works of art. He was a competent watercolourist, and he illustrated many of his own works. An exhibition of his watercolour sketches took place in London in 1902.

Hare enjoyed society and when in England spent much time visiting country houses, where he was well known as a raconteur of ghost stories. His large circle of distinguished friends included Oscar II, king of Sweden, who decorated him with the order of St Olaf in 1878. His *The Story of my Life* (6 vols., 1896–1900) was described in 1912 as 'a long, tedious, and indiscreet autobiography' (*DNB*). By the late twentieth century, however, Hare was undergoing something of a revival. A society of enthusiasts and collectors of his works was formed: a one-volume condensed edition of his autobiography was edited by A. Miller and J. Papp in 1995, and it and the original proved a useful source for those interested in country-house life in the later nineteenth century. The play *Eminent Victorian* by James Roose-Evans (1996) is based on the life of Hare. He died, unmarried, on 22 January 1903 at Holmhurst, and was buried in the graveyard of All Saints' Church, Herstmonceaux, Sussex.   ELIZABETH BAIGENT

Sources *DNB* · *The Athenaeum* (31 Jan 1903), 147 · *The Times* (23 Jan 1903) · *The Times* (27 Jan 1903) · *The Times* (28 Jan 1903) · S. Leslie, *Men were different* (1937) · *WW* (1903) · *Peculiar people: the story of my life: Augustus Hare*, ed. A. Miller and J. Papp (1995) [condensed edn of his 6 vol. autobiography] · *Augustus Hare in Italy*, ed. G. Henderson (1977) · augustus-hare.tripod.com, 9 May 2001 · www.umilta.net/hare.html, 9 May 2001 · M. Barnes, *Augustus Hare* (1985)
Archives E. Sussex RO, personal inventory; sketchbooks | Borth. Inst., corresp. with second Viscount Halifax · Royal Palace, Stockholm, letters to Gustav V
Likenesses G. da Pozzo, portrait, University College, Oxford · woodburytype photograph, NPG

Wealth at death £22,157 17s. od.: probate, 17 April 1903, *CGPLA Eng. & Wales*

Hare, Augustus William (1792–1834), Church of England clergyman, second son of Francis Hare-Naylor (1753–1815) of Herstmonceaux, Sussex, and his first wife, Georgiana (c.1755–1806), daughter of Jonathan Shipley, was born at Rome on 17 November 1792. He received his names from his godfathers, Prince Augustus Frederick and Sir William Jones. At five years old he was adopted by Anna Maria (d. 1829), Sir William's widow, his mother's eldest sister, and his parents took him to England to place him in her care. Henceforward his home was entirely with his aunt at Worting House, near Basingstoke, and he paid only occasional visits to his parents.

After boarding at Revd L. M. Stretch's school at Twyford, Lady Jones sent Hare to Winchester College as a commoner in 1804, and he went into college at election 1806. Weak health prevented his especially distinguishing himself, but in 1810 he was elected to a vacancy at New College, where he held a fellowship until 1829. With his schoolfriends he established one of the first Oxford debating clubs, the Attic Society, whose members included Thomas Arnold. Lady Jones wished him to qualify himself for the rich family living of Herstmonceaux by taking orders, and he incurred her extreme displeasure by the repugnance he felt to such a step. In the last years of his undergraduate life he offended the college authorities by an attempt to extinguish the privileges of founder's kin at Winchester and New College, and he printed an attack, in the form of a letter to his friend George Martin, on the exceptional privilege which permitted New College men to graduate without examinations. Hare himself graduated BA in 1814 and MA in 1818.

After a long absence in Italy, Hare returned to New College as a tutor in 1818. In June 1824 he published a defence of the gospel narrative of the resurrection, entitled *A Layman's Letters to the Authors of the 'Trial of the Witnesses'*. In 1825 he was ordained in Winchester College chapel. In 1827 with his brother Julius Charles *Hare he published *Guesses at Truth, by Two Brothers*, a collection of essays and aphorisms inspired by Coleridge and Wordsworth.

On 2 June 1829, having been recently appointed to the college living of Alton-Barnes, Wiltshire, Hare married Maria, daughter of Revd Oswald Leycester, rector of Stoke upon Tern. In his tiny parish, isolated in the corn-plains at the foot of the Wiltshire downs, he spent the next four years as the loving father and friend of his people. He spoke in the familiar language of ordinary life, making use of apt illustrations drawn from his parishioners' simple surroundings. After his death many of his sermons were widely read, through the two volumes known as *The Alton Sermons, or, Sermons to a Country Congregation*, first published in 1837 and frequently reprinted. On the death of an uncle in 1831 the family living of Herstmonceaux fell vacant, and was offered to him by his eldest brother, but he could not bear to leave his quiet home at Alton. He continued to lead with his devoted wife an ideally happy existence until his failing health obliged them to go for the winter to Italy, where he died at Rome on 18 February 1834. He was buried at the foot of the pyramid of Caius Cestius, in the old protestant cemetery. His widow, who lived until 13 November 1870, took up residence in the parish of her brother-in-law Julius, and was buried in Herstmonceaux churchyard.

A. J. C. HARE, *rev.* M. C. CURTHOYS

Sources A. J. C. Hare, *Memorials of a quiet life*, 2 vols. (1872–3) · letters of Mrs Hare-Naylor to Lady Jones; corresp. between Augustus Hare and Lady Jones · *GM*, 2nd ser., 1 (1834), 664 · Foster, *Alum. Oxon.* · J. F. Waller, ed., *The imperial dictionary of universal biography*, 3 vols. (1857–63) · N. M. Distad, *Guessing at truth: the life of Julius Charles Hare (1795–1855)* (1979) · *Hist. U. Oxf.* 6: *19th-cent. Oxf.*
Likenesses J. S. Agar, stipple, pubd 1836 (after marble bust by J. Gibson), BM, NPG

Hare, Dorothy Christian (1876–1967), physician, was born on 14 September 1876 at 1 Lansdown Place, Bath, the third of four daughters and seventh of eight children of Major Edward Hare (d. 1897), formerly of the Indian Medical Service, and his wife, Mary Ann, *née* Wood (1835–1889). As their father disapproved of formal education and careers for girls, Dorothy and her sisters were educated by governesses and given generous bequests in case they never married. Dorothy decided to read medicine, went to Cheltenham Ladies' College in 1897, passed the London intermediate science examinations in 1899 and 1900 with honours, and entered the London (Royal Free Hospital) School of Medicine for Women in 1900. She graduated MB BS in 1905 and MD in 1908, received the DPH at Cambridge in 1912, and was admitted MRCP in 1920. In 1936 she became only the third woman elected a fellow of the Royal College of Physicians.

Dorothy Hare practised initially in London, as casualty house surgeon at the New Hospital for Women (renamed the Elizabeth Garrett Anderson Hospital in 1917) and as house physician at the Royal Free Hospital. A clinical student recalled the 'sculptural correctness of her features, calm and impressively confident manner, obvious intellectual ability and respect with which she was treated by her Chief' (*BMJ*, 559). After appointments as assistant clinical pathologist at the Royal Free and assistant medical officer at Kingswood Sanatorium she then practised privately in Cambridge (1910–16).

Responding to the War Office's urgent appeal, Dorothy Hare next served in Malta from 1916 to 1918, first in association with the Royal Army Medical Corps. The clinical experience was valuable but conditions of service were deplorable. From April 1918 to October 1919 she was chief medical officer of the newly formed Women's Royal Naval Service (WRNS), ranked as assistant. Her work was largely administrative, with tours of inspection of all naval establishments employing women in various duties. In 1920 she was invested CBE for her distinguished services. While with the medical corps she became gravely concerned by the plight of women with venereal diseases, rare in the WRNS but rife in the other services. Dismissed from the forces, often rejected by their families, and, if pregnant, refused admission to homes for mothers and babies, they faced poverty and long and painful treatment without rehabilitation.

After a temporary post at the South London Hospital for Women, Dorothy Hare was successively medical registrar at the Royal Free (from 1921), and clinical assistant and physician to the Royal Free and Garrett Anderson hospitals from 1929 to 1937. Contemporaries remember her as reserved and soberly dressed, an encouraging teacher and a splendid trainer of her juniors. She demanded careful history-taking and clinical examination, accurate records, and judicious selection of special investigations. On ward rounds she greeted every patient by name, and her kindness was memorable, especially to young patients suffering from ulcerative colitis, then an illness with a very high mortality rate. She played a significant and generous part in establishing three hostels and long-term follow-up and rehabilitation for women with venereal diseases. With the advent of penicillin the need for the hostels passed, but she never forgot the almoner (social worker) responsible for aftercare and left her a small legacy.

Dorothy Hare produced relatively few publications but they were succinct and comprehensive. The three most important were *Simple instructions for diabetic patients. With prescription sheet for the use of patients, nurses and practitioners* (1933) and two presidential addresses to the section of therapeutics and pharmacology of the Royal Society of Medicine, entitled 'Therapeutic observations on non-specific ulcerative colitis' (1935) and 'Therapeutic trial of raw vegetable diet in chronic rheumatic conditions' (1936).

Dorothy Hare retired to Falmouth and shared her house with a long-standing friend, Dr Elizabeth H. Lepper, former pathologist at the Elizabeth Garrett Anderson Hospital. She travelled widely, visiting former students and young relatives, skilfully illustrating the letters and diary of her two-year trip round the world. She arranged art exhibitions with the help of the Arts Council and supported the Royal Cornwall Polytechnic and amateur operatics, painting scenery and acting as property manager and stage carpenter. Friends of all ages 'were legion and [her] interest in their doings, successes and problems [was] inexhaustable. The cold grey eyes which daunted students became the bright and eager eyes of a wonderful old lady' (*Lancet*, 1213). As her strength gradually failed her cousin Ewan Hare and his wife, Elsie, invited her to their home, 1 Castle Park, Appleby, Westmorland, where she died peacefully after a cerebral thrombosis on 19 November 1967. She was buried on 22 November in the graveyard of the Anglican church of St Lawrence, Appleby, at which she had been a regular attender.

RUTH E. M. BOWDEN

Sources private information (2004) [Mrs Elsie Hare, B. Corden, E. Gilchrist, A. Milne] · *BMJ* (2 Dec 1967), 559 · *The Lancet* (2 Dec 1967), 1213 · archives, Cheltenham Ladies' College · archives, Royal Free Hospital school of medicine for women · archives, Royal Free Hospital [minutes of weekly board and annual reports] · L. Fairfield, *Journal of the Medical Women's Federation*, 492 (1967), 99–102 · b. cert. · d. cert. · L. Leneman, 'Medical women at war, 1914–18', *Medical History*, 38 (1994), 160–77 · *Medical Directory*

Archives priv. coll., family archives and memorabilia | Royal Free Hospital, London · Wellcome L., Medical Women's Federation archive
Likenesses photograph, London (Royal Free Hospital) School of Medicine for Women, archives of centenary exhibition · photograph · photographs, priv. coll.
Wealth at death £32,967: probate, 6 Feb 1968, *CGPLA Eng. & Wales*

Hare, Francis (1671–1740), bishop of Chichester, was born on 1 November 1671 in London, the son of Richard Hare (*b.* 1636) of Leigh, Essex, and of his second wife, Sarah, daughter of Thomas Naylor. Hare was educated at Eton College, where he was elected fellow in October 1712. He was admitted to King's College, Cambridge, on 16 April 1689 and graduated BA in 1692, MA in 1696, and DD in 1708. He was a fellow of King's from 1692 to 1706. At Cambridge he was tutor to Anthony Collins and, more usefully, to the future Sir Robert Walpole and John, marquess of Blandford, son of the first duke of Marlborough. His friendship with Charles Townshend, later Viscount Townshend, dates from this period.

In the autumn of 1709 Hare married his cousin Bethia Naylor. They had one child, who as Francis Hare-Naylor inherited an estate from his uncle George Naylor, which included Herstmonceux Castle, near Battle, Sussex. Hare raised his son at Herstmonceux, 'making him speak Greek as his ordinary language' (Cole, fol. 101a), and himself residing there occasionally at least until 1736. A second marriage, in April 1728, to Mary Margaret, daughter and coheir of Joseph Alston of Edwardstone, Suffolk, and Easthamstead, Berkshire, produced five daughters and two sons, the eldest of whom, the Revd Robert Hare, was godson to Sir Robert Walpole and succeeded his half-brother to the Hare-Naylor name and estate. This second marriage brought Hare property in Suffolk, Norfolk, and Buckinghamshire, where he principally resided, during his later years, at The Vache, near Chalfont St Giles. Hare's preference for London during the parliamentary season prompted William Whiston to criticize him and other 'political Bishops' neglectful of their dioceses; Hare's letters, however, show that he was attentive to his duties in Chichester.

Hare was named chaplain-general to Marlborough's army in 1704. His letters describe some of the principal battles of the War of the Spanish Succession; a manuscript 'Account of his grace the duke of Marlborough's expedition into Germany' (1704–5), possibly misattributed to Hare (Horn, 154, n. 19), contains more detailed accounts. Hare's *Life and Glorious History of John D. and E. of Marlborough* (1705) was probably written in fulfilment of the duke's wishes. His sermon *The Charge of God to Joshua* (1711), preached two months before the duke's dismissal, criticized tory demands for peace; it was denounced in *A Learned Comment upon Dr. Hare's Sermon* (1711) by Delariviere Manley and by Jonathan Swift, who also attacked Hare in *The Examiner*. Hare remained loyal to Marlborough after the duke's fall; his other publications on Marlborough's behalf include *Bouchain* (1711); the four instalments of *The Management of the War* (1711); *The Conduct of the Duke of Marlborough* (1712); and *The Allies and the Late Ministry Defended*

(1711–12), a four-part response to Swift's *The Conduct of the Allies* (1711).

Hare's tenure with Marlborough initiated his rapid rise in church and state. On 20 July 1707 he was named canon-residentiary of St Paul's and prebendary of Portpool in St Paul's Cathedral; he held the prebend until his death. He received a royal chaplaincy under Queen Anne and was reappointed in that capacity by George I. Hare was rector of Barnes, Surrey, from 1713 until 1723, and on 29 April 1715 he was made dean of Worcester, in which capacity he continued until 26 October 1726, when he was elected to the more lucrative deanery of St Paul's. In 1722 Walpole appointed him usher to the exchequer; Henry Pelham, then a lord of the Treasury, estimated the worth of the position at £800–£1000 annually, even if executed by proxy. On 17 December 1727 Hare was made bishop of St Asaph; Queen Caroline, a supporter of Hare, almost certainly, but unsuccessfully, promoted Hare's candidacy for the bishopric of Bath and Wells about this time (Nichols, *Lit. anecdotes*, 97–8). On 25 November 1731 Hare was translated to the see of Chichester.

Not unfairly portrayed by John Toland as fancying himself 'a Drawcansir in Controversy' (Toland, fol. 44b), Hare was involved in polemical exchange throughout his adult life. The ironic and antideistic *Difficulties and Discouragements which Attend the Study of the Scriptures* (1714) led Whiston to accuse Hare of 'Scepticism' (Whiston, 109) and prompted a more forgiving contemporary to remark that at this date Hare's 'Credit in Point of Orthodoxy stood in no very good Light in the Eye of the World' (Cole, fol. 98a). The work was censured by convocation but eventually printed in eleven editions; Whiston claims that Hare unsuccessfully attempted to deny its authorship (Whiston, 116). Hare's involvement in the Bangorian controversy produced three anti-dissent pamphlets, including *Church-Authority Vindicated* (1719), which appeared in five editions within two years. Benjamin Hoadly, bishop of Bangor, and Richard Steele were among those who answered Hare.

Hare's scholarly pursuits were also marked by controversy. A friendship with Richard Bentley, who had dedicated his *Remarks upon a Late Discourse of Free-Thinking* (1713) to Hare and had in turn been dedicatee of Hare's *The Clergyman's Thanks to Philoleutherus* (1713), soured when Hare published an edition of Terence (1724) that drew on Bentley's annotations for his own intended edition. Bentley's edition appeared in 1726; in it Hare was repeatedly criticized. By adding to this volume a hastily prepared edition of the *Fables* of Phaedrus, Bentley pre-empted an edition on which Hare was then at work. Hare responded with a furious *Epistola critica* (1727) against Bentley's sloppy Phaedrus. One account of the spat over Terence, perhaps apocryphal, has Sir Isaac Newton wondering why two divines were 'fighting with one another about a play-book' (Monk, 235). Hare returned to textual criticism in 1736, when he published an edition of the Psalms in Hebrew. The edition of Plautus that he was preparing toward the end of his life was never published.

Hare's acquaintance with William Warburton proved less tempestuous, perhaps because Hare was able to play the patron to the younger scholar, if testily at times. His admiration for Warburton's *The Alliance between Church and State* (1736) prompted Hare to recommend Warburton to Queen Caroline, whose death prevented her from patronizing Warburton. Warburton's dedication to Hare of the second part of the second volume of *The Divine Legation* (1741), earlier instalments of which Hare had praised, illustrates both the fulsomeness with which Warburton often addressed Hare and the respect that he had for Hare's learning.

Hare compromised his reputation in 1732, when, commemorating the death of Charles I, he preached a sermon before the House of Lords, praising the dead king more profusely than Hanoverian custom allowed and criticizing dissent more stridently than the government's apologists generally did. Fourteen pamphlets and newspaper leaders were published on the sermon; Hare's detractors included the Walpolite journalist Thomas Gordon. Probably worried by accusations that he had embraced a high-church and thus anti-whig doctrine Hare reasserted his loyalty by aggressively supporting his old patron Thomas Pelham-Holles, duke of Newcastle, in the 1734 elections. Walpole's twentieth-century biographer believes that Hare was writing for the pro-government *Daily Courant* around this time (Plumb, 315). Walpole continued faithful to Hare; John, Lord Hervey, claimed that only his intervention prevented Walpole from appointing Hare archbishop of Canterbury in 1737. Letters to Newcastle and Edmund Gibson, bishop of London, demonstrate that Hare was a committed Walpolite until the end of his life, seeking to mend a rift between Newcastle and Walpole, defending the government's troubled foreign policy, and criticizing the coalescent 'patriot' opposition.

Hare died at his home, The Vache, on 26 April 1740 after a thirteen-month illness contracted, according to his widow, 'by being too free in walking in the garden' and exacerbated by the unusually cold winter of 1739–40 (*Buckinghamshire MSS*, 258). In his final days he 'suffered much with a fever, cough and swelling in his hand, and side' (ibid.). He was buried at the parish church, Chalfont St Giles, on 3 May 1740 in a vault ordered by his widow for him and for three of their children previously buried at St Paul's. Hare bequeathed approximately £50,000 to the sons of his second marriage upon the decease of their mother.

Because Hare refused to sit for portraits no likenesses remain. Hervey, perhaps fancifully, remembers that 'Dr Hare had the cruel, sharp, dark-lanthorn, stiletto countenance of an Italian assassin' (Horn, 162). Hare's impressive record of preferment attests to his associations with prominent whigs as well as to his talents as a cleric. In 1763 the *Critical Review* remembered Hare as 'the tool of a faction' with 'little else to recommend him … but blind zeal for his party' (83); but Alexander Pope, no friend to whig faction, complimented Hare's preaching in the third book of his expanded *Dunciad* (1743).   ALEXANDER PETTIT

Sources W. Cole, 'A catalogue of all the provosts, fellows & scholars … in King's College in Cambridge', 1750, BL, Add. MS 5817, fols. 97a–103a • *The manuscripts of the earl of Buckinghamshire, the earl of Lindsey ... and James Round*, HMC, 38 (1895) • *DNB* • F. Hare, letter to Thomas Pelham-Holles, duke of Newcastle, 8 Nov 1739, BL, Add. MS 32692, fols. 450a–450b • F. Hare, letters to Edmund Gibson, 1737–9, Hunt. L. [uncatalogued volume of Gibson's correspondence] • Burke, *Gen. GB* (1972), vol. 3 • *Fasti Angl.* (Hardy) • W. Whiston, *Memoirs of the life and writings of Mr William Whiston: containing memoirs of several of his friends also* (1749) • A. Pettit, 'The Francis Hare controversy of 1732', *British Journal for Eighteenth-Century Studies*, 17 (1994), 41–53 • R. D. Horn, 'Marlborough's first biographer: Dr Francis Hare', *Huntington Library Quarterly*, 20 (1956–7), 145–62 • J. Hervey, *Memoirs of the reign of George the Second*, ed. J. W. Croker, 3 vols. (1884), vol. 2 • J. H. Monk, *The life of Richard Bentley, DD*, 2nd edn, 2 (1833) • Nichols, *Lit. anecdotes*, vol. 5 • *Critical Review*, 15 (1763), 81–90 • J. S. Watson, *The life of William Warburton, D.D.* (1863) • J. Toland, comments on F. Hare's *Scripture vindicated from the misrepresentations of the bishop of Bangor*, 1721, BL, Add. MS 4295, fols. 44a–47b • F. Hare, letters to Thomas Pelham-Holles, duke of Newcastle, 1733–4, BL, Add. MS 32688, fols. 135a–136b • F. Hare, letters to Thomas Pelham-Holles, duke of Newcastle, 1733–4, BL, Add. MS 32689, fol. 220a • F. Hare (?), 'An account of his grace the duke of Marlborough's expedition into Germany', 1704–5, BL, Add. MS 9114 • F. Hare, 'Notes design'd for an ed. of Plautus', BL, Add. MSS 5171, 5172 • J. H. Plumb, *Sir Robert Walpole*, 2 (1960) • N. Sykes, *Church and state in England in the XVIII century* (1934) • W. Sterry, ed., *The Eton College register, 1441–1698* (1943)

Archives BL, collections, journal of Marlborough's campaigns, and literary MSS, Add. MSS 5171–5172, 9114 • GL, corresp. and household accounts • NRA, priv. coll., family and personal corresp. | BL, Cole MSS • BL, letters to Henry Watkins, Add. MS 3225

Wealth at death approx. £50,000 left to sons; also large fortune in the estates of Newhouse in Suffolk, the ancient manor of Hos-Tendis near Skulthorpe in Norfolk, and The Vache near Chalfont St Giles in Buckinghamshire: *DNB*; BL, Add. MS 5817, fol. 103a

Henry Hare, second Baron Coleraine (*bap.* 1636, *d.* 1708), by unknown engraver, 1703

Hare, Henry, second Baron Coleraine (*bap.* 1636, *d.* 1708), antiquary and architect, was baptized on 21 April 1636 at Totteridge, Hertfordshire, the eldest son of Hugh *Hare, first Baron Coleraine (1605/6–1667), and his wife, Lady Lucy (*d.* 1682), daughter of Henry *Montagu, first earl of Manchester, and his wife, Catherine Spencer. Henry Hare visited Italy in the late 1650s or the 1660s and translated a work of 1656 by Giovanni Francesco Loredano as *The Ascents of the Soul, or, David's Mount*. Completed in 1665, it was dedicated to his mother but not published until 1682, after her death. He married in or before 1667 Constantia, daughter of Sir Richard *Lucy (1592–1667), of Broxbourne, Hertfordshire; they had three children, Hugh *Hare (*bap.* 1668, *d.* 1707), Lucius (*d.* 1699), and Constantia. From about 1667 Hare, who became second Baron Coleraine that year, sat on the commission of the peace for Hertfordshire. The following year he became deputy lieutenant for Wiltshire and a gentleman of the privy chamber. In the 1679 parliament he was MP for Old Sarum, close to his Wiltshire residence and once represented by his father-in-law; he was a fairly active member, who probably opposed the exclusion of the duke of York from the succession. Although his privy chamber office ended with the death of Charles II, he continued to hold some local offices in Middlesex and Wiltshire through the 1680s and 1690s, but his candidature in 1690 for one of the Wiltshire county seats was unsuccessful.

Coleraine's first wife having died in 1680, he married secondly, by licence dated 17 July 1682, Sarah (1632–1692), daughter and coheir of Sir Edward *Alston and his wife, Susan Hussey, and widow successively of George Grimston (*d.* 1655) and of John Seymour, duke of Somerset (*d.* 1675). They subsequently separated, and he married thirdly, on 4 August 1696 at the Charter House chapel in Middlesex, Elizabeth (*c.*1646–1732), daughter of John Portman, a London goldsmith, and widow of Robert Reade of Cheshunt, Hertfordshire. Coleraine lived most of his life at Tottenham, Middlesex, the four manors of which his father had purchased in 1626. He remodelled the family house, Bruce Castle, adding a two-storey porch and clock tower with cupola, which still survived at the end of the twentieth century. In carrying out this work Coleraine was guided by the antiquarian principles that dictated his life, relating in his manuscript 'The history and antiquities of the town and church of Tottenham' (1705) how 'in respect to its great antiquity more than conveniency, I keep the old brick tower (of the earlier house) in good repair'. This history, which deals with the etymology of Tottenham's name, the parish church, and the parochial charities, was Coleraine's principal written work but he also compiled accounts of his other antiquarian observations, including his inspection in 1675 of the skeleton of the medieval bishop of London, Robert Braybrooke, while in 1694 he wrote the 'Longford Inventory', a poem celebrating Longford Castle, bought by his father in 1641, where he appears to have completed the rebuilding of the domestic offices, begun by his father, after damage in the civil war. He also corresponded regularly with other antiquaries, among them Walter Charleton and John Woodward, and was a noted collector of medals.

Coleraine's taste for the romantic is clearly seen in his instruction to workmen in 1690 to pin back the roots of ivy torn from the tower of Tottenham church, an idea drawn from Longford, in order to increase its picturesque effect, but a more permanent contribution was his addition in 1697 'at his own only and great expence' of a vestry/mausoleum at the east end of the church, a large circular structure of classical form with blind niches, pilasters, frieze, and cornice surmounted by a ribbed lead dome with tapering obelisk. His will (made in 1702 and disposing of assets of over £6000) left £100 to be invested in land for the repair of this building with the surplus to be used for the benefit of the parish but in 1875 the vestry was demolished and the family burials reinterred. He died at Tottenham on 4 July 1708 and was buried on 15 July in the mausoleum he had built, the barony passing to his grandson, Henry *Hare (1693–1749).   NICHOLAS DOGGETT

Sources GEC, *Peerage* · J. P. Ferris, 'Hare, Henry', HoP, *Commons, 1660–90* · H. Hare, 'The history and antiquities of the town and church of Tottenham', 1705, Bodl. Oxf., MS Gough Middx. 5 [clerk's copy; also printed as appx to H. G. Oldfield and R. H. Dyson, *History and antiquities of the parish of Tottenham High-Cross* (1790)] · D. Lysons, *The environs of London*, 3 (1795) · W. Robinson, *The history and antiquities of the parish of Tottenham High Cross, in the county of Middlesex*, 2nd edn, 2 (1840), vol. 2, frontispiece, 8, 10, 215–22 · M. Robbins, *Middlesex* (1953), pl. 1 · *VCH Middlesex*, 5.327, 351, 379 · R. C. Hoare, *The history of modern Wiltshire*, 3 (1834–5), 26, 32, 34 · R. G. [R. Gough], *British topography*, [new edn], 1 (1780), 542, 567 · Nichols, *Lit. anecdotes*, 5.348, 699; 9.762 · J. Granger, *A biographical history of England, from Egbert the Great to the revolution*, 2nd edn, 3 (1775), 229–30; 4 (1775), 195 · J. L. Chester, ed., *The marriage, baptismal, and burial registers of the collegiate church or abbey of St Peter, Westminster*, Harleian Society, 10 (1876), 230 · N. Luttrell, *A brief historical relation of state affairs from September 1678 to April 1714*, 2 (1857), 602 · *The manuscripts of Shrewsbury and Coventry corporations*, HMC, 47 (1899), 170–72
Archives BL, corresp., Add. MSS 3322, 3961, 3962, 4039, 4040, 4062, 4075 · BL, account of Bishop Braybrooke's skeleton, Add. MS 5833, fol. 120 · BL, account of the duchess of Cleveland's visit to Bishop Braybrooke's skeleton, Add. MS 1055, fol. 16 · BL, notes, Lansdowne MS 827 (15) | BL, corresp. with William Charleton, Sloane MS 3962 · BL, 'Longford inventory', Add. MS 39167, fol. 91
Likenesses mezzotint, 1703, BM, NPG [*see illus.*] · W. Faithorne, line engraving (after Lord Coleraine, 1681), BM, NPG; repro. in *Ascent of the soul* (1681) [trans. of Lauredanus] · W. Faithorne and G. Vertue, line engraving, BM, NPG; repro. in E. Evans, *Catalogue of a collection of engraved portraits*, 1 (1853)
Wealth at death approx. £6000: will, PRO, PROB 11/503, sig. 184

Hare, Henry, third Baron Coleraine (1693–1749), antiquary, was born at Blechingley, Surrey, on 10 May 1693, the eldest son of the Hon. Hugh Hare (*bap.* 1668, *d.* 1707), landowner, and his wife, Lydia, daughter of Matthew Carlton, merchant, of Edmonton, Middlesex. In 1707 his father died, and when the following year his grandfather, Henry *Hare, second Baron Coleraine, died, he succeeded to the title. He also inherited the family seat known as Bruce Castle at Tottenham, Middlesex. He was educated at

Henry Hare, third Baron Coleraine (1693–1749), by George Vertue, 1740

Enfield by a Dr Uvedale, and subsequently matriculated from Corpus Christi College, Oxford, in February 1712. At the university he was tutored by John *Rogers (*bap.* 1678, *d.* 1729), a fellow of Corpus Christi College, who in 1716 married Coleraine's sister, Lydia. On 20 January 1718 Coleraine married Anne (1699–1754), the only daughter of John Hanger, merchant and sometime governor of the Bank of England, and his wife, Mary Coles. Anne brought her husband an inheritance of some £100,000, but the marriage was not a success. In October 1720 Lady Coleraine left her husband; there were no children and they were never reconciled.

In 1723 Coleraine undertook his second tour of Italy (the date of the first is unknown) with Conyers Middleton, during which he made a collection of prints and drawings of the antiquities, buildings, and paintings. Coleraine was proficient in Latin and Greek, and was admitted to the Republica Litteraria di Arcadia, a learned society promoting Italian poetry. He was included by Maurice Johnson and Browne Willis in the circle of antiquaries who met frequently at the Temple, Exchange, Fountain, and other taverns and coffee houses around the Temple in London during 1709 and 1710, and which was the genesis of the revived Society of Antiquaries established in 1718. He is listed among the founders of the society, and on 18 May 1727 was elected vice-president. The following year he was made grand master of the freemasons, and he was also a member of William Stukeley's Brazen-nose Society of Stamford, and from 18 May 1727 of the Spalding Gentlemen's Society. He became a close friend and patron of George Vertue, the Society of Antiquaries' official engraver, and together they made a number of antiquarian tours around England. Although a keen collector of coins, medals, and other antiquities, as well as paintings and drawings, Coleraine did not publish anything on antiquarian subjects. His grandfather had preserved a collection of material relevant to the history of Tottenham, and the bookseller Thomas Osborne's posthumous catalogue of Coleraine's library included 'A MS history of Tottenham High Cross', by the second Lord Coleraine, 'curiously written, and neatly bound, with his lordship's arms on the cover' (Nichols, *Lit. anecdotes*, 3.650). In 1731 Coleraine met the antiquary Thomas Hearne in Oxford, who described him as 'a very sober, studious, regular man. His Grandfather and Father were likewise men of great Learning and Virtue'. Hearne also observed that Coleraine was a devoutly religious man. Though Hearne did not know the reason for Coleraine's separation from his wife, he recorded a possibly telling anecdote: 'It is said that he was so studious that when his Lady and he lived together, he would (as he lay in bed with her) have one [of his servants] come up to him at midnight and read Greek to him' (*Remarks*, 423–4). From 1730 to 1734 he sat in the Commons as a tory MP for Boston.

In 1740 Coleraine contracted an unorthodox and legally unrecognized conjugal arrangement with Rose Duplessis, or du Plessis (1710–1790), the daughter of Francis Duplessis, a French clergyman. In his will Coleraine recorded that 'about the beginning of April 1740, I employed James West, esq. of Lincoln's Inn' to offer terms of reconciliation to Lady Hare. He stated that he was not led to this act 'by the lucre of that ample provision her father left her', and was doing it in spite of her 'most obstinate, though undeserved, hatred and contempt of me' (Nichols, *Lit. anecdotes*, 5.351). Lady Coleraine refused this solicitation and on 29 April 1740 Coleraine entered with Rose 'into a solemn, mutual engagement to take each other for husband and wife'. They had a daughter, Henrietta Rosa Peregrina, who was born at Crema, Italy, on 12 September 1745, during Hare's third and final tour of Italy. Vertue recorded meeting Coleraine in London in September some time between 1745 and 1748, and observed that he 'looks mighty well after his travels, and invites me to Tottenham' (Nichols, *Lit. anecdotes*, 6.151). But Coleraine died at Bath on 4 August 1749, of unknown causes, and was buried in the family vault at Tottenham on 24 August. His 'marriage' contract and generous bequests to his mistress—including two annuities worth in total £660 a year—together with the bequest of his estates to their illegitimate daughter led to a complex legal entanglement. As foreign born, his daughter was not legally entitled to inherit her father's estate. Joseph Ames recorded meeting Coleraine's lawyer, James West, in September 1749, and talked with him regarding 'the affair of Lord Colerane, who appear'd to be a very bad man' (Nichols, *Illustrations*, 8.604). It seems that the bulk of Coleraine's estate was inherited by his wife, as it was only following her death on 10 January 1754 that his collection of antiquities and paintings was sold at auction, in March 1754, for £904 13s. 6d., and his library of books was bought

by Thomas Osborne. His collection of drawings from his Italian tours was bequeathed to Corpus Christi College, Oxford, and those of the antiquities and buildings of Britain were left to the Society of Antiquaries. Though this last bequest was declared void, as the society was then unchartered and legally unable to accept endowments, the drawings were eventually presented to the society by Rose Duplessis. The complications arising from this bequest was one of the prompts that led the Society of Antiquaries to petition for and obtain a royal charter in 1751. On 2 May 1763 Coleraine's daughter married James Townsend, an alderman of London, and a grant to him from Coleraine's estates was subsequently obtained. The title of Baron Coleraine passed to Gabriel Hanger, the third son of Lady Coleraine's uncle, Sir George Hanger, in 1762. Rose Duplessis died on 30 March 1790.

DAVID BOYD HAYCOCK

Sources Nichols, *Lit. anecdotes*, esp. 5.347–52 · Nichols, *Illustrations*, 8.604 · *Remarks and collections of Thomas Hearne*, ed. C. E. Doble and others, 10, OHS, 67 (1915) · *GM*, 1st ser., 24 (1754), 47 · *GM*, 1st ser., 19 (1749), 380 · *DNB* · GEC, *Peerage* · P. Watson, 'Hare, Henry', HoP, *Commons, 1715–54* · Foster, *Alum. Oxon.*
Likenesses G. Vertue, watercolour drawing, 1740, BM [*see illus.*] · J. Richardson, oils (as a young man), S. Antiquaries, Lond.

Hare, Hugh, first Baron Coleraine (1605/6–1667), royalist nobleman, was the grandson of John Hare of Stow Bardolph, Norfolk, and the son of John Hare (1546–1613) and Margaret (d. 1653), daughter of John Crowch of Cornbury in Buntingford, Hertfordshire. Hugh's father, John, a London citizen and resident of Fleet Street, was called to the Inner Temple bench in 1591, was treasurer of the inn in 1605, and was member of parliament for Horsham in 1587. Hugh Hare had an uncle of the same name, also a bencher of the Inner Temple, who became master of the court of wards and died in March 1620 leaving more than £30,000 to his fortunate nephew.

Hare followed his father and uncle into the Inner Temple, where he was admitted as a student in November 1620. On 26 April of that year his mother remarried; her husband was Sir Henry Montague, lord chief justice of king's bench and later first earl of Manchester. Hare himself married, before 1636, Lucy (d. 1682), Montague's second daughter by his first wife, Catherine, daughter of Sir William Spencer of Yarnton, Oxfordshire. Admitted to court and advancing quickly in the royal favour, on 31 August 1625 Hare was created Baron Coleraine of Coleraine. From this time, he 'continued ever afterwards a faithful adherent of the king' (GEC, *Peerage*, 3.365–6). Unable or unwilling to attend the parliament in Ireland, he displayed his loyalty by allocating his proxy to Viscount Loftus of Ely, the lord chancellor, whose authority to use it was accepted by the Lords on 30 July 1634. The exercise of a further proxy was accepted in May 1641.

Also in 1641 Coleraine bought the manor and castle of Longford, near Salisbury, Wiltshire, from Edward, Lord Gorges, who was deeply in debt. The following year this must have appeared a fortunate stroke, since at the outbreak of the civil war many royalists in parliamentarian areas had to abandon their estates and Coleraine, who suffered sequestration in Middlesex and Hertfordshire, and who also had property at Barking, was no exception. But he met little but trouble in Wiltshire. First, as his chaplain, Pelate, reported, he found Longford 'so encumbered that he spent in a very short time £18,000 to secure his title in suits of law'. Then, in April 1644, he was compelled to surrender the place to the king as a garrison. By then he had 'too great a family of young children (to abide with them among soldiers)', but he was concerned to keep an eye on his impressive new property, and moved into his steward's house at nearby Britford. In these months, adds Pelate, he suffered 'barbarous usage' at the hands of Colonel Barnabas Pell, royalist governor of Longford, who determined 'with spiteful intent to dismantle the comeliness as well as the strengths of the place' (*Shrewsbury and Coventry MSS*, 171). Military necessity must have played a role in the changes. Clarendon reported that while the king marched to engage Waller, who lay at Andover, he arranged for his large cannon to be secured at Longford Castle.

Some time in 1645, probably after Naseby, Coleraine tired of watching his house used as a barracks. Obtaining permission from Charles to leave Wiltshire, he arrived back at Totteridge before the surrender of Longford to Cromwell on 18 October 1645. Now the castle came under the control of 'a knavish committee of clowns of neither fortune nor understanding'; in May 1646 parliament and the county committee decided that it must be slighted. Longford was preserved through the influence of Coleraine's brother-in-law, now the earl of Manchester. In 1650, however, on revisiting his mansion, Hare found there 'nothing but filthiness and desolation' (*Shrewsbury and Coventry MSS*, 172).

On 12 February 1655 it was reported that despite his prominence among the king's supporters, no evidence had been found that Coleraine had compounded for delinquency. Nothing is known of his activities during the interregnum, and it may be that he went abroad. *The Ascents of the Soul*, a translation of a work by Loredano published in 1681 or 1682, bound with a book called *La scala sancta*, contains material written in the 1650s. It reports the translator's travels in Italy, but it is probably to be attributed to Coleraine's eldest son, Henry *Hare (*bap.* 1636, *d.* 1708). It contains poems in praise of Coleraine's wife, Lucy, who evidently inspired much love and respect, and who died in 1682. The marriage produced at least five boys and three girls. Coleraine is reported to have been an enthusiast of heraldry, a lover of art and music, and 'a great florist' or landscape gardener (Nichols, *Lit. anecdotes*, 5.348).

Coleraine's enormous fortune was proof against all catastrophes. He told his chaplain that he had lost £40,000 through the misfortunes of war, but was still able at an unknown date to 'set about levelling the ditches and mounds, and rebuilding the offices, which he in a good measure restored' (Hoare, 34). On 6 May 1661 a proxy was accepted from him, since he was too ill to attend the upper house of the Irish parliament. He died suddenly at his house at Totteridge on 2 October 1667, aged sixty-one, and was buried there on 9 October. His will was dated 18 January 1653, and probate was granted on 11 November 1667 to Henry, his son and successor to the barony of Coleraine.

STEPHEN WRIGHT

Sources *The manuscripts of Shrewsbury and Coventry corporations*, HMC, 47 (1899), 170–72 [summary of, and extracts from, the 'History of Longford' by Henry Pelate, chaplain to Hugh Hare] • GEC, *Peerage*, new edn, 3.365–6 • R. C. Hoare, *The history of modern Wiltshire*, 3/5: *Hundred of Cawden* (1835) • VCH *Hertfordshire*, vol. 3 • VCH *Middlesex*, vol. 5 • *CSP Ire.*, 1633–47 • M. A. E. Green, ed., *Calendar of the proceedings of the committee for compounding … 1643–1660*, 5 vols., PRO (1889–92) • G. F. Loredano, *The ascents of the soul, or, David's mount towards God's house*, trans. H. Hare, 2 vols. (1682) [It. orig., *Gradi dell'anima* (1656)] • H. Chauncy, *The historical antiquities of Hertfordshire* (1700); repr. in 2 vols., 2 (1826)

Hare, Hugh (*bap.* 1668, *d.* 1707), translator, baptized at Totteridge, Hertfordshire, on 2 July 1668, was the eldest surviving son of Henry *Hare, second Baron Coleraine (*bap.* 1636, *d.* 1708), and his first wife, Theodosia (*d.* 1680), daughter of Sir Richard Lucy, baronet, of Broxbourne, Hertfordshire. He lived at East Betchworth, Surrey, and married Lydia, daughter of Matthew Carlton of Edmonton, Middlesex; they had four children. On being appointed chairman of the general quarter sessions for Surrey, held at Dorking on 5 April 1692, Hare delivered a 'religious, learned, and loyal' charge, which he published by request in 1692. In the following year there appeared his translation from the Italian of Agostino Mascardi, *An historical relation of the conspiracy of John Lewis count de Fieschi, against the city and republick of Genoua in the year 1547*. He was also one of 'several eminent hands' who helped in the four-volume translation of the *Works of Lucian* (1710–11), to which is prefixed a life by John Dryden. Hare's precise death date is unknown; however, he was buried at Tottenham on 1 March 1707 with his wife. He was survived by his son Henry *Hare (1693–1749) who became the third Baron Coleraine on his grandfather's death in 1708.

GORDON GOODWIN, rev. PHILIP CARTER

Sources GEC, *Peerage* • PRO, PROB 11/493, fols. 331v–335v [will]
Likenesses G. Kneller, oils, 1685, Lancaster House, London

Hare, James (*bap.* 1747, *d.* 1804), social celebrity and politician, was baptized on 9 April 1747 at Somerton, Somerset, the second son of Joseph Hare, an apothecary at Wells, and his wife, Frances. For many years he was wrongly identified as the son of one Richard Hare of Limehouse and as having been educated at Oxford University. In fact he attended Thomas Hodgkinson's school in Exeter and Eton College between 1760 and 1765. In the latter year he matriculated at King's College, Cambridge, where he was a fellow (1768–74), and in April 1768 he entered Lincoln's Inn. It was at Eton and Cambridge that Hare met Charles James Fox, Frederick Howard, fifth earl of Carlisle, and William Cavendish, fifth duke of Devonshire, whose friendship ensured his elevation into the sophisticated and privileged whig society centred on Devonshire House. With a growing reputation for scholarly excellence, wit,

James Hare (*bap.* 1747, *d.* 1804), by Sir Joshua Reynolds, *c.*1774–5

and social polish, during the early 1770s he became a much sought-after guest within this circle.

In May 1772 Hare was elected MP for Stockbridge, Hampshire, whereupon there was considerable interest in how this most eloquent and entertaining man would address the house: 'Wait till you hear Hare', Fox was rumoured to have said on being praised for his own maiden speech in 1769. However, Hare's early political career was characterized by diffidence and taciturnity, and there is no record of his having attempted to speak during the two years that he sat for Stockbridge. On 21 January 1774 he married Hannah (1752–1827), the daughter of Sir Abraham Hume. The union, which, according to Nathaniel Wraxall, was financially highly advantageous to Hare, produced one daughter, but broke down soon after. His new wealth was directed to financing Hare's lavish metropolitan lifestyle, in which, as with many members of his set, gaming featured prominently. Although he was never as indulgent as richer friends such as Fox, Hare's extravagance ensured that his financial situation remained precarious, prompting a concerned correspondence between his whig associates.

After a failed bid to become MP for Pontefract in 1774, Hare spent several years pursuing a diplomatic career. Carlisle's influence with the prime minister, Lord North, secured him the post of minister-plenipotentiary in Poland, though Hare twice delayed his departure for Warsaw on account of the unresolved state of his affairs in London. In June 1780, having failed to meet his second departure, he resigned the position. During this period Hare continued to balance his desire for financial security with his love of Brooks's gaming table, to which he was easily led

by Fox (whose house in St James's Street, London, he shared). In July 1781 he was elected as MP for Knaresborough in the interest of the duke of Devonshire. Hare held the seat until his death, though he was from the start never an assiduous parliamentarian. 'I had much rather … remain out of Parliament', he wrote to Lord Carlisle on 13 February, 'and the privilege of freedom from arrests is the only one I care a farthing for' (Namier). Hare's preference for political dealing at Brooks's Club rather than in the chamber irritated some members of whig society, who noted the inappropriateness of such actions from someone of modest social origins. However, his reputation for tactfulness and sincerity in an otherwise gossipy and distrustful society made him a valued friend and confidant of the duke of Devonshire and especially of the duchess, Georgiana, whom he frequently attended at Chatsworth.

Despite voting with Fox against the North administration in 1780, Hare did not gain office under Rockingham or Shelburne, or indeed during the Fox–North coalition. Thereafter he sided with Fox for the opposition. Despite his sympathy for Burke's *Reflections on the Revolution in France* (1790), he again fell behind Fox, to whom he remained committed as the whig party split over the question of war with revolutionary France. While he was celebrated for his social ease and gentlemanly wit, Hare was rather less impressive on first meeting. He was, in Sir Alexander Clifford's view, 'the thinnest man I ever saw', with a face so pallid that it resembled a 'surprised cockatoo' (Stokes), and often gave him the appearance of being nearer death than life.

In August 1802 Hare travelled to Paris to join other members of the whig club. Here he suffered from an attack of asthma, a condition made worse by his imprisonment following the resumption of war with Britain in May 1803. He suffered a relapse in his health soon after his return to England. His death at Bath on 17 March 1804 was marked with warm praise from Charles James Fox, his friend of forty years, and the duchess of Devonshire, whose verses on Hare were reprinted in the *Gentleman's Magazine* (76, 1806, 512).   PHILIP CARTER

Sources L. B. Namier, 'Hare, James', HoP, *Commons, 1754–90* · W. Stokes, 'Hare, James', HoP, *Commons, 1790–1820* · Venn, *Alum. Cant.* · *GM*, 1st ser., 76 (1806), 513 · A. Foreman, *Georgiana, duchess of Devonshire* (1998) · Walpole, *Corr.* · L. G. Mitchell, *Charles James Fox and the disintegration of the whig party, 1782–1794* (1971) · P. Ziegler and D. Seward, eds., *Brooks's: a social history* (1991)

Archives Castle Howard, Yorkshire, letters to Lord Carlisle · Chatsworth House, Derbyshire, letters to duke and duchess of Devonshire

Likenesses J. Reynolds, oils, *c.*1774–1775, unknown collection; copyprint, NPG [*see illus.*] · J. Nollekens, bust, 1802, Woburn Abbey, Bedfordshire · S. W. Reynolds, mezzotint, pubd 1804 (after J. Reynolds), BM · oils (after J. Reynolds), Hardwick Hall, Derbyshire

Hare, Sir John [*real name* John Joseph Fairs] (1844–1921), actor and theatre manager, was born on 16 May 1844, probably at Giggleswick, Yorkshire, the son of Thomas Fairs, a London architect. Very little is known of his boyhood years, although they were spent in London. His parents apparently died while he was young, and an uncle became

Sir John Hare (1844–1921), by Sir John Everett Millais, 1893

his guardian. He managed to see some leading contemporary actors (such as Charles Kean at the Princess's Theatre) by pretending to visit a fictitious aunt living in Brixton. He was educated partly at Loudoun House, St John's Wood, before his uncle sent him to Giggleswick grammar school, where the headmaster was J. R. Blakiston, his uncle's personal friend and a noted teacher. Blakiston prepared the boy for an intended career in the civil service, but in the meantime he was invited to participate in some private theatricals in Settle, Yorkshire, and quickly found himself directing a play and stepping into the leading role at the last minute. His first public appearance was in an amateur benefit performance for the Lancashire Distress Fund on 29 January 1863, when one of his roles was Box in F. C. Burnand's *Cox and Box*. This experience confirmed his ambition to be an actor, and Blakiston persuaded his guardian to allow him to go on the stage. So for six months the ailing Henry Leigh Murray (1820–1870), an accomplished, versatile actor and excellent mimic, became his drama coach. Murray also secured a first engagement for him at the Prince of Wales's Theatre, Liverpool, and accompanied him for the ordeal.

One of Fairs's early acquaintances at Liverpool was Squire Bancroft, and they became lifelong friends. His first minor role was as the fop Smallpiece in Ben Webster the younger's *A Woman of Business* on 28 September 1864, with J. L. Toole (eventually another intimate) in the lead. On the first night he suffered stage fright and forgot his

lines, but, despite the audience hissing him, he quickly recovered. Another star visitor, recreating his London successes, was E. A. Sothern, and he too offered encouragement. The part of an old man in Charles Reade's *The Lyons Mail* revealed a particular talent for make-up. However, Fairs aspired to more than a career in the provincial theatre and set his sights on London. But before securing an engagement he married, on 12 August 1865, his childhood sweetheart, Mary Adela Elizabeth Hare-Holmes (*d.* 1931), part of whose surname he immediately adopted as his stage name. Their happy marriage lasted over fifty years, and in his will Hare called her his 'helpmate, best friend, and wisest counsellor'. They had one son, Gilbert (1869–1951), who became a well-known actor, and two daughters, one of whom, Effie, married the actor George Pleydell Bancroft, the son of Squire Bancroft.

The desired London engagement materialized at the Prince of Wales's Theatre, the newly renamed and refurbished home of Marie Wilton and H. J. Byron. (Squire Bancroft, soon to be Marie Wilton's husband, had also joined the same theatre.) So the second and most influential phase of Hare's career began with the role of Short in the anonymous *Naval Engagements* (25 September 1865). However, he did not attract critical notice until 11 November 1865, when he performed Lord Ptarmigant in *Society* by T. W. Robertson, with whose plays he became particularly associated. Even though Ptarmigant was a small role, Hare's thorough attention to detail reformed the way in which old male characters were recreated on stage. His achievement was also a reflection of the Bancrofts' managerial policy, which emphasized ensemble acting and realistic stage presentation. Other Robertson roles he created were Prince Perovsky in *Ours* (1866), Sam Gerridge in *Caste* (1867), Hon. Bruce Fanquehere in *Play* (1868), Beau Farintosh in *School* (1869), and Dunscombe Dunscombe in *MP* (1870). For these roles he was complimented repeatedly for his thorough impersonation, polish, refinement, costume, and make-up. He also scored hits as Sir John Vesey in Bulwer-Lytton's *Money* (1872) and Sir Peter Teazle in *The School for Scandal* (1874), his final part for the Bancrofts. Even though he was unhappy with his performance, he killed the tradition of making Teazle a figure of low rather than high comedy. After nine years with the Prince of Wales's company, Hare had established his own distinguishing niche in the London theatre as a character actor; however, he also harboured the desire to manage a theatre on his own account.

For this third phase of his career, Hare secured the Court Theatre with William Hunter Kendal as his silent partner. Kendal's wife, Madge, provided a further connection with T. W. Robertson, since she was one of his younger sisters, and she played the title role in Charles Coghlan's *Lady Flora*, Hare's first managerial production, on 18 March 1875. Hare hoped to foster original modern English comedies and so extend the Robertsonian tradition. However, original plays by Coghlan and W. S. Gilbert were not as successful as Coghlan's French adaptation, *A Quiet Rubber*, which opened on 8 January 1876, and provided Hare with one of his most enduring stage triumphs. J. Palgrave Simpson's adaptation of Sardou's *Les pattes de mouche*, entitled *A Scrap of Paper* (1876), was also successful, and notable for Hare's settings, which were praised as realities rather than mere imitations. A revival of an older English comedy, *New Men and Old Acres* (1876), by Tom Taylor and A. W. Dubourg, also succeeded. As an actor–manager, Hare did not believe he should always be in the spotlight, and indeed one of his major triumphs was W. G. Wills's adaptation of Goldsmith's *The Vicar of Wakefield*, entitled *Olivia* (30 March 1878), in which he did not have a role. He frequently contented himself with the demands of stage management, which Ellen Terry admired. If any criticism of his tenure of the Court Theatre could be made it would be that (as with *Olivia*) he allowed a play's dramatic merits to be overwhelmed by the stage decoration. His management of the Court concluded on 19 July 1879, not with an original English work, but with Robertson's adaptation of a Scribe and Legouvé play, *The Ladies' Battle*.

After a brief three-month hiatus, Hare joined with Kendal again to manage the St James's, considered at the time to be an unlucky theatre. They aimed both to amuse and to improve public taste, in which they succeeded by providing a mixture of French adaptations and original English plays. Their first production on 4 October 1879 was a revival of G. W. Godfrey's *The Queen's Shilling*. More significant, some sixteen months later, was *The Money Spinner* (1881), the first of several of Pinero's plays Hare and Kendal presented. The play was regarded as rather unconventional and a risky venture, but it caught on with the public. In it Hare created one of his most famous roles, Baron Croodle, a disreputable but delightful old reprobate and card-shark. Other plays by Pinero included *The Squire* (1881), with Hare as the Revd Paul Dormer (and additionally notable because Pinero was accused of plagiarizing Hardy's *Far from the Madding Crowd*), *The Ironmaster* (1884), *Mayfair* (1885), and *The Hobby Horse* (1886), in which Hare played Spencer Jermyn. His sole excursion into Shakespeare, *As You Like It* (1885), was somewhat controversial and was criticized for being overdone—his Touchstone was considered by some to be the worst ever seen. When the management terminated on 21 July 1888, Hare and Kendal had produced twenty-one plays, fairly evenly divided among English plays, French adaptations, and revivals. However, their tenancy was distinguished by the Pinero productions.

A year later Hare was again a manager, this time of the Garrick, a handsome theatre which W. S. Gilbert had built at a cost of £44,000. The initial production, *The Profligate* (24 April 1889), with Hare as Lord Dangars, continued the association with Pinero and was a great success (especially given Pinero's serious theme in the play). Two other Pinero plays followed: *Lady Bountiful* (1891), and *The Notorious Mrs Ebbsmith* (1895), the latter consolidating Mrs Patrick Campbell's earlier success in Pinero's *The Second Mrs Tanqueray* (1893). Two other outstanding productions at the Garrick were Sydney Grundy's *A Pair of Spectacles* (1890), in which Hare was more than memorable as Benjamin Goldfinch (another 'dear old man' role), and a revival

of *Diplomacy*, with a magnificent cast that included the Bancrofts and Johnston Forbes-Robertson. Hare closed his career as a manager on 15 June 1895 with single reprise performances of *A Pair of Spectacles* and *A Quiet Rubber*.

Thereafter, and perhaps surprisingly, Hare did not venture into management again, and his career became rather unfocused. He visited America in 1895 and again in 1897, re-creating his successful London roles in *The Notorious Mrs Ebbsmith*, *A Pair of Spectacles*, and *A Quiet Rubber*. In addition he toured the provinces extensively. His major new roles were Quex in Pinero's *The Gay Lord Quex* (1899) and the earl of Carlton in J. M. Barrie's *Little Mary* (1906). His knighthood in 1907 was a fitting and well-received accolade. From 1907 until his actual retirement in 1917, he undertook an extended series of farewell tours, and gave several royal command and benefit performances, playing his signature roles.

On 21 December 1921 Hare fell ill with influenza and then pneumonia, and died as a result on 28 December 1921, at his home, 187B Queen's Gate, London. After a funeral service at St Margaret's, Westminster, he was buried in Hampstead cemetery on 31 December; the ceremonies were attended by his children and numerous leading members of the theatrical profession, including Bancroft and Pinero. His wife of fifty-six years was unable to attend because she, too, was suffering from influenza.

Hare was said to have modelled his acting on François Joseph Regnier (1807–1885), whom he had studied closely in Paris, but the influence of the Bancrofts at the Prince of Wales's is also undeniable. Hare was a polished and subtle actor and he understood his somewhat limited capabilities. The roles he tackled were memorable because of his mastery of impersonation, and he was particularly adept at expressing gentle emotions with perfect simplicity. He strived for natural deportment and facial expression, and never degenerated into caricature. As a manager he encouraged English dramatists and actors and generally improved the stage. His choice of repertory was governed by a secure taste and vivified by finished, polished stage management. Although he was modest and retiring, he could as a director be strict and peppery, and even sarcastic. However, this slight man, with a remarkable stage presence, was suffused with personal charm and was both respected and loved by his profession.   J. P. WEARING

Sources T. E. Pemberton, *John Hare, comedian, 1865–1895* (1895) • *Who was who in the theatre, 1912–1976*, 4 vols. (1978) • D. Barrett, 'John Hare's Court Theatre, 1875–1879', *Nineteenth Century Theatre Research*, 8 (1980), 71–86 • T. E. Pemberton, *The Kendals* (1900) • C. E. Pascoe, ed., *The dramatic list*, 2nd edn (1880) • D. Mullin, ed., *Victorian actors and actresses in review: a dictionary of contemporary views of representative British and American actors and actresses, 1837–1901* (1983) • B. Duncan, *The St James's Theatre: its strange and complete history, 1835–1957* (1964) • m. cert. • d. cert.

Likenesses W. H. Kendal, process print, 1881, NPG • Barraud, photograph, 1890, NPG; repro. in Barrett, 'John Hare's Court Theatre' • J. E. Millais, oils, 1893, Garr. Club [*see illus.*] • W. & D. Downey, woodburytype photograph, 1894, NPG • H. G. Riviere, oils, 1908, Garr. Club • E. A. Abbey, pencil, Garr. Club • H. Ashdown, photograph, repro. in Pemberton, *John Hare* • W. & D. Downey, photograph, Harvard TC; repro. in W. Downey and D. Downey, *The cabinet* *portrait gallery* (1890–94) • Elliott & Fry, photographs, repro. in Pemberton, *John Hare* • A. Ellis & Walery, photograph, repro. in J. Parker, ed., *The green room book, or, Who's who on the stage* (1907) • Falk, photograph, Harvard TC • H. Furniss, pen-and-ink sketch, NPG; repro. in H. Furniss, *The Garrick Gallery of caricatures* (1905) • London Stereoscopic Co., carte-de-visite, NPG • E. Matthews & Sons, lithograph, NPG • J. E. Millais, photogravure, Harvard TC • Spy [L. Ward], chromolithograph caricature, NPG; repro. in *VF* (1 March 1890), pl. 462 • Walker & Boutall, photograph, Harvard TC • Window & Grove, photographs, repro. in Pemberton, *John Hare, comedian* • lithograph, Harvard TC • photograph, repro. in Pemberton, *John Hare* • two woodburytype cartes-de-visites, NPG

Wealth at death £30,066 5s. 6d.: probate, 1 March 1922, *CGPLA Eng. & Wales*

Hare, John Hugh, first Viscount Blakenham (1911–1982),

politician, was born in London on 22 January 1911, the third of four sons and the third of six children of Richard Granville Hare, fourth earl of Listowel (1866–1931), and his wife, Freda (1885–1968), daughter of Francis Vanden-Bempdé-Johnstone, second Baron Derwent. After schooling at Eton College he worked for two years on Wall Street. Shortly after his return he married, on 31 January 1934, the Hon. (Beryl) Nancy (1908–1994), daughter of Weetman Harold Miller Pearson, second Viscount Cowdray. They had a son and two daughters.

John Hare's eldest brother, William Francis *Hare, fifth earl of Listowel, supported the Labour Party (and served as a junior minister in the Attlee government); his father-in-law had been a Liberal MP. But Hare himself was a Conservative with paternalistic views and a strong desire to contribute to public life. From 1937 to 1952 he served as an alderman on London county council, and at the time of his first election he was its youngest member. He was opposition leader on the London county council's housing committee, and became chairman of the London Municipal Society (1947–52), which ran the Conservative Party's local government activity in London.

Despite Hare's career in London politics, he was based in Suffolk, where he had a 600 acre dairy farm. During the Second World War he served with the Suffolk yeomanry, seeing action in north Africa and taking part in the Salerno and Anzio landings in Italy. A brave soldier who was mentioned in dispatches, he ended the war with an OBE and the US Legion of Merit. By then he had been promoted to lieutenant-colonel.

At the general election of 1945 Hare was returned as MP for the safe Conservative seat of Woodbridge (from 1950 Sudbury and Woodbridge), which he represented until 1963. He was not an inspiring speaker, and when his party regained office in 1951 he did not obtain a ministerial post. Instead he was given special responsibility for the Conservative Party candidates' list, as a deputy chairman of the party under Lord Woolton. This proved to be an inspired appointment. In the wake of the Maxwell-Fyfe reforms, and the much-praised 1950 intake of MPs, the party needed to maintain its drive to field candidates more representative of the general public. Hare was an extremely shrewd judge of character, and was prepared to champion talented recruits who did not conform to the traditional profile of Conservative MPs.

After the general election of 1955 Hare received his first government appointment as minister of state for colonial affairs. In October 1956 he was promoted to secretary of state for war, and was plunged almost immediately into the Suez crisis. He made clear his opposition to the adventure, but chose not to resign at a time when the survival of the government was at stake. By January 1958 he had proved his administrative capabilities, and he was moved again to a more congenial post. With his farming background he was a natural minister for agriculture, fisheries, and food, but the fact that he often knew more about the issues than his officials could sometimes be a handicap. After two and a half years at agriculture he was moved again, reaching the cabinet as minister of labour in July 1960.

Hare's new task was crucial for the government of Harold Macmillan. The prime minister was preparing a more interventionist strategy in the hope of reversing Britain's relative economic decline, for which good relations with the trade unions were essential. He worked closely with his friend, the chancellor of the exchequer Selwyn Lloyd, in promoting the National Economic Development Council ('Neddy'), which brought government, industry, and unions together in a tripartite forum. Hare was present at its first meeting on 7 March 1962. He also introduced legislation (the Contracts of Employment Act) which established minimum standards for conditions at work. He had a particular interest in industrial training, initiating some of the earliest efforts to establish industrial training boards with government assistance. But although Hare was an emollient character, the trade unions did not share his desire for constructive co-operation. In 1962 a record number of workers (more than 4 million) were involved in industrial disputes, and he found himself having to fend off demands from within the party to remove some of the trade unions' legal immunities.

Hare was personally involved in the events which led to Macmillan's downfall. During the 'night of the long knives' in July 1962 he had contemplated resigning in support of Selwyn Lloyd following the latter's dismissal; instead, he sought an undertaking from Macmillan that Lloyd's budgetary policy would be maintained. Hare was also a close friend of the disgraced secretary of state for war, John Profumo. The immediate effect of Macmillan's departure in October 1963 was congenial to Hare, who admired the new prime minister, Alec Douglas-Home. Originally Hare had supported Lord Hailsham, but changed his mind when the latter's conduct at the party conference provoked adverse comment. In the ensuing reshuffle Hare left the Ministry of Labour and took over as party chairman from Iain Macleod and Oliver Poole, retaining his seat in the cabinet as a sign of the prime minister's special trust. He left the Commons, taking a hereditary peerage in November 1963 as Viscount Blakenham (the name commemorated his home in Suffolk).

Blakenham had a difficult period as Conservative Party chairman. Almost immediately the Conservatives lost Luton in a by-election (on the day that Home survived his own electoral test at Kinross and West Perthshire). On

Blakenham's advice, the prime minister decided against a general election in the spring of 1964. But although the gap in the opinion polls narrowed just before October's general election, the Conservatives were always trailing Labour. The party's task was not helped by the abolition of resale price maintenance, which Blakenham opposed; but the new prime minister, Harold Wilson, proved a more serious handicap. Even if Blakenham had been a master of public relations he could not have sold Home to a modern electorate. During the campaign Blakenham dutifully attacked the opposition, but he seemed ill-suited to the new demands of a television age.

Blakenham resigned as party chairman in January 1965, against Home's wishes. His personal sense of failure was unjustified; always a popular figure at central office, he had worked tirelessly to keep up morale and in view of the party's handicaps the organization had performed extremely well in confining Labour's overall majority to four. Ironically, although Blakenham might not have worked smoothly with Edward Heath, who took over from Home in August 1965, his own successor as chairman, Edward du Cann, was even less congenial to the new leader.

Blakenham was not quite fifty-four when he resigned, but he never returned to front-line politics. Instead he devoted himself to his farming, and undertook various charitable works. He was on the council of Toynbee Hall (where Profumo was also active) from 1966. He had a great love of gardening and cultivated a woodland garden at his home, Cottage Farm, Little Blakenham. After 1971 he was treasurer of the Royal Horticultural Society, for which he was awarded the society's Victoria medal of honour in 1974. But his health in his final years was poor. He died in London on 7 March 1982.   MARK GARNETT

Sources DNB · *The Times* (9 March 1982) · W. Whitelaw, *The Times* (13 March 1982) · private information (2004) · K. Young, *Sir Alec Douglas-Home* (1970) · J. Ramsden, *The age of Churchill and Eden, 1940–1957* (1995) · J. Ramsden, *The winds of change: Macmillan to Heath, 1957–1975* (1996) · A. Horne, *Macmillan*, 2: *1957–1986* (1989) · D. R. Thorne, *Selwyn Lloyd* (1989) · Burke, *Peerage*
Archives U. Birm. L., corresp. with Lord Avon
Likenesses group portrait, photograph, 1963, Hult. Arch. · Bassano, vintage print, NPG
Wealth at death £1,656,711: probate, 9 Aug 1982, CGPLA Eng. & Wales

Hare, Julius Charles (1795–1855), author and Church of England clergyman, was born on 13 September 1795 at Valdagno, Italy, the third of five children of Francis Hare-*Naylor (1753–1815), author, and his first wife, Georgiana Shipley (c.1755–1806), daughter of Jonathan *Shipley, bishop of St Asaph. He was baptized on 12 October 1795; his siblings were three brothers and a sister.

Hare was almost four when his parents moved to England from Italy, the country to which they had eloped and where they had found congenial shelter for their genteel poverty and republican views. His bluestocking mother tutored him for five years, until he briefly attended Tonbridge School from January to March 1804. In 1804 he accompanied his family to Weimar, where they met Goethe, Schiller, and fellow expatriate Henry Crabb

Julius Charles Hare (1795–1855), by John Henry Robinson, pubd 1852 (after George Richmond, 1850)

Robinson. There Julius's eldest brother, Francis, began teaching him German and Greek. After his mother's death in 1806 Hare attended Charterhouse School in London until 1812. There he received a solid, albeit narrow, education in the classics. His father's remarriage in 1807 and sale of the family's estate at Herstmonceaux, Sussex, led to some estrangement, and strengthened the attachment of the children to their maternal aunt, Lady Jones, the widow of the orientalist Sir William Jones.

At Michaelmas 1812 Hare matriculated as a pensioner at Trinity College, Cambridge, with a knowledge of German—then uncommon in England—and a passionate devotion to German literature and scholarship. His closest friends at Trinity, and for many years after, were Connop Thirlwall and William Whewell. At Cambridge Hare adopted some small spelling 'reforms', which he was said to have 'cherisht till he parisht', despite their failure to win wide acceptance. He succeeded, however, in inducing a circle of friends to study German, independent of the curriculum; thus began his pioneering efforts to promote German thinkers and writers. Familiarity with German ideas greatly influenced the careers of Hare, Thirlwall, and Whewell, but this foreign dimension in their work offended many critics. One of Hare's surviving manuscript commonplace books testifies to his devotion to classical and German writers, his wide reading of English literature and theology, and his deep admiration for the works of William Wordsworth and Samuel Taylor Coleridge. Despite his excellence as a classicist, Hare's disdain for mathematics excluded him from highest honours when he graduated BA in 1816. In October 1818 he was elected a fellow of Trinity. This provided a modest income, but long-term tenure of a fellowship would have required him to take holy orders and maintain celibacy. During a holiday spent in Paris that year, his eldest brother persuaded him to study law. In 1819, without his customary zeal, he took up residence in Hare Court, Middle Temple, and began desultorily reading for a career at law.

In 1822 Hare won a reprieve when Whewell obtained a classical lectureship for him. Hare's excellence as a teacher was attested by many students. Lecturing on Whewell's side, Hare taught only one-third of Trinity's undergraduates, but they included some remarkable students. Some, such as J. F. D. Maurice and John Sterling, became Hare's close friends. Both were Apostles, as members of the Cambridge Conversazione Society were known. As Charles Merivale, another Apostle, reminisced: 'Coleridge and Wordsworth were our principal divinities, and Hare and Thirlwall were regarded as their prophets.' Hare instilled respect in his students for literature as a serious pursuit, impelled some to the study of German thinkers and scholars, and inspired some to pursue scholarly careers. In 1825 Hare sought the regius professorship of Greek. While ideally qualified for the post, the religious partisanship of his own college's master blocked his election, and his best chance of devoting his life to the university. Hare's fellowship and lectureship supported his bibliomania, which produced a collection of 12,000 volumes. In 1825 Crabb Robinson judged it 'the best collection of modern German authors I have ever seen in England'. Lack of independent means, however, bound Hare to the college. Over the years this forced him to terminate two lengthy betrothals. He eventually married Jane Esther Maurice (1814–1864), younger sister of J. F. D. Maurice, on 12 November 1844; they had no children. His ordination as priest in 1826 was necessary both to retain his fellowship and to satisfy Lady Jones, from whom he expected a legacy. However, she died intestate in 1829.

While still at the inns of court Hare had begun a literary career which provided a distraction from the law and yielded some profit, without which, he explained to publisher Charles Ollier, he could ill spare the time to write. His rendering of Fouqué's Gothic tale *Sintram, and his Companions* appeared in 1820. Other translations and criticism appeared in *Ollier's Literary Miscellany*, *London Magazine*, *Quarterly Magazine*, and *The Athenaeum*; the latter was briefly run by former Cambridge students, including members of the Apostles led by Maurice and Sterling. Hare acted as editor and agent for Walter Savage Landor, and demonstrated his capacity for devoted friendship by supervising publication of Landor's *Imaginary Conversations* (1824–9). With his elder brother Augustus Hare, he compiled *Guesses at Truth* (1827), which went through at least twenty editions. *Guesses* also brought him the friendship of Daniel and Alexander Macmillan, whose bookselling and publishing business was founded upon a loan from Hare of £500. The Macmillans later reciprocated by buying up Hare's copyrights, and keeping many of his books in print for decades. Hare also assisted with publication of Thirlwall's translations of Schleiermacher's controversial essay on the gospel of St Luke (1821) and stories

by Ludwig Tieck (1825), and together they founded and edited the *Philological Museum* (1831–3) to promote the study of classical history and philology. Hare's largest, and perhaps most significant, scholarly work, also produced with Thirlwall, was a translation of the first two volumes of Barthold Niebuhr's history of Rome (1828–32). Thus they introduced English-speaking readers to prime examples of the German higher criticism in theology and historiography. This gained a foothold as the 'Germano-Coleridgean' school, whose exponents included several Trinity men and Apostles, as well as Hare's friend Thomas Arnold of Rugby. Unfortunately, in the eyes of many, these contributions tainted Hare and Thirlwall with German heterodoxy, and thus limited their opportunities for advancement in the church.

In 1832 the Hare family living of Herstmonceaux fell vacant. His brother Augustus refused it, so Julius became rector, but not before undertaking a nine-month tour of the continent with Landor, and acquiring valuable additions to his collection of Italian paintings. Hare's diffidence about his ability to communicate with common people was borne out in his parish career; his lengthy sermons went well over the heads of his parishioners and were the 'detestation' of Hare's hostile nephew and first biographer, A. J. C. *Hare.

Hare's main contribution to the church stemmed not from the cure of souls, but from his administrative work as archdeacon of Lewes, a position which he held from 1840 until his death, his non-partisan leadership, and his pursuit of his vision for the future of the Church of England. He strove for a truly national church, comprehending a broad spectrum of belief and theological opinion. The narrow partisanship of the high and low factions of the Church of England were so repellent to Hare and those who, like his brother-in-law, Maurice, shared his ideals that they vehemently rejected the label of 'broad-church party' which was later attached to them. Equally repugnant to Hare were Benthamites, Malthusians, and political economists, whose anti-Christian theories he denounced for arrogant self-righteousness in his best-known sermon, 'The Children of Light' (1828). Hare's commitment to religious toleration is best illustrated in his association with Henry Edward Manning, archdeacon of Chichester. Within their diocese they worked in harmony to build and restore churches, abolish pews, and establish schools. Hare sought to accept Manning's Tractarian sympathies and to minimize their doctrinal differences, while Manning emphasized them. However, Manning's later conversion to Rome even Hare could not rationalize. Hare's zeal for church reform and projects for reunion led him to promote the revival of convocation and rural deaneries, and to collaborate with his friend, Prussian diplomat and scholar Baron Christian J. K. Von Bunsen, to create in 1841 a protestant bishopric of Jerusalem, sponsored by the British and Prussian governments.

While Hare persisted in viewing Manning as an ally, he had no such illusions about J. H. Newman, who cast doubt on Arnold's Christianity. Newman's later attacks upon

Luther, of whose works Hare was an avid collector and student, elicited spirited rebuttals in Hare's *The Victory of Faith* (1840) and *The Mission of the Comforter* (1846). (The latter prompted the king of Prussia to award Hare his government's gold medal of science, which only confirmed Hare's critics in their hostility.) Hare's career as polemicist had begun somewhat earlier, in 1829, when his *Vindication of Niebuhr's History* appeared in response to criticisms in the *Quarterly Review*. Thomas De Quincey's criticism of Coleridge in 1834 elicited from Hare a passionate defence. His outraged sense of justice later prompted him to write defences of Bunsen, Bishop Hampden, and Sterling. No labour pained him more than the last, for his biography of Sterling, prefixed to his edition of Sterling's *Essays and Tales* (1848), started the controversy by publicizing Sterling's religious doubts. (Sterling named Hare and Thomas Carlyle as his literary co-executors.) Displeasure with Hare's work inspired Carlyle's better-known *Life of John Sterling* (1851). This is precisely what Hare had hoped to prevent. Hare's admirers have regretted that he dissipated his energy upon polemics, but these expressed the passionate side of his temperament. They also reinforced the impression that Hare, Maurice, and others—whose common bond was a shared dream of a national church and a non-literal reverence for the Bible—were a formal church party. By his pen Hare became, in the view of Thirlwall and others, both the archetype for, and principal defender of, the broad church.

Maurice's dismissal from King's College, London, in 1853 marked a watershed; it was clear that the broad-church advocates of toleration would not be tolerated within the church establishment. On this occasion, though Hare lent his support to an organized protest, he wrote no vindication. His health had broken down, and he was haunted by the idea that his defence of Sterling had done more harm than good. Despite ill health and the sight of friends subjected to calumnies within an increasingly divided church, Hare maintained a stoic optimism. Crabb Robinson noted that Hare was 'consistent, to a degree I envy, in his faith that all will end well'. Hare took pleasure in his appointment as a royal chaplain in June 1853, but regretted that his health left him unable to execute his duties. Suffering with chronic erysipelas, he died on 23 January 1855, and on the 30th of that month was buried in Herstmonceaux churchyard.

Twentieth-century scholarship, including that focused upon Maurice and his theology, retrieved Hare from obscurity: in the nineteenth his role as influential teacher, proponent of German literature and scholarship, and defender of broad-church ideals were obscured by Maurice's failure to produce a promised memorial biography and by Hare's own, perhaps too diffuse, labours. In the end, Hare's example, friendships, and influence on others form his most lasting claim to remembrance.

N. MERRILL DISTAD

Sources N. M. Distad, *Guessing at truth: the life of Julius Charles Hare (1795–1855)* (1979) · A. J. C. Hare, *Memorials of a quiet life*, 13th edn, 3 vols. (1872–6) · [A. P. Stanley], 'Archdeacon Hare', *QR*, 97 (1855), 1–23; repr. in J. C. Hare, *Victory of faith*, 3rd edn, ed. E. H. Plumptre (1874), xc–cxxxii · J. F. D. Maurice, 'Introduction', in J. C. Hare, *Charges to the clergy of the archdeaconry of Lewes*, 3 vols. in 1 (1856), i–lxiii [repr. as 'Essay on Archdeacon Hare's position within the church' in J. C. Hare, *Victory of faith*, 3rd edn (1874), xvii–lxxxix] · E. H. Plumptre, 'Memoir', in A. W. Hare and J. C. Hare, *Guesses at truth*, new edition (1866), xvii–liv · *The life of Frederick Denison Maurice*, ed. F. Maurice, 2 vols. (1884) · J. C. Thirlwall jun., *Connop Thirlwall: historian and theologian* (1936)

Archives JRL, letters · Trinity Cam., Baden-Powell family MSS, commonplace book and diary of continental tour [copies; originals in priv. coll.] | BL, Flaxman, Kingsley MSS · BL, corresp. with Macmillans, Add. MS 55109 · Bodl. Oxf., corresp. with H. E. Manning · CUL, Add. MSS · DWL, Crabb Robinson MSS · Hunt. L., F. J. Furnivall MSS · JRL, Landor MSS · JRL, Stanley MSS · JRL, Taylor MSS · Lancing College, Lancing, Sussex, corresp. with Nathaniel Woodard · N. Yorks. CRO, Havelock-Allen MSS · NYPL, Berg collection, corresp. with John Taylor · St Mary of the Angels, Bayswater, London, Manning archive · Trinity Cam., Thirlwall MSS · Trinity Cam., corresp. with W. Whewell · U. Leeds, Brotherton L., Thomas Arnold MSS · V&A, Forster MSS · W. Sussex RO, diocesan cause MSS, diocesan records

Likenesses G. Richmond, portrait, *c*.1832 · J. H. Robinson, stipple, pubd 1852 (after G. Richmond, 1850), BM, NPG [see illus.] · T. Woolner, white marble bust, after 1855, Trinity Cam. · W. Taylor, lithograph (after S. Laurence), NPG · engraving (after G. Richmond), Trinity Cam.

Hare, Sir Nicholas (*c*.1495–1557), lawyer and speaker of the House of Commons, was the first son of John Hare of Homersfield, Suffolk, and Elizabeth Fortescue. He was a pensioner of Gonville Hall, Cambridge, in 1509, and was admitted to the Inner Temple on 4 February 1515, probably after studying in one of the inns of chancery. He occupied chambers in the Outer Temple in the 1520s. Already by 1523 he was reckoned among the eighteen members of his inn liable to pay the poll tax, and was assessed as having £40 in goods. Later in the 1520s he was one of Wolsey's legal advisers. He was elected to parliament in 1529, 1539, 1545, and 1547, serving as speaker in 1539. He was married by 1528 to Katherine (*d.* 1557), daughter of Sir John Bassingbourne of Woodhall, near Hatfield, Hertfordshire, with whom he had three sons. In 1531 he was appointed counsel to the city of Norwich and a justice of the peace for Norfolk, becoming recorder of Norwich in 1536, perhaps in each case through the patronage of the third duke of Norfolk. His own home remained in Suffolk, however, and he established his seat at Bruisyard Hall in 1539.

When in 1532 Hare became a bencher of the Inner Temple, he touched in his reading on the topical subject of ecclesiastical jurisdiction, doubtless an indication that he was already bent on the royal service. The first principal appointment came in 1537, when he was made a stipendiary member of the king's council, or master of requests, and knighted. He held this judicial position until 1553, apart from an interval between 1540 and 1545 when he was chief justice of Chester. The latter post may have been a form of demotion following an incident in February 1540 when, together with Sir Humphrey Browne and William Coningsby, he was committed to the Tower by Star Chamber for advising Sir John Shelton on a means of avoiding the revenue consequences of the Statute of Uses, an event which led directly to the penning of the Statute of Wills of 1540. This was evidently considered to be a breach of his oath to serve the king. Only a few months later, however, he addressed the throne as speaker of the Commons upon the dissolution, comparing the English constitution to the microcosm, in which the king was the head, the peers the body, and the Commons the rest of the machine. His speech was received by the king with a gracious nod. Hare was also about this time steward of the Marshalsea. His favour with the king is evident from a mention in his will of a gilt pot 'of the sorte that king Henrye the eight gave me'.

On 18 September 1553 Mary I appointed Hare to be master of the rolls in place of Sir Robert Bowes, with a retrospective grant of the profits of the office from 1 April. Considered one of Mary's most trusted advisers, he is nevertheless said to have opposed her marriage to Philip of Spain. In 1554 Hare was one of the commissioners for the trial of Sir Nicholas Throckmorton in Westminster Hall for high treason, and had several angry exchanges with the accused. Throckmorton mortally offended him by stating that it was from him that he had learned to mislike the Spanish match, and Hare retaliated injudiciously by refusing to examine one of his witnesses. Throckmorton was acquitted. In 1555 Hare sat on a commission for the trial of certain conjurors charged with compassing the queen's death by unlawful arts. In November of the same year he was for a short time sole commissioner of the great seal after the death of Stephen Gardiner.

Hare died in office on 31 October 1557 and was buried on 8 November in Temple Church, where there was formerly a monument with his arms. His wife died on 22 November the same year. He left the profits from a meadow in Homersfield 'to be yerely converted for evermore into deedes of charitie ... for my freendes soules and all christen soules', and £5 to the Inner Temple for church ornaments. His three sons, Michael, Robert *Hare (d. 1611) (the antiquary and member of parliament), and William were all to be recusants in the time of Elizabeth I; all died without issue, and the family estates passed to the descendants of Nicholas's younger brother John, a mercer of London and of Stow Bardolph, Norfolk. Three of John's sons became benchers of the Inner Temple and gave their name to Hare Court there. John's grandson Hugh Hare (d. 1667) was created Lord Coleraine in the peerage of Ireland in 1625, and another grandson, Ralph Hare, was created a baronet in 1641.   J. H. BAKER

Sources HoP, Commons, 1509–58, 2.296–7 · HoP, Commons, 1558–1603, vol. 2 · Foss, Judges, 5.374–6 · Sainty, Judges, 150 · F. A. Inderwick and R. A. Roberts, eds., A calendar of the Inner Temple records, 1 (1896) · will, PRO, PROB 11/39, sig. 46 · W. Hervey, The visitation of Suffolk, 1561, ed. J. Corder, 2, Harleian Society, new ser., 3 (1984), 247 · inquisition post mortem, PRO, C 142/114/31 · The reports of Sir John Spelman, ed. J. H. Baker, 2, SeldS, 94 (1978), 2.351 · BL, Harleian MS 5158, fol. 93v · W. Dugdale, Origines juridiciales, or, Historical memorials of the English laws, 3rd edn (1680), 178, 186 · Cooper, Ath. Cantab., 1.172 · W. R. Williams, The history of the great sessions in Wales, 1542–1830 (privately printed, Brecon, 1899) · D. MacCulloch, 'The Vita Mariae Angliae Reginae of Robert Wingfield of Brantham', Camden miscellany, XXVIII, CS, 4th ser., 29 (1984), 181–301, esp. 208

Hare, Robert (c.1530–1611), antiquary and benefactor of Cambridge University, was the second of the three sons of Sir Nicholas *Hare (d. 1557), master of the rolls, and Katherine, daughter of Sir John Bassingbourne. He matriculated as a fellow-commoner of Gonville Hall, Cambridge, on 12 November 1545, the same day as his elder brother, Michael. Like many of his station he did not graduate but was admitted to the Inner Temple (his father's inn) on 2 February 1548. In 1551 Hare may have been travelling on the continent: he acquired in that year a copy of Thomas Netter's Doctrinale, previously owned by the Carmelites of Ghent, and another manuscript of northern French provenance, but he was back in England by 15 July 1555, when he was one of the gentlemen appointed to bear the bannerols at the funeral of Anne of Cleves. Three years later he was in the service of William Paulet, marquess of Winchester, lord high treasurer to Mary and Elizabeth, and on Paulet's nomination he was admitted, on 14 June 1560, clerk of the pells, and was returned as MP for Dunwich to the parliament which met on 11 January 1563. Shortly afterwards he was again on his travels, buying manuscripts in Louvain in 1563 and in Paris in 1564 and 1565.

Thus far Hare's career had closely followed his father's, but whereas his father had risen to enjoy high offices of state Robert resigned the clerkship of the pells in 1570 or 1571 and thereafter devoted his life entirely to antiquarian activities. The pursuit of manuscripts was not unusual among gentlemen of his background, and he was certainly well known to his contemporary antiquaries, being at various times recorded as giving assistance to, or receiving it from, such scholars as Michael Heneage, Arthur Agarde, and John Stow. However, an additional reason for his withdrawal from public life may well have been Hare's recusancy and, in particular, the abortive rising of the Catholic families of East Anglia in 1570. In 1577 he, his brothers, and two others featured in the list for the Inner Temple in the diocesan return for recusants in England and Wales as 'not of a longe tyme continued emongst us but [to be] publikyelye noted to be verie backward in religion' (Ryan, 105), and in October the following year he was reported among the papists resorting for mass to the house in Spitalfields of Lord Chidiock Paulet, brother of his patron, the marquess of Winchester. It has been suggested that he maintained connections with the exchequer which helped protect East Anglian recusants from fiscal pressure. On 23 January 1601 Cambridge University voted to write to the chancellor, Sir Robert Cecil, praying that Hare be not hindered in his good works towards the university, which suggests that he was in trouble of some kind. As executor of William Mowse, sometime master of Trinity Hall, who died in 1588, Hare had increased by £600 Mowse's bequest of £1000 for the improvement of the highways, still evidenced today by the two men's arms on the first and sixteenth milestones on the road to Barkway.

Hare's other remarkable benefaction to Cambridge was his Liber privilegiorum et libertatum universitatis Cantebrigiensis, comprising transcripts of charters and letters patent relating to the university and, in one case, the town. This survives in three copies, of two, three, and four volumes respectively, the first, presented in 1590, magnificently illuminated. A similar set was presented to Oxford, but Hare's working papers for the Cambridge volumes (BL, Cotton MS Faustina c.iii), which also contain some original documents, including a letter from the university to Thomas Cromwell, suggest that he at one time contemplated a full-scale history of the university, meticulously sourced. It is alleged that Hare was prompted to this work by Dr Copcot, vice-chancellor in 1587 and master of Corpus Christi from 1588, but Hare seems to have started work on the project far earlier than the 1580s. He also wrote, between 1556 and 1557, 'A treatise on military discipline, and rules to be observed in time of war' (BL, Cotton MS Julius, fol. v).

Hare amassed a considerable collection of manuscripts, all of which he seems to have disposed of during his lifetime. In 1594 he returned to Cambridge University the collection of university records made by Thomas Markaunt, proctor in 1417/18, and presented manuscripts to several colleges, twelve of them to Trinity Hall, including Thomas Elmham's *Speculum Augustiniensis* of about 1414. Many of his printed books are also to be found in Cambridge libraries.

On 11 April 1611 Hare's brother Michael died and Robert inherited the estate at Bruisyard, Suffolk, formerly a Franciscan nunnery, which had been bought by his father in 1539. He did not enjoy it for long, however, for on 1 July following, describing himself as 'of greate age joyned with some infirmitye of bodye' he drew up his will (PRO, PROB 11/118, fol. 234). Hare's note in his manuscript of Elmham records how he had obtained it after the dissolution of St Augustine's, Canterbury, and provides for its restitution thither 'if hereafter, by God's favour, the monastery should happen to be rebuilt' (McKisack, 60–61), and his will, too, is a defiantly Catholic document, dedicating his soul to 'our blessed Ladie St Marie the virgin Mother of Christe my Savyoure, to St Michael the Archaungell and to all the holie Aungells and Archaungells and to the Rest of the glorious Company of heaven' and requesting the prayers of his friends. He had never married, but maintained links with his nephews, nieces, and cousins, ten of whom received bequests. Several of them were recusants like himself. One of the latter was 'my welbeloved neiphue Nicholas Tymperley the elder of Hintlesham esquire', who not only was made Hare's sole executor and residuary legatee, but also received the bequest of silver spoons and 'all my paynted pictures of Kynges Queenes Bishopps and other greate personages'. Hare's first named beneficiary was William Sebright, town clerk of London, 'my deere and steadfast freind in all my adversitie and trouble', and he also remembered his attorney in the exchequer and his solicitor. His will records the names of six servants, who were left cash bequests totalling £135, household goods, and the proceeds of the sale of his printed books. £5 were left to the parson of Bruisyard, 40s. to the poor of the parish. Most of the other legatees were to receive pieces of plate or gold coins, the latter often in the form of 'ducketts' or 'portugues'.

Hare died at Bruisyard on 2 November 1611 and was buried in St Paul's Cathedral, having obtained the grant of his burial place, at the west end of the nave, twenty years earlier. His will was proved four days after his death.

ELISABETH LEEDHAM-GREEN

Sources BL, Cotton MSS Julius, fol. 5; Faustina c.iii; Faustina c.vii · CUL, Hare A; Hare B; Hare C; Buxton MS 5/1 · S. Bentley, *Excerpta historica* (1831) · CSP dom., addenda, 1566–79, pp. 550–51 · Cooper, *Ath. Cantab.*, 3.47–9 · C. Crawley, *Trinity Hall: the history of a Cambridge college, 1350–1975* (1976) · A. W. W. Dale, ed., *Warren's book* (1911) · will, PRO, PROB 11/118, fol. 234 · D. MacCulloch, *Suffolk and the Tudors: politics and religion in an English county, 1500–1600* (1986) · A. G. Watson, 'Robert Hare's books', *The English medieval book: studies in memory of Jeremy Griffiths*, ed. A. S. G. Edwards, V. Gillespie, and R. Hanna (2000), 209–32 · M. McKisack, *Medieval history in the Tudor age* (1971) · P. Ryan, ed., 'Diocesan returns of recusants for England and Wales, 1577', *Miscellanea, XII*, Catholic RS, 22 (1921), 1–114
Archives BL, treatise on military discipline, Cotton MS Julius, fol. 5 · CUL, Hare A, Hare B, Hare C | BL, Cotton Faustina c.iii; Faustina c.vii · Gon. & Caius Cam., 391, 392
Wealth at death cash bequests of £149 10s.; 7 ducats and 2 'portugues'; much plate; pictures; household goods: will, PRO, PROB 11/118, fol. 234

Hare, (John) Robertson (1891–1979), actor, was born on 17 December 1891 at the family home, 26 Cloudesley Street, Islington, London, the younger child and only son of Frank Homer Hare, an accountant and later a newspaper manager, and his wife, Louisa Mary, *née* Robertson. He was educated at Margate College in Kent and was then coached for the stage by Lewis Cairns James. His first professional stage appearance was in 1911 when he played the Duke of Gallminster in a provincial production of *The Bear Leaders*. The following year he made his London début as one of the crowd in the Covent Garden production of *Oedipus Rex*, and in 1913 he had his first part in a metropolitan production, as Kaufman in *The Scarlet Band* at the Comedy Theatre. He then toured the provinces for a number of years, notably in the title role of *Grumpy*, which thereafter remained his favourite part. It commanded considerable success on tour during the early years of the First World War. He served for the last two years of the war with the army in France, having married (Alice) Irene Mewton (1890/91–1969), daughter of Samuel Mewton, on 16 December 1915. They had one daughter.

1922 was the crucial year of Hare's career. He played James Chesterman in *Tons of Money* at the Shaftesbury Theatre in London under the joint management of Tom Walls and Leslie Henson. In February 1924 he transferred, with the same management, to the Aldwych, where he opened as William Smith in *It Pays to Advertise*. This inaugurated the era of the famous Aldwych farces, and, for over ten years, the outrageous comedies of Ben Travers offered their contribution to the madcap climate of the twenties and early thirties in London. Chief among Hare's parts were the Revd Cathcart Sloley-Jones in *A Cuckoo in the Nest* (1925), Harold Twine in *Rookery Nook* (1926), Hook in *Thark* (1927), and Ernest Ramsbotham in *A Cup of Kindness* (1929). In all, he featured in twelve consecutive farces at the Aldwych between 1924 and 1933. The pattern of his career was by then firmly established. Apart from an occasional appearance in revue—*Fine Fettle*, for instance, in 1959—or in period farce in 1963, as Erronius in *A Funny Thing Happened on the Way to the Forum*, he was fairly strictly typecast as the nervy and fussy innocent, continually trapped in awkward situations. Between 1933 and 1960 he created such a character in over twenty more farces, several of them at the Strand Theatre. Herbert Holly (*Aren't Men Beasts!*, 1936), Humphrey Proudfoot (*One Wild Oat*, 1948), and, very successfully, Willoughby Pink (*Banana Ridge*, 1938) are perhaps his best-remembered roles from this period. During the sixties his extraordinarily active stage appearances began to diminish as he rested on his well-earned laurels, though he toured in *Arsenic and Old Lace*—a rare example of his playing in a comedy already well tried—and, after opening in the play at the Lyric in 1968, he visited South Africa as Dr Simmons in *Oh, Clarence!* in 1970, when he was almost eighty years old.

Hare's cinema work was of early vintage. In 1929 Herbert Wilcox, production chief of British and Dominion Studios at Elstree, began the straightforward and uncomplicated filming of several of the Aldwych farces, and Hare also made a few film appearances in the post-war years. *Thark* (1932) is usually regarded as the best cinematic translation of a Travers comedy. Hare wrote, not too successfully, a couple of plays and then, late in life, turned energetically to television. To the seventies' generation, who would scarcely have recognized him as a stage performer, he was best-known for his playing of the archdeacon in *All Gas and Gaiters*, a creditable comedy series with a clerical orientation, starring Derek Nimmo as Noote, a young and naïve clergyman.

Hare created a cosily familiar style and was identified completely with, in effect, one part, that of the prissy little man, constantly in a state of unease and agitation, invariably sucked into some maelstrom of domestic upset and dislocation, unfailingly compromised and often trouserless. The bald dome, with brows furrowing anxiously beneath it; the spectacles, emphasizing the shock and bewilderment with which he responded to his travails; the jerky, staccato movements as his distress grew—these made him a highly recognizable stage figure. In concert with the worldly wise Tom Walls and the affable Ralph Lynn and, later, in alliance, on stage or screen with the likes of Gordon Harker or Alfred Drayton, he became one of the premier exponents of English farce, particularly in the period between the wars. Above all, there was the somewhat archdeaconal, tremulous, and vacillating (though, from an audience stance, always clearly intelligible) voice. Rarely has a comic actor become so intimately associated with one word. Hare, faced with disaster, was wont to warble the five syllables of 'Oh, calamity' in a characteristic kind of plainchant. It is fitting that many should remember and identify him thus, and that 'Oh, calamity' should have passed into popular usage. *Yours Indubitably*, his autobiography, was published in 1957. He was appointed OBE just before he died in London on 25 January 1979.   ERIC MIDWINTER, *rev.*

Sources *The Times* (16 Nov 1979) • J. Parker, ed., *Who's who in the theatre*, 6th edn (1930) • I. Herbert, ed., *Who's who in the theatre*, 16th edn (1977) • personal knowledge (1986) • m. cert. • *DNB*

Archives FILM BFI NFTVA, propaganda film footage (ministry of information) • BFI NFTVA, performance footage | SOUND BL NSA, performance recordings
Likenesses photographs, 1933–54, Hult. Arch.

Hare, Thomas (1806–1891), political reformer, born on 28 March 1806, was the illegitimate son of Anne Hare (*d.* 1853) of Leigh, Dorset; Hare later recorded his father as being Thomas King, a farmer (m. cert.). On 14 November 1828 he was admitted as a student of the Inner Temple, and on 22 November 1833 he was called to the bar. He married on 7 August 1837 Mary (*d.* 1855), daughter of Thomas Samson, farmer, of Kingston Russell. He practised in the chancery courts and from 1841 reported in Vice-Chancellor Wigram's court. With Henry Iltid Nicholl and John Monson Carrow he edited the first two volumes (1840 and 1843) of *Cases Relating to Railways and Canals in the Courts of Law and Equity, 1835–1840*. His reports of cases adjudged by Wigram were published in eleven volumes (1843–58), and were regarded as authoritative. He published in 1836 *A Treatise on Discovery of Evidence by Bill and Answer in Equity*. A second edition, 'adapted to the supreme court of judicature acts and rules 1873 and 1875', was published by his eldest son, Sherlock Hare, in 1876. In 1872 he was elected a bencher of his inn.

Hare was appointed an inspector of charities on 22 October 1853, and on 7 December 1872 was created assistant commissioner with a seat at the board. He married, secondly, on 4 April 1872, Eleanor Bowes Benson (1833–1890), second sister of Edward White Benson. On 21 December 1887 he retired from official life. During these years he was engaged in reporting on the charities of the United Kingdom; his reports on London charities filled, in a collected form, the third volume of the reports of the royal city charities commission. He was well known for his hard work, wide interests in life, and clearness of intellectual vision. He belonged to the Athenaeum and Political Economy clubs, and until his death was actively interested in their proceedings.

Hare's principal fame rests in his efforts to devise a system of proportional (or, as he put it, personal) representation of all classes and opinions in the United Kingdom, including minorities, in the House of Commons and other electoral assemblies. His views, sharpened by the 1857 election, which saw the defeat of the opponents of the Crimean War, Liberal radicals and Peelite tories, were set out at first in *The Machinery of Representation* (1857, 2 edns), and they were afterwards more fully developed in his *Treatise on the Election of Representatives, Parliamentary and Municipal* (1859, 1861, 1865, and 1873). This was a very technical work setting out machinery (including a national constituency comprising thousands of candidates) that was generally regarded as too complicated for practical operation, but 1500 copies of the treatise were sold by 1875, and many societies were formed for its propagation. Hare's views received powerful endorsement when John Stuart Mill commended them in the second edition of *Thoughts on Parliamentary Reform* (1859) and he helped Henry Fawcett in

Thomas Hare (1806–1891), by Lowes Cato Dickinson, 1867

the preparation of the latter's pamphlet *Mr Hare's Reform Bill, Simplified and Explained* (1860). Fawcett thought Hare's scheme offered 'the only remedy against the great danger of an oppression of minorities' (Stephen, 170). With the aid of Mill, Fawcett, G. J. Holyoake, and Max Kyllmann, Hare had some success in popularizing the scheme of personal representation among the working class, and he formed the Representative Reform Association with George Howell and Edmond Beales. Through Mill, Hare also became involved in the co-operative movement (he was on the committee of the 1869 congress and delivered a paper there) and joined Mill's Land Tenure Reform Association, serving on the executive committee in 1873.

Hare's other works included: a pamphlet in support of the relaxation of the navigation laws, published in 1826 at the request of his early mentor, William Huskisson; *The Development of the Wealth of India* (1861), a reprint from *Macmillan's Magazine*; *Usque ad coelum: Thoughts on the Dwellings of the People, Charitable Estates, Improvement and Local Government in the Metropolis* (1862); *The Distribution of Seats in Parliament* (1879); and *London Municipal Reform* (1882), which contained many papers he had previously published on that subject. He contributed to Alfred Hill's volume of *Essays upon Educational Subjects* (1857) a paper on 'Endowments created for the apprenticeship of children'. He was also a regular contributor to the *Fortnightly Review* between 1865 and 1885.

Hare died at his London home, Carlyle Mansions, Chelsea, on 6 May 1891, and was buried at Hook, near Surbiton,

Surrey, on 9 May. Of the eight children by his first marriage, the eldest daughter, Marian, wife of the Revd William Ryton Andrews, wrote under the pseudonym Christopher Hare. The second daughter, Alice, married John Westlake. The only child of his second marriage, Mary Eleanor (1874–1883), predeceased him.

W. P. COURTNEY, *rev.* MATTHEW LEE

Sources *The Times* (7 May 1891) · L. Courtney, *The Athenaeum* (16 May 1891), 635–6 · J. Westlake, *The Academy* (16 May 1891), 465–6 · J. Hart, *Proportional representation: critics of the British electoral system, 1820–1945* (1992) · L. Goldman, *Henry Fawcett and British liberalism* (1989) · F. Parsons, 'Thomas Hare and the Victorian proportional representation movement, 1857–1888', PhD diss., U. Cam., 1990 · M. Lee, 'John Stuart Mill, George Jacob Holyoake and the "social question": themes of continuity in mid-nineteenth century radicalism and socialism', PhD diss., U. Cam., 1996 · *Wellesley index* · L. Stephen, *Life of Henry Fawcett* (1886) · *CGPLA Eng. & Wales* (1891) · private information (2004) [family] · m. cert.
Likenesses L. C. Dickinson, oils, 1867, NPG [*see illus.*] · A. Westlake, pencil drawing, *c.*1885, NPG
Wealth at death £10,593 15s. 5d.: probate, 28 May 1891, *CGPLA Eng. & Wales*

Hare, William (*b.* 1792/1804). *See under* Burke, William (1792–1829).

Hare, William Francis, fifth earl of Listowel (1906–1997), politician, was born on 28 September 1906 at 37 Wilton Crescent, London, the eldest child in the family of four sons and two daughters of Richard Granville Hare, Viscount Ennismore, and later fourth earl of Listowel (1866–1931), and his wife, Freda (1885–1968), younger daughter of Francis Vanden-Bempde-Johnstone, second Baron Derwent. His younger brothers all served with distinction in their chosen fields. Richard Gilbert Hare (1907–1966) became professor of Russian literature at the University of London; John Hugh *Hare (1911–1982) was Conservative MP for Woodbridge, Suffolk, from 1945 to 1963 and chairman of the Conservative Party from 1963 to 1965, and was ennobled as the first Viscount Blakenham in 1963; and Alan Victor Hare (1919–1995) served in MI6 before becoming chairman of the *Financial Times*.

At the time of his birth, Hare's family, an Anglo-Irish offshoot of the ancient Hares of Norfolk, owned estates in Ireland and London; the latter included Kingston House, his grandparents' residence in Knightsbridge, and Ennismore Gardens. Young Billy (as he was universally known) grew up with his younger siblings at 14 Bryanston Square, spending holidays with his Derwent grandparents at Hackness Hall, near Scarborough in Yorkshire. Most unusually for someone of his background and upbringing, he became a socialist during his schooldays at Eton College, having been deeply affected by the sight of ragged children playing barefoot in the street near Bryanston Square. From that time, he said, he viewed the Labour Party as 'the standard bearer of radical social change' (private information). The only other person at Eton thought to share his views was the headmaster's wife, Mrs Alington. From Eton, he went up to Balliol College, Oxford, to read politics, philosophy, and economics. But his father removed him after a year, having read newspaper reports of his socialist opinions (discussion of party politics was banned at home), and wrongly suspecting that the left-wing master of Balliol, A. D. Lindsay, was to blame for them. A place was found for him at Magdalene College, Cambridge, where he switched to reading English. After Cambridge—where his political views, and his preference to be known as Mr W. F. Hare rather than Viscount Ennismore (a courtesy title to which he became entitled in 1924 when his father became fourth earl of Listowel) continued to attract press interest and to infuriate his father—he went to the Sorbonne in Paris to study aesthetics under Professor Victor Basch, later developing his research into a well-received doctoral thesis at London University. It was published as *A Critical History of Modern Aesthetics* in 1933; a revised edition was published as *Modern Aesthetics: an Historical Introduction* in 1967.

In 1931 Hare's father died, disinheriting him and his next brother, Richard (an intellectual who had failed to show any interest in sport), in favour of his brothers John and Alan. Nevertheless he succeeded his father in both the Irish earldom of Listowel and the UK barony of Hare, under which title he took his seat among the handful of Labour peers in the then entirely hereditary House of Lords, and there he soon made an impression as a knowledgeable and earnest debater. Perceiving the growth of European fascism to pose a dire threat to his hopes for social reform, he made several visits to the continent at this period. In 1934 he and the Labour MP Ellen Wilkinson were censured by the national executive of the Labour Party for acting without authority in visiting Spain to protest about the maltreatment of miners in the Asturias. The pair had eventually been escorted to the French frontier by the national guard. With the outbreak of war in 1939, Listowel—who had by then been sitting on the Labour front bench in the Lords for three years—joined up as a private in the Royal Army Medical Corps. Shortly afterwards, because he knew some German, he was transferred to the intelligence corps and commissioned, along with A. J. Ayer, the Oxford philosopher, as a second lieutenant. But in 1941 he was required by his leader in the Lords, Lord Addison, to return to civilian life as opposition chief whip.

Listowel's involvement with India began in October 1944, when he became deputy leader (to the marquess of Salisbury) in the Lords and under-secretary of state at the India Office, under Leo Amery. Three years later, when the Labour government had resolved on independence for India and appointed Mountbatten as viceroy, the latter requested that Listowel, by then postmaster-general, be appointed secretary of state. He took up this post (which included responsibility for Burma) in April 1947. The India Independence Bill was introduced into the Commons on 4 July 1947, and Listowel then steered it through the Lords, unamended, by the end of the month. With parliament's summer recess impending, any amendment would have jeopardized the timetable for independence on 15 August. While honours were then showered on Mountbatten, Listowel was simply thanked by the king and by the prime minister, Clement Attlee. He remained as secretary of state for Burma until January 1948, when Burma became an independent republic and left the Commonwealth.

In January 1948 Listowel was given a post outside the cabinet as minister of state for the colonies. He went to Malaya for the inaugural session of the federal legislative council, and to Barbados to preside at a meeting of all the governors in the region (the first such meeting of its kind). In British Guiana he was surprised to find Amerindian children learning English from a book which began 'The Scottish nobleman strode out from his castle into the snow' (private information). His last ministerial post was as joint parliamentary secretary at the Ministry of Agriculture and Fisheries, from November 1950 to October 1951—an odd post, he once observed, for someone who had never tended more than a window-box in London. In March 1957 he was appointed, at Kwame Nkrumah's request, governor-general of Ghana. He was scrupulous in remaining above politics, restored relations between Nkrumah and the Asantahene, and in later life would remember his three years in Accra with particular pleasure. He returned to England when Ghana became a republic within the Commonwealth in July 1960. Labour regained power in 1964, and the next year he was appointed chairman of committees and deputy speaker of the House of Lords. Thereafter, until retiring in 1976, he adhered strictly to the non-party line demanded, and by his patience, acuity, and attractive manner never failed to achieve a consensus. He was sworn of the privy council in 1946, and was appointed GCMG in 1957. By the time of his death he was the longest-serving member of both the House of Lords and the privy council.

Listowel was thrice married. He married first, on 24 July 1933, Judith de Marffy-Mantuano, only daughter of Raoul de Marffy-Mantuano, Hungarian diplomat and politician, and herself a prominent political activist, though of a different political persuasion from Listowel. There was one child of the marriage, Deirdre Mary Freda (b. 1935), which ended in 1945 in divorce. Listowel married second, on 1 July 1958, Stephanie Sandra Yvonne Currie, otherwise known as Stevie Wise, jazz singer, daughter of Sam Wise of Toronto, and former wife of Hugh Currie. There was one daughter of this marriage, Fiona Eve Akua (b. 1960), which also ended (in 1963) in divorce. Listowel then married third, and happily, on 4 November 1963, Pamela Mollie Reid, hairdresser, daughter of Francis Day, bus driver, of Croydon, and former wife of John Alexander Reid, middleweight boxer. There were three children of this marriage, Francis Michael (b. 1964), Diana France (b. 1965), and Timothy Patrick (b. 1966).

Mild-mannered and unassuming, but nevertheless tenacious in his political beliefs, Listowel was held in great affection by all who came across him. He died in London of heart failure on 12 March 1997, and was survived by his third wife and his five children. He was succeeded as sixth earl of Listowel by the older son of his third marriage.

GEORGE IRELAND

Sources earl of Listowel [W. F. Hare], *Memoirs* (privately printed, 1995) • *The Times* (13 March 1997) • *The Independent* (13 March 1997) • *Daily Telegraph* (13 March 1997) • *The Guardian* (14 March 1997) •

WWW [forthcoming] · Burke, *Peerage* (1970) · private information (2004) · personal knowledge (2004) · b. cert. · *CGPLA Eng. & Wales* (1997)
Archives priv. coll. | BL OIOC, corresp. with Lord Mountbatten, Sir H. E. Rance · Bodl. RH, Fabian Bureau papers
Likenesses B. Organ, oils, 1995?, priv. coll. · photograph, repro. in *The Times* · photograph, repro. in *The Independent* · photograph, repro. in *Daily Telegraph* · photograph, repro. in *The Guardian*
Wealth at death £5482: probate, 1 Aug 1997, *CGPLA Eng. & Wales*

Harewood. For this title name *see* Lascelles, Henry, second earl of Harewood (1767–1841); Lascelles, Henry George Charles, sixth earl of Harewood (1882–1947).

Harflete, Henry (*b.* 1580), writer, was the eldest son of Henry Harflete of Hills Court, Ash-next-Sandwich, Kent, and Mary, daughter and heir of George Slaughter of Ash. His was an old Kentish family, traceable to the reign of Henry II. About 1620 he married Dorcas, daughter of Joshua Pordage of Sandwich; they had six sons and four daughters. Henry's eldest son, also called Henry, was born on 27 September 1633, remained unmarried in 1663, and was buried at Ash in 1679, and with him the line expired.

Harflete inherited his father's law books in 1608 and in 1630 was admitted to Gray's Inn. Like some of his more famous contemporaries, he found the law tiresome and fulfilled himself instead in literary pursuits. In 1632 he published *The Hunting of the Fox, or, Flattery Displayed*. He treats this Jonsonian theme intelligently, noting, for instance, that flattery kills 'two at a blow; the flatterer, and the flattered' (p. 12), and his prose occasionally rises to an impressive combination of clarity and suggestiveness.

Harflete is better known for his next and very different work, *Vox coelorum: Predictions Defended*, in which he aligns himself with the controversial astrologer William Lilly, and argues for the dignity of astrological science, quoting scripture, appealing to experience, and seeing in the heavens the designing hand of God. The date of 1645 written in the British Library copy is too early, for it contains references (pp. 55, 58) to Lilly's almanac for 1646. There is a distinct note of personal disappointment. Harflete addresses a supposedly indifferent reader and contends that the world is in its Iron Age, the position of intellectuals precarious. Lilly, the author of *Monarchy and No Monarchy* (1651), was a republican: Harflete observes in his preface that he has himself 'laboured day and night in the Parliaments service'.

In his prefatory epistle to *Vox coelorum*, Harflete had signed himself 'a well-wisher to the Mathematicks' and in 1653 he brought out an almanac for Sandwich and Dover praising and deploying the new decimal arithmetic. He also published in that year *A Banquet of Essayes*, consisting of seven prose pieces on one of Owen's epigrams, in which there are frequent translations from Horace, Owen, and others. Lately the defender of learning, Harflete now emerges as the opponent of pedantry. 'The world is a sea', he writes, 'upon which the theoretical reader floates in the pinnace of self-opinionated praise, driven by the winde of vaine-glory' (p. 12). Again the note of frustrated hopes is heard, but tempered now by a lofty resignation. Harflete admits, 'I have little sought to winde

my selfe into the worlds favour, since I have experienced its ficklenesse' (p. 76), and his sixth essay disclaims praise. And yet, from the beginning there had been a strain of *contemptus mundi* in his writings, as well as an undercurrent of more particular misogyny. The preface to *The Hunting of the Fox* had favourably quoted St Gregory's comparison of this world to 'a rotten nut, which being opened with the knife of verity, you shall find nothing within but rottenness, and vanity'. It is not known when Harflete died.						EWAN FERNIE

Sources *DNB* · J. R. Planché, *A corner of Kent* (1864) · H. Harflete, *The hunting of the fox* (1632) · H. Harflete, *Vox coelorum* [n.d.] · H. Harflete, *A banquet of essayes* (1653)

Harford family (*per. c.*1700–1866), merchants, brass manufacturers, and bankers, came to prominence with Charles Harford (1631–1709). He and his immediate descendants were Quakers. Charles Harford, the first Harford to enter trade in Bristol, was the son of Mark Harford (1570–1652) of Marshfield in Gloucestershire. He was active in soap-boiling in the 1680s and 1690s, and in plans to set up a brassworks in 1700. In an eventful life he was among many Bristol Quakers imprisoned for not attending national worship, and in 1691 he was fined heavily for customs fraud. By his first marriage in 1656, to Mary Bushe (*d.* 1667), Charles Harford had six children. His second son, Charles Harford the younger (1662–1725), merchant, was the father of Trueman Harford (1704–1750), father of James *Harford (1734–1817), iron and tin-plate manufacturer. His eldest son, Edward, was the head of the three branches of the family in brass-making and banking.

Edward [i] **Harford** (1658–1705) continued in his father's trade of soap-making and married Elizabeth Jones (1670–1729) in 1689; they had ten children. He expanded into the tobacco trade, and became part-owner of a ship. His three grandsons in the separate Blaise Castle, Stapleton, and Stoke Bishop lines became especially prominent.

The Stoke Bishop line was the branch most intimately involved with brass-making. It began with Mark [i] Harford (1700–1788), eighth child of Edward [i] Harford and Elizabeth Jones. Mark [i] Harford was a haberdasher of small wares who became connected with the brass trade through his marriage to Love Andrews, granddaughter of one of the founders of the Bristol Brass Company. The company was begun as the Bristol Brass Wire Company in 1702 by Quaker merchants including John Andrews, Nehemiah Champion, Thomas Coster, Abraham Darby, and Edward Lloyd, and it dominated the British brass trade for nearly a century. Mark [i] Harford's only child, **Mark** [ii] **Harford** (1738–1798) of Stoke Bishop, increased the family's stake in the company by marrying Sarah (*d.* 1798), daughter of Samuel Lloyd, in 1762, and became its leader. In the following years it became one of the most important industrial enterprises in the world, owning copper mines, smelters, and brassworks, in Cornwall, Bristol and its environs, Esher in Surrey, Lower Redbrook in the Wye valley, and Swansea. Mark [ii] Harford headed a committee of nine, on which sat five Harfords, including his first cousins Edward [iii] and Joseph, of the Blaise Castle and Stapleton branches. He reorganized the company in 1788 as the Harford and Bristol Brass and Copper Company with additional capital of £100,000 and ten members, of whom six were Harfords.

Mark [ii] Harford retired in 1796, and leadership of the company passed for six years to his cousin Joseph Harford of Stapleton before returning to his second son, Mark [iii] Harford (*b.* 1768). In 1799 it could still be described by its chief rival, Thomas Williams, as 'perhaps the most considerable brass house in all Europe' (Day, 112). However, it was already declining and was managed largely as a static investment. The company continued to use slow methods to make traditional goods such as brass ingots and wire, copper sheets, and battery-ware pans and kettles. By contrast the Birmingham industry was developing new techniques and products such as gas fittings and machine components. The industrial empire began to fall apart, and even its central sites were allowed to decay. Woodborough battery mill was derelict by the 1790s, Weston battery mill was sold about 1811, and Baptist Mills was abandoned around 1814. All smelting had ceased by 1820. From 1833 the company was simply a property owner, with its remaining premises leased for £500 per annum; it was sold by the Harford family in 1862.

The Stapleton line originated with Charles Harford (1704–1746), grocer, youngest child of Edward [i] Harford and Elizabeth Jones. Charles married Mary (*d.* 1742), the daughter of Joseph Beck of Frenchay and niece of one of the partners in the Old Bank. Their sons were Trewman Harford (*fl.* 1727–1761), merchant, and **Joseph Harford** (1741–1802), born at Frenchay, Bristol. Joseph Harford's commercial interests were based upon his father's wholesale grocery business in Queen's Square, but he extended into important new areas. He was a founding partner of the New Bank in 1786 and a partner in the bank of Ames, Cave & Co. from 1786 to 1798. He was a member of Merchant's Hall, and master of the Society of Merchant Venturers in 1796. His industrial interests centred on the Bristol Brass Company, of which he was a committee member, and leader from 1796 to 1802, but he also had interests in the iron, tin, and glass trades, and financed Richard Champion's Bristol China Works in 1768.

Joseph Harford aggrandized the family by marrying in 1763 Hannah (*d.* 1811), daughter of Joseph Kill of Stapleton Grove, near Bristol, where they took up residence. He became a justice of the peace, treasurer of Bristol Infirmary, promoter of the Bristol Library Society, and chairman of the Bristol slavery abolition committee. He was prominent in Bristol politics during the radical campaign of 1769 and was in 1771 one of Edmund Burke's two sponsors to become a member of parliament, opening his campaign with a subscription of £300. Burke said, 'You could not have a better man than Mr Harford. He has a great bottom for confidence. He has a firm Integrity; very enlarged notions; and one of the most solid and well cultivated understandings I have met with' (Underdown, 137). Harford himself was elected to Bristol common council in

1779 and acted as high sheriff on three occasions. The Society of Friends disavowed him for taking his oath, resulting in his conversion to the Church of England. Joseph Harford died at Stapleton Grove on 11 October 1802.

The Blaise Castle descendants of Edward [i] Harford and Elizabeth Jones sprang from their son Edward [ii] Harford (1691–1779), merchant, who married Elizabeth Lloyd, daughter of Edward Lloyd of the Brass Company. Edward [ii] expanded his father's mercantile and industrial interests, beginning to import tobacco from Virginia in 1724 and owning a ship, taking a partnership in a glassworks in 1724, and holding membership of the Brass Company. His business was carried on by his only child, **Edward [iii] Harford** (1720–1806) of Frenchay, merchant, who joined the committee of the Brass Company. Unlike his father, he became a Merchant Venturer and was progenitor of the family's lucrative banking interests, leading the six original partners in creating the Harford Bank in 1769. In 1747 he married Sarah Scandrett (1725–1776) of Birmingham, the daughter and heiress of John Scandrett (*d.* 1730), who was also related to the Lloyds. Of their seven children, only one survived him: **John Scandrett Harford** (1754–1815).

John Scandrett Harford ensured the transition of his line from commerce to landed gentry; this was to be consolidated by the conversion of his son John Scandrett *Harford the younger (1787–1866) to the Church of England, as well as the latter's advantageous marriage and literary concerns. The elder J. S. Harford maintained the family's industrial interests as a committee member of the Brass Company, and as an iron merchant and a partner in Lydney ironworks in Gloucestershire. He continued as the leading partner of Harford's Bank until his death. In 1782 he was warden, and in 1798 master, of the Bristol Merchant Venturers' Guild. He married another Quaker, Mary Gray (*d.* 1830) of Tottenham, Middlesex, in 1780, and they had nine children. By his death he was said to have trebled the fortune inherited from his father nine years earlier, and left nearly £300,000. He lived at Brunswick Square, Bristol, until 1789, when he purchased the Blaise Castle estate, near Bristol; this signified perhaps the greatest single step in the gentrification of the Harfords. He built a grander house to designs by William Patey about 1795, and commissioned additions by John Nash, Humphrey Repton, and George Stanley Repton. He is best remembered for Blaise Hamlet, the estate pensioners' houses built by Nash in 1810–11 at a cost of £3800, one of the most successful examples of picturesque architecture in England now in the care of the National Trust. J. S. Harford the elder died at Blaise Castle on 23 January 1815.

The Harford family, through its principal Bristol branches, formed a major business empire. This advanced fastest in the generation of the mid- to late eighteenth century led by the first cousins Joseph Harford (1741–1802) of Stapleton, Edward [iii] Harford (1720–1806) of the Blaise Castle line, and Mark [ii] Harford (1738–1798) of Stoke Bishop. Each of these made considerable fortunes in their different sections of the mercantile, banking, and brass trades, and they were linked by their Quakerism, kinship, and common interests. They built upon several generations of expertise and capital, which increased in parallel with the commercial and industrial revolutions. They handed on substantial fortunes to their children, who entered the landed gentry, and for the most part left industry and commerce behind.

The Harford businesses developed over several generations, and included the major brass-making company of the eighteenth century, mercantile activities, and banking interests which provided capital and credit for the second port of the kingdom. The family progressed from trade to industry, finance, and eventually gentrification. It was the chief among several interrelated Quaker families in Bristol who began as grocers or ironmongers and became wealthy business leaders, including the Champions, Goldneys, Andrews, Scandretts, Truemans, and Lloyds.   PETER WAKELIN

Sources A. Harford, *Annals of the Harford family* (1909) · J. Day, *Bristol brass: a history of the industry* (1973) · A. Raistrick, *Quakers in science and industry* (1950) · A. Harford, *A supplement to the annals of the Harford family* (1958) · S. Harding and D. Lambert, eds., *Parks and gardens of Avon* (1994) · P. T. Underdown, 'Burke's Bristol friends', *Transactions of the Bristol and Gloucestershire Archaeological Society*, 77 (1958), 127–50 · C. H. Cave, *A history of banking in Bristol from 1750 to 1899* (privately printed, Bristol, 1899) · C. E. Harvey and J. Press, eds., *Studies in the business history of Bristol* (1988) · J. Summerson, *The life and works of John Nash, architect* (1980) · H. Lloyd, *The Quaker Lloyds in the industrial revolution* (1975)
Archives Bristol RO, Cardiganshire and Gloucestershire deeds, family and estate papers · NL Wales, Cardiganshire deeds, manorial records, family and estate papers · NL Wales, Peterwell estate papers
Likenesses J. Singleton, portrait, 1812 (John Scandrett Harford the elder), priv. coll.; photograph, Blaise Castle House Museum, Bristol

Harford, Edward (1658–1705). *See under* Harford family (*per. c.*1700–1866).

Harford, Edward (1720–1806). *See under* Harford family (*per. c.*1700–1866).

Harford, Edward (1837/8–1898), railwayman and trade unionist, was born in Bristol on 21 March 1837 or 1838, the son of Edward Harford, a policeman. When he was five years old the family moved to Tiverton in Devon and Edward was educated until the age of fourteen at the Tiverton factory school from which he was apprenticed to the confectionery trade. He disliked this employment and after enduring it for five years, transferred to the recently established Devonshire county constabulary. In Hatherleigh, on 26 October 1857, he married Fanny Ann Reed Sanders, a domestic servant; they had five sons and two daughters.

Shortly after this Harford began his railway career as a porter employed by the Bristol and Exeter Railway Company. For nearly twenty years thereafter he was employed in a variety of grades in the goods departments, first of the Midland and then of the Manchester, Sheffield, and Lincolnshire Railways. Harford became a keen trade unionist and on 24 June 1872 represented Grimsby at the first great delegate meeting of the Amalgamated Society of Railway Servants (ASRS), held in London. In 1873 colleagues in the

Sheffield area persuaded him to become a full-time, locally paid, organizer. He accepted the proposal, but subscriptions from the branches were so uncertain that for some months he felt obliged to take employment in an iron foundry. However, by 1881 he was again active for the union as joint secretary of the movement for a nine-hour working day.

At that time union organization presented many difficulties. The directors of the railway companies, with the partial exception of the North Eastern Railway, were vehemently opposed to union recognition. Victimization was widespread and it was not until the annual general meeting of October 1889 that delegates decided to give their personal, as well as their branch name, to reporters. In 1882 Harford was appointed by the union's executive as paid national organizer, and in February 1883, when his predecessor, Frederick Evans, had a nervous breakdown and deserted his post, he was chosen as the only person legally qualified to be general secretary. Apart from this, his good organizing abilities and his wide range of experience in railway employment ensured his succession.

Harford's policy after election was to increase the union's membership and hence its bargaining strength. He detested strikes, declaring at a public meeting in Birkenhead on 12 February 1897 that strikes would be a thing of the past as soon as every man was a member of his trade society. He campaigned vigorously for reduced working hours in the belief that overwork was an important cause of the horrendous level of railway accidents. He gave well-prepared evidence to both the royal commission on labour of 1890 and the select committee on railway servants' hours of labour of 1890–91.

Harford played an active role in the establishment of the labour electoral committee in 1886, and served as its treasurer. His union decided in 1892 that it should be represented in parliament through the general secretary, and Harford subsequently stood as a Liberal for Northampton in the general election of 1895, but was defeated because of a split opposition vote. He served on the parliamentary committee of the TUC from 1887 to 1892 (chairman in 1890) and from 1894 to 1897.

By 1898 the union was in a much stronger position than it had been when Harford took over in 1883. Membership had risen from 8077 to 54,426, and reserve funds had grown from £37,000 to nearly £200,000. It was well established in Ireland and strong in the north-east and Scotland, following the merger of the Scottish ASRS with the main body after the defeat of the Scottish rail strike in 1892. Above all it had become an industrial organization, or, as Harford described it, 'a trade union with benefit funds, not a friendly society with a few mutual protection benefits' (Bagwell, 1.149).

In 1897 Harford defied his executive by settling disputes with the boards of the North Eastern Railway and the London and North Western Railway. He was also drunk at an important stage of negotiations. The union dismissed him in October 1897 with a pension of £100 a year. Harford died of pneumonia on board the SS *St Paul* on 4 January 1898 while returning from a conference in the USA. His funeral took place in Abney Park cemetery in London on 11 January 1898, and was attended by large numbers of railway workers walking beneath their banners. Harford was survived by his wife.   PHILIP S. BAGWELL

Sources J. Bellamy and A. Holt, 'Harford, Edward', DLB, vol. 5 · private information (2004) · G. Alcock, 50 years of railway trade unionism (1922) · Railway Review (16 Feb 1883) · Railway Review (11 May 1883) · Railway Review (14 Jan 1898) · P. S. Bagwell, The railwaymen: the history of the National Union of Railwaymen, [1] (1963) · P. S. Gupta, 'Railway trade unionism in Great Britain, c.1880–1900', Economic History Review, 2nd ser., 19 (1966), 124–53 · H. A. Clegg, A. Fox, and A. F. Thompson, A history of British trade unions since 1889, 1 (1964) · R. M. Martin, TUC: the growth of a pressure group, 1868–1976 (1980) · R. J. Irving, 'The profitability and performance of British railways, 1870–1914', Economic History Review, 2nd ser., 31 (1978), 46–66
Archives National Union of Rail, Maritime and Transport Workers, Unity House, 205 Euston Road, London, archives · People's History Museum, Manchester, Labour Party archives
Wealth at death £227 13s. 7d.: probate, 22 Jan 1898, CGPLA Eng. & Wales

Harford, James (1734–1817), iron and tin plate manufacturer and merchant, was the son of Truman Harford (1704–1750), merchant and manufacturer, and Mary Taylor of Baldock, Hertfordshire, and grandson of Charles Harford (1662–1725), a merchant, of Bristol [see Harford family]. He developed a powerful network of tin plate- and iron-making interests and was the foremost among many Bristol merchants who became industrial entrepreneurs in south Wales. He lived at Felindre, Melingriffith, near Cardiff, and at his estate at Chew Magna in Somerset. In 1756 he married Anne Summers, daughter of his business partner, Richard Summers; they had six sons and four daughters.

Harford developed industrial interests while maintaining his connections in Bristol, where he was a member of the Society of Merchant Venturers and part of an extensive Quaker merchant family. He succeeded by linking and developing existing enterprises rather than establishing new ventures, and was one of the few ironmasters to prosper in the eras of both charcoal and coke fuel. His numerous interests included the Pen-tyrch, Ebbw Vale, Nant-y-glo, Sirhowy, and Caerphilly smelting works in south-east Wales; Redbrook furnace, Monmouth forge, Newent forge, and New Weir forge in the Wye valley; and the Machen and Basaleg forges near Newport, Monmouthshire.

Harford's central industrial concern was the Melingriffith forge and tin plate works near Cardiff, which was established by Bristol merchants about 1750. He became a partner about 1768, along with the noted ironmaster Richard Reynolds, Richard Summers, and a number of others. By the 1770s he was in partnership with John Partridge sen. (fl. 1730s–1770s) and John Partridge jun. (c.1736–1816), Quaker ironmasters of Ross, Herefordshire, and Monmouth. In 1795 Harford and his younger brother John Harford (1736–c.1816), with James's sons Richard Summers Harford [see below] and Samuel Harford (1766–1838), were major figures in the enterprise. At this time Melingriffith was the largest tin plate works in the world. The main products were tin plate, and wrought-iron bars, sheets,

rods, and hoops, but the company also dealt in cast-iron pots, frying pans, anvils, hammers, and spades, some purchased from other manufacturers. Goods were exported under the auspices of James Harford & Co., merchants, of Bristol. In 1805 the nearby Pen-tyrch furnace was bought, and both enterprises were enlarged. However, in 1808 the partnership was dissolved, as the Harfords concentrated on more recently acquired, larger ironworks. They left Felindre, their local residence, in 1810 and Melingriffith and Pen-tyrch were transferred in 1812 to a group led by Richard Blakemore (b. 1775), the grandson of John Partridge sen.

Of the other ironworks interests, most were intended initially to complement the existing business, such as Redbrook furnace and Lydbrook forge, brought into the group through partnership with the Partridges. Caerphilly furnace was acquired in 1781 with a rolling and slitting mill. Although a blowing engine was installed in 1793, the furnace remained charcoal-fuelled and output in 1796 was only 600 tons. It was out of blast by 1805, made obsolete by the larger coke-fuelled works the Harfords had acquired.

The acquisitions which carried the Harfords into the production of bulk iron began in the 1790s. The only new venture was the ironworks at Nant-y-glo, promoted in 1792 with Thomas Hill, already a successful ironmaster at Blaenafon. Unfortunately, Hill complained that £485 was spent above his £10,000 capital and refused to let production start, even though Harford, Partridge & Co. had spent £16,381. The company was obliged simply to smelt material in stock, and the works lay idle from 1796 until 1802, when Hill returned with different partners.

Immediately before this débâcle, however, Harford, Partridge & Co. had become partners of Jeremiah Homfray at Ebbw Vale ironworks, introducing capital for expansion. It became the sole owner in 1796. This was the first element in what was to become one of the most powerful ironworks enterprises in south Wales. James Harford as senior partner and his brother John as managing partner expanded Ebbw Vale from one blast furnace to four. Then, around the time of James's death in 1817, the company acquired the adjacent Sirhowy works (much to the anger of another ironmaster, Richard Fothergill, who had confided his own plans to renew the lease). This site too was expanded, from two furnaces to five. The period of greatest growth in the Harford iron fortunes ensued, under the management of Richard Summers Harford. Output at Ebbw Vale in 1805 had been 3664 tons; but from the two combined works it was 10,425 tons in 1823 and 26,020 in 1830. The capital value in 1820–21 was over £62,000 and rising rapidly.

As the possessor of an extensive industrial empire, James Harford was an enthusiastic promoter of improvements to transport. In 1785 he became a trustee of the turnpike from Merthyr Tudful to Tongwynlais, which brought iron to Melingriffith. When the Glamorganshire Canal Company was established in 1790, he was its first honorary treasurer and he and his sons were among the largest shareholders. Richard Crawshay, the Merthyr iron-master, was constantly at loggerheads on the canal committee with Harford, whom he described as 'a rude, selfish Jew Quaker', insolent, and 'a mercenary fellow who must be treated as Circumstances require' (*Letterbook*, xx, 92). Harford, Partridge & Co. and James Harford were also leading shareholders in the Monmouthshire Canal Company.

Harford's interests in education and workers' welfare were demonstrated at Melingriffith. From about 1775 the works had a scheme for medical attendance, as well as a reading-room. In 1786 a friendly society, the Melingriffith Benefit Club, was established, one of the earliest in south Wales. In 1798 there were sixty-three members, including John Harford, the employees at Melingriffith, and other local people. The club provided social activities, benefits, and pensions, and similar ones were started at Caerphilly in 1787 and at Ebbw Vale. A school for workers and their children existed at Melingriffith before 1786, and in 1807 James Harford invited Joseph Lancaster to address a meeting which resulted in the establishment there by subscription of a Lancastrian school for boys and girls.

James Harford's sons and grandsons continued in the iron industry. His eldest son, Truman Harford (1758–1803), took the lease of Caerphilly furnace with his father and Philip Crocker in 1789 and dealt with iron orders at Melingriffith in the 1790s, but he established himself also as a brewer in Limehouse, London. Samuel, his fourth son, participated at Melingriffith. John Harford (1768–1851), his fifth son, and his daughters Elizabeth Harford (*d.* 1836) and Sophia Harford (*b.* 1779) lived at Gelliwastad, Machen, about 1816 and may have overseen Caerphilly furnace and Machen forge.

However, it was James's second son, **Richard Summers Harford** (1763–1837), iron manufacturer, who became his effective heir. Richard established Nant-y-glo ironworks and lived nearby at Trosnant until 1799, and continued to operate associated collieries until 1801. He was increasingly involved at Ebbw Vale, which became the focus of the Harford interests, and he built a three-storey mansion, Ebbw Vale House, in 1817. He led the company from the time of his father's death in 1817 until his own in 1837. He followed his father into the Society of Merchant Venturers in 1825 and inherited the Chew Magna estate. In 1792 he married Jane Lloyd Perkins; their sons, Summers Harford and Charles Lloyd Harford, appear subsequently to have taken responsibility for the works. Their iron business was severely damaged by defaults on credits in Maryland, USA, which led to the bankruptcy of Harford, Davies & Co. of Ebbw Vale in 1842. Significantly, the meeting of creditors was held in Bristol. Although Ebbw Vale continued to expand under new owners, this ended almost a century of the Harfords' leadership in the iron trade of south Wales.

PETER WAKELIN

Sources A. Harford, *Annals of the Harford family* (1909) • P. Riden, *A gazetteer of charcoal-fired blast furnaces in Great Britain in use since 1660*, 2nd edn (1993) • L. Ince, *The south Wales iron industry, 1750–1885* (1993) • C. Hadfield, *The canals of south Wales and the border*, 2nd edn (1967) • A. H. John, *The industrial development of south Wales, 1750–1850: an essay* (1950) • G. Rattenbury, *Tramroads of the Brecknock and Abergavenny canal* (1980) • *The letterbook of Richard Crawshay, 1788–* 1797, ed. C. Evans, South Wales and Monmouth RS, 6 (1990) • P. McGrath, *The merchant venturers of Bristol: a history of the Society of Merchant Venturers of the city of Bristol from its origin to the present day* (1975) • E. L. Chappell, *Historic Melingriffith* (1940) • A. Raistrick, *Quakers in science and industry* (1950) • W. Rees, *Industry before the industrial revolution*, 2 vols. (1968) • A. Gray-Jones, *A history of Ebbw Vale* (privately printed, Ebbw Vale, 1970)

Archives Carmarthenshire RO, Trostie collection, 19–49 • Glamorgan RO, Cardiff, Melingriffith deeds and documents • Gwent RO, Cwmbrân, Ebbw Vale papers • NL Wales, E. L. Chappell MSS

Harford, John Scandrett (1754–1815). *See under* Harford family (*per. c.*1700–1866).

Harford, John Scandrett (1787–1866), biographer, was born at Bristol on 8 October 1787, the second son of the banker and manufacturer John Scandrett Harford (1754–1815) [*see* Harford family] of Blaise Castle, Henbury, Gloucestershire, and Mary (*d.* 1830), daughter of Abraham Gray of Tottenham, Middlesex. He was educated under the Revd Lloyd at Peterley House, Buckinghamshire, later studying for several terms at Christ's College, Cambridge. The death of his elder brother, Edward Gray Harford, on 25 April 1804, produced deep religious impressions, which continued throughout his life. His parents were members of the Society of Friends, but he left that connection and was baptized at Chelwood church, Somerset, in 1809. He became a firm supporter of the Church Missionary Society and the Bible Society, and assisted at the formation of the Bristol branches of those associations in 1813. He was a close friend of Hannah More from 1809, and of William Wilberforce from 1812, and he was the model for the hero of Hannah More's novel *Coelebs in Search of a Wife* (1809).

On 31 August 1812 Harford married Louisa Davies, eldest daughter of Richard Hart Davies, MP for Bristol. The following year he visited Ireland with his wife, and his subsequent 'Letter on the state of Ireland', addressed to William Wilberforce, was published in the *Christian Observer* (June 1813). On the death of his father in 1815 Harford succeeded to the family estates, and was made a magistrate and a deputy lieutenant for Gloucestershire and Cardiganshire. While in Rome in 1815 he obtained an interview with Pius VII and requested his influence in putting down the Spanish and Portuguese slave trade. He possessed considerable taste in art and literature, and during visits to Paris and other European cities in 1815–17 laid the foundation of a valuable collection of pictures which adorned the walls of Blaise Castle. About 1821, on the death of his brother-in-law, Hart Davies, formerly MP for Colchester, he came into the Peterwell property, Cardiganshire, where he made improvements and took in tracts of waste land.

In 1822, on the advice of Thomas Burgess, bishop of Salisbury, Harford and his brother donated the site of the castle of Lampeter for the foundation of a college in south Wales. The same year, the University of Oxford created him honorary DCL, and he was elected FRS on 29 May 1823. In 1824 he was appointed high sheriff for Cardiganshire. On the completion of St David's College in 1827 Harford was appointed sub-visitor and watched over its interests with great care.

In January 1841 Harford was present in Bristol at a discussion between John Brindley and Robert Owen, when he strongly denounced socialism. He was elected Conservative MP for the borough of Cardigan on 6 July 1841, but as a result of the loss of a poll book a double return was made to parliament and on a petition his name was erased from the roll on 18 April 1842. He contested the same place again on 12 February 1849, without success. For fifteen years he acted as president of the Bristol Infirmary. He contributed towards the restoration of the cathedrals of Llandaff and St David's, and at Lampeter he drained the Gorsddu bog, and made it into cottage garden allotments, while also providing a supply of pure water for the town. During two visits to Italy, in 1846 and 1852, he collected materials for his best-known literary work, the *Life of Michael Angelo* (1857); he also had a copy of the ceiling of the Sistine Chapel made at his own expense. After the loss of his sight in 1862 he found employment in dictating to his wife his *Recollections of W. Wilberforce* (1864) from notes of conversations and correspondence in his possession. He died, childless, at Blaise Castle on 16 April 1866, and was buried on 23 April. He was succeeded by his nephew, John Battersby Harford.

G. C. BOASE, *rev.* CHARLES BRAYNE

Sources GM, 4th ser., 1 (1866), 770 · *Christian Observer* (1866), 489–98 · G. F. Waagen, *Treasures of art in Great Britain*, 3 (1854), 187–95 · *The Welshman* (20 April 1866), 5 [Carmarthen] · Venn, *Alum. Cant.*
Archives Bristol RO, corresp. and papers
Likenesses portrait, St David's University College, Lampeter
Wealth at death under £70,000: probate, 3 Aug 1866, CGPLA Eng. & Wales

Harford, Joseph (1741–1802). *See under* Harford family (*per.* c.1700–1866).

Harford, Mark (1738–1798). *See under* Harford family (*per.* c.1700–1866).

Harford, Richard Summers (1763–1837). *See under* Harford, James (1734–1817).

Hargood, Sir William (1762–1839), naval officer, youngest son of Hezekiah Hargood, a purser in the navy, was born on 6 May 1762. In 1773 he was entered on the books of the *Triumph*, flagship in the Medway, but had his first experience of sea life in March 1775, on the *Romney*, going to Newfoundland as flagship of Rear-Admiral Robert Duff. On her return to England in the winter, Hargood was appointed to the *Bristol*, carrying the broad pennant of Sir Peter Parker, an old family friend, under whose care he went to North America, and was present in the attack on Sullivan's Island on 28 June 1776. In the following September he followed Parker to the *Chatham*, and then, in December 1777, back to the *Bristol*, which was shortly afterwards sent to Jamaica. Hargood continued in her, under the direct patronage of Parker, until January 1780, when he was promoted lieutenant of the sloop *Port Royal*, in which he was actively engaged in the unsuccessful defence of Pensacola, captured by the Spaniards in May 1781. By the terms of the surrender, he and the rest of the prisoners were sent to New York, from where he returned to England. He was immediately appointed to the *Magnificent* (74 guns),

which sailed from Spithead in February 1782, and joined Rodney in the West Indies in time to take part in the actions to leeward of Dominica on 9 and 12 April; he was then with Hood in the Mona passage on 19 April, when he assisted in the capture of a scattered detachment of French ships.

On the peace of 1783 the *Magnificent* returned home, and in May 1784 Hargood was appointed to the frigate *Hebe* with Captain Edward Thornbrough, in which ship, in 1785, Prince William Henry (later William IV) served as a junior lieutenant. In 1786, when the prince was appointed to the command of the *Pegasus*, Hargood, at his request, was appointed one of his lieutenants; in the same way, in 1788, he was appointed first lieutenant of the *Andromeda*, which the prince paid off in April 1789. Two months afterwards Hargood was promoted commander, and in the following December was appointed to the sloop *Swallow* from which, after a year on the coast of Ireland, he was advanced to post rank on 22 November 1790. In April 1792 he commissioned the frigate *Hyaena* (24 guns) for service in the West Indies, where she was captured off Cape Tiberon on 27 May 1793 by the *Concorde*, a powerful French frigate of 44 heavy guns. Hargood and the other officers were landed on their parole at Cape François, Haiti; but on 20 June, on the outbreak of the insurrection there, they escaped for their lives on board the *Concorde*, where the commanding officer declined to receive them as prisoners, but allowed them to take a passage for Jamaica. There was some disposition to blame Hargood for surrendering to the *Concorde* without sufficient resistance; but as the *Hyaena* was partially dismasted, and under the guns of a frigate of at least four times her force, supported by a couple of 74-gun ships and three other frigates in the offing, she could offer no effective defence, and Hargood was honourably acquitted by the court martial held at Plymouth on 11 October 1793.

In April 1794 Hargood was appointed to the frigate *Iris*, and employed in convoy service in the North Sea, to the coast of Africa, and to North America, until, in August 1796, he was transferred to the *Leopard* (50 guns), one of the ships involved in the mutiny of the following year. On 31 May Hargood was put on shore at Yarmouth, Isle of Wight, by the mutineers; but ten days later those of his officers who had been kept on board succeeded in regaining possession of the ship and taking her into the River Thames under heavy fire from the mutinied ships. Hargood did not resume the command, and on 12 July was appointed to the *Nassau* (64 guns), which during the next two months formed part of the North Sea Fleet under Duncan; but having received serious damage in a gale, it was sent to Sheerness to refit in the early days of October. In February 1798 Hargood was appointed to the *Intrepid* (64 guns), and on 30 April he sailed for China in charge of a convoy, afterwards joining the flag of Vice-Admiral Peter Rainier, then commander-in-chief in the East Indies.

Hargood returned to England in the spring of 1803, and in the following November was appointed to the *Belleisle* (80 guns), then off Toulon, under the command of Nelson. Hargood joined her in March 1804, and continued under

Nelson's orders during that year and the next, taking part in the watch off Toulon through 1804, and in the pursuit of the allied fleet to the West Indies and back, from April to August 1805. On joining the Brest fleet under Cornwallis, the *Belleisle* was ordered to Plymouth to refit, which was done only just in time to enable her to join the fleet off Cadiz on 10 October and take part in the battle of Trafalgar; following in the wake of the *Royal Sovereign*, she was one of the ships earliest in action. She lost thirty-three men killed and ninety-four wounded, besides being totally dismasted and having her hull much damaged. She was sent home the following January to be refitted. In February she was again commissioned by Hargood, and in May joined the squadron sent to the West Indies under Sir Richard John Strachan. On 18 and 19 August the squadron was scattered by a hurricane south of Bermuda. Hargood sailed northward, and being joined on 5 September by the *Bellona* and the frigate *Melampus*, continued cruising off the mouth of the Chesapeake, where on 14 September he fell in with the French ship *Impétueux*, jury-rigged, having been dismasted in the storm which had scattered the French squadron as well as the British. The *Impétueux*, in no condition to resist or escape, ran herself ashore. She was captured and burnt, her officers and crew being sent on board the British ships. This action was a breach of neutrality; but it seems to have passed unnoticed by the United States government, and was approved by the Admiralty. In November 1806 the *Belleisle* returned to England, and, after being docked and refitted, was again sent out to the West Indies, where Sir Alexander Cochrane hoisted his flag on board her, Hargood changing into the *Northumberland* (74 guns) and taking home a large convoy. After this he joined the fleet at Lisbon under the command of Sir Charles Cotton, and was employed in the blockade during the summer of 1808, under the immediate orders of Rear-Admiral Purvis, until, after the sudden change of alliances in July, the *Northumberland* joined the flag of Lord Collingwood, who sent her into the Adriatic, to co-operate with the Austrians. In October 1809 Hargood again joined the admiral, and in the following summer returned to England. Shortly afterwards, in 1811, he married Maria, daughter of T. S. Cocks, banker; they had no children.

On 7 August 1810 Hargood was promoted rear-admiral, and hoisted his flag at Portsmouth as second in command, which post he held until 13 March, when he took command of the squadron at the Channel Islands. He was promoted vice-admiral on 4 June 1814, and admiral on 22 July 1831. In January 1815 he was made a KCB, and in September 1831 a GCB. He had previously (22 March 1831) been specially made a GCH by the king, who had kept up a personal correspondence with Hargood throughout his career. From March 1833 to April 1836 he was commander-in-chief at Plymouth. He died at Bath on 11 September 1839. Admiral William Hargood, who died in 1888, was his nephew. J. K. LAUGHTON, *rev.* ROGER MORRISS

Sources J. Allen, ed., *Memoir of the life and services of Admiral Sir William Hargood, GCB, GCH* (1841) • O'Byrne, *Naval biog. dict.* • commission and warrant books, PRO • W. James, *The naval history of Great Britain, from the declaration of war by France in 1793, to the accession of George IV*, [4th edn], 6 vols. (1847) • P. Mackesy, *The war in the Mediterranean, 1803–1810* (1957) • R. Muir, *Britain and the defeat of Napoleon, 1807–1815* (1996)

Likenesses F. R. Say, oils, *c.*1835, NMM • J. Thomson, stipple, NPG • engraving (after F. R. Say), repro. in Allen, ed., *Memoir*

Hargrave, Francis (1740/41–1821), legal writer, was the son of Christopher Hargrave (*c.*1710–1787), a chancery solicitor. He was admitted to Lincoln's Inn in 1760, and his father was admitted to the same inn two years later. Francis was not called to the bar until 1771, having presumably practised below the bar for several years. But within a year of call he attracted wide attention and admiration for his successful argument on behalf of the escaped slave James Somerset upon his application for habeas corpus. Hargrave's learned argument, which was printed in 1772 and several times reprinted, drew upon recondite sources such as the medieval law of villeinage to persuade Lord Mansfield that no one could be a slave in England.

Hargrave's practice at the chancery bar was chiefly in chambers, as a draftsman and writer of opinions, and from 1781 to 1789 he was parliamentary counsel to the Treasury. He was also retained to prepare arguments for the use of others, doubtless because he was less gifted in the oral part of advocacy. Among those who benefited from his assistance were Edward Thurlow, for whom he devilled when he was attorney-general and after he became lord chancellor, and Charles Jenkinson, later first earl of Liverpool. In 1776 he drafted the statute 16 Geo. III c.43, a criminal law amendment act which allowed convicts to be employed in cleaning the Thames. His own speeches, though painstakingly accurate, were prolix and tortuous, and Lord Erskine once related how he had benefited professionally from the overnight adjournment of a case in 1778 after a long-winded speech by Hargrave which 'tired the court' (Townsend, 1.406). Hargrave had to leave the court once or twice during that speech because of 'strangury', and ill health pressed severely upon him in the years to come. In 1785, after completing about half of his important new edition of *Coke upon Littleton*, he retired from the task, saying that he could no longer sustain the weight of the labours involved, for personal reasons which it might be 'improper and disgusting' to particularize. He nevertheless continued to work when he was able; he was a commissioner of bankrupts, became recorder of Liverpool in 1797 and a bencher of Lincoln's Inn in 1802, and in 1806 he was given a silk gown by Lord Erskine. He published many of his own speeches and opinions in *Juridical Arguments* (1797–9) and *Jurisconsult Exercitations* (1811–13), the latter a three-volume collection chiefly of reprinted matter. Hargrave had intended to continue the *Exercitations* in at least three further volumes, but the 1813 instalment was delayed by 'causes beyond his power of controuling … a subject involving much of delicacy' (Hargrave, *Exercitations*, vol.3, preface), and it was the last. The unspoken reason was an increasing failure of his mental faculties. Probably his last professional function was to serve as treasurer of Lincoln's Inn in 1813–14.

Hargrave married Diana, the daughter of the Revd Mr Fountaine of Marylebone, on 4 November 1776. She made

Francis Hargrave (1740/41–1821), by Sir Joshua Reynolds, 1787

a public appearance in 1813 when she petitioned parliament for assistance, her husband's selfless contributions to jurisprudence having left him in debt and unable to support her; and by vote of the House of Commons on 1 July his law library was purchased for the nation for £8000 and placed in the British Museum. Besides 499 manuscripts, still kept as a separate collection (catalogued in 1818 by Sir Henry Ellis), more than 100 printed books contain annotations in his hand. Some further manuscripts, mostly containing unpublished works by Sir Matthew Hale, were purchased by Lincoln's Inn in 1843 from one of his sons.

Hargrave pioneered the editing of modern legal manuscripts, 'which hitherto have either been confined to the small circle of those few who visit public repositories of books, or have been destined to occupy private libraries in a state nearly dormant except to the particular proprietors' (Hargrave, *Tracts*, preface). In 1776 he published eleven volumes of state trials from the reign of Henry IV to 1769, and this formed the basis of the vulgate edition by T. B. Howell. His *Collection of Tracts Relative to the Law of England* (1787) contained eleven previously unpublished items, from the time of James I to his own day, beginning with Hale's *De jure maris*, edited from a manuscript given to him by George Hardinge of the Middle Temple. It was followed by *Collectanea juridica: Consisting of Tracts Relative to the Law and Constitution of England*, which first appeared in periodical parts in 1791–2 and included an important edition of William Hudson's *Treatise on the Star Chamber*. It combined edited texts with opinions, articles, case notes, and lists of recent publications, and may be considered to have provided a model for the law journal of later times.

In 1796, in pursuance of his keen interest in the unpublished writings of Sir Matthew Hale, he produced an edition of Hale's *Jurisdiction of the Lords' House of Parliament*.

Hargrave died on 16 August 1821, and was buried in the undercroft of Lincoln's Inn chapel a week later in the presence of Lord Eldon. He left at least two sons—the second of whom, Francis Albany James, was called to the bar by Lincoln's Inn in 1809—and a daughter, Fanny Maria.

J. H. BAKER

Sources W. P. Baildon, ed., *The records of the Honorable Society of Lincoln's Inn: admissions*, 2 vols. (1896) · W. P. Baildon and R. Roxburgh, eds., *The records of the Honorable Society of Lincoln's Inn: the black books*, 5 vols. (1897–1968) · J. Cradock, *Literary and miscellaneous memoirs*, 1 (1828), 79–80 · W. C. Townsend, *The lives of twelve eminent judges*, 1 (1846), 406 · Sainty, *King's counsel* · *JHC*, 68 (1812–13), 944–5 · *GM*, 1st ser., 46 (1776), 530 · *GM*, 1st ser., 91/2 (1821), 282 · *Annual Register* (1821), 238 · *The Times* (27 Aug 1821) · *The correspondence of Edmund Burke*, 3, ed. G. H. Guttridge (1961), 251 · F. Hargrave, *Jurisconsult exercitations*, 3 vols. (1811–13) · F. Hargrave, *Collection of tracts relative to the law of England* (1787) · D. Lemmings, *Professors of the law* (2000), 256, 259, 261, 338

Archives BL, legal MSS · Inner Temple Library, London, legal MSS · Lincoln's Inn, London, MS collections | Beds. & Luton ARS, corresp. with Samuel Whitbread

Likenesses oils, c.1771, priv. coll. · J. Reynolds, oils, 1787, Lincoln's Inn, London [see illus.] · J. Jones, engraving, 1793 (after Reynolds, 1793)

Hargrave, John Gordon (1894–1982), writer and illustrator, was born on 6 June 1894 at Midhurst, Sussex, the son of Gordon Hargrave, landscape painter, and his wife, Babette, *née* Bing. He attended Hawkshead grammar school in Lancashire for a short time and when he was fifteen illustrated Swift's *Gulliver's Travels* and Thackeray's *The Rose and the Ring*. Two years later he was appointed chief cartoonist of the *London Evening Times* and in 1914 joined the staff of C. Arthur Pearson Ltd.

On the outbreak of the First World War Hargrave enlisted in the Royal Army Medical Corps and later served with the 10th (Irish) division at Gallipoli and in Salonika. Having been invalided from the army at the end of 1916, he became art manager of C. Arthur Pearson Ltd from 1917 to 1920. On 28 November 1919 he married Ruth Clark (b. 1899/1900), daughter of William Clark, engineer; they had one son. The marriage ended in divorce in 1952. He continued his work as a cartoonist over the next thirty years and in 1952 created the animal character Bushy for *The Sketch*.

At the age of fourteen Hargrave had joined the Boy Scout movement, recently formed by Robert Baden-Powell, and by 1921 he was commissioner for woodcraft and camping. In that year, however, he left the movement, having inaugurated in 1920 the Kindred of the Kibbo Kift (an old Scottish term meaning a feat of strength). The purpose of this organization was to encourage youth 'to seek health of body, mind, and spirit' and to become expert at woodcraft and other open-air pursuits while believing in disarmament and the brotherhood of man. In its early years the Kibbo Kift, whose members wore a woodcraft costume of cloak, hooded jerkin, and shorts, numbered only a few hundred, but it was supported by such eminent people as H. Havelock Ellis, Julian

Huxley, H. G. Wells, and Emmeline Pethick-Lawrence. After 1931, when the movement developed into the Green Shirts, a paramilitary organization, the membership increased to thousands.

In the meantime Hargrave had met and come under the influence of Clifford Hugh Douglas, the originator of the theory of social credit. In brief, the ideas of Douglas were based on the premiss that the economic problems of his time were caused by a shortage of purchasing power which stemmed from a flaw in the system of price-fixing. To remedy these defects he advocated the issue of additional money to consumers or of subsidies to producers to enable them to set prices below the costs of production. Hargrave had sufficient influence with his followers to persuade the movement of which he was the leader to adopt these theories in opposition to the prevailing banking and financial structure of the capitalist system. Although Hargrave and the Green Shirts were opposed to the activities of Sir Oswald Mosley and his Black Shirt fascists, both movements were equally affected by the Public Order Act of 1937 which banned the wearing of political uniforms; and two years later the outbreak of the Second World War effectively brought to an end the activities of both organizations. After the war Hargrave attempted to revive the Green Shirts, but his efforts ended in failure, and in 1951 the organization was dissolved.

In 1936–7 Hargrave had been honorary adviser to the Alberta government planning committee which was seriously concerned with the introduction of the social credit system into that province of Canada. The Alberta government, led by William Aberhart, accepted the theories set out in the report, in the preparation of which Hargrave had played an influential part, but never succeeded in putting its plans into effect as, in the last resort, the governor-general declared them to be unconstitutional.

Hargrave was indefatigable in setting out his ideas in writing. By 1913 he had written *Lonecraft* and five other books on camping and similar outdoor activities. His *Social Credit Clearly Explained* (1934) gave chapter and verse for his theories on that subject, and in other publications, such as *Professor Skinner, alias Montagu Norman* (1939), he castigated mercilessly the exponents of monetarism and other policies of contemporary financiers. *The Confession of the Kibbo Kift* (1927) explained the purpose of that movement; he also wrote *Words Win Wars* (1940).

Hargrave demonstrated his versatility in many other books, including *Summer Time Ends* (1935) and five other novels. He was also a lexicographer and published his *The 'Paragon' Dictionary* in 1953; he wrote *The Life and Soul of Paracelsus* (1951), the German-Swiss physician and alchemist on whom he was a recognized authority; and his wartime experiences led to *The Suvla Bay Landing* (1964). In 1968 he married Gwendoline Florence Gray, an actress.

Another aspect of the career of this extraordinary man, with his intense personal enthusiasms and keen, if unorthodox opinions, was Hargrave's invention of an automatic navigator for aircraft which he claimed to be the basis for equipment used in Concorde and other supersonic aeroplanes. These claims were argued in *The Facts of the Case Concerning the Hargrave Automatic Navigator for Aircraft* (1969) but he failed to win his case in a public inquiry held in 1976. Hargrave died on 21 November 1982 at his home, Branch Hill Lodge, Branch Hill, Hampstead, London. H. F. OXBURY, *rev.*

Sources *The Times* (25 Nov 1982) · m. cert. [J. G. Hargrave and R. Clark] · d. cert. · J. G. Hargrave, *Lonecraft* (1913) · J. G. Hargrave, *Social credit clearly explained* (1934) · J. G. Hargrave, *Professor Skinner, alias Montagu Norman* (1939) · J. G. Hargrave, *The confession of the Kibbo Kift* (1927) · J. G. Hargrave, *Words win wars* (1940) · J. G. Hargrave, *The Suvla bay landing* (1964)
Archives BLPES, papers, incl. copies of research material, and original MS

Hargraves, Edward Hammond (1816–1891), gold prospector in Australia, the third son of John Edward Hargraves, a lieutenant of the Sussex militia, and his wife, Elizabeth Whitcombe, was born at Stoke Cottage, Gosport, Hampshire, on 7 October 1816. His schooling was at Brighton and Lewes. In 1832 he emigrated to the colony of New South Wales, where for about sixteen years he followed a variety of pursuits, which included in 1835 several months' work on a cattle property near Bathurst. On 26 December 1836 he married Eliza Mackie (1815–1863), the daughter of a leading Sydney merchant.

Cattle-raising had been Hargraves's business. From 1836 to 1839 he worked his 100 acre property near Wollongong; he then sold it to settle at Brisbane Water in East Gosford, where his wife owned residential properties. For about three years he was agent for the General Steam Navigation Company, but when the British downturn of the 1840s carried the New South Wales economy into depression he was again forced to run cattle, having leased pasture land along the Manning River. By the time of the 1848 California gold discoveries he was still struggling.

Hargraves joined the rush to California, but failed to improve his lot. Its terrain, however, had 'very forcibly impressed' on him that in 1835 he had been in a gold region near Bathurst. He returned to Sydney in January 1851; he was penniless, but confidently borrowed the finance so as to test his belief. He knew that shepherds had picked up isolated pieces of matrix gold in the Bathurst region, and his Californian experience had taught him that it was likely alluvial deposits of gold should also exist.

On 12 February an exuberant Hargraves, accompanied by a local lad, John Lister, panned five specks of gold. Then, aided by an experienced bushman, James Tom, they made a determined but inconclusive search of the inhospitable inland waterways for payable gold. After supervising the construction of a gold cradle by William Tom, the brother of James, Hargraves returned to Sydney where, on 3 April, he hopefully lodged a personal claim for a reward as the discoverer of an 'extensive goldfield'.

While Hargraves was attending to his own affairs, William Tom and Lister, between 7 and 9 April, had arrived at 'the grand desideratum': ground which produced payable gold. When informed, Hargraves hurried back and took the equally shared 4 ounces of gold to Bathurst, whose citizens, stirred by Californian events and buoyed by the local discoveries of copper, had become awakened to the mineral potential of their district. After Hargraves's lecture many rushed to Ophir, where Tom and Lister had dug the gold. This event, in the middle of May 1851, marked the beginning of the Australian gold rush.

The tall, heavily built, and well-connected Hargraves was fêted by business and rewarded by governments; he received initially £10,000 from New South Wales and £2381 from Victoria. He had made no representations on behalf of the aggrieved Lister and the Tom brothers, nor had he confided in them. He argued that he had taught them the mining techniques, such as cradling, and stimulated their enthusiasm for prospecting; and, although he had referred to them in correspondence as 'colleagues', he regarded them merely as his 'guides'. At first Hargraves stated he had dug the historic gold himself; then, when challenged, shifted his ground and asserted that its role in the rush was not important.

In 1854 Hargraves toured England as the 'Gold Discoverer'. The following year his polemical publication, *Australia and its Gold Fields*, appeared. Having returned to Australia and spent his money, between 1862 and 1865 he unsuccessfully prospected for gold, employed by the governments of Western Australia, South Australia, and Tasmania. He died at his home, Mertonville, 64 Westmoreland Street, Forest Lodge, Sydney, on 29 October 1891, leaving two sons and three daughters. He was buried in Waverley cemetery on 31 October.   BRIAN HODGE

Sources New South Wales Legislative Council, *Votes and proceedings* (1853) · Deas Thomson MSS, Mitchell L., NSW · W. B. Clarke MSS, Mitchell L., NSW · 'Correspondence relative to the discovery of gold in Australia', *Parl. papers* (1852–3), 64.1, no. 1607; 64.465, no. 1684; (1854), 44.179, no. 1719; (1854–5), 38.107, no. 1859; 38.321, no. 1978; (1856), 43.565, no. 2030; 43.651, no. 2138; (1857), session 2, 28.181, no. 2283 · *Bathurst Advocate* (1849) · *Bathurst Free Press and Mining Journal* (1850–53) · *Sydney Morning Herald* (1851–3) · G. Blainey, 'Gold and governors', *Historical Studies: Australia and New Zealand*, 9 (1959–61), 337–50 · diary of Samuel Stutchbury, Mitchell L., NSW, MS A2639 · S. Davison, *The discovery and geognosy of gold deposits in Australia* (1860) · W. B. Clarke, *Researches in the southern goldfields of N. S. W.* (1860) · E. H. Hargraves, *Australia and its gold fields* (1855)
Wealth at death under £375: *AusDB*

Hargreave, Charles James (1820–1866), judge and mathematician, was born at Wortley, near Leeds, Yorkshire, in December 1820, the eldest son of James Hargreave, woollen manufacturer, and his wife, of whom little is known. He was educated at Bramham College, near Leeds, and at University College, Dublin (1836–8), graduating LLB in the University of London.

Hargreave spent several months working for a solicitor at the beginning of his studies, and afterwards was the pupil of Richard James Greening, and then of the conveyancer Lewis Duval. He was called to the bar at the Inner Temple on 7 June 1844, and, before his own practice began to take off, helped Jonathan Henry Christie as his draughtsman. In 1843 he was appointed professor of jurisprudence in University College, a position which he held until he left London in 1849.

Following the great famine in Ireland and the passing of the Encumbered Estates Act in 1849, a court was established in Dublin to receive applications for the sale of the estates. Hargreave was appointed as one of the three commissioners who made up the court, at a salary of £2000 a year, and in August 1849 took up residence in Dublin. For the next nine years his official duties kept him fully occupied, although he did find time on 3 September 1856 to marry Sarah Hannah, daughter of Thomas Noble of Leeds. The amount of work accomplished by the court during this period was very large. The commissioners were involved in the reading of titles, statements, petitions, and affidavits, and protecting the rights of absent persons, infants, and others. They dealt with 4413 petitions and the sale of the estates produced £25,190,389. Hargreave was of the opinion that no mistake of consequence was ever made by the court. After the Conservatives came to power in 1858 a new measure for establishing the court in perpetuity, under the designation of landed estate court, was passed; Hargreave was appointed one of its judges, and held this position until his death.

Hargreave was made a bencher of the Inner Temple in 1851, master of the library in 1865, reader in 1866, and had he lived would have succeeded to the office of treasurer. In 1852 he was created a QC. Hargreave was given charge of the judicial business arising out of the Record of Title Act 1866 (29 & 30 Vict. cap. xcix), an act which he conceived in order to establish a registry of Irish titles. Thus, Hargreave will be remembered as having masterminded the introduction of registration of title into Ireland, but was prevented from carrying out his later duties by his last illness. He was also interested in the subject of the registering of the title of QC.

In addition to his legal work, Hargreave was also deeply interested in mathematics, and published a number of scholarly papers in the field. One of his earliest mathematical essays, 'On the solution of linear differential equations' (*PTRS*, 138, 31–54), obtained the gold medal of the Royal Society, and on 18 April 1844 he was elected a fellow of the Royal Society. Other papers included 'General methods in analyses for the resolution of linear equations in finite differences' (ibid., 140, 1850, 261–86); 'On the problem of three bodies' (*PRS*, 1857–9, 265–73); 'Analytical researches concerning numbers' (*London and Edinburgh Philosophical Magazine*, 35, 1849, 36–53); 'On the valuation of life contingencies' (ibid., 5, 1853, 39–45); 'Applications of the calculus of operations to algebraical expansions and theorems' (ibid., 6, 1853, 351–63); 'On the law of prime numbers' (ibid., 8, 1854, 14–22); and 'Differential equations of the first order' (ibid., 27, 1864, 355–76).

Hargreave was awarded the honorary degree of LLD by the University of Dublin in 1852. In 1866 his attention was again drawn to a new method of solving algebraic equations, and he began to write an essay on this problem. Exhaustion and brain fever were thought to have killed him: he died at Bray, co. Wicklow, on 23 April 1866. He was survived by his wife.   G. C. BOASE, *rev.* SINÉAD AGNEW

Sources C. Knight, ed., *The English cyclopaedia: biography*, suppl. (1872), 645 · *Law Times* (5 May 1866), 460 · *Law Times* (12 May 1866), 479 · *Law Times* (29 Sept 1866), 814 · *Law Magazine*, new ser., 21

(1866), 220–35 · [T. T. Shore], ed., *Cassell's biographical dictionary* (1867–9), 752 · Boase, *Mod. Eng. biog.* · Allibone, *Dict.* · *PRS*, 16 (1867–8), xvii–xviii · *The Times* (24 April 1866), 12 · *CGPLA Eng. & Wales* (1866)

Wealth at death under £30,000: probate, 6 July 1866, *CGPLA Eng. & Wales*

Hargreaves [*née* Liddell], **Alice Pleasance** (1852–1934), prototype of the character Alice, was made famous by Lewis Carroll (Charles Lutwidge *Dodgson) in *Alice's Adventures in Wonderland* (1865) and *Through the Looking-Glass* (1872). She was the second daughter of Henry George *Liddell (1811–1898) and his wife, Lorina Hannah (1826–1910), daughter of James Reeve of Lowestoft. Alice was born at 19 Dean's Yard, Westminster, on 4 May 1852, while her father was headmaster of Westminster School. In 1855 he was appointed dean of Christ Church and the family moved to Oxford, where Alice and her sisters were educated by a governess, Mary Prickett, at their home within the college walls, the spacious, handsome deanery, fronting on Tom Quad and backing on a large private garden. As the girls grew they received additional instruction in art from John Ruskin and in foreign languages and music. In later years Alice recalled that, although she and her sisters were compelled to take a cold bath every morning, it was at the deanery that 'we spent the happy years of childhood' (A. and C. Hargreaves).

Mrs Liddell, according to W. M. Thackeray, Liddell's schoolboy friend, was 'a 3d rate provincial lady' but 'first rate in the beauty line' (*Letters and Private Papers*, 2.641–2). She transformed the staid deanery into a grand social venue with her musical evenings and dinner parties, and the children came to know some of Britain's most eminent personalities, even Queen Victoria, who stayed at the deanery when the prince of Wales was an undergraduate at Christ Church.

On the afternoon of 25 April 1856 Alice, not quite four, first met Charles Dodgson, then aged twenty-four and in his second year as mathematical lecturer at Christ Church. He had come to the deanery with his friend Reginald Southey to take a photograph of the cathedral, and although their efforts failed they encountered Alice, her older sister, Lorina, and her younger sister, Edith, in the garden: 'we became excellent friends', Dodgson recorded. 'We tried to group them in the foreground of the picture, but they were not patient sitters' (Dodgson, *Diaries*, 1.83). Photography, the new rage, provided Dodgson the entrée to the deanery and he became a regular visitor, not only taking photographs but also playing croquet with the children in the garden, inventing and playing other games with them in the nursery, telling them stories, and, in good weather, taking them on river picnics up and down the Isis. On 4 July 1862, on one of these picnics, he invented the story of Alice in Wonderland. The real Alice was then aged ten and pleaded with him to write Alice's adventures down for her, which he carefully did, supplying his own illustrations, in a green notebook that has become one of the most cherished literary manuscripts in the British Library.

Alice Pleasance Hargreaves [Liddell] (1852–1934), by Lewis Carroll (Charles Lutwidge Dodgson), 1858 [*The Beggar-Maid*]

The friendship between the Oxford don and the dean's daughter flourished until the following summer, when an unexplained incident that some assume was a marriage proposal exiled Dodgson from the deanery. Polite relations were later re-established, but the earlier warmth was gone for ever. Marriage proposal or no, Mrs Liddell would not consider Dodgson, a mere don with a stammer and a deaf right ear, an appropriate suitor for her daughters. She destroyed all the letters that Dodgson wrote to the children and kept her eye trained on the titled and the rich. She even kept any mention of Dodgson and the *Alice* books out of the authorized biography of her husband, published in 1899.

A beautiful child and young woman, Alice attracted numerous eligible men including, in the mid-1870s, the queen's youngest son, Leopold, duke of Albany, who, like his brother, had been sent to be educated at Christ Church. But the queen insisted upon royal consorts, and Alice was rejected. From the shadows emerged another dashing Christ Church undergraduate, Reginald (Regi) Gervis Hargreaves (1852–1926), the sporting scion of landed gentry. He wooed and won Alice, aged twenty-eight, for his bride. They were married in Westminster Abbey on 15 September 1880. Although Dodgson sent a wedding present, his name does not appear in the list of gift givers. Relations with his 'dream-child' then became formal; the few letters he wrote to her in later life are addressed to 'Mrs Hargreaves'.

The newly-weds moved into the Hargreaves's family home, Cuffnells, a Georgian mansion at Lyndhurst in the New Forest surrounded by 160 lush acres, and Alice, as chatelaine, sought to reproduce the grand parties she had grown accustomed to at the deanery. The couple had three sons and named the third Caryl. They lived comfortably, but were devastated by the deaths of their two eldest sons in the First World War. The crumbling estate, moreover, no longer sustained itself, and Regi was forced to sell off outlying lands. After he died in 1926 and Caryl inherited the property, Alice continued to live there, virtually alone, berating her servants, objecting to her son's extravagant London lifestyle, and criticizing his decision to marry a widow. In 1928 she tried to alleviate another financial crisis by selling at public auction the manuscript booklet of *Alice's Adventures* and other books and memorabilia that Lewis Carroll had given her as a child. In 1932, the centenary of Carroll's birth, the lonely woman was invited, with a sister and her son, to New York to receive an honorary degree at Columbia University, to be fêted, interviewed, filmed, and written about. She succumbed, but on her return confessed that she was 'tired of being Alice in Wonderland' (A. Hargreaves to C. Hargreaves, Liddell-Hargreaves Collection). Alice died at The Breaches, Westerham, two years later, on 15 November 1934, at the age of eighty-two; her ashes were buried at Lyndhurst. Cuffnells continued to decay, and after the Second World War was demolished.　　　　　　MORTON N. COHEN

Sources A. Clark, *The real Alice* (1981) · [A. Hargreaves and C. Hargreaves], 'The Lewis Carroll that Alice recalls', *New York Times* (1 May 1932) · C. Hargreaves, 'Alice's recollections of Carrollian days, as told to her son', *Cornhill Magazine*, [3rd] ser., 73 (1932), 1–12 · A. C. Amor, *Wonderland come true to Alice in Lyndhurst* (1995) · *The diaries of Lewis Carroll*, ed. R. L. Green, 2 vols. (1953) · *The letters of Lewis Carroll*, ed. M. N. Cohen and R. L. Green, 2 vols. (1979) · M. N. Cohen, *Lewis Carroll: a biography* (1995) · *The letters and private papers of William Makepeace Thackeray*, ed. G. N. Ray, 4 vols. (1945–6) · Christ Church Oxf., Liddell-Hargreaves Collection
Archives Christ Church Oxf. · Morgan L. · priv. coll. | FILM priv. coll., print of newsreel film of Mrs Hargreaves's arrival in New York in 1932
Likenesses L. Carroll [C. L. Dodgson], photograph, 1858, NPG [*see illus.*] · C. L. Dodgson, drawing, BL; repro. in Dodgson, *'Alice's adventures underground'* · C. L. Dodgson, photograph, BL; repro. in Dodgson, *'Alice's adventures underground'* · W. B. Richmond, group portrait (*The sisters*), priv. coll. · photographs, Princeton University · photographs, Ransom HRC · photographs, Mansell Collection · photographs, Christ Church Oxf. · photographs, Morgan L. · photographs, New York University
Wealth at death £13,471 10s. 1d.: administration, 4 Feb 1935, CGPLA Eng. & Wales

Hargreaves, Alison Jane (1962–1995), mountaineer, was born on 17 February 1962 at 67 Brisbane Road, Mickleover, Derbyshire, the younger daughter and second of three children of John Edward Hargreaves, a senior scientific officer at British Rail, and his wife, Joyce Winifred, née Carlile, a teacher. Her family moved to Belper, Derbyshire, in 1971, and often went hillwalking. She began rock climbing with school groups in 1975, and soon led 'very severe' climbs. She broke her leg when another climber knocked her off a cliff in 1977, and the following year she began part-time work at an outdoors shop in Matlock Bath. On her eighteenth birthday she left home and moved to Meerbrook Lea, Whatstandwell, outside Matlock Bath, to live with James Herbert Ballard, son of Albert Ballard, a naval ordnance inspector. Jim Ballard, an extroverted Yorkshireman sixteen years her senior, had recently separated from his wife, Jean, and owned the outdoors store where Hargreaves worked. Hargreaves had previously applied to study geography at universities near climbing centres, but then scored too low on her A levels to gain admission. She began producing climbing equipment for her own label and making rock climbs of increasing difficulty, both of which led to a modest reputation among the climbing *cognoscenti*.

After attending a 'meet' for women climbers in 1982 Hargreaves began to consider herself a professional mountaineer. In 1986 she went to the Himalayas with Bill O'Connor to attempt Ama Dablam, and appeared in *Games Climbers Play*, a film. She joined an American expedition led by Jeff Lowe in 1987, when she and Mark Twight ascended a new route on the north-west face of Kantega (22,240 ft). Spending most of her time at home, however, she was isolated from the mainstream climbing community and suffered from low self-esteem. She also lacked the distinctive profile of other contemporary women climbers, such as the feminism of Jill Lawrence or the *savoir-faire* of Catherine Destivelle. She first attracted public attention by combining mountaineering and motherhood. After deciding to have children, she married Ballard at the register office in Belper on 23 April 1988. His divorce had been made final only months previously. Hargreaves (who retained her maiden name) then climbed the north face of the Eiger while five-and-a-half months pregnant. Although her ascent was the first by a British woman, it was her pregnancy that made it newsworthy. She told the ITV television programme 'Women of Today' (27 July 1989) that her 'bump' made it difficult to tie her boots at a bivouac; she confided to her diary that she felt the foetus kicking before and during the climb. She gave birth to a son, Tom, in October 1988, and a daughter, Kate, in March 1991. During this period she spent less time climbing in order to concentrate on raising the children.

Ballard's outdoors business had been struggling financially for years, and when it went bankrupt in 1993 their home was repossessed. They fled creditors and moved to the Alps to pursue a multi-year plan for Hargreaves to make solo climbs of north faces in the Alps and a solo ascent of Everest. Their only income was Hargreaves's £600 a month sponsorship from an outdoor clothing manufacturer. Ballard and the children camped at the foot of each peak while Hargreaves became the first person to climb solo, in a single season, six classic north faces: Grandes Jorasses, Matterhorn, Eiger, Piz Badile, Petit Dru, and Cima Grande di Lavaredo. In her book, *A Hard Day's Summer* (1994), she claimed that the elapsed time climbing these faces was just twenty-four hours. Climbing snobs sneered that her achievements were exaggerated by taking easy routes on the Eiger and the Grandes Jorasses. To answer her critics, she became the first woman to climb solo the formidable Croz Spur of the Grandes Jorasses, in November 1993.

In the autumn of 1994 Hargreaves attempted to climb Everest 'alone' in affiliation with a British medical expedition while her family stayed at base camp in Nepal. She turned back at 27,600 ft to prevent frostbite. In 1993 Rebecca Stephens, a journalist, had become the first British woman to climb Everest, receiving the lucrative endorsements that still eluded Hargreaves. Hargreaves replaced Ballard as her agent with Richard Allen, a retired executive, and developed an ambitious new plan to climb the world's three highest peaks—Everest, K2, and Kanchenjunga—all in one year. In 1995 she returned to Everest without her family to attempt the north-eastern ridge from Tibet unsupported by porters and without supplemental oxygen. On 13 May she reached the summit and radioed a message to her children: 'To Tom and Kate, I am on the highest point in the world and I love you dearly' (BBC, 9 Feb 1996). After Everest she spent two weeks at home in the media spotlight, escaping only for a few days with the children, and bought a new home in the Great Glen beneath Ben Nevis in Scotland. A book contract paid off her debts and covered the cost of her next expedition, to K2.

After several unsuccessful attempts on K2 in July 1995 Hargreaves was minutes away from returning home when she resolved to try again. During a brief period of calm weather she reached the summit of K2 on 13 August; on the descent, a savage storm killed her and six other climbers, among them Americans, Spaniards, and a New Zealander. When their deaths were reported several days later, Ballard suggested to their children, then aged six and four, that they visit 'mum's last mountain'. Their arduous trip to K2 in the autumn of 1995 resulted in a BBC television programme, 'Inside Story: Alison's Last Mountain' (9 Feb 1996), and Ballard's book, *One and Two Halves to K2* (1996). Commentators debated whether the voyeuristic scenes of her grief-stricken children in bereavement counselling on the K2 trek were ghoulish or moving. A wider debate in the press centred on whether a mother should climb. Some considered Hargreaves self-centred or foolhardy for leaving her children for Everest and K2, while others noted that male climbers who died and were fathers were not subject to the same criticism. Her personal motives were at least as complex as the commentary. A biography by David Rose and Ed Douglas, based on extensive interviews and diaries she started in 1973, reported that her relationship with Ballard had been tempestuous and at times violent. She often considered leaving him, but was frequently indecisive: she even died intestate. She told friends and relatives that she planned to divorce Ballard but feared that courts would not give her custody of her children if she continued to climb. Since climbing was her only means of support, she could not stop until she attained financial security. She believed the ascent of Everest and K2 would provide this, and her diaries record the anguished conflict between her desire

to be with the children and her obsession with climbing K2.

Hargreaves was petite, standing 5 feet 4 inches tall, with a wide, round face, wavy, dark blonde hair, and a warm smile. Friends admired her terpsichorean grace on rock, her stamina and organizational skill at high altitudes, and her devotion to her children. Tom and Kate built small memorial cairns in sight of K2, and the government of Pakistan erected a plaque in her honour in the Skardu valley. A memorial service was held at Belper in November 1995. She was posthumously awarded a doctorate by the University of Derby in 1996.   PETER H. HANSEN

Sources D. Rose and E. Douglas, *Regions of the heart* (1999) · J. Ballard, *One and two halves to K2* (1996) · P. Hansen, 'Mum's last mountain: Alison Hargreaves in historical perspective', unpublished paper, 1996, priv. coll. · A. Hargreaves, *A hard day's summer* (1994) · newscuttings, Alpine Club library archives, A69 · *Sunday Times* (3 Dec 1995) · *Climbing* (Sept–Dec 1995) · *Climbing* (Feb–March 1996) · *The Independent* (15–16 May 1995) · *The Independent* (18 May 1995) · *The Independent* (20–21 May 1995) · *The Independent* (20 June 1995) · *The Independent* (1 July 1995) · *The Independent* (18–21 Aug 1995) · *The Independent* (4 Sept 1995) · *The Independent* (16 Oct 1995) · *The Independent* (31 Oct 1995) · *The Independent* (10 Feb 1996) · *The Guardian* (18–21 Aug 1995) · *The Times* (18–21 Aug 1995) · *The Times* (27 Jan 1996) · 'Alison's last mountain', *Inside story*, BBC, 9 Feb 1996 · *Women of today*, ITV, 27 July 1989 · *High* (July–Aug 1986) · *High* (July 1993) · *High* (Jan 1994) · *High* (July 1995) · *High* (Oct 1995) · *On the Edge* (June 1995) · *On the Edge* (Oct–Nov 1995) · *On the Edge* (Dec 1995–Jan 1996) · *On the Edge* (May 1996) · b. cert. · m. cert.
Archives Alpine Club, London, archives | FILM BFI NFTVA, *The slot*, Channel 4, 24 Aug 1995 | SOUND National Public Radio, Washington, DC
Likenesses photograph, repro. in *The Times* (18 Aug 1995) · photograph, repro. in *The Independent* (18 Aug 1995) · photograph, repro. in *The Times* (21 Aug 1995) · photograph, repro. in *The Independent* (21 Aug 1995) · photographs, repro. in Rose and Douglas, *Regions of the heart*

Hargreaves, James (*bap.* 1721, *d.* 1778), inventor of the spinning jenny, was born in Oswaldtwistle, Lancashire, and baptized at Church Kirk on 8 January 1721. His exact birthplace is unknown, and apart from the fact that he became a hand-loom weaver, little has been discovered of his early life. His parents had one other child, Elizabeth, who was three years younger than James. On 10 September 1740, Hargreaves married Elizabeth Grimshaw at Church Kirk. Both were described as 'of Oswaldtwistle'. They had six sons and six daughters. About 1762, while living at Stanhill, on the outskirts of Oswaldtwistle, Hargreaves helped his neighbour, Robert Peel, the calico printer and grandfather of the future prime minister, to construct an improved carding machine. In the mid-1760s he invented the spinning jenny, having observed a spinning-wheel overturned on the ground, when both the wheel and the spindle continued to revolve. The spindle having thus exchanged a horizontal for an upright position, it seems to have occurred to him that if a number of spindles were placed upright and side by side several threads might be spun at once.

The spinning jenny was invented at a time when it was urgently needed. The fly shuttle, invented by John Kay, and supposed to have first come into general use in cotton manufacture about 1760, had doubled the productive power of the weaver, while that of the worker on the spinning-wheel remained much the same. The spinning jenny at once multiplied eightfold the productive power of the spinner, and because of its form could be worked much more easily by children than by adults.

Very soon after the jenny came into use, other inventors sought to make it more efficient, replacing the horizontal driving wheel with the vertical one familiar from most illustrations. The original machine was suitable only for spinning cotton, but once improved, it was widely adopted in the woollen industry. Samuel Crompton combined the principles of the jenny and Arkwright's water frame in his mule. The earliest description of the jenny—a northern word for engine—occurs in a letter in the September 1807 issue of Aitkin's *The Athenaeum*. The writer states that Hargreaves made his first machine 'almost wholly with a pocket knife. It contained eight spindles, and the clasp by which the thread was drawn out was the stalk of a briar split in two' (September 1807, 221–2).

Hargreaves's daughter, Mary Burgess, who dated the invention at 1766, said the machine enabled Hargreaves to dispense with hand spinners. This aroused the interest of his employers, Jonathan Haworth and Robert Peel, who were allowed to inspect the machine. 'When they saw my father spin upon it, Mr Peel said, "James, if you do not make this public we shall", though he had previously pledged his word and honour he would not make the invention known' (Aspin, 120–21).

Shortly afterwards the family moved to Ramsclough, a farm on the edge of Oswaldtwistle Moor, where Hargreaves set up a workshop. Mary Burgess stated that local people who feared the jennies 'would ruin the country … came to our house and burnt the frame work of 20 new machines which were in the barn, and all the working implements.' Not wishing to risk further hostility, Hargreaves became a bookkeeper for Peel, but within a year accepted an invitation to make jennies in Nottingham for the merchant hosiers Shipley, Rawson, Heath, and Watson.

In 1770 Hargreaves became a partner in a new mill at Hockley on the outskirts of Nottingham, and for the rest of his life he lived in a house close by. His partners were Thomas James, a machine maker; William Sadlier, a framework knitter; and Thomas Marlow, a hosier. On 12 June 1770 Hargreaves applied for a patent, which was granted. In the patent he stated that 'after much application and many trials' he perfected a method of making 'a wheel or engine of an entire new construction … [that] will spin, draw and twist sixteen or more threads at one time by a turn or motion of the hand and the draw of other' (patent no. 962, 1770). A threat by the partners to prosecute anyone infringing the patent caused alarm in Lancashire, where many jennies were in use. Hargreaves is said to have refused an offer of £3000 from a delegation representing the manufacturers, but his plans to prosecute the pirates were frustrated when it was shown that he had sold jennies before leaving Lancashire.

Hargreaves died at Nottingham on 18 April 1778, and was buried four days later at St Mary's Church there. John James, son of Thomas James, said that he paid Elizabeth Hargreaves £400 for her husband's share in the business (Baines, 163), and this seems to have been the bulk of his estate. He left 2 guineas to each of his nine surviving children. There is no known portrait of Hargreaves, and the only description is that left by John James: 'a stout, broad-set man, about five feet ten inches high, or rather more' (Aspin and Chapman, *James Hargreaves*, 22).

CHRISTOPHER ASPIN

Sources C. Aspin and S. D. Chapman, *James Hargreaves and the spinning jenny* (1964) · C. Aspin, 'New evidence on James Hargreaves and the spinning jenny', *Textile History*, 1 (1968–70), 120–21 · 'Further remarks on the inventions in cotton-spinning', *Athenaeum: a Magazine of Literary and Miscellaneous Information*, 2 (1807), 221–3 [letter] · E. Baines, *History of the cotton manufacture in Great Britain* (1835) · *Drewry's Derby Mercury* (1 May 1778) · parish registers (baptism, marriage), Church Kirk, Lancashire
Archives Peel Park Library, Salford, Brotherton MSS
Wealth at death £400–£500: Baines, *History*, 163; Aspin, 'New evidence'; Aspin and Chapman, *James Hargreaves*, 70

Hargreaves, James (1768–1845), Baptist minister, was born near Bacup, Lancashire, on 13 November 1768. His family was poor: he began work at the age of seven, and between the ages of thirteen and eighteen was employed in his uncle's public house. He became a keen student of the Bible and began to preach in 1791, the year he married. He joined Bacup Baptist Church in 1794, became active in its work, and was chosen pastor at Bolton in 1795 and at Ogden in 1798, where he remained until 1822. The congregation's poverty compelled him to keep a school at Ogden in addition to his pastoral duties. While at Ogden he was a frequent speaker at the meetings of the Lancashire and Yorkshire Baptist Association, and twice wrote its circular letter. He compiled a catechism for younger Sunday school children, and wrote a biography of his Bacup pastor, John Hirst, and a 300-page history of the Bacup Baptist Church, which is a model of its kind.

Hargreaves removed to Little Wild Street Chapel, London, in 1822 and to the Baptist church at Waltham Abbey Cross, Essex, in 1828. He was active in the affairs of the Baptist Board and the London Baptist Building Fund, and in home and overseas missionary work generally. He wrote on religious subjects from a moderate Calvinistic standpoint: his *Essays and Letters on Important Theological Subjects* was published in 1833. He was an active member of the Peace Society (founded 1816), being for a time its secretary, and was not averse from using the pulpit to express his peace sentiments. After 1822 he kept in close touch with his north-country brethren, thereby linking them more closely with Baptist life in the capital, and may also be regarded as a link between the anti-war stance of many Baptists in the 1793–1815 period and the denomination's peace testimony in the Victorian age. He died at his home in Waltham on 16 September 1845. IAN SELLERS

Sources P. J. Saffrey, *Baptist Magazine*, 39 (1847), 197–201, 273–7 · W. T. Whitley, *The Baptists of Yorkshire and Lancashire* (1913) · E. C.

Starr, ed., *A Baptist bibliography*, 10 (1965) • P. R. Dekar, 'Baptist peacemakers in nineteenth-century peace societies', *Baptist Quarterly*, 34 (1991–2), 3–12

Hargreaves, James (1834–1915), chemical manufacturer and inventor, was born in May 1834, at Hoarstones, Pendle Forest, Lancashire, the eldest of the seven sons of John Hargreaves, a schoolmaster. Hargreaves's education began at his father's school in Slaithwaite. In 1844 his father left schoolmastering to become a druggist and Hargreaves was introduced to medicine and chemistry. In 1856 he turned to technical chemistry, especially the problem of recovering sulphur from alkali waste. John Mercer persuaded him to contact William Gossage, who had been experimenting on similar lines, and in 1859 Hargreaves joined Gossage's soap works. Here he invented methods for recovering chromates used for bleaching oils and fats in soap manufacture and bleaching common brown soap. He was also the first to prepare blue mottled soap.

After leaving Gossage in 1865, Hargreaves worked for two other soap manufacturers in Runcorn and Liverpool. In 1871 he and his youngest brother, John, set up as consulting chemists in Widnes. Turning to metallurgy, James proposed a modification of the Bessemer process for the manufacture of steel, using sodium nitrate instead of air. James Heaton of Widnes tried this on a small scale at Langley Mill, Nottinghamshire, but the cost proved too high. Hargreaves also devised a method for recovering phosphorus from blast-furnace slag; the by-product, ferric chloride, was converted into ferric oxide and chlorine.

About 1872 Hargreaves, with Thomas Robinson, an iron-founder, invented a process and plant for making salt-cake from salt without using sulphuric acid. The Atlas Chemical Company, Widnes, was formed in 1873 to make salt-cake and hydrochloric acid by Hargreaves's method. Hot gases from pyrites burners, mixed with steam, were passed over small blocks of moulded salt, a process which worked successfully for many years; the works was absorbed by the United Alkali Company in 1890 and the last Hargreaves–Robinson salt-cake plant closed in 1918.

With Thomas Bird, an electrical engineer, Hargreaves about 1893 invented an electrolytic process for decomposing common salt, using an asbestos diaphragm. After trials the General Electrolytic Alkali Company was established in 1899 with Hargreaves as a director, and production began at Cledford Bridge near Middlewich in 1901. In 1914 the company was reorganized as Electro-Bleach and By-products Ltd. The process, which was highly efficient, was extensively adopted in Europe and America.

Hargreaves's inventions were numerous and diverse; besides his innovations in the soap, alkali, metallurgical, and electrochemical industries, his 'thermo-motor' anticipated the idea of the diesel engine, and he was among the first to advocate the use of gaseous chlorine for treating sewage. Shrewd in business, he had a ready wit and a distinctive appearance, with a full beard and piercing eyes.

The name of Hargreaves's wife and the date of their marriage is unknown but they had one son and five or six daughters. Hargreaves died at 32 Sayce Street, Widnes, on 4 April 1915.   N. G. COLEY, *rev.*

Sources *Journal of the Society of Chemical Industry*, 24 (1915), 409 • *Widnes Examiner* (5 April 1915) • *Widnes Guardian* (5 April 1915) • D. W. F. Hardie, *A history of the chemical industry in Widnes* (1950) • P. J. T. Morris and C. A. Russell, *Archives of the British chemical industry, 1750–1914: a handlist* (1988), 85–6 • d. cert.
Likenesses portrait, repro. in Hardie, *History of the chemical industry*

Hargreaves [Hargraves], **Thomas** (1774–1847), miniature and portrait painter, was born on 16 March 1774 in Castle Street, Liverpool, and baptized on 7 April at St Nicholas's, the son of Henry Hargreaves, a woollen draper of Castle Street. He entered the Royal Academy Schools in London on 29 March 1790, possibly on the advice of Sir Thomas Lawrence, to whom he served an apprenticeship from 10 May 1793 until he returned to Liverpool because of ill health in August 1795. He went back to London in October 1797 and exhibited intermittently at the Royal Academy between 1798 and 1843 and at the Society of British Artists (of which he was a founder member) between 1824 and 1831. By 1803 he had established a practice in Liverpool where he also assisted his father in his drapery business until 1818. He built up a large clientele in Cheshire and Lancashire and in 1810 was elected a founder member of the Liverpool Academy, exhibiting there between 1810 and 1835.

Hargreaves worked primarily, and, during his final years, only, in miniature, and 785 sketches for his miniatures became part of the collections of the local history department of the City of Liverpool Library. Among those whose portraits he painted in miniature were Mr John Gladstone, Mrs Gladstone, W. E. Gladstone and his sister as children (all at Hawarden Castle, Flintshire), Sir Thomas Lawrence (exh. 1865, South Kensington Museum, London), the comedian Richard Suett, and the singer James Bartleman (Victoria and Albert Museum, London). Some of his miniatures were engraved. The Athenaeum Library and the Walker Art Gallery, Liverpool, both have important collections of his work. With Sophia Shaw Hargreaves had seven children. At least two of his sons, George Hargreaves (1797–1870) and Francis Hargreaves (1804–1877), became miniature painters and assisted in the family miniature-painting business, Hargreaves & Co., conducted in Bold Street, Liverpool, from about 1834. Thomas Hargreaves died on 5 January 1847 in Liverpool.

V. REMINGTON

Sources M. Bennett, *Liverpool painters, people and places* (1978), 108–9 • H. C. Marillier, *The Liverpool school of painters: an account of the Liverpool Academy from 1810 to 1867, with memoirs of the principal artists* (1904), 132–4 • *Art Union*, 9 (1847), 137–8 • B. Stewart and M. Cutten, *The dictionary of portrait painters in Britain up to 1920* (1997) • D. Foskett, *Miniatures: dictionary and guide* (1987), 246, 271, 273–4, 557 • B. S. Long, *British miniaturists* (1929), 191–2 • L. R. Schidlof, *The miniature in Europe in the 16th, 17th, 18th, and 19th centuries*, 1 (1964), 333 • S. C. Hutchison, 'The Royal Academy Schools, 1768–1830', *Walpole Society*, 38 (1960–62), 123–91, esp. 151 • Graves, *RA exhibitors* • K. Garlick, ed., *Sir Thomas Lawrence: a complete catalogue of the oil paintings* (1989), 25 • parish register, Liverpool, St Nicholas, 1774, no. 175 [baptism] • census returns for Liverpool, 1841

Likenesses T. Hargreaves, self-portrait, watercolour on ivory, 1824; Christies, 9 Feb 1993 · T. Hargreaves, self-portrait, watercolour on paper, Walker Art Gallery, Liverpool

Wealth at death many old masters and some eighteenth-century paintings from estate sold after death

Hargrove, Ely [*pseud.* E. H. Knaresborough] (1741–1818), topographer, born on 19 March 1741, was the son of James Hargrove of Halifax, Yorkshire, and his wife, Mary, daughter of George Gudgeon of Skipton in Craven in the same county. In February 1762 he settled at Knaresborough, Yorkshire, as a bookseller and publisher. A few years later he opened a branch business at Harrogate. On 25 October 1762 he married Christiana Clapham (*bap.* 1743, *d.* 1780), daughter of Thomas Clapham of Firby, near Bedale, Yorkshire. They had twelve children.

In 1769 the first edition of Hargrove's *History of the castle, town, and forest of Knaresborough, with Harrogate and its medicinal waters* appeared anonymously. This was frequently republished, latterly with Hargrove's name on the title-page. The York edition of 1789 contains plates and woodcuts by Thomas Bewick. An 'Ode on Time' is appended to the sixth edition, later reprinted in William Hargrove's *York Poetical Miscellany* of 1835 (pp. 60–61). Hargrove also wrote *Anecdotes of Archery from the Earliest Ages to the Year 1791*, which contained details on the life of Robin Hood. A revised edition of this with new material, including an account of the principal existing societies of archers, a life of Robin Hood, and a glossary of terms used in archery, by Alfred E. Hargrove, was published in 1845.

Hargrove was also author of *The Yorkshire Gazetteer* (1806), and he provided an account of Boroughbridge for the fifth volume of Abraham Rees's *New Cyclopaedia*. He was a contributor to the *Gentleman's Magazine* on the topography and antiquities of Yorkshire under the signature of E. H. Knaresborough (*GM*, 1st ser., 59/1, 1789, 438). His manuscript collections on Yorkshire history filled sixteen folio and quarto volumes. Following his wife's death in 1780, he married Mary Bower (*d.* 1825), daughter of John Bower of Grenoside Hall, near Sheffield. They had four children, the youngest of whom was the historian and newspaper proprietor William *Hargrove.

Hargrove died at Knaresborough on 5 December 1818, and was buried in the churchyard there. His widow died at York in April 1825 and was buried at Knaresborough.

GORDON GOODWIN, *rev.* J. A. MARCHAND

Sources *GM*, 1st ser., 88/2 (1818), 645 · C. R. J. Currie and C. P. Lewis, eds., *English county histories: a guide* (1994), 435 · private information (1890) · [D. Rivers], *Literary memoirs of living authors of Great Britain*, 2 vols. (1798) · *IGI* · W. Boyne, *The Yorkshire library* (1869), 141

Hargrove, William (1788–1862), historian and newspaper proprietor, born at Knaresborough, Yorkshire, on 16 October 1788, was the youngest of the four children of the topographer Ely *Hargrove (1741–1818) and his second wife, Mary (*d.* 1825), daughter of John Bower of Grenoside Hall, near Sheffield. Being intended for the church, he was placed in the care of his godfather Robert Wyrell, curate of Knaresborough, who recommended that his pupil should be trained as a journalist. He was accordingly apprenticed

to a Mr Smart of Huddersfield and, after the expiration of his articles, returned to Knaresborough. In 1813 Hargrove and two partners purchased the *York Herald*, a weekly newspaper. He moved to York on 1 July of that year, and the first issue of the newspaper under his management was published on the following 13 July. For the next thirty-five years he was an energetic editor, taking over rival newspapers and installing up-to-date machinery. He added to the staff a verbatim and descriptive reporter, engaged a special correspondent in nearly every town in the shire, and in 1848 bought the shares in the business possessed by his two sleeping partners. In 1818 he published a two-volume *History and Description of the Ancient City of York; Comprising All the most Interesting Information Already Published in Drake's 'Eboracum', with much New Matter and Illustrations*. In October of the same year Hargrove entered the corporation as a common councilman. He defended Queen Caroline in the *York Herald*, and announced her acquittal in 1820 by torchlight from the steps of the Mansion House. In 1827 he successfully promoted, with Charles Wellbeloved (1769–1858), a scheme for the erection of a mechanics' institute, of which he became the first secretary and treasurer. In 1831 he was elected a sheriff of York. He married, on 2 September 1823, Mary Sarah, daughter of William Frobisher, banker, of Halifax, with whom he had several children; in 1855 he took his eldest sons, Alfred Ely and William Wallace Hargrove, into the management of his newspapers.

Much of Hargrove's leisure was devoted to antiquarian studies; he wrote a regular column for his newspapers and produced a pocket guide to the city in 1842. He collected the Roman and medieval remains excavated in and around York, and in 1846–7 he transferred the entire collection to the museum of the Yorkshire Philosophical Society. Hargrove died at York on 29 August 1862; his wife survived him.

GORDON GOODWIN, *rev.* WILLIAM JOSEPH SHEILS

Sources *GM*, 3rd ser., 13 (1862), 784 · J. M. Biggins, *Historians of York* (1956) · W. K. Sessions and E. M. Sessions, *Printing in York from the 1490s to the present day* (1976) · private information (1890, 2004) · *CGPLA Eng. & Wales* (1862)

Wealth at death under £3000: probate, 2 Dec 1862, *CGPLA Eng. & Wales*

Harington [*formerly* Poë], **Sir Charles** [Tim] (1872–1940), army officer, was born Charles Poë at Oaklands, Chichester, on 31 May 1872, the youngest son of Emanuel Thomas Poë (*d. c.*1900), of London, an indigo planter of Behar, India, and his wife, Isabella Jane Crowdy. When Charles was four years old his father adopted his own mother's maiden name and thereafter the son became known as Charles Harington. He entered Cheltenham College in 1886, before passing into the Royal Military College, Sandhurst, in 1890; he was commissioned into the Liverpool (later the King's) regiment, alternating thereafter between regimental and staff duty overseas and at home. Harington was appointed DSO (1900) for service on the staff during the Second South African War. There followed in 1903 a tour as instructor at Sandhurst and qualification (1906) at the Staff College, Camberley. On 7 January

1904 he had married Gladys Norah, eldest daughter of Brigadier O'Donnel Colley Grattan of the King's regiment. They had no children. During these early years, as later, he excelled at all games, especially cricket and hockey, possibly because hunting was beyond his means. When he was in his fifties he swam the Hellespont and back and in his sixties he was still playing high class cricket.

Shortly after the outbreak of the First World War Harington, then a major, was appointed general staff officer, grade 2 (GSO2) to 3rd corps in France. Early next year he was promoted GSO1 (the sole regular staff officer) to the 49th (West Riding) division, territorials newly arrived from England. Towards the end of 1915 he became brigadier-general, general staff, to the Canadian corps, then being formed and in the line near Messines. With them he first became known as a staff officer who was always out and about near the front line.

In June 1916 he was selected major-general, general staff of the Second Army, whose commander was General Plumer. Together they made a splendid team, Harington's brilliant staff work complementing Plumer's powers as a commander.

The first and major test of this partnership occurred in June 1917 when the Second Army's hundred battalions made a successful assault on the Messines Ridge. It began with the explosion of nineteen gigantic mines, dug over more than a year in anticipation of such an attack. Each assaulting unit had been intensively trained in its role. In the first stages the fire of the entire artillery, numbering 2266 weapons, was concentrated under a single commander. Control of the air was complete; 154 mobile workshops supported 12,500 motor vehicles. Tanks had learned how to co-operate with the infantry. Morale was high, largely due to the excellence of the arrangements. By this meticulous and imaginative planning, the first major British victory of the war had been won with comparatively modest casualties.

The subsequent autumn losses and stalemate at Passchendaele were largely due to general headquarters' failure to follow up this Messines victory before the weather broke. For this disaster Harington's staff work was never blamed.

The respective contributions of Harington and Plumer to the successes of the Second Army continue to intrigue historians, hampered as they have been by the fact that both men destroyed their papers. In the plethora of condemnation of First World War leaders, the reputation of neither man has suffered. Harington was especially noteworthy for the way in which his meticulous attention to detail ensured the co-ordination of the various arms and the well-being of the men. He was also well ahead of his time in his relations with the press, whom he habitually took into his confidence. In his somewhat fulsome biography, *Plumer of Messines* (1935), Harington took no credit for his own achievements.

Shortly after Passchendaele Plumer and Harington were ordered to Italy; but they returned to the Second Army at Kassel in March 1918, where the situation had deteriorated. Three months later during the great German spring

offensive Harington was appointed deputy chief, Imperial General Staff, but was allowed to remain in Flanders until the situation became stabilized. In May 1918 he took up his new duties at the War Office. In October 1920 he was promoted lieutenant-general and left for Constantinople as general officer commanding-in-chief the army of the Black Sea.

In Constantinople, in the aftermath of the treaty of Sèvres, Harington became commander-in-chief of the allied forces of occupation in Turkey. There he encountered what was to become known as the Chanak crisis, the most serious challenge of his career.

The occupation by Greek troops of Smyrna (Izmir) and their subsequent ill-judged drive into the heart of Anatolia led to their ignominious defeat by resurgent Turkish troops. The result was the burning of Smyrna with its accompanying horrors. In charge of the Turks was General Mustafa Kemal (later Kemal Atatürk, the modernizer of Turkey).

After crushing the Greeks, Kemal turned to expelling the meagre allied forces occupying Constantinople and the Dardanelles. By September 1922 Kemal had deployed some 50,000 men against Chanak, on the southern shore of the Dardanelles, held by six British battalions. With the leading Turkish troops jeering at the British soldiers from the further side of their barbed wire defences, the start of another war seemed imminent. This Harington was determined to avoid. Doubtful whether the Turks wanted war or would press matters to a conclusion, he had for some time been trying to establish personal contact with Kemal; in so doing he had well exceeded his strictly military duties.

On 29 September 1922, as tension rose, Lloyd George's coalition government instructed Harington to give the Turks an hour's notice to withdraw from the vicinity of Chanak; if they failed to comply, his forces were to open fire. This instruction Harington failed to obey, concerned that it was an order both foolish and dangerous. On 4 October, accompanied by the other allied commanders, he met Kemal's senior representatives, still with his government pressing him to take offensive action. A week later he had achieved success: agreement was reached that the Turks would withdraw. With fine courage, skill, and diplomacy, Harington had avoided what could well have become another major war. It would have been fought with neither allied nor dominion support.

The immediate aftermath was the collapse of the already unpopular and divided coalition government, in which Winston Churchill had both encouraged and supported the prime minister while Curzon, the foreign secretary, had sought peace. The general election that followed brought Bonar Law's Conservative government into office.

Harington, who loathed personal publicity, had by directly disobeying orders become a public figure. He wrongly assumed that his military career was at an end, although he never achieved the position of chief of the Imperial General Staff, generally thought to have been his due.

He returned home in December 1923 to become general officer commanding-in-chief, northern command, at York. There he spent the next three and a half years, and he was promoted general in March 1927. He was sent to India the following October as general officer commanding-in-chief western command, where he spent an uneventful but happy few years at Quetta. In 1931 he became general officer commanding-in-chief, Aldershot, and was made aide-de-camp general to the king (1930–4). He accepted the governorship of Gibraltar in 1933. Here he found life very pleasant until the outbreak of the Spanish Civil War in 1936 with its problems of refugees and neutrality.

Ill health necessitated Harington's retirement and in October 1937 he settled in Sussex. There he occupied himself with many varied interests. He was appointed CB in 1917, KCB in 1919, GBE in 1922, and GCB in 1933. The honorary degree of DCL was conferred upon him by Oxford University in 1924, and he was given the freedom of the city of York in 1927. He founded and became first president of the army sports control board.

Harington was 'a spare, highly strung man, with a charming manner and remarkable clarity of vision' (*DNB*). A deeply religious person, he had a great sense of humour and was liked everywhere. He died at Cheltenham on 22 October 1940, the year in which his autobiography, *Tim Harington Looks Back*, was published.

GEOFFREY S. POWELL

Sources DNB · *The Times* (24 Oct 1940) · C. Harington, *Tim Harington looks back* (1940) · D. Walder, *The Chanak affair* (1969) · G. Powell, *Plumer: the soldiers' general* (1990) · Lord Kinross [J. P. D. Balfour], *Atatürk: the rebirth of a nation* (1964) · P. Gibbs, *Realities of war* (1920) · J. F. Maurice and M. H. Grant, eds., *History of the war in South Africa, 1899–1902*, 4 vols. (1906–10) · J. E. Edmonds, ed., *Military operations, France and Belgium, 1918*, 4–5, History of the Great War (1947) · D. L. George, *The truth about the peace treaties*, vol. 2 (1938), chaps. 25–6 · *CGPLA Eng. & Wales* (1941)

Archives King's Lond., Liddell Hart C., map of Middle East · Lpool RO, corresp. and papers | IWM, corresp. with Sir Henry Wilson · King's Lond., Liddell Hart C., corresp. with Sir B. H. Liddell Hart

Likenesses W. Stoneman, photograph, 1918, NPG · photographs, repro. in Harington, *Tim Harington looks back*

Wealth at death £1880 7s. 4d.: probate, 27 Jan 1941, *CGPLA Eng. & Wales*

Harington, Sir Charles Robert (1897–1972), biochemist and medical administrator, was born on 1 August 1897 at Llanerfyl, north Wales, the elder son (there were no daughters) of the Revd Charles Harington (1862–1921), and his wife, Audrey Emma, daughter of the Revd Robert Burges Bayly, vicar of Hampton Bishop, Herefordshire.

In 1906 Harington went to a preparatory school at Malvern Wells, Worcestershire. The next year, however, he developed tuberculosis of the hip, which left him with a permanent severe limp, and for the following six and a half years he was immobilized at home. Despite this, he won a scholarship to Malvern College, from which in 1916 he won an exhibition to Magdalene College, Cambridge. In 1919 he took a first class in part one of the natural sciences tripos. Having developed an interest in the chemical aspects of pharmacology, in 1920 he went to the department of medical chemistry in Edinburgh under George

Barger, and subsequently to the department of therapeutics under J. C. Meakins, where he acquired a PhD in 1922. In 1923 he married Dr Jessie McCririe, younger daughter of the Revd James Craig, minister of Kirkpatrick Durham, near Dalbeattie; they had a son and two daughters.

On Barger's strong recommendation Harington was appointed lecturer in charge of the new department of chemical pathology at University College Hospital medical school in London. He arrived there in 1923, after a year at the Rockefeller Institute in New York, began research on the internal secretions of the thyroid gland, and only four years later succeeded in establishing the chemical constitution of the prototype, thyroxine, and effecting its synthesis. For this he was elected FRS in 1931 and promoted professor (he had become reader in 1928). He was editor of the *Biochemical Journal* from 1930 to 1942.

Harington's research expanded rapidly, so that by the end of the decade his achievements put him in the first rank of biochemists. It was not this, however, that accounted for his growing reputation in wider circles, but the range of his understanding in the biomedical field. Thus, in his book *The Thyroid Gland: its Chemistry and Physiology* (1933) he covered not only the gland's chemistry but also its physiology, pathology, and the clinical features of its disorders. In 1938 he was appointed a member of the Medical Research Council (and in 1941–5 of the Agricultural Research Council), and in 1942, despite his lack of medical qualifications, he was chosen to succeed Sir Henry Dale as director of the National Institute for Medical Research.

Both professionally and temperamentally Harington was well suited to direct a major multidisciplinary research institute. Because of his wide knowledge of biomedical subjects, he was capable of appraising its activities both individually and collectively. He saw that, without overall direction, such an institute could easily become a collection of self-centred interests. To counteract this tendency he paid close attention to the balance of effort within the institute, and its continuing relevance to developments in biomedical knowledge and the fields in which these found practical expression. On this basis he formed his decisions or recommendations to the Medical Research Council on the recruitment of staff, the initiation or expansion of particular lines of work, and the contraction or closing down of others.

When Harington took over the institute he found that it would be impossible to combine, as his predecessor had done, the post of director with that of head of one of its divisions, in his case biochemistry, because of the expansion of its programme and staff. He therefore devoted himself to his job as director. Harington retired in 1962; however, he agreed to act as consultant adviser to the secretary of the Medical Research Council on non-clinical matters. This he did for five years with objectivity and insight. Thereafter his health declined.

In 1944 Harington gave the Croonian lecture and won the royal medal of the Royal Society. In 1951 he was elected FRSE and in 1959 honorary FRSM. He was knighted in 1948 and appointed KBE in 1962. In 1963 he was elected honorary FRCP, one of the first two non-medical men (the other was Austin Bradford Hill) to be accorded this honour. He was awarded honorary doctorates by Paris (1945), Cambridge (1949), and London (1962). Harington died on 4 February 1972 at Mill Hill, London.

HAROLD HIMSWORTH, *rev.*

Sources H. Himsworth and R. Pitt Rivers, *Memoirs FRS*, 18 (1972), 267–308 · personal knowledge (1986) · Burke, *Peerage* (1924) · *CGPLA Eng. & Wales* (1972) · *DNB*
Wealth at death £45,586: probate, 19 April 1972, *CGPLA Eng. & Wales*

Harington, Sir Edward (1754–1807), traveller and essayist, was born on 27 February 1754 in Wells, Somerset, the only son of Henry *Harington MD (1727–1816), musician and author, and his wife, Martha Musgrave. He was knighted on 27 May 1795, when, as mayor of Bath, he presented to the king a congratulatory address from the corporation on his escape from the attempt of Margaret Nicholson. He was twice married: first, on 10 February 1800 at St Marylebone, Middlesex, to Frances Boote, and then, on 13 February 1804 at St James's, Bath, to Frances Wake with whom he had a number of children; one of his sons, Edward (1774–1811), was father of Edward Charles *Harington (1804–1881). Harington was described as clever, but eccentric. His writings include *A schizzo on the genius of man, in which … the merit of Thomas Barker, the celebrated young painter of Bath, is particularly considered* (1793) and *Remarks on a letter relative to the late petitions to parliament for the safety and preservation of his majesty's person, and for the more effectually preventing seditious meetings and assemblies …* (1796). He died at his lodgings in London on 18 March 1807, aged fifty-three.

GORDON GOODWIN, *rev.* REBECCA MILLS

Sources Foster, *Alum. Oxon.* · [D. Rivers], *Literary memoirs of living authors of Great Britain*, 1 (1798), 238 · F. Townsend, *Calendar of knights … from 1760 to the present time* (1828), 30 · W. Shaw, 'The knights of England', *Heraldry Today*, 2 (1971), 302 · *IGI* · *GM*, 1st ser., 77 (1807), 486

Harington, Edward Charles (1804–1881), Church of England clergyman, born on the Isle of Man, was the only son of the Revd Edward Harington (*d.* 1811) and his wife, Frances, daughter of John Boote of Fifield House, Oxfordshire. Sir Edward Harington was his grandfather. He traced an unbroken descent from John Harington of Kelston, near Bath, father of Sir John Harington. He appears to have been educated privately, and entered Worcester College, Oxford, on 6 July 1824, aged nineteen, where he graduated BA in 1828 and MA in 1833. After entering orders, he became incumbent of St David's, Exeter, and having come to the attention of Bishop Phillpotts of Exeter was made a prebendary of Exeter in 1845, and in 1847 chancellor of the church. He resigned his incumbency and concentrated on diocesan work, especially education. He persuaded contending parties within the church to co-operate in establishing the diocesan training college for teachers in church schools. For many years he taught at the college, and was a generous contributor to its endowment.

In 1856 Harington became canon residentiary of Exeter, and was energetic in turning the cathedral into 'a house of prayer'. He spent £15,000 on the repairs of the fabric, and

£1000 in providing seats in the nave. A wealthy man, he was munificent in private charity, sending poor clergymen with their wives and families to the seaside for weeks, and paying all expenses. He shared Bishop Phillpotts's taste for religious controversy, in which he took a high-church position, producing pamphlets and sermons on the history of the Scottish church (1843) and apostolical succession (1844), and several rebuttals of Roman Catholic claims (1846–56).

Harington was shy, retiring, and somewhat eccentric in manner, living at first with his sisters and afterwards alone. He always attended the turning of the first sod of every new railway in England. Though not a great scholar he was a man of considerable learning, and collected a fine library. On 4 July 1881 he was attacked by apoplexy while attending a meeting at the guildhall of Exeter of the Society for the Prevention of Cruelty to Animals, and died at his canon's lodgings, the close, Exeter, on 14 July 1881. He was buried with his ancestors at Kelston, near Bath, to the poor of which parish he left £300. By his will he bequeathed his library to the dean and chapter of Exeter, with £2000 for a librarian. He left many legacies to church institutions and to poor dependants.

RICHARD HOOPER, *rev.* M. C. CURTHOYS

Sources personal knowledge (1890) · private information (1890) · Boase, *Mod. Eng. biog.* · Foster, *Alum. Oxon.*
Likenesses oils, deanery, Exeter
Wealth at death £31,936 2s. 5d.: probate, 2 Aug 1881, *CGPLA Eng. & Wales*

Harington, Henry (1727–1816), composer and physician, was born at Kelston, Somerset, on 29 September 1727, the son of Henry Harington and his wife, Mary Backwell. He was descended from Henry VIII's treasurer of the army, Sir John Harington (*d.* 1553). He matriculated at the Queen's College, Oxford, on 17 December 1745, graduating BA in 1749 and MA in 1752. At Oxford he joined the Club of Gentlemen Musicians, founded by Dr William Hayes; he both sang and played the flute. On 7 December 1752 he married Martha Musgrave; they had at least one daughter and two sons, Sir Edward *Harington (1754–1807) and Henry *Harington (1754/5–1791). Abandoning the idea of taking holy orders, in 1753 Harington established himself as a physician at Wells. He took the degrees of MB and MD at Oxford in 1762, and in 1771 moved to Bath, where he continued his medical practice. He was an alderman and magistrate of Bath, and the town's mayor in 1793, and was appointed physician to the duke of York.

Harington devoted his leisure to composition and music, and in 1784 was appointed 'composer and physician' to the newly founded Harmonic Society of Bath. He was one of the leading composers of glees of his day, and published four collections of glees and songs (that of 1800 was edited by his daughter Susanna Isabella Thomas) in addition to many single items. His most popular works were a round, 'How great is the pleasure', and a duet for two sopranos, 'How sweet in the woodlands'. His satirical catches, such as 'The Alderman's Thumb', have been judged 'particularly successful' (*New Grove*). He also wrote some sacred music, poetry, *A Treatise on the Use and Abuse of*

Musick, and *The Geometrical Analogy of the Doctrine of the Trinity Consonant to Human Reason* (1806). Harington died at Bath on 15 January 1816 and was buried in the chancel of Kelston church. A subscription was raised for a monument to his memory in Bath Abbey (occasioning five celebratory stanzas in the *Gentleman's Magazine*, 86/1, 1816, 352); his collection of music was sold by auction.

GORDON GOODWIN, *rev.* K. D. REYNOLDS

Sources New Grove · Foster, *Alum. Oxon.* · *GM*, 1st ser., 86/1 (1816), 185–6, 352, 640 · IGI · J. D. Brown, *Biographical dictionary of musicians: with a bibliography of English writings on music* (1886)
Likenesses C. Turner, mezzotint, pubd 1799 (after T. Beach), BM, NPG · lithograph (after J. Slater), BM

Harington, Henry (1754/5–1791), antiquary and Church of England clergyman, was born at Wells, Somerset, the younger son of Henry *Harington (1727–1816), physician and composer, and Martha Musgrove. He matriculated at Queen's College, Oxford, on 2 July 1770, aged fifteen, proceeding BA (1774), MA (1777), and BD and DD (1788). He married Esther Lens at Norwich on 3 April 1782. Following ordination he became rector of North Cove with Willingham, Suffolk; rector of Heywood, Norfolk; prebendary of Bath and Wells on 1 May 1787; minor canon of Norwich Cathedral; and assistant minister of St Peter Mancroft, Norwich.

From an early age Harington began to use family papers belonging to his father to compile the collection of literary pieces and historical notes known as *Nugae antiquae*. The volumes deal chiefly with the life and writings of Sir John Harington (1560–1612) and his father. The first volume appeared in 1769, without the editor's name; a second volume (1775) bore his name on the title-page, and was dedicated to Lord Francis Seymour, dean of Wells. A second enlarged edition in three volumes, dated 1779, was dedicated to Charles, bishop of Bath and Wells. The work was re-edited by Thomas Park in 1804 in two volumes. Harington died at St Giles, Norwich, on 25 December 1791.

SIDNEY LEE, *rev.* J. A. MARCHAND

Sources Foster, *Alum. Oxon.* · *GM*, 1st ser., 61 (1791), 1237 · *Fasti Angl.* (Hardy), 1.205 · IGI

Harington, Sir John (d. 1553), administrator, was the eldest son of Sir John Harington of Exton, Rutland (d. 1524), and Alice, daughter of Henry Southill. By the terms of his marriage settlement of January 1513 to Elizabeth, daughter and heir of Robert Moton of Peckleton, Leicestershire, the ward of Sir Richard Sacheverell (d. 1534), Harington established an independent estate in Leicestershire, Lincolnshire, Nottinghamshire, and Suffolk.

The death of Harington's father placed him among the prominent gentry of the kingdom. Beginning in 1520 he was four times sheriff of Rutland, and sheriff once each of Lincolnshire, and Warwickshire and Leicestershire. Harington was junior knight of the shire for Rutland in the parliament of 1529, and senior knight in 1539 and 1542. He was among the first to oppose the Pilgrimage of Grace and was subsequently made esquire of the body to the king (1539) and knighted (16 January 1542). Local honours, offices, and responsibilities multiplied, including the

commissions for the survey of the monasteries (1536) and church goods (1553), stewardship of Stamford, bailiffship of Leicester, keepership of Beaumanor Park, and receivership of the duchy of Lancaster for Leicester honour (1537–53).

On 30 August 1542 Harington was appointed treasurer of war for the autumn campaign against Scotland of Thomas Howard, duke of Norfolk, and was responsible for disbursements of £60,129. He repeated this service in 1543 for Charles Brandon, duke of Suffolk, warden of the Scottish marches, but was replaced as treasurer of war in the north by Sir Ralph Sadler in February 1544. Harington became vice-treasurer of the army in France for the king's campaign of 1544 when he contributed 10 horsemen and 100 foot, and then was treasurer of the expedition to France of 1546 led by Edward Seymour, earl of Hertford. In October 1549 Harington became a royal councillor to Henry Manners, earl of Rutland, as warden of the east and middle marches against Scotland.

Harington purchased extensive property, profiting considerably from the dissolutions of the religious houses and more than doubling his inheritance. He had a reputation for litigiousness and was implicated in the malfeasance of his former treasurer's clerk in France, John Bradford, the Marian martyr. Harington himself appears to have been a religious conservative. He made his will on 20 August 1553 and died on 28 August in the parish of St Helen, Bishopsgate, London. Extensive masses and dirges were conducted upon his death, and he was buried in Exton on 8 September following. By his marriage to Elizabeth Moton he had five sons and four daughters, including his heir Sir James Harington (d. 1592) of Exton and the MP Edward Harington of Ridlington, Rutland. His grandson, Sir John Harington (d. 1613), the guardian of Princess Elizabeth, daughter of James I, was created Baron Harington of Exton on 21 July 1603.

J. D. ALSOP

Sources HoP, *Commons, 1509–58* · R. Hughey, *John Harington of Stepney: Tudor gentleman* (1971), 6–7 · will, PRO, PROB 11/37, sig. 1 · *LP Henry VIII* · *CPR, 1547–53* · R. Somerville, *History of the duchy of Lancaster, 1265–1603* (1953), 567, 571 · PRO, SP 15/3, fols. 117–22 · PRO, E 165/9, fol. 105 · PRO, E 351/212 · J. Foxe, *The acts and monuments*, 8 vols. (1965), vol. 7, pp.143, 162, 278–9; vol. 8, p. 747 · G. J. Armytage, ed., *The visitation of the county of Rutland in the year 1618–19*, Harleian Society, 3 (1870), 38 · J. Strype, *Ecclesiastical memorials*, 3/2 (1822), 366–7 · HoP, *Commons, 1558–1603* · *The diary of Henry Machyn, citizen and merchant-taylor of London, from AD 1550 to AD 1563*, ed. J. G. Nichols, CS, 42 (1848), 43 · *Report on the manuscripts of the late Reginald Rawdon Hastings*, 4 vols., HMC, 78 (1928–47), vol. 1, p. 307 · *The manuscripts of his grace the duke of Rutland*, 4 vols., HMC, 24 (1888–1905), vol. 4

Harington, John (c.1517–1582), courtier and writer, was the son of Alexander Harington (d. 1539), and a member of the northern, staunchly Yorkist branch of the family which flourished under Edward IV but forfeited much of its land as a result of Richard III's defeat in 1485. His father, who was son of James, dean of York, settled in Stepney. John Harington had entered the service of Henry VIII by 1538. He studied music under Thomas Tallis, and wrote an anti-monastic hymn which the king liked to sing.

Probably in 1547 Harington married Ethelreda (also

known as Esther or Audrey) Malte, supposedly the natural daughter of Henry VIII, who had been passed off as the illegitimate daughter of a tailor named John Malte in exchange for grants of land and revenues. Through this match Harington received dissolved monastic estates in Berkshire and Somerset, among them the manor of Kelston, which he would later make the family's country seat. By the spring of 1546 he had entered the service of Sir Thomas Seymour, and his life was much affected by his master's rise and fall in the reign of Edward VI. Thanks to Seymour's influence, he sat in the parliament of 1547 as the member for Pembroke. After Seymour's arrest in January 1549, Harington was imprisoned and questioned about his master's relationship with the young Princess Elizabeth, and about his own part in negotiations to marry Edward VI to Lady Jane Grey.

Harington remained in the Tower until the spring of 1550, long after his master's execution. There he took advantage of spare time and distinguished company (including that of Sir Thomas Smith) to learn French and to translate a French version of Cicero's *De amicitia* into English; this text was published in 1550 with a dedication to Catherine Willoughby, duchess of Suffolk (a second edition appeared in 1562). He may also have caught a first glimpse of his future second wife, Isabell, daughter of the lieutenant of the Tower, Sir John Markham, and one of the maids in attendance on Princess Elizabeth. However, Harington's first wife was still alive when he was imprisoned again in 1554, this time for suspected involvement in Wyatt's rebellion; both John and Ethelreda attended Princess Elizabeth during her confinement in the Tower. Ethelreda was still alive in early 1556, and they had a daughter, Esther, probably born about 1549; she is last heard of in 1568. Ethelreda evidently died some time before the end of 1559, the year in which Harington married Isabell Markham, who served as a lady of the queen's privy chamber until her death in London in 1579.

After Elizabeth's accession Harington's fortunes recovered. As 'the queen's servant', he obtained two exchequer posts and various land grants. Elizabeth stood godmother to his son John *Harington, baptized on 4 August 1560; his second son, Francis, was probably born in 1562 or 1563. On 12 February 1569 he received a grant of arms, and on 5 August 1570 he received the reversion of the Harington estates forfeited at Bosworth, although he was never to obtain them. Harington represented Old Sarum in the parliament of 1559 and sat for Caernarfon in 1563 (he had been appointed constable of Caernarfon Castle in June 1551, a post he held until his death). He died at Stepney, 'at a Prebende house neere the Bishop's Palace of London', on 1 July 1582 and was buried alongside Isabell in St Gregory by Paul, London.

Harington stands out as a vigorous champion of the vernacular, both in his own poetry and in poems by others which he collected. Thirty poems, some of which were printed in Tottel's *Songes and Sonettes* of 1557, can be attributed to him with confidence; these include a translated stanza from Ariosto's *Orlando Furioso* which his son John incorporated into his complete English translation of that poem. He also played an important role in preserving the works of Wyatt and Surrey, copying their poems, along with many by their contemporaries and successors, into a verse miscellany which was continued by his heir, and which is now in the library at Arundel Castle. Harington's biographer, Ruth Hughey, sums up his significance by describing him as 'a representative gentleman of the new order in the Tudor age' (Hughey, *John Harington*, 4), a scholar–courtier who negotiated the reigns of four monarchs and whose reformed learning assisted his rise from relative obscurity to considerable wealth.

JASON SCOTT-WARREN

Sources R. Hughey, *John Harington of Stepney: Tudor gentleman* (1971) · HoP, *Commons, 1509–58* · R. Hughey, 'The Harington manuscript at Arundel Castle and related documents', *The Library*, 4th ser., 15 (1934–5), 388–444 · R. Hughey, ed., *The Arundel Harington manuscript of Tudor poetry*, 2 vols. (1960) · P. Beal and others, *Index of English literary manuscripts*, ed. P. J. Croft and others, [4 vols. in 11 pts] (1980–), vol. 1, pt 2 · J. D. Alsop, 'A manuscript copy of John Harington's *Of the death of Master Deuerox*', *Manuscripta*, 24/3 (1980), 145–54 · A. Stewart, *Close readers: humanism and sodomy in early modern England* (1997), chap. 4

Archives BL, family archive, Add. MSS 46366–46384 · TCD, Blage MS 160 | Hatfield House, Hertfordshire, Cecil MSS, depositions in Seymour investigation

Likenesses C. Warren, line engraving, pubd 1822 (after drawing by J. Thurston), BM; repro. in B. W. Proctor, *Effigies practicae, or, The portraits of the British poets* (1824) · oils, probably Victoria Art Gallery, Bath; repro. in Hughey, *John Harington*, 53

Harington, John, first Baron Harington of Exton (1539/40–1613), courtier and landowner, was the eldest son of Sir James Harington (*c*.1511–1592), landowner and administrator, of Exton Hall, Rutland, and his wife, Lucy (*c*.1520–*c*.1591), daughter of Sir William Sidney and his wife, Anne. His family held the most extensive estates in Rutland during the late sixteenth century and, with the Digbys of Stoke Dry and the Noels of Brooke, monopolized the parliamentary representation of the county throughout Elizabeth I's reign. In 1558 Harington entered the Inner Temple, where his future father-in-law, Robert *Keilwey, surveyor of the court of wards, was treasurer.

Harington represented Rutland in parliament in 1571, his father being unable to sit as MP because he was sheriff. About this time he married Anne (*c*.1554–1620), daughter and heir of Keilwey and his wife, Cecily; through Anne he acquired Combe Abbey, Warwickshire, on her father's death in 1581. They had two sons and two daughters. Harington divided his time between Exton in Rutland, which had been magnificently renovated by his father, and his newly acquired property at Combe Abbey. He was placed on the commission of the peace for Kesteven, Lincolnshire, from about 1559 until 1593, probably through family influence, and became JP for Rutland and Warwickshire from about 1579 and 1583 respectively. These and other local appointments enhanced his influence and power. Harington also had a service relationship with the Dudleys, who were the dominant family in the west midlands. He exchanged gifts and hospitality with Robert Dudley, earl of Leicester, served under him in the Netherlands in 1585, was an assistant mourner at his funeral, and keeper of Kenilworth Castle, Warwickshire, from 1588 to

John Harington, first Baron Harington of Exton (1539/40–1613), by unknown artist, 1592

1590 for Ambrose Dudley, earl of Warwick. He served as sheriff for Warwickshire in 1582–3, was knighted in 1584, and was county MP in 1586. He was more active in this and subsequent parliaments. In September 1586 he was chosen to accompany Mary, queen of Scots, through Warwickshire on her way to Fotheringhay in Northamptonshire.

In 1592 Harington succeeded his father and was MP for Rutland in 1593 and 1601 as the senior member. His county prestige was advanced further with his appointment as deputy lieutenant of Rutland and Warwickshire during the 1590s. He shared the former position with Sir Andrew *Noel, the husband of his sister Mabel. In 1597 ill health prevented him from standing for parliament and shortly after his cousin Sir John *Harington, the writer, described him and Thomas Cecil, first earl of Exeter and second Baron Burghley, together at Bath, suffering from gout: 'It gave me some comfort to hear their religious discourse and how each did despise his own malady and hold death in derision, because both did not despair of life eternal' (Harington, 1.236). Harington was replaced as MP by his younger brother James Harington of Ridlington, continuing the family's parliamentary influence. The political unity of Rutland was broken during the 1601 parliament when a dispute over the second seat led to a rift with Noel and brought the 'bane of faction' to the county (Neale, 131).

At the end of Elizabeth's reign Harington was one of the leading knights in the country, whose wealth equalled that of many barons. He was considered a suitable candidate, based on wealth and service, for elevation to the peerage. In 1602 John Chamberlain described him as keeping a 'royal Christmas' with Edward Russell, third earl of Bedford, who had married his daughter Lucy *Russell, Roger Manners, fifth earl of Rutland, William Herbert, third earl of Pembroke, Sir Robert Sidney, and others (CSP dom., 1601–3, 271). On the accession of James I, Harington took care to consolidate his position, travelling to Yorkshire with his brother James to meet the king and subsequently entertaining him to dinner at Burley on the Hill,

his second Rutland residence. In June 1603 Princess Elizabeth stayed at Combe Abbey on her journey south. In July Harington was raised to the peerage at the coronation as first Baron Harington of Exton and in October he was appointed Elizabeth's guardian. His daughter Lucy meanwhile established herself as the constant companion of the queen, Anne of Denmark, and his son John *Harington, later second Baron Harington, joined the intimate circle of Henry, prince of Wales. Elizabeth and her entourage were established at Combe, from where members of the Gunpowder Plot intended to abduct her in 1605. Hearing a report of a raid on the stable at Warwick Castle, however, Harington removed his charge to the safety of Coventry with only a few hours to spare. The strong protestant beliefs espoused by Elizabeth throughout her life were undoubtedly influenced by the godly piety of her guardian and his wife, who continued to control her household until her marriage to Frederick V, elector palatine.

The vagaries of Jacobean royal accounting and his unwillingness to defraud the king led Harington to incur substantial costs in maintaining Elizabeth's household and in 1612 he petitioned for the privilege of coining brass farthings for three years in recompense. These coins were known as Haringtons. This grant was agreed before his wife and he accompanied his former charge and her husband to Germany in April 1613 at their own expense. In Heidelberg Harington spent four months arranging the princess's financial and household affairs. During the return journey he died of fever at Worms on 23 August 1613, aged seventy-three. His widow returned his body to Exton for burial. His elder son, Kelway, having died in infancy, he was succeeded by his younger son, John, who survived him by little more than six months. This dynastic accident prevented his family from recovering the costs of their involvement with the royal family. Despite an income of £5000–£7000, the family debt stood at £30,000–£40,000. Lucy, countess of Bedford, dying without children, the family survived only through Anne, the child of Harington's younger daughter, Frances, and her husband, Sir Robert Chichester.   JAN BROADWAY

Sources HoP, Commons, 1558–1603, 2.257–8 · J. E. Neale, The Elizabethan House of Commons (1963), chap. 6 · B. Burke, A genealogical history of the dormant, abeyant, forfeited and extinct peerages of the British empire, new edn (1883), 264–5 · GEC, Peerage · CSP dom., 1603–10, pp. 81, 191, 241–2, 534, 557, 611; 1611–18, pp. 141, 167, 170, 174–5, 180, 184, 215 · J. Harington, Nugae antiquae, ed. T. Park and H. Harington, 2 vols. (1804)
Archives Bodl. Oxf., letter to Sir Julius Caesar about Princess Elizabeth's financial affairs
Likenesses oils, 1592, Parham, West Sussex [see illus.] · Passe, line engraving, BM, NPG; repro. in H. Holland, Heröologia Anglica (1620)
Wealth at death approx. £30,000–£40,000 in debt

Harington, Sir John (bap. 1560, d. 1612), courtier and author, was the first of two sons of John *Harington (c.1517–1582), courtier, and his second wife, Isabell Markham (d. 1579). He was baptized in the church of All Hallows, London Wall, on 4 August 1560. Thanks to his parents' high favour, his godparents were Queen Elizabeth and William Herbert, second earl of Pembroke. By 1570 he was at Eton College, where he and his schoolfellows translated into Latin the story of Elizabeth's sufferings during the reign of Mary Tudor, from Foxe's book of martyrs; the resulting volume, no longer extant, was presented to the queen. The queen sent 'Boye Iacke' a copy of her 1576 end-of-session speech to parliament defending her right to celibacy, telling him that although 'it cannot be suche striplinges have entrance into Parliamente Assemblyes as yet', he would if he studied her words 'perchance, fynde some good frutes hereof when thy godmother is oute of remembraunce' (*Nugae antiquae*, 2.154). Harington matriculated at King's College, Cambridge, in 1576, graduated BA in 1578, and proceeded MA in 1581. While at Cambridge he received advice on his studies from the lord treasurer, William Cecil, and acknowledged the support of the secretary of state, Sir Francis Walsingham. In November 1581 he was admitted to Lincoln's Inn, but his time there was cut short by the death of his father; he took possession of the family estate in Kelston, near Bath, in June 1583. On 6 September of the same year he married Mary (*d.* 1634), daughter of George Rogers (*c.*1528–1582) of Cannington, Somerset, and granddaughter of Edward Rogers (*c.*1500–1568), a prominent office-holder under Henry VIII, Edward VI, and Elizabeth I.

The translator of Ariosto Harington refused to subscribe to the 1584 bond of association, believing it prejudicial to James VI's claim to the English throne. In 1586, in the company of his brother-in-law Edward Rogers, he visited Ireland with an eye to participating in the plantation of Munster. Probably he began to sit as justice of the peace around this time, initiating an involvement in county government which would continue throughout his life. But in general the 1580s are a poorly documented part of Harington's life. This is doubtless because 'some yeeres, & months, & weeks, and dayes' (*Letters*, 176) of this decade were devoted to the huge task which earned him his place in literary history, the first complete translation into English of Ludovico Ariosto's epic romance poem *Orlando Furioso*. A celebrated anecdote (first recorded in the late eighteenth century) relates that these labours were a penance; when his godmother the queen caught him circulating a translation of the lewd tale of Fiametta from canto 28 of the *Orlando* among her ladies-in-waiting, she banished Harington from the court until he had translated all thirty-three thousand lines of it. The folio volume, published by Richard Field in 1591, was a triumph of book design, lavishly illustrated and indexed, each canto furnished with highly individual, gossipy notes. It was dedicated to Elizabeth, but Harington also presented large-paper copies, some of them hand-coloured, to potential patrons, including James VI, William Cecil, and Sir Thomas Coningsby; the work's title-page, incorporating portraits of the translator and of his beloved dog Bungay, covertly advertised Harington's desire for public office. The translation was reprinted, with revisions, in 1607; a third edition appeared in 1634. Although Ben Jonson's damning judgement that Harington's Ariosto 'under all translations was the worst' (C. H. Herford and P. Simpson, eds., *Ben Jonson*, 11 vols., 1925–52, 1.133) has coloured much

subsequent commentary, the work has won admirers and is often seen as part of a key moment in the history of Anglo-Italian literary relations, alongside Spenser's *Faerie Queene* (1590–96) and Fairfax's translation of Tasso's *Gierusalemme liberata* (1600).

The Metamorphosis of Ajax Harington's next published work grew out of a convivial gathering at Wardour Castle in Wiltshire, home of the fanatical horse-lover Sir Matthew Arundell; the company included Henry Wriothesley, earl of Southampton, and his sister Mary. The conversation turned to matters of sanitary technology, and the idea of keeping a permanent cistern of water above a privy, with a primitive flushing mechanism, was conceived. Harington outlined the design (with illustrations supplied by his servant, the emblematist Thomas Combe) in his *New Discourse of a Stale Subject, called the Metamorphosis of Ajax* (1596). 'Ajax' played on 'a jakes', meaning 'a privy', a device here transformed in the manner of Ovid's Ajax. The punning title gives some idea of the work that follows, a complex blend of scatological comedy, moral reflection, and social satire. Although Harington wrote the *New Discourse* under the pseudonym Misacmos ('hater of filth'), he dropped many clues to his identity throughout, so that he became known as Sir Ajax Harington. On the basis of his first two publications, critics have speculated about his relevance to the Jacques and Orlando of his contemporary Shakespeare's *As You Like It*. As a result of the *New Discourse*'s satire, Harington was threatened with Star Chamber suits; for a derogatory remark about the earl of Leicester, 'the great Beare that caried eight dogges on him when Monsieur [the duke of Alençon] was here' (*New Discourse*, 171), he languished for some time in royal disfavour. Harington avowed to Elizabeth Russell that his aim in writing the pamphlet was to 'give some occasion to have me thought of and talked of' (*Letters*, 66), and in this he was undoubtedly successful. The work enjoyed considerable if short-lived popularity, going through four editions in 1596 and attracting an anonymous response in an animadversion entitled *Ulysses upon Ajax*. Although the *New Discourse* was merely an octavo pamphlet, there is evidence that Harington tried to use it to further his career. In the final section of the book (the 'Apologie') he created a complex fictional vehicle which allowed him to flatter potential patrons and to promote the toleration of conformist recusants such as his friend Ralph Sheldon and his uncle Thomas Markham. And Harington's water-closet itself became a gift in the patronage economy; he installed one at the royal palace of Richmond and sent another to Robert Cecil for use at Theobalds.

In 1599 Harington returned to Ireland, this time with the army sent to crush the rebellion of Hugh O'Neill, second earl of Tyrone. Robert Devereux, earl of Essex, newly appointed lord lieutenant, wrote directly to Harington appointing him to lead a mounted troop under the command of the earl of Southampton. On 30 July Harington became one of the scores of soldiers knighted by Essex in the course of his ill-fated campaign. From Ireland he sent letters describing the English military defeat at the Curlew Mountains in Connaught, and recounting his meeting with Tyrone in the company of Sir William Warren. He recalled proudly that he had presented Tyrone's sons with a copy of his *Orlando* and, asked by the earl to read a section aloud, turned '(as it had been by chance)' to the beginning of canto 45, a passage describing how fortune's wheel raises men up and throws them down again. Then they had breakfasted together on Tyrone's 'fern table and fern forms, spread under the stately canopy of heaven' (*Letters*, 78). Harington returned to England 'in the very heat and height of all displeasures' (ibid., 79), sharing in the wrath which Elizabeth vented at Essex. Soon, however, he was granted a private audience and restored to favour.

Throughout the 1590s Harington had been engaged in writing epigrams in imitation of Martial, and on 19 December 1600 he made two manuscript collections of them. He sent one to Lucy, countess of Bedford, the daughter of Sir John Harington of Exton. In it his poems followed three psalm paraphrases by Mary Sidney, attending them 'as a wanton page is admitted to beare a torche to a chaste matrone' (*Letters*, 87). The other, larger collection Harington gave to his widowed mother-in-law, Jane Rogers; here the epigrams followed a copy of the *Orlando*, with printed and manuscript sections joined in an elaborate gold-tooled binding. For this collection Harington chose those poems he had written on domestic occasions, recapitulating a troubled history of relations between the courtier, his wife, Mall, and her mother. Harington decreed that the gift should descend through the female line, a stipulation which betrays the book's part in his broader project to oust his scapegrace brother-in-law Edward as Lady Rogers's heir. In this he appears to have been successful. Jane Rogers died on 19 January 1602, naming as her executors Mary Harington and Francis Rogers; the latter, Edward's eldest son, was a minor. The events which followed her death were hotly disputed in Star Chamber between December 1603 and July 1604. Harington claimed that Edward Rogers had besieged him in Lady Rogers's house at Cannington, subsequently locking him up for nine hours and ransacking his personal belongings. Edward claimed that Harington had conferred with a physician in order to predict the likely date of his mother-in-law's death, and that he had kept the news of that event under wraps while he carried away her possessions. The terms of the arbitrated settlement of the dispute remain obscure.

The search for patronage Meanwhile Harington had also been speculating about his godmother's death and, although discussion of the question was prohibited by law, he completed a substantial *Tract on the Succession to the Crown* in 1602. This work adduced writers from the three most populous sects, 'Papists, protestants, and purytans', in order to convince the whole spectrum of confessional opinion of the justice of the Stuart claim to the English throne. The work survives in a single manuscript copy in the chapter library at York, among the books of Archbishop Tobie Matthew. Matthew, at this time bishop of Durham, was known to be hostile to James's claim, and Harington may well have given him the manuscript to

win him round. The *Tract* was one of several gestures which Harington made in anticipation of James's accession. In 1602 he sent the Scottish king a richly symbolic lantern, comparing himself with the good thief crucified alongside Christ and asking his lord to 'remember me when you come into your kingdom'. He also sent James a manuscript of his epigrams, which were now over four hundred in number, arranged into four books. Before the death of Elizabeth, Harington made contact with Sir William Maurice, a vociferous supporter of union between England and Scotland in the early Jacobean parliaments.

On 14 April 1603, as the nation awaited the arrival of its new king, Harington bade 'Farewell to his muse' at Eton. Ironically, he saw her off in verse, and less than a fortnight later he was in Rutland, presenting the new king and queen with 'gratulatorie Elegies'. But his hopes of gaining public office in the dawn of a new regime were dashed by extreme misfortune. In the summer of 1603 he was incarcerated in the Gatehouse prison, Westminster, as guarantor of a £4000 debt incurred by his uncle Thomas Markham. In this period of enforced *otium* he revised a translation he had made of the sixth book of Virgil's *Aeneid*, which he presented to King James in June 1604 for use in the instruction of Prince Henry. From this point forward Henry became the focus of Harington's search for patronage. In 1605 he gave him a collection of his epigrams, and in 1608 he presented him with a weighty quarto volume containing Bishop Francis Godwin's printed *Catalogue of the Bishops of England* (1601), to which he had added marginalia, two indexes, and a 'Supplie or addicion', a substantial supplement updating Godwin with colourful biographies of the Elizabethan episcopate. Harington claimed that his work was a defence of the established church hierarchy, written in response to a prophecy which ran:

Henry the 8. pulld down Abbeys and Cells
But Henry the 9. shall pull down Bishops and bells.

None the less, Harington's opposition to clerical marriage, which he argued out in correspondence with Bishop Joseph Hall around this time, gave a critical edge to many of his portraits. The *Catalogue* was first printed by Harington's grandson John Chetwind in 1653 as a justification for the dismantling of episcopacy. Harington's support for the ecclesiastical hierarchy is perhaps best evidenced by his extraordinary attempt to join it. In 1605 he sent Robert Cecil and Charles Blount, earl of Devonshire, manuscript copies of a 'short relation … contayning my humble and zelows offer for his Majesties sarvyce in Ierland' (*Letters*, 118). Having heard that the lord chancellor of Ireland, Adam Loftus, was sick, Harington applied for his job in a treatise outlining his solutions to Anglo-Irish conflict; and with it he asked for Loftus's other position, as archbishop of Dublin. This extraordinary request was perhaps inspired by the example of Prince Henry's tutor Adam Newton, a layman whose successful bid for the deanery of Durham Harington had supported. Harington's suit was rejected. Yet it was part and parcel of his behaviour under James. He seems to have viewed the accession of an adult male monarch, after decades of 'anomalous' rule by women and children, as a return to Henrician values, with courtiers as bishops and humanists in high office. In his final years Harington remained active, completing a metrical paraphrase of the psalms and pursuing a scheme to persuade Thomas Sutton, the richest commoner in England, to declare Prince Charles his heir. He died on 20 November 1612, and was buried at Kelston on 1 December; his wife, Mary, died in 1634. Their eldest son, John (1589–1654), became a noted parliamentarian and diarist.

Thanks largely to the care of his descendants, whose pride in their ancestry led to the publication of the historical miscellany *Nugae antiquae* (1769–75; 2nd expanded edn 1779), Harington is one of the best-documented writers of his age. The printer's copy for large sections of the *Orlando* and *New Discourse* survives; we also have memoranda, first drafts, reworkings, and texts customized for presentation. From the last few years of his life we have two remarkable booklists, one of which shows that he owned a large collection of printed playtexts. Combined with this documentary wealth, the fact that he devoted so much effort to publicizing himself in his writings makes him seem an unusually knowable figure. Since his self-presentation was always designing, it is unreliable; indeed, much of the foregoing biographical narrative should be treated with caution, since Harington is often our only source for what we 'know' about him.

Assessment Historical estimates of Harington are divided; some dismiss him as a failed careerist and minor writer, others celebrate him as a maverick figure, the licensed fool of Queen Elizabeth and King James. His letters, which offer cool analyses of the machinations of these monarchs from the perspective of a disaffected suitor, are enduringly fascinating. Equally involving is the sheer intricacy of his attempts to win favour and public office through textual transactions, involving sophisticated exploitation of the media of manuscript and print. But Harington was far from being merely self-interested; he had a humanistic concern for 'the commonweal', and his works promote many causes, from the restoration of Bath Abbey to religious toleration. He had a strong leaning towards Catholicism, although he called himself a 'protesting Catholicke Puritan' (*New Discourse*, 263). The complex blend of 'high' and 'low' cultural elements in his writings made them broadly popular. His epigrams, particularly those which satirized 'puritans', circulated widely in manuscript in the seventeenth century; partial (and censored) collections were printed in 1615 and 1618. His *Englishmans Docter*, a translation of the medieval medical poem *Regimen sanitatis Salernitanum*, went through five editions between 1607 and 1624, only the last of which bore Harington's name; it may well have reached print without his knowledge.

Harington justified his references to friends and kinsfolk in the notes to his *Orlando* by recalling that Plutarch had criticized Homer for leaving no account of himself; his translation, 'a worke that may perhaps last longer then a better thing' (*Letters*, 15), would not be thus blamed. In the event, it is the unashamedly personal element in Harington's writings which has made them last.

JASON SCOTT-WARREN

Sources *The letters and epigrams of Sir John Harington*, ed. N. E. McClure (1930) · J. Harington, *Nugae antiquae*, ed. H. Harington, 2nd edn, 3 vols. (1779) · D. H. Craig, *Sir John Harington* (1985) · *Sir John Harington's A new discourse of a stale subject, called the metamorphosis of Ajax*, ed. E. S. Donno (1962) · J. Harington, *A tract on the succession to the crown* (AD 1602), ed. C. R. Markham (1880) · J. Harington, *A supplie or addicion to the catalogue of bishops to the yeare 1608*, ed. R. H. Miller (1979) · *Ludovico Ariosto's Orlando furioso, translated into English heroical verse by Sir John Harington* (1591), ed. R. McNulty (1972) · *The sixth book of Virgil's Aeneid, translated and commented on by Sir John Harington*, ed. S. Cauchi (1991) · *A short view of the state of Ireland*, ed. W. D. Macray (1879) · P. Beal, *Index of English literary manuscripts*, ed. P. J. Croft and others, 1/1–2 (1980) · J. Scott-Warren, 'Sir John Harington as a giver of books', PhD diss., U. Cam., 1997 · S. Cauchi, 'Recent studies in Sir John Harington', *English Literary Renaissance*, 25 (1995), 112–25 · R. Hughey, *John Harington of Stepney* (1971) · *CSP Ire., 1600*, 233–4 · will of George Rogers, PRO, PROB 11/64 · will of Mary Harington, PRO, PROB 11/173

Archives BL, family archive, Add. MSS 46366–46384 · BL, Add. MS 27632 · Hatfield House, Hertfordshire, corresp. and MSS

Likenesses attrib. H. Custodis, oils, *c*.1590–1595, Ampleforth College, York; on loan · T. Cockson, line engraving, BM, NPG; repro. in L. Ariosto, *Orlando furioso*, trans. J. Harington (1591), title-page · attrib. H. Custodis, double portrait, oils (with his wife); Sothebys, 11 July 1983, lot 52 · attrib. H. Custodis, oils, NPG

Harington, John, second Baron Harington of Exton (*bap.* 1592, *d.* 1614), courtier, was baptized at Stepney, Middlesex, on 3 May 1592, the only surviving son of John *Harington (1539/40–1613) and his wife, Anne (*c*.1554–1620), daughter and heir of Robert Keilway of Minster Lovell, Oxfordshire. He may have been the 'Mr Harington' listed as a page to the countess of Rutland (his second cousin) in 1600, but if so he was presumably withdrawn from service when the earl of Rutland was arrested for his part in the rebellion of Robert Devereux, second earl of Essex, in February 1601.

Although Harington's father cultivated relations with Sir Robert Cecil, his links with Essex's faction meant that he did not return to favour until the accession of James I in 1603, when he received a peerage as Baron Harington of Exton and the governorship of the king's daughter Princess Elizabeth. Harington himself was created a knight of the Bath on 5 January 1604 and became one of the aristocratic companions of the king's eldest son, Prince Henry, two years his junior, encouraging the latter in his studies and developing a close relationship best illustrated by a joint portrait of the two men on a stag hunt. In 1607–8 Harington spent a year at Sidney Sussex College, Cambridge, which his father had helped to found a decade earlier, and in the summer of 1608 he and his tutor, John Tovey, a former master of Coventry Free School, embarked on an eighteen-month grand tour on the continent. Prince Henry, who interceded with the king in person to secure Harington's passport, was then beginning to develop his own network of policy advisers and his friend's itinerary was clearly intended to provide the prince with eyewitness reports of most of the potential diplomatic flashpoints of western Europe.

Having left England with an entourage of ten gentlemen, Harington met Archduke Albert and his wife, Isabella, at Brussels and attended lectures at Heidelberg and Basel before travelling to Florence, where he just missed the nuptials of Grand Duke Cosimo de' Medici. He sent Prince Henry a printed copy of the wedding celebrations and stated his intention to travel home through France, but changed his plans, heading for Rome upon an invitation from the Catholic exile Sir Anthony Standen. Fearing that Tovey would be arrested by the inquisition Harington went instead to Venice, where he arrived a few days before Christmas 1608 and was warmly recommended to the doge by the English ambassador, Sir Henry Wotton, who claimed that 'being the right eye of the Prince of Wales, this world holds that he [Harington] will one day govern the kingdom' (CSP Venice, 1607–10, 216).

Harington spent six months in Venice 'to study the form of this government', informing Prince Henry about the criticisms of Rome which had been circulating within the city since the papal interdict of 1606. Attending the church of San Lorenzo, he reported that 'every day during Lent a Brother Fulgenzio [Micanzio] of the Servite order has preached the word of God purely and without intermixture', an assessment which owed much to the fact that the sermons denigrated papal claims to temporal authority and supported the English line in the oath of allegiance controversy. The Venetians expressed their regard for Harington by giving him dispatches to take to their ambassador at the imperial court in Prague upon his departure from the city in July 1609.

Harington returned homewards via Vienna and Prague, reporting to Prince Henry about the looming conflict between Archduke Mathias and the estates of Lower Austria, then on to Frankfurt, where he commented upon the Jülich–Cleves succession crisis, and Paris, where he observed the French king's increasing resolve to intervene in Germany. He probably returned to England in the entourage of the Venetian ambassador, arriving a few days after the performance of the masque The Barricades, which Prince Henry used to lay claim to the leadership of the protestant cause. Six weeks after his return Harington was returned to the Commons at a by-election for Coventry, undoubtedly at his father's behest. Although named to a number of committees, he made no recorded speeches.

The death of Prince Henry in November 1612 had a major impact on Harington's long-term prospects but he was able to maintain his position at court with an annuity of £1000 from his father and a reversion to the clerkship of common pleas, an enormously lucrative sinecure. Tipped for the governorship of Guernsey, his plans changed when his father died suddenly in August 1613 leaving an estate burdened with debts of £30,000. Harington's father had hoped to marry him to Salisbury's only daughter, and at the end of his life he was spoken of as a match for one of the daughters of the ninth earl of Northumberland, but he was still unmarried when he was struck down by smallpox at Kew, where he died on 26/27 February 1614. There was widespread grief at his early demise, particularly among the godly clergymen he had patronized, while John Donne observed 'thou dids't intrude on death, usurps't a grave' (J. Donne, 'Obsequies to the Lord Harrington', line 192). Harington was buried at Exton, Rutland, on 31 March 1614. His funeral sermon, delivered by Richard Stock, the rector of All Hallows, Bread Street, London, and published as The Churches Lamentation for the Losse of the Godly (1614), portrayed him as a model of puritan piety.

Harington's mother paid off many of the family's creditors by selling the family's main estate at Exton to Sir Baptist Hicks. The remainder of the family's lands were dispersed by his childless sister, Lucy *Russell, countess of Bedford, before her death in 1628.   SIMON HEALY

Sources I. Grimble, The Harington family (1957) • T. Birch, ed., The life of Henry, prince of Wales (1760) • CSP Venice, 1607–10 • R. Stock, The churches lamentation for the losse of the godly (1614) • The letters of John Chamberlain, ed. N. E. McClure, 2 vols. (1939) • The life and letters of Sir Henry Wotton, ed. L. P. Smith, 2 vols. (1907) • HoP, Commons, 1604–29 [draft] • GEC, Peerage • G. J. Armytage, ed., The visitation of the county of Rutland in the year 1618–19, Harleian Society, 3 (1870) • IGI • DNB
Archives Leics. RO, Exton MSS | BL, Harley MSS 7007, 7011 • BL, Lansdowne MSS 91, 108
Likenesses R. Elstrack, line engraving, BM, NPG • Passe, line engraving, BM, NPG; repro. in H. Holland, Herōologia Anglica, 2 vols. (1620) • line engraving, BM • portrait, repro. in Grimble, Harington family • portrait, repro. in Stock, Churches lamentation, frontispiece • woodcut, BM; repro. in R. Stock, The churches lamentation for the losse of the godly: delivered in a sermon, at the funerals of … John Lord Harington (1614)
Wealth at death £60,000: Exton MSS, Leics. RO

Harington, John Herbert (1764/5–1828), administrator in India and Persian scholar, obtained a writership in the East India Company's service in Bengal in 1780 and in 1781 was made assistant in the revenue department. By 1783 he had mastered Persian sufficiently to be appointed Persian translator to the revenue department and thereafter to begin work on his two-volume edition of The Persian and Arabick Works of Sadi, published in Calcutta in 1791 and 1795.

Harington was briefly employed in the secret department, but most of his career was given over to the internal administration of British India. In 1796 he became registrar of the sadr diwani and nizamat adalats and in 1799 fourth member of the board of revenue. In 1801 he was appointed puisne judge of the sadr diwani and nizamat adalats, being further promoted in 1811 to chief judge. He married Amelia Johnston in Calcutta on 4 June 1808. Two of their five children died in infancy.

Harington was an enthusiastic educationist and, although of an earlier generation of civil servants, he welcomed the establishment in 1800 of the new training college of Fort William, Lord Wellesley's proposed 'Oxford of the East', and became the college's law specialist and a member of the Persian department. In 1809 he presided over the college council and throughout his time in India always defended the college against intermittent calls for its abolition. In turn, in its law classes the college promoted Harington's principal work, An Elementary Analysis of the Laws and Regulations Enacted by the Governor General in Council, published in three volumes by the company's press in Calcutta, 1805–17.

In the emerging debate about Indian education Harington pursued a moderate course between the orientalist and Westernizing extremes. He favoured the reinvigoration of classical Indian scholarship and the promotion of the vernaculars, but he also wanted Indians to be exposed to European knowledge and the English language. An evangelical, he liberally supported the missionaries' educational experiments in Bengal and variously held office in the Calcutta School Society, the Calcutta School Book Society, the Church Missionary Society (of which he was an honorary life governor), the British and Foreign Bible Society, and the Society for the Propagation of Christian Knowledge. He was also an active member of the Asiatic Society of Bengal and was instrumental in the society's decision to build a permanent home for itself in Calcutta.

In 1819 Harington took furlough, returning to India in 1822 on his provisional appointment to the supreme council. In 1823 he became senior member of the board of revenue of the Western Provinces and agent to the governor-general at Delhi. In April 1825 he joined the supreme council and became president of the board of trade. He went home to England again in 1827 on absentee allowance and died in Bloomsbury Square, London, on 9 April 1828. KATHERINE PRIOR

Sources M. A. Laird, *Missionaries and education in Bengal, 1793–1837* (1972) · D. Kopf, *British orientalism and the Bengal renaissance* (1969) · Dodwell [E. Dodwell] and Miles [J. S. Miles], eds., *Alphabetical list of the Honourable East India Company's Bengal civil servants, from the year 1780 to the year 1838* (1839) · *GM*, 1st ser., 98/1 (1828), 379 · C. E. Buckland, *Dictionary of Indian biography* (1906) · ecclesiastical records, East India Company, BL OIOC
Archives BL OIOC, Home Misc. series

Harison, Anthony (1563–1638), Church of England clergyman and episcopal secretary, son of William Harison, was born on 18 November 1563, at Over, Cambridgeshire. He matriculated sizar from King's College, Cambridge, at Easter 1580, but apparently did not graduate. Nevertheless, he acquired legal expertise, became a notary public and, according to his own notebooks, a solicitor and attorney of the university. In May 1603 he was chosen by John Jegon, the newly appointed bishop of Norwich, as his secretary, a post he filled until Jegon's death in 1618. In 1609 he was ordained and presented to the rectory of Catfield, Norfolk, a living which was in two medieties, one held by the king and one by the bishop. After 1618 he retired to Catfield but continued to be consulted by subsequent bishops of Norwich about the temporal affairs of the see. On his appointment in 1603 Harison found the financial affairs of the bishopric in disarray with alarming gaps in the estate records: many of the latter he claimed had been embezzled after Bishop Redman's death. He made it his life's work to bring order to this chaos, first to help Jegon to improve his income, subsequently to strengthen the long-term financial position of the bishopric. A few years before his death he reflected that he had long been 'a diligent observer and preserver of all matters which did concern the Bishop of Norwich' (*Registrum vagum*, 1.11).

Harison's observations were kept in a series of meticulously detailed notebooks, mainly concerned with the leasing of the episcopal estates, which show a thorough grasp of every possession of the see. His published *Registrum vagum* reveals the broader nature of his work as episcopal secretary. Its charm derives from its eclecticism: it records diocesan and national religious business but includes personal letters and poems, and is as much commonplace book as precedence text. Jegon's successors angered Harison by being insensitive to the fiscal needs of the see: Bishop Samuel Harsnett, who carried 'court holy water' (*Registrum vagum*, 1.12), particularly offended by appropriating some of Harison's notebooks, though they were subsequently reconciled.

Harison was married twice. The name of his first wife is unknown; his second, Margaret, was named with several of his five surviving children in leases made to him at Ludham. One son, Oliver, became a clergyman and another, Joshua, was a student at Trinity College, Cambridge, in 1616. Harison died at Catfield on 17 September 1638 and was buried there the next day: his successor recorded in the register that 'he was a man of admirable parts both of nature and grace' (*Registrum vagum*, 1.15). Oddly for so punctilious a man, Harison seems to have left no will. FELICITY HEAL

Sources *The Registrum vagum of Anthony Harison*, ed. T. F. Barton, 2 vols., Norfolk RS, 32–3 (1963–4) · CUL, MS Dd. 12. 43 · A. Harison, ledger, CUL, MS Mm. 3. 12 · Harison's ledger, Bodl. Oxf., MS Tanner 228 · Venn, *Alum. Cant.* · F. Heal, *Of prelates and princes: a study of the economic and social position of the Tudor episcopate* (1980) · parish register (burial), Catfield, 18 Sept 1638
Archives Bodl. Oxf., ledger, Tanner MS 228 · CUL, ledger, Dd. 12. 43; Mm. 3. 12; Mm. 6. 8 · LPL, ledger, Tenison MS 887 · Norfolk RO, HAR/1–3, MSC/1

Harkeley, Henry. See Harclay, Henry (c.1270–1317).

Harker, Alfred (1859–1939), petrologist, was born on 19 February 1859 at Kingston upon Hull, Yorkshire, the son of Hull corn merchant Portas Hewart Harker, and Ellen May Harker (*née* Tarbotton). His schooling was at the Hull and East Riding College, and then Clewer House School, Windsor. Even in his teens, Harker contributed articles on a variety of scientific topics, some geological, to the *English Mechanic* and *Design and Work*. He went up to St John's College, Cambridge, as a sizar in 1878, and while a student secured an exhibition and then a foundation scholarship. Eighth wrangler in 1882, he received a first in the natural science tripos the same year, and in physics in 1883. Even before his finals he was demonstrating in mineralogy and petrology, and he became demonstrator in petrology in January 1884. The following year he was elected to a fellowship at St John's. In 1904 he was appointed university lecturer, and in 1918 he became reader in petrology, a position he held until his retirement in 1931. Harker was a notable teacher, his *Petrology for Students* passing through seven editions in his lifetime.

Harker's first research field was concerned with slaty cleavage, for which he received the Sedgwick prize in 1888. In the following two years, in company with John Marr, Harker worked at Carrock Fell and Shap, broaching the problem of igneous masses of composite composition. Analogous investigations were subsequently made in Skye. The question was whether there was more than one kind of 'primeval' magma in the earth's interior, or whether magmas self-differentiated during crystallization. Harker came to the view that fractional crystallization was the principal process, but he also described what he took to be hybrid admixtures, arising from the intrusion of magma into a still-hot igneous mass of different composition.

In the early 1890s there was a major controversy between Archibald Geikie and John Judd regarding the order of emplacement of the basic rocks of the Cuillins and the acidic rocks of the adjacent Red Hills in Skye. The solution was to be found by detailed field-mapping and Harker, by then the country's leading petrologist, was invited by Geikie to map the region for the geological survey, being seconded part-time from Cambridge for the purpose. This work, began in 1895 and completed with the publication of *The Tertiary Igneous Rocks of Skye* (1904), vindicated Geikie's view that the Red Hills were younger than the Cuillins; but more importantly Harker produced a magnificent set of geological maps, superseded only in the late twentieth century. Harker's empirical and theoretical work at Blá Bheinn, the mountain where the Cuillins and the Red Hills meet, is particularly renowned.

With his work in Skye, Harker developed a great love for the Hebrides, which he revisited, year after year, into old age. His *Geology of the Small Isles of Inverness-Shire* (1908) was another major contribution. However, *The Natural History of Igneous Rocks* (1909) was Harker's principal monograph; it was followed by *Metamorphism* (1932). Perhaps his major theoretical suggestion was that the general character of different regions of igneous rocks might be related to the tectonic environment—the conditions of temperature and pressure under which the rocks were formed. Following the studies at Shap, Harker showed that the rocks surrounding the Shap granite had been reconstituted without significant changes in bulk composition. In subsequent years he was disinclined to adopt the views of those who advocated fundamental changes induced by percolating hot liquors (metasomatism).

Harker was elected FRS in 1902 and received a royal medal in 1935. He was president of the Geological Society (1916–18), and received its Murchison medal (1907) and Wollaston medal (1922). He was awarded an honorary LLD by McGill University in 1913 and an honorary DSc by Edinburgh University in 1919. Harker's whole academic life was based at St John's, where he was for several years senior fellow. He did not marry, and was somewhat reclusive. He was, however, a keen cricketer, and liked the occasional game of billiards, poker, or tennis. One of his most important gifts to Cambridge University was his collection of some 40,000 thin sections of rocks. Harker died in the Evelyn Nursing Home in Cambridge on 28 July 1939, mourned by numerous former students who attested to his gifts as a teacher.   DAVID OLDROYD

Sources A. C. Seward and C. E. Tilley, *Obits. FRS*, 3 (1939–41), 197–216 • 'Eminent living geologists: Alfred Harker', *Geological Magazine*, new ser., 6th decade, 4 (1917), 289–94 • A. C. S. [A. C. Seward], *The Eagle*, 51 (1938–9), 273–85 • S. J. Shand, 'Memorial to Alfred Harker', *Proceedings of the Geological Society of America for 1939* (1940), 207–9 • A. C. Seward, 'Alfred Harker (1859–1939)', *The west highlands and the Hebrides: a geologist's guide for amateurs by Alfred Harker*, ed. J. E. Richey (1941), xvii–xxiii • *CGPLA Eng. & Wales* (1939)
Archives U. Cam., Sedgwick Museum of Earth Sciences, field notebooks
Likenesses H. Lamb, pencil drawing, 1936, St John Cam. • R. Guthrie, pen-and-ink drawing, 1939, U. Cam., Department of Mineralogy • R. Guthrie, pencil drawing, 1939, U. Cam., Department of Mineralogy • Elliott & Fry, photograph, repro. in 'Eminent living geologists' • Lafayette, photograph, repro. in A. C. S., *The Eagle* • photograph, repro. in Shand, 'Memorial to Alfred Harker'
Wealth at death £33,962 18s. 4d.: probate, 24 Nov 1939, *CGPLA Eng. & Wales*

Harker, (William) Gordon (1885–1967), actor, was born at 60 Fullerten Road, Wandsworth, London, on 7 August 1885, the second among six sons of Joseph Cunningham Harker (1855–1927), a successful designer and scenic artist, and his wife, Sarah Elizabeth Hall. Like four of his brothers, who later became notable scene painters in their own right, young Gordon was initially apprenticed in his father's Horsley Street studio in south-east London, but his own ambitions lay elsewhere. After enjoying performing in a school play during his education at Ramsey grammar school, Isle of Man, in the late 1890s, he was intent on a more active theatrical career, and as a first step persuaded the actor–manager Fred Terry to employ him as prompter for a provincial tour in 1902. Joining Fred's celebrated older sister Ellen Terry during her management of the Imperial Theatre, Harker made his London début on 23 May 1903 by walking on in her production of *Much Ado about Nothing*, directed by her son Gordon Craig and co-starring Oscar Asche. Harker was then engaged by the latter when he took the lease of the Adelphi Theatre in 1904, and acted with the company for nine years, throughout Asche's joint managements of other West End theatres with his wife Lily Brayton and their overseas tours of Australia and South Africa—a solid grounding of supporting roles in a mixed, but predominantly Shakespearian, repertory.

Early in the First World War Harker enlisted in the 8th Hampshire regiment and served with it in Gallipoli and Palestine, but in 1917 he was so badly wounded as to be pronounced unfit for action and was left with a permanent limp (which he later exploited for theatrical effect). Invalided out in 1919, he rejoined Asche briefly to understudy in his long-running musical fantasy *Chu-Chin-Chow* at His Majesty's before appearing in the British première of Robert Hichens's *The Garden of Allah* at Drury Lane in June 1920, both productions designed by his father. Over the next five years Harker was cast in a motley collection of plays, including a revival of J. M. Barrie's *Quality Street* (Haymarket, 1921), John Drinkwater's *Robert E. Lee* (Regent, 1923)—challengingly, as the ineffectual Confederate president Jefferson Davis—and modern comedies by Seymour Hicks, Ian Hay, Arnold Bennett, and Eden Phillpotts, but did nothing which caught the public's imagination. In 1926, however, he was introduced to Sir Gerald Du Maurier, who was looking for a resourceful Cockney actor to play Sam Hackitt, the 'old lag', in his production of Edgar

Wallace's *The Ringer* at Wyndham's, and Harker's phenomenal success in this role catapulted him to fame. The encounter proved crucial for both author and performer, helping to determine their subsequent theatrical fortunes: Harker went on to appear in a succession of similar crime and mystery plays, written by (or adapted from) Wallace and containing parts intended specifically for him, on either the right or wrong side of the law but always to provide comic relief—*Persons Unknown* (Shaftesbury, 1929), *The Calendar* (Wyndham's, 1929), *The Case of the Frightened Lady* (Wyndham's, 1931), *The Frog* (Princes, 1936), and *Number Six* (Aldwych, 1938)—as well as a stage version of Sapper's detective novel *Bulldog Drummond* (Adelphi, 1932) and other comedy-thrillers. He was also constantly in demand for light or romantic comedies, and enjoyed a close collaboration in the thirties with the expatriate American playwright–producer Walter Hackett, starring in three of his plays, *Road House* (Whitehall, 1932), *Afterwards* (Whitehall, 1933), and *Hyde Park Corner* (Apollo, 1934).

At the same time Harker was building a solid (and profitable) reputation in the cinema. Produced quickly and cheaply in studios in or near London, his films were not difficult to combine with his stage work; indeed, many were merely adaptations of his theatrical successes, making the process simpler still. In the twelve years between his screen début in Alfred Hitchcock's silent *The Ring* in 1927 and the outbreak of war in 1939 Harker appeared in no fewer than fifty films, all targeted at the home market, playing an assortment of rough diamonds, likeable rogues, and ponderous policemen. The coming of sound served to redouble his popularity, adding to the familiar, rather solemn-looking face a rich, husky-voiced East End accent and slick verbal timing, which endeared his comic creations to filmgoers throughout the country; in 1933 he acknowledged its importance by contributing an article, 'Cockney humour on the screen', to a national film magazine.

Harker remained active throughout the Second World War, registering particular success with two comedies—Frank Harvey's *Saloon Bar* (Wyndham's, 1939) and Denis and Mabel Constanduros's *Acacia Avenue* (Vaudeville, 1943)—the thriller *Once a Crook* by Evadne Price (Aldwych, 1940), and Vernon Sylvaine's spy drama *Warn that Man* (Garrick, 1941), all of which were subsequently filmed. He also added one more to his formidable repertory of policemen, borrowing from a popular radio programme the character of Inspector Hornleigh, who featured in three films between 1939 and 1941. Harker's film career continued uninterrupted until 1959, when he made his last film—*Left, Right and Centre*, for Sydney Gilliat—though his post-war stage appearances became more intermittent. His final performance, at seventy, as an ageing waiter artfully resisting replacement by a young waitress, in Rex Frost's comedy *Small Hotel* (St Martin's, 1955), afforded opportunities for amusing characterization in a suitably valedictory role. Harker had married comparatively late in life, on 18 July 1938, the young actress Grace Underwood (stage name Christine Barry; 1911–1964); she

appeared with him in several West End productions before their marriage, but predeceased him by three years. His own last days were spent quietly, and he died at his home—11 Carlyle Mansions, Cheyne Walk, Chelsea—on 2 March 1967.

Harker was a gifted and highly original comedian of few pretensions. That he could respond so well to more complex and demanding characters like the truculent Bill Walker of George Bernard Shaw's *Major Barbara* (Wyndham's, 1929) or Alfred Doolittle in his *Pygmalion* (Embassy, 1951), may indicate untapped imaginative potential, but for most of his career he seemed content to inhabit a regular comic persona of blunt, dry-humoured understatement. Capitalizing on his hooded eyes, crooked nose, and protrusive underlip, and ringing occasional changes on a largely deadpan expression, now morose, now sardonic or pugnacious, this persona was one in which audiences found him inimitable.　　DONALD ROY

Sources *The Times* (3 March 1967), 14 · *The Guardian* (3 March 1967), 6 · *WWW, 1961–70* · *Who was who in the theatre, 1912–1976*, 2 (1978) · E. M. Truitt, *Who was who on screen*, 3rd edn (1983) · S. D'Amico, ed., *Enciclopedia dello spettacolo*, 6 (Rome, 1959) · M. Lane and E. Wallace, *The biography of a phenomenon* [1938] · *The Times* (6 June 1967) · D. Gifford, *The British film catalogue, 1895–1970* (1973) · D. Quinlan, *Quinlan's illustrated directory of film stars*, 4th edn (1996) · C. Winchester, ed., *The world film encyclopedia: a universal screen guide* (1933) · J. Walker, ed., *Halliwell's filmgoer's companion*, 10th edn (1993) · L. Clynton, 'The Cockney king of the screen', *Film Weekly* (19 Dec 1931) · G. Harker, 'Cockney humour on the screen', *Film Weekly* (15 Dec 1933) [as told to R. Pollock] · B. McFarlane, ed., *An autobiography of British cinema* (1997) · E. Katz, *The Macmillan international film encyclopedia*, 3rd edn (1998) · *Ramsey Courier and Northern Advertiser* (26 May 1899) · *CGPLA Eng. & Wales* (1967) · b. cert. · m. cert. · d. cert.

Likenesses Stage Photo Co., photograph (as Det. Sgt Totty in *The case of the frightened lady*), repro. in *Play Pictorial*, 356 (1931) · Swarbrick Studios, photograph (as George Hawkins in *Warn that man*), repro. in *Theatre World* (Feb 1942) · J. Vickers, photograph (as Mr Robinson in *Acacia Avenue*), repro. in *Theatre World* (Dec 1943) · photograph (in middle age), repro. in *The Times* (3 March 1967) · photograph (as Jefferson Davis in *Robert E. Lee*), repro. in *ILN* (14 July 1923) · photograph (as Hillcott in *The calendar*), repro. in *Play Pictorial*, 332 (1929) · photograph (as William Ambrose in *Afterwards*), repro. in *Theatre World* (March 1934) · photograph (as Joe Harris in *Saloon bar*), repro. in *Theatre World* (Dec 1939)

Wealth at death £31,023: probate, 3 May 1967, *CGPLA Eng. & Wales*

Harker, Joseph Cunningham (1855–1927), scene painter and theatrical designer, was born on 17 October 1855 in Levenshulme, Lancashire, the third of the three children of William Harker and his wife, Maria O'Connor. When Harker was three years old, his father, a well-known character actor in Manchester, died, and his mother, an actress, toured the provinces to support her children. Although Harker spent these early years performing occasionally in child roles, he showed more interest in scene design, and by the age of twelve he began building and painting his own toy-theatre models. In 1870 he moved to London, where his uncle, John O'Connor, a principal scene painter at the Haymarket Theatre, arranged for him to be apprenticed as a scene painter's assistant at the Globe for Thomas W. Hall, whose daughter, Sarah Elizabeth, Harker married on 10 May 1877. During this period,

Harker gained further experience through his occasional work for his uncle at the Haymarket, Albert Callcott at the Alhambra, and Ada Cavendish at the Olympic. In 1874 he ended his apprenticeship, and for the next eight years his freelance work at various London theatres included supervising scenes for *The Ring* at Her Majesty's Theatre, painting in its entirety the scenery for *Parsifal* at Covent Garden, and painting scenery for George Sanger's pantomimes at Astley's and Augustus Harris's spectacular pantomimes and melodramas at Drury Lane. Harker's many years of freelancing at various studios under the supervision of prominent London scene designers afforded him a breadth of training that greatly enhanced his proficiency in both designing and painting according to different styles and for different genres, ranging from Shakespeare to musical comedy.

After spending six years in Scotland, Dublin, and the United States—where he was employed to paint the backgrounds for large panoramas (open-air pictures) which were very much in vogue—Harker returned to London in 1888 and secured his first significant commission, which paved the way for the development of his professional career. In the autumn of 1888 he was hired to paint several scenes for Henry Irving's Lyceum production of *Macbeth*. Shortly afterwards, Irving, who had befriended Harker's father while the two had performed together in Edinburgh, furnished Harker the money to open his own painting studio and offered him work in subsequent Lyceum productions. From 1888 until Irving relinquished management of the Lyceum in 1899, Harker designed and painted dozens of sets for the Lyceum, including scenery for *King Lear*, *Cymbeline*, and *Henry VIII*.

Harker's prestigious position as a principal scenic artist for Irving garnered him other commissions during the 1890s from some of London's prominent theatre managers, including George Alexander at the St James's Theatre, Richard D'Oyly Carte at the Savoy, and Herbert Beerbohm Tree at the Haymarket. By 1900 he had secured a reputation as one of the leading scene painters and designers for the British stage. Because he preferred to work as an independent scene artist and not as a stock artist for any one particular house, he received commissions to design scenery from almost every London theatre manager. In addition to providing scenery for more than half of Beerbohm Tree's sixty-odd productions at Her Majesty's Theatre between 1898 and 1917, Harker also designed scenery for Otho Stuart at the Adelphi and the Court, John Vedrenne at the Comedy and the Savoy, George Grossmith at the Shaftesbury and Winter Garden, and George Edwardes at the Gaiety and Daly's. His prolific output as an independent scenic artist was aided by his collaboration with his four sons, who joined the scene studio some time after 1910, and their partnership earned special recognition for their expert designs of oriental settings, including those for *Kismet* (1914), *Cleopatra* (1925), and *Chu-Chin-Chow* (1916), the latter regarded by Harker's contemporaries as his finest work. By the time of his death in 1927, his studio (which was later named Harker,

Homan, and Bravery Studios Ltd, and continued in business until the 1950s) had provided scenery for most of London's major theatres and managers.

As a master scenic artist of the Victorian and Edwardian eras, Harker, like the other prominent contemporary scene designers with whom he was ranked (Hawes Craven, Walter Hann, and William Telbin), worked according to a scenographic tradition of pictorial realism, which equated the proscenium arch to a frame in which the painted setting represented 'real' environments and locales. Applying the principles of realistic scene painting required that Harker depend on visual source material based on direct observations of natural and geographical environments or on research in historical and archaeological facts, but his designs were not merely photographic realism *per se*, for they were governed by his careful selection and manipulation of compositional details that created stage pictures that served myriad illustrative ends, from showing character psychology to vivifying dramatic atmosphere. Harker, believing in the primacy of the scene painter in creating visual effects, preferred to design and paint sets without three-dimensional pieces, advocating instead the use of drops painted to simulate three-dimensional detail. He excelled particularly in painting realistic exterior settings with vibrant colours and sunlight effects; J. Comyns Carr, recalling Harker's designs, remarked that 'the foliage of the trees seems actually to move in the breeze' (Harker, 198).

Towards the end of Harker's career, the pictorial aesthetic that had long governed his profession and dominated the Victorian and Edwardian theatres was being challenged by the new stagecraft of Poel, Appia, and Craig, who advocated non-illusionistic, non-representational settings. Harker remained a strong proponent of traditional stagecraft, and in 1924, when the new scenography was gaining increasing supporters, he wrote his memoirs, *Studio and Stage*, devoting over half of it to criticism of the new stagecraft and a defence of scenic realism and scene painting.

Harker died on 15 April 1927 at his home at 4 Lyndhurst Road, Hampstead, and his ashes were interred on 19 April at Golders Green crematorium.   B. A. KACHUR

Sources J. Harker, *Studio and stage* (1924) · J. Gardner, 'Hawes Craven, William Telbin and Joseph Harker', PhD diss., Florida State University, 1977 · J. P. Wearing, *The London stage, 1890–1899: a calendar of plays and players*, 2 vols. (1976); *The London stage, 1900–1909*, 2 vols. (1981); *The London stage, 1910–1919*, 2 vols. (1982); *The London stage, 1920–1929*, 3 vols. (1984) · b. cert. · m. cert. · d. cert. **Archives** Harker, Homan and Bravery Studios Ltd, London | Bristol University, Theatre Collection, Beerbohm Tree archive **Likenesses** R. Harker, drawing, repro. in Harker, *Studio and stage* **Wealth at death** £10,937 7s. 2d.: probate, 23 June 1927, CGPLA Eng. & Wales

Harkes, Garbrand (*fl.* 1539–1590). *See under* Garbrand, John (1541/2–1589).

Harkey, Joan (*d.* 1550), prioress of Ellerton, may well have come from a parish gentry family in the North Riding of Yorkshire. At an unknown date she became a Cistercian nun and subsequently prioress of the very small convent of Ellerton in Swaledale. At least one other of her nuns derived from a similar background, Agnes Aslaby being possibly able to claim descent from William Aslaby, one of the putative founders of the priory in the late twelfth century. Life cannot have been easy in the early Tudor period for a tiny community of only six religious in an inadequately endowed house which could count on an income of no more than £15 10s. per annum, and the nuns had difficulty in observing the rule. At their visitation in February 1536 Cromwell's commissioners reported that Cecily Swale had given birth to a child and was seeking release from her vows. Ellerton immediately became vulnerable on the passing of the act authorizing the dissolution of religious houses with an annual income of less than £200 per annum, and on 18 August 1536 Joan Harkey surrendered her house to the crown. At this early stage of the dissolution only heads of houses qualified for compensation, with pensions calculated in proportion to the total revenues of the house, with the result that the prioress gained a very meagre allowance of £3 per annum and the rest of her sisters nothing at all. It may partly have been because of this lack of provision for the rest of the community that several of the Ellerton nuns chose to move to larger Yorkshire nunneries which had won a temporary respite; Agnes Aslaby and Elizabeth Parker transferred to Nun Appleton Priory, and Cecily Swale, despite her alleged desire to abandon the religious life, joined the nunnery at Swine.

On losing her office Joan Harkey moved to the nearby town of Richmond where she lived in retirement for a further fourteen years. On 8 April 1550 she made her will as Dame Joan Harkey of Richmond, consigning her soul to almighty God, and beseeching the Virgin Mary and all the saints in heaven to pray for her before requesting burial in the parish church. She gave 6d. to every priest in Richmond, double that to Sir John More and Sir Gabriel Loftus, a former monk of Kirkstall Abbey, and 20d. each to Sir Cuthbert Hutchinson and Sir William Loftus. Her natural family did not concern her overly much at this time: Christopher Harkey's son, perhaps her nephew, received 20d., Cecily Conyers a silver spoon, and her daughter Emmot a spruce coffer. Instead her thoughts turned to her former community and she bequeathed 12d. each to four of her sisters in religion, Dame Alice Tomson, Dame Cecily Swale, Dame Agnes Aslaby, and Dame Elizabeth Parker, and appointed as her executor another former nun, and possibly also a one-time member of Ellerton Priory, Dame Margaret Dowson, whom she charged with disposing of the residue of her estate for the health of her soul. Her possessions, which included two brass pots, some pans and pewter dishes, a basin and ewer, two little chests and a coffer, fire irons, a chair and three cushions, an 'evil' feather bed and bedding, an ambry, a kirtle, a coat, and other linen gear, were valued at a mere £3 12s. 4d. She had died before 22 July 1550 when grant of probate was made.

CLAIRE CROSS

Sources will and inventory, Leeds RO, RD/AP1/43/19 · J. Raine, ed., *Wills and inventories from the registry of the archdeaconry of Richmond*, SurtS, 26 (1853), 69–70 · J. W. Clay, ed., *Yorkshire monasteries: suppression papers*, Yorkshire Archaeological Society, 48 (1912), 17, 108–9 · *LP Henry VIII*, 10.142 · G. W. O. Woodward, *The dissolution of the monasteries* (1966), 156, 161–2 · C. Cross and N. Vickers, eds., *Monks, friars and nuns in sixteenth century Yorkshire*, Yorkshire Archaeological Society, 150 (1995), 560–62, 583, 592 · *VCH Yorkshire*, 3.160–61 · PRO, LR6/116/1 m.5
Wealth at death £3 12s. 4d.: will and inventory, W. Yorks. AS, Leeds, RD/AP1/43/19

Harkness, Edward Stephen (1874–1940), philanthropist, was born on 22 January 1874 in Cleveland, Ohio, USA, the second son and youngest of the four children of Stephen Vanderburg Harkness (d. 1888), businessman, and his second wife, Anna M. Richardson (d. 1926) of Dalton, Ohio. Stephen Harkness, one of the six original stockholders in John D. Rockefeller's Standard Oil Company, had amassed a large fortune, and after his death his widow moved with her family to New York city. Harkness was educated at St Paul's School, Concord, New Hampshire, and after graduating from Yale University in 1897 he joined his brother, Charles, in New York, helping him to administer the family investments. In 1904 he married Mary (d. 1950), daughter of Thomas Edgar Stillman, lawyer, of Brooklyn, New York. There were no children.

The Commonwealth Fund was set up in 1918 by Anna Harkness with an endowment of $10 million, in order to pursue humanitarian goals, with Edward as president (Charles had died in 1916). Harkness was particularly interested in child welfare, and the fund helped to establish child guidance clinics in a number of large cities to finance research into child psychology and to train teachers in child guidance work. It also helped to build rural hospitals from 1926.

Harkness had become interested in medical research, convinced that medicine should prevent disease and not just cure it. Elected to the board of trustees of Presbyterian Hospital in New York in 1910, he offered a $1,300,000 endowment to enable the hospital to affiliate with Columbia University College of Physicians and Surgeons, in order to create a medical centre combining the services of a large hospital with medical education and research—a very new idea at the time. The two institutions were affiliated in 1911, and Harkness and his mother later bought a 22 acre site on Washington Heights for the new Columbia-Presbyterian Medical Center, which opened in 1928, when Columbia University conferred an honorary LLD on him. He continued to make donations, including a $4½ million endowment for the medical centre in 1930, and $5 million for the construction and endowment of the Institute of Ophthalmology, which opened in 1933.

Another major beneficiary of the Harkness fortune was education. Harkness, concerned at the growing size of American colleges, wanted to create small residential units on the lines of Oxford and Cambridge colleges. The presidents of Harvard and Yale had been thinking along similar lines, but had found it difficult to persuade their trustees. After his offer of funds was turned down by Yale, the 'house plan' was launched at Harvard by President Lowell in 1928, with the help of $10 million of Harkness

Edward Stephen Harkness (1874–1940), by James Russell & Sons

money, making Harkness the greatest benefactor to Harvard in the history of the college. In 1930 Yale accepted $16 million from Harkness to build eight residential quadrangles. He also gave $5 million to Phillips Exeter Academy, a leading boys' boarding-school, to enable the reorganization of the school curriculum according to the 'conference' system of teaching, with students seated around what came to be known as Harkness tables.

Harkness was very proud of his Scottish ancestry—he was descended from William Harkness, who left Dumfries for Massachusetts in 1716—and had great admiration for the people and institutions of the British Isles. He was convinced that the future of civilization depended on better understanding between Britain and the United States, and to this end in 1925 the Commonwealth Fund established twenty two-year fellowships, to be awarded annually to British or Commonwealth graduates from British universities for postgraduate study and travel in the United States, intended to parallel the Rhodes scholarships offered to Americans. The scheme was later extended to British civil servants. The London Child Guidance Clinic and the Child Guidance Council were also set up by the Commonwealth Fund.

The Pilgrim Trust, based in Britain, was established in 1930 with a £2 million gift from Edward Harkness. He imposed no conditions on how the gift was to be spent, although he did appoint the original trustees, and the first chairman, Stanley Baldwin. The first grant was to help the Educational Settlement Association extend its work in areas of high unemployment, and social service continued to be one of the main beneficiaries, with grants to boys' clubs, training ships, children's homes, and day nurseries. The other main activity was the preservation of Britain's heritage, with grants for the repair and restoration of churches, including the lady chapel in Ely Cathedral, and the housing of archives, including the conversion of the monastic kitchen in Durham Cathedral into a muniment room.

Harkness gave generously to various British institutions, including the Shakespeare Memorial Theatre at Stratford upon Avon, Oxford University, and the University of St Andrews, where he helped to restore the collegiate system, and was awarded an honorary LLD in 1926. In recognition of his generosity to Great Britain, Harkness was invited to the coronation of George VI, and was received at Buckingham Palace.

A modest, unassuming man, Harkness hated publicity. He devoted his life to spending his vast inheritance for the benefit of mankind, giving all proposals his personal attention. Although he disapproved of reckless spending—'a dollar misspent is a dollar lost, and we must not forget that some man's work made that dollar' (Irvine, 7)—he also once said, 'what's the use of having money if you can't have the fun of spending it' (Lamb, 333). Harkness gave away $130 million during his lifetime. He died on 29 January 1940 at his New York home, 1 East 75th Street, and was buried at Woodlawn cemetery, New York. His wife survived him. He was believed to have left more than $100 million.   ANNE PIMLOTT BAKER

Sources A. R. Lamb, *The Presbyterian Hospital and the Columbia-Presbyterian Medical Center, 1868–1943* (1955) • J. C. Irvine, 'Edward Stephen Harkness', *9th annual report of the Pilgrim Trust* (1939), 5–11 • J. W. Wooster, 'Harkness, Edward S.', *DAB*, suppl. 2 • W. A. Nielsen, *The big foundations* (1972), 254–62 • B. M. Kelley, *Yale: a history* (1974), 373–6 • S. E. Morison, *Three centuries of Harvard* (1936); repr. (1946), 476–7 • R. Chernow, *Titan: the life of John D. Rockefeller Sr* (1998) • *Annual Report of the Commonwealth Fund* (1939) • *The Times* (31 Jan 1940) • *Annual Report of the Commonwealth Fund* (1940) • *The Times* (8 Feb 1940) • *Who was who in America*, 1 (1943) • E. B. Reed, *The Commonwealth Fund fellows and their impressions of America* (1932) • *CGPLA Eng. & Wales* (1942)
Archives NL Wales, corresp. with Thomas Jones
Likenesses J. Russell & Sons, photograph, priv. coll. [*see illus.*] • drawing, repro. in Lamb, *Presbyterian hospital*, facing p. 74 • photograph, repro. in Irvine, 'Edward Stephen Harkness', frontispiece
Wealth at death over $100,000,000 in USA: *The Times*, 8 Feb 1940 • £128 9s. 6d. effects in England: administration with will, 24 Aug 1942, *CGPLA Eng. & Wales*

Harkness, Margaret Elise (1854–1923), author and journalist, was born on 28 February 1854 at Great Malvern, Worcestershire, the second of five children of Robert Harkness (1826–1886), a Church of England clergyman, and Elizabeth Bolton Toswill (1821–1916). At the time of her marriage to Robert Harkness, Elizabeth, whose maiden name was Seddon, was a widow with a daughter. Margaret's mother was related to the family of Beatrice Potter, later Webb; Margaret and Beatrice were second cousins. Her father's family was related through marriage to George Henry Law, bishop of Bath and Wells, and this connection may be in part responsible for Margaret

Harkness's decision to adopt the pen name of John Law for most of her published work.

Harkness was educated at home, although at the age of twenty-one she was sent to Stirling House, a finishing school in Bournemouth. From there she went to London in 1877 to be trained as a nurse at Westminster Hospital. On completion of her training she took up a post at Guy's Hospital, although letters of the time suggest she had little aptitude for the nursing profession. Some time early in the 1880s, therefore, she decided to try to earn her living by her pen, perhaps prompted by Beatrice Potter, who, with her sister Kate, helped Harkness financially and introduced her to a circle of intellectuals whose chief meeting-place was the reading-room of the British Museum.

Harkness now began to take an increased interest in radical politics, and her direct experience of poverty in London's East End, together with her friendship with such women as Eleanor Marx and Annie Besant, helped shape her growing conviction that socialism offered a solution to the problems of social inequality, poverty, and hardship which she saw about her. She was for a short time a member of the Social Democratic Federation, and through her membership met Henry Champion (1859–1928), John Burns, and Tom Mann, with all of whom she would work during the London dock strike of 1889. Her major contribution to the strike was her visit to Cardinal Manning on 5 September 1889, which may have been instrumental in persuading him to intervene. When she came to write of her experiences of working in the labour movement, in *George Eastmont: Wanderer* (1905), she dedicated the book to 'the memory of His Eminence Cardinal Manning with whom the author was associated during the Great Dock Strike of 1889'.

By the time of the strike Harkness was the author of two novels. The first, *City Girls* (1887), had drawn favourable comments from Engels, to whom she had sent a copy. Her second and finest novel, *Out of Work* (1888), is concerned with key events in London during jubilee year, especially the famous occasion of 'bloody Sunday', the march of the unemployed on 13 November 1877 which ended with police charging the crowd that had assembled in Trafalgar Square. One man was killed, many injured, and Burns was arrested and then sentenced to six weeks' imprisonment. Harkness puts the occasion to good use in her novel.

In 1888 Harkness also published in book form a series of articles she had edited for the *British Weekly: a Journal of Social and Christian Progress* on the temptations awaiting young men and women in London. From this came her best-known work, originally called *Captain Lobe: a Story of the Salvation Army* and republished two years later under the title by which it is still known, *In Darkest London*. In 1890 she published *A Manchester Shirtmaker*, based on a short stay in that city. She also worked in Scotland in 1887 and 1888 as a contact for Champion with the Scottish miners' leader Keir Hardie. Other trips took her out of England, to Germany, and then in 1891 to New Zealand and Australia, where, after a brief return, she seems to have stayed for some years.

After that Harkness's movements become increasingly difficult to trace. From 1906 until the outbreak of the First World War she appears to have spent most of her time in the Indian subcontinent. Annie Besant seems to have introduced her to Theosophy, which led her to attend the annual convention in Madras in 1907. However, she soon became more interested in Indian nationalism and set out to explore Indian life: *Glimpses of Hidden India* (1909), revised and reissued under a new title, *Indian Snapshots* (1912), tells something of her wanderings. By now she had abandoned socialism—conjecturally as a result of the failure of her relationship with Henry Champion—in favour of the ideals of the Salvation Army. Her last known work, *A Curate's Promise: a Story of Three Weeks, September 14–October 5 1917* (1921), recounts a curate's decision to join the Salvation Army rather than become an army chaplain. During her last years she lived in France and then Italy. She died at the Pensione Castagnoli in Florence on 10 December 1923.

JOHN LUCAS

Sources J. Bellamy and B. Kaspar, 'Harkness, Margaret Elise', *DLB*, vol. 8 · B. Kirwan, introduction, in J. Law [M. Harkness], *Out of work* (1990) · b. cert. · private information (2004) **Archives** BLPES · Working Class Movement Library, 51 The Crescent, Salford | Passmore College, Beatrice Webb collection

Harkness, Robert (1816–1878), geologist, was born at Ormskirk, Lancashire, on 28 July 1816, the son of Richard and Ellen Harkness. He was educated at Dumfries high school and Edinburgh University (1833–4) where he studied under Robert Jameson and J. D. Forbes. Between 1834 and 1848 he lived in Ormskirk, where he investigated the geology of south Lancashire. In the latter year he and his father moved to Dumfries.

Harkness's first scientific paper, read before the Manchester Geological Society in April 1843, was entitled 'The climate of the Coal epoch'. However, much of his work centred on south-western Scotland, where he discovered Permian reptile footprints in the local breccias and sandstones. In the Lower Palaeozoic rocks of the southern uplands he discovered fourteen new species of graptolites. Indeed, Harkness worked out the structure of the southern uplands of Scotland and the north of England as well as identifying the metamorphic rocks of northwestern Ireland and Scotland. In conjunction with Professor H. A. Nicholson, he did much to clarify the structure of the graptolitic deposits of the Coniston series.

In 1853 Harkness was appointed professor of geology in Queen's College, Cork. In 1854 he was elected fellow of the Royal Society of Edinburgh, and in 1856 of the Royal Society of London. In 1876 he was required to add substantially to his teaching load, and this seriously damaged his health. He had just resigned his chair, and was on his way to visit his sister in Penrith when he died, unmarried, on 5 October 1878, in a Dublin hotel. He was buried in Penrith. Harkness was a sound reasoner, an acute observer, an excellent teacher, and an enthusiast in his work, and was valued as a cheerful and generous colleague. He published more than sixty papers.

BERYL AMBROSE-HAMILTON

Sources *Geological Magazine*, new ser., 2nd decade, 5 (1878), 574–6 · *Nature*, 18 (1878), 628 · H. C. Sorby, presidential address, *Quarterly Journal of the Geological Society*, 35 (1879), 41–4 · *CGPLA Eng. & Wales* (1878) · *IGI*
Archives GS Lond., drawings and maps | U. Edin. L., letters to Sir Archibald Geikie · U. Edin. L., letters to Sir Charles Lyell
Likenesses J. B. Brenan, oils, 1854, Department of Geology, Cambridge · portrait, repro. in *Geological Magazine*, p. 575, pl. XIV · wood-engraving (after photograph by C. Voss Bark), NPG; repro. in *ILN* (26 Oct 1878)
Wealth at death under £6000 effects in England: probate, 5 Dec 1878, *CGPLA Eng. & Wales*

Harland, Sir Edward James, baronet (1831–1895), shipbuilder, was born on 15 May 1831 in Scarborough, the fourth of six sons (the third of whom died in infancy) and seventh of ten children of Dr William Harland, physician, a close friend of the engineer George Stephenson, and his wife, Anne, daughter of Gowan Peirson of Goathland, Yorkshire. He was apprenticed to Robert Stephenson & Co. at Newcastle from 1846 to 1851. Through his uncle, Dr Thomas Harland, he got to know Gustav Christian Schwabe, a partner in the Liverpool shipping company of John Bibby & Sons. Schwabe arranged for him to work for the Clyde engineering and shipbuilding firm of J. and G. Thomson, who were building ships for Bibby. He returned to the Tyne in 1853 to manage a shipyard, leaving the following year to take up a similar post at Robert Hickson's shipyard in Belfast. Here he quickly became notorious for his stern management, which turned the shipyard round, allowing it to survive the financial embarrassment of the owner in 1855. Two years later he recruited Gustav Wilhelm Wolff, Gustav Schwabe's nephew, as his personal assistant. In 1858 he purchased the yard, renaming the business Edward James Harland & Co. Immediately Bibby placed a contract for three boats. They were so pleased with these that they ordered a further six vessels in 1860 of novel long design, with a narrow beam and flat bottom, which earned them the nickname of 'Bibby's coffins'. Harland and Wolff went into partnership in 1861 to form the company of that name.

Over the next thirty years the shipyard prospered. Building on the technical success of the Bibby ships, the partners established a strong relationship with the White Star Line of Thomas Ismay, Cunard's principal competitor on the north Atlantic. In 1879–80 the partners added an engine works to their enterprise and the following year equipped the yard to handle the newly introduced open-hearth steel. By this time most of the contracts were being negotiated by William James Pirrie, who had become a partner in 1874. During the home rule crisis in 1885, Harland made secret preparations to withdraw to mainland Britain if the situation became intolerable. This proved unnecessary and massive investment followed to provide facilities for the construction of the latest generation of Atlantic liners. In 1891, when shipbuilding was distressed, Harland was persuaded to introduce a system of cost plus contracts for favoured customers which secured a large volume of business over the next four years.

The success of the shipyard depended on improvement to the Lagan waterway made by Belfast harbour commissioners. Harland served as a commissioner from 1875 and was chairman from 1875 to 1885. Although a unionist in politics, he tried to pursue a policy of non-discrimination in the shipyard, strained by the sectarian troubles in 1864 and in 1884–5. He was mayor of Belfast in 1885–7 and helped co-ordinate the campaign against the Home Rule Bill. He was elected MP for North Belfast in 1887, moving to London but rarely speaking in parliament. He was knighted in 1885 and created a baronet later the same year.

A Presbyterian, Harland was a member of the First Congregation in Rosemary Street, Belfast. In January 1860 he married Rosa Matilda, of Vermont, near Belfast, the daughter of Thomas Wann, a stockbroker and insurance agent. They had no children and the baronetcy became extinct when Harland died on Christmas eve 1895 at his Irish home, Glenfarne Hall, near Enniskillen, co. Leitrim.

MICHAEL S. MOSS, *rev.*

Sources M. Moss and J. R. Hume, *Shipbuilders to the world: 125 years of Harland and Wolff, 1861–1986* (1986) · W. Johnson and F. Geary, 'Harland, Sir Edward James', *DBB* · *CGPLA Eng. & Wales* (1896)
Wealth at death £67,438 5*s*. effects in England: Irish probate sealed in London, 22 Oct 1896, *CGPLA Ire.*

Harland, Henry (1861–1905), novelist and journal editor, mythologized his origins, claiming a St Petersburg birthplace. The son of Thomas Harland (1830–1900), then a journalist on the *New York World*, and Irene Jones Harland (1839–1925), and the only one of three children to survive childhood, he was born in Brooklyn on 1 March 1861. Young Harland attended Brooklyn city schools, then from 1877 the College of the City of New York, leaving without a degree to study briefly at Harvard divinity school (1881–2). Further fabricating his past, he later claimed a *baccalauréat* from the University of Paris.

Harland's first employment was as tutor to two boys in Manhattan, after which he travelled abroad. In Rome he became, at least emotionally, a Roman Catholic. Returning home he became a clerk, writing in his spare time: his novel *Grandison Mather* (1889) exploits that experience. His attraction to Jewish life in New York, which he saw as exotic and picturesque, led to his earliest efforts in fiction. Despite unpromising prospects he married on 5 May 1884 the musically talented Aline Herminie Merriam (1860–1939). They had no children. Her interests were reflected in Harland's first novel, *As it was Written: a Jewish Musician's Story* (1885), published under a seemingly Jewish pseudonym, Sidney Luska. Its earnings enabled the couple to divide their time between New York and Paris, during which period Harland wrote two further 'Jewish' novels, *Mrs. Peixada* (1886), and *The Yoke of the Thorah* (1887). Exposure of his identity ended his career as Sidney Luska.

Late in 1889 the Harlands moved to London, where Harland began to write, one acquaintance quipped, as 'a lemonade Henry James'. Fame followed a chance meeting with Aubrey Beardsley in the offices of a physician treating both men for tubercular symptoms. In collaboration they devised a hard-cover quarterly, the *Yellow Book*, which would display what they saw as the quintessence of contemporary art and literature, with the gifted Beardsley creating as well as acquiring the art, and Harland procuring and editing the letterpress portion. John Lane of the Bodley Head became the publisher, and the first number appeared to great acclaim in April 1894. From the beginning Harland demonstrated his shrewdness as editor in the writers he solicited as contributors, who ranged from the eminent and safe to the upcoming and experimental. Although the quarterly opened with a novella by Henry James and art by J. S. Sargent, critics sniffed scandal in the yellow covers, used in France for racy novels, and in the artifice of Max Beerbohm and Beardsley himself. Other writers who appeared during its abbreviated life were such representatives of respectability as Edmund Gosse, William Watson, Richard Garnett, and George Saintsbury, and, as their modish antithesis, George Moore, Frederick Rolfe (Baron Corvo), John Davidson, and Arthur Symons.

The *Yellow Book* might have lived down abuse as precious and depraved, had Oscar Wilde not been described on his arrest a year later as carrying 'a yellow book'. The Bodley Head offices were stoned, and Beardsley—who had refused Wilde a place in the publication—was sacked by Lane to save the journal.

When the *Yellow Book* expired in 1897, Harland, now jobless, resumed writing novels, often suffused with Romanism. He and Aline were received into the Roman Catholic church in 1898, inspiring his novel *The Cardinal's Snuff-Box* (1900). Its popular success financed stays in France and Italy as Harland's tuberculosis worsened. Two novels with a Roman Catholic ambience followed, *The Lady Paramount* (1902) and *My Friend Prospero* (1903), with fashionable ladies and transparent questions of identity.

Slight, moustached, and bearded in mid-life, as he was drawn by Beardsley, Harland at the end was wan, spectacled, and clean-shaven. His last novel, *The Royal End* (1909), unfinished at his death in San Remo, Italy, on 20 December 1905, was completed by his widow. Aline added a further fiction by referring to her late husband as Sir Henry, and to herself as Aline, Lady Harland. After initial burial in San Remo cemetery the day he died, Harland was reburied on 1 March 1906 at Yantic cemetery, Norwich, Connecticut.

Harland's enduring claim to significance lies in his packaging of a publication that, although no manifesto of a movement, became the model for future reflections of aesthetic moments in time. The *Yellow Book*, as exemplar of later periodicals with similar ambitions, has, as a metaphor, remained alive.   STANLEY WEINTRAUB

Sources K. Beckson, *Henry Harland: his life and work* (1978) · K. L. Mix, *A study in yellow: the Yellow Book and its contributors* (1960) · S. Weintraub, *The London Yankees* (1979) · J. G. Nelson, *A view from the Bodley Head* (1971) · *The letters of Aubrey Beardsley*, ed. H. Maas, J. L. Duncan, and W. G. Good (1970)
Archives Boston PL, letters · Col. U. · NYPL, Berg collection · Queen Mary College, London, Westfield College archives | Connecticut College, Aline Harland MSS · Pennsylvania State University, Pattee Library, K. L. Mix MSS · Ransom HRC, corresp. with John Lane

Likenesses photograph, 1900, NPG · F. Hollyer, photograph, c.1902, repro. in *The Critic*, 44 (1904), 108 · A. Beardsley, sketch, repro. in *The early work of Aubrey Beardsley* (1899) · M. Beerbohm, caricature, repro. in M. Beerbohm, *Caricatures of twenty-five gentlemen* (1896) · photograph, repro. in *The Lamp*, new ser., 26 (April 1903), 227
Wealth at death seemingly little; widow sent begging letters to publishers

Harland, John (1806–1868), journalist and antiquary, was born at Hull on 27 May 1806, the eldest child of John Harland and his wife, Mary, the daughter of John Breasley of Selby. He was apprenticed to Messrs Allanson and Sydney, the proprietors of the *Hull Packet* newspaper, in 1821 to learn letterpress printing. He quickly achieved promotion, taught himself shorthand, and became a reporter. In 1825–6 he designed his own system of shorthand and became the most expert shorthand writer in the country at that time. This brought him to the notice of John Edward Taylor of the *Manchester Guardian*, who travelled to Hull to secure his services; he moved to Manchester in November 1830.

Harland soon placed the *Guardian* at the head of the provincial press because of his full and reliable reporting. He exhibited remarkable endurance in the pursuit of his profession, undertaking long journeys and writing out the notes of the day in the stagecoach. He presided over the reporting staff of the *Guardian* until 1860, when he retired, owing to lameness. He had for several years used crutches.

Harland was married twice, first in 1833 to Mary (d. 1840), the daughter of Samuel Whitfield of Birmingham, and then in 1852 to Eliza, daughter of Joseph Pilkington of Manchester. He had four children by his first marriage and five by his second. Although raised as a member of the Church of England, he became a Unitarian in 1828 and was for some time a Sunday school teacher.

Harland possessed an extensive knowledge of early English history, was skilled at medieval Latin, and was at that time one of the foremost antiquaries in Lancashire. He was elected a fellow of the Society of Antiquaries and was on the council of the Chetham Society, for which he edited fourteen volumes, mostly relating to Manchester. He was also a founder member of the brotherhood of Rosicrucians. He published independently a collection entitled *Ballads and Songs of Lancashire* (1865) and, in conjunction with T. T. Wilkinson of Burnley, *Lancashire Folklore* (1867). He was in the process of a major revision of Edward Baines's *Lancashire* at the time of his death. Harland died on 23 April 1868 at Bride Oak Street, Cheetham, Manchester, and was buried at Rusholme Road cemetery.

RICHARD GARNETT, *rev.* ZOË LAWSON

Sources *Manchester Guardian* (25 April 1868) · E. Baines and W. R. Whatton, *The history of the county palatine and duchy of Lancaster*, rev. edn, ed. J. Harland and B. Herford, 2 (1870) [reliquary] · *CGPLA Eng. & Wales* (1868)
Archives Chetham's Library, Manchester, antiquarian commonplace book; indexes and annotations to John Palmer's collections · Man. CL, antiquarian notes, collections, and papers, incl. some relating to Rosicrucian Society of Manchester
Wealth at death under £9000: probate, 12 May 1868, *CGPLA Eng. & Wales*

Harland, Sir Robert, first baronet (*c*.1715–1784), naval officer, son of Captain Robert Harland RN, entered the service on 10 February 1729 as a volunteer per order in the *Falkland* (50 guns). After serving as able seaman, master's mate, and midshipman in the *Dreadnought*, *Suffolk*, *Hector*, *Greyhound*, and *Romney* on the home, Lisbon, and Mediterranean stations he passed his lieutenant's examination on 11 July 1735. He was at this time described as 'upwards of 20' but it may be assumed that he was, in fact, under age, since his father was one of his examiners.

Harland's first commission appears not to have been until 25 February 1742 when he became third lieutenant of the *Weymouth*; from her he was appointed to the *Princessa*, in which he was present in the action off Toulon on 11 February 1744; and a few days afterwards he moved into the *Namur* as first lieutenant. On 4 January 1745 he was promoted to the command of the fireship *Scipio*; and on 19 March 1746 he became captain of the *Tilbury* (60 guns), in which he took part in Hawke's engagement with *L'Étenduère* off Cape Finisterre on 14 October 1747. He was then appointed to the *Nottingham* (60 guns), in succession to Captain Philip Saumarez, who had been killed in the 14 October action.

On 31 January 1748, while with Hawke's squadron off Ushant, Harland in the *Nottingham* and Captain Charles Stevens in the *Portland* (50 guns) intercepted and, after a six-hour engagement, captured the French ship *Magnanime* (74 guns) limping back to Brest after being dismasted in a gale.

During the peace after 1748 Harland commanded the *Monarch* guardship at Portsmouth. On 1 November 1749 he married a daughter of Colonel Rowland Reynold, with a fortune of £40,000. They had three daughters and a son, Robert.

After the outbreak of hostilities Harland was again at sea, from 20 March 1755, in the *Essex*, cruising in the channel and the Bay of Biscay. On 23 May 1758 he was appointed to the *Conqueror* (70 guns), and the following year he was sent into the Mediterranean with Boscawen. At Gibraltar he exchanged into the *Princess Louisa* (60 guns), in which he took part in the battle of Lagos on 18 August 1759.

On 18 October 1770 Harland was promoted rear-admiral of the blue, and in the following March he was created a baronet, and, with his flag in the *Northumberland*, went out to the East Indies as commander-in-chief, a post which he held until 1775. On 7 December 1775 he became vice-admiral of the blue, and in 1778 vice-admiral of the red. He hoisted his flag on board the *Queen* (90 guns) as second in command of the Channel Fleet under Admiral Augustus Keppel at the battle of Ushant on 27 July 1778, during which Harland commanded the van, and Palliser the rear, and in the October cruise. On 10 May 1779, after siding with Keppel at the time of his and Palliser's courts martial, he resigned his command. Under Lord Sandwich's administration he had no further command, but on the change of ministry he was appointed on 27 March 1782 to the Board of Admiralty under Keppel. On 8 April he became admiral of the blue. He quitted the Admiralty,

with Keppel, on 28 January 1783, and on 21 February 1784 he died at Sproughton, near Ipswich. His son, Robert (1765–1848), succeeded to the baronetcy.

J. K. LAUGHTON, *rev.* RANDOLPH COCK

Sources Register of commissions and warrants, PRO, ADM 6/14, 16, 17, 18, 19, 20, 21 · lieutenant's passing certificates, 1713–45, PRO, ADM 107/3 fol. 288 · W. L. Clowes, *The Royal Navy: a history from the earliest times to the present*, 7 vols. (1897–1903) · *GM*, 1st ser., 16 (1746), 45 · *GM*, 1st ser., 18 (1748), 41 · *GM*, 1st ser., 19 (1749), 285, 524 · *GM*, 1st ser., 40 (1770), 488 · *GM*, 1st ser., 52 (1782), 207, 360 · *GM*, 1st ser., 53 (1783), 804 · *GM*, 1st ser., 54 (1784), 154 · J. Charnock, ed., *Biographia navalis*, 6 vols. (1794–8) · Burke, *Peerage* · N. A. M. Rodger, *The insatiable earl: a life of John Montagu, fourth earl of Sandwich* (1993) · B. Tunstall, *Naval warfare in the age of sail: the evolution of fighting tactics, 1650–1815*, ed. N. Tracy (1990)
Archives BL OIOC, corresp. relating to India, Home misc. series
Likenesses attrib. D. Heins, oils, 1747–8, NMM · R. Earlom, mezzotint, pubd 1788 (after H. Dance), BM

Harland, Sydney Cross (1891–1982), agricultural botanist and geneticist, was born on 19 June 1891 at Snainton, near Scarborough, the son of Erasmus Harland and his wife, Eliza. He was educated at the municipal secondary school in Scarborough and at King's College, London, where he graduated in 1912 with honours in geology. He then took a job as a schoolmaster in the Danish colony of St Croix (later part of the US Virgin Islands). Within a year he became assistant to the director of an agricultural experiment station on the island, where he was given responsibility for investigating hybrids between local and North American cottons. So began a career which advanced understanding of the genus *Gossypium*, and successfully applied that knowledge to the breeding of improved varieties.

In 1915 Harland married Emily Wilson Cameron; the couple later had two daughters. Also in 1915 he moved to St Vincent as assistant agricultural superintendent. His studies on the genetics of cotton continued, and his published work from this period was recognized by the award of the London DSc degree. He returned to England in 1920 as head of botany at the British Cotton Industry Research Association (the Shirley Institute) in Manchester, but in 1923 he returned to the West Indies as professor of botany and genetics at the Imperial College of Tropical Agriculture, Trinidad. Here he resumed his field studies on cotton, and also became a skilled teacher.

Harland's reputation now attracted the attention of the Empire Cotton Growing Corporation (ECGC) and from 1926 to 1935 he took charge of cotton genetics at their new Trinidad research station. The outstanding success of his work during these years came from Harland's vision and originality, but it was also helped by the freedom and independence allowed him by the corporation. He gained an extensive knowledge of the world's cottons and established a classification of *Gossypium* based on genetic criteria, thus providing a new basis for breeding strategies. His achievements were academic as well as agricultural. He made contributions to the understanding of evolutionary processes and of speciation; his paper 'The genetical conception of the species' (1936) was of crucial importance. It was followed in 1939 by his only book, *The Genetics of Cotton*, in which he described the results of his own research.

In 1934, after his first marriage had ended in divorce, Harland married Olive Sylvia Atteck, daughter of a prominent Trinidad family, and they had a son who later became professor of child health in the University of the West Indies.

Harland was affable and respected by close colleagues, but he could also be outspoken and obstinate. His contract with the ECGC came to an end during a time of disagreement in 1935, and he moved to Brazil as general adviser to the state cotton industry. In 1940 he went to Peru as director of the Institute of Genetics at Lima, and in 1949 he was appointed reader in genetics at Manchester University; he became professor of botany there in 1950. By this time his most productive research had been done, but he continued to travel widely to cotton growing regions in an advisory capacity. Within the university he insisted that genetics should feature largely in the curriculum of any student of biology in its broadest sense, and the introduction of genetical teaching for students of medicine and psychology was largely due to his influence.

Harland received many honours, including FRS (1943), FRSE (1951), honorary fellowship of the Textile Institute (1954), and an honorary DSc from the University of the West Indies (1973). He was also president of the Genetical Society from 1952 to 1955. He retired in 1958 and lived for some years on a small private estate in Peru where he bred tropical crops. But he never ceased to be a Yorkshireman at heart, and he finally returned to Snainton, his birthplace, where he died on 8 November 1982.

J. N. HARTSHORNE, rev.

Sources J. Hutchinson, *Memoirs FRS*, 30 (1984), 299–316 · personal knowledge (1990) · *CGPLA Eng. & Wales* (1983)
Archives John Innes Centre, Norwich, corresp., scientific notebooks, and research papers
Wealth at death £56,668: probate, 29 March 1983, *CGPLA Eng. & Wales*

Harlaw, William (*c.*1500–1578), Church of Scotland minister, was born in Edinburgh, where he became a tailor in the Canongate. He was associated with the early stages of the movement for religious reform in Scotland and fled to England, where he is said to have been ordained a deacon. However, it is quite certain that he was never appointed a chaplain to Edward VI, as has also been claimed. Probably he has been confused with John Harley, later bishop of Hereford. Harlaw returned to Edinburgh on the death of Edward VI, unlike some of the more prominent Scottish reformers who fled to the continent. There he became one of the ministers who conducted services privately in the homes of evangelicals. Later he also preached in public, and, as the number of unofficial congregations grew, he travelled widely throughout the country. Denounced for preaching at Dumfries in 1558, he was summoned to appear before the lord justice at Stirling on 10 May 1559, when he was proclaimed a rebel along with Paul Methven, John Christison, and John Willock, for usurping the authority of the church in taking into his own hands the ministry within the burgh of Perth and places nearby. He

may have come to know John Willock and other Scottish exiles during his stay in England; he certainly held similar theological views to theirs, which were greatly influenced by Zwingli and Bullinger.

Harlaw became minister of St Cuthbert's, Edinburgh, in 1560, and was a commissioner for St Cuthbert's along with Robert Fairley of Braid at the first general assembly, which began on 20 December that year. He was also present at the assembly of June 1562, his last recorded appearance there. He does not appear to have ever been appointed by a general assembly to undertake any duties on behalf of the church, but concentrated on his ministry within Edinburgh. On 25 June 1566, a supplication was presented to the assembly on behalf of Robert Stewart, commendator of Holyrood Abbey and patron of the benefice, for the appointment of a former canon of Holyrood as minister of St Cuthbert's in place of Harlaw. The assembly summoned some of the elders of the parish, who opposed this proposal because—according to the order of admission of ministers to parishes—the congregation had to 'elect' the presentee. The congregation was not prepared to do this, and Harlaw remained minister there. Following the death of the vicar, Archibald Hamilton, who had been in possession since at least 1547, Harlaw was presented to the vicarage under the privy seal on 6 February 1573. From 1574, however, he was overshadowed by the appointment of Robert Pont, one of the outstanding ministers of that era, as his junior colleague. On his death in 1578 Harlaw was succeeded by Pont. Nothing is known of Harlaw's wife, but she may have been English, as their grandson William, the son of Nathaniel, minister of Ormiston, became a minister in the Church of England.

DUNCAN SHAW

Sources *Fasti Scot.*, 1.93 · C. H. Haws, *Scottish parish clergy at the Reformation, 1540–1574*, Scottish RS, new ser., 3 (1972), 214 · D. Hay Fleming, *Was Knox a royal chaplain?* (1924) · D. Calderwood, *The history of the Kirk of Scotland*, ed. T. Thomson and D. Laing, 8 vols., Wodrow Society, 7 (1842–9), vol. 1, pp. 303, 333, 343; vol. 2, p. 45 · *John Knox's History of the Reformation in Scotland*, ed. W. C. Dickinson, 1 (1949), 118, 125, 148, 161 · T. Thomson, ed., *Acts and proceedings of the general assemblies of the Kirk of Scotland*, 3 pts, Bannatyne Club, 81 (1839–45), pt 2, pp. 13, 78, 204, 266

Harlech. For this title name *see* Gore, William George Arthur Ormsby-, fourth Baron Harlech (1885–1964); Gore, (William) David Ormsby-, fifth Baron Harlech (1918–1985).

Harley, (John) Brian (1932–1991), geographer and map historian, was born on 24 July 1932 in Ashley, Bristol, and spent some of his infant years in Oxford. On 15 March 1935 he was adopted by John Jack Harley (*b.* 1883), farmer, and his wife, Emily Louise Rogers (1890–1963), who lived in rural Staffordshire. He was given the name John Brian Harley. To his great delight, a few years before he died he met his natural mother, whom he had last seen on his fifth birthday. From 1943 to 1950 he attended the grammar school at Brewood near Wolverhampton, where the children exploited his family circumstances to make him miserable. However, he excelled at Brewood, gaining the school essay prize and representing the school at cross-country running and football.

Harley's two years of national service from 1950 to 1952

were spent in the army in Trieste, Egypt, and Cyprus and were a character-forming experience which surfaced occasionally in hilarious stories. Harley was not a favourite of the officer class: the army taught him to type as a punishment. Life at school and in the army left Harley with a strong sympathy for the underdog and contempt for those with status he felt they did not merit.

In 1952 Harley gained a place at Birmingham University. Personal distractions robbed him of his expected first in geography in 1955 but he won the W. A. Cadbury prize. Perhaps uncertain of an academic future, Harley decided to teach, gaining his DipEd from University College, Oxford, in 1956. He then returned, however, to Birmingham for graduate work on the historical geography of medieval Warwickshire under the supervision of Harry Thorpe, whose speciality was to study past landscapes through maps. He took inspiration from Rodney Hilton, then working on the social structure of medieval Warwickshire, and whose Marxism suited Harley's own political ideology. Harley graduated PhD in 1960, publishing an important paper on population and agricultural trends as seen through the hundred rolls of 1279 in the Economic History Review the year before.

Harley married Amy Doreen (1921/1922–1983), daughter of Frederick Chatten, a welder, at St Clement's Church, Nechells, Birmingham, on 14 December 1957. In the following September he began teaching at Queensbridge School, Moseley, but in the same month he was offered an assistant lecturership in geography at Liverpool University and took up the post in January 1959.

In Liverpool Harley turned to the history of cartography. His book Christopher Greenwood, County Map-Maker (1962), written at Hilton's suggestion, was a landmark in English map history. With the significant exceptions of one further paper on medieval Warwickshire and a chapter on 'England in 1850' in H. C. Darby's New Historical Geography of England (1973), virtually all his subsequent output was on maps and map makers. At first he concentrated on English mapping, mostly of the eighteenth and nineteenth centuries. His work on the Ordnance Survey gave him a reputation beyond the academic realm. He was influenced and supported by R. A. (Peter) Skelton, head of the map room at the British Museum, who pointed him towards the mapping of North America, notably during the American War of Independence, and through the career of William Faden.

Harley formed lasting associations at Liverpool: as he wrote soon after leaving, 'I shall always remember that the really formative years of my life were spent at Liverpool' (letter to Robert Steel, 7 Oct 1969). He even admitted to 'occasionally missing the very different world enshrined somewhere between the Senior Common Room and the last night of a field week', but in 1969 Harley resigned from Liverpool to become sponsoring editor with the publishers David and Charles in Newton Abbot. This was a bold move for a man with a wife and three children. Harley commissioned a substantial number of works in fields entirely new for David and Charles; yet he hankered after the academic life, and by March in the following year a chance to return presented itself.

The death of the Montefiore reader in geography at the University of Exeter in 1970 left a vacancy for a historical geographer which Harley was appointed to fill, initially as a lecturer but from 1972 as the Montefiore reader. His writing at Exeter was dominated by the history of the Ordnance Survey. His notes on the popular David and Charles reprints of the old series one-inch maps (with A. G. Hodgkiss) led to more substantial syntheses in a series of co-authored regional volumes of facsimiles, text, and carto-bibliography. He wrote Ordnance Survey Maps: a Descriptive Manual (1975) and wrote a substantial part of the official history of the Ordnance Survey, which appeared in 1978. In 1985 Harley graduated DLitt by accumulation from the University of Birmingham, an achievement of which he was particularly proud.

From the early 1980s Harley turned his attention to a philosophical view of maps and their meanings. By 1986 he had virtually completed a book-length manuscript, 'The map as ideology'. In contributions to journals, books, conferences, and symposia he revised his ideas and, shortly before he died, proposed a new book combining a selection of these essays with a guide to the map philosophy they expounded. This was published in 2001 under his own title, The New Nature of Maps (ed. P. Laxton). Harley showed how the map is more than a skilfully constructed artefact with geographical outlines. Absorbing ideas from art history and literary criticism, he revealed their hidden agendas: 'silences' that speak, names that have other levels of meaning, signs and icons with subliminal messages; some reflecting deliberate propaganda, most reflecting cultural values unacknowledged by either the map maker or his society. Harley showed maps to be not just passive mirrors of landscape and society but potent agents of governments and tools of propaganda.

Yet despite Harley's obvious distinction and notwithstanding a huge international body of admirers, he failed to secure promotion and recognition in the British academic world. His perceptive, often blunt, and sometimes angry observations on academic life gained him an unjustified reputation as a difficult colleague, despite his success in forming scholarly partnerships and his being a good administrator who served on the councils of several learned societies, including the Institute of British Geographers (1971–4). To professional frustrations were added personal tragedy: in 1983 his wife, Amy, died, followed less than a year later by his son John. Harley began to think of a new life in the USA. He was familiar with the country through fellowships and invitations to lecture (notably the Kenneth Nebenzahl lectures at the Newberry Library, Chicago, in 1974), but the main attraction was that in 1977 he and David Woodward, of the University of Wisconsin at Madison, had persuaded Chicago University Press to publish a multi-volume History of Cartography (1987–). This dominated the rest of Harley's life, particularly after 1986 when he was appointed full professor of geography at Madison's Milwaukee campus. This multi-disciplinary project involving some 130 scholars worldwide is the first comprehensive history of maps in world cultures, a synthesis of existing and new research.

Harley continued his cartographic research outside the confines of the *History*. He was involved in controversies over the Columbus celebrations. He broadcast on the topic and wrote *Maps and the Columbian Encounter* (1990), the interpretative guide to a travelling exhibition of maps. He was due to give twelve public lectures on the topic in 1992.

Harley said that he wished to go out in full flood while lecturing. He did die suddenly and unwarned, of a heart attack as he arrived at his Milwaukee office on 20 December 1991. He was survived by his three daughters. He was cremated in December 1991 in Milwaukee, and his ashes were interred on 16 March 1992 at Highweek, Newton Abbot, Devon, after a memorial service. Harley's death deprived the *History of Cartography* project of his vision and panache, which would have come especially into their own in the volumes covering the eighteenth and nineteenth centuries, periods in which his authority was supreme. Bearded and with alert eyes, Harley was an utterly single-minded, formidably hard-working scholar. He judged people by the quality of their discourse and their capacity for conviviality. Beneath his strongly held views lay a characteristic uncertainty, covered by a self-mocking modesty which failed to hide his enthusiasm for both the chase and the writing. He always wrote well with an unfailing nose for the comic and tragic sides of early cartographic projects, and his lectures turned potentially abstruse subjects into an eye-opening delight.

PAUL LAXTON

Sources personal knowledge (2004) · P. Laxton, *The Independent* (27 Dec 1991) [additional comment by Lionel M. Munby, 29 Feb 1992] · P. D. A. Harvey, *The Guardian* (28 Dec 1991) · [W. Ravenhill], *The Times* (30 Dec 1991) · A. R. H. Baker, *Daily Telegraph* (7 Jan 1992) · R. Lawton, *Journal of Historical Geography*, 18 (1992), 210–12 · R. R. O. [R. R. Oliver], 'Brian Harley, 1932–1991: historian of the ordnance survey—and much else', *Sheetlines*, 33 (1992), 5 · D. Woodward, 'John Brian Harley, 1932–1991', *Imago Mundi*, 44 (1992), 120–25 · W. Ravenhill, 'John Brian Harley, 1932–1991', *Transactions of the Institute of British Geographers*, new ser., 17 (1992), 363–9 · E. M. J. Campbell, *GJ*, 158 (1992), 252–3 · F. Ormeling, 'Brian Harley's influence on modern cartography', *Cartographica*, 29 (1992), 62–5 · M. H. Edney, 'J. B. Harley (1932–1991): questioning maps, questioning cartography, questioning cartographers', *Cartography and Geographic Information Systems*, 19 (1992), 175–8 · D. Woodard and others, *Map Collector*, 58 (1992), 40–41 · W. Ravenhill and others, *A celebration of the life and work of J. B. Harley* (1992) [incl. photograph, c.1970, taken in the department of geography, University of Exeter] · *New York Times* (27 Dec 1991) · R. Lawton, address delivered at Harley's memorial service and interment of ashes at Highweek church, Newton Abbot, Devon, 16 March 1992 · J. Crampton, *Harley's critical cartography: in search of a language of rhetoric*, Department of Geography, University of Portsmouth, working papers, 26 (1993) · P. Gould and A. Bailly, eds., *Le pouvoir des cartes: Brian Harley et la cartographie* (1995), 1–9, 53–8 · J. H. Andrews, 'Meaning, knowledge and power in the map philosophy of J. B. Harley', in J. B. Harley, *The new nature of maps: essays in the history of cartography*, ed. P. Laxton (2001), 1–32 [introduction] · *CGPLA Eng. & Wales* (1992)

Archives BL

Likenesses photograph, repro. in *Daily Telegraph* (30 Dec 1991) · photographs, priv. coll.

Wealth at death £63,702—in England and Wales; most property presumably in America: probate, 11 June 1992, *CGPLA Eng. & Wales*

Harley [*née* Conway], **Brilliana**, **Lady Harley** (*bap.* 1598, *d.* 1643), parliamentarian gentlewoman, was baptized in 1598 at the English garrison at Brill, Netherlands (hence her unusual forename), the second daughter of Edward *Conway, first Viscount Conway and first Viscount Killultagh (*d.* 1631), of Ragley, Warwickshire, and Dorothy (*d.* 1612), daughter of Sir John Tracy of Toddington, Gloucestershire, the widow of Edward Bray of Great Barrington, Gloucestershire. Brilliana's father was lieutenant-governor of the cautionary town of Brill at the time of her birth and she, her sisters, Heilwaie and Mary, and brother, Ralph, were naturalized by private act of parliament in 1606.

Brilliana was the third wife of Sir Robert *Harley (*bap.* 1579, *d.* 1656) of Brampton Bryan, Herefordshire, whom she married in July 1623. The couple had three sons, Edward *Harley (1624–1700), Robert (1626–1673), and Thomas (*b.* 1628), and four daughters, Brilliana (*b.* 1629), Dorothy (*b.* 1630), Margaret (*b.* 1631), and Elizabeth (*b.* 1634), the sole child to die young. Little is known about Lady Harley's life before her marriage, but the survival of approximately 375 letters written mainly to her husband from 1623 and to her eldest son, Edward, from 1638 until her death in October 1643 provides a rich illustration of her married life. The letters have been widely cited as evidence of her domestic and maternal concerns, but as a staunch puritan and parliamentarian Lady Harley was also engaged in the religious and political debates of the time. Her letters constitute the most detailed single source of information about the outbreak of the civil war in Herefordshire from 1640 to 1643. They also record the active political role that she played as the senior representative of the Harley family in the county during the early 1640s.

Her letters reveal Lady Harley to have been a literate woman, well read in contemporary religious works, by her own account more at ease with reading French than English, and able to teach her sons Latin when the schoolmaster proved unreliable. With her letters she dispensed medicines, advice about health to her family, and gifts of food. When her husband attended parliament in the 1620s and the early 1640s, Lady Harley kept him informed about his family and estates as well as local political affairs. She also used her letters to pass on her own puritan beliefs to her children and as a vehicle for the transmission of news. Her letters to Edward at Oxford in the late 1630s reveal her disapproval of Laudian innovations in ceremonial and church decorations. The debates of the Long Parliament encouraged her to believe that the church would finally be fully reformed and in June 1641 she rejoiced at the progress of the root and branch bill to abolish episcopacy.

Lady Harley also organized the Harley family's response as local governors to national events during her husband's absence as one of Herefordshire's representatives to the Long Parliament. In the winter of 1640–41 she orchestrated the collection of information about the parish clergy in Herefordshire for the House of Commons committee for scandalous ministers. In June 1642, on the instructions of Sir Robert, Lady Harley tried unsuccessfully to buy up arms from the royalist Croft family on behalf of the parliamentary commission for Irish affairs. As the civil war progressed she played an active role in maintaining the Harley estates and family influence in the county, including her successful resistance to the royalist siege of her home in the summer of 1643, which lasted for nearly seven weeks.

From the outbreak of the civil war in 1642 Herefordshire remained largely under royalist control and Lady Harley had to protect her family and dependants. In March 1643 she received the first formal demand from the sheriff to surrender Brampton Bryan Castle and its armaments to the royalists, which she refused. The siege was commenced under the command of Sir William Vavasour in late July 1643. Throughout it Lady Harley conducted a series of negotiations by letter, parley, and a petition to the king, in which she maintained that she and her family were faithful subjects, and that Vavasour should withdraw. These protestations were not entirely truthful, since she had arranged for the delivery of two horses and £500 worth of family plate to her husband for the parliamentary war effort in the summer of 1642. In June 1643 her elder sons, Edward and Robert, had joined Sir William Waller's forces in the west of England and Lady Harley had encouraged local recruits to join them, furnishing one man with a horse worth £8. She had also offered refuge at Brampton to local parliamentarians, and had taken some fifty soldiers into the house for her own defence, in effect turning it into a garrison.

Lady Harley's strategy of spinning out the negotiations was successful and in early September Vavasour's men were called away to the siege of Gloucester. Sir Robert then advised his wife to leave Brampton, but she was unwilling to do so without a guarantee of safe conduct. Instead Lady Harley took decisive action to forestall a renewal of the siege. The troops under her command compelled her tenants to level the earthworks raised by the royalists, neighbours who had been active supporters of the siege were plundered for 'necessities', and Lady Harley ordered forty of her soldiers to attack a royalist camp 4 miles away at Knighton. In one of her last letters to her husband, in October 1643, Lady Harley described the foundation of her resistance to the royalists as the desire to defend Harley property and to preserve the influence of the godly in Herefordshire. She died at Brampton Bryan on 29 October 1643. Lady Harley's actions were a response to the demands of civil war in the mid-seventeenth century, but they were also an integral part of the political and social role of élite women, which can be traced back to the later middle ages, if not earlier.

JACQUELINE EALES

Sources *Letters of the Lady Brilliana Harley*, ed. T. T. Lewis, CS, 58 (1854) · letters to Sir Robert Harley, BL, Add. MSS 70001, 70003, 70004, 70110 · Lady Harley's commonplace book, 1622, U. Nott. L., Portland MSS, London collection · J. Eales, *Puritans and roundheads: the Harleys of Brampton Bryan and the outbreak of the English civil war* (1990) · J. Eales, 'Patriarchy, puritanism and politics: the letters of Lady Brilliana Harley (1598–1643)', *Women's letters and letter writing in England, 1450–1700*, ed. J. Daybell and C. Brown [forthcoming] ·

Calendar of the manuscripts of the marquis of Bath preserved at Longleat, Wiltshire, 5 vols., HMC, 58 (1904–80), vol. 1, pp. 1–39 · *DNB* · GEC, *Peerage* · PRO, SP9/95, fol. 188a · private bills, HLRO, 3 Jac 1, cap 50 **Archives** BL, Add. MSS 70001, 70003, 70004, 70110 · BL, corresp., loan 29 · NRA, priv. coll., files of letters | BL, letters to Sir Robert Harley, Add. MS 70110 · U. Nott. L., Portland MSS, London collection, commonplace book **Likenesses** portrait, priv. coll.

Harley, Sir Edward (1624–1700), politician and parliamentarian army officer, was born on 21 October 1624 at Brampton Bryan, Herefordshire, and baptized there on 24 October. He was the third but first surviving son of Sir Robert *Harley (*bap.* 1579, *d.* 1656), politician, and the first son with his third wife, Brilliana, Lady *Harley, *née* Conway (*bap.* 1598, *d.* 1643), parliamentarian gentlewoman, the second daughter of Edward Conway, first Viscount Conway. After attending school in Shrewsbury and Gloucester, Edward Harley matriculated in 1638 from the puritan Magdalen Hall, Oxford. He took with him as his servant George Griffiths, who later became a noted Welsh divine. In 1640 he left Oxford to join his father in London, and in 1641–2 he attended Lincoln's Inn.

By 1643 Harley had joined the parliamentarian army under Sir William Waller, commanding a troop of horse, and by the following year he had raised and taken command of a regiment of foot. He distinguished himself particularly in the conflict at Redmarley, near Ledbury, on 27 July 1644, where, according to John Corbet, he routed the enemy's cavalry and captured nearly all the foot, receiving a wound in the process. Having been appointed governor of Monmouth in the same year, he was given command of a foot regiment in the New Model Army in April 1645. In the conflict between Prince Rupert and Colonel Massey in Ledbury that same month he was once again wounded. Appointed governor of Canon Frome, a garrison near Hereford, in August 1645, he was recommended in the following January to the committee of both kingdoms to hold some command or employment worthy of him in that county. Consequently he was soon made general of horse for the counties of Hereford and Radnor, and he later served as one of the commissioners appointed to treat for the surrender of Exeter and Oxford.

On the removal from the Commons of Humphrey Coningsby, member for Herefordshire, Harley was elected in his place in November 1646, defeating Colonel John Birch, governor of Hereford. In September that year he had backed a plan to disband Birch's Herefordshire forces. He strongly resisted the growing influence of the military in politics and achieved notoriety in the eyes of his army colleagues on 29 March 1647 when he informed the Commons of the continued circulation of an army petition of grievances condemned by Westminster, prompting parliament's declaration of dislike against the army. His attempt to win his regiment to service in Ireland having failed, he had resigned his command by June. In the same month and on grounds of his behaviour in March, he was among the eleven presbyterian MPs against whom the army presented charges of impeachment, and with those MPs he withdrew from the Commons. Having retaken his

Sir Edward Harley (1624–1700), by Samuel Cooper

seat in the following year, he was excluded and arrested, alongside his father, at Pride's Purge in December 1648. Released in February 1649, both men remained objects of suspicion to the Cromwellian regime.

In August 1650 Edward was summoned by letter from Major Stephen Winthrop at Leominster to appear at Hereford before the commissioners of the militia. His papers were searched, and after appearing before the authorities in London he was briefly detained and banished from Herefordshire. Even so in 1654 he was appointed to the county's committee for scandalous ministers and made a JP two years later. On 26 June 1654 he married Mary, daughter and coheir of Sir William Button of Parkgate, Tawstock, Devon, with whom he had four daughters. He rebuilt the church at Brampton Bryan, which had been damaged during the civil war, in 1656 and augmented the living there and at Leintwardine, Wigmore, Leinthall Lingen, Knighton, and Stow, where following his father he promoted puritan ministers. At the elections for the second protectorate parliament in 1656 he was again returned for Herefordshire, despite the combined efforts of the local sheriff and major-general to rig the contest. Nevertheless when parliament met in September he was promptly purged by Cromwell as one of the members who had signed a remonstrance against the protector's rule. In February 1660 he resumed his seat in the Long Parliament with the secluded members and was elected to the council of state.

Having been returned for Herefordshire to the Convention Parliament in April 1660, Harley met Charles II at Dover in May, and on the recommendation of General Monck was appointed governor of Dunkirk. During the short time he held the office he much improved and strengthened the town, aware that the French intended to take it by surprise. He strenuously opposed the mooted sale of the port to the French and proposed an act of parliament to declare it inalienable. With the government well aware that he would never willingly hand over the port, he was honourably discharged from the post in May 1661, the king having acknowledged his prudent management. It was said that Harley had supported the garrison at his own expense, and he informed Charles that the stores he left were worth more than the £500,000 the French were to pay for the port in the following year. According to family tradition he was offered a peerage in the coronation honours in April 1661 but preferred to be made a knight of the Bath. On 25 February 1661 he married Abigail, daughter of Nathaniel Stephens of Eastington, Gloucestershire. The couple had four sons and a daughter: Robert *Harley, first earl of Oxford and Mortimer (1661–1724), Edward *Harley (1664–1735), Nathaniel (1665–1720), Brian, who died in infancy, and Abigail (1664–1726).

Soon after 1660 Harley built a new brick house at Brampton Bryan, adjoining the ruined castle. He also reclaimed the ancient deer park, which had been 'wholly laid open and destroyed' during the civil wars (*Letters*, ed. Lewis, 230). Further damage had been inflicted during the storm which coincided with the death of Oliver Cromwell on 3 September 1658. He reportedly complained:

> I wish the devil had taken him any other way than through my Park, for not content with doing me all the mischief he could while alive, he has knocked over some of my finest trees in his progress downwards. (Sidebotham, 21)

Looking back in 1673 he referred to the many years when his estate was a 'waste region of the shadow of death' but now restored to 'a goodly heritage' (*Letters*, ed. Lewis, 245). Together with his sons he took considerable pains to establish a fine garden adjoining his new house and in 1692 contemplated employing a royal gardener, George London, to 'make a draught of what he thought the place capable of' (*Portland MSS*, 3.494). He was a fellow of the Royal Society from 1663 to 1685; the beginnings of the family's antiquarian interests can be traced back to 1671 when he lent the Wormsley priory ledger book to Sir William Dugdale, who used it for his *Monasticon*. Sir Edward duly received a copy of the book in 1673.

Harley sat in all the parliaments of Charles II's reign, representing the borough of New Radnor in 1661 and March 1679, and Herefordshire in October 1679. Although a regular attender he was not a prominent committeeman or orator during the Cavalier Parliament, though he helped secure an act in 1662 (and again in 1695) which rendered the River Wye navigable. He personally conformed to the established church but vigorously opposed acts passed against dissenters and regarded the Clarendon code as a 'national sin' (*Portland MSS*, 5.642–3). Richard Baxter spoke of him as 'a sober and truly religious man', and Harley lamented the 'incomparable' Baxter's death in 1691 (*Reliquiae Baxterianae*, ed. M. Sylvester, 1696, 59–60).

His support for nonconformity saw him draw closer to the earl of Shaftesbury, who noted him as 'thrice worthy' in 1677, and he duly voted for the First Exclusion Bill in 1680. In the following year he wrote a tract on religious comprehension, attacking the imposition of rites and ceremonies, and attended the third Exclusion Parliament at Oxford. To his opponents Harley was a presbyterian rogue and naturally suffered during the tory reaction, being removed from all local office in 1682 and briefly imprisoned during Monmouth's rebellion three years later. Because he was identified as an obvious opponent of James II attempts were made to win him over by restoring him to local office, but he urged the bishop of Hereford not to read the declaration of indulgence, and neither he nor any of his family ever took an oath to the king. Acting on behalf of his constituents he concerned himself with improving road communications between Hereford and London and fought to preserve the chartered rights of the city of Hereford. It was during James II's reign that he set aside a 'greater part of one day' a week to pray that 'the storm which seemed then to be falling on the nation might be averted' (*Letters*, ed. Lewis, xxxvi).

In 1688 Harley and his sons took up arms on behalf of William of Orange. Although into his sixties, he raised a troop of horse and rode to Worcester to hold the city for the prince. Elected without opposition for Herefordshire in 1689 to William III's first parliament, he avoided party connections and helped obtain an act for the abolition of the court of the Welsh marches. He was defeated at the general election the following year but returned to the Commons for Herefordshire in 1693 and 1695. As a former parliamentarian and proponent of exclusion he was a natural supporter of the king. However, he did not find the new regime particularly appreciative of his services, and his support for William gradually waned as the wars against Louis XIV saw increased taxation and the extension of the power of the state. Along with his eldest son, Robert, he became a leading figure in the country whig opposition determined to resist the growing encroachment of the executive upon the ancient liberties of the political nation. He retired from public life in the final years of his life, and died on 8 December 1700 at Brampton Bryan, where he was buried in the church two days later. His son Robert succeeded him.

Although never a figure of national political importance Harley was of significant stature within his county, relying on his character rather than his moderate territorial power in securing support. Herbert Aubery, a political opponent, could write to him 'That you are kind and good all persons own' (Helms and Rowlands, 3.496). Although Brampton Bryan Castle suffered estimated damage of £60,000 during the civil wars he refused the offer of the sequestered estate of Sir Henry Lingen, the commanding officer who had laid siege to the castle, instead returning the estate to Lady Lingen. His love of his country was also renowned, George Monck describing him as 'a man of public spirit, firm to the interests of his country', while other admirers called him '*ultimus Anglorum*' (*Letters*, ed. Lewis, xxiv, xxviii). His son Edward referred to his habit throughout his life of constant reading of the scriptures, and Brampton Bryan in Harley's time perhaps epitomized the ideal of the spiritual puritan household.

GORDON GOODWIN, *rev.* DAVID WHITEHEAD

Sources *Letters of the Lady Brilliana Harley*, ed. T. T. Lewis, CS, 58 (1854) · J. Hutchinson, *Herefordshire biographies* (1890) · *The manuscripts of his grace the duke of Portland*, 10 vols., HMC, 29 (1891–1931), esp. vols. 3, 5 [see vol. 5, pp. 641–69 for 'memoirs'] · A. Collins, *Collections of noble families* (1752) · A. McInnes, *Robert Harley, puritan politician* (1970) · D. Underdown, *Pride's Purge: politics in the puritan revolution* (1971) · *JHC*, 4 (1644–6) · J. Eales, *Puritans and roundheads* (1990) · G. Nuttall, *The Welsh saints, 1640–1660* (1957) · G. Townsend, *The town and borough of Leominster* (1863) · J. Webb, *Memorials of the civil war … as it affected Herefordshire*, ed. T. W. Webb, 2 vols. (1879) · C. J. Robinson, *The castles of Herefordshire and their lords* (1869) · A. Sidebotham, *Brampton Bryan church and castle* (1950) · M. W. Helms and E. Rowlands, 'Harley, Edward', HoP, *Commons, 1660–90*, 2.494–7 · Foster, *Alum. Oxon.* · bishop's transcripts, Herefs. RO

Archives BL, corresp. and papers, Add. MS 61989 · BL, corresp. and papers, Add. MSS 70002–70019, 70062, 70112–70140, 70223–70225 · BL, corresp. and papers, loan 29 · Brampton Bryan Hall, Herefordshire, archives · Herefs. RO, letters, AK43 · Notts. Arch., accounts and papers relating to governorship of Dunkirk · U. Nott. L., corresp. and papers | BL, Add. MS 5834 · BL, Harley MS 1545; Stowe MS 597 · BL, letters to Robert Harley, Add. MS 40621 · BL, Portland loan · Longleat House, Warminster, Portland MSS, X

Likenesses G. Vertue, line engraving, 1749 (after S. Cooper), BM, NPG · S. Cooper, miniature, priv. coll. [*see illus.*] · S. Cooper, portrait, Brampton Bryan Castle, Herefordshire · engraving (after S. Cooper), repro. in Collins, *Collections*

Harley, Edward (1664–1735), politician, was born at Brampton Bryan, Herefordshire, on 7 June 1664, the second son of Sir Edward *Harley (1624–1700), politician, and his second wife, Abigail, the daughter of Nathaniel Stephens of Eastington, Gloucestershire. Robert *Harley, first earl of Oxford, was his elder brother. He was probably educated at Westminster School and was called to the bar at the Middle Temple. About 1683 he married Sarah Foley (d. 1721), the daughter of Thomas Foley of Witley, Worcestershire; they had three sons and one daughter.

Harley took an active part in the transactions which preceded and accompanied the landing in England of William of Orange in 1688. With a fellow Herefordian, Colonel John Birch, he met the prince at Salisbury, where he organized the approach to London, suggesting a crossing of the Thames at Wallingford. With his father and brother he later declared for the prince at Worcester. He was a staunch Presbyterian with close connections with several London dissenting congregations and was one of the executors of Richard Baxter's will. He was first elected to parliament in 1695 for Droitwich in Worcestershire but afterwards he was closely associated with the town of Leominster, and held the office of recorder there from 1692 until 1732; from 1698 until 1722 he served as its MP. There was a bitter feud between the Harleys and Thomas, Lord Coningsby, of Hampton Court, Herefordshire. When the latter tried to undermine the Harley interest in Leominster about 1720 by challenging the borough's charter in parliament, Harley repelled the assault at considerable cost to himself. He was long remembered in Hereford for his endeavours in parliament and the courts for the passage of the Wye Navigation Act in 1696. Although his parliamentary activity is difficult to distinguish from that of his brother he was responsible for inaugurating several bills, among them the legislation to confirm the privileges of the Hudson's Bay Company (1698). In 1702, through his brother Robert's good offices, he obtained the office of auditor of imprest, an ancient department of the Admiralty. In this position, which he held for life, he is said to have 'acted with care, integrity and ability' (Hutchinson, 57), earning him the name 'Auditor Harley'. This brought him close to the Marlborough–Godolphin administration and his actions in parliament between 1702 and 1708 show his support for the government. However, on a list of 1708 he is classed as a tory and he followed his brother Robert into opposition in this year. When Robert returned to office as chancellor of the exchequer in 1711, Harley worked hard to organize financial support for the continuing war, playing an important role in raising £1,500,000 via the lottery. He also helped frame the act which established the South Sea Company, becoming one of its founding directors. He was a strong supporter of the Hanoverian succession, and on Queen Anne's death signed the proclamation of George I. Harley remained in parliament, notwithstanding the collapse of his brother's interest in the 1715 election.

Harley was a most ardent advocate of his brother, collecting documentation of the latter's achievements and providing a generous tribute in his unpublished memoir of the Harley family. During moments of stress, Robert Harley frequently sought his brother's counsel: Edward negotiated the details of Robert's second marriage, looked after his London and Herefordshire property, and, according to McInnes, 'deliberately sacrificed his chances of a front line political career in order to smooth his brother's pathway in every way he could' (McInnes, 184). In parliament the lord treasurer could always rely upon his brother's assistance. During the treason crisis of 1708, Robert's impeachment by Lord Coningsby in 1715, and in the later struggle with Bolingbroke, Harley was always very visible in his brother's defence. Characteristically, he attributed Robert's success to divine 'dispensations' and their 'excellent parents'. Harley's own career was in danger in 1717, when he was accused of having embezzled the funds of the state as auditor; however, he proved that, while £36 million passed through his hands each year, his accounts were correct to within 3s. and 4d., and that this sum had been mischarged through the neglect of a clerk. Priding himself on his own financial probity, he regularly complained in his letters of court extravagance and blamed many of the ills of society on immorality and profanity.

On his own account Harley purchased considerable property in west Herefordshire and the adjoining counties of Wales, and established himself at Eywood in the parish of Titley, where he built a new house about 1705. With James Brydges, duke of Chandos, a political ally of the Harleys, he sponsored attempts to find coal and copper in south Shropshire and mid-Wales. Also with Brydges, between 1717 and 1721 he was joint developer, on behalf of his young nephew Edward Harley, of the Cavendish–Harley estate in the West End of London, and, having planned a new garden at Brampton Bryan in 1693, he was directly involved in the layout of Cavendish Square. He was a patron of nonconformist education, and maintained schools at Titley, Brampton Bryan, and in Wales. In 1714 he spoke in the Commons against the Schism Act, which was aimed at the closure of nonconformist schools, and in 1725 was chosen as chairman of the trustees of charity schools in London. He was also the author of a number of pious works of a puritan character, including *An Essay for Composing a Harmony between the Psalms and other Parts of the Scripture* (1724). He died on 30 August 1735 in his chambers in the New Square, Lincoln's Inn, and was buried on 15 September in Titley churchyard, where his monument with its long inscription remained legible at the end of the twentieth century. He was survived by his eldest son, Edward *Harley (*bap.* 1699, *d.* 1755), who succeeded Robert's son, also Edward Harley (1689–1741), as third earl of Oxford. The third earl was the father of Thomas Harley (1730–1804), lord mayor of London.

GORDON GOODWIN, *rev.* DAVID WHITEHEAD

Sources *The manuscripts of his grace the duke of Portland*, 10 vols., HMC, 29 (1891–1931), vols. 2–10 · A. McInnes, *Robert Harley, puritan politician* (1970) · G. Townsend, *The town and borough of Leominster* (1863) · Harley letters, C64, Herefs. RO, Kinsham Court MSS, A77; deeds · Brampton Bryan Hall, Brampton Bryan MSS · C. J. Robinson, *A history of the mansions and manors of Herefordshire* (1872) · J. Summerson, *Georgian London*, rev. edn (1962) · C. H. Baker and M. Baker, *James Brydges, first duke of Chandos* (1949) · E. S. Roscoe, *Robert Harley, earl of Oxford, prime minister 1710–1714* (1902) · J. Hutchinson, *Herefordshire biographies* (1890) · will, PRO, PROB 11/673, sig. 188 · D. W. Hayton, 'Harley, Edward', HoP, *Commons, 1690–1715*, 4.233–40

Archives BL, account book as auditor, Add. MS 70092 · BL, corresp., loan 29 · BL, memoir of the family and first Lord Oxford, Add. MSS 70088–70089, 70142 · U. Nott., department of manuscripts and special collections, corresp. | BL, letters to first Lord Oxford, Add. MSS 40621, 70236 · BL, corresp. with second Lord Oxford, Add. MSS 70380–70381 · Herefs. RO · Worcs. RO

Likenesses G. Vertue, line engraving, 1751 (after J. Richardson), BM, NPG · J. Richardson, oils, Brampton Bryan, Herefordshire

Harley, Edward, second earl of Oxford and Mortimer (**1689–1741**), book collector and patron of the arts, was born on 2 June 1689, the only son of Robert *Harley, first earl of Oxford and Mortimer (1661–1724), politician, and his first wife, Elizabeth (*d.* 1691), daughter of Thomas Foley of Witley Court, Worcestershire. He was educated at Westminster School and at Christ Church, Oxford, from 1707; he graduated MA on 2 January 1712 and DCL on 4 June 1730. He left university in 1711 to become the MP for Radnor, but lost the seat in 1714. He was MP for Cambridgeshire from 1722, but entered the House of Lords on 21 May 1724 upon succeeding to his title. He became FRS on 20 March 1711.

On 31 August 1713 Harley married Lady Henrietta Cavendish Holles (1694–1755) [*see* Harley, Henrietta Cavendish], only daughter and heir of John *Holles, first duke of Newcastle upon Tyne (1662–1711), and his cousin Lady Margaret Cavendish. She had a reputed fortune of £500,000, as well as Wimpole Hall in Cambridgeshire, which the

Edward Harley, second earl of Oxford and Mortimer (1689–1741), by Michael Dahl

couple made their principal home. In 1716 they inherited Welbeck Abbey in Nottinghamshire from the duchess of Newcastle. However, their early married life was troubled by a legal dispute, over her father's will, with the Pelham family (who succeeded to the Newcastle title and some of his estates). This dispute was resolved by act of parliament in 1719, involving substantial payments from Harley's resources. The Harleys had a daughter, Margaret Cavendish (1715–1785), who married William Bentinck, second duke of Portland, on 11 June 1734 [see Bentinck, Margaret Cavendish]; a son was born on 18 October 1725 but died four days later.

Unlike his father, Edward Harley took no significant part in public affairs: 'He loved the society of men of letters and of learning; he dabbled in archaeology; he patronised the arts; he made the collecting of manuscripts, of books, and of coins, medals and miniatures the consuming passion of his life' (Turberville, 1.344–5). Jonathan Swift, who had been a protégé of Robert Harley, continued to correspond with and visit his son. Alexander Pope was also a frequent guest at Wimpole, and benefited from Harley's patronage in many ways; he made use of Harley's influence in publishing the second edition of the *Dunciad*, and was helped to avoid threatened lawsuits. They maintained an extensive correspondence between 1721 and 1739. However, Harley was closest to the diplomat and poet Matthew Prior, who had been left destitute

following his impeachment and imprisonment (1715–17). Harley helped to arrange for the publication of Prior's *Poems*, which earned him £4000 and a lasting literary reputation. He also patronized and corresponded with many other scholars and antiquaries, and frequently assisted the publication of their works; these included William and Elizabeth Elstob, John Anstis, and Zachary Grey, who wrote a memoir of Robert and Edward Harley. Likewise Harley helped Thomas Tudway publish his collection of early ecclesiastical music. He subscribed to large numbers of contemporary works, frequently in multiple copies—such as twelve copies of John Covel's account of the Greek church. Many of these duplicate copies were subsequently donated to libraries and literary societies. William Warburton described Harley as 'the most distinguished Patron and Friend of Letters that this age can boast of' (ibid., 1.349).

Harley also patronized architects and artists, employing James Gibbs to design extensions to Wimpole Hall, and acting as agent for the purchase of pictures by continental artists such as Carracci and Lorrain. He gave commissions to the engraver George White, and the painters John Wootton and Christian Zincke. Above all he was the close friend and constant patron of the antiquary and engraver George Vertue, who made frequent use of Harley's library and accompanied him on tours of the south-eastern counties in 1738 and East Anglia in 1739. These extended annual tours throughout different parts of Britain during the summer months were a regular feature of Harley's life from 1723 onwards, and gave rise to lively accounts, written by Harley and his guests, among the Welbeck and Portland manuscripts. In other respects he was 'utterly indifferent to society, in which he played little or no part, and by which he was in consequence looked upon as an eccentric if harmless outsider' (Lees-Milne, 169).

Harley is principally remembered for the library that bears his family's name. Indeed he devoted most of his energies and fortune into turning his father's already substantial collections of manuscripts, charters, and rare books into the finest private library of the time. He assumed partial control over the collection in 1711, when his father became lord treasurer, but took over full control in July 1715 upon his father's impeachment and imprisonment in the Tower of London. At this time there were only 3000 printed and manuscript books, but the 13,000 charters represented 'the largest collection known to be anywhere', and the unbound manuscripts and state papers represented 'much the best and most valuable and numerous of any now in England, excepting only that of Sir Robert Cotton' (*Diary of Humfrey Wanley*, 1.xxviii). The collection was then primarily genealogical, heraldic, and political in coverage. Edward expanded the existing collection 'enormously both in range and bulk, guided largely by the advice and knowledge of his library-keeper Humfrey Wanley' (ibid., 2.450). He also absorbed the library of the duchess of Newcastle at Welbeck Abbey into his own in 1718, and incorporated many manuscripts from his family's ancestral home at Brampton, Herefordshire, following the death of his father in 1724. He continued collecting manuscripts with 'incessant Assiduity and at an immense expense' (*Catalogue of the Harleian Manuscripts*, 1.7), employing agents to seek out and purchase collections on the continent. He also had extensive dealings with London booksellers, notably Nathaniel Noel, who was for many years his principal supplier and agent. Among many other significant purchases were the collections of Greek manuscripts of John Covel (1716) and an important collection of Italian manuscripts from Conyers Middleton, librarian of Cambridge University. When his agent John Bagford died, Harley purchased his collections relating to the history of printing. He likewise amassed a substantial collection of Hebrew and oriental manuscripts from individual collectors, merchants, or the consuls and chaplains of the Levant Company. Ultimately his library contained 7639 manuscript volumes and 14,236 original rolls, charters, deeds, and other legal documents, as well as extensive collections of antiquities, coins, medals, and other items of historical significance or curiosity.

Yet it was principally in the area of printed books and pamphlets that Harley devoted his energies and resources. These were held at his home in Wimpole Hall, whereas the manuscripts and charters remained at his Dover Street house in London. The number of printed books grew to 'upwards of 12 thousand' (Wright, 'Portrait', 161) by 1717, and 50,000 by the time of his death. He had by then also collected 350,000 printed pamphlets and 41,000 prints. Harley's printed books 'were the most choice and magnificent that were ever collected in this Kingdom' (Collins, 213), including some of the earliest-known examples from many European countries. These were used extensively by Michael Maittaire in the compilation of his *Annales typographici*, the second volume of which was dedicated to Harley. The collection was particularly strong with respect to items from Caxton's and de Worde's presses in England and those of Sweynheym and Pannartz, Jenson, and Aldus on the continent. Many of these were used by Joseph Ames to illustrate his *Typographical Antiquities*. According to C. E. Wright 'every conceivable subject was represented; the collection of Bibles, in all the languages of Europe, was immense' (Wright, 'Portrait', 172–3). Harley likewise spent considerable sums upon the binding of the books in his collection. As an undergraduate he had developed a taste for expensive tooled bindings in what Wanley later described as 'My Lord's Marocco Leather' (*Diary of Humfrey Wanley*, 1.120). For many years he retained a binding workshop in Dover Street where he insisted that his most valuable works should be bound.

Collecting on this scale, combined with Harley's generosity and his want of attention to everyday business affairs, inevitably damaged his finances. He had been warned several times about his extravagance, and as early as 1726 he needed to raise £16,000 to meet his creditors. Wanley died in the same year, and after 1728 Harley was guided by William Oldys, his literary secretary. In June

1728 he confessed to his wife that the state of their financial affairs was 'in very great measure due to my own Folly and my neglect in looking into them as I ought to have done' (Turberville, 1.384). In spite of resolutions to reform, matters deteriorated throughout the 1730s until he was forced to sell his house at Wimpole to Lord Chancellor Hardwicke for £86,740 and move to Dover Street in 1740. The shock of the sale was so great that Harley sought increasing solace in drink. His health rapidly deteriorated until his death, at his home, on 16 June 1741. He was buried in the duke of Newcastle's vault in Westminster Abbey on 25 June 1741.

The library was left to Harley's widow during her lifetime and thereafter to their daughter. The antiquities, coins, medals, and pictures were sold by auction on 8 March 1742. Later in the same year the printed books were sold to the bookseller Thomas Osborne for £13,000, a price that was somewhat less than the cost of binding them. They were catalogued by Oldys and Samuel Johnson (who wrote an account of the library) and dispersed in various sales until 1748. Many of the rare pamphlets were reprinted in the *Harleian Miscellany*, also edited by Oldys and Johnson (1744–6). The manuscripts were retained until 1753, when the family agreed to sell them to the nation for £10,000 (a fraction of their contemporary value). They now form one of the foundation collections of the British Library.

Edward Harley's reputation suffered following his death, when he was unfavourably compared with his father and criticized for his want of financial prudence. The earl of Orrery, writing to Swift, spoke of his having sacrificed £400,000 to 'indolence, good-nature, and want of worldly wisdom' (*Correspondence of Jonathan Swift*, 206), and Horace Walpole wrote of the 'rubbish' in his collection, implying that he was an extravagant and mediocre dilettante (Walpole, 17.357–8). However, the Harleian library was both well used and loved by its owner, and was made available to a generation of scholars, including William Stukeley, Richard Bentley, Thomas Tanner, and Richard Fiddes, who both used and valued its resources. The public preservation of Harley's invaluable manuscript collection is now a fitting monument to his life.

DAVID STOKER

Sources A. S. Turberville, *A history of Welbeck Abbey and its owners*, 2 vols. (1938) • C. E. Wright, 'Portrait of a bibliophile, VIII: Edward Harley, 2nd earl of Oxford, 1689–1741', *Book Collector*, 11 (1962), 158–74 • *The diary of Humfrey Wanley, 1715–1726*, ed. C. E. Wright and R. C. Wright, 2 vols. (1966) • R. Maxwell, 'Robert Harley, first earl of Oxford and Edward Harley, second earl of Oxford', *Pre-nineteenth-century British book collectors and bibliographers*, ed. W. Baker and K. Womack, DLitB, 213 (1999) • J. Lees-Milne, *Earls of creation: five great patrons of eighteenth-century art*, another edn (1986) • *A catalogue of the Harleian manuscripts in the British Museum*, 4 vols. (1808–12) • *The correspondence of Jonathan Swift*, ed. H. Williams, 5 vols. (1963–5) • S. Johnson, W. Oldys, and M. Maittaire, eds., *Catalogus bibliothecae Harleianae*, 5 vols. (1743–5) • W. Oldys, ed., *The Harleian miscellany*, 8 vols. (1744–6) • Walpole, *Corr.* • *The correspondence of Alexander Pope*, ed. G. Sherburn, 5 vols. (1956) • A. Collins, *Historical collections of the noble families of Cavendishe, Holles, Vere, Harley and Ogle* (1752) • W. Weber, 'Thomas Tudway and the Harleian collection of "ancient" church music', *British Library Journal*, 15 (1989), 187–205 •

Letters of Humfrey Wanley: palaeographer, Anglo-Saxonist, librarian, 1672–1726, ed. P. L. Heyworth (1989) · *Johnson's proposals for printing Bibliotheca Harleiana, 1742* (1926) · *An act to render more effectual the agreements that have been made between Thomas Holles, duke of Newcastle, Henry Pelham, Esq., Edward Lord Harley, and the Lady Henrietta, his wife* (1719) · H. M. Nixon, 'Harleian bindings', *Studies in the book trade in honour of Graham Pollard*, ed. R. W. Hunt, I. G. Phillip, and R. J. Roberts (1975), 153–94 · C. E. Wright, *Fontes Harleianae* (1972) · *DNB* · GEC, *Peerage*

Archives BL, corresp. and papers, Add. MSS 70237, 70372–70471, loan 29 · BL, lists of books and notes thereon, Add. MSS 19746–19757, 70077–70078 · BL, literary corresp., Harley MSS 7523–7526 · Longleat House, Wiltshire, corresp. and related papers · LPL, corresp. · Notts. Arch., personal and estate accounts · NRA, priv. coll., executor's papers · U. Nott. L., corresp. | BL, Portland MSS · Bodl. Oxf., letters to Thomas Hearne · Notts. Arch., Portland MSS **Likenesses** G. Kneller, oils, *c*.1716, Christ Church Oxf. · attrib. J. Richardson, oils, *c*.1725, NPG · G. Vertue, line engraving, 1745 (after M. Dahl), BM, NPG · G. Vertue, line engraving, 1746 (after M. Dahl), BM, NPG · mezzotint, pubd 1809 (after M. Dahl), NPG · M. Dahl, black chalk drawing, BM [*see illus.*] · M. Dahl, oils, BM · M. Dahl, oils, S. Antiquaries, Lond. **Wealth at death** approx. £100,000; had squandered £400,000: *Correspondence of Jonathan Swift*, 206

Harley, Edward, third earl of Oxford and Mortimer (*bap.* 1699, *d.* 1755), politician, was baptized on 27 August 1699, the eldest of the four children of 'Auditor' Edward *Harley MP (1664–1735), and his wife, Sarah (*d.* 1721), the daughter of Thomas Foley and his wife, Elizabeth. He was educated at Westminster School, and progressed in 1717 to Christ Church, Oxford, where he became the first gentleman commoner in the eighteenth century to be awarded the degree of honorary MA. Harley's serious, even priggish, character was already apparent during his student days, as was his passion for politics and his indulgence in the two family vices, drink and books. Little is known about his activities in the years immediately after he left Oxford, but he seems to have acted as a man of business for his father and uncle. On 16 March 1725 he married Martha (*d.* 1774), the daughter of John and Martha Morgan of Tredegar, Monmouthshire. Their closeness and affection is revealed in numerous letters written while Harley was attending parliament or electioneering. Together they had five sons and two daughters. The eldest, Edward, Lord Harley (1726–1790), served as MP for Herefordshire before succeeding his father as fourth earl of Oxford and Mortimer. The third son, John Harley (1728–1788), became bishop of Hereford, while the fourth, Thomas *Harley (1730–1804), set up as a wine merchant in London and served as lord mayor in 1767–8.

By the time Harley entered parliament as MP for Herefordshire, in 1727, he had emerged as the representative of the political legacy bequeathed to him by his father and, above all, his uncle, Robert *Harley, first earl of Oxford and Mortimer—his first recorded speech was a defence of the latter's ministry during the Dunkirk debate in February 1730. It was, without doubt, the Harley name which enabled him to emerge so quickly as one of the leading members of the tory party in the House of Commons. In the year of his election he founded a board of like-minded tory MPs, which met at the Cocoa Tree Coffee House in Pall Mall and which soon developed into 'a vital and durable

component of tory organization' (Colley, 86). Harley's principles were those of country toryism. During the 1741 elections he prided himself on his 'plain Frock', in contrast to the 'fine Laced Cloaths' of the 'Courtiers' (Taylor and Jones, 255). Throughout his parliamentary career he was a consistent and enthusiastic advocate of the country programme of reforms which aimed at securing the independence of parliament and its members from the corrupt influence of the ministry. On issues such as place and pension bills he was able to work closely with opposition whigs. But he always distrusted the 'patriots', from whom he was separated above all by his high Anglican beliefs and his unwavering commitment to the preservation of the rights and privileges of the established church. However, he was never an extremist. He distrusted the extreme high flyers, describing their champion, the preacher Henry Sacheverell, as 'a coxcomb' (*Portland MSS*, 5.587), and there is no evidence that he ever dabbled in Jacobitism.

Harley's greatest political achievement was the Jury Bill of 1730, which he piloted through the House of Commons and onto the statute book. The bill, which aimed to combat the corrupting of jurors by establishing new procedures for their selection, reflects the interest of many country MPs in law reform. Crucial to the success of this particular measure, however, was Harley's ability to construct an alliance in its support which included not only tories and opposition whigs but also a fair number of government supporters. Harley commemorated his success by commissioning a painting, which still hangs over the staircase at the family home, Brampton Bryan, Herefordshire, in which he is portrayed, with two of his children, holding a copy of the act. For contemporaries, however, his distinctive brand of toryism was probably revealed most clearly in the debate which took place in February 1741 on Samuel Sandys's motion for an address to the king to dismiss his prime minister, Robert Walpole. In a short speech, which Earl Nugent still recalled forty-five years later, Harley, referring explicitly to his uncle's impeachment, stated that he would not censure anyone without 'Facts and Evidence'. He then walked out of the chamber and refused to vote, a course of action in which he was joined by many other tories who shared his abhorrence of arbitrary 'Bills of Pains and Penalties' (Taylor and Jones, 50).

A few months later, on 16 June 1741, Harley's cousin died and Harley moved to the House of Lords as third earl of Oxford and Mortimer. Between this date and his death he was one of the senior figures in the tory party. He remained one of the whig ministry's most persistent and vocal critics in the upper house, entering his protest in the *Journals of the House of Lords* more frequently than any other opposition peer. It is a measure of his prominence that he was talked of as a possible candidate for the chancellorship of that bastion of high-church toryism, Oxford University. After the death of Henry Pelham in March 1754, however, there is some evidence of negotiations between Oxford and the ministry. Little over a year later, on 11 April 1755, Oxford himself died at Bath, so it is impossible to say where these overtures may have led. But they hint at the process which facilitated the return to court of his son, together with representatives of many other old tory families, at the accession of George III. The third earl himself was buried at Brampton Bryan on 18 April 1755.

STEPHEN TAYLOR

Sources Tory and whig: the parliamentary papers of Edward Harley, third earl of Oxford, and William Hay, MP for Seaford, 1716–1753, ed. S. Taylor and C. Jones (1998) · L. J. Colley, 'The Loyal Brotherhood and the Cocoa Tree: the London organization of the tory party, 1727–1760', HJ, 20 (1977), 77–95 · The manuscripts of his grace the duke of Portland, 10 vols., HMC, 29 (1891–1931), vol. 5 · C. Nugent, Memoir of Robert, Earl Nugent (1898) · E. G. W. Bill, Education at Christ Church, Oxford, 1660–1800 (1988) · GM, 1st ser., 25 (1755), 187 · GEC, Peerage · BL, Add. MS 70079 · Old Westminsters, vols. 1–2 · Foster, Alum. Oxon. · parish register (marriage), 16 March 1725, St Anne's, Soho, London · parish register (burial), Brampton Bryan, Herefordshire, 18 April 1755 · faculty office, marriage allegations, LPL, 15 March 1725
Archives BL, corresp., loan 29 · BL, family corresp., Add. MSS 70237, 70381, 70497 · BL, general corresp., Add. MS 70498 · Brampton Bryan, Herefordshire, Harley MSS · CUL, parliamentary journal, MS Add. 6851 | BL, Hardwicke MSS, Add. MSS 35588, 35590, 35602–35604 · BL, Newcastle MSS, Add. MSS 32707–32708 · BL, Portland MSS, Add. MSS 70001–70523 · Herefs. RO, Brydges MSS, A81/IV · PRO, Rodney MSS, PRO 30/20
Likenesses oils, c.1731, Brampton Bryan, Herefordshire · G. Hamilton, group portrait, oils, 1736 (with family), Brampton Bryan, Herefordshire; repro. in E. Einberg, Manners and morals: Hogarth and British painting, 1700–1760 (1987) [exhibition catalogue, Tate Gallery, London, 15 Oct 1987–3 Jan 1988]

Harley, George (1791–1871), watercolour painter and drawing-master, worked in many parts of England. He exhibited two London scenes at the Royal Academy in 1817 and showed one painting at the Society of British Artists in 1865. He painted landscapes, and topographical and architectural subjects. He did some lithographs, Lessons in Landscape (1820–22), for a series of lithographic drawing-books published by Rowney and Forster. In 1845 he published a small Guide to Landscape Drawing in Pencil and Chalk. Two of his watercolour drawings are in the collection of the British Museum's department of prints and drawings, one of which is a view of Maxstoke Priory, Warwickshire. A watercolour of Fulham church and Putney Old Bridge, London (1837) is in the Victoria and Albert Museum. Harley died on 10 January 1871 at his home, 27 Church Terrace, Kentish Town, London. He was survived by his wife, Elizabeth.

L. H. CUST, rev. ANNE PIMLOTT BAKER

Sources Mallalieu, Watercolour artists, vol. 1 · Wood, Vic. painters, 3rd edn · Graves, RA exhibitors · Boase, Mod. Eng. biog. · J. Johnson, ed., Works exhibited at the Royal Society of British Artists, 1824–1893, and the New English Art Club, 1888–1917, 2 vols. (1975), 206 · L. Lambourne and J. Hamilton, eds., British watercolours in the Victoria and Albert Museum (1980), 172–3 · CGPLA Eng. & Wales (1871)
Wealth at death under £450: probate, 14 Feb 1871, CGPLA Eng. & Wales

Harley, George (1829–1896), physician and physiological chemist, was born on 12 February 1829 at Harley House, Haddington, East Lothian, the only son of George Barclay Harley (1766–1832), a landowner, and his wife, Margaret, née Macbeath (1788/9–1845). His father was sixty-three at the time of his birth, and his mother was forty. After his

father's death he was raised by his mother and maternal grandmother. He received his early education at the Haddington burgh schools and at the Hill Street Institution, Edinburgh, and subsequently proceeded to the University of Edinburgh, where he matriculated at the age of seventeen and graduated MD in August 1850.

After acting for fifteen months as house surgeon and resident physician to the Royal Infirmary, Harley spent two years in Paris learning physiological chemistry in the private laboratories of Charles Dollfus, François Verdeil, and Charles Adolph Wurtz. Among the most notable of his early researches were the recognition of iron as a constant constituent of human urine, and the observation that the cherry colour of normal urine was due to urohaematin (urobilin). He next worked in the physiological laboratory of the Collège de France under Claude Bernard, whose publications on the influence of the liver in the production of diabetes led Harley to undertake research as to the effects of stimulation of nerves on the production of sugar by the liver. He remained a strong advocate of vivisection in medical research. During his two years' residence in Paris, Harley was almost entirely occupied by physiological researches, and in 1853 he was elected president of the Parisian Medical Society. He subsequently spent two years in Germany to study microscopy and clinical chemistry with R. A. Kölliker and J. J. Scherer at the University of Würzburg, followed by further advanced studies at the universities of Giessen, Berlin, Vienna, and Heidelberg. When he was studying in Vienna, during the height of the Crimean War, he attempted to join the army of Omar Pasha as a civil surgeon, but travelling with an irregular passport he was arrested and narrowly escaped being shot as a spy.

The exceptional depth of Harley's foreign studies and continental contacts well qualified him for the lectureship in practical physiology and histology at University College, London, to which he was appointed on his return from Padua in 1855. He was also made curator of the anatomical museum at University College, and in 1856 he started medical practice in Nottingham Place. In 1858 he was elected a fellow of the Chemical Society and fellow of the College of Physicians of Edinburgh, and he read at the Leeds meeting of the British Association a paper in which he showed that pure pancreatin was capable of digesting both carbohydrates and fats. In 1859 he was founder editor of an annual report on the progress of medicine brought out by the New Sydenham Society. In the same year he replaced Alfred Carpenter as professor of medical jurisprudence at University College, and in 1860 he was appointed physician to University College Hospital. He held these appointments until a retinal haemorrhage and glaucoma brought on by his histological studies obliged him to resign them in 1868. Although he recovered his eyesight after nearly two years of wearing dark glasses and living in a dark room, he spent the remainder of his life in private practice, the living embodiment of his own aphorism: 'True science is the key to wise practice' (Tweedie, 345).

In 1861 Harley married Emma Jessie, youngest daughter

of the Liverpool alkali manufacturer, James Muspratt of Seaforth Hall. They had one son, Vaughan, who eventually became professor of pathological chemistry at University College, and two daughters. Under her married name, Mrs Alec Tweedie [see Tweedie, Ethel Brilliana], their daughter Ethel published over fifty books, including a biography of her father in 1899. In 1862 Harley received the triennial prize of 50 guineas from the College of Surgeons of Edinburgh for his researches into the anatomy and physiology of the adrenal glands.

While at Heidelberg, Harley had spent much time in studying gas analysis in the laboratory of Robert Bunsen. After his return to England he began research on the chemistry of respiration. Some of the results were published in the *Philosophical Transactions* and resulted in his election to the fellowship of the Royal Society in 1865. In 1864 he was elected fellow of the Royal College of Physicians; he afterwards held the post of examiner in anatomy and physiology in the college. Fluent in French, German, and Italian, he also became a corresponding member of numerous foreign scientific societies. In 1864 Harley took an active share in the work of the committee of the Royal Medical and Chirurgical Society appointed to study the subject of suspended animation by drowning and hanging. The experiments were carried out in his laboratory at University College, as were those for the committee of the same society on chloroform anaesthesia (1864), of which Harley was also a member. Harley made careful researches into the action of strychnine, and of the ordeal bean. In 1863 and 1864 he read papers to the British Association on the botanical and therapeutic characters of the ordeal bean and one entitled 'Poisoned arrows of savage man', in which he demonstrated the nature of some of the poisons used. He was the first physiologist to demonstrate that strychnine and wourali (arrow poison) have the property of reciprocally neutralizing the toxic effects of each other. During the years 1864 and 1865 Harley was one of a small group of London doctors who gave Elizabeth Garrett private lessons to forward her ambition to enter the medical profession.

Harley contributed a large number of papers to various scientific periodicals. His most important publications concerned the diseases of the liver. In 1863 he published *Jaundice, its Pathology and Treatment*, replacing it in 1883 by the more comprehensive *Diseases of the Liver*. Both books stressed the role of chemical and physiological knowledge in diagnosis. In 1885 he published a pamphlet *Sounding for Gall Stones*, and in the following year a book, *Inflammation of the Liver*, in which he advocated puncture in congestive liver induration and hepatic phlebotomy during acute hepatitis. In 1868 his former pupil George T. Brown published Harley's lectures and demonstrations as *Histology*. When blind he dictated to an amanuensis *Urine and its Derangements* (1872), which was translated into French and Italian.

Harley had many hobbies. He invented a microscope, which by a simple adjustment could be transformed from a monocular into a binocular, or into a polarizing instrument, either of high or low power. He tried hard to reform

English spelling, and published a book entitled *The Simplification of English Spelling* (1877), in which he advocated the total omission of redundant duplicated consonants and mute letters from all words except personal names.

In July 1876 Harley was left lame following a spell of rheumatic gout. He died suddenly from rupture of a coronary artery and haemorrhage on 27 October 1896 at his house, 25 Harley Street. His body was cremated at Woking on 30 October, and the remains buried at Kingsbury Old Church on the same day. Religious, without being sectarian, and a great socializer, Harley always wore a walrus moustache. Although ill health robbed him of the chance of high academic honours, he was an important figure in bringing laboratory medicine to bear on British medical education and practice.

W. W. WEBB, rev. W. H. BROCK

Sources Mrs Alec Tweedie, ed., *George Harley, F.R.S.: the life of a London physician* (1899) · W. M., *PRS*, 61 (1897), v–x · Munk, *Roll*, 4.141 · bap. reg. Scot.
Archives UCL, lecture notes · Wellcome L., papers
Likenesses lithograph, 1873, Wellcome L. · photograph, repro. in Tweedie, ed., *George Harley*, frontispiece · photogravure, Wellcome L. · photogravure, NPG · wood-engraving (after photograph by Jerrard), NPG; repro. in *ILN* (7 Nov 1896)

Harley, George Davies (d. 1811), actor and writer, was probably born in the late 1760s in London, and was originally known as George Davies. While working as an insurance clerk he formed a friendship with the actor John Henderson of Covent Garden. Inspired and taught by Henderson, he added Harley to his surname and went on the stage. He made his début at the Theatre Royal, Norwich, in April 1775, playing Richard III. In the next four years he took a succession of major roles there, including Macbeth, Lear, and Othello, and in August 1788 he played Dumont to Sarah Siddons's Jane Shore, on her only appearance in Norwich.

Henderson had died as Harley began his career. Loyal to his teacher's memory, Harley frequently recited William Cowper's 'John Gilpin', a poem which Henderson had made famous, and he published and performed a monody on his death. On 4 March 1788 he married Elizabeth Griffith. They had at least three children, one of whom died in infancy. When Harley died his property was left to a second wife, Susanna, and in his will he expressed concern that his two surviving children should not disturb her possession of it.

Harley was recruited by Thomas Harris for Covent Garden and made his début there in September 1789, again as Richard III. During his first season he took a number of other major roles—Iago, Shylock, Lear, and Jacques—as well as lesser parts by other writers. His salary rose from £2 to £5 per week in the 1790–91 season, and to £6 in 1793–4, but reached no higher—half the amount of the highest paid actors in the company. High success had escaped him. His Lear was criticized for seeming too young, and his relationship with Henderson was characterized by Anthony Pasquin in the lines:

By HENDERSON tutor'd, whom GARRICK had made,
He is but the shadow at best of a shade.

By 1796 his major roles had become fewer; in the spring he played Kent, rather than King Lear, for instance. That summer, after a short season at the Haymarket, he left London for the provinces, where he remained with rather more success for the rest of his career. He worked at Bath, Bristol, Birmingham, Manchester, and elsewhere in a wider range of parts, including those of old men in comedy. In 1802 he supported Mrs Siddons again, on her farewell visit to Dublin.

Harley had written and published poetry from his Norwich days. His last was a descriptive account of the battle of Trafalgar. The quality of his work is typified by the opening lines of one of his elegies:

> Alas, poor DASH! Thou wert no vulgar dog;
> Nor were thy merits of the common kind.

He also wrote a prose biographical sketch of the life of William Henry West Betty. Harley died at Leicester on 28 October 1811. An obituary in the *Gentleman's Magazine* described him as 'a poet of some eminence, and a comedian of much provincial celebrity' (*GM*, 1st ser., 81/2, 1811, 491) and noted his reputation for integrity.

JOHN LEVITT

Sources C. B. Hogan, ed., *The London stage, 1660–1800*, pt 5: *1776–1800* (1968) · Highfill, Burnim & Langhans, *BDA* · [J. Haslewood], *The secret history of the green rooms: containing authentic and entertaining memoirs of the actors and actresses in the three theatres royal*, 2 vols. (1790) · *Theatrical biography, or, Memoirs of the principal performers of the three Theatre Royals*, 2 vols. (1772) · *Norfolk Mercury* (1759–65) · G. D. Harley, *Poems* (1796) · *GM*, 1st ser., 81/2 (1811), 491 · A. Pasquin [J. Williams], *The children of Thespis*, 13th edn (1792) · Genest, *Eng. stage*

Likenesses S. De Wilde, pencil and watercolour drawing, 1794, V&A · S. De Wilde, oils (as Caleb, in *The siege of Damascus*), Garr. Club · portrait (after G. Clint), NPG · theatrical prints, BM, NPG

Harley [*née* Holles], **Henrietta Cavendish**, **countess of Oxford and Mortimer** (1694–1755), patron of architecture, was born on 4 February 1694 at Newcastle House, Clerkenwell, Middlesex, the only child of John *Holles, duke of Newcastle upon Tyne (1662–1711), and his wife, Lady Margaret Cavendish (1661–1716), third daughter of Henry *Cavendish, second duke of Newcastle upon Tyne. After the deaths of his sons, Henry Cavendish had caused family controversy by leaving his estate to Margaret at the expense of her sisters, and her husband was on this basis allowed to take the title of Newcastle on being made a duke in 1694. To Henrietta, then, descended the wealth and castles of the Cavendish and Ogle families in Derbyshire and Northumberland, and Welbeck Abbey in Nottinghamshire. Henrietta was acutely conscious of her ancestry and also inherited her family's traditional passion for horses; Horace Walpole described her homage to the 'great families from which she descended, and which centred in her' (Walpole, *Corr.*, 35.271). Her great-grandfather William Cavendish, first duke of Newcastle, had written the standard English work on horsemanship. His great-granddaughter's dun mare appears with her in portraits, and she is thought to have been the only woman whom the sporting artist John Wootton ever depicted in the saddle.

Henrietta too endured a complicated family wrangle. In

Henrietta Cavendish Harley, countess of Oxford and Mortimer (1694–1755), by Sir Godfrey Kneller, 1714

1711 she inherited much property from her father—unfairly, according to her mother—and it was during an estrangement lasting until just before Margaret's death that Henrietta married Edward *Harley (1689–1741), son of the tory first minister Robert *Harley, first earl of Oxford and Mortimer. The wedding, 'in the Drawing Room at Wimple' on 31 August 1713, was followed the next day by the nervous dispatch of letters to 'the Dutchess of Newcastle' (BL, Add. MS 70440, 31 Aug/1 Sept 1713) informing her. Wimpole Hall, the Harley house in Cambridgeshire, expanded to form a setting for Edward Harley's famous collections, was sold in 1740 to pay debts. The couple had one surviving child, another Margaret (1715–1785) [*see* Bentinck, Margaret Cavendish], who married William Bentinck, second duke of Portland. The Cavendish inheritance therefore passed through the female line yet again, from the Harley to the Bentinck family.

Henrietta's husband inherited the earldom of Oxford and Mortimer in 1724 but not his father's interest in politics, concentrating instead on his extensive collection of books and manuscripts. Following her husband's death in

1741, Henrietta dispersed his collection, the transactions culminating in the sale of the manuscripts to the nation for £10,000, such a low price that it ranked as a tremendous gift, and she has often been criticized for her implied ignorance of the collection's value. In fact, her daughter communicated her spirited refusal to 'bargain with the publick' (*Bath MSS*, 2.183) to the House of Commons. Henrietta was a great reader herself, as the books in the library at Welbeck marked in her handwriting 'daer tuo' (Goulding, 14: 'read out' backwards) attest.

Henrietta's common reputation for being somewhat stiff-necked stems from a letter of Mary Pendarves (later Mrs Delany) of 1734 saying she was 'afraid Lady O. would have come' to join a party, and that 'her formality would not by any means have agreed with the liberty of this constitution' (*Autobiography … Mrs Delany*, 2.230). This view survived in her description as a 'dull, worthy woman' in the *Dictionary of National Biography*. But Henrietta's supporters included her devoted correspondent Lady Mary Wortley Montagu, who would round on detractors, saying, 'Lady Oxford is not shining, but she has more in her than such giddy things as you and your companions can discern' (*Letters and Works*, 1.66). Jonathan Swift's high-flown verses on Henrietta's marriage contrast with his private view, in his journal, that she was 'handsome, and has good sense, but red hair'.

'I live as retired here as I can in this country where my ancestors had lived so long', Henrietta wrote from Welbeck Abbey to Lady Mary on 21 January 1747, 'but must see more company than I chuse' (BL, Add. MS 70432). Her widowhood was spent in furious activity improving the house for her grandson, William Henry Cavendish Cavendish-*Bentinck, the future third duke of Portland. Walpole described her 'doing ten thousand right and just things … collecting and monumenting the portraits and reliques' of her family and their ancestors (Walpole, *Corr.*, 35.271). Her account books for 'the Repairing Beautifying & Ornamenting the Ancient Seat of the Cavendishe Family at Welbeck' (Nottinghamshire Archives, MS DD. P5.6.1.1) have been preserved. They record the reconstruction of the west wing of the abbey, and inside the creation of medievalizing masterpieces such as the 'Gothic Hall', whose fantastic ceiling still survives. Marble fireplaces were based—unusually for the period—on her great-grandfather's Jacobean models at Bolsover Castle, another ancestral house which she repaired. The architect John James helped with the work until 1746, and in 1750 Henrietta reported her impatience with its progress. 'I have now above a hundred men employ'd, and entend to have more', she wrote to her grandson, 'The stuco men work by candle light night and morning' (Goulding, 32).

Henrietta's interests included the family documents collected by Arthur Collins, and her husband's librarian Humfrey Wanley himself was her devoted servant. She reorganized the pictures at Welbeck to create a veritable shrine to horses and to her ancestors. 'Oh! portraits!' swooned Walpole in 1756, shortly after her death:

I went to Welbeck. It is impossible to describe the bales of Cavendishes, Harleys, Holleses, Veres, and Ogles: every

chamber is tapestried with them; nay, and with ten thousand other fat morsels; all their histories inscribed; all their arms, crests, devices, sculptures on chimneys of various English marbles in ancient forms (and, to say truth, most of them ugly.) (Walpole, *Corr.*, 35.270–71)

Henrietta's death at Welbeck on 9 December 1755 of 'an apoplexy and palsy' (*Autobiography … Mrs Delany*, 3.383) reunited her with her ancestors, for she was buried on 26 December 'in the old Duke of Newcastle's vault' (Chester, 389) at Westminster Abbey. Far from being a dull cipher as was once thought, she became through her intense family pride a vigorous and eccentric architectural innovator, despite—or perhaps because of—her reclusive later life.

LUCY WORSLEY

Sources J. L. Chester, ed., *The marriage, baptismal, and burial registers of the collegiate church or abbey of St Peter, Westminster*, Harleian Society, 10 (1876) · A. Collins, *Historical collections of the noble families of Cavendishe, Holles, Vere, Harley and Ogle* (1752) · DNB · R. W. Goulding, 'Henrietta countess of Oxford', *Transactions of the Thoroton Society*, 27 (1923), 1–41 · *Calendar of the manuscripts of the marquis of Bath preserved at Longleat, Wiltshire*, 5 vols., HMC, 58 (1904–80), vol. 2 · *The manuscripts of his grace the duke of Portland*, 10 vols., HMC, 29 (1891–1931), vol. 9 · C. Jones, 'The Harley family and the Harley papers', *British Library Journal*, 15 (1989), 123–33 · *The autobiography and correspondence of Mary Granville, Mrs Delany*, ed. Lady Llanover, 1st ser., 3 vols. (1861); 2nd ser., 3 vols. (1862) · *The journal to Stella, 1710–1713*, ed. F. Ryland (1905), 277 · Walpole, *Corr.* · A. S. Turberville, *A history of Welbeck Abbey and its owners*, 2 vols. (1938–9), vol. 1 · *The letters and works of Lady Mary Wortley Montagu*, ed. Lord Wharncliffe, 3 vols. (1837), vol. 1, p. 66; vol. 3, pp. 205–37 · will, PRO, PROB 11, sig. 228 · London Metropolitan Records Centre, MS P76:JS1:16

Archives BL, corresp. and papers, Add. MSS 70426–70433 · BL, papers | Longleat House, Wiltshire, Portland Collection · Notts. Arch., direct deposit Portland · U. Nott., Portland collection

Likenesses G. Kneller, oils, 1714, priv. coll. [*see illus.*] · J. Wootton, oils, 1716, priv. coll.

Harley, John (*d.* 1557/8), bishop of Hereford, is said by Wood to have been a native of Herefordshire; however, an alternative tradition names Newton Pagnell in Buckinghamshire as his birthplace. He was educated at Magdalen College, Oxford, from where he graduated BA on 5 July 1536, proceeded MA on 4 June 1540, and was admitted BTh before 1550, and where he was a probationary fellow from 1537 to 1542. Ordained deacon and priest on 20 February 1541, between 1542 and August 1548 he was the usher of Magdalen College School. His learning became such as to earn him an encomium from John Leland. A man of strong evangelical sympathies, during Lent 1547 Harley preached a vehemently protestant sermon in St Peter-in-the-East, attacking the pope and upholding the doctrine of justification by faith alone. Delivered at a sensitive moment, shortly after the death of Henry VIII, the sermon unnerved the university authorities, who in self-defence had Harley summoned to London to be examined on a charge of heresy. However, as it became clear that he had the support of the king and of Protector Somerset, he was allowed to return to Oxford without hindrance. Even so he may have found it advisable to leave the university, for probably in 1548 he became chaplain to John Dudley, earl of Warwick, and tutor to his children.

Harley's ecclesiastical career flourished under Edward VI. On 9 May 1550 he became rector of Upton-on-Severn, and on 30 September following vicar of Kidderminster, both in Worcestershire, while on 30 September 1551 he was recorded as incumbent of Maiden Bradley, Wiltshire. On 2 July 1551 he was presented by the king to the ninth prebend in Worcester Cathedral, and in December that year he was one of six men appointed royal 'chaplains ordinary', with the intention that they should undertake evangelizing tours of those parts of the realm (especially the north) regarded as insufficiently attuned to the new religious dispensation. In 1552 he was considered likely to succeed Owen Oglethorpe as president of Magdalen, but reportedly failed to secure election through laziness and love of money; it seems more likely, however, that his religious views were out of step with those of a mostly conservative fellowship. Indeed, the outspokenness with which he attacked the shortcomings of the king's government earned him a stiff rebuke from his former employer Dudley, now duke of Northumberland.

Nevertheless in October 1552 Harley was named for the see of Hereford. That he was not consecrated until 26 May 1553 may have been due to his reluctance to pay the government's price for his elevation. In any case his appointment was short-lived. He was imprisoned in September 1553 for leaving church at the elevation of the host, and formally deprived on 15 March 1554 on the grounds of his having married (his wife's name is unrecorded). Thereafter, according to Wood:

> Harley absconding for a time, did at length go from place to place in an obscure condition, to consolate the poor remnant of protestants, and confirm them in their belief, but died soon after in his wandring to and fro in England. (Wood, *Ath. Oxon.*, 2.769)

He probably died in 1557, and certainly by June 1558; his wife survived him.

GORDON GOODWIN, rev. ANDREW A. CHIBI

Sources Emden, *Oxf.*, 4.266–7 · J. R. Bloxam, *A register of the presidents, fellows ... of Saint Mary Magdalen College*, 8 vols. (1853–85) · *Hist. U. Oxf.* 3: *Colleg. univ.* · P. Collinson, *Archbishop Grindal, 1519–1583: the struggle for a reformed church* (1979) · Foster, *Alum. Oxon.*, *1500–1714*, 2.651 · C. Litzenberger, *The English Reformation and the laity: Gloucestershire, 1540–1580* (1997) · L. B. Smith, *Tudor prelates and politics* (Princeton, NJ, 1953) · T. Fuller, *The worthies of England*, ed. J. Freeman, abridged edn (1952) · D. MacCulloch, *Thomas Cranmer: a life* (1996) · J. Strype, *Memorials of the most reverend father in God Thomas Cranmer*, 2 vols. (1848) · Wood, *Ath. Oxon.*, new edn, 2.768–71 · *Fasti Angl., 1541–1857*, [Ely] · *Reg. Oxf.* · Rymer, *Foedera*, 1st edn · J. Leland, *Encomia* (1589)
Archives PRO, SP 10/15

Harley, John Laker [Jack] (1911–1990), botanist, was born on 17 November 1911 in Old Charlton, London, the elder son and second of four children of Charles Laker Harley, civil servant in the Post Office, and his wife Edith Sarah Smith, daughter of an armament artificer. His early childhood was spent in various parts of London. When he was twelve the family moved to Leeds, where his father took a post at the labour exchange. Harley entered Leeds grammar school, originally intending to become a classicist, but switched to science in the sixth form. Three outstanding teachers made him interested and successful at biology, and he entered for the Oxford entrance examination.

The hard work needed for this, combined with being prefect and house captain as well as playing first-fifteen rugby, taught him the efficient use of time and how to work early in the morning, a lesson he never forgot, to the later consternation of research collaborators, who found he often began preparing for experiments at dawn.

In 1930 Harley won an open exhibition to Wadham College, Oxford, but was unsure whether to read botany or zoology. He chose the former because the interviewers for the latter did not attract him. His undergraduate career was crowned with the awards both of a first-class honours degree (1933), and the Christopher Welch research scholarship, which financed the first four years (1933–7) of his postgraduate research on the mycorrhizas of the beech tree (mycorrhizas are very common and widespread symbiotic associations between fungi and the underground organs of plants, and the principal route for mineral nutrients such as phosphate to pass from soil to roots). This topic was chosen because he had carried out notable researches as an undergraduate into both fungi and plant ecology, but he was very dissatisfied with the outcome and, after his DPhil (1936), switched to studying the physiology of fungi, having been awarded an 1851 studentship. In 1939 he became a departmental demonstrator in the botany department. In 1938 he married (Elizabeth) Lindsay, daughter of Edward McCarthy Fitt, civil engineer. They had a son and a daughter.

War service intervened from 1940 to 1945, and Harley was commissioned in the Royal Signals. He joined the army operational research group no. 1 in 1943, serving first in the Burma theatre, and then in Ceylon as a staff officer at supreme allied command headquarters, ending the war with the rank of lieutenant-colonel. His experiences left a marked impression, and the military way of life had some appeal for him. He returned to Oxford in 1945 as a university lecturer in the botany department, moving to the agriculture department in 1958. He was reader in plant nutrition from 1962 to 1965. He became a research fellow of Queen's College in 1946 (full fellow in 1952), a happy association which ended in 1965 when he moved to Sheffield University as a professor of botany. He returned to Oxford in 1969 as professor of forest science and fellow of St John's, a post he held until his retirement in 1979.

Harley's major contribution to science was that, over a period of nearly forty years after the war, he oversaw a pioneering series of researches into tree mycorrhizas which put the experimental study of these ecologically important symbioses firmly on the map; before his work, no one had a clear idea of their role. The initial stimulus to his studies was an invitation to write a review on mycorrhizas in 1947, which then inspired research with a succession of talented collaborators, many of whom were his own students. Two outstanding books were published, the second written with his daughter, herself an international expert on mycorrhizas: *The Biology of Mycorrhiza* (1959) and (with S. E. Smith) *Mycorrhizal Symbiosis* (1983).

Harley was elected a fellow of the Royal Society in 1964,

and had honorary degrees from the universities of Sheffield (1989) and Uppsala (1981). He was president of the British Mycological Society (1967), the British Ecological Society (1970–72), and the Institute of Biology (1984–6), and had honorary fellowships of Wadham College, Oxford (1972), Wye College, London (1983), and the Indian National Academy of Sciences (1981). He was appointed CBE in 1979 and won the gold medal of the Linnean Society in 1989. His excellent analytical judgement benefited many national bodies, including the Agricultural Research Council, the Lawes Agricultural Trust, and the *New Phytologist*, the largest journal of general botany in Europe, which he served as both editor (1961–83) and a trustee.

Harley inspired intense loyalty and affection from his students and collaborators. Beneath his bluff, rather military style lay a remarkably perceptive and compassionate person, who combined courage and honesty with a zany sense of humour. He was 6 feet tall, erect, and slim, although he put on weight later in life. Harley died on 13 December 1990 at his home, The Orchard, 20 Oxford Road, Old Marston, Oxford.   DAVID SMITH, *rev.*

Sources D. C. Smith and D. H. Lewis, *Memoirs FRS*, 39 (1994), 157–75 · personal knowledge (1996) · *CGPLA Eng. & Wales* (1991) · D. Smith, *The Times* (28 Dec 1990) · D. Lewis and D. Smith, *New Phytologist*, 119 (Sept 1991), 5–7
Archives Bodl. Oxf., corresp. and papers | University of Sheffield, corresp. with Arthur Roy Clapham
Wealth at death £250,062: probate, 26 March 1991, *CGPLA Eng. & Wales*

Harley, John Pritt (1786–1858), actor, the son of John Harley, a draper and silk mercer, and his wife, Elizabeth, was born in February 1786 and baptized in the parish church of St Martin-in-the-Fields, London, on 5 March. At the age of fifteen he was apprenticed to a linen draper in Ludgate Hill, and while there became friends with William Oxberry, afterwards a well-known actor, and in conjunction with him appeared in 1802 in amateur theatricals at the Berwick Street private theatre. His next employment was as a clerk to Windus and Holloway, attorneys, in Chancery Lane. In 1806 and the following years he acted at Cranbrook, Southend, Canterbury, Worthington, Brighton, and Rochester. At Southend, where he remained for some time, he acquired a complete knowledge of his profession. His comic singing rendered him a favourite, and being extremely thin he was satirically known as 'Fat Jack'. From 1812 to 1814 he was in the north of England, and appeared at York in 1813, but after obtaining an engagement from Samuel John Arnold he went to London, and made his first public appearance there on 15 July 1815 at the English Opera House, as Marcelli in *The Devil's Bridge*. His reception was favourable, and in the roles of Mingle, Leatherhead, Rattle, and Pedrillo he increased his reputation as an actor and singer. On 16 September 1815 he was first seen in Drury Lane Theatre, and acted Lissardo in Susannah Centlivre's *The Wonder*.

As John Bannister had retired from the stage, Harley not only succeeded to his parts, but had also to take the characters which would have fallen to the latter in the new pieces; he was consequently continually before the public and played the comic heroes of all the operas. His voice was a countertenor. He had a considerable knowledge of music and a good ear, and he executed cadenzas with grace and effect. When Bannister, with whom Harley was on the most intimate terms, died in 1836, he gave him his Garrick mourning ring and his Shakespearian jubilee medal. Harley remained at Drury Lane, with occasional summer excursions to the provinces and engagements at the Lyceum, where he for some time was stage-manager, until Braham opened the St James's Theatre on 14 December 1835, when he joined the company at that house. However, he soon returned to his old quarters at Drury Lane. He was with W. C. Macready at Covent Garden in 1838, and afterwards with Madame Vestris and Charles Mathews when they opened the same establishment two years later. From 1841 to 1848 he was under Alfred Bunn at Drury Lane, and finally, when Charles Kean attempted to restore the fortunes of the legitimate drama at the Princess's Theatre in 1850, Harley became a permanent member of the company. He was master and treasurer of the Drury Lane Theatrical Fund after the retirement of Edmund Kean in 1833.

In humour and versatility Harley almost equalled Bannister. In 1816, when Ben Jonson's *Every Man in his Humour* was revived in order that Edmund Kean might play Kitely, Harley sustained the part of Bobadil, and was thought the best exponent of the character that had appeared since Henry Woodward. In the Shakespearian clowns he had a rich natural humour peculiar to himself. Not even Joseph Munden or John Liston excited more general merriment. On Friday 20 August 1858 he acted Lancelot Gobbo at the Princess's Theatre; as he reached the wings on leaving the stage he was seized with paralysis, and he died at his home, 14 Upper Gower Street, London, on 22 August. His last words were a quotation from *A Midsummer Night's Dream*: 'I have an exposition of sleep come upon me.' He was buried at Kensal Green cemetery on 28 August. Eccentric and thrifty to all outward appearance, he died penniless: his estate was administered by one of his creditors. He had a passion for collecting walking sticks and canes, and after his death more than three hundred varieties were included in the sale of his personal effects.

G. C. BOASE, *rev.* KATHARINE COCKIN

Sources *The biography of the British stage, being correct narratives of the lives of all the principal actors and actresses* (1824) · *Oxberry's Dramatic Biography*, 1/5 (1825) · Hall, *Dramatic ports.* · J. Cumberland, *British theatre* (1829) · H. Valentine, *Behind the curtain* [1848] · E. Stirling, *Old Drury Lane*, 2 vols. (1881) · J. W. Cole, *The life and theatrical times of Charles Kean ... including a summary of the English stage for the last fifty years*, 2nd edn, 2 vols. (1860) · *Macready's reminiscences, and selections from his diaries and letters*, ed. F. Pollock, new edn (1876) · *ILN* (27 March 1858), 321 · *The Era* (29 Aug 1858), 9–10 · *Illustrated News of the World* (4 Sept 1858), 145, 147
Archives LMA, diary
Likenesses S. De Wilde, watercolour and chalk drawing, 1816, Garr. Club · G. Clint, group portrait, oils, 1820, Garr. Club · H. Watkins, albumen print, 1855–60, NPG · G. Clint, oils, Garr. Club · likeness, repro. in *Metropolitan Magazine* (Oct 1836), 126–31 · likeness, repro. in *Era*, 9, 10 · likeness, repro. in Stirling, *Old Drury Lane*, vol. 2, p. 115 · likeness, repro. in Cole, *The life and theatrical times of*

Charles Kean (1860), 2.12, 307–12 · likeness, repro. in *Macready's reminiscences* (1876), 254, 282, 376, 377 · portrait, repro. in *Oxberry's Dramatic Biography*, 69–77 · portrait, repro. in *Theatrical Inquisitor* (Sept 1815), 163–4 · portrait, repro. in *British Stage* (July 1821), 201–2 · portrait, repro. in J. Cumberland, *British theatre*, 14 (1828), 7–8 · portrait, repro. in J. Cumberland, *British theatre*, 18 (1828), 6–7 · portrait, repro. in *Actors by Daylight* (5 May 1838), 73–5 · portrait, repro. in *Dramatic Mirror* (14 April 1847), 5 · portrait, repro. in *Theatrical Times* (4 Dec 1847), 377 · portrait, repro. in Valentine, *Behind the curtain*, 38–42 · portrait, repro. in *Tallis's drawing-room table book* (1852), pt 14 · portrait, repro. in *ILN*, 321 · portrait, repro. in *Illustrated News of the World*, 145, 147 · portrait, repro. in *Illustrated Sporting and Dramatic News* (13 Sept 1879), 629–30 · portrait, repro. in J. R. Planché, *Extravaganzas, 1825–1871*, ed. T. F. D. Croker and S. Tucker, 2 (1879), 63 · prints, Harvard TC · prints, BM, NPG · watercolour (as Somno in *The sleepwalker*), Garr. Club · watercolour and pencil, NPG

Wealth at death under £300: administration, 5 Nov 1858, *CGPLA Eng. & Wales*

Harley, Lady Margaret Cavendish. *See* Bentinck, Margaret Cavendish, duchess of Portland (1715–1785).

Harley, Sir Robert (*bap.* 1579, *d.* 1656), politician, was born probably at Wigmore Castle, Herefordshire, the only surviving child of Thomas Harley (*c.*1543–1631) of Brampton Bryan Castle, Herefordshire, and his first wife, Margaret Corbet, daughter of Sir Andrew Corbet of Moreton Corbet, Shropshire. He was baptized at Wigmore on 1 March 1579. In 1597 he entered Oriel College, Oxford, where he was under the tutelage of Cadwallader Owen. He graduated BA in July 1599 and entered the Middle Temple, where he remained until at least February 1603, when he married Ann (*d.* 1603), daughter of Charles Barrett of Belhouse, Essex, and granddaughter of Sir Walter Mildmay, the puritan founder of Emmanuel College, Cambridge. Ann died in childbirth on 1 December 1603, and she and the child, a son, Thomas, were buried at Cuxton, near the home of her stepfather, Sir John Leveson of Halling, Kent. Harley next married Mary (*d.* 1622), daughter of Sir Andrew Newport of High Ercall, Shropshire. The children of this union did not survive infancy. In July 1623 he married for a third time; his wife, Brilliana *Harley (*bap.* 1598, *d.* 1643), was the daughter of the secretary of state, Sir Edward Conway of Ragley Hall, Warwickshire. This marriage produced three sons, Edward *Harley (1624–1700), Robert (1626–1673), and Thomas (1628–1692?), and four daughters, Brilliana (1629–1660), Dorothy (*b.* 1630), Margaret (*b.* 1631), and Elizabeth (*b.* 1634), the sole child to die young.

These three marriages allowed the Harley family to consolidate their power within Herefordshire. Ann Barrett's dowry of £2300 was used for the purchase of the manor and borough of Wigmore, which was conveyed with the advowsons of Brampton Bryan and Wigmore to the use of Robert Harley for life. This not only provided an income for him, but also enhanced his social standing. The success of this policy was reflected in a series of royal grants and local appointments. In July 1603 he was made a knight in the Order of the Bath at James I's coronation. In the spring of 1604 he was returned to parliament as burgess for Radnor and at about the same time was appointed as a justice of the peace for Herefordshire. In the same year he received a crown grant of the keepership of the forests of Bringwood and Prestwood. In 1606 he served as sheriff of Radnor and was appointed deputy to Charles, earl of Nottingham, as itinerant justiciar in the royal forests, chases, parks, and warrens in Herefordshire, and by 1619 he was acting as a deputy lieutenant. He did not serve in parliament again until 1624 and 1626, when he was returned for Herefordshire on both occasions. In 1628 he was elected as burgess for Evesham through the influence of his father-in-law, Viscount Conway.

During the 1620s Harley acted as Conway's aide in the Commons, repeatedly speaking, for example, in favour of the payment of subsidies without conditions or delay. In 1626 he opposed the impeachment of Conway's patron, the duke of Buckingham, and in 1628 tried to shield the duke from parliamentary censure. Harley's support for Buckingham was, however, not uncritical, and he undoubtedly regarded his primary allegiance as lying with Conway and not the duke.

Harley's marriage to Brilliana Conway in 1623 had been brokered by her aunt, Mary, Lady Vere, but it was also a love match strengthened by the couple's shared puritan beliefs. Harley had accepted the reduced sum of £1600 as a dowry for Brilliana and his father had conveyed the remainder of his estates, including his main seat at Brampton Bryan, to the use of his son and daughter-in-law. The Harleys placed considerable importance on the union, in part because of the political contacts offered by Secretary Conway. On 30 June 1623 Harley was admitted as a member of the council in Wales, and in 1626 he was appointed master of the mint through Conway's influence. In 1627 he was granted the monopoly for discovering abuses in the manufacture of gold and silver thread. He was forced to forfeit the mastership of the mint in 1635 because the previous master still had a legal interest in the office. The death of Conway in 1631 and Harley's religious beliefs were also important factors, and he was not compensated for his loss. He was reinstated as master in 1643 by order of parliament, but resigned after the execution of Charles I. He believed that his support for nonconformist clergymen, including John Stoughton and John Workman, was responsible for his loss of the mastership in 1635.

Harley's puritan beliefs were first probably inculcated by his mother and then by his Oxford tutor, Cadwallader Owen. Between 1613 and 1615 Harley was at odds with his father over Harley's choice of the moderate puritan, Thomas Pierson, as rector of Brampton Bryan. Pierson and Harley introduced a new style of evangelical piety into what was a religiously very conservative region and Thomas Harley represented a considerable body of traditional opinion within the parish and surrounding areas. Pierson was undoubtedly responsible for influencing his patron's religious beliefs and in 1621 Harley drew up a 'character' of a puritan in which he criticized episcopacy and emphasized the moderate puritan position against separation from the Church of England. He also cultivated a wide circle of puritan clerics outside the county, including William Gouge, the lecturer at the Blackfriars, where Harley took lodgings in 1611 and 1612, Thomas Gataker, rector of Rotherhithe, who preached at his marriage to Brilliana Conway, Julines Herring, the lecturer at St Alkmond's, Shrewsbury, who was suspended and fled to Amsterdam in the 1630s, and John Cotton, the minister of Boston, Lincolnshire, who emigrated to America in 1633.

Harley's puritan and Calvinist beliefs strongly coloured his actions as a member of parliament. In the 1620s he supported Buckingham's policy of war against Spain primarily on religious grounds. He also took a strongly anti-Catholic position, calling for strict measures against recusants and the Jesuits. In 1626 he extended his concerns to include the English Arminians, when he joined the Commons' attempts to censure the publications of Richard Mountague. During the personal rule of the 1630s he came to regard himself as a country gentleman rather than a courtier, and the Short Parliament of 1640 gave him the opportunity to demonstrate his opposition to ship money, the Laudian church innovations, and the Scottish war. He continued this stance as a member of the Long Parliament with the support of the Herefordshire county élite, but during the next eighteen months enthusiasm for reform waned and a strongly royalist party emerged in the county in the summer of 1642. His house and estate at Brampton Bryan were severely damaged during the course of two royalist sieges in 1643 and 1644. The death of Lady Harley in October 1643 represented not only a personal blow to him, but also the loss of a perceptive observer, who had kept him fully informed about local political developments.

At Westminster Harley was one of the most active supporters of the reforming middle group led in the Commons by Pym, St John, and Hampden, who favoured a policy of effective war against Charles I. In September 1643 he took the solemn league and covenant, which sealed the military alliance between parliament and the Scots, and prepared the way for the introduction of a presbyterian church system in England. He also undertook much of the routine committee work needed to secure the middle group's policies. In January 1642 he replaced Pym as chairman of the standing committee for Irish affairs and after Pym's death, in December 1643, took his place on the important committee for the assembly of divines engaged in reform of the church. He also chaired the committee for the destruction of superstitious and idolatrous monuments set up in 1643 and the committee for elections. His sympathy for the Scots and his religious presbyterianism meant that from 1645 he was increasingly drawn into alliance with the political 'presbyterian' party led by Denzil Holles. After the capture of Hereford in December 1645 by parliamentarian forces led by colonel John Birch, Harley set about restoring Harley family influence in the county. In 1646 he was appointed steward of Hereford and embarked on a power struggle with the newcomer Birch.

During the political crisis in the summer of 1647 Harley's son Edward was one of the eleven members indicted by the army for plotting to restore the king to power and Harley was anonymously charged with financial and electoral corruption. He withdrew from the Commons and did not return until the spring of 1648. In the autumn of that year he was a member of the joint committee which formulated the terms offered by parliament to the king at Newport. He also steered the new militia ordinance through its committee stage in the Commons. On 6 December 1648, as a result of his support for a settlement with the king, he and Edward Harley were excluded from taking their seats in the Commons by Pride's Purge. They remained imprisoned by the army until after Charles I's execution, which marked the effective end of Sir Robert's political career; in May 1649 he resigned his office as master of the mint. In 1654 he was named to the commission for the ejection of scandalous ministers in Herefordshire, but was not active in local politics. He died on 6 November 1656 in Ludlow and was buried on 10 December at Brampton Bryan.   JACQUELINE EALES

Sources J. Eales, *Puritans and roundheads: the Harleys of Brampton Bryan and the outbreak of the English civil war* (1990) · BL, Add. MSS 70105–70109 · BL, Add. MSS 70001–70007 · *Letters of the Lady Brilliana Harley*, ed. T. T. Lewis, CS, 58 (1854) · T. Froysell, *Yadidah, or, The beloved disciple* (1658) · J. Eales, 'Thomas Pierson and the transmission of the moderate puritan tradition', *Midland History*, 20 (1995), 75–102 · J. Eales, 'Sir Robert Harley KB (1579–1656) and the "character" of a puritan', *British Library Journal*, 15 (1989), 134–57 · monument, St Michael's Church, Cuxton, Kent
Archives BL, corresp. and MSS, Add. MS 61989 · BL, corresp. and papers, Add. MSS 70001–70007, 70062, 70105–70111 · BL, corresp. and papers, loan 29 · BL, letters and MSS, Add. MSS 70001–70007 · BL, letters and MSS, Add. MSS 70105–70109 · U. Nott. L., corresp.
Likenesses P. Oliver, miniature, *c.*1620–1629, priv. coll. · G. Vertue, line engraving, 1737 (after P. Oliver), BM, NPG

Harley, Robert, first earl of Oxford and Mortimer (1661–1724), politician, was born on 5 December 1661 in Bow Street, London, and baptized on the following day at St Paul's, Covent Garden. He was the eldest son of Sir Edward *Harley (1624–1700) of Brampton Bryan, Herefordshire, and his second wife, Abigail, *née* Stephens.

Early life and marriage Harley's father was a prominent Presbyterian who had played a conspicuous part on the parliamentary side in the civil war. Although he conformed to the Anglican church at the Restoration he sent Robert in 1671 to be educated at a school run by Samuel Birch, a dissenter, at Shilton in Oxfordshire. This upbringing led to some distrust later when Harley associated with high-church tories. Thus in 1710 the dean of Christ Church called him the 'spawn of a Presbyterian' (Feiling, 421). After Shilton he attended a school in London established by a Huguenot, Monsieur Foubert, but left it after a year, aged nineteen, apparently appalled at the moral danger he was exposed to there. In 1682 he was admitted as a member of the Inner Temple. On 14 May 1685 he married Elizabeth Foley (d. 1691) of Witley Court, Gloucestershire, the daughter of a whig ally of Robert's father. They had four children: Edward *Harley (1689–1741), who succeeded him as second earl of Oxford; Robert, who died in infancy in 1690; Elizabeth, who married Peregrine Hyde Osborne, second marquess of Carmarthen, in 1712 and died in November 1713; and Abigail, who married George Henry Hay, second earl of Kinnoull, who died on 15 July 1750. Harley's second wife, Sarah Middleton, whom he

Robert Harley, first earl of Oxford and Mortimer (1661–1724), by Sir Godfrey Kneller, 1714

married on 18 September 1694, died on 17 June 1737. This marriage was childless.

Country politician, 1689–1700 During the revolution of 1688 Harley and his father raised a troop of horse and went to Worcester, which they took for William, prince of Orange. Afterwards Harley complimented William on the success of his undertaking. In April 1689 he entered the House of Commons for the first time, at a by-election for Tregony. There he immediately revealed his zest for parliamentary activity, becoming one of the most assiduous members in the house. He was to acquire unrivalled experience and knowledge in the ways of procedure, which contributed considerably to his political advancement. As John Macky noted, 'no man knows better all the Tricks of the House' (*Memoirs of the Secret Services*, 84). It was for these skills that he became known as Robin the Trickster. Once at a whig dinner party he raised a glass to propose the toast of 'Love and Friendship and everlasting Union' and lamented that there was no Tokay to drink it in. This prompted Lord Cowper to remark that clear white Lisbon was more appropriate than the cloudy Hungarian wine, a remark which was a deliberate reference to:

> that humour of his, which was never to deal clearly and openly, but always with reserve, if not dissimulation or rather simulation; and to love tricks even when not necessary, but from an inward satisfaction he took in applauding his own cunning. If any man was ever born

under a necessity of being a knave, he was. (*Private Diary of … Cowper*, 30)

In 1690 Harley identified himself with the whigs, voting for the Sacheverell clause. He was consequently blacklisted as a 'Commonwealthsman' in the general election of 1690. Harley stood at New Radnor, where the returning officer declared that an opponent, Rowland Gwynne, had been duly elected. He petitioned against Gwynne's return and succeeded in replacing him as member for Radnor in November. The success of his petition in a predominantly tory Commons indicates that he was supported by tories as well as whigs, and this suggestion is reinforced by his being elected to the commission of public accounts on 26 December 1690 since the commission brought together back-bench whigs and tories. The commissioners were paid £500 per annum out of public funds and sat all year, in parliamentary recesses as well as sessions. Harley seems to have been the most constant attender, and presented the commission's reports, which helped him to emerge as the leader of the commission after being first elected to it with the lowest number of votes. Initially it was intended to be a back-bench watchdog on public expenditure, but when the government frustrated its enquiries it became more a political weapon in the hands of the opponents of the ministry. Since these consisted of tories such as Sir Thomas Clarges and Sir Christopher Musgrave, as well as whigs such as Harley and his ally Paul Foley, it was wielded by country opponents of the court party. As Harley's brother Edward observed, 'Whigs and Tories unite against the court in endeavouring to be frugal by good management' (*Portland MSS*, 3.481). Harley adopted a typical country stance in his support of place bills to eliminate placemen from the Commons, which the court managed to defeat in the Lords, and measures for more frequent elections, which eventually succeeded with the passage of the Triennial Act in 1694.

After the general election of 1695 Harley became the acknowledged leader of the court's opponents, receiving the highest number of votes cast for the commissioners of public accounts. He advocated the setting up of a Board of Trade by methods similar to those used to elect the commission, making it directly dependent upon parliament. The court managed, however, to ensure that, when the newly formed board was established in 1696, it was appointed by the crown and not by the Commons. Harley also proposed the creation of a land bank to cater for the landed interest as the Bank of England did for the monied interest. Although it was not financially unsound, as its critics claimed, it was launched at an inappropriate time, when the recoinage was affecting liquid capital adversely, and the subscription had to be abandoned through lack of support. A further setback to the country cause was the discovery of the assassination plot against William III, which created tensions between tories and whigs, especially over the pressure to join associations in defence of the king. Harley urged tories to join, and later opposed the attainder against Sir John Fenwick. These activities finally alienated him from the junto whigs who by then controlled the ministry. They also temporarily shattered the country alliance, and the junto were able to get their own nominees elected to the commission of public accounts in 1697, which effectively ended its career.

In the summer of 1697, however, the signing of the treaty of Ryswick ending the Nine Years' War presented Harley with an opportunity to revive the country opposition's fortunes. He undertook to ensure a major demobilization of troops in English pay against the court's efforts to keep as many on foot as possible. Anticipating his leading role in the standing army controversy, the court apparently approached him to offer the post of secretary of state, but he refused to be bought off. In the session of 1697–8 he successfully spearheaded the move to reduce the forces to 10,000 men. Following the general election of 1698, which was fought mainly over this and other issues dividing court from country, Harley was able to obtain a further reduction of the armed forces to 7000. His success is often seen as a triumph for what was called the new country party. By this time, however, Harley and his supporters were little more than the country whig tail which wagged a tory dog. Most whigs supported the court, while most tories were in opposition. Harley's gradual move towards the tory camp was consolidated in 1698 when he forged a political partnership with Lord Godolphin. Thus, when he sponsored a bill in 1700 to resume grants made by the king in Ireland, it was seen as a tory measure by ministers. The death that summer of the duke of Gloucester, Princess Anne's only surviving child, persuaded William that further arrangements for the succession were necessary. He was also convinced that this must be done by a change of ministry and in a new parliament.

Court politician, 1701–1706 The king alone with Harley thrashed out the conditions for the succession of the house of Hanover after Anne's death. The ministerial changes were negotiated with Harley and his tory ally Godolphin in concert with the earl of Rochester, Anne's uncle. Godolphin became lord treasurer, Rochester was appointed lord lieutenant of Ireland, and Harley accepted the court nomination for the speakership of the Commons.

Parliament was dissolved and a general election took place early in 1701. When parliament met in February Harley was elected speaker by 249 votes to 125 cast for a whig rival. As one observer noted, 'his six years' opposition to the Court followed by such a sudden turn to that side is made use of by his enemies to his disadvantage' (Bodl. Oxf., MS Ballard 6, fol. 35). The first major business before the house was the indictment of those whig members of the previous ministry who had advised the king to conclude partition treaties dividing the Spanish empire between Bourbon and Habsburg claimants. The main targets of the attack were the members of the junto, and Harley took a partisan role in it, especially in committees of the whole house, which allowed the speaker to participate in debate. As a country whig noted at the time, he 'was the principall man that had all along contrived their ruin' (*Diary of Sir Richard Cocks*, 158). This marked the parting of the ways between Harley and the whig leaders, who never forgot or forgave his attempt to impeach them. He

took the lead in guiding the Bill of Settlement through the house, which placed restrictions upon the powers of the crown before conferring it on to the house of Hanover.

When the Commons proved reluctant to vote supplies for a war which was becoming increasingly imminent, especially when Louis XIV recognized James II's son as king of England on James's death, William became increasingly impatient with his new ministers. In the summer of 1701 he negotiated the grand alliance to combat Bourbon claims to the whole Spanish inheritance and on his return to England dissolved parliament. Godolphin resigned in protest, and Harley made it clear that, while he was prepared to continue as speaker, he did not wish to do so as the court nominee. When the new parliament met in December he succeeded in retaining the speakership, albeit by the narrow margin of 216 votes to 212 cast for his rival, who was supported by the court. He again displayed flagrant partiality against the junto. Henry St John, already a henchman after a year in parliament, moved that the Commons had not had right done them by the Lords in the matter of the impeachments. Harley in committee spoke out against the Lords' defence of the junto. The session did not last long, however, for on 8 March 1702 William died and Anne became queen.

The accession of Queen Anne brought to the innermost circles of government Harley's close colleague Godolphin and his friends the duke and duchess of Marlborough. These formed the so-called Cockpit group, which included Harley by association. He was not immediately offered a major ministerial post, perhaps because Anne expressed a preference for staunch Anglicans to be her servants at this time. For although Harley attended the established church he also took his family to chapel. He none the less was the inevitable choice for speaker when the parliament elected in the summer of 1702 met. He also had a hand in drafting the queen's speech to parliament at the opening of the session. And by 1703 he was having meetings twice a week with Marlborough and Godolphin discussing matters to be decided by the cabinet. So close were the three men that they were referred to as 'the triumvirate'.

The 'triumvirs' were more attached to the queen than to a party. They acted as brokers between her and tory leaders, such as the earl of Nottingham, on the one hand and the whig junto on the other. Where Anne had preferred high-church tories in her first ministerial appointments, she quickly became disillusioned with them. Rochester resigned in 1703, to be followed by Nottingham in 1704. In the ministerial reconstruction that ensued Harley played a key role. Although he would have preferred to appoint moderate men who would support the court rather than a party, he accepted that there were not enough of them to govern without employing whig or tory leaders. In taking them into partnership with the court, however, they were to be treated as junior partners. Ministerial appointments at cabinet level were to be reserved as far as possible for men whose loyalty to the queen, like that of the triumvirs, was stronger than their ties to a party. Party zealots were to be admitted only into less influential posts. Harley himself replaced Nottingham, becoming secretary of state for the north. His henchmen Sir Thomas Mansell and Henry St John were promoted to the positions of comptroller of the household and secretary at war. St John was far from being a moderate, having espoused such high-church tory causes as the bills to outlaw occasional conformity, introduced into the Commons in the first two sessions of this parliament.

Occasional conformity bills to this effect had passed the Commons in the first two sessions of Anne's first parliament, but had been thwarted in the Lords. To obviate the opposition of the whig majority in the upper house to the measure, the high-church tories planned to tack it to a supply bill in the third session. The defeat of the tack in November 1704 was a major example of Harley's expert parliamentary management. An urgent note from Simon Harcourt warning him that the tack might succeed if he did not exert himself galvanized him into a canvass of moderate tories to ensure that they would oppose it. In his own words, 'thus this noisy, mischief-making, party-driving, good for nothing bill came to be utterly lost' (Harley, 'Faults on Both Sides', in Somers, ed. Scott, 12.691). Harley was so jubilant at this outcome not only on account of his own sympathy for dissent, but also because he hoped it would divide the tories permanently between tackers and those who opposed the tack, and that the latter could be relied on to support the court in future even in collaboration with moderate whigs. He himself initiated a move to recruit a moderate whig, the duke of Newcastle, to the ministry, and obtained his appointment to the post of lord privy seal in March 1705. He also expected to sustain the coalition through the general election of spring 1705, writing to the duke of Marlborough in April: 'I am more concern'd how to deal with them when they are chosen, than under doubt of having a great majority for the Queen and the public good' (BL, Add. MS 61123, fol. 142).

In the event the court's efforts to keep tackers out of parliament were not as successful as Harley had anticipated, for of the 134 tories who had voted for the tack no fewer than ninety were returned. Moreover, tory ranks closed during the election campaign. So, far from there being a great majority of moderate men prepared to support the court, the result was effectively a hung parliament, with the placemen holding the balance between whigs and tories. In the view of Godolphin this necessitated a greater *rapprochement* with the whigs than Harley felt to be desirable or necessary. He went along with the choice of a whig, John Smith, to replace himself as speaker of the Commons. But he was chagrined by the appointment of Lord Cowper as lord keeper. This caused the first breach in his relationship with the treasurer, which was to culminate in its complete breakdown early in 1708. The fissure really became a chasm in December 1706, when Marlborough and Godolphin obtained the secretaryship of state for the south for the earl of Sunderland despite the queen's protests, backed by Harley.

Meanwhile Harley played a major role in the forging of the union with Scotland. He himself became a commissioner for the union in April 1706 and employed Daniel Defoe as an agent to feed back reports to him about the state of feeling north of the border. He later took a cynical view of the negotiations which brought about the articles of union, saying of the Scots simply: 'we bought them' (*George Lockhart's Papers*, 1.327). Harley was ill during the debates on the articles and the Ratification Bill, having had what appeared to be a stroke ('estoit tombé dans une espece d'apoplexie'; *Correspondance diplomatique*, 6.248–9). He returned to the Commons in time to take part in a dispute about the effects on trade of the union when it came into effect on 1 May 1707. On that date customs duties were to become uniform in the new united kingdom of Great Britain, and in anticipation of that some merchants had imported goods into Scotland to take advantage of the lower rates there, intending to take them to England after 1 May. A petition was presented to parliament protesting against this, and Harley supported the protest and a measure to penalize the practice. This issue created a dispute between the Commons and the Lords, since the upper house regarded it as a breach of the union. Harley's stance on it has been seen as further evidence of his growing antagonism to Godolphin but in fact seems to have been a genuine objection to unfair trading, for at the same time he left his sickbed to rebut a tory motion critical of the subsidies paid to the Habsburg claimant to the Spanish throne. He was taken ill as he spoke and said that if he died he wanted it engraved on his tombstone that he was one of those who advised the queen to give these subsidies. The grants were vindicated by 254 votes to 105. Had they not been it would have been Godolphin (the real target of the tory proposal) who faced censure. Harley was therefore going out of his way to defend the treasurer on this issue.

In 1707 the first suspicions that Harley was actively obstructing their policies occurred to Marlborough and Godolphin over the appointment of bishops to the vacant sees of Chester and Exeter and Norwich. The fact that they wished to fill them with whig candidates offended Anne as a usurpation of her prerogative. Although Harley supported her in this stance he was not in fact responsible for advising her to promote tory clergymen to the vacancies. Nor was he as closely involved with the intrigues of Anne's new favourite, Abigail Masham, as the duumvirs feared. But that they suspected his scheming against them in the summer of 1707 shows how far their relationship was breaking down before the fall of Harley.

Out of office Harley's fall from office came about in February 1708 for reasons which remain mysterious. He was certainly making overtures to tories with a view to reconstructing the ministry and reversing the drift to the whigs. But this seems to have been done to some extent with Godolphin's knowledge if not his approval. The most plausible reason for the treasurer's charge of treachery against Harley, therefore, is that he at least did nothing to stop a virtual vote of censure on the government's handling of the war in Spain, and possibly helped to bring it about. The resolution of the Commons on 29 January, that of

29,000 men voted for the Spanish theatre only 8660 were present at the battle of Almanza the previous April, was aimed directly at his fellow secretary Sunderland and indirectly at the treasurer. On 7 February the duke of Marlborough wrote to Anne offering his resignation, protesting at 'the false and treacherous proceedings of Mr. Secretary Harley to Lord Treasurer and myself' (Coxe, 2.191). Next day the duumvirs absented themselves from the cabinet. Harley tried to address business there, but the duke of Somerset said: 'if her Majesty suffered that fellow … to treat affairs of the war without the advice of the General he could not serve her; and so left the council' (*Correspondence of Jonathan Swift*, 1.70). After the meeting broke up Anne was pressured by at least four cabinet ministers to dismiss Harley or they would resign. On 9 February further pressure was exerted by the whigs in parliament. In the Lords, Wharton moved an enquiry into the security in Harley's office at the Cockpit, where a clerk, William Gregg, had been caught sending copies of official correspondence to France. A select committee of seven staunch whigs was set up to investigate the affair. The implication was clear that Harley was to be impeached, and well he might have been if Gregg had not resisted the temptation to implicate him. Anne now admitted that the game was up and informed Marlborough that she would ask Harley to resign. On 11 February he resigned, and three of his close associates left office with him: Sir Simon Harcourt, the attorney-general; Thomas Mansell, comptroller of the household; and Henry St John, secretary at war. They immediately joined with the ministry's tory opponents. On 24 February the Almanza business came to a conclusion with a tory motion that the deficiencies of English troops at the battle were due to a lack of timely recruits. Harley, who ostentatiously read a book during the debate and said not a word, voted for the motion. The court, however, was able to defeat it by 230 votes to 175.

The tories hoped to make headway against the court after the general election of 1708 despite the fact that it had resulted in a whig majority. This was because the whigs were split, even grooming rival candidates for the speakership over the summer. There was talk of Harley standing again for the chair as the tory candidate, but in the event the tories rallied round William Bromley. Harley dropped any pretensions he might have entertained and assured Bromley that he would serve him heartily. The death of Anne's husband, Prince George, however, brought the whig divisions to a temporary close. Once they had agreed on a single candidate for the speakership there was no way the tories could carry one against him.

Although he had allied with the tories since his fall, Harley did not commit himself entirely to them. At some time in the spring of 1708 he was in correspondence with the whig duke of Shrewsbury, who had returned from a self-imposed exile in Italy in 1706. Harley's strategy seems to have been to get his revenge on the duumvirs and their immediate henchmen, such as Sunderland, rather than to overthrow the entire ministry. He spelt out his objections to 'the family', as he called them in a draft pamphlet written in the summer of 1708, 'Plain English to all who are honest or would be so if they knew how'. They were deliberately prolonging the war for their own personal gain and keeping up party divisions artificially in order to retain their hold on power. Harley is often seen as scheming constantly with the queen from his fall in 1708 until his return to power in 1710. In fact he appears to have lain low, and to have seen her rarely, though they did correspond. He seems to have bided his time until an opportunity arose to bring down the duumvirs. This did not occur until the ill-fated decision of the whig ministers to impeach Dr Sacheverell in November 1709. Harley, who had not even bothered to leave Herefordshire for the start of the session, arrived in London in January 1710 determined to exploit the changed political situation for his own advantage. His hand can be seen behind the ministerial changes which ensued on the virtual acquittal of Sacheverell. The very first beneficiary was his ally Shrewsbury, who became lord chamberlain in April. Sunderland followed in June. Anne was reluctant to get rid of Godolphin, making Harley impatiently note in a memorandum for an audience with her on 3 July: 'get quit of him' (Hill, 128). Yet it was not until 8 August that she did.

Prime minister The Treasury was then put into commission, filled with Harleyites, Harley himself being one. He also became chancellor of the exchequer. And that was probably where the ministerial revolution of 1710 would have ended if Harley had had his way. For he intended 'only the removal of the treasurer and his immediate dependents, with some others, to make room for his own friends, and then to have continued the parliament and the war with the duke of Marlborough in the command of it' (*Bishop Burnet's History*, 6.13). Certainly Harley made overtures even to members of the whig junto at this time, urging them not to resign despite the changes that were afoot. Moreover they were prepared to entertain his approach, at least in the short run. They did not resign even when Sunderland, one of their own, was dismissed in June. Lord Halifax was the most responsive to Harley's appeal, and indeed the two sustained a curiously friendly relationship long after the negotiations collapsed. The whigs, however, declined to come into his scheme when he could not give guarantees that there would not be a dissolution of parliament that year. Their resolve stiffened by Thomas, earl of Wharton, who was the least inclined to listen to Harley's assurances, they broke off the communications. Harley had then to turn more to the tories than he had wished. Thus, although the earl of Nottingham was kept out of office, the earl of Rochester became president of the council. On 21 September Anne dissolved parliament, and in the ensuing elections the tories got more seats than Harley desired. For he was determined to maintain a whig presence at all levels of his administration. Even the cabinet contained the duke of Newcastle until his death in 1711 and the duke of Somerset until his dismissal in 1712.

This caused concern among some back-bench tories, who organized themselves early in 1711 into the October Club, pledged among other aims to purge whigs from posts in the government from top to bottom. They were thrown a sop with the dismissal of Robert Walpole from the treasurership of the navy. They also felt the strain of direct taxation and sought a speedy peace. One of their first successes was to defeat a measure laying a tax on leather. War weariness and objections to the tax burden had already caused a credit crisis, due to a reduction in the revenues received by the Treasury. Harley, to whom the passage of this bill was vital, managed to retrieve the situation by the dubious procedural device of reintroducing it immediately as a tax on hides and skins. He also contrived to lay the blame for the financial straits he faced on the previous ministry by getting supporters in the Commons to claim that there was £35 million unaccounted for. This gave the October Club a hare to chase, but financial stability had to be achieved by more serious measures. Harley managed to improve revenues by raising money from lotteries in the spring of 1711. The crisis was finally resolved by his successful launching in May of the South Sea Company, which assumed the unfunded debt in exchange for trading privileges to be negotiated in the peace treaties ending the War of the Spanish Succession.

Harley's success was crowned by his being promoted to the position of lord treasurer and by his elevation to the peerage as earl of Oxford and Mortimer on 23 May 1711. His personal prestige was never higher than at this time, for he had survived an assassination attempt by a French spy, the marquis de Guiscard, on 8 March. Guiscard was being examined by the lords of the committee—the cabinet meeting without the queen's being present—when he produced a knife and stabbed the prime minister. Only the heavy gold-thread embroidery, lovingly sewn to his coat by his devoted sister Abigail, prevented the blow from being fatal, for it broke the blade of the knife. Even then a second stab with the broken blade seriously wounded Harley, and he was obliged to take to his bed for six weeks. His confinement generated considerable sympathy, so much so that Henry St John jealously let it be spread abroad that the blow was intended for himself.

Relations with St John St John indeed began in February 1711 to exploit the October Club's frustration with Harley's moderation to build it up into a power base for himself. The two had drifted apart following their joint departure from the ministry in 1708, and in the ministerial revolution of 1710 Harley had not at first intended to give St John a major post. Although in the event he did become secretary of state he resented the initial slight. Thus began a rivalry between them which was to bedevil politics for the rest of the reign. When Harley was recuperating from Guiscard's attack St John had to play a greater part in government than had previously been the case. Above all he was let into the secret of the negotiations with France towards peace which Harley and Shrewsbury had kept to themselves. While maintaining publicly Britain's commitment to the war aims of the grand alliance, they had been discussing privately with the French government through the informal agency of the earl of Jersey terms which were inconsistent with those aims. Thus the allies had been committed since 1703 to ensuring that Spain and the Spanish West Indies went

to the Habsburg candidate. But after the allied defeat at Almanza in 1707, and above all at Brihuega in 1710, they accepted that this was no longer achievable. Nor with the death of the emperor in April 1711, and the prospect of the Habsburg candidate's succeeding to the Austrian territories of the family, was it even desirable any more. For the whole War of the Spanish Succession had been fought to prevent either the Bourbons or the Habsburgs obtaining the lion's share of the Spanish empire and consolidating it with their own possessions. Once he was privy to the dual nature of the peace negotiations, St John was prepared to be more open than Harley about dropping the slogan 'No peace without Spain' and to risk alienating the Dutch by encouraging public criticism of them such as Jonathan Swift's *The Conduct of the Allies*. But the notion that St John took over responsibility for negotiating a treaty from Oxford is a myth. The prime minister remained in charge throughout the summer of 1711 in the discussions conducted by Matthew Prior in France, which culminated in the preliminaries which were signed in London on 27 September. While he did not attack the Dutch openly, 'he often played Walrus to St John's Carpenter, meekly bemoaning … the Dutch morsels which St John was wolfing down in the Commons' (MacLachlan, 211).

The use by some historians of the term 'the Harley–St John ministry' for the government at this time is an even bigger myth. That Oxford was prime minister he demonstrated in the ministerial changes of that year, when he persuaded the queen to appoint Lord Jersey to the post of lord privy seal, made vacant by the death of the duke of Newcastle. Ironically Jersey died on the very day he was to assume his duties, and the position then went to John Robinson, the bishop of Bristol, in a typically Harleyite coup. It brought into the cabinet a tory churchman and took some of the sting out of the failure to bring in the earl of Nottingham. Nottingham himself was driven to desperation. In the winter he allied with the whig junto to oppose the peace preliminaries in return for their support for an Occasional Conformity Bill. The result was that, while the terms were passed comfortably by the Commons, a motion that no peace could be safe or honourable which ceded Spain and the Indies to the Bourbon candidate was passed, despite all Oxford's managerial skills, by one vote in the Lords. Among those who voted in the majority against the government was the captain-general Marlborough. To add to Oxford's discomfort the queen, who attended the debate, was led from the house by the duke of Somerset, who, like Marlborough, though a member of the government, had voted for the whig motion. As the prime minister said to Swift: 'the hearts of kings are unsearchable' (Swift, *Journal*, 2.434).

But Anne's unsteadiness was short-lived, and over the Christmas recess Oxford persuaded her not only to dismiss peers in her service who had voted against the preliminaries, including Marlborough, but also to create twelve new lords to give his ministry a majority in the upper house. He himself drew up a list of twenty men from which Anne chose the famous dozen. It was very much a Harleyite team. The prime minister had reasserted his control over the ministry and over the Lords, as the majority for the government's motion to adjourn when the house resumed its sitting on 2 January revealed. Despite problems with the October Club, he had retained the support of the Commons, where a motion similar to the one on the peace preliminaries which had passed in the Lords was easily defeated. Now he rewarded the backbench tories by encouraging resolutions against Marlborough and Walpole, accusing them of corruption. Walpole was consequently expelled from the Commons and spent some time in the Tower. Oxford in fact had so far ingratiated himself with the October Club that a hard core of its membership, disturbed by the way he had undermined its independence, seceded and formed the March Club on 24 March 1712. They also differed from the rank-and-file Octobrists by suspecting that the prime minister was prepared to conclude a dishonourable peace and even to open up the possibility of restoring the direct Stuart line on Anne's death. By contrast, the main body of the October Club yearned for peace at almost any price, while some were out-and-out Jacobites.

Although Oxford had no intention of pursuing either end, his natural inclination to cloud issues and keep options open fed these suspicions, so that even some modern historians have been misled into suspecting him of Jacobitism. In fact his proudest achievement as speaker was piloting the Act of Settlement through the Commons, and he had his portrait painted holding the statute in his hand. And in March 1712 he sent his cousin Thomas Harley to Hanover, taking with him an act giving the house of Hanover precedence in the British peerage. Any hints he gave Jacobite tories that he would promote the Pretender's interests were deliberately intended to dupe them. On the peace issue, however, he was more vulnerable. He continued to intrigue with the French privately even after the peace conference opened at Utrecht in January. Previously his whole strategy had been to wage a vigorous war in order to keep the pressure on the French during the negotiations. But with the dismissal of Marlborough and his replacement by the duke of Ormond the pressure was undoubtedly eased, especially when the new commander was given so-called restraining orders to avoid engaging the enemy. Yet a parliamentary effort to condemn both the orders and the negotiations ended in a triumph for the prime minister. He rewarded those who had supported his strategy by promotions at the end of the session, which brought the ministry nearer to being dependent upon the tory party by the summer of 1712 than he had intended two years previously.

Oxford had recovered from the near fatal setback of the vote on the peace preliminaries to a position of apparently impregnable strength. Yet it was at this time that St John, who had begun to cultivate the frustrations of backbench tories against his former 'master' in February 1711, chose to make his first challenge to him. Lord Bolingbroke, as St John became at the end of June, was chagrined at being elevated to the peerage as a mere viscount, which he blamed on Oxford but which in fact was due to the queen's dislike of his libertinism. On 28 September he opposed the prime minister in cabinet, recommending the immediate signing of a separate peace with France. Although Oxford outmanoeuvred him, the clash was so violent that Anne was reduced to tears. The protraction of the peace negotiations in order to make the subsequent settlement at Utrecht a general treaty kept parliament prorogued for ten months. During the prorogation Oxford tried to maximize support for the treaty, even assuring whigs that: 'if we were at the Gates of Paris, we could not have a better Peace than what we were now to have' (*Private Diary of … Cowper*, 54).

The treaty was eventually signed on 31 March 1713. When parliament finally met on 9 April there was a majority in both houses in favour of the general terms of the peace, which in any case did not need the sanction of parliament. But a commercial treaty with France which formed articles 8 and 9 needed the approval of the Commons, and here disaster struck for the ministry. On 18 June a rebellion by tory back-benchers, known as whimsicals, defeated the bill to ratify the clauses by 194 to 185 votes. Meanwhile Oxford had come close to losing control of the Lords, upon a motion by disgruntled Scottish peers on 1 June to bring in a bill to dissolve the union. Their disgruntlement, and that of the forty-five Scots in the Commons, arose from a measure laying a uniform duty on malt throughout Great Britain in flagrant disregard of the principle of equitable taxation guaranteed at the union. A motion to set aside a day to debate the bill failed by only four votes.

Bolingbroke's challenge The end of the session, and the approach of a general election required by the Triennial Act, brought the rivalry of Bolingbroke and Oxford to a head as each jockeyed to be in position to exploit the parliamentary situation. Oxford emerged ahead of his rival, having reconstructed the ministry over the summer in ways which demonstrated his continued mastery. Thus his close ally William Bromley was made secretary of state for the north in place of Dartmouth, and Bolingbroke was moved to the southern secretariat, where he no longer had responsibility for dealings with the Dutch. Although Bolingbroke wanted rid of Dartmouth, he scarcely wished him to be replaced by a leading high-church tory whose loyalty lay with Oxford rather than with himself. Besides, Dartmouth's loyal services were retained, as he obtained the post of lord privy seal. The duke of Shrewsbury was made lord lieutenant of Ireland, where he would be out of harm's way after having flirted alarmingly with Bolingbroke's rash ambitions. Another blow to Bolingbroke's aspiration to put himself at the head of the tories was Oxford's coup in persuading Sir Thomas Hanmer to be speaker in the new parliament. The only sop to Bolingbroke's tory cronies was the promotion of Sir William Wyndham to the chancellorship of the exchequer, though that did not give him a seat in the cabinet. Thus the reconstructed ministry which fought the general election of 1713 was more Harleyite in its composition than ever.

At the polls the tory victory was greater than in 1710, returning a majority of more than 200 over the whigs. But the tories were by now seriously divided between Hanoverians and Jacobites, while their opponents were united behind the protestant succession. To some extent the divisions in the tory ranks reflected that in the ministry between the staunchly Hanoverian Oxford and a Bolingbroke more and more inclined to reopen the option of a second Stuart restoration, as prospects for the tories looked bleaker and bleaker in the next reign. The dilemma was brought home in December 1713, when Anne fell gravely ill for over a month.

Oxford, who had been riding high in the summer, felt his influence eclipsed by Bolingbroke in the closing months of 1713. In September he made the fatal mistake of asking for a dukedom for his son, who had just married the daughter of the late duke of Newcastle. Anne, who was jealous of her prerogative of ennobling men, despite, or perhaps even because of, being forced to create twelve new peers in 1712 at Oxford's behest, and was particularly concerned to preserve the nobility's highest ranks against new creations, refused. Oxford himself regretted the 'never enough to be lamented folly' of requesting the title (*Portland MSS*, 5.466). In November his daughter, the marchioness of Carmarthen, died, and her death was a devastating blow to him. Prostrated with grief, he left off attending the queen even in her illness. He also seems to have taken to drink for solace at this time, so that even when he did appear at court Anne was offended by his being under the influence of alcohol. Meanwhile Bolingbroke ingratiated himself with the queen, indulging her dread of having any member of the house of Hanover residing in England while she lived. He also won over Lady Masham and used her intimacy with the queen to promote his own interests against those of Oxford.

By March 1714 Oxford was sufficiently depressed by these developments to contemplate resignation. Something of his confused state of mind at that time comes through a bizarre motion he made in the Lords on 17 March to bring in a bill to make it high treason to introduce foreign troops into the kingdom. As the whigs pointed out, this would affect the house of Hanover as well as the Pretender, and the prime minister withdrew the motion. These proceedings also highlighted the fact that the succession was very much in the minds of politicians when parliament assembled in March for the first time since the general election. It informed the debate in the Commons to censure Sir Richard Steele for claiming in print that it was in danger under Oxford's ministry. Although Steele was duly censured and expelled from the house, a significant minority of Hanoverian tories voted in his favour. Moreover, the main thrust of his charge, that the succession was in danger under the present administration, was repeated by the whigs in the Lords on 5 April. The court replied with a motion that the succession was not in danger under her majesty's government. During the debate Oxford put his hand on his heart and challenged any peer present to question his own zeal for the protestant succession. Nevertheless the motion was carried by only twelve votes, leading one whig to claim that Oxford had been saved by his dozen. A similar vote in the Commons on 15 April was carried for the ministry by only forty-eight votes, revealing that a great many tories as well as all the whigs were worried about the prospects for the protestant succession when Anne died.

Meanwhile the whigs had kept up the momentum by encouraging the Hanoverian envoy to apply to the lord chancellor for a writ summoning the electoral prince to the House of Lords in his capacity as duke of Cambridge. Anne took umbrage at his not applying to her first, and Oxford used this lapse in protocol to demand the envoy's being summoned to return to Hanover. The duke of Cambridge did not take his seat after all. As Oxford himself said, were he to do so it would 'drive every body to the wall' (Oxford to Cowper, 12 May 1714, Herts. ALS, Panshanger MSS). But the issues raised by the incident caused the last breach between the prime minister and the queen, who believed that Oxford himself was responsible for engineering the request for the writ. Though this was utterly untrue it led her to suspect his loyalty to her, suspicions which Bolingbroke and Lady Masham sedulously fostered. This brought the quarrel between the two leading ministers out into the open. By the middle of May, rival tory factions in parliament openly sided with either the prime minister or the secretary of state. At court Oxford felt his influence with the queen being superseded by that of Bolingbroke. The most conspicuous sign of this was the appointment in June of the Jacobite earl of Clarendon as envoy-extraordinary to Hanover instead of his own nominee, Lord Paget. Sensing that his days in office were numbered, Oxford made overtures to the whigs in an endeavour to secure the protestant succession in the event of a Jacobite ministry headed by Bolingbroke.

Bolingbroke tried to hasten his downfall by promoting the so-called Schism Bill, outlawing the separate educational establishments of the dissenters. He felt sure that this measure would wrong-foot the prime minister. For if Oxford opposed it he would complete his alienation from Anne, while if he supported it his lines of communication with the whigs would be severed. His immediate reaction to the dilemma was to begin on 6 June to draw up a 'very brief account of her Majesty's affairs' (*Portland MSS*, 5.464–6), which was clearly intended to be his personal vindication on leaving office. Yet he got off the hook by supporting a whig amendment to the bill, which minimized its impact by reducing the proposed penalties while not opposing the measure in principle. As one whig put it, 'he castrated the Bill' (Holmes). Oxford used his unrivalled mastery of parliamentary tactics not only to emasculate the Schism Bill but also to prolong the session as long as possible in order to put a brake on Bolingbroke's schemes. Just as his rival had hoped to discredit him by sponsoring the Schism Act, so he took the offensive by persuading the cabinet to approve a proclamation placing a price on the Pretender's head. Bolingbroke managed to restrict the reward to £5000 at that juncture, but Oxford outmanoeuvred him in parliament by getting the Commons to increase it to £100,000. The debate aligned Oxford's supporters with Hanoverian tories and whigs against the Jacobite tories. This combination in both houses kept the pressure on Bolingbroke for the rest of the session, pursuing an enquiry that he had been corrupt in his dealings with the South Sea Company and the concessions obtained for it from Spain in the commercial treaty he had negotiated with that country. Oxford was so convinced that his rival would be completely discredited that on 3 July he advised the queen to dismiss him.

Anne, however, stood by the secretary, and put an end to the session on 9 July. Oxford realized that his own days were numbered too, but determined to be dismissed rather than resign. The blow fell on 27 July. The queen made public her reasons for dismissing the prime minister:

> that he neglected all business; that he was seldom to be understood; that, when he did explain himself, she could not depend upon the truth of what he said; that he never came to her at the time appointed; that he often came drunk; lastly, to crown all, he behaved himself towards her with bad manners, indecency and disrespect. (*Correspondence of Jonathan Swift*, 2.86)

Some of these charges ring true. Oxford's characteristically opaque way of speaking and writing did make him hard to understand, bewildering and even infuriating contemporaries. He was generally unpunctual. Since the death of his daughter he had sought solace in the bottle. But others were contrived. As Geoffrey Holmes observes: 'few Lord Treasurers had ever shown more personal deference to their sovereign than Oxford, and few had discharged their financial responsibilities more conscientiously' (Holmes). As Lord Dartmouth wrote of his ministry, it represented 'a four years cessation from plunder' (Burnet, 6.50). Bolingbroke's triumph was short-lived. On 30 July the queen collapsed. The privy council was summoned, and Oxford took his seat on it the following day. He therefore played his part in the contingencies made for the peaceful accession of the house of Hanover in the event of Anne's death, which indeed occurred on 1 August.

Later life Despite his efforts on behalf of the protestant succession, Oxford found himself *persona non grata* on the accession of George I. He was associated with the peace of Utrecht, which in the new king's view had been a betrayal of the allies—of which the electorate of Hanover was one. Consequently he was stripped of all his remaining offices—his deputy lieutenancies of Herefordshire and Radnorshire, his post as *custos rotulorum* of the latter county, even the stewardship of Sherwood Forest. His disgrace was completed in 1715 with his impeachment by the triumphant whigs. Where Bolingbroke reacted to being impeached by fleeing to France, Oxford with characteristic phlegm stayed to face his accusers. As he told his brother, he had decided to resign himself to Providence, 'and not either by flight or any other way to sully the honour of my Royal Mistress, though now in her grave, nor stain my own innocence even for an hour' (*Portland MSS*, 5.663). On 9 July the Commons brought sixteen articles of impeachment against him. He defended himself robustly, warning the Lords that, 'if ministers of state, acting by the immediate commands of their Sovereign, are afterwards to be made accountable for their proceedings, it may one day be the case of all the Members of this august assembly' (Cobbett, *Parl. hist.*, 7.106). This did not stop them from committing him to the Tower nor the Commons from producing six further articles against him. Where the previous articles had mostly concerned the making of the treaty of Utrecht, these accused him of Jacobitism. Though there were rumours that he dabbled in Jacobite intrigue while in the Tower, these were never substantiated. Oxford indeed was never attracted to the Pretender's cause, and in 1721 wrote to Lord Foley that 'we enjoy liberty, property and the Protestant Succession' (Hill, 234). The articles of impeachment were never pressed, and when Oxford petitioned for his trial to be brought on in June 1717 they were dropped. He was thereby acquitted. The king, however, never forgave him. He was omitted from the Act of Grace and forbidden to appear at court. Nevertheless he appeared in the House of Lords and contributed to debates, taking a leading role in the opposition to the Mutiny Bill in 1718 and the Peerage Bill in 1719.

Library and writings Oxford left behind him one of the largest collections of manuscripts of the English Augustan age. His own papers are voluminous, for he seems to have kept everything from cabinet minutes to his claret bills. In addition he acquired a large corpus of medieval and later manuscripts which form the Harleian collection, now housed, like most of his private papers, in the British Library. By 1721 the Harleian collection numbered some 6000 volumes, 14,000 charters, and 500 rolls. Humphrey Wanley, his librarian, began the catalogue of these in 1708. They included the collections of Sir Simonds D'Ewes, John Foxe the martyrologist, and John Stow the surveyor of London. Oxford also collected books, and by 1715 owned a library of some 3000 volumes, many of them expensively bound in leather or velvet. He was also a writer himself, composing occasional verse and political pamphlets such as *Faults on Both Sides*, published in 1710.

Oxford was one of the first politicians to be aware of the importance of journalism, a relatively new phenomenon, in the political system which emerged after the revolution of 1688. In 1704 he was instrumental in getting Defoe to write for the ministry in his *Review*, and he renewed his professional relationship with him when he became prime minister in 1710, though by then he was also engaging Swift to support his administration in *The Examiner*. His political instincts were well developed in other respects, for in many ways he was the most completely professional politician of his age. It was virtually a new profession, for a career as a member of parliament could be followed only after the revolution, when the House of Commons itself became a permanent institution with annual sessions. Harley grasped the implications of this novel situation quicker than most. At parliamentary management he became the consummate craftsman. This skill did not depend upon oratory, for he was not a good speaker. Rather it relied on endless hours of patient work building up an astonishing range of contacts who could be used to defend or oppose developments in parliament. Although his deviousness created enemies at the time and critics ever since, he could also inculcate the warmest friendships and command respect for his abilities from historians. In many ways he was the most significant individual in the tortuous politics of what is widely known as the first age of party.

Following his prominent role in opposing the Peerage Bill, Oxford took little part in debates, but entered a steady decline in his health. He died at Albemarle Street, London, on 21 May 1724 and was buried at Brampton Bryan church, Herefordshire. **W. A. SPECK**

Sources BL, Harley MSS · Longleat House, Wiltshire, Harley MSS · U. Nott., Harley MSS · G. Holmes, 'The great ministry, 1700–1714', typescript to be deposited at IHR · *The manuscripts of his grace the duke of Portland*, 10 vols., HMC, 29 (1891–1931), vols. 3, 5 · B. W. Hill, *Robert Harley: speaker, secretary of state and prime minister* (1988) · *The private diary of William, first Earl Cowper, lord chancellor of England*, ed. [E. C. Hawtrey], Roxburghe Club (1833) · *The parliamentary diary of Sir Richard Cocks, 1698–1702*, ed. D. W. Hayton (1996) · K. Feiling, *A history of the tory party, 1640–1714* (1924) · *Memoirs of the secret services of John Macky*, ed. J. M. Grey, Roxburghe Club (1895) · W. A. Speck, *The birth of Britain: a new nation, 1701–1710* (1994) · J. A. Downie, *Robert Harley and the press* (1979) · A. McInnes, *Robert Harley: puritan politician* (1970) · W. A. Speck and J. A. Downie, 'Introduction' to R. Harley, 'Plaine English to all who are honest', *Literature and History*, 3 (1976), 100–10 · J. Swift, *Journal to Stella*, ed. H. Williams, 2 vols. (1948) · *The correspondence of Jonathan Swift*, ed. H. Williams, 5 vols. (1963–5) · *Bishop Burnet's History* · R. Harley, 'Faults on both sides', *A collection of scarce and valuable tracts … Lord Somers*, ed. W. Scott, 2nd edn, 12 (1814), 678–707, esp. 691 · *Correspondance diplomatique et militaire du duc de Marlborough, du grand-pensionnaire Heinsius, et du trésorier-général des Provinces-Unies, Jacques Hop*, ed. G. G. Vreede (Amsterdam, 1850) · W. Coxe, *Memoirs of John, duke of Marlborough, with his original correspondence*, 3 vols. (1818–19) · A. D. MacLachlan, 'The road to peace, 1710–1713', *Britain after the glorious revolution*, ed. G. Holmes (1969), 197–215 · Harley correspondence, Herts. ALS, Panshanger MSS · BL, Add. MS 61123, fol. 142 [Harley correspondence] · Bodl. Oxf., MS Ballard 6, fol. 35 · Cobbett, *Parl. hist.*, 7.106 **Archives** BL, corresp. and papers, Add. MSS 18249–18265; Add. MSS 70011–70051, 70088, 70382–70383, 70419 · BL, Harley MSS 7523–7526 · BL, list of books and notes thereon, Add. MSS 70077–70078 · Longleat House, corresp. and papers · U. Nott., Harleian MSS | BL, Cavendish-Bentinck MSS · BL, letters to James Dayrolle, Add. MS 15866 · BL, letters to son-in-law, third duke of Leeds, Egerton MS 3385A · BL, letters to John Robinson, Add. MS 34677 · BL, corresp. with Alexander Stanhope, Stowe MSS 223–248, *passim* · BL, corresp. with George Stepney, Add. MSS 61142–61144, 61502 · BL, corresp. with Charles Whitworth, Add. MSS 37352–37356 · CKS, corresp. with Alexander Stanhope · Herts. ALS, letters to first Earl Cowper **Likenesses** P. Angelis, group portrait, oils, *c*.1713 (Queen Anne and the knights of the garter), NPG · G. Kneller, oils, 1714, NPG [*see illus.*] · J. Richardson, oils, *c*.1718, Christ Church Oxf. · attrib. J. Richardson, portrait, Longleat House, Wiltshire · oils (after G. Kneller), NPG

Harley, Robert (1828–1910), mathematician and Congregational minister, was born on 23 January 1828 at Seacombe, near Liverpool, the third son of Robert Harley of Dunfermline, Fife, merchant and Wesleyan minister, and his wife, Mary Stevenson, daughter of William Stevenson and niece of General Stevenson of Ayr.

As a child he detested arithmetic but his mathematical aptitude developed rapidly while he was at school at Blackburn. At the age of sixteen he became a mathematics master at Seacombe. In 1845 he returned as head assistant master to his old school at Blackburn, kept by William Hoole, a notable mayor of the town.

In 1851 Harley became a divinity student at Airedale Independent college, Bradford, and on completing his course entered the Congregational ministry at Brighouse, Yorkshire. On 17 November 1854 he married Sara Stroyan (1820/21–1905) of Burnley, daughter of James Stroyan, a draper, and a niece of William Hoole. They had four children. While at Brighouse Harley preached with William Booth, later famous as the founder of the Salvation Army. Concurrently, he served as professor of mathematics and logic at Airedale (1864–8). He was a notable admirer of the mathematician George Boole, who visited Brighouse frequently. After Boole's death in 1864 Harley gave several lectures on Boole's logic and produced a masterly biographical sketch for the *British Quarterly Review* (1866).

Harley's lifelong devotion to mathematics began in 1844 with attempts to solve problems posed in the *Lady's and Gentleman's Diary*. In this context he made the acquaintance of James Cockle, later a distinguished mathematician and judge. His first full paper was on the subject of impossible equations (1851), and he focused thereafter on the study of algebraic equations of the fifth degree. He and Cockle were in almost daily correspondence on the subject, particularly from 1858 to 1862. The basic problem of their research was the determination of a certain sextic equation (termed a 'resolvent'), upon which the solution of the quintic equation would depend. They were unaware of G. Malfatti's and C. G. Jacobi's earlier and similar attempts. Partly coinciding with Cockle's conclusions, Harley's independent results, published principally in the *Memoirs of the Manchester Literary and Philosophical Society* and in the *Quarterly Journal of Mathematics* (1860–62), immediately impressed Arthur Cayley and Boole, who made their own additions to his theory. Boole was particularly attracted by Harley's connection between algebraic and differential equations. With their support, Harley was elected a fellow of the Royal Society in 1863.

In 1868 Harley left Brighouse to serve as a pastor in Leicester (1868–72), and then moved to Mill Hill, near London, as vice-master of Mill Hill School. There he supervised the erection of a public lecture hall, opened by his friend, Earl Stanhope. From 1882 to 1886 he was principal of Huddersfield College, Yorkshire, and from 1886 to 1890 minister of the Congregational church at Oxford. On arrival in Oxford he was made an honorary MA by the university and he later took part in the foundation of the Oxford Mathematical Society. He also lectured before the Ashmolean Society on Boole's 'Laws of thought'.

About 1891 Harley was offered a permanent position as minister to a Congregational church in Sydney, Australia. However, he stayed for only eight months, feeling the need to return to his family in Britain. In 1895, after serving as pastor at Halifax, he retired and settled at Forest Hill, London. His energy and industry were unimpaired to the last; he fulfilled preaching engagements in London and the provinces, and was unceasing in the public advocacy of temperance. The only project he left incomplete was a treatise on quintics. He was a versatile man, of merry conversation, and he delivered his last sermon just a few days before his death. He died at the age of eighty-two, at his home, Rosslyn, 15 Westbourne Road, Forest Hill, on 26 July 1910, and was buried in Ladywell cemetery.   H. T. M. BELL, rev. MARIA PANTEKI

Sources P. A. M., *PRS*, 91A (1915), i–v · R. H. [R. Harley], *PRS*, 59 (1895–6), xxx–xxxix [obit. of Sir J. Cockle] · D. MacHale, *George Boole, his life and work* (1985) · m. cert. · d. cert.
Archives RAS, letters to RAS
Wealth at death £1271 18s. 7d.: probate, 21 Sept 1910, *CGPLA Eng. & Wales*

Harley, Thomas (1730–1804), politician and banker, was born at Eywood, Herefordshire, on 24 August 1730, the fourth son of five among the seven children of Edward *Harley (*bap.* 1699, *d.* 1755), a politician, who in 1741 succeeded his cousin as third earl of Oxford and Mortimer, and his wife, Martha (*d.* 1774), the eldest daughter of John Morgan of Tredegar, Monmouthshire. He was educated at Westminster School (1738–48). As 'the Hon. Thomas Harley', he was apprenticed in 1749 to the merchant Edmund Bockin of Size Lane, London, for the unusually large premium of £735. On 15 March 1752 he married Anne (*d.* 1798), the eldest daughter of Edward Bangham, a politician, who had served as deputy auditor of the imprest under Harley's paternal grandfather, Edward *Harley (1664–1735). They had two sons and five daughters. After his marriage Harley used his wife's considerable fortune to set up as a wine merchant at 152 Aldersgate Street. During the Seven Years' War he diversified, purveying clothing to militia regiments, and in 1761, as a freeman of the Goldsmiths' Company, he was backed by the merchants' committee as parliamentary candidate for London. Having succeeded in a contested election in April 1761, he was elected alderman for the Portsoken ward the following month and admitted to the livery of the Goldsmiths' Company, of which he served as prime warden from 1762 to 1763. He first spoke in the Commons on 11 March 1762, and was listed as favourable to the peace preliminaries. An opponent of the cider tax in 1763, he spoke in favour of the Grenville ministry's general warrants to apprehend the authors and publishers of seditious libels on 14 February 1764, but voted against, under pressure from his constituency, on 18 February. He was then a sheriff of London, and had been thanked by parliament for carrying out its orders to burn no. 45 of the *North Briton* at the Royal Exchange the previous December, when a mob had broken his coach glass, scratching his forehead. A mayoral casting vote thwarted a bid to carry a vote of thanks to him from the corporation then, but on 21 February 1764 the common council voted thanks to the London MPs for their opposition to general warrants. On 22 February 1766, Harley voted against the repeal of the Stamp Act, reviled by the American colonies, and he supported the Chatham ministry except on the land tax.

Harley was a precocious choice as lord mayor of London in Michaelmas 1767, and had to deal with a weavers' riot early in 1768 which he assuaged by distributing fish. In March 1768 he was re-elected, head of the poll, for London, defeating John Wilkes. Two sarcastic letters addressed to him by a fellow alderman were published in consequence. A mob broke the Mansion House windows in his absence when Wilkes petitioned for the Middlesex seat in May 1768. Harley's fearless confrontation of them earned him a laudatory address from both houses of parliament to the king, and the offer of a knighthood and a pension. These he declined in favour of the exceptional honour of being sworn of the privy council on 27 May. Though lampooned in the satirical *Rape of the Petticoat* of 3 May 1768, he was the subject of an admirer's *Epistle* in 1769. A year later, however, a mob frustrated his attempt to present a loyal address to George III on the birth of Princess Elizabeth. He had voted with the ministry for Wilkes's expulsion from the house on 3 February 1769, but against them, under pressure, on the seating of Wilkes's opponent Luttrell on 15 April. In general a supporter of Lord North's ministry, he was regarded as the leader of the party loyal to the establishment in the City. In 1772 he was chairman of the secret committee on East Indian affairs but held no stake in the company. Although expected to succeed, he declined to stand again for London in the 1774 election. Instead he contested Herefordshire on the family interest, only to be defeated. He was successful in a by-election there in 1776.

In November 1768 Harley had obtained a share in a contract to remit funds to America, and during the War of Independence he was involved as well in supplying clothing and blankets to British troops. To facilitate this he became a partner in the bank of Sir Charles Raymond, Harley, Webber & Co. of George Street in 1778. He was sensitive about his integrity as a contractor, and all but one of his subsequent speeches in the house to 1782 were in vindication of his probity. He abstained in the division on Shelburne's peace preliminaries, but there was some doubt about his allegiance to North in March 1783, and he went on to oppose Fox's East India Bill in November. After belonging to the group of MPs anxious to unite Fox and William Pitt, he proceeded to support Pitt's administration, except on the Irish commercial treaty of 1785.

In May 1785 Harley switched his London aldermanic ward to Bridge Without, being by then senior alderman or father of the City. He had acquired various other London honours: colonel of the Yellow regiment of the London militia (1771–94); president of the Honourable Artillery Company (1772–80), of the London Lying In Hospital, Aldersgate Street (1764), and of St Bartholomew's Hospital (1769); collector of the London orphans' coal duties (1789); president of the patrons of St Paul's charity schools; and governor of the Irish Society (1793–7). By 1775, however, he had acquired a country estate at Berrington, Herefordshire, purchased from the Cornewall family. Henry Holland jun. was the architect of Berrington Hall, built between 1778 and 1781, and it was hailed in 1784 as a model of elegance. Harley held local offices, being recorder of Leominster (1780–1802) and later high steward; he was also mayor of Shrewsbury (1784), lord lieutenant of Radnorshire (1791–1804, during the minority of his nephew Edward Harley, fifth earl of Oxford), and captain in the Herefordshire militia (1794). He faced only one further contest for the county seat, in 1796, when he headed the poll, and was also influential in Leominster elections. In 1790 he procured the return of his son-in-law David Murray for New Radnor. He occasionally exploited his loyalty to Pitt by asking for patronage for his friends. In 1795 he chaired the committee for William Lushington's candidature in the London by-election, and on 3 December he presented the Aldersgate ward petition in favour of the legislation against sedition, for which he had previously guaranteed City support. His current banking partnership of Harley, Cameron & Co. collapsed in March 1797 during the run on the Bank of England, but he paid his liabilities in full before withdrawing from business. In 1798 he declined the City chamberlainship in favour of Richard Clark. By now he was a widower, for his wife had died at Berrington Hall on 15 January 1798, aged sixty-six. His retirement from parliament was expected as early as January 1800, and late in 1801 he divulged it privately, stating his infirmity as the reason. Both his sons, Thomas and Edward, had died young, as had one of his daughters, Henrietta, and so he made his then eldest daughter, Anne, the widow of George, second Baron Rodney, heir to his estate. He died at Berrington Hall on 1 December 1804, leaving an estate valued at under £45,000.   ROLAND THORNE

Sources HoP, Commons • DNB • A. Collins, The peerage of England: containing a genealogical and historical account of all the peers of England • apprenticeship indentures index, Society of Genealogists, 18/176 • Walpole, Corr., vols. 22–3, 38 • GM, 1st ser., 74 (1804), 1175, 1237–40 • J. L. Milne, Berrington Hall (1991) • will, PRO, PROB 11/1419 • The Sun (27 Feb 1795) • Morning Chronicle (28 Nov 1795) • The Times (24 March 1797) • J. Almon, ed., The parliamentary register, or, History of the proceedings and debates of the House of Commons, 17 vols. (1775–80); repr. (1802) • J. Stockdale, ed., The debates and proceedings of the House of Commons: during the sixteenth parliament of Great Britain, 19 vols. (1785–90) • J. Almon, ed., The parliamentary register, or, History of the proceedings and debates of the House of Commons, 17 vols. (1775–80) • W. Cobbett, Parliamentary debates (1803–20) • GM, 1st ser., 68 (1798), 88 • estate duty register, PRO, IR 26/95
Archives PRO, Chatham MSS, 30/8/142 • Royal Bank of Scotland, London, Royal Bank of Scotland archive, papers relating to payment of troops in America
Likenesses F. Bate, portrait, 1836 (after pen-and-ink drawing, c.1768), probably Berrington Hall, Herefordshire • J. Hall, stipple (after portrait by H. Edridge), BM, NPG
Wealth at death under £45,000: PRO, death duty register, IR 26/95

Harliston, Richard (d. after 1495), administrator, was born at Humberstone, Lincolnshire, and brought up in the household of Richard, duke of York. After the accession of Edward IV he became a yeoman of the king's chamber, and in that capacity received a joint grant for life of the manor of Walton, Surrey, on 30 September 1464. He was described as 'yeoman of our chamber' and 'yeoman of the corone' when granted exemption from parliamentary Acts of Resumption (RotP, 5.537; 6.84, 87). Harliston was also employed in a naval capacity. In February 1468 he was commissioned to take ships and sailors for the king's fleet,

and in April was one of the four captains sent out to attack French shipping. The English fleet, which also carried 500 soldiers, subsequently landed on Jersey, where under the command of Harliston and Edmund Weston its men helped Philip de Carteret de St Ouen to capture the castle of Mont-Orgueil from the French, who had occupied the Channel Islands in 1461. The successful conclusion of the siege in September completed the English recovery of Jersey. Harliston was afterwards made captain of the islands of Jersey, Guernsey, Sark, and Alderney, by a patent dated 3 January 1477, and was the first to bear the title of captain-in-chief of the islands. He remained in office until 1487, and is reported by the late sixteenth-century *Chroniques de Jersey* to have been a popular governor, encouraging the natives to practise the use of the longbow.

Nevertheless, after the fall of Richard III Harliston is said to have tried to make himself lord of the islands, under the protection of the French and of Duchess Margaret of Burgundy, and to have been thwarted by local resistance. He was attainted for joining John de la Pole, earl of Lincoln, in Lambert Simnel's rising of 1486, but was granted a general pardon on 4 September of that year, when he was described as 'late of the island of Jersey, esquire' (Campbell, 2.30). In the following year Henry VII named Matthew Baker as governor of the Channel Islands, and Harliston took refuge with Margaret of Burgundy. In July 1495 he was one of Perkin Warbeck's supporters who attacked the Kentish coast at Deal, and was subsequently attainted, being now described as 'late of London, knight'. There is, however, no certain evidence for his having been knighted. Harliston remained in Margaret's service thereafter, and when he died in Flanders, at an unknown date some time after 1495, received honourable burial there at her expense. He had a daughter, possibly illegitimate, named Margaret; she married Philip de Carteret, grandson of her father's old ally, with whom she had twenty-one children.   E. L. O'BRIEN

Sources S. de Carteret, Chroniques des Iles de Jersey, Guernsey, Aurigny et Sark, ed. G. S. Syvret (1832) • P. Falle, An account of the island of Jersey, [new edn.] (1837) • P. Falle, Caesarea, or, An account of Jersey, the greatest of the islands remaining to the crown of England of the ancient Dutchy of Normandy, [new edn.] (1797) • C. L. Scofield, The life and reign of Edward the Fourth, 2 vols. (1923) • A. J. Eagleston, The Channel Islands under Tudor government, 1485–1642, ed. J. Le Patourel (1949) • Chancery records • RotP, vols. 5–6 • W. Campbell, ed., Materials for a history of the reign of Henry VII, 2 vols., Rolls Series, 60 (1873–7) • DNB

Harlow, George Henry (1787–1819), painter, was born on 10 June 1787 in St James's Street, London, the youngest child and only son of a merchant of Canton, China, who died in February 1787, four months before he was born.

Early years and education Harlow was brought up by his mother, Elizabeth (1759/60–1809), who was widowed at the age of twenty-seven; of his five sisters only one survived to adulthood. From a young age he attended Dr Barrow's classical school in Soho Square, London; then he was sent to a Mr Roy in Burlington Street before his interest in drawing led to his being placed with the landscape draughtsman Henry de Cort. Next he became the pupil of

George Henry Harlow (1787–1819), self-portrait, 1818

the painter Samuel Drummond and, having rejected the offer made by friends of his father of a writership in India, when about fifteen entered the studio of the celebrated portrait painter Thomas Lawrence. A memorandum of an agreement dated 9 December 1803 made between Lawrence and Elizabeth Harlow records that from that day for one year Harlow would 'faithfully serve and assist' Lawrence 'in his art or profession of a portrait painter', and that in return Lawrence would 'to the best of his abilities teach and instruct … Harlowe in the Art or profession of a portrait painter' and 'at his own expence find and provide … Harlowe with all such Canvas colours paints brushes and other ingredients' (Lawrence papers, RA, Law 1/105). On the same day Joseph Farington noted in his diary that 'Lawrence has got a young pupil of 15 years of age, who draws, Lane says, better than *He does*. His name is Harlow' (Farington, *Diary*, 5.1943).

With his mother, who 'spoiled her good-looking boy' (Redgrave, *Artists*, 198), and two surviving sisters Harlow left Queen Street, Mayfair, to lodge with a Mr Hamilton in Dean Street, Soho. Two years later Mrs Harlow retired to the country leaving Harlow, aged seventeen, with one sister in London. Described by J. T. Smith, biographer of the sculptor Joseph Nollekens, as 'naturally vain', Harlow 'became ridiculously foppish, and by dressing to the extreme of fashion, was often the laughing-stock of his brother artists' (Smith, 2.410). John Knowles, biographer of Henry Fuseli, who supported Harlow when others remained critical, also noted that:

Harlow proved himself, on many occasions, to be among the vainest of men … It is said that he had affected a sort of swagger in his gait, and unlicensed audacity in speech, from a belief that they became him, and that it was proper to

mark out a man of genius from the … crowds. (Cunningham, 5.286, 288)

His foibles led his friends to give him the nickname Clarissa Harlowe (many later references to Harlow include the final 'e' to his surname). Following a breach with Lawrence about a painting, Harlow stayed at the Queen's Head, Epsom, where, to discharge his bill, he painted a signboard in a style caricaturing that of his master which he signed 'T. L., Greek Street, Soho' (ibid., 279). After this rupture Harlow did not seek further instruction but went on to paint 'at a low price many of the actors of the day, and thus fell into their society, and being of an easy, careless disposition, soon became embarrassed in his affairs' (Redgrave, *Artists*, 198).

Portraits of artists From 1804 Harlow had sent works for exhibition at the Royal Academy, where in 1806 he exhibited a drawing of his mother, who died in 1809 when Harlow was twenty-two. After completing a few historical pictures including *Bolingbroke's Entry into London* and *Queen Elizabeth Striking the Earl of Essex* (exh. RA, 1807) he turned his attention to portraits. He was an excellent draughtsman and his portraits, whether in oils, pencil, chalk, or crayon, show much sensitivity. Redgrave notes that:

in 1815 he commenced a series of small size [portraits], of eminent painters and some of the notorieties of the day; they are refined, yet broadly finished, and full of character. He also made portrait sketches in chalk, slightly tinting the face, many of them admirable in taste and manner. Several of his portraits were engraved.   (Redgrave, *Artists*, 198)

They included one of Benjamin West, president of the Royal Academy (exh. RA, 1815; Sothebys, 9 November 1994, lot 62), who appears to have shown some encouragement to Harlow. In June 1817 Joseph Farington recorded that 'West last night, was at the British Institution and had *Harlowe* under His care & introduced Him to many of the principal people there' (Farington, *Diary*, 14.5029). At the end of that month he noted, 'Lord Abercorn sitting to Harlowe' (ibid.). Harlow also made a portrait of Colonel George Wyndham, first Baron Leconfield, eldest son of the third earl of Egremont, the munificent patron of J. M. W. Turner and other notable contemporary artists. In 1816 Harlow exhibited portraits of two Royal Academicians, James Northcote and Sir William Beechey, and the following year another of Northcote and one of Henry Fuseli (Yale U. CBA, Paul Mellon collection), which was commissioned by John Knowles and subsequently reproduced in his biography of Fuseli. He also made a drawing of the sculptor Peter Turnerelli and another of Thomas Rowlandson (1814; Hunt. L.). There is an oil sketch of Thomas Stothard at Petworth House, Sussex, showing, in the background, Stothard's *Mars and Venus*. Of two self-portrait drawings one, signed and dated 1810, is in the National Portrait Gallery and another, signed and dated 1813, is in a private collection. J. T. Smith commented:

of the immense number of portraits painted of Northcote, perhaps the one by Harlow may be fairly appreciated as the best likeness … [He] also made a highly spirited beginning of a portrait of Nollekens [and] produced one of the most dignified and characteristic likenesses of Fuseli, for which that artist threw himself into a position, and gave the

Painter every possible advantage, by affording him numerous sittings … From its richness of colouring, grandeur of effect, and exquisite finish [it may be] fairly considered as the *chef-d'œuvre* of that highly-talented Artist, though perhaps most improvident of men.   (Smith, 2.410)

Financially dependent, as most artists then were, on portrait commissions, and seeking further patronage through the exhibition of his work at the Royal Academy, Harlow evidently sought also to redeem his early loss of position as Lawrence's pupil by seeking the notice of other academicians and thus to gain a stronger foothold within the academy. His series of artists' portraits was done 'con amore and gratis' (*Literary Gazette*, 202). In 1816, however, his candidacy for associate status within the academy received only one vote (from Fuseli, who commented, 'I voted for the talent—not for the man!' (Cunningham, 5.281)).

Portrait drawings   Of Harlow's portrait drawings that of Haydon reproduced as the frontispiece to *The Autobiography and Memoirs of Benjamin Robert Haydon* (1926) is similar in format to several others, including a fine one of William Godwin, signed and dated 1816 (priv. coll.), and the elegant and highly finished chalk drawing of Lord Byron (*c*.1815; priv. coll.) engraved by Henry Meyer for the *New Monthly Magazine* (July 1815). The fashionable fencing master Henry Angelo recollected that 'Harlow … whom I had known from a boy, made two drawings (through my recommendation), one of his lordship, another of his sister' (Angelo, 131). While staying with Charles Madryll Cheere at Papworth Hall, Cambridgeshire, Harlow wrote on 8 August 1815 to Henry Colburn, publisher of the *Monthly Magazine*, stating, 'We are all great admirers of Lord Byron here and it would be very gratifying to give away a print or two of him to my friends' (Michael Silverman sale catalogue). Harlow's obituarist recorded that 'Mr Harlow was in the habit of drawing, and depositing in a book, the likenesses of eminent persons with whom he was struck on meeting them in company. These are among the most precious of his remains.' (*Literary Gazette*, 202) Of those mentioned many are signed with Harlow's initials G. H. H. or sometimes G. H. Harlow and dated with the day, month, and year. Other sitters included the Gothic novelist M. G. (Monk) Lewis (engraving by J. Hollis, repr. in *Finden's illustrations to … Byron*, 1834); Horace and James Smith, authors of *Rejected Addresses* (1812); and the actors Elizabeth Inchbald (1814), Robert Elliston (1814), John Kemble, and Charles Mathews (first two, Garrick Club, London). Others are listed in the catalogue of the posthumous sale of 'a few capital original pictures, studies and drawings, the works of G. H. Harlow' held 'by Mr Christie' on 3 June 1820 (*Catalogue*).

Theatrical portraits   Of Harlow's other known portraits in oil, those of actors form a distinctive group. These include *Robert Elliston* (*c*.1808), *John Philip Kemble as Coriolanus* (*c*.1808), *A Group of Portraits of Mr Mathews in Private, and in Various Characters* (exh. RA, 1814; engraved Henry Meyer 1817, and W. Greatbach for Mathew's *Memoirs*, 1838), *Sarah Siddons as Lady Macbeth* (*c*.1813), another *Sarah Siddons as Lady Macbeth* (*c*.1814), and *Catherine Stephens as Diana Vernon*

(*c*.1818; all Garrick Club, London, all repr. in Ashton). All these portraits were formerly in the collection of the actor Charles Mathews, who was a close friend of Harlow's. A small bust-length portrait in a painted oval of Catherine Stephens, afterwards countess of Essex (engraved by W. Say, 1816), is at Petworth. For portraits such as the small whole length of Sarah Siddons as Lady Macbeth, Harlow charged 20 guineas.

The picture for which Harlow became celebrated when it was exhibited at the Royal Academy in 1817 was entitled *Court Scene for the Trial of Queen Katharine: Queen, 'Lord Cardinal, to you I Speak.'—Henry VIII* (priv. coll.), an indication that it was as a theatrical rather than a historical picture that Harlow intended it to be received. A reduced autograph replica is in the Royal Shakespeare Company collection, Stratford upon Avon (repr. Solkin, 122). It was originally commissioned by Thomas Welsh, the singer and composer, for 100 guineas, as a portrait from memory of Sarah Siddons as Queen Katherine; the actress subsequently, and at Welsh's request, gave Harlow a sitting and he then expanded the portrait into the trial scene. Exhibited five years after Siddons's official retirement:

[that] Harlow's picture was one of the most enduring theatrical images of the 19th century is demonstrated by the fact that most subsequent productions of *Henry VIII* during that century used it as the basis for their arrangement of the trial scene. Even 70 years later, Ellen Terry based her interpretation of Queen Katherine on that of Sarah Siddons and her trial scene on Harlow's picture.   (Ashton, 393)

In April 1817 Farington noted that 'Sir G. & Lady Beaumont were strongly impressed with the excellence of a picture by Harlowe, representing the *Kemble family* in characters forming a Scene in the Play of Henry 8th' (Farington, *Diary*, 14.4998), but that 'it was certainly a work which approached towards vicious art, finery & ostentatious display' (ibid., 5008). Intended for display on the densely hung walls of the academy's great room where exhibited works competed for the attention of a large crowd of viewers, this work, with the melodramatic expressions and gestures of its characters, heightened by rich colouring and a composition that conveys an impression of deep three-dimensional space, was nevertheless highly successful as a theatrical genre painting. Fuseli advised Harlow on compositional details, including the placing of the two page boys in the foreground 'to throw the eye of the spectator into the picture' (Cunningham, 5.285). Harlow included in the painting a self-portrait; he is standing immediately to the left of the cross behind the cardinal. The copyright to a plate for engraving the painting was sold for 500 guineas, and the mezzotint by George Clint further enhanced its popularity.

Visit to Italy   Following the exhibition of three of his works at the Royal Academy in 1818 Harlow left on 22 June for Italy accompanied by his servant, William Gravely. During the early part of his visit he made a second drawing of Byron (John Murray, London) that is inscribed in Byron's handwriting 'Byron. Venizia Ao 6. 1818'. That Harlow visited Byron at the Palazzo Mocenigo, Venice, where he also made a pendent drawing of Byron's housekeeper,

Margarita Cogni, *La Fornarina* (John Murray, London), suggests a degree of intimacy between sitter and artist that went beyond the conventions of a formal portrait sitting. It was at Byron's instigation that Countess Benzoni provided a letter of introduction for Harlow ('forwarded to Mr. H. Poste Restante Florence') to the celebrated Italian sculptor Antonio Canova in Rome (Christies autograph letter sale catalogue, 22 October 1980, lot 126). At Rome, Harlow worked extremely hard: in eighteen days he made a copy of Raphael's *Transfiguration* (1517–20; Pinacoteca, Vatican, Rome). Earlier, at Venice, he had copied Tintoretto's *Crucifixion* (1565; Scuola Grande di San Rocco, Venice). From his lodgings at '4 Piazza Rosa, secundo piano in casa di Polidori, Roma' he wrote on 23 November 1818 to a friend in London, Mr Tomkisson, a musical instrument maker in Dean Street, Soho, 'I shall send the Transfiguration, which I think will make a stare in England, with other pictures, sketches, and prints' (*Literary Gazette*, 203). After exhibiting his painting *Wolsey Receiving the Cardinal's Hat in Westminster Abbey* together with other works at Canova's house, he presented *Wolsey* to the Accademia di San Luca, Rome, and sent the finished sketch to England (Tabley House, University of Manchester). He was elected to the Rome academy, and invited to submit his own portrait (1818) to the Uffizi Gallery in Florence. Painted in the bravura style of Lawrence, this self-portrait leaves no doubt of Harlow's intention to claim the mantle of his master. To Tomkisson, Harlow noted further that he 'was much pleased with Naples, stayed ten days; went to Portici, Herculaneum, and Pompeii, and ascended Mount Vesuvius … red hot ashes came tumbling down continually where I stood sketching' (Smith, 2.412). Canova 'expressed the highest admiration for Harlow' and introduced him to Pope Pius VII (*Literary Gazette*, 202):

> I am to be presented to the Pope either on the 2d or 3d of next month … I leave Rome directly after; perhaps the next day—a day that I most sincerely dread, for I have become so attached to the place and the people, that I expect a great struggle with myself. (Smith, 2.413)

After his triumphal visit to Rome, Harlow was elected a member of the Florence academy on his way home and landed at Dover on 13 January 1819 with a sore throat. His complaint soon became more serious and he took to his bed at his home, 83 Dean Street, Soho, London, where he died on 4 February 1819. He was buried on 16 February in St James's Church, Piccadilly, where his funeral was attended by Sir William Beechey RA and the enamellist Henry Bone. Joseph Farington confided to his diary on 27 February that John Aytoun, who had seen Harlow shortly before he died, had spoken to him of Harlow's death:

> He had an external swelling in His throat, which [was] supposed to be the *Mumps*. It increased to a very large size & so disfigured Him that He would only admit to His room, Mr. Andrews, a Medical friend and a Servant, so unwilling was he to be seen under such an appearance … Such was His situation when He died, that had not Tijou, the frame maker, come forward to take charge of his funeral, He must have been buried at the expence of the Parish. (Farington, *Diary*, 15.5333)

Reputation 'That Genius must have panted for posthumous fame' (Lawrence to Farington, 20 March 1819, RA, Law 3/19, fol. 7). Lawrence's comment comes at the end of a letter written from Vienna—where, before proceeding to Rome, he was painting portraits of sovereigns, statesmen, and generals which form part of his brilliant series done for 'His late Majesty [George IV] FOR THE WATERLOO GALLERY AT WINDSOR' (Millar, 1.xxxv). Replying to Joseph Farington's letter bearing news of Harlow's death, Lawrence's letter covers three folio sheets in closely written small handwriting, and is wholly devoted to his reflections on his former pupil. Though, to his close friend, he referred candidly to Harlow's former 'defects' he averred that:

> No one I believe appreciated his Genius more highly than myself … I for one, had prepared myself for many an arduous struggle with him hereafter. … When I heard that he had copied the Transfiguration at Rome … it confirmed my Impression of his Genius, and the superiority of his Taste. … While he was with me his application was unremitting; and although every now and then he was disquieting to his Profession, at so early an Age … [he] had more than the usual follies of Youth to combat … So rare as is the appearance of *great* power in Art, one must wonder … that it is given to the World so suddenly to be withdrawn. (Lawrence to Farington, 20 March 1819, RA, Law 3/19, fol. 7)

Farington replied, 'He appears to have been sadly and strangely neglected during his illness, and, if better attended and with proper medical advice, might probably have recovered' (Farington to Lawrence, 6 April 1819, RA, Law 3/26). An 'Exhibition of paintings and drawings of the late Mr George Henry Harlow' held at 87 Pall Mall, London, in 1819, which included his sketches and sketchbooks, helped to discharge Harlow's debts to creditors of whom Welsh was the principal. Two sales held at Fosters on 21 June 1819 and Christies on 3 June 1820 comprised paintings and drawings by Harlow, including his Italian studies, the original sketch for *Wolsey*, and casts from antique sculpture which he acquired in Italy.

Although expressive of a different facet of Romanticism, like those of his contemporary, the landscape painter Thomas Girtin, who died at twenty-seven, Harlow's late works, for example, *The Proposal* (c.1819; ex Christies, New York, 11 January 1995, lot 36), demonstrate an assurance of style and interpretation in which his artistic future is clearly evident. He was celebrated for his own 'unrivalled brilliance' and 'incomparable ability' (Millar, 1.xxxiii), and Lawrence's opinion of Harlow's 'Genius' acknowledges his pupil's ascendancy and confirms that, had he lived, Harlow's success at Rome would undoubtedly have consolidated his position at home among the first painters of his age. ANNETTE PEACH

Sources Lawrence papers, RA · G. Ashton, *Pictures in the Garrick Club*, ed. K. A. Burnim and A. Wilton (1997) · A. Peach, 'Portraits of Byron', *Walpole Society*, 62 (2000), 1–144 · D. H. Solkin, ed., *Art on the line* (2001) · G. Ashton, *Pictures in the Garrick Club*, ed. K. A. Burnim and A. Wilton (1997) · G. Perry, 'The spectacle of the muse: exhibiting the actress at the Royal Academy', *Art on the line*, ed. D. H. Solkin (2001), 111–26 · photographs, sale catalogues, archive notes, NPG, Heinz Archive and Library · Farington, *Diary* · *Literary Gazette* (27 March 1819), 187–8, 201–4, 266 · Graves, *RA exhibitors* · J. T. Smith,

Nollekens and his times, 2 vols. (1828), vol. 2, pp. 408–14 · A. Cunningham, *Lives of the most eminent British painters*, 2nd edn, 6 vols. (1830–33) · Redgrave, *Artists* · O. Millar, *The later Georgian pictures in the collection of her majesty the queen*, 2 vols. (1969) · L. Cust, 'DNB notebooks', NPG, Heinz Archive and Library, Cust papers · A. Burton and J. Murdoch, *Byron* (1974) [exhibition catalogue, V&A] · C. H. Collins Baker, *Catalogue of pictures at Petworth House* (1920) · *A catalogue of a few capital and original pictures, studies and drawings, the works of G. H. Harlow, Esq* (3 June 1820) [sale catalogue, Christies] · R. Walker, *National Portrait Gallery: Regency portraits*, 2 vols. (1985) · Foster sale catalogue (21 June 1819) · *Exhibition of paintings & drawings of the late Mr G. H. Harlow at no. 87 Pall Mall* (1819) [exhibition catalogue] · [J. Murdoch, D. H. Solkin, and A. Puetz], *Art on the line* (2001) [exhibition catalogue, Courtauld Inst., 18 Oct 2001 – 20 Jan 2002] · *The diary of Benjamin Robert Haydon*, ed. W. B. Pope, 5 vols. (1960–63), vol. 2, p. 22 · *The autobiography and memoirs of Benjamin Robert Haydon*, ed. T. Taylor, new edn, 2 vols. (1926), frontispiece [introduction by A. Huxley] · J. Timbs, *Anecdote biography*, 2nd ser. (1860) · *GM*, 1st ser., 89/1 (1819), 186–7 · *DNB* · H. Angelo, *Reminiscences of Henry Angelo, with memoirs of his late father and friends*, 2 vols. (1828–30) · Michael Silverman sale catalogue no. 20, 2002, Michael Silverman, London

Archives RA, letters to Thomas Lawrence

Likenesses G. H. Harlow, self-portrait, drawing, 1810, NPG · G. H. Harlow, self-portrait, chalk drawing, 1813, Hunt. L. · G. H. Harlow, self-portrait, drawing, 1813, priv. coll. · G. H. Harlow, self-portrait, oils, exh. RA 1817 (*The court for the trial of Queen Katharine: Queen, 'Lord Cardinal, to you I speak.' - Henry VIII*), priv. coll.; autograph replica, Royal Shakespeare Memorial Theatre Museum, Stratford upon Avon · G. H. Harlow, self-portrait, oils, 1818, Uffizi Gallery, Florence [see illus.]

Harlow, Thomas (*d.* 1741), naval officer, was appointed on 19 March 1690 to command the *Smyrna Merchant*, a hired ship. Later he commanded the *Burford* (70 guns), first in 1691 in the Grand Fleet under Admiral Edward Russell, and again in 1692, when he took part in the battle of Barfleur, being then in the division of Vice-Admiral Sir Ralph Delavall.

In the *Burford*, in the *Humber*, and afterwards in the *Torbay* (80 guns), Harlow continued to serve with the Grand Fleet during the course of the Nine Years' War. On 14 August 1697, while in command of a small squadron cruising in the Soundings, he fell in with and engaged a somewhat superior French squadron, under the command of M. de Pointis, homeward bound from the West Indies. The French were to windward, and after a three-hour contest, finding they gained no advantage, and probably unwilling to risk their very rich cargo, they hauled their wind and made sail. The British followed as best they could, but were not able to prevent the enemy's retreat. After his return to England Harlow was charged with having permitted the French to escape. He was tried by court martial on 29 November, but was acquitted. The court martial was remarkable both for the distinction and the number of its members: Sir George Rooke, admiral of the fleet, sat as its president; Sir Cloudesley Shovell, Matthew Aylmer, Sir David Mitchell, and John Benbow were among its sixty-one members. Proceedings focused on tactical principles, the charge virtually amounting to an assertion that Harlow should have cut through the enemy's line and so forced the fighting. His decision not to do so was accepted by all of the senior officers of the navy. Furious passions raged over the matter, arising probably from anger that

the rich prize should have escaped; the court martial's decision did not bring an end to a wider debate on Harlow's actions, much of this prompted by the extent of the French prize to have eluded the British forces. Despite Charnock's claim that he had no further employment under William III, Harlow was appointed to the *Grafton* on 14 February 1701. In 1702, still in the *Grafton*, he took part in the expedition to Cadiz, and was prominently engaged at Vigo in support of Vice-Admiral Hopsonn. He returned to England with Shovell in November, and the following April was appointed master-attendant at Deptford Dockyard. In February 1705 he was appointed a commissioner of victualling, in which position he continued until November 1711. In May 1712 he was again appointed master-attendant of Deptford Dockyard. The date of his retirement is unknown. He died 'at a very advanced age' in 1741, having been for several years the senior captain on the list. J. K. LAUGHTON, *rev.* NICHOLAS TRACY

Sources J. Charnock, ed., *Biographia navalis*, 6 vols. (1794–8) · D. Syrett and R. L. DiNardo, *The commissioned sea officers of the Royal Navy, 1660–1815*, rev. edn, Occasional Publications of the Navy RS, 1 (1994)

Harlowe, Sarah (1765–1852), actress, was probably born in London, and it is thought that her original name was Wilson. She evidently had some theatrical experience when she became a member of the summer company based at Richmond under Francis Godolphin *Waldron (*bap.* 1743, *d.* 1818). He was prompter of the Haymarket Theatre, a bookseller, a playwright, and an occasional actor. Her theatrical career was allied to his during the 1780s, although the extent of their early relationship remains unclear. The *Secret History of the Green Rooms* (1790) claimed that she took the name Harlowe because she thought it would look good on a playbill.

Sarah Harlowe's first recorded London appearance was on 19 July 1786 as Kitty Sprightly in *All the World's a Stage*, at the Windsor Castle inn, King Street, Hammersmith. The following summer she was again with the Richmond company, and was soon engaged at Sadler's Wells, reputedly through Waldron's influence. Apparently the two began living together about this time (they never married), and she continued performing under the name Harlowe.

After gaining some celebrity as a singer, actress, and performer in pantomimes, Harlowe secured an engagement at Covent Garden, and made her first appearance there on 4 November 1790 in *The Fugitive*. She remained there for two seasons, and sustained the characters of smart chambermaids, romps in breeches, shrews, and old women, and was hired to portray a similar line at the Haymarket. She retained a place in that theatre until 1799, and travelled in the provinces during the winter months.

Harlowe's engagement at Drury Lane, which lasted twenty-six years, began on 2 February 1801, when she played Cora in Sheridan's *Pizarro*. *Oxberry's Dramatic Biography* described her as being of 'middle size' and as having a face with 'an air of vulgarity and impudence', but with an upturned nose that was inviting. It evidently suited her cast of second- and third-ranking comic characters such as Lucy in Sheridan's *The Rivals*, the Widow Warren in

Sarah Harlowe (1765–1852), by Samuel De Wilde, 1805 [as Beatrice in *The Anatomist, or, The Sham Doctor* by Edward Ravenscroft]

Thomas Holcroft's *The Road to Ruin*, and old Lady Lambert in Isaac Bickerstaff's *The Hypocrite*. Waldron died in March 1818, and his will left the bulk of his property to Sarah Harlowe in trust for their four children, Sarah Elizabeth, Frances Ann, Francis, and William Waldron.

In 1826 Harlowe retired from the stage, having on 21 February in that year played Mrs Foresight in the farce of *John Bull*. One of the original subscribers to the Drury Lane Theatrical Fund, she received from 1827 an annuity of £140 per annum, which was reduced in 1837 to £112. She died of heart failure at her lodgings, 5 Albert Place, Gravesend, Kent, on 2 January 1852, aged eighty-six, and her death was registered as that of 'Sarah Waldron, annuitant'.

G. C. BOASE, rev. K. A. CROUCH

Sources Highfill, Burnim & Langhans, *BDA*, 7.109–13 · C. B. Hogan, ed., *The London stage, 1660–1800*, pt 5: 1776–1800 (1968) · Genest, *Eng. stage* · J. Roach, *Roach's authentic memoirs of the green room* (1796) · [J. Haslewood], *The secret history of the green rooms: containing authentic and entertaining memoirs of the actors and actresses in the three theatres royal*, 2 vols. (1790) · *Oxberry's Dramatic Biography*, 3/46 (1825) [incl. engraving] · *GM*, 2nd ser., 37 (1852), 308–9 · Mrs C. Baron-Wilson, *Our actresses*, 2 vols. (1844)

Likenesses S. Harding, watercolour, in or before 1794, Garr. Club · W. Wellings, watercolour, 1795, Garr. Club · S. De Wilde, pencil and watercolour, 1805, Royal Collection [*see illus.*] · S. De Wilde, group portrait, oils, exh. RA 1810, Garr. Club · G. Clint, group portrait, oils, exh. RA 1823, Garr. Club · Barlow, double portrait, engraving (as Jenny, with Harriet Grist as Sophia, in *The road to ruin*), repro. in Highfill, Burnim & Langhans, *BDA* [entry on Harriet Grist] · J. Rogers, engraving, repro. in *Oxberry's Dramatic Biography* · three prints, Harvard TC

Harman, Sir Charles Eustace (1894–1970), judge, was born in London on 22 November 1894, the second son of John Eustace Harman (1861–1927), an eminent junior of the Chancery bar and a popular bencher of Lincoln's Inn. His mother was Ethel Frances, daughter of Henry Birch, a housemaster at Eton College who had been tutor to Edward VII. Throughout his life Harman retained a strong filial attachment to his father's memory and admiration for his professional skill and wisdom.

Harman won the third scholarship in the 1908 election at Eton where he played the wall game both for college and the school; for some years after 1918 he used to return regularly as a vociferous and savage player for the bar. He gained a classical scholarship at King's College, Cambridge, and went up in autumn 1913, but the outbreak of war interrupted his career. He was commissioned in the Middlesex regiment and after the battle of Loos in 1915 he was a prisoner until 1918, a time in which he acquired fluent French, good Italian, and some Russian. He returned in 1919 to Cambridge, where by his own account he spent much time in recreating the undergraduate life and institutions he had known before the war. For the Marlowe Society he gave a memorable performance as Falstaff in Shakespeare's *Henry IV Part I*. He won the university's Winchester reading prize and the Charles Oldham Shakespeare scholarship and, reading for a war degree, was in the first class in both parts of the classical tripos, graduating in 1920.

Harman was called to the bar by Lincoln's Inn in 1921, and quickly attracted business at the Chancery bar. He took silk in 1935. In 1947 he was appointed a judge of the Chancery Division with the customary knighthood, and in 1959 was promoted to the Court of Appeal and sworn of the privy council. As an advocate Harman's style had sometimes an abrasive quality which was not endearing, but he was a careful and conscientious counsel; solicitors knew that a client's case would be thoroughly and firmly presented. As a judge he proved much more patient and urbane than many of his friends had expected. He was ever ready to listen attentively to a well-presented argument. His judgments were robust and clear, showing a deep respect for legal scholarship combined with common sense. His style was lucid and his vocabulary flexible, as befitted a classical scholar and wide reader. Although his interlocutory remarks were sometimes characterized by a disconcerting judicial waywardness, he was not inclined to lace his judgments with wit or epigrams, but the language in which he clothed them, particularly his extempore judgments, lent them a peculiar vigour. To his cases he brought a forceful combination: a powerful mind and a wide knowledge of and profound respect for orthodox law.

At the end of every sitting Harman would be on the first available boat-train to Holyhead. All his vacations were spent at Tully, his home on the west coast of co. Mayo, and the setting of holidays from early boyhood. There he devoted himself mainly to outdoor pursuits. As a naturalist he had studied and knew his country intimately. He was a good shot and a first-class fisherman, whose happiest hours were spent on the river which flowed past, and occasionally under, his front door.

Harman developed a gruff and sometimes intimidating manner to cover a shy disposition, but his asperities were matched by great kindliness to others. Although in some respects a solitary man, he nevertheless delighted in good talk, good company, and good living. He gave devoted service to Lincoln's Inn, of which he was appointed a bencher in 1939 and treasurer in 1959. As he strolled back to the courts after lunching at the bench in Lincoln's Inn, he caught the eye. 6 feet 4 inches tall, broad and upstanding, wearing a tall silk hat and an overcoat of elegantly Edwardian cut, with a military moustache and a monocle appropriately slung on a length of fishing line, he was a striking figure; and the manner matched the man.

On 30 July 1924 Harman married Helen Sarah, daughter of Colonel Herman Le Roy-Lewis; they had two sons, one of whom, Jeremiah, followed his father to the Chancery bar and was appointed a queen's counsel in 1968 and a judge in the Chancery Division of the High Court in 1982. The other, Nicholas, became a well-known writer and broadcaster on economic and political subjects.

In June 1970 failing sight and hearing compelled Harman to retire, and he died in London on 14 November 1970. He was buried by his own wish in the churchyard of his Irish parish church. DENYS B. BUCKLEY, rev.

Sources *The Times* (16 Nov 1970) · *The Times* (21 Nov 1970) · personal knowledge (1981) · private information (1981) · **Archives** CUL, letters to Edward Dent · **Likenesses** J. Pannett, portrait, priv. coll. · D. Rolt, portrait, priv. coll. · **Wealth at death** £29,368 in England: probate, 10 May 1971, *CGPLA Eng. & Wales*

Harman, Edmund (*c*.1509–1577), barber, was born in Ipswich, the second son of Robert Harman, and of merchant stock. In 1530 he became free of the Barbers' Company and able to practise in the City. Although the trade was a manual one and of low social standing, not normally offering great rewards, in Harman's case it did so through his entry to the king's household by 1533, perhaps through the intervention of Sir William Sabyn, an Ipswich merchant and serjeant-at-arms to the king, or by Thomas Vicary, a surgeon to Henry VIII from 1528 and five times master of the Barbers' Company. From 1533 until the king's death Harman was a member of the small and intimate privy chamber which attended to the king's comfort and safety. Described variously as a groom of the privy chamber, one of the pages of the privy council, or one of the king's barbers, he was, according to a grant of 1546, 'one of those accustomed to be lodged within the King's Majesty's house'. The last of these posts, which he shared with two others, demanded the greatest trust by the king in view of the lethal nature of razor and scissors, and equally, discretion and confidence on Harman's part. He was required to be ready with his water, basins, and implements when the king rose in the morning in order to wash and trim his hair and beard, and contact with diseased or unclean persons, who might cause the royal person to become infected, was to be prevented. Harman's other posts included keeper of the wardrobe, and by September 1536 he had become one of the common packers at the Port of London, a position of importance, for in 1540, upon the complaint of the French ambassador, he was ordered to release lead belonging to a Rouen merchant which had been retained at London. The wages from the crown were £10 yearly, but his status also entitled Harman to a superior diet and personal attendants; four horsemen and eight footmen escorted him when he went with the king on the Boulogne expedition in 1544. His reliability had also been demonstrated in the previous year when the king had pardoned him following an accusation of heresy. The Barbers' Company elected him master as early as 1540, and he also appears with the king as one of the assistants of the company in Holbein's painting commemorating its establishment in that year.

Devotion to the king was rewarded by numerous grants of offices and land, the first of which was the post of bailiff of the manor of Hovington in the North Riding of Yorkshire in February 1536, to be followed by land in Middlesex, Gloucester, and Oxfordshire. By the time of the king's death Harman was a man of considerable wealth, and also a beneficiary from the king's will, which he witnessed, to the extent of 200 marks. His position enabled him to benefit others, including his brother James, who was granted a post in 1546 'at Mr Harman's suit'. Harman married, about 1540, Agnes, daughter of Edmund Silvester of Burford, who was buried on 30 March 1576; of their sixteen children only two survived into adulthood. On 16 November 1576 Harman married again. His second wife, of whom no other details are known, was called Katherine. He died only four months later at Burford on 19 March 1577, and was buried at Taynton church, Oxfordshire, on 10 April. In his will Harman had described himself as 'of Burford' where he had retired after the king's death. Thus he rose from a mere barber to wealth and status in only thirteen years through loyal service at court, and his 'countless blessings' were celebrated by a monument he erected to himself in Burford church in 1569. It features strangely modern-looking carvings of South American Indians, perhaps indicating an awareness of the expanding world.

I. G. MURRAY

Sources D. Power, 'Some notes on Edmund Harman, king's barber', *Proceedings of the Royal Society of Medicine*, 9 (1915–16), 67–88 · M. Balfour, *Edmund Harman barber and gentleman* (1988) · *LP Henry VIII* · W. H. Turner, ed., *The visitations of the county of Oxford … 1566 … 1574 … and in 1634*, Harleian Society, 5 (1871), 137 · register of freedom admissions, 1522–1665, Barbers' Company Archives, C/4/1

Likenesses H. Holbein the younger, group portrait, *c.*1541 (*Henry VIII and the company of barbers and surgeons of London*), Barber Surgeons' Hall, Monkwell Square, London

Wealth at death many thousands of acres, revenue-bearing offices, and plate to reward heirs

Harman, Sir George Byng (1830–1892), army officer, born in Chester Square, London, on 30 January 1830, was the son of John Harman of Chester Square and Moor Hall, Cookham, Berkshire. He was educated at Marlborough College (1844–6), and was commissioned as ensign in the 34th regiment on 18 September 1849, being promoted lieutenant on 21 June 1850 and captain on 19 June 1855. He serving with his regiment in the Ionian Islands, Gibraltar, the West Indies, and the Crimea, and took part in the assault of the Redan on 18 June 1855, where he received seven severe wounds. He was mentioned in dispatches, and awarded the medal with clasp, the Mejidiye (fifth class), and a brevet majority on 2 November 1855.

Harman served with the 34th in India during the mutiny, and was present at Windham's action with the Gwalior contingent at Cawnpore, and at the siege and capture of Lucknow. He was given half-pay unattached majority on 4 June 1858, and was assistant inspector of Volunteers from 18 February 1860 to 8 March 1865, when he was made brevet lieutenant-colonel. He served on the staff in the West Indies from 10 June 1866 to 30 April 1872, first as assistant military secretary, and afterwards as deputy adjutant-general. In 1868 he married Helen, daughter of John Tonge of Starborough Castle and Edenbridge, Kent; she survived him. Harman became brevet colonel on 2 June 1871. On 1 May 1872 he was given an unattached lieutenant-colonelcy, and was appointed to the command of a brigade depot at Pontefract on 1 April 1873.

On 18 December 1874 Harman was made assistant adjutant-general at Aldershot, and on 1 January 1878 he went to Ireland as deputy adjutant-general. He was promoted major-general on 14 November 1881, and placed on the staff of the expeditionary force in Egypt on 3 September 1882. He commanded the garrison of Alexandria. On 18 April 1883 he was appointed deputy adjutant-general at headquarters, and on 1 November 1885 military secretary. He was made CB on 24 May 1881 and KCB on 21 June 1887, and was promoted lieutenant-general on 1 April 1890. Harman was still serving on the staff at headquarters when he died at his home, 64 Courtfield Gardens, South Kensington, on 9 March 1892.

E. M. LLOYD, *rev.* JAMES FALKNER

Sources *The Times* (10 March 1892) · L. W. James, ed., *Marlborough College register: 1843–1952*, 9th edn (1952), 16 · *Army List* · *Hart's Army List*

Likenesses lithograph, BM

Wealth at death £48,642 12s. 5d.: probate, 29 April 1892, *CGPLA Eng. & Wales*

Harman, Sir John (d. 1673), naval officer, was possibly one of the Suffolk Harmans, some of whom were involved in shipowning. His brother was said to be 'an upholsterer at Cornhill' (*Le Neve's Pedigrees*, 3), presumably the Philip Harman who was related by marriage to Samuel Pepys. John Harman entered parliament's naval service in 1646,

Sir John Harman (d. 1673), by Sir Peter Lely, c.1665–6

commanding the hired merchantman *Falcon*. He gained his first command of a state's ship in the 36-gun *Welcome* in 1652, commanding her at the battles of Portland and the Gabbard. He was captain of the *Diamond* between August 1653 and 1655 and of the *Worcester* between 1656 and 1657. In the latter he served in Blake's fleet and took part in the successful attack on the Spanish plate fleet in Santa Cruz. Harman commanded the *Torrington*, part of Montagu's fleet in the Baltic, in 1659. Despite the Baptist faith to which he had adhered openly during the 1650s, Harman survived the Restoration, conformed to the Church of England, and returned to sea in September 1664 as captain of the *Gloucester*, prompting Sir William Coventry's barbed remark that Harman had both served the state 'and served himself' (Bath MSS, Coventry MS 98, fol. 67). He moved to the *Royal Charles* on 26 March 1665 to serve as flag captain to the lord high admiral, James, duke of York. After the battle of Lowestoft on 3 June 1665, Harman allegedly received a message from one of James's retinue, Henry Brouncker, conveying the duke's orders to shorten sail during the night. This 'order'—or else Brouncker's insistence, said to have been inspired by the duchess of York, on not endangering James's life—was blamed for allowing the Dutch to escape further punishment, and would return to haunt Harman after the war. In the short term, however, he benefited directly from the battle, being appointed rear-admiral of the white on 13 June with his flag in the *Resolution*. He moved to the Blue squadron on 2 July. Harman transferred to the *Revenge* in October 1665, convoying home the Göteborg trade. He served once more as rear-admiral of the blue for the 1666 campaign, flying his flag in the *Henry* and transferring to the white when the fleet was divided prior to the Four Days' Battle (1–4 June 1666). The *Henry* bore the brunt of a concerted Dutch attack on the first day of that engagement. Harman was seriously wounded by a falling spar, and his ship had to fight off three separate fireship attacks, which 'singed both her sides and her sails', while 'above 40 of the men leaped overboard, and drowned themselves for fear of burning' (Powell and Timings, 238). Despite the damage Harman refitted the *Henry* overnight at Harwich and rejoined the fleet on the next day. He gave up his command on 9 June, presumably to convalesce, and was knighted about this time.

In February 1667 Harman was appointed to command the *Lion* and to serve as admiral of a squadron bound for the West Indies, where Dutch and French forces had been attacking the English colonies. Arriving in June, Harman joined the local forces under Captain John Berry, which had already successfully defeated a Franco-Dutch fleet off Nevis. Together they sailed for St Kitts, intending to recapture it, but the attack failed. However, they immediately received intelligence that about two dozen French ships were lying at Martinique, and Harman ordered an attack on this new target. Although the French were guarded by shore batteries, a series of assaults finally resulted on 25 June in the destruction of all but two or three of the enemy ships, at a cost of about eighty English lives. Harman then sailed for Cayenne, capturing it on 15 September, and Paramaribo in Surinam, forcing its surrender on 8 October. On his return to Barbados on 10 November, however, Harman found that peace had been concluded three months earlier at Breda—a peace which confirmed Dutch possession of Surinam. Harman returned to England in April 1668 and was immediately summoned to appear before the House of Commons, which had been investigating the shortening of sail after the battle of Lowestoft three years before. Harman's first examination, on 17 April, reflected badly on him—hardly surprising, either because he had only just returned from sea and had little grasp of the political circumstances, or because, as Pepys suggested, he had been carousing with his crew the night before—and he was ordered to be detained pending re-examination. By the time he returned to the house on 21 April Henry Brouncker had panicked and fled, and Harman took the opportunity to shift all the blame onto him, appearing to the MPs as 'a very gallant man, and very humble and modest' (*Diary of John Milward*, 270). Harman commanded the *Defiance* briefly in the summer of 1668, then took command of the *Saint David* in April 1669 as rear-admiral of the fleet under Sir Thomas Allin engaged against the corsairs of Algiers. Harman returned to England in April 1671 and in the following year became rear-admiral of the blue, then of the red, for the first campaign of the Third Anglo-Dutch War, flying his flag in the *Royal Charles*. He served in the battle of Solebay on 28 May 1672, engaging De Ruyter's flagship *Zeven Provincien* for two hours. With his main mast severely damaged, Harman transferred to a ketch and then to the *Cambridge*, returning to the *Charles* for the remainder of the 1672 campaign.

In the following year Harman took the *London* for his flagship, serving initially as vice-admiral of the blue and then of the red, and fought in all three major engagements (the battles of the Schooneveld on 28 May and 4 June and of the Texel on 11 August 1673). Already seriously ill, apparently with gout, it was said that Harman issued his orders from a chair on the quarterdeck throughout the last battle, during which he and his division closely supported Rupert against De Ruyter's attacks. The death of Sir Edward Spragge led to Harman's appointment as admiral of the blue, a flag which he hoisted on 14 August, and at the end of the month he succeeded Prince Rupert as commander-in-chief of the fleet. He did not enjoy the supreme command for long; he died in London on 11 October 1673 and was buried in the churchyard of St Mary Magdalen, Bermondsey.

It is not known when Harman married, but his widow, Dame Katherine (d. 1696), received a pension of £500 per annum, which at least partly offset the common belief that Harman had died relatively poor. He had at least three sons: James, William, who served as a lieutenant in the Third Anglo-Dutch War and died in command of the *Guernsey* in an engagement with Algerine corsairs in December 1677, and John, who commanded a ship in the West Indies in 1669 and served as his father's lieutenant in 1672–3. There was also a daughter, Katherine (d. 1718), who married Dauntsey Brouncker (d. 1693). Dame Katherine's will was proved in 1696: she asked to be buried alongside her husband and made bequests to Katherine and her daughters, and to a nephew, William Palmer.

J. D. DAVIES

Sources PRO, ADM MSS · R. C. Anderson, ed., *Journals and narratives of the Third Dutch War*, Navy RS, 86 (1946) · J. R. Powell and E. K. Timings, eds., *The Rupert and Monck letter book, 1666*, Navy RS, 112 (1969) · B. Capp, *Cromwell's navy: the fleet and the English revolution, 1648–1660* (1989) · J. D. Davies, *Gentlemen and tarpaulins: the officers and men of the Restoration navy* (1991) · J. Baltharpe, *The straights voyage*, ed. J. S. Bromley, Luttrell Society (1959) · *The diary of John Milward*, ed. C. Robbins (1938) · *Le Neve's Pedigrees of the knights*, ed. G. W. Marshall, Harleian Society, 8 (1873) · Pepys, *Diary* · *CSP col.*, vol. 5 · PRO, PROB 11/435, fols. 37–8 [Katherine Harman] · J. M. Collinge, *Navy Board officials, 1660–1832* (1978) · Longleat House, Wiltshire, Bath MSS, fol. 67

Archives PRO, ADM MSS

Likenesses P. Lely, oils, c.1665–1666, NMM [see illus.] · P. Lely, oils, second version, NPG

Wealth at death died poor: Capp, *Cromwell's navy*, 400n.

Harman, Thomas (*fl.* 1547–1567), writer on vagabonds, was grandson of Henry Harman, clerk of the crown under Henry VII, who obtained about 1480 the estates of Ellam and Maystreet in Kent. Thomas's father, William Harman, added to these estates the manor of Mayton, or Maxton, in the same county. As his father's heir Thomas inherited all this property and lived at Crayford, Kent, continuously from 1547. He writes that he was 'a poore gentleman', detained in the country by ill health. He found some recreation in questioning the vagrants who begged at his door as to their modes of life, and paid frequent visits to London with the object of corroborating his information. He thus acquired a unique knowledge of the habits of thieves and beggars. Occasionally his indignation was so roused by the deception practised by those whom he interrogated at his own door that he took their licences from them and confiscated their money, distributing it among the honest poor of his neighbourhood.

Before 1566 Harman had composed an elaborate treatise on vagrants, and travelled to London to superintend its publication. He lodged at 'the Whitefriars within the Cloister', and continued his investigation even while his book was passing through the press. The title of the book runs, *A Caveat or Warening for Common Cursetors Vulgarely called Vagabones*, and it went through two editions in 1566–7. Its popularity was at once so great that Henry Bynneman and Garrad Dewes were both fined by the Stationers' Company in 1567 and 1568 respectively for attempting to circulate pirated copies. The work begins with a dedication by Harman to his neighbour, Elizabeth, countess of Shrewsbury, who had a house in the parish of Erith, nearby. The 'epistle to the reader' is followed by exhaustive little essays on each class of the thieves' and tramps' fraternity to the number of twenty-four, and by a list of names of the chief professors of the art 'lyvinge nowe at this present'. A vocabulary of 'their pelting speche' or cant terms concludes the volume, which is embellished by a few woodcuts, including one of 'an upright man, Nicolas Blunt', and another of 'a counterfeit cranke, Nicolas Genynges'. Harman borrowed something from *The Fraternitye of Vacabondes*, by John Awdely, which was probably first issued in 1561, although the earliest edition now known is dated 1575. Harman's information, however, is far fuller and fresher than that of Awdely, who does not record the underworld vocabulary and whose tone is much more condemnatory. Harman's book was used extensively by later writers. *The Groundworke of Conny-Catching* (1592), which makes use of illustrations from earlier books by Robert Greene, and has on occasions been assigned to him, reprints the greater part of Harman's book. Thomas Dekker, in his *Belman of London* (1608), made free use of it, and Samuel Rowlands exposed Dekker's theft in his *Martin Mark-All, Beadle of Bridewell* (1610). Dekker, in the second part of his *Belman*, called *Lanthorne and Candlelight* (1609), conveyed to his pages Harman's vocabulary of thieves' words, which Richard Head incorporated in his *English Rogue* (1671–80). Harman's vocabulary is the basis of the later slang dictionaries (see, among others, that forming the appendix to *Memoires of John Hall* (d. 1707), 1708). Another edition of Harman's *Caveat* appeared in 1573, and this was reprinted by Machell Stace in 1814. A carefully collated text of the second edition was edited by Viles and Furnivall for the Early English Text Society in 1869. They exalt Harman in a somewhat panegyric introduction as a 'wise and practical man' and a 'keen inquiring Social Reformer'.

Harman married Millicent Leigh, daughter of Nicholas Leigh, from Addington in Surrey, and had three daughters, Anne, Mary, and Bridget, and also perhaps a son, William. It is not known when he died.

SIDNEY LEE, *rev.* CHRISTOPHER BURLINSON

Sources T. Harman, *Caveat*, ed. E. Viles and F. J. Furnivall, EETS (1869) • E. Hasted, *The history and topographical survey of the county of Kent*, 1 (1778) • *STC, 1475–1640* • Arber, *Regs. Stationers* • R. S. Luborsky, 'Telling a book by its cover, or, How Harman masquerades as Greene', *American Notes and Queries*, new ser., 5 (1992), 100–03 • T. Robinson, *The common law of Kent, or, The custom of gavelkind* (1741) • A. L. Beier, *Masterless men: the vagrancy problem in England, 1560–1640* (1985) • C. J. Ribton-Turner, *A history of vagrants and vagrancy and beggars and begging* (1887)

Harmar, John (*c.*1555–1613), Greek scholar, was born at Newbury in Berkshire of unknown parentage. In 1569 he entered Winchester College. In 1572 he became a scholar at New College, Oxford, where he matriculated on 10 January 1575, graduated BA on 21 January 1577, and became a fellow. Anthony Wood records that he was accounted 'a subtle Aristotelian' in his youth (Wood, *Ath. Oxon.*, 2.138). His first published work, an English translation of Calvin's sermons on the ten commandments, appeared in 1579 and again in 1581. He dedicated this translation to Robert Dudley, earl of Leicester. The preface records that Leicester's patronage allowed him to study at Winchester and Oxford.

It appears that Harmar travelled on the continent some time before 1585, perhaps after he graduated MA on 18 June 1582. He stayed at Geneva, where he attended Theodore Beza's lectures and sermons and 'found him no lesse than a father unto me in curtesie & good will' (*Sermons*, trans. Harmar, sig. 3r). He acknowledged this debt at Oxford in 1587 with an English translation of Beza's French sermons on the Song of Songs, also dedicated to Leicester. Wood states that Harmar disputed at Paris with Catholic theologians.

On 25 March 1585 Harmar was appointed regius professor of Greek at Oxford. He held the position for five years. In 1586 he was responsible for the first Greek book printed at Oxford: an edition of six sermons of John Chrysostom from New College manuscripts, dedicated to Sir Thomas Bromley, lord chancellor. In 1590 he used manuscripts at New College to produce the first edition of the Greek text of twenty-two of Chrysostom's sermons to the people of Antioch, and he supplied his own Latin version of the nineteenth sermon. This work he dedicated to Bromley's successor, Sir Christopher Hatton.

From 1588 until 1595 Harmar was headmaster of Winchester College. The following year he was elected warden of the college, a post he held until his death. He was installed as a prebendary at Winchester on 10 January 1595; he became rector of Compton in Hampshire the same year and of Droxford in 1596. In 1604 he was one of the Oxford scholars assigned to work on the translation of the gospels, Acts, and Revelation for the English Bible of James VI and I. In recognition of this role he was made BD and DD on 16 May 1605. Sir Henry Savile was a fellow Bible translator, and Harmar may have contributed to his important edition of the works of Chrysostom, printed at Eton in 1610–13. Harmar's will bequeaths a copy of this edition to Winchester College.

Harmar died on 11 October 1613. He was married to Elizabeth, who survived him; they had no children. He did, however, make numerous bequests to relatives, friends, and dependants. He left many of his Greek books to New College and gave his collection of foreign-language bibles to Winchester College. He was buried in the chapel of New College, where his epitaph was placed. His nephew John *Harmar (1593x6–1670), also regius professor of Greek at Oxford, promised Wood an account of his uncle's life for the *Athenae*. This, unfortunately, was never delivered. P. BOTLEY and N. G. WILSON

Sources will, PRO, PROB 11/123, sig. 7 • *Sermons of M. John Calvin, upon the x. commandements of the lawe, given of God by Moses, otherwise called the Decalogue*, trans. J. Harmar (1581) • *D. Ioannis Chrysostomi archiepiscopi Constantinopolitani, homiliae sex, ex manuscriptis codicibus Novi Collegii*, ed. J. Harmar (1586) • *Master Bezaes sermons upon the three first chapters of the Canticle of Canticles*, trans. J. Harmar (1587) • *Ioannis Chrysostomi archiepiscopi Constantinopolitani homiliae ad populum Antiochenum, cum presbyter esset Antiochae, habitae, duae & viginti*, ed. J. Harmar (1590) • Wood, *Ath. Oxon.*, new edn, 2.138–9 • *DNB*
Wealth at death approx. £427—plus several properties and his library: will, PRO, PROB 11/123, sig. 7

Harmar, John (1593x6–1670), Church of England clergyman and Greek scholar, was, according to Wood, born at Churchdown, near Gloucester, eldest son of Arthur Harmar. He entered Winchester School probably about 1606 and was elected to a scholarship there in 1608 aged twelve, during the wardenship of his uncle, also John *Harmar (c.1555–1613). In 1610 he was elected to a demyship at Magdalen College, Oxford, being, according to Wood, of about a year's standing; his age was given then as sixteen. He was admitted BA on 15 December 1614 and MA on 28 June 1617. In 1616, with fifteen other BA demies, he was deprived of commons for a week for dining in hall with a hat instead of a cap, contrary to the vice-president's injunctions. On graduating MA Harmar took holy orders and became usher at Magdalen College School, where he was again deprived of commons, this time for a day, for speaking contumeliously of his superior, and it appears that he was already something of a figure of fun: Heylyn's diary records under 12 April 1624: 'Jack Harmar went towards London in the wagon, on which ... I made a knavish song to make merry withal' (*Memorial*, xviii). In 1626 he was appointed master of St Alban's Free School and, in a letter to the mayor and burgesses there, boasted of the orations made by his pupils on a visit there by Charles I. He supplicated for the MB on 4 July 1632 (and a tract, *De lue venerea*, is doubtfully attributed to him). He left St Alban's for the under-mastership of Westminster School in 1632, and in 1649 he addressed to Lambert Osbaldeston the headmaster, a defence of John Williams, archbishop of York. In 1650 he was intruded as regius professor of Greek at Oxford and in 1659 was, through the influence of Richard Cromwell, presented to the donative rectory of Ewhurst, Hampshire.

Harmar wrote grammatical texts for Magdalen College School and for St Alban's, and his *Lexicon etymologicum linguae Graecae* (1637) was many times reprinted as an appendix to Scapula's *Lexicon Graeco-Latinum*. He also published Greek and Latin verses on religious themes *Christologia metrike, sive, Hymnus ad Christum, vitam ejus enarrans Latine redditus et in lucem emissus opera et cura J. Harmari* (1658), which was reprinted several times as an appendix to his Greek and Latin translation of the shorter

catechism of the Assembly of Divines (1659). Wood reports that Harmar translated one or more of the plays of Margaret, duchess of Newcastle, but there is evidence only of his being considered as a possible translator; however, it is conceivable that he was the anonymous translator of her biography of her husband.

Though Harmar's scholarship and his skill in Latin and Greek composition were never questioned, and he was credited with the revival of Greek learning at Oxford, his indiscriminate flattery of those in power made him a laughing-stock to his contemporaries: he published verses in praise of Oliver and Richard Cromwell and of Charles II, and was the dupe of a hoax, delivering a solemn Greek oration before a London merchant visiting The Mitre inn at Oxford who was represented to him as a Greek patriarch. His *Oratio steliteutica* of 1658, directed against the speeches of the *terrae filios* and other jesters, while flattering the presbyterian and independent heads of the university, also reflects his own treatment at the hands of his juniors.

On 14 September 1660 Harmar was deprived of his chair by the commissioners for non-appearance, and he retired to Steventon, in Hampshire, where, according to Wood, he lived largely on the jointure of his wife, who was probably Joan Orpwood (d. 1670). In 1662 he published a Latin life of Cicero. He died at Steventon on 1 November 1670 and was buried there on the following day partly at the cost of the lexicographer, Nicholas Lloyd.

ELISABETH LEEDHAM-GREEN

Sources Wood, *Ath. Oxon.*, new edn, 1.xxxviii; 3.918–21 • Wood, *Ath. Oxon.: Fasti* (1820), 332 • J. R. Bloxam, *A register of the presidents, fellows ... of Saint Mary Magdalen College*, 8 vols. (1853–85), vol. 3 • W. D. Macray, *A register of the members of St Mary Magdalen College, Oxford*, 3 (1901) • *Reg. Oxf.*, vol. 2 • *Hist. U. Oxf.* 4: *17th-cent. Oxf.* • T. F. Kirby, *Winchester scholars: a list of the wardens, fellows, and scholars of ... Winchester College* (1888), 163 • N. Carlisle, *A concise description of the endowed grammar schools of England and Wales* (1818) • P. Heylyn, *Memorial of Bishop Waynflete*, ed. J. R. Bloxam (1851) [incl. partial transcription of Bodl. Oxf., Wood MS E.4] • *Calamy rev.*

Harmar, Samuel (*fl.* 1642), educational reformer, probably lived in Gloucestershire. Virtually nothing is known of his life, though he may have belonged to the Harmer family in that county, various members of which were mill owners and clothiers in the area around Stroud. If Samuel Harmar attended Oxford or Cambridge, he did not earn a degree. In 1642 Harmar was one of the earlier proponents of virtually universal education. His tract, *Vox Populi, or, Glostersheres Desire*, printed in London for Thomas Bates, sought to redress what he deemed to be the greatest evils in the land—ignorance, profaneness, and idleness. To cure these problems Harmar called on parliament to appoint an honest, religious schoolmaster in every parish capable of maintaining one. He envisaged teachers as allies of godly ministers, sharing the task of educating every child to read, write, and understand religious principles. Apparently alluding to the grand remonstrance's call for a general synod, Harmar wanted a 'learned synod' and parliament to approve a catechism. One goal of catechetic instruction was religious uniformity, an ideal that situates Harmar among the more conservative puritans, and the importance he attached to such instruction reflects Gloucestershire's general interest in catechisms; among those known to have been in use in the county were John Sprint's *The Summe of the Christian Religion* (1613), Richard Webb's *A Key of Knowledge for Catechizing Children in Christ* (1622), John Geree's *A Catechisme in Briefe Questions and Answeres* (1629), and, later, William Sheppard's *A New Catechism* (1649). The Westminster assembly issued its shorter catechism for similar use in 1647.

To finance the schools Harmar recommended a tax similar to the poor rate; he wanted those without children to pay more because they too benefited from widespread education. He suggested that someone with an annual income of £20 10s. a year. Tax-supported education, he averred, would reduce the dependence of poor parents on parishes for assistance in raising their children. He also recommended that parents require each child to earn a penny before school and another afterwards by spinning, knitting, working with flax or hemp, or engaging in other forms of productive labour; similar programmes were later advocated by Samuel Hartlib, William Petty, and Henry Robinson.

For Harmar the schoolmaster should be a disciplinarian, 'a terror to the malicious [students], because he would be always resident like a magistrate' to hear complaints against his charges (Harmar, *Vox populi*, A4r). In addition to instruction in reading and writing, students would learn to be godly and well mannered. Harmar framed the curriculum in terms of four 'laws', which would be read twice weekly in every school with the intent of reforming children's hearts. Focusing on God and the sabbath, the first rule prohibited swearing and called for appropriate behaviour on Sundays, with a ban on playing games, gadding about, or acting wantonly. The second stressed love and obedience to parents, elders, and superiors, while the third concentrated on loving, considerate behaviour toward siblings, servants, neighbours, and fellow pupils. The last rule dealt in a catch-all manner with reading, writing, care of apparel, and correct behaviour. Reading in a humming manner or nasally was eschewed, as were writing outside the lines and using uneven letters or irregular spacing between words. Clothing was to be clean and not torn, stockings gartered, and shoes pointed. Proper conduct included doffing one's hat, civil greetings, and courtesy. Violating a rule brought blows with a rod on a child's hand, four times for an infraction of the first regulation, three for any of the others. Harmar believed that students who embraced these rules in their hearts would be like little preachers, rebuking and persuading obstinate and servile children to reform. His tract thus reflects the puritan concern with making basic education widespread, combining study with productive labour, and using schools to buttress the catechetic instruction of ministers. The date of Harmar's death is not known.

RICHARD L. GREAVES

Sources S. Harmar, *Vox populi, or, Glostersheres desire* (1642) · VCH *Gloucestershire*, vols. 10–11 · J. Morgan, *Godly learning: puritan attitudes towards reason, learning, and education, 1560–1640* (1986) · I. Green, *The Christian's ABC: catechisms and catechising in England,* c.1530–1740 (1996) · C. Webster, *The great instauration: science, medicine and reform, 1626–1660* (1975) · W. A. L. Vincent, *The state and school education, 1640–1660, in England and Wales* (1950) · R. L. Greaves, *The puritan revolution and educational thought: background for reform* (1969)

Harmer, James (1777–1853), lawyer and local politician, was born in London, the son of a Spitalfields weaver. Left an orphan at the age of ten, he was articled to an attorney in 1792, but left because of an early marriage. He later transferred to Messrs Fletcher and Wright of Bloomsbury, and went on to practise for himself in 1799, with considerable success. His practice was chiefly in the criminal courts, and the experience he gained there made him a strong advocate of reform in criminal procedure. His evidence before the committee for the reform of the criminal law was declared by Sir James Mackintosh to be unequalled in its effect: he was held to have had great influence on both public opinion and parliamentary decision.

Harmer exposed the shortcomings of witnesses, and especially the mode of obtaining evidence against Holloway and Haggerty, who were (most probably wrongly) executed in 1807 for the murder of a Mr Steele. He was also instrumental in procuring the abolition of the blood money system. He energetically investigated cases where he considered that prisoners had been wrongly committed. He wrote pamphlets on behalf of Holloway and Haggerty in 1807, on the case of George Mathews in 1819, and in 1825 on behalf of Edward Harris.

In 1833 Harmer was unanimously elected alderman of the ward of Farringdon Without, which he had represented since 1826 in the common council, and gave up his legal practice, which was said to have been worth £4000 a year. He was sheriff of London and Middlesex in 1834. He resigned his alderman's gown in 1840, when his election to the mayoralty, which would normally have been automatic as senior alderman, was successfully opposed on the ground of his being proprietor of the *Weekly Dispatch*, which then advocated very advanced liberal and independent religious and political views.

Harmer was president of the Newsvendors' Benevolent Provident Institution, making liberal contributions to their funds. He took a leading part in establishing the Royal Free Hospital in Greville Street, in 1828. He was a member of the Guild of Spectacle Makers. He lived in Kent, where he built a mansion, Ingress Abbey, at Ingress Park, near Greenhithe, chiefly of stone procured from old London Bridge on its demolition. He died at the house of his friend Adam Steele, Oakland House, Cricklewood, Middlesex, on 12 June 1853, after an illness of seven weeks, and was buried on 16 June in Kensal Green cemetery. He left a large fortune to his granddaughter.

CHARLES WELCH, rev. BETH F. WOOD

Sources *ILN* (25 June 1853), 507 · *GM*, 2nd ser., 40 (1853), 201–2 · J. Grant, *The newspaper press: its origin, progress, and present position*, 3: *The metropolitan weekly and provincial press* (1872) · A. B. Beaven, ed., *The aldermen of the City of London, temp. Henry III–[1912]*, 1 (1908), 165, 334 · A. B. Beaven, ed., *The aldermen of the City of London, temp. Henry III–[1912]*, 2 (1913), 144, 204 · Ward, *Men of the reign* · *The Times* (13 June 1853), 9 · *Annual Register* (1819) · Boase, *Mod. Eng. biog.*

Likenesses T. Wright, stipple, pubd 1820, Bm, NPG · Wivell, engraving, repro. in Evans, *Catalogue*, no. 16870 · oils, Gravesend town hall, Kent

Wealth at death £70,000–£300,000

Harmer, Sir Sidney Frederic (1862–1950), zoologist and university teacher, was born in Heigham, Norwich, Norfolk, on 9 March 1862, the second son among the five children of Frederic William Harmer, wool merchant and manufacturer, and his wife, Mary Young Lyon. He was educated at Amersham Hall, Reading, and at seventeen won a mathematical scholarship to University College, London, where he studied natural sciences. He subsequently went to King's College, Cambridge, where he had a distinguished career as exhibitioner, scholar, and fellow. He obtained first classes in both parts (1882 and 1883) of the natural sciences tripos.

In 1885 Harmer became university lecturer in advanced invertebrate morphology, and five years later became superintendent of the University Museum of Zoology. As a teacher he was highly respected for his industry, patience, and accuracy in observation, his clarity and precision in recording, and his ability to impart knowledge. Throughout his life he inspired affection by his gentleness, courtesy, and kindness.

In 1891 Harmer married Laura Russell, daughter of Arthur Pearce Howell of the Bengal civil service. They had two sons and two daughters (a son and a daughter predeceased him).

Harmer was appointed keeper of zoology at the British Museum (Natural History) in 1907 and from 1919 to 1927 was its director. His industry was prodigious and he left to the museum a volume of files, indexes, and notebooks filled with accurate and methodically arranged taxonomic work, together with his exceptionally fine library of works on Polyzoa and whales.

At Cambridge Harmer's research centred on the embryology, anatomy, and taxonomy of Polyzoa and *Cephalodiscus*, for which he was the first of the Cambridge zoologists to use the binocular microscope. He also developed an interest in whales, and worked at the Stazione Zoologica in Naples and the Plymouth laboratory of the Marine Biological Association, with which he was long connected. His first three volumes on *The Polyzoa of the Siboga-Expedition* were published in 1915, 1926, and 1934, and the material for the fourth was prepared by 1941. Harmer published numerous influential papers on the Cetacea and enhanced the collections. His equanimity led to good relationships with the trustees of the British Museum (Natural History), and he steered the museum smoothly through a difficult time with tact and judgement.

Harmer had a long connection with the Museums Association, of which he was president in 1904, becoming an honorary member in 1922. For thirty-one years he was a fellow of the Linnean Society, serving on the council in 1921–4 and 1927–32, and being vice-president in 1931–2 and president in 1927–31. In 1934 he received the Linnaean medal. Harmer was elected a fellow of the Royal Society in 1898, served on the council, and was a vice-president.

Other honours included being made a foreign member of the Norwegian and Swedish academies and an honorary member of the Boston Society of Natural History and the Société Zoologique de France. He was appointed KBE in 1920.

Harmer travelled extensively, was fond of music, and was a competent pianist. He was a keen cyclist on the high bicycle until quite late in life, and was always an enthusiastic and knowledgeable gardener. Harmer died at his home, 5 Grange Road, Melbourn, Cambridgeshire, on 22 October 1950.   NEIL CHALMERS, *rev.*

Sources W. T. Calman, *Obits. FRS*, 7 (1950–51), 359–71 · W. T. Stearn, *The Natural History Museum at South Kensington: a history of the British Museum (Natural History), 1753–1980* (1981) · *The Times* (24 Nov 1950) · A. B. Hastings, *Proceedings of the Linnean Society of London*, 163rd session (1950–51), 250–52 · J. G. Kerr, 'Sir Sidney Harmer, KBE, FRS', *Nature*, 166 (1950), 888–9

Archives Marine Biological Association of UK, Plymouth, letters, papers, press cuttings · NHM, corresp. and bibliography of polyzoa and drawings · U. Cam., Museum of Zoology, corresp. and papers | BL, corresp. with Macmillans, Add. MS 55223 · King's AC Cam., letters to Oscar Browning · Linn. Soc., corresp. with Herbert Forrest · NHM, letters to A. C. L. G. Gunther · NL Scot., corresp. with Sir J. M. Wordie and corresp. relating to the *Discovery* committee · Scott Polar RI, letters to Apsley Cherry-Garrard

Likenesses photograph, repro. in *Obits. FRS*, 359

Wealth at death £25,972 16s. 9d.: probate, 30 March 1951, CGPLA Eng. & Wales

Harmer, Thomas (1714–1788), Independent minister and church historian, was born at Norwich in 1714, probably in October. From 1730 to 1734 he attended Moorfields Academy, where he was trained for the ministry by Thomas Ridgley and John Eames. While a student at Moorfields he gained a reputation as a preacher of considerable promise, and this led in July 1734 to his being invited to become minister of the Independent church at Wattisfield, Suffolk. Although he moved to Wattisfield in September 1734, he declined to accept pastoral responsibility of the congregation until he had become of age. As a consequence he was not ordained until 7 October 1735.

Harmer proved to be a popular and industrious preacher, as well as a man of considerable learning, especially in oriental customs and history, and 'one of the most eminent and influential ministers of his day' (Duncan, 22). His reputation as a scholar and useful writer rested originally upon his *Observations on Divers Passages of Scripture, Illustrated by Accounts of Travellers in the East*, which was published initially in a single volume in 1764, but by 1787 had been extended to four volumes. A fourth edition, edited and revised by Dr Adam Clarke, appeared in 1808. However, Harmer is probably better remembered for his histories of the dissenting churches of East Anglia. He compiled or collected in manuscript form brief accounts of almost all the dissenting churches in Norfolk and Suffolk down to 1774. Although never published, this manuscript formed the basis for Browne's *Memorials* (1877) and Harmer's own *Remarks on the Ancient and Present State of the Congregational Churches in Suffolk and Norfolk*, published originally in 1777 but reprinted in 1823, together with some letters and minor works and with a memoir of his life by William Youngman.

Harmer remained minister at Wattisfield for fifty-four years, during which time he missed only one Sunday service through illness. He married, on 27 October 1741 at Allhallows, London, Catherine Burwood, schoolteacher, of Woodbridge; they had a daughter, Elizabeth, who was born in 1745. Harmer died suddenly at Wattisfield on 27 November 1788 and was buried on 7 December, when his funeral sermon was preached by his friend John Mead Ray of Sudbury.   ALEXANDER GORDON, *rev.* M. J. MERCER

Sources T. J. Hosken, *History of Congregationalism and memorials of the churches of our order in Suffolk* (1920) · J. Browne, *A history of Congregationalism and memorials of the churches in Norfolk and Suffolk* (1877) · J. Duncan, 'Rev. Thomas Harmer, 1714–1788: pastor at Wattisfield, 1734–1788', 1959, DWL [typescript] · C. A. Jolly, *The story of Wattisfield Congregational Church, 1654–1949* (1949) · J. M. Ray, *The conflict and the crown of the faithful ministers. A sermon … on the occasion of the death of the Rev. T. Harmer* (1789) · C. Surman, index, DWL · J. Aikin and others, *General biography, or, Lives, critical and historical of the most eminent persons*, 10 vols. (1799–1815) · W. Youngman, introduction, in *The miscellaneous works of the late Rev. Thomas Harmer* (1823) · A. Clarke, 'Memoir', in T. Harmer, *Observations on divers passages of scripture*, 4th edn (1808) · S. W. Rix, ed., 'Historical and biographical accounts of the dissenting churches in the counties of Norfolk and Suffolk', 1774, Norfolk RO · *IGI*
Archives DWL
Likenesses T. Wright, stipple (after portrait by unknown artist), BM, NPG; repro. in *Lives of eminent and remarkable characters … of Essex, Suffolk and Norfolk* (1820) · portrait, Wattisfield church

Harmsworth, Alfred Charles William, Viscount Northcliffe (1865–1922), journalist and newspaper proprietor, was born at Sunnybank, Chapelizod, near Dublin, on 15 July 1865, the eldest son of Alfred Harmsworth (1837–1889), barrister, and his wife, Geraldine Mary (1838–1925), daughter of William Maffett, a land agent from co. Down. The family background was therefore Anglo-Irish, but the Harmsworths moved to London two years later in the hope of improving their prospects. Declining fortunes necessitated another move, from St John's Wood to Hampstead.

Early years and journalism Alfred began his education at Stamford grammar school, Lincolnshire, in 1876 and went as a day boy to Henley House School, Hampstead, in 1878, where he showed an early interest in journalism by publishing the school magazine. The family continued to decline, thanks to Alfred's father's fondness for alcohol, and Alfred set out to earn his living; by 1880 he was an occasional reporter on the *Hampstead and Highgate Express*. He diversified his experience, composing articles for *The Cyclist* and *Wheeling*, by no means a minor job, for this was the great age of the bicycle, and he also wrote for *The Globe* and various boys' and girls' papers published by James Henderson, whom Alfred described as his first journalistic sponsor. His education took another, and rather unusual, turn when he embarked on a continental tour with E. V. R. Powys, third son of the third Lord Lilford; but his personal life was thrown into disarray when he made a maidservant pregnant, and his mother obliged him to leave the family home and take lodgings. In 1882 he took rooms in the Temple at 6 Pump Court, and abandoned any thoughts

Alfred Charles William Harmsworth, Viscount Northcliffe (1865–1922), by Philip A. de Laszlo, 1911

of going to Cambridge (a somewhat vague notion floated before his continental tour).

There is no specific reason why the young Harmsworth chose to make his career in journalism, except that it was a profession in which the less than completely educated could make their way if they showed sufficient talent and made the right contacts. Harmsworth wrote for *The Globe*, the *Morning Post*, the *St James's Gazette*, and the various publications of Cassell & Co., and for the rising man of popular journalism, George Newnes. His freelance work enabled him to make vital contacts, and alerted him to what he described in a conversation with Max Pemberton on the steps of the British Museum as the need to offer 'less British Museum and more life' (Taylor, 11). He was impressed by what the editor of *Tit-Bits*, Newnes, was doing to cater for those whom Harmsworth described as the products of the British schools: 'thousands of boys and girls … who are aching to read. They do not care for the ordinary newspaper. They have no interest in society, but will read anything which is simple and is sufficiently interesting' (ibid., 12). Harmsworth was only nineteen when he edited *Youth* for £2 a week. A bout of pneumonia brought on by cycling from Bristol in the rain and with insufficient food resulted in his doctor's ordering him in 1885 to leave London for a while, and he moved to Coventry, where he worked for Iliffe & Sons, a publishing house which owned the *Midland Daily Telegraph* and *Bicycling News*. But Harmsworth maintained his connection with London journalism, writing two books for George Newnes, *One Thousand Ways to Earn a Living*, and *All about Railways*. He was offered a partnership in the Iliffe firm before he was twenty-one, but by now he had recovered his health and saved £1000, and he returned to London in 1887. Harmsworth had now the experience and the capital to found his own newspaper business, which he did at 26 Paternoster Square, and from there issued a number of magazines, including the celebrated *Answers to Correspondents*. The first issue came out on 16 June 1888, a 'storehouse of interesting knowledge' (ibid., 14). It was eye-catching, for it asked questions and supplied answers which still intrigue: for example, 'How madmen write' (ibid., 15). In 1890 he launched *Comic Cuts*, a pictorial magazine which was not aimed at children but at adults who had read little or nothing previously. Harmsworth was joined in this enterprise by his financially astute brother Harold *Harmsworth, and together they built up the Amalgamated Press Company, whose profits soon reached £50,000 a year; within five years *Answers* alone was recording net weekly sales of more than 1 million copies.

Harmsworth was an impetuous man. On 11 April 1888, much to his mother's disapproval, he married Mary Milner (1867–1963), daughter of Robert Milner of Kidlington, Oxfordshire, a merchant with West India interests. They had no children, which Harmsworth seems to have regretted, but there was plenty to absorb his energy, because he was becoming a man to notice in the world of journalism when it was about to enter a new and vital stage in its development. The 'new journalism' of the 1890s was by no means entirely new: its economic and technological foundations had been laid in the previous decades, with improved machinery, the use of illustrations, investigative reporting, and the employment of news agencies. To these were now added short paragraphs, more space for human interest stories, and catchy headlines. Another important development was the wider range of distribution which created truly national newspapers for a population which was ready for the 'busy man's newspaper' in what the politician and journalist T. P. O'Connor called in 1889 'an age of hurry' (A. Jones, 134). Harmsworth and his brother were in the forefront of popular publishing with their magazines, which included *Boys' Home Journal*, *Marvel*, *Boys' Friend*, *Home Sweet Home*, and *Home Chat*. By 1892 the firm's combined weekly sales figure was 1,009,067, the largest of any magazine company in the world. The Harmsworths now moved into daily journalism when in 1894 William Kennedy *Jones persuaded them to buy the derelict *Evening News* for £25,000; with Kennedy Jones's help they made it into a profitable newspaper. Harmsworth now briefly showed an interest in politics, standing unsuccessfully as Unionist candidate for Portsmouth in the general election of 1895. A year later he revealed where his real talents lay.

On 4 May 1896 Alfred Harmsworth showed that he had the ability and the nerve to take the new journalism at the tide, when he launched the *Daily Mail*, a perfect example of the newspaper for the busy man in the age of hurry.

The *Daily Mail* and *The Times* The *Mail's* appearance was conservative by the standards of today's tabloids. It was not, as used to be supposed, a working man's paper, but a paper for the lower middle classes, the clerks and other City workers who needed something to read on their way to and from work. Harmsworth used the techniques that had turned the *Evening News* round: the insertion of eye-catching items; the improvement of the distribution of the paper, with selected sales points where most potential readers were to be found; the use of a net sales certificate to attract advertising; a women's page. Moreover, Harmsworth realized the importance of careful preparation: more than sixty-five dummy runs of the *Mail* were made, beginning on 15 February 1896. Harmsworth was sure of the kind of readership he wished to reach. The *Mail* was described as 'The busy man's paper' (Pound and Harmsworth, 202), and Harmsworth developed the means to satisfy their reading needs by using the new technology which could cut, fold, and count copies as well as printing them; between 48,000 and 90,000 copies an hour were produced. The first issue sold 397,213 copies, and net sales peaked at 989,255 in 1900, never falling below 713,000. Harmsworth knew too that a commercial enterprise must never stand still, but must forever expand. In 1902 he set up a Manchester office, using a system of coding that enabled his staff to telegraph from London to Manchester letterpress, headings, and positions. He established two printing presses and twelve linotype printing machines, which applied the principle of the typewriter to the automatic casting of type, in an empty schoolroom in Manchester, thus doing away with hand compositors. In 1897 he took advantage of the telegraphic link between London and New York, and in 1898 established a wire from his headquarters to the end of the ocean cable on Valentia Island off the Irish coast. In 1902 the firm moved into Carmelite House and there Harmsworth installed eight linotype 3 small rotary presses in the basement, producing savings of 35 per cent; this enabled him to sell his paper for half the price of his nearest competitors. He arranged a telegraph between the *Mail* in London and *Le Journal* in Paris.

But Harmsworth's genius did not lie only in his appreciation of the potential of the technological revolution of the late nineteenth century. He was a supreme exponent of popular journalism, with an instinctive flair for getting inside the mind of the common man. The third marquess of Salisbury dismissed the *Mail* as 'a newspaper run by office boys for office boys' (Pound and Harmsworth, 211), but this was an unfair description of Harmsworth's talents. He understood the middle classes of England, appreciating that they did not necessarily want 'four leading articles, a page of Parliament, and columns of speeches' (Taylor, 32). Harmsworth was not an easy man to work for. He searched the *Mail* for ways of perfecting its style, and he was savage in his criticism of what he saw as failures among his staff—if they did not produce good pictures or print a woman's page, for example. But it would be wrong to dismiss him as a trivializer. He still harboured political desires, and he urged the patriotic line. In 1897 he warned of the German 'threat' to the British empire. The Second South African War of 1899–1902 gave him a perfect canvas on which to paint his political beliefs. He called for more guns, better generalship; he criticized the Conservative cabinet as inefficient, old, and prone to panic. He printed vivid—and uncompromisingly realistic—accounts of combat and the battlefield. By the end of the war Harmsworth had no doubt that his newspaper made him politically significant. In 1904 he wrote to St Loe Strachey:

> The most unfortunate part of the circulation of my paper is the fact that the immense number of people who see everything that appears in it and the comment they make magnifies every utterance. We have been obliged to reduce the tone and colour of the paper to far below that of any morning newspaper except the 'Times'. (Northcliffe to St Loe Strachey, 18 Nov 1904, St Loe Strachey MSS, HLRO, S/11/4/16)

The position, he went on, 'is a new and difficult one for a newspaper owner'. He gave examples of how recently, in a small savings bank collapse, he had been obliged to 'leave things alone' after he was inundated with letters and telegrams from bankers all over the country.

The Harmsworth empire expanded, though not always quite so successfully. On 2 November 1903 he founded the *Daily Mirror* as a women's paper with—a great innovation—an all-female staff; this failed, but characteristically Harmsworth ordered a relaunch in January 1904 as the *Illustrated Daily Mirror*, and sales recovered. His national reputation was acknowledged on 23 June 1904 when he was made a baronet. He always liked to claim that when he wanted a peerage he would 'buy one, like an honest man' (Taylor, 85), but he was satisfied to accept one on 9 December 1905, taking as his title Baron Northcliffe of the Isle of Thanet. He liked to style himself N to advertise his role as the Napoleon of Fleet Street. Northcliffe exemplified popular journalism; but he also aspired to buy a quality newspaper, and in 1905 he acquired *The Observer*, which was added to his Associated Newspapers group. But he quarrelled with its editor, J. L. Garvin, and sold it to Waldorf Astor in 1912. By then he had realized his ambition by buying *The Times* on 16 March 1908 for £320,000, following a complex financial and political campaign in which he outmanoeuvred his rival, C. Arthur Pearson. Northcliffe was more acceptable to the Conservative Party leader, A. J. Balfour, and he was able to portray Pearson as a young adventurer. He always claimed that he allowed the paper independence, but its editor, Geoffrey Dawson, saw eye to eye with him on protectionist and unionist politics, otherwise the relationship would not have worked. Northcliffe wanted to save the paper as a kind of national asset, and even contemplated leaving it in his will to a national committee like that which ran the British Museum. He also wanted to make it more commercially viable by attracting advertising and making its coverage of the news more topical, however much he protested that it should not be run 'as a profit-making

machine' (Koss, 96). When sales dipped below 41,000 in 1913 Northcliffe took appropriate action, reducing the price by one third to 2*d.*, though the net gain in sales of 6000 did not offset the loss in revenue. On 16 March 1914 he again took bold action, reducing the price to 1*d.* Average sales rose to 145,000. He also introduced pictorial advertisements, purged inefficient staff, enlivened the typography, offered discounted advertising and subscription rates, and appointed a penny-pinching day editor, Hugh Chisholm, on the assumption that a Scotsman would save him money.

Private life Northcliffe's private life at this time could be described as one not unnatural for a newspaper magnate, with plenty of money, power, and the glamour of success. He already had an illegitimate son, Alfred Benjamin Smith, the product of his youthful indiscretion, who was raised by his grandmother and whom Northcliffe apprenticed to a carpenter. From 1900 he and his wife grew apart, and he kept a regular mistress, Kathleen Wrohan (d. *c.*1923), an Irishwoman with whom he had three children, two sons and one daughter, all of whom he provided for. The first son was born on 25 August 1912 at 2 Brick Lane, London, and Northcliffe gave £1000 a year for the first three years of the boy's life and £6000 a year thereafter. In 1912 his daughter, Geraldine, was born and on 14 August 1914 a second son, Harold. All were generously provided for. Likewise he was good to his employees, provided they satisfied his relentless journalistic standards, and he gave generously to them, especially those who named their sons after him, all of which suggests that his lack of family with his wife was deeply disappointing to him. In 1902 he took a second mistress, his secretary Louise Owen (also Irish), and he had an affair with the Baroness Betty von Hutten, a popular novelist. By 1914 Northcliffe had made his mark on British cultural history. He was supposed to possess political power, but no one knew for sure how powerful he really was. Politicians did not like to take chances; in 1909 Lloyd George showed him his draft budget proposals, telling him to make what he liked of the information in the *Daily Mail*. In 1910 he was offered £1000 from Unionist Party funds to produce an extra million copies of a special edition of the *Mail* for provincial distribution, a plan which came to nothing, but which illustrated the important links between press and politicians. But Northcliffe was not for sale, unlike many of his journalist contemporaries. And it was the coming of the First World War that gave him his chance to play a key role on the political stage. He had always taken the patriotic line. In 1913 he urged the country to support Lord Roberts's idea of a national service league to put the country on a war footing. He had always predicted that Germany was the enemy of Britain and her empire, with 'preparations … quietly and systematically made' (Taylor, 141). He lobbied MPs, especially Winston Churchill, to alert them to the German threat.

Northcliffe at war When the European crisis broke in August 1914, however, Northcliffe did not want to send an army to Europe: 'What about our own country?' (Taylor,

144). But he quickly threw himself heart and soul into the allied cause, claiming that the *Daily Mail* was the paper that foretold the war, and setting himself up as the personal advocate of soldiers' interests. At the end of August the *Mail* offered to pay for letters sent to their families by serving soldiers. He campaigned against official secrecy, and on 26 August Hamilton Fyfe wrote graphically of the British wounded, adding that they 'had no trenches, no cover of any kind' (ibid., 149). He was keen to identify German 'atrocities'. He called on the government to declare cotton as contraband. Above all, he exposed the 'shells scandal' in April 1915 when he alleged, and with good cause, that the want of sufficient high explosive shells was 'fatal' to the British offensive at Festubert (ibid., 157). On 21 May the *Mail* printed the headline 'The Tragedy of the Shells; Lord Kitchener's grave error' (ibid., 157). This had the unexpected result of causing a dip in the *Daily Mail* sales, with Northcliffe described as the ally of the Hun; but it also contributed to the crisis which ended with Asquith reconstructing his government and taking the Unionist opposition into the cabinet. Northcliffe's reputation rested on the assumption that he could, and did, wield power; and this was enhanced by the political manoeuvres of December 1916, which ended with the replacement of Asquith as prime minister by Lloyd George. The role of the press is still disputed, but there is no doubt that at the time Northcliffe was given the credit. When his younger brother Cecil Harmsworth asked Northcliffe 'who killed cock robin?', he answered his own question: 'you did' (McEwen, 63). On 4 December *The Times* carried a leading article written by its editor, Dawson, criticizing Asquith, disclosing much of the detail behind the 'war council' which Lloyd George and Andrew Bonar Law proposed on 21 November consisting of three men, and in effect sidelining the prime minister. On 5 December Asquith backed out of his earlier assent to the council, and matters were now set on a collision course. But Asquith was possibly looking for an excuse to retreat from his earlier concession, and Lloyd George denied that he had seen *The Times* article, adding that failure to implement the proposed agreement would only reward Northcliffe who 'frankly wants a smash' (Koss, 305). But the outcome enhanced Northcliffe's reputation as a kingmaker.

Northcliffe always, and sincerely, prided himself on his independence from the political parties, and indeed his financial success enabled him to detach himself from them, unlike most newspaper proprietors and editors. He quickly dispelled any notion that he might be inveigled into the new administration: 'Ah-h, wouldn't they like to get me out of Fleet Street' (Koss, 306). Therefore, although Northcliffe agreed to go to the United States of America as head of the British war mission in May 1917, which he found a frustrating experience as he was rebuffed by the British ambassador, Spring Rice, and accepted a viscountcy on his return, he still maintained his independence. He accepted the post of director of propaganda in enemy countries in February 1918, insisting that his choice of the term director rather than minister reflected his freedom from politicians' clutches.

Such declarations of independence were unwelcome to politicians and journalists alike. When on 16 November 1917 Northcliffe publicly stated, in a letter to *The Times*, ostensibly in reply to a reader, that he was highly dissatisfied with the conduct of the war, and would not join any administration, the Liberal editor, A. G. Gardiner, asserted that 'the message of it all' was that 'The democracy, whose bulwark is Parliament, has been unseated, and mobocracy, whose dictator is Lord Northcliffe, is in power' (Willis, 245). Lloyd George acted for the politicians when he claimed that the press must be either squashed or squared. When faced with criticism for appointing Northcliffe as director of propaganda in enemy countries Lloyd George replied that he was 'safe as long as he was occupied' (Koss, 327). When the war ended, unexpectedly Lloyd George was anxious to continue squaring Northcliffe, asking for his support in the forthcoming general election. Northcliffe's response gave some substance to the charge of megalomania: 'I do not propose to use my newspapers and personal influence … unless I know definitely, and in writing, and can consciously approve, the personal constitution of the Government' (ibid., 338). Lloyd George smartly rebuffed him, but Northcliffe's ambitions took an even more bizarre turn when he published an article in the *Daily Mail* on 4 November 1918, 'From war to peace', which was taken as a bid for a seat at the Versailles peace conference. In the general election campaign Northcliffe called for the most punitive peace to be imposed on Germany, and called on Lloyd George to take a firm stand on reparations. In April 1919 Lloyd George, having earlier warned Northcliffe not 'to be making mischief' (ibid., 346), turned on the press lord. In the House of Commons on 16 April 1919 he denounced Northcliffe's 'diseased vanity', accusing him of trying to sow dissent between the allies, and asserting that 'not even that kind of disease is a justification for so black a crime against humanity' (*Hansard 5C*). The implication was that Northcliffe was suffering from mental illness, and Lloyd George tapped his head as he spoke to make the point clear. The rumour that Northcliffe was indeed going insane was spreading, but Northcliffe wrote calmly to Louise Owen that Lloyd George should be dealing with the world's problems, not attacking him: 'No ordinary man like myself should at this time figure so prominently before the world' (Taylor, 200).

Last years Northcliffe's health was now in decline. He suffered from a cough and a sore throat. He continued to use his newspapers to campaign for political causes, against waste of public money by government, for an Irish peace settlement. But he appeared to have lost his journalistic touch when his campaign for the 'Sandringham hat' (which Winston Churchill wore) failed. Yet he showed that the old performer had not forgotten his skills when he persuaded Dame Nellie Melba to sing in the first wireless concert in history at Marconi Place, Chelmsford, and the next day, 20 June 1920, editorialized on the importance of the wireless set as a means not only of business and government, but of entertainment. He showed his abiding interest in technology by installing a wireless set in *The Times* offices to speed up news delivery. He also appreciated the importance of air travel, as shown in the Alcock and Brown flight from Newfoundland to Ireland in June 1919. His interest in what made people into newspaper readers remained undimmed: 'Smiling pictures make people smile … I personally, prefer short leading articles … People like to read about profiteering. Most of them would like to be profiteers if they had the chance' (Taylor, 204–5). In the summer of 1921 he went on a world cruise, though prematurely aged, and was besieged by admirers wherever he went. He returned looking more unwell in February 1922 and although he appeared in London at several public functions, and even went to Germany (where he was hated during the war for his propaganda there, and where he suspected that he had been poisoned), he displayed alarming symptoms of ill health. His condition was a blood infection, possibly from his teeth, which invaded the brain and then damaged the valves of the heart, and it caused his behaviour to become more erratic. He was rude, delirious, and often insensible, and this appeared to give substance to the false claim by Wickham Steed, *The Times*'s editor in 1922, that he was suffering from syphilis. This rumour persisted until 1954, when definitive medical analysis contradicted it.

Northcliffe died on 14 August 1922 at his house, 1 Carlton Gardens, London, and was given a funeral at Westminster Abbey. He was buried at North Finchley, Middlesex, on 17 August. He left two messages before he died: one was that he wished to be laid to rest as near his mother (who outlived him by three years) as possible at North Finchley 'and I do not wish anything erect from the ground or any words except my name and the years I was born and this year upon the stone'. The second was truly magnificent: 'In *The Times* I should like a page reviewing my life-work by someone who really knows and a leading article by the best man on the night' (Pound and Harmsworth, 881–2). These last words sum up Northcliffe better than any other tribute or criticism. Northcliffe sought political power, and used his independence from the political parties, which subsidized and suborned newspapers, to pursue his aim as self-appointed tribune of the people. This pleased neither politicians nor political journalists. It also missed the point that Northcliffe was essentially a great newspaperman, who exercised a profound influence on popular culture. This is not to deny that Northcliffe exercised a certain kind of political power; when conditions were right, when governments were weak, or politicians made vulnerable for other reasons, then the Northcliffe press could and did exert influence on the workings of high politics. Contemporaries in the political world seemed to fear him; but it was hard to judge the extent of their fear, for it was always useful for politicians to have as their stock-in-trade the argument that press power was too great and that press lords were over-mighty subjects. Northcliffe's uncomplicated patriotism, springing no doubt from his Anglo-Irish roots, strikes the modern observer as extreme; his determination to drive Lord Haldane from office as lord chancellor in 1915 arose from what Northcliffe regarded as Haldane's brushing aside

Northcliffe's insistence on the importance of the aeroplane in modern warfare, but it was a brutal campaign. Northcliffe saw Ireland and Irish politics in terms of their relationship to the well-being of the British empire, and he had no sympathy for the Ulster resistance to Irish home rule, except insofar as it must be resolved for the good of empire.

But Northcliffe's importance lay in his instinctive knowledge of what the modern newspaper could be, and of the potential it had to gather in a mass readership. His understanding of the importance for the press of technological developments was unrivalled. No detail of the world of newspaper production escaped him. In 1905 he founded the Anglo-Newfoundland Development Company to purchase 3100 square miles of territory to produce wood pulp for his newspapers. In all this he was supported by his brother Harold, whose financial acumen perfectly matched Northcliffe's bold and imaginative strokes.

Northcliffe's last years were almost grotesque: his illness, his incoherence, the decline in his appearance from beautiful young man to a prematurely aged one with heavy, even ugly features, his overweening political ambitions culminating in Lloyd George's denunciation in no doubt carefully chosen words of his 'diseased vanity', all bear witness to his physical and mental deterioration. But Northcliffe's career must not be judged in terms of his final collapse, even though his last wish to be buried beside his mother is resonant of Orson Welles's classic film *Citizen Kane*. Northcliffe, in his grasp of the principles and techniques of modern journalism and of the nature of its readers, was the greatest figure who ever walked down Fleet Street: the Chief.   D. GEORGE BOYCE

Sources R. Pound and G. Harmsworth, *Northcliffe* (1959) · S. J. Taylor, *The great outsiders: Northcliffe, Rothermere and the 'Daily Mail'* (1996) · S. E. Koss, *The rise and fall of the political press in Britain*, 2 (1984) · P. Ferris, *The house of Northcliffe* (1971) · A. P. Ryan, *Lord Northcliffe* (1953) · L. Andrews and H. A. Taylor, *Lords and labourers of the press* (1970) · W. K. Jones, *Fleet St. and Downing St.* (1916?) · J. M. McEwen, 'The press and the fall of Asquith', *HJ*, 21 (1978), 863–83 · F. Williams, *Dangerous estate: the anatomy of newspapers* (1957) · A. G. Gardiner, 'Two journalists: C. P. Scott and Lord Northcliffe: a contrast', *Nineteenth Century and After*, 111 (1932), 247–56 · I. C. Willis, *England's holy war* (1928) · A. Jones, *Powers of the press: newspapers, power, and the public in nineteenth-century England* (1996) · L. Owen, *Northcliffe: the facts* (1931) · [A. C. W. Harmsworth] and Lord Northcliffe, *At the war* (1916) · *The Times* (15 Aug 1922) · *Hansard 5C* (1919), 114.2935 · J. Lee Thompson, *Northcliffe: press baron in politics, 1865–1922* (2000) · *CGPLA Eng. & Wales* (1922) · J. Lee Thompson, *Politicians, the press and propaganda: Lord Northcliffe and the great war, 1914–1919* (1999)

Archives BL, corresp. and MSS, Add. MSS 62153–62397 · Bodl. Oxf., bulletins to the *Daily Mail*, MSS Eng. Hist d. 303–305 [copies] · Daily Mail and General Trust plc, London, archives · News Int. RO, MSS | BL OIOC, letters to Lord Reading · HLRO, corresp. with Lord Beaverbrook; letters to David Lloyd George; corresp. with John St Loe Strachey · Houghton Hall, King's Lynn, letters to Sir Philip Sassoon · Lpool RO, corresp. with seventeenth earl of Derby · NA Scot., letters to Philip Kerr · NMM, corresp. with Dame Katharine Furse · Norfolk RO, corresp. with H. W. Massingham · PRO, corresp. relating to British war mission, FO800 · PRO NIre., corresp. with Edward Carson · U. Aberdeen, account of Scottish tour with W. E. Carson · U. Leeds, Brotherton L., letters to Edmund Gosse | FILM BFI NFTVA, documentary footage · BFI NFTVA, news footage · BFI NFTVA, other film footage | SOUND BL NSA, documentary recording · BL NSA, recorded talk

Likenesses E. A. Bell, bronze plaque, 1900, NPG · P. A. de Laszlo, oils, 1911, priv. coll. [*see illus.*] · J. Lavery, oils, 1921, Municipal Gallery, Dublin · Lady Hilton Young, bronze bust (posthumous), St Dunstan's Church in the West, Fleet Street, London, forecourt · B. Partridge, caricature, watercolour and pen and ink, NPG; repro. in *Punch Almanack* (1922) · Spy [L. Ward], lithograph, NPG; repro. in *VF* (16 May 1895) · photographs, repro. in Pound and Harmsworth, *Northcliffe*

Wealth at death £2,000,000: administration, 8 Sept 1922, *CGPLA Eng. & Wales*

Harmsworth, Esmond Cecil, second Viscount Rothermere (1898–1978), newspaper proprietor, was born in London on 29 May 1898, the third and youngest son (there were no daughters) of Harold Sidney *Harmsworth, first Viscount Rothermere (1868–1940), and his wife, Mary Lilian (d. 1937), daughter of George Wade Share, of Forest Hill. The first viscount, younger brother of Alfred Charles William *Harmsworth, Viscount Northcliffe (1865–1922), was the financial genius behind the rise of the Harmsworth press. Educated at Chatham House (Ramsgate) and at Eton College, Esmond Harmsworth was commissioned into the Royal Marine Artillery in 1917. Both his elder brothers were killed in the war, and he became heir to his father's peerage and newspaper properties which after the death in 1922 of Northcliffe included, under the umbrella of the Associated Newspapers Group, the *Daily Mail* and many other papers. In 1919 he accompanied David Lloyd George as his aide-de-camp at the Paris peace conference. In the same year on 15 November he won a by-election in the Isle of Thanet as a Conservative 'Anti-Waste' candidate. Aged only nineteen, he was 'the baby of the House'. His political career was not helped by an over-zealous father who in 1922 told Andrew Bonar Law that he would withdraw his newspapers' support unless Esmond was given cabinet office—a threat which the prime minister disregarded. He was also handicapped because of his father's eccentric right-wing views, for which he was sometimes regarded as a mouthpiece; in fact his own attitude was conservative but far more liberal.

In 1929 Harmsworth abandoned parliament and concentrated on his business interests. In 1932 he became chairman of Associated Newspapers. He created a chain of provincial papers and under his regime the flagging fortunes of the *Daily Mail* revived in the 1930s and 1940s. In 1934 he was elected, surprisingly young, to succeed Lord Riddell as chairman of the Newspaper Proprietors' Association (NPA)—a post he retained until 1961. He was an able and tactful negotiator, praised widely for his dealings over the allocation of newsprint in the war and with the printing unions after it. He was chairman of the Newsprint Supply Company from 1940 to 1959.

From his youth Harmsworth moved easily in the social world—the slightly raffish post-war society patronized by the prince of Wales and censured by George V and Stanley Baldwin. He was tall (6 feet 4 inches), slim, fair-haired, blue-eyed, and very handsome with great charm of manner. Women fell for him 'like ninepins'. He was an excellent player of tennis, both lawn and real. He preserved his looks and athletic skill long into old age. He was a friend of the prince and Mrs Simpson, and in the autumn of 1936 played an important part in keeping the press silent for so long about their friendship. It was he who suggested to Baldwin that the abdication crisis might be solved by a morganatic marriage. This required legislation. Baldwin had little love for the Harmsworth family but he felt obliged to consult the cabinet and the dominion governments. There was no support for the proposal.

In 1940 Harmsworth succeeded his father. From then onwards he and Lord Beaverbrook were, until the latter's death, the two leading, though friendly, rival owners of the British mass-circulation press. He greatly strengthened Associated Newspapers by diversification into television (though he sold out too soon), property, and North Sea oil exploration. He also had wide interests in the Canadian paper-making industry. He was the first chancellor of the Memorial University of Newfoundland from 1952 to 1961. In 1952 he took over the ailing *Daily Sketch* from Lord Kemsley and in 1960 reached the high point of his Fleet Street career when the *News Chronicle* and the *Star*, despite their Liberal affiliations, felt obliged to accept amalgamation with the *Daily Mail* and its companion, the *Evening News*. Rothermere was a strong supporter of press freedom and was much concerned with the journalists who worked under him. It was sad that in 1970 the decline of Fleet Street obliged him to accept economies and redundancies which were not well handled and aroused bitter protest. The following year he retired in favour of his son Vere.

Though an unwavering Conservative, Rothermere never engaged in the direct intervention in his papers publicly disclaimed but privately practised by Beaverbrook in his. Like his father, he was more concerned with finance than journalism. He had many interests—farming, racing, and history, in which he was widely read. He had something of a scholar's disposition and at times something of the indecisiveness which can go with it. He was a connoisseur of books and art. In 1946 he bought Daylesford, near Chipping Norton, Oxfordshire, the former seat of Warren Hastings. He filled it with Hastings memorabilia. The house was sold and its contents dispersed in 1977 shortly before he died. He also owned the crown lease of a part of St James's Palace—Warwick House—given by his father as a birthday present in 1923. The generous and courteous hospitality extended in both houses was famous.

Rothermere was married three times, first in 1920 to Margaret Hunam, daughter of William Redhead, of Carville Hall, Brentford; they had a son and two daughters. The marriage ended in divorce in 1938. In 1945 he married Ann Geraldine Mary (1913–1981) [*see* Fleming, Ann Geraldine Mary], widow of Shane Edward Robert O'Neill, third Baron O'Neill, and daughter of the Hon. Guy Lawrence Charteris. He divorced her in 1952, and she married in the same year the author Ian Fleming. His third marriage was in 1966 to Mrs Mary Ohrstrom, of Dallas, Texas, daughter of Kenneth Murchison; they had one son. Rothermere died in London on 12 July 1978 and was succeeded in the viscountcy by his elder son, Vere Harold Esmond *Harmsworth (1925–1998).   ROBERT BLAKE, *rev.*

Sources *Daily Mail* (13 July 1978) · *The Times* (13 July 1978) · F. Donaldson, *Edward VIII* (1974) · A. J. P. Taylor, *Beaverbrook* (1972) · personal knowledge (1986) · private information (1986) · *CGPLA Eng. & Wales* (1978)
Archives HLRO, corresp. with Lord Beaverbrook · King's Lond., Liddell Hart C., corresp. with Sir B. H. Liddell Hart · Nuffield Oxf., corresp. with Lord Cherwell | FILM BFI NFTVA, news footage
Likenesses group photograph, *c.*1915, Hult. Arch. · photograph, 1963, Hult. Arch.
Wealth at death £4,072,870: probate, 21 July 1978, *CGPLA Eng. & Wales*

Harmsworth, Harold Sidney, first Viscount Rothermere (1868–1940), newspaper proprietor, was born on 26 April 1868 at Hampstead, London, the second son of Alfred Harmsworth (1837–1889), and his wife, Geraldine Mary Maffett (1838–1925). He was of Anglo-Irish stock: his father was an Englishman who had qualified as a barrister at the Middle Temple, and his mother was the daughter of a land agent from co. Down, who was then living in Pembroke Place, Dublin. His elder brother was Alfred *Harmsworth, first Viscount Northcliffe, who was first to make his mark in the newspaper industry with his popular publications *Answers* and *Comic Cuts*. Harold Harmsworth was educated at Marylebone grammar school, which he left 'at an early age' (*The Times*) to become a clerk in the mercantile marine office of the Board of Trade. In 1888 he joined his brother's newspaper enterprise, showing a flair for financial management; in 1894 he and his brother purchased the *Evening News* for £25,000; it soon became a valuable property.

Although Harmsworth showed shrewd business sense in the newspaper world, the same cannot be said of his private life. In 1893 he married Mary Lilian Share (*d.* 1937), the daughter of George Wade Share, a bankrupt City hardware merchant. The marriage was not fulfilling. Harmsworth lavished gifts on his wife, but she had an affair with his younger brother, St John, and there were even rumours that one of his sons, Esmond, was St John's. Harmsworth, for his part, also found other personal attractions: he had many women friends, and a number of mistresses. Little is known about the latter, but he had a relationship for fourteen years (possibly platonic) with a ballet dancer called Alice Nikitina (whose real name was Hilda Munnings). However, he never considered divorcing his wife.

In 1896 Harmsworth and his elder brother launched the *Daily Mail*, which is regarded as marking the beginning of the 'new journalism'; it was a daily newspaper for the lower middle-class clerks and office workers travelling daily to the City. They went on to found the *Daily Mirror*, which by 1914 Alfred had turned over to Harold. In 1910 Harmsworth acquired the *Glasgow Record and Mail*, and in 1915 the *Sunday Pictorial*. By 1921 he owned the *Daily Mirror*, *Sunday Pictorial*, *Glasgow Daily Record*, *Evening News*, and *Sunday Mail*, and shared ownership of Associated Newspapers with Northcliffe. When Northcliffe died in 1922 Harmsworth acquired his controlling interest in Associated

Harold Sidney Harmsworth, first Viscount Rothermere (1868–1940), by Philip A. de Laszlo, 1930

Newspapers, for £1.6 million, selling *The Times*. The following year he bought the Hulton newspaper chain, and thus brought under his control three national mornings, three national Sundays, two London evening papers, four provincial dailies, and three provincial Sunday newspapers. A few months after buying the *Evening Herald* in 1922 Rothermere (as he had become) resold a 51 per cent interest in it to Lord Beaverbrook, obtaining in return a 49 per cent interest in the latter's *Daily Express* and *Sunday Express*. In 1926 he sold Amalgamated Newspapers (his magazine empire) to the Berry brothers. He then moved into the field of provincial newspapers, challenging the supremacy of the Berry brothers (later lords Camrose and Kemsley). In 1928 he formed Northcliffe Newspapers Ltd and declared his intention of starting a chain of evening papers in the main provincial cities. There followed the 'newspaper war' of 1928–9, which ended in Rothermere's founding new evening papers in Bristol and Derby, and obtaining a controlling interest in Cardiff's newspapers. By the end of 1929 his empire consisted of fourteen daily and Sunday newspapers, with a substantial holding in another three. The 1949 royal commission on the press declared that newspaper production had become a 'major industry' which 'had no relation to journalism as such' (*Royal Commission on the Press*, 14–15); but Rothermere, like the other great press lords of his day, saw himself as representing a constituency, his readers, with authority to speak on their behalf.

Politicians both courted and disliked the press lords, but

great newspapermen tended to rise in the honours lists. In 1910 Harmsworth became a baronet; in 1914 Baron Rothermere. The First World War gave him further opportunities to enter the world of politics. In 1916 he accepted the director-generalship of the royal army clothing department, and in 1917 he was appointed air minister. He found himself at odds with Sir Hugh Trenchard, who resigned as chief of the air staff in March 1918, but although Lloyd George took Harmsworth's side in the House of Commons Harmsworth resigned on 25 April 1918. The war, which elevated him to ministerial office, and to the privy council in 1917, also cost him great personal loss. Two of his three sons, Harold Vyvyan St George and Vere Sidney Tudor, were killed; Harmsworth founded university chairs in their memory. In November 1918 he was invited to a Downing Street luncheon by Winston Churchill to gather press support for Lloyd George. He was made a viscount in 1919, but by 1922 was growing to distrust the Lloyd George coalition. Party political consistency was not the hallmark of the press lord. In 1922 he was believed to be seeking a step in the peerage as the price of his support for a Conservative government led by Andrew Bonar Law. In 1928 he refused to serve the publicity needs of the Conservative Party, but he did declare himself an 'anti-socialist' (*The Times*), and his *Daily Mail* was responsible for publishing the celebrated 'Zinoviev letter' on 25 October 1924 which purported to reveal a plot to pressurize the Labour Party to ratify a treaty between the United Kingdom and the Soviet Union which would prepare the way for red revolution. The letter was exposed as a forgery in the 1960s, but although its impact on Labour in the general election was exaggerated, the incident seemed to reveal the power of the press.

It was this apparent power, or its abuse, that Stanley Baldwin attacked in 1931, when Rothermere supported Beaverbrook's campaign for empire free trade. Beaverbrook put up candidates for his 'crusading party', one of whom split the Conservative vote in East Islington. Baldwin denounced newspapers which were 'engines of propaganda for the constantly changing policies, desires, personal wishes, personal likes and personal dislikes' of their controllers who exercised 'power without responsibility' (Political and Economic Planning, 178–9). Baldwin spoke at the beginning of a decade that saw a period of contraction in the press, as the newspaper industry paid the price for its competitive marketing era. In 1931 Rothermere sold his interest in Beaverbrook's papers, and in 1937 he handed over control of Associated Newspapers to his son Esmond Cecil *Harmsworth, second Viscount Rothermere (1898–1978). But the 1938 Political and Economic Planning *Report on the British Press* noted that Rothermere 'issues general instructions to his editors and gives massive broadsides in the form of articles in the *Daily Mail* which are duly reproduced by other papers in the group' (ibid., 177). Two themes in particular were selected: Rothermere's support of a revision of the treaty of Trianon (which followed the end of the First World War) in Hungary's favour; and his support of Oswald Mosley's British Union of Fascists. Rothermere's interest in Hungary began in 1927 when he made the acquaintance of Princess Sophie Hohenlohe, a Hungarian beauty. In return for championing Hungary, Rothermere was offered the Hungarian crown, which he declined, instead allowing Esmond to accept an honorary degree from Szeged University in May 1928.

Rothermere's involvement in politics sprang from his sense of the deep European as well as British crises that threatened to open the way to Bolshevism. This drove him to the right, and his support for the British Union of Fascists led him to describe them as a 'well-organized party of the Right seeking to take over responsibility for national affairs with the same directness of purpose and energy of methods' (Koss, 537) that Hitler and Mussolini displayed. He defended the tough response of the blackshirts to their opponents at the meeting at Olympia of 7 June 1934, but he subsequently put some distance between himself and Oswald Mosley, though he never completely broke with him. Rothermere was anxious to avert war between the states of western Europe, a war that could only be of advantage to the Soviet Union, which he hated. He supported what he called Germany's natural desire to recover her role as a major European power, and in his advocacy of appeasement he did not differ from many, perhaps most, Englishmen of his day. Where he did differ from them was in his personal links with Hitler, and his frequently expressed admiration for his methods.

Rothermere was convinced, and his newspaper publicized his views, that aerial bombardment must reduce a country to ruin within a short time. Therefore, while he supported the controversial Hoare–Laval pact, which proposed to allow Mussolini what amounted to a free hand in Abyssinia, he also called for Britain to rearm. In March 1934 he commissioned the construction of an airplane (the 'Britain First') which he offered in August 1935 to the Royal Air Force as a 'peace gift'; it later became the Blenheim bomber. He argued strenuously that standing up to Italy and Germany was folly, given Britain's unprepared defences, especially her deficiency in aircraft; he used his close contacts with Germany to pass on information to the government. He established close relations with Winston Churchill, but his anxiety to walk a careful line between appeasement and surrender was revealed in his frantic drafting and redrafting of his ghosted book, *Warnings and Predictions* (September 1939) when he was 'in a panic about its seeming too pro-Nazi' and 'scuppered two chapters and added a purely patriotic ending' (*Fleet Street*, 242). On 24 September 1939 he had his close colleague and 'ghost', Collin Brooks, draft a letter to Neville Chamberlain urging the futility of trying to save Poland and warning that 'whether victorious or not, Britain will emerge from such a conflict with her social and economic fabric destroyed', which could mean 'a revolution of the Left in these islands, which might be more deadly than the war itself' (ibid., 291). But the letter was never sent (despite Rothermere's fear that Britain was 'finished'), because of the 'national mood and temper' (ibid., 292); a nice example of the would-be opinion leader and press baron being led by the public itself. Rothermere offered his services to the nation, and Lord Beaverbrook, minister of aircraft production, telegrammed him on 15 May 1940 asking him to go to America, where his services were needed, and his aviation experience would be put to good use. But by now Rothermere was very ill. He suffered a fall while in America, and died in the King Edward VII Memorial Hospital, Paget, Bermuda, on 26 November 1940. He was buried in St Paul's churchyard, Paget, on 28 November, and was succeeded as viscount by his son, Esmond Cecil Harmsworth.

Rothermere's wife had predeceased him in March 1937, having been estranged from him for more than twenty years. Rothermere was described by contemporaries as a handsome man, but his photographs, at least from middle age, are almost the caricature of the plutocrat: corpulent, with bulging eyes and a heavy lower lip above which sat a walrus moustache. But he was generous to his wife, and he was capable of philanthropic acts, some of which, like his gift to the Middle Temple of £40,000, could be construed as self-seeking (he was elected an honorary bencher in return), while others appear to be simply well meaning, such as his purchase of the old Bethlem Hospital for a playground in memory of his mother, and his donation to a fund for saving the Foundling Hospital.

Although reputed to be one of the three richest men in Britain, Rothermere left only a few hundred thousand pounds, thus proving Beaverbrook's point that newspapers run for propaganda purposes were expensive indulgences.   D. GEORGE BOYCE

Sources S. J. Taylor, *The great outsiders: Northcliffe, Rothermere and the 'Daily Mail'* (1996) • G. Boyce, J. Curran, and P. Wingate, eds., *Newspaper history: from the seventeenth century to the present day* (1978) • S. E. Koss, *The rise and fall of the political press in Britain*, 2 (1984) • Viscount Rothermere [H. S. Harmsworth], *Warnings and predictions* (1939) • Viscount Rothermere [H. S. Harmsworth], *My fight to rearm Britain* (1939) • *Report on the British press*, Political and Economic Planning (1938) • 'Royal commission on the press, 1947–49: report', *Parl. papers* (1948–9), vol. 20, Cmd 7700 • *The Times* (27 Nov 1940), 7 • B. Morris, *The roots of appeasement: the British weekly press and Nazi Germany during the 1930s* (1991) • 'Real old Tory politics': the political diaries of Sir Robert Sanders, Lord Bayford, 1910–1925, ed. J. Ramsden (1984) • *Fleet Street, press barons and politics: the journals of Collin Brooks, 1932–1940*, ed. N. J. Crowson, CS, 5th ser., 11 (1998) • *DNB* • *CGPLA Eng. & Wales* (1941)
Archives Daily Mail and General Trust plc, London, archives | CAC Cam., corresp. with Henry Page Croft • HLRO, corresp. with Lord Beaverbrook; letters to David Lloyd George • NA Scot., corresp. with Lord Elibank • NA Scot., corresp. with Lord Lothian • Nuffield Oxf., corresp. with Lord Cherwell | FILM BFI NFTVA, news footage • Northcliffe House, London, film footage, 1938 | SOUND BL NSA, documentary recording
Likenesses P. A. de Laszlo, portrait, 1930, Courtauld Inst. [see illus.] • P. A. de Laszlo, oils, 1936, Middle Temple, London • J. Cope, oils, priv. coll. • J. Epstein, bronze bust, RAF Museum, Hendon, London • J. Epstein, bust, priv. coll. • P. A. de Laszlo, oils, Parliament House, Budapest
Wealth at death £335,308 5s. 2d.: probate, 24 April 1941, *CGPLA Eng. & Wales*

Harmsworth, Patricia Evelyn Barbara, **Viscountess Rothermere** (1928/9–1992). *See under* Harmsworth, Vere Harold Esmond, third Viscount Rothermere (1925–1998).

Harmsworth, Vere Harold Esmond, **third Viscount Rothermere** (1925–1998), newspaper proprietor, was born on 27 August 1925 at Warwick House, Stable Yard, Strand, London, the son of Esmond Cecil *Harmsworth, second Viscount Rothermere (1898–1978), a newspaper proprietor, and his first wife, Margaret Hunam Redhead (1897–1991). His family background was unhappy. His parents separated when he was five and he shared a suite of rooms at Claridge's with his mother. Later he and his two elder sisters were ferried by a French governess between their mother's house in Dorset and their father's London house in St James's. His education was equally disrupted. He spent a year at Eton College before being evacuated in 1940 to the United States, where he attended Kent School, Connecticut. In 1944 he returned briefly to Eton, and was then conscripted into the army. He failed the officer selection board and served in the ranks. He later claimed that this gave him insight into the people—a sentiment of which his great-uncle Lord Northcliffe would have approved. In 1948 he began his business career, working in the Anglo-Canadian paper mills in Quebec before joining the family firm, Associated Newspapers, in Fleet Street in 1951, where he worked in every department.

The newspaper world which Harmsworth entered was dominated by the three groups that had consolidated their position in the previous decade. Lord Beaverbrook led the market with 16 per cent of the overall circulation; Associated Newspapers (Rothermere's empire) was next with 14 per cent; and Kemsley had 13 per cent. But Fleet Street never stood still, and new powers were emerging: the International Publishing Corporation (IPC), headed by Cecil King, and Roy Thompson, who was beginning his successful career and in 1959 bought the Kemsley chain. The Rothermere flagship, the *Daily Mail*, was suffering competition from Beaverbrook's *Daily Express*, and Vere Harmsworth's father showed little flair for beating this off. *Mail* editors came and went, and a merger with the *News Chronicle* failed to lift sales. He was forced to close the loss-making *Sunday Dispatch*. In 1956 Vere Harmsworth began a lifelong friendship with the *Daily Sketch*'s features writer, David English, with whom he launched a 'win a pub' competition—a publicity stunt in the best traditions of the Northcliffe house.

Harmsworth was a man about town, and on 21 March 1957 he married a Rank Organization starlet, who used the name Beverley Brooks. **Patricia Evelyn Barbara** [Pat] **Harmsworth**, Viscountess Rothermere (1928/9–1992) was the daughter of John William Matthews, a Hertfordshire architect, and his wife, Doris. She went to drama school, and married Captain Christopher John Brooks, a guards officer. She began a career on the stage, and was spotted by Rank at the Edinburgh Festival; her only significant film role was in *Reach for the Sky* (1956). She divorced Brooks in 1956, having had a daughter, and the following year married Harmsworth. Rothermere settled £2.75 million on Harmsworth on his marriage; Pat Harmsworth repaid the investment, becoming a noted and inveterate society hostess. She was given the nickname Bubbles by *Private Eye*, and it was universally adopted. She disliked it,

Vere Harold Esmond Harmsworth, third Viscount Rothermere (1925–1998), by Nils Jorgensen, 1993

because it implied that she was superficial. She described herself as a simple person, but was shrewd enough to appreciate that 'I didn't just marry a man. I married an empire' (*The Times*, 14 Aug 1992). The couple had two daughters and a son.

Vere Harmsworth inherited the business in 1971, seven years before his father's death. An internal report the previous year had shown that the company had a projected loss over five years of £32 million. By the mid-1970s the balance of power within the British press swung towards the new men: King, Thompson, and most notably Rupert Murdoch. Between them Reed International, News International, and the Thompson organization commanded 55.6 per cent of the market. Harmsworth was a risk taker. He merged the *Daily Mail* with the *Sketch* in a tabloid format, with drastic staff cuts. The new *Daily Mail* was not an immediate success, but its eventual rise seems to have been due largely to the readership that Lord Northcliffe always sought: women. The pressures of the business began to take their toll on Harmsworth's private life. He moved to Paris to escape ever higher personal taxation, increasingly living apart from the flamboyant Bubbles, though without formally separating. In Paris he met the Japanese-born Korean Maiko Joeong-shun Lee, but he refused to divorce his wife and he did not marry Maiko until a year after Bubbles died, from an accidental overdose of sleeping tablets on 12 August 1992, in Cap-d'Ail,

France. She was buried in Holy Trinity Church, High Hurstwood, Sussex, on 21 August 1992.

In 1978 his father died, and Rothermere continued to modernize his business. In 1980 he made a deal with Beaverbrook newspapers, agreeing to merge Associated Newspapers' *Evening News* with the Express group's *Evening Standard*. The *News* ceased publication, but by the terms of the transaction Associated Newspapers assumed full ownership of the *Standard* when the Express group was taken over by United Newspapers in 1986. Rothermere wanted a Sunday newspaper and in May 1982 he launched the *Mail on Sunday*, but it was a failure. A relaunch in October, with a colour magazine and comics, cost more than the original launch, but Rothermere's risk proved successful, attracting younger readers. The price of newspaper success was eternal vigilance. In 1986 Robert Maxwell, another buccaneer businessman, began recruiting staff to launch what he said would be a 24-hour-a-day newspaper, the *Daily News*, aimed primarily at Rothermere's *Evening Standard* monopoly. Rothermere responded by reviving the *Evening News* at half the price of the Maxwell paper and won the price war within four months.

Rothermere enjoyed besting his rivals; he always tried to keep in tune with his readers, whom he defined as probably having at least some GCSEs or O levels and maybe an A level or two, holding what were seen as the 'current family values of Middle England' (Snoddy, 120–1). Newspaper statisticians confirmed that his *Mail* readership came mainly from social classes B, C1, and C2 (middle class to skilled working class). He rode the revolution which saw Fleet Street move to new areas. In 1987 a new printing centre was opened in Surrey Docks and new premises occupied in Kensington. He also moved with the political times, supporting Margaret Thatcher in the 1980s, with a brief flirtation with the Social Democratic Party in 1987, and then endorsing Tony Blair's 'new' Labour in the 1990s, though still calling reluctantly in 1995 for voters to vote Conservative because of that party's greater Euroscepticism. He sat on the Labour benches in the Lords in 1997, believing that Blair's call for a new social mobility was a return to the family values crusade.

Rothermere believed that the press reflected public taste and public fashions and standards. But he moved with the times, and developed the concept of the newspaper as necessarily part of a larger economic conglomerate: he had interests in London Broadcasting Company, Herald-Sun TV (Australia), Plymouth Sound radio, the Wyndham Theatre and Harmsworth House Publishing (USA). He was part of the twentieth-century trend towards more newspaper titles in fewer hands, while viewing the press as a watchdog on the public's behalf. He retained personal control of the business, owning most of the voting stock, and averting criticism by providing profits. He was a member of the Oxford University Court of Benefactors, a patron of the London School of Economics, and a fellow of the Royal Society of Arts. He was awarded the order of merit by various countries, including Hungary, which had offered its crown to his grandfather in the 1930s.

Rothermere died of a heart attack in St Thomas's Hospital, London on 1 September 1998 and was cremated on 8 September. His funeral, at St Bride's, Fleet Street, was attended by the prime minister, the leader of the opposition, and his professional competitor Rupert Murdoch. He was a man of handsome, patrician style, with something of the appearance of Lord Northcliffe about the lower face. His photographs suggest a reflective, even introspective nature, but he was a newspaper businessman who succeeded in an environment remarkable, even by its own Darwinian standards, for its ruthless competition. D. GEORGE BOYCE

Sources *The Guardian* (3 Sept 1998) • *The Times* (3 Sept 1998) • J. Thomas, 'A bad press? Popular newspapers, the labour party and British politics from Northcliffe to Blair', PhD diss., U. Wales, Swansea, 1999 • R. Bourne, *Lords of Fleet Street: the Harmsworth dynasty* (1990) • C. Seymour-Ure, *The British press and broadcasting since 1945* (1991) • R. Snoddy, *The good, the bad and the unacceptable: the hard news about the British press* (1992) • 'Royal commission on the press', *Parl. papers* (1961–2), vol. 21, Cmnd 1811; vol. 22, Cmnd 1812-4 • 'National newspaper industry', *Parl. papers* (1975–6), vol. 41, Cmnd 6433 [interim report; royal commission on the press]; (1976–7), 40.1, Cmnd 6810; 40.321, Cmnd 6810-I [final report] • *The Times* (14 Aug 1992); (25 Aug 1992); (25 Sept 1992) [Viscountess Rothermere] • *Sunday Times* (16 Aug 1992) [Viscountess Rothermere] • Burke, *Peerage* (1999) • b. cert.
Likenesses N. Jorgensen, photograph, 1993, Rex Features Ltd, London [*see illus.*] • photograph, repro. in *Daily Telegraph* (3 Sept 1998) • photograph, repro. in *The Guardian* • photograph, repro. in *The Times*
Wealth at death £60,219,897—gross; £58,883,918—net: probate, 27 Aug 1999, *CGPLA Eng. & Wales* • £4,099,960—Patricia Harmsworth: probate, 8 April 1993, *CGPLA Eng. & Wales*

Harness, Sir Henry Drury (1804–1883), army officer, son of John Harness MD, commissioner of the transport board, was born on 29 April 1804. William *Harness was an elder brother. Harness passed high out of the Royal Military Academy (RMA) at Woolwich in 1825, but had to wait two years for a commission; meanwhile he studied mining engineering at the silver mines of Mexico. On being commissioned second lieutenant in the Royal Engineers on 24 May 1827, Harness returned to England and went through the usual Chatham course.

In 1828 Harness married Caroline, daughter of Thomas Edmonds of Cowbridge, Glamorgan; they had at least one daughter. In 1829 he went with his company to Bermuda. He was promoted lieutenant on 20 September 1832, and on his return home in 1834 was appointed an instructor in fortification at the RMA. There he remained for six years, and compiled a textbook used at the RMA for the next twenty years. In 1840 he was appointed instructor in surveying at Chatham, and was promoted second-captain on 30 June 1843. In 1844 Harness went back to the RMA as professor of fortification. The next year he was appointed inspector of Welsh roads, assisting the county authorities in the rearrangement of the public roads following the abolition of turnpikes. In 1846 he was appointed joint secretary with the Hon. F. Bruce to the new railway commission. When this commission became merged in a department of the Board of Trade, Harness remained as sole secretary.

Under an act to provide for the transport of the royal mails by railway the remuneration to the railway companies was to be fixed by agreement, and Harness was appointed arbitrator for the Post Office, a difficult duty, which he carried out with a result beneficial to the Post Office. He was promoted first captain on 20 February 1847.

Harness was next called upon to reform the Royal Mint. The master of the mint in 1850 was a political officer whose responsibilities were limited to his parliamentary duties, and when Harness was made deputy master he became virtually the head of the establishment. The mechanical operations of coining were at that time a matter of contract between the deputy master and certain melters, assayers, and moneyers, who, besides enjoying considerable emoluments, claimed also a vested interest in the appointment of their successors. Harness had to substitute for this system a government department. During these reforms the master, a Mr Sheil, was appointed British minister at Florence. Sir John Herschel succeeded him, with no parliamentary responsibility. On the completion of the reorganization in 1852 Herschel said that but for the resource and energy of Harness he could not have carried out the reforms so efficiently.

Before Herschel's appointment Harness had been promised the mastership when the proposed abolition of a political head took place. He therefore considered himself superseded and resigned the position of deputy master, although Lord Aberdeen, the prime minister, personally pressed him to remain. After declining the governorship of New Zealand, he accepted the appointment of commissioner of public works in Ireland, and remained there two years. In addition to his ordinary duties he, as a special commissioner, carried on an inquiry into the works of arterial drainage, and was a commissioner for the abolition of turnpike trusts.

On 20 June 1854 Harness was promoted brevet major and on 13 January 1855 lieutenant-colonel. He was then brought back to England to take charge of the fortification branch of the War Office, under the inspector-general of fortifications, an office he held until the close of the Crimean War, when he was appointed commanding royal engineer at Malta.

On the outbreak of the Indian mutiny Harness was given the command of the Royal Engineers of the force under Lord Clyde. He took part in the operations at Cawnpore, the siege and capture of Lucknow, and the subsequent operations in Rohilkhand and Oudh. He was mentioned in dispatches, thanked by the governor-general in council, and made a CB (July 1858).

In 1860, after his return from India, Harness was appointed director of the Royal Engineer Establishment at Chatham (later the School of Military Engineering), which he raised to a high standard. He became a full colonel on 3 April 1862 and a major-general on 6 March 1868. On leaving Chatham he was appointed a member of the council for military education.

Shortly after the outbreak of the cattle plague in 1866 Lord Granville invited Harness to become head of a new temporary department in the council office. According to the clerk of the council, Sir Arthur Helps, the privy council heard more plain truths from Harness than they were accustomed to. He declined the governorships of Bermuda and Guernsey. He was made KCB in May 1873, and was awarded a good service pension. He was promoted lieutenant-general and made a colonel-commandant of the Royal Engineers in June 1877, and retired in October 1878 as a full general. He died on 10 February 1883 at his home, Barton End, Headington, Oxfordshire. On his death George Robert Gleig, chaplain-general to the forces, wrote: 'I never found one in whose society I so much delighted as in his. … I invariably heard from him something which I loved to carry away. He was so gentle, so pure-minded, so simple in his tastes, so just in his estimate of character.' R. H. VETCH, *rev.* JAMES LUNT

Sources corps records, royal engineers, Institution of Royal Engineers, Chatham · T. B. Collinson, *A memoir of General Sir H. D. Harness, K.C.B.* (1883) · Boase, *Mod. Eng. biog.* · *CGPLA Eng. & Wales* (1883)
Archives NRA, letters
Likenesses Archer, portrait, Royal Engineers, Brompton barracks, Chatham, Kent · oils, Royal Engineers, Pasley House, Chatham, Kent · portrait, repro. in Collinson, *Memoir of General Sir H. D. Harness*
Wealth at death £763 19s. 0d.: probate, 25 April 1883, *CGPLA Eng. & Wales*

Harness, William (1790–1869), literary scholar, was born near Wickham, Hampshire, on 14 March 1790, the second son of Dr John Harness, commissioner of transports, and his wife, Sarah, *née* Dredge (*b.* 1765). He was the brother of General Sir Henry Drury *Harness (1804–1883) who was fourteen years his junior. As a toddler his foot was crushed by 'an old oaken bedstead' so that 'he always felt a slight pain in walking; but such was his spirit and perseverance that in after-life he became a good pedestrian' (L'Estrange, 7). From 1796 to 1799 he lived in Lisbon, his father serving as physician to Admiral Hood's fleet.

Harness entered Harrow School in 1802, and was immediately befriended by Byron, who, although three years his senior, empathized with his disability and declared: 'if anyone bullies you, tell me, and I'll thrash him if I can' (*Byron's Letters and Journals*, 1.47). Initial friendliness ended in March 1805, when Harness supported Dr Butler, Byron's enemy Pomposus, in replacing Joseph Drury as headmaster; and 'traduced [Byron's] poetry in an English exercise' (L'Estrange, 6). Amity revived in 1808 when Byron, sending Harness a copy of *English Bards and Scotch Reviewers*, revealed that 'the *first Lines* I ever attempted at Harrow were addressed to *you*' (*Byron's Letters and Journals*, 1.156). Louis Crompton notes: 'Byron's letters to him are the only surviving examples of … his sentimental correspondence with schoolboy friends' (Crompton, 184). He was among the 'most intimate Schoolfellows' whose miniatures Byron had painted before going abroad in 1809. Their friendship peaked in late December 1811, when he and the Revd Francis Hodgson stayed at Newstead while Byron was revising the first two cantos of

Childe Harold. As Harness planned to take holy orders, Byron decided against dedicating the poem to him, so as not to 'injure him in the profession to which he was about to devote himself' (*Byron's Letters and Journals*, 1.348). Of this visit Harness recalled: 'nothing could be more quiet and regular than the course of our days' (Duncan-Jones, 16). His surviving letters to Byron show that he disliked J. C. Hobhouse's 'pedantry', and abhorred C. S. Matthews: 'a would be wit, a varmint Man, and an *Atheist*!!!' But he defended Southey and eulogized Robert Bland. Byron told Hodgson 'Master William Harness and I have recommenced a most fiery correspondence; I like him as Euripedes liked Agatho, or Darby admired Joan, as much for the past as the present' (*Byron's Letters and Journals*, 2.140). He addressed Harness 'My dearest', 'Child', and 'mio Carissimo Amico' (ibid., 142), confessing that 'The latter part of my life has been a perpetual struggle against affections which embittered the earlier portion' (ibid., 148); Crompton observes that this 'must have puzzled' Harness, 'but it is just as likely he had in mind his rejection by Mary Chaworth' (Crompton, 185). Although Harness wrote praising 'The Giaour' on publication in December 1813, and 'The Corsair' in February 1814, no communication of Byron's to him after December 1811 survives. In September 1821 Byron unemotionally mentioned Harness to John Murray as someone who might possess letters of biographical interest (*Byron's Letters and Journals*, 8.228).

'He had no taste whatever for mathematics, and he found that at Cambridge they were everything' (L'Estrange, 14), but, none the less, Harness graduated BA from Christ's College in 1812. He was briefly curate of Kilmeston, Hampshire, followed by Dorking until 1816. That year he took his MA degree, progressing to the position of preacher at Trinity Chapel and minister and evening lecturer at St Anne's, Soho. He was appointed Boyle lecturer at Cambridge 'to satisfy such real scruples as any may have concerning matters of religion, and to answer such new objections and difficulties as may be stated'; one of his first duties was to counter-attack Byron's 'Cain', which he did with conviction. As André Maurois wrote, 'From Kentish Town to Pisa, clergymen preached against this calvinistic Prometheus' (Maurois, 349), but it is remarkable that one such clergyman had recently been so close a friend. The two lectures were published as *The Wrath of Cain* (1822).

In 1824 Harness quarrelled with W. S. Macready over the rewriting of Mary Russell Mitford's 'Rienzi'. Harness and Mitford had been friends since childhood, and she later dedicated her *Country Stories* (1837) to him. He relented and forgave Macready only on their meeting personally for the first time in 1839. During 'a time without regular employment' (Duncan-Jones, 19) Harness produced his greatest work, the eight-volume edition of Shakespeare, first published in 1825, including a 'Life', transcript of the will, chronology of plays, editions, list of 'plays ascribed to', portraits and poems on Shakespeare, as well as 'Prefaces' by Rowe, Pope, and Johnson. In 1826 he became both private chaplain to the dowager Countess De La Warr and first incumbent of Regent Square Chapel, where 'Mrs Siddons was not the only one … deeply moved by his preaching' (L'Estrange, 36). Nearby stood Edward Irving's Catholic Apostolic church, which Harness once attended, witnessing what he termed 'horrid Gibberish', that is, speaking in tongues. He also corresponded with John Henry Newman, but Harness's biographer L'Estrange defines him as 'an old-fashioned High Churchman'.

Harness's 'Reverses', a comic story with Goldsmithian and Byronic elements, was published in *Blackwood's Magazine* in 1827 and enjoyed great popularity. Harness knew Henry Crabb Robinson, William Makepeace Thackeray, and Charles Dickens: he is depicted as overcome by emotion in the Maclise drawing showing Dickens reading aloud 'The Chimes' (December 1840). He also befriended Samuel Rogers, Robert Southey, and William Wordsworth, the latter of whom he visited in the Lake District in 1835. Although appointed clerical registrar to the privy council by Lord Lansdowne (1841), with a salary of £420 p.a., he felt obliged to write requesting preferment from Harrow contemporary and prime minister Robert Peel in 1842 and again in 1845. He received short, polite, but firm rejections. Visiting Stratford upon Avon in 1844, Harness personally paid £3 to have Shakespeare's family monuments refurbished, including restoring the words 'witty above her sex' to that of his daughter Susannah Hall. That year, as Presbyter Catholicus, he published a controversial attack on the bishop of London's proposals for charitable reform, *Visiting Societies and Lay Readers*. He was minister of Brompton Chapel (1844–7) and Holy Trinity, Knightsbridge (1848–9), while raising funds to build All Saints, Ennismore Gardens, where he became perpetual curate. Henry Manning, then bishop of Chichester, preached at its opening. In 1865 Harness revisited Newstead Abbey which he hardly recognized after Thomas Wildman's alterations.

Harness's last appointment was as Rugmere prebendary at St Paul's, in 1866. On 11 November 1869 he was killed falling down a stone staircase while on a visit to the deanery at Battle, where he is buried. His life of Mary Russell Mitford was published posthumously and anonymously in 1870, and his annotated *Literary Remains of Catherine Maria Fanshawe* appeared six years later. The Harness prize for Shakespeare studies remains to his memory at Cambridge. He never married, but lived with his sister Mary, the sole beneficiary of his will.   RALPH LLOYD-JONES

Sources *Byron's letters and journals*, ed. L. A. Marchand, 1 (1973) · *Byron's letters and journals*, ed. L. A. Marchand, 2 (1973) · *Byron's letters and journals*, ed. L. A. Marchand, 8 (1978) · *Letters and journals of Lord Byron, with notices of his life*, ed. T. Moore, 2 vols. (1830) · L. Crompton, *Byron and Greek love: homophobia in nineteenth-century England* (1985) · C. M. Duncan-Jones, *Miss Mitford and Mr Harness: records of a friendship* (1955) · A. G. K. L'Estrange, *The literary life of the Rev. William Harness* (1871) · A. Maurois, *Byron*, trans. H. Miles (1930) · Hants. RO

Archives Shakespeare Birthplace Trust RO, Stratford upon Avon, journal of visit to Stratford upon Avon [typescript copy] | BL, Add. MSS 37189, fol. 380; 37191, fol. 398; 37199, fol. 171 (Babbage); 40514, fols. 260, 262 (Peel); 40561, fols. 252, 259 (Peel) · John Murray, London, letters to Byron

Likenesses E. Greenwood, drawing, 1815 (aged twenty-five), priv. coll. · B. Holl, stipple, pubd in or before 1828 (after T. C. Wageman), BM · J. R. Jackson, mezzotint (after H. W. Phillips), BM · G. Lance, oils, V&A · portrait (in later life), priv. coll.; repro. in Duncan-Jones, *Miss Mitford*

Wealth at death under £6000: resworn probate, 25 Nov 1869, *CGPLA Eng. & Wales*

Harnett, Cornelius (1723–1781), merchant and revolutionary politician in America, was born on 20 April 1723 in Chowan county, North Carolina, the son of Cornelius (*d.* 1742), colonial official, planter, and tavern-keeper, and Elizabeth Harnett. With his family Harnett moved in 1726 to Brunswick Town in Craven (later New Hanover) county in the lower Cape Fear region of North Carolina. In 1748, during King George's War (War of the Austrian Succession), Harnett and other residents of Brunswick Town repulsed a Spanish invasion of the town. Two years later the royal governor of North Carolina appointed Harnett a justice of the peace, a position that he retained at least until 1776.

By 1750 Harnett had moved to the town of Wilmington in New Hanover county. In addition to mercantile activities, in partnership Harnett owned a rum distillery, wharf, warehouse, and schooner, the *Mary*, and purchased a plantation, Poplar Grove, about 10 miles north-east of Wilmington. Residents of Wilmington elected Harnett a town commissioner in 1750–51, 1754, 1756–7, and 1768–70. When Wilmington briefly assumed borough status in 1760, Harnett was named one of the original eleven aldermen. In provincial governmental affairs Harnett represented the town of Wilmington in the North Carolina general assembly in every session of the legislature from 1754 to 1775, and became unquestionably one of the most important leaders in the colony's general assembly during the years before the revolution.

From the passage of the Stamp Act (1765), by which parliament implemented internal taxes on the Americans, Harnett headed the opposition to British policies in the lower Cape Fear region. He confronted royal governor William Tryon in 1766 in an action that thwarted the implementation of the Stamp Act in the region, and served as chairman of the local Sons of Liberty, an American patriot organization. According to a visitor from Massachusetts in 1773, Harnett was the 'Samuel Adams of North Carolina' (M. A. D. Howe, 'Journal of Josiah Quincy, Jun.', *Massachusetts Historical Society Proceedings*, 49, June 1916, 458).

Local committees of safety spearheaded the drive to revolution in North Carolina. Upon the organization of the Wilmington safety committee on 23 November 1774, Harnett was unanimously elected chairman of that body. When the Wilmington committee merged with the New Hanover committee on 4 January 1775, Harnett chaired the joint group. He remained chairman until October 1775, and a member of the committee until February 1776, by which time the importance of the safety committees had declined. Under his leadership the Wilmington–New Hanover committee was one of the most energetic in the colony. Living up to his reputation as an opponent of British authority, Harnett, together with John Ashe, in

1775 led some 300 men to burn British-occupied Fort Johnston in Brunswick county. When the British general Sir Henry Clinton in 1776 offered a general pardon to the American revolutionaries in the lower Cape Fear, only Harnett and Robert Howe were excluded from the grant.

Meanwhile, North Carolina held five provincial congresses from 1774 to 1776. Out of the colony when the first convened, Harnett represented the town of Wilmington during the ensuing three congresses and Brunswick county in the last congress. When the third congress, in 1775, created a government for the colony headed by a provincial council, Harnett was chosen president of the council. During the fourth congress, in 1776, Harnett chaired the committee that produced the Halifax Resolves, a document stating that the colonies should declare their independence from Great Britain. He also served as president of the council of safety in 1776 which replaced the provincial council, becoming *de facto* the first chief executive of a North Carolina that was independent of the crown. In the last provincial congress in 1776, of which he was vice-president, Harnett served on the committee that wrote the constitution for the independent state of North Carolina, and was elected to the first council of state, which advised the governor.

Harnett resigned his seat on the council of state in 1777 upon his election to the continental congress, in which he represented North Carolina until 1780. He worked tirelessly to support the articles of confederation, the document that bound the thirteen independent colonies, and helped persuade the North Carolina legislature to ratify it. Yet he chafed under the tedium of public business, and welcomed the opportunity to return to Wilmington in 1780. After the British invaded Wilmington in 1781, Harnett fled, but was captured, returned to the town, and imprisoned. His health declined rapidly, and, though paroled, he died in Wilmington soon thereafter, on 28 April 1781.

At some point Harnett married Mary Holt (*d.* 1792), daughter of Martin Holt, and afterward lived at Maynard (later called Hilton), just north of Wilmington, a highly sophisticated, two-storey Georgian frame structure that commanded a view of the north-east Cape Fear River. Harnett was worshipful master of St John's Lodge in Wilmington, the first masonic lodge in North Carolina. Although a reputed deist, Harnett was a vestryman of St James's parish (Church of England) in New Hanover county, and upon his death was interred in the graveyard of St James's Episcopal Church in Wilmington, where his grave may currently be seen. His wife, Mary, died in New York in April or May 1792. They had no known children.

ALAN D. WATSON

Sources R. D. W. Conner, *Cornelius Harnett: an essay in North Carolina history* (1909) · A. D. Watson, D. R. Lennon, and D. R. Lawson, *Harnett, Hooper and Howe: revolutionary leaders of the lower Cape Fear* (1979) · D. T. Morgan, 'Cornelius Harnett: revolutionary leader and delegate to the continental congress', *North Carolina Historical Review*, 49 (1972), 229–41 · J. G. Coyle, 'Cornelius Harnett', *Journal of the American Irish Society*, 29 (1930–31), 146–58 · W. L. Saunders and W. Clark, eds., *The colonial records of North Carolina*, 30 vols. (1886–1907), vols. 1–26 · A. M. Walker, ed., *New Hanover county court minutes, 1738–1800*, 4 vols. (1958–62) · D. R. Lennon and I. B. Kellum, eds., *The Wilmington town book, 1743–1778* (1973) · L. H. McEachern and I. M. Williams, eds., *Wilmington–New Hanover safety committee minutes, 1774–76* (1974)

Archives University of North Carolina, Chapel Hill, southern historical collection, letters · Raleigh, North Carolina, North Carolina State Archives, papers

Harney, (George) Julian (1817–1897), Chartist and journalist, was born on 17 February 1817 at Deptford, Kent, the son of George Harney, sailor, and his wife. Brought up in poverty, he was educated at dame-schools and by his own reading. In 1828 he entered the Boys' Naval School, Greenwich, to train as a merchant seaman; but the ill health that dogged him throughout his life—he suffered from congenital quinsy and impaired hearing—kept him in the infirmary for much of the time and, after six months as a cabin-boy, he quit in 1831 and became a pot-boy in London. He joined the National Union of the Working Classes, worked as a shop-boy for Hetherington, and completed his education in what he was to describe as the 'radical school of the 'thirties' (Schoyen, 6). He served three prison sentences, lastly at Derby for six months in 1836, for selling unstamped papers. His major intellectual influence—his 'guide, philosopher, and friend' (ibid., 12)—was Bronterre O'Brien, yet whereas O'Brien was drawn to Robespierre, Harney came to identify with Marat, frequently signing himself, throughout the Chartist years, as L'Ami du Peuple or A Friend of the People. Harney also learned from the group of old Spenceans and in 1837 formed with some of them the East London Democratic Association, which the following year was reorganized as simply the London Democratic Association in opposition to the Working Men's Association.

One result of this conflict was that in the first Chartist convention Harney sat not for London but for Norwich, Derby, and Newcastle. It was his opinion, in December 1838, that 'as the Gallic Convention of 1793 required a jacobin club to look after it, so will the British Convention of 1839 require the watchful support of the Democratic Association' (Goodway, *London Chartism*, 31); but his efforts to swing the convention behind physical force and immediate preparations to take power failed, earning him the censure of other delegates and a reputation among some historians as a mindless hothead. During his extensive travels outside London in 1838–9 this still very young man, recognized as the foremost spokesman of the most radical, physical-force Chartism, was permanently admitted to the hearts of the new movement's rank and file. He was of 'ruddy complexion, of medium height', with 'grey eyes, and a plentiful shock of dark-brown hair' (Cole, 299); and Gammage, while criticizing him for vanity and vindictiveness, conceded that to 'those whom he considered his friends no man could be more warmly or devotedly attached' (Gammage, 30).

In April 1840 the case against Harney for a seditious speech at Birmingham the preceding May was dropped; and, equally paradoxically, he failed to be implicated in the conspiracies culminating in and following the Newport rising. As he admitted in January, 'he was much wiser

(George) Julian Harney (1817–1897), by unknown engraver, pubd 1894

in the year 1840 than he had been at the commencement of 1839' (Schoyen, 97). After his acquittal he spent almost a year in Scotland, and in September 1840 married Mary Cameron, of Mauchline, Ayrshire, 'tall, beautiful, and of high spirit' (Holyoake, 1.106) and the daughter of a radical weaver. It was a meeting of minds and an immensely happy union (although there were to be no children). On his return to England he worked as full-time Chartist organizer in Sheffield, and acted as local correspondent for the *Northern Star*; he moved to Leeds in 1843 to become sub-editor, and was formally appointed editor two years later. This was Harney's finest and most influential period: he was until 1850 the great editor of a great newspaper. Throughout the 1840s Chartism cohered around the weekly *Northern Star*; and under Harney its unrivalled coverage of domestic working-class affairs was supplemented by an authoritative presentation of international radicalism and revolutionary movements, together with a strong emphasis on literature. Harney himself was a bibliophile and a voracious reader, especially of poetry, above all that of Byron.

The *Northern Star* moved to London in 1844 and Harney proceeded to build up the Fraternal Democrats, a London society (with country members) of Chartists and European exiles, and his new revolutionary internationalism exercised a much broader appeal, attracting key Chartist militants, than had the sterile Jacobinism of 1838–9. His concern with foreign affairs led him to contest Tiverton, Palmerston's seat, in 1847, dissecting in a two-hour speech on the hustings the policy of the foreign secretary, who responded with what was judged the 'most lengthy and plain-spoken account of his stewardship ever given to the British public' (Schoyen, 151). In 1843 Engels visited Leeds to meet Harney; they became lifelong friends and Engels a contributor to his journals. From 1848 Harney, with Ernest Jones, was instrumental in moving the Chartist left to a socialist position. Still editor of the *Northern Star*, he brought out his own *Democratic Review* (1849–50) until the inevitable break with O'Connor. He then edited the *Red Republican* (1850), in which the first English translation of the *Communist Manifesto* appeared. This became the *Friend of the People*, absorbed into the *Northern Star* when Harney acquired it in 1852, but by the end of the year the resulting *Star of Freedom* had folded. Mary Harney died on 11 February 1853; and in December Julian was obliged to move to Newcastle and compromise by assisting Joseph Cowen with his *Northern Tribune* (1854–5).

In 1855, aged only thirty-eight, Harney left Britain and working-class politics to settle in the Channel Islands, where he edited the Jersey *Independent* (1856–62). Here in 1859 he married, secondly, Marie Le Sueur Métivier (*née* Le Sueur), widow of a prosperous shopkeeper, and acquired a stepson, James (*b.* 1853). The family emigrated in 1863–4 to the United States, where, in Boston, Harney edited briefly his final newspaper, the abolitionist *Commonwealth*, and then spent the remainder of his working life as a clerk in the secretary's office at the Massachusetts State House. He returned permanently to England in 1888 to live by himself, but nine years later his wife nursed him in his final illness. The last surviving member of the 1839 convention, he died on 9 December 1897 at Richmond, Surrey. He was buried in Richmond cemetery.   DAVID GOODWAY

Sources A. R. Schoyen, *The chartist challenge: a portrait of George Julian Harney* (1958) · F. G. Black and R. Métivier Black, eds., *The Harney papers* (1969) · M. Hambrick, *A chartist's library* (1986) · G. D. H. Cole, *Chartist portraits* (1941) · R. G. Gammage, *History of the Chartist movement, 1837–1854*, new edn (1894) · G. J. Holyoake, *Sixty years of an agitator's life*, 2 vols. (1892) · J. Saville, introduction, 'The red republican' and 'The friend of the people', ed. G. J. Harney, facs. edn, 2 vols. (1966) · W. E. Adams, *Memoirs of a social atom*, 2 vols. (1903) · D. Goodway, *London Chartism, 1838–1848* (1982) · D. Goodway, 'The Métivier collection and the books of George Julian Harney', *Bulletin of the Society for the Study of Labour History*, 49 (1984), 57–60 · W. H. Maehl, ed., *Robert Gammage* (1983) · CGPLA Eng. & Wales (1898)

Archives priv. coll. | Bodl. Oxf., letters to Bertram Dobell · International Institute of Social History, Amsterdam, Marx-Engels Archive, letters to Friedrich Engels

Likenesses engraving, repro. in *Reynolds's Political Instructor* (16 Feb 1850) · photograph, repro. in Adams, *Memoirs of a social atom*, vol. 1, facing p. 218 · woodcut, repro. in Gammage, *History of the chartist movement*, facing p. 29 [see illus.]

Wealth at death £273 1s. 8d.: probate, 2 Feb 1898, CGPLA Eng. & Wales

Harold I [*called* Harold Harefoot] (*d.* 1040), king of England, was allegedly the son of *Cnut, king of England, of Denmark, and of Norway (*d.* 1035), and *Ælfgifu of Northampton (*fl.* 1006–1036), daughter of Ealdorman Ælfhelm of Northumbria. His mother's association with Cnut began no later than 1015, Harold and his brother Swein apparently having been born by 1017, when Emma of Normandy [*see* Emma [Ælfgifu]] is said by her encomiast to have married Cnut on condition that his existing sons would not succeed if she had male offspring. They and Ælfgifu do not witness royal charters during his reign, but had some sort of recognized position, as Ælfgifu and Swein were eventually sent to rule Norway. Harold's sobriquet Harefoot, indicating fleetness of foot according to late medieval chroniclers, appears first as Harefoh or Harefah in the twelfth-century history of Ely Abbey, perhaps through confusion with the Norwegian king Harold Fairhair.

Harold I (d. 1040), coin

If Cnut made arrangements for the succession they are obscure. The German chronicler Adam of Bremen stated in the 1070s that Cnut intended Harold to have England and Emma's son *Harthacnut, Denmark, while Symeon of Durham thought c.1100 that Cnut made Harold king of England; the encomiast of Emma, on the other hand, asserts that England was pledged to Harthacnut. At Oxford, late in 1035, Earl Leofric of Mercia, almost all the thegns north of the Thames, and the professional troops in London elected Harold regent to hold England for himself and Harthacnut (then in Denmark). Emma, who was supported at this stage by Earl Godwine, was to live in Winchester and hold Wessex for Harthacnut. Relevant manuscripts of the Anglo-Saxon Chronicle express reservations about Harold's parentage, text C denying that he was Cnut's son with Ælfgifu, text D initially calling him 'his son Harold' and then (in a passage possibly added later) denying it, and text E reporting that some claimed it, while many were incredulous. The encomiast reports a belief that Harold was not Cnut's son, but a servant's baby whom Ælfgifu passed off as such, and John of Worcester had heard similar tales which made Swein a priest's and Harold a shoemaker's offspring. Probably untrue, these stories suggest, paradoxically, that Harold was a recognized son of Cnut, although the doubts expressed by the Anglo-Saxon Chronicle may mean that he had no public position before 1035. Adam of Bremen says clearly that Swein and Harold were Cnut's sons with a concubine.

When Cnut died, on 12 November 1035, Harold sent to Winchester and took his father's best treasures from Emma. He probably owed his support north of the Thames to Ælfgifu and her midland origins. She had returned to England by 1036, and early in that year Emma's son Alfred Ætheling arrived from Normandy to attempt to take the throne, after an abortive attack on the south coast by his brother Edward (later king, as Edward the Confessor). Alfred was intercepted by Godwine,

brought before Harold (who, the encomiast says, duped him into coming by sending a forged letter in Emma's name), and condemned to a blinding from which he died. Godwine was clearly prepared to support Harold, even if he had not yet abandoned Harthacnut. Had the latter appeared in 1036 the country might have been divided, with Harthacnut taking Wessex and Harold the rest; but he did not, and in 1037 Harold was 'everywhere chosen as king', and Emma exiled (ASC, s.a. 1037, text C).

Numismatic evidence broadly mirrors this sequence of events: a few pennies of Cnut's final type, Short Cross, are known in Harold's name, the succeeding Jewel Cross issue being initially produced for him at mints north of the Thames only, while those south of it and a few to the north issued for Harthacnut; mints on the river (London, Oxford, Southwark, Wallingford) struck for both; but production in Harthacnut's name was apparently short-lived, all moneyers thereafter issuing for Harold. Probably in 1037, after his recognition as sole king, the diademed bust of Jewel Cross was replaced by the diademed and armoured bust, with a sceptre, of Harold's next and final type, Fleur de Lys.

Evidence on Harold's government is scanty. The Anglo-Saxon Chronicle says that sixteen ships of the navy were paid at 8 marks a rowlock, as in Cnut's day. No royal charters have survived, although a Canterbury Cathedral document, incorporating the text of a royal writ, describes how he took the port of Sandwich from them, only restoring it on his deathbed. This may be connected with the encomiast's story that Æthelnoth, archbishop of Canterbury, had earlier refused to consecrate Harold king, and with a desire to control an important port at a time when Harthacnut threatened invasion.

Harold died at Oxford on 17 March 1040 and was the first king interred in Westminster Abbey; his corpse was exhumed on Harthacnut's orders and flung into a marsh and then, according to John of Worcester, the Thames, whence it was extracted by a fisherman and buried in a Danish cemetery in London (perhaps at St Clement Danes). There is inconclusive continental evidence that he had a wife, Ælfgifu, and son, Ælfwine. M. K. LAWSON

Sources ASC, s.a. 1035–7, 1040 [text C]; s.a. 1035–6 [text D]; s.a. 1036, 1039 [text E] · A. Campbell, ed. and trans., Encomium Emmae reginae, CS, 3rd ser., 72 (1949), 32–3, 38–47 · Magistri Adam Bremensis gesta Hammaburgensis ecclesiae pontificum, ed. B. Schmeidler, 3rd edn, MGH Scriptores Rerum Germanicarum, [2] (Hanover, 1917), 134 · John of Worcester, Chron. · 'Historia regum', Symeon of Durham, Opera, 2.158 · English historical documents, 1, ed. D. Whitelock (1955) · A. J. Robertson, ed. and trans., Anglo-Saxon charters, 2nd edn (1956), 174–9 · F. E. Harmer, ed., Anglo-Saxon writs, 2nd edn (1989), 542 · E. O. Blake, ed., Liber Eliensis, CS, 3rd ser., 92 (1962), 160 · T. Talvio, 'Harold I and Harthacnut's Jewel Cross type reconsidered', Anglo-Saxon monetary history: essays in memory of Michael Dolley, ed. M. A. S. Blackburn (1986), 273–90 · W. H. Stevenson, 'An alleged son of King Harold Harefoot', EngHR, 28 (1913), 112–17 · F. Barlow, Edward the Confessor (1970), 42–8

Likenesses coin, BM [see illus.]

Harold II [Harold Godwineson] (1022/3?–1066), king of England, was probably born in 1022 or 1023, and was the second son of the most powerful nobleman in England,

*Godwine, earl of Wessex (*d.* 1053), and his wife, *Gytha (*fl. c.*1022–1068) [*see under* Godwine].

Family background Godwine had been earl in Wessex for four or five years by the time Harold was born. The origins of this parvenu are extremely obscure. In spite of his brilliant marriage and important office, Godwine was the quintessential new man, described as such even by his family's apologist, the author of the life of King Edward. There is some evidence to suggest that Godwine was the son of the late tenth-century renegade and pirate Wulfnoth of Sussex, who had rebelled spectacularly against Æthelred the Unready and had purloined his fleet; and judging from the location of Godwine's estates it does appear that the family had long been established as thegns in Sussex and Hampshire. Harold's mother, unlike her husband, came from a distinguished Danish family. She was the sister of Cnut's loyal follower Earl Ulf, who was himself the husband of Cnut's sister Estrith. The union between Gytha and Godwine produced at least eight children who survived to adulthood, and almost all of them came to hold important positions at court and large tracts of land in the shires. Harold's sister *Edith, born either just before or just after him, became *Edward the Confessor's wife in 1045. His elder brother *Swein was earl of the south-west midlands in 1043; his younger brother *Tostig became earl of Northumbria in 1055; *Leofwine was made earl of the south-east by 1057; and *Gyrth was earl of East Anglia and Oxfordshire by 1057 or 1058. Only two of Harold's siblings could not be found at the centre of the kingdom's court and politics. One was apparently a nun and the other a professional hostage at the ducal court in Normandy.

Earldom and rebellion During Harold's childhood his father was positioned at the heart of politics, helping, along with two of Cnut's other favourites—Earl Siward of Northumbria and Earl Leofric of Mercia—to govern England during the king's extended absences. The three together were centrally involved in keeping the kingdom and its administration intact during the short and lacklustre reigns of Cnut's sons. Godwine himself was the supporter of Cnut's youngest son, King Harthacnut, and it was Godwine who engineered and smoothed the way for the return in 1041 of King Æthelred's son Edward the Confessor, an atheling long exiled in Normandy. Godwine subsequently supported the Confessor's succession to the throne in 1042 at Harthacnut's death; and he proved himself more than willing to manage the Confessor's affairs when the new king began his rule as a returning exile. As a result of these circumstances Godwine's family prospered. Within twenty months his eldest son was made an earl, and his eldest daughter was married to the new king. And Harold himself, now a man in his early twenties, came into an earldom in eastern England, probably extending across East Anglia, Essex, Huntingdonshire, and Cambridgeshire. While Harold acted as earl in eastern England, he formed important lifelong relations with the region's ecclesiastical establishments and prelates, its great thegns and middling sokemen. It was during this period that Harold doubtless took as his concubine Edith Swanneck (Swanneshals). She is probably identical with

Harold II (1022/3?–1066), embroidery (Bayeux Tapestry) [enthroned, with (right) Stigand, archbishop of Canterbury]

*Eadgifu the Fair, also known as the Rich, one of the largest landholders in eastern England. Such relationships, in spite of increasing pressures from a reforming church, were common. Cnut himself had had a concubine, and William the Conqueror was a product of just such a union. Harold and Edith had at least five children. This 'Danish marriage', as contemporaries called it, must have bound Harold closely through ties of kinship and marriage to many Anglo-Scandinavian lords settled in his earldom. Stigand and his brother Æthelmær, who both, in their turn, served as bishops of Elmham, were also allies of Harold, although these bonds may have been fostered as much in the royal court as in the shire-courts of Norfolk and Suffolk. Harold also cultivated ties with some of the religious communities of his earldom. He was a patron of Peterborough Abbey, and Peterborough's abbot, Leofric, fought with him at Hastings. Harold also had proprietary interests in a newly founded community at Waltham Holy Cross in Essex. Ely Abbey, too, seems to have had ties with the earl, and it may have given Harold a gift of relics as a token of friendship or gratitude. But it was not only with the region's élites that Harold formed bonds of association. By 1066 Harold and his brother Gyrth, who followed him as earl in East Anglia, had freemen commended to them in almost two hundred East Anglian villages.

Within a few years Harold's earldom and his responsibilities were broadened. His brother Swein, a reckless man, abducted the abbess of Leominster in 1046, and within a year, for this and other, more obscure, crimes, he fled to Bruges and then to Denmark. His earldom was divided between Harold and his cousin *Beorn Estrithson, and eventually a share was given to the Confessor's nephew Ralph of Mantes. When Swein returned to England in 1049, in hopes of a pardon and the restoration of his earldom, Harold and Beorn opposed him. Swein, in unclear circumstances, retaliated by murdering his cousin. This was a shocking crime. He was declared a *nithing* by the king and the army and was forced once again into exile. Although he was pardoned the next year and back in England, it was Harold who was now his father's most important son and chief lieutenant. In 1050 and 1051 Godwine had need of a steady son, because relations between the family and the king had chilled. Both the monks of Canterbury and the Godwinesons supported the candidacy of one of Godwine's kinsmen for archbishop of Canterbury, but in the spring of 1051 the king appointed Robert of Jumièges, the Norman bishop of London. Robert was one of the family's implacable enemies, and once he became archbishop he accused Godwine of stealing Canterbury land and of murdering, many years before (1037), the Confessor's younger brother Alfred. Then, in September 1051, the king's brother-in-law, Eustace, count of Boulogne, came to England. As he passed through Dover, one of the most important urban communities in Godwine's earldom, the count and his men got into a deadly altercation with some of the burgesses there. When Eustace complained, the king ordered Godwine to punish the town. Godwine, however, refused, in the words of the Anglo-Saxon Chronicle, to 'carry war into Kent' (*ASC*, text E, s.a. 1048, *recte* 1051). Godwine was called to court to answer for his actions. In the weeks that followed Godwine and his sons on the one hand, and the king and his remaining earls on the other, gathered their armies; but Godwine's men in the end lost their nerve. The family was outlawed and deprived of its lands and offices. Harold's parents and three of his brothers fled to Flanders. Harold, accompanied by his brother Leofwine, sailed from Bristol to Ireland to the court of Diarmait mac Máel na mBó, king of Leinster. His sister the queen, who had not produced an heir, was put into a nunnery. In their year of exile, the family (except for Swein, who instead walked barefoot to Jerusalem and died on the journey home) recruited ships' crews from around the northern world—in Scandinavia, Flanders, and Ireland; and in 1052, with their newly raised fleet and the aid of their English allies at home, they forced the king to take them back. The queen was returned to court, Harold and his father were given back their earldoms, and their greatest enemies, including Robert of Jumièges and a number of Edward's other Norman favourites, were driven from the kingdom. The king never challenged the family's power again. The following year, at the king's Easter court (1 April), Earl Godwine died of a stroke. Harold, now thirty, succeeded his father as earl of Wessex. In the next few years, with Harold as the most important secular lord at the royal court, his family, long rich and powerful, became both the dominant office-holding kindred in England and its dominant landholder. Three of Harold's younger brothers, over the course of the next half-decade, received earldoms, twice at the expense of the families of earls Leofric and Siward.

Harold's family, rich since the 1020s, became enormously wealthy over the course of the 1050s. Much is known about their landed resources during these years, because they were systematically recorded in the great 1086 survey, Domesday Book. The bulk of the family's holdings, and the bulk of Harold's, lay in the south-west and south-east of the kingdom, but they had, none the less, substantial interests in English Mercia, East Anglia, Lincolnshire, and Yorkshire. Together their land produced something like £8500 a year. They controlled over twice the amount of land held by the family of Earl Leofric, the next wealthiest kindred in England, and twenty times as much as the kingdom's wealthiest thegnly families. More disturbing for the king, the value of the Godwinesons' estates dwarfed his own. In all, the Confessor's lands rendered almost £2500 less revenue each year than those of his brothers-in-law.

Secular and ecclesiastical patronage Harold's vast territorial interests allowed him to alienate property to thegns and housecarls (household troops) hungry for land; and his central role in the governance of the realm enabled him to proffer aid in court and help his dependants stave off attacks from neighbours and competitors. Men flooded to his affinity during these years. Many were the wealthiest thegns in England, men like Asgar the Staller, Æthelnoth Cild of Kent, Eadmær Atre, Eadnoth the Staller, Leofwine Cild, and Thorkill the White. All of these thegns were powerful men of at least regional importance and all held lands valued at over £40 per annum, the amount according to the *Liber Eliensis* that set apart lesser thegns from the more important magnates. Furthermore, some of these men, such as Æthelnoth Cild, Asgar the Staller, and Eadmær Atre, held hundreds of hides of land and had large retinues of their own, and attended the Confessor regularly at court. Harold also formed close alliances with important ecclesiastics during these years. His family had long-standing relations with the sees of Worcester, York, and Canterbury, and Harold continued to foster them. Wulfstan, bishop of Worcester, was a friend and confidant of the earl, and the author of the life of Wulfstan says that Harold often journeyed miles out of his way to see the saintly bishop. Harold and Ealdred, first bishop of Worcester and later archbishop of York, often worked in concert, and Ealdred travelled to the continent on more than one occasion in the company of Harold or his brothers. Ealdred also gave Harold an impressive collection of relics. Stigand, the former bishop of Elmham, now bishop of Winchester and archbishop of Canterbury, was also an ally of the family, and he allowed Harold to maintain advantageous leases on large tracts of archiepiscopal land that his father, Godwine, had held.

Anglo-Norman historians often portray Harold as an impious man and as the despoiler of monks; and it is true that Harold, by 1066, was holding an unseemly amount of church land—estates belonging to the bishops of Exeter, Hereford, Rochester, Wells, and Worcester, the archbishop of Canterbury, and the nuns of Shaftesbury. Some of these holdings were the result of predation pure and simple, but others represented loans of land by religious communities in return for political favours. Such sharp practices were not Harold's invention, but were common English custom. On the eve of the Norman conquest many great lords, both lay and ecclesiastical, could be found operating in a similar fashion. And in spite of some angry claims and a handful of lawsuits, the memory of Harold and his family was cultivated after the conquest by monks and canons in Abingdon, Canterbury, Durham, Peterborough, Winchester, and Worcester.

Harold's particular locus of benefaction, however, was the small community of Waltham Holy Cross that he refounded in these years. He built a beautiful stone church for the community and its wonder-working stone crucifix, and he was at its dedication on the feast of the Invention of the Cross in 1060. King Edward, as a mark of his favour, lent Harold support in this endeavour: he, too, was present at the dedication, and two years later the king gave Waltham a golden-lettered confirmation of Harold's donations that was kept, in the later middle ages, with the community's other relics. The king also sent the clerks of Waltham a blue cloak, which they remade into a chasuble. While there may have been more logical places for the earl of Wessex to build a church, Harold still had wide interests in Essex. King Cnut's follower Tovi the Proud, from whom Harold had inherited Waltham, had had woods for hunting there and an impressive hall, and Harold probably continued to travel to Waltham to hunt, to

pray, and to visit both the dean and the master of the canons, men Harold admired. Waltham, moreover, was only a day's journey from London, a place of increasing importance to the royal court, and a centre of Godwineson power and influence. Harold's interest in the community was also doubtless an indication of his devotion to the cult of the cross. This was particularly strong in Anglo-Scandinavian court circles across the eleventh century and from Cnut's time on there are many indications that the king, his great men, and their wives did much to sponsor and encourage it. By the mid-eleventh century many communities had life-sized crucifixes and large collections of crosses which had been given to them by Anglo-Danish noblemen, and Harold's brother Tostig and his brother's wife, Judith, were major patrons of the cult.

When Harold refounded Waltham, he made it into a college of secular canons. Although men of Harold's station in the tenth century had often been drawn to the reformed Benedictine monasticism of their own day, many of the great men of Cnut's and Edward's court preferred the more worldly and pragmatic piety of the secular canons. Many English noblemen, moreover, including Harold himself, had visited reformed communities of canons in Lotharingia and were impressed with what they saw. Siward, earl of Northumbria, for example, founded a church for secular canons in York; Harold's womenfolk appear to have done the same in Exeter, and Harold's friend and ally Archbishop Ealdred was the patron of a house of canons at Beverley. Harold, moreover, had come of age in the royal household, a *familia* full of clerks. The kind of sophisticated and cosmopolitan piety they sponsored must have appealed to Harold, but so too did their utility. If Harold's own household was modelled on the king's, which seems likely, he would have had use for a college of secular canons to serve as a place to train clerks for his own chapel and for his writing office. Indeed, Harold appointed Adelard, a learned German who had studied at Utrecht, as *magister* at Waltham.

Harold gave lavishly to his foundation, both at the dedication and after his victory at the battle of Stamford Bridge. In the late twelfth century the community angrily recalled that William Rufus had despoiled the abbey of many of Harold's gifts, including seven jewel-encrusted shrines and four of its books. Two of Harold's other books, however, both gospels, remained at Waltham in spite of their elaborate decorations and valuable covers, because they were written in Old English, and were, therefore, of little utility to Norman monks. Both were still at Waltham in the sixteenth century when the community was dissolved. The large number of beautiful books at Waltham suggests that Harold, like his sister-in-law Judith and a number of other late Anglo-Saxon nobles, was a patron of deluxe manuscripts. Indeed it appears as if Harold himself owned an elaborate book on falconry. Harold also gave Waltham a large number of relics, which he apparently collected himself. A number of these were of English provenance, and had either been taken from monastic communities, or more likely given by them to Harold as payment for support or to ensure his favour. Ely, Shaftesbury, Cerne, Winchester, and Christ Church, Canterbury, all appear to have contributed to Harold's collection. Harold had also been to Rome, and a number of Waltham's relics—including a piece of St Peter's chain and hair from his beard—were probably acquired there. Other relics were probably collected during his trip to Flanders and Germany: they came from Rheims, Noyon, St Riquier, St Amand, Metz, and Cologne. Harold's taste in relics was cosmopolitan and eclectic, and exhibits a fondness both for English saints and for saints whose churches he had visited on his travels. And some, like the relic of St Nicholas, suggest that Harold shared a passion for the same eastern saint that so many of his Norman contemporaries did.

Beyond England Between 1053 and the Northumbrian revolt late in 1065, Harold, besides consolidating his power at home, spent much of his energy pursuing alliances abroad or punishing foreign enemies, acting, as the author of the life of King Edward puts it, as David to Edward the Confessor's Solomon. Wales in the first half of the 1050s was dominated by two great Welsh princes—Gruffudd ap Llywelyn in Gwynedd and Powys and Gruffudd ap Rhydderch in Deheubarth. Both raided deep into English territory, and both built alliances with the enemies of England. Then, in 1055, Gruffudd ap Llywelyn helped to bring about the death of his namesake, and Welsh power was ominously unified. That autumn Gruffudd routed the Confessor's nephew Earl Ralph (henceforth known as the Timid) and other Frenchmen who had been settled along the Welsh march to protect the kingdom from just such attacks. Harold, as a result, reorganized the march. In early 1056 one of his clerks, the moustache-wearing warrior Leofgar, was made bishop of Hereford, but in less than three months the bishop and his army were defeated and slaughtered by Gruffudd. Gruffudd continued to cause problems. In 1058 he made common cause with his father-in-law, Ælfgar, the exiled earl of Mercia. By 1063 Harold had had enough. In the early months of that year he led a raid deep into Welsh territory in an unsuccessful attempt to capture his nemesis. In May Harold and his brother Tostig assaulted Wales simultaneously from the south and the north. Many Welsh noblemen sued for peace. On 5 August Gruffudd was killed by his own men, and his head and the beak of his ship were sent to Harold. The earl took oaths, hostages, and tribute from the Welsh, and installed two more congenial men as kings in Wales. Harold's victories were stunning, and according to Gerald of Wales large numbers of standing stones could still be found up and down the Welsh march in the late twelfth century, inscribed with the words *hic fuit victor Haroldus* ('here Harold was the victor').

Harold travelled outside Britain during these years as well. He journeyed once to Rome on a pilgrimage and is thought to have gone abroad on two other occasions, on trips which, since the Norman conquest, have generally been characterized as diplomatic missions concerning the English succession. He certainly travelled to Flanders in the autumn of 1056, and then on to Germany. Although there is no explicit evidence for the reason for this journey, it has often been suggested that Harold made the trip to negotiate the return of Edward the Exile, son of Edmund Ironside, who was living in Hungary, and that he may have seen Edward as another Confessor, an adult princeling raised in exile, without much experience of war or governance, and incapable of ruling without the help of Harold's family. Whatever the hopes vested in him, however, Edward died in 1057, soon after his arrival in England, leaving his young son Edgar to uphold a claim to the throne with little or no support from the English aristocracy.

Harold is also said to have gone to Normandy, probably in 1064. While no contemporary or near-contemporary English source records this, the story being picked up there only in the twelfth century, it does appear in Norman sources written immediately after 1066. According to these, Harold was sent by Edward to confirm that the king had made William his heir. The story tells of an ill-fated trip on which Harold was shipwrecked on his way to Normandy and held captive by Guy (I), count of Ponthieu. He was redeemed by William and then joined the duke on his Breton campaign, accepting arms from him and, these Norman sources allege, taking an oath of fealty to William, promising to protect the duke's claim to the English throne: an act vividly depicted on the Bayeux tapestry. A narrative that accepts that this expedition took place might further envisage that it was then, in his only personal encounter with the Norman duke, that Harold determined that William was no Edward the Confessor, and that as king he would neither need nor bear the Godwinesons. A hint that the oath-taking, at least, might be factual appears in the life of King Edward, a not obviously pro-Norman work written in 1066–7, which, albeit in a different context, laments that Harold was 'rather too generous with oaths (alas!)' (*Life of King Edward*, 53). Whatever the truth, any arrangements made in 1064 were certainly disregarded, by both Edward and Harold, when the Confessor lay on his deathbed at the beginning of 1066.

Kingship and death In October 1065, while Harold's brother Tostig was with the king in Wiltshire, the thegns of Northumbria revolted against Tostig's harsh, or more likely efficient, rule. The rebels wanted Morcar, grandson of the old Mercian earl Leofric, as Tostig's replacement. Harold, at the expense of his brother, struck a deal with *Morcar, his brother *Eadwine [see under Ælfgar], and the thegns of Northumbria. Tostig was driven into exile and Morcar was made earl of Northumbria in his place. Probably to solidify their alliance, and in anticipation of the king's death, which now seemed imminent, Harold married *Ealdgyth, sister of his new Mercian allies and a woman once married to Gruffudd ap Llywelyn. By the time of the battle of Hastings, she had produced a son—Harold Haroldson—a boy both families would have wanted, one day, to become king. After Tostig's exile, the Confessor became ill, so ill that he could not attend the consecration of his life's work, the new abbey of Westminster, on 29 December. The king died on 4 or 5 January. Although bequest of the kingdom to a successor not of the royal line appears to have no place in the English tradition of royal succession, English sources record that on his deathbed Edward designated Harold Godwineson as his heir, and the Norman sources do not dissent. Harold's election by the magnates and anointing, by Archbishop Ealdred of York, on the day immediately following the death of his predecessor also seem to have been unprecedented, as well as having been achieved with unseemly haste, a point noted by one near-contemporary commentator. While the claims of Edgar Ætheling were ignored, Harold became the first English king to be crowned at Westminster Abbey.

Recording the beginning of Harold's ten-month reign, the Anglo-Saxon Chronicle states ominously 'he met little quiet in it as long as he ruled the realm' (*ASC*, s.a. 1065, texts C, D). Much of it was spent preparing for war against the various claimants to the English throne and his old Welsh enemies. Coins with Harold's likeness were issued from more than forty mints. Romney, Chester, and York, however, were especially productive, suggesting that the king was minting money to prepare himself for war in regions where troublemakers and claimants to the throne were most likely to challenge him: Harald Hardrada, king of Norway, now in league with Tostig, in the north; the Welsh in the north-west; and the duke of Normandy on the south coast. In September Harald Hardrada and Tostig invaded with three hundred ships. They fought the Northumbrians at Gate Fulford and routed them. Harold hurried north, and on 25 September, at the battle of Stamford Bridge, he annihilated the invaders. Harald Hardrada, the greatest warrior of his generation, was killed, and so too was Earl Tostig. Three days later Duke William crossed the channel. Harold, in a strategy that had served him well in the north, immediately moved south, and on 14 October, 7 miles from Hastings, he fought against William and his men. It was the third major battle in a month. Harold's army, fighting on foot behind a wall of shields, turned back the Norman cavalry most of the day under a heavy barrage of Norman arrows, but at the end of a hard day's fight King Harold and his brothers Gyrth and Leofwine were dead. The Bayeux tapestry shows Harold's death—apparently pierced in the eye by an arrow. Whether he did, indeed, die in this manner (a death associated in the middle ages with perjurers), or was killed by the sword, will never be known.

Although one Norman account claims that Harold's body was buried, after Hastings, in a grave overlooking the Saxon shore, it is more likely that he was buried in his church of Waltham Holy Cross. According to Waltham tradition, Harold's handfast wife, Edith Swanneck, brought the king's mutilated body from Hastings to Waltham. Waltham sources, moreover, record that before 1177 the king's body was translated within the church three times, and it is just possible that before the reform of Waltham Abbey by Henry II a cult was developing around Harold's body. Very soon after the conquest the notion emerged—in Norman sources, at least—that Harold had never been king. On the one hand, the Conqueror's biographer William of Poitiers and, following

him, the Bayeux tapestry, asserted that Harold had been crowned by Stigand, the usurping archbishop of Canterbury: in reality, Ealdred of York had been selected to crown Harold, as he later crowned William, precisely because of Stigand's unsuitability. On the other hand, 'with the exception of two slips in proof-reading' (Garnett, 72), Domesday Book never treats Harold as a king, not even a perjured one. Notions of the illegitimacy of his rule persisted for centuries. Not all, however, had been persuaded that King Harold had died at Hastings. By the twelfth century a number of legends, all no doubt spurious, were in circulation, that Harold had indeed survived the battle. In one version, Harold spent two years recovering from his wounds in Winchester. After he was restored to health he left England for Germany, and spent many years wandering as a pilgrim. As an old man he returned to England, and after living ten years as a hermit in a cave outside Dover, he travelled to Chester, where he lived once again as a hermit. As he lay dying, he confessed that although he went by the name of Christian, he had been born Harold Godwineson.

Apart from various versions of this story, accounts of Harold written in the later middle ages differ only over details (for example, the place where he swore the oath to William and the location of his burial). All agree on the fundamental point, dating from the earliest Norman sources, that in accepting the crown of England Harold had perjured himself. Literary interest in Harold revived in the nineteenth century, with the publication of the historical novel *Harold, the Last of the Saxon Kings* by Edward Bulwer-Lytton (1848) and of the play *Harold* by Alfred, Lord Tennyson (1876). Rudyard Kipling wrote a grimly impressive story, 'The tree of justice', which concludes his *Rewards and Fairies* (1910), describing how a very old man who turns out to be Harold is brought before Henry I and his courtiers. Serious revision of the historical Harold began with E. A. Freeman's *History of the Norman Conquest of England* (1870–79: esp. vols. 2 and 3), which put him forward as one of the great heroes of English history. At the end of the twentieth century, his ability and courage as ever unquestioned, Harold's reputation remains bound up, as it has always been, with differing and ultimately subjective views of the rightness or wrongness of the Norman conquest.

ROBIN FLEMING

Sources *ASC*, s.a. 1048, i.e. 1051 [text E]; 1065 [texts C, D] · A. Farley, ed., *Domesday Book*, 2 vols. (1783) · L. Watkiss and M. Chibnall, eds. and trans., *The Waltham chronicle: an account of the discovery of our holy cross at Montacute and its conveyance to Waltham*, OMT (1994) · F. Barlow, ed. and trans., *The life of King Edward who rests at Westminster*, 2nd edn, OMT (1992) · D. M. Wilson, ed., *The Bayeux tapestry* (1985) · *Vita Haroldi: the romance of the life of Harold, king of England*, ed. and trans. W. de Gray Birch (1885) · *Willelmi Malmesbiriensis monachi de gestis regum Anglorum*, ed. W. Stubbs, 2 vols., Rolls Series (1887–9) · John of Worcester, *Chron.* · Guillaume de Poitiers [Gulielmus Pictaviensis], *Histoire de Guillaume le Conquérant / Gesta Gulielmus ducis Normannorum et regis Anglorum*, ed. R. Foreville (Paris, 1952) · *AS chart.* · *The Vita Wulfstani of William of Malmesbury*, ed. R. R. Darlington, CS, 3rd ser., 40 (1928) · F. E. Harmer, ed., *Anglo-Saxon writs* (1952) · E. A. Freeman, *The history of the Norman conquest of England*, 2nd edn, 6 vols. (1870–79), vol. 2 · R. Fleming, *Kings and lords in conquest England* (1991) · F. Barlow, *Edward the Confessor*, 2nd edn

(1979) · G. Garnett, 'Conquered England, 1066–1215', *The Oxford illustrated history of medieval England*, ed. N. Saul (1997), 61–101 · N. Rogers, 'The Waltham Abbey relic-list', *England in the eleventh century* [Harlaxton 1990], ed. C. Hicks (1992), 157–81 · A. Thacker, 'The cult of King Harold at Chester', *The middle ages in the north-west* (1995) · F. Barlow, *The English church, 1000–1066: a history of the later Anglo-Saxon church*, 2nd edn (1979) · M. Ashdown, 'An Icelandic account of the survival of Harold Godwinsson', *The Anglo-Saxons: studies in some aspects of their history and culture presented to Bruce Dickins*, ed. P. Clemoes (1959), 122–36 · P. Grierson, 'A visit of Earl Harold to Flanders in 1056', *EngHR*, 51 (1936), 90–97 · E. C. Fernie, 'The Romanesque church of Waltham Abbey', *Journal of the British Archaeological Association*, 138 (1985), 48–78 · B. Hudson, 'The family of Harold Godwinsson and the Irish Sea province', *Journal of the Royal Society of Antiquaries of Ireland*, 109 (1979), 92–100 · C. R. Dodwell, *Anglo-Saxon art: a new perspective* (1982) · W. Winters, *The history of the ancient parish of Waltham Abbey or Holy Cross* (1888)

Likenesses Dermon, silver penny, 1066 (after Theodoric), BM, NPG · embroidery (Bayeux Tapestry), Bayeux, France [*see illus.*]

Harold, Francis (*c*.1617–1685), Franciscan priest and historian, was born in Limerick, the nephew and cousin respectively of prominent Franciscans Luke Wadding and Bonaventure Baron. Thomas Harold, a leading disciple of Peter Walsh, was also a cousin, and two other Franciscans shared his name, one a nephew. After education in Ireland he began his studies in St Isidore's College, Rome, under Baron, on 9 January 1639, and was ordained on 22 December 1640. About this time he compiled a large 'Index sanctorum' for his uncle, transcribed into two large volumes by an amanuensis in 1647. Later Alexander VII (1655–1667) ordered two copies of this, while Harold also supplied him with copies of manuscripts, including sermons of St Bernardino of Siena OFM. He lectured in philosophy in Prague (1642–5), and in theology in Vienna and then in Graz (*c*.1650–51). He was recalled to Rome to be lecturer and librarian, assisting and then succeeding Wadding in 1655 as chronicler and historian of the Franciscan order. The appointment was renewed by papal brief in 1671 and 1675. In 1666 he was one of the Franciscan procurators in Rome, looking after the interests of the Irish province. His failure to be elected guardian of St Isidore's College because he was from the province of Munster was a disappointment.

Harold's output, of which he left a list, was not as voluminous as that of his uncle, Wadding, nor of his cousin, Baron. Wadding had chronicled the history of the Franciscan order up to 1540 in eight folio volumes, published in small editions. There was a great demand for them and Harold had to bring out an *Epitome annalium ordinis minorum* (Rome, 1662) in two folio volumes, containing 2462 columns of text and 63 pages of a closely printed index, prefaced with a life of Wadding which includes a description of Hugh Ward's projected hagiography of Irish saints. In 1680–82 Sylvester Castet OFM published an 'Epitome annalium' in French that seems to have been a translation of Harold's. His work for the continuation of Wadding's annals was later used by Giovanni De Luca OFM and appeared, without acknowledgement, in volume 18 of the Fonseca edition in 1740. Harold's life of Wadding was prefixed to the later editions of the annals, and his tract on the Holy Land was inserted into the *Epitome*. His

Lima limata, on the province of Lima, Peru, as limned or portrayed in the works of Archbishop Turibio Alfonso de Mongrovejo, was published in 1673, six years before the archbishop was beatified, a sort of legitimate interlude in the drama of work as annalist (as he said in the introduction) undertaken at the request of a 'vir reverendus', to help with the process of beatification. In 1680 Harold published a life of the Blessed Turibio, who was canonized in 1726, and would become the patron saint of Peru. Both works have a dedication to a cardinal penned by the postulator of the cause of Turibio, who may have been the 'vir reverendus' in question. Harold wrote a life and edited the letters of the Blessed Albert of Sarteano OFM, published after his death by Patrick Duffy OFM in Rome in 1688. He also wrote about three cardinals, Borromeo, Albergati, and Ximénes, and annotated some works of the Franciscans Bonaventure, Scotus, John of Wales, Wadding, and Bonaventure John of Mantua. He wrote too about the Irish Franciscan province, Irish bishops and churches, and the Trinitarians in Ireland, and gave help to the Bollandist Daniel Papebroch SJ. He died at St Isidore's College, Rome, on 18 March 1685, and was buried at the college.

IGNATIUS FENNESSY

Sources G. Cleary, *Father Luke Wadding and St Isidore's College, Rome* (1925) · B. Jennings, ed., 'Miscellaneous documents, 1588–1715 [pt 2]', *Archivium Hibernicum*, 14 (1949), 1–49 · B. Pandžić, 'Gli *Annales minorum* di Luca Wadding', *Archivum Franciscanum Historicum*, 70 (1977), 656–66 · J. H. Sbaralea, *Supplementum … ad scriptores … S. Francisci*, 3 vols. (Rome, 1908–36), vol. 3 · T. Sweeney, *Ireland and the printed word: a short descriptive catalogue of early books … relating to Ireland, printed, 1475–1700* (Dublin, 1997) · Killiney, co. Dublin, Ireland, Franciscan Library, MSS D 5, D 17, D 18 · *The whole works of Sir James Ware concerning Ireland*, ed. and trans. W. Harris, rev. edn, 2 vols. in 3 (1764) · B. Egan and others, 'Irish students ordained in Rome, 1625–1710', *Irish Ecclesiastical Record*, 5th ser., 61 (1943), 116–24 · I. Fennessy, 'The B manuscripts in the Franciscan Library Killiney', *Dún Mhuire, Killiney, 1945–95*, ed. B. Millett and A. Lynch (1995) · *DNB* · F. Grannell, 'Letters of Daniel Papebroch to Francis Harold, 1665–1690', *Archivum Franciscanum Historicum*, 59 (1966), 385–455 · C. Giblin, 'Documents on the Irish Trinitarians, 1621–71', *Collectanea Hibernica*, 27–8 (1985–6), 11–43 · R. M. Huber, *A documented history of the Franciscan order, 1182–1517* (1944) · B. Millett, *The Irish Franciscans, 1651–1665* (1964)

Archives Franciscan Library, Killiney, co. Dublin, MSS D 5, D 17, D 18 · St Isidore's College, Rome, MSS

Likenesses fresco, St Isidore's College, Rome, Aula Maxima

Harper, Sir Edgar Josiah (1860–1934), land valuer and civil servant, was born on 15 January 1860 at 11 Beaumont Square, Mile End, London, the third son of Henry Harper, a merchant's clerk, and his wife, Mary Ann, *née* Burletson (*b*. 1826?). He was educated privately in Bexley Heath. Effectively a self-made man, Harper showed an early aptitude for statistics. Beginning at the age of eighteen as a clerk in the architect's department at the Metropolitan Board of Works, he progressed rapidly to become an assistant valuer in the estate and valuation department. While employed in that position he married on 8 September 1887 Jessie Anne Wood (1844–1927), the daughter of Hugh Wood and Jessie McKinnon, and sister of Thomas McKinnon Wood (1855–1927), who became leader of the

Progressive Party on the London county council (LCC), secretary for Scotland in 1912, and financial secretary to the Treasury during the First World War.

Harper came to believe strongly in the need to replace the long-established rating system with a single system based on the rating of all land, excluding structures and improvements. His expertise was such that in 1889 he gave persuasive evidence to the LCC's special committee on the valuation of land. He then joined the new London county council, being appointed in 1891 assistant valuer—in which capacity he was concerned primarily with matters of rating and valuation—and within a few years he had oversight of much of the new council's property. From 1895 to 1896 he carried out a pilot valuation of London, his zeal impressing Sydney Webb, who invited him to become one of the first lecturers at the London School of Economics. As an acknowledged expert by now, he gave evidence to the royal commission on local taxation of 1898, again advocating the separate valuation of land and houses as a cheap and easy process, and his contribution was particularly noted in the commission's special report in 1901 on urban rating and site values.

In 1901 Harper was appointed statistical officer to the LCC, and in view of his expertise, an immediate reorganization brought a transfer of the work connected with rating and assessment from the estates and valuation department. By 1905–6 a new, more analytical, and comprehensive series of London Statistics appeared, compiled by Harper. But inter-departmental rivalries were set in train by such actions, and as a covert single-taxer he also became strongly associated with the Liberal government's land campaign. His information and opinions were highly regarded by radical Liberal politicians, but any such advice had to be covert while he remained an LCC official. By December 1908 he was helping Lloyd George, by then chancellor of the exchequer, to frame the necessary legislation for a national tax on land values, writing a paper, 'The imposition of a national tax on land values', for the chancellor's cabinet colleagues. Following the political furore surrounding the 'people's budget' of 1909, when these ideas were put forward by Lloyd George but rejected by the House of Lords, such a tax, together with the necessary valuation of all land, was introduced via the Finance (1909–10) Act of 1910.

At this time Harper became involved in a minor political storm. It had been assumed within the LCC that Harry Haward, the council's comptroller and senior financial officer, who was well versed in local taxation matters, would be asked to join the departmental committee on local taxation, set up to investigate developments since the royal commission report of 1901, as a London representative. In fact, Lloyd George asked for Edgar Harper, and a 'warm interchange' ensued between the council and the government, which was resolved by Harper's resignation from the LCC in April 1911, enabling him to take up the committee appointment. Lloyd George told the House of Commons that Harper would not tolerate the public snub administered to him by the LCC, and, as a very independent man, had unconditionally resigned. Hayes

Fisher (leader of the Municipal Reform Party, afterwards Lord Downham) noted Harper's 'very pronounced and extreme views on the questions of Land Values Taxation' as being the real reason for Lloyd George's choice, adding that Harper would be on the committee as a 'Government wolf in the left-off clothing of a county council lamb' (Hansard 5C, 25, 11 May 1911, 1459–60).

In August 1911 Harper moved on again, succeeding Sir Robert Thompson as chief valuer of the new Inland Revenue valuation department at Somerset House, and assuming responsibility for the valuation of land, a task finally completed in autumn 1915. By 1912 his well-known agenda for the assessment of site values was being pushed forward, and by December 1913 he was again preparing a cabinet paper for Lloyd George, designed to attract substantial revenue from vacant land and empty properties, especially in urban centres, which traditionally had escaped taxation. But the scheme was confused and poorly designed, and the proposal in Lloyd George's budget of 1914 came to nothing.

The First World War now overtook much of Harper's work, and the taxation of land values was finally abandoned in the Finance Act of 1920. His confidence had perhaps been misplaced, and in retrospect he blamed overcomplex drafting, the impact of the war, a cumbersome appeals procedure, and insufficient time. While this was true, he cannot be absolved. Possibly he was too ambitious, and other leading civil servants were more sceptical. Never a good communicator, and possibly encumbered by his social origins in comparison with those of Treasury and revenue officials, he had to accept defeat. Nevertheless, in the same year that the taxes were repealed, he was knighted for public and professional services. He was also appointed to the air raid compensation committee set up by the Board of Trade.

Harper retired from the chief valuer's post at the age of sixty-five in 1925. Thereafter, associated with various interest groups, he continued to speak at national and international gatherings, and to write on the subject of land values during the later 1920s. He was a fellow of the Surveyors' Institution and of the Royal Statistical Society, and an honorary fellow of the Auctioneers' Institute. He was president of the College of Estate Management in 1929, and was a governor of the City of London College. After the death of his first wife, he married on 22 April 1930 Mary Richardson Burge (b. 1877) of Streatham, the widow of Arthur C. Burge, and daughter of William Henry Twine. There were no children by either of his marriages.

Having been born in the East End of London, Harper lived all his adult life in the growing south-eastern suburbs, at South Croydon, Denmark Hill, Blackheath, Upper Norwood, and finally Peckham; during his last long illness he was resident at 112 Peckham Road, Peckham, Surrey, where he died from heart disease and bronchopneumonia on 23 January 1934. His widow survived him for many years.   BRIAN SHORT

Sources The Times (24 Jan 1934), f. 6d · A. Offer, Property and politics, 1870–1914 (1981) · B. Short, Land and society in Edwardian Britain (1997) · b. cert. · m. certs. · d. cert. · CGPLA Eng. & Wales (1934) ·

Report of the special committee on the valuation of land (London county council, 1889) · 'Select committee on land values', *Parl. papers* (1920), 19.753, Cmd 556 · *WW* (1910–34) · *WWW* · H. Haward, *The London county council from within* (1932) · 'The valuation office, 1910–1985: establishing a tradition', Inland Revenue, 1985

Archives LMA, LCC/MIN/6270 | Valuation Office Agency, Carey Street, London, inland revenue, chief valuer's library

Likenesses group photograph, 1912, repro. in 'The valuation office 1910–1985' · photograph, 1913, Valuation Office Agency, Carey Street, London

Wealth at death £4037 11*s*. 5*d*.: probate, 23 Feb 1934, *CGPLA Eng. & Wales*

Harper, Elizabeth. *See* Bannister, Elizabeth (1757–1849).

Harper, Sir George Montague (1865–1922), army officer, was born on 11 January 1865 in Batheaston, Somerset, the son of Charles Harper RN, physician and surgeon, and his wife, Emma (*née* Skinner). Having received his education at Bath College and the Royal Military Academy, Woolwich, he was commissioned in the Royal Engineers in July 1884. He was promoted captain on 1 October 1892, and became adjutant, 2nd Yorkshire (West Riding) Royal Engineer volunteers—an appointment he held until 1898. During this period he met and married (19 September 1893) the Hon. Ella Constance Jackson, second daughter of the first Baron Allerton. They had no children.

In 1898 Harper returned to his regiment and, in October 1899, on the outbreak of war with the Boers, he went to South Africa. His first war experiences were at Spion Kop and in operations leading to the relief of Ladysmith. He was also at Vaal Krantz, Tugela Heights, and Pieters Hill before being invalided home in October 1900, having contracted enteric fever. He received the DSO for his services.

Harper completed his training at the Staff College, Camberley, in 1901, and secured promotion to major on 1 April of that year. His qualities as a staff officer were obvious and he was immediately appointed general staff officer, grade 2 (GSO2), mobilization branch, at the War Office; subsequently he became deputy assistant quartermaster-general (DAQMG). During his five years at the War Office (1902–7) his work came to the attention of Brigadier-General Henry Wilson, assistant director of staff duties. When Wilson became commandant of the Staff College in 1907, Harper's appointment as an instructor soon followed, together with promotion to lieutenant-colonel (1 January 1907). In June 1911, returning to the War Office as GSO1 in charge of the operations section, he was reunited with his patron, Wilson—now director of military operations (DMO). He assisted Wilson in planning details of embarkation and concentration of the British expeditionary force (BEF) in the event of a European war. These plans and schedules, used so successfully in August 1914, were meticulously detailed and their creators were rightly praised.

Harper became a full colonel on 19 July 1911. He accompanied the BEF to France in August 1914 as GSO1 with general headquarters staff. An energetic staff officer, he succeeded Wilson as DMO at general headquarters and was promoted temporary brigadier-general on 7 November 1914. In 1915 he was created CB. On 7 February 1915 he took command of 17th infantry brigade, a position he held until 25 September 1915 when promoted to command the 51st (Highland) division and given the rank of temporary major-general. For the next thirty months he moulded its character and earned credit as the maker of the division.

Harper became inextricably associated with the division. Establishing an intense *esprit de corps* and ensuring a level of organization the division previously lacked, Harper laid the foundations upon which a tremendous self-belief among its officers and men could be built. A thorough trainer, he believed in developing the individual soldier's initiative—a view expressed in his brief work *Notes on Infantry Tactics and Training* (1919), published after the war. His nickname—Uncle—indicated the regard in which he was held. Avuncular in appearance, with a shock of white hair, he seemed to show due regard to the views of all ranks and appeared to have their welfare fundamentally at heart. However, he suffered from a certain blinding stubbornness and an inability to express his thoughts clearly, preferring to declare his views abruptly rather than expounding them in detail.

On assuming divisional command Harper used the extensive period in which the division was not engaged in large-scale offensive operations to develop fighting skills and an aggressive raiding policy. Nevertheless the division's part in the Somme battles was limited until 13 November 1916 when, in a much-praised operation, the capture of Beaumont Hamel village saw his methods bear fruit. In 1917 the Highland division was used three times in the battle of Arras. On each occasion the task given was of particular difficulty. Between 9 and 12 April it operated against the southern end of Vimy Ridge, while on two occasions—23 April and again between 13 and 17 May—it was heavily engaged in Roeux and the adjacent chemical works. Whether operating offensively or defensively the division performed creditably.

On the opening of the third battle of Ypres (31 July 1917) the division was in the successful 18th corps, advancing as far as the Steenbeek Stream. Later, in the Flanders campaign on 20 September, it took part in Plumer's successful limited operation—the battle of the Menin Road Ridge—securing limited objectives and inflicting heavy casualties on counter-attacking German units.

During the battle of Cambrai, which opened on 20 November 1917, the division's chief first-day objective was the village of Flesquières, in the centre of the attack. Conspicuously it failed to take this—a fact attributable in some part to the failure of tank–infantry co-operation in the attack. The extent to which this failure can be ascribed to Harper has been exaggerated. Harper's stubborn refusal to accept instruction from above on employment of infantry with tanks only compounded problems encountered by the attacking units suffering as a consequence of decisions by army and corps.

Promotion to temporary lieutenant-general and command of 4th corps came on 11 March 1918. Only 10 days later, as part of the Third Army, 4th corps took the full force of the great German attack on the western front, but survived—retreating stubbornly. The corps returned to the offensive in August 1918, playing a significant part in operations north of the Ancre and being almost continuously engaged until the war ended.

After the war Harper was created KCB (1918) and on 1 January 1919 he was made a substantive lieutenant-general. He continued to command 4th corps until becoming general officer commanding, southern command, in June 1919. On 15 December 1922, while driving from Sherborne, Dorset, to Bradford Abbas, Harper was killed and his wife injured when their car overturned. His funeral was on 19 December at Salisbury Cathedral, where he was buried and commemorated by a bronze plaque.

BRYN HAMMOND

Sources *Army List* · *Hart's Army List* · B. Hammond, 'General Harper and the failure of 51st (highland) division at Cambrai, 20 Nov 1917', *Imperial War Museum Review*, 10 (1995) · O'M. Creagh and E. M. Humphris, *The distinguished service order, 1886–1923* [1923]; repr. (1978) · *The Army Quarterly* (1923), 7–10 · F. W. Bewsher, *The history of the 51st (highland) division* (1921) · *The Times* (16 Dec 1922) · *The Times* (20 Dec 1922) · J. E. Edmonds, ed., *Military operations, France and Belgium*, 14 vols., History of the Great War (1922–48) · W. N. Nicholson, *Behind the lines* (1939) · *In good company: the First World War letters and diaries of the Hon. William Fraser*, ed. D. Fraser (1990) · divisional commanders database, U. Birm. · *DNB* · *Debrett's Peerage* · *CGPLA Eng. & Wales* (1923)
Archives FILM IWM FVA, news footage
Likenesses photograph, 1917, repro. in Hammond, 'General Harper' · W. Stoneman, photograph, 1918, NPG · photograph, 1921?, repro. in Bewsher, *History of the 51st* · bronze relief portrait, Salisbury Cathedral
Wealth at death £17,776 12s. 7d.: administration with will, 3 Feb 1923, *CGPLA Eng. & Wales*

Harper, James (1795–1879), theologian and minister of the United Presbyterian church, was born at Lanark on 23 June 1795, the younger son of Alexander Harper (c.1768–1832), a minister in the Burgher church there, and his wife, Janet Gilchrist (d. c.1834). The family was descended from Sir John Harper, sheriff of Lanarkshire in the time of Charles II. He was educated at Cartland village school and at the grammar school in Lanark before going on to Glasgow University, where he attended classes from 1810 to 1813. In the autumn of 1813 he began to study at the Associate Synod Divinity Hall in Selkirk, under George Lawson. As this occupied only two months of the year he also attended medical classes at Edinburgh University.

Harper was licensed by Lanark presbytery on 3 April 1818 and received calls from congregations at Stonehouse, Lanarkshire, and North Leith. The synod preferred the claims of the latter, and he was ordained on 2 February 1819. He married, on 22 November 1820, Barbara, daughter of a Secession minister, James *Peddie of Bristo Street, Edinburgh. She outlived him, as did thirteen of their family of eight daughters and seven sons.

Harper soon established his reputation as a preacher and a pastor, and from 1826, when he assumed the editorship of the *Edinburgh Theological Magazine*, the organ of the United Secession church, he addressed a wider audience. He clashed with Andrew Thomson in the course of the Apocrypha controversy (over the inclusion of the Apocrypha in missionary Bibles) and was prominently involved

in other religious controversies of the time. In 1840 he was elected moderator of synod. Three years later he was appointed professor of pastoral theology, and in that year received the degree of DD from Jefferson College, Pennsylvania. Harper transferred to the chair of systematic theology after Robert Balmer's death in 1844, and after the union with the Relief church in 1847 he held the chair of systematic and pastoral theology in the United Presbyterian church. From 1850 Harper edited the *United Presbyterian Magazine*. In 1860 he was moderator of synod for a second time and in 1876, on the remodelling of the United Presbyterian Divinity Hall, he became its first principal. Harper was convener of the committee on union which negotiated with the Free Church (1863–73), the object of which was frustrated by opposition within the latter. He was also senior convener of the committee on subordinate standards; its 'declaratory statement' awaited final acceptance at the time of his death. Glasgow University belatedly honoured him with the degree of DD in 1877.

A tall, slim figure, whose receding hair emphasized a lofty brow, Harper grew more distinguished with age. When not engaged in the work of his church, he was actively involved with a number of philanthropic and political movements, and was a much sought-after platform speaker. A Liberal in politics, he was passionately opposed to the corn laws. The consequence of such a busy life was that Harper produced no publication of substance. The appointment of a colleague in North Leith in 1864 freed him from congregational duties but he retained his connection to the end. Harper died on 13 April 1879, after a short illness, at Leith Mount, the house at 46 Ferry Road which members of his congregation had purchased for him some thirty years earlier. He was buried, amid crowds, in Rosebank cemetery, Edinburgh, on 18 April.

LIONEL ALEXANDER RITCHIE

Sources A. Thomson, *Life of Principal Harper DD* (1881) · *The Scotsman* (14 April 1879) · *The Scotsman* (19 April 1879) · *United Presbyterian Magazine*, new ser., 23 (1879), 226–7, 241–9, 297–9 · R. Small, *History of the congregations of the United Presbyterian church from 1733 to 1900*, 1 (1904), 505–6 · J. Smith, *Our Scottish clergy*, 3rd ser. (1851), 338–45 · personal knowledge (1890) [*DNB*] · *DSCHT* · *DNB*
Likenesses etching (in later life), repro. in Thomson, *Life*
Wealth at death £7903 5s. 6d.: confirmation, 20 May 1879, *CCI*

Harper, John (d. 1742), actor, may have been the Mr Harper mentioned in 1714 among the acting company of the duke of Southampton and Cleveland, and can be confidently identified as the performer of a drunken man dance at Southwark fair on 5 September 1719. He continued to perform at London's summer fairs at least until 1733, latterly as a popular booth manager: an engraving by Hogarth of Southwark fair (1733/4) gives central placing to the Lee and Harper booth. Harper's drunken man dance also featured during his seasons with John Rich's company at Lincoln's Inn Fields (1719–21).

The popular appeal of a fat man dancing has been exploited by comedians throughout the history of the stage, and Harper is one of the links in a chain from Will Kemp to Oliver Hardy, Fred Emney, and beyond. He made his first appearance as Falstaff at Drury Lane in 1723, and played the part often during an association with that theatre that lasted more or less continuously from 1721 to 1738. His bulk made him the natural choice for such roles as Sancho Panza, Sir Tunbelly Clumsy in John Vanbrugh's *The Relapse*, and the pig-woman Ursula in Ben Jonson's *Bartholomew Fair*. Plump Jack was, however, a willing servant of his managers. If required, he would turn from clowning as Sir Epicure Mammon in Jonson's *The Alchemist* to play straighter roles, such as Casca in *Julius Caesar* or Pinchwife in William Wycherley's *The Country Wife*. It may well have been this willingness, allied to a natural timidity, that led to Harper's being undervalued. It was not until his success opposite Kitty Clive as Jobson in Charles Coffey's *The Devil to Pay* in 1731 that his weekly salary was raised to £4, in line with that of other prominent members of the Drury Lane company, and it was almost certainly his latest manager's belief that Harper could easily be intimidated that led to his imprisonment in November 1733. The dispute between John Highmore, newest of the Drury Lane patentees, and a group of disgruntled actors, vehemently led by Theophilus Cibber, had been the talk of the town since May 1733. Harper was among the group of Cibber's rebels who, in September, set up at the Haymarket in competition with the rump of the company at Drury Lane. Having failed in his attempt to impose an embargo on the seceders, Highmore decided to make an example of one of them, and the one he chose was Harper. On 12 November, costumed as Falstaff, Harper was arrested at the Haymarket under the terms of the Vagrant Act of 1713 and incarcerated in Bridewell. Highmore's case collapsed when Harper was shown to be a householder in Westminster and a freeholder in Surrey, but it was not until February 1734 that he was formally discharged. The defeated Highmore sold his shares to Charles Fleetwood, and the seceders returned to Drury Lane in March 1734.

Harper appeared for the last time at Drury Lane, as the Falstaffian Cacafogo in John Fletcher's *Rule a Wife and Have a Wife*, on 21 October 1738. He was paralysed by a stroke then, or shortly afterwards, but survived until 1 January 1742. He was buried at St Paul's, Covent Garden, on 29 January having bequeathed, by a will dating from August 1737, all his periwigs to his brother William and the residue of his estate to his widow, Ann Harper. During his long years of incapacity that estate had dwindled sufficiently to encourage David Garrick to mount a second benefit for Harper's widow following the disappointing financial outcome of the first benefit. The young Garrick, in his first Drury Lane season, was already a sufficient draw to attract receipts of £240 on 11 May to add to the £50 taken ten days earlier.   PETER THOMSON

Sources Highfill, Burnim & Langhans, *BDA* · *DNB* · W. W. Appleton, *Charles Macklin: an actor's life* (1961) · R. Paulson, *Hogarth*, 3 vols. (1991–3)
Likenesses A. Miller, mezzotint, 1739 (after drawing by G. White), BM, NPG · W. Hogarth, portrait (as Falstaff)
Wealth at death possibly Westminster house, value £50, and modest Surrey holdings: Highfill, Burnim & Langhans, *BDA* · widow received profits to two Drury Lane benefits in May 1742

Harper, John (1809–1842), architect, was born on 11 November 1809 at Dunkenhalgh Hall, near Blackburn, Lancashire, and was probably the son of John Harper, estate agent, of Blackburn. He was a pupil of Benjamin and Philip Wyatt, and helped them to prepare their designs for Apsley House, York House, and the Duke of York's Column. In 1835 he submitted a design in the competition for rebuilding the Houses of Parliament.

Harper lived and practised in York for many years, and worked for the duke of Devonshire at Bolton Abbey, and for Lord Londesborough and others. Most of his buildings were in the Gothic style. They included St Peter's School, York (1838), St Marie's, Bury, a Roman Catholic church (1841), and All Saints, Elton, near Bury (1841–3).

Harper was a close friend of the painters William Etty, David Roberts, and Clarkson Stansfield. Etty particularly admired Harper's architectural sketches and also painted his portrait, which, together with nearly all the sketches, passed into the possession of his brother Edward Harper, of Brighton. While travelling and studying art in Italy, Harper died, apparently unmarried, of malaria on 18 October 1842 in Naples.

ALBERT NICHOLSON, *rev.* ANNE PIMLOTT BAKER

Sources Colvin, *Archs.* · Redgrave, *Artists* · A. Gilchrist, *Life of William Etty, R.A.* (1855), 2.139–42
Archives W. Yorks. AS, Calderdale, letters to Anne Lister
Likenesses W. Etty, portrait; known to be in family possession, 1890

Harper, Samuel (1732–1803), librarian, was born in London on 28 December 1732 and baptized at Lincoln's Inn Chapel, Holborn, on 12 January 1733, the second son of Robert Harper (c.1700–1772) and his wife, Elizabeth. His father was the eldest son of Samuel Harper, of Farnley, near Leeds, and was admitted to Lincoln's Inn in March 1717. He was not called to the bar until February 1735, having in the meantime built up a lucrative practice as a conveyancer and a parliamentary agent. He became a bencher of Lincoln's Inn in 1746. Samuel was educated at Mr Croft's school in Fulham and in March 1750 was admitted to Trinity College, Cambridge, whence he graduated BA (1754) and MA (1757). Ordained a deacon in June 1756 (and priest in March 1757), he became curate of Gamston, Nottinghamshire, but only held this post for a short time because in the summer of 1756 he became an assistant librarian in the newly founded British Museum. In 1775 he became vicar of Rothwell, near Leeds, but employed a curate to look after the parish because his duties in the museum kept him in London. Previously, in 1769, he had officiated at the marriage at St George's, Hanover Square, of the second duke of Kingston to Elizabeth (*née* Chudleigh) who had been secretly married in 1744 to Augustus John Hervey, later third earl of Bristol. Harper gave evidence for the prosecution at her trial in 1776 when she was found guilty of bigamy.

At about the time that Harper joined the staff of the museum he married his wife, Jane, and their first child, also called Jane, was baptized in April 1758. By 1789 when he made his will both his wife and this daughter were dead. The children referred to in his will were Samuel (*b.*

1760), who became a law stationer, Robert John (1764–1846), who entered the duchy of Lancaster office and retired as deputy clerk of the duchy council in 1826, and Elizabeth.

When in 1757 the collections of the British Museum were organized into three departments—manuscripts, printed books, and natural and artificial productions—each under the care of an under-librarian and an assistant librarian, Harper became assistant librarian of the department of printed books. The prime duty of the under- and assistant librarians was to escort visitors round the museum, but Harper also helped to arrange the collections of his department, and compiled a catalogue of the Old Royal Library which had been presented by George II in 1757. In 1765 the under-librarian of the department of printed books, Matthew Maty, transferred to the department of natural and artificial productions, and Harper became under-librarian of printed books. He held this post until his death. In April 1766 he was elected FRS. In the eighteenth century the British Museum was not a very active organization, but Harper was conscientious in carrying out his duties. Apart from showing members of the public round the collections, he selected duplicate books to be sold (to raise funds for the chronically under-financed museum), recommended items to be purchased (far too few, because of lack of money), checked material presented (such as the collection of early English plays which was bequeathed by David Garrick in 1779), gave directions to the binders, and (in response to subpoenas) took books to the lawcourts to be used as evidence.

Harper's major task, however, was to supervise the compilation of a catalogue of the collection of printed books. In 1771 the trustees of the museum gave orders that such a catalogue was to be prepared, and the work was eventually published in two folio volumes in 1787. It contained about 63,000 entries for the 70,000 or so volumes in the collections. It was not a very good catalogue but to produce such a work at all with only some temporary help for the two permanent members of the staff of the department was a considerable achievement. Harper also put in hand a rearrangement of the collections of printed books. In 1757 Maty and he had recommended that these should be shelved primarily by collectors. Thirty years later the advantages of arranging the books in subject order had become very apparent, and on Harper's orders Samuel Ayscough drew up his scheme for a 'synthetical arrangement'. Work began on moving books to their new locations about 1790 and continued until 1805. By this time Harper was dead. Since 1766 he had been reader at the Foundling Hospital, but in 1801 his health declined, and he was replaced in this office. The next year he sold his library through Leigh, Sotheby & Son. This included a large collection of the petitions and private bills which his father had acquired in connection with his work as a parliamentary agent. These were bought for the British Museum.

Harper died on 13 July 1803, probably in his residence at the museum, and was buried on 18 July in the vault under the chapel of the Foundling Hospital. His body remained there until the hospital was demolished in 1927, and the remains in the vault were transferred to Kensal Green cemetery.　　　　　　　　　　　　　P. R. HARRIS

Sources *GM*, 1st ser., 73 (1803), 697 • BM • S. Lambert, *Bills and acts* (1971) • Venn, *Alum. Cant.* • diary of S. Harper, 1765–82, BL, Add. MS 45873 • P. R. Harris, *A history of the British Museum Library, 1753–1973* (1998) • P. R. Harris, ed., *The library of the British Museum* (1991) • W. P. Baildon, ed., *The records of the Honorable Society of Lincoln's Inn: admissions*, 2 vols. (1896) • W. P. Baildon and R. Roxburgh, eds., *The records of the Honorable Society of Lincoln's Inn: the black books*, 5 vols. (1897–1968) • LMA, P82/GEO 1/14, St George's, Bloomsbury [index of baptisms, 1730–99] • LMA, A/FH/A14/4/4 [burials in the Foundling chapel] • PRO, PROB 11/1397, q. 706 [will] • R. H. Nichols and F. A. Wray, *The history of the Foundling Hospital* (1935) • *A catalogue of the ... library of the Rev. Samuel Harpur* (1802) [sale catalogue, London, 1802] • *The record of the Royal Society of London*, 4th edn (1940) • L. Melville, ed., *Trial of the duchess of Kingston* (1927)
Archives BL, official diary, Add. MS 45873 • BM, MSS

Harper, Thomas (1786–1853), trumpeter, was born at Worcester on 3 May 1786. As early as 1798 he was in London, where he studied the trumpet and the horn under Eley, and soon joined the East India Company band, of which his teacher was director. Harper was subsequently appointed inspector of musical instruments to the company, a post he held until his death. He played in small London theatre orchestras until, in 1806, he was engaged as principal trumpet at Drury Lane and at the English Opera House (Lyceum Theatre). In 1820 he distinguished himself at the Birmingham festival. The following year he succeeded John Hyde as the principal trumpet at the Concerts of Ancient Music and at the Italian Opera, and from this time took part in every important orchestral concert and music festival in both London and the provinces. Harper was an active member of the Royal Society of Musicians from 1814, was first trumpet at the Philharmonic Concerts until 1851, and played for the rival New Philharmonic Society in 1852.

Contemporary reports present Harper as a very fine instrumentalist, referring to his purity and delicacy of tone and his unrivalled facility of execution. He played the slide trumpet throughout his life, making important contributions to its development. Harper's Improved Model continued to be made by J. A. Köhler & Son of London at a time when valved instruments were coming into vogue. Most of the space in Harper's tutor, *Instructions for the trumpet, with the use of the chromatic slide, also the Russian valve trumpet, the cornet à pistons ... and the keyed bugle* (c.1835), is given over to the slide trumpet, and he compiled a number of books of selections for the instrument (though he also made arrangements of airs for the bugle). His own instrument, which has a very large mouthpiece, is housed at the Royal College of Music.

Harper was seized with illness at Exeter Hall in London during a rehearsal of the Sacred Harmonic Society on 20 January 1853. He died a few hours later at the house of the conductor Joseph Surman, a friend of his, who lived very close to the hall. The cause of death was reported as an 'abnormal condition of the aorta, of some standing' (*Musical World*, 5 Feb 1853).

Harper's eldest son, Thomas John Harper (1816–1898), was a trumpeter and violinist and succeeded his father as the principal trumpeter of the day; he wrote a method entitled *School for the Cornet à Pistons* (1865). Harper also left a daughter and two other sons, Charles Abraham (1819–1893), a successful horn player, and Edmund (*c*.1821–1869), a horn player, pianist, and organist.

L. M. MIDDLETON, *rev.* DAVID J. GOLBY

Sources *Musical World* (22 Jan 1853), 56 • J. Surman, letter, *Musical World* (5 Feb 1853), 83–4 • [J. S. Sainsbury], ed., *A dictionary of musicians*, 2 vols. (1824) • W. H. Husk and E. Tarr, 'Harper, Thomas', *New Grove* • C. Ehrlich, *First philharmonic: a history of the Royal Philharmonic Society* (1995), 98
Likenesses L. Hague, lithograph, BM • lithograph, repro. in *New Grove*, 3.404

Harper, Sir William (1496–1574), mayor of London, was born at Bedford, the son of William Harper of Bedford, a man of humble circumstances. After moving to London with no significant education to recommend him, he served his apprenticeship (*c*.1510–1520) and was admitted a freeman of the Merchant Taylors' Company in 1533. Harper became master of the company in July 1553. Though nominated sheriff in 1552 by the lord mayor, Sir George Barne, his financial circumstances did not permit him to accept the responsibility at that time, but Harper promised to serve in the future if elected. On 14 November 1553 he succeeded Sir John Ayloffe as the second alderman of Bridge Without ward, in the borough of Southwark. He moved to Dowgate ward in 1556, became sheriff in June 1556, and on 29 September 1561 Harper was chosen lord mayor.

On 28 October 1561 Lord Mayor Harper, scarlet-cloaked aldermen, and the London crafts in their livery sailed on barges toward Westminster for a riverine celebration of feasting, shooting, and trumpeting; later that same day the Merchant Taylors' Company hailed his election with an equally impressive pageant in St Paul's Churchyard. On 1 November Harper went in state to hear a sermon at St Paul's by Edmund Grindal, then bishop of London, and in January 1562 in his capacity as mayor he entertained the privy councillor Thomas Howard, fourth duke of Norfolk, at the Guildhall. According to custom, he was knighted by Elizabeth I at Westminster on 15 February 1562. In September 1562 Mayor Harper and the aldermen, as part of the annual survey of the city's water supply, visited the conduit heads west of the city where they hunted hare in neighbouring fields. After dining at the lord mayor's banqueting house, the party went fox-hunting at the end of St Giles's. Towards the close of his term of office Harper personally raised a band of soldiers for service in Normandy.

Harper was pragmatic in his religious and political life. During the reign of Mary I, he professed devotion to Roman Catholicism and in June 1556, as sheriff, after attempting to persuade a group of thirteen condemned protestants to recant, directed that their collective burning be carried out at Stratford-le-Bow. Under Queen Elizabeth, however, Harper 'conformed to the Protestant church and was zealous for the faith' (Wyatt, 16–17). Harper's philanthropy was extraordinary. During his mayoralty, together with his first wife, Alice Harrison, *née* Tomlinson, whom Harper married on 18 November 1547, he established the Merchant Taylors' grammar school in his native Bedford, refounding a school closed there after the dissolution of the monasteries. The Harpers granted the premises by indenture along with 13 acres of meadowland in the parish of St Andrew's, Holborn, to the mayor and corporation of Bedford. The land, which originally belonged to the Charterhouse, was described in the deed of gift as being by Little Conduit-shot, the priory and convent of Chapter House, Bloomsbury Field, and bounded by several ditches. Harper had purchased the property from Dr Caesar Adelmare, physician to Queen Mary. Harper's munificence provided relief of poverty and increased opportunity for many men; his praises were recited with justifiable pride in published tracts for generations to come as his charity became a model for subsequent merchant leaders in London to emulate.

Alice Harper died in October 1569 and was buried in St Mary Woolnoth, the Harpers' London parish, her tomb adjacent to their regular pew. The widow of Richard Harrison of Shropshire and mother of one daughter, Beatrice Prestwood, before she wed Harper, Alice Harper had no children with Sir William. On 13 September 1570 Harper married Margaret Lethers, a native of Bedford and daughter of William Lethers. According to Clode, Harper died on 27 February 1573 in London, but his will is dated 27 October 1573 and was proved on 6 April 1574, making the date of his death 27 February 1574 in the new style. He was buried in the chancel of St Paul's, Bedford. According to the terms of his will, he left money to the Merchant Taylors for a cup to be made in his memory but no other bequests to the company. The remainder of his property went to his widow, sole executor of Harper's estate, who had possession of the company's house in Lombard Street, which had been granted to Sir William and his first wife for use during their lifetimes. When the second Lady Harper would not vacate the house, proceedings in the lord mayor's court were initiated against her by Nicholas Foljambe, the common clerk charged by the company with recovering the house. After prolonged negotiations (during which Foljambe died of plague) and intercession on her behalf by Lord Burghley, the widow withdrew from the house with generous compensation awarded to her from the company for her new accommodations. Margaret Harper died in 1591.

ELIZABETH LANE FURDELL

Sources C. M. Clode, *The early history of the Guild of Merchant Taylors of the fraternity of St John the Baptist, London*, 2 vols. (1888) • J. Wyatt, *The Bedford schools and charities of Sir William Harper* (1856) • *The diary of Henry Machyn, citizen and merchant-taylor of London, from AD 1550 to AD 1563*, ed. J. G. Nichols, CS, 42 (1848); repr. (1968) • *DNB* • will, PRO, PROB 11/56, sig. 14 • J. Stow, *The survey of London* (1912) [with introduction by H. B. Wheatley] • A. B. Beaven, ed., *The aldermen of the City of London, temp. Henry III–[1912]*, 2 vols. (1908–13) • W. K. Jordan, *Philanthropy in England, 1480–1660* (1959) • J. G. Nichols, *Transactions of the London and Middlesex Archaeological Society*, 3 (1865–9), 16–17 • R. Cooke, *Visitation of London, 1568*, ed. H. Stanford London and S. W. Rawlins, [new edn], 2 vols. in one, Harleian Society, 109–10 (1963)

Harper, William (1806–1857), poet and biographer, was born in Manchester, the son of William and Frances Harper. He was originally intended for the ministry but, discouraged by friends, he turned to commercial pursuits, becoming a yarn merchant in Pall Mall, Manchester. He also assisted the local Conservative association in the organization of Sunday schools and of evening classes for working people. For many years he contributed verses to the Conservative *Manchester Courier*, an Anglican publication for the upper and middle classes; he also wrote the weekly trade article in the same paper. In 1840 he published his first volume, *The Genius and other Poems*, and a second collection was entitled *Cain and Abel: a Dramatic Poem, and Minor Pieces* (1844). He was also the author of a *Memoir of Benjamin Braidley* (1845). Harper was well known outside Manchester as one of the better Lancashire poets; his obituary in the *Manchester Courier* praises the elegance and power of his poetry. He was remembered as 'a firm friend' and an honest man, unsuited for the commercial life; he had a withdrawn look, despite the 'unnatural brilliancy' of his dark eyes (Procter, 121). Harper died on 30 January 1857 at Lever Street, Lower Broughton, Manchester, where he had lived with his parents and several sisters.   C. W. SUTTON, *rev.* SARAH BROLLY

Sources Boase, *Mod. Eng. biog.* • R. W. Procter, *Literary reminiscences and gleanings* (1860) • G. Milner, 'Reminiscences of a Manchester poet—William Harper', *Manchester Quarterly*, 31 (July 1889), 248–53

Harpsfield, John (1516–1578), religious writer and Roman Catholic priest, was born about 31 May 1516 in St Mary Magdalen parish, Old Fish Street, London. His father, John Harpsfield (*d.* 1550), was a gentleman and a mercer; an uncle, Nicholas, had studied at Winchester College, New College, Oxford, and the University of Bologna, and became an official of the archdeaconry of Winchester. Elder brother by three years to Nicholas *Harpsfield, later archdeacon of Canterbury, John was admitted as a scholar at Winchester College in 1528. He became a scholar of New College, Oxford, in November 1532, having received a scholarship from his father's company. He was elected a perpetual fellow in 1534, graduated BA in February 1537, and proceeded MA in theology in April 1541. Harpsfield became Oxford's first regius professor of Greek, and lectured there from 1541 to about 1545. He translated Simplicius's commentary on book 1 of Aristotle's *Physics* into Latin and dedicated it to Henry VIII (BL, Royal MS 12 F V); he also translated book 1 of Virgil's *Aeneid* into Greek, in a manuscript that later belonged to Thomas Cranmer (BL, Royal MS 16 C VIII).

John Harpsfield's position under Edward VI was not without ambiguities. Ordained priest on 9 April 1547 he contributed a sermon, 'Of the misery of all mankynde', to the official collection of homilies published that year, stressing mankind's dependence for salvation on divine grace and Christ's passion. And whereas his brother Nicholas fled to Europe rather than accept the protestantism of the new regime, John remained a fellow of New College

until 1551, when he became a bursal prebendary of Chichester Cathedral, collated by the conservative Bishop George Day. He had been made vicar of Berkeley, Gloucestershire, in 1550. Under Mary, however, he swiftly rose to prominence. At the October 1553 convocation he called for Catholic renewal in an opening sermon which was published later that year as *Concio quaedam admodum*. In 1554 he became archdeacon of London, and chaplain to Bishop Edmund Bonner, his 'kindred spirit' (Strype, *Cranmer*, 3. 72), as well as being made a prebendary of St Paul's and rector of St Martin Ludgate. He also proceeded DTh at Oxford. On 9 November 1556 he was elected warden of New College, but did not take up office. In 1558 he became dean of Norwich and also succeeded his brother Nicholas as rector of Laindon, Essex.

Harpsfield was a leader in the Marian campaign to extirpate protestantism. In April 1554 he had debated with Cranmer and Nicholas Ridley in Oxford, in the former case as part of the procedure whereby he took his DTh degree, though with a certain amount of theological animus thrown in, and in the following February he 'was intimately involved in Cranmer's last days', preaching at his disgrading on the 14th and assisting Bonner in questioning the former archbishop (MacCulloch, 585). As archdeacon he interrogated John Bradford and John Philpott before they were burnt for heresy in 1555. Yet John Foxe describes Nicholas, not John, as the greatest persecutor among archdeacons, and notes John's relatively gentle approach in dealing with protestants.

A noted spokesman for Catholicism, Harpsfield preached variously before Philip of Spain shortly after the restoration of the rood in St Paul's, at the public penance of married priests, the funerals of prominent citizens, and the feast of the Assumption of the Virgin. To the controversialist John Bale he was 'Dr Sweetlips' because of 'his smooth words and fair discourse' (Strype, *Ecclesiastical Memorials*, 175). A number of his sermons were printed, including *A Notable and Learned Sermon made upon Saint Andrewes Day* (1556), which defended papal primacy while commemorating England's 1554 reconciliation with Rome.

Harpsfield's chief contribution to Catholic reform, however, consisted of his nine sermons in Bonner's frequently reprinted thirteen *Homilies* (1555), which set forth the central teachings of Marian Catholicism. Five of them, 'Of the creation and fall of Man', 'Of the misery of all mankynde' (a revision of his sermon in the 1547 Edwardian homilies, but with the passages denigrating the role of human merit in justification excised), 'Of the redemption of Man', 'How the redemption in Chryste is apliable to Man', and 'Howe daungerous a thinge the breake of charitie is', present salvation as arising both from humanity's dependence upon divine grace and from free human co-operation with grace through virtuous living. It is in the Catholic church, 'the onely scoole, for all men to come and repayre unto, … for the attaynynge of everlasting lyfe', that Christians receive grace (*Homilies*, 18). 'An homelye of the Primacy, or supreme power, of the highest governor of the militant churche', and 'Another homelye of the Prymacye', along with his 1556 sermon, proclaimed Harpsfield a principal champion of papal authority. Two more homilies, 'Of the true presence of Chrystes body and blud in the sacrament of the Aultare' and 'Of transubstantiation', defend Christ's corporeal presence in the eucharist and the sacrament's centrality in the church. All give emphasis to Christ and his passion, 'a consistent characteristic of the Marian church' (Duffy, 536/7).

Harpsfield's position collapsed under Elizabeth I. He was a leader in the January 1559 convocation which affirmed Catholic doctrine, and participated in the Westminster disputation between Catholic and protestant churchmen. He refused to conform to Elizabethan protestantism, was deposed as archdeacon and dean in 1559, and had been deprived of his other preferments by 1560. From 1559 to 1574 both Harpsfields were held in London's Fleet prison. Hoping for sympathy from fellow humanists, in 1574 John composed letters in Greek to Burghley and Sir Thomas Smith, the secretary of state, requesting leave for Nicholas and himself to go to Bath to regain their health. The privy council does not seem to have granted permission, fearing the Harpsfields might 'lure' others into Catholicism; rather they were released to live under close surveillance, and frequently had to present themselves before the council. In his commonplace book John noted staying with George Monnox of Walthamstow, Middlesex, in March 1575; his writings from this time included a metrical history of the English church and a chronicle from the flood to 1559. Nicholas Harpsfield died in 1575, and in 1577 John was placed in the custody of Thomas Cooper, bishop of Lincoln. In 1578 he again requested to go to Bath. He died in London on 19 August that year and was buried in St Sepulchre parish church, London. Letters of administration were subsequently granted to his niece Anne Worsopp, the daughter of his sister Alice.

WILLIAM WIZEMAN

Sources R. W. Chambers, 'Life and works of Nicholas Harpsfield', in N. Harpsfield, The life and death of Sr Thomas Moore, knight, ed. E. V. Hitchcock, EETS, original ser., 186 (1932), clxxv–ccxiv • J. Foxe, Actes and monuments (1563), 3rd edn, 2 vols. (1576) • J. Strype, Ecclesiastical memorials, 3 vols. (1822), vol. 3 • APC, 1558–78 • The diary of Henry Machyn, citizen and merchant-taylor of London, from AD 1550 to AD 1563, ed. J. G. Nichols, CS, 42 (1848) • E. Bonner, J. Harpsfield, and H. Pendleton, Homilies sette forthe by … Edmunde byshop of London (1555) • J. Harpsfield, A notable and learned sermon made upon Saint Andrewes day (1556) • J. Strype, Annals of the Reformation and establishment of religion … during Queen Elizabeth's happy reign, new edn, 1 (1824) • J. Strype, Memorials of the most reverend father in God Thomas Cranmer, 3 vols. in 4 (1848–54), vols. 2–3 • Foster, Alum. Oxon., 1500–1714, 2.652 • Mercers' Company, acts of court, Mercers' Hall, London, vol. 2 • D. MacCulloch, Thomas Cranmer: a life (1996) • E. Duffy, The stripping of the altars: traditional religion in England, c.1400–c.1580 (1992) • Emden, Oxf., 4.267–8 • BL, MS Royal 8BXX • Wood, Ath. Oxon., new edn, 1.439–41

Archives BL, commonplace book, letters, and papers, Royal MSS 8, 12, 16 | BL, Lansdowne MS 27

Harpsfield, Nicholas (1519–1575), religious controversialist and historian, was born in the parish of St Mary Magdalen, Old Fish Street, in the city of London. His father, John Harpsfield, was a mercer, while his uncle Nicholas,

who had been educated at Winchester College, New College, Oxford, and then the University of Bologna, was a doctor of canon law and an official of the archdeacon of Winchester. The identity of his mother is unknown.

Early life and connections It appears that the young Nicholas Harpsfield was destined from an early age to follow in his uncle's footsteps; he was admitted as a scholar of Winchester College in 1529. (His elder brother John *Harpsfield had been admitted to Winchester in the preceding year.) Nicholas proceeded to New College (as had his brother John before him), where he was elected fellow in January 1535 and perpetual fellow three years later. (Both John and Nicholas had received scholarships for their university education from their father's company.) Nicholas Harpsfield was a student of canon and civil law and he received his BCL on 4 June 1543. The next year he became principal of White Hall in Oxford, a hostel chiefly attended by students of civil law, which stood on the site of present-day Jesus College.

It was almost certainly during his years at Oxford that Harpsfield came into the orbit of the family of Sir Thomas More, particularly of More's son-in-law, William Roper. In the dedication to Roper of his biography of More, Harpsfield hailed Roper as his patron and went on to declare to Roper that 'by your long and great benefits and charges employed and heaped upon, toward the supporting of my living and learning, have most deeply bounde me, or rather bought me, to be at your commandment during my life' (Harpsfield, The Life and Death of … More, 3). The fact that Harpsfield was an archdeacon, and a considerable power in the Marian church, when he wrote this, serves only to underscore his gratitude towards Roper.

Up until Edward VI's accession, Harpsfield's rise in Oxford had been steady and smooth. The new king's religious policies, however, made Oxford an uncongenial place for Harpsfield and in 1550 he migrated overseas to Louvain; a year later he matriculated at the university there. During his sojourn in Louvain, Harpsfield stayed with Antonio Bonvisi, a wealthy merchant who had been one of More's closest friends; members of More's family were also living in the Bonvisi household at the time.

It was probably now that Harpsfield wrote all, or part of, his biography of More. (This was finished only at the end of 1556 or in 1557; it was probably delayed, however, to supplement William Rastell's great edition of More's works, which was printed in 1557.) Harpsfield wrote his biography at Roper's request (in fact, Roper's celebrated memoir of his father-in-law was originally written as a source for Harpsfield's use). It is a striking sign of Roper's close relationship with Harpsfield that such an important task was entrusted to a novice author. In the event, Harpsfield did a good job; his work has been praised as the first complete biography of More as well as for (when allowance is made for bias) its scrupulous accuracy. In the biography Harpsfield adumbrated some of the concerns which motivated his own career and writings: he emphasized and praised More's controversial works and his persecution of heretics, while at the same time venerating More as a martyr for the faith.

Catholic activist It is quite likely that Harpsfield's ties to Bonvisi, and to the More family, recommended him to Cardinal Reginald Pole. In any event, Harpsfield's rise in the English church, after his return home from exile at the start of Mary's reign, was little short of spectacular. On 31 March 1554 he was admitted archdeacon of Canterbury. On 27 April he was collated to the prebend of Harleston in St Paul's Cathedral, and a succession of other livings followed. Although he had resigned his fellowship at New College in 1553, Harpsfield took the degree of DCL at Oxford on 16 July 1554 and practised as a proctor in the court of arches. His legal career, however, was extinguished under the load of ecclesiastical responsibilities placed upon him. In the months before Pole's arrival in England, in November 1554, Harpsfield was the new archbishop's principal agent in the diocese of Canterbury; a correspondent of Richard Thornden, Pole's suffragan, wrote that Thornden's authority in the diocese was second only to Harpsfield's. The archdeacon, whose brother John had been made archdeacon of London, was also appointed vicar-general of the capital. Between November 1554 and March 1558, Harpsfield conducted a sweeping visitation of London which tried around four hundred offenders. The targets of the visitation were well chosen, for in addition to some conspicuous disturbers of the peace, many active and zealous protestants were caught in Harpsfield's net. Although no heresy charges resulted, the punishments imposed—in most cases fines and penances—were substantial, and the visitation intimidated London's evangelical lay élite.

But it was in the diocese of Canterbury, where Pole left the enforcement of the Marian reaction to his subordinates, that Harpsfield made his greatest mark. He presided over numerous heresy trials and conducted repeated and rigorous visitations of the diocese. John Foxe, in the first edition of his martyrology, characterized Harpsfield as being among 'the sorest and of leaste compassion' of all the Marian archdeacons, charging that by his 'unmercifull nature and agrest disposition, very many were put to death in that dioces of Canterbury' (Foxe, *Actes and Monuments*, 1563, p. 1546). Foxe even claimed that, as Mary lay dying, Harpsfield hurried back from London in order to execute heretics in Canterbury before they could be reprieved by the new regime. Undoubtedly there is some exaggeration in these stories, but there is a core of truth to them as well. There is nothing to suggest that Harpsfield was particularly bloodthirsty, but his interrogation of suspected heretics was probing and intense, while his zeal in eradicating heresy was unquestioned.

Pole appreciated both this zeal and the abilities which accompanied it. On 28 October 1558 Harpsfield was made dean of the court of arches and dean of the peculiars. Two days later Pole issued a commission authorizing Harpsfield to conduct a visitation of All Souls College, Oxford. (Apart from giving the archdeacon a virtual stranglehold on the administration of the diocese of Canterbury, these appointments extended his jurisdiction over heresy into London and Oxford.) On 1 November 1558 Pole also appointed Harpsfield to the fourth prebend in Canterbury Cathedral. But a little more than two weeks later, both the cardinal and Queen Mary were dead.

Attacks on Cranmer During Mary's reign, Harpsfield battled against heresy with the pen as well as the stake. In addition to his biography of More, he wrote two other books before Elizabeth came to the throne. The first of these was *Cranmer's Recantacyons*, an account of the former archbishop's imprisonment, trial, and execution. The book is anonymous and its authorship has been disputed, but a manuscript life of Cranmer, written in Latin, was found in the possession of William Carter, Harpsfield's amanuensis and printer, in 1582. Carter confessed to the authorities that Nicholas Harpsfield had written the work, which from its description was almost certainly *Cranmer's Recantacyons*. Moreover, the sole surviving copy of the *Recantacyons*, now Paris, Bibliothèque Nationale, Latin MS 6056, contains extensive corrections in Harpsfield's handwriting. The book was probably designed to supplement the official version of Cranmer's recantations printed in 1556 by John Cawood. Harpsfield stated that he was commanded to write the work; this was very probably Pole's order. Cranmer's well-publicized heroism at his execution made the project problematic and, alone among Harpsfield's major works, *Cranmer's Recantacyons* remained obscure and nearly forgotten until it was eventually printed in the nineteenth century.

The last book Harpsfield wrote during Mary's reign, his *Treatise on the Pretended Divorce*, may well have been intended, at least in part, to replace *Cranmer's Recantacyons* as an attack on the archiepiscopal martyr. Two-thirds of the work is a rebuttal of the canon law case for Henry VIII's divorce from Katherine of Aragon; the remaining part of the treatise is a narrative history of the divorce marked by an intense animus against Cranmer, 'the pillar of the Divorce'. In fact, much of the character assassination of the archbishop contained in *Cranmer's Recantacyons* is repeated in the *Pretended Divorce*, including the evergreen story of Cranmer's transporting his wife in a box equipped with breathing holes. Harpsfield's treatise remained in manuscript until 1878 (the accession of Elizabeth made a book denying her legitimacy and raking up scurrilous stories about the Boleyns too dangerous to print). Nevertheless, the *Pretended Divorce* had a considerable impact, for it supplied much of the substance of Nicholas Sander's extraordinarily influential history of the English Reformation, *De origine et progressu schismate Anglicana* (1573).

Prisoner The nearly simultaneous deaths of Mary and of Cardinal Pole were disastrous for Harpsfield. He was, however, undaunted, and wasted little time in displaying his hostility to the new regime. On 9 February 1559 he was summoned before the privy council; two days later the council sent a letter to officials in Canterbury ordering the investigation of charges that Harpsfield was inciting the townspeople to sedition and stockpiling arms in the cathedral. During that summer Harpsfield, joined by leading citizens of Canterbury, defiantly led a religious procession which, in turn, provoked a counter-demonstration by the town's protestants. On 1 August 1559 Harpsfield led a majority of the members of the Canterbury chapter in their refusal to attend the election of Matthew Parker; he was pronounced contumacious for his recalcitrance. On 11 August Nicholas Harpsfield, in his capacity as a prebend of St Paul's, joined his brother John in defying the royal commissioners during their visitation of the cathedral and in refusing to subscribe to the prayer book and the queen's injunctions. During the autumn of 1559 Nicholas Harpsfield was stripped of all of his ecclesiastical offices and livings. Both Harpsfield brothers were later committed to the Fleet prison for refusing to swear to the oath of supremacy, and on 28 July 1562 the privy council instructed the warden of the Fleet not to allow certain prominent Catholic prisoners, including the Harpsfield brothers, to receive visitors. The brothers would remain in prison for the next twelve years.

The defence of the faith Yet incarceration did not end Nicholas Harpsfield's unrelenting battle against heresy. In 1566 a massive book, about 1000 pages long, was published in Antwerp, under the title *Dialogi sex contra summi pontificatus, monasticae vitae, sanctorum, sacrarum imaginum oppugnatores, et pseudomartyres*. This huge work, although published under the name of Alan Cope, was written by Harpsfield, and it was nothing less than the detailed rebuttal of two of the greatest protestant historical works of the era, the *Historia ecclesiae Christi*, known as the Magdeburg Centuries, and John Foxe's *Acts and Monuments*, the first edition of which was published in 1563. The first five dialogues are devoted largely to Magdeburg Centuries, attacking the Centuriators's treatment of papal primacy, monasticism, and the veneration of saints and images, although criticisms are also made of other protestant writers, especially Johann Sleidan, John Bale, and John Jewel. The last and longest of the dialogues, totalling about a quarter of the entire book, is an acerbic critique of the martyrologies of John Foxe and, to a lesser extent, Jean Crespin. This last dialogue, the first sustained and systematic attack on Foxe's book, is of considerable importance for two reasons. The first is that Harpsfield's criticisms were repeated by other Catholic controversialists, especially Thomas Stapleton and Robert Persons, through whom Harpsfield's criticisms of Foxe were to become staples of English Catholic polemical as well as historical writing.

The second reason for the importance of the *Dialogi sex* was the influence it had on the *Acts and Monuments* itself. Foxe took Harpsfield's criticisms very seriously and emended the next edition in order to counter them. While this sometimes led to the deletion of incorrect or embarrassing material, it also resulted in an enormous expansion of Foxe's text as material rebutting Harpsfield was added to it. To take merely one example, Harpsfield's (accurate) claims that Foxe had misrepresented Oldcastle's rebellion of 1414 provoked a thirty-four-page answer from the martyrologist which drew upon extensive research in the parliament rolls (Foxe, *Actes and Monumentes*, 1570 edn, 676–700). Although it was hardly his intention, Harpsfield forced his adversary to increase the scope and quality of his research, thus improving dramatically subsequent editions of the *Acts and Monuments*. A second edition of the *Dialogi sex*, with only a very modest amount of additional material, was printed three years after the publication of the second edition of the *Acts and Monuments*.

A few years before this, Harpsfield had extensively edited, to the point of actually rewriting, a treatise attacking the legitimacy of Elizabeth's claim to the throne and upholding the claim of Mary Stuart, which was published in 1571 under the name of Morgan Philipps (ESTC 15506). At some time during his imprisonment, Harpsfield also penned his final work, the *Historia Anglicana ecclesiastica*. This book is divided into two parts. The first part presents a history of each English diocese, emphasizing the apostolic succession of the bishops, the preservation of true doctrine, and the growth of monasticism. The second part, in contrast to this history of the true church, is a 'Historia haeresis Wiccliffianae'. This is a skilful synthesis of the fourteenth- and fifteenth-century historical works of Henry Knighton, Thomas Netter, and Thomas Walsingham, which had depicted Lollardy as a continuation of ancient heresies and as a source of anarchy and rebellion. Although not published until 1622, the *Historia* circulated widely in manuscript; apart from numerous copies now extant in England, there were manuscripts of the work in the English College at Rome and in the Vatican, while Cardinal William Allen gave a copy to the English College at Douai. The *Historia* became one of the foundations of English Catholic interpretations of the Reformation; in fact, Persons's ambitious history of the English Reformation, the *Certamen ecclesiae Anglicanae*, was intended as a continuation of Harpsfield's history.

Death and legacy On 19 August 1574 both Harpsfield brothers were released on bail, on the grounds of ill health. On 18 December 1575 Nicholas Harpsfield died in London. In addition to the works discussed above, he wrote a 'Life of Christ' in Latin: a translation survives in the Lambeth Palace Library (MS 446). Anthony Wood claimed that another work by Harpsfield, an 'Impugnatio contra bullam honorii papae primi ad Cantabrigiam' survived in manuscript; the whereabouts of this work, if it still survives, are unknown.

Although he was an active and successful cleric and lawyer, Harpsfield's historical writings were his enduring legacy. Through these works, and those of writers such as Stapleton, Sander, and Persons who drew liberally from them, Harpsfield established the basis of the Catholic interpretations of the English Reformation. When this is added to Harpsfield's profound, if inadvertent, influence on Foxe's *Acts and Monuments*, he must be regarded as one of the greatest, and most influential, historians of the Reformation in England. THOMAS S. FREEMAN

Sources R. W. Chambers, 'Life and works of Nicholas Harpsfield', in N. Harpsfield, *The life and death of Sr Thomas Moore, knight*, ed. E. V. Hitchcock, EETS, original ser., 186 (1932), clxxv–ccxiv · BL, Add. MS 48029, fols. 58r–59r · N. Harpsfield, *Dialogi sex contra summi pontificatus, monasticae vitae, sanctorum, sacrarum imaginum oppugnatores, et pseudomartyres* (1566) · N. Harpsfield, *A treatise on the* *pretended divorce between Henry VIII and Catharine of Aragon*, ed. N. Pocock, CS, new ser., 21 (1878) · *Bishop Cranmer's recantacyons*, ed. R. M. Milnes and J. Gairdner (1877–84) · N. Harpsfield, *Historia Anglicana ecclesiastica*, ed. R. Gibbons (1622) · LMA, DL/C/614 · L. E. Whatmore, ed., *Archdeacon Harpsfield's visitation, 1557*, 2 vols., Catholic RS, 45–6 (1950–51) · J. Foxe, *Actes and monuments* (1563) · J. Foxe, *The first volume of the ecclesiasticall history contayning the actes and monumentes of thynges passed*, new edn (1570) [RSTC 11223] · D. MacCulloch, *Thomas Cranmer: a life* (1996), 584–607 · S. Brigden, *London and the Reformation* (1989), 562–71 · T. S. Freeman, 'The importance of dying earnestly: the metamorphosis of the account of James Bainham in *Foxe's Book of Martyrs*', *The church retrospective*, ed. R. N. Swanson, SCH, 33 (1997), 267–88 · P. Collinson, P. N. Ramsay, and M. Sparks, eds., *A history of Canterbury Cathedral* (1995), 164–6 · A. K. Dillon, 'The construction of martyrdom in the English Catholic community to 1603', PhD diss., U. Cam., 1998 · Emden, *Oxf.*, 4.268–9 · Bibliothèque Nationale, Paris, MS latin 6056 · BL, Royal MS 8 B.xx, fol. 162v · APC, 1558–75 · Mercers' Company, acts of court 2, Mercers' Hall, London, fol. 207r · B. Carier, *A copy of a letter … to some particular friends in England* (1615) · J. Strype, *The life and acts of Matthew Parker*, new edn, 3 vols. (1821), vol. 1 · J. Strype, *Annals of the Reformation and establishment of religion … during Queen Elizabeth's happy reign*, new edn, 1 (1824) · Westm. DA, A XII · BL, Harleian MS 421, fols. 94r–95r

Archives BL, corrected copy of *Historia Anglicana ecclesiastica*, MS Stowe 105 and MS Arundel 73 | BL, MS Arundel 72

Harpur, Charles (1813–1868), poet, was born on 23 January 1813 at Windsor, New South Wales, the third of seven children of Joseph Harpur (*d.* 1842) of Kinsale, co. Cork, and Sarah Chidley (*d.* 1866) of Somerset. Both parents were former convicts, Joseph having arrived on the *Royal Admiral* on 22 November 1800, and Sarah on the *Alexander* in August 1806. Joseph Harpur made good in the colony, becoming parish clerk and schoolmaster at Windsor, and retiring on a government pension of £50. Charles Harpur gave his date of birth as 1817, possibly because his parents were not married until 16 June 1814, and possibly from a wish to emulate the youthfulness of Chatterton, the subject of the long poem *Genius Lost*. As he explained in a note to 'To the Lyre of Australia', Harpur decided in his teens to be a poet, making a choice that brought him 'hunger and rags'. He allied himself with the native-born in the colony, the 'native youth' or the 'currency lads' as they called themselves, and styled himself 'Charles Harpur, an Australian'. He was sympathetic to the plight of the Aborigines, and used Aboriginal terms in his writing.

Poems by Harpur appeared in the Sydney newspapers from 1833 onward, and *The Tragedy of Donohoe*, a blank verse play on the bushranger of that name, was published in selections in *The Monitor* in 1835. Harpur found employment in Sydney as a post office clerk in 1836, but resigned to avoid dismissal on 10 October 1839. Although he continued to spend time in Sydney, where his mother had remained in Parramatta after his father's death in 1842, Harpur for the next twenty years lived a life of hardship on the Hunter River, where his elder brother Joseph had established a farm. He was located at Patrick's Plains and then at Jerry's Plains, where he deputized for his brother in the post office store, and acted as pound-keeper and as agent for the Sydney papers. At Jerry's Plains in 1843 Harpur met Mary Ann Doyle (1820–1899), who was in part the inspiration of the sonnet series to 'Rosa' (later 'Nora').

She was the daughter of a more prosperous family in the district, who frowned on the match, but the pair eventually married on 2 July 1850. After unsuccessful ventures as a schoolmaster at Black Creek and at Muswellbrook, Harpur returned to sheep farming at Doyle's Creek, probably with the assistance of his wife's family.

In the 1840s and 1850s Harpur had increasing contact with the nascent literary circles in Sydney, especially with Henry Halloran, D. H. Deniehy, and N. D. Stenhouse. He was praised by Henry Parkes, who in 1843 made him a gift of the six-volume edition of Shelley. These years on the Hunter were Harpur's most productive, not only for some of his identifiably 'Australian' poems, but also for polemical pieces in verse and prose on such issues as convict transportation, land reform, and self-government.

Harpur's feeling that the world owed him a living was answered in August 1859, when he was appointed gold commissioner for the Goulburn and Araluen districts. He proved effective in this office, and selected land and built a house (the 'Euroma' of the later poems) for his family at Eurobodalla. This property was hardly adequate to support him when the goldfields appointment lapsed in July 1866, and ruinous floods came the year after. Harpur died on 10 June 1868 of 'induration (hardening) of the lungs'. He was buried at Euroma, beside his second son Charlie, killed in a shooting accident in 1867.

Apart from the occasional pamphlet offprinted from a poem appearing in the press such as *The Tower of the Dream* (1865), Harpur's published volumes were two: *Thoughts: a Series of Sonnets* (1845) with a dedication to Wordsworth, and *The Bushrangers* (1853), a reworking of *The Tragedy of Donohoe*, with 'other poems'. As the posthumous *Poems* (1883) were substantially abridged and 'improved' by H. M. Martin, there was no comprehensive text of Harpur until the 1984 edition by Elizabeth Perkins, who is preparing a definitive text. Harpur's manuscripts occupy some twenty-five volumes in the Mitchell Library, Sydney, offering multiple versions of the poems, annotations sometimes as extensive as the text, and much writing in prose.

Harpur has been seen as the poet who brought Australian landscape into Australian verse. It was already there, in W. C. Wentworth's *Australasia* (1823) and Charles Tompson's *Wild Notes, from the Lyre of a Native Minstrel* (1826), but these were in the cultivated eighteenth-century manner, which seemed to later readers to mask the features of the Australian scene. Harpur was more recognizably a Romantic, and 'A Mid-Summer Noon in the Australian Forest' was gratefully seized on by the anthologists. This misrepresented his work. Although particular observations were not lacking (the 'rush of startled kangaroo', 'the upland growths of wattles'), Harpur more often saw the Australian bush as vast and overwhelming and unknown—to some extent recording an Australia which has passed. He typically responds to the natural world in its larger, sometimes more threatening movements, as in a bushfire, a storm in the mountains, or in the darkness enveloping those who are lost in the bush. This is the quality of 'The Creek of the Four Graves', 'The Kangaroo Hunt', and 'Lost in the Bush'. Harpur is also sensitive to the distinctive effects of light, especially in glare and haze, and he made an antipodean analysis of the 'dancing' of the sun.

Like Wentworth and Tompson before him, and his admirer Henry Kendall after, Harpur saw himself as laying claim to the English poetic tradition, and as giving it individual expression. The projected edition of his poems in 1867 was dedicated 'to the People of England'. From the autobiographical 'The Dream by the Fountain' to the more ambitious 'The World and the Soul' and 'The Witch of Hebron', his work is informed by his conviction of the peculiar sensibility and mission of the poet. He becomes his own hero, meeting adversity with a melancholy satisfaction. Harpur's achievement otherwise is to have conveyed the immensity and the menace of the Australian bush more effectively in larger poetic structures, where the local faults may be overtaken in the general impression. G. A. WILKES

Sources Mitchell L., NSW, Harpur MSS, MSS 947, A87–A97, B78, C376–C386 · A. Gray, 'The collected poems of Charles Harpur', MA diss., University of Sydney, 1965 [3 vols.] · C. Harpur, *Poetical works*, ed. E. Perkins (1984) · J. Normington-Rawling, *Charles Harpur: an Australian* (1962) · C. W. Salier, 'Harpur and his editors', *Southerly*, 12 (1951), 47–54 · A. Mitchell, ed., *Charles Harpur* (1973) · J. Wright, *Charles Harpur*, rev. 2nd edn (1977) · R. Dixon, 'Charles Harpur and John Gould', *Southerly*, 40 (1980), 315–29
Archives Mitchell L., NSW | Mitchell L., NSW, James Normington-Rawling MSS
Likenesses photograph, Mitchell L., NSW; repro. in Normington-Rawling, *Charles Harpur*, frontispiece

Harpur, Joseph (1773–1821), literary scholar, was born in Motcombe, Dorset, the son of Joseph Harpur. He matriculated at Trinity College, Oxford, on 10 March 1790, and proceeded BCL in 1806 and DCL in 1813. After a long absence he returned to the university about 1806, and held for many years the office of deputy professor of civil law. He wrote *An Essay on the Principles of Philosophical Criticism Applied to Poetry* (1810). He and his wife, Mary Jane, who survived him, had at least one son, also Joseph. Harpur died in his lodgings in Clarendon Street, Oxford, from an attack of paralysis on 2 October 1821, and was interred in the churchyard of St Michael's parish.

FRANCIS WATT, *rev.* MEGAN A. STEPHAN

Sources Foster, *Alum. Oxon.* · [J. Watkins and F. Shoberl], *A biographical dictionary of the living authors of Great Britain and Ireland* (1816) · Watt, *Bibl. Brit.* · *GM*, 1st ser., 91/1 (1821), 381 · *N&Q*, 3rd ser., 4 (1863), 190, 278 · will, PRO, PROB 11/1648, sig. 549
Wealth at death see will, PRO, PROB 11/1648, sig. 549

Harpur, Richard (*d.* 1577), judge and law reporter, was the son or grandson of Henry Harpur of Rushall, Staffordshire, son of the MP John Harpur (*d.* 1464). He came to the attention of Sir John Port (*d.* 1540), justice of the king's bench, at whose instance he was admitted to the Inner Temple in 1537 from Barnard's Inn. Not long after Port's death he married Jane, daughter of Sir George Fynderne and Elizabeth Port (the judge's daughter), and thereby acquired estates in Derbyshire, where he settled at Swarkestone. He was closely associated with the younger John

Port in various transactions, and referred to him in his will as 'my deare frend'.

Harpur's vacation practice was chiefly in Derbyshire and Staffordshire, though he was also connected with Port's native city of Chester and became an alderman there. In 1543 he acquired the clerkship of assize on the Oxford circuit in succession to John Port the younger, and held that office until he took the coif. He was elected a bencher of the Inner Temple in 1552, and two years later autumn reader, becoming a serjeant-at-law at the first general call of Elizabeth I's reign in April 1559. He was well known as a reporter of cases in the common pleas from at least the 1550s until the 1570s, and his reports survive in numerous manuscripts. The texts associated with Harpur commonly begin in 1546, though with respect to the first twelve years or so it has proved difficult to separate his work from that of William *Dalison (*d.* 1559).

On 18 May 1567 Harpur was appointed a judge of the common pleas in succession to Sir Anthony Browne, and he also followed Browne on the northern circuit. He made his will on 9 July 1576. After ten years as a judge, he died on 29 January 1577; he was buried in accordance with his testamentary wishes in Swarkestone church, where there is a full-length recumbent alabaster effigy in judicial robes and collar of SS—a distinction apparently still sometimes worn by puisne justices—with his wife lying beside him, and a ribbon between their hands inscribed 'Cogita mori' ('Think on dying'), the motto of his mourning rings. Besides Swarkestone Harpur left a farm at Milton and extensive estates in Derbyshire and neighbouring counties. His libraries at Swarkestone and Serjeants' Inn were divided between his sons John and Richard. John (*d.* 1622), the eldest, was member of parliament for Derbyshire in 1597 and 1604, and knighted in 1603; John's son Henry was created a baronet in 1626. The seventh baronet assumed the additional surname of Crewe. J. H. BAKER

Sources L. W. Abbott, *Law reporting in England, 1485–1585* (1973), 122–41 · *The notebook of Sir John Port*, ed. J. H. Baker, SeldS, 102 (1986), xxii–xxiii · Sainty, *Judges*, 73 · will, PRO, PROB 11/59, sig. 9 · inquisition post mortem, PRO, C142/176/28 · HoP, *Commons, 1558–1603*, 2.258 · Foss, *Judges*
Likenesses alabaster effigy on monument, Swarkestone church, Derbyshire

Harraden, Beatrice (1864–1936), novelist and suffragist, was born at 32 St John's Wood Park, South Hampstead, London, on 24 January 1864, the youngest child in the family of two sons and two daughters of Samuel Harraden, musical instrument importer, and his wife, Rosalie Harriet Eliza Lindstedt. Educated in Dresden, and at Cheltenham Ladies' College, she went on to Queen's and Bedford colleges in the University of London, where she studied English literature, Latin, and Greek, and was awarded a first in the bachelor of arts degree in 1884.

Harraden's entry into London literary life in the 1890s was as a protégée of Eliza Lynn Linton, who introduced her as 'my little B.A.' to her Sunday afternoon soirées. Short and slight, with an olive complexion and luminous dark eyes, Harraden appears in most photographs with short hair in a fringe, looking clever and serious.

Harraden's first published story appeared in *Belgravia* after it was rejected by *Blackwood's Edinburgh Magazine*, and she published her first book, a children's story, *Things will Take a Turn*, in 1889. Her first novel, *Ships that Pass in the Night* (1893), coined the phrase and, despite William Blackwood's rejection as 'too sad to suit the public taste', was an instant success and made a fortune for her publishers, Lawrence and Bullen (George Gissing's publisher). Unfortunately she saw none of the profits, as, in her inexperience, she had sold them the copyright for a pittance. It was translated into most European languages, and Japanese, and none of her later books achieved similar success.

Most of Harraden's literary productions feature an almost mystical emphasis on the significance of a fleeting encounter between two strangers. Some of her contemporaries attributed this to her having fallen deeply in love with a man who falsified his clients' accounts and whose body was found soon after on a Swiss glacier. It was something which she neither confirmed nor denied, but she never married.

In 1894 Blackwood's published Harraden's contributions to its magazine under the title *In Varying Moods* and, in 1897, her *Hilda Strafford*. This was written in San Diego, on one of her several visits to the United States, where she stayed on a ranch recuperating from the ill health which dogged her all her life. The seventeen novels she produced between 1891 and 1928 often reflected her suffragist sympathies. Thus in *Interplay* (1908) she portrayed an independent woman and in *The Growing Thread* (1916) a woman who escapes a restrictive marriage. She herself regarded *The Fowler* (1899) as her best work, with one of the characters supposedly based on her beloved father.

Devoting only 90 minutes a day to her writing, Harraden worked diligently with other prominent women suffragists to secure the vote for women, participating and speaking at public meetings of the Women's Social and Political Union (WSPU) as well as contributing regularly to its journal, *Votes for Women*. Speaking in Manchester in 1910 she declared:

> I have always been interested in the militant Suffragists. … They appealed to my imagination … [if] they did not always appeal to my brain. … [As] time went on … [w]hat I had judged to be a mistake on their part … invariably turned out to be a successful move … having quite unexpected and far-reaching consequences. (*Votes for Women*, 3, 1909–10, 27)

Harraden was steadfast in her dedication to the 'cause' and, when denied the vote for parliament in 1910, refused to pay income tax. When, on 22 April 1913, her household goods were sequestered by bailiffs and auctioned under destraint for income tax, they were bought by her friends. While attempting to hold a public meeting following the auction, she was injured in the eye when the police permitted between 300 and 400 schoolchildren to throw missiles at her and two supporting suffragist friends. Later that year she published a moving account of the funeral of the suffragist 'martyr' Emily Davison.

Harraden served on the executive committee and as vice-president of the Women Writers' Suffrage League, and worked as an active member of the London Graduates' Suffrage Society and such organizations as the Lyceum, Halcyon, and Writers' clubs. The First World War made its mark on her novel *Where Your Treasure Is* (1918) and inspired her to serve on the Commission for Belgian Relief and to publicize its work in the *Bedford College Magazine* during 1915. At the behest of her friends Dr Elizabeth Garrett Anderson and Dr Flora Murray she also worked as librarian at the Endell Street Military Hospital in London.

In 1929 Harraden was elected a governor of Bedford College and in the following year was awarded a civil-list pension of £100. She died of delirium tremens on 5 May 1936 at the Grove Nursing Home, Grove Road, Barton-on-Sea, Hampshire.   FRED HUNTER

Sources Royal Holloway College, Egham, Surrey, MSS AS 200/1/2, AR 201, AR 220/1/1, AR 386/1/3 · J. Todd, ed., *British women writers: a critical reference guide* (1989), 313–14 · *Cheltenham Ladies' College Magazine* (1936) · S. A. Tooley, 'Some women novelists: Miss Beatrice Harraden', *Woman at Home*, 5 (Dec 1897) · B. Harraden, 'A writer's correspondence', *Cheltenham Ladies' College Magazine* (1901), 178–82 · 'General gossip of authors and writers', *Current Literature* (July 1900), 40 · letters to Blackwood's, NL Scot., MSS 4001–4734x; MS Acc. 309 · *DNB* · *CGPLA Eng. & Wales* (1936) · b. cert. · d. cert. · Cheltenham Ladies' College Archives, Cheltenham
Archives Royal Holloway College, Egham, Surrey, papers · Royal Literary Fund, London, case files, 2768/2791 | Bodl. Oxf., letters to Arthur St John Adcock · Bodl. Oxf., letters to Evelyn Sharp · NL Scot., letters to Blackwood's · Queen's University, Belfast, letters to Otto Kyllmann · U. Leeds, Brotherton L., letters to Clement Shorter · Women's Library, London, letters to Miss Solomon
Likenesses wood-engraving, 1897 (after photograph by M. Asquith), NPG; repro. in *ILN* (20 March 1897)
Wealth at death £1187 13s. 5d.: probate, 24 July 1936, *CGPLA Eng. & Wales*

Harraden, Richard (1756–1838), topographical draughtsman and printmaker, was born in London, the son of a physician who came from Flintshire. Little is known of his life, although Robert Willis believed that he lived for some time in Paris but left on the fall of the Bastille in 1789; however, no work survives to support this supposition. In London Harraden practised from 16 Little Newport Street. He specialized in topographical draughtsmanship and executed most of his designs in etching or aquatint. This was the case with the series of six large views of colleges which he published from his new premises in Great St Mary's Lane, Cambridge, in 1797. Aquatinted by a variety of engravers, including Harraden himself, these folio plates were designated a coherent series by their ornamental title-page with its heavy aquatint border bearing the words 'Views of Cambridge Drawn by Rd Harraden' in a 'stopped-out' script that was intended to evoke a monumental inscription. Indeed, after he opened this print shop in Cambridge, the recurrent subject of Harraden's work was Cambridge and the university.

Harraden sent five views of the town for exhibition at the Royal Academy in 1799 and two to the British Institution in 1823. There was much demand for Harraden's skills as a topographical draughtsman and in the first decade of the nineteenth century he contributed a number of designs, as well as finished aquatint plates, to a variety of drawing books and art primers. While 1803 marks the year in which he executed aquatints for Thomas Girtin's *Views of Paris*, it was also then that he produced a series of etched costume plates of Cambridge academic dress; focused on the human figure as a mannequin for the relevant robes, these reveal Harraden's weakness in anatomy, which can be contrasted with his usually more confident handling of landscape and architectural elevations. His best-known series again exploited the ready market among Cambridge academics or graduates. *Cantabrigia depicta* (1809–10) comprised twenty-four plates engraved after Harraden's designs by a variety of hands, including J. Hassel, J. Cartwright, and **Richard Bankes Harraden** (1778–1862), the artist's son, who was also an artist and a printmaker who favoured topographical views.

Published in the name of Harraden & Son of Cambridge, *Cantabrigia depicta* was evidently a success. This can be assumed as Richard Bankes Harraden continued to exploit the market for views of Cambridge in his own *Illustrations of the University of Cambridge* (1830). Also, as twenty-four of the fifty-eight plates in this series of 'engravings of architectural and picturesque Views' had already been published in *Cantabrigia depicta*, the younger Harraden was evidently sensitive to the continuing taste for them.

Robert Willis held that these plates were of 'no great artistic merit' (Willis, cxvii), and on comparing their works it is evident that the son had greater skill as an artist than his father. Although Richard Bankes Harraden did execute a few views of other locations, such as St Ives and the Isle of Wight, he concentrated mainly on Cambridge, which he published in the name of Harraden & Son until his father died at Trumpington, near Cambridge, on 2 June 1838.

Little else is known of Richard Bankes Harraden except that he was one of the first members of the Society of British Artists after its foundation in 1823. He subscribed to the society from 1824 until 1849, and, although he was never a prominent member, he submitted more than twenty antiquarian and picturesque landscapes (mostly of Cambridge) to the exhibitions they arranged to rival those of the Royal Academy and the British Institution. He died in Cambridge on 17 November 1862 at the age of eighty-four.   J. W. CLARK, *rev.* LUCY PELTZ

Sources J. R. Abbey, *Scenery of Great Britain and Ireland in aquatint and lithography, 1770–1860* (1952); repr. (1972) · Boase, *Mod. Eng. biog.* · M. Bradshaw, ed., *Royal Society of British Artists: members exhibiting, 1824–1892* (1973) · D. Bank and A. Esposito, eds., *British biographical archive*, 2nd series (1991) [microfiche] · Graves, *RA exhibitors*, 5.168 · H. Hubbard, *An outline history of the Royal Society of British Artists* (1937) · letter to the third earl of Hardwicke from Harraden & Son, 8 Nov 1813, BL, Add. MS 35689 · Redgrave, *Artists* · R. Willis, *The architectural history of the University of Cambridge, and of the colleges of Cambridge and Eton*, ed. J. W. Clark, 4 vols. (1886)

Archives BL, letters to Lord Hardwicke, Add. MS 35689, fol. 384, and 35690, fol. 92

Harraden, Richard Bankes (1778–1862). *See under* Harraden, Richard (1756–1838).

Harrap, George Godfrey (1868–1938), publisher, was born on 18 January 1868 at 11 Woodville Grove, Islington, London, the son of Frederick James Harrap, a former warehouseman, and his wife, Jemima, *née* Godfrey. He was educated at West Ham model school, leaving at the age of fourteen with an already keen love of reading. His first post, which would endure for nineteen years, was an appointment as an assistant with the publishing house of Isbister & Co. in Tavistock Street, Covent Garden, London, the office of *Good Words* and the *Sunday Magazine*. Here Harrap neglected no opportunity for improving on his somewhat scanty formal education, and secured early advancement into a field that provided opportunities for him to capitalize on his gifts as a lover of literature and as an enterprising businessman. Progress, however, did not keep pace with his ambition, and he was obliged to seek other outlets for his talents. He developed a particular interest in the educational publications of D. C. Heath & Co. of Boston, Massachusetts, for whom Isbister were the London agents, and a personal friendship with Heath himself followed. This association enabled him to introduce Heath's books to English teachers. It was at about this time that Harrap also became London representative for the publishing house of Thomas Y. Crowell, New York.

On 6 September 1890 Harrap had married his first wife, Christine Mary Steward (1869–1923), the daughter of the late Walter Steward, a timber merchant. The marriage took place at Stepney parish church, and the couple lived at 126 Carr Street, off Salmon Lane, Stepney, London. They had four children: George Steward Harrap, Walter Godfrey Harrap, Violet Christina Harrap, and Heath Stanley Harrap, this last named by way of compliment to D. C. Heath.

In 1901 Harrap started his own publishing business, concentrating at first on the production of modern language and other textbooks. The publication that year of Heath's *Practical French Grammar* gave a new direction to the teaching of French in Britain, and a general success in this field led to Harrap's decision to produce *Harrap's Standard French Dictionary*, the first volume of which, however, appeared only in 1934, fifteen years after its inception. The firm that subsequently bore his name, George G. Harrap & Co. Ltd, came formally into being in 1905, when Harrap brought G. Oliver Anderson into partnership.

Christine Harrap died on 3 June 1923, and on 10 September 1935, at the church of All Souls, Langham Place, London, Harrap married his second wife, Jessie Marguerite Pittman, the widow of J. J. Pittman and daughter of the late Benjamin Addley Bourne. There were no children of this marriage. Harrap himself was now living at 29 Langham Street, in the West End of London, but the couple made their home at his new wife's house, Corner Cottage, Tadworth, Surrey.

Harrap retired from his now flourishing publishing business in the year of his second marriage, leaving an account of his venture in an autobiographical account, *Some Memories, 1901–1935*. Another publication was *Love Lyrics from Five Centuries*, testifying to his fondness for foreign travel. Other interests, apart from books, which played as large a part in his domestic life as in his professional, were motoring and golf, the latter on a mostly modest scale. Harrap's convivial nature also brought him a wide circle of friends. He was a member of the Stationers' Company and the City Livery Club.

Following an operation to remove gallstones, George Harrap died on 29 October 1938 of bronchopneumonia at 20 Devonshire Place, London, apparently survived by his second wife. The publishing house founded by him was directed by the Harrap and Anderson families until 1971. Harrap's second son, Walter Godfrey Harrap (1894–1967), joined his father's business in 1913 and became the firm's managing director in 1950. His grandson, Paull Harrap (1917–1985), son of George's eldest son, George Steward Harrap, entered the family business in 1936 and became its chairman in 1971, on the retirement of Olaf Anderson.

ADRIAN ROOM

Sources WWW · *Everyman's encyclopedia*, 6 (1978) · private information (2004) · b. cert. · m. certs. · d. cert.
Wealth at death £63,084: resworn probate, 9 Jan 1939, *CGPLA Eng. & Wales*

Harrel, Sir David (1841–1939), police officer and civil servant, was born at Downpatrick, co. Down, Ireland, on 25 March 1841, the youngest son of David Harrel of Mount Pleasant, co. Down, who was agent for the Ker estate in that county, and his wife, Jane, daughter of James Wharton of Belfast. He was educated at the Royal Naval School, Gosport, intending to enter the Royal Navy, but was over age at the examination date and became a midshipman in the Dunbar Shipping Company. He left the merchant navy in order to enter the Royal Irish Constabulary in 1859. In 1863 he married Juliana (1839/40–1931), daughter of Richard Nugent Horner, rector of Killeeshill, co. Tyrone, with whom he had a family of three sons and two daughters.

Harrel became interested in the Irish land question when, as a young police officer, he witnessed unfair treatment of tenants and evictions, and wrote a letter to Gladstone, stating what he had seen. In later years Harrel followed with constant interest the successive remedial measures which led to the settlement of the land question. He was appointed resident magistrate in 1879, serving during the Land League days in co. Mayo, where his fairness and generous character established a mutual trust and affection with the local people. He was chief commissioner of the Dublin Metropolitan Police from 1883 to 1893 and was an active member of the congested districts board, which brought much improvement to the poor western districts of Ireland. An Ulster protestant, he worked for the Irish peasantry in co-operation with Roman Catholic clergy, with whom his relations were always good. In 1895 he was made KCB and in 1900 KCVO.

Although the two administrations represented differing political outlooks, Harrel, serving as under-secretary for Ireland (1893–1902) while John Morley and George Wyndham were chief secretaries, maintained a lasting friendship with each statesman. In 1912 his views on the prospects of Ulster resistance were sought by Augustine Birrell, Liberal chief secretary, and considered by the cabinet. Birrell attached great weight to Harrel's opinions on the Ulster question and was encouraged by his view that a major problem would not arise. After his retirement from Irish office, owing to ill health, he acted as chairman and member of various arbitration and conciliation boards dealing with industrial disputes in England. Harrel died at his home, 1 Lansdown Crescent, Bath, on 12 May 1939. His second son, William Vesey Harrel (1866–1956), became assistant commissioner of the Dublin Metropolitan Police and was in charge of the attempted disarming of Irish Volunteers in 1914, when he brought in troops. He was censured by an inquiry chaired by Lord Shaw of Dunfermline and removed from the service.

PAMELA HINKSON, *rev.* DAVID HUDDLESTON

Sources *The Times* (13 May 1939), 16 · *WW* (1939) · K. Tynan, *The years of the shadow* (1919) · P. Jalland, *The liberals and Ireland* (1980) · L. Ó'Broin, *The chief secretary Augustine Birrell in Ireland* (1969) · *Dod's Peerage* (1904), 461 · Burke, *Peerage* (1921) · private information (1949) · personal knowledge (1949)
Archives BLPES, memoirs | HLRO, corresp. with fifth Earl Cadogan · TCD, letters, etc.
Likenesses W. Stoneman, photograph, 1918, NPG
Wealth at death £31,028 16s. 0d.: probate, 7 July 1939, *CGPLA Eng. & Wales*

Harries, Henry (*bap.* 1821, *d.* 1849). *See under* Harries, John (*c*.1785–1839).

Harries, John (*c*.1785–1839), astrologer and physician, was born possibly at Pant-Coi, Cwrtycadno, Carmarthenshire, the eldest son of Henry Jones Harries (1739–1805), and his wife, Mary Wilkins. He was educated until he was ten years old at The Cowings, Commercial Private Academy, Caeo, and then boarded at Haverfordwest grammar school until he was eighteen; when his father died in 1805 he inherited the estate of Cwrtycadno.

It is not known where Harries studied medicine, but he later established a practice in Harley Street, London, with his astrologer friend Robert Cross Smith (alias Raphael; 1795–1832), before returning to Caeo to establish a practice there when he was in his forties. He was certainly a popular physician with a large practice:

> The sick and sorrowful came to enquire of his oracles from all parts of Wales, and from the testimony of the oldest people in the district, he was eminently successful in his cures. Lunatics were brought to him from parts of Pembrokeshire and Radnorshire, and he had a wonderful power over them. The course of treatment would include what he would term the water treatment, the herbs treatment, and the bleeding treatment. One of his chief methods was, he would take the afflicted to the brink of the river, and fire an old flint revolver; this would frighten his patient to such a degree that he would fall into the pool. He assumed the power of charming away pain, and was so successful that people believed thoroughly that he was in league with the evil one. (Price, 54)

Harries has been described as being 6 feet 2 inches tall, and well built in middle age, with 'Short dark hair … Mutton-chops sideboards. Medium sized forehead. Very straight nose. Mouth wide, slight jaws. At 53 years of age, beginning of a double chin. Blue, wistful thinking eyes' (Vaughan-Poppy, 4). It has been claimed that he married Elizabeth Emily Lewis, a lawyer's daughter from Fishguard. However, a marriage licence for 8 August 1821, records that John Harries, surgeon, and significantly a bachelor of Caeo parish, was married to a Lettice Rees. Their son **Henry Harries** (*bap.* 1821, *d.* 1849), it has been suggested, was born on 30 June 1816, though the Caeo parish baptismal entry for Harry, the eldest son of John and Lettice Harries of Pant-Coi, was recorded on 7 November 1821. He was described in later life as having 'a pale face, very dark hair, hanging down in ringlets over his narrow shoulders, grey eyes, and a very high narrow forehead …. His health was very delicate, owing to a weak chest' (Price, 56). Henry followed his father's footsteps and was educated at The Cowings and at Haverfordwest grammar school before attending London University. Between 1839 and 1842 Henry lived with his mother at Aberdâr, a house on their estate, while Pant-Coi was being rebuilt. During this period he met Hannah Marsden, a teacher at Caeo, and the daughter of a workman on the Pant-Coi estate, and on 4 November 1842 they were married at Caeo church. The marriage, however, was viewed with horror by Henry's family as it was felt that he had married beneath his social status, and allegedly the marriage turned out to be an unhappy one. Harries nevertheless accepted his fate and stated, 'I cannot help it. I must marry her. I dare not cross my planet' (NL Wales, MS 11119B). They had three children: Victoria Letitia, born in March 1843; John, born in March 1844; and Henry Harri Harries, born in April 1846.

Although the Harries family were recognized as doctors, they gained notoriety with their ability to predict future events, recover lost or stolen property, fight witchcraft, and invoke benign spirits. Henry Harries issued the following proclamation shortly before his father's death describing his work as that of a Dyn Hysbys ('cunning man') in Carmarthenshire. He suggested that he could, without seeing the person, determine:

> Temper, disposition, fortunate or unfortunate in their general pursuits, honour, riches, journeys and voyages (success therein, and what places best to travel in or reside in), friends and enemies, trade or profession best to follow, and whether fortunate in speculation, viz: lottery, dealing in foreign markets, etc.
>
> Of marriage, if to marry. The description, temper, disposition of the person, rich or poor, happy or unhappy in marriage, etc.
>
> Of children, whether fortunate or not, etc., deduced from the influence of the sun and moon, with the planetary orbs at the time of birth.
>
> Also judgement and general use in sickness and disease, etc.   (Price, 56)

Tales of supernatural events involving both father and son have long found their way into Welsh folklore and are quite numerous and varied. One of the most famous incidents involving John Harries concerned the disappearance of a local girl and the recovery of her body at Maes-yronnen—the precise location where Harries had informed the police that they would find the corpse of the young girl who had been murdered by her boyfriend. This led to Harries being charged as an accessory to the crime and the penning of a popular verse:

> Awn yn alarus
> At Doctor Harries
> Am ei fod yn hysbys,
> I 'mofyn hanes hon;
> Dywedai ei bod yn gorwedd

> Gerllaw Maes yr on;
> Mae ceu-bren mawr o wenwyn
> Yn tyfu bwys y lle,
> A nant yn rhedeg heibio
> Lle'i lladdwyd ganddo fe.

> We go concerned
> To Doctor Harries
> Because he is 'Hysbys'
> To ask her history;
> He said that she was lying
> Near Maes yr on;
> There is a tree full of bees
> Growing by the place,
> And a stream runs near
> Where she was murdered by him.
> (NL Wales, MS 11119B and translation)

The details of the case were passed on to Llwyd Glansefin and Gwyn Glan Bran, two magistrates at Llandovery, who called Harries before them and accused him of the crime. Harries was prepared to demonstrate his talent for second sight as part of his defence by suggesting to the magistrates 'Dywedwch chwi yr awr y daethoch chwi i'r byd, Mi ddywedaf finnau yr awr yr ewch chwi allan ohono' ('You tell me which hour you came into the world, and I will tell you the hour you will depart from it'; Bosse-Griffiths, 16). The two magistrates not wishing to pursue this line of questioning and possibly unwilling to know their fate proceeded to set Harries free.

Aspects of the supernatural involving both John and Henry Harries have underlined the importance of these men in Welsh folklore. In the Cwrtycadno collection (Pantcoy MSS) at the National Library of Wales there are various personal items, particularly astrological data, medical ledgers, and a book of incantations, which showed how the Dyn Hybsys could 'obtain the Familiar of the Genius or Good Spirit and cause him to appear' (J. C. Davies, 'Ghost-raising', 328). There are a considerable number of other tales which concern the Harrieses, notably the recovery of lost cows on Carmarthen Bridge and wedding rings, and the punishments meted out to people who had committed an act of ill will. John Harries died on 11 May 1839 aged fifty-four in a fire which also destroyed the family home at Pant-Coi, and on 13 May he was buried at Caeo churchyard. The character of his death, however, was unusual. He had a premonition that he would die by accident on 11 May 1839 and to avoid this happening he stayed in bed throughout the day. During the night, he was awoken by people crying out that the house was on fire. In his haste to dowse the flames he slipped from the ladder he was standing on and was killed. Henry Harries died aged twenty-eight from consumption, on 16 June 1849, and was buried three days later.

Other family members also had some ability in predicting the future as 'there was also a daughter who was rather clever in the "art"', as well as John Harries, who 'dabbled in it but never shone' (NL Wales, MS 11119B). These are probably references to Anne and John, the daughter and son or grandson of John Harries. The following letter from J. Williams of The Court, Brecon, on 21

March 1863, addressed to John Harries, shows the continuing role of the Harries family in Welsh social life:

> I have written to ask if you would oblige me by ruling my planet. I have long had a wish to have it done and when I heard of your truly wonderful gift I determined to write. I wish to know something relating to my marriage and particular friends. (NL Wales, MS 11717B)

This was certainly not an isolated case, as the fame of Cwrtycadno spread quickly throughout Wales and led to a number of distinguished visitors. These included the actress Sarah Siddons and her colleagues, and the writer George Borrow, who spent a day at Pant-Coi in 1854.

RICHARD C. ALLEN

Sources notes on Harries, Cwrtycadno, NL Wales, 14876B · parish register, Cynwyl Gaeo, NL Wales [birth, marriage, burial] · entry of death, c.1839, NL Wales, facs. 374 · I. Vaughan-Poppy, 'The Harries kingdom—wizards of Cwrtycadno', 1976, NL Wales · J. E. Lloyd, R. T. Jenkins, and W. L. Davies, eds., Y bywgraffiadur Cymreig hyd 1940 (1953), 317–18 · DWB, 338 · E. Gruffydd, Gwrachod Cymru (1980), 91–101 · K. Bosse-Griffiths, Byd y Dyn Hysbys – Swyngyfaredd yng Nghymru (1977), 15–43, 90–93, 133–4 · A. Mee, Magic in Carmarthenshire: the Harrieses of Cwrt-y-Cadno (1912) · F. S. Price, History of Caio (1904), 54–7 · M. Trevelyan, Folk-lore and folk-stories of Wales (1909), 215–23 · E. Jones, 'A Welsh wizard', Carmarthen Antiquary, 2 (1945–51), 47–8 · J. F. Jones, 'Harries of Cwrt-y-Cadno', Carmarthen Antiquary, 4 (1962–3), 102–3 · J. C. Davies, 'Ghost-raising in Wales', Folklore, 19 (1908), 327–31 · J. C. Davies, Folk-lore of west and mid-Wales (1911), 230–64 (231–4, 236–8, 240, 246, 252–63) · J. Rowland, 'Dr Harries Court y Cadno, the Carmarthenshire conjuror', Carmarthenshire notes, antiquarian, topographical and curious, ed. A. Mee, 1 (1889), 29–30 · A. T. Davies, Crwydro Sir Gâr (1955), 51–4 · G. Thomas, 'The witches of the southern counties of Wales', Cymru Fu: Notes and Queries Relating to the Past History of Wales and the Border Counties, 1 (1888), 117–18 · E. Hanmer, 'A parochial account of Llanidloes', Montgomeryshire Collections, 10 (1876–7), 231–312, esp. 235–7 · Curiosus, H. Watney, and D. R. Phillips ('Beili Glas'), 'A Welsh Archimago', Red Dragon, 10 (1886), 184–5, 282–3, 373–4 · 'Iorwerth', 'Llyfr Cwrtycadno', Yr Haul, 4 (1839), 142–5 · 'Llyfr Cwrtycadno', Yr Haul, 4 (1839), 142–5 · Hedd Molwynog [J. H. Davies], 'Dyn Hysbys Cwrt y Cadno', Cymru, 13 (1897), 215–19 · M. L. Lewes, Stranger than fiction: being tales from the by-ways of ghosts and folk-lore (1911), 196–8 · G. P. Jones, 'Folk medicine in the eighteenth century', Folklife: Journal of the Society for Folklore Studies, 7 (1969), 63–4 · J. H. Davies ('Penardd'), Rhai o hen Ddewiniaid Cymru (privately printed, London, 1901), 42, 52, 134, 137, 145–7, 154–7, 217 · S. J. Williams, Y Dyn Hysbys: Comedi mewn tair act (1935) · G. H. Jenkins, 'Popular beliefs in Wales from the Restoration to Methodism', BBCS, 27 (1976–8), 440–62 · E. Owen, Welsh folk-lore (1896), 255, 262 · D. Owen ('Brutus'), 'Tynghedfeniaeth', Brutusiana (1853), 315–19 · A. R. Wallace, My life: a record of events and opinions, 2 vols. (1905), vol. 1, p. 219 · 'Three Carmarthenshire conjurors', Bye-Gones Relating to Wales and the Border Counties, 2nd ser., 5 (1897–8), 209 · 'The Cwrtycadno Library', Transactions of the Carmarthenshire Antiquarian Society, 23 (1932), 46 · Yr Haul, 5 (1840), 286 · 'Harries, Court-y-Cadno', Caermarthenshire Miscellany and Notes and Queries for South-West Wales, 2 (1890), 61–2 · NL Wales, MS 11119B
Archives NL Wales, papers | NL Wales, Pantcoy MSS
Likenesses M. D. Bourne, photographs on glass, c.1838, NL Wales, Picture Collection

Harrild, Robert (1780–1853), printer and engineer, was born in Bermondsey, London, on 1 January 1780; the identity of his parents is unknown. In 1801 he set up the Bluecoat Boy Printing Office in Bermondsey in partnership with Edward Billings, whose sister Elizabeth he married in that year. The office printed books and commercial stationery, from 1807 under Harrild's sole direction, until 1832, when he ceased printing. He maintained business contact with Billings, however, and his daughter Sarah married into the Billings family.

By 1809 Harrild was also manufacturing printers' materials, his best-known product being his 'composition' rollers for inking type, introduced in 1810 to replace the ancient method of applying ink with balls of hide. Harrild's rollers were made from the unlikely combination of animal glue and molasses, which set into a soft yet firm texture; in later years carbonate of soda was added. His contracts with the major newspaper printing houses to supply, maintain, and renovate these rollers brought him good profits.

In 1819 Harrild moved north of the river to 20 Great Eastcheap, then in 1824 to 25 Friday Street. In 1827 he added 10, and later 11, Distaff Lane, adjacent to Friday Street, ultimately connecting all these premises into one large manufactory. His sons Robert (b. 1808) and Horton (b. 1813) joined him, and by 1832 Harrild & Sons were advertising as printers' brokers, manufacturers of presses, and suppliers of all kinds of printers' equipment, both new and secondhand. By the middle of the century they were well known throughout England and on the continent, and Harrild's display at the 1851 Great Exhibition was much admired.

Harrild's philanthropy found an outlet when he acquired the old press which Benjamin Franklin had operated while in London in 1725–6. In 1841 Harrild presented this press to an American, J. B. Murray, who removed it to the United States. Harrild paid for its transport to Liverpool and its public exhibition there, and visitors were invited to contribute to the Printers' Pension Society. So small a sum was collected that Harrild added to it over the years, and bequeathed £1000 on his death, enabling the society to endow a 'Franklin pension' of 10 guineas per year to needy printers. He was one of the first parish guardians appointed after the passing of the Poor Law Act and retained that office for many years. At Sydenham, Kent, where his last years were spent, he contributed generously towards the conversion of what had previously been a wild common into a populous and wealthy neighbourhood. Harrild died at his home, Round Hill Villa, Sydenham, on 28 July 1853. His descendants continued the business for a century after his death.

R. E. ANDERSON, rev. ANITA MCCONNELL

Sources E. Liveing, The house of Harrild, 1801–1948 (1949) · GM, 2nd ser., 40 (1853), 320 · E. C. Bigmore and C. W. H. Wyman, A bibliography of printing, 3 vols. (1880–86); repr. (1969), 1.232, 234, 306 · d. cert.
Likenesses portrait, repro. in Liveing, House of Harrild, frontispiece

Harriman, Sir George William (1908–1973), motor vehicle manufacturer, was born in Coventry on 3 March 1908, the son of George Harriman, a motor machinist, and his wife, May Victoria, formerly Cooper. At the age of fifteen and a half he became an apprentice at the Hotchkiss works, Gosford Street, where his father was a general foreman. This factory was taken over in May 1923 by William Morris for the manufacture of engines; it was, at this time, an important centre of innovation in production engineering. Frank Woollard, who became Morris's manager there, enhanced the existing capabilities of the workshops by reorganizing the flow of work. Within a few months he raised weekly engine production from fewer than 300 units to 1200. By 1924 the factory was making 2000 engines per week, with only limited extensions of the work space and labour force (Lewchuk, 167–70). During his apprenticeship Harriman made the acquaintance of Leonard Lord, who was then working in the drawing office. By 1938 Harriman was assistant works manager at the new Courthouse Green engine works in Coventry.

Two years later Harriman followed Lord to the Longbridge, Birmingham, works of Austin, where he became machine shop superintendent responsible for engine production. During the early part of the war he worked closely with Lord, who had been appointed as government controller of Boulton and Paul Aircraft Ltd, to expedite production of Defiant night fighters. For this work Harriman was appointed OBE in 1943. In the following year he became production manager at Austins.

In 1948 Harriman accompanied Lord on a visit to the United States, where he developed a broader appreciation of American production methods. Under his direction Austins pioneered in Britain the introduction of automated transfer machines for engine manufacture. An innovative assembly building, designed by an American architect, was opened at Longbridge in 1951. Harriman's role in the company was recognized by his appointment as general works manager in 1945 (with a seat on the board), and his elevation to deputy managing director in 1950 and deputy chairman in 1952.

When Austin and Morris merged to form the British Motor Corporation (BMC) in February 1952, Harriman's responsibilities expanded. He was very successful in rationalizing engine production and to a lesser extent the range of models built. The total volume of output was raised from 279,000 in 1952–3 to 656,000 in 1959–60 with only a modest increase in factory space, labour force, and capital investment. Harriman was appointed deputy chairman and joint managing director of BMC in 1956.

When Sir Leonard Lord retired as chairman and managing director in 1961, Harriman was the obvious successor. Over the next five years BMC's production base was extended by new factory development such as the new truck and tractor plant in Bathgate, Scotland, opened in 1961, and by acquisitions such as the Pressed Steel Company in 1965 and Jaguar in the following year. Harriman became chairman of British Motor Holdings Ltd (BMH), formed in 1966 and the fourteenth largest industrial corporation outside the USA. With assets of £210 million, 114,000 employees, 32 factories worldwide, and some 6000 dealers, the new organization had a production capacity of 1.1 million vehicles. In addition to making cars, trucks, and tractors, BMH also made buses, fork-lift trucks, and domestic appliances.

The enlarged corporation had, however, many inherent points of weakness. The 1966–7 financial results showed a loss of £3.2 million, partly a result of the costs of the merger but, more seriously, a reflection of declining productivity and profitability. Future product development was limited. As later critics have noted, there were no real successors to the innovative Mini and 1100/1300 range designed by Alec Issigonis in the late 1950s. A strategy for the European market was only in the early stages with the development of small assembly operations in Belgium, Italy, and Spain.

BMH, in common with other British motor manufacturers, was being undermined by more volatile conditions in the industry especially in labour relations, annual sales, and worldwide export competition. Informal talks between Leyland and BMC about a possible merger had started as early as 1964 but, except for some limited joint ventures overseas, nothing happened. A dinner for Donald Stokes of Leyland and Harriman, hosted by the prime minister, Harold Wilson, at Chequers in October 1967, moved the merger discussions closer to a climax. Final terms were agreed in January 1968 and the formation of the British Leyland Motor Corporation was announced the following month. Harriman became the first chairman but his influence was limited, as Leyland men and outside appointments dominated. In 1969 Stokes took over the chairmanship and Harriman became honorary president. Until his retirement aged sixty-five, in March 1973, Harriman had a very minor role in the direction of the company.

As a key figure in the post-war British motor industry, Harriman was essentially a production engineer, at his best grappling with the problems of engineering, factory layout, and vehicle production. He was adept at expanding output with fairly minimal capital investment, a policy which worked well in the 1950s but one which compromised the future possibilities of higher productivity and profits. In the company Harriman was well liked by fellow executives and workers on the shop floor.

Harriman was important in modernizing the firms created by the first generation of motor magnates, Austin and Morris, but he was less comfortable in the new era of corporate administration where larger strategies in finance, marketing, and organized research were critical. While BMC managed to retain a home market share of about 38 per cent from the early 1950s to the mid-1960s, the merger of the original Austin and Morris interests was never completed. Both companies retained separate boards of directors and books until 1966 and separate lines of dealers were retained until even later. The informal methods of BMC in administration, precise costing of vehicles, and market research contrasted with the rigorous organization of Ford.

Most of Harriman's working life was spent as a company executive. His wider contribution to the British motor industry was recognized by the Society of Motor Manufacturers and Traders, which he served as president in 1967–9. He was made CBE in 1951 and was knighted in 1965 for services to exports. In his earlier years he was an active sportsman and later found relaxation in golf and trout fishing. He never lived far from the factories he managed, first in Coventry, then for many years in Solihull and latterly in the nearby village of Knowle. Harriman was very reticent about his private life; all that is recorded is that he was survived by a widow and one daughter (Josephine Marie). He died at his home, Dial House, Chadwick End, Knowle, of cardiac failure, on 29 May 1973.

G. T. BLOOMFIELD

Sources G. T. Bloomfield, 'Harriman, Sir George William', *DBB* · M. Adeney, *The motor makers: the turbulent history of Britain's car industry* (1988) · K. Williams, J. Williams, and D. Thomas, *Why are the British bad at manufacturing?* (1983), case study no. 3 · G. Turner, *The Leyland papers* (1971) · G. Turner, *The car makers* (1963) · W. Lewchuk, *American technology and the British vehicle industry* (1987) · d. cert. · *WWW*
Wealth at death £42,109: probate, 11 July 1973, *CGPLA Eng. & Wales*

Harriman, John (1760–1831), botanist, was born at Maryport, Cumberland, son of a family of German extraction named Hermann. At seventeen he became a medical student, but after two years he turned to classical studies. He never graduated. In 1787 he was ordained a deacon and became assistant curate at Bassenthwaite. Thence he passed to Barnard Castle, Eggleston, near Middleton in Teesdale (1795–1801), and Gainford, all in co. Durham. On 19 April 1808 he married Ann Ayre (1773–1862) of Gainford. They had no children. After a period at Long Horsley in Northumberland, he returned to co. Durham, serving at Heighington, Croxdale, and, lastly, in the perpetual curacies of Ash and Satley.

Harriman's early botanical ambitions sometimes made him unscrupulous in his tactics, as is evident from his correspondence with James Sowerby (1757–1822), Nathaniel Winch (1768–1838), and James Edward Smith (1759–1828). Nevertheless, he was elected a fellow of the Linnean Society on 18 December 1798, and his original work on lichens rivals that of Smith and Dawson Turner (1775–1858). Indeed, Turner described him as 'a man of real talents' (London, Linn. Soc., Winch MSS, W2.065). But for his financial circumstances, his temperament, and his geographical isolation, Harriman would probably have published some important work on lichens.

Together with his fellow botanists William Oliver (1760–1816), John Binks (1766–1817), and Edward Robson (1763–1813), Harriman discovered many of the 'Teesdale rarities', including *Gentiana verna* L., new to Britain. He contributed to Sowerby and Smith's *English Botany* (1790–1814), and he was also an active mineralogist. He died on 3 December 1831 at Croft in the North Riding of Yorkshire, where he was buried next to his friend the Revd James Dalton (1764–1843). Erik Acharius (1757–1819) named the lichen *Verrucaria harrimanii* after him. F. HORSMAN

Sources F. Horsman, *Botanising in Linnaean Britain: a study of upper Teesdale in northern England* [forthcoming] · NHM, Sowerby MSS · Linn. Soc., Winch papers · Linn. Soc., Smith papers · Trinity Cam., Dawson Turner MSS · *Durham County Advertiser* (27 Oct 1905) · E. Acharius, *Lichenographia universalis* (1810), 284 · *Annual Register* (1834), 249 · *DNB*

Archives Liverpool Museum, herbarium | Linn. Soc., Smith corresp.; Winch corresp. · NHM, Sowerby corresp. · Trinity Cam., Dawson Turner corresp.
Wealth at death under £450: will

Harriman [*née* Digby; *other married names* Churchill, Hayward], **Pamela Beryl** (1920–1997), adventurer and diplomatist, was born on 20 March 1920 at Farnborough, Kent, the eldest of three daughters and oldest of the four children of Edward Kenelm Digby, eleventh Baron Digby (1894–1964), and his wife, (Constance) Pamela Alice (1895–1978), youngest daughter of Henry Campbell Bruce, second Baron Aberdare. A brave, boisterous, auburn-haired child, with a tendency to dumpiness, she spent her infancy in Australia, where her father (who had won the DSO and two MCs in the First World War) was military secretary to the governor-general. Thereafter she grew up at Minterne Magna, the family house near Dorchester in Dorset. Her upbringing was provincial, with an emphasis on sporting pursuits. Her formal education at home was by convention similarly limited. Glamour was in short supply, but those glimpses she had of it, such as staying with her wealthy aunt Eva, countess of Rosebery, proved the spur that would take her from rural England to the heart of American political life, via the bedrooms of some of the richest men in the world. It was a career that evoked comparison with that of her ancestor Jane Digby, who had scandalized Georgian society with her love affairs, become mistress to King Ludwig I of Bavaria, and finally wife to a sheik. Her great-great-niece often pointed to parallels between their two lives.

In 1935 Pamela Digby went to Downham School, Hertfordshire, for a year and then to Paris and Munich to be 'finished'. On coming out into society in 1938 she was taken up by the American hostess Lady Baillie, who recognized and fostered her ability to attract, please, and organize the lives of powerful men—the art of the courtesan. Her talents in this field, however, were not immediately apparent to her contemporaries. While one remembered her as 'hot stuff, a very sexy young thing' (*Daily Telegraph*, 6 Feb 1997), most concurred with the unkind judgement of one of John F. Kennedy's sisters, that she was 'a fat, stupid little butterball' (*The Times*, 6 Feb 1997). She remained without a genuine suitor until the outbreak of war in 1939. Then, on the first evening that they met, she received and accepted a proposal of marriage from Randolph Frederick Edward Spencer *Churchill (1911–1968), journalist and politician, only son of Winston Leonard Spencer *Churchill. Churchill had already made a good number of somewhat panicky wartime proposals, but despite warnings on all sides the couple were married within three weeks, on 4 October 1939. Pamela Churchill, however, quickly established excellent relations with her parents-in-law, Winston and Clementine, and sealed the bond with the birth on 10 October 1940 of her first and only child, also Winston, later Conservative MP for Davyhulme. When her father-in-law became prime minister in 1940, Pamela Churchill leapt at an offer to live at 10 Downing Street.

Less happy were Pamela Churchill's dealings with her

Pamela Beryl Harriman (1920–1997), by Diana H. Walker, 1977

husband who, though he possessed the breezy self-confidence that she found attractive in a man, was adulterous and argumentative, and drank too much. The marriage had got off to a sticky start when he insisted on reading Gibbon aloud to her on honeymoon, and deteriorated rapidly under the weight of his gambling debts. Soon both parties began to look elsewhere for amusement, and Pamela Churchill formed liaisons with several visiting American dignitaries, among them Jock Whitney, later ambassador in London, Bill Paley, the president of CBS, and his star broadcaster, Ed Murrow. Her most important conquest was (William) Averell Harriman (1891–1986), heir to the Union Pacific Railway fortune and President Roosevelt's choice to supervise the lend-lease programme; she was twenty-one, he forty-nine. The affair was promoted by Lord Beaverbrook and, by some accounts, condoned by the prime minister, who saw it as a useful informal channel for smoothing misunderstandings between allies. The relationship came to an end when Harriman was posted to Moscow in 1943.

Randolph and Pamela Churchill were divorced in 1946, although she continued to use the surname (which became an asset in her amorous adventures) for much of the rest of her life. For a time she worked as a gossip writer for Beaverbrook's *Evening Standard*, but post-war England, and English men, were not to her taste, and in 1947 she moved to France, where she soon took up with Prince Aly Khan. When he left her for Rita Hayworth the next year,

she speedily reattached herself to Gianni Agnelli, the owner of Fiat.

Aside from her gifts of vitality and self-discipline, Pamela Churchill's great skill as a mistress lay in her malleability. She made every man at whom she set her cap feel that he and his cares were the sole object of her attention, and to this end she dressed as they liked, decorated houses according to their taste, cultivated their friends, aped their politics, learnt their languages, and even changed her religion; in 1950, in the vain hope that Agnelli would marry her, she became a Roman Catholic. At times she overreached herself in ambition and extravagance, but she took no outward heed of criticism or shame and, with supreme resilience, simply marched on to the next consuming interest of her life. She was at heart, perhaps, a frustrated romantic. Any such vexation can only have been increased by her repeated failure to turn her status as mistress into that of wife. Despite running Agnelli's household for five years, and nursing him after a serious car crash, he looked elsewhere for a wife and so, after a fling with the Greek shipping magnate Stavros Niarchos, in 1954 Pamela Churchill became *maîtresse en titre* to Baron Elie de Rothschild, the French banker.

When it became clear that Rothschild would not leave his wife for her, in 1960 Pamela Churchill turned to America and captured Leland Hayward (1902–1971), producer of Broadway shows such as *The Sound of Music*, who had already married five times. They married on 4 May 1960, the marriage lasting until his death in March 1971. 'The Widow of Opportunity', as she became known, then made eyes at Frank Sinatra before bringing the wheel full circle that same year by marrying, on 28 September, Averell Harriman, himself now a widower and formerly governor of New York state. In December 1971 she took American citizenship. By instinct a conservative, she now became, like her husband, a pillar of the Democratic Party, prized by it for her skill as a fundraiser and political hostess at her home in Georgetown, Washington, DC, which served as the party's unofficial headquarters during the Reagan and Bush administrations. Although never an intellectual, she also took care to familiarize herself thoroughly with policy issues.

Harriman died in July 1986, leaving his wife some $115 million, as well as Van Gogh's *White Roses*. She soon gave her backing to two aspiring presidential candidates, Bill Clinton and Al Gore, and when Clinton was elected in 1992, he rewarded her the next year by making her ambassador in Paris. Her time in France was broadly a success. She approached her briefs with the energy, hard work, and determination that had characterized her career hitherto, and brought an aura of power and glamour to her office, 'more than making up in style what she may have lacked in detailed diplomatic knowledge' (*The Times*, 6 Feb 1997). If the English still carped at her past behaviour, the French were impressed by her looks (which had been improved by time and surgery) and her social adroitness, and the Americans respected what she had to offer as a public servant. Her reconciliation of differences between these two last nations helped finalize the General Agreement on Tariffs and Trade in 1993. Her later years at the embassy, however, were overshadowed by her need to settle a lawsuit brought by her Harriman stepchildren, who alleged that she had squandered $21 million left in trust for them.

Pamela Harriman died on 5 February 1997 at the American Hospital, Neuilly-sur-Seine, after suffering a cerebral haemorrhage while swimming at the Hôtel Ritz, Paris. She was buried, after a service at Washington National Cathedral conducted with the protocol of a state funeral, on 14 February at Arden, the Harriman estate near Harriman, New York. She was survived by her only child, Winston Churchill.   JAMES OWEN

Sources S. Bedell Smith, *Reflected glory: the life of Pamela Churchill Harriman* (1996) · C. Ogden, *Life of the party* (1995) · *Daily Telegraph* (6 Feb 1997) · *The Times* (6 Feb 1997) · *The Independent* (6 Feb 1997) · *The Scotsman* (6 Feb 1997) · *The Observer* (9 Feb 1997) · Burke, *Peerage*
Archives CAC Cam. | Foundation Center Library, Washington, DC, W. Averell and Pamela C. Harriman Foundation · L. Cong., W. Averell Harriman MSS · NYPL, Leland Hayward collection | SOUND BL NSA [as Pamela Harriman]
Likenesses photograph, 1938, repro. in *The Tatler* (22 June 1938) · photograph, 1939, Hult. Arch.; repro. in *The Independent* · C. Beaton, photographs, 1941, Sothebys, London · J. Swope, photograph, c.1948, repro. in *The Observer* · two photographs, 1971–96, repro. in *The Scotsman* · D. H. Walker, photograph, 1977, Hult. Arch. [see *illus.*] · photographs, CAC Cam. · photographs, Hult. Arch.

Harrington. For this title name *see* individual entries under Harrington; *see also* Stanhope, William, first earl of Harrington (1683?–1756); Stanhope, William, second earl of Harrington (1719–1779) [*see under* Stanhope, William, first earl of Harrington (1683?–1756)]; Stanhope, Charles, third earl of Harrington (1753–1829); Stanhope, Charles, fourth earl of Harrington (1780–1851); Stanhope, Leicester Fitzgerald Charles, fifth earl of Harrington (1784–1862); Foote, Maria [Maria Stanhope, countess of Harrington] (1797–1867).

Harrington family (*per. c.*1300–1512), magnates, claimed descent from Osulf, whose son was a benefactor of St Bees Abbey, Cumberland, in the reign of Richard I. The family was originally of Flimby, Cumberland, and acquired Aldingham, Lancashire, in the late thirteenth century through the marriage of Robert Harrington to Agnes, daughter of Richard Cansfield and heir of her childless brother William. As well as Aldingham, which became the home of the main family line, Agnes brought the Harringtons Tunstall, Westmorland, and Farleton, Lancashire. The son of Robert and Agnes, **John Harrington**, first Lord Harrington (*c.*1281–1347), was a minor at his father's death in 1297 and his wardship was granted for five years to William Dacre. To judge by the heraldry on their tomb in Cartmel Priory church, John's wife, Joan, was Dacre's daughter. John was an adherent of Thomas, earl of Lancaster, receiving a pardon in 1313 for his complicity in the death of Piers Gaveston. But he avoided Boroughbridge, and was serving under Andrew Harclay on the Scottish border in June 1322. Harclay's disgrace the following year brought Harrington's outlawry, but he submitted and was pardoned, and in 1326 received a personal summons to parliament, by which he is deemed to have become the first Lord Harrington.

John's eldest son, Sir Robert Harrington, married Elizabeth, sister and coheir of John Moulton, who brought the Harringtons land in Ireland as well as in Suffolk and Lincolnshire. Robert died, and his widow remarried Walter Birmingham, in or before 1334. At John's death on 2 July 1347 the Harrington lands passed to Robert's eldest son, John Harrington (*c.*1328–1363), while a younger son of John (*d.* 1347), another John Harrington (*d.* 1359), founded the Harringtons of Farleton and Hornby, Lancashire.

The Harringtons of Aldingham John Harrington, second Lord Harrington (*c.*1328–1363), probably married a kinswoman of his stepfather, Walter Birmingham. His younger brother, Robert (*d.* 1399), was the ancestor of the Harringtons of Fleet, Lincolnshire, and Exton, Rutland. John died at the manor house he had built at Gleaston, Lancashire, on 28 May 1363. The wardship of his heir, **Robert Harrington**, third Baron Harrington (1356–1406), then aged six, was granted to the king's daughter Isabel. He came of age in 1377, his first intended wife, Alice Greystoke, having died *c.*1376. About 1383 he married Isabel (*d.* 21 Aug 1400), the widow of Sir William Cogan of Huntspill, Somerset, and the daughter and coheir of Sir Neil *Loring (*d.* 1386). She brought the Harringtons extensive lands in Devon, Cornwall, and Somerset. Robert died at Aldingham on 21 May 1406.

John Harrington, fourth Baron Harrington (1384–1418), Robert's son and heir, secured a decisive broadening of Harrington horizons through his marriage (perhaps arranged by his father) to Elizabeth, the daughter of Edward Courtenay, earl of Devon, who was lord of much of the land that the Harringtons had acquired through Isabel Loring. John accompanied Henry V on his French campaign in 1415, but was among those invalided home from Harfleur. In June 1417 he made his will, as part of his preparations for returning to France, and it was presumably on campaign that he died, childless, on 11 February 1418. He was buried in the church at Porlock, Somerset.

William Harrington, fifth Baron Harrington (*c.*1392–1458), John's brother and heir, pursued a military career with more success than his brother. He was in the duke of Gloucester's contingent on the campaign of 1415, and also fought in all the major campaigns between 1418 and 1421. He married Margaret, the daughter of Sir John Hill, a justice of the king's bench with strong links to the Courtenays. But Margaret was not Hill's heir and the marriage, arranged certainly before 1432 and probably before William inherited the barony, did not greatly benefit the Harringtons. William was a low-profile figure in both the north and the south-west. He died in 1458 and was buried with Margaret, who predeceased him, at Conishead, Lancashire. Their only child, Elizabeth, had married, in or before 1442, William *Bonville, the stepson of William Harrington's sister-in-law Elizabeth, but had died by 1458. The Harrington heir was her sixteen-year-old son William Bonville, who died with his father at the battle of Wakefield in 1460. The arms of the Harringtons of Aldingham were sable, a fret argent.

The Harringtons of Farleton and Hornby The Harrington family of Farleton and Hornby, Lancashire, were a junior branch of the Harringtons of Aldingham. The family was founded by **Sir John Harrington** (*d.* 1359), the second son of John Harrington, first Lord Harrington (*d.* 1347). At John's marriage to Katherine, daughter of Adam Banaster of Bolton-le-Moors, his father settled on the couple the manor of Farleton in Lonsdale, Lancashire. John died on 1 August 1359, to be followed less than two years later by two sons: Robert, who died in late January or early February 1361, and Thomas, who died in the following May, both, apparently, 'in parts beyond the sea' (*CIPM*, 11, no. 251). Their heir was their younger brother **Sir Nicholas Harrington** (*b.* 1345/6, *d.* in or before 1404), aged fifteen, whose wardship was sold by John of Gaunt, duke of Lancaster, to Sir James Pickering. Nicholas was to make his career in Gaunt's service, although he is first to be found, in 1369–70, serving in Ireland under William Windsor, husband of the king's mistress, Alice Perrers. Back in England Nicholas's career was marked by violence. In 1373 he was involved in an attack on the Cumberland estates of Ralph, Lord Dacre, and in 1375 was the accomplice of Dacre's brother Hugh in the murder of Lord Ralph in his bed. Neither episode seems to have interrupted Nicholas's public career, which included representing Lancashire in parliament five times and being sheriff of the county from 1379 to 1384.

Nicholas married twice. His first wife was Isabel, the younger daughter of Sir William English, who was the mother of his three sons: William, James (the ancestor of the Harringtons of Wolphege), and Nicholas. Sir Nicholas took as his second wife Joan Venable, widow of Sir Thomas Lathom and Roger Fazakerley (reputedly Joan's lover before her first husband's death). Joan had control of her first husband's lands in Huyton and Knowsley, and she and Sir Nicholas seem to have taken up residence at the latter until Sir Nicholas's death some time before February 1404.

Sir Nicholas's heir, his eldest son, **Sir William Harrington** (*d.* 1440), continued the tradition of service to the house of Lancaster. He served the future Henry V while he was still prince of Wales, and after his accession became one of the king's knights and his banner-bearer—a duty he performed at Agincourt and again at the siege of Rouen in 1419, where he was seriously wounded. He was made a knight of the Garter in 1417. William married Margaret, the daughter of Sir Robert Neville of Hornby, Lancashire, and Farnley, Yorkshire, the lord of the Harringtons' manor of Farleton in Lonsdale. At the time of the marriage Margaret was not an heiress. She had a brother, whose daughter (also called Margaret) was married to the youngest of the Beauforts, Thomas, duke of Exeter. But the younger Margaret died childless, and on her widower's death in 1426 Margaret Harrington and her nephew John Langton, son of her sister Joan, became heirs to the Neville inheritance. Part of the land, including Farnley but excluding Hornby, had already been demised to Sir William by Exeter before his death, but in the final division ratified by the king's council in 1433 that share of the land

went to Langton, while the Harringtons took Hornby itself.

Even before his acquisition of the Neville lands Sir William Harrington had begun to play an active role in Yorkshire (where he was sheriff four times from 1408), presumably on the strength of land that made up Margaret's marriage settlement. But he retained his Lancashire interests, receiving extensive office within the duchy of Lancaster which culminated in his appointment as chief steward in the north parts in 1428. An earlier sign of royal favour had come on the death of Thomas, Lord Dacre, in 1419, when William was granted the wardship of Dacre's daughter Elizabeth, whom he promptly married to his heir **Thomas Harrington** (*d.* 1460), thereby securing the Dacre manors of Tatham and Heysham, Lancashire. Thomas followed his father into royal service in France. He was with Henry VI on his only visit to France in 1430, served in Picardy in 1436, and was one of those responsible for escorting Margaret of Anjou to England in 1445. He also took over a number of his father's lesser duchy of Lancaster offices after his death in 1440. It was probably the duchy connection that helped to draw Thomas into the orbit of the Nevilles, for in the 1440s he was acting as deputy to the earl of Salisbury as steward of Amounderness. In the northern unrest of 1454–5 he was active on their behalf against the duke of Exeter and Lord Egremont.

As civil war began to look increasingly likely, Thomas gave thought to the future. Early in 1459 'rememberyng hymselfe off the grete werres and trobles likelie to fall emong suche mightie princes' he enfeoffed his lands to a group of Lancastrian supporters, including the earl of Shrewsbury and Lord Clifford,

> to thintent that for the same lords war myghty and in consorte with the contrari partie [they] sholde be faire meaynes if God fortuned the feld in the sayde werres to goo ageyne that partie that the seide Sir Thomas was open ... [to] safe hys landes unforfeited.   (Whitaker, 2.261–2)

Thomas Harrington and his second son, James, were captured in the aftermath of Bloreheath and imprisoned at Chester, where they stayed until the Yorkist victory at Northampton restored them to lands and favour. On 30 November 1460 the prior of Durham wrote to Thomas Harrington, 'thankyng God that ye are past the trouble that ye were in' (Roskell, 186). On 29 December Thomas and his eldest son, John, were with the duke of York at the battle of Wakefield and both died there.

Their death embroiled the surviving Harringtons in a bitter dispute over the descent of their land. John left two daughters from his marriage to Matilda Clifford, but in 1463 the feoffees who had been appointed by Thomas in 1459 handed over all the land to John's eldest surviving brother, **James Harrington** (*d.* 1485?), who, according to a later claim, kept his two nieces in custody. In October 1466 Thomas, Lord Stanley, intervened, securing a grant of the Harrington lands and of the two girls. In 1468 a commission found that the girls were indeed the heirs to the estates, but the dispute dragged on until 1475, when Edward IV imposed a compromise. Both James and his brother Robert Harrington were in the service of Richard, duke of Gloucester, and his accession raised their hopes of reopening the case. By 1485 Richard may have been sufficiently mistrustful of the Stanleys to countenance the idea, but his death at Bosworth supervened. Both Harringtons were attainted for their part in the battle, and the family tradition was that James died there. This may well have been true, for the only firm references to a James alive after 1485 are to Robert's son, who was attainted for his part in the rebellion of 1487, or to their kinsman James Harrington of Wolphege (d. 1497), who was descended from a younger son of Sir Nicholas Harrington. But even if James senior survived, the family had been extinguished as a force. James's son John died soon afterwards, reputedly poisoned. Robert's son James secured a pardon for his involvement at Stoke, and died as dean of York in 1512. The arms of the Harringtons of Farleton and Hornby were as Harrington of Aldingham, differenced.

ROSEMARY HORROX

Sources Chancery records · I. Grimble, The Harington family (1957) · GEC, Peerage, new edn · J. S. Roskell, The knights of the shire for the county palatine of Lancaster, 1377–1460, Chetham Society, new ser., 96 (1937) · HoP, Commons, 1386–1421 · VCH Lancashire · 'A brief account of the re-grants made by K. Hen. VIII and Q. Elizabeth to the Haringtons of Wolphege', Miscellanea Genealogica et Heraldica, new ser., 3 (1880), 236–7, 269–72 · T. D. Whitaker, A history of Richmondshire, 2 vols. (1823) · R. Somerville, The duchy of Lancaster, 1 (1953) · S. Walker, The Lancastrian affinity, 1361–1399 (1990) · M. Jones, 'Richard III and the Stanleys', Richard III and the north, ed. R. Horrox (1986) · R. Horrox, Richard III: a study of service (1989) · J. C. Dickinson, 'Three pre-Reformation documents concerning south Cumbria', Transactions of the Cumberland and Westmorland Antiquarian and Archaeological Society, new ser., 86 (1986) · M. Halliday, a description of the monument and effigies in Porlock church, Somerset (1882)
Likenesses effigies (John Harrington and Joan Dacre), Cartmel Priory, Cumbria · effigies (John Harrington and Elizabeth Courtenay), Porlock parish church, Somerset

Harrington, James (d. 1485?). See under Harrington family (per. c.1300–1512).

Harrington, James [formerly Sir James Harrington, third baronet] (bap. 1607, d. 1680), politician, was baptized on 30 December 1607 at Merton in Oxfordshire, the first son of Sir Edward Harrington, second baronet (d. 1653), of Ridlington, Rutland, and Margery (c.1578–1658), daughter and coheir of John D'Oyley of Merton. Nothing is known of his early years or education but he was knighted in 1628. On 2 August 1632 he married Catherine (1617–1675), daughter and coheir of Sir Edmund Wright of Swakeleys, Middlesex, one-time lord mayor of London. They had seven sons and nine daughters. In 1639 the privy council ordered that Harrington be placed in custody for default of muster, doubtless indicating his opposition to the war with the Scots. This act of opposition did not manifest itself in a political vacuum. Harrington's family had some relation by marriage to the Huntingdonshire Montagues, a very prominent political dynasty. Sir James evidently also enjoyed significant connections with City politics, which came to the fore when he sided with the parliament on the outbreak of civil war in 1642. By 1643 he was major-

general in command of a brigade of five regiments comprising up to 4000 citizen soldiers drawn from London and Westminster. The force had a hand in the victory at the second battle of Newbury. Some years later Harrington, several of whose fifteenth-century ancestors had proud warlike histories, had a medal struck in commemoration of his victorious active military service, which depicted him in full armour.

Harrington's recruitment to the House of Commons for the county of Rutland in July 1646 is difficult to locate in terms of factional politics. The previous year had seen the publication of a highly eirenic tract entitled Noah's Dove which he wrote as a plea for unity among presbyterian and Independent parliamentarians. Within months of his election he was one of the commissioners for the king's journey south from Newcastle and his residence at Holdenby, during which time Harrington and Charles I debated matters of religion and conscience of prime significance to the tortuous progress of the quest for settlement in England. Perhaps in reflection of his own misgivings about the king's firm adherence to the authority of the episcopal church, Harrington dissented early from the vote of 5 December in favour of further peace talks, and on that basis has been described as a revolutionary. However, he cannot realistically be comprehended among that small band of Rump politicians such as Henry Marten and Thomas Grey who wished, for various reasons, to implement sweeping changes in the ancient constitution of England. On 4 January 1649 he was certainly among those who moved the impeachment of those lords who had rejected the ordinance for trial of the king two days earlier. But he probably saw this as a way of deflecting demands that the upper house be shut down altogether. He attended both meetings of the high court of justice which took place on 23 January, and probably also the third, at which the prospect of sentence was delayed by the decision to hear witnesses to the king's crimes, but appeared at no other time during the judicial proceedings against Charles I. Harrington had no hand in the condemnation of the king, and at his appointment to the first Commonwealth council of state in February 1649 he refused to endorse his execution.

Harrington's behaviour during the early years of the parliamentary Commonwealth reflected the essentially eirenic outlook of one who was tolerant, but no tolerationist. He supported the maintenance of tithes, and oversaw the passage of the Adultery Act. In 1651 he was prominent among those MPs who sought to deflect the fury of the Rump against the presbyterian plotter Christopher Love. Harrington was a prominent member of the Rump regime, five times councillor of state, and president in September 1652. He also became joint master of the mint—gaining the opportunity to strike the medals commemorating his military achievements. He succeeded his father as third baronet on 19 May 1653. He had no hand in the affairs of the Commonwealth from the fall of the Rump in 1653 to its restitution in 1659, whereupon he returned to the helm—acting as first president of the new council of state in May—and remained there (even serving on the committee of safety in October that year) until the readmission of the secluded members in February 1660.

He was treated very roughly at the Restoration, despite the best efforts of his kinsman the earl of Lauderdale; for his single day's attendance in the high court of justice Harrington was singled out for confiscation of his estate, degradation of his titles, imprisonment, and even the indignity and immense discomfiture of a sledging. In evasion of these penalties he was concealed for a while by William Dugard, in gratitude for Harrington's own kindness in restraining the punishment meted out to the printer for his role in the publication of the *Eikon basilike* in 1649. But eventually flight became his only option. Harrington passed his exile on the continent, partly at Antwerp. He died in April 1680, in which year his heir, also James, assumed the baronetcy. His spiritual meditations, or *Horae consecrae*, written during these long years, were published posthumously in 1682. Harrington may or may not have been buried surreptitiously at Merton, to the resumption of which, her own inheritance, Lady Harrington had most resourcefully applied herself after her husband's disgrace.   SEAN KELSEY

James Harrington (1611–1677), after Sir Peter Lely, c.1658

Sources GEC, *Baronetage*, 1.53 · I. Grimble, *The Harington family* (1957) · B. Worden, *The Rump Parliament, 1648–1653* (1974) · S. Kelsey, *Inventing a republic: the political culture of the English Commonwealth, 1649–1653* (1997) · CSP dom., 1649–53 · E. Hawkins, *Medallic illustrations of the history of Great Britain and Ireland to the death of George II*, ed. A. W. Franks and H. A. Grueber, 1 (1885); repr. (1978), 406

Likenesses medal, 1653, repro. in Hawkins, *Medallic illustrations*, ed. Franks and Grueber, vol. 1, p. 406 · portrait, repro. in Grimble, *Harington family*

Wealth at death own assessment of estate in 1661 suggested annual income, after service of debt, of £284; however property forfeit to crown for life: Grimble, *Harington family*, 227

Harrington, James (1611–1677), political theorist, was born on 3 January 1611 at Upton, Northamptonshire, the eldest son of Sir Sapcote Harrington of Rand in Lincolnshire (d. 1629) and Jane (d. 1619), daughter of Sir William Samwell (or Samuell) of Upton. His immediate family was a minor branch of the ancient and far-flung Harrington family, which had included royal favourites and generations of civic dignitaries and was related to the high nobility by either descent or marriage; his first biographer, John Toland, cited a seventeenth-century antiquary to the effect that eight dukes, three marquesses, seventy earls, twenty-seven viscounts, and thirty-six barons were descended from or related to his great-grandfather (Toland, para. 1). He was the grandson of Sir James Harrington, first baronet, of Ridlington, and was the cousin of Sir James Harrington, third baronet, of Ridlington (unhelpfully for historians, most Harrington eldest sons were called either James or John); the second of these James Harringtons was a prominent parliamentarian MP, a military commander during the civil war, and a member of a parliamentary commission which supervised the captivity of Charles I and some of his transfers between residences. He attended the early sessions of the high court of justice which tried Charles (even though he was neither present when it passed sentence, nor one of

the signatories to his death warrant), and served several times as member and twice as president of the council of state. Several other Harringtons were also associated with the parliamentarian side, and a letter survives to suggest that Clarendon viewed the whole extended Harrington family with hostility, particularly on account of the activities of this Sir James Harrington (H. Harington, *Nugae*, 200). But although both Sir James and his cousin were with the king at Carisbrooke, there is no suggestion of any personal closeness between them.

Education, foreign travel, interests, and personality The James Harrington who is the subject of this article was never knighted and held no public office. Little is known of his financial circumstances, but he seems to have been comfortably off from inherited properties. He was able to live as a private scholar on his estates and, from the mid-1650s until his death, in a house named Little Ambry near Dean's Yard, Westminster, and to provide for his brother and three sisters, as well as his stepmother, two half-brothers, and two stepsisters, his father having married again after the death of James's mother. The family was remarkably close. Two of his sisters who married well, Elisabeth into the Assheton (or Ashton) family and Anne into the Evelyn family, were especially devoted to him. He made his brother William's children his heirs at his death; he himself died childless. In 1675, only two years before his death, he married a Mrs Dayrell, his 'old sweetheart' (*Brief Lives*, ed. Dick, 285), the daughter of Sir Marmaduke Dayrell (or Dorell) of Buckinghamshire. In person he was reckoned very good company, an excellent conversationalist, amiable, and generous. He had no personal enemies and many devoted friends, and was highly gregarious. One of his friends, the diarist John Aubrey, described him as 'of middling stature', thick-set, with bright eyes and 'thick, moist curled hair' (*Brief Lives*, ed. Clark, 1.293). He shared the enthusiasm of his times for tobacco, coffee, and (it appears) Rhenish wines.

Nothing definite is known of Harrington's childhood, except that it was spent at the family's manor at Rand, a hamlet about 10 miles from Lincoln, or of his education, except that he attended Trinity College, Oxford, as a gentleman commoner for two years, going up at what was then the relatively late age of eighteen in 1629 and leaving without a degree. Archbishop Laud became chancellor of Oxford during this time, and William Chillingworth was briefly Harrington's tutor, but Harrington does not seem to have attached significance to either event. He subsequently registered at the inns of court, but left after a few weeks. Harrington had no interest in law or in academic jurisprudence, and his antipathy to lawyers was very marked in his later writings: his *Oceana* even excluded them from parliament. He inherited his father's estate in 1629 while legally still a minor but the indulgence of his guardian, his grandmother Lady Samwell, allowed him to travel abroad in 1631 and to remain there for several years. He first enlisted in an English volunteer regiment in the Netherlands to sustain the cause of the elector palatine, whose wife, Elizabeth, daughter of James I and VI, had been tutored by a distant relation of his. Harrington seems to have seen no fighting and the enterprise itself was fruitless, but he evidently made a good impression at the court of the elector since he not only accompanied him to Denmark, but at the age of twenty-one became in effect his agent in England. He later acted the same part for the elector's son Charles, successfully petitioning parliament in 1644 for funds for the latter's 'urgent Necessities' (Blitzer, 22). He subsequently travelled in the Netherlands and in Germany, France, and Italy. According to Herbert, Harrington spoke German, Italian, and French, presumably having become competent in these languages during his travels. In Italy on a visit to Rome in either 1634 or 1636 he refused to kiss the pope's foot (according to Toland, para. 4); he also visited Venice. No personal records remain of any impressions he may have gathered on his travels, and there is no evidence to show whether his interests at that time were already political, or what (if any) books he purchased. Confident assertions to the contrary made by later commentators all rest only on Toland, whose account is not implausible but is unsupported by any evidence, from him or anyone else, and is in at least one instance avowedly conjectural. Harrington did, however, stress the importance of travel as well as the study of history for the understanding and practice of politics. Although he 'retired to his library' for years on end, no inventory of its contents at any point remains. He was unquestionably highly erudite in *humaniores litterae*, even publishing a translation of Virgil's *Aeneid* (2 vols., 1658 and 1659); according to Aubrey, Harrington's close friend Henry Neville dissuaded him from further efforts at poetry. By the 1650s he had an extensive knowledge of the history and political literature of the Italian republics, especially Venice, and in time became very familiar with British and continental 'antiquities'. He was also extremely well-versed in Old Testament history. Conversely he seems to have known and cared nothing about contemporary neo-scholastic political theory or its Grotian offshoots; although he cited Hugo Grotius frequently in his writings, it was almost invariably as a theologian and an authority on scripture.

Career before writing *Oceana* Neither the date of Harrington's return from the continent (perhaps as late as 1636)

nor his activities during Britain's critical political period until 1647 are known; he is, however, said to have twice lent substantial sums of money to parliament in 1641 and 1642 (Blitzer, 21). An unconfirmed story (Toland, para. 4) has him accompanying Charles I to Scotland during the first bishops' war in 1639 as gentleman of the privy chamber extraordinary; another (Wood, *Ath. Oxon.*, 3.1115) is that he offered to stand for Stamford in the parliamentarian interest; he was perhaps collecting money for the parliamentarian cause in Lincolnshire in 1645, but it seems entirely unlikely that he was parliamentary commissioner for Holland in Lincolnshire in 1647 and 1648 (Blitzer, 23). Toland, apparently the last person with access to Harrington's papers, knew of no public office of any kind held by Harrington, and his assertion that 'his natural inclination to study kept him from seeking after any public employments' (Toland, para. 8) was perhaps his attempt to explain why Harrington in this respect did not follow either family tradition or the practice of his relatives. Certainly, however, he became with Sir Thomas Herbert a gentleman groom of the royal bedchamber, attending on Charles I during his captivity at Holmby House from May 1647 to the end of that year, and again at Carisbrooke and at Hurst Castle in 1648. He was among the king's servants who bravely stood up to Cornet Joyce's attempt to remove the king from Holmby to London by force.

Charles, to whom Harrington was personally devoted, greatly valued his company and conversation but there is no independent evidence for the topics of their conversations, and Aubrey's assertion that 'the Kinge would not endure to heare of a Commonwealth' (*Brief Lives*, ed. Dick, 282) is not supported by any independent evidence. In his *Memoirs* Herbert (admittedly mostly infuriatingly vague about Harrington) says nothing of it, although he might have been expected to allude to the fact in view of Harrington's subsequent reputation. He mentions only that the king asked Harrington and himself for their verdict on his translation of Dr Saunderson's *De juramentis*, all three of them being very considerable linguists. According to Toland's reworking of the story they talked politics (which seems inevitable) but not of commonwealths. Nothing whatever is reliably established about Harrington's opinions at this time, except that he freely expressed favourable opinions on the king in general, and his conduct over the treaty of Newport in particular, and it was because of this that some parliamentarians doubted his reliability and secured his dismissal from Charles's attendance, to the latter's chagrin. According to Toland and also an otherwise unknown royalist, J. Lesley, who condemned him as a traitor to his monarch, family, and class for his republicanism, Harrington was present with Charles on the latter's scaffold on 31 January 1649, but no contemporary account mentions anything of the sort, and according to Herbert, who attended Charles almost to the end, only Bishop Juxon was present (Herbert, 134–5; H. Harington, *Nugae*, 82). The execution, however, unquestionably distressed Harrington immeasurably. Aubrey records both his 'zeal and passion' in his frequent references to the king (presumably in the later 1650s), and also his claim that he 'contracted a disease', perhaps some mental breakdown, as a result of the execution (*Brief Lives*, ed. Dick, 283).

Harrington had by this time returned to live at Rand. Nothing more is known until 1656, by which time he had recently moved to Little Ambry in Westminster, and had (according to his own account) been working somewhat under two years on his masterpiece, *Oceana*. The work appeared between September and November 1656, in two editions published simultaneously, both in London: one 'printed by J. Streater, for Livewell Chapman', the other 'printed for D. Pakeman'; each edition has a second title-page with Harrington's name and a dedication to Oliver Cromwell. Harrington claimed that political obstruction hindered the book's publication, and according to Toland it was the intercession of Cromwell's favourite daughter that eventually made publication possible (Toland, para. 14). While the approximate ideological context of *Oceana* can be satisfactorily reconstructed, Harrington's personal and political connections at this time cannot. By 1658 his circle included persons associated with the Good Old Cause, anti-Cromwellians, and even the former Levellers John Wildman and Maximilian Petty, as well as the radical John Streater, one of the publishers of *Oceana*. Harrington counted Henry Neville MP, Andrew Marvell, and Aubrey himself among his close friends but it is not known when or how his association with them began. Perhaps Neville encouraged him to write *Oceana*, but Aubrey is again the sole witness for his claim that Thomas Hobbes suspected Neville of actually having had a hand in its composition; Aubrey gives no evidence for his claim, though there is no reason why he should have invented it. Hobbes's *Behemoth* (written about 1668), however, betrays no knowledge of *Oceana* and does not mention Neville. There is nothing to suggest that Harrington was not the sole author.

Oceana and Harrington's career during the late interregnum
Oceana, on which Harrington's contemporary and much more his posthumous reputation rested, earned him not only disciples but also critics, although not as many of the latter as he seems to have wished. Hobbes, whom he had attacked in *Oceana* (albeit highly respectfully) for having failed, among other faults, to distinguish between authority and power, never replied. Harrington thought of his critics as principally clerics and Oxford men, although the most able of them, Matthew Wren, was neither. Harrington answered him in *The Prerogative of Popular Government* (1657), and again in *Politicaster*, a much slighter work of 1659. During the confused period following Oliver Cromwell's death on 3 September 1658, Harringtonian opinions about the political order conducive to a permanent settlement for England were frequently voiced in Richard Cromwell's parliament in 1659, but to no avail: Harrington's main concern at this time was to prevent the restoration of anything like a hereditary House of Lords or a nominated replacement, but the parliament voted for the restoration of the Lords. The 'republicans' in this parliament included a few supporters of 'classical republican'

ideas like Harrington's (eight or ten according to *Brief Lives*, ed. Dick, 284) out of perhaps fifty opponents of the continuation of military oligarchy, or monarchy, or a restored House of Lords, but they could not agree.

Harrington's most intensive period of publication, as well as his most direct participation in Commonwealth politics, began after the dissolution of this parliament by the army and the restoration of the Rump Parliament in May 1659. On 6 July 1659 Harrington's circle presented to the restored Rump *The Humble Petition of Divers Well-Affected Persons*. It advocated a 'senate' (an upper house) of 300 members, one-third of them subject to election annually (the favourite Harringtonian idea of 'rotation'), and a much larger popular assembly. Both parts of this bicameral legislature were to be elected by ballot (another favourite Harringtonian idea) in equal constituencies. Parliament politely ignored the proposal. Some of the most ardent republicans such as Sir Henry Vane were bitterly opposed to Harringtonian ideas, especially since Harrington rejected the republic ruled by the godly advocated by Vane and Milton (against whom Harrington also intended to write) as much as any other kind of permanent oligarchy. Harrington propagated his ideas, which were sufficiently well known to be derided in pasquills and newsbooks, in the 'Rota', a sort of club or select debating society which met from October 1659 in Miles's Coffee House at the Turke's Head, New Palace Yard, on the Thames Embankment. Aubrey remarks on the high quality of the discussions, the numbers and salience of those attending, and also on the fact that proposals were formally voted on; Samuel Pepys was prepared to pay to become a member.

Harrington's political theory Harrington professed himself a devotee and a restorer (following in Machiavelli's footsteps) of what he termed 'ancient prudence', by which he meant the political institutions and wisdom of the ancient Greeks, Romans, and Israelites that constituted a 'government of laws, not of men'. According to Harrington, ancient prudence taught that freedom and political stability depend crucially on a strict separation of tasks between the people and its 'natural aristocracy'—that is, those in a state or any other association whose moral authority and superior competence the rest will readily acknowledge. The natural aristocracy must have the exclusive right to 'debate', in other words to deliberate, advise, and propose what is to be done. The people must have an equally exclusive right of 'result', that is, to decide on law and policy without discussion. Any confusion between the two roles of 'debate' and 'result' would be fatal, not least because this institutional separation for Harrington guaranteed that the self-interest of each assembly would be neutralized by its dependence on the other.

According to the subtle historical analysis which Harrington used to substantiate his 'model' (or blueprint) of a new political order in *Oceana* and later writings, England from the time of Henry VII onwards had neither the concentrations of property nor (consequently) of political and especially military power that either a stable absolute monarchy or a hereditary aristocracy required. Harrington regarded the redistribution of property following the dissolution of the monasteries as particularly significant. Nor was there now any reason to attempt to restore the always inherently unstable modern (or 'Gothic') balance of monarchy, aristocracy, and democracy, characteristic especially of feudal monarchy, which Harrington dismissively called 'modern prudence'. Its instability had merely been disguised during Queen Elizabeth's reign by her 'love-tricks' with her people. The current 'balance' of property ownership ruled out monarchy. It also precluded aristocracy, which could in any event never survive without a hereditary monarchy, and even then only as the 'perpetual wrestling match' which passed for 'modern prudence'. Only an 'equal commonwealth' offered any prospect for a political order that would be permanent, indeed 'immortal', in that it had no internal causes of decay, and would not be subject to external defeat either. Harrington, like Machiavelli, held that a popular commonwealth must be expansionist and martial.

The central institution of Harrington's model is the bicameral parliament, composed of a deliberative 'senate' of the prudent with 300 members, and a much larger assembly of the people ('the prerogative tribe') as the supreme legislature and judiciary. One of Harrington's more fanciful notions was that the latter, composed of well over 1000 representatives, was to vote without any kind of debate on proposals from the senate. Both chambers were to be indirectly elected by means of the 'ballot', an immensely complicated system combining selection by lot of voters who then elected delegates, beginning with the parishes and thence via the hundreds to the counties, which in turn elected the senators and representatives. The model entirely ignored the boroughs apart from London and Westminster. The executive of the commonwealth was to be elected by and from the senate for one-year terms, and was to consist of two chief magistrates ('consuls'), various commissioners, two 'censors' (who were also to serve as the chancellors of the two universities), and four councils (of state, of war, of religion, and of trade). The whole order was to be defended by a civic militia, divided according to property into cavalry and foot, and by age into a Home Guard and marching regiments; its officers were to be elected, but with an age qualification in addition. All administrative and judicial officials for local government were also to be elective, their elections and those of the parliamentarians and officers of the militia taking place at the same time. All public offices were subject to 'rotation', and all holders of public office were to be salaried. Underpinning the whole order was to be an 'Agrarian Law' limiting how much property any individual might acquire or inherit, in order to prevent excessive concentrations of property (discussed in detail in Davis, *Utopia*). His terms 'foundation' and 'superstructure' (the institutional order), and his assertion that Oceana's public order was free from 'contradictions' have acquired misleading connotations. In fact the 'foundation' or 'fundamental laws' of Oceana were the ballot and

the agrarian law; the 'property' that concerned Harrington was property in land; and the link between political power and property was the latter's capacity to sustain a 'militia', in other words, military might.

Harrington's particular animus was directed against any permanent oligarchy, whether clerical (in which regard he recognized himself, as others recognized him, as having much in common with Hobbes), godly, military, or hereditary. He presented himself as an aggressive advocate of 'popular government' (or even 'democracy') and 'equality' at a time when these were virtually synonymous with disorder. His use of these terms and of the whole vocabulary of classical republicanism was, however, idiosyncratic and perhaps deliberately provocative. His model commonwealth was 'popular' and 'equal' in the sense that citizens were rulers and ruled by turns, and that all authority ultimately reposed on popular consent. In any other sense it was markedly aristocratic and hierarchical at every level from local government to the councils of state. Higher property qualifications governed eligibility for the senate, the cavalry, and all high office, as compared to those demanded for representatives, the foot, and minor local offices; some property was, however, a prerequisite even for the franchise. 'The people' of Harrington's 'popular' commonwealth excluded not only women, but also the vague and broad category of 'servants'; divines, lawyers, and bachelors were entitled to vote but not to be elected, as lacking the necessary civic spirit. And the commonwealth was free in that it excluded oppression, but in every other respect the entire purpose of the institutions of Oceana was to place all citizens and office-holders in a position in which they had no alternative but to be virtuous. The design of his model was to ensure that 'no man or men … can have the interest, or, having the interest, can have the power to disturb [the commonwealth] with sedition'. Even former royalists could therefore be safely admitted to citizenship. His preoccupation was not with individual autonomy but with political stability. In his 'government of laws, not of men', the 'laws' ('orders') were the institutional order, and their purpose was to immunize the commonwealth for ever against private interests and factions ('men'), and against any political conflict whatever. And the participation of ordinary citizens was a highly stylized ritual, for there was nothing for them to do, apart from designating holders of public office: the 'orders' were entirely comprehensive and set in stone. For all Harrington's ostentatious classical republicanism, the centrality of representation in his commonwealth was entirely unclassical, he denied any right of resistance and freely acknowledged the need for a sovereign in any commonwealth, he at no point placed any reliance upon the unsecured civic virtue of anyone, and the contemporary whom he most resembles in preoccupations was Hobbes, whom Harrington admired as 'the best writer at this day in the world' (*Political Works*, 423).

Writings after *Oceana* and activities after the Restoration For reasons best known to its author *Oceana* was presented as a fictitious history of the foundation of the commonwealth of Oceana, with lengthy orations, pseudonyms (mostly classical and/or facetious) for places, persons, offices, and institutions, and an elaborate humanist apparatus of citations from authorities, especially regarding Venice, which in many ways served Harrington as a model, notably for the complicated system of balloting to which he was addicted. The fictional format in no way implied that Harrington's proposals were not intended seriously or that he thought of himself as writing some kind of speculative utopia: on the contrary his analysis of the basis of 'empire' (government) in general provided in his view the only grounds on which any proposal for a permanent settlement for England, and indeed Scotland and Ireland, might be sustained. But in the last year of the Commonwealth Harrington issued numerous pamphlets, now expressly addressed to England, describing the new order he was advocating in the precise detail crucial to a political theory which relied heavily on the apt ordering of institutions to secure the well-being and permanence of the polity, but now without any of the prolixity, allegories, or 'fancy' of his *magnum opus*. And whereas in *Oceana* he had appeared to cast Cromwell in the role of a classical lawgiver, in these writings he offered to the public at large all the knowledge that was essential to *The Art of Lawgiving* (the title of one of the pamphlets, 1659), in the form of a model: as for example in his *Brief directions, showing how a fit and perfect model of popular government may be made, found or understood* (1659), *Aphorisms Political*, (2nd edn, 1659), and *The Rota, or, A Model of a Free State or Equall Commonwealth* (1660). His other concern in these writings was to defend his interpretation of the Israelite commonwealth as by divine institution a popular commonwealth, depending entirely on human prudence like the other commonwealths of ancient prudence; so does the Christian commonwealth, which is as firmly subordinated to the secular (but now popular) polity by Harrington as it was by Hobbes. Harrington proposed an inclusive national church without bishops, with salaried ministers selected for parishes by the two universities and accepted or rejected by their congregations after a period of probation. Equally, however, there was to be freedom of conscience for all Christians except Roman Catholics.

In February 1660, after the arrival of General Monck in London, the Rota ceased to meet. Harrington also ceased to publish. He was, however, presumably still working on *A System of Politics*, his only political work that remained unpublished in his lifetime. It evidences no diminution in his intellectual powers, but also no sense on his part of any need to revise his previous ideas in the light of the Restoration, which he had not anticipated before 1660. Even in 1660 he thought it would be impermanent if it were to take place. He was not molested at the Restoration, and is even said to have outlined a model for a restored monarchy for the use of the royal court. But on 28 December 1661 he was arrested and his papers were seized. This was perhaps because of the malice of Clarendon against the Harringtons generally. Harrington's sisters claimed that the arrest was based on a (very unlikely) confusion, since the warrant was in the name of Sir James Harrington

(Toland, para. 32); the latter had been specifically exempted from the Act of Indemnity, condemned in 1661 to life imprisonment and forfeiture of all his possessions, and was then in hiding. But more probably Harrington was arrested on suspicion of complicity with the Bow Street circle of Commonwealthsmen 'plotters' which included John Wildman and Praisegod Barebone. He was imprisoned without trial in the Tower and badly treated there until his sisters Elizabeth, Lady Assheton, and Anne Evelyn bribed the lieutenant. He was interrogated by Lauderdale (who acknowledged that he was a remote 'kinsman' of Harrington) and others to establish any recent contacts with the plotters; Harrington's record of the interrogation was published by Toland. His sisters obtained a writ of habeas corpus in April 1662, but to frustrate it he was spirited away to St Nicholas Island, off the coast of Plymouth. After his brother and his uncle posted a bond for the enormous sum of £1000 (Toland says £5000), he was released to the fort at Plymouth because of his gravely deteriorated mental and physical health. Apparently treatment with guaiacum, an addictive drug in vogue at the time, which he took in his coffee, made his mental condition much worse. As a result of a petition by the earl of Bath to Charles II on account of Harrington's alarming physical and mental condition, a warrant was issued for his release.

Harrington lived for another fifteen years in Little Ambry, but very little is known about this period of his life. Robert Hooke, who was taken by Aubrey to visit him, thought him simply 'mad' (*Brief Lives*, ed. Dick, 100). Toland treats Harrington's late marriage as evidence that he 'was not himself' (Toland, para. 41). He certainly suffered from intermittent delusions, notably that his perspiration turned into flies, but was otherwise rational and sociable, according to Aubrey who continued to visit him. He was looked after by his 'true friend' Henry Neville. He never recovered his health, suffering from gout and palsy, and in his last year he was paralysed by a stroke. Wood claims that after his release from imprisonment he travelled in Italy, but this seems highly unlikely, given his uncertain health, and is mentioned by no one else, though Echard embroidered Wood's story into the claim that he was 'seeking out new Models of Government' there (Echard, 3.439). Harrington died at Little Ambry on 10 September 1677, according to the Westminster Abbey burial register, and was buried in St Margaret's Church, Westminster. An epitaph composed by Andrew Marvell was not used; the one that was used records him (inaccurately, it seems) as dying on the seventh day of September, in his sixty-sixth year, AD 1677.

Such of Harrington's papers as remained were kept by his sister Elizabeth Assheton, and subsequently by Dorothy Bellingham, his half-sister, who made them available to Toland; their subsequent fate is unknown. Virtually nothing in his own hand is still extant. Knowledge of Harrington's life derives principally from John Toland's introduction to the first edition of his *Oceana … and other Works*, and from John Aubrey, to whose *Brief Lives* Toland did not have access except via Wood, whom Aubrey had supplied with many details.

Posthumous reputation and reception Wood claims that after the Restoration Harrington was 'reputed no better than a whimsical and crack'd brain'd person' (Wood, *Ath. Oxon.*, 3.1120), and Montesquieu regarded him as a utopian. Hume, however, thought much better of his work. Nevertheless Harringtonian themes already re-emerged during the exclusion crisis, and in the eighteenth century Harrington became one of the principal authorities in England and especially in America for Commonwealthsmen; the publisher of Toland's first edition had already inserted advertisements for the works of two other Commonwealthsmen heroes, Algernon Sidney and Milton. From Toland onwards Harrington's principle that 'Empire follows the balance' was regarded as a scientific natural law. He was especially valued for the intimate link he had asserted between liberty and civic virtue, and conversely between corruption and arbitrary government. Ironically, Harringtonian themes figured prominently in the defence of the restored and hereditary upper house as a 'screen and bank' against monarchical tyranny and corruption, and in the eighteenth-century attack on what Harrington had regarded as impossible, namely 'standing (that is to say professional and permanent) armies in time of peace', funded out of taxation as instruments of arbitrary government.

More dramatically, perhaps, Harrington was clearly being read by radical lawyers during the French Revolution, and the French constitution of 1799 (at least until it was subverted by Napoleon) was clearly modelled on parts of the *Oceana*. He was not one of the English radicals of the revolution lionized by nineteenth-century progressives. But he was invoked by R. H. Tawney in a highly influential British Academy lecture as the spokesman for 'the operation of impersonal, constant and, it might be measurable, forces, which, to be controlled, needed to be understood'—of social engineering no less (R. H. Tawney, 'Harrington's interpretation of his age', *Studies in History: British Academy Lectures*, ed. L. Sutherland, 1966, 243). His restoration as a pioneer in applying the theories of Machiavelli and of other civic humanists to English political society and social conditions had to wait until the appearance of the first critical edition of his writings in 1977, edited by J. G. A. Pocock as *The Political Works of James Harrington*.

H. M. HÖPFL

Sources J. Toland, 'Life of James Harrington', in *The 'Oceana' of James Harrington, and his other works*, ed. J. Toland (1700), xi–xxxvi • *Aubrey's Brief lives*, ed. O. L. Dick (1949); repr. (1976) • *Brief lives, chiefly of contemporaries, set down by John Aubrey, between the years 1669 and 1696*, ed. A. Clark, 2 vols. (1898) • T. Herbert and others, *Memoirs of the two last years of the reign of … King Charles I* (1702) • Wood, *Ath. Oxon.*, new edn • *The political works of James Harrington*, ed. J. G. A. Pocock (1977) • I. Grimble, *The Harington family* (1957) • C. Blitzer, *An immortal commonwealth: the political thought of James Harrington* (1960) • H. F. Russell Smith, *Harrington and his 'Oceana': a study of a seventeenth-century utopia and its influence in America* (1914) • J. C. Davis, *Utopia and the ideal society* (1981), chaps. 8–9 • J. Scott, 'The rapture of motion: James Harrington's republicanism', *Political discourse in early modern Britain*, ed. N. Phillipson and Q. Skinner (1993), 139–63 • G. Burgess, 'Repacifying the polity: the responses of Hobbes and Harrington to the "crisis of the common law"', *Soldiers, writers and statesmen of the English revolution*, ed. I. Gentles and others (1998), 202–28 • J. C. Davis, 'Equality in an unequal commonwealth: James Harrington's republicanism and the meaning of equality', *Soldiers, writers and statesmen of the English revolution*, ed. I. Gentles and others (1998), 229–42 • J. Harington, *Nugae antiquae*, 2 vols. (1769–75); 2nd edn in 3 vols., ed. H. Harington (1779) • L. Echard, *History of England from the Restoration of King Charles II* (1718), vol. 3 of *History of England*

Likenesses attrib. A. Van de Venne, oils, c.1635, NPG • oils, c.1658 (after P. Lely), NPG [*see illus.*] • W. Hollar, etching (after P. Lely, c.1658), BM; repro. in J. Harrington, *Discourses* (1660) • P. Lely, portrait; now lost • J. Marchi, mezzotint (after unknown artist), BM, NPG • M. Vandergucht, engraving (after P. Lely), repro. in J. Harrington, *Works* (1700)

Harrington, James (1664–1693), lawyer, was born in 1664, probably at Waltham Abbey, Essex, the younger son of James Harrington (*fl.* 1660–1665). He may well be the James Harrington who was baptized on 24 April 1664 at St Andrew's, Holborn, and whose mother's name was Anne. He was educated at Westminster School, where he was elected a king's scholar in 1679, and whence he was further elected to a studentship at Christ Church Cathedral, Oxford, matriculating from the college on 17 December 1683. (Shortly afterwards, probably in 1684, he was admitted to the Inner Temple.) In Oxford he supplemented his income by writing verses and composing speeches for undergraduates to deliver when seeking their degrees. He took his BA on 28 May 1687, his MA on 8 May 1690.

Harrington was called to the bar at the Inner Temple on 2 June 1690. His reputation preceded him: in 1689, for example, he had been employed to oversee, and to act as solicitor in, the celebrated case of Henry Wildgoose, a dispute between the university and the city of Oxford (Wildgoose was an Oxford tradesman who attempted to avoid undertaking city office by being matriculated as a privileged servant of the university). Sir John Holt, the lord chief justice, found emphatically in favour of the city, but this Williamite snub to the university had little to do with Harrington's efforts; indeed, through his private practice on the Oxford circuit, and in London, and his participation in a series of local disputes in the 1690s, he soon began to acquire a reputation for his considerable abilities in the common law. Although he was the author of a poem in Latin hexameters on the death of Charles II, published in the second volume of *Musarum Anglicanarum analecta* (1699), many of his appearances in print were prose tracts occasioned by religious, political, or legal controversies.

Harrington's *Some Reflexions upon a Treatise call'd 'Pietas Romana & Parisiensis'* (1688) was thus a response to the account that Abraham Woodhead, the absentee Catholic fellow of University College, had published in 1687; *A Letter from a Person of Honour* (1690) supported the candidacies of Montagu Venables-Bertie, who as Lord Norris was heir to the earl of Abingdon, and Sir Robert Jenkinson, bt, for election as knights of the shire; *Roger L'Estrange's Queries Considered* (1690) replied, and was appended, to the tory journalist's anonymous pamphlet, *Some Queries Concerning* the *Election of Members for the Ensuing Parliament* (1690), an imprint frequently attributed to Harrington himself; and two works, one a broadsheet, both entitled *The Case of the University of Oxford* (and both published in 1690), concerned a bill before parliament to confirm the colleges' charters. The longer tract, 'Presented to the honourable House of Commons on Friday Jan. 24. 1689/90', according to the title-page, was also included in *A Defence of the Rights and Priviledges of the University of Oxford* (1690), another publication often ascribed to Harrington but the bulk of which was by Gerard Langbaine. Harrington was further engaged in negotiating with the Stationers' Company on behalf of the university in a dispute over the privilege of receiving a copy of every book published, and about which he wrote in *Reasons for Reviving and Continuing the Act for the Regulation of Printing* (1692).

By January 1691 Harrington was sufficiently trusted to make routine motions on behalf of the university in king's bench. The actions related to the involved quarrel between Arthur Bury, the rector of Exeter College, the hostile response to whose theologically controversial work *The Naked Gospel* (1690) coincided with his no less disputed ejection of James Colmer, a fellow of the college, and its visitor, the Rt Revd Jonathan Trelawney, the bishop of Exeter. These separate, but coeval and inevitably associated, affairs, and the pamphlets they attracted, Harrington considered in *An Account of the Proceedings of the … Bishop of Exeter* (1690), *A Vindication of Mr James Colmar* (1691), and *A Defence of the Proceedings of the … Visitor and Fellows of Exeter College* (1691). Harrington also edited the Revd George Stradling's *Sermons and Discourses upon Several Occasions* (1692), to which edition he added a life of the minister, and contributed the preface to the first volume, and the introduction to the second volume, of the first edition of Anthony Wood's *Athenae Oxonienses* (1691–2). And in 1692 Harrington was employed to argue at a hearing before Holt, the lord chief justice, opposing the recently appointed solicitor-general, Thomas Trevor. Four or five months before his death Harrington moved to Lincoln's Inn. His contemporaries spoke highly of his abilities, his honesty, and generosity. Warmly anti-Catholic, and suspicious of non-conformity, he appeared to have a successful career at the bar, to say the least, ahead of him.

Harrington died on 23 November 1693 within the precincts of Lincoln's Inn, and was buried on 30 November in the north transept of Christ Church Cathedral, Oxford.

JONATHAN PRITCHARD

Sources Wood, *Ath. Oxon.*, new edn, 4.392–5 · Wood, *Ath. Oxon.: Fasti* (1815), 400, 409 · *Old Westminsters*, 1.428 · Foster, *Alum. Oxon.*, 1500–1714, 2.653–4 · J. Harrington, 'preface to the first edn', Wood, *Ath. Oxon.*, new edn, 1.clvii–clxi · D. Lemmings, *Gentlemen and barristers: the inns of court and the English bar, 1680–1730* (1990), 114–15, 120 · A. Crossley, 'City and university', *Hist. U. Oxf.* 4: *17th-cent. Oxf.*, 105–34 · N. Tyacke, 'Religious controversy', *Hist. U. Oxf.* 4: *17th-cent. Oxf.*, 569–620 · G. V. Bennett, 'Against the tide: Oxford under William III', *Hist. U. Oxf.* 5: *18th-cent. Oxf.*, 31–60 · G. V. Bennett, 'University, society and church, 1688–1714', *Hist. U. Oxf.* 5: *18th-cent. Oxf.*, 359–400 · E. G. W. Bill, *Education at Christ Church, Oxford, 1660–1800* (1988), 230 · will, PRO, PROB 11/418, sig. 34

Archives BL, corresp. and papers, Add. MS 36707 · Bodl. Oxf., corresp., Ballard MS 22 | York Minster, papers on Scottish succession and 'Apologie for poetrie'

Wealth at death £40 specific bequests; many small items of jewellery worth 10s. each; number of further bequests of books, clothes, and personal effects: will, PRO, PROB 11/418, sig. 34

Harrington, John, first Lord Harrington (c.1281–1347). *See under* Harrington family (*per.* c.1300–1512).

Harrington, Sir John (d. 1359). *See under* Harrington family (*per.* c.1300–1512).

Harrington, John, second Lord Harrington (c.1328–1363). *See under* Harrington family (*per.* c.1300–1512).

Harrington, John, fourth Baron Harrington (1384–1418). *See under* Harrington family (*per.* c.1300–1512).

Harrington, Sir Nicholas (b. 1345/6, d. in or before 1404). *See under* Harrington family (*per.* c.1300–1512).

Harrington, Robert, third Baron Harrington (1356–1406). *See under* Harrington family (*per.* c.1300–1512).

Harrington, Robert (1751–1837), surgeon and writer on science, was born in Carlisle, the eighth of nine children of Robert Harrington (d. 1753), a surgeon and apothecary, and his wife, Jane, the daughter of Henry Hall, a former alderman of the city. He was baptized on 26 August 1751. Harrington was admitted to the Carlisle grammar school in 1760 and later claimed to have studied at Edinburgh University, naming Joseph Black as one of his teachers. He became a member of the Company of Surgeons of London some time before 1781, and was described as 'MD' on his marriage to Margaret Benson on 28 September 1789. The marriage produced at least one child, a son, Henry, who was baptized on 23 February 1793 and died in 1815. Harrington lived almost all his life in Carlisle, where he practised surgery from his residence in Abbey Street. He became an honorary freeman of the city in 1785.

Harrington wrote a series of inelegant and idiosyncratic works on chemistry, medicine, and natural philosophy, between 1781 and 1819. His first book, *A Philosophical and General Enquiry into the … Principles of Animal and Vegetable Life* (1781), established the pattern of his writings and their poor reception among his contemporaries. He assumed a version of the phlogiston theory, claiming that phlogiston ('fixed fire') was the principle of life, and insisting (against the prevailing views of Joseph Priestley and others) that it was removed from air in the course of respiration. A critic in the *Monthly Review* took the author to task for interpreting phenomena through the distorting lens of a preconceived hypothesis, and for lacking the laboratory experience that was necessary to ground such theories. His next book, the anonymously published *Thoughts on the Properties and Formation of the Different Kinds of Air* (1785), was quickly attributed by a reviewer to Harrington, on the basis of its 'uncouthness of literary composition, [and] … loose, desultory, inconclusive mode of reasoning' (Chisholme, *Thoughts*, 449).

In the *Letter Addressed to Dr. Priestley, Messrs. Cavendish, Lavoisier, and Kerwan* [sic] (1786), Harrington continued to uphold his peculiar version of the phlogiston theory, which he accused Priestley, Henry Cavendish, and Richard Kirwan of having stolen from him and then abandoned. Having failed to gain a hearing for his work under his own name, he published *A Treatise on Air* (1791) under the pseudonym Richard Bewley, though this disguise too was easily penetrated by the critics. His campaign against contemporary chemists—increasingly turned against the new theories of Antoine Lavoisier—continued to unfold in rambling and unstructured books, where experimental remarks were punctuated by passages of colourful invective: *Chemical Essays* (1794), *Some New Experiments … upon Heat* (1798), and *The Death-Warrant of the French Theory of Chemistry* (1804).

In *A New System on Fire and Planetary Life* (1796) Harrington resuscitated the cosmological dimension of his speculations, which had already been present in his first work. He developed Sir William Herschel's vision of the sun and planets as habitable domains, sharing the same provision of life-giving fire. *Some Experiments and Observations on Sig. Volta's Electrical Pile* (1801) showed him as an electrical experimenter, convinced that electricity was a compound of fire with an acid. On this basis, he disputed the claim that the voltaic pile acted to decompose water into its constituent gases, thereby again putting himself at odds with the leading experimenters of his day. In his final book, *An Elucidation and Extension of the Harringtonian System of Chemistry* (1819), he attacked Humphry Davy at some length; his mastery of the voltaic pile as an instrument of analysis led Harrington (p. 81) to dub him a 'chemical Hercules'.

Harrington was evidently not dismayed by his contemporaries' unwillingness to accept his theories; in 1804 he wrote: 'I stand alone, insulated in an obscure corner of the kingdom; but, I hope, *firm as a rock*, upon the pedestal of Truth' (R. Harrington, *The Death-Warrant of the French Theory of Chemistry*, 1804, 133). The one exception to the general indifference was the view taken by the short-lived journal, *The Medical Spectator* (1792–3), published in two volumes under the editorship of the Enfield physician Dr John Sherwen. Sherwen dedicated the first volume to Harrington, whose theory that the atmosphere supplied a vital fire to living things he hailed as a significant contribution toward understanding the causes of disease. A correspondent in the journal was, however, obliged to admit that Harrington's writings were 'destitute of the charms of elegance and arrangement' (*Medical Spectator*, 1.117). Harrington died in Carlisle on 14 January 1837.   JAN GOLINSKI

Sources C. R. Hudleston, 'Notes on Dr Robert Harrington of Carlisle', *Transactions of the Cumberland and Westmorland Antiquarian and Archaeological Society*, new ser., 46 (1947), 116–25 · *Medical Spectator*, 1–2 (1791–3) · [W. Bewley], review of Harrington, *Philosophical enquiry into animal and vegetable life*, *Monthly Review*, 66 (1782), 98–102 · [A. Chisholme], review of Harrington, *Thoughts on different kinds of air*, *Monthly Review*, 74 (1786), 449–51 · [A. Chisholme], review of Richard Bewley [pseud.], *Treatise on air*, *Monthly Review*, new ser., 6 (1791), 435–9
Archives BL, corresp. with Sir Joseph Banks, Add. MS 33979

Harrington, Thomas (*d.* 1460). *See under* Harrington family (*per.* c.1300–1512).

Harrington, Timothy Charles (1851–1910), Irish nationalist, was born at Castletown Bere, co. Cork, the son of Denis Harrington and Eileen O'Sullivan. His early education was at a national school, and he was briefly a schoolteacher. In partnership with his brother Edward, he established the *Kerry Sentinel* newspaper in 1877. He began the study of law at Trinity College, Dublin, in 1884, but by then was active in public affairs and did not graduate. Called to the Irish bar in 1887, it was as a barrister that he earned his livelihood. In 1892 he married Elizabeth, second daughter of Dr Edward O'Neill of Dublin.

Actively involved in the Land League from 1880, Harrington was briefly its secretary in 1882. He was Irish nationalist MP for County Westmeath from 1883 to 1885 (having been elected while a prisoner in Mullingar gaol) and for the Harbour division of Dublin from 1885 until his death. He was one of the three secretaries of the Irish National League from its inception in 1882, and was joint author of its constitution. He helped define the pledge by which members of Parnell's party bound themselves to party discipline. One of Parnell's closest advisers in the management of the nationalist movement, his early reputation had been established on the basis of his organizing abilities and his clear political judgement. In 1884–5 he played a leading role in seeking redress for the execution for the Maamtrasna murders of a man almost certainly innocent. Generally credited with the authorship in 1886 of the article from which it took its name, he played a leading role in the Plan of Campaign. He was counsel for Parnell, under Sir Charles Russell, in the Parnell commission of 1888–9.

In 1890 Harrington had no hesitation in taking Parnell's side in the crisis which arose out of the O'Shea divorce case. Deeply attached personally to Parnell, he also recognized the importance politically of the issues on which Parnell chose to fight. However, unlike others of his Parnellite colleagues, he was quick to recognize that Parnell's death in 1891 made a substantive difference to their position. He soon separated himself from them and, in association with the anti-Parnellite William O'Brien, undertook the work of reconstructing the nationalist movement through the United Irish League, formed in January 1898. In doing this, he split the Parnellite faction, especially at its grass-roots level, and highlighted the continued commitment to factionalism of its leader, John Redmond. However, when it came to the nationalist reunion of January 1900, Harrington did not countenance any isolation of Redmond because of his opposition to the new organization, and he played a central role in ensuring that the reunited party was as inclusive as possible. One of the effects of this was to stereotype the membership of the new party in terms of the old, with longer-term consequences for which Harrington must bear part of the responsibility.

Harrington was lord mayor of Dublin from 1901 to 1903. Partly because of this, he was selected as a member of the

Timothy Charles Harrington (1851–1910), by James Russell & Sons, 1887

conference responsible for the agreement on which the Land Act of 1903 was based. He was an ideal choice for this task, which required understanding of the tenant perspective, a grasp of legal detail, and a high reputation among nationalists. Harrington's abilities and political imagination merited a more prominent place in the nationalist movement than he was ever given. Financial difficulties caused conflict between public life and his profession and interfered with his attachment to the idea of personal independence in politics. Despite this, he gave generously of his time and professional skills in defence of colleagues and supporters who appeared before the courts. Imprisoned twice in the 1880s under the coercion laws and fined £500 for contempt during the Parnell commission, he had himself experience of the wrong side of the law. His effectiveness as a speaker put him in demand for public meetings, especially during the early years of the United Irish League, but it was with pain that he had often to seek reimbursement of his expenses. He was deeply committed to his nationalist ideals, and adhered to them even against his personal interests; he refused as lord mayor to attend the coronation of Edward VII and successfully opposed an address from the corporation on the king's visit to Dublin in 1903. He was both liked and respected by his colleagues, regardless of political divisions which from time to time separated him from them. He died in Dublin, at his home at 70 Harcourt Street, on 12 March 1910 and was buried in Glasnevin cemetery. He was survived by his wife and five children.   Philip Bull

Sources C. C. O'Brien, *Parnell and his party, 1880–90* (1957) • F. S. L. Lyons, *Charles Stewart Parnell* (1977) • P. J. Bull, 'The United Irish League and the reunion of the Irish parliamentary party, 1898–1900', *Irish Historical Studies*, 26 (1988–9), 51–78 • R. B. O'Brien, *The life of Charles Stewart Parnell*, 3rd edn, 2 vols. (1899) • M. Davitt, *The fall of feudalism in Ireland* (1904) • *Irish Independent* (14 March 1910) • *WWW, 1897–1915* • *WWBMP*, vol. 1 • *Dod's Parliamentary Companion* (1883–1910) • J. S. Crone, *A concise dictionary of Irish biography*, rev. edn (1937) • *DNB*

Archives NL Ire., corresp. and papers | NL Ire., letters to John Redmond • TCD, corresp. with John Dillon

Likenesses J. Russell & Sons, photograph, 1887, NPG [*see illus.*] • S. P. Hall, group portrait, pencil, 1889 (*Parnell's reception in the Great Hall of the Royal Courts of Justice*), NG Ire. • A. Mancini, portrait, 1901–3, City Hall, Dublin • S. P. Hall, group portrait, pencil (*Counsel for Parnell standing at the luncheon bar*), NG Ire. • S. P. Hall, pencil, NG Ire.

Wealth at death £1598 19s. 2d.: administration, 1 June 1910, CGPLA Ire.

Harrington, Sir William (d. 1440). *See under* Harrington family (*per. c.*1300–1512).

Harrington, William, fifth Baron Harrington (*c.*1392–1458). *See under* Harrington family (*per. c.*1300–1512).

Harrington, William (d. 1523), Catholic priest and author, son of William Harrington of Newbiggin, Cumberland, and Joanna, daughter of W. Haske of Eastrington, Yorkshire, was born at Eastrington, and educated at Cambridge and Bologna (where he studied civil law). He was ordained priest on 10 March 1498. He held several ecclesiastical appointments: prebendary of Islington (collated 8 July 1497), vicar of Darrington, Yorkshire (1496–1504), rector of St Anne, Aldersgate (1505–10), and canon of Wells from 1509. His tomb was built in St Paul's Cathedral shortly before his death. Harrington was presumably dead by November 1523, when his prebend was recorded as vacant.

Harrington is remembered chiefly as the author of *The Commendations of Matrimony*, a guide for clergy in the legal and pastoral teachings of the church on marriage. The work is divided into three sections, which outline the benefits of marriage, the manner in which the marriage ceremony should be conducted, and impediments to marriage. Harrington defends marriage as a divine institution (Harrington, sig. Aiiv); details the duty of married couples to bear children and educate them in the laws of God and man (ibid., sig. Aiiiv); and upholds the death penalty for male adultery (ibid., sig. Dir). Marriage is to be contracted only with the express consent of both parties, although the wife is to be obedient to her husband, whose duty it is to correct and discipline her (ibid., sigs. Aiiir, Cviiiv). The work also includes a lengthy analysis of the impediments to marriage, with tables of affinity and consanguinity (ibid., sigs. Bir, Bviir, Ciir). The *Commendations*, dedicated to Polydore Vergil, was printed by John Rastell ('at the instance of Mayster Polydore Virgil') in 1515, and reprinted in 1517 and 1528 (*STC, 1475–1640*, 12798.5–12800).   H. L. Parish

Sources W. Harrington, *In this booke are conteyned the 'Commendations of matrimony'* (1528) • K. M. Davies, 'Continuity and change in literary advice on marriage', *Marriage and society: studies in the social history of marriage*, ed. R. B. Outhwaite (1981), 58–80 • R. Newcourt, *Repertorium ecclesiasticum parochiale Londinense*, 1 (1708) • J. Weever, *Ancient funerall monuments* (1631) • Emden, *Cam.* • *STC, 1475–1640* • *DNB*

Harriot, Thomas (*c.*1560–1621), mathematician and natural philosopher, was born in the city or county of Oxford. All that is known for certain of his family is that his father was a commoner, he had a married sister, he had relatives in Berkshire, and he did not marry. He matriculated at

Oxford on 29 December 1577 as a member of St Mary Hall, and was awarded a BA degree at Easter 1580.

The art of navigation Harriot soon developed a high reputation for the mathematical and instrumental skills necessary for astronomical navigation, stimulated in these studies, perhaps, by the prevailing enthusiasm for exploration and colonies in America. By 1584 at the latest he was employed 'at a most liberal salary' by the queen's favourite, Sir Walter Ralegh (c.1552–1618), to teach Ralegh and his sea captains at Durham House in London the sciences of navigation, and to serve him in various other capacities, in preparation for Ralegh's first enterprise to establish a settlement in America. Harriot—but not Ralegh—was a member of the short-lived colony which landed on Roanoke Island, Virginia, in June 1585 and returned to England with Sir Francis Drake in June 1586. Before the voyage Harriot had studied the local language from two Algonquian Indians who had been taken to England in 1584 by a reconnaissance expedition. He even invented a phonetic alphabet to represent the language, and used his knowledge in Virginia to study local social and religious customs, together with plants, animals, and produce. Harriot published a summary of his survey, largely to defend Ralegh's enterprise, as a pamphlet in 1588 entitled *A Brief and True Report of the New Found Land of Virginia*. At a time of brutal violence between colonists and native inhabitants the text is remarkable for its sympathy towards Algonquian beliefs and customs. It also contains what may be the first printed promotional literature in English for tobacco by an English writer, and Harriot and Ralegh were subsequently credited with the introduction of pipe tobacco smoking into England from Virginia. The *Report* was much published subsequently.

Following his return from Virginia, Harriot participated in Ralegh's colonizing enterprise in Munster and was granted title to Molanna Abbey near Youghal. He was definitely living there in August, 1589, although by early 1590 he was back in Durham House. From at least 1591 Harriot became increasingly involved in the circle of another controversial figure, Henry Percy (1564–1632), the ninth and so-called 'Wizard' earl of Northumberland, a close friend of Ralegh. In 1590 Harriot is reported as being at work examining existing navigational tables for Ralegh. He discovered that 'eclipses happen an houre and sometimes more out and sometimes little less, after the time they are foretold' (Roche, 251). To reform these tables Harriot constructed the largest astronomical instrument in sixteenth-century England, a 12 foot device which may have been an astronomer's cross-staff. The observations and calculations which he carried out between 1590 and 1594, his lost navigational manuscript 'Arcticon', his innovations in mathematical cartography, and his improved instruments and observing practices provided Ralegh with the best navigational expertise then available in Europe, which he made use of during his voyage in 1596 to Guiana in search of El Dorado. Perhaps Harriot's most advanced achievement in map theory during this period was his construction of a table which allowed a navigator to set a fixed compass course when sailing between two ports—offering a solution to the so-called 'Mercator problem'. He completed this work by 1614, developing very sophisticated mathematical techniques in the process.

Political misfortunes Ralegh's star began to wane at court in 1592 following the queen's discovery of his secret marriage to Elizabeth Throckmorton. He was also accused in print in the same year of maintaining a school of atheism led by Harriot. Both men were mentioned in the evidence gathered to prove the 'scorn of Gods word' by the free-thinking playwright Christopher Marlowe (1564–1593), who was murdered in 1593 (Shirley, *Biography*, 181–3). This led to hearings on atheism in Dorset by an ecclesiastical commission which met in 1594 at Cerne Abbas, near where Ralegh then lived. Although much hearsay evidence was presented against Ralegh and Harriot the investigation went no further. Indeed, Harriot's published papers and manuscripts reveal an intelligent piety and contain little which might be interpreted as irreligion; even so, he acquired a damaging reputation for impiety, which was reinforced by his support for atomism—long associated with atheism—and his phrase *ex nihilo nihil fit* ('from nothing, nothing is made') echoing the ancient atomists. However, soon after, he found a powerful new patron: during the mid-1590s Henry Percy granted him rents from an estate in co. Durham, the use of an estate house in the grounds of Syon House, Isleworth, and a pension of £80 a year which he received for the rest of his life. Harriot maintained a library and a research workshop at Syon, and was looked after by three servants and craftsman. He appears to have had no formal duties, was able to pursue his theoretical and practical researches in a most encouraging environment, and maintained a close involvement with Ralegh and with navigational matters. Harriot's most important achievement during his early years at Syon was his discovery in 1601 of the correct mathematical law according to which light is refracted when it passes from one transparent medium into another—the sine law of refraction. He also recognized that red, yellow, and blue light are refracted differently and measured their refractions. Johann Kepler (1571–1630) heard of Harriot's discovery and wrote to him in 1606 for information. Harriot sent Kepler some refraction data but did not reveal the law, hoping, perhaps, to achieve proper recognition in print: perplexingly, however, Harriot never published a discovery which would have secured his reputation in the history of science, nor was any of his work in optics, mechanics, astronomy, mathematics, navigation, or cartography published in his lifetime—causing considerable distress to his friends. Harriot's other interests during this period included the study of ordnance, and chemical experiments. The former studies seem to have led him to an advanced mathematical treatment of falling bodies and projectiles, and of collisions between bodies. He also read widely in the learned literature of his day.

Harriot must have felt very secure in June 1603, when King James visited Syon House as part of his progress through the realm and showed clear marks of favour to Northumberland. In July, however, Ralegh was arrested on suspicion of involvement in a plot to kill the king and taken to the Tower, where he attempted suicide. Harriot assisted Ralegh's preparation for his trial and was mentioned by Lord Chief Justice Popham as an atheist and evil influence when passing a judgment of treason on Ralegh. Although the king stayed the execution, Ralegh was not pardoned: after his release in 1616 he undertook a disastrous voyage to Guiana and on his return was beheaded in 1618, an event witnessed by Harriot. Misfortune also struck Harriot's second patron, Henry Percy, who was rumoured to be aware of the Gunpowder Plot of 1605. He was interrogated and imprisoned in the Tower. In November 1605 Harriot was incarcerated in the Gatehouse prison for at least three weeks, his house at Syon was searched, and he and his close friends Nathaniel Torporley (1564–1632) and Sir William Lower (c.1570–1615) were interrogated. In a controversial trial of 1606 Northumberland was convicted of various offences connected with the Gunpowder Plot, stripped of offices, fined £30,000 and imprisoned in the Tower at the king's pleasure. Until his release in 1621 he lived in the Tower, from where he managed his estates and continued to support Harriot at Syon. Harriot, of course, saw his situation as precarious and, in a letter to Kepler in 1608, stated that 'we still stick in the mud' (Kepler, 15.172).

A tradition developed in the early seventeenth century that Ralegh and the earl maintained a kind of academy (the 'School of Night') in the Tower, with Harriot as its master and including the mathematicians Walter Warner (d. before 1644) and Robert Hues (1553–1632). The antiquary John Aubrey (1626–1697) in his *Brief Lives* reports that 'these 3 were usually called *the earle of Northumberland's three Magi*' (*Brief Lives*, 1.286). Although Warner and Hues were connected with the earl of Northumberland there is no evidence for any such association based in the Tower. Nevertheless, during the first two decades of the seventeenth century Harriot was the leading figure in a network of scholars which, together with Percy, Ralegh, Warner, and Hues, included the poet and scholar George Chapman (1557–1634), Sir William Lower, member of parliament for Lostwithiel in Cornwall, Thomas Aylesbury (d. 1658), secretary to the earl of Nottingham, Torporley, mathematician and clergyman, and Lord Harrington (1592–1614).

Mathematics and astronomy Harriot's will and surviving manuscripts make it clear that he thought of himself primarily as a mathematician. He was, perhaps, the most able mathematician in Europe between François Viète (1540–1603) and René Descartes (1596–1650), but he failed to publish any mathematics in his lifetime. In 1631 Walter Warner edited and published posthumously a limited selection of Harriot's papers dealing with algebra, with the title *Artis analyticae praxis*. The mathematician John Wallis (1616–1703) was so impressed by this text that, in a publication of 1685, he accused Descartes of failing to acknowledge Harriot as the source of most of his innovations in algebra, provoking a long dispute with French mathematicians. It seems unlikely that Harriot had found Descartes's 'rule of signs' about the positive and negative zeroes of a polynomial, but Wallis claimed it for him, and

his name was and is often associated with it. A more sober assessment of Harriot's *Artis analyticae praxis* shows that it developed the algebra of Viète into a fully symbolic form—dropping all verbal expressions of relations and operations—and expanded considerably the problems dealt with by Viète's methods. This was an achievement of the first importance. The text also introduced inequality symbols for the first time in print, it used italic lower-case notation systematically for the first time to represent algebraic equations, and it gave Viète's algebra a numerical rather than a geometrical interpretation. By contrast, Descartes's algebra (*La géometrie*, published in 1637) was interpreted geometrically.

By 1610 Harriot was a Copernican and rejected the crystalline spheres of the ancients. He anticipated Kepler by conjecturing that the motions of planets were not perfect circles and he immediately accepted Kepler's theory of elliptical orbits. He also anticipated Galileo in conjecturing that other planets besides the earth have satellites. Speculations, however, are not discoveries, and Harriot was not a dedicated theoretical or observational astronomer, although he made astronomical observations for some thirty years. He used a cross-staff to measure the angular distances to neighbouring stars of Halley's comet during its return in 1607, and Friedrich Bessel (1784–1846) found his data sufficiently accurate to calculate its orbit. Harriot also observed the comet of 1618. On 26 July 1609 Harriot observed the moon through his telescope—the first was possibly bought in the Low Countries, though lenses were subsequently apparently ground and constructed by himself and his craftsman Christopher Tooke (1572–1630)—and sketched the lunar surface. Harriot's first recorded observation of sunspots was on 28 November 1610. Although this was undoubtedly an independent observation, Harriot may not have observed them before Galileo. Harriot's most sustained programme of observations contains some 100 nightly logs of Jupiter's satellites between 17 October 1610 and 26 February 1612. These led him to a remarkably accurate value for the period of Io, the first satellite. Harriot's papers contain records of various observations of lesser importance, including the determination of planetary positions, the exact moment of occurrence of the first quarter of the moon, and the study of the phases of Venus.

In his day Harriot had something of a European reputation but his failure to publish meant that his positive contributions to European science, which may have been transmitted through his personal contacts, are difficult to establish. The commitment to publication often brings a scholar's work to maturity. This failure was in part due to Harriot's reputation for impiety and his close association with Ralegh and Northumberland, but it is difficult to see how publications in navigational science or of maps, mathematics, optics, mechanics, or astronomy could have been other than beneficial to his position. It is difficult, also, to form a clear picture of Harriot the person. His friend Sir William Lower speaks of his 'too great reservednesse' (Shirley, *Biography*, 400). In 1615 the king's physician Theodore de Mayerne examined Harriot for a cancerous tumour of the nose and describes him as 'a man somewhat melancholy' (ibid., 433). There are indications, however, that he had a restrained, scholarly humour. Also, he had many loyal friends and showed considerable loyalty himself in dangerous circumstances.

Death and revaluation Harriot died of his tumour at a house in Threadneedle Street, London, on 2 July 1621, a month before Henry Percy was released from the Tower, and he was buried in the nearby church of St Christopher-le-Stocks. His will, dictated three days previously, reveals that, although Harriot owned no landed property, he possessed a substantial library, much scientific equipment, including many telescopes and alchemical furnaces, and savings of about £300. He bequeathed his papers to the earl, which explains why so many have survived. The memorial plaque erected to Harriot in the church was destroyed in the great fire of 1666 but its wording was preserved. In 1971 a bronze plaque with the same Latin inscription was unveiled on a wall in the Bank of England, as close to the site of Harriot's grave as could be determined.

Many volumes of Harriot's working mathematical papers survive. An examination of them shows that he made other important innovations in mathematics, including the application of algebra to the analysis of conic sections, a study of binary numbers, the discovery of an algorithm for computing the area of a spherical triangle, and the development of logarithmic tangents.

Harriot's astronomical papers received considerable publicity following the rediscovery by Frans Xavier Zach (later Baron von Zach; 1754–1832) in 1784 of Harriot's manuscripts at Petworth House, Sussex, where they had remained since the death of Henry Percy in 1632. Von Zach, who was particularly interested in astronomy, claimed priority for Harriot over Galileo in the discovery of sunspots and Jupiter's satellites. This caused considerable controversy until a systematic study of Harriot's astronomical papers was undertaken and published in 1833 by Stephen Peter Rigaud (1774–1839), Savilian professor of astronomy at Oxford. Rigaud attempted to refute von Zach's claims for Harriot's priority but, as he himself admitted, he had not the opportunity to study all of Harriot's manuscripts bearing on this subject. Nor did Rigaud have access to Harriot's will which sheds significant light on his astronomy. The latter was discovered before 1885 by Henry Stevens (1819–1886) of Vermont. Except for von Zach's selection of papers and some others which remain at Petworth—a total of more than 1000 folios—the bulk of the Harriot manuscripts—more than 4000 folios—were deposited in 1810 in the British Museum by Lord Egremont, who held title to Petworth House. The Harriot manuscripts received considerable scholarly attention in the twentieth century, mainly as a result of some forty years of pioneering historical research by John W. Shirley of the University of Delaware and owing to the scholarship, stimulus, and financial support of Cecily Young Tanner of Imperial College, London.

J. J. ROCHE

Sources J. W. Shirley, *Thomas Harriot: a biography* (1983) [incl. bibliography] · D. B. Quinn, ed., *The Roanoke voyages, 1584–1590: documents to illustrate the English voyages to North America under the patent granted to Walter Raleigh in 1584*, 2 vols., Hakluyt Society, 2nd ser., 104, 105 (1955) · J. Jacquot, 'Thomas Harriot's reputation for impiety', *Notes and Records of the Royal Society*, 9 (1951–2), 164–87 · R. C. H. Tanner, 'Thomas Harriot as mathematician: a legacy of hearsay', *Physis*, 9 (1967), 235–92 [includes Harriot's will] · J. Wallis, *A treatise of algebra both historical and practical* (1685) · J. A. Lohne, 'Thomas Harriot, 1560–1621: the Tycho Brahe of optics', *Centaurus*, 6 (1959), 113–21 · J. W. Shirley, 'Thomas Harriot's lunar observations', *Science and history: studies in honor of Edward Rosen*, ed. E. Hilfstein and others (1978), 283–308 · J. W. Shirley, ed., *A source book for the study of Thomas Harriot* (1981) · T. Harriot, *A briefe and true report of the new found land of Virginia* (1588) · Petworth House, Harriot MSS, MS HMC, 240 i–v; 241 i–x · BL, Add. MSS 6782–6789 · *Johannes Kepler: Gesammelte Werke*, ed. W. von Dyck and M. Caspar, 15–17 (München, 1951–9) · J. J. Roche, 'Harriot's "Regiment of the sun" and its background in sixteenth-century navigation', *British Journal for the History of Science*, 14 (1981), 245–61 · *Brief lives, chiefly of contemporaries, set down by John Aubrey, between the years 1669 and 1696*, ed. A. Clark, 2 vols. (1898) · J. W. Shirley, ed., *Thomas Harriot: Renaissance scientist* (1974) · matriculation register, Oxford
Archives BL, corresp. and mathematical calculations, Harley MS 6083; Add. MSS 6782–6789 · Petworth House, West Sussex, astronomical and mathematical notes, MS HMC 240 i–v and 241 i–x | BL, Sloane MS 2292
Wealth at death approx. £300: will, Archdeaconry court of London

Harriott, Diana. *See* Hill, Diana (d. 1844).

Harriott, John (1745–1817), magistrate and a founder of the Thames police, was born on 14 June 1745 at Broomhills, Great Stambridge, Essex. His father was a seafarer whose forebears had been tanners and copyhold tenants in Brigstock, Northamptonshire. It is difficult to establish family details from surviving evidence but Harriott was probably the eldest of at least seven siblings. He joined the Royal Navy, aged thirteen, as a midshipman at the height of the Seven Years' War. The war ended too quickly for him: he had insufficient active service to qualify for a commission and without influential patrons could not expect to remedy the deficiency in peacetime. A lack of connections also blighted his subsequent merchant navy career. In 1768 he joined the East India Company and embarked for Madras. In April 1772 he was wounded and returned to Broomhills, arriving in England in July 1773.

In December 1773 Harriott married. According to his memoirs his wife was named Sarah; they were probably the John Harriott and Sarah Eaton who married at St Mary Magdalen, Old Fish Street, London, on 23 December 1773. His wife was buried at Great Stambridge on 5 January 1775. He married again the following September. His second wife, Ann, was buried, also in Great Stambridge, on 29 January 1785. He married Elizabeth Wood of Great Bursted on 11 August 1785.

From 1773 to 1790 Harriott pursued various occupations. Under the tutelage of his uncle John Staples, whom he had assisted between voyages, he became an underwriter. He also traded in wine and spirits and took up farming. He became a minor public figure, serving as a magistrate for Rochford hundred, and promoting several local causes. Despite his apparently assured position, Harriott's finances were precarious. He suffered heavy losses in the late 1770s as a result of his father-in-law's bankruptcy and had a large family to support (at least seven children survived into early adulthood). In 1790 Broomhills was destroyed by fire; in 1791 flooding destroyed another major investment, 200 acres of reclaimed land. A voluntary agreement with his creditors prevented bankruptcy, and in 1793 he emigrated to the USA, where he found the work of day-to-day farming incompatible with his gentlemanly pretensions. He returned to England in 1795 and settled in east London.

Staples, who had twice offered to take Harriott into partnership as an underwriter, was then a stipendiary magistrate with extensive experience of river crime. In 1797 he again tried to help Harriott by recommending him as a stipendiary at Shadwell police office. The ensuing discussions awakened Harriott to 'the great advantages that would result to all concerned in the shipping commerce of the Port of London if a River Police was established. I soon formed an outline and consulted my relation who much approved of it' (Harriott, *Struggles*, 2.109). Police reform was a fashionable topic of discussion: Patrick Colquhoun had published the first two editions of his *Treatise on Police* in 1796 and had gained further publicity for his ideas from the report of the select committee on finance (1798). Harriott sent his plan to the lord mayor of London and to the home secretary in October 1797, but it was Colquhoun's backing that secured the support of the West India merchants and the initial finance that got the scheme off the ground in the summer of 1798.

Harriott's appointment to the Thames police office relieved him of his most pressing financial problems, but did not entirely dispel them. He continued to dabble in business, although he preferred not to associate his name with so ungentlemanly an activity, for fear of 'letting down the magistrate' (Harriott, Letter books, vol. 1, fols. 42–42b). Among his enterprises was a small factory to build ships' pumps according to his own design, patented on 31 October 1797; another of his patents, registered in 1802, was an engine for raising weights and working mills. The failure of his partners, Hurry & Co., in 1807 brought renewed losses at a time when he was already worried about the cost of establishing his two youngest children in creditable situations and about the debts of an older son. The following year he published the first of three editions of his autobiography, *Struggles through Life*, which proved to be satisfyingly profitable. It remains the major source for details of his life. His other works included a work on improving landed estates, and *The Religion of Philosophy* (1812).

Harriott was a strong-minded man who regularly found himself involved in disputes with relatives and colleagues. He took advantage of his position at the Thames police office, among other things using the boats for occasional pleasure trips and contracting maintenance work to Hurry & Co. In 1809 his dismissal of two Thames police clerks for accounting irregularities rebounded when they reported his own conduct to the home secretary. Harriott was horrified to learn that he would be prosecuted in the king's bench, 'the very odium of which would sink one to the earth' (Harriott, letter-books, vol. 2, fol. 16). In 1810 he was acquitted of all but one charge: that of concealing his name as a partner in Hurry & Co. The jury expressly vindicated his integrity. He returned to his post resentful of the ingratitude of 'those above' and determined not to 'make myself the slave to it I have hitherto done' (ibid., fol. 7b).

By 1811 Harriott, who had always boasted of his robust constitution, was expressing concern about his declining physical health and mental agility. His melancholy was exacerbated by the deaths of three of his adult children, further business losses, and illness. Yet he could still be as energetic and enthusiastic as ever. He played a leading role in the investigation of the Ratcliffe Highway murders (1811), rescued an old acquaintance from a madhouse (1814), and organized a grand military display in aid of the Waterloo subscription (1816). During 1816 an enlarged prostate caused an illness so painful that, despite his strong religious beliefs, he contemplated suicide. During a remission he put his affairs in order, signing his will on 14 December 1816. He killed himself on 13 January 1817 at the Thames police office. A sympathetic coroner's jury, aware that his condition was terminal and mindful of the social and legal penalties attached to suicide, returned a verdict of death by natural causes. He was buried at Great Stambridge on 22 January 1817. His estate at death was valued at £6000. He was survived by his third wife, Elizabeth, two of his sons, John Staples and George, a daughter, Dorothy Hannah, and several grandchildren; he may have had thirteen children in all, but most of them predeceased him. RUTH PALEY

Sources J. Harriott, *Struggles through life*, 3rd edn (1815) · letter-books of J. Harriott, NL Scot., MSS 5066–7 · parish register, Great Stambridge, Essex RO, D/P 218 [marriage, burial] · police entry books, series 1, PRO, HO65 · U. Nott. L., Portland MSS · *Annual Register* (1817) · parish register, St Mary Magdalene, Old Fish Street, London, 23 Dec 1773 [marriage]
Archives NL Scot., corresp. and MSS, 5066, 5067 | LMA, Thames police letter-books, PS/TH/CO1/1–4
Likenesses H. Cook, line engraving (after H. Hervé), NPG · H. Cook, stipple (after H. Hervé), BM, NPG · Page, stipple, BM; repro. in *The lives of eminent and remarkable characters in the counties of Essex, Suffolk and Norfolk* (1820) · portrait, repro. in Harriott, *Struggles through life*, frontispiece
Wealth at death £6000: PRO, death duty registers IR 26/709, fol. 53

Harriott, (Arthurlin) Joseph [Joe] (1928–1973), saxophonist, composer, and bandleader, was born on 15 July 1928 in Linstead, St Catherine, Jamaica, the first son and the eldest of the three children of Raphael Garfield Harriott, a professional gambler, and Muriel Scarlet or Scarlett (d. 1932). His parents were Jamaican. His father moved to Kingston, leaving the family to be brought up by their mother, but when she died following the birth of another child (Harriott's half-sister) Harriott and his younger brother were placed in a children's home, Maxfield Park. About 1940 they were sent to Alpha Cottage School in Kingston, an industrial school and orphanage renowned for its musical tuition. There Harriott trained as a bookbinder and shoe-repairer and studied music. He played

(Arthurlin) **Joseph Harriott (1928–1973)**, by Val Wilmer, 1960

clarinet in the school's marching and dance bands, impressing the saxophonist Eric Deans, a professional musician attached to the school. In 1945 Deans enlisted Harriott for his own band, where the youngster remained for three years, playing baritone and tenor saxophones and learning to play Latin-American music and jazz. By 1948 he was playing bebop, the new modern jazz, with the trumpeter Sonny Bradshaw. He came to wider public attention in the nightclub band of the pianist Baba Motta and concentrated on the alto saxophone. In 1948 he formed a relationship with Edith Mary Grant (*b.* 1931); they lived together in Kingston, and their daughter Pauline Theresa Harriott was born there in 1951, shortly before Harriott left Jamaica for Britain with the pianist Ozzie Da Costa.

At London's Sunset Club, where music enthusiasts socialized with Caribbean settlers, Harriott was heard by the drummer Laurie Morgan, who took him to a jam session at the Feldman Club. There he amazed the cognoscenti with his technical ability and passion; returning with his own quartet later that month, he was advertised as 'sensational' (*Melody Maker*, 30 Sept 1951). Harriott soon became one of the most respected musicians in London's modern jazz circles. He joined the group led by a fellow Jamaican, the trumpeter Pete Pitterson, and the racially mixed big band led by the singer and percussionist Leon Roy, and associated also with musicians from an earlier era such as the Barbadian swing trumpeter Dave Wilkins. In 1953 he toured in variety with the Harlem All-Stars, led by the Guyanese pianist Mike McKenzie, and began to record.

Harriott raised his jazz profile by joining both the quartet of the drummer Tony Kinsey and Ronnie Scott's big band, and he worked prolifically with other prominent groups before forming his own quintet. This developed a healthy following during an extended residency at the Marquee Club in Oxford Street (beginning in 1957), but the uncertainties of the jazz life proved damaging to a man without a robust constitution. In 1958 he collapsed and was hospitalized with bronchial pneumonia, pleurisy, and a lung infection. He spent three and a half months in a sanitorium, a period of reflection during which he rethought his musical direction. He emerged with a new concept he named 'free form'. His idea was that the music's participants should not be limited by conventional structures but feed off one another, taking whatever direction the music itself dictated. It was an approach that had parallels with what the saxophonist Ornette Coleman was doing in the United States, except that, while Coleman's music generally retained a swinging rhythm section, Harriott's often dispensed with this and included space, silence, and unaccompanied solos as part of the abstract picture.

In the early 1960s Harriott's quintet performed their new music, interspersed with conventionally organized pieces, at several European festivals. Their recordings *Free Form* (1960) and *Abstract* (1961–2) were critically acclaimed in the United States, but the comparison with Coleman would dog Harriott, and controversy over his place in musical history continued after his death. The American saxophonist Jackie McLean, visiting London in 1961, recognized his exceptional attributes: 'This abstract thing … [has to] come naturally. I think Joe Harriott is the only London band making a move in that direction' ('Jackie McLean talks to Valerie Wilmer', 4). In his free form he juxtaposed moments of Romantic impressionism with Caribbean rhythms and musical references. His reputation was of a purist, dedicated only to jazz, yet he maintained populist links in the 1950s, performing for Caribbean dancers at the Sunset and elsewhere and even recording with Trinidadian calypso musicians such as Lord Kitchener. He retained his Jamaican nationality, too, and his quintet played for the Jamaica high commission's independence celebrations in 1960. The same year he was named *Melody Maker*'s musician of the year.

Harriott was comfortable in any musical context. He made guest appearances with traditional jazz groups, played in big bands, recorded with strings, and toured with the Modern Jazz Quartet. He played for poetry and jazz concerts and in other settings devised by the pianist Michael Garrick, then in 1965 began collaborating with the Indian violinist and composer John Mayer for a series of Indo-jazz fusions, a synthesis of Indian and Western music that presaged the later interest in such cultural exchanges. He was an outstanding, resourceful musician with an unlimited flow of ideas. An obvious early debt to Charlie Parker diminished in significance when he added his own emphasis, playing in a fierce, spiky manner that reflected his own personality. A tall, lean man whose long face and wispy beard gave him a Moorish appearance, he radiated acute personal tension and projected this on to his music, but could also play with great warmth and sensitivity: 'Joe has always played beautiful love and hate songs' (Grime, 10).

Harriott has been called the father of European free jazz, yet in his lifetime he never achieved the success that the posthumous regard for his contribution might suggest. Despite his originality and extraordinary musical ability, he could not make a living playing jazz, and in his last years lived an itinerant life. He travelled around Britain, playing with local musicians, and it was while staying in the Southampton area in 1972 that he discovered he had cancer of the spine. He was treated in the Royal South Hampshire Hospital and died in the Wessex Radiotherapy Unit there on 2 January 1973; he was buried ten days later at Bitterne church, near Southampton. He was unmarried, but was survived by his four children, his first daughter and Theresa Harriott (b. c.1959), Christopher Cornelsen (b. 1961), and Amber Copp (later Avstreih; b. 1964). In 1986 Harriott was one of twenty-seven black figures acknowledged by Lambeth Council, a recreation hall in Norwood being renamed in his honour.   VAL WILMER

Sources R. Cotterrell and B. Tepperman, *Joe Harriott memorial bio-discography: his life in music* (1974) • V. Wilmer, 'Joe Harriott: jazz abstractionist', *Down Beat* (25 Sept 1964), 12, 37 • C. Blackford, 'Joe Harriott: forgotten father of European free jazz', *Rubberneck*, no. 25 (1997) • C. Sheridan, 'Harriott, Joe', *The New Grove dictionary of jazz*, ed. B. Kernfeld, 2nd edn (2001) • S. Atkin, 'Joe Harriott—past master', *Third World Impact* [n.d.], 46, 48 • I. Carr, D. Fairweather, and B. Priestley, *Jazz: the essential companion* (1987) • 'Jackie McLean talks to Valerie Wilmer', *Jazz Journal* (July 1961), 4 • 'Jamaican "unknown" returns as star', *Melody Maker* (1 Sept 1951), 7 • *Melody Maker* (30 Sept 1951) • K. Grime, 'In review: Joe Harriott at the Ronnie Scott club', *Jazz News* (20 Sept 1961), 10 • J. Chilton, *Who's who of British jazz* (1997) • personal knowledge (2004) • private information (2004) • d. cert.
Likenesses P. Gwynne-Jones, photographs, 1960, repro. in Cotterrell and Tepperman, *Joe Harriott*, front and back cover • V. Wilmer, photograph, 1960, priv. coll. [*see illus.*] • V. Wilmer, photograph, 1963, priv. coll.; *see illus. in* Keane, Ellsworth McGranahan (1927–1997) • M. Joseph, photographs, 1966, priv. coll. • T. Cryer, photographs, c.1969, priv. coll. • photographs, priv. coll.

Harris, Alexander (*fl.* 1619–1621), prison warden, of whose personal circumstances very little is known, and whose origins are unknown, did not attend university or any of the inns of court. He is known entirely as a result of the complaints made against him by a number of prisoners to the privy council while he was warden of the Fleet prison, London. It seems that the prisoners originally made fourteen complaints in 1619 which were investigated by a number of judges including Sir Julius Caesar (a copy survives in his papers). These were later expanded to nineteen and presented as a petition before the parliament of 1621, where it was debated in the Commons as to whether he should be punished. A committee was formed to investigate the complaints and Harris was called to the bar to be questioned, as were a number of witnesses. It was ordered to prepare charges to be put before the House of Lords, but the parliament was adjourned before any action could be taken.

The prisoners accused Harris of charging excessive rates for lodgings in the prison, putting impositions on meat and fuel bought privately by prisoners, breaking open prisoners' trunks, theft of money from two prisoners, and 'close and cruel' imprisonment of prisoners of high status without cause. In response to the prisoners' charges, Harris wrote a defence which he entitled *The economy of the Fleete, or, An apologeticall answeare of Alexander Harris (late warden there) unto xix articles sett forth against him by the prisoners*. It survived in the form of scribal manuscripts in the possession of the duke of Westminster without any indication of a particular addressee, and was published in 1879. Problems between the wardens of the Fleet and its prisoners were inevitable given that the wardenship was an office which was held for profit through earnings from fees the prisoners had to pay for food and lodging. Harris himself claimed that the profits of his wardenship should have been £4000 which he justified by claiming that he was able to collect only £2200 of this and had to spend much of it defending himself against the prisoners' law suits and violence. He did not say how much he had to pay for the office, but the purchase price must have meant he was fairly wealthy. However, the unusual and dangerous conditions of the job would not have made it a particularly attractive position. As Harris implied, fees had to be earned from prisoners for debt, often of a higher social status than the warden, who already owed thousands if not tens of thousands of pounds to others, so the likelihood of default was great. There were various orders from the beginning of Elizabeth's reign concerning the constitution of how the prison should be governed, and what fees the prisoners should be charged, but to make up losses from unpaid debts successive wardens, including Harris, raised their fees to levels which prisoners complained were extortionate.

Such matters came to public prominence in 1619–21 because of a riot against the warden by a number of élite recusants including Sir Francis Englefeild, bt, and Sir John Whitbrook. This involved one of the warden's servants being stabbed, and Harris being hit on the head with a hammer. Harris's defence provides a detailed, if one-sided, narrative of these events containing one of the best descriptions of conditions within an early modern prison, where many prisoners carried stilettos, and decayed debtors of élite status continued to run up debts by entertaining, it was said, 40–50 people at a time in their rooms, and also kept their families with them in the prison.

Harris provided a convincing defence, but by the time he wrote it he was no longer warden. Members of the House of Commons certainly took the prisoners' complaints seriously, and determined that Harris's witnesses' affidavits were false. Considering that the complaining prisoners were Catholics, and that the privy council had admonished some of them as riotous two years previously, this suggests that Harris was probably more guilty of hard practices than indicated by his defence.

CRAIG MULDREW

Sources *The economy of the Fleete, or, An apologeticall answeare of Alexander Harris*, ed. A. Jessopp, CS, new ser., 25 (1879) • W. Notestein,

F. H. Relf, and H. Simpson, eds., *Commons debates, 1621*, 7 vols. (1935) · *APC, 1619–20* · BL, Add. MS 12504, fols. 279–83
Archives BL, MSS of Sir Julius Caesar, Add. MS 12504

Harris, Sir Arthur Travers, first baronet (1892–1984), air force officer, was born on 13 April 1892 in Cheltenham, the second youngest in the family of four sons and two daughters of George Steele Travers Harris (*b.* 1852), an engineer and architect in the Indian Civil Service, and his wife, Caroline Maria (1863–1922), the daughter of William Charles Elliot, a surgeon in the Madras cavalry. The second son died in 1917, and the youngest died as an infant. Educated at Gore Court, Sittingbourne, Kent, and Allhallows, Honiton, Devon, while his parents were in India, Harris soon became exceptionally self-reliant. At the age of seventeen, against the wishes of his father, who wanted him to join the army, he went out to Rhodesia, where he tried his hand at goldmining, coach-driving, and farming.

First World War In October 1914 Harris joined the newly formed 1st Rhodesian regiment as a bugler (he had acquired the skill while at school in Devon). He took part in the successful operations against German South-West Africa, and on the disbanding of the regiment in 1915 returned to Britain to enlist. Unable to find a posting in the cavalry or artillery, he was helped by an uncle to join the Royal Flying Corps (RFC). Half an hour's tuition at Brooklands qualified him as a civilian pilot. He was awarded his licence by the Royal Aero Club on 10 November 1915, and was commissioned as a second lieutenant.

In the RFC Harris became a night pilot assigned to anti-Zeppelin defence and was given command of 38 squadron. Posted to 70 squadron in France, he was invalided home after a crash, but he returned in May 1917 for fighter work with 45 squadron. Here he displayed many of his later qualities as a commander. He proved to be a cool and effective pilot and was attributed with five aerial victories. He constantly searched for ways to improve the tactical or technical performance of his squadron. He was also a strict officer, with high standards that he imposed on those around him. During 1918 he commanded a night-training and night-fighting squadron (44) in England and was awarded the AFC.

Harris married, on 30 August 1916, Barbara Daisy Kyrle, the daughter of Lieutenant-Colonel Ernle William Kyrle Money, of the 85th King's Shropshire light infantry, with whom he had a son and two daughters. The marriage was dissolved in 1935. On 17 June 1938 he married Thérèse, known as Jill (1915–1987), the daughter of Major Edward Patrick Hearne, Carlow, Éire, with whom he had a daughter.

RAF officer: inter-war appointments In August 1919 Harris was offered a permanent commission in the new Royal Air Force as a squadron leader. From 1919 to 1925 he successively commanded 2 flying training school at home, 31 squadron in India (with operations on the north-west frontier against Afghanistan), and 45 squadron in Iraq, where he successfully adapted his troop-carrying Vernons for day and night bombing. He spent two and a half years

Sir Arthur Travers Harris, first baronet (1892–1984), by Howard Coster, 1941

in Iraq before returning for a course at the Army Senior Officers' School, then from 1925 to 1927 commanded 58 squadron at Worthy Down. He made the squadron one of the most efficient in the service and undertook the intensive training of crews by night. In 1927 he was appointed OBE.

During 1928–9 Harris attended the Army Staff College at Camberley, where he was taught by, among others, Bernard Montgomery. He refused the offer to stay on as an instructor at the college, and was posted for two years to serve on the air staff in Cairo. In 1933 he returned again to Britain to command 210 (flying-boat) squadron, a year Harris later described as his 'most enjoyable year' in the RAF (Harris, *Bomber Offensive*, 25). Six months as deputy director of operations and intelligence at the Air Ministry followed, after which he served as deputy director of plans (1934–7). Here, as a member of the chiefs of staff joint planning subcommittee, he was much concerned with national defence policy as a whole. As an airman he urged the development of mines for aircraft to lay at sea, and he was an enthusiast for the new generation of four-engined 'heavy' bombers which the RAF had under review. He was a key figure in the decisions to adopt the models that formed the later backbone of Bomber Command during the Second World War. Harris took the view that air power was a short-cut to victory, avoiding what he saw as the pointless carnage of the western front. He also argued in 1936 for bombers that could reach targets in the Soviet

Union, marking him out as one of the earliest 'cold warriors'.

Harris left the ministry in 1937 to command the newly formed 4 (bomber) group, following the reorganization of the RAF into separate commands based on function (bomber, fighter, and so on). During the year he was promoted air commodore. In 1938 he was sent to the United States to study aircraft and aircraft equipment and to recommend purchases. He and his small staff selected the Lockheed Hudson (a twin-engined aircraft) for general reconnaissance and the North American Harvard (a single-engined monoplane) advanced trainer.

Harris's next appointment was as air officer commanding Palestine and Transjordan (1938–9). In his task of helping to restrain the growing hostility between Jews and Arabs he co-operated smoothly with the army and devised what he called the 'air-pin'—pinning down villagers by the threat of bombing from patrolling aircraft until the army could get to the scene and root out the trouble makers, a policy he first exploited in Afghanistan and Iraq in the 1920s. During the course of this posting Harris was promoted air vice-marshal (1939) and mentioned in dispatches.

Second World War: Portal's deputy Shortly after the outbreak of war in 1939 Harris was given command of 5 (bomber) group, with headquarters at Grantham, Lincolnshire. The group's Handley Page Hampden twin-engined light bombers proved too vulnerable for daylight operations, and, like most of Bomber Command aircraft, were forced to fly at night, something that Harris had encouraged since the First World War, in contrast to common practice in the force. His group contributed to the anti-invasion operations against German shipping concentrations and airfields close to the channel ports and began the task of mine-laying in German waters, which Harris developed extensively later in the war. Harris was respected as a tough and efficient organizer in the command, and he introduced a number of important innovations, including thorough operational training. In 1940 he was appointed CB.

In November 1940 Sir Charles Portal summoned Harris to serve with him in the Air Ministry as deputy chief of the air staff. Harris agreed to do so, but found bureaucratic work in the vastly swollen ministry apparatus uncongenial after so many years in active command. In May 1941 Portal sent Harris to the United States as head of the RAF delegation to try to speed up the supply of aircraft and engines from American industry, many of which had been on order since 1939. Though Harris succeeded in speeding up delivery, and made some good friends among American airmen, his views on the United States were characteristically acerbic. He took the view that his hosts 'are not going to fight' unless pushed into war, and disliked having to deal with 'a people so arrogant' that they simply refused to listen to technical advice from the British (Harris Papers, H98). In February 1942, following the sacking of Sir Richard Pierse in January, Harris was recalled from Washington to be appointed commander-in-chief of Bomber Command, a post he held without interruption until the end of the war. He was formally appointed on 23 February 1942.

Commander-in-chief, Bomber Command Harris's appointment came at a time when Bomber Command was in crisis. Under Pierse's uninspiring leadership there was growing talk of ending bombing and allocating bombers to help the Royal Navy and the army. The new commander was least likely to give way to such pressure. The choice of Harris was recognition of his long experience, enormous capacity for work, organizational capabilities, and clear-mindedness. It also came despite his less flattering reputation as a man who spoke his mind bluntly, who would suffer fools not at all, and who had often in the past allowed his candour to get the better of his sense of responsibility. Though many in the Air Ministry regarded him as gruff and unapproachable, he was also able to inspire intense loyalty in those who served with him. The force of fewer than 400 operational bombers that Harris inherited had only a handful of the new four-engined aircraft, and was capable of only the most modest and inaccurate attacks on areas of western Germany. Harris transformed the command during the course of 1942, improving its striking power, its tactical procedures, and the morale of its crews. Only in 1943 did Bomber Command under Harris become a serious threat to the enemy.

Harris has often been accused of initiating and prosecuting a policy of so-called area bombing of German cities, deliberately targeting residential areas and causing the death of more than 400,000 German civilians, even when it was possible by the end of the war to attack smaller economic targets with greater accuracy. Harris did not originate the plan to bomb German cities. During the course of 1941 it became clear that Bomber Command could not hit military and economic targets with any accuracy, and the Air Ministry moved to a policy from July 1941 of attacking German morale by hitting industrial cities and 'de-housing' the industrial workforce. When Harris assumed command the directive had already been issued calling for attacks on civilian morale by bombing a selected list of German cities.

Harris did not have the authority to overturn these directives, and the order to attack the important cities of Germany remained in force down to the end of the war. He did not disagree with the aim of destroying German urban areas, but he did not think that morale on its own was a worthwhile target. His aim throughout the war was to destroy Germany's capacity to make war by eliminating the industries, infrastructure, and amenities of German industrial areas. In discussions with the Air Ministry he was candid about a campaign which in his view was designed for 'the destruction of German cities, the killing of German workers and the disruption of civilised community life' (Harris Papers, H53). Unlike many in the Air Ministry and Britain's other services, Harris was convinced that a bombing campaign properly mounted could 'knock Germany out in six weeks' (ibid.). He remained hostile to the idea that any single target, or 'panacea' target, would be enough on its own to cripple Germany, and was not enthusiastic even about the 'dambusters' raid' in

May 1943 against the Möhne, Eder, and Sorpe dams in Germany. He judged that the enemy would be flexible enough to cope with a threat to just one element in the war effort—such as oil—but would be worn down by a more general programme of attrition of the urban industrial area.

When Harris assumed command, Bomber Command was capable of nothing on this scale. Bomber aircraft made up just 11 per cent of front-line aircraft based in Britain, and bombers were called upon to perform a wide variety of roles in addition to the bombing of Germany. Despite Harris's own beliefs about the need for concentration of effort and strategic efficiency, well over 50 per cent of bombing effort was devoted to other targets, particularly the war at sea, while other bombers were sent to the Mediterranean theatre. During 1942 and 1943 bomber aircraft were called on for mine-laying, attacks on the Atlantic submarine pens (with negligible results), and attacks in support of ground offensives in Italy. All of these diversions Harris regretted, but, though he sometimes hovered on the edge of insubordination, he never refused to accept orders once given.

Before he could argue a case for the massive bombing of Germany, Harris had to transform the command. He was greatly assisted by his deputy, Air Marshal Robert Saundby, who had to match Harris's onerous daily routine. Harris had a sound understanding of the nature and limitations of the technology with which he was working. The introduction of four-engined Lancaster and Halifax bombers was speeded up and conversion training organized. Improved bombs and navigational aids were promoted in order to rectify the poor tactical performance earlier in the war. Harris favoured the introduction of specialized vanguard units to lead in the main force and accurately mark the target. Though he would have preferred each bomber group to develop its own skilled target finders, the Air Ministry overruled him, and in August 1942 the élite 'pathfinder' force was introduced, made up of specially trained pilots whose task it was to illuminate the target for the oncoming bomber stream. With the introduction of the Oboe and Gee radio navigation systems in 1942, and the H2S radar navigation equipment during 1943 and 1944, Bomber Command was much better equipped to find and bomb industrial areas with increasingly devastating effect.

The bombing campaign Harris also recognized that the morale of the command was poor when he joined it in 1942. There were strong voices in the army and navy calling for the diversion of Bomber Command to the support of surface forces and the scaling down of bomber procurement. Harris, with the support of the prime minister, Winston Churchill, defended his force vigorously. In May 1942 he decided on the first 1000 bomber raid to boost the flagging spirits of his crews and to demonstrate in a spectacular way the efficacy of bombing strategy. The results of the raid on Cologne were modest by the standards later in the war, but the impact in Britain was important for Harris, who always had to fight two battles—against the German air defences and against domestic critics of

bombing. His staff came to appreciate that he would stoutly defend their position, and the crews, despite very high levels of attrition, came to feel a respect and affection for Harris that had been shown to none of the earlier commanders-in-chief. He worked tirelessly from his bunker headquarters in High Wycombe, even through bouts of ill health, and took not a single day of holiday throughout the war.

In winter 1942–3 Bomber Command was joined by the American 8th Air Force operating from British bases. Harris hoped to persuade American air leaders, with whom he was on very good terms, that they should join him in night bombing, but at the Casablanca conference in January 1943 Roosevelt and Churchill approved a new directive for a combined bomber offensive in which the RAF would bomb by night and the US 8th Air Force by day. The directive, which was finally issued as operation Pointblank in June 1943, called on bomber forces to achieve 'the progressive destruction and dislocation of the German military, industrial and economic system' as well as 'undermining the morale of the German people' (Webster and Frankland, 4.153). Harris began the new campaign with the battle of the Ruhr, waged between March and June 1943, and an assault on Hamburg in July which created the first firestorm and killed 40,000 people in three days.

German defences improved steadily during 1943 and the toll on Harris's force grew. In the winter of 1943–4 he ordered the battle of Berlin, but losses were so high that in the spring of 1944 attacks had to be suspended. This setback coincided with the decision by the Anglo-American combined chiefs of staff to use the bomber forces to prepare the way for the planned invasion of France in 1944. The RAF took part in attacks to weaken German aircraft production, the so-called big week attacks in February 1944. Harris resisted the plan on the grounds that the best contribution his command could make would be to continue the attack of German cities and slow up the flow of supplies to German forces. Nor did he want to relinquish command to the invasion force air commander, Air Marshal Trafford Leigh-Mallory. A compromise was reached which brought Harris under the direct command of the American General Eisenhower, the supreme commander, with whom he eventually established a good working partnership.

Despite his reservations, Harris carried out the support role with great efficiency, and Bomber Command contributed substantially to the destruction of German transport in north-west Europe and the disruption of the German air force. In September 1944 command over bomber forces was returned to Harris, and the final programme of destruction, aimed at oil, transport, and industrial areas (operations Hurricane I and Hurricane II), began in full. By this stage the force Harris commanded bore no relation to the one he had inherited. It was composed only of four-engined bombers, equipped with modern radio and radar navigation aids, and escorted by long-range night fighters, and the obliteration of German cities and infrastructure now became a possibility. In January 1945 the combined chiefs of staff ordered an operation codenamed Thunderclap, to attack the cities of central and eastern Germany to help speed up the Soviet advance from the east and prevent German forces from consolidating in the central areas of the country.

It was during operation Thunderclap that the notorious attack was made on Dresden on 13–14 February 1945 by the RAF and the US 8th Air Force which caused the death of around 40,000 people. The city was not high on the list of Harris's area targets, but was attacked as part of a concerted disruption of the German front line facing the Red Army. The targets were suggested by Eisenhower's supreme headquarters in Paris, after pressure from the Soviet side to do something to accelerate the destruction of German resistance in the east. After the attack Churchill wrote to the Air Ministry criticizing bombing for the sake of mere terror, even though he had played a major part in encouraging the attacks in eastern Germany. Harris reacted angrily to the charge by arguing that he had 'never gone in for terror bombing' (Harris Papers, H98), and that city bombing was still justified in order to speed up surrender and avoid further allied casualties. He had already crossed swords with the chief of air staff, Portal, in December 1944, over his preference for city attacks over attacks on specific target systems. The new arguments angered and puzzled him. After the war he continued to argue with vigour that the Dresden attack was his operational responsibility but not his choice of target.

The debate about bombing Since the end of the war there has been widespread argument about the impact of bombing. The official history, published in 1961, was critical of some aspects of the campaign, and Harris resented what he saw as a conspiracy to label him as the man responsible for destroying German cities regardless of civilian casualties. In fact much of the debate has been concerned not with issues of morality, but with the direct results. The conclusions of the post-war bombing surveys suggested that German production had not been significantly dented by bombing, and that area bombing in particular had done relatively little to undermine economic performance. More recent assessments have demonstrated that bombing, both British and American, had much wider consequences for the outcome of the war than the official view suggested.

As Harris intended, bombing did disrupt German social and economic life to an exceptional degree. By the end of 1944 8 million Germans had been evacuated from the major cities, and the cumulative strain on the welfare services and food supply, as well as the dispersal of much of the German female workforce, prevented Germany from exploiting domestic resources to the full. The impact on production through destruction was not negligible and forced an expensive and incomplete underground dispersal. Interruptions to communications again prevented Germany from maximizing production at the critical stage of the war in 1943–4. Although German military output did increase threefold between 1941 and 1944, bombing placed a very real ceiling on the capacity of the German economy, which persistently performed below the

level that might have been expected from the resources and labour available.

Equally important were the military consequences. Bombing forced the diversion of very large and unanticipated resources to air defence in Germany. Some 2 million potential workers were manning defences and clearing up bomb damage by 1944; by early 1944 two-thirds of the German fighter force was in Germany, and only 17 per cent on the eastern front, while bomber output fell to only one-fifth the number of fighters; 20 per cent of all ammunition, one half of all electro-technical equipment, and one-third of all optical equipment went into air defence. One-third of all artillery output was kept in the Reich for anti-aircraft units. The bombing war proved to be a genuine 'second front', soaking up resources and denuding the front line in Italy, France, and the USSR of the aircraft, manpower, and equipment which might have produced a military stalemate between the two sides. Bomber support for the invasion of France helped to make a hazardous operation more certain. Bombing helped to constrain and then weaken German fighting power, just as Bomber Command policy under Harris had intended. Loss rates in Bomber Command were high, but no higher than those sustained by the spearhead of allied forces in the invasion of France. The total losses of 55,000 men over six years were modest compared with the losses in a few weeks on the western front in 1916–17. Harris's enduring belief during the war that bombing would in the end save the allied nations a very high bloodletting was vindicated.

The moral argument against bombing was seldom heard during the war. Harris had little time for it, complaining in 1942 about the few 'weaker sisters' in his own command (Harris Papers, H51), and telling the Air Ministry in 1943 that 'the sentimental and humanitarian scruples of a negligible minority' should be ignored (ibid., H47). At the end of the war Harris found himself the butt of much official criticism in circles where bombing was viewed as a strategy inappropriate for a liberal state. He was sufficiently cynical not to be surprised by it, but resented the absence of proper recognition for those who had served under him which he perceived to be the consequence of such criticism.

Honours, retirement, and reputation Harris himself was not short of recognition. In 1943 he was promoted air chief marshal, a year after appointment as KCB. An abundance of foreign honours descended on him: the Soviet order of Suvorov in 1944 and then in 1945 the order of Polonia Restituta, the Brazilian national order of the Southern Cross (grand cross), the French Légion d'honneur (grand officer), and the Croix de Guerre with palm. In 1946 came the US Distinguished Service Medal. There was much speculation that he was passed over for a peerage at the end of the war, but Harris later claimed that he had not wanted it ('a Lord in South Africa was a joke'; Harris Papers, Misc. Box B, Folder 5), and much preferred his promotion to marshal of the Royal Air Force in 1946 because it brought enhanced salary after years when there had not been sufficient money. There was talk that he would be appointed military governor of the British zone of occupied Germany, a singularly inappropriate choice, which came to nothing. When Churchill became prime minister again in 1951 Harris was asked if he wanted a peerage, but he refused. In January 1953 he accepted a baronetcy instead.

In 1946 Harris retired from the RAF, after writing a detailed dispatch on the period of his command, which was circulated in the Air Ministry in autumn 1945 and occasioned a good deal of critical comment. In 1947 he published his memoir of the war, *Bomber Offensive*, which gave a robust defence of his actions. After the war he returned, as he had always wanted to do, to southern Africa. Here with a friend he started up, as a subsidiary of a larger concern, a shipping firm, the South African Marine Corporation. He ran this until 1953, when he returned to England to settle down in Goring-on-Thames. Here he entertained regularly. He had a reputation for hospitality during the war which belied the widespread perception that his was a gruff and prickly personality. With those he trusted or respected he was affable and generous of spirit. The Bomber Command veterans remained staunchly loyal to their wartime commander, affectionately nicknamed Bomber Harris (or Bert to his colleagues, from the naval habit of referring to all Harrises as Berts). Between 1953 and his death Harris was, in his turn, a loyal defender of the command he had led and of the strategy it had pursued. In numerous articles and lectures he sustained his beliefs in the efficacy of bombing and the justness of his wartime cause.

Harris's post-war reputation nevertheless remained mixed. He was without question a commander of real stature, single-minded, hard-working, intelligent, and practical, who contributed in substantial ways to allied victory in 1945. Yet his association with the bombing of cities and the killing of civilians invited a chorus of criticism. From the 1980s bombing came increasingly to be viewed in Germany and elsewhere as a war crime and Harris therefore as a potential war criminal for mass murder. When it was decided to erect a statue to Harris to stand next to Lord Dowding outside the RAF church of St Clement Danes in the Strand in London, there were widespread objections. The statue was unveiled in 1992, amid scenes of noisy protest, and was regularly defaced thereafter. Harris was a controversial figure in his own lifetime, and controversy over his wartime reputation and intentions flourished even more after his death, at his home, Ferry House, Goring-on-Thames, on 5 April 1984. He was buried at Burntwood cemetery, Goring, on 11 April.

R. J. OVERY

Sources Royal Air Force Museum, Hendon, London, Harris papers • PRO, AIR 8, AIR 9, AIR 14, AIR 20 • *DNB* • H. Probert, *Bomber Harris: his life and times: the biography of Marshal of the Royal Air Force, Sir Arthur Harris, the wartime chief of bomber command* (2001) • A. T. Harris, *Bomber offensive* (1947) • A. T. Harris, *Despatch on war operations* (1995) • D. Saward, *'Bomber' Harris* (1984) • C. Messenger, *'Bomber Harris' and the strategic bomber offensive* (1984) • R. J. Overy, *Bomber command, 1939–1945* (1997) • C. Webster and N. Frankland, *The strategic air offensive against Germany*, 4 vols. (1961) • S. Cox, ed., *The strategic air war against Germany, 1939–1945: the official report of the*

British bombing survey unit (1998) • O. Groehler, *Bombenkrieg gegen Deutschland* (Berlin, 1990) • S. Garrett, *Ethics and air power in World War II* (1993) • A. J. Levine, *The strategic bombing of Germany, 1940–1945* (1992)

Archives Royal Air Force Museum, Hendon, corresp. and papers | Nuffield Oxf., corresp. with Lord Cherwell • PRO, AIR 8, AIR 9, AIR 14, AIR 20 | FILM IWM, newsreel material | SOUND IWM, interviews and speeches

Likenesses W. Stoneman, photograph, 1940, NPG • H. Coster, photograph, 1941, NPG [*see illus.*] • L. McCombe, photograph, 1943, Hult. Arch. • photograph, *c*.1945, NPG • bronze statue, 1992, St Clement Danes Church, London • E. Kennington, crayon, IWM • H. A. Olivier, double portrait (with General Anderson), priv. coll. • H. A. Olivier, oils, Royal Air Force Museum, Hendon • P. Taylor, bronze head, Royal Air Force Museum, Hendon • A. Zinkeisen, portrait, Strike Command Headquarters, High Wycombe

Wealth at death under £40,000: probate, 24 Aug 1984, *CGPLA Eng. & Wales*

Harris, Augustus Frederick Glossop [Augustus Glossop Harris] (1826–1873), actor and theatre manager, was born at Portici, Naples, on 12 June 1826. His father, Joseph Glossop, built the Coburg Theatre (later known as the Royal Victoria and nicknamed the Old Vic), and was at various times manager of La Scala, Milan, and the San Carlo in Naples. His mother, Elizabeth Glossop was an opera singer, known on the stage as Madame Feron. Harris's début was made in America, at about the age of eight, as a fairy coachman in the opera *Cinderella*. In London he played with Thomas Robson at the Bower Theatre in Stangate in the comic parts of Harlequin, Pantaloon, and Clown, and in 1843 appeared as Snobbington Duprez in a farce at the Princess's Theatre, under the management of J. M. Maddox. On 17 February 1846 Harris married Maria Ann Bone, a theatrical costumier. Eventually they had three daughters, Patience, Ellen, and Maria, and two sons, Sir Augustus Henry Glossop *Harris and Charles, all of whom were later connected with the stage.

In 1859, after the retirement of Charles Kean from the Princess's, Harris became the manager. He opened on 24 September 1859, with Oxenford's adaptation *Ivy Hall*, and during his lesseeship introduced Charles Albert Fechter to the London stage. His management closed on 16 October 1862. Harris is known principally as a manager of opera and ballet. He had an admirable eye for colour and a great capacity for stage arrangement. He was connected, with only one break, for twenty-seven years with the stage and general management of the Royal Italian Opera, Covent Garden, and he undertook the stage direction of opera in St Petersburg, Madrid, Paris, Berlin, and Barcelona. During the last four years of his life he gave Christmas spectacles at Covent Garden. He died on 19 April 1873, at his home, 2 Bedford Place, Russell Square, and was buried on the 25th at Brompton cemetery.

JOSEPH KNIGHT, rev. NILANJANA BANERJI

Sources *The Era* (27 April 1873) • P. Hartnoll, ed., *The concise Oxford companion to the theatre* (1972) • P. Hartnoll, ed., *The Oxford companion to the theatre* (1951); 2nd edn (1957); 3rd edn (1967) • *The life and reminiscences of E. L. Blanchard, with notes from the diary of Wm. Blanchard*, ed. C. W. Scott and C. Howard, 2 vols. (1891) • private information (1891) • m. cert. • d. cert.

Likenesses H. Watkins, albumen print, 1855–60, NPG

Wealth at death under £5000: resworn probate, June 1878, *CGPLA Eng. & Wales* (1873)

Harris, Sir Augustus Henry Glossop (1852–1896), actor and theatre manager, was born on 18 March 1852 in the rue Taitbout, Paris, one of five children of the theatre manager Augustus Glossop *Harris (1826–1873) and his wife, *née* Maria Ann Bone, a theatrical costumier.

Harris's early life is mostly unrecorded. As a child, prima donnas petted and kissed him as he sat in the wings of Covent Garden Theatre, where his father was stage manager. He attended a school in London, and when he was eleven years old went to the École Niedermeyer, Paris, where he rubbed shoulders with fellow student Gabriel Fauré and, apocryphally, acted Hamlet. A brief spell in Hanover to learn German completed his education before he began work in commerce for Emile Erlanger & Co. On his father's death Harris turned to his and his family's first love, the theatre: his grandfather Joseph Glossop had built the Coburg (later the Old Vic), and his father had been stage manager at the Théâtre Italien in Paris when Harris was born.

Harris's début was as Malcolm in *Macbeth* in September 1873 at the Theatre Royal, Manchester, which was followed by juvenile and light comedy roles at the Amphitheatre, Liverpool, with Barry Sullivan. During that engagement 'Colonel' Mapleson hired him as an assistant stage manager and, with his brother, Charles, as *régisseur* (producer), he toured the provinces with Mapleson's company. Their mother supplied the costumes, which they guarded closely to ensure she received payment. Harris's efforts at staging opera at the Theatre Royal, Bath, resulted in his quick promotion to stage-manager. In 1876 Lord Newry sent him to Paris to engage the Odéon company for the St James's Theatre, where it performed *The Danischeffs* successfully. Harris gained additional experience producing E. L. Blanchard's pantomime *Sinbad the Sailor* at the Crystal Palace (21 December 1876) for Charles Wyndham. Wyndham subsequently cast Harris as Henry Greenlanes in James Albery's *The Pink Dominos* (31 March 1877), a role he played for 555 consecutive performances.

While not a talented actor, Harris was ambitious: in 1876 he proposed running the Philharmonic, Islington, as a first-class music-hall featuring ballets. Then, in 1879, he happened to pass the vacant Drury Lane and, although virtually penniless and but twenty-seven years old, he applied for the lease. He found backing by badgering William Edgecombe Rendle and some friends for £2750, the minimum needed to begin production. (Harris married Rendle's daughter Florence Edgecombe (*d.* 1914) on 9 November 1881; they had one daughter, Florence Nellie. Florence Harris remarried in 1904; her new husband was Edward Terry.)

Harris had a straightforward management policy: to gauge public taste precisely and satisfy the demand. That was the only way to fill the cavernous Drury Lane and make it pay. The theatre's vastness required commensurately massive, spectacular, and lavish productions. The result was a three-part season, with a pantomime as its money-making centrepiece, preceded by a melodrama,

Sir Augustus Henry Glossop Harris (1852–1896), by Walery, before 1891

and followed by other 'high-brow' productions sustained by the pantomime's profits.

As he was not ready with his first production, Harris sublet Drury Lane in November 1879 to George Rignold, who produced *Henry V*—which incidentally confirmed that legitimate drama could not pay. Harris's first pantomime was Blanchard and Greenwood's *Bluebeard* (26 December 1879), which established his lavish, spectacular (and successful) style. A brief Shakespeare season given by Marie Litton intervened before Harris's first melodrama, *The World* (31 July 1880), which he co-wrote, staged, and acted in (he never took things lightly). The production opened nearly two months before the traditional season began, which signalled Harris's intention of attracting more than a society audience to Drury Lane. This strategy lengthened the period for profits to accrue and for the pantomime to be prepared. Although the plot of *The World* was baffling, audiences (though not every critic) were enthralled and almost overwhelmed by the stupendous staging and effects. So the pattern of Harris's tenancy at Drury Lane was set. *The World* was followed by similar melodramatic extravaganzas, whose titles were as short as their plots were long and bewildering—*Youth* (1881), *Pluck* (1882), *Pleasure* (1887), and *The Derby Winner* (1894). First nights, often four hours long, became attractions in themselves: the complex staging often resulted in confusion and disarray, and subsequent performances had to be abbreviated somewhat. Nevertheless, virtually all were successful, as were the pantomimes into which Harris introduced numerous music-hall stars (Kate Santley, Arthur Roberts, Fred Storey, Little Tich, Marie Lloyd, Vesta Tilley), and, even more notably, the comedians Dan Leno and Herbert Campbell. A hallmark of both pantomimes and melodramas was enormous processions: the 1892 pantomime included one procession representing twenty-one sports and pastimes and another depicting twenty-eight nursery rhymes, while the then Major Kitchener was engaged to supervise marching scenes in the 1885 melodrama, *Human Nature*.

In the spring of most years Harris offered 'high art'. The Saxe-Meiningen company appeared in 1881, and its expert handling of supernumeraries, particularly in the crowd scenes in *Julius Caesar*, influenced not only Harris in directing the 500 to 600 performers in his own processions, but the young F. R. Benson. There were seasons of German opera (with Hans Richter conducting), which included the first English performance of *Die Meistersinger* (30 May 1882) and the first production outside Germany of *Tristan und Isolde* (20 June 1882). From 1883 to 1887 Harris nurtured the Carl Rosa Opera Company, whose purpose was to produce opera in English (an 1884 production of *Carmen* featured scenery based on a real cigarette factory in Seville). Its 1887 season celebrated Queen Victoria's jubilee by featuring the opera sensation of the time, Jean de Reszke, whom Harris hired. It was an artistic and social success, but lost £10,000. Serious drama was represented by Madame Ristori in *Macbeth* (1882), the Comédie-Française (1893), Eleonora Duse (1895), and the ducal court company of Saxe-Coburg and Gotha (1895).

His success with opera at Drury Lane convinced Harris—popularly known as 'Druriolanus'—to tackle Covent Garden, and, with the backing of society friends, he launched his first season there in May 1888, which included the inauspicious début of Nellie Melba. (The same year Harris bought the *Sunday Times* to retaliate against often cruel criticisms of his efforts levelled by other newspapers.) He engaged many other great singers, paid close attention to the visual aspects of the operas, and eventually produced operas in their original language. This innovation was greeted as a bold experiment; previously they had been sung, rather arcanely, only in Italian. This led to 'Italian' being dropped from the theatre's name in 1892, when it became the Royal Opera House. The same year Harris began to widen his audience by attracting city merchants and members of London's German colony. Other highlights of his management included the débuts of Emma Eames (1891) and Emma Calvé (1892), and visits by Leoncavallo, Mascagni (1893), and Puccini (1894). Command performances at Windsor Castle were given in 1893 and 1894. And Harris, always adept in handling divas, also induced Adelina Patti to return to the stage for a final series of performances in 1895.

Outside the theatre, Harris was a member of the London county council (1890), and sheriff of London (1890–91), for which he was knighted during the 1891 visit of the German emperor. As part of his shrieval duties he once attended court and discovered the Pantaloon from an earlier pantomime charged with bigamy.

Harris's myriad exertions eventually proved fatal: suffering from exhaustion, diabetes, and cancer, he died on 22 June 1896 at the Pavilion Hotel, Folkestone. He was then only forty-three, quite portly, bearded, and closely resembled the prince of Wales. A genial, gregarious man, Harris had the knack of surrounding himself with clever assistants and friends. His spectacular Drury Lane productions had become legendary and he rejuvenated Covent Garden, making it a world-class opera house. His funeral on 27 June 1896 at Brompton cemetery was attended by several thousand people of all classes, a final grand procession he would have surely enjoyed.   J. P. WEARING

Sources *The Times* (23 June 1896) · *New York Times* (23 June 1896) · J. M. Glover, *Jimmy Glover: his book* (1911) · J. Stottlar, '"A house choked with gunpowder and wild with excitement": Augustus Harris and Drury Lane's spectacular melodrama', *When they weren't doing Shakespeare: essays on nineteenth-century British and American theatre*, ed. J. L. Fisher and S. Watt (1989), 212–29 · H. Rosenthal, *Two centuries of opera at Covent Garden* (1958) · W. J. Macqueen Pope, *Theatre Royal, Drury Lane* (1945) · W. J. Macqueen-Pope, *Pillars of Drury Lane* (1955) · A. Harris, 'The National Theatre', *Fortnightly Review*, 44 (1885), 630–36 · *Five years at Old Drury Lane, 1879–1884: being a record of the productions at the national theatre during the past five years of the management of Augustus Harris* (1884) · H. Klein, 'Modern musical celebrities', *Century Magazine*, 66 (1903), 268–83, 461–71 · F. M. Coggin, 'The pantomimes of Augustus Harris: Drury Lane 1879–1895', PhD diss., Ohio State University, 1973 · M. R. Booth, *Victorian spectacular theatre, 1850–1910* (1981) · d. cert.

Archives BL, letters · University of Rochester, New York, corresp.

Likenesses Walery, photograph, before 1891, NPG [*see illus.*] · S. Kent, lithograph, 1894, NPG · A. Beardsley, pen-and-ink caricature, Tate collection; repro. in J. Davidson, *Plays* (1894) · A. M. Broadley, pen-and-ink sketch, NPG · A. Bryan, caricatures, repro. in *Entr'acte* (1881–90) · A. Bryan, drawing, repro. in Glover, *Jimmy Glover* · E. J. W., sketch, Harvard TC · H. Furniss, pen-and-ink sketch, NPG · Hay, watercolour, NPG · H. C. Merrill, photograph, repro. in Klein, 'Modern musical celebrities' · Spy [L. Ward], chromolithograph caricature, Harvard TC, NPG; repro. in *VF* (28 Sept 1889) · bronze bust, Drury Lane Theatre, London · pen-and-ink, NPG · photographs, Harvard TC · photographs, repro. in B. Dobbs, *Drury Lane: three centuries of the Theatre Royal, 1663–1971* (1972)

Wealth at death £23,677 2s. 9d.: probate, 2 July 1896, CGPLA Eng. & Wales

Harris, Benjamin (*c*.1647–1720), publisher and bookseller, was born in London, the son of William Harris, citizen and barber–surgeon. Apprenticed to a bookseller on 6 April 1663, he gained his freedom from the Stationers' Company on 1 August 1670. His first known publication (with Robert Clavell), in 1673, was of the work of Particular Baptist divine Benjamin Keach, whose religious beliefs he shared. Harris continued to publish Keach's writings together with a medley of religious controversy and potboilers, including an astrological guide by William Lilly and Hannah Wolley's *The Accomplished Ladies Delight* (1675), a successful cookery book.

1679 marks the turning point in Harris's career. He was part of a publishing syndicate for the *Narrative and Impartial Discovery of the Horrid Popish Plot* by William Bedloe, a tract which marks his entry into the religious and political turmoil of the years 1679–81. During that time he published at least a dozen pamphlet titles, including works by John Bunyan as well as ballads, a pack of playing cards depicting the Popish Plot, and anti-popish prints. In July 1679, with characteristic ingenuity and appreciation of the market, Harris was the first to exploit the new press freedom by starting a bi-weekly newspaper, the *Domestick Intelligence*, which he may also have written in collaboration with Nathaniel Crouch and Robert Claypole; his protest in 1681 that 'he was never the author of anything he ever published' can be interpreted as a denial of single authorship made at a time when he was struggling to avoid prison. Although 'published to prevent false reports', the *Domestick Intelligence* was packed with anti-Catholic venom written in lively prose. Its success brought rivals, most notably Nathaniel Thompson's paper of the same name which began in August and deliberately sought to scoop Harris's readers.

Harris soon found himself in trouble for publishing a tract, *The Appeal from the Country to the City*, probably written by Charles Blount, which was circulating in London in October 1679. It was remarkable on two counts. First, it contained a vivid depiction of the rape and pillage associated with an imagined Catholic massacre of protestants. As if the prose was not graphic enough, two years later Harris issued *A Scheme of Popish Cruelties*, which included copperplate images closely linked to the *Appeal's* imagery. Second, the *Appeal* was unique in its open support for the succession of Charles II's illegitimate son, James Scot, duke of Monmouth, on the grounds that 'he who has the worst title makes the best king' (*Appeal*, 25). Throughout the autumn of 1679 Harris reported on Monmouth's exile and in 1681 he was to dedicate a work to Monmouth's son. Harris claimed he had merely republished 'to get money' a tract that had already been running 'up and down the town' (*State trials*, 928); but it was he who 'bore all' (Luttrell, 1.36) when the government singled him out for prosecution. The publisher of the original copy has been a matter of dispute. Harris's enemy Nathaniel Thompson is one candidate, especially since his wife was arrested for dispersing the tract; Roger L'Estrange, the former licenser of the press, thought Langley Curtis was responsible; but it may ironically have been Harris himself who introduced the first copies, since customs officials had discovered a box of 'treasonable papers' sent direct to Harris from Flanders. In any case, Harris was brought to trial on 5 February 1680. The prosecuting counsel, James Jeffreys, and the presiding judge, Lord Chief Justice Scroggs, refused to allow Harris to speak in his own defence and made it clear that Harris was regarded by the government as 'factious'. The jury originally returned a verdict that he was guilty only of selling the book, prompting 'a very great and clamorous shout' in what was evidently a packed courtroom, but Scroggs condemned Harris to imprisonment, a promise of good behaviour for three years, and a £500 fine (*State trials*, 929, 931). When, a week later, Harris stood in the pillory his friends and wife 'hollowed and whooped and would suffer nothing to be thrown at him' (Luttrell, 1.34); but although he had

boasted that 'he had above a thousand persons who would stand by him in whatsoever he did' (*State trials*, 926–7) he was unable to pay the fine and languished in prison. His newspaper carried on without him but ceased publication on 16 April, having shortly beforehand published an erroneous report that Lord Chief Justice North had said that the laws against absentees from church should only be enforced against the papists. Crouch tried to continue the paper with a slightly different title, prompting the imprisoned Harris to disclaim in print any responsibility for the new venture.

Harris petitioned the House of Commons on 19 November 1680 and the Lords on the 24th. Both houses considered his case, the peers debating whether the excessive fine contravened Magna Carta, and the Commons resolving on 22 December that king's bench had acted arbitrarily and illegally. Harris was set free (on dubious authority) and immediately published *The Triumph of Justice over Unjust Judges*, a vituperative attack on Scroggs. On 28 December he was again first in the field—after a proclamation in May had silenced the periodical press—in resuming his newspaper, with the express hope that 'it may not give offence to any, not in the least intending to meddle with any thing, that may be any ways prejudicial to State-Affairs or any private Persons, but to proceed with all Modesty and Moderation imaginable'. But in January 1681 he changed its title to the *Protestant (Domestick) Intelligence*, largely to distinguish it from the Catholic Nathaniel Thompson's paper, and started another, short-lived, paper, the *Weekly Discoverer Strip'd Naked*, on 16 February 1681. Harris had now become a public butt of satire. A Catholic tract abusing the duke of Monmouth and the earl of Shaftesbury was published with Harris's imprint on it, forcing him to run to the lord mayor to disown the piece. Equally humiliating was the ridicule heaped on him, in a ballad called *The Protestant Cuckold*, for the alleged adultery of his wife, Ruth, with whom he had three children by 1681 but about whom no further details are known. Once parliament had been dissolved, privy council launched an inquiry into why Harris had been released and ordered him back into custody on 11 February 1681. His friendship with the republican Slingsby Bethel can hardly have endeared him to the government, which was also amassing evidence that Harris was one of Shaftesbury's printers. Harris's paper had also become more daring: it was accused in March 1681 of having invented one of the so-called 'instructions' to MPs which Shaftesbury was supposed to have promoted at the general election. The paper ceased publication on 15 April 1681.

In June 1681, presumably as proof of good behaviour, the imprisoned Harris sent the secretary of state papers 'of a pernicious consequence' (*CSP dom., 1680–81*, 335) which had been sent to him for publication. In September he petitioned the king, protesting that he was 'heartily sorry' for his 'folly', confessing that he could not pay the fine, and that when free he would give the king an account of the *Appeal* (Muddiman, *N&Q*, 149). Yet it was not until November or December 1682 that he finally recovered his liberty. In March 1683 he registered his *Domestick Intelligence*, to be 'published gratis every Thursday for the promoting of Trade', but no copies appear to have been issued. He was nevertheless back in trouble in August 1683 when he attempted to sell seditious libels at Bristol fair. A warrant was issued for his arrest and although he escaped he was forced to lie low in disguise. He continued to promote the nonconformist cause in print but was increasingly cautious, publishing less critical pieces such as *Regall Power Asserted agt. Papall and Popular Userpation* and, in May 1684, *The Pious Politician*, a collection of the maxims of 'that incomparable prince' Charles I. Yet, perhaps because of his earlier support for Monmouth, Harris was a figure of suspicion in 1685 when James II came to the throne, and his house was searched. Among the materials seized in November were 'seventy reams of a seditious book entitled *English Liberties*' (*CSP dom.*, 1685, 382), a radical statement of the rights of a freeborn subject written by Henry Care. Although Harris had not published the pamphlets, despite having bought the title in June 1683, and even proved to the Stationers' Company that he was already 'selling them for waste paper' (Myers, 209), the raid was enough to frighten him. He later claimed that his assertion of the laws and liberties of England had won him so many inveterate enemies that 'to save my life and family from ruin, I was compell'd to be an exile from my native country, for above eight years' (*Intelligence, Domestick and Foreign*, 1, 14 May 1695).

Harris went to Boston, Massachusetts, in 1686 where he resumed publishing in 1687 and, continuing a trade he appears to have entered during the succession crisis, set up the London Coffee House. He was accompanied by one of his children, Vavasour. His newspaper experience and his eye for the main chance led him to publish, on 25 September 1690, the first (and last) unlicensed issue of *Publick Occurrences*, which has been hailed as the first American newspaper. Its novelty lay partly in its intended periodical nature—it was to be 'furnished once a moneth (or if any Glut of Occurrences happen, oftener)'. But in style and content it was also revelatory. The paper promised to cover 'memorable occurents of divine providence', domestic and foreign public affairs so 'that people every where may better understand' them and 'assist their Businesses and Negotiations', and finally to do something 'towards the Curing, or at least Charming of that Spirit of Lying, which prevails amongst us, wherefore nothing shall be entered, but what we have reason to believe is true'. To achieve the latter aim the paper claimed it would 'expose the name' of anyone who maliciously raised a false report. The statement of high ideals was followed by some characteristically lively reports of disasters, a suicide, and fires, but also a racy report that Louis XIV slept with his daughter-in-law and another provocative item about the failure of 'miserable' Indian allies to deliver their promises. The governor and council of Massachusetts believed the paper contained 'reflections of a very high nature; as also sundry doubtful and uncertain reports' and suppressed it and any other unlicensed print. The influential puritan Cotton Mather was suspected as its author, particularly since Harris's partner and printer Richard Pierce was related by marriage to him, but in a private letter Mather disowned any large hand in it, suggesting that 'the Publisher had not one Line of it; only as accidentally meeting him on the high-way, on his Request, I show'd him how to contract & express the Report of the Expedition at Casco & the East'. Indeed Mather claimed the publisher 'pick't up here & there what hee inserted' and that Harris had his information from 'three or four … Ingenious men'. Even so, Mather's support for the publication, which he regarded as 'a very Noble, useful and Laudable Design', was clear and he may have been right that the suppression had been aimed at him as much as at Harris (Paltsis, 85–8).

Harris's other claim to fame in America was his publication, again in 1690, of the often reprinted *New England Primer*. While in England, Harris had fused his protestant zeal, propagandizing genius, and an interest in the education of the young with the publication in 1679 of *The Protestant Tutor*. This has suggested to some that Harris was the author of the Boston publication. As with some of his other works the extent to which Harris was copying rather than innovating is not always clear. Even before Harris had arrived, a *New England Primer* had been published by John Griffin; but in 1685 Griffin had himself published a *Protestant Tutor* which lifted its catechism against popery and one other item from Harris's work of that name.

Harris prospered in Boston and in 1691 he set up a profitable partnership with John Allen, another refugee from London who had previously printed several of Increase Mather's works. In December 1692 the partners won the right to publish the Massachusetts *Acts and Laws* as printers to the governor, though they lost this the following year.

Harris is thought to have visited England in January 1688 and again in November 1688, but he did not finally return to London until late in 1694 or early in 1695, perhaps tempted back by the final lapse of the Licensing Act. Although he resumed publishing tracts, including works by Keach, he once more ventured into newspapers. On 14 May 1695 he published the *Intelligence, Domestick and Foreign*, 'to please and divert my older Protestant friends', changing its title in June to the *Pacquet-Boat from Holland*. But he was arrested the following month 'for printing false news' (Luttrell, 3.497), probably because of a misleading account of the war against France. He had more success in June 1699 when he began the *London Slip of News* which, after changing its title on the second issue to the *London Post*, continued in a whig vein until 1705. Before its closure Harris used the paper to attack his erstwhile friend John Dunton, who in happier days had described him as 'the most Ingenious and Innocent Companion that I had ever met with' (*Life and Errors*, 216–17). Dunton in turn now condemned Harris as a liar: 'his employment, or rather livelihood, is to blast other men's credit and to steal their copies. He is a mere F—y for slander, falsehood, tricking' (ibid., 466). After another unseemly tangle with the astrologer (and former fellow supporter of Monmouth)

John Partridge, whose almanac he pirated, Harris was forced to close his 'thievish paper ... for want of receivers' (ibid., 474). The quarrel with Partridge nevertheless rumbled on, for as late as 1713 Partridge observed that 'two or three poor printers and a bookbinder, with honest Ben' would counterfeit his work (Muddiman, *King's Journalist*, 255). As this suggests, Harris's fortunes were, and had been since the 1690s, in decline. Indeed, he spent his last years as a quack seller of Angelical Pills and other patent medicines.

Aside from the two sons, Vavasour and Benjamin, who were apprenticed to their father, it is possible that the publisher John Harris who began entering titles in 1685, and Sarah Harris who issued Benjamin's titles in 1688–90, were also relatives. Harris died intestate, probably shortly before July 1720 when an administration order was granted to Anne, his second wife.   MARK KNIGHTS

Sources W. C. Ford, 'Benjamin Harris, printer and bookseller', *Proceedings of the Massachusetts Historical Society*, 57 (1923–4), 34–68 • J. G. Muddiman, 'Benjamin Harris, the first American journalist', *N&Q*, 163 (1932), 129–33, 147–50, 166–70, 223, 273–4 • J. G. Muddiman, *The king's journalist, 1659–1689* (1923), 211–55 • *The life and errors of John Dunton*, [rev. edn], ed. J. B. Nichols, 2 vols. (1818) • *CSP dom.* • *State trials*, 7.926–32 • V. H. Paltsis, 'New light on *Publick Occurrences*', *Proceedings of the American Antiquarian Society*, 59 (1949), 75–88 • N. Luttrell, *A brief historical relation of state affairs from September 1678 to April 1714*, 6 vols. (1857); repr. (1969) • *Intelligence, Domestick and Foreign*, 1 (14 May 1695) • PRO, PROB 6/96, fol. 113 • R. Myers, *The Stationers' Company archive: an account of the records, 1554–1984* (1990) • *The manuscripts of the House of Lords*, 4 vols., HMC, 17 (1887–94), vol. 1, pp. 212–13 • *Memories of the life of Anthony, late earl of Shaftesbury* (1683), 6 • *The protestant cuckold* (1681) [ballad]

Harris, Benjamin Randell (1781–1858), soldier and shoemaker, was born in 1781 in Portsea, Hampshire, and was baptized on 28 October 1781. He was the eldest of the two sons of Robert Harris, a shepherd, and his wife, Elizabeth, *née* Randell (d. 1788). Robert Harris married again following Elizabeth's death and had two more children.

Harris had no formal education and was illiterate. As a boy and young man he helped his father as a shepherd until he was recruited by the 66th regiment on 27 August 1803. While on an exercise in Ireland he was recruited by the 2nd battalion of the 95th rifles, attracted by the regiment's reputation for accuracy. Harris's first active service with the 95th was on the British operation to capture the Danish fleet, to deny it to the French. The regiment arrived in Denmark on 10 August 1808 and following the bombardment of Copenhagen and the capture of the Danish warships they arrived back in England on 16 November. Harris then left for Portugal in July and fought at the battle of Roliça on 17 August 1808 and at the battle of Vimeiro, where the riflemen caused substantial French losses.

Harris must have trained as a cobbler as his skills were employed during the war to mend other soldiers' boots and shoes. During the march to Salamanca in November 1808 Harris saw men whose boots had worn completely away. Later in 1808 the 95th was part of the British retreat towards Corunna. Exhaustion claimed the lives of many soldiers and of the wives and families who were allowed to travel with them. Harris nearly died when he was too weak to keep marching and was left behind in the village of St Domingo-Flores in January 1809. He was helped by a rifleman named Brooks and then sheltered with a Spanish family before catching up with the 95th. They reached the port of Vigo on 12 January 1809.

Back in Britain, Harris helped recruit for the regiment and in May 1809 they left for Dutch Zeeland. They arrived in Walcheren on 1 August 1809 only to be struck down by malaria. Harris became ill on the ship back to Dover. He had £200 saved from shoemaking and bought wine and food which he believed saved him. Of the 39 riflemen who were hospitalized, only Harris survived. He never went on active service again. He joined the 8th veteran battalion and was discharged in July 1814. He devoted his time to shoemaking and possibly owned premises in Soho in the mid-1830s before moving to 4 Upper James Street, Golden Square, London, about 1848.

There is no evidence that Harris married, though it is likely. He certainly became close to two women during the war. He proposed to a Mrs Cockayne, the widow of a rifleman killed in the battle of Roliça, but was refused. After the battle of Vimeiro he met a Spanish girl whose family offered her in marriage. Harris declined on grounds of religion, and fears of court martial.

Harris told his story to Henry Curling, an officer of the 52nd regiment. Curling first published the *Recollections of Rifleman Harris* in 1848. The emphasis was on Harris's career as a soldier and there is very little personal information, especially about his later life. Harris's purpose was to portray the courage of the rifleman, as he felt true bravery was only shown by men at war.

Harris died in Poland Street workhouse, London, on 10 December 1858. He had been declared insane, and the cause of death was diagnosed as illness of the prostate. In the twentieth century there were more editions of Harris's recollections and a revival in interest in him, which reached a peak towards the end of the century with Bernard Cornwell's Sharpe novels, and an ensuing television series.   ROSY LYNE

Sources E. Hathaway, *A Dorset rifleman—the recollections of Benjamin Harris* (1995) • *The recollections of Rifleman Harris: as told to Henry Curling*, ed. C. Hibbert (1996) • *Recollections of Rifleman Harris*, ed. H. Curling (1848)
Archives City Westm. AC, parish registers and census returns for St Anne's, Soho • Dorset RO, Blandford Forum militia MSS • Dorset RO, parish registers for Stalbridge • PRO, Chelsea Hospital registers • PRO, 95th rifle brigade MSS

Harris, Charles Amyand (1813–1874), bishop of Gibraltar, was born at Christchurch, Hampshire, on 4 August 1813, the third son of James Edward Harris, second earl of Malmesbury (1778–1841), and his wife, Harriet Susan (1783–1815), daughter of Francis Bateman Dashwood of Well Vale, Lincolnshire. James Howard *Harris, third earl of Malmesbury, was his eldest brother. He matriculated from Oriel College, Oxford, on 5 May 1831, graduating BA in 1835, with fourth-class honours in classics and second in mathematics, and MA in 1837. He was fellow of All Souls College from 1835 until his marriage on 20 May 1837 to

Katherine Lucia (*d.* 1865), youngest daughter of Sir Edward O'Brien, bt. They had an only son who died in childhood.

In 1834 Harris was entered as a student of the Inner Temple, but, after changing his mind about his profession, was ordained deacon in 1836 and priest in 1837. He acted as rector of Shaftesbury, Dorset, during 1839–40. In the latter year he was appointed to the rectory of Wilton in Wiltshire, which had attached to it the rectory of Bulbridge and the vicarage of Ditchampton. On 16 August 1841 he was nominated prebendary of Chardstock in Salisbury Cathedral, and made a domestic chaplain to the bishop of the diocese. His health failed in 1848, when he resigned his livings. After some years of rest he became in 1856 the perpetual curate of Rownhams, Southampton, where Lord Herbert, in conjunction with the widow of Major Colt, had built a new parish church. In 1863 he succeeded the Revd Henry Drury as archdeacon of Wiltshire, when he was also made vicar of Bremhill-with-Highway, near Chippenham. He was an active parish priest and a valued assistant to his bishop, Walter Kerr Hamilton, who had a high regard for his business capacity.

In 1868 Harris was nominated to the bishopric of Gibraltar, and consecrated on 1 May. His kindly manner, gentle bearing, knowledge of languages, and long experience fitted him for his new duties. He gave accounts of his work on Gibraltar at the meetings of the Society for the Propagation of the Gospel. In 1872 he was taken ill with fever; he returned to England, resigned his bishopric in October 1873, and settled at Torquay. Harris died there on 16 March 1874, and was buried at Bremhill on 19 March by the side of his wife. By his will he left considerable sums to episcopal societies, besides legacies to his relatives.

G. C. BOASE, rev. M. C. CURTHOYS

Sources *Salisbury and Winchester Journal* (21 March 1874), 8 · *Guardian* (25 March 1874), 355 · *ILN* (4 April 1874), 331 · W. H. Jones, *Fasti ecclesiae Sarisberiensis, or, A calendar … of the cathedral body at Salisbury* (1879), 177, 372 · Boase, *Mod. Eng. biog.*
Archives Hants. RO, corresp. and papers | U. Edin. L., special collections division, letters to Sir Charles Lyell · U. St Andr. L., corresp. with James Forbes
Wealth at death under £25,000: probate, 25 March 1874, *CGPLA Eng. & Wales*

Harris, Sir Charles Herbert Stuart- (1909–1996), virologist, was born at 1 High Street, King's Heath, King's Norton, Birmingham, on 12 July 1909, the son of Charles Herbert Harris (*d.* 1913), a general practitioner, and his wife, Helen, *née* Parsons; the hyphen between Stuart and Harris was introduced later. He won scholarships to King Edward's School, Birmingham, and later to St Bartholomew's Hospital medical school, London. His ability was clear, and he graduated MB BS with two gold medals in 1931 and MD in 1933; he was admitted MRCP in 1934. He was house physician to Professor Sir Francis Fraser and demonstrator in pathology at St Bartholomew's Hospital from 1933, and he moved with Fraser to become first assistant in the department of medicine at the newly established British Postgraduate Medical School at Hammersmith Hospital in west London in 1935.

In 1935 Stuart-Harris was awarded a fellowship valued at

Sir Charles Herbert Stuart-Harris (1909–1996), by unknown photographer

£55 a year from the bequest of Sir Henry Royce (of Rolls-Royce) which enabled him to undertake research into the cause and cure of influenza at the National Institute for Medical Research, where Wilson Smith, Christopher Howard Andrewes, and Sir Patrick Playfair Laidlaw had made the first isolation of human influenza virus two years earlier using ferrets which had developed a respiratory tract infection. A laboratory infection enabled Smith and Stuart-Harris to show that influenza A virus that had been through a number of ferret passages was still infectious to man. Stuart-Harris also succeeded in adapting influenza A virus to mice by serial intracerebral passage. In the USA two other researchers, Francis and Magill, had made separate isolations of influenza B virus, and Stuart-Harris next spent a period at the Rockefeller Institute in New York working with Thomas Francis on influenza B virus. After returning to England he continued his influenza virus studies supported by a Foulerton research fellowship of the Royal Society, awarded in 1938. In the previous year, on 4 September 1937, he had married Marjorie Winifred (*b.* 1915), younger daughter of Fred Robinson of Dulwich.

The outbreak of the Second World War interrupted his active research on respiratory tract infections, and Stuart-Harris next served the Royal Army Medical Corps as a pathologist, by 1945 with the rank of colonel. His laboratory background led to his involvement in the development of a typhus vaccine, during which he contracted the disease, but he made a full recovery and later took part in field trials of the vaccine in north Africa. He contributed to the Medical Research Council's Special Report on typhus, published in 1946. He also served in Italy, India, and the Far East, where he was concerned with the medical problems of released prisoners of war in Singapore. Later, in Germany, the somewhat different problems of survivors of concentration camps came under his care.

Returned to civilian life, Stuart-Harris in 1946 became the first full-time professor of medicine at the University of Sheffield, an appointment that initially caused surprise that a pathologist should be given a clinical chair. Any reservations concerning his suitability were quickly dispelled, however, as he gradually built up a department with a high reputation for both teaching and research.

Somewhat austere by nature Stuart-Harris was quietly spoken, though firm in his dealings with students and staff. He seldom missed a ward round or an outpatient or teaching session. He was nicknamed 'the Smiling Tiger' by medical students, reflecting his intolerance of laziness or loose thinking, but he was immensely supportive of creative ability wherever he found it. The Christmas parties he and his wife hosted for members of staff were warmly remembered as features of the Sheffield year. The Medical Research Council set up a research unit at Lodge Moor Hospital, Sheffield, under his charge. Direct personal involvement in laboratory research evolved into teamwork with a succession of handpicked assistants, several of whom later went on to senior appointments elsewhere. Research on influenza and other respiratory infections, notably chronic bronchitis and pertussis, continued, and one of the first clinical trials of oral poliovirus vaccine was carried out in Sheffield.

Highly esteemed by both patients and staff in Sheffield, Stuart-Harris's rare combination of broad clinical and laboratory skills meant that his advice was sought far beyond that city. He served on the board of the Public Health Laboratory Service (1954–66); the Medical Research Council (1957–61); and the University Grants Committee (1968–77), being chairman of the medical subcommittee (1973–7). He became a fellow of the Royal College of Physicians in 1944 and gave the Goulstonian lecture in 1945, the Croonian lecture in 1962, and the Harveian oration in 1974. He wrote many original papers and contributions to textbooks and reviews, most of them relating to respiratory tract infections. He was much in demand outside the UK and was visiting professor of medicine at Albany Medical College in 1953, and at Vanderbilt University, Tennessee, in 1961. As Sir Arthur Sims Commonwealth travelling professor he visited the University of Southern California, Los Angeles, in 1962. He gave the Henry Cohen lecture at the Hebrew University of Jerusalem in 1966 and was Waring professor at the University of Colorado and Stanford University, California, in 1967. He was president of the Association of Physicians of Great Britain and Ireland in 1971, and honorary member of the Association of American Physicians and of the Infectious Diseases Society of America. He was awarded honorary degrees by the University of Hull in 1973 and by Sheffield University in 1978. He was appointed CBE in 1961 and knighted in 1970.

After retirement in 1972 Stuart-Harris continued his service to Sheffield University as postgraduate dean of medicine until 1977. Overseas he acted as medical adviser to the new Chinese medical school in Hong Kong, and he also advised the National Institutes of Health in Bethesda, Maryland, on viral vaccines. His wisdom and dedication to his work were clear to all his associates, and he continued with an office in the medical school until he was eighty-five. Less apparent was the strength he drew from the support of his wife and the peaceful family life they enjoyed with their daughter, who became an educational psychologist, and their two sons, one of whom became an accountant in Sheffield and the other of whom became a

professor of oncology in Australia. Stuart-Harris died on 23 February 1996, and was survived by his wife and three children.   JAMES S. PORTERFIELD

Sources WWW · *The Times* (20 March 1996) · *BMJ* (22 March 1997), 906–7 · private information (2004) [D. A. J. Tyrrell] · Munk, *Roll* · b. cert. · m. cert.
Archives University of Sheffield, casebook, ref. MS 182
Likenesses photograph, News International Syndication, London [*see illus.*] · photograph, repro. in *BMJ*
Wealth at death £192,909: probate, 26 April 1996, *CGPLA Eng. & Wales*

Harris, Sir Charles Joseph William (1901–1986), civil servant, was born on 10 June 1901 at his parents' home, 249 Upper Street, Islington, London. His father, William Harris, was a stud groom and came from Thornaugh, near Wansford in Northamptonshire; his mother, Edith Elizabeth Goldsmith, was a lady's maid and came from Ramsgate in Kent. Because his parents were in domestic service in London he was brought up by his grandmother and his aunt Anne Goldsmith in Ramsgate. He was educated at Christ Church School there, but he left at fourteen and worked in a greengrocer's shop. As a boy scout at the beginning of the war he helped out at the naval base in Ramsgate and there attracted the attention of Lieutenant-Commander Dudley Ward MP, a former and a subsequent Liberal whip. In October 1917 Ward arranged for Harris to be considered for a clerical job in the whips' office at 12 Downing Street. He was accepted and stayed there for forty-four years, starting as office boy to Freddie Guest, the National Liberal chief whip (during the coalition there were joint chief whips). He soon became involved in the setting up of the Coalition Liberal organization for the 1918 election and the allocation of 'coupons' to trustworthy Lloyd George candidates.

In 1919 Harris started to work for Lord Edmund Talbot (later Viscount Fitzalan), the Conservative chief whip, at £100 per annum; he became active in the organization of parliamentary business, with a desk in the whips' office in the Commons. When Leslie Wilson became chief whip in the 1922 Bonar Law government, he formally appointed Harris as his private secretary at £400 per annum. Harris married, on 7 June 1924, Emily Kyle Thompson (b. 1902/3), to whom he was introduced by her uncle George Thompson, who was Freddie Guest's agent. She was the daughter of John Drysdale Thompson, a cabinet-maker. They had one son and two daughters.

In 1924 and again in 1929, when the Conservatives went into opposition, Harris continued to work as private secretary to their chief whip. It was only in 1939 that, with the agreement of the leader of the opposition, he became a fully established civil servant, as 'assistant to the parliamentary secretary to the treasury' with a salary of £850 per annum. Clement Attlee wrote 'Mr Harris would be an admirable man for the post' (Attlee to Sir James Rae, 14 Feb 1939, priv. coll.). In 1945, when Labour came to power, the new chief whip, William Whiteley, took it for granted that Charles Harris would continue in the job. He found the transition from Conservative employee to civil servant entirely easy, although he felt that some looked askance at the move. When Harris retired in July 1961, Hugh Gaitskell observed that the post-war Labour government 'had no more faithful servant than Sir Charles Harris' (Butler).

When Harris started in the whips' office there were no records. Harris later wrote, 'I can modestly claim to have endeavoured to secure method, planning and arrangement to the business of the House … The new "age" was taking hold. The easy-going gentlemanly methods were giving place to more exact planning' (priv. coll.). He was responsible for helping the chief whip in his task of organizing the legislative programme for the session, assessing what could reasonably be achieved. He knew that all governments were 'too ambitious', and that they put into the queen's speech their 'impossible hopes— legislation which they will have no hope of passing or intention of implementing'.

R. H. S. Crossman wrote that 'Sir Charles Harris was for years and years an absolutely key figure … a little round ball-bearing linking Government and Opposition Offices … [running] the Speaker and also, to some extent, the Opposition'. He was 'hugely influential'; his exact memory led him to be described as 'a flesh-and-blood storehouse of Parliament's own case-law' (Crossman, 2.23). Crossman commented:

> The Chief Whip and the Leader don't spend much time on the Parliamentary time-table. This is completely in the hands of the Chief Whip's Secretary. Partly this is inevitable and healthy because the goodwill of the Opposition is required and this is most easily attained when they spend their time talking to a non-partisan, non-political civil servant. (ibid., 366–7)

Few papers are preserved by the whips' office and fewer are ever released. There are hardly any events in which the role played by Sir Charles Harris is explicitly recorded; anecdotes are hard to come by but there is no doubt that his competence and discretion established the post of secretary to the chief whip as an essential, if unknown, part of the government of the country. The orderly arrangement of parliamentary business is conducted through 'the usual channels'. It was Sir Charles Harris's genius to see that affairs almost always flowed smoothly through those channels. When inter-party communications broke down during the general strike and at the time of Suez, he continued to provide a discreet link. He and his successors have developed a role that has become central to Westminster politics. Peter Hennessy notes:

> Occasionally Harris surfaces in the more sensitive documents at the Public Record Office. For example, in the file dealing with the royal prerogative and the dissolution of Parliament during the run-up to the October 1959 General Election, Freddie Bishop, the Prime Minister's Principal Private Secretary, minuted Harold Macmillan that 'I have consulted Sir Charles Harris about the precedents'. Harris was quite simply *the* collective memory by that stage of his career and the first person called upon when, as it were, the written precedents ran out or were contradictory. (Hennessy, letter in priv. coll.)

Charles Harris was appointed CBE in 1927 (at the age of twenty-six). One letter of congratulation (from a civil servant, Douglas Veale) ran 'The way you carry out your intricate and harassing work without any friction whatever has always been a marvel' (3 June 1927, priv. coll.). Another from a junior clerk ran, 'You are undoubtedly the most popular person in the House with MPs, Press and staff, all grades' (priv. coll.). He certainly managed his complex task with immense amiability. He was a handsome man, 6 foot tall and dark-haired, modest but with a sure confidence in his own ability, his prodigious memory, and his feel for politics and politicians. He was the most discreet and sure-footed of political operators. Harris was knighted in 1952 and raised to KBE in 1961. He died at Bushey and District Hospital, Hertfordshire, on 14 January 1986. A granddaughter (Julia Drown) became a Labour MP in 1997.   DAVID BUTLER

Sources D. Butler, *The Times* (17 Jan 1986) · priv. coll., Harris MSS · R. H. S. Crossman, *The diaries of a cabinet minister*, 3 vols. (1975–7) · private information (2004) · b. cert. · m. cert. · d. cert.
Archives priv. coll.
Likenesses portrait, 12 Downing Street
Wealth at death £73,384: probate, 1 July 1986, *CGPLA Eng. & Wales*

Harris, David (1754–1803). *See under* Hambledon cricket club (*act. c.*1750–*c.*1796).

Harris, Dame (Muriel) Diana Reader (1912–1996), educationist, was born at 83 The Peak, Hong Kong, on 11 October 1912, the only daughter and elder child of Montgomery Reader Harris (*b.* 1884), a lawyer, and his wife, Frances Mabel, *née* Wilmot Wilkinson. She returned to England with her mother, who died suddenly of meningitis when she was two. Her father remained in the Far East, leaving the children to be brought up by their Aunt Dorothea who provided them with emotional stability. Dorothea's marriage to Godfrey Buxton some seven years later brought Reader Harris into the orbit of the Pentecostal movement. Godfrey Buxton became principal of the Missionary Training Colony in Upper Norwood, London. This appointment meant that household conversation often centred on what they referred to as 'the importance of going out into the uttermost parts of the world to bring Christian education': a concept which was to become central to Reader Harris's own life.

Initially taught by a governess, at the age of eight Reader Harris was sent to Francis Holland School, London, and then in 1925 to Sherborne School for Girls in Dorset—an association she retained for the rest of her life. She was offered a place at Newnham College, Cambridge, to read English, but her father interpreted the lack of a scholarship offer as a sign that she was not suited to university life and refused her financial support. Instead she studied at home for an external degree from London University, graduating with a first-class degree in English in 1934. In the same year she joined the staff of Sherborne School, becoming a housemistress two years later. In the 1930s she established camps which mixed public school girls with Girls' Club members. For three years during the war she accompanied girls whose parents wished them to be evacuated to Toronto, Canada, returning in 1943. At this point she decided to broaden her experience and joined the National Association of Girls' Clubs, gaining valuable administrative experience and an insight into the lives of young working-class women.

Reader Harris rejoined Sherborne as headmistress in 1950, remaining there until her retirement in 1975, being made DBE in recognition of her services to education and the church in 1972. As head she considered it her responsibility to bring out the best in every pupil: 'Everyone has something of value to give, a better nature to be appealed to' (Williams, 91). At school she operated an open door policy and had the ability to retain personal information about pupils and staff long after they had left, leaving them with a sense of self-worth and purpose. Throughout her life she was an enabler, with an affirming presence and a personality which made people want to work with her and for her. Those who knew her all commented on her physical beauty, with an inner radiance illuminating her presence. She had the ability to combine the different strands of her professional experience; on becoming president in 1964 her speeches to the Association of Headmistresses brought together her knowledge of the independent sector in education with her real understanding of the needs of young women from her earlier youth work. She emphasized the importance of recognizing the individual and the need for variety in education.

Reader Harris's tireless energy and her speed at grasping essentials allowed her to combine work as headmistress with a growing number of outside bodies, without the organizations with which she was associated registering a sense of having only part of her attention. While she was still headmistress she served as a member of the Independent Television Authority, the council of the National Youth Orchestra, the council of the Outward Bound Trust, and numerous other committees. Her long-standing Christian beliefs led to her joining the council of the Church Missionary Society (CMS) in 1953 and serving as its president from 1969 to 1982, a period of huge changes. A committed advocate of the Brandt report, she led the society as it re-examined its role within the Church of England and reformulated the aims of the society to enable it to work with the aspirations of local communities. She travelled widely abroad, sometimes in unstable or even dangerous areas (including Uganda under Idi Amin), gathering information and more importantly fostering good relationships between the centre and localities. The strength of her leadership at CMS led the board of Christian Aid to co-opt her and she subsequently became chairman (1978–83). For Christian Aid, her experience in education and youth work combined with the depth of her spiritual beliefs and her personal qualities made her an ideal leader to expand its work in development education.

After serving on the council from 1975, Reader Harris was also invited to become chairman of the Royal Society of Arts (RSA). Her period of office (1979–81) has been described as significant since she brought together her experience in education with her world perspective. Her inaugural address in November 1980 discussed the problems of trade inequalities between 'developed' and 'undeveloped' countries, and the importance of the links that the RSA was promoting to try to resolve some of the key threats to health and agriculture. On completion of her term as chairman she continued as an effective member of the environment committee, vice-president from 1981 to 1989, and vice-president emerita thereafter.

In her own home Reader Harris was a superb hostess and cook. She kept detailed notes in her diaries of her menus, matching guests and dishes very carefully, with some wonderfully exotic recipes. Her diaries too kept note of the daily kindnesses she received. She never learned to drive, and her journeys were made mainly by public transport, even the bus conductors occasionally being mentioned in the diaries. She was a vivid and observant correspondent: her letters to her aunt and uncle revealed both a keen eye and insights into local conditions. She was a practical Christian, able to explain her faith simply. Her radio talks drew appreciative letters: she was much in demand as a speaker at lunches, and over the years she gave many sermons, appearing at Canterbury Cathedral as well as small village churches. She was a keen supporter of ordination for women, and after moving with her widowed sister-in-law Henrietta (d. 1995) to the close at Salisbury in 1983 she became a lay canon.

In her last years Diana Reader Harris's sight deteriorated badly, giving her much anxiety, especially as her ability to recognize people was so important to her. During this time she was cared for by Susan Bowser, a friend who shared her religious convictions and her love for Iona. She died at her home, 35 The Close, Salisbury, on 7 October 1996. She was cremated, and her ashes interred in Cloister Garth, Salisbury. She was unmarried.

CAROLINE M. K. BOWDEN

Sources private information (2004) [S. Bowser and others] · B. Williams, *So many opportunities: a historical portrait of Sherborne School for Girls* (1998) · *WWW* · *The Times* (9 Oct 1996) · *Daily Telegraph* (9 Oct 1996) · *The Independent* (10 Oct 1996) · b. cert. · d. cert. · *CGPLA Eng. & Wales* (1996)
Archives priv. coll. | U. Warwick Mod. RC, Association of Headmistresses
Likenesses B. Bury, portrait, 1978, Christian Missionary Society · photograph, repro. in *The Times* · photograph, repro. in *Daily Telegraph* · photograph, repro. in *The Independent*
Wealth at death £441,780: probate, 1996, *CGPLA Eng. & Wales*

Harris, Edmund Robert (1803–1877), lawyer and benefactor, was born on 6 September 1803, probably at Preston, Lancashire, one of four children (three boys and a girl) of Robert Harris (1764–1862), a Cambridge graduate and vicar of St George's Church, Preston (1798 to death), and headmaster of Preston grammar school (1788–1835), and his wife, Nancy (1774–1837), daughter of Edmund Lodge and Elizabeth Eccleston. He was probably educated at his father's school before he and his younger brother, Thomas (the oldest brother, Robert, died in infancy), were articled to their uncles Edmund and Jonathan Lodge's firm of solicitors in Chapel Street, Preston; the practice eventually passed to the two brothers. A solicitor from 1827, in 1848 Edmund Robert was appointed deputy prothonotary to the court of common pleas for Lancashire, which gave him responsibility for the general official business of the court. One of the superior courts in the county and sitting at the Lancaster assizes, the court of common pleas dealt with actions concerning lands, personal actions of Lancashire residents, and actions against corporations in the county. In 1865 Harris became the court's acting prothonotary and associate, assuming full title four years later. However, his responsibilities were reduced as new offices for the court were opened in Liverpool and Manchester, presumably in response to an expansion in business at a time of marked population growth. He was left in charge of the court's Preston office, with jurisdiction for the county's northern division.

On the death of their father in 1862 Edmund Robert Harris and his brother Thomas, neither of whom had married, moved from Ribblesdale Place in Preston to the town's newly emerging suburb of Ashton-on-Ribble. There they resided at Whinfield, an imposing, classical-style detached house in extensive grounds, with kitchen garden, orchard, fowl yard, and aviary. By the early 1870s, however, Robert Edmund's health was beginning to fail—he suffered from bronchial and heart problems—and before his retirement in 1874 he relinquished some of his more demanding duties. He died at his home on 27 May 1877 in his seventy-fourth year, and was buried on 1 June in St Andrew's churchyard, Ashton, Preston.

According to Harris's close and long-standing friend the Revd C. H. Wood, Harris was a most punctilious man with regard to business matters, always paying very close attention to detail and following established procedures—ideal qualities, Wood believed, for a lawyer. Harris was also a very private man, preferring to go about his work in a quiet, unostentatious manner and shunning public office, though, in 1854, he did become a member of the general committee for establishing a free library in Preston. Not least through his charitable bequests he was regarded as a benevolent person, as well as a kind and considerate employer.

Harris's death caused considerable interest in Preston, not only because he was the last in his family line—neither his brother nor sister had children—but also because he was very wealthy. He had inherited money from his parents, uncles, and siblings, pursued a successful legal career, and acquired railway stock and real estate. Rumour abounded as to how the proceeds from realizing his estate, thought to be worth £250,000, would be spent. He had already made numerous charitable bequests, including £7000 to erect an infectious disease ward at Preston Infirmary, and though some people believed that the bulk of his fortune would be left to Queen Anne's Bounty for augmenting the livings of poor clergy, others anticipated that local charities and local people would be the main beneficiaries. The will stipulated that the Harris money was to be used to establish educational and/or charitable institutions in Preston, which would perpetuate the memory of the Harris family. During the 1880s and 1890s the Harris bequest financed three such institutions,

namely the Harris Orphanage (1888), the Harris Free Library and Museum (1893), and the Harris Technical School (1897). The orphanage and technical school eventually became part of the University of Central Lancashire. In 1912 it was reported that the solicitors of the Harris trustees estimated that the value of the benefactions made to Preston under Harris's will amounted to no less than £311,000.   J. GEOFFREY TIMMINS

Sources J. Convey, *The Harris Free Library and Museum, Preston, 1893–1993* (1993) · 'Death of Mr E. R. Harris', *Preston Guardian* (30 May 1877) · 'Funeral of the late E. R. Harris, esq', *Preston Guardian* (2 June 1877) · 'Funeral sermon of the late E. R. Harris, esq', *Preston Guardian* (6 June 1877) · 'The will of the late E. R. Harris', *Preston Guardian* (6 June 1877) · 'To honour his father's name', *Lancashire Daily Post* (6 March 1933) · plan of Whinfield, Ashton-on-Ribble, by Messrs T. Dewhurst and Son, auctioneers, Preston, July 1895 · will, proved, Lancaster, 12 June 1877 · H. W. Clemesha, *A history of Preston in Amounderness* (1912) · A. Hewitson, *History (from AD 705 to 1883) of Preston in the county of Lancashire* (1883); facs. repr. as *A history of Preston* (1969) · E. Baines, *History, directory and gazetteer of the county palatine of Lancaster*, 1 (1824) · Boase, *Mod. Eng. biog.* · Venn, *Alum. Cant.*
Wealth at death under £250,000: probate, 12 June 1877, *CGPLA Eng. & Wales*

Harris, Sir Edward Alfred John (1808–1888). *See under* Harris, James Howard, third earl of Malmesbury (1807–1889).

Harris, Elizabeth (*fl.* 1655/6–1663), Quaker missionary, whose place and date of birth are unknown, arrived in Maryland, North America, as an adult some time between late 1655 and mid-1656. Whether she was the first Quaker to reach American shores is debatable, since Ann Austin and Mary Fisher arrived in Boston in 1656, but she was the first Quaker minister to gain converts in America. The Quaker account book of 1656 in which return fares for Austin and Fisher are recorded notes that £2 5s. was expended for 'books to Virginia' (a reference to the Chesapeake region), which must have been intended for those convinced by Harris. Owing to her personal gifts and the liberty she enjoyed—in contrast to the constraints placed on her New England counterparts—Harris was profoundly effective, both in terms of the numbers convinced and the depth of her proselytes' devotion. While in Newgate prison in London in 1663, Charles Bayly remembered his own Maryland convincement: while 'seeking in my heart a man of love, or a people in whom one might put confidence', God sent 'one of his dear servants into those parts, whose name was *Elizabeth Harris*, who soon answered that which was breathing after God in me' (Bayly, 11).

Harris ministered to English colonists sprinkled in settlements along Maryland's shores who were predominantly puritan. William Fuller, charged by parliament with the government of Maryland from the 1654 seizure of power from Lord Baltimore until 1658, was among Harris's more notable converts. Other important Maryland figures convinced by her included William Durand and Robert Clarkson. With the assent and protection of these individuals, Harris's Maryland ministry was unencumbered by the persecutions levelled against her contemporary co-religionists in New England.

Although her departure date from Maryland is unknown, Harris is considered to be the subject of Gerrard Roberts's report of 9 July 1657 to George Fox: 'the ffrend who went to Virginey is Returned in a pretty Condition: and There shee was Gladly Recd by Many who meet together: the Governey is Convinsed' (Carroll, 102). From Maryland, Clarkson wrote Harris an extensive update, assuring her that books she had sent were being well used and that many of her converts 'abide convinced' (ibid., 104). Within several months Elizabeth Harris had taken on another mission, this time to Italy with Elizabeth Coward. They were in Venice in April 1658, and had returned to London by August. Harris continued to preach publicly in London, Cambridge, and Manchester, sometimes appearing in 'steeple-houses in sackcloth', which apparently troubled fellow Friends who were tending away from such displays (Jones, 266n.).

In February 1661 Harris visited Friends in a Salisbury prison and was herself arrested for refusal to swear an oath. Her remaining years are clouded. Evidence suggests that she sympathized with the schismatic John Perrot in his disagreement with Fox. Harris was upset at being frowned upon for her sackcloth ranting and Perrot favoured the unfettered following of one's inner spirit. A tract by another Perrot supporter, John Harwood, entitled *To All People that Profess the Eternal Truth of the Living God* (1663), criticized Fox for a written attack on Elizabeth Harris, who appears to have returned via Barbados to Maryland where converts Fuller and Bayly were also Perrot partisans. What then became of Harris is indefinite: a William Harris, whose wife was named Elizabeth, purchased land in Anne Arundel county, Maryland, in 1662; in 1665, an Elizabeth Harris was arrested in England and banished to Jamaica on charges of attending unauthorized meetings; and in 1672, an Elizabeth Harris was released from a Northampton prison, where she had been for at least six years.   STEVEN C. HARPER

Sources K. L. Carroll, 'Elizabeth Harris, the founder of American Quakerism', *Quaker History*, 57 (1968), 96–111 · C. Bayly, *A true and faithful warning to the upright-hearted and unprejudic'd reader* (1663) · P. Mack, *Visionary women: ecstatic prophecy in seventeenth-century England* (1992) · R. M. Jones, *Quakers in the American colonies* (1911), 263–301 · 'Dictionary of Quaker biography', RS Friends, Lond. [card index]

Harris, Emanuel Vincent (1876–1971), architect, was born on 26 June 1876 at 3 Lambert Street, Devonport, Devon, the son of Major Emanuel Harris and Mary Vincent. He was educated at Kingsbridge grammar school and in 1893 was articled to James Harvey, architect, of Plymouth. Harris then moved to London to study at the Royal Academy Schools while working in several offices. He was first with E. Keynes Purchase, then with Leonard Stokes, and finally with Sir William Emerson for three years before joining the architects' department of the London county council, which was then erecting the buildings connected with its electric tram system. Harris was assistant architect for the generating station at Greenwich and designed several transformer stations which were also characterized by the use of an austere and monumental

neo-classical style in yellow brick. The station in Upper Street, Islington, was evidently inspired by Newgate prison, the masterpiece of George Dance junior, which was demolished in 1902.

Harris was awarded the gold medal and travelling studentship at the Royal Academy Schools in 1903 and the following year set up in practice. He was placed sixth in the competition for the Wesleyan Methodist hall in London and second in that for Torquay town hall before winning the competition for the Glamorgan county hall in Cardiff in 1908 in partnership with Thomas Anderson Moodie (1875–1948), who had spent the preceding five years as architect to the Central South African Railway. The executed design 'achieved the Roman scale he was to maintain in his work throughout his life' (Stuart Gray), and this success launched Harris on his uniquely successful and prolific career as an architect of public buildings reflecting the contemporary taste for the grand manner as an expression of civic pride and expansion. It was a career described by C. H. Reilly as 'a series of raids all over England, and mostly carried out single handed. No one of his age … has tackled so many competitions, and at the same time been placed in so many' (Reilly, 393). In 1914 Harris won that for the new offices of the Board of Trade in London, although two world wars were to pass before his much simplified version of 'the Whitehall Monster' (Summerson, 424) was completed on the site in 1959 for the Ministry of Defence.

After the First World War, E. Vincent Harris (as he was known) won a series of open competitions for public buildings owing to his firm grasp of planning combined with his assured handling of a monumental classical language. These included Sheffield city hall (1920–34), Braintree town hall (1926–8), Leeds civic hall (1930–33), Somerset county hall at Taunton (1936), and Nottingham county hall (1937–46). In 1927 Harris won two separate competitions for two important adjacent buildings in Manchester, and while the circular central library is classical, the town hall extension is in a subtle hybrid style which respects the vigorous Gothic of Alfred Waterhouse's Victorian pile. Other departures from the pure classic included Messrs Atkinson's premises in Bond Street, London, and some of the buildings in an abstracted Tudor manner (designed with Sidney K. Greenslade) for the University College of the South West (later Exeter University), for which he had prepared a master plan in 1931.

For Sheffield, Harris looked to H. L. Elmes's St George's Hall in Liverpool for inspiration, while in Leeds there are echoes of Wren, but his later civic buildings were designed in a simpler Georgian manner in brick, influenced by the work of Sir Edwin Lutyens. The long, curved council house at Bristol was designed in 1935 but not completed until after the Second World War. The Kensington Central Library (1955–60) was designed when the architect was almost eighty years of age and was the object of one of several public demonstrations against such conservative traditional architecture, organized by a pressure group calling themselves the Anti-Uglies.

Harris did not only handle public buildings; he designed

a church at Stewartby, Bedfordshire, and his versatility was demonstrated by the screen wall and racquets court in Carlos Place, London (1924), shielding the courtyard of 47 Grosvenor Place for Stephen Courtauld. Harris considered his best building to be 2–3 Duke Street, St James's (1910–12). His own house in Fitzroy Park, Highgate, of 1932–4 (which he gave to the London borough of Camden when he retired to Chard, Somerset) was largely designed by Donald McMorran, one of several talented architects who assisted him in his busiest years. Others included E. Berry Webber, who went on to design Southampton civic centre and Hammersmith and Dagenham town halls, and Arthur Bailey.

Short in stature and taciturn, Harris was respected rather than liked. He wrote to McMorran in 1942 that 'we both know there is only one thing that really matters and that is "the work". All the rest is vanity though it does sweeten labour' (private information). Arthur Bailey recalled that

> This man was completely dedicated to classical architecture to the exclusion of all other interests and he expected and received the same approach from his staff, not only quality of work, but an austerity which would not be acceptable today; no smoking, no tea or extended public holidays, the whole office closing for the summer recess … He had no time for letters, meetings or officialdom. (*The Times*, 13 Aug 1971)

Harris was very conscientious; in 1929 Reilly noted that, 'as an indication of the pains he takes with his actual buildings when he has won them, there is the fact that he has been three times to America, each time to study some particular type he was about to build' (Reilly, 393).

Harris was awarded the royal gold medal for architecture in 1951. He was elected FRIBA in 1914 and RA in 1942, and later served as treasurer of the Royal Academy; he was appointed OBE in 1950 and was awarded an honorary DLitt. by the University of Exeter. In 1913 he married Edith Maule, the daughter of William Maule MD of Southport; she died in 1965 and there were no children. Harris died at the Cranhill Nursing Home, Weston Road, Weston, Bath on 1 August 1971 and was buried in the churchyard of St Michael and All Angels at Chaffcombe, near Chard, under a stone designed by Arthur Bailey. The RIBA holds some of Harris's drawings, presented to them in 1967.

GAVIN STAMP

Sources C. H. Reilly, 'Eminent living architects and their work: E. Vincent Harris', *Building* (Sept 1929), 393–9 · J. Summerson, 'Recent work of Mr E. Vincent Harris', *Country Life*, 75 (1934), 423–6 · 'The royal gold medallist, 1951', *RIBA Journal*, 58 (1950–51), 149–52 · *The Times* (2 Aug 1971) · *The Times* (13 Aug 1971) · G. Stamp and G. Boyd Harte, *Temples of power* (1979) · A. S. Gray, *Edwardian architecture: a biographical dictionary* (1985) · *WWW* · private information (2004) · biography file, RIBA BAL · fellowship nomination form, 1913, RIBA BAL · MS, priv. coll. · F. H. W. Sheppard, ed., *The Grosvenor estate in Mayfair, 1: General history*, Survey of London, 39 (1977) · *CGPLA Eng. & Wales* (1971) · *CGPLA Eng. & Wales* (1975) · d. cert.
Likenesses photograph, repro. in Reilly, 'Eminent living architects and their work: E. Vincent Harris', p. 393
Wealth at death £549,426: probate, 27 Oct 1974, *CGPLA Eng. & Wales*

Harris, Francis (1829–1885), physician, the son of John Rawlinson Harris, a hat manufacturer and in 1830 MP for Southwark, was born on 1 December 1829 at Winchester Row, Southwark, London, and was baptized in St Saviour's, Southwark. He was educated at Dulwich and at King's College, London, and matriculated in 1848 at Gonville and Caius College, Cambridge, where he graduated BA in 1852 and, after studying medicine in London at St Bartholomew's Hospital, MB in 1854.

Harris lived for a time in Gray's Inn, London, and in November 1856 he became house surgeon to the nearby Sick Children's Hospital in Great Ormond Street. In 1857 he became a member of the Royal College of Physicians, and then continued his studies in Paris, and afterwards in Berlin under Rudolf Virchow. After a year abroad, concluding with a short visit to Prague and Vienna, he returned to London and, seeing no other alternative, began to practise obstetrics. However, in 1858 he was additionally elected demonstrator of morbid anatomy at St Bartholomew's Hospital, and in May 1859 he became assistant physician to the Sick Children's Hospital in Great Ormond Street. In that year he took his MD degree at Cambridge. His thesis, which was later published, was entitled 'On the nature of the substance found in the amyloid degeneration of various organs of the human body'. In this he described two cases of amyloid disease of the liver and two of the kidneys, which were the only cases he had encountered in sixty post-mortems made at St Bartholomew's; these were the first elaborate descriptions of the disease by an English morbid anatomist. He achieved some reputation from this work, but published nothing else.

In 1861 Harris abandoned obstetrics and was elected assistant physician to St Bartholomew's Hospital and lecturer on botany. In August 1861 he married his second cousin, Marianne Harris, and in 1865 he bought The Grange, an estate at Lamberhurst, Kent, a district he had liked from boyhood. Here his many guests and all his neighbours used to enjoy his hospitality and conversation. A fellow of the Linnean Society, he cultivated pineapples, oranges, and orchids. A *dendrobium* and a *calanthe* 'Harris' hybrid orchid, which he produced, are called after him. He also kept beagles.

Harris began to suffer from bronchitis, and he resigned his physiciancy in 1874. He became more and more of a valetudinarian and eventually, having caught cold while fishing in Hampshire, died at his London house, 24 Cavendish Square, of pneumonia of both lungs, on 3 September 1885. He was buried in the churchyard of Brenchley, Kent. Harris's astuteness as a physician was well known, and his kindness to younger physicians and qualities as a teacher made him one of the more popular physicians among students. His hair had begun to turn grey when he was sixteen, and by the time of his final illness he looked an old man.

NORMAN MOORE, *rev.* PATRICK WALLIS

Sources Munk, *Roll* · *BMJ* (3 Oct 1885), 674 · Venn, *Alum. Cant.* · *The Lancet* (26 Sept 1885), 601
Wealth at death £15,160 13s.: probate, 10 Nov 1885, *CGPLA Eng. & Wales*

Harris, Frank. *See* Harris, James Thomas (1856?–1931).

Harris, Geoffrey Wingfield (1913–1971), physiologist and endocrinologist, was born on 4 June 1913 in Acton, Middlesex, the elder child and only son of Thomas Harris, physicist, from Oxfordshire, who worked at University College, London, at the ballistics department at Woolwich arsenal, and later at Cambridge, and his wife, Winifred Irene, *née* Stiles, of Buckinghamshire. He was educated at Dulwich College, and for a few months at University College, London, before he went in 1932 to Emmanuel College, Cambridge, where he was awarded a double first in the natural science tripos, 1934 and 1935. He chose St Mary's Hospital, London, for his clinical training and gained the Cambridge degrees of MB (1939), MD (1944), and ScD (1950). His life's work led to the creation of neuroendocrinology, of which he is regarded as the father figure.

In 1936 Harris married Georgina Mary Birnie, daughter of a Scottish engineer. They had a son who qualified in medicine. This marriage ended in a divorce in 1951. In the same year Harris married Margaret (Peggy), daughter of Dr Michael John O'Kane, general practitioner, of Cushendall, Northern Ireland. They had two daughters.

From 1940 to 1947 Harris was demonstrator in anatomy at Cambridge, in 1947–8 lecturer in anatomy, and from 1947 to 1952 lecturer in physiology. In 1952 he became head of the laboratory of experimental neuroendocrinology at the Maudsley Hospital, London, and in 1953 professor of physiology at the University of London. From 1962 until his death he was Dr Lee's professor of anatomy in Oxford, honorary director of the Medical Research Council's neuroendocrinology unit in the university, and fellow of Hertford College, Oxford. He was also an honorary consultant in psychiatry at the Littlemore Hospital, Oxford. He played an important part in establishing the new physiological sciences honour school, in which neuroendocrinology was one of the options.

To understand the significance of Harris's work, it is necessary to realize that until the mid-1930s the connection between the nervous system and the endocrine glands was unknown. In the early 1930s, however, Francis Marshall of Cambridge—who had an immense influence on the young Harris—pointed out that the great majority of animals have a more or less definite season when they breed, raising the question of what it is that controls breeding seasons and how the body is able to react to environmental signals.

While still an undergraduate, Harris took this as his starting point and developed the idea that the seasonality of breeding might be controlled by the transmission of stimuli from the brain to the anterior lobe of the pituitary gland. It was a brilliant insight which led to what is possibly his best known work, *Neural Control of the Pituitary Gland* (1955), in which he established that environmental stimuli, acting through the nervous system, led to the release of what later became known as releasing factors from the hypothalamus. These factors travel through a portal system of blood vessels (so called because of the analogy with the hepatic portal circulation), which links the under surface of the hypothalamus and the anterior pituitary, and controls the release of pituitary hormones. Later he showed that this mechanism was common to a wide range of vertebrates, suggesting that it must have a very important functional role. It was this which led to the establishment of neuroendocrinology as a new and rapidly expanding discipline.

Although his ideas were accepted by most of his contemporaries, Harris had his opponents, most notably Solly Zuckerman—an extremely powerful figure in the world of science—who, on the basis of a single flawed experiment on one ferret, decided Harris was wrong and described his work in 1952 as 'an edifice of speculation … that has been erected because of an urge to explain the incomprehensible' (Vogt), a view which Zuckerman held throughout his life, although everyone else knew that Harris's findings were so firmly based as to be incontrovertible.

Harris then showed that there was a link between the central nervous system and other endocrine glands. For example, he showed that the control of the secretions of the adrenal cortex was mediated through the release of ACTH (adrenocorticotrophic hormone) by the anterior pituitary when it received the appropriate signals from the hypothalamus. Further research by Harris was concerned with the effect of gonadal hormones on sexual differentiation of the brain during neonatal life, and the isolation of hypothalamic releasing factors.

It has been said that 'Harris put the brain into the endocrine system' (Raisman). Certainly his work was immensely broad and influential. It has led to an understanding of the neural mechanisms which underlie cycles of birth, growth, reproduction, and death in the animal kingdom. In medicine it has clarified a whole range of clinical conditions, and it has increased our understanding of the physiological changes associated with stress, emotional trauma, and jet lag.

Harris was a large, powerfully built, and energetic man, a keen boxer and rugby player in his youth, who continued to play squash into his fifties, often beating much younger players. He was an excellent teacher and generous and helpful colleague; his outstanding success was based on the combination of an excellent operative technique, a continual bubbling flow of ideas, and a huge capacity for work. His publications included chapters in more than twenty texts, and over a hundred original papers. He was elected FRS in 1953, received an Oxford DM in 1962, was appointed CBE in 1965, and received the Dale medal of the Endocrine Society in 1971. Harris died at the Radcliffe Infirmary, Oxford, on 29 November 1971, survived by his wife. His ashes were later buried in Bladon churchyard. The Physiological Society established a lecture in memory of Harris in 1986. IRVINE LOUDON

Sources M. L. Vogt, *Memoirs FRS*, 18 (1972), 309–29 • G. Raisman, 'An urge to explain the incomprehensible: Geoffrey Harris and the discovery of the neural control of the pituitary gland', *Annual Review of Neuroscience*, 20 (1977), 533–66 • private information (1996) • *BMJ* (4 Dec 1971), 628 • J. D. L., *The Lancet* (11 Dec 1971), 1328–9

Archives Bodl. Oxf., corresp., notebooks, papers · Wellcome L. | FILM U. Oxf., department of human anatomy, a film made by the subject on 'milk ejection'
Likenesses photograph, repro. in Vogt, *Memoirs FRS* · photograph, U. Oxf., department of human anatomy · photographs, priv. coll.
Wealth at death £19,648: probate, 10 Feb 1972, *CGPLA Eng. & Wales*

Harris, George (*bap.* **1721**, *d.* **1796**), lawyer, was baptized at St Martin-in-the-Fields, Westminster, on 5 September 1721, the only child of John Harris (1680–1738) and his wife, Ann Duckett (*d.* 1754). Harris's father, originally from Milford Haven, Pembrokeshire, in 1729 became bishop of Llandaff, where he promoted the restoration of Llandaff Cathedral, and was reckoned to be an assiduous prelate in the eighteenth-century manner, often absent from his diocese to tend to his lesser cures, and his prebend at Canterbury.

George Harris entered Westminster School, aged seven, in 1729, and on 23 June 1738 matriculated from Oriel College, Oxford. From there he graduated BCL in 1745 and DCL in 1750, when he was admitted as a member of the College of Advocates. In 1752 he anonymously issued a pamphlet, *Observations upon the English Language, in a Letter to a Friend*, who was not named.

On 28 February 1756 Harris married from Doctors' Commons at St Benet Paul's Wharf Hannah Price of the same parish. A few days earlier he had completed his edition of the emperor Justinian's *Institutes*, containing a translation from the Latin and notes. That work opened with a fawning dedication to the leading advocate and opposition politician, Sir George Lee, stating, 'I have the honour to attend those courts [of arches and the prerogative court of Canterbury], in which you so eminently preside' (Harris, iv). He failed to succeed to such posts after Lee's death in 1758. Instead, Harris practised conscientiously and lucratively in the civil law which was his pride, describing it as 'universally allowed to be the Master-work of human policy' (ibid., viii). He was an advocate—unlike Lee, not a principal—of the court of arches, chancellor of the dioceses of Durham, Hereford, and Llandaff, and commissary of Essex, Hertfordshire, and Surrey, administering those counties' ecclesiastical affairs when the respective bishops were away. A second edition of his *Institutes* appeared in 1761, later editions of the work being published in the next century. The most notorious episode in his career came in 1776, when he appeared in Westminster Hall as a prosecuting counsel against Elizabeth Chudleigh, duchess of Kingston, for bigamy.

By April 1796, when Harris made his will, his mental confusion was such that several deponents had later to swear to that will's legal validity. In two codicils, he declared, 'I sleep much with druggs; for God's sake let me not be buried alive', and 'I cannot keep myself awake' (PRO, PROB 11/1275/257). He died at his house in Doctors' Commons on 19 April, or on 16 April according to the deponents. The will makes no mention of his wife, Hannah, who had presumably already died without children. Most of his considerable fortune went to charitable causes, including £40,000 to St George's Hospital, London, £20,000 to Heterington's Charity for the Blind, and £15,000 to Westminster Lying-in Hospital.

T. A. B. CORLEY

Sources DNB · Venn, *Alum. Cant.* · Foster, *Alum. Oxon.* · *Old Westminsters* · G. Harris, *D. Justiniani Institutionem libri quatuor* (1756) · *The Times* (19 April 1796) · *GM*, 1st ser., 66 (1796), 358, 437 · will, PRO, PROB 11/1275/257 · *N&Q*, 12th ser., 2 (1916), 190 · *N&Q*, 12th ser., 11 (1922), 233 · *GM*, 1st ser., 8 (1738), 490 · will, PRO, PROB 11/692/235 (do.) [John Harris] · C. L. Shadwell, *Registrum Orielense*, 2 (1902) · G. Williams, ed., *Glamorgan county history*, 4: *Early modern Glamorgan* (1974) · *IGI* · W. A. Littledale, ed., *The registers of St Bene't and St Peter, Paul's Wharf, London*, 3, Harleian Society, register section, 40 (1911)
Wealth at death very wealthy: bequeathed at least £80,000 to charities: will, PRO, PROB 11/1275/257

Harris, George, **first Baron Harris** (**1746–1829**), army officer, the eldest son of George Harris (*d.* 1759), curate of Brasted, Kent, and his wife, Sarah, the daughter of George Twentyman of Braintree, Cumberland, was born in London on 18 March 1746. He was educated at Westminster School and on 1 January 1759, through the good offices of Lord George Sackville, a school contemporary of his father, entered the Royal Military Academy, Woolwich. Although Sackville's disgrace after the battle of Minden lost Harris his patron, fortunately Lord Granby had been at Cambridge with his father, and through him, on 23 June 1762, Harris was appointed lieutenant fireworker in the Royal Artillery. In the following month Granby transferred Harris to an ensigncy in the 5th foot, explaining that his artillery battalion faced imminent disbandment. Having joined his new regiment in Ireland, Harris purchased a lieutenancy in 1765 and was appointed adjutant in 1767. He travelled in France in 1768, purchased his company in 1771, and went with his regiment to America in 1774. As captain of the grenadier company he fought at Lexington, where he lost half his men as casualties. On 17 June 1775, at Bunker Hill, the 5th again suffered heavily and Harris received a head wound which required trepanning. After recruiting in England he rejoined his regiment in July 1776 and served throughout the New York campaign. During the Philadelphia campaign the following year he was wounded in the leg at Iron Hill, and on 7 October 1777, having taken temporary command of the 5th, he was promoted major.

In November 1778 Harris sailed from New York for the West Indies with General James Grant's expedition. He commanded a provisional battalion of grenadiers at the capture of St Lucia, and on 18 December acted as second in command to General William Medows during the heroic repulse of an overwhelming French counter-attack against the post of La Vigie. After a period aboard the fleet in the Caribbean as a marine, Harris returned to England, and on 9 December 1779 he married Anne Carteret Dickson (1759–1833), the daughter of Charles Dickson of Bath. They had four sons and six daughters.

Harris was promoted lieutenant-colonel on 29 December 1780 and served for the next six years with the 5th in

Ireland. When his regiment was ordered to North America he resolved to sell his commission, but a chance meeting with General Medows saw him offered the post of secretary and aide-de-camp to his old comrade in arms, who had just been appointed governor of Bombay. On 12 October 1787 he transferred to the 76th foot, a new regiment raised for service in India. He reached Bombay in September 1788 and then followed Medows to Madras, where he was promoted colonel on 18 November 1790. He fought throughout the Third Anglo-Mysore War of 1790–92 under first Medows and then Lord Cornwallis.

Following a year's leave in England, Harris was promoted major-general on 3 October 1794 and appointed commandant of Fort William at Calcutta. In January 1797, with the local rank of lieutenant-general, he succeeded to the command of the Madras army. A dispute with the governor of Madras, Lord Hobart, over civil interference in military patronage was unresolved at the time of Hobart's departure in February 1798, and until the arrival in August of his replacement, Lord Clive, Harris was acting governor. As such, he responded to the order of the new governor-general in Bengal, Richard Wellesley, earl of Mornington, that preparations be undertaken to renew war against Tipu Sultan's Mysore. Money was short, however, and the need to gather sufficient supplies while also securing the military support of the nizam of Hyderabad meant that it was not until February 1799 that Harris could lead a 40,000 strong army against Mysore. His advance thereafter was slow but sure—the army was encumbered with a large siege-train and more than 100,000 camp followers. On 27 March an attack by Tipu's forces was beaten off at Mallavalli. Tipu nevertheless hoped that scorched-earth tactics would deny the British the necessary fodder for their bullock transport, stopping Harris's advance. Harris, however, surprised him by finding a ford and crossing the River Cauvery to the south, where forage was plentiful. On reaching the Mysorean capital, Seringapatam, he then surprised Tipu again by directing his siege works against the fortress's western side, rather than its east. A breach was made and on 4 May an assault launched. Seringapatam was captured and Tipu Sultan killed.

Harris's real difficulties then began. General David Baird, who had led the storming of Seringapatam, wrote in an insubordinate fashion, implying that Harris had shown favouritism to Colonel Arthur Wellesley (Lord Mornington's younger brother and the future duke of Wellington) by appointing him governor of the newly conquered city. Out of consideration for Baird, the resulting correspondence was at the time suppressed by Harris, but in 1829 the letters were published by Baird's biographer, Theodore Hook, which in turn prompted Harris's son-in-law Stephen Lushington to write a biography of Harris which refuted Hook's ungenerous conclusions. But, more seriously, Harris also became embroiled in controversy over the allocation of £1,143,216 of prize money for the capture of Seringapatam. Having consulted Mornington, Harris left the task to a prize committee of the army. Its verdict, however, generated such rancour

that excluded parties—as well as the president of the prize committee, General John Floyd—resorted to publishing pamphlets, in the process quoting confidential documents and making contentious claims about the army's supply situation immediately before the fall of Seringapatam. Mornington blamed Harris for negligently permitting publication, and relations between the two men were temporarily strained. The court of directors of the East India Company, meanwhile, came to the view that a coterie of general officers had appropriated too much of the prize money to themselves and retrospectively tried to restrict their entitlement. The share of Harris as commander-in-chief was to be cut from one-eighth to one-sixteenth, in line with naval practice but at variance with both prior and subsequent custom in India.

It was perhaps official disapproval of the alleged rapacity of the conquerors of Seringapatam that led to the withholding from them of significant honours, although Harris on his return to England was offered an Irish peerage, which he declined, and in February 1802 was made colonel of the 73rd highlanders. For his part, Harris maintained that malevolent influences prevented him receiving his due. This included a 'Scotch party' which had taken against him 'for bringing an Officer to a proper sense of his duty who's flatterers having taught him to imagine he had taken Seringapatam, thought he was to have everything his own way' (Harris to Richard, Marquess Wellesley, 24 Feb 1802, BL, Add. MS 13729, fols. 247–8). Even more gallingly for Harris, the court of directors went so far as to support a chancery suit to force repayment of a proportion of the Seringapatam prize money. The suit lasted until 1807, when it was dismissed, and was followed by an appeal to the privy council, where the plea was again rejected.

Although Harris had received promotions to lieutenant-general in 1801 and full general in 1812, in 1815 he was persuaded to address a public memorial to the prime minister and commander-in-chief of the army calling for full recognition of his achievements. He received an English peerage as Baron Harris on 11 August 1815 and was appointed GCB in May 1820; he was made governor of Dumbarton Castle in 1824. According to the *Gentleman's Magazine*, he 'was in the frequent habit of boasting that he had been the architect of his own fortune' (*GM*, 1st ser., 99/2, 1829, 81). He was a tory, and with the duke of Clarence, later William IV, signed a protest against the abandonment of proceedings against Queen Caroline. Harris died at his seat, Belmont Park in Throwley, Kent, on 19 May 1829 and was buried in nearby Throwley church. He was succeeded by his eldest son, William George *Harris (1782–1845), also an army officer.   ALASTAIR W. MASSIE

Sources S. R. Lushington, *The life and services of General Lord Harris* (1840) · Harris papers, CKS, U624 · correspondence and papers relating to the Seringapatam prize cause, 1799–1808, BL OIOC, Home misc. 83, 504, 437 · BL, Add. MS 13627; Add. MS 13729, fols. 243, 247–8 · *GM*, 1st ser., 99/2 (1829), 80–82 · E. Ingram, ed., *Two views of British India* (1970) · T. Hook, *The life of General, the Right Honourable Sir David Baird*, 2 vols. (1833) · J. Weller, *Wellington in India*

(1972) • L. H. Thornton, *Light and shade in bygone India* (1927) • GEC, *Peerage* • *Old Westminsters*, vol. 1

Archives BL, corresp., Add. MSS 13665, 13727–13729 • BL OIOC, corresp. and papers relating to India • CKS, corresp. and papers | CKS, letters to Charles Polhill

Likenesses J. Chapman, stipple, pubd 1799, NPG • T. Hickey, charcoal and chalk drawing, 1800, Stratfield Saye, Hampshire • S. W. Reynolds, mezzotint, pubd 1824 (after A. W. Devis), BM, NPG • G. Rennie, statue, 1835, St Michael and All Angels Church, Throwley, Kent • W. Evans, stipple (after A. W. Devis), BM, NPG; repro. in *European Magazine* (1800) • W. Theed junior, bust, Royal Military Academy, Sandhurst, Camberley, Surrey

Wealth at death under £90,000: will, June 1829, *GM*; GEC, *Peerage*

Harris, George (1794–1859), Unitarian minister, was born on 15 May 1794 at Maidstone, Kent, the eldest child of Abraham Harris (*d.* 1820), Unitarian minister of the Presbyterian chapel, Maidstone, and his wife, Hannah (1766–1853), only child of John Polhill of Southwark. He was educated at Thomas Pine's school and at Maidstone grammar school. In 1808 he entered the warehouse of Manchester relatives in Cheapside, London. He was immediately drawn into London Unitarian life at Essex Street Chapel, where Thomas Belsham was minister. Belsham gave him a free ticket to a Unitarian Fund dinner when Richard Wright, the Unitarian missionary, was speaking. Wright so inspired Harris that he decided to become a Unitarian minister.

Harris entered John Evans's academy, Islington, but in November 1812 went to Glasgow University for three years on a Dr Williams's scholarship. He never graduated because his enthusiasm for Unitarian Christianity absorbed him. In July 1813 he helped organize the Scottish Unitarian Association and under its auspices started a Unitarian congregation in Greenock and Port Glasgow. In a tradition more often noted for erudition than popular appeal Harris combined a simple Bible-centred Unitarian Christianity with a warm universalism and a fearless demand for liberty and social justice. He remained largely unaffected by the intuitive trends in Unitarian theology which would soon emerge around him. He was a populist with a melodic voice, a handsome appearance, and a convivial personality.

While fundraising in England for the Greenock and Port Glasgow congregation Harris received an invitation from Renshaw Street Chapel, Liverpool. His Liverpool ministry began in 1817 and ended in 1821. It was followed with ministries at Moor Lane, Bolton (1822–5), Union Street, Glasgow (1825–41), St Mark's, Edinburgh (1841–5), and Hanover Square, Newcastle upon Tyne (1845–59). He married Elizabeth Agnes Auchinvole (1798–1865) of Glasgow in 1821. Of their eight children, all born in Glasgow, six survived. A grandson, Leopold George Harris Crook (1862–1895), was Unitarian minister at Ilkeston (1890–91) and Wolverhampton (1892–5), and a great-granddaughter, Margaret Brackenbury Crook, Unitarian minister at Norwich (1918–20) and professor of religion at Smith College, Massachusetts (1921–54).

For Harris, theological controversy was an opportunity to make Unitarian Christianity better known. When orthodox Liverpool clergy replied to his lecture series *Unitarianism and Trinitarianism Contrasted* (1820), Harris responded with the assertion that Unitarianism was the only religion that could become universal. Also, the chapel walls attracted supportive graffiti like 'Harris kill the Devil!' A quarter of a century later, when a Methodist minister in Newcastle negatively reviewed twenty-one of his published addresses, Harris still replied with his usual vigour.

This militant Unitarianism made the more staid Unitarians uncomfortable. Harris's Liverpool congregation as good as sought his resignation. At a ministers' meeting at Bury, in 1823, less militant colleagues dined at a separate inn; and at an 1824 dinner in Manchester honouring John Grundy, Harris's remarks sparked the Manchester Socinian controversy, from the disastrous consequences of which Unitarians were rescued only by the Dissenters' Chapels Act (1844).

Harris combined his vigorous preaching and lecturing with missionary zeal. He made a tour of central Lancashire while at Liverpool, and in Scotland this became a regular activity. Dubbed The Unitarian Bishop, he was the catalyst for about sixty Unitarian groups in central and east Scotland. His Liverpool congregation resented the time he spent away; at Glasgow a growing congregation was more tolerant. But at Edinburgh the Unitarian congregation needed for itself the time and effort which Harris spent elsewhere. Only at Newcastle upon Tyne, where his crowning glory was the new church of the Divine Unity, opened in 1854, did Harris really give his all to one congregation. In fact, his capacities as a Unitarian proselytizer were carefully balanced with other capacities for human friendship, such that George Hope of the Edinburgh congregation reported that every time he met Harris, he would ask after every person connected with that body: 'he lost sight of none, rich or poor'.

Harris's evangelistic endeavours were supplemented by two other significant contributions to Unitarianism. He was one of the first to recognize the importance of religious journalism as a tool of communication, and he established three Unitarian magazines. At Liverpool, with F. B. Wright, brother of Richard Wright, he started the *Christian Reflector* (1820–9). The other two magazines, the *Christian Pioneer* (1826–45) and the *Christian Pilot* (1847–51), he founded, edited, and managed himself.

Secondly, Harris made an indivisible relationship between Unitarian faith and social justice. In the years leading to Peterloo he befriended several British Unitarian emigrés passing through Liverpool to America. He collected 3470 signatures in ten days to support the repeal of the Test and Corporation Acts. He preached gratefully for the 1832 Reform Act. He opposed slavery, upheld national education, supported church voluntaryism, preached and practised teetotalism, and was a provocative and early voice against hanging. His 1835 protest (*Christianity and Church-of-Irelandism*), after nine people were killed at Rathcormack, Ireland, at the seizure of a widow's goods for non-payment of church tithes, reached four editions in one week. Irish Catholics, in particular, fêted him. In New-castle he visited ragged schools and attended 2000 homes during a cholera epidemic.

Exhausted by his strenuous activity, Harris collapsed in 1859. The Newcastle congregation sent him to North Ber-wick for three months. He returned to Newcastle and died in harness on Christmas eve, 24 December 1859. He was buried in Jesmond cemetery, Newcastle upon Tyne.

ANDREW M. HILL

Sources J. Gordon, 'George Harris: a memoir', *Christian Reformer, or, Unitarian Magazine and Review*, new ser., 16 (1860), 193–201, 261–73, 393–408, 479–91, 620–31, 668–79, 717–38 · G. E. Evans, *Record of the provincial assembly of Lancashire and Cheshire* (1896) · W. I. Addison, ed., *The matriculation albums of the University of Glasgow from 1728 to 1858* (1913) · A. Holt, *Walking together: a study in Liverpool non-conformity, 1688–1938* (1938) · J. Birt, ed., *The Manchester Socinian controversy* (1825)
Archives Bank Street Chapel, Bolton, records of Moor Lane Uni-tarian Chapel · Divine Unity Unitarian Chapel, Newcastle upon Tyne, records · Lpool RO, records of Renshaw Street Unitarian Chapel, Liverpool, 288 ULL · Mitchell L., Glas., Strathclyde Regional Archives, records of Union Street Unitarian Chapel, Glas-gow, TO 978/1–17 · NA Scot., records of St Mark's Unitarian Chapel, Edinburgh, CH 15/1
Wealth at death under £1000: administration, 5 April 1860, *CGPLA Eng. & Wales*

Harris, George (1809–1890), author, was born at Rugby on 6 May 1809, the eldest son of George Harris (d. 16 Jan 1856), a solicitor of that town, and his wife, Christabella, only daughter of Rear-Admiral William Chambers. At birth he was so weak that he was baptized immediately. Still a deli-cate child, on 6 May 1820 he entered Rugby School, where he suffered from rough treatment. He left school to join the *Spartiate*, the flagship of Admiral Sir George Eyre, as a midshipman. He was not strong enough for life on board ship, however: he became ill before the vessel sailed and gave up the idea of entering the navy. After some unpleas-ant experiences at a private school at Totnes in Devon he was articled to his father in 1825. On the expiry of his art-icles in 1832 he was admitted attorney, and in January 1834 became a partner in his father's firm. Life at Rugby, how-ever, did not suit him; he had literary ambitions and on 22 June 1838 he gave up his position and moved to London.

After staying in London for little more than a year, dur-ing which he wrote for the *British and Foreign Review* and other journals, and entered at Trinity Hall, Cambridge (in April 1839), he accepted the post of editor of the *Hull Times* on 11 September 1839. An attack on the Hull railway line led to his resignation on 21 September 1840, and he decided to prepare for the bar. He had entered the Middle Temple in December 1839, and was called to the bar on 13 January 1843. He joined the midland circuit, but was not very successful. In 1847 he published his *Life of Lord Chancel-lor Hardwicke*, on which he had been working for nearly three years. It was dedicated to the prince consort, who had taken some interest in the progress of the book; it was favourably received by the critics, but did not sell well. Harris had neglected his practice at the bar during the preparation of the work; he was disappointed in hopes of patronage from the earl of Hardwicke, who had taken a

great interest in the book; and he had lost money in rail-way speculations. He consequently found himself in great financial difficulties, which were only resolved by his mar-riage on 12 December 1848 to Elizabeth, daughter of George Innes, master of Kings' School, Warwick, and rec-tor of Hilperton, Wiltshire, who had baptized Harris in his infancy. He became sincerely attached to his wife.

In April 1853 Harris became deputy county court judge of the Bristol district, and early in 1861 he became acting judge of the county court at Birmingham. In 1862 he was appointed registrar of the court of bankruptcy at Man-chester, a post which he retained until 1868, when ill health compelled him to retire on a pension.

In the meantime Harris had turned his attention to the possibility of rendering accessible manuscripts and his-torical documents scattered throughout the country in private hands. He had himself had experience of the diffi-culties of historical research while compiling his *Life of Hardwicke*, and gradually formed the idea of an official commission to investigate and catalogue manuscripts of historical interest in private collections. In October 1857 he first brought forward his idea in a paper read at Bir-mingham before the Law Amendment Society, entitled *The Manuscript Treasures of this Country, and the Best Means of Rendering them Available*. The paper was published in the *Transactions of the National Association for the Promotion of Social Science*, a society founded under the patronage of Lord Brougham in 1857, of which Harris was an original member. In this paper Harris suggested the formation of a committee for the purpose of cataloguing and arranging manuscripts in private hands. The project was taken up by Lord Brougham, and Harris himself worked to promote it. The matter was presented to Palmerston on 9 July 1859 by a deputation with Harris as spokesman. Palmerston was interested, but the project met with much opposition, and the commission was not finally formed until 2 April 1869, after which the work of investigation proceeded steadily. Harris, however, had little or no connection with the pro-ject after its temporary failure in 1859.

In 1868 Harris was deprived of a powerful friend and pat-ron by the death of Lord Brougham. He contributed a 'Memoir of Lord Brougham', compiled partly from per-sonal recollections, to the *Law Magazine* and *Review*. It was afterwards separately published in 1868. In 1876 he brought out his *Philosophical Treatise on the Nature and Consti-tution of Man*, a work on which he had been engaged inter-mittently for forty-three years. While many of his theories were novel, his general treatment of the subject reverted to the principles and terminology of the medieval school-men, and he completely ignored the methods and conclu-sions of contemporary scientific psychology.

Harris was an active member of the Anthropological Society of London, and in 1871 was chosen as vice-president, a position which he retained on the formation of the Anthropological Institute in that year by the union of the Anthropological Society and the Ethnological Soci-ety. In 1875, thinking that the Anthropological Institute 'did not give sufficient attention to psychological sub-jects', he joined Edward William Cox in founding the

Psychological Society, of which he became a vice-president.

In 1888 Harris issued his egotistical *Autobiography* for private circulation. It consists chiefly of extracts from his diary, which he kept regularly from 1832, and contains a preface by his friend Benjamin Ward Richardson. Harris died at Northolt in Middlesex on 15 November 1890, at his residence, Iselipps, an old manor house which he had bought and enlarged.

Besides the works already mentioned, Harris was the author of several other works on legal, political, and anthropological subjects. He contributed many papers to the *Journal of the Anthropological Society* and to *Modern Thought*. He wrote numerous legal biographies for the *Law Magazine* and *Law Review*, including those of Lord Westbury, Lord Cranworth, Lord Chief Baron Pollock, and Lord Wensleydale.

E. I. Carlyle, rev. Catherine Pease-Watkin

Sources G. Harris, *The autobiography of George Harris* (privately printed, London, 1888) · *Journal of the Anthropological Institute*, 20 (1890–91), 199–200 · *Biograph and Review*, 4 (1880), 95–100 · *Rugby school register* (1884), 141 · *Men of the time* (1887) · Chambers, *Short memoir of George Harris (the elder)* (1856) · *CGPLA Eng. & Wales* (1891)
Archives PRO, corresp. and papers relating to foundation of Historical Manuscripts Commission
Likenesses engraving, repro. in Harris, *Autobiography*, frontispiece
Wealth at death £1313 18s. 5d.: probate, 14 April 1891, *CGPLA Eng. & Wales*

Harris, George Francis Robert, **third Baron Harris** (1810–1872), colonial governor, was born at Belmont, Throwley, near Faversham, Kent, on 14 August 1810, the eldest son of General William George *Harris, second Baron Harris (1782–1845), and his first wife, Eliza Selina Anne (d. 1817), daughter of William Dick of Tullymet House, Perthshire. General George *Harris, first Baron Harris, commander of the East India Company's forces in the Fourth Anglo-Mysore War (1799), was his grandfather. Harris was educated at Eton College and privately with the Revd John Shaw at Potton, Bedfordshire, before going up to Oxford in 1829. He matriculated at Merton College but shortly thereafter transferred to Christ Church, graduating BA in 1832. His contemporaries at Christ Church included the future lords Elgin, Dalhousie, and Canning, the last of whom he had already met and befriended while studying under John Shaw.

After his graduation Harris was beset by poor health and resided for a time at Pau, France, where he received a testimonial from the British residents for services in connection with the work of the Church of England. He succeeded to the peerage in 1845; in the following year he was appointed governor of Trinidad, holding the post until his promotion in 1854 to the governorship of Madras. Midway through his term as governor of Trinidad, on 16 April 1850, he married Sarah (d. 1853), younger daughter of George Cummins, archdeacon of Trinidad, with whom he had a daughter and a son.

Harris, like many of his contemporaries, viewed Trinidad's freed slaves as half-savage, childlike creatures; nevertheless, as governor he implemented legislation that laid the foundations for Trinidad's cosmopolitan society of the future. The achievement in which he took most pride, although there was still little to show for it at the time of his departure, was the introduction of a rigorously secular system of primary education which was based upon a parish rate and open to any child of a rate-payer.

To meet the plantation owners' incessant cries for labour Harris initiated the importation of indentured labourers from India, and was one of the first to recognize that these workers would become a permanent part of Trinidadian society. Although it was initially only rarely used, he put in place the mechanism whereby Indians could stay on after their period of indenture, taking a grant of crown land in lieu of their return passage home. More generally, he enabled the purchase of crown land in small lots and offered a virtual amnesty on crown land squatters, two measures which were intended to bridge the gulf between Trinidad's labourers and plantation owners by promoting a small-holding culture and the creation of village communities. His plans were handicapped by an empty treasury and numerous executive blunders and he appointed far too many of his own men—the 'Harristocracy'—to government jobs, yet he was one of Trinidad's most energetic and interested colonial governors, rivalled only by Arthur Hamilton Gordon, governor from 1866 to 1870.

When Harris arrived in Madras, in April 1854, he was astounded by the size and political complexity of his new territory. Moreover, after nine years of virtual gubernatorial autocracy in Trinidad, he was dismayed to discover the number of interest groups in Madras politics that needed to be placated and the paperwork and meetings that they generated.

Early on in his term Harris decided that there was no rural police force worthy of the name and embarked on a radical overhaul of its administration, putting in its place a two-tiered force of unarmed constables and paramilitary reserves modelled respectively on the London Metropolitan Police and the Irish constabulary. In turn this arrangement, encompassing a civil force and a military force under the one authority, became the model for all the provincial police forces of India and was continued after independence. After the relative tranquillity of Trinidad, Harris was stung by the belligerent independence of Madras's Anglo-Indian press, and shortly before the uprising of 1857 he published a minute which accused the Madras newspapers of being the worst of a bad lot: 'disloyal in tone, un-English in spirit, and wanting in every principle'. In spite of the patriotic fervour of his complaints, however, his hostility to the press stemmed from his recognition that the government was dangerously isolated from its subjects and could not tap into the sources of information open to Madras's editors. Indeed, part of his inspiration for remodelling the police force, in addition to the desire to enhance the security of property and the reputation of British authority, had been to secure better information about the state of the country. When the uprising broke out in 1857 Harris was quick to forward troops to his old schoolfriend Canning in the north, and denuded his presidency of all but a skeleton force. He was subsequently lauded in British histories of the rising for his unselfish action in putting imperial considerations before local ones.

In 1859 Harris's term as governor expired and he returned to England, where he was made GCSI. In 1860 he was appointed lord-in-waiting to the queen and in 1863 (as a result of a request of the late Prince Albert) chamberlain to the princess of Wales. He was a whig but did not take an active part in politics. For a time he served as the deputy chairman of the London, Chatham and Dover Railway. Harris died at the family seat, Belmont, on 23 November 1872. His only son, George Robert Canning *Harris (1851–1932), succeeded him as fourth Baron Harris.

KATHERINE PRIOR

Sources D. Wood, *Trinidad in transition: the years after slavery* (1968) · J. J. Higginbotham, *Men whom India has known: biographies of eminent Indian characters*, 2nd edn (1874) · D. Arnold, *Police power and colonial rule: Madras, 1859–1947* (1986) · *ILN* (7 Dec 1872) · *DNB* · BL OIOC, Wood MSS · Burke, *Peerage* · Foster, *Alum. Oxon.* · H. E. C. Stapylton, *The Eton school lists, from 1791 to 1850*, 2nd edn (1864)
Archives CKS, corresp. and papers | BL, corresp. with W. E. Gladstone, Add. MSS 44362–44782 · BL OIOC, Wood MSS · Lpool RO, corresp. with fifteenth earl of Derby · U. Durham L., corresp. with third Earl Grey · U. Nott. L., letters to J. E. Denison · W. Yorks. AS, Leeds, letters to Lord Canning
Likenesses R. Beard, daguerreotype, 1840–49, NPG · F. Grant, oils, 1859, Government House, Madras · attrib. Hill & Saunders, photograph, 1863, NPG
Wealth at death under £35,000: probate, 27 Jan 1873, *CGPLA Eng. & Wales*

Harris, George James (1896–1958), chocolate and confectionery manufacturer, was born at 383 Paisley Road West, Govan, Glasgow, on 8 August 1896, the son of Charles Harris, an engineer's draughtsman, and his wife, Agnes, *née* Brownlie. He was educated at Ayr Academy, from 1914 served in the Royal Flying Corps as a pilot and, after being shot down, transferred to the King's Liverpool regiment. He fought at most of the western front's bloody battles, was mentioned in dispatches, won an MC and bar, and left the military at the age of twenty-three as a major and acting colonel. After the war he studied mathematics at the London School of Economics, but left before completing his degree in order to qualify as a chartered accountant with Deloitte & Co. In 1923 he married Friede Rowntree, a member of the famous cocoa and chocolate family, and was by custom offered a position at Rowntree & Co., where, as secretary of the quality research groups, he co-ordinated the analysis of products and production issues.

Harris moved to the sales department in 1925, and spent an unsuccessful year in the United States attempting to launch a line of sweet gums; he returned as the company's London sales manager. His appointment to the post of marketing manager for bar chocolate products in January 1931 was one of many concurrent managerial changes throughout Rowntree. The recent recession had exposed the company's weak product range and highlighted rival Cadbury's growing dominance of the British confectionery industry, and Rowntree had to tackle a very real threat to its viability. It was Harris's drive and insight which inspired his firm's renaissance in the 1930s: his marketing concepts and techniques underwrote the introduction of Black Magic in 1933; he directly oversaw the launch of Kit-Kat and Aero in 1935, Dairy Box in 1937, and Smarties in 1938; and, although another nine years passed before it was placed on sale, Polo had been conceived by 1939. Harris's career reflected these successes: he became marketing director in 1936, chairman of Rowntree's executive board in 1938, and company chairman in 1941.

The Second World War, with its consequent shortages and rationing, forestalled the commercial potential of Rowntree's new products. Reluctantly, Harris turned his attentions to the industry as a whole. From 1941 to 1946 he was chairman of the Cocoa, Chocolate and Confectionery Alliance and chairman of the Cocoa and Chocolate War-Time Association, which undertook the wartime organization of the industry on behalf of the Ministry of Food. Harris was seriously ill in 1946 and 1947, and medical advice was offered as the explanation for his retirement in January 1952. In fact there was dissension within Rowntree, and the prospect of publicity over Harris's legal defence of a minor traffic offence appeared to some indicative of declining judgement. It was a sad end to a brilliant business career—all the sadder because Rowntree did not fully benefit from its most recent product innovations until confectionery rationing was lifted in 1953.

It was Harris's role as a pioneer of British marketing which makes his career so notable. As a person he was reserved, laconic, and determined, setting the highest standards of effort and achievement for himself and for others. After his unsuccessful year in the United States in 1925–6 he had returned with knowledge of the latest developments in marketing thought, and over the following decade he proved himself an innovator in creative marketing. He was distinguished by his clear perception of how to develop unique products that could command consumer confidence, and during the 1930s he introduced to Rowntree marketing principles which were to become commonplace in British industry. A mixture of branding, intensive advertising, and statistically testable consumer research enabled the company to discover and respond and appeal to consumer wishes; in creating a marketing-orientated business, Harris transformed Rowntree's prevailing corporate culture.

Fascinated by commercial enterprise, suspicious of employees with outside interests, and dismissive of a Rowntree family engrossed by various public works, Harris was determined to professionalize his company. Unlike the previous chairmen, Joseph and Benjamin Seebohm Rowntree, he was uninterested in personnel issues, and it was his overriding concern with marketing and product innovation that created a company of high quality and high-profile brands, a fact denied by none of his successors. This single-mindedness, when combined with illness towards the end of his career, may have made Harris more reclusive and subject to mood changes, but he had always been impatient of corporate politics and procedures, preferring to work entrepreneurially with a selected staff. He died at his home, Bossall Hall, near York, on 11 September 1958, survived by his wife and three daughters.   ROBERT FITZGERALD

Sources R. Fitzgerald, *Rowntree and the marketing revolution, 1862–1969* (1995) · *Confectionery Journal* (2 Oct 1958), 485 · *Cocoa Works Magazine* (Easter 1952) · *Cocoa Works Magazine* (autumn 1958) · *The Times* (2 Oct 1958), 14 · private information (2004) · Borth. Inst., Rowntree archives · b. cert.
Archives Borth. Inst., Rowntree archives
Likenesses portrait, Borth. Inst., Rowntree archives
Wealth at death £10,421 0s. 4d.: probate, 16 Dec 1958, *CGPLA Eng. & Wales*

Harris, George Robert Canning, fourth Baron Harris (1851–1932), cricketer and administrator in India, was born at St Ann's, Trinidad, on 3 February 1851, the only son of George Francis Robert *Harris, third Baron Harris (1810–1872), governor of Trinidad, and his wife, Sarah (d. 1853), younger daughter of George Cummins, archdeacon of Trinidad.

Harris entered Eton College in 1864 and soon revealed a talent for cricket. He was in the school eleven for his last three years and captained the team in 1870. Although in maturity he often extolled the ennobling qualities of cricket's spirit of fair play, as a schoolboy he was not above slyness. In 1870, in a match against Harrow School, Harris, coming in to bowl, observed that the batsman at his own bowling end was out of his crease and, instead of releasing the ball, whipped off the bails and stumped him, an unorthodox form of dismissal which helped Eton to a slim victory of twenty-one runs. Harris was reportedly unfazed by the Harrovian jeers, an early sign, perhaps, of the disdain for public opinion he was to show in later life. In 1871 he went up to Christ Church, Oxford, where he graduated BA in 1875, and for three years (1871, 1872, and 1874) was in the university eleven. Although now beginning to show talent as a batsman, his scores for the university were usually modest.

In 1872, on his father's death, Harris succeeded as fourth Baron Harris. Two years later, on 8 July 1874, he married Lucy Ada (d. 1930), second daughter of Carnegie Robert John Jervis, third Viscount St Vincent.

Upon leaving Oxford, Harris focused his cricketing energies on his home county club of Kent. He was captain of Kent from 1875 to 1889, playing in most of the matches, and came to be regarded as one of the best amateur batsmen in England. He also played a prominent part in early matches with Australia, captaining an English touring side there in the winter of 1878–9. No test matches were played and a certain amount of bad feeling was generated by the tour, in particular by a notorious incident in which the crowd rushed onto the Sydney cricket ground to contest an umpiring decision. In 1880 when an Australian side next visited England, a string of unprestigious fixtures seemed set to continue the sour tone between the two countries until, in the interests of colonial cricketing relations, it was decided that Harris should assemble a full-strength English team to play the Australians. The game, which England won by five wickets, was played at the Oval

George Robert Canning Harris, fourth Baron Harris (1851–1932), by Arthur Hacker, 1919

in the first week of September 1880 and is recognized as the first test match played on English soil. In 1884 Harris again captained England in two test matches, one at Lord's which England won, and the other, a huge run-getting affair at the Oval, which was drawn.

Harris retired from first-class cricket in 1889, the year he was appointed governor of Bombay. Before this he had accumulated extensive administrative experience; he had been under-secretary for India (from June 1885 to February 1886) and under-secretary for war (1886–9), a job he found particularly arduous. But he always regarded his official work as a distraction from cricket, albeit a necessary one, and was at best a reluctant colonial governor. He remained in Bombay from 1890 to 1895, a turbulent era marked by nascent nationalism and sectarian riots. An arch conservative, he decried any attempt to apply democratic principles to India, arguing that it was the role of the British to protect India's agricultural masses from the self-interested clamour of educated Indians. He disapproved of the 1892 Councils Act, which promised a minute degree of electoral responsibility to Indians, and tried to use it instead to marginalize politicians from Poona, at that time home to western India's most radical and articulate nationalists, among them Bal Gangadhar Tilak. Ironically, Tilak was able to capitalize on Harris's dislike of the 'Poona Brahmans' by accusing his administration of being anti-Hindu, a charge which incensed Harris. Particularly after outbreaks of sectarian rioting in 1893 and 1894, Harris saw himself as an umpire in India, deploying the rules of fair play to balance the competing interests of Hindus, Muslims, and Parsis.

While governor, Harris promoted cricket in Bombay, especially among school and college boys, and in 1892 secured the first visit to India of a representative team from England, captained by his friend Lord Hawke. To his numerous critics in the Indian press who added the frivolity of cricket playing to his crimes, Harris replied grandly that cricket afforded a far superior means of inculcating the spirit of patriotism than noisy politicking.

Harris left Bombay in 1895 and upon his return to England began a long connection with the City of London as chairman and director of various South African undertakings. He served in the Second South African War as assistant adjutant-general with the imperial yeomanry. In retirement he devoted himself to cricket and for many years was chairman of Kent County Cricket Club. He was also a member of the Marylebone Cricket Club for over sixty years, serving as its president in 1895, and as treasurer from 1896 until his death in 1932. He published several substantial books on cricket, including an autobiographical account entitled *A Few Short Runs* (1921), and *The History of Kent County Cricket* (1907), and contributed numerous prefaces to other works. He was appointed GCIE in 1890, GCSI in 1895, and CB in 1918. Harris died at his home, Belmont, near Faversham, on 24 March 1932, and was succeeded as fifth baron by his only surviving son George St Vincent (1899–1984).   KATHERINE PRIOR

Sources R. I. Cashman, *The myth of Lokamanya* (1975) · H. S. Altham, *A history of cricket* (1926) · Lord Harris [G. R. C. Harris], *A few short runs* (1921) · Burke, *Peerage* · BL OIOC, Harris MSS · Foster, *Alum. Oxon.* · *The Times* (26 March 1932) · *CGPLA Eng. & Wales* (1932)
Archives BL OIOC | BL OIOC, Elgin MSS · BL OIOC, letters to Lord Wenlock, MS Eur. D 592 · Bodl. Oxf., corresp. with Lord Kimberley · CAC Cam., corresp. with Lord Randolph Churchill · CKS, letters to Edward Stanhope · CUL, corresp. with Lord Hardinge
Likenesses J. Brown, stipple, 1880 (after photograph by W. & D. Downey), NPG; repro. in *Bailey's Magazine* (1880) · W. Stoneman, two photographs, 1918–31, NPG · A. Hacker, oils, 1919, Marylebone Cricket Club, Lord's, London [*see illus.*] · H. von Herkomer, portrait, County Hall, Maidstone, Kent · W. Hoare, oils, Borough of Faversham, Kent · Spy [L. Ward], chromolithograph caricature, NPG; repro. in *VF* (16 July 1881)
Wealth at death £57,152 7s. 11d.—except settled land: probate, 11 Aug 1932, *CGPLA Eng. & Wales* · £55,709 4s. 6d.—limited to settled land: further grant, 9 Nov 1932, *CGPLA Eng. & Wales*

Harris, Harry (1919–1994), geneticist, was born on 30 September 1919 at 1 Marshall Place, Cheetham, Manchester, the eldest son of Solomon (Sol) Harris, garment manufacturer and secretary of a friendly society, and his wife, Sarah, *née* Chazan, whose father was a religious bookseller. Harris was educated first at the Grecian Street elementary school in Salford and then at Manchester grammar school, where he excelled in science and went on to win an open scholarship to Trinity College, Cambridge, in 1938. He obtained a first in the natural sciences tripos in 1941 and then moved to the Royal Infirmary in Manchester to complete his medical training. He qualified as a doctor in 1943 and worked as a house officer in hospitals in Sunderland for the next two years before joining the Royal Air Force. There, as a medical officer, he held the rank of flight lieutenant and served in Britain and the Far East. Fortunately there was little serious medical work to be done in the RAF in the immediate post-war period and Harris used this unlikely opportunity to launch a lifelong study of human genetic variation.

This was an unusual career choice since genetics was scarcely mentioned in any of the medical textbooks of those days and it was well before DNA had been shown to hold the secrets of the genetic code. Harris later recorded that he was greatly stimulated at the time by the growing literature on the complex genetics of human blood groups (in particular the Rh or rhesus system) and also by J. B. S. Haldane's *New Paths in Genetics*, published in 1941. These elements, together with a history of premature baldness on his father's side of the family, led Harris to undertake a large scale study of the genetics of baldness in a consecutive series of more than 900 servicemen. He wrote up his results and was delighted to have his first paper accepted for publication in a scientific journal edited by Professor Lionel Penrose at the Galton Laboratory, University College, London. This early link with the Galton and University College proved to be decisive in the development of Harris's career. On demobilization from the RAF in 1947 he joined the Galton Laboratory as a research assistant, and indeed returned as Galton professor eighteen years later when Penrose retired. His first three years at the Galton, followed by three years as a lecturer in the biochemistry department in University College, allowed him to put down his roots and establish the main directions of his life's work. In 1948 he married Muriel Hargest; they had one son, Toby.

Harris's first laboratory work involved devising a method to distinguish people by their ability to taste bitter/sweet substances and to show that tasting was a genetically determined characteristic. These basic experiments were a pointer to developments during the next forty years, and his subsequent comprehensive analysis of variation in normal healthy individuals and families using simple chemical and biochemical techniques. Harris proved that genetic variation in man was not rare and unusual and always associated with a dreadful disease, the widely held view of those days, but was commonplace and usually harmless. Harris was the first to draw attention to the fact that we are all individually different in our genetic constitution and, using a range of laboratory tests, was able to demonstrate that no two individuals (except for identical twins) are exactly alike in their biochemical make-up. This work prepared the ground for many new concepts and applied procedures which became well known in later years, such as the identification of individuals by genetic 'fingerprints', the use of genetic markers to map genes on to human chromosomes, and the prenatal diagnosis of disorders using genetic markers. His basic research work also anticipated the extensive genetic heterogeneity of inherited disease, revealed in later years by molecular analysis at the level of the DNA.

In addition to being a dynamic force in the laboratory Harris was also a prolific and popular author. He was most successful with his excellent, crystal clear, student text

The Principles of Human Biochemical Genetics, which first appeared in 1970 and went through two further editions and four foreign language (Italian, Russian, German, Chinese) versions. Altogether, he published nearly 400 scientific papers in mainstream journals and eight books in the field.

All of Harris's research in England was carried out in London. Following appointments as a university lecturer in biochemistry at University College, London, and at the London Hospital medical college (1950–60) Harris served as professor and head of the department of biochemistry at King's College, London, from 1960 to 1965. In 1961 he established the Medical Research Council human biochemical genetics research unit and was its director until 1976. In 1965 he was appointed Galton professor of genetics and biometry at University College and stayed there until 1976. Then, with an unexpected final flourish, Harris left England to take up the Harnwell chair in human genetics at the University of Pennsylvania, where he worked and published papers on a wide variety of topics until he retired with great reluctance in 1990.

Harris was widely honoured and recognized for his major contributions to genetics. He was elected a fellow of the Royal Society in 1966, a fellow of the Royal College of Physicians in 1973, a foreign associate of the National Academy of Sciences (USA) in 1976, and doctor *honoris causa* by the Université René Descartes, Paris, in 1976. He also received the William Allen memorial award from the American Society of Human Genetics in 1968. Harris had an outstanding career which was devoted to science but sadly shortened by chronic diabetes, from which he died in Philadelphia on 17 July 1994. He was survived by his wife and son.   D. A. HOPKINSON

Sources D. A. Hopkinson, *Memoirs FRS*, 42 (1996), 153–70 · citation for the William Allen memorial award, *American Journal of Human Genetics*, 21 (1969), 107–8 · *American Journal of Human Genetics*, 58 (1996), 896–8 · D. J. Kevles, *In the name of eugenics* (1985); pbk edn (1995) · Munk, *Roll* · *The Independent* (22 July 1994) · personal knowledge (2004) · WWW · b. cert.
Likenesses photograph, repro. in *Memoirs FRS*, 153 · photograph, repro. in *The Independent* · photograph, repro. in *American Journal of Human Genetics*

Harris, Henry (1633/4–1704), actor and engraver, was said on 12 November 1691 to be fifty-seven, which means that he was born in 1633 or 1634. Although his early career is obscure, it is clear that by the Restoration he had already acquired considerable standing, for in 1660 he was party to the formation of the Duke's Company of actors under Sir William Davenant. His designation 'of the Citty of London, painter' (Highfill, Burnim & Langhans, *BDA*), and the sum of £5000 in which he was bound, suggest that initially he took particular responsibility on the production side. Later, however, it was as an actor that he made his mark. Despite a brush with the authorities in July 1662 when he and others attempted to stop the office of the revels preventing them from performing, Harris had a good season, seemingly his first, in 1661–2. Indeed, 'the King and everybody else crying him up so high', as Samuel Pepys recorded, 'he grew very proud and demanded 20 *l*

Henry Harris (1633/4–1704), by John Greenhill, 1664 [as Cardinal Wolsey in *Henry VIII* by William Shakespeare]

for himself extraordinary there, [more] then Batterton or anybody else, upon every new play, and 10 *l* upon every Revive—which, with other things, Sir W Davenant would not give him' (Pepys, 4.239). For a while he toyed with the idea of joining the King's Company of actors, but in the event, 'by the Duke of Yorkes persuasion' (Pepys, 4.347), he stayed with Davenant on the terms he had originally demanded. His subsequent performance as Cardinal Wolsey in *Henry VIII* was considered outstanding, and it is in this role that he is depicted in his surviving portrait (possibly the first of a Shakespearian character) by John Greenhill, versions of which are in the Ashmolean Museum, Magdalen College, Oxford, and the Garrick Club.

With Harris's successes on the stage, in a wide variety of roles, came social preferment. In 1663 he was made yeoman of the revels, a post he was to keep for the rest of his life and which placed on him the responsibility of keeping the vestments and trappings for court masques and disguisings. In the following year he was said to have had lodgings at court. Although the original intention seems to have been to give him board wages and house rent as well as a money allowance, in practice it was this last which he received at the rate of 6*d*. per day, back-dated to 1660. By January 1667 Harris had become acquainted with Pepys, who found him 'a very curious and understanding person in all, pictures and other things—and a man of fine conversation' (Pepys, 8.29), and later a warm friendship developed. In the following year, on the death of Davenant, Harris took over, with Thomas Betterton, with whom he had acted from the start, the direction of the Duke's

Company. In June 1671 he gave his last performance at the Lincoln's Inn Fields playhouse, where he had been since 1661, and in November acted at the new Dorset Garden Theatre, which he had been instrumental in creating and near which he went to live, in Salisbury Court. There followed a string of performances, including that of Ulysses in John Dryden's *Troilus and Cressida* (1679), before his retirement in 1681. Thereafter Harris remained a shareholder in the company, but from March 1687 he did not receive his rightful income, and at the time of his death litigation concerning the outstanding sums was still unresolved.

In addition to that from his theatrical career, Harris enjoyed another income as engraver of public seals. At first sight this seems a distinct improbability and, indeed, the *Dictionary of National Biography* was innocent of it. However, the connection is clearly made in a letter of 1675 from the committee of trade and plantations instructing 'Mr. Harris at the Duke's Play House to hasten the seal for St. Christopher's' (*CSP col.*, 9, no. 651) and another in 1678 requesting Henry Slingsby, master worker of the Royal Mint, to appraise a seal 'cut by Mr. Harris of the Play House' (*CSP col.*, 10, no. 812). Harris had been granted the office of engraving the king's signets, arms, and seals on 11 November 1670, at £50 per annum (plus piece-rates for every item done), possibly through the patronage of Lord Arlington, for whom Harris had produced in 1665 a cipher of initials. Certainly, according to an account itemizing the seals which Harris had produced in January and February 1666, it was under Arlington's direction that the work had been undertaken. The dating of the account obviously indicates that Harris had begun his engraving duties some time before his formal grant, while the inclusion in it of a claim for two great seals for Providence Island, a commission which still lay unfinished on 24 February 1667, suggests that 1666 should be taken as old style.

Despite his activities in respect of the plantations and some of the English courts, Harris was not responsible for all government seals in the later 1660s and 1670s. It is quite unclear what work, if any, he did in the 1680s, until William and Mary made him engraver of seals in 1689. From that time until his death he took on a whole range of commissions, both for the colonies and for the English and Irish offices of state. Notwithstanding his declaration in his petition of 1690 to the lords of the Treasury that he had been 'educated in the art' of die cutting (*Calendar of Treasury Papers, 1557–1696*, 108), no signed work by Harris is known; the presumption must be that, throughout his long connection with seal making, he left the practical part of his work to deputies.

Although it has been claimed that Harris entered the mint as an assistant engraver in 1680, there is no mention of him in the mint accounts until 1690, when he succeeded George Bowers as chief engraver. All in all, Harris was remunerated in this post, at £325 per annum, from 25 March 1690 until 31 August 1704, and during this time he took as his deputies, first, the Roettier brothers, James and Norbert, jointly from 1690 to 1695, and then James alone until 1697. In that year, when the great recoinage of silver

was in full swing and each of the five country mints had its own deputy engraver, John Croker became his deputy at the Tower at the rate previously paid to the Roettiers, £175 per annum, and he brought in eight others to help out in die or letter making, labouring, and smithying. Two of these went on to enjoy more extended careers in the mint—Richard Fletcher becoming smith and Samuel Bull assistant to Harris's successor as chief engraver. In 1698—on the instruction of the Treasury—the mint took on as his assistant Thomas Silvester, a smith, to assist in the sinking, filing, and polishing of dies. For the tin issue of 1690 to 1691 Harris was appointed, with James Roettier, engraver at £100 per annum and then from 1691 to 1693 sole engraver at £200 per annum. Just how tenuous was Harris's grasp on minting affairs during this time may be seen from the report of a committee set up in 1697 to inquire into irregularities concerning the coinage dies. Captain Harris, it was admitted, was indeed 'the Patent Officer, and ought to have the Inspection of the Dyes, yet … Roteer [that is, Roettier] would never suffer him to come into the House where the Press and Dyes are kept' (*JHC*, 11, 686). The explanation of why, in this and other contemporaneous sources, Harris was termed 'Captain' seems to lie in the decision by the lords of the Treasury on 5 February 1697 to recommend him for military employment, but why this should have been so is obscure. Earlier on, in 1691, Harris had become with Thomas Neale, master worker at the mint, one of the assistants in the Company of Tapestry Makers, and later, from 1694 to 1702, he drew a salary of £300 as a commissioner of stamps.

Harris was married by 1672, though to whom is uncertain, and had one daughter, Elizabeth, who married George Furness, a London merchant. It was Elizabeth who took responsibility for the completion of various seals for the plantations which were unfinished at Harris's death; it was she to whom he bequeathed half his estate; and it was her children, Henry, George, and Elizabeth, who were the beneficiaries of the rest. Harris died on 3 August 1704 and was buried on 6 August at St Paul's, Covent Garden, the parish in which he had lived since his retirement.

W. W. WROTH, *rev.* C. E. CHALLIS

Sources Highfill, Burnim & Langhans, *BDA* · C. E. Challis, 'Mint officials and moneyers of the Stuart period', *British Numismatic Journal*, 59 (1989), 157–97 · *CSP dom., addenda, 1660–85* · W. A. Shaw, ed., *Calendar of treasury books*, [33 vols. in 64], PRO (1904–69), esp. vols. 3, 9–22 · *CSP col.*, vols. 7, 9–23 · PRO, T1/7 no. 69, 83 no. 83; PROB 11/478 sig. 183; SP 44 no. 40, fol. 236 · BL, Add. MS 18,757 · J. Redington, ed., *Calendar of Treasury papers*, 6 vols., PRO (1868–89), vols. 1, 3 · W. Van Lennep, 'Henry Harris, actor, friend of Pepys', *Studies in English theatre history* (1952), 9–23 · Pepys, *Diary* · *Journal of the commissioners for trade and plantations*, [vol. 1]: *From April 1704 to February 1708/9* (1920) · *JHC*, 11 (1693–7), 686

Likenesses J. Greenhill, pastel, 1664 (as Cardinal Wolsey), Magd. Oxf. [*see illus.*] · J. Greenhill, coloured chalk and wash (as Cardinal Wolsey), AM Oxf. · J. Greenhill, oils (as Cardinal Wolsey), Garr. Club

Harris, Howel (1714–1773), evangelist, was born on 23 January 1714, at Trefeca, near Talgarth, in Brecknockshire, the youngest of the five children born to Howel ap Howel alias Harris (1672?–1731), carpenter, and his wife, Susannah (d. 1751), daughter of Thomas Powell. Surviving knowledge about his youth comes from *A Brief Account of the Life of Howell Harris, Esq.* (1791; Welsh version 1792). The book contains exaggerated descriptions of early sinfulness. From boyhood he was talented and ambitious, as were his surviving brothers, Joseph *Harris (*bap.* 1704, *d.* 1764), mathematician, navigational expert, and from 1748 assay-master at the Royal Mint, and Thomas *Harris (*bap.* 1705, *d.* 1782) [see under Harris, Joseph], tailor and landowner. He was also haughty and undirected. His education at several local schools and at Llwyn-llwyd, a dissenting academy of note, was more than adequate to enable him from 1732 to keep schools of his own. In 1735, at Joseph's insistence, he entered St Mary Hall, Oxford, but within a week he left 'this Mother Harlot of Laud' (Beynon, *Visits to London*, 169), and returned home to continue the unauthorized semi-public round of meetings of prayer and exhortation he had started that midsummer after experiencing a profound spiritual conversion. Unease about the condition of his soul, unrelieved by the study of moral treatises such as *The Whole Duty of Man* (1658) and *The Practice of Piety* (2nd edn, 1612), was dispelled by his conviction that at communion on Whit Sunday, 25 May 1735, he had been pardoned 'on account of [Christ's] blood', a conviction 'sealed' on 18 June when he felt his heart melt inside him 'of love to God my Saviour' (*Hanes ferr o fywyd Howell Harris yscwier*, 12–13).

Immediately Harris began to counsel others, initially in and around Talgarth, later further afield, gathering converts whom in 1736 he began to organize into private societies. In 1737 he met Daniel *Rowland, a curate whose preaching had created similar spiritual remorse and excitement in Cardiganshire. Now well known in south Wales, by 1738 Harris was venturing northwards too. In 1736, and thrice in 1739, the church refused him holy orders. By then Harris, with his genius for fiery, extempore preaching and for organizing his followers, was, with Rowland, the chief instrument of what became known as the Welsh Methodist revival (but the name 'Methodist' he repeatedly repudiated).

Consulting God on all matters, without regular means of sustenance, for the next twelve years Harris worked unsparingly in this cause. He travelled on average about 6000 miles a year, preaching three, four, sometimes five times a day, establishing private societies, creating an association to oversee their welfare, examining his soul, and making daily entries in his journal. From 1739 he also worked annually in England at the behest of the leaders of revivalism there, George Whitefield and John Wesley. The visits to London put him in touch with the Moravians, for some of whose beliefs and practices Harris had a good deal of sympathy. London also allowed him to feed his conceit and pride and 'bondage to cloathes' (Beynon, *Visits to Pembrokeshire*, 134). But his exertions were so demanding and his persecutions so damaging that, at thirty years of age, all his finery could not disguise the fact that he looked 'old and decaying' (Beynon, *Visits to London*, 45) and that his voice was permanently hoarse. Harris's career as revivalist was extraordinarily heroic.

In this spiritual career, paradoxically, position and title meant much to Harris. In 1743 he was elected 'General Superintendent or Father of all the work in Wales, wholly unsought for by me' (Beynon, *Reformer and Soldier*, 123). Although he was then general superintendent to only a few thousand people in a few hundred societies, the office was deserved and the title correct; but the adverbial clause is a defensive fiction. From the beginning the relationship between Harris and Rowland had not been smooth. Both aspired to leadership, both were self-assertive. Enmity was inevitable; a division most likely. The friction between them was compounded by a long drawn-out theological argument, the last of many, on the nature of Christ's person, and by Harris's insistence on preaching 'God's blood'; also by his claim that Madam Sidney *Griffith, the estranged wife of a Caernarvonshire squire, was his urim, his prophetess, 'the first that God raised to raise me' (ibid., 68), and by his determination to allow her to accompany him on preaching tours and to association meetings. In the rift that followed, Welsh society members became 'Rowland's people' or 'Harris's people'. The two leaders were reunited only after a second revival, the Llangeitho revival of 1762, had occurred and a new momentum was created. Harris again undertook preaching tours, now and again in a carriage with verses painted on its sides, and visited societies, bringing to them order and discipline. But the new converts were rarely his, and in the association's success he felt 'as it were laid aside' (ibid., 231). A stridently faithful Anglican (when it suited him), he sensed a growing distance between Methodism and the church. He also disapproved of the building of new chapels for society members—and yet at home he fully supported Lady Huntingdon's plans to establish a college for evangelical preachers in Trefeca Isaf. He was still his irrational, wilful, commandeering self.

In many ways the post-1762 years were the formative years of Welsh Methodism: it was the period of Williams Pantycelyn's major and influential publications and of Daniel Rowland's dedication to Capel Gwynfil and the cause; but were it not for the fifteen years Harris had dedicated to 'his rounds' (as he called them) between 1735 and 1750 there would not have been a second period. In that crucial first period he had been Boanerges, Wales's spiritual awakening personified.

Left with his diminishing band, after 1750 Harris decided to start a new venture and to create an establishment not dissimilar to the communities at Halle and Fulneck. Between 1752 and 1760 he transformed Trefeca, rebuilding and extending the old house, planning orchards and avenues, and building a chapel, a kiln, an infirmary, a bakehouse, a printing shop, and several other workshops; in 1765 he began to build a greater house. By 1755 over 100 of his followers had settled there, half of them of necessity lodging in neighbouring farmhouses, living a regulated life of great devotional and commercial discipline. Harris's reputation and expertise as an agricultural pioneer was such that in 1756 he was elected an honorary member of the Brecknockshire Agriculture Society. At the height of the Seven Years' War he joined the county's militia, taking with him twenty-four young men from the Family: he was made an ensign and called himself esquire.

The Trefeca press printed Harris's *Last Message and Dying Testimony* in both Welsh and English in 1774 as well as a selection of his letters and hymns in 1782. A few of his hymns had been published earlier, in 1740 and 1742. Extracts from his journals were published in 1791 and 1792, and in several twentieth-century books, but the massive bulk of the contents of his 300-odd volumes of journals, like most of his 3000 letters, his self-testimony, and literary memorial, remain in manuscript form only. His historical memorial was the transformation of pre-Methodist Wales.

For this great, difficult man neither marrying nor marriage was easy. After years of indecision and divine consultation about several possible partners, including Mrs Elizabeth James, who eventually married Whitefield, Harris finally married Anne Williams, daughter of John Williams, of Skreen, in the parish of Llansteffan, Brecknockshire, on 18 June 1744, his spiritual birthday. Of two daughters born to them only one, Elizabeth (*b.* 1749), unruly and headstrong like her father, survived. His wife died in 1770. Harris died on 21 July 1773 and was buried in Talgarth church. DEREC LLWYD MORGAN

Sources *A brief account of the life of Howell Harris, esq.* (1791) · *Hanes ferr o fywyd Howell Harris yscwier* (1792) · G. M. Roberts, *Portread o ddiwygiwr* (1969) · T. Beynon, ed., *Howell Harris's visits to London* (1960) · T. Beynon, ed., *Howell Harris, reformer and soldier (1714–1773)* (1958) · G. M. Roberts, ed., *Selected Trevecka letters (1742–1747)* (1956) · G. M. Roberts, ed., *Selected Trevecka letters (1747–1794)* (1962) · G. F. Nuttall, ed., *Howel Harris, 1714–1773: the last enthusiast* (1965) · R. T. Jenkins, *Yng nghysgod Trefeca* (1968) · IGI · T. Beynon, ed., *Howell Harris's visits to Pembrokeshire* (1966)

Archives NL Wales, MSS | Trevecca College, Trefeca, artefacts
Likenesses engraving, repro. in J. M. Jones and W. Morgan, *Y tadau Methodistaidd*, 1 (1895), 71

Harris, James (1709–1780), philosopher and musical patron, was born on 24 July 1709, probably at the family home in the close, Salisbury, now called Malmesbury House. He was the eldest of three sons of James Harris (1674–1731) and his second wife, Elizabeth (*c.*1682–1744), daughter of Anthony Ashley Cooper, second earl of Shaftesbury, and his wife, Dorothy; he had an older half-sister from his father's first marriage to Catherine Cocks. Harris was educated at Salisbury grammar school, under its master Richard Hele, and matriculated from Wadham College, Oxford, in 1726. He left, without taking a degree, in 1729, when he entered Lincoln's Inn, although probably with no intention of following a legal career. His father's death in 1731 left him with sufficient resources to devote his life to philosophy, literature, and music, and in its last twenty years to politics. In 1732 he toured the Low Countries and parts of France and Germany for four months; diaries of the tour compiled by Harris and by his servant James Gibbs survive in the family archive. This appears to have been his only visit abroad.

Harris's philosophical and literary studies centred on the classical writers, and his many friends helped to track

James Harris (1709–1780), attrib. Frances Reynolds, *c.*1777

down both manuscripts and printed texts and to obtain copies; the area of search was extended when his son embarked on his diplomatic career abroad. A more recent and particularly strong influence was his uncle the moral philosopher Anthony Ashley Cooper, third earl of Shaftesbury, whom he never knew but whose son, the fourth earl, was a frequent and intimate correspondent. Four major works by Harris were published: *Three Treatises* (concerning art; music, painting, and poetry; and happiness) in 1744; *Hermes, or, A Philosophical Inquiry Concerning Universal Grammar* in 1751; *Philosophical Arrangements* in 1775; and *Philological Inquiries*, published posthumously in 1781. The first two were later published in German and French, and the second provided him with the nickname by which he was frequently known, Hermes Harris.

On 8 July 1745 Harris married Elizabeth (1722–1781), daughter of John Clarke and his wife, Catherine. Clarke had an estate at Sandford in Somerset but the family was from Salisbury. The marriage was outstandingly happy and Elizabeth Harris springs to vibrant life in her regular letters to her son. Of five children, three survived babyhood: James *Harris, later first earl of Malmesbury (1746–1820); Gertrude (1750–1834), who married the Hon. Frederick Robinson after surviving shipwreck off the coast of the Netherlands on her unaccompanied return from Russia in 1779; and Louisa (1753–1836), who became a distinguished amateur singer.

Music was a major passion for Harris, and much of his energy throughout his life was expended on maintaining regular concerts in Salisbury, with gentlemen amateurs playing alongside professionals from the cathedral and elsewhere, and in building up the annual St Cecilia celebrations into what became the Salisbury festival. Harris and many of his relatives and friends were passionate admirers of George Frideric Handel and his correspondence is full of previously unknown details about the composer, including an account of a visit by Handel to Harris's Salisbury home in 1739. Harris was responsible for the first draft of the libretto for Handel's *L'allegro, il penseroso ed il moderato*, based on Milton's poems and brought to its final form by Charles Jennens. He supplied the catalogue of Handel's works appended to John Mainwaring's *Memoirs of the Life and Writings of George Frederic Handel* (1760) and owned an important collection of manuscript texts of Handel's works. His brother Thomas Harris (1712–1785), a legatee of the composer, acquired Philippe Mercier's fine portrait of Handel.

Harris wrote other librettos also and set them to music adapted from the works of various composers. *Daphnis and Amaryllis*, performed at Salisbury in 1761, was adapted the following year at the request of David Garrick and performed at Drury Lane Theatre under the title *The Spring*. A collection of Harris's musical adaptations, *Sacred Music*, was published by the Salisbury Cathedral organist Joseph Corfe about 1800.

In 1761 Harris was elected MP for Christchurch, Hampshire, and held the seat until his death. As a supporter of George Grenville he served as a commissioner of the Admiralty from January to April 1763 and of the Treasury from April 1763 until Grenville's fall from power in 1765. In 1774 he was appointed secretary and comptroller to Queen Charlotte, a post which brought him into close contact with the king as well as the queen and which he held until his death. Whether in or out of office Harris was a committed MP, rarely absent from London when parliament was sitting and working hard for his constituents, soliciting places and favours for them. He made detailed memoranda of all significant political conversations that he witnessed and of the various political crises of the day. Similarly he recorded all his conversations with the king and queen and kept separate diaries of his social and cultural life in London.

Harris was elected a fellow of the Royal Society in 1763 and served as a trustee of the British Museum from 1765 until his death. His friends and correspondents include most scholars and writers of the day. Henry Fielding, a Salisbury neighbour, was a particularly close friend; Harris helped Fielding's sister Sarah with her published translation *Xenophon's Memoirs of Socrates* (1762) and wrote an unpublished memoir of Fielding, following his death.

Harris's published works were highly regarded in his own day. His diaries are an important source for the political, social, and cultural history of the time. But the lasting impression from a study of his archive is of a man with a genius for friendship. Samuel Johnson's intemperate but much quoted description of Harris as 'a prig and a bad prig' (Boswell, *Life*, 3.245) must be set against innumerable warm comments. Fanny Burney in 1775 found him 'a charming old man, well bred even to humility, gentle in

his manners, & communicative & agreeable in his conversation', adding on another occasion, 'I like him amazingly' (*The Early Journals and Letters of Fanny Burney*, ed. L. E. Troide, 2, 1990, 130, 174). Harris died on 22 December 1780 at his house in the close, Salisbury, and was buried six days later in the cathedral; a memorial including a portrait medallion is in the south transept.

ROSEMARY DUNHILL

Sources Hants. RO, Harris (Malmesbury) archive · *Music and theatre in Handel's world: the family papers of James Harris, 1732–1780*, ed. D. Burrows and R. Dunhill (2002) · third earl of Malmesbury, ed., *A series of letters of the first earl of Malmesbury, his family and friends*, 1 (1870) · C. T. Probyn, *The sociable humanist: the life and works of James Harris, 1709–1780* (1991) · *DNB* · Salisbury Cathedral register, 10 Aug 1709 [baptism]
Archives Hants. RO, corresp.; household accounts · PRO, corresp., PRO 30/43 · Wilts. & Swindon RO, letters | BL, letters to first and second earls of Hardwicke and Charles Yorke, Add. MSS 35592–35692, *passim* · BL, letters to Jonathan Toup, Add. MS 32565 [copies] · Bodl. Oxf., letters to J. Williams · Hants. RO, corresp. with John Thomas Batt · NL Scot., corresp. with Lord Monboddo
Likenesses J. Highmore, oils, 1740, priv. coll. · F. Bartolozzi, engraving, 1776 (after drawing by F. Bartolozzi), repro. in J. Harris, *Philological inquiries*, pts 1–2 (1781) · F. Reynolds, portrait, *c*.1777, NPG [*see illus.*] · J. Reynolds, oils, 1777, priv. coll. · G. Romney or J. Reynolds, oils, *c*.1777, Wadham College, Oxford; version, NPG · J. Barry, group portrait, oils, 1777–82 (*The Society for the Encouragement of Arts*), RSA · Bacon, marble medallion on monument, 1781, Salisbury Cathedral · F. Bartolozzi, line engraving (aged sixty-seven), BM · C. Bestland, stipple (aged sixty-seven; after wax model by I. Gosset, 1776), BM, NPG · C. Bestland, stipple (aged thirty-one; after J. Highmore), NPG · W. Evans, stipple (after drawing by W. Evans, *c*.1769), BM, NPG; repro. in *Works of R. O. Cambridge* (1803) · oils, NPG

Harris, James, first earl of Malmesbury (1746–1820), diplomatist, was born on 21 April 1746 in St Ann's Gate House in the close at Salisbury, the eldest and only surviving son of James *Harris (1709–1780), MP and philosopher, and his wife, Elizabeth Clarke of Sandford, Somerset.

Education and early career Born into a long-established Wiltshire family, Harris rose spectacularly to become the leading British diplomatist of the final quarter of the eighteenth century and an important adviser to government. Educated first in Salisbury Cathedral school and then at Winchester College (1757–62), he went up to Merton College, Oxford, in June 1763. His two years at university established important future connections, especially those with Charles James Fox and William Eden, but were untroubled by serious scholarly achievement. This changed when he left Oxford in 1765 and quite deliberately began to prepare himself for a career in diplomacy. He first spent a year at the leading Dutch university of Leiden, learning the Dutch language—an unusual accomplishment which proved significant in his later diplomatic career. He studied the history of Europe, international relations, and the republic's distinctive constitution, while improving his social and linguistic skills by circulating within high society at The Hague and Amsterdam and establishing a firm friendship with the British ambassador, Sir Joseph Yorke. Harris then set off on a grand tour, unconventionally focused upon northern rather than southern Europe. Having returned first to the

James Harris, first earl of Malmesbury (1746–1820), by Sir Thomas Lawrence, 1806

Dutch republic, he travelled through Prussia and Poland and finally back to Paris. Once back from France, he was soon appointed secretary of embassy, the first step on the diplomatic ladder, to Sir James Gray, ambassador in Madrid from 1767 to 1769.

Harris arrived in Spain in December 1768. The three years which he spent at the Spanish court launched his career. When Gray left in August 1769, Harris became chargé d'affaires at the age of twenty-three, and acted in this role during a serious Anglo-Bourbon crisis in 1770–71 over the distant Falkland Islands. At a key moment in this confrontation Harris won the admiration of his superiors: ordered to leave his post by the British government, in a crude attempt to put pressure upon Madrid, he lingered some 60 miles north of the Spanish capital, so that he was able to make a rapid return when the crisis was resolved and his own instructions were countermanded. The reason for this convenient delay was not diplomatic finesse but the pursuit of a Spanish lady, but that did not prevent Harris reaping his reward: promotion, first as minister-plenipotentiary in Madrid (1771–2) and then as envoy-extraordinary in Berlin (1772–6), to which he was appointed at the age of twenty-five. The four years which he spent in Prussia revealed both his limitations as a diplomatist and his real abilities. Within a month of arriving in Berlin on 21 February 1772, he achieved a great coup: he was the first foreign diplomat to discover the intention of Frederick the Great and his ally Russia to partition Poland, a convention having been signed two weeks earlier. Yet after this impressive début the envoy's four years at the Prussian court were lacking in solid achievements.

Though he won the plaudits of the court and the esteem of the Prussian king (who asked for him to be reappointed), there was no significant improvement in relations, which remained cool and distant as they had been since the alienation at the close of the Seven Years' War (1756–63).

The year after Harris returned from Berlin he married, on 27 July 1777, Harriet Maria (1761–1830), the youngest daughter of the MP Sir George Amyand (1720–1766) and his wife, Anna Maria Corteen. There were four children of this marriage: two sons, James Edward (1778–1841), who succeeded his father as second earl, and Charles Amyand, together with two daughters. During his career as a diplomatist Harris was MP for Christchurch (1770–74; 1780–88), but his membership of the House of Commons was nominal, and he attended only during the few months after he returned from St Petersburg in autumn 1783.

At this stage in his career, Harris had obvious strengths as a diplomatist and some equally apparent shortcomings. An able man who was a born intriguer, he could penetrate the cocoons of secrecy behind which rulers and their ministers carried out important negotiations: as in his discovery of the Prusso-Russian plan to partition Poland, or of the existence of a secret Russo-Austrian alliance through skilful bribery in 1781. His handsome bearing, social talents, and linguistic aptitude made him a popular member of the diplomatic corps in every capital in which he served, gaining him privileged access to the entourage of the ruler. His impressive fluency in French, the language of monarchical and aristocratic Europe, was here important. But he was still youthful and relatively inexperienced, dangerously prone to snap judgements and given to private initiatives, as became apparent in his mission to Russia during the War of American Independence (1775–83).

Missions to St Petersburg and The Hague In autumn 1777 Harris set off for St Petersburg, which he reached in December. He was accompanied by his young wife and his sister, both ladies losing their wardrobe on the difficult journey through a northern European winter. He served as envoy-extraordinary to Catherine II's Russia from the close of 1777 until September 1783. His rapid and erroneous conclusion that the empress's leading foreign policy adviser, the pro-Prussian Nikita Panin, was anti-British, and the warm personal relations which he quickly established with G. A. Potyomkin, would shape his whole mission. A wily intriguer, Potyomkin, Catherine's favourite in 1774–6 and probably her morganatic husband, was the leader of the pro-Austrian faction at the Russian court. He led the gullible Harris by the nose, using him as a pawn in his struggle for ascendancy. From the outset Britain's envoy transmitted Potyomkin's view of men and events back to London, and this undermined his own diplomacy during these years. He failed to conclude the long-desired Russian alliance, which was more elusive than ever by the close of his mission. He was equally unable to prevent Catherine II's League of Armed Neutrality in 1780, a wide-ranging association of states in defence of maritime neutral trade in time of war which compounded Britain's problems during the closing stages of the American conflict.

Harris's Russian mission had conferred experience and seniority: though only in his later thirties, he was clearly Britain's leading professional diplomatist of his generation, recognized in the award of a KB during his sojourn in St Petersburg. Hitherto a supporter of Charles James Fox, he joined the Portland whigs upon his return from Russia. His pre-eminence secured his appointment as envoy-extraordinary and plenipotentiary to The Hague, a post for which he was ideally suited through his knowledge of the country and mastery of its language. His mission saw Harris at the peak of his powers. His ruthlessness and professionalism were reinforced by established social skills which were essential for any successful eighteenth-century diplomatist. With his striking appearance, white hair, and brilliant eyes he was a formidable adversary: his opponent Mirabeau styled him 'rusé et audacieux' ('cunning and daring') in 1786. Harris arrived at The Hague in December 1784, at a vital moment for the republic and the ruling house of Orange. The shattering defeats in the fourth Anglo-Dutch War (1780–84) had further weakened the stadholderate, while strengthening the patriot movement, which wished to extend the degree of participation in the republic's oligarchical political life. Harris's formal instructions prescribed support for the unimpressive William V and a restoration of British control over the republic's external policy. By the mid-1780s, however, the patriots—now backed by France—were beginning to gain the upper hand. In November 1785 a Franco-Dutch treaty of friendship and alliance was signed, revealing the extent of France's new-found ascendancy. In response Harris moved on to the offensive, setting about rescuing William V and organizing the Orangist party. Ruthless and resourceful, his tactics blended bribery with intimidation and contributed to the onset of crisis in 1787.

Forging the triple alliance Britain's foreign secretary from 1783 to 1791 was the incompetent marquess of Carmarthen. Harris, however, had been skilfully cultivating the prime minister, William Pitt, who effectively took control of foreign policy from late 1786. With the two men meeting frequently, in spring 1787 the envoy convinced Pitt of the French threat in the Low Countries, a traditional British strategic bogey, and gained funds and political support for an active policy in the republic. Harris shared the common British failing of assuming the absolute pre-eminence of Anglo-French rivalry within both international relations and Dutch domestic politics, and had exaggerated the extent of Versailles's commitment and its actual control over the patriots. In the event Britain played little direct part in the resolution of the crisis. In autumn 1787 the Prussian king, Frederick William II, now confident of British support, sent an army to free his sister, the wife of William V, who had been detained by the patriots. With patriot resistance melting away, this force restored the authority of the stadholderate. Yet Harris and Pitt had contributed to the triumph, and Britain enjoyed the diplomatic benefits: a renewed Anglo-Dutch alliance (April 1788), converted into a triple alliance through the conclusion of a separate treaty with Prussia (August 1788). On a visit to the republic, Harris had personally negotiated the alliance with Frederick William II, who was visiting his sister and staying at Het Loo. It ended a quarter-century of British diplomatic isolation, which had lasted since the Seven Years' War.

Harris once more reaped the rewards of his success. In February 1788 he was promoted to the rank of ambassador, while a month after the definitive Anglo-Prussian alliance he was ennobled as Baron Malmesbury, a title which was subsequently (December 1800) raised to an earldom. In late 1788, having returned from The Hague in October at the close of his mission, he was considered for the Paris embassy, in rank the equivalent of a cabinet post and testimony to his pre-eminence in the British diplomatic corps; following normal practice, however, the post was filled by an aristocratic amateur. In the following year his conduct during the Regency crisis, when he supported his old friend Fox and voted against the government, cost him Pitt's favour. His political eclipse lasted until early 1793, when against the background of Louis XVI's trial and execution and an anticipated war with France he rallied to the government's support.

The war against France Malmesbury's standing as Britain's leading diplomatist ensured that he was soon re-employed. Although he was never again a resident ambassador, during the next four years he was sent by the Pitt government on a series of special missions for which his seniority, experience, and political connections made him particularly appropriate. In late 1793 and 1794 he carried out an extended and wide-ranging mission to the continent, nominally to Berlin (December 1793–October 1794), but with a month at The Hague (March–April 1794) and a protracted period at the Prussian army's military headquarters in the field. Its purpose was to negotiate Dutch and especially Prussian participation in an anti-French coalition, as Britain sought to put allies into the field against the forces of the French Revolution. Although a subsidy treaty was formally signed with Berlin (April 1794), Prussia, with further Polish gains in view, dragged her feet in the west, while the responsibility of all the allies to contribute to the £2 million subsidy promised to Frederick William II was a fertile source of difficulties. Austria in particular resented what she viewed as the unilateral and pro-Prussian conduct of Britain's representative. By late October 1794 Malmesbury was summoned home when it became clear that the Prussian king's priority was a final partition of Poland, carried out in the following year. In December 1794 Malmesbury was sent to Brunswick-Wolfenbüttel, where he negotiated the prince of Wales's marriage to the duke's daughter, Princess Caroline, and in the next year he escorted her to England for the formal betrothal.

Malmesbury's final missions were linked to the search for peace with France in 1796–7. Britain's quintessential *ancien régime* diplomatist now encountered the very different methods and practices of the French revolutionaries. While the outward forms of the old diplomacy were observed, the blunter, less flexible style of the republican negotiators, who set out and then stuck to their demands, was a shock to Malmesbury, used to the give and take of diplomatic negotiations. He also found the sharp reduction in the number of social events, at which diplomacy could be pursued by other means, an obstacle to his established way of conducting discussions. He was forced to pursue his aims entirely in a series of formal conferences. In mid-October 1796 he landed in France and, because of the bad state of the roads, made his way slowly to Paris. Edmund Burke, the opponent of any compromise with the hated revolution, sardonically observed that the journey took so long because 'he went the whole way on his knees' (Ehrman, 2.645). Within two months it was clear that no settlement could be concluded. Negotiations were broken off by Britain in December and Malmesbury was recalled. In the following summer, despite a recent illness, he was sent back to France, this time to Lille, where he arrived in early July 1797. His task was doubly complicated—by divided counsels at home over the wisdom of any agreement, and by uncertainties about whether the Directory government genuinely wished to conclude a settlement. After two months of futile discussions, matters were resolved by the *coup d'état* of 18 Fructidor (4 September 1797), which purged the Directory of those moderates who wanted to continue peace negotiations. Within a week the new French delegation adopted a tougher stance; another week passed and Malmesbury was recalled, breaking off the discussions at Lille.

Final years This brought down the curtain on Malmesbury's career as a diplomatist, and his increasing deafness was now an obstacle to any public role. His prestige ensured that he remained influential, and he was periodically considered for further posts. In summer 1799 a reluctant foreign secretary, Lord Grenville, briefly contemplated sending him back to The Hague, but a further bout of illness made this impracticable. In 1800, and again three years later, he was mentioned as a potential foreign secretary in projected ministerial reshuffles. Malmesbury retained important connections in the ministry and at court, but he was now in honourable retirement. A final reminder of his linguistic skills came on a Sunday in 1805, when government offices were closed and when he obliged Pitt by translating an article in a Dutch newspaper. Two years later he became lord lieutenant of Hampshire, an office he held for the rest of his life. He divided his final years between Henley and London, where he died in his house at Hill Street, Berkeley Square, Mayfair, on 21 November 1820; he was buried in Salisbury Cathedral. Talleyrand famously described him as 'le plus habile Ministre que vous aviez de son temps' ('the cleverest minister of his age'). Malmesbury's influence was enduring, as the leading British diplomatist of his generation. He was mentor to George Canning during the latter's apprenticeship as an under-secretary in the Foreign Office during the later 1790s, and subsequently gave the young Palmerston his first lessons in statecraft. His diaries and correspondence, published in 1844 by his grandson the third earl of Malmesbury, are a valuable source for the political and diplomatic history of the period. H. M. SCOTT

Sources *Diaries and correspondence of James Harris, first earl of Malmesbury*, ed. third earl of Malmesbury [J. H. Harris], 4 vols. (1844) · I. de Madariaga, *Britain, Russia and the armed neutrality of 1780: Sir James Harris's mission to St Petersburg during the American Revolution* (1962) · A. Cobban, *Ambassadors and secret agents: the diplomacy of the first earl of Malmesbury at The Hague* (1954) · J. Ehrman, *The younger Pitt*, 3 vols. (1969–96) · GEC, *Peerage*

Archives Hants. RO, family, official, and personal corresp., diaries, and papers · Merton Oxf., family corresp. · NRA, priv. coll., family corresp. · PRO, family corresp. and papers, PRO 30/43 · PRO, letter-books, FO 353 | Beds. & Luton ARS, corresp. with Lord Grantham · Beds. & Luton ARS, corresp. with Frederick Robinson · BL, corresp. with Lord Auckland, etc., Add. MSS 33539–33557, 33412–33456, Egerton MSS 2700–2703, *passim* · BL, corresp. with Charles James Fox, Add. MS 47562 · BL, letters to Lord Grenville, Add. MS 59019 · BL, letters to Thomas Grenville, Add. MSS 41855–41856 · BL, letters to Sir Robert Keith, Add. MSS 35434, 35504–35540, *passim* · BL, letters to duke of Leeds, Add. MSS 28060–28067, Egerton MS 3500 · BL, letters to Lord Northington, etc., Add. MSS 33090–33133, *passim* · CKS, letters to William Pitt · Hants. RO, corresp. with John Thomas Batt; corresp. with William Bingley · Hunt. L., letters to Grenville family · NL Scot., letters to Hugh Elliot · NL Scot., corresp. with Sir Robert Liston · NL Scot., corresp. with Lord Minto and Lady Minto · NRA, priv. coll., letters to Sir John Stepney · PRO, corresp. with first Earl Granville, PRO 30/29 · PRO, corresp. with William Pitt, PRO 30/8 · U. Nott. L., letters to duke of Portland · U. Southampton L., corresp. with Lord Palmerston · Wilts. & Swindon RO, corresp. with Lord Pembroke

Likenesses C. Watson, stipple, pubd 1786 (after J. Reynolds), BM, NPG · T. Lawrence, oils, 1806, priv. coll. [*see illus.*] · C. Bestland, miniature, 1807 (after T. Lawrence, 1806), NPG · F. Chantrey, marble statue, Salisbury Cathedral · B. Granger, stipple (after R. Corbould), BM, NPG; repro. in *English Magazine* (1797) · C. Picart, stipple (after H. Edridge), BM, NPG; repro. in *Contemporary portraits* (1814) · print (after J. Reynolds), BL; repro. in Cobban, *Ambassadors and secret agents*

Wealth at death under £25,000 in 'personals': GM, 91/2 (1821), 190

Harris, James Howard, third earl of Malmesbury (1807–1889)

, politician, was born at Spring Gardens, London, on 25 March 1807, the eldest son of the second earl, James Edward Harris (1778–1841), and his wife, Harriet Susan (1783–1815), daughter of a Lincolnshire squire, Francis Bateman Dashwood of Well Vale. The earldom had been created for the eminent diplomat Sir James Harris, whose *Diaries and Correspondence* (1844) his grandson edited. James Howard Harris, styled Viscount FitzHarris from 1820 until he succeeded his father in 1841, went from a small private school to Eton College and Oriel College, Oxford (BA, 1828), where as someone with a limited interest in learning he claimed to have ragged his tutor, John Henry Newman, a claim denied by Newman after the publication of his old pupil's memoirs. From his father FitzHarris inherited his toryism, 5000 acres lying mainly in Hampshire (a modest estate for his rank), and a taste for country pursuits. He married first, on 13 April 1830, Lady Corisande Emma Bennet (1807–1876), daughter of the fifth earl of Tankerville and his countess, Armandine de Gramont, whose brother the duc de Gramont was Napoleon III's foreign minister for a few months in 1870. After her death, on 1 November 1880 he contracted another childless marriage with Susan (1854–1935), daughter of John Hamilton, formerly Crosse, seated at Fyne Court, Somerset.

James Howard Harris, third earl of Malmesbury (1807–1889), by William Walker, c.1867

Pleasure and politics, 1830–1852 After leaving Oxford, Fitz-Harris lived the life of a man of fashion for several years. Continental travel was a habit that never left him; so, too, was a weakness for the ladies. In Italy FitzHarris met Byron's last mistress, Countess Teresa Guiccioli, and through her became familiar with the atmosphere of aristocratic liberalism under governments which he as an English tory, with the libertarianism of his kind, found 'despotic' (Malmesbury, 18). At Rome he struck up a friendship with the exiled Prince Louis Napoleon, the future Napoleon III, not yet head of the house of Bonaparte. On the other hand, he absorbed, through his first wife's Gramont relatives, something of their legitimist outlook. At home his tory instincts were strengthened by the experience of helping to put down the agricultural labourers' revolt of 1830 in Hampshire. The political excitement of the thirties made an indelible impression on him, as it did on others of his class: 'The country was in a delirium', he later wrote (ibid., 30). He did not succeed in entering the Commons before 1841, when his brief representation of the surviving pocket borough of Wilton was cut short by succession to his father's peerage. By his own admission the years before 1846 were largely devoted to pleasure. But if his diary for the period illustrates the *douceur de vivre* of an early Victorian nobleman, its pages reveal a growing attraction to politics. His sympathy with the losing side in the Carlist War was expressed in a pamphlet of 1837 critical of Palmerstonian policy in Spain. Later he spent two

years editing his grandfather's papers in four volumes. It was, he recalled, an indispensable education in the methods and language of diplomacy (ibid., 239).

Though not quite a backwoodsman, Malmesbury was one of those tories shocked into making a political career by Peel's precipitate abandonment of protection. A friend of the protectionist leader, Stanley, he emerged as the rebellious tories' whip in the Lords. He spoke well at rallies organized to defend the landed interest in the widest sense, where he predicted national ruin from the abolition of the corn laws. It was not until later, when a cabinet place was in the offing, that he approached Stanley's intellectual son Edward for a reading list on political economy, a subject he had never yet studied (*Disraeli, Derby and the Conservative Party*, 56, 15 March 1851). By then, it had become clear, protection was a lost cause. Malmesbury and the elder Stanley had more than their politics in common. A passion for shooting united them, and Malmesbury was a regular guest at Knowsley, his leader's Lancashire seat, for the autumn battues. As Stanley's closest political associate (Stewart, *Politics of Protection*, 145), he, with Disraeli, made the future prime minister attend to the social duties of party leadership in that age, giving dinners to his parliamentary followers. He urged Stanley to accept Disraeli as his lieutenant in the Commons, convinced that there was no alternative to that gifted politician (ibid., 137). Like Disraeli, he was exasperated when Stanley's refusal to form a government without the Peelites enabled a dying whig administration to struggle on for another year. 'There is not a woman in London who will not laugh at us', exclaimed Malmesbury in the presence of his leader and their principal colleagues (ibid., 178). The party, strong in both houses of parliament, did not relish being told by their chief that they lacked the talent to fill a cabinet (Malmesbury, 207–8, 1 March 1851).

The Foreign Office, Disraeli, and the party, 1852–1858 When Stanley, now the fourteenth earl of Derby, did form a minority government in February 1852, the appointment of Malmesbury to the Foreign Office (he was sworn of the privy council on 27 February 1852) attracted fierce criticism. Beside the whig Palmerston and the Peelite Aberdeen, he was the merest amateur, and had unsuccessfully pleaded his unwillingness to spend the time in London which the job required (Malmesbury, 227, 21 Feb 1852). More seriously, a hostile press accused him of partiality for reactionary Austria and Louis Napoleon's dictatorship in France. Malmesbury differed from his whig predecessors in letting it be known that his was to be an 'exclusively *English* policy', and not one that sought to export the distinctive institutions of his country, regardless of history and national character (*Letters of Queen Victoria*, 2.375, 27 Feb 1852). 'The ablest foreigners', he informed the British minister to liberal Sardinia, 'can never perfectly apprehend the principles of constitutional liberty' (Malmesbury, 256, 8 June 1852). He stood up to Austria when her ambassador made a scene about asylum in Britain for political refugees: no British government could afford to yield on that question. Malmesbury surprised those who condemned him out of hand as 'ignorant and mediocre' (*Greville Memoirs*, 6.335, 26 March 1852) by the competence with which he preserved continuity in the negotiations he inherited and carried through, notably an international settlement of the Schleswig-Holstein dispute. He embraced free trade round the world in Palmerstonian fashion as being in everybody's interest, and especially Britain's.

Malmesbury presented a deliberate contrast to Palmerston in his far milder diplomatic style, but they were agreed on the importance of a good working relationship with the France of Louis Napoleon. Malmesbury's friendship with the prince president had endured through the latter's years in English exile and a French prison. He visited Louis Napoleon in captivity after his abortive coup of 1840, and did his best to persuade Peel, then in power, to intercede with the Orléanist regime on the prince's behalf. Later, as ruler of France, Louis Napoleon was accessible to someone who had befriended him in adversity and now counted for something in opposition politics. A Bonapartist restoration naturally excited lively fears across the channel, which 'I stand alone ... in disbelieving', wrote Malmesbury to Derby as his foreign secretary (Malmesbury, 272, 8 Oct 1852). Though it was only sensible to ensure that the navy could repel an attempt at invasion, his personal knowledge of Louis Napoleon made him think that the prince was sincere in his desire to co-operate with his maritime neighbour. Long before he realized his apparently hopeless ambition to rule France, he had always told his English friend that the great mistake of his uncle Napoleon I had been to make an enemy of Britain. Malmesbury must be given some of the credit for the improvement in Anglo-French relations that preceded the Crimean alliance. Well aware of the prince's plans to 'remodel everything' (ibid., 180, 30 March 1849) on the map of Europe, he was satisfied that Louis Napoleon '*means* to try *peace* with us' (ibid., 273, 8 Oct 1852). While his French legitimist connections made him mildly scornful of the imperial style that was to be assumed in December 1852—it would be 'a masquerade of mummers' (ibid., 244, 29 March 1852)—he was enough of a liberal to sympathize with a good deal of what Napoleon III hoped to do. In particular, the overweening influence of Tsar Nicholas I's Russia, the embodiment of reaction and a threat to the British position in the East, needed to be challenged.

In opposition, to which the tories returned at the end of 1852, Malmesbury welcomed the eventual resort to arms after the tsar invaded the Ottoman empire: 'To stop the modern Attila is a great and sound game' (Monypenny & Buckle, 1.1339). He, and Disraeli, deplored Derby's failure to persist with his efforts to form a war administration in February 1855 on the collapse of the Aberdeen coalition. Malmesbury attributed Derby's loss of 'nerve ... courage and energy' (Malmesbury, 350, 9 Feb 1855) to bad health, and thought the government that Palmerston constructed and reconstructed ought to be supported. Yet he loyally followed Derby in trying to bring down the ministry later in the session. 'We had no case', he reflected after a first defeat (ibid., 362, 12 May 1855). Derby and Disraeli

omitted to consult him, or anyone else, when they renewed the attack and nearly succeeded. Malmesbury regretted the peace of 1856 as premature; but his advice to make common cause with the more bellicose Liberals against terms forced on Palmerston by France was rejected (Monypenny & Buckle, 1.1423-4). These differences did not affect his fidelity to Derby, or to a toryism which, he felt, possessed strengths overlooked by friend and foe.

Disraeli, it seems, would have liked the Foreign Office for himself in 1852. The resulting coolness between the two men was a factor in their subsequent disagreements over policy and party organization. In the 1850s Derby's ambitious lieutenant used his own journal—'the cursed *Press*', as Malmesbury called it (Monypenny & Buckle, 1.1423-4; to Derby, 23 Nov 1855)—to promote independent initiatives. The *Press* built up Disraeli amid talk of putting him or Derby's son Edward at the head of the party. Malmesbury crushed the go-between who sounded him about a change in April 1856 (Malmesbury, 379, 26 April 1856); but before the year was out he took it on himself to warn the leader that his political lethargy and Disraeli's activities were seriously damaging the party (Monypenny & Buckle, 1.1458; to Derby, 7 Dec 1856). He was Derby's emissary to the remaining Peelites in March 1857, when Palmerston survived an adverse vote on his China policy by appealing to the electorate. In the aftermath of that sharp electoral setback there was more friction with Disraeli, whose mouthpiece infuriated Malmesbury by some unwise criticism of one of the heroes of the Indian mutiny. 'The *Press*', he complained crossly, 'must needs let a fart at the present idol of England, Havelock' (Malmesbury to Disraeli, 6 Dec 1857, Hughenden MS B/XX/Hs). At this stage of his career Disraeli's opportunism was unpopular with tories, but Malmesbury was one of the two colleagues—Edward Stanley was the other—who shared his concern to modernize tory thinking somewhat (Monypenny & Buckle, 1.1298-9).

Malmesbury was ahead of most tories in contemplation of the next instalment of parliamentary reform, with which the parties were wrestling from the early 1850s. He believed, with some reason, that the unskilled labourers were instinctively conservative, unlike the shopkeepers and artisans just above them, and was therefore inclined to prefer universal manhood suffrage to the £5 franchise under discussion in 1853. He sat on the not very efficient committee that endeavoured to give some central direction to tories organizing themselves for elections, and recommended Disraeli to pay more attention than he usually did to such mundane matters, stressing that 'really it is on this *mechanical* element that our *avenir* rests', adding that all his talents, multiplied infinitely, would be useless without better preparations for the polls. Malmesbury went on to caution him against the temptation to ally with the radicals in parliament, who were influential, though few in numbers: 'Our men will never follow them' (Malmesbury to Disraeli, 22 July 1855, Hughenden MS B/XX/Hs). While his tone did not spare his correspondent's feelings, it should be remembered that the earl spoke for solid, but not unreflecting, tories. Many years passed before they saw Derby's successor in the exotic figure of Disraeli. Malmesbury often referred to his party simply as 'Derbyites', and he was always one himself. He pressed their leader to exercise his undoubted authority and make Disraeli conform to an agenda for each session (Monypenny & Buckle, 1.1331). This amateur in politics had a natural grasp of the management of party and public opinion to which Derby was temperamentally reluctant to condescend. He was also remarkably disinterested, being one of three ministers who offered to retire from the tory cabinet in 1852 in favour of weightier selections from other political groupings.

Britain, the great powers, and the war of 1859 Malmesbury has been judged on his performance in the crisis leading to war between France, allied with Sardinia, and Austria over the future of Italy. His mediation failed; but he may be said to have succeeded in his national aims. He went back to the Foreign Office in February 1858 in alarming circumstances. At their first interview, the French ambassador shouted 'C'est la guerre! C'est la guerre!', while Malmesbury listened impassively, 'the best way of meeting such explosions from foreigners' (Malmesbury, 425, 14 March 1858). His sixteen months in office were devoted to buying time for the modernization and expansion of the British fleet, the superiority of which to the French navy had been dangerously eroded by professional complacency and technological change. When the second Derby ministry fell in June 1859, the country was safer, at any rate, and Palmerston took over from there. In the process the tension with Disraeli increased: he found Malmesbury's diplomacy wanting in the assertiveness which he thought was the mark of a great power. 'The policy of insisting and threatening is Palmerstonian', replied Malmesbury. It would commit them to the French or the Austrian camp and diminish British influence in Europe where 'they are now *bidding* for our friendship'. He likened Britain in his person to 'a respectable clergyman co-trustee with five horse-dealers', the other powers professing their desire to maintain the continental peace (Monypenny & Buckle, 1.1628–9 [1859]).

Nevertheless, British policy under Malmesbury remained essentially Palmerstonian. The Palmerston government, enjoying a large majority after the 1857 election, had been overthrown by Derby's opportunistic decision to support a Liberal rebellion on the Conspiracy to Murder Bill directed at refugees who plotted assassinations abroad. Public opinion turned against this legislative gesture to appease French indignation following the recent attempt on Napoleon III's life by conspirators based in Britain. After as before Palmerston fell, Malmesbury was convinced that appeasement could not be avoided: 'we are not in a position to have war with anyone' (Malmesbury, 415, 1 Feb 1858). In addition to the anxiety about the state of the navy, suppression of the Indian mutiny had denuded Britain of regular troops. The attitude of the French military was openly menacing; but Malmesbury put his trust in personal friendship with the emperor and

in Napoleon's 'undoubted disposition' to stand well with the old enemy. He hoped and believed the liberal Bonaparte would be able to control those about him who were more or less hostile to Britain (ibid., 448, 24 Feb 1858). The tories were, in principle, committed to the Conspiracy to Murder Bill, and their abandonment of it as impossible to carry was difficult to justify to the French. In effect, Malmesbury threw himself on the emperor's mercy: his crucial dispatch was edited '*sub rosa*' by the French ambassador, who discussed the wording with his government before the British foreign secretary was permitted to send it off (Steele, 147). Napoleon exacted a price for sparing a weakened Britain national humiliation and saving the ministry.

'I have not moved … without information, explanation, and invitation given spontaneously. I do not see how consistently with the honour of England I can have … shown more deference to an ally', wrote Malmesbury in 1859, looking back on a string of concessions to France (Steele, 147). When Portugal was subjected to French intimidation for co-operating with the British against a thinly disguised revival of the African slave trade under the tricolour, he did not encourage her to resist. 'A shot at Lisbon … and France would have been mistress of the Channel', he commented after the French navy's show of force in the Tagus (27 Oct 1858, Malmesbury MS 9M73/1/5). One of his difficulties was the public inability to realize the extent of British weakness. The 'free emigration' of Africans incurred the wrath of the powerful anti-slavery lobby. Malmesbury was obliged to appeal to it for restraint and to the emperor for understanding of his predicament, warning the first of the danger of war and offering the second a supply of indentured coolie labour from India for the French sugar colonies. The substitute, he admitted to Bishop Samuel Wilberforce, was far from ideal—'there may be suffering more or less'—but he begged him to use his considerable influence in favour of the compromise 'upon which I really believe peace with France depends' (ibid., 11 Nov 1858). He chose his envoys to Constantinople and Madrid, and shaped his policy all over Europe and beyond, to please Napoleon as far as he could without jeopardizing British interests. If he exaggerated the peril in which his country stood, others, including Disraeli, were sometimes more frightened.

Napoleon's designs on the Austrian presence in Italy, secretly concerted with the Sardinian minister Count Cavour at Plombières in July 1858, were quite unacceptable to Malmesbury when they leaked out over the next four months. In writing to the queen, whose sympathies were decidedly Austrian, he alluded to Italy's splendid past and her 'present degradation': the 'romantic feelings' which her plight had inspired in him and Napoleon as young men were not dead in either of them (*Letters of Queen Victoria*, 3.273, 7 March 1858). He was not prepared, however, to back the emperor in disturbing the territorial settlement of the peninsula, a part of the European order that depended on respect for the Vienna treaties of 1814–15. On the other hand, he refused to entertain the idea of going to war for the patchwork of Italian states threatened by France. It would be humbug for a British government to join in condemning the Austrian domination that saved Italy from Latin American anarchy. 'How can we who have conquered Ireland and hold all India by the sword in common decency be the Quixote of Italy', he asked in a letter written for communication to the emperor. These points, which he repeated in the Lords, offended Liberals who perceived a qualitative distinction between British and Habsburg imperialism (Malmesbury to Cowley, 7 Feb 1858, Malmesbury MS 9M73/1/5; Steele, 148). Malmesbury tried to avert the impending clash by urging Austria and France to combine in reforming the papal dominions, the worst administered and most discontented of the Italian states, with moral support and even some unspecified material help from Britain. The proposal was almost an irrelevance, and his continuing mediation was no more successful.

Malmesbury sent Cowley, the ambassador in Paris, to Vienna with a plan of the latter's devising to reduce both French and Austrian involvement in Italy, and isolate Sardinia. It had the effect of giving Austria the impression that Britain would fight beside her, despite Malmesbury's statement to the contrary. At the same time, Malmesbury's soundings in Germany led Napoleon to suspect him of inciting Prussia and other German states not to the exercise of moral pressure but to war. Malmesbury foresaw these failures: but his was 'the duty of every honest man to prevent the scourge which … unprincipled men would inflict on mankind for their personal profit'. While he anticipated the 'folly … perfectly inconceivable' of the Austrians, who were to emerge as the technical aggressors, his trust in Napoleon was destroyed (Malmesbury, 459, 2 Jan 1859). The emperor's weaknesses, personal and political, had been clearly exploited by Cavour, for whom Malmesbury reserved his harshest strictures. The war which opened in April 1859 was as bloody as he feared; but Britain, Prussia, and Russia were determined to localize the conflict. To call Malmesbury's diplomacy 'futile' (Taylor, 108) is to ignore the realities. Britain could not abstain from the great power politics that produced and limited the war. The risks of closer involvement were illustrated after the fighting started when, in the middle of an election called over the fate of the government's Reform Bill, Disraeli and other ministers spoke of the difficulty of remaining neutral. Disraeli suggested sending an expeditionary corps to Germany to await developments, and a new French ambassador talked excitedly to Malmesbury of an alliance with Britain 'to conquer all Europe'. As he reminded the queen, public opinion was squarely behind Malmesbury's policy of neutrality, which had Lord Derby's full support (Steele, 30–31, 149).

Yet Malmesbury, and the government with him, were labelled pro-Austrian. The charge was their undoing in the new parliament where, still in a minority, they lost a vote of confidence on their policy. Malmesbury blamed Disraeli as leader in the Commons for failing to ensure that the house had the blue book containing his official correspondence in time for the debate. It showed how he had striven to hold the balance between France and Austria. Why the blue book was not ready has never been satisfactorily explained. 'Disraeli *never reads a word of my papers*', Malmesbury had complained. On his side, Disraeli's antagonism was barely concealed: 'Malmesbury must go', he told Derby on the day the Commons voted (Monypenny & Buckle, 1.1624, 1659, 7 Jan 1859, 10 June 1859). Typically, he appears to have thought the foreign secretary's policy lacked the colour and dash which he could have given it. Malmesbury had no illusions and no regrets: accepting a GCB (15 June 1859) from Derby as the government went out he said that if he deserved the honour, it was for gaining time to rebuild the navy's strength. He was glad to escape from office, and from Disraeli '*who always lied*' (Steele, 160, 5 June 1859).

'His real claims are very far above his reputation' These words are taken from Edward Stanley's character sketch of Malmesbury written in 1856, which controverted the view, then and later, that he was a political lightweight and a society figure (*Disraeli, Derby and the Conservative Party*, 351). In the mid-1860s the former foreign secretary might have had the Foreign Office for a third time when the tories came in again. He stepped aside, serving Derby and then Disraeli as lord privy seal from 1866 to 1868 and from 1874 to 1876. Although the social round, shooting, and travel took up much of his year, he retained his interest in politics. He deputized for the gout-stricken Derby in the Lords, and acted as his intermediary in promising tory assistance for Palmerston's policies. When he became prime minister in 1868, Disraeli considered dropping him from the cabinet but kept him on to lead the upper house for the short remainder of that parliament. A shrewd judge of what the public wanted and what the party would stand, he had encouraged Disraeli to commit himself to household suffrage in March 1867 when three of their cabinet colleagues were poised to resign in protest. He watched disapprovingly as the Commons stripped the new franchise of its accompanying safeguards. After the party lost the 1868 election, he gave up the leadership of the tory peers; but his old admiration for Disraeli had revived, and there was a place for him in the government formed in 1874 until age and deafness compelled him to retire. He died at Heron Court, his Hampshire seat, on 17 May, and was buried in the priory church, Christchurch, in the same county, on 22 May 1889. The earldom devolved on his nephew Lieutenant-Colonel Edward James Harris, eldest son of his second brother, Admiral Sir Edward Harris [see below].

Malmesbury's *Memoirs of an ex-Minister* consist mainly of his edited diaries and include selections from his private correspondence. Indiscreet by the standards of the day, and not always accurate, they are none the less a useful source, and a frequently amusing one. Even superficially, they do not bear out Palmerston's description of him, in an angry moment, as 'lazy, useless and supremely ignorant' at the Foreign Office (Monypenny & Buckle, 1.1629). Stanley, who had been his under-secretary in 1852, fairly remarked that Malmesbury was handicapped by a late start in ministerial life without the lengthy apprenticeship in minor office that others served. If he did not have Palmerston's appetite for unremitting toil, he applied himself conscientiously (*Disraeli, Derby and the Conservative Party*, 351). He was excellent company, and, as a minister, capable of satirizing himself and his colleagues, anonymously, in *Punch*. More a man of ideas and less pragmatic than Stanley supposed, he often masked a serious purpose with a jest. 'Nothing can be more agreeable to a foreign minister though perhaps not to an active mind like yours than the dormant state of politics', he told a British ambassador. 'It is **my** *beau idéal* of foreign affairs' (Malmesbury to Loftus, 10 Nov 1858, Malmesbury MS 9M73/1/5). Like many men who enjoy slaughtering the animal creation, he had an acute sense of the folly and waste of war: to provoke it deliberately was 'intolerable'. By no means the least effective of Victorian foreign secretaries, he was the kind of tory who rated peace and security above the political benefits of cutting a figure in the affairs of Europe (Malmesbury to Cowley, 13 Jan 1859, Malmesbury MS 9M73/1/5).

Sir Edward Alfred John Harris (1808–1888), naval officer and diplomatist, Malmesbury's second brother (Charles Amyand *Harris was the third), was born on 20 May 1808, and went from Eton College to the Royal Naval College, Portsmouth, in 1822. A midshipman in 1823 and lieutenant in 1828, he was not employed again after attaining the rank of captain in 1841; but his subsequent promotions eventually made him a full admiral on the reserve list in 1877. On 4 August 1841 he married Emma Wylie or Wylly (d. 1896), daughter of Captain Samuel Chambers RN, with whom he had seven children. He entered parliament as a tory in 1844 at a by-election for Christchurch, a small Hampshire borough where his family's influence was strong. When his party split in 1846, he, like his brother, adhered to the protectionist majority and was a beneficiary of Malmesbury's patronage as foreign secretary in 1852 and 1858–9. Harris left the Commons in 1852 to become consul-general in Denmark and, later that year, chargé d'affaires and consul-general in Peru, a post which he exchanged in 1853 for its equivalent in Chile. Malmesbury brought him back to Europe in 1858 to be consul-general at Trieste, and he was promoted minister to Switzerland almost at once. The next tory foreign secretary, Lord Stanley, moved Harris to the Netherlands as minister in 1867 and, on his retirement in 1877, wrote that he was 'no loss to the service … a kindly good-natured sort of man who … did no more than he could help' (*Diaries of E. H. Stanley*, 437). Created KCB in 1872, Harris died at his home in Kent, Sandling Park, on 17 July 1888 and was buried in the priory church, Christchurch, Hampshire. His eldest son, Edward, succeeded as the fourth earl of Malmesbury in 1889.   DAVID STEELE

Sources J. H. Harris [third earl of Malmesbury], *Memoirs of an ex-minister: an autobiography*, new edn (1885) · Hants. RO, Malmesbury MSS · Bodl. Oxf., Dep. Hughenden · W. F. Monypenny and G. E. Buckle, *The life of Benjamin Disraeli*, rev. G. E. Buckle, 2nd edn, 2 vols. (1929), vol. 1 · E. D. Steele, *Palmerston and liberalism, 1855–1865* (1991) · *Disraeli, Derby and the conservative party: journals and memoirs of Edward Henry, Lord Stanley, 1849–1869*, ed. J. R. Vincent (1978) · R. Stewart, *The politics of protection: Lord Derby and the protectionist party, 1841–1852* (1971) · D. E. D. Beales, *England and Italy, 1859–60* (1961) · K. Weigand, *Österreich, die Westmächte und das europäische Staatensystem nach dem Krimkrieg, 1856–1859* (1997) · R. Blake, *Disraeli* (1966) · A. J. P. Taylor, *The struggle for mastery in Europe, 1848–1918* (1957) · R. Stewart, *The foundation of the conservative party, 1830–1867* (1978) · *The letters of Queen Victoria*, ed. A. C. Benson and Lord Esher [R. B. Brett], 3 vols., 1st ser. (1907) · *The diaries of E. H. Stanley, 15th earl of Derby, 1869–1878*, CS, 5th series, 4 (1994) · *The Greville memoirs, 1814–1860*, ed. L. Strachey and R. Fulford, 8 vols. (1938) · *Dod's Parliamentary Companion* · GEC, *Peerage* · CGPLA Eng. & Wales (1889) · *The Times* (18 July 1888) [Sir Edward Alfred John Harris]

Archives Hants. RO, corresp. and papers | BL, corresp. with W. E. Gladstone, Add. MSS 44387–44388 · BL, corresp. with Lord Westmorland [microfilm] · Bodl. Oxf., corresp. with Sir John Fiennes Crampton · Bodl. Oxf., corresp. with Benjamin Disraeli · Bodl. Oxf., Hughenden MSS · Bodl. Oxf., corresp. with Lord Kimberley · LPL, corresp. with A. C. Tait · Lpool RO, letters to fourteenth earl of Derby · Lpool RO, corresp. with fifteenth earl of Derby · Norfolk RO, corresp. with Sir Henry Lytton Bulwer · NRA, priv. coll., letters to S. H. Walpole · NRA, priv. coll., corresp. with Lord Wemyss · PRO, letters to Lord Cairns, PRO 30/51 · PRO, corresp. with Stratford Canning, FO 352 · PRO, corresp. with Lord Cowley, FO 519 · PRO, corresp. with Lord John Russell, PRO 30/22 · PRO, corresp. with Odo Russell, FO 918 · Som. ARS, letters to Sir William Jolliffe, DD/H7 · W. Sussex RO, letters to fifth duke of Richmond; letters to sixth duke of Richmond · W. Yorks. AS, Leeds, letters to Lord Canning

Likenesses R. J. Lane, lithograph, 1840 (after Count D'Orsay), BM, NPG · J. G. Middleton, oils, 1852, Hughenden Manor, Buckinghamshire; version, Gov. Art Coll. · W. Walker, photograph, c.1867, NPG [*see illus.*] · Ape [C. Pellegrini], chromolithograph caricature, NPG; repro. in *VF* (25 July 1874) · H. Gales, group portrait, watercolour (*The Derby cabinet of 1867*), NPG · W. Roffe, stipple and line engraving (after photograph by H. R. Barraud), NPG

Wealth at death £91,762 6s. 9d.: probate, 1 Aug 1889, CGPLA Eng. & Wales · £8516 4s. 11d.—Sir Edward Alfred John Harris: probate, 12 Sept 1888, CGPLA Eng. & Wales

Harris, James Rendel (1852–1941), biblical scholar and palaeographer, was born in Plymouth on 27 January 1852, the second son of Henry Marmaduke Harris, a house decorator, and his wife, Elizabeth Carter, *née* Budd. Educated at Plymouth grammar school, he entered Clare College, Cambridge on 9 June 1870, where he was a scholar and was deeply influenced by the teaching of F. J. A. Hort. He graduated BA and third wrangler in 1874 and proceeded MA in 1877.

Elected a fellow of Clare College in 1875, Harris was mathematical lecturer there until 1882, when he was appointed to teach New Testament Greek at Johns Hopkins University in Baltimore, Maryland. Here he began his long series of works on early Christian documents, whose originality and learning assured for him a place at the forefront of New Testament studies. He had converted from Congregationalism to the Society of Friends in 1880, partly under the influence of the mystic Madame Guyan and the second evangelical revival, but mainly owing to his marriage in that year to Helen, *née* Balkwill (d. 1914), a Quaker, also from Plymouth. Harris was soon in difficulties at Johns Hopkins through his denunciations of vivisection, and he then accepted an invitation to join the Quaker University of Haverford College, Pennsylvania, where he was professor of biblical languages and literature from 1885 to 1892. His first publication, *The Teaching of the Apostles and the Sibylline Books*, appeared in 1885 and was followed in 1887 by his essay, *The Origin of the Leicester Codex*.

On his first visit to the monastery of St Catherine on Mount Sinai in 1889, Harris came across the Syriac version of the lost Apology of Aristides. This was published in 1891 and in the same year his study of the Codex Bezae appeared in print. He called for a revaluation of the western text, asserting that modern textual critics had overstated their case; Hort, although impressed with his former student's find, felt that his theoretical gifts were rather limited, and that his arguments did not take a sufficiently broad analytical view of the evidence.

In 1893 Harris returned to Cambridge as lecturer in palaeography. Specialist studies followed in quick succession, among them *The Origin of the Ferrar Group* (1893), *Stichometry* (1893), and *Hermas in Arcadia* (1896). In 1893 he again visited Mount Sinai to assist Agnes Lewis and her sister in deciphering the Sinai Palimpsest. In 1896 he and his wife spent six months organizing relief for Armenian refugees in Asia Minor and publicized their plight in *Letters from the Scenes of the Recent Massacres in Armenia* (1897). In 1912, during the Balkan War, he again took up the cause of the Armenians, travelling to Constantinople to attempt to help to influence their fate.

In 1903 Harris was invited to become professor of early Christian literature and New Testament exegesis at the University of Leiden, but he chose instead to become the first director of studies of Woodbrooke, a Quaker settlement for religious and social study in Selly Oak, Birmingham. Addresses belonging to his early Cambridge period were published as *Memoranda sacra* in 1892; some delivered after his return appeared in *Union with God* (1895); and many addresses given at Woodbrooke were published in *The Guiding Hand of God* (1905) and in later volumes. In 1909 Harris discovered in one of his manuscripts a Syriac version of the lost Odes of Solomon, a find which rivalled in interest that of the Apology of Aristides. A last visit to the Middle East and Mount Sinai in 1922–3 did not result in any great discovery, but Harris acquired some papyri in Egypt of which a selection was edited by J. Enoch Powell and published as *The Rendel Harris Papyri* (1936).

During the First World War Harris had two narrow escapes from drowning. He was sailing to join his friend J. H. Moulton in India, when his ship was torpedoed. Again, on the return voyage, his boat was torpedoed and Moulton died from exposure. Having survived the war, in 1918 Harris was appointed curator of eastern manuscripts at the John Rylands Library, Manchester, where he studied folklore. Before leaving Cambridge in 1903 he had lectured on the Dioscuri in Christian legend. He had become interested in twin-lore and became more radical in his speculations. At Woodbrooke he had written *Boanerges* (1913), which argued that there was more than one pair of twins among the apostles. At Rylands he also produced many studies of the origins of Greek gods. His research into early Christian controversies with Jews over the use of passages from the Old Testament resulted in two books, entitled *Testimonies* (1916 and 1920), in which Vacher Burch

collaborated. The tercentenary in 1920 of the sailing of the Pilgrim Fathers to America on the *Mayflower* also led Harris to advance the theory that the barn at Jordans, next to the Friends' meeting-house there, was built from the timbers of the ship.

In 1925 Harris retired, his sight beginning to fail him, to Birmingham, where he became interested in tracing the spread of Egyptian culture in the millennia before Christ. During his career he had received the honorary degrees of LittD from Dublin (1892), of LLD from Haverford (1900) and Birmingham (1909), of DTheol from Leiden (1909), and of DD from Glasgow (1914). He was an honorary fellow of Clare College, Cambridge, from 1909, and was elected FBA in 1927. He was a leader among free churchmen and was president of the National Free Church Council in 1907–8. Harris died at his home, 2 King's Mead Close, Selly Oak, Birmingham, on 1 March 1941.

H. G. Wood, rev. Sinéad Agnew

Sources *The Times* (3 March 1941), 7 • *The Friend* (7 March 1941) • Venn, *Alum. Cant.* • *WWW, 1941–50* • Allibone, *Dict.*
Archives priv. coll. • U. Birm., Orchard Learning Resources Centre, corresp. and papers • Woodbrooke Quaker Study Centre, Birmingham, papers | Bodl. Oxf., corresp. with Gilbert Murray • JRL, letters to J. H. Moulton • NL Scot., corresp. with publishers
Likenesses P. Bigland, portrait, Woodbrooke Quaker Study Centre, Birmingham • J. Russell & Sons, photograph, NPG • photograph, repro. in *The Times*
Wealth at death £1514 19s. 0d.: probate, 5 April 1941, *CGPLA Eng. & Wales*

Harris, James Thomas [Frank] (1856?–1931), journalist and rogue, was probably born on 14 February 1856, in a thatched cabin at Galway, third son and fourth of the five children of Thomas Vernon Harris (1814–1899), a mariner, and his wife, Anne (1816–1859/60), daughter of James Hughes Thomas, a Baptist missionary. He endured a mean, miserable, and loveless childhood, in which he resented alike the puritanical severity of his father and the discipline of his masters at the Royal School in Armagh and, later, Ruabon grammar school in Denbighshire (1869–71). Emigrating to the USA in 1871, he joined his brother in Lawrence, Kansas, where he enrolled at the university in 1874 and passed the Douglas County bar examinations in 1875. During these years he phased out use of his baptismal names and, by his return to Europe, had adopted Frank as the forename by which to be known.

Harris worked as French tutor at Brighton College in Sussex (1875–7) before marrying at Paris, on 17 October 1878, Florence Ruth (1852–1879), daughter of Thomas Bell Adams, maltster, of Ware, Hertfordshire. She died of tuberculosis after ten months, and he settled in London on her bequest of £1000. Lecherous, bawdy, and bombastic, with a thundering bass voice, he joined the Social Democratic Federation before seeking glory through literary journalism. By the favour of Lord Folkestone (who remained one of the few friends whom Harris did not cross or denigrate) he was appointed in 1883 as editor of the *Evening News*. He engineered several circulation stunts, and fancied himself as a journalistic Robin Hood, running campaigns against poverty and intervening in society

James Thomas [Frank] **Harris** (1856?–1931), by Alvin Langdon Coburn, 1913

scandals in a mischievously anti-aristocratic spirit. The publicity that he gave to Lord Garmoyle's breach of promise of marriage to an actress in 1884 may have first raised his reputation as a blackmailer. He was dislodged from his job in 1886, but swiftly obtained the editorship of the *Fortnightly Review*.

Harris married second, on 2 November 1887, Emily Mary (1839–1927), daughter of James Remington, captain in the Bengal army, and widow of Thomas Greenwood Clayton, a manufacturer. He intended to use her fortune of £90,000 and small house on Park Lane as the foundations of a political career, but he was too unsteady in his aim. In 1889, shortly after becoming secretary of the Father Damien Fund for leprosy research, he was adopted as prospective Conservative candidate in South Hackney. However, he withdrew his candidature in 1891, after unrest at his neglect of constituency business and his espousal of the cause of C. S. Parnell in the O'Shea divorce. From the time of his second marriage until about 1892 he maintained an American mistress, and after this arrangement broke up he was so flagrant and boastful in his infidelities that his wife separated from him in 1894. Henceforth he was always in financial straits.

During his eight-year tenure Harris transformed the *Fortnightly Review* from suffocating gentility into vivacious modernity: George Bernard Shaw and then Max Beerbohm were his drama critics. He was disorganized, unpunctual, and slipshod about editorial details yet craved prestige and money. Though denigration of aristocracy was one consistent theme of his life, he enjoyed the company of plutocrats, and commissioned vigorous articles on the City. '"I'm a blackmailer", he announced time and again, and represented himself as a terrible wolf among financiers' (Wells, 521). Harris was dislodged from the editorship of the *Fortnightly Review* in 1894, supposedly after accepting for publication a sensational article by an anarchist praising political murder as 'propaganda … by deed' (Charles Malato, 'Some anarchist portraits', *Fortnightly Review*, 62, Sept 1894, 315). But this was a pretext. His brigand manners and sexual bluster had become intolerable to his proprietors. It was about this time that in the

Café Royal dining room he boomed to the duc de Richelieu, 'No my dear duke, I know nothing of the joys of homosexuality. You must speak to my friend Oscar about that'. A profound silence descended upon the room. 'And yet', Harris mused, in a more subdued but still reverberating tone, 'if Shakespeare had asked me, I would have had to submit' (Kingsmith, *Harris*, 70–71).

Soon after losing the editorship of the *Fortnightly Review* Harris bought the Conservative *Saturday Review*. Here he pursued a virulently anti-German and anti-American editorial policy. As it became clear that literary glory would evade him, he turned to high finance with the intention of securing the awe and authority commanded by millionaires. He visited the South African mining districts in 1896, and acted with Ernest Terah Hooley in several company promotions until the latter's ruin in 1898. His facile criticisms of Milner's policy in South Africa persuaded Cecil Rhodes and Alfred Beit to buy Harris's interest in the *Saturday Review*, which he ceased to edit (1898). Though he needed the money from this sale, this was a fatal turning point in his career. 'His dominating way in conversation startled, amused and then irritated people', according to H. G. Wells.

> That was what he lived for, talking, writing that was loud talk in ink, and editing. He was a brilliant editor, for a time, and then the impetus gave out, and he flagged rapidly. So soon as he ceased to work vehemently he became unable to work. He could not attend to things without excitement. As his confidence went, he became clumsily loud. (Wells, 523–4)

In 1898 Harris was maintaining a *ménage* at St Cloud with an actress named May Congden, with whom he had a daughter, together with a house at Roehampton containing Nellie O'Hara, with whom he possibly also had a daughter (who died young). He seems to have had other daughters with different women. O'Hara (*d.* 1955) was his helpmate and *âme damnée* for over thirty years. Apparently the natural daughter of Mary Mackay and a drunkard named Patrick O'Hara, she was a clumsy schemer, battening onto Harris in the hope of millions but encouraging him in self-destructive and rascally courses. During 1898 he bought and luxuriously improved the Palace Hotel, situated in an unfashionable side street of Monaco. He also built an elegant restaurant and hotel, La Réserve, overlooking the Riviera coast at Eze. Simultaneously Harris began translating Shakespeare into French, tried to launch an *Automobile Review*, talked of making his fortune by exporting French motor cars to England, and struggled to establish himself as an agent or dealer for Rodin. These schemes all failed by Harris's indiscipline, bad luck, poor judgement, and ill timing. His chief rule of life was fatally self-infatuated:

> The first commandment is: be yourself; never conform; be proud of yourself and wilful; for there is no-one in the world like you, and never has been, and your unlikeness to all others is the reason for your existence, and its solitary justification. ('Thoughts on morals', *English Review*, 8, June 1911, 442)

Harris published his first short story (about the adulterous desires of a Baptist minister) as late as 1891, and his first book, *Elder Conklin and other Stories*, in 1894. Written under the influence of Maupassant and Balzac, these stories about small-minded materialistic provincials living in the western United States evoked 'a picture as unlovely and barbaric as it is powerful and convincing' (*The Athenaeum*, 8 Dec 1894, 785–6). Other vivid and ardent stories are contained in *Montes the Matador* (1900). His play *Mr and Mrs Daventry* (the plot of which he bought from Wilde) betrays his preoccupation with adultery and sexually emancipated women and contains a self-idealization in the character of Ashurst. Opening at the Royalty Theatre in 1900 with Mrs Patrick Campbell and Gerald du Maurier, it seemed 'the most daring and naturalistic production of the modern English stage … at once repellent and fantastic' (*The Athenaeum*, 3 Nov 1900, 587). The most notable of his other plays, *The Bucket Shop*, was produced at the Aldwych Theatre in 1914. Offering a brazenly authoritative account of company promoters and City chancers, Harris in his egotistical and self-justifying way preached that the world comprised fools and rogues. The leading rogue of the play was a successful womanizer with exemplary coolness, courage, and tenacity. Harris's first long novel, *The Bomb* (1908), set in Chicago, was 'highly charged with an explosive blend of socialistic and anarchistic matter, wrapped in a gruesome coating of "exciting" fiction … crowded with swindled workmen, callous employers, brutal police, inhuman millionaires' (*Times Literary Supplement*, 3 Dec 1908, 446). In a subjective, self-centred way he wrote repeatedly about Shakespeare, including *The Man Shakespeare* (1909), a play *Shakespeare and his Love* (1910), and *The Women of Shakespeare* (1911).

In May 1901 Harris first published his weekly society magazine, the *Candid Friend*, which expired in August 1902. Later in 1902 his career as a hotelier collapsed when creditors seized the properties. Harris was henceforth an increasingly querulous, jealous, melodramatic, valetudinarian schemer, with no capital but his energy, and an insatiable need of sexual and other flattery. He and O'Hara were constantly obliged to shift from house to house. During 1905 he acted as a sort of literary agent for Winston Churchill. He edited (in the interest of the Dunlop Tyre Company) an unsuccessful motorists' society magazine called *Motorist and Traveller* (1905–6). In January 1907 he revived *Vanity Fair*, but his formula as a society editor and anecdotalist was becoming stale, and his journalistic campaigns more truculent and eccentric. Among much litigation, his reputation was particularly injured by a lawsuit which he brought in 1908 against Arthur du Cros. He sold his shares in *Vanity Fair* in 1909. For some months in 1911–12 he edited a ladies' paper, *Hearth and Home*.

In August 1913 the first issue of a penny-paper gossip-sheet called *Modern Society* appeared under Harris's editorship. Enid *Bagnold (1889–1981) was employed to rewrite Maupassant articles under her own name and to trace the legs of girls from *La Vie Parisienne*. Having deflowered her in an upper room of the Café Royal, Harris told her, 'Sex is the gateway to life' (Bagnold, 92). In old age she wrote of him,

He *was* an extraordinary man. He had an appetite for great things and could transmit the sense of them. He was more like a great actor than a man of heart. He could simulate anything. While he felt admiration he could act it, and while he acted it, he felt it. And 'greatness' being his big part, he hunted the centuries for it, spotting it in literature, in passion, in action. (Bagnold, 87)

Their idyll ended when Harris was committed to Brixton prison on 3 February 1914 for contempt of court following a scurrilous, sneering article on Earl Fitzwilliam, who had been cited as a co-respondent in the Leslie-Melville divorce. When bailiffs occupied Harris's offices, Bagnold let his Shakespeare 'first folio' out of the window on a rope, and kept it. Feeling dismal after his release in March, Harris became entangled with the countess of Warwick in efforts to raise or extort money on her intimate letters from Edward VII.

Shortly after the outbreak of the First World War he sailed for New York, where his war articles (collected in 1915 as *England or Germany?*) attacked Britain's war aims, legal and prison systems, philistinism, snobbery, and prudery. His paranoia increased when he was branded a traitor. Desperate for money, in 1915 he published *Contemporary Portraits*: there is a bitter, jealous tone to this book, except in the chapters on John Davidson and Richard Middleton, two unappreciated poets who were driven to suicide, with whose disappointment he sympathized. Four later volumes of these pen-portraits are vivid and ebullient. In 1916 he published a biography of Oscar Wilde which has impressionistic value despite factual vagaries: the most admirable feature of Harris's life was his patient kindness and loyalty to Wilde.

During Harris's editorship of *Pearson's Magazine* (1916–22) he repeatedly clashed with American censorship and made many enemies with his rude, unpredictable, and arrogant conduct. He was naturalized as a United States citizen in April 1921. The onset of sexual impotence about 1920 was a cruel disablement for a man who had always been both priapic and desperately needing of women's admiration. In 1921–7 he dictated his immense serial autobiography (containing innumerable senescent erotic fantasies), which was published in various editions from 1922 as *My Life and Loves*. Nothing in these volumes is to be trusted without independent corroboration; but when such corroboration is available Harris proves a sharp and sometimes accurate observer. He settled permanently at Nice in 1923, and entered a slow decline; a long-standing and egocentric obsession with Jesus Christ became more pronounced. Very soon after the death of his second wife he married, on 15 October 1927, Nellie O'Hara. In 1930 he contracted to write a biography of George Bernard Shaw, which was published posthumously in 1931. Shaw had already memorialized his biographer in an unforgettable *bon mot*: 'He is neither first-rate, nor second-rate, nor tenth-rate. He is just his horrible unique self' (Kingsmith, *Harris*, 174).

Harris died of heart failure, following bronchitis, on 26 August 1931, at his home, 9 rue de la Buffa, Nice. His remaining friends raised the money for his burial in the British cemetery at Caucade. Harris figures as Hardfur

Huttle in W. W. and G. Grossmith's *Diary of a Nobody* (1892), the eponymous hero of Frederic Carrel's *The Adventure of John Johns* (1897), Alfred Butteridge in H. G. Wells's *The War in the Air* (1908), Ralph Parker in Hugh Kingsmill's *The Will to Love* (1919), Baxendale Strangeways in Sir Harry Johnston's *The Gay-Dombeys* (1919), Jim Galway in Kate Stephens's *Life in Laureltown* (1920), and Jack Fordham in Aleister Crowley's *The Diary of a Drug Fiend* (1923).

RICHARD DAVENPORT-HINES

Sources P. Pullar, *Frank Harris* (1975) · H. Kingsmith, *Frank Harris* (1932) · H. Kingsmith, *After puritanism* (1929), 111–67 · A. I. Tobin and E. Gertz, *Frank Harris* (1931) · H. G. Wells, *Experiment in autobiography: discoveries and conclusions of a very ordinary brain (since 1866)*, 2 (1934), 519–29 · E. Bagnold, *Enid Bagnold's autobiography (from 1889)* (1969), 87–99 · H. Pearson, *Modern men and manners* (1921), 102–32 · H. L. Mencken, *Prejudices*, 3rd ser. (1923), 182–9 · S. Roth, *The private life of Frank Harris* (1931) · E. M. Root, *Frank Harris* (1947) · V. Brome, *Frank Harris* (1959) · G. Cumberland, *Set down in malice* (1919), 32–46
Archives NYPL · Ransom HRC | BL, Dilke MSS · BL, Shaw MSS · L. Cong., Elmer Gertz MSS · PRO NIre., Stewart MSS
Likenesses W. Rothenstein, oils, 1895, NPG · M. Beerbohm, caricature, 1896, repro. in M. Beerbohm, *Twenty-five gentlemen* (1896) · M. Beerbohm, caricature, drawing, c.1898, U. Texas · M. Beerbohm, caricatures, 1898, repro. in M. Beerbohm, *More theatres* (1898) · M. Beerbohm, caricature, drawing, c.1910, U. Texas · M. Beerbohm, caricatures, c.1910, repro. in Sir R. Hart-Davis, *A catalogue of the caricatures of Sir Max Beerbohm* (1972), 214, pl. 51, 52 · J. D. Fergusson, brush and ink, 1911–13, NPG · A. L. Coburn, photogravure, 1913, NPG [*see illus.*] · M. Beerbohm, caricatures, 1914, repro. in M. Beerbohm, *Modern society* (1914) · Owl, mechanical reproduction, NPG; repro. in *VF* (12 Nov 1913)
Wealth at death virtually penniless: Pullar, *Frank Harris*

Harris, John (1587/8–1658), college head, was the son of Richard Harris, rector of Hardwick, Buckinghamshire. He entered Winchester College as a scholar at the age of eleven in 1599. He proceeded to New College, matriculating on 26 October 1604; he was a fellow from 1606 until 1622. He graduated BA on 13 April 1608 and proceeded MA on 23 January 1612. On 11 April 1617 he was elected junior proctor of the university. On 17 July 1619 he graduated BD. From 1619 to 1622 he was regius professor of Greek. In 1621 he became rector of North Crawley, Buckinghamshire, and on 1 July the next year he was licensed DD. On 2 October following he was collated to the prebend of Combe XII in Wells Cathedral; this he exchanged for the prebend of Whitchurch by Archbishop Abbot's *pro hac vice* presentation of 6 February 1627. He resigned the stall by 26 May 1631. On 14 May 1628 he was collated to a canonry in Winchester Cathedral. That year appeared his only published sermon—on Sodom—and he contributed the memoir of Arthur Lake which prefaces the bishop's *Sermons*, published in 1629.

In September 1630 Harris was elected warden of Winchester College. The alternative candidate (Edward Stanley, the head master) had secured the king's recommendation, but a free election was nevertheless allowed, in which Harris's scholarly credentials and personal connections held more sway with the fellows. He was admitted on 28 September. On 7 February 1631 Bishop Neile collated him to the rectory of Meonstoke, Hampshire, vacated by the death of Nicholas Love. Harris's lasting

memorial at Winchester is the sick house, which he provided in 1640, the first addition to the college buildings since the foundation. With the onset of the civil war he helped to preserve Winchester from the fate of the cathedral corporations by fostering contacts with Wykehamists in parliament, notably Nicholas Love the younger, and by accepting the presbyterian regime. In 1649 he protested that the replacement of ejected fellows of New College by non-Wykehamists was a 'great prejudice and discouragement' to Winchester scholars (Leach, 347). Early in 1650 Winchester was itself visited by parliamentary commissioners. Fourteen allegations were presented against the warden's conduct: he was accused of bowing to the altar and other proscribed rituals (though his abandoning these was the object of a further charge of timeserving); his fondness for 'organicall music in the Quire' was particularly deprecated; and he was said to have prevented his wife, of whom nothing more is known, from reading an improving book. More seriously, Harris was indicted for supporting the king's cause with prayer and plate. Harris acknowledged that he served the prevailing system, and accounted it no fault. His friends among the visitors (including Love) sensed that their chairman, Sir Henry Mildmay, was over-zealous to secure the wardenship for himself, and accepted Harris's defence.

Harris died in office on 11 August 1658 and was buried in the college chapel. He left three sons, John, Thomas, and Richard, all of whom went to Oxford and followed the law. The two younger sons received £1000 apiece in their father's will, which also mentions his brother Samuel and sister Phoebe, their children, and the children of apparently deceased siblings Josiah, Nathaniel, Dorothy, Elizabeth, and Mary. Harris left £20 to New College for plate, and his divinity books to Winchester. Other books went to Thomas, as well as his sermon notes and papers (on condition nothing was published unless Harris gave further order while he lived).

C. S. KNIGHTON

Sources T. F. Kirby, *Winchester scholars: a list of the wardens, fellows, and scholars of … Winchester College* (1888), 158 · T. F. Kirby, *Annals of Winchester College, from its foundation in the year 1382 to the present time* (1892), 316–17, 336–41 · A. F. Leach, *A history of Winchester College* (1899), 334, 338, 345–8, 350–51 · Foster, *Alum. Oxon.* · Wood, *Ath. Oxon.*, new edn, 3.455 · *Reg. Oxf.*, 2.276, 360; 3.277 · *Fasti Angl., 1541–1857*, [Canterbury], 103 · *Fasti Angl., 1541–1857*, [Bath and Wells], 48, 96 · A. Lake, *Sermons with some religious and divine meditations* (1629) · *CSP dom.*, 1629–31, 338, 340, 344, 346 · PRO, PROB 11/280, fols. 330r–331r
Likenesses oils, Winchester College; copy, New College, Oxford
Wealth at death land at Nuffield, Oxfordshire; £1000 to each of two younger sons; approx. £150 in other specified bequests: will, PRO, PROB 11/280, fols. 330r–331r

Harris, John (c.1666–1719), writer and lecturer on science, was reportedly the son of Edward Harris, or possibly Fitzharris (c.1648–1681), an army lieutenant. He entered Trinity College, Oxford, as a scholar in 1683, and graduated BA in 1686 and MA at Hart Hall in 1689. Shortly after the revolution he was made vicar of Icklesham, Sussex, entered on the cure of Winchelsea St Thomas by the order of the bishop of Chichester, and on 14 February 1691 was made

John Harris (*c.*1666–1719), by Bernard (III) Lens, 1707

rector of Winchelsea. He may have graduated BD from Cambridge in 1699, and was made DD at Lambeth in 1706. Throughout his early career he benefited from connections among the whigs, particularly with William Cowper, lord keeper of the great seal and later lord chancellor. Harris became Cowper's chaplain, and through Cowper's influence obtained a prebend in Rochester Cathedral in February 1708, and the united parishes of St Mildred, Bread Street, and St Margaret Moyses, both London, in the same year. By right of his prebendal stall he also became perpetual curate of Strood, Kent, on 29 August 1711 and rector of East Barming, Kent, in 1715. He was particularly active in pursuing preferment, notably in the influence of the whig bench, especially of Archbishop William Wake. His persistence, however, was often regarded as troublesome.

During the last few years of Queen Anne's reign Harris was particularly close to the whig Charles Cox (1660–1729), MP for Southwark. Cox joined those who demanded Sacheverell's impeachment for a sermon attacking the Godolphin ministry and 'false bretheren' in the church. Much to Cox's dismay, Sacheverell had procured a chaplaincy at St Saviour's, Southwark; and when he delivered and then published his famous sermon, Harris complained about the conduct of high-church zealots in his own sermon *The Evil and Mischief of a Fiery Spirit* in February 1710. The Sacheverell affair turned into an electoral disaster for the whigs and led directly to the tory triumph in the summer of 1710. After the death of Queen Anne in 1714, Harris supported the concerns of the court of George I about high-church attitudes and closet Jacobites, and he

gave vehement sermons in defence of the Hanoverian succession. In his *Picture of a Highflying Clergyman* (1716), written in the aftermath of the Jacobite rising, Harris reported the public expression of Stuart sympathies as sufficient grounds for the dismissal of the Revd Charles Humphreys as lecturer at St Mildred. Humphreys was an associate of Sacheverell and soon found a place with him in St Andrew's, Holborn, where they encountered the antagonism of the Revd William Whiston, zealous whig, Newtonian, and natural theologian.

Harris exhibited an early interest in natural theology and scientific matters, and became engaged in the defence of Dr John Woodward in the controversy, provoked by the works of the Revd Thomas Burnet (1635–1715), surrounding the deluge. In 1697 Harris published one of many reflections on the subject in his *Remarks on some late papers relating to the universal deluge, and to the natural history of the earth*. The previous year he had been elected a fellow of the Royal Society and published a paper in the *Philosophical Transactions* on microscopical observations of animalcula. By 1698 he was appointed to one of the lectures established by the will of Robert Boyle for the confutation of atheism. His sermons at St Paul's were published as *The atheistical objections against the being of God, and his attributes, fairly considered and refuted*.

Since the revolution Harris had privately taught mathematics at his home in Amen Corner, by St Paul's, and with Charles Cox, the Southwark brewer, organized a set of mathematical lectures delivered gratis by Harris in Southwark from 1698, and later at the Marine Coffee House near the Royal Exchange. He dedicated to Cox his translation of Ignatius Gaston Pardies, *Short, but yet Plain Elements of Geometry and Plain Trigonometry* (1701), which was intended, along with *The Description and Uses of the Celestial and Terrestrial Globes* (1702), for his students. By 1704 Cox's financial support for the lectures was uncertain, and Harris found himself with rivals such as the experimentalist and mathematician James Hodgson FRS, who ultimately succeeded him at the Marine in 1707 and who was followed in turn by Humphry Ditton, whose work Harris assisted. Harris found sufficient subscribers to continue his lectures, which evolved to include the experimental and mechanical philosophy then promoted by the disciples of Newton. Harris also published by subscription the first volume of his famous *Lexicon technicum, or, An Universal English Dictionary of Arts and Sciences* (1704), which became one of the first books to display the importance to the public of Newton's science, and which has since been regarded a prototype of the more famous dictionaries and encyclopaedias of the Enlightenment. This was followed in 1710 by a successful second volume (with 1200 subscribers) in which mathematics was emphasized as 'the only Solid Foundation on which a Useful Enquiry into Nature and all Physical Learning can possibly be built'.

Harris promoted utility and took a special interest in the scientific instruments, such as the air-pump, that provided the Royal Society with many experiments, as well as in the technology of the Savery engine and in the practical problems of navigation. His high-church rivals predictably dismissed the *Lexicon* as of little consequence. In 1705 he was employed by London booksellers in compiling *Navigantium atque itinerantium bibliotheca, or, A compleat collection of voyages and travels, consisting of above four hundred of the most authentick writers*. Harris's involvement in the Royal Society continued throughout Anne's reign, though he served only briefly as secretary (1709–10), having been caught up in a dispute between the physicians John Woodward and Hans Sloane. He maintained his concern in scientific affairs, and during the summer of 1718 was engaged in experiments before the society with the lecturer John Theophilus Desaguliers in which the power of combustion of Villette's concave burning glass was demonstrated. In 1719 Harris published *Astronomical Dialogues between a Gentleman and a Lady*.

Harris was involved in several early insurance promotions, such as the Company of London Insurers or the Sun Fire Office under Charles Povey, which began its operations near St Paul's in 1709–10. From 1699 Harris had been among the trustees of the Society of Assurance for Widows and Orphans, but of equal consequence may have been his involvement in 1709–10 in the court of assistants of the mines royal and mineral and battery works, of which Newton was deputy governor. Both Cox and Harris were among the petitioners for a charter for the Amicable Society for a Perpetual Assurance Office, and in 1716 they were directors of the Union or Double Hand in Hand Fire-Office for Goods.

At his death in 1719 Harris was in the process of printing an undistinguished, but handsomely subscribed, first volume of *The History of Kent*, which he had been compiling for many years. His interest was undoubtedly induced by Kent connections and by the curacy of Strood and prebendary of Rochester Cathedral. Certainly his reputation was such that Thomas Hearne, the Oxford antiquary, dismissed him as 'a most rank whigg, & a sad, vile, loose Wretch' (*Remarks*, 7.46). Harris died on 7 September 1719 at Norton Court, Kent, and his manuscripts came into the hands of his friend John Godfrey, at whose expense, apparently, he was buried, at Norton Court. The rumour that he died an absolute pauper was first aired by Nichols in his *Literary Anecdotes* (1815) and has been reproduced ever since. While he was hardly wealthy, as many of his insurance promotions were unsuccessful, it must be doubted that he was destitute, for he left several books and instruments, including globes, telescopes, and a barometer, along with his furnishings and, suitably, a statue of King William. Harris was a widower and was survived by a daughter, Elizabeth, then a minor.

LARRY STEWART

Sources L. R. Stewart, *The rise of public science: rhetoric, technology, and natural philosophy in Newtonian Britain, 1660–1750* (1992) · R. H. Kargon, 'Harris, John', *DSB* · Venn, *Alum. Cant.* · *Remarks and collections of Thomas Hearne*, ed. C. E. Doble and others, 11 vols., OHS, 2, 7, 13, 34, 42–3, 48, 50, 65, 67, 72 (1885–1921), vol. 4, p. 164; vol. 7, p. 46 · Nichols, *Lit. anecdotes*, 9.769–75 · G. Carr-Harris, 'The ancestry of John Harris (1667–1719)—father of the encyclopaedia', *N&Q*, 223 (1978), 19–23 · D. McKie, 'John Harris and his *Lexicon technicum*', *Endeavour*, 4 (1945), 53–7 · A. Bardwell, 'Arts and science in English encyclopedias', MA diss., University of Toronto, 1976 · E. G. R. Taylor, *The mathematical practitioners of Tudor and Stuart England* (1954) · E. G. R. Taylor, *The mathematical practitioners of Hanoverian England, 1714–1840* (1966) · M. P. Southwark, 'Cox, Charles (1660–1729)', HoP, *Commons* [draft] · L. E. Bradshaw, 'John Harris's *Lexicon technicum*', *Notable encyclopedias of the seventeenth and eighteenth centuries*, ed. F. A. Kafker, Studies on Voltaire and the eighteenth-century, 194 (1981), 107–21

Archives Trinity College, Oxford, MS autobiography | BL, Wake letters, Add. MS 6117 · CUL, Flamsteed corresp. · LPL, William Wake diary · RS, Flamsteed-Sharp corresp., council minutes, journal books

Likenesses Bernard (III) Lens, miniature, 1707, Yale U. CBA [*see illus.*] · G. Vertue, line engraving (after A. Russel), BM, NPG; repro. in J. Harris, *History of Kent* (1719) · G. White, line engraving (after R. White), BM, NPG; repro. in J. Harris, *Lexicon technicum* (1704)

Wealth at death see inventory, PRO, PROB 3/17/86

Harris, John (d. 1743). *See under* Harris, Renatus (c.1652–1724).

Harris, John (*fl.* 1700–1740), engraver and draughtsman, appears to have originated in Northamptonshire. This can be judged from an inscription on a map of Northampton in John Morton's *The Natural History of Northamptonshire* (1712) where Harris described himself as 'a Native'. No other details are known of his life, and his biography can only be reconstructed from his work, though this can be equally problematic on account of the number of artists with the name John Harris at work in the eighteenth century. Although Strutt and Dodd both believed him to be the engraver of a 1686 print of the royal army encampment on Hounslow Heath, this attribution seems unlikely. Harris's first certain plates date from the early years of the eighteenth century. Like his plan of Buckinghamshire for Morden's *The New Description and State of England* in 1701, they were mostly plans and maps; throughout his career he specialized in such large-scale engravings of topography, cartography, and architecture. One of his earliest achievements was a fourteen-sheet survey of Cornwall, which was the first large-scale map of any county to be published. This was based on the survey by Joel Gascoyne, who was evidently impressed with Harris's work, as he later employed him to engrave the six sheets for his *An actuall survey of the parish of St Dunstan Stepney alias Stebunheath being one of the ten parishes in the county of Middlesex London* (1703). For this Harris received half of 'the Sum of One Hundred Pounds for the defraying the Charge of the said Plate & Survey', paid by St Dunstan's Church (Ravenhill, 9). In the first decade of the eighteenth century he also engraved maps and plans of Ireland, Scotland, and Cambridgeshire. The size and scale of much of this work suggest that he was a specialist engraver, working at the top end of the market and producing large multi-sheet plates for didactic or decorative purposes.

In 1711 Harris began to engrave architectural plates and bird's-eye views, many of which survive because they were gathered into or reissued for various collections, such as David Mortier's *Britannia illustrata* (1720). As some of these architectural elevations and prospects of gentlemen's country houses were signed 'Io^n. Harris delin.:et fecit', we know that Harris, evidently a surveyor, travelled round the country, drawing and engraving houses to order. Undoubtedly, however, Harris is best known for his folio-sized engravings, after Wenceslaus Hollar, of each of the prospects of old St Paul's Cathedral, which were published in the second edition of William Dugdale's *The History of St Paul's Cathedral in London* (1716). At the same time he engraved four plates of the new cathedral, after the designs of J. King, which were intended to celebrate its inauguration.

Given the many county plans and maps that Harris engraved during his career he must have travelled extensively around England in the course of his work. He engraved prospects of Rochester for Thomas Badeslade in 1720, of Leeds for the Buck Brothers in 1721, of Northampton for Richard Collins in 1732, and of Scarborough for John Settrington in 1735. Despite his having executed several plates of American prospects for the publisher William Burgis between 1719 and 1721, there is no other suggestion that Harris visited that country. Such plates of foreign places afford evidence of Harris's skill at working from the designs of others.

Harris also worked directly for book publishers, producing more circumscribed illustrations—often for architectural treatises. He engraved twenty-eight plates for Leoni's edition of Andrea Palladio's architectural designs between 1715 and 1719, and produced plates for Leoni's edition of Alberti's work in 1726 as well as for James Gibb's *Book of Architecture* (1728). Later in his career he capitalized on his skill with surveys and topography, and gained much work providing illustrations for antiquarian county histories. This was the case with the illustrations for Dr John Harris's *History of Kent* (1719) and for Francis Drake's *Eboracum, or, The History and Antiquities of the City of York* (1736). Although the signature is uncharacteristic, the last-known print that might be attributed to this John Harris also appears in an antiquarian context: *A Ground Plot of Stonehenge*, signed 'Harris sc.', appears in William Stukeley's *Stonehenge* of 1740.

L. H. CUST, rev. LUCY PELTZ

Sources B. Adams, *London illustrated, 1604–1851* (1983) · private information (2004) [David Alexander] · T. Dodd, 'Memoirs of English engravers, 1550–1800', BL, Add. MS 33401, fol. 214 · D. Bank and A. Esposito, eds., *British biographical archive*, 2nd series (1991) [microfiche] · [R. Gough], *Anecdotes of British topography*, 2 vols. (1768) · J. Morton, *The natural history of Northamptonshire* (1712) · W. Ravenhill, 'Joel Gascoyne's engraved maps of Stepney', *London Topographical Society*, 150 (1995) · Redgrave, *Artists* · J. Strutt, *A biographical dictionary, containing an historical account of all the engravers, from the earliest period of the art of engraving to the present time*, 2 vols. (1785–6) · Vertue, *Note books*

Harris, John (1756–1846), publisher and bookseller, was apprenticed to Thomas Evans, a London bookseller, and worked for him for fourteen years. Nothing else is known about his education or early life. In 1784 he spent a year managing a bookshop in Bury St Edmunds, but some time in 1785 he returned to Evans's employ in London. He then worked briefly for John Murray. He married Maria (date unknown) and they had three children.

In 1801–2 Harris purchased Elizabeth Newbery's business, having apparently worked for her for some time

before becoming her manager in 1797. Harris's talents and initiative ensured the continued success of the firm, which under John Newbery had been the first to specialize successfully in publishing books for children. Harris published adult works—including the *Gentleman's Magazine*—but his shop was Harris's Juvenile Library. He maintained a general list, including moral tales, school books, and stock from other publishers. Among his children's book authors were Lady Eleanor Fenn, Barbara Hofland, Sarah Trimmer, and Elizabeth Turner. In 1805 he published *The Comic Adventures of Old Mother Hubbard and her Dog*. He boasted that in a few months he had sold 10,000 copies of the small book of engraved text and plates. The design appealed to children and adults accustomed to the engraved narrative illustrations of Hogarth and Rowlandson. He followed this with a picturebook version of a light-hearted poem by William Roscoe, *The Butterfly's Ball* (1807), illustrated by William Mulready. It was enormously popular and was imitated repeatedly throughout the nineteenth century. Harris went on to publish a series of attractive and elegant small, square picturebooks, Harris's Cabinet of Amusement and Instruction (1807–9). These represent his principal contribution which was in the development of picturebooks.

In 1819 John Harris jun. joined his father in business. The two brought out a second Cabinet series of more than fifty titles including the first known book of limericks, *Sixteen Wonderful Old Women* (1820). In 1824 Harris retired and in 1843 his son sold the business to Grant and Griffith. Harris died at his home, 2 York Place, Walworth, London, on 2 November 1846, and was probably buried at St Peter's, Walworth. He left upwards of £30,000 in invested capital and bequests to his family, including his grandson, John Newbery Harris. He also left bequests to his servants, the Booksellers' Provident Retreat, and other book trade charities, and the poor of the parish. The *Gentleman's Magazine* obituary described him as 'the very worthy successor to Mrs. E. Newbery, at the corner of St. Paul's Church-yard (whence so many prettily-gilt, clever, and interesting books have taught the young of many generations)' (*GM*).

JILL SHEFRIN

Sources M. Moon, ed., *John Harris's books for youth, 1801–1843: being a checklist* (1976) · *GM*, 2nd ser., 26 (1846) · M. Moon and B. Alderson, *Childhood re-collected: early children's books from the library of Marjorie Moon* (1994) · W. West, *Fifty years' recollections of an old bookseller* (privately printed, Cork, 1835; repr. (New York, 1974) · Nichols, *Illustrations*, vol. 8 · d. cert.
Wealth at death £16,000 in bequests in 3 percents; £14,409 outright bequests; bequests to daughter and grandchildren of unspecified amounts: will, Moon, *John Harris's books*

Harris, John (1767–1832), watercolour painter and illustrator, was born in London on 5 June 1767, the second son of Moses *Harris (1730–c.1788), the artist and entomologist. He was brought up at Deptford, which gave him a taste for marine subjects. He was articled c.1780 to the entomologist Thomas Martyn, whose Academy for Illustrating and Painting Natural History was in Great Marlborough Street. Until about 1789 he also worked for James Edwards, the bookseller in Pall Mall, colouring prints and books. He exhibited landscapes and topographical subjects in watercolour at the Royal Academy from 1797, when he was living at Amelia Street, Walworth, to 1815, by which time he had moved to 27 Mansion House Row, Kennington.

In collaboration with his son, John *Harris (1791–1873), Harris published illuminated versions of early statutes and Magna Carta in 1816, and they lithographed a number of portraits of prominent masons in 1825. According to a memoir by the son, which is tipped in a Bible now at the Houghton Library, Harvard, 'as an Artist in the painting of Subjects of natural History Viz Insects, Shells &c &c He was I Believe, without a rival' (Weimerskirch, 249); but it is for the illustrating and ornamenting of books that he is best remembered. This Bible, with over 700 original watercolour illustrations, is perhaps his *magnum opus*. He died at his home in Wandsworth Road in May 1832 and was buried at Kennington New Church, now St Mark's, on 1 June. He was a widower, and there were several children besides the younger John. There are examples of the work of the elder Harris in the British Museum, London, and the Exeter Museum; in the Bridewell Library of the Southern Methodist University, Dallas, Texas, there is a Book of Common Prayer with a double fore-edge painting thought to be by him.   HUON MALLALIEU

Sources P. J. Weimerskirch, 'John Harris, sr., 1767–1832: a memoir by his son', *Book Collector*, 42 (1993), 245–52 • Graves, *RA exhibitors* • Mallalieu, *Watercolour artists* • Thieme & Becker, *Allgemeines Lexikon*
Archives Harvard U., son's memoirs
Likenesses J. Harris, self-portrait, drawing, repro. in Weimerskirch, 'John Harris, sr'; copy by J. H. junior

Harris, John (1791–1873), artist and facsimilist, was born on 17 November 1791 in Kennington, London, the son of the watercolour painter John *Harris (1767–1832), with whom he has often been confused. His grandfather was the entomologist and illustrator Moses *Harris.

Harris occasionally exhibited at the Royal Academy between 1810 and 1834. As an academy student he specialized in portrait miniatures, and with his father he executed the illuminations in the British Library vellum copy of John Whittaker's 1816 gold-printed Magna Carta. Harris worked for Whittaker, a printer and bookbinder, from 1815 until about 1820. By then he had also begun to produce the facsimile work for which he is principally remembered. Both Thomas Grenville and G. J. Spencer (second Earl Spencer) were among the collectors who employed him, and in 1854 Harris described himself in a manuscript memoir of his father as 'an Artist following a variety of branches connected with the Fine Arts, but priding himself more particularly upon executing fac-simile Leaves for perfecting rare old books' (Harvard U., Houghton L., Bi 65.820F*).

Harris married his wife, Mary, on 13 February 1820, and about the same time began his long association with the British Museum, where, in addition to supplying facsimiles, he served as an attendant in the reading rooms. In his memoirs Robert Cowtan described an incident in which the librarian Anthony Panizzi, along with two others, was unable to identify the facsimile leaves in a rare volume,

and called in Harris to distinguish his own work, which he was able to do only after considerable examination of the book. On 8 July 1843, following this episode, the museum trustees at Panizzi's request ordered that Harris in future sign any leaf he restored with the formula 'This is by J. H.'; other signatures used on facsimiles include 'F. S. J. H.', 'by H', and 'J. H.'. Harris's unsigned work is often difficult to distinguish from an original, and his minute signature is sometimes overlooked, as when the British Museum for many years reproduced as genuine a signed Harris facsimile of the printer's device of William Caxton.

In 1851 Harris showed his facsimiles at the Great Exhibition; his own brief account of his technique and early work appears in the 1852 *Reports by the Juries*. By August 1856 he had become totally blind, and in 1858 an appeal for contributions on his behalf was launched in the advertisement columns of *Notes and Queries*. Two years later Harris and his wife became residents of the Royal Masonic Benevolent Institution for Aged Freemasons in Croydon; he had been an active freemason since 1818, and in 1849 had published a set of designs for lodge tracing boards, which became standard for many years. While resident at Croydon, where he died on 28 December 1873, Harris published two poems, *Lines on the Royal Masonic Benevolent Institution*, sold in aid of the Freemasons' Life Boat Fund in 1871, and *Lines on the Fiftieth Anniversary of the Wedding Day of John and Mary Harris* (1870). He left a daughter, Helen Caroline Martin, and a son, John Alfred, who for a time continued his father's business of supplying facsimiles.

JANET ING FREEMAN

Sources R. Cowtan, *Memories of the British Museum* (1872) • [W. Roberts], 'John Harris, facsimilist', *TLS* (23 Jan 1919), 48 • B. Gaines, 'A forgotten artist: John Harris and the Rylands copy of Caxton's edition of Malory', *Bulletin of the John Rylands University Library*, 52 (1969–70), 115–28 • P. J. Weimerskirch, 'John Harris, sr., 1767–1832: a memoir by his son', *Book Collector*, 42 (1993), 245–52 • *CGPLA Eng. & Wales* (1874) • *The Freemason* (17 Jan 1874), 39
Wealth at death under £200: probate, 14 Jan 1874, *CGPLA Eng. & Wales*

Harris, John (1802–1856), Congregational minister and college head, was born on 8 March 1802 at Ugborough, Devon, the eldest son in the family of eight children of William Harris, a tailor and draper, and his wife, Elizabeth. He was a studious child, and was nicknamed Little Parson Harris. About 1815 his parents moved to Bristol, where he worked during the day in his father's shop and spent the evenings studying. As a member of the Bristol Itinerant Society he began to preach in villages around the city and became very popular, known as the 'boy preacher'. After studying under the Revd Walter Scott of Rowell, in 1823 he entered Hoxton Academy. After completing his course he became minister of the Congregational church at Epsom in 1825, and here established a reputation as a preacher. Although neither a fluent nor a theatrical speaker, he attracted large audiences.

Soon after the publication of his first work, usually regarded as his best, *The Great Teacher* (1835), Harris won a prize of 100 guineas offered by Dr John Trickey Conquest for the best essay on the sin of covetousness. His essay,

Mammon, or, Covetousness the Sin of the Christian Church (1836), sold over 100,000 copies. Its plain speaking offended some theologians, and James Ellaby, Algernon Sydney Thelwall, and others published criticisms of the book. He then won a prize awarded by the British and Foreign Sailors' Society for the best essay on missions to seamen, published in 1837 as *Britannia, or, The Moral Claims of Seamen*. After publishing sermons and other addresses, in 1835 he won 200 guineas for his essay on Christian missions, published as *The Great Commission* (1842).

In 1838 Harris became president of Cheshunt College and professor of theology. Also in that year he married Mary Anne Wrangham, daughter of W. Wrangham and a niece of Archdeacon Francis Wrangham. He was awarded a DD by Brown University, Rhode Island in the United States, in 1838. Following the amalgamation of the Independent colleges of Highbury, Homerton, and Coward into New College, London, in 1850, he became principal and professor of theology in 1851. He was elected chairman of the Congregational Union of England and Wales in 1852.

As a theologian Harris tried to make doctrine more accessible, while at the same time some of his works show profound analysis of metaphysical theology. He had a limited readership in Great Britain, but in America his writings became very popular. His published works included *Union, or, The Divided Church Made One* (1837), *The Importance of an Educated Ministry* (1843), and *The preAdamite Earth* (1846), a discussion of problems arising from advances in the science of geology. He was one of the editors of the *Biblical Review*, and was a regular contributor to the *Congregational Magazine* and the *Evangelical Magazine*. Harris died on 21 December 1856 at New College, St John's Wood, London, and was buried in Abney Park cemetery.

G. C. BOASE, *rev.* ANNE PIMLOTT BAKER

Sources *Congregational Year Book* (1858), 207–9 · E. E. Cleal, *The story of congregationalism in Surrey* (1908), 44–5 · *GM*, 3rd ser., 2 (1857), 240 · Boase, *Mod. Eng. biog.* · Allibone, *Dict.* · *Eclectic Review*, 4th ser., 4 (1838), 303–19 · *Eclectic Review*, 4th ser., 21 (1847), 137–54 · *Eclectic Review*, 4th ser., 26, 612–25 · *IGI*
Archives DWL, corresp. and papers

Harris, John (1820–1884), poet and miner, was born at Six Chimneys Cottage, Bolennowe Hill, Camborne, Cornwall, on 14 October 1820, the eldest of the ten children of John Harris (*d.* 1848), miner and farmer, and his wife, Christianna Smith (*d.* 1881). The only formal education he received was at small local schools. He worked from the age of nine, first on a farm owned by a distant relative, then as a tin streamer. From the age of ten he worked at Dolcoath mine, near Camborne, dressing copper ore. At about the age of twelve he went underground in Dolcoath mine with his father. By this time he had begun to compose verses, which he would sometimes recite to his fellow labourers in the mine. He composed a dirge on the death of some men who were killed in Carn Brea mine, which was printed, and sung by a blind man in the streets of Camborne. Hugh Rogers, rector of Camborne, and others lent him books, which helped him to gain a knowledge of English poetry.

From 1841 to 1843 Harris kept a journal which reveals details not included in his autobiography. He appears to have fallen in love with Eliza Thomas, six years his senior. Although she shared his interest in literature, she eventually married another man and died young, probably of tuberculosis. This early rejection, combined with many other personal tragedies and hardships, doubtless contributed to the preoccupation with mortality which was one of the major influences on Harris's poetry. By 1844 he had become a tributor in Dolcoath mine and had managed to save £200, with a portion of which he built a house with his own hands in his spare time. On 11 September 1845 he married Jane Rule (1821–1911), daughter of James Rule of Troon, Cornwall. They had four children: Jane (*b.* 1 April 1846), Lucretia (*b.* 1849), James Howard (*b.* 1857), and John Alfred (*b.* 1859). Their daughter Jane later emigrated to the United States; Lucretia died of pneumonia in 1855; James (writing as John Howard Harris) wrote a biography of his father, *John Harris, the Cornish Poet*, published in 1884; and John Alfred, who was born with a spinal defect which forced him to work from a prone position, illustrated his father's works with woodcuts and was an accomplished photographer.

Harris's first volume of poems, *Lays from the Mine, the Moor, and the Mountain*, was printed by subscription, with the help of George Smith, in 1853, with a second edition published in 1856. In August 1857 Edward Bastin secured him a small appointment as scripture reader in Falmouth, which enabled him to give up working as a miner. (He had long been a local preacher among the Wesleyans and had taught Sunday school from the age of sixteen.) From this time he issued a volume nearly every year, publishing ten in all, in addition to his *Autobiography* (1882). In 1864 he entered a poetry competition in honour of Shakespeare's tercentenary and obtained the first prize; this allowed him to make his first and only trip out of Cornwall, to Stratford upon Avon. He received grants from the Royal Literary Fund in 1872 and again in 1875, while Lord Beaconsfield in 1877, and Gladstone in 1881, each secured him £200 from the Royal Bounty Fund. Harris was struck with paralysis on 14 April 1878, which confined him to his room for two months. At the end of 1883 he fell backwards off a step, which led to spasmodic asthma attacks. He died at his home, Killigrew Terrace, Falmouth, on 7 January 1884 and was buried at Treslothan, Cornwall, on 10 January. His wife survived him.

Harris wrote extensively about nature and Cornish legends, as well as contributing to religious periodicals and tract society publications. Contemporary critics described his poetry as 'homely and ennobling', possessing 'freshness, vigour, and beauty' (J. Harris, 128). His best work shows strong emotion, exploring his concerns about death and 'man's brutal relish for war and drink', while demonstrating an intense spirituality and positive faith (Drabble, 139).

MEGAN A. STEPHAN

Sources P. Newman, *The meads of love: the life and poetry of John Harris (1820–84)* (1994) · J. Harris, *My autobiography* (1882) · J. H. Harris, *John Harris, the Cornish poet, by his son* (1884) · Boase & Courtney, *Bibl.*

Corn., 1.208–9 · G. C. Boase, *Collectanea Cornubiensia: a collection of biographical and topographical notes relating to the county of Cornwall* (1890), 321–2 · J. Gill, *John Harris, the Cornish poet: a lecture on his life and works* [1884] · M. Drabble, ed., *The Oxford companion to English literature*, rev. edn (1995), 443

Likenesses J. A. Harris, photograph, 1882, repro. in Harris, *My autobiography*, frontispiece · portrait, repro. in Harris, *John Harris*, frontispiece

Wealth at death £1098 14s. 7d.: probate, 15 March 1884, CGPLA Eng. & Wales

Harris, Sir John Hobbis (1874–1940), campaigner against slavery, was born on 29 July 1874 at Grove Street, Wantage, the son of John Hobbis Harris, plumber (and later a builder), and his wife, Elizabeth Emily Saunders. An earnest Christian, young John Harris spent all his free time doing evangelical social work in the common lodging houses under the leadership of F. B. Meyer of Christ Church, Westminster Bridge Road, London. While working as a twenty-year-old in the City of London for Cooks, the gentlemen's outfitters, he also began to train to become a Baptist missionary in central Africa. Together with his wife, Alice (1870–1970), daughter of Alfred Seeley, a silk works manager, whom he had just married (on 6 May), Harris sailed for the Congo in May 1898. They had two sons and two daughters.

At first Harris concentrated on learning the language and customs of the people of his part of the Congo Free State, and in teaching basic skills such as housebuilding. But very soon he was forced to witness such abominations in the treatment of the local people by agents of King Leopold II of the Belgians that, instead of bringing Christ to pagan Africa, Harris had to respond to the revelation that it was the Christians who were now the crucifiers. He watched horrified as Africans were lashed mercilessly with a long whip of twisted hippopotamus hide by other Africans who would be flogged themselves if they refused to obey European orders. Shortly afterwards he and his wife were shown the amputated hand and foot of a five-year-old girl by her distraught father. The source of all this horror was King Leopold's insatiable demand for rubber and ivory which his company extracted from the Congo, ostensibly via a 'civilizing' mission but in fact by slavery, hostage-taking, the torture and mutilation of women and children, the burning of whole villages, and, when necessary, mass murder. The Harrises realized that they must abandon private protest for public action. The British consul, Roger Casement, and the investigative journalist E. D. Morel joined with John Harris to inform the British government of the atrocities and to urge it to intervene. But at first no one in high places responded except Charles Dilke, Lord Lansdowne, and H. R. Fox Bourne. In 1903–4 John and Alice Harris supplied E. D. Morel's Congo Reform Association with a detailed account, attested by Alice Harris's photographic evidence, of the deliberate system of atrocity being perpetrated. In December 1904 John Harris was asked by the local Africans to represent their case and translate their submissions to King Leopold's (packed) commission of enquiry. Its reluctant, shameful, findings were eventually published in October 1905, but without any of Harris's damning evidence. John Harris himself

then published the pamphlet *Rubber is Death: the Story of the Bonguronga Rubber Collectors*, enumerating case after case, giving the names of the victims and their families, many of them known to him personally. 'Again and again when these horrors have been brought to our notice, we have been ashamed that our skin is white … Has the conscience of Christian England gone to sleep?' (Harris, 21).

Despite the fact that they had to leave behind their own small children in Britain, and at real risk not only to their health but to their lives, Alice and John Harris continued 'to march round the world … laying before the public the evidence [of] … the barbarous nature of the system' (*Anti-Slavery Reporter and Aborigines' Friend*, April 1911). Supported by the evidence of the actual whips and chains used and the sixty photographs of both victims and perpetrators taken by Alice Harris (made into lantern slides), the Harrises spoke in the cause of Congo reform at well over 600 public meetings in Britain, Europe, and the United States before 1910. In 1911 they travelled 5000 miles, on river steamer, by canoe, or on foot through almost impenetrable tropical forests, on a fact-finding investigation of current conditions in central and west Africa.

John Harris became a political crusader against white capitalist imperialism in general, advocating a system of genuine, international trusteeship in the interests of all native peoples on every continent. Between 1910 and 1940 he produced a number of important articles and books on the topic, including *Dawn in Darkest Africa* (1912), *Africa, Slave or Free?* (1919), and *Slavery or 'Sacred Trust'?* (1926). In these he identified usurpation of land as the root of the evil that then led to forced labour in order to exploit the mineral resources and products of the soil. Harris redefined contract labour and debt bondage as neo-slavery; he insisted that the native should see some benefit for all his taxation and, unlike most of his contemporaries at the beginning of the twentieth century, he believed that the native races had as much right to self-determination as any one else.

From 1910 to 1940 John Harris was parliamentary secretary to the amalgamated Anti-Slavery and Aborigines' Protection societies. In 1923 he was elected Liberal MP for Hackney North, but lost his seat at the next election in 1924. As a member of the national executive of the League of Nations Union, he visited Geneva every year and added international lobbying on behalf of all the native races to his workload. In 1933 John Harris was knighted in acknowledgement of his part in getting the League of Nations to accept British proposals for the suppression of slavery world wide. According to Lord Lytton, 'It was the *thing* slavery, not merely the *word*, which he worked to abolish' (*Anti-Slavery Reporter and Aborigines' Friend*, July 1940). Therefore Harris also tackled the abuse of *mui tsai*— 'adopted daughters'—in domestic servitude in Hong Kong, Malaya, and Ceylon; he placed questions in parliament to challenge the use of ten-year-old African children as labourers in British Kenya; he investigated and criticized the endemic, systematic oppression of black people both in the southern states of America and in southern

Africa; and he was one of the earliest to monitor and criticize white Australia's racist oppression of the Aborigines. In addition, John Harris would never refuse a request to help individual Africans finding themselves in difficulties in London. Not surprisingly he wore himself out.

Sir John Harris died suddenly from bronchitis and a cerebral haemorrhage on 30 April 1940, at Stonelands, Bath Road, Frome, Somerset. Obituaries glow with regard for the meticulous integrity of his research, and for his tireless, courageous altruism: 'He was afraid of nobody', wrote Gilbert Murray (*Anti-Slavery Reporter*, October 1941). According to Charles Roden Buxton, 'He was a truly lovable man' (*The Friend*, 10 May, 1940). The burial, probably on 6 May, and memorial services were conducted by the Society of Friends, which Harris had joined after the First World War.   SYBIL OLDFIELD

Sources W. R. Louis, 'Sir John Harris and "Colonial Trusteeship"', *Bulletin des Séances de l'Académie Royal des Sciences d'Outre Mer*, 14 (1968), 832–56 · A. Hochschild, *King Leopold's ghost* (1999) · P. B. Rich, *Race and empire in British politics* (1986) · K. Grant, '"A civilised savagery": British humanitarian politics and European imperialism in Africa, 1884–1926', PhD diss., U. Cal., Berkeley, 1997 · b. cert. · m. cert. · d. cert. · *WWW* · *The Times* (2 May 1940) · *The Times* (8 May 1940) · *The Times* (3 Dec 1970) · *Anti-Slavery Reporter and Aborigines' Friend* (April 1911) · *Anti-Slavery Reporter and Aborigines' Friend* (July 1940) · *Anti-Slavery Reporter and Aborigines' Friend* (Oct 1941) · Bodl. RH, Harris MSS · J. Harris, *Rubber is death: the story of the Bonguronga rubber collector* (1905) · *The Friend* (10 May 1940) · *CGPLA Eng. & Wales* (1940)

Archives Bodl. RH, autobiography, corresp., and papers · Bodl. RH, corresp. and papers, incl. MS 'A century of emancipation' | BLPES, corresp. with E. D. Morel · Bodl. Oxf., corresp. with Gilbert Murray · JRL, letters to the *Manchester Guardian* | SOUND BBC WAC

Likenesses photograph, Anti-Slavery International, Thomas Clarkson House, London

Wealth at death £11,252 18s. 7d.: probate, 8 July 1940, *CGPLA Eng. & Wales*

Harris, John Mortimer Green (1864–1939), department store manager, was born on 21 March 1864 at 164 Field Street, Everton, Liverpool, the son of David Stephen Harris, draper's assistant, and his wife, Anne Green. He was of Welsh descent. Little is known about his early life, but he worked for a department store in Liverpool until 1908, when he was asked to become a director of Browns of Chester, as manager of the drapery department. Harris married Mary Roberts, and they had a son and a daughter.

In 1908 the store became a private limited company under the chairmanship of Harry Brown but Harris ran Browns (it was first referred to as 'Browns of Chester' in 1913) for over thirty years, and developed it from an old family business into a large modern department store. He successfully promoted Chester, with its black and white timbered medieval houses, as the alternative to the industrial grime of Liverpool and Manchester, and persuaded county people from the Wirral and north Wales to drive into Chester in their motor cars to do their shopping. The store continued to specialize in French fashions (advertisements were often priced in francs), and the first fashion show to be put on outside London was held by Browns in the ballroom of the Grosvenor Hotel, Chester, in 1913.

Expansion continued after the war, and, when the fashion designer Lucy Duff Gordon gave a talk 'Dress—what to wear and how' in 1924, she told the *Daily Sketch* that Browns was 'one of the most up-to-the-minute department stores I have ever been in. … I've never seen a shop as good as this anywhere in England' (Willcock, 192). Browns of Chester claimed to be the 'Harrods of the North', and as the mayor of Chester said when opening the new four-storey building in 1926, Browns was Chester, and Chester was Browns.

On the death of Harry Brown in 1936, Harris became chairman, and Harry Brown's son, S. H. Brown, became a director, thus ensuring the continued involvement of members of the Brown family in the business. John Mortimer Harris died on 10 August 1939 at Brookfield Nursing Home, Brookfield Gardens, West Kirby, Hoylake, Cheshire.

His son, **Leonard Mortimer Harris** (1903–1989), department store manager, also made a career with the firm. Born on 24 August 1903 at The Elders, Grosvenor Road, Hoylake cum West Kirby, Cheshire, he began work as a drapery apprentice with Marshall and Snelgrove in London, and then worked for Harrods before becoming a freelance advertising agent. In 1924 he was invited to take up the temporary post of advertising manager at Browns of Chester, and remained there for the rest of his working life.

L. M. Harris was put in charge of publicity, and it was he who was responsible for making Browns a fashionable place to do one's shopping. The restaurant opened in 1926, and the roof tea garden in 1927, while the 'salon de beauté' was followed by a palmistry service in 1932. When the new building opened in 1926 there was an exhibition of Roman antiquities discovered during the excavations. Messrs Bees, the seed merchants, held the first of their annual flower shows there in 1926, with talks on flowers and plants by their horticultural experts.

In 1929 Harris was made a director, and, when in 1934 Browns faced a financial crisis as a result of the depression, he became general manager, and took over day-to-day control of the business. On the death of his father in 1939 he was appointed chairman and managing director. In 1943 Harris commissioned the first of several surveys by Mass-Observation Ltd, a public opinion research organization, with the aim of making Browns more appealing to a wider clientele. He later became a director of Mass-Observation Ltd. From 1948 to 1950 he was chairman of both the Drapers' chamber of trade and the Association of Retail Chambers of Trade, and from 1950 to 1951 he was president of the appeal for the Linen and Woollen Drapers' cottage homes, devoting six working days a month to this. Harris was married to the fashion buyer for Browns, Dorothy Freda (1899–1988), daughter of James Parker.

After the war Browns was able to expand again, and in 1950 annual turnover reached £1 million for the first time. In order to compete, the store had to cater for a middle-class market, and in the 1950s the French fashion parades were revived. In October 1950 the Paris collection of Jean Dessés was flown over to Browns, the first time a complete Paris collection had been shown in a British store. In 1953 the famous Paris milliner Mlle Andrée Fosse spent a week at Browns designing and making hats for customers, and in 1956 and 1960 Pierre Balmain's winter collection was presented. In 1959 Mme Ginette Spanier, directrice of the House of Balmain, described Browns of Chester as one of the best stores in the world.

In December 1960 the firm became part of the Peter Robinson department store, sector of the Montague Burton Group. In consequence Harris retired as chairman but turned to writing again. In the 1930s he had been interested in philosophy and psychology, and published a number of books and pamphlets. In the 1940s he had also begun lecturing widely on retail business efficiency, and from 1957 he developed the idea of unit cost accounting, a new method of pricing. He published *Profit and Personality in Retailing* (1961), with Ulric M. Spencer, and *Buyer's Market: How to Prepare for the New Era in Retailing* (1963), written with Mass-Observation Ltd. He also published, again with Mass-Observation, *Long to Reign over Us: the Status of the Royal Family in the Sixties* (1966). A fellow of the Royal Economic Society, Harris was appointed a JP in 1955. He was a member of the Liberal Party, serving on the national executive as well as working for the party in the north-west. He and his wife spent the last years of their lives in Monte Carlo. Harris died on 30 January 1989 at 133 avenue du Petit Juas, Cannes, France.   ANNE PIMLOTT BAKER

Sources H. D. Willcock, ed., *Browns and Chester: a Mass-Observation survey* (1947) · L. M. Harris, personal letters, 1940–60, U. Sussex, TC 24/5/C, vols. 9–22 · B. Lancaster, *The department store: a social history* (1995) · *Chester Chronicle* (28 Jan 1961) [report on retirement of L. M. Harris] · *Fashion and Fabrics* (Sept 1950) [profile of L. M. Harris. repr. in vol. 12 of *Personal letters*] · A. Adburgham, *Shops and shopping, 1800–1914: where, and in what manner the well-dressed Englishwoman bought her clothes*, 2nd edn (1981) · b. cert. · b. cert. [Leonard Mortimer Harris] · d. cert. · private information (2004)
Likenesses photograph (Leonard Mortimer Harris), repro. in *Chester Chronicle* · photographs (Leonard Mortimer Harris), repro. in Harris, *Personal letters* · portrait, priv. coll.; presented to Harris in 1938 · portrait (Leonard Mortimer Harris), Hans Galleries, London; presented, 1951
Wealth at death £13,545 2s. 10d.: probate, 30 Jan 1940, *CGPLA Eng. & Wales*

Harris, John Ryland [*pseud.* Ieuan Ddu o Lan Tawy] (1802–1823), author, was born at Swansea on 20 December 1802, the only son of Joseph *Harris (Gomer) (1773–1825), Baptist minister, author, and founder of the first Welsh-language newspaper. When nine years old he persuaded his parents to allow him to be apprenticed to a printer, and for the next four years he served as a compositor; in 1818 and 1819 his tasks included the printing of his father's newspaper, the *Seren Gomer*, and other works of importance. After this he attended a 'high-class' school and studied Latin, Greek, Hebrew, German, French, and Italian. His progress, however, was effected at the expense of his health, which had never been strong.

Harris's first literary effort, made when he was between eleven and twelve, was *Cymorth i chwerthin* ('Aids to laughter'), and it passed through two editions. His contributions to *Seren Gomer* from 1818 until 1823 were numerous and striking. They appeared anonymously, embraced a great variety of subjects, and soon arrested considerable attention. In 1819 W. O. Pughe sent him, in consideration of their merits, a copy of his *Coll gwynfa*, the Welsh translation of Milton's *Paradise Lost*, long passages of which Harris committed to memory. This probably induced him later on to undertake the translation of *Paradise Regained*, specimens of which appeared in the *Cambro Briton* and met with great approval.

In 1821 Harris carried on a warm controversy in the *Cambrian* concerning the Welsh language, which he passionately loved, and this brought him correspondence from many men of letters. He wrote two of the hymns in his father's hymn-book, and one of them long remained popular. An article of his appeared in the *Monthly Magazine* on the Welsh sounds 'ch' and 'll.' His last published work was *Grisiau cerdd arwest*, a guide to the reading of music which he type-set personally. Two large editions were speedily sold. At the time of his death he had a Welsh and English dictionary on a large scale in preparation, and had made some progress with his *Geirlyfr barddonol*, a kind of rhyming dictionary.

Harris died of consumption on 4 December 1823, when barely twenty-one. The memoir (*Cofiant Ieuan Ddu*) by his father is one of the most touching in the Welsh language.   R. M. J. JONES, rev. CLARE L. TAYLOR

Sources T. R. Roberts, *Eminent Welshmen: a short biographical dictionary* (1908)

Harris, John Wyndham Parkes Lucas Beynon [*pseud.* John Wyndham] (1903–1969), writer, was born at Dorridge, Knowle, Warwickshire on 10 July 1903, the elder son of George Beynon Harris (d. 1934), a barrister of Welsh descent, and his wife, Gertrude Parkes (d. 1953), the daughter of a Birmingham ironmaster. The younger son, Vivian Beynon Harris, became the author of four light novels published between 1948 and 1951. Because his parents separated when he was eight, John gained a wide experience of English preparatory schools before being sent to Bedales School from 1918 to 1921.

Wyndham became a handsome, tweedy kind of man. He tried his hand at several careers, including his father's profession of law, farming, commercial art, and advertising, but a small private income—coupled with something in his temperament—made it difficult for him to settle to anything. He began to write short stories, and an early affection for the novels of H. G. Wells prompted him towards science fiction. He sold a slogan to an American science-fiction magazine in 1930 and, encouraged by this minor success, wrote fiction published in American magazines like *Wonder Stories* and *Amazing Stories*, under the name of John Beynon Harris.

Honour demanded an attempt at the English market. The *Passing Show*, in its third midsummer double number for 20 July 1935, launched a new serial in nine parts, *The Secret People*, under the name John Beynon. Harris had gone, as Beynon sounded more literary. His was an unlikely tale of a man and woman captured by pygmies under a Sahara which was being flooded to create the New Sea; it was published as a book in 1936. It was successful enough to encourage both Wyndham and the magazine to try again for, in May 1936, the *Passing Show* began serialization of 'Stowaway to Mars', published as a book (*Planet Plane*) in the same year. Both these novels were reprinted in the 1970s.

The war brought a halt to this stop–go career. Wyndham became a civil servant and worked as a censor; later, in 1943, he joined the Royal Corps of Signals, working in a cipher office with the rank of corporal, and playing his part in the Normandy landings. After the war, Wyndham had to start again. He was a familiar figure at the Penn Club in Bedford Place, just off Russell Square in London, and knew the publisher Robert Lusty, then a director of Michael Joseph Ltd. With some diffidence and nonchalance, he consulted Lusty on the manuscript which Michael Joseph published in 1951, as *The Day of the Triffids*. In the same year it was serialized in five parts in *Collier's* magazine and from then on Wyndham's was a famous name—for he had shuffled through his generous supply of forenames and arrived at John Wyndham. His story of the perambulating vegetable menace which takes over a Britain stricken with blindness was an immediate success. The inferior MGM film version (1963) starred Howard Keel, and a BBC television adaptation appeared in 1981. The novel sold as well and steadily as a Penguin book as did any title by Agatha Christie.

The Kraken Wakes was published in 1953. The story is one of interstellar invaders who settle on the sea-bed and flood the land. It provides a chance for the type of mild surrealism—motor boats chugging up Oxford Street—which Wyndham enjoyed, and it increased his popularity. Wyndham's success sprang from portraying civilization under stress, while at the same time deploying middle-class values (the role of women and of the working class) which were already being questioned. His mild ironies serve as no defence against such critics as John Scarborough, who calls his work 'candidly anti-intellectual' (Scarborough, 223). Edward James, on the other hand, claims Wyndham was 'actually a disturbingly subversive voice' (James, 80). Wyndham's most powerful novel, *The Chrysalids*, was published in 1955; a puritanical post-nuclear war community in Labrador oppresses its children, exiling any with the slightest physical abnormalities. A group of children, however, develop telepathic powers and break free. A similar theme, this time with the children unsympathetically cast, emerged in *The Midwich Cuckoos* (1957), the story of a sleepy English village where all the women are astrally impregnated at the same time. The novel was filmed with notable success as *Village of the Damned* (1960), starring George Sanders. A sequel followed, *Children of the Damned* (1963), which owed less to Wyndham and more to commerce. *The Outward Urge* appeared in 1959. This time Wyndham had found a collaborator, Lucas Parkes, using up his two remaining forenames. This story depicted an English family, the Troons,

venturing into space, but Wyndham was less successful when operating in Arthur C. Clarke territory. Although *Trouble with Lichen* (1960) has its supporters, it is an indecisive attempt to tackle the debating point of 'Immortality: is it democratic?' *Chocky*, published in 1968—and ominously serialized in the magazine *Good Housekeeping*—was a too cosy account of a boy taken over by an interstellar something. An ITV television series was produced in 1984; two sequels followed. *Web*, a novel dealing with a Wyndham phobia, giant spiders, was published posthumously in 1979.

Among Wyndham's many short stories, collected in such volumes as *Jizzle* (1954) and *The Seeds of Time* (1956), special mention must be made of the collection *Consider her Ways* (1961), a strikingly nasty glimpse of a future world where men are extinct and gigantic breed mothers perpetuate the species.

On 26 July 1963 Wyndham married Grace Isabel Wilson (b. 1904), a teacher and long-term member of the Penn Club. They had no children. Wyndham died on 11 March 1969, at his home, Oakridge, Mill Lane, Steep, Petersfield, Hampshire.

As this critic has remarked elsewhere, Wyndham was the master of the 'cosy catastrophe' (Aldiss, 293). Although that vogue has passed, Wyndham's importance in the rebirth of British science fiction after the Second World War was second to none. His very English style ('the Trollope of science fiction', according to one reviewer), coupled with the Wellsian gift for exploring emotive ideas, brought him international success and encouraged others to strike out in the same way. Writers as diverse as John Christopher, Charles Eric Maine, J. G. Ballard, and Christopher Priest are in his debt. Indeed, it can be claimed that, however hesitatingly, Wyndham established a flourishing school of writers.

BRIAN W. ALDISS

Sources D. Tuck, *The encyclopaedia of science fiction and fantasy*, 1 (1974) · R. Lusty, *Bound to be read* (1974) · J. Scarborough, 'John Wyndham, 1903–1969', *Science fiction writers: critical studies of the major authors from the early nineteenth century to the present day*, ed. E. F. Bleiler (1982), 219–24 · N. Ruddick, *Ultimate island* (1993) · personal knowledge (2004) · E. James, *Science fiction in the twentieth century* (1994) · B. W. Aldiss, *Billion year spree: the history of science fiction* (1973) · b. cert. · d. cert. · *CGPLA Eng. & Wales* (1970) · m. cert.
Archives U. Lpool, Science Fiction Foundation
Wealth at death £70,799: probate, 6 Nov 1970, *CGPLA Eng. & Wales*

Harris, Joseph (*fl.* 1684–1703), actor and playwright, is of unknown origins. His first recorded roles date from the repertory of the United Company in 1684–5, probably at Drury Lane, London, when he doubled Duprete and the Yeoman of Sellar (cellar), according to the 1686 edition of John Fletcher's *Rollo, or, The Bloody Brother*. Harris seldom played anything but minor parts, twenty-five of which have been enumerated (see Highfill, Burnim & Langhans, *BDA*), and no doubt he appeared as an unrecorded supernumerary in many plays. When he did have a named character, his lines were usually few (for example Captain Noysey in Aphra Behn's *Luckey Chance*, the Music Master who begins Thomas Southerne's *Wives Excuse*) or none

(Guillamar in the Dryden–Purcell *King Arthur*). The level of Harris's roles suggests that he would not have been paid more than £2 per week, so he would probably have needed to supplement his earnings with other jobs. The turn to playwriting kept him in the theatre. Unfortunately, none of his three plays pleased his audience. In the preface to his tragicomedy *The Mistakes, or, The False Report* (acted 1690; published 1691), Harris acknowledged help from his colleague William Mountfort, who cut one scene and wrote another for him. Langbaine mentioned the 'Young Author' in the appendix to his *Account of the English Dramatic Poets* (1691), but was not encouraging about his prospects. Persevering, Harris was sworn in as a comedian-in-ordinary to the king and queen on 2 March 1692 (PRO, LC5/151, p. 35), a status not easily understandable from the traces of him that survive. In 1694 he signed the petition to the lord chamberlain protesting about the treatment of actors by a new management. On 2 March 1695 a Mr Sharples asked permission to sue Harris for a £6 unpaid note of hand (PRO, LC5/192, fol. 98).

Beginning in the spring of 1695, the newly licensed actors' co-operative at Lincoln's Inn Fields employed Harris as a hireling (Milhous and Hume, no. 1513). They mounted his version of John Webster's *Cure for a Cuckold* in March 1696, as *The City Bride, or, The Merry Cuckold*. It appears as one of several plays by actors in a list of those 'Damn'd', according to *A Comparison between the Two Stages*. In March 1699 Harris offered *Love's a Lottery, and Woman the Prize*, but neither the play nor the masque it included, *Love and Riches Reconcil'd*, seems to have been well received. Harris's name continued to turn up in new cast lists about once a year. His most extensive roles were those of the priest Feodor in Mary Pix's *Czar of Muscovy*, a failure, and the Duke in George Granville's *Jew of Venice*, which he played as late as 1703. However, the 'Mr Harris' in casts at other theatres between 1705 and 1715 was probably another person, nor can Joseph Harris be connected with certainty to the minor singer Mrs Harris. There is no documentable link between the actor and the panegyric poetry published between 1703 and 1714 by a Joseph Harris. The early part of his career is often entangled with those of the actors William Harris and Henry Harris. Joseph was identified by Gildon, probably inaccurately, as a brother of the organ builder Renatus Harris. Although Joseph Harris sustained a twenty-year career, much of it fell during a lull in the popularity of theatre, and he was not important enough to leave much trace.

JUDITH MILHOUS

Sources Highfill, Burnim & Langhans, *BDA*, vol. 7 · J. Milhous and R. D. Hume, eds., *A register of English theatrical documents, 1660–1737*, 2 vols. (1991) · J. Milhous, 'United Company finances, 1682–1692', *Theatre Research International*, 7 (1981–2), 37–53 · G. Langbaine, *An account of the English dramatick poets* (1691), appx · [C. Gildon], *The lives and characters of the English dramatick poets ... first begun by Mr Langbain* [1699] · S. B. Wells, ed., *A comparison between the two stages* (Princeton, 1942), 18 · PRO, LC5/151, p. 35, LC 5/192, fol. 98 · 'The London Stage', BM, Q1696 841.c.8[3] [copy] · T. Otway, *Venice preserv'd*, MS cast, BM, 841.c.8[3]

Harris, Joseph (*bap.* 1704, *d.* 1764), astronomer and assayer, the eldest son of Howel ap Howel, alias Harris

(1672?–1731), carpenter, and his wife, Susannah, *née* Powell (*d.* 1751), of Trefeca, Brecknockshire, was baptized at Talgarth on 16 February 1704. After being trained by his maternal uncle, Thomas Powell, the local blacksmith, he moved to London in May 1724 with a commendation to the astronomer royal, Edmond Halley, for mathematical proficiency. He went to sea the following year, probably as a teacher of navigation. His magnetic and eclipse observations made in Vera Cruz in 1726 and 1727 were published by the Royal Society, to whom they were submitted by Halley. At the request of the lord commissioners of the Admiralty, Halley examined and approved Harris's *Treatise of Navigation* (1730), which criticized navigation as conventionally taught for not reflecting shipboard realities. Harris's proposed design changes for the azimuth compass and the forestaff were ignored by manufacturers. His elementary exposition *The Description and Use of the Globes and the Orrery ... [and] of the Solar System* (1731) was reprinted fourteen times by 1793. A work on optical instruments was begun in 1742; two of four proposed parts were published posthumously in 1775.

Having been engaged by Colin Campbell FRS, Harris sailed for Jamaica early in 1731 'to assist him in his design of erecting an observatory for the improvement of Astronomy and the promoting of other parts of natural knowledge in that island' (J. Bradley, *Philosophical Transactions of the Royal Society*, 38, 1733–4, 307). Ill health forced his early return to London, but a series of magnetic observations made at sea were published by the Royal Society. Unsuccessful in his application for the mastership of the navigational school at Portsmouth (March 1733), Harris became tutor in the household of John Knight MP. In 1736 he gained employment at the Royal Mint, and in April 1737 was appointed deputy assay master to Hopton Haynes. He succeeded to the post of master's assay master in 1748 and king's assay master the following year. Soon after joining the mint Harris married Anne (*d.* 1763), the daughter of Thomas Jones of Tredustan.

Harris was convinced of the economic importance of maintaining the gold value of specie. His *Essay upon Money and Gold Coin* (1757–8) was highly regarded. When the Political Economy Club reissued the work, it was described as 'one of the best and most valuable treatises on the subject of money that has ever seen the light' (J. R. McCulloch, ed., *A Select Collection of Scarce and Valuable Tracts on Money*, 1856, xii). Harris's skill and ability were formally recognized by the mint in 1757, when he was granted a personal salary increase from £200 to £500 and allowed a deputy.

Harris was involved in comparisons between standard weights for the Royal Society in 1743, and in 1758–9 he advised and assisted the parliamentary committee chaired by John Proby, first Baron Carysfort, which tried to resolve the correct level and legal basis of metrological standards. Reference weights were made for Carysfort by Harris and adjusted against mint standards and others, and one of these (a troy pound of 1758) was adopted by parliament in 1824 as the primary British weight standard under the new imperial system.

Harris retained strong connections with Wales.

Although he was averse to the Calvinistic Methodism of his youngest brother, Howel *Harris, he supported the latter's endeavours, and remained a valued confidant. In later life he took an active interest in the Brecknockshire Agricultural Society, founded in 1755, to which he was elected an honorary member (1756). A long period of convalescence in 1761 was spent at Trefeca, where he observed the transit of Venus. He died in London on 26 September 1764, survived by an only child, Nanny (Hannah, or Annie, Maria), and was buried within the precincts of the Tower, where he had been living.

A second brother, **Thomas Harris** (*bap.* 1705, *d.* 1782), baptized at Talgarth on 6 January 1705, left Trefeca in 1728, and worked as a journeyman tailor in Bath before moving to London to join an uncle, Solomon Price. He had set up in business in his own right by 1732. In 1736, unable to finance an extravagant lifestyle, he went to Paris, but by 1738 was back in London. Social contacts with the fashionable set brought him lucrative contracts to supply clothing to the army, enabling him to buy land and property in and around Trefeca in 1763. Despite Howel Harris finding Thomas 'shut against truth', he nevertheless ordered militia uniform from him, and paid rent for land used by the Trefeca 'family'. Thomas had a house built at Tregunter and was sheriff of Brecknockshire in 1768. After his death on 23 September 1782, his estates passed to Joseph Harris's daughter, and not to his own three illegitimate children by a Miss or Mrs Robinson. The actress Mary Robinson married the feckless younger illegitimate son, Thomas Robinson, and their first daughter was born under Howel Harris's roof at Trefeca.

R. M. J. JONES, rev. D. J. BRYDEN

Sources M. H. Jones, 'Joseph Harris: an assay master of the mint', *Journal of the Welsh Bibliographical Society*, 3 (1929), 256–67 • M. H. Jones and R. T. Jenkins, eds., *The Trevacka letters* (1932) • T. Beynon, ed., *Howell Harris, reformer and soldier (1714–1773)* (1958) • T. Jones, *A history of the county of Brecknock*, 2 (1809), 334–7 • D. J. Bryden, 'The Jamaican observatories of Colin Campbell, FRS, and Alexander Macfarlane, FRS', *Notes and Records of the Royal Society*, 24 (1969–70), 261–72 • C. E. Challis, ed., *A new history of the royal mint* (1992) • 'Report from the committee appointed … to inquire into the original standards of weights and measures in this kingdom', *Reports from Committees of the House of Commons*, 2 (1737–65), 411–51, 453–63 [26 May 1758, 11 April 1759] • 'An account of a comparison lately made … of the standard of a yard, and the several weights … with the original standards of measures and weights in the exchequer', *PTRS*, 42 (1742–3), 541–56 • W. H. Miller, 'On the construction of the new imperial standard pound and its copies of platinum', *PTRS*, 146 (1856), 753–946
Archives BL, Add. MS 4435 • NL Wales, corresp.

Harris, Joseph (*c.*1745–1814), organist and composer, was born at Birmingham. He matriculated at Magdalen College, Oxford, on 16 March 1773, and took his BMus a week later, submitting the 'pleasantly unambitious' (Wollenberg) *Ode to May* as his examination exercise. Between 1766 and 1772 several of his vocal works were performed at the Holywell Music Room. In 1787 he was appointed organist of St Martin's, Birmingham. He published two collections of songs and one of music for harpsichord. He died in Liverpool in 1814.

L. M. MIDDLETON, rev. K. D. REYNOLDS

Sources A. Loewenberg, 'Harris, Joseph', *New Grove* • S. Wollenberg, 'Music and musicians', *Hist. U. Oxf.* 5: *18th-cent. Oxf.*, 865–87 • J. T. Bunce, *History of old St Martin's, Birmingham* (1875)

Harris, Joseph [*pseud.* Gomer] (**1773–1825**), Baptist minister, author, and journal editor, was born in 1773, probably in August, the eldest son of William Harris, a farm bailiff, at Llantydewi, Pembrokeshire. Harris was educated at local schools. A Baptist like his father, who had converted from the Anglican church, he was baptized at the Llangloffan Baptist Church in 1792 or 1793, where, two years later, at the height of the 1795 religious revival, he began to preach. He published a Baptist hymnbook in 1793, with a supplement in 1796. He married Martha Symons of Little Newcastle. Ordained in 1800, he assumed pastoral duties at the Back Street Chapel, Swansea. To improve his English he attended a one-year course at the Baptist academy in Bristol, but returned to Swansea after only four months. He published his *Bwyell Crist yn nghoed Anghrist* (1804) in an effort to resist a drift towards Arminianism in his congregation. He also opened a bookshop, kept a day-school, and produced a series of influential works in defence of Baptist theology, including *Pechod anfaddeuol* (1812) and *Traethawd ar briodol dduwdod ein harglwydd Iesu Grist* (1816–17).

In 1806 Harris, with Titus Lewis (1773–1811), launched *Y Drysorfa Efengylaidd*, a nonconformist magazine. He spent part of 1811 preaching in London, and attended the debate at the House of Lords at which Lord Sidmouth moved his motion to restrict the rights of nonconformists. This he reported in detail, in English, and is a fine example of his skill as a news reporter. His most significant contribution to the literature of Wales was made on 1 January 1814 when he first edited and published *Seren Gomer*, the first weekly newspaper ever to appear in the Welsh language (ten years after *The Cambrian*, the first Welsh newspaper in English, had appeared, also in Swansea). *Seren Gomer* was intended to provide a voice for nonconformity in the form of a popular newspaper and to defend the Welsh language 'against its enemies', seeking both to create a new readership and to 'purify and reform' the written language. *Seren Gomer* appeared weekly for eighty-five numbers until 9 September 1815, when it was discontinued due to lack of support, as a consequence of which it has been estimated that Harris and five other proprietors lost about £1000. One month earlier, in August 1815, he had been honoured by the Gwyneddigion Society in London with a medal for his services to Welsh literature. Harris returned to journalism in 1817 with a Baptist magazine, *Greal y Bedyddwyr*, and in January 1818 *Seren Gomer* reappeared as a fortnightly, non-denominational, nonconformist journal. It was discontinued in 1983, having been closely associated with the Baptists since 1859. The death of his only son, John Ryland *Harris, in 1823 prompted the publication in the same year of his tribute to him, *Cofiant Ieuan Ddu*. His final work was the publication of a bilingual Welsh and English Bible (1825). Harris died in Swansea on 10 August 1825.

ALED G. JONES

Sources *DWB* • T. M. Bassett, *The Welsh Baptists* (1977) • D. ap Rhys Stephen, *Gweithiau Awdurol y Diweddar Barch: Joseph Harris (Gomer)*

(1839), esp. iii–xxxii • E. Edmunds, 'Gomer', *Seren Gomer* (1897), 10–53 • E. W. Richard, 'Joseph Harris', *Y Traethodydd*, 1 (1845), 233–63 • T. Shankland, 'Joseph Harris a chychwyniad llenyddiaeth gyfnodol yng Nghymru', *Trafodion Cymdeithas Bedyddwyr Cymru* (1912–13), 9–58 • W. C. Williams, 'Gomer a'r dadeni llenyddol', *Seren Gomer* (1919), 26–38 • J. Samuel, *A sketch of the life, character and labours of the Rev. J. Harris … also an elegy* (1825) • DNB

Archives NL Wales, William Roberts (Nefydd) collection
Likenesses W. T. Fry, stipple, in or before 1826, NPG • portrait, NL Wales, MS 12,353D p.290

Harris, Joseph John (1799–1869), organist and composer, was born in London. For seven years he was in the choir of the Chapel Royal, St James's, under John Stafford Smith, and in 1823 he was appointed organist of St Olave's Church, Southwark. He held a similar position at Blackburn, Lancashire, from February 1828 to 1831, when he became singing-master and assistant organist at the Manchester collegiate church, now the cathedral. On 25 March 1848 he succeeded William Sudlow as organist and choirmaster of the cathedral. He was also for many years director of the Gentlemen's Glee Club and other societies in Manchester. He published *A selection of psalm and hymn tunes, adapted to the psalms and hymns used in the church of St Olave, Southwark* (1827), *The Cathedral Daily Service* (1844), and *The Musical Expression: a Guide for Parents* (1845), as well as anthems, glees, sacred songs, and piano pieces, including arrangements of operas by Weber and Rossini. Six chants and three arrangements for responses to the commandments are included in Joule's *Collection of Chants* (2nd edn, 1861). Harris died of congestion of the lungs at Manchester on 10 February 1869, leaving a widow, Elizabeth Mary Harris, of 11 Edward Street, Broughton Lane, Manchester.

Joseph Harris's son, **Joseph Thorne Harris** (1828–1868), was born in Bow, London. He was reputedly a musician of great talent and ability, a brilliant pianist and a prolific composer, some of whose works were published. He died at 4 Ebor Terrace, Sussex Street, Manchester, on 29 July 1868, about seven months before his father.

C. W. SUTTON, rev. DAVID J. GOLBY

Sources W. H. Husk, 'Harris, Joseph (John)', Grove, *Dict. mus.* (1954) • *Manchester Courier* (12 Feb 1869) • private information (1891) • d. cert. [Joseph Thorne Harris]
Wealth at death under £450: probate, 10 March 1869, CGPLA Eng. & Wales

Harris, Joseph Macdonald (1789–1860), composer, was born in London. He was a chorister at Westminster Abbey, and remained there until his voice broke, 'when he received from the dean and chapter a marked testimony of their approbation of his conduct' (*A Biographical and Historical Dictionary*, 332). He then studied under Robert Cooke, organist of the abbey. Harris published a number of songs, some duets and trios, glees, and piano music; and arranged Burgoyne's *Collection of Psalms and Hymns* (1827). He also taught the piano and singing, and conducted both public and private concerts. He was apparently confined in a lunatic asylum in 1843, and he died on 20 May 1860 at 1 Penton Street, Newington, Surrey.

L. M. MIDDLETON, rev. DAVID J. GOLBY

Sources [J. S. Sainsbury], ed., *A dictionary of musicians*, 2 vols. (1824), 332 • Brown & Stratton, *Brit. mus.* • J. D. Brown, *Biographical*

dictionary of musicians: with a bibliography of English writings on music (1886) • d. cert.

Harris, Joseph Thorne (1828–1868). *See under* Harris, Joseph John (1799–1869).

Harris, Leonard Mortimer (1903–1989). *See under* Harris, John Mortimer Green (1864–1939).

Harris, (Frederick) Leverton (1864–1926), politician and art collector, the eldest son of Frederick William Harris (1833–1917), shipowner of Norwood, London, and his wife, Elizabeth Rachel, daughter of Peter Macleod Wylie, was born at Norwood on 17 December 1864. His family were of Quaker background. The traveller Walter Burton Harris was his younger brother. He was educated at Winchester College (1878–81) and then at Gonville and Caius College, Cambridge (1881–4), where he gained a second class in the natural sciences tripos. He then joined his father's firm, Harris and Dixon, long established coal factors and shipowners in London. In 1886 he married Gertrude, daughter of John G. Richardson, of Moyallon, co. Down, and Bessbrook, co. Armagh; they had no children.

In 1900 Leverton Harris entered parliament as the Conservative member for Tynemouth, Northumberland, and held the seat for six years. He next sat for Stepney in London as a Unionist from 1907 to 1910, and then succeeded Austen Chamberlain as the member for East Worcestershire from 1914 to 1918. He was an old family friend of the Chamberlains and, as an enthusiastic supporter of Joseph Chamberlain's tariff reform campaign, he sat on the tariff commission formed by Chamberlain in 1904. He was also a member of the London county council from 1907 to 1910.

Shipping and trade were Harris's main areas of policy expertise and interest. He strongly, and successfully, opposed the attempts to have enshrined in legislation limits on the powers to search vessels at sea suspected of carrying contraband, as agreed to in the international declaration of London (1909).

With the outbreak of the First World War, Leverton Harris joined the trade division of the Admiralty with the honorary rank of lieutenant, Royal Naval Volunteer Reserve. He was made adviser in commerce and promoted commander in February 1915, and in 1916 was sworn of the privy council. In June 1916 he was placed in control of the Restriction of Enemy Supplies Department under the Foreign Office, and from December 1916 to January 1919 he was under-secretary to the ministry of blockade. He was very effective in this role. He developed schemes for diverting supplies of cotton from Germany before it had been declared contraband, and for stopping her imports of copper and meat. After visiting Norway in July 1916 and meeting its leading fish exporters he succeeded in diverting to Britain 85 per cent of all Norwegian fish and fish oil, although this was offset by the 'extraordinary activity' of parts of the Danish fishing fleet which still supplied Germany (Bell, 606). The American ambassador of that time described Leverton Harris as: 'The man who really makes the blockade … He and Lloyd George are the two most energetic men that I know of in this kingdom. ... This gentle, resolute, quiet man sits guardian at all the gates of Germany' (*Life and Letters of Walter Hines Page*, 3.311).

But Harris's career was badly damaged by political scandals which erupted in June 1918 regarding both him and his wife. First, Gertrude Harris was accused of visiting in prison an interned German, Baron Leopold Plessen, and of being 'the medium of carrying correspondence or parcels' to him (*The Times*, 16 Nov 1926, 16), which she denied. Mrs Harris explained that the baron's mother was an old family friend and that 'the boy, until the war broke out, was an undergraduate at Oxford' (Searle, 253). But the furore increased four days later when Leverton Harris was also accused of having, when at the trade division of the Admiralty, secured favourable treatment for his family firm. Although denying the charge, Harris offered his resignation, but after his chief at the blockade ministry, Lord Robert Cecil, threatened also to resign in support, Harris remained in his post. He declined, however, to stand again at the general election later that year, because of his concern, he said, that 'the contest would be fought on personal lines' (*The Times*, 16 Nov 1926, 16). Cecil expressed his regret that Harris's 'sensitiveness to unjust attack cut short a career of great public usefulness' (Searle, 255).

In 1919 Harris succeeded Cecil as chairman of the economic council in Paris. He was made an officer of the Légion d'honneur in France, and of the order of Sts Maurice and Lazarus in Italy, and was confirmed in the rank of honorary captain, Royal Naval Volunteer Reserve, for the Tyne division.

Outside his public career Harris was also a noted collector of art and antiques. His substantial collection of maiolica, which he began to form during a pre-war visit to Siena with Austen Chamberlain, provided an extremely important historical representation of the development of this type of decorated earthenware. This was later the basis for the great expansion of the maiolica collection of the Fitzwilliam Museum at Cambridge. In a bequest to the museum he also left £10,000, which established the Leverton Harris fund and was used for further important purchases. In 1906 Harris had been left by his uncle the property Camilla Lacey in Dorking, the former home of the eighteenth-century writer Fanny Burney, and which still housed many of her possessions and manuscripts, and a collection of antiques, to which Harris added greatly. But in a 'personal catastrophe' for Harris in 1919 (Poole, xviii), the house and its contents were destroyed in a fire. But Harris began to form another major collection, which upon his death was dispersed to the Victoria and Albert and British museums, and the National Portrait Gallery as well as the Fitzwilliam.

Harris was honorary secretary of the Contemporary Art Society from 1923 until his death, and he served on the sites committee of the office of works from 1922 to 1924. During the last six years of his life he began to paint, studied at the Slade School, and in April 1926 an exhibition of fifty of his oil paintings was held at the Goupil Gallery, although they received only faint praise. On 14 November

1926 Harris died from angina pectoris at his home at 70 Grosvenor Street, London. His funeral took place four days later at St George's, Hanover Square.

H. S. EDE, rev. MARC BRODIE

Sources *The Times* (16 Nov 1926) · *The Times* (19 Nov 1926) · G. R. Searle, *Corruption in British politics, 1895–1930* (1987) · J. E. Poole, *Italian maiolica and incised slipware in the Fitzwilliam Museum, Cambridge* (1995) · A. C. Bell, *A history of the blockade of Germany* (1937) · *Life and letters of Walter Hines Page*, ed. B. J. Hendrick, 3 (1926) · J. B. Wainewright, ed., *Winchester College, 1836–1906: a register* (1907) · *WWW* · Venn, *Alum. Cant.* · B. K. Murray, *The people's budget, 1909/10: Lloyd George and liberal politics* (1980)

Archives BLPES, letters to Tariff Commission · HLRO, corresp. with Andrew Bonar Law | FILM BFI NFTVA, documentary footage

Likenesses W. Stoneman, photograph, 1923, NPG · Spy [L. Ward], caricature, Henschel-colourtype, NPG; repro. in *VF* (30 Dec 1909)

Wealth at death £265,108 6s. 8d.: resworn probate, 15 Feb 1927, CGPLA Eng. & Wales

Harris, Margaret Frances (1904–2000). *See under* Motley (*act.* 1921–c.1975).

Harris, Maria (*fl.* 1769–1796). *See under* Smith, Theodore (*fl.* c.1765–c.1810x23).

Harris, Moses (1730–c.1788), entomologist and artist, was born in Churchyard Alley, Holborn, London, on 15 April 1730, the son of Joseph Harris and his wife, Mary. He had at least two brothers, William and John, the latter a harpsichord maker who emigrated to America in 1767. From an early age Harris showed great enthusiasm for entomology, which was encouraged by an uncle of the same name who was a member of the Society of Aurelians. In 1742 Harris's own application to join the society was, not surprisingly, rejected on grounds of his youth (he was twelve) and lack of 'sufficient Sagacity'. Tragically, the society's meeting-place, the Swan tavern in Cornhill, London, was destroyed by fire on 25 March (new year's day) 1748 and all its property lost; the new society, formed in 1762 with Harris as secretary, lasted only four years.

In 1744 Harris was apprenticed to the geographer Charles Price. However, he did not complete his apprenticeship and with his wife travelled to Halifax, Nova Scotia, aboard the *Winchelsea*, one of the thirteen transports carrying the colony's first settlers. He arrived in June 1749 and was soon drawing the pictures of Halifax plants that were later reproduced in the *Gentleman's Magazine*. He may also have been active in drawing plans of the proposed new settlement and its environs—his name appears as that of the surveyor of 'a view of HALIFAX Drawn from ye Topmasthead' dated October 1749, published by Edward Ryland and afterwards by Thomas Jeffreys. There is no evidence that Harris stayed long in Canada, and it is likely he remained there less than a year before returning to London to pursue his interests in natural history and art.

On his own admission Harris lacked a liberal education, but he was a clever practical entomologist as well as an accurate artist, who drew, engraved, and coloured all his own works; he was also a miniature painter of some renown. *Proposals* (1758) for the publication of his *magnum opus*, *The Aurelian, or, Natural History of English Insects*, included various addresses in London for the receipt of or, *The Aurelian's Pocket Companion* (1775), which contained much advice not previously comprehensively published; it invariably accompanied him on his frequent collecting trips. He also executed a number of illustrations for natural history works of other authors, probably the best known being Dru Drury's three-volume *Illustrations of Natural History* (1770–82), of which Harris signed most of the 150 fine plates.

Harris died *c*.1788, survived by his wife and at least one child, John *Harris (1767–1832), who with his son John *Harris (1791–1873) achieved great distinction in branches of the fine arts. ROBERT MAYS

Sources A. A. Lisney, 'Moses Harris', *A bibliography of British lepidoptera, 1608–1799* (1960), 156–75 · D. Drury, 'Letters to John and Moses Harris, 1768–1770', Letterbook, 1761–1783, NHM, entomology library · P. J. Weimerskirch, 'John Harris, sr., 1767–1832: a memoir by his son', *Book Collector*, 42 (1993), 245–52 · M. Harris, *The Aurelian, or, Natural history of English insects*, ed. R. H. Mays (1986) · R. S. Wilkinson, 'English entomological methods in the seventeenth and eighteenth centuries': pt 3, 'Moses Harris' *The Aurelian*', *Entomologist's Record*, 80 (1968), 193–200 · R. S. Wilkinson, 'Another fascicule of Moses Harris' *An exposition of English insects*', *Entomologist's Record*, 92 (1980), 143–4 [1776] · H. Hagan, 'Moses Harris', *Weekly Intelligencer*, 10 (1861), 181–3 · *Bibliotheca Entomologica*, 1 (1862) · F. J. Buckell, 'History of butterfly classification', *Entomologist's Record*, 4 (1893), 315–16 · E. Kilmurray, *Dictionary of British portraiture*, 2 (1979), 102 · E. R. Goffe, 'The Syrphidae (Diptera) of Moses Harris, 1776', *Entomologist's Monthly Magazine*, 82 (1946), 67–86 · R. L. Coe, 'On the Syrphidae (Diptera) of Moses Harris', *The Entomologist*, 83 (1950), 149–61 · E. R. Goffe, 'The Syrphidae (Diptera): described by Moses Harris in 1776', *The Entomologist*, 84 (1951), 195–204 · parish register, Holborn, St Andrew, 27 April 1730 [baptism] · *Journal of the commissioners for trade and plantations*, [vol. 8]: *From January 1741/2 to December 1749* (1930), esp. 1748–9 · T. B. Akins, ed., *Selection from the public documents of the province of Nova Scotia* (1869), 513 · apprentice records of Merchant Taylors' Company, GL, 273
Likenesses M. Harris, self-portrait, etching, 1780, AM Oxf., BM; repro. in M. Harris, *An exposition of English insects* (*c*.1780) [*see illus.*] · etching, BM; repro. in M. Harris, *The Aurelian, or, Natural history of English insects* (1766)

Moses Harris (1730–*c*.1788), self-portrait, 1780

subscriptions, but his residence at that time is unrecorded; however, in 1768 he was known to be living in Deptford, near Greenwich. He moved shortly afterwards to Crayford, Kent, to the irritation of his patron and fellow entomologist Dru Drury, who in 1770 pleaded with him to move closer to London. Publication of *The Aurelian* commenced in December 1758. Finally completed in 1766, it was issued in parts, of which only parts 1 to 4 have been separately located. There were forty-one plates, and four more (the 'Supplement') were added in the second issue (*c*.1773). Later editions, with issues of various dates and contents, were dated 1778, 1794, and 1840 (ed. J. O. Westwood). In 1986 the first edition was reproduced with a new introduction and commentaries.

Contemporary with production of *The Aurelian* Harris published the pioneering *Natural System of Colours* (1766), which Thomas Martyn edited in 1811; a facsimile of the extremely rare original edition was published in America in 1963. A scarce and scientifically important treatise followed (*c*.1767), entitled *An Essay Precedeing a Supplement to 'The Aurelian'*: it established a classification of Lepidoptera based on wing venation and included eight coloured engraved plates. This was incorporated in *Exposition of English Insects* (dated 1776, but not published until 1780), considered by many Harris's principal scientific work. It was of particular value to dipterists, and notable also for the author's self-portrait at the age of forty-nine (dated 1780). There was also an issue of 1781, a second edition in 1782, and finally an issue of 1786. Thirty years' experience was gathered in his popular handbook *The English Lepidoptera*,

Harris, Paul. *See* Green, Paul (*b.* 1573?, *d.* in or after 1642).

Harris, Sir Percy Alfred, first baronet (1876–1952), politician, was born at 197 Queen's Gate, London, on 6 March 1876, the younger son of Wolf Harris (1834–1926) and his wife, Elizabeth (*d.* 1928), daughter of David Nathan, general dealer, of Auckland, New Zealand. He was educated at Harrow School (where Winston Churchill was a slightly older contemporary) and at Trinity Hall, Cambridge, where he obtained a third class in the historical tripos in 1897. Two years later he was called to the bar by the Middle Temple, but never practised. On 1 April 1901 he married Marguerite Frieda (*d.* 1962), younger daughter of John Astley Bloxam, a well-known London surgeon. She was an artist of merit. They had two sons.

Harris was for some years engaged in the prosperous wholesale and manufacturing firm of Bing Harris, which his father had co-founded in New Zealand. Harris first helped to look after the London office, then spent three years in New Zealand. His lifelong interest in that country found expression in his book *New Zealand and its Politics* (1909).

Harris returned to England in 1903. Thenceforward his

Sir Percy Alfred Harris, first baronet (1876–1952), by unknown photographer

main interest was in politics, where he took his stand firmly on the Liberal side. These were the years leading up to the great Liberal triumph of 1906, when Harris contested Ashford; but this was a Conservative stronghold and he was narrowly defeated. In 1907 he was elected a Progressive (Liberal) member of the London county council for South-West Bethnal Green, thus beginning a close association with the borough which lasted until the end of his life. His success coincided with his party's loss of the control over London's government which it had held since the council's establishment in 1889 but was never to enjoy again. Nevertheless, he played an important part in the work of the council, becoming chief Progressive whip in 1912 and deputy chairman in 1915–16. His book *London and its Government* (1913, rewritten 1931) was considered a standard work of its kind. His special interest and knowledge were in those matters which particularly concerned his constituents, although some of these problems, such as education, housing, and unemployment, were of nationwide as well as local significance.

After defeat at Harrow in January 1910 Harris entered parliament at a by-election at Market Harborough in 1916. In the intervening period he had taken a lead in the formation of the Volunteer Training Corps in 1914, bringing him to national attention. His main work in the short remainder of the wartime parliament was as a member of the select committee on national expenditure, of which he was also a member during the Second World War. In the election which followed the armistice in 1918 he suffered for his loyalty to Asquith, and the refusal of the 'coupon' by the coalition leaders was sufficient to ensure his defeat.

In 1922 Harris returned to parliament as member for South-West Bethnal Green, a constituency he had been offered as long ago as 1911. Amid the rising and more often falling hopes of a Liberal revival he won affection and respect as an industrious, knowledgeable, and independent-minded member. He was created a baronet in January 1932, and was chief Liberal whip between 1935 and 1945. In 1940, on Churchill's recommendation, he was sworn of the privy council. He was acting leader of the Liberal Party from 1940 to 1945 while Sir Archibald Sinclair

held a government post. He was also secretary of the Inter-Parliamentary Union from 1935 to 1945 and, in 1940, established the Liberal Party's committee on post-war reconstruction, the first of its kind.

Perhaps Harris's most remarkable feat was to hold Bethnal Green against all comers in six successive general elections; for years his constituency was the only Liberal seat in or within 100 miles of London. He did so by assiduously building up voluntary organizations such as the Bethnal Green Men's Institute and by holding weekly surgeries, as a result of which Harris's agent, George Holmes, became known as the 'poor man's lawyer' (*The Star*). These activities were not innovations in Bethnal Green's political life but were later claimed as antecedents of Liberal community politics.

Harris's defeat in 1945 was not the end of his association with Bethnal Green, for in the next year he won back the seat on the London county council, which he had unexpectedly lost in 1934. In 1949 he was the only Liberal returned to that body in an election which resulted in the two main parties having an equal number of supporters. David Low produced a cartoon depicting him as the dictator of London, but any hopes or fears in this respect were quickly dissipated when the allocation of aldermanic seats took place. Nevertheless, he campaigned tirelessly on education matters and spoke out against the construction of tower blocks.

Percy Harris was a big, rubicund, extrovert man, who seemed to meet most people and situations with a beaming smile. It could not be claimed that he was either an orator or an original political thinker. The guiding principles of his career were an unfailing sympathy for the oppressed and the unlucky, and an inflexible loyalty to the Liberal cause. During his party's long decline many members of its radical wing found their way into the Labour camp, but he showed no inclination to follow. He died at 31 Queen's Gate, London, on 28 June 1952, and was buried on 2 July at St Nicholas's Church, Chiswick Mall, Chiswick.   FRANK MILTON, *rev.* ROBERT INGHAM

Sources P. Harris, *Forty years in and out of parliament* (1946) · *The Times* (30 June 1952) · *WWW, 1951–60* · Burke, *Peerage* (1939) · Venn, *Alum. Cant.* · T. Cowley, *Liberator*, 210 (Jan 1993) · *Bethnal Green Special* (7 March 1946) [Bancroft Road Library, Tower Hamlets, London, press cutting boxes 320.2, 321.4, 321.5] · *East End News* (4 July 1952) [Bancroft Road Library, Tower Hamlets, London, press cutting boxes 320.2, 321.4, 321.5] · *East End News* (11 July 1952) [Bancroft Road Library, Tower Hamlets, London, press cutting boxes 320.2, 321.4, 321.5] · *East London Advertiser* (4 July 1952) [Bancroft Road Library, Tower Hamlets, London, press cutting boxes 320.2, 321.4, 321.5] · *The Star* (20 Feb 1937) [Bancroft Road Library, Tower Hamlets, London, press cutting boxes 320.2, 321.4, 321.5] · *East London Observer* (24 Oct 1936) [Bancroft Road Library, Tower Hamlets, London, press cutting boxes 320.2, 321.4, 321.5] · *Jewish Chronicle* (4 July 1952) · D. Brack and M. Baines, eds., *Dictionary of liberal biography* (1998) · H. Pelling, *Social geography of British elections, 1885–1910* (1969)

Archives HLRO, MSS | HLRO, letters to Lloyd George | FILM BFI NFTVA · Reuters, London, news footage

Likenesses D. Low, cartoon, 1949 · photographs, repro. in Harris, *Forty years in and out of parliament* [see illus.]

Wealth at death £56,400 3s. 1d.: probate, 11 Sept 1952, CGPLA Eng. & Wales

Harris, Sir Percy Wyn- (1903–1979), colonial governor and mountaineer, was born at 1 Cumberland Road, Acton, Middlesex, on 24 August 1903, the eldest of the three sons and the second of the five children of Percy Martin Harris, managing director of a firm of builders' merchants and JP, and his wife, Catherine Mary Davies. He was educated at Gresham's School and at Gonville and Caius College, Cambridge, where he obtained a second class in part one of the natural sciences tripos in 1925. At Cambridge he gained a half-blue for cross-country running and was secretary of the Mountaineering Club, which pioneered the guideless climbs then frowned on by the alpine establishment. He aspired to a career in business, but having found vacation work in a cement works and, on going down, employment as a moulder in the family iron foundry far too dull, he applied for the Sudan political service and for the colonial service.

Accepted for the latter and posted to Kenya in 1926, Harris (he added the hyphen in 1953, having been named Wynne on his birth certificate) was to spend the next twenty years in district administration, rising steadily from district officer to settlement officer for Kikuyu land claims in 1939–40 generated by the Carter commission of 1932, to district commissioner among nomadic Turkana, in crowded Kakamega, urban Nairobi, in Kitui and Nyeri, and to provincial commissioner in 1945. In 1944–6 he was labour commissioner (his department's memorandum was one of the administration's earliest proposals to solve the squatter problem), and from 1947 to 1949 he was chief native commissioner and member for African affairs on the governor's executive council. His appointment as governor of the Gambia in 1949 was to result in its longest governorship since the turn of the twentieth century. He quickly galvanized the place, for he was, as Elspeth Huxley once said, 'not the sort to paddle backwards' (Huxley, 11).

On retirement to Suffolk in 1958, it was not long before Wyn-Harris's profound and sympathetic experience of African administration was re-invoked. In 1959 he was appointed as a member of the commission of inquiry led by Sir Patrick Devlin into the disturbances which had rocked Nyasaland and resulted in the arrest of the nationalist leader Hastings Banda. When it came to drafting the report (*Parl. papers*, 1958–9, 10, Cmnd 814), Wyn-Harris, 'torn between loyalty to the Service of which he had long been a distinguished member' and the apparent disloyalty of submitting a separate opinion (Baker, 146), disagreed with Devlin's final section in which Sir Robert Armitage's government was condemned for abuse of power. His fellow commissioner E. T. Williams eventually talked him out of submitting a minority report, though, as he acknowledged many years later, it was a case of getting Wyn-Harris to 'agree to the report which turned his back on his whole career' (ibid., 149). It was perhaps ironic that, had the Colonial Office not changed its mind on who should succeed Sir Geoffrey Colby as governor of Nyasaland in 1956, it could well have been Wyn-Harris standing in Armitage's shoes.

No sooner was this difficult task completed than Wyn-

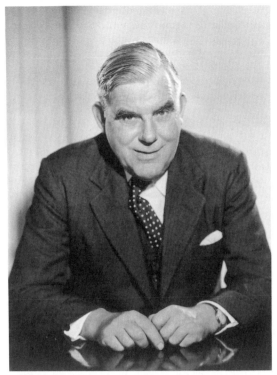

Sir Percy Wyn-Harris (1903–1979), by Walter Bird, 1959

Harris was again called upon, to take on the post, unique in decolonizing Africa, of Britain's administrator of the northern Cameroons during the interim period of the United Nations-supervised plebiscite on the future of the trust territory areas of Northern Nigeria, from October 1960 to June 1961. His relationships with some of the expatriate administrators as well as the political leaders of Nigeria, by then an independent country, required all Wyn-Harris's gifted combination of correctness, courage, and courtesy.

But if Wyn-Harris made his mark as a notable colonial administrator, he also made his name as a distinguished mountaineer. Taking advantage of his posting to Kenya, he profited from his local leaves and in 1929, along with Eric Shipton, at that time a young settler, he made a successful ascent of the Batian peak of Mount Kenya, only the second such climb since Halford Mackinder reached the summit in the 1890s; they also became the first mountaineers to scale its other peak, Nelion. Two years later another first came Wyn-Harris's way, his visit to North Island on Lake Rudolf. Then, despite the routine of district life in Kenya, he earned a place among the fourteen picked for the 1933 assault on Mount Everest led by Hugh Ruttledge. With the blessing of the colonial government but without pay, he and L. R. Wager, another newcomer to the Himalayas, participated in the first ascent, reaching an altitude of 28,000 feet. It was Wyn-Harris who retrieved the ice axe, probably that of G. L. Mallory, from the site of the 1924 disaster. When the 1936 Everest expedition was assembled, again led by Hugh Ruttledge, Wyn-Harris's reputation at once ensured his nomination. On both expeditions he narrowly missed death on the slopes. Subsequently Sir John Hunt, who led the triumphant 1953 Everest expedition, was to number him among the 'stout spirits' of the Everest saga (Hunt, 9).

If Wyn-Harris's transfer from mountainous Kenya to sea-level Gambia spelt finis to one recreation, it was not to end his prominence as a sportsman. In the Atlantic-swept estuary off Bathurst he took up sailing, long a second string to his recreational bow (in Nairobi, he had built his own boat in his garden). He spent his leaves in the discomfort of a 4 ton yawl, sailed single-handed to Accra to attend Ghana's independence celebrations, and in his retirement was to fill the years 1962–9 unhurriedly circumnavigating the world in nothing more solid than a 12 ton sloop, the *Spurwing*. As chief commissioner in Kenya, he had already exploited his ability to fly solo by making sudden safaris to outlying bomas. Determined and adventurous rather than a master of do-it-yourself (he was, in fact, all fingers and thumbs in his construction work), and an amateur photographer who had filmed the 1933 Everest expedition, Wyn-Harris was an obvious choice to tour the dominions as the special representative of the duke of Edinburgh's award in 1962–3. Wyn-Harris was twice married. On 22 December 1932 he married Mary Moata (Mo; *b.* 1897/8), daughter of Ranald Macintosh Macdonald CBE, civil engineer, of Christchurch, New Zealand. She died in 1976, and on 7 September that year he married Jacoba Julie Daniela Gunning-Scheltema (*b.* 1902/3), daughter of Hugo Scheltema, a tobacco merchant, and widow of Maximiliaan Frederik Gunning, a Dutch naval architect and member of the Royal Institution of Naval Architects. From the first marriage there was one son, Timothy, born in 1934.

Quick of speech and friendly, yet with a positive sense of authority in his build (that of the ideal mountaineer) and manner, P. Wyn, as he was widely known, was tough, stocky, and 'packed with Welsh pugnacity and vigour. ... The quality of leadership is there' (Huxley, 11, 29). A glutton for work, he was intolerant of slovenly standards and disloyalty to the service. His own deep loyalty to that service was boldly displayed in his rejection of the first draft of the Devlin commission's conclusions.

Wyn-Harris was appointed MBE in 1941 and CMG in 1949, being advanced to KCMG in 1952. He was made knight of the order of St John of Jerusalem in 1950. Wyn-Harris died at his home, Little Hawsted, Steep, Petersfield, Hampshire, on 25 February 1979.

A. H. M. KIRK-GREENE

Sources P. W. Harris, autobiography, Bodl. RH · *The Times* (23 Nov 1979) · *The Times* (17 Dec 1979) · *West Africa* (19 Nov 1949) · C. Baker, *State of emergency: crisis in central Africa, Nyasaland, 1959–1960* (1997) · E. Huxley, *Four guineas: a journey through west Africa* (1954) · J. Hunt, *The ascent of Everest* (1953) · W. H. Murray, *The story of Everest* (1953) · C. Chevenix Trench, *Men who ruled Kenya* (1993) · A. H. M. Kirk-Greene, *A biographical dictionary of the British colonial governor* (1980) · *CGPLA Eng. & Wales* (1979) · b. cert. · m. certs. · d. cert. · private information (1986)
Archives Bodl. RH
Likenesses W. Bird, photograph, 1959, NPG [*see illus.*]

Wealth at death £203,747: probate, 25 June 1979, *CGPLA Eng. & Wales*

Harris, Reginald Hargreaves [Reg] (1920–1992), cyclist, was born Reginald Hargreaves at 7 Garden Street, Bury, Lancashire, on 1 March 1920, the son of Elsie Hargreaves, cotton weaver. He acquired the surname Harris following his mother's marriage to Joseph Harris, engineer and businessman. His first job was as an apprentice motor mechanic but he soon moved from the workshop to the showroom, which also sold cycles. He joined the Bury branch of the Cyclists' Touring Club and then the Lancashire Road Club, where his promise produced an invitation to train with the club star. He was soon cycling in every free moment, half-day closing afternoon, summer evenings, and Sundays. He began to enter competitions such as 100 mile reliability trials, and to win prizes at local events. His employers were obviously impressed because they gave him a new bike, but he soon moved to a slipper factory, where the pay was better and then to a paper mill where, with plenty of overtime, he calculated that he could earn enough during the winter to allow him to concentrate on his cycling in the summer. His first sprint races were on Lancashire grass tracks in 1936, and he began to compete successfully against men ten years older than himself. With the overtime and the sale of the prizes that he was beginning to collect he bought new and better machines, and in 1937 gave up his job in the paper mill to concentrate full-time on the cycling season.

In 1938 Harris joined the Bury athletics club and won half a dozen races in the north of England, including the Wells bequest trophy, the first time he had beaten some of the best of the opposition. In 1939 he changed clubs again, to the prestigious Manchester Wheelers, and although disappointed by his performance in the British championship he was still selected for the world championships to be held in September in Milan. The team was withdrawn on the outbreak of the Second World War.

Harris liked to say that he was one of the few people who came out of the army less fit than he went in. He drove a tank for the 10th hussars in north Africa but was wounded, invalided home, and transferred to the Royal Army Service Corps. He was then discharged from the army as medically unfit, but barely a year later he had won three titles at the national cycling championship in 1944: the 1000 yards, 5 miles, and quarter-mile. In 1945 he repeated the feat by winning the 1000 yards and quarter-mile on the track and the half-mile on grass. He was invited to race in Paris, where he excited the crowd and won several big races. It was after these successes that Claud Butler, the lightweight cycle manufacturer, agreed to provide him not only with all his equipment but also with a job. This was pushing up against the sports amateur–professional boundaries in Britain. But it paid off for both of them when Harris won the world title in 1947 in Paris, the first British rider to do so since Harold Johnson in 1922.

Harris thought he might win three gold medals in the Olympic games in London in 1948, but three months

Reginald Hargreaves Harris (1920–1992), by Bert Hardy, 1947

before they were due to begin he fractured two vertebrae in his back in a car accident. Determined to get fit after several weeks in hospital he began training, racing, and winning, only to fracture an elbow after a fall in a 10 mile race at the Fallowfield track. Though still very sore, he continued to train with the elbow in a plaster cast and (perhaps to show his rivals and the selectors) rode a kilometre time-trial in the rain and equalled the British empire games record. But he had to be satisfied with Olympic silver medals in both the individual and tandem sprints.

The next step for Harris was to turn professional, even though he was already running a Mark IV Jaguar as an amateur. He signed up with the Raleigh Cycle Company for £1000 a year, a £100 bonus if he became world champion, £50 for every grand prix victory, and £25 every time he broke the British record. He probably earned £12,000 a year from racing in the early 1950s. He won the world sprint title in 1949, the first Englishman to win a professional title and the first man ever to do it in his professional début season. He also won in 1950, 1951, and 1954. In 1952 the rules were changed to allow three finalists instead of two, and in the final of that year the Swiss rider Oskar Plattner blocked Harris so that 'the flying Dutchman' Arie Van Vliet could win. At the end-of-season meeting of champions at Herne Hill, Harris destroyed Plattner in a revenge match before an ecstatic crowd. He retired in 1957 but returned in 1971 at fifty-one, and won the British title again in 1974, just to show what he thought of the younger generation of cycle racers.

All forms of sport reached new levels of popularity in the years immediately following the Second World War,

but British cycling had no great competitive tradition until Harris established one more or less single-handed. His physique was phenomenal, his training routines ferocious, and his will to win formidable. He had an indomitable spirit, and returned as sharp as ever after accidents that would have daunted lesser men. His five world records set as a professional stood for many years. Two years running he was named sportsman of the year, a star whose name was as familiar to the British and European public as Stanley Matthews or Stirling Moss. His debonair good looks dominated Raleigh's advertising campaigns for a decade. His sporting achievements were recognized with an OBE in 1958. Nevertheless he had little patience with what he saw as the amateurish administrators of British cycling.

Harris married, first, on 7 April 1945, Florence Stage (b. 1923/4), the daughter of William Stage, licensed victualler, of Bury. The marriage ended in divorce, and on 29 March 1955 he married, second, Dorothy Hadfield (b. 1926/7), secretary, and the daughter of Henry Hadfield, master fruiterer. This marriage also ended in divorce, and on 25 September 1970 he married, third, Jennifer Anne Geary, née Brazendale (b. 1944/5), daughter of James George Brazendale, electrical engineer. Following his retirement from professional cycling he had a number of businesses, including running a garage and a cycle-building company, and becoming a director of a firm making plastic foam. His individualism made him a somewhat erratic businessman, with little taste for delegating or negotiating. He smoked a pipe and liked a glass of wine, but cycling was the most important thing in his life. Even at seventy-two, after an operation for a snapped ankle tendon, he was on his bike when he had a minor stroke. Two days later, on 22 June 1992, he died of another stroke, at Macclesfield District General Hospital. He was survived by his third wife, Jennifer.

TONY MASON

Sources R. Harris, *Two wheels to the top: an autobiography* (1976) · G. Houston Bowden, *The story of the Raleigh cycle* (1975) · *The Guardian* (24 June 1992) · *The Independent* (23 June 1992) · *The Times* (23 June 1992); (4 July 1992) · b. cert. · m. cert. · d. cert.

Likenesses B. Hardy, photograph, 1947, Hult. Arch. [*see illus.*] · photograph, 1956, repro. in *The Independent* · photograph, repro. in *The Times* (23 June 1992) · photograph, repro. in *The Times* (4 July 1992)

Harris, Renatus [René] (*c.*1652–1724), organ builder, was born in Brittany, the second of four children of **Thomas Harrison** (*fl.* 1652–1674) and his wife, Katherine, daughter of the organ builder Thomas *Dallam, both English exiles in France during the Commonwealth. Soon after the Restoration they returned to England, and by January 1662 Thomas Harrison, who followed the same trade as his father-in-law, claimed to have worked in Windsor, Salisbury, and Winchester and to have built up a supply of new materials. Shortly after this the family changed their name to Harris.

Renatus Harris, or René, as he was sometimes known, began a career in which he built at least seventeen new organs, repaired at least fourteen others, and worked in more than sixty cathedrals and churches, collaborating with his father on projects principally in the west country. Two of their earliest joint instruments were at Worcester in 1666 and Gloucester in 1673–4, and they may have been at Salisbury in 1668. In 1672 they enlarged the organ at Magdalen College, Oxford. Harris was a recusant Catholic, and in 1674 agreed to let the dean and chapter of Gloucester know his address every six months.

In 1677 Harris was convicted in the court of king's bench of trying to shift the responsibility for a bastard child onto a Mr Jacobson. On 16 September in the same year he married Joan Hiett at St Martin-in-the-Fields. They had four children, Renatus, Clarissa, Abigail, and John [see below], and lived a more settled life in London, based at Wine Office Court. Harris first signed a contract on his own behalf in 1681, when he took on work for St Dunstan and All Saints, Stepney.

Harris's Catholicism may have fuelled his rivalry with the protestant organ builder Bernard Smith. This reached its peak in a competition over the organ of the Temple Church in London, in which Harris was favoured by the Inner Temple and Smith received the support of the Middle Temple. In February 1682 each builder was asked to provide an organ, the instruments to be judged, and the best one to be erected in the Temple Church. By June 1683 Harris's organ was ready, before that of his rival, Smith. Harris was allowed to erect his organ in the Temple Church, and by June 1685 both builders' instruments were in working order in the church. Smith's was finally allowed to stand there, and a bill of sale for the organ was signed with the Middle Temple on 21 June 1688. Renatus Harris finally cut his losses in February 1691, when he signed a quitclaim with the Inner Temple.

Another dispute between Smith and Harris, in 1698, concerned the latter's claim to be able to divide half a note into fifty gradual and distinguishable parts. Harris invited all organists and others with 'nice ears' to his house to see this demonstrated. He may have been experimenting with different tuning systems or may perhaps have devised a way of altering the volume level of a note on the organ. Although division to this degree seems unlikely, Harris apparently followed up this demonstration with a further subdivision into 100 parts.

Lawyers and legal disputes formed a considerable part of Harris's life. In 1702 at the court of arches he made an unsuccessful attempt to make a student lawyer of the Inner Temple, Mr Lingard, marry his daughter Abigail after having a child with her. In the records of the trial much is made of his Catholic religion and that he was prepared to pay a £1000 dowry with his daughter. In May 1703 he took his employee Mr Mitchell to court over the carving for the organ case at St Andrew's, Holborn, which he claimed was unsatisfactory. He had various minor disputes, sometimes making his own instruments unplayable in an attempt to extract payment for them.

In 1722 Harris was responsible for the construction of an organ at St Dionis Backchurch. This instrument, with a comprehensive specification including characteristic solo stops in a vigorous and bold chorus with prominent mutation and mixture stops, and an emphasis on tierce sounding ranks, is characteristic of Harris's work. The specification of twenty-five stops includes eight reeds and is evidence of his skill with these. He is also noted for developing the mechanical device known as 'communication', which made the stops of one manual of an organ playable on another. By 1722 Harris was living in Bristol. He died in the city and was buried in St Nicholas's parish church on 21 November 1724.

John Harris (d. 1743), son of Renatus Harris and his wife, Joan, worked with his father in 1722, when he made twenty-one of the stops at St Dionis Backchurch. He lived in Red Lion Square, Holborn, and had a contract in his own name to build an organ for St John, Clerkenwell, in 1724. He soon set up in partnership with his brother-in-law John Byfield (c.1694–1751) and by 1726 it was Harris and Byfield jointly who signed the contract for the substantial new organ in St Mary Redcliffe, Bristol. The partnership still allowed each party to sign contracts in their own right, for example John Harris at St George's, Doncaster (1738), and John Byfield at the Temple Church in 1741. The latter may not be surprising after the earlier history of the Harris family and this church. Byfield continued building organs in the Harris style, and is known for the high quality of his reed stops. They also did much work extending existing instruments, often by adding swelling organs. At a date unknown Harris married Catherine. In 1733 he was living in the parish of St George the Martyr, Middlesex. He died in 1743.   DAVID S. KNIGHT

Sources D. Knight, 'Renatus Harris organ builder', MMus diss., U. Reading, 1995 · B. Matthews, 'The Dallams and the Harrises', *Journal of the British Institute of Organ Studies*, 8 (1984), 59–68 · D. Knight, 'The battle of the organs, the Smith organ at the Temple and its organist', *Journal of the British Institute of Organ Studies*, 21 (1997), 76–99 · B. Matthews, 'The organs of St. Andrew Holborn', *Journal of the British Institute of Organ Studies*, 13 (1989), 67–73 · A. Freeman, 'Renatus Harris's proposed St. Paul's organ and his puzzling invention', *The Organ*, 10 (1930), 74–7 · L. Stone, *Uncertain unions and broken lives: marriage and divorce in England, 1660–1857* (1995) · D. Knight, 'The development of the swell organ in the eighteenth century', MMus diss., U. Reading, 1995 · N. Plumley, 'The Harris Byfield connection: some recent findings', *Journal of the British Institute of Organ Studies*, 3 (1979), 108–34 · certificates as to papists, 1706, GL, MS 9800/1 · Bristol RO, FCP/St.N/R/1(j)2, frame 44 · GL, MS 11276/A

Harris, Richard (1557/8–1621), Church of England clergyman and author, was the son of Roger Harris, a Shrewsbury draper. Educated from 1571 at Shrewsbury School, he matriculated at St John's College, Cambridge, at Easter 1576. He played the role of Nuntius when Thomas Legge's tragedy *Richardus tertius* was performed at St John's in March 1580. Harris graduated BA in 1580 and was admitted a fellow of his college in 1581. He proceeded MA in 1583 and was probably the man of this name who was incorporated MA of Oxford in July 1584. He subsequently held a series of college offices, which suggests that he enjoyed the favour of the controversial master of St John's, William Whitaker. Appointed college lecturer in Hebrew in 1588, Harris became a college preacher in 1589, proceeded BD in

1590, became a senior fellow in 1593, and proceeded DD in 1595.

Whitaker's patronage may explain how Harris became a chaplain to Robert Devereux, second earl of Essex, by 1593. Harris's association with Essex and Whitaker clearly aided his appointment as town lecturer (or common preacher) at Colchester in August 1593. As lecturer, he received an annual stipend of 100 marks and was expected to deliver regular public sermons. Harris soon fell out with influential members of the town corporation. This ill will may have been occasioned by his increasingly strident criticism of nonconformity and his insistence on obedience to episcopal authority. By 1597 he believed that his pay was being deliberately kept in arrears. In October 1599 he gained an outside income when he was appointed by the crown to the rectory of Gestingthorpe, Essex, through the intercession of Dr Mountford. In 1604, Harris's attacks on local Brownists prompted his enemies to circulate libels against him as a persecutor of the godly. This prompted an inquiry and the prosecution of the ringleaders in Star Chamber. This affair further weakened his position in Colchester. In 1605 the corporation demanded that he return his patent of appointment and he was dismissed outright in 1608.

Harris ventured into international religious controversy in 1612 when he published *Concordia Anglicana* (translated in 1614 as *The English Concord*), in which he sought to offer a definitive reply to criticisms of the Church of England by the Jesuit Martin Becanus in his *Controversia Anglicana* (1612). This work demonstrated that Harris's dislike of protestant nonconformity was matched by a violent anti-Catholicism. Perhaps as a reward for this intervention, Harris was preferred by the crown in February 1613 to the lucrative Essex living of Bradwell-juxta-Mare, valued at £400 a year by a survey of 1609. In 1617 he contributed commendatory verses to *The Arithmeticall Jewell* (sig. A 7r) by his fellow St John's man William Pratt.

Harris died aged sixty-three in Colchester between 17 September and 6 October 1621, and was buried in St Nicholas's Church, Colchester, where the curious wording of his funeral monument suggested that he remained a controversial figure to the last. It is unclear whether he married. A pedigree of 1612 records that Barbara, daughter of Thomas Crochrode of Toppsfield, Essex, was 'married to Doctor Harris of Cambridge' (Metcalfe, 1.185), but there is no mention of a wife or children in Harris's will, drawn up on 17 September 1621 and proved on 6 October, although a brother (George Harris) and a niece and nephew are named. The will contained bequests totalling approximately £2000, the largest being £500 'together with my bookes and apparell whersoever' to one Samuel Bettar, a student at Cambridge (PRO, PROB 11/138, fol. 124r). Harris's executor was Henry Barrington, an alderman of Colchester.   PAUL E. J. HAMMER

Sources PRO, PROB 11/138, fol. 124r · PRO, STAC 8/177/5 · J. R. Davis, 'Colchester, 1600–1662: politics, religion and office-holding in an English provincial town', PhD diss., Brandeis University, 1980 · G. W. Fisher, *Annals of Shrewsbury School* (1899) · Venn, *Alum. Cant.* · Essex RO, D/B, Gb1, Gb2 · Essex RO, Colchester collections MS, acc. C28b · Hatfield House, Cecil MSS, 53/32, 53/96 · Bodl. Oxf., MS Tanner 179, fol. 44r · R. Newcourt, *Repertorium ecclesiasticum parochiale Londinense*, 2 vols. (1708–10) · T. Baker, *History of the college of St John the Evangelist, Cambridge*, ed. J. E. B. Mayor, 2 vols. (1869) · *VCH Essex*, vols. 2, 9 · H. C. Porter, *Reformation and reaction in Tudor Cambridge* (1958) · Foster, *Alum. Oxon.* · W. C. Metcalfe, ed., *The visitations of Essex*, 2 vols. (1878–9) · R. J. Lordi, *Thomas Legge's 'Richardus tertius'* (1979) · PRO, E334/12, fol. 139r; E334/14, fol. 222r · L. M. Higgs, *Godliness and governance in Tudor Colchester* (Ann Arbor, MI, 1998)
Wealth at death approx. £2000: 1621, PRO, PROB 11/138, fol. 124r

Harris, Richard (d. **1734**), slave trader and lobbyist, is of obscure ancestry. He was in St Kitts in the West Indies in 1694, where he observed that French privateers, by intercepting provisions from British North America, caused Barbados planters 'to suffer much & their Negroes perish for want' (PRO, CO 137/8, 40). After establishing himself as a merchant in London he began sending cargoes to Africa, and from 1702 to 1712 he dispatched the second highest valuation among London merchants. From 1718 to 1734 eleven vessels owned by him transported slaves to Jamaica, Barbados, Virginia, and Buenos Aires, in the notorious 'triangular trade'.

Harris early developed an interest in the Jamaica trade (importing slaves and exporting sugar). In 1709, concerned about wartime security, he advised the Board of Trade: 'What seems absolutely necessary, especially for Jamaica, is to remove the French from among our settlements in America' (CSP col., 24.319). As the Royal African Company undertook its long quest to recover its monopoly over trading in Africa, lost in 1698, Harris united with London merchants in opposition. They proposed that the trade be vested in a regulated company. Parliament refused to renew the African Company monopoly, but failed to establish a regulated company until 1750.

By 1708 Harris stood to the fore among London slave merchants; the Board of Trade that year wrote to Harris enclosing queries to be communicated to the separate traders to Africa. Jamaica legislators and merchants employed Harris's services in petitioning for an open trade to Africa, asserting that 'Jamaica hath been better supplied with negroes by the seperate traders to Affrica than at any time by the Affrican Company' (CSP col., 25.336). In a quest for information the Board of Trade in 1731 wrote to 'Mr. Harris, one of the principal Separate Traders to Africa', requesting him to 'communicate to some others of the Principal Separate Traders, and let their Lord's have your and their answers' (PRO, CO 389/28, 447). Marketing slaves in American colonies encountered obstacles in the shape of colonial duty laws. Recognizing that the laws interfered with the slave trade, the crown in 1717 prohibited the passage of laws imposing a duty on importation of Africans. Jamaica and Virginia, where Harris held an economic interest in the trade, were major offenders. Harris persistently protested against the existing laws, only to find that the colonial legislatures no less persistently maintained them.

Harris won greater success in other measures. London

merchants faced impediments to the recovery of colonists' debts. Colonial laws exempted houses and lands from liability for debts. Although Harris and others reminded the Board of Trade that such exemption defied English law and royal instructions, the board, noting the laws were of long standing, recommended that the privy council not interfere. The merchants then turned to parliament and pushed through the Credit Act of 1732, a triumph described as 'the Palladium of Colony credit, and the English Merchant's grand security' (Sheridan, 288–9). The act made lands, tenements, and slaves owned by colonial debtors liable to be seized for repayment of debts. The following year the passage of the Molasses Act had Harris's support. He had earlier advised the Board of Trade that, 'if the French sugar colonies were not supplied with provisions and lumber from our northern colonies, it would not be possible for them to carry on their sugar trade in the manner they do' (*Journal of the Commissioners*, 1728–34, 253).

To the end of his life Harris pursued his long career as a slave trader. In 1733 the Board of Trade appealed to 'Mr. Harris, one of the most ancient traders to the West Indies', for information (*CSP col.*, 40.52). Six weeks after his death his ship *Antelope* imported 286 Africans from Angola into Virginia. On 14 September 1734 *Read's Weekly Journal* recorded: 'Last Tuesday Night [10 September] died at his House on Tower-Hill, Mr. Richard Harris, who for many Years was an eminent Trader to the Coast of Africa, and the West Indies'.

For three decades Harris, without any official capacity, probably wielded more influence in shaping slave-trade policy than any other Briton. He enjoyed the esteem of London merchants and the Board of Trade, and testified frequently on the policy. He had the satisfaction of seeing free trade in slaves won, colonial exclusionary laws opposed, and two significant parliamentary measures—the Credit Act and the Molasses Act—made law. He also foretold the imperial policy of evicting France from North America. JAMES A. RAWLEY

Sources CSP col., vols. 24–5, 36–41 · Journal of the commissioners for trade and plantations, [14 vols.] (1920–38) [April 1704 – May 1782] · PRO, CO 137/8, 388/25, 389/28, T70.T70/354, 1119 · J. A. Rawley, 'Richard Harris, slave trader spokesman', Albion, 23 (1991), 439–58 · L. F. Stock, ed., Proceedings and debates of the British parliaments respecting North America, 5 vols. (1924–41), vols. 3, 4 · JHC, 16 (1708–11), 71, 160, 235, 246, 300, 310, 312, 317–20 · JHC, 17 (1711–14), 164–5, 319 · JHC, 21 (1727–32), 522–3 · JHC, 22 (1732–7), 845–6 · W. L. Grant and J. F. Munro, eds., Acts of the privy council of England: colonial series, 3: 1720–1745 (1910) · K. G. Davies, The Royal African Company (1957); repr. (1970) · R. B. Sheridan, Sugar and slavery: an economic history of the British West Indies, 1623–1775 (1974) · BL, Add. MS 14034 · The manuscripts of the House of Lords, new ser., 12 vols. (1900–77), vol. 10 · slave trade database, Harvard U., W. E. B. Du Bois Institute · Read's Weekly Journal, or, British Gazetteer (14 Sept 1734), 4

Harris, Robert (1580/81–1658), college head, was born at Broad Campden, Gloucestershire, probably one of at least five sons of John Harris, whose family originated in Shropshire, and his wife, Elizabeth (*née* Hyron). He attended the free school of Chipping Campden, where his unhappy experiences 'brought such a trembling and sadness of spirit upon him that he could not be quite rid of so long as he lived' (Durham, 2–3). Later he attended Worcester Free School. He matriculated from Magdalen Hall, Oxford, on 10 June 1597, aged sixteen. There he applied to be placed under the tutelage of Stephen Goffe, whose academic talents he admired, but who was also a puritan. Robert Lister, the college principal, disapproved of the choice, but eventually allowed it. Harris learned both Hebrew and religious principles from Goffe, who won him to the need for regular bible study and discussion of sermons. Harris graduated BA on 5 June 1600. The chief authority for his life, William Durham, tells us that he also proceeded MA, though the university has no record of this.

Harris left Oxford when plague reached the city in 1604, and was offered hospitality by a Mr Doyly (perhaps Sir John Doyley of Chiselhampton), where he assisted during the illness of the minister, Mr Prior. Nearby at Banbury lived William Whately, lecturer and vicar from 1604 to 1639. On 20 May 1606 Harris married Whately's sister, Joane (*bap.* 1588), and on 16 June 1607 the couple baptized a son, Malachi, at Banbury church. They had many other children, of whom several died in infancy; Durham wrote of Harris as a model father. Joane evidently shared her husband's deep interest in religious matters and was intimately familiar with Foxe's book of martyrs. It seems that in later life she began to suffer obsessive guilt feelings, to the eventual loss of her sanity.

By early 1607 Sir Anthony Cope MP, a fierce opponent of Archbishop Bancroft's drive to impose conformity among the clergy, had presented Harris to the rectory of Hanwell, Oxfordshire, in succession to the deprived incumbent, the eminent puritan preacher and writer, John Dod. The latter supported Harris's candidature, not least because they had been in the habit of studying together, though it seems that there was resentment among the congregation at the loss of their old pastor. However, Bancroft then nominated a candidate of his own. A furious Cope descended upon Lambeth, with Harris, Whately (his nominee for Banbury), and at least one other MP in tow. In response Bancroft was forced to accept Sir Anthony's right of presentation, but ordered an examination of both Whately and Harris in order to test their sufficiency and conformity. When Harris eventually came before Bishop William Barlowe, this enthusiastic student of Greek was agreeably surprised to find that Harris was his equal in that language: 'so long they both Greeked it, till at last they were both scoted, and to seek of words, whereupon they both fell a laughing, and so gave up' (Durham, 14). Harris was instituted to the rectory probably some time before the issue of his *Absalom's Funeral* (1610), with a preface signed from Hanwell on 25 August 1610.

While teaching students at his house Harris continued to study theology at Oxford and on 5 May 1614 he proceeded BD. The same year he acquired the Spittal estate near Banbury from Thomas Whately—William's father—who had bought it from the Copes. That year Sir Anthony died, and it was Robert Harris who preached his funeral sermon, published as *Samuels Funeral* (1618). The preface contains the first reference to the illnesses which seem to have dogged him: 'the Lord hath already stript me of the poor man's portion, health'. The revenues of Hanbury did not justify the claim of poverty, but as Harris refused preferment the modesty of his lifestyle appears to have been voluntary. The biographer Samuel Clarke described him as a man 'grave without affectation, pleasant without levity' (S. Clarke, *A Collection of the Lives of Ten Eminent Divines*, 1662, 305), who did not make a show of his great learning. The title of *The Drunkard's Cup* (1630) might suggest a stereotypical puritan, raging against the evils of loose living, and the work certainly contains its share of dire warnings. But it also discusses the causes of drunkenness: gentlemen not only set a bad moral example in patronizing taverns, but also made it harder in practice for the magistrates to police them. There was criticism of those who 'work the husbandman out of his dwelling (either by turning him to a rack rent, or by sending him to look for a dwelling in some market town), and what becomes of him? Either he turns badger or maultster' (R. Harris, *The Drunkard's Cup*, 1630, preface).

Durham tells us that Harris rarely ventured out of his home parish, but for a time gave fortnightly sermons at Stratford which attracted both leading laymen and other preachers. On 30 June 1622 at Paul's Cross he preached a sermon later published as *God's Goodness and Mercy*, dedicated to Sir Baptist Hickes. Harris was also involved in the combination lecture at Deddington, 6 miles south of Banbury, and was well acquainted with local puritan preachers, including Robert Cleaver, deprived rector of Drayton, and his successor, Henry Scudder. But it is likely that he was closest to his brother-in-law, William Whately, vicar of Banbury. Whately's death on 10 May 1639 brought to an end a friendship of over thirty years.

Harris was reluctant to declare for either side in the civil war. The respect for authority and fear of political conflict evident in his 1622 sermon was also manifested in the preface to a sermon given in May 1642 before the House of Commons:

> Mens consciences are miserably perplexed between command and command. … Let me assure you, the case betwixt pastor and flock will be very sad if there be not a timely settlement. But things of this nature I had rather speak in private than in press or pulpit.   (*A Sermon*, M3v)

This proved not to be a sustainable position. Already, on 8 August, cavalier troops arrived at his Hanwell home, 'outed him and his family, took possession of his house on Sunday night, and made him wander for his lodging' (*Proceedings at Banbury*, 5). After the battle of Edgehill close by (on 23 October 1642), Harris is reported to have suffered again at the hands of the royalist victors. Buffeted by the winds of military fortune in this exposed part of Oxfordshire, he seems to have protested neutrality in vain. Harris was called as a delegate to the assembly of divines, but stayed at Hanwell as long as he could. Finally convinced by military threats to seek a place of safety he chose London, rather than Oxford, and in 1644 was instituted as rector of St Botolph without Bishopsgate. Probably his choice stemmed at least in part from the confluence in London of

so many godly ministers of his own presbyterian convictions, but at the assembly he was careful to 'hear all and say little' (Durham, 33).

In 1647 Harris was appointed one of the parliamentary visitors to the University of Oxford. During the six-month period before the purge of royalist and high-church fellows commenced, Harris was among the new preachers to be heard in Oxford. At about this time Harris and his colleagues were challenged by the radical William Erbury to a debate at the university church of St Mary's concerning the validity of their ordination by the bishops. Harris seems not to have spoken in the dispute, but did agree 'that he would begin the work with prayer' (Durham, 39). He was more eloquent on 4 June when 'the length of Mr Harris's visitation sermon made his colleagues so late' that Dean Samuel Fell of Christ Church 'seized the opportunity of dissolving the convocation' (Blakiston, 136) and politely taking his leave. On 1 April 1648, after several attempts at evading the authority of the visitors, President Hannibal Potter of Trinity College was ousted from his lodgings by the chancellor, Philip Herbert, fourth earl of Pembroke, and was replaced by Harris, 'who had been created DD the previous day' (Blakiston, 137). Harris does not seem to have used his newly acquired authority in any vindictive spirit, writing of Oxford soon afterwards:

> I love the place, I honour divers there who are of a different judgement in some things, and could heartily wish, that they would have prevented our journey thither, and task there, by a timely reformation of themselves and free concurrence with the parliament in that necessary work.   (Harris, 8)

Anthony Wood asserted that Harris and his wife laid false claim to £200 found in the college about this time, and in April 1648 a hostile pamphleteer, signing himself Basilius Philomusus, accused Harris of pluralism and greed, listing his benefices with inflated estimates of their worth. Harris denied this in *Two Letters* (1648), stressing that at Hanwell his belongings had been 'pillaged' and buildings 'turned to ashes by the fury of fire and sword' (Harris, 3). He had been officially invited to the other livings, to St Botolph by parliament, to Hanborough by the Oxfordshire committee, and to Buriton and Petersfield by the committee of Hampshire. He had never received as much as £300 p.a. from livings, let alone the £1500 suggested by his accuser.

On 30 September 1647 Matthew Unite and Thomas Wilday had been appointed as delegates of Trinity by Harris and the other visitors, and they retained effective control of the college government after his appointment as president. On 1 April 1652 Harris attended the first visitors' meeting at which John Owen was present, but this commission was dissolved soon afterwards by the Rump. In June 1653 a more radical commission appointed by Cromwell under Owen's leadership met for the first time, and Harris was not a member. But when, on 2 September 1654, another commission was instituted, he and two other original visitors were restored. In this year too, were published two bulky volumes of his sermons. During the 1650s Harris lectured at All Souls, and preached a weekly sermon at Garsington, the parsonage attached to Trinity.

Now over seventy, he confided to his friends that he found this last burden too much, 'being a man very much addicted to privacy and his book' (Durham, 44). He died, probably of pleurisy, in Oxford on 11 December 1658 and was buried in the chapel of Trinity College next day.

STEPHEN WRIGHT

Sources W. D. [W. Durham], *The life and death of … Robert Harris* (1662) • H. E. D. Blakiston, *Trinity College* (1898) • Foster, *Alum. Oxon.* • Wood, *Ath. Oxon.*, new edn • M. Burrows, ed., *The register of the visitors of the University of Oxford, from AD 1647 to AD 1658*, CS, new ser., 29 (1881) • B. Worden, 'Cromwellian Oxford', *Hist. U. Oxf. 4: 17th-cent. Oxf.*, 733–72 • A. Beesley, *The history of Banbury* (1841) • J. S. W. Gibson, ed., *Marriage register of Banbury*, 1: *1558–1724*, Banbury Historical Society, 2 (1960) • J. S. W. Gibson, ed., *Baptism and burial register of Banbury, Oxfordshire*, 1: *1558–1653*, Banbury Historical Society, 7 (1965–6) • J. Walker, *An attempt towards recovering an account of the numbers and sufferings of the clergy of the Church of England*, 2 pts in 1 (1714) • *The proceedings at Banbury since the ordinance went down* (1642) • *Pegasus, or, The Flying Horse from Oxford* [1648] • R. Harris, *Two letters written by Mr Harris in vindication of himself from the known slanders of an unknown author* (1648) • M. Maclure, *The St Paul's Cross sermons, 1534–1642* (1958) • *Walker rev.* • *N&Q*, 148 (1925), 201–2, 299–300

Likenesses M. Droeshout, line engraving, BM; repro. in R. Hobson, *The arraignment of the whole creature* (1631); engraved title lent dated 1632 • T. Metcalfe, black watercolour drawing, Trinity College, Oxford

Harris, Robert (1809–1865), naval officer, son of James Harris of Wittersham Hall, Kent, and, on his mother's side, grandson of Sarah Kirby *Trimmer, was born on 9 July 1809; Sir William Cornwallis *Harris was his elder brother. Robert Harris entered the navy in January 1822, and, serving almost continuously in the Mediterranean, was a midshipman of the frigate *Euryalus* during the little war with Algiers in 1824, and of the *Cambrian* at the battle of Navarino, on 20 October 1827, and when she was wrecked at Carabusa on 31 January 1828. After his return to England early in 1829 he was on the books of the yacht *Royal George*, when he was in fact serving on the tenders *Onyx* and *Pantaloon*, on the coast of South America, in the West Indies, on the coast of Spain and Portugal, or in the channel and on the coast of Ireland. On 21 May 1833 he was promoted lieutenant, and the following December was appointed to the gunnery training ship *Excellent*, at Portsmouth, under the command of Captain Thomas Hastings (1790–1870). From her he was appointed in January 1836 to be gunnery lieutenant of the *Melville* with Captain Douglas, and, later on, with Richard Saunders Dundas, under whose command he served in China, and was promoted commander on 8 June 1841 for his services in the Canton River, and particularly at the capture of the Bogue (Humen) forts on 26 February 1841. During 1842, while on half pay, he studied at the Royal Naval College at Portsmouth; in 1843 he married Priscilla Sophia, daughter of Captain Penruddocke of the fusilier guards; they had a son, Robert Hastings, who become an admiral, and two daughters.

From September 1844 to May 1846 Harris commanded the *Flying Fish* on the west coast of Africa. In March 1848 he was appointed commander of the *Ganges* in the Channel Fleet with Captain Henry Smith, and from her was promoted to the rank of captain on 19 October 1849. In March 1851 he was appointed to the *Prince Regent*, also in the Channel Fleet, as flag captain to Commodore William Fanshawe Martin, but left her in May 1852 on Martin's being relieved by Rear-Admiral Corry. His service under such officers as Hastings, Dundas, and Martin established his peculiar fitness for the appointment which he received in January 1854 to the *Illustrious* (72 guns), then commissioned as a training ship for landsmen entering the navy, according to a plan of Sir James Graham's (they consequently became generally known as 'Jemmy Graham's novices'); he put his own son through the training.

Harris displayed such ability and resource in his discharge of his new and exceptional duty that when, in 1857, it was determined to give effect to a long-mooted scheme for improving the education and training of young officers, he was selected for the task. Initially the cadets entered the *Illustrious*, but on 1 January 1859 Harris and the cadets were moved to the larger *Britannia* (120 guns); the ship was then in Portsmouth harbour, but in November 1861 was sent to Portland. Harris continued to hold this difficult and important post until October 1862, during which time the shipboard system of education of naval cadets, which lasted until early in the twentieth century, was fully established. He had no further employment, and died at his home in Southsea, Portsmouth, on 16 January 1865; his wife survived him.

J. K. LAUGHTON, *rev.* ANDREW LAMBERT

Sources O'Byrne, *Naval biog. dict.* • personal knowledge (1891) • R. Taylor, 'Manning the Royal Navy: the reform of the recruiting system, 1852–1862', *Mariner's Mirror*, 45 (1959), 46–58 • W. N. Calkins, 'Notes on "Manning the Royal Navy"', *Mariner's Mirror*, 46 (1960), 65–6 • E. Rasor, *Reform in the Royal Navy* (1976) • private information (1891)

Wealth at death under £5000: probate, 7 March 1865, *CGPLA Eng. & Wales*

Harris, Sir Ronald Montague Joseph (1913–1995), civil servant, was born on 6 May 1913 at 41 Cornwall Gardens, Kensington, London, the only son and the youngest of the three children of the Revd (Joseph) Montague Harris (1864–1964), a Church of England clergyman, and his wife, Edith Annesley, *née* Malcolmson (1874–1957), the fourth daughter of George Forbes Malcolmson, merchant and banker. Through his maternal grandmother he was descended from King Edward I. His father was rector of St Nicholas's Church, Colchester, from 1913 to 1928.

After his education at West Downs School, Winchester (1922–6), at Harrow School (1926–32), and at Trinity College, Oxford (1933–6), to which he won a scholarship and from which he graduated with first-class honours in modern history, Harris passed into the administrative class of the civil service in 1936. His first appointment, at the India Office, was in the department dealing with the affairs of Burma, and when in 1937 the office of secretary of state for Burma (held in plurality with that of secretary of state for India) was created, he was one of the six staff serving that office. On 14 January 1939 he married (Margaret) Julia Wharton (1914/15–1955), the daughter of John Robert

Wharton, an engineer, of Haffield, Ledbury, Herefordshire; they had three daughters and a son.

Also in January 1939 Harris moved to the Cabinet Office as private secretary to the secretary of the cabinet, Sir Edward Bridges, where he served until July 1943. Harris described it as a unique apprenticeship: a period of sustained hard work for long hours under intense pressure, working directly for a master whom he served with devotion, admiration, and affection. Bridges was always for him one of the two outstanding men whom he served. Harris (who was made MVO in 1943) remained in the War Cabinet Office for a further year, first organizing administrative arrangements for the British delegation to the first Quebec Conference, then working as civilian staff officer in London for Lord Mountbatten, the newly appointed supreme allied commander in south-east Asia, and also serving Sir Archibald Rowlands, the adviser to the viceroy of India on war administration. He returned to the India Office in October 1944 to serve as principal private secretary to the secretary of state for India (Lord Pethick-Lawrence from September 1945, the earl of Listowel from April 1947).

After spending 1948 at the Royal College of Defence Studies, Harris moved to the Treasury as an assistant secretary, in charge for two and a half years of an establishments division and then for eight months of the 'supply' division dealing with the departments concerned with overseas affairs. Then in May 1952 he was summoned back to the Cabinet Office to serve as one of the two deputies to the secretary of the cabinet, Sir Norman Brook. In July 1955 he was appointed permanent commissioner of crown lands in succession to Christopher Eastwood (who had been transferred to other duties following the Crichel Down affair), to manage the reorganization of the crown lands commission as the crown estate commission, with a part-time first commissioner, Sir Malcolm Trustram Eve, and a full-time executive second commissioner, which Harris became. Eve was the second of those whom Harris regarded as the two outstanding men with whom he served. The reorganization was successful, and Harris enjoyed supervising the management of the crown estate, and in particular the rural parts of the estate. He was made CB in 1956. On 3 October 1957 (his first wife having died two years previously), he married Marjorie Tryon (1913–1986), the widow of Captain Julian Guy Tryon (with whom she had a son and a daughter) and the eldest of the eight children of Sir Harry Calvert Williams Verney, fourth baronet, who had been Liberal MP for North Buckinghamshire from 1910 to 1918.

In 1960, newly made a KCVO, Harris returned to the Treasury to supervise the divisions responsible for overseas expenditure, pay, and conditions of the armed services, the 'law and order departments', and—especially congenial to him—arts and sciences. There was then no department for the arts; the Treasury was directly responsible for grants to the Arts Council, to the national museums and galleries, to the Royal College and the Royal Academy of Music, to the Royal College of Art, and to the Royal Opera House, Covent Garden. Harris much enjoyed dealing with these institutions, and for them he was an understanding and well-disposed 'friend at court'. In this capacity Harris was responsible for advising the government on the decision to establish a national theatre.

Although Harris had elected not to follow his father and grandfather into the priesthood, he was sustained throughout his life by a strong Christian faith and an abiding commitment to the Church of England. When therefore in spring 1964 the archbishop of Canterbury asked him to be secretary of the church commissioners, he welcomed the opportunity. The appointment was the more welcome to him because it meant once again working with Lord Silsoe (the former Sir Malcolm Trustram Eve), the first church estates commissioner, until he himself succeeded Lord Silsoe in that office in May 1969. Harris sought both to increase the commissioners' income, which provides a substantial part of the stipends and pensions of the clergy, and to encourage larger contributions from dioceses, with the result that over his thirteen years as first commissioner the average clergy stipend rose, in line with inflation, by some 350 per cent, and the average pension rose fivefold (an increase of some 50 per cent in real terms), together with greatly improved provision for the housing of retired clergy. He also set himself to improve the commissioners' relations with the general synod and with the central administration of the church in Church House—so much so, that in 1978 he was appointed chairman of the central board of finance, while continuing as first commissioner until his retirement in November 1982.

Harris was a man of wide intellectual and artistic interests, but music was of special importance. He sang for some years in the Bach Choir. His home in later years was in Stoke D'Abernon, near Cobham, Surrey, close to the Yehudi Menuhin School, in whose affairs he became closely involved. The school was his chief outside interest after his retirement: he had chaired the friends of the school from 1972, and served on its board of governors from 1976 to 1990 (as vice-chairman from 1984 to 1989 and as chairman for a year thereafter). He converted an Elizabethan barn on his property for it to use as a concert hall.

Harris was relatively tall, with an open and friendly countenance. He had a lively, engaging, and enthusiastic personality, and was notable particularly for his urbanity and his bow-ties. His volume of personal recollections, *Memory—Soft the Air* (1987), described both his professional and his personal life, and articulated the basis of his Christian faith. He died of myelomatosis on 22 January 1995 at his home, Slyfield Farm House, Stoke D'Abernon, survived by the four children of his first marriage and by the stepdaughter of his second marriage. A memorial service was held in Southwark Cathedral on 24 May 1995, at which his stepson-in-law, the Very Revd Colin Slee, provost of Southwark, officiated, and at which the Right Revd Lord Runcie gave an address.   ROBERT ARMSTRONG

Sources R. Harris, *Memory—soft the air* (1987) · *The Times* (24 Jan 1995) · *The Times* (26 May 1995) · *The Independent* (11 Feb 1995) ·

WWW, 1991–5 • Burke, *Peerage* • personal knowledge (2004) • private information (2004) • b. cert. • m. certs. • d. cert.
Likenesses photograph, repro. in *The Times* (24 Jan 1995) • photograph, repro. in *The Independent*

Harris, Samuel (1682–1733), Church of England clergyman, was born on 9 December 1682 and baptized the following day at St Christopher-le-Stocks, London, the son of Samuel and Mary Harris. He entered Merchant Taylors' School, London, on 11 September 1694 and proceeded to Peterhouse, Cambridge, whence he matriculated in 1701. He graduated BA (1704), proceeded MA (1707), and was elected Parke fellow in 1706 and Ramsay fellow in 1709. He was Craven scholar of the university in 1701. Ordained deacon in May 1708 and priest in June 1708, he was rector of Intwood and Keswick, in Norfolk, from 1708 to 1720.

In October 1724 Harris was admitted first regius professor of modern history at Cambridge. The chair had been founded by George I in the previous May, with an annual stipend of £400. Harris's inaugural lecture (in Latin) was printed but he gave no further lectures. His only other publication was a lengthy, learned commentary on the fifty-third chapter of Isaiah, which his widow, Mary, issued in 1735, two years after his death, and dedicated to Queen Caroline. He was made a fellow of the Royal Society in 1722 and proceeded DD in 1728. He died on 21 December 1733. SIDNEY LEE, *rev.* S. J. SKEDD

Sources Venn, *Alum. Cant.* • C. J. Robinson, ed., *A register of the scholars admitted into Merchant Taylors' School, from AD 1562 to 1874*, 1 (1882), 333 • C. H. Cooper and J. W. Cooper, *Annals of Cambridge*, 5 vols. (1842–1908), vol. 4, pp. 182, 185 • T. A. Walker, ed., *Admissions to Peterhouse or St Peter's College in the University of Cambridge* (1912) • will, PRO, PROB 11/663, sig. 34

Harris, Sir Sidney West (1876–1962), civil servant and film censor, was born on 10 October 1876 at the family home, 85 Crawford Street, Marylebone, London, the son of George Harris, a builder (later a builder's merchant), and his wife, Kezia, *née* West. After attending St Paul's School he entered Queen's College, Oxford, as a scholar in 1895, and took a second class in classical moderations (1897) and a third class in *literae humaniores* in 1899. Joining the Post Office in 1900, he moved to the Home Office in 1903, and was secretary to the royal commission on mines from 1906 to 1909. On 13 April 1909 he married Emily Mary Wilson (1880/1881–1940) of Darlington, the daughter of George David Wilson, a coal and coke merchant. From 1909 to 1910 he was private secretary to the permanent under-secretary of state and was subsequently private secretary to six successive home secretaries from 1910 to 1919. He was promoted to assistant secretary in 1914 and assistant under-secretary of state at the Home Office in 1932. He was appointed CB in 1916 and CVO in 1918.

From 1919, during a period when the civil service possessed effective initiative in policy development, Harris's main responsibility was the children's branch and he was involved in significant developments affecting the welfare of children. A member of the committee on adoption set up in 1924 and chaired by Mr Justice Tomlin, he was involved in drafting and promoting the Adoption Act of 1926, which created legal adoptions. From 1927 he championed what became the wide-ranging Children and Young Persons Act (1933). While trying but failing both to abolish judicial whipping for children and to achieve the intended degree of procedural distinctiveness for children's proceedings, it established the welfare model for juvenile justice, and welded reformatory and industrial schools into a single system of approved schools. Harris promoted the contribution of the children's branch in a series of publications on its work from 1923. He was himself—unusually for an official—appointed in 1934 to chair the departmental committee on social services in the courts of summary jurisdiction, which reported in 1936. The outcome was a uniform, professional probation service with its own inspectorate.

The reputation of its children's work was one of the factors which persuaded the cabinet in 1947 to locate the new central responsibility for the welfare of children in the Home Office rather than in the ministries of Education or Health. Although Harris had by then retired (having been retained during the war long beyond normal age), throughout the Whitehall discussions from 1943 (and before) he had persistently urged consolidating on the Home Office the services then scattered across government. His own reputation (which had benefited also from his work from 1922 on social questions with the League of Nations and the United Nations) added weight to his views. Following his retirement in 1946, he chaired in 1947 the committee that recommended the grant system for supporting marriage guidance.

In April 1947 Harris, who was knighted on his retirement from the Home Office, succeeded Lord Tyrrell to become president of the British Board of Film Censors (BBFC). This was not a random appointment: he had been associated with film censorship since attending the home secretary's seminal 1912 meeting with the trade; the subject had been among his responsibilities since 1919; and he had urged sponsoring the arrangements that had—much to ministers' advantage—emerged. When during 1947 the government was instituting the Wheare committee on children and the cinema at a time of post-war unease about the behaviour and handling of the young, Harris—well known to the trade and to the long-serving BBFC secretary (J. Brooke Wilkinson), and knowledgeable about film and other forms of censorship—was the natural candidate. His background and reputation were ideal both to help the system through an awkward review and to handle any unwelcome recommendations and resulting legislation (the Cinematograph Act of 1952) that emerged. In the event, Harris set up voluntary consultative arrangements, which saw off recommendations that would have separated censorship from classification.

Harris was a 'working' president, albeit at a time when the secretary's role became more prominent. Under Harris the BBFC negotiated the shifting tastes of the times and was normally successful in sustaining the appearance of satisfactory norms of social control that is at the heart of the censorship requirement. If certificating *No Orchids for Miss Blandish* (1948) was controversial, classifying *Room at the Top* (1958) 'A' rather than 'X' was not. He continued to view films at the BBFC two or three days a week until, at the age of eighty-three, he was succeeded in 1960 by Lord Morrison of Lambeth. His time as a conscientious Surrey county governor of King's College School, Wimbledon (1939–60), included his active support for a creative film society.

Harris and his wife (she was reputedly dominant in the marriage) had two sons (the elder was lost at sea in 1940) and three daughters. His wife died in 1940. A long-time resident of Wimbledon, he died at Wimbledon Hospital from heart failure on 9 July 1962.

Harris was bespectacled, short, and stocky. Colleagues thought him conspicuously self-effacing and shy: 'It was an affectionate jest among those who worked for him that he would bid you "Good morning" and then wonder if he had gone too far' (C. P. Hill, *The Times*, 27 July 1962). Some deprecated his tentative habit of first submitting minutes to superiors in draft, his way no doubt of managing them. Other people found him unassuming and kindly. It was perhaps his longevity in post at the Home Office, and his thoughtfulness and persistence, rather than any startling personal qualities, that resulted in his accumulated child-welfare reputation. At the BBFC, his 'safe pair of hands' were reassuring equally to the trade and central and local government. Overall, Harris represented the quintessentially decent public servant of his time who chose to remain with duties that gave him opportunities over nearly sixty years usefully to contribute to, and shape, policy and practice when state welfare provision and public tastes were rapidly changing.   R.M. MORRIS

Sources *The Times* (10 July 1962); (27 July 1962) · private information (2004) [Lord Allen of Abbeydale; Bert Mayall; K. B. Paice; Jack Smith] · b. cert. · m. cert. · d. cert. · Home Office List, 1933, Home Office Library · PRO, HO 45/12642 [Tomlin Committee and Adoption Act, 1926] · PRO, HO 45/14714, 45/14802, 45/14804 [Children and Young Persons Act, 1932, consolidated into 1933 Act] · PRO, HO 45/14188 [first to fifth reports of the children's branch, 1923–38] · PRO, MH 102/1384, 102/1393, 102/1394 [cabinet discussions, 1945–7, about location within government of responsibility for policy on children] · PRO, HO 45/10551 [film censorship, 1912] · PRO, HO 45/17080 [departmental committee on social services in the courts] · PRO, HO 45/22250 [memorandum on social questions, 28 Jan 1946] · PRO, HO 45/25201 [Wheare committee on children and the cinema, report Cmd 7945, 1950] · S. M. Cretney, *Law, law reform and the family* (1998) · J. C. Robertson, *The British Board of Film Censors: film censorship in Britain, 1895–1950* (1985) · N. M. Hunnings, *Film censors and the law* (1967) · A. Aldgate, *Censorship and the permissive society* (1995) · G. Phelps, *Film censorship* (1975) · T. D. P. Mathews, *Censored* (1994) · A. Travis, *Bound and gagged* (2000) · J. Trevelyan, *What the censor saw* (1973) · C. Mallet, *Lord Cave: a memoir* (1931) · *CGPLA Eng. & Wales* (1962)
Archives PRO, papers
Likenesses photograph, repro. in *The Times* (10 July 1962)
Wealth at death £18,699 3s. 9d.: probate, 7 Sept 1962, *CGPLA Eng. & Wales*

Harris, (Audrey) Sophia (1900–1966). *See under* Motley (*act.* 1921–c.1975).

Harris, Thomas (*bap.* 1705, *d.* 1782). *See under* Harris, Joseph (*bap.* 1704, *d.* 1764).

Harris, Thomas (*d.* 1820), theatre manager, came from a 'respectable' family, and was brought up with a view to a career in trade. The *Thespian Dictionary* described him as the recipient of a liberal education and as being fond of literature. Harris acquired his fortune in the soap-manufacturing business. In autumn 1767 he joined with John Rutherford, William Powell, and George Colman the elder to buy the patent and property of the Theatre Royal, Covent Garden, from the heirs of John Rich, at the price of £60,000. Powell suggested that George Colman the elder join them. Colman assumed that he would manage the theatre, but Harris, Rutherford, and Powell never legally ceded authority to him. The house opened on 14 September 1767. During the first season there was a violent quarrel between Harris and Colman concerning the actress Jane *Lessingham (1738/9–1783), with whom Harris lived, and whom Harris thought was discriminated against when Colman allocated parts. Colman, with whom Powell sided, barricaded the theatre, and Harris, supported by Rutherford, broke it open forcibly and made off with books, music, and costumes. Legal proceedings and a pamphlet war followed. In July 1770 a legal decision of the commissioners of the great seal reinstated Colman as acting manager, subject to the advice and inspection, but not the control, of his fellows. Powell meanwhile had died, on 3 July 1769, and Rutherford had sold his shares. About 1771 Harris left Lessingham, and from then on he enjoyed a better relationship with Colman.

On Colman's resignation in May 1774 Harris became manager of the theatre, and remained so until his death, acting as senior partner to a succession of shareholders. He was accused of sacrificing to spectacle the best interests of the drama, as he liked pantomimes, exhibitions, and popular entertainment. This strategy secured the financial health of Covent Garden, and avoided the debts run up at Drury Lane. Harris also sought to extend his theatrical activities. In 1778 he and Richard Brinsley Sheridan acquired the King's Theatre and its opera company for £22,000, but following the bankruptcy of William Taylor, Sheridan's successor as Harris's partner, Harris sold the theatre to John Gallini without making a return on his investment. In 1782 Harris again joined Sheridan in a plan to build a new London theatre, the Prince of Wales, on land behind Grosvenor Place owned by the architect Henry Holland, but they failed to attract sufficient subscribers. In 1784 he apparently took a company including John Philip Kemble and others to Paris.

Harris was reputedly generous to actors and had a good reputation and some personal popularity; he regularly increased the salaries of those actors who did well, although he endured a dispute over salaries and benefit payments with his company in 1800. He also encouraged the plays of unknown authors and introduced them at his theatre; however, he did not pay new authors well. In 1797 Thomas Holcroft complained that the sum Harris had paid for a play—£400, with £150 for the copyright—barely reflected Harris's takings. Successful playwrights received more—in 1807 Holcroft, by then established, received £1000 from Harris for a play. Harris built up a substantial collection of theatrical paintings, among them several portraits by Gainsborough Dupont, subsequently in the Garrick Club.

Harris was presumably married but, if so, nothing is known of his wife. He had a daughter, who died in 1802 aged fifteen, and four sons, including Henry Harris, later manager at Covent Garden, and George Harris, who became a captain in the Royal Navy. He was probably the father of three of Jane Lessingham's sons, Thomas, Charles, and Edwin. His sister married into the family of the Longmans, the well-known publishers. Harris died on 1 October 1820 at his cottage near Wimbledon, and was buried in his family vault at Hillingdon, near Uxbridge, where his daughter was also buried.

JOSEPH KNIGHT, rev. NILANJANA BANERJI

Sources Highfill, Burnim & Langhans, *BDA* · C. Price, 'Thomas Harris and the Covent Garden theatre', *Essays on the eighteenth-century English stage*, ed. K. Richards and P. Thomson (1972), 105–22 · *The thespian dictionary, or, Dramatic biography of the present age*, 2nd edn (1805) · *London Magazine*, 2 (1820), 527 · *GM*, 1st ser., 90/1 (1820), 374–5 · Genest, *Eng. stage* · B. Victor, *The history of the theatres of London and Dublin*, 3 (1771) · *Boswell's Life of Johnson*, ed. G. B. Hill, 6 vols. (1887)
Likenesses J. Opie, oils, Garr. Club

Harris, Thomas (1829/30–1900), architect, is of unknown parentage, and details of his education and early career remain obscure. He was established in independent practice in London by 1851, when he was elected an associate of the Royal Institute of British Architects. In 1860, however, he published the pamphlet *Victorian Architecture*, which energetically engaged contemporary debate about the need for a modern architectural style rather than the prevailing historicism. Historical examples, Harris argued, should be studied for their spirit and principles, not merely copied; architects should seek a style to embody the revolutionary technological progress that typified modernity. The difficulty of achieving this appears in Harris's accompanying design for an apartment block, supposedly in the new 'Victorian' style but actually an undisciplined effort in the eclectic Gothic of the period. In 1862 Harris edited, and largely wrote, *Examples of the Architecture of the Victorian Age*, which similarly advocated a distinctive 'Victorian' style, and enthused about the iron and glass construction of railway stations and the Crystal Palace. Illustrations included two central London shops by Harris in a forceful, highly simplified Gothic that made some structural use of iron. Even more functionalist was a warehouse on Lisson Grove he designed in 1873, its rectilinear brick and girder construction given vestigial Renaissance styling.

Away from commercial buildings, Harris's career, and his style, developed more conventionally. His 1869 competition design for Bradford town hall, though unsuccessful, led to important contacts in the town, where he may have had family connections: Bradford's largest bankers, closely involved in architectural development, had the same surname. Harris's first two major houses were for local magnate families: the dramatically composed Gothic pile of Milner Field, Bingley (1871–3; dem.) for a son

of Sir Titus Salt, founder of Saltaire; and the many-gabled timber-framed Belstone Court, Shropshire (1884), for the Ripleys, woollen manufacturers and dyers. This latter commission probably led to his third great house, the nearby Jacobean-style mansion of Stokesay Court (1889), designed for a glove maker. Similar stylistic historicism characterizes the commissions Harris undertook in London, including the remodelling of Marylebone parish church (1883), houses in Shaftesbury Avenue and Wardour Street (1889), and the Holborn shop of the publisher Batsford (c.1889).

Yet Harris remained ideologically committed to the need for a new style. Returning to print with *Three Periods of English Architecture* (1894), he argued that the structural inheritance of Gothic represented indigenous tradition, and its revival was the prelude to an architectural awakening through a future style based on metal construction. His ideas were little regarded, and passed over in the brief obituaries following his death aged seventy-one at his home, 54 Carlton Hill, St John's Wood, London, on 10 July 1900. He was unmarried. Since then, however, his writings have been seen as anticipating the modernist movement, even as his career exemplified the Victorian dilemma of style. CHRIS BROOKS

Sources T. Harris, *Victorian architecture* (1860) · T. Harris, ed., *Examples of the architecture of the Victorian age* (1862) · T. Harris, *Three periods of English architecture* (1894) · D. Harbron, 'Thomas Harris', *ArchR*, 92 (1942), 63–6 · P. F. R. Donner, 'A Harris florilegium', *ArchR*, 93 (1943), 51–2 · H. S. Goodhart-Rendel, 'Rogue architects of the Victorian era', *RIBA Journal*, 56 (1948–9), 251–9 · N. Pevsner, *Some architectural writers of the nineteenth century* (1972) · J. Franklin, *The gentleman's country house and its plan, 1835–1914* (1981) · M. Girouard, *The Victorian country house*, rev. edn (1979) · D. Linstrum, *West Yorkshire: architects and architecture* (1978) · *The Builder*, 79 (1900), 39 · *Building News*, 79 (1900), 40 · *RIBA Journal*, 7 (1899–1900), 450 · *London: north-west*, Pevsner (1991) · *London: the cities of London and Westminster*, Pevsner (1973) · *Shropshire*, Pevsner (1958) · *Yorkshire: the West Riding*, Pevsner (1967)
Likenesses T. R. Davison, drawing, repro. in Harbron, 'Thomas Harris', 66

Harris, Thomas Lake (1823–1906), millenarian and mystic, was born on 15 May 1823 at Fenny Stratford, Buckinghamshire, the only son of Thomas Harris, an auctioneer, and his wife, Annie (*née* Lake), who died when her son was only nine. In 1828 the family emigrated to Utica, New York, where they kept a grocery store. At about the age of eighteen Thomas dissociated himself from the Calvinism of his father, who was a deacon in a Baptist church, and went to live in the home of the Universalist minister at Utica, whose creed was more suited to Harris's romantic and poetic spirit. After some tentative journalism he began preaching in the Mohawk valley. In 1845 he married Mary Van Arnum (d. 1850) and they had two sons, John Hampden and Thomas Lake. In December 1845 he became pastor of the Fourth Universalist Society of New York city, but in 1847 he became a spiritualist. After a brief association with the Swedenborgian medium Andrew Jackson Davis, he learnt of the latter's affair with a married woman and organized his own Independent Christian Society in New York, where one of his sermons, *Juvenile*

Depravity and Crime in our City (1850), led to the founding of the New York Juvenile Asylum.

The death of his wife in 1850 led Harris to retire to Mountain Cove, Fayette county, Virginia, with another medium, James D. Scott of Auburn, New York; together they edited the *Mountain Cove Journal* and gathered a small community. It was at this time that Harris claimed to be the medium of epics which were suggested to him by such poets as Byron and Coleridge, and dictated to an amanuensis while Harris was in a trance. They were later published as *A Lyric of the Golden Age* (1856). In 1853 he returned to New York but visited New Orleans in 1855, where he married Emily Isabella Waters (*d.* 1885). Even before this, in 1854, he had begun to formulate his ideas of 'conjugal angels' and spiritual or 'counterpartal marriages'—a belief which would soon become a distinctive part of his philosophy. From May 1857 to August 1861 he edited the *Herald of Light*, in which he presented himself as Swedenborg's heir, a prophet with a messianic mission to introduce the world to the mysteries of 'spiritual respiration'. Most Swedenborgians rejected Harris's *Arcana of Christianity* (1858), in which he claimed to be a 'pivot' on which revolved the divine plan for the world's redemption, but as his ideas evolved during the next forty years his debt to Swedenborg was always apparent.

Furnished with introductions from the founder of the *New York Tribune*, Horace Greeley, who was also a member of his congregation, Harris arrived in England in May 1859, at a time when revivalism was in vogue. His reticence at this stage about his perception of himself in a messianic role meant that many orthodox Christians welcomed his preaching in London, Manchester, and Edinburgh. After returning to America in 1861 Harris bought a farm at Wassaic, Dutchess county, New York, and established a small community, which he called the Use, and which he regarded as a visible expression of a new universal society, the Brotherhood of the New Life. In 1863 the farm was sold and the community's resources were pooled to purchase a mill, where they settled, 4 miles up the valley, in Amenia. The communist ideal now became a family partnership, and in due course a patriarchy, with Harris as Father. He established the 'first national bank' of Amenia, with himself as president, and experimented in viticulture. In the community each member was given a new name and was expected to be unquestioningly obedient to Harris who was known as Faithful. Many members had earlier suffered financial or other disappointment, and, in other cases, had been casualties of the civil war, but now they all accepted a severe regime of manual labour. Most of them were of Baptist origin, some having been ministers and others professional people. Laurence Oliphant, who had been impressed by Harris in 1860, visited Amenia in 1865, and his widowed mother became a member of the community.

Lady Oliphant's wealth made possible the purchase in 1867 of a new site for the community, at Brocton, near Dunkirk, beside Lake Erie, where their grape cultivation and winemaking under the direction of Dr J. W. Hyde of Missouri were more successful. Harris, a shrewd business

man, named the settlement Salem-on-Erie to publicize the new Salem grape in which he had invested heavily. He opened a restaurant at the local railway station to encourage the drinking of the community's wine, claiming that it (together with the smoking of tobacco) was beneficial to the community's practice of 'open breathing', by which the divine breath (or Holy Spirit) was thought to enter their bodies. He further propounded this idea in *The Breath of God with Man* (1867). Another distinctive feature at Brocton was Harris's insistence that his followers (including those who were married) should abstain from sexual relations so as to leave them free to be united with their 'celestial counterparts'.

Harris's influence over Laurence Oliphant in particular is fascinating. For a while Oliphant was encouraged by Harris to work in Europe as a correspondent for *The Times* and Harris visited him in Paris during a journey to Europe in 1871–2. Nevertheless Oliphant had to return to Brocton from time to time, and when Harris reluctantly approved of Oliphant's marriage to Alice le Strange in 1872 she had first to pledge her obedience to Harris and place her property unreservedly in his hands. Even after Oliphant's irrevocable break with the community in 1881, his description of Harris (who is the eponymous character of Oliphant's novel *Masollam*) is far from being unremittingly hostile.

Initial reactions from the local population at Brocton had been favourable, but some complaints probably led to the Brotherhood's removal in 1875 to Fountain Grove near Santa Rosa, California, where Harris's conduct became still more eccentric. He had often claimed to be near to total exhaustion from his interior struggle with the natural forces of evil and from his efforts to be fully united with his 'heavenly counterpart', but in 1885 he reckoned that he had achieved this and that he was immortal. This may have been connected with the death on 1 October 1885 of his much neglected wife, whose condition, for some time, had been regarded by many as near to insanity.

Harris had repeatedly proclaimed the imminent demise of the natural world but in one of his later books, *The New Republic* (1891), an expansion of a lecture given in San Francisco, he favoured some recent ideas of utopian socialism, advocating a form of 'theosocialism' which would usher in the final denouement. In December 1891 a critical account by Alzire A. Chevaillier in the *San Francisco Chronicle* included suggestions of impropriety between Harris and Jane Lee Waring (*c.*1829–1916), one of the earliest and most trusted members of the community. To the surprise of Harris's followers, in spite of his long-standing criticism of the married state as a hindrance to spiritual development, on 27 February 1892 he married Miss Waring, who was the daughter of George Edwin and Sarah (*née* Burger) Waring, and the sister of a distinguished police commissioner in New York city. The couple left for a short holiday in Wales but then settled in New York, spending some winter months in Mohawk, Florida. Their life was comparatively secluded, though Harris continued to write and publish. When he died on 23 March 1906 at his home, 308

West 102nd Street, New York city, and was cremated on the 26th, the fact was kept a secret for some months, as his followers preferred to think that he was asleep. His widow died in San Diego in 1916.

It is hard to distinguish Harris the eccentric from Harris the impostor. For each genuine acquaintance who denounced him as a financial or sexual opportunist, there were others who were ready to rebut the charges. To the uninitiated, the rambling mysticism of his prose and verse seems a torrent of deluded self-indulgence, but to dismiss him merely as a manipulative charlatan fails to do justice to a significant body of testimony. Even Oliphant believed that Harris was honest at the start. His gaunt and imposing bearing made a lasting impression—something which cannot really be said about his poetry or his philosophy, which generally seem to be banal, derivative, or impenetrable.　　　　Timothy C. F. Stunt

Sources H. W. Schneider and G. Lawton, *A prophet and a pilgrim: being the incredible history of Thomas Lake Harris and Laurence Oliphant* (1942) • A. Taylor, *Laurence Oliphant (1829–1888)* (1982), 115–45, 163–5 • P. Washington, *Madame Blavatsky's baboon: a history of the mystics, mediums, and misfits who brought spiritualism to America* (1995), 18–24 • M. F. Bednarowski, 'Harris, Thomas Lake', *ANB*

Archives Col. U., Rare Book and Manuscript Library, corresp. and papers • L. Cong.

Likenesses four photographs, repro. in Schneider and Lawton, *A prophet and a pilgrim*

Harris, Thomas Maxwell (1903–1983), palaeobotanist, was born on 8 January 1903 in Leicester, the first of the four children, and only son, of Alex Charles Harris, engineer and inventor, and his wife, Lucy Frances, daughter of Arthur Evans of Leicester. He attended Wyggeston grammar school, Northampton grammar school, and Bootham School, York. He went on to University College, Nottingham, in 1919, where he obtained a London University pass degree of BSc in chemistry, physiology, and botany. While at Nottingham, he obtained a scholarship to Christ's College, Cambridge, and in 1922 he embarked on a science tripos, graduating with a BA in botany two years later. Contact with the palaeobotanist Albert Seward brought him the chance of a studentship from the Department of Scientific and Industrial Research (1924) to investigate the Triassic fossil plants of east Greenland, research which led to the award of his PhD in 1927. In 1926 Harris went to Greenland with a party led by the Dane Lauge Koch, and overwintered on the east coast. His energetic and meticulous collecting, together with his exploitation of fossil cuticle preparation, gave the most comprehensive picture of a Mesozoic flora then known. The flora was published in five parts (1931–7) in *Meddedelser om Grønland*. In 1927 Harris married Katherine Massey (d. 1984), daughter of Harold Massey and his wife, Margaret MacKennall. They had met on an excursion to the Lake District, during a meeting of the British Association at Leeds. She was a lecturer in botany at Manchester, with a research interest in algae that she maintained throughout her life. They had four children.

Harris's main research was on the Jurassic flora of Yorkshire, and was carried out over a period of nearly forty years. He started this research soon after becoming professor of botany at Reading University, (a post he held from 1934 to 1968) and published the final volume of *The Yorkshire Jurassic Flora* in 1979. During this period Harris changed the ethos of palaeobotanical research. He believed that a palaeobotanist should collect his own material rather than waiting for it to be brought to him by geologists, since he alone would know what was worth collecting. He eschewed large eye-catching specimens of fossil plants, demonstrating that these could often be less scientifically rewarding than the small scraps which could be made to yield vital details of the living plant. His goal was always to reassemble 'the whole plant' using microscopic features of detached fragments, and their associated occurrence in many localities, to link the separated parts. By such detective work he radically changed the knowledge of many groups of Mesozoic plants, most notably the Caytoniales, the cycads, the Czeckanowskiales, and the genus *Pentoxylon*.

Harris's approach to palaeobotany was always practical, and often unconventional. Over the years he must have walked and cycled many hundreds, probably even thousands, of miles across Yorkshire on his collecting excursions. He experimented with the process of fossilization, burying rubber balls in grass clippings to see how pollen grains behave in a rock matrix, and fed his goat and ducks pollen grains to see how they survived passage through the gut. He burnt dead plant material, and even a beetle, buried in sand, to study the formation of fossil charcoal. Harris regarded the occurrence of charred wood as evidence for the occurrence of forest fires in the Mesozoic. In this, he rejected the view of Marie Stopes and others that such fusainized plant material could be formed biologically, without involving fire (a process which has not been found to occur in any modern environment).

Harris's approach to teaching was equally forthright and enterprising. He led many student parties on ecological excursions to Cadair Idris in north Wales, camping and cooking with the minimum of facilities. He regarded this combination of a physical and intellectual 'assault course' as a vital element in university education. He travelled widely, lecturing and encouraging aspiring young palaeobotanists in many parts of the world, most notably in India. He was elected to the Royal Society in 1948, and was a foreign member of both the Danish and the Swedish academies of science. He died following a heart attack on 1 May 1983, at his home, 74 Bird Hill Avenue, Reading. He left his body for science and his remains were subsequently cremated.　　　　William G. Chaloner

Sources W. G. Chaloner, *Memoirs FRS*, 31 (1985), 229–60 • *The Times* (3 May 1983) • personal knowledge (2004) • private information (2004) • *CGPLA Eng. & Wales* (1983)

Archives NHM, papers • RS | sound RS, tape of lecture reminiscing on his life and contemporaries, 1977

Likenesses photograph, repro. in K. L. Alvin, P. D. W. Barnard, and W. G. Chaloner, eds., 'Studies on fossil plants', *Journal of the Linnean Society, Botany*, 61 (1968), 1–226 • three photographs, repro. in Chaloner, *Memoirs FRS*

Wealth at death £166,759: probate, 15 July 1983, *CGPLA Eng. & Wales*

Harris, Tomás Joseph (1908–1964), artist, art dealer, and intelligence officer, was born on 10 April 1908 at 21 Lymington Road, Hampstead, London, the youngest son and sixth of the seven children of Lionel Harris (*d*. 1943) and his Spanish wife, Enriqueta Rodriguez. His father had founded the Spanish Art Gallery in Bruton Street and was responsible for importing almost all the important works of art which came from Spain into England in the years before and after the First World War. Tomás was educated at University College School and at the age of fifteen won the Trevelyan-Goodall scholarship to the Slade School of Fine Art where he studied from 1923 to 1926, concentrating mainly on sculpture. He continued his studies in the arts by spending a year at the British Academy in Rome, but in 1928 he decided to become an art dealer. He set up a small gallery of his own, first in Sackville Street and then in Bruton Street, but after a short time moved it to join his father at the Spanish Art Gallery. He continued to run the latter after his father's death in 1943. He was also a talented amateur musician, and played the piano, the saxophone, and other wind instruments. On 10 August 1931 he married Hilda (*b*. 1919/20), daughter of Ernest Campbell Webb, of London; there were no children of the marriage.

As a dealer Harris continued the policy of his father and brought to Britain not only Spanish paintings, including works by El Greco, whose importance was only just beginning to be recognized, but also medieval tapestries, Oriental carpets, Renaissance jewellery, and other *objets d'art* in which the palaces and religious houses of Spain were rich. He had an astonishing instinct for discovering works of art in unexpected places, and on one occasion bought a group of panels from a fifteenth-century German altarpiece which were among the contents of an outhouse at a country sale in England. He had a reputation for absolute probity which sometimes aroused the jealousy of his less successful competitors.

At the beginning of the Second World War, Harris joined a branch of intelligence which was later dissolved and in 1940 was transferred to the security service, where his intimate knowledge of Spain was of great value. His greatest achievement in this field was as one of the principal organizers of operation Garbo, which was the most successful double-cross operation of the war and which seriously misled the Germans about allied plans for the invasion of France in 1944. The success of the operation, which was described by a senior commander as worth an armoured division, was mainly due to the extraordinary imaginative power with which Harris directed it. In 1945 he was appointed OBE.

Even during the war Harris did not completely relinquish his activities as an artist and in 1943 he held a one-man show at the galleries of Reid and Lefèvre in King Street. After the war he gradually freed himself from his commitments as a dealer and spent more and more time in Spain, first at Malaga and then in Majorca where he designed and built a house at Camp de Mar. Here he was able to paint as much as he wanted, and he also experimented with making ceramics and stained glass and

designing tapestries, three of which were woven at the royal tapestry factory at Madrid. His great versatility enabled him to master all the technical problems involved in these activities with astonishing ease.

At the same time Harris devoted much time to collecting, concentrating first on drawings by the two Tiepolos (which were shown by the Arts Council in 1955) and later on the engravings of Dürer and the etchings of Rembrandt. His greatest achievement was, however, to form a magnificent collection of etchings and lithographs by Goya which in 1979 was accepted in part payment of death duties and is now in the British Museum. Finding that the standard works on Goya were seriously misleading he decided to write a book about the etchings himself and the result was the two volumes published in 1964 which became the standard work. In writing *Goya: Engravings and Lithographs* he was helped by Juliet Wilson.

Harris was notable for his warmth, his generosity, and the enthusiasm with which he threw himself into any undertaking. He died in a motor accident at Lluchmayor, Majorca, on 27 January 1964. In 1975 an exhibition of his work was held at the galleries of the Courtauld Institute, to which his widow and sisters had presented a fine collection of textiles formed by his father and himself.

ANTHONY BLUNT, *rev.*

Sources private information (1981) · personal knowledge (1981) · A. Blunt, *Tomás Harris, 1908–1964: paintings, dry-points, lithographs, tapestries, stained glass and ceramics* (1975) [exhibition catalogue, Courtauld] · b. cert. · m. cert.
Likenesses T. Harris, self-portrait, drypoint drawing, *c*.1954, NPG · T. Harris, self-portrait, Courtauld Inst.
Wealth at death £600,213 effects in England: probate, 29 April 1965, *CGPLA Eng. & Wales*

Harris, Walter (1647–1732), physician, the son of Walter Harris, was born in Gloucester. A scholar at Winchester College, he matriculated from New College, Oxford, on 22 February 1667 and became a fellow of the college. He received a BA degree on 10 October 1670, but following his conversion to Roman Catholicism about 1673, he studied medicine in France and obtained a medical degree from Bourges on 20 July 1675. Moving to London in 1676, Harris turned his attention to translating French medical manuals into English. His first effort was Nicolas de Blégny's book about curing venereal diseases with mercury; it was followed by Nicolas Lémery's popular *Cours de chymie*, which contained descriptions of various chemical medicines used by continental physicians, with suggestions for their easy preparation. Harris later (1680) wrote an appendix to the Lémery text.

However, Harris's Catholicism remained an impediment to his medical career, and amid the turmoil of the Popish Plot he renounced catholicism and published *Farewell to Popery* in 1679. The pamphlet is in the form of a letter to John Nicholas, vice-chancellor of Oxford University and a warden of New College, justifying Harris's return to the Church of England. He was consequently incorporated MD by Cambridge University in 1680 and became a fellow of the Royal College of Physicians in 1682. He was appointed physician-in-ordinary to Charles II in 1683, but was out of favour with Catholic James II. When James confiscated the college's charter, and in 1687 imposed a new one that increased its membership, Harris's name was omitted; he was restored the next year. Harris supported in 1695 the college's controversial pharmaceutical dispensary, created to reduce competition from London apothecaries for patients and income. Active in the college's governance, he served as its treasurer from 1714 to 1717, consiliarius from 1711 until his death, and censor five times (1688, 1698, 1700, 1704, and 1714). Harris delivered the Harveian oration on four occasions (1699, 1707, 1713, and 1726), and was Lumleian lecturer from 1710 until 1732. His 1707 oration was published in 1720 as *De morbis aliquot gravioribus observationes*. Two of the lectures appeared in print: *De peste dissertatio* (1721) and *Dissertationes medicae et chirurgicae habitae in amphitheatro collegii regalis medicorum Londiniensium* (1725).

After the revolution of 1688 the archbishop of Canterbury, John Tillotson, recommended Harris's expertise to William III; Harris became physician-in-ordinary to William and Mary, and attended Mary during her fatal bout of smallpox in 1694. He was also present at her autopsy and described the royal demise in his *De morbis aliquot gravioribus*. Harris disagreed with Richard Lower's advice to the indisposed queen to take Venice treacle, an opiated sudorific and popular panacea since Roman times, and reported that he had warned her not to provoke a permanent fever with an intensely hot medicine. Following the queen's death Harris accompanied William to the Netherlands, where he was much impressed by Dutch gardens. In 1699 he wrote *A Description of the King's Royal Palace and Garden at Loo*; it also included Harris's observations about diseases in the Netherlands. A protégé of the great Thomas Sydenham, whom he praised profusely in his Lumleian lectures, Harris often asked him for guidance in his continuing medical education. Sydenham purportedly suggested that he should read *Don Quixote* and learn how knowledge comes through observation.

In 1683 Harris published his most famous work, *Pharmacologia anti-empirica, or, A Rational Discourse of Remedies both Chymical and Galenical*, on the six great medications: mercury, antimony, vitriol, iron, quinine bark, and opium. It included discussion of superstitious cures, such as broth in which gold has been boiled, amulets, and charms. In his chapter on gout Harris emphasized the prevention of acute attacks, rejected a rigid diet in the management of the ailment, and remarked on the higher incidence of gout among men of intellect. He also justified the concentration by a physician on one disease. Harris hoped to vindicate 'natural remedies' in the book, which additionally lambasted 'diverse empiricks and mountebanks'. Calling for a judicious and methodological administration of medicine, buttressed by interventionist authorities, Harris ridiculed Paracelsus as an impetuous chemist who wrote like a heathen and never said his prayers.

In 1689 Harris produced his most noteworthy contribution to medicine, a treatise in Latin on acute diseases in infants, *De morbis acutis infantum*, first translated into English in 1693 by William Cockburn. Reprinted in 1705, 1720, 1736, 1741, and 1745, the work became the standard paediatric monograph for a century and was translated into French and German. Harris addressed the difficulties of diagnosing and treating young patients; he also estimated the effect of heredity on disease in children and the importance of correct diet in infancy. He was particularly concerned about the noxious effects of childhood acidosis, attributing the aetiology of various digestive troubles to intestinal acid. He recommended first neutralizing the acidity with powdered oyster shell, followed by a rhubarb purge to rid the body of abnormal elements. He was dropped as physician-in-ordinary in 1701. A parishioner at St George the Martyr, Queen Square, London, Harris penned a religious tract, *The Works of God*, in 1727. He was married and had one daughter, Mary Aubrey Harris, to whom he left his worldly goods when he died on 1 August 1732 at his home in Red Lion Square, London. Harris was buried at St George the Martyr.

ELIZABETH LANE FURDELL

Sources DNB · Munk, *Roll* · J. Ruhräh, 'Walter Harris: seventeenth-century pediatrist', *Annals of Medical History*, 2 (1919), 228–40 · RCP Lond., *Mutual admiration* (1989) · will, PRO, PROB 6/108, fol. 144 · Venn, *Alum. Cant.* · W. Harris, *Farewell to popery* (1679)
Archives Bodl. Oxf., letters to Edward Harris
Wealth at death see will, PRO, PROB 6/108, fol. 144

Harris, Walter (1686–1761), historian, was the son of Hopton Harris of Mountmellick in Queen's county, Ireland, an army officer who served in William III's militia against James II's forces in Ireland (1690–91). Walter Harris was educated at Kilkenny School from 1701 and was admitted in 1704 to Trinity College, Dublin, where he obtained a scholarship in 1707, but was soon after expelled for having joined with other students in a disturbance; afterwards, in 1753, he received the honorary degree of doctor of laws. He was called to the bar in 1713, and in November 1716 married Elizabeth, daughter of the Revd Thomas Waye of Killree, co. Kilkenny. She died in the following month, and Harris subsequently married Elizabeth Ware, a greatgrandchild of the antiquary and historian Sir James Ware. This marriage appears to have sparked the plan, which occupied him for many years, of publishing an English edition of Sir James's Latin works relating to Ireland. In 1739 Harris issued *The whole works of Sir James Ware concerning Ireland, volume one, containing the history of the bishops of that kingdom*. He not only translated Ware's account of the bishops, but enlarged it and continued it through the protestant succession to 1739. The first part of the second volume appeared in 1745, and contained a revised and enlarged version in English of Ware's treatise, *De Hibernia et antiquitatibus eius*. Harris published the volume's second part a year later as *The writers of Ireland, in two books: I Of such writers who were born in Ireland; II Of such writers who, though foreigners, enjoyed preferments or offices in Ireland, or had their education in it*. As before, Harris made a number of, often inferior, additions to the original work, which he also brought up to date with a discussion of Jonathan Swift.

Harris's other works, all published in Dublin, included *Historiographorum aliorumque scriptorum Hiberniae commentarium, or, A history of the Irish writers* (1736) and part one of *Hibernica, or, Some Ancient Pieces Relating to the History of Ireland* (1747). In the following year he received a pension of £100 from the Irish government to continue his historical researches. A second part of the *Hibernica* appeared in 1750, and a third was prepared for the press but never published. His *History of William III* was printed anonymously in 1747 in four volumes. Complaints from the author that his work had been published in a curtailed form were followed in 1749 by an unabridged history of the king's life and reign, dedicated to the earl of Harrington, lord lieutenant of Ireland. In the first part of *Hibernica* Harris had spoken of the need and extant materials for a history of Ireland. In 1755 he presented a petition to the House of Commons at Dublin, requesting assistance to allow him to publish such a work. Reports from the parliamentary committee were favourable and calculations were made to establish the cost of producing 750 copies of the study. However, the scheme was not carried out and Harris's transcripts were subsequently purchased by parliament and presented to the Dublin Society.

Harris was appointed vicar-general of the Church of Ireland bishop of Meath in 1753. He died in Dublin on 26 July 1761. A collection of his papers was published posthumously as *The History and Antiquities of the City of Dublin* (1766).   PHILIP CARTER

Sources DNB · J. T. Gilbert, R. M. Gilbert, and J. F. Weldrick, eds., *Calendar of the ancient records of Dublin*, 18 vols. (1889–1922) · *Faulkner's Dublin Journal* (1739–61) · *The journal of the House of Commons … of Ireland, 1613–1800*, 21 vols. (1796–1802)
Archives Armagh Public Library, papers

Harris, William (c.1546–1602), Roman Catholic priest, was born in Lincoln diocese. He was educated at Lincoln College, Oxford, where he graduated BA on 26 January 1565 and was elected to a fellowship in 1567. Admitted MA on 4 July 1570 Harris was made college bursar in 1571. A few years later he 'left the College, his friends, religion and the little all he had' (Wood, *Ath. Oxon.*, 1.724) in order to study at Louvain. He arrived at Douai apparently already a priest, and was admitted to the English College in 1574. Harris was sent to the English mission in 1575.

In a confession by Robert Gray to Richard Topcliffe, Harris is referred to as being at Cowdray, Sussex, the seat of Viscount Montague, in 1590, when he is described as 'a tall man, blackish hair of head and beard' (*CSP dom.*, 1591–4, 380). In 1591 he is said to have returned to Douai, where, as acting principal in the absence of Richard Barret, he received Edward Pemberton, who reported that 'Mr Harris, principal of the English College at Douay, has been over and returned'. In September 1593 Topcliffe confirmed that Harris, Sir Robert and Lady Dormer's 'traitorous seminary priest', had lodged at Buxton (ibid., 372).

Writing of Harris, Fuller states that 'his writings were much esteemed' by Catholics, and that he was as 'obscure among Protestants as eminent with the Popish party' (Fuller, 2.419; 5.257). He wrote a work of ecclesiastical history in ten parts entitled 'Theatrum, seu, Speculum verissimae et antiquissimae ecclesiae magnae Britanniae'. The work survives in manuscript at the Bibliothèque Municipale, Douai (MS 920). Like similar contemporary studies, in his ecclesiastical history Harris set out to defend the historically close relationship of the English church with the see of Rome. The author died in England in 1602.   J. ANDREAS LÖWE

Sources J. Pits, *Relationum historicarum de rebus Anglicis*, ed. [W. Bishop] (Paris, 1619), 801 · Wood, *Ath. Oxon.*, new edn, 1.724 · Foster, *Alum. Oxon.* · T. F. Knox and others, eds., *The first and second diaries of the English College, Douay* (1878), 7, 24 · G. Anstruther, *The seminary priests 1: Elizabethan, 1558–1603* [1966], 150 · Wood, *Ath. Oxon.: Fasti* (1815), 164 · T. Fuller, *The church history of Britain*, ed. J. S. Brewer, new edn, 6 vols. (1845)
Archives Bibliothèque Municipale de la ville de Douai, 'Theatrum, seu, Speculum', MS 920

Harris, William (1675–1740), Presbyterian minister, may have been born in Southwark. Nothing is known about his parents or early life; his widowed mother is thought to have been living in Southwark in 1692. Serious from an early age, Harris was a member of a religious society for young men, as was his lifelong friend and fellow minister Benjamin Grosvenor. He was educated for the Presbyterian ministry at Timothy Jollie's academy at Attercliffe, near Sheffield, and from June 1692, probably until late 1694, at John Southwell's academy at Newbury. It is believed that he also attended the academy kept by James Waters at Uxbridge. He was preaching by the mid-1690s and was assistant to Henry Read at Gravel Lane Chapel, Southwark, in 1697. In 1698 he was appointed minister at Crutched Friars, London. He hesitated about accepting, possibly because his appointment was contested.

> It was about this time that he got the Keys of this Place, and coming here, all alone, he spent the whole Day in Fasting, and Prayer to God, for Directions and Blessings in that Work which he took upon himself with so much Fear and Trembling. (Grosvenor, 27)

Harris soon established himself as one of the leaders of liberal dissent, both as a speaker and a writer.

> His preaching was always clear and distinct … his voice strong, though somewhat interrupted by a hoarseness at the outset of his speaking; this however gradually cleared itself till he made his audience glow with the same warmth he himself felt towards the application, which was always pathetic and affecting. (Wilson, 1.68)

He published much, especially sermons, but his works also include at least two volumes of biblical exposition. According to Walter Wilson, Harris 'was reckoned the greatest master of the English tongue among the Dissenters' (ibid., 1.72). From 1708 he was one of the Friday evening lecturers at the Weighhouse, Eastcheap, and from 1712 the Merchants' lecturer at Salters' Hall. He was made DD by Edinburgh in 1728 and by King's College, Aberdeen, on 23 December 1728. He was an active dissenter, and his friend Benjamin Grosvenor wondered 'how could he have sufficient time and strength for what he did' (Grosvenor, 71). Grosvenor also testified to his toleration in theological matters: 'To me he seemed to be of no party; he was fond of no denomination but Christian' (ibid., 70).

Harris died on 25 May 1740 at Goodman's Fields, London, and was buried on 30 May in Dr Daniel Williams's vault in Bunhill Fields. No children of his marriage to Elizabeth (d. 1743) were alive at the time of his death. In his will he made bequests of South Sea stocks and annuities and Bank of England stocks with a nominal value of £2900. He also bequeathed his library of nearly 2000 items to Dr Williams's Trust and Library, of which he had been a trustee since 1716, part of which was later loaned to the second and third Exeter Academies, and found its way into the Warrington Academy Library; it is now held in Harris Manchester College in Oxford. From the wording of the will it would seem that Harris owed most of his wealth to his wife, whom he described as 'the dear and agreeable companion of my life' (will, PROB 11/703, fol. 87v).

ALAN RUSTON

Sources B. Grosvenor, *God's eternity the mourner's comfort—a sermon … on the death of … Dr W. Harris* (1740) · W. Wilson, *The history and antiquities of the dissenting churches and meeting houses in London, Westminster and Southwark*, 4 vols. (1808–14), vol. 1, pp. 66–75 · N. Lardner, *A sermon occasioned by the death of W. Harris* (1740) · C. Surman, index, DWL · *GM*, 1st ser., 10 (1740), 262 · *Protestant Dissenter's Magazine*, 6 (1799), 466–7 · *DNB* · W. D. Jeremy, *The Presbyterian Fund and Dr Daniel Williams's Trust* (1885), 113–14 · will, PRO, PROB 11/703, sig. 171 · Presbyterian Fund board minutes, vol. 1, 1 July 1690–26 June 1693, DWL, MS OD 67, fols. 93r, 98r · Presbyterian Fund board cash books, DWL, MS OD 114–115 · 'An account of the dissenting academies from the Restoration of Charles the Second', DWL, MS 24.59, pp. 31–3 · P. Morgan, *Oxford libraries outside the Bodleian: a guide*, 2nd edn (1980)
Likenesses engraving, repro. in Wilson, *History and antiquities of dissenting churches*, 1 (1808) · oils, DWL
Wealth at death stocks and annuities to value of £2900: will, PRO, PROB 11/703, sig. 171

Harris, William (1720–1770), biographer and Presbyterian minister, was born at Salisbury, Wiltshire, the son of a nonconformist tradesman of that city. He was educated for the Presbyterian ministry at Henry Grove and Thomas Amory's academy at Taunton, Somerset. He first officiated at Looe in Cornwall, and was afterwards invited to another congregation at Wells, Somerset, where he was ordained on 15 April 1741. He then married Elizabeth Bovet of Honiton, Devon, and moved to his wife's home town. The couple had no children. Thereafter his ministerial labours were confined to a very small congregation at Luppitt, near Honiton. Harris's literary career was dedicated to commemorating the historical struggles of the nonconformists in the cause of religious and civil liberty. His first biography was a study of the seventeenth-century New England independent minister Hugh Peter (or Peters) that appeared anonymously in 1751. In this and in subsequent biographies Harris professed to follow 'the manner of Mr. Bayle', illustrating the text with copious notes. In 1753 he published his *Life of James I*, which was followed by three historical accounts: he wrote on Charles I in 1758, on Cromwell in 1762, and on Charles II four years later. He was assisted in his researches by Thomas Birch and Thomas Hollis; Hollis recommended Harris to Glasgow University to receive a DD degree that was duly conferred in 1765.

Harris intended to complete his biographical services

with a life of James II, but this was interrupted by an illness from which he died on 4 February 1770. A five-volume collection of his works, together with a life of the author, was published in 1820. In his will he gave his collection of historical documents to Dr Williams's Library, and in 1832 a catalogue of Harris's books appeared. He was survived by his wife. GORDON GOODWIN, *rev.* PHILIP CARTER

Sources 'Life of William Harris', W. Harris, *Works*, 5 vols. (1820) · Nichols, *Lit. anecdotes* · *GM*, 1st ser., 40 (1770), 95 · A. Chalmers, ed., *The general biographical dictionary*, new edn, 32 vols. (1812–17)

Harris, William (1775×7–1830), Independent minister, was educated at Hoxton Academy, and ordained at Kingston upon Thames on 8 April 1801. He was pastor of the church in Downing Street, Cambridge, from about 1805, until he was appointed divinity tutor at Hoxton Academy in 1818. He became minister of the meeting-house in Church Street, Stoke Newington, at Michaelmas 1820, and subsequently theological tutor of Highbury College when Hoxton Academy moved to its new buildings at Highbury in 1826. He died on 3 January 1830, aged fifty-three or fifty-four, and was buried on 11 January in Bunhill Fields. He left a widow and nine children; the property he left was not enough to sustain them, and a fund was launched to help them.

Harris was made an LLD. He published *Grounds of Hope for the Salvation of All Dying in Infancy: an Essay* (1821) and ten other titles. He is to be distinguished from William Harris (*fl.* 1840), minister of the Congregational church at Wallingford in Berkshire, author of numerous pamphlets and discourses. GORDON GOODWIN, *rev.* R. TUDUR JONES

Sources J. Bowden, *The Christian minister …: a charge delivered … April 8, 1801, at the ordination of the Rev. William Harris* (1801) · *Congregational Magazine*, 13 (1830), 110–11, 165–6 · H. McLachlan, *English education under the Test Acts: being the history of the nonconformist academies, 1662–1820* (1931), 240 · *Evangelical Magazine and Missionary Chronicle*, 29 (1821), 341 · *GM*, 1st ser., 100/1 (1830), 280
Likenesses Freeman, stipple, pubd 1820, NPG · T. Woolnoth, stipple, pubd 1826 (after Uwins), NPG · stipple, BM; repro. in *Evangelical Magazine* (1823)
Wealth at death left some property; fund launched to help dependants: *Congregational Magazine*, 111, 116

Harris, Sir William Cornwallis (*bap.* 1807, *d.* 1848), army officer and traveller, the son of James Harris of Wittersham, Kent, was baptized on 2 April 1807. Robert *Harris (1809–1865) was a younger brother. After attending a military college Harris was appointed to the Bombay establishment (Engineers) in 1823. His commissions were: second lieutenant (18 December 1823), lieutenant (1 May 1824), captain (8 August 1834), and major (16 August 1843). He was appointed assistant superintending engineer at Bombay on 9 September 1825, and executive engineer at Khandesh in November 1825 and at Deesa in October 1830. In 1836 Harris was invalided to the Cape Colony for two years by a medical board.

On the voyage to the Cape, Harris, who from a very early age had been keen on shooting, made the acquaintance of Richard Williamson of the Bombay civil establishment, a noted hunter, and the two arranged an expedition into the African interior in search of big game. After conferring with Dr Andrew Smith, the African naturalist, then just returned from the interior, Harris and his friend started by ox-wagon from Algoa Bay, by way of Somerset and the Orange River, and travelled in a north-easterly direction until they reached the regions of the formidable Matabele (Ndebele) chief Mzilikaze. He proved friendly, and permitted the travellers to return to the Cape by a new and previously closed route by summer of 1837.

Their absence from India extended from March 1835 to December 1837, and on his return to India Harris was appointed executive engineer at Belgaum in January 1838, and field engineer to the Sind force in December of the same year. In December 1840 he was made superintending engineer to the southern provinces, and in September 1841 was sent in charge of a mission to establish relations with the ancient Christian kingdom of Shoa in the highlands of Ethiopia. He returned to England with a commercial treaty with that state, and was knighted for his services (June 1844). Harris was highly regarded in his role as executive engineer at Dharwar Dion in 1846 and at Poona in February 1847, and on 5 February 1848 was appointed superintending engineer, northern provinces. He died of malignant fever at Surwur, near Poona, on 9 October 1848.

Harris submitted an account of his travels in southern Africa to the Royal Geographical Society, London, and the Geographical Society of Bombay. He published a further account, *Wild Sports in South Africa* (1841). Under the title 'Wild sports in South Africa, being a narrative…', the same work appeared in London in 1841. Harris, a competent artist, also published *Portraits of the Game Animals of Southern Africa, Drawn from Life in their Natural Haunts* (1840) and *Highlands of Ethiopia: a Narrative of a Mission to the Kingdom of Shoa* (1844). He also published papers in the Zoological Society's *Transactions* and *Proceedings*, the Linnean Society's *Proceedings*, and elsewhere.

H. M. CHICHESTER, rev. JAMES FALKNER

Sources *Indian Army List* · *The Times* (24 Nov 1848) · W. Harris, *An expedition in South Africa* (1838) · *LondG* (7 June 1844) · Bodl. RH
Likenesses attrib. R. R. Reinagle, oils, c.1823, NPG · attrib. F. Howard, oils, c.1830, NAM · O. Oakely, watercolour, 1845, Johannesburg Public Library, South Africa, Africana Museum

Harris, William George, second Baron Harris (1782–1845), army officer, eldest son of George *Harris, first Baron Harris, and his wife, Anne Carteret (d. 30 July 1833), daughter of Charles Dickson of Bath, was born at Limerick on 19 January 1782. After education at a private military academy in Chelsea under Captain Reynolds, Harris was appointed ensign in the 76th regiment in May 1795, and the year after was promoted to lieutenant in the 74th highlanders, which he joined at Walajapet, Madras, in 1797. With that regiment he served in the army commanded by his father throughout the campaign of 1799 against Tippu Sahib, and at the capture of Seringapatam was one of the storming party and among the first to enter the fortress, for which he was commended by General David Baird. He was sent home in charge of the captured Mysorean and French standards, which he presented to George III.

Promoted to a company in the 49th regiment (16 October 1800), Harris joined it in Jersey, and later embarked with the regiment (serving as marines) on board the fleet under Sir Hyde Parker and Nelson. He was on board HMS *Glatton* at the battle of Copenhagen and in the Baltic cruise. In 1802 he accompanied his regiment to Canada, and won the confidence of Sir Isaac Brock, colonel of the regiment. Promoted major in the 73rd highlanders, he was on his way to join the regiment in India when the expedition under Baird was dispatched in the autumn of 1805 for the recapture of the Cape. Harris joined Baird as a volunteer, and was present at the landing and action with the Dutch at Blue Berg. On his arrival in India he found his regiment had returned to England where, after visiting China, he followed it.

In 1809, when about to embark with the regiment for New South Wales, Harris was instead posted to the command of the newly raised 2nd battalion in England. A tory, in September 1812 he stood as MP for Coventry, but retired in favour of Joseph Butterworth. In 1813 he was embarked with his battalion on 'a particular service', but was ordered to join the troops under General Gibbs sent to Stralsund in Swedish Pomerania. Harris was then detached with his battalion into the interior to establish communication with the army under Lieutenant-General Count Walmoden. Moving cautiously with his small force between the strong army corps under Davout and other French marshals then in Pomerania, Mecklenburg-Schwerin, and Hanover, Harris succeeded in reaching Walmoden, and contributed significantly to the victory at Göhrde in Hanover on 16 September 1813, when, after the German hussars had been repulsed, he charged with his battalion, capturing a French battery in gallant style and causing a panic among the defenders. In November the battalion re-embarked at Warnemünde in the Gulf of Lübeck, and on arriving at Yarmouth was ordered to join the army at Antwerp under Sir Thomas Graham. During the succeeding operations Harris distinguished himself in the presence of the duke of Clarence (later William IV) by storming and capturing the village of Merxem.

Harris remained with his battalion in the Low Countries after the peace of 1814, and in May 1815 joined Wellington's army. The 2nd battalion 73rd was brigaded with the 2nd battalions 30th and 69th and the 33rd regiments, under Sir Colin Halkett, and suffered heavily at Quatre Bras and Waterloo. At Waterloo, Harris was shot through the right shoulder. He returned home with the battalion, and soon after went on half pay of the Bourbon regiment. On his retirement the officers of the 73rd presented him with a splendid sword. Harris became a major-general in 1821, and held a staff command in Ireland from May 1823 to June 1825, and commanded the northern district in England from 1825 to July 1828, where he suppressed disturbances in the manufacturing districts. He became colonel of the 86th (Royal County Down) regiment in 1832, colonel of the 73rd in 1835, and lieutenant-general in 1837. He was a CB (1815), KCH (1833), and a knight of Wilhelm the Lion in the Netherlands.

In his early years Harris was an expert athlete and swimmer. As a commanding officer he was strict but kind, and was reportedly well-liked by both his soldiers and his officers. After succeeding to the peerage as second Baron Harris in 1829, he lived in retirement on his estate at Belmont, near Faversham, Kent. He was twice married: first, on 17 October 1809, to Eliza Selina Anne (d. 25 Jan 1817), daughter of William Dick MD, of Tullymet House, Perthshire, with whom he had two sons and one daughter; second, on 28 May 1824, to Isabella Helena (d. January 1861), only daughter of Robert Handcock-Temple of Waterstown, county Westmeath, with whom he had three sons and one daughter. Harris died at Belmont, after a short illness, on 30 May 1845, and was succeeded by his eldest son by his first wife, George Francis Robert *Harris, third Baron Harris.

H. M. CHICHESTER, rev. JAMES FALKNER

Sources Army List · J. Philippart, ed., The royal military calendar, 3 (1816) · R. Cannon, ed., Historical record of the seventy-third regiment (1851) · Hart's Army List · Annual Register (1845) · GM, 2nd ser., 24 (1845), 76–8 · GEC, Peerage
Archives CKS, corresp. and papers
Likenesses T. Hickey, charcoal and chalk drawing, 1799, Stratfield Saye, Hampshire · W. Salter, group portrait, oils (Waterloo banquet at Apsley House), Wellington Museum, London · W. Salter, oils, NPG

Harris, Sir William Henry (1883–1973), organist and composer, was born on 28 March 1883 in Tulse Hill, London, the first of the three children of William Henry Harris (1864–1958), Post Office official and amateur organist, and his wife, Alice Mary Clapp (1861–1946). His early musical training was overseen by the organist Herbert Morris at St David's Cathedral, and he passed the fellowship examination of the Royal College of Organists in 1899. In the same year he entered the Royal College of Music as a scholar, studying under Sir Walter Parratt, Charles Wood, and Walford Davies, and later publishing his own hymn harmonizations in the 1906 English Hymnal. Service in the Artists' Rifles during the First World War interrupted his early career as assistant organist at Lichfield Cathedral (1911–19) and as a teacher at the Birmingham and Midland Institute in collaboration with Granville Bantock. In 1913 Harris married Kathleen Doris Carter (1889–1968), youngest daughter of James Perrins Carter JP, a merchant, of Redland, Bristol; they had two daughters.

Harris moved to Oxford in 1919 where he served first as organist at New College, in succession to Hugh Allen, and then as organist of Christ Church (1928–33), in succession to Noel Ponsonby. In 1923 he took the Oxford BA and MA to become a full member of the university, even though he already held the degrees of BMus (1904) and DMus (1910). During his time at the university he directed the Balliol concerts (1925–33), and conducted the amateur Oxford Bach Choir (1926–33) and the Opera Club. With the latter, which he was instrumental in founding, he conducted the famous production of Monteverdi's Orfeo staged by the young Jack Westrup in 1925.

In March 1933 Harris took up the position of organist at St George's Chapel, Windsor, in succession to Charles

Hylton Stewart. At Windsor, he provided music for the funeral of George V in 1936 and the coronation of George VI in 1937, and he later participated in the musical education of Princess Elizabeth and Princess Margaret; he also instituted an annual Festival of Church Music. Other royal commitments included the provision of music for the funeral of George VI and service as assistant conductor at the coronation of Elizabeth II in 1953. Harris retired from St George's in 1961, having also served as professor of organ and harmony at the Royal College of Music (1923–53), as president of the Royal College of Organists (1946–8), and as director of musical studies at the Royal School of Church Music (1956–61). He was appointed CVO and FRCM in 1942, KCVO in 1954 and honorary RAM in 1955.

As a composer Harris was an impressive heir to the conservative tradition of Anglican music represented by the work of Sir C. H. H. Parry, by whom he was initially strongly influenced. Among the most celebrated and enduring of Harris's works is the a cappella double-choir anthem 'Faire is the heaven' (1925), with its thrilling antiphony between the two performing groups (the decani and cantoris sides of the traditional Anglican chapel); the choice of a text by Spenser was typical of the composer's refined literary tastes. Equally fine, and still widely performed, is the anthem 'Bring us, O Lord God', first heard at Windsor on 29 October 1939. Harris composed several major concert works, including the skilfully crafted and expansive cantata The Hound of Heaven (1919, to a poem by Francis Thompson), which received a Carnegie award. In 1935 he composed a further cantata, Michael Angelo's Confession of Faith (to a poem by Morna Stuart, after Wordsworth), for the Three Choirs festival at Worcester; in this score bold rhetorical gestures, colouristic harmony, and unpredictable rhythms serve to enliven solid contrapuntal choral writing derived from the style of Sir C. V. Stanford. Harmonic richness and rhythmic subtlety were to remain Harris's most significant contributions to what Erik Routley termed 'the rehabilitation of orthodox cathedral music' in the first half of the twentieth century. Harris made a modest contribution to the solo organ repertory, and he composed a full-scale organ sonata in 1938. His mature hymn tunes include 'Alberta' (Songs of Praise, 1926) and 'North Petherton' (Hymns Ancient and Modern, 1950). Harris died peacefully at Petersfield, Hampshire, where he lived, on 6 September 1973 and he was cremated there on 11 September; his ashes were interred together with those of his wife at the foot of the organ-loft stairs in St George's Chapel, Windsor, at a memorial service held on 9 October 1973.

MERVYN COOKE

Sources DNB · private information (2004) [M. Brockway] · C. Palmer, 'Harris, Sir William', New Grove · H. W. Shaw, The succession of organists of the Chapel Royal and the cathedrals of England and Wales from c.1538 (1991), 352 · E. Routley, Twentieth-century church music (1964) · J. Buxton and P. Williams, eds., New College, Oxford, 1379–1979 (1979) · H. C. Colles and J. Cruft, The Royal College of Music: a centenary record, 1883–1983 (1982) · The Times (8 Sept 1973) · CGPLA Eng. & Wales (1973)
Archives Royal College of Music, London, MSS · St George's Chapel, Windsor, MSS

Likenesses photographs, St George's Chapel, Windsor · photographs, Royal College of Music, London
Wealth at death £10,763: probate, 14 Nov 1973, *CGPLA Eng. & Wales*

Harris, Sir William Snow (1791–1867), natural philosopher, was born on 1 April 1791 at Plymouth, the only son of Thomas Harris, solicitor, and Mary (*d. c.*1839), daughter of William E. Snow. Educated at Plymouth grammar school, he studied medicine at Edinburgh University, 1811–12, attending Thomas Hope's chemistry lectures. He became a member of the Royal College of Surgeons of London in late 1813 and served as a militia surgeon before becoming a general practitioner in Plymouth. In 1824 he married Elizabeth Snow Thorne (*d.* 1886), eldest daughter of Richard Thorne of Pilton, near Barnstaple. They had two daughters and one son. Harris converted the ceiling of their nursery into a planetarium and the floor into a compass card. The marriage settlement allowed him to give up medical practice, though he treated a few select friends, such as the actor Charles Mathews.

Instead Harris pursued his strong scientific interests in electricity and magnetism. He invented an improved compass and the disc electrometer. But his work on lightning conductors on ships was the most significant. He had a great love of the sea and was a very competent yachtsman. In 1820 he invented a lightning conductor for ships' masts connected to their copper sheeting. This conductor, Harris asserted, would prevent damage to ships when struck by lightning. In 1823 a committee appointed by the Royal Society to investigate Harris's conductors agreed with his conclusions. This view was not universally shared, and two decades passed before lightning conductors were installed in Royal Navy ships. Thomas Byam Martin ascribed this delay to the obstinacy of the secretary at the Admiralty, John Barrow. While Barrow did play a role in delaying their installation, there were sound reasons for so doing. First, it was not clear whether the presence of conductors would attract lightning to the ships, and second, there was no agreed theory to explain how lightning occurred.

Much of Harris's work from the mid-1820s was devoted to pursuing two strategies to overcome these problems. First, he compiled and published in the *Nautical Magazine* and elsewhere meticulous records of ships damaged or destroyed by lightning to show the seriousness of the problem. Second, he worked experimentally on the theory of high tension, static, electricity. In a *Philosophical Transactions* paper of 1834 Harris provided experimental evidence against Coulomb's mathematical law of electrical action; this work drew some criticism from William Whewell and others which Harris felt keenly. Harris's work gained him election to fellowship of the Royal Society in 1831 and the Copley medal in 1835; he was the society's Bakerian lecturer in 1839. Furthermore, during the 1830s, Harris gave three Friday evening discourses at the Royal Institution.

In 1839 the Admiralty appointed a committee to investigate lightning conductors, which reported favourably.

Sir William Snow Harris (1791–1867), by J. Dickson

Yet, despite the strong support of George Cockburn, one of the lords of the Admiralty, it was not until 1843 that a full programme of installation commenced. Harris's work was recognized by the government with the award in 1841 of a civil list annuity of £300, the conferral of a knighthood in 1847, and a grant of £5000 in 1854. The Russian navy had installed lightning conductors on its ships before the Royal Navy, and Tsar Nicholas I, in gratitude, presented Harris with a ring and vase in 1845. He was further recognized in England by election to the Naval Club at Plymouth in 1850 and to the Royal Yacht Club at Cowes in 1854.

Following his success with ships Harris turned his attention towards buildings. He compiled lists of buildings damaged by lightning, though these were less detailed than for ships. He had to struggle less to gain acceptance for the terrestrial use of lightning conductors. In 1855 parliament voted £2314 for the installation of lightning conductors in the new houses of parliament which was supervised by Harris. Later he oversaw lightning conductors at royal palaces, powder magazines, and the Royal Mausoleum at Frogmore.

Although Harris had to spend some time in London lobbying for lightning conductors, most of his activities were centred on Plymouth. He was a member of the Plymouth Institution, founded in 1812, which had built the Plymouth Athenaeum in 1819, where Harris gave many lectures on scientific topics, mainly electrical, but also on subjects such as gravitation or atmospheric railways. The museum of the Plymouth Institution was completed in

1829 and Harris was curator of apparatus almost continuously until 1851, apart from 1847–8 when he was president; he was president again in 1853–4. In 1829 he was one of the founders of the Blue Friars, a dining club whose members wore monkish garb of serge blue cloth when they dined three or four times a year to discuss intellectual matters and enjoy an entertaining evening; the club seems to have dissolved about 1846. Using the provincial ideology of the British Association (of which he was a local secretary in 1841), Harris was able to gain their support for making hourly meteorological observations in Plymouth. During ten years from 1832 the British Association granted him more than £300 with which he oversaw the making of more than 120,000 observations.

Harris was also active in the larger community serving, for instance, as a justice of the peace. He had a great love of music which, through concerts held in his drawing room where he played the piano or harp, was passed on to his children. In 1851 he was one of the founders of a philharmonic society in Plymouth which for two or three years attracted eminent singers from London.

Although Harris was well known and respected, both locally and nationally (Charles Darwin dined with him a month before the *Beagle* set sail), his studies of static electricity became increasingly old fashioned during his lifetime. He did not investigate current electricity where most research effort came to be concentrated. In August 1861 he suffered an attack of iritis which eventually led to the loss of sight in one eye and impaired severely the vision in the other. Despite deteriorating health he completed his *Treatise on Frictional Electricity* (published posthumously). He died, survived by his wife and children, on 22 January 1867, at his home, 6 Windsor Villas, Plymouth, and was buried in Plymouth cemetery on 28 January.

FRANK A. J. L. JAMES

Sources C. Tomlinson, 'Biographical notice of the author', in W. S. Harris, *A treatise on frictional electricity* (1867), vii–xxii · *Western Daily Mercury* (23 Jan 1867), 3a · *Western Daily Mercury* (29 Jan 1867), 3b · W. H. K. Wright, *The Blue Friars: their sayings and doings, being a new chapter in the history of old Plymouth* (1889) · R. Anderson, *Lightning conductors: their history, nature, and mode of application* (1880) · PRO, Admiralty Lightning Conductor Committee MSS, ADM 1/607 · *Letters and papers of Admiral of the Fleet Sir Thos. Byam Martin, GCB*, ed. R. V. Hamilton, 1, Navy RS, 24 (1903) · *Annual Reports* [Plymouth Institution and Devon and Cornwall Natural History Society] · *Report of the British Association for the Advancement of Science* · J. Morrell and A. Thackray, *Gentlemen of science: early years of the British Association for the Advancement of Science* (1981) · *PRS*, 16 (1867–8), xviii–xxii · records, U. Edin. · records, RCS Eng. · *The correspondence of Charles Darwin*, ed. F. Burkhardt and S. Smith, 1 (1985)

Archives Lambton Park, Chester-le-Street, co. Durham, corresp. | BL, letters to Charles Babbage, Add. MSS 37193–37197, *passim* · Lpool RO, letters to fourteenth earl of Derby · PRO, Admiralty MSS · RS · Trinity Cam., letters to William Whewell · U. St Andr. L., corresp. with James Forbes

Likenesses J. Dickson, lithograph, RS [*see illus.*] · photograph (in old age), repro. in Wright, *Blue Friars*, facing p. 73

Wealth at death under £2000: probate, 23 Feb 1867, *CGPLA Eng. & Wales*

Harris, (Henry) Wilson (1883–1955), journalist and author, was born on 21 September 1883 at 3 Eton Place, Plymouth, the elder son of Henry Vigurs Harris (*b.* 1850), who

carried on a family business as a house-decorator, and his wife, Fanny Wilson. The theologian James Rendel Harris was his uncle. Harris's parents being devout Quakers, their son was brought up in that persuasion. He was educated at Plymouth College and St John's College, Cambridge, where he was a foundation scholar. In 1905 he was elected president of the Cambridge Union and obtained a second class in part one of the classical tripos. After leaving Cambridge he contemplated being called to the bar, and also thought of making teaching his career; but in 1908 his literary gifts and his sympathy for Liberal principles led him to join the staff of the *Daily News*, edited by A. G. Gardiner. He served on that paper successively as news editor, leader writer, and diplomatic correspondent. On 7 May 1910 he married Florence, daughter of Alfred Midgley Cash, medical practitioner of Torquay. They had one daughter.

Harris attended a great many international gatherings from the peace conference in 1919 onwards, acquiring a considerable knowledge of foreign affairs. He made his name as an author with *President Wilson: his Problems and his Policy* (1917) and *The Peace in the Making* (1919). From the start he was a convinced supporter of the League of Nations movement and soon decided to devote himself to the cause of peace and international friendship. It was said of him that he 'did more than any other writer to build up informed and popular support for the League' (*The Times*, 19 Jan 1955, 10), producing several pamphlets and books, including *What the League of Nations is* (1925). In 1923 he joined the staff of the League of Nations Union, editing its journal *Headway*, and speaking at meetings up and down the country. But his attempts to 'encourage a lively diversity of opinion' in the journal were restricted by an executive committee eager to avoid controversy, and after a frustrating period he left the post in 1932 (Birn, 134).

Harris's journalistic curiosity was allied to a Quaker concern to find Christian solutions for the world's political and social problems. So when, in the year he left the League of Nations Union, Sir Evelyn Wrench offered him the editorship of *The Spectator*, he accepted readily. He commented that *The Spectator* 'alone among secular weeklies ... has always had quite definitely a religious side' (Harris, 242). Harris in fact broadened the paper's coverage of religious issues significantly, taking responsibility for much of this himself. He said that having 'some concern for the things of the spirit myself, I was not willing that all that vital aspect of human affairs should, so far as *The Spectator* was concerned, be dealt with by hands other than mine' (ibid.). Describing himself politically as of the 'Left Centre' he 'had voted for all three parties at different times' (Harris, 246), and saw himself, like his paper, as independent and concerned more with moral than political issues. He wrote fine character sketches of public figures for the paper and in columns under the pseudonym Janus was a 'witty and incisive commentator on public affairs' (*The Times*, 13 Jan 1955). A selection of his articles was published under the title *Ninety-Nine Gower Street* (1943).

During the Second World War years of 1939–45 Harris

found time to write a short book, *The Daily Press* (1943); a survey, *Problems of the Peace* (1944); and biographies of Caroline Fox (1944) and J. A. Spender (1946). In 1945 he accepted an invitation to stand as an independent parliamentary candidate for Cambridge University and was elected after a close contest with J. B. Priestley for the second seat. This gave him the opportunity to debate in the national forum issues of social or moral concern without the constraints of party discipline or constituency pressures. The abolition of the university seats brought his parliamentary career to a close in 1950; his editorship of *The Spectator* came to an end in 1953. In the last two years of his life he wrote under his pseudonym Janus in the columns of *Time and Tide*.

Tall, upright, spare of figure, with clear-cut features, genial and brisk in manner, Harris worked rapidly, and in his leisure hours was a voracious reader and a keen traveller and motorist. Being 'by nature a teacher, and something of a preacher' (*The Times*, 13 Jan 1955), he gave *The Spectator* a moral authority which was widely respected across the political spectrum. The reputation and the circulation of the paper were both enhanced during his long editorship. If the counterpart of his many great qualities was a certain stubbornness and narrowness of outlook, he was remembered as a journalist of deep integrity active for the common good. He was a member of the council of the Royal Institute of International Affairs, a governor of the Leys School, and in 1953 received the honorary degree of LLD from the University of St Andrews. He died in a nursing home at 10 Eaton Gardens, Hove, Sussex, on 11 January 1955 and was cremated at the Downs crematorium, Brighton, on 14 January. His wife survived him.

Derek Hudson, *rev.* Marc Brodie

Sources W. Harris, *Life so far* (1954) · *The Times* (13 Jan 1955) · personal knowledge (1971) · private information (1971) · D. S. Birn, *The League of Nations Union, 1918–1945* (1981) · S. E. Koss, *The rise and fall of the political press in Britain*, 2 (1984) · WWBMP · CGPLA Eng. & Wales (1955)
Archives Bodl. Oxf., corresp. with Gilbert Murray · Bodl. Oxf., corresp. relating to Society for Protection of Science and Learning · JRL, corresp. with James Ramsey MacDonald
Wealth at death £36,902 3s. 11d.: probate, 29 March 1955, CGPLA Eng. & Wales

Harrison family (*per.* 1715–*c.*1790), gun-founders, came to prominence with **William Harrison** (*d.* 1745). He and his sons, Andrews and John, were the main suppliers of guns and shot in Britain in the mid-eighteenth century. The origins of William Harrison are unknown, but he is mentioned in Board of Ordnance records in 1715 acting first as surety for Richard Jones, iron-founder in Southwark, then completing his contracts for him. In 1717 he lodged a bond for £1000 with the Treasury before delivering his guns and two years later he was put on the same footing as other contractors. Within a short time he became the most important founder, supplying guns, shot, or cast-iron wheels to the board almost every year until his death. From 1718 until 1744 Harrison had a virtual monopoly selling guns and ammunition to the East India Company. A large part of his business was supplying guns for the company's ships, as well as for other merchantmen; and he

also bought old guns from the East India Company and the board, indicating he had access to an air furnace to melt them down.

Harrison had a wide network of partners. Early on he worked with Richard Jones, Samuel Gott, and Stephen Peters, and with William Jukes he leased Robertsbridge furnace, Sussex. He is frequently mentioned in John Fuller's letters, selling guns which had failed proof or lending others to complete contracts for payment. In 1741 Harrison formed a partnership with Samuel Remnant, master smith at Woolwich and Fuller's agent, and John Legas and William Gott of Lamberhurst, between them controlling five wealden furnaces: Lamberhurst, Waldron, Brede, Conster, and Hamsell. Remnant got the most profitable contracts for his partners and the least for Fuller. With so many orders, the partners were able to plan casting programmes, using the capability of each furnace, always having at least one furnace working all year with access to the sea while another was devoted to producing shot. In 1743, out of a total of 752 guns supplied to the board, 591 were from the partners and the following year 324 out of 519. Moreover, since the board paid for the actual weight of iron, Harrison made his guns as heavy as possible within the acceptable limits to maximize his profits. Although owning property in Sussex, Harrison remained in London, living at New Broad Street and leasing Stone Wharf, Southwark, from which he carried out his trade in guns.

William Harrison died in London in January 1745 at New Broad Street, and under his will Remnant and Legas looked after the business interests of his two sons, while Harrison's clerk, Robert Bagshaw, was named guardian. The elder son, **Andrews Harrison** (1725–*c.*1786), was born in London on 14 November 1725. His brother **John Harrison** (*b.* 1729, *d.* before 1792) was also born there, in November 1729. Their father's partnership was dissolved when John came of age in 1750. The board began prosecuting Remnant for stealing iron over many years and accused Legas and the Harrisons of colluding with him to keep the price of iron artificially high. From then on the Harrisons were only employed by the board in time of war. Having also lost their father's monopoly of East India Company business, they concentrated on guns for the export and merchant market.

When the Seven Years' War started in 1756 the board was forced to order guns, shot, and trucks from the Harrisons, now in partnership with Bagshaw and Richard Tapsell, Legas's nephew, because they still controlled more furnaces than anyone else. The Harrison business reached its apogee in 1760, supplying 864 guns out of 1991. Again the numbers derived from intelligent use of several furnaces, rather than from any technical improvements, although they were the only founders willing to cast the very large 42-pounder guns.

At the end of the war the board was in a financial crisis, delaying payments to contractors. Tapsell was declared bankrupt and the Harrisons began to withdraw from casting iron, and let go their furnaces to concentrate on selling instead. This mirrored what was happening generally in the iron industry, where a shortage of skilled labour had led to a slowdown in the spread of gun-founding on a large scale, and caused the closure of many wealden furnaces after the end of the Seven Years' War. This gave competitors a chance to recruit skilled founders, and the war marked the end of the dominance of the wealden gun-founders. For the first time Welsh and midlands founders supplied ordnance. The board believed that again the iron-founders had conspired to keep the cost of iron up, and used the low price offered by the Carron Company of Scotland to force other gun-founders to lower their price. The Harrisons refused to do this.

In the 1770s the business took new directions; the Harrison brothers formed a new company with Samuel Ambrose and Joseph Stanley. They used their old contacts in an important new venture; by 1775 they became agents for John Wilkinson (1728–1808) and his new solid-bored guns with both the Board of Ordnance and the East India Company. During the American War of Independence Wilkinson became one of the most reliable suppliers of guns, consistently producing high-quality guns in large numbers. However the company suffered when the board abruptly cancelled orders, and yet again drastically lowered the price for iron guns at the end of the war. Again the Harrisons refused on behalf of Wilkinson to lower their prices to those offered by the *Walker family of Rotherham, and again lost the contracts.

During the same period the business changed direction and became increasingly involved in wrought-iron production, taking on new premises in Deptford for anchor making and in Skinnerburn, north-east England, for nail-making. It continued to have some part in the gun trade through its ships' chandlery business at Lime Street, near the Thames. By 1786 a member of the Gordon family replaced Ambrose as a partner. By this time the Harrisons were playing a smaller part in the business; Andrews died about 1786 and John was dead by 1792. The new firm of Gordon and Stanley continued to represent John Wilkinson until 1797, after which it gave up the gun trade. It remained in maritime ironmongery, and under the name of Gordon Brothers it was able to enter the new industry of building iron ships at its yards in Deptford from 1828 until 1843.   RUTH RHYNAS BROWN

Sources R. R. Brown, *British gunfounders and their marks* [forthcoming] • R. R. Brown, 'Identifying 18th century trunnion marks', *International Journal of Nautical Archaeology*, 18 (1989) • [J. Fuller], *The Fuller letters: guns, slaves and finance, 1728–1755*, ed. D. Crossley and R. Saville, Suffolk RS, 76 (1991) • board of ordnance minute books, PRO, series WO47 • board of ordnance bill books, PRO, series WO51 • Harrison partnership records, GL, MSS 3736, 6482, 6483 • East India Company ledgers, BL, 101C • H. C. Tomlinson, 'Wealden gunfounding: an analysis of its demise', *Economic History Review*, 2nd ser., 29 (1976) • C. Evans, 'Manufacturing iron in the north east during the eighteenth century: the case of Bedlington', *Northern History*, 28 (1992), 178–96, esp. 186, n. 22
Archives GL, Harrison partnership | BL OIOC, East India Company ledgers • PRO, board of ordnance papers, minute books series WO47, bill books series WO51

Harrison, Agatha Mary (1885–1954), industrial welfare reformer and unofficial diplomat, was born on 23 January

1885 at Sandhurst in Berkshire, the youngest daughter of Charles Harrison, a Methodist minister, and his wife, Elizabeth, *née* Tilt. She was educated at Jersey Ladies' College and at Redland School, Bristol, but her schooling was interrupted after her father died in 1898, though she continued her studies for a time as a pupil teacher, and obtained the Froebel certificate, which qualified her to teach young children.

She entered industrial welfare work with Boots the Chemist in Nottingham, and in 1915 moved to the Metal Box Company in Hull, where she made a deep impression with her vigorous championship of women workers' rights. One employee recalled that he 'never knew a woman that could get her own way as well as Miss Harrison' (Harrison, 19). In 1917 the London School of Economics appointed her to the first academic post in Britain concerned with industrial welfare. This work led to her appointment in 1921 by the Young Women's Christian Association as an investigator into industrial conditions in China. There she became particularly concerned with the issue of child labour, and her often successful efforts to persuade industrialists to dispense with it gave her valuable experience in negotiating in adverse conditions.

From 1925 to 1928 she worked in the USA for the YWCA's education and research division, after which she returned to Britain to work for the Women's International League for Peace and Freedom. In 1929 she joined the Whitley commission on labour in India, serving as personal assistant to the only woman member, Beryl Power. Her six months in India fostered her sympathy with Indian nationalism, as well as her conviction that conflicts could best be resolved by patient listening and quiet firmness.

When the round-table conference on India was held in London in 1931, she helped with the arrangements made for Gandhi by sympathizers, and he—evidently impressed by her strong personality—asked her to commit herself to working for a better understanding between India and Britain. She became secretary of the India Conciliation Group, working with C. F. Andrews and Quakers like Carl Heath and Horace Alexander. This organization lobbied actively for Indian independence throughout the 1930s. She spent three extended periods in India in those years, and came to know Gandhi well, acting as an intermediary for him during his Rajkot fast in 1939.

This direct experience sustained her work through the difficult years of the Second World War, 1939–45, and enabled her to return to India after the war to help in the background as the cabinet mission from the new Labour government negotiated with nationalist leaders. Her skills in mediation were also helpful in the conflicts that followed the partition of the subcontinent.

In 1940 she joined the Society of Friends (Quakers) and thereafter took an active part in its various international committees. In 1950 she joined the small Quaker team of observers at the United Nations' general assembly, and applied herself to improving contacts between the western powers and the communists. Her distinctive mode of operation—an impeccable courtesy coupled with a sense that she believed totally in the integrity of those with whom she was dealing—was of immense service in this daunting task. She had great dignity: a colleague who knew her at the London School of Economics said that she looked like 'a tragedy queen'; and she would even dress for dinner in the inappropriate setting of the Quaker Centre in Calcutta. But this grave formality was qualified by an impish sense of humour which she skilfully exploited in stressful situations.

In Geneva in 1954, at the conference to end the war in Indo-China, she prepared the way for informal contacts between the Chinese diplomats there and non-communist representatives. She died in Geneva from a heart attack on 10 May; her remains were cremated in Geneva, where her ashes remain.

GEOFFREY CARNALL

Sources I. Harrison, *Agatha Harrison: an impression by her sister* (1956) · RS Friends, Lond., Harrison papers
Archives RS Friends, Lond., papers | JRL, letters to the *Manchester Guardian*
Likenesses photograph, repro. in Harrison, *Agatha Harrison*, frontispiece

Harrison, Alice [*known as* Dame Alice] (*c*.1680–*c*.1765), schoolmistress, was born at Fulwood Row, near Preston, Lancashire, and was brought up in the Church of England. She came into early contact with Roman Catholic literature and, while still a minor, became a Catholic against her parents' wishes. Treated by them with great severity for this conduct, she remained firm in her convictions, but was eventually forced to leave home.

Edward Melling, a Catholic priest serving the hamlet of Fernyhalgh, near to Alice Harrison's parental home, together with other Catholics in the neighbourhood, took her under their protection. About 1708 they encouraged her to set up a school for the boys and girls of the district, notwithstanding the penal laws prohibiting Catholics from practising as teachers. This she duly did, in a house with a large, adjoining barn, both of which still stand, at Haighton Top, Durton Lane, Fernyhalgh.

That Alice Harrison was saved from prosecution during her long period of over fifty years as schoolmistress at Fernyhalgh is attributable both to the strength of Catholicism in the area and to the fact that she accepted children of all religious backgrounds. Once her school was fully established her pupils numbered between 100 and 200 at any given time and these came not simply from the immediate neighbourhood, but also from the Fylde, Liverpool, Manchester, London, and all parts of England. They lodged either with the dame or else in cottages and farmhouses in the district, paying £5 per annum for their board and 1*s*. 6*d*. per quarter for their tuition. With her assistants, whose names, apart from one Mary Blackburn or Backhouse, are not recorded, Alice Harrison offered a curriculum ranging beyond the use of the hornbook and the art of spelling. She daily took her pupils to the Catholic chapel at Ladywell in Fernyhalgh and to the adjoining pre-Reformation holy well and shrine to the Virgin Mary. At such times her protestant pupils were allowed to absent themselves from prayers if they wished.

Such was the solid grounding in religious education provided by Dame Alice that a steady stream of boys began to proceed from Fernyhalgh to the English College at Douai, many of them subsequently continuing to holy orders. Her many students included the future priests Alban Butler (1709–1773), author of *Lives of the Saints*; Thomas Southworth (1749–1816), president of Sedgley Park; John Daniel (1745–1823), last president of the English College, Douai; John Gillow (1753–1828), president of Ushaw College; and the layman Peter Newby (1745–1827), poet and schoolmaster, who carried on the dame's educational work at Haighton after her death.

The venerable dame continued her school until she was very advanced in years, having by that time under her care the children and grandchildren of her earliest pupils. About 1760 she retired from her work and she was provided for in her last years by the Gerard family of Haighton, and, subsequently, as she became increasingly feeble, by the main branch of the Gerard family at their seat, Garswood Hall, near Ashton in Makerfield. She died at Garswood about 1765, though the precise date of her death is not known. She was buried in an unmarked grave at the Catholic churchyard at Windleshaw, near St Helens, Lancashire, where a modern plaque, in the tower of the ancient, ruined chantry chapel there, briefly records her life.

Alice Harrison may be seen as the archetypal Catholic schoolteacher of the recusant period. Diminutive in stature, and living in a tiny hamlet in the depths of rural Lancashire, not a single letter from her pen is known to survive, yet her undisputed and amply recorded influence on the several generations of her pupils who rose to become leading eighteenth-century English Roman Catholics, clerical and lay, at home and in continental Europe, is accompanied, even today, by an enduring folk memory of the schoolmistress in the farmsteads of the Fernyhalgh area.

MAURICE WHITEHEAD

Sources Gillow, *Lit. biog. hist.*, 3.145–8 · *Catholic Magazine and Review*, 2 (1832), 482–5 · B. C. Foley, *Some people of the penal times (chiefly 1688–1791)* (1991), 51–7 · Oscott College, Birmingham, Kirk MSS, 'Collectanea Anglo-Catholica', vol. 3, fols. 1123–1126 · memorial plaque, Windleshaw Catholic churchyard, near St Helens, Lancashire, ruined chantry chapel

Harrison, Andrews (1725–*c*.1786). *See under* Harrison family (*per*. 1715–*c*.1790).

Harrison, Arthur (1868–1936), organ builder, was born on 21 February 1868 in College Street, Rochdale, Lancashire, the second of the seven children of Tom Hugh Harrison (1839–1912), organ builder, and his wife, Elizabeth Ann, *née* McDowell (*d*. 1921). In 1872 the family moved to Durham, and in 1882, after attending Durham School, Harrison followed his father into the craft of organ building, serving as an apprentice and eventually, in 1893, becoming his partner. The firm's business took him to many parts of the British Isles, but Durham remained his base for the rest of his life. On 24 January 1895 he married Elizabeth Jane Henderson (1869–1946), daughter of the Revd James Henderson, rector of Wallsend. They had three daughters.

Harrison's first notable instrument, the organ at St Nicholas's, Whitehaven, was completed in 1904 to a design influenced by Lieutenant-Colonel George Dixon, a wealthy amateur who became a close friend. Thanks partly to Dixon's influence, by the outbreak of the First World War Harrison had completed a series of instruments which, through their distinctive tonal qualities, mechanical reliability, and immaculate finish, established the firm of Harrison and Harrison as the foremost organ builder of the day. The organs at Durham and Ely cathedrals (1905, 1908), All Saints, Margaret Street, London (1911), and St Mary Redcliffe, Bristol (1912), were outstanding in the pre-war period. Outstanding in the postwar period was his work at the Caird Hall, Dundee (1923), the Royal Albert Hall, London (1925–33), and King's College, Cambridge (1934). Throughout his career he built small organs of distinction, too, such as those at St John's, Keswick (1912), and All Saints, Maidenhead (1931).

Harrison's conception of the organ had crystallized by the time of the Ely contract, and there was little essential difference between his Edwardian organs and those he built in the 1920s and 1930s. A romantic conception, developed at a time when organists habitually played orchestral transcriptions, it was influenced by the work of Henry Willis and, in points of detail, by the work of continental builders such as Schulze and Cavaillé-Coll, and progressive builders such as Casson and Hope-Jones. It was, moreover, a conception intense in its particularity, and every realization of it called for Harrison's personal involvement. The finishing of an organ was a task Harrison almost invariably undertook himself, to prevent the slightest departure from the proud, highly polished norm. His perfectionism must have made him a demanding colleague, and photographs of him suggest a stern outlook; but portraiture has its conventions, and neither his working practices nor the unsmiling features then demanded by the camera should be allowed to obscure his fine personal qualities. There is humility of a genuine and touching kind in the sentence with which in 1929 this master organ builder at the height of his powers concluded a letter to a small church in Berkshire:

> We should very much like to build this organ for your Church, and I promise you that I would give it my careful personal attention and do everything possible to make it successful. (Archive of Harrison and Harrison Ltd, Durham)

His final letter to George Dixon testifies to a capacity for warm and intimate friendship, and Elvin's account of the reaction to his death suggests that he was widely admired throughout the world of music. As one who enjoyed the patronage of the Church of England, the older universities, and a number of town and city councils, Harrison became something of an establishment figure himself, involved as he was with diocesan bodies and with the Federation of Master Organ Builders, of which he was for a time president. A diplomatic, socially sophisticated man, he moved easily among his clients.

In November 1936 Harrison interrupted the finishing of the organ at Westminster Abbey in order to undergo an operation for a suspected ulcer. Inoperable cancer was discovered, and he died on 14 November at 16 Fitzroy Square, London. The funeral took place at St Margaret's, Durham, on 18 November, and in 1937 a memorial window was placed in the chapter house of Durham Cathedral.

Harrison's style of organ building has withstood the twists and turns of fashion, so that instruments built under his auspices, especially those that survive unaltered, are highly regarded, both in Britain and abroad. That he was mainly concerned with tonal design and voicing has tended to obscure the vitally important contribution of his younger brother, Harry Shaw Harrison (1871–1957), who concentrated upon mechanical design. The battleship construction and consequent reliability of Harrison organs and their characteristically elegant, comfortable consoles were, however, an integral (and much appreciated) part of the overall concept, and it was for these things that Harry was responsible. His early career followed very closely that of Arthur; it fell to him to oversee the completion of the Westminster Abbey organ and steer the firm through the vicissitudes of the Second World War. He retired in 1945.   RELF CLARK

Sources b. cert. • m. cert. • d. cert. • personal knowledge (2004) • private information (2004) • Harrison and Harrison Ltd, Durham, archive • L. Elvin, *The Harrison story* (1974) • S. Bicknell, *The history of the English organ* (1996)

Archives Harrison and Harrison Ltd, Durham, archive

Likenesses photographs, Harrison and Harrison Ltd, Durham

Wealth at death £23,197 0s. 6d.: probate, 16 Jan 1937, *CGPLA Eng. & Wales*

Harrison, Austin Frederic (1873–1928), journalist and journal editor, was born on 27 March 1873 at 1 Southwick Place, London, the second of four sons and a daughter of the positivist writers Frederic *Harrison (1831–1923) and his wife, Ethel Bertha *Harrison (1851–1916). His first lessons, with his older brother, Bernard, were given by their parents until December 1880. Then, to the boys' delight, their father employed as their tutor the struggling young novelist George Gissing. His visits to the Harrisons' comfortable house at 38 Westbourne Terrace, Bayswater, continued for three years, after which Austin spent three years at St Paul's School, London, and three at Harrow School. He then studied languages in Lausanne, Marburg, and Berlin to prepare for the Foreign Office examination. After failing it in 1896, he was hired by *The Times* as a favour to his father, and sent to its Berlin office. Its formidable chief, George Saunders, soon had him dismissed, and he was then sent by the *Manchester Guardian* to the Hague Peace Conference to assist W. T. Stead, who also eased him out. He fared better at Reuters news agency in Berlin, rising to office manager.

By 1904 the German foreign office's control of information and Reuters' prohibition against opinion in dispatches so frustrated Harrison that he resigned from Reuters and documented his apprehensions about the Kaiser in *The Pan-Germanic Doctrine* (1904). In London he did freelance journalism until his book caught the eye of Sir Alfred Harmsworth (later Lord Northcliffe), who suddenly installed him as political editor of his prestigious Sunday

Observer. Besides weekly leaders, Harrison wrote eye-witness accounts of St Petersburg after 'bloody Sunday' (22 January 1905) and of German political developments in 1906, reprinted as *England and Germany* in 1907. Towards the end of that year, the unpredictable Harmsworth replaced him with J. L. Garvin, naming Harrison *The Observer's* literary editor and drama critic of the *Daily Mail*.

Finally, at the end of 1909 Harrison attained the position that made his reputation. Sir Alfred Mond (later the first Baron Melchett) invited him to edit the *English Review*, a literary and political monthly which Mond had just purchased. Aware that mismanagement had doomed it under its founding editor, Ford Madox Hueffer (later Ford), Harrison displayed Nietzsche's admonition in his office: 'Be hard, my brothers'. His editorial practices irritated some, but contrary to what is often asserted the *English Review* maintained its high standards for years. Indeed, Harrison published many of Ford's contributors—for example, Joseph Conrad, D. H. Lawrence, H. G. Wells, and Norman Douglas, who became his literary sub-editor. He opened the review to women, continental writers, and promising unknowns. By challenging conventional attitudes towards sexuality with the work of writers like Frank Harris he ran afoul of the Vigilance Society, newsagents, and libraries. *The Spectator* accused him of 'dumping garbage on the nation's doorstep' (8 July 1911). Harrison defended his 'adult review' in a petition signed by fifty well-known writers. *The Everlasting Mercy* by John Masefield created another storm, but caused the circulation to jump to 18,000. Reducing the magazine's price from 2*s*. 6*d*. to 1*s*. in 1912 proved advantageous, and Harrison was able to buy out Mond in 1915.

Under Harrison the *English Review* supported liberal reforms and military preparedness. When his fears of Germany were validated in 1914, he reprinted his earlier warnings in a best-seller for Stanley Unwin, *The Kaiser's War* (1914). The death of Harrison's youngest brother in the battle of Festubert (1915) made him especially bitter about the scandal of shortage of munitions. He supported the coalition war cabinet, but was so opposed to Lloyd George's punitive peace terms that he stood quixotically against the prime minister in his own Welsh constituency in 1918. He was an early proponent of a league of nations.

In 1923 Harrison sold the *English Review*, which was then in decline. Having helped found PEN, an international society of writers, he wished to write books himself. While engaged in newspaper journalism, mainly for the *Sunday Pictorial*, he published *Lifting Mist* (1924), a novel about school life; *Pandora's Hope* (1925), speculations about women; and his one enduring book, *Frederic Harrison: Thoughts and Memories* (1926), a loving portrait of his father. They had resolved their differences over Austin's marriage on 30 April 1914 to the American-born Mary Medora Greening (1880–1980) after her divorce from the pianist Evlyn Howard-Jones. Harrison took a great interest in the education of his children, two daughters and a son. He died at his home, Lychgate House, Seaford, Sussex, of bronchial pneumonia on 13 July 1928, and was cremated on 17 July at Golders Green.   MARTHA S. VOGELER

Sources A. Harrison, *Frederic Harrison: thoughts and memories* (1926) · BLPES, Harrison MSS · 'Celebrities at home', *The World* (22 April 1913), 257–72 · 'Touchstones of genius', *Daily News and Leader* (21 Jan 1912), 12 · M. S. Vogeler, *Frederic Harrison: the vocations of a positivist* (1984) · M. S. Vogeler, 'Pulling strings at Printing House Square', *Papers for the millions: the new journalism in Britain, 1850s to 1914*, ed. J. H. Wiener (1988) · B. A. White, 'The English Review', *British literary magazines*, ed. A. Sullivan, [3]: *The Victorian and Edwardian age, 1837–1913* (1984), 125–9 · H. R. Winkler, *The League of Nations movement in Great Britain, 1914–1919* (1967) · register of sacraments, London positivists, BL, Add. MS 43844, 10 Feb 1874 · *The Times* (16 July 1928) · *The Times* (18 July 1928) · *The Observer* (15 July 1928) · m. cert.
Archives priv. coll., corresp. | BL, Macmillan Co. MSS · BL, corresp. with Lord Northcliffe, Add. MS 62174 · BL, corresp. with George Bernard Shaw, Add. MS 50538 · BL, corresp. with Marie Stopes, Add. MS 58497 · BLPES, Frederic Harrison MSS · North-western University, Illinois, J. B. Pinker MSS · NYPL, Berg collection, MSS of Joseph Conrad, J. B. Pinker, Thomas Burke · State University of New York, Buffalo, Edgar Jepson MSS · State University of New York, Buffalo, Richard Middleton MSS · State University of New York, Buffalo, Henry Savage MSS · U. Edin. L., corresp. with Charles Sarolea · U. Reading, George Allen and Unwin MSS · U. Reading, Macmillan Co. MSS · U. Texas, Aleister Crowley MSS · U. Texas, F. S. Flint MSS · U. Texas, Edward Garnett MSS · U. Texas, J. L. Garvin MSS · U. Texas, Thomas Hardy MSS · U. Texas, Frank Harris MSS · U. Texas, PEN MSS
Likenesses group portrait, photograph, *c*.1907 (with family), repro. in Vogeler, *Frederic Harrison* · R. Haines, photograph, 1915, repro. in *The letters of D. H. Lawrence*, ed. J. T. Boulton, 7 vols. (1979–93) · H. Murchison, photograph, repro. in 'Touchstones of genius' · photograph, repro. in *ILN* (21 July 1928)
Wealth at death £9801 6*s*. 3*d*.: probate, 16 Aug 1928, CGPLA Eng. & Wales

Harrison, Beatrice Bohun (1892–1965), cellist, was born on 9 December 1892 in Roorkee, in the North-Western Provinces of India, the second of the four daughters of Colonel John H. C. Harrison RE (d. 1936), at that time principal of the College of Sappers and Miners, and his wife, Annie (d. 1934), daughter of Charles Martin, a civil engineer. All four daughters were musical, as was their mother, who had been a pupil of George Henschel, and two others besides Beatrice became professional musicians: May (1890–1959), a violinist, and Margaret (1899–1995), a violinist and later a pianist. Shortly after Beatrice's birth, the family returned to England, where Colonel Harrison was given the command of the home battalion of the Royal Engineers at Chatham barracks, and also took charge of the band of the Royal Engineers. In 1902 he retired in order to devote his life to his family.

The girls were educated at home, starting music lessons at a very early age, but Beatrice did not begin to learn the cello until she was nine, when her mother gave her a full-size cello, taller than she. After being awarded the gold medal of the Associated Board of the Royal Schools of Music at the age of ten, in 1904 she won an exhibition to the Royal College of Music, London, where she studied with William Whitehouse, and a scholarship in 1907; in the latter year she made her début at the Queen's Hall, playing the Saint-Saëns cello concerto no. 1 in A minor under Henry Wood. After playing to King Edward VII at a private dinner party she became a close friend of Princess Victoria, a good pianist, and it was she who paid for her cello (Pietro Guarneri, 1739) after her American benefactress died. In 1908 the whole family moved to Berlin so that she could have lessons with Hugo Becker at the Hochschule für Musik, where in 1910 she was the youngest student ever to win the Mendelssohn prize, and she made her European début in Berlin in 1910.

After returning to England in 1910 Beatrice Harrison embarked on a solo career, with many tours to Europe and North America. In the United States, in 1913, she was the first woman cellist to play at Carnegie Hall, and the first to play with the Boston Symphony Orchestra. It was after a performance in Manchester in 1914, with her sister May, of the Brahms double concerto with the Hallé orchestra under Thomas Beecham, that she first met Frederick Delius, who became a close friend of the Harrison family. Delius greatly admired Beatrice's passionate playing and full tone, and she played an important part in introducing Delius's works to American audiences. Delius wrote his double concerto (1915) for Beatrice and May Harrison, encouraging Beatrice to make any alterations she wished to the solo cello part; he wrote these into the definitive score, and they gave the first performance in the presence of the composer at the Queen's Hall in 1920. She gave the first performance of his cello sonata (1916), dedicated to her, with Hamilton Harty at the Wigmore Hall, and the British première of his cello concerto (1921), which Delius had begun to compose in the Harrisons' garden, in 1923. She performed the serenade from Delius's incidental music to *Hassan*, arranged by Eric Fenby in 1929 for solo cello and chamber orchestra, in Boston in 1930, and Delius wrote *Caprice and Elegy* (1930) for her for this American tour. It was Beatrice Harrison's recording of *Caprice and Elegy*, made for HMV, that was played by the BBC after Neville Chamberlain's broadcast on 3 September 1939 announcing that England was at war with Germany. After Delius's death in France in 1934 the Harrisons arranged for his body to be taken to England in 1935, and he was reburied in Limpsfield churchyard in Surrey, close to the Harrison family grave.

Beatrice Harrison became closely associated with the Elgar cello concerto (1919), recording first an abridged version for HMV in 1919, with a complete recording, conducted by Elgar, following in 1928, and it was thanks to her many performances that it became so popular. Elgar felt she conveyed the spirit of the work as he had intended it, and always used her as the soloist when he conducted the work. She performed works by other contemporary British composers, many of whom were inspired to write for her: Arnold Bax became a close friend, and she commissioned a cello sonata (1923) from him, which she first performed in 1924 with Harriet Cohen. He wrote *Rhapsodic Ballad* (1939) for her, and she gave many performances of his cello concerto (1934), including two at the Promenade Concerts during the Second World War. Roger Quilter's cello solo 'L'amour de moy' and John Ireland's cello sonata (1923) were written for her, and her recording of an old Irish folk tune, 'The Lament of Fanaid Grove' (1926), arranged by the Irish composer Herbert Hughes and dedicated to her, became very famous. She also gave the first performances in Britain of Kodály's sonata for unaccompanied cello (1915) and, with her sister Margaret, Ravel's sonata for cello and violin (1920–22).

But to the wider public Beatrice Harrison was known for her famous nightingale broadcasts. She had discovered while playing her cello in the woods at night in the garden of the Harrisons' house, Foyle Riding, in Surrey, that she could make a nightingale sing with her, and in 1924 persuaded John Reith, general manager of the BBC, to arrange an outside broadcast. At midnight on 19 May 1924 over a million people listened while she played a duet with the nightingale, and for the next twelve years the BBC broadcast her nightingale concerts in May. Thousands of visitors flocked to Foyle Riding during the nightingale season; the Harrisons entertained musicians and friends, and chartered buses to bring families from the East End, giving them tea and beer until midnight. The broadcasts gave her a good deal of publicity, and the nightingale was depicted on her concert posters and embroidered on her concert dresses.

Her mother's death in 1934 was a great blow. Beatrice had always lived at home with her parents and sisters, and had never led an independent life. Her mother had organized all her concert tours and usually accompanied her on them. Her youngest sister Margaret took over their mother's role, often also accompanying Beatrice on the piano. Beatrice continued to perform regularly until the 1950s, and her last public performance was a televised recital in 1958 to raise money for the rebuilding of Coventry Cathedral.

Beatrice Harrison died on 10 March 1965 at Smallfield, near Horley, Surrey, and was buried on 16 March. She was unmarried. Strikingly beautiful with dark auburn hair, she had many suitors, but she devoted her life single-mindedly to the cello. The leading British cellist of her generation, she was also the first British cellist to win an international reputation. Her autobiography, *The Cello and the Nightingales*, was published in 1985. To mark the centenary of her birth, a radio play, *The Cello and the Nightingale*, by Patricia Cleveland-Peck, was broadcast in 1992.

ANNE PIMLOTT BAKER

Sources B. Harrison, *The cello and the nightingales: the autobiography of Beatrice Harrison*, ed. P. Cleveland-Peck (1985) · *Delius Society Journal*, 87 (autumn 1985) [Harrison sisters issue] · *The Strad*, 103 (1992) [B. Harrison issue] · L. Carley, *Delius: A life in letters*, 2: 1909–1934 (1988) · L. Foreman, *Bax* (1983) · G. Moore, *Am I too loud?* (1962) · E. Cowling, *The cello* (1975), 181–2 · R. Threlfall, *A catalogue of the compositions of Frederick Delius* (1977) · R. Threlfall, *Frederick Delius: a supplementary catalogue* (1986) · *The Times* (11 March 1965) · *WW* · *New Grove*, 2nd edn · *Edward Elgar: letters of a lifetime*, ed. J. Northrop Moore (1990)

Archives FILM BFI NFTVA, performance footage | SOUND BBC WAC · BL NSA, performance recordings

Likenesses double portrait, photograph (with May Harrison), repro. in *The Strad*, 1176 · double portrait, photograph (with Elgar), repro. in *The Strad*, 1175 · photograph, repro. in Harrison, *Cello and the nightingales* · photograph, repro. in *The Strad*, cover

Harrison, Benjamin (*c*.1726–1791), planter and revolutionary politician in America, was probably born at Berkeley, the family residence, in Charles City county, Virginia, the oldest surviving son of Benjamin Harrison (1701–

Benjamin Harrison (c.1726–1791), by unknown artist

Acts'. He was elected a delegate to the first continental congress soon thereafter, as he was to the second in 1775. In that capacity he was a signer of the Declaration of Independence. John Adams insisted that he was of 'no use in Congress' (*Diary and Autobiography*, 3.367–8), but, in fact, he appears to have been an effective member and served subsequently in 1777. Harrison was reported never 'to utter any [un]truth' and this, with 'his frankness' and sound judgement, recommended him to his constituents and to his colleagues in Virginia's new house of delegates, where he served almost continuously from 1776 until 1791. He was speaker of the house from 1778 until 1781 and again in 1785. In December 1781 he was elected governor.

Harrison proved to be a competent, cautious executive, who was resistant to change. His three years in office, in the aftermath of war, were difficult, and the time thereafter was not a happy one. He sought to represent Charles City in the house of delegates in 1785, but was defeated. He then ran and was elected from Surry county, where he owned property. He soon regained his Charles City seat, and in 1788 was elected to the convention to consider the proposed constitution. Harrison opposed ratification on the grounds that too much power was given to the central government. After ratification he became a supporter. He continued to serve in the legislature, but his health declined. He died on 24 April 1791 at Berkeley, where he was buried.

EMORY G. EVANS

1744/5), a prosperous planter, and Anne Carter (*b. c.*1699), the daughter of Robert 'King' *Carter of Corotoman in Lancaster county. Little is known of his early years. His father and two of his sisters were killed by lightning while he was a student at the College of William and Mary. Heir to a large estate, which included land in at least four counties, a fishery, and a grist mill, he took over its management in 1745. Over time, and in addition to tobacco planting, he added grist mills and a shipyard. But he was not a good businessman: as early as the mid-1750s he was heavily in debt, largely to British merchants, and debt remained a problem.

Harrison married, between 1745 and 1750, Elizabeth, daughter of William Bassett of New Kent county. There were to be eight children from this union, seven of whom survived to maturity, including William Henry Harrison, who was elected president of the United States in 1840. At Berkeley the Harrisons maintained a generous, hospitable, and rich lifestyle which was typical of the Virginia élite at mid-century. A tall, 'muscular' man, in later years he became 'corpulent' because he so 'enjoyed the pleasures of the table'. Convivial, and fond of a 'good joke' (Sanderson, 8.168), his colourful language was later to offend John Adams.

Harrison was elected to the house of burgesses from Charles City county in 1748, and served continuously until 1776. He quickly assumed a prominent role in that body, and in the 1760s he was twice recommended, but never selected, for a coveted seat on the council. Conservative politically, he was on the committee of the general assembly which drafted the memorial protesting against the proposed stamp act, but he was certainly in that group of older members in the house of burgesses who were shocked by Patrick Henry's attack on George III and some of his proposals concerning American rights.

Over time, Harrison, whose 'talents seem to have been rather useful than brilliant' (Sanderson, 8.168), began to take a firmer position with respect to British measures. By 1774 he was among those who strongly protested against the closure of the port of Boston and other 'Intolerable

Sources H. W. Smith, *Benjamin Harrison and the American revolution* (1977) • J. Sanderson, *Biography of the signers of the Declaration of Independence*, 9 vols. (1820–27), 8.127–72 • *Virginia Magazine of History and Biography*, 30 (1922), 196–202, 408–12 • *Virginia Magazine of History and Biography*, 31 (1923), 83–7, 180–82, 277–83, 380 • *Virginia Magazine of History and Biography*, 32 (1924), 92–103, 199–202, 298, 304, 313–16 • *Virginia Magazine of History and Biography*, 33 (1925), 413–16 • *Virginia Magazine of History and Biography*, 34 (1926), 90–92, 97, 205, 212, 410 • *Virginia Magazine of History and Biography*, 35 (1927), 89–93 • C. Dowdey, *The great plantation: a profile of Berkeley Hundred and Plantation Virginia, from Jamestown to Appomattox* (1957) • H. R. McIlwaine, ed., *Official letters of the governors of the state of Virginia*, 3 vols. (1926–9), 3.103–461 • H. R. McIlwaine and J. P. Kennedy, eds., *Journals of the house of burgesses of Virginia, 1619–1776*, 13 vols. (1905–15) • *Journal of the house of delegates of Virginia, 1776–1790* (1827–8) • E. Randolph, *History of Virginia*, ed. A. H. Schaffer (1970) • W. J. Van Schreeven, R. L. Scribner, and B. Tarter, eds., *Revolutionary Virginia: the road to independence*, 7 vols. (1973–89) • P. H. Smith and others, eds., *Letters of delegates to congress, 1774–1789*, 26 vols. (1976–2000) • *Diary and autobiography of John Adams*, ed. L. H. Butterfield and others, 3 (1964) • N. Risjord, *Chesapeake politics, 1781–1800* (1978) • R. Corbin, letterbook, 1758–68, Colonial Williamsburg Foundation • E. Jenings, letterbook, 1753–69, Virginia Historical Society • American loyalist claims, John T. Warre for the executors of Farrell and Jones, PRO, T79/30 • N. Risjord, 'Harrison, Benjamin', *ANB* • T. E. Buckley, *Church and state in revolutionary Virginia, 1776–1787* (1977)

Likenesses miniature, oils, Virginia Historical Society, Richmond [see illus.]

Wealth at death heavily in debt but still large estate

Harrison, Benjamin (1771–1856), hospital administrator and philanthropist, was born on 29 July 1771 at West Ham, Essex, the fourth son of Benjamin Harrison (1734–1797), treasurer of Guy's Hospital. His formal education is obscure, but he was well prepared for his life's work by living from the age of fourteen with his father in the treasurer's house at Guy's. There he became familiar with hospital administration and well acquainted with the governors and important members of staff. Harrison was elected a governor in 1793 and succeeded his father as treasurer in 1797. That same year he married Mary Pelly, daughter of Henry Hinde Pelly (1744/5–1818) of Upton and Aveley, Essex, and Sally Hitchen; Mary was sister to Sir John Henry *Pelly, chairman of the Hudson's Bay Company. There were three sons (the eldest, Benjamin *Harrison, became archdeacon of Maidstone) and six daughters (the eldest of whom married W. Cripps, MP for Cirencester from 1841 to 1848 and a lord of the Treasury).

For more than fifty years, to 1848, Harrison devoted his energy and executive skills to every aspect of Guy's Hospital and its medical school. His initial reforms aimed to improve the financial condition of the hospital, the cleanliness of its wards, and the recruitment of its nursing staff. His ambition for Guy's soon caused more land to be bought in order to expand hospital facilities and improve the surrounding areas. Harrison encouraged the training of several talented young men, notably Thomas Addison and William Gull. In 1825, abetted by Sir Astley Cooper, he achieved the separation of the medical school from St Thomas's, and under his direction Guy's medical school soon became the premier medical school in London. Harrison also supported the publication of *Guy's Hospital Reports*, thereby helping to advance medical science. In 1829 his friend and fellow governor William Hunt bequeathed more than £180,000 to the hospital. Additional land was acquired and new buildings constructed, more beds became available, and departments of ophthalmology, gynaecology and obstetrics, and diseases of children were added at the medical school.

Harrison was viewed as an autocratic, even a despotic, administrator by contemporaries who referred to him as King Harrison. Popular caricatures show him seated upon a throne, surrounded by obedient courtiers and frightened subjects; he issued strict rules regarding the behaviour of staff and patients, appointed the lecturers, and ensured that hospital physicians and surgeons were selected according to his wishes. Many of his decisions seemed completely arbitrary, yet his fellow governors invariably accepted his recommendations, including the denial of promotion to Thomas Hodgkin as assistant physician. Hodgkin, along with Thomas Addison and Richard Bright, was one of the 'great triumvirate of Guy's' (Cameron, 127). As long as Harrison was treasurer, writers for the medical journal *The Lancet* were excluded from Guy's, primarily because of the criticisms of the hospital published during the Bransby Cooper scandal.

Harrison deeply resented the Charity Commission's investigation into his administration in 1837. The inquiry was instigated by the House of Commons, which called for a government-appointed committee to examine the conduct of all charities. The commission report of 1840 made only minor suggestions for change at Guy's but strongly criticized the extensive powers of the treasurer.

Although no abuse was found in 'the extraordinary delegation of authority to this gentleman' (*Report of Charity Commissioners*, 1837), the commission did discuss Harrison's unilateral decision making and warned that his successor might not be equally honourable. As a voluntary member of the Guy's Hospital board of governors, Harrison received no salary for his additional responsibilities as treasurer, though he was provided with a spacious residence, coach house, and stables. He was, however, personally wealthy and frequently contributed large sums to the hospital's funds. Part of his wealth came from manufacturing bottles at an establishment he owned in Newcastle upon Tyne.

In contrast with his authoritarian reputation at Guy's, Harrison was also known for his philanthropy and public service. He was associated with the evangelical Clapham Sect. As a member of the committee of the Hudson's Bay Company from 1809 onwards and later as deputy governor, Harrison advocated the distribution of religious tracts and appointment of clergymen in the Canadian wilderness. He also supported an Indian mission in the Red River settlement as well as a school of industry for orphan children of white settlers there. He was also a deputy governor of the South Sea Company and chairman of the exchequer loan board. During his long service in the latter post, he approved allocation of £14 million for local loans. A fellow of the Society of Antiquaries, he was one of three appeal commissioners for the City of London on the initial imposition of an income tax.

Following his retirement in 1848 Harrison moved to Clapham Common in south London, where he died on 18 May 1856. He was commemorated in Canada by the Harrison Islands and other geographical features.

AMALIE M. KASS

Sources H. C. Cameron, *Mr Guy's Hospital, 1726–1948* (1954) · S. Wilks and G. T. Bettany, *A biographical history of Guy's Hospital* (1892) · E. E. Rich, *The history of the Hudson's Bay Company, 1670–1870*, 2: 1763–1870 (1959) · A. M. Kass and E. H. Kass, *Perfecting the world, the life and times of Dr. Thomas Hodgkin, 1798–1866* (1988) · *DNB* · D. M. Lewis, ed., *The Blackwell dictionary of evangelical biography, 1730–1860*, 2 vols. (1995)
Archives LMA, Guy's Hospital archives · Provincial Archives of Manitoba, Winnipeg, Hudson's Bay Company Archives
Likenesses oils (after G. Richmond), Guy's Hospital Medical School, London

Harrison, Benjamin (1808–1887), Church of England clergyman, was born on 26 September 1808, probably in London, one of the three sons of Benjamin *Harrison (1771–1856), treasurer of Guy's Hospital, and his wife, Mary Pelly. He matriculated at Christ Church, Oxford, on 17 May 1826, and was elected a student in 1828. He took his BA in 1830, and his MA in 1833. Harrison had a distinguished career at Oxford, where he was a contemporary of W. E. Gladstone, among others. He was placed in the first class for classics and in the second class for mathematics; and gained the Ellerton theological essay prize, the Kennicott and the Pusey and Ellerton Hebrew scholarships in 1831–2, and the chancellor's English essay prize in 1832. The subject of the last was 'The study of different languages as it relates to the philosophy of the human mind' (printed in Oxford, 1833).

Harrison took part in the early stages of the Oxford Movement, acting as a link between the older high-churchmen of the Phalanx and the younger Tractarians. He wrote tracts 16, 17, 24, and 49 of the Tracts for the Times, mostly on the scriptural authority for the episcopalian organization of the church. However, his conservative temperament and steady preferment kept him firmly within the mainstream of traditional Anglicanism; his moderation was evidenced in 1845 by his *Historical Inquiry into the True Interpretation of the Rubrics*, which sought to reconcile a number of more extreme interpretations. He was select preacher to the university (1835–7), domestic chaplain to William Howley, archbishop of Canterbury (1843–8), and canon of Canterbury and archdeacon of Maidstone (1845–87). In 1841 he married Isabella, daughter of Henry Thornton MP of Battersea Rise. They had no children.

Harrison was a fine Hebrew scholar, as his *Prophetic outlines of the Christian church and the antichristian power as traced in the visions of Daniel and St. John* (1849) and his inclusion among the revisers of the Bible issued in 1885 showed. At Canterbury he proved to be an energetic and popular archdeacon. Friendly to the clergy and regular in his attendance at cathedral services, he was actively involved in church societies and keenly participated in secular gatherings, such as those of the Canterbury cricket week or the meetings of the agricultural and archaeological societies. He inherited from Howley a valuable library, which his widow later presented, with the addition of a collection of Bibles and liturgical works made by his father, and many other books acquired by himself, to Canterbury Cathedral, where it forms the Howley–Harrison Library. He was intimate with Dean Stanley during his tenure of a canonry at Canterbury, and to him Stanley dedicated the *Historical Memorials of Canterbury* (1854).

Harrison published sermons and charges, as well as an edition (1857) of the sermons of William Grant Broughton, bishop of Sydney, and *Christianity in Egypt: Letters and Papers Concerning the Coptic Church* (1883). He died on 25 March 1887 at 7 Bedford Square, London, a house which he had inherited from Sir Robert Inglis, MP for Oxford University, a relative by marriage.

W. H. FREMANTLE, *rev.* GEORGE HERRING

Sources Boase, *Mod. Eng. biog.* · P. Schaff and S. M. Jackson, *Encyclopedia of living divines and Christian workers of all denominations in Europe and America: being a supplement to Schaff-Herzog encyclopedia of religious knowledge* (1887) · Foster, *Alum. Oxon.* · Crockford (1887) · *CGPLA Eng. & Wales* (1887)
Archives Pusey Oxf., corresp. | BL, corresp. with W. E. Gladstone, Add. MS 44204 · Bodl. Oxf., letters to H. E. Manning · LPL, letters to Edward Benson · LPL, Howley MSS · LPL, corresp. with A. C. Tait
Likenesses C. Holl, stipple (after G. Richmond), NPG · Spy [L. Ward], chromolithograph caricature, NPG; repro. in *VF* (6 June 1885)
Wealth at death £46,222 5s.: resworn probate, April 1888, *CGPLA Eng. & Wales* (1887)

Harrison, Charles (1835–1897), politician, was born on 1 August 1835 in Muswell Hill, Middlesex, the third of five

Charles Harrison (1835–1897), by James Russell & Sons, pubd 1898

sons of Frederick Harrison (1799–1881), a wealthy stockbroker, and his wife, Jane Brice, daughter of a Belfast granite merchant. Educated at King's College School and King's College, London, and also privately, in 1858 he became a solicitor in the prosperous law firm of his uncle, Charles Harrison, at 19 Bedford Row, London, as did his younger brother, Sidney. Their clients included the London, Chatham, and Dover Railway, the Law Fire Insurance Society, and many leaseholders, in whom Harrison took a special interest. He testified before the parliamentary select committee on town holdings in 1886 that, having bought and sold leasehold property valued at over £2 million, he agreed with the supplementary report of the royal commission on the housing of the working class (1884–5), which held the existing system of building leases of under ninety-nine years responsible for much bad construction and for deterioration of the property towards the close of the lease. The corrective he urged was leasehold enfranchisement (the right of tenants to purchase the property they occupied at a price determined by the ground rent, not the market value)—already a central radical tenet and soon to be official Liberal policy.

Meanwhile, the creation of the London county council (LCC) in 1888 refocused Harrison's reforming zeal. Elected for South West Bethnal Green, he allied himself with the Progressives, who, outnumbering the Moderates, placed their own candidates (including his elder brother Frederic *Harrison) in nineteen of the twenty seats allotted to aldermen. He immediately took a commanding position as chairman of the Progressive Party and of the LCC's parliamentary committee, and from 1892 to 1895 he served as the council's vice-chairman. Membership on standing committees dealing with finance and with local government and taxation enabled him to press his reform proposals. He argued, for example, that the ground landlord should share the burden of local taxation, and that LCC street improvement schemes should embody the betterment principle, by which rates would be increased on property benefiting from the action of public authorities. By insisting that LCC loans to the school board and vestries should be repaid according to the annuity principle, he caused the chairman of the finance committee to resign. Appointed to represent the council on the Thames Conservancy Board, he studied the history of the London docks and called for sweeping changes, including their municipalization; and as chairman of the council's committee to prepare recommendations to the royal commission on the amalgamation of the City and the county of London, he helped to shape the commission's report in 1894 recommending unification. On all these complex and controversial issues he wrote forcefully in the press and periodicals (including the *Fortnightly Review* and the *Liberal Magazine*), acquiring a reputation for unrivalled mastery of fact.

'When are the times and seasons at which Mr Charles Harrison takes food or sleep?' once asked Lord Rosebery, first chairman of the LCC. Yet Harrison was no drudge. At school he excelled at cricket and rowing, and later he travelled extensively in Europe and the Near East, sometimes indulging historical and archaeological interests. Besides belonging to several learned societies, he commissioned some 800 photographs of art and antiquities in the British Museum, which he arranged to be sold at cost, and in 1872 published a catalogue of them to illustrate the progress of civilization. By the 1880s he was sailing his own 120 ton yacht in Mediterranean waters. Socially and politically his life was enhanced by his marriage on 7 January 1886 to Lady Harriet, widow of Francis Barlow and sister of the earl of Lanesborough.

After unsuccessfully standing for parliament as a Liberal in 1885 and 1892, Harrison was narrowly returned for Plymouth in 1895, while retaining his LCC seat. In the Commons he questioned government policies leading to the Jameson raid (publishing an article on it in the *Contemporary Review*, 69, 1896), and applied his expert knowledge of public finance to such issues as London sewers, naval estimates, voluntary schools, light railways, and clerical incomes. His copious objections to a rating bill favouring agricultural interests led Conservatives to shout him down three times in four days. But on 24 December 1897 his voice—a 'hoarse guttural' according to Beatrice Webb—was suddenly stilled by heart failure following laryngitis. He died at his home, 29 Lennox Gardens, London, and following an Anglican service, his body was cremated and the ashes interred in the family vault at Brookwood cemetery, Woking.   MARTHA S. VOGELER

Sources Boase, *Mod. Eng. biog.* · *The Times* (27 Dec 1897) · *The Times* (31 Dec 1897) · *The Times* (9 March 1898) · A. T. C. Pratt, ed., *People of the period: being a collection of the biographies of upwards of six thousand living celebrities*, 1 (1897) · W. Saunders, *History of the first London county council, 1889, 1890, 1891* (1892) · Progressive Party minute books, LCC, LMA · LCC minutes, London County Council Archives · K. Young and P. L. Garside, *Metropolitan London* (1982) · J. Davis, *Reforming London* (1988) · G. Gibbon and R. W. Bell, *History of the London county council, 1889–1939* (1939)

Archives BLPES, corresp. | BLPES, F. Harrison MSS · BLPES, Webb MSS

Likenesses J. Russell & Sons, photograph, NPG; repro. in *ILN* (7 Jan 1898) [*see illus.*] · photograph, repro. in *Law Gazette* (5 March 1891), 227

Wealth at death £65,196 7s. 5d.: probate, 7 March 1898, *CGPLA Eng. & Wales*

Harrison, Sir Cyril Ernest (1901–1980), cotton industrialist, was born on 14 December 1901 at Sileby gas works, near Leicester, the son of Alfred John Harrison, a gas works manager, and his wife, Edith, *née* Perry. He was educated at Padiham Wesleyan school and Burnley grammar school, the family having moved to east Lancashire.

Harrison's early career was far from smooth. In 1917, through the influence of his father, he was appointed office boy at Herbert Noble's Perseverance Mill, Padiham, under the impression that he was serving an apprenticeship for a managerial position, but he was soon pushed out to make room for Noble's sons. For a time, Harrison trained as a weaver—a lowly occupation—and then as a fabric dealer on the Manchester Cotton Exchange. On 4 June 1927 he married Ethel (1901/2–1971), daughter of Edward Wood FCA JP, a leading Burnley accountant. The couple had two sons. Having learned the trade, Harrison and a friend, Ralph Harling, set up their own fabric merchanting business, C. E. Harrison & Co., in 1928. After further vocational studies, Harrison qualified as a fellow of the Chartered Institute of Secretaries, and in the 1930s he took an interest in the deliberations of the Burnley chamber of commerce.

Harrison's potential was spotted in 1939, and he was appointed manager of the yarn sales division of English Sewing Cotton (ESC), Britain's second largest producer of cotton thread. It was not considered unusual at that time for someone without a technical or managerial degree to fill an important post in a major company. Harrison's skill at selling thread was not, however, to be put to the test. When war broke out in 1939, market forces in the textile industry were gradually replaced by a system of planning. In 1940 ESC sent Harrison to work for the official Cotton Control, which supervised the rationing of raw cotton supplies, and ensured that each mill gave priority to essential orders. ESC granted Harrison a directorship in 1942, and he became managing director in 1948, and vice-chairman in 1952. The late 1940s were halcyon days for Lancashire; with Japanese and continental European mills temporarily out of contention, British firms could make large profits with ease. Harrison rose to the top at a time when ESC was not exposed to the discipline of market forces, and in 1950 he remained an untried man.

Under Harrison's vigorous leadership, ESC adopted a policy of modernization, investing £4 million in new machinery and other facilities between 1945 and 1955, reforming its manning practices, and revitalizing its marketing procedures. Significant gains were made in productivity. Harrison introduced a pension scheme for operatives, and enjoyed an excellent relationship with the unions. But Lancashire faced a daunting struggle in the 1950s against competition from countries with lower labour costs, and men such as Harrison could do no more than mount a spirited rearguard action. In 1963, Harrison became chairman of ESC. This was a year of crisis in the cotton industry. Courtaulds and ICI, Britain's main producers of man-made fibres, were about to embark on a series of acquisitions of large textile companies and had set their sights on ESC and another firm, Tootal. Harrison was in favour of the creation of larger, multi-process textile groups, but did not relish the prospect of ESC's being absorbed by a bigger firm. As a compromise, he arranged for ESC to purchase Tootal, and for Courtaulds and ICI to accept minority stakes in the enlarged company. Then, in 1968, in order to frustrate a takeover bid by Viyella, and shortly before Harrison's retirement from the chair, ESC merged with the Calico Printers Association, the dominant firm in the textile finishing sector, and adopted the name English Calico. Harrison had saved ESC from extinction, but English Calico was financially weak and unable to compete internationally, a situation not unrepresentative of the Lancashire textile industry as a whole. It would be unfair to blame Harrison for the problems of ESC in the 1960s; it is, of course, much harder to succeed in a declining industry than in one which is expanding.

Harrison was a busy man with many interests. He was active in the Cotton Board, the umbrella organization representing the Lancashire interest, and led a Cotton Board trade mission to Australia and New Zealand in 1959; he was president of the Shirley Institute, the cotton industry's research association; between 1958 and 1960 he was president of the Manchester chamber of commerce. He then served as president of the Federation of British Industries, 1961–3, proving that his performance at ESC in the 1950s was held in high regard in other industries, and he thereafter remained on the grand council of the Confederation of British Industry (CBI). He was a member of the National Economic Development Council and the British National Export Council. He was knighted for his services to industry in 1963. Between 1965 and 1972, he was a deputy chairman of William and Glyns Bank, and joined the board of the Royal Bank of Scotland in 1966. He was a member of the North West Electricity Board, sat on the governing council of Manchester University (receiving an honorary MA in 1961), and served on the council of the Manchester Business School. In 1959, he was appointed chairman of the Christie Hospital in Manchester, which specialized in cancer research, and between 1966 and 1974 was chairman of governors of the United Manchester Hospitals. He declined an invitation to become high sheriff of Lancashire in 1970, due to the illness of his wife, who died in 1971. Harrison was a deacon and secretary of Wilmslow Congregational Church for many years. Sir Cyril Harrison died at his home, 8 Harefield Drive, Wilmslow, Cheshire, on 14 March 1980, aged seventy-eight.   JOHN SINGLETON

Sources I. Harrison, 'Harrison, Sir Cyril Ernest', *DBB* • C. E. Harrison, 'A company's policy in the ten post war years', *The Cotton Board Conference* [Harrogate 1955] (1955) • *The Times* (18 March 1980), 15 • J. Singleton, *Lancashire on the scrapheap: the cotton industry, 1945–70* (1991) • J. A. Blackburn, 'The British cotton textile industry since World War II: the search for a strategy', *Textile History*, 24 (1993), 235–58 • d. cert. • m. cert. • b. cert.

Archives U. Warwick Mod. RC, papers as president of Federation of British Industries

Likenesses D. Groves, portrait, repro. in Harrison, 'Harrison, Sir Cyril Ernest'

Wealth at death £53,291: probate, 1 Sept 1980, *CGPLA Eng. & Wales*

Harrison, Edmund (*bap.* 1591, *d.* 1667), embroiderer, was born in London, the son of Christopher Harrison (*d.* 1611), merchant taylor, and his wife, Elizabeth, daughter of Thomas Cook of Wakefield. He was baptized at St Margaret's, Westminster, on 23 May 1591. From 1599 to 1604 he was a pupil at Merchant Taylors' School. Nothing is known of his apprenticeship as an embroiderer, but the intimate association of his name with those of William Broderick (*d.* 1620), king's embroiderer to James I, and his son-in-law, John Shepley or Shipley (*d.* 1631), embroiderer to Charles I as prince of Wales, suggests he was trained by one of them. He must have been working for James I in 1618, when he is referred to as king's embroiderer in the diary of his friend, Thomas Godfrey (1586–1664) of Sellinge, Kent, but he only bore the title officially from 1621, sharing it with Shepley until about 1626, when it became his alone. From 1623 he often served as churchwarden at St Benet Paul's Wharf, the church closely associated with the Broderers' Company, and in 1628 he became warden of the company for the first time, presenting a parcel gilt cup on that occasion.

On 13 September 1630 Harrison married Jane (1615–1688), eldest daughter of Thomas Godfrey and his second wife, Sarah Iles of Hammersmith. In 1622 he had stood godfather to one of her younger brothers, later the magistrate Sir Edmund Berry Godfrey. By 1630 he had moved from Grub Street in the parish of St Giles Cripplegate, to Knightrider Street in that of St Benet Paul's Wharf, which was nearer to the great wardrobe. According to his own reckoning, twenty children were born to him and his wife, but only three sons and two daughters were living at his death.

The civil war temporarily ended Harrison's career as king's embroiderer. By 1651 he had moved to Hartshorne Lane (now Northumberland Avenue), where he engaged in the coal trade from an adjacent wharf. That year he also acted for one of the syndicates of the king's creditors, buying numerous paintings and other items at the sales of the king's goods. These included royal portraits and important works such as Rubens's *Peace and War* (now in the National Gallery, London) and pictures by Mantegna (in the Brera Gallery, Milan) and Titian (in the Prado, Madrid). He also acquired Henry VIII's richly embroidered table carpet from the paradise chamber at Hampton Court, and the cloth of state with the arms of James I, which he himself had embroidered for the banqueting hall at Whitehall in 1638. His production of these at the Restoration in 1660, and a certificate from the Broderers' Company testifying to his skill as 'the ablest worker living', helped to get him reinstated as king's embroiderer. He retained the position until his death.

None of Harrison's official work remains, but the accounts of the great wardrobe and master of the robes detail numerous suits, masque costumes, horse trappings, cloths of state, heralds' tabards, liveries, Bible and prayer book covers, banners and armorials embroidered by him. Elias Ashmole's book of 1672 on the Order of the Garter describes and illustrates two examples: the seal bag and the cover of the red book of the order. For Charles

I he also executed rich figure embroidery on altar cloths and hangings. This is closest to his surviving work, a set of embroidered pictures of the life of the Virgin, of which five are now known (preserved in the Victoria and Albert Museum, London, Fitzwilliam Museum, Cambridge, and Royal Museums of Scotland, Edinburgh). Unique of their kind in Britain, in being worked entirely in the technique of gold embroidery known as *or nué*, these were commissioned either by Lady Alethea Talbot (*d*. 1654), wife of Thomas Howard, earl of Arundel (1586–1646), or their third son William Howard, Lord Stafford (1611–1680). Also attributed to Harrison are an embroidered altar frontal with the last supper in the same technique, and an associated pulpit hanging of 1633 with the arms of Sandys of the Vyne.

Edmund Harrison died of a stroke on 9 January 1667. He was buried at St Giles Cripplegate, where a monument (now lost) was erected to him at the behest of his eldest son Godfrey (1635–1677). PATRICIA WARDLE

Sources P. Wardle, 'The king's embroiderer: Edmund Harrison (1590–1667)', *Textile History*, 25 (1994), 29–59; 26 (1995), 139–84 · C. Holford, *A chat about the Broderers' Company* (1910) · 'The domestic chronicle of Thomas Godfrey, Esq', ed. J. G. Nichols, *The topographer and genealogist*, 2 (1853), 450–67 · E. Ashmole, *The institution, laws and ceremonies of the most noble order of the Garter* (1672), 247–8, 250 · O. Millar, ed., 'The inventories and valuations of the king's goods, 1649–1651', *Walpole Society*, 43 (1970–72), 1–432 · J. J. Baddeley, *An account of the church and parish of St Giles, without Cripplegate* (1888), 93
Wealth at death approx. £6946 10s.: inventory, PRO, PROB 4/19423

Harrison, Edward (*bap.* 1766, *d.* 1838), physician, was baptized on 5 November 1766 in Sefton, Lancashire, the son of Edward Harrison. He studied medicine in London, Paris, and Edinburgh (MD, 1784), before settling in Lincolnshire, first in Louth and then in Horncastle, where he founded the Horncastle Dispensary. One of the first physicians to recognize the parlous state of medical education and the practice of physic, he was persuaded in 1804 by the Lincolnshire Medical Benevolent Society (which he had founded) to investigate medical practice in Britain. His findings, which included a vivid account of the scandalous extent of quackery, were published in 1806 as a pamphlet entitled *Remarks on the ineffective state of the practice of physic in Great Britain; with proposals for its future regulation and improvement*. This caused such a stir that Harrison threw himself into the cause of medical reform.

Harrison's proposals for reform of the education and organization of all medical practitioners had much merit. He moved to London where, with the backing of Sir Joseph Banks and the support of many influential physicians and members of parliament, a bill for medical reform was drawn up. William Pitt, the prime minister, promised his support but died before anything could be done. When success was near, however, the Royal College of Physicians, fearing loss of countenance and despising Harrison as an 'outsider' from the provinces, succeeded in defeating the bill.

Bitterly disappointed, Harrison abandoned medical reform, but his ideas lived on to provide a solid basis for future important developments, which culminated in the Medical Act of 1858. From 1817 Harrison specialized in the treatment of spinal disorders, a subject on which his unorthodox views (*Pathological and Practical Observations on Spinal Diseases*, in 1827, and *Observations on Spinal Diseases*, about 1832) were initially derided; they were, however, accepted after his death. A disappointed man, Harrison, who appears to have been unmarried, died on 6 May 1838, while travelling between Marlborough and Devizes, on his way to see a patient with a spinal affliction. He had recently given £300 to the North London Hospital.

IRVINE LOUDON, *rev.*

Sources *British and Foreign Medical Review*, 6 (1838), 289 · *Journal of Health and Disease*, 3 (1847–8), 65–9 · *The Lancet* (19 May 1838), 262–3 · *GM*, 2nd ser., 9 (1838), 670

Harrison, Elizabeth (*fl.* 1724–1756), writer, is an obscure figure. She first appears as the author of *A letter to Mr. John Gay; on his tragedy call'd The captives. To which is annex'd a copy of verses to her royal highness, the princess* (1724). This brief but detailed review of Gay's play is complemented by a poem in honour of the princess of Wales on her patronage of *The Captives*.

The friendly instructor, or, A companion for young ladies and young gentlemen … in plain and familiar dialogues was first published in 1741 and is generally attributed to Harrison. The preface by the Revd Philip Doddridge (1702–1751) provides the only biographical information on the author: 'they were written by a Lady, with whose valuable character I have been acquainted many years, and who has been long employed in the education of children' (Harrison, iii). This didactic work consists of numerous fictional dialogues between children on issues such as the death of a child, diligence and obedience, parents, religion, and friendship. This clearly popular work was expanded in 1770 with a second part and woodcut illustrations, and went through thirteen editions by 1804, with further new editions throughout the nineteenth century in England and America.

The last available record of Harrison is the *Miscellanies on Moral and Religious Subjects, in Prose and Verse*, published in 1756 financially to aid Harrison's ageing parent. It follows the conventional structure of religious miscellanies, offering biblical instruction on sin and virtue through a selection of short moral fables, fictional letters, hymns, and psalms. Some of the pieces in prose and verse, indicated by three asterisks as signature, can be attributed to the hymn writer Joseph Grigg (1728?–1768). Despite the impressive list of subscribers that includes Elizabeth Singer Rowe and Samuel Johnson, the *Literary Magazine* speculated that *Miscellanies* was not published for a general readership. It highlights Harrison's indebtedness to Elizabeth Singer Rowe's work, in attempting to fuse elements of romance fiction with religious doctrine: 'The authors of the essays in prose seem generally to have imitated or try to imitate the copiousness and luxuriance of Mrs. *Rowe*' (*Literary Magazine*, 7, 1756, 282). Two letters in the volume, 'From Laura to Aurelia', are presented as a direct sequel to Rowe's *Letters Moral and Entertaining* (1728–32). The review ends by reprinting a selection of verses and dialogues. The

Monthly Review charitably refrained from 'any criticism that might tend, in the least, to obstruct the progress of so worthy an intention' (*Monthly Review*, 15, Oct 1756, 537). The 1756 edition advertises a further volume, *Meditations upon various subjects, religious and moral. In a train of visions, chiefly design'd for persons in younger life*, but its publication remains unconfirmed.   NICOLE POHL

Sources [E. Harrison], *The friendly instructor, or, A companion for young ladies and young gentlemen* (1741) · J. Julian, ed., *A dictionary of hymnology*, rev. edn (1907) · J. Grigg, *Hymns on divine subjects* (1861)

Harrison, Ethel Bertha (1851–1916), positivist and essayist, was born at Highgate Hill, London, on 27 October 1851, the only daughter of William Harrison (1805–1883), a wealthy West India merchant, and his wife, Anne Tonge Lake (1819–1876), who had four older sons. Ethel grew up in Claybury, a Georgian house near Chigwell, Essex, and was educated by French and English governesses and music teachers, with periods in London and France. Her reading was guided by her first cousin, Frederic *Harrison (1831–1923), twenty years her senior, whom she married on 17 August 1870.

Her intellectual and political interests enabled Mrs Harrison to fit easily into her husband's social and radical circles. She gossiped wittily about writers and politicians with Beatrice Potter, discussed servants with George Eliot, and cautioned Rosalind Howard, the future countess of Carlisle, against undermining her health in the temperance cause. Her own health suffered following the birth of four sons between 1871 and 1877—Bernard, Austin *Harrison, Godfrey, and René—and she had to relinquish her plan to take charge of their early education. Bernard and Austin were tutored by the young George Gissing, who admired their mother's Pre-Raphaelite dark beauty and enjoyed hearing her play the piano.

Sharing her husband's commitment to the positivist movement, Mrs Harrison was appointed to the parent group in Paris, and at the Newton Hall centre which her husband headed in London from 1881 to 1902 she organized a women's guild and conducted homemaking classes and social events for neighbourhood residents. To enhance the Sunday worship of Humanity she founded and directed a choir and produced *The Service of Man*, a hymnal of inspirational verses, including twelve of her own.

The Harrisons lived in London, first at 1 Southwick Place, and later at 38 Westbourne Terrace, their affluence made possible by their generous parents. Holidays were spent in rural England or on the continent, and after the birth of their daughter Olive in 1886 they retired for long periods to Blackdown Cottage on the Sussex Downs, partly so that she could have a country childhood like her mother's.

Only in the 1890s did Mrs Harrison begin writing for publication. She proved adept at different literary genres. The *Positivist Review*, founded in 1893, welcomed her thoughts on such topics as education, patriotism, women, and the empire. Her husband assigned her the entries in his *New Calendar of Great Men* on Thomas à Kempis, Bunyan, Madame de la Fayette, Fénelon, and Maria Edgeworth, and she translated from the French a lecture on his friend John Ruskin. In the *Cornhill Magazine* and the *Nineteenth Century* she recalled her experiences of France and of Paris commune refugees in the 1870s, and compared family life in her parents' generation and her own, showing special interest in the relation of mothers and daughters and the need to improve the treatment of servants. She expressed her views on the education of girls in an imaginary conversation for the *Fortnightly Review*, and used dialogue in vignettes of village life for *Temple Bar* and sketches of London scenes for the *Westminster Gazette*.

Like her husband, Mrs Harrison was a prominent opponent of women's suffrage. Biological and Comtist theories had persuaded them that women were unsuited to political activities, which in any case would compromise their functions as wives and mothers. In 1889 she solicited signatures from notable women for an influential *Nineteenth Century* appeal against franchise reform. When the Women's National Anti-Suffrage League was founded in 1908, she served on its executive committee; she organized its first branch, in Hawkhurst, Kent, where the Harrisons had settled in 1902, and wrote *The Freedom of Women*, a much noticed pamphlet. She also composed songs for league meetings, though a heart condition kept her from attending most of them.

In 1912 the Harrisons moved to 10 Royal Crescent, Bath. Her health improved, and when war broke out she and Olive helped to equip a military hospital. Bernard and René served in France, where René was fatally wounded in the battle of Festubert. Mrs Harrison died at home the next year, on 6 June 1916, following a cerebral embolism, and was cremated at Brookwood cemetery, Woking. Her grieving husband published her bibliography and a short memoir of her life; her ashes were later mingled with his in Wadham College chapel.   MARTHA S. VOGELER

Sources F. Harrison, *Memoir and essays of Ethelbertha Harrison* (1917) · F. Harrison, 'A bibliography: published and signed writings of Mrs Frederic Harrison, 1890–1916', *Positivist Review*, 24 (1916), 178–9 · E. B. Harrison, 'A woman's charter', *The Nation* (25 Jan 1908), 605–6 · E. B. Harrison, *The Times* (15 Aug 1908), 14c · E. B. Harrison, *The Times* (22 March 1912), 6b · A. Harrison, *Frederic Harrison: thoughts and memories* (1926) · M. S. Vogeler, *Frederic Harrison: the vocations of a positivist* (1984) · S. H. Swinny, *Positivist Review*, 24 (1916), 162–5 · *Positivist Review*, 24 (1916), 169–77 · *Anti-Suffrage Review* (Sept 1910) · E. B. Harrison, 'The place of women in politics', *Anti-Suffrage Review* (Dec 1910), 4–5 · B. Harrison, *Separate spheres: the opposition to women's suffrage in Britain* (1978) · Mrs F. Harrison [E. B. Harrison], 'A thinking woman's verdict: "liberal standpoint"', *The Standard* (9 Oct 1911), 13 · parish register, Christ Church, Lancaster Gate, London, 17 Aug 1870 [marriage]

Archives BLPES, Frederic Harrison and London Positivist Society MSS · Bodl. Oxf., corresp. with F. S. Marvin · Castle Howard, Yorkshire, letters to Rosalind Howard, ninth countess of Carlisle

Likenesses photograph, 1889, priv. coll. · group photograph, *c.*1907 (with family), priv. coll. · W. B. Richmond, portrait, 1913, repro. in Vogeler, *Frederic Harrison*, 1984, no. 17 · portraits, repro. in Vogeler, *Frederic Harrison*, nos. 14, 16, 17

Wealth at death £2799 8*s.* 11*d.*: probate, 11 July 1916, *CGPLA Eng. & Wales*

Harrison, Francis Llewelyn [Frank] (1905–1987), music scholar, was born on 29 September 1905 in Dublin, the second son in the family of four sons and two daughters of Alfred Francis Harrison, an accountant with the Great Southern Railway and a talented amateur singer, and his wife, Florence May Nash, who was of Welsh descent on her mother's side, and, on her father's (William Nash, of Kilrush, co. Clare, craftsman in inlaid wood), of mixed English and Hiberno-Norman. Both sides of his family belonged to the protestant, urban tradition of Irish society. The young Harrison showed a precocious talent for music, and was educated at the choir school of St Patrick's Cathedral, from which he won one of the two annual cathedral scholarships to Mountjoy School. He continued studies part-time at the Royal Irish Academy of Music, where he won prizes for organ, piano, and composition, and later at Trinity College, Dublin (MusB 1926, MusD 1930). After a short spell as organist at Kilkenny Cathedral (1929) he emigrated to Canada in 1930.

Harrison was to spend two decades on the other side of the Atlantic. His first posts were within the church music sphere in which he had established himself in Ireland. Alongside this he built up a flourishing career as a private music teacher, organist, and composer. In 1933 he studied with Marcel Dupré in France, and in 1943 he won the Canadian Performing Right Society's composers' award. But from 1935, when he was appointed resident musician to Queen's University, Kingston, Ontario, his career was to be chiefly within academic institutions. In 1940 he opened the university's new music department. After spending 1945–6 as Bradley-Keeler fellow at Yale, studying with Paul Hindemith and Leo Schrade, and posts at Colgate University, New York (1946–7), and Washington University, St Louis (1947–50), he went to England in 1950 and settled in Oxford, as lecturer in music in 1952–6, senior lecturer in 1956–62, and reader in the history of music from 1962 to 1970. From 1965 to 1970 he was a senior research fellow of Jesus College.

The decade in Canadian and North American universities was responsible for changing the focus of Harrison's musical interests. Composition seems to have been virtually abandoned after he went to Oxford, and his appearances as a performer became sporadic. For a highly imaginative man, the challenge of devising humanities curricula from scratch, in a climate suffused with left-wing cultural politics, had left an indelible mark. The need to understand how processes of artistic production, and those of music in particular, related to social structures and assumptions was to be the mainspring of his work for the rest of his life. In Oxford he immersed himself in a study of pre-Reformation insular liturgical music—then an uncharted field—and rapidly established himself as an expert of international repute. His *Music in Medieval Britain* (1958) is a remarkable combination of both encyclopaedic positivism, using mainly manuscript sources alongside liturgical evidence then rarely admitted into musicology, and a rigorous concern to establish the music's comprehensibility in terms of its context. He was also involved with two major editorial projects: *Polyphonic*

Music of the Fourteenth Century, published by Oiseau-Lyre, from 1962 to 1986, and the *Early English Church Music* project initiated by the British Academy at his instigation (1961–72). Among his other publications was *The Eton Choirbook* (3 vols., 1956–61). By nature restlessly inquisitive, Harrison was not content with ploughing a single furrow. During the 1960s, while consolidating his reputation as a medievalist (he was elected a fellow of the British Academy in 1965), his interest in what he dubbed 'anthromusicology' led him to explore musical culture more widely, and he undertook important fieldwork in Latin America. This expansion of his activities led in 1970 to the offer of the chair in ethnomusicology at Amsterdam, which he held until 1976. In Amsterdam Harrison's formidable capacity for hard work was stretched in numerous directions. While establishing his department on a new footing and moulding it as a centre of international academic excellence, he also engaged in fieldwork on the music of Latin America and the Celtic peoples, as well as continuing research on medieval Europe. Throughout the 1970s he continued to accept visiting posts abroad, particularly in North America, where he was much in demand. On a return to Queen's University, Kingston, Ontario, in 1974 he was awarded an honorary degree of LLD, and was present at the inauguration of the Harrison–Le Caine concert hall, named in his honour.

Harrison was a stocky energetic figure, who spoke in tones that recalled both his homeland and his years in North America, and who always took great care with his appearance. A gregarious character, with personal as well as academic interest in people and their activities, he had a wide international circle of friends. As an émigré he carried with him a capacity to make a home almost anywhere, and he was an informed enthusiast for international cuisine. In 1927 he married Norah Lillian, daughter of William Thomas Drayton, antique dealer; they had two daughters. The marriage was not a happy one and there was a divorce in 1965. In 1966 he married Joan, daughter of Edmund Thomas Rimmer, schoolmaster. She had been since 1960 his companion in his exploration of the world's music. There were no children of the second marriage. Harrison died in Canterbury, Kent, where they retired, on 29 December 1987. DAVID CHADD, *rev.*

Sources D. F. L. Chadd, 'Francis Llewelyn Harrison, 1905–1987', *PBA*, 75 (1989), 361–80 • personal knowledge (1996) • private information (1996)

Harrison, Frederic (1831–1923), positivist and author, was born at 17 Euston Square, London, on 18 October 1831, the son of Frederick Harrison (1799–1881), a stockbroker whose father was a prosperous builder from Leicestershire, and his wife, Jane, daughter of Alexander Brice, a Belfast granite merchant. He was baptized in the new St Pancras Church, Euston, and shortly afterwards the family settled in suburban Muswell Hill. His parents undertook his early education and that of his four brothers, born at two-year intervals: Lawrence and Robert Hichens Camden, who would enter their father's firm; and Charles *Harrison and William Sidney, later partners in a firm of solicitors. In 1840 the family moved to 22 Oxford Square,

Frederic Harrison
(1831–1923), by
unknown
photographer

Hyde Park, a house designed by Harrison's father. On the advice of Richard Bethell (Lord Westbury), a family friend, Harrison entered Joseph King's day school in St John's Wood. He did so well that when he went on to King's College School, Strand, in 1843, again on Bethell's recommendation, he was placed with boys older than himself.

Education Given considerable freedom by his teachers, Harrison developed a love of the classics, and on holidays in France an interest in its history and architecture. Stocky in build and energetic, he excelled at sports, especially cricket. He won prizes for Latin and English composition, and performed in school recitations, though he would never speak as well as he wrote. Among his schoolfriends, the most helpful in later years was William Stebbing, an editor of *The Times*, to which Harrison contributed a number of commissioned articles and over 200 letters.

Second in his school when he left, Harrison entered Oxford in 1849 with a scholarship at Wadham College. He found intellectual companionship with Edward Spencer Beesly, John Henry Bridges, and George Earlam Thorley, who would become warden of Wadham. Harrison later said that he had arrived at Oxford with 'the remnants of boyish Toryism and orthodoxy', and left 'a Republican, a democrat, and a Free-Thinker' (*Autobiographic Memoirs*, 1.95). This transformation owed something to the theories of Auguste Comte, which he encountered in works by John Stuart Mill and George Henry Lewes, among others, and later learned were influencing his tutor, Richard Congreve.

Harrison gained only a second class in moderations in 1852, but earned a first in the final school of *literae humaniores* the next year. Ineligible for honours in the new law and history school, he nevertheless took the examination and received an 'honorary' fourth class. He stayed on to assume the tutoring responsibilities relinquished by Congreve, who settled in London to further the cause of Comte's positivist philosophy and Religion of Humanity. Harrison, awarded a fellowship, grew close to such Oxford liberals as A. P. Stanley, Goldwin Smith, Mark Pattison, and Benjamin Jowett.

Lawyer and teacher The summer of 1855 was a turning point in Harrison's life. He arranged an interview with Comte in Paris and was impressed by his insistence upon science as the basis of his new philosophy, outlined in *Cours de philosophie positive*. Back in London, Harrison tried in a small way to make up for the absence of science in his education. More pressing was his study of law at Lincoln's Inn in fulfilment of a promise to his parents, with whom he lived until his marriage, mostly at 10 Lancaster Gate. His distaste for the practical aspects of the profession was offset by his fascination with Roman law and jurisprudence, which he read with Henry Maine. When Maine's lectures were published as *Ancient Law* (1861), Harrison praised them in John Chapman's *Westminster Review* as scientific.

Called to the bar in 1858, Harrison took chambers at 7 New Square, Lincoln's Inn, but spent much of his time on polemical journalism. In 1859 he and Beesly urged British support for Napoleon III's Italian campaign against Austria, and after peace was declared, Harrison visited northern Italy to report for British papers on the aftermath. Later he compared the Risorgimento heroes Cavour and Garibaldi in the *Westminster Review*. For the same periodical he also released his pent-up antagonism towards the growing latitudinarianism in the church. Why should clergymen who believed hardly more of the creeds than did Congreve continue to enjoy the perquisites of their offices? he asked himself. At Chapman's urging, he wrote 'Neo-Christianity' (1860) with the aim of showing that the liberal theology of *Essays and Reviews*, whose authors included Jowett and Pattison, was inconsistent with the beliefs of most churchmen. In the controversy that followed, one of the bitterest in the Victorian church, he became notorious.

Meanwhile, Harrison had begun teaching history and Latin at the London Working Men's College founded by the Christian socialists in Bloomsbury. His proposal to recast the history syllabus along Comtean lines led the school's founder, F. D. Maurice, to force his resignation. He then taught briefly for the secularist George Jacob Holyoake and at his own expense published his lectures as *The Meaning of History* (1862), reprinted in *The Meaning of History and other Historical Pieces* (1894). He was also associated with secularists and Christian socialists in efforts on behalf of the working class. Holyoake provided introductions to friends in Lancashire, whom Harrison visited in 1861 to assess working-class conditions, and again in 1863 to report on the cotton famine resulting from the American Civil War. With Maurice's colleagues Thomas Hughes and J. M. Ludlow he wrote to London newspapers justifying the aims of the striking building trades. In the mid-1860s he defended the 'new model' unions of skilled workers against the political economists. His articles in the *Fortnightly Review* much impressed George Eliot, who enlisted his help with legal issues in several of her novels. In 1867 Harrison was appointed to the royal commission on trade unions and wrote its minority report, recommending a secure legal status for unions and protection of their funds, changes in the law that were soon largely enacted. His prestige among labour leaders survived his later criticism of their policies.

Among the political causes that engaged Harrison's pen in the 1860s were Polish independence, the union's position in the American Civil War, and the case against Governor Eyre in Jamaica. Joining a committee headed by Mill, Harrison condemned Eyre's use of military authority against civilians in 1865, employing arguments that he later directed against British forces in Afghanistan in 1879 and in South Africa during the Second South African War. He opposed the suspension of *habeas corpus* in response to the violence of the Fenians, and helped to draw up a petition to parliament demanding that they be treated as political prisoners rather than criminals. In *International Policy* (1866), a collection of essays edited by him, he called for closer ties with France, and in an essay in *Questions for a Reformed Government* (1867) he criticized the government's attempt to influence the course of the American Civil War as a betrayal of public sentiment. He made the case for parliamentary reform in working-class papers, but wrote his liveliest essays for the middle-class readers of the *Fortnightly Review*: 'Our Venetian constitution' (March 1867), deriding Walter Bagehot's conservative theories of government; and 'Culture: a dialogue' (November 1867), satirizing Matthew Arnold's fear of democracy. Arnold had provoked Harrison's witty dialogue by depicting him as a dangerous radical, once imagining him in a London garden 'in full evening costume, furbishing up a guillotine' (*Pall Mall Gazette*, 22 April 1867, 3).

Though he denigrated the future High Court judge James Fitzjames Stephen for 'thrusting his huge carcass up the ladder of preferment' (F. Harrison to John Morley, 28 July 1873, London School of Economics, Harrison MSS), Harrison himself advanced in his profession partly through connections. In 1869 Lord Westbury appointed him secretary to the royal commission for the digest of the law. The next year, on Maine's recommendation, the Council of Legal Education appointed him examiner in jurisprudence, Roman law, and constitutional history; and from 1877 to 1889 he was professor of jurisprudence, international law, and constitutional law for the council. Essays derived from his lectures appeared in the *Fortnightly Review* and were reprinted in his *On Jurisprudence and the Conflict of Laws* (1919).

The positivist Harrison considered 1870 his *annus mirabilis*. In that year he found his vocation as a positivist and on 17 August married eighteen-year-old Ethel Bertha *Harrison, his first cousin. She supported his decision to join Bridges, Beesly, and the twins Vernon and Godfrey Lushington with others in founding England's first positivist centre, under Congreve. At 19 Chapel Street (now 20 Rugby Street), not far from the working men's college, they offered a smaller version of its free classes. They were especially eager to provide English lessons to refugees from the Paris commune, which the positivists had defended in defiance of middle-class British outrage. They

also published a joint translation of Comte's four-volume *Système de politique positive* (1875–7). Harrison undertook the second volume (*Social Statics*), to the dismay of his father and of Matthew Arnold, who deplored the waste of his literary gifts. At Chapel Street, Congreve introduced an attenuated form of Comte's ritual. The positivists dated letters by Comte's calendar, and it provided the Harrisons with names for their sons, born between 1871 and 1877 and 'presented' to the positivist community: Bernard Oliver, Austin Frederic *Harrison (1873–1928), Godfrey Denis, and Christopher René. Though the Religion of Humanity was commonly ridiculed as a parody of Christianity, to Harrison it represented the rational final stage of mankind's long religious evolution.

In 1876 Harrison moved his family from their first home, at 1 Southwick Place, London, to 38 Westbourne Terrace. Part of each summer was spent at the elder Harrisons' country house, Sutton Place, a Tudor mansion in Surrey, whose architectural and historical riches Harrison depicted in *Annals of an Old Manor House* (1893; abridged 1899). From 1888 to 1897 there were also long periods at Blackdown Cottage, Haslemere, Surrey.

In the 1870s Harrison wrote regularly on British and French politics in the *Fortnightly Review*. Its editor, John Morley, a good but not uncritical friend, helped him plan his first substantial book, *Order and Progress* (1875), which advocated a strong government but assigned religion, education, and morality to the private sphere. This Comtean division of authority lay behind Harrison's opposition to censorship and his participation in the Liberation Society's campaign to disestablish and disendow the Church of England.

In 1878 long-smouldering dissatisfaction with Congreve's leadership led Harrison, Bridges, Beesly, James Cotter Morison, and the Lushingtons to break with him. Three years later they opened their own positivist centre in Fetter Lane, off Fleet Street, and named it Newton Hall. Pierre Laffitte, head of Comte's Paris disciples, designated Harrison president of the London positivist committee. For two decades Harrison delivered the most important addresses, gratified by the occasional attendance of friends such as Morley, Thomas Hardy, or Wilfrid Blunt. Though repudiating the title of priest, he led prayers to humanity and administered Comte's sacraments, as well as co-ordinating educational and recreational activities, handling funds, and contributing to the French positivists' *Revue occidentale* and Beesly's *Positivist Review*. For years he laboured over a vast compendium of biographical sketches of the historical figures named in Comte's calendar, writing 136 of the 599 entries himself. Outside Newton Hall, *The New Calendar of Great Men* (1892) was largely derided or ignored, but Harrison declared that its selectivity gave it an advantage over his friend Leslie Stephen's *Dictionary of National Biography*, 'an interminable snake' (F. Harrison to John Morley, 31 Jan 1891, London School of Economics, Harrison MSS). No empire-builder, he maintained only loose relations with several small positivist groups in other parts of Britain. Though he made sparks fly with his witty sallies in controversies over positivism with Huxley, James Fitzjames Stephen, John Ruskin, and Herbert Spencer, he could not halt the decline in Newton Hall's small membership after its first decade.

Later writings During the last twenty years of the century Harrison was a familiar figure at the Athenaeum and in Liberal circles. A home-ruler, he stood unsuccessfully as a Gladstonian Liberal for London University in the general election of 1886. Local politics proved more congenial. The first London county council elected him alderman in 1889, and as a member of its Progressive Party, led by his brother Charles, he served for five years on important committees, one of which produced early plans for Kingsway. A far-sighted urbanist, he published articles on the London county council's accomplishments and his conception of the ideal city. The Harrisons' views on the family, which reflected both their class and their positivism, led them to help organize a petition against women's suffrage for the *Nineteenth Century* in 1889, and two years later Harrison debated the issues with Millicent Fawcett in the *Fortnightly Review*.

In 1880 Harrison befriended the then unknown George Gissing and engaged him as tutor for the two older Harrison boys, though in the end he failed to appreciate Gissing's best novels. Harrison's judgements and reminiscences of other writers are found in *The Choice of Books* (1886), *Studies in Early Victorian Literature* (1895), and *Tennyson, Ruskin, Mill and other Literary Estimates* (1899). Invited by Macmillan, the publisher of these volumes, to write the popular studies *Oliver Cromwell* (1888) and *William the Silent* (1897), he proved adept at assimilating secondary sources. When his last child, a girl, was born in 1886, he named her Olive. Later he helped organize celebrations honouring Gibbon and Alfred the Great. Trips to France, Italy, and the Mediterranean yielded essays informed by his wide historical knowledge. After a lecture tour in the United States he published *George Washington and other American Addresses* (1901).

In 1902 Newton Hall's lease expired and the Harrisons settled at Elm Hill, Hawkhurst, Kent. Others carried on a diminished positivist programme in hired rooms. Harrison's attention lay elsewhere. He became a JP and held offices in the Royal Historical Society, the Sociological Society, the Eastern Question Association, and the London Library. *John Ruskin* appeared in 1902, and *Chatham* in 1905. His only novel, *Theophano: the Crusade of the Tenth Century* (1904), and a drama in blank verse, *Nicephorus: a Tragedy of New Rome* (1906), were unsuccessful offshoots of research on Byzantine history for his Rede lecture at Cambridge in 1900. Between 1906 and 1908 he compiled six volumes of essays, including his recollections of mountaineering, *My Alpine Jubilee, 1851–1907* (1908). His *Autobiographic Memoirs* appeared in 1911, informative but disappointing as literature. *Among my Books* (1912) reprinted essays from the *English Review* of his son Austin, and much of *The Positive Evolution of Religion* (1913) originated in the *Positivist Review*.

In 1912 the Harrisons moved to 10 Royal Crescent, Bath. During the war Harrison published *The German Peril*, which embodied fears dating back to the 1860s. His youngest son died in France of battle wounds in 1915, with his father at the bedside. Ethel died in 1916. Harrison, still vigorous and opinionated, went on to produce four more volumes of reprinted essays and commentary on current affairs. He died suddenly from heart failure at his home in Royal Crescent on 14 January 1923. He had received honorary degrees from three universities—Cambridge (1905), Aberdeen (1909), and Oxford (1910)—and the freedom of the city of Bath (1921). Wadham had made him an honorary fellow in 1899, and after his death an urn containing his ashes, mingled with Ethel's, was placed in the college ante-chapel.   MARTHA S. VOGELER

Sources F. Harrison, *Autobiographic memoirs*, 2 vols. (1911) [with bibliography of articles to 1910 not in bks] · A. Harrison, *Frederic Harrison: thoughts and memories* (1926) · M. S. Vogeler, *Frederic Harrison: the vocations of a positivist* (1984) · J. Saville, 'Harrison, Frederic', *DLB*, vol. 2 · *DNB* · F. Harrison, *The creed of a layman* (1907) · *Early life and letters of John Morley*, ed. F. W. Hirst, 2 vols. (1927) · R. Harrison, *Before the socialists: studies in labour and politics, 1861–1881* (1965) · J. E. McGee, *A crusade for humanity: the history of organized positivism in England* (1931) · W. M. Simon, *European positivism in the nineteenth century* (1963) · C. Kent, *Brains and numbers: élitism, Comtism and democracy in mid-Victorian England* (1978) · H. R. Sullivan, *Frederic Harrison* (1983) · T. R. Wright, *The religion of humanity* (1986) · parish register (marriage), 17 Aug 1870, Christ Church, Lancaster Gate, London · private information (2004) · *The Times* (15 Jan 1923) · *The Times* (20 Jan 1923) [cremation] · *The Times* (24 Jan 1923) [memorial service] · *The Times* (19 March 1923) [positivist memorial service] · *The Times* (7 June 1923) [placing of ashes] · *Positivist Review*, 31 (1923), 75–7 · BLPES, Harrison MSS

Archives BL, Positivist MSS · BLPES, London Positivist Society MSS, corresp. and literary papers · NL Scot., letters, incl. to Sir Patrick Geddes and Lord Rosebery | Bishopsgate Institution, London, letters to George Howell · BL, corresp. with Richard Congreve, Add. MS 45228 · BL, letters to Sir Charles Dilke, Add. MS 43898 · BL, corresp. with Macmillans, Add. MSS 55035–55037 · BL OIOC, letters to Sir Mountstuart Grant-Duff, MS Eur. F 234 · Bodl. Oxf., letters to Herbert Asquith · Bodl. Oxf., letters to Francis Marvin and Edith Marvin · Bodl. Oxf., corresp. with Gilbert Murray · Castle Howard, letters to Lord and Lady Carlisle · CUL, letters to Lord Acton · Dorset County Museum, Dorchester, Thomas Hardy corresp. · Hunt. L., letters, mainly to Richard Watson Gilder · King's Cam., letters to Oscar Browning · L. Cong., Andrew Carnegie corresp. · Maison d'Auguste Comte, Paris, letters to Constant Hillemand · Maison d'Auguste Comte, Paris, letters to Charles Jeanmolle · Maison d'Auguste Comte, Paris, letters to Pierre Laffitte · Maison d'Auguste Comte, Paris, letters to A. Vaillant · Mitchell L., Glas., letters to John Lane · U. Birm. L., corresp. with Joseph Chamberlain · U. Edin., Lord Rosebery corresp. · U. Edin. L., corresp. with Charles Sarolea · U. Leeds, Brotherton L., letters to Sir Edmund Gosse · UCL, letters to A. Beesly and E. S. Beesly · W. Sussex RO, letters to F. A. Maxse · Yale U., Beinecke L., George Eliot corresp.

Likenesses Nadar, photograph, c.Sept 1862, repro. in Vogeler, *Frederic Harrison*, 1; priv. coll. · photograph, 1880, repro. in *The collected letters of William Morris*, ed. N. Kelvin, 2 (1987), 7 · six photographs, 1885–1919, repro. in Vogeler, *Frederic Harrison*; priv. coll. · E. Walker, photograph, 1901, repro. in Harrison, *Autobiographic memoirs* · E. Walker, photograph, 1908, repro. in Harrison, *Autobiographic memoirs*, 2 · W. R. Sickert, pencil, 1912, NPG · photograph, c.1913, maison d'Auguste Comte, Paris; repro. in Vogeler, *Frederic Harrison* · Ape [C. Pellegrini], watercolour, NPG; repro. in *VF* (23 Jan 1886) · G. C. Beresford, two prints, NPG · W. & D. Downey, woodburytype, NPG; repro. in W. Downey and D. Downey, *The cabinet portrait gallery*, 2 (1891) · B. Harrison, oils, Wadham College, Oxford · photograph, NPG [see illus.]

Wealth at death £34,076 2s. 1d.: probate, 22 Feb 1923, CGPLA Eng. & Wales

Harrison, Sir George (1767–1841), civil servant, was born on 19 June 1767, the fourth of the five sons of Thomas Harrison (1736–1792), attorney and advocate-general of Jamaica, and his first wife, Dorothy, daughter of Edmund Buntingfield of Stockton-on-Tees, co. Durham. Nothing is known of his early education. He entered Lincoln's Inn in 1789 and was called to the bar in 1800. On 23 September 1791 he married Dorothy (d. 1802), daughter of Tomlinson Bunting of Middleton Lodge, York, with whom he had two sons, only one of whom lived to maturity.

Harrison early established a reputation as an authority on tax and revenue law. This led the prime minister, William Pitt the younger, to appoint him register and counsel to the commission for the redemption of the land tax in 1798. To this he added the part-time post of counsel to the War Office in 1804. On 19 August 1805 Pitt appointed him assistant secretary to the Treasury. This was a new office created as part of wide-ranging reorganization of the business of the Treasury. The assistant secretary ranked immediately after the two joint secretaries and took over many of their departmental duties, thus enabling them to concentrate on their political and parliamentary roles. Harrison's duties were to take the minutes of the board and to ensure that its decisions were carried into effect, as well as to supervise and discipline the clerical establishment. Until 1816 he also occupied the position of law clerk, in which capacity he was expected to assist in the preparation of bills for parliament and to report on questions of law.

Unlike the joint secretaries the assistant secretary was specifically barred from parliament. The post did not, however, guarantee security of tenure and thus its occupant was theoretically at risk whenever there was a change of administration. However, such were Harrison's abilities and assiduity that he made himself indispensable as the linchpin of the new organization. In his hands the assistant secretaryship rapidly evolved from a superior clerkship into the role of confidential adviser to successive prime ministers and chancellors of the exchequer. Perceval and, more particularly, Liverpool relied on his counsel on a wide range of matters, including the organization of departments connected with the Treasury, dealings with the Bank of England, and City interests. The value placed on his services was such that his salary, originally £2000 a year, was progressively increased until it reached £3500 in 1815. Harrison held office for over twenty years until his retirement on 7 April 1826 on grounds of ill health. It was not until 1867 that the title 'permanent secretary' was applied to the post which he had held, but it was he who had laid the foundations for the later development of this pivotal office, with all that this implied for the evolution of the modern higher civil service.

Harrison had been appointed auditor of the duchy of Cornwall in 1823. On his retirement from the Treasury he obtained the additional office of auditor of the duchy of Lancaster. He held both positions until his death and wrote several legal works on the revenues of the royal duchies. In 1834 he published *Fragments and Scraps of History*. On 13 April 1831 he was made knight grand cross of the Royal Guelphic Order. He was married a second time, in 1829, to Ann (d. 1840), widow of William Hill, his successor as assistant secretary of the Treasury. Harrison died on 3 February 1841 at 4 Spring Gardens Terrace, London, and was buried at St Martin-in-the-Fields on the 11th.

J. C. SAINTY

Sources J. R. Torrance, 'Sir George Harrison and the growth of bureaucracy in the early 19th century', *EngHR*, 83 (1968), 52–88 · H. Roseveare, *The treasury: the evolution of a British institution* (1969) · *Miscellanea Genealogica et Heraldica*, new ser., 4 (1884), 118–24 · W. P. Baildon, ed., *The records of the Honorable Society of Lincoln's Inn: admissions*, 2 vols. (1896) · *The heritage of Great Britain and Ireland* (1841) · *GM*, 2nd ser., 15 (1841), 328 · parish records (burial), St Martin-in-the-Fields, Westminster, 11 Feb 1841
Archives BL, official corresp., Add. MSS 29472–29474 · CUL, papers relating to Scilly Isles | BL, corresp. with Jeremy Bentham, Add. MSS 33544–33545 · BL, letters to T. C. Brooksbank, Add. MSS 38253–38292, *passim* · BL, letters to Lord Grenville, Add. MS 58969 · BL, corresp. with J. C. Herries, Add. MSS 57372–57373 · BL, corresp. with Lord Holland, Add. MS 51535 · BL, corresp. with Lord Liverpool, Add. MSS 38253–38320, 38573, *passim* · BL, letters to Robert Peel and others, Add. MSS 40215–40605, *passim* · Derbys. RO, letters to Sir R. J. Wilmot-Horton · Herts. ALS, notes to William Plunkett · U. Nott. L., letters to Lord William Bentinck, etc.
Likenesses C. Turner, mezzotint, pubd 1816 (after T. Barber), BM, NPG · portrait, priv. coll.; known to be in possession of A. R. W. Harrison, warden of Merton College, Oxford, in 1968

Harrison, George Bagshawe (1894–1991), university teacher and literary scholar, was born on 14 July 1894 at 6 Brunswick Place, Hove, Sussex, the fourth (and second surviving) of the five children of Dr Walter Harrison (1860–1939), dental surgeon, and his wife, Ada Louisa (b. 1861), daughter of John Bagshaw, wholesale grocer, and his second wife, Martha. Walter's father, James George Harrison, had become the proprietor of the Concert Hall in West Street, Brighton, and his brothers and sisters had a wide range of musical and literary interests. Walter Harrison was well qualified, as a licentiate in dental surgery (England) (1882) and a doctor of medical dentistry (Harvard University) (1885), and in 1903 became president of the British Dental Association.

Education and war service G. B. Harrison (as he was known) was educated at Crescent House preparatory school, Brighton (1901–7), Brighton College (1907–13), and Queens' College, Cambridge (1913–14). Short-sighted, he took little pleasure in team sports, and at Brighton College he became an active debater, going on later to participate in debates in the Cambridge Union, which he found admirable training in organized thought and in the skills of public speaking.

Soon after the First World War broke out, in August 1914, Harrison volunteered for service in the Territorial Army. Having been a colour-sergeant in the Officers' Training Corps (junior branch) unit at Brighton College, in September he was commissioned as a subaltern in the 5th battalion Queen's Royal West Surrey regiment. As a territorial unit, in November it went off to Lucknow in India to release a regular battalion for service in France. In December 1915 it was sent to Mesopotamia as part of the force

George Bagshawe Harrison (1894–1991), by Howard Coster, 1939

which occupied the southern area and which unsuccessfully attempted to relieve the siege of General Townsend's army by the Turks at Kut al-Amara. In February 1916, north of Nasiriyyah, while trying to do battle with some noisy half-wild cats in the night, Harrison tripped over a tent rope and re-fractured his right forearm, badly set following a riding accident in India, and was sent back there to recover. He rejoined his regiment in October, taking charge of a signals section, in time to take part in much of General Maude's campaign which captured Baghdad and then advanced as far as Haditha on the Aleppo Road by the end of March 1917, effectively ending Turkish power in Mesopotamia. In mid-1918 he took up a junior staff position, and ended the war as staff captain to General F. S. Lucas, who commanded the 42nd Indian infantry brigade and the 'Ramadi area'. As a student part-way through a degree, Harrison had a high priority for demobilization, and he arrived back in Brighton as a civilian on 3 March 1919.

On 9 April 1919 Harrison married Dorothy Agnes Barker (1894–1986), whom he had first met as the sister of a schoolfriend, at Dunsby rectory in Lincolnshire, where her father, the Revd Thomas Barker, was curate-in-charge. They had four children: Joan (b. 1920), Maurice (1921–1942), Michael (1923–1968), and Anthony (1926–1947). Harrison returned to Queens' College, Cambridge, for the summer term of 1919. Originally having studied for the classical tripos, he could now enrol for the recently introduced English tripos, and in 1921 he gained a BA and MA with a first-class pass. Outstanding lecturers he had at the

time included I. A. Richards, E. M. W. Tillyard, Mansfield Forbes, and Sydney Roberts. He took pride in having been Richards's first student. With little employment then offering in university English departments, he taught for two years (1921–3) at Felsted School, Essex, and for one year at St Paul's Training College, Cheltenham, Gloucestershire, before gaining appointment in 1924 as an assistant lecturer in English literature at King's College, University of London. Here he progressed through to lecturer (1927–9) and reader in English literature (1929–43).

Shakespearian scholar Already, while at Felsted, Harrison had perceived that to get ahead he would need to publish, and had written his first book, a popularizing work, *Shakespeare: the Man and his Stage* (1923), in collaboration with E. A. Greening Lamborne. He followed it with *Shakespeare's Fellows* (1923), on the actors of Elizabethan London. Seeing a need and a market for inexpensive, old-spelling reprints of important Elizabethan background texts, between 1923 and 1926 he organized the publication of fifteen volumes of them, as Bodley Head Quartos. At Cheltenham he had also seen the need for editions of Shakespeare, designed for teachers and students, which would be more 'reader-friendly' than those available, and arranged with the publisher George G. Harrap to edit *The New Reader's Shakespeare*, of which twenty volumes were published between 1925 and 1929, with introductory text preceding scenes and a minimum of annotation.

Harrison's most ambitious venture, however, was the Elizabethan and Jacobean Journals series, which was made up of compilations of sixteenth- and seventeenth-century everyday news and gossip, of value as contexts to the literature of the time. The *First volume of the Elizabethan journal, being a record of those things most talked of during the years 1591–94* was published in 1928. Two more volumes, published in 1931 and 1933, brought this journal through to 1603; and two volumes of the *Jacobean Journal*, published in 1940 and 1959, covered the first years of James I's reign, up to 1610. A third volume remained uncompleted.

In 1928 Harrison was awarded a University of London PhD for his first *Elizabethan Journal*, and for a scholarly paper, 'The Stationers' register', as contributions to learning. That year being the tercentenary of the birth of John Bunyan, he published an edition of *The Pilgrim's Progress and The Life and Death of Mr. Badman*, as well as one of *The Church Book of Bunyan Meeting, 1650–1821*, and a short study of Bunyan. In 1929 he spent the summer session at the University of Chicago, as the Frederic Ives Carpenter visiting professor of English, and in 1933 he lectured at the Sorbonne in Paris.

At King's College in the mid-1930s Harrison helped to run the London University Diploma for Journalism, and tutored in this course, which could have become Britain's first journalism degree but for the Second World War. He also contributed to the production of a series of Shakespeare plays in modern dress. He served for years as secretary to the Shakespeare Association under the presidencies of Professor Sir Israel Gollancz and then from late 1929 of Harley Granville-Barker, with whom he edited the *Companion to Shakespeare Studies* (1934), contributing a chapter on 'The national background'. He participated in the first series of Shakespeare summer schools at Stratford upon Avon (1937–9), contributed to a documentary film about Shakespearian imagery by Gaumont-British Instructional, and spoke about Shakespearian topics on radio and, in 1938, on public television.

In 1935 Allen Lane, the head of the Penguin publishing firm, broached the project of producing inexpensive paperback editions of Shakespeare, and Harrison undertook to edit them in consultation with Granville-Barker. The first six plays appeared in 1937, and twelve more by 1939; after the Second World War he resumed this project, with the rest of the plays and the poems appearing between 1947 and 1959. However, in that post-war period he was simultaneously working on an edition of Shakespeare's works for the American publisher Harcourt Brace, with *Twenty-Three Plays and the Sonnets* appearing in 1948 and *The Complete Works* in 1952. When Penguin wished to extend sales of its Shakespeares to the United States, he could not agree to this, as he felt that this would violate the spirit of his contract with Harcourt. Penguin, therefore, embarked on a new series of editions by separate editors, to which American publication would not be a barrier.

Harrison enlisted in 1940 in the supply branch of the Royal Army Service Corps and helped administer stores depots at Inverness and Thurso in Scotland. In October 1941 he transferred to the intelligence corps, serving successively in Liverpool docks, in Lisburn, near Belfast, in the War Office, and in its recruitment section in London. Underemployed, however, as a middle-aged officer, he sought university positions in Canada. Offered the post of professor and head of the English department at Queen's University, Kingston, Ontario, he gladly took it, obtaining his release from the army, and moving, in July 1943. Queen's had limited resources in comparison to those he had enjoyed in London; none the less its vacations provided scope to pursue his editing of Shakespeare. The Harcourt Brace Shakespeare was by far the most ambitious of his editions, with extensive introductions, annotations, and illustrations, and twenty-eight appendices.

In July 1942 Harrison's eldest son, Maurice, who had first gone to Southern Rhodesia as a farm-trainee, had died in India of transverse myelitis. In 1947, on the night of 11–12 January, his youngest son, Anthony, who was serving in the British army in Palestine, was killed in an accident. The profound shock of this second loss induced Harrison and his wife to seek what they felt to be a more spiritually sustaining form of Christian worship than the Church of England; and they turned towards the Roman Catholic faith, being received into that church on 14 June 1947.

Professor in the United States In mid-1949 Harrison took up a professorial post in the department of English at the University of Michigan, Ann Arbor, a large, high-quality department with many students and supported by a first-class university library. As part of his duties he became faculty adviser to Catholic students. At this time he also acted as general editor for Harcourt Brace's two-volume anthology, *Major British Writers* (1954), which was used extensively by American universities for about fifteen years. Other books included *Profession of English* (1962), an endeavour to establish a rationale for English literature studies, and *The Fires of Arcadia* (1963), a novel about breeding humans with animals. Honorary degrees awarded him during this period included LittDs from Villanova University in Pennsylvania (1960), Holy Cross College, Worcester, Massachusetts (1961), and Marquette University, Milwaukee, Illinois (1963), and an honorary LLD from Assumption University, Windsor, Ontario (1962). In 1964 he retired from the University of Michigan, at the age of seventy, as an emeritus professor, permitted to teach a single course for the next three years.

Also in 1964 Harrison became involved in the large-scale project for the establishment of a uniform translation into English of the Catholic liturgy. Following on from the decisions of the Second Vatican Council of 1962, the International Commission on English in the Liturgy (ICEL) was set up to bring this about. Harrison had published an article on this issue and hence was appointed as one of the two lay members of the ICEL's advisory committee, which organized and oversaw the translation process. In due course he became part of its central working group, and its general editor. He completed his work for the ICEL in 1970 and on 23 April, in New York, was awarded the Campion medal for long and eminent service in the cause of Christian literature. He retained an active interest in the problems of introducing the English liturgy, editing the three-volume *Lectionary for Mass, for Sundays of the Year Annotated for Reading* (1973–5) and co-authoring, with John McCabe, *Proclaiming the Word: a Handbook of Church Speaking* (1976). In June 1981 he was included by Pope John Paul II as one of those 'chosen as Knights of the Order of St Gregory the Great' (Harrison, *One Man in his Time*, 283).

In 1967 Harrison finally ended his connection with the University of Michigan and moved to Santa Fe, New Mexico, for four years. His surviving son, Michael, was working as a doctor in Oundle, Northamptonshire, but in 1968 his cancer recurred and on 1 September he died. Harrison and his wife were doing a lot of international travelling and spent much time with their son and, later, with his widow and six children. They moved from Santa Fe to Honolulu in 1971 to join their daughter, Joan, and her husband, Dr John McIntosh, an academic biochemist. After eighteen months there they tried living in Oundle for several years, but in 1976 they shifted to Palmerston North, New Zealand, where John McIntosh now had a post in the department of chemistry and biochemistry at Massey University. Here Harrison wrote *One Man in his Time: the Memoirs of G. B. Harrison, 1894–1984* (1985). Dorothy Harrison died on 4 October 1986, and Harrison himself on 1 November 1991, at the age of ninety-seven, at Brightwater rest home, 69 Brightwater Terrace, Palmerston North. He was cremated on 7 November at Palmerston North. Of his children, only his daughter Joan survived him. She had trained as a nurse and midwife in London, and then as a medical doctor, and had married John McIntosh at Elgin, Ontario, in 1960. They had two daughters, Anne and Frances.

Achievement During his lifetime Harrison was the author of twenty-five books and edited three editions of Shakespeare, as well as nineteen other works, or series. He also wrote several articles and delivered many public or visiting lectures. While he may not have been in the highest rank of academic literary scholars, he successfully pursued three major ideas: that to understand English literary works of the past required detailed knowledge of the literary, social, and political (and for plays, theatrical) contexts out of which they were written; that the textual editing of literary works should reproduce as closely as possible the substantives and most of the accidentals of a single authoritative text; and that 'cheap, popular and portable' editions of Shakespearian plays and of background texts, based upon sound scholarship but accessible and inviting to the reader, should be made available to students and serious-minded general readers. These notions might not sound startling today, but in the 1920s and 1930s English literature studies as a discipline was still evolving, and Harrison played a vital pioneering role.

Harrison did much to pioneer the publication of reprints or facsimiles of primary texts, of minor literary or 'background' contextual importance for the study of Elizabethan and Jacobean literature, and to foster contextual studies, even though his own reprints have since been superseded. His studies of Elizabethan drama and theatre have likewise generally been superseded, except for his Elizabethan and Jacobean journals; and these are of lasting interest and value. As an editor of Shakespeare his conservative faithfulness to a quarto or folio version, as opposed to eclectic editing, and his insistence that Shakespeare's later plays were written not in a basic iambic pentameter but in a form of free verse, punctuated for speaking, were far ahead of his time.

As a university teacher Harrison's particular stresses were upon contextual understanding of dramatic texts and upon the importance of their oral dimension. One of his students at Michigan paid tribute to his erudition, his impeccable preparation, and his classroom decorum. Robert Neale, who had been a junior colleague at the University of Michigan, recalled that:

> Initially I found him to be a remote senior professor who was not very forthcoming. On further acquaintance, however, I found him to be a kind and generous man and very intelligent. He was one of half a dozen of the most knowledgeable men in his field and a great man of his time. (private information)

The *Times* obituary praised his Shakespeare editions and his Elizabethan and Jacobean journals, citing Rose Macaulay's praise of 'Harrison's fictional diarist' as '"learned, inquisitive, and remarkably well informed"', with an '"urbane, anecdotal pen"' (12 Nov 1991).

JOHN C. ROSS

Sources G. B. Harrison, *One man in his time: the memoirs of G. B. Harrison, 1894–1984* (1985) · G. B. Harrison, typescript drafts for autobiography, priv. coll. · *The Times* (12 Nov 1991) · *British Dental Journal*, 67 (1939), 576–7 [Walter Harrison] · letter from James Packard to G. B. Harrison, 28 Nov 1989, priv. coll. · *WW* · private information (2004) [Mrs B. Holmes, Mr R. Neale] · *The Independent* (25 Nov 1991) · records, Thomas Griggs & Son, funeral directors, Palmerston North, New Zealand
Archives priv. coll., incl. typescripts, letters, and press cuttings of reviews and obituaries · U. Mich., Bentley Historical Library, corresp., diaries, and papers · U. Mich., corresp.
Likenesses photographs, 1901–85, repro. in Harrison, *One man in his time* · H. Coster, photograph, 1939, NPG [*see illus.*]

Harrison, George Henry (1816–1846), painter, was born in Liverpool, the second son in the family of twelve children of William Harrison (*d.* 1861), businessman, and his wife, Mary *Harrison (1788–1875), a flower painter, daughter of William Rossiter of Stockport. He was baptized at St Peter's Church, Liverpool, on 23 January 1823, as too was his brother Robert [*see below*]. Another brother, William Frederick *Harrison (1815–1880), was also a painter. In 1830 he moved with his mother to London, where he studied anatomy at the Hunterian School in Windmill Street, while earning a living making anatomical drawings. Encouraged by John Constable, Harrison began to paint watercolour landscapes, and was one of many artists who went to the Farne Islands in 1838 to paint Grace Darling and the wreck of the *Forfarshire*; an engraving of his painting is in the British Museum. He exhibited fourteen paintings at the Royal Academy from 1840, and was elected an associate of the Society of Painters in Water Colours in 1845. Harrison gave weekly outdoor sketching classes during the summer months, and when the family moved to Paris for the sake of his health he gave similar classes there. Many of his later paintings are of the palaces and gardens of Fontainebleau and St Cloud, in the style of Watteau and Boucher, including *Fontainebleau, in the Days of Henri quatre* (exh. Society of Painters in Water Colours, 1846). He also painted a number of scenes of Gypsies, such as *Gypsy Children* (exh. Suffolk Street, 1836). Two of his watercolours are in the Victoria and Albert Museum. His sketch of Hinchinbrook House, Huntingdonshire, was engraved for S. C. Hall's *The Baronial Halls and Picturesque Edifices of England* (1848). Harrison died in Paris on 20 October 1846, and was buried in Kensal Green cemetery.

Harrison's younger brother **Robert Harrison** (1820–1897), librarian, was born on 26 November 1820 in Liverpool. He worked for a bookseller in High Holborn, London, before moving to Paris, and from there to St Petersburg in 1844, where he spent nine years as tutor to the family of Prince Demidov, and as a lecturer at St Anne's School. He married in Russia, but brought his family back to England before the outbreak of the Crimean War, and later published *Notes of a Nine Years' Residence in Russia, 1844–1853* (1855).

Robert Harrison was librarian of the Leeds Library from 1854 to 1857, before his appointment as librarian of the London Library. He remained there until his retirement in 1893, and was responsible for the fifth edition of the catalogue (1888), with a preface on the history of the library. One of the founders of the Library Association in 1877, he served as treasurer until 1889, sat on several committees, and contributed papers to its *Transactions*, including 'On the elimination of useless books from libraries' (1881). He was elected president for 1891–2.

Harrison wrote ninety articles for the *Dictionary of National Biography* between 1885 and 1891 for the editor, Leslie Stephen, who was to succeed Tennyson as president of the London Library in 1892. He also helped Sir Henry Montague Hozier with *The Franco-Prussian War* (1870–72), wrote, with Joseph Gostwick, *Outlines of German Literature* (1873), and translated Alfred von Reumont's *Lorenzo de Medici the Magnificent* in 1876. Robert Harrison died on 4 January 1897 at his home in Christchurch Avenue, Brondesbury, Middlesex, and was buried in Kensal Green cemetery on 8 January.   ANNE PIMLOTT BAKER

Sources J. L. Roget, *A history of the 'Old Water-Colour' Society*, 2 (1891), 296–9 • *The Royal Watercolour Society: the first fifty years, 1805–1855* (1992) • L. Lambourne and J. Hamilton, eds., *British watercolours in the Victoria and Albert Museum* (1980) • J. Johnson, ed., *Works exhibited at the Royal Society of British Artists, 1824–1893, and the New English Art Club, 1888–1917*, 2 vols. (1975) • C. Smedley, *Grace Darling and her times* (1932), chap. 22 • Graves, *RA exhibitors* • F. Beckwith, *The Leeds Library, 1768–1968* (1994), 50–55 • J. Minto, *A history of the public library movement in Great Britain and Ireland* (1932) • J. Wells, *Rude words: a discursive history of the London Library* (1991) • *Art Union*, 9 (1847), 44 • *The Times* (7 Jan 1897) • IGI • DNB • *Art Union*, 8 (Nov 1846)
Likenesses G. Browne, drawing, 1880 (Robert Harrison), London Library; repro. in Beckwith, *Leeds Library*, pl. IX
Wealth at death £2056 3s. 1d.—Robert Harrison: probate, 4 Feb 1897, CGPLA Eng. & Wales

Harrison, Henry (c.1785–c.1865), architect, was born in London, the son of John Harrison, a builder and surveyor. His brother George was also a builder–developer, and Henry seems to have engaged in the business on his own account. Harrison averred that he had been 'brought up as a builder and architect', and his family were indeed at the heart of the London building trade (*Report from the Select Committee on the Office of Works and Public Buildings*, 1828). Between 1803 and 1809 Harrison exhibited a number of views at the Royal Academy, including a 'design for a temple' in 1806. His first documented work as an architect seems to have been Richmond Terrace, Whitehall, which his brother George built 1822–5. Harrison in fact adapted this from a design by Thomas Chawner, supplying the working drawings himself. Its severe Greek revival style is of the mainstream for its date, though Harrison's use of yellow stock brick and Bath stone, instead of stucco, imparts a warmer quality to the building. The General Lying-in Hospital on York Road, Lambeth (1828), is in the same idiom, severe and well designed, with a portico in antis of giant Ionic columns.

In the 1820s Harrison established a wealthy clientele, almost all of them from the landed aristocracy or gentry, building or altering numerous town houses in Mayfair or St James's, most of these in the Italianate style then favoured by the Grosvenor estate. His clients included the second Viscount Hampden at 61 Green Street (1824), the earl of Kinnoull at 51 Grosvenor Street (1826), and the earl of Carysfort at 46 Upper Grosvenor Street (1827). Harrison's prosperity at the time, and his connections with Mayfair, were alike expressed in the construction of his own house, 31 Park Street, Grosvenor Square, built 1825–6, and occupied by Harrison 1828–39. The most eminent of all these jobs was the reconstruction, c.1821, of Bath House, 82 Piccadilly (dem. 1963), for Alexander Baring, first Lord Ashburton. Harrison's work in Mayfair has suffered from very heavy losses; notable survivals are the Greek revival rear elevation of 61 Green Street (1824 and later) and three Italianate houses at 10–11 Upper Grosvenor Street and 62 Park Street (1843–4).

In the 1820s Harrison managed to establish valuable connections in Cornwall, where he carried out a good deal of work over the period 1825–34. These probably began with work for the second earl of St Germans at Port Eliot. Sir John Soane had remodelled the house 1804–6; Harrison added a new entrance front and adjacent service wing, in the plainest Tudor gothic, as severe and symmetrical as any of his Grecian buildings, in 1825–9. This was followed by work at Heligan, where Harrison made alterations for J. H. Tremayne (1830); at Carclew, near Mylor, where he made additions for Sir Charles Lemon (c.1830; burnt), and at Enys, near Mylor, where he built a severely plain granite house for J. S. Enys (1833). The new house at Enys was exceptional; most of Harrison's commissions consisted in refurbishment or alteration, and relatively few involved designing from scratch. Nevertheless, he had already demonstrated at Port Eliot that he could design in the gothic style, and used this again in almshouses (1829–33) at Saffron Walden, Essex, for the local magnate, Lord Braybrooke of Audley End, and in alterations to a house called Pendarves in Cornwall (1832; dem. 1955).

From around 1823 Harrison was surveyor to the Holland estate in west London, and thus had an important role in the development of this area. He produced the general layout plans, and also took a number of plots as builder-developer on Kensington High Street. The most important element of these was the ambitious St Mary Abbot's Terrace (1825–30; dem. c.1960), a series of pairs of four-storey houses, with a grand pedimented centre, similar to that at the General Lying-in Hospital. Harrison's activities as a builder-developer ended in bankruptcy in 1840. There are fewer known works from after 1840, though one of his finest and most prestigious buildings, the new Guards' Club at 70 Pall Mall, in a fashionable Italianate style, dated from 1848–9; this, too, has been demolished. Harrison does not seem to have recovered fully from the bankruptcy, for in 1856, around the age of seventy, he applied (unsuccessfully) for the post of architect to the Metropolitan Board of Works. In 1864 he was resident in Bedford Square; thereafter his name disappears from the London Post Office directories. He does not seem to have received an obituary in the architectural press.   STEVEN BRINDLE

Sources Colvin, *Archs.*, 463–5 • F. H. W. Sheppard, ed., *Northern Kensington*, Survey of London, 37 (1973), 103–7 • C. Hussey, 'Port Eliot, Cornwall [pts 1–2]', *Country Life*, 104 (1948), 778–81, 828–31 • Graves, *RA exhibitors* • *Cornwall*, Pevsner (1970) • will, LMA, Middlesex land registry, 1828/1/794 [John Harrison]
Archives Cornwall RO, letters to John Hawkins, mainly relating to Bignor Park

Harrison, Henry (1867–1954), Irish nationalist and writer, was born at Holywood, co. Down, on 17 December 1867, the son of Henry Harrison JP DL and his wife, Letitia Tennent, who after her husband's death married the author

Hartley Withers. Harrison was educated at Westminster School, of which he became a Queen's scholar, and at Balliol College, Oxford, where he obtained a third class in classical honour moderations (1888) and captained the cricket and football elevens.

While still an undergraduate Harrison developed what was to be a lifelong interest in Irish politics. He was honorary secretary of the Oxford University Home Rule Group, and in 1889 crossed to Ireland with his tutor Godfrey Benson to visit the scene of the Gweedore evictions in Donegal. While there Harrison had the first of several clashes with the police and John Morley afterwards spoke out against the severity of the police action towards 'this stripling'. It was a curious misnomer for a very large and powerful young man who generally gave as good as he got, but the Stripling nevertheless became his nickname and he was a nationalist celebrity overnight. The next year Charles Stewart Parnell invited him to stand as member for Mid-Tipperary, which had become vacant. He left Oxford to contest the seat, and was returned unopposed in May 1890.

Harrison joined the Irish Parliamentary Party just as it was about to be torn asunder by the petition of W. H. O'Shea for a divorce from his wife, Katharine, on the grounds of her adultery with Parnell, whom she later married. In the famous 'split' Harrison was a devoted and uncompromising Parnellite, partly because of his instinctive faith in Parnell's honour as a gentleman and partly because he genuinely believed that for Irish nationalists to throw over their leader, under pressure from Gladstone and the Liberal Party, was both disloyal and imprudent.

After the party broke in two in December 1890, Harrison campaigned with his chief in Ireland, constituting himself a bodyguard and aide-de-camp. After Parnell's death in October 1891 Harrison, young though he was, hastened to Brighton to put his services at the disposal of Parnell's widow. It was then that he heard from her a very different account of the circumstances surrounding her divorce from that given in court. This indicated that O'Shea's evidence had been completely untrustworthy, that he had apparently connived for a long period at Parnell's relations with his wife, from whom he himself had virtually separated, and that his motives had been a mixture of political ambition and financial greed. Harrison felt unable to publish this story until those most likely to be affected were dead.

Harrison retired from his Mid-Tipperary seat in 1892, though he contested Limerick West at the general election the same year and Sligo North in 1895. In that year he married Maie, daughter of J. C. Byrne, of New York; they had a son. For the next ten years he disappeared from public view, but re-emerged after the outbreak of war in 1914. Though nearly fifty years of age, Harrison gained a commission as a second lieutenant in the Royal Irish regiment in March 1915. He was sent to France in 1916 and served on the western front with conspicuous gallantry and dash. He was awarded the MC in December 1916 and a bar in February 1918, and was subsequently invalided out of the war

and appointed OBE (mil.) in 1919. His son was seriously wounded at Gallipoli and died soon after the war.

When the war was over Captain Harrison, as he was always to be known thereafter, threw himself eagerly into the affairs of the newly established Irish Free State. For a short period (1920–21) he was secretary of the Irish Dominion League and was closely associated with Sir Horace Plunkett. He supported the Anglo-Irish treaty and regarded dominion status as an acceptable compromise in the quest for Irish independence, though he opposed partition. From 1922 to 1927 he was Irish correspondent of *The Economist*, combining this between 1924 and 1927 with the editorship of a Dublin weekly, *Irish Truth*.

Harrison next turned to what was to be the major work of his life—the rehabilitation of his beloved Parnell. In 1931 he published *Parnell Vindicated: the Lifting of the Veil*, which not only embodied the account Mrs Parnell had given to him, but was also based on intensive and original research. Although not all of Harrison's conclusions have been accepted by scholars, his work significantly changed the attitude of historians towards the *cause célèbre*. A notable exception was J. L. Garvin, the early volumes of whose biography of Joseph Chamberlain ignored Harrison's findings. Harrison responded with a second book, *Parnell, Joseph Chamberlain and Mr. Garvin* (1938), which had the double aim of exposing the deficiencies of Garvin's biography and of implicating Chamberlain in a 'conspiracy' to bring about Parnell's downfall. The first object was easily enough achieved, but Chamberlain's complicity, despite some plausible evidence, was never conclusively proved.

Harrison continued his defence of Parnell's reputation to the end of his life, and he took issue in particular with the chapter 'Parnellism and crime' in the third volume of *The History of The Times*, published in 1947. This hinted that not all of the letters secretly purchased by *The Times* from Richard Pigott, and used in 1887 as material for a series of damaging articles on Parnell, were in fact forgeries. Harrison was able to quote directly from the Parnell commission of inquiry to show that they were. So authoritative were his comments on the chapter that a four-page *corrigenda*, written by him, was included as an appendix in the fourth volume of the *History* (1952). Characteristically, he celebrated his victory with a pamphlet, *Parnell, Joseph Chamberlain and The Times* (1953).

In that same year Harrison made his last public appearance when he received an honorary LLD from Dublin University. He died at Sir Patrick Duns Hospital, Dublin, a few months later on 20 February 1954, leaving to those who knew him the recollection of a warm and vital personality, an acute intelligence, vigorous and uninhibited conversation, and a memory for long past events so copious and exact as to make the man himself almost as valuable a historical source as his books.

F. S. L. LYONS, *rev.* MARK POTTLE

Sources *The Times* (22 Feb 1954) · *The Times* (23 Feb 1954) · *The Times* (25 Feb 1954) · H. Harrison, *Parnell vindicated* (1931) · personal knowledge (1971) · private information (1971) · [S. Morison and others],

The history of The Times, 3 (1947) • [S. Morison and others], *The history of The Times*, 4/2 (1952) • *CGPLA Eng. & Wales* (1954)
Archives SOUND BL NSA, current affairs recording; performance recording
Likenesses S. C. Harrison, oils, 1931, NG Ire.
Wealth at death £1894: probate, 4 Aug 1954, *CGPLA Éire* • £1156 14s. 2d.: probate, 21 Oct 1954, *CGPLA Eng. & Wales*

Harrison, James Jonathan (1857–1923), traveller and author, was born on 8 July 1857 at Park House, Selby, Yorkshire, the son of Jonathan Stables Harrison (*c*.1837–1917), landowner and magistrate, and his wife, Eliza Jane, *née* Whitehead (*c*.1825–1905). Educated at Harrow School and at Christ Church, Oxford (although he did not graduate), he became a lieutenant in the Princess of Wales's Own Yorkshire hussars on 19 July 1884 and remained with that élitist yeomanry regiment, experiencing no war service, until 3 September 1904 when, a major, he retired with the honorary title of lieutenant-colonel.

Harrison visited Bermuda, Canada, and South Africa, and published *A Sporting Trip through India; Home by Japan and America* in 1892. His home, The Hall, Brandesburton, near Hull, was filled with trophies from his almost annual hunting trips, including those to central Africa (1896), Ethiopia and Uganda (1899), and the Congo (1904). In mid-1905 Harrison brought six pygmies to England from the Congo to be displayed at the London Hippodrome for fourteen weeks. Harrison's plans led to criticism and opposition from the foreign secretary, Lord Lansdowne, who disliked the exploitation but, as the Africans were not British subjects, he could not stop Harrison. The Africans spent the autumn of 1905 appearing in major cities in England and Scotland, then travelled to Germany. From mid-1906 they appeared in resorts including Bridlington, Southend, Eastbourne, Whitby, and Blackpool, and spent the summer of 1907 at a London exhibition. Harrison's *Life among the Pygmies of the Ituri Forest, Congo Free State* (1905), picture postcards, posters, handbills, and gramophone recordings promoted the group, whose activities were detailed in the national and local press. 'Objects of curiosity to amusement-seeking Londoners', 'the poor little wretches are somewhat repulsive', 'great attractions', and 'a revelation in strange humanity' were among the early reviews of the exhibition. Publicity statements from Harrison: 'the nearest thing to a human monkey', 'strange ape-like people', and 'half-way between Anthropoid Apes and Man' were quoted. The Africans, armed with spears and poisoned arrows, went with Harrison to a garden party at Buckingham Palace and to parliament within days of arriving in London; their role as 'savages' was a carefully constructed image. That image, however, had drawn British audiences of 1 million by the time they departed from Hull in October 1907.

Harrison returned to the Congo twice more, but ceased travelling when he married Mrs Mary Clarke, *née* Stetson (1866–1932), an American, on 19 November 1910. After Harrison's death at Brandesburton on 12 March 1923 she returned to America, and the spacious and ugly hall became a mental hospital.

A gaunt man, whose love of cricket endeared him to Brandesburton villagers, Harrison is a footnote in natural history, with a pygmy antelope, a chestnut-headed sparrow lark, and a painted or woolly bat having carried his name. Harrison's letters to London newspapers and the British government (1904–5) disputed claims by E. D. Morel and Roger Casement over misrule in the Congo—the personal possession of Leopold, king of the Belgians. Harrison is depicted in literature as Colonel Grindle in Osbert Sitwell's poem 'Wrack at Tidesend' (1952).

Harrison gained his income from a trust (whose farms were sold in the 1940s), and his travelling and taxidermy expenses are thought to have led to the commercial exploitation of the African pygmies. They lived at The Hall when not touring, and into the 1990s were recalled locally with affection and respect, as was Harrison.

JEFFREY GREEN

Sources NHM, Harrison MSS • J. J. Harrison, *A sporting trip through India; home by Japan and America* (1892) • J. J. Harrison, *Life among the pygmies of the Ituri forest, Congo Free State* (1905) • *Yorkshire Post* (21 Nov 1910), 8 • memorial stone, St Mary's Church, Brandesburton • b. cert.
Archives Museum of Natural History, Scarborough
Likenesses B. Stone, photograph, 1905, NPG
Wealth at death £17,123 4s. 3d.: probate, 4 June 1923, *CGPLA Eng. & Wales*

Harrison, Jane Ellen (1850–1928), classical scholar, was born on 9 September 1850 at Cottingham, near Hull, Yorkshire, the third daughter of Charles Harrison, a timber merchant, and his first wife, Elizabeth Hawksley Nelson, who died soon afterwards. Her father was an affectionate but a reserved and absent-minded parent, who entrusted her early education to a series of governesses. One of these, a fervent Welsh revivalist, became her stepmother, and her insistence that the children must be born again and that 'God must have their whole hearts or nothing' had much to do with Jane Harrison's loss of Christian faith, which was completed when, like Nietzsche, she read Darwin at the age of twenty.

Early achievements From the first Jane Harrison read avidly, and with one of the governesses attacked German, Latin, the Greek testament, and even a little Hebrew. In 1868 she went to Cheltenham Ladies' College, and in 1870 obtained honours in the London University examination for women. For four years after that she remained at home, teaching her brothers and sisters, but in 1874 she won a scholarship on the results of the Cambridge local examination and went up to Newnham College, Cambridge.

Here Jane Harrison was happy, reading for the classical tripos and being at the centre of a group of friends that included Mary Paley, who married Alfred Marshall, Margaret Merrifield, who married A. W. Verrall, and Ellen Crofts, who married Sir Francis Darwin. Jane Harrison was not beautiful, but she was tall and had a splendid figure; she became an elegant dresser in the fashion of the current avant-garde. At this time her favourite painter was Rossetti and her favourite poet Swinburne. It is clear that the great personal charm which later helped to make her

Jane Ellen Harrison (1850–1928), by Augustus John, 1909

such a successful lecturer and teacher was already in evidence in these early years. Newnham under Anne Jemima Clough offered interesting social opportunities, and as an undergraduate she met Turgenev, Ruskin, Gladstone, and Marian Evans (George Eliot). She had a passion for languages, and is said to have known something of about sixteen of them, but she never managed to learn Greek with the accuracy that would have come with a strict classical education. In the tripos she obtained second-class marks, and though she applied for the lecturership in classics that Newnham advertised in 1879, the post was given to Margaret Merrifield.

Student of Greek art Jane Harrison now settled in London, and studied archaeology at the British Museum under the direction of Sir Charles Newton. She made a special study of Greek vase-painting, and made a reputation as a lecturer on that subject, speaking, among other places, at Eton and Winchester. She made several visits to Italy and Germany, where Wilhelm Klein, then professor at Prague, introduced her to several eminent archaeologists, including Wilhelm Dörpfeld. Jane Harrison had a good knowledge of German, and later often took part in the archaeological tours in Greece organized by Dörpfeld. In 1882 she published *The Odyssey in Art and Literature* and in 1885 *Introductory Studies in Greek Art*. These were attractively written books, but have no great scientific value, so that no injustice was done when she failed to be elected to succeed Newton in the Yates chair of archaeology at London University in 1888.

During this period Jane Harrison became acquainted with D. S. MacColl, who is said to have proposed marriage to her, but to have been rejected; she seems to have realized early that the life of a wife in those Victorian times was not for her. But MacColl had a decisive influence upon her career, for he poured contempt on her very successful but in his view effusive manner of lecturing, and cured her decisively of her early *fin de siècle* aestheticism. Emerging from a severe depression, she began to examine objects of Greek art more exactly and more objectively, and to pay attention to things which earlier she might

have despised as 'primitive'. Visiting Greece with MacColl in 1888, she came away with a strong sense of the cults that lay behind the myths; later she wrote that she came from art to religion because she had become aware that the religion which she found displayed by early works of art did not correspond with the Olympian religion known from later art and literature.

In 1890 Jane Harrison published two books which show her moving in a new direction. One was a *Manual of Mythology in Relation to Greek Art*, a translation from the French of Maxime Collignon, a work that gives attention to archaic art as well as classical; the other was *Mythology and Monuments of Ancient Athens*, which consisted of a translation of the first book of Pausanias by Mrs Verrall with a commentary by Miss Harrison. In this work she wrote that 'in many, even in the large majority of cases, *ritual practice misunderstood* explains the elaboration of myth' (Preface, iii).

In 1894 Jane Harrison was again a candidate for the Yates chair, but was defeated by E. A. Gardner. But in 1898 she was given an opportunity much better suited to the kind of work on which she had now embarked when she was elected to a research fellowship at Newnham College. She greatly enjoyed college life, and had many friends in Cambridge, several of them scholars with whom she could profitably discuss her subject. One of her friends was R. A. Neil, who like MacColl was a Scot and a thoroughly sound scholar, a better counsellor for Miss Harrison than the over-speculative Verrall.

Jane Harrison is said to have been engaged to Neil when he died in 1901 at the age of forty-nine, but one wonders whether she would have married him. In 1900 she met Gilbert Murray, then living near Churt after resigning from the chair of Greek at Glasgow. At about the same time she became acquainted with F. M. Cornford, then an undergraduate. These people were the main members of the group which has come to be known as the 'Cambridge ritualists'. A. B. Cook is often counted among their number, and he and Jane Harrison were friends, but his Christian monotheism to some degree conditions his learned book on Zeus, and in several ways their outlooks differed. The same may be said of another Cambridge scholar active in related fields at the same time, Sir James Frazer.

Student of Greek religion Between 1899 and 1904 Jane Harrison published in the *Journal of Hellenic Studies* three substantial articles on Greek religion, much of whose content was repeated or summarized in her first major work, *Prolegomena to the Study of Greek Religion* (1903; 2nd edn, 1908; 3rd edn, 1922). During the classical period, Miss Harrison argued, Greek religion appears in literature as 'a thing of joyful confidence', and its watchword is *do ut des* ('I give that you may give'); but she is concerned to acquaint her readers with another kind of religion, whose watchword is *do ut abeas* ('I give that you may go away'), since its central element is not that of tendence, but that of aversion. Even in classical times the Greeks distinguished between the gods of heaven (*Ouranioi*) and the gods beneath the earth (*Chthonioi*), and even during the classical period the Greeks took account of certain shadowy powers which in

Miss Harrison's view helped one to get a notion of the kind of spirit the ancestors of the Greeks had been trying to placate. Pointing out that worship in many localities centred on a single special deity, Miss Harrison argued that monotheism existed before polytheism, and that at a certain stage the gods of different localities were artificially brought together.

So far Jane Harrison can be seen to have made a striking contribution to the difficult attempt to guess at the early stages of religion; but other contentions are more questionable. In her attempt to show that all or most myths grew out of rituals Miss Harrison was not successful; when a ritual can be seen to be connected with a myth, one usually finds that the myth was invented to explain the ritual. Nor is her attempt to show that the early religion was dominated by goddesses, reflecting the nature of a matriarchal—later she would have said 'matrilinear'—society, convincing. Much of the book is devoted to an account of the worship of Dionysus which is in several ways open to attack: Miss Harrison failed to distinguish between the violent maenadism of literature and the harmless maenadism of cult, and in speaking of the way in which maenads are depicted as tearing apart animals and eating their raw flesh, she repeatedly uses the Christian term 'sacrament', in the belief that the worshippers of Dionysus imagined that they were eating the flesh of their god. She believed that Orpheus was not a mythical singer but a real man, who founded mysteries in which the soul of the initiate became identical with Dionysus.

But these weaknesses do not do away with the fascination and the importance of the book. Its elegant and highly individual style mark it off from the work of most scholars; its use of art as well as literature to explain religion, a practice in which few later writers have followed its example, lends it a special quality; and, building on the German work of the preceding century, it introduced its English readers to a side of Greek religion of which few of them could previously have had much notion.

Jane Harrison had developed a close relationship with Francis Macdonald Cornford (who wrote her memoir in the *Dictionary of National Biography*), and their daily bicycle rides together were the occasion of a fruitful exchange of ideas. His marriage in 1909 to Frances Darwin caused her great emotional distress. Mrs Cornford, who was the daughter of her early friend Ellen Crofts, was devoted to Miss Harrison, and wished the rides to continue; but the resulting strain was great, and is reflected in the splendid portrait of Miss Harrison which Augustus John painted in the same year, and which is now in the combination room of Newnham College. There are grounds for suspecting that Jane Harrison did not entertain ordinary sexual feelings; but emotional intimacies such as those that played a great part in her life can also give rise to jealousy and distress. In the same year of 1909 there came up to Newnham Hope Mirrlees, the last of the persons to whom Jane Harrison became devoted, whom she called her spiritual daughter.

Themis During this period Jane Harrison maintained intense intellectual activity, and her sensitivity to new impressions became almost febrile. First, she was carried away by Henri Bergson's *L'évolution créatrice*, which appeared in 1907; then in 1909 lectures given in Cambridge by A. R. Radcliffe-Brown made her acquainted with the work of Émile Durkheim; and in the same year she was powerfully impressed by Sigmund Freud's *Totem and Taboo*. All these authors influenced her second major work, *Themis*, which appeared in 1912 (2nd edn, 1927). The difficult Greek word *themis* means 'divine justice', or 'divinely instituted order'; according to Hesiod the personified Themis was the earliest consort of Zeus. The book derived its initial impetus from the discovery at Palaicastro in eastern Crete of a stone inscribed with a Greek hymn; the inscription dates from the second century AD, but the hymn must be much earlier, written perhaps in the fourth century BC and containing religious notions that are much earlier. The hymn is addressed to Zeus, but this Zeus is very different from the classical Greek Zeus; he is a fertility god, who has disappeared during the winter months, and is now urged to return and to leap into flocks, houses, cities, ships, citizens, and into Themis. This encouraged Miss Harrison to believe that all Greek gods had started as fertility spirits. The Zeus of the hymn is described as leading his followers, and Miss Harrison argued that he is the projection of his band of worshippers, and that in the same way Dionysus is the projection of his band, his *thiasos*. Those initiated into the mysteries of the band experience a kind of death and rebirth; and Miss Harrison goes on to identify not only Zeus and Dionysus but *all* Greek gods and heroes with the spirit of the year, the *Eniautos Daimōn*, putting together two words which are not found together in any Greek text. 'Ritual', she wrote, 'is the utterance of an emotion, a thing felt in *action*, myth in words or thought'; and later 'it is when religion ceases to be a matter of feeling together, when it becomes individualized and intellectualized, that doubts gather on the horizon'.

One sees here the influence of Durkheim's theory of totemism, now generally rejected, and of his opinion that belief in supernatural beings was a comparatively late development. But the book was not welcomed by the school of Durkheim, since its Bergsonian element was little to their taste. The extreme claims made for the spirit of the year, despite the powerful support of Gilbert Murray, have been generally rejected.

During the First World War, Jane Harrison threw herself into work designed to alleviate the sufferings of Russians, and became preoccupied with Russia and its language. In all these activities, Hope Mirrlees was her partner. In the second edition of *Themis* she wrote that for ten years she had never opened a Greek book, and she destroyed many of her papers, including all Gilbert Murray's letters.

In 1921, however, Jane Harrison brought out her *Epilegomena to Greek Religion*, in which she set out 'to summarize as briefly as possible the results of many years' work on the origins of Greek religion, and to indicate the bearing of these results on religious questions of today'. In this work totem, taboo, and exogamy are presented as closely linked facets of group unity, and the importance of initiation rites is strongly stressed. The group comes to be dominated by one person, the medicine man or king-god, and thus there comes into being the spirit, later the god. Fertility rituals lead to the creation of tragedy and comedy, as Murray and Cornford had tried to show. But curiously enough Jane Harrison proclaims that 'the core and essence of religion today is the practice of asceticism'; 'religion turns not to the impulsion of life but its betterment, and the betterment of life involves asceticism'. Renate Schlesier has acutely observed that Jane Harrison 'is at once attracted and repelled by ecstasy and asceticism' (Schlesier, 224); it would seem that the Russian influence is responsible for this final victory of the ascetic Orpheus over the ecstatic maenads who tore him to pieces. Miss Harrison adds that the kind of asceticism she means is not mere negation; it must be consistent with the cultivation of the Bergsonian *élan vital*.

In 1922 Jane Harrison surprised her friends by leaving Cambridge and taking up residence, together with Hope Mirrlees, in Paris, where they remained for three years, staying at the American Women's Club and making contact with French and Russian intellectuals. But in 1925 they returned to England to live in London in a very small house, 11 Mecklenburgh Street in Bloomsbury. There Jane Harrison died on 15 April 1928; she was buried on 19 April in St Marylebone cemetery, East Finchley.

For some fifty years after the First World War the work of Miss Harrison and that part of the work of her collaborators that stood in close relation with her was not highly valued by students of Greek religion. Some members of the school of Durkheim were influenced by her treatment of groups of worshippers and initiates, and other schools of thought shared her concentration on ritual rather than myth. But the leading scholars were averse to the ethnological preoccupation she and her associates shared, and Wilamowitz wrote to Murray, who had sent him a copy of *Themis*, that he 'was not disposed to explain the perfect structure by the embryo nor Plato by the superstitions of his grandmother' (G. Murray, 'Memories of Wilamowitz', *Antike und Abendland*, 4, 1954, 12). But during the 1960s scholars renewed the attempt to understand the early stages of Greek religion. Walter Burkert in *Homo necans* (1972; English translation, 1983) wrote that after Miss Harrison he had introduced functionalism to the study of Greek religion, and even evinced some sympathy for the theory of Dionysus as representing the Eniautos Daimon or the dying king. Both he and the French school of Jean-Pierre Vernant and Pierre Vidal-Naquet look back at Miss Harrison as an honoured predecessor, and Gilbert Murray's remark in 1955 that while few people would accept the whole of her conclusions nobody could write about Greek religion without being influenced by her work continues to be true.　　　　　　　　　　HUGH LLOYD-JONES

Sources J. E. Harrison, *Reminiscences of a student's life* (1925) · J. Stewart, *Jane Ellen Harrison: a portrait from letters* (1959) · R. Ackerman, 'Jane Ellen Harrison: the early work', *Greek, Roman and Byzantine Studies*, 13 (1972), 209–30 · R. Schlesier, 'Prolegomena to Jane Harrison's interpretation of early Greek religion', *The Cambridge ritualists reconsidered: First Oldfather Conference* [Urbana-Champaign, IL 1989], ed. W. M. Calder (1991), 185–226 · H. Lloyd-Jones, 'Jane Ellen Harrison, 1850–1928', *Cambridge women: twelve portraits*, ed. E. Shils and C. Blacker (1996), 29–72 · S. Arlen, *The Cambridge ritualists: an annotated bibliography of the works by and about Jane Ellen Harrison, Gilbert Murray, Francis M. Cornford, and Arthur Bernard Cook* (1990) · *The Times* (20 April 1928)

Archives Bodl. Oxf., letters and notes · McMaster University, Hamilton, Ontario, William Ready division of archives and research collections, letters to Bertrand Russell · U. Glas. L., special collections department, letters to D. S. MacColl

Likenesses photograph, 1877–1920, repro. in Stewart, *Jane Ellen Harrison*, frontispiece, facing p. 97 · A. John, oils, 1909, Newnham College, Cambridge [see illus.] · T. Van Rysselberghe, pencil drawing, 1925, NPG

Wealth at death £8607 10s. 8d.: probate, 6 July 1928, *CGPLA Eng. & Wales*

Harrison, Joan Mary (1907–1994). *See under* Ambler, Eric Clifford (1909–1998).

Harrison, John (*bap.* 1579, *d.* 1656), benefactor, was born at Pawdmire, Briggate, Leeds, and baptized at Leeds parish church on 16 August 1579, the only son of John Harrison (*d.* 1601), clothier, and his wife, Elizabeth Marton (*d.* 1602), daughter of Henry Marton of Leeds. After attending one of the local schools, probably the free grammar school, where (on the evidence of his letters) he received a sound classical education, Harrison eventually inherited the family business as one of a new generation of Leeds merchants whose buccaneering methods of trading brought them rich rewards and extensive influence. Success also brought him membership of the self-perpetuating cabal that ruled the town after the grant of the first royal charter of incorporation in July 1626. Following appointment as deputy to the first alderman, Sir John Savile, from July to Michaelmas 1626, Harrison was elected to succeed him.

A year after the death of his mother Harrison married Elizabeth (*bap.* 1576, *d.* 1631), daughter of Thomas Foxcroft of New Grange, Headingly, and some time after 1628 moved from his father's burgage house at the northern end of Briggate, known as Pawdmire, to a more impressive dwelling in Briggate opposite the east end of Boar Lane where, according to Thoresby, there were holes cut in the wainscot 'to allow the free passage of cats', for which he had a 'strange inclination' (Thoresby, 12).

Harrison embarked on an apparently disastrous venture in April 1626 when he was commissioned as one of the collectors for the West Riding of the so-called privy seal loan. Though his share of the charge amounted to £725 6s. 8d., the perquisites to which he was entitled—10 per cent commission and personal immunity from assessment—were extremely attractive. But the poor response he received soured his relationship with Sir John Savile, who would neither allow him his commission nor send him a discharge for the sum remitted (£425). Four years later he fell victim to another of Charles I's money-raising schemes, the fines for distraint of knighthood.

Described as 'a man of intellectual power, energy and inspiration' (H. Heaton, *The Yorkshire Woollen and Worsted Industries*, 1920, 99), Harrison's standing in the town was due not only to his commercial acumen but also to the generosity with which he devoted his wealth to civic improvement, whether as one of a small group who purchased the manor of Leeds from the corporation of London (1628) and subsequently conveyed five-ninths of the bailiwick to feoffees to the use of the corporation (W. Yorks. AS, DB 149/8, 18), or for the munificence of his provision for the needy, for local education, and for religion: a munificence made possible, no doubt, because he and his wife were childless. Having purchased the estates of the Rockleys and Falkinghams to the north of the town, he built there, between 1620 and 1640, a new street, known as New Briggate (whose rents he assigned to the use of the poor), the beautiful church of St John the Evangelist, a row of almshouses to accommodate forty poor persons, and a new building on an attractive site for the free grammar school, hitherto housed in a former chantry chapel in Lady Lane. By a deed of settlement of 1638 a house and 71 acres of glebe was vested in trustees to the use of the minister of St John's together with an annual stipend of £80. The church was consecrated in September 1634, as Harrison was about to enter his second term as alderman, by Richard Neile, archbishop of York; a puritan divine, Robert Todd, was appointed to the curacy. Harrison himself once remarked that he had laid out £6000 on these and other charitable causes, either specified or distributed privately (Whitaker, appx, 1; Thoresby, 27).

The civil war was a catastrophe for the royalist principal burgesses. Harrison, it seems, was an unwilling, even niggardly, collaborator, whose faint-heartedness earned him the contemptuous observation by Adam Baynes that he was 'a timorous man', who 'when my Lord Fairfax's drums did beat in Leeds … was troubled and afraid and went to Otley-side' (W. Yorks. AS, DB 204/1, 35). Insignificant as his delinquency was, however, it provided his enemies, including two of the sequestrators for the wapentake of Skyrack, Francis Allanson and William Marshall, the latter hitherto a close friend, with a pretext for betraying and tormenting him. Excluded from the reconstituted corporation of 1646 and desperate to preserve his fortune for the endowment of his charities, Harrison's vexatious battle with the compounding authorities ended in 1654 in a fine of £464 18s. Anguish, indeed, may be the explanation for his relentless pursuit of Roger Portington—also facing a crippling penalty—for the recovery of a substantial debt.

Already bedridden by 1651, Harrison was by then a lonely, tragic figure. Widowed since the death of his wife in 1631, his final years were riven by discord between himself and Robert Todd, who incited his presbyterian clique at St John's to virulent denunciation of Harrison's loyalty to Anglicanism. He died, probably at Briggate, on 29 October 1656. Sadly, his funeral on 8 November 1656 was held in the old parish church rather than in the church he had built. His remains, thought to have been interred in an orchard—possibly belonging to the house opposite the eastern end of Boar Lane where he was living in April 1653 when his will was drawn up (Whitaker, appx, 15–19)—were in 1658 transferred to St John's under a monument with an epitaph composed by the vicar of Leeds, Dr John

Lake, later bishop of Chichester. The full-length portrait presented by his nephew, Dr John Robinson, still hangs above his tomb.   JOAN KIRBY

Sources letters and MSS relating to John Harrison, W. Yorks. AS, Leeds, DB 204/1 · J. W. Kirby, 'Leeds elite: the principal burgesses of the first Leeds corporation', *Northern History*, 20 (1984), 88–107 · J. W. Kirby, 'The rulers of Leeds: gentry, clothiers and merchants, c. 1425–1626', *The Thoresby Miscellany*, 18, 22–49, Thoresby Society, 59 (1985), 22–49 · R. Thoresby, *Ducatus Leodiensis, or, The topography of … Leedes* (1715) · T. D. Whitaker, *Loidis and Elmete* (1816), appx, 1–19, 28 · M. A. Hornsey, 'John Harrison, the Leeds benefactor, his life and times', *Publications of the Thoresby Society*, 33 (1935), 103–47 · J. W. Clay, ed., *Yorkshire royalist composition papers*, 3, Yorkshire Archaeological Society, 20 (1896) · J. P. Cooper, ed., *Wentworth papers, 1597–1628*, CS, 4th ser., 12 (1973) · D. Hirst, 'The fracturing of the Cromwellian alliance: Leeds and Adam Baynes', *EngHR*, 108 (1993), 868–94 · P. G. Holiday, 'Royalist composition fines and land sales in Yorkshire, 1645–1665', PhD diss., U. Leeds, 1965 · *Leeds parish church registers, 1: 1572–1612*, ed. S. Margerison, Thoresby Society, 1 (1891) · G. D. Lumb, ed., *The registers of the parish church of Leeds, from 1612 to 1639*, Thoresby Society, 3 (1895) · G. D. Lumb, ed., *The registers of the parish church of Leeds, from 1639 to 1667*, Thoresby Society, 7 (1897) · J. Wardell, *The municipal history of the borough of Leeds* (1846) · M. Oxley, 'John Harrison and St John's Church, Leeds', *Stuart England*, ed. B. Worden (1986), 88–9

Archives BL, accompts and memoranda, Add. MSS 4273B, 4275 · W. Yorks. AS, Leeds, letters and MSS, DB 204/1

Likenesses W. Holl, stipple, pubd 1816 (after oil painting), BM, NPG · engraving (after portrait), BM, NPG; repro. in R. Thoresby, *Ducatus Leodiensis*, 2nd edn (1816), facing p. 12 · oils, St John's Church, Leeds

Wealth at death see will, repr. in Whitaker, *Loidis and Elmete*, appx 15–19

Harrison, John (*d.* 1641x52), commercial and political agent in Morocco and author, first appears when, at the accession of James I, he became a member of the privy chamber of Prince Henry. In May 1610 he sailed on the first of eight voyages to Morocco, 'in the behalfe of the Barbarie merchants' (Castries, *Sources … d'Angleterre*, 2.449). He returned in April 1611 accompanied by Samuel Pallache, Morocco's agent in the Netherlands. As a result of meeting with a significant Jewish population in Morocco, Harrison wrote the *Messiah Already Come, or, Profes of Christianitie* (1619) in an attempt to convert Pallache and his co-religionists. Throughout his career Harrison revealed a deep evangelical zeal, both toward the Jews as well as the Morisco exiles in north Africa.

Harrison's second voyage began in May 1614 and coincided with a Moroccan–Dutch attempt to dislodge English pirates from their naval base in Mamoura. Harrison facilitated their settlement elsewhere, and later discussed with Mawlay Zaydan, sultan of Morocco, a possible Dutch–English alliance against Spain. The third voyage was uneventful, and so was the fourth, 1616–18, during which he had to await Mawlay Zaydan's permission to land for two winters. Disappointed in the lack of royal support Harrison went to Germany seeking the patronage of James I's son-in-law Frederick, elector palatine. When the latter departed for Prague to take up the throne of Bohemia, Harrison published *A Short Relation* (1619) on the subject which he dedicated to him, and a year later he published, as *Bohemica jura defensa*, a defence of Bohemian laws. The defeat of Frederick at the battle of the White Mountain in

1620 frustrated Harrison's hopes, and he now turned his eyes to America where he became, as he later wrote, 'governour of the Sommer Ylands', that is, Bermuda (Castries, *Sources … d'Angleterre*, 2.595).

In 1625 England declared war on Spain, whereupon Harrison proposed to the secretary of state, Sir Albertus Morton—who agreed—that he raise an army of 10,000 anti-Spanish Moriscos in Morocco. He began his fifth voyage in July 1625, and from Tetouan he wrote to Mawlay Zaydan for assistance: 'now is the tyme or neaver, both for the Englishe and Moores, to right themselves against theire [Spanish] enimies' (Castries, *Sources … d'Angleterre*, 2.572). In his letter to the commander of the British fleet he confirmed the offer of Moroccan soldiers, explaining that such co-operation would hasten the 'plantation' of Christianity 'in these partes' (ibid., 2.579). After Cadiz was attacked by the English, with little Moroccan participation, Harrison returned to England in May 1626.

On his sixth voyage, which started in January 1627 and ended in May, Harrison took cannon and ammunition to Salé and effected the release of British captives there. Three years later, in April 1630, he sailed on his seventh voyage to Salé with letters to the Moriscos there as well as to the new Moroccan sultan, Mawlay ʿAbd al-Malik. Sidi Muhammad al-Ayashi, the marabout leader, asked Harrison to assist him navally against the Spanish garrison of Mamoura; although Harrison was eager to do so, King Charles refused to sanction such co-operation. Harrison's last voyage in September 1631 was again to Salé and then to Marrakesh where he met the new ruler, Mawlay al-Walid.

Harrison returned to England in May 1632 and in 1633 he published *The Tragical Life and Death of Muley Abdala Malek*, and dedicated it to Charles Louis, the new elector palatine of the Rhine, in the hope of patronage. Despite being favourably mentioned by Barbary merchants and the privy council in 1635 and 1641, and despite being the most widely informed Englishman about the history, society, religious tradition, and administration of the Moroccan region, Harrison was excluded from England's naval and commercial involvement in the Mediterranean. By 1638 he had incurred such a huge debt that he and his wife, Elizabeth (about whom nothing else is known), separately petitioned the king for payment of his arrears, lest, as she wrote, her husband go to gaol or flee the country. By 1652 he was dead, as the third edition of the *Messiah* showed.

In addition to ransoming hundreds of captives, Harrison laid the foundations for England's commercial and ideological relations with Morocco. Throughout his 'imployments into Barbarie' he wrote voluminously. A large amount of that material has been published by Henri de Castries; the rest is preserved among the state papers. NABIL MATAR

Sources CSP dom., 1603–39 · H. de Castries, P. de Cenival, and P. de Cossé Brissac, eds., *Les sources inédites de l'histoire du Maroc, 1 série, Dynastie Saʿdienne: archives et bibliothèques d'Angleterre*, 3 vols. (Paris, 1918–35) · H. de Castries, ed., *Les sources inédites de l'histoire du Maroc, 1 série, Dynastie Saʿdienne: archives et bibliothèques des Pays-Bas*, 6 vols. (Paris, 1905–23) · writings by J. Harrison, PRO, SP 71/12

Archives PRO, travel writings, SP 71/12

Harrison, John (1614–1670), clergyman and ejected minister, was the eldest son of Peter Harrison of Hindley, near Wigan in Lancashire. He is probably the John Harrison who was educated at Trinity College, Dublin, graduating BA, before his admission at Emmanuel College, Cambridge, as pensioner in October 1634. His degree was incorporated at Cambridge, where he proceeded MA in 1636. At some date he married; possibly his wife was Elizabeth Hollinprieste, whose marriage to a John Harrison was recorded in the parish register for Manchester on 11 January 1634. Harrison and his wife had at least two children: a daughter, Lydia, who was buried at Ashton under Lyne in Lancashire on 14 June 1655, and a son, Maurice, baptized at Bolton on 24 October 1636.

John Harrison was first appointed curate at Walmsley near Bolton, and subsequently minister at Ashton under Lyne in 1642, where he signed the protestation. In 1648 he signed the harmonious consent of ministers at Manchester. He had the reputation for being 'an orthodox, painfull, able minister' (Fishwick, 21–2). He was one of a circle of devout presbyterians in Manchester, described by Adam Martindale as 'very zealous (usually called Rigid) Presbyterians, that were for setting up the governance of the Church of Scotland amongst us' (*Life of Adam Martindale*, 63). From the inception of the first Lancashire classis, which met for the first time at Manchester on 2 October 1646, Harrison was an active member and regularly officiated as moderator until the final (163rd) meeting on 14 August 1660.

In common with many presbyterians Harrison appears to have deplored the execution of Charles I and surrounding events, as well as the divisive effect of radical religion and the influence of the army. He was actively involved in the debate about national events and policies. Martindale considered him to be one of 'three great knockers for disputation' in Manchester, which was the heartland of presbyterianism in the north-west (*Life of Adam Martindale*, 93). It is not clear at this period whether debate ever developed into direct action. Nevertheless, in September 1651, Harrison was called to account upon suspicion of having entered into correspondence with Charles II. He was imprisoned at Liverpool with other Manchester presbyterians John Angier, Richard Hollinworth, and William Meek.

Between this date and 1659 Harrison appears to have confined his activities to parochial work and attendance at the classis. However, in July 1659 he signed the agreement between presbyterian and Independent ministers, in company with Henry Newcome, John Tyldsley, John Angier, and other Lancashire presbyterians, as a gesture of orthodox co-operation in the light of rising religious and political radical activity in the region. Unlike his cautious friend and colleague Newcome, Harrison clearly did not fear to express his opinions and at this time became actively involved in political action. In August 1659 he was arrested and imprisoned for his part in Sir George Booth's ill-fated Cheshire rising. Following the Restoration, in December 1660 he signed a petition to the king of sixty ministers of the gospel in Lancashire, which sought moderation in the church settlement and provision for ministers deprived of their income. Again, in March 1662, he petitioned the king, on this occasion apparently regarding the proposed Act of Uniformity.

Harrison was ejected from Ashton under Lyne in 1662 and the next year was in trouble for repeating sermons and was arrested. Yet again, in February 1664, he came under suspicion with Angier and others for plotting against parliament for the failure to honour the declaration of Breda. However, no charge appears to have been made. Following the Five Mile Act he moved to Salford, but returned to Ashton under Lyne where he died, aged fifty-six, at about four o'clock on the afternoon of 31 December 1670, and was buried on 2 January 1671. Henry Newcome recorded: 'A precious man of God, learned, sound, zealous and pious, one that feared God above many, and suffered much in many ways with great courage and patience. He had languished long, and now entered into rest' (*Autobiography*, 194). Harrison's will was proved at Chester in 1671, but in common with many Chester wills for the 1670s it has not survived.

Elizabeth Harrison outlived her husband and continued to live in Ashton under Lyne, where she was buried on 14 August 1679. Maurice Harrison, who had been educated at Manchester grammar school, entered St John's College, Cambridge, where he graduated BA in 1659 and MA in 1664. He conformed at the Restoration and became vicar of St Julian's in Shrewsbury. He died in 1689.

CATHERINE NUNN

Sources *The autobiography of Henry Newcome*, ed. R. Parkinson, 2 vols., Chetham Society, 26–7 (1852) · *The diary of the Rev. Henry Newcome, from September 30, 1661, to September 29, 1663*, ed. T. Heywood, Chetham Society, 18 (1849) · *The life of Adam Martindale*, ed. R. Parkinson, Chetham Society, 4 (1845) · W. A. Shaw, ed., *Minutes of the Manchester presbyterian classis*, 3 vols., Chetham Society, new ser., 20, 22, 24 (1890–91) · *Oliver Heywood's life of John Angier of Denton*, ed. E. Axon, Chetham Society, new ser., 97 (1937) · *Calamy rev.* · W. M. Bowman, *England in Ashton-under-Lyne* (1960) · B. Nightingale, *Lancashire nonconformity*, 6 vols. [1890–93] · Venn, *Alum. Cant.* · H. Fishwick, ed., *Lancashire and Cheshire church surveys, 1649–1655*, Lancashire and Cheshire RS, 1 (1879) · G. R. Abernathy, *The English presbyterians and the Stuart restoration, 1648–1663* (1965) · parish register, Manchester [marriage], 11 Jan 1634 · parish register, Ashton under Lyne [burial], 2 Jan 1671

Archives CUL, sermons

Harrison, John (*bap.* 1693, *d.* 1776), horologist, was born at Foulby in the parish of Wragby, Yorkshire, where he was baptized on 31 March 1693, the eldest of five children of Henry Harrison (1665–1728) and his wife, Elizabeth, *née* Barber. His father was a joiner and was said to have worked for Sir Rowland Winn (*d.* 1721) at Nostel Priory, Wragby. In 1696 or 1697 the family moved to Barrow upon Humber, Lincolnshire, where Winn owned other estates. Henry Harrison was appointed parish clerk soon after his arrival. The younger Harrison was mainly self-taught, but a visiting clergyman lent him a copy of Nicholas Saunderson's lectures on natural philosophy, from which he made his own copy. These lectures introduced Harrison to the science of Sir Isaac Newton which his analytical mind enabled him to grasp. He was also interested in the

John Harrison (*bap.* 1693, *d.* 1776), by Thomas King, 1765–6

theory of music and wrote extensively on the subject later in life. On 30 August 1718 he married Elizabeth Barrel at Barrow upon Humber; she died on 18 May 1726, and on 23 November that year he married Elizabeth Scott at Hampstead, Middlesex. She died in 1777. Two sons, John (1719–1738) and William (1728–1815), survived infancy.

Harrison had been brought up to be a carpenter and joiner, and made very few clocks before he started his lifetime work on the development of the marine timekeeper. His earliest extant clock, signed and dated 1713, is in the collection of the Clockmakers' Company, London; one dated 1715 is in the Science Museum, London; and a third, dated 1717, is at Nostel Priory. All his early clocks are very similar and of an all-wood construction, a practice he followed until 1730. A fine extant turret clock was made by him about 1722 for Brocklesby, Lincolnshire. His experience with this clock led Harrison to his innovative ideas of escapement design, and ways to reduce friction, which were further developed in the precision longcase clocks of 1725–8 from which he claimed an accuracy of rate to within one second a month. These clocks included two of his greatest inventions: the 'gridiron' temperature compensated pendulum which consisted of a grid of five steel rods and four brass rods, and the 'grasshopper' escapement which provided an impulse to the pendulum with very low friction. The wooden wheels had brass pivots running in bushes of lignum vitae, a tropical hardwood containing naturally lubricating resin, and the clocks consequently required no extra lubrication, which eliminated problems caused by the poor oils of the period. In 1726 Harrison first heard of the 1714 Longitude Act (12 Anne c. 15), offering to reward anyone who could provide a method for determining longitude at sea within certain prescribed limits on a trial to the West Indies. The prizes were £10,000 for a determination to within 60 geographical miles, £15,000 to within 40 geographical miles and £20,000 to within 30 geographical miles.

In 1730 Harrison described his recently made precision clocks, with a proposal to adapt this technology for a portable 'sea clock'. He travelled to London and presented his proposal to the astronomer royal, Edmond Halley, who persuaded him to visit the eminent clockmaker George Graham. The latter was amazed at Harrison's claims but appreciated the potential and gave encouragement and support, persuading Harrison to construct his design. Harrison returned to Barrow and completed the sea clock, a large machine of more than 72 lb, now referred to as 'H1', by 1735. When he took it back to London H1 became the fascination of scientists and the talking point of society. A certificate was signed by Halley, Graham, and three other fellows of the Royal Society suggesting that Harrison deserved public encouragement and that H1 should be given a sea trial. In 1736 he was sent on a voyage with H1 to determine the longitude of Lisbon. He was able to correct the ship's reckoning by nearly one and a half degrees, a success which resulted in the very first meeting of the commissioners of the board of longitude, on 30 June 1737. At this meeting Harrison was awarded £500 in two payments to enable him to make a further improved sea clock. By 1739 this clock, H2, a little larger and considerably heavier, was ready, but it was never tested at sea. A third sea clock, the lightest of these early timekeepers, was finished in 1759, having been beset by many technical problems. During this period, in 1749, the Royal Society awarded Harrison the Copley gold medal for his experimental work.

During these same years Harrison set a size standard for all future marine timekeepers when finally in 1760 he produced his fourth timekeeper, his masterpiece, H4, the size of a large pocket watch with a diameter of 5.2 ins and weighing only 3 lb. This was sent on a trial to Jamaica in 1761 where, during the 81 day voyage, the watch lost 5.1 sec. after applying a 'rate' (an allowance made for the known daily performance of a timekeeper before a voyage, taken into account when making the final calculations). Unfortunately Harrison failed to mention this hitherto unknown practice of applying a rate before the voyage, which nullified the results of the trial, but the board of longitude was sufficiently impressed to award him £2500 to be paid in full subsequent to a second trial. In addition the board wanted him to divulge the technicalities of H4 and also required him to make two more watches. Harrison objected to these additional demands but a second trial was arranged in 1764, this time with an agreed rate for the watch of a gain of 1 sec. a day. The trial to Barbados was a resounding success, the error of the watch during the outward voyage of 47 days computed to 39.2 sec., equal to 9.8 geographical miles. This was three times better than required to win the full £20,000. The board could not believe the accuracy of the watch and insisted that it should be dismantled before a committee

and that Harrison should explain the technology, which would then be published. It further stipulated that all the marine timekeepers made by Harrison were to be handed over to the board and that H4 was to be duplicated by an independent craftsman. Harrison would then be granted the balance of the first £10,000. They also reiterated that he would have to make two more watches before he could be awarded the second half of the prize. Despite considerable acrimony, in August 1765 the committee met at Harrison's house; he explained the intricacies with working drawings, satisfied the board, and eventually received the agreed sum of £7,500. Harrison was determined to get the further £10,000 to which he was already entitled. He was refused access to H4, which was being duplicated by the watchmaker, Larcum Kendall (1721–1795), but despite this Harrison completed another large watch, H5, in 1770.

Harrison was now seventy-seven and considered that to make yet another watch as demanded by the board of longitude was asking too much and also beyond the terms of the Longitude Act of 1714. The board refused to yield. Kendall's copy, K1, completed in 1769, was recognized as of exceptional craftsmanship. It was taken by Captain James Cook on his second and third voyages of discovery and underpinned Cook's cartographic surveys in the southern hemisphere. Harrison, determined to settle his claim, appealed to George III in 1772. With the king's support H5 was put on test at the Royal Observatory at Kew for ten weeks resulting in a rate of less than 0.33 sec. a day. With these results Harrison approached the board of longitude again, but the commissioners refused to acknowledge the Kew trial.

An appeal by Harrison to the prime minister, Lord North, eventually resulted in a further act of parliament (George III c. 77), whereby Harrison was awarded a final settlement of £8750 which, including all the payments over the years, came to a total of more than £20,000. Harrison was able to enjoy the recognition of his life's work for less than three years before his death, reputedly on his birthday, on 24 March 1776, in London. He was buried at St John's Church, Hampstead.

The bestselling book *Longitude* (1996) by Dava Sobel and its subsequent television adaptation (1999), starring Michael Gambon and Jeremy Irons, brought Harrison's achievements to a wider audience.   ANDREW KING

Sources W. J. H. Andrewes, ed., *The quest for longitude: the proceedings of the Longitude Symposium* [Harvard U. 1993], 2nd edn (Cambridge, MA, 1998) · parish register (baptisms), Wragby, Yorkshire, 31 March 1693 · Library of the Worshipful Company of Clockmakers, London, Harrison MSS · priv. coll., The Martin MSS · minutes of the Board of Longitude, CUL, RGO ser. · H. Quill, *John Harrison: the man who found longitude* (1966) · R. T. Gould, *The marine chronometer: its history and development* (1923); repr. (1960), 40–70 · *Annual Register* (1777) · parish register (marriages), Barrow upon Humber, Lincolnshire, 30 Aug 1718 · parish register (marriages), St John, Hampstead, Middlesex, 23 Nov 1726 · parish register (deaths), St John, Hampstead, Middlesex, 24 March 1776 · parish register (burials), St John, Hampstead, Middlesex, 2 April 1776 · will, PRO, PROB 11/1018
Archives GL, drawings and papers · Library of the Worshipful Company of Clockmakers, London · Lincs. Arch., memorial on marine timepiece

Likenesses T. King, oils, 1765–6, Sci. Mus. [*see illus.*] • W. Holl, stipple, NPG; repro. in C. Knight, *Gallery of portraits* (1835) • B. Reading, engraving, repro. in *European Magazine* (Oct 1789) • J. R. Smith, mezzotint (after J. Wright), BM, NPG • J. Tassie, paste medallion, NPG

Wealth at death £6500 plus clocks, watches, scientific instruments, and contents of studio workshop: will, PRO, PROB 11/1018

Harrison, John (*b.* 1729, *d.* before 1792). *See under* Harrison family (*per.* 1715–*c.*1790).

Harrison, John (*fl.* 1762–1781), purser in the Royal Navy, deserves to be remembered for his pioneering use, on the voyage of the Royal Navy sloop *Dolphin* round the world in 1766–8, of the lunar-distance method for finding longitude at sea. He should not be confused with his contemporary and namesake John *Harrison (*bap.* 1693, *d.* 1776), whose timepieces first made practicable the 'rival' chronometer method. It may be surmised from the pattern of his appointments as a purser that he was successively in the patronage of admirals Pocock and Rodney, but no evidence, it seems, now survives of the details of his origins, life, or death. His talent, and his role in early scientific navigation, are known from only two sources: his captain on the *Dolphin*, Samuel Wallis (1728–1795), who recorded that it was through Harrison's means that 'we took the Longitude by taking the Distance of the Sun from the Moon and Working it according to Dr. Masculine's Method [that of Nevil Maskelyne, the astronomer royal] which we did not understand' (Beaglehole, 119 n.), and William Wales (1734?–1798), astronomer on the *Resolution* with James Cook (1728–1779), who asserted that

> the lunar observations that were made on board the *Dolphin*, in her second voyage, under the command of Captain Wallis, were all made by Mr Harrison, the Purser: they were also computed by him; and it is but justice to his merit to say that they have every appearance of being exceeding good ones. It is also much to his credit as an astronomer, that I have found but one error of any importance in all his computations, notwithstanding he had not the advantage of a Nautical Almanac [not published until November 1767], but had all the places of the sun and moon to compute from the tables. (Wales, ii)

This talent led J. C. Beaglehole, the scholar of James Cook's life and work, to postulate that Harrison was actually an astronomer, and was rated purser in the *Dolphin* only as an administrative convenience. However, Harrison was in fact a purser by profession, serving in that capacity through eleven appointments to nine different naval vessels between 2 April 1762 (his appointment to the bomb-vessel *Grenado* at St Kitts in the West Indies) and his discharge from the *Sandwich* (90 guns), Rodney's flagship, on 5 November 1781. This makes his achievement all the more remarkable, as 'computing these observations was, at that time, an arduous task' (Wales, ii), involving about four hours of complex mathematical calculation for each determination of longitude.

As Harrison's was the first voyage of discovery to employ a practicable method of accurately determining longitude at sea, he was able to plot the positions of each of the *Dolphin's* discoveries in the Pacific with far greater precision than ever before achieved by any maritime explorer. Most significantly, Matavai Bay in Tahiti was located at 149°35′ west of London, only six minutes or about 5 miles from the true position. This enabled James Cook in the *Endeavour*, also using the lunar-distance method but now with the advantage of the *Nautical Almanac*, to find it again in April 1769 when sent there to observe the transit of Venus.

It is while he was at Tahiti that we catch the only glimpse we have of Harrison's personality and his activity as an astronomer: George Robertson, the master, recorded that, together with 'our good merry friend the purser', he and midshipman George Pinnock observed a solar eclipse, and derived from it a second value for the longitude of the island (9 July 1767). RANDOLPH COCK

Sources W. Wales, *Astronomical observations made in the southern hemisphere* (1788) • *The journals of Captain James Cook*, ed. J. C. Beaglehole, 1, Hakluyt Society, 34a (1955); repr. (1968) • *The discovery of Tahiti: a journal of the second voyage of HMS Dolphin round the world … written by her master George Robertson*, ed. H. Carrington, Hakluyt Society, 2nd ser., 98 (1948) • R. Cock, 'Precursors of Cook: the voyages of the *Dolphin*, 1764–8', *Mariner's Mirror*, 85 (1999), 30–52 • commission and warrant books, PRO, AOM 6/19–22 • original warrants by Cs-in-C overseas, PRO, ADM 6/63 • officers appointed by the navy board, PRO, ADM 106/2898 • muster books of *Grenado*, *Juno*, *Nottingham*, *Dolphin*, *Sandwich*, PRO, ADM 36/5691, 5886, 6215, 7580, 8863–8865

Harrison, John (*b.* 1786, *d.* after 1830). *See under* Cato Street conspirators (*act.* 1820).

Harrison, John Heslop- (1920–1998), botanist, was born on 10 February 1920 at 181 Abingdon Road, Middlesbrough, North Riding of Yorkshire, one of the three children of John William Heslop Harrison (1881–1967), a distinguished scientist who held posts variously at the universities of Newcastle upon Tyne and Durham in both zoology and botany, and his wife, Christian Watson (*née* Henderson).

Heslop-Harrison was educated at Chester-le-Street grammar school and King's College, University of Durham, where he read botany, zoology, and chemistry. In 1941, before being able to embark on an academic career, he was called up for war service in the army. He spent time on Orkney working on the development of radar, and later was attached to the Supreme Headquarters Allied Expeditionary Force, where he helped in the evaluation of the technical capabilities of the German armed forces. In 1945, at the end of the war, he returned to King's College as lecturer in agricultural botany, and then a year later moved as lecturer in botany to the Queen's University of Belfast, with a special interest in the reproductive physiology of plants; he obtained his PhD degree there. On 23 September 1950 he married Yolande Massey (*b.* 1918/19), a university lecturer in botany at Newcastle.

A move to University College, London, allowed Heslop-Harrison to develop research interests in modern plant systematics, and he became reader in taxonomy in 1953. In the following year he returned to Belfast to take up the chair of botany, where he remained until 1960. He was then appointed to the Mason chair of botany at Birmingham, where he was active in the establishment of the school of biological sciences, the first of its type in the country, with the integration of teaching and research across several biological disciplines. At Birmingham, too, he developed the then relatively new technique of electron microscopy, especially its application to plant reproductive studies.

Between 1967 and 1971 Heslop-Harrison was based at the University of Wisconsin, Madison. He took whatever opportunities were open to him within the United States and internationally to promote his concerns about the erosion of biological diversity, and the importance of fostering environmentally sensitive agriculture.

In 1971 Heslop-Harrison returned to Britain as director of the Royal Botanic Gardens, Kew, a remarkable and significant appointment in many ways. Kew had long been a pre-eminent centre of taxonomic studies, albeit largely traditional, but with Heslop-Harrison as director it was suddenly at the forefront of the 'new taxonomy'. At Kew he worked closely with his wife. He gradually found central government, then responsible for the funding of Kew, frustratingly unwilling to support fully his plans for the new direction in which he wished the Royal Botanic Gardens to go. Uniquely for a Kew director, therefore, he resigned in 1976 to become Royal Society research professor at the University College of Wales, Aberystwyth, based at the Welsh Plant Breeding Station. Freed of much administrative labour, there the Heslop-Harrisons made important and extensive studies of the fertilization process in plants and the interaction of the pollen tube with the female floral parts, work that was technically exacting as well as significant. Heslop-Harrison remained there until his formal retirement in 1985, when he continued his studies, at first in Aberystwyth and later from the basement of his home in Leominster.

Heslop-Harrison's legacy in the understanding of the flowering process and reproductive physiology in plants is immense, his publication list voluminous, and his students legion; many subsequently progressed to senior professional posts themselves. He had an immense grasp of the entire subject of botany, both modern and historic. He possessed the rare attributes of being a brilliant lecturer and highly gifted technically. His contributions were formally recognized in many ways, most notably with his election to fellowship of the Royal Society in 1970 and receipt of its Darwin medal in 1976 and its royal medal in 1996. Among other awards were the Linnean medal for botany from the Linnean Society in 1976, the Navashin medal of the Komarov Institute of the USSR Academy in 1991, the Erdtman international medal for palynology in 1971, and honorary doctorates from the universities of Belfast, Bath, Edinburgh, and Hull.

Heslop-Harrison was a big man, tall and physically very imposing, and in his company there was never any doubt that one was in the presence of a powerful and forceful intellect. Notwithstanding this, he was a man of much humour, who always had time for students, no matter how junior or inexperienced, and was always willing to listen carefully to the other's argument before making a decision or reaching a conclusion. John Heslop-Harrison

died on 7 May 1998 following a heart attack at his home, The Pleasaunce, 137 Bargates, Leominster, Herefordshire; his wife survived him.　　　　　　　STEFAN BUCZACKI

Sources WW · *Daily Telegraph* (11 July 1998) · S. J. Owens, *The Times* (29 July 1998) · personal knowledge (2004) · b. cert. · m. cert. · d. cert.

Likenesses W. Vanderson, photograph, 1971, Hult. Arch. · portrait, repro. in *The Times*

Wealth at death £271,113—gross: probate, 1999, *CGPLA Eng. & Wales* · £268,652—net: probate, 1999, *CGPLA Eng. & Wales*

Harrison, John Vernon (1892–1972), geologist and explorer, was born on 16 March 1892 at Bloemfontein, Orange Free State, the son of J. Frederick Harrison, a civil engineer. Of Scottish parentage, he was educated at George Watson's College, Edinburgh, and Allan Glen's School, Glasgow, before proceeding to Glasgow University where the inspiration provided by the great explorer professor John Walter Gregory was to set the pattern for Harrison's whole professional life.

Harrison graduated in 1914, and became an explosives chemist before being commissioned in the Royal Engineers, where he was concerned with water-supply problems in Mesopotamia. In late 1918 he was seconded to the Anglo-Persian Oil Company, joining their staff on demobilization and remaining with the company for the next twenty years. During this period he undertook geological exploration in Central and South America, Borneo, and the West Indies, as well as the work in Persia for which he became best-known. Harrison's gifts of observation coupled with vivid geological imagination enabled him to visualize in three dimensions the large-scale geological structures with which he was confronted, particularly in the Zagros Mountains, and the sometimes singular processes which had given rise to them. Striking results emerged from arduous fieldwork carried out in the roughest of terrains; it is said that many mules died nobly in Harrison's service in Persia. Among some forty published papers, those with G. M. Lees on salt dome emplacement and with N. L. Falcon on gravitational tectonics long retained classic status.

In 1938 Harrison accepted a university demonstratorship in geology at Oxford where he undertook all the undergraduate teaching in structural geology and in petrology. The field classes he led, clad in a kilt of no recognized tartan, to Arran, Skye, and Assynt became legendary and he played a major role in the training of many geologists. His outstanding research record, as well as his qualities as a teacher, stressing rigour and accuracy, were recognized by his election to a readership *ad hominem* in 1956. Harrison's Oxford years saw no diminution in his urge to continue geological exploration in remote regions, and he surveyed thousands of square kilometres of the Peruvian Andes in a series of summer expeditions on which he was often accompanied by one or two of his students, who would return exhausted, but with vivid travellers' tales.

Harrison (universally known simply as 'J. V.'), believing that any young geologist who married was placing fetters upon his activities to the extent of being unfaithful to his science, did not himself marry until 1939 when, predictably, he married another Scottish geologist, Janet Mitchell Dingwall. They were active churchgoers and a devoted couple until her death following a road accident in 1971.

Harrison was tall and spare of build, with a short pointed beard. On first acquaintance he could seem cold, austere, remote; the humanity, together with a keen wit and acid sense of humour, became apparent later. He was fond of music and was an enthusiast for Scottish dancing. But the predominant passion of Harrison's life remained exploration geology in remote places, carried out under the most arduous conditions that could be arranged.

Harrison's work was recognized by his election to FRSE in 1934, by the award of the Lyell medal by the Geological Society in 1961 and by his appointment in 1957 as a grand officer of the Order al Merito por Servicios Distinguidos by the Peruvian government. He died at Oxford on 31 July 1972. E. A. VINCENT

Sources *Proceedings of the Geologists' Association*, 84 (1973), 114–18 · E. A. Vincent, *Geology and mineralogy at Oxford, 1860–1986* (1994) · W. S. McKerrow, *Year Book of the Royal Society of Edinburgh* (1972–3) · B. Kummel, *Geological Society of America, Bulletin*, 1973 [with bibliography] · *WWW* · personal knowledge (2004)
Archives BGS · Oxf. U. Mus. NH, corresp., diaries, notebooks, papers
Likenesses photographs, repro. in Vincent, *Geology and mineralogy*
Wealth at death £108,787: probate, 25 Oct 1972, *CGPLA Eng. & Wales*

Harrison, Joseph (*bap.* 1798?, *d.* before 1861), horticulturist and writer, was born in Sheffield, Yorkshire, and was possibly the son of Charles Harrison and his wife, Ann, *née* Wightman, who was baptized on 16 November 1798. He was for some years gardener to Lord Wharncliffe at Wortley Hall, near Sheffield. In 1830 he and Richard Gill Curtis were granted a patent (no. 6007) for a new method of glazing, which gave a plane surface, presumably intended for horticultural glasshouses. In 1831 Harrison and Joseph Paxton edited the *Horticultural Register*, which abstracted and reviewed articles from other journals. In 1833, the year that Harrison was elected an honorary member of the Doncaster, Bawtry, and Retford Horticultural Society, he commenced publication of the *Floricultural Cabinet*, a monthly magazine. Claiming to embrace everything useful in horticulture, natural history, and rural economy, it was an immediate success, and was said to have sold 59,000 copies in the first nine months of its life. Twenty-seven volumes had appeared by 1859, when it became the *Gardener's Weekly Magazine*. His magazine *The Gardener's and Forester's Record* was restricted to information of practical use to gardeners; more general material was published in *The Garden Almanack*, later *The Gardener's and Naturalist's Almanack*, from 1852.

In 1837 Harrison left Yorkshire to begin business as a florist at Downham in Norfolk, where George Harrison, perhaps a relative, was in business at Lynn Road between 1833 and 1836. Joseph Harrison was still there in 1850, but he subsequently moved to Larkfield Lodge, Kew Road, Richmond, Surrey, where he traded as a florist and nurseryman while continuing his writing and publication. It

is not known when he married Louisa, who came from St Marylebone in London; their eldest son, Charles W. Harrison, an electrical engineer, and his wife, Eliza, and their four young children, also lived at Larkfield Lodge, as did Joseph's younger sons, Joseph J. and Edward Harrison, both following their father as nurserymen and writers. It is not known when or where Joseph Harrison died; by the time of the 1861 census Larkfield Lodge had passed into other hands. ANITA McCONNELL

Sources census returns, 1851, 1861 · directories, Richmond, 1851 and 1853 · W. White, *History, gazetteer, and directory of Norfolk* (1836) · *Horticultural Register* (1831) · *Floricultural Cabinet* (1833–59) · G. E. Fussell, 'Joseph Harrison, sometime florist', *Gardeners' Chronicle*, 3rd ser., 128 (1950), 6

Harrison, Julius Allan Greenway (1885–1963), conductor and composer, was born on 26 March 1885 in Bewdley Road, Lower Mitton, Worcestershire, the eldest in the family of four sons and three daughters of Walter Henry Harrison (*b.* 1852), grocer and candle maker, and his wife, Henriette Julien Schoeller (1860–1936), who came from Heidelberg, Germany. His parents had met while his mother was working in England as a governess. He grew up in a musical household: his father conducted the Stourport Glee Union, and he was taught the piano by his mother before taking organ and violin lessons from the organist of Wilden church. He also sang in the church choir, where the future prime minister, Stanley Baldwin, was a fellow chorister.

Educated at Queen Elizabeth's School, Hartlebury, from 1903 to 1907 Harrison trained at the Midland Institute School of Music in Birmingham, where Granville Bantock was principal. From 1905 to 1908 he was organist at Hartlebury parish church, and after winning first prize in the composition class at the 1908 Norwich musical festival for his cantata *Cleopatra*, he moved to London to work as a freelance musician. While working for the Orchestrelle Company, correcting and editing piano rolls for player-pianos, he gained conducting experience with amateur musicians, including the Dulwich Philharmonic Society and the Hampstead Opéra Comique. He was also organist of the Union Chapel, Highbury, where he had the opportunity to write music for the choir, including *Harvest Cantata* (1910) and *Christmas Cantata* (1911). He found time for composing other works, including the tone poem *Night on the Mountains* (1910), which Hans Richter invited him to conduct at a London Symphony Orchestra concert. On 16 December 1913 he married (Florence) Mary (*b.* 1886/7), a singer, of Eastbourne, Sussex, daughter of Joseph Cooper Eddison; they had two daughters.

Harrison's career as an opera conductor began in the autumn of 1913, when he was engaged to conduct for the season at Covent Garden, London; he had worked as pianist and coach for the German opera there in the spring, when he was able to observe Arthur Nikisch rehearse Wagner's *Ring* cycle. At the end of the season he visited Bayreuth to hear Hans Richter conduct, and in 1914 he went to Paris as a member of the Covent Garden syndicate, which was promoting a German opera season there, to rehearse Wagner's *Parsifal* and *Tristan und Isolde* for

Nikisch, and *Die Meistersinger* for Felix Weingartner. He was one of the conductors for the Beecham Opera Company, formed by Thomas Beecham, during its existence from 1915 to 1919, and although he was called up in 1916 and was commissioned into the Royal Flying Corps his postings, first to Northolt to supervise the testing of aeroplane engines and then to the Royal Flying Corps's depot in Regent's Park, allowed him to continue to work for the opera company. In 1920 he was appointed conductor of the Bradford Permanent Orchestra, a post he held until 1927, and from 1920 to 1923 he was also co-conductor, with Landon Ronald, of the Scottish Orchestra, which had a three-month summer season in Glasgow. When Beecham founded the British National Opera Company in 1922, he invited Harrison to be a principal conductor; Harrison worked for several seasons at Covent Garden, specializing in Wagner operas and conducting twenty-two performances of *Tristan und Isolde*. He left the company in 1924, when appointed director of opera and professor of composition at the Royal Academy of Music, and for five years prepared the opera class for the academy's annual opera week at the Scala Theatre. He was divorced from his first wife in 1929, and on 28 October that year married Dorothy Helen (*b.* 1904/5), a musician, of Baldock, Hertfordshire, daughter of Francis William Henry Langston Day; she had been a member of his harmony class at the academy. They had one son.

In 1930 Harrison was appointed conductor of the Hastings Municipal Orchestra, a post that involved organizing an annual festival and conducting as many as twelve concerts a week during the summer season. After the orchestra was disbanded in 1940, he was director of music at Malvern College until 1942, when he became a conductor of the BBC Northern Orchestra in Manchester. As his deafness grew more severe, however, he accepted fewer conducting engagements, and after conducting the final concert of the Malvern Elgar Festival, of which he was artistic director in 1947, he was forced to give up conducting altogether.

Harrison had always resented having to earn his living by conducting, and he was now able to devote most of his time to composition, while doing some teaching at Trinity College of Music and the Birmingham School of Music. Although he had been composing all his life, he had destroyed most of his early unpublished works, and his orchestral *Worcestershire Suite* (1917), first performed in 1920, was his first work to attract widespread attention. This was followed by *Requiem of Archangels for the World* (1920) for chorus and organ, but it was not until 1938, with *Autumn Landscape* for string orchestra, written after the death of his elder daughter in 1935, that Harrison began to emerge as a mature composer with his own voice. Traditional in style, and strongly influenced by the works of Brahms, he was never interested in modernism, and hated the avant-garde. Harrison began working on his mass in C in 1936, as a memorial to his daughter, but this was not finished until 1947. It was performed regularly in his lifetime—he heard twenty-eight performances—and

the BBC broadcast it in 1955 in celebration of his seventieth birthday. Other important works include *Bredon Hill* (1942), a rhapsody for violin and orchestra often compared to Vaughan Williams's *The Lark Ascending*, with the score headed by lines from A. E. Housman's poem 'Here of a Sunday Morning'; the viola sonata (1946); and *Missa liturgica* (1950). From 1947 to 1957 he was writing his Requiem, dedicated to Sir Edward Elgar and first performed at the Worcester festival in 1957, the year of the Elgar centenary.

Although he never wrote a symphony himself, Harrison was an expert on the form, and published the monograph *Brahms and his Four Symphonies* (1939). He contributed the chapter on Dvořák's orchestral music to *Antonín Dvořák: his Achievement* (1943), edited by Viktor Fischl, and wrote four chapters for Robert Simpson's symposium *The Symphony* (1967), which was dedicated to his memory. He also began an autobiography, 'The Red Earth of Worcestershire', which was completed by his wife but never published.

A quiet, gentle, and sensitive man, Harrison suffered ill health for much of his life. The stress of overwork led to the development of a duodenal ulcer in early middle age at the same time as the onset of deafness, which was possibly caused by his work during the First World War. He died on 5 April 1963 at his home, The Greenwood, 28 Ox Lane, Harpenden, Hertfordshire.   ANNE PIMLOTT BAKER

Sources G. Self, *Julius Harrison and the importunate muse* (1993) · L. Foreman, *From Parry to Britten: British music in letters* (1987) · *New Grove*, 2nd edn · *The Times* (6 April 1963) · *WW* · b. cert. · d. cert. · *CGPLA Eng. & Wales* (1963) · m. certs.

Likenesses photograph, 1929, repro. in Self, *Julius Harrison*, facing p. 46

Wealth at death £10,180 16s. 6d.: probate, 6 Aug 1963, *CGPLA Eng. & Wales*

Harrison, Kathleen (1892–1995), actress, was born on 23 February 1892 at 500 Whalley New Road, Little Harwood, Blackburn, Lancashire, the daughter of Arthur Harrison, assistant engineer to Blackburn corporation, and his wife, Alice Maud, *née* Parker. From the age of five, when her father became borough engineer for Southwark, she was brought up in London. She was educated at Clapham high school before training at the Royal Academy of Dramatic Art (1914–15), where she won the Du Maurier bronze medal. While rehearsing her role as Eliza Doolittle for a production of *Pygmalion* there the play's writer, George Bernard Shaw, visited and gave her advice that would help her in her subsequent career: 'Go out into the Old Kent Road and just listen to the women talking' (*The Independent*).

Although she appeared in the film *Our Boys* (1915) on leaving drama school, Harrison married John Henry Back (*d.* 1960), of the Western Telegraph Company, in the following year, and lived with him in Argentina and Madeira for eight years. When he became unemployed they returned to Britain, and Harrison made her stage début as Mrs Judd in *The Constant Flirt*, at the Pier Theatre, Eastbourne, in 1926. The next year she appeared in the West End as Winnie in *The Cage*, at the Savoy Theatre. This was the start of a fifty-year stage career in which she became notable for playing cockney mothers, maids, and charwomen. Her subsequent West End plays included *A Damsel in Distress* (1929), *The Merchant and Venus* (1930), *Lovers' Meeting* (1931), *Line Engaged* (1934), *The Corn is Green* (1938), and *Flare Path* (1942–4), but it was her role as the comic cook, Mrs Terence, in Emlyn Williams's chiller *Night must Fall*, at the Duchess Theatre in 1935, that established her as a star, and she reprised it in the 1937 film version. She toured north Africa and Italy with Emlyn Williams's Entertainments National Service Association company in 1944. After the war she played, to great acclaim, on stage and screen, the role of Violet, the excitable maid, in Terence Rattigan's *The Winslow Boy* (Lyric Theatre, 1946, adapted two years later for the cinema) and took over from Peggy Mount the lead part of fearsome mother Emma Hornett in *Watch it Sailor!* (1960). On stage she also played a blunt former chorus girl in Noël Coward's *Nude with Violin* (Globe Theatre, 1956) and Mrs Hardcastle in *She Stoops to Conquer* (Young Vic Theatre, 1972), one of her rare classical roles.

In the cinema Harrison was usually seen in the same types of role, playing cockney domestics. Her early films included *The Man from Toronto* (1932, as Jessie Matthews's maid), *The Ghoul* (1933, alongside Boris Karloff), *Home from Home* (1939, as comedian Sandy Powell's wife), and Noël Coward's wartime masterpiece *In which we Serve* (1942). Screen fame came to her in middle age, when she starred as London East End cleaner Ma Huggett in *Holiday Camp* (1947), featuring the fictional Huggett family enjoying a post-war leisure innovation. With Jack Warner as her screen husband, the film was so popular that Rank capitalized on its success by making the sequels *Here Come the Huggetts* (1948), *Vote for Huggett* (1949), and *The Huggetts Abroad* (1949). These portrayals of the 'common man'— and woman—were panned by the critics but such was the public's love for the family that their adventures continued on BBC radio in the serial *Meet the Huggetts* (1953–62).

Harrison was recognized as one of the greatest British film character actresses of the 1940s and 1950s, and made notable appearances in *Oliver Twist* (1948, as Mrs Sowerby), *Scrooge* (1951, with Alastair Sim), *The Pickwick Papers* (1952, as Miss Wardle), *Lilacs in the Spring* (1954, as Anna Neagle's dresser), *The Big Money* (1956, as Ian Carmichael's mother), and *Alive and Kicking* (1958, appearing with Sybil Thorndike and Estelle Winwood as three lively old ladies escaping from a home).

After acting in the films *On the Fiddle* (1961, as Stanley Holloway's wife) and *West 11* (1963, as Alfred Lynch's mother), Harrison found new fame on television, as the star of *Mrs Thursday* (1966–7), a comedy-drama written specially for her by Ted Willis and running to two long series. She played a warm-hearted cockney charwoman, Alice Thursday, who inherits from her late employer £10 million, a mansion, the controlling interest in a property empire, and a Rolls Royce, while his four wives are left nothing. The programme was the most popular series of 1966 and toppled *Coronation Street* from the top of the television ratings week after week. Her other small-screen appearances included parts in BBC serializations of *Our Mutual Friend* and *Martin Chuzzlewit* (Charles Dickens was her favourite novelist). Her final screen appearance was in the Disney comedy *The London Connection* (1979).

Throughout her career Harrison knocked six years off her age, revealing her true age only with the approach of her hundredth birthday, in 1992. She died at her home, 30 Cottenham Park Road, Merton, London, on 7 December 1995. She was survived by a son and daughter, her husband and a son having predeceased her.

ANTHONY HAYWARD

Sources A. Hayward and D. Hayward, *TV unforgettables* (1993) • *The Independent* (8 Dec 1995) • *The Times* (8 Dec 1995) • *The Guardian* (8 Dec 1995) • D. Quinlan, *Quinlan's illustrated directory of film stars*, 4th edn (1996) • T. Vahimagi, ed., *British television: an illustrated guide*, 2nd edn (1996) • R. Taylor, *The Guinness book of sitcoms* (1994) • *WWW*, 1991–5 • b. cert. • d. cert.
Likenesses photographs, 1947–60, Hult. Arch. • photograph, repro. in *The Times* • photograph, repro. in *The Independent* • two photographs, repro. in *The Guardian*
Wealth at death £125,111: probate, 23 April 1996, *CGPLA Eng. & Wales*

Harrison, Lawrence Whitaker (1876–1964), venereologist, was born on 2 April 1876 at Regent Street, Haslingden, Lancashire, youngest son of Jonathan Atkinson Harrison, physician, and his wife, Margaret, formerly Whitaker. Educated at Manchester grammar school and the University of Glasgow, Harrison was awarded the medical degrees of MB BCh in 1897. A student private in the Volunteer Medical Staff Corps, he joined the Army Medical Services in 1898 and remained in the military until the end of the First World War. He always retained thereafter the title of colonel.

Harrison served as a medical officer in South Africa during the Second South African War (1899–1902). Thereafter he was posted to India in 1903, and it was here that his interest in venereal disease began to take shape. Echoing the discarded practices of the controversial Cantonment Act of 1864, which had regulated prostitution in military cantonments, Harrison retained infected prostitutes in the cantonment hospital for treatment. When that failed to reduce the high rate of venereal disease among soldiers, he arranged for daily disinfection of women sexually servicing British soldiers, claiming that this was an effective solution. Harrison was back in London in March 1905 for his marriage on 7 March to Mabel Alice, daughter of Colonel Edward James Fairland. They returned to India, where they raised two sons and two daughters. As a father Harrison was stern rather than affectionate, always formal in his bearing. His son Douglas followed him into the army.

Harrison remained at Sialkot cantonment in the Punjab until 1908 when he returned to Britain as assistant to the professor of military medicine at Queen Alexandra Hospital, Millbank, London. He was promoted captain in 1902, and major in 1911. In 1909, he was appointed pathologist at Rochester Row Military Hospital, where he began to monitor the use of the newly available treatment for syphilis, the arseno-benzoid Salvarsan. Harrison was one of the very first doctors to make use of the drug in Britain, pioneering significant modifications in its use as a result of his observations of patient progress. He also refined the new Wassermann test which demonstrated the presence of syphilis in the bloodstream. The Harrison–Wyler Wassermann method became an internationally recognized alternative in the inter-war period. He was also deeply involved in experimental treatments for gonorrhoea.

On the outbreak of war in 1914 Harrison was posted to France. When rising venereal disease rates among British troops proved difficult to control he took over command of a hospital at Le Havre dedicated to its treatment, finding ingenious ways to circumvent the dwindling supplies of German-manufactured Salvarsan. He was promoted to lieutenant-colonel in 1915, and in 1916 returned to Britain as adviser to the War Office on venereal diseases in western Europe, as well as chief physician at the Rochester Row Hospital. He was promoted to brevet-colonel in 1917, receiving the DSO for his wartime services.

Appointed honorary physician to the king in 1917, Harrison's civilian career was a mix of medical and policy positions, always combining his interests with a private medical practice. As a member of the 1919 Ministry of Health committee, chaired by Waldorf Astor, to investigate infectious diseases and demobilization, he was critical of its reluctance to disseminate clear information about prophylaxis. In 1919 he accepted a position as lecturer in the venereal diseases at Edinburgh University with charge of the venereal diseases department at the Edinburgh Royal Infirmary. Before he could take up the position he was invited to become the first technical adviser to the new Ministry of Health on venereal diseases, a post he had, as a member of the Astor committee, recommended establishing. Remaining in London, Harrison worked concurrently as adviser to the ministry and as director of the department of venereal diseases at St Thomas's Hospital, running a clinic funded by the London County Council under the new Venereal Disease Act of 1916. He and his family settled in Eccleston Square. He remained with the Ministry of Health until 1947, retiring from his position at St Thomas's in 1936. At the ministry he explored schemes for better organizing the venereal disease clinics established after 1917, though budgetary limitations were a constant source of frustration. At the time of his retirement from St Thomas's, Harrison accepted an honorary post at the postgraduate medical school, Hammersmith. In the early 1940s he designed Defence of the Realm Act regulation 33B which introduced the principle of contact tracing in cases of venereal infection. He maintained international connections, collaborating on clinical experiments with the Toronto Public Health Laboratory and, from 1928, as a member of the League of Nation's health organization committee of experts on syphilis and cognate subjects. In the 1950s he was a member of the World Health Organization's advisory panel on serology.

In the 1920s and 1930s Harrison was a leading figure in the development of British venereology, writing three major textbooks and helping to found in 1922 the Medical Society for the Study of Venereal Diseases (of which he was president from 1923 to 1925, and again from 1938 to 1942). He was central to the launching of the *British Journal of Venereal Diseases* in 1925, and was its editor from 1925 to 1942, sharing the editorship with E. R. T. Clarkson until the latter's death in 1939, and then continuing as sole editor. He contributed a substantial number of articles to its pages, as well as to other pertinent journals. A firm believer in education, he was closely associated with the Institute of Venereal Disease Technicians. He was elected fellow of the Royal College of Physicians of Edinburgh in 1925, and received in 1946 both the CB and the William Freeman Snow award of the American Social Hygiene Association for distinguished services to humanity.

Harrison's military mien was not always popular, but his staff showed him affection as well as respect. He died at his home, 6 Witton Court, 59 Eccleston Square, London, on 9 May 1964.   PHILIPPA LEVINE

Sources L. W. Harrison, 'Half a lifetime in the management of venereal diseases', *Medicine Illustrated*, 3 (1949) · *The Lancet* (16 May 1964), 1113 · *The Times* (11 May 1964), 14f · A. King, 'The life and times of Colonel Harrison', *British Journal of Venereal Diseases*, 50 (1974), 391–403 · L. W. Harrison, 'Some lessons learnt in fifty years practice in venereology', *British Journal of Venereal Diseases*, 30 (1954), 184–90 · L. W. Harrison, 'A history of the Medical Society for the Study of Venereal Diseases', *British Journal of Venereal Diseases*, 37 (1961), 2–15 · J. D. Oriel, *The scars of venus: a history of venereology* (1994) · b. cert. · m. cert. · d. cert. · *CGPLA Eng. & Wales* (1964)

Likenesses photographs, 1913, repro. in King, 'Life and times of Colonel Harrison', 393, 399, 401

Wealth at death £83,463: probate, 27 Aug 1964, *CGPLA Eng. & Wales*

Harrison, Lucy (1844–1915), headmistress, was born on 17 January 1844 at Birkenhead, the youngest of the eight children of Daniel Harrison and his wife, Anna (*née* Botham) of Uttoxeter. The Harrisons were an old Yorkshire Quaker family and Anna was also brought up as a Quaker although she later converted to the Church of England. About 1849 the family moved to Springfield, Egremont, in Cumberland. The Harrison children had a happy country childhood in a home which valued diversity of opinion and in which Quaker and Anglican beliefs co-existed peaceably. In 1854 the family moved to Marshalls, a manor house in Romford, Essex, where Lucy was taught at home by her eldest sister. She was a pretty child with light blonde hair and blue eyes; though reserved and shy she could be amusing in the company of family and friends. She loved animals and practical hobbies. Octavia Hill, who had worked with one of Lucy's sisters, visited the family at Marshalls and remarked on their relaxed Yorkshire hospitality. About 1857 Lucy and three of her sisters travelled to Heidelberg, where they studied German. In 1859 the girls, now accompanied by their parents, moved to Dieppe, where they stayed for a year. Lucy attended a good Catholic school and learned French.

They returned to England about 1861 and the family settled in Highgate, Middlesex. Lucy attended Bedford College for two years, studying Latin, history, and English literature. She was befriended by Dr George MacDonald, who taught her English literature. She impressed him with her feeling for Shakespeare, though his children remembered her for skills as a carpenter. After leaving college Harrison lived with her family in Leicester for several years. Apparently contented, she amused herself by making humorous topical sketches and by learning wood-carving, a craft she later taught to schoolgirls, poor boys, and the women who attended the Working Women's College in London. The family moved to Shirley House, Beckenham, about 1864, where they enjoyed a rich social and intellectual life. Although Lucy's shyness often kept her at home, she was bursting with energy; this she discharged by riding and skating, reading, studying Latin, acting in home-made plays, and attending lectures at her old college in London.

Lucy Harrison came to teaching by accident. In 1866 the head of Bedford College School asked her to fill in for an ill teacher and the post was quickly made permanent. She taught Latin, English, and natural history. A natural teacher, she learned rapidly and loved the work. In 1868 the school became independent of Bedford College, and in 1870 Harrison became a partner in the newly named Gower Street School. She left her family to live in Gower Street and in 1875 became the school's sole head. She flourished in her new role and under her direction the school grew, acquiring an excellent academic reputation. In addition to her duties as headmistress, she continued to contribute to the Working Women's College and to help Octavia Hill with her housing projects. She furthered her own education, studying Anglo-Saxon, sitting an examination in 1880 in which she was placed first class with distinction. She published a book on Spenser (1883) and was one of the first to join the new professional associations, the Schoolmistresses' Association and the Teachers' Guild.

In 1885, after suffering a severe bout of ill health, Harrison resigned as headmistress of Gower Street School. She decided to build herself a little house near her father's birthplace at Bainbridge in Wensleydale; remaining in London while the house was being built, she formed a warm and devoted friendship with her successor, Amy Greener. In her memoir of Harrison, Greener recalled that, although she had never wished to be married, the self-sufficient Harrison was lonely and craved the love of an undemanding friend. Although Greener's work at Gower Street meant that the friends lived apart for several years, they became inseparable and remained so for the rest of Harrison's life.

By 1889 Harrison's health was so much improved that friends suggested she apply for the post of headmistress of the Mount School, York. She took up the position in 1890 and, despite initial shyness and self-doubt, successfully led the school for twelve years. Under her leadership, the Mount developed into a modern school with high academic standards and a modern communal life. She abolished outmoded customs such as the obligatory 'crocodile walk', replacing it with organized sports. Under her direction a number of new student societies were established—she used to accompany the Archaeology Society on trips to historical sites in and around York. She raised the intellectual standard by appointing only university graduates to teaching posts, as well as by her own teaching of English literature. Sometimes the standard she set

was, if anything, too high—some students commented that her erudition was more appropriate to a college than a school—but they idolized her and tried to absorb her teaching, such was the force of her personality. Under her direction a new building programme gave the school a new wing, gymnasium, library, and junior school.

Harrison came into her own at the Mount. Although she never lost her innate shyness and reserve, she was at ease among the girls, who remembered her not only for her high intellectual and ethical standards but for her calm good sense and great sense of humour. Whether she was giving a demonstration of bad table manners, laughing heartily when a frightened pupil confessed to a mishap with the ink bottle, or whistling (which she did beautifully), Harrison was relaxed, at home, and utterly in command. Perhaps her intellectual standards stood in her way at times—one student remarked that she sometimes seemed to prefer animals because they did not think, and therefore draw wrong conclusions (Sturge and Clark, 167). Nevertheless she found an attentive and devoted, if not always knowledgeable, audience at the Mount, and for her gentleness, justice, and good humour was both respected and loved.

In 1902, suffering from a heart problem that had plagued her since she had rheumatic fever in 1891, Harrison retired to a small house in York, from which she continued to teach her English literature classes. Amy Greener had joined her in 1895 and the two kept close ties with the Mount. In 1907 they returned to Bainbridge, where Harrison continued to read and to write on a variety of subjects from Shakespeare to Tagore, to garden and to do carpentry and household repairs. She always had a dog or two and was a supporter of animal welfare—she opposed hare- and fox-hunting and addressed the York Antivivisection Society in 1909. She supported the women's suffrage campaign although she deplored the violent methods of the militants. The two friends organized community activities for young people and Harrison tried always to attend the annual meeting of the Old Scholars of the Mount.

They were attending a conference in Stratford upon Avon when war was declared in 1914. A performance of *Henry V* was hastily substituted for the planned evening's entertainment and perhaps this affected Harrison's mood, for she became preoccupied with the war and the sufferings of its victims. Work with Belgian refugees did not satisfy her and she diverged from many fellow Quakers by supporting the war. She was restless and her nights were disturbed—in 1915 she seemed to fail and in April that year underwent an operation for appendicitis from which she never recovered. She died at Bainbridge, Wensleydale, on 2 May 1915 and was buried near the Friends' meeting-house at Bainbridge on 6 May.

Harrison's staff and students at the Mount remembered their first sight of her, a pleasant-faced woman with short curly hair, a tailored black suit and white blouse, simple, practical, unfashionable—'but fashion did not dictate to

Lucy Harrison'. The school quickly accepted her as 'just herself' and let their original, witty, and intellectual head get on with the business of transforming a small Quaker school into a modern centre for women's education (Sturge and Clark, 165).   ELIZABETH J. MORSE

Sources A. Greener, *A lover of books: the life and literary papers of Lucy Harrison* (1916) • H. W. Sturge and T. Clark, *The Mount School, York, 1785 to 1814, 1831 to 1931* (1931) • G. Darley, *Octavia Hill* (1990)
Likenesses photogravure, 1890, repro. in Greener, *Lover of books*, frontispiece • photogravure, 1901, repro. in Greener, *Lover of books*

Harrison [*née* Rossiter], **Mary P.** (1788–1875), flower painter, was born in Liverpool, the daughter of William Rossiter, a prosperous hat manufacturer of Stockport and Liverpool. On 3 August 1814 she married at St James's, Westminster, William Harrison, businessman (*d.* 1861), and on her honeymoon in France she took up watercolour painting. Her first son, William Frederick *Harrison (1815–1880), was born at Amiens, and she had to return home in haste in 1815. Back in Liverpool William Harrison became a partner in a brewery, in which he lost all his capital, and became an invalid. Mary then turned to painting as a means of support for her family, which eventually comprised twelve children. She became a popular teacher in Liverpool, Chester, and the surrounding district. In 1829 she moved to London, and she was a founder member in 1831 of the New Society of Painters in Water Colours. She exhibited there from 1833 until her death. She also exhibited at the Royal Academy and the Society for British Artists, altogether over 320 works being shown.

Mary Harrison's art, though of limited scope, was of a very delicate and refined nature. Her fruit and flower pieces bore unmistakable marks of taste, feeling, and close observation of nature. Her early work followed the fashion of the time in representing detached specimens of fruit or cut sprigs of garden flowers, or a branch of blackberry blossom lying near a bird's nest. As she progressed, the beauty of growing plants, especially of wild flowers set in a natural habitat, engaged her attention. Because of her groups of violets, cowslips, wood anemones, primroses, snowdrops, crocuses, and the most beautiful roses, she became known as the 'rose and primrose painter'. In 1862 she painted her most famous work, *History of a Primrose*, depicting primroses in three panels; 'Infancy', 'Maturity', and 'Decay'. Her *Basket of Flowers* (1864) and *Vase of Flowers* are both in the Walker Art Gallery, Liverpool. Her work was much sought after in France, where she met George Sand and other notables.

After ensuring her paintings for the 1875 winter exhibition were ready for dispatch, Mary Harrison died at Chesnut Lodge, Squires Mount, Hampstead, London, on 25 November 1875. Four of her children were fine painters: William Frederick Harrison (1815–1880), George Henry *Harrison (1816–1846), Maria (*fl.* 1845–1893), and Harriet. Another son, Robert *Harrison [*see under* Harrison, George Henry], was a librarian.
                    ROBERT HARRISON, *rev.* D. J. MABBERLEY

Sources E. M. Routh, 'Harrison [*née* Rossiter], Mary P.', *The dictionary of art*, ed. J. Turner (1996) • Wood, *Vic. painters*, 206 • *The Athenaeum* (4 Dec 1875), 758 • d. cert. • *IGI*

Harrison [*née* Kingsley], **Mary St Leger** [*pseud.* Lucas Malet] (1852–1931), novelist, was born at her father's rectory at Eversley, Hampshire, on 4 June 1852, third of the four children of the novelist Charles *Kingsley (1819–1875), and his wife, Frances Eliza (*d.* 1892), daughter of Pascoe Grenfell, of Taplow, Buckinghamshire. Henry Kingsley (1830–1876) was her uncle. After being educated at home and taken on several extensive trips on the continent, in America, and in the East, she studied at the Slade School of Fine Art under Edward Poynter. However, she abandoned her artistic career on her marriage in 1876 to the Revd William Harrison (*d.* 1897), a curate of her father's. After a short period spent at Wormleighton, Warwickshire, her husband was appointed to the living of Clovelly in north Devon. Although the two separated amicably shortly after their marriage, it appears that Mary Harrison continued to live at Clovelly.

Mary Harrison's first literary success came with the appearance of her second novel, *Colonel Enderby's Wife* (1885), dealing with the failed marriage of a middle-aged man and his young, heartless wife. It was written, like all her books, under the pseudonym Lucas Malet, a name formed from the surnames of two families related to the Kingsleys, and chosen because she did not want to profit from her family's literary fame. In 1891 she published *The Wages of Sin*, a novel dealing partly with artistic circles in London, partly with the fishing people of her own home at Clovelly. The book was stigmatized by many critics as being both daring and unpleasant, as it displayed the consequences of a cross-class pre-marital relationship. *The History of Sir Richard Calmady* (1901) provoked an even louder storm of criticism, partly owing to the book's treatment of deformity, and partly because it deals with the emotional contacts that three women have with the same man. Such work excited the admiration of Henry James and the critic W. L. Courtney, who became two of Mary Harrison's closest friends.

In 1897 William Harrison died, and in 1902 Mary Harrison was received into the Roman Catholic church. She revised her earlier writings to conform to her new sense of religious faith, published a religious novel, *The Far Horizon* (1906), and also purchased a house in her father's old parish of Eversley. There, she said, she 'developed the characters, disentangled the plot, and completed the story' of her father's unfinished manuscript, *The Tutor's Story*, written just before *The Water Babies*, and published in 1916. Her post-conversion fiction continued to shock, however, a case in point being *Adrian Savage* (1911), which a *Times Literary Supplement* reviewer called 'ugly and brutal'. It dealt with a romantic triangle of a widow, her daughter, and a young poet, and ended with the daughter's suicide.

Mary Harrison spent much of her time travelling abroad with her cousin and adopted daughter, Gabrielle Vallings, and felt especially at home in France, where she had many friends among the artists of the day. She was a handsome woman and an excellent conversationalist; her knowledge of French literature was extensive and she had a particular admiration for Flaubert. She lived in London throughout the First World War, but in 1924 she moved to Montreux, where she made one of a literary circle that included such luminaries as Romain Rolland, Robert Smythe Hitchens, Cyril McNeile (Sapper), and Louis N. Parker. It was at this time that her most successful novels were published, *The Survivors* (1923) and *The Dogs of Want* (1924), both of which won immense commercial success, as did her earlier collection, *Da Silva's Widow and other Stories* (1922).

Mary Harrison spent part of each year in England, and it was during one of these visits that she was taken ill, dying some eighteen months later at a friend's house, 18 The Norton, Tenby, Pembrokeshire, on 27 October 1931. The previous year she had been awarded a civil-list pension in recognition of her literary work.

GEORGINA BATTISCOMBE, rev. KATHARINE CHUBBUCK

Sources S. J. Kunitz and H. Haycraft, eds., *Twentieth century authors: a biographical dictionary of modern literature* (1942) · *The Times* (29 Oct 1931) · B. Colloms, *Charles Kingsley: the lion of Eversley* (1975) · S. Chitty, *The beast and the monk: a life of Charles Kingsley* (1974) · J. Sutherland, *The Longman companion to Victorian fiction* (1988) · P. Schlueter and J. Schlueter, eds., *An encyclopedia of British women writers* (1988)
Likenesses S. A. Lindsey, two miniatures; formerly, priv. coll. · photograph, repro. in Kunitz and Haycraft, eds., *Twentieth century authors*
Wealth at death £150: probate, 12 Nov 1932, *CGPLA Eng. & Wales*

Harrison, Peter (1716–1775), merchant and architect, was born on 14 June 1716 in or near York, the last of four children of Thomas Harrison (1670–1737), a Quaker, and his wife, Elizabeth Dennyson (1683–1753), of York. Although no record has been found of formal architectural training, Harrison appears to have studied informally with the York architect and builder William Etty (1675–1734) and his son John (1705–1738). At the age of twenty Harrison understood that architecture was not a lucrative profession, so he attached himself to his elder brother, Joseph (1709–1789), a merchant sea captain.

In most of the ports he visited, whether as Joseph's assistant or as a captain in his own right, Harrison offered to design buildings in the neo-Palladian style and, as a result, designs attributable to him appeared in Gibraltar, Barbados, Georgia, South Carolina, North Carolina, Virginia, Maryland, Pennsylvania, Rhode Island, Massachusetts, and Cape Breton Island, before he was arrested at sea by the French privateer Pierre Morpain in 1744, and taken as a prisoner of war to Louisbourg on Cape Breton Island. Thanks to his earlier work there, Harrison was not incarcerated but became the guest of the architect Colonel Étienne Verrier, and he secretly copied Verrier's plans of the Louisbourg fortress. Released on a prisoner exchange late in 1744, he smuggled the plans to Massachusetts governor William Shirley, who used them to persuade his legislature to permit him to attack and capture Louisbourg in 1745. Shirley apparently felt the capture of Louisbourg forestalled the French from invading British America, and provided a bargaining counter at the 1748 Anglo-

French peace conference in which the fort was traded for the large portion of British-controlled India captured by the French.

Shirley urged British colonies around the world to show gratitude for Harrison's part in saving them from the French by engaging him to design any important buildings required, and Harrison was deluged with commissions. About 1745 he became a member of the Church of England, and married on 6 June 1746 the wealthy but pregnant Elizabeth Pelham (1721–1784) of Newport, Rhode Island, kinswoman of Shirley's wife and of Henry Pelham, the prime minister. Harrison therefore no longer needed to follow the sea or charge money for the architecture he loved to design. He and his wife lived at Leamington Farm, Newport, where they had four children, only one of whom, Elizabeth Ludlow (1759–1790), had descendants. In 1766 Harrison moved to New Haven, Connecticut, where he was appointed customs collector, but the mild-mannered architect, loyal to the crown, soon fell foul of the local American patriots. He died of apoplexy on 30 April 1775 when a mob intended to lynch him after hearing of the opening of British–American armed hostilities at the battle of Concord. Shortly afterwards the mob, led by Isaac Sears, burnt all Harrison's papers at his house. Consequently firm documentation for his career is rare. He was buried on 10 May at Trinity Church, New Haven, but his stone has been lost.

Only nineteen Harrison designs can be documented, including the steeple of Christ Church, Philadelphia; King's Chapel, Boston; Christ Church, Cambridge, Massachusetts; Redwood Library, Brick Market, Touro Synagogue, and St John's Masonic Hall, Newport; St Paul's Chapel, New York city; Trinity Church, Brooklyn, Connecticut; and Dartmouth College, New Hampshire. Also attributable to Harrison on circumstantial grounds are over 200 buildings in England, Ireland, Gibraltar, India, China, and America from Newfoundland and Hudson Bay to Tobago, including All Saints' Church, Gainsborough, Lincolnshire (his first design); Drayton Hall, South Carolina; British America's first domes, many statehouses, governors' mansions, markets, churches, synagogues, and private houses. Many were built posthumously. Harrison was influenced by Gibbs, Burlington, and his own extensive library of pattern books, but his architecture was fresh and far ahead of his contemporaries in the colonies. He also appears to have designed furniture, including John Goddard's 'French-style' pieces.

JOHN FITZHUGH MILLAR

Sources C. Bridenbaugh, *Peter Harrison, first American architect* (Chapel Hill, NC, 1949) · C. Bridenbaugh, 'Peter Harrison, addendum', *Journal of the Society of Architectural Historians*, 18 (1959), 158–9 · M. B. Woods, 'Harrison, Peter', *ANB*
Archives priv. coll., family papers
Likenesses N. Smibert, oils, c.1750, priv. coll.; copy, Redwood Library, Newport, Rhode Island
Wealth at death see inventory, 28 June 1775, Hartford, Connecticut State Library, town of New Haven, 1775, no. 4710

Harrison, Ralph (1748–1810), Presbyterian minister and tutor, was born on 30 August 1748 at the minister's house in Buxton, Derbyshire, the eighth of ten children of William Harrison (1708–1783), nonconformist minister successively at Stand, Buxton, and Chinley, and his wife, Ann Cooper (1710–1782), daughter of John Cooper, minister of Hyde Chapel. After schooling in Buxton, Chinley, and Chapel-en-le-Frith, he entered Warrington Academy on 6 October 1763 to train for the ministry with a grant from the Presbyterian Fund. His tutors included John Aikin and Joseph Priestley. He preached for the first time at Allostock on 27 September 1767, before supplying the congregation at Hale for two years. In August 1769 he accepted an invitation to become Joseph Fownes's assistant at Shrewsbury. In November 1771 he was chosen as co-pastor with Robert Gore of Cross Street Chapel, Manchester, following the death of Joseph Mottershed, at a stipend of 100 guineas p.a. On Gore's death in 1779 Thomas Barnes became Harrison's colleague. Their friendship had begun at Warrington while students and continued uninterrupted until Barnes's death over thirty years later.

In 1774 Harrison opened a private grammar school in Manchester, which enjoyed considerable success and was patronized by the marquess of Waterford among others. His pupils included the chemist Dr William Henry. Dr Thomas Percival, a Manchester physician who was a fellow pupil of Harrison's at Warrington, considered Harrison as 'peculiarly gifted with a knowledge of the juvenile character; … and more than ordinarily skilful in exercising and varying the direction of the mental powers' (Harrison, iii). His abilities as a classics scholar were praised by the Revd Gilbert Wakefield. On 6 March 1775 at Manchester collegiate church he married Ann Touchet (1747–1797), daughter of John Touchet, with whom he had several children. He gave up his school when appointed the first tutor in classics and *belles-lettres* at the Manchester Academy in 1786, but resigned his tutorship in September 1789 after only three years for health reasons. According to Joseph Hunter, he was much involved in business. Harrison's own diary discloses that in 1788 he was regularly visiting his quarry at Heyrod, Derbyshire. Unlike his colleague Thomas Barnes, he appears to have played only a small part in late eighteenth-century reform. Following his wife's death in 1797, Harrison married Rebecca Hinde (d. 1835) on 18 February 1806 at St Mary's, Lancaster.

Harrison published his *Institutes of English Grammar* (1777; 2nd edn, 1816) for the use of children, which found considerable popularity in America as *Rudiments of English Grammar* (1787; 11th edn, 1812), with a new edition by John Comly as late as 1815; a book of geographical exercises (the first to have a blank atlas without references); and a series of geographical cards. A skilful musician, he published *Sacred Melodies* (1786), a collection of ancient and modern psalm tunes, which was generally adopted by dissenters and found favour even with the established church. He composed several hymn tunes, of which 'Warrington' remains popular. His remaining works were a sermon upon the establishment of the Manchester Academy and a biographical tribute to John Seddon, one of his predecessors at Cross Street. Harrison is said to have been less orthodox in doctrine than Barnes, who was an

Arian, but his sermons were 'plain, serious and practical', avoiding controversy. His delivery 'though not highly animated' was serious and impressive, but at least one of his hearers found his voice in later years 'so low that he could not be heard distinctly' (BL, Add. MS 24867, fol. 247*v*). Harrison died of dropsy in Manchester on 24 November 1810 after a long illness, and was buried in the Cross Street Chapel, Manchester. His son William (*d.* 1859), who was minister at Blackley, Lancashire, published a memoir of his father, together with his sermons, in 1813.

DAVID L. WYKES

Sources family correspondence, including part of Harrison's diary (Sept 1787–Nov 1788), JRL, Unitarian College collection, B1³⁰, 7ff. • W. Harrison, 'A biographical memoir of the author', in R. Harrison, *Sermons on various important subjects* (1813) • E. Axon, 'Harrison Ainsworth's maternal ancestors', *Transactions of the Lancashire and Cheshire Antiquarian Society*, 29 (1911), 103–53, esp. 141–2 • 'Cross Street Chapel, Manchester', Harris Man. Oxf., Aspland MS, 30 • *GM*, 1st ser., 80 (1810), 592–3 • *Monthly Repository*, 5 (1810), 592–3, 601–2 • collections on ministers and churches, DWL, Walter Wilson MS A. 11, fols. 33–8 [drawn largely from *Sermons on various important subjects*] • H. McLachlan, *English education under the Test Acts: being the history of the nonconformist academies, 1662–1820* (1931), 217, 224, 256–7 • T. Baker, *Memorials of a dissenting chapel* (1884) [incl. bibliography] • B. Smith, ed., *Truth, liberty, religion: essays celebrating two hundred years of Manchester College* (1986) • G. E. Evans, *Record of the provincial assembly of Lancashire and Cheshire* (1896), 114 • minutes of proceedings of the committee of the Manchester Academy, 1786–1810, Harris Man. Oxf., MSS M.N.C. Misc. 65, fols. 1–2, 11, 30–31 • 'Britannia Puritanica, or outlines of the history of the various congregations of Presbyterians and Independents which arose out of the schism in the Church of England of 1662', BL, Add. MS 24484, fol. 116*r* • J. Darbishire jun. to J. Hunter, 8 April 1811, BL, Add. MS 24867, fol. 247*v* • *DNB* • parish register, Chinley Chapel, Derbyshire, 3 Sept 1759 • will, proved 4 June 1813, Chester

Archives JRL, Unitarian College collection, B1³⁰

Likenesses miniature (at the time of his marriage), Man. CL • silhouette, repro. in Baker, *Memorials*

Wealth at death under £3500: will, proved at Chester, 4 June 1813

Harrison, Reginald (1837–1908), surgeon, was born on 24 August 1837 at Hodnet rectory, near Market Drayton, Shropshire, the eldest son of Thomas Harrison, vicar of Christ Church, Stafford, and his wife, Mary *née* Lloyd. He was educated at Rossall School, and after a short period of probation at the Stafford General Hospital, he entered St Bartholomew's Hospital, London. He was admitted MRCS on 15 April 1859. Also in 1864 he obtained the licence of the Society of Apothecaries. He was then appointed house surgeon at the Northern Hospital, Liverpool, and shortly afterwards he moved to the Royal Infirmary, Liverpool, as senior house surgeon (1860–62), a post which carried with it the duty of attending the city lunatic asylum. He was surgeon to the Cyfarthfa ironworks at Merthyr Tudful (1862–4).

Returning to Liverpool in 1864 Harrison became assistant to E. R. Bickersteth; he practised as a surgeon, first at 18 Maryland Street, and in 1868 in Rodney Street. Also in 1864 he married Jane, only daughter of James Baron of Liverpool. They had one son and two daughters. In 1864 Harrison was appointed both surgeon to the Liverpool Blue

Coat school and demonstrator of anatomy at the Royal Infirmary school of medicine. He became lecturer on descriptive and surgical anatomy in the school in 1865, and in 1872 he became lecturer on the principles and practice of surgery. On 13 December 1866 he was admitted FRCS. He was surgeon to the Northern Hospital at Liverpool (1867–8); quarantine officer to the port of Liverpool; assistant surgeon to the Royal Infirmary (1867–74); and full surgeon at the infirmary from 1874 until he moved to London in 1889. In October 1889 he was elected surgeon to St Peter's Hospital for stone and other urinary diseases, Henrietta Street, London, following the resignation of Walter Coulson.

At the Royal College of Surgeons, Harrison was a member of the council (1886–1902) and vice-president (1894–5). He was Hunterian professor of surgery and pathology (1890–91) when he delivered a course of lectures on urological diseases. In 1896 he was Bradshaw lecturer, taking as his subject vesical stone and prostatic disorders. In 1903 he visited Egypt officially, on behalf of the college, to inspect the school of medicine at Cairo. He was president of the Medical Society of London in 1890, having delivered the Lettsomian lectures there in 1888, on the surgery of the urinary organs. Harrison retired from active professional work in April 1905, when he resigned his post at St Peter's Hospital.

Harrison helped to make the Royal Infirmary school of medicine at Liverpool into a well-equipped medical faculty of the University of Liverpool. In 1869 the private school of the infirmary became a joint-stock company; money was raised and new laboratories were built. Harrison as secretary-manager sought to supply each lectureship as it fell vacant with a young and energetic doctor who was not distracted by the demands of private practice. The school, thus improved, became University College, Liverpool, which existed as a separate body from 1882 to 1903, when it was merged with the university.

Harrison also helped to establish the street ambulance system (already current in America) which made Liverpool remarkable among British cities. He was active in promoting the Street Ambulance Association which aimed to develop the system throughout England. He published work on the practice of surgery, urology, and the ambulance service. Harrison died on 28 February 1908 at his home, 6 Lower Berkeley Street, Portman Square, London, and was buried at Highgate cemetery.

D'A. POWER, rev. B. A. BRYAN

Sources The Lancet (14 March 1908), 822–3 · BMJ (7 March 1908), 601–3 · Liverpool Medico-Chirurgical Journal (July 1908), 251 · WWW · b. cert. · d. cert.
Likenesses portrait, repro. in BMJ
Wealth at death £18,642 6s. 9d.: probate, 25 March 1908, CGPLA Eng. & Wales

Harrison, Sir Reginald Carey [Rex] (1908–1990), actor, was born on 5 March 1908 in Huyton, Lancashire, the youngest of three children and only son of William Reginald Harrison, stockbroker, and his wife, Edith Mary

Sir Reginald Carey [Rex] **Harrison** (1908–1990), by Anthony Buckley, 1950 [in *The Cocktail Party* by T. S. Eliot]

Carey. At the age of ten he adopted the name Rex, by which he was known for the rest of his life. He was a sickly child and a bout of measles left him with poor sight in his left eye. He was educated at Birkdale preparatory school and Liverpool College. His appearances in school plays, and regular visits to the Liverpool Playhouse, confirmed an early desire to be an actor. At sixteen he was taken on at the playhouse and after a year backstage made his acting début in 1924 in *Thirty Minutes in a Street*. After two and a half years playing small roles, he left Liverpool for London, where in 1927 he landed a part in a touring production of *Charley's Aunt*. Thus began six years of touring and repertory, in which he learned his craft. It was a five-month run as a caddish explorer in *Heroes Don't Care* in 1936 that provided his breakthrough. The critic of *Theatre World* proclaimed him 'one of the best light comedians on the English stage' and he maintained this position until his death.

On the basis of *Heroes Don't Care*, the producer Alexander Korda signed a contract with Harrison at London Films, and he was launched on a cinematic career, which he was to continue henceforth in tandem with his stage career. He achieved an early success in the delightful comedy *Storm in a Teacup* (1936), where as a crusading reporter he was taught by the director Victor Saville how to relax in front of the camera. He consolidated his theatrical reputation with long runs in *French without Tears* (1936), *Design for Living* (1939), and *No Time for Comedy* (1941). From 1942 to 1944 he served in the Royal Air Force volunteer reserve as a flying-control liaison officer. Emerging from the forces, he established himself as a major British film star in the screen version of *Blithe Spirit* (1945) and in *The Rake's Progress* (1945), in which he was excellent as a charming, feckless, parasitic playboy, who expiates a worthless life with a heroic death on the battlefield.

Hollywood inevitably beckoned and Harrison signed a seven-year contract with Twentieth Century Fox. They saw him not as a light comedian but as a character actor. The vehicles they provided for him, if not always to his taste, were invariably superbly mounted and stretched him as an actor. In *Anna and the King of Siam* (1946), Harrison was both comic and touching as the capricious but dedicated King Mongkut. In *The Ghost and Mrs Muir* (1947), playing the spirit of an old sea dog, he took to being blasphemous and bad-tempered with evident glee. In *Unfaithfully Yours* (1948) he played an autocratic and egocentric orchestral conductor with a memorable line in vituperation. But his continuing unhappiness in Hollywood, his unflattering comments on the film capital, poor box-office returns on his later Fox films, and an unsavoury scandal surrounding the suicide of actress Carole Landis, with whom he was having an affair, led Harrison and Fox to terminate the contract by mutual consent. He returned to Broadway to play Henry VIII in Maxwell Anderson's *Anne of the Thousand Days* (1948) at the Shubert Theatre, New York, and promptly won a Tony award as best actor. Then in London and on Broadway he did John Van Druten's play *Bell, Book and Candle* (1950) and directed and starred in Peter Ustinov's play *The Love of Four Colonels* (1953). He won the 1961 Evening Standard best actor award for his performance in Anton Chekhov's *Platonov* at the Royal Court Theatre in 1960.

Harrison resolutely avoided Shakespeare, but became the supreme interpreter of the plays of Bernard Shaw, bringing the necessary quality of civilized intelligence to his performances both on stage (*Heartbreak House*, 1983; *The Devil's Disciple*, 1977) and film (*Major Barbara*, 1940–41). He will for ever be associated with the role of Professor Henry Higgins in *My Fair Lady*, the Lerner and Loewe musical based on Shaw's *Pygmalion*. Harrison played the part for three years on stage in New York and London (1956–9), winning a second Tony award, and an Oscar for his performance in the film version (1964). So much did he make the part his own that he later said: 'For years I could never bear to see anyone else do it—Higgins has become so much a part of me and I, of him.'

Harrison's success in *My Fair Lady* made him a major international star and led to appearances in several screen epics in the 1960s. There was more than a touch of Shaw's Julius Caesar in his drily witty and very human performance as the Roman conqueror in *Cleopatra* (1963). When Caesar expired half-way through, so did the film. The ponderous film about Michelangelo, *The Agony and the Ecstasy* (1965), was almost redeemed by Harrison's engaging interpretation of Pope Julius II as an urbane schemer.

In the late 1960s there was a string of expensive flops— *The Honey Pot* (1965), *Doctor Doolittle* (1966), *A Flea in her Ear* (1967)—and in the 1970s and 1980s Harrison's film appearances were mainly cameos, though he played Don Quixote in a notable 1973 BBC television production. He concentrated his energies on the stage, displaying his gifts in London and New York in a series of Edwardian revivals: *Heartbreak House* (1983), *Aren't we All?* (1984–5), *The Admirable Crichton* (1988), and *The Circle* (1989). He was appearing in *The Circle* when his final illness was diagnosed. Harrison was married six times, and allegedly mistreated all his wives. His first wife (1934) was the fashion model Collette Thomas (her real name was Marjorie). They had one son, the actor and singer Noel Harrison (b. 1935), and were divorced in 1943. His second wife was the émigré German Jewish actress Lilli Palmer (1914–1986) (whose real name was Lilli Peiser), whom he married on 25 January 1943. They had one son, the playwright Carey Harrison (b. 1944), and were divorced in 1957. His third wife (23 June 1957) was the English actress Kay *Kendall (1927–1959), who died of leukaemia at the age of thirty-two. Their relationship was the basis of the play *After Lydia*, by Sir Terence Rattigan, in which Harrison starred on Broadway in 1974, playing the role based on himself. He married his fourth wife on 21 March 1962, the Welsh actress Rachel *Roberts (1927–1980), daughter of the Revd Richard Rhys Roberts. They divorced in 1971 and she committed suicide in 1980. His fifth wife (26 August 1971) was Mrs (Joan) Elizabeth Rees Harris (b. 1936), daughter of David Rees Rees-Williams, first Baron Ogmore, and ex-wife of actor Richard Harris. They divorced in 1976. He married finally on 17 December 1978 an American, Mercia Tinker. Harrison wrote two volumes of autobiography and three of his wives left their impressions of him in their autobiographies.

Harrison was a man of enormous charm and this often compensated for the personal and professional self-centredness and perfectionism that sometimes tried the patience of colleagues and associates. He was perhaps the last Edwardian, compeer of Sir Gerald Du Maurier, Sir Charles Hawtrey, and Sir (E.) Seymour Hicks, actors who contrived to give the impression that they had just popped into the theatre for a spot of acting on the way to the club. Harrison had admired and closely studied the style and technique of the great Edwardians and had come to embody the same combination of elegance, authority, wit, and grace. He was appointed commendatore of Italy's order of merit in 1967, awarded an honorary degree by the University of Boston in 1973, and knighted in 1989. He died of cancer of the pancreas in New York on 2 June 1990. He was cremated and his ashes were scattered over the sea near Portofino, Italy, where he had owned a villa from 1949 to 1976.   JEFFREY RICHARDS, rev.

Sources R. Harrison, *Rex* (1974) · R. Harrison, *A damned serious business* (1990) · A. Eyles, *Rex Harrison* (1985) · N. Wapshott, *Rex Harrison* (1991) · A. Walker, *Fatal charm* (1992) · L. Palmer, *Change lobsters and dance* (1976) · R. Roberts and A. Walker, *No bells on Sunday* (1984) · E. R. Harris, *Love, honour and dismay* (1976) · P. Garland, *The incomparable Rex* (1998) · H. Vickers, *The Independent* (4 June 1990)

Likenesses Baron, photograph, c.1950, Hult. Arch. · A. Buckley, photograph, 1950, NPG [*see illus.*]

Harrison, Sir **Richard John** (1920–1999), anatomist and marine biologist, was born on 8 October 1920 at 30 Carson Road, Norwood, London, the son of Geoffrey Arthur Harrison, reader in chemical pathology at London University (St Bartholomew's), and Theodora Beatrice Mary, née West. From Oundle School he entered Gonville and Caius College, Cambridge, in 1939, as a major scholar, to read natural sciences (medicine). In 1941 he took part one of the tripos and was placed in the second class. Under wartime emergency regulations this was a sufficient qualification for the BA degree, and he proceeded immediately to London as a clinical student at St Bartholomew's Hospital (Bart's) medical school.

At Bart's Harrison met and, while still a clinical student, married on 22 December 1943 Joanna Gillies (b. 1917/18), a daughter of the eminent pioneer plastic surgeon Sir Harold Delf *Gillies, and a civil servant. They had two sons and a daughter. He qualified medically as LRCP (London) and MRCS (England) in 1944, and graduated MB BChir (Cambridge) soon afterwards. There was a brief spell as a house surgeon at Bart's, but he soon became demonstrator in anatomy there, under Professor W. J. Hamilton.

In 1946 Harrison moved to a lectureship in anatomy at Glasgow (where Hamilton had become regius professor), and there received the degree of DSc in 1948. In 1950 he followed Hamilton to Charing Cross Hospital medical school, where he held a readership and gained the Anatomical Society's Symington prize for research. In 1951, still not quite thirty-one, he became head of the department of anatomy at the London Hospital medical college, for three years as reader and then as professor. He continued at the London until, on J. D. Boyd's death in 1968, he was elected to the chair of anatomy at Cambridge, and a fellowship of Downing College, where he stayed until retirement in 1982.

Harrison was a lively teacher, unconventional and entertaining, and he was a good examiner. Sometimes his deep knowledge of human anatomy was called on to help in solving a colleague's forensic problems. At one stage he and Gillies were concerned in the anatomical minutiae of sex-change surgery. He made useful contributions to human anatomy and embryology. His distinction was recognized by his appointment as president of the Anatomical Society of Great Britain and Ireland (1978–9), president of the twelfth International Congress of Anatomists (London, 1983), and president of the International Federation of Associations of Anatomists (1985–7), and by honorary membership of the American Association of Anatomists and of the Societa Italiana Anatomica. He was elected FRS in 1973, became an honorary fellow of Downing College in 1982, and was knighted in 1984.

In parallel with this successful conventional career in human anatomy went a much wider-ranging, more adventurous one, that had started in boyhood with an enthusiasm for natural history. It led to Harrison's distinguished researches in comparative mammalian reproduction (the field of his work for the MD, 1954) and, especially, in the biology of marine mammals. He was appointed Fullerian professor of physiology at the Royal Institution

(1961–7), Wooldridge lecturer of the British Veterinary Association (1983), chairman of the Farm Animal Welfare Advisory Committee of the Ministry of Agriculture, Fisheries and Food (1974–9), member of the Farm Animal Welfare Council (1979–88), president of the European Association for Aquatic Mammals (1974–6), a trustee of the British Museum (natural history) (1978–88) and chairman (1984–8), and a member of the council of the Zoological Society (1974–8 and 1980–83). There were important publications on the biology of marine mammals, and he was invited to Wuhan, China, to advise on the plight of the beiji (Yangtze (Yangzi) river dolphin), one of the most endangered mammals in the world.

Heir to an ancient tradition in which nearly all human anatomists were medically qualified—and had been required, meticulously, to dissect the whole human body in fine detail—Harrison was proud to call himself 'a fundamental olecranologist—somebody who does indeed know his arse from his elbow'. This was no pub pleasantry but a serious reaffirmation that a knowledge of gross anatomy is important for the proper understanding of function. In Britain for the first half of the twentieth century there had been a disastrous decline in respect for topographical anatomy, partly because such powerful figures as Daniel John Cunningham, Sir William Turner, and Sir Alexander Macalister, men of immense learning and attention to detail, had concentrated too narrowly on formal descriptive anatomy to the relative exclusion of functional concerns and wider biological problems. Harrison's command of comparative gross anatomy, central to his researches in aquatic mammalogy, attracted the respect of his colleagues internationally.

His marriage to Joanna Gillies having ended in divorce, Harrison married on 30 March 1967 Barbara Jean Fuller (1930/31–1988), an editorial assistant. On 3 March 1990 he married Gianetta Phyllis Drake, née Lloyd (b. 1921/2), a widow whom he had known for half a century; she survived him, with the three children of his first marriage. Michael M. Bryden wrote, in *The Times* obituary (3 November 1999):

> Outwardly reserved, Richard Harrison had a lively wit and enjoyed the company of friends. Many a research idea was hatched and collaboration developed over a drink in the pubs of London and Cambridge. He enjoyed a whisky and a cigar, but nothing so much as a robust argument about biological principles, animal welfare, the British Open golf championship or the fight for the Ashes.

It is also believed that Harrison helped his friend and near contemporary the author Richard Gordon (Dr Ostlere) in collecting and devising jokes for *Doctor in the House*. He died on 17 October 1999 at his home, 58a High Street, Barkway, Hertfordshire.   GORDON WRIGHT

Sources *The Times* (3 Nov 1999) · *WWW* · private information (2004) [Dennis Austin McBrearty] · personal knowledge (2004) · b. cert. · m. certs. · d. cert. · *CGPLA Eng. & Wales* (2000)

Wealth at death £800,537—gross; £796,960—net: probate, 18 May 2000, *CGPLA Eng. & Wales*

Harrison, Robert (d. c.1585), Brownist and writer, is of unknown origins. Nothing is known of his life before he matriculated as a pensioner of St John's College, Cambridge, on 4 October 1564; he later moved to Corpus Christi College and, having graduated BA in 1567, proceeded MA in 1572. In July 1573 he applied for the post of master of the grammar school of Aylsham, Norfolk, being recommended to Bishop Parkhurst by the mayor and certain of the aldermen of Norwich. The recommendation endeavoured to excuse Harrison for having raised an objection to the use of the prayer-book service at his marriage, which took place at Aylsham, Norfolk, in 1573. The bishop at first refused to appoint him, alleging that he was young, that he had recently suffered 'with a frenzy' (Strype, 2.335), and that his offence in the matter of his marriage had been committed in spite of the warning of the vicar, Lancelot Thexton, and the schoolmaster, Greenwood. The bishop finally gave way, in response to an appeal from the chief inhabitants of Aylsham, but within a month of his appointment Harrison requested that changes might be made in the baptismal service on the occasion of his being godfather to an infant, and he was in consequence removed by the bishop in January 1574.

Harrison afterwards went to Cambridge with a view to taking orders. He was dissuaded by Robert *Browne, whom he had known previously. Subsequently he became master of a hospital in Norwich, probably that of St Giles, or the Old Men's Hospital, which had some connection with Aylsham. Browne visited him at Norwich, and lodged and boarded with him and his wife. In *A True and Short Declaration, &c.* Browne gives an elaborate account of the origin and growth of his friendship with Harrison, whom he puts first in the list of his helpers and disciples. In 1580 both men signed a 'Supplication of Norwich men to the queen's majesty', urging her to institute a 'holie Eldership' in her church and remove nonpreaching ministers (Peel, *Seconde Parte*, 1.157–60). Later, according to Browne's narrative, Harrison somewhat reluctantly came completely over to his views, and the two spent all their energies in preaching and collecting a gathered and covenanted congregation at Norwich. In April 1581 Bishop Freake of Norwich, as part of an energetic campaign against nonconformity in East Anglia, sent formal articles of complaint against Browne and Harrison to Burghley, and the whole congregation decided to migrate to Middelburg in Zeeland in the spring or summer of 1582. Harrison, according to his own account (in the preface to his *Little Treatise* of 1583), suffered persecution and imprisonment before leaving England.

Prior to his departure Harrison wrote a censorious letter to Edward Fenton, rector of Booton, Norfolk, sternly rebuking him for his failure to separate from the established church and defending Thomas Wolsey, another separatist leader. This letter forms the second portion of a two-part manuscript titled 'A treatise of the church and the kingdome of Christ'. The entire manuscript was published, with the rest of Harrison's writings, by Peel and Carlson in 1953. Harrison may have written the first part of the manuscript as well, but the question of its authorship is unclear, for Henry Barrow may also have penned it. Its text closely parallels 'Profes of aparant churche', which

Carlson included in his edition of the works of Henry Barrow, published in 1962. If Harrison was indeed the author of this portion of the manuscript, it would constitute his most significant work. It considers the characteristics of the true church versus the false church, the question of true preachers, the proper form of church government, and the kind of communicants who should participate in the sacraments.

At Middelburg the refugees endured illness and poverty, but enjoyed freedom of worship. They also wrote tracts explaining their views, which were shipped over to England and distributed in large quantities. Two men were hanged in 1583 for distributing them, and a royal proclamation was issued against them in June of that year (misnaming Harrison as Richard). Harrison wrote two of the books: *A Little Treatise uppon the Firste Verse of the 122nd Psalm* (1583, reprinted at Leiden, 1618), which states in its preface that the book is a fragment of a more elaborate work on church government, which illness and the cost of printing have prevented Harrison from completing; and *Three Formes of Catechismes, Conteyning the most Principal Pointes of Religion* (1583). The cost of printing these Brownist tracts was apparently borne largely by Harrison.

Grave internal dissensions soon arose among the members of the Middelburg congregation, and factions formed. Harrison and Browne quarrelled, and the latter sailed for Scotland with a few followers late in 1583. Harrison was now the head of the congregation, and made an unsuccessful effort to join it to the church of English merchants presided over by Thomas Cartwright and Dudley Fenner. He apparently addressed a formal letter to Cartwright, who in his reply spoke in high terms of Harrison, but no union of the two groups occurred. Browne replied to Cartwright in a tract titled *An Answere to Master Cartwright* (n.d. [1585?]). Harrison died about 1585 at Middelburg. He and his wife had children, for Browne mentions that least some of them had died there during the congregation's dissensions. Harrison remains a shadowy figure. His early death left open the possibility that he, like Browne, might have eventually returned to the established church. However, it is also possible that, had he lived, he might have emerged as a better-known separatist leader.   RONALD BAYNE, *rev.* MICHAEL E. MOODY

Sources A. Peel and L. Carlson, eds., *The writings of Robert Harrison and Robert Browne* (1953), 1–15, 396–429 · A. Peel, *The Brownists in Norwich and Norfolk about 1580* (1920) · *The writings of Henry Barrow, 1587–1590*, ed. L. H. Carlson (1962), 68–70 · S. Ofwod, *Advertisement* [1632], 40 · G. Johnson, *A discourse* (1603), 7 · A. F. S. Pearson, *Thomas Cartwright and Elizabethan puritanism, 1535–1603* (1925), 215–23 · A. Peel, ed., *The seconde parte of a register*, 1 (1915), 157–60 · H. Dexter, *Congregationalism of the past 300 years, as seen in its literature* (1880), 61–128 · D. MacCulloch, *Suffolk and the Tudors: politics and religion in an English county, 1500–1600* (1986) · J. Strype, *The life and acts of Matthew Parker*, new edn, 3 vols. (1821), vol. 2, p. 335

Harrison, Robert (1714/15–1802), natural philosopher and linguist, son of Robert Harrison, was born in Durham, where he was baptized on 1 March 1715 at St Nicholas's Church. He was a king's scholar at Durham School, practised law in Yarm, and married Anne Hett (1716/17–1799) of

Darlington. He was gifted with a very remarkable memory. In 1751 he abandoned his legal practice and moved to Newcastle upon Tyne, where he taught classical and oriental languages, mathematics, and science in a local school. In 1752, the year the Gregorian calendar was introduced in Britain, he published a popular guide to it. In 1754 he commenced lecturing on elementary mathematics and physics for the lecture courses established in Newcastle by the printer Isaac Thompson. In 1757 he published jointly with Thompson *A Short Account of a Course on Natural and Experimental Philosophy*.

In 1757 Harrison was appointed master of the navigation school of Trinity House in Newcastle. His salary was £20, with the perquisite of preparing private pupils for careers such as the armed forces or the legal profession. His reputation attracted many wealthy pupils, among them the two sons of William Scott, who later became lords Stowell and Eldon. His distinguished appearance and attire earned him the nickname Beau, and his lectures the alternative Philosopher Harrison.

Harrison became a member of Newcastle Literary and Philosophical Society. In 1767 he resigned his post at Trinity House, and until 1778 taught at a private school in Newcastle, where he gave advanced legal training. His tutoring success enabled him to retire to Durham in 1778. There he spent much time in literary pursuits, interacting with many of the literati of the day. Latterly his cultivated eccentricities of dress extended to growing an unfashionable beard, and he was ejected from his club for smoking. From about 1779 to 1796 he was Cosin librarian at Durham Cathedral.

After the death of his wife in 1799 Harrison became almost reclusive. He died aged eighty-seven at Durham on 29 October 1802, and was buried beside his wife at Darlington on 2 November. An obituary notice described him as highly distinguished for his literary acquirements, benevolence, and piety. F. R. STEPHENSON

Sources R. Welford, *Men of mark 'twixt Tyne and Tweed*, 3 vols. (1895) · M. A. Richardson, ed., *The local historian's table book … historical division*, 5 vols. (1841–6), vol. 2, p. 242; vol. 3, p. 21 · R. V. Wallis and P. J. Wallis, eds., *Biobibliography of British mathematics and its applications*, 2 (1986), 395 · D. R. Moir, *The birth and history of Trinity House, Newcastle upon Tyne* (1959), 27 · Trinity House, Newcastle upon Tyne, records · *Newcastle Courant* (6 Nov 1802) · *Newcastle Chronicle* (6 Nov 1802)

Likenesses W. Bell, oils, c.1791, NPG · ink drawing, repro. in Welford, *Men of mark*

Harrison, Robert (1820–1897). *See under* Harrison, George Henry (1816–1846).

Harrison [*née* Winsten], **Ruth** (1920–2000), animal welfare campaigner, was born at 15 Edith Villas, Fulham, London, on 24 June 1920, the second of three children of Stephen Winsten, author, and his wife, Clare, *née* Birnbury, artist. She was educated at Parliament Hill School and Bedford College, London University, where she read English. She was a member of the Society of Friends and worked during the Second World War in the Friends' Ambulance Unit based in Hackney and, subsequently, with displaced persons in Schleswig-Holstein and Bochum in Germany. After

Ruth Harrison (1920–2000), by unknown photographer

returning to Britain she attended the Royal Academy of Dramatic Art, where she was coached by George Bernard Shaw (an advocate of the rights of animals) and was complimented on her production of *An Inspector Calls* by its author, J. B. Priestley. Later she worked for a firm of architects, Harrison and Seel, marrying its senior partner, (Donald) Dex Harrison (1909/10–1987), on 6 August 1954. They had two children, Jonathan (*b*. 1955) and Jane (*b*. 1956).

It was the chance delivery of a leaflet on factory farming put through her door by the Crusade Against All Cruelty to Animals that started Ruth Harrison on her life's work. In 1964 she published her book, *Animal Machines*, in which she attacked the developing practices of industrialized farming, drawing attention to the callous treatment of animals which many in the industry had come to regard merely as mechanisms for the production of profit. Veal calves and pregnant pigs were being kept in crates, usually unable even to turn around. Egg-laying hens were cramped five to a cage, unable to spread a wing. The book's foreword was by Rachel Carson, whose *Silent Spring* (1962) had warned of the dangers to wildlife of the escalating use of chemicals in agriculture. Harrison's work appeared at a time when some in British government circles were becoming anxious for such matters to receive greater public examination. Almost immediately, a technical committee was established by the government under the chairmanship of Professor F. W. R. Brambell, of which Harrison was invited to become a member. The Brambell committee's report was published in 1965 and led in 1968 to the passage of the Agriculture (Miscellaneous Provisions) Act, which provided a framework of regulation for the welfare of animals used in agriculture. In 1966 the British government set up the Farm Animal Welfare Advisory Committee, which was subsequently reorganized and renamed as the Farm Animal Welfare Council. Harrison was invited to serve on both bodies. She constantly drew to the attention of these committees the latest relevant research. She also contributed to the deliberations of the Council of Europe which, in 1976, produced its convention on the protection of animals kept for farming purposes, and she continued to offer effective advice to its standing committee until a few months before her death.

The British animal welfare movement after the 1960s led the way for the rest of the world and Harrison's influence on the treatment of farm animals was considerable and widespread. Although wary of ethical argument in general, and overtly suspicious of the concept of animal rights, Harrison was meticulously careful to ascertain the facts. She did not care for political campaigning of a public nature but availed herself of her 'insider' position.

Harrison was a director or member of many organizations including the council of the Royal Society for the Prevention of Cruelty to Animals (RSPCA), the Conservation Society, the Soil Association, the Animal Defence Society, and the World Society for the Protection of Animals. She also founded and chaired the Farm Animal Care Trust from 1967. Although *Animal Machines* was her only complete book, she published articles and contributed chapters to several books including the seminal *Animals, Men and Morals* (ed. Stanley Godlovitch, Rosalind Godlovitch, and John Harris, 1971). Ruth Harrison was awarded the OBE in 1986 and the RSPCA's Richard Martin award in 2000. For most of her life she lived at 34 Holland Park Road, Kensington, London. After bravely fighting cancer for many years, she died there on 13 June 2000 and was cremated. A memorial meeting, organized by the Farm Animal Care Trust, was attended by representatives from seven countries.

RICHARD D. RYDER

Sources *The Times* (8 July 2000) · *The Guardian* (6 July 2000) · *The Independent* (21 June 2000) · *Animal Welfare Institute Quarterly*, 49/4 (2000) · *International Society for Applied Ethology Newsletter* (winter 2001) · personal knowledge (2004) · private information (2004) · b. cert. · m. cert. · d. cert.
Archives Carleton College, Minnesota
Likenesses photograph, repro. in *The Guardian* · photograph, News International Syndication, London [*see illus.*]
Wealth at death £240,268—gross; £238,024—net: probate, 6 Oct 2000, *CGPLA Eng. & Wales*

Harrison, Samuel (1760–1812), singer, was born on 8 September 1760 at Belper, near Duffield, Derbyshire. His first teacher was one Burton, a bass singer in the Drury Lane oratorio performances. Harrison was trained as a boy at the Chapel Royal, and sang soprano solos at the Ancient Concerts and at the Society of Sacred Music in 1776. He was engaged for the 1778 Three Choirs festival at Gloucester, but his voice broke on the day the festival opened. After George III heard him sing at one of Queen Charlotte's musical parties at Buckingham House, he arranged for Harrison to sing the opening recitative and aria in *Messiah* at the 1784 Handel Commemoration festival in Westminster Abbey. He had made his first appearance at the Three Choirs festival as principal tenor in 1781, at Gloucester. From 1786 until 1808 he sang at each of the Hereford meetings, and from 1801 to 1808 was a principal at Gloucester and Worcester as well. The 1811 festival was managed by Harrison with others.

In London Harrison was a member of the Catch Club, and performed at the Professional Concerts from about

1783, at Saloman's from 1786, and at the Society of Sacred Music from 1785 until 1790 (when Michael Kelly succeeded him). Together with John Ashley, Harrison conducted (and sang in) oratorios at Covent Garden Theatre during Lent 1791. He sang in the Drury Lane oratorios in 1794, and at the Lenten concerts at the King's Theatre in 1795.

Harrison was principal tenor at the Ancient Concerts from 1785 until 1791, when he left to found the Vocal Concerts at Willis's Rooms with Charles Knyvett and James Bartleman, the first of which took place on 11 February 1792. Although ten excellent concerts a year were given, with glees and catches performed by Harrison, the two Knyvetts, and Bartleman, they ceased to be popular after a few seasons, and Harrison returned to the Ancient Concerts in 1794. In 1801 the Vocal Concerts were revived on a much larger scale than before, with an orchestra, and were very successful until newer musical attractions drew the public away. On 8 May 1812 Harrison repeated some of his most popular performances, including Pepusch's *Alexis* and Handel's song 'Gentle airs' at his benefit concert. His voice was pure and sweet, but lacked power. One reviewer compared it to the sound of musical glasses (*Quarterly Musical Magazine and Review*, 1818).

Harrison married, on 6 December 1790, a Miss Cantelo, a soprano. Before her marriage she sang at the Ancient Concerts and at the Three Choirs festivals, and she also performed at the Handel Commemoration of 1784. The couple often appeared together. They had one son and two daughters. Harrison died of internal inflammation on 25 June 1812 at Percy Street, London. He was buried in St Pancras old churchyard, where his tombstone includes extracts from an ode on Harrison composed by the Revd T. Beaumont.

L. M. MIDDLETON, rev. ANNE PIMLOTT BAKER

Sources *New Grove* · D. Lysons and others, *Origin and progress of the meeting of the three choirs of Gloucester, Worcester and Hereford* (1895) · 'Mr Harrison', *Quarterly Musical Magazine and Review*, 1 (1818), 81–5 · 'Memoirs of Harrison and Bartleman', *The Harmonicon*, 8 (1830), 181–2 · J. Crosse, *A sketch of the rise and progress of musical festivals in Great Britain* (1825), 25–6 · Grove, *Dict. mus.*
Likenesses W. Daniell, soft-ground etching, pubd 1814 (after G. Dance), BM, NPG · print, Harvard TC

Harrison, Sarah. *See* Bembridge, Sarah (c.1794–1880).

Harrison, Stephen (*fl.* 1604–1605), joiner and architect, was living at the sign of the Snayle, Lime Street, London, in 1604. In that year he published a slim folio volume of his designs for the seven *Arches of Triumph* erected for James I's passage through London on 15 March 1604, engraved by William Kip. These arches were the stages upon which the tableaux of songs and orations composed for the pageant by the leading dramatists of the day, Ben Jonson, Thomas Dekker, and Thomas Middleton, were performed. They were between 40 and 70 feet tall (according to Harrison's scale), lavishly bedecked with intricate, emblematic ornaments in a Flemish mannerist style, and provided with platforms and niches for the singers, players, and musicians.

According to Dekker's account of *The Magnificent Entertainment* (1604), the triumphal arches were constructed by over 250 artificers

over whom, Stephen Harrison, Joyner was appoynted chiefe; who was the sole inventor of the Architecture, and from whom all directions, for so much as belonged to Carving, Joyning, Molding, and all other works in those five Pageants, of the Citie (Paynting excepted) were set downe [the other two being erected by the Italian and Dutch merchants].
(*Dramatic Works*, 302–3)

Harrison's *Arches of Triumph* is the first set of designs for English civic pageant ever to be published. Though his drawings do not agree in every detail with the written descriptions given by the dramatists, they 'stand', as he intended them to, 'as perpetuall monuments' to the 'great Triumphall Bodies' that were erected at great expense for only one day and then 'disjoynted and taken in sunder' (S. Harrison, *The Arches of Triumph*, 1604, sig. K). The committees in charge of the pageant were ordered by the City on 27 May 1604 to 'consider of the paines and travell taken by Stephen Harrison … in drawing of certaine plottes and moddells of the same pageante and putting them in printe in a booke to bee kept by Mr Chamblen' to the Cittyes use' and to give him reasonable 'consideracion and allowaunce for doing the same' (Robertson and Gordon, xxxiii). The book was reissued without the text *c*.1613 and in 1662 under new imprints, from which Harrison's name was removed.

The only other record of Harrison is as a joiner at Syon House, Isleworth, Middlesex, in 1604–5 (Percy Archives, Alnwick Castle, U.1.13). EILEEN HARRIS

Sources D. M. Bergeron, *English civic pageantry, 1558–1642* (1971), 71–85, 245–6 · A. M. Hind, *Engraving in England in the sixteenth and seventeenth centuries*, 2 (1955), 19–21, 27–9 · E. Harris and N. Savage, *British architectural books and writers, 1556–1785* (1990), 229–31 · *The dramatic works of Thomas Dekker*, ed. F. Bowers, 2 (1955) · D. M. Bergeron, 'Harrison, Jonson and Dekker: the magnificent entertainment for King James (1604)', *Journal of the Warburg and Courtauld Institutes*, 31 (1968), 445–8 · J. Robertson and D. J. Gordon, eds., 'A calendar of dramatic records in the books of the livery companies of London, 1485–1640', *Malone Society Collections*, 3 (1954), xxxiii · J. Peacock, *The stage designs of Inigo Jones: the European context* (1995), 63 · P. Palme, 'Ut architettura poesis', *Figura, Acta Universitatis Uppsaliensis*, new ser., 1 (1959), 105 · G. Parry, *The golden age restored* (1981), chap. 1 · Alnwick Castle, Northumberland, Percy Archives

Harrison, Susannah (1752–1784), poet, probably born at Ipswich, of poor parents, entered domestic service when she was sixteen. Four years later illness permanently invalided her. Although without regular education, she taught herself to write, and developed much poetic power and piety. She reluctantly consented to the publication of the verses which she sang at home while awaiting death and called *Songs in the Night* (after Job 35:10). In the first edition (1780) they are stated to be 'by a young woman under deep afflictions', and were edited by Dr John Conder, a Congregationalist minister. A second edition was issued in 1781, with eleven additional pages. Dr Conder supplied several pages of 'Recommendation', and Susannah added an acrostic to show her name. The fourth edition (Ipswich,

1788) was augmented with twenty-two pages of posthumous verses, and twelve more recounting her resignation and giving admonitions to her friends before she died. She died on 3 August 1784 in Ipswich, and was buried in Tacket Street burial-ground there, with an inscription recording that 'she wrote "Songs in the Night"'.

Susannah Harrison's poems reached a fifteenth edition in 1823. In addition to this, her poems went through six American editions. All that she wrote is characterized by religious enthusiasm. Her versification is smooth, although sometimes defaced by grammatical blunders. The influence of Thomas Ken's hymns is apparent in her earlier pieces, and that of William Cowper and John Newton afterwards. It is evident that she had read John Milton's 'Ode on the Nativity'.

A portrait (a silhouette) of Susannah Harrison forms the frontispiece of the first edition. She also wrote *A Call to Britain*, seemingly a broadside, of which many thousands were sold in a short time.

M. G. WATKINS, *rev.* REBECCA MILLS

Sources J. Fulland, ed., *British women poets, 1600–1800* (1990) · S. Harrison, *Songs in the night*, 4th edn (1788) · J. Todd, ed., *A dictionary of British and American women writers, 1660–1800* (1985) · Blain, Clements & Grundy, *Feminist comp.*, 495 · Watt, *Bibl. Brit.*, 1.470d
Likenesses silhouette, repro. in S. Harrison, *Songs in the night*, 1st edn (1780), frontispiece

Harrison, Thomas (1555–1630), biblical scholar, was born in London, the son of John Harrison. He received his early education at the Merchant Taylors' School, London, which he left in 1572 to study for a BA at Cambridge. A later contemporary attested that while at school 'he was second only to Lancelot Andrewes, later Bishop of Winchester, who … could not have been more intelligent and learned' (Dalechamp, 5). Harrison matriculated as a pensioner, or privately funded student, at Trinity College in Michaelmas term 1573, and was elected to a scholarship two years later. Having received his BA in 1577, he was elected to a fellowship at Trinity in 1579. In 1581 he took his MA and was given leave to undertake further studies toward the degree of BTh, to which he was admitted in 1588. At Trinity he held the offices of senior dean (1593–4) and vicemaster (1611–30). From 1596 to 1630 he was possibly also incumbent of St Andrew's Church, Great Cornard, Suffolk.

Harrison was a distinguished Greek scholar and prominent Hebraist. William Whitaker, the puritan regius professor of divinity and later master of St John's College, Cambridge, noted his talent at an early age, and also spoke of him as a 'proficient poet' (Dalechamp, 6). Harrison was a supporter of puritanism. Archbishop Richard Bancroft, a stern opponent of the puritan cause, attested that Harrison took part in a synod held at St John's College in 1589 at which a number of Cambridge puritans allegedly sought to adopt John Knox's first Book of Discipline (1560) for the reorganization of the Church of England.

Harrison was appointed one of the eight Cambridge translators of the Authorized Version of the Bible and, alongside three successive regius professors of Hebrew of the university, helped translate the two books of Chronicles, Ezra, Nehemiah, Esther, Job, and the Song of Solomon. He died in 1630 and was buried in the chapel of Trinity College, Cambridge.   J. ANDREAS LÖWE

Sources CUL, department of manuscripts and university archives, vice-chancellor's court, MS UA VCC I.52, fol. 187r · C. Dalechamp, *Harrisonus honoratus* (1632) · [R. Bancroft], *Daungerous positions and proceedings* (1593), 3.97 · Mrs E. P. Hart, ed., *Merchant Taylors' School register, 1561–1934*, 2 vols. (1936) [Harrison, Thomas (–1572)] · Venn, *Alum. Cant.*, 1/2.317 · W. W. Rouse Ball and J. A. Venn, eds., *Admissions to Trinity College, Cambridge*, 2 (1913), 97 · O. S. Opfell, *The King James Bible translators* (1982), 49

Harrison, Thomas (*bap.* 1616, *d.* 1660), parliamentarian army officer and regicide, was baptized on 16 July 1616 in Newcastle under Lyme, Staffordshire, the second of four children and the only son of Richard Harrison (*bap.* 1587, *d.* 1653), butcher, burgess, and four times mayor of the town, and his wife, Mary. He was probably educated at a local grammar school, and then became a clerk to an attorney of Clifford's Inn.

The first civil war In 1642, aged twenty-six, Harrison enlisted in the earl of Essex's lifeguard to wage war against the king. The following year he went with Charles Fleetwood to fight in the earl of Manchester's army in the eastern association, evidently because the religious atmosphere there was more to his liking. 'Look', wrote an angry presbyterian, 'on Col. Flettwoods regiment with his Major Harreson, what a cluster of preaching offecers and troopers ther is' (D. Masson, ed., *The Quarrel between the Earl of Manchester and Oliver Cromwell*, CS, new ser., 12, 1875, 72). He fought at Marston Moor (2 July 1644), and was sent after the battle to report to the committee of both kingdoms, and, to the annoyance of the Scots, 'to trumpett over all the city' the praises of Cromwell and the Independents (R. Baillie, *Letters and Journals*, ed. D. Laing, 3 vols., 1841, 2.209).

Harrison joined the New Model Army at the time of its founding in early 1645. He saw action at Naseby and Langport, at the captures of Winchester and Basing, and at the siege of Oxford. At Langport Richard Baxter stood beside Harrison on a hill opposite the New Model horse and musketeers who were driving Goring's army from its positions. He heard him 'with a loud voice break forth into the praises of God with fluent expressions, as if he had been in a rapture' (*Reliquiae Baxterianae*, 54). At the storming of Basing Harrison killed with his own hands Major Cuffle, 'a notorious papist', and 'one Robinson, son to the clowne of Blackfriers playhouse, … as they were getting over the workes' (J. Sprigge, *Anglia rediviva*, 1647, 139; *Mercurius Civicus*, 9–16 Oct 1645, 1202). A royalist writer later accused Harrison of shooting Major Robinson with a pistol after he had laid down his arms, saying 'cursed is he that doeth the work of the Lord negligently' (J. Wright, *Historia histrionica*, 1699, 7–8). Given the New Model Army's usual respect for the laws of war the story is implausible.

In 1646 Harrison was elected to the Long Parliament as recruiter MP for Wendover. In the same year he married his cousin Catherine Harrison, the daughter of his father's brother Ralph Harrison, a woollen draper in Watling Street, London. Although Harrison and his wife settled in Highgate, they attended the church of St Ann Blackfriars, which by 1650 housed a Fifth Monarchist congregation. Their three children were buried there in 1649, 1652, and 1653.

The army revolt of 1647 By 1646 Harrison's military reputation had risen to such a height that when Lord Lisle was appointed lord lieutenant of Ireland he asked for Harrison to serve under him. Within four months he had returned to England, and was thanked by the Commons for his services. But when parliament provoked a revolt in the army by ordering the soldiers to disband or be shipped to Ireland with only a token payment of their arrears, Harrison sided with his comrades. He signed the letter of the officers to the City of 10 June 1647 and was one of those appointed by Fairfax to treat with the parliamentary commissioners. When Colonel Sheffield opted to back parliament in this conflict Fairfax gave the command of his horse regiment to Harrison. Harrison was absent from the debates of the army's general council at Putney in late October and early November. He was, however, named to the committee that drew up the army's engagement for Sir Thomas Fairfax to present to the three rendezvous of the army in mid-November. He used the opportunity to testify that it 'lay upon his spiritt … that the king was a man of bloud' who ought to be prosecuted for his crimes (Firth, *Clarke Papers*, 1.417). It was not the first time that this label had been applied to Charles I, but it contributed to the king's decision to flee Hampton Court for the relative safety of the Isle of Wight. Harrison further disclosed his radical political views by opposing further negotiations with the king and speaking against the veto power of the House of Lords.

The second civil war, the Levellers, and religion During the second civil war Harrison served in the northern army under Major-General John Lambert. On 17 July 1648 he exhibited notable bravery when Langdale surprised Lambert's quarters at Appleby. With a few troopers he checked the enemy's advance, 'and being more forward and bold then his men did second him; having hold himself of one of his enemy's horse colours he received three wounds' (Rushworth, 7.1201). By November he was actively negotiating with John Lilburne a reconciliation between the army leaders and the Levellers, and agreed on behalf of the officers to the Leveller proposal for a committee of sixteen to draft a second version of the *Agreement of the People*. For the moment he supported the projected constitution for England, but was acutely conscious of the conflict between the effort to settle the state in the light of human prudence and his own conviction that it was God's evident purpose to supersede all merely 'carnal' government. He attempted to persuade the Levellers that before the agreement could be perfected it was necessary for the army to invade London and prevent parliament from concluding a treaty with the king. Such a treaty would entail the disbandment of the army, with the consequence 'that you will be destroyed as well as we' (Lilburne, 32). Moreover, he was sure that eventually the agreement would prove unsatisfactory to God's purpose. 'Our Agreement shall bee from God, and nott from men' (Firth, *Clarke Papers*, 2.186).

Religion is the key to understanding both Harrison's military and political careers. A puritan of the most zealous, millenarian stamp, he would emerge in the 1650s as a leader of the Fifth Monarchist movement. Baxter relates that when he attempted to argue against antinomianism and Anabaptism with him:

> he would not dispute with me at all, but he would in good discourse very fluently pour out himself in the extolling of Freegrace, which was savoury to those that had right principles, though he had some misunderstandings of freegrace himself. (*Reliquiae Baxterianae*, 54)

Harrison shared the Fifth Monarchist readiness to take up arms to usher in the kingdom of heaven on earth. To Edmund Ludlow he quoted the apocalyptic book of Daniel (7: 18) that 'the saints … shall take the kingdom', 'to which he added another to the same effect, "That the kingdom shall not be left to another people"' (*Memoirs of Edmund Ludlow*, 2.7–8).

The trial and execution of Charles I Few men were more bent on destroying the king than Harrison. He personally escorted Charles from Hurst Castle to London to stand trial. Charles, who had heard a report that Harrison wanted to assassinate him, was none the less attracted by his soldierly bearing and his fine clothes. Harrison assured the king that the report was untrue; what he had really said was 'that the law was equally obliging to great and small, and that justice had no respect of persons' (Herbert, 142). Appointed to the high court of justice, Harrison attended nearly every meeting, and signed the death warrant [*see also* Regicides]. He also supervised the king's funeral, and was paid £100 to cover his expenses (BL, Add. MS 63788B, fol. 60). Publicly he never doubted the justness of his action, and went to his death proclaiming that God had willed the king's execution. One may wonder if Harrison the providentialist, or his wife, might have entertained private doubts about the regicide, given that his first-born son died and was buried at almost the same time as the king.

The republic, 1649–1653, and the monarchy of Christ At the army's prayer meeting prior to the departure of Cromwell's expedition to Ireland Harrison 'expounded some places of scripture excellently well and pertinent to the occasion' (Whitelocke, 3.66). He did not travel to Ireland on this occasion but remained in England, where he was entrusted with high military and political responsibility for the next four years. General Fairfax appointed him commander-in-chief of the Commonwealth's forces in the counties of Monmouthshire, Glamorgan, Brecknockshire, Radnorshire, Cardiganshire, Carmarthenshire, Herefordshire, and parts of Gloucestershire. In 1650 he was given command of the forces in England during Cromwell's absence in Scotland, and in July of the same year was made lieutenant of the ordnance. He was nominated to the council of state when it was first constituted in

January 1649, though he was not actually elected to it until 10 February 1651. In June 1650 he was one of those designated by the council of state to persuade Fairfax to lead the expedition to Scotland. When Fairfax demurred and Cromwell had to be sent instead, Harrison wrote the latter a letter which illustrates the intimate friendship between the two men. 'I know yow love me', he declared, and then cited scriptural authority for faith and prayer as the 'cheife engines' of military success, witnessed by 'the ancient Worthies [who] through Faith subdued Kingdomes, out of weakness were made strong, waxed valiaunt in fight, and turned to flight the armies of the Aliens' (Ellis, 3.353–4).

On 22 October 1650 Harrison reviewed the newly raised militia forces in Hyde Park. The following March rumours of plots in the north prompted the council of state to dispatch him to the border with 2500 fresh cavalry of doubtful quality.

In the summer of 1651 Charles II marched into England at the head of a Scottish army. Cromwell instructed Harrison to 'attend the motions of the enemy, and endeavour the keeping of them together, as also to impede his march' (Cary, 2.294). On 13 August Harrison joined Lambert and the cavalry detached from Cromwell's army at Preston, and attempted unsuccessfully to stop the royalists at Knutsford. He then took part in the battle of Worcester (3 September) and was given the job of pursuing the fleeing royalists. He completed the assignment so energetically and skilfully that few royalists escaped.

Like Cromwell, Harrison interpreted the crushing victory at Worcester as a mandate for 'establishing the ways of righteousness and justice, yet more relieving the oppressed, and opening a wide door to the publishing the everlasting gospel of our only Lord and Saviour' (Cary, 2.375). His own appetite for justice had been revealed in 1650 when he obtained the expulsion of Edward, Lord Howard of Escrick, from parliament for taking bribes to excuse royalists from sequestration and composition fines. More contentiously, he took the lead in having Gregory Clement excluded for adultery in May 1652. These actions lost him a number of political friends.

For his part Harrison grew more and more hostile to the Rump, as the Long Parliament was coming to be known. In December 1651 he attended the conference on the settlement of the kingdom organized by Cromwell, and he was one of the promoters of the army's blueprint for reform: its petition to parliament of August 1652. Among other things the petition called for law reform, the more effective propagation of the gospel, the elimination of tithes, and speedy elections for a new parliament. When the Rump failed to act on these items, Harrison began to press for its dissolution. He was too avid for Cromwell's taste. Harrison 'is an honest man, and aims at good things', Cromwell was heard to say, 'yet from the impatience of his spirit will not wait the Lord's leisure, but hurries me on to that which he and all honest men will have cause to repent' (*Memoirs of Edmund Ludlow*, 1.346). Harrison himself explained to Ludlow some years later that he had assisted in the expulsion of the Rump 'because he was fully persuaded they had not a heart to do any more good for the Lord and his people' (ibid., 2.6). The last straw for him was the Rump's refusal, on 1 April 1653, to renew the mandate of the commission for the propagation of the gospel in Wales. The commission had been created in 1650 under the leadership of Harrison, a number of other zealous army officers, and several tirelessly evangelical Welsh pastors, most notably Vavasour Powell. Among its achievements were the rooting out of royalist and scandalous clergy and the planting of a preaching ministry in their place, the extension of English law and culture, and the propagation of millenarian ideas. Proof of the subduing of Welsh royalism was Harrison's feat of recruiting a large local militia from the Welsh saints in 1651 for the battle of Worcester. In contrast to the first civil war, when the Welsh had almost formed the backbone of Charles I's infantry, they supplied almost no recruits for the invading army of his son. But by 1653 parliament had become darkly suspicious of Harrison's power base in Wales, and was alarmed by rumours that he had 'underhandedly listed 40,000 men and … sworn them to be true to him' (Bodl. Oxf., MS Clarendon 45, fol. 206).

Parliament's decision to jettison the Welsh commission was decisive in swinging Harrison over to the militant wing of the Fifth Monarchist movement, which wanted to do away with parliaments as well as princes. What brought Cromwell to the same position with regard to parliament was its decision to proceed with elections for a new representative without any of the safeguards deemed essential by the army. When Cromwell arrived in the middle of the debate on the morning of 20 April Harrison was already 'most sweetly and humbly' exhorting the MPs to lay aside the bill for new elections (*Parliamentary or Constitutional History*, 20.130). Just as the question was about to be put on the bill Cromwell leaned over to Harrison and whispered, 'This is the time I must do it' (*Memoirs of Edmund Ludlow*, 1.352). Harrison later maintained that he had not known of Cromwell's intention until then, but contemporary accounts give the impression that the two men were already hand in glove at this moment (*Moderate Publisher*, 15–22 April 1653, 813; *Several Proceedings in Parliament*, 14–21 April 1653, 2944). After Cromwell had delivered his tirade against the Rump he shouted to Harrison to 'call them in', and twenty or thirty musketeers filed in to clear the house, with Harrison pulling Speaker William Lenthall by the gown to make him vacate his seat (*De L'Isle and Dudley MSS*, 6.615).

Authority was now temporarily vested in the hands of a small council of thirteen persons nominated by the officers, with Harrison acting as its president during the third week of its existence. It was during these months that he attained the zenith of his political influence. In the debate over how to reshape the sovereign power in the wake of the Long Parliament's demise he argued for an assembly of seventy, on the Old Testament model of the Jewish Sanhedrin. In the event the officers of the army summoned a body twice that large, augmented by five co-opted members, of whom Harrison was one. He had been instrumental in the nomination of several Welsh saints and four

members of his own Fifth Monarchist sect, as well as getting himself elected to the new council of state, both in July and December. Known as Barebone's Parliament, the nominated assembly grappled with several of Harrison's favourite issues: tithes, law reform, the excise tax, and the war with the Netherlands. He pressed for the immediate abolition of tithes, but was unable to avert the question being shunted into a committee. In August the house passed resolutions for the abolition of the court of chancery and the framing of a completely new body of law. Harrison was appointed to the committee to embody these resolutions into statutes, but no statutes materialized. He was also named to the excise committee, in the expectation that the tax would soon be eliminated, but the expectation was never fulfilled.

There are several reasons for the failure of the radical agenda in Barebone's Parliament, but among them must be counted Harrison's lack of political aptitude, his impatience with committee work, and his reluctance to undertake the hard slogging required to accomplish significant change. His record of attendance, in both the council of state and parliament, was spotty. More exciting to him than tedious parliamentary debates were the Monday prayer meetings at St Ann Blackfriars, where the fiery preaching of Christopher Feake and John Rogers furnished heady inspiration. More appealing than boring meetings of the council of state were the Fifth Monarchist gatherings at Arthur Squibb's house in Fleet Street to plot political strategy. Inflamed by the millenarian vision of the imminent overthrow of Antichrist, Harrison and his friends campaigned for the continued prosecution of the war against the Dutch. It was their conviction that the civil war in England had merely begun the overturning of Antichrist, and that England's duty was to carry the struggle across the lands of Europe until Rome itself had fallen. The Netherlands, because of its materialism and pursuit of wealth, had betrayed this calling, and so they called down the wrath of God upon that nation. In the words of a royalist news-writer, Harrison 'choaked the poore cittizens' with propaganda, preaching that 'when we have beaten the Dutch … the whole world should saile into this Commonwealth; … the Dutch must be destroyed; and we shall have an heaven upon earth' (Bodl. Oxf., MS Clarendon 45, fol. 380v). Cromwell, because he desired peace with the Netherlands, also became the target of radical vituperation. By late November 1653 he and Harrison were near to an open breach. Cromwell sent for Harrison several times in early December, but Harrison was deaf to his overtures.

The protectorate and political exile, 1654–1659 The decision by the moderate majority in Barebone's to surrender its authority to Cromwell was fiercely opposed by Harrison and his faction. Barebone's dissolution also marked the effective end of his political career. Before the end of December 1653 he had been deprived of his military commission, and two months later he was ordered to retire to Staffordshire.

In spite of his various shortcomings, few apart from the Levellers and Lucy Hutchinson ever questioned Harrison's integrity. Never found guilty of peculation or dishonest dealing of any kind, he was nevertheless labelled a 'gilded' hypocrite by John Lilburne for his initial encouragement of the Levellers, followed by his part in crushing them at Burford in May 1649, and then his acceptance of the honorary degree of master of arts at Oxford for his reward (Lilburne, 31). Mrs Hutchinson scolded him for exhorting his fellow MPs to dress in sober puritan garb to welcome visiting ambassadors and then turning up the next day fitted out 'in a scarlett coate and cloake, both laden with gold and silver lace, and the coate so cover'd with clinquant that scarcely could one discerne the ground, and in this glittering habit sett himselfe just under the Speaker's chaire' (Hutchinson, 197).

Like many leading revolutionaries Harrison took advantage of his position to enrich himself. With his own and other soldiers' arrears debentures he acquired three crown properties: part of Marylebone Park and the manor of Tottenham, in Middlesex, and the manor of Newcastle under Lyme in his native Staffordshire. He also acquired dean and chapter land and crown fee farm rents in Middlesex and Staffordshire respectively. The total value of confiscated lands which he is known to have bought and kept during the interregnum was well over £13,000.

With the adoption of the 'Instrument of government' in December 1653 Harrison effectively became an exile within his own country. Looking back later on the six years from the beginning of the protectorate until the Restoration he explained:

> when I found those that were as the apple of mine eye to turn aside, I did loathe them and suffer'd imprisonment many years. Rather than to turn as many did, that did put their hands to the plough, I chose rather to be separated from wife and family than to have compliance with them, tho' it was said 'sit at my right-hand' and such kind expressions. (Hargrave, 1.320)

In the elections to the first protectorate parliament Harrison was said to have been chosen in eight different constituencies. Fifth Monarchists planned to circulate a petition in the army and then have Harrison present it to parliament. The petition stated that the protectoral regime was worse than that of Charles I, exhorted parliament to extirpate the new tyranny, and called for a 'state of perfect liberty' (Bodl. Oxf., MS Clarendon 49, fols. 58v, 59). Cromwell had Harrison arrested, to be released a few days later with a friendly warning 'not to persevere in those evil ways whose end is destruction' (Thurloe, *State papers*, 2.606).

In February 1655 an informer told the government that Harrison, Feake, and Rogers were involved in a fresh plot against it. Cromwell summoned them before him, but, far from pledging not to attack the government, they asserted that 'armes may bee taken upp againste it' (Firth, *Clarke Papers*, 2.244). After being placed under house arrest for a few days Harrison was lodged in Portland Castle. In March 1656 he was released and allowed to live at Highgate with his family. In the parliamentary elections of that year, despite the pressures of the major-generals, Harrison was apparently elected, though not permitted to sit.

Fifth Monarchist agitation continued in 1657, Harrison's house being one of the main rendezvous, although he was not directly implicated in Venner's conspiracy. Again placed under arrest, Harrison was this time sent to Pendennis Castle. In July he was released again and freed from all remaining restrictions.

In February 1658, however, a more dangerous plot came to light, in which Harrison was allegedly embroiled, and he was again sent to the Tower. In the summer of 1659, with the overthrow of the protectorate, the Fifth Monarchists experienced a sudden accession of strength. There were rumours of an intended insurrection in which Harrison was said to be deeply implicated. The restored Rump had barred him from office as punishment for his role in their fall in 1653; nevertheless, he appears to have taken no part in politics during the year leading up to the Restoration. His inactivity may have been due to declining health brought on by his wounds and bouts of imprisonment.

Trial and execution On the eve of the Restoration Harrison refused to pledge not to disturb the government or to save his life by flight. He was accordingly arrested at his house in Staffordshire and taken to the Tower of London. One of seven people originally excepted from Charles II's promised Act of Indemnity, he was among the first to be brought to trial.

Harrison's trial and execution were the climactic episode of his life. At his trial he asserted that he had acted in the name of the parliament of England and by their authority. 'Maybe I might be a little mistaken, but I did it all according to the best of my understanding, desiring to make the revealed will of God in his holy scriptures as a guide to me' (Hargrave, 320). Convicted and condemned to the gruesome death reserved for traitors, he remained unshaken in his confidence that the overthrow of the revolution was but a temporary setback for the godly. On 13 October 1660 he was taken on a sledge to Charing Cross, the place appointed for his sufferings. 'Where is your good old cause now?', jeered a bystander on the way. 'With a cheerefull smile [Harrison] clapt his hands on his brest and sayd, Heere It Is, And I Goe To Seale It With My Blood' (E. Ludlow, *A Voyce from the Watch Tower: Part Five, 1660–1662*, ed. A. B. Worden, CS, 4th ser., 21, 1978, 215). Speaking from the scaffold, he refused to explain away his part in the regicide, boldly affirming that 'being so clear in the thing, I durst not turn my back, nor step a foot out of the way, by reason I had been engaged in the service of so glorious and great a God'. 'The finger of God', he went on:

> hath been amongst us of late years in the deliverance of his people from their oppressors, and in bringing to judgement those that were guilty of the precious blood of the dear servants of the Lord … Be not discouraged by reason of the cloud that now is upon you, for the Sun will shine and God will give a testimony unto what he hath been doing in a short time. (W. S., 17, 19, 21)

Pepys, who was there, commented on the cheerfulness with which he suffered, while a royalist observer was dismayed by his hardness of heart. His hands and knees were seen to tremble on the scaffold, but Harrison explained that 'It is by reason of much blood I have lost in the wars, and many wounds I have received in my body' (ibid., 18). According to Ludlow the sentence of hanging, drawing, and quartering 'was so barbously executed, that he was cut down alive, and saw his bowels thrown into the fire' (*Memoirs of Edmund Ludlow*, 2.305). According to another account, as he was being quartered he struggled to his feet and boxed the executioner about the ears. In order to terrify the next condemned regicides Harrison's decapitated head was placed on the sledge which drew John Cook to his execution three days later. It was then stuck on a pole in Westminster Hall, while each of his quarters was fastened to one of the City's gates.

Harrison's fearlessness at the end enhanced his reputation as a martyr in radical circles, and a report spread that he was soon to rise again, judge his judges, and restore the kingdom of the saints. He continues to stir the imagination of later centuries not only because of his courage, but also because of his decisiveness as a man of action and his integrity. A convinced regicide, he was motivated by a profound religiosity, which found expression in a millennial yearning for the reign of Christ on earth. In conscious opposition to Levellers and republicans he proclaimed his belief in the theocratic rule of the saints. The closest he came to realizing that vision was in 1653 with the calling of Barebone's Parliament. However, his deficiencies as a political leader, added to his lack of patience for administrative routine, helped to condemn the experiment in theocracy to failure. His enduring mark on the historical record derives from his key role in bringing one king to the scaffold, and his fearless surrendering of his life in defiance of the next.   Ian J. Gentles

Sources C. H. Firth, 'A memoir of Major-General Thomas Harrison', *Proceedings of the American Antiquarian Society*, new ser., 8 (1893), 390–464 · B. S. Capp, *The Fifth Monarchy Men: a study in seventeenth-century English millenarianism* (1972) · I. Gentles, *The New Model Army in England, Ireland, and Scotland, 1645–1653* (1992) · *The memoirs of Edmund Ludlow*, ed. C. H. Firth, 2 vols. (1894) · J. Lilburne, *The legall fundamentall liberties of the people of England* (1649) · *Reliquiae Baxterianae, or, Mr Richard Baxter's narrative of the most memorable passages of his life and times*, ed. M. Sylvester, 1 vol. in 3 pts (1696) · Bodl. Oxf., MSS Clarendon 45, 49 · W. S., *A compleat collection of the lives, speeches … letters and prayers of those persons lately executed* (1661) · F. Hargrave, ed., *A complete collection of state-trials*, 4th edn, 11 vols. (1776–81), vol. 1 · *The Clarke papers*, ed. C. H. Firth, 1, CS, new ser., 49 (1891) · *The Clarke papers*, ed. C. H. Firth, 2, CS, new ser., 54 (1894) · *Report on the manuscripts of Lord De L'Isle and Dudley*, 6, HMC, 77 (1966) · J. Rushworth, *Historical collections*, new edn, 7 (1721) · exchequer, certificates of the sale of crown land, PRO, E 121/3/4/39, 40; E 121/4/6/112 · exchequer, deeds of sale, fee farm rents (interregnum), PRO, E 307, box 11/H4/5 · chancery close rolls, PRO, C 54/3545/38; 54/3713/11 · crown estate office, surveyor-general's books of constats, 1660–61, PRO, CRES 6/2, fols. 224–6 · L. Hutchinson, *Memoirs of the life of Colonel Hutchinson*, ed. J. Sutherland (1973) · T. Herbert, *Memoirs of the two last years of the reign of King Charles I*, another edn (1813) · H. Cary, ed., *Memorials of the great civil war in England from 1646 to 1652*, 2 vols. (1842) · BL, Civil War MSS, Add. MS 63788B, fol. 60 · B. Whitelocke, *Memorials of English affairs*, new edn, 4 vols. (1853) · H. Ellis, ed., *Original letters illustrative of English history*, 2nd ser., 3 (1827) · *Moderate Publisher* (15–22 April 1653), 813 · *Several Proceedings in Parliament* (14–21 April 1653), 2944 · Thurloe, *State papers* · *The parliamentary or constitutional history of England*, 2nd edn, 24 vols. (1751–62), vol. 20 · C. H. Firth and G. Davies, *The regimental history of Cromwell's army*, 2 vols. (1940) · T. Pape, *Newcastle-under-Lyme in Tudor and early Stuart times*, Publications of the University of Manchester, no. 261: Historical Series, 75 (1938) · F. J. Varley, *Major-General Thomas Harrison* (1939) · I. Gentles, 'The debentures market and military purchases of crown land, 1649–1660', PhD diss., U. Lond., 1969

Likenesses M. van der Gucht, pubd 1713, BM, NPG; repro. in Ward, *History of the rebellion* (1713) · engraving, BL, Civil War MSS, Add. MS 63788A, fol. 9 · portrait, repro. in E. Hyde, earl of Clarendon, *History of the rebellion and civil wars in England* (1717)

Wealth at death none, as a convicted traitor; before conviction, approx. £17,000—capital value of lands (crown, dean and chapter, and fee farm rents): exchequer, certificates of the sale of crown land, PRO, E 121/3/4/39, 40; E 121/4/6/112; chancery, close rolls, PRO, C 54/3545/38; 54/3713/11; exchequer, deeds of sale, fee rents (interregnum), PRO, E307, box 11/H4/5; crown estate office, surveyor-general's books of constats, 1660–61, PRO, CRES 6/2, fols. 224–6

Harrison, Thomas (1617/18–1682), clergyman and ejected minister, was born at Hull, Yorkshire, the son of Robert Harrison, merchant. After studying at Hull under James Burney, Harrison matriculated as a pensioner at Sidney Sussex College, Cambridge, on 12 April 1634, aged sixteen, and graduated BA in 1638. By 1640 he had gone to Virginia, where the people of Sewell's Point, Lower Norfolk, chose him as their minister on 25 May, paying a salary of £100 per annum. He also served as a chaplain to the governor, Sir William Berkeley, though he was dismissed after adopting puritan views about 1644. For refusing to baptize according to the Book of Common Prayer Harrison was indicted by a grand jury in 1645. By 1647 he was preaching in neighbouring Nansemond county, founding a congregation that soon numbered more than a hundred. For refusing to use the Book of Common Prayer he was banished from Virginia in 1648. With an elder, William Durand, he went to Boston in October, having previously corresponded with the Massachusetts governor, John Winthrop. Responding to a petition from Harrison's congregation at Nansemond, the English council of state, on 11 October 1649, ordered Winthrop to restore Harrison, 'an able man of unblameable conversation' (*CSP col.*, 1.330), but he never went back. Harrison married Dorothy Symonds, daughter of Samuel Symonds, in New England in 1648.

By 1650 Harrison had returned to England, where he joined Philip Nye, John Owen, Sidrach Simpson, and other ministers in endorsing Samuel Eaton's *The Mystery of God Incarnate* (1650), a defence of Christ's divinity against the Socinian John Biddle and the Arian John Knowles. The following year Harrison accepted appointments as minister of St Dunstan-in-the-East, in London, and as Thomas Goodwin's successor as pastor of an Independent church in the same parish. That November he signed *A declaration of divers elders and brethren of congregationall societies in and about the city of London* (1651), opposing any limitation on voting or standing for parliament to members of gathered churches. In February 1652, after Owen, Nye, Simpson, and John Dury had condemned the Racovian catechism at the bar of the House of Commons, the latter appointed a committee to discuss the issue with ten ministers, including Harrison, George Griffith, and William Greenhill. Harrison maintained his interest in the colonies, petitioning the council of state in July on behalf of various residents of Virginia and Maryland. In November 1652 the council instructed him to produce the commission for an officer's position in America recently granted to Sir William Davenant by Prince Charles. Harrison's first publication, *Old Jacobs Accompt Cast up and Owned by one of his Seed, a Young Lady*, a sermon preached on 13 February 1655 at Lady Susanna Reynolds's funeral, appeared the same year. Taking Genesis 47:9 as his text, Harrison focused on the evil days that afflict godly and ungodly alike.

Harrison's interest in Ireland was sparked by Nathaniel Brewster, the Independent rector of Alby-cum-Thwaite, Norfolk, during a return voyage from America. In the summer of 1651 commissioners in Dublin invited Harrison to visit the country, hoping he would encourage New England settlers to migrate there as planters. He declined the invitation, but by June 1655 he had accepted an appointment as one of thirteen ministers assigned to accompany Henry Cromwell to Ireland, where he served as a chaplain in Cromwell's household. At the council's behest, Sir Gilbert Pickering and Colonel William Sydenham examined his preaching certificate before his departure. Harrison was in Dublin by 21 July, when he received instructions to take turns preaching at Christ Church. Two days later he was also assigned to preach at St John's. Stephen Charnock succeeded him there after Harrison became the regular Sunday morning preacher at Christ Church on 8 September 1655. Harrison's stipend of £300 was the largest paid to any minister in Ireland during the 1650s. As he explained to secretary of state John Thurloe, he was optimistic about Ireland's future, for 'the nation lyes like clay upon the wheele, ready to receive what forme authority shall please to give it' (Thurloe, 3.715). However, he was soon frustrated by the Baptists' refusal to join the Independents in public worship; the principal stumbling block, as Christopher Blackwood explained, was disagreement over baptism, though Blackwood also opposed psalm singing and honorific titles. In December Harrison reported criticism of Oliver and Henry Cromwell to Thurloe—a matter of concern because he linked his welfare to theirs.

On 4 April 1656 the Irish council instructed Harrison to consult the committee for the approbation of ministers, to which he was formally appointed on 22 December. The same year he visited London, where his 'adversaries' detained him for a time. Harrison accepted an appointment in 1657 as a trustee for five schools to be founded with a bequest from Erasmus Smith, though nothing came of this until 1669. During the spring of 1658 Harrison unsuccessfully opposed Jeremy Taylor's move to Ireland at Lord Conway's invitation. About early 1659 Harrison and Dr Henry Jones agreed to support a grant of land to supply income for Samuel Hartlib, but this project came to naught with the collapse of the interregnum government. Harrison's work at Christ Church resulted in two publications, *Topica sacra: Spiritual Logic* (1658), a devotional handbook, and *Threni Hybernici* (1659), a sermon on Lamentations 5:16 in commemoration of Oliver Cromwell, England's Josiah; further reformation, Harrison

insisted, was necessary. About 1658–9 he received the DD degree from Trinity College, Dublin. With Charnock, Samuel Winter, and two other ministers he examined a shipment of Quaker books from London in 1659 and ordered that they be burnt.

Some time before 1660 Harrison's first wife died. By early 1660 he had returned to England, for on 28 February he married Katherine (*d.* 1672), daughter of Edward Bradshaw, at St Oswald's, Chester. He was vicar there from 1661 until his ejection the following year. For illegally preaching at Chester with William Cook, he was imprisoned in 1663. On 21 April of the same year the government issued a warrant for his arrest on charges of having removed some of Charles I's books from St James's Library while Hugh Peter was caretaker. Harrison was still residing in Chester in 1663–4, when he was taxed on five hearths. For holding a conventicle (attended by approximately a hundred worshippers) he was arrested and fined in July 1665. Two months later he was imprisoned at Chester. In 1669 he was holding conventicles at Bromborough, Cheshire, probably with the support of the Hardware family. Lord Arlington learned in May 1670 that Harrison had vowed to continue such meetings and submit to whatever penalties were imposed. He received a licence to travel to London the following October, though for what purpose is unclear. He reportedly went to Ireland the same year at the invitation of Dublin's mayor. Under the declaration of indulgence (1672) Harrison was licensed to preach in Chester, but he soon returned to Dublin. There he and Daniel Rolls contributed an epistle to the pseudonymous *Lemmata meditationum* (1672), a collection of pious soliloquies. He apparently finished but never published a 'System of divinity' in a large folio volume. The congregation to which Harrison now ministered, which met in Winetavern Street and then, beginning in 1673, in Cooke Street, included Presbyterians and Independents, among them the countess of Donegal and Lord Massereene. Despite the differences in polity, according to Edmund Calamy 'he managed all matters with that discretion, temper and moderation, that there never was the least clashing or danger of a faction' (*Nonconformist's Memorial*, 1.262). After Harrison's death in Dublin on 22 September 1682, Daniel Williams preached his funeral sermon. Harrison's renowned oratory—he preached from memory—is reflected in Lord Thomond's comment that 'he had rather hear Dr. *Harrison* say grace over an egg, than hear the bishops pray and preach' (ibid., 1.262).   RICHARD L. GREAVES

Sources *Calamy rev.* • *The nonconformist's memorial … originally written by … Edmund Calamy*, ed. S. Palmer, 1 (1775), 261–2 • St J. D. Seymour, *The puritans in Ireland, 1647–1661* (1912) • *CSP col.*, 1.330, 386 • *CSP dom.*, 1651–2; 1655; 1660–61; 1663–5; 1670; 1672 • Thurloe, *State papers*, 3.751; 4.90–91, 349 • Venn, *Alum. Cant.* • R. L. Greaves, *God's other children: protestant nonconformists and the emergence of denominational churches in Ireland* (1997) • T. C. Barnard, *Cromwellian Ireland: English government and reform in Ireland, 1649–1660* (1975) • P. A. Bruce, *Institutional history of Virginia in the seventeenth century*, 2 vols. (1910) • G. F. Nuttall, *Visible saints: the congregational way, 1640–1660* (1957) • E. MacLysaght, ed., 'Commonwealth state accounts, 1650–6', *Analecta Hibernica*, 15 (1944), 227–321, esp. 274–5 • S. G. Drake, *The history and antiquities of the city of Boston* (1854)

Archives BL, Lansdowne MSS 821, 822 • PRO, state papers 29

Harrison, Thomas (*fl.* 1652–1674). *See under* Harris, Renatus (*c.*1652–1724).

Harrison, Thomas (1693–1745), Particular Baptist minister and Church of England clergyman, was the son of Thomas Harrison (1667–1702), minister of the Baptist church at Loriners' Hall, London. He was first invited to preach at Little Wild Street, London, in April 1714, but was not called to be minister until March 1715 after the call had been refused by another. He had already published a sermon to mark the accession of George I, giving thanks for the providential deliverance of the protestant succession, which included a hymn written specially for the occasion. He was a founder of the Particular Baptist fund (1717), and was an orthodox subscriber at the Salters' Hall controversy in 1719. His earliest publications were sermons, principally funeral sermons for prominent lay members of his church, but after the manner of Isaac Watts he published his *Poems on Divine Subjects* (1719; repr. 1721) which consisted of forty-one poems in two books. Several of them became popular as hymns and were frequently reprinted. He also published a dramatic poem, *Belteshazzar, or, The Heroic Jew* (1727), which is his most notable work.

His ministry appears to have been successful, with a number of wealthy families as members, and his preaching was described as popular in 1727 (*Correspondence and Diary*, 2.379). In March 1729 he preached a funeral sermon for Dame Mary Page, who belonged to Devonshire Square Baptist Church, a service which he claimed he undertook at the request of her executor, apparently because of doubts about the abilities of her minister, Thomas Richardson, for the task. One critic accused Harrison of slighting Richardson's efforts, that they might be 'stifled in the Embryo, … the above doctrines not being agreeable to the taste of the polite part of the town' (Gill, 37). His conduct was censured by the Baptist ministers who met at Blackwell's Coffee House, for having damaged Richardson's reputation as a minister.

In January 1729 Harrison sought an assistant to preach on Sunday mornings, and told the church that he could not preach twice a day because of the state of his health. The church agreed to an assistant without reducing his salary, but soon learnt that Harrison spent his Sunday mornings attending the Church of England with the intention of conforming. Shortly afterwards it was reported that he was going to stay at the fashionable watering place of Tunbridge Wells, and when he returned he 'would come up to London in canonical robes' (Ivimey, 3.569). His intended conformity was reported in *Fog's Weekly Journal* on 10 July 1729. He resigned on 31 July, telling his congregation that his sentiments had changed, particularly regarding infant baptism, and that he no longer had any scruples about conforming. His conformity occurred at the same time as that of a number of younger ministers, who together caused considerable concern to dissenters (Calamy, 2.504). Harrison claimed to have left his congregation, where he was handsomely provided for, 'without any offer to encourage me' and, despite his conformity, to have kept his former congregation's affection (Harrison, *A Sermon Deliver'd*, 13). He was ordained deacon on 7 September 1729 and priest on 21 September at St Paul's Cathedral by the bishop of London, probably to the title of a chaplainship to Lady Culepeper. He had preached a recantation sermon at St Leonard, Foster Lane, on 14 September. This was later answered by the celebrated 'Orator' Henley, in *A Child's Guide for the Reverend Mr Thomas Harrison* (1729), who ridiculed Harrison's scholarly pretensions and arguments: 'he has not given one reason that obliged his conscience to conform, … only some of his reasons … why he *might*' (Henley, 4). Harrison was presented to the vicarage of Ratcliffe on the Wreake, Leicestershire, a crown living, on 28 November 1730. In his first sermon there he laid down the duties he expected of his parishioners, which for a rural parish were demanding and included monthly communion: expectations which perhaps owed something to his nonconformist background. He died on 30 March 1745, and was buried at St Peter's churchyard, St Albans. His wife, Mary (1693/4–1747), survived him.   DAVID L. WYKES

Sources J. Ivimey, *A history of the English Baptists*, 4 vols. (1811–30), vol. 3, pp. 500–501, 568–73 · W. Wilson, *The history and antiquities of the dissenting churches and meeting houses in London, Westminster and Southwark*, 4 vols. (1808–14), vol. 1, p. 383; vol. 2, p. 558 · D. E. Baker, *Biographia dramatica, or, A companion to the playhouse*, rev. I. Reed, new edn, rev. S. Jones, 3 vols. in 4 (1812) · J. Nichols, *The history and antiquities of the county of Leicester*, 3/1 (1800), 382 · E. Calamy, *An historical account of my own life, with some reflections on the times I have lived in, 1671–1731*, ed. J. T. Rutt, 2nd edn, 2 (1830), 504 · T. Harrison, *A sermon preach'd the 20th of January 1714/15* (1715) · T. Harrison, *Poems on divine subjects in two parts* (1719) · T. Harrison, *Belteshazzar, or, The heroic Jew: a dramatic poem* (1727) · T. Harrison, *A funeral sermon occasioned by the death of Dame Mary Page* (1729) · [J. Gill], *An essay on the original of funeral sermons, orations and odes* (1729) · T. Harrison, *A sermon deliver'd in the parish-church of St Leonard's, Foster-Lane, on September 14, 1729* (1729) · J. Henley, *A child's guide for the Reverend Mr Thomas Harrison* (1729) · T. Harrison, *The mutual duties of clergy and laity considered* (1730) · *The correspondence and diary of Philip Doddridge*, ed. J. D. Humphreys, 5 vols. (1829–31) · will, 20 March 1744, PRO, PROB 11/739
Wealth at death see will, 20 March 1744, PRO, PROB 11/739

Harrison, Thomas (*bap.* 1744, *d.* 1829), architect, was baptized on 7 August 1744 at Richmond, Yorkshire, the son of Thomas Harrison and his wife, Anne Brittel. His father was a carpenter, but little else is known of his family. He probably attended Richmond grammar school from *c.*1755 to *c.*1759. In 1769 he was sent to Rome with his friend George Cuitt, a landscape painter, by Sir Lawrence Dundas of Aske. There he studied Roman antiquities and in 1770 submitted to Pope Clement XIV a design for converting the Vatican Cortile del Belvedere into a museum for antique sculptures; this proposal seems to have brought him to the attention of Piranesi and Mengs. In 1773 he entered the Concorso Balestra of the Accademia di San Luca, for which the theme was the replanning of the piazza del Popolo. Harrison's design, the only one of his Roman projects to survive, was later exhibited at the Royal Academy in 1777. It shows a more accomplished performance than that of his Italian competitors: the handling of elements is more severe and archaeological, the components more clearly delineated. It was the most neo-classical of the designs submitted, though it was not yet in the simplified manner of Harrison's mature style. When he found that he had been passed over, he petitioned the pope and was presented with gold and silver medals before being created Accademico di Merito in June 1773. The pope later commissioned him to alter the sacristy of St Peter's but died (22 September 1774) before work could begin. In 1776 Harrison visited the temple of Augustus at Pula, Istria, on his way back to Britain; his later works suggest that he may well have visited Paris as well, to admire French neo-classical architecture.

After a short stay in London, Harrison returned to Richmond from where he sent further exhibits to the Royal Academy: a national monument (exhibited 1779) and two elevations of a bridge across the Thames (exhibited 1780). In 1782 he built the cupola of the old town hall, Lancaster. In 1783 he moved to Lancaster after winning the competition for the Skerton Bridge. From then on bridge building occupied him for the rest of his career, allowing him to combine his engineering and architectural skills; he had an excellent understanding of masonry construction and a talent for the handling of massive forms. The Skerton Bridge (completed 1783) had elliptical arches and a level road surface across the river, a device never before used in England on a large scale but pioneered in France by Jean-Rodolphe Perronet with his celebrated bridge at Neuilly-sur-Seine, Paris (1768–74; des. 1939). Probably because of its success, Harrison was subsequently commissioned to rebuild St Mary's Bridge, Derby (1788–93), and the Stramongate Bridge, Kendal (1791–7), both more modest interpretations of the same theme. In addition he held an unofficial appointment as bridge master of Lancashire (from at least 1792) and worked on several Cheshire bridges between 1800 and 1805; he was appointed county surveyor of Cheshire in 1815 after having carried out the duties for fifteen years. He also experimented with laminated timber constructions of his own devising at Warrington (1812; dem. before 1837) and Cranage (1816; dem.). Although neither was a practical success, they were daring works and the first of their type to be built in England; such structures were not developed until John Green (1787–1852) considered them for his Scotswood Bridge over the Tyne in 1827–8. Harrison's final and greatest engineering work was the Grosvenor Bridge (1827–33), Chester, then the largest single-span masonry arch in the world, measuring 200 feet across. It appears almost too weak to bear its load but the slender beauty of its proportions is a merit rather than a defect. Harrison's opinions were respected and he was consulted in several important commissions including the Eden Bridge, Carlisle (1805), the Strand (later Waterloo) Bridge (1809), and the Ouse Bridge, York (1810). This made him known to engineers, including Jesse Hartley, John Rennie, William Jessop, and Thomas Telford, as well as to architects.

Harrison's most important public work, which he won in competition in February 1786, was the rebuilding over almost thirty years (1788–1815) of Chester Castle in an innovatory Greek revival style. The work included felons' and debtors' gaols, the shire hall and offices, armoury, barracks, and a grand propylaeum, during the building of which (1795) he moved to Chester. The polygonal plan of the felons' goal, an outstanding solution to reformed prison design, was based on William Blackburn's Northleach bridewell, Gloucestershire (1785); the shire hall portico was the first large-scale application in Britain of a baseless, unfluted primitive Greek Doric order, here modelled freely on the Tuscan order as described by Vitruvius and remarkable for its gigantic proportions. The interior hemicycle was inspired by the design of Jacques Gondoin for the École de Chirurgie (1769–86) in Paris, although Harrison introduced a simplified Ionic Ilyssus order. Expressing clearly the fourfold purpose of the building—administrative, judicial, penal, and defensive—Chester Castle's exterior was notable for its sobriety (akin to that of contemporary French grand prix architectural designs), for its long low silhouette, and for the powerful handling of masonry. Each separate part of the building was clearly defined, yet Harrison succeeded in reconciling a prison with the façade of a sessions house. The riverside elevation of the castle, sublimely terrible with its dramatic massing of layers of cells, must have been particularly compelling in its original setting of small houses and warehouses.

At about the same time (1786–99) Harrison was working on the reconstruction of Lancaster Castle in a Gothic revival style to complement the existing buildings. The shire hall (c.1791–2) is a Gothic rendering of the same building at Chester, and the male felons' prison (1792–3) is a hybrid of the polygonal and radial gaol plans used by Blackburn. Harrison's reputation as a public architect was made with these and other structures, including three early instances of Greek revival buildings: the Liverpool lyceum (1800–03), and the portico library (1802–6) and the exchange (1805–9), both in Manchester.

Domestic architecture was a small but important part of Harrison's practice. His houses, apart from the triangular castellated Hawkstone Citadel, Shropshire (1824), are generally of two types. Some are in a plain fashionable style like that of Samuel Wyatt, characterized by finely cut masonry, minimal motifs, tripartite windows, and domed bows; these include, for example, Kennet House (1793–4; dem. 1967). Others are of the idyllic stucco villa type with wide eaves, resembling the work of John Nash and Henry Holland: a fine example is St Martin's Lodge, Chester (1821–3), which he built for himself. His plans developed from the villa type favoured by Robert Adam and the Wyatts into more informal arrangements with the principal rooms disposed asymmetrically. His only executed large-scale house was Broomhall, Fife (1796–9), for Thomas Bruce, seventh earl of Elgin; Harrison's suggestion that Elgin use his embassy in Constantinople to gather details of Greek architecture and sculpture resulted in the eventual acquisition of the Elgin marbles.

Harrison was the leading Greek revivalist in the northwest, pioneering the baseless Doric and a simplified Ionic order with great assurance. His public works are characterized by a sense of construction, pure geometrical shapes, and a limited number of refined and simplified motifs; his domestic works are of great external simplicity. C. R. Cockerell noted 'it is in the great intelligence of the masonry that Harrison's merit lies' (diary, 4 March 1828, RIBA BAL, COC/1013). His first biographer, Canon Blomfield, later praised him as 'almost, if not quite, the first architectural genius in the kingdom, with a more clear apprehension of the principles of the art and a more accurate knowledge of it than, perhaps, any man of his day' (Blomfield). A man of apparently quirky humour and disposition, Harrison achieved national standing. Because of his retiring nature, however, he remained in the northwest, where his major works ensured a long-lived reputation.

In 1785, at the priory church, Lancaster, Harrison married Margaret Shackleton; the couple had three surviving children, a son, John (1789–1802), and two daughters. He died on 29 March 1829 at his home, St Martin's Lodge, 54 Nicholas Street, Chester, opposite the castle, and was buried in the churchyard of St Bridget's, Chester, on 6 April. His wife and daughters survived him. He was reinterred at Blacon, near Chester, when St Bridget's churchyard was cleared, about August 1964.   MOIRA RUDOLF-HANLEY

Sources M. A. Rudolf Ockrim, 'The life and work of Thomas Harrison of Chester, 1744–1829', PhD diss., Courtauld Inst., 1988 • Colvin, *Archs.* • A. Blomfield, 'Harrison of Chester, architect', *The Builder*, 21 (1863), 203–5 • *GM*, 1st ser., 99/1 (1829), 460, 468–70 • F. Milizia, *Lettere al Conte Francesco di Sangiovanni* (1827), 41–3 • L. Pirotta, 'Thomas Harrison, architetto inglese Accademico di San Luca per sovrano motu', *Strenna dei Romanisti*, 21 (1960), 257–63 • J. M. Crook, 'The architecture of Thomas Harrison [pts 1–3]', *Country Life*, 149 (1971), 876–9, 944–7, 1088–91 • D. Stillman, 'British architects and Italian architectural competitions, 1758–1780', *Journal of the Society of Architectural Historians*, 32 (1973), 43–66 • Faringdon, *Diary*, vols. 1–4, 7–9 • M. A. Ockrim, 'Thomas Harrison and the rebuilding of Chester Castle: a history and reassessment', *Journal of the Chester Archaeological Society*, 66 (1983), 57–76 • parish register, Richmond, Yorkshire, 7 Aug 1744 [baptism] • parish register, Richmond, Yorkshire, 26 Nov 1743 [marriage] • parish register, Chester, St Bridget, 6 April 1829 [burial] • *Cheshire Sheaf*, 3rd ser., 59 (1964), 48–50 • parish register, Lancaster, Priory Church [marriage]

Archives RIBA | Broomhall, Fife, Elgin family MSS • Ches. & Chester ALSS, plans and drawings • Chester and Cheshire Museums Service • Chester City RO, plans and drawings • Cumbers House, Gredington, Kenyon family MSS • Cumbria AS, Carlisle, plans • Denbighshire RO, Ruthin • Flintshire RO, Hawarden • Grosvenor Museum, Chester, drawings • Lancs. RO, proceedings of Lancaster Castle • Shrops. RRC • Weaver Hall Museum, Nantwich

Likenesses J. Downman, chalk, *c.*1815, Grosvenor Museum, Chester • J. Downman, drawings, 1815, Grosvenor Museum, Chester • J. Downman, watercolour, 1815, Grosvenor Museum, Chester • H. Wyatt, oils, *c.*1820, Grosvenor Museum, Chester • H. Wyatt, oils, *c.*1822, Ches. & Chester ALSS • A. R. Burt, stipple, pubd *c.*1824, NPG • engraving, pubd 1824 (after A. R. Burt), Grosvenor Museum, Chester; copy, Chester City Library • silhouette, after 1832 • bronzed plaster cast, 1839 (after marble bust by G. Cauldwell, *c.*1823), Gov. Art Coll., Manchester • plaster cast, 1839 (after marble bust by G. Cauldwell, *c.*1823), Portico Library, Manchester • M. Gauci, lithograph (after H. Wyatt, *c.*1822), Chester City Library

Wealth at death £6000: will, 1829, Ches. & Chester ALSS

Harrison, Thomas Elliot

Harrison, Thomas Elliot (1808–1888), civil and mechanical engineer, was born on 4 April 1808 in Fulham, Middlesex, the son of William Harrison, an official at Somerset House. Shortly after his birth his father moved to Sunderland in order to establish a shipbuilding firm and promote local mineral railways. Thus Thomas was educated in Durham, a county for which he had great affection throughout his life, at Houghton-le-Spring grammar school. Later, during an apprenticeship with William and Edward Chapman, civil engineers of Newcastle, he gained experience in dock construction for the coal trade.

Harrison's first connection with railways came as an assistant to T. L. Gooch (1808–1882) who was surveying part of the route of the London and Birmingham Railway for Robert Stephenson (1803–1859). In 1832 Harrison became the engineer, with the support of Stephenson as consulting engineer, of the Stanhope and Tyne Railway and, two years later, of the Durham Junction Railway. The outstanding Victoria Bridge over the River Wear was erected to Harrison's designs on the latter line between Penshaw and Washington. This experience laid the foundations of his career and qualified him for the role of resident engineer under Robert Stephenson in the completion of the east coast rail route in England through the construction of the Newcastle and Darlington Junction and Newcastle and Berwick railways. According to Stephenson, Harrison carried the main responsibility for the building of not only the lines but also the high level bridge across the Tyne and the Royal Border Bridge, Berwick.

With the amalgamation in 1849 of these and other lines, Harrison received the appointment of chief engineer and general manager of the York, Newcastle, and Berwick Railway. In 1854 the York, Newcastle, and Berwick, York and North Midland, and Leeds Northern companies were consolidated into the North Eastern Railway, for which he was made chief engineer; he held the post for the rest of his life.

In the years that followed Harrison played a significant part in creating the largest railway territorial monopoly in the country through his contributions to the negotiations and parliamentary enquiries that accompanied the North Eastern's crucial mergers with the Newcastle and Carlisle (1862) and Stockton and Darlington (1863) companies. In addition to the absorption of existing railways, the North Eastern further strengthened its position by providing improved services to the public in the form of new lines, such as the Team Valley and York to Doncaster, via Selby. Harrison planned these and other lines, and the designs and estimates for the station at York, the company's administrative headquarters.

Harrison's performance as a mechanical engineer was less impressive than were his achievements in the field of civil engineering. The rope and pulley device which he produced in the 1860s to provide communication between the passengers and crew of a moving train proved a failure. More reprehensible, he submitted a paper to the royal commission on railway accidents of 1874–7 advising that the block system of signalling should be confined to junctions, sidings, and stations. His opinion ran counter to the unequivocal advice of the railway inspectorate. Further, the North Eastern was among the slowest of the major railways to replace its iron rails with steel. In contrast to this comparative failure in some areas of mechanical engineering, under Harrison's guidance the North Eastern was in the vanguard among British railways in its use of both the Smith vacuum and Westinghouse air brakes. Moreover, he demonstrated the advantages of hydraulic power in his designs for the gates of Tyne Dock, Jarrow, and the large swing bridge over the River Ouse on the direct line between Hull and Doncaster.

Harrison also sat on the royal commission on water supply, 1867–9, and gave evidence to the royal commission on railways, 1865–7. He was consulting engineer of the London and South Western Railway and was much in demand as an arbitrator in disputes between railway companies. A career in politics had no interest for him and the honour he valued above all others was his election as president of the Institution of Civil Engineers in 1873. He married twice: first to a Miss White of Whitburn and then to Sophia Jane Collinson, daughter of the Revd Collinson, rector of West Boldon. There were two surviving sons and five daughters.

In his methodical and cautious approach, 'Honest Tom' Harrison was the embodiment of the principles that prevailed in the management of the North Eastern and, to the benefit of a company whose position insulated it from many competitive pressures, he provided valuable links with the wider railway scene. He died at home in Whitburn, near Sunderland, on 20 March 1888 of a heart attack, his second wife surviving him. At the time of his death, Harrison was heavily involved in the designs for the Forth Bridge.   DAVID BROOKE

Sources PICE, 94 (1887–8), 301–13 · Institution of Mechanical Engineers: Proceedings (1888), 261–3 · D. Brooke, 'Harrison, Thomas Elliot', DBB · W. W. Tomlinson, The North Eastern railway: its rise and development [1915] · K. Hoole, North east England [1965] · J. Marshall, A biographical dictionary of railway engineers (1978) · 'Royal commission to inquire into … accidents on railways', Parl. papers (1877), 48.1, C. 1637; 48.173, C. 1637-I; 48.1335, C. 1637-II
Archives PRO, records of the North Eastern Railway, PRO RAIL 527
Likenesses W. W. Ouless, oils, 1884, Railway Offices, York; made at request of North Eastern Railway shareholders · W. W. Ouless, oils, c.1884, Inst. CE · goupilgravure (after photograph), repro. in PICE
Wealth at death £133,748 0s. 2d.: resworn probate, March 1890, CGPLA Eng. & Wales (1888)

Harrison, William (1535–1593), historian and topographer, was born in the 'house next to the Holy Lamb toward Cheapside', in Cordwainer Street, London, at 'hora 11, minut 4, Secunde 56', on Sunday 18 April 1535, the son of John and Anne Harrison, whom he described as 'honourable citizens' in his brief Latin autobiography written about 1565 in his copy of John Bale's Scriptorum illustrium majoris Brytannie … catalogus (1559); this volume is now in the Derry Diocesan Library. His father was probably not John Harrison the elder, one of the printers of Holinshed's Chronicles, but a merchant adventurer of that name. Harrison attended St Paul's School in the 1540s, and describes himself as an 'unprofitable grammarian' at Westminster School under the protestant humanist Alexander Nowell,

probably in the reign of Edward VI. He entered Christ Church, Oxford, in 1554 and graduated BA in 1557. He became a probationary fellow of Merton College, Oxford, in July 1557 and was ordained in April 1558.

Harrison resigned the Merton fellowship some time before July 1558 to become household chaplain to the leading protestant magnate, William Brooke, Lord Cobham, who presented him to the rectory of Radwinter, Essex, on 16 February 1559. He held adjacent Wimbish from January 1571 to autumn 1581. The dean and chapter of St Paul's, noted for preferring zealous preachers in their London peculiars, presented him to St Olave, Silver Street (1567–71), and St Thomas the Apostle (1583–7). Harrison's pluralism ensured that he had an adequate but not spectacular clerical income. He proceeded MA at Oxford in June 1560, and BD at Cambridge in 1571. He assured Gabriel Harvey that he left unfinished the Cambridge exercises for his DTh degree not from presbyterian scruples but from lack of 'will, skill, and [to] beare it out'. Some time in the 1560s he married Marion Isebrand (d. 1593), a refugee from Andern in the Calais pale. Of their four children, their daughter Anne married George Downham, the leading Cambridge Ramist, and Church of Ireland bishop of Derry in the reign of James I. Their son Edmund graduated BD from Cambridge in 1603 and held livings in Derry diocese, where his books, added to those of his father and Downham, became the core of the diocesan library. Harrison's son William predeceased him, and an unnamed daughter is mentioned in his will.

Harrison's autobiography ascribed his conversion from popish 'insanity' to the preaching of the Oxford martyrs, Thomas Cranmer, Hugh Latimer, and Nicholas Ridley. He fitted this experience into a historical scheme that increasingly directed his writing. The preaching of the martyrs and much protestant controversial writing, including Bale's Catalogus, in which Harrison wrote his own life, convinced him that all of history witnessed an unceasing conflict between the true church, descending through the spiritual generations of the elect since Adam, and the church of Cain, descending from that first apostate and shaped by Satan through paganism into a parody of the true religion. Harrison claimed that contemporary popery perpetuated this pagan debasement under antichristian forms, and he felt deep shame at his 1558 ordination as 'a shaven worshipper of Baal'.

Following his conversion to a variety of protestantism that appeared radical in the England of the 1560s, Harrison attached new importance to the study of time, in which religious conflict was conducted and fulfilled in accordance with God's will. Thus by 1565 he had written 'Chronological computations from the beginning of the world to his own times', which was expanded by the 1570s into 'The great English chronology'. This demonstrates his Pauline conception of history, newly acquired through his BTh studies at Cambridge, as the precise chronological and historical demonstration of God's care for his elect, applied to galvanize individual Christians and to build up Christ's church in the present. The discovery in 1977 at Trinity College, Dublin, of the first version of this manuscript, dating from about 1570, reveals Harrison's immersion in this strange world of chronological complexities. It also depicts a mind utterly alien to the genially prolix Harrison of a historiographical tradition created by F. J. Furnivall's selective mining of the picturesque, 'Merry England' sections of Harrison's *Historicall Description of the Island of Britain* prefaced to Holinshed's *Chronicles*. The Trinity manuscript describes lost works on the rulers of monarchies and empires (of which the British section appeared in the 1587 *Description*), and on linking eclipses to chronological calculations. It lists works revising the date of the incarnation, precisely dating the creation at the first moment of Leo in 3966 BC and synchronizing the Hebrew sabbath cycle with the Julian year, and relating the calendar of English and foreign rulers to scriptural prophecy. Harrison also wrote discriminating 'annotations' on the prophecies of Merlin, and 'The antiquities of this land', in the manner of William Lambarde and William Camden, both now lost.

The 'Chronology' through its myriad revisions demonstrates Harrison's 'most exquisite diligence', as Holinshed described it, in wrestling with the chaotic record of time. Harrison wrote the 'Chronology' at Radwinter, Essex, and at Wimbish, from a library of sixty-five manuscripts, none extant, and more than 500 printed authors, of which 165 titles survive in Derry Diocesan Library and in the Ipswich Town Library. He also used the libraries of Gabriel Harvey, Alexander Nowell, John Stow, St Paul's Cathedral, several Cambridge and Oxford colleges, and Reginald Wolfe, who was the inspiration behind a projected 'Universal cosmography' only partially realized in Holinshed's *Chronicles*. Until 1576 Harrison worked independently of Holinshed, who remained ignorant of the 'Chronology' until after Wolfe's death in December 1573, and who only commissioned Harrison to write the *Description* in June or July 1576. Initially Harrison refused because the work might interfere with the 'Chronology', but after vague promises of publishing the 'Chronology' in the *Chronicles* he hurriedly concocted from printed, oral, and personal information three engrossing books on the history and physical and social geography of Britain. Much promised information never materialized, and Harrison could only glance at the 'Chronology' for material on the former nations of Britain, its ancient names, the evidence for giants, its former languages, kingdoms, and religions, which better fit his chosen title of *Historical Description*. Holinshed cited the 'Chronology' sixty-one times in his *Chronicles*, often as a radical contrast to current interpretations.

Harrison's work on the *Description* exposed him to the censure of London's narrowly scripturalist protestants, who reinforced the arguments of his Radwinter curate, Richard Rogers, that civil histories were unfitting for divines. He therefore abandoned the 'Chronology' until the autumn of 1578, but about 1583 he rewrote it as an even larger manuscript in three volumes organized around the four monarchies of the book of Daniel. The last volume of these, from 1066 to 'the year of expectation which is of grace 1588 expired wherin the age of the world runneth

all by fire', but in fact continuing until Harrison's death in 1593, is now in the British Library. It reveals Harrison's increasing obsession with Satan's plots against Elizabethan England, whether through Roman Catholic missions and Spanish power or more covertly through courtly conspiracies against church endowments, masked by presbyterian agitation. Harrison argued that these plots fitted into the historical pattern of commonwealths ruined by the destruction of learned preaching. This concern, supplemented by his fears of war and economic and social unrest, led him to abandon his earlier sympathy for further reformation, and Harrison became an unflinching defender of the established church because of its pastoral effectiveness.

This outlook underlies Harrison's revisions of the *Description* published in the second edition of Holinshed's *Chronicles* (1587). He drew more heavily on the protestant, prophetic world-view of the 'Chronology' for historical parallels that would warn his countrymen to avoid God's repeated judgments by following the true church and purifying their commonwealth of the evils of enclosure, excessive consumption, and church corruption. His despair at England's failure to emulate the social ideals of protestant humanism clouded his last years until his death, perhaps of the plague, on 9 November 1593 at St George's Chapel, Windsor, where he was buried.

GLYN PARRY

Sources G. J. R. Parry, *A protestant vision: William Harrison and the Reformation of Elizabethan England* (1987) · G. J. R. Parry, 'William Harrison and Holinshed's *Chronicles*', *HJ*, 27 (1984), 789–810 · G. J. R. Parry, 'Trinity College Dublin MS 165: the study of time in the sixteenth century', *Historical Research*, 62 (1989), 15–33 · W. Harrison, 'The great English chronology', TCD, MS 165 · W. Harrison, 'The fourth and last part of the great English chronology', BL, Add. MS 70984 · G. Edelen, 'William Harrison (1535–1593)', *Studies in the Renaissance*, 9 (1962), 256–72 · Bale, *Catalogus*, Derry Diocesan Library [Harrison's copy incl. autobiography] · muniments, St George's Chapel, Windsor, Berkshire

Archives BL, 'The fourth and last part of the great English chronology', Add. MS 70984 · Derry diocesan library, autobiography written in copy of Bale, *Catalogus* · TCD, 'The great English chronology', MS 165

Harrison, William (1553–1621), Roman Catholic archpriest, was born in Staffordshire, Warwickshire, or Derbyshire. He entered the English College at Douai in 1575. He was ordained to the diaconate at Cambrai on 6 April 1577 and on 2 August 1577 was sent to the English College at Rome, where he was ordained at an unknown date but before the institution of the college oath on 23 April 1579. There is some disagreement when he took the oath. Gillow claims that he was among the first, the same day that the oath was instituted. He left Rome on 26 March 1581, arrived in Rheims on 13 May 1581, and left for England on 22 May 1581. Soon afterwards he is mentioned as being at the house of Henry Sacheverell at Hopwell Hall, Derbyshire. The Rome register lists him as a confessor which implies that he was imprisoned for the faith.

According to Dodd, Harrison returned to the continent and studied civil and canon law at Paris in 1587. Allegedly he left the college on 10 January 1591 to supervise a small

English school established by Robert Persons at Eu in Normandy. Harrison remained at the school until its closure as a result of the French wars of religion. There is a reference to Harrison's running the school in 1591 in an interrogation of a recusant in the Gatehouse prison, but Dodd's assertion lacks confirmation: Persons never mentioned Harrison in his correspondence, and references in the Douai diaries do not support Dodd. While a connection between Persons and Harrison would have been interesting in ascertaining the future archpriest's attitude to Jesuits in England, the story seems to be unfounded. We do know that he rematriculated at Douai University about 1592, proceeded STD, and was on the staff by the end of 1594. He served at Douai as professor, vice-president, and bursar until his transfer to Rome in 1603.

Harrison arrived in Rome on 21 August 1603 to serve as Roman agent for the English archpriest George Blackwell during the appellant controversy during which certain secular clergy protested first the appointment of an archpriest in 1598, and then the treatment and harassment of their agents. Persons considered Harrison a moderate or, indeed, an opponent of the appellant clergy. Philip Hughes described Harrison as so hostile to them that he had informed Pope Paul V that the recently condemned oath of allegiance (1606) embodied ideas disseminated by the appellant clergy. During his stay in Rome, Harrison acquired a non-residential benefice in the diocese of Liège. He returned to Douai on 29 October 1608 and departed for England on 19 June 1609. By 1610 he was in Sussex. By August 1613 he was an assistant to Archpriest George Birket. The archpriest died in December 1614 and Harrison was appointed his successor in February 1615. Whatever his relations with Jesuits prior to his appointment Harrison pursued policies independent from, and at times positively opposed to, Jesuit plans and projects. He removed the Jesuit confessor at Douai in 1619 and sought to establish classes in the humanities within the English College itself so that seminarians would not have to attend the Jesuit schools. He favoured the restoration of regular ecclesiastical governance through the appointment of a bishop. He sent John Bennet, a secular priest, to Rome in 1621 to petition for a bishop who would improve the pastoral good of English Catholics deprived of some of the sacraments, correct scandals and dissensions within the English church, and restore ordinary discipline. The presence of a bishop might prevent future conspiracies (as it might have prevented the Gunpowder Plot).

Harrison died, aged sixty-eight, on 11 May 1621. He was described as 'short of stature and very decent of body and behaviour, his head of flaxen colour cut short, very fair of countenance' (Talbot, 209). His request for a bishop was answered by the appointment of William Bishop as bishop of Chalcedon and vicar apostolic of England in June 1623.   JOHN J. LaROCCA

Sources G. Anstruther, *The seminary priests*, 1 (1969) • F. Fabre, 'The English College at Eu', *Catholic Historical Review*, 37 (1951), 257–80 • Gillow, *Lit. biog. hist.* • L. Hicks, 'The foundation of the College of St. Omers', *Archivum Historicum Societatis Jesu*, 19 (1950), 146–80 • C. Talbot, ed., *Miscellanea: recusant records*, Catholic RS, 53 (1961) • *Letters of William Allen and Richard Barret, 1572–1598*, ed. P. Renold, Catholic RS, 58 (1967) • W. B. Ullathorne, *History of the restoration of the Catholic hierarchy in England* (1871) • *DNB* • W. M. Brady, *The episcopal succession in England, Scotland, and Ireland, AD 1400 to 1875*, 3 (1877) • C. Dodd [H. Tootell], *The church history of England, from the year 1500, to the year 1688*, 3 vols. (1737–42) • *Dodd's Church history of England*, ed. M. A. Tierney, 5 vols. (1839–43), vol. 5 • C. Aléthleus, *A specimen of the amendments candidly proposed to the compiler of a work which he calls, 'The church history of England from the year 1500 to the year 1688'* (1741) • T. F. Knox and others, eds., *The first and second diaries of the English College, Douay* (1878) • M. C. Questier, *Newsletters from the archpresbyterate of George Birkhead*, CS, 5th ser., 12 (1998) • P. Hughes, *Rome and the Counter Reformation in England* (1942)

Harrison, William (1685–1713), poet and diplomat, was born in the parish of St Cross, Winchester, the son of Dorothy and William Harrison (*d.* 1694), rector of Cheriton, Hampshire, from 1672 until his death. He attended nearby Winchester College in 1698 and subsequently New College, Oxford, where he was given a scholarship in 1704 and a fellowship in 1706. Addison befriended Harrison and obtained for him the post of governor to a son of James Douglas, second duke of Queensberry and first duke of Dover, at a salary of £40 per annum. Addison also recommended him to Swift, who wrote to Stella that:

> There is a young fellow here in town we are fond of ... one Harrison, a pretty little fellow, with a great deal of wit, good sense and good nature; has written some mighty pretty things ... I love the fellow and am resolved to stir people up to do something for him: he is a Whig. (Swift, *Journal*, 1.54–5)

Harrison had already earned a reputation as a poet through his 'Woodstock Park' (1706), published when he was only twenty-one, 'On his Grace the Duke of Marlborough Going for Holland' (1707), and 'To Mrs. M.M. with a Bough of an Orange Tree' (1709). He subsequently wrote 'The Passion of Sappho' (1711), which was set to music, and several minor poems.

Harrison is better known for his continuation of *The Tatler* which he undertook with the backing of Swift and Henry St John, a relative. Swift, 'afraid the little toad has not the true vein for it' (Swift, *Journal*, 1.164), doubted that it would succeed. Harrison produced fifty-two issues, twice a week between 13 January and 19 May 1711. The paper failed notwithstanding the efforts of Swift, who met Harrison two evenings a week to help him edit the news sheet. Swift, in a characteristic fit of pique, stormed that 'I'm tired of correcting his trash' (Swift, *Journal*, 1.162). At this time St John secured Harrison's appointment as secretary to Thomas Wentworth, Baron Raby, ambassador-extraordinary and plenipotentiary to the United Provinces, and subsequently second plenipotentiary to the peace congress at Utrecht. Harrison left for The Hague on 20 April 1711. In 1712 he succeeded Henry Watkins as queen's secretary to the embassy at Utrecht. His letters are full of ironic asides in which he pokes fun at his own inexperience, his short stature, and his drinking habits.

At the end of January 1713 Harrison was sent to London with a copy of a new barrier treaty. Swift, 'who longed to see the little Brat', found him at his doorstep, without a shilling in his pocket, having not been paid since late spring 1712, though Swift had 'teazed their hearts out for it' (Swift, *Journal*, 2.611). Harrison soon caught cold and fell desperately ill. Swift had the young man moved to Knightsbridge where the air was said to be better. Swift got 30 guineas and a £100 Treasury note for him from Bolingbroke and went to deliver the money on 14 February 1713. Swift, dreading the worst, was afraid to knock. Harrison had died an hour before. 'No loss ever grieved me so much', Swift confided (Swift, *Journal*, 2.619). His finely honed sense of humour and good nature had endeared Harrison to those around him. Lady Strafford (Wentworth's wife) wrote that Mr Harrison was 'very much lamented by all that knew him' (Cartwright, 319). His fellow poets, Addison, Swift, and Ambrose Philips, buried him. Edward Young, who was at his bedside when he died, described him as 'a little brisk man, quick, and passionate; rather foppish in appearance, a pretty look and quick eye' (Spence, 354). Young memorialized his friendship with the 'partner of my soul' in 'An Epistle to Lord Landsdowne' (E. Young, *Complete Works, Poetry and Prose*, ed. J. Nichols, 1854, repr. 1968, 1.311).

W. P. COURTNEY, *rev.* LINDA FREY *and* MARSHA FREY

Sources *Observations from The Hague and Utrecht: William Harrison's letters to Henry Watkins, 1711–1712*, ed. L. Frey, M. Frey, and J. C. Rule (1979) · R. C. Elliott, 'Swift's "Little" Harrison, poet and continuator of the *Tatler*', *Studies in Philology*, 46 (1949), 544–59 · J. Swift, *Journal to Stella*, ed. H. Williams, 2 vols. (1948) · J. J. Cartwright, ed., *The Wentworth papers, 1705–1739* (1883) · *Letters and correspondence, public and private, of … Henry St John, Lord Viscount Bolingbroke, during the time he was secretary of state to Queen Anne*, ed. G. Parke (1798) · *The correspondence of Jonathan Swift*, ed. H. Williams and [D. Woolley], rev. edn, 5 vols. (1965–72) · J. Spence, *Observations, anecdotes, and characters, of books and men*, ed. J. M. Osborn, new edn, 2 vols. (1966) · *The correspondence of Edward Young, 1683–1765*, ed. H. Pettit (1971) · T. F. Kirby, *Winchester scholars: a list of the wardens, fellows, and scholars of … Winchester College* (1888) · *VCH Berkshire* · Foster, *Alum. Oxon., 1500–1714* · G. A. Aitken, *The life of Sir Richard Steele*, 2 vols. (1889) · S. Johnson, *Lives of the English poets*, ed. G. B. Hill, [new edn], 3 vols. (1905) · *GM*, 1st ser., 47 (1777) · *GM*, 1st ser., 50 (1780)
Archives BL, letters to Bolingbroke, Add. MS 31137, fols. 236r–236v · Ohio State University, Columbus, letters to Henry Watkins
Wealth at death penniless: *Journal to Stella*, ed. Williams, 2.611, 619–20

Harrison, William (*d.* 1745). *See under* Harrison family (*per.* 1715–*c.*1790).

Harrison, William (1802–1884), antiquary, son of Isaac Harrison, hat manufacturer and merchant, was born at Salford, Lancashire, on 11 December 1802. As a young man he worked in merchant shipping in Manchester, leaving his business for more than a year from 1831 to travel extensively in South Africa, where he made contact with his friend, the missionary Robert Moffat (1795–1883), whom he had known as a student in Manchester. He returned home some months before his marriage in 1832 to Mary Sefton Beck of Upton Priory, Macclesfield.

Harrison retired to the Isle of Man in 1842 and settled at Rockmount, a small estate at St Johns, near Peel. He was a member of the unreformed, self-elected House of Keys from 1856 until its dissolution in 1867, captain of the parish of German, and in 1872 a justice of the peace. A prime mover in the foundation in 1858 of the Manx Society for the Publication of National Documents, he served it as council member and honorary secretary, and was the editor of thirteen out of the thirty-three volumes that it published. He developed a wide scholarly expertise, extensive contacts, and a deep interest in Manx history, folklore, and customs; his own eight works, particularly his pioneering *Bibliographical Account of Works Relating to the Isle of Man* (1861, 1866) and the comprehensive *Account of the Diocese of Sodor and Man* (1879), are still valuable sources. He occasionally contributed articles on antiquarian matters to the *Manchester Guardian* and other papers. He died in the Isle of Man, at Rockmount, on 22 November 1884 and was buried in Peel cemetery.   A. M. HARRISON

Sources 'William Harrison: scholar and antiquary', *Journal of the Manx Museum*, 4/57 (1938) · W. Cullon, *A bibliographical account of works relating to the Isle of Man, with bibliographical memoranda and copious literary references*, 2 vols. (1933–9) · *Manchester Guardian* (27 Nov 1884)
Archives Manx Museum Library, The Manx Society MSS · U. Edin. L., special collections division, Halliwell-Phillipps MSS, corresp. with James Halliwell-Phillipps
Likenesses M. Wane, photograph, 1864, Manx Museum Library, Douglas, Isle of Man

Harrison, William (1812–1860), merchant navy officer, son of a master in the merchant service, was born at Maryport, Cumberland, in October 1812. He was apprenticed to Mr Porter, a Liverpool shipowner, and went to sea in October 1825. On the expiry of his articles he was given command of a vessel, and served in the East and West Indies, and on the coast of South America. In the course of the numerous disagreements among the rival powers on the American coast, he was more than once in action, and acquitted himself with credit. In 1834 he transferred his services to Barton, Erlam, and Higgonson, and took charge of vessels on the Barbados line.

From 1842 to 31 December 1855 Harrison was connected with the Cunard Line of packet-boats trading between Liverpool and America; he crossed the Atlantic more than 180 times, and was one of the most popular commanders on that route. In January 1856 he was selected by the directors of the Eastern Steam Navigation Company out of 200 competitors to take command of Brunel's huge steamship, the *Great Leviathan*, then building at Millwall in the Thames. In the following years he was appointed to superintend the arrangements for internal accommodation and navigation. The ship, being at last completed after great delay, and renamed the *Great Eastern*, was sent on a trial trip from Deptford to Portland Roads. When it was off Hastings on 9 September 1859 an explosion of steam killed ten firemen and seriously injured several other people. Harrison showed prompt courage and resourcefulness, and brought the vessel into Portland, though in a badly damaged state. The *Great Eastern* was then put into winter quarters near Hurst Castle. On 21 January 1860 Harrison, sailing with others from Hythe to Southampton in the ship's gig, was capsized during a squall near the Southampton Dock gates, and when taken from the water was found to be dead. Doctors considered that 'Captain Harrison's sudden relinquishment of the struggle for life was caused by apoplexy induced by the intense cold' (*Annual Register*, 1860, 12). He was buried in St James's cemetery, Liverpool, on 27 January, when more than 30,000 people followed his body to its grave. Some time previously he had become surety for a friend, by whose sudden death all his savings were lost. A subscription was therefore raised for his aged mother, wife, Martha, and three children.

G. C. BOASE, *rev.* ROGER MORRISS

Sources *ILN* (6 Nov 1858), 435 · *ILN* (28 Jan 1860), 83 · *ILN* (4 Feb 1860), 116 · *Annual Register* (1859), 136–40 · *Annual Register* (1860), 10–12 · D. J. Pound, ed., *The drawing room portrait gallery of eminent personages*, 3rd ser. (1860) · *The Times* (23–31 Jan 1860) · *The Times* (9 March 1860) · *Pall Mall Gazette* (31 Aug 1888), 5–6 · Boase, *Mod. Eng. biog.* · *GM*, 3rd ser., 8 (1860), 308 · *CGPLA Eng. & Wales* (1860)

Likenesses D. J. Pound, stipple and line engraving (after photograph by Mayall), NPG; repro. in *The drawing room portrait gallery*, pl. 31 · portrait, repro. in *ILN* (6 Nov 1858), 435 · portrait, repro. in *ILN* (4 Feb 1860), 116

Wealth at death under £3000: administration, 5 Aug 1860, *CGPLA Eng. & Wales*

Harrison, William (1813–1868), singer and opera manager, the son of a coal merchant, was born at Marylebone, Middlesex, on 15 June 1813. After studying at the Royal Academy of Music he appeared from 1837 as a professional singer there and at the Sacred Harmonic Society, as well as in a mediocre Covent Garden opera company. On 2 May 1839 he sang the tenor lead in W. M. Rooke's *Henrique*. He was tall and handsome, a good actor, with a sweet voice, but 'quite unequal' to a heroic part opposite Adelaide Kemble in *Norma* (1841). For some years he confined himself to lighter parts; at Drury Lane he sang the leads in the two new English works that came closest to establishing themselves as repertory operas, Balfe's *The Bohemian Girl* (1843) and Vincent Wallace's *Maritana* (1845). His significance for the history of both English opera and opera in English was enhanced in 1854, when he and the soprano Louisa Pyne took a nucleus of British singers to New York. They opened on 9 October with a repertory drawn from the lighter Italian and French operas (in English), *The Bohemian Girl* and *Maritana*, and *The Beggar's Opera*. Their success was enormous (in 1855 a 125-night run in their New York summer season alone) and they toured from Montreal to New Orleans for nearly three years, adding some heavier operas such as Donizetti's *Lucia di Lammermoor*. On their return home (1857) they carried on their venture through successive winter seasons at Covent Garden or the Lyceum until 1864. Their repertory was much as before, with, in addition, a dozen new English operas, including six by Balfe (notably *The Puritan's Daughter*, 1861), Wallace's *Lurline* (1860), and Julius Benedict's *The Lily of Killarney* (1862). Harrison seems to have been thought an effective and honest manager; he and the other singers worked hard, often performing six nights a week. After the first few years, however, the undertaking began to lose money—a notion, perhaps ill-founded, that the prince consort might help it to a parliamentary subsidy was cut short by his death—and by 1861 there were grumbles about artistic quality. In 1864–5 Harrison alone managed a season of opera in English (including Gounod's *Faust*) at Her Majesty's. His voice by then was

weakening and he tried himself out as a straight actor, as Charles Surface in scenes from Sheridan's *The School for Scandal*. His last appearance was at Liverpool, in May 1868, as Fritz in Offenbach's *The Grand Duchess of Gerolstein*. He married, at an unknown date, Ellen, daughter of the actress Maria Clifford; his home life was 'curiously removed from the theatre'. Of their two sons, William, rector of Clovelly, married Charles Kingsley's youngest daughter, and Clifford became a professional reciter. Harrison died of pneumonia at his home, 33 Gaisford Street, Kentish Town, London, on 9 November 1868, and was buried at Kensal Green cemetery.

C. L. KINGSFORD, *rev.* JOHN ROSSELLI

Sources J. E. Cox, *Musical recollections of the last half-century*, 2 (1872), 128, 147, 351 · G. C. D. Odell, *Annals of the New York stage*, 15 vols. (1927–49), vol. 6 · C. Harrison, *Stray records*, 2 vols. (1892), 1.95–115 · C. L. Kenney, *A memoir of Michael William Balfe* (1875), 185, 192, 202, 246 · H. Phillips, *Musical and personal recollections during half a century*, 2 (1864), 213 · *The Times* (11 Nov 1868) · E. W. White, *A history of English opera* (1983) · d. cert.

Likenesses C. R. Bone, lithograph, BM · D. J. Pound, engraving, repro. in Odell, *Annals*, 342 · D. J. Pound, stipple and line print (after photograph by Mayall), BM, NPG · lithograph (after sheet music of Balfe's *Satanella*), repro. in *New Grove dictionary of opera* · lithographs, repro. in P. Hope-Wallace, *Opera* (1959)

Harrison, William Frederick (1815–1880), watercolour painter, was born at Amiens, Picardy, France, in March 1815, three months before the battle of Waterloo. He was the eldest of the twelve children of William Harrison (*d.* 1861), a businessman from Liverpool, and his wife, Mary P. *Harrison (1788–1875), the daughter of William Rossiter, a hat maker of Stockport, Cheshire. His mother was a flower painter and his brother George Henry *Harrison (1816–1846) was also a watercolourist. His brother Robert *Harrison [*see under* Harrison, George Henry], was a librarian. Harrison worked for the Bank of England for over forty years and was never a full-time artist. He exhibited marine subjects at the Royal Academy, the Dudley Gallery, London, and elsewhere. He died, unmarried, at his home, Goodwick, near Fishguard, Pembrokeshire, on 3 December 1880.

ANNE PIMLOTT BAKER

Sources Mallalieu, *Watercolour artists*, vols. 1–2 · E. M. Routh, 'Harrison [*née* Rossiter], Mary P.', *The dictionary of art*, ed. J. Turner (1996) · Wood, *Vic. painters*, 3rd edn · Boase, *Mod. Eng. biog.* · *CGPLA Eng. & Wales* (1881) · *DNB*

Wealth at death under £2000: administration, 8 Jan 1881, *CGPLA Eng. & Wales*

Harrison, William George (1827–1883), lawyer, was born on 15 January 1827, the fourth son of Charles and Charlotte Harrison, of Sackville Street, Piccadilly. He was educated at King's College, London, before entering St John's College, Cambridge, as a sizar, in 1846. He became a scholar in 1849. He distinguished himself as a speaker on the Conservative side at the university union, and graduated as eighteenth wrangler in 1850. He entered the Middle Temple on 12 April 1850, and was called to the bar by that society on 26 January 1853. He married Caroline Mary Wilkinson; they had two sons, Charles and Harold.

The rise of 'Devil Harrison', as he was known to his contemporaries, was very slow, but he gradually acquired a considerable reputation as a commercial lawyer, and many pupils attended his chambers. He was the co-author, with G. A. Capes, of *The Joint Stock Companies Act* (1856). He was also a prominent freemason, and in April 1882 was appointed one of the senior grand deacons of the grand lodge. He became a bencher of his inn and a QC in 1877. His practice continued to increase until his death at South Lodge, Little Stanmore, Edgware, on 5 March 1883.

FRANCIS WATT, rev. JOANNE POTIER

Sources *Law Times* (10 March 1883), 344 · *The Times* (7 March 1883) · *The Times* (8 March 1883) · *The Times* (12 March 1883) · *Solicitors' Journal*, 27 (1882–3), 319 · Venn, *Alum. Cant.* · H. A. C. Sturgess, ed., *Register of admissions to the Honourable Society of the Middle Temple, from the fifteenth century to the year 1944*, 2 (1949) · J. B. Williamson, ed., *The Middle Temple bench book*, 2nd edn, 1 (1937)

Wealth at death £30,369 1s. 9d.: administration with will, 17 April 1883, *CGPLA Eng. & Wales*

Harrison, Sir William Montagu Graham- (1871–1949), parliamentary draftsman, was born William Montagu Harrison on 4 February 1871 at Charlton, Kent, the youngest child of Captain Thomas Arthur John Harrison, Royal Artillery, then stationed at Woolwich, and his wife, Mary Elizabeth Thompson. From Wellington College he went in 1891 to Magdalen College, Oxford, where he took a first in jurisprudence three years later. Election to a fellowship at All Souls and the Vinerian law scholarship in 1895 led Harrison to consider an academic career, yet he preferred to prepare for legal practice as a pupil of Charles Sargant.

Called to the bar by Lincoln's Inn in 1897, Harrison spent a year in the chambers of Robert John Parker before being invited back to help Sargant. Legal scholarship continued to engage him: he assisted Sir William Anson with an edition of *Principles of the English Law of Contract* and Sir Kenelm Digby with *An Introduction to the History of the Law of Real Property* (1897). In 1900 he changed his surname to Graham-Harrison when on 29 May he married Violet Evelyn Cecilia Graham, daughter of the late Sir Cyril Clerke Graham, fifth baronet, of Kirkstall. They had a daughter and two sons, one of whom later became an Anglican clergyman, while the other, Francis (1914–2001), reached a high grade in the Home Office.

Graham-Harrison was elected to the London school board in 1900 but resigned his seat in 1903 on leaving the bar and joining the civil service. He became an assistant in the office of the parliamentary counsel to the Treasury, then housed at 18 Queen Anne's Gate, Westminster. This small élite department, staffed exclusively by lawyers, was responsible for drafting bills for all government ministries. Working under Arthur Thring and Frederick Liddell, Graham-Harrison grew particularly friendly with the latter, another fellow of All Souls previously in Sargant's chambers. A very fastidious draftsman, G-H (as he was known to colleagues) maintained that a major bill needed three months for proper preparation. Before the First World War it was possible to uphold this ideal in most cases. His duties extended to co-editing the 1907 edition of the *Manual of Military Law*.

In 1912 Graham-Harrison was temporarily assigned to the nascent National Health Insurance Commission to alleviate the burden on its secretary Claud Schuster by acting as legal adviser. Having helped introduce the complex new contributory system—involving close co-operation between the government, insurance companies, friendly societies, and trade unions—he left Wellington House in 1913 to succeed Sir Nathaniel Highmore as solicitor to HM customs and excise, in which capacity he devised the drastic Trading with the Enemy Act of 1914.

Graham-Harrison was appointed second parliamentary counsel in May 1917, returning to work with Liddell in offices now located within the Treasury building in Whitehall. Each of the three counsel turned his hand to legislation of all sorts, taking charge of new bills according to the government's timetable, but it was natural that G-H should specialize in financial matters, given his grasp of national insurance and indirect taxation. He turned down the chance to be Chichele professor of international law and diplomacy at Oxford in 1922 despite being chosen by the electors, who mistakenly assumed his withdrawal to be a gesture of modesty. (The chair went to J. L. Brierly.) Though respected by his peers, he had an ascetic appearance and austere public demeanour which strangers could find off-putting. His knighthood (KCB) in July 1926 followed a CB in January 1920.

As first parliamentary counsel from July 1928, Graham-Harrison earned £2500 per annum and lived at 36 Sloane Gardens, Chelsea. He made a point of drafting the annual Finance Bill himself, a piece of legislation in a class of its own as regards pressure of time, intricacy, and importance, whose slow passage through a committee of the whole house required his lengthy attendance in the official gallery of the Commons. Characteristically, he set great store by mapping out a bill in a logical sequence of parts, clauses, and schedules before commencing on its wording. The Crown Proceedings Bill of 1928 (which aimed to make the crown liable to be sued at tort) and the Pharmacy and Poisons Act of 1933 were rated fine examples of his skill.

A painstaking regard for accurate statement made Graham-Harrison a hesitant witness before parliamentary committees, however great his mastery of the subject. He was wont to remark that the longer a man devoted himself to the science of legislative expression, the more inarticulate he became. The constitutional issues raised by the growth of delegated legislation exercised him a good deal. In a notable memorandum submitted to the committee on ministers' powers in 1930 he argued that, if acts of parliament had to be self-contained (dispensing with departmental rules and orders), it would be quite impossible to produce the amount and kind of legislation that parliament desired to pass. This was also the underlying message of his DCL thesis, called *Notes on the Delegation by Parliament of Legislative Powers* (1931).

Illness forced Graham-Harrison to retire from the parliamentary counsel's office in November 1933. However, having become a KC in 1930, he resumed his practice at Lincoln's Inn and was briefed in March 1936 before the privy council in the Belfast Corporation case, which challenged the Northern Ireland Finance Act of 1934. He sat on the legal board of the church assembly and was chancellor of the dioceses of Durham (1934–40), Truro (1935–40), Gloucester (1937–49), and Portsmouth (1938–40). In addition he served as British member of the Institut pour l'Unification du Droit Privé at Rome and chaired the national merchandise mark committee from 1937, the national committee of investigation under the Coal Mines Act of 1930 from 1936, and the Northern Ireland civil service committee from 1937. His official activities were effectively suspended in 1939, however, when the outbreak of war found Sir William and Lady Graham-Harrison on a rest-cure in Switzerland. There they remained, isolated and in poor health, as long-term residents of the Hotel du Lac at Vevey.

Graham-Harrison was taken home to Great Britain on 27 October 1949. Two days later, on 29 October 1949, he died suddenly at 9 Mandeville Place, St Marylebone, London. Following a funeral at Magdalen College, of which he had been an honorary fellow since 1938, his body was buried on 2 November 1949 at Wolvercote, near Oxford.

JASON TOMES

Sources *DNB* · *The Times* (31 Oct 1949) · H. S. Kent, *In on the act* (1979) · W. M. Graham-Harrison, *Notes on the delegation by parliament of legislative powers* (1931)
Archives All Souls Oxf., letters to Sir William Anson
Likenesses W. Stoneman, photograph, 1930, NPG · H. Collison, oils, priv. coll.
Wealth at death £15,446 8s. 9d.—in England: probate, 27 Feb 1950, *CGPLA Eng. & Wales*

Harrisson, Tom Harnett (1911–1976), ornithologist, museum curator, and co-founder of the Mass-Observation social survey project, was born in Buenos Aires, Argentina, on 26 September 1911, the elder of the two children of Brigadier-General Geoffry Harnett Harrisson (1881–1939) and his wife, Marie Ellen (Doll; 1886–1961), daughter of William Eagle Cole, a Norfolk naturalist, and his wife, Rachel, a Liverpool heiress. He spent his early years in Concordia, Entre-Ríos, Argentina, a British railway-building community where his engineer father, who had gone to South America in 1907 to make his fortune, was now the manager. Young Harrisson spoke no Spanish, had no friends, and received virtually no parental attention. His brother, William Damer Harrisson, born in 1913, was his only playmate. In 1914 his father took the family back to England and joined the army; he earned the DSO for building light railways near the front at Gallipoli, and retired in 1918 with the honorary rank of brigadier-general. In the Itchin Valley, Hampshire, the boys' nanny, Kitty Asbury, took them for long walks and their naturalist grandfather sometimes went along; Harrisson became a keen walker and birdwatcher. Their mother, a hypochondriac, gradually degenerated into alcoholism.

In 1919 Harrisson's parents returned to Argentina, leaving both boys at Eastacre junior preparatory school, Winchester, where their ignorance of 'games' made them pariahs. While at Eastacre, and later, at Winton House preparatory school, Winchester, they spent their holidays at down-at-heel vicarages with assorted Danes and other 'foreign' children. In 1922 the general took them back to

Concordia, for the best year of Harrisson's childhood. He made an aviary and kept notes of bird behaviour. His father taught him to hunt with a gun, fly-fish, and climb mountains. This was the high point of his relations with his father. Back at Winton House in 1923, Harrisson felt more a foreigner than ever but later credited his 'feeling of belonging to England and *not* belonging to it' for helping him see his 'home' country clearly.

Ornithology and early expeditions At Harrow School (1925–30) Harrisson was allowed by an enlightened housemaster to wander for miles (on foot) to gather material for a monograph on birds of the Harrow district. He took part in several bird censuses and in 1930–31, with another public schoolboy, he enlisted 1300 volunteer birdwatchers in a census of the great crested grebe; updating this census afterwards became a fixture of British birdwatching.

Harrisson went to Pembroke College, Cambridge, in 1930, where the pedestrian teaching of the natural sciences bored him. By then he was already recognized by the Oxford naturalists Charles Elton and Max Nicholson as a pioneering ornithologist, having served in that capacity on the Oxford University expedition to St Kilda in summer 1930. Before turning twenty-one he was ornithologist on two more Oxford expeditions: to Norwegian Lapland (1931), and, in 1932, to Sarawak, northern Borneo. He organized the Sarawak expedition and found, for once, that he liked and was liked immediately by a group of people, the longhouse dwellers of north-central Borneo. Ever after, he fitted in better with 'primitive' people abroad and with working-class people in England than with members of his own class.

Before leaving for Borneo, Harrisson had a final row with his father (who later disinherited him in favour of his brother). His father could not forgive him for quitting Cambridge (late in 1931), after more than a year of neglecting his studies and engaging in drunken escapades in the company of young literati (including the novelist Malcolm Lowry and the journalist John Davenport) as given to drinking and brawling as he. His failure to take a university degree proved a lifelong obstacle to obtaining the recognition which he craved and may have deserved. For the rest of his life he pioneered in various fields, full of fresh ideas, energy, and not always pent-up rage.

Harrisson's fourth Oxford expedition (1933–5) was to the New Hebrides. When the rest of the Oxford party left Santo Island for home in 1934, Harrisson got to Malekula, where cannibalism was still widespread. Unarmed, barefoot, with no money, he made friends with the cannibals and took censuses that helped to disprove the then popular thesis that the islanders were dying out from a morbid despair caused by culture shock; he found instead that their numbers were increasing. Harrisson's focus had shifted from birds to people. In his best-selling book, *Savage Civilisation* (1937), he defended the cannibals' way of life and their rights to their own land. He spoke before the Royal Geographical Society and appeared frequently in the press, and on BBC radio and television.

Mass-Observation Late in 1936 Harrisson decided to practise his birdwatching and 'cannibal-watching' techniques on the working poor of the north of England. Installed in Bolton, Lancashire, he claimed that he could, without disguising his accent, blend in with his cotton mill co-workers. While there and, next, as a lorry driver, ice-cream vendor, and shop assistant, he discreetly took notes on the people around him. This remained his fieldwork method. He focused on what people did, not what they said; he claimed that the best field equipment was a pair of earplugs. Thus he made an asset of his chief handicap as an anthropologist: his lack of foreign languages. (Malay, his best foreign language, he never spoke beyond the bazaar level.)

In 1937 Harrisson joined forces with some English surrealists in London who were seeking to do 'anthropology at home' (C. Madge, H. Jennings, and T. H. Harrisson, letter, *New Statesman*, 30 Jan 1937). Alongside the poet Charles Madge he took charge of the effort; they called it Mass-Observation (M-O). This is the work for which Harrisson became best known in Britain. Based, respectively, in Bolton (Worktown) and in London, he and Madge induced small teams of M-O unpaid researchers to collect data by covertly observing people and asking open-ended questions. This data, together with contributions by hundreds of volunteer diarists whose anonymity was protected to encourage frank comment, helped M-O pioneer in fields that market research later took on: bathing habits, burial customs, smoking, drinking, sexual behaviour, attitudes towards current events, etc. Harrisson saw this as a way of letting the ordinary people speak for themselves. A Harrisson–Madge bestseller, *Britain by Mass-Observation* (1939), showed how damage to public morale was caused by the lack of dialogue between the people and their leaders at the time of the prime minister Neville Chamberlain's decision to seek 'peace in our time' at Munich. With this book Mass-Observation became a household word, although its methodology was condemned by academic social scientists, chiefly for its lack of statistical rigour.

In 1940 Madge left M-O and Harrisson found new headquarters for it at the London home of his new paramour, Betha (Biddy) Wolferstan Clayton, *née* Pellatt (1907–1961), a wealthy upper-class wife and mother. Immediately after Biddy's divorce, they married on 25 June 1940 at St Ethelburga's, Bishopsgate. Harrisson's only child (and Biddy's second), a son, was born three months later. By then Harrisson had moved his family to Letchworth, Hertfordshire, to escape the blitz, while he stayed in London.

From 1939 the ministry of information had engaged M-O to provide feedback on its (lamentable) efforts at propaganda to improve civilian morale. In 1940 Harrisson and his team observed people during and after heavy aerial bombardments; M-O colleagues noticed that he seemed to have no fear. M-O's frank reports were unwelcome at Whitehall, especially when published as books and in the popular press, but John Godfrey, director of naval intelligence, then engaged M-O to monitor morale in the blitzed southern ports.

In 1942 Harrisson was called up and joined the King's Royal Rifle Corps, later receiving a commission. On the side he wrote radio criticism for *The Observer*, the first journal to have such a column. Until 1944 he contributed 122 weekly 'Radio' columns. They display his gift for recognizing talent and things of durable interest.

Borneo and Sarawak In 1944 Harrisson was approached by Special Operations Executive, then looking to help its Australian equivalent obtain intelligence on Borneo in advance of an allied invasion. On 25 March 1945 Major Tom Harrisson and his seven seasoned Australian special operatives parachuted onto a hidden plateau in north-central Borneo. Harrisson's unit produced, in terms of damage to the enemy in relation to its own casualties, by far the best results of any Second World War Australian special operations unit. Harrisson provided behind-the-lines intelligence and recruited a thousand blow-piping headhunters who killed or captured 1500 Japanese, losing only a handful of Borneans. Harrisson won the DSO (1946) and dozens of his men received honours.

After the war, lacking credentials for a good job in Britain, Harrisson abandoned his English wife and family, acquired, seriatim, two Kelabit tribeswomen as concubines, and made his home in Sarawak for the next twenty years. Biddy continued a trend towards alcoholism; she divorced Harrisson for desertion in 1954.

As government ethnographer and museum curator of Sarawak (1947–66) Harrisson defended, and recorded the details of, inland Bornean societies before outside influences had transformed them. In 1958 one of his television films about Borneo, *Birds' Nest Soup*, won the Cannes prize for documentaries. He wrote about Borneo in myriad scholarly journals and in the British press. The best-known of his dozen books, *World Within* (1959), describes pre-war life among his favourite tribespeople, the Kelabits, and gives an account of his wartime exploits.

Harrisson explored large portions of Borneo, receiving the prestigious founder's medal of the Royal Geographical Society (1962). In Sarawak's Great Cave of Niah, in 1958 his diggers found a skull of *Homo sapiens sapiens* (modern man), at a level carbon-dated to 40,000 years BP. Lacking stratigraphic methodology, Harrisson faced scepticism from many archaeologists. His reputation as an amateur and limelight seeker, and his violent quarrels with noted anthropologists, helped to keep the Niah skull from receiving the credence it may have deserved.

Harrisson pioneered techniques for saving endangered species, such as the green sea turtle and the Philippine tamaraw, which are still in use. His best collaborator was his next wife, Barbara Brunig, *née* Guttler (b. 1922), a German who had accompanied her first husband to Sarawak and divorced him to marry Harrisson. Married on 14 March 1956, they gained custody of Harrisson's son in 1957, and tried, unsuccessfully, to make a home for the boy in Kuching. The couple pioneered raising orphan orang-utans and reintroducing them to the wild, via a protected half-way house in the jungle. They continued to organize digs in Sarawak, Brunei, and Sabah, and made the Sarawak Museum in Kuching (founded in the nineteenth century by the second white rajah) a model of its kind.

Later years After Harrisson's retirement from the British colonial service at the mandatory age of fifty-five, the couple went in 1967 to Cornell University, Ithaca, New York, where he was appointed senior research fellow. They were active in the species survival activities of the World Wildlife Fund and made annual trips to Brunei, as guests of the sultan. Tragically, Harrisson was permanently banned from Sarawak in 1967 because of rumours and press stories, never substantiated but spread by his many enemies, that he had misused his position in Sarawak to smuggle out Borneo treasures.

In the late 1960s, as US support for south-east Asian studies diminished, Harrisson sought work in Britain. The historian Asa Briggs, then vice-chancellor of Sussex University, invited him to install the Mass-Observation archive at Sussex, with Harrisson as visiting professor. There would be no salary, but Harrisson resolved his money problem by entering into a passionate affair with Christine Forani, *née* Madeleine Lucie Antoinette Bonnecompagnie (1916–1976), a Belgian heiress and Second World War heroine parachutist, widow of an Italian baron, who adopted Christine as her *nom de guerre*. In 1969 he left Barbara for Brussels and his baroness. After his divorce at the end of 1970, they married in London on 9 January 1971. Christine, a sculptor, could be as wild as Harrisson. When the two were not being thrown out of restaurants, or having a riotous good time, or travelling throughout the Far East and north Africa, he worked on the first book to emerge from the revived M-O. The result, *Living through the Blitz* (1976), was, according to Stephen Spender, 'not quite the masterpiece by a man of immensely independent mind—Churchillian, Lawrentian—which one hoped it would be' (*The Guardian*, 29 July 1976). It was, none the less, wrote C. P. Snow, 'the best account of the 1940–41 Blitz ever written' (*Financial Times*, 5 Aug 1976).

Before the book appeared, its author had been killed. Harrisson and his wife died on 16 January 1976, in a collision of their minibus with a timber lorry on a Thai road north of Bangkok. Cremation later that month at the That Thong *wat* in Bangkok was followed by interment of his ashes alongside Christine's in the cemetery of Uccle, Brussels, on 2 February, in the tomb of her first husband, Baron Antonio Forani. A memorial meeting for Harrisson at the Royal Society of Arts in London on 17 March 1976 brought together notables from British media, ornithology, and animal conservation, with sprinklings of politicians and literati.

Rarely able to control his temper or his drinking, Tom Harrisson made many enemies but was a sincere, effective advocate for, and protector of, the common people, whether in London's East End, Bolton, or the tropical bush. He bullied his subordinates but gave them interesting work, the training to do it and, behind the scenes, got them recognition and promotion. His museum staff stayed with him for twenty years. A dreadful husband, father, son, and brother, he was often a loyal friend. He

brought fresh ideas to many fields: fauna conservation, ornithology, sociology, archaeology, and anthropology, through hundreds of articles, scholarly and popular. Despite careless editing, some of his books remained in print and readable decades after his death. He believed in transmitting knowledge in a form that anybody could use. Two words he hated were 'obvious'—nothing is—and 'vulgar'—everything should be. JUDITH M. HEIMANN

Sources J. M. Heimann, *The most offending soul alive* (1999) repr. (2002) · Harrisson MSS, U. Sussex, Mass-Observation archive · T. Green, *The adventurers* (1970) · Harrisson MSS, Australian War Memorial Library, Canberra · Harrisson MSS, National Archives of Malaysia, Kuala Lumpur · personal knowledge (2004) · T. Harrisson, *World within* (1959) · T. Harrisson, *Savage civilisation* (1937) · private information (2004)

Archives Australian War Memorial, Canberra, MSS, AWM 3 DRL 6502, AWM file no. 419/35/25 · National Archives of Malaysia, Kuala Lumpur, MSS · NRA, papers relating to studies on Asia and relating to nature conservation · RGS, letters · U. Oxf., Edward Grey Institute of Field Ornithology, ornithological diary and papers · U. Sussex, papers relating to Mass-Observation archive | FO, Hanslope Park, Buckinghamshire, western Pacific archive, New Hebrides files, WHPC 1935 · Granada, London, Lord Bernstein corresp. · NL Aus., MS 7132 · PRO, SOE files · PRO, director of naval intelligence (DNI) files, ADM 223, especially ADM 223/476/XC/18749 and ADM 223/47b/XL/18749 and HS1/253 · Trinity Cam., letters to J. O. Trevelyan · U. Sussex, Mass-Observation archive, Mary Adams MSS · U. Sussex, Mass-Observation archive, Charles Madge MSS · U. Warwick Mod. RC, Richard Crossman archive · University of East Anglia Library, Norfolk, Lord Zuckerman archive · University of Melbourne, department of history and philosophy of science, Jock Marshall MSS | FILM Cornell University, southeast Asia program library, copies of six documentary films about Borneo by Harrisson and Hugh Gibb, edited by David Attenborough in 1957 and shown on BBC television in 1958 · Granada, London, three TV films about, respectively, Borneo's rainforest, swamp, and caves, made in 1959–60 by Tom and Barbara Harrisson | SOUND BL NSA, BBC 'People Today' (Stewart Wavell, interview with), 17 Aug 1960

Likenesses K. Hutton, photograph, 1942, Hult. Arch. · photographs, repro. in Heimann, *Most offending soul alive*

Wealth at death £5549: probate, 18 Feb 1976, CGPLA Eng. & Wales

Harrod, Charles Digby (1841–1905), grocer and tea dealer, was born on 25 January 1841 at 4 Cable Street, Whitechapel, second child and eldest son of Charles Henry *Harrod (1799–1885), grocer and tea dealer, and his wife, Elizabeth Digby (1810–1860). He left school at sixteen, was apprenticed to a City grocer, and trained as a commercial clerk.

In 1861 Harrod purchased the family grocery shop (8 Middle Queen's Buildings, later 105 Brompton Road) from his father. Brompton Road was being redeveloped and wealthier people were moving into the district, enabling Harrod to build up a good counter trade, repaying his father's sale price within three years. He developed a substantial business which ultimately became Harrods Ltd.

On 25 March 1864 Harrod married Caroline (1841?–1922), daughter of James Godsmark, grocer, of 4 Percy Terrace, Gloucester Grove West; they had seven daughters and one son. Harrod was a kindly man, very firm about honesty and punctuality. A devoted Anglican and family man, after retirement he maintained an involvement bumper Christmas trade resulted from the publicity. Harrod provided a staff member, taken ill rescuing some accounting books from the fire, with invalid fare until he recovered. Trade continued from premises nearby until the grand new Brompton Road store opened in September 1884.

Although not teetotal, Harrod would not seal a business deal with a drink or accept gifts from business associates. He personally interviewed staff, and paid a half sovereign to each going on holiday. Latecomers were fined but, unusually, he would pay overtime. Harrod presided over an annual dinner for staff on the premises. The quality of staff played an essential part in the success of the business, as did Harrod's hard work and integrity.

According to Amy Menzies, many customers asked to be served personally by Harrod, described as a 'good looking young man' serving behind the counter and 'most obliging' (Menzies, 55). In addition he was known occasionally to help customers in dire straits, charging their orders to his account. As the store became fashionable his customers ranked from 'the Peer to the peasant', and Harrods traded worldwide ('Local industries', 4).

In his final years Harrod suffered from arteriosclerosis and retired, in poor health, in 1889. He sold the firm for cash to the newly floated Harrods Stores Ltd, recognizing he would not retire completely if he retained any interest. However the Harrod name was retained by the new firm in recognition of the quality of his business. On retirement, Harrod became involved in politics in Somerset, where he also served as a JP; and then after moving to Sussex in 1902 he was elected a Liberal member of the Sussex county council. While living at Culverwood, a house he purchased at Cross in Hand, Sussex, Harrod served as chairman of the local schools attendance council. Harrod died on 15 August 1905 at the Grosvenor Hotel, London, and was buried on 19 August at Waldron parish church.

N. HANSEN

Charles Digby Harrod (1841–1905), by unknown photographer

with children through Sunday schools, even giving parties for children from all denominations at his home. Grandchildren recollected happy times in the close family circle. Harrod's younger brother Henry worked with him in the early 1860s, moving to Old Compton Street with his father in 1866.

Unlike most grocers, who allowed extended credit to households (even bribing servants to patronize their shops), Harrod advertised his goods for cash (with free delivery), at a very low margin of profit. This risky strategy worked and he competed successfully with the co-operative stores. People were curious after seeing the advertisements, came, appreciated the quality of the goods, purchased, and returned. As business expanded, more commercial space was needed and a first step was for the family to move from the house. Then Harrod roofed over the garden of 105 Brompton Road, acquired numbers 101 and 103, and, in 1883, a large block of land behind them. Continuous rebuilding increased the premises. By 1883 there were six departments, selling food and household items, staffed by 200 assistants.

On 6 December 1883 the shop caught fire, destroying everything, including packed Christmas orders. The purchase of new goods, repacking, and delivery began immediately. Harrod was determined that everyone should be supplied for Christmas. The press wrote admiringly, the public in turn were impressed by their reports, and

Sources 'Founder of Harrods stores: beginnings of a great commercial colony', newspaper cutting (obit.), 17 Aug 1905, Harrods Ltd, London · 'Local industries, no. 10. Cash v. credit. Mr C. D. Harrod', *Chelsea Herald* (30 Aug 1884), 4 · *Sussex Express* (22 July 1905) · *Sussex Express* (12 Aug 1905) · *Sussex Express* (19 Aug 1905) · *Sussex Express* (30 Sept 1905) · G. Frankau, research notes and draft of an unpubd book on the history of Harrods, 1944, Harrods Ltd, London · *Harrodian Gazette* (Aug 1913), 13 · *Harrodian Gazette* (June 1923), 136–7, 153 · *Harrodian Gazette* (May 1928), 133–40 · *Harrodian Gazette* (June 1928), 184 · *Harrodian Gazette* (Sept 1930), 348 · *Harrodian Gazette* (Oct 1955), 435 · Miss Condor, 'The story of Mr C. D. Harrod', text of a talk by the granddaughter of C. D. Harrod, 26 Jan 1932, Harrods Ltd, London · corresp., Harrods Ltd, London [incl. corresp. of Dr R. Harrod, P. Harrod, Mr B. Heather, and Mr Godsmark] · A. C. B. Menzies, *Modern men of mark* (1921), 55–7 · Post office and trade directories, 1830–1915, Guildhall Library and Metropolitan archives · T. Dale, *A palace in Knightsbridge* (1995) · F. H. W. Sheppard, ed., *Southern Kensington: Brompton*, Survey of London, 41 (1983) · b. cert. · m. cert. · d. cert. · *CGPLA Eng. & Wales* (1905)

Archives Harrods Ltd, London

Likenesses oils, priv. coll. · photograph, Harrods Ltd, London [*see illus.*]

Wealth at death £147,494 17s. 7d.: probate, 21 Sept 1905, *CGPLA Eng. & Wales*

Harrod, Charles Henry (1799–1885), tea dealer and grocer, was born on 16 April 1799, at Lexden, Essex, the son of William Harrod and his wife, Thamar, but little else is known about his early life. However, as he became a grocer and tea merchant, it can be presumed he had at least a rudimentary education.

By 1834 Harrod had a business at 4 Cable Street, Whitechapel. The East India Company had just lost its monopoly on the control of tea pricing and individual grocers were able to move into this lucrative trade. Harrod opened new wholesale premises at 38 Eastcheap in 1849, the same year he is thought to have become involved in a small retail grocery shop at 8 Middle Queen's Buildings, Knightsbridge. He ran this one-room shop in conjunction with his city business. He retired from the shop in 1864, having sold it to his son Charles Digby *Harrod in 1861. He ran another grocery at 40 Old Compton Street from 1866, which another son, Henry Digby Harrod, took over.

Harrod married Elizabeth Digby (1810–1860), daughter of a pork butcher from Birch, Essex, in 1830. They had four sons, the youngest of whom died in infancy, and a daughter, who died of measles, aged four. Harrod subsequently moved his family into the house behind the little shop at 8 Middle Queen's Buildings in 1853, as conditions there were better for the children than the City. Scrupulously fair with his sons, Harrod gave each equal help during his life, and equal shares in his estate on death. The Harrods were a close-knit family and when Elizabeth died in 1860, a niece from Birch helped Harrod with the household. After he retired another member of his wife's family cared for him. Harrod died of old age on 3 March 1885 at 2 Oxford Terrace, Wellesley Road, Chiswick, Middlesex, and was buried at Brompton cemetery.

His son, Henry Digby Harrod, later wrote that 'I should like my Father's name … honoured before all other things as he was the person … the principal factor in the making of success, for without his Father's help my brother could have done nothing' (H. D. Harrod to W. Kibble, Harrods archives). Harrod's hard work laid the groundwork for Charles Digby Harrod to build a world-renowned grocery and department store business. N. HANSEN

Charles Henry Harrod (1799–1885), by unknown photographer

Sources T. Dale, *A palace in Knightsbridge* (1995) · private information (2004) · A. Turton and M. Moss, *A legend in retailing: the House of Fraser* (1989) · post office and trade directories, 1830–1915, Guildhall Library and Metropolitan archives · G. Frankau, research notes and draft of an unpubd book on the history of Harrods, 1944, Harrods Ltd, London · letter, Harrods, London, Henry Digby Harrod to William Kibble · d. cert. · *CGPLA Eng. & Wales* (1885)

Archives Harrods Ltd, London

Likenesses oils, Harrods Ltd, London · photograph, Harrods Ltd, London [see illus.]

Wealth at death £3436 9s. 10d.: probate, 18 May 1885, *CGPLA Eng. & Wales*

Harrod, Henry (1817–1871), antiquary, was born at Aylsham, Norfolk, on 30 September 1817, and educated at Norwich. He was admitted an attorney in Michaelmas term 1838, and for many years was in practice at Norwich. He was for twelve years secretary to the Norfolk and Norwich Archaeological Society, and contributed many papers to their *Transactions*. During this period he collected the information which in 1857 he published in *Gleanings among the Castles and Convents of Norfolk*, illustrated with his own drawings. On 16 March 1854 he was elected a fellow of the Society of Antiquaries, for whose *Proceedings* he wrote some articles, principally on matters connected with Norfolk. He was also a contributor to *Archaeologia*, his first paper, read on 3 May 1855, being 'On some horse-trapping found at Westhall' (*Archaeologia*, 36, 454–6). In 1862 he moved to Marlborough, and entered into partnership with Richard Henry Holloway, solicitor; then in 1865 he moved to 4 Victoria Street, Westminster, London, where he became a professional antiquary. He was remarkable for his skill in deciphering old documents, and was employed in arranging the records of Norwich, Lynn, and other boroughs. The New England Historic and Genealogical Society elected him a corresponding member. His wife, Mary Jane, was the eldest daughter of Colonel Franklin Head. Harrod was busy at work on a monograph on the Tower of London when he died at his home, 2 Rectory Grove, Clapham, London, on 24 January 1871, his wife surviving him.

G. C. BOASE, rev. H. C. G. MATTHEW

Sources *Proceedings of the Society of Antiquaries of London*, 2nd ser., 5 (1870–73), 141–3 · *Solicitors' Journal*, 15 (1870–71), 294 · *CGPLA Eng. & Wales* (1871)

Archives priv. coll., corresp. and papers relating to King's Lynn borough records

Wealth at death under £600: administration, 1 June 1871, *CGPLA Eng. & Wales*

Harrod, Sir (Henry) Roy Forbes (1900–1978), economist, was born in London on 13 February 1900, the only child of Henry Dawes Harrod (d. 1918), a solicitor and a member of the London metals exchange, and his wife, Frances Marie Desirée, who was one of the eleven children of John Forbes-Robertson, art critic and journalist, and the younger sister of Johnston Forbes-Robertson, the actor.

Sir (Henry) Roy Forbes Harrod (1900–1978), by Walter Bird, 1963

Frances Harrod, aided by her literary and artistic gifts and her maternal determination, exercised an immense influence on her son, overshadowing that of her husband, whose later years were darkened by his bankruptcy (after misinvesting his remaining capital in a copper mine in Anglesey, he was 'hammered' on the metals exchange in 1907 and remained an undischarged bankrupt until 1917, the year before his death).

Roy Harrod won a scholarship to St Paul's School (from its preparatory school, Colet Court), but stayed there for only two years. His mother insisted that he move to Westminster School, which he duly entered as a king's scholar at the second attempt in 1913. Five years later he won a history scholarship to New College, Oxford. After a period from September 1918 in the Royal Garrison Artillery, he went to Oxford and obtained a first in *literae humaniores* in 1921, despite a discordant relationship with his philosophy tutor, H. W. B. Joseph, and another first, in modern history, only twelve months later. He was elected by Christ Church, Oxford, to a lectureship in 1922, and in 1924 to a studentship (that is, fellowship) in modern history and economics, which he held for forty-three years until he retired in 1967, combining it for the final fifteen years with the Nuffield readership in international economics. He was a fellow of Nuffield College, Oxford, from 1938 to 1947 and from 1954 to 1958. From 1945 to 1961 he was joint editor of the *Economic Journal*.

Apart from some study of British currency, banking, and public finance in the context of the Oxford modern history school, Harrod's immersion in economics began after his election to Christ Church. His principal mentors

in the subject were J. M. Keynes and colleagues (with whom, at King's College, Cambridge, he spent the autumn of 1922 as part of two terms' leave before embarking on his tutorial responsibilities at Christ Church), and F. Y. Edgeworth, Drummond professor of political economy at Oxford. His own principal contributions to economics, dating mostly from the 1930s, covered three main areas of theory: the firm; aggregate demand; and economic growth and fluctuations.

Under the first head, Harrod was an originator of the marginal revenue curve, clarified the relation between short-period and long-period cost curves, and helped to develop the theory of pricing and output decisions of imperfectly competitive producers, that is, those that are in some degree 'price-making'. His papers on these topics were reprinted in *Economic Essays* (2nd edn, 1972). As regards aggregate demand, Harrod's *International Economics* (1933; 4th edn, 1957) and *The Trade Cycle* (1936) pioneered the application of the 1931 'multiplier' concept of R. F. Kahn to an economy engaging in foreign trade. Harrod showed how an increase in exports would, in the presence of underutilized resources and inflexible prices, expand total output and employment up to the point at which imports had risen to match the new level of exports. Keynes's use of the multiplier mechanism in *The General Theory of Employment, Interest and Money* (1936) followed Kahn in concentrating on the closed economy, where it was investment and savings, rather than exports and imports, that were brought into balance through changes in income.

The relationship between investment and savings was also of central importance in Harrod's path-breaking formulation of a one-sector growth model—'An essay in dynamic theory' (*Economic Journal*, 1939), later incorporated in *Towards a Dynamic Economics* (1948; 2nd revised edn, 1973)—in which he sought to analyse the macroeconomic properties of a long-run expansion path. In the so-called Harrod–Domar model (the Russian-American economist Evsey Domar having produced in 1946 a model similar in important respects to Harrod's) the odds were overwhelmingly against the attainment of steady-state growth. This finding initiated a spate of theoretical literature on macroeconomic growth models in the 1950s and 1960s.

Harrod's own economic writings after the Second World War concentrated mainly on questions of policy, especially British economic management (*Are these Hardships Necessary?*, 1947; *Topical Comment: Essays in Dynamic Economics Applied*, 1961; *Towards a New Economic Policy*, 1967) and international monetary issues (*The Dollar*, 1953, and *Reforming the World's Money*, 1965). Following the Keynesian revolution and the post-war development of 'growth economics', Harrod became a persistent and somewhat extreme advocate of fiscal and monetary expansion, arguing that an economy must be run under strong demand pressure if it was to realize its full growth potential, and that inflation and balance-of-payments deficits should be curbed not through general restraints on demand but through direct intervention—namely, incomes policy in the case of inflation, and export subsidies and import restrictions in the case of payment deficits. Internationally, Harrod favoured a rise in the official price of gold to enhance the volume of international reserves. His insistence on expansionary policies at all points owed something to his belief that, even in the post-Keynesian era, it was easier to maintain economic activity at a high level than it would be to restore it after another slump.

Besides his economic writings, Harrod made noteworthy contributions to biography and to philosophy. His official *Life of John Maynard Keynes* (1951), though criticized for undue obtrusion of its author's personality in selecting and presenting material, was a compelling and magisterial account of Keynes's career and achievements. *The Prof* (1959), his memoir of F. A. Lindemann, Viscount Cherwell, was a slighter work, more in the nature of an extended essay, recalling the author's own disappointingly short period of service in Winston Churchill's 'S branch' in the early part of the Second World War as well as painting a sympathetic portrait of the aloof and controversial figure of Cherwell.

In philosophy, Harrod's most ambitious venture, and one to which among all his work he himself attached particular importance, was *Foundations of Inductive Logic* (1956). This attempted—unsuccessfully, in the opinion of professional philosophers—to refute Hume by providing a strictly logical justification for induction, that is, for assuming that 'because the sun has risen every day so far, it will do so again tomorrow'. But his most influential philosophical work was a paper in *Mind* (1936) entitled 'Utilitarianism revised', which sought to defend the utilitarian approach against certain criticisms by elaborating the doctrine. Harrod argued, first, that morality is concerned with means rather than ends, that is, with the promotion of whatever ultimate goals are sought by the greatest number of people, and, second, that utilitarian principles call for adherence to universal rules of conduct (rather than case-by-case decisions) in matters (for example, promise-keeping) where repetition and predictability are themselves socially beneficial.

Harrod combined originality of mind with breadth of interest, and immense power of assimilation and concentration with a fluent and sometimes picturesque writing style. Although not averse to lecturing or orating (including political campaigning, to which he gave considerable energy through much of the inter-war period), he preferred to write (including memoranda and letters to his colleagues on college or university business, characteristically marked 'Immediate' on the envelope). He was of lean physique and above-average height; even in later years, when he had a stoop, his manner retained an Olympian element. He was irresistibly discursive with pupils, to whom he conveyed a sense of contact with great minds and grand decisions, and unfailingly courteous to all.

Harrod was made FBA in 1947 and knighted in 1969. He received honorary degrees from the universities of Aberdeen, Glasgow, Warwick, Pennsylvania, Poitiers, and Stockholm. In 1962–4 he was president of the Royal Economic Society. He was an honorary student of Christ Church (1967) and an honorary fellow of Nuffield College (1958) and New College (1975).

In 1938 Harrod married Wilhelmine Margaret Eve (Billa), daughter of Captain Francis Joseph Cresswell, of the Norfolk regiment, and Lady Strickland DBE, of Old Hall, Snettisham, Norfolk. They had two sons. Harrod died at the family home, the Old Rectory, Holt, Norfolk, on 8 March 1978.   P. M. OPPENHEIMER, *rev.*

Sources H. Phelps-Brown, 'Sir Roy Harrod: a biographical memoir', *Economic Journal*, 90 (1980); repr. in *PBA*, 65 (1979) · personal knowledge (1986) · private information (1986) **Archives** BL, corresp., Add. MSS 71181–71197 · BL, corresp., deposit 9333 · BL, corresp. and papers · BLPES, corresp. and MSS relating to Royal Economic Society | BLPES, corresp. with J. E. Meade · BLPES, corresp. with Lady Rhys Williams · CAC Cam., corresp. with Sir Ralph Hawtrey · Georgetown University, Washington, DC, letters to Christopher Sykes · JRL, letters to the *Manchester Guardian* · McMaster University, Hamilton, Ontario, corresp. with Bertrand Russell · Nuffield Oxf., corresp. with Lord Cherwell · Trinity Cam., corresp. with Sir D. H. Robertson · U. Birm. L., corresp. with Lord Avon · U. Sussex, corresp. with Leonard Woolf | SOUND BL NSA, performance recording **Likenesses** W. Bird, photograph, 1963, NPG [*see illus.*] · *Oxford Mail*, photograph, repro. in Phelps-Brown, 'Sir Roy Harrod: a biographical memoir' **Wealth at death** £81,612: probate, 12 June 1978, *CGPLA Eng. & Wales*

Harrod, William (*bap.* 1753, *d.* 1819), topographer and printer, was baptized on 15 February 1753 at Market Harborough, Leicestershire, the eldest of five children of William Harrod (*bap.* 1730, *d.* 1805) and his wife, Deborah (*c.*1723–1806). His father was a printer and bookseller who served as master of Smith's charity school in Market Harborough from 1780 to 1805 and was the author of a poem in honour of his native Sevenoaks, Kent, published in 1753, and of *The Patriot: a Tragedy* (1769). After attending school at Market Harborough, probably at Smith's charity school, Harrod worked as a journeyman printer in London before opening a business as printer, bookseller, and stationer in the High Street, Stamford, Lincolnshire, in 1776. He married his first wife, Deborah Heather (*c.*1748–1808), in her home parish of Bromley, Kent, on 8 February 1779. They had six children, one of whom died in infancy. Compelled to purchase the freedom of the borough of Stamford in 1776, Harrod was elected to the council on 30 August 1781. In 1785 he published his first work, *The Antiquities and Present State of Stamford and St. Martins, Including Burghley*, in two volumes, adding his own notes on contemporary life to the antiquarian writings of the Revd Francis Peck. He was assisted in this and his next venture by a local apothecary, John Lowe (*d.* 1803). In 1788 he began republishing James Wright's *History and Antiquities of Rutland* (1684) with his own additions, but was unable to secure enough subscriptions for more than two issues. These were reprinted in 1790 but his copperplates and manuscripts were subsequently purchased by John Nichols. From 1793 until 1795 Harrod edited and printed his own newspaper, the *Stamford Herald, or, The Lincolnshire, Rutland, Leicestershire, Huntingdonshire and Northamptonshire Advertiser*, later renamed *Loyal Intelligencer etc.*, which was intended as a whig rival to the established *Stamford Mercury*. It lacked sufficient financial backing and was eventually brought to an end by the increase in stamp duty. A catalogue of *Harrod's Circulating Library* was published in 1790.

In 1799 Harrod moved to Mansfield in the hope of better trade and here he commenced collaboration with the local antiquary Major Hayman Rooke. In 1801 he published *The history of Mansfield and its environs in two parts. I: Antiquities including a description of two Roman villas … discovered by H. Rooke esq. 1786, and II: The 'present state' by W. Harrod*. Short of work, he decided to concentrate on printing handbills and billheads, debating for a while whether to move to London. Some time after 1801 he moved to Nottingham to set up in partnership with printers named Turner. During the turmoil surrounding the election in Nottingham in 1803, he printed several pamphlets, including *Harrod's Defence, or, The Battle of the Printers*. All the material was later republished in a compilation entitled *Coke and Birch: the paper war carried on at the Nottingham election, 1803; containing the whole of the addresses, songs, squibs, etc., circulated by the contending parties, including the books of accidents and chances*.

Harrod returned to Market Harborough after his father's death in 1805 and in 1808 published his final history, *The History of Market Harborough in Leicestershire and its Vicinity*, in which he used material from John Nichols's history of Leicestershire. Rowland Rowse, who had provided most of the material for Nichols in the first place, was greatly angered by this publication, particularly since he had intended to publish his own history. After his wife's death in 1808, Harrod married again at the age of fifty-nine. He and his second wife, Jane, had two children. Little more is known of his activities except that he left Market Harborough in 1818. It has been suggested that he left to escape domestic troubles but it is just as likely that the shortage of money which had been a constant problem throughout his life culminated in the failure of his business. He died in obscurity at Birmingham on 1 January 1819 and was buried on 6 January at St Mary's Church, Whittall Street, Birmingham.

Although by no means an erudite scholar, Harrod enjoyed the respect of his contemporaries. His books received kind reviews despite his eccentric and quite often waggish style. Perhaps Nichols defined him best when, reviewing *The History of Market Harborough* in 1808, he described Harrod as the town's 'jolly and facetious historian … an honest, civil and intelligent printer and bookseller' (*GM*, 1st ser., 78/1, 1808, 329).   JESS JENKINS

Sources A. Broadfield, 'John Nichols as historian and friend', unpublished MS, 733–8 · Market Harborough parish registers, 1753–1816, Leics. RO, DE 1587/1–6, 29 · Bromley marriage register, 1779, Bromley Borough Archives · parish register, Stamford, St Michael, 1779–88, Lincs. Arch., 1/7 and 1/8 [baptism] · J. Simpson, 'Harrod the topographer', *Leicestershire and Rutland Notes and Queries*, 3 (1893–5), 185–7 · *GM*, 1st ser., 89/1 (1819), 584–5 · J. Nichols, *The history and antiquities of the county of Leicester*, 2/2 (1798), 501 · R. Gordon, ed., *Newsplan: report of the Newsplan project in the east midlands, 1987–8* (1989), 239 · J. P. Briscoe, 'A historian of Mansfield', *Mansfield and North Notts. Advertiser* (26 Dec 1879) · D. Pullar, Greater Birmingham burial index · parish register, Sevenoaks, 24 April 1730 [baptism] · *DNB*

Archives Bodl. Oxf., corresp. with John Nichols

Wealth at death impoverished; died in obscurity: *GM*

Harrop, Joseph (*bap.* **1727**, *d.* **1804**), newspaper proprietor and printer, was baptized on 1 October 1727 at Manchester Cathedral, the second of the eight children of James Harrop (*c*.1700–1754), joiner, of Manchester, and his wife, Sarah Dickons (*d.* 1763). He was admitted to Manchester grammar school on 15 November 1736 and later served an apprenticeship with Robert Whitworth, proprietor and publisher of the *Manchester Magazine*. On 11 April 1749 he married Ellen Williamson (*c*.1727–1772) at Manchester Cathedral; they had one child, Harrop's successor, James. Ellen died from consumption on 12 January 1772. Two years later, on 5 July 1774, Harrop married, as his second wife, Mary Bury (*c*.1745–1801), daughter of John Bury (*d.* 1785), brewer and timber merchant of Salford, and his wife, Frances Hanford (*d.* 1788), at St Anne's, Soho. The couple had six children: Frances, John Bury, Sarah Ann, Mary, William Bury, and Joseph; only the two youngest daughters survived into adulthood. Their mother died from dropsy on Christmas day 1801.

Whitworth's whig-orientated *Manchester Magazine* had enjoyed a monopoly in Manchester for several years. In 1752, however, with the assistance of the Revd John Clayton and others, Harrop established a formidable rival. The first number of *Harrop's Manchester Mercury* was issued on 3 March 1752. With the ninth number the title changed to *Harrop's Manchester Mercury and General Advertiser*; later it was called the *Manchester Mercury and Harrop's General Advertiser*. Published every Tuesday—Manchester's main market day—at the sign of the printing press, opposite the exchange, the *Mercury* was to become the longest-running venture of its type in the eighteenth century. The final number, 3672, was issued on 28 December 1830, seventy-eight years after its first publication. A loyal and patriotic paper, advocating tory politics, it supported the government during the period of the American War of Independence. Occasionally Harrop issued supplementary sheets containing war news, noted for their 'expressiveness' of language (Swindells, 'Harrop's "Manchester Mercury"', 201). The popularity of Harrop's paper owed much to his individual enterprise. By meeting the mail at Derby he brought London and foreign news express to Manchester, thereby increasing circulation. He also published various weekly instalments, most notably a *New History of England*, which extended to 778 pages, at a personal cost of 100 guineas.

Harrop was the most prolific Manchester printer and publisher of his day, producing numerous books, tracts, sermons, and bills. He also sold books and patent medicines. Among his most famous imprints are the large paper copies of John Byrom's *Miscellaneous Poems* (1773) and Elizabeth Raffald's *The Experienced English Housekeeper* (1769). He retired from business in 1788 in favour of his son James, although he did serve as borough reeve of Salford in 1792. Harrop died at his home, 1 Bury Street, Salford, on

Friday morning, 20 January 1804. The *Manchester Mercury* (24 January 1804) paid tribute to its former proprietor, a man 'highly esteemed among an extensive circle of acquaintance'. He was buried, with his first and second wives, at St John's churchyard, Byrom Street, Deansgate, Manchester, on 23 January 1804. Harrop's will included cash bequests in excess of £8000; his son James inherited the remainder of the estate. Chetham's Library, Manchester, holds a selection of correspondence relating to the *Manchester Mercury*. JULIE RAMWELL

Sources T. Swindells, 'Harrop's "Manchester Mercury"', *Manchester Streets and Manchester Men*, 3rd ser. (1907), 197–202 • T. Swindells, 'An old newspaper: the enterprise of a Manchester printer and publisher in 1769', *Manchester Evening Chronicle* (12 Sept 1912) • *Manchester Mercury* (24 Jan 1804) • F. Leary, 'History of the Manchester periodical press', 1899, Man. CL, MS f 052 L161 • W. E. A. Axon, ed., *The annals of Manchester: a chronological record from the earliest times to the end of 1885* (1886), 88–9, 96, 132 • J. E. Bailey, 'Manchester booksellers', 19th cent., Chetham's Library, Bailey MSS, XI, MUN. C.7.19 • J. E. Nodal, ed., *Manchester Notes and Queries* (1885–6) [repr. from *Manchester City News*, 6.134, 284] • unpub notes, 1996, Man. CL, biographical cuttings file • J. F. Smith, ed., *The admission register of the Manchester School, with some notices of the more distinguished scholars*, 1, Chetham Society, 69 (1866), 6, 183, 220–21 • C. H. Timperley, *A dictionary of printers and printing* (1839), 682, 817 • *Prescott's Manchester Gazette* (9 July 1774) • W. H. Thomson, *History of Manchester to 1852* (1966), 190–1 • R. W. Proctor, *Memorials of Manchester streets* (1874), 199–200 • R. W. Proctor, *Memorials of bygone Manchester with glimpses of the environs* (1880), 6, 127 • J. Everett, *Wesleyan methodism in Manchester and its vicinity* (1827), 121 • parish register, Manchester, 1 Oct 1727 [baptism] • parish register, Manchester, 11 April 1749 [marriage] • parish register, Manchester, June 1754 [burial] • parish register, Manchester, St John, Byrom Street, Deansgate, 25 Dec 1801 [burial] • parish register, Manchester, St John, Byrom Street, Deansgate, 23 Jan 1804 [burial] • memorial inscriptions, St John's Church, Byrom Street, Deansgate, Manchester [Ellen Williamson, Mary Bury]
Archives Chetham's Library, Manchester, James Crossley collection, accounts, and notes on accounts and printing; advertisements for the *Manchester Mercury*, Mun. E.3.6 and A.7.37
Likenesses engraving, Man. CL
Wealth at death over £8000—cash bequests: will, proved 7 Oct 1802, Chester

Harrowby. For this title name *see* Ryder, Nathaniel, first Baron Harrowby (1735–1803) [*see under* Ryder, Sir Dudley (1691–1756)]; Ryder, Dudley, first earl of Harrowby (1762–1847); Ryder, Dudley, second earl of Harrowby (1798–1882); Ryder, Dudley Francis Stuart, third earl of Harrowby (1831–1900).

Harry. *See* Hary (b. *c*.1440, d. in or after 1492).

Harry, George Owen. *See* Owen, George (b. *c*.1553, d. in or before 1614).

Harry, Nun Morgan (1800–1842), Independent minister, was born on 9 June 1800 in Llanbedr Felffre, Pembrokeshire, the third in a family of four sons. After his father's death in 1804 the family moved to live with his grandfather, David Harry, who gave them a good education. In 1817 he joined the Independent church at Henllan, and in 1822, with the patronage of Lady Barham, entered the college at Newport Pagnell, Buckinghamshire, where he studied for four years.

Harry became pastor of the Independent church at Banbury, and was ordained on 25 April 1827. He remained there nearly seven years. In 1828 he married Eliza, eldest daughter of William Warlow, minister of the Tabernacle, Milford. They had five children. On 15 August 1832 he became pastor of the Independent church in New Broad Street, London, remaining there until his death. He became closely associated with the work of the London Peace Society, and in 1837 he was elected one of its honorary secretaries, becoming editor of the *Herald of Peace*. He also published a series of twelve lectures entitled *What Think ye of Christ?* (1832). Harry died on 22 October 1842 in London, and was buried on 31 October in Abney Park cemetery. R. M. J. JONES, *rev.* ANNE PIMLOTT BAKER

Sources C. Morris, *A discourse occasioned by the death of the Rev N. M. Harry* (1843) • E. H. Rowland, *A biographical dictionary of eminent Welshmen who flourished from 1700 to 1900* (privately printed, Wrexham, 1907) • *Herald of Peace* (Jan 1843) • *DWB*

Harsnett, Adam (1579/80–1639?), Church of England clergyman, was born at Colchester, the eldest son of Adam Harsnett (*c*.1550–1612), a joiner, who from 1601 was sergeant at mace of Colchester, and his wife, Mercy (d. 1640). He matriculated as a sizar from Pembroke College, Cambridge, about 1597, graduated BA in 1601, proceeded MA from St John's in 1604, and took his BD from Pembroke in 1612. On 22 December 1605, aged twenty-five, he was ordained as a priest in the diocese of London.

Harsnett obtained three appointments in Essex. Probably first he acted as curate of Shenfield, where his father's cousin Samuel Harsnett, the future archbishop, was rector in April 1604; on 16 May 1606 Samuel was instituted to the vicarage of Hutton, and when he resigned in 1609 Adam Harsnett succeeded him there. On 8 September 1612, on the presentation of John Petre, Lord Petre, he was instituted to the rectory of Cranham. Harsnett retained both these livings until his death, but seems to have lived chiefly at Cranham, for it was from here that he signed his works and his will. The living was not poor, for in 1640 Ignatius Jordan, Harsnett's successor, provided Ralph Josselin, then the assistant curate, with an income of £24 p.a. Harsnett was married twice, first to Mary, daughter of the celebrated Richard *Rogers (1551–1618), preacher at Wethersfield, and widow of William Jenkins, minister at Sudbury, and second to Mary, widow of John Dawson, of Benham.

In November 1629 Harsnett was one of forty-five clergymen to petition Bishop William Laud against the removal of Thomas Hooker, the lecturer at Chelmsford, proclaiming him to be 'for doctrine, orthodox, and for life and conversation, honest, and for his disposition, peaceable, no ways turbulent or factious' (Davids, 154); later in the month their views were controverted by a second petition of forty-one Essex ministers. Harsnett was acquainted with several among the local puritan gentry. The second edition of his book, *A Touch-Stone of Grace*, contained a preface signed from Cranham on 3 October 1635, to his former parishioners, George Pitt and his wife, Mary, now of Harrow on the Hill, in which he thanks them for their 'constant and continued kindnesses to me and mine'

(A3r). *A Cordial for the Afflicted* (1638) contained a dedicatory epistle to Joan, Lady Barrington, the wife of Sir Francis, and to Mary, Lady Eden, wife of Sir Thomas Eden of Ballingdon Hall; the posthumously published *God's Summons unto a Generall Repentance* (1640) was dedicated to Sir Richard Saltonstall.

Harsnett died between signing his will on 30 November 1638 and the institution of his successor at Cranham on 2 September 1639. Both his wife and his mother, Mercy, survived him. Probate was granted on 16 September 1639. Harsnett named as his executors 'his dear and loving brothers' John Pope of London, salter, and Samuel Harsnett, grocer, enjoining them to 'have a care of my poor orphans as (God knows) I would have had of theirs if I had been put in trust of them'. Harsnett's five children, all under twenty-one, were extremely well provided for. John, the eldest son, inherited property at Much Badow and £500, there was £400 for Ezekiel (who also received his father's books), £300 for Nathaniel and Abigail, and £250 for Anne.   STEPHEN WRIGHT

Sources Venn, *Alum. Cant.* · PRO, PROB 11/181 · W. Benham, 'Pedigree of Archbishop Samuel Harsnett', *Essex Review*, 40 (1931), 105–15 · W. Waller, 'Notes on the Harsnett family', *Essex Review*, 21 (1912), 21–6 · R. Newcourt, *Repertorium ecclesiasticum parochiale Londinense*, 2 vols. (1708–10) · T. W. Davids, *Annals of evangelical nonconformity in Essex* (1863) · 'Liber scholae Colcestriensis: entries concerning sons of the clergy admitted into the Royal Grammar School, Colchester, during the headship of William Dugard, 1637–1642', *Transactions of the Essex Archaeological Society*, new ser., 2 (1879–83), 251–8, esp. 256 · *VCH Essex*, vol. 7

Wealth at death over £2000: will, PRO, PROB 11/181

Harsnett, Samuel (*bap.* 1561, *d.* 1631), archbishop of York, was born at Colchester, Essex, and baptized at St Botolph, Colchester, on 20 June 1561, the son of William Haselnoth (*d.* 1574) and his wife, Agnes. His parents were noted among the twelve Colchester protestants indicted for heresy in 1556 for attending the conventicles led by Thomas Putto, an itinerant preacher from London with a track record for religious radicalism. William Haselnoth was cited as a tallow chandler. Unusually he later changed occupation: in his will of 16 March 1574 he is a baker. The hot gospeller Joan Dybney, mentioned by John Foxe for her sufferings under Mary, left money in her will to provide books for Samuel's education.

Early career in Cambridge and the diocese of London, 1579–1605 Whether this background in strict protestantism led Samuel to change his family name is not clear. He was admitted, as Harsnett, as a sizar at King's College, Cambridge, at Easter 1579, five years after his father's death, but subsequently became a scholar of Pembroke College, where he graduated BA in 1581, became a fellow on 27 November 1583, and proceeded MA in 1584. Soon afterwards he was ordained and, probably on 27 October 1585, he preached at Paul's Cross a sermon on Ezekiel 23: 11 (later published as an appendix to R. Steward, *Three Sermons*, 1656), against a narrowly Calvinist reading of the doctrine of predestination, much as had Richard Hooker in the same pulpit in 1581. Harsnett attacked the doctrine that 'God should design many thousands of souls to Hell before they were' as an opinion 'grown huge and monstrous' and he concluded with an aspiration that formed his lifelong creed:

> Let us take heed & beware, that we neither (with the Papists) rely upon our free will; nor (with the Pelagians) upon our Nature: nor (with the Puritan) Curse God and die, laying the burthen of our sins on his shoulders, and the guilt of them at his everlasting doores.   (R. Steward, *Three Sermons*, 1656, 133, 165)

Archbishop Whitgift silenced him at the time but later Harsnett took delight in claiming that even Archbishop Abbot's brother, Robert, had exonerated him in print. It may be that at this period he remained true to some of his parental leanings. He also drew censure for his failure to wear a surplice in college: this he regarded as a matter of conscience, claiming to the bishop that to do so would be to bring his ministry into contempt. The upshot of the incident is unclear.

In March 1587 Harsnett was appointed master of the free school in Colchester but he did not much enjoy teaching and resigned eighteen months later, returning to Pembroke College to study for his higher degrees in divinity. In 1592 he was elected junior proctor and he became an intimate of the ceremonialist Lancelot Andrewes, the new master of Pembroke, although he had himself supported the candidacy of a Peterhouse man, Mark Sadlington. Andrewes, Harsnett, and John Overall of St John's were among those who supported Professor Peter Baro's criticism of the 1595 Lambeth articles and declined to condemn him for his views.

Ten days after his enthronement as bishop of London on 4 June 1597, Richard Bancroft presented Harsnett with the vicarage of Chigwell in his diocese; Harsnett also became one of his chaplains. The two men became firm friends and much of Harsnett's early promotion was due to the connection with Bancroft, who made him overseer of his will of 28 October 1610 and commanded him to preach his funeral sermon at Lambeth. In March 1598 Harsnett sat on the commission that condemned John Darel for pretending to exorcise devils. Harsnett's *A Discovery of the Fraudulent Practises of John Darel* (1599) gave him a certain reputation in adjudicating matters of alleged witchcraft and in 1605 he was involved in the case of Anne Gunter, the teenage daughter of Brian Gunter of North Moreton, Berkshire, whom he found had acted mischievously. On 5 August 1598 he was installed prebendary of Mapesbury in St Paul's Cathedral and in 1599 he became rector of St Margaret's, New Fish Street Hill, London. As bishop's chaplain Harsnett was also a licenser of books for the press. The decision to publish his college friend John Hayward's *The First Part of the Life and Raigne of King Henrie IIII* was therefore his responsibility. The book appeared in print with an interpolated eulogy to the disgraced earl of Essex in the dedication. This cost Hayward, otherwise known only for devotional works, his liberty. Harsnett only escaped degradation by writing craven letters to the attorney-general, Sir Edward Coke. He weakly alleged that he was 'only a poor divine, unacquainted with books and arguments of state'. In a letter of 20 July 1600 he further claimed that his wife was still in her childbed and 'since your messenger has been at my house, she has neither eaten, drunk, nor slept for fear' (PRO, SP 12/275/31). Some years before he had married a Suffolk girl, Thomazine, widow of William Kempe and the elder daughter of William Walgrave and his wife, Elizabeth, daughter of Richard Poley of Boxted. Thomazine died early in 1601, and was buried at Chigwell on 3 February, leaving an only daughter, also Thomazine, the child born the previous July, who apparently did not live long.

As a childless widower, on 17 January 1603 Harsnett was collated to the archdeaconry of Essex to serve Bancroft in the diocese of London. In the first year of the new reign he published by command of the privy council *Popish Impostures*, an attack on the Jesuit Father Edmunds, alias Weston, and other recusants. On 16 April 1604 Sir Thomas Lucas presented him to the living of Shenfield, Essex, and he resigned his London rectory that autumn. Harsnett remained a close friend of Lucas and his family: twenty years later he asked secretary of state Edward Conway and Archbishop Abbot to help the family to arrange wardship payments for the younger Lucas, who was living in France.

Master of Pembroke College and bishop of Chichester On 5 November 1605 Harsnett was elected to succeed Andrewes as master of Pembroke College. The following year he served as vice-chancellor of Cambridge and he introduced much-needed university statutes. Years later he was remembered for using his rigorist statutes to oppress even the Stationers' Company's privilege. In 1606 he obtained his DD by special grace. His theses treated of double predestination (BL, Harley MS 3142, fols. 54–61). He resigned his much-loved vicarage at Chigwell in 1605 and on 16 May 1606 became vicar of Hutton, also in Essex, which he later ceded to his relative, Adam Harsnett. On 3 November 1609 Bancroft informed Lord Salisbury that the king had bestowed on Harsnett the see of Chichester. Again following in the footsteps of Lancelot Andrewes, Harsnett was consecrated on 3 December by Bancroft. Although he was allowed to retain *in commendam* the Essex living of Stisted, obtained only on 28 September (when he resigned his prebendal stall in St Paul's to the archbishop's nephew, John, later Bishop Bancroft), he gave up his archdeaconry. He also resigned the Lucas rectory of Shenfield to Dr John Childerley, rector of St Dunstan-in-the-East and another of Archbishop Bancroft's chaplains.

In the diocese, as earlier in the parish, Harsnett was a noted preacher. He later claimed, in self-defence, that as vicar he:

> preached every Sabbath in the Morning, catechised in the afternoon: and that he continued the like in Preaching in *Chichester* when he was Bishop there. That in *Norwich* he never missed the public Place, and even preached there against Popery.

He further maintained 'that Popery is a Fire; which will never be quiet; he hath preached a Thousand sermons since, and nothing of Popery can be imputed unto him out of any of them' (*JHL*, 3.389, 19 May 1624). He took a close personal interest in the diocese and conducted in person successive visitations of the cathedral. In the dean, William Thorne (1601–1629), and subdean, John Meredith, Harsnett faced implacable enmity and distrust and in his 1616 cathedral visitation Harsnett pointedly inquired how often 'hath the dean preached in your cathedrall church or any other church of the diocese during the time of 6 or 7 years last past' (Fincham, 1.139–41). Dean Thorne had advanced his protégé to be subdean on 20 July 1616 ahead of the visitation. Although Harsnett suspended Meredith from preaching he resumed once the visitation was over, on Thorne's authority.

Preaching on 11 March 1610 at the outset of his parliamentary career, the new bishop caused grave offence by supporting the civilian lawyer John Cowell, whose *The Interpreter* (1607) had been censured by the Commons. Cowell was a long-standing friend of Archbishop Bancroft and he supported claims for royal absolutism. The king, it was said, ordered Harsnett's sermon to be burned and on 21 March set out his own views on royal duty and civil obligation in a two-hour speech to the house. The matter did not end there, and in the next session Harsnett was himself denounced in the House of Commons by Richard Martin MP for talking up the royal prerogative. In a sermon on Matthew 22: 21 ('Give unto Caesar') Harsnett had preached, as Martin recalled on 10 November, that 'it was not to give but to render, and made subsidies, not gifts but duties' (BL, Add. MS 48119, fol. 204). Martin's theological reading, that the verse clearly commends free giving and not duteous extortion, was a political reading that followed the contemporary translation in the Genevan Bible, later set aside by Andrewes and those responsible for the Authorized Version of 1611. Although there is no formal notice in the parliamentary record of either house of any action taken against Harsnett, he ceased to attend the session after the sitting of 27 October, having assiduously attended the first seven sittings. The affair may have marred Harsnett's early relations with parliament and in the 1614 session (April–June) he rarely attended. As a result he was not sitting when Bishop Richard Neile faced censure in both houses.

As his interest shifted from academe to cloister and court Harsnett found less and less time to attend to business in college, leaving it to two junior fellows, his chaplain John Pocklington and Thomas Muriell. As early as July 1612 Andrewes reported to secretary of state Sir Thomas Lake that Harsnett was keen to resign the mastership to Muriell. Considering Muriell unworthy, and no doubt recalling that in 1599 he had been examined before the university for suspected popery, Andrewes proposed another Pembroke fellow, Nicholas Felton. However, Harsnett not only remained master, but was also re-elected vice-chancellor 1614–15, when he showed himself zealous in maintaining the university's prerogative against the king's desire to grant higher degrees promiscuously to members of his court. But he was eventually subjected to a vote of no confidence from the fellowship; Matthew Wren, Walter Balcanquhall, and Nicholas Felton were among the signatories to the fifty-seven articles complained against him in the so-called *Querela Pembrochiana*.

He was forced to resign in 1616. At the same time the fellows denounced Pocklington for his usurpation of seniority in college and for interpreting the loss of social values in the contemporary world 'to be an evident signe how acceptable the Romish Religion was to God' (CUL, MS Mm.I.46, p. 388).

Bishop of Norwich and 1620s' parliaments   One of Harsnett's supporters in this affair was Thomas Howard, second earl of Arundel, who as a lord lieutenant of Sussex had known Harsnett as his bishop and entrusted to him his son William's education. In seeking the earl's assistance for Pocklington on 22 September 1617, Harsnett disclaimed any interest in higher preferment for himself, but when, following the death of John Overall in 1619, he was translated to the diocese of Norwich, it seems to have been largely due to Arundel's patronage. Overall had died in his first year at Norwich, before his primary visitation. Harsnett hastened to take control, devising in 1620 visitation articles without parallel in the Jacobean church: he specifically inquired whether any lecturers maintained doctrines contrary to the articles of religion or were 'not conformable to the discipline and governement ecclesiasticall within the Church of England, but schismatically and phantastically affected to novelties and innovations' (Fincham, 1.216).

As at Chichester, Harsnett also concerned himself with the fabric of Norwich's cathedral and episcopal buildings. He paid some £2000 from his own money to repair both the house at Ludham and the palace at Norwich. He found himself facing the perennial problem of the stranger churches and of lectureships operating at the limits of episcopal control. In response to his September 1621 report the privy council reached a compromise on 10 October. All English-born members of the Walloon congregation were allowed to continue as members of that church and to submit to its discipline. Harsnett apparently gained an ally locally when in 1625 Muriell was appointed archdeacon of Norwich; he served in the office until 1630.

Harsnett took little active part in the opening session of the parliament of 1621, even after 1 March, when Archbishop Abbot gained the agreement of the Lords not to sit on Wednesdays and Fridays when convocation met. When Harsnett was granted leave of absence it was to preach at Paul's Cross on 18 February, but no other reason is alleged for his missing so many sittings in the first session. In contrast, during the second session (November 1621 – February 1622) he became something of a parliamentary manager, missing only one day's sitting, and he was added to a number of parliamentary committees. He was also among the lords spiritual who on 20 November granted a dispensation to Archbishop Abbot following his accidental killing of his gamekeeper, Peter Hawkins.

In the first month's sittings of the 1624 parliament Harsnett was routinely absent. When he was granted leave of absence on 1 and 5 March, it may have been for him to remain in Norwich to meet the increasing criticisms of the citizenry. In July 1622 he had suspended a lecturer at Ipswich in place of a more conformable preacher and he had also attacked Samuel Ward for popularly celebrating

protestantism in his play *The Double Deliverance* (Amsterdam, 1621). Harsnett's 1620 articles had insisted that women who came to be churched should be veiled. Elizabeth Shipden, who had taken exception to this new insistence on decency, had been excommunicated. In Trinity term 1622 her husband Thomas Shipden, a sheriff and alderman, sought a prohibition against this in the king's bench, which was taken to the archbishop and six bishops. Although the Shipdens lost their claim, such a prominent case more than rankled.

Late in 1623, 300 citizens had presented a petition to the mayor against Harsnett, in particular criticizing his decision to suspend Sunday morning sermons across the city. With thirty-four churches whose likely population was 40,000, all could not easily worship in the cathedral 'where Two or Three Thousand only could hear' (*JHL*, 3.388). The complaints were taken up by Edward Coke and were enlarged in the Commons to six points, which on 19 May 1624 the Lords agreed to hear. Harsnett not only 'inhibited and disheartened preachers on the Sabbath-day in the forenoon', but also countenanced that 'images were set up in the churches and one of the Holy Ghost fluttering over the font' (ibid.). Francis Nethersole had written to Sir Dudley Carleton on 15 May that Harsnett had also excommunicated 'those not turning to face east to pray which is a usurpation of a papal power' (PRO, SP 14/164/86).

These charges allowed Harsnett the opportunity to defend the anti-Calvinist opinions prevalent among some of the higher clergy and to justify himself from any continuing suspicion of popery in the wake of the widespread suspicions raised by the Spanish match. Confident that it was a calumny, Harsnett made light of the charges and answered to the satisfaction of the Lords, although the prince of Wales spotted that he had failed to answer 'touching the Paraphrase of the Catechism taken away by him' (*JHL*, 3.390). Largely at Harsnett's own insistence the case was transferred to the court of high commission from which Abbot would report back. At the close of the session (29 May 1624) James VI and I exonerated both Harsnett and George Mounteigne. He told his parliament that he 'would rather commend than punish the Bishops of Norwich and London for setting up & adorning images in churches and putting down popular lay lecturers' (PRO, SP 14/167/10), but he added that he would not condone the suppression of popular ministers. Lord Keeper John Williams was worried that the king had been too conciliatory. He insisted that the king's speech should not be reported, 'because of passages not very pleasing to Puritans' (PRO, SP 14/167/17) and the official parliamentary record omits it. Those who later complained against Harsnett were to be bound over, as William Locke reported to Sir Dudley Carleton on 12 June.

In the first parliament of the new reign Harsnett attended more frequently, both in London and in the August sessions in Oxford. He was enrolled on the grand committee of privileges and on several committees to hear bills, including that which set out to explain the 1606 act for the 'better discerning & repressing of Popish Recusants' (*JHL*, 3.485, 10 Aug 1625). Work on this halted two days later at the dissolution of parliament. In the 1626 parliament (6 February – 15 June) Harsnett attended almost daily, with only a few short periods of absence. He sat on numerous committees and was one of the parliamentary managers of the conference with the Commons that led the way to the impeachment of Buckingham. His most important ecclesiastical work was undertaken on the committee for the act for 'the further reformation of sundry abuses committed on the Lord's Day, commonly called Sunday'. In November 1617 he was one of the lords spiritual in high commission who heard the case of adultery brought against Sir Edward Coke's daughter, Viscountess Purbeck, and the fifth son of the first earl of Suffolk.

In the 1628 parliament Harsnett was much more active and attended every recorded sitting. With Lord Keeper Williams he led the support of the petition of right with Lord Saye and Sele, Lord Spencer, and the earl of Clare. A copy of Benjamin Rudyerd's speech in favour of republishing Magna Carta and his proposed bill to prevent imprisonment for those who refused to pay loans exacted under the privy seal survives in the bishop's handwriting (PRO, SP 16/102/43). The five propositions sent by the Lords to the Commons 'concerning the great business' on 25 April 1628 were also penned by him (PRO, SP 16/102/14; JHL, 3.769, 770). The petition of right was presented on 2 June 1628. It did no harm to Harsnett's career: the king immediately pardoned those in the Lords who had been involved in the matter and restored Harsnett to favour.

Archbishop of York At the death of George Mounteigne later that year Charles I appointed Harsnett archbishop of York, giving royal assent on 11 December. Thomas Fuller noted in *The History of the Worthies of England* (1662) that it was said that this was on the advice of his long-term friend Arundel; the earl had certainly observed of Harsnett the previous year that 'I am sensible of his extraordinary love' (BL, Add. MS 15970, fol. 5). Many of Harsnett's former colleagues at Pembroke who had been so prompt to criticize him in 1616 now wrote to congratulate him on his eminence in the church. Almost his first task as archbishop was to assist Bishop William Laud of London in drafting the royal declaration for the peace of the church. Composed in December 1628, it prefixed the articles of religion of 1563, which it enjoined as containing 'the true doctrine of the Church of England, agreeable to Gods word', and was available at Epiphany 1629 (T. Birch, ed., *The Court and Times of Charles the First*, 2 vols., 1848, 2.3, 5). It sought to restrict discussion of the niceties of doctrine to the higher clergy and proscribed discussion in the universities. Harsnett, who may have also had a hand in writing the earlier directions to preachers (1622), was in his element.

Harsnett attended each day's sittings in the 1629 session of parliament. In addition to serving on all the usual committees, for privileges, customs, petitions, the increase of trade, and the king's better revenue, he was involved in trying to maintain the ministry and 'prevent decay of churches, chancels and chapels and to support curates' (JHL, 4.31, 16 Feb 1629). He also served on a committee that sought to establish an academy 'for the educating of the children of the nobility, and of the gentry of worth of this kingdom' (JHL, 4.39, 23 Feb 1629). A couple of months later, on 13 April, he founded two schools of his own, in Chigwell, by way of a personal thanksgiving for his eminence in the church.

As soon as Harsnett entered the northern province he set out a familiar pattern of visitation and inquiry to redress several abuses. In his diocese he distributed a circular in 1629 that set out his concerns. Following Bishop Mounteigne's lead he was concerned at the 'great irreverence, openly shewed in your churches and chappels during the time of divine service' when 'yong men mis-led by the example of their elders, doe sit covered with their hats on their heads' (S. Harsnett, *Orders Set Down*, 1629, 1); he also much decried talking before and after service. He was worried that some archdeacons had extorted fees for books and that fees were not regulated. In 1630 he issued metropolitan articles of inquiry for the province that shared some of these considerations. They largely followed those of Archbishop Tobie Matthew (1622–3) but Harsnett added a further sixteen articles, attending to the decay of church fabric, concealed glebe lands, the abuse of surgery and of sorcery, and church-gadding. He visited both the diocese of Carlisle and the diocese and cathedral of Chester (23 June 1630). Bishop John Howson of Durham, who resisted his authority as a visitor, was reported at Michaelmas 1630 to have been excommunicated. Harsnett's appointment to York was evidently not widely popular even among fellow churchmen. Cotton Mather used to tell how he had been prayed against, while some puritans believed Harsnett had died on his way back to York 'at a blind House of Entertainment', as a result of their intercession with God (C. Mather, *Magnalia Christi Americana*, 3 vols., 1704, 3.44). Harsnett's failing health had led him to take the waters at Bath, and it was on his way back northwards that he died in Gloucestershire at Moreton in Marsh on 25 May 1631. He was buried on 7 June without pomp or solemnity at the foot of his wife's grave in Chigwell, as he had requested. The brass that was placed over the tomb, designed by Harsnett himself, depicts him in rochet, chimere, and cope and is the only post-Reformation brass of a bishop depicted in cope and mitre, with crosier and Bible. The inscription makes no reference to his thirty years of widowerhood. He bequeathed his own library to the corporation of Colchester for the use of the clergy. It contains none of his own printed works.

NICHOLAS W. S. CRANFIELD

Sources JHL, 2–4 (1578–1642) · JHC, 1 (1547–1628) · Colchester Court Rolls, Essex RO, 2x3 Mary and 1x2 Eliz m.4 · PRO, SP 14/109/126; 14/110/57; 14/112/128; 14/123/21; 14/123/113; 14/123/118; 12/275/31; 14/49/7; 14/70/15; 14/27/59; 14/49/14; 14/51/11; 14/80/51; 14/132/51; 14/134/20; 14/134/75; 14/142/13; 14/132/59; 14/164/46; 14/164/86; 14/185/29; 14/165/2; 14/165/21; 14/167/10; 14/167/17; 14/167/50; 14/169/16; 14/176/1, 2, 3; 16/6/105; 16/7/27; 16/27/2; 16/64/71; 16/65/78; 16/102/14; 16/102/43; 16/120/8; 16/122/34; 16/123/46; 16/124/81; 16/132/13; 16/132/14; 16/136/66; 16/149/24; 16/152/23; 16/159/23; 16/160/55; 16/160/68; 16/182/8; 16/187/46 · GL, MS 9531/14 · BL, Add. MS 5873, fols. 37, 44 · G. Goodwin, *Catalogue of the Harsnett Library at Colchester* (1888) · J. Strype, *The life and acts of John Whitgift*, new edn, 3 vols. (1822) · *The works of the most reverend father in God, William Laud*, ed. J. Bliss and W. Scott, 7 vols. (1847–60) · K. Fincham, ed., *Visitation articles and injunctions of the early Stuart* *church*, 2 vols. (1994–8) • W. Sussex RO, Ep III/4/9; Ep I/17/16 • R. W. Ketton-Cremer, *Norfolk in the civil war: a portrait of a society in conflict* (1969) • parish register, St Botolph, Colchester, 20 June 1561, Essex RO [baptism] • parish register, Chigwell, Essex, 3 Feb 1601, Essex RO [burial of Thomazine Harsnett] • memorial, Chigwell parish church • parish register, Chigwell, Essex, 7 June 1631, Essex RO [burial] • Venn, *Alum. Cant.*

Archives BL, letters and papers | Arundel Castle, West Sussex, letters to earl of Arundel

Likenesses brass effigy on monument, 1631, St Mary's Church, Chigwell, Essex; repro. in M. Clayton, *Catalogue of rubbings of brasses* (1968), pl. 57

Hart, Aaron [Uri Feibusch, Uri ben Rav Hirz Hamburger] (**1670–1756**), rabbi, was born at Breslau, Silesia, the son of Hartwig Moses Hart (Naphtali Herz), rabbi at Breslau and later at Hamburg. He studied at *yeshivot* in Poland, and probably went to England after 1697, following his younger brother **Moses Hart** [*known as* Moses Bressler] (**1675–1756**), merchant, who had moved to London from Breslau in 1697 and set up in business with the help of the magnate Benjamin Levy, perhaps his cousin or uncle. During the War of the Spanish Succession, Moses Hart was employed in financial dealings on behalf of the Godolphin–Marlborough administration. Moses Hart and Abraham of Hamburg, another prominent Jewish businessman, saw Aaron Hart as a potential replacement for Jehuda Loeb ben Ephraim Anschel, then rabbi of the German and Polish (Ashkenazi) Jewish community in London, whose synagogue was at Shoemaker's Row, London, and would become the Great Synagogue. Aaron Hart succeeded Jehuda as rabbi in 1705 following Jehuda's disgrace when he was found to be officiating wearing a defective prayer shawl.

In 1706 Hart prepared a conditional *get* (bill of divorce) for a member of his congregation, Ascher Ensel Cohen (or Katz), who was leaving for the West Indies to escape his creditors, designed to free Cohen and his wife to marry other partners should Cohen neither return nor write. The decision was challenged by Marcus Moses, whose attempt to set up a *beth midrash*, or study house, in London had been frustrated by Hart's supporters on the grounds that it would count as another place of worship, and its establishment would compromise Hart's dignity. In doing so Marcus Moses ran the risk of being perpetually excommunicated under a twelfth-century ruling for those who questioned rabbinical decisions in divorce cases. Hart initially offered mediation, but then excommunicated Marcus Moses under pressure from Abraham. Marcus Moses appealed to rabbis outside Britain, who agreed that his excommunication should not stand, but Hart rejected their opinions. Marcus Moses then recognized his children's tutor, Johanan Holleschau, as rabbi of a new synagogue, which evolved into the Hambro Synagogue. Hart defended his conduct in his only book, *Urim v'tumim* (1707), the first book printed in Hebrew in London. Holleschau replied in *Ma'aseh rav* (a Hebrew pun meaning 'great event' or 'rabbi's story'), published in 1707 in Amsterdam, which circulated widely and was translated into German. The Hambro Synagogue prospered despite Hart's excommunication of its adherents.

Aaron Hart (1670–1756), by James Macardell, 1751 (after Bartholomew Dandridge)

In 1721 Aaron Hart's synagogue moved to a new building constructed at the expense of his brother on Duke's Place, Aldgate, a site adjacent to its old one on Shoemaker's Row. The expansion of the rival Hambro Synagogue led to a legal battle before the lord mayor and court of aldermen of London in 1725. Moses Hart led the petitioners from his brother's synagogue, but could not prevent the Hambro Synagogue establishing itself on its new site in Magpie Alley, Fenchurch Street. The two communities were not reconciled until after the excommunication of the Hambro community was rescinded in 1750.

Moses Hart married Prudence Heilbruth and had six children, including the philanthropist Judith *Levy (1706–1803); two other daughters married leading Jewish businessmen, the brothers Isaac Franks and Aaron Franks. His place of business was in St Mary Axe, and prosperity allowed him to acquire a mansion at Isleworth. Moses Hart received letters of denization, recognizing him as a British resident, in 1722. In 1744 Moses Hart and Aaron Franks petitioned George II, requesting that he intervene in favour of the Jewish community from Prague expelled from the city in 1744. The king granted them an audience and encouraged his ministers to take the lead in a campaign, co-ordinated with other European powers, aimed at the reversal of the expulsion, which was achieved in 1748. Moses Hart was later involved in the campaign for the Jewish Naturalization Bill of 1753.

Aaron Hart remained at his synagogue until his death. His final years were made more wearisome by visits from Edward Goldney, who campaigned to convert Jews to

Christianity and concentrated on the community's leaders; in Goldney's account Aaron Hart referred him to the writings of William Whiston on miracles, and on his religion stated that 'if it had been his fortune to have been born and bred a Mahometan, or in the principles of any other religion, he should have continued as such' (Katz, 254–5). Aaron Hart died in London during 1756, and was followed by his brother Moses, who died on 19 November the same year. Both brothers were buried at Alderney Road cemetery, London.

Aaron Philip Hart [Moshe Uri ben Yechezkel] (1724–1800), merchant, was born in London on 5 May 1724, the son of Ezekiel Hart (b. 1690?), and may have been related to Aaron and Moses Hart. He went to Jamaica in 1742 and is said to have accompanied Sir Frederick Haldimand and Colonel Bouquet on a visit to New York in 1752. His name appears on a certificate of membership issued by a masonic lodge in New York city, dated 10 June 1760, making him one of the first Jews to become a mason in America. Later that year he accompanied the commissariat of an English battalion that entered Montreal in 1760. He was one of the first British merchants and perhaps the first Jew to settle in the former French colony of Quebec. By 1761 he was established at Trois-Rivières, and in the following years established an interest in the fur trade and began to acquire property. Not wishing to marry outside his faith, he returned to London and on 2 February 1768 married his cousin Dorothy Catherine Judah (1747–1827). Although he was a founding member of Shearith Israel, the Sephardic synagogue at Montreal, in 1768, he was an Ashkenazi Jew who kept his records in Yiddish. Hart sought to establish a dynasty as well as a business empire, and through his dealings with the remaining aristocracy of New France built up immense landholdings. Some of these lands carried titles of lordship, making him *seigneur* of Bécancour and of St Marguerite, and *seigneur* or *marquis* of Le Sablé, as well as feudal dues (*cens et rentes* and *lods et ventes*), which along with the dues from fiefs bought by his sons were valued at the time of their extinction (fifty-seven years after his death) at $86,293.05 p.a.

At his death on 28 December 1800 at Trois-Rivières Hart was reputed to be the wealthiest man in the British colonies, an impression borne out by the detailed inventory of his estate. He bequeathed his businesses, vast lands, and the attached titles to his sons Moses (1768–1852), who acquired the seigneurie of St Marguerite and the marquessate of Le Sablé, and Ezekiel [see Hart, Ezekiel], who inherited the seigneurie of Bécancour, and the other six of his eleven children who survived him; the titles were extinguished along with seigneurial tenure in 1857. His many descendants took various paths, including leading roles in the Jewish community as well as assimilation to the protestant and Catholic populations.

ANDREW COLIN GOW

Sources D. S. Katz, *The Jews in the history of England, 1485–1850* (1994) • C. Roth, *History of the Great Synagogue* (1950) • G. W. Busse, 'The Herem of Rebenu Tam in Queen Anne's London', *Transactions* [Jewish Historical Society of England], 21 (1968), 138–47 • H. Adler, 'The chief rabbis of England', *Papers read at the Anglo-Jewish exhibition* (1888), 230–78 • E. Goldney, *A friendly epistle to deists and Jews* (1759) • S. Godfrey and J. Godfrey, *Search out the land: the Jews and the growth of equality in British colonial America, 1740–1867* (Montreal and Kingston, 1995) • D. Vaugeois, *Les juifs et la Nouvelle France* (Trois-Rivières, 1968) • A. D. Hart, *The Jew in Canada* (Montreal, 1926) • R. Douville, *Aaron Hart, récit historique* (Montreal, 1938) • Archives du Séminaire de Trois-Rivières, fonds Hart • H. Biron, *Index du fonds Hart* (Trois-Rivières, 1950) • American Jewish Historical Society Archives, Waltham, Massachusetts, Hart family papers • early Hart family papers, McCord Museum, Montreal, Canada, M21359 • R. J. Brym, W. Shaffir, and M. Weinfeld, *The Jews in Canada* (1993) • D. Vaugeois, 'Hart, Aaron', *DCB*, vol. 4 • *GM*, 1st ser., 26 (1756), 595 • private information (2004) [family]

Archives American Jewish Historical Archives, Waltham, Massachusetts, family MSS • Archives du Séminaire de Trois-Rivières, Trois-Rivières, Quebec, fonds Hart • McGill University, Montreal, McCord Museum, family MSS | BL, petition to George II, 1744, Add. MS 23819, fol. 63

Likenesses J. Macardell, mezzotint, 1751 (after B. Dandridge), BM, NPG [see illus.] • B. Dandridge, oils (Aaron Hart), Jewish National and University Library, Jerusalem, Israel, Schwadron collection • oils (Moses Hart), repro. in *Encyclopedia Judaica*, 7 (1971), 1356; formerly in boardroom, Great Synagogue, Aldgate, London • portrait (Aaron Philip Hart), repro. in Godfrey and Godfrey, *Search out the land*

Hart, Aaron Philip (1724–1800). *See under* Hart, Aaron (1670–1756).

Hart, Adolphus Mordecai (1814–1879). *See under* Hart, Ezekiel (1770–1843).

Hart, Sir Andrew Searle (1811–1890), mathematician, was born on 14 March 1811 at Limerick, the youngest son of the Revd George Vaughan Hart of Glenalla, co. Donegal, and Maria Murray, daughter of the Very Revd John Hume, dean of Derry. He entered Trinity College, Dublin, in 1828, graduated BA in 1833, and proceeded MA in 1839, and LLB and LLD in 1840. While a student he was a close friend of Isaac Butt, later leader of the Home Rule Party, but then still a Conservative. Their friendship continued even after their political views diverged. Hart was elected a fellow of Trinity College, on 15 June 1835, was co-opted senior fellow on 10 July 1858, and was elected vice-provost in 1876.

In 1840 Hart married Frances, daughter of Henry MacDougall, QC, of Dublin; she died in 1876. They had two sons: George Vaughan, who became a barrister, and Henry Chichester, of Carrablagh, co. Donegal. Hart took an active interest in the affairs of the Irish church, and was for many years a member of the general synod and Representative Church Body. He obtained a considerable reputation as a mathematician, and published treatises on mechanics (1844, 1847) and the theory of fluids (1846, 1850). Between 1849 and 1861 he contributed valuable papers to the *Cambridge and Dublin Mathematical Journal*, to the *Proceedings of the Irish Academy*, and to the *Quarterly Journal of Mathematics*, principally on the subject of geodesic lines and on curves. On 25 January 1886 he was knighted at Dublin Castle by the lord lieutenant, Lord Carnarvon, 'in recognition of his academic rank and attainments'. He died suddenly at Kilderry House, Kilderry, co. Donegal, the residence of his brother-in-law, George Vaughan Hart, on 13 April 1890.

G. C. BOASE, rev. JULIA TOMPSON

Sources *Freeman's Journal* [Dublin] (26 Jan 1886), 5 · *Dublin Gazette* (29 Jan 1886), 94 · *The Times* (15 April 1890), 6 · Burke, *Gen. GB*
Likenesses J. B. Yeats, oils, TCD
Wealth at death £3114 4s. 7d.: probate, 7 June 1890, *CGPLA Ire.*

Hart, Andro (*b.* in or before **1566**, *d.* **1621**), bookseller and printer, whose parentage, date and place of birth, and education are unknown, first appears as a merchant burgess of Edinburgh in February 1587, when it is assumed that he was at least twenty-one, and as a bookseller soon after. His bookshop and printing house were located separately on the same close on the north side of the High Street of Edinburgh, opposite the burgh cross. He became the most successful and important Scottish book merchant and book importer before the Restoration.

Hart's career had both business and political dimensions. He emerges as a major book merchant in 1590 when he and the London bookseller John Norton successfully petitioned the Scottish privy council for the right to import books free of custom, they having 'interprisit twa yeiris syne or thairby the hamebringing of volumis and buikis furth of Almanie and Germanie' to avoid expensive importing via London (*Reg. PCS*, 4.459). These activities were to bring Hart into conflict with the London trade. None the less, acting for Norton and his partners, Hart arranged in 1601 for English printers to travel to Dort to produce bibles for England and to circumvent the monopoly of Robert Barker, England's royal printer. Subsequently, to reduce Scottish Bible printing and importing, the king's printers in London came to agreements with Hart, and later his son John, to supply cheap London bibles for the Scottish market. From 1601 to 1603 Hart also commissioned printings from Amsterdam and Leiden as well as Dort. He also commissioned the London press, as in 1605 when the London printer Richard Field agreed to produce for him an edition of the Psalms of David in metre. In 1610 type set and ready for printing was held for Hart by the Rotterdam typefounder Gabriel Guyot. In 1614 Hart attempted to secure a monopoly on printing overseas and importing into Scotland, but although he purchased such a gift from the king, the privy council refused to ratify the monopoly in a landmark ruling that secured commercial freedom for the book trade.

Hart appears to have been printing from 1607, when he was contracted to print in partnership with the booksellers Richard Lawson and James Cathkin, and from 1608 he was acting as master to printing apprentices. In 1610 he acquired the materials of the Edinburgh royal printer Robert Charteris, but was passed over in favour of Thomas Finlason when a new royal incumbent was appointed two years later. His first major printing project was his great Geneva Bible of 1610, the second Bible edition to be printed in Scotland, which was so accurate it became the template for numerous editions printed in the Low Countries. Thereafter his output was extensive and varied.

Hart was an intellectual and made a considerable contribution to literary publishing, producing volumes by contemporary poets such as William Drummond of Hawthornden and Sir William Alexander. He also continued the Scots vernacular 'revivalism' championed by his predecessor Henry Charteris, and issued various editions of the epic poems of Bruce and Wallace, as well as the work of the poet–dramatist Sir David Lindsay. He published an edition of Bacon's essays, for which he was labelled a pirate by later scholars, an inaccurate description, given the separate copyright regime in Scotland, and also Elizabeth Melville's *Ane Godly Dreame*, a pious volume in Scots verse and one of the most popular presbyterian works of the time. However, Hart's most significant publication other than his Bible was John Napier's *Mirifici logarithmorum canonis constructio* (written in 1614 and published in 1619), which was read throughout Europe.

Although he was the publisher of court favourites like Alexander, Hart was a fervid presbyterian who, as a young man, had come under the influence of Andrew Melville and his supporters. With the booksellers Edward and James Cathkin, Hart was arrested in December 1596 for participating in presbyterian riots in Edinburgh, although his accuser was an opportunistic debtor to John Norton; Hart had acquired, with Edward Cathkin, Norton's Edinburgh stock and debts earlier that year. By then Hart had been recruited by Sir Robert Cecil as an English 'puritan' spy at a time when King James's religious policies were of great concern to Queen Elizabeth and of relevance to the succession question. This surreptitious role may account for Hart's subsequent failure to become royal printer. Hart was in fact connected by a network of marriages and apprenticeships to the main presbyterian book traders of the next four decades, the Cathkins, Richard Lawson, John Wreittoun, John Threipland, and James and Robert Bryson. In 1617 Hart and James Cathkin are found acting as witnesses in favour of the banished presbyterian cleric David Calderwood. Thus the 1619 government investigation into the distribution of Calderwood's *Perth Assembly*, a book critical of innovations in church ritual, saw Hart's, Lawson's, and Cathkin's booths and homes raided and searched. Lawson and Cathkin suffered internal banishment while the ageing Hart received only a severe reprimand. As the publisher of Elizabeth Melville, Hart was undoubtedly sympathetic to the manifestos of Calderwood and he distributed much else of a presbyterian flavour.

Hart was married three times, first on 22 February 1597 to Jonet (Janet) Mitchelhill (*d.* 1604), with whom he had three sons: Samuel (*b.* 1598), John (*b.* 1600), and Edward (*b.* 1601), and one daughter, Janet (*b.* 1602); second on 9 January 1605 to Elizabeth McNacht (McNaught; *d.* 1605), who may have died in childbirth; and third on 26 December 1605 to Jonet (Janet) Kene (*d.* 1642), with whom he had at least three sons: Andrew (*b.* 1606), who died young, John (*b.* 1608), and another Andrew, and four daughters: Margaret (*b.* 1610), Elizabeth (*b.* 1613), Janet, and Rachell.

Hart died in Edinburgh in December 1621. His will and testament survive, dated 12 December, as do those of his first and third wives, and the inventories confirm his huge stockholding of home-produced and imported stock, especially Latin imports. Hart was wealthy in Scottish terms and at his death his estate was valued at nearly £20,000 Scots. His place of burial is unknown.

Hart's widow continued the business with the aid of their sons, principally Samuel and John. Printing as the 'Heirs of Andro Hart', Widow Hart was a formidable book merchant in her own right, printing a variety of texts including the special edition of poems *Eiscodia musarum Edinensium in Carole* presented to Charles I to commemorate his coronation visit in 1633. The previous year she unsuccessfully opposed the appointment of the London printer Robert Young as king's printer for Scotland, taking her case directly to parliament. A. J. MANN

Sources D. Laing, ed., *The Bannatyne miscellany*, 2, Bannatyne Club, 19a (1836), 237, 241–9, 257 · *Reg. PCS*, 1st ser., vols. 4–5, 10–12 · J. D. Marwick, M. Wood, and H. Armet, eds., *Extracts from the records of the burgh of Edinburgh*, 14 vols., Scottish Burgh RS (1869–1967), vol. 5, pp. 80, 172 · D. Calderwood, *The history of the Kirk of Scotland*, ed. T. Thomson and D. Laing, 8 vols., Wodrow Society, 7 (1842–9), vols. 5, 7 · m. reg. Scot. [Jonet Mitchelhill, wife] · m. reg. Scot [Jonet Kene, wife] · m. reg. Scot. [Elizabeth McNacht, wife] · C. B. B. Watson, ed., *Roll of Edinburgh burgesses and guild-brethren, 1406–1700*, Scottish RS, 59 (1929), 238–9 · H. Paton, ed., *The register of marriages for the parish of Edinburgh, 1595–1700*, Scottish RS, old ser., 27 (1905), 309 · register of deeds, NA Scot., NAS. RD. 1/313, 267–8 · W. Cowan, 'Andro Hart and his press with a hand list of books', *Publications of the Edinburgh Bibliographical Society*, 1/12 (1890–95) [whole issue] · NL Scot., Wodrow MS 43 · H. G. Aldis and others, *A dictionary of printers and booksellers in England, Scotland and Ireland, and of foreign printers of English books, 1557–1640*, ed. R. B. McKerrow (1910); repr. (1968), 127–9 · A. Mann, 'Embroidery to enterprise: the role of women in the book trade of early modern Scotland', *Women in Scotland, c.1100–c.1750*, ed. E. Ewan and M. M. Meikle (1999), 136–47 · PRO, SP 94/7/232–3 · *APC, 1601–4*, 14–15 · W. A. Jackson, ed., *Records of the court of the Stationers' Company, 1602 to 1640* (1957), 15 · [M. Sparke], *Scintilla, or, A light broken into darke warehouses* (1641)
Wealth at death £19,528 Scots: will, Scott, Laing, and Thomson, eds., *Bannatyne miscellany*, vol. 2, pp. 241–9

Hart, Sir Anthony (1757–1831), lord chancellor of Ireland, was born on 17 April 1757 in the island of St Kitts, West Indies, the fourth son of William Hart of St Kitts and his wife, Sarah Johnson. He followed two of his brothers to Tonbridge School, appearing on the school lists between 1765 and 1770. He is then said to have been for a short time a Unitarian preacher at Norwich. He was admitted a student of the Middle Temple in 1776, and was called to the bar in 1781. On 7 June 1786 he married Martha Jefferson (d. 1819). He practised in equity work, including bankruptcy. In 1807 he was appointed a king's counsel, and in the same year was elected a bencher of his inn. In 1816 he was made solicitor-general to Queen Charlotte, and in 1827 was appointed vice-chancellor of England in the place of Sir John Leach. Having been admitted to the privy council and knighted, he took his seat in the vice-chancellor's court on 4 May.

Hart was appointed later that year to succeed Thomas Manners-Sutton, first Baron Manners, as lord chancellor of Ireland by the government of Frederick Robinson, Viscount Goderich. He accepted office 'as an Equity judge, not as a politician' (Kenny, 146) and promised not to take sides on the issue of Catholic emancipation. He was sworn in on 5 November 1827, and took his seat in the court of chancery the following day. He was described at the time

as having 'all the appearance of a hale constitution, and a placidity of temper … His eye is piercing yet kindly; his features are strong but not harsh; his countenance is marked with the mingled traits of deep thought and good-humour' (*Irish Law Recorder*, 10 Nov 1827).

Hart's appointment had been criticized by members of the Irish bar, many of whom thought that an Irishman should have held the post. His critics were unaware that the main Irish contender for the chancellorship, William Conyngham Plunket, had been consulted on the appointment. Hart's character and actions soon conciliated his critics. He introduced various reforms, and endeavoured to shorten equity pleadings, which he considered were too prolix. On his appointment he made an order that all petitions in the court of chancery should henceforth be directed to the chancellor, not the master of the rolls, restricting an assumed right of the master of the rolls to appoint a secretary separate from that of the chancellor, and of any such secretary to charge separate fees. When the existing secretary of the master of the rolls brought a petition to set aside the order the chancellor held that the master of the rolls in Ireland was not a judicial officer by prescription having a right to decide a case litigated between the king's subject (as was the case in England), but that the judicial functions of the office had simply been created by statute in 1801.

In 1829, after receiving a memorial on the subject that had been adopted at a meeting of the bar, the chancellor informed the magistrates in Bruff, co. Limerick, that:

> it is the privilege of [His Majesty's] subjects to be heard by counsel in all his courts, for supporting and defending their civil rights; and the rule laid down in the court where you preside precluding that privilege is illegal and must be rescinded. (Burke, 206)

This meeting and the chancellor's communication arose out of an incident in that court in which the magistrates had denied counsel a right of audience in accordance with a rule they had adopted of declining to hear professional persons as representatives of parties. The bar protested at this rule, which reflected a more widespread practice on the part of magistrates in the south of Ireland. The chancellor's action ensured that this right of representation in the petty sessions courts was thereafter respected.

Hart was an amiable man, a sound lawyer, and a patient and urbane judge. His judgments were both able and impartial, and were delivered in a quiet lucid manner. He was continued in office under the duke of Wellington, but retired on the formation of Lord Grey's administration. He sat as lord chancellor for the last time on 22 December 1830, and was succeeded the next day by Plunket. He died in Cumberland Street, Portman Square, London (although his residence at the time was in Upper Harley Street), on 6 December 1831, and was survived by a daughter. Two volumes of Hart's judgments as lord chancellor were edited by Philip Molloy and published in Dublin in 1832 and 1833. DAIRE HOGAN

Sources J. R. O'Flanagan, *The lives of the lord chancellors and keepers of the great seal of Ireland*, 2 vols. (1870) · *Irish Law Recorder* (1827–30) · F. E. Ball, *The judges in Ireland, 1221–1921*, 2 vols. (1926) · Foss, *Judges*, vol. 9 · *The public and private life of Lord Chancellor Eldon, with selections* *from his correspondence*, ed. H. Twiss, 3 vols. (1844) • *GM*, 1st ser., 101/2 (1831), 566 • *Dublin Morning Post* (23 Dec 1830) • O. J. Burke, *The history of the lord chancellors of Ireland from AD 1186 to AD 1874* (1879) • *Annual Register* (1831) • C. Kenny, 'Irish ambition and English preference in chancery appointments, 1827–1841', *Explorations in law and history*, ed. W. N. Osborough (1995) • W. G. Hart, ed., *The register of Tonbridge School from 1553 to 1820* (1935)

Likenesses stipple and etching with watercolour, *c.*1800, NG Ire. • line engraving, 1827 (after T. Cahill), BM, NG Ire.; repro. in *Irish Law Recorder*, frontispiece

Wealth at death over £20,000; left £20,000 to trustees for daughter; plus estates in St Kitts, West Indies

Sir Basil Henry Liddell Hart (1895–1970), by Howard Coster, 1939

Hart, Sir Basil Henry Liddell (1895–1970), military thinker and historian, was born on 31 October 1895 at 4 rue Rosquépine, near the place St Augustin, in Paris (8th arrondissement). He was the younger son of Revd Henry Bramley Hart (1860–1937), the Wesleyan Methodist minister in Paris, and his wife, Clara Liddell (1862–1954). Bramley Hart came from Westbury-on-Severn, Gloucestershire, of yeoman stock. His mother's family was more distinguished, hailing from Cornwall and among its early railway pioneers. Clara's father, Henry Liddell, was assistant general manager of the London South-Western Railway. However, though the young Basil identified socially with his mother's family, he developed a strong bond with his broad-minded and shrewd father; his sour and contrary mother was a much less important figure in his life. Basil had an elder brother, Ernest Ravensworth Hart (1888–1932), who became an eye surgeon. Basil did not enjoy robust health as a child, and was rather indulged as a result.

Education and military service The Harts returned to England in 1901. Basil attended school briefly in Folkestone, but thereafter he was educated privately by governesses, not attending school until he was sent to Edgeborough School (1904–7) aged almost nine. He moved to Willington School (1907–10) before his parents selected a day school, St Paul's School (1911–13), in preference to boarding at Haileybury College, because of his delicate health. During these years he spent much time at home reading voraciously, giving free rein to his romantic imagination, and writing. An adolescent passion of his was aviation, and by the age of sixteen he was writing confident letters to magazines such as *The Aeroplane*.

Bored by school, Hart persuaded his parents to allow him to go up to Corpus Christi College, Cambridge, eighteen months early, and take the history tripos. He was uninterested in medieval and constitutional history, and scraped a third in his qualifying examination in May 1914. Preoccupied with his hobbies, he recalled later, 'I was content to let the future take care of itself until I graduated' (Liddell Hart, 1.10); but this casual attitude was swept aside by the outbreak of the First World War in August. In December 1914 Liddell Hart (a surname he did not adopt until 1921) was gazetted second lieutenant in the King's Own Yorkshire light infantry (KOYLI). He saw three tours of duty on the western front, concluding with active service with 9 KOYLI during the battle of the Somme in July 1916. On 18 July he was gassed in Mametz Wood. While recovering he wrote a short book extolling the qualities of British commanders. He was promoted captain in April 1917 and served as adjutant of the 4th battalion Gloucestershire volunteer regiment in Stroud. Here he met and on 24 April 1918 married at Stroud parish church his first wife, Jessie Douglas (1895–1977), the youngest daughter of J. J. Stone, a stockbroker. They had one son, Adrian John (1922–1990).

Liddell Hart had moved to Cambridge in January 1918 and codified his experiments in training soldiers in a short book, *New Methods of Infantry Training* (1918). Encouraged by this first step, he began to submit articles to military journals. In March 1920 he sent a long paper on mobile offensive tactics to General Sir Ivor Maxse, general officer commanding, northern command. This move inaugurated a technique that Liddell Hart would deploy skilfully, that of impressing his superiors by sending them copies of his writings. General Maxse introduced him to his brother, Leo Maxse, editor of the *National Review*. Liddell Hart's paper was published in this periodical in two parts, as 'The "Man-in-the-dark" theory of war', and 'A new theory of infantry tactics'. Also through Maxse, Brigadier-General Winston Dugan requested that Liddell Hart serve on the staff of 10th infantry brigade headquarters. He was asked to write the manual *Infantry Training*, which was completed in September 1920. He sent parts of the draft to Colonel J. F. C. Fuller and started their long friendship. In October 1920 Liddell Hart delivered the Royal United Service Institution's opening lecture, 'The expanding torrent system of attack'. These important lectures and papers consolidated Liddell Hart's growing reputation as an intelligent interpreter of the operational experience of 1918: distilling its essential principles for training purposes, and then relating them perceptively to mobility and command in a novel way. However, frustrated by the army's doctrinal 'vetting' process that sandpapered his conclusions, Liddell Hart published his unadulterated views in *The Framework of Infantry Tactics* (1921); a revised edition was entitled *A Science of Infantry Tactics* (1923, 1926).

Liddell Hart's career on the staff seemed assured, as he

enjoyed the patronage of Maxse and Dugan. They suggested he transfer to the Royal Army Education Corps; in 1921 he was given a regular commission, but the medical board refused to pass him fit (he had experienced two mild heart attacks in 1921 and 1922). In 1923 he was selected for the Royal Tank Corps, until his medical record was scrutinized; then in July 1923 he was placed on half pay, but he was not officially retired until 1927, with the rank of captain, on the grounds of 'ill health caused by wounds'.

Career in journalism The early 1920s were years of struggle as Liddell Hart faced up to the disappointments resulting in the end of his military career and he tried to find another. His experiments in writing fiction and film screenplays came to nothing. He wrote to Lord Northcliffe asking for a job, but was refused. His first success was in sports journalism, covering Wimbledon for *American Lawn Tennis* and several national newspapers. In 1926 he published a collection of his tennis writings as *The Lawn Tennis Masters Unveiled*. His first opportunity came in 1924 when he accepted the post of lawn tennis correspondent and assistant military correspondent of the *Morning Post*. On 10 July 1925, thanks to the intercession of General Maxse (a director), Liddell Hart was appointed military correspondent of the *Daily Telegraph*. 'I decided to make it a platform', he averred, 'for launching a campaign for the mechanisation of the Army' (Liddell Hart, 1.76). In addition, in the autumn he was selected military adviser (later he was to be editor) to the *Encyclopaedia Britannica*, a stimulus to his study of military history.

Liddell Hart quickly established himself as a journalist of formidable talent. Affable, knowledgeable, and reliable, he soon forged relations of trust with progressive soldiers. He developed an enormous network of contacts and was very well informed; consequently his reports were authoritative, and his judgement was trusted; he was granted privileged access to the War Office. When the chief of the Imperial General Staff designate, General Sir George Milne, wished to signal his desire to reform the army in August 1925, he met Liddell Hart in Arundel. No military journalist before or since has attained comparable influence.

Liddell Hart's early books were written from the perspective of improving war-fighting techniques, and reveal the powerful influence of J. F. C. Fuller. His most notable early success was *Paris, or, The Future of War* (1925), which argued that technological improvement of weapons would enable psychological paralysis of armies and nation states to occur and reduce the destructive time-scale of war. His historical works stress the importance of the great individual, *A Greater than Napoleon: Scipio Africanus* (1926), *Great Captains Unveiled* (1927), and *Reputations: Ten Years After* (1928), complementing the theoretical ideas advanced in *The Remaking of Modern Armies* (1927). He argued that the Napoleonic strategy of confronting the enemy directly in great strength at the earliest moment in order to effect his destruction was obsolescent because of improvements in weapons, especially the machine gun. Scipio's campaigns had shown that 'the moral objective

was the aim of all plans, whether political, strategical or tactical' (Reid, 219). With the exception of *Scipio* these early books were essentially collections (or extended essays), at which journalists excel. They were certainly didactic, confident, and written with great flair. Their reception abroad was not retarded by a trip that Liddell Hart undertook to France and Italy in the autumn of 1926, during which he met Mussolini. Liddell Hart's first impressions of fascism were not unfavourable.

Growing reputation By the late 1920s Liddell Hart had acquired an international reputation as a military critic. He began to develop as a thinker and move beyond the confines of a talented journalist. He worked confidently in assembling larger theoretical and historical structures. The influence of Fuller was less pervasive and his books bear his own distinct voice. Liddell Hart began to take some of Fuller's theorems in new, more radical directions, and indeed began to surpass him in influence. It was perhaps no coincidence that tensions erupting between their two wives in 1928 spilled over into a quarrel in 1929 about American Civil War generals, although they were quickly reconciled. Liddell Hart had championed William T. Sherman as a practitioner of what he later termed the strategy of the indirect approach. His biography, *Sherman: Soldier, Realist, American* (1929), appeared at the same time as Fuller's study of Ulysses S. Grant. Liddell Hart himself believed that the concept of the indirect approach was his major contribution to military theory, and claimed that it was the outgrowth of a general, philosophical outlook on life that valued reason, detachment, urbane 'civilized' good manners, and honest, moderate objectives. In military terms, it was based on movement, deception, and surprise, resulting in the 'dislocation of the enemy's psychological and physical balance' which forms 'the vital prelude to a successful attempt at his overthrow' (B. H. Liddell Hart, *The Decisive Wars of History*, 1929, 5). T. E. Lawrence quickly replaced Fuller as his guru and served 'as the living embodiment' of the theory (Reid, 167). Significantly also, his writings on the First World War, *The Real War* (1930), enlarged as *A History of the World War, 1914–1918* (1934), and *Foch: Man of Orleans* (1931), began to exhibit a critical, hectoring tone, especially in the chapters on the western front.

With these substantial books Liddell Hart took his place as a leading member of the liberal intelligentsia. Thanks to General Sir Ian Hamilton he was elected a member of the Athenaeum. He moved beyond military social circles, consorting with Gilbert Murray, John Buchan, and Maurice Bowra. In the spring of 1930 he was invited as a lecturer to attend the Hellenic travellers cruise, along with Murray, H. A. L. Fisher, and Canon Wigram. He became consumed by 'the truth' and in the years 1930–35 entered a philosophical phase, most apparent in 'T. E. Lawrence' in *Arabia and After* (1934). By comparison with his exalted ideals, Liddell Hart became increasingly impatient with soldiers. His private reflections were littered with complaints about 'military trades-unionism' and wilful blindness to 'truth' (Holden Reid, 175–6).

Indeed, in truth, Liddell Hart's dedication to mechanization and the cause of the Royal Tank Corps always implied much more than an interest in the tank or even armoured warfare. It was a means to an end—the revival of generalship as an art. Liddell Hart's pioneering stress on strategy was initially viewed through the prism of operations. At a lecture given at the Royal United Service Institution in January 1931 Liddell Hart posited a 'British way in warfare'. This essay was included in a book of that title published the following year and subsequently enlarged as *When Britain Goes to War* (1935). British strategy, Liddell Hart argued, had traditionally rested on commercial pressure imposed by naval power. In 1932–3 Liddell Hart delivered the Lees Knowles lectures at Trinity College, Cambridge, published as *The Ghost of Napoleon* (1933). He denounced the Prussian theorist Carl von Clausewitz as the 'Mahdi of Mass'. He blamed him (unfairly) as the source of the brutal, unimaginative, and bloody frontal attacks in 1914–18. The more Liddell Hart stressed the operational potential of armoured warfare, criticized conscription, and stressed the need for lighter, more flexible infantry tactics, as in *The Future of Infantry* (1933), the more his logic seemed to demand a grand strategy that could fit his scenario for a more limited form of war. In 1932 Liddell Hart visited the disarmament conference in Geneva, and advocated a reduction in the size of tanks and calibre of artillery—foreshadowing a new defensive twist to his thinking.

Leading military and public opinion In March 1935 Liddell Hart joined *The Times* as defence correspondent. His appointment conferred not only prestige but a lofty platform from which to expound his views on policy. Throughout 1935–7 he advised the secretary of state for war, Duff Cooper. By this date he had become outraged by revelations concerning the conduct of the First World War that had emerged through private briefings from the official historians, as well as from recently published diaries and memoirs. A further catalyst to Liddell Hart's critical perspective on the war was the help he gave in 1934–6 to Lloyd George when preparing his *War Memoirs*. Liddell Hart thus denounced British generalship harshly in *The War in Outline, 1914–1918* (1936) and *Through the Fog of War* (1938). He came to believe passionately that the continental commitment to France was a colossal error that should never be repeated. In two books, *Europe in Arms* (1937) and *The Defence of Britain* (1939), Liddell Hart advocated a policy of 'limited liability', restricting military commitments to air and naval forces, supported by two high-quality armoured divisions. He assumed a position to advance this case after he became unofficial adviser to Cooper's successor, Leslie Hore-Belisha. He helped introduce many reforms that modernized the officer's career structure and improved training, drills, and living conditions for the troops. The army council was purged of older generals who were replaced by more dynamic men. However, many felt that Liddell Hart had become too powerful and that the army should not be run by journalists. His influence waned and the 'partnership' ended in July 1938.

Liddell Hart's hectic schedule became even more frantic

as he began a round of public-speaking engagements warning against the dangers of fascism, which he detested—leading to an estrangement with Fuller (1937–42)—and opposing both appeasement and war. The confluence of public despair and private sorrow was reached in August 1938 when he separated from his wife, Jessie. His relations with the pro-appeasement editors of *The Times* had also deteriorated, and he left the paper at the end of 1939. In any case Liddell Hart suffered a major heart attack in June 1939 coupled with a nervous breakdown. He moved to Devon to convalesce, nursed by Kathleen Nelson (*née* Sullivan; *b.* 1904), who in 1942 became his second wife, his divorce from his first wife having taken place earlier that year.

Discredited by events Liddell Hart's fall from grace was rapid. The reasons are complex. Throughout the years 1925–37 he had reflected and led public opinion, especially on the First World War. In 1938–9 opinion began to change, but Liddell Hart consistently defended his original stance, and he became out of step. The spectre of war had concentrated Liddell Hart's mind, and his strategic concepts were based less on operations and more on deterrence, containment, collective security, and an 'armed truce'; this structure was cemented by a concept that almost destroyed his reputation: the primacy of the defence. However, Liddell Hart's underestimation of the ruthless exercise of military power was punished savagely by the allied collapse in the West in May–June 1940, leaving him vulnerable to the charge of being a canting false prophet. His self-confidence never quite recovered from this experience. He wrote freelance for the *Daily Mail* and *Sunday Express*. Yet the taint of defeatism stuck, especially after his calls for a compromise peace with Hitler and his criticisms of Churchill's strategy. In 1940 Lord Beaverbrook warned him that his name was a byword in the House of Commons for defeatism. Some MPs had 'stated that you sympathise on occasion with Mosley and his fascist movement' (Beaverbrook MSS, C/159, 15 Feb 1940). As a consistent anti-fascist Liddell Hart must have been stung by this letter, but his attitude to the war inevitably meant that he could not be offered a senior official position.

Liddell Hart's health recovered slowly, but his reputation only fitfully. In 1941 he moved to the Lake District. His wartime books, *Dynamic Defence* (1940), *The Current of War* (1941), and *This Expanding War* (1942), are tedious apologias that somehow miss their mark. His dedication to 'moderation' in *Why Don't We Learn from History?* (1944) seems misguided. Liddell Hart never quite grasped the true nature of the Nazi regime in Germany; and his dedication to limited forms of war is attested in *Thoughts on War* (1944). In the spring of 1943 he still believed that an allied victory was only 'a possibility' (Bond, 147). His contract with the *Daily Mail* ran out in February 1945 and was not renewed. In 1946–7 he seriously contemplated abandoning his military studies and writing full time on (and designing) ladies' fashion, one of his private passions.

Reputation restored None the less, Liddell Hart had laid the foundations for rebuilding his career, and as before

1939 they rested on a combination of historical and contemporary analysis. The strategic concepts that Liddell Hart had explored in the late 1930s were better suited to the cold war. *The Revolution in Warfare* (1946) absorbed the atomic bomb into his thinking, and was followed up by *The Defence of the West* (1950). While still living in the Lake District he interviewed captured German generals in a neighbouring prisoner-of-war camp. His *The Other Side of the Hill* (1948, 1951) discussed their view of their campaigns in the Second World War. Although a valuable source for many years, this book underestimated the generals' allegiance to the Nazi regime. Liddell Hart followed this up with an edition of *The Rommel Papers* (1953). Further, he campaigned indefatigably on behalf of the German generals, rather relishing his minority position, demanding an improvement in their living conditions, and arguing that they should not be tried as war criminals. By the 1950s he had received a number of glowing tributes (for instance, from Heinz Guderian) as the 'creator' of modern armoured warfare. These claims have been disputed, but there can be little doubt that he exerted a general stimulus or inspiration. However, Liddell Hart tended to exaggerate the extent to which his ideas were neglected in Britain and taken up in Germany; and his later choice of the ideas he deemed important from the 1930s was highly selective.

However, Liddell Hart's version of events was accepted, and his rehabilitation coincided with his move back to the home counties, first in 1946 to Tilford House, Farnham, Surrey, and then to Wolverton Park in 1949, and then a decade later to States House, Medmenham, Buckinghamshire. He assumed the role of sage, entertained generously, and surrounded himself with younger 'pupils', drawn not just from western Europe and the United States, but also Israel. He still endured disappointment. His failure in 1946, for instance, to be appointed to the Chichele chair in the history of war at Oxford wounded him deeply. However, by 1960 Liddell Hart's reputation had not just been restored but enhanced, as he was fêted by distinguished foreign admirers, and John F. Kennedy was photographed holding a copy of his *Deterrent or Defence* (1960), which called for a more flexible NATO strategy. When in 1960 he visited Israel he received more attention than any other foreign visitor save Marilyn Monroe. In 1963 he was awarded (with Fuller) the Royal United Service Institution's Chesney gold medal, and a year later he received an honorary DLitt degree from Oxford.

Liddell Hart also emerged as something of a man of the left. His most extravagant admirers in civilian circles tended to be socialists who found much to approve of in his denunciation of the incompetence of the British army (especially in 1916–17) and his trenchant criticisms of its social ethos. His political allegiance if not his sympathies had been kept vague for much of his career. Hore-Belisha had been a National Liberal, and Liddell Hart had been consulted by both the Liberal and Labour parties; during 1938 both agreed to support him as a Progressive candidate for the Rye division. After 1945 he supported the Labour Party, and made contact with defence intellectuals

on the left, like John Strachey and Denis Healey. He was not a Conservative, and his relations with Churchill after 1940 were cool; they united only once, in 1954–5, to denounce Richard Aldington's 'debunking' biography of their mutual friend T. E. Lawrence, a campaign which Liddell Hart orchestrated brilliantly. In 1966 Harold Wilson's Labour government rewarded him with a knighthood for services to military thought.

The years 1965–6 formed Liddell Hart's apogee. He was visiting distinguished professor at the University of California, Davis. A Festschrift, edited by Michael Howard, *The Theory and Practice of War* (1965), appeared, and in the same year two volumes of his *Memoirs*. However, while in Davis he suffered a painful swelling of the prostate and had to return to England early. Yet he was not deflected from his remorseless labours: replying to his huge correspondence, commenting on international events such as the 1967 Six Day War, scrutinizing the book manuscripts of others, and preparing his own *History of the Second World War*, which was published posthumously in 1970. He regularly took an annual holiday after Christmas with Field Marshal Montgomery, at the Carlton Hotel, Bournemouth. He died suddenly at his home in Medmenham, shortly after returning from holiday, on 29 January 1970. He was buried at the parish church in Medmenham on 2 February.

Liddell Hart was a bundle of contradictions. He was self-confident but insecure, vain and sometimes arrogant, but he was remarkably tolerant and open to argument. Despite a rather glamorous air (a man who dined with film stars, as well as famous military men, scholars, and writers) he was fundamentally an Edwardian rationalist and gentleman. He was self-made, however, and could be mendacious in defence of his reputation, but his overriding sincerity and abundant generosity contributed to a tremendous talent for making (and keeping) friends. He had real but untapped gifts as a teacher. For all his weaknesses (which sprang from his journalistic background), Liddell Hart made a massive contribution to British intellectual life, not least in introducing the study of war into its mainstream, and making war studies a respectable province for scholarly endeavour.   BRIAN HOLDEN REID

Sources B. Bond, *Liddell Hart: a study of his military thought* (1977) • B. H. Liddell Hart, *The memoirs of Captain Liddell Hart*, 2 vols. (1965) • B. Holden Reid, *Studies in British military thought: debates with Fuller and Liddell Hart* (1998) • A. Gat, *The fascist and liberal visions of war: Fuller, Liddell Hart, Douhet and other modernists* (1998) • A. Danchev, *Alchemist of war* (1998) • J. J. Mearsheimer, *Liddell Hart and the weight of history* (1988) • B. Bond, ed., *The First World War and British military history* (1991) • J. Luvaas, *The education of an army: British military thought, 1815–1940* (Chicago, IL, 1964) • King's Lond., Liddell Hart C., Liddell Hart MSS • HLRO, Beaverbrook papers • *CGPLA Eng. & Wales* (1970)

Archives King's Lond., Liddell Hart C., corresp. and MSS • News Int. RO, MSS as military correspondent for *The Times* | Bodl. Oxf., corresp. with Gilbert Murray • CAC Cam., corresp. with Monty Belgion; corresp. with M. P. A. Hankey; corresp. with E. L. Spears • HLRO, corresp. with Lord Beaverbrook • IWM, corresp. with Sir Michael Carver [photocopies] • JRL, corresp. with E. E. Dorman O'Gowan • King's Lond., Liddell Hart C., corresp. with Robert Graves; corresp. with John North; letters and articles to Don Russel, editor of the *Chicago Daily News*; corresp. with E. L. Spears;

corresp. with R. W. Thompson; corresp. with Sir Andrew Thorne · NRA, priv. coll., corresp. with John Strachey · Queen's University, Kingston, Ontario, corresp. with John Buchan | FILM IWM FVA, actuality footage | SOUND BL NSA, 'Scipio and Hannibal', 8 Oct 1960, B302365 · BL NSA, documentary recordings · IWM SA, oral history interview

Likenesses H. Coster, photographs, 1930–39, NPG [*see illus.*] · S. Botzaris, drawing, 1938, priv. coll. · H. Heckroth, oils, 1939, NPG · E. Kennington, portraits, 1943, priv. coll. · W. Bird, photograph, 1966, NPG · J. Pannett, chalk, 1966, NPG · M. Fitzgibbon, bronze bust, 1978, King's Lond., Liddell Hart C. · M. Fitzgibbon, bronze bust, IWM · Joss, cartoon, repro. in *The Star* (6 April 1936) · R. Searle, cartoon, repro. in *Punch* (7 April 1954) · Vicky, cartoon, repro. in *New Statesman* (4 Jan 1958)

Wealth at death £63,161: probate, 23 Sept 1970, *CGPLA Eng. & Wales*

Hart, Charles (*bap.* 1625, *d.* 1683),

actor, was baptized on 11 December 1625 in St Giles Cripplegate, London, the son of William Hart (*d.* 1650), probably the minor actor and theatrical functionary of that name with the King's Men. There is no evidence that he was the grandson of Shakespeare's sister Joan Hart, as was once commonly believed. Although Joan Hart did have a son named William, that man died a bachelor in Stratford in 1639. While still in his teens Charles Hart became an apprentice actor with the King's Men. Wright says in *Historia histrionica* that:

> Hart and Clun, were bred up Boys at the *Blackfriers*; and Acted Womens Parts, Hart was [Richard] *Robinson's* Boy or Apprentice: He Acted the *Dutchess* in the Tragedy of the *Cardinal*, which was the first Part that gave him Reputation. (Wright, 3)

James Shirley's *The Cardinal* was licensed for production by the King's Men in 1641, when Hart was fifteen years old, a typical age for a Caroline apprentice actor. Hart is probably also the 'Charles' who is listed as playing Euphrasia, another female role, in a manuscript cast list for a production of *Philaster* by the King's Men about 1640.

When the theatres closed and civil war broke out in 1642 Hart briefly became a lieutenant of horse under Sir Thomas Dallison in Prince Rupert's regiment. However, he soon joined a company of English actors who went into exile on the continent, performing in The Hague in 1644 and before Prince Charles in Paris in 1646. They returned to London in 1647, and on 27 December 1648 Hart and nine other actors signed a contract making upholsterer Robert Conway a sharer in their company in exchange for his financial backing. But only five days later, on 1 January 1649, the authorities raided several London theatres and arrested the actors in their costumes, effectively sending them into exile again for the next decade. Hart and his fellows began to act more openly just before the Restoration, performing at the Red Bull and the Cockpit in 1659–60. On 5 November 1660 they officially became the King's Men under the management of Thomas Killigrew, and soon afterwards they opened their Vere Street theatre in a converted tennis court. Hart became a sharer in the company and one of its leading members, playing such prominent roles as Amintor in *The Maid's Tragedy*, Rollo in *The Bloody Brother*, and Michael Perez in *Rule a Wife and Have a Wife*.

Between December 1661 and spring 1663 the King's Company planned and built the first completely new Restoration theatre, the Theatre Royal in Bridges Street. Hart paid a total of about £130 for a one-eighteenth share in the building, and he also appears to have acted as financial manager for his fellow actors. About 1663 Killigrew appointed Hart, Michael Mohun, and John Lacy co-managers of the company, paying their salary with three-quarters of an acting share taken from the minor actors. Dissension within the ranks soon scuttled this plan, but Hart (often with Mohun) continued to be a figurehead for the company in legal matters.

Although Hart never married, in the mid-1660s he carried on an affair with Nell Gwyn, the popular actress with whom he co-starred in numerous productions [*see* Gwyn, Eleanor (1651?–1687)]. In summer 1667 Nell was lured from the playhouse (and from Hart) by Charles Sackville, Lord Buckhurst, and upon returning in September she was spurned by the actors, with Pepys reporting in his diary that 'Hart, her great admirer, now hates her' (Van Lennep, 113). By the following spring, Hart was having a passionate affair with Barbara *Palmer, countess of Castlemaine (*bap.* 1640, *d.* 1709), onetime mistress of Charles II. Pepys reported in his diary for 7 April 1668 that Castlemaine was 'mightily in love' with Hart, and that 'he is much with her in private, and she goes to him, and do give him many presents' (ibid., 133). However, Lady Castlemaine eventually abandoned Hart in favour of another actor, Cardell Goodman.

Throughout the 1660s and 1670s Hart maintained his reputation as one of the finest actors in the King's Company. He often played kings, princes, and other roles requiring a dignified presence, but he was also a quite capable comedian. Some of his later roles included Alexander in Lee's *The Rival Queens*, Mark Antony in Dryden's *All for Love*, and Horner in Wycherley's *The Country Wife*. The prompter John Downes, after listing some of Hart's tragic roles, wrote that:

> if he Acted in any one of these but once in a Fortnight, the House was fill'd as at a New Play, especially Alexander, he Acting that with such Grandeur and Agreeable Majesty, That one of the Court was pleas'd to Honour him with this Commendation; That Hart might Teach any King on Earth how to Comport himself. (Downes, 16)

Thomas Rymer praised Hart's ability to breathe life into even inferior material, writing that 'to the most wretched of Characters he gives a lustre and brilliance which dazzles the sight, that the deformities in the Poetry cannot be perceiv'd' (Rymer, 5).

In January 1672 the Bridges Street theatre was destroyed by a fire which also claimed the costumes and scenery of the King's Company. The company moved temporarily to the Lincoln's Inn Fields Theatre, which had just been abandoned by the rival Duke's Company, but soon set about building a new theatre of their own in Drury Lane, which opened on 26 March 1674. Because the project had run sixty per cent over budget, Hart and his fellow sharers were forced to pay excessive rents to their investors during their first few years in the new venue.

Soon afterwards renewed dissension arose between the

King's Company and its management. Thomas Killigrew installed his son Charles to manage the company in 1675, with Hart being granted an annual salary of £100, the highest among all the actors. But when the elder and younger Killigrews fell out, the lord chamberlain appointed Hart, Michael Mohun, Edward Kynaston, and William Cartwright co-managers of the company on 9 September 1676. Hart was later made sole manager, but the plan did not work out and on 22 February 1677 Charles Killigrew was again put in charge of the company.

By this time the King's Company was fading fast and losing ground to the younger and more popular Duke's Company. The newer players were bitter at the company's elders for taking the best parts, and so a new agreement was drawn up on 30 June 1680, Hart and Mohun being replaced as sharers by younger actors. Hart was acting only rarely by this time anyway. After a disastrous season in 1680–81, during which the King's Company performed only sporadically, Hart sold his company stock to the rival Duke's Company on 14 October 1681, secretly agreeing to work towards a merger of the two companies. When this union was accomplished in spring 1682 Hart officially retired with a pension of 40s. a week.

Hart retired to Great Stanmore, Middlesex, where he died of kidney failure on 18 August 1683, and was buried on 20 August. In his will he distributed most of his goods among various friends and servants, leaving his share in Drury Lane to his fellow actor Edward Kynaston. The only apparent relative named in the will is an unnamed daughter of Matthew Hart, late clerk of St Botolph without Bishopsgate, to whom Hart gave £20. An elegy printed shortly after Hart's death (Wing, STC, E368) praises his acting highly and names some of his most famous roles.

DAVID KATHMAN

Sources Highfill, Burnim & Langhans, BDA • W. Van Lennep and others, eds., The London stage, 1660–1800, pt 1: 1660–1700 (1965) • J. Milhous and R. D. Hume, 'New light on English acting companies in 1646, 1648, and 1660', Review of English Studies, new ser., 42 (1991), 487–509 • J. Wright, Historia histrionica (1699) • J. Downes, Roscius Anglicanus, or, An historical review of the stage (1708) • T. Rymer, The tragedies of the last age (1678) • D. George, 'Early cast lists for two Beaumont and Fletcher plays', Theatre Notebook, 28 (1974), 9–11 • H. J. Oliver, 'The building of the Theatre Royal in Bridges St.: some details of finance', N&Q, 217 (1972), 464–6 • IGI • E. A. J. Honigmann and S. Brock, eds., Playhouse wills, 1558–1642: an edition of wills by Shakespeare and his contemporaries in the London theatre (1993), 221–5
Archives PRO, signature, CP 40/2751, rot. 317
Wealth at death £95 cash; one share in Drury Lane Theatre; twenty-three gold rings worth 20s. apiece; miscellaneous goods of undetermined value: Highfill, Burnim & Langhans, BDA, 152; will, PRO, PROB 10/1142

Hart, Charles (1797–1859), organist and composer, was born in London on 19 May 1797. He became a pupil at the Royal Academy of Music under William Crotch and was awarded a prize there in 1827. After leaving the academy he was successively organist of Essex Street Chapel, St Dunstan and All Saints, Stepney (1829–33), Trinity Church, Mile End, and St George's Church, Beckenham. He published Twenty-Six Hymns (1820), for the use of the congregation of Essex Street Chapel, Anthems (1830), dedicated to Crotch, a Jubilate and Te Deum (1832), which gained the

first of the yearly Gresham prizes (a gold medal) in December 1831, Sacred Harmony, a collection of hymns set to the music of various composers, including some tunes of his own (1841), and Congregational Singing with Chants (1843). His oratorio Omnipotence was first performed under his own direction at the Hanover Square Rooms, London, in April 1839. This was later published in piano score; Mendelssohn was among the subscribers. Hart died at his home, 148 Bond Street, London, on 29 March 1859. His wife predeceased him, but he was survived by his daughter Emily Rhodes Hart.

L. M. MIDDLETON, rev. NILANJANA BANERJI

Sources Grove, Dict. mus. • Brown & Stratton, Brit. mus. • J. D. Brown, Biographical dictionary of musicians: with a bibliography of English writings on music (1886) • D. Baptie, A handbook of musical biography (1883) • GM, 1st ser., 102/1 (1832), 545 • concert announcement, Musical World (21 March 1839), 188 • review, Musical World (4 April 1839), 216 • CGPLA Eng. & Wales (1859)
Wealth at death under £200: administration, 12 July 1859, CGPLA Eng. & Wales

Hart, Edith Tudor [née Edith Suschitzky] (1908–1973), photographer, was born in Vienna on 28 August 1908. Her father was the radical bookseller and publisher Wilhelm Suschitzky (1877–1934), a campaigner for a variety of progressive causes. Her mother, Adele Bauer (1878–1980), worked in the home. The two of them, together with her brother, Wolf, provided Edith with a lively and educated background, rather than with a particularly affluent one.

Suschitzky imbibed that atmosphere, and was remembered by those who knew her in her youth as immensely vivacious, amusing, curious, and gifted. On visiting Sweden in 1919–20, a trip hosted by the Swedish government for central European children afflicted by the First World War, she found she enjoyed both travel and languages. She also had a natural affection for children and undertook her first training in progressive nursery teaching in Vienna in 1925. Two years later she took a course in London with the pioneer educator Maria Montessori.

By the end of the 1920s, however, and led by her increasingly left-wing politics, Suschitzky decided that the nascent field of photojournalism was the relevant means for her to document social ills. After a course of study at the Bauhaus from October 1929 to April 1930, Edith was ready to use her camera less for creating artful compositions—such as her early geometric perspective through the Prater ferris wheel, which was to feature so significantly in the film of Graham Greene's novel The Third Man—and more for showing people, often children, in pitiful slum housing or living on the streets. Austria was still reeling from the effects of the loss not only of a war but of an empire. Suschitzky's series on street beggars, mostly the war wounded, Gypsies, and blind or deaf people, remains utterly harrowing: all are attempting to earn a living with an instrument or a few stray articles for sale; all are dressed in rags, some lacking even shoes or protection against the cold. Other images illustrate the lives of those without domestic water and power, without a bathroom or furniture. Whole families exist on bomb sites or rubbish tips. By contrast, there are heroic pictures of May day

Edith Tudor Hart (1908–1973), by Wolfgang Suschitzky, 1937

parades (shot from above) and demonstrations by the unemployed with the already sinister figures of the special police forces set against barbed-wire barricades in the background.

Suschitzky travelled to Paris and London at the end of the 1920s, and in 1932 to Italy, where she took a series of photographs of Gypsies at Montefalcone. In 1925 she met an idealistic young British doctor called Alexander Tudor Hart (d. 1992), who had gone to Vienna to study orthopaedics under the famous surgeon Professor Boehler. They married at the British consulate in Vienna in 1933, and determined to return to London. Edith's family were Jewish and her brother, Wolf, left for Amsterdam in 1934. Already a member of such organizations as the Artists' International Association (AIA) and the Workers' Film and Photo League, Tudor Hart became involved in curating and contributing to such exhibitions as the AIA's 'The social scene' (1934) and 'Artists against fascism and against war' (1935).

Following their wedding and the move, the Tudor Harts did not remain long in London. Sharing Edith's left-wing politics and motivated by humanitarian concerns, Alexander Tudor Hart determined to use his skills among the miners and steelworkers of the Rhondda valley in Wales. Tudor Hart documented a great many of her husband's patients and their children, living conditions, home and working lives. By 1936 their own child, Tommy, was born and Alexander Tudor Hart enlisted as a surgeon on the government (republican) side in the Spanish Civil War. By the time he returned at its end Edith had to accept that their marriage was effectively over. They were finally divorced in 1945.

Thus from the mid-1930s until her death in 1973, Tudor Hart had to provide not only for herself but also for a son who, it gradually emerged, suffered from autism. A dual dedication to Tommy, for whom she attempted every kind of restitution to health, from psychoanalysis to a residential home, and to her own uncompromising style of photography inevitably put her under severe strain. The outlets for her work, never large nor lucrative, were dwindling, particularly with the post-war demise of *Lilliput*, the *News Chronicle*, and especially *Picture Post*. Even the non-paying but morally supportive left-wing press took a while to recover its circulation—paradoxically afflicted by the combination of a Labour Party victory and higher standards of living. She wrote several features on women, health, and work, including *Working Class Wives*, published as an imprint in 1939, and in 1952 produced a book for the Ministry of Education entitled *Moving and Growing*.

Tudor Hart's situation was made more difficult by the British security services' belief that she was a Communist Party spy. Tudor Hart believed they pursued her to the point where, by the 1960s, she felt bound to destroy not only a very great number of prints but also her negatives. She attempted a variety of semi-commercial ventures, from the Sun Studio in the West End (where she worked as a photographic assistant) to a small antiques shop in Brighton, without finding one that thrived. After a long illness she died at Copper Cliff, Redhill Drive, Brighton, of stomach cancer on 12 May 1973, leaving virtually no estate but her remaining negatives to her brother. She was cremated in Brighton on 15 May.

The best testament to Edith Tudor Hart's work is her 'Photography as a profession', written for the magazine *Housewife*:

> In the hands of the person who uses it with feeling and imagination, the camera becomes very much more than the means of earning a living, it becomes a vital factor in recording and influencing the life of the people and in promoting human understanding. (Hart, 4–5)

AMANDA HOPKINSON

Sources D. Nishen, *The eye of conscience: Wolf Suschitzky* (1987) · N. Rosenblume, *A history of women photographers* (1994), 128, 141, 145 · V. Williams, *Women photographers: the other observers, 1900 to the present* (1986) · E. T. Hart, 'Photography as a profession', *Housewife* (June 1945), 4–5 · d. cert. · private information (2004)
Likenesses W. Suschitzky, photograph, 1937, priv. coll. [*see illus.*]
Wealth at death £3054: administration, 18 Jan 1974, *CGPLA Eng. & Wales*

Hart, Eliakim ben Abraham [Jacob] (1745x50–1814), writer in Hebrew on religion and science, was born in London probably between 1745 and 1750, the son of Abraham Hart. The name of Hart's mother is unknown, but his paternal grandfather had come from Eisenstadt in Hungary, and was of a rabbinical family. Hart married his wife Rachel in or before 1769; their eldest daughter Hannah (d. 1846) was born then or in 1770, and was followed by two others daughters, Ann and Frances, and three sons, Eliezer, Abraham (who died in childhood), and Asher Angel. Hart was treasurer of the Hambro Synagogue in 1784, but in 1797 was one of the founders of the Denmark Court Synagogue, signing the lease as Jacob Hart, the name by which he was known outside the Jewish community, and identifying his profession as a jeweller with a business on the Strand. Hart was also a freemason and a member of Hiram's Lodge, Swan Street. In 1801 he is listed in the lodge's directory, along with his age (given as forty-five, although the date of the birth of his first child suggests that he was older) and profession (silversmith).

Hart wrote Hebrew books on a wide variety of subjects including grammar, mathematics, natural philosophy, and the cabbala. His major intellectual project was a planned series of ten relatively modest works entitled *Asarah ma'amarot* (*Ten Essays*), of which only five were printed. The first, *Milḥamot Adonai* (*Wars of the Lord*), on the subject of Newtonianism, was published in London in 1794 and is clearly his most important work. A year later he also published in London *Binah la-itim* (*Chronology*), an explication of the Daniel prophecies in light of past chronologies and contemporary political events. His other works include a summary and commentary of part of the work of Joseph Delmedigo, a seventeenth-century Hebrew writer on the cabbala and science. He also completed another summary of cabbala, a work on the Hebrew vowels, and a Hebrew grammar, all published in Germany. His other works, which were apparently never printed, dealt primarily with cabbala, especially the system of the sixteenth-century cabbalist Isaac Luria and on mystical speculations concerning the secrets of numbers. Hart's entire works betray the links between natural philosophy and mystical theosophy that existed in his mind, in a manner reminiscent of a similar integration in the writings of Delmedigo, Newton, and some of his disciples.

Hart's relative obscurity as a writer is surely related to the esoteric subjects he elected to treat, to the relative brevity and unfinished nature of his planned works, but mostly to the fact that he chose to write in Hebrew, essentially excluding any potential readership among Jews or Christians in England and focusing instead on Hebraists living in central or eastern Europe. In one instance, the well-known Polish-Jewish author of a Hebrew encyclopaedia, Pinhas Elijah Hurwitz, cited him approvingly.

The *Milḥamot Adonai* is ostensibly a polemic against four groups who corrupt the beliefs of traditional Jews and impugn the sanctity of their sacred revelation: ancient pagan chroniclers who claim that other cultures preceded that of the Hebrews, Aristotle and his followers, Descartes and his followers, and Newton and his more radical students. The most sustained part of the polemic is his treatment of Newton whom he initially praises for his scientific contributions as well as for his commitment to the truth of biblical prophecy. Hart's explicit mention of Newton's commentary on the book of Daniel suggests that it was probably the model for Hart's own commentary as well.

Hart offers a cursory description of Newton's principal scientific accomplishments regarding the laws of motion, especially gravitation, as well as his optical experiments with the prism. He quickly interrupts this description, however, to summarize the conservative critique of Newton by Robert Greene, fellow of Clare College, Cambridge, and staunch opponent of the latitudinarian interpreters of Newton. Unlike most high-churchmen, Greene had familiarized himself with Newtonian philosophy, especially in its 'holy alliance' with the latitudinarians, and maintained that it imperilled the Christian faith by allowing nature to be controlled by seemingly random forces rather than the direct providential hand of the creator. In selecting Greene as his chief source of criticism of Newtonianism, Hart appropriated an informed battery of arguments against the cosy relationship between Newtonianism and the Jewish faith previously articulated by such Anglo-Jewish writers as David Nieto and Mordechai Gumpel Schnaber Levison. It was also a powerful antidote to the negative example of David Nieto's own disciple, Jacob Sarmento, who as a Newtonian had deserted the Jewish faith. For Hart, the gushing enthusiasm of Newton's supporters who triumphantly proclaimed the new merger of science and faith could ultimately threaten Jewish notions of divine providence and revelation. Greene offered him the brake on the excesses the latitudinarian and deist followers of Newton were espousing. Like Greene, Hart could extol Newton's glorious achievements while distancing himself from his more radical interpreters. Hart spent his entire life in London except for the period between 1800 and 1804, when he may have received rabbinical ordination in Germany; he first refers to himself as rabbi in 1805. Hart died on 30 April 1814. His home at the time of his death was probably on Plumbtree Street (later Grape Street), near Drury Lane. He was buried on 1 May 1814 at Lauriston Road cemetery, which he had helped to found. At the time of his death he was in dispute with some other leading members of Denmark Court Synagogue, and consequently did not leave the synagogue any money, although his business had enabled him to support it generously in the past. Three coaches were sent to the synagogue at his funeral at double the usual cost, an indicator of the social and financial position Hart enjoyed in the early nineteenth-century Jewish community in London. His widow died on 23 November 1833 and was buried at Lauriston Road cemetery. DAVID B. RUDERMAN

Sources A. Barnett and S. Brodetsky, 'Eliakim ben Abraham (Jacob Hart): an Anglo-Jewish scholar of the eighteenth century', *Transactions of the Jewish Historical Society of England*, 14 (1935–9), 207–23 • D. Ruderman, 'On defining a Jewish stance toward Newtonianism: Eliakim ben Abraham Hart's *Wars of the Lord*', *Science in context*, 10 (1997), 677–92 • D. Ruderman, *Jewish thought and scientific discovery in early modern Europe* (1995) • J. Gascoigne, *Cambridge in the age of the Enlightenment* (1989) • D. B. Ruderman, *Jewish enlightenment in an English key: Anglo-Jewry's construction of modern Jewish thought* (2000) • directory of Hiram's Lodge, Swan Street, Masonic Grand Lodge, London

Hart, Ernest Abraham (1835–1898), medical journalist, was born on 26 June 1835 at Knightsbridge, London, the second son of Septimus Hart, dentist, and his wife. He was educated at the City of London School (1848–1852) where he had a brilliant academic career, gaining numerous school prizes, the school captaincy, and, in competition with John Seeley, the Lambert Jones scholarship. This

Ernest Abraham Hart (1835–1898), by Camille Silvy, 1866

scholarship entitled the holder to a place at Queens' College, Cambridge, but, as a Jew, and therefore subject to the University Test Acts, Hart decided against university entry and secured permission to use the award to study medicine. He pursued his medical studies in London at St George's Hospital and at Samuel Lane's school of medicine in Grosvenor Place, where he won many more prizes. As a student, at the time of the Crimean War he was prominent in the campaign to improve the shipboard conditions of naval assistant surgeons.

Hart married twice: in June 1855 and on 19 July 1872. His first wife, Rosetta, daughter of Nathaniel Levy, died in suspicious circumstances in November 1861. Even though a coroner's inquest found that she had been 'accidentally poisoned' there were persistent rumours that her death was due to her husband's negligence, incompetence, or criminality; Hart was thought to be the model for Frank Danby's eponymous *Dr Phillips: a Maida Vale Idyll* (1887). Hart's second marriage was to Alice Marian, daughter of Alexander William Rowland, a merchant of Sydenham. She survived him. Alice Hart, who was medically trained, proved an able collaborator in much of her husband's work. Both marriages were childless.

Hart qualified MRCS in 1856 and became house surgeon at St Mary's Hospital, London. For a short time he was also in practice with William Coulson in Frederick Place, Old

Jewry. For two years he was surgical registrar and demonstrator of anatomy at St George's Hospital. In February 1859 he was appointed junior surgeon at the West London Hospital, and he became full surgeon in September 1860 before resigning in 1863. In 1861 Hart played an important part in founding the Medical Society of London, a body which encouraged the discussion of medical subjects by students and the newly qualified. In the same year he returned to St Mary's, where he became a successful ophthalmic surgeon (1861–8), aural surgeon (1865–8), and dean of the medical school (1863–8). During his time as a practising surgeon Hart introduced a new technique for treating aneurysm of the popliteal artery. As a practitioner he had a high income at an early stage in his career, earning an average of over £2000 per annum during his first five years of practice.

Hart had contributed articles to periodicals from a relatively early age, but his journalistic career really began in 1858 when he joined the staff of *The Lancet*. His duties included writing leading articles to order, proof-reading, and running the medico-parliamentary column. In 1865–6 he participated in two important *Lancet* inquiries: into the cholera outbreak at Theydon Bois in Essex and into London's workhouse infirmaries, the findings of which contributed to the passage of the Metropolitan Asylums Act. In 1866 Hart's contract with *The Lancet* was abruptly terminated as the result of a quarrel with the editor, James Wakley, probably over Hart's unavailing demand to be made joint editor. Later that year the council of the British Medical Association (BMA) appointed Hart editor of the *British Medical Journal* (*BMJ*). He took up the post in January 1867 at an initial salary of £250 per annum. In making this appointment, it was later suggested, the BMA 'had caught the editorial *leprechaun*, actually bought up the life and soul of the opposition establishment' (*Medical Press and Circular*, 5 May 1869, 375). Although Hart remained editor of the *BMJ* at the time of his death, his tenure of office was interrupted for about a year during 1869–70. The reason for his departure, while not entirely clear, appears to have been connected with the fact that a large part of the payments to *BMJ* contributors found its way into Hart's pocket.

Hart's achievement as editor of the *BMJ* was to transform it from a comparatively modest, obscure, low-circulation, and impecunious medical weekly, into a large, prosperous, highly respected, and mass-circulation journal, on the success of which the BMA rose to national and international prominence as a professional body. As editor Hart intervened effectively in a number of socio-medical questions including baby farming, public health, military and naval medicine, vivisection, compulsory vaccination, medical education for women, the diet of the working classes, and several aspects of poor-law medicine. In addition to editing the *BMJ*, which he did on a part-time basis, Hart played a prominent part in BMA affairs. He chaired the BMA's important parliamentary bills committee (1872–97), was secretary to the scientific grants committee, and served as the association's honorary librarian (1887–97).

Hart had many professional and public interests outside the BMA. He was adviser on medical literature to the publisher Smith Elder, and he edited two of the firm's weekly journals, the *London Medical Record* (1873–87) and the *Sanitary Record* (1874–87). It was Hart who first brought notice of the possibilities of developing the Apollinaris spring waters in Germany to the attention of the head of the firm, George Smith. Hart was founder and first chairman of the Medical, Sickness, and Life Assurance Society (1883–92), president of the Harveian Society (1868), chairman of the National Health Society (1877–96), and an executive member of several other bodies; he was much involved in the smoke-abatement, temperance, and cremation movements. He gave evidence to official inquiries into the protection of infant life (1871), the Medical Act (1879), and poor-law schools (1894). He stood, unsuccessfully, as a Liberal parliamentary candidate in 1885. Aside from his contributions to the journals he edited, Hart wrote numerous articles, pamphlets, lectures, and reports on medical and other subjects. Some of his writings in the *BMJ* were collected elsewhere and published in book form. The University of Durham awarded him an honorary DCL degree in 1893.

Hart had little time for leisure activities though he travelled extensively, including to the Americas and the Far East, often combining vacations with long overseas trips on BMA business. Until he sold it shortly before his death, he possessed an outstanding collection of ancient Japanese art. He was a rose grower, skilful at chess, and active in dog and pigeon breeding. In appearance Hart was short, slight, and frail. He smoked heavily, suffered frequent bouts of depression, and aged prematurely. He had a forceful personality, being ambitious, opinionated, egotistical, self-confident, and inclined to intolerance. While many admired his intellectual, organizational, and other abilities, he gained numerous enemies, including within the BMA. On several occasions attempts were made to deprive him of his *BMJ* editorship, notwithstanding his acknowledged editorial achievements. At least in part, the antipathy towards him was antisemitic, for Hart was staunch and outspoken in his Jewish faith. But even his admirers admitted that he had serious personality defects.

From the early 1880s, when diabetes was diagnosed, Hart's health declined steadily. In 1897 his right foot was amputated as a result of herpetic spots, which were ulcerating and turning gangrenous. Hart died at 16 Brunswick Terrace, Hove, Sussex, on 7 January 1898. After cremation at Woking, his ashes were interred on 11 January in the Jewish cemetery at Willesden in north London.

P. W. J. BARTRIP

Sources *BMJ* (15 Jan 1898) · *The Lancet* (15 Jan 1898) · P. Bartrip, *Mirror of medicine: a history of the British Medical Journal* (1990) · *Jewish Chronicle* (14 Jan 1898) · *Medical Press and Circular* (5 May 1869) · *Medical Press and Circular* (12 Jan 1898) · *WWW* · [H. Barnett], *Canon Barnett: his life, work, and friends*, 2 vols. (1918) · Boase, *Mod. Eng. biog.* · *Medical Times and Gazette* (16 Nov 1861), 509 [death notice of Mrs Hart] · *The Practitioner*, 60 (1898), 117–18 · J. Leyland, ed., *Contemporary medical men and their professional work: biographies of leading*

physicians … from the 'Provincial Medical Journal', 2 vols. (1888) · m. cert. · d. cert. · *DNB*

Archives British Medical Association · Wellcome L., corresp. | Bodl. Oxf., corresp. with Sir Henry Burdett

Likenesses C. Silvy, photograph, 1866, NPG [*see illus.*] · A. P. Tilt, group portrait, 1882, Wellcome L. · F. Holl, oils, 1883 · G. R. Fitt, photograph, Wellcome L. · S. Soloman, group portrait, photograph (*An octave for Ernest Hart*), Wellcome L. · cartoon, repro. in *Punch* (29 July 1876) · photograph, repro. in *BMJ* · photograph, repro. in *Medical Press and Circular* (12 Jan 1898) · photographs, British Medical Association

Wealth at death £15,966 6s. 11d.: probate, 24 March 1898, *CGPLA Eng. & Wales*

Hart, Ezekiel (1770–1843), landowner and politician, was born in Trois-Rivières, Quebec, Canada, on 15 May 1770, one of the sons of Aaron Philip *Hart (1724–1800) [*see under* Hart, Aaron], merchant, and his wife, Dorothy Catherine Judah (1747–1827). In 1792 he was based in Albany, New York, assisting his father in the fur trade. In February 1794 he married Frances Lazarus (1768/9–1821) of New York city, then returned to Trois-Rivières, where from 1796 he joined his brothers Moses and Benjamin in the M. and E. Hart Company, which had interests in brewing and the manufacture of potash. He sold his share to Moses Hart soon after their father's death in 1800, when he inherited the seigneurie of Bécancour.

Hart is best remembered as the first Jew elected to the assembly of Lower Canada. (Samuel Hart was the first Jewish public office-holder in Canada; he was elected to the assembly of Nova Scotia in 1791, but took the Christian oath and later became an Anglican.) In 1807 Hart was elected in a by-election at Trois-Rivières, supported by the French Catholic majority which sought to increase the number of non-protestant legislators in order to weaken British hegemony. He was denied the right to take his seat by both the French Catholic delegates and the British colonial administration, both of which saw the election of a Jewish member to the assembly as a potential threat to their identity and authority, and to a lesser extent shared an antisemitism based on their religious beliefs. After several months of hesitation, Hart eventually appeared at the opening of the legislative assembly on 29 January 1808 and took the oath on the Old Testament, but did not take the oath of abjuration 'on the true faith of a Christian'; following protests by some members of the assembly he was expelled on 20 February. He was re-elected in the general election of 17 May 1808, and when the house met in April 1809 he took the Christian oath, kissed the New Testament, and took his seat. However, the assembly again decided that he could not take his seat as he was Jewish.

The executive council of the province decided that the assembly had been wrong to reject Hart, but the governor, Sir James Craig, did not enforce their recommendation and instead dissolved the assembly, hoping that the new composition would allow Hart to take his seat. Before it could meet, in September Robert Stewart, Viscount Castlereagh, the British colonial secretary, ruled that a Jew could not sit in the assembly. Hart chose not to stand again in the election of November 1809, leaving the seat to his brother Moses, who was unsuccessful. Hart returned to his business affairs, but in 1830 his son Samuel Bécancour Hart petitioned the assembly to remove the obstacles that prevented Jewish Canadians from holding public office, and a bill to that effect received the royal assent in 1832.

Hart had been admitted to the 8th battalion of the Trois-Rivières militia as an ensign in 1803. The Canadian colonies ignored the requirement that militia officers were required to take a Christian oath, and in 1813 Hart was promoted lieutenant. In 1816 he became a captain in the 1st battalion of Trois-Rivières, and on 16 May 1830 was promoted colonel of the Saint-Maurice militia.

Hart died in Trois-Rivières on 16 September 1843, and was buried in the Prison Street cemetery there on the same day. According to Le Canadien he 'worked honestly and worked for the welfare of his friends and his country'. During his funeral the 'stores were closed; the Court of King's Bench, then in session, was suspended to permit the judges to follow the cortège; officers of the 81st regiment attended in full dress' (Joseph, 205). His remains were moved to the Mount Royal cemetery, Montreal, in 1909. His sixth child, Aaron Ezekiel Hart (1803–1857), was a barrister and the first Jewish lawyer in British North America, although he took the necessary oath 'upon the true faith of a Christian'.

Hart's thirteenth child and sixth son was **Adolphus Mordecai Hart** [pseud. Hampden] (1814–1879), lawyer and writer on history and politics, born in Trois-Rivières on 11 April 1814. Following a legal training spent in part as a clerk in the office of Charles Richard Ogden, attorney-general of Lower Canada, he was called to the bar of Lower Canada on 19 May 1836. During this period he was active in the campaign to allow Jews the same rights as non-Jews in Canada. On 12 December 1844 he married his first cousin Hannah Constance Hatton Hart (1826–1898), daughter of Benjamin and Harriot Judith Hart. He was an attorney-at-law in Canada, and published many studies on Canadian history and politics, including pamphlets and books written under the pseudonym Hampden. He also wrote on American subjects, and published in the United States. He resided in New York state from 1850 to 1857, where he was active in the Democratic Party, and wrote for the gubernatorial campaign of Horatio Seymour in 1854. He returned to Canada in 1857. He was denied a judgeship in Trois-Rivières because he was neither a Catholic nor a French Canadian, and in his writings opposed interference by the Catholic church in the Canadian electoral process. He died on 23 March 1879 in Montreal, a few days after suffering a stroke while pleading a case in court, and was buried in the Prison Street cemetery, Trois-Rivières. His remains were moved to Montreal in 1909. YITZCHAK KEREM

Sources M. Brown, Jew or juif? Jews, French Canadians, and Anglo-Canadians, 1759–1914 (1986) · A. Joseph, Heritage of a patriarch: Canada's first Jewish settlers and the continuing story of these families in Canada (1995) · G. Tulchinsky, Taking root: the origins of the Canadian Jewish Community (1992) · S. J. Godfrey and J. C. Godfrey, Search out the land: the Jews and the growth of equality in British colonial America, 1740–1867 (1995) · J. Kage, With faith and thanksgiving: the story of two hundred years of Jewish immigration and immigrant aid effort in Canada (1760–1960) (1962) · M. Solomon, Aaron Hart, sieur de Bécancour: la vie mouvementée du premier juif établi au Québec au XVIIIe siècle, roman (Montreal, 1992) · M. C. Cohen, The member from Trois-Rivières, based on the life of Ezekiel Hart, the fist Jew to be elected to public office in Canada (1959) · D. Vaugeois, 'Hart, Ezekiel', DCB, vol. 8 · D. Rowe, 'Hart, Adolphus Mordecai', DCB, vol. 10
Archives Archives du Séminaire de Trois-Rivières, Quebec, family papers · Archives Nationales du Québec, Montreal, will of Dorothea Hart · McGill University, Montreal, McCord Museum, papers | McGill University, Montreal, McCord Museum, Gerald E. Hart papers
Likenesses portrait, repro. in Godfrey and Godfrey, Search out the land
Wealth at death property in Trois-Rivières, Quebec, Canada: Joseph, Heritage, 205

Hart, George Vaughan (1752–1832), army officer and politician, was the fourth son of Edward Hart (c.1713–1793), of Lynsfort, co. Donegal, later rector of Desertegny, and his wife, Elizabeth, the daughter of John Ramsay, rector of Stranorlar, also in co. Donegal. After being commissioned in 1775 as ensign in the 46th foot he served in North America as aide-de-camp to General Vaughan in the failed attack on Charlestown and fought at Long Island, Brandywine, and Germantown. He was promoted lieutenant in 1777 and saw further action at Monmouth and during the raid on Newhaven. In 1779, while serving in the West Indies, he became a captain in the 55th foot. He was later aide-de-camp to General William Medows at the Cape (1781) and Madras (1782).

After five years in England Hart returned to India in 1788 as military secretary and adjutant to Medows in Bombay. In 1790 he moved with Medows to Madras, where he became deputy paymaster and, in defiance of the supreme council, insisted on accounting only to the pay office. He served thereafter in the campaigns against Tipu Sultan in Mysore. In 1792 Hart became deputy paymaster for India. The same year, on 22 July, he married at Calcutta Charlotte (d. 1827), the daughter of John Ellerker of Ellerker, Yorkshire; they had five sons and four daughters. He was invalided home in 1795, but returned to India in 1798 as colonel of the 75th foot, a regiment in which he had served the previous eleven years as both major and lieutenant-colonel. For his very active part in the last campaign against Tipu Sultan he earned a bounty of £4000. Having failed to become deputy paymaster in Ceylon, and obtaining only the command of Kanara (1799), he returned home, only to be charged with peculation as commissary of grain for Mysore. He was suspended by court martial and, in 1801, dismissed by the East India Company. He was then on the Irish staff (northern district), and became major-general in 1805.

Hart's wish to clear his name led him into politics. On the death of a kinsman, the MP for co. Donegal, he unsuccessfully fought the by-election in 1808. He then solicited further employment, and, though he became lieutenant-general in 1811, lost his place on the Irish staff in June; he retrieved it in 1812 on appeal to the prime minister, Spencer Perceval. Further ministerial support secured his return for the county later that year.

At Westminster Hart was an occasional speaker, chiefly on Irish affairs. On 2 March 1813 he disingenuously voted for a committee on Catholic relief, with the intention of fully exposing the danger of their demands; later he opposed them. He criticized some Dublin Castle measures, such as collective district fines for illicit distillation: these fines, followed by overpopulation, he described as Ireland's greatest evil. In 1816 he was expected to retire on grounds of ill health, but he persisted. After 1818 the ministry granted him an equal share, with Lord Conyngham, in county patronage, and in 1820 he became governor of Londonderry and Culmore. He was promoted general in 1825. Hart retained his parliamentary seat until 1831, and died at his home, Kilderry, co. Donegal, on 14 June 1832. He had inherited the Kilderry estate from his father and Ballynagard from his brother John in 1815, a year after he had resisted a ministerial offer of £10,000 compensation for his Indian setback.   ROLAND THORNE

Sources PRO NIre., Hart MSS, D 3077 · GM, 1st ser., 102/2 (1832), 180 · P. J. Jupp, 'Hart, George Vaughan', HoP, Commons, 1790–1820 · Burke, Gen. GB · Hansard 1 (1812–20) · Hansard 2 · Hansard 3 (1830–32) · C. H. Philips, The East India Company, 1784–1834 (1940), 204–6 · H. T. Hart, The family history of Hart of Donegal (1907), 47, 114, 125
Archives BL OIOC · PRO NIre., military and family papers; Indian corresp. and papers | BL, corresp. with Sir Robert Peel, Add. MSS 40231–40397, passim · PRO NIre., Abercorn MSS
Wealth at death £13,300 incl. £300 in Canterbury, rest in Ireland: PRO, death duty registers, 1832, fol. 81 · left £24,000 in bequests to his children: will, 1832

Hart, Heber Leonidas (1865–1948), judge and jurist, was born on 31 March 1865 at 5 Binfield Road, Clapham, the youngest of several sons and one of eight children of Percy Matthew Hart, company registrar, of Wimbledon, and his wife, Sarah Ann Stillwell. He was named Heber after Bishop Reginald Heber (1783–1826), author of the hymn 'From Greenland's Icy Mountains', and, at the suggestion of the clergyman officiating at his baptism, was given the second name Leonidas in preference to his parents' original choice of Leonard. Both his forenames provoked mirth in others but were 'a prolific source of lifelong annoyance' to Hart (Hart, Reminiscences, 54). 'Heber Hart' also suggested that he was of Jewish or German-Jewish origin, whereas, as he often felt obliged to make clear, he was 'absolutely English' (ibid., 58) and of pious Anglican parentage. Educated at private schools, he graduated at the University of London as a bachelor of laws with first-class honours in 1886. He was called to the bar of the Middle Temple in 1887 and joined the southeastern circuit, taking the further degree of doctor of laws at London University in 1893. In 1894 he helped to establish the general council of the bar.

As a junior Hart had a large general practice and frequently appeared in headline catching cases. He was led by many of the most eminent counsel of the day, a galaxy which included Sir Edward Clarke; Sir Charles Russell (later lord chief justice), who impressed Hart with his 'overmastering natural eloquence' (Hart, Reminiscences, 23); Sir Frank Lockwood; W. O. Danckwerts (later lord justice), 'easily the most masterful of leaders' (ibid., 29); the often 'irascible' (ibid., 20) Sir Robert Reid (later Lord Chancellor Loreburn); Henry Herbert Asquith, the future prime minister, whom he found 'neither genial nor attractive as

a leader' (ibid., 146); F. E. Smith (later Lord Chancellor Birkenhead); and Sir Edward (later Lord) Carson, 'a model leader' (ibid., 27). Of all the orators whom he heard in a lifetime's experience, however, none in Hart's view compared for 'psychic power' with Sir Henry Irving, whom at the age of twelve he saw perform in The Bells.

Specializing in commercial law, Hart wrote The Law Relating to Auctions (1895) and was elected first honorary member of the Auctioneers' and Estate Agents' Institute; he followed this with The Law of Banking (1904), which ran to three further editions in 1906, 1914, and 1931, and became Gilbart lecturer in banking at London University in 1922. He took silk in 1913. In 1915 Lord Chancellor Haldane appointed him recorder of Ipswich, a position which he occupied until his retirement in 1936. He became a bencher of the Middle Temple in 1923, and was reader in 1931 and treasurer in 1937.

From 1920 the foreign secretary, Lord Curzon, appointed Hart as the British member of the mixed arbitral tribunals established under the post-war peace treaties with Germany, Austria, Hungary, and Bulgaria. The task of the tribunals, which sat in London, was to resolve suits in contract and tort between British litigants and subjects of former enemy states in circumstances where the legal effects of war would otherwise have denied redress to either side. Each tribunal had unlimited jurisdiction to decide on fact and law, including complex questions of international law, and its decisions were final and not subject to appeal. Issues of fact ranged 'from the value of the world-wide concerns of great industrial companies to the items of a tailor's bill' (Hart, Reminiscences, 39). Hart adjudicated together with a representative of the relevant state and a neutral president, but it was invariably he who took the lead in giving judgment. The workload was immense: some 10,000 cases fell to be decided by the Anglo-German tribunal alone. Hart sat from 1920 to 1931 until the work was complete, and he personally drafted most of the judgments, now in the Public Record Office. The strain of responsibility took its toll in insomnia and 'cardiac and nervous exhaustion' (ibid., 41).

Hart was a Liberal, an active partisan of the imperialist wing of the party. He stood unsuccessfully as a parliamentary candidate for the Isle of Thanet in 1892, South Islington in 1895, and Windsor in 1910. In 1900 he founded the Imperial Liberal Council, whose aim was empire federation, and he criticized the Statute of Westminster (1931) for severing the constitutional ties between Britain and the dominions. From 1916 he was chairman of the Eighty Club, whose purpose was to further the Liberal cause in parliament, and from 1918 to 1923 he was chairman of what became known as the 1920 Club, founded to promote the cause of the Coalition Liberals under Lloyd George and to advocate their fusion with the Conservatives in a national centre party.

Hart's professional career did not match his promise. His appointment to the mixed arbitral tribunals cut short his progress as a leader and may have cost him the high judicial promotion for which his gifts seemed to mark him out. While many of the advocates who appeared before him at the tribunals were raised to the Court of Appeal and House of Lords, his own services went unrewarded. Yet his contribution to the tribunals was distinguished, important, and original. 'I had a free hand in preparing what appeared to me the simplest and best rules of procedure' (Hart, *Way to Justice*, 8), and in general the 'unique experience' (ibid.) gave scope to his extensive learning, his judicial flair, his creative ingenuity, and reforming zeal. He seized the opportunity to cut through 'the thraldom of archaic formalism' (ibid., 69), especially the rules of evidence, and to reduce the technicalities of English law to its underlying principles and to those of continental jurisprudence, which he saw as essentially akin. 'The entire laws of contracts and torts', he wrote, 'may be viewed as respectively expansions of two deep-seated imperatives of the ethics of civilised peoples, namely, "Keep your promise" and "Injure no man"' (Hart, *Mixed arbitral Tribunals*, 13–14).

The 'experiment' of the tribunals stimulated Hart's appetite for law reform generally. Holding that 'our legal system is grievously at fault' and 'may be the worst in western Europe' (Hart, *Way to Justice*, 8, 26), he aired his views in a hard-hitting little book, *The Way to Justice: a Primer of Legal Reform* (1941), published when he was over seventy-five. In the spirit of Bentham, whom he quotes at length, he attacked the English legal system root and branch. He held that a bench of three judges should be the norm in every court of first instance, arguing for the abolition, both in civil and criminal cases, of trial by jury, or what he called 'a fortuitous assemblage of twelve people unacquainted with law or legal procedure, and not improbably including one or more persons of indifferent character or intelligence or unjudicial mind' (ibid., 55). He deplored the two-tier appellate system from Court of Appeal to House of Lords as a lottery—arbitrary, unfair, and prohibitively costly for the loser—calling for a single supreme court of appeal. He questioned the principle of the presumption of innocence and the rule against self-incrimination, arguing that both were outweighed by the need to protect the community from crime. He urged the abolition of most rules of evidence. Above all he condemned the very basis of the English legal system, reliance on precedent, and called for the law to be codified in order to 'obviate the enormous waste of time, labour and money now involved in the search for relevant authorities, and their examination, citation and discussion' (ibid., 35), after which 'every volume of law reports … might then be burnt' (Hart, *Reminiscences*, 357). Such radical proposals 'received attention and also some criticism' (*The Times*, 5 Feb 1948). Whatever their merits, some of the issues which they raise only began to receive serious consideration half a century after his death.

A founding member of the Romilly Society (1898), established to encourage penal and prison reform, Hart opposed both capital and corporal punishment, believing that sentencing should be 'neither retaliatory, vindictive nor retributive' (Hart, *Reminiscences*, 325). As recorder of Ipswich he put his ideals into practice, to his own satisfaction but not without controversy. He chose to err on the side of mercy, imposing whenever possible a bind-over rather than a custodial sentence. In consequence of what he called 'my notorious leniency' (ibid., 34), defendants appearing before him regularly pleaded guilty, so that few cases came to trial. In the interests of impartial justice he held that recorders and judges should not have local allegiances in the area to which they are appointed and should not socialize with the lay magistrates with whom they sit on appeal. At the swearing-in of new justices he would remind them that a magistrate should 'comport himself towards the accused as he would feel it right to be treated himself if their relative positions were reversed' (ibid., 98). These admonitions still bear repeating.

Hart was a Christian philanthropist, who believed that 'underneath the shows of life there lies … the brotherhood of man' (Hart, *Reminiscences*, 326). He championed the Church Army and the nascent Salvation Army at a time when General Booth's ideas, publicized in *In Darkest England* (1890), met with 'opposition and ridicule' (ibid., 78). He admitted to 'my own excessive religiosity—a morbidly developed sense of accountability to an unseen Power' (ibid., 176). There was something in Hart of a late Victorian individualist, combining personal eccentricities with strong convictions. As secretary of the London University defence committee from 1894 to 1900, he took part in the long controversy surrounding the university's reorganization. He played a 'prominent part' (ibid., 81) in opposing women's suffrage. He opposed boxing, fox-hunting, and the compulsory teaching of the classics; he advocated decimal coinage and the metrification of imperial weights and measures. He regarded reform of English spelling on phonetic lines as 'a truly urgent matter' (ibid., 356). He argued against pacifism—during the First World War he served as a special constable, and became company commander of the Stepney battalion of the London volunteer regiment, receiving the post-war rank of honorary captain—but he also wrote *The Bulwarks of Peace* (1918) in support of a League of Nations.

Hart was indifferent to sport, and particularly contemptuous of golf; his one physical recreation was sea voyages. He was cultivated and well read, becoming president of the Johnson Club in 1943. His acquaintances included the Victorian critic Theodore Watts-Dunton, the friend of Swinburne, whose cure from dipsomania was first effected at The Pines, 9 Putney Hill, London, where Hart himself lived continuously from the age of seventeen. He was a member of the Reform Club. A bachelor until the age of seventy-six, on 31 October 1941 he married Mabel Neal (*b.* 1891/2), a spinster more than twenty-five years his junior, the daughter of Thomas Neal, agriculturist. Hart died at his Putney home on 4 February 1948 of heart disease and arteriosclerosis, and was survived by his wife. He was cremated at Putney Vale on 7 February and his ashes were interred in the family vault at Putney Vale cemetery two days later.　　　　　　　　　　　　A. LENTIN

Sources H. L. Hart, *Reminiscences and reflections* (1939) · H. L. Hart, *The way to justice: a primer of legal reform* (1941) · H. L. Hart, *The mixed arbitral tribunals: an experiment in legal procedure* (1932) · *Men and women of the time* (1899) · *The Times* (5 Feb 1948) · *The Times* (10 Feb

1948) · J. B. Williamson, ed., *The Middle Temple bench book*, 2nd edn, 1 (1937) · *WWW*, 1941–50 · H. C. G. Matthew, *The liberal imperialists: the ideas and politics of a post-Gladstonian élite* (1973) · b. cert. · m. cert. · d. cert.
Likenesses J. Russell & Sons, photograph, repro. in Hart, *Reminiscences and reflections*, frontispiece
Wealth at death £17,710 8s. 11d.: probate, 5 April 1948, *CGPLA Eng. & Wales*

Hart, Henry. See Harte, Henry (d. 1557).

Hart, Henry George (1808–1878), army officer and founder of *Hart's Army List*, belonged to the old Dorset family of Hart of Netherbury, and was the third son of Lieutenant-Colonel William Hart, who served in the Royal Navy, the Dorsetshire militia, and the 111th regiment, and went out to the Cape in 1819, where he died in 1848. Henry George, the third son, born on 7 September 1808, accompanied his father to the Cape, and was on 1 April 1829 appointed ensign in the 49th (Princess of Wales's) regiment, then stationed in the colony. His regimental service was all in the 49th. His subsequent commissions were: lieutenant, 19 July 1832; captain, 1 December 1842; major, 15 December 1848; lieutenant-colonel, 30 May 1856; colonel, 27 December 1860; major-general, 6 March 1868; and lieutenant-general, 4 December 1877.

Hart was noted for his professional enthusiasm and his thirst for accurate military information. At that period, except for Philippart's *Royal Military Calendar* of 1820, then out of print, there was no collective account, official or otherwise, of the war services of army officers. Hart meticulously compiled for himself a large number of these services from military histories, personal accounts, and other sources. Very basic information was then all that was given by the official army lists. Hart gradually added to his own interleaved copies until, while still a subaltern, he had accumulated so much information that he decided to publish an improved and more detailed army list of his own. Aided by his wife in this laborious work Hart, in February 1839, with the approval of the military authorities, published the first edition of his *Quarterly Army List*. It was favourably received by the queen, the duke of Wellington, and other senior officers of the army. Hart was allowed access to the official records of officers' services, and in 1840 published his first *Annual Army List*, containing supplementary information of interest, in addition to the contents of the quarterly lists. He also proposed a military biographical dictionary, specimen pages of which he issued, but never found sufficient time to complete the work. From the first appearance of *Hart's Army List* until 1915 the annual and quarterly volumes regularly appeared. The original form was little altered, although the book went to over 200 editions. Of particular value were the detailed footnotes giving the active service details and campaign awards for each officer although, as much of the information was provided by the subjects themselves, it should be treated with care.

Hart married in 1833 Alicia, daughter of the Revd Holt Okes, and their family included three sons, who all served in the army: General A. Fitzroy Hart, East Surrey regiment (later editor of *Hart's Army List*), Colonel Reginald Clare

Hart, Royal Engineers, and Major Horatio Holt Hart, Royal Engineers.

Hart never allowed his compilation to interfere with his army work, and was a competent regimental officer and a respected and popular staff officer. He rendered enlightened and valuable services as a poor-law inspector in Ireland during the famine of 1845–6. In July 1856, when in temporary command of the depot battalion at Templemore, by his energy and wisdom he suppressed a dangerous mutiny of the North Tipperary militia with little bloodshed, and saved the town of Nenagh from rioting, bloodshed, and pillage. He received the thanks of Lord Seaton, commander of forces in Ireland, for his control and forbearance in the face of the armed insurgents. Hart died at Biarritz, France, on 24 March 1878.

H. M. CHICHESTER, rev. JAMES FALKNER

Sources *Army List* · Burke, *Gen. GB* · Royal Berkshire Regiment Museum, records · *Hart's Army List* · Boase, *Mod. Eng. biog.* · private information (1891)
Archives PRO, corresp. and papers relating to *Army List*, WO 211
Wealth at death under £3000: probate, 12 April 1878, *CGPLA Eng. & Wales*

Hart, Henry George (1843–1921), headmaster, was born on 16 April 1843 at Poona, India, of northern Irish descent, the second child and eldest son of William Hart (c.1816–1904), East India Company servant—fifth son of General George Vaughan *Hart (1752–1832) of Kilderry, co. Donegal—and his wife, Frances Anne (d. 1898), daughter of Edward Frere of Llanelli, Brecknockshire, and sister of Sir (Edward) Bartle *Frere (1815–1884). Hart was educated at a day school in Bath and a boarding-school near Taunton, neither of which he liked, and from February 1858 to summer 1862 at Rugby School under Frederick Temple (headmaster 1857–69), to whom he became devoted. Lastingly influenced by the school's Arnoldian values, he enjoyed and was successful at Rugby. He played football—even when an adult he displayed his 'Big Side' cap in his study—and became head of School House. In later years he 'used to speak with less enthusiasm of his university than of his school' (Coulton, *Victorian Schoolmaster*, 55). In October 1862 he went to St John's College, Cambridge (admitted pensioner May 1862, scholar 1864), with a Rugby exhibition. He had £110 a year in scholarships and an allowance from his father. A 'reading man', he worked hard, rowed, played football, edited the college magazine, *The Eagle*, and was 'a man of high moral influence and of bright and attractive personality' (ibid., 53). In 1866 he was seventh classic (BA 1866, MA 1869), and was a fellow from 1867 until his marriage in 1873.

At Rugby he had wanted to become a cavalry officer, but in 1866, invited by the headmaster of Haileybury College, Arthur Gray Butler, old Rugbeian and Hart's master at Rugby, Hart became a classics master at Haileybury, the public school recently established in the buildings of the former East India College where Hart's father had been educated. His salary was £150 plus accommodation and extras, and he again played football. A keen fisherman, from 1867 to 1914 he holidayed and fished in Norway, and he learned Norwegian. On 9 August 1873 he married Honoria Letitia (1850–1923), orphaned only surviving daughter of Sir Henry *Lawrence (1806–1857). From 1873 to 1879 Hart was a classics master at Harrow School, with an income of over £500 a year. Fair-haired, hazel-eyed, short, and of apparently frail build, he greatly impressed contemporaries by his character: his goodness, sincerity, dedication, and earnestness. A devout Anglican—though as a young man he had serious doubts and was 'a very broad Churchman' (Coulton, Fourscore Years, 215)—he believed Christianity crucial to education. According to his biographer, 'his every action was consciously and deliberately guided by religion' (Coulton, Victorian Schoolmaster, 138). Daily with his wife he read a portion of The Imitation of Christ.

The free grammar school of King Edward VI at Sedbergh, remote in the West Riding of Yorkshire, was founded about 1525 and munificently endowed with land in Yorkshire. After various vicissitudes it reached a nadir in the 1860s under the disastrous headmastership of the Revd Henry George Day (1830–1900, headmaster 1861–74), who by incapacity and neglect reduced the school to thirteen pupils: in 1865 no new pupil joined. Following scathing reports by the Taunton commission and others, there was a proposal to end the school and use its endowments elsewhere, but in 1874 it was reconstituted by the endowed schools commission. Day was pensioned off, and lived as a parasite on the resources of the school he had so nearly destroyed. The new governors appointed as headmaster the Revd Frederick Heppenstall (c.1835–1879). He revived Sedbergh, increasing its numbers, but died suddenly of an incurable disease in July 1879: Hart said he 'had restored the School from nothing into a School' (Clarke and Weech, 150).

From 1880 to 1900 Hart was headmaster of Sedbergh. He was successful, and contemporaries thought him 'a remarkable man' (Coulton, Fourscore Years, 213) and 'a great headmaster' (Coulton, Victorian Schoolmaster, 183), but essentially he was neither original nor innovative. Rather he transferred Arnoldian traditions and the normal externals of a public school to Sedbergh, ran the school well, inspired confidence in it, increased the numbers of its pupils—to about 200, he did not want more—and masters, improved its buildings and facilities, and gained examination successes. He worked hard, teaching and without clerical assistance except from his wife. Self-sacrificing and generous, he subsidized the school. He himself paid for masters and house scholars from 1891 to 1900 £3878. He won the respect and affection of masters and boys. The latter nicknamed him Daddy, soon abbreviated to Da. His achievement was made possible by the support and generosity of the governors, and especially Sir Francis Sharp Powell, first baronet (1827–1911), old Sedberghian, Conservative MP, chairman of the governors from 1884, and a munificent benefactor whose donations included the sanatorium and the gymnasium. Hart introduced rugby football, the wearing of caps and gowns by masters, and in the Arnoldian tradition initiated the building of a chapel where he preached. In 1883 he was licensed as a lay reader. His assistant masters included H. W. Fowler and G. G. Coulton. In 1891 his health broke down and he spent the Lent term of 1892 away recuperating. He resigned in 1900. Under him Sedbergh had become a successful, if lesser, public school. Typically he gave his large testimonial sum to the school, and it was spent on the drawing school. In 1901 he published Sedbergh School Sermons.

Hart had broken from his family's traditional Conservatism and become a Liberal, supporting Irish home rule and women's suffrage, but he gave up overt political activity lest it harm Sedbergh. He was reportedly a member of both the Peace Society and the National Service League.

Hart moved in 1901 to Wimbledon, where he named his house Sedbergh. He visited India and Ceylon, was a temporary Board of Education secondary school inspector and an inspector for the Oxford and Cambridge Board, worked on the Wimbledon Guild of Help, was a governor of Wimbledon high school, and from 1904 to 1919 was an 'invaluable member' (Wimbledon Boro' News, 2) of the Wimbledon education committee. In the First World War he was a volunteer Norwegian translator at the War Office. Paralysed from late 1918, he died on 12 January 1921 at his home, Sedbergh, Hillside, Wimbledon, Surrey. On 17 January a funeral service at St John's, Wimbledon, was followed by cremation at Woking crematorium; the remains were interred at Sedbergh School chapel.

ROGER T. STEARN

Sources G. G. Coulton, A Victorian schoolmaster: Henry Hart of Sedbergh (1923) · H. L. Clarke and W. N. Weech, History of Sedbergh School, 1525–1925 (1925) · B. Wilson, The Sedbergh School register, 1546–1909 (1909) · F. J. Salt and F. T. Dallin, eds., Rugby School register, 1858–1891, rev. edn (1952) · Venn, Alum. Cant. · WWW, 1916–28 · Burke, Gen. GB (1878) · Burke, Gen. GB (1937) · Burke, Peerage (1999) · HoP, Commons, vol. 4 · Sedbergh School and its chapel (1897) · G. G. Coulton, Fourscore years: an autobiography (1944) · J. R. de S. Honey, Tom Brown's universe: the development of the Victorian public school (1977) · B. Gardner, The public schools: an historical survey (1973) · VCH Yorkshire, vol. 1 · J. Lawrence, Lawrence of Lucknow: a story of love, ed. A. Woodiwiss (1990) · Wimbledon Boro' News (21 Jan 1921), 1–2

Likenesses M. Girardot, portrait, c.1892, repro. in Coulton, Victorian schoolmaster, following p. 195 · P. A. Thomas, photograph, c.1896, repro. in Coulton, Victorian schoolmaster, following p. 195 · Swaine, photograph, 1916, repro. in Coulton, Victorian schoolmaster, following p. 195

Wealth at death £9891 5s. 1d.: probate, 30 June 1921, CGPLA Eng. & Wales

Hart, Herbert Lionel Adolphus (1907–1992), legal philosopher, was born at Harrogate, Yorkshire, on 18 July 1907, the third of four children of Simeon Hart (1871–1953), master tailor and furrier, and his wife, Rose (1874–1953), who helped him in the business. She was the daughter of Samuel Samson and his wife, Fanny (née Rosenthal). His father came of a Jewish family descended from Polish and German immigrants of the nineteenth century named Zadek, who were in the clothing trade in the East End of London. In 1900 the family moved to Harrogate. They had three sons and a daughter. Herbert, as he was known to his friends, always published as H. L. A. Hart.

Early years and education, 1907–1929 Hart's family wished their son to have an education suited to orthodox Jews. He

Herbert Lionel
Adolphus Hart
(1907–1992), by
Steve Pyke, 1990

was therefore sent to Cheltenham College, a boarding-school with a separate house for Jewish boys, from 1918 to 1921. He looked back on these years as the only unhappy period of his life. The school seemed dull, class-ridden, and obsessed by athletics. He disliked being labelled a Jew, though in later life he came to value his part in the Jewish heritage. Religion did not attract him. Despite a gift for languages he found Hebrew unpalatable.

In 1921 a family set-back came to the rescue. Hart's father, whose business had gone downhill, could no longer afford to keep his son at Cheltenham. Herbert was sent instead to Bradford grammar school. In contrast with Cheltenham he found the school exciting. Good teaching and friendly companionship stimulated an expansion of thought and feeling, with freedom to explore the town and walk in the beautiful countryside on its borders. From E. H. Goddard, the classics master, an admirer of Spengler, he absorbed, along with an interest in the minutiae of language, a taste for large generalizations. In retrospect this period at Bradford (1921–6), where he became head boy, seemed a very happy one. Hart's passionate but opposite reactions to life at the two schools was in character, for he responded strongly to people, ideas, and places.

At Gilbert Murray's suggestion Hart tried successfully in 1926 for a classical scholarship at New College, Oxford. He found the college a place of ravishing beauty, a joy in which to study and, later, teach. He was fairly well off, since his father's fortunes had revived. A tall, lean youth, with fine, intellectual features, rumpled clothes, and awkward gait, his appearance and way of life changed little over the years. Easy in conversation, with never a trace of vanity, his vitality and humour would light up almost any topic. Douglas Jay, a contemporary, noted his strong Yorkshire accent, later lost, and formed a friendship that lasted for more than sixty years. Hart found in H. W. B. Joseph a stimulating tutor, who steered his mind towards Plato and realism. H. A. L. Fisher, the warden of New College, invited him for walks and introduced him to such figures as Lloyd George, Virginia Woolf, and Dean Inge. With Jay and other friends he talked about history and philosophy; at times his friends got more from him than from their tutors. But with an eye to the examinations, in which he needed to prove his worth, he kept a notebook with secret nuggets of information. He had his reward, for in 1929 Hart

obtained the best first class of the year in classical Greats. At the Jowett Society, of which he became president, he met in Isaiah Berlin another able young man who was to be a lifelong friend. Berlin was quick to appreciate what was rare in someone of his gifts: complete honesty; for Hart was always ready to modify his assertions, and later, to disavow his writings, in the face of what seemed valid objections.

Law and philosophy, war and marriage, 1930–1952 Hart made up his mind to become a barrister. He joined the Middle Temple and from 1932 until 1940 practised at the Chancery bar along with Richard Wilberforce, John Sparrow, and Duff Dunbar. Of this brilliant quartet Hart emerged as the front runner. The growth of his practice was continuous and increasing, and he much enjoyed the opera, hunting, and travel abroad that his earnings at the bar made possible. But war clouds were gathering and he did not share the prevailing illusions. As Wilberforce records (private memoir):

> In 1938 we were together when the news came that Mr Chamberlain was returning with 'Peace for our time'. There was applause; there was talk of going to the airport to cheer him home. We just looked at each other with tears in our eyes—it was unnecessary to speak.

When war broke out Hart was turned down for military service owing to a mitral murmur, which turned out not to be serious. By then he had fallen in love with Jenifer Williams, a civil servant in the Home Office since 1936. Born in 1914, she was the third of five daughters of Sir John Fischer *Williams (1870–1947), an international lawyer who had been a member of the British panel on the Permanent Court of Arbitration at The Hague. In May 1940 Hart was recommended at Williams's instance to MI5, in which he served throughout the war. He worked on the Ultra material and made an important contribution to the D-day disinformation plan in 1944. During lulls, when there was nothing to decipher, he made buttons in a factory. His devotion to the work of MI5 was absolute. No whisper of what he was doing escaped him.

Hart, who had to overcome a feeling that he was not really heterosexual, became committed to Jenifer Williams from 1937 onwards and married her in 1941. They had a daughter and three sons. During the war Hart and Jay were for a time living in the same house, and he also saw something of the philosophers Gilbert Ryle and Stuart Hampshire. His interest in philosophy was rekindled. At the same time his political views moved closer to those of his wife, which were left-wing. He came to feel that his life should not be spent at the bar, minimizing the tax liability of the rich. He became a Labour Party supporter— a democratic socialist with liberal leanings—and remained one for the rest of his life.

These developments led Hart in 1945 to accept what he had rejected before the war, the offer of a philosophy fellowship at New College. The warden of the college, A. H. Smith, engineered Hart's fellowship without advertisement because he saw in him a bulwark against the radical empiricism that was then fashionable. But he was mistaken, for Hart had, under the influence of J. L. Austin, come to abandon Joseph's views and to believe that linguistic analysis was of central importance in philosophy. He was a founder member of the discussion group led by Austin that, from 1947, met on Saturday mornings to discuss such topics as rules. For the first eighteen months at New College he agonized over his capacity to teach philosophy but by 1947, when his wife settled in Oxford, he was committed to academic life. They lived first in New College Lane, then from 1952 at 11 Manor Place, Oxford. Hart was an excellent tutor, who believed that his special gift was for smoothing the path of weaker students. The truth behind this modest self-assessment was that he esteemed clarity the chief intellectual virtue and was notably patient with pupils, whatever their ability. His method was to rub their noses in the two questions 'How do you know?' and 'What do you mean?'. But he was reluctant to commit himself to print until quite certain that what he had to say was correct. In these seven years he published only three papers and two book reviews.

Hart's first paper (1948–9), 'The ascription of responsibility and rights', foreshadowed his later concern with legal philosophy. Its novel ideas, though he later rejected them, struck a chord both in Britain and the United States. In 1952, at the urging of J. L. Austin, he was persuaded to think of himself as a possible successor to Arthur Goodhart as Oxford professor of jurisprudence. He was not sure that he was good enough as a pure philosopher. Nor did the admiration that came to him later dissipate his doubts about the correctness of his views. His self-critical spirit accounted for the corrections and recorrections, scrawled-over notes, and bundles of paper held together by clips that cluttered his rooms. But he had come to see that many philosophical distinctions could be applied to law and that, given his practice at the bar, he was the person to apply them. Conversely, examples drawn from the law suggested new paths for philosophy to explore.

Professor of jurisprudence Hart was elected to the chair of jurisprudence at Oxford in 1952 by a slender majority, on what was by any standards a thin contribution to the subject: three articles and two reviews, one of each being about law. But the choice was inspired. During his tenure of the chair (1952–68) Hart rescued English jurisprudence from its century-long decline and restored it to a central position in moral and political philosophy. He revitalized the positivist tradition stemming from Hume, John Austin, and Bentham. His writings in turn provoked restatements of other currents of opinion. R. M. Dworkin revived the eighteenth-century philosophy of rights that underlay the United States constitution, J. Finnis the still older natural law tradition. Along with positivism went a measured liberalism in political philosophy. Echoing J. S. Mill, Hart called in question the right of the state to force the individual to conform to even the most strongly held moral views of the majority.

As a professor Hart had to overcome his natural diffidence and to lecture and publish more freely. In his mature years the intellectual vigour of his talks could electrify an audience. It did not matter that his notes might be jottings on the back of a chequebook. In the long

vacation of 1952, staying at his wife's family property in Cornwall, the new professor scribbled the first draft of the lectures that came out nine years later as *The Concept of Law*. Reflection on John Austin's view that a law was the command of a sovereign habitually obeyed led Hart to question the value of definition in law. It prompted his inaugural lecture in 1953, 'Definition and theory in jurisprudence'. Instead of trying to define terms such as 'law', 'right', and 'corporation' one did better to explain the conditions under which sentences in which they occur are true. He came later to think that this lecture was flawed, but it swept away much futile debate.

In 1952–3 Hart laid the foundations for nearly all his later work. He lectured on rights and duties. The lectures were crowded and were heard with rapt attention, though with some apprehension, as the audience saw the lecturer shuffle from distance to reading glasses, wipe them, mislay them and rediscover their whereabouts, all the while expounding a complex argument. But he was never willing to publish his lectures on rights since, while rejecting the view of Austin and Bentham that only law could create rights, he could not see his way through to a satisfactory alternative.

Another project begun in this year was the study of causation. To take this concept, so central in philosophy, and see how it looked within the law, was the sort of enterprise that had attracted Hart to the chair of jurisprudence. He and A. M. Honoré gave seminars on causation in this year and the next, and together wrote a book that came out in 1959 as *Causation in the Law*. They wrote separate chapters, but mulled over each other's drafts until they agreed on every detail. The work defends common-sense causal distinctions inside and outside the law against the philosophical reproach of being unscientific and the scepticism of some lawyers. *Causation*, though a joint enterprise, was Hart's first and largest book and, in retrospect, one of the most substantial volumes to emerge from linguistic philosophy. A second edition, which has been translated into Japanese, was published in 1985. The themes it incorporates have since been taken further by Honoré. In the same year Hart began a discussion group in A. R. N. (Rupert) Cross's rooms in Magdalen College, which alerted many members of the law faculty to their stultifying neglect of theory. In 1954 he published an edition of John Austin's 1832 classic, *The Province of Jurisprudence Determined*, in the introduction to which he insisted on the central place of rules, and the acceptance of rules, in the law.

Hart's visit to the United States in 1956–7 at the invitation of Harvard was a landmark in his career. He was welcomed equally by lawyers and philosophers, who in the past had had little contact. America stimulated him—the noisy, unregulated life of cities; the students, unblasé, with a vast desire for knowledge; the disdain of Americans for privacy and precision of language; their passion for taking part in decision making. These and other aspects of life in the New World relaxed his neuroses. Five papers stemmed from his US visit. The most important was the Oliver Wendell Holmes lecture at Harvard in April

1957, 'Positivism and the separation of law and morals'. A *succès de scandale*, recognized at once as an enduring contribution to legal philosophy, it drew from Lon Fuller an eloquent critical response. The two were published together in the *Harvard Law Review* in 1958. Hart was a positivist only in the limited sense which insists that laws need not reproduce the demands of morality. He thought it essential, in the interests of clarity, to distinguish between law as it is and as it ought to be. Demonstrably iniquitous laws are still laws. But Fuller pointed in reply to an internal morality of law, to which it typically conforms, so that laws that violate this morality are not fully law.

Law and morality In 1959–60 Hart was president of the Aristotelian Society, a signal honour for a law professor. In the same year two other debates were launched, both concerned with the functions of criminal law. In September 1957 the Wolfenden committee had recommended that homosexual practices between consenting adults should cease to be criminal. Sir Patrick Devlin, giving the Maccabaean lecture in jurisprudence in 1958, widened the debate by attacking the committee's view that there was a realm of private conduct that was not the law's business. A community had the right to defend the morality which bound it together against attempts to undermine it. Hart counter-attacked with a talk on the BBC, published in *The Listener* for 30 July 1959. He reformulated J. S. Mill's argument that the only purpose for which power could rightfully be exercised over a member of a civilized community was to prevent harm to others. Thus began a wide-ranging debate about the proper limits of both criminal and civil law. Hart's views, effectively confined to the criminal law, were developed in two short books, *Law, Liberty and Morality* (1963), delivered at Stanford in 1962, and *The Morality of the Criminal Law* (1965), given in Jerusalem in 1964. He was moved by a dislike of cruelty masquerading as moral rectitude, which led him to be specially severe on attempts to enforce sexual morality—a view that struck a chord with the young.

The controversy with Devlin made Hart a public figure in Britain. Each was well equipped to fight his corner and their contest has become a classic. But Hart never sought publicity and he eschewed public honours apart from those honorary degrees traditionally conferred on scholars. In 1966 he declined a knighthood. In private debate he was tenacious, but his manner was courteous and impersonal. He excelled in the demanding skill of presenting an opponent's argument cogently. The same quality made him an excellent research supervisor. He read and reread his pupils' drafts with close attention and made dozens of critical comments, but at the same time knew how to foster the promise inherent in their line of thought. A consequence of his intellectual detachment was that Hart's pupils, though deeply influenced by him, never formed a school. Instead they displayed an engaging spectrum of views, ranging from J. M. Finnis's *Natural Law and Natural Rights* (1980) to W. J. Waluchow's *Inclusive Legal Positivism* (1993).

Hart's 'Prolegomenon to the principles of punishment' was also published in 1959. The paper argued that the general aim that justified punishment, that of keeping deviance within bounds, should be distinguished from the conditions in which it was proper to punish a given individual, which should include the fact that the offender had knowingly chosen to break the law. In 1968 eight of his papers on criminal responsibility were collected and published in a volume entitled *Punishment and Responsibility: Essays in the Philosophy of Law*. These masterly essays owed a good deal to his friend Rupert Cross, Vinerian professor of English law at Oxford (1964–79). Cross, with his energetic mind and buoyant character, was his closest colleague among lawyers. Hart wrote a memoir of his friend for the *Proceedings of the British Academy* (70.405–37).

The concept of law From 1960 to 1974 Hart was a delegate of the Oxford University Press. Here his most important initiative was to set up a new series of law books, the Clarendon Law Series. He was struck by the lack of works that introduced students in untechnical language to the problems of the subjects they were to study. The series did much to fill this gap. Hart took great trouble with the manuscripts submitted, and would suggest dozens or hundreds of additions and corrections.

The impulse that led Hart to found the Clarendon Law Series induced him to publish in 1961, under the title *The Concept of Law*, the general course of lectures he had been giving for the last eight years. His aim was to give beginners in jurisprudence a book that was more than a catalogue of great names spiced with superficial comments on their theories. Instead they would be introduced to the main issues in the subject, of which two stood out: the relation of law to brute force on the one hand and to morality on the other. Judged by the pragmatic test of sales *The Concept of Law* was a brilliant success. Some 150,000 copies were bought over the next thirty years. The work aroused interest in many countries and has been or is being translated into more than a dozen languages. Its influence extended to people who were not specially interested in law. For Anglo-Saxon writers on jurisprudence criticism of Hart at once replaced criticism of John Austin as the starting point of their thinking.

The Concept of Law belongs to the genre 'general jurisprudence'. It seeks to lay bare the structure of modern legal systems and to show what it is that separates them from other forms of social control such as morality or brute coercion. The central concept is that of a rule. Rules have internal and external aspects, and every legal system needs a rule by which other legal rules can be recognized. *The Concept of Law* is in no sense a work of linguistic philosophy. It concentrates instead on behaviour, on people's attitudes towards rules and their violation. Critics argue that an account of a legal system in terms of behaviour cannot be adequate, for laws at least *purport* to be morally binding. Hart disagreed. To him legal duties and obligations need be duties and obligations only from the legal point of view.

In 1961–2 Hart spent a year at the University of California at Los Angeles and gave the Harry Camp lectures at Stanford. In November 1961 he met and debated with the octogenarian legal philosopher Hans Kelsen (1881–1973) at Berkeley. They tackled three topics, including the question whether legal and moral norms can conflict. Kelsen was thought to have had the better of the debate, but Hart made some telling points. At one stage he was so startled by Kelsen's insistence, in stentorian tones, that norms were norms and nothing else that he fell over backwards.

In 1964 Hart delivered the Lionel Cohen lectures in Jerusalem. For this, his first visit to Israel, he was at the height of his powers, a dominant figure in legal and political philosophy and the standard-bearer of moral liberalism. He now came to appreciate the richness of Jewish culture. He was captivated by Jerusalem, one of the four cities, he thought, which had made modern culture what it was, the others being Constantinople, Athens, and Rome. Without them 'life for me at any rate would be a howling wilderness' (Wilberforce). Hart was intellectually anchored to the British empirical tradition and, though he loved Greece and Italy for their luminous, southern qualities, he was passionately attached to the English countryside. But his Jewishness shone through in his personal warmth, his sense of humour, and a rich, earthy, unsnobbish view of the world. On this visit he met Joseph Raz, later his doctoral student and the legal philosopher who has succeeded him as the standard-bearer of legal positivism.

Administration and Bentham, 1967–1978 Not a natural administrator or committee man, Hart threw himself with zest into those offices that presented an intellectual challenge. From 1967 to 1973 he was a member of the Monopolies Commission. On it his intelligence and legal acumen were much appreciated. He regretted his lack of training in economics, but filled the gap as best he could by reading. He put searching questions to those who appeared before the commission. These could be disconcerting both for their complexity and from Hart's habit of lowering his head as the question unfolded.

In 1968 Hart was asked by Oxford University to chair a commission on relations with junior members. Lord Franks's commission on the university, reporting in 1966, had dismissed student affairs in three lines. Two years later students were in uproar throughout the Western world. Even in Oxford there were sit-ins, though the *enragés* were neither particularly numerous nor able. Hart's left-wing views commended him to the student body, his intellectual rigour to the university authorities. He turned the inquiry into a miniature royal commission, to which some 30 dons and 200 students gave evidence. The report suggested reforms of the disciplinary system and the creation of standing joint committees of students and dons, the students to have access to but not membership of the decision-making bodies. Hart wrote a penetrating appendix on student revolt, in itself a significant contribution to political theory. The report was implemented and helped to bring students peacefully into the governance of Oxford, though the unrest would largely have died down in any case, as it did elsewhere.

By the time the commission reported in 1969 Hart had resigned from the chair he had held for sixteen years in order to devote more time to editing the *Collected Works* of Jeremy Bentham. He had already begun work on the text of Bentham, poring over his predecessor's scrawl with an enormous magnifying glass. He and J. H. Burns published in 1970 new editions of Bentham's *An Introduction to the Principles of Morals and Legislation* and *Of Laws in General*. He wanted to make available to a wider public the work of his great predecessor. For the next twelve years he concentrated on Bentham, on whom he planned a big book. This did not come about, but in 1982 he published *Essays on Bentham*, containing ten essays. It seemed odd that Hart should be devoted to the man whom Marx pilloried as the pedantic, leather-tongued oracle of bourgeois intelligence. But he was fascinated by Bentham's willingness to plunge into enormous detail to promote a proper understanding of the greatest happiness principle. While Hart turned his attention to Bentham, his successor as professor of jurisprudence in Oxford, R. M. Dworkin, proved a formidable critic of his legal philosophy, though in an epilogue to the second edition of *The Concept of Law* published posthumously (1994) Hart contends that Dworkin misrepresents his views.

A number of Oxford colleges made approaches to find out whether Hart would consider presiding over their affairs. In 1973 he accepted an offer from Brasenose College, of which he was principal for the next five years. He enjoyed the new role, and threw himself with energy into the wide range of activities it called for. His brief reign made a mark on the college, whose fellows were at the time rather demoralized. Hart labelled them 'Old Turks and Young Fogeys'. He was made uneasy by what, with his austere temperament, he saw as the 'Lucullan feasts' enjoyed by the fellows. But he liked talking to the students and was quick both to see their point of view and to take steps to widen their intellectual horizons. Supervising research by a relative of the Tanner family he won the admiration of Obert C. Tanner of Salt Lake City, founder of the Tanner Trust for Human Values. Tanner consequently established an annual lectureship at Oxford to be attached to Brasenose College. The series continues and has been a success.

The last years, 1978–1992 After he retired from Brasenose in 1978 Hart resumed his association with University College, of which he was an honorary fellow, and where he had a room until his death. The 1980s were for him a period of honour interspersed with distress. As early as 1960 Hart had received his first honorary degree in Stockholm. It was followed by twelve other such honours, including two in Israel, three in the United States, and one in Mexico. The Tanner trustees established at University College an annual lecture on jurisprudence and moral philosophy in his honour, the first being given in 1985. A series of essays in his honour, entitled *Law, Morality and Society*, edited by P. M. S. Hacker and J. Raz, had been published in 1977. A volume edited by Ruth Gavison, *Issues in Contemporary Legal Philosophy: the Influence of H. L. A. Hart*, containing papers for a conference given in his honour in Jerusalem in March 1984, was published in 1987. In 1983 seventeen of his essays were collected and published under the title *Essays in Jurisprudence and Philosophy*.

But Hart was not to enjoy an untroubled old age. His wife, more radical than he, a member of the Communist Party from 1935, had by the outbreak of war become disillusioned with communism, to which Hart was strongly opposed. In the early 1980s the press and the BBC, matching her pre-war communism to his wartime work for MI5, wounded them both by imputations of disloyalty. The distress this caused Hart, together with groundless worries about the provision he had made for his youngest son, who was brain damaged at birth, led to a nervous breakdown in 1983. He recovered, but it was a sad ordeal for a loyal citizen who had done sterling work during the war, had always been opposed to communist totalitarianism, and held in contempt the activities of Philby and Blunt, when it emerged what they had done. Moreover by the late eighties arthritis and injuries suffered in cycling and motor accidents made him less mobile, and brought to an end the long country walks that had meant so much since his schooldays. He died peacefully at Oxford on 19 December 1992, at the age of eighty-five, and was buried in Wolvercote cemetery, Oxford.

Conclusion Hart doubted the value of his contributions to legal and political philosophy. Introduced at a gathering in the United States as an 'intellectual giant' he told his audience that he did not feel like an intellectual giant. By the highest standards the doubts were justified. His achievement was to develop the ideas of Hume, Bentham, John Austin, and J. S. Mill in original and ingenious ways. If his work was less profound than that of Bentham or Kelsen, the two legal philosophers whom he thought most worth studying, in clarity he surpassed them. Critical studies of his work have been or are being published in America, Scotland, Ireland, Germany, Japan, Argentina, Italy, and Poland. Those who came across him as pupils, friends, or colleagues, at lectures, in seminars, or reading what he wrote might suddenly find their view of the world transformed. Almost to the end he retained a boyish enthusiasm for new experiences. He liked people and their foibles, appreciated natural beauty, was widely read in fiction and poetry, and enjoyed classical music. A man of the Enlightenment, his mind was firm and clear, unshakeably hostile to intellectual muddle and the political oppression it fosters. With this uncompromising rigour went the gift of pure human goodness. The intellectual and moral qualities were inseparable. There were of course weaknesses. Hart was naturally inaccurate; at times his enthusiasm for a person or idea led him astray. He was untidy and absent-minded beyond the professional norm. But these were the faults of a man of generous mind, impatient with trivia, who was by common consent the outstanding British legal philosopher of the twentieth century. TONY HONORÉ

Sources J. Hart, *Ask me no more: an autobiography* (1998) • T. Honoré, 'Herbert Lionel Adolphus Hart, 1907–1992', *PBA*, 84 (1994), 295–321 • Lord Wilberforce, private memoir • H. L. A. Hart, interview with M. Brock and B. Harrison for *HUOxf. 8: 20th cent.* [unpublished transcript] • H. L. A. Hart, 'Alfred Rupert Neale Cross', *PBA*, 70

(1984), 432–3 • N. MacCormick, *H. L. A. Hart* (1981) • R. Gavison, ed., *Issues in contemporary legal philosophy: the influence of H. L. A. Hart* (1987) • P. M. S. Hacker, 'Preface', *Law, morality and society: essays in honour of H. L. A. Hart*, ed. P. M. S. Hacker and J. Raz (1977) [with bibliography to 1976] • P. M. S. Hacker, chapter 1, *Law, morality and society: essays in honour of H. L. A. Hart*, ed. P. M. S. Hacker and J. Raz (1977) [with bibliography to 1976] • H. Eckmann, *Rechtspositivmus und sprachanalytische Philosophie: der Begriff des Rechts in das Rechtstheorie H. L. A. Harts* (1969) • personal knowledge (2004) • S. L. Paulson, 'A bibliography of H. L. A. Hart', *Ratio Juris*, 8/3 (Dec 1995), 397–406

Archives SOUND BL NSA, current affairs recordings • BL NSA, documentary recording

Likenesses D. Hill, oils, *c*.1977, Brasenose College, Oxford • S. Pyke, photograph, 1990, NPG [*see illus.*] • photograph, repro. in Hacker and Raz, eds., *Law, morality and society*

Wealth at death £318,084: probate, 20 April 1993, *CGPLA Eng. & Wales*

Hart, Horace Henry (1840–1916), printer, was born on 23 March 1840 in Ballingdon, Sudbury, Suffolk, the son of William Hart (*b*. 1829), a shoemaker and schoolmaster, and his wife, Caroline Elizabeth, *née* Clark. At fourteen he became a reading boy at the publishers Woodfall and Kinder in London. He worked as a proof-reader and cashier, and was appointed manager at the age of twenty-six. He took over the management of Savill, Edwards & Co. for the Edinburgh printers Ballantyne, Hanson & Co. in 1878, and joined Clowes & Son two years later. In 1883 he became controller of the Oxford University Press; this newly created post made Hart general manager at Walton Street in Oxford, and he remained there until his retirement.

Hart came to Oxford as a modernizer. Benjamin Jowett had become vice-chancellor of the university in 1882, and, like the delegates of the press, Jowett was determined to abolish the unprofitable share partnership in the printing business. Hart's appointment led to the end of the partnership, as Jowett dismissed Edward Pickard Hall, the senior printer, and the delegates regained all shares in the press. With their guarded support Hart set out to reorganize Oxford's printing, and to regulate the different practices within its two sides, the learned press and the Bible press. Oxford's London office remained under its publisher, Henry Frowde. Jowett established a committee to investigate printing standards, and Hart reported to it. He favoured retaining the foundry—the sheer variety of language and type size in Oxford's output rendered other possibilities absurd—and obtaining fresh stocks from Europe. As Hart pointed out, this was precisely the course John Fell had followed when building up Oxford's printing in the seventeenth century. Hart toured Germany during 1887, and brought back thirty new founts. He introduced new casting machines and enlarged the ink factory in 1888, and a collotype department was established in 1890. Folding and stitching machinery was purchased a year later, establishing the bindery. Monotype keyboards and casters arrived in 1903, and soon became vital to Oxford's work.

Hart's love of printing led to the two works for which he is best remembered. In 1900 he published *Notes on a Century of Typography*. Charles Daniel had revived John Fell's types in 1876, and Hart used the neglected collection for Robert Bridges' works, notably the *Yattendon Hymnal*. Hart decided then 'to save the ancient printing materials belonging to the University from a state of rust and confusion' (Hart, xiii), and he cleaned, preserved, and catalogued Oxford's vast holding of matrices and punches. The *Notes* presented comprehensive specimens from this treasure trove; a beautiful limited edition, it reached a wider audience when reprinted in 1970. Hart put the rediscovered Fell to good use in his acclaimed facsimile reprints of Tudor and Stuart works, and in printing the order of service for the coronation in 1902. Hart's second major work was *Rules for Compositors and Readers*. It was issued privately in 1893, but demand was so great that Hart published the booklet in 1904. Intended as house rules for Oxford printers, it became the accepted authority on English grammar, punctuation, and disputed spellings. It was through the *Rules* that the spelling 'Shakespeare' entered standard usage.

As controller Hart printed such volumes as Max Müller's edition of the Rig-Veda, and early parts of James Murray's *New English Dictionary*. His broader concerns made him first chief officer of the press fire brigade in 1885, and led to his founding the Clarendon Press Institute in 1893. Hart married twice. With his first wife he had two daughters, Agnes and Beatrice. With his second wife, Susan Ellen, from whom he separated in 1914, he had a son, Harold Raven Hart, and a daughter, Daisy. A series of nervous breakdowns forced Hart to retire from the press in 1915, and he committed suicide by drowning in Youlbury Lake near the home of one of his daughters in Boars Hill, near Oxford, on 9 October 1916. He was buried at St Peter's, Wootton, Berkshire. It was a tragic end to a successful career. Staff at the press had revered him, and in the course of his work there he had preserved the heritage of the press, while also thoroughly updating its procedures. Under him, Oxford won an unprecedented grand prix for books and printing at the Paris Exhibition of 1889, and weathered recession and competition from Cambridge in the 1890s. The university awarded him an MA *honoris causa* in 1897, and although the merger of learned and Bible sides in 1906 somewhat dented his prestige, nevertheless, at Hart's retirement, the press was modern, profitable, and much admired.　　　　　　　　　　　　　　MARTIN MAW

Sources C. Batey, 'Horace Hart and the university press, Oxford, 1883–1915', *Signature*, new ser., 18 (1954), 5–22 · P. Sutcliffe, *The Oxford University Press: an informal history* (1978) · *The Times* (10 Oct 1916) · N. Barker, *The Oxford University Press and the spread of learning, 1478–1978* (1978) · H. Hart, *Notes on a century of typography at the University Press, Oxford, 1693–1794* (1900); facs. edn with introduction by H. Carter (1970) · *DNB* · Oxford University Press, archives · *The Periodical* [OUP literary magazine], 6/89, 85–7 · *Oxford Times* (14 Oct 1916) · *CGPLA Eng. & Wales* (1916) · b. cert. · d. cert.
Archives Bodl. Oxf., papers, MSS Eng. lett c.466–467; Eng. misc. e 971–972 · Oxford University Press, guard books, scrapbooks, working MSS, etc. | LPL, corresp. with John Wordsworth, MS 2165
Likenesses photograph, c.1897, Oxford University Press · photograph, repro. in Sutcliffe, *Oxford University Press*
Wealth at death £14,881 11s. 7d.: resworn probate, 2 Dec 1916, *CGPLA Eng. & Wales*

Hart, James (d. 1639), physician, was a native of Edinburgh and a nephew of Sir William Hart (d. 1617?) of Preston and Levilands, king's advocate and justice-depute of Scotland. He was perhaps the James Hart who graduated MA at Edinburgh University in 1599. Between about 1605 and 1610 he travelled and studied on the continent of Europe; incidental references in his writings give clues to his movements. He spent more than two years in France, at Paris, Fontenay-le-Comte in Poitou, and probably elsewhere. In November 1608 he matriculated at the University of Basel, and he graduated MD there on 21 February 1609. His printed thesis *Positiones de pleuritide*, dated 30 January, is dedicated to his uncle, as patron of his studies. He was still in Basel on 13 November 1609, when he signed the *Stammbuch* of Caspar Bauhin (1560–1624), but he also spent some time in Germany and mentions particularly a journey from Meissen in Saxony to Prague in April 1610. He must have returned to England soon afterwards, as he mentions cases seen in London in 1610 and 1611. By 1612 at the latest he was settled as a physician at Northampton, where he lived for the rest of his life and apparently succeeded in practice. He never belonged to the College of Physicians. Hart was a strong puritan, an appellation which he adopts more than once in his writings, and prominent in the local puritan community.

Hart's first published work was *The Arraignement of Urines* (1623), an abridged translation of *De incerto, fallaci, urinarum judicio* (1589) by Pieter van Foreest. This was followed in 1625 by *The Anatomie of Urines … or, The Second Part of our Discourse on Urines*. Both works are dedicated to Charles I, then prince of Wales; they expose the fallacies of diagnosis by means of an examination of urine at the hands of ignorant persons, and attack three kinds of trespassers on the medical domain—unlicensed quacks, meddlesome old women, and, above all, clergymen. A third work, entitled *A discourse of the lawlesse intrusion of parsons and vicars upon the profession of phisicke with the absurditie of the same*, 'was intended to bee printed with the others: but could by noe means bee licenced'. Two holograph manuscript copies survive, one, perhaps the earlier, in the Bodleian Library (MS Rawlinson D146), the other in the British Library, in the department of printed books (C.54.b.6), bound up with the other two works. Hart incorporated much of the work into his *Klinikē* (1633); the full text has been edited for publication by David Harley.

Hart obtained letters of denization in October 1626 and married Elizabeth Ward, a widow, at Horton, Northamptonshire, on 13 October 1635. His principal work is *Klinikē;, or, The Diet of the Diseased*. This 'fruit of twenty years' experience' is an attempt, in the Hippocratic tradition, to prescribe the proper regimen and physical conditions in disease as well as in health, dealing with health, air, exercise, and the like, though not with drugs. It includes a detailed discussion of all kinds of food and drink, much of it from personal observation. In rationality and freedom from the tyranny of therapeutic routine it is far in advance of most medical works of the time, and apart from its professional interest presents instructive pictures of contemporary manners and customs, both in Britain and on the continent. The work also contains much of Hart's *Discourse of the Lawlesse Intrusion*, perhaps inserted surreptitiously after licensing, since the approbation of the College of Physicians refers only to having 'read some part of this booke'.

Hart died intestate at Northampton in 1639 and was buried there on 2 August. Administration of his estate was granted to his brother John, of the city of Westminster (perhaps John Hart, groom of the robes, granted letters of denization on 12 July 1627). JOHN SYMONS

Sources private information (2004) [Northants. RO; M. Steinmann, University of Basel] · D. Harley, 'James Hart of Northampton and the Calvinist critique of priest physicians', *Medical History*, 42 (1998), 362–86 · P. Elmer, 'Medicine, religion, and the puritan revolution', *The medical revolution of the seventeenth century*, ed. R. French and A. Wear (1989), 10–45 · J. H. Raach, *A directory of English country physicians, 1603–1643* (1962) · D. Laing, ed., *A catalogue of the graduates … of the University of Edinburgh*, Bannatyne Club, 106 (1858) · H. G. Wackernagel and others, eds., *Die Matrikel der Universität Basel*, Bd III, 1601/2–1665/66 (1962) · F. Husner, 'Verzeichnis der Basler medizinischen Universitäts-schriften von 1575–1829', *Festschrift für Jacques Brodbeck-Sandreuter* (1942), 137–269 · DNB

Hart, James (1663–1729), Church of Scotland minister, was the son of James Hart, provost of Jedburgh. He studied at the University of Edinburgh, graduating with an MA degree on 11 July 1687. On 4 July 1692 he was ordained as minister of Ratho, near Edinburgh, and on 4 August he married Margaret Livingston. After her death he married Mary, daughter of James Campbell of Kilpont, with whom he had thirteen children, nine of whom survived him. On 19 August 1702 he became minister of Old Greyfriars, Edinburgh, as successor to Gilbert Rule. During the early years of his pastorate he strongly opposed the idea of a union of parliaments with England. From the pulpit he denounced William Carstares, principal of the University of Edinburgh, long-time counsellor to William of Orange, and a powerful advocate for union, as an enemy to his country and a traitor to the church. He was speedily reconciled to the change in political affairs after the Union of 1707, however, and in the autumn of 1714 was among those appointed by the general assembly of the Church of Scotland to congratulate George I on his accession to the throne. George appointed him king's almoner in August 1726. Robert Wodrow described Hart as 'a worthy, good man, and one whose sermons were much haunted. He was naturally a little warm and keen, but of considerable gravity and prudence with it' (Wodrow, 4.62). When Richard Steele visited Scotland in 1718, he met Hart while endeavouring to bring about a union between the Presbyterian and Episcopal churches, and was much impressed by his character. He noted the contrast between Hart's affability and benevolence in private and his fierce public preaching against sin and the doom awaiting the sinner, and he later referred to him as 'the hangman of the Gospel'.

In 1703 Hart published *A Sermon Preached in the New-Church before the Honourable Magistrates of the City of Edinburgh*, which was reprinted in 1749 as *The Qualifications of Rulers, and the Duty of Subjects Described*. He died in Edinburgh on 10 June 1729. A century later John Lee, principal of the University of Edinburgh, edited for publication *The Journal of Mr. James Hart in 1714* (1832).

A. H. MILLAR, *rev.* MICHAEL JINKINS

Sources *Fasti Scot.*, new edn · R. Wodrow, *Analecta, or, Materials for a history of remarkable providences, mostly relating to Scotch ministers and Christians*, ed. [M. Leishman], 4 vols., Maitland Club, 60 (1842–3)
Archives U. Edin. L., journal and sermons

Hart, John (c.1501–1574), herald and phonetician, belonged to a family of tenant farmers long settled at Northolt, near London; his father, John Hart, died about 1500. There are no records of his baptism and education, but his writings demonstrate that he was a well-read man, acquainted not only with classical languages, but also with several contemporary vernaculars. He may have spent some time at the University of Cambridge, since he had intellectual or personal links with three Cambridge scholars, two of whom, Sir Thomas Smith (*d.* 1577) and Sir John Cheke (*d.* 1557), were (like Hart) active in promoting spelling reform; a third, Sir William Cecil (*d.* 1598), was described by Hart as his 'specially good master'. As a powerful figure in government circles, Hart's 'master' was in a good position to act as his patron, and he became by the 1550s a diplomatic courier, then in the 1560s an official of the court of wards and liveries and a herald pursuivant. He was finally promoted in 1567 to the highly prestigious rank of Chester herald at the College of Arms in London.

Hart wrote three treatises on spelling reform; the first (1551) was not published at the time; the second, *An Orthografie* (1569), was a more sophisticated version of this manuscript; and the third, *A Methode* (1570), instructs learners in the use of the 'phonetic' alphabet which Hart devised. A fourth work intended to provide a simpler alphabet was not completed. Hart proposed to reform English spelling because it was both inconsistent and irregular. A fairly standardized orthography had been developed in the fifteenth century by chancery scribes, whose obligation to send out legal documents, by now in English, to all parts of the country, and to speakers of regional dialects, required them to use a generally regular and comprehensible spelling system. But when Caxton set up his printing press in 1476, he abandoned the regularized orthography of the scribes—possibly because he had to employ foreign compositors—and his successors, even as late as 1551, were no more systematic.

Hart hoped to reform English orthography because it was an obstacle to the acquisition of literacy by, for example, protestants anxious to read the Bible for themselves in their quest for salvation. Furthermore, literate foreigners needed assistance in coping with the vagaries of English spelling, which were such a deterrent to comprehension. Hart's aim was to match graphs and sounds, taking as his standard the speech of the court and of London and its environs. Where necessary he provided new graphs where single characters representing single sounds were lacking in the existing alphabet, as with, for example, <sh> and <th>. In Hart's system, one graph represented one sound and vice versa. He also explained, for the benefit of speakers of other dialects who needed to be conversant with the sounds of the standard language, how individual sounds were articulated. Consequently, he not only became a spelling reformer, but also developed into a phonetician of outstanding intelligence and insight.

Whereas the study of orthography in the classical tradition was based on the written representation of vowels, diphthongs, semi-vowels, and consonants (including a sub-category of mutes), Hart based his phonetic script on the spoken language, noting for the first time by any scholar several features of connected English speech, such as elision, assimilation, stress, and intonation; and in his study of individual sounds, he noticed such features as the aspiration which follows initial voiceless plosives, represented by Hart as <h> in, for example, *pheip*, for 'pipe'. These features are clearly visible in the phonetic transcription of some forty pages of text included in *An Orthografie*.

Hart was not the first English scholar to publish his ideas on spelling reform, since he was forestalled by Sir Thomas Smith, who published his *De recta et emendata linguae anglicae scriptione* in 1568, but he was the first (in 1551) to deal with it so subtly. Unfortunately his work did not meet with the lasting success it deserved, possibly because Richard Mulcaster published, in 1582, *The First Part of the Elementarie*, a proposal for reforming English spelling, without using new characters. It was based as far as possible on traditional and established spellings, and proved extremely popular, superseding Hart's more academic works.

Hart died in London on 16 July 1574, leaving a widow, Mary. She was still alive in 1578, when she presented a petition to Lord Burghley.   VIVIAN SALMON

Sources *DNB* · B. Danielsson, ed., 'John Hart's works on English orthography and pronunciation, 1551, 1569, 1570; I: Biographical and bibliographical introductions, texts, and index verborum', *Stockholm Studies in English*, 5 (1955) · B. Danielsson, ed., 'John Hart's works on English orthography and pronunciation, 1551, 1569, 1570; II: Phonology', *Stockholm Studies in English*, 11 (1963) · R. Lass, 'John Hart', *Lexicon grammaticorum*, ed. H. Stammerjohann (1996), 393–5 · V. Salmon, 'John Hart and the beginnings of phonetics in 16th-century England', *Perspectives on English*, ed. K. Carlon, K. Davidse, and E. Rudzka-Ostyn (1994), 2–20
Archives BL, 'Opening of the unreasonable writing of our Inglish toung', Royal MS 17 c vii

Hart, John (d. 1586), Roman Catholic priest and Jesuit, was the son of William Hart, a recusant gentleman living in the precincts of the former abbey at Eynsham, Oxfordshire. According to Anthony Wood he was educated at the University of Oxford, but there is no mention of him in any college register. He and his younger brother William (1561–1584) were both sent abroad by their father. John Hart received minor orders at the English Hospice in Rome in May 1575 and after proceeding to the University of Douai in 1576 graduated STB there in 1578. He was ordained at Cambrai on 29 March 1578.

In 1580 Hart was sent on the English mission, but was arrested on landing at Dover on 5 June, separated from his companions, and was escorted to Nonsuch to be interviewed by Sir Francis Walsingham, who treated him with exceptional favour; Hart was allowed 'libertie of conference at home, first in my owne countrie, and afterward in prison' (Rainolds, iv). He was set at liberty to confer with theologians at Oxford, and then committed to the Marshalsea prison, from which he was moved to the Tower on 24 December 1580 for formal interrogation. After being sentenced to death on 21 November 1581 he was brought out for execution along with Edmund Campion and others on 1 December only to be reprieved at the last moment. The same day he wrote to Walsingham offering to use his intimacy with William Allen as an informer in government service. He argued that as a survivor of the Tower and of the rack ('though I endured nothing therein, but that is unknown to him') he would be privy to all Allen's secrets (Harrison, 163–5). This apostasy was not known to his fellow Catholics or to Allen, who described him as a 'brave athlete of God', who had conducted himself 'heroically' (Knox, 114, 199). Subsequently Hart claimed to have repented of his treachery. He was due a second time to have been executed, on 28 May 1582, but again the execution was stayed 'for certain good considerations' (*APC*, 13.428), and he accepted Walsingham's proposal that he should confer with John Rainolds, the leading puritan divine at Oxford. Their lengthy discussions in the Tower were published in 1584 with a preface in which Hart acknowledged the text to be a true record. Though he defended the fundamentals of Catholic doctrine, protestant polemicists claimed that he had denied the right of the pope to depose monarchs, perhaps on the basis of his statement that the pope had 'the fatherhood of the Church, not the princehood of the world' (Rainolds, iv). Rainolds told Walsingham that Hart was taking part in the exercise—stage-managed by the government in order to present an image of clemency and toleration—only to obtain a reprieve.

In January 1585, after four years in the Tower, Hart was deported to France with twenty other priests. He made his way to Rome, where he was formally received into the Society of Jesus on 14 November 1585, having earlier applied for admission in 1583, while still in prison. His prison journal, sometimes erroneously attributed to Edward Rishton, was incorporated into the second edition of Nicholas Sander's *De origine ac progressu schismatis Anglicani*, published at Rome in 1586. The fact that this 'Diarium rerum gestarum in Turri Londinensi' was dropped from the third edition (1587) by the editor, Robert Persons, may indicate that Persons had discovered Hart's secret. The diary, with its details about the martyrs imprisoned and tortured in the Tower, may have been presented by Hart in Rome to establish his credentials. In April 1586 he was sent by his superiors to Poland, where he died at Jarosław on 19 July, soon after his arrival. The annual letters of the Jarosław college for 1594 recorded the wonder aroused there when, seven years after Hart's death, his body 'once racked for the faith', was found to be incorrupt (Lukács). His younger brother William, a student at the English College in Rome, joined the Society of Jesus there in 1582 and died in August 1584.

G. MARTIN MURPHY

Sources G. Anstruther, *The seminary priests*, 1 (1969), 153–5 · B. A. Harrison, *A Tudor journal: the diary of a priest in the Tower, 1580–1585* (2000) · T. M. McCoog, *English and Welsh Jesuits, 1555–1650*, 2, Catholic RS, 75 (1995), 203 · J. Morris, ed., *The troubles of our Catholic forefathers related by themselves*, 2 (1875), 28–34 · *The letters and memorials of William, Cardinal Allen (1532–1594)*, ed. T. F. Knox (1882), vol. 2 of *Records of the English Catholics under the penal laws (1878–82)* · J. Rainolds, *The summe of the conference between John Rainoldes and John Hart* (1609) · C. Talbot, ed., *Miscellanea: recusant records*, Catholic RS, 53 (1961), 212 · T. F. Knox and others, eds., *The first and second diaries of the English College, Douay* (1878) · *Calendar of the manuscripts of the most hon. the marquis of Salisbury*, 24 vols., HMC, 9 (1883–1976), vol. 13, p. 272 · H. Foley, ed., *Records of the English province of the Society of Jesus*, 7 (1882–3), 338 · A. F. Allison and D. M. Rogers, eds., *The contemporary printed literature of the English Counter-Reformation between 1558 and 1640*, 1 (1989), 136, no. 973 · M. C. Questier, 'English clerical converts to protestantism, 1580–96', *Recusant History*, 20 (1990–91), 455–77, esp. 456–8 · L. Grzebień, *Encyklopedia wiedzy o jezuitach na ziemiach Polski i Litwy, 1564–1995* (Krakow, 1996) · *CSP dom.*, *1581–90*, 59 · *Documenta Romana historiae Societatis Iesu in regnis olim corona Hungarica unitis*, 3, ed. L. Lukács (1967), 637 · BL, Add. MS 48029, fol. 58a
Archives BL, 'Thomas Norton's Chayne of treasons', Add. MS 48029, fols. 58ff. · BL, Hart's answer to interrogations, Add. MS 48035, fols. 179r–182v · LPL, MS 402

Hart, John (*c*.1690–1740), army officer and colonial governor, was born at Crover, co. Cavan, the son of Merrick Hart (*d. c*.1681) and his wife, Lettice, daughter of Thomas Vesey and sister of John Vesey, archbishop of Tuam. Hart had two brothers and five sisters. The family was of English origin, but Hart's grandfather Henry, a soldier who served in Ireland, had been granted land in the plantation of Ulster.

Hart spent his early career as a military officer, serving in Spain and Portugal during the War of the Spanish Succession and achieving the rank of captain. During this period he made the acquaintance of Benedict Leonard Calvert, son of the third Baron Baltimore. At Calvert's recommendation, on 17 January 1714 the crown commissioned Hart as Maryland's fifth royal governor; Hart, in return, agreed to pay Calvert £500 from the profits of his Maryland offices. In addition to the governorship, which Hart continued to hold after restoration of proprietary authority in 1715, these included the positions of chancellor (1715–20) and surveyor-general of both the eastern and western shores (1717–20).

Hart's governorship was marked by generally cordial relations with both houses of the general assembly. None the less, Hart's effectiveness, and ultimately his security in office, was threatened by contentious personal disputes. A militant protestant, Hart found himself at odds with two formidable Irish-born adversaries, the Roman Catholic Charles Carroll (1691–1755) and Thomas Macnemara. Hart opposed Carroll's attempt to hold public offices, to which the proprietor appointed him in 1716, without taking the oath of abjuration, and he vehemently resented Carroll's attempt to control all provincial revenues, including those designated for the governor's support. In this dispute Hart had the backing of both the council and the proprietor, who revoked Carroll's commission in 1717. Hart was less successful in asserting his authority over Macnemara: in fact his criticism of proprietary support for Macnemara eventually led to termination of his own commission as governor.

In December 1719 Lord Baltimore relieved Hart of his post, ordering him to leave Maryland no later than May 1720. Although the personal conflicts that marked his tenure resulted in the breach with the proprietor, they did not precipitate a similar rupture of relations with British authorities. Instead Hart received an appointment as royal governor of the Leeward Islands, which he held from 1721 until 1727. Little is known of Hart's life after he left the islands, but he was apparently in London in 1732, when Herman van der Myn painted his portrait. Hart appears to have settled, however, at Wardfield Hall in Berkshire.

Hart's first wife was his cousin Mary (*b*. 1681, *d*. before 1710), daughter of Colonel Henry Hart and widow of Captain Francis Purefoy. John Hart next married Anne (surname unknown) about 1710; the couple had two sons and a daughter. Hart died on 30 December 1740 at his Berkshire home. He survived his wife, and in his will he left his daughter, Marylanda, one half of her mother's personal property and £5000. The balance of his personal estate and all his land in England, Ireland, and overseas colonies Hart bequeathed to his elder and sole surviving son, Thomas.

Until recently the assessment of Hart's tenure in Maryland characterized him as a fanatic who saw popish plots everywhere. According to A. C. Land he was a man of 'immense energy and modest talent', who presided over 'provincial leaders far superior … in native ability' and who confronted 'forces he could not grasp' (Land, 'Provincial Maryland', 29). Ronald Hoffman and R. J. Rockefeller, however, hold a more balanced view of his performance, recognizing the challenge to his authority and to Maryland statutes posed by the actions of Carroll and Macnemara. In these assessments Hart emerges as an able governor, with '[p]ersonal conflicts, tainted with religious bigotry', rather than ineptitude, eventually leading to his downfall (Rockefeller, 309). JEAN B. RUSSO

Sources E. C. Papenfuse and others, eds., *A biographical dictionary of the Maryland legislature, 1635–1789*, 1 (1979), 430; 2 (1985), 945 · J. H. Pleasants, research notes, Maryland State Archives, Annapolis, MSA S1259-131-1010 · R. J. Rockefeller, 'Their magistrates and officers: executive government in eighteenth-century Maryland', PhD diss., University of Maryland, 1998 · R. Hoffman, *Princes of Ireland, planters of Maryland: a Carroll saga, 1500–1782* (2000) · C. N. Everstine, *The general assembly of Maryland, 1634–1776* (1980) · D. M. Owings, *His lordship's patronage: offices of profit in colonial Maryland* (1953) · A. C. Land, 'Provincial Maryland', *Maryland: a history*, ed. R. Walsh and W. L. Fox (1983), 29–31 · A. C. Land, *Colonial Maryland: a history* (1981) · R. J. Brugger and others, *Maryland: a middle temperament, 1634–1980* (1988) · will, PRO, PROB 11/707, sig. 12
Likenesses H. van der Myn, oils, 1732, Government House, Annapolis, Maryland

Wealth at death personal property, incl. £5000, left to daughter; balance of personalty and land in England, Ireland, and 'plantations abroad' to son; also government securities, money, plate, and jewels: will, PRO, PROB 11/707, sig. 12

Hart [*formerly* Herriot], **John** [*known as* Captain Hart] (1809–1873), merchant and politician in Australia, was born in Devon on 25 February 1809, the son of John Herriot and his wife, Mary, *née* Granville. He went to sea at the age of twelve and gained immense experience, and visited Hobart in September 1828 as a sailor on the *Magnet*. He was one of the earliest whaling captains at Portland Bay and entered the coastal trade. In November 1829 he was second mate on the *Britannia* to Western Australia, and he soon became fully familiar with the south coast of the continent. In 1832 he was master of the *Elizabeth*, owned and built by John Griffiths at Launceston. He often visited Kangaroo Island, where he traded in seal and wallaby skins and salt. In 1833 he conveyed Edward Henty from Launceston to Portland and returned with whale oil. He sailed to New Zealand for pine and potatoes, reconnoitred St Vincent's Gulf, and stood on the future site of Adelaide in advance of the first settlers. His prior knowledge of the territory made him especially valuable as an adviser to the new colonists.

In 1835 Hart visited England to buy a ship for Griffiths; he supplied vital local knowledge and information to the South Australian colonial commissioners and gave Colonel William Light sailing directions. He returned with the *Isabella* to Launceston on 11 January 1837, with J. B. Hack and his family, then left with livestock for Hack to Adelaide. He apparently shipped the first livestock to the colony—developing the trade by sea and overland through the Wimmera. The *Isabella* was wrecked off Cape Nelson on 30 March and Hart lost everything, though he found his way back to Adelaide. Hack came to his rescue and set him up as the skipper of a schooner in the new coastal trade. Hart became harbour master at Encounter Bay in December 1838 and in the following year the two men joined forces in a whaling enterprise at Encounter Bay which Hart managed for £500 per annum. In November 1840 he became director of the Adelaide Auction Company, but the financial crisis soon after curbed his activities. Hack fell bankrupt in 1841 and Hart later engaged him as his own accountant. Hart continued the whaling station from 1841 to 1846 with new partners. His finances revived and he bought two larger ships. In 1843 he took to the sea again and sailed to England aboard the *Augustus*, in which he owned a two-thirds interest. He visited Britain twice; in 1845 he married Margaret Gillmor Todd of Dublin and returned to settle in South Australia. Throughout his life he was known as Captain Hart.

Hart gave up the sea in 1846 to devote himself to commerce, and eventually settled down to manage flour mills, which produced some of the finest brands of Australian flour. He started the Mercantile Marine Insurance Company, and was a director of the Union Bank of Australia. He settled in Adelaide and bought and leased land across the colony. He ran cattle and acted as agent for absentee owners. In 1845–8 he invested in copper at Burra and several other mines. He was a director of the Forest Iron Smelting and Steam Sawing Company and of a copper-smelting venture in Port Adelaide. In 1849 he helped form the Adelaide Marine Association Company and an aborted project for a railway to Port Adelaide. His new flour mill at Port Adelaide was built (in 1855) at a cost of £3750 and demonstrated his faith in the colony as the granary of Australia. He was much involved in the Kapunda copper mines and acted as agent for British investors. In 1860 he was caught up in the great northern copper-mining scandal but was exonerated in the investigation by the select committee. He was a shareholder in the National and Union banks.

In 1851 Hart was elected to the legislative council for the district of Victoria (with only sixty-eight voters); he resigned in 1853 to visit England and was re-elected in 1854. In the house of assembly he represented first Port Adelaide (1857–9, 1862–6), then Light (1868–70), then Burra (1870–73). He filled various positions—notably as treasurer under Baker (1857), Hanson (1857–8), Ayres (1863, 1864), and Blyth (1864–5). He was chief secretary in 1863. He formed his own ministries in 1865–6, 1868, and 1870–71, the last being his most influential stint, during which he introduced the title 'premier'. He was regarded as a conservative and tough politician and something of a schemer.

Hart saw himself as primarily representing port and shipping interests. He adopted a severely *laissez-faire* attitude and was opposed to government railways, declaring that the only duties of government were to protect society from foreign aggression and internal disorders. Nevertheless he was instrumental in developing a reliable water supply to the city from the Adelaide hills. He advocated the abolition of customs (the revenue to be replaced by direct taxes) and opposed state-aided religion and free education. He inaugurated the bonded debt policy, which proved important for state finances. He thought that public service was an honour and should be paid for only in terms of the time forgone. He brought to the colony a cargo of coolies in 1853 and advocated immigration from China, India, and Britain particularly for the development of the Northern Territory, where he held company interests. In office he planned Goyder's survey expeditions and the Northern Territory telegraph to Darwin.

Hart was made CMG in 1870. He was provincial grand master of freemasons. He built Granville House at Semaphore, where he died suddenly of apoplexy, after addressing a meeting of the Mercantile Marine Insurance Company, on 28 January 1873. His wife and a family of seven children survived him. He was buried in the North Road cemetery on 30 January.

C. A. HARRIS, *rev.* ERIC RICHARDS

Sources W. H. Baynes, 'John Hart: the public record, 1831 to 1872', BA hons. diss., University of Adelaide, 1961 · D. Pike, *Paradise of dissent: South Australia, 1829–1857*, 2nd edn [1967] · *Adelaide Observer* (24 March 1853) · *AusDB* · W. J. Ruediger, *Border's land* (1980) · J. Blacket, *History of South Australia* (1911) · *Adelaide Observer* (1 Feb 1873) · V. Smith, ed., *Brief biographical notes on the lives of some of those sailing*

ship captains of the Semaphore (1952) · G. D. Combe, Responsible government in South Australia (1957) · South Australian Register (30 Jan 1873) · T. F. Bride, ed., Letters from Victorian pioneers (1898)
Wealth at death over £50,000: AusDB

Hart, Joseph (1711/12–1768), Independent minister and hymn writer, was born in London. Little is known about his early life except that his parents were Independents and that he had a classical education. He taught classics in a London school and published translations of *Phocylides* (1744) and *Herodian* (1749). About 1752 he married Mary (1726–1790), who may have been the sister of the Revd John Hughes. They had five children.

Hart suffered much spiritual turmoil over many years. In 1741 he published *The Unreasonableness of Religion* in reply to an attack by John Wesley on Whitefield's emphasis on predestination. For Hart, religion received no support from reason, but was diametrically opposed to reason. On Whit Sunday 1757 he was converted after hearing a sermon on Revelation 3: 10 preached at the Moravian chapel in Fetter Lane, London. From 1760 until his death he was the minister of a large congregation at Jewin Street Chapel, London. He published an account of his conversion as the preface to his extensive hymn collection, *Hymns &c Composed on Various Subjects*, which went through many editions. Dr Johnson recorded his disapproval of Hart's Calvinism when he related how he once gave a poor girl money, 'though [he] saw Hart's hymns in her hand' (Johnson, 1.79). Most of the hymns are strongly Calvinist, but three are still included in many widely used hymnals.

Hart died at his house at the sign of the Lamb, near Durham Yard, London, on 24 May 1768, aged fifty-six. He was buried in Bunhill Fields, where 20,000 people are said to have listened to Andrew Kinsman's funeral oration. His widow and their young children survived him, but were left destitute; consequently subscriptions were raised among friends and John Hughes's funeral sermon on Hart was published for their benefit.

J. M. RIGG, rev. JOHN S. ANDREWS

Sources J. Hart, 'The author's experience', *Hymns &c composed on various subjects* (1759) [with autobiographical preface] · T. Wright, *Joseph Hart* (1910) [incl. bibliography] · J. Julian, ed., *A dictionary of hymnology*, rev. edn (1907), 492–3, 1511, 1764 · W. Wilson, *The history and antiquities of the dissenting churches and meeting houses in London, Westminster and Southwark*, 4 vols. (1808–14), vol. 3, pp. 342–7 · *Memorial to Mr. Joseph Hart … with memoir and Mr. Hart's experience* (1877) · E. Routley, *I'll praise my maker* (1951), 243–8, 278 · *Hymn quest: a dictionary of hymnody*, 1 (1997) · S. Johnson, *Works*, ed. E. L. McAdam, 2nd edn, 1 (1960), 79 · D. M. Lewis, ed., *The Blackwell dictionary of evangelical biography, 1730–1860*, 2 vols. (1995)
Wealth at death wife and family left destitute

Hart, Joseph Binns (1794–1844), composer, born in London on 5 June 1794, was a chorister at St Paul's Cathedral under John Bernard Sale from 1801 to 1810, and during those years had lessons on the organ from Samuel Wesley and Matthew Cook, and on the piano from J. B. Cramer. At the age of eleven Hart often played as deputy for Thomas Attwood, the organist of St Paul's. In 1810 he was elected organist of Walthamstow church, Essex, and joined the earl of Uxbridge's household as organist for three years. Hart was elected, after severe competition, organist of

Tottenham church, Middlesex. On the introduction of the quadrille at the fashionable dances at Almack's by Lady Jersey after 1815, Hart, who was described as a teacher and pianist at private balls, began his long series of adaptations of national and operatic airs to the fashionable dance measures. His most notable achievement was the compilation in 1819 of the tunes of 'The Lancers' Quadrille'. From 1818 to 1821 Hart was chorus master and pianist for the English opera at the Lyceum Theatre, and wrote the songs for *Amateurs and Actors* (1818), *The Bull's Head*, and *A Walk for a Wager* (both 1819), *The Vampyre* (1820), and other musical farces and melodramas. From 1829 until his death Hart lived at Hastings, where he opened a music shop, conducted a small band, and played the organ at St Mary's Chapel. He died on 10 December 1844 at Hastings, aged fifty.

Some of Hart's most successful quadrilles were based on the music of *Don Giovanni* (1818), Matthew Locke's *Macbeth*, and various English, Irish, and Scottish melodies. He composed forty-eight sets of quadrilles, waltzes, and gallopades. *An Easy Mode of Teaching Thorough Bass and Composition* was also ascribed to him.

L. M. MIDDLETON, rev. NILANJANA BANERJI

Sources Grove, *Dict. mus.* · Brown & Stratton, *Brit. mus.* · *Sussex Advertiser* (17 Dec 1844) · T. Busby, *A complete dictionary of music* (1827), 333

Hart [née Ridehalgh], **Judith**, Baroness Hart of South Lanark (1924–1991), politician, was born at 51 Ennismore Street, Burnley, Lancashire, on 18 September 1924, the daughter of Harry Ridehalgh, linotype operator, and later secretary of a mechanics' institute, and his wife, Lily, née Lord, schoolteacher and Baptist lay preacher. Baptized Constance Mary, at the age of twelve she adopted the name Judith. She was educated at Burnley primary school and Clitheroe Royal Grammar School, where she was head prefect, before a scholarship took her to the London School of Economics (LSE). The mass unemployment she had witnessed in 1930s Lancashire converted her to socialism and at eighteen she joined the Labour Party, becoming secretary of the Cambridge University Labour Club during the LSE's wartime evacuation to Cambridge. After receiving a first-class degree in sociology in 1945 and teaching briefly at a training college in Portsmouth she married Dr Anthony Bernard (Tony) Hart (1917–1999), research chemist, on 17 April 1946; they later had two sons. They had met at a meeting where he gave a speech against the nuclear bomb. His similar political views (he was later a Richmond borough councillor) and support for her career were important to her throughout her life. Soon after their marriage his work took them to Dorset where she became a researcher for the Ministry of Health and a co-opted member of the Dorset county council public health committee.

Hart entered politics in Dorset, running unsuccessfully for Parkstone municipal council at twenty-five and for the parliamentary constituency of Dorset West in 1951. Four years later, after the Harts had moved to Scotland, she reduced Lady Tweedsmuir's majority in the hard-fought

Judith Hart, Baroness Hart of South Lanark (1924–1991), by unknown photographer, 1968

'battle of the housewives' in Aberdeen South, where her beauty was the source of some comment. During this time she made broadcasts on BBC's *Woman's Hour*, wrote articles on Scottish affairs for *The Tribune* (she was an early devolutionist), and lectured in sociology. When offered the more promising constituency of Lanark she decided that she could do more for people's welfare as an MP than as a lecturer.

After Judith received the nomination for Lanark, Tony withdrew as PPC for Glasgow Hillhead to campaign for his wife. She was elected in October 1959 and her family eventually joined her in London, where her mother-in-law helped raise her two sons. Although her own mother had died when Hart was fifteen she had imparted to her a strong pacifist philosophy, and the issue of disarmament dominated Hart's early parliamentary career. She served on the national committee of the Campaign for Nuclear Disarmament, joined the first Aldermaston march, and tried to initiate parliamentary debates on the Christmas Island nuclear tests and the police raid on the offices of the controversial anti-nuclear Committee of 100. The *Glasgow Herald* retracted its claim that she belonged to the committee after she sued the editors, but some still found such views as her opposition to Britain's membership of NATO immoderate.

None the less when Labour came to power in October 1964 Prime Minister Harold Wilson appointed Hart a joint parliamentary under-secretary of state for Scotland, partly as she had been one of the few Scottish MPs to support him for the leadership over George Brown. Her responsibilities included health, children, and education and she energetically promoted school-building in Scotland, but she felt it was important to have responsibility for areas outside women's traditional sphere in order to be seen as a credible politician. One of her interests was decolonization, and after Labour's re-election in April

1966 she was made minister of state at the Commonwealth Office. As minister she sought African leaders' support for sanctions against Rhodesia, and assured her party that the government would not capitulate to Rhodesia's illegal white minority regime. After only one year in this portfolio she became minister of social security, in July 1967, to implement spending cuts resisted by her predecessor, Margaret (Peggy) Herbison. She surprised colleagues with criticism of 'work-shy young people who think they are God's gift to poetry and guitar playing' (*Daily Telegraph*, 9 Dec 1991). Her role at social security caused ill-feeling in Lanarkshire, where Herbison was her very popular constituency neighbour.

In October 1968 Hart entered the cabinet as paymaster general, but frequently quarrelled with Wilson and especially irked him with her assertion that she had overall responsibility for government announcements (Crossman, 3.368). Following her attack on the government's plan for union reform, *In Place of Strife*, she was dropped from the cabinet in October 1969 and was moved to the Ministry of Overseas Development, which Wilson had created in 1964. Her decision to award pensions to expatriate colonial officers living in former dependencies won praise, but she served for less than a year before Labour was defeated in June 1970. The election also ended her brief tenure as first co-chair of the Women's National Commission.

In opposition Hart retained the overseas development portfolio and published *Aid and Liberation* (1973), based on her first-hand research in the Third World, where she became known and respected. This book called for 'socialist' aid to replace 'neo-colonial' aid, the cancellation or rescheduling of Third World debt, and an end to private investment in the Third World which primarily benefited the investors. She warned about the impact of EEC membership on British aid, and tried to amend the European Communities Bill to safeguard Britain's more generous aid programme.

After returning to her old ministry in March 1974 Hart spent over 200 hours negotiating with her EEC counterparts to achieve the Lomé convention, signed in 1975. This provided for aid from members of the community to forty-six of the world's poorest countries, and was her foremost accomplishment. Her book, *Aid and Liberation*, had also recommended using aid to support left-leaning governments and destabilize oppressive right-wing governments, and she was instrumental in cancelling aid to Chile after Labour's return to power. She welcomed many Chilean refugees into her home and hosted the widow of the slain Marxist president, Salvador Allende, but her association with communists and her speech at a rally organized by the *Morning Star* in 1974 attracted the interest of MI5. Her telephones were tapped, partly because of confusion with a communist, Mrs Tudor Hart, but nothing was uncovered which Wilson felt warranted her dismissal. He did demand an assurance that she and two colleagues would uphold the principle of collective ministerial responsibility after they had supported resolutions of the party's national executive committee (NEC) criticizing the government over arms sales to Chile and a joint naval exercise with South Africa.

To a certain extent Hart's interest in overseas affairs came at the expense of attention to local concerns, and despite her sympathy with radical and left-wing causes some felt that she lacked the common touch, though many constituents still remembered her fondly. Contemporaries described her as cool and efficient, though sometimes as aggressive and strident in public speeches, lacking in humour, and elegant in appearance and dress. In Richard Crossman's view 'she is a competent, efficient woman, not tremendously creative in mind, lacking many good ideas and a bit slapdash, but she is dashing, courageous, with a good political instinct for being on the right side' (Crossman, 3.311). Her sometimes grand manner and sense of self-importance led her to disregard the Foreign Office when making policy, which contributed to her department's being brought under its auspices. Although she had demonstrated how Britain could co-operate with European partners she urged withdrawal from the EEC in the referendum of June 1975, warning that it would lead to a federal Europe and threatened parliamentary sovereignty. Shortly after the referendum Wilson demoted the anti-marketeers in a cabinet shuffle and she refused to accept the Ministry of Transport. Her subsequent personal statement to the house was emotional and defensive, though from the backbenches she was now free to criticize the government over spending cuts and the abandonment of plans for a new town at Stonehouse near Lanark in 1976.

Yet Hart remained influential within the party and the NEC, on which she served from 1969 to 1983, and returned to the overseas development portfolio in February 1977 under Prime Minister James Callaghan. During her final term she increased both the quantity and the quality of aid, converting interest-free loans into permanent grants for countries which met a minimum standard of human rights. However, she did not establish similar criteria when she chaired the Labour Southern Africa Solidarity Fund, and there was criticism over its backing of Marxist guerrillas. She replied that the violence used by dictatorships could not be equated with that used by freedom fighters.

To a mixture of amusement and dismay Hart became a dame of the British empire in the government's resignation honours list in May 1979, as recognition for her work for the Lomé convention but perhaps also in compensation for her failure to attain more senior office. No doubt her talents could have taken her even further had it not been for her independent streak and her tendency to annoy her superiors. She continued as party spokesman on overseas aid until 1980 and was appointed an honorary fellow of the University of Sussex's Institute of Development Studies in 1985. During her final years in the Commons she chaired the NEC (1981–2) and remained one of the voices of the Labour left, opposing the Falklands War and the expulsion of the 'militant tendency' from the party. She left the Commons at the general election of 1987. In 1988 she was elevated to the House of Lords as Baroness Hart of South Lanark and delivered her maiden speech on the security services before ill health prevented her from taking any further active part. Shortly after the end of the Pinochet regime she was to receive the order of merit from the new Chilean government, but before it could be presented she died of cancer at Queen Mary's University Hospital, Roehampton, London, on 7 December 1991. She was survived by her husband and their two sons.

DUNCAN SUTHERLAND

Sources M. Phillips, *The divided house* (1980) • E. Vallance, *Women in the house: a study of women members of parliament* (1979) • *The Times* (9 Dec 1991) • *The Telegraph* (9 Dec 1991) • *The Guardian* (9 Dec 1991) • *The Scotsman* (9 Dec 1991) • *The Independent* (9 Dec 1991) • *The Times* • M. Falkender, *Downing Street in perspective* (1983) • J. Mann, *Women in parliament* (1962) • P. Brookes, *Women at Westminster: an account of women in the British parliament, 1918–1966* (1967) • S. Dorril and R. Ramsay, *Smear! Wilson and the secret state* (1991) • R. H. S. Crossman, *The diaries of a cabinet minister*, 3 vols. (1975–7) • *WWW*, 1991–5 • private information (2004) • b. cert. • m. cert. • d. cert. • *CGPLA Eng. & Wales* (1994)

Archives JRL, Labour History Archive and Study Centre, corresp. and papers • Mitchell L., Glas., Glasgow City Archives, constituency papers | SOUND BL NSA, Bow dialogues, 2 March 1971, C812/29 C20 • BL NSA, current affairs recordings • BL NSA, documentary recordings • BL NSA, party political recordings • BL NSA, recorded lecture

Likenesses photographs, 1968–74, Hult. Arch. [*see illus.*] • photograph, 1969, repro. in *The Guardian* • photograph, repro. in *The Times* • photograph, repro. in *Daily Telegraph* • photograph, repro. in *The Independent* • photograph, repro. in *The Scotsman*

Wealth at death £72,310: probate, 1 Nov 1994, *CGPLA Eng. & Wales*

Hart, Julia Catherine Beckwith [née Julia Catherine Beckwith] (**1796–1867**), novelist, was born on 10 March 1796 in Fredericton, New Brunswick, Canada, the eldest daughter of Nehemiah Beckwith (*d.* 1815), a loyalist who had become a trader and shipbuilder, and Julie Le Brun Duplessis, who had been governess to the children of Thomas Carleton, lieutenant-governor of the province. Educated at home by her mother, Julia enjoyed a financially comfortable childhood, spending time with her parents' relations in Nova Scotia and her mother's native Quebec. It was during these visits that she collected stories and recorded impressions that figured in her first novel.

After the shock caused by the robbery and murder of Julia's father in 1815, the family were left in financial difficulties, and Julia moved to Kingston, Ontario, to live with her aunt, the mother of the Quebec historian Abbé Ferland. She supported herself by working as a teacher, applying for her licence in 1816. But her fame rests upon her first novel, the two-volume romance *St Ursula's Convent, or, The Nun of Canada*, which she had begun to write at seventeen, perhaps influenced by her mother's Roman Catholic background (Julie Duplessis became a Methodist on marriage). Published anonymously in Kingston, Ontario, in 1824, it remains the earliest recorded novel published in Canada by a native-born author. Aimed primarily at younger readers, the novel has a melodramatic content which belies its sedate title and features a sensational, plot-driven narrative that includes shipwrecks, kidnappers, changeling babies, false priests, and a highly sentimental conclusion. Though a commercial success, with 175 out of the first edition of 200 books sold by subscription before its appearance in May 1824, *St Ursula's Convent* was too faithful to the conventions of popular fiction to be critically acclaimed. Today, however, with only six copies remaining at Canadian libraries, the novel is considered a landmark in early Canadian literature, and provides an example of the fiction that appealed to the reading public in early nineteenth-century Canada.

Two years before its publication, on 3 January 1822, Beckwith had married George Henry Hart, a bookbinder from England, with whom she had seven children: a daughter (Julia) and six sons. The couple established a girls' boarding-school in Kingston before moving to Rochester, New York, in 1824. There Julia published her second two-volume romance, *Tonnewonte, or, The Adopted Son of America* (1824–5), under the pseudonym 'an American', which ran to three editions in the United States. Set in France and upper-state New York, the novel patriotically demonstrates the many advantages of New World democracy compared with the class divisions of France during the Napoleonic period and, like *St Ursula's Convent*, incorporates descriptions of North American history and landscape.

In 1831 Julia Beckwith Hart returned with her husband to Fredericton, where he became a civil servant in the crown land department of New Brunswick. Julia remained in Fredericton for the rest of her life, contributing fiction to the *New Brunswick Reporter* and *Fredericton Advertiser* and writing her third (unpublished) novel, 'Edith, or, The Doom', the manuscript of which is preserved in the University of New Brunswick archives. She died in Fredericton on 28 November 1867, and remains a pioneer of early Canadian literature, and a celebrated native of New Brunswick.   EMMA PLASKITT

Sources W. Toye, ed., *The Oxford companion to Canadian literature* (1983), 336–8 · Blain, Clements & Grundy, *Feminist comp.*, 496 · new-brunswick.net/new-brunswick/fame.html [website on famous natives of New Brunswick], 23 Sept 2002 · biographical article on Julia Beckwith, nlc-bnc.ca [*National Library News*, 30/6 (June 1998)], 23 Sept 2002 · www.sfu.ca [Simon Fraser University database; Julia Beckwith Hart] · Early Canadiana online, www.canadiana.org/eco/english/collection_eng_lit.html, 23 Sept 2002 · J. Beckwith, *St Ursula's convent, or, The nun of Canada*, 2 vols. (1824); see online at digital.library.upenn.edu/women/_generate/CANADA.html · J. Beckwith, *Tonnewonte, or, The adopted son of America: a tale containing scenes from real life*, 2 vols. (1824–5)
Archives University of New Brunswick, archives

Hart, Moses (1675–1756). *See under* Hart, Aaron (1670–1756).

Hart, Philip (*d.* 1749), organist and composer, was the son of James Hart (1647–1718), a gentleman of the Chapel Royal and composer. He was appointed assistant organist at St Andrew Undershaft, London, in 1696, becoming sole organist the following year and remaining there until his death. He was also organist of St Michael Cornhill (1704–23) and of St Dionis Backchurch (1724–49). Sir John Hawkins considered him a 'sound musician', uninfluenced by the innovations introduced by the Italian opera, and he

had a considerable reputation as an organist, although Hawkins criticized his excessive use of the shake. His compositions included a number of keyboard pieces published in 1704 as *Fugues and Lessons*, many songs and duets, and his masterpiece, the *Ode to Harmony*, which was probably the official St Cecilia's day ode for 1702 and was performed at Stationers' Hall on 3 March 1703. They were held in low repute in the nineteenth century—'no more than respectable' (*DNB*)—but he was later considered to rank among 'those who brought distinction to English music between the death of Purcell and the arrival of Handel' (*New Grove*). Hart died on 17 July 1749 at an advanced age in the parish of St George the Martyr, and was buried at St Andrew Undershaft on 22 July, leaving his property to his nephew William Hart.

L. M. MIDDLETON, *rev.* K. D. REYNOLDS

Sources *New Grove* · Grove, *Dict. mus.* (1927) · J. Hawkins, *A general history of the science and practice of music*, 5 vols. (1776)

Hart, Sir Raymund George (1899–1960), air force officer, was born on 28 February 1899 at Northcote, Kingston Road, Merton, Surrey, the son of Ernest Joseph Hart, a commercial traveller, and his wife, Emily Caroline Simmons. Following his education at the Simon Langton School, Canterbury, he enlisted in the Royal Flying Corps in 1916. He was commissioned in 1917 and afterwards flew with 15 squadron on the western front. Hart had a short but distinguished period of service in France, and won the MC for his part in a historic air battle over Bouzincourt on 11 April 1918. His RE8-type two-seater aircraft was engaged in an artillery observation patrol when it was attacked by four German fighters. Although his plane was hit, Hart managed to take evasive action, enabling his observer to shoot down three of the enemy before the RE8 itself crashed, wounding both occupants. Hart returned to England to convalesce, and on his recovery he joined the school of technical training. He was demobilized early in 1919.

Hart then joined the Imperial College of Science and Technology and obtained his ARCS with a second class in physics in 1921. In 1924 he was appointed a flying officer in the Royal Air Force on the reserve, and in 1926 he transferred to the active list. He qualified as a flying instructor and as a signals officer and with another British officer was sent to study at the Éole Supérieur d'Électricité in Paris, where the pair of them passed out at the head of their group. Hart was a qualified French interpreter. On 12 May 1927 he married Katherine Gwenllian (*b.* 1899/1900), the daughter of Charles Penman Wiltshier, of Canterbury; they had one son.

Between 1929 and 1935 Hart served on signals and flying duties at home and in India, being promoted flight lieutenant in 1930. In 1936 he was promoted squadron leader and posted to Fighter Command for staff signals duties. He was attached to the team of scientists then engaged on the development of what became known as radar, with a responsibility to ensure the incorporation of service requirements in the systems. He worked in close co-operation with Sir Henry Tizard and Robert Watson-

Watt in the establishment set up at Bawdsey for the purpose of applying the radar potential to the air defence of Great Britain. Hart continued in this work until the outbreak of war in 1939, and his contribution played a large part in ensuring that a radar-based defence system was by then available to the Royal Air Force.

Shortly after the outbreak of war Hart was posted for special duties to Fighter Command headquarters, where he organized the systems necessary for the operational use of the information obtained by radar. He perceived the need for 'filter rooms', in which the information from a number of radio direction finding (RDF) stations could be collated and made intelligible to those who had to take operational decisions. He also saw the need for the decentralization of this system, as soon as the technology was available, to allow the interpretation of radar information directly at the source. Hart was promoted wing commander in 1940, and in the following year he was posted to the ministry air staff as deputy director of signals and later deputy director of radar. There he worked closely with Lord Dowding in the development of airborne radar, then a vital requirement for the defence against the enemy night bomber offensive.

In 1943 Hart was appointed chief signals officer at Fighter Command headquarters, and later that year he took up the same post with the headquarters of the allied expeditionary air force. He was involved in planning the air signals and radar operations for the invasion of Europe and in 1944 went to France with that headquarters, where he remained until the end of the war. He then served in Germany as chief signals officer until early 1946, when he was appointed air officer commanding 27 group in the United Kingdom. The next year he joined the Air Ministry as head of technical service plans—the first of three spells there: later he served as director-general of engineering (1951–5) and as controller of engineering and equipment (1956–9). In between he was air officer commanding 90 (signals) group (1949–51) and of 41 group (1955–6).

Hart was gazetted air vice-marshal in 1953 and air marshal in 1957 and placed on the retired list in 1960. In the meantime, in February 1959, he had been appointed director of the Radio Industry Council, where he applied himself to co-ordinating the work of the industry to develop internationally accepted standards.

Hart was technically and operationally qualified by his early training, as an engineer and an experienced pilot, to contribute a major part in the development and application of radar to the needs of the Royal Air Force, first in the air defence of Britain and later in the bombing of Germany and in the anti-submarine offensive. His knowledge of the practical requirements of the Royal Air Force was invaluable to the scientists developing radar, and they were spurred on by his enthusiasm and encouragement. His approach to the many problems that were encountered was blunt and direct, but his friendly personality enabled him to obtain the results he was striving for without undue friction.

Hart was appointed OBE in 1940, CBE in 1944, KBE in 1957, and CB in 1946. He was mentioned in dispatches three times and was a commander of the United States Legion of Merit and a chevalier of the Légion d'honneur. He died on 16 July 1960 as the result of an accident while using an electric lawnmower at his home, The House on the Green, Aston Rowant, Oxfordshire.

VICTOR TAIT, *rev.* MARK POTTLE

Sources private information (1971) · personal knowledge (1971) · *The Times* (19 July 1960) · b. cert. · m. cert. · d. cert.
Likenesses W. Stoneman, two photographs, 1945–58, NPG
Wealth at death £17,240 4s. 10d.: probate, 25 Nov 1960, CGPLA Eng. & Wales

Hart, Sir Robert, first baronet (1835–1911), official in the Chinese service, was born on 20 February 1835 in Portadown, co. Armagh, Ireland, the eldest of the ten children of Henry Hart (1806–1875), a retail merchant ('spirit grocery') and a devout convert to Wesleyan Methodism, and Ann Edgar (1809–1874), second daughter of John Edgar of Ballybray, both of protestant stock dating to the plantation and to fourteenth-century Scottish incursions respectively. Educated at Methodist schools in Taunton and Dublin, Hart attended the non-denominational Queen's College, Belfast, and graduated BA from Queen's University in 1853. The following year he received his college's nomination to a Foreign Office appointment as a student interpreter (Chinese) in the consular service. On 25 July 1854 he reached Hong Kong, and thus, at the age of nineteen, began a residence in China which, but for two short leaves in 1866 and 1874, would last fifty-four years.

Assigned to the Ningpo (Ningbo) vice-consulate in September, Hart, while resisting missionary efforts to recruit him, obtained his firm grounding in conversational and classical Chinese. More exceptionally, he began to document, understand, and, as appropriate, act consistently with Chinese patterns of etiquette. The new Treaty Port system of open ports and foreign residence with extraterritorial rights was in a constant state of challenge and adjustment, and thus Hart was from the first performing complex consular duties in a highly charged context of local administrative and political crises.

In 1858 Hart was transferred to Canton (Guangzhou), where he was appointed secretary to the allied (British and French) commissioners then governing through detained Chinese officials. Hart, as interpreter, moved between the two parties, understanding the Chinese position and, through his knowledge of the language and his tact, winning their appreciation and trust.

Meanwhile developments in Shanghai would radically alter Hart's career. In 1854, with secret societies in control of the city, the Chinese customs commissioner, unable to function, requested assistance from the foreign consuls. The task fell eventually on Vice-Consul Horatio Nelson Lay (b. 1832), who became the first inspector-general of the new foreign inspectorate of the Chinese maritime customs (CMC).

The success of the foreign inspectorate was noted in Canton, and Hart was invited by the governor to develop a similar system. Hart, however, knew of plans to establish a centrally co-ordinated inspectorate in all the open ports. Declining appointment by Canton-based officials, he

Sir Robert Hart, first baronet (1835–1911), by Sir Benjamin Stone, 1908

wrote to Lay advising him on local customs policies. Lay, impressed, offered Hart the deputy commissionership of customs in Canton; Hart accordingly resigned from the consular service, taking over his new duties as a Chinese official on 1 July 1859.

Known by the Chinese for his aggressive lack of tact Lay, contrary to instructions from Peking, left for England on medical leave in 1861, first appointing Hart one of three officiating inspectors-general based in Shanghai. Deputed to visit Peking, Hart, who was already translating texts on international law, held discussions with Yixin (1833–1898), Prince Gong, the powerful head of the newly established office in charge of foreign affairs, the Zongli Yamen, and his colleague the influential grand councillor, Wenxiang (1818–1876), convincing them both of his trustworthiness and ability. Prince Gong consequently supported Hart's proposal for a revived Tongwenguan, the predecessor of Peking University.

Aware of the need to protect coastal shipping, Hart designed plans, approved by Prince Gong, for a foreign-officered naval fleet organized along the lines of Charles 'Chinese' Gordon's (1833–1885) Ever Victorious Army. Lay unilaterally and unacceptably changed the terms under which the intended commander, Sherard Osborn, would operate, making him a virtually independent force. Hart attempted diplomacy, Prince Gong held firm, and the fleet

returned to Europe; Lay was discharged, and on 15 November 1863 Hart was appointed his successor.

In 1864, on orders of the Zongli Yamen, Hart moved to Peking, where he would reside until 1908. As to the CMC, he issued circulars detailing the basic regulations and further integrated the service. On the diplomatic front, he reconciled 'Chinese' Gordon with Li Hongzhang (1823–1901), who, as acting governor of Kiangsu (Jiangsu), was planning his final operations against the Taiping insurgents. As a recognized adviser to the Zongli Yamen, Hart submitted a memorandum entitled 'A bystander's view', arguing, in the style of a censor's memorial, for administrative reform in terms compatible with the aspirations of those Chinese officials attempting a Confucian dynastic 'restoration', but focused additionally on the unfamiliar problems of foreign relations. Hart, often described as the right man at the right time, had become an active partner in the Chinese quest for 'wealth and power'.

After twelve years in China, Hart took home leave, accompanied by his three 'wards' (his illegitimate children), whom he placed with foster parents. On his initiative the Zongli Yamen sent with him the first Chinese overseas delegation, which, though it lacked official diplomatic status, was well received in the capitals of Europe.

Hart continued to Ireland, where he met, wooed, and on 22 August 1866 married Hester Jane, aged nineteen, the eldest daughter of Edward Bredon MD of Portadown. They were to have a son and two daughters. On their first anniversary, Hart noted that he 'could not have a better wife … at the same time, matrimony does interfere with a man's work.' (Hart, *China's Early Modernization*, 365). In 1881 Lady Hart left China for a London residence; Hart focused on his many tasks.

Hart's lasting contribution would be the foreign inspectorate of the CMC, a model of an empire-wide organization, centralized in Peking, administered efficiently and honestly, which *The Times* (10 January 1899) rightly declared 'one of the most striking monuments ever produced by the genius and labour of any individual Englishman'.

Charged with facilitating trade, Hart initiated schemes which effected significant reforms without the involvement of as yet unprepared Chinese officials. He built lighthouses, made harbour and waterways improvements, and initiated a statistical service, the collection of medical and scientific data, and participation in international exhibitions. In 1896 his customs' postal service became national and was recognized as such internationally. The same year Hart, an amateur violinist, cellist, and composer, established a customs' band, the 'mother of bands' in north China.

When Hart became inspector-general in 1863 the CMC was operating in seven open ports; in 1907 it was operating in 57, and 76 native customs stations were under his administration or guidance. Hart presided over the servicing of 182 lights, various other navigational aids, and 2800 post offices. His staff included 11,970 persons, of whom 1345 were foreigners. In sterling equivalents, the annual maritime customs expenditure for 1907 totalled approximately £25,900. Meanwhile China's trade had increased from 1863's £38.9 million to £111.7 million, and customs revenue from £2.3 million to £3.3 million, a formidable contribution to the revenues of the Chinese empire.

Hart was a son of northern Ireland and retained the work ethic learned in youth. In an 1874 self-assessment, he wrote, 'I'm a safe sort of hardworking, modestly-gifted, many sided, equal-tempered, and inwardly God fearing & heaven-seeking man' (Hart, *China's Early Modernization*, 408–9). Hart was an administrative genius with a flair for detail. 'The I.G.-ship', Hart wrote his successor just weeks before his death, 'does not admit of either partnership, advice, or interference, but must be its own guide and its own master!' (Wright, 852). But the CMC outgrew even his talents, and the expectations of a hard-working 'boss' could lead to apparently unreasonable and arbitrary demands on subordinates. The majority probably understood the restraints under which he acted, but the complaints are on record. Accused of nepotism, Hart was beset by diplomatic complications in the assignment of his multinational staff, the customs being under constant threat of international intervention. And after the Boxer uprising there was ill health and old age.

As adviser to the Zongli Yamen, Hart was successfully involved in negotiations relative to the Chefoo (Yantai) agreement (1876), the Sino-French treaty of 1885, and, with his brother James (1847–1902), the Sikkim–Tibet conventions (1886, 1893). Hart was on occasion over-optimistic. He supported the visionary Burlingame mission (1868) and the favourable terms found in the unratified Alcock convention (1869). His attempts to resolve the status of Macau (Macao) were unsatisfactory to both sides—he even offered, during the Portuguese financial crisis of 1891, to buy back the territory for $1 million.

Hart recognized that China's creditworthiness would be dissipated by unco-ordinated foreign borrowing. By requiring an imperial edict for loans secured by the customs revenues, such borrowing could be controlled by government in Peking, advised by Hart as inspector-general. Although responsible for occasional key negotiations, Hart was never in full control; his efforts and the role of the CMC were nevertheless a major factor in preserving China's territorial integrity and sovereignty.

In 1885 Hart accepted appointment as British minister to China. Sensing the preference of the Chinese, and concerned as always about the future of the CMC, Hart, with the approval of the Salisbury government, determined to remain with the customs and to resign the appointment before actually taking office.

China, moreover, was coming under mounting foreign pressure. There was always a crisis, and Hart felt he could not in good conscience abandon China. The CMC remained Chinese, but it took all Hart's diplomatic skills to keep it so. British success in assuring to itself the succession and the organizational *status quo* of the CMC, in Hart's strongly stated opinion, undermined the integrity of the service as a sovereign Chinese operation and invited other imperialistic demands.

Hart's services were recognized by both China and the foreign powers he advised. His honours included the prestigious peacock's feather (1885) and the ancestral rank of the first class of the first order for three generations (1889), and from Britain the KCMG (1882), GCMG (1889), and a baronetcy of the United Kingdom (1893); Hart became a grand officer of the order of the Légion d'honneur (France, 1885), and there were awards from eleven other countries as well as recognition by museums and professional societies.

The ferocity of the Boxer uprising of 1900 was unexpected, and, with other foreigners, Hart was besieged in the legation quarter of Peking, and his home fired. In London a premature obituary was published in *The Times*. Personally, his steady, even heroic behaviour received general commendation. The siege raised, Hart successfully urged the return of Yikuang, Prince Qing, to negotiate for the dynasty, the ever-optimistic Hart assuming the Qing government could still reform itself. Hart's subsequent series of articles, collected as *These from the Land of Sinim* (1901), which urged understanding and moderation, led many to brand him an apologist for a decadent, alien (Manchu) regime.

Still Hart could not abandon China, not until he had urged more moderate demands for indemnity or made proposals for tariff reform, an improved land tax, a central mint, and improved facilities to be provided by the CMC. In an audience with the empress dowager, Cixi (Empress Xiaoqin; 1835–1908), Hart, now aged seventy, was urged to continue his services to China.

But reform was coming from 'Young China', and Hart foresaw the end of extraterritoriality, warning that if the lesson of the Boxers were not heeded, eventually 'millions of Boxers … with the latest weapons will make foreign living in China impossible' (*The Times*, 16 Nov 1900, 4d). In 1905 Hart nevertheless again postponed retirement on news that his wife and youngest daughter would, after an absence of twenty-five years, be visiting Peking. Then in 1906, without warning, Hart and the CMC became responsible not directly to the post-Boxer foreign ministry but to a joint revenue council, the Shuiwu ju. Britain protested ineffectively, the council argued there would be no real change, but Hart understood. It was at last time to go; yet paradoxically he could not go. Britain determined the crisis required his presence.

His health deteriorating, Hart in 1907, facing Chinese refusal to permit his retirement, obtained instead a succession of one-year leaves. This fortuitously permitted him to delay an unfavourable decision as to his successor, requesting the Chinese appoint his deputy inspector-general and brother-in-law, Sir Robert Edward Bredon (1846–1918), acting inspector-general despite British opposition. Not until 1910 did he accept the inevitable; the Chinese then appointed Bredon to a sinecure and, from a list of five submitted by Hart, selected Sir Francis Arthur Aglen (1869–1932), the son of an old school friend from Taunton days, as officiating inspector-general.

Sir Robert Hart left Peking on 13 April 1908 on a not entirely fictitious leave. There were first the honorary degrees and the freedom of several cities to enjoy. But the hoped-for peerage never came; the succession controversy had soured relations. Hart then rested at his home at Fingest Grove, near Great Marlow, Buckinghamshire, writing of an early return to Peking, keeping abreast of CMC developments, and sending advice and instructions. Hart died at his home on 20 September 1911 suffering cardiac decline following a bout of pneumonia. He was buried on 25 September at Bisham, Berkshire, and was survived by his wife, their three children, and by two of his 'wards'. He was awarded posthumously the title of grand guardian of the heir apparent, an honour never before (or after) bestowed on a foreigner. Three weeks later the dynasty he had served faced the Chinese nationalist revolution.

Eulogized by the contemporary British press, Hart's role has been criticized by commentators with other perspectives applied ahistorically. Hart's own attitude is best explained in a letter to his successor, 'See the questions from the Chinese point of view—hold on to the common sense side of stipulations, regulations, and precedents' (Hart to Aglen, March 1910, Aglen MS 211081), sentiments consistent with those of President Eliot of Harvard as inscribed below the statue erected on the Shanghai Bund (Wright, 865):

> Inspector-General of the Chinese Maritime Customs, Founder of the Chinese Lighthouse Service, Organizer and Administrator of the National Post Office, Trusted Counsellor of the Chinese Government, True Friend of the Chinese People, Modest, Patient, Sagacious, and Resolute, He overcame formidable Obstacles, and Accomplished a work of Great Beneficence for China and the World.

FRANK H. H. KING

Sources *Robert Hart and China's early modernization: his journals, 1863–1866*, ed. R. J. Smith, J. K. Fairbank, and K. F. Bruner (1991) · R. Hart, *Entering China's service: Robert Hart's journals, 1854–1863*, ed. K. F. Bruner, J. K. Fairbank, and R. J. Smith (1986) · *Archives of China's imperial maritime customs: confidential correspondence between Robert Hart and James Duncan Campbell, 1874–1907*, ed. Chen Xiafei and Han Rongfang, 4 vols. (1990–93) [compiled by Second Historical Archives of China, Institute of Modern History, CASS] · R. Hart, '*These from the land of Sinim': essays on the Chinese question* (1901); repr. with additional chap. 'China, reform, and the powers' (1903) · S. F. Wright, *Hart and the Chinese customs* (1950) · J. Bredon, *Sir Robert Hart: the romance of a great career* (1909) · SOAS, Francis Arthur Aglen MSS · Robert Hart, correspondence, Hatfield House, Hertfordshire, Salisbury MSS · P. King, *In the Chinese customs service*, rev. edn (1930) · C. Drage, *Servants of the Dragon Throne, being the lives of Edward and Cecil Bowra* (1966) · F. H. H. King, *The history of the Hongkong and Shanghai Banking Corporation*, 2 (1988) · Chan Lau Kit Ching, 'The succession of Sir Robert Hart at the Imperial Chinese Maritime Customs Service', *Journal of Asian History*, 9 (1975), 1–33 · S. Bell, *Hart of Lisburn* (1895) · R. Hart, *Chu-wai p'ang-kuan chih lun* [A bystander's view], *Ch'ou-pan i-wu shih-mo* [A complete account of the management of barbarian affairs], 130 vols. (Beijing, 1929–31), vol. 40, pp. 13b–22a · *The Times* (22 Sept 1911) · *The Times* (21 Sept 1911), 3 · *The Times* (26 Sept 1911), 7a · China, Chinese Customs Service, *Documents illustrative of the origin, development, and activities of the Chinese customs service*, 7 vols. (Shanghai, 1940) · J. K. Fairbank, K. F. Bruner, and E. M. Matheson, eds., *The I.G. in Peking: letters of Robert Hart, Chinese Maritime Customs, 1868–1907*, 2 vols. (1975) · H. B. Morse, *The international relations of the Chinese empire*, 3 vols. (1910–18), 3.470–71

Archives Administration of the Second Historical Archives of China, Nanjing (?), archives of China's Imperial Maritime Customs, incl. 3,528 confidential letters between Hart and Campbell, 4,496 confidential telegrams, and 30 pictures of major figures associated with the Customs · Queen's University Library, Belfast, Northern Ireland, journals and correspondence | BL, MSS of the Peking Legation, Add. MS 46499 · Bodl. Oxf., miscellaneous letters and MSS, MSS Eng. lett. and Eng. misc. · Harvard U., Houghton L., Cambridge, Massachusetts, Morse collection · Hatfield House Archives, Hatfield, Hertfordshire, correspondence, 3M/A38/34, 36, 39 · Hong Kong University Library, Hart MSS, special collections · NL Wales, Aberystwyth, Department of MSS and Records, correspondence with Lord Rendel, 1880–1910 and 1882–1900, MSS 19440–19467, 20569–20572 · PRO, correspondence with Sir E. M. Satow, 1901–6, 30/33/10/3 · SOAS, Archives of the Library, correspondence with Sir Francis Aglen and Sir Frederick Maze

Likenesses photograph, 1866, repro. in Bredon, *Sir Robert Hart* · photograph, 1878, repro. in *Archives*, vol. 1 · photograph, 1878, repro. in Bredon, *Sir Robert Hart* · photograph, 1891 (in his office), repro. in *Archives*, vol. 1 · photograph, after 1900 (Robert Hart feasts German envoy), repro. in *Archives*, vol. 2 · photograph, after 1900 (Robert Hart's brass band), repro. in *Archives*, vol. 2 · photograph, 1907 (with Yikuang, Prince Qing [*Wade-Giles*, I-k'uang, Prince Ch'ing] and others), repro. in *Archives*, vol. 3 · F. McKelvey, portrait, 1908, Queen's University, Belfast, Great Hall · B. Stone, photograph, 1908, NPG [*see illus.*] · photograph, 1908, repro. in *Archives*, vol. 3 · photograph, 1908 (leaving China), repro. in *Archives*, vol. 3 · photograph, 1908, repro. in Bredon, *Sir Robert Hart* · portrait, 1908 (members attending the China Association dinner for Hart), University of Hong Kong Library, Hart Collection, Special Collections · H. Pegram, statue, 1914, repro. in *Archives*, vol. 3 · Imp, cartoon, chromolithograph (in Chinese dress), NPG · J. M. Price, sketch (standing at his famous standing desk), repro. in *ILN*, 99 (19 Sept 1891) · B. Stone, photograph, print, Birmingham Reference Library · photograph (with colleagues of Maritime customs in the garden at his residence), repro. in *Archives*, vol. 2 · photograph (Robert Hart and Kate Carl, etc.), repro. in Bredon, *Sir Robert Hart* · portraits (including also family members, especially children and grandchildren, eminent Chinese, Hart's servants, Hart's customs band, members of the customs service, and prominent foreign residents on the China coast), University of Hong Kong Library, Hart Collection, Special Collections

Wealth at death £140,260 4*s.* 6*d.*: probate, 18 Nov 1911, *CGPLA Eng. & Wales*

Hart, Solomon Alexander (1806–1881), historical genre painter, was born in April 1806 in Plymouth, son of Samuel Hart (*fl.* 1785–1830), a Jewish engraver and teacher of Hebrew. Hart's mother died when he was young and his father married again. Two brothers are known, Charles John Hart and Mark Mordecai Hart (*fl.* 1836–1839), an engraver. At the age of seven Hart attended a school in Exeter for a year but, as Jews were barred from the grammar school in Plymouth, was tutored thereafter by a Unitarian minister, the Revd Israel Worsley, for about five years. Hart's family moved to London in 1820. Samuel Hart wanted his son to become an engraver but could not afford the premium. In 1821, with the encouragement of the painter James Northcote, Hart began drawing from antique marbles in the British Museum and in due course was admitted to the Royal Academy Schools on 15 August 1823. His time for studying was limited, however, as he had to support himself and his father by colouring theatrical prints and copying old masters on ivory.

Hart's first exhibit at the Royal Academy in 1826 was a portrait miniature of his father. His first real success came

Solomon Alexander Hart (1806–1881), self-portrait

in 1830 with a more ambitious painting exhibited at the Society of British Artists, *Interior of a Polish Synagogue at the Moment when the Manuscript of the Law is Elevated* (Tate collection). One of Hart's best works, it successfully combines the details of the interior of an Amsterdam synagogue with numerous figures. However, Hart wished to avoid 'the imputation of being the painter of merely religious ceremony' and sought to express 'something of a more definite character in the expression of human emotion and strong dramatic action' (Hart, 13). Thus in 1834 he exhibited *The Quarrel between Wolsey and Buckingham* (*Art Journal*, 1873, opposite p. 104), a scene from Shakespeare's *Henry VIII*, in which historical details of the interior and the costume were carefully observed but the figures were somewhat stiffly painted.

In the 1830s Hart supported himself by supplying drawings for wood-engravings for the publisher Charles Knight and contributed illustrations to various volumes including G. N. Wright's *Landscape-Historical Illustrations of Scotland* and the *Waverley Novels* (2 vols., 1836–8). In 1835 he exhibited *King Richard I of England and Soldan Saladin* (Walker Art Gallery, Liverpool), based on a dramatic moment in Walter Scott's *Talisman*. It was this painting which Hart believed to have secured his election as ARA on 2 November 1835. To obtain election as a Royal Academician he worked for a year on the nearly 14 feet square *Lady Jane Grey at the Place of her Execution on Tower Hill* (1839; Guildhall, Plymouth). He was duly elected RA on 10 February 1840, the first Jew to be thus honoured.

Hart painted a small number of portraits, including *David Salamons* (c.1856; Guildhall, London). He received a fortunate commission from the Jews' Hospital in Mile End, London, to paint the duke of Sussex. The sitter advised Hart to travel and provided him with letters of introduction; Hart left England on 1 September 1841, visiting Italy for a year. He made a series of drawings of architectural details and interiors, examples of which can be found in the Royal Academy Library. Although originally intended for publication as engravings, they were incorporated instead into paintings of Italian history and into architectural interiors including *The Feast of the Rejoicing of the Law at the Synagogue in Leghorn, Italy* (1850; Jewish Museum, New York). Hart also worked in watercolour, a fine example being the brilliantly hued *Othello and Iago* (1857; V&A), which he considered 'the *best* watercolour drawing I have ever done' (RA archives MIS/HA14).

Hart was professor of painting from 1854 to 1863 at the Royal Academy and his lectures were highly regarded. He also wrote for *The Athenaeum* and the *Jewish Chronicle*. He was librarian at the Royal Academy from 1864 to 1881 and was extremely active in this post, greatly expanding the library and putting together a fine collection of books on historical costume. According to his obituarist in *The Athenaeum* 'he found chaos and left a library'.

Hart was an observant Jew. To his friends he 'exhibited a strong vein of humour [and] … was a confirmed punster' (*Jewish Chronicle*). In appearance he had somewhat hooded eyes and a great amount of dark wiry hair. He continued to exhibit until his death but in later years his failing eyesight meant that his work lost its power and his reputation suffered. He died unmarried at his home at 36 Fitzroy Square, London, on 11 June 1881 and was buried at Brompton Jewish cemetery on 14 June.   HELEN VALENTINE

Sources *The reminiscences of Solomon Alexander Hart, R.A.*, ed. A. Brodie (1882) · *Jewish Chronicle* (17 June 1881) · *The Times* (13 June 1881) · *The Athenaeum* (18 June 1881), 821 · N. Savage, 'The academician's library: a selection not a collection', *Apollo*, 128 (1988), 258–63 · D. Foskett, *A dictionary of British miniature painters*, 1 (1972) · R. Parkinson, ed., *Catalogue of British oil paintings, 1820–1860* (1990) [catalogue of V&A] · S. A. Hart, letters to William Smith, RA, MIS/HA/1–12 · artist's file, archive material, Courtauld Inst., Witt Library · Hart members' file, RA

Archives RA, draft lectures given when professor of painting; letters and MSS | RA, letters to William Smith, MIS/HA/1–12 · V&A, corresp. with T. Williams

Likenesses C. Lear, pencil drawing, 1845, NPG · C. Birch, pencil and watercolour, 1853, NPG · J. & C. Watkins, photograph, 1860–69, RA · C. Cope, drawing, c.1862, NPG · Elliott & Fry, photograph, 1870–79, RA; repro. in Brodie, ed., *Reminiscences* · S. A. Hart, self-portrait, oils, 1870–79, RA · E. Edwards, photograph, NPG; repro. in L. Reeve, ed., *Men of eminence*, 1 (1863) · S. A. Hart, self-portrait, oils, Royal Albert Memorial Museum, Exeter [*see illus.*] · J. & C. Watkins, carte-de-visite, NPG · wood-engraving, NPG; repro. in *ILN* (25 June 1881)

Wealth at death £12,561 16s. 1d.: probate, 11 July 1881, *CGPLA Eng. & Wales*

Hart, Thomas John (1907–1970), marine biologist, was born on 17 September 1907 at Cintra Lodge, Little Shelford, near Cambridge, the eldest of the four sons of John Henry Arthur Hart (1876–1952), theological lecturer and librarian of St John's College, Cambridge, and later a clergyman, and his wife, Katherine Mary Gwatkin (1873–1961), who was an occasional schoolteacher in biology.

The family had wide-ranging interests, especially in natural history and the sea, and spent holidays on their converted coal barge beached on Blakeney Point, Norfolk. Hart was educated at Lady Manners School, Bakewell, and Leeds University, where he graduated with first-class honours in zoology in 1929. Subsequently he was awarded the degrees of MSc in 1934 and DSc in 1935. On 17 June 1931 he married Edith Angood (1907–1989), also a graduate in zoology from Leeds University. They later had three sons.

Immediately after graduating in 1929 Hart had joined the *Discovery* investigations, established by the Colonial Office for marine research around the Falkland Islands. He served on Royal Research Ship (RRS) *Discovery II* in the Southern Ocean on her first, third, and fifth commissions (1929–31, 1933–5, and 1937–9). He also served on RRS *William Scoresby* in 1936–7 and 1950. During the Second World War he was commissioned for a short time as lieutenant RNVR but was invalided out and continued his *Discovery* investigations work at Plymouth in the laboratories of the Marine Biological Association. In 1949 *Discovery* investigations were transferred to the newly established National Institute of Oceanography and Hart remained a member of its staff at Wormley until his death.

Hart's task on joining *Discovery* investigations was to continue work begun by A. C. Hardy on the phytoplankton of the Southern Ocean. His two major *Discovery* reports, 'On the phytoplankton of the south-west Atlantic and the Bellingshausen Sea, 1929–31' (1934) and 'Phytoplankton periodicity in Antarctic surface waters' (1941), provided the foundations for subsequent investigations of phytoplankton ecology in Antarctic seas. In his later work he used the newly developed technique of colorimetric estimation of chlorophyll as a measure of total phytoplankton. The importance of his observation that dense phytoplankton growth followed the stabilization of the water column by melting of ice was fully recognized four decades later.

Hart distinguished different types of water by their diatom floras and described how a particular species could be used to trace water movements. A report 'On the diatoms of the skin film of whales' (1935) showed that whales accumulate these films only in Antarctic waters and that their density is an index of the condition of the animal. Another *Discovery* report by Hart, on behalf of his late colleague E. R. Gunther, dealt with trawling surveys on the Patagonian continental shelf. A later paper, 'Some observations on the relative abundance of marine phytoplankton populations in nature' published in *Some Contemporary Studies in Marine Science* (1966) summarized much information from his previous studies, together with that from ships' meteorological logbooks. In all Hart published some twenty-two scientific papers. In 1930 Hart and H. E. Marshall were the first people to land on Thule Island in the South Sandwich group. During the war Hart pressed for the continuation of work in the Antarctic and his efforts helped result in the establishment of the Falkland Islands dependencies survey. His last major work at sea was as scientist in charge of a whale-marking expedition

in RRS *William Scoresby* in 1950, but he had to leave the ship early because of ill health.

Hart was a quiet, retiring man with a dry sense of humour, whose wide knowledge of marine science and Antarctic affairs was always available to others. Outside his work he enjoyed rowing, football, cricket, sailing, choir singing, chess, and woodwork. He was awarded the polar medal in 1940 and Hart Rock, off Laurie Island, South Orkneys, was named after him. He died of heart failure at his home, Sherborne, Petworth Road, Witley, Surrey, after returning from work on 4 May 1970. His ashes were consigned to the north Atlantic from RRS *Discovery*.

G. E. FOGG

Sources P. M. David, *Polar Record*, 15 (1970–71), 555–6 · *Marine Observer*, 41 (1971), 41–2 · J. Coleman-Cooke, *Discovery II in the Antarctic: the story of British research in the southern seas* (1963) · b. cert. · d. cert. · private information (2004)
Archives Southampton Oceanography Centre, National Oceanographic Library
Wealth at death £35,577: probate, 6 Aug 1970, *CGPLA Eng. & Wales*

Hart, Sir William Ogden (1903–1977), local government administrator and legal writer, was born on 25 May 1903 at 5 Lawson Road, Ecclesall Bierlow, Sheffield, the son of Sir William Edward Hart (1866–1942), a solicitor, who was town clerk of Sheffield (1913–31) and was knighted in 1929, and his wife, Jane Elizabeth, *née* Ogden. He was educated at Rugby School and then at New College, Oxford, where he took firsts in jurisprudence (1924) and in the BCL (1925). Elected a fellow of Wadham College, Oxford, in 1926, on 15 July 1927 he married Dorothy Eileen (b. 1901/2), the daughter of Douglas Wilfred Churcher, lieutenant-colonel in the Royal Irish Fusiliers; they had three sons and one daughter. Hart was called to the bar by Lincoln's Inn in 1928 but did not practise, becoming bursar of Wadham in 1928 and law tutor in 1934.

In 1934, following the Local Government Act of 1933, Hart collaborated with his father in the publication of *An Introduction to the Law of Local Government and Administration*, assuming full responsibility for seven out of eight subsequent editions (which were titled *Hart's Introduction*). The work was the leading authority on the subject, the local government practitioners' bible.

Hart's own first direct experience of local government came as a member of Oxford city council from 1935 to 1939, when he contributed to *A Survey of Social Services in the Oxford District* (2 vols., 1938–40). During the Second World War he joined the Ministry of Shipping (1940–41), then joined the British merchant shipping mission in Washington, USA, serving as head of the mission from 1944 to 1946.

Hart was one of a number of able and mature men who at the beginning of the war left academic life to work in the public service and developed considerable aptitude and taste for public administration, and remained in the public service after the war. Relinquishing his fellowship and tutorship in 1947, he moved into local government, and played a prominent part in the developments in the post-war new-town era. He was general manager of Hemel Hempstead development corporation from 1947 to 1955.

In 1956 Hart was appointed to the top job in local government, clerk to the London county council, and subsequently, on local government reorganization, director-general and clerk to the Greater London council (GLC) from 1964 to 1968. This reorganization, involving the abolition and truncation of many authorities and welding them into the new much larger body, required sympathetic understanding, unerring diplomacy, and calm judgement, all of which Hart had in good measure, and the whole operation was achieved with minimum discord and maximum co-operation. His advice on local government matters was widely sought, and he became the doyen of the local government scene. He was knighted in 1961.

Hart had a formidable intellect, a superbly ordered mind, very wide administrative experience, and the willingness to delegate. With his strong skills as chairman of a meeting and his unfailing courtesy he always inspired confidence in colleagues and staff, and in agencies and people with whom he had to deal. He was described as a fine, loyal, and devoted public servant, kindly, courteous, respected, popular, held indeed in affection by many who knew him.

Hart became an honorary fellow of the Royal Institute of British Architects and of the Royal Town and Planning Institute. In retirement from the GLC he was appointed chairman of the Northampton New Town Development Corporation (1968–77) and of the commission on broadcasting of the general synod of the Church of England (1971–3). He was a member of the Social Science Research Council (1965–70) and in business served on the board of the National Bus Company (1968–71). He lived at Turweston Lodge, Brackley, Northamptonshire, and died in the Radcliffe Infirmary, Oxford, on 29 April 1977.

ALEC SAMUELS

Sources *The Times* (3 May 1977) · *The Times* (5 May 1977) · *WWW*, *1971–80* · b. cert. · m. cert. · d. cert. · personal knowledge (2004)
Wealth at death £48,509: probate, 20 Sept 1977, *CGPLA Eng. & Wales*

Hartcliffe, John (1651/2–1712), Church of England clergyman, was born at Harding near Henley-on-Thames, Oxfordshire, the eldest son of John Hartcliffe, a graduate of Corpus Christi College, Oxford, and subsequently described as of Windsor, clergyman. His mother was the daughter of Henry Owen, vicar of Stadhampton, Oxfordshire, and sister of John Owen (1616–1683), the intruded dean of Christ Church. Hartcliffe was admitted to Eton College as a scholar in 1664 at the age of twelve. He matriculated at Oxford as a servitor of Magdalen College on 29 March 1667, but at once migrated to St Edmund Hall as a commoner. In Easter term 1669 he moved to King's College, Cambridge, as a scholar, and matriculated that year. He became a fellow of King's in 1671, graduated BA in 1673, and proceeded MA in 1676. In 1681, seemingly by the recommendation of his uncle Dr Owen, he was appointed headmaster of Merchant Taylors' School. Among his pupils there were future archbishops of Armagh (Hugh

Boulter) and York (William Dawes), and the historian Edmund Calamy.

In 1686 Hartcliffe resigned and returned to Cambridge. Following the death of Provost Coplestone in 1689 the fellows of King's were determined to reassert their right to elect a successor, a freedom latterly denied them by the crown. No doubt they hoped William III would be unfamiliar with these matters. Hartcliffe, however, took it upon himself to ride at once to court and inform the king of the vacancy, and of the practice of his recent predecessors in nominating to the provostship. As an exercise in self-advancement this was of limited success; William recommended Hartcliffe to the university for the degree of BD (17 September) but named Stephen Upman, fellow of Eton, for the provostship of King's. The fellows rejected the royal *mandamus* on the plausible grounds that Upman was a professed Jacobite. The king then nominated Sir Isaac Newton, whom the fellows legitimately disallowed as an alien. A third *mandamus* (2 September) was dispatched to Cambridge, at last in Hartcliffe's favour, but the fellows, knowing this to be on its way, shut their doors against the king's messenger, who was obliged to leave the document on the hall table, from where it was mysteriously removed by night and tossed over the college wall. The fellows then proceeded to hold their election, in which Hartcliffe received one vote (presumably his own). He gave up his fellowship in the following year. He had let it be known that he was 'very well contented to wait for some other mark of his Majesty's favour' (*CSP dom.*, *1689–90*, 281). On 14 May 1691 William obliged by granting him a canonry of St George's, Windsor, where he was installed on 8 June. He retained his stall to his death; from 1708 he was also vicar of Twickenham, Middlesex.

Hartcliffe had some renown as a preacher, though an attempt to address Charles II had been unsuccessful: 'not being able to utter one word of his sermon, he descended from the pulpit as great an orator as he went up' (Wood, *Ath. Oxon.*, 1.791). He found a less intimidating auditory in the corporation of London, before whom he preached at St Bride's, Fleet Street, on 11 April 1694. On 30 January 1695 (when the annual commemoration of Charles I's execution was compounded by mourning for Mary II) he preached to the House of Commons in St Margaret's, Westminster. These two and another sermon were published. He also wrote *In veritate rerum* (1678), *A Discourse Against Purgatory* (1685), publicly burnt in France, and *A Treatise of Moral and Intellectual Virtues* (1691).

Hartcliffe died on 16 August 1712 and was buried in St George's Chapel, Windsor, apparently next day. According to Sterry (p. 161), Hartcliffe had a wife, Elizabeth; neither she nor any child is mentioned in his will, dated 24 October 1704, and there may have been a confusion with the sister Elizabeth who was bequeathed all Hartcliffe's leases, bonds, bank stock, and Treasury notes. Her son John received a life annuity of £14. Her daughters Elizabeth and Hester were Hartcliffe's principal legatees, receiving annuities of £14 and £30 respectively, and marriage portions of £1000 each. All Hartcliffe's books (save the manuscripts) were to be sold—not by auction, which had been the fate of his uncle's collection, but after individual valuation, with the proceeds added to his nieces' legacies.   C. S. KNIGHTON

Sources W. Sterry, ed., *The Eton College register, 1441–1698* (1943), 161 · Venn, *Alum. Cant.*, 1/2.320 · Wood, *Ath. Oxon.*, new edn, 4.790–91 · S. L. Ollard, *Fasti Wyndesorienses: the deans and canons of Windsor* (privately printed, Windsor, 1950), 159 · H. C. Maxwell Lyte, *A history of Eton College, 1440–1898*, 3rd edn (1899), 280–81 · F. W. M. Draper, *Four centuries of Merchant Taylors' School, 1561–1961* (1962), 80, 85–8 · J. R. Bloxam, ed., *Magdalen College and James II, 1686–1688: a series of documents*, OHS, 6 (1886), 272–3 · *CSP dom.*, 1689–90, 229–30, 239, 259, 280–81; 1690–91, 374 · Wing, *STC* · PRO, PROB 11/528, fols. 256v–257v

Wealth at death see will, PRO, PROB 11/528, fols. 256v–257v

Harte, (Francis) Bret [*formerly* Francis Brett Hart] (1836–1902), author, was born on 25 August 1836 in Albany, New York, the third child of Henry Philip Hart (1800–1845), who conducted a private school in his home, and Elizabeth Ostrander Hart. His paternal grandfather was Bernard Hart, an English Jew who had emigrated to New York via Canada and married, in 1799, Catherine Brett, of English and Dutch ancestry. They separated after their only son was born.

Henry Hart added an 'e' to his surname and moved to wherever he could find paying pupils. Young Frank claimed to have attended eight different schools in eight cities before dropping out in New York city at thirteen to work, as his father had died and his mother could no longer afford the luxury of tuition. When she remarried in 1854 (her new husband was a Californian, Andrew Williams), Bret—as he now called himself—followed the family across the United States to Oakland.

Seeking employment at eighteen, Harte drifted in and out of jobs—some of which he later may have invented—as tutor, typesetter, goldminer, and 'shot-gun' on a stage coach, penning poetry all the while. He confided to his diary that he intended to make a livelihood by writing. His opportunity came while he was a 'printer's devil'—compositor—for the weekly *Northern Californian* in Uniontown, where he filled empty spaces with his own verse and prose, often using Western dialect. Composing sketches while typesetting, he recalled, compressed his style. His six years along the Humboldt River, source of a lifetime of material, would turn that segment of the West, in the popular mind, into 'Bret Harte country'.

When, as the *Californian*'s sub-editor, Harte denounced a massacre of peaceable Indians by local 'diggers' in early 1860, the ire of the white establishment cost him his job, but his frontier experience shaped his writing. His stories and verse would scorn the greed, corruption, lawlessness, brutality, and hypocrisy of miners and ministers, bankers and sheriffs, merchants and politicians. Gamblers, prostitutes, and other social outcasts, open in their ways, were by contrast more worthy.

In San Francisco he contributed to the weekly *Golden Era*, often under the pseudonym the Bohemian, and also worked as compositor for this journal. In 1868 he moved to the *Overland Monthly* as its first editor. One paper for

(Francis) Bret Harte (1836–1902), by Frederick Hollyer

which he wrote, the San Francisco *Call*, employed a writer, Samuel Clemens (Mark Twain), who claimed, before the two had a falling out, that he learned his craft from Harte.

Irony with a realistic texture, yet softened by sentimentality, was the hallmark of Harte's style. Typical of his best fiction was his nativity parable 'The Luck of Roaring Camp' (August 1868), published in the second issue of the *Overland Monthly*. In a mining camp a prostitute, Cherokee Sal, dies in childbirth, leaving an infant christened by the miners Thomas Luck. For the boy, who is being bottle-fed with ass's milk, they import a rosewood cradle. A metamorphosis begins. They wash, plant flowers, eschew profanity. The 'Ingin' baby survives into spring, when melting snow and rain inundate the foothills. A flash flood sweeps away the cabin in which Kentuck, a miner, is sleeping with 'The Luck' in his arms. Vanished also may be the brief moment of civilization.

Harte's verse is remembered for 'Plain Language from Truthful James' (*Overland Monthly*, September 1870), popularly known as 'The heathen Chinee'. In a satiric condemnation of racism—Chinese immigrant labour was abused in the West—the inscrutable Ah Sin confounds the prejudices of narrator and reader by outwitting at euchre two 'Anglo' card-sharks. Although Harte would dismiss it as 'possibly the worst poem anyone ever wrote' (Stewart, 181), it was widely reprinted.

Early success had brought Harte into contact with local worthies eager to sponsor him. He received two regional sinecures—with the surveyor-general and then with the United States mint. His rising status led to his marriage, on 11 August 1862, to Anna Griswold, who was four years his elder. With local fame came mannerisms at odds with his uncouth subject matter. So transformed, Harte would not have been out of place in a London club in Pall Mall; he wore elegant clothes and affected a nasal voice.

Publication in the eastern USA led to an invitation from Fields, Osgood & Co. of Boston for Harte to furnish a minimum of twelve contributions annually to its magazines, which included the *Atlantic Monthly*. The $10,000 contract was the most lucrative up to that time in American publishing. When he left California with his family he was at the top of his form, but like Antaeus of Greek mythology he would be enervated by separation from the vital soil. He overspent, resorting then to fictional formulas which seemed parodies of past writings. His agreement was not renewed, compelling him to concoct sketches often refused by once-eager editors. He took up lecturing from 1872 to 1875 to augment his dwindling earnings, delivering 'The argonauts of '49' —on gold rush California—150 times, but receiving little over expenses. Simultaneously, he struggled to create stage vehicles from his stories, but the plays were stillborn. One, *Ah Sin*, based upon his 'heathen Chinee' character and with Mark Twain as collaborator, also failed. Mutual recriminations ended their association.

With his career reduced to desperate hack work, Harte appealed to influential acquaintances for a diplomatic post in the tradition of Washington Irving, Nathaniel Hawthorne, and James Russell Lowell, even ridiculing his own efforts in the pages of the New York *Sun* as the Office-Seeker. He floated, the Boston *Traveller* quipped, 'on the raft made of the shipwreck of his former reputation'. Rescue came via an appointment as consul in the Rhenish town of Crefeld on the Rhine. On 28 June 1878 he left his wife, two sons, and two daughters in New Jersey, never to return to the USA.

Crefeld regenerated Harte's pen. While he sent his salary 'home' to his wife, whom he had all but divorced, he wrote clichéd frontier stories as well as fiction about an American innocent abroad in 'Sammstadt'. The Germans were enthusiastic. In translation he would become one of the most popular American-born writers there. Yet he did not learn German and appealed for a post where English was spoken. Despite his unconcealed absenteeism he was transferred in August 1880 to Glasgow, where he would encounter even gloomier weather than that of which he had complained in Crefeld, and impenetrable English. (Harte would call Glasgow 'a damp cellar'.) He would also abandon business to aides, spending so much time in London that 562 letters and telegrams from him to his Glasgow office are recorded during the five years of his assignment.

Harte's plunge in reputation in the United States had not affected his esteem in Europe. He had already appeared, on 1 May 1880, at the Royal Academy's annual meeting to reply to the toast to literature. In his writings in Britain, where he would live out his remaining years, Glasgow became 'St Kentigern'. London editors, however, preferred his more exotic frontier tales, and commissioned them. Eager for further income once his consular salary ceased in 1885—for he had to send maintenance payments to Anna—he turned again to the theatre. Plays promised continuing receipts; stories earned only a fee. Assisted by Marguerite Van de Velde, the wife, then widow, of a Belgian diplomat in whose home at 74 Lancaster Gate in London he usually lived, he collaborated, between 1882 and 1885, upon three plays based upon his fiction—*Thankful Blossom*, *The Luck of Roaring Camp*, and *A Frontier Penelope*. Up until 1897 he wrote eight other plays, mostly with T. E. Pemberton, a knowledgeable stage technician. One, *Sue*, an adaptation of Harte's 'The Judgment of Bolinas Plain', actually had twenty-eight performances at the Garrick Theatre beginning on 29 June 1898, following earlier brief runs in Boston and New York.

Harte continued to collect in book form his increasingly benign short stories, many featuring his favourite character, Colonel Culpepper Starbottle. His fiction written in London, like his plays, increasingly betrayed his distance in time and place from 'Bret Harte country'. Yet whatever his inaccuracies, his vision of the gold rush days in the West had mapped it for countless English readers.

Parody remained Harte's métier. In 1867 he had published *Condensed Novels and Other Papers*, influenced by Thackeray's parodies in *Punch*. Perhaps his cleverest was 'Lothaw' (1870), mocking Disraeli's *Lothair*. *Condensed Novels, New Burlesques* (1902), in which his later parodies were collected, satirized, among others, Conan Doyle, Kipling, Caine, Marie Corelli, and, in 'Rupert the Resembler', Anthony Hope's *The Prisoner of Zenda*. Stoical in his last illness (throat cancer after decades of smoking strong cigars), he warned his wife, who had finally sailed to England in 1898 but whom he declined to see, that his income was 'precarious' and that she could expect little. He wrote anxiously for the McClure syndicate in the United States, which supplied Sunday supplements—and dollars— though in London his work was still welcome in such prestigious monthlies as the *Cornhill Magazine* and *The Strand*.

An exploratory operation in March 1902 confirmed that Harte's cancer was inoperable, and he returned to the care of Marguerite Van de Velde. On 17 April he rallied enough to begin 'A Friend of Colonel Starbottle'. It remained a fragment. Following his death on 5 May 1902 at the Red House, Camberley, Surrey, he was interred in the churchyard at Frimley, Surrey, where Marguerite Van de Velde arranged the obsequies and ordered the tombstone. Also at the funeral, however, and uncontested now, was Anna Harte. To her, Harte left all his assets—his copyrights and £360.

His English writings were less deft than his brilliant early fiction, but Harte never abandoned his rude West, merely rearranging his familiar characters within their recognizable settings. Beginning as a frontier Dickens, he faded with failed ambition into inadvertent self-parody. Still, the vision of the frontier he defined remained potent enough to leave its impact upon fiction, drama, and film thereafter. Five years after his death the melodrama *Salomy Jane*, drawn from his 'Salomy Jane's Kiss', was a long-running West End hit. Film after film in the silent era emerged from his fiction, and his characters have since stereotyped the mythical West.

STANLEY WEINTRAUB

Sources G. Scharnhorst, *Bret Harte* (1992) · R. O'Connor, *Bret Harte* (1966) · G. R. Stewart, *Bret Harte: argonaut and exile* (1935) · T. E. Pemberton, *The life of Bret Harte* (1903) · *Letters of Bret Harte*, ed. G. B. Harte (1926) · *CGPLA Eng. & Wales* (1902) · *Selected letters of Bret Harte*, ed. A. Scharnhorst (1997) · A. Nissen, *Bret Harte: prince and pauper* (2000)
Archives Hunt. L. · U. Cal., Berkeley, Bancroft Library · U. Cal., Los Angeles, Charles E. Young Research Library · University of Virginia, Charlottesville, Alderman Library · Yale U., Beinecke L. | Richmond Local Studies Library, London, Sladen MSS
Likenesses W. J. Linton, engraving, 1871, repro. in Stewart, *Bret Harte* · photograph, 1880, repro. in Pemberton, *Life of Bret Harte* · J. Pettie, portrait, 1890, repro. in *McClure's Magazine* (4 Dec 1894) · Bradley and Hodgson, photograph, U. Cal., Berkeley, Bancroft Library, Mark Twain Project · F. Hollyer, photograph, V&A [*see illus.*] · J. R. Osgood, engraving, repro. in *Harper's Weekly* (28 May 1892), 508 · Spy [L. Ward], cartoon, repro. in *VF* (1879)
Wealth at death £360 6s. 9d.: administration, 31 Dec 1902, *CGPLA Eng. & Wales*

Harte [Hart], **Henry** (d. 1557), religious radical, was probably a native of Pluckley, Kent, where a Harte family is recorded as owning property at the end of the fifteenth century. His own parentage is unknown, and nothing is recorded of his life before 29 April 1538, when Archbishop Thomas Cranmer wrote to Thomas Cromwell asking for relief for Harte and five other Kentishmen, all from Pluckley or nearby Smarden, who had been indicted at Canterbury quarter sessions for unlawful assemblies. Their offence, according to Cranmer, lay in their favouring 'God's word' and their being regarded as supporters of 'the new doctrine, as they call it' (Penny, 45). The precise purpose of these gatherings is unclear, and Harte himself disappears from the historical record for the next ten years, though he may very well have been the Henry Harte who is regularly listed as residing in Holborn in the returns from this decade of aliens living in London.

It was at London that in 1548 Harte published *A godly new short treatyse instructyng every parson howe they shulde trade theyr lyves in the imytacyon of vertu, and shewing of vyce, and declaryng also what benefyte man hath receaved by christe, through the effusyon of hys most precyons bloude* (STC 12887). In 1549 he followed this up with a more extensive work, published at Worcester, *A consultorie for all Christians, most godly and ernestly warnyng al people to beware lest they beare the name of Christians in vayne* (STC 12564). Themes common to both tracts include an insistence on a biblical literalism, a rejection of the teaching of 'learned men', and an emphasis on the need for Christians to lead a virtuous life. In *A consultorie* Harte emphasizes the importance of giving 'diligent ear to the voice of wisdom', telling his readers to 'Refuse not his [Christ's] worde which teacheth yo al wisdom. Come to her bookes, [and] drinke of her conduite, for wisdom hath cast out floudes' (Bii). The precise nature of the views expressed in these tracts has given rise to considerable debate. Thus J. W. Martin has argued that they embody a call to separate from the national church, while

M. T. Pearse has commented that Harte's work lacks sufficient theological precision to allow any but the most general comments to be made about it. But the most accurate account of Harte's views is probably that of W. K. Jordan, who comments that '*A Godly New Short Treatyse* and *A Consultorie* display no particularly incendiary views. The latter work is especially impressive, being a treatise of piety, almost devotional in nature and cast roughly in the form of a sermon' (Jordan, 228–9).

On 3 February 1551 five men from Kent and seven from Essex came before the privy council and were examined about irregular religious meetings that apparently had been taking place in those counties, and especially in Bocking in Essex. Their arrest and examination should be seen as part of the Edwardian government's attack on religious radicalism. Harte himself is mentioned in a number of depositions. John Grey, for example, stated that 'henry harte' had affirmed that 'ther was no man so chosen that he mighte dampne hime selfe Nether yet anye man soo reprobate that he mighte kepe goddes Comaundementes', while Laurence Ramsey claimed that 'harte saide that lernyd men were the cause of grete Errors' (Burrage, 1–6).

During the period 1554–6 Harte was involved in the debates which took place in the king's bench prison between the so-called freewillers and such orthodox Edwardian protestants as John Bradford and John Careless concerning predestination. Bradford, who was executed in 1555, and then Careless engaged in heated arguments with a number of other prisoners who rejected this doctrine and stressed instead the importance of human free will as a means to salvation. Henry Harte was viewed by Bradford as a leading freewiller although it is unclear if he was ever actually imprisoned at this time. The debate started in the summer of 1554 and became more heated as the year went on. It reached a crescendo around Christmas and continued throughout 1555. Bradford in his letters relating to the disputes between his supporters and the freewill men in the king's bench consistently refers to Harte.

John Strype prints a letter entitled *A pious letter against complying with idolatours worship in Q. Maries days* that may have been written by Henry Harte since it contains a number of puns on his name, for example that 'God will have a free wylling Harte, and not an unwilling Harte come unto him' (Strype, 115). Harte was also involved at some level in the ultimately unfruitful negotiations between John Trew and John Careless over the holding of a joint service for all the prisoners in king's bench for Christmas 1555. He secured a copy of a doctrinal statement apparently drawn up by Careless as part of these discussions and wrote a number of brief but highly critical comments on it (this document is now Cambridge, Emmanuel College Library, MS 260, fol. 87).

Early in 1557 Stephen Morris wrote to Bishop Edmund Bonner of London informing him that:

> John Kempe and Henry Harte: these two lie at the bridge-foot, in a cutler's house whose name is Curle; and namely Henry Harte, is the principal of all those called free-will men; for so they are termed by the Predestinators. And he hath

drawn out thirteen articles to be observed amongst his company, and, as far as I do learn, there come none to their brotherhood except he be sworn. (Foxe, 1605)

Later that year Harte was reported as dead to Archdeacon Nicholas Harpsfield's visitation of the diocese of Canterbury. He appears to have died intestate and his son John was named as the administrator of his property.

Harte may have been the author of a tract, now lost, entitled the *Confutation of the errors of the careless by necessity*. Its contents are now known only from the numerous quotations from it contained in John Knox's reply, *The answer to a great number of blasphemous cavillations written by an Anabaptist and adversary to God's eternal predestination*.

TOM BETTERIDGE

Sources H. Harte, *A godly new short treatyse* (1548) · H. Harte, *A consultorie for all Christians* (1549) · *APC*, 1550–52 · J. Strype, *Ecclesiastical memorials*, 3 vols. (1822) · M. T. Pearse, *Between known men and visible saints: a study in sixteenth-century English dissent* (1994) · D. A. Penny, *Freewill or predestination: the battle over saving grace in mid-Tudor England* (1990) · W. K. Jordan, *Edward VI, 1: The young king* (1968) · C. Burrage, *The early English dissenters in the light of recent research (1550–1641)*, 2 vols. (1912) · J. Foxe, *Actes and monuments* (1563) · J. W. Martin, 'English protestant separation at its beginnings: Henry Harte and the free-will men', *Sixteenth Century Journal*, 7 (1976), 55–74 · Emmanuel College Library, Cambridge, MS 260 · L. E. Whatmore, ed., *Archdeacon Harpsfield's visitation, 1557*, 1, Catholic RS, 45 (1950)

Harte, Henry Hickman (1790–1848), mathematician, was born in co. Limerick, Ireland, the son of a solicitor. He obtained a scholarship in 1809, and a fellowship ten years later, at Trinity College, Dublin. In 1831 he accepted the college living of Cappagh, diocese of Derry, Tyrone. He left his mark on science by English translations of major works by two leading French figures of his time, Laplace and Poisson. In 1822 and 1827 the house of Milliken in Dublin put out the first two volumes of his annotated translation of the first two books of P. S. Laplace's *Traité de mécanique céleste*, which had appeared as one volume in 1799. At this rate the full translation that he planned would have taken about twelve volumes, but no more appeared, perhaps for financial reasons; at all events the edition became forgotten, especially when the American Nathaniel Bowditch put out a similar translation of Laplace's first four volumes between 1829 and 1839.

Harte's two other annotated translations with Milliken gained more success. In 1830 they published *The System of the World*, translated from the fifth edition (1824) of *Système du monde*, Laplace's more popular account of astronomy. Then in 1842 came two volumes of the *Treatise of Mechanics*, translated from the second (1833) edition of S. D. Poisson's *Mécanique*. These works performed a valuable service in acquainting English readers with leading texts. Harte died on 5 April 1848, having preached on the same day in his church, where he was also buried.

WILLIAM REYNELL, *rev.* I. GRATTAN-GUINNESS

Sources I. Grattan-Guinness, 'Before Bowditch: Henry Harte's translation of books 1 and 2 of Laplace's *Mécanique céleste*', *Schriftenreihe für Geschichte der Naturwissenschaften Technik und Medizin*, 24 (1987), 53–5 · private information (1891)

Harte, Walter (1708/9–1774), writer, was the son of Walter Harte, one-time fellow of Pembroke College, Oxford, who in 1684 became vicar of St Mary Magdalen, Taunton, prebendary of Ashill (diocese of Bath and Wells), and canon of Bristol, was deprived on 1 February 1691 as a nonjuror, lived later at Chipping Norton, Oxfordshire, and died at Kintbury, Berkshire, in February 1736, aged eighty-five. The son was educated at Marlborough grammar school under John Hildrop, and at St Mary Hall, Oxford, where he matriculated 22 July 1724, aged fifteen. As an undergraduate he was introduced to Pope (perhaps by Joseph Spence). He proceeded BA in 1728 and MA on 21 January 1731; he was ordained deacon on 21 December 1729 and priest on 13 March 1731.

Harte published his *Poems on Several Occasions* by subscription in May 1727, receiving £30 from Bernard Lintot for the copyright in addition to subscriptions. The collection consists mostly of imitations and translations from Greek and Latin; it is dedicated to Charles Mordaunt, earl of Peterborough, in whose family Harte was tutor at some time. (One of Spence's *Anecdotes*, dated 28 February 1727, says that Harte wrote 'a history of Lord Peterborow', but no such work has been traced.) Harte said that Pope, who is complimented in *Poems on Several Occasions*, and who subscribed for four copies, had corrected every page of the volume. Harte helped Pope revise the third edition of James Gardiner's translation of Rapin's *De hortis* (1728) and praised Pope again in a verse *Essay on Satire* (1731). The mutual admiration of the two men was ridiculed as late as 1743 in the anonymous *Mr. P—pe's Picture in Miniature*, where it is said that Pope 'flatters *Hart* for Praise' and that Harte is an 'Under-Trumpeter to Mr. *P*'.

According to Joseph Warton, Pope inserted many good lines in Harte's next poem, *An Essay on Reason* (1735), and, when pressed by Edward Young to write on the side of revelation, replied that Harte had already done this. When the theology of *An Essay on Reason* reappeared in Harte's sermon *The Union and Harmony of Reason, Morality, and Revealed Religion* (1737), he was accused of Socinianism: he was satirized in more general terms in the anonymous *Epistle to the Author of the Essay on Reason* (1735).

In December 1734 Harte became rector of Gosfield, Essex, in the gift of Pope's friend Mrs Knight, whose son had recently been in residence at St Mary Hall under the tutelage of David Mallet and Harte. Pope was unsuccessful in his several attempts between 1728 and 1737 to obtain other academic and ecclesiastical preferments for Harte, of whom he wrote (24 November 1732):

My Zeal for him was not only moved by his Ingenuity & Morals, but by his great Piety to his Parents both whom he has maintain'd in their old age upon the whole of his small Income by pupils in the university: & left himself nothing but his Clothes & Commons many years. (*Correspondence of Alexander Pope*, 3.332)

In 1740 Harte was elected vice-principal of St Mary Hall, where he attained great reputation as a tutor.

Between June 1746 and the end of 1750 Harte was travelling tutor to Philip Stanhope, Lord Chesterfield's illegitimate son, and, for part of that time, to Edward (later Lord)

Eliot; but 'Harte's partiality to Greek and Latin, German law, and Gothic erudition rendered him rather remiss in other points'; long accustomed to college life, he 'was too awkward both in his person and address to be able to familiarise the graces with his young pupil' (Maty, 1.171, 192). Nevertheless Chesterfield spoke highly of Harte and Harte spoke highly of his pupil in regular progress reports from France, and the German and Italian states.

Whatever the effect on his charges, Harte improved himself on their travels: he wrote poetry, made sketches, and took note of continental agricultural methods; he collected materials for and partly wrote his *History of the Life of Gustavus Adolphus*. More tangible rewards accrued when, in 1750, Chesterfield obtained for him a prebend of Windsor, worth £450 p.a., and the rectory of Creed, Cornwall, to which was added in 1758 the valuable nearby crown living of St Austell and St Blazey. He cultivated the glebe: Harte's *Essays on Husbandry* (1764) derives from his own experiments as well as his correspondence with other gentleman farmers and observation of European methods.

Harte's ambitious *History of the Life of Gustavus Adolphus* was published in April 1759 and, according to Horace Walpole, was universally decried for its style. Chesterfield agreed that the style is execrable, though the book is full of good matter. Johnson said the book's defects 'proceeded not from imbecility, but from foppery', but commended Harte 'as a scholar, and a man of the most companionable talents he had ever known' (Boswell, *Life*, 3 Dec 1763). In the preface to the second edition Harte apologized for his 'words of foreign growth' and explained that the first edition 'was chiefly written in foreign countries' (p. xxvii).

About 1759 Harte retired to Bath, suffering from jaundice, melancholy, and other unnamed distempers, real and imaginary. His last publications, *Essays on Husbandry* (1764) and *The Amaranth, or, Religious Poems; Consisting of Fables, Visions, Emblems, &c.* (1767), had been conceived and mostly written many years earlier. Two of the religious poems, for instance, were written in 1749 in the Tyrol and were illustrated by Harte's own drawings 'made on the spot'. Of a visit to 'my very excellent friend' Harte in Bath, Arthur Young wrote, 'His conversation on the subject of husbandry is as full of experience and as truly solid as his genuine and native humour, extensive knowledge of mankind, and admirable philanthropy are pleasing and instructive' (Young, 153). Harte suffered strokes in 1766 and 1768, which left him paralysed and hardly able to speak intelligibly, but he lingered until May 1774, when he died in Bath; his will was proved on 22 June. Harte, who never married, was small of stature (*Letters of ... Chesterfield*, 1.310).   JAMES SAMBROOK

Sources *The letters of Philip Dormer Stanhope, fourth earl of Chesterfield*, ed. B. Dobrée, 6 vols. (1932) • *The correspondence of Alexander Pope*, ed. G. Sherburn, 5 vols. (1956) • J. Spence, *Observations, anecdotes, and characters, of books and men*, ed. J. M. Osborn, new edn, 2 vols. (1966) • M. Maty, 'Memoirs', in *Miscellaneous works of the ... earl of Chesterfield*, ed. M. Maty, 2nd edn, 1 (1779) • A. Young, *Six weeks' tour through the southern counties* (1768) • J. Warton, *An essay on the genius and writings of Pope*, 5th edn, 2 vols. (1806) • Boswell, *Life* • Walpole, *Corr.*, vols. 15–16 • Boase & Courtney, *Bibl. Corn.*, 1.211 • D. F. Foxon, ed., *English verse, 1701–1750: a catalogue of separately printed poems with notes on contemporary collected editions*, 2 vols. (1975) • *Fasti Angl., 1541–1857*, [Bristol] • Foster, *Alum. Oxon., 1715–1886* • Nichols, *Lit. anecdotes*, 8.296 • Bodl. Oxf., MS Rawl. 4º3, fols. 426–30 • *GM*, 1st ser., 44 (1774), 286

Likenesses Hibbart, etching (after Seeman)

Hartgill, George (*b.* in or before **1555**, *d.* in or before **1597**), astronomer and astrologer, was the son of Thomas Hartgill and Anne Harvey. His family, based at Kilmington, Somerset, were minor landowners in Somerset and Dorset; his paternal grandfather, William Hartgill, steward to William, sixth Baron Stourton, and his uncle, John Hartgill, were both murdered by Charles, seventh Baron Stourton, on 12 January 1557. (Stourton was hanged at Salisbury on 6 March 1557.) Little else is known of Hartgill's early life. He was the author of *Calendaria, sive, Tabulae astronomicae universales* (1594), a comprehensive set of astronomical tables designed mainly for astrological use, also published in English as *Generall Callendars, or, Most Easie Astronomicall Tables* (1594). He had previously published a *Prognostication* calculated for Bristol for the year 1581, of which only the title-page is extant. He was a client of William Paulet, third marquess of Winchester (1533–1598), to whom he dedicated all three of his works.

Hartgill's tables took partial account of the reform of astronomy since Copernicus. The main reason he is still known today is that the astrological reformer John Gadbury, together with an otherwise unknown T. Gadbury, brought out a revised and updated edition of his tables in 1656, together with commendations by Lilly, Booker, and Wharton. Their clear intention was to make Hartgill a respectable Elizabethan predecessor for their cause, that of a thoroughly heliocentric system of astrology.

Hartgill may have been a protestant preacher. In his commendation Lilly described him as 'a painful *Preacher*, a very reverend *Divine*, a most excellent *Mathematitian*, a profound student in *Astrology*', before going on to admit that his tables were often both obscure and faulty. Nevertheless there are some hints in Hartgill's original edition that may substantiate Lilly's claim: its title-page, built around the theme 'Christian Philosopher', identifies him as 'minister of the word of God' and represents him iconographically as holding out an armillary sphere (in one hand) and (with the other hand) clutching a book entitled *Verbum dei* to his heart. His dedication shows him to be familiar with the works of continental protestant theologians and respectful of Calvin, who is included among those whose criticism of astrology would condemn them, if not for the fact that they 'in other respects have deserved well of the church'.

Hartgill married Dorothy Ashcome on 24 June 1580. The following year he became rector of Steepleton Iwerne, Dorset, and in 1582 added the rectorship of West Chickerell, Dorset. Chickerell was a living that belonged to Paulet, and *Calendaria* was signed 'from my study at your Lordshippes Manor of Chickerell'. For a country rector he was unusually well informed on developments in astronomy and astrology both in Britain and on the continent, and he had a respectable private library. It might be speculated that he frequently travelled to London; it is also possible that he was one of the protestant refugees who studied abroad during the reign of Mary, though there is no evidence to support this. He is presumed to have died in or before 1597, when new incumbents were installed at his livings. JOSEPH GROSS

Sources P. Morgan, 'George Hartgill: an Elizabethan parson-astronomer and his library', *Annals of Science*, 24 (1968), 295–311 · *STC, 1475–1640* · GEC, *Peerage* · B. S. Capp, *Astrology and the popular press: English almanacs, 1500–1800* (1979)

Likenesses woodcut, 1594, BM · R. Gaywood, etching, 1656, BM

Harthacnut [Hardecanute] (*c.*1018–1042), king of England and of Denmark, was the only son of *Cnut, king of England, of Denmark, and of Norway (*d.* 1035), and Emma of Normandy [*see* Emma [Ælfgifu]]. He was the brother of Gunnhild, first wife of the later emperor Heinrich III of Germany; the half-brother on his father's side of Swein and *Harold I (Harold Harefoot); and on his mother's side of *Edward the Confessor, *Alfred Ætheling, and Godgifu.

Harthacnut ('tough-knot') was probably named after his Danish great-grandfather King Gorm, who is called Hardecnudth Vurm by the German chronicler Adam of Bremen. According to Emma's encomiast, he was born not long after his parents' marriage in July/August 1017. He accompanied Emma at the translation of the relics of St Ælfheah from London to Canterbury in June 1023, and so is unlikely to have been the son given by Cnut to his adversary Thorkell the Tall in Denmark earlier the same year unless the source—the Anglo-Saxon Chronicle—has jumbled the sequence of events. Cnut had probably already had Swein and Harold Harefoot with *Ælfgifu of Northampton when he married Emma; and the encomiast says that Emma refused to proceed with the match until Cnut swore that her male offspring would have precedence in the succession. The same source states that when Harthacnut grew up Cnut pledged the entire kingdom to him, secured oaths of loyalty from the nobles, and sent him to rule Denmark.

By the time of Cnut's death in 1035 Harthacnut had probably been in Denmark for some years, and had struck coins with the title REX. Whether he was intended to have England too is unclear, given that the encomiast had every reason to write what suited his patron, Queen Emma, and that such arrangements as Cnut made are otherwise obscure. Adam of Bremen thought that Harthacnut was supposed to take Denmark and Harold England, and certainly at the Oxford meeting which followed Cnut's death on 12 November 1035 the E text of the Anglo-Saxon Chronicle says that Harold received much support from the magnates north of the Thames; however, Harthacnut was promoted by his mother and Earl Godwine of Wessex, and it was agreed that Harold should act as regent for both, and that Emma should hold Wessex for Harthacnut. Had he appeared immediately the country might have been divided between them, and it is probably a reflection of some sort of formal arrangement that mints south of the Thames produced silver pennies in his name, while those

Harthacnut (*c.*1018–1042), coin

to the north minted almost entirely for Harold (although pennies of Harthacnut are known from Cambridge, Gloucester, Hertford, Lincoln, Stamford, Warwick, and York) and those on the river (London, Oxford, Southwark, and Wallingford) struck for both. However, Harthacnut's issues probably ceased fairly quickly, and in 1037 Harold was accepted everywhere as king.

Meanwhile, Harthacnut remained in Denmark, probably because of the threat to its security posed by Magnus Olafson, who now ruled Norway after expelling Cnut's son Swein. According to later Scandinavian sources they eventually made a treaty which provided that if either died without an heir his kingdom should go to the other, and this may have freed Harthacnut to turn his attention to England. In 1039, with ten ships, he sailed to meet his mother in Bruges, fortified on the way by a vision assuring him that Harold Harefoot would soon die. This he did, in March 1040, and envoys quickly crossed the channel to offer Harthacnut the throne. He had by then assembled an invasion force, and eventually landed at Sandwich with sixty-two ships on 17 June.

Harthacnut's reign is criticized by the C and E texts of the Anglo-Saxon Chronicle, the former recording that he had Harold's body disinterred and flung into a marsh, and stating that he never did anything worthy of a king. Both texts complain about the severity of the taxation required to pay his fleet, which text E says amounted to £21,099, while £11,048 was afterwards given to thirty-two ships (probably indicating that he doubled the size of the standing navy from the sixteen vessels of Harold's time). The first sum was handed over in 1041, is said to have alienated his supporters, and caused trouble in Worcestershire, where on 4 May two of the housecarls collecting it were killed by the inhabitants. Harthacnut reacted angrily, sending an army led by his earls and including most of the élite housecarls, with orders to burn Worcester, devastate the shire, and slaughter all the men. The destruction began on 12 November and on the fifth day, after burning the city, they retired with much booty, although without having killed or captured many of the population, who had received warning of their arrival and fled in all directions. Then, says the Worcester chronicler John, writing c.1120, Harthacnut's wrath was appeased.

The same source records how the previous year Harthacnut had also been angry with Earl Godwine and Lyfing, bishop of Worcester, over the death of his half-brother Alfred in 1036. Godwine was evidently tried, swore together with many important men that in dealing with Alfred he had acted on Harold Harefoot's orders, and gave to the king 'for his friendship' (John of Worcester, *Chron.*, s.a. 1040) a ship with a gilded prow crewed by eighty magnificently equipped men. Lyfing's bishopric was transferred to Archbishop Ælfric of York, one of his accusers, but Harthacnut returned it in 1041 after Lyfing made his peace. The same year he guaranteed the safety of Earl Eadwulf of Bernicia, who was seeking reconciliation, and then colluded in his murder by Earl Siward of Deira; the latter (a Dane) was subsequently made earl of all Northumbria. One might discern here a policy of strengthening northern England against the Scots by giving authority over the whole of it to a trusted follower, and Harthacnut presumably also expected a degree of loyalty from the cleric Eadred, who paid him to be appointed bishop of Durham.

But little is known of Harthacnut's government of England. Pennies of Harold's 'Fleur de Lys' type were briefly produced in his name before being replaced by that known today as 'Arm and Sceptre', which has a bust of Harthacnut facing left, wearing a diadem and holding a sceptre in his left hand; a similar portrait may have appeared on his seal, now lost. Only three royal charters have survived: one to the abbey of Bury St Edmunds, which is almost certainly a later forgery; another granting land in Berkshire to the monks of Abingdon and of dubious authenticity; and a probably genuine transfer in a contemporary hand of an estate in Hampshire to Bishop Ælfwine of Winchester. In addition there are two writs, both to Ramsey Abbey and probably authentic, although surviving in later copies. One confirms to Abbot Æthelstan a property in Thetford which he had held in Cnut's time; in the second, Harthacnut and his mother give land at Hemingford, Huntingdonshire, for the sake of Cnut's soul and their own. The twelfth-century Ramsey chronicle, which not surprisingly speaks well of Harthacnut's generosity to churches and of his character generally, says that he also gave them an estate at 'Gilling'.

In 1041 Harthacnut sent to Normandy for his halfbrother Edward: the encomiast states that Harthacnut wished them to hold the kingdom together, and the C text of the Anglo-Saxon Chronicle says that Edward was sworn in as king. This may mean that Edward was recognized as heir of Harthacnut, who had neither wife nor children, and who is said by the slightly later Norman historian William of Poitiers to have suffered from frequent illness; the likely truth of this is suggested not only by his sudden death the following year, but also because it is otherwise

difficult to see why a man in his early twenties with a normal life expectancy should have acted so. He was perhaps moved by brotherly love, as the encomiast alleges, but one might also discern the influence of Emma, keen to maintain her own position by ensuring that one kingly son should be followed by another. The copy of her encomium which she probably received contains a drawing of her accepting the work, while two figures—doubtless Harthacnut and Edward—look on. Harthacnut is thus one of the few pre-conquest kings depicted in a contemporary manuscript.

Harthacnut died at Lambeth on 8 June 1042, after collapsing when drinking at the feast celebrating the marriage of Gytha, daughter of Osgod Clapa, to Tovi the Proud; both Osgod and Tovi were old henchmen of Cnut. He was buried next to Cnut in the Old Minster, Winchester. Harthacnut is a remote figure: the little that is known suggests that, both ruthless and feared, he possessed at least two of the requisites of a successful medieval king. But in the event, his death was more significant than his life. He was the last of the dynasty established by the Danish conquest of 1016, and the succession of Edward proved the prelude to the much more significant Norman victory of 1066. Had Harthacnut not died young, that conquest might never have happened, with considerable implications for later English history.   M. K. LAWSON

Sources A. Campbell, ed. and trans., *Encomium Emmae reginae*, CS, 3rd ser., 72 (1949), 6–8, 32–4, 38–52 · *ASC*, s.a. 1037, 1039–42 [text C]; s.a. 1023 [text D]; s.a. 1036–7, 1039–41 [text E] · John of Worcester, *Chron.* · *AS chart.*, S 982, 993–7, 1068, 1106 · F. E. Harmer, ed., *Anglo-Saxon writs* (1952), 245–6, 256–7, 471 · *Magistri Adam Bremensis gesta Hammaburgensis ecclesiae pontificum*, ed. B. Schmeidler, 3rd edn, MGH Scriptores Rerum Germanicarum, [2] (Hanover, 1917), 134–5 · *The Gesta Guillelmi of William of Poitiers*, ed. and trans. R. H. C. Davis and M. Chibnall, OMT (1998) · W. D. Macray, ed., *Chronicon abbatiae Rameseiensis a saec. x usque ad an. circiter 1200*, Rolls Series, 83 (1886), 151–2 · T. Talvio, 'Harold I and Harthacnut's Jewel Cross type reconsidered', *Anglo-Saxon monetary history: essays in memory of Michael Dolley*, ed. M. A. S. Blackburn (1986), 273–90 · F. Barlow, *Edward the Confessor* (1970), 42–60 · P. Stafford, *Unification and conquest* (1989), 76–82 · F. M. Stenton, *Anglo-Saxon England*, 3rd edn (1971), 404–6, 420–23

Likenesses coin, BM [*see illus.*] · drawing (with his mother, Emma, and brother Edward), BL, 'Encomium Emma reginae', Add. MS 33241, fol. 1v, frontispiece; *see illus. in* Emma (*d.* 1052)

Hartington. For this title name *see* Cavendish, Spencer Compton, marquess of Hartington and eighth duke of Devonshire (1833–1908).

Hartlepool [Hertelpoll], **Hugh of** (*c.*1245–1302), Franciscan friar and theologian, presumably originated at Hartlepool, co. Durham, where a Franciscan house had been established by 1240, and must have read theology at Oxford in the 1270s. His identity with the secular master Hugh of Hartlepool, who appears in northern deeds in 1262 and 1271, is doubtful. He appears first together with another northern master, Master William Meynill, as the agent of Dervorguilla de Balliol (*d.* 1290), lady of Galloway, in the grant of statutes to Balliol College on 22 August 1282. The statutes authorized the two masters to act as trustees, with authority over the principal and fellows, and consequently a succession of external masters, of whom one was often a friar, played a prominent part in Balliol affairs until the new statutes of 1340. Hugh of Hartlepool seems to have been succeeded in this role by another Franciscan, Richard of Slickburn (or of Durham), who was appointed on 16 April 1284. He became the twentieth lector or regent master of the Franciscan school in Oxford about 1287; some evidence of his teaching survives. He preached university sermons on 25 January, 2 February, and 20 April 1291. He was elected minister provincial, in succession to Roger Marston, not long before April 1299, and therefore took responsibility for implementing the provisions for licensing friars to act as preachers and confessors made by Boniface VIII in *Super cathedram* (1300); his attempt to have twenty-two confessors licensed in the Oxford convent alone was frustrated by John Dalderby, bishop of Lincoln, and he was compelled to make do with only eight (7 August 1300). He attended the general chapters of his order at Lyons in 1299, Genoa in 1301, and (probably no longer as provincial) Assisi in 1302, with subventions from Edward I: the king also summoned him to the Lincoln parliament of January 1301, and on 9 September 1302 commissioned him to negotiate for peace with Philippe IV of France at the Roman court. By the time of this last commission he was already in Italy; he died at Assisi on 11 September, and was buried in the Sacro Convento there. His sepulchral stone survives.

Four of Hartlepool's disputed questions survive in Assisi notebooks, together with three university sermons in another notebook from Worcester. They expound traditional Franciscan teaching, while the sermons show a light and imaginative touch. His lectures were also cited by William of Nottingham, OFM, in his *Sentences* commentary of c.1312.   JEREMY CATTO

Sources 'Quaestiones', Biblioteca Comunale, Assisi, MS 158, fols. 310r, 329r–330v · 'Quaestiones', Biblioteca Comunale, Assisi, MS 196, fols. 67r–74r · 'Quaestiones', Worcester Cathedral, MS Q.46, fols. 129r–131r, 159v–161v, 254v–256v · William of Nottingham, gospel commentary, Gon. & Caius Cam., MS 300, fol. 166v · H. E. Salter, ed., *The Oxford deeds of Balliol College*, OHS, 64 (1913), 277–80 · *Calendar of chancery warrants*, 1: 1244–1326 (1927), 121 · *CPR, 1301–7*, 62 · H. Pouillon, 'Le manuscrit d'Assise, Bibl. Comm. 196', *Recherches de Théologie Ancienne et Médiévale*, 12 (1940), 347 · A. G. Little and F. Pelster, *Oxford theology and theologians*, OHS, 96 (1934), 88, 127–8, 156–7, 192–204 · J. C. Russell, 'Dictionary of writers of thirteenth century England', *BIHR*, special suppl., 3 (1936) [whole issue], esp. 51 · Emden, *Oxf.*, 2.920 · A. G. Little, *The Grey friars in Oxford*, OHS, 20 (1892)
Archives Biblioteca Comunale, Assisi, MSS 158, 196 · Worcester Cathedral, MS Q. 46, fols. 129r–131r, 159v–161v, 254v–256v

Hartley, Arthur Clifford (1889–1960), oil engineer, was born at Springbank, Hull, on 7 January 1889, the elder son of George Thomas Hartley, surgeon, and his wife, Elizabeth Briggs. From Hymers College, Hull, and after a brief period of engineering studies at Hull Technical College, Hartley went to the City and Guilds College, the engineering school of the Imperial College of Science and Technology at South Kensington, London. He graduated BSc in 1910 with a third-class honours degree in engineering, and then undertook practical work at the North Eastern Railway Company's docks at Hull. After gaining mechanical engineering experience, he became works superintendent with a London company producing asphalt.

In the war of 1914–18 Hartley was commissioned in the Royal Flying Corps, where he qualified as a pilot, and earned the OBE (1918) and the substantive rank of major. After Hartley joined the armaments section of the Air Board (where he worked under Bertram Hopkinson) it became clear that technical invention was his forte. He was responsible for the development of the Constantinescu interrupter gear which enabled a Vickers machine-gun to be synchronized so that the pilot could fire straight ahead between the propeller blades. After the war Hartley spent five years as a partner of a firm of consulting engineers, until in 1924 he joined the Anglo-Persian Oil Company as assistant manager of its rapidly expanding engineering division, becoming chief engineer in 1934.

After the outbreak of the Second World War, Hartley was seconded by Anglo-Iranian (as the company was now called) to the Ministry of Aircraft Production and worked on developing the stabilized automatic bomb-sight which Bomber Command used to sink the *Tirpitz*. In 1942 he was appointed technical director of the petroleum warfare department. The most pressing problem facing Hartley and his team, at the express command of Air Chief Marshal Arthur Harris, was the need to devise a means of clearing fog from airfields, so as to reduce crashes and allow bombing operations to continue whatever the weather. The fog investigation dispersal operations, code-named FIDO, involved the laying of oil burners alongside runways. Successfully installed at fifteen airfields in Britain, they allowed more than 2500 aircraft to land safely with adequate visibility during foggy conditions.

Hartley's most important technical contribution to the war effort, however, came through his association with the pipeline under the ocean (code-named PLUTO). The idea of laying a pipeline across the channel to supply an invasion force with petrol was first proposed by Lord Louis Mountbatten, then chief of combined operations; but it was Hartley and other talented engineers who overcame the technical problems. Following D-day and the securing of the Cherbourg peninsula, several hundred miles of submarine three-inch cable were laid, through which petrol could be pumped. Two lines were laid from the Isle of Wight to Cherbourg, followed by nineteen lines from Dungeness to Calais: petrol was pumped through this system at the rate of a million gallons a day during the advance of the allied armies into Nazi Germany. After the war Hartley received £9000 in recognition of his contribution to PLUTO on the recommendation of the Royal Commission on Awards to Inventors. In 1944 he was appointed CBE.

Although Hartley retired from Anglo-Iranian in 1951, his inventive nature continued to bear fruit. He became an engineering consultant (with Rendel, Palmer and Tritton) and, most notably, he devised the Hartley hoister. This allowed oil tankers to be loaded offshore, and was first used successfully off Kuwait in January 1959.

Hartley married Dorothy Elizabeth Wallace, daughter of a Shanghai-based marine engineer, in 1920; they had two sons. Dorothy died in 1923, and four years later Hartley married Florence Nina Hodgson; they also had two sons.

Within his own profession Hartley undertook a number of responsible offices. He was elected president of the Institution of Mechanical Engineers in 1951, and was also an honorary fellow of the City and Guilds Institute and of Imperial College, London. In 1959 he received the Redwood Medal of the Institute of Petroleum. He was elected president of the Institution of Civil Engineers in 1959, but died at St Thomas's Hospital, London, on 28 January 1960, less than three months afterwards. His second wife survived him.   A. C. VIVIAN, *rev.*

Sources PICE, new ser., 15 (1959–60), 477–9 · *Obituaries from the Times* (1979), 338 · A. C. Hartley, 'Fog dispersal from airfield runways', in *The civil engineer in war: a symposium of papers on war-time engineering problems*, Institution of Civil Engineers, 3 vols. (1948), vol. 1 · A. C. Hartley, 'Operation PLUTO', in *The civil engineer in war: a symposium of papers on war-time engineering problems*, Institution of Civil Engineers (1948), vol. 3 · *The Central*, 43 (June 1948) · D. J. Payton-Smith, *Oil: a study of wartime policy and administration* (1971) · J. H. Bamberg, *The history of the British Petroleum Company, 2: The Anglo-Iranian years, 1928–1954* (1994) · personal knowledge (1971)
Archives University of Warwick, British Petroleum archives
Likenesses J. Codner, oils, RIBA · J. Codner, portrait, Inst. CE
Wealth at death £72,779 6s.: probate, 22 April 1960, CGPLA Eng. & Wales

Hartley, Sir Charles Augustus (1825–1915), civil engineer, was born at Hedworth, co. Durham, on 3 February 1825, the second of three sons of William Augustus Hartley (d. 1844) and his wife, Lillias, daughter of Andrew Todd of Bo'ness, Linlithgow. William Augustus was a manufacturer, agent, and dealer in iron, active in Durham, Northumbria, and southern Scotland. He moved house frequently and Charles attended schools in Gateshead, Bishop Auckland, and Darlington. In 1843, after several informal attachments, he was accepted as apprentice with George Leather & Sons of Leeds, civil engineers, only to have to withdraw when his father died. He was fortunate to find good and regular employment with the Scottish Central Railway, and when that ended in 1848 he immediately found work at Plymouth harbour. During 1855 and 1856 he served in the Crimean War in the Anglo-Turkish contingent with the rank of captain, and constructed some defence works at Kerch.

Hartley's connection with the Near East did not end when peace came in 1856. One article of the treaty of Paris established the European commission of the Danube, whose purpose was to improve navigation of the lower Danube by clearing a channel through the mud and sand encumbering the estuary. (The commission was subsequently empowered by the treaty of Berlin in 1878 to exercise its powers independently of the Ottoman government.) To this commission Hartley was appointed chief engineer in 1856, his first task being to decide which of the three principal estuaries of the Danube—the Kilia, the Sulina, or the St George—was best adapted for improvement. He visited the mouths of the Oder and Vistula, on the Baltic coast, to see the effects of recent coastal works there, and advised that provisional works should be undertaken to improve the harbour at the Sulina mouth

by utilizing the natural scour of the river. These works consisted of two piers forming a seaward prolongation of the fluvial channel. They were begun in April 1858 and completed in July 1861, having the effect of doubling the depth of the channel to 16 feet or more. Hartley was appointed to the order of the Mejidiye, but under British regulations was obliged to decline; he was given a knighthood in 1862. The provisional piers were replaced by permanent solid structures in 1871, making the Sulina, formerly known as 'the grave of sailors', into one of the best harbours on the Black Sea. In later years its depth was further increased, to accommodate the increasing draught of vessels using the channel.

Equal success was achieved in dealing with the course of the Danube above the Sulina mouth. In 1880 construction of a new entrance from the Toulcha Channel commenced, in accordance with plans designed by Hartley in 1857. This work was completed by 1882, and by 1886 the St George branch also was made navigable. In consequence the Danube as far as Braila was navigable by steamers of 4000 tons, as compared with vessels of 400 tons before the improvements were begun.

In 1862 Hartley toured Egypt, going as far south as Aswan and visiting Suez to inspect the works then under way for the Suez Canal. He retained his appointment as chief engineer until 1907 and returned each year to oversee progress on the Danube, meanwhile occupying himself on projects elsewhere in western Europe, in Russia, and in India. An eager traveller, his inspection and report of river works on the Mississippi, for which he had been consulted by the president of the United States, gave him the opportunity to tour the USA and Canada in 1873–4, and he regularly visited members of his family scattered throughout England and Scotland. From 1884 he was a member of the technical commission of the Suez Canal, on which he served for twenty-two years. He was created KCMG in 1884, and he received Romanian and other decorations. He became an associate of the Institution of Civil Engineers in 1856 and a member in 1862; all his published works appeared in their proceedings.

Hartley enjoyed a lifelong friendship with Sir John *Stokes (1825–1902) of the Royal Engineers, whom he met in the Crimea and who was later the British commissioner on the European commission of the Danube, and he came to regard Stokes's family as an extension of his own. In 1887 he seriously considered marrying Stokes's daughter Edith and went so far as to ask her father's permission before admitting that he was unlikely to be faithful after so many years of bachelor freedom. Until 1890, when he was increasingly afflicted by a hand-tremor, he continued to enjoy travel and golf; in his latter years he found comfort and pleasure among members of his own and Stokes's families. He died, unmarried, at his residence, 26 Pall Mall, London, on 20 February 1915 and after a funeral at St James's, Piccadilly, was buried in Highgate cemetery.

     E. I. CARLYLE, *rev.* ANITA MCCONNELL

Sources PICE, 200 (1914–15), 1–3 · *The Times* (22 Feb 1915), 10d · *The Times* (25 Feb 1915), 11e · H. Trotter, 'Danube', *Encyclopaedia Britannica*, 11th edn (1910–11) · C. W. S. Hartley, *A biography of Sir*

Charles Hartley, civil engineer (1825–1915): the father of the Danube, 2 vols. (1989) · *Journal of the Royal Society of Arts*, 63 (1914–15), 322 · *CGPLA Eng. & Wales* (1915) · IGI

Archives Inst. CE, corresp., diaries, notebooks, and other papers **Likenesses** photograph, repro. in Hartley, *Biography of Sir Charles Hartley* **Wealth at death** £59,037 7s. 1d.: probate, 22 Dec 1915, *CGPLA Eng. & Wales*

Hartley, David (*bap.* 1705, *d.* 1757), philosopher and physician, was baptized on 21 June 1705 at St John's, Halifax, Yorkshire. His father was David Hartley (1674–1720), BA 1695, Lincoln College, Oxford, a clergyman who served at Luddenden (1698–1705); Illingworth, Halifax (1705–17); and Armley, Leeds, where he died. Hartley's mother, Evereld Wadsworth (*bap.* 1676, *d.* 1705) of Elland, Yorkshire, gave birth to a daughter, Elizabeth, in 1704, and died three months after the birth of her son.

Early medical career After attending Bradford grammar school Hartley was admitted sizar to Jesus College, Cambridge, on 21 April 1722. He received his BA in 1726 and MA in 1729. At Cambridge he met Nicholas Saunderson, the blind Lucasian professor of mathematics, and later helped raise the subscription to publish Saunderson's *Elements of Algebra* (1740). Although the orphaned son of a poor clergyman, himself in line for the church, Hartley would not sign the Thirty-Nine Articles. Instead, by Easter 1730 he had become the first layperson to be master of Magnus Grammar School, Newark. A few months later, on 21 May 1730, Hartley married Alice Rowley (*bap.* 1705, *d.* 1731), at Saffron Walden, Essex. The couple then moved to Bury St Edmunds. Alice Rowley died there giving birth to their son, David *Hartley (1731–1813). She was buried on 22 July 1731.

While in Newark Hartley began to practise medicine, and there he became an advocate of variola inoculation for smallpox. This led to the publication, in 1733, of *Some reasons why the practice of inoculation ought to be introduced into the town of Bury at present*. Of interest is Hartley's use of probability theory to argue for the new and controversial procedure. While in Bury, Hartley met his second wife. Elizabeth Packer (1713–1778) was the fifth child and only daughter of Robert Packer and Mary Winchcombe, of Donnington Castle and Bucklebury, near Newbury, Berkshire. Mary Winchcombe was the daughter of Sir Henry Winchcombe, bt. Her sister Frances had married Henry St John, Viscount Bolingbroke. According to David and Elizabeth's daughter Mary, 'Her family were much against the match, and did for some time retard it' (Warner, 107). The prospective husband was a former charity student, unorthodox in religion, a doctor without a medical degree, and the father of a young son. One can imagine the reaction. None the less, the couple married on 25 August 1735 at Nowton, Suffolk, after they had signed away control of the £5000 that had been willed to Elizabeth by her father. Later that year they moved to Prince's (now Wardour) Street, near Leicester Fields, London, where Hartley built up a medical practice that included Thomas Pelham-Holles, duke of Newcastle. In London,

David Hartley (*bap.* 1705, *d.* 1757), by James Heath, pubd 1809 (after John Shackleton)

David and Elizabeth had two children, Mary (1736–1803) and Winchcombe Henry (1740–1794).

The lithontriptic In a letter of 15 May 1736 to his lifelong friend John Lister, Hartley affirmed 'that a Man … who entirely abandons Self-Interest & devotes his Labours to the Service of Mankind … is sure to meet with private Happiness' (Allen, 44). In addition to his medical practice and to participation in the Royal Society, Hartley sought to serve mankind through various philanthropic projects. He laboured to promote his friend John Byrom's shorthand, which he hoped would become the standard for written communication.

Hartley also devoted himself to discovering a lithontriptic, a medication that would disintegrate bladder stones. The standard treatment was to cut open the patient's bladder and pick out the stone. But lithotomy could kill. In *Ten cases of persons who have taken Mrs. Stephens's medicines for the stone* (1738) Hartley suggested that Joanna Stephens might have developed an effective lithontriptic. His interest was hardly casual. *Ten cases* contains a diary of his own harrowing course of treatment, starting on 18 July 1737. Hartley records that on 28 November 1737 'I walk'd abroad as far as the Custom-house, having confined myself for Twenty Weeks, taking the Medicines regularly, without stirring out of Doors'. Hartley's diary is remarkably forthright: unlike the other nine cases, and after twenty weeks of excessive pain, Hartley does not claim that Stephens's medicines have cured him. Hartley's *Ten cases*, along with the proposal to raise a £5000 subscription to pay Stephens for her formula, sparked a controversy. One critic charged that Hartley would be 'deemed only a Puff-scribbler in Favour of an old Woman's Quack-medicine, if you continued to publish the Cases of Persons only, who received Benefit from those Medicines' (Allen, 56). Hartley responded by publishing *A view of the present evidence for and against Mrs. Stephens's medicines, as a solvent for the stone* (1739). The work contains 155 cases of people treated by Stephens.

The subscription failed, but Hartley and his allies succeeded. An act of parliament instructed a group of trustees, headed by the archbishop of Canterbury, to award the £5000 to Stephens, provided that they verified that the medicine worked. Stephens disclosed her 'secret' in June 1739 and received the reward the following March. During these months Hartley, working with Stephen Hales, set about analysing Stephens's concoction. The two also corresponded with the chemist Claude-Joseph Geoffroy and Sauveur-François Morand, chief surgeon at the Invalides. Hales published his results in *An account of some experiments and observations on Mrs. Stephens's medicine for dissolving the stone* (1740). Geoffroy and Morand read their own positive reports to the Académie Royale des Sciences in December 1739 and November 1740 respectively, and Morand published a translation of Hales's *Account* in the same year. In 1741 Hartley's Latin account of his search for a solvent, *De lithontriptico*, was published in Leiden and Basel. The results of the research were now available to physicians throughout Europe.

Hartley and Hales considered themselves to be conducting a scientific analysis of a promising folk remedy. They employed the chemical theory that Hales had developed in his *Statical Essays* (1733)—a theory based on the Newtonian concept of forces of attraction and repulsion and on the experimental observation that many solid concretions, including bladder stones, have large quantities of 'air' locked within. According to the theory, such concretions would disintegrate if the repulsive force of the air within them could be released through chemical reactions. Hartley and Hales were looking for an ingestible chemical that would initiate such a reaction.

In May 1742 the Hartleys moved 'on account of the many illnesses … which my wife has had in town' to Bath, to 'a very pleasant house in the new Square' (Trigg, 262). In Bath, Hartley again conducted a busy medical practice. Four years later, in 1746, Elizabeth's two brothers both died unmarried, and the Packer and Winchcombe estates passed to David and Elizabeth's son, Winchcombe Henry. Thereafter the family lived at their home in Bath and at their estates at Donnington and Bucklebury, and Great and Little Sodbury, Gloucestershire.

The *Observations on Man* From the mid-1730s Hartley had been at work writing on religious, moral, and scientific subjects. Byrom read 'Dr. Hartley's paper upon benevolence' in June 1735 (*Private Journal*, 1.2.634). On 2 December 1736 Hartley mentioned 'two small Treatises' to Lister, titled 'The progress of happiness deduced from reason—& from scripture' (Trigg, 236). On 23 November 1738 Hartley sent Lister part of 'An introduction to the history of man … considering him in his corporeal, mental, moral, and religious capacities' (Trigg, 244–5). The final result was his *Observations on Man, his Frame, his Duty, and his Expectations* (1749).

The *Observations* is, in one aspect, a seminal attempt to extend Newtonian science to the study of human nature. We should assume, Hartley writes, that the body's component particles are 'subjected to the same subtle laws' (Hartley, 1, prop. 9) as are all other material entities. The subtle laws are those Newton hinted at in the 'Queries' to his *Opticks*, and upon which Hales based his chemical theory. Hartley's doctrine of vibrations is thus a neurophysiology constructed on the basis of Newtonian speculative physics: when sound strikes the eardrum or light the eye, the spheres of attraction and repulsion surrounding the particles in the relevant nerves vibrate, and the vibrations move along the nerves and into the brain, where the signals travel both to the region dedicated to the sensory modality and also to regions that are associated with it. This last point is crucial, for without such 'joint impression' of signals from different sensory modalities, an organism would be unable to co-ordinate vision with hearing or either with movement.

Commentators have habitually linked Hartley's name with the phrase 'the association of ideas' and have viewed him as the precursor of the school of association psychology. However, the term is misleading to the extent that it suggests that Hartley took ideas to be pre-existing entities that association connects. Rather, the psychological chemistry of association fuses sensory stimuli, emotional responses, cognitive and semantic elements, and physical movements into new compounds. 'It was reserved for Hartley', wrote John Stuart Mill, 'to show that mental phenomena … may form a still more intimate, and as it were chemical union—may merge into a compound, in which the separate elements are no more distinguishable as such, than hydrogen and oxygen in water' (Mill, 294). In Hartley's theory a neurological process of association generates 'ideas'—that is, perceptions, concepts, and actions. A person learns to identify the notes on a clef; with practice, the person perfects repertoires of complex actions, such as those that link visual and auditory perceptions with hand movements, so that they become 'secondarily automatic'; and these repertoires enable the person to perform what Hartley termed 'decomplex' actions, such as playing a piano sonata.

Hartley's contemporaries commonly contrasted mind to body, emphasizing the unity of consciousness and the freedom of the will. In contrast, Hartley advocated the 'mechanism of the mind' (Hartley, 1, Conclusion), and, by so doing, he abandoned the idea that mind acts independently of nerves and brain. It does not, however, follow that words such as 'choice', 'belief', and 'intent' have no meaning. To state this positively: that complex actions go from being deliberately learned to being secondarily automatic, and then become the basis for the voluntary performance of decomplex actions illustrates that the mechanism of the mind is more an achievement than a given. Our capacities to choose when and how to perform skilled (decomplex) actions depend upon the perfection of the complex actions that enter into them. As Hartley put it in a key formulation, 'All our voluntary powers are of the nature of memory' (Hartley, 1, prop. 90). For me to choose what to do, my body must remember how.

Hartley also offers a model of psychological development in his 'six classes of intellectual pleasures and pains'. These divide into two groups. The first group consists of imagination, the orientation toward objects as sources of pleasure or displeasure; ambition, whereby pleasure or pain derives from one's awareness of being an object of attention; and self-interest, the ego which tries to accommodate imagination and ambition. The second group consists of sympathy, the orientation of personal intersubjectivity, and theopathy, the person's relationship with the divine. (Like 'decomplex', the word 'theopathy' appears to be Hartley's invention.) Hartley calls the last orientation, the moral sense, the 'monitor' of sympathy and theopathy, their 'substitute upon emergent occasions' (Hartley, 2, prop. 74).

The self thus defined is epigenetic and transformative. Hartley states that the earlier orientations 'model' the ones that follow, and in turn the later orientations 'new-model' the earlier. Just as there are imaginative and ambitious forms of sympathy and theopathy, there are also sympathetic and theopathic forms of imagination and ambition. Which forms predominate depends upon the orientation that serves as the person's 'primary pursuit'. And given enough time, Hartley believes, sympathy and theopathy will become primary pursuits and new-model the self. Hartley thus offers a psychological account that supports his belief in universal salvation. Although liberation may take place only in a future life, no person is locked within selfishness—that is, in hell—forever.

The opening chapters of the *Observations* speak the language of Newtonian science. But as one progresses into the work, one encounters references to the 'everlasting gospel', 'perfect self-annihilation', and 'the pure love of God', recommendations of 'mental prayer', and quotations of select biblical passages, especially the promise of becoming 'partakers of divine nature' (2 Peter 1:4). All these place Hartley within the worlds of pietism and mysticism. In this aspect, his *Observations* is a religious epic that tells of the restoration of a fallen, fragmented, and self-alienated humanity to perfect manhood, in which all people, as members of the mystical body of Christ, will become 'new sets of senses, and perceptive powers, to each other, so as to increase each other's happiness without limits' (Hartley, 2, prop. 68). In writing this epic Hartley seeks to show that association 'has a tendency to reduce the state of those who have eaten of the tree of the knowledge of good and evil, back again to a paradisiacal one' (Hartley, 1, prop. 14). His theme is paradise regained.

Reception of the *Observations* Joseph Priestley wrote that studying Hartley's *Observations* was 'like entering upon *a new world*', and he confessed himself 'more indebted to this one treatise, than to all the books I ever read beside; the scriptures excepted' (Priestley, *Examination*, xix). In the century that followed Priestley's sense that Hartley had opened up a new world was shared by other scientific, social, and religious reformers. But the quality of their indebtedness drew on different aspects of the *Observations*.

For some, Hartley was the first to assay the science of psychology; others, especially Unitarians, revered Hartley as a moralist; Coleridge looked to Hartley both for inspiration and confirmation of his own early religious beliefs. Such was the range of response to a book that one can, with good reason, put on one's shelf next to James Mill's *Analysis of the Phenomena of the Human Mind* (1829)—or William Blake's 'Jerusalem'.

However, Priestley also lamented that 'many excellent articles … in this great work have been … lost to the world, in consequence of being published as parts of so very extensive a system' (Priestley, *Hartley's Theory*, v). As psychology and philosophy separated into academic specializations the extensiveness of the *Observations* made it difficult for the whole work to be fitted comfortably into either. In each case, if some of Hartley's ideas were accepted as properly psychological or philosophical, others were overlooked. But his observation that 'all our voluntary powers are of the nature of memory' should identify a central issue for both: that the mind–body of a person skilled at performing decomplex actions differs from that of an unskilled infant. Hartley's 'great work' thus calls the separation of psychology and philosophy into question. It also draws attention to academic psychology's aphasia concerning religion. Hartley's model of the self suggests that a science of human nature, to be complete, must be observant of the theopathic dimension of human experience.

Hartley died in Bath on 28 August 1757, probably from the stone. He was buried on 2 September 1757 in Old Sodbury church, Gloucestershire. RICHARD C. ALLEN

Sources R. C. Allen, *David Hartley on human nature* (1999) • D. Hartley, *Observations on man, his frame, his duty, and his expectations* (1749) • W. B. Trigg, 'The correspondence of Dr David Hartley and the Rev. John Lister', *Transactions of the Halifax Antiquarian Society* (1938), 230–78 • D. Hartley and J. Lister, correspondence, Calderdale Central Library, Halifax • *The private journal and literary remains of John Byrom*, ed. R. Parkinson, 2 vols. in 4 pts, Chetham Society, 32, 34, 40, 44 (1854–7) • J. S. Mill, review of Alexander Bain, *The senses and the intellect* and *The emotions and the will*, *EdinR*, 110 (1859), 287–321 • J. Priestley, *An examination of Dr Reid's 'Inquiry into the human mind on the principles of common sense', Dr Beattie's 'Essay on the nature and immutability of truth', and Dr Oswald's 'Appeal to common sense in behalf of religion'* (1774) • J. Priestley, *Hartley's theory of the human mind* (1775) • R. Warner, *Original letters, from Richard Baxter, Matthew Prior, Lord Bolingbroke, Alexander Pope, Dr. Cheyne, Dr. Hartley, etc.* (1817) • parish register (baptism), St John's, Halifax, 21/6/1705 • parish register (baptism, marriage), Saffron Walden • parish register (burial), St Mary, Bury St Edmunds, 22/7/1731 • parish register (marriage), Nowton, Suffolk, 25/8/1735 • parish register (burial), Gloucestershire, Old Sodbury, St John the Baptist, 2 Sept 1757
Archives priv. coll., family MSS | W. Yorks. AS, Calderdale, corresp. with John Lister
Likenesses J. Heath, stipple, pubd 1809 (after J. Shackleton), NPG [*see illus.*] • W. Blake, line engraving (after portrait by J. Shackleton), BM, NPG; repro. in Hartley, *Observations on man* (1791)
Wealth at death see will, PRO, PROB 11/832/346

Hartley, David (1731–1813), politician and inventor of fireproofing systems, was born in Bury St Edmunds, the eldest son of David *Hartley (*bap.* 1705, *d.* 1757), philosopher and physician, and only child of his first wife, Alice Rowley (*bap.* 1705, *d.* 1731), who died giving birth to him.

He had a half-brother and a half-sister from his father's second marriage, in 1735, to Elizabeth Packer (1713–1778). Hartley was educated privately and then at Sherborne School, Dorset. He matriculated on 6 April 1747 from Corpus Christi College, Oxford, where he studied medicine, science, and classics, and obtained his BA in 1750. From August 1753 he became a lifelong fellow of Merton College, Oxford; and in 1757 he studied medicine at Leiden in the Netherlands. In 1759 he joined Lincoln's Inn as a student, and in London he met Benjamin Franklin, who became a close and trusted friend.

In the 1760s Hartley started publishing pamphlets, and his first, *The Right of Appeal to Juries* (1763), was followed by a short series in which he attacked George Grenville's government. In 1765 he declined the position of Treasury secretary in Lord Rockingham's administration, declaring an aversion to office work; but as an expert on public finance, he still prepared a financial plan for Rockingham to follow. In 1768 he stood with John Bentinck for the parliamentary seat of Callington in Cornwall, but honourably withdrew on realizing that bribery would be required to win. Encouraged by his friend Sir George Savile, in 1774 he stood again for parliament, and was elected as a member for Hull, a position he held until 1780, when he lost the seat. Two years later he was re-elected and served the city until 1784, when on defeat he retired from politics and continued his political writings. These included *Thoughts on the Kingdom of Ireland* (1785) and *Argument on the French Revolution* (1794). He also edited two editions (1791 and 1801) of his father's *Observations on Man*.

In parliament Hartley was a consistent supporter of the Rockingham (later Fox) faction, the self-styled whig party. He made nearly one hundred speeches, and between 1775 and 1779 presented eight motions concerning the conciliation of the colonies. Some of his speeches were exceedingly long—one lasted over four hours—and it was said that 'his rising always operated like a dinner-bell' (*Memoirs of … Wraxall*, 3.124), and that 'he was unnecessarily minute in his details, feeble in his arguments and languid in his delivery' (*Bath Chronicle*, 23 Dec 1813). His opposition to the American War of Independence was robust, and from 1775 to 1777, in several speeches concerning America, he introduced proposals which he hoped would lead to the ending of slavery; an objective he always pursued, and which William Wilberforce, his fellow MP for Hull, finally achieved in 1807. After France entered the war, North sent commissioners in 1778 to treat for peace in Paris. Hartley, whose important *Letters on the American War* (1778) set out his views on the confrontation, also went to Paris, but unofficially and with no powers to negotiate. Although he met Franklin and Vergennes, the French foreign minister, he failed to realize that America would stand by its treaty with France. On his return he declared he had found a negotiable policy, naïvely expecting America to come back into the fold; but the war continued.

When Rockingham took office again in 1782, Sir George Savile, Hartley's political patron in Hull, asked him to include Hartley in the peace negotiations, but when Rockingham offered him a suitable position, Hartley turned it

down. After Rockingham's death, in 1782, Lord Shelburne's administration drew up a preliminary peace treaty, which Hartley opposed. Then in 1783, after long discussions with Lord North, whose coalition government had come to power, Hartley was sent to act as plenipotentiary in Paris. Negotiations followed and agreement was eventually reached, but with many concessions to America. The final treaty, which basically ratified the preliminary treaty, failed to fulfil all Hartley's hopes, especially on trade reciprocity. Nevertheless the document was signed in Paris on 3 September 1783 by Hartley, Franklin, and other signatories.

Apart from politics, Hartley was interested in science, and in 1774 he published his ideas on fireproofing in *An account of the method of securing buildings and ships against fire*. He received a grant of £2500 to experiment with a three-storey house which he built at Putney Heath, Surrey. Six trials were held in 1776. George III and members of the court attended one trial, and the lord mayor of London, City officials, parliamentary members, and the public were spectators at the others. Hartley's method was to sandwich thin sheets of iron between two layers of floorboards. He then set fire to various parts of the house, including a room below or beside one where his visitors could remain in reasonable comfort and safety. As the system worked, Hartley was granted the freedom of the City of London in 1777, and a commemorative obelisk was erected near the house, on Putney Heath. In 1792 he published *Proposals for the security of spectators in any public theatre against fire*, which probably led to the installation of the first theatre safety curtain.

Hartley never married and was somewhat eccentric in dress and habit. While an MP in the 1780s he rented a house in Golden Square, London. He also owned a house in Bath and one at Little Sodbury in Gloucestershire, both of which had previously been his father's. He was a politician whose ideas were often far-sighted but whose political judgement was sometimes deficient. He died at home in Belvedere, Lansdown, Bath, Somerset, on 19 December 1813, and was buried in the family vault at Little Sodbury, Gloucestershire, on 27 December.

CHRISTOPHER F. LINDSEY

Sources G. H. Guttridge, 'David Hartley, MP: an advocate of conciliation, 1774–1783', *University of California Publications in History*, 14/3 (1926), 231–340 · 'Some account of the public trials made by David Hartley, esq., member of parliament for Kingston upon Hull to evince the efficacy of a new, cheap and early method invented by him, for preserving houses, ships etc. built with the most combustible materials, from fire', *Annual Register* (1776), 244–8 · *GM*, 1st ser., 84/1 (1814), 95 · *N&Q*, 5th ser., 6 (1876), 177, 217 · inscription, Hartley fireproof house memorial obelisk, Kingston Road, Putney Heath, London · Foster, *Alum. Oxon.* · J. Pollock, *Wilberforce* (1977) · *DNB* · J. Brooke, 'Hartley, David', HoP, *Commons, 1754–90* · will, PRO, PROB 11/1552, fols. 160a–165 · J. J. Norwich, *The architecture of southern England* (1985), 28 · D. Gerhold, ed., *Putney and Roehampton past* (1994), 49–50 · St James's, Piccadilly, 1782, Rate Book D 803, 45 · private information (2004) [Merton Oxf.] · *Bath Chronicle* (23 Dec 1813) · *Bath Chronicle* (30 Dec 1813) · J. Black, *War for America: the fight for independence, 1775–1783* (1998) · *The historical and the posthumous memoirs of Sir Nathaniel William Wraxall, 1772–1784*, ed. H. B. Wheatley, 5 vols. (1884) · D. Gerhold, *Villas and mansions of Roehampton and Putney Heath* (1997)

Archives Berks. RO, corresp. and papers · BL, letters · L. Cong., MSS · U. Mich., Clements L., corresp. | American Philosophical Society, Philadelphia, Franklin MSS · Harvard U., Arthur Lee MSS · Harvard U., Sparks MSS · L. Cong., Franklin MSS · LRO · N. Yorks. CRO, corresp. with Christopher Wyvill · Notts. Arch., corresp., mainly with John Hewett, incl. testimonial of Sir George Savile · U. Nott. L., letters to duke of Portland

Likenesses G. Romney, portrait, 1783, probably priv. coll. · L. Vaslet, pastel drawing, 1789, Merton Oxf. · J. Walker, mezzotint (after G. Romney), BM · portrait (after engraving by J. Walker; after G. Romney, 1783), Hull Corporation

Wealth at death probably very wealthy: will, PRO, PROB 11/1552, fols. 160a–165

Hartley, Dorothy Rosaman (1893–1985), historian, was born on 4 October 1893 at the grammar school, Skipton, Yorkshire, the youngest of the three children of the Revd Edward Tomson Hartley (1849–1923) and his wife, Amy Lucy Eddy (1853–1932). The Revd Hartley was headmaster of the grammar school; his wife came from Froncysylltau, near Llangollen in north Wales, where the family owned quarries and property. Dorothy was educated at a convent in Skipton until 1904, when her father retired through failing sight and became rector of a country parish at Rempstone, Nottinghamshire. She then went to Loughborough high school and afterwards to Nottingham Art School. Her education was interrupted by the First World War, when she worked in a munitions factory, but in 1919 she entered the Regent Street Polytechnic in London where she was a prize pupil; she returned to Nottingham Art School as a teacher in 1920–22 and subsequently taught in London.

During this period Dorothy Hartley began writing. Batsford published her six-volume *Life and Work of the Peoples of England*, written with M. M. V. Elliot, between 1925 and 1931, and in 1930 Knopf published the *Old Book*, a medieval compilation. She had a restless curiosity, and in her 1931 book, *Medieval Costume and Life*, not only recreated the clothes of peasants depicted in old manuscripts, but used pictures of herself wearing them. She temporarily abandoned English rural life in 1931 to travel by car from Cairo to the Congo, and the photographs which she took on her journey were exhibited at the Imperial Institute.

Between 1932 and 1936 Dorothy Hartley toured the British Isles by bicycle and car, with pen, pencil, and camera, writing weekly articles for the *Daily Sketch* on country people and their trades. Her articles covered such themes as horse-ploughing, bread making, and clog making. They used the calendar months as their basis, and were strongly influenced by the sixteenth-century agricultural writer and poet Thomas Tusser. Dorothy Hartley was a keen photographer, developing and printing her own photographs. The material gleaned on these travels went into her many other books and articles, which eventually covered many aspects and periods of English rural life. Medieval culture always held a particular fascination for her and she toured Ireland in the footsteps of the twelfth-century prelate Gerald of Wales. This led to her book *An Irish Holiday* (1938).

In 1933 Dorothy Hartley made her home in a cottage at Froncysylltau and this estate remained her base thereafter. Yet, despite her long residence in Wales, and apart from one book on her Irish journey, she dealt only with English life. During the Second World War she contributed to the publications of the United Nations and began work on the book for which she is probably best known, *Food in England* (1954), a treasury of information on the gathering, storing, and cooking of food from the twelfth to the twentieth centuries. The clarity and detail of text and her charming illustrations made it accessible to a wide public.

In the post-war years she also taught at University College and Goldsmiths' College in London, performed on television with Philip Harben, and advised on the BBC *Archers* programmes. In between these professional activities she juggled with the maintenance of her house in Froncysylltau and its six cottages which were occupied by a constant stream of tenants and visitors. In 1964 she published a major book, *Water in England*. This remarkable work is full of valuable information on all manner of related phenomena such as holy springs, well digging, leather jugs, spa hotels, and suchlike.

Dorothy Hartley never married; living alone and in a remote place and coming from a generation more accustomed to communicate by the pen than by telephone, letters became her principal form of contact with the wider world. Much of her thought and writing was engaged with the minute details of the relationship between an object and its function—the scythe to the height of wheat cut, the exact width of a linen sheet to the dimensions of the linen press. Part of the great strength of her major books lay not only in her own very exact, decorative yet diagrammatic explanatory drawings, but in the ways these were allied to her text. Her own collections of documents and illustrations of early agricultural life led ultimately to a monumental photographic bequest to the Reading Museum of English Rural Life, reflecting the pleasure that she had from her correspondence with the keeper and her visits to the centre, from its pre-war conception to her death. Dorothy Hartley died from cancer at Fron House, Froncysylltau, on 22 October 1985.

During her lifetime Dorothy Hartley acquired an unrivalled knowledge of the life, work, and food of people living in England since medieval times. She proceeded to document this field through her writings, drawings, and photographs. In a number of books, which have become minor classics, Hartley produced some of the most absorbing and readable accounts of the history and folklore of country life and food ever published. Arguably her best work, and the one for which she will be remembered, is *Food in England*. This book has continued to be republished, and is as full of magic and potions as any medieval herbal.

MARY WONDRAUSCH

Sources private information (2004) · b. cert. · d. cert. · D. Hartley, *Food in England* (1954) · *The Times* (6 Nov 1985)
Archives Centre of English Rural Life, Reading, Berkshire, photographs | priv. coll., letters · priv. coll., letters and documents
Wealth at death £42,842: double probate, 7 Sept 1986, *CGPLA Eng. & Wales*

Hartley [*née* White], **Elizabeth** (1750/51–1824), actress, was born in Berrow, Somerset, in 1750 or early 1751, the daughter of James and Eleanor White. According to a memoir in the *London Magazine* (October 1773), she was a chambermaid in a gentleman's house and became the mistress of a Mr Hartley, who persuaded her to take up acting in order to supplement their income. There is no record of a marriage to Hartley, and Mrs Hartley resumed her family name of White on her retirement from the stage in 1780. Little is known of her early stage career until her first appearance in Edinburgh, on 4 December 1771, when she appeared as Monimia in Thomas Otway's *The Orphan*. In the summer of 1772 she made her début at Bristol in the title role of Nicholas Rowe's *Jane Shore*. David Garrick had become interested in employing her at Drury Lane, and sent the actor John Moody to watch her perform. On 26 July 1772 Moody wrote to George Garrick:

> Mrs. Hartley is a good figure, with a handsome, small face, and very much freckled; her hair red and her neck and shoulders well turned. There is not the least harmony in her voice; but when forced (which she never fails to do on every occasion) is loud and strong, but such an inarticulate gabble that you must be acquainted with her part to understand her … there is a superficial glare about her that may carry her through a few nights; but be assured she cannot last long. (*Private Correspondence*, 1.476)

In fact Moody's appraisal of her work was of little consequence to Mrs Hartley, since she was already engaged at Covent Garden, where she made her début on 5 October 1772, as Jane Shore. The *Town and Country Magazine* said, 'She is deserving of much praise, her figure elegant, her countenance pleasing and expressive, her voice in general melodious, and her action just' (*Town and Country Magazine*, 1772, 545). In her first London season she also played Queen Catherine in *Henry VIII* (6 November 1772), the title role in the original production of William Mason's *Elfrida* (21 November 1772), Orellana in Arthur Murphy's *Alzuma* (23 February 1773), and Rosamund in Thomas Hull's *Henry II* (1 May 1773). William Hawkins wrote that, on her début, 'She was received with respectable marks of applause by a very brilliant audience', and went on to say:

> She is the finest figure on the London Stage: therefore it is not to be wondered a lady endued with such requisites for this profession should gain great applause, had she absolutely little or no merit. But this is not Mrs. Hartley's case … I believe [she] has given the public incontestable proofs of her rising genius. The only fault I can discover in this Lady is, her voice is somewhat harsh, and she is sometimes apt to wind it beyond the bounds of harmony. (Hawkins, 52)

She remained popular with audiences throughout her career. According to Leslie and Taylor, 'The crowd flocked to see Mrs. Hartley kneel in *Elfrida* as they flocked to see Mrs. Siddons walk in her sleep as Lady Macbeth' (Leslie and Taylor, 41). She was the subject of a number of paintings by Sir Joshua Reynolds, who complimented her on her beauty when she sat for him. She responded with laughter, saying, 'Nay, my face may be well enough for shape; but sure, 'tis as freckled as a toad's belly' (ibid.). She retired at the end of the 1779–80 season, and died at King Street, Woolwich, on 26 January 1824, in 'easy circumstances', at the

Elizabeth Hartley (1750/51–1824), by Sir Joshua Reynolds, 1771 [*Nymph with Young Bacchus*]

age of seventy-three, 'her merits, during her public services, having procured her a handsome inheritance' (*New Monthly Magazine*, 12, 1824, 425). She was buried at the Union Chapel graveyard, Woolwich, on 6 February. An obituary claims that 'Her extreme beauty and the truth and nature of her acting attracted universal admiration, and caused her to rank the highest (as a female) in her profession previous to the appearance of Mrs. Siddons'.

C. CONROY

Sources Highfill, Burnim & Langhans, *BDA* · W. Hawkins, *Miscellanies in prose and verse, containing candid and impartial observations on the principal performers belonging to the two Theatres-Royal, from January 1773 to May 1775* (1775) · W. C. Russell, *Representative actors* [1888] · *Illustrated Sporting and Dramatic News* (12 April 1879) · Theatre Museum, London, Jan 1824; 2 Feb 1824 · *The thespian dictionary, or, Dramatic biography of the present age*, 2nd edn (1805) · T. Marshall, *Lives of the most celebrated actors and actresses* [1846–7] · Genest, *Eng. stage* · *The private correspondence of David Garrick*, ed. J. Boaden, 2 vols. (1831–2) · *London Magazine*, 42 (1773), 471–2 · *London Magazine*, 9 (1824), 336 · C. R. Leslie and T. Taylor, *Life and times of Sir Joshua Reynolds*, 2 vols. (1865) · *Town and Country Magazine*, 4 (1772) · *The letters of David Garrick*, ed. D. M. Little and G. M. Kahrl, 3 vols. (1963) · *Memoirs of Mrs Inchbald*, ed. J. Boaden, 2 vols. (1833) · H. Bromley, *A catalogue of engraved British portraits* (1793) · playbills, The Theatre Museum, Tavistock Street, London · parish register, Union Street chapel, Woolwich, London [burial]

Archives BL, MSS

Likenesses J. Reynolds, oils, 1771, Tate collection [*see illus.*] · R. Houston, mezzotint, pubd 1774 (after H. D. Hamilton), BM, NPG · S. W. Reynolds, mezzotint, pubd 1834 (after J. Reynolds), BM · R. Cosway, portrait (*Venus Victrix*) · A. Kauffman, oils, Garr. Club · J. Roberts, drawings, BM · theatrical prints, BM, NPG

Wealth at death easy circumstances: *New Monthly Magazine*, 12 (1824), 425

Hartley, Sir Frank (1911–1997), pharmacist, was born on 5 January 1911 in Nelson, Lancashire, the son of Robinson King Hartley (d. c.1916), a plumber, and his wife, Mary, née Holt. He attended Nelson municipal secondary school and in 1926 obtained the northern universities' school certificate. His ambition was to be a schoolteacher but his bursary from the county council was withdrawn when it was discovered that he was deaf in one ear. On the advice of his physics teacher he entered pharmacy and served a three-year apprenticeship with J. Hayhurst in his shop in Railway Street, Nelson. At the end of his apprenticeship he competed for three scholarships—the Leverhulme, Manchester, and Jacob Bell—taking first place in each. He accepted the Jacob Bell award, which enabled him to study for the diploma of pharmaceutical chemist at the School of Pharmacy in Bloomsbury Square, London. He qualified as a pharmacist in 1932. He then acted as a demonstrator at the School of Pharmacy while studying for a degree in chemistry at Birkbeck College, University of London, from where he graduated with first-class honours in 1936. On 22 December 1937 he married Lydia May England (1909/10–1996), daughter of Mark England, a carpenter, of Hadleigh, Essex. They had two sons.

Following his marriage, Hartley continued to teach at the School of Pharmacy and worked for the PhD degree under the supervision of Professor W. Linnell and Professor S. Sugden. His doctorate was awarded in 1941. In 1940 he became chief chemist at the British laboratories of Organon, a Dutch company involved in the manufacture of steroids. In 1943 he was appointed secretary to the Therapeutic Research Corporation, which had the important wartime task of maximizing penicillin production and initiating research into antibiotics. He also acted as secretary to the penicillin committee of the Ministry of Supply.

By the end of the Second World War Hartley had gained sufficient experience to take an active role in dealing with the challenges and problems following the introduction of antibiotics and chemotherapeutic agents. He embarked on a career that did much to advance pharmaceutical science and education in the new era of medicine. In 1946 he became director of research and scientific services at British Drug Houses, involved in research into the chemistry of vitamin B12 and the first generation of contraceptive steroids. His experience with the clinical assessment of oral contraceptives drew his attention to the problem of the adverse reactions of drugs, and he became deeply involved in matters concerning the quality and safety of medicines. He became a member of the Poisons Board in 1958 and in 1963 he joined Sir Derrick Dunlop's committee on the safety of drugs. He was appointed to the Medicines Commission which was established by the Medicines Act of 1968 and became its vice-chairman in 1974. In 1970 he was the first pharmacist to be appointed chairman of the British Pharmacopoeia Commission. Between 1964 and 1980 he was the UK delegate to the European pharmacopoeia commission. In each of these posts he exhibited his considerable knowledge of the wide range of sciences involved in the composition of

a pharmacopoeia. His expertise in matters related to the safety of medicines was often called upon. In 1972 he served on a committee dealing with the prevention of microbial contamination of pharmaceuticals and on a committee of inquiry on contamination of infusion fluids, following a number of patient deaths.

In 1962 Hartley returned to academic life, succeeding W. H. Linnell as dean of the School of Pharmacy, which had become a school of the University of London. He was appointed chairman of the scientific advisory committee of the Pharmaceutical Society of Great Britain in 1964, and a year later was elected president of the Royal Institute of Chemistry. He took an active role in the affairs of the University of London. He became a member of the senate and a member of the court, was elected deputy vice-chancellor in 1973, and was made vice-chancellor in 1976. In 1979 he became the first pharmacist to be made an honorary member of the Royal Society of Physicians and he was similarly honoured a year later by the Royal College of Surgeons. He received the charter gold medal of the Pharmaceutical Society, was elected an honorary fellow of the Imperial College of Science, and received honorary degrees from the universities of Warwick, Strathclyde, and London. He was appointed CBE in 1970 and was knighted for services to pharmacy in 1977.

Hartley served on numerous committees and boards, always exhibiting a mastery of the subject in hand and an ability to confront the major issues involved. He was a good-humoured man but could be an overpowering chairman, invariably living up to his reputation for prolixity. He died of heart failure at his home, 16 Town Thorns, Easenhall, Rugby, Warwickshire, on 26 January 1997. He was survived by his sons, Peter (a canon of the Church of England) and Frank (a chemist and vice-chancellor of Cranfield University), his wife, Lydia, having predeceased him by a month.   M. P. EARLES

Sources WWW · *Pharmaceutical Journal*, 258 (1997), 164 · H. Grainger, *Pharmaceutical Journal*, 258 (1997), 238 · J. Stenlake, *Pharmaceutical Journal*, 258 (1997), 266 · *Pharmaceutical Journal*, 212 (1974), 463 · *The Independent* (15 Feb 1997) · *The Times* (25 Feb 1997) · m. cert. · d. cert.
Likenesses photograph, repro. in *Pharmaceutical Journal* · photograph, repro. in *The Independent* · photograph, repro. in *The Times*
Wealth at death £222,174: probate, 24 July 1997, *CGPLA Eng. & Wales*

Hartley, Sir Harold Brewer (1878–1972), physical chemist and industrial consultant, was born on 3 September 1878 in London, the only son of Harold Thomas Hartley, a mineral water manufacturer and later a partner in the publishing firm of Emmot, Hartley & Co., of Fleet Street, and his wife, Katie, daughter of Francis Brewer. After schooling at Mortimer College and three years at Dulwich College, where he was a pupil of the Balliol chemist H. B. Baker (1862–1935), in 1897 he entered Balliol College, Oxford, on a Brackenbury scholarship. In 1900 he graduated with first-class honours in natural science (chemistry and mineralogy), and in 1901 was appointed tutorial fellow of Balliol in the place of his tutor, Sir John Conroy, who had just died.

Sir Harold Brewer Hartley (1878–1972), by Bassano, 1947

Besides the usual tutorial and lecturing duties Hartley had the responsibility of teaching in the Balliol–Trinity laboratory which the two colleges had jointly set up twenty years earlier. In 1904 it was arranged that the laboratory should develop for the university a course in the then novel subject of physical chemistry, and this later achieved a notable reputation. In 1906 Hartley married Gertrude Mary Forster Smith (d. 1970), daughter of the historian Arthur Lionel *Smith, later master of Balliol. They had one son, Air Marshal Sir Christopher Hartley, and one daughter.

At the outbreak of the First World War Hartley joined the 7th Leicestershire regiment. In June 1915, when there was great anxiety over the lack of an adequate defence against German gas attacks and a decision was made to appoint three chemists as specialist advisers to the three fighting armies, he was promoted to captain and chosen as chemical adviser to the Third Army. His responsibilities were varied, and included the interpretation of intelligence on the chemical capacities of the enemy and participation in planning chemical warfare operations, as well as the more mundane tasks connected with anti-gas defence. In 1917, having been promoted to lieutenant-colonel he was made assistant director gas services (ADGS), a senior position at the army's general headquarters. As ADGS he issued a monthly bulletin, *Gas Warfare*, which was circulated to officers and civil servants concerned with chemical warfare, and which later came to form a valuable part of the historical record. He was three times mentioned in dispatches, won an MC (1916), and was appointed OBE. He attained the rank of brigadier-general in 1918, was created CBE in 1919, and was appointed controller of the chemical warfare department at the Ministry of Munitions.

In 1919 Hartley was one of the members of the Holland committee, charged with advising the government on the future of chemical weapons. Throughout the inter-war years he was the senior scientific adviser to the government on issues relating to chemical weapons and chemical defence, serving on the chemical warfare board until 1950. He was sceptical about the more far-reaching claims made for the military potential of chemical weaponry, contending that with effective defence mechanisms and good training most chemical attacks could be withstood. By the same token, however, he disagreed with the widely held view that chemical warfare was qualitatively different from previous, supposedly more 'civilized', methods of warfare.

Hartley returned to Oxford in 1919, keen to start work in physical chemistry, and was fortunate in having as pupils a succession of able young Balliol scholars. Most notable was Cyril Hinshelwood, later to receive a Nobel prize and to become president of the Royal Society. In the 1920s Hartley realized that science teachers in schools had little opportunity to learn physical chemistry, or how to teach it. For several years, therefore, he organized summer schools at Balliol with lectures and laboratory work on the subject. These were a great success and helped to raise teaching standards throughout the country.

Hartley conducted undergraduate tutorials in a rather unorthodox manner. No formal instruction was given; he expected his students to instruct him. He combined his senior fellowship at Balliol with a job as director of research at the Gas Light and Coke Company (later the North Thames Gas Board); this meant that his tutorials were given in the early hours of the day or late in the evening. He directed his students towards the history of chemistry in its growth to a rational subject and stressed the need for technique and precision in measurements. This appealed to him more than speculative theories. Mathematical treatments of any complexity were a closed subject, and he often relied on his more able pupils for an introduction to the rapid post-war developments. In spite of this handicap his powers of judgement on broader aspects and his ability to concentrate on essential issues prevented him from falling behind during the 1920s.

In research Hartley returned to an earlier interest in the electrical conductivity of solutions. The subject then appeared to many as one already supplied with enough useful data, but the situation was transformed in 1923 by the publication of the Debye–Hückel theory. Realizing that a study of non-aqueous solutions afforded the best test, Hartley began a systematic series of conductivity measurements of salts dissolved in alcohols and other organic solvents. This body of work made a substantial contribution towards the understanding of ionic solutions, for which Hartley was in 1926 elected a fellow of the Royal Society.

In 1919 and again in 1921 Hartley served on official missions to Germany, to investigate the chemical side of German wartime activities and to debrief its leading practitioners. He was impressed by the high scientific qualifications of the leading German industrial chemists and the level of organized government support for the industry. The development of chemical industry now seemed to him to be of vital importance to Britain; in 1922 he joined the Society of Chemical Engineers and he stayed on the board of the Gas Light and Coke Company until 1945, being deputy governor during the Second World War. The efficient use of fuels occupied his mind, and in 1929 he joined the Fuel Research Board of the Department of Scientific and Industrial Research, acting as chairman from 1932 to 1947.

In 1930 Hartley decided to resign from his tutorial fellowship and to accept a full-time post of vice-president and director of research of the railway system which had been reorganized as the London, Midland, and Scottish Railway Company. His motives for the move were complex, involving the possibility that his electrochemical researches offered few new lines of enquiry, as well as his position within Balliol College, with which he was less happy than he had been, and his desire to work to unite science and industrial technology. In 1934 he was appointed chairman of the newly formed Railway Air Services. This led to the chairmanship of British European Airways (1946–7) and the British Overseas Airways Corporation (BOAC) (1947–9), and a lifelong interest in air travel. To his regret he was removed from the BOAC post by the then minister, and then became the first chairman of the Electricity Supply Council (1949–52), continuing (later as deputy chairman) until 1954. He attracted distinguished scientists on to the council, and later, as consultant to the Central Electricity Generating Board, he was active in furthering its research.

Hartley constantly urged the upgrading of British chemical engineering. In 1951–2 and 1954–5 he was an active president of the Institution of Chemical Engineers and was awarded its Osborne–Reynolds medal (1954). The Society of Instrument Technology elected him president (1957–61), and a Hartley medal and lecture were introduced. The construction firm John Brown appointed him adviser (1954–61), and enabled him to develop his views of the importance of replacing batch chemical and biochemical processes by continuous plant, and of the need for high-level studies of methods of precise control. Between 1935 and 1950 Hartley was chairman of a number of World Power conferences and associated meetings and organizations.

Hartley had a long connection with the Goldsmiths' Company and became its prime warden in 1941–2. Through his influence the company provided powerful support for historical research in science and the preservation of instruments and records. He had always been attracted by the problems facing nineteenth-century chemists, for whom he had great admiration, and whose work he described in various publications. He was a particularly active editor of *Notes and Records of the Royal Society* from 1952 to 1970.

As a judge of character Hartley was quick to distinguish the efficient from the inefficient. He never argued with opponents, but faced them with a blank blandness. His numerous chairmanships were efficiently conducted, and it needed unusual strength and persistence among members of a meeting to prevent agreement on the proposals he would put forward. His friends coined the verb 'to hartle' to describe his manner of getting his way with others. While those who agreed with him admired his abilities, others sometimes felt that they had been treated with a degree of intolerance. He was knighted in 1928 and created KCVO in 1944, GCVO in 1957, and CH in 1967.

Hartley's activities persisted undiminished almost until his death. His *Studies in the History of Chemistry*, said to have been commissioned in 1901, was finally published in 1971. For the last thirty years of his life he suffered increasing arthritic trouble in the legs, until he was finally confined to a bedroom in a London nursing home. This he treated as an office, writing and interviewing with an energy and clarity which astonished his colleagues. He appreciated objects of neatness, symmetry, and colour. As a young man he enjoyed demonstrating the brilliant colours of thin crystals in polarized light, skilfully using a projection microscope with a heating stage, and he once entertained Kelvin and Stokes with such a show, while he was still an undergraduate. However, his increasingly busy later life did not allow much time for these interests. Hartley died on 9 September 1972.   E. J. BOWEN, rev. K. D. WATSON

Sources A. G. Ogston, *Memoirs FRS*, 19 (1973), 349–73 · R. V. Jones, 'Harold Brewer Hartley, 1878–1972', *Notes and Records of the Royal Society of London*, 27 (1973), 181–4 · L. F. Haber, *The poisonous cloud: chemical warfare in the First World War* (1986) · 'The Royal Society club dinner … in celebration of … Sir Harold Hartley', *Notes and Records of the Royal Society of London*, 24 (1969), 146–55 · *CGPLA Eng. & Wales* (1972)

Archives Balliol Oxf., corresp. and papers · CAC Cam., corresp. and papers · NRA, priv. coll., notebooks | CAC Cam., corresp. with A. V. Hill; corresp. with R. V. Jones · CUL, corresp. with Gordon Sutherland · ICL, corresp. with Dennis Gabor · Rice University, Houston, Texas, Woodson Research Center, corresp. with Julian Huxley · RS, letters to Christina Colvin · U. Oxf., physical chemistry laboratory · U. Reading L., corresp. with E. J. Russell | SOUND RS, sound recordings

Likenesses W. Stoneman, photograph, 1946, RS · Bassano, photograph, 1947, NPG [*see illus.*] · C. Hinshelwood, oils, c.1958 (after photograph?), RS · portrait, Worshipful Company of Goldsmiths; repro. in Ogston, *Memoirs FRS*, facing p. 349; copy, RS · two photographs, RS

Wealth at death £48,406: probate, 7 Nov 1972, *CGPLA Eng. & Wales*

Hartley, Henry Robinson (1777–1850), eccentric and philanthropist, was born on 12 November 1777 in Southampton, second and only surviving child of Henry Hartley (1731–1800) and his wife, Susanna, *née* Lavender (1742–1821). His father inherited a prosperous wine business from a childless uncle, George Robinson, and, despite intermittent service as mayor of Southampton and as a justice of the peace, appears to have been a taciturn and retiring individual. The atmosphere in the Hartley home was strict, probably reflecting a strong Calvinist faith.

Hartley attended Southampton grammar school (from about 1787) where he exhibited pronounced intellectual talents, although he did not attend a university. Scholarly interests were to dominate his life and he showed little aptitude for other occupations. Upon leaving school, in 1794 or 1795, Hartley lived at home, chafing at its restraints. He adopted, and briefly practised, a philosophy of libertinism, possibly based on the French *philosophes'* conception of personal liberty, fuelling an adolescent rebellion against a puritanical father (Anderson, 77). This phase of Hartley's youth left him with a distaste for the restrictions of English society and with a severe venereal infection which would cause him great suffering throughout his life and may have increased his susceptibility to depression.

On 24 November 1798 Hartley married Celia Ann Crowcher (1779–1848), a chance acquaintance, over the objections of his parents. The failure of this marriage further encouraged him to emigrate, but ill health and a deep attachment to his native Southampton made him hesitate. The marriage was annulled in 1802, after Celia had given birth to a daughter. The child was almost certainly not Hartley's and was never acknowledged by him.

Upon the death of his mother in 1821, Hartley inherited a considerable fortune and continued to live a reclusive and scholarly existence in his family home in Southampton. Unable to accept any change in his neighbourhood and irritated by the presence of small businesses in his district, Hartley quarrelled with his neighbours, closed his house, and travelled to Calais in 1825, where he lived until 1838. Unable to settle, he returned to England, living in Southwark, London, between 1838 and 1846. In 1842 he made a will leaving the bulk of his estate to the city of Southampton to preserve his house as a museum and to promote the study of his favourite subjects: natural history, astronomy, antiquities, classics, and oriental literature.

In 1846 Hartley returned to Calais where his health continued to deteriorate. He died there on 24 May 1850 of cardiac ailments and complications of a stricture of the urinary tract which had afflicted him since his youth. He was buried in London in a vault in New Bunhill Fields, a burial-ground for dissenters.

Hartley's biographer describes him as an eighteenth-century scholar and dilettante, alienated by the commercial and industrial expansion of the nineteenth century (Anderson, 202). His existence was certainly unhappy and would have remained obscure were it not for the bequest to Southampton. The estate was valued at approximately £110,000. The will was contested in chancery, principally by Celia Hartley's daughter, Sarah. The claimants eventually accepted a settlement but the sum remaining to the corporation of Southampton was less than half the original amount.

After much debate, the city used the bequest to establish the Hartley Institution (1862) which combined a museum, library, and venue for public lectures. The institution evolved in a pattern familiar in the nineteenth century, becoming Hartley College (1896), Hartley University College (1902), University College of Southampton (1914), and the University of Southampton (1952). Notwithstanding the intentions of his bequest, Hartley's house was demolished and, except in his association with the university, Hartley has been largely forgotten, even in his native Southampton.   ELIZABETH J. MORSE

Sources A. Anderson, *Hartleyana: being some account of the life and opinions of Henry Robinson Hartley, scholar, naturalist, eccentric and founder of the University of Southampton* (1987) · A. T. Patterson, *The University of Southampton: a centenary history of the evolution and development of the University of Southampton, 1862–1962* (1962) · *Annual Register* (1850)
Archives U. Southampton L. | PRO, affidavit of William Devereux, C 31/1179/69 · PRO, examination of Elizabeth Froggett, C 121/271
Likenesses portrait (aged nine), U. Southampton L.
Wealth at death £83,000: Anderson, *Hartleyana*

Hartley, James (1745–1799), army officer in the East India Company, had a brother, Samuel, and a sister, Mary, but little else is known of his family. He entered the military service of the Bombay presidency in 1764. In 1765 he took part in expeditions against the piratical strongholds of Rairi and Malwan on the Malabar coast. By 1768 he had reached the rank of lieutenant, and in October 1770 he was made aide-de-camp to the governor of Bombay. He superintended the disembarkation of the detachment which took Broach in November 1772, and in July 1774 he gained the rank of captain and the command of the fourth battalion of Bombay sepoys.

The interesting part of Hartley's career began with the First Anglo-Maratha War. In February 1775 he was sent to co-operate with Colonel Keating in Gujarat. But the Bengal government put an end to the war in August, and Hartley, with the rest of the English forces, returned to Bombay. Three years later hostilities were resumed. The Bombay government now sent an army into the Konkan (the coastal strip south of Bombay), with orders to march up the ghats to attack Poona, the capital of the Maratha confederacy, 70 miles inland from Bombay. An advance party of six companies of grenadier sepoys under Captain Stewart first took possession of the Bhor Ghat (the pass up onto the Deccan plateau), where they were joined by the main army under Colonel Charles Egerton. Hartley had been offered the post of quartermaster-general to the army, but he preferred to take his place at the head of his battalion. On 4 January 1779 Captain Stewart was killed in a skirmish at Karli, and Hartley was appointed to succeed him in command of the six companies of grenadiers. On 9 January the army continued their march, and reached Talegaon, only 18 miles from Poona. But John Carnac, a former general in Bengal but now a member of the Bombay council and civil commissioner with the Bombay expeditionary force, became increasingly alarmed at the increasing numbers of Marathas, and determined on a retreat. Hartley objected to this proposal, but was overruled, and the retreat began on 11 January. Hartley's reserve was directed to form the rear guard. At daybreak on 12 January the Marathas attacked the retreating army in force. The main energy of their attack was directed at the rear, where Hartley's sepoy grenadiers stoutly covered the retreat; the

Maratha commander, Sindhia, described them admiringly as 'a red wall, no sooner beaten down than it was built up again' (Cadell, 95). Hartley in vain protested against the convention of Wadgaon, by which the Bombay expeditionary force was allowed to retire unmolested in exchange for the surrender of their ally Raghunath Rao. When Hartley arrived in Bombay in the spring of 1779, he was universally regarded as having saved the army from annihilation. He was raised to the rank of lieutenant-colonel, preceding two majors, and was appointed to the command of the European infantry on the Bombay establishment. However, the convention was repudiated by the supreme council at Calcutta, and the war with the Marathas was resumed. In December 1779 Hartley was sent north to Gujarat with a small detachment to act under Colonel Thomas Goddard, who commanded an expeditionary force sent from Bengal to aid Bombay. Hartley led the storming party which captured Ahmadabad on 15 February 1780. In May he was recalled to Bombay, from where he was sent to screen the exits from the ghats in the Konkan against Maratha incursions while Goddard continued the campaign in the north. Twice during 1780 Hartley's force drove back vastly superior numbers of Marathas (2000 against 20,000). In December he was ordered to hold the Marathas off while Goddard besieged Bassein, a strategically vital fortified town 30 miles north of Bombay on the coast. Hartley successfully held the line, defeating a Maratha attempt to raise the siege on 10–12 December, and killing the enemy general in the process.

Hartley continued to act as military commandant of the Konkan when a dispatch arrived from London acknowledging his services but declaring his recent promotion as lieutenant-colonel informal, and that this commission would be suspended until those who were his seniors should have been first promoted. Hartley quit the army, deeply hurt, and in December 1781 started for England to lay his case before the court of directors. The court refused to make any concession, but ultimately recommended him to the king, who gave him the lieutenant-colonelcy of the 75th regiment of foot in the royal army.

In April 1788 Hartley returned to India with his regiment; he was appointed quartermaster-general of the Bombay army and a member of the military board. On the outbreak of war with Tipu Sultan of Mysore in 1790 he received command of a detachment sent to the coast of Cochin to aid the East India Company's ally the raja of Travancore. In May Hartley received orders to invest Palghatcherry, an important fortress dominating the pass which led through the Western Ghats into Mysore. On arriving within 40 miles of the place, Hartley heard that it had already surrendered to the Madras army under General Meadows. He none the less continued his march, and occupied himself partly in collecting supplies for the main army at Trichinopoly, and partly in watching any movement of Tipu's troops to the south-west. On 10 December, with small losses to his own force, he inflicted a crushing defeat on vastly superior forces under Hussain Ali, Tipu's general, at Calicut. The remnant of the beaten army was pursued to the fortress of Ferokh, where it surrendered.

In January 1791 Hartley joined General Robert Abercromby, now commanding the company and king's troops in the west, to march up the ghats to assist the governor-general and overall commander-in-chief, Lord Cornwallis, in besieging Tipu's capital at Seringapatam. However, the siege had to be suspended because supplies for the besiegers could not be sustained, and the Bombay troops retired to Cannanore. Hartley was present when the siege was resumed in December 1791, and on 22 February 1792 he took part in defeating a sortie specially directed against Abercromby's position on the north side of the fortress. Peace was concluded on 25 February and Hartley, in recognition of his local knowledge, was made commander of the forces in the south-west provinces ceded by Tipu.

On the outbreak of war with France in 1793 Hartley commanded the expedition which captured the French settlement of Mahé on the Malabar coast. In March 1794 he was promoted colonel and returned for a time to England. In May 1796 he was made a major-general, and appointed to the staff in India. He returned to Bombay in 1797. In addition to his military rank, he was now made a supervisor and magistrate for the province of Malabar. In 1799 war again broke out with Tipu, and it was resolved to attack Seringapatam again from east and west. A Bombay force of 6420 under General Stuart, with Hartley as second in command, mustered on the Malabar coast at Cannanore and set out across the mountains of Coorg on the nearest road for Tipu's capital. On 5 March the advanced guard of three sepoy battalions under Colonel Montresor at Seedaseer was attacked by a division of the Mysore army. Hartley had gone forward early in the morning to reconnoitre. He was thus the first to perceive the serious nature of the attack, and, after sending a message to General Stuart, remained himself with the beleaguered battalions. As the main body was at Siddapur, 8 miles off, the advanced line was compelled to fight off overwhelming numbers for six hours. At last Stuart came up with reinforcements, and Tipu's army retreated. This victory rendered possible the investment of Seringapatam from the western side. Hartley was present at the storming of Tipu's capital on 4 May 1799. He then returned to resume his civil duties in Malabar, but died, unmarried, after a very short illness, on 4 October 1799 at Cannanore.

G. P. MORIARTY, rev. G. J. BRYANT

Sources P. Cadell, *History of the Bombay army* (1938) · BL OIOC · Fortescue, *Brit. army* · Dodwell [E. Dodwell] and Miles [J. S. Miles], eds., *Alphabetical list of the officers of the Indian army: with the dates of their respective promotion, retirement, resignation, or death ... from the year 1760 to the year ... 1837* (1838) · J. Philippart, *East India military calendar*, 3 vols. (1823–6) · J. G. Duff, *A history of the Mahrattas*, 3 vols. (1826) · PRO, PROB 11/1351, fols. 81–2

Wealth at death £3140; plus emerald ring and unknown residue of estate: will, PRO, PROB 11/1351, fols. 81–2

Hartley, Jesse (1780–1860), civil engineer, was born on 21 December 1780 in or near Pontefract, Yorkshire, the second son of Bernard Hartley (c.1745–1834), builder and architect, and his wife, Mary. His father was from 1797 surveyor of bridges to the West Riding of Yorkshire, and Hartley was probably apprenticed to him as a mason on the construction of John Carr's design for the bridge at Ferrybridge on the Great North Road over the River Aire, completed in 1804. Father and son worked together as architect and builder respectively to construct the bridge at Castleford which was completed in 1808.

By 1809 Hartley was in Ireland, working for the sixth duke of Devonshire at Dungarvan in co. Waterford, in the vicinity of Lismore. The introduction to this job may have come from John Carr who himself worked at Chatsworth and Lismore and who knew Devonshire's architect, William Atkinson. During his period in Ireland, Hartley built a bridge and a long causeway across the Colligan estuary at Dungarvan and directed the construction of the market square in the town. While in Ireland he met and married Ellenor (later known as Ellen) Penney; their only son, John Bernard, was born there in 1814, and two daughters, Mary and Fanny, were born later. On returning to England in 1819 Hartley was engaged for two years on the repair of bridges in the hundred of Salford, Lancashire. He was subsequently appointed bridge master of the hundred at an annual salary of £200.

In 1824 the Liverpool dock trustees advertised the vacancy of the new post of deputy surveyor, in the hope that the introduction of an independent outsider would put an end to the irregularities practised by 'individuals who, with injustice to the tradesmen of the town at large had, for so many years, monopolised the supplying of the dock estate so as to have almost considered it as their own exclusive property'. It is likely that Hartley's conspicuous honesty and administrative skills as well as his engineering competence persuaded the trustees that he was the best of the fourteen applicants for the job; two weeks after the appointment of the new deputy, the dock surveyor, John Foster (1759–1827), and his clerk and measurer all resigned, leaving Hartley in sole charge. His annual salary in 1825 was £1000.

Hartley remained in post for thirty-six years, during which period he was responsible for designing and carrying out the construction or alteration of nearly all of the docks in the Port of Liverpool, increasing the area of the docks by more than 450 per cent. This work was carried out mainly by a large direct labour force, operating from a number of dockyards which included purpose-built foundries, sawmills, and boilermakers' and millwrights' shops. Granite masonry for the dock works was supplied from the Kirkmabreck quarry, Kirkcudbrightshire (leased to the dock trustees), and shipped to Liverpool in the trustees' own vessels. Hartley kept meticulous accounts of his department's expenditure, which averaged about £250,000 a year; he analysed management costs, monitored productivity, and supervised a workforce which had an exceptionally good safety record.

While being careful never to absent himself from the dock estate at spring tides, Hartley accepted a number of outside consultancies, including commissions relating to Littlehampton harbour (1825), Grosvenor Bridge, Chester (1826), the Liverpool and Manchester Railway (1827), the Manchester, Bolton, and Bury Canal (1832), and the Carlisle Canal (1835). From 1840, however, he was required to devote his whole attention to his job in Liverpool. Hartley, who was possibly descended from Hugh Hartley, a mason and architect active in Yorkshire during the reign of George II, was styled 'architect' when he worked in Ireland. In Liverpool he designed not only dock and harbour works but also a great number of beautifully constructed, functional buildings such as gatemen's huts, engine houses, and multi-storey warehouses. His best-known monument in Liverpool is the Albert Dock (opened 1845) and its five huge stacks of 'fireproof' warehouses built of incombustible materials. His remarkable six-faced clock tower at the entrance to Salisbury Dock became another distinctive landmark, typical of his idiosyncratic style.

Hartley attended his office until just three days before his death, on 24 August 1860, at his home in Derby Road, Bootle, outside Liverpool. He died prosperous, having earned a salary of £3500 a year from 1845, and possessed of an extensive library, some good paintings, and a gold medal which had been presented to him by Prince Albert. Ellen Hartley had died in 1836; she was buried at the churchyard of St Mary's, Bootle, under a slab of the granite which was the material so favoured by Hartley for its permanence and strength. Hartley himself was buried next to his wife under a matching stone, next to which now lies a third, blank slab which was clearly intended to mark the grave of John Bernard (who was, in fact, buried in Stirlingshire). St Mary's Church was destroyed by German bombs in May 1941, but the three gravestones survived.   NANCY RITCHIE-NOAKES

Sources PICE, 33 (1871–2), 216–23 [obit. of John Bernard Hartley] · N. Ritchie-Noakes, *Liverpool's historic waterfront: the world's first mercantile dock system*, Royal Commission on Historical Monuments, suppl. ser., 7 (1984) · V. Burton, ed., *Liverpool shipping trade and industry* (1989) · A. Jarvis, *Liverpool central docks* (1991) · *Liverpool Daily Post* (25 Aug 1860), 5 · *The Times* (25 Aug 1860), 9 · *Liverpool Mercury* (25 Aug 1860), 5 · F. E. Hyde, *Liverpool and the Mersey: an economic history of a port, 1700–1970* (1971) · 'An account of the new or Grosvenor Bridge over the River Dee at Chester', PICE, 1 (1837–41), 207–14 · N. Ritchie-Noakes, *Jesse Hartley: dock engineer to the port of Liverpool* (1980) · CGPLA Eng. & Wales (1860) · d. cert. · parish register (baptisms), Pontefract, Yorkshire, 18 Feb 1781 · gravestone, St Mary's churchyard, Bootle, Liverpool

Archives National Museums and Galleries on Merseyside, Liverpool, Mersey Docks and Harbour Board collection | Athenaeum Library, Liverpool, Robert Gladstone, no. 37 · Lancs. RO, county bridge surveyor's accounts · NL Ire., Lismore, Devonshire, and Dungarvan MSS · West Yorkshire RO, Wakefield, quarter sessions bridge index

Likenesses M. Noble, portrait, Walker Art Gallery, Liverpool

Wealth at death under £25,000: probate, 17 Sept 1860, CGPLA Eng. & Wales

Hartley, John (1839–1915), dialect poet and writer, was born on 19 October 1839 at 7 Bedford Street, Halifax, the youngest of the five children of John Hartley, tea dealer and travelling draper, and his wife, Rachel, *née* Riley. His paternal grandparents were members of the choir at St Mary's Church, Illingworth, and had 'more than ordinary musical talent' (Waddington, 4), but little is known about the cultural influences of his childhood. He received an elementary education at a local dame-school and at John Farrar's academy in Halifax before serving his apprenticeship as a textile designer at James Akroyd & Sons, worsted spinners, in 1851. In his early twenties he joined the Beacon Club, a young men's literary and musical club which met at the Corporation Arms inn, Gibbet Street, Halifax, where he found an audience for his developing literary aspirations.

Hartley's first published poem, 'Bite Bigger', a poignant story of an encounter with two young street urchins in a Yorkshire mill town and issued as a penny broadsheet, was a phenomenal success, selling thousands of copies. It was directly influenced by Edwin Waugh's Lancashire dialect piece 'Come whoam to thi childer an me'. It resulted in Hartley's appointment in 1866 as editor of the *Original Illuminated Clock Almanack*, which provided a vehicle for his prolific output of dialect poetry and prose. Under his editorship, which extended over almost half a century, the almanac became Yorkshire's most popular and enduring dialect magazine, achieving annual sales of 80,000 by 1887 and continuing publication until 1957. A radical Liberal, Hartley combined in his writing sentimentality and social realism, spiced with an earthy Yorkshire humour and reflecting a strong sense of community. He also displayed an extraordinary versatility in his writing, choosing subjects ranging from simple tales to abstract philosophical themes, and utilizing a variety of forms of literary expression. Many of his stories were based on the fictional, semi-autobiographical character of Sammywell Grimes, and he was both a brilliant essayist and a master of the pithy aphorism. His homespun observations included such classics as 'A chap 'ats nivver had to struggle doesn't know his strength' and 'If yo say nowt, tho' yo know nowt, folk'll credit you wi' wisdom' (Waddington, 4). A contemporary bibliophile, J. Horsfall Turner, writing in 1906, concluded that 'undoubtedly' Hartley had 'the greatest popularity of any Yorkshire writer' (Turner, 134).

Hartley supplemented his income from writing with a business dealing in and designing carpets and upholstery, but his career displayed some enigmatic twists and some imprudent commercial decisions. Having temporarily handed over responsibility for editing the almanac to others he made a disastrous trip to North America between 1872 and 1875. During this visit he invested most of his money in the hire of a public hall in Quebec for the purpose of giving a public recital; but he failed to attract an audience and he then moved up the St Lawrence to Montreal, where he tried his hand variously as a newspaper canvasser, painter and decorator, theatre manager, and even a circus acrobat. Moreover, in 1875, on his return to England, he foolishly sold the copyright of his *Yorkshire Ditties* to his publisher. On a later, twelve-year sojourn in North America he enjoyed some success as a businessman in Philadelphia, but by the turn of the century he was poor, even though the *Illuminated Clock Almanack* continued to record buoyant sales. In 1904 some of his readers petitioned for a civil-list pension for him, but without success, and in 1909 he was presented with a purse of 100 guineas at a seventieth birthday dinner at the Great Northern Hotel in Bradford.

Hartley's often precarious financial situation failed to subdue his genial, optimistic, warm-hearted character. Photographs and sketches reveal a man of sturdy build, with dark hair combed back, sparkling eyes, an aquiline nose, and a patriarchal beard. He married three times. His first wife, Martha, whom he married at Halifax parish church on 23 May 1859, bore him five children, but died following the birth of the youngest, Percy, in 1878 or 1879. His second wife was Sophia Ann Wilson, the daughter of Alfred Wilson, a Halifax hatter and the originator and publisher of the *Illuminated Clock Almanack*. They married in 1880 and she featured as Mally Grimes in many of his stories. After her death in January 1915 Hartley married, on 21 September 1915, a widow and former schoolteacher, Annie Spencer (*b.* 1859), daughter of Thomas McCandlish, a safe and bedstead salesman. Shortly after his third marriage Hartley died of a cerebral haemorrhage, pneumonia, and heart failure on 18 December 1915 at his home, 11 Seaview Avenue, Wallasey, Cheshire. He was survived by his wife. A small private funeral service was held in Wallasey on 23 December 1915, conducted by the Revd Dr Gasking of Walton.

JOHN A. HARGREAVES

Sources *Halifax Guardian* (24 Dec 1915) · J. H. Waddington, *John Hartley* (1939) · P. Joyce, *Visions of the people: industrial England and the question of class, 1848–1914* (1991) · I. Hargreaves, 'The Yorkshire poet who found fame by accident', *Bradford Telegraph and Argus* (15 March 1976) · *Evening Courier* [Halifax] (20 Aug 1993) · *Halifax Courier* (8 May 1969) · *Halifax Courier* (2 Nov 1967) · J. H. Turner, *Halifax books and authors* (1906) · b. cert. · m. cert. [Annie Spencer] · d. cert. · E. Webster, 'The Halifax Original Clock Almanack (1865–1957)', *Transactions of the Halifax Antiquarian Society*, 10 (2002)
Archives Calderdale Central Library, Halifax, Horsfall Turner collection, collection of *Clock Almanacks*, poetry, and prose
Likenesses A. Comfort, line drawing, repro. in *Halifax Courier* (23 Sept 1989) · photograph, repro. in *Halifax Guardian* · photograph, Calderdale Libraries
Wealth at death poor by early 1900s; readers' request for civil-list pension rejected 1904; Bradford presented purse of 100 guineas at seventieth birthday dinner, 1909

Hartley, Leslie Poles (1895–1972), novelist and essayist, was born on 30 December 1895 at Whittlesey in Cambridgeshire, the second of the three children of Harry Bark Hartley (1860–1954), solicitor and director of a brickworks, and his wife, Mary Elizabeth Thompson (1863–1948), the daughter of William James Thompson, a Crowland farmer. Until his thirteenth year, Hartley was educated at the family home, Fletton Tower, Peterborough, where his parents were respected Liberals and Methodists. Here he was much under the influence of his elder sister, Enid Mary (1892–1968), and the stultifying love of his mother; his younger sister was Annie Norah (1903–1994). In 1908 he managed a happy transition to Northdown Hill, a preparatory school in Thanet, and in 1910 was briefly at Clifton College, Bristol, where he probably first met his lifelong friend, the novelist Clifford Kitchin. He was soon moved to Harrow, where he won an exhibition to Balliol College, Oxford, in 1915. Despite his mother's attempts to keep him out of the war, he enlisted in April 1916, but never saw active service. He was invalided out of the army

Leslie Poles Hartley (1895–1972), by Mark Gerson, 1954

in September 1918 by Sir Frederick Treves, who told him, 'My poor boy, you have done your utmost for King and Country' (Hartley). Returning to Balliol, he began an intense friendship with Lord David Cecil, and was dismayed when Cecil announced his engagement to Rachel MacCarthy: to Hartley, it was an act of betrayal, from which he may never have recovered.

Aldous Huxley introduced Hartley to Ottoline Morrell at Garsington, and Kitchin led him to the Asquiths at The Wharf, marking the beginning of Hartley's fascination with the higher reaches of society, to which he longed to be attached. Much of his life was spent in a seemingly ceaseless grand tour of the houses of the rich and famous. Lacking intimates, he had strong associations with, among others, Lady Cynthia Asquith, Christabel Aberconway, Osbert and Edith Sitwell, Henry Lamb, and Molly, countess of Berkeley.

Hartley published eighteen novels and six volumes of short stories, as well as a book of essays. His first short stories appeared in the undergraduate magazine *Oxford Outlook*, which he also edited. Some of these made up *Night Fears* (1924), his first collection, which typically contained several ghost stories of which Hartley was a capable writer. A novella, *Simonetta Perkins* (1925), about the sexual infatuation of an American girl with a Venetian gondolier, remains one of his most distinctive and dangerous works. Neither book became a popular success but Hartley was encouraged in his writing by a sympathetic aunt, the novelist Kathleen Lund. To supplement his substantial private income, derived from the fortunes of the brickworks, he turned to reviewing, establishing himself for the next twenty years as an assiduous and much respected critic.

Venice became a necessity to Hartley: it distanced him from his mother and Fletton Tower (where he always felt ill at ease) and was to inspire much of the best in his writing. For part of each year until 1939 he made his home there, mainly in San Sebastiano, and was at his happiest when 'gondoling', for the stillness of water intrigued him. He never forgave England for the dissatisfaction he felt on his enforced return in 1939, a year he blamed for 'the Great Divide', just as he had blamed the end of Edwardian perfection on the coming of jazz. He did not settle easily, renting houses on the river at Lower Woodford, near Salisbury, and at Rockbourne in Hampshire, the home of the Cecils, but, encouraged by the publisher Constant Huntington, he determined to become a novelist. In 1944 he published *The Shrimp and the Anemone*, a novel that had its roots in his memories of family holidays at Hunstanton in Norfolk. Begun in 1925 as an unpublished short story, 'Back to Cambo', this account of the childhood of Eustace and his domineering elder sister Hilda owed much to the relationship between Enid and Hartley, a fact only admitted after Enid's death. The first of a trilogy, the novel was followed by *The Sixth Heaven* (1946) and *Eustace and Hilda* (1947).

In 1946 Hartley bought his first home, Avondale, a substantial house on the banks of the Avon at Bathford, where he was attended by his faithful servant Charlie Holt. The rambling epic novel of wartime England, *The Boat* (1949), owed much to his experiences with his domestic staff at Lower Woodford; relationships with his servants (of which he had a bewildering number until his death) became an obsession. He was in Venice, working on his science fiction novel *Facial Justice* (1960), when he wrote the opening line of a new book: 'The past is a foreign country; they do things differently there.' *The Go-Between* (1953) was inspired by Hartley's visit to Bradenham Hall, Norfolk, in the summer of 1909, and was testament to the theme of childhood trauma destroying emotional development. Such thoughts also dominate *The Brickfield* (1964), Hartley's account of his Fenland childhood with its thinly disguised cast of family members. Among his other novels, *The Hireling* (1957) offers an astounding discussion of its author's fear of love.

Throughout the 1960s Hartley's output increased in quantity as it decreased in quality, a fact often regretted by his long-suffering publisher Hamish Hamilton. Increasingly, it was a platform for Hartley's detestation of the state and his strongly reactionary views on modern life (he advocated hanging and the branding of criminals, but did not hesitate to poison some troublesome swans that upset his rowing on the Avon). Avondale offered repose, but he never felt completely happy there. He bought a London flat at Rutland Gate in Knightsbridge and subsequently shared his time between Bathford and London. In 1967 he published *The Novelist's Responsibility*, a collection of essays and lectures, including a lengthy appreciation of one of his literary mentors, Nathaniel Hawthorne; other pieces confirmed his fastidious, moral attitude to his writing.

Mild-mannered, socially charming, and walrus-like with rolling chins and a widening girth—captured by Derek Hill's oil portrait—Hartley (often unwillingly) served his profession on the management committee of the Society of Authors and as president of the English PEN Club. In his last years, alcohol muddled his talent. He was always in confusion about the doings of his many, often sinister, servants, and his flat was strewn with manuscripts for several novels in various stages of composition. From the disorganization his typist and friend Joan Hall helped him to rescue *The Harness Room* (1971), a novella about the love between a chauffeur and his employer's adolescent son: here, the underlying fact of homosexual adoration that had been hinted at in so much of his work found full expression. It was a last effort to capture the finest of Hartley's talent: a gift for an understanding of the human heart by a man who could not participate in its wonder.

Created a CBE in 1956, Hartley received a final honour in 1972 when he was made a companion of literature, but the morning after the ceremony he could remember nothing of it. In his last years he visited Avondale less and less and lived only to write. 'I seem to have become part of my past', he told David Cecil (MS letter, 10 March 1972). His writing looked back to an England for which he had admiration and fondness, but his reputation as a writer was hindered by the sometimes evident unevenness of his work and its increasing lack of relevance to anything resembling real life. Never having revealed whether he had suffered the trauma that so affected the adult lives of many of his characters, Hartley died, unmarried, of myocardial degeneration and cirrhosis of the liver, at his home, Flat 10, 53 Rutland Gate, London, on 13 December 1972, and was cremated at Golders Green.

ADRIAN WRIGHT

Sources A. Wright, *Foreign country: the life of L. P. Hartley* (1996) · family MSS from Fletton Tower, JRL · L. P. Hartley, 'Three wars', unpublished essay, priv. coll. · d. cert. · b. cert.
Archives JRL, MSS and corresp. · JRL, letters · Ransom HRC, corresp. · University of Bristol, corresp. | BBC WAC, corresp. with BBC staff · BL, letters to Lady Aberconway, Add. MSS 60382–60383 · Bodl. Oxf., corresp. with R. B. Montgomery; letters to Cecily Margaret Piggott · Royal Society of Literature, London, letters to Royal Society of Literature · U. Birm., letters to Jessica Brett Young · U. Reading, corresp. with Bodley Head · U. Sussex, corresp. with Leonard Woolf | SOUND BL NSA
Likenesses H. C. Pilsbury, oils, 1916, priv. coll. · H. Lamb, oils, 1938, NPG · M. Gerson, photograph, 1954, NPG [*see illus.*] · D. Hill, oils, priv. coll.
Wealth at death £377,503: probate, 20 March 1973, CGPLA Eng. & Wales

Hartley [*née* Laffan], **Mary** [May] (*c.*1850–1916), novelist and short-story writer, was born in Dublin, the elder daughter of Michael Laffan, custom house officer of Blackrock, co. Dublin, and his wife, Ellen Fitzgibbon, who was related to Gerald *Fitzgibbon (1793–1882). Not much of her earlier life is known. The family was Catholic and probably middle-class, and she was brought up in Blackrock and educated at a convent school. Throughout her life she seems to have been called May rather than Mary.

May Laffan began publishing anonymously in June 1874 with an attack on her Catholic education in an essay in *Fraser's*. Her first novel, *Hogan, M.P.* (1876), the story of the rise and fall of a political opportunist, gave a detailed and satirical insight into Dublin society. It also strongly criticized Catholic education as detrimental to social climbing, leading to petty intrigues, social manoeuvres, gossip, and scandal. One reviewer commented that:

> if instead of refined, delicate and pungent satire, there is too much of rather broad and coarse caricature in the filling up, still we must admit that the descriptions generally have truth and point, more especially in the sketches of society … (*Dublin University Magazine*)

Apparently the book caused a stir in Dublin, since it dealt with contemporary events, and it was assumed that it had been written by a man.

Laffan's next novel, *The Hon. Miss Ferrard* (1877), was an attack on a typical Irish middle-class household, exposing its vulgarity, pretension, and extravagance. In *Christy Carew* (1878) she criticized the Catholic church's discouragement of mixed marriages. *Flitters, Tatters and the Counsellor* (1879) contained four stories: the first two about Dublin slum children, the third about Glasgow slum life, and the last about conspiracy and murder in a county district. These stories are characterized by their social realism, and show the brutalizing effect of poverty and slum life. It is her most acclaimed work (John Ruskin admired it) and went through three Irish editions before being published in England. The Tauchnitz edition of 1881 had three extra stories. 'The Game Hen' and 'Baubie Clark' had been published separately in 1880. In 1880 Laffan produced *No Relations*, a translation of a French novel by Hector Malat.

On 4 July 1882 May Laffan married a protestant, Walter Noel Hartley (1846–1913), the distinguished professor of chemistry at the Royal College of Science in Dublin who was knighted for his services to science in 1911. When he lectured at King's College, London, the couple lived in London. May Hartley published *A Singer's Story* in 1885. Her last novel was *Ismay's Children* (1887), a fictional account of the lives of a group of men who join the Fenian movement.

Hartley was described as 'a most witty and delightful woman' (*Irish Book Lover*). But she suddenly stopped publishing, probably because of public anger about and strong clerical opposition to her criticism of the Catholic education system and her support for mixed marriages. There were also rumours of a nervous breakdown and a separation from her husband. The obituaries in *The Times* and *Irish Times* for Sir Walter, who died on 11 September 1913 at Braemar, did not mention his family at all, which does point to an estrangement. However, an unpublished memorandum on education from about 1895 shows that she continued writing.

Mary Hartley died on 23 June 1916 at her home, 10 Elgin Road, Dublin, shortly after her only son was killed at Gallipoli. The death notice in the *Irish Times* declared that the funeral was private. It did not mention her literary achievements, and there was no obituary. It seems that the life and work of this powerful social critic of Irish Catholic life had already been forgotten, and some ninety years later her works continued to be neglected by writers on Irish literature.

BRIGITTE ANTON

Sources R. Hogan, ed., *Dictionary of Irish literature*, rev. edn, 1 (1996) · S. J. Brown, *Ireland in fiction*, 2nd edn, 1 (1969) · R. Welch, ed., *The Oxford companion to Irish literature* (1996) · review of Hogan, MP, *Dublin University Magazine*, 88 (1876), 254–6 · *CGPLA Eng. & Wales* (1913) · *CGPLA Eng. & Wales* (1916) · *Irish Times* (26 June 1916), 1 · *The Times* (12 Sept 1913), 1, 9 · *Irish Times* (12 Sept 1913), 7 · *WWW, 1897–1915* · R. O'Raghallaigh, 'Three centuries of Irish chemists', *Journal of the Cork Historical and Archaeological Society*, 2nd ser., 46 (1941), 53 · 'Notes and queries—*Flitters, tatters and the counsellor*', *Irish Book Lover*, 20 (1932), 137 · R. J. Hayes, ed., *Manuscript sources for the history of Irish civilisation*, 11 vols. (1965), vols. 2–3 · R. J. Hayes, ed., *Manuscript sources for the history of Irish civilisation: first supplement, 1965–1975*, 1 (1979) · R. J. Hayes, ed., *Manuscript sources for the history of Irish civilisation*, 2 (1965) · Women's Commemoration and Celebration Committee, ed., *10 Dublin women* (Dublin, 1999), 96 · m. cert. · Blain, Clements & Grundy, *Feminist comp.*
Archives CUL, memorandum on education in Ireland, MS Add. 6553
Wealth at death £262 14s. 10d.: resworn probate, 1916, *CGPLA Eng. & Wales*

Hartley, Thomas (1708/9–1784), religious writer and translator, son of Robert Hartley, a London bookseller, was born in London. He was educated at Mr Tower's school in Kendal, and at the age of sixteen was admitted on 10 May 1725 as a subsizar at St John's College, Cambridge, graduating BA in 1728 and MA in 1745. Ordained on 24 September 1732 he soon afterwards became curate at Chiswick, Middlesex. On 8 September 1741 he was appointed vicar of East Claydon, Buckinghamshire, a living which he relinquished in 1745, a year after he had become rector of Winwick, Northamptonshire. He was probably never resident in either of these parishes.

Hartley's early theological sympathies were with the evangelical school represented by James Hervey and George Whitefield, and he may have owed his advancement in the church to Selina, countess of Huntingdon. However, his admiration for mystical writers, such as William Law and Jakob Boehme, is demonstrated in his 'discourse on Mistakes concerning religion, enthusiasm', which was prefixed to his volume of collected sermons (1754), dedicated to Lady Huntingdon. These interests appear further developed in a millenarian treatise, *Paradise Restored* (1764), which included a 'defence of the mystic writers against Warburton'.

Hartley began his acquaintance with the Swedish mystic Emanuel Swedenborg by at least 1769, in which year Swedenborg wrote him a letter, declining an offer of pecuniary aid, and supplying autobiographical particulars. He visited Swedenborg at Cold Bath Fields, in company with the Quaker preacher William Cookworthy, who was later a follower of Swedenborg. In 1770 Hartley published *A Theosophical Lucubration on the Nature of Influx*, which was a translation of Swedenborg's *De commercio animae et corporis* (1769). It was in response to Hartley's 'nine questions' that Swedenborg briefly formulated his view of the doctrine of the Trinity, published by Hartley in 1785 as *Quaestiones novem de trinitate … ad E. Swedenborg propositae … tum illius responsa*, followed by an English version, *Nine Queries* (1786). Hartley paid frequent visits to Swedenborg, but when Swedenborg sent for him in his last illness in March 1772 Hartley did not respond, to his subsequent great regret. He also revised and wrote a preface for Cookworthy's 1778 translation of Swedenborg's *De coelo … et de inferno*. A letter from him to the Swedenborgian John Clowes is inserted in the preface to Clowes's 1781 translation of Swedenborg's *Vera Christiana religio*.

Hartley remained outside the organized society for propagating the doctrines of Swedenborg, started in 1783 by Robert Hindmarsh. Apart from his translations of Swedenborg's works, he published various sermons, and *God's Controversy with the Nations* (1756). During some part of his life he resided in Hertford, but from early in 1772 he lived at East Malling, Kent, where he died on 11 December 1784, aged seventy-five, and was buried.

ALEXANDER GORDON, rev. JON MEE

Sources A. E. Beilby, *Rev. Thomas Hartley, A.M., rector of Winwick in Northamptonshire* (1931) · Venn, *Alum. Cant.* · *GM*, 1st ser., 55 (1785), 76 · R. Hindmarsh, *Rise and progress of the New Jerusalem church*, ed. E. Madeley (1861)

Hartley, William (1857–1924), showman and medicine vendor, was born on 8 August 1857 at Marsh Southowram, near Halifax, Yorkshire, the son of Alfred Hartley, described as a flag facer, and his wife, Sarah Ann (*née* Peel) (1832/3–1910). Of his early life nothing is known. Hartley came to public notice in 1887 as the promoter of, and chief actor in, a travelling 'American medicine-show', which started in Portsmouth in September 1887, and which is next recorded in 1888 in Brighton and then in Dublin. His professional title was Sequah, and he was also known as William Henry Hartley.

The American medicine-show was an American adaptation of an older European way of selling medicines through *commedia dell'arte* shows and the telling of traveller's tales. The protagonist of the American version would entertain crowds with fictitious accounts of his travels in the Wild West, display his knowledge of secret Native American medicinal lore, draw teeth on stage with incredible speed, and effect apparently miraculous cures by rubbing the limbs of lame or rheumatic patients with supposed Indian botanic remedies. The whole performance would be heightened by brass bands, circus acts, and the presence of people supposed to be Native Americans ('Redskins'), dressed in full tribal war-dress, and would culminate in the sale of medicines to the public from a stage or wagon.

Hartley had probably had experience of such operations in America before 1887, when he formed a partnership in London with two opticians from Chicago (Alfred Danziger and Leon Kokocinski) to import the American medicine-show format unchanged into England under the name Sequah. This name was derived partly from the name of the Cherokee leader Sequoyah, and partly from a design to confuse customers of a rival American medicine troupe, the Kickapoo Indian Medicine Firm, active in the USA, which sold a medicine called Sagwa. At his crowded meetings in the great industrial cities of Britain in 1888–90 Hartley, alias Sequah, met with sensational success, selling vast quantities of two main medicinal preparations—Sequah's Prairie Flower, for internal use, and Sequah's Indian Oil, for external application, as well as various other branded products such as a Sequah denti-frice. The internal medicine was alleged by competitors to be made of fish oil flavoured with marjoram and alcohol, with the external one made from aloes, capsicum, and carbonate of potash.

In 1889 the three members turned their partnership into a small joint-stock company, Sequah Ltd, which was floated on the London stock exchange in 1890. Hartley was the managing director and the dominating figure in the company, and he was the main beneficiary of the flotation, which brought him about £100,000 in cash. Hartley's enrichment from a 'quack medicine' company may have contributed to the theme of H. G. Wells's novel *Tono Bungay* (published in 1909 but set in the 1890s). Soon after the flotation no fewer than twenty-three teams, each headed by its own Sequah, were operating simultaneously in Great Britain, with gilded wagons, German brass bands, and troops of Redskin Indians. In September 1890 the company started to expand overseas, to India, Venezuela, the West Indies, Spain, the Netherlands, and elsewhere. A Sequah was even sent to North America to compete with the original American medicine-show companies on their own ground. Hartley provided the commercial flair and the entrepreneurial spirit of the company. One of the Sequahs who worked for him at this time represents him (in a private letter) as a callous and ruthless swindler.

Sequah Ltd could not maintain its initial success, for several reasons. Since the beneficiaries of the flotation were the founding partners (Hartley, Danziger, and Kokocinski) rather than the company, the latter had no capital with which to finance its operations. The British government disliked the civil disturbance caused by the company's mass gatherings in market places, commons, and waste grounds, objected to the non-payment of stamp duty on its medicines, and passed an act (53 Vict. c. 8) requiring sales of medicines to take place only from a set of premises, not from a vehicle or a stage. There were objections to the company's price-fixing policy, and its many charitable donations did not pacify those who disliked its use of extreme commercial methods in an ethically sensitive market. European governments took action against Sequah's unorthodox interventions in their traditional controlled markets for pharmaceuticals, and in North America public interest in the (by then) old-fashioned routine of the American medicine-show had begun to fade. In 1895 Sequah Ltd went into liquidation. The numerous Sequahs went back to their original occupations—herbalist, dentist, music-hall artist, and so on—but how Hartley himself spent the rest of his life is not known; it was possibly in yacht broking. He died at his home, 7 Sherwood Street in Soho, London (later the site of the Piccadilly Theatre), on 16 January 1924, leaving £734.

WILLIAM SCHUPBACH

Sources W. Schupbach, 'Sequah: an English "American medicine"-man in 1890', *Medical History*, 29 (1985), 272–317 · b. cert. · *CGPLA Eng. & Wales* (1924)
Archives Wellcome L., Sequah archive, CMAC/GC/69
Likenesses Grossmann of Dover, portrait, priv. coll. · oils, Wellcome L.; repro. in Schupbach, 'Sequah: an English "American medicine"-man', pl. 1, 2 · portrait, repro. in Schupbach, 'Sequah: an English "American medicine"-man', 287
Wealth at death £734: probate, 1 Aug 1924, *CGPLA Eng. & Wales*

Hartley, Sir William Pickles (1846–1922), jam manufacturer and philanthropist, was born on 23 February 1846 at Colne, Lancashire, the only surviving child of John Hartley, a whitesmith, and his wife, Margaret Pickles. He attended a local British and Foreign School Society school, and then Colne grammar school for a year before leaving at fourteen. Prevented from training as a chemist, he threw his energies into developing his mother's grocery business. Within two years he was running the shop himself and had begun to hawk grocers' sundries round adjoining towns and villages. He soon controlled one of the largest wholesale enterprises in Lancashire.

In 1866 Hartley married Martha O'Connor, the youngest daughter of Henry Horsfield, grocer, of Colne. They had a son and eight daughters, one of whom died in infancy. He valued, but did not always follow, her common-sense advice, grounded on a thorough knowledge of grocery. He was led into manufacturing when a local grocer failed to fulfil a contract for supplying jam; having won the subsequent arbitration case, Hartley decided to take up jam making himself. In 1874 he opened a factory at Bootle, near Liverpool, almost bankrupting himself as for some years the cost of his borrowings exceeded profits. Then in 1885, after the factory had been enlarged twice and profits had reached £18,000 a year, he registered William Hartley & Sons Ltd with a nominal capital of £100,000.

In 1886 Hartley decided to move operations to Aintree, which was better served by the railway network. The high quality of his ingredients, the absence of preservatives, and the reasonable prices of his products secured him a substantial market in the north of England and the midlands. To supply the steadily growing demand further south, in 1901 he opened a factory at Southwark in London. The two works had a joint capacity of 1000 tons a week, with storage space for 5–6 million jars.

Hartley, a Primitive Methodist, consistently applied Christian principles to business. In 1888 he built a model village at Aintree; the following year he introduced a profit-sharing scheme, the results each year being announced at a special ceremony, with music and speeches. He claimed that the wages he paid to women and girls—four-fifths of the workforce—were appreciably higher than those of his competitors; he also provided free medical treatment. He personally chose his managers and trained them, sending them on advanced chemistry courses at his own expense.

From 1877 onwards Hartley devoted a tenth of his income to philanthropy, later raised to one-third; his benefactions totalled nearly £300,000. He preferred to donate part of any sum requested, so as to encourage others to give. He endowed a number of hospitals in Colne, Liverpool, and London, and financed departments at Liverpool and Manchester universities. Equally generous to Primitive Methodism, he supported an organization for building chapels, acted as treasurer of its missionary society, and converted the old Holborn Town Hall into its national headquarters. He propagated his ideas in his only published work, *The Use of Wealth* (n.d.). Uniquely for a layman, he was elected president of the Primitive Methodist conference in 1909.

Hartley was apt to undertake himself tasks which others could have done equally effectively. Until more scientific methods were introduced, after each boiling at the Aintree factory he used his delicacy of touch on the paper covers to test the consistency of selected samples. Likewise, he is said personally to have scrutinized each employee's work record annually, together with the head of department, to fix the profit-sharing bonus. His public services were thus necessarily limited. In 1893 he became JP for Lancashire, and he served as a Liberal on Liverpool city council from 1895 to 1898. He was also vice-president of the British Temperance League. Appropriately, he gave his recreations in *Who's Who* as 'none except driving'.

Knighted in 1908, Hartley was one of those who were consulted on financial policy in the opening days of the First World War by the chancellor of the exchequer, Lloyd George. Hartley generously supported war charities, but chafed at the official demands and restrictions during the conflict. As the post-war years brought further problems to the company, he suffered increasing attacks of angina, from which he died at his home, Horsfield Cottage, 11 Oxford Road, Birkdale, Lancashire, on 25 October 1922. He was buried at Trawden, near Colne. His wife survived him.   T. A. B. CORLEY

Sources A. S. Peake, *The life of Sir William Hartley* (1926) · D. J. Jeremy, 'Hartley, Sir William Pickles', *DBB* · *The Times* (26 Oct 1922) · *WWW* · D. J. Jeremy, *Capitalists and Christians: business leaders and the churches in Britain, 1900–1960* (1990) · D. A. Simmons, *Schweppes, the first 200 years* (1983) · W. H. Beable, 'Hartley's', *Romance of great businesses*, 1 (1926) · *CGPLA Eng. & Wales* (1923)

Archives Cadbury-Schweppes, Birmingham, archives, records of company

Likenesses photograph, repro. in Peake, *Life of Sir William Hartley* · photograph, repro. in Beable, *Romance of great businesses*

Wealth at death £1,099,935 19s. 0d.: probate, 5 Feb 1923, *CGPLA Eng. & Wales*

Hartlib, Samuel (*c*.1600–1662), educational reformer and writer, was born at Elbing, the Baltic town that was then part of western Poland. Hartlib described his father as 'a merchant, but no ordinary one' (Hartlib papers, 26/1/1A). The family claimed 'very ancient extraction in the German empire' as privy councillors to the emperor and syndics of the cities of Augsburg and Nuremberg. Hartlib's father, however, had followed in the family's fortunes as a factor for the English Eastland Company in the Baltic trade. The profits enabled him to fund the construction of a church in Posnán and, in due course, he moved to Elbing. There he built one of its most elegant town houses, set up a dye-works, and married into the Polish nobility. After the death of his second wife, however, he married for a third time, this time an English lady. Her family name is not known but she evidently had good connections, for one of her two sisters married Sir Richard Smith, who would become a wealthy privy councillor to James I. Samuel Hartlib was their son, born at an unknown date but probably (working backwards from the

details of his education) about 1600. Although Samuel Hartlib spent the majority of his adult life in England, he remained in touch with his Baltic family, especially through his brother Georg, who is mentioned as studying at the University of Heidelberg in several matriculation registers from 1612 to 1620 and who became the rector at the *Gymnasium* at Vilna until persecution drove him out in 1639.

Samuel Hartlib also received an extensive education. After a period at the *Gymnasium* in Brieg, it is just possible that he spent some time thereafter at the University of Königsberg, where an entry in its matriculation register for the year 1614 refers to one 'Samuel Gartelieb, Elbingensis Borussus' (Turnbull, *Samuel Hartlib*, 5). From the surviving drafts of letters that he wrote from Cambridge, he certainly was studying at the university there in the years 1625–6, apparently as a protégé of John Preston, master of Emmanuel College, and he may in fact have been there from about 1621. At all events, he neither matriculated nor graduated but perfected his knowledge of Latin and English to add to his native German and working capability in Polish. After a brief period back in Elbing, he retreated to London in the summer of 1628 in the face of the capture of Mecklenburg and Pomerania by the imperial Habsburg armies and the siege of Stralsund. The withdrawal of the privileges accorded to the English merchants in Elbing that year probably also sounded the death knell for the staple trade that had sustained the Hartlib family fortunes.

London Within a year of his arrival in London, Samuel Hartlib married Mary Burningham (*d*. 1658), on 20 January 1629 at St Dionis Backchurch, London. His first venture thereafter was establishing a private academy for gentlefolk at Chichester, Sussex, in 1630, which is where he came to know John Pell and William Speed. When this collapsed, it was the latter who advised Hartlib to retire to London, where Hartlib hoped God would 'provide me some commodious house' in which he might maintain himself with 'some borders and scollars', probably intending to establish another school (Hartlib papers, 7/16/5B). By the summer of 1631 he was living in a house at Duke's Place 'by the Living Vine' amid the City of London's merchant rich. He stayed there until early 1650, when he moved to 'Charing Cross, over against Angel Court' (Turnbull, *Samuel Hartlib*, 42). In his latter years, after his wife's death, he went to live with his son Sam in Axe Yard, Westminster, a near neighbour of Samuel Pepys, who later recalled that he had been 'much below Hartlibb in all respects' before the Restoration (Pepys, 5.30).

It was at Duke's Place that Hartlib began to cultivate an international network of correspondents. On his return to Elbing in 1627 he had made the acquaintance of John Dury, the Calvinist minister there from 1625 to 1630. Dury would become 'a most dear and precious friend', with whom he became 'a Co-agent' (Dury, 1). Together they had shared an intoxicating vision of reconciling protestant divisions, and became associated with a fraternity whose goal was to establish a model godly community (referred to as Antilia) by colonizing a Baltic island. In due course Hartlib would become the London agent for John Dury's peregrinations in search of ecclesiastical pacification that began in 1631. Dury went to 'settle a way of Correspondency' between protestant divines so that 'they may be able to communicate in all spiritual things' (BL, Sloane MS 654, fols. 247–9). He promised to 'gather, to elaborat, and to observe severall things of great profitt' (ibid.) as he went and send them back to Hartlib—information about rare books, inventions, scientific developments, and technological innovations. Dury remained one of Hartlib's main sources for information but he had many others, especially among the protestant refugee networks of central Europe. This was the basis on which Hartlib started a manuscript newsletter service in the 1630s, providing international intelligence to the protestant (mainly puritan) English political élite that had become alienated from the Stuart court. At the same time, Hartlib's house provided shelter to various scholars from abroad who made it to London. His manuscript diary (or 'Ephemerides') for the years 1634–5 and 1639–43 reveals his fascination with the processes of learning that had already led him to admire and reflect on the works of (among others) Francis Bacon. His correspondence with the Czech educationist Jan Amos Komenský (Comenius) had begun at least as early as 1632, and the transhipment of Baconian materials to Comenius was an early subject of their letters. By 1634 Hartlib was collecting money for Comenius to engage a secretary to advance his ambitious pansophical projects and to visit London. Although Comenius declined to make the journey in 1636, Hartlib was undeterred, and published (albeit without the author's permission) the manuscript sketch of pansophy that Comenius had sent him under the title *Conatuum Comenianorum præludia* (Oxford, 1637). The work was distributed around Hartlib's contacts at home and abroad with a request for comments and an appeal for funds. Support and scepticism were expressed in roughly equal measure to the pansophical design, and financial contributions dribbled in. Hartlib published a second, expanded edition of Comenius's blueprint, the *Pansophiæ prodromus* (London, 1639), and the stage was set for Comenius's arrival in London on 21 September 1641, after which he stayed, lodging with Hartlib, for nine months.

Intelligencer The involvement with Comenius established Hartlib's reputation as an imparter of scientific ideas and information. He was on the way to becoming an 'intelligencer'—an agent for the dissemination of news, books, and manuscripts. He was encouraged by his (and Dury's) belief that Christian solidarity arose out of relations of exchange, or communication (the term 'communicatio' having a religious signification, since it was the Latin rendering of the Greek 'koinonia' or 'shared communion'). Their shared sense was that God had given all human kind a 'talent' that should not be 'hidden under a bushel' but placed at the disposal of the common weal. Those talents would be best released by a reformation of learning (or 'Reformation of schooles' as Hartlib entitled the translation into English of Comenius's *Prodromus* in

1642). That reformation would be best engaged by the establishment of a model college of learning, a 'Solomon's House' as envisaged in Bacon's *New Atlantis*. Hartlib saw Chelsea College, whose reform was a matter of current debate before the Long Parliament, as a possible institution, and Comenius as its ideal director. The possibilities of such a reformation of learning had been publicly preached before the House of Commons in a sermon on 29 November 1640 by Dr John Gauden. It had both practical and utilitarian as well as millenarian implications. In October 1641 Hartlib published a small utopian treatise that he entitled *Macaria* (after an off-shore island of Utopia). Its authorship used to be ascribed to him, but it was evidently drafted by his projector friend Gabriel Plattes. In it, the contentious debates of church and state (that were about to recommence in the second session of the Long Parliament) were replaced by a commonwealth whose government and people collaborated in prosperity generated by the practical application of diffused knowledge. Pansophy was an encyclopaedic project whose ultimate goal was a millennial recovery of the knowledge that mankind had lost when expelled from the Garden of Eden. In a remarkable pact or 'Foederis fraterni ad mutuam in publico Christianismi bono promovendo ædificationem sanctè in conspectu Dei' ('Fraternal pact in the sight of God for mutual advancement in the promotion of the public good of the Christian religion'), drafted by Comenius and signed by himself, Hartlib, and Dury on 3 March 1642, they pledged themselves to a secret fraternity devoted to the advancement of religious pacification, education, and the reformation of learning (Hartlib papers, 7/109/1A–2B). It was a pledge that would overshadow Hartlib for the rest of his life.

During the English civil war Hartlib remained in London, acting as an unofficial agent for the parliamentary cause. He sponsored military innovations such as novel siege tanks and assisted in the importation of Swedish 'leathern' guns while publicly advocating in *A Faithfull and Seasonable Advice* (1643) and *The Necessity of Some Nearer Conjunction and Correspondency* (1644) the 'necessity' for the parliamentarians to make common cause with protestantism elsewhere. His proposed reformation of learning induced Milton to write his treatise *On Education* (1644), which was dedicated to Hartlib. His advocacy of a world of correspondency unfettered by monopolist restraint was one of the stimuli to Milton's composition of the *Areopagitica* (1644), with its criticism of censorship tempered by a defence of authorial rights. He received parliamentary grants of £50 (on 14 January 1645) and £100 (on 25 June 1646) in respect of his services, and 'some place at Oxford … for his future Support' was discussed.

The 'Hartlib circle' Following the parliamentary victory in 1646 Hartlib devoted himself to establishing an 'Office of Address' with elements borrowed from the model of the 'Bureau d'Adresse' set up by Théophraste Renaudot in Paris. The initial pamphlet in which he advertised his scheme, *Considerations Tending to the Happy Accomplishment of Englands Reformation in Church and State* (1647), was published to coincide with the parliamentary vote of £300 to him 'in Consideration of his good Deserts, and great services' and the recommendation that he be given 'some Place of Benefit in the University' of Oxford (*JHC*, 5.131–3). The novel scheme combined two elements, the first being an 'Office of Address for Accommodations', or labour exchange, based in London and directed by Henry Robinson, which sought to ameliorate the economic dislocations after the civil war. The second was the 'Office of Address for Communications', based in Oxford around Hartlib, whose purpose was to maintain registers of information on 'Matters of Religion, of Learning and Ingenuities' and to act as a 'Center and Meeting-place of Advices, of Proposalls, of Treaties and of all Manner of Intellectual Rarities' (Hartlib, *Considerations*, 46, 48). The proposal created comment and spawned imitators but it was never officially instituted. Instead, Hartlib was voted an annual pension of £100 a year for 'the Advancement of Arts and Learning' on 26 April 1649, although securing warrants for its actual payment in the 1650s proved time-consuming and frustrating (*JHC*, 6.227).

It was on this basis that Hartlib felt himself 'obliged to becom a conduit pipe … towards the Publick' (Weston, sig. A4a). He employed scriveners and translators to copy portions of letters and treatises for circulation to others, seeking in turn their own comments and intelligence on a remarkably diverse range of practical scientific matters, including chemistry, medicine, engineering, colonization, horticulture, charitable endeavour, the 'natural history' of Ireland, and agronomy. At the same time, he did not neglect to pursue the possibilities afforded by the new regime to reform the universities, establish new instruments of learning, and seek the conversion of the Jews to Christianity. What is sometimes now regarded as the 'Hartlib circle' was, in reality, a diverse and self-selecting group of enthusiasts or 'ingenui', whose interests in the possibilities of technical change were supported by a shared viewpoint in which the potential of free and 'real' knowledge to benefit the commonwealth was contrasted with the greed of individual monopolists and the obfuscation of old institutions and learning. His surviving papers were purchased after Hartlib's death by Lord Brereton and were last heard of in his Cheshire house in 1667 before being recovered in a London solicitor's office by G. H. Turnbull in 1933. Through them, it is possible to estimate the extent of Hartlib's informal communicative energies both at home and abroad. It is evident that his reputation among contemporaries as 'born and framed to be an Instrument of God for stimulating, sharpening and uniting men's inborn talents' (Comenius), 'that painfull and great instrument' (Petty), 'the incitement of great good to this Iland' (Milton), and 'the greatest instrument of public edification' (Dury) was not entirely misplaced (*Complete Prose Works of John Milton*, 2.363; Petty, 1; Turnbull, *Hartlib, Dury and Comenius*, 67). Hartlib had a hand in over half the patents for new inventions issued by the English government during the Commonwealth and protectorate period, was on good terms with the secretary of the council of state, and attended audiences with Lord Protector Cromwell.

The most visible impact of Hartlib's circle lay in the numerous pamphlets that he published. A reasonably complete list of sixty-five publications associated with Samuel Hartlib is to be found in G. H. Turnbull, *Hartlib, Dury and Comenius*. Hartlib's most substantial publications, *Samuel Hartlib his Legacie* (1651 and subsequent editions), *Chymical, Medicinal, and Chyrurgical Addresses* (1655), and *The Reformed Commonwealth of Bees* (1655), were, in reality, offshoots of his scribal network. They comprised letters and treatises solicited or received from individuals in his circle upon a particular subject, which had then been circulated for additional comments, the results edited, and then launched upon the public (often without the express consent of the original author), anticipating utility and inviting comment and amendment. Less than 5 per cent of the copy was generated by Hartlib himself, generally as prefaces, his talents being more as an editor and publisher. He used Richard Wodenothe and William Dugard as his preferred printers in the 1650s. His treatises spread a solvent of new ideas in a variety of contexts, but they were particularly successful in husbandry. He publicized the advantages of planting new leguminous crops, experimenting with fertilizers and manures, and using seed drills and new ploughs, and advocated the possibilities of apiculture, rabbit farming, fruit-tree propagation, and silk cultivation (in Virginia). His network included a group of innovative farmers willing to experiment. But his pamphlets should also be read as ideas, models, or patterns as to how the processes of reformation would occur. In the case of the *Commonwealth of Bees* (1655), for example, the analogy was particularly evident. The bees are Hartlib's correspondents, collecting the pollen of information in a providentially bountiful and free nature and bringing it back in a spirit of public service to the hive of the office of address.

It is difficult to determine Hartlib's own overall intellectual dimensions with precision. He readily adopted the dominant ideas and language of others, and his agenda evolved over time. He was a self-effacing individual, receding even in his own diary behind a kind of anagram of his name (Albureth) that Dury had derived for him. There is no known portrait of him. Francis Bacon's blueprint for a reformed natural philosophy became Hartlib's, as did Comenius's pansophical designs. He regularly supported the laudable but ultimately unrealistic efforts of John Dury to be the peacemaker among Europe's divergent protestant traditions. He took a keen interest in Paracelsian chemical medicine and Helmontian chemistry. But Hartlib's adoption of other people's ideas also involved conscious thought and adaptation, and the common thread that linked them was his perception that through the dissemination of knowledge the public good would be served and the coming of the millennium achieved. His commitment to that dissemination gave him a distinctive voice, even though it was a goal that would be eventually articulated in very different ways by the Royal Society of London.

Final years Hartlib's later years were overshadowed by illness, penury, and disappointment. He began to suffer from a kidney stone as early as October 1642; by 1656 it kept him confined to his house. His papers document numerous remedies, but they probably contributed more to his suffering rather than its relief. In 1653 he began to complain of his eyesight, with cataracts in both eyes. His wife died in early November 1658, but he continued to raise money for the exiled Czech brethren around Comenius in Leszno in 1658 and 1659. He had a stroke towards the end of 1660, and moreover a household fire in 1662 destroyed some of his papers. His financial circumstances had never been entirely secure, and the Restoration in 1660 removed his pension. His petition to parliament in 1660, which alluded to his reduced circumstances, went unanswered. The new age reasserted gentry civilities as the means by which knowledge should be circulated and truth validated. Hartlib was readily parodied as a fanatic and a 'projector', someone seeking to make a quick fortune at the public expense. He died on Monday 10 March 1662 in Axe Yard, Westminster, where he had been living since 1658, and was buried on the following Wednesday at St Martin-in-the-Fields, although there is a suggestion in Evelyn's correspondence that he had permitted his body to be used for anatomical dissection.

By the time of Hartlib's death, there were three surviving children. Samuel (Sam) was probably the eldest. He was an officer in the excise who was employed as the London agent for Berwick upon Tweed in 1653, and, in 1656, appointed a solicitor for the Merchant Adventurers of Newcastle upon Tyne. Of only modest abilities, he later became a drinking companion of Samuel Pepys and was accused of corruption as one of the collectors of hearth money in 1667. He escaped imprisonment but was dismissed from office. On 6 January 1672 a warrant for his arrest was issued 'for seditious speeches and for publishing libels' and he was rescued only by the intervention of friends in high places (*CSP dom.*, *1672*, 70). Eventually, perhaps later that same year, he fled England for the Netherlands to escape his debts and never returned. Mary, probably the eldest daughter, married Frederick Clodius, a chemical laborant who came to live with the Hartlibs. Clodius attempted to treat his father-in-law's illness with chemical remedies and probably thereby abused the naïve trust that Hartlib had placed in him. Nan Hartlib, Mary's sister, married a wealthy Fifth Monarchist from Utrecht, Jan Roth (Roder), gaining a dowry the equivalent of £6000, and went to live in the Netherlands.

M. GREENGRASS

Sources Sheffield University, Hartlib papers · G. H. Turnbull, *Samuel Hartlib: a sketch of his life and his relations to J. A. Comenius* (1920) · G. H. Turnbull, *Hartlib, Dury and Comenius: gleanings from Hartlib's papers* (1947) · C. Webster, *The great instauration: science, medicine and reform, 1626–1660* (1975) · C. Webster, ed., *Utopian planning and the puritan revolution: Gabriel Plattes, Samuel Hartlib and Macaria* (1979) · M. Greengrass, M. Leslie, and T. Raylor, eds., *Samuel Hartlib and universal reformation: studies in intellectual communication* (1994) · *The Hartlib papers*, ed. J. Crawford and others, 2nd edn (2002) [[2nd edn, HROnline, Sheffield, 2002]; CD-ROM] · *The diary and correspondence of Dr John Worthington*, ed. J. Crossley, 1, Chetham Society, 13 (1847) · 'The letters of Sir Cheney Culpeper, 1641–1657', ed. M. J. Braddick, *Camden miscellany*, XXXIII, CS, 5th ser., 7 (1996), 105–402 · J. L. Chester, ed., *The reiester booke of Saynte De'nis Backchurch

parishe … begynnynge … 1538*, Harleian Society, register section, 3 (1878) · Pepys, *Diary* · J. Dury, *The unchanged, constant and single-hearted peace-maker* (1650) · *JHC*, 5–6 (1646–51) · *JHL*, 1 (1509–77) · *CSP dom.*, 1672 · [S. Hartlib], *Considerations tending to the happy accomplishment of Englands reformation in church and state: humbly presented to the piety and wisdome of the high and honourable court of parliament* (1647) · W. Petty, *The advice of W. P. to Mr Samuel Hartlib for the advancement of some particular parts of learning* (1648) · *Complete prose works of John Milton*, ed. D. Wolfe, 8 vols. in 10 (1953–82), vol. 2 · [R. Weston], *A discours of husbandrie used in Brabant and Flanders, shewing the wonderfull improvement of land there; and serving as a pattern for our practice in this common-wealth* (1650) · J. Dury, 'The purpose and platform of my journy into Germany', BL, Sloane MS 654, fols. 247–9 · 1900, Harleian Society Publications, p. 161

Archives BL, corresp. and papers, Add. MSS 4364–4365 · University of Sheffield, corresp. and papers | BL, letters to John Evelyn, Add. MS 15948 · BL, corresp. with John Pell, Add. MSS 4279–4280, 4377, 4408, 4431 · BL, Sloane MSS, corresp. and papers · Chetham's Library, Manchester, corresp. with John Worthington · CUL, letters to John Worthington [copies] · Yale U., Osborn MSS, corresp. and papers

Hartman, Dame (**Gladys**) **Marea** (1920–1994), sports administrator, was born on 22 June 1920 at 33 Honeybrook Road, Clapham, London, the daughter of Ernest George Hartman and Esther Brook, who both worked in the hotel catering trade and eventually rose to senior positions at the Savoy and the Waldorf respectively. She became a regular runner at her local track and was invited to join the mainly male Spartan athletic club by its founder, Terry Knowles. She won a gold medal as a sprinter for Surrey, and attended the international meeting in Cologne in 1939, six days before the Second World War broke out. During the war she served in the army welfare division. Her fiancé was killed in the war and she never married. Although she achieved modest success as an athlete, it was as an administrator that she achieved international sporting fame. Shortly after the war the Spartan club asked her to become its treasurer, and her career in that field was launched.

In 1950 Hartman was appointed honorary treasurer of the Women's Amateur Athletic Association (WAAA), a post she held for a decade. During her regime she secured sponsorship for the women's annual championships from companies such as Bovril, Kraft, and Sunsilk, capitalizing on the attractiveness of the female performers. Indeed throughout her career she understood the value of publicity for her sport. In 1961 she became honorary secretary, effectively chief executive, of the organization, a position that she held for thirty years. She was initially an opponent of a merger between the men's and women's AAAs, but eventually came round to support the idea. She was unanimously elected the first president of the Amateur Athletic Association of England in 1991.

In 1956 Hartman was appointed manager of the British women's athletics team and took them to the Melbourne Olympics. She retained this position for twenty-two years, leading the team to five further Olympic games and as many European championships and Commonwealth games, as well as numerous international team competitions. In 1958 she became a member of the women's commission of the International Amateur Athletics Federation, and served as chairman from 1968 until 1981. While in this role she was presented with the Prince Chichibu award in recognition of her work in fostering athletics for women in Japan. Other posts included serving on the executive committee of the Central Council of Physical Recreation (representing the main national sporting bodies) from 1972 and becoming both the council's deputy chairman and its honorary treasurer. As chairman of the British Amateur Athletic Board (1989–91), she was instrumental in the creation of its replacement body, the British Athletics Federation.

As a manager Hartman was a firm but flexible disciplinarian. She is alleged never to have imposed a curfew on the women in her charge, preferring to organize entertainment and hospitality for the group as a whole, and accompanying them on their evenings out. Her regard for 'her girls' was epitomized in her establishment of a trophy in memory of the 400 metres runner Lillian Board, who died of cancer in 1970, two years after the Mexico Olympics. Hartman had been at Board's bedside when she died. Nevertheless not all she did was regarded as positive. She brought embarrassment to her sport by banning padded brassières as giving an unfair advantage in a close finish, and her attempt in 1969 to recruit intelligent 'big girls' to combat the East German women was notably unsuccessful. Following a dismal British athletic performance at the Montreal Olympics in 1976, she was criticized as being out of touch with modern athletics. She survived a vote of no confidence but in 1978 lost her position as manager of the women's team.

Perhaps Hartman's major contribution to women's sport was her long and ultimately successful campaign to increase the number of track and field events open to female athletes in Britain—from five in the 1950s to twenty at the time of her death. Her greatest regret was the decision of 1975 to combine the men's and women's AAAs championships into a single event, a move that she had strenuously resisted. An ebullient personality, she met problems with determination and humour, had a taste for Campari and soda, and always a ready smile for the cameras. She cited her recreations as music, reading, and the theatre, but essentially she devoted her life to sports administration. For over thirty years she was personnel officer at Bowaters, the paper manufacturers. They were extremely tolerant, given that much of her time was devoted to nurturing female athletics and athletes. All her work for sport was unpaid. She was appointed MBE in 1967, advanced to CBE in 1978, and DBE in 1994, for services to women's sport. Despite suffering from cancer, she attended the AAA championships in 1994 but was too ill to leave her Wimbledon home to go to the Commonwealth games in Canada. She died of cancer at the Harestone Marie Curie Centre, Harestone Drive, Caterham, Surrey, on 29 August 1994. A memorial service was held at St Martin-in-the-Fields, London, on 28 November 1994.

WRAY VAMPLEW

Sources *The Times* (31 Aug 1994) · *The Independent* (31 Aug 1994) · *The Guardian* (31 Aug 1994) · *Daily Telegraph* (2 Sept 1994) · *Sunday Telegraph* (4 Sept 1994) · *WWW*, *1991–5* · b. cert. · d. cert.

Likenesses photograph, repro. in *The Times* · photograph, repro. in *The Independent*
Wealth at death £128,000: probate, 14 Dec 1994, *CGPLA Eng. & Wales*

Hartnell, Sir Norman Bishop (1901–1979), fashion designer, was born on 12 June 1901 at 2 Streatham Hill, Streatham, London, the only son and younger child of Henry Bishop Hartnell, hotelier, and his wife, Emma Mary Coulson, *née* Polley. He had three half-sisters. He was educated at Mill Hill School and, from 1921, Magdalene College, Cambridge, which he left after two years. While at Cambridge he joined the Footlights dramatic club where he acted and designed the costumes and sets. His creations were acclaimed, and on leaving Cambridge he sought a job in London's high fashion industry. After initial difficulties he and his sister, with some financial help from their father, opened, in 1923, a couture establishment at 10 Bruton Street. The business survived and prospered. Apart from society ladies his clients increasingly included many of the leading actresses of the day such as Gertrude Lawrence, Mistinguett, Evelyn Laye, and Alice Delysia. He also designed dresses for many of the shows produced by Charles Cochran, the André Charlot reviews, and the plays of Noël Coward. Hartnell was best known for his lavishly embroidered, romantic evening and bridal gowns. In 1935 he was requested by Lady Alice Montagu-Douglas-Scott to produce her wedding gown for her marriage to the duke of Gloucester. He was also asked to produce the dresses for the bridesmaids, among whom were the princesses Elizabeth and Margaret. The wedding dress was a great success and shortly afterwards he was asked to produce some designs for the duchess of York (the future Queen Elizabeth the queen mother).

However, the pre-war highlight of Hartnell's career came in 1938 when he was asked to design the clothes for the queen's state visit to Paris. At the request of the king he based his designs on the crinoline gowns depicted in the 1860s portraits by F. X. Winterhalter at Buckingham Palace. The court was in mourning and it was Hartnell's suggestion that the clothes, which became the subject of worldwide admiration, be in white, a lesser-used colour of summer mourning. In spring 1938 Hartnell presented crinoline gowns in his own collection and this style was to become his signature. For Hartnell's services to fashion the French government made him an officier d'Académie (1939). In 1940 he received his first royal warrant of appointment to the queen.

The war brought about two developments in Hartnell's career. First he started to design utility dresses for the mass market, and then became a founder member of the Incorporated Society of London Fashion Designers (established 1942), a couture body which was formed to deal with government departments and to promote British fashion talent at home and abroad. He became its second chairman with his period of office lasting from 1947 to 1956.

The year 1947 was excellent for Hartnell. He was asked to design the wedding dress for Princess Elizabeth together with the dresses for her bridesmaids, the maid of

Sir Norman Bishop Hartnell (1901–1979), by Snowdon, 1968

honour being Princess Margaret. In the same year he received the prestigious American Neiman-Marcus award given annually for an outstanding contribution to world fashion.

In 1953 Hartnell produced the coronation robe for Elizabeth II. This again proved to be a resounding success and he was appointed MVO. He then designed wardrobes for the queen's royal tours to Australasia and other parts of the Commonwealth and for state visits to the capital cities of Europe. He increasingly became known as the royal dressmaker. He was a much loved man with great personal charm who made a major contribution to enhancing the prestige of élite British fashion.

Hartnell was a talented and versatile designer whose work was disseminated to a broad market. From 1949 he introduced ready-to-wear garments and during the 1950s he designed for Berkertex and conceived a range of paper patterns for *Women's Illustrated* magazine. Hartnell also designed for the services: in 1949 his anonymous design was selected for a uniform (in lovat green) for the officers of the Women's Royal Army Corps; he subsequently designed the uniform for the British Red Cross and in 1967 was invited to design a new uniform for Metropolitan policewomen.

In 1977, the year of the queen's silver jubilee, Hartnell was appointed KCVO, the first knighthood conferred for services to fashion. Shortly afterwards his health began to deteriorate and he died at King Edward VII Hospital, Windsor, on 8 June 1979 and was buried at Claydon, Sussex. He was unmarried. Collections of dress designed by Hartnell are in the Royal Ceremonial Dress Collection (the Royal Collection), the Victoria and Albert Museum, the Museum of London, and the Museum of Costume, Bath.

EDWARD RAYNE, rev. AMY DE LA HAYE

Sources N. Hartnell, *Silver and gold* (1955) • N. Hartnell, *Royal courts of fashion* (1971) • A. de la Haye, ed., *The cutting edge: 50 years of British fashion, 1947–1997* (1997) [exhibition catalogue, V&A, March 1997] • b. cert. • *CGPLA Eng. & Wales* (1980) • M. Pick, *The life of Norman Hartnell* [forthcoming] • *Norman Hartnell, 1901–1979* (1985) [exhibition catalogue, Royal Pavilion Art Gallery and Museums, Brighton]

Likenesses Snowdon, photograph, 1968, priv. coll. [*see illus.*] • photographs, Hult. Arch.

Wealth at death £208,434: probate, 22 Jan 1980, *CGPLA Eng. & Wales*

Hartnell, William Henry (1908–1975), actor, was born at 24 Regent Square, St Pancras, London, on 8 January 1908, the son of Lucy Hartnell of that address, a commercial clerk, and an unnamed father. He was enrolled at the Italia Conti Stage School with the assistance of his unofficial guardian, Hugh Blaker. Conti herself had been a member of the repertory company of actor–manager Sir Frank Benson and Hartnell followed in her footsteps, joining in 1924. Billy Hartnell, as he was known at this time, could often appear in eight plays in a single week, especially those of Shakespeare, for the production of which the Benson company was well known. He was also keen to be offered comedy roles so he could try to emulate his hero, Charlie Chaplin.

In 1928 Hartnell appeared in a romantic comedy by R. N. Stephens and E. Lyall Swete, *Miss Elizabeth's Prisoner*, with an actress called Heather McIntyre (*d.* 1984) of Chelsea. She was born Amy Heather Miriam Armstrong McIntyre in 1906 or 1907, the daughter of Thomas McIntyre, a company director, and was later a playwright. They married on 9 May 1929 at the Chelsea register office; they had one daughter.

Hartnell made his first appearance on the London stage in 1932 but his first feature film, *School for Scandal*, was in 1930. Still appearing as Billy Hartnell (until the mid-1940s), he was the star of a handful of films in the 1930s (*Follow the Lady* and *I'm an Explosive*, 1933; *Seeing is Believing* and *Swinging the Lead*, 1934; *Nothing Like Publicity*, 1936). Such films, though, were often made very quickly and with cheap production values. After the outbreak of war Hartnell was drafted into the tank corps. He was invalided out after eighteen months after suffering a nervous breakdown. Returning to acting he had his first major success as Sergeant Fletcher in Carol Reed's film tribute to the British army, *The Way Ahead* (1944); the role made him a leading actor. In 1940 he had toured, and appeared in the West End, with Richard Attenborough in the play of Graham Greene's novel *Young Scarface*. In 1947 they were reunited in John Boulting's screen version, Hartnell playing Dallow. His theatrical appearances became much less frequent after the war, but he did star in the West End again in 1950 in Hugh Hastings's long-running comedy-drama, *Seagulls over Sorrento*.

In films Hartnell alternated starring roles in lesser films (*Murder in Reverse*, 1945; *Appointment with Crime*, 1946; *Temptation Harbour*, 1947; *Date with Disaster*, 1957; *On the Run*, 1958) with leading roles in better films (*Odd Man Out*, 1947; *Now Barabbas was a Robber*, 1949; *The Dark Man*, 1951; *Yangtse Incident*, 1957; *The Mouse that Roared*, 1959) and featured roles in major films (*The Magic Box*, 1951; *The Pickwick Papers*, 1952; *Private's Progress*, 1956; *Hell Drivers*, 1957; *Shake Hands*

William Henry Hartnell (1908–1975), by Harry Todd, 1964 [with two extra-terrestrials during filming for *Doctor Who*]

with the *Devil*, 1959; *Heavens Above*, 1963). In 1957–8 he appeared on television as Sergeant-Major Bullimore, an unpopular, aggressive character, in the series *The Army Game*. He left the series to make perhaps his best-known film, *Carry on Sergeant*, the first in the famed series of British comedies. In perhaps a third of his films Hartnell played figures of authority, often in the police force or the services, but here, as Sergeant Grimshawe, he was able also to display a softer side to his usual harsher character. Despite beginning to feel typecast in what he referred to as 'bastard roles', he returned to *The Army Game* for a further season in 1960–61.

One of Hartnell's best film roles was one of his last, as the old rugby league talent scout, Johnson, in Lindsay Anderson's *This Sporting Life* (1963), written by David Storey. As a result of this role in the same year he was offered the lead in *Doctor Who*, a new BBC television series. His Doctor was a quirky, even irascible, time-traveller, with long white hair and eccentric clothes, who travelled the universe in a time machine which was not only bigger inside than out but took the form of an everyday blue police telephone box. Although the series included the head of drama at BBC television, Sydney Newman, as one of its devisers, some other BBC executives had little confidence in its future, but Hartnell was convinced it would be hugely successful and, thanks largely to him, it was. He played the part for three years (1963–6) in 134 episodes; at one point the viewing audience numbered over twelve million. Seeing the role as 'manna from heaven' after playing so many tough army types, he sought to bring out the element of magic in the Doctor. In so doing he became a national celebrity and a hero to thousands of children, and attracted a huge personal fan mail, not just from them but from adults too. It was a great disappointment for him to have to leave the series owing to a combination of poor health (he suffered from arteriosclerosis) and disputes with the new producer. That he went straight into touring with the pantomime *Puss in Boots* suggests that the latter reason was predominant.

Despite continuing ill health, occasional television appearances punctuated the next few years for Hartnell. He even returned to the stage in 1968 (in *Brother and Sister*); but the roles he could now manage were few and he made his last major television appearance in 1970. Since leaving *Doctor Who* he had become known for playing that one role, despite his theatre background and over sixty film appearances, so it was perhaps fitting that he reprised it in his final appearance when he managed to record a few scenes for a tenth anniversary episode featuring the other two Doctors to that date. He had retired to Marden in Kent but his health was now in serious decline and his wife became his full-time nurse. He was admitted to Linton Hospital, Coxheath, near Maidstone, for a short time in August 1974 and in December was admitted permanently. Following a series of strokes he died there on 23 April 1975. He was survived by his wife, who died in December 1984, and his daughter.   ROBERT SHARP

Sources *The Times* (25 April 1975), 18g • J. Carney, 'Who's there?' (1996) [a biography by his granddaughter] • www.uk.imdb.com • b. cert. • m. cert. • d. cert. • *Celestial Toyroom* (Feb 1985)
Archives FILM BFI NFTVA, performance footage
Likenesses photographs, 1944–64, Hult. Arch. • H. Todd, photograph, 1964, Hult. Arch. [*see illus.*]

Hartnup, John Chapman (1806–1885), astronomer, was born on 7 January 1806 in Hurst Green, Sussex. Nothing is known of his life before 1831, when he became an assistant to John (later Lord) Wrottesley at the latter's private observatory in Blackheath, Kent. Wrottesley's ambition was to use a transit telescope to measure the right ascensions of some 1318 specially selected stars. The observing programme lasted from May 1831 to July 1835, and the resulting catalogue contained over 12,000 observations; in 1839 it won for Wrottesley the gold medal of the Royal Astronomical Society (RAS). In fact, the observations were secured by Hartnup, and provided him with a very solid grounding in positional astronomy and set the course for his career.

After leaving Wrottesley's employment, Hartnup became a supernumerary computer at the Royal Observatory, Greenwich. In March 1838 he became assistant secretary to the RAS. His basic yearly salary was £80, although he supplemented this with commissions for collecting subscriptions and selling the society's *Memoirs*. He had married Elizabeth Furness on 7 January 1837 at St Mary, Lewisham, Kent. While working for the RAS, he resided in its apartments in Somerset House, and it was here that his son John was born; the child was baptized on 7 February 1841 at St Mary-le-Strand.

In November 1843, on the recommendation of G. B. Airy, the astronomer royal, Hartnup was appointed as the first director of the Liverpool observatory. During the 1830s there had been in Liverpool a strong local feeling that an observatory should be founded to serve the interests of its rapidly growing port. After much discussion, involving, among others, the British Association for the Advancement of Science, various commercial interests, and private individuals, the Liverpool Dock Act of 1841 was passed with a section relating to the establishment of an observatory. This act enabled the town council to erect an observatory and meet the expenses out of dock dues. The observatory building was opened on Waterloo Dock in 1845. There was a residence for the astronomer, and the observatory apparatus included a transit instrument, an equatorially mounted refracting telescope, and associated clocks and meteorological instruments. The choice, design, and construction of the instruments owed much to Airy: the large refracting telescope, with an object glass of 8½ inches by Merz of Munich, was erected on an 'old English' mounting entirely under his superintendence.

As director of the Liverpool observatory, Hartnup was given three main tasks: to determine the longitude of Liverpool with as much accuracy as possible; to give accurate time to the port (this was to be done by use of a time-ball like that at Greenwich); and, most importantly, to test and rate chronometers. It was the third area that consumed the bulk of Hartnup's efforts and led to his invention of the 'Hartnup balance'.

Through his chronometer work at Liverpool, Hartnup soon focused on the so-called middle temperature error, which was inherent in the standard compensation balance employed in chronometers. To pursue this matter he designed a gas-heated oak box to test chronometers at a range of temperatures. In 1847 he conceived of a new sort of balance and his design was put into effect by William Shepherd, a Liverpool chronometer maker. Hartnup's balance, however, suffered various drawbacks, which meant it was not widely employed despite its definite advantage in terms of maintaining very close to the same rate at a wide range of temperatures.

As the port of Liverpool's business continued to expand, so Hartnup's chronometer work became ever heavier. This, together with advancing age, at first cut down and eventually curtailed his more directly astronomical pursuits. However, he had taken some excellent photographs of the moon in 1854. In Hartnup's earlier years at Liverpool Richard Sheepshanks, secretary of the RAS, had encouraged him to make extensive use of the refracting telescope to observe the positions of comets and minor planets. Good and large refractors were then so few that this work was important.

In 1863 the observatory was transferred from the Waterloo Dock to nearby Bidston on the Wirral. Shortly before the move, Hartnup's son had become an assistant to his father. In failing health, Hartnup resigned the directorship in May 1885, handing it over to his son, and moved to London in search of medical advice. He died suddenly on 20 October 1885 at his then home, 20 Langham Street, Portland Place, from causes that, according to the death certificate, derived from several years' senility. Seven years later, on 21 April 1892, Hartnup's son was killed when he fell from the observatory roof while making meteorological observations.　　　ROBERT W. SMITH

Sources *Monthly Notices of the Royal Astronomical Society*, 46 (1885–6), 188–91 · J. C. Poggendorff and others, eds., *Biographisch-literarisches Handwörterbuch zur Geschichte der exacten Wissenschaften*, 3 (Leipzig, 1898) · 'Reports of the Liverpool observatory', *Monthly Notices of the Royal Astronomical Society*, 6–47 (1843–86) · R. W. Smith, 'The Hartnup balance', *Antiquarian Horology and the Proceedings of the Antiquarian Horological Society*, 14 (1983–4), 39–45 · *Monthly Notices of the Royal Astronomical Society*, 28 (1867–8), 64–8 [obit. of John Wrottesley, second Baron Wrottesley] · *Monthly Notices of the Royal Astronomical Society*, 53 (1892–3), 218 · d. cert.

Archives BM · National Museums and Galleries on Merseyside, artefacts, log books · RAS, letters to Royal Astronomical Society | RAS, Lassell MSS · RAS, letters to Richard Sheepshanks

Wealth at death £6201 14s. 11d.: probate, 21 Nov 1885, *CGPLA Eng. & Wales*

Hartog, Numa Edward (1846–1871), campaigner for Jewish rights, was born at 55 Mansell Street, Whitechapel, London, on 20 May 1846, the elder son among the five surviving children of Alphonse Hartog (c.1815–1904), a native of France and professor of French in London, and his wife, Marion, *née* Moss (c.1821–1907), a writer and teacher. Philip Joseph *Hartog was his youngest brother. Educated by his father and then at Dr Pinches' City Commercial School, Hartog was later enrolled at University College School, whence he proceeded to University College, London. His remarkable intellectual powers were soon reflected in the award of numerous monetary prizes, and his University of London BSc degree, awarded to him at the age of eighteen, was gained 'with honours and emoluments for proficiency in mathematics, classics, French and German' (*The Times*, 21 June 1871, 9).

In October 1865 Hartog was admitted to Trinity College, Cambridge, to read for the mathematical tripos. Elected a foundation scholar the following year, he was judged senior wrangler—that is, top in his year—in January 1869, thus becoming the first professing Jew to gain this distinction. Hartog declined to be admitted to his degree using the Christian form of words then prescribed, and a 'special grace' was passed, unanimously, by the Cambridge Senate on 29 January 1869 to enable the vice-chancellor to admit him in a manner which did not offend his religious sensibilities.

Legislation enacted in 1854 had made it possible for professing Jews to take the bachelor's degree at Oxford University; in 1856 this right had been extended to Cambridge. However, higher degrees, fellowships, and offices at these universities were still barred to them. Hartog was thus unable to benefit from the customary practice whereby the senior wrangler was elected to a Trinity College fellowship more or less automatically. Instead, he had to make do with a post in the Treasury, subsequently entering the office of the parliamentary draftsman, Henry Thring, having been admitted to the Inner Temple in 1864.

But his fate became a *cause célèbre*, a test of the reality of the civic emancipation which the Jews of Britain were supposed to have won a decade earlier. The case was taken up by Gladstone's Liberal government, and a bill was introduced to abolish religious tests at the ancient universities; Hartog's disability was frequently quoted in the many parliamentary debates which followed. In 1869 and again in 1870, bills passed by the Commons were vetoed by the Lords. But on 3 March 1871 Hartog himself appeared before a select committee of the House of Lords established to inquire into 'university tests'; his evidence was said to have made a particular impact, and was perhaps decisive in persuading the upper house that it should endorse the legislation, which received the royal assent on 16 June.

Hartog, tragically, did not live long enough to be able to benefit from it. He contracted smallpox (for the second time), and died, unmarried, at his home, 15 Belsize Square, Hampstead, on 19 June 1871; he was buried on 20 June. His younger brother, Marcus Manuel Hartog (1851–1924), followed him in 1870 to Trinity College, Cambridge, where he obtained first-class honours in the natural sciences tripos and graduated BA in 1874 and MA in 1878; he subsequently became professor of zoology at University College, Cork.   GEOFFREY ALDERMAN

Sources The Times (21–2 June 1871) · Jewish Chronicle (23 June 1871) · DNB · Venn, Alum. Cant. · Boase, Mod. Eng. biog. · d. cert. · b. cert.
Archives Jewish Museum, Woburn House, Upper Woburn Place, London, corresp. and papers · LUL, notebooks
Wealth at death under £300: administration, 27 July 1871, CGPLA Eng. & Wales

Hartog, Sir Philip Joseph (1864–1947), educationist, was born in London on 2 March 1864, the third son of Alphonse Hartog (c.1815–1904) and his wife, Marion (c.1821–1907), *née* Moss. The family was poor but its members were distinguished. Alphonse Hartog, who belonged to a Jewish Dutch family which had settled in Paris in the late eighteenth century, had come to London to teach French in 1845 and was married to Marion Moss, daughter of Joseph Moss and member of one of the oldest Jewish families in Portsmouth, whom he met while she was teaching in London. Marion Moss was a writer and an accomplished teacher who, with her husband, ran schools for Jewish children. Their pupils included Philip Hartog's cousin Sarah Marks, who became the physicist Hertha Ayrton in later life. As neither parent possessed a flair for business the schools failed to prosper.

The Hartogs had seven children of whom five survived. Philip (named Philippe at birth) was the youngest, born when his mother was past forty. His eldest brother was the brilliant Numa Edward *Hartog, whose untimely death at the age of twenty-five occurred when Philip was only seven. The family never ceased to grieve for Numa but the surviving brothers and sisters supported one another emotionally and materially, focusing much attention on Philip and planning for him a distinguished career in the mould of the lost brother.

From 1875 Philip attended University College School, London, where his fees were paid by the Baroness Mayer de Rothschild, who had helped Numa; this arrangement ended abruptly in 1878 when her daughter cancelled the gift, stating that Hartog showed insufficient promise. His horrified family managed the final year at University College School before sending him to live with his brother Marcus, then an assistant lecturer in biology at Owens College, Manchester. Philip became a pupil of Sir Henry Roscoe and graduated BSc of Victoria University in 1882 at the age of eighteen. When Marcus was appointed professor at the University of Cork, Philip went to Paris to live with the family of his sister Helena and her husband, the philologist Arsène Darmesteter. In that cultured household he acquired an interest in language that was to last a lifetime, although he continued to pursue a scientific career, working on the composition of sulphites with Professor Berthelot at the Collège de France, and was placed first in his class for the degree of licencié-ès-sciences. The Darmesteters then paid for Philip to spend a year at Heidelberg University working with Bunsen. Hartog graduated BSc (London) with second-class honours in chemistry in 1885 and lived happily in Paris until his brother-in-law's sudden death. Faced with the necessity of helping his widowed sister, in 1889 Philip obtained a Bishop Berkeley fellowship in chemical physics at Victoria University of Manchester, where he became assistant lecturer in chemistry in 1891.

Hartog lived in Manchester from 1889 to 1903, a happy period of friendship with the academic circle that surrounded T. F. Tout and with C. P. Scott of the *Manchester Guardian*. In this period his contentment was marred only by his failure to obtain the London degree of DSc in 1890, a growing suspicion that he would never distinguish himself as a research chemist, and a persistent lack of money, as he contributed to the support of his parents and sister. To earn extra money he wrote book reviews and scientific articles for the *Manchester Guardian* and Tout introduced him to writing for the *Dictionary of National Biography*. His wife wrote that in 1891 he was entrusted with the biographies of Macadam, Mayow, and Mercer 'and he eventually wrote the biographies of all the chemists from the letter "M" onwards', nearly forty altogether (Hartog, 22). This work gave him a lucid prose style and an interest in Priestley, to which he would return in later life.

Philip Hartog was a natural teacher and a popular lecturer (he was flattered to be chosen to lecture in chemistry at the Manchester High School for Girls until he found out that the headmistress was looking for a homely lecturer to avoid distracting the girls). In 1895 Principal Ward offered him the post of secretary of the extension committee, of which Tout was chairman. This fortunate partnership called forth both Hartog's talent for teaching and a previously unrecognized genius for administration. His extension work led to friendship with Michael Sadler, and Sadler's influence led Hartog to accept that, for him, teaching and administration were to be of greater importance than research. He worked at the Ancoats settlement and was a respected member of its short-lived Ruskin Hall. This work gave him an abiding interest in clear expository writing; he was to publish two influential books on the subject, notably *The Writing of English* (1907). From 1902 to 1903 he was secretary of Alfred Mosely's commission to study educational methods in the USA.

Despite his happiness at Manchester, Hartog realized that advancement was unlikely there. With the support of Roscoe, Schuster, and the physicist Will Ayrton (who had married Hartog's cousin) he applied for the post of and was appointed academic registrar of the University of London. He served in this post from 1903 to 1920 and was instrumental in organizing and drafting statutes for the newly reorganized university. Both his talent for administration and his innate courtesy served him well in this position, in which he exerted considerable influence.

In 1905 Hartog became secretary of a committee of London University to reorganize oriental studies. He brought to the project, which resulted in the foundation of the school of oriental studies (1916), an 'almost missionary enthusiasm' (*Bulletin*, 491). The undertaking required his best diplomatic and managerial skills; when the school came into being he regretfully declined to be its first head in preference to a recognized oriental studies scholar. He continued to serve the school for thirty years as crown member of its governing body. He was appointed CIE in 1916 for his work for the school and in old age it was his delight to hear himself described as its founder.

Hartog's parents died early in the twentieth century; he remained close to his two sisters until their deaths in 1940. On 9 April 1915 Hartog married Mabel Hélène (*d.* 1954), daughter of Henry Joseph Kisch. She was to write several books on India, together with her husband's biography. They had three sons. The family were enthusiastic walkers and climbers, and Hartog continued to climb until at least his early seventies.

Despite his domestic felicity, Hartog was restless during the war years, longing for work of national importance. Despite his age, he tried unsuccessfully to get himself sent to France as an interpreter. In 1917 Sadler invited him to join a commission on the University of Calcutta. Six months' work turned to eighteen months, but, despite personal inconveniences (his second son was born during his absence), for Hartog the work was stimulating, calling for both his meticulous attention to detail and his qualities of tact and good humour. It led to an involvement with India that would continue for the rest of his life.

In 1920 Hartog was appointed first vice-chancellor of the new University of Dacca, created to serve the Muslim community of Bengal. He and his family spent five happy years in Dacca, where he was instrumental in establishing the university as a residential, tutorial body, with a staff engaged in serious research and a mission to train its students for life and citizenship, a model unfamiliar in existing Indian universities but one which proved highly popular with students and community alike. Despite communal disturbances and almost routine criticism in the local press, Hartog kept the university open and secured it reliable funding, leaving it in 1925 well established with harmonious relations between its Muslim and Hindu students. His own reputation as an academic administrator was enormously enhanced; he received the honorary

degree of LLD of the university in 1925 and a knighthood in 1926 for services to India.

Hartog returned to England in 1925 but felt unoccupied and quickly returned to India as a member of the newly created Indian public service commission. In 1928 and 1929 he chaired a commission on the growth of education in India which exposed appalling wastage in elementary education, especially among girls. In 1930 Hartog resigned from the public service commission eighteen months early, wishing to spend more time with his wife and young sons, and he was appointed KBE.

People who knew Hartog remarked on how little he seemed to age and how much he accomplished after what is generally thought of as the age of retirement. In the 1930s Eleanor Rathbone enlisted Hartog, who had championed women's suffrage at the University of London, to chair a group pressing for women's franchise in the new constitution of India; he debated with Gandhi, refuting Gandhi's claim that literacy had declined in British India; he returned to his study of Joseph Priestley; and he became an active member of the Academic Assistance Council, working to help displaced academics from Nazi Germany.

Hartog had a long-standing interest in the operation of examinations and in 1931 he was appointed as director, under Sadler, of an international committee, the International Institute Examinations Enquiry, whose object was to promote objective and scientific methods of examining. With Gladys Roberts he conducted two major surveys of the intelligence tests used by local authorities in the United Kingdom. His studies with E. C. Rhodes, published as *An Examination of Examinations* (1935) and *The Marks of Examiners* (1936), helped to secure recognition of the distinction between examinations designed to test mastery of specific skills and those that tested educational progress.

Hartog was a deeply religious individual, in Manchester a member of the Reform synagogue, and later a member of the council of the Liberal Jewish synagogue in London. He worked for various Jewish organizations, including the Liberal Jewish movement led by C. J. Goldsmid-Montefiore. Although never a Zionist, Hartog came to see Palestine as a refuge against persecution and in 1933 chaired a small committee to report on the organization of the Hebrew University of Jerusalem. He worked hard to establish its department of English and served on its board of governors.

During the Second World War Hartog chaired a committee to create a register of linguists available for war work, hoping to avoid the waste of talent he remembered from the First World War. He slowly completed his last work in defence of rhetoric, *Words in Action: the Teaching of the Mother Tongue for the Training of Citizens in a Democracy* (1947), which he hoped would replace the meaningless prose compositions then still assigned in many schools. He coined the phrase 'intellectual conscience' to describe the critical habits of mind that made individuals resistant to propaganda. His health declined early in 1946 and he died at 5 Collingham Gardens, Kensington, London, on 27 June

1947. Mabel Hartog was killed in a mountaineering accident in 1954.

Hartog was a small man; his wife described him in Manchester days as 'short and dark with [a] small head, rather like an eager little bird, inconspicuous though not easily forgotten' (Hartog, 159). He was by nature kind, modest, and unassuming, of a legendary absent-mindedness which often led to his arriving home with alien articles of clothing. He himself said his life was never dull because he had 'a constitutional interest in and liking for people' (ibid., 159). The universities of Manchester, London, Dacca, and Jerusalem, the Jewish communities in London and Palestine, and the educational systems in England and India as a whole benefited from his formidable administrative talents. He was remembered not just for these talents but also for his belief in the liberating possibilities of clear writing and his gift for friendship.

ELIZABETH J. MORSE

Sources DNB · M. Hartog, *P. J. Hartog: a memoir by his wife* (1949) · *Bulletin of the School of Oriental and African Studies*, 12 (1948), 491–3 · D. McKie, *JCS* (1948), 901–3 · T. Kelly, *Outside the walls: sixty years of university extension at Manchester, 1886–1946* (1950) · *WWW* · M. A. Rahim, *The history of the University of Dacca* (1981) · M. D. Stocks, *Fifty years in every street: the story of the Manchester University settlement* (1945) · G. Sutherland and S. Sharp, *Ability, merit and measurement: mental testing and English education, 1880–1940* (1984) · E. Ashby, *Universities: British, Indian, African* (1966) · *CGPLA Eng. & Wales* (1947)
Archives BL OIOC, corresp. and MSS, MSS Eur. D 551, E 221 · JRL, corresp. and MSS | Bodl. Oxf., corresp. relating to Society for the Protection of Science and Learning · CAC Cam., corresp. with A. V. Hill · JRL, letters to *Manchester Guardian* · UCL, Pearson MSS, letters to Karl Pearson
Likenesses W. Stoneman, photograph, 1931, NPG · H. Darmesteter, oils, SOAS · photograph (in late middle age), repro. in Hartog, *P. J. Hartog* (1949), facing title-page
Wealth at death £18,571 4s. 2d.: probate, 31 Oct 1947, *CGPLA Eng. & Wales*

Hartopp, Sir John, third baronet (*bap.* 1637, *d.* 1722), politician, was baptized on 31 October 1637, the only surviving son of Sir Edward Hartopp, second baronet (*d.* 1658), landowner, and Mary, daughter of Sir John *Coke of Melbourne, Derbyshire. He matriculated from St John's College, Oxford, on 25 July 1655, but did not graduate; he was admitted on 19 June 1656 to Lincoln's Inn. He succeeded as third baronet in March 1658, inheriting his father's estate at Freatby, Leicestershire. In 1664 his mother married the former republican general Charles *Fleetwood and went to live with him in Stoke Newington, Middlesex. On 8 November 1666 Sir John Hartopp married Elizabeth (*d.* 1711), Fleetwood's daughter from his first marriage.

In September 1673 the churchwardens of Stoke Newington presented Hartopp and Charles Fleetwood 'for not coming to their said parish church nor receiving the sacrament at Easter last past nor since to this day' (Cliffe, 84). Hartopp worshipped at the Leadenhall Street congregation of the Independent minister Dr John Owen; after the death of Joseph Caryl in 1672 his followers and those of Owen joined forces to form 'one of the most aristocratic of the London Nonconformist congregations', meeting at Bury Street in the parish of St Mary Axe (Whiting, 78). Hartopp made shorthand notes of Owen's sermons and as a result thirteen were published for the first time in 1756.

Hartopp represented Leicestershire in the three Exclusion Parliaments of 1679 and 1681. He was an exclusionist, but was otherwise inactive in the first parliament; following his re-election in October he sat on eight committees, including those charged to 'inquire into the conduct of Sir Robert Peyton, into abhorring, and the proceedings of the judges. He was also among those instructed to bring in bills to regulate parliamentary elections, to unite Protestants, and to reform the Post Office' (Cruickshanks). Though he was returned unopposed in 1681, he appears once more to have lapsed into inactivity. In April 1686 fines totalling £7000 were levied on Hartopp and Charles Fleetwood on the grounds that they were guilty of holding conventicles at Stoke Newington, though it appears that some of this was recovered following legal objections.

According to Isaac Watts, his chaplain for five years, Hartopp:

> had a taste for universal learning; and ingenious arts were a delight from his youth ... mathematical speculations and practices were a favourite study with him in his younger years; and even to his old age he maintained his acquaintance with the motions of the heavenly bodies ... But the Book of God was his chief study, and his divinest delight. His bible lay before him night and day. (Watts, 242–3)

Hartopp himself gave sermons: 'he entertained his family in the evening worship on the Lord's day with excellent discourses' (ibid., 250). In addition to his Stoke Newington mansion he had a house in Epsom, and Watts sometimes preached in the adjoining Independent chapel. He also stayed at the family's property at Freatby near Melton Mowbray, acting there as tutor to Mary Hartopp, probably Sir John's daughter.

Hartopp died at Stoke Newington on 1 April 1722 and was buried on the 11th in Stoke Newington church beside his wife, who had died on 9 November 1711 and had been buried on 26 November. He left £10,000 for the training of dissenting ministers, but his heirs used a legal technicality to appropriate the bequest; it seems that eventually nearly half the money was restored to its intended purpose. Sir John and Elizabeth Hartopp had a family of four sons and nine daughters. Of these Frances married Nathaniel *Gould of Stoke Newington (1661–1728), a director of the Bank of England (1697) and later MP for Shoreham. She died on 15 November 1711, six days after her mother. The eldest boy, John (1680?–1762), married Sarah, the daughter and coheir of the wealthy Sir Joseph Woolfe of Hackney, an alderman in 1705 and brother of Sir John Woolfe (sheriff of London, 1696–7). Soon after this union, Sir John Hartopp handed over the estate to his son, with the proviso that the young man should settle £500 per annum on each of his six unmarried sisters, who all lived in the Fleetwood house and died between 1739 and 1764.

STEPHEN WRIGHT

Sources E. Cruickshanks, 'Hartopp, Sir John, 3rd bt', HoP, *Commons, 1660–90* · I. Watts, *Death and heaven, or, The last enemy conquered ... in memory of Sir John Hartopp and his lady deceased* (1722) · A. Shirren, *The chronicles of Fleetwood House* (1951) · J. T. Cliffe, *The* *puritan gentry besieged, 1650–1700* (1993) · W. Robinson, *The history and antiquities of Stoke Newington* (1842) · C. Whiting, *Studies in English puritanism* (1931) · A. B. Beaven, ed., *The aldermen of the City of London, temp. Henry III–[1912]*, 2 vols. (1908–13) · W. P. Baildon, ed., *The records of the Honorable Society of Lincoln's Inn: admissions*, 1 (1896) · Foster, *Alum. Oxon.* · GEC, *Baronetage*

Archives DWL, transcripts of sermons, etc.
Likenesses attrib. G. Kneller, drawing, Morgan L. · oils, Abney Congregational church, Stoke Newington

Hartree, Douglas Rayner (1897–1958), mathematician and theoretical physicist, was born on 27 March 1897 in Cambridge, where his father, William Hartree, a grandson of Samuel Smiles, was a member of the teaching staff of the engineering laboratory; he retired in 1913, but thereafter continued to do scientific work, much of it as assistant to his son. Hartree's mother, Eva Rayner, was the daughter of a prominent Stockport physician and sister of E. H. Rayner, who for many years was superintendent of the electricity division of the National Physical Laboratory. She was herself active in public affairs, serving as president of the National Council of Women and as mayor of Cambridge.

Douglas Hartree was the eldest of three sons, but alone survived to manhood. He was educated first in Cambridge, then at Bedales School, in Petersfield, from 1910 to 1915, where the excellent teaching of mathematics shaped his chief interests in later life. In 1915 he entered St John's College, Cambridge, as a scholar, but after a year he abandoned his studies for work in a team under A. V. Hill developing the new science of anti-aircraft gunnery. After the war Hartree completed his university courses and was awarded a PhD in 1926. In 1923 he had married Elaine, daughter of Eustace and Beatrice Charlton of Keswick, and an ex-pupil of Bedales School. They had one daughter and two sons. Hartree was elected fellow of St John's (1924–7) and of Christ's College (1928–9). He was appointed to the chair of applied mathematics (1929–37) and of theoretical physics (1937–45) in the University of Manchester. In 1946 he became Plummer professor of mathematical physics at Cambridge, a chair which he held until his death, and was again a fellow of Christ's. He was elected FRS in 1932.

The main scope of Hartree's work was largely determined by his early experiences in anti-aircraft gunnery. The calculation of trajectories involved much numerical work with pencil and paper, a type of mathematics in which he became expert; already at the age of twenty he had introduced outstanding improvements into the calculation of trajectories. He continued to develop this kind of work all through his life, and he came to be regarded as a world leader in computation, called in as consultant in many countries.

In the 1920s Hartree applied his methods to the solution of problems associated with the new quantum theories of the structure of the atom, particularly wave mechanics. In this field his most conspicuous work was the invention of the method of the self-consistent field. This made possible the practical solution of a problem which, if exactly treated, would have a quite impossible degree of complexity. Ten years later numerical methods were much changed by the invention of the differential analyser by Vannevar Bush in America. Hartree visited him at Massachusetts Institute of Technology in the summer of 1933 and gained both theoretical knowledge and valuable practical experience with the analyser. After returning to Britain Hartree first constructed (with graduate student Arthur Porter) a model of Bush's machine using the children's construction toy, Meccano. Successful operation of the model machine to solve differential equations allowed Hartree to persuade philanthropic benefactor and Manchester University deputy treasurer, Sir Robert McDougall, to fund a full-scale machine. This differential analyser, built by Metropolitan-Vickers, was widely used for military and scientific calculations. Hartree also became a leader in developing methods of automatic control for many complicated processes of manufacture: for example, his three term controller, used in chemical engineering plants, was a significant new technique of automation.

Hartree was also involved in the development of the digital electronic computer, which emerged from wartime attempts to automate calculation further, and was to replace differential analyses as the means of rapid solution of equations. In 1946 Hartree's advice was sought in the application of the United States army's ENIAC (electronic numerical integrator and computer) to the production of ballistic tables. A process which previously took a team of workers several days could now be done in thirty seconds. The first electronic digital stored program computer, based on the ideas of the ENIAC designers, was built at Manchester University in 1948, but Hartree had left for Cambridge two years previously.

Hartree's distinction as a scientist was not so much in the depth of his researches as in their breadth. With the new methods it became possible to attack many problems in a great variety of subjects which had before been insoluble, and it was he who largely led the way in this new attack. His book, *Numerical Analysis* (1952), came to be regarded as a classic of the subject. He was remembered as a good lecturer and brilliant at clarifying a subject by an intuitive knowledge of the level of understanding of his listener.

From boyhood Hartree had a strong interest in railways and their signalling methods, and in later life this proved useful to the railway companies in relation to their complicated traffic problems. He served on a committee of the British Transport Commission and showed how to use the high-speed computing machines to solve traffic problems which had previously taken months of calculation. Music was among his other interests: he played the piano and other instruments and also conducted an amateur orchestra. Hartree died of heart failure in Addenbrooke's Hospital, Cambridge, on 12 February 1958. He was survived by his wife. C. G. DARWIN, *rev.* JON AGAR

Sources C. G. Darwin, *Memoirs FRS*, 4 (1958), 103–16 · M. V. Wilkes, introduction, in D. R. Hartree, *Calculating machines* (1984), ix–xvi · M. D. Bowles, 'US technological enthusiasm and British technological skepticism in the age of the analog brain', *IEEE Annals of the History of Computing*, 18 (1996), 5–15 · L. Owens, 'Vannevar Bush and the differential analyzer: the text and context of an early computer', *Technology and Culture*, 27 (1986), 63–95 · National Archive for the History of Computing, Manchester · *CGPLA Eng. & Wales* (1958)

Archives Christ's College, Cambridge, corresp. and scientific papers · University of Manchester, National Archive for the History of Computing, working papers, etc. | American Institute of Physics, College Park, Maryland, Niels Bohr Library, corresp. with Niels Bohr · Duke U., Perkins L., corresp. with F. London · U. Leeds, Brotherton L., corresp. with E. C. Stoner

Likenesses W. Stoneman, photograph, 1944, NPG · photograph, repro. in Darwin, *Memoirs FRS* · photograph, repro. in Wilkes, 'Introduction'

Wealth at death £55,691 2s. 0d.: probate, 14 May 1958, *CGPLA Eng. & Wales*

Hartry, Malachy [*formerly* John] (*b.* 1580?, *d.* in or after 1651), historian, was born in Waterford city, Ireland, soon after 4 July 1580 of 'respectable parents', whose names do not survive (Hartry, 293). He was educated in the humanities at the Irish College, Lisbon, and became a Cistercian monk at the abbey of Palacuel in Spain. In 1619 Hartry returned to Ireland to work in Cistercian communities at Holy Cross, co. Tipperary, Kilkenny, Drogheda, Mothel, co. Waterford, and Waterford city. As an essential part of his missionary work, he devoted himself to investigating the history of the Irish branch of the order.

Of Hartry's many Latin writings, under the name Malachy, only two substantial pieces survive. One, entitled 'Triumphalia chronologica de coenobio sanctae crucis sacri ordinis Cisterciensis in Hibernia', is dated 4 July 1640, and contains an autobiographical note in which the author describes himself as nearly sixty. It comprises an account of the establishment of Holy Cross Abbey, with notices of its relics and administrators. The other, entitled 'De Cisterciensium Hibernorum viris illustribus' and completed on 18 April 1651, contains over forty biographical sketches of illustrious members of Irish Cistercian houses. Both were edited and published in 1891 under the title of the 1640 piece. Among Hartry's works which do not survive was a biography of the Irish Cistercian monk Thomas Lombard.

Hartry's corpus made a significant contribution to the ecclesiastical historiography of Ireland in the late medieval and immediate post-Reformation periods. The leading Cistercian historians on the continent, Juan Crisostomo Henriquez and Angelus Manrique, knew and thought highly of Hartry, and made use of his researches in their own work. Hartry died some time after 18 April 1651, at a date and place unknown. COLM LENNON

Sources M. Hartry, *Triumphalia chronologica de coenobio sancta crucis sacri ordinis Cisterciensis in Hibernia*, ed. D. Murphy (1891), lxx–lxxi, 214–15, 292–7 · C. Conway, 'Three unpublished Cistercian documents', *Louth Archaeological Society Journal*, 13 (1953–6), 252–78 · *Cause for the beatification and canonisation of the servants of God, Richard Creagh, archbishop, who died in England, and companions who died in Ireland in defence of the Catholic faith, 1572–1655*, 2 vols. (1998), 1.133–6, 311–13 · *DNB* · B. Jennings, ed., *Wadding papers, 1614–38*, IMC (1953), 232 · J. C. Henriquez, *Menologium Cisterciense, annotationibus illustratum* (1630), 389 · M. Gonçalves da Costa, ed., *Fontes inéditas Portuguesas para a história de Irlanda* (Braga, 1981), 408

Hartshorn, Vernon (1872–1931), trade union leader and politician, was born at Cross Keys, Pont-y-Waun, Monmouthshire, on 16 March 1872, the elder son of Theophilus Hartshorn, coalminer, and his wife, Helen Gregory, daughter of a farm labourer. He began work in the mines before taking employment as a clerk in a colliery company's office at Cardiff docks. Having returned to work at Risca, he was elected by the miners as their checkweighman. In 1899 he married Mary Matilda, daughter of Edward Winsor, a Somerset coalminer. They had two sons and a daughter.

Hartshorn, whose political career developed from his early commitment to Primitive Methodism, was one of the pioneers of the Independent Labour Party in Wales. In 1905 he was elected miners' agent of the Maesteg district of the South Wales Miners' Federation. In 1911 he was elected to its executive council and to the national executive council of the Miners' Federation of Great Britain, one of a number of young radicals who displaced more established figures, following the Cambrian combine strike of 1910–11. He took a leading part in the minimum wage strike of 1912 and was prominent in local government business.

During the First World War, Hartshorn served on the coal trade organization committee, the coal controllers' advisory committee, and the industrial unrest committee in south Wales, and his services were recognized by his appointment as OBE in 1918. At the general election of 1918 Hartshorn, who had in 1910 twice unsuccessfully contested the Mid-Glamorgan division as an independent socialist candidate, was returned unopposed as the first member for the newly formed Ogmore division of Glamorgan, and he held the seat until his death. Notwithstanding parliamentary duties, he aided the miners in their strike in 1920, but he resigned from both the miners' executive councils to which he belonged because of a disagreement over the tactics employed in the strike. He returned to both councils from 1922 to 1924, having been elected president of the South Wales Miners' Federation.

In parliament Hartshorn was elected chairman of the Welsh Labour group in 1923, and in the first Labour administration in 1924 he was postmaster-general and sworn of the privy council. In 1927 he was appointed to the seven-man Indian statutory commission, which he later considered to have achieved outstanding results. The chairman, Sir John Simon, stated that those portions of the commission's report which dealt with the franchise and the method of election were especially due to Hartshorn.

On the formation of the second Labour administration, in 1929, the prime minister announced that a place for Hartshorn would be found as soon as the commission had completed its work. Accordingly, in 1930 he was appointed lord privy seal with special responsibility for the government's policy on employment. Hartshorn showed great promise in this post, earning Ramsay MacDonald's high praise for a report he handed to the prime minister after two months in office; but he was prevented from fulfilling this early promise by death.

Vernon Hartshorn (1872–1931), by Bassano, 1924

Hartshorn owed his rise to his detailed knowledge of the mining industry, his outstanding ability as a negotiator, and his moderation and pragmatism. He died at Hill Crest, Maesteg, Glamorgan, on 13 March 1931, survived by his wife.   W. L. COOK, rev. ROBERT INGHAM

Sources The Times (14 March 1931) · DLB · R. Gregory, The miners and British politics, 1906–1914 (1968) · H. A. Clegg, A. Fox, and A. F. Thompson, A history of British trade unions since 1889, 2 (1985) · DWB · WWBMP · A. Morgan, J. Ramsay Macdonald (1987)
Archives JRL, Labour History Archive and Study Centre, corresp. | JRL, corresp. with James Ramsay Macdonald
Likenesses Bassano, photograph, 1924, NPG [see illus.] · photograph, repro. in The Times
Wealth at death £2278 15s. 9d.: probate, 4 Aug 1931, CGPLA Eng. & Wales

Hartshorne, Albert (1839–1910), archaeologist, was born on 15 November 1839 at Cogenhoe rectory, Cogenhoe, near Northampton, one of the eight children of Revd Charles Henry *Hartshorne (1802–1865), antiquary, and his wife, Frances Margaretta (d. 1892), younger daughter of Revd Thomas *Kerrich (1748–1828), sometime president of Magdalene College, Cambridge, and principal librarian of the university library at Cambridge. After attending Westminster School (1854–7) he completed his education in France and at Heidelberg. In 1872 he married Constance Amelia (d. 1901), younger daughter of Revd Francis MacCarthy of Ballyneadrig and Lyradane; they had no children.

Hartshorne's antiquarian curiosity was unsurprising given his family background; both his father and maternal grandfather had earlier studied church monuments, which became one of his chief interests. His major work on The Recumbent Monumental Effigies in Northamptonshire was published in parts between 1867 and 1876, with illustrations made by photographing ink copies of original pencil drawings which had been prepared to scale on the spot. In their faithful likeness to the original sculptured figures, showing details of armour, dress, and jewellery at actual size, the drawings and descriptions of the individual dated monuments contained useful information of costume history, which Hartshorne himself developed in later studies of sword belts (1891) and portraiture (1899). His draughtsmanship also included measuring and planning buildings, together with drawing Anglo-Saxon pottery and other objects. His interest in artefacts extended to more recent items, and he wrote a monograph on drinking glasses from early times to the end of the eighteenth century, published as Old English Glasses (1897).

Hartshorne was twice secretary of the Royal Archaeological Institute of Great Britain and Ireland, between 1876 and 1883 and from 1886 to 1894, and during that time also edited its annual proceedings, the Archaeological Journal, from 1878 to 1892. He was elected a fellow of the Society of Antiquaries of London in 1882 and served for a time on its council, as well as becoming the local secretary for Derbyshire. He remained active in national archaeological affairs and frequently contributed papers to meetings in London, as well as continuing to publish historical research until his death. In later life Hartshorne lived chiefly at Bradbourne Hall, Derbyshire, but died at his home at 7 Heene Terrace, Worthing, on 8 December 1910, and was buried in Holdenby churchyard, Northamptonshire, where his father had been appointed rector in 1850.   BRIAN DIX

Sources The Times (10 Dec 1910) · Proceedings of the Society of Antiquaries of London, 2nd ser., 23 (1910–11), 436 · DNB · CGPLA Eng. & Wales (1911)
Archives Haverford College, Pennsylvania, corresp., family papers · Northants. RO, corresp. and antiquarian collection
Likenesses S. Lucas, sketch, 1888; in possession of H. R. P. Wyatt in 1912
Wealth at death £2378 7s. 11d.: resworn probate, 18 Feb 1911, CGPLA Eng. & Wales

Hartshorne, Charles Henry (1802–1865), antiquary, was born in Broseley, Shropshire, on 17 March 1802, the only child of John Hartshorne (1759–1805), known probably from involvement in the local trade as 'the ironmaster', and his wife, Frances, née Holleyshead (1777–1849). The Hartshornes had long been settled at Broseley and neighbouring Benthall. His father's premature death impaired Hartshorne's early prospects. He entered Shrewsbury School late, aged sixteen, in 1818 and was advised by the judge Sir James Alan Park that exertion was essential and that the expense of studying for the bar (£250–£300 a year) was likely to be prohibitive. Hartshorne soon 'fixed upon the Church', Park urging him in letters to aspire to be a learned divine, to strive for perfection of character, and to avoid the 'quicksand' of fanaticism, enthusiasm, and

Methodism. Hartshorne was admitted pensioner at St John's College, Cambridge, in 1821, graduated BA in 1825, and proceeded MA in 1828.

Hartshorne's earliest source of antiquarian and bibliophilic inspiration was Thomas Frognall Dibdin, though a more important—and more fateful—contact was Richard *Heber, the bibliophile and MP for Oxford University, whom he had met before going up and visited a number of times while at Cambridge. Heber brought him into the circle of the Roxburghe Club and introduced him to Frederick North, fifth earl of Guilford. North, who was chancellor of the University of Corfu, invited Hartshorne to accompany him there; he travelled through Italy and also toured the Levant. An account of this journey was one of his many uncompleted literary projects.

On returning to England in September 1826, Hartshorne discovered that a rumour had been circulating for some time of a homosexual relationship between himself and Heber, and that this had been referred to by innuendo in the muck-raking magazine *John Bull* during the previous May. Heber had since gone abroad, and could not be prevailed upon to return to rebut the charges; it seems likely that there was nothing to hide in this case, but he may have wanted to avoid scrutiny of other episodes in his private life. Hartshorne accordingly sought, and was granted, a criminal information against *John Bull* in king's bench, and its editor was fined £500. But Heber's exile effectively ended Hartshorne's hopes of obtaining a post in the British Museum or the civil service. He was ordained deacon in 1827, becoming curate of Benthall, Shropshire, near his family home. He was ordained priest in 1828 and was curate of nearby Little Wenlock from 1828 to 1836. On 10 December 1828 Hartshorne married Frances Margaretta, younger daughter of the Revd Thomas *Kerrich, principal librarian of the University of Cambridge, who had died earlier that year. She brought with her a considerable fortune, and they had fourteen children, four of whom died in infancy. By 1829 Hartshorne's mother had been widowed again, and the indefatigable Park (letter of 10 June, Hartshorne MSS) was rejoicing over the power her late husband's kindness had left her, 'of providing handsomely for you'.

After two years in Leamington, Warwickshire, 'which everything intellectual shuns', Hartshorne took charge of Cogenhoe church, Northamptonshire, in 1838, rejoicing to find it, as he told his fellow antiquary Albert Way, 'hoary with grey lichen … the natural abode of an Antiquary' (Hartshorne MSS). A few years later he was conscious of being more antiquary than divine, having to confess that he was 'woefully deficient' in books 'on my own profession'. Nevertheless his mention of 'Oxford poison' suggests that he was armed against enthusiasm of a non-Methodist kind (letter to Way, ibid.). He was elected a fellow of the Society of Antiquaries in 1839 and became a member of the Roxburghe Club, belatedly, in 1861. He was honorary chaplain to the seventh and eighth dukes of Bedford, and in 1850, during the premiership of the seventh duke's brother Lord John Russell, he was presented to the crown living of Holdenby rectory, Northamptonshire.

Hartshorne's publications include *Ancient Metrical Tales, Printed Chiefly from Original Sources* (1829), referred to by Scott in his introduction (1830) to *Ivanhoe*; *Sepulchral Remains in Northamptonshire* (1840); *Salopia antiqua, or, An Enquiry into the Early Remains in Shropshire and the North Welsh Borders* (1841), including a glossary of the 'Provincial Dialect' of Shropshire; *Historical Memorials of Northampton* (1848); and *Memoirs Illustrative of the History and Antiquities of Northumberland* (1858), a useful contribution to the history of the borders. He contributed an article, 'The Latin plays acted before the University of Cambridge', to the *Retrospective Review* and was a frequent writer in the *Archaeological Journal*. His archaeological papers cover the architectural history of medieval towns and castles, various medieval parliaments, the royal councils of Worcester, the obsequies of Katherine of Aragon, early remains in the great isle of Arran, the itineraries of Edward I and II, and domestic manners in the reign of Edward I. He was also author of papers on the drainage of the New Valley, and subjects connected with social science. *Salopia antiqua*, a genuinely original archaeological synopsis which may still be consulted with profit, was founded on an extensive and vigorous exploration of his native county: in 1837 he wrote (to Way) describing long tramps, of 30–50 miles daily, over the Shropshire hills. The book was in some respects pioneering, for example in its inclusion of material on dialect and place names which were anticipations of later, more systematic work by Georgina F. Jackson and others. Much of his work, however, contains errors and internal inconsistencies, and is characterized, according to one modern assessment, by 'wide learning and shallow scholarship' (Hunt, 31).

Hartshorne died of heart disease at Holdenby on 11 March 1865, a week short of his sixty-third birthday. His library was sold at Sothebys, but owing to the water damage caused to many items following a fire, the sale prices were disappointing. His wife survived him; his third son, Albert *Hartshorne, achieved distinction as an archaeologist, and a daughter, Emily Sophia, was the author of *Memorials of Holdenby* (1868) and three other books.

GEORGE C. BAUGH

Sources DNB · E. Glasgow, *Hartshorne, Charles Henry* [1984] · correspondence, Northants. RO, Hartshorne collection, pt 3 · Venn, *Alum. Cant.*, 2/3.274 · H. I. Longden, *Northamptonshire and Rutland clergy from 1500*, ed. P. I. King and others, 16 vols. in 6, Northamptonshire RS (1938–52), vol. 6, p. 189 · *VCH Shropshire*, 10.256, 287 · A. Hunt, 'A study in bibliomania: Charles Henry Hartshorne and Richard Heber', *Book Collector*, 42 (1993), 25–43, 185–212 · d. cert. · *IGI* · *CGPLA Eng. & Wales* (1866)

Archives Northants. RO, antiquarian and family corresp. · Northants. RO, corresp. and antiquarian collection | BL, rubbings of sepulchral brasses, Add. MS 34806 A–C · Bodl. Oxf., corresp. with Sir Thomas Phillipps · U. Edin. L., letters to James Halliwell Phillipps · U. Edin. L., letters to David Laing

Likenesses photograph, c.1850, repro. in Glasgow, *Hartshorne*

Wealth at death under £3000: probate, 10 Jan 1866, *CGPLA Eng. & Wales*

Hartstonge, John (1659–1717), Church of Ireland bishop of Derry, was born on 1 December 1659 at Catton, near

Norwich, the second son of Sir Standish Hartstonge (*d.* *c.*1702), one of the barons of the Irish exchequer, and his first wife, Elizabeth (*d.* 1663), daughter of Francis Jermy of Gunton in Norfolk. Having attended schools at Charleville and Kilkenny, he entered Trinity College, Dublin, on 20 May 1673, and graduated BA in 1677 and MA in 1680. Meanwhile he had entered Gonville and Caius College, Cambridge, on 19 June 1676, where he took his MA in 1680. After travelling for a year until he had reached the canonical age, he took orders and was elected a fellow of Caius in 1681. He became chaplain to the first duke of Ormond, and through his influence was collated to the archdeaconry of Limerick on 24 June 1684. He served as chaplain to the second duke of Ormond during his campaigns in Flanders, and in 1693 was appointed bishop of Ossory (patent 8 April, consecrated 2 July).

In the reign of Anne, Hartstonge emerged as a militant member of the tory and high-church party. In 1704 he was one of three bishops whom the primate, acting through his chaplain, condemned as 'incendiaries'. When convocation in 1709 became involved in a conflict with the lord lieutenant, Wharton, Hartstonge was one of two bishops sent to London to appeal against his authority. Later, in 1711, Dominic Langton, a renegade friar who had come forward with wild allegations of treasonable conspiracy among the whig gentry of co. Westmeath, claimed immunity from arrest as Hartstonge's chaplain. In January 1713 Swift reported that Hartstonge was not to succeed to the see of Hertford, 'to the great grief of himself and his wife' (Swift, *Journal to Stella*, 597–8). He was appointed bishop of Derry on 3 March 1714. In May 1715 his agent, a Mr Jeffreys, was arrested carrying what were held to be treasonable papers addressed to Swift and others. According to Archbishop William King the packages included 'two letters of the bishop of Derry that were not very prudent I confess, but there being nothing directly against his majesty we ordered them to be restored' (*Correspondence of Jonathan Swift*, 5.232).

Swift, who saw Hartstonge regularly when they were both in London in 1711, described him to Stella as 'the silliest, best natured wretch breathing, of as little consequence as an egg shell' (Swift, *Journal to Stella*, 424). Hartstonge died in Dublin on 30 January 1717 and was buried in St Andrew's Church. He left lands in co. Kilkenny, Hertfordshire, and Radnorshire, as well as £10,000 to a daughter aged under ten.   S. J. CONNOLLY

Sources J. B. Leslie, *Ossory clergy and parishes* (1933) · H. Cotton, *Fasti ecclesiae Hibernicae*, 6 vols. (1845–78) · *The whole works of Sir James Ware concerning Ireland*, ed. and trans. W. Harris, rev. edn, 2 vols. in 3 (1764) · *The correspondence of Jonathan Swift*, ed. H. Williams, 5 vols. (1963–5) · J. Swift, *Journal to Stella*, ed. H. Williams, 2 vols. (1948) · Burtchaell & Sadleir, *Alum. Dubl.*, 2nd edn · F. E. Ball, 'Some notes on the Irish judiciary in the reign of Charles II [pts 1–4]', *Journal of the Cork Historical and Archaeological Society*, 2nd ser., 7 (1901), 26–42, 90–104, 138–49, 215–27 · F. E. Ball, 'Some notes on the Irish judiciary in the reign of Charles II [pt 5]', *Journal of the Cork Historical and Archaeological Society*, 2nd ser., 8 (1902), 179–85 · F. E. Ball, 'Some notes on the Irish judiciary in the reign of Charles II [pt 6]', *Journal of the Cork Historical and Archaeological Society*, 2nd ser., 9 (1903), 85–94

Archives BL, letters to John Ellis, Add. MSS 28877–28926 · TCD, corresp. with William King
Wealth at death £10,000—lands

Hartwell, Abraham (*b.* 1541/2, *d.* in or before 1585), Latin poet and translator, was educated at Eton College and was admitted to King's College, Cambridge, on 25 August 1559, aged seventeen. He became a fellow of King's College in August 1562 and graduated as BA in 1563 and MA in 1567, in which year he resigned his fellowship. He was a protégé of Sir Walter Haddon, the influential statesman and controversialist, created regius professor of civil law at Cambridge in 1550/51 and master of requests in 1558. Hartwell wrote his most important work, *Regina literata* (1565), for Haddon.

As an active Cambridge University Latin poet, Hartwell wrote verses for the rehabilitation, soon after the accession of Queen Elizabeth, of the protestant martyrs Paul Fagius and Martin Bucer. These verses were later printed on page 954 of Bucer's *Scripta Anglicana*, published in Basel in 1577, and take the form of a poem of some eighty lines consisting of a dialogue between Bucer and the university. Hartwell also wrote prefatory or commendatory verses for Walter Haddon's collection of speeches, letters, and poetry, the *Lucubrationes* (1567), and for the 1570 edition of John Foxe's *Acts and Monuments*. There are a few unpublished verses by Hartwell extant in Cambridge manuscripts. He translated from Latin into English one of Haddon's refutations of the Portuguese controversialist Osorius da Fonseca as *A Sight of the Portugall Pearle* (1565). Some poems by Hartwell also appear in Gabriel Harvey's *Gratulationes Valdinenses* (1578), including a poem on Lord Burghley and one on Robert Dudley, earl of Leicester, in which he urges the latter's suitability as a husband for the queen.

Hartwell's reputation as a Latin poet rests principally on the *Regina literata* of 1565. The poem, handsomely printed by William Seres (a printer favoured by Lord Burghley), is almost 1400 lines long, and is an account of Queen Elizabeth's ceremonial visit to the University of Cambridge in August 1564, which lasted for five days. Hartwell supplies many details of the university's elaborate arrangements to celebrate this occasion, including, in fluent elegiac couplets, such matters as the composition of the greeting parties, where the queen slept, her apparel and demeanour, plot summaries of the plays which she saw during her visit, the Latin disputations which she attended, and the speeches made both by and to Elizabeth at the colleges she visited. The poem celebrates the queen as a learned protestant monarch, ably discharging the responsibilities of the sovereign. The *Regina literata* concludes with some further verses by Hartwell—an acrostic poem on Elizabeth, a few epigrams, and a series of nineteen distichs which versify biblical observations on the nature of monarchy.

Hartwell was ordained deacon in London on 13 October 1566. He became rector of Stanwick, Northamptonshire, in 1568, of Toddington, Bedfordshire, in 1570, and of Tingrith, also in Bedfordshire, in 1572. He must have died in or before 1585, the year in which his widow, Anne, remarried; Thomas Newton in his *Illustrium aliquot Anglorum encomia* (1589, p. 124) speaks of him as having died recently.

J. W. BINNS

Sources J. W. Binns, 'Abraham Hartwell, herald of the new queen's reign', *Ut granum sinapis: essays on neo-Latin literature in honour of Jozef IJsewijn*, ed. G. Tournoy and D. Sacré (1997), 292–304 · Venn, *Alum. Cant.* · F. S. Boas, *University drama in the Tudor age* (1914) · J. W. Binns, *Intellectual culture in Elizabethan and Jacobean England: the Latin writings of the age* (1990) · T. Harwood, *Alumni Etonenses, or, A catalogue of the provosts and fellows of Eton College and King's College, Cambridge, from the foundation in 1443 to the year 1797* (1797) · DNB

Hartwell, Abraham (1553/4–1606). *See under* Society of Antiquaries (*act.* 1586–1607).

Harty, Sir (Herbert) Hamilton (1879–1941), conductor and composer, was born on 4 December 1879 in Main Street, Hillsborough, co. Down, Ireland, the fourth of ten children of William Michael Harty (1852–1918), organist of Hillsborough church, and his wife, Annie Elizabeth, daughter of Joseph Hamilton Richards, soldier, from Bray, co. Dublin. Harty was raised in the Anglican faith.

Educated mainly at Hillsborough local school, Harty studied the organ, piano, and viola with his father. Though he also benefited from playing the viola in the family string quartet, his father's extensive music library was the basis for much of his early musical education. Having had no formal training as a musician, Harty used these scores to develop his skills as both composer and executant. In 1894 he was appointed organist at Magheragall, and in November 1895 he became organist at St Barnabas's Church, Belfast. There he continued to play the viola, joining chamber music groups and becoming a member of an orchestral society. But he was unimpressed by the industrial character of the city and applied for, and was appointed to, the post of organist at Christ Church, Bray. Being close to Dublin, Harty sought musical guidance from Michele Esposito (1855–1929), professor of piano at the Royal Irish Academy of Music. Though never a formal pupil, he was influenced heavily by him. Encouraged by his mentor to further his skills as a piano accompanist, Harty found that his reputation as a sympathetic musical partner soon flourished: with Ella Russell he played for Queen Victoria, and in 1900 he worked as an accompanist at the Feis Ceoil (Dublin). It was there that he had an early success as a composer: he was awarded a prize for his string quartet, op. 1.

Limited by the opportunities available to him in Ireland, Harty moved to England. After resigning from his post at Bray in January 1901, he was appointed organist at All Saints' Church, Norfolk Square, London, but his tenure there lasted for only one week. Now unemployed as an organist, he earned his living by playing the piano at soirées and working as an accompanist at both the Boosey ballad concerts and the South Place Sunday popular concerts. But he never severed his links with Ireland, and he continued to submit works to the Feis Ceoil during the first decade of the twentieth century. Among the compositions entered was his 'Irish' symphony, with which he made his début as a conductor in 1904. He later revised the

Sir (Herbert) Hamilton Harty (1879–1941), by Harold Speed, 1905

symphony twice and made it a regular feature of his concert programmes.

It was on 15 July 1904 that Harty married the singer **Agnes Helen Nicholls** (1877–1959). Born at Cheltenham on 14 July 1877, she studied at the Royal College of Music. After performances of Purcell's *Dido and Aeneas* at the Lyceum Theatre in 1895, she sang privately for Queen Victoria. She made her Covent Garden début in 1901 and continued to perform at that theatre until 1924. A principal of the British National Opera Company, she later became a director of that organization. But it was her professional relationship with the Hungarian conductor Hans Richter that was of greatest importance to Harty. After performing in Wagner's *Der Ring des Nibelungen* under Richter in 1908, she approached him on her husband's behalf. And it was through this connection that Harty secured his first important conducting engagement: a performance of his tone poem *With the Wild Geese* with the London Symphony Orchestra in March 1911. The performance was a success, and he was engaged to conduct the orchestra again during its 1912–13 season. Hoping to reinforce his status as a composer–conductor, Harty gave the first performance of his *Variations on a Dublin Air* with the same orchestra in February 1913. Unfortunately, neither the critics nor the public shared his enthusiasm for his music: his concerts made a loss and he was not invited back for the following season. Nevertheless, his reputation as a conductor continued to grow, and he was invited to perform Wagner's *Tristan und Isolde* and Bizet's *Carmen* at Covent Garden in 1913. But he had little sympathy with opera, preferring, instead, symphonic music. In January 1914 he conducted the Liverpool Philharmonic Orchestra, and in April he made his début with the Hallé Orchestra of Manchester. His career was interrupted briefly by the First World War: in June 1916 he joined the Royal Naval Volunteer Reserve and was posted for duties in the North Sea, and he rose to the rank of lieutenant in 1917 before leaving in June 1918. In December he substituted for an indisposed Sir Thomas Beecham at a performance of Handel's *Messiah* with the Hallé Orchestra, and on 27 March 1919 he again replaced Beecham at a performance of J. S. Bach's mass in B minor.

Harty was appointed permanent conductor of the Hallé Orchestra in 1920, at a time of financial difficulty, and he participated fully in the management of the ensemble. But his primary responsibilities were musical, and, with the benefit of tenure, he was able to explore his interests thoroughly. In an interview with the *Musical Times* that was published shortly after his appointment, he set out his thoughts on music in general. For him, Berlioz and Mozart were 'deities', whose works reflected their abilities as 'intuitive composers'. Conversely, he argued that with Wagner he 'sometimes [felt that] a mechanical process [was] at work', causing him to 'rate him below Berlioz'. Harty liked Stravinsky and Ravel, but had reservations about the music of Franck, Brahms, and Skryabin. His preference for all-male orchestras proved most controversial: he claimed that the inclusion of women precluded a homogeneous orchestral style and caused logistical difficulties on tour. At a time when the role of women in the workplace was an important social and economic issue, this argument was difficult to sustain. Though challenged widely, he maintained his position and appointed only one woman to the orchestra: the harpist. Because of his responsibilities with the Hallé Orchestra, Harty's activities as a composer diminished during his Manchester period. Even so, he continued to compose and to arrange, completing his transcriptions of Handel's 'Water Music' and 'Music for the Royal Fireworks' in 1920 and 1923 respectively. A keen chamber musician, Harty was the driving force behind the Manchester chamber concerts in 1921 and later the Harty chamber concerts. Having improved the Hallé Orchestra's standard of playing, he took the ensemble to London during the 1924–5 season, its first visit to the capital since 1913. It returned regularly to London thereafter and undertook the Hamilton Harty symphony concerts at the Queen's Hall in the 1929–30 and 1930–31 seasons. Though successful musically, the concerts were a financial disaster: Harty, acting as promoter, was responsible for a deficit of £3000. But his troubles were more than financial: his reluctance to perform works from music's cutting edge also caused concern. In his lecture 'Some problems of modern music' (1929) he raised the question: had contemporary music 'wandered aside into barren and unfruitful wastes?' Yes, he said; but he was forced to review his position, and in his last three seasons with the Hallé Orchestra he included works by

Prokofiev, Bartók, Walton, and Krenek. In 1931 and 1932 he toured North America, and on his return from his second tour it was announced that he had been appointed artistic adviser and conductor-in-chief of the London Symphony Orchestra. Although his agreement with the Hallé Orchestra was not exclusive, the Hallé Concerts Society decided to end his contract after the season of 1932–3. Distressed by their decision, Harty announced his resignation on 5 February 1933 and appeared for the last time as permanent conductor at Preston on 30 March 1933.

As conductor of the London Symphony Orchestra, Harty was scheduled to lead eight concerts and two tours during the season of 1933–4. But it soon became clear to the directors that he was not the right man for the job. At Manchester he exercised influence and power, but this approach was unsuitable for a self-governing orchestra. It was agreed, therefore, that Harty's contract should be terminated after 1934. But that year was not a complete disaster for the conductor: he performed in Australia and toured the USA twice. Triumphant in North America, he returned there in 1935 and 1936. But he also maintained a heavy schedule in Britain, conducting the first complete performance of Walton's symphony no. 1 and the première of Bax's symphony no. 6 on 6 and 21 November 1935 respectively.

Harty's health began to deteriorate sharply in 1936: a malignant brain tumour was discovered and surgery was required. After both the growth and his right eye were removed, Harty convalesced in Ireland and Jamaica during 1937 and 1938. Unable to conduct, he returned to composing: he set five Irish songs and wrote his last original composition, *The Children of Lir*, during his convalescence. Following two studio concerts with the BBC Symphony Orchestra in December 1938 and February 1939, Harty returned to the Queen's Hall on 1 March 1939, directing the première of *The Children of Lir* with the BBC Symphony Orchestra. And after another period of convalescence in the summer of 1939 he undertook a full programme of concerts during the 1939–40 season. But his illness continued to trouble him, and he conducted for the last time on 1 December 1940.

Remembered primarily for recordings that only partially reflect his interests and abilities, Harty was an executant of influence and standing. His achievements with the Hallé Orchestra compare favourably with those of Hans Richter but are less important historically than those of Sir John Barbirolli. His skills as an accompanist have been likened to those of Gerald Moore, but his talents as a creative artist are less convincing. A self-taught composer, Harty often used derivative methods, and his works soon fell from the standard repertory. Only his transcriptions of Handel's 'Water Music' and 'Music for the Royal Fireworks' were heard regularly after his death, but these too have fallen from favour and are performed rarely. His work was recognized formally in 1925 when he was knighted. After being made a fellow of the Royal College of Music in 1924, he received honorary doctorates from several universities and on 22 November 1934 was awarded the gold medal of the Royal Philharmonic Society. The Hamilton Harty chair of music was established at the Queen's University, Belfast, in 1951; from 1952 an annual Hamilton Harty memorial concert, at which one of his major works was to be performed, was given at that university. Because of Harty's estrangement from his wife, who died in London on 21 September 1959, the conductor was nursed through his final illness by his secretary and intimate friend, Olive Elfreda Baguley, who survived him. Harty died at 3 Palm Court, 33 Brunswick Square, Hove, on 19 February 1941; after cremation his ashes were placed at Hillsborough parish church.

RAYMOND HOLDEN

Sources T. Beecham, *A mingled chime* (1944) · *WWW*, 1929–40 · Grove, *Dict. mus.* (1954) · 'C', 'Hamilton Harty', *MT*, 61 (1920), 227–30 · N. Cardus, *Autobiography* (1947) · N. Cardus, *Talking of music* (1957) · R. W. Clarke, *The Royal Albert Hall* (1958) · Grove, *Dict. mus.* (1927) · C. Ehrlich, *First philharmonic: a history of the Royal Philharmonic Society* (1995) · R. Elkin, *Royal Philharmonic: the annals of the Royal Philharmonic Society* (1946) · R. Elkin, *Queen's Hall, 1893–1941* [1944] · H. Foss and N. Goodwin, *London Symphony Orchestra* (1954) · D. Greer, ed., *Hamilton Harty: his life and music* (1978) · D. Greer, ed., *Early memories: Hamilton Harty* (1979) · J. Hunt, *More musical knights: Harty, Mackerras, Rattle, Pritchard* (1997) · M. Kennedy, *Barbirolli: conductor laureate* (1971) · M. Kennedy, *The Hallé tradition: a century of music* (1960) · M. Pearton, *The LSO at 70: a history of the orchestra* (1974) · C. B. Rees, *100 years of the Hallé* (1957) · C. Reid, *John Barbirolli* (1971) · C. Rigby, *John Barbirolli: a biographical sketch* (1948) · H. Rosenthal, *Two centuries of opera at Covent Garden* (1958) · J. Russell, 'Hamilton Harty', *Music and Letters*, 22 (1941), 216–24 · *New Grove* · B. Shore, *The orchestra speaks* (1938) · J. Szigeti, *With strings attached: reminiscences and reflections* (1949) · J. R. Thackrah, *The Royal Albert Hall* (1983) · m. cert. · d. cert. · *CGPLA Eng. & Wales* (1941) · J. B. Steane, 'Nicholls, Agnes', *New Grove*

Archives Queen's University, Belfast · Manchester, archive of the Hallé Orchestra | SOUND BL NSA, documentary recordings · BL NSA, performance recordings · BL NSA, *Great British conductors*, 5

Likenesses H. Speed, crayon drawing, 1905, NG Ire. [*see illus.*] · W. Weatherby, caricature, Indian ink and wash, 1926, Man. City Gall.

Wealth at death £6865 25s. 0d.: probate, 24 June 1941, *CGPLA Eng. & Wales*

Harty, (Fredric) Russell (1934–1988), television broadcaster, was born on 5 September 1934 in Blackburn, Lancashire, the only son and elder child of Fred Harty, greengrocer (who, his son claimed, introduced Blackburn to the avocado pear), and his wife, Myrtle Rishton. He was educated at Queen Elizabeth's Grammar School, Blackburn, and Exeter College, Oxford, where he read English and was taught by Nevill Coghill, who noted of an early essay, 'Sex in the *Canterbury Tales*', 'Energetic and zealous but very naïve'. He took a third-class degree (1957) and taught briefly at Blakey Moor secondary modern school in Blackburn before moving in 1958 to Giggleswick School in Yorkshire. Giggleswick was a school and a village with which he was to have close connections for the rest of his life. In 1964 there followed a spell at City College, New York, and at Bishop Lonsdale College of Education, Derby, but with many of his friends and contemporaries busy in the theatre and broadcasting he was increasingly dissatisfied with teaching.

In 1966 Harty made his first foray into television, an inglorious appearance as a contestant on Granada TV's *Criss Cross Quiz*; the only question he answered correctly was on Catherine of Braganza. It was such a public humiliation that his mother refused to speak to him. Still, it was a beginning and in 1967 he was taken on by BBC radio as an arts programmes producer, his hankering to perform whetted by the occasional trip to the studio down the corridor whenever *Woman's Hour* wanted a letter read in a northern accent.

As an undergraduate Harty had invited Vivien Leigh round for drinks and this precocious appetite for celebrity stood him in good stead when, in 1969, he became producer and occasional presenter of London Weekend TV's arts programme, *Aquarius*. He might not have seemed the best person to film Salvador Dalí, but the elderly surrealist and the boy off Blackburn market took to one another and the programme won an Emmy award; in another unlikely conjunction he set up an encounter on Capri between the eminent Lancashire exiles Sir William Walton and Gracie Fields. Harty was never abashed by the famous (his critics said that was the trouble), but it was his capacity for provocative half-truths and outrageous overstatement, which made him such a good schoolmaster, that now fitted him for a career as the host of a weekly talk show (*Eleven Plus* and later *Russell Harty*) and made him one of the most popular performers on television. Plump, cheerful, and unintimidating, he was particularly good at putting people at their ease, deflating the pompous, and drawing out the shy.

In 1980 Harty returned to the BBC, but his output remained much as it had been for the last ten years, the same mixture of talk shows varied by occasional films like *The Black Madonna*, and his *Grand Tour*, shown in 1988. He wrote regularly for *The Observer* and the *Sunday Times*, publishing a book of his television interviews, *Russell Harty Plus* (1976) and also *Mr Harty's Grand Tour* (1988). He was a regular broadcaster on radio besides presenting the Radio 4 talk show *Start the Week*.

'Private faces in public places are wiser and nicer than public faces in private places' (W. H. Auden) did not anticipate television, where the distinction is not always plain. For his friends Harty was naturally a private face but for the public he seemed a private face too and one that had strayed on to the screen seemingly untouched by expertise. That was why, though it infuriated his critics, so many viewers liked him and took him to their hearts as they never did more polished performers. He giggled, he fumbled, and seldom went for the right word rather than the next but two, and though his delivery could be as tortured as his mother's on the telephone, it did not matter. It was all part of his ordinariness, his deficiencies, his style.

Harty never made much of a secret of his homosexuality. He did not look on it as an affliction, but he was never one for a crusade either. His funniest stories were always of the absurdities of sex and the ludicrous situations it had led him into, and if he was never short of partners, it was because they knew there would always be laughs, sharing a joke being something rarer than sharing a bed.

In the second half of the 1980s the spread of AIDS

enabled the tabloid press, and in particular those newspapers owned by Rupert Murdoch, to dress up their muckraking as a moral crusade, and they systematically trawled public life for sexual indiscretion. Harty, who had not scrupled to question his more celebrated interviewees about their sex lives, knew that he was in a vulnerable situation. Early in 1987 a young man who had had a previous fling with Harty was wired up with a tape recorder by two *News of the World* reporters and sent to call on Harty at his London flat. To the reporters' chagrin nothing newsworthy occurred, but the paper fell back on printing the young man's account of the previous association, thus initiating a campaign of sporadic vilification in the tabloid press which ended only with Harty's death just over a year later.

The cause of Harty's death was liver failure, the result of hepatitis B, but in the hope that he was suffering from AIDS the press laid siege firstly to his home at Rose Cottage, Giggleswick, and then to St James's Hospital in Leeds, where he was in intensive care. A telescope was trained permanently on the window of his ward and a reporter tried to smuggle himself into the ward disguised as a junior doctor, in order to look at his case notes. When Harty was actually on his deathbed one of the journalists responsible for the original 'scoop' could not be restrained from retelling the tale of her exploits on television. Harty died in Leeds on 8 June 1988 and was buried in Giggleswick, the gravestone evidence of the vulgarity from which he never entirely managed to break free.

ALAN BENNETT, *rev.*

Sources personal knowledge (1996) · private information (1996) · *The Independent* (9 June 1988) · 'Extracts from an autobiography', *Sunday Times* (16 June 1988) · *CGPLA Eng. & Wales* (1988)
Archives FILM BBC · ITV [LWT] |SOUND BBC
Likenesses photographs, 1973–85, Hult. Arch.
Wealth at death £430,887: administration with will, 19 Oct 1988, *CGPLA Eng. & Wales*

Harty, William (1781–1854), physician, was born in Kilkenny, the son of Timothy Harty, gentleman. He entered Trinity College, Dublin, as a pensioner on 27 April 1797, became a scholar two years later, and graduated BA in 1801, MB in 1804, and MD in 1830, with a thesis on the Dublin bills of mortality. Harty was an unsuccessful candidate for the chair of botany at the university in 1808. He became a licentiate of the King and Queen's College of Physicians in Ireland in 1818, a fellow in 1824, and a censor in 1826. He resigned his fellowship in the following year, for reasons which are now unknown, but was made an honorary fellow in 1833.

Harty was a staunch Anglican, familiar with scripture and with Irish church history, and evinced a strong commitment to the poor throughout his professional career. Shortly after graduation he became one of the physicians to the Sick Poor Institution in Dublin's teeming Liberties district, where the most common illnesses were fevers and diseases of the chest, stomach, and bowels, as well as rheumatic and dropsical complaints. Harty and others attributed the prevalence of these ailments to the wretched living conditions of the poor. In January 1818 he

was one of the founders of the Association for the Suppression of Street-Begging in Dublin, commonly known as the Mendicity Association. The economic crisis that followed the fall of Napoleon was responsible for an upsurge in mendicancy and vagrancy throughout Ireland and triggered off a fever epidemic which may have affected as many as 1,500,000 individuals. Harty's *Historic sketch of the causes, progress, extent and mortality of the contagious fever epidemic in Ireland during the years 1817, 1818, and 1819*, which appeared in 1820, is his most notable published work. In it Harty criticized the government's role as reactive and remedial rather than preventive, contending that the adoption of temporary expedients for the suppression of fever was useless; the evil itself had to be rooted out. This could only be achieved, Harty believed, by direct government intervention—by changing the social conditions that gave rise to disease and in effect ridding the country of pauperism.

Harty depicted fever as Ireland's greatest scourge and dysentery as its close companion. A revised edition of his 1805 pamphlet *Observations on the History and Treatment of Dysentery* appeared at the beginning of 1847, when the country was again racked by famine and its attendant diseases. Fifteen years earlier, he had also contributed a characteristically polemical article on the fearful cholera epidemic to the *Dublin Journal of Medical and Chemical Science* (3.1833). Harty's interest in infectious diseases may have stemmed from his involvement with a number of Dublin institutions. In addition to his dispensary work in the Liberties, he served as physician to the King's Hospital, or Blue Coat School, and to the prisons of Dublin, for more than forty years. About 1820 he acquired Finglas House, a private lunatic asylum in co. Dublin, which, under an act of 1843, was licensed for eighteen inmates. Ownership of this institution involved Harty in a number of legal wrangles over the detention of patients and the rights of the insane.

Early in 1851 Harty committed Henry William Mathew, a 25-year-old student at Trinity College, Dublin, to Swift's Hospital for the Insane. In the following December, Mathew sued Harty for assault and false imprisonment, and damages were laid at £5000. The defence pleaded that Mathew was a dangerous lunatic who had to be confined for his own protection and treatment. The revelation on the fourth day of the trial that he was Harty's natural son caused a sensation; the jury found a verdict for the plaintiff for £1000 damages and 6d. costs. It was stated during the course of the trial that Harty was married and had a legitimate family. A son, William, had been born in 1814, had entered Trinity College, Dublin, as a pensioner in July 1830, had graduated BA in 1835, and had been called to the Irish bar in 1838. His half-brother, Henry Mathew, graduated BA in 1855.

Harty did not long survive his public humiliation in the courts. He died at Ballickmoyler, Queen's county, on 30 March 1854.

LAURENCE M. GEARY

Sources *Authentic report of the most important and interesting trial of Mathew v. Harty and Stokes, before the Right Hon. the lord chief baron and a special jury, on Thursday, December 11, 1851, and the following days*

(1852) • Burtchaell & Sadleir, *Alum. Dubl.*, 2nd edn • minutes, Royal College of Physicians of Ireland, 5.122, 472; 6.163, 256, 273 • *Medical Times and Gazette* (22 April 1854), 419

Likenesses T. C. Thompson, portrait, exh. Royal Hibernian Academy 1827

Harvard, John (1607–1638), educational benefactor, was baptized on 29 November 1607 at St Saviour's Church, Southwark, Surrey, the fourth of the nine children of Robert Harvard (d. 1625), butcher, and the second with his second wife, Katherine (1584–1635), the daughter of Thomas Rogers, yeoman and alderman, of Stratford upon Avon, Warwickshire. An active resident of his parish, Robert Harvard held a series of influential local offices, including vestryman, churchwarden, overseer of the poor, and governor of the parish grammar school, which his son John almost certainly attended, probably beginning in or about 1615.

John Harvard was seventeen years old in the summer of 1625 when his father died of the plague, a disease which also carried off a half-sister from his father's first marriage and two brothers. Since four other siblings and half-siblings had already died of other causes, only his mother and his brother Thomas survived to share in a comfortable inheritance. Katherine Harvard took a second husband, John Elletson, a cooper of Middlesex, in January 1626; after Elletson died five months later, in June 1626, she married Richard Yearwood, a grocer of Southwark, in 1627, each marriage significantly increasing the family resources.

Harvard had not continued his education following the completion of grammar school, but after the deaths of his father and most of his siblings, as the family assets became concentrated in increasingly fewer hands, the opportunity for further learning opened to him. He was entered pensioner at Emmanuel College, Cambridge, on 19 December 1627, responsible for his own charges without college assistance. In 1632 he graduated BA, and three years later, in 1635, he proceeded MA. Harvard's selection of Emmanuel offers a clear indication why he resumed his education. Sir Walter Mildmay had endowed the college in 1584 specifically for the education of a preaching ministry. The obvious reason for entering Emmanuel was to prepare to take holy orders, and only those who were attracted to its strict faith chose this stronghold of puritanism.

Katherine Yearwood died in July 1635, and less than two years later Harvard's last surviving sibling, Thomas, a cloth worker, died in the spring of 1637. Their deaths left John Harvard the primary heir to family assets worth some £2000. These included money, rental properties, and an inn, the Queen's Head, in Southwark. By now, Harvard had married: on 19 April 1636 he had taken as his wife Ann (b. 1614), the daughter of John Sadler, minister of Ringmer, Sussex, and the sister of John *Sadler (1615–1674), a close college friend.

In the 1630s and early 1640s Emmanuel College furnished thirty-five emigrants to puritan New England—more than a quarter of the 130 university men who arrived before 1646—and the Harvards prepared to join this stream during the spring of 1637. John had apparently already taken holy orders; although generations of assiduous researchers have failed to find a record of his ordination either in England or New England, by 1635 several surviving documents, including his mother's will, referred to him as 'John Harvard Clarke' (Morison, 212). Harvard was still in England in late May 1637 when he laid claim to a debt of about £300; by 1 August he and his wife were living across the harbour from Boston in Charlestown, Massachusetts, where this town of perhaps 150 families accepted him as a freeman. The couple had probably sailed from London in early June and spent a month or more at sea, arriving in Massachusetts Bay at some point in July. Their impedimenta had included his large personal library of about 400 books on subjects both sacred and secular.

Churches in early Massachusetts frequently called two clergymen—a pastor and a teacher—and the church in Charlestown had recently lost the services of its teacher, Thomas James, who had been too choleric for his parishioners. Harvard succeeded James as colleague to the church's pastor, Zechariah Symmes, an Emmanuel man. Surviving records do not indicate when Harvard took up the teacher's duties, but on 6 November 1637 John and Ann were admitted to membership in the church.

The Harvards lived in Charlestown for slightly more than thirteen months before John died there of consumption, childless, on 14 September 1638, and was buried in the town. During those months they built or bought a substantial house, and in April 1638 Harvard served on a town committee to assist in drafting a legal code for the colony. A leader in the community from his arrival, he received large portions on several occasions in recognition of his station when the town divided common lands. When he preached and prayed in public he spoke 'with teares [of] affection strong' (Morison, 218).

While the Harvards were establishing themselves in their new home, the college that would bear the family name was being organized a few miles away in Newtown (renamed Cambridge in 1638). Authorized on 28 October 1636 and granted £400 by a vote of the colony's general court, the school opened under the mastership of Nathaniel Eaton, a college contemporary of Harvard, some time between early June and 7 September 1638. John Harvard's only claim to lasting recognition results from his bequest to this infant institution. The beneficiary of several inheritances himself, by nuncupative will he left the college about £800—half of his monetary estate—as well as his entire library. In money alone, the bequest was about twice the size of the legislature's original grant. Six months later, on 13 March 1639, the general court voted 'that the college agreed upon formerly to bee built at Cambridge shalbee called Harvard College'. Harvard's widow, who received the remainder of the estate, married Thomas Allen, his successor as the teacher of the Charlestown church.

A fire in 1764, which destroyed the college library, consumed all but one of the books in John Harvard's bequest. Aside from it and his signature in a volume of records at

Emmanuel College, no Harvard artefacts have survived. A seated statue of him by Daniel Chester French, now located in Harvard Yard, is an idealization, not a likeness.

CONRAD EDICK WRIGHT

Sources S. E. Morison, *The tercentennial history of Harvard College and University, 1636–1936*, 1: *The founding of Harvard College* (1935) • H. C. Shelley, *John Harvard and his times* (1907) • H. F. Waters, 'John Harvard and his ancestry', *New England Historical and Genealogical Register*, 39 (1885), 265–84 • A. M. Davis, *John Harvard's life in America* (1908) • [W. Rendle], *Old Southwark and its people* (1885) • H. W. Foote, 'The church in which John Harvard was married', *Harvard Alumni Bulletin* (22 Jan 1932), 301–34, 472–8 • J. L. Hotson, 'New light on John Harvard', *Publications of the Colonial Society of Massachusetts*, 26 (1927), 229–33 • A. C. Potter, *Catalogue of John Harvard's library* (1919), 190–230 • H. J. Cadbury, 'John Harvard's library', *Publications of the Colonial Society of Massachusetts*, 34 (1937–42), 353–77 • J. G. Bartlett, 'The landed possessions of John Harvard', *Harvard Alumni Bulletin*, 26 (1924), 751–6

Likenesses D. C. French, statue, 1884, Harvard Yard, Cambridge, Massachusetts

Wealth at death approx. £ 1600; plus 400 books: Morison, *Founding of Harvard College*, 222

Harvel, Edmund (*d.* in or before **1550**), merchant and diplomat, was probably the gentleman of that name of Besford and Cowley, Worcestershire, who appears on the pardon roll at the accession of Henry VIII and in a genealogical table in a Worcestershire heralds' visitation of 1564. Little else is sure about his family and early life, except that he had a brother, a London merchant, who visited him in Venice in 1539. This man was almost certainly the Richard Harvel who was an exile in Zürich and Geneva in the reign of Mary I. Edmund Harvel was in Venice by 1524, when he acted as an agent for the Paduan philosopher Niccolò Leonico Tomeo. He was by then a friend to Tomeo's circle of English students, which numbered Thomas Lupset, Reginald Pole, and Thomas Starkey. He developed particularly strong relations with Starkey and Pole, and in the 1530s came to be on close terms with Starkey's associate Richard Morison, and with one of Pole's servants, Bernardino Sandro. By the 1540s a succession of English students and tourists were in contact with him as a potential aid and protector in Venice, and several of them, including Thomas Hoby and John Denny, stayed in his home.

Harvel's semi-official activities on behalf of Henry VIII date at the latest from 1530, when he acted as an agent for Richard Croke and John Stokesley, who were in Italy to find solutions to the problem of the royal divorce. He transmitted money from England to Croke in Venice, and sent back to the king Croke's letters and writings, activities for which he received royal grants in 1530 and 1531. It was probably through Thomas Starkey—who was back in England by 1534, and with whom Harvel carried on a regular correspondence in the mid-1530s—and through Thomas Winter, Cardinal Wolsey's illegitimate son, that Harvel became known to Thomas Cromwell, who offered him employment in 1535 and advised him to move back to England. At this time Starkey was himself in Cromwell's service as an intelligencer for Italian affairs, and was working to persuade Reginald Pole to come to terms publicly with Henry VIII's divorce and royal supremacy.

Although Harvel wrote to Starkey in 1535 communicating his plans to return to England as soon as he had tied up his business affairs in Italy, and reassuring him that Pole would satisfy the king, it appears that Harvel was misleading Starkey. In the autumn of 1535, while Pole stayed in his house in Venice, Harvel visited Sicily. This journey, apparently made to settle his business interests, was at least in part a mission on Pole's behalf to Charles V, then in Palermo, probably intended to persuade the emperor to take action against the schismatic king of England. In April 1536 Pole, whose passionate denunciation of Henry VIII had by then reached England, still regarded Harvel as one of his clients, claiming to his friend Alvise Priuli that he could not send Harvel again to Charles V without causing suspicion in England. This material explains why Harvel in the event thought it prudent not to return to England, instead marrying Apollonia Uttinger, the daughter of an Augsburg merchant resident in Venice, in 1538. Uttinger brought a substantial dowry worth 1500 Venetian *ducati* to the union.

Harvel's work for Pole also testifies to his skills of concealment: in 1537 he entered government service and through Cromwell was granted a stipend from the crown and a licence to export wool from England. Thereafter he sent regular newsletters to Cromwell until the latter's death in 1540. But his diplomatic status remained ambivalent. From the English side he was not yet an official agent in 1538, when Richard Morison begged Cromwell to make him so. By 1539 he was specifically instructed as an intelligencer by Cromwell 'under the colour of his feate and trade of merchandise, keping this Commission secrete from all men'. His task was to include spying on the papacy and on Reginald Pole; fostering evangelical and antipapal sentiment among 'notable and honest persons'; and secretly conveying the king's favourable disposition to the duke of Urbino, who was under threat of invasion from the pope (Merriman, 2.167–75). His letters to Cromwell also include extensive reports on Mediterranean and Turkish matters. After Cromwell's fall Harvel wrote directly to Henry VIII, or occasionally to Thomas Wriothesley and William Paget.

From the Venetian government Harvel gained some, but not total, diplomatic recognition. In 1542 he was granted permission for his thirteen servants, four of them English, to carry arms, and the authorities gave him retrospective exemption from taxes on the basis of his ambassadorial status in 1545. On the other hand, although permitting him a grand funeral in 1550, partially paid for by the state, the signoria did not follow the procession because Harvel was considered more of an 'envoy' and 'vice-ambassador' than a full ambassador. Although most of his business activities remain obscure, they included trade in corn in Sicily and, more importantly, the export of wool from England to Venice and elsewhere. The Venetian republic's traditionally warm relations with England were maintained in this period because of the wool trade in particular, and some of Harvel's diplomatic dealings reveal the Venetian authorities' anxieties not to alienate Henry VIII because of this. For example, the republic was reluctant to act against the Bolognese *condottiere* Ludovico dalle Armi, accused of various criminal activities in the 1540s, in part because he was in the employment of the king; Harvel acted as a negotiator over this matter, helping to postpone dalle Armi's execution until after Henry VIII's death.

Harvel's marriage to a German probably reflected his religious sympathies. His connections in the late 1530s and 1540s with Italian evangelicals, Lutherans, and critics of the established church were wide-ranging. His physician (Girolamo Donzellino) and his secretary (Baldassare Altieri) were both noted heretics, while he maintained relations with Pietro Aretino, Antonio Brucioli (whom he recommended to Cromwell as a potential spy in Rome in 1539), Ortensio Lando (who dedicated to him his *Lettere di molte virtuose donne* in 1548), and, possibly, Michelangelo Florio and Vincenzo Maggi. Harvel used his diplomatic position to protect evangelicals in Venice and to foster protestant connections between England and Italy, but apparently always with sufficient prudence and discretion not to come under suspicion himself.

It was indeed for his prudential qualities that Harvel was highly regarded by the Venetian government as a diplomat. He also gained a reputation for kindness, friendship, and learning. By the 1540s his household was a substantial one and the inventory of his goods, drawn up after his death, indicates possessions (including 170 books) valued at 930 Venetian *ducati*. From this, 446 *ducati* and 12 *grossi* were spent on paying off his servants and on his funeral in the church of San Geremia and burial in the church of Santi Giovanni e Paolo; these took place before 7 January 1550. His wife, by whom he was deeply mourned, inherited the remainder as the return of her dowry.

JONATHAN WOOLFSON

Sources H. F. Brown, ed., 'The marriage contract, inventory, and funeral expenses of Edmund Harvel', *EngHR*, 20 (1905), 70–77 · *CSP Venice, 1534–54* · *LP Henry VIII* · *Life and letters of Thomas Cromwell*, ed. R. B. Merriman, 2 (1902), 167–75 · T. F. Mayer, *Reginald Pole* (2000)
Archives BL, corresp., Cotton MSS
Wealth at death 930 Venetian ducati: 1550 post-mortem inventory, repr. in Brown, ed., 'Marriage contract'

Harvey, Alexander [Alex] (1935–1982), popular singer, was born on 6 February 1935 at 40 Govan Road, Kinning Park, Glasgow, the first of the two children of Leslie Harvey (*d.* 1992) and his wife, Greta. A son of the infamous violent era of Glasgow, he left school at fifteen and had reputedly had thirty-six jobs by the age of twenty-two. He was married twice: first to Mary Martin (*d.* 1999), with whom he had a son, Alex, and, after their divorce, to Trudy, with whom he had another son, Tyro.

Harvey's first musical engagement was as a trumpeter at a wedding, but his break came in 1957, when he won a newspaper contest. The *Sunday Mail* had been looking for 'Scotland's Tommy Steele' and found it in Alex, 'a first-rate rock'n'roll singer with unlimited vitality' (*Sunday Mail*, 10 April 1957). His reputation quickly spread—especially as he had friends appearing in ballrooms all over Scotland pretending to be him. After some years in skiffle and folk outfits, he created the Big Soul Band by asking musicians

if they wanted to get into debt. They supported many chart acts of the time in Scotland, then travelled to Hamburg, where they released *Alex Harvey and his Soul Band* (1964). On returning to Britain, Harvey worked with his brother, Les, on *The Blues* (1965). Another stint on the Scottish circuit led to several unsuccessful singles and to disillusionment, which led Harvey to move to London, where he joined the band of the cult musical *Hair* for five years. After the release of *Roman Wall Blues* (1969) he became disillusioned again and dropped out of music altogether.

Along with having witnessed Jimi Hendrix's early appearances, the death of his brother is credited with inspiring Harvey's return to work: Les Harvey was electrocuted on stage in May 1972. Close friends said Alex never really recovered from the experience. He joined up with Zal Cleminson (guitar), Hugh McKenna (keyboards), Ted McKenna (drums), and Chris Glen (bass), and the Sensational Alex Harvey Band first performed on 29 June 1972. They released eight albums in five years: *Framed* (1972), *Next* (1973), *The Impossible Dream* (1974), *Tomorrow Belongs to me* (1975), *Live* (1975), *The Penthouse Tapes* (1976), *SAHB Stories* (1976), and *Rock Drill* (1978). The band had two hit singles: 'Delilah' (1975) and 'Boston Tea Party' (1976).

The Sensational Alex Harvey Band became noted for powerful live performances. Harvey was older than the rest of the band and the audiences, but commanded their respect. He took to wearing a pink-and-black striped jumper, and discarded the crooning soul voice in favour of his gravelly Glaswegian accent. Theatrical presentation was a priority: Harvey said he always wanted to be a director. He played various parts during the shows: a street thug during 'Framed'; a private detective for 'Man in the Jar'; a drunkard in 'Gamblin' Bar Room Blues'. The rest of the band had roles too—notably Zal, who performed as a harlequin. The interplay between the Harvey and Cleminson characters became a trademark.

Regarded by many as the 'oldest punk in the world' (a description apparently coined by the *New Musical Express*), Alex went to lengths to exact a response from every audience. When Slade were the biggest band in Britain, the Sensational Alex Harvey Band were the only outfit who dared to support them and they thrived on the mixed reactions. Harvey once invaded the Tubes' stage and drowned out their show with two bagpipers; and he performed 'I was Framed' in Germany dressed as Hitler. On and off stage his dominant personality was difficult to ignore: as his drummer, Ted McKenna, noted, 'Alex could dominate a room just by entering it'. The theme of violence followed Harvey through his career. He stopped performances if trouble broke out in the audience, and even stopped fights himself, often saying: 'Don't make any bullets, don't buy any bullets, don't shoot any bullets ... and don't pish in the water supply'. Despite this, he failed to escape the image of backstreet Glasgow. He regarded himself as a conscientious objector, as his father had been; but he was fascinated by military history, and collected books, toy soldiers, and memorabilia.

Contrary to his public image, Harvey was often racked

by personal doubt, and would ask friends, 'What do they want from me?' He did not find an answer to his recurring disillusionment. The death of his manager, Bill Fehilly, in 1976 shook him dramatically, and during rehearsals for the *Rock Drill* tour in late 1977 he announced his retirement. One year later he returned with a new band and released 'The Mafia Stole my Guitar' (1979), which had no more success than his pre-Sensational Alex Harvey Band material. On tour with his new Alex Harvey Band he died of a heart attack in Zebrugge, Belgium, on 5 February 1982. He was survived by his second wife and his two sons. The respect he held in the public eye was reflected by Charles Shaar Murray's obituary six days later in the *New Musical Express*: 'I've lost my sergeant'.

MARTIN KIELTY

Sources *Sunday Mail* (10 April 1957) · *New Musical Express* (11 Feb 1982) · M. Kielty, 'SAHB story', www.sahb.co.uk · private information (2004)
Archives FILM BBC WAC | SOUND BBC WAC
Likenesses photographs, priv. coll.

Harvey, Beauchamp Bagenal (1762–1798), barrister and Irish nationalist, was born at Bargy Castle, co. Wexford, the son of Francis Harvey (d. 1792), barrister and landowner, of Bargy Castle, and Martha, daughter of the Revd James Harvey of Killan. He was tutored by Mr Ball as a boy and entered Trinity College, Dublin, in February 1771. He graduated BA in 1775 and, after studying at the King's Inns, was called in 1782 to the Irish bar, where he hoped to emulate his father's successful legal career. His Trinity contemporary and circuit associate Sir Jonah Barrington claimed that Harvey was a popular, courageous, and generous young man. In 1792 Harvey inherited his father's estates in Wexford and Waterford, which provided him with an annual income of £3000. Like many liberal protestants he supported Catholic emancipation and campaigned for the reform of parliament. His interest in politics evidently dated from 1782 and by 1792 he was prominent in Wexford's influential Catholic committee. He was also then a leading member of the republican Dublin Society of United Irishmen, over which he occasionally presided. An experienced duellist, he defended the honour of the society by wounding Ambrose Hardinge Giffard on 8 May 1794.

In March 1795 a meeting of Wexford freeholders selected Harvey, Edward Hay, and Cornelius Grogan to deliver a petition supporting the retention of Earl Fitzwilliam as viceroy. Harvey's journey to England on this business aroused the extreme hostility of Wexford's powerful conservative interest. As a comparatively moderate United Irishman he had little contact with the clique attached to Lord Edward Fitzgerald that actively sought French military aid and plotted insurrection in Ireland. Instead his closest United Irish associates included Hay, John Henry Colclough, William Hatton, and Mathew Keugh, who, like him, were not deeply concerned with the military side of the Wexford organization prior to the 1798 rising. In 1797 he reputedly married Judith Steevens of Arklow.

The mass arrest of republican leaders at Oliver Bond's house in March 1798 may have enhanced Harvey's importance in the movement and his name was linked to senior conspirators in neighbouring co. Wicklow during this period. He hosted a famous dinner party during the April assizes attended by the Sheares brothers; Barrington was one of the few non-United Irishmen present and inferred from the guarded conduct of other guests that an insurrection was imminent. Martial law was imposed on Wexford in April 1798, and although Harvey's former activism attracted suspicion the authorities' failure to penetrate the security of the county leadership shielded him until the rising began. On 23 May 1798 he continued to feign loyalty by complying with a proclamation demanding the surrender of arms. He brought a cartload of his tenantry's weapons to Wexford town and was at lodgings near by that night when arrested by Captain James Boyd.

Harvey was in Wexford gaol when fighting spread to the county on 26–7 May. The battles of Oulart Hill and Enniscorthy turned the tide of the rising in favour of local insurgents who menaced Wexford town from Forth camp on 30 May. Harvey was requested to use his influence to safeguard the lives and properties of the pro-government community and was unharmed when the unnerved garrison abandoned the town later that day. On the night of 31 May he entertained United Irish leaders Edward Hay and Edward Fitzgerald of Newpark in his town house but was disturbed when a crowd demanded that they send out Edward Turner. Turner, a liberal magistrate, was subsequently imprisoned and Harvey realized that it would be difficult to defend such men from those wishing to avenge loyalist atrocities. The same night a meeting of rebel officers at Windmill Hill unexpectedly appointed Harvey rather than Fitzgerald as commander-in-chief of Wexford forces. Informed observers considered Harvey a compromise candidate whose protestantism reassured his co-religionists that they had nothing to fear from the nascent Wexford republic. Dissension within the county command structure arising from regionalism and tactical arguments remained unresolved and Harvey consequently lacked supreme authority. His was a largely honorary position in what remained a committee-led irregular army.

The delay of south Wexford insurgent forces in attacking the strategic border town of New Ross has been attributed in part to Harvey's indecision and complacency. The insurgents left Carrickbyrne on the night of 4 June and took up positions overlooking New Ross at Corbet Hill. Harvey established his headquarters in the local mansion and dined well ahead of what he assumed would be a short battle. His planned three-pronged attack on the town on 5 June using 10,000 men was tactically sound but was cancelled when an insurgent emissary was shot under flag of truce. A poorly executed assault, commenced at dawn, eventually drove the garrison from their positions but his failure to consolidate this costly victory exposed him to severe criticism when the army's counter-attack succeeded. He was also dismayed by reprisals taken against loyalist prisoners at Scullabogue and his last act in the field was to issue a proclamation threatening the abetters of such crimes with death.

Harvey stood down, or was deposed, as commander of the dwindling insurgent forces on 7 June and accepted another largely honorary position as 'president' of the administration in Wexford town. His attempt to open negotiations with government on 14 June was frustrated by hardliners, and the dispatch of a delegation to General Lake on the 21st also ended in failure the following day. Harvey decided to flee via Bargy Castle to Great Saltee Island off the Wexford coast with John Henry Colclough, probably intending to escape abroad at a later stage. They were seized on the information of Dr Richard Waddy on 23 June by a landing party of the revenue cutter *Rutland* and committed to Wexford gaol the following morning. Harvey was tried for eight hours on 26 June and defended himself with claims that he had accepted command only to encourage restraint. Capital conviction for treason was almost a formality and Harvey was executed on 27 June on Wexford Bridge, a structure he had helped finance in 1795. His body was thrown into the river and his head spiked on Wexford court house. He left no children. An act of attainder against Harvey's estate received royal assent on 6 October 1798 but was not effected. The lands were instead leased to Harvey's brother James who received their formal regrant in 1810 before their ultimate restoration to his older brother, John.   RUÁN O'DONNELL

Sources R. R. Madden, *The United Irishmen: their lives and times*, 2nd edn, 4 vols. (1857–60) · J. Barrington, *Personal sketches of his own times*, 3 vols. (1827–32) · C. Dickson, *The Wexford rising in 1798* (1955) · T. Cloney, *A personal narrative of those transactions in the county Wexford … during the awful period of 1798* (1832) · D. Gahan, *The people's rising: Wexford, 1798* (1995) · R. Roche and O. Merne, *Saltees, islands of birds and legends* (1977) · *Report of the Deputy Keeper of the Public Records in Ireland*, 59 (1962)
Wealth at death Wexford and Waterford estates, town house in Wexford, Bargy Castle

Harvey, Charles Barnet Cameron [Roscoe] (1900–1996), army officer and racing administrator, was born on 19 July 1900 in Sarawak, the son of Charles David Harvey, merchant of the Borneo Company. Following his father's death in 1901 he came to England with his mother. She rode to hounds with the Beaufort and Harvey learned to ride at an early age and fox-hunted throughout his youth. Despite inherited myopia which forced him to wear thick spectacles he was an outstanding games player and fine amateur rider. His first ride was at Cheltenham, when he fell off at the last fence while lying fourth. He also took up showjumping and lost the King George V Cup at the royal international horse show only after a jump off. He was known as Charles until one day in 1921 when he rode 2 pounds overweight at an Irish steeplechase; a fellow officer likened him to the film star Roscoe (Fatty) Arbuckle and the sobriquet stuck.

Educated at Downside, where he scraped through his school certificate, and at Sandhurst, where he required an interview to compensate for his poor entrance exam, Harvey joined the 10th hussars in 1920. After a spell at the Weedon Cavalry School he was appointed regimental equitation officer. On 25 October 1926 he married Iris

Daphne (Biddy) Mylne (b. 1902/3), daughter of Ernest Mylne, merchant. There was one son and one daughter of the marriage, which ended in divorce. In 1929 Harvey went with his regiment to Egypt, where he spent his leisure time organizing a racing stable. He was then posted to Meerut in India, where he took up polo to international standard, tent-pegging, and pig-sticking, in which he reached the final of the Kadir cup, the blue riband of that sport. Later he was involved in the mechanization of his squadron and, wearing a red hat rather than the official tin one, he proved a dashing, front-line leader of armour in the Second World War, in which he was awarded three DSOs. In May 1940 he embarked for France as second in command of the 10th hussars and fought several brisk actions in tanks which, in his own words, 'wouldn't even stop a rifle bullet' (*The Times*, 30 March 1996) before being evacuated from Brest in June. He served in the Middle East in 1941 and for the final stages of the north African campaign he was commander of the 8th armoured brigade. On one occasion his thirty tanks, most of which were destroyed, engaged 160 Panzers of the German Afrika Korps and halted the German advance long enough for the British army to retreat behind the Alamein line. He also found time to organize horse-races in the sands of Tripoli. Later he took the 11th armoured division into France, where it fought its way across the Orne. Despite heavy casualties Harvey's vigorous leadership kept morale high. He spearheaded the recapture of Antwerp and was the British officer responsible for liberating Belsen. His men also captured William Joyce—Lord Haw Haw—and Heinrich Himmler, the SS chief. He once told Montgomery that 'being a master of hounds is a damn sight more difficult than being a general' (*Daily Telegraph*, 29 March 1996). In Schleswig-Holstein at the end of the war he organized a series of race meetings with commandeered German thoroughbreds.

At the age of forty-six Harvey decided to leave the army, though he later became colonel of the 10th hussars. He wrote to his friend at the Jockey Club, Sir Humphrey de Trafford, enquiring about becoming a stipendary steward. On leaving the army in 1946 he was appointed a stewards' secretary, becoming senior stewards' secretary five years later. In this position he had a major role in controlling the discipline of British racing for two decades, though generally he aimed to prevent malfeasance rather than to punish it. As in his army days his humour and imperturbability concealed a determined and imposing character. He owned and bred National Hunt horses at Oddington Top, his Cotswold home near Moreton in Marsh, Gloucestershire. For three years he was also a member of the British Boxing Board of Control. On 23 February 1966 he married Betty Stoddard Horn (1905/6–1980), a widow, and daughter of Louis Ezekiel Stoddard, financier. On Harvey's retirement in 1970 he was elected a member of the Jockey Club. Although he modestly claimed that he continued as senior steward for so long 'because he couldn't do anything else', champion jockey Sir Gordon Richards acknowledged him as 'the greatest man racing has known in my lifetime' (*Daily Telegraph*, 29 March 1996). He died at his Gloucestershire home, Oddington Top, Oddington, on 28 March 1996 of bronchopneumonia, a few months after taking the salute from his wheelchair at the VJ parade at Stow on the Wold. He was survived by the daughter of his first marriage, Marion Jennefer Matthey.

WRAY VAMPLEW

Sources *The Times* (30 March 1996) · *The Independent* (29 March 1996) · *Daily Telegraph* (29 March 1996) · *The Guardian* (3 April 1996) · R. Mortimer, R. Onslow, and P. Willett, *Biographical encyclopedia of British flat racing* (1978) · m. certs. · d. cert.
Likenesses photograph, repro. in *The Independent* · photograph, repro. in *Daily Telegraph* · photograph, repro. in *The Times* · photograph, repro. in *The Guardian*
Wealth at death £3,344,582: probate, 18 July 1996, CGPLA Eng. & Wales

Harvey, Christopher (1597–1663), Church of England clergyman and poet, was the son of the Revd Christopher Harvey (*d*. 1601) of Bunbury in Cheshire, a clergyman, and his wife, Ellen. He probably attended Bunbury grammar school, where his father had been headmaster, until his widowed mother married Thomas *Pierson and moved to Brampton Bryan in Herefordshire. He was enrolled as a batteler at Brasenose College, Oxford, in 1613, graduated BA on 19 May 1617, and was licensed MA on 1 February 1620. Having taken holy orders, by 1630 he was working in the parish of Whitney in Herefordshire, where the baptism of a daughter was recorded on 13 March and where he was appointed rector on the death of the incumbent in December. He was the first headmaster of Kington grammar school in Worcestershire from September 1632 until March 1633, when he resumed his duties in Whitney. On 14 November 1639 he was instituted into the vicarage of Clifton-on-Dunsmore in Warwickshire. According to a dedication in Pierson's *Excellent Encouragements Against Afflictions* (1647), which Harvey edited after his stepfather's death, he owed these livings to the patronage of Sir Robert Whitney. His wife, Margaret, bore nine children, five baptized at Whitney between 1630 and 1639 and four, including twin daughters, baptized between 1642 and 1645 at Clifton.

Harvey is best-known as the author of *The Synagogue*, a collection of religious poems first published anonymously in 1640 and bound with the sixth edition of *The Temple* by George Herbert. Subtitled 'The shadow of the temple', it was originally conceived as a modest imitation of a revered master but the ecclesiastical reforms of the 1640s led to a change of emphasis in later editions. Groups of poems on church festivals and church utensils added in 1647 indicate a determination to defend the doctrines and practices of the established church against puritan attack, and new poems on church offices in the third edition of 1657 were part of 'a canny political campaign' during the interregnum 'for the restoration of high Anglicanism' (Bell, 268–9). His main literary ally was Izaak Walton, who quoted Harvey's poem on the outlawed Book of Common Prayer in the second edition of *The Compleat Angler* (1655). Harvey contributed a commendatory poem to this volume

and Walton reciprocated in the 1657 edition of *The Synagogue*. There was no further expansion of Harvey's collection, which continued to be issued as an appendage to *The Temple* at regular intervals up to 1709. The two were still yoked together when an eleventh edition came out in 1799, and there were further joint editions in the nineteenth century. Alexander Grosart eventually issued the poetic works of Harvey as a separate volume in the Fuller Worthies' Library in 1874, which was the last edition of *The Synagogue* to appear.

Harvey's other venture into verse, *Schola cordis*, published anonymously in 1647, was an emblem book adapted from the Latin of Benedict van Haeften. His explications of forty-seven engravings depicting the spiritual travails of the human heart exploited the 'mixture of literalness and symbolism' (Freeman, 135) made popular by Francis Quarles and, in spite of a statement in the third edition of 1674 that it was 'by the author of the *Synagogue*', the work was later ascribed to Quarles and reprinted with his emblem books. Harvey's 'predictable, stolid didacticism' (Bell, 274) and 'piety served up with a sauce of wit' (Dundas, 98) have not appealed to modern taste but Walton praised *The Synagogue* as a true picture of the poet's mind, Grosart discerned here and there 'an imaginative faculty in *kind* resembling Herbert and Vaughan's' (Harvey, xxxvi), and Freeman found 'considerable variety in metre and in treatment' in the adaptations of van Haeften (Freeman, 137).

In his edition of Pierson's *Excellent Encouragements* (1647) Harvey expressed an 'obstinate resolution never to send mine own name to the presse' unless it were 'to bring to light another mans labours' (sig. aa2r) but he acknowledged his authorship of two early prose works when they were printed towards the end of his life. *Self-Contradiction Censured, or, A Caveat Against Inconstancy* (imprimatur 14 June 1662) exposes the deceitfulness of 'Phanatick spirits' (title-page) and defends the 'sacred secrecie' of royal government (p. 148) in the form of a dialogue between Affection and Judgement. Harvey claims in a dedicatory letter that it was 'penned in the year 1642, under the borrowed name of Irenaeus Philalethes' and permitted to circulate in manuscript, 'not without approbation from some, both loyal Subjects of the Crown, and obedient sons of the Church of England' (sig. A3r).

The Right Rebel: a Treatise Discovering the True Use of the Name by the Nature of Rebellion (1661), which was reissued in 1663 as *Faction Supplanted, or, A Caveat Against the Ecclesiastical and Secular Rebell*, is said in a preface to have been completed on 3 April 1645 and made public in two manuscript copies because no printer could be found for it in London. In a postscript dated 11 March 1661 Harvey states that he was 'a constant sufferer' for his 'loyalty and conformity' so long as 'any usurpers of pretended authority were in power' (p. 173) and regrets that he has had to set aside two other intended treatises, *Logick for Loyalty* and *A Motion for Moderation*, because of age and infirmity (pp. 175–6). Harvey died at his vicarage at Clifton-on-Dunsmore, and was buried at Clifton on 4 April 1663.

ROBERT WILCHER

Sources *The complete poems of Christopher Harvey*, ed. A. B. Grosart, Fuller Worthies' Library (1874) • A. C. Howell, 'Christopher Harvey's *The synagogue* (1640)', *Studies in Philology*, 49 (1952), 229–47 • *DNB* • Wood, *Ath. Oxon.*, new edn, 3.538–9 • I. Bell, 'In the shadow of the temple', *Like season'd timber: new essays on George Herbert*, ed. E. Miller and R. Di Yanni (1987), 255–79 • R. Freeman, *English emblem books* (1948); repr. (1967), 134–7 • J. Dundas, 'Levity and grace: the poetry of sacred wit', *Yearbook of English Studies*, 2 (1972), 93–102

Harvey, Daniel Whittle (1786–1863), politician, newspaper proprietor, and police administrator, was born on 10 June 1786 in Witham, Essex, the son of Matthew Barnard Harvey of Witham, a merchant and banker, and his wife, a daughter of Major John Whittle of Feering House, Kelveden, Essex. Harvey trained as a lawyer; he was articled first in Colchester and subsequently with a law firm in Chancery Lane, London. In 1807 he took possession of his maternal estate, Feering House, and began to practise as a country solicitor in the Colchester district. In partnership with his father he also began speculating in the buying and selling of estates. On 23 May 1809 he married Mary, the only daughter of Ebenezer Johnston of Bishopsgate Street in London, who reputedly brought a dowry of £30,000.

Harvey's various business ventures brought him into conflict with other local attorneys, in particular with Thomas Andrew. Between 1808 and 1814 Harvey was involved in three court actions. The first was a case of slander against Andrew following accusations of theft and fraud. The other two also indirectly involved Andrew. Harvey lost on each occasion. On 7 November 1810 he was admitted as a student of the Inner Temple, and in 1819, with the intention of taking up the post of recorder of Colchester, he applied to be called to the bar. His application was refused on the grounds of the stigma of defeat in the slander case against Andrew. When Harvey's appeal was heard in February 1822 the judges, as visitors to the inn, upheld the decision of the benchers. Twelve years later, in 1834, the benchers heard the appeal again, and confirmed their original decision; and when, later that year, a select committee of the House of Commons investigated the case and exonerated Harvey entirely, the benchers continued to reject him.

Harvey served as a member of the common council of the City of London for the Bishopsgate ward from 1808 to 1818, and from early on he sought an active involvement in national politics. He canvassed Maldon, Essex, in 1807. In 1812 and again in a by-election in 1818 he unsuccessfully contested Colchester. In the general election of June 1818, however, after a particularly expensive campaign, Harvey was elected. In 1820 he was unseated when his election was declared void, but he successfully contested the seat again in 1826. The Reform Act of 1832 changed the nature of the constituency, leading Harvey to sense that his seat was under threat from the tories. In the general election of 1835 he stood down in Colchester and was elected for Southwark; he held this seat until 1840. In parliament Harvey was an eloquent advocate of radical causes, notably religious toleration, and reform of both parliament and the established church.

Financial problems, exacerbated by his own extravagance, dogged Harvey's career. His lawsuits cost him considerable sums. In 1814 the Rochford and Billericay Bank, owned by his father and uncle, collapsed, and while Harvey succeeded in paying off his own creditors, he was left with very little. In 1822, in settlement of a debt, he acquired the ownership of the new *Sunday Times*. An article in the edition of 9 February 1823 declared George IV to be mad, like his father. The suggestion had already been made elsewhere in the press, but Harvey was singled out as an example. Prosecuted for a libel, he was found guilty, fined £200, and imprisoned for twelve months in the king's bench. Yet the *Sunday Times* was a considerable success, due in no small measure to Harvey's ideas and innovations such as the use of wood-engravings and of advertising in agricultural and sporting supplements. Within five years Harvey was able to sell the paper at a profit, and, over the next few years, he sought to repeat its success. He ran the daily *True Sun* from 1833 to 1837, the *Weekly True Sun* from 1833 to 1839, and *The Statesman, or, The Weekly True Sun* from January to December 1840. The *True Sun* was a London evening paper which attempted to mediate between working-class and middle-class radicalism, and was in the forefront of the campaign to repeal newspaper stamp duty. But, like its weekly offshoot, it was not a commercial success.

It was financial difficulties which encouraged Harvey to accept the office of registrar of metropolitan carriages in February 1839. The offer of the post, however, appears to have been a ploy to oust him from his Southwark constituency. The post of registrar was held by some to be an office of profit under the crown and thus incompatible with a seat in parliament. Writs were issued for a by-election. Harvey contested the charge against him, and was re-elected for the borough. A similar issue occurred later in the year when Harvey sought the newly created office of commissioner of the City of London police. He had strong backing from members of the corporation, and he intended to combine the office with his duties as an MP. However, a disqualifying clause was inserted in the bill establishing the City police; allegedly, this was aimed specifically at Harvey. Peel, then leader of the opposition in parliament, supported the government's proposal, pointing out that the commissioners of the Metropolitan Police were similarly barred, and warning against the possibility of a police commissioner sitting in the Commons and challenging the home secretary on police matters. The disqualifying clause was passed, together with a clause which limited the power of the court of common council in police management largely to finance. The common council, furious that it would have only a limited say in the appointment of a commissioner and none at all in his retention of office or dismissal, responded by slashing the salary for the post from £1000 a year to £800. Harvey considered withdrawing his candidacy, but was urged by his supporters that the move would be dishonourable. He was sworn in as the first commissioner of the City of London police on 11 November 1839.

Harvey never appears to have given up hope of returning to national politics. In 1847 he was nominated Liberal candidate for Marylebone, and he promised his supporters there that he would give up his police post. However, dependence on his City salary meant that, in the event, he had to stand down since his parlous financial state would not have allowed him to take a seat in the Commons. Whatever his hopes, Harvey continued to serve as commissioner until his death. While he had no experience of police work, or of commanding men, in many respects his career as commissioner can be judged a success. He was inflexible in the way that he controlled and directed his men; nevertheless he established and maintained a body of men as disciplined and effective as any other police force during the period. As in the earlier stages of his life, he clashed publicly and damagingly with others. There were lengthy disputes with the City's police committee and common council over his official residence and his determination that he alone should make decisions regarding the deployment and management of his men. This latter was in keeping with the 1839 legislation, but it was not the way in which policing had traditionally been organized in the City.

Harvey died on 27 February 1863 after a short illness, beginning with a carbuncle in his mouth which was rapidly followed by erysipelas. He was buried in the grounds of the Unitarian chapel at Hackney. The City police paid for a monument to be erected over his grave. His wife, disabled long before by a fall sustained crossing a road, survived him by a year.   CLIVE EMSLEY

Sources D. Rumbelow, *I spy blue: the police and crime in the City of London from Elizabeth I to Victoria* (1971) · M. E. Speight, 'Politics in the borough of Colchester, 1812–1847', PhD diss., U. Lond., 1969 · R. Ainslie, *Discourse on the death of D. W. Harvey* (1863) · L. Taylor and R. G. Thorne, 'Harvey, Daniel Whittle', HoP, *Commons, 1790–1820* · D. Griffiths, ed., *The encyclopedia of the British press, 1422–1992* (1992) · H. Hobson, P. Knightley, and L. Russell, *The pearl of days: an intimate memoir of the Sunday Times, 1822–1972* (1972) · J. H. Wiener, *The war of the unstamped* (1969)

Archives CLRO, minutes and papers of police committee
Likenesses G. Shade, mezzotint, pubd 1836 (after E. H. Latilla), NPG · G. Hayter, group portrait, oils (*The House of Commons, 1833*), NPG · lithograph, BM · portrait, Guildhall, London, Coll. of City of London

Harvey, Edmund (c.1601–1673), regicide, was the first son of Charles Harvey (*fl.* 1600–1634), merchant, of London and his wife, Alice, daughter of Ralph Houghton of Houghton, Leicestershire. Harvey's grandfather had moved to London from the west country and his father was a London citizen and member of the Fishmongers' Company. Edmund Harvey followed his father into trade, being apprenticed in 1619 and becoming a freeman of the Drapers' Company in 1627. On 8 December 1629 he married Elizabeth, daughter of Samuel Gott of London. They had at least three sons. A silk merchant in partnership with Alderman Edward Sleigh, Harvey contributed with him £300 towards equipping the naval force raised to aid suppression of the Ulster rising in 1642. At the outbreak of civil war he was commissioned as a colonel of the city horse. He was probably the 'one Harvey' referred to by

Clarendon as 'a decayed silkman, who from the beginning had become one of the most confided in' and whose troops in 1643 dispersed 'with sad inhumanity … as an enemy worthy of their courage … a rabble of women' (Clarendon, *Hist. rebellion*, 3.139) presenting the House of Commons with a peace petition.

Harvey had acquired property in Suffolk, where he was a deputy lieutenant in 1643, receiver-general for the county in 1644, and an assiduous member from 1643 to 1645 of the parliamentary committee there, signing many orders. He was at the siege of Gloucester in the summer of 1643 and later served in the north, to be accused afterwards of plundering there. In May 1644 he resisted the instruction of the committee of both kingdoms to march with the earl of Essex unless his men's and his own arrears were first paid. The committee was thereupon ordered to 'secure his horse and arms, discharge his quarters, take his muskets and despatch his pay' (*JHC*, 3.490, 505). By an ordinance of 3 March 1647 he was paid £1448 in settlement of his arrears.

In 1646 Harvey had been recruited MP for Great Bedwyn, Wiltshire. He was an active MP, being named to many committees: he was particularly involved with the issues of indemnity and confiscated lands, and by January 1647 he was chairman of the indemnity committee. In July 1648 he opposed the motion that the king be taken at his word that he would not try to escape, arguing that Charles I could not be trusted. Throughout the 1640s he evidently managed skilfully and profitably to exploit the opportunities thrown up by the war and his contacts to his own profit, sliding into speculation, if not embezzlement. A summation as 'a time serving profiteer and a dishonest racketeer' seems not unjust (Underdown, 87, 134–5). When bishops' lands were sold off during 1647 and 1648 he was able to find £7617 2s. 10d. to acquire the manor of Fulham, £674 10s. for other land in the same area, and a fee farm rent out of the manors of Burton and Holnest, Dorset. Other purchases included the great tithes of the see of London and the episcopal palace at Fulham, where he lived over the next decade in great style and comfort. An enemy later wrote that on Harvey's purchase of bishops' lands he was transformed 'from a furious Presbyter to a Bedlam Independent' (F. T. K.). Edward Walker names him 'late a poor silkman' among a list of MPs and army officers obtaining, contrary to the self-denying ordinance, money, offices, and land.

Harvey sat as a commissioner for the trial of Charles I and was on a committee to prepare the final charge, but though present on 27 January 1649, did not sign the death warrant. This, however, did him no harm under the Commonwealth. Still 'Colonel', he became first commissioner of the customs, was on the navy committee, and continued in office into the protectorate. It is not known when Harvey's first wife died but he probably married Judith (d. 1668), daughter of George Langham of London and widow of Thomas Bales of London, in the early 1650s. They had at least ten children before Judith's death in September 1668. Harvey's career began to decline when, on 7 November 1655, only two days after lavishly entertaining

Cromwell at Fulham, he was committed close prisoner (along with his brother-in-law Henry Langham), charged with divesting state funds to his own use, estimated at £57,000. On 13 November his papers were ordered to be examined, but on 27 November, reported as ill by his wife, he was given the liberty of the Tower. Dismissed from his offices, on 24 December he was allowed, on security of £10,000, to live at Fulham for a month. In January 1656 proceedings against him were started in the exchequer. In February 1657 a remarkably low charge of £326 6s. 8d. was levied on his goods and chattels and he was released from custody.

Though out of office, Harvey was still financially active, notably on behalf of Bulstrode *Whitelocke, then a commissioner of the treasury, with whom he had been involved in arranging the purchase of the City house of the divine Cornelius Burgess. Harvey's son Samuel, 'a sober young man', married Whitelocke's youngest daughter, Cecilia, in September 1658 and Fulham Palace was settled on them. On the recall of the Rump in 1659 Harvey returned to parliament but his committee appointments were generally confined to those considering private petitions. After the restoration of Charles II in 1660, Whitelocke was negotiating on Harvey's behalf the palace's return to Gilbert Sheldon, the new bishop of London, when troops were suddenly sent in to search it on 24 December. The place was ransacked, a traumatic experience for Harvey's daughter-in-law, who was pregnant, and Whitelocke somewhat implausibly blamed this incident for the premature deaths less than two years later of Samuel, Cecilia, and the child (b. June 1661).

Harvey, having surrendered himself, was excepted from the Act of Indemnity and Oblivion as to life and property. Tried on 16 October 1660, he was spared his life. In November Whitelocke was still working to secure him a pardon but Harvey was sent to Pendennis Castle, Cornwall, in 1661 and died there in June 1673; he was buried in Falmouth parish churchyard. His son Samuel was survived by a younger brother, Charles.

IVAN ROOTS and S. M. WYNNE

Sources CSP dom., 1644–61 · C. H. Firth and R. S. Rait, eds., Acts and ordinances of the interregnum, 1642–1660, 3 vols. (1911) · The diary of Bulstrode Whitelocke, 1605–1675, ed. R. Spalding, British Academy, Records of Social and Economic History, new ser., 13 (1990) · R. Spalding, Contemporaries of Bulstrode Whitelocke, 1605–1675 (1990) · B. Worden, The Rump Parliament, 1648–1653 (1974) · D. Underdown, Pride's Purge: politics in the puritan revolution (1971) · Clarendon, Hist. rebellion · G. E. Aylmer, The state's servants: the civil service of the English republic, 1649–1660 (1973) · G. Edwards, The last days of Charles I (1998) · State trials, vol. 5 · I. Gentles, The New Model Army in England, Ireland, and Scotland, 1645–1653 (1992) · S. Barber, Regicide and republicanism (1998) · T. Verax [C. Walker], Anarchia Anglicana, or, The history of independency, pt 2 (1649) · K. Roberts, 'Citizen soldiers: the military power of the city of London', London and the civil war, ed. S. Porter (1996) · F. T. K., 'Harvey, Edmund', HoP, Commons, 1640–60 [draft]

Harvey, Edmund George

Harvey, Edmund George (1828–1884), author and composer, was born on 20 February 1828 at Penzance, the eldest son of **William Woodis Harvey** (1798–1864) and his first wife. The father was born in Alverton Vean, Penzance, on 15 June 1798. He was educated at a school in Market Jew

Street, Penzance, and then at a Wesleyan school. He was a Wesleyan missionary in Haiti between about 1818 and 1824. In 1825 he married Sarah, daughter of William Morgan of Penzance. Encouraged by the vicar of Penzance to attend university, he matriculated at Queens' College, Cambridge, in 1824, graduated BA in 1828, and proceeded MA in 1835. He was ordained in the Church of England and was curate of St Mary's, Penzance (1828–30), and of King Charles the Martyr, Falmouth (c.1834–1838), before becoming rector of St Mary's, Truro (1839–60). In 1846, after the death of his first wife, he married Frances Fox, of Penn Cottage, Penn, Buckinghamshire. He was the author of Sketches of Hayti (1827) and various sermons, and he edited John Wesley's minor works. He died on 5 October 1864 at Alverton, near Torquay.

Edmund George, his eldest son, entered Queens' College, Cambridge, in 1845 and graduated BA in 1850. He afterwards lived for a few years on the continent, and made a pair-oar expedition through France and Prussia, which he described in Our Cruise in the 'Undine'. He was ordained deacon in 1851 and priest in 1855, and he became in 1859 curate, and in 1860, rector, of St Mary's, Truro. From 1865 to 1884 he was vicar of Mullion, Cornwall.

Edmund George Harvey published very widely on topics ranging from sermons and devotional works to antiquarian works relating to Cornwall, but particularly on music. He was honorary secretary of the Cornwall Association of Church Choirs and wrote hymns and pointed psalms for local use. His secular music included dances, parlour songs, and folk tunes. The music fairly soon fell into obscurity.

Harvey died at the vicarage at Mullion on 21 June 1884, and was buried at Truro. He left a son, but nothing is known of his wife, Sarah.

L. M. MIDDLETON, rev. ELIZABETH BAIGENT

Sources Venn, Alum. Cant. · GM, 3rd ser., 17 (1864), 662 [obit. of Revd William Woodis Harvey] · Clergy List (1855–65) · CGPLA Eng. & Wales (1864) · CGPLA Eng. & Wales (1884) · Boase & Courtney, Bibl. Corn., 1.212

Wealth at death £745: administration, 1 Aug 1884, CGPLA Eng. & Wales · under £30,000—William Woodis Harvey: probate, 29 Oct 1864, CGPLA Eng. & Wales

Harvey, Sir Edward

Harvey, Sir Edward (1783–1865), naval officer, was the third son of Captain John *Harvey (1740–1794) and his wife, Judith, daughter of Henry Wise of Sandwich, Kent; he was a younger brother of Admiral Sir John *Harvey. He was with his father as a first-class volunteer on board the Brunswick (74 guns) in the battle in the north Atlantic on 1 June 1794; he was afterwards with his brother John in the Prince of Wales (98 guns); then, in the frigate Beaulieu (40 guns), he was at the battle of Camperdown; and was again with his brother in the Southampton (32 guns) and Amphitrite (28 guns). In July 1801 he was made lieutenant; and after continuous service, mostly in the North Sea and Mediterranean, was promoted in January 1808 to command the sloop Cephalus (18 guns) in the Mediterranean. On 18 April 1811 he was posted to the frigate Topaze (36 guns), which he brought home and paid off in 1812.

From 1830 to 1834 Harvey commanded the Undaunted

(46 guns) on the Cape of Good Hope and East India stations; in 1838 the *Malabar* (74 guns) in the West Indies; and from 1839 to 1842, the *Implacable* (74 guns) in the Mediterranean, where he took part in the operations on the coast of Syria, including the bombardment of Acre in 1840. He attained his flag on 17 December 1847, and from 1848 to 1853 was superintendent at Malta, with his flag in the *Ceylon*. He became vice-admiral on 11 September 1854, was commander-in-chief at the Nore from 1857 to 1860, and was promoted admiral on 9 June 1860; he was made a KCB on 28 June 1861, and a GCB on 28 March 1865, a few weeks before his death at his residence at Walmer, Kent, on 4 May 1865. He had married Miss Cannon of Deal, and they had six children, one of whom was Henry, a captain in the navy, who died in the West Indies in 1869, while in command of the *Eclipse*.

J. K. LAUGHTON, rev. ROGER MORRISS

Sources O'Byrne, *Naval biog. dict.* · *GM*, 3rd ser., 18 (1865), 804 · *Navy List* · private information (1891) · P. Mackesy, *The war in the Mediterranean, 1803–1810* (1957) · R. Muir, *Britain and the defeat of Napoleon, 1807–1815* (1996) · *CGPLA Eng. & Wales* (1865)
Wealth at death under £14,000: probate, 23 May 1865, *CGPLA Eng. & Wales*

Harvey, Sir Eliab (1758–1830), naval officer and politician, was born on 5 December 1758 at Chigwell, Essex, the fourth but second surviving son of William Harvey (1714–1763), MP for Essex, and his wife, Emma (b. *c*.1729), daughter of Stephen and Emma Skynner of Walthamstow. William Harvey, the discoverer of the circulation of the blood, was his great-great-uncle. Eliab was educated at Westminster School (1768–9) and at Harrow School for most of the period 1770–74; meanwhile on his fourteenth birthday his name was sagaciously entered on the books of the yacht *Mary*. He spent the summer of 1773 in the *Orpheus* (32 guns) and from May 1774 served in the sloop *Lynx* for two years in the West Indies. In September 1776 he returned to North America in the *Mermaid* (28 guns), before transferring to Lord Howe's flagship, the *Eagle* (64 guns), in the following July. In December 1777 he was lent to the *Liverpool* (28 guns), in which he was wrecked in heavy surf off Long Island in February 1778. He rejoined the *Eagle*, returned home in her in October, and was then ashore for three years.

On 25 February 1779 Harvey was promoted lieutenant of the *Resolution*, which he did not join. In April, on the death of his elder brother, William, he succeeded to the family's very handsome property. He wasted no time in making his mark as a man about town and a reckless plunger. Soon after his twenty-first birthday he lost £100,000 at hazard to

an Irish gamester, Mr O'Byrne, who said 'you can never pay me'. 'I can', answered Harvey; 'my estate will sell for the debt.' 'No', said O'Byrne, 'I will win £10,000; you shall throw for the odd ninety.' They did, and Harvey won. (Walpole, *Corr.*, 25.12)

He was, however, still £10,000 short.

In May 1780 Harvey was elected MP for Maldon, Essex, a seat he held until 1784, though he returned to sea in September 1781 for four months as lieutenant of the *Dolphin*

(44 guns) in the Downs. After promotion to commander on 21 March 1782 he commanded the sloop *Otter* until his speedy advancement to captain (20 January 1783). He was then unemployed until 1790. On 15 May 1784 he married Louisa (d. 1841), younger daughter and coheir of Robert, first Earl Nugent. They had six daughters and two sons; the elder son was killed at the siege of Burgos in 1812.

From May 1790 Harvey commanded the *Hussar* (28 guns) for six months in the Spanish armament. When war broke out in 1793 he was appointed to the *Santa Margarita* (38 guns), serving under Vice-Admiral John Jervis (later earl of St Vincent), and took part in the capture of Martinique and Guadeloupe in March and April 1794. After returning to England in May the *Santa Margarita* joined the Channel Fleet and on 23 August was one of the squadron under Sir John Borlase Warren which drove a French frigate and two corvettes ashore in Brittany. In August 1795 Harvey took command of the *Valiant* (74 guns) and went to the West Indies with Sir Hyde Parker's squadron.

In February 1797 ill health obliged him to return home and in the following year he commanded the sea fencibles in Essex. In 1800 he was appointed to the *Triumph* (74 guns), serving in the channel and off Brest until the peace of Amiens. He was elected MP for Essex in June 1802, and represented the county until 1812; in November 1803 he commissioned the *Temeraire* (98 guns).

After fifteen months off Brest and the Bay of Biscay the *Temeraire* formed part of Nelson's fleet at Trafalgar. As second ship of the weather column, closely astern of the *Victory*, she was soon in action and, as Harvey was to write to his wife (23 October 1805), for 'more than three hours two of the enemy's line of battleships were lashed to her, one on each side' (Jackson, 2.223). Although herself much damaged, the *Temeraire* forced both French ships to strike to her deadly broadsides. 'Nothing could be finer', wrote Vice-Admiral Cuthbert Collingwood of the *Temeraire's* part; 'I have not words in which I can sufficiently express my admiration of it' (PRO, ADM 1/5396, Collingwood to Harvey, 28 Oct 1805). Unfortunately Harvey's subsequent bragging irritated his fellow captains. Joseph Turner's painting of *The Fighting Temeraire* hangs in the National Gallery.

On 9 November 1805 Harvey was promoted rear-admiral of the blue, and in March 1806 he hoisted his flag in the *Tonnant* (80 guns) in the channel and off Finisterre under St Vincent; later he hoisted it under Admiral James Gambier.

In April 1809 Harvey returned from two months' leave to rejoin his commander-in-chief, Lord Gambier, off Basque Roads where preparations were in hand for an attack on the French fleet by fireships. Harvey was so angry that the Admiralty had appointed Captain Lord Cochrane and not him to command the fireships that he went to the flagship, marched into Gambier's cabin, and 'used vehement and insulting language to Gambier ... showed great disrespect to him ... and treated him in a contemptuous manner' (PRO, ADM 1/5396, minutes of court martial, 22, 23 May 1809). He then spoke disparagingly of Gambier in public on the flagship's quarterdeck.

For this he was court martialled and dismissed the service. His behaviour was evidently in line with his reputation: 'His intemperate manner is such', wrote Lord Gardner to Joseph Farington (26 May 1809), 'that, had I been told the circumstance without a name being given, I should have supposed it to be Admiral Harvey' (*Farington Diary*, ed. Greig, 5.173).

On 21 March 1810 Harvey was, in consideration of his long and meritorious service, reinstated in his rank and seniority, but he was never employed again. He was promoted vice-admiral on 31 July 1810, created KCB in January 1815, and advanced to admiral on 12 August 1819 and GCB in 1825. In 1820 he was again elected MP for Essex, and he held the seat until his death on 20 February 1830 at his home, Rolls Park, Chigwell, Essex. He was buried on 27 February in the family mausoleum at Hempstead church.

J. K. LAUGHTON, rev. C. H. H. OWEN

Sources minutes of court martial, PRO, ADM 1/5396, 22, 23 May 1809 · admiralty documents, PRO, ADM 9/1, 36, 37, 51, 52, 107/7 · *GM*, 1st ser., 100/1 (1830), 365–6 · J. Marshall, *Royal naval biography*, 1/1 (1823), 273–6 · J. Ralfe, *The naval biography of Great Britain*, 2 (1828), 432–4 · T. S. Jackson, ed., *Logs of the great sea fights, 1794–1805*, 2, Navy RS, 18 (1900), 223 · M. M. Drummond, 'Harvey, Eliab', HoP, *Commons, 1754–90* · W. Stokes and R. G. Thorne, 'Harvey, Eliab', HoP, *Commons, 1790–1820* · Walpole, *Corr.* · *The Farington diary*, ed. J. Greig, 8 vols. (1922–8)

Archives Essex RO, Chelmsford, family corresp. and papers | BL, letters to second Earl Spencer · NL Wales, letters to Louisa Lloyd; letters to William Lloyd

Likenesses L. F. Abbott, oils, *c*.1806, NMM · Hudson?, oils, City University of New York, Queen's College

Wealth at death £120,000: PRO, death duty registers, IR 26/1227, no. 75

Harvey, Sir Ernest Musgrave, first baronet (1867–1955), banker, was born on 27 July 1867 at 1 Oak Hill, Hampstead, London, the third son of the Revd Charles Musgrave Harvey, curate of St John's Church, Hampstead, and later rector of Acton and vicar of Hillingdon, Middlesex, and his wife, Frances Harriet, *née* Brewster. He was educated at Marlborough College, and in 1885 obtained a clerkship in the Bank of England. In 1896 he married Sophia Paget (1871–1952); they had a son and three daughters.

During fifty years at the Bank of England Harvey— among the first of a new breed of central banker—became only the second of its officials to be elected a director and the first to enter the ranks of 'governors'. Appointed deputy chief cashier in 1902 at the early age of thirty-five, from 1914 he played a large part in the bank's tasks of arranging massive war loans and then post-war monetary reconstruction for Britain and its European allies. For these services he was decorated by the French and Belgian governments, made a CBE in 1917, and knighted in 1920. He succeeded Sir Gordon Nairne as chief cashier in 1918 and again as comptroller in 1925, before joining him as a director in 1928.

These promotions of senior officials to a court of directors traditionally composed of merchant bankers introduced a new professionalism to the Bank of England's highest levels as part of wider organizational reforms arising from its recognition that, amid post-war financial dislocations, central banking had become a much more active and complex function. The customary two-year rotation of governors was also abandoned. Just as Montagu Norman was the first modern, long-term governor, so Harvey in 1929 became the first modern deputy governor.

Harvey's great strength was his thorough knowledge of the Bank of England's organization and practices, making him 'the perfect permanent secretary' for Norman by relieving him of responsibilities for administration and co-ordination (Sayers, 2.622–3, 635, 650–52). He was also unusually articulate in expounding his understanding. On trips to European capitals, and in a visit to Australia in 1927, he was an apostle of the bank's conception of central banking principles under the restored gold standard. With Norman absent through illness in late 1929, Harvey gave the bank's long opening evidence to the Macmillan committee of finance and industry, impressing even Keynes with what remains the most comprehensive and lucid source for the inter-war Bank of England.

Another of Norman's illnesses left Harvey as the bank's acting head during the sterling crises of August and September 1931. He not only orchestrated defensive actions by the City, the Treasury, and American and French banks, but with his fellow director Sir Edward Peacock became a principal adviser to successive governments, even attending cabinet committees. Calling for urgent balancing of the budget as the best means to restore international confidence, they contributed to the pressures which fatally divided the second Labour cabinet. Consequently they figured prominently in accusations of forming a 'bankers' ramp' against a socialist government, although Harvey had scrupulously left discussion of specific taxes and expenditure cuts to the politicians. Under the emergency all-party National Government they criticized Conservative efforts to force a general election, and believed these helped to precipitate the final collapse of confidence. After two months of strenuous struggle, Harvey had to preside over the Bank of England's decision to advise abandonment of the gold standard, announced on 21 September 1931.

What then seemed a catastrophe was soon accepted as an economic relief. One result was the implementation in June 1932 of the long-prepared plans of Harvey and Sir Richard Hopkins of the Treasury for a great war loan conversion, which inaugurated the 'cheap money' that assisted Britain's economic recovery in the 1930s. Harvey also participated in Bank of England rescues of commercial banks and in its novel industrial reorganization schemes, notably of the Lancashire Cotton Corporation. From 1934 he chaired the R. M. and E. D. Realisation Companies, the Bank of England-led arrangements for liquidating the failed Royal Mail–Elder Dempster shipping combine. Harvey was created a baronet in 1933. He retired from the Bank of England in 1936, but during the Second World War was a member of the General Claims Tribunal. He died at his home, Pennings, Mildenhall, Marlborough, on 17 December 1955.

PHILIP WILLIAMSON

Sources *The Times* (19 Dec 1955) · *WWW* · R. S. Sayers, *The Bank of England, 1891–1944*, 3 vols. (1976) · P. Williamson, *National crisis and*

national government: British politics, the economy and empire, 1926–1932 (1992) · P. Clarke, *The Keynesian revolution in the making, 1924–1936* (1988) · b. cert.
Archives Bank of England, London, deputy governor's MSS
Likenesses O. Birley, oils, 1936, Bank of England, London
Wealth at death £39,112 2s. 1d.: probate, 23 Feb 1956, *CGPLA Eng. & Wales*

Harvey, Sir Francis (*c.*1568–1632), judge and politician, was a younger, but the eldest surviving, son of Stephen Harvey (*d.* 1606), an auditor of the duchy of Lancaster, of Cotes, Cotton End, Hardingstone, Northamptonshire, and his wife, Anne (*d.* 1590), daughter of Richard Greene of Broughton, Hertfordshire. Admitted to the Middle Temple in 1582 from Barnard's Inn, with which a family connection possibly existed (Brooks, 147), Harvey then matriculated at Cambridge University as a pensioner of Christ's College in March 1583. He took his BA from Corpus Christi in 1586, graduated MA from the newly founded Emmanuel College in 1589, then contrived to be called to the bar in 1591. His first marriage, to a widow, Elizabeth James, *née* Heming, probably took place about 1596. A second wife, Christian, survived him. Although his father's duchy connections may have secured his return as member for Aldeburgh in the 1597 parliament, Harvey's recorded role in the Commons' proceedings was confined to possible attendance at one committee meeting.

Harvey's subsequent professional advancement was assisted by Henry Hastings, fifth earl of Huntington, whose steward Thomas Harvey was a kinsman, and by the influential Montagu family, whose intervention may have secured his appointment as counsel to the town of Northampton in 1602. In 1609 he was promoted to the bench of the Middle Temple. He succeeded Augustine Nicolls, another Northamptonshire resident, as recorder of the borough of Leicester in 1612, but declined invitations to become one of the town's MPs two years later. He was promoted serjeant-at-law in the general call of 1614 and delivered a brief three-day reading that August on the statute 21 Hen. VIII c. 13 (non-residency), some notes from which survive in manuscript. He then moved on to Serjeant's Inn, Fleet Street. Among the busier and most widely practised serjeants-at-law during the second decade of the seventeenth century, Harvey was constantly on the move; asked whether he would be in London for Hilary term 1617, he brusquely replied that he did indeed so intend, 'for from thence came his living' (*Buccleuch MSS*, 3.198).

In October 1624 Harvey became a justice of common pleas; according to Lord Keeper Williams the king recognized him as eminent in his profession, 'grave, discreet and religious', and a good governor in his own country (*Diary of Sir Richard Hutton*, 54). Knighted in July 1626, when Westminster Hall flooded in October 1629, Harvey rode in on horseback to adjourn his court. Next year he retorted to an assize sermon attacking judicial corruption 'that we can use conscience in our places, as well as the best clergie man of all' (*Diary of John Rous*, 62). After his death at Hardingstone, Northamptonshire, on 2 August 1632 a judicial colleague memorialized Harvey as 'reverend and learned … temperate, patient and upright, a man of good courage

… honoured, beloved and respected' (*Diary of Sir Richard Hutton*, 92). He was buried, as he had desired, in the family aisle of Hardingstone parish church, where he still kneels in effigy beside his first wife and their children.

WILFRID PREST

Sources J. Hasler, 'Harvey, Francis II', HoP, *Commons, 1558–1603*, 2.266–7 · C. H. Hopwood, ed., *Middle Temple records*, 1–2 (1904) · Venn, *Alum. Cant.* · *The diary of Sir Richard Hutton, 1614–1639*, ed. W. R. Prest, SeldS, suppl. ser., 9 (1991) · W. R. Prest, *The rise of the barristers: a social history of the English bar, 1590–1640*, 2nd edn (1991) · Baker, *Serjeants* · J. C. Cox and C. A. Markham, eds., *The records of the borough of Northampton*, 2, ed. J. C. Cox (1898) · *Records of the borough of Leicester*, 4: *1603–1688*, ed. H. Stocks (1923) · will, PRO, PROB 11/162, sig. 88 · *Report on the manuscripts of his grace the duke of Buccleuch and Queensberry … preserved at Montagu House*, 3 vols. in 4, HMC, 45 (1899–1926), vol. 3 · *Diary of John Rous*, ed. M. A. E. Green, CS, 66 (1856) · C. W. Brooks, *The admission registers of Barnard's Inn, 1620–1689* (1995) · J. Bridges, *The history and antiquities of Northamptonshire*, ed. P. Whalley, 2 vols. (1791) · W. A. Shaw, *The knights of England*, 2 vols. (1906) · W. C. Metcalfe, ed., *The visitations of Northamptonshire made in 1564 and 1618–19* (1887)
Archives CUL, notes of serjeant's reading, MS E.e.6.3 · Hunt. L., Hastings papers, payments to subject for legal services, Lit. 3, box 6, accounts uncatalogued
Likenesses effigy, parish church, Hardingstone, Northamptonshire
Wealth at death £15,000—left to widow: J. H., 'Harvey, Francis II'; will, PRO, PROB, 11/162, sig. 88

Harvey, Frederick William (1888–1957), poet and army officer, was born on 26 March 1888 at Murrel's End, Hartpury, Gloucestershire, the eldest of the five children of Howard Harvey (1853–1909), a farmer and horse dealer, and his wife, Matilda (Tillie), *née* Waters (*d.* 1945). In 1891 the family moved within Gloucestershire to Minsterworth and took up residence in a large Georgian farmhouse, The Redlands, where Harvey, known as Will, spent his youth and acquired his love of the countryside.

From the age of nine Harvey attended King's School, Gloucester, where he met and became a close friend of Ivor Gurney. At fourteen he was sent by his parents to Fleetwood, Lancashire, to board at Rossall School. His musical abilities came to the fore and he was considered a fine singer, offering concert recitals, performing solo in competitions, and winning a school prize in 1905, the year he left Rossall.

Following the advice of a phrenologist, Harvey's family decided he should study law and he became articled to a Gloucester solicitor, Frank Treasure. He qualified in 1912 and then moved to Chesterfield to become a solicitor's assistant. Here, despite his Anglican upbringing, he first began to consider the possibility of joining the Roman Catholic church.

Harvey, who felt that the church would bring order and discipline to his life, eventually became a Roman Catholic in 1914, just after he joined the fifth battalion of the Gloucestershire regiment, along with his brother Eric, on 8 August. On 29 March 1915 the 1st battalion 5th Glosters sailed from Folkestone for Boulogne and then marched to the front-line trenches at Ploegsteert. Soon after the battalion's arrival in France a trench newspaper, the *Fifth Glo'ster Gazette*, was founded, and Harvey became a regular contributor. In 1915 he gained promotion to lance corporal and days afterwards he participated in a night reconnaissance for which he was decorated with a Distinguished Conduct Medal. He also gained a commission, and after returning to France following an officer-training course on Hayling Island, he was captured while reconnoitering alone in 1916. Over the next two years he experienced seven different German prison camps and gained the title of the Poet for his essays, lectures, and verse.

Harvey's uncensored poems home were published in two volumes by Sidgwick and Jackson: *A Gloucestershire Lad at Home and Abroad* (1916) and *Gloucestershire Friends* (1917). On returning from solitary confinement he saw that a fellow prisoner had drawn a picture of a duck in a pool over his bed, and this inspired Harvey's most famous poem, named in the title of his third collection, *Ducks and other Verses* (1919).

Physically and mentally exhausted, Harvey convalesced at The Redlands following his return to England in spring 1919. Here he wrote an account of his prison-camp experiences, published as *Comrades in Captivity* in 1920. In the following year he married an Irish nurse, (Sarah) Anne Kane, at the Holy Rood Church in Swindon on April 30.

Also in 1921 a further volume of verse was published, *Farewell*. Harvey and his wife moved from Swindon back to Gloucestershire, acquiring a cottage in Cranham Woods. They had two children: Eileen Anne, born in 1922, and Patrick, born in 1925. Sidgwick and Jackson published *September and other Poems*, Harvey's finest collection, in 1925, and there the influence of Edward Thomas is clear. He also decided in this year to set up on his own as a solicitor in Lydney, but he was not particularly successful and the 1930s saw him sell the practice. Still troubled by his war experiences, he became increasingly withdrawn. Two further books of his poetry were published in 1926, the year in which he made his final move, to Yorkley, in the Forest of Dean: *In Pillowell Woods and other Poems* and *F. W. Harvey in the Augustan Books of English Poetry* edited by Humbert Wolfe. Harvey served in the Home Guard in the Second World War. An anthology of his poetry was published by Oliver and Boyd in 1947, entitled *Gloucestershire*. He died of cardiac failure at High View, Yorkley, on 13 February 1957, and was buried in the family grave at Minsterworth; his wife survived him. Having come to be known as the 'laureate of Gloucestershire', Harvey was commemorated by a slate memorial tablet on the south transept of Gloucester Cathedral in 1980.　　　　　PETER CHILDS

Sources A. Boden, *F. W. Harvey: soldier, poet*, rev. edn (1998) · F. Townsend, *The laureate of Gloucestershire* (1988) · E. Wysall, *The Gloucestershire regiment in the war, 1914–18* (1931) · d. cert.
Archives Glos. RO, scrapbook, incl. poems and notes · Gloucester Public Library, local history collection | Gloucester Public Library, Gurney archive
Likenesses photographs, repro. in Boden, *F. W. Harvey*
Wealth at death £762 9s. 7d.: probate, 28 May 1957, CGPLA Eng. & Wales

Harvey, Gabriel (1552/3–1631), scholar and writer, was born at Saffron Walden, Essex, the eldest son of Alice (d.

1613) and John Harvey (d. 1593), a yeoman farmer and master rope maker who was a prominent member of the town's corporation. Richard *Harvey and John *Harvey were his younger brothers. Gabriel was educated first at Saffron Walden grammar school and then, the first of four sons sent to study at nearby Cambridge, matriculated as a pensioner at Christ's College on 28 June 1566, and proceeded BA in 1569–70, coming ninth in the order of seniority. On 3 November 1570, thanks in part to the patronage of another worthy of Walden, the statesman Sir Thomas Smith, he was elected a fellow of Pembroke College.

Early Cambridge career and friendship with Spenser It was at Pembroke in 1573 that the first of many storms in Harvey's career blew up. A group of fellows led by Thomas Neville, later master of Trinity and dean of Canterbury, attempted to obstruct Harvey's admission as master of arts. His colleagues levelled a variety of charges against him, chiefly relating to his intellectual singularity (in particular his devotion to the writings of Peter Ramus, and consequent disparagement of Aristotle) and his arrogant, unsociable demeanour. Harvey defended himself vigorously in letters to Pembroke's master, John Young, who forced through his admission later in 1573; this time he was placed first in seniority. There followed another brief fracas over Harvey's appointment as the college's Greek lecturer. But Harvey soon recovered from these setbacks, becoming junior treasurer of the college by the end of 1573 and senior treasurer in 1575. In April 1574 he was appointed university praelector of rhetoric, lecturing at least four days a week to halls which were (by his own account) packed. Among his earliest published works were his opening spring-term orations for 1574 and 1575, printed as *Rhetor*, and his Easter-term oration for 1576, printed as *Ciceronianus*. The former maps out the pathway to true eloquence, via 'nature', 'art', and 'practice'. The latter describes the author's realization (upon reading Ramus's *Ciceronianus*) that superficial imitation of Cicero is not enough; the orator's style must, like Cicero's, grow out of his broad expertise in all fields of human knowledge. Harvey's efforts to attain such expertise are attested by his library, which he had begun to gather by the early 1570s, and which receives explicit mention in the *Ciceronianus*. Harvey's orations appeared in print in 1577, two years after his first publication, an elegy to Ramus entitled *Ode natalitia*.

At some point early in his Cambridge career Harvey made the acquaintance of his close contemporary Edmund Spenser, who had entered Pembroke College as a sizar on 20 May 1569. Their friendship, which would last until the poet's death in 1599, is first documented in 1578, when Spenser gave Harvey a number of books. In 1579 Harvey starred in *The Shepheardes Calender* as Colin Clout's 'especiall good freend Hobbinol'; he was also the addressee of E. K.'s dedicatory epistle to the volume, which urged him to defend the new poet's work 'with your mighty Rhetorick and other your rare gifts of learning'. A year later the public was granted a deeper insight into the Spenser–Harvey relationship in *Three proper, and wittie, familiar letters: lately passed betwene two universitie men, touching the earthquake in Aprill last, and our English refourmed versifying.* The letters (which he later, somewhat implausibly, claimed had been published without his consent) offered Harvey an opportunity to display his scholarly talents in analysing the causes of a recent English earthquake; they also demonstrate the friends' shared interest in applying classical, quantitative versification to vernacular poetry, and tell of their devotion to the courtier poets Philip Sidney and Edward Dyer. Along with many tantalizing references to lost and possibly fictitious works by the two writers, the letters also contain the earliest (somewhat deprecating) notice of Spenser's *Faerie Queene*, the first part of which would appear a decade later.

Harvey was a firm believer in the superiority of the active to the contemplative life, and across the course of the 1570s he worked to realize his aspirations for public office by cultivating court connections, in particular to the circle of the stridently protestant earl of Leicester. Some time between October 1576 and February 1577 he was engaged by Leicester's nephew Philip Sidney, about to set out on an embassy to the emperor Rudolph II, as a professional reader of the Roman historian Livy (a role he had already performed in 1571 for Sir Thomas Smith's son, who was preparing for a colonial venture in Ireland). Early in 1578 there were plans for Harvey himself to travel abroad on official business, as part of a deputation of English scholars and courtiers joining the conference of protestant princes at Schmalkalden; the project never came to fruition. On 26 July of the same year Harvey was among the Cambridge scholars who disputed before Queen Elizabeth at Audley End; he took advantage of the occasion to present four large folio manuscripts of Latin verse to monarch and courtiers. Then, in September 1578, he published the poems in expanded forms as *Gratulationes Valdinenses*, and presented them to the queen again, this time at Hadham Hall, Hertfordshire, home of Harvey's friend Arthur Capel. In their revised versions the poems noted several details of Elizabeth's dealings with Harvey at Audley End (she permitted him to kiss her hand, and told him he had the look of an Italian); they may also have attempted (in veiled terms) to strike a blow against the proposed marriage of the queen to the Catholic duke of Alençon. Harvey's support for the pro-Leicester camp was made evident in the *Three Letters* of 1580, the third of which contained a poem entitled 'Speculum Tuscanismi', which was taken (probably with some justice, although Harvey denied it) as a libel on Sidney's enemy Edward de Vere, earl of Oxford. Oxford was alerted to the poem by his client, the writer John Lyly, and Harvey endured a brief spell in the Fleet prison which ended when he convinced the peer of his innocence. (This was apparently the second 'Fleeting' Harvey received for the *Letters*, which had also offended the controller of the queen's household, Sir James Croft.)

The death in August 1577 of Harvey's esteemed patron and role model, Sir Thomas Smith, spurred him to write a set of Latin elegies, published as *Smithus, vel, Lachrymae musarum* in 1578. It also, indirectly, sparked off a new round of academic feuding. Smith's widow and her co-executors had given Harvey 'certaine rare manuscript books' from his library. Preaching the funeral oration was Andrew Perne, vice-chancellor of Cambridge University, an inveterate bibliophile who wanted the manuscripts for himself. Perne, 'between jest, and earnest', called Harvey a fox, to which the younger man replied, 'betweene earnest, & jest, I might haply be a Cubb, as I might be used, but was over young to be a Fox, especially in his presence' (Stern, 38). Perne was apparently silenced by Harvey's witticism at the time, but he took ample revenge later, opposing his candidacy for the university oratorship in 1579 and intervening to prevent him from becoming master of Trinity Hall in February 1585. Harvey had jumped ship to Trinity Hall in 1578, pursuing his plan to train as a civil lawyer. This seems to have been just one of several options the perennially hard up academic was considering at this time (in April 1579, for example, he had asked Leicester to procure a prebend of Lichfield for him). For five months, from May 1583, he was appointed by the college as deputy proctor of the university. In 1584 he completed his legal training and obtained his LLB, but for reasons which remain unclear he was not subsequently inaugurated and he eventually incepted doctor of civil law at Oxford in July 1585. (Spenser's sonnet to 'HARVEY, the happy above happy men', may have commemorated this event.) Although Harvey retained his Trinity Hall fellowship until 1591–2, and possibly received a stipend from the college still longer, he moved to London at some point between about 1586 and 1588 to take up legal practice in the court of arches. Doubtless he viewed the law as another step on the ladder to a career at court.

Controversy with Nashe Unfortunately, Harvey was to enter the public eye by another, altogether more problematic route. Shortly after his move to London, he became embroiled in a seemingly interminable series of vernacular print controversies with some of the most significant pamphlet writers of his day. Several factors conspired to force this new role on Harvey. First, there was the reputation he had acquired in certain quarters of the university for arrogance and singularity. He had for many years been the butt of poetic and dramatic satires, chief among which was *Pedantius*, a play performed at Trinity College on 6 February 1581, about a Ciceronian orator whose overblown ambitions in love and at court end in humiliation. Second, there was his family. Gabriel's fortunes were closely tied to those of his brothers, and especially Richard, another devotee of Ramus, who attracted much mockery for his publication, in 1583, of an astrological pamphlet predicting that dramatic and apocalyptic upheavals would follow the conjunction of Saturn and Jupiter in April of that year. Third, there were the celebrated 'Marprelate tracts', a radical protestant attack on the established ecclesiastical hierarchy, written by the pseudonymous 'Martin Marprelate'. When John Lyly, fighting back on behalf of the authorities in his *Pap with a Hatchet*, hinted that Harvey or someone associated with him might lie behind Marprelate, the new print war was poised to begin.

Although Gabriel wrote an immediate reply to Lyly,

entitled 'An advertisement for Pap-hatchet, and Martin Mar-prelate', he held back from publishing it, for reasons unknown. Richard Harvey, however, weighed into the controversy with two tracts, both probably published in 1590. One of these made the mistake of criticizing the 22-year-old Thomas Nashe for 'peremptorily censuring his betters at pleasure' in his preface to Robert Greene's *Menaphon* (1589). Among the 'betters' named were Sir Thomas More, Roger Ascham, and 'my brother Doctor Harvey' (Stern, 89). Greene retaliated in his *Quip for an Upstart Courtier* (1592) by pillorying the Harvey brothers and their father, a 'knave' whose 'cheefe living is by making fatal instruments, as halters and ropes, which divers desperate men hang themselves with' (ibid., 92). (Perhaps fearing lawsuits or punishment in the hereafter, Greene excised the satirical passage from later editions of the *Quip* before his death in September 1592.) In the same year Nashe published his *Pierce Pennilesse*, which (without naming him) poured scorn on Richard Harvey, the 'son of a ropemaker' (ibid., 93) who had grown into an overweening critic of Aristotle and an astrologer mocked for his prognostications by the likes of the clown Richard Tarlton and the balladeer William Elderton. At this point, Richard fell silent, and Gabriel stepped in on his brother's behalf, publishing his *Foure letters, and certain sonnets: especially touching* Robert Greene, *and other parties, by him abused* shortly after Greene's death. 'Wedded … to private study, and devoted … to publike quietnesse' (sig. G2r), he claimed that he was venturing into print most unwillingly, duty bound to defend his family's honour. In his judgement, 'the Print is abused, that abuseth' (sig. H1r). Despite this professed aversion to controversies, Harvey used his pamphlet to denigrate Greene, patronize Nashe, and praise himself, 'a very excellent generall Scholler' (sig. A3r) who might be a great asset to the commonweal.

Spotting an opportunity, Nashe quickly produced a mock-scholarly commentary on Harvey's *Foure Letters* entitled *Strange newes, of the intercepting certaine letters, and a convoy of verses, as they were going privilie to victuall the Low Countries* (entered in the Stationers' register in January 1593). In sprightly, conversational prose, this pamphlet punctures Harvey's every pretension and leaves his often sophisticated argumentative and stylistic manoeuvres looking clumsy and amateurish. Such a vicious assault could not go unanswered, and Harvey energetically defended his credit in *Pierces Supererogation, or, A New Prayse of the Old Asse* (probably completed by the summer of 1593). Here he turns Nashe's sarcasm back on him, mocking his voguish satire as shallow and unprofitable, while continuing to lament his own embroilment in the very thing he condemns. (Perceiving the similarity of Nashe's style to Marprelate's, Harvey bulked out this already lengthy book with the 1589 'Advertisement for Pap-hatchet' mentioned above.) In September 1593 Harvey wrote another attack on Nashe, prompted by the latter's attempt to call a truce in the preface to his *Christ's Tears over Jerusalem*. Realizing the error of his ways, Nashe now attributed 'all acknowledgements of aboundant Schollership, courteous well governed behaviour, and ripe experient judgement'

(Stern, 111) to Harvey. Harvey's *New Letter of Notable Contents* weighed Nashe's repentance in the balance and deemed it hollow. The impulse to go on railing may not have been all his own; it is quite possible that Harvey's printer, John Wolfe, with whom he was probably living and working at about this time, was responsible for prolonging an altercation which both parties felt had run its course.

Stung by the *New Letter*, Nashe returned to the offensive in a revised epistle prefacing the 1594 edition of *Christ's Tears*; in the same year he may have taken another swipe at Harvey via the figure of the university orator in *The Unfortunate Traveller*. Finally, in 1596, he published a substantial counter-blast to *Pierces Supererogation*, entitled *Have with you to Saffron-Walden, or, Gabriell Harveys Hunt is up*. His delay in producing this riposte was, Nashe declared, due to his desire of obtaining 'perfect intelligence of [Harvey's] life and conversation' (sig. E2v) for the fantastically embroidered biography of the 'eldest sonne of the Halter-maker' which formed the work's centrepiece. This comic *tour de force* is accompanied by a full-length woodcut portrait which purports to be 'The picture of Gabriell Harvey, as hee is readie to let fly upon Aiax' (sig. F4r) ('Aiax' being 'a jakes', a water-closet); this is almost certainly a recycled image rather than a genuine attempt at a likeness. Nashe insists that his repeated assaults on his enemy's 'humble' origins are motivated not by any snobbery of his own, but rather by Harvey's denial of his background; being the son of a rope maker would not be 'anie such hainous discredit simply of it selfe, if his horrible insulting pride were not' (sig. 12v–13r). An anonymous reply to *Have with You*, entitled *The Trimming of Thomas Nashe*, appeared in 1597; although it has frequently been attributed to Harvey, it is almost certainly not his work. Thus ended the Nashe–Harvey controversy, which received dishonourable mention in the ban on satire decreed by Archbishop John Whitgift of Canterbury and Bishop Richard Bancroft of London in 1599. It ordered that 'all Nasshes and Doctor Harvyes bookes be taken wheresoever they maye be found and that none of theire bookes bee ever printed hereafter' (Stern, 129).

Final years and reputation In the last three decades of his life, Harvey largely disappears from view. He had left London several years before Nashe struck his final blows (the *New Letter* of 1593 was dated from Saffron Walden), and there is no evidence of his residence in the capital thereafter. It has been suggested that the motives for his withdrawal were chiefly financial. Nashe reports having lodged in the same Cambridge inn as Harvey, unbeknownst to him, some time in 1595–6, and in 1598 Gabriel wrote a long letter to Robert Cecil, bidding unsuccessfully to replace the grievously ailing Thomas Preston as master of Trinity Hall. Thereafter Harvey seems to have lived retired in the town of his birth. In 1608 his sister Marie and her husband sued him in chancery for £60 which she was due by the terms of their father's will; the dispute appears to have been resolved amicably. In 1626 Harvey, 'aged threescore and thirteene yeres or thereaboutes' (Eccles, 61), testified in the town on behalf of Thomas Byrd, a member of a local family. There is some evidence to suggest that Harvey put his lifelong interest in medicine into practice in the final years of his life, and his last literary work may have been an epitaph on an apothecary of Hadleigh, Suffolk, dated 1630 and initialled 'G. H.'. Harvey died in Saffron Walden on 7 February 1631 and was buried there on the 11th.

Aside from his friendship with Spenser and his paper-wars with Greene and Nashe, Harvey's interest today lies chiefly in his books. Although there is no catalogue of his library, which was dispersed after his death, it is likely to have been one of the most substantial of its day; more than 180 extant volumes from it have so far been identified in collections around the world. Furthermore, Harvey was one the most assiduous annotators in an age of annotation. His books are instantly recognizable from the sheer density of his marginal commentary, which sometimes tells of several readings conducted across the course of decades. He often used every scrap of available white space to record his thoughts on the printed text, employing astrological symbols to note the subject under discussion (Mercury for eloquence, Mars for war, and so on), and making repeated references to a mysterious cast of characters (with names like 'Axiophilus', 'Angelus Furius', 'Eudromus', and 'Eutrapelus') who may represent aspects of himself, or may refer to as-yet-unidentified acquaintances.

Attitudes to Harvey's annotations reflect broader divisions of opinion over his reputation. Some historians are inclined to see his marginal ruminations as 'self-therapy' (Stern, 180), and to view Harvey as little more than a fantasist, over-assured of his own capabilities and blind to his failings, who came nowhere near to attaining the position of authority he sought. Their case is strengthened by some of the more bizarre contents of Harvey's letter-book of the 1570s, including a series of missives relating to the attempted seduction of his sister Mercy by an unnamed nobleman, identifiable as Philip Howard, earl of Arundel; the drama, in which Gabriel plays a prominent role, may well be entirely the product of his imagination. Critics have also frequently echoed Nashe's attacks on Harvey, condemning his repetitious, 'euphuistic' style and accusing him of trying to lead Spenser into the literary cul-de-sac of quantitative metrics. But for others, Harvey's marginalia merely reflect the fact that his books were a semi-public resource, which needed to be customized in order to be useful. It is known that Harvey made them available for loan to friends and colleagues, and that he employed them in his capacity as a 'professional reader' to those (like Sir Philip Sidney) who needed the wisdom they enshrined. In this light, Harvey appears as a paradigmatic Elizabethan man of letters, a humanist who sought to bring ancient learning to bear on modern problems and who believed, like many of his contemporaries, that the best route to power was through knowledge.

JASON SCOTT-WARREN

Sources V. F. Stern, *Gabriel Harvey: his life, marginalia, and library* (1979) · M. Eccles, 'Gabriel Harvey', in 'Brief lives: Tudor and Stuart authors', *Studies in Philology*, 79/4 (1982), 61–3 · *The letter-book of Gabriel Harvey, AD 1573–1580*, ed. E. J. L. Scott (1884) · G. C. Moore Smith, *Gabriel Harvey: marginalia* (1913) · A. Grafton and L. Jardine, '"Studied for action": how Gabriel Harvey read his Livy', *Past and Present*, 129 (1990), 30–78 · J. Nielson, 'Reading between the lines: manuscript personality and Gabriel Harvey's drafts', *Studies in English Literature*, 33 (1993), 43–82 · J. W. Binns, *Intellectual culture in Elizabethan and Jacobean England: the Latin writings of the age* (1990) · L. Jardine, 'Gabriel Harvey: exemplary Ramist and pragmatic humanist', *Revue des Sciences Philosophiques et Théologiques*, 70 (1986), 36–48 · P. Collinson, 'Andrew Perne and his times', *Andrew Perne: quatercentenary studies*, ed. P. Collinson and others (1991) · D. Attridge, *Well-weighed syllables: Elizabethan verse in classical metres* (1974) · L. Hutson, *Thomas Nashe in context* (1989)
Archives BL, autograph notes, Add. MS 42518 · BL, commonplace book, Add. MS 32494 · BL, letter-book, Sloane MS 93 · Pembroke Cam., marginal notes to *Compendium Romanae historiae*
Likenesses portrait, Essex RO, I/Pb/8/9

Harvey, Sir George (1806–1876), figure and landscape painter, was born at St Ninians, Stirlingshire, on 1 February 1806, the son of George Harvey (d. 1835), a watchmaker, and his wife, Elizabeth Jeffrey. Shortly after his birth the family settled in Stirling where Harvey attended the high school before being apprenticed to a bookseller. At the age of eighteen his devotion to art took him to Edinburgh, where he studied for about two years at the Trustees' Academy under Andrew Wilson and then William Allen. In 1826 he exhibited his first picture, *The Village School* (exh. Edinburgh Institution for the Encouragement of the Fine Arts in Scotland, 1826; NG Scot.), its subject continuing the tradition of David Wilkie. In the same year he became one of the original associates of the Scottish Academy, to whose first exhibition in 1827 he contributed seven works. In 1829 he became a full member of the academy, to whose interests, in its early days of struggle, he devoted himself unweariedly. Treasurer in 1843, he succeeded Sir John Watson Gordon as president in 1864, and received the honour of a knighthood in 1867. His *Notes on the Early History of the Royal Scottish Academy* (1870) gives curious particulars regarding its foundation and progress.

From the late 1820s Harvey devoted himself to figure painting, the subjects of which were mainly derived from the history and the daily life of Scotland. He became best-known for his series depicting scenes from the covenanting period, including *Covenanters Preaching* (1829–30, exh. Royal Scottish Academy, 1830; Glasgow Art Galleries and Museum) and *The Covenanters Communion* (exh. Royal Scottish Academy, 1840; NG Scot.). Although sentimental, such works dealt with contemporary concerns. Along with genre pieces like *The Curlers* (exh. Royal Scottish Academy, 1835; NG Scot.), and *The Schule Skailin* (exh. Royal Scottish Academy, 1846; NG Scot.), his work became widely popular through engravings. His history paintings included *Shakespeare before Sir Thomas Lucy* (1836–7, exh. Royal Scottish Academy, 1837; Royal Scottish Academy) and *First Reading of the Bible in the Crypt of St. Paul's* (1839–40, exh. RA, 1846). However, owing to his use of bitumen, many of his works have now deteriorated. He produced a small number of portraits, such as *Professor John Wilson* (exh. Royal Scottish Academy, 1851) and *David Ramsay Hay* (Royal Scottish Academy). However, it was as a landscape painter that Harvey excelled; his execution was singularly spontaneous and unlaboured in the expression of the very spirit of border landscape and of the quiet sublimity of great stretches of rounded grassy hills. His landscapes were mostly the work of his later life and many are now lost. Among the finest of them are *The Enterkin, Leadhills* (exh. Royal Scottish Academy, 1846) and *Glen Falloch* (exh. Royal Scottish Academy, 1868; NG Scot.). The *Art Journal* called *Glen Dhu, Arran* (exh. Royal Scottish Academy, 1861) 'one of the grandest landscapes ever produced by the Scottish School' (*Art Journal*, 1861, 86).

On 2 July 1839 Harvey married Elizabeth Margaret Carstairs, with whom he had two daughters, Ellen and Elizabeth. Following Elizabeth's early death in 1844 or 1845, he married Margaret Muir on 6 April 1847. In 1867 Harvey was elected a fellow of the Royal Society of Edinburgh, to which he delivered, on 21 December 1868, a paper, 'On the colour of aërial blue'. He died peacefully at his home, 21 Regent Terrace, Edinburgh, on 22 January 1876, in the jubilee year of the Royal Scottish Academy, whose interests he had made his own. His wife predeceased him.   J. M. GRAY, *rev.* AILSA BOYD

Sources A. Lindesay and N. Walsh, *Sir George Harvey P.R.S.A., 1806–76* [1985] [exhibition catalogue, Smith Art Gallery and Museum, Stirling, Aug 1985] · *The Portfolio*, 18 (1887), 152 · *Art Journal*, 12 (1850), 341 · *Art Journal*, 20 (1858), 73–5 · *Art Journal*, 38 (1876), 105 · *Art Journal*, new ser., 24 (1904), 392 · *Art Journal*, 14 (1852), 134 · J. Turner, ed., *The dictionary of art*, 34 vols. (1996) · Wood, *Vic. painters*, 3rd edn · A. L. Simpson, *Harvey's celebrated paintings: a selection from the work of Sir George Harvey, P.R.S.A.* (1870) · *Recollections of Sir George Harvey* (1880) · P. J. M. McEwan, *Dictionary of Scottish art and architecture* (1994) · W. Hardie, *Scottish painting, 1837 to the present* (1990) · J. L. Caw, *Scottish painting past and present, 1620–1908* (1908) · S. Cursiter, *Scottish art to the close of the nineteenth century* (1949) · Bryan, *Painters* (1908) · *Transactions of the Royal Society of Edinburgh* (1867–8) · d. cert. · m. reg. Scot.

Archives Royal Scot. Acad., letters

Likenesses Hill and Adamson, photographs, 1843–6, Scot. NPG · A. R. Hill, marble bust, 1867, Smith Art Gallery, Stirling · R. Herdman, oils, 1874, Scot. NPG · J. Ballantyne, oils, 1889?, Scot. NPG · J. Hutchison, marble bust, Scot. NPG · J. Moffat, photograph, carte-de-visite, NPG · R. and E. T., woodcut (as an old man; after T. Scott), BM · photographs, Royal Scot. Acad. · wood-engraving, BM; repro. in *ILN* (12 Feb 1876) · woodcut, BM; repro. in *Art Journal*, 12 (1850), 341

Wealth at death £8319 5s. 11d.: probate, 23 Feb 1876, *CCI* · £3100: eik additional estate, 3 April 1876, *CCI*

Harvey, Gideon (1636/7–1702), physician, was born in the Netherlands, the child of John Harvey and his wife, Elizabeth. His parents were probably Dutch, although two of Harvey's siblings, Frances and Nathaniel, also later lived in England. He was educated in the Low Countries before coming to England and matriculating at Exeter College, Oxford, on 31 May 1655. He left Oxford without a degree and entered Leiden University on 4 January 1657, aged twenty, where he studied medicine, anatomy, and botany. According to his account in *Casus medico-chirurgicus*, while in Leiden he was also instructed in surgery, chemistry, and pharmacy by practitioners outside the university. He apparently then travelled to Paris, where he studied at the hospitals before making the *petit tour* of Europe, during which he claimed to have taken his MD, although he never specified the university. On reaching Paris again he

Gideon Harvey (1636/7–1702), by Pierre Philippe, pubd 1663

assisted the surgeon at one of the hospitals, observed anatomies, and studied chemistry.

Harvey then returned to the Netherlands, where he became a fellow of the College of Physicians of The Hague. He did not, however, remain in The Hague for long, and soon went to London. In July 1659 his name was put forward to the committee of public safety by John Desborough as a candidate for the post of physician to Dunkirk, which had recently been taken by the English, but he had not left London in January 1660 and it is unclear if he actually went. Following the Restoration he apparently spent some time as physician to the army in Flanders, and then travelled through Italy and Germany before returning to take up practice in London. In December 1661 he successfully petitioned for denization. Harvey never joined the College of Physicians, but seems to have established a successful practice with several aristocrats among his patients. In 1664 he married Elizabeth Leigh of St Matthew's, Friday Street, London, with whom he had at least two children, Elizabeth and Gideon Harvey [*see below*].

It was as a medical author and controversialist that Harvey was most prominent over the next three decades. He was a prolific writer with a lively and witty style. His earliest published work, *Archelogia philosophica nova*, appeared in 1663, and he followed it with a series of books on a variety of diseases, including plague, scurvy, venereal disease, and fevers. Although he recommended many chemical medicines and questioned the validity of humoural medicine, the core of Harvey's physic appears to have remained largely traditional and rationalist. His main emphasis throughout these works was on the (slightly self-serving) importance of experience and expertise, and the dangers of credulity and conformity to unsubstantiated traditions. One of his most direct assaults on contemporary medicine, *The Art of Curing Diseases by Expectation* (1689), in which he railed against the cunning 'sects' of physicians who impress their patient with shows of activity while waiting for nature to cure the disease, earned the patronage of Georg Ernst Stahl, who published a Latin version on the continent with notes of his own. Harvey also published several medical handbooks for lay use containing critical discussions of contemporary practice and recommendations for treatments, and, in *The Family Physician and House Apothecary*, details of the costs of ingredients so that readers could calculate for themselves 'what the *Apothecary* deserveth for his pains' (sig. A5v). Harvey was also a strong opponent of the use of Peruvian bark.

Harvey's writing took on a more confrontational tone in 1678 with the publication of *Casus medico-chirurgicus, or, A most Memorable Case of a Noble-Man, Deceased*. His relationship with the College of Physicians appears to have been amicable to this point, and two years earlier he had written a strongly worded defence of several of its members against the 'clandestin scurrilous Cabal' of apothecaries who were attacking them (*Accomplisht Physician*, 91). Now, however, he appears to have fallen out with the college over the treatment of Lord Mohun, one of Harvey's patients, who had died after the unsuccessful treatment of a duelling wound, first by several college physicians and then by Harvey. In the work he defended his treatment of Mohun and lambasted the other physicians who had attended him, barely disguising their names. His attack on the college was even stronger in *The Conclave of Physicians* (1683), in which he ridicules their pretences to learning—particularly through anatomy and experiment—and avaricious practices. Anonymous replies lacking Harvey's satirical bite appeared in verse (*Gideon's Fleece*, 1684, attributed to Thomas Guidott) and prose (*A Dialogue between Philiater and Momus*, 1686).

Despite these controversies Harvey won the patronage of the crown and acquired land in Middlesex and Cambridge. He was appointed physician to the Tower of London and possibly served as physician-in-ordinary to the king. He moved to Sawley, Middlesex, and died in 1702.

Gideon Harvey (*c*.1671–1755), physician, son of Gideon Harvey and his wife, Elizabeth Leigh, entered St John's College, Oxford, in May 1686. He left without taking a degree and entered Leiden University on 12 May 1688, where he graduated MD in May 1690 with a thesis entitled 'De febre ardente', dedicated to Robert Lucas, Lord Shenfield, governor of the Tower of London. In 1698 he was created MD at Cambridge by royal letters.

By this time Harvey was already settled in London and practising there. He had been licensed to marry Mary Fothergill of St Dunstan-in-the-West in September 1695, when he was apparently living in Westminster. The year after receiving his MD he became a candidate of the Royal College of Physicians, and was elected a fellow in March 1703. He held a number of college offices in subsequent years, serving as censor twice, consiliarius on numerous occasions, and elect in 1716, and was father of the college at his death. Little is known of his practice and he never published, but it is clear that his career was supported by court patronage. In February 1702 he was made physician to the Tower of London in succession to his father, a position he held for the following half century, despite having been appointed as a compromise after a dispute between two rivals who expected him to die shortly. Harvey died on 24 April 1755 in Petty France, London.

PATRICK WALLIS

Sources Foster, *Alum. Oxon.* · R. W. Innes Smith, *English-speaking students of medicine at the University of Leyden* (1932) · Munk, *Roll* · G. Harvey, *Casus medico-chirurgicus* (1678) · A. Cunningham, 'Thomas Sydenham and the "good old cause"', *The medical revolution of the seventeenth century*, ed. R. French and A. Wear (1989), 164–90 · H. A. Cantlie, 'Gideon Harvey', *Annals of Medical History*, 3 (1921), 205–37 · *CSP dom.*, 1659–60, 9; 1661–2, 309; 1698, 107–8; 1700–02, 358; 1702–3 · will, PRO, PROB 11/467, fol. 68 · *DNB*

Likenesses A. Hertocks, line engraving, 1672, BM, NPG, Wellcome L.; repro. in G. Harvey, *Great Venus unmasked*, 2nd edn (1672) · P. Philippe, line engraving, BM, NPG, Wellcome L.; repro. in G. Harvey, *Archelogia philosophica nova, or, New principles of philosophy* (1663) [*see illus.*]

Harvey, Gideon (*c*.1671–1755). *See under* Harvey, Gideon (1636/7–1702).

Harvey, Henry (*d.* 1585), civil lawyer and college head, was the son of Robert and Joan Harvey of Stradbroke, Suffolk. He graduated LLB from Trinity Hall, Cambridge, in 1538 and LLD in 1542. An active and successful ecclesiastical lawyer, Harvey was admitted to the court of arches on 10 November 1549 and as an advocate of Doctors' Commons on 27 January 1550. About 1550 he became vicar-general to Bishop Ridley of London; he was vicar-general of Canterbury in 1551 and Ely in 1559/60. He became dean of the court of arches and president of Doctors' Commons in 1567, and a master in chancery in 1568. Harvey secured a lease from the dean and chapter of St Paul's for the mortuary house in the parish of St Benet Paul's Wharf, which was then maintained by Trinity Hall for the use of Doctors' Commons. He also secured Trinity Hall as the home of Cambridge's regius professorship in civil law. Under Elizabeth I most of the advocates in Doctors' Commons were supplied by the university.

Harvey was elected master of Trinity Hall about 1557–8, before Mary I's death. He succeeded Stephen Gardiner, who had been master since 1525 (save under Edward VI, when he had been replaced by first Walter Haddon and then William Mowse). Mowse was removed in 1553, allowing Gardiner to be reinstated. Mowse himself was then reinstated upon Gardiner's death in 1555, but forced to resign within two years for religious reasons. Harvey became master following this tumultuous period, making him 'the first fully home-bred Master since Walter Hewke', and the last clerical master until the nineteenth century (Crawley, 56). He openly held conservative religious commitments, but his moderate approach allowed Trinity Hall to enjoy a peaceful existence and avoid the doctrinal battles that other Cambridge colleges endured during Elizabeth I's reign. Harvey's success was partly a result of the college's constituency. After 1535, when the degree of canon law was abolished and civil lawyers became the exclusive practitioners for ecclesiastical courts, he continued Stephen Gardiner's work of establishing Trinity Hall as the 'nursery for civilians'—and this at a time when most other colleges were concentrating on training parish clergy. Although only one Marian exile, Christopher Southhouse, became a fellow at Trinity Hall during Elizabeth's reign, the college included several 'Catholic-minded fellows', prompting Cambridge puritans to complain that 'he hath scarce chosen one Protestant Fellow these twelve years' (Strype, *Parker*, 2.175). However, this variety helped Harvey to achieve relative peace in the college.

Harvey fulfilled a variety of other roles at Cambridge. In 1556 Cardinal Pole placed him on the commission assigned to root out protestant books and heresy in Cambridgeshire. He actively participated in the visitation of the university by Pole's delegates in January and February 1557. At the opening of the visitation (11 January) he exhibited the cardinal's letters of authority to the assembly in King's College chapel, and gave a short speech in Latin. On 23 January he provided the visitors with a copy of the university statutes, which he had previously been commissioned to revise, along with the composition for the election of proctors. He was one of the four doctors to bear the canopy over the sacrament in the great procession of 8 February. In 1560 he became vice-chancellor to the university, the first to be identified with Trinity Hall. On 27 November 1564 the privy council commissioned him in an effort to establish perpetual concord between the university and town. In 1570 he again assisted Whitgift in revising the university statutes and in settling disputes. Bishop Cox used him during his visitation that year to frame new statutes, and the next year as a visitor for St John's College in 1576. He helped compile new statutes for St John's the same year.

Harvey served in a number of ecclesiastical posts. He was archdeacon of Middlesex between 1551 and 1554, when Bonner made him precentor at St Paul's (12 April 1554). He held the sinecure rectory of Littlebury, Essex, from 12 March 1554; the prebend of Oxton in Southwell Minster (7 September 1558); the stall of Curborough in Lichfield Cathedral (1559–60); and the prebend of Torleton in Salisbury Cathedral (25 October 1559). He was commissioned to visit Ely, York, Durham, Carlisle, and Leicester cathedrals in 1559, and was also collated to the canonry of Ely on 27 June 1567. As a benefactor Harvey created a scholarship and supported building projects for Trinity Hall and various sites around the university; Emmanuel College also benefited from his generosity. In 1561 he was part of the commission to repair the great bridge in Cambridge. It is noteworthy that in 1558 he presided over a deposition in an enclosure case regarding lands claimed by the hospital of St John and Mary Magdalen, Ely. He was subsequently listed as one of the parties to whom Edward Leeds, then master of the hospital and of Clare College, conveyed the lands and rents of that hospital in 1562 to endow Clare College.

Harvey died on 20 February 1585, and his will shows a generous man who left considerable sums to care for the poor. He made provision for scholars at Trinity Hall, willed gifts to all of the college heads at Cambridge and to his family, and endowed Trinity Hall with ceilings of oak and wainscot. Four coats of arms are attributed to him.

JOHN F. JACKSON

Sources C. Crawley, *Trinity Hall: the history of a Cambridge college, 1350–1975* (1976) · Cooper, *Ath. Cantab.*, 1.505–7 · Venn, *Alum. Cant.*, 1/2.323 · G. D. Squibb, *Doctors' Commons: a history of the College of Advocates and Doctors of Law* (1977) · G. D. Squibb, *The high court of chivalry* (1959) · *Fasti Angl., 1541–1857*, [Ely] · *CPR, 1550–53*, 355 · J. Strype, *Annals of the Reformation and establishment of religion … during Queen Elizabeth's happy reign*, new edn, 2 (1824) · J. Strype, *The life and acts of John Whitgift*, new edn, 3 vols. (1822), vol. 3 · J. Strype, *The life and acts of Matthew Parker*, new edn, 3 vols. (1821), vol. 2 · *DNB* · Clare College Archives, Cambridge, cupboard 5/58, safe c/610

Wealth at death see will, Cooper, *Ath. Cantab.*, 1.505–7

Harvey, Sir Henry (1737–1810), naval officer, was born in July 1737, the second son of Richard Harvey of Eastry, Kent, and Elizabeth, *née* Nichols. The Harvey family, long settled in the county, was connected by marriage with Captain Peircy Brett who was later knighted for his services to the navy. Henry received his early education in France and entered the navy in May 1751 with Captain Cosby on the *Centaur*. In her, and three years later in the *Nightingale*, the greater part of his junior time was served on the North American station. On 10 March 1757 he was promoted third lieutenant of the *Hampshire*, in which he served on the channel, North American, and West India stations; and from her he was moved as first lieutenant to the *Hussar*, which was wrecked off Cape François on 23 May 1762.

Harvey was released on parole and returned to England in the *Dragon*, on which he made the acquaintance of one of the ship's lieutenants, the Hon. Constantine Phipps (later Lord Mulgrave and a lord of the Admiralty). In April 1763 Harvey was first lieutenant of the *Mermaid*, again on the coast of North America; and in 1764–5 he commanded the schooner *Magdalen*, employed in the Gulf of St Lawrence for the prevention of smuggling. From August 1768 to April 1771 Harvey commanded the revenue cutter *Swift* in the channel and North Sea; and in March 1773, after two years on half pay, he was invited by Phipps (now Captain Phipps) to go with him as first lieutenant of the *Racehorse* on his voyage of discovery towards the north pole. On the return of the expedition he was promoted commander (15 October 1773).

In January 1776 Harvey was appointed to the sloop *Martin* in which he served under Commodore Charles Douglas at the relief of Quebec. In July 1776 he joined the squadron under Admiral John Montagu at Newfoundland, and in May 1777 he was promoted to the command of the frigate *Squirrel*, which was employed for the next eighteen months on convoy duty.

In December 1778 Harvey was appointed to the *Convert* (32 guns) and in May 1779 he assisted at the relief of Jersey under Captain Gideon. Subsequently he commanded a small squadron sent off the Isle of Man to look for the American revolutionary naval officer John Paul Jones; convoyed the trade to Quebec and home; and was in

December 1779 sent out to join the flag of Sir George Rodney in the West Indies. Here the *Convert* was chiefly employed in active cruising and scouting, but was with the fleet in the action off Dominica on 12 April 1782. In the following August she was sent home with convoy. In March 1786 Harvey was appointed to the frigate *Rose*, but he was shortly afterwards ordered to take temporary command of the *Pegasus*, fitting for Newfoundland and the West Indies. At this time Prince William Henry was her first lieutenant, and it was understood that when she was ready for sea he was to take command. Harvey discharged this delicate duty with 'such discretion as secured to him the lasting friendship of His Royal Highness' (NMM, MS 81/041, fol. 12). He afterwards rejoined the *Rose*, and in August the two ships sailed together for Newfoundland. In 1788 the *Rose* returned to England, and in 1789 she was paid off.

During the Spanish armament (1790) Harvey for a few months commanded in succession the *Alfred* and the *Colossus*; and in 1793 he was appointed to the *Ramillies*, which joined the Channel Fleet under Lord Howe. Through her relief of the *Brunswick* (commanded by Harvey's brother John *Harvey) the *Ramillies* played a distinguished part in the battle of 1 June 1794. On 4 July of that year Harvey was promoted rear-admiral, and was immediately ordered to take command of a small squadron in the North Sea. In January 1795 he hoisted his flag on the *Prince of Wales*, attached to the Channel Fleet, and on 23 June he took part in the action off Lorient; he remained through the winter to cover the landing in Quiberon Bay, under Sir John Borlase Warren.

In April 1796 Harvey was appointed commander-in-chief in the Leeward Islands, and in the following February, jointly with Sir Ralph Abercromby, he took possession of Trinidad, after capturing one and destroying three ships of the line. An attempt on Puerto Rico in April failed, owing to the unexpected strength of the defences. In July 1799 Harvey resigned the command to Lord Hugh Seymour, and returned to England in the frigate *Concorde*. He had been already nominated a KB, and was invested with the insignia of the order in January 1800. In the summer he hoisted his flag in the *Royal Sovereign* as second in command of the Channel Fleet, under Lord St Vincent, and in this post he remained until the peace of Amiens, with which his active service terminated. He attained the rank of admiral on 23 April 1804, and died at Walmer, Kent, on 28 December 1810. Harvey had married Elizabeth Boys (1739/40–1823), daughter of the naval officer William Boys; they had five children.

Harvey was survived by his wife, who died on 4 March 1823, aged eighty-three. Three of their five children—Henry, Richard, and Thomas *Harvey—entered the navy. Henry drowned in 1788 while serving in the *Rose*.

J. K. LAUGHTON, *rev.* CHRISTOPHER DOORNE

Sources 'Historical memoirs of Admiral Sir Henry Harvey', NMM, MS 81/041 · J. Ralfe, *The naval biography of Great Britain*, 2 (1828) · W. James, *The naval history of Great Britain, from the declaration of war by France, in February 1793, to the accession of George IV in January 1820*, 5 vols. (1822–4), vols. 1–3 · PRO, commission and warrant books, ADM 6/18 (1751–8), ADM 6/19–22 (1758–82), ADM 6/24–25 (1789–96), ADM 6/27–28 (1799–1804) · R. Beatson, *Naval and military memoirs of Great Britain*, 2nd edn, 6 vols. (1804) · *Steel's Original and Correct List of the Royal Navy* (1793–1802) · N. Tracy, ed., *The Naval Chronicle: the contemporary record of the Royal Navy at war*, 5 vols. (1998–9) · W. L. Clowes, *The Royal Navy: a history from the earliest times to the present*, 7 vols. (1897–1903); repr. (1996–7), vol. 4
Archives BL, corresp. with Frederic Haldimand, Add. MS 21800
Likenesses Bartolozzi, Landseer, Ryder and Stow, group portrait, line engraving, pubd 1803 (*Commemoration of the victory of June 1st 1794; after Naval victories* by R. Smirke), BM, NPG

Harvey, Hildebrand Wolfe (1887–1970), marine biologist, was born on 31 December 1887 in Streatham, London, the elder son of Henry Allington Harvey, paint manufacturer in the firm of Foster, Mason, and Harvey of Mitcham, Surrey, and his wife, Laetitia, daughter of Peter Kingsley Wolfe. After attending Gresham's School at Holt in Norfolk from 1902 to 1906 he entered Downing College, Cambridge, to read natural sciences. He gained a second class in both parts of the tripos (part one in 1909 and part two—specializing in chemistry—in 1910). During the First World War Harvey—a keen sailor—served in minesweepers and patrol vessels in the Royal Naval Volunteer Reserve. His skill at navigating these in stormy waters in all seasons, including northern winter nights, became legendary. In 1921 he joined the staff of the Marine Biological Association of the United Kingdom in Plymouth as administrative and hydrographical assistant. Two years later he married Elsie Marguerite Sanders. The marriage was later dissolved.

Harvey's early work at the Marine Biological Association was on the physical oceanography of the western English Channel. At that time useful measurements were largely confined to salinity and temperature and the theory for interpreting these in shallow seas was much behind that available for the waters of the deep ocean. Though Harvey quickly saw that an understanding of biological productivity which his colleagues sought needed a more biochemical approach, it took him a decade to develop a quantitative method. His first success was a method for analysing nitrate, which he considered that marine plants were likely to need. Though no more than semi-quantitative and using a highly corrosive medium it was immediately and widely used by expedition ships. The broad picture of distribution in the world oceans which it yielded was confirmed by the far better methods developed since. The publication in 1928 of Harvey's monograph on the biological chemistry and physics of sea water illustrated the ordered and economical way in which he carried through all his researches. In 1933 Harvey published his classic paper on the rate of diatom growth. In the same year he married Marjorie Joan Sarjeant. The couple later had a son.

Harvey succeeded in enlisting the help of three specialist colleagues to produce a seminal paper on plankton production and its control, in which the methods of physics, chemistry, plant physiology, and zooplanktology were applied to the waters of the English Channel for a year. He also wrote two further books.

The words in which the Murray committee of the

United States National Academy of Sciences recommended the award of the Agassiz medal in 1952 to Harvey convey the seminal value of his work:

> H. W. Harvey … has been the leading student for many years of the changes in the chemical constituents of sea water brought about through the agencies of plants and animals and also of how the availability of nutrient chemicals determines the fertility of the sea.

His field observations were mainly limited to the English Channel, but many of his conclusions applied to the whole biologically active zone of the marine environment. Indeed, Harvey's talent lay in recognizing untilled fields ready for strategic research and cultivating those fields with maximum production of pertinent knowledge. In 1945 he was elected to fellowship of the Royal Society, and in 1958 he was appointed CBE.

Harvey had a combination of qualities rarely found in one man. He was a gifted synthesizer of existing knowledge, from which he constructed powerful hypotheses. This was combined with the patience to undertake meticulously designed experimental work needed to test these hypotheses. He was a master of the experimental method, able to minimize the time spent on experiment by his intuitive flair for rejecting work likely to be unproductive.

Harvey was a kindly man who taught quietly by precept. Always considerate, he once offered a colleague a lift in his car, to receive the reply 'No thank you, Dr Harvey, I am in a hurry'. And so he drove through life. He died in Freedom Fields Hospital, Plymouth, on 26 November 1970.

L. H. N. COOPER, rev.

Sources L. H. N. Cooper, *Memoirs FRS*, 18 (1972), 331–47 · *Journal of the Marine Biological Association of the United Kingdom*, 52 (1972), 773–5 · private information (1981) · personal knowledge (1981) · *CGPLA Eng. & Wales* (1971)
Archives Marine Biological Association of the United Kingdom, Plymouth, notebooks and papers
Wealth at death £70,132: probate, 15 Feb 1971, *CGPLA Eng. & Wales*

Harvey, Jane (*bap.* 1771, *d.* 1848), writer, baptized at Gateshead on 8 July 1771, was probably the daughter of William Harvey, wharfinger (*b.* c.1738), and his second wife, Jane, daughter of James Marshall. According to *The Feminist Companion to Literature in English* she was the daughter of Lawrance and Elizabeth Harvey of Barnard Castle, but there seems no evidence to connect her with this place.

Harvey's earliest known work is *A Sentimental Tour through Newcastle*, by 'A Young Lady', published in 1794. This takes the form of a guide to various aspects of the city 'certainly in no way inferior to any provincial town in England' visited by the 'young lady'. As well as more typical sights the tour takes in the infirmary and the prison, with digressions, including political comment, on fishing and the coal trade. Her second book, *Poems on Various Subjects*, appeared in 1797.

Harvey continued to publish poetry throughout her life, including two collections for children—*Sacred Hymns* and *Poems Original and Moral*—both in 1818, but she is probably better known for her romantic novels, especially *The Castle of Tynemouth* (1806). Her books enjoyed wide currency and

are represented in surviving catalogues of a number of private and circulating libraries. However, contemporary critical reaction was not always kind. The annual publication *The Flowers of Literature*, for example, says of *The Governor of Belleville* (4 vols., 1808) that 'there are two volumes too much of it' and describes the author as 'lamentably deficient in the knowledge of character'.

Little is known of Harvey's life but her obituary published in several Newcastle newspapers states that she ran a circulating library in Tynemouth for some years. At the time of her death, on 4 March 1848 in Saville Row, she was living in Brunswick Place, Newcastle upon Tyne. She was buried in the Newcastle general cemetery, at Jesmond, on 6 March. She was unmarried.   E. A. REES

Sources Blain, Clements & Grundy, *Feminist comp.* · [A. Myers], *Myers' literary guide: the north east* (1995) · obituary, Newcastle Central Library [unpublished typescript, 1915; kept from c.1800 to 1860 by Matthew Forster, solicitor, Newcastle upon Tyne, and from 1860 to 1870 by his son Jonathan Langstaff Forster, with additions by Richard Welford JP, of Gosforth] · *Newcastle Journal* (11 March 1848) · *IGI* · parish register, Gateshead, St Mary, 8 July 1771 [baptism]; 29 June 1769 [marriage: William Harvey and Jane Marshall] · d. cert. · register, Newcastle upon Tyne general cemetery, Jesmond · census returns, 1841 · J. Belanger and others, 'British fiction, 1800–1829: a database of production and reception, phase II, the flowers of literature', www.cf.ac.uk/encap/corvey/articles/database/flowers.html [Centre for Editorial and Intertextual Research Project Report, 7 (2001)] · D. Blakey, *The Minerva Press, 1790–1820* (1939)

Harvey, John (*bap.* 1564, *d.* 1592), astrologer, was baptized at Saffron Walden, Essex, on 13 February 1564, the third son of John Harvey (*d.* 1593), a prosperous master rope maker and farmer, and his wife, Ales (Alice; *d.* 1613). Like his older brothers Gabriel *Harvey and Richard *Harvey, he attended the local grammar school before proceeding to Cambridge, where he matriculated pensioner of Queens' College in June 1578, graduating BA in 1581 and MA in 1584. Thomas Nashe, a fierce enemy, claimed later that Harvey had been notorious for his trysts with 'the wenches in Queenes Colledge Lane' (*Works of Thomas Nashe*, 3.81), but he was also clearly an assiduous scholar. On leaving university he became a tutor in the household of Thomas Meade of Wendon Lofts, near Walden, a justice of the queen's bench, whose son had been a school and college friend. Subsequently he 'stole away' and married Meade's daughter Martha (ibid.), probably in 1583 when he was still only nineteen, though he was soon reconciled to his new father-in-law. In 1587 Cambridge granted him a licence to practise medicine and he became a successful practitioner at King's Lynn where, according to his brother Gabriel, he was highly respected among the Norfolk gentry.

Harvey's first publication was *An Astrologicall Addition* (1583), a supplement to his brother Richard's notorious *Astrological Discourse* on the great conjunction of Saturn and Jupiter in 1583. The dedication, to Meade, was dated 1 April 1583. To this work Harvey appended a translation of the *Iatromathematica* of Hermes Trismegistus, a guide to astrological medicine, undertaken at the request of a friend he identified only as M. Charles P., and one of the earliest hermetic writings to appear in English. Harvey shared his brother's conviction that the conjunction of 1583 heralded dramatic woes. He speculated that an Antichrist or new Mahomet might appear, or 'some Turkish Martiall Tyrant' (Harvey, *Addition*, sig. C5), but promised that God would protect the faithful and thought a great new monarchy could arise to restore peace.

Harvey commenced a series of almanacs in 1584 to monitor these developments. The first, *Leap Year*, was dedicated to Meade, and subsequent editions to the lord chancellor, Sir Thomas Bromley, and his successor, Sir Christopher Hatton. The failure of the astrological prophecies concerning the great conjunction brought a flood of ridicule and abuse against the two younger Harvey brothers, and led John to reassess his position. In 1588 he published *A Discursive Probleme Concerning Prophesies*, completed in August 1587 and dedicated to Hatton, in which he distinguished sharply between astrological and other predictions. The prophecies of Merlin, the Sibyls and other ancient seers were dismissed as 'flimflams packed up in pedlers prose' and he demanded, 'Who laugheth not at their ... beggerly trumperie?' (Harvey, *Discursive Probleme*, 65). Harvey also now took a far more critical approach to the astrological prophecies of Regiomontanus, Leowicz (Leovitius), and others concerning the conjunction of 1583, wholly rejecting their apocalyptic claims. 'I cannot sufficiently marvell', he remarked, 'what mooved so famous learned men in this facultie, to ascribe, or attribute so exceeding much unto that silly Conjunction' (ibid., 110). He passed over his own and his brother's earlier sensational writings on the subject. Harvey still defended judicial astrology itself, however, citing Ptolemy as a sound guide on the effects of eclipses, and he also endorsed a 'true, and right Naturall Magique' (ibid., 79). His almanac for 1589 stressed that astrological predictions were at best contingent.

Harvey died at King's Lynn in July 1592, aged only twenty-eight, after a short illness, and was survived by his wife and their two young daughters. The settlement of the estate generated a fierce dispute. Martha had brought a dowry of £300, in return for which John and his father promised her £600 in the event of his death, with the house and land at Saffron Walden as security. Relations between the couple appear to have been strained; Martha repeatedly asked, in vain, for a formal jointure on the terms agreed verbally and urged him to make a will confirming the settlement. After his death, intestate, she asked his brother Gabriel to handle the administration on her behalf, and later claimed that he cheated her of everything. In May 1593 she petitioned Sir John Puckering, the lord keeper, for redress and commenced an action in chancery against Gabriel and his father, though the matter seems eventually to have been compounded. Nothing further is known of her or her children.

John Harvey shared both the intellectual energy and the pugnacious temperament of his two more celebrated brothers. All three were the targets of merciless attacks by Nashe and Robert Greene. Harvey's *Discursive Probleme*

was none the less a significant contribution to intellectual debate, and all the more striking for its author's readiness to review his previous position in the light of experience.

BERNARD CAPP

Sources V. F. Stern, *Gabriel Harvey* (1979) · *The works of Thomas Nashe*, ed. R. B. McKerrow, 5 vols. (1904–10); repr. with corrections and notes by F. P. Wilson (1958) · J. Harvey, *A discursive probleme concerning prophesies* (1588) · J. Harvey, *An astrologicall addition* (1583) · G. Harvey, *Foure letters* (1592) · D. C. Allen, *The star-crossed Renaissance: the quarrel about astrology and its influence in England* (1979) · W. H. B. Stone, 'Shakespeare and the sad augurs', *Journal of English and Germanic Philology*, 52 (1953), 457–79 · M. Aston, 'The fiery trigon conjunction: an Elizabethan astrological prediction', *Isis*, 61 (1970), 159-87 · B. S. Capp, *Astrology and the popular press: English almanacs, 1500–1800* (1979)

Harvey, John (1740–1794), naval officer, was born on 9 July 1740, at Elmton, Kent, the third son of Elizabeth, *née* Nichols, and Richard Harvey of Eastry, Kent. His younger brother was Sir Henry *Harvey, who also achieved distinction in the navy. In 1754 John Harvey joined the *Falmouth* (50 guns) with Captain William Brett. Under the patronage of Admiral Francis Holbourne and Sir Peircy Brett (a distant family relation) he was promoted lieutenant on 30 January 1759, and appointed first to the sloop *Hornet* (18 September) and then in March 1761 to the frigate *Arethusa*. With the conclusion of the peace in 1762 Harvey came ashore, and on 27 September 1763 he married Judith, daughter of Henry Wise of Sandwich; the couple had a large family.

In November 1766 Harvey was appointed to command the cutter *Alarm* on the coast of Scotland, a duty he performed until his promotion to the rank of commander in 1768 when he was placed on half pay. In January 1776 he was appointed to the sloop *Speedwell*; and in September 1777, as war loomed with France, he was posted from her to the *Panther* (60 guns) as flag-captain to Rear-Admiral Robert Duff in the Mediterranean. Harvey distinguished himself in the defence of Gibraltar during the early part of the siege in 1779–80, latterly as senior officer after the departure of Duff and of his successor Commodore Elliot. In July 1780 the *Panther* sailed for England, and in November she was sent to the West Indies in the squadron under Sir Samuel Hood; from here she returned in the following summer.

Early in 1782 Harvey was appointed to the *Sampson* (64 guns), which formed part of the Channel Fleet, and he was present at the relief of Gibraltar and the encounter off Cape Spartel. During the interlude of peace between the American War of Independence and that occasioned by the French Revolution, Harvey continued in employment. In 1787 he was regulating captain at Deal and from 1788 to 1792 he commanded the guardship *Arrogant* at Sheerness.

In February 1793, following the outbreak of war with France, Harvey was appointed at the special request of Admiral Lord Howe to the *Brunswick* (74 guns), one of the Channel Fleet. In the battle of 1 June 1794 she was stationed second astern of Howe's flagship, *Queen Charlotte*, but was separated from her by the close order of the French line astern of the *Jacobin*.

Harvey attempted to force an opening ahead of the

John Harvey (1740–1794), by Gilbert Stuart

Vengeur, when the *Brunswick*'s starboard anchor hooked in the *Vengeur*'s forechains and dragged the *Vengeur* along with her. The master proposed to cut her free. 'No', said Harvey, 'as we've got her we'll keep her.' The two ships remained firmly grappled through a great part of the battle. Towards the close other English ships came to the *Brunswick*'s help; and the *Ramillies*, commanded by Harvey's brother, poured two tremendous raking broadsides into the *Vengeur*. The grappling had been cut away, but after a short time the *Vengeur*, dismasted and with the water pouring in through her smashed side, surrendered. Without a seaworthy boat the *Brunswick* was unable to take possession, and the *Vengeur*, dropping astern, endeavoured to make off when she was brought to by the *Culloden* and *Alfred*. Every effort was made to remove her men, but she sank with more than half her crew still on board. The *Brunswick*, severely damaged, had fallen far to leeward, and being unable to rejoin the fleet bore up, and reached Spithead on 12 June with a loss of 44 men killed and 114 wounded.

Early in the action Harvey's right hand had been shattered by a musket-ball; afterwards he was stunned by a heavy splinter striking him in the small of the back; and a round shot afterwards smashed his right elbow. He was landed at Portsmouth, where he died on 30 June 1794. He was buried at Eastry; a monument, jointly to his memory and to that of Captain John Hutt of the *Queen*, who also died of his wounds on 30 June, was erected in Westminster Abbey. Two of Harvey's sons, Sir John *Harvey and Sir Edward *Harvey, also entered the navy.

J. K. LAUGHTON, *rev.* NICHOLAS TRACY

Sources *Naval Chronicle*, 3 (1800), 241 · logbooks, 1792–4, NMM, LOG/N/B/16–17 · *Kentish Gazette* (11 July 1794) · 'Historical memoirs of Admiral Sir Henry Harvey', NMM, MS 81/041
Archives NMM, logbooks | NMM, MS 81/041
Likenesses Bartolozzi, Landseer, Ryder and Stow, group portrait, line engraving, pubd 1803 (*Commemoration of the victory of June 1st 1794*; after *Naval victories* by R. Smirke), BM, NPG · Stuart, stipple, 1803 (engraved by Ridley), NMM · J. Bacon jun., medallion on monument, 1804, Westminster Abbey · G. Stuart, portrait, NMM [*see illus.*]

Harvey, Sir John (1772–1837), naval officer, was the second son of Captain John *Harvey RN (1740–1794) and his wife, Judith, daughter of Henry Wise of Sandwich. Sir Edward *Harvey was his younger brother. After serving as midshipman of the frigate *Rose* with his uncle, Sir Henry Harvey, he was promoted lieutenant on 3 November 1790; on 5 September 1794 to command the sloop *Actif* in the West Indies; and on 16 December to be post captain, as a tribute to the memory of his father. In January 1795 he was chosen by his uncle as his flag-captain in the *Prince of Wales* (98 guns), in which he was present in the action off Lorient, in the operations on the coast of Brittany in the following winter, and in the West Indies, including the capture of Trinidad, when he was sent home with dispatches. He afterwards commanded the *Southampton* (32 guns) and the *Amphitrite* in the West Indies and off Cadiz; the *Agamemnon* (64 guns) in Robert Calder's action off Cape Finisterre; the *Canada* (74 guns) in the West Indies; and the *Leviathan* (74 guns) and *Royal Sovereign* (110 guns) in the Mediterranean. He became rear-admiral on 4 December 1813. From 1816 to 1819 he was commander-in-chief in the West Indies; he was made vice-admiral on 27 May 1825, KCB on 6 June 1833, and admiral on 10 January 1837. He married in 1797 his first cousin, daughter of William Wyborn Bradley of Sandwich; they had one daughter. He died at Upper Deal, Kent, on 17 February 1837.

J. K. LAUGHTON, *rev.* ROGER MORRISS

Sources J. Marshall, *Royal naval biography*, 1/2 (1823), 613–14 · *GM*, 2nd ser., 7 (1837), 436 · A. B. Rodger, *The war of the second coalition: 1798–1801, a strategic commentary* (1964) · R. Muir, *Britain and the defeat of Napoleon, 1807–1815* (1996)

Harvey, Sir John (1778–1852), army officer and administrator in Canada, was born on 23 April 1778 in England. Complete mystery surrounds his background. Rumours that he was an illegitimate son of the first marquess of Anglesey are undoubtedly untrue. Nothing certain is known about his youth except that he was brought up in Dronfield, Derbyshire, by the vicar, the Revd John Russell. On 18 September 1794 he became an ensign in the 80th regiment of foot, and from 1794 to 1802 he served in the Netherlands, at the Cape of Good Hope, in Ceylon, and in Egypt. From 1803 to 1807 he was in India, where he joined the staff of the commander-in-chief, Lord Lake, whose daughter, Elizabeth (*d.* 1851), he married on 16 June 1806. They had five sons and one daughter. On 15 July 1798 Harvey became a lieutenant, on 9 September 1803 a captain, and on 28 January 1808 a major. After being employed in England during the first half of 1808 as an assistant quartermaster-general, he was stationed in Ireland from July 1808 to 1812.

On 25 June 1812 Harvey became a lieutenant-colonel and deputy adjutant-general in Upper Canada. By travelling overland from New Brunswick on snowshoes, he arrived in Upper Canada early in 1813 and played a conspicuous part in the Anglo-American War of 1812–14. On 6 June 1813, at the battle of Stoney Creek, he attacked and drove back an American force five times larger than his own. In November 1813 he earned a medal at the battle of Crysler's Farm, and he was wounded during the siege of Fort Erie on 6 August 1814. Although he went on half pay in 1817, he became knight commander of the Royal Guelphic Order in 1824 and in May 1825 was made a colonel. Through seniority he rose to the rank of major-general in January 1837 and lieutenant-general in November 1846.

Without private means Harvey desperately needed a civil appointment. In 1825–6 he served on the commission to determine the price of crown land in Upper Canada and from 1828 to 1836 as one of the four inspectors-general of the newly formed Irish constabulary, with responsibility for Leinster. During the tithe wars of the 1830s Leinster was the centre of agitation: Harvey did everything in his power to promote compromise and avoid bloodshed and won recognition for his moderation. In 1832 he gave evidence to the House of Commons select committee on Ireland and recommended the solution to the tithes question that was eventually adopted. In April 1836 the Irish constabulary was reorganized and his post abolished, but he was compensated with the position of lieutenant-governor of Prince Edward Island.

In 1767 the whole of Prince Edward Island had been divided into townships, distributed by lottery to landlords in Britain, and on his arrival in August 1836 Harvey was confronted by an assembly controlled by a popular party demanding confiscation of the estates, a policy opposed by the Colonial Office. Harvey sought to take the initiative out of the hands of the escheat party by persuading the landlords resident in Britain to make concessions to their tenants, and he supported a measure to increase the taxes paid by non-resident landlords. These measures temporarily restored a degree of tranquillity to the island and won Harvey considerable popularity and a reputation for being able to handle recalcitrant assemblies. This reputation was later enhanced in New Brunswick, where he was transferred in May 1837 to succeed lieutenant-governor Sir Archibald Campbell, who was at loggerheads with his assembly. By surrendering to the assembly control over the rapidly increasing revenues derived from the sale of crown lands, and reconstructing his executive council to include the leaders of the colony's reform movement, Harvey established a harmonious working relationship with the majority in the assembly and ensured New Brunswick's loyalty during the Canadian uprising of 1837–8. In 1838 he was created KCB for his services and he was fulsomely praised in the Durham report in 1839 and by Governor-General Lord Sydenham in 1840.

Harvey was less successful in resolving the Maine–New Brunswick boundary dispute. Although he prevented friction along the border from evolving into a serious conflict, he was not sufficiently aggressive in upholding the British claims, and in 1841 he was abruptly dismissed, although later that year he was reassigned as governor of Newfoundland. In Newfoundland sectarian violence between the predominantly English and protestant urban middle class in St John's and the largely Irish and Roman Catholic majority in the outports had led to the suspension of the constitution. The new constitution imposed by the Newfoundland Act of 1842 was opposed by the largely Catholic Reform Party, but Harvey again showed his remarkable abilities as a conciliator. He put an end, at least temporarily, to the sectarian violence and won the respect of the colony's Roman Catholics, although in 1846 he could not convince the reformers to agree to a renewal of the Newfoundland Act. None the less, his sojourn in Newfoundland was not a particularly happy one. He went deeply into debt maintaining a lifestyle he could not afford, and he was reprimanded by the Colonial Office for borrowing money from his colonial secretary.

In August 1846 Harvey was given the more lucrative post of lieutenant-governor of Nova Scotia. His instructions were to engineer a coalition between the colony's Conservatives, who dominated the assembly and the executive council, and the reformers, who were likely to win the next election and were demanding the introduction of responsible party government. Despite his best efforts, Harvey was unable to construct a coalition, and following the election of August 1847 he had no option but to dismiss the Conservatives and admit the reformers to office. On 2 February 1848 he therefore reluctantly presided over the introduction of the first formally responsible party ministry in the British empire. The transition did not prove easy. A stream of petitions was sent to London accusing Harvey of identifying himself with the new reform administration, and he lost the confidence of the secretary of state for the colonies, the third Earl Grey, who was unwilling to accept the full implications of the new system and criticized Harvey for not restraining the partisanship of his new advisers. Harvey suffered a shattering blow when his wife died on 10 April 1851, and his health rapidly deteriorated. He began a six-month leave of absence in May, but on his return was incapable of performing even routine tasks. On 22 March 1852 he died at Government House, Halifax, Nova Scotia, and was buried in the military cemetery in Halifax alongside his wife.

Harvey was lucky in that the long wars against France opened up unusual opportunities for the promotion of officers like himself who had neither family connections nor large personal fortunes. Repeatedly he won recognition for acts of daring and bravery: but most of his military service was spent in backwaters. During the Anglo-American War of 1812–14 Harvey became one of the best-known military officers in British North America, but after the war he was just one of a vast number of young officers with an uncertain future. After a false start in Ireland, at the age of fifty-eight he began a new career as a colonial administrator and eventually served in more British North American colonies than any other governor. Partly because his origins were humble, he did not find exile among the colonists as tedious as did most of his contemporaries, and everywhere he served he won popular support. Noted for his tolerance and flexibility, he was the ideal colonial administrator during a period when the role of the governor was undergoing a fundamental transformation.   PHILLIP BUCKNER

Sources P. Buckner, 'Harvey, Sir John', *DCB*, vol. 8 • P. A. Buckner, *The transition to responsible government: British policy in British North America, 1815–1850* (1985)
Archives NA Canada, corresp. and papers | NA Scot., corresp. with Lord Dalhousie • NRA, priv. coll., corresp. with Sir John Colborne • PRO NIre., letters to Lord Gosford • University of New Brunswick, letters to Lord Durham
Likenesses portrait, Legislative Assembly building, Fredericton, New Brunswick

Harvey, John Hooper (1911–1997), architectural and garden historian, was born on 25 May 1911 in St John's Wood, London, the only child of William Harvey (1883–1962), architect, and his wife, Alice Mabel Wilcox (1874–1958). He attended St John's School, Leatherhead, from 1923 to 1927. In 1928 he joined the office of Sir Herbert Baker, architect, and while there went to the Regent Street Polytechnic (1929–32) to study architecture, in both cases following in his father's footsteps. He spent the years 1933 to 1935 with his father in Palestine assisting in the compilation of survey reports on ancient buildings. In 1934 he returned to marry, on 24 February, (Sarah) Cordelia Story (1903–1996). They had two sons, Richard (b. 1938) and Charles (1940–2000), and one daughter, Eleanour (b. 1945).

Harvey entered the office of works in 1936. As he refused all forms of war work 'on aesthetic and historical grounds' (private information), he was imprisoned in Wormwood Scrubs for six months in 1942. After release he joined his father—now living in Bookham, Surrey—in identifying buildings of historic interest at risk from enemy action. This early 'listing' of buildings was resumed on a more general footing in 1947, and Harvey briefly became one of its investigators in 1949. He was appointed consultant architect (for conservation matters) to Winchester College (1947–64), and this gave him the experience needed to become in 1950 the lecturer in the first dedicated conservation course at the Bartlett school of architecture at University College, London (until 1959). In 1972 he published *The Conservation of Buildings*. For over thirty years from 1960 he sat on the council of the Ancient Monuments Society.

In 1930 Harvey had begun to compile biographical information about medieval architects, and it became his mission to celebrate their work and enhance their status in the eyes of history. A short biography, *Henry Yevele* (1944), was followed over the next thirty years by a constant stream of articles and an overlapping series of books, including *Gothic England: a Survey of National Culture* (1947); *The Plantagenets* (1948); *Tudor Architecture* (1949); *The Gothic World* (1950); *The Mediaeval Architect* (1972); *Mediaeval Craftsmen* (1975); *The Black Prince and his Age* (1976); and *The Perpendicular Style* (1978). Although the range of scholarship displayed in all these books was impressive, the most significant was *English Mediaeval Architects: a Biographical*

Dictionary Down to 1550 (1954, with contributions by Arthur Oswald). This work of reference rapidly became indispensable: as Eric Fernie wrote, it 'demolishes the idea of medieval architectural anonymity' (Fernie). An expanded edition was published in 1984, funded by subscription. This won Harvey the Alice Davis Hitchcock medallion of the Society of Architectural Historians of Great Britain in 1987. Of his other works, *The Perpendicular Style* contained the fullest account of his researches.

Throughout this body of work Harvey sought to establish the artistic importance of England in the fourteenth and fifteenth centuries. He wanted to demonstrate that in this period the visual arts cohered to form a national style, analogous to the national language used by Chaucer. For Harvey, the fortunes of this artistic movement were closely bound up with those of the later Plantagenets. It was their wish to foster national identity through architecture which had made the Perpendicular 'the most important phenomenon of English art' (J. Harvey, *The Perpendicular Style*, 1978, 13) with Yevele as 'our greatest architect' (J. Harvey, *Henry Yevele*, 1944, vii). While the depth of his scholarship was freely acknowledged, many contemporaries were not convinced by these central ideas. Younger scholars have, however, vindicated his methods and confirmed the concept of artistic identity in this period.

In the later stages of this campaign Harvey was living (from 1963) in York, where he was employed by the Royal Commission on Historical Monuments (England) as an editor (1963–70). In 1975 the family moved to Frome in Somerset. Although he maintained his wide interests concurrently, in these later years he moved increasingly into the field of garden history, which he pursued through a similar attention to neglected sources and an interest in the techniques and materials available to English gardeners. *Early Gardening Catalogues* (1972) and *Early Nurserymen* (1974) were crucial texts in establishing the story of how plants were introduced, propagated, and diffused. Many articles, mostly published in *Garden History*, examined this story in greater detail and supplied the background to introductions from other countries, especially in the Islamic world, where he delighted to travel. In 1981 he published *Mediaeval Gardens*. He became a leading figure in the Garden History Society and was president from 1982 to 1985; in addition to his articles, the society published his *Availability of Hardy Plants of the Late Eighteenth Century* in 1988.

Contemporaries were dazzled by the breadth and authority with which Harvey wrote, and he was elected a fellow of the Society of Genealogists (1939), the Royal Society of Literature (1945), and the Society of Antiquaries (1949). The University of York conferred an honorary doctorate in 1976. He was a shy man, and of unbending principle; he could seem reserved and austere. The prodigious, almost obsessive labours by which he transformed medieval architectural studies were driven by a faith in the past, and hatred of much of modern life, which set him apart from most of his contemporaries, although to his inner circle he was jovial and to all who sought information he was punctiliously generous. He died at his home, 32 Christchurch Street East, Frome, on 18 November 1997 of heart failure, and was cremated at Bath crematorium. He was survived by his three children, his wife having predeceased him.   DAVID BROCK

Sources *The Independent* (25 Nov 1997) · *Daily Telegraph* (4 Dec 1997) · J. Harvey and A. Oswald, *English mediaeval architects: a biographical dictionary down to 1550*, 2nd edn (1984), lii–lvii · A. Clifton-Taylor, 'John Harvey: a decade of letters', *Transactions of the Ancient Monuments Society*, new ser., 25 (1981), 27–37 · J. H. Harvey, 'Listing as I knew it in 1949', *Transactions of the Ancient Monuments Society*, new ser., 38 (1994), 97–104 · J. H. Harvey, 'The origins of listed buildings', *Transactions of the Ancient Monuments Society*, new ser., 37 (1993), 1–20 · J. Harvey, *The conservation of buildings* (1972), preface · R. Gorer, 'John Harvey and garden history', *Transactions of the Ancient Monuments Society*, new ser., 25 (1981), 38–46 · L. S. Colchester, 'Bibliography of John H. Harvey', *Transactions of the Ancient Monuments Society*, new ser., 25 (1981), 47–52 · [L. S. Colchester], 'Bibliography of John H. Harvey: additions', *Transactions of the Ancient Monuments Society*, new ser., 26 (1982), 249–52 · J. H. Harvey, 'Published writings by John Hooper Harvey (1911–97) on garden history and related topics', *Garden History*, 26/1 (1998), 102–5 · P. Kidson, review of *The Perpendicular Style*, *Antiquaries Journal*, 62 (1982), 167–8 · E. Fernie, 'Contrasts in the methodology and interpretation of medieval ecclesiastical architecture', *Archaeological Journal*, 145 (1988), 344–64 · personal knowledge (2004) · private information (2004) [Eleanour Harvey]
Archives Borth. Inst., papers on garden history · Guildford Museum, Surrey Archaeological Society, papers on history and topography of Surrey · priv. coll., papers on architectural history · priv. coll., personal papers
Likenesses G. Hall, photograph, 1978, repro. in Harvey, 'Published writings by John Hooper Harvey'
Wealth at death under £180,000: probate, 17 March 1998, *CGPLA Eng. & Wales*

Harvey, Sir John Martin- (1863–1944), actor and theatre manager, was born in Wivenhoe, Essex, on 22 June 1863, the eldest son to survive infancy and the fourth of the seven children of John Harvey, naval architect and builder of yachts, and his wife, Margaret Diana Mary, daughter of the Revd David George Goyder, a Swedenborgian minister. His mother died while he was still a child, and he was cared for temporarily by family friends in Paisley, Renfrewshire, where he attended the grammar school before continuing a sound if largely unprofitable education at Linton House, Colchester, and King's College School, London. Expected to inherit the family business, he was apprenticed as a shipwright in his father's yard at fifteen, but despite a gift for draughtsmanship he evinced little interest in the work, and his response to a chance visit to a London theatre persuaded an indulgent parent to enrol him for acting lessons with the veteran tragedian John Ryder. After making his stage début in a walk-on part at the Court Theatre on 24 September 1881, he had one of his father's yachting clients, W. S. Gilbert, to thank for a brief engagement with Charles Wyndham. In September 1882 a letter of introduction from a friend of his maternal grandfather's who knew Henry Irving brought him employment as a 'Lyceum gentleman', a secure position though little more than a 'super'.

Harvey remained at the Lyceum for fourteen years without playing any parts of substance except during Irving's provincial and American tours or during the company's annual summer break, when with other young colleagues he formed a small touring group calling itself the Lyceum Vacation Company. But it proved a crucial apprenticeship, enabling the novice to assimilate both the art of acting and the business of management, and thereafter he freely acknowledged his indebtedness to Irving by referring to him always as 'the master'. At the Lyceum, too, he met his future wife, Angelita Helena Margarita (Nina; *d.* 1949), daughter of Don Ramón de Silva Ferro, a Spanish diplomat and businessman of distinguished parentage. After their marriage on 24 January 1889 she was his devoted helpmate, managerial partner, and leading lady for the rest of his life. They had two children, a son, Jack Seaforth Elton, and a daughter, (Margaret) Muriel de Melfort, who also became a well-known actress.

After leaving the Lyceum in 1896 Harvey was a freelance actor for three years, notably as Osric in *Hamlet* with Johnston Forbes-Robertson, Erhart in Ibsen's *John Gabriel Borkman* for the New Century Theatre Society, and Pelléas to Mrs Patrick Campbell's Mélisande in the British première of Maeterlinck's drama. He then ventured into management at the Lyceum in February 1899 with *The Only Way*, an adaptation from Dickens's *A Tale of Two Cities*; both husband and wife had a hand in fashioning it into a vehicle for their respective talents, and its phenomenal success helped to determine their entire career. Not only did it ensure their continuing prosperity, registering over 5000 performances in forty years and still featuring in their farewell tour of 1938–9, but it afforded a melodramatic template for subsequent additions to their standing repertory, such as *Rouget de Lisle* (1900), *A Cigarette-Maker's Romance* (1901), *Eugene Aram* (1902), *The Exile* (1903), *The Breed of the Treshams* (1903), *Boy O'Carroll* (1906), and *The Last Heir* (1908). Amid all this costumed romance and swashbuckling adventure he presented his first *Hamlet* in 1904, *Richard III* in 1910, *The Taming of the Shrew* in 1913, and a revival of *Pelléas and Mélisande* in 1911. In 1912, with conspicuous daring and at vast expense, he mounted a revolutionary production of *Oedipus rex*, using Gilbert Murray's recent translation and with Max Reinhardt as director; he accommodated the elements of a classical Greek theatre to the stage and auditorium of Covent Garden, then compounded his ambition by touring the production to provincial theatres as well.

With comparable enterprise Harvey marked Shakespeare's tercentenary in 1916 with a five-week season at His Majesty's Theatre. This added *Henry V* to the three works already in his repertory, and demonstrated four radically different approaches to Shakespearian staging: the archaeological, the fit-up, the expressionistic, and the quasi-Elizabethan. His aim was to exemplify what might be accomplished through the establishment of a national theatre, a cause that he constantly promoted in public lectures. During the war years he also staked his personal popularity on producing two new plays bearing uncomfortably on the current conflict—Stephen Phillips's *Armageddon* (1915) and Maeterlinck's *The Burgomaster of Stilemonde* (1918). He delivered recruiting speeches, spent a month at the front line giving dramatic recitals to the troops, and raised handsome sums for the Red Cross and various war charities. For this fundraising as much as for his services to the theatre he was knighted in 1921. On 28 October of that year he assumed by deed poll the additional surname Martin.

After the war Martin-Harvey premièred fewer new plays, Rafael Sabatini's *Scaramouche* (1927) and Frederic Jackson's *The King's Messenger* (1931) being notable exceptions; as he disarmingly admitted in his autobiography: 'I could find little work by authors of the day which would satisfy that taste for the purely dramatic which audiences expected from me. I was rather hoist on my own petard of "stardom"' (Martin-Harvey, 527). Instead he resorted again to *The Corsican Brothers*, which he had already revived in 1906, and to two of Irving's other Lyceum triumphs, *The Lyons Mail* (1927) and *The Bells* (1932). He appeared in film versions of four of his own successes—*A Cigarette-Maker's Romance* (1913), *The Breed of the Treshams* (1920), *The Only Way* (1925), and *The Lyons Mail* (1931)—while *The Burgomaster of Stilemonde* was broadcast by the BBC. Recognition for a lifetime's theatrical achievement came in 1938 with the conferment of an honorary doctorate of laws by Glasgow University. He died peacefully at his home, Primrose Cottage, 31 Fife Road, East Sheen, Surrey, on 14 May 1944, and was buried on 17 May at East Sheen cemetery.

The longevity of Martin-Harvey's career served at last to make his style of acting seem magnificently old-fashioned, though for a practitioner so firmly rooted in late-Victorian tradition he was surprisingly receptive to new ideas, some of his original scenic designs showing the influence of his friend Gordon Craig, Reinhardt, or Willam Poel, while alone among his peers he attempted to acclimatize contemporary Spanish drama to the English stage, with pieces by José Zorrilla, José Echegaray, and Angel Guimera. Accustomed to deploying *The Only Way* and similar stand-bys to subsidize performances of Shakespeare and Sophocles, he was prepared to lose money on other plays he considered worthy of presentation: drawn by a Swedenborgian upbringing (he later joined the Church of England), or perhaps the untimely loss of his mother, to the spiritual and homiletic, he essayed *Great Possessions*, a morality play from the German of Carl Rössler in 1907, and challenged the hedonistic twenties with *Via crucis* (1922), an adaptation of Hofmannsthal's *Jedermann*. That he never had a regular West End base and spent most of his time 'on the road' in the provinces or North America (especially Canada, where he was lionized) made it easier for metropolitan critics to ignore or patronize him, but the so-called 'last of the romantics' was also a manager of great resourcefulness and an actor capable of tragic grandeur.   DONALD ROY

Sources J. Martin-Harvey, *The autobiography of Sir John Martin-Harvey* (1933) · [R. N. Green-Armytage], ed., *The book of Martin Harvey* (1930) · M. Willson Disher, *The last romantic: the authorised biography of Sir John Martin-Harvey* (1948) · G. Edgar, *Martin Harvey: some pages from his life* (1912) · [R. De Cordova], *Parts I have played: a photographic and descriptive biography* (1909) · H. Pearson, *The last actor-managers* (1950), 47–53 · *The Times* (15 May 1944) · *The Times* (18 May 1944) · J. T. Grein, *ILN* (15 Jan 1921), 76 · A. Williamson, 'Martin-Harvey', *Theatre World*, 11/234 (July 1944), 23–4 · *The Times* (19 May 1944) · *Who was who in the theatre, 1912–1976*, 2 (1978) · *DNB* · *WWW, 1951–60* · J. M. Harvey, *Character and the actor* (1908) · B. Hunt and J. Parker, eds., *The green room book, or, Who's who on the stage* (1906–9) · P. Hartnoll, ed., *The Oxford companion to the theatre*, 3rd edn (1967) · M. Banham, ed., *The Cambridge guide to world theatre* (1988) · B. Sobel, ed., *The new theatre handbook and digest of plays* (New York, 1959) · S. D'Amico, ed., *Enciclopedia dello spettacolo*, 7 (Rome, 1960) · *CGPLA Eng. & Wales* (1944)

Archives Harvard U., corresp. and papers · Theatre Museum, London, letters · University of Bristol, Theatre Collection, corresp. and papers | Bodl. Oxf., corresp. with Gilbert Murray · NL Scot., letters to Katherine Kay · Theatre Museum, London, letters to Lord Chamberlain's licensee · University of Kansas, Lawrence, Kenneth Spencer Research Library, MSS relating to production of L. Binyon's *Arthur*

Likenesses G. Frampton, bronze bust, 1900, Royal Shakespeare Theatre, Stratford upon Avon · Histed, photograph, c.1905, NPG; repro. in Hunt and Parker, eds., *Green room book*, 1 (1906) · A. Hacker, oils, c.1917, London Museum; repro. in Green-Armytage, *Book of Martin Harvey* · C. Buchel, chalk drawing, 1918, NPG · Capstack, photograph, c.1925, Blackpool; repro. in Green-Armytage, *Book of Martin Harvey* · F. O. Salisbury, oils, c.1925, Garr. Club; repro. in Martin-Harvey, *Autobiography* · W. Stoneman, photograph, 1933, NPG · C. Beatson, portrait (as Lieut. Reresby), repro. in Edgar, *Martin Harvey* · B. Munns, oils (as Richard III), Royal Shakespeare Theatre, Stratford upon Avon · cigarette card, NPG · photographs, NPG; repro. in *Daily Herald* · Rotary photo, photograph, NPG

Wealth at death £12,737 12s. 7d.: probate, 26 Aug 1944, *CGPLA Eng. & Wales*

Harvey, Laurence [*real name* Hirsch Moses Skikne] (1928–1973), actor and film director, was born on 1 October 1928 in Joniskis, Lithuania, the youngest of the three sons of Orthodox Jewish parents, Ber Skikne (1895/6–1974) and his wife, Ella Zotnickaita (1897/8–1974). In 1929, endeavouring to improve his prospects as a building contractor, his father emigrated to South Africa, where the family followed in 1934 and settled in a Jewish suburb of Johannesburg. Educated initially at the Earl of Athlone High School, young Skikne proved a rebellious, unscholarly pupil and was sent away to Meyerton College, Meyerton, Transvaal, a private boarding-school, to be taught discipline. At the age of fourteen he absconded and, claiming to be an orphan, enlisted in the South African navy. After being brought home to Johannesburg he took desultory jobs while studying architecture part-time and found a ready escape into counterfeit reality by joining a semi-professional theatre group and affecting the stage names Larushka Mischa or Larry M. Skikne. In 1943, again having lied about his age, he was recruited into an infantry regiment and soon posted to an entertainment unit, which toured north Africa and Italy giving variety performances to front-line troops.

Aided by an ex-service grant, Skikne travelled to London in 1946 and auditioned successfully for the Royal Academy of Dramatic Art, but he abandoned his training after one term to take up a four-month engagement from January 1947 with André van Gyseghem's newly established Library Theatre in Manchester. Among other leading parts he played Konstantin in Anton Chekhov's *The Seagull*, the

Warrior in Jean Giraudoux's *Amphitryon 38*, and Aimwell in George Farquhar's *The Beaux' Stratagem*. By arranging his parents' naturalization in South Africa he acquired the status of British subject, while a further change of name served to conceal his Slav-Hebrew origins and, through association with the Knightsbridge store of Harvey Nichols, enhanced the suave English image he now sought to project. As Laurence Harvey he made his West End début at the Cambridge Theatre in May 1951 in the role of Rafi, King of the Beggars, in an ill-fated revival of James Elroy Flecker's *Hassan*. He had also become the constant companion of Hermione Baddeley, who introduced him to London theatrical circles, and whose brother-in-law Glen Byam Shaw, co-director of the Shakespeare Memorial Theatre, invited him to join the company for the 1952 season. He appeared as Aufidius in *Coriolanus*, Malcolm in *Macbeth*, and Castrone in *Volpone*, and his tall, good-looking, sensitive Orlando in *As You Like It* was much admired. On his return to Stratford upon Avon in 1954 he confounded expectations by offering a 'contemporary', aggressively demotic Romeo (likened by one reviewer to a Berwick Street barrow boy) and a virile but woefully unpoetic Troilus. A foray to New York in October 1955, to play Angelo in the American première of Ugo Betti's *Goat Island*, also miscarried. He fared better in 1956 with two traditional comedies, both his Jack Absolute in R. B. Sheridan's *The Rivals* at the Saville in February and his Horner in William Wycherley's *The Country Wife* at the Royal Court in December being well received, and he achieved an unlooked-for triumph in the title role of *Henry V* during the Old Vic's American tour of 1958–9.

Meanwhile Harvey had been pursuing a parallel career in cinema: under contract first to Associated British Pictures, then to the Woolf brothers' Romulus Films, he appeared in more than fifty films in twenty-five years. Beginning in 1948 with *House of Darkness*, he played an assortment of criminal or unsavoury characters in low-budget British second features before graduating via the lead in a British-Italian *Romeo and Juliet* and the playboy protagonist of *The Good Die Young* (both 1954) to Christopher Isherwood in *I am a Camera* (1955), Johnny Jackson, the unscrupulous showbiz agent in *Expresso Bongo* (1959), and, more resourcefully still, Joe Lampton, the social-climbing north-country anti-hero of Jack Clayton's *Room at the Top* (1959), a performance which earned him an Oscar nomination. This, and the film's commercial success in America, promptly made him *persona grata* in Hollywood, and there followed a decade of extraordinary 'bankability', when he was cast in a rapid succession of leading roles in major films on both sides of the Atlantic, notably *The Alamo* (1960), *Butterfield 8* (1960), *The Long and the Short and the Tall* (1961), *Summer and Smoke* (1961), *Walk on the Wild Side* (1962), *The Manchurian Candidate* (1962)—arguably his best screen performance, as a brainwashed Korean War veteran—*The Running Man* (1963), *The Outrage* (1964), *Of Human Bondage* (1964), *A Dandy in Aspic* (1968), and *WUSA* (1970). He also appeared frequently on television. It was a period of ceaseless activity, most acutely in the autumn of 1964, when he shot *Darling* with John Schlesinger by day while at night playing King Arthur in the Lerner and Loewe musical *Camelot* at Drury Lane. Commuting by jet between film studios and locations, he surrounded himself with the accoutrements of stardom—luxury homes, expensive clothes, vintage wines—wherever he went, amassed a fleet of classic cars, and found time to set up a business selling antique furniture.

Imputations of bisexuality notwithstanding, Harvey was married three times. His first two marriages, to the West End actress Margaret *Leighton (1922–1976) from 1957 to 1961, and from 1968 to 1972 to Joan Perry Cohn, the widow of the former head of Columbia Pictures, doubtless benefited his career, although both ended in divorce. His third wife, and the mother of his daughter, Domino, was the London model Paulene Stone (*b.* 1942), whom he married on new year's eve 1972 and who published a memoir of their life together, *One Tear is Enough*, in 1975.

When the offers from Hollywood dwindled, Harvey continued to make films elsewhere: *The Magic Christian* (1969) and *Night Watch* (1973) in Britain, *Kampf um Rom* (1968–9) in Germany, *Rebus* (1968) in Lebanon, *L'assoluto naturale* (1969), which he also produced, in Italy, *Escape to the Sun* (1972) in Israel, and Orson Welles's multinational co-production *F for Fake* (1973) in Yugoslavia. He returned to the theatre spasmodically but with inveterate bravado: undeterred by criticism of his posturing and vocally mannered Leontes in *The Winter's Tale* at the 1966 Edinburgh festival, he contributed a provocatively un-Shavian, albeit effective, Sergius to *Arms and the Man* at Chichester in 1970, while at the same time co-producing Siobhan McKenna's touring one-woman show *Here are Ladies*, and abortively challenged the West End in March 1971 with Robert Marasco's melodramatic *Child's Play* at the Queen's, in which he made his last stage appearance as a suicidal Catholic schoolmaster. Enterprisingly, he also produced and directed two independent films, *The Ceremony* (1963), a thriller with overtones of political allegory set in Franco's Spain, and *Welcome to Arrow Beach*, dubbed by him 'a Gothic tale of romance and cannibalism', which he shot and edited while terminally ill and in constant pain. Harvey died of stomach cancer at his home in Kidderpore Avenue, Hampstead, on 25 November 1973, survived by his third wife, Paulene. He was cremated at Golders Green later that month.

Harvey's career was one of vaulting ambition and wayward focus, a paradox embodied in his conflicting desires to be taken seriously as a stage actor and renowned as an internationally successful film star. His genuine appetite for artistic advancement was matched, if not exceeded, by a compulsive need for material rewards and a free-spending lifestyle. After welcoming his early promise, critical reaction to his performances became increasingly cool or unsympathetic, and he inspired widespread animosity among professional colleagues, alienating many by an element of detachment, not to say egotism, in his playing, though he could be congenial and engagingly witty in company. A driven man, impatient with under-achievement yet masking insecurity behind a display of aloof self-sufficiency, he was continually moving from project to project, and dissipating a real if circumscribed talent through a restlessness of temperament.

DONALD ROY

Sources D. Hickey and G. Smith, *The prince: being the public and private life of Larushka Mischa Skikne, a Jewish Lithuanian vagabond player, otherwise known as Laurence Harvey* (1975) · P. Stone, *One tear is enough: my life with Laurence Harvey* (1975) · *Who was who in the theatre, 1912–1976*, 4 vols. (1978), vol. 2 · *The Times* (27 Nov 1973) · *The Guardian* (27 Nov 1973) · C. Moritz, ed., *Current Biography Yearbook* (1961), 195–6 · W. Rigdon, ed., *The biographical encyclopaedia & who's who of the American theatre* (1966) · A. Stanbrook, 'Happy as Larry', *Plays and Players* (May 1964), 42–6 · D. Shipman, *The great movie stars: the international years*, rev. edn (1980) · www.us.imdb.com · D. Thomson, *A biographical dictionary of film* (1994) · D. Quinlan, *Quinlan's film stars*, 4th edn (1996) · R. Pickard, *The Oscar stars from A–Z* (1996) · B. McFarlane, ed., *An autobiography of British cinema* (1997) · S. D'Amico, ed., *Enciclopedia dello spettacolo, suppl. 1955–1965* (Rome, 1966) · E. Katz, *The international film encyclopedia* (1980) · E. M. Truitt, *Who was who on screen*, 3rd edn (1983) · *WWW, 1981–90* · L. Maltin, *Leonard Maltin's movie encyclopedia* (1994) · *CGPLA Eng. & Wales* (1975)
Likenesses A. McBean, photograph, 1954, repro. in *Plays and Players* (Aug 1954) · film stills, repro. in D'Amico, ed., *Enciclopedia dello spettacolo*, 3 (1956), supplement, 1955–65 · film stills, repro. in Hickey and Smith, *The prince* · film stills, repro. in Stone, *One tear is enough* · photograph, repro. in Quinlan, *Quinlan's film stars* · photograph, repro. in *The Times* · photograph, repro. in *The Guardian* · photographs, repro. in Hickey and Smith, *The prince* · photographs, repro. in Stone, *One tear is enough* · photographs, Hult. Arch.
Wealth at death £34,349 in England and Wales: Bahaman administration sealed in England, 16 July 1975, *CGPLA Eng. & Wales*

Harvey, Margaret (1768–1858), poet, was the daughter of John Harvey, surgeon, of Sunderland. During the early years of her life she lived with her two younger sisters, Ann and Jane, in the care of an aunt, a Miss Ilderton, in Mosley Street, Newcastle upon Tyne. About 1812, after the death of their aunt, the Harvey sisters moved to a house at the White Cross, and it was here that Margaret Harvey wrote her first poem, at about the age of thirty-six. *The Lay of the Minstrel's Daughter: a Poem in Six Cantos* was published by subscription in 1814, and her *Monody on the Princess Charlotte* was published in 1818. About this time Margaret Harvey moved to Bishopwearmouth, co. Durham, where she assisted in keeping a ladies' school, and published *Raymond de Percy, or, The Tenant of the Tomb: a Romantic Melodrama* (1822). In the preface she invokes the spirit of Garrick. The piece was performed at Sunderland in April 1822, and some accounts maintain that she and her sisters lived in Sunderland for a time. Margaret Harvey wrote some other minor poems. She was described as 'endowed with remarkable energy of character', and 'slightly marked by the smallpox' (*N&Q*, 4th ser., 10.260). She died at 27 Villiers Street, Bishopwearmouth, on 18 June 1858.

Margaret Harvey's sister Jane was a painter of miniatures on ivory; Andrew Morton (1802–1845), the portrait painter, was her pupil.

FRANCIS WATT, rev. M. CLARE LOUGHLIN-CHOW

Sources *N&Q*, 2nd ser., 11 (1861), 389 · *N&Q*, 4th ser., 9 (1872), 469 · *N&Q*, 4th ser., 10 (1872), 93 · *N&Q*, 4th ser., 10 (1872), 260 · *GM*, 3rd ser., 5 (1858), 202 · Boase, *Mod. Eng. biog.* · d. cert.

Harvey, Sir Nicholas (c.1491–1532), diplomat, was the third son of William Harvey (d. 1538) of Ickworth, Suffolk, and Joan, daughter of John Cokett of Ampton, Suffolk. Descended from a leading Bedfordshire family, Nicholas Harvey's grandfather had settled in Suffolk, near Bury St Edmunds. By 1512, probably soon after he came of age, Harvey had married Elizabeth, daughter of Sir Thomas Fitzwilliam of Aldwark, Yorkshire, and the widow of Sir Thomas Mauleverer; they had at least one son, Thomas. About 1519, following the death of his first wife, Harvey apparently enjoyed the king's support in an (unsuccessful) attempt to wed an unknown widow; he subsequently married Bridget, daughter of Sir John Wiltshire of Stone Castle, Kent, and widow of Sir Richard Wingfield (d. 1525) of Kimbolton, Huntingdonshire. They had at least three sons and two daughters.

Having received the manor of Ickworth from his father in 1511, the young Harvey left Suffolk to seek his fortune. In 1513 he fought at Tournai under his kinsman Sir George Harvey, who probably introduced him to royal service. A member of the king's household by 1521, Harvey joined the garrison at Berwick soon afterwards. While serving there he regularly commanded men in border raids, and in 1523 was entrusted by Thomas Howard with urgent messages for the king concerning threats anticipated from Scotland. As reward for his military service, in May 1522 the king granted him the Bedfordshire manor of Backenho. By 1527 Harvey was once again at court, where he jousted to entertain the French ambassador, and in 1529 he was chosen first knight of the shire for Huntingdonshire in the Reformation parliament, reflecting his new standing in that county following his marriage to Lady Wingfield. By this time he had also been formally knighted.

Harvey's attendance at Westminster was cut short, however, for in June 1530 he was dispatched as English ambassador to Charles V, on the recommendation of his former commander Thomas Howard (now duke of Norfolk). He was a wise choice: the imperial ambassador Chapuys described the new envoy as 'well acquainted with the French and Flemish tongues, besides his being a man of great integrity, incapable of intriguing or lying', but also as a strong partisan of Anne Boleyn (*CSP Spain, 1529–30*, 586). Both Harvey and his wife were friends of Anne, and sympathetic to the evangelical cause. Harvey travelled first to Augsburg, where the emperor had convened a diet, arriving there early in July. The court remained until late November, before returning to Flanders. Harvey proved an adept defender of his royal master's Great Matter; he later related to the chronicler Edward Hall how at Ghent he had confounded a Spanish nobleman in debating the king's case. Despite such success, Harvey was replaced early in 1531 by Sir John Hacket, leaving Brussels on 12 February. The reason for his recall is unknown, but perhaps reflected the urgent need in parliament for defenders of the divorce proceedings.

Upon his return Harvey continued to promote Henry's cause, and it was while attending the king during a visit to Ampthill, Bedfordshire, where Queen Katherine resided, that Harvey fell ill and died on 5 August 1532. He was buried in Ampthill church, where a brass commemorates him. Although he left a will, it is now lost. His widow married Robert Tyrwhitt and probably died *c.*1535. But she was cited posthumously as a source of evidence against Queen Anne in 1536.

P. R. N. CARTER

Sources *LP Henry VIII*, vols. 1–5 · HoP, *Commons, 1509–58*, 2.310–11 · *CSP Spain, 1529–30* · D. MacCulloch, *Suffolk and the Tudors: politics and religion in an English county, 1500–1600* (1986) · *VCH Bedfordshire*, vol. 3 · E. Hall, *Henry VIII*, ed. C. Whibley, 2 (1904) · E. W. Ives, *Anne Boleyn* (1986) · brass sculpture, Ampthill parish church, Bedfordshire

Likenesses brass sculpture, Ampthill parish church, Bedfordshire · portrait?, Ickworth House, Park and Garden, Suffolk

Harvey, Oliver Charles, first Baron Harvey of Tasburgh (1893–1968), diplomatist and diarist, was born on 26 November 1893 at Rainthorpe Hall, near Norwich, the only son of Sir Charles Harvey, second baronet (1849–1928), landowner, and his second wife, Mary Anne Edith (*d.* 1929), daughter of G. F. Cooke, of Holmewood, Norwich. There were two half-sisters and a half-brother from his father's first marriage. Harvey was educated at Malvern College and at Trinity College, Cambridge, where he obtained a first in part one of the historical tripos in 1914. He served throughout the war in the Norfolk regiment, in France, Egypt, and Palestine, and was mentioned in dispatches.

After the war Harvey began his career in the diplomatic service, from 1920 in partnership with his wife, Maud Annora (Maudie; *d.* 1970), daughter of Arthur Watkin Williams-Wynn, landowner, of Coed-maen, Montgomeryshire, a woman of taste and accomplishment, whose Matisse-like sketch of her husband (reproduced in his *Diplomatic Diaries*) sympathetically captures his owlish mien. He served as second secretary in Rome from 1922 to 1925, and as first secretary in Athens from 1929 to 1931. In the latter year he found his niche in Paris, where he remained five years as head of chancery, and was a discriminating student of all things French. His path thereafter was an alternation between Paris and London, punctuated by Boswellian periods as private secretary and confidant to the temperamental Anthony Eden (1936–8 and 1941–3), then in his crown prince phase—a difficult and significant achievement.

Harvey served Eden with a devotion to which his posthumously published diary bears eloquent witness. 'Eden gave me his confidence most fully and I endeavoured to return it in the same spirit, loyally and to the best of my ability'. The diary itself, written 'hot' at the time, as he said, 'by one who then held a privileged position as observer and confidant', is a fascinating chronicle—hotter indeed than the diarist's equable exterior—a catalogue of the folly and foible of high stakes and high politics (*Diplomatic Diaries*, 11–12). It is especially illuminating on his beloved 'AE', and, by way of baleful counterpoint, on the ungovernable Winston Churchill:

> Really the PM is a lunatic: he gets in such a state of excitement that the wildest schemes seem reasonable. I hope to goodness we can defeat this one. AE believes the Cabinet and finally the King will restrain him, but the

Oliver Charles Harvey, first Baron Harvey of Tasburgh (1893–1968), by Walter Bird, 1958

Cabinet are a poor lot for stopping anything. (*War Diaries*, 70)

As private secretary to the foreign secretary, and as a convinced anti-appeaser, Harvey interpreted his duties widely, often proffering advice on matters of policy in terms critical of the prime minister and of his interference in foreign affairs. After Eden's resignation in February 1938, Harvey continued to offer unofficial advice to his former chief. His personal relations with Eden's successor, Halifax, were good but unenthusiastic; he noted that the new foreign secretary was less inclined to rely on his private secretary for political counsel, and more in the habit of resorting to the conventional channel, via the permanent under-secretary, for any advice on policy. Harvey remained at his post, with diminished influence, until he became minister in Paris in the dismal December 1939.

There Harvey's time was brief but eventful. France fell within a few months and Harvey was involved in the embassy's odyssey from Paris, via Touraine to Bordeaux, and evacuation in a British warship. He worked briefly at the Ministry of Information in charge of propaganda to the occupied countries of Europe, but it was no surprise that when Eden returned to the Foreign Office in December 1940 he took the first opportunity of reappointing his old private secretary, although Harvey was by now well above the rank normal for the post. 'What a signal justification of his previous period there', commented Harvey.

'He now succeeds his own successor who leaves with a very dusty reputation' (*War Diaries*, 10). From then on Harvey was closely involved in all the complicated issues which beset the Foreign Office during the war. He accompanied Eden on three trips to Moscow, the first at the dramatic moment when the Germans had been halted a bare 20 miles away in December 1941, and once to the United States. He was closely involved too in the controversies over the employment of Darlan and Giraud, the struggle over the recognition of the national committee of De Gaulle, the difficulties with the exiled Polish government, and the like. In all these questions his advice was forward looking, realistic, and on the side of the new forces which he believed would emerge in the open at the end of the war. His admiration for Eden in this period was not unqualified, though he continued to hope for his succession as prime minister, discouraging him from accepting the viceroyalty of India proffered by Churchill in 1943. That same year Harvey finally left Eden's service to become assistant under-secretary, and in 1946 deputy under-secretary (political) at the Foreign Office, where he worked closely with Ernest Bevin, whom he much admired.

In 1948 Harvey was appointed ambassador in Paris in succession to Duff Cooper. His intimate acquaintance with European and in particular French problems made the appointment natural, almost inevitable; his long tenure extended until 1954. Harvey's embassy was a very different one from the dazzling display of Duff and Diana Cooper, a display which he did not seek to emulate; but he was skilfully alert to the temper of the times. Strict in excluding from the embassy anyone tainted by collaboration with the Germans, he filled the beautiful house in the Faubourg St Honoré with carefully-selected parties of leading Frenchmen, mainly politicians. The food was delicious, the Harveys's distinguished collection of modern paintings ornamented the salon vert, and the discriminating style of their entertaining was exactly suited to the ethos of the Fourth Republic, whose leading statesmen were mostly men of refinement. To this ethos Harvey was almost ideally suited. His tenure marked one of the least acrimonious periods of Anglo-French relations in recent history.

In 1954, on retirement, Harvey was created a baron; in the same year he succeeded his half-brother as fourth baronet. He had been appointed CMG in 1937, CB in 1944, KCMG in 1946, GCMG in 1948, and GCVO in 1950. He took little part in the debates in the House of Lords although he attended with some regularity, sitting on the cross-benches and normally voting on the Labour or Liberal side. His retirement, spent in London with winters in the south of France, was peaceful and uneventful. He enjoyed his trusteeship of the Wallace Collection, and was active in the Franco-British Society, of which he became chairman. He died, at 37 Parkside, Knightsbridge, on 29 November 1968. His elder son, Peter (b. 1921), succeeded to the baronetcy and the barony; his younger son, John (b. 1923), edited the diary for publication, according to his father's wishes:

Its whole value, if it has a value, lies in its 'hotness', in the immediate impression and atmosphere. I am the first to recognise how many of the first reactions and impressions and judgements were proved wrong and would be admitted wrong by myself now, but that is not the point. This is how we saw things at the time. ... The more light that can be shed on the circumstances in which impressions were formed, decisions and actions taken, the better.   (*Diplomatic Diaries*, 11–12)

It is a fitting final testament.   ALEX DANCHEV

Sources DNB · *The diplomatic diaries of Oliver Harvey, 1937–40*, ed. J. Harvey (1970) · *The war diaries of Oliver Harvey*, ed. J. Harvey (1978) · *The Times* (30 Nov 1968) · *CGPLA Eng. & Wales* (1969)
Archives BL, diaries and papers, Add. MSS 56379–56402 | BL, corresp. with P. V. Emrys-Evans, Add. MSS 58235, 58268 · CAC Cam., corresp. with Duff Cooper, DUFC · U. Birm. L., corresp. with Lord Avon, AP 23/26
Likenesses W. Stoneman, photograph, 1947, NPG · W. Bird, photograph, 1958, NPG [*see illus.*] · MAH [M. A. Harvey], pencil? and charcoal?, repro. in J. Harvey, ed., *Diplomatic diaries*
Wealth at death £134,209: probate, 25 Feb 1969, *CGPLA Eng. & Wales*

Harvey, Sir (Henry) Paul (1869–1948), civil servant and writer of reference books, was born on 1 October 1869 in Paris, France, the only child of Henri Joseph François de Triqueti, baron de Triqueti (1804–1874), a respected French sculptor, whose commissions included the cenotaph of Prince Albert in the Albert Memorial Chapel, Windsor Castle. Orphaned at an early age, Paul was brought up in Paris and at the Château de Varennes, near Montargis, Loiret, by Blanche Lee Childe, *née* de Triqueti, a cultivated Frenchwoman married to an expatriate American. When she died in 1886 her friend (Isabella) Augusta, Lady Gregory (later a dramatist), took responsibility for Harvey (the surname by which he was known), then at Rugby School. He took a first in *literae humaniores* after studying at New College, Oxford, from 1888 to 1892. Early adversity, thought Lady Gregory, had moulded a character of rare gentleness and rectitude.

Harvey entered the civil service in February 1893 as a clerk in the War Office. His talents were soon recognized, for he became first assistant private secretary and then private secretary to the secretary of state for war (1895–1900), Lord Lansdowne, who had him appointed a CB in 1901. Harvey, who longed for marriage and a home of his own, enjoyed matrimonial advice from the novelist Henry James, another friend of Mrs Lee Childe. On 6 August 1896 he married Ethel Frances Persse (1873–1966), niece of Lady Gregory. Their only child, Susan (b. 1897), grew up to be a *Picture Post* photographer, publishing as Merlyn Severn.

In 1902 Harvey was appointed auditor of the 2nd army corps. His subsequent career was financial rather than military in its focus. He moved to Athens in 1903 as the British delegate to the International Commission for the Control of Greek Finance. After the indemnity imposed at the end of the Graeco-Turkish War (1897) drove Greece into bankruptcy, the great powers had taken control of Greek indirect tax revenues in order to service foreign debt. He then represented Britain on the rather more controversial International Commission for the Control of

Macedonian Finances, created in May 1905 as part of the Mürzteg reforms of Turkey in Europe to manage the budgets of the troubled provinces of Kosova, Salonika, and Monastir. While living in Salonika (Thessaloniki), he held the local rank of counsellor with the British embassy in Constantinople.

Having displayed tact and ability in handling the Ottoman Turks, Harvey replaced Sir Vincent Corbett as financial adviser to the Egyptian government in October 1907. Egypt, while nominally part of the Ottoman empire, had been occupied by British forces since 1882, so the financial adviser was effectively a senior imperial official. Harvey looked the part: tall and handsome with a large moustache. He faced an Egyptian economy in severe recession. The *entente cordiale* (1904), by mollifying French creditors of Egypt, had allowed a fiscal relaxation that began a speculative bubble—and now it had burst. He pursued a tough retrenchment policy and suggested extending the Suez Canal Company's concession (due to end in 1968) by another forty years in return for £4 million in Egyptian currency. Though Egyptian nationalists blocked this revenue-raising scheme, he had succeeded in balancing the budget by 1911, when he became Sir Paul Harvey KCMG. However, after Kitchener, the new British agent and consul-general, proposed a land reclamation programme that Harvey deemed too costly, a swift battle of wills ended in Sir Paul's resignation in 1912.

Back in London, Harvey acted as the chief auditor of the National Health Insurance Commission from 1912 until 1918. He represented Britain (1913–14) on the International Commission for the Settlement of Financial Questions arising out of the Balkan War, directed the prisoners of war information bureau (1914–16), and went to the USA in October 1915 to administer the Anglo-French war loan on behalf of the Treasury. His efforts to boost a flagging bond market were hindered by friction with J. P. Morgan & Co., who saw his presence as a slight on their own performance as American financial agents of the British government. In February 1916 Harvey was appointed secretary of the new Air Board, an advisory body intended to deal with the competing demands of the Royal Naval Air Service and the Royal Flying Corps. He opined in private that its first chairman, Lord Curzon, merely exacerbated disagreement. A new Air Ministry superseded the board in January 1918.

Harvey returned to Cairo as financial adviser in September 1919, when, despite serious political unrest, the Egyptian economy was enjoying the tail-end of a wartime boom. A year later he chose to retire, receiving the order of the Nile to add to his earlier Ottoman honours. Although not in the best of health—he endured fierce headaches—he was finding time heavy on his hands by the late 1920s. After indexing *The Persian Gulf* by Sir Arnold T. Wilson in 1927, he asked Oxford University Press if it had any other work for him. Kenneth Sisam of the press offered to pay £500 for a large new A–Z reference book to contain short biographies of English authors, synopses of major works, and explanations of literary allusions. The

Oxford Companion to English Literature, 866 pages long, appeared in 1932. Harvey had written nearly all of it himself, being both highly industrious and well read. The entries derived a semblance of objectivity from the deliberate conventionality of their judgements. Sales exceeded expectation, and Oxford University Press persuaded him to follow it up with *The Oxford Companion to Classical Literature* (1937). Much of *The Oxford Companion to French Literature* (1959) was also his work. Harvey, who latterly lived at Bierton House, Midhurst, Sussex, died on 30 December 1948 at Pendean, West Lavington, Sussex. The body was cremated. His companion to English literature became a standard reference volume and passed through four editions before being supplanted by a new version in 1985.

JASON TOMES

Sources P. Sutcliffe, *The Oxford University Press: an informal history* (1978) • *Lady Gregory's diaries, 1892–1902*, ed. J. Pethica (1996) • Lord Lloyd, *Egypt since Cromer*, 1 (1933) • P. Mellini, *Sir Eldon Gorst* (1977) • K. Burk, *Britain, America and the sinews of war, 1914–1918* (1985) • 'New year honours', *The Times* (2 Jan 1911) • *Lady Gregory's journals*, ed. D. Murphy, 2 vols. (1978–87) • m. cert. • d. cert. • J. Foster, *Oxford men, 1880–1892: with a record of their schools, honours, and degrees* (1893) • J. Turner, ed., *The dictionary of art*, 34 vols. (1996)

Archives Oxford University Press, archives • PRO, Balkan Commission papers, FO 800 | PRO, FO files; War Office files • U. Durham L., corresp. with Sir Reginald Wingate

Likenesses photograph; http://www.oxfordreference.com/pub/views/6B04.html, accessed 31 Oct 2002

Wealth at death £16,206 6s. 7d.: probate, 16 Feb 1949, CGPLA Eng. & Wales

Harvey, Richard (*bap.* 1560, *d.* 1630), astrologer and polemicist, was born in Saffron Walden, Essex, and baptized there on 15 April 1560, the second son of John Harvey (*d.* 1593), a prosperous master rope maker, and his wife, Ales (Alice; *d.* 1613). Like his elder brother, Gabriel *Harvey, and younger brother John *Harvey, he attended the local grammar school and went on to Cambridge, matriculating at Pembroke College as a pensioner on 15 June 1575. He proceeded BA in 1578, and MA in 1581, when he was also elected a fellow and appointed university praelector in philosophy. Harvey shared his elder brother's pugnacious disposition as well as his diminutive stature, and his university career was marked by controversy. His enemy, the writer Thomas Nashe, who dubbed him 'Pigmey Dicke' (*Works of Thomas Nashe*, 1.270), pronounced him 'a notable ruffian with his pen' (ibid., 3.81) and declared he was always 'in hate' (ibid., 3.82). Harvey was a zealous champion of the reformed logic of Peter Ramus against Aristotelian methods and, according to Nashe, once 'set [an effigy of] Aristotle, with his heeles upward, on the Schoole gates at Cambridge, and asses eares on hys head' (ibid., 3.85). Not surprisingly, such behaviour provoked much resentment. The students of Clare College devised a satirical college play about the three Harvey brothers, and another college play at Peterhouse, entitled *Duns Furens: Dick Harvey in a Frensie*, so enraged its victim that he smashed the college windows in protest and was put in the stocks as punishment. Harvey promoted Ramist dialectics in more seemly fashion in

Ephemeron (1583), a collection of fifteen short Latin dialogues dedicated to the court favourite, Robert, earl of Essex.

In the spring of 1583 Harvey achieved far greater notoriety with his first and only publication on astrology. *An astrological discourse upon the great and notable conjunction of the two superiour planets, Saturne and Iupiter*, entered in the Stationers' register on 22 January, commented on the conjunction itself and on prophecies concerning the year 1583 by the Bohemian astrologer Cyprian Leowicz (Leovitius) and Regiomontanus. Harvey predicted dramatic and apocalyptic upheavals. A great wind would spring up at noon on Sunday 28 April 1583 (the precise moment of the conjunction), heralding great woes which might culminate within a few years in the final dissolution or total reconstitution of the world. Harvey had discussed his ideas with John Young, bishop of Rochester, and Dr Lewen, son-in-law to John Aylmer, bishop of London, and he dedicated his tract to Aylmer, who received it graciously. The text itself is addressed to his brother Gabriel, who was far more sceptical about judicial astrology. Despite the sober tone of the work, its sensational message provoked widespread alarm and controversy. In March Harvey's younger brother John published *An Astrologicall Addition* to answer the critics, while at the end of the month the astrologer and mathematician Thomas Heth rushed out a formidable *Confutation* of Harvey and other English and continental writers on the conjunction. Bishop Aylmer, no doubt now highly embarrassed, felt it necessary to preach against Harvey's work in a sermon at Paul's Cross. The total failure of the predictions brought a storm of ridicule, both in Cambridge and in London. Richard Tarleton mocked Harvey on the stage while William Elderton composed derisive ballads. Even before publishing the *Discourse*, Harvey had decided to pursue an ecclesiastical career, and he was to write nothing more on astrology.

Given his combative nature, it was unlikely that Harvey would be able to avoid controversy for long, and at the end of the 1580s he intervened in the pamphlet war raging over the radical puritan squibs published under the name of 'Martin Marprelate'. In *Plaine Percivall, the Peacemaker of England* (1589), published anonymously, Harvey condemned both the so-called Martinists and their opponents and called for peace between them. Despite the work's eirenic professions, its pugnacious style was calculated to inflame passions rather than still them. It certainly irritated Thomas Nashe, who had published several pieces against the Martinists, and he alluded to it dismissively in his *First Parte of Pasqvils Apologie* (1590). Harvey's *A Theologicall Discourse of the Lambe of God and his Enemies* (1590), dedicated to the earl of Essex, was a much longer and more wide-ranging work, based on sermons he had given earlier at Cambridge. It staunchly defended the established church against its puritan critics, whom he condemned as subversive hypocrites. Though much of the work was relatively restrained in tone, Harvey included a long, intemperate attack on Marprelate, branding him 'a bloudy massacrer and cutthroat in iesters

apparell'. In a provocative epistle added as an afterthought he also attacked Nashe, whom he dubbed an insolent upstart tilting at authority in the literary world just as Marprelate did in the church. Nashe had to some degree provoked this snub, which was to trigger a celebrated literary row. In a preface to Robert Greene's *Menaphon* (1589), which itself contained a verse ridiculing the Harvey family, Nashe had lavishly praised Greene while naming Gabriel Harvey among the literary pygmies of the age. The fact that Richard Harvey and Nashe held very similar views on the Martinists was ignored in the storm which now broke.

It was not, however, Richard Harvey but his brother Gabriel who took up the cudgels to defend the family's honour. Richard did not reply in print to the abuse Nashe flung at him, and his later years are poorly documented. He was appointed rector of Chislehurst, Kent, in 1586 and remained as minister there for over forty years until his death. Marlowe allegedly dismissed him as 'an asse, good for nothing but to preach of the Iron Age' (*Works of Thomas Nashe*, 3.85). His father died in 1593, leaving him an annuity of £20 payable on the death of his mother. 1593 also saw Harvey's last publication, *Philadelphus, or, A Defence of Brutes, and the Brutans History*, dedicated again to the earl of Essex. In this curious patriotic tract he defended the traditional account of Brute's escape from Troy and settlement in England against the criticisms of the Scottish historian George Buchanan, and offered moral reflections on early English history as recounted by Geoffrey of Monmouth. In 1593 Nashe referred contemptuously to Harvey as 'a blind Vicar' (ibid., 1.262) with 'decayed eyes, … starke blinde' (ibid.), and it is at least possible that physical disability explains the subsequent silence. In a letter addressed to Essex in 1598, Richard Harvey (or a namesake) complained of his remote living and the hostility of his bishop. Certainly Harvey progressed no further in the church, and the death of Essex in 1601 deprived him of his main patron.

Harvey never married. Several contemporary anecdotes touched unflatteringly on his private life, however, and Nashe described a comically bungled attempt to seduce a Cambridge milkmaid. He alleged too that Harvey had preached against dancing while secretly admiring his 'wench' dancing on the green. Robert Greene claimed that Harvey's parishioners resented him for being too familiar with their wives, a smear Gabriel Harvey angrily repudiated in his *Foure Letters* (1592). Richard Harvey died in 1630, some time before 10 June. In his will, drawn up in 1625, he left bequests to his surviving nephews and nieces, and his aged brother Gabriel acted as executor. Nashe claimed that Harvey was also the author of *A Defence of Short Haire* (entered in the Stationers' register in 1593 but now lost), and that in his early years he 'was wont to pen Gods iudgements upon such and such and one, as thicke as Water-men at Westminster bridge' (*Works of Thomas Nashe*, 3.84). Though neither claim is impossible, there is nothing to confirm them.

BERNARD CAPP

Sources R. Harvey, *A theologicall discourse of the lambe of God and his enemies* (1590) · *The works of Thomas Nashe*, ed. R. B. McKerrow, 5 vols.

(1904–10); repr. with corrections and notes by F. P. Wilson (1958) • G. Harvey, *Foure letters* (1592) • V. F. Stern, *Gabriel Harvey* (1979) • E. A. Webb, G. W. Miller, and J. Beckwith, eds., *The history of Chislehurst: its church, manors, and parish* (1899) • will, CKS, DRb PW 28 • Bishop of Rochester's register book, CKS, DRb Arl/16 • J. Harvey, *An astrologicall addition* (1583)

Harvey, Stephen

Harvey, Stephen (1655–1707), lawyer and poet, was born on 20 October 1655 at Walthamstow, the son of Stephen Harvey (1622–1688), of East Beechworth, a barrister of the Middle Temple, and his wife, Dorothy (1631–1694), daughter of William Conyers, of Walthamstow, sergeant-at-law. He had two younger sisters, Dorothy and Elizabeth. After attending Merchant Taylors' School, 1668–71, he matriculated as Merchant Taylor fellow and Sir Thomas White scholar at St John's College, Oxford, on 27 June 1671, was admitted to the Middle Temple on 12 February 1673, and was called to the bar on 21 May 1680. He married his cousin Anne, daughter of John Harvey, of St Mary-at-Hill, on 15 August 1693. They had seven children: John, admitted to the Middle Temple on 17 May 1709, Elizabeth, Stephen, born at East Beechworth on 14 February 1700, Ann, Dorothy, Frances, Martin, and William.

Harvey made three contributions as a verse translator to the publishing ventures of Jacob Tonson. His translation of Juvenal's notorious ninth satire appeared in *The Satires of Decimus Junius Juvenalis, Translated … by Mr. Dryden and Several other Eminent Hands* (1693 [i.e. 1692]). His translation of 'The Passion of Byblis' from the ninth book of Ovid's *Metamorphoses*, which borrows some phrases from John Oldham's translation of the same episode, and of 'Jupiter and Europa' from the fourth book, both appeared in *The Annual Miscellany: for the Year 1694* (1694). All three poems treat of an unusual sexual situation without prurience, and Harvey shows himself to be a fluent versifier whose competence occasionally rises to excellence.

Harvey's friendship with John, Baron Somers, led to his being appointed steward of the royal manor of Reigate when it was granted to Somers on his becoming lord chancellor in 1697, and the following year he became MP for the borough of Reigate, holding both positions until his death. Harvey acted as deputy steward or steward for other manors, including John Evelyn's Surrey estates, where he is recorded as serving as steward in September 1701. In May 1706 he was appointed a puisne justice of the Anglesey circuit, and on 25 October that year he became a master of the bench of the Middle Temple. Harvey died on 24 May 1707.　　　　　　　　　　ALEXANDER LINDSAY

Sources *The satires of Decimus Junius Juvenalis, translated into English verse, by Mr. Dryden and several other eminent hands* (1693), 175–88 [i.e. 1692] • [J. Dryden], ed., *The annual miscellany, for the year 1694: being the fourth part of miscellany poems* (1694), 202–16, 254–8 • H. F. Brooks, 'Dryden's Juvenal and the Harveys', *Philological Quarterly*, 48 (1969), 12–19 • J. B. Whitmore and A. W. Hughes Clarke, eds., *London visitation pedigrees, 1664*, Harleian Society, 92 (1940), 74, 164–5 • J. Aubrey, *The natural history and antiquities of the county of Surrey*, 4 (1718), 276 • Mrs E. P. Hart, ed., *Merchant Taylors' School register, 1561–1934*, 2 vols. (1936) • H. A. C. Sturgess, ed., *Register of admissions to the Honourable Society of the Middle Temple, from the fifteenth century to the year 1944*, 1 (1949), 186 • J. B. Williamson, ed., *The Middle Temple bench book*, 2nd edn, 1 (1937), 151 • O. Manning and W. Bray, *The history and antiquities of the county of Surrey*, 1 (1804), 292; 2 (1809), 208 • J. E. Smith, *Parliamentary representation of Surrey, 1290 to 1924* (1927), 105 • Evelyn, *Diary*, 5.478 • BL, Add. MS 38484, fol. 249

Archives Bodl. Oxf., transcripts | BL, Add. MS 38484, fol. 249

Harvey, Sir Thomas

Harvey, Sir Thomas (1775–1841), naval officer, was fourth son of Admiral Sir Henry *Harvey (1737–1810) and his wife, Elizabeth (1739/40–1823), daughter of Captain William Boys RN. He entered the navy in 1787, served as master's mate of the *Ramillies*—then commanded by his father—in the action in the north Atlantic of 1 June 1794, and was promoted lieutenant in the following October. As lieutenant of the *Prince of Wales* (98 guns), with his father and cousin Sir John *Harvey (1772–1837), he was present in the action off Lorient on 23 June 1795. He was promoted commander in July 1796, commanded the sloop *Pelican* at the capture of Trinidad in February 1797, and was advanced to post rank on 27 March 1797. He afterwards commanded the frigates *Lapwing* and *Unité* in the Mediterranean and West Indies; upon returning to England in the latter, he joined the squadron in the Thames under Nelson, who for a short time hoisted his flag on board the *Unité*.

Towards the end of 1805 Harvey was appointed to the *Standard* (64 guns), which joined Lord Collingwood's flag in the Mediterranean, and which, in February 1807, was one of the squadron under Sir John Thomas Duckworth in the Dardanelles, and was specially engaged in the destruction of the Turkish squadron at the entrance to the straits. In the return passage she was struck by one of the huge stone shot, 2 feet or more in diameter and weighing 800 pounds, which broke through to the lower deck, caused an explosion of cartridges which wounded several men, and set the ship on fire. After returning to England in the autumn of 1808, Harvey was appointed early in the following year to the *Majestic* (74 guns), attached to the fleet in the Baltic; he afterwards commanded the *Sceptre* (74 guns) in the North Sea. In June 1815 he was made a CB, and from 1819 to 1821 he commanded the guardship *Northumberland* (74 guns) at Sheerness, from which he was superseded on attaining his flag on 19 July. In April 1833 he was made a KCB; he became vice-admiral on 10 January 1837, and in March 1839 was appointed commander-in-chief in the West Indies, a post previously held by his father and his cousin John.

Harvey married on 28 March 1805, his first cousin Sarah, youngest daughter of Captain John *Harvey (1740–1794); they had five daughters and three sons, of whom Thomas, born in 1810, died a rear-admiral in 1868, and Henry, born in 1812, died an admiral in 1887; the third, William, was in holy orders. Harvey, during his tenure of office, died at Admiralty House, Clarence Hill, Bermuda, on 28 May 1841; he was buried in Bermuda.

J. K. LAUGHTON, *rev.* ROGER MORRISS

Sources J. Marshall, *Royal naval biography*, 1/2 (1823), 797–804 • O'Byrne, *Naval biog. dict.* • *United Service Journal*, 3 (1841), 101 • *GM*, 2nd ser., 16 (1841), 204 • P. Mackesy, *The war in the Mediterranean, 1803–1810* (1957) • R. Muir, *Britain and the defeat of Napoleon, 1807–1815* (1996)

Archives NMM, journals and papers

Harvey, Thomas (1812–1884), philanthropist, was born on 15 March 1812 at Barnsley in Yorkshire, the second of five children of William Harvey, a linen manufacturer, and his wife, Susanna, *née* Atkinson. Both parents were Quakers. He was educated at a dame-school and Barnsley grammar school before being sent to the Quaker school at Ackworth, Yorkshire, in 1822, where he remained about three years, followed by a further year at William Simpson's school at York. Shortly after leaving school he was apprenticed to W. and T. Southall, chemists and druggists of Birmingham, and during his apprenticeship made the acquaintance of Joseph Sturge. He subsequently commenced business as a pharmacist in Leeds.

From his youth Harvey took great interest in philanthropic movements, and in 1836 he accompanied Sturge to the West Indies to make inquiries into the condition of the former slaves, visiting Antigua, Montserrat, Dominica, St Lucia, Barbados, and Jamaica. He returned in the following year, and in 1838 published, together with Sturge, a lengthy report calling for the termination of the unpaid apprenticeship system which had replaced slavery. He gave much time to promoting measures for the relief of the former slaves. On 16 October 1845 he married Sarah Grace, daughter of Joseph Fryer of Rastrick, a Quaker. They had three children.

In the autumn of 1856 Harvey accompanied Sturge to Finland. While the British fleet was stationed in the Baltic during the Crimean War much damage had been done to property, and the tsar's Finnish subjects endured considerable hardship. Sturge and Harvey published a report of this visit in the same year, and they formed a committee which raised, chiefly from Quakers, the sum of £9000 for distribution in Finland. In 1866 Harvey again visited Jamaica, accompanied by Thomas Brewin, to inquire into the Gordon riots, which had been suppressed with great harshness in 1865, and to distribute among the sufferers funds subscribed by the British Quakers. In 1867 the two men published a narrative of their tour. In that year, accompanied by Isaac Robson, Harvey travelled to the colonies of Mennonites in southern Russia, which had been persecuted for their pacifism. Harvey and other Quakers superintended the resettlement of many Mennonites in Canada.

In the same year Harvey retired from business and devoted himself to religious, philanthropic, and charitable work in Leeds and elsewhere. He was recorded as a Quaker minister in 1868. He retained his interest in slavery, publishing a volume on the Polynesian slave trade in 1872, and was a dedicated worker for temperance and international peace. For many years he acted as honorary secretary of an institution for blind, deaf, and deaf mute people. During his early years in business Harvey was hard-pressed financially, but later he contributed substantially to his charities with the help of funds bequeathed by his brothers. In May 1884 the Quaker yearly meeting appointed Harvey, J. B. Braithwaite, William Robinson, and Thomas Pumphrey as a deputation to their

co-religionists in Canada, among whom there existed doctrinal differences. The labour injured Harvey's already feeble health. He died on 25 December at Ashwood, his residence at Headingley Hill, near Leeds. His condition was diagnosed as pneumonia acting on a chronically weakened heart. He was buried four days later in the Quaker burial-ground at Adel, near Leeds. His wife survived him.

Harvey was a man of considerable scientific acumen, a good classical and Hebrew scholar, and a conscientious student even in his old age. He was as remarkable for severe integrity in business as for his gentleness and refinement in private life. He was a member of the Leeds school board during its earlier years, and was always a zealous promoter of education. A clear and simple speaker and efficient preacher, he also wrote on scriptural themes and was a frequent contributor to the Quaker and secular periodical press.

A. C. BICKLEY, *rev.* ALEX TYRRELL

Sources S. G. Harvey, *Memorials of Thomas Harvey: compiled from a short autobiography, and from his own writings and letters* (1886) · *Leeds Mercury* (26 Dec 1884) · *The Friend*, new ser., 25 (1885), 3–4 · *British Friend*, 43 (Jan 1885) · A. Tyrrell, *Joseph Sturge and the 'moral radical party' in early Victorian Britain* (c.1987) · m. cert. · CGPLA Eng. & Wales (1885)

Archives RS Friends, Lond.

Likenesses engraving, repro. in Harvey, *Memorials of Thomas Harvey*

Wealth at death £48,061 3s. 10d.: probate, 13 Feb 1885, CGPLA Eng. & Wales

Harvey, William (*d.* 1567), herald, is first referred to on 8 December 1540, when he was sent with dispatches to Bishop Gardiner on embassy to Emperor Charles V. Nothing is known of his origins or parents, but one sibling, Thomas, a London grocer, is recorded. Harvey joined the College of Arms on his appointment as Hampnes pursuivant, 5 February 1541, at a salary of 8d. per day. On 18 June 1544 he was promoted to the office of Bluemantle pursuivant, and by patent dated 28 September 1545 he was created Somerset herald. During these years his employment was mainly in France and the Low Countries, attending particularly the embassy of William (afterwards Lord) Paget, who became his patron. Other diplomatic missions took him to Denmark, Spain, and several times to Germany. In August 1547 he was attached to the army sent against the Scots. By patent dated 4 February 1550 Edward VI created him Norroy king of arms. In the same year he became a member of the Skinners' Company, and on 10 June 1560 he was elected a warden of the company, marking the occasion with a most lavish feast. Queen Mary deputed him to declare war on France at Rheims on 7 June 1557, with a reward of £20. Having created him Clarenceux king of arms on 6 September 1557 following the death of Thomas Hawley, the queen herself set a crown upon his head in a ceremony at St James's on 21 November.

Harvey's visitations were more extensive and thorough than those of his predecessors. It was while he held the office of Clarenceux that the practice of visiting individual gentlemen in their own houses was superseded by a more judicial system of summoning groups of gentry to appear before him on specified days. As Norroy he made a visitation of the north (1552), and as Clarenceux he visited in person or by deputy fifteen southern counties, an intensive campaign continued by his successor Robert Cooke. He was similarly energetic in granting arms and in undertaking the ceremonial arrangements for funerals. His learning and integrity, however, not only attracted the strictures of J. H. Round (who demolished a number of his pedigrees), but were also the subject of vicious attacks from his contemporary, Gilbert Dethick, Garter king of arms. The rivalry between the two appears to have reached its height in 1562, in an unseemly quarrel over the funeral of the first Lord Mordaunt, in the course of which Harvey claimed that rather than give up his official books to Dethick 'he would stoppe Jakesses with them' (Coll. Arms, Vincent MS 92, p. 488). In June 1565 the earl marshal imposed a temporary prohibition on Harvey from visiting his province. Dethick's petition to the earl marshal listing complaints against Harvey alleged the granting of false or incorrect arms and impropriety over Harvey's executorship of Thomas Hawley's will. The will was declared invalid, but Harvey nevertheless appears to have secured the prized bequest of Hawley's books.

With his wife, Etheldreda (surname perhaps Welles) Harvey had at least two daughters: Anne, who married John Sackville esquire, and Meldred, whose baptism on 24 July 1562, in the parish of St Bride's, was attended by godparents Sir William Cordell, master of the rolls, Lady Bacon, and Lady Cecil, evidence of the strength of Harvey's connections. One indication of his material prosperity, even early in his career, is the grant to him on 4 July 1548, following the surrender of a £20 life annuity, of Trinity Hall and other property of the dissolved fraternity of the Holy Trinity in Aldersgate. He died at Thame, on 27 February 1567, while on a visitation of Oxfordshire, and was buried there. The administration of his goods was granted to his widow on 26 March.   ANN PAYNE

Sources *DNB* · W. H. Godfrey, A. Wagner, and H. Stanford London, *The College of Arms, Queen Victoria Street* (1963) · *The diary of Henry Machyn, citizen and merchant-taylor of London, from AD 1550 to AD 1563*, ed. J. G. Nichols, CS, 42 (1848) · *LP Henry VIII*, vols. 16–21 · *CSP dom.*, 1547–58; 1601–3, addenda, 1547–65 · *CPR*, 1547–53 · Rymer, *Foedera*, 3rd edn, 6/3.172–3, 179, 181; 6/4.60 · Coll. Arms, Vincent MS 92, pp. 482–90 · officers of arms, Coll. Arms, vol. 2, pp. 397–8, 403 · partition book 1, 1528–82, Coll. Arms, fols. 265r, 283r · Coll. Arms, Brooke's collection, I. C. B. 82, fols. 122–3 · GL, MSS 5141; 13474; 30727/3; 30728/1, fol. 10v; 31693; Add. MSS 110, 111 · L. Campbell and F. Steer, *A catalogue of manuscripts in the College of Arms collections*, 1 (1988), 5–7, 17–19, 483, 563 · A. R. Wagner, *The records and collections of the College of Arms* (1952), 56, 68–9, 78–9 · A. Wagner, *Heralds of England: a history of the office and College of Arms* (1967), 171–2, 182–7, 206, 209 · M. Noble, *A history of the College of Arms* (1805), 129, 144, 153, 168–9 · [F. W. Dendy], ed., *Visitations of the north*, 1, SurtS, 122 (1912) · P. Basing, ed., *Parish fraternity register: fraternity of the Holy Trinity and SS. Fabian and Sebastian in the parish of St Botolph without Aldersgate*, London RS, 18 (1982), xxv · J. H. Round, *Studies in peerage and family history* (1901), 134–44

Archives BL, Harley MSS, charters and rolls · BL, Harley MSS, visitations · BL, charters and rolls, Add. MSS · BL, heraldic collections and papers, Add. MSS 4969, 19816, 59865 · Coll. Arms, MSS owned by him, L and M series · Coll. Arms, visitations · Devon RO, visitation of Devon · GL, Skinners' Company material, and grants relating to property of the Holy Trinity fraternity · Plymouth and West Devon RO, visitation of Wiltshire, bound with arms of Devon gentlemen emblazoned by J. Goff · S. Antiquaries, Lond., records of arms in Suffolk and Essex churches and houses · Suffolk RO, Ipswich, visitation of Suffolk

Likenesses engraving (after illuminated initial), repro. in J. Dallaway, *Inquiries into the origin and progress of the science of heraldry in England* (1793), pl. 12 · illuminated portrait initial, BL, Blenheim papers, Add. Charter 76069 · illuminated portrait initial, BL, Add. MS 59865

Harvey, William (1578–1657), physician and discoverer of the circulation of the blood, was born on 1 April 1578 at Folkestone, Kent. His father, Thomas (1549–1623), and his second wife, Joan (1556–1605), *née* Halke, had two daughters, Sarah (1580–1591) and Amy (b. 1596), and six other sons, John (b. 1582), Thomas (b. 1585), Daniel (b. 1587), Eliab (b. 1590), and the twins Michael and Matthew (b. 1593). William was thus the couple's eldest child. There was also a daughter from Thomas's previous marriage. Thomas was a farmer and a carrier with a business between Folkestone and London; Harvey's birthplace was accordingly known as 'the Post House'. Harvey's brothers succeeded as merchants, or at court, and were able to assist him in his career in a material way. Harvey was short, with black hair, as a young man, and bright brown eyes; John Aubrey thought him 'very cholerique'.

Education, marriage, and early career Details of Harvey's early education are sketchy; however, by 1588 he was attending the King's School, Canterbury. Here he learned his Latin, which was businesslike rather than elegant, and occasionally idiosyncratic. He went on to Gonville and Caius College, Cambridge, to which he was admitted on the last day of May 1593. The old Gonville Hall had been refounded by John Caius in 1567, who was its master on his death in 1573. Caius was a notable scholar who had studied medicine under Montanus and who had shared lodgings with the anatomist Vesalius; possibly his college was attractive to those with an eye on medicine as a career, for one of Caius's innovations was to procure the bodies of executed criminals for dissection. These anatomies were probably still performed in Harvey's day, although his tutor was not a medical man but George Estey, a clergyman who taught Hebrew.

In Michaelmas 1593 Harvey was awarded a Matthew Parker scholarship. The intention of its founder, the archbishop, was that his endowment should enable a man born in Kent and educated at the King's School to study medicine. Harvey graduated BA in 1597 and continued to receive his annual stipend of £3 0s. 8d. until 1599; clearly he was taught the bulk of his natural philosophy and medicine in Cambridge.

In early 1600 Harvey was in Padua, an understandable choice for an ambitious medical student. He furthered his anatomical education with Girolamo Fabrizi of Acquapendente (Fabricius) who was carrying out original anatomical research in a manner derived from Aristotle. This was to be of great importance to Harvey. Little more than two years after arriving in Padua, Harvey was awarded his MD degree on 25 April 1602. He was incorporated at Cambridge in the same year. On his return to England, Harvey

William Harvey (1578–1657), attrib. Daniel Mytens, *c.*1627

took a house in the parish of St Martin Ludgate, London, and sought to be admitted to the College of Physicians, in order to be able to practise in the capital. He was first examined on 4 May 1603 but not admitted, although he was allowed to practise. He was examined a second time nearly a year later and a third on 11 May 1604, when he was approved for a candidateship. Further rituals of admission followed in August, and finally on 5 October he was sworn in as a licentiate. Harvey was now in a position to marry, and he did so the following month, the marriage licence being dated 24 November 1604. His wife was Elizabeth Browne (*d.* 1645×52), daughter of Lancelot *Browne (*d.* 1605), physician to James I and an important fellow of the College of Physicians. William and Elizabeth had no children; all that we know of her from Harvey's own words was that she kept a parrot. Before his death Browne tried unsuccessfully to secure a position for his son-in-law as physician to the Tower of London. Nevertheless Harvey became known at court, perhaps through the good offices of his brother John, who was in the king's service, and ultimately Harvey became physician to St Bartholomew's Hospital, on 14 October 1609.

Harvey pursued his career in the College of Physicians with vigour. He was appointed a censor in 1613 and reappointed in 1625 and 1627. Therefore, on the eve of publishing a book that demonstrated the circulation of the blood and undermined the theories of Galen, he was examining applicants to the college on the orthodoxy of their Galenism. He became an elect of the college in 1627 and treasurer in 1628.

Discovery of the circulation of the blood When, in 1615, Harvey was elected to the Lumleian lectureship in the College of Physicians he made detailed preparations for his course

of lectures (the notes survive). He had no special interest in the heart, but was aware that for several centuries its primacy in the body, asserted by Aristotle and defended by scholastic philosophers, had been challenged by the medical men, who based their views on Galen (who believed that the brain was the primary organ). Two things were important in Harvey's approach to the heart. First, his notion of anatomy was the Aristotelian one that knowledge of a part of the body was primarily knowledge of its function. Second, as a pupil of Fabricius in Padua he saw that this function could be seen most clearly in a range of examples: that is, in different animals. Whatever it was that hearts did, their characteristic and identifying action must be present in all cases.

Harvey's preparation for his lectures included vivisectional experiments. There was nothing new about this, especially in the case of the heart, as its motion was unique: being involuntary, very obvious, immediately necessary for life, and not muscular (since all muscles were held to move with voluntary motion). Harvey's first concern was to identify the two traditional phases of the heart's action, systole (contraction) and diastole (expansion). He could not do so. The exposed heart of a living animal rose up vigorously and then subsided, without obvious change in size. Harvey tackled the matter from theory. The vigorous erection of the heart seemed like its purposeful action. In Galenic theory the purpose of the heart was to initiate the pulse, a flow of arterial blood into the arteries. It accordingly expanded vigorously, drawing in blood from the large veins, and then subsided as a wave of forcible expansion—the pulse—passed down the arterial coats, drawing blood from the collapsing heart. Harvey sought confirmation of this view by puncturing the principal artery and observing how the spurting of blood from it correlated with the rise and fall of the heart. He found that as the heart rose up with its vigorous motion, so the blood leapt from the hole in the artery. This was inconsistent with the Galenic doctrine that blood moved into the arteries as the heart passively contracted after its forcible diastole. Harvey concluded that the active phase of the heart's action was a forceful systole—its rising up in the vivisected animal—which produced the pulse by pushing the blood into the arteries as it contracted.

Harvey was proud of his new doctrine about the forceful systole and pulse and argued in the lectures that it corrected an ancient mistake. He continued with his experiments while giving the first few lectures, as his modifications in his notes show. His new doctrine was a radical departure from the accepted professional Galenism of the college and not all the members accepted it. Harvey represented himself as conducting an academic disputation on the topic, with the president of the college, John Argent, acting as the presiding master. Harvey strove to convince his audience by emphasizing the force of blood emerging from the heart, and his emendations to his notes for the lectures show that he now chose a stronger verb for the spurting of the blood from the punctured artery.

Harvey also emphasized the quantity of blood emerging from the forceful systole. He made a rough estimate of the amount of blood contained in the left ventricle of the relaxed—expanded—heart, and of the amount ejected as the ventricle contracted. However modest he made his estimate of the amount ejected at every beat, he soon saw, given a heart beating more than seventy times a minute, that in a whole day the total would be impossibly large. Impossible, that is, because Galenic theory held that the arterial blood from the heart was absorbed as necessary by the tissues; and that venous blood was supplied to the heart by the conversion of ingested food into blood in the liver. No amount of food could supply this amount of venous blood and the arterial blood was emerging from the heart in quantities too great to be absorbed by the tissues.

In his efforts to convince his audience of his new doctrine of the forceful systole Harvey had been led into a crisis. He could not say where all the arterial blood went, nor whence came the venous. As he sought for an answer he had in mind the newly discovered structures in the veins which seemed to slow down the centrifugal flow of blood from the liver to the parts of the body so that it would not accumulate there. These structures looked like valves, and Galen had argued that valves were open in one direction and allowed a small, controlled, flow in the other. In the case of the valves in the veins the controlled flow was towards the parts of the body from the central liver. Harvey suddenly saw that the open direction of the valves was towards the centre of the body, and that the motion of the blood was from the ends of the arteries to the beginnings of the veins, which terminated in the vena cava, returning blood to the heart.

The De motu cordis Harvey had given the first of the Lumleian lectures in 1616 and the changes he made in his notes for them, indicating his discovery of the forceful systole and circulation, seem to date from the second delivery of the lectures in 1618. For more than nine years he argued in favour of the circulation with his colleagues and demonstrated it in the lectures. The conventional academic procedures of the day meant that this discussion took the shape of a disputed question, in which his opponents had the opportunity to challenge the form of his arguments, his authorities, and the status of his observations.

This process prepared Harvey for the writing of the book in which he announced the discovery of the circulation. It appeared in 1628, printed by Fitzer in Frankfurt. Harvey was not on hand to see it through the press, and there were many errors in the set type. The erratum sheet that accompanied some copies is now rare. Harvey called his book *Exercitatio anatomica de motu cordis et sanguinis in animalibus*. As this title suggests it is a formal academic exercise about two things, the motion of the heart and that of the blood. That the context is the animal world indicates that this was a philosophical enquiry, not medical. His philosophy was derived from Aristotle and Fabricius and was directed at discovering what hearts are and what they do.

Harvey knew how radical his new doctrine was and that its reception in the College of Physicians had been mixed.

He was obliged, both in the lectures and in the book, to proceed with great care in putting his case. Only rigorous and agreed academic procedures would convince physicians educated in a university. Conventionally in anatomical commentary any novel finding was located almost in the last place, so that the reader was already familiar with the authorities and their arguments before judging the new finding. Had Harvey *begun* his book by announcing the discovery he would have lost much of the force of his argument. He began, therefore, with an account of his first discovery, the forceful systole and true nature of the pulse. This was both logically and historically prior to the circulation. The first half of *De motu cordis* is therefore devoted to establishing the forceful systole. Then Harvey takes the reader through the moment of crisis that had occurred after he had made his calculations of the amount of blood leaving the heart and explains how he resolved the crisis. He states the thesis about circulation formally, with propositions that are shown to have certain consequences. The remainder of the book is taken up with certain observations that could be explained best on the assumption of circulation.

Reactions As in the College of Physicians, so in the world at large, reactions to the doctrines of the forceful systole and pulse were mixed. Almost no one accepted both in the way Harvey wanted them to. The two doctrines were generally separated, and accepted or rejected on their own. Yet when Harvey died some sort of consensus about the fact of circulation had been reached and produced the biggest change in medical theory since the Alexandrian discovery of the nervous system, about a thousand years earlier.

But the arguments about Harvey's doctrines were not simply between those who could see the truth and those who could not. The main argument against Harvey was that circulation had no medical use. This argument was used at two levels. First, medical philosophers like Caspar Hofmann asserted that circulation had no purpose, no Aristotelian final cause: it was therefore incapable of proper demonstration in a philosophical sense. Hofmann concluded that Harvey was not a philosopher, but a mere accountant, totting up quantities (of blood leaving the heart); philosophers, with Aristotle, thought that mathematics could not uncover essences. At the second level educated medical practitioners, like Harvey's countryman James Primrose and the French anatomist Jean Riolan, found that a Galenic understanding of how the body worked served them fairly well in practice. If the blood circulated the basis of practice would be destroyed as the humours of the body would be mixed together and could not be changed or evacuated separately, and there would be no basis for the letting of blood.

Harvey understood these objections. Although an Aristotelian, he could not give a final cause of circulation and was driven to say that it had to be enough to show that a thing is, despite being unable to say what it is for. He had no convincing answer to the charge of destroying the basis of medical practice. Harvey's doctrine, because radical, was isolated; opponents such as Primrose could use all the authority and arguments of Galenic physiology and its vehicle, an Aristotelian natural philosophy, that reached and explained all the phenomena of the physical world.

There were a number of factors that contributed to the eventual consensus. One was generational. Students were attracted to the idea of circulation, partly because it was radical. When they became teachers themselves the notion that the blood circulated was more popular. Many of these students were anyway being educated at a time when attacks were being made on the old orthodoxies of natural philosophy on which the theory of medicine rested, and Harvey could be seen as part of those attacks. More important, René Descartes, the greatest of the neoteric philosophers, accepted that the blood circulated. It seemed to him that the circulation was an excellent example of how the body worked in a purely mechanical way and indeed he used it in his *Discourse on Method* (1637) as his most important example of mechanism. He was obliged to deny Harvey's account of the forceful systole because the parts of the contracting heart seemed to move closer to each other by attraction, a species of motion impermissible in mechanism. He substituted a heat driven forceful diastole in which the blood entering the heart was vaporized. The vapour expanded the heart and forced its way into the arteries, where it condensed. Descartes' works were very widely read, and this transformed version of Harvey's doctrine of circulation must have reached a bigger audience than it would otherwise have done, ironically in tandem with a neoteric philosophy that Harvey despised.

Court business Harvey's abilities were not limited to experimental anatomy. Before or early in 1618 he was appointed physician-extraordinary to James I; his senior colleague was Sir Theodore Turquet de Mayerne. When James died in 1625 Harvey's appointment continued under Charles I, and the two men developed a friendship. Harvey was able to demonstrate to Charles a virtually exposed beating heart in the young Viscount Montgomery, and Charles provided deer which Harvey dissected while working on his book on animal reproduction. In 1630 Charles ordered Harvey to accompany the young duke of Lennox on a grand tour, and while we know that Harvey was in Paris in September, he was back in London in October and December. In February 1632 he was in Spain, and recorded the destructive effects of war that he had seen on his travels. When Charles progressed to Scotland in 1633 for his coronation Harvey went with him as royal physician, and was perhaps a witness when Charles demonstrated his royal line by touching for the king's evil. It was court business too when in the following year Harvey examined some 'witches' of Burnley. The historical literature here does not always distinguish the English term 'witch' from older European terms relating to intelligences less material than man. James I had in 1597

published in Edinburgh a dialogue about 'demons', a category universally accepted in pre-Reformation Europe, but not one necessarily co-terminous with the English word 'witch'. Possibly Calvinist Scotland entertained different ideas about witches than did early seventeenth-century London; at all events Charles showed less antagonism to them than his father might have done and ordered a medical enquiry, under Harvey, to investigate their physical normality or abnormality. The point at issue was largely to determine whether they had supernumerary nipples to feed their familiars. Harvey, William Clowes, Alexander Read, and the midwives who conducted the examination concluded that they were normal. The women were pardoned by Charles.

It was court business too when the king in 1635 ordered Harvey to perform an autopsy on the body of Old Parr, probably a Shropshire tenant of Thomas Howard, the earl of Arundel. Parr was reputed to have been born in 1483 and so to have lived through the lives of ten sovereigns (and the Reformation) when Arundel brought him to London for the amusement of the king. He appeared vigorous for a man of 152, joked about doing penance for adultery at 100, carefully evaded questions as to his religion, and died before the year was out. Harvey dissected the body in the presence of some important physicians of the time and declared that the cause of Old Parr's death was removal to London and his way of life rather than anything pathological in the body.

In April 1636 Harvey left England as part of an embassy to the emperor Ferdinand under the earl of Arundel. The purpose was to secure the rights of Charles's nephew, Prince Charles Louis, as elector, and Harvey was chosen as physician to the large retinue, probably because of his friendship with both Charles and the earl. On 11 May the party reached Nuremberg and on the 18th Harvey gave a demonstration of the circulation of the blood before Caspar Hofmann, his principal opponent after Riolan. Hofmann was not convinced and it was here that he argued that Harvey's quantitative argument was a mere accountant's trick and not a philosophical demonstration; like all of Harvey's opponents he argued that a doctrine of circulation had no medical use, either in theory or practice.

Charles I's favours to Harvey culminated in Harvey becoming physician-in-ordinary on 6 December 1639. His duties included accompanying the king on three journeys to Scotland and caused him to be absent on many occasions from the College of Physicians and St Bartholomew's Hospital. Harvey does not seem to have been much interested in religion or politics, but had bitter words to say about would-be revolutionaries, whether in philosophy or civil life. He accompanied the king as he gathered his army and was present at the battle of Edgehill. Harvey had charge of the young prince of Wales and duke of York, and is said to have read a book under a hedge until the artillery came uncomfortably close. At Oxford with the king, Harvey was incorporated DM on 7 December 1642, and in the following year was by royal command made warden of Merton College following the departure of Sir Nathaniel Brent. After the surrender of Oxford in

1646 Harvey returned to London and lived with his brothers.

In 1649 Harvey made his only printed reply to his opponents in the form of two addresses to Riolan. It was prompted by two publications in which Riolan denied circulation in Harvey's sense and claimed as his own a much reduced doctrine of a circulation through anastomoses of the major vessels only. Harvey's reply, the *Exercitatio anatomica de circulatione sanguinis*, reviewed the history of the controversy and offered some new experiments; he recognized, however, Riolan's need to defend the professional Galenism of the medical corporations.

De generatione animalium Harvey's other major work was on what we call animal reproduction, the *Exercitationes de generatione animalium* of 1651. He had been working on it for many years, though would probably not have published it but for the determination of his friend George Ent. Like the book on the pulse and circulation this is an academic exercise, or rather a series of small, formal, exercises, each limited in scope to an aspect of the whole topic. It is again Aristotelian in its methods, and Harvey says that his starting point is the adult animal and that the investigation will be into the causes that make the adult possible. Again Harvey used a large number of animals and where before he had sought for a common understanding of the heart, he was now looking for the essence of the egg.

By the time he was writing the final version of the book on the generation of animals, Harvey's thoughts had changed on a topic central to both generation and circulation: the blood. While at Oxford with the king he continued to work on fertilized eggs and doubtless reflected on the reception accorded to his doctrine of circulation. He had shown that it was the *same* blood that circulated, and that arterial blood was not produced in the heart from venous blood by the addition of spirits as traditional medicine held. Harvey was no mechanist, but he could not allow that the blood contained spirit, or that the vital or natural faculty of the soul moved the heart, as so many of his opponents said. What prompted the heart into action, he came to think, was the blood itself. It was the blood too that was the first thing to be seen in the developing egg, in a pulsating point that was at first so small that it disappeared as it contracted. A primal active blood was at the beginning of the cycles both of generation and circulation; it was vital and constantly moving with an expansive force for which Harvey even used the Aristotelian analogy of boiling potage. This took him dangerously close to arguments used against him that denied his quantitive argument on the assumption that the blood merely expanded and contracted within the heart without leaving it. Despite the danger Harvey retained the analogy because he could use Aristotle's definition of nature as an internal principle of motion. If he could, Harvey always used Aristotle's principles (and so was traditionalist in a sense) even though in working them out to the level of practice he disagreed with Aristotle's conclusions (that is,

Harvey was also 'a modern'; although it is not a terminology that Harvey adopted).

By now, preparing the final version of the book on generation, Harvey had seen a great deal of the controversy over the circulation and had failed to convince major figures like Riolan and Hofmann. He had come to despair of philosophical sceptics and the neoteric philosophers. As an old man he now wanted to defend his method of acquiring knowledge—what we would call research—which he believed had helped him in his discovery of the circulation and which he felt to be threatened as Aristotle's natural philosophy was vanishing from the schools. Accordingly a part of *De generatione animalium* was given over to a consideration of how many observations of sensory particulars could lead to the creation of a universal in the mind. Harvey now argued that philosophical induction could indeed lead to universals, which could in turn produce a kind of demonstration.

There were still some Aristotelian philosophers who would have agreed with him, but the new natural philosophers believed in a particulate, mechanical world quite devoid of local purposeful action (they did not deny that God had originally made purposeful action in it). In such a world there could be no final cause and no demonstrative knowledge. It was now often argued that medicine was an art, not a science, thus swinging the pendulum to one side of a debate that had been initiated with the successful search for the new Aristotle of the late twelfth century and the new Galen of the late thirteenth. Intellectual systems, like that of Aristotle, came under suspicion because rationality was uncorrected by observation. Sensory observation gave conviction but the knowledge it provided was only probable, that is, that which could not be built up into a rational system.

Experiment was a special case of sensory observation, and here Harvey played a more important role than his discussion of method in *De generatione animalium* would suggest. The medical experiment had been a method of demonstration since medieval physicians and philosophers had read of Galen's demonstrations in Rome in the second century. Anatomists demonstrated hollow organs by inflation and injection, and Harvey knew in detail the work of sixteenth-century anatomists who, on the Galenic model, had vivisected animals to show movements that were invisible in the dead animal. They showed the development of embryos in the uterus by vivisection of pregnant bitches and illustrated Galen's doctrines by exposing and sometimes excising the beating heart. Harvey differed in having a research programme and making systematic dissections and vivisections in order to understand the heart. The medical experiment was central to experimental philosophy. Harvey drew upon an old medical tradition and argued the case for the forceful systole and circulation experimentally. The European battle for and against Harvey was most often experimental. Medical experiments and apparatus influenced wider and often later philosophical experiments. Even the great rationalist Descartes struggled to prove his version of Harvey's doctrines by means of experiments drawn from the medical tradition.

Last days and reputation The old Harvey did not fit comfortably into the new Commonwealth. Early in the civil war his lodging had been ransacked and the loss of notes from much work on the generation of 'insects' was a great blow to him. He was temporarily banished from London by parliament because of his connections with the king. His royalist brothers, Daniel and Eliab, with whom he was now lodging, were fined large amounts of money. Disliking the political atmosphere of Cambridge, Harvey chose to be remembered in the College of Physicians, though even here there were some who preferred to ignore him. Harvey's gift to the college, a library, was completed on 2 February 1654; a statue of him had already been erected. He was elected to the presidency of the college on 30 September 1654, but declined because of his age. In 1656 Harvey gave his estate at Burmarsh, Romney Marsh, Kent, to the college. Harvey died, apparently from a stroke, on 3 June 1657 at a house of his brother Eliab, either at Roehampton, or at Cockaine House in London. According to Aubrey, Harvey prepared himself for death on finding himself unable to speak. His last acts were to indicate to his apothecary to let blood from his tongue (a therapy inconsistent with the circulation) and to give the watch which he had used in experiments to one of his nephews. He was buried on 26 June 1657 in the family vault at Hempstead church, in Essex. On 18 October 1883 (St Luke's day) his body was moved and placed in a sarcophagus in the Harvey chapel of Hempstead church, where a memorial was set on the north wall of the transept. The Royal College of Physicians commemorates Harvey with an annual oration.

Harvey has been justly celebrated as the author of a major medical discovery. Nineteenth-century historians tended to assess Harvey according to contemporary ideals and saw Harvey as a 'scientist', either patiently accumulating evidence or endowed with early but authentic scientific spirit. He was universally admired for overcoming the dead weight of ancient authority and revealing the truth. His contemporaries were assessed on their ability or failure to recognize this truth when presented with it. In contrast, scholarship has since the 1950s been more inclined to explain Harvey's work by treating it in its historical context. Harvey discovered something which became accepted as a physical truth; however, this was far from the case during his own time. Then his work had no value at all for the many intelligent and earnest men who opposed him. Much scholarship at the end of the twentieth century was therefore concerned with the processes by which the validity of Harvey's discovery came to be accepted, and its immense significance acknowledged.

ROGER FRENCH

Sources G. Keynes, *The life of William Harvey*, [new edn] (1978) · R. French, *William Harvey's natural philosophy* (1994) · R. G. Frank, *Harvey and the Oxford physiologists* (1980) · G. Whitteridge, *William Harvey and the circulation of the blood* (1971) · G. Whitteridge, ed., *The anatomical lectures of William Harvey* (1964) · D. G. Bates, 'Harvey's account of his "discovery"', *Medical History*, 36 (1992), 361–78 · J. Bylebyl, ed., *William Harvey and his age* (1979) · G. Keynes, *A bibliography of the writings of William Harvey, 1587–1657*, 2nd edn (1953) · *DNB*

Archives BL, prescriptions and papers, Sloane MSS 230A, 260A, 486, 520; Add. MS 36308 · RCP Lond., papers | Bodl. Oxf., prescriptions for John Aubrey · RCP Lond., letters to Lord Feilding · RCP Lond., corresp. relating to B. Harvey

Likenesses attrib. D. Mytens, oils, *c.*1627, NPG [*see illus.*] · attrib. R. Gaywood, etching, after 1649, BM, RCP Lond., RCS Eng. · possibly by W. van Bemmel, oils, 1656, U. Glas., Hunterian College · oils, before 1666, RCP Lond. · E. Marshall, bust on monument, 1719, St Andrew's Church, Hempstead, Essex · W. Faithorne, bust on pedestal, BM, NPG · attrib. R. Gaywood, etching, priv. coll. · R. Gaywood, line print (with Lord Bacon), BL; repro. in *Eighteen books of the secrets of art and nature* (1660) · line print (after bust by W. Faithorne), repro. in *De generatione animalium* (1653) · oils (after etching attrib. R. Gaywood), NPG

Wealth at death considerable; left £1800 in bequests and annuities totalling £136; remainder to brother: will

Harvey, William (1796–1866), wood-engraver and book illustrator, was born on 13 July 1796 at Newcastle upon Tyne, where his father was keeper of the public vapour baths and swimming pool outside the west gate of the city wall. He was one of Thomas Bewick's favourite pupils [*see* Bewick, Thomas, apprentices] and 'came on Tryal' to him on 27 November 1809. On 1 January 1810 he was bound apprentice, a few months younger than the usual fourteen years, and he first appeared on the wages in January 1813 at 5s. per week (this rose to 8s. in his last year). His contribution to Bewick's *Fables of Aesop and Others* (1818) was considerable, and, unusually, his initials appear against named engravings in the workshop records from July 1811 onwards. But the claim of earlier authorities that he copied onto the wood the drawings of a former apprentice, Robert Johnson, who had died in 1795, can relate to only a small number. Bewick, in a letter of 29 January 1816 to Robert Pollard, described how he himself prepared his designs for the *Fables* by drawing directly on the wood with the highest degree of finish, 'otherwise my Boys cou'd not cut them'; their work required 'close superintendance' and a subsequent 'going over'. Harvey's apprenticeship ended on 1 January 1817, and on 9 September following he left for London. Desperate to complete the printing of the *Fables*, and not having heard from his pupil, Bewick feared that some blocks he had prepared—'with the finish of miniature paintings'—had been taken to London by Harvey 'to make a blaze' about their being of his doing, at Bewick's expense (letter, 5 Feb 1818). He was ever quick to suspect an injury, but such an action would have been at odds with what is known of Harvey's honest nature. In his *Memoir*, Bewick described Harvey as one of 'the first in excellence ... who both as engraver & designer stands pre-eminent at this day' (*Memoir*, 200).

When Harvey arrived in London in 1817 he would have been overwhelmed and preoccupied with the search for work, although within a year Bewick was worried that he had taken on more than he could accomplish. One of his earliest commissions was a small tailpiece for *Puckle's Club*, published in that year as an elaborate display of the skills of the printer John Johnson and the principal wood-engravers of the day. In its list of engravers Harvey is noted as being a pupil of Bewick.

In a letter of 11 February 1818, the painter William Bewick, a native of Durham (and, although acquainted, not a relative of the engraver), sent a letter to his brother in Newcastle through his friend Harvey: 'a very clever fellow' whom he had found in an obscure part of the town, with very few acquaintants, and in need of 'bringing forward' (Landseer, 40–41). It was thus that Harvey was introduced to the Landseers, Edwin and Thomas, sons of the engraver John Landseer, and with them became a fellow student of figure painting under Benjamin Robert Haydon; for the study of anatomy they were taught by Sir Charles Bell. From this association came Harvey's remarkable *Assassination of Dentatus*, after Haydon. A greatly ambitious large multiple block of 15 inches by 11, published in 1821 after three years' work, it was intended to rival copper but wavers in its mixture of the wood-engraver's white line and its imitation of the copper-engraver's black and crossed line. The block joints failed to hold, and sound impressions are rare. But the work showed Harvey's mastery to the full, as did his designs and engravings for Henderson's *History of Ancient and Modern Wines* (1822) and his portrait of the printer John Johnson engraved for the latter's *Typographia* (1824).

On the death of John Thurston in 1822 the mantle of leading draughtsman to the London wood-engravers soon fell to Harvey, who almost completely abandoned the graver and by 1839 was reckoned to have completed more than 3000 drawings for the trade. As a practical wood-engraver, he always made his drawing sympathetic to the process and helpful to those who worked to his drawings.

Of the principal books for which Harvey produced designs, apart from the many publications of Charles Knight, note should be made of Northcote's *Fables* (first and second series, 1828 and 1833); *The Tower Menagerie* (1829); *The Gardens and Menagerie of the Zoological Society Delineated* (1830–31); *The Children in the Wood* (1831); and Lane's *Arabian Nights* (1840), for which he provided some 600 illustrations. Harvey's drawing was well observed but later prone to mannerism, a trait which no doubt stemmed from his swift facility and which was to curtail his employment by the Revd J. G. Wood for his *Illustrated Natural History* (1851–3). He was good with natural history, but often his animals displayed a curious daintiness of posture, and something of this is also seen in a few of his early watercolour drawings. The backgrounds to his natural history figures were often reduced to light pencillings, thus giving added emphasis to the principal subject, rather in the manner of the steel-engraved plates in such works as Jardine's *Naturalist's Library* (1840–).

Harvey established no school of engravers, although he employed assistance, and it is recorded that John Jackson came to him from Bewick to finish his time. He was described by the engraver F. W. Fairholt, who worked for him, as honest and unpretentious, free from vanity or jealousy, and of fertile invention and rapid hand; only by noticing his penetrating eye might one be aware of his active mind and great powers of observation (*Art Journal*, 1866, 179–80). He was infinitely generous to the aspiring young. In the words of the Dalziel brothers, 'William Harvey was a great and highly gifted artist, a true man, a friend and a counsellor to us from the time of our earliest efforts to the day of his death' (G. Dalziel, *The Brothers Dalziel: a Record of Work*, 1901, 14). He died, unmarried, at Prospect Lodge, Richmond, Surrey, his home for many years, on 13 January 1866, and was buried in Richmond cemetery.

IAIN BAIN

Sources *A memoir of Thomas Bewick written by himself*, ed. I. Bain (1975); rev. edn (1979) [first full transcript of original MS with chronology and bibliography] • R. Welford, *Men of mark 'twixt Tyne and Tweed*, 3 vols. (1895) • T. Landseer, *Life and letters of William Bewick* (1871) • MS correspondence, priv. coll. • Beilby–Bewick workshop records, Tyne and Wear Archives Service, Newcastle upon Tyne, 1269 • R. Robinson, *Thomas Bewick: his life and times* (1887) • J. Boyd, *Bewick gleanings* (1886) • W. Chatto and J. Jackson, *A treatise on wood engraving* (1839) • memorial, St Nicholas, Newcastle upon Tyne • gravestone, Richmond cemetery, Surrey • [G. Dalziel and E. Dalziel], *The brothers Dalziel: a record of fifty years' work … 1840–1890* (1901)
Archives V&A NAL, family and business corresp., L3250–3262 | Cherryburn, Northumberland, family and business corresp. • Newcastle Central Library, Laing Gallery collection, family and business corresp. • Newcastle Central Library, Natural History Society of Northumbria collection, family and business corresp. • Newcastle Central Library, Pease Bequest collection, family and business corresp. • priv. coll., family and business corresp. • Tyne and Wear Archives Service, Newcastle upon Tyne, family and business corresp., 1269 [incl. the Beilby–Bewick workshop account books] • UCL, corresp. with Society for the Diffusion of Useful Knowledge
Likenesses engraving, repro. in Dalziel, *The brothers Dalziel*, 15 • wood-engraving, NPG; repro. in *ILN* (1866)
Wealth at death under £600: probate, 1866 • under £800: probate, resworn, 1866, *CGPLA Eng. & Wales*

Harvey, William Henry (1811–1866), botanist, was born at Summerville, Limerick, on 5 February 1811, the eleventh and youngest child of Joseph Massey Harvey (1764–1834), a Quaker merchant, and Rebecca Mark (d. 1831). He went to Newtown School, Waterford, and thence to Ballitore Quaker school, co. Kildare, before joining his father's business, as he himself described it, 'exchanging the dross of Mammon for the store of Ceres' (Nelson, 'Juvenile correspondence', 58).

Harvey's interest in natural history can be traced to his days at Newtown School where he helped assemble a natural history collection. As a boy he collected shells on the coast at Miltown Malbay, co. Clare, and there also developed his fascination for cryptogamic plants, especially seaweeds. In the summer of 1831 Harvey collected the minute moss, identified as *Hookeria laetivirens*, in two places near Killarney, co. Kerry, and this discovery prompted him to write to Professor William Jackson Hooker, after whom the moss was named, at the University of Glasgow. The subsequent correspondence between Harvey, then calling himself 'a very young Cryptogamist' (Fisher, 21), and Hooker developed into a close, lifelong friendship.

Following his father's death Harvey was listless and thought about travelling abroad. In 1835, through political patronage and a bungled warrant, his brother Joseph

(1793–1836) was appointed treasurer of Cape Colony; William was the intended appointee although he had no experience of government or financial affairs. Unable to correct the warrant, William accompanied Joseph to the Cape of Good Hope where he commenced studying the flora of southern Africa. Joseph was unfit for his duties and resigned after seven months; he died at sea on 26 April 1836 during their return voyage. William petitioned to fill the vacant post and was quickly appointed. He returned to Cape Town and served two short terms as colonial treasurer but he too was unable to fulfil his duties and twice was sent home suffering from 'aberration of the mind' (most probably acute depression; Dr S. Bailey RN, 6 Dec 1841, PRO, CO 48/214). When he recovered Harvey resigned the colonial treasurership and began to pursue his outstanding career in botany. The retirement of Professor William Allman (1776–1846) left the chair of botany in the University of Dublin vacant, and as a result of Dr Thomas Coulter's death in 1843 the university's herbarium was without a curator. Harvey canvassed for the combined positions, which were within the School of Physic, but his lack of medical qualifications precluded his election. The university overcame this legal difficulty by awarding him an honorary degree (MD, 20 March 1844). This caused much debate, and eventually Harvey was offered only the curatorship. His appointment took effect on 30 March 1844. In 1856, however, he was elected to the again vacant chair of botany, succeeding Professor George James Allman (1812–1898).

While Harvey spent most of his working life in Trinity College, Dublin, in 1848 he was elected professor of botany to the Royal Dublin Society and thus effectively he became director of the society's botanic gardens at Glasnevin. He took no part in the gardens' administration, but gave public lectures and helped to identify plants. In 1854, when the Royal Dublin Society's professorships were transferred to the Museum of Irish Industry, Harvey's links with Glasnevin diminished.

Harvey was an acknowledged authority on marine algae by 1836 when he contributed to J. T. Mackay's *Flora Hibernica*. Subsequently he published many papers and books on phycology, including *Manual of British Algae* (1841), *Phycologia Britannica* (1846–51), *Nereis Australis* (1847), *Nereis boreali-Americana* (1852–8), *Phycologia Australica* (1858–63), and one popular work, *The Seaside Book* (1849). He also published numerous papers on flowering plants and, most notably, seminal works on the flora of southern Africa, particularly *The Genera of South African Plants* (1838) and, with O. W. Sonder, the first three volumes (1859, 1862, 1865) of *Flora Capensis*. Harvey drew and often also lithographed hundreds of illustrations for his publications, and thus must be counted among the most accomplished botanical artists.

Harveya, a genus of root parasites native in Africa, is a beautiful, witty memorial for this impishly witty man. 'All I have taste for is natural history, and that might possibly lead in days to come to a genus called Harveya, and the letters F. L. S. after my name, and with that I shall be content,' he wrote (Fisher, 6). He was indeed elected a fellow of the Linnean Society of London (1857) and also of the Royal Society of London (1858), and was a member of the Royal Irish Academy (1844).

Harvey had been brought up as a member of the Society of Friends and remained a Quaker until 1846 when he converted to the Anglican Church of Ireland. He published his religious views in the form of a pseudonymous letter to his friend Josiah Gough, entitled *Charles and Josiah, or, Friendly Conversations between a Churchman and a Quaker* (1862). Deeply held religious views and his work as a naturalist combined to cause Harvey to dismiss Charles Darwin's work *On the Origin of Species* (1859). 'It strikes me that there is fallacy at the very base of Mr. Darwin's argument', Harvey wrote in the preface to a 'serio-comic squib', printed privately under the title *An Inquiry into the Probable Origin of the Human Animal, on the Principles of Mr. Darwin's Theory of Natural Selection, and in Opposition to the Lamarckian Notion of a Monkey Parentage* (1860). By publishing this, Harvey's mischievous sense of humour evidently overwhelmed his common sense, and Darwin commented that the pamphlet was not worthy of its author. Harvey seems to have had second thoughts, for one of the copies of this work, in the National Library of Ireland, Dublin, was inscribed 'This is *rubbish*—merely got up to amuse an evening meeting of a *private* society. W. H. H.', and another copy has, again in Harvey's distinctive handwriting, '(To be burned when read) (Suppressed by the Author)' on the title page.

On 2 April 1861, in Limerick, Harvey married Elizabeth Lecky Phelps (1804/5–1895). Symptoms of pulmonary tuberculosis appeared shortly afterwards and from that time until his death Harvey rarely enjoyed good health. He died in the home of Lady Hooker, at Torquay, Devon, on 15 May 1866, and was buried in Torquay.

E. CHARLES NELSON

Sources [L. Fisher], *Memoir of W. H. Harvey, M.D., F.R.S.* (1869) · E. C. Nelson, 'William Henry Harvey as colonial treasurer at the Cape of Good Hope: a case of depression and bowdlerized history', *Archives of Natural History*, 19 (1992), 171–80 · E. C. Nelson, 'The juvenile correspondence of William Henry Harvey', *Quakers in natural history and medicine in Ireland and Britain* [Glasnevin 1994], ed. E. C. Nelson (1996), 55–61 · E. C. Nelson, 'William Henry Harvey: a portrait of the artist as a young man', *Curtis's Botanical Magazine*, [6th ser.], 13 (1996), 36–41 · D. A. Webb, 'William Henry Harvey, 1811–1866, and the tradition of systematic botany', *Hermathena*, 103 (1966), 32–45 · E. C. Nelson and E. M. McCracken, *The brightest jewel: a history of the National Botanic Gardens, Glasnevin, Dublin* (1987) · M. Gunn and L. E. Codd, *Botanical exploration of southern Africa* (1981), 179–81 · S. C. Ducker, *The contented botanist: letters of W. H. Harvey about Australia and the Pacific* (1988) · private information (2004) · death notice (E. L. Harvey, *née* Phelps), NL Ire., E. P. Wright MSS · Representative Body Library

Archives National Botanic Gardens, Dublin, papers · RBG Kew, papers · TCD, corresp. | American Philosophical Society, Philadelphia, letters · Harvard U., Arnold Arboretum, letters to Asa Gray · RBG Kew, corresp. with Sir W. Hooker · Sheff. Arch., letters from Margaret Gatty

Likenesses J. Barry, group portrait, etching and line engraving, 1791, NG Ire. · D. Macnee, crayon, c.1835, RBG Kew · F. W. Burton, chalk drawing, c.1850, NG Ire. · F. W. Burton, portrait, c.1850, TCD, department of botany · T. H. Maguire, lithograph, 1851, BM · A. C. Cooper, photograph, RS · Maull & Polyblank, photograph, RS ·

line engraving, NPG · photographs, repro. in Ducker, *The contented botanist* · stipple, NPG

Harvey, William Wigan (1810–1883), Church of England clergyman, was born at Great Stanmore, Middlesex, on 17 February 1810, the second son of George Daniel Harvey, barrister and commissioner of bankruptcy, and his wife, Mary, daughter of William Wigan. A king's scholar at Eton College, he matriculated at King's College, Cambridge, in 1829, graduating BA in 1832, MA in 1836, and BD in 1855. He was elected a fellow of King's in 1831, holding office as divinity lecturer from 1836 to 1844 and algebra lecturer from 1837 to 1844. He was ordained deacon in 1833 and priest in 1834, holding curacies in Cambridge parishes before his institution in 1844 to the rectory of Buckland, near Royston, Hertfordshire, a living in the gift of King's. He became a magistrate for Hertfordshire. His fellowship was vacated on his marriage in 1844 to Anne, youngest daughter of the Revd Fairfax Francklin, rector of Attleburgh, Norfolk, with whom he had at least two sons.

Harvey, who had gained the Tyrwhitt Hebrew scholarship at Cambridge in 1833, devoted much of his time to preparing works of orthodox theology. He published an account of the Anglican articles, *Ecclesiae Anglicanae vindex Catholicus* (3 vols., 1841–3), *History and Theology of the Three Creeds* (2 vols., 1854), an edition of the works of St Irenaeus (2 vols., 1857), and *Sermons upon the Doctrines and Evidences of the Christian Religion* (1859). In 1867 he was an unsuccessful candidate for the Gresham professorship of divinity, when his churchmanship was likened to that of John Kaye, the old high-church bishop of Lincoln, 'equally removed from the Puritan and Romanising parties of the time' (*Hansard 3*, 209, 1872, 1695).

Harvey would have remained a comparatively obscure, scholarly clergyman, but for the political row early in 1872 following his presentation by the prime minister, Gladstone, to the rectory of Ewelme, Oxfordshire. He had become oppressed by 'the raw airs of the winters' (BL, Add. MS 44431, fol. 170) at his Hertfordshire rectory and in 1871 approached Gladstone, an Eton contemporary and occasional correspondent in the intervening years, angling for a cathedral stall on the strength of his opinions in favour of cathedral reform. Gladstone seems to have considered his claims insufficient for a stall, and thought him unsuited for the vacant crown living of Southam, which, with its large population, called for a younger man. Instead Harvey was offered Ewelme, a small country parish that had already been declined by one claimant for preferment, W. E. Jelf. Earlier in 1871 Ewelme had been severed by act of parliament from the regius chair of divinity at Oxford and in compensation to the university, at Gladstone's own suggestion, a proviso was inserted in the act stipulating that the incumbent should be a member of the university convocation, to ensure that an Oxford man would always receive the presentation (Gladstone, *Diaries*, 7.465). Gladstone now indicated that this restriction could be circumvented by Harvey incorporating at Oxford, and brushed aside Harvey's misgivings about the proposed subterfuge (ibid., 8.8). He was duly incorporated at Oriel College, Oxford, on 10 October 1871,

keeping the requisite forty-two days' residence in Oxford before being admitted a member of convocation on 22 November 1871. Presented on 15 December 1871, he was unable to attend his formal institution to the living for several weeks owing to ill health.

Harvey's appointment, following that of R. P. Collier to a judicial position in similarly dubious circumstances, was a clear violation of the spirit of the act of parliament. Gladstone's justification of it, during the long debate on 8 March 1872 in response to a question in the House of Commons raised by Sir John Mowbray, MP for Oxford University, amply confirmed some contemporaries' view of his casuistry and obduracy. It was regarded as a scandal, though by later standards it was trifling: Harvey was a tory, he had no particular familiarity with the prime minister, his personal qualities were not in question, and no issue of financial gain was involved. More than once he offered to stand down to avoid the embarrassment which his appointment had caused. Harvey proved an active parish priest at Ewelme, carrying out repairs to the church, while continuing his antiquarian researches, being elected FSA in 1881. His eldest son, Charles Wigan Harvey, served for a while as his curate. Harvey died at Ewelme on 7 May 1883 and was buried on 11 May in the churchyard.

M. C. CURTHOYS

Sources Boase, *Mod. Eng. biog.* · Venn, *Alum. Cant.* · J. Morley, *The life of William Ewart Gladstone*, 3 vols. (1903) · Gladstone, *Diaries* · *Hansard 3* (1872), 209.291–2, 772, 1153, 1673–1720, 1946 · J. A. Dodd, *A historical guide to Ewelme church* (1916)
Archives BL, corresp. with W. E. Gladstone
Wealth at death £14,663 15s. 1d.: probate, 4 Aug 1883, *CGPLA Eng. & Wales*

Harvey, William Woodis (1798–1864). *See under* Harvey, Edmund George (1828–1884).

Harward, Simon (*fl.* 1572–1607), Church of England clergyman and author, was probably related to the Hawarde (or Harward, or Heyward) family of Tandridge, Surrey, though the nature of that relationship is unclear. He was sufficiently wealthy to matriculate as a pensioner from Christ's College, Cambridge, in December 1572, graduating BA early in 1575. In 1577 Harward was incorporated in that degree at Oxford and in 1577 was appointed chaplain of New College there, proceeding MA the following year. In 1579 he acquired the rectory of Warrington, Lancashire. On 4 July 1581 a Michael Johnson MA was instituted to the rectory, but there is no record of his having paid the first fruits. On 8 May 1582 Harward signed from Warrington a preface to two sermons recently preached in Manchester, where on 25 September that year he married Mary, daughter of its sometime reeve Robert Langley. It was apparently as a minister of Warrington (and not as master of the Boteler School there) that he acted as one of the moderators of the thrice-yearly exercises or synods of the Lancashire clergy which originated in October 1582. It may be that Harward actually remained in occupancy at Warrington for some time, perhaps until the institution to the rectory of John Ashworth on 3 June 1589.

Using Harward's published sermons Wood assembled a list of places at which he preached, strongly implying that he was an itinerant priest or that he had many temporary appointments, having 'a rambling head'. There was an element of truth in this assessment of his character, for Harward was encouraged to issue *The Solace for the Souldier and Saylor* (1592), as the preface reveals, by 'certain godly and valiant Captains and ship masters, with whom being on the Spanish seas, under the conduct of the most noble earl of Cumberland' he had for some time served, before October 1592, apparently as a naval chaplain and perhaps also as a doctor. This phase of Harward's career had not met with universal approval: Harward recalls the 'obloquies and reproachful speeches of many, which have not sticked to affirm, that these my voyages upon the seas have been some blot and discredit to the doctrine which is or shall by me be delivered upon the land'; in reply he did not shrink from condemning 'seditious malcontents' in their 'unnatural refusing to help their country' in time of war.

However, Wood's evaluation of Harward's career should be revised. He was not a preacher at Bletchingley, Surrey, a place which, as he himself reported in 1607, he had never visited. He certainly preached at Crowhurst, Surrey, on 9 July 1598 but signed his preface to the published version, *The Danger of Discontentment*, from Tandridge, about 3 miles distant, only two days later. This preface was addressed to Sir Edward Bower, a Surrey JP, and John his brother, who had been among the congregation and with whom Harward had been acquainted for some years. William Cole reported that Harward had been recommended by Archbishop Whitgift as master of a school at Tandridge, and it was from Tandridge that he signed his *Enchirideon morale* (December 1596, dedicated to Whitgift), his *Phlebotomy* (August 1601), and his *A Discourse Containing the Soule and Spirit of Man* (December 1603), which contains another dedication to Sir Edward Bower. It was in Tandridge and Crowhurst that he preached in 1597 two of his *Three Sermons* (1599). It seems likely that from 1596, and possibly since his return to England in 1592, Harward was master at Tandridge School, and that he remained so until 1604. This may in turn suggest that he was related, possibly as a nephew, to Henry Heyward, alderman and fishmonger of London and his wife, Agnes, whose son and heir John Hawarde was a barrister of the Inner Temple, and who had purchased substantial properties in Surrey, including Tandridge Hall. It may be that Simon Harward stayed there as a guest.

Harward's *Phlebotomy, or, A Treatise of Letting of Blood*, is of particular interest. In its preface the author deplored the fact that, while in London there were many learned and competent physicians and surgeons, in the country towns far too many thoughtlessly bled their patients. This caused them 'more hurt and danger than ease and succour', for if 'rashly and inconsiderately attempted, the spirits and blood are spent and wasted, the natural heat is plucked away and dispersed … [to the] unrecoverable destruction of their health and life' (sigs. A2v–A3r). It seems, therefore, that the tradition that the schoolteacher also practised medicine at Tandridge and elsewhere may be well founded, and that he preached only

occasional sermons, delivered at the invitation of resident parsons and the local authorities. In 1604 Harward was instituted to the rectory of Banstead, Surrey. From there he signed his *Discourse … written by occasion of a fearful lightning which … did in a very short time burn up the spire steeple of Blechingly in Surrey, and in the same melt into infinite fragments a goodly ring of bells*, an event which occurred on 17 November 1606 and which is attributed by the author to God's judgment on the inhabitants of the place. After the publication of this account in 1607 nothing further is heard of Simon Harward.

STEPHEN WRIGHT

Sources Wood, *Ath. Oxon.*, new edn · Venn, *Alum. Cant.* · J. Peile, *Biographical register of Christ's College, 1505–1905, and of the earlier foundation, God's House, 1448–1505*, ed. [J. A. Venn], 1 (1910) · Foster, *Alum. Oxon.* · S. Harward, *The solace for the souldier and saylor* (1592) · R. C. Richardson, *Puritanism in north-west England: a regional study of the diocese of Chester to 1642* (1972) · E. Baines and W. R. Whatton, *The history of the county palatine and duchy of Lancaster*, new edn, ed. J. Croston and others, 4 (1891) · W. P. Baildon, introduction, in *Les reportes del cases in camera stellata, 1593 to 1609, from the original ms. of John Hawarde*, ed. W. P. Baildon (privately printed, London, 1894) · A. B. Beaven, ed., *The aldermen of the City of London, temp. Henry III–[1912]*, 2 vols. (1908–13)

Harwood, Basil (1859–1949), organist and composer, was born on 11 April 1859 at Woodhouse, Olveston, Gloucestershire, the eighth son and youngest of the nine children of Edward Harwood (1818–1907), a banker and JP, and his first wife, Mary (1840–1867), the daughter of Young Sturge of the Bristol Quaker family. He was brought up in strict accordance with Quakerism until 1869, when, following his father's marriage to an Anglican, the family began to attend Olveston church.

Harwood was educated first at Walton Lodge preparatory school, Clevedon. He returned home from Clevedon in 1863, when he started to take piano lessons from Joseph Roekel. He entered Charterhouse School in 1864, and in 1876, with a scholarship, entered Trinity College, Oxford, where he gained a second class in classical moderations (1879) and a third in modern history (1881). He took the Oxford BMus degree in 1880, studying theory with C. W. Corfe, choragus to the university. After leaving Oxford he travelled to Leipzig and spent a year studying composition with S. Jadassohn and the organ with H. Papperitz. On returning to England he took further lessons with George Riseley, organist of Bristol Cathedral, and secured his first employment, as organist of St Barnabas's Church, Pimlico, London. In 1887 he moved on to Ely Cathedral, succeeding E. T. Chipp. Five years later he was appointed organist at Christ Church, Oxford (succeeding Charles Harford Lloyd), which proved to be his last professional position. On 27 December 1899 he married a former pupil, Mabel Ada Jennings (1871–1974), the daughter of George Jennings, of Castle Eve, Parkstone, Dorset, and Ferndale, Clapham. They had two sons, John Edward Godfrey (*b.* 1900) and Basil Anthony (*b.* 1903).

While at Oxford, Harwood entered fully into the musical life of the university. Besides his duties at Christ Church, he was precentor at Keble College (1892–1903) and conductor of the Oxford Orchestral Association

(1892–8). In 1896 he helped to found the Oxford Bach Choir and became its first conductor, a post he retained with distinction until 1900. On Hubert Parry's appointment as Heather professor of music at Oxford in 1900, he became choragus, a position he held until his retirement. He took the Oxford DMus in 1896, submitting his setting of Psalm 86, *Inclina domine*, op. 9.

As a composer Harwood belongs firmly within the diatonic 'English' tradition established by S. S. Wesley, John Stainer, Parry, and C. V. Stanford. He produced several works for chorus and orchestra, including *Inclina domine*, op. 9 (Gloucester, 1898), 'As by the streams of Babylon', op. 20 (Oxford, 1907), 'Thy boundless love to me', op. 22 (St Paul's Cathedral, 1909), *Ode on May Morning*, op. 27 (Leeds, 1913), and 'Love incarnate', op. 37 (composed 1922, performed Gloucester, 1925), and a concerto for organ and orchestra, op. 24, in which he appeared as soloist (Gloucester, 1910). Harwood's most important contribution, however, was to the repertories of Anglican liturgical music and the organ. Several anthems, such as 'O how glorious is the kingdom', op. 12 (1898) and 'When the son of man shall come', op. 13 no. 2 (1900, published in 1902), show an originality of thought, while his service in A♭, more conservative in style, has remained popular among cathedral and church choirs. Arguably his finest music is for the organ. While at St Barnabas's Church, Pimlico, he completed his organ sonata no. 1 in C♯ minor, op. 5 (1886), a symphonic work of Germanic proportions and treatment, suggesting the influence of Rheinberger. A second sonata, in F♯ minor, op. 26 (1912), dedicated to Charles Harford Lloyd, shows a similar boldness in the handling of climax and registration. Harwood's organ style is distinctive and technically challenging; he was a fine pianist and this is amply reflected in his dexterous writing for manuals. The scope of his musical thought, even in the shorter pieces, tends to demand a large instrument, as is demonstrated by *Paean*, op. 15 no. 3 (first played by Sir Walter Parratt at the opening of the new rebuilt organ in York Minster in 1902), the fantasia *Christmastide*, op. 34, and the rhapsody, op. 38.

Many of Harwood's organ works and anthems reveal his love for plainchant and hymn tunes. This is particularly evident in the quasi-improvisatory finale of the organ sonata no. 1 and in shorter pieces such as the *Short Postlude for Ascensiontide*, op. 15 no. 4, where hymn or plainsong melodies serve as an important structural feature. Harwood published numerous hymn tunes, edited *The Oxford Hymn Book* (1908), and lectured on the whole manner of hymn singing, notably to the church congress at Liverpool in 1904. Among his best-known tunes are 'Thornbury' ('Thy hand, O God, has guided'), written at the request of Sir George Martin for the London Church Choir Association's twenty-fifth annual festival in 1898, 'Luckington' ('Let all the world in every corner sing'), and 'St Audrey' ('Sing ye faithful, sing with gladness').

Harwood, a deeply religious individual, had a quiet, gentle, and reserved personality. In 1907 his father died, having outlived all his other children. Harwood, who was

faced with the dilemma of whether to continue his career in music or to manage the family estate in Gloucestershire, decided on the latter and retired in 1909 after his work as music editor of *The Oxford Hymn Book* was completed. It was a decision made to the dismay and sorrow of his colleagues. On moving back to Olveston he participated actively in the musical life of Bristol. He was president of its musical club and the Madrigal Society (1914–19).

In 1936 Harwood and his wife left Woodhouse in charge of tenants and moved to London. When war broke out in 1939 they moved away temporarily, and lived first in Bournemouth and then at Shiplake, near Reading. After war was over they returned to London, where they settled at 50 Courtfield Gardens, Kensington. Harwood died there eight days before his ninetieth birthday, on 3 April 1949. His ashes were interred under a memorial tablet in St Barnabas's Church, Pimlico, where he had held his first appointment.   JEREMY DIBBLE

Sources V. Ruddle, *The life and hymn tunes of Basil Harwood* (1996) • H. W. Shaw, *The succession of organists of the Chapel Royal and the cathedrals of England and Wales from c.1538* (1991) • J. A. Fuller Maitland and H. C. Colles, 'Harwood, Basil', Grove, *Dict. mus.* (1927)
Archives Bodl. Oxf. • Christ Church Oxf.
Wealth at death £72,128 3s.: probate, 17 Aug 1949, *CGPLA Eng. & Wales*

Harwood, Sir Busick (*bap.* 1750, *d.* 1814), anatomist, the fourth son of Mary and John Harwood, was born in Newmarket, Suffolk, and baptized on 15 December 1750. Educated at a private school, he was apprenticed to a Newmarket apothecary and later to William Forfitt, a surgeon at Uppingham, from 1766 to 1771. In January 1772 he became a dressing pupil at the London Hospital. Leaving for India on 22 April 1773 as surgeon to the Indiaman *Harcourt* (a brother was already in the country), he joined the Indian Medical Service (IMS) and was appointed assistant surgeon in Bengal. On 29 April 1776 he was posted as surgeon to officers deputed to serve the nawab of Oudh and benefited financially from treating members of the Oudh court. He resigned on 4 February 1778 and returned to England.

On 22 September 1779 Harwood was admitted a fellow commoner at Christ's College, Cambridge, to read medicine. Maintaining a connection with the London Hospital, and concerned about the teaching of medicine, he helped William Blizard raise money for the London Hospital medical college, built by 1783, where he gave a course of lectures on botany. Harwood's pupils gave him a silver cup in thanks for the lectures and his help in establishing the college. At the formal opening in 1785 he gave a lecture on 'The utility of physic in general'. On 10 June 1782 Harwood obtained an MD by examination from St Andrews University. Described as 'well versed in History, particularly that of oriental nations and many other parts of curious and useful learning' (society minutes, 3 April 1783, S. Antiquaries, Lond.), he was elected a fellow of the Society of Antiquaries on 3 April 1783. He was elected a fellow of the

Royal Society on 22 April 1784, being 'well versed in various branches of natural history and particularly in Botany' (Royal Society election certificate IV. 114, RS). Harwood graduated MB at Cambridge with a thesis on blood transfusion in 1785 and was appointed professor of anatomy at Cambridge in succession to Charles Collignon; in 1786 he was granted a licence to practise and became a physician at Addenbrooke's Hospital. Having moved to Emmanuel College he graduated MD in 1790.

Cambridge University provided little for the very few who chose to read medicine each year. Harwood published synopses of his lectures (the only medical lectures in Cambridge) and the third edition, published in 1792, outlined a very adequate course of anatomy and related physiology. He demonstrated the transfusion of blood from sheep to blood-depleted dogs under differing experimental conditions. Student annotated copies of the synopsis record relevant comments from all fields of medicine and indicate that Harwood possessed an extensive knowledge of contemporary medical research. Having failed to get attendance at lectures and dissections made compulsory, Harwood gave up public dissections because nobody came to them. In 1796 he published *A System of Comparative Anatomy and Physiology*, volume 1, dealing with the brain and sense organs, particularly the olfactory organ, suggesting that their development in different animals was affected by their dependence on a sense of smell to find food. He received no encouragement to continue this work, though a German translation was published in 1799. On 21 July 1798 he married Elizabeth Maria (*d.* 1836), daughter of the Revd Sir John Peschell (*d.* 1778) of Horsley; there were no children from the marriage. First they lived in St Andrew's Street, Cambridge, but by 1803 had moved to Bartlow House, Bartlow, Cambridgeshire, 20 miles away. In 1800 Harwood was elected Downing professor of medicine though continuing as professor of anatomy. His lectures now concentrated on comparative anatomy supported by preparations, made mainly by himself, of which he published a catalogue in 1803 of those preserved in spirit. A full catalogue was prevented by serious illness. An 1807 synopsis of his Downing lectures, open to members of the university, covered domestic medicine and the treatment of infectious diseases.

Harwood was also concerned to reform the examination system for MDs at Cambridge. MBs could proceed after five years to an MD, desirable because only MDs of Oxford and Cambridge could become fellows of the Royal College of Physicians. Harwood fought for the strict enforcement of the regulations governing the award of the degree as the examination of candidates' medical knowledge was not taking place (Winstanley). He raised the problem with Sir Lucas Pepys, president of the Royal College of Physicians, hoping that he also would exert pressure for reform, but Sir Isaac Pennington, the regius professor of medicine and fellow of the college, had sufficient influence to prevent reform as it was he who awarded the MD degree. Harwood once challenged Pennington to a duel which he refused to accept.

Harwood was knighted in 1806 partly for having raised

and captained a volunteer corps in 1798. Expanding further his anatomy course, he published in 1812 *A synopsis of a course of lectures on the philosophy of natural history and the comparative structure of plants and animals*. Having sold Bartlow House in 1810 he moved into East Lodge, Downing College, assigned to the professor of medicine, where he died on 10 November 1814. His will left everything to his wife and a request to be buried in the college grounds. Permission having been obtained from the bishop of Ely, he was buried where it had originally been proposed to build the chapel. His grave was marked by a stone set in the grass. Though Henry Gunning gave an unfavourable account of Harwood in his *Reminiscences of … Cambridge* (1854), he was generally well liked in the university, being witty and sociable. He did his best to improve Cambridge medicine against much opposition. Easy financial circumstances enabled him to endow an annual scholarship of £10 for a medical student at Emmanuel.   HELEN BROCK

Sources Christ's College archives, Cambridge · Emmanuel College archives, Cambridge · Downing College archives, Cambridge · Royal London Hospital archives, Whitechapel Road, London · D. G. Crawford, *A history of the Indian medical service, 1600–1913*, 2 (1914) · J. Ellis, *LHMC, 1785–1985: the story of the London Hospital medical college* (1986) · S. Antiquaries, Lond. · private information (2004) · U. St Andr. L. · R. Williamson, 'Sir Busick Harwood: a reappraisal', *Medical History*, 27 (1983), 423–33 · B. Towers, 'Anatomy and physiology in Cambridge before 1850', *Cambridge and its contribution to medicine* [Cambridge 1969], ed. A. Rook (1971), 65–77 · B. Harward, correspondence with L. Pepys and I. Pennington, RCP Lond., MSS 109/112–119 [re: the Cambridge MD degree] · H. Gunning, *Reminiscences of the university, town, and county of Cambridge, from the year 1780*, 2 vols. (1854) · E. J. C. Kendall, 'Sir Busick Harwood', *Aspects of Downing history*, ed. S. French (1982) · D. A. Winstanley, *Unreformed Cambridge: a study of certain aspects of the university in the eighteenth century* (1935) · *GM*, 1st ser., 84/2 (1814), 605 · election certificate, RS, IV.114

Archives CUL, UPI, 178, 180 · RCP Lond., corresp. and MSS · U. Cam., department of plant sciences, lecture notes | BL, letters to Lord Hardwicke, Add. MSS 35644–35733, *passim*

Likenesses W. N. Gardiner, line engraving, 1790, Wellcome L. · W. N. Gardiner, stipple, pubd 1790 (after S. Harding), BM, NPG · J. Jones, mezzotint, pubd 1791 (after S. Harding), BM · J. Jones, mezzotint, 1791, Wellcome L. · G. Engleheart, miniature; copy, Emmanuel College, Cambridge · J. Smart, miniature; Sothebys, 1975; copy, Emmanuel College, Cambridge · T. Uwins, watercolour drawing, BM · oils, Christ's College, Cambridge

Harwood, Sir Edward (*c.*1586–1632), army officer, was the eldest son of William Harwood of Thurlby, Lincolnshire, and his wife, Eliza (*née* Grenham). Harwood went to the Netherlands in 1599 as a page, possibly joining Colonel Sir John Ogle, who came from nearby Pinchbeck. He spent most of the rest of his career in the service of the Dutch republic.

After good service at Ostend in 1602 Harwood was consistently promoted until by 1607, still very youthful, he was captain of a company of 150 foot. About this time he attracted the favour of Prince Maurice of Nassau, captain-general of the United Provinces, becoming one of the prince's 'servant[s] … in the privy chamber': a great honour (*Downshire MSS*, 3.83). It may well have been at Maurice's behest that he was knighted, which, as Henry Peacham records, he had been by the time of the Cleves-

Jülich campaign of 1614 (Peacham, sig. D3). After the earlier Jülich campaign of 1610 Harwood and General Sir Edward Cecil (nephew of James I's chief minister Robert Cecil, earl of Salisbury), had 'exchanged as much bitterness as rage and malice can think'. Maurice prevented a duel and, it was reported, 'studieth to compound' the dispute, yet it still dragged on into 1613. Eventually a panel of English nobility was appointed to judge its rights and wrongs (*Downshire MSS*, 3.82–3, 98, 4.205–6).

By 1620 Harwood was a lieutenant-colonel and by 1626 he was colonel of an English regiment (one of only four in Dutch pay) 1820 strong. Harwood had thus become one of the premier English soldiers of the day. He was one of the colonels in the disastrous English expedition to Cadiz in 1626 (commanded by Cecil) and got the rearguard away safely. He then returned to the Netherlands where he served for the rest of his life. Harwood was mortally wounded at the siege of Maastricht in June 1632 'pierced through by three successive bullets' (Knight, 72). In his will he requested that, if 'my Leutenant Coll. [Sir Henry Herbert] shall thinke good some small superscription of the time of service and the charges I have borne' be made (PRO, PROB 11/162, fol. 225r); in 1636 Herbert and one of Harwood's captains, Nicholas Byron, erected a monument to his memory in The Hague, where he had been buried at Maurice of Nassau's command.

Harwood was known for his courage, both on the battlefield and in sieges. He was unquestionably a supporter of 'godly' religion. He opposed a Spanish marriage for Prince (later King) Charles; he used his influence with Maurice to have the exiled puritan William Ames appointed professor of divinity at Franeker University; and in his will he bequeathed £100 'to piouse uses to be disposed of by my brother by such Ministers advise as he knowes I most respecteth' and left jewels and medals to the exiled queen of Bohemia's family (PRO, PROB 11/162, fol. 225r). Harwood also made several bequests to his officers. This, together with their loyalty to his memory and his ability to charm the prickly Maurice, suggests he was very personable. He never married and left the bulk of his possessions to the family of his brother, George, a London merchant who, in 1642, published a manuscript treatise by his brother on the appropriate defence policy for England, *The Advice of that Worthy Commander, Sir Ed. Harwood*. It included a memoir of his life and death by the celebrated puritan minister Hugh Peter, who stressed Harwood's military skill, bravery, and reformed godliness, declaring: 'Religion, fidelity, and prowesse met in him' (Harwood, sig. B2v). It is an admirable summary of Sir Edward Harwood's character and career.   D. J. B. TRIM

Sources PRO, PROB 11/162, sig. 94 • H. R. Knight, C. R. B. Knight, and R. S. H. Moody, *Historical records of the Buffs, east Kent regiment, 3rd foot*, 4 vols. (1905–51), vol. 1 [1572–1704] • *The advice of that worthy commander, Sir Ed. Harwood, Collonel … Also a relation of his life and death. Whereunto is also annexed divers remarkable instructions, written by the late, and ever-famous earle of Essex* (1642) • *The visitation of London, anno Domini 1633, 1634, and 1635, made by Sir Henry St George*, 1, ed. J. J. Howard and J. L. Chester, Harleian Society, 15 (1880) • Nationaal Archief, The Hague, Archief van de Staten-Generaal, 8043–8044 • Nationaal Archief, The Hague, Archief van de Raad van State,

1244 • *Report on the manuscripts of the marquis of Downshire*, 6 vols. in 7, HMC, 75 (1924–95), vols. 3–4 • C. R. Markham, *The fighting Veres* (1888) • H. Peacham, *A most true relation of the affaires of Cleve and Gulick* (1615) • *CSP dom., 1611–18* • N. Tyacke, *The fortunes of English puritanism, 1603–1640* (1990)

Wealth at death approx. £500: will, PRO, PROB 11/162, sig. 94

Harwood, Edward (1729–1794), Presbyterian minister and biblical scholar, was born at Darwen, Lancashire, but his parentage is not clear. W. A. Abram believed he belonged to the Lower Darwen branch of the Harwood family and suggested that he was probably the son of Edmund Harwood (*d.* 1764) and the grandson of William Harwood (*d.* 1741), both of whom are described as yeoman farmers and trustees of the Presbyterian chapel in Lower Darwen. Harwood received his early education at the school in Darwen run by Mr Belsborrow, where he learned Latin and Greek. In 1745 he proceeded to Blackburn grammar school, then under the direction of Thomas Hunter, who tried to persuade him to enter Queen's College, Oxford, with a view to becoming an Anglican clergyman; but Harwood's father, being a strict Presbyterian, would, according to Harwood, 'have died if he had seen me in a surplice' (*GM*, 63/2, 1793, 994). He instead became a student in 1748 at the academy managed by the Coward Trust in Wellclose Square, London, where he was trained for the nonconformist ministry by David Jennings, the principal and theological tutor, and the Revd Samuel Morton Savage, the classical and mathematics tutor. He remained there for five years, but found unrewarding the strict adherence to Calvinist orthodoxy insisted on by Jennings and the Coward trustees. He later criticized the theology taught there as 'a gloomy heavy Dutchman's divinity', a reference to Johannes Marck's *Medulla*, the standard divinity textbook at the academy, and described his time there as 'the only blank in my life; for what systems of ethics and divinity I learned, I afterwards took pains to unlearn' (ibid., 994).

On leaving Wellclose Square in 1753 Harwood became a tutor at a boarding-school in Peckham and preached occasionally for George Benson in Poor Jewry Lane, Crutchedfriars. He also gained the friendship and respect of two other notable London divines, Nathaniel Lardner and Samuel Chandler, and soon after married Chandler's youngest daughter, possibly Elizabeth. In 1754 he moved to Congleton, Cheshire, where he taught at the grammar school run by William Turner and preached on alternate Sundays at Wheelock, Cheshire, and Leek, Staffordshire. While in Cheshire, Harwood became a friend and associate of two local dissenting luminaries, Joseph Priestley, minister at Nantwich (1758–61) and afterwards a tutor at Warrington Academy, and John Taylor, the first principal of that academy. How far Harwood deviated from orthodox Calvinism is not clear, but he certainly belonged to the rational wing of dissent. He associated and corresponded with many leading Arians and Socinians of his day and in 1785 he defended Priestley's Socinianism against the attacks of the Revd Samuel Badcock, a former Socinian turned Anglican clergyman. Yet he always denied being an Arian or a Socinian, preferring to label himself 'a moderate and candid dissenter' (*GM*, 63/1, 1793, 409) and dismissed accusations that he had become a Deist as 'mean illiberal malice' (ibid., 53/2, 1783, 691).

In 1765 Harwood accepted the invitation to succeed John Wright as pastor at the Presbyterian chapel in Tucker Street, Bristol. He was ordained on 16 October 1765 at Samuel Chandler's meeting-house in Old Jewry, London, where the ordination sermon was preached by Thomas Amory, the former principal of the academy at Taunton. While at Bristol, Harwood continued his classical studies and became an authority on the Greek language and the Greek fathers of the first three centuries. He was awarded in 1768 the degree of DD by Edinburgh University for the textual criticism outlined in his *Introduction to New Testament Studies* (1767). His detractors, however, claimed the award owed more to the influence and intercession of his father-in-law, Samuel Chandler, than to Harwood's scholarship. Harwood's ministry at Bristol was bitter and acrimonious. His heterodox views revealed in *The Melancholy Doctrine of Predestination* (1768) and his publication of a second edition of William Williams's *On the Supremacy of the Father* made him locally unpopular and led to his castigation in the Bristol press as an Arian, a Socinian, and a Deist. Charges of immorality, which he was never able satisfactorily to answer, were also preferred against him. So his congregation dwindled and with it his income. Over twenty years later he still smarted over what he considered to be an unwarranted desertion by members of his congregation. 'About twenty years ago', he wrote in May 1793, 'I was extremely ill used by a very small society whose subscription, though I had a wife and numerous family, was continually dwindling' (*GM*, 63/1, 1793, 409).

Harwood resigned in 1772 and moved to London where, after failing to obtain a position at the British Museum, he was able to support himself and his family by private tuition and by his literary endeavours. However, in 1782 he suffered a severe stroke which in his own words, 'instantly deprived me of the use of my left side, confined me to the sick room for many months and hath eversince rendered me a helpless cripple' (*GM*, 53/2, 1783, 691). Henceforth he lived in much straitened circumstances. He appears to have relied upon charitable donations and was one of the first individuals to whom the benefits of the Literary Fund were extended.

Harwood was a prolific writer and author of numerous religious and biblical treatises and classical works. He once claimed to have written more books than anyone then living with the exception of Joseph Priestley. Of these the one which contributed most to his reputation as a scholar was *A View of the Various Editions of the Greek and Roman Classics* (1775), which by 1790 had run to four editions and had been translated into German (1778) and Italian (1780 and 1793). Another important work was *A New Introduction to the Study of the New Testament*, the first volume of which appeared in 1767, a second in 1771, and a second edition in 1773. His reconstructed text of the Greek New Testament, published under the title *New Testament Collated with the most Approved MSS with Select Notes in English*

(1776), was remarkable for the independent critical judgement it displayed. In the preface he hoped

> that the Text of the inspired writers here exhibited will approve itself to every Scholar who is a Judge of sacred criticism, to be as near to the original autograph of the Evangelists and Apostles as any hitherto published in the world.

He certainly departed from the *textus receptus* in countless passages and according to Metzger pre-empted 'the epoch-making critical edition of Lachman published in the nineteenth century' (Metzger, 117). Another of his biblical works to attract attention was *A Liberal Translation of the New Testament* (2 vols., 1767), which was well received by rational dissenters but to the orthodox traditionalists it was 'more the New Testament of Dr. Harwood than of the apostles' (Allibone, *Dict.*, 1.798). Notwithstanding the interest these works aroused, his biblical studies never gained the recognition his scholarship deserved. This was in part due to the author's turgid style but also owed much to the lack of encouragement from his fellow dissenters. After the deaths of Chandler (1766) and Lardner (1768) he had few influential friends to commend his work.

From August 1793 Harwood was confined to his bed. He died at his home, 6 Hyde Street, Bloomsbury, on 14 January 1794. His wife had died on 21 May 1791. A Latin epitaph to their memory was written by their eldest son, Edward *Harwood (d. 1814), a distinguished naval surgeon and numismatist, and was published appropriately in the periodical to which Harwood had regularly written, the *Gentleman's Magazine* (64/1, 1794, 185).   M. J. MERCER

Sources *GM*, 1st ser., 64 (1794), 184 · *GM*, 1st ser., 63 (1793), 409 · *GM*, 1st ser., 53 (1783), 691 · *GM*, 1st ser., 63 (1793), 994 · C. Surman, index, DWL · W. A. Abram, *A history of Blackburn, town and parish* (1877) · *DNB* · E. Baines and W. R. Whatton, *The history of the county palatine and duchy of Lancaster*, rev. edn, ed. J. Harland and B. Herford, 2 vols. (1868–70) · E. R. Matthews, ed., *Bristol bibliography* (1916) · J. Aikin and others, *General biography, or, Lives, critical and historical of the most eminent persons*, 10 vols. (1799–1815) · M. Caston, *Independency in Bristol: with brief memorials of its churches and pastors* (1860) · lists of students at Wellclose Square Academy, DWL, L54/3/63, L54/3/72 · B. M. Metzger, *The text of the New Testament: its transmission, corruption and restoration*, 3rd edn (1992) · W. Urwick, ed., *Historical sketches of nonconformity in the county palatine of Cheshire, by various ministers and laymen* (1864) · H. McLachlan, *English education under the Test Acts: being the history of the nonconformist academies, 1662–1820* (1931) · W. Beckett, *A universal biography*, 3 vols. (1835–6) · Allibone, *Dict.*

Harwood, Edward (d. 1814), numismatist, was the eldest son of Edward *Harwood (1729–1794), Presbyterian minister and biblical scholar, and his wife (possibly called Elizabeth), who was the youngest daughter of Samuel *Chandler and died in 1791. He was for many years a surgeon in the navy, and served under Captain (afterwards Admiral) William Bligh on board the *Providence* in 1791–4. He was a collector of ancient coins, specializing in the large bronze and copper coinage of Rome and the Greek world. He assisted John Pinkerton with the third edition of his *Essay on Medals* (1808), and in 1812 he himself published *Populorum et urbium selecta numismatica Graeca ex aere descripta*, with brief notes and a list of places that issued autonomous and Greek imperial coins. The work was dedicated to his friend the barrister and coin collector Philip Le Neve.

For a period Harwood lived at Castle Hedingham, in Essex, but he was living in Kirby Street, Hatton Garden, London, when he died there, unmarried, on 6 January 1814. Le Neve was one of his two executors. His coins and books were sold by auction at Leigh and Sothebys on 28–30 April 1814; the first seven lots were the coins illustrated in the plates of his book. He is described in his obituary notice in the *Gentleman's Magazine* as combining 'the warmest affections of a kind, benevolent friend, and the taste of a deep, elegant scholar' (*GM*, 84/1).

C. E. A. CHEESMAN

Sources *GM*, 1st ser., 63 (1793), 994 · *GM*, 1st ser., 84/1 (1814), 200 · will, with grant of administration, Feb 1814, LMA, London Consistory Court, DL/C/379, p. 129 · death duty entry on subject's estate, 1814, PRO, IR 26/611, fol. 37 · J. Pinkerton, *An essay on medals*, 3rd edn (1808) · *DNB*

Wealth at death under £3500: PRO, death duty registers, IR 26/611, fol. 37

Harwood, Elizabeth Jean (1938–1990), singer, was born on 27 May 1938 at Hawnby, Markton Lane, Barton Seagrave, Kettering, Northamptonshire, the daughter of Sydney Curtis Harwood, local government officer, and his wife, Constance Read. Her mother had herself been a professional soprano (after studies at the Royal Academy of Music, London) and gave Elizabeth her first childhood singing lessons. Harwood was educated at Skipton Girls' High School and went on to the Royal Manchester College of Music, the family having moved to Yorkshire. As a vocal student there of Elsie Thurston she was encouraged by the college principal, Frederic Cox, to involve herself in opera; he had recognized that with her alluring blonde glamour and outgoing personality Harwood, a soprano, was a 'natural' for the stage.

After graduating in 1960 Harwood won the Kathleen Ferrier memorial prize and joined the Glyndebourne Festival Chorus, making her début there as Second Boy in Mozart's *Die Zauberflöte*. In the following year she was engaged by Sadler's Wells Opera in London, where she was first cast in coloratura roles and won success as Gilda (*Rigoletto*), Zerbinetta (*Ariadne auf Naxos*), and Constanze (*Die Entführung aus dem Serail*). Colin Davis, then music director of the company, was a strong influence on her stage development, while audiences much enjoyed the sense of fun she regularly imparted in her singing.

Harwood's international reputation developed after she was joint winner of the 1963 international Verdi competition at Busseto, Italy, and in 1965 she toured Australia in starring roles with the Sutherland–Williamson company, an *ad hoc* ensemble formed primarily to showcase Joan Sutherland's return to her native country as an international celebrity and for whom Harwood was engaged as the alternate soprano for specific performances. These included the title role in *Lucia di Lammermoor* (Donizetti) and the leading roles in *La sonnambula* (Bellini) and *L'elisir d'amore* (Donizetti), parts that Harwood then also sang after her return to England. In the year after the Australia tour, on 15 January 1966, she married Julian Adam Christopher Royle (*b.* 1937/8), a company director, with whom she shared a happy home life in the Essex countryside, becoming an accomplished horsewoman and keen swimmer. They had a son.

During the next decade Harwood was probably heard at her best, although not always on first nights, while recurring throat infections forced her to cancel some performances altogether. She nevertheless became a famously memorable partner to Janet Baker in productions of *Così fan tutte* and *Der Rosenkavalier* for Scottish Opera (their complementary eloquence and style in both Mozart and Richard Strauss were an enduring memory). Harwood further enhanced her reputation with engagements at the major festivals of Aix-en-Provence in 1967–9, while also making her Covent Garden début in 1968 as the Fiakermilli in *Arabella* (Strauss). Here she went on to sing Gilda, Teresa in *Benvenuto Cellini* (Berlioz), and, in a rare excursion into contemporary opera, Bella in *The Midsummer Marriage* (Tippett).

At Aix-en-Provence Harwood was heard in *Don Giovanni* by the conductor Herbert von Karajan, who engaged her for the prestigious Salzburg Festival in 1970; she regularly returned there until 1976, mainly singing Mozart roles. Meanwhile she made her début at the Metropolitan Opera, New York, in 1972 as Fiordiligi (*Così fan tutte*), and returned there in subsequent seasons, also making successful guest appearances in Hamburg, Stuttgart, and Paris and at La Scala, Milan. In 1975 she captured Viennese hearts as Rosalinde in *Die Fledermaus*, and even persuaded listeners that an Englishwoman could successfully become the quintessentially Viennese operetta heroine, Hannah Glawari, in the title role of Lehár's *Die lustige Witwe* (*The Merry Widow*) with the recording she made under Herbert von Karajan, treasured by many for the infectious vocal character she brought to the role.

Harwood was often described as 'bubbly', an apt epithet for her offstage persona, which was warm and friendly, even to a professional critic whom she was not averse to accompanying to a concert that interested her. She also brought endearing vocal character to her varied oratorio and song performances, of which several recordings fortunately constitute a living legacy, and she liked to organize musical evenings at home as well as bringing the benefit of her experience to aspiring young singers, whom she greatly enjoyed musically 'mothering'. She died after a long struggle against carcinomatosis and cancer of the breast at her home, Masonettes, Fryerning, Ingatestone, Essex, on 22 June 1990, aged fifty-two. Her husband survived her.

NOËL GOODWIN

Sources M. Kennedy, 'Elizabeth Harwood—an appreciation', *Opera*, 41 (1990), 932–4 · *WW* (1990) · *The Times* (23 June 1990) · S. Sadie, ed., *The new Grove dictionary of opera*, 4 vols. (1992), vol. 2 · personal knowledge (2004) · b. cert. · m. cert. · d. cert.

Archives FILM BFI NFTVA, performance footage | SOUND BL NSA, performance recordings

Likenesses photograph, 1963, Hult. Arch. · photograph, repro. in *The Times* · two photographs, repro. in *Opera*, 933; priv. coll.

Wealth at death £16,118: probate, *CGPLA Eng. & Wales* (1990)

Harwood, Francis (1726/7–1783), sculptor, worked primarily in Italy. Of his place of birth and his parents, nothing is known. At Easter 1752, when he was twenty-five, he was living at the Palazzo Zuccari, Rome. In Rome he shared accommodation with Sir Joshua Reynolds and Simon Vierpyl. In the following year he was working with the sculptor Joseph Wilton in Florence. He was admitted to the Florentine Academy on 11 January 1755 as a 'pittore Inglese' but he matriculated as a 'scultore'. There is evidence that soon afterwards Harwood worked with Giovanni Battista Piamontini (b. c.1690) in a studio near SS Annunziata. In 1758 both sculptors were among those contracted to decorate Porta San Gallo, where Harwood's statue *Equity* was installed the following year. After Piamontini's death Harwood acquired his studio. Before long his stock in trade was to provide the grand tourist market with copies after the antique; Lord Northampton was among the first to buy a selection. Using more imagination, Harwood sculpted a bust of Cromwell (1759) and a black person (1758; Getty Museum, Malibu, California), which shows exceptional ability. In 1767 he carved an elaborate monument showing Virtue pointing to heaven and to a cherub holding a portrait medallion of William, second Earl Cowper (Hertingfordbury church, Hertfordshire).

In 1768 Thomas Patch made an etching of Harwood which endorses his reputation as 'a drunken Englishman' and in the following year, writing to Thomas Banks, Joseph Nollekens described him as 'knocking the marbil about like feway & belive he has got more work to do than any One Sculptor in England' (Whitley, 41). He was able to meet the growing demand for his work by employing Pietro Pisani (whom he also taught), Pietro Bastianelli, and Niccolò Kindermann as assistants, and his work shows a consequent reduction in quality. From the late 1760s his output began to include garnitures and chimney-pieces. There are records of Harwood providing vases and other items for Charles Townley (1768), Sir Watkin Williams Wynn (1768), the earl of Shelburne (1772), and Sir John Griffin Griffin (1772; Audley End, Essex). He also provided chimney-pieces for Pietro Leopold II (Salone Celesti, Palazzo Pitti, Florence), Catherine the Great (Tsarskoye Selo, near St Petersburg), and Patrick Home (1774–5; Wedderburn Castle, Berwickshire). Others were made after designs by George Dance for Sir William Mainwaring (c.1761; Peover Hall, Cheshire) and, after a design by Sir William Chambers, for the earl of Charlemont (1768; Casino, Dublin). Sir Lawrence Dundas commissioned both fireplaces and other objects (1768–9; Aske Hall, Yorkshire). In 1776 Harwood contributed one of the copies of a Harpy after Giambologna for the Isolotto in the Boboli Gardens, Florence. By 1779 Harwood's success was envied by the young Canova, who remarked on the large number of assistants in his studio and his extensive stock of plaster models, materials, and sculpture. Harwood converted to Catholicism shortly before his death in Florence in December 1783.   HUGH BELSEY

Sources J. Fleming and H. Honour, *Festschrift Ulrich Middeldorf* (1968), vol. 1, pp. 510–16 · R. Cremoncini, 'Alcune note su Francis Harwood', *Gazzetta Antiquaria*, 22–3 (1994), 68–74 · H. Belsey, 'Newly discovered work by Francesco Harwood', *Burlington Magazine*, 122 (1980), 65–6 · R. Gunnis, *Dictionary of British sculptors, 1660–1851* (1953) · J. Ingamells, ed., *A dictionary of British and Irish travellers in Italy, 1701–1800* (1997) · R. R. Villani, 'Il "Busto di Negro" di Francis Harwood del J. Paul Getty Museum di Malibu', *Paragone*, 42 (1991), 68–74 · C. O'Connor, 'Furnishing for the Casino at Marino, co. Dublin', *Burlington Magazine*, 128 (1986), 670–72 · R. R. Villani, 'La decorazione … di Porta San Gallo', *Paragone*, 37 (1986), 53–67 · W. T. Whitley, *Art in England, 1821–1837* (1930)

Likenesses T. Patch, etching, 1768, BM; Hunt. L., Yale U. CBA

Harwood, Harold Marsh (1874–1959), businessman and theatre manager, was born at Ellesmere Park, Barton, near Manchester, on 29 March 1874, the son of George Harwood (1845–1912), cotton spinner and Liberal MP for Bolton from 1895, and his wife, Alice, *née* Marsh. The family's fortune was based on the cotton firm of Richard Harwood & Sons, founded by Harold's grandfather in 1860. Harold was educated at Marlborough College, Trinity College, Cambridge, and St Thomas's Hospital, London, where he gained his MD. Harwood later claimed that it was at Marlborough that it was determined by a 'high power', meaning his father, that he should become a doctor. After a brief spell as a house physician at St Thomas's he set up his own practice at Throgmorton Avenue in the City of London. Harwood acknowledged that his choice of location might 'appear a queer place for a young doctor to start' but he wanted a practice where there would be no calls at night, and he could indulge a passion that was to shape the rest of his life—writing plays. At Throgmorton Avenue, Harwood wrote two plays, and although neither was produced he was encouraged by Sir John Hankin to continue writing. Certainly Harwood did not see his future in the medical profession, and had been lobbying his father to join the family firm at Bolton. In 1900 Harwood's father gave way, and at the age of twenty-six Harold began his career in business. He started learning the cotton trade just at the time when the Lancashire industry entered a phase of export boom, and found the work so demanding that within two years his health broke down. He took a year's complete rest from the business, returning to the firm in 1903.

As part of his recovery Harwood again turned to writing, and helped set up the Bolton Amateur Dramatic Company, where he produced two or three plays a year. During this period he also wrote a one-act play called *The Mask*, an adaptation of a short story written by his future wife, Fryn Tennyson Jesse, and *The Interloper*, a play produced in 1913. The outbreak of the First World War meant for Harwood a temporary return to medicine. He joined the Royal Army Medical Corps, reached the rank of captain, and served in France and Egypt. Even war, however, did not prevent Harwood from maintaining his link with the theatre and in 1916 a play he had written two years previously, *Please Help Emily*, ran with Gladys Cooper in the lead role. This was followed by *Theodore and Co.* at the Gaiety Theatre with Harwood's play put to the music of Ivor Novello. On 9 September 1918 he married Fryniwyd Tennyson (Fryn) *Jesse

(1888–1958), the daughter of Eustace Tennyson, a clergyman, and the great-niece of the poet Tennyson; they collaborated on a number of theatrical projects throughout their married life.

In the inter-war years Harwood was a man of the theatre and his contact with the cotton trade was kept to a minimum. He achieved considerable artistic success, producing an English version of *The Marriage of Figaro* for Sir Thomas Beecham, being invited to Hollywood as a script writer in the early 1930s, writing and producing numerous plays, and entering management at the Ambassador Theatre. His plays were generally in the genre of light comedy, and, while popular with audiences, only one from this period achieved serious critical acclaim: *The Grain of Mustard Seed*. This was written and produced in 1920, and Harwood, departing from type, used comedy as a vehicle for exploring the world of politics. Its success established Harwood as a West End playwright, and expressed his commitment to the liberal individualism which had run deeply in his own family's politics and was subsequently to shape his opposition to the business policies of the post-war Labour government. Harwood added to his reputation with three further successful plays in the 1920s. A somewhat uneven period followed with disappointing productions in 1927, and two rather thin comedies written in collaboration with R. Gore Brown, before he returned to form in 1932.

Following the outbreak of the Second World War Harwood relinquished his theatrical interests and once more became actively engaged in the cotton trade. In 1920 the family firm had been absorbed by the Fine Spinners' and Doublers' Association and Harwood became an ordinary director of the association. His role before 1940 was passive; indeed in 1936 Harwood offered the association the family's preference shares. But within four years there was a dramatic turn of events: Harwood was elected vice-chairman of the association in April 1940, and within four months, following the death of the incumbent, was chairman of one of the largest firms in the cotton industry. Harwood set himself two basic objectives as chairman of Fine Spinners: to return the group to profitability, and to project himself as champion of the small shareholder and staunch defender of the private enterprise system. In his first year as chairman the long-suffering preference shareholders received their first dividend for nearly a decade. Later he implemented a rationalization programme and this, coupled with a capital reorganization scheme, delivered profits of over £1 million by 1950, while the company gained a reputation as a progressive innovator, particularly in the field of new product development.

Harwood aspired to be something more than a company chairman, and sought to present himself as a defender of the private enterprise system against the encroachment of the state. As early as 1942 he had warned shareholders that profits would be reduced because of the imposition of state controls, and he was particularly critical of the 1944 white paper on employment. He believed it threatened the survival of the small shareholder, a group which for him was crucial to the well-being of industry in Britain, and he repeatedly returned to his theme that businessmen should be left to control their own affairs. By the late 1940s opinion seemed to be moving in Harwood's direction as a series of political and economic problems weakened the authority of the Labour government. In 1947 he was elected to the grand council of the Federation of British Industry, and in the following year he used the occasion of Fine Spinners' jubilee to attack what he considered to be the apologetic attitude towards profit making. For Harwood profit making was a wholly useful activity that had helped make Britain a great international power. He espoused a business philosophy which assumed the superiority of the private enterprise system over state planning, and towards the end of his chairmanship could draw on the satisfaction that his views were no longer out of fashion.

For most of the 1940s Harwood's theatrical activities were restricted but in 1948 he and his wife wrote *A Pin to See the Peepshow*, a play based on a book written by his wife in 1934 about an actual murder case. The play embroiled Harwood in a controversy when the lord chamberlain refused to grant a licence for its public performance. It was shown privately in London in 1951, and gained its first public production on Broadway, but it received mixed notices, and had only a short run. It was eventually shown in Britain on television in 1979.

Outside business and the theatre Harwood was a keen yachtsman, a passion he shared with his wife; they sailed in the Mediterranean, and along the coast of Africa. Harwood retired from business on 22 July 1950. He died at his home, Pear Tree Cottage, 11 Melina Place, Marylebone, London, on 20 April 1959, a year after his wife.

ROGER LLOYD-JONES

Sources R. Lloyd-Jones, 'Harwood, Harold Marsh', *DBB* • business records of Fine Spinners and Doublers, Courtaulds plc, Northern Division, Manchester • *Who's who in the theatre*, various edns • *Jubilee distaff: Fine Spinners and Doublers Ltd (1898–1948)* (1948) • *Manchester Guardian* (21 April 1959) • A. A. Rogow, *The labour government and British industry, 1945–1951* (1955) • *Skinners cotton trade directory* (1923) • J. R. Vose, ed., *Bolton: its trade and commerce* (1919) • P. Johnson-Smith, *For the love of books* (1934) • *CGPLA Eng. & Wales* (1959) • b. cert. • m. cert. • d. cert.

Archives Courtaulds plc, Northern Division, Manchester, Fine Spinners and Doublers business papers; minute books of board of directors and executive directors | BL, corresp. with League of Dramatists, Add. MS 63396 • U. Sussex, corresp. with B. W. Levy

Wealth at death £34,899 7*s.* 10*d.*: probate, 19 June 1959, *CGPLA Eng. & Wales*

Harwood, Sir Henry Harwood (1888–1950), naval officer, was born in London on 19 January 1888, the son of Surtees Harwood Harwood, barrister, of Ashman's Hall, Beccles, Suffolk, and his wife, Mary Cecilia Ullathorne, a distant relative of Archbishop Ullathorne. He was educated at Fosters School, Stubbington, and, choosing the navy as a career, he became a cadet in the *Britannia* in 1903. He soon displayed his intellectual capacity by gaining first-class certificates in all subjects in his examinations for lieutenant. In 1911 he specialized in torpedo and thereafter served as torpedo officer in a number of ships. He did not see action in the First World War, although his service in

Sir Henry Harwood Harwood (1888–1950), by Walter Stoneman

the Grand Fleet was recognized when he was made an OBE in 1919.

Harwood's first post-war service was a two-year commission in the South American squadron, during which he gained a working knowledge of Spanish which was of use to him again twenty years later. His subsequent peacetime service was largely in staff posts and included periods at the Naval Staff College, the Admiralty plans division, the Imperial Defence College, on the staff of the senior officers' war course, and as fleet torpedo officer in the Mediterranean. He was promoted to commander in 1921 and to captain in 1928. In 1924 he married Joan, who survived him, daughter of Selway Chard, of West Tarring, Sussex. They had two sons, both of whom entered the Royal Navy.

In 1936 Harwood was appointed commodore in command of the South American division of the America and West Indies station. With the outbreak of war in 1939 reinforcements were sent to this station and then, after some weeks, arrived the news that the German pocket battleship the *Admiral Graf Spee*, with heavier guns and thicker armour than any of his own ships possessed, was operating in the south Atlantic. Harwood went in search with the three cruisers *Ajax*, *Exeter*, and *Achilles*, and by skilful estimation of her movements sighted the enemy off the River Plate early on 13 December. Harwood had planned at length for such an engagement. He was said at the time, and in later reports, to have 'handled his ships brilliantly' in the engagement, splitting his force in two and attacking from widely different angles (Grove, 350), although recent historical accounts have suggested that

his general approach to the encounter was relatively pedestrian and timid, and his tactics a 'sensible compromise' on the options (Stephen, 30). The German captain stood his ground for about twenty minutes and then made for the land. Harwood followed, but although the action was pressed for more than another hour, with much damage on both sides, the *Admiral Graf Spee* had not been crippled before shortage of ammunition compelled Harwood to break off the fight and resort to shadowing. The German ship was thus able to reach Montevideo about midnight. The British were able to convince the Germans that a much larger force was waiting outside the harbour, and on 17 December the *Admiral Graf Spee* emerged only to blow herself up rather than be interned.

This British success could not have been more timely or welcome, for it gave Hitler his first rebuff and was of immense propaganda value. Harwood, by wireless, was appointed KCB and promoted to rear-admiral. It is likely, however, that his elevation 'may have placed him higher than his abilities merited' (Stephen, 30).

A year later Harwood was taken home to be an assistant chief of the naval staff at the Admiralty, where he became 'a favourite of Churchill's' (Grove, 366), and in 1942 the latter appointed him commander-in-chief, Mediterranean, in succession to Sir Andrew Cunningham. For a rear-admiral to receive such a post was almost unknown in modern times. But he was less than successful. A number of failed naval operations through late 1942 and January 1943 caused the army commander, Montgomery, and Churchill to lose confidence in Harwood and he was relieved of his command soon after. He held the less exacting Orkneys and Shetlands command for some months before being finally invalided from the navy in 1945 with the rank of admiral.

Harwood had received honours from many quarters. He was appointed to the Chilean order of merit for earthquake rescue work and received the Greek war cross. He received in 1940 the freedom of Exeter; the Gosport council gave his name to a road on its Bridgemary estate, an avenue was called after him in the new town of Ajax, Ontario, and in South America two streets were named after him, one in Punta del Este and one near Carrasco, Montevideo.

A keen sportsman, Harwood was an excellent shot, a fine fisherman, and had a golf handicap of seven at Sandwich. His personality played no small part in his success. A natural geniality and charm of manner brought out the best in his subordinates and smoothed his relations with others, notably in the South American countries where these qualities, reinforced by his command of Spanish, had already earned him much goodwill among influential civilians when his victory off the Plate made him the most popular British figure for generations.

He died at his home, White Cottage, Goring-on-Thames, Oxfordshire, on 9 June 1950. After his death public requiem masses were said for him—for he was a Roman Catholic—in the cathedral at Montevideo and in the basilica at Buenos Aires.

RUSSELL GRENFELL, *rev.* MARC BRODIE

Sources *The Times* (13 June 1950) • M. Stephen, *The fighting admirals: British admirals of the Second World War* (1991) • E. J. Grove, 'A service vindicated', *The Oxford illustrated history of the Royal Navy*, ed. J. R. Hill (1995) • M. H. Murfett, ed., *The first sea lords: from Fisher to Mountbatten* (1995) • D. Pope, *The battle of the River Plate* (1956) • *WWW* • personal knowledge (1959) • S. W. Roskill, *The war at sea, 1939–1945*, 3 vols. in 4 (1954–61) • *CGPLA Eng. & Wales* (1950)
Archives FILM IWM FVA, news footage | SOUND IWM SA, oral history interview
Likenesses O. Birley, oils, *c.*1945–1948, Royal Naval College, Greenwich • W. Stoneman, photograph, NPG [*see illus.*] • D. Wales-Smith, oils (after photograph), NMM
Wealth at death £14,676 5*s.* 1*d.*: probate, 13 Aug 1950, *CGPLA Eng. & Wales*

Harwood, Isabella Neil (1837?–1888), novelist and playwright, probably born on 14 June 1837, was the daughter of Philip *Harwood (1811–1887), Unitarian minister, journalist, and editor of the *Saturday Review* from 1868 to 1883, and his wife, Isabella Neill or Neil (*d.* 1899), of Scottish descent and daughter of Robert Neill, a solicitor and member of the Edinburgh congregation. At the time of Isabella's birth the Harwoods were resident in Bridport, Dorset, where Philip Harwood was minister of a Unitarian congregation. They later settled in London. Little is known about Isabella Harwood's education or early life.

Harwood began her literary career as a reviewer. From 1864 to 1870 she wrote several successful novels, published anonymously, including *Abbot's Cleve* (1864), *Carleton Grange* (1866), *Raymond's Heroine* (1867), and *The Heir Expectant* (1870). Harwood adopted some conventions associated with the popular genre of sensation fiction in her novels; *Carleton Grange*, for example, relies on the familiar sensational devices of complex plotting and mistaken identity. Some critics found her fiction to be 'excessively wholesome' (Sutherland, 283), although *The Heir Expectant* contains some interesting departures from contemporary fictional norms. It features an intellectual, independent heiress, Olivia Egerton, who remains defiantly unmarried until the end of the third volume, and suggests that the love between brother and sister may be stronger than that between husband and wife.

Under the masculine pseudonym Ross Neil, Harwood published a number of blank verse dramas, including *Lady Jane Grey* and *Inez* (1871), *Elfinella* (1876), *Tasso* (1879), and *Andrea the Painter* (1883). *Elfinella* was produced at the Princess's Theatre, Edinburgh, in 1875, and at the Princess's Theatre, London, on 6 June 1878. *Inez* was produced as *Loyal Love* at the Gaiety Theatre in 1887. Such so-called 'poetical dramas' were out of fashion at the time. Although contemporary critics felt that Harwood brought 'engaging freshness' to familiar issues, and wrote about historical subjects like Lady Jane Grey in a style 'completely free from affectation', her dramatic works did not enjoy great popular success (*Saturday Review*, 2 June 1888, 644; 16 Dec 1871, 782).

Editing a selection of Harwood's works for *The Poets and Poetry of the Nineteenth Century* (1907), Richard Garnett observed that, like Joanna Baillie a generation earlier, Harwood 'kept the torch of the poetical drama alight without the power to send it abroad'. Although he praised her

'intellectual ability, singular elegance of diction, and accurate delineation of character', he considered her dramas to be 'too manifestly works of reflection' (Garnett, 147).

Harwood never married, and lived with her father in London and then in Hastings until his death in 1887. She shared not only his interest in literature, but also his musical taste and proficiency. She did not long survive him, dying of breast cancer at her home, South Bank, Baldslow Road, Saint Mary-in-the-Castle, Hastings, on 29 May 1888.   MEGAN A. STEPHAN

Sources Blain, Clements & Grundy, *Feminist comp.* • J. Sutherland, *The Longman companion to Victorian fiction* (1988) • *Saturday Review* (2 June 1888), 644 • R. Garnett, 'Isabella Harwood ("Ross Neil")', *The poets and poetry of the nineteenth century*, ed. A. H. Miles (1907) • 'Ross Neil's two dramas', *Saturday Review* (16 Dec 1871), 782–3 • 'Ross Neil's plays', *Saturday Review* (9 May 1874), 595–7 • Allibone, *Dict.* • Boase, *Mod. Eng. biog.* • S. J. Kunitz and H. Haycraft, eds., *British authors of the nineteenth century* (1936), 280 • R. L. Wolff, *Nineteenth-century fiction: a bibliographical catalogue based on the collection of R. L. Wolff*, 5 vols. (1982), 2.198

Harwood, Philip (1811–1887), Unitarian minister and journal editor, was born in Worcester on 22 March 1811, the second son and fifth child (of eight) born to William Harwood (1773?–1848) and his wife, the former Abigail Hawley (*d.* 1847). Following their marriage in Shrewsbury in 1802 the Harwoods moved to Worcester, and soon after Philip's birth settled in Bristol. There William Harwood, who lived in Portland Square, may well have joined Harwood, Hawley, and Holden, sugar refiners and wholesale grocers in Counter Slip. By 1825, with his eldest son (also William), he was operating a business dealing in raw sugar.

The religious background of the family was quite possibly Baptist—Harwoods and Holdens appear as subscribers at Broadmead Chapel, Bristol—but no Harwood is entered in the registers of Baptist chapels in Shrewsbury or Worcester. In the Lewin's Mead records for 1831, William Harwood, presumably Philip's brother, is noted as a pew renter, and Philip was recorded as having contributed half a guinea. That connection supports the assertion (not otherwise confirmed) of Alexander Gordon (1841–1931), the dissenting historian (notes for a history of St Mark's, Edinburgh), that Philip Harwood was educated in the well-known school of Lant Carpenter, the minister of the Unitarian chapel in Lewin's Mead. It seems more likely, however, that Philip, articled to a solicitor, attended the much renowned informal classes that Carpenter conducted for young people in the congregation.

In 1833 Philip Harwood and his youngest brother, Reynold (1816–1889), entered the divinity course at the University of Edinburgh. The Lewin's Mead connection seems to falsify the assertion of one obituarist (*The Inquirer*, 24 Dec 1877) that his intention was to enter the Baptist ministry, while lending credence to the report that he was appalled by lectures on the atonement given by Thomas Chalmers, the celebrated evangelical who was then professor of divinity, although neither brother's name appears on Chalmers's class list. After withdrawing from the university in his first year, Philip Harwood came under the influence of George Harris, minister at Glasgow, and Bartholomew Teeling Stannus, minister at Edinburgh; he preached at the Unitarian chapel in Young Street during Stannus's absence in England in 1834–5.

In 1835 Harwood became minister of the small, distinguished Unitarian congregation at Bridport, Dorset, where he grew increasingly heterodox. On 26 April 1836 he married Isabella (d. 1899), the daughter of Robert Neill, a solicitor and a leading member of the Edinburgh congregation, newly housed and renamed St Mark's; their only child, Isabella *Harwood, became a novelist and playwright. In 1839, during a visit to Edinburgh, he preached several times at St Mark's. His views, which by then included rejection of gospel miracles, alienated the minister, R. E. B. MacLellan, and split the congregation; one faction, led by Harwood's father-in-law, set up a separate church which in time became associated with Owenite socialism.

A gap in the minute books of the Bridport congregation prevents direct confirmation of a reported disagreement there over Harwood's theological views. However that may be, in 1840 he became (in the phrase used in the South Place records) 'co-adjutor' to W. J. Fox, who was by then formally separated from the Unitarians, in his chapel in South Place, Finsbury. In 1841, with warm expressions of appreciation from the South Place congregation, he moved to the Beaumont Institution, a museum, reading-room, and chapel opened in east London a year earlier by the wealthy insurance merchant J. T. Barber Beaumont; a list of the lectures delivered by Harwood and his colleague Thomas Wood, an Anglican turned Unitarian, appears in Harwood's *The Object of the Sunday Lectures at the Philosophical Institution, Beaumont Square* (1842).

From the institution's founding, many in the audience came 'from the antipodes of Mile End' (Hennell, 52–3). Among them was the diarist Henry Crabb Robinson, who noted others in attendance and commented on the lectures: although he was often favourably impressed, he thought on one occasion that Harwood's message was that of 'an inferior Carlyle' (Robinson, diary, 6 Aug 1841) and often expressed grave doubts about his theology. Harwood was also in close touch with Charles Christian Hennell, the Unitarian biblical critic; the memoir of Hennell by his sister throws much light on the Beaumont period.

Harwood's published sermons and lectures, in Bridport and London, cover a wide range of topics. In one he condemned religious 'materialism', by which he meant devotion to forms, and in another argued for 'church extension' dedicated to moral and cultural improvement. His call, no doubt influenced by Coleridge, for a broadly based national church to accomplish these ends provoked a stern rebuke from his old mentor George Harris (*Christian Pioneer*, 555–7) for his apparent abandonment of the voluntary principle. An ethical utilitarian and a political liberal, Harwood threw himself into the free-trade agitation, arguing that the corn laws were unbiblical. His most important contribution, however, was six lectures at South Place published as *German Anti-Supernaturalism*

(1841), one of the earliest public expositions in England of the religious views of David Friedrich Strauss (1808–1874), whose *Leben Jesu* (1835–6) had advanced a mythic explanation of Christian appeal.

Thomas Wood soon left the institution, and in 1842 Harwood was dismissed because Beaumont's son and heir found his views unacceptable. Introduced by Fox to John Forster, the drama and literary critic of *The Examiner*, in 1843 Harwood became sub-editor on the paper. In 1844 he published a sympathetic *History of the Irish Rebellion of 1798*. He subsequently moved to *The Spectator*, and in 1849 became sub-editor at the *Morning Chronicle*, then a Peelite organ edited by John Douglas Cook (1808?–1868). He followed Cook to the *Saturday Review*, begun in November 1855, a weekly journal whose able contributors and brashly brilliant style placed it among the most influential periodicals for more than thirty years. He was by repute 'the best sub-editor who ever lived' (Bevington, 352), and the obituary in that journal gives a glimpse into his methods. On Cook's death in 1868 he succeeded to the editorship, in which he was successful, if less brilliantly so than his predecessor.

The anonymity of Harwood's later years reflected both personal choice and professional principle; he wrote little, even for his own journal. Outwardly shy, but genial and amusing with friends and steadily encouraging to his writers, he found his deepest interests in music—he played the violin—and politics, though his early radicalism had substantially abated. The obituary in the *Saturday Review* names Sir Stafford Northcote and Lord Hartington as his favourite politicians, and Richard Garnett, the British Museum librarian and W. J. Fox's biographer, recalled that Harwood's terrier, Moses, would show 'vehement demonstrations of disapproval' at the mention of Gladstone and Bright (Garnett, 217–18).

Troubled by illness from 1881, Harwood resigned in 1883, retiring to Hastings, where he died of bronchitis at his home, South Bank, Baldslow Road, on 10 December 1887. The obituarist in *Christian Life* (17 December 1887), who claimed to know him well, said that he had become a high-churchman—the strongly held position of the *Saturday Review*'s proprietor, Alexander Beresford Hope (1820–1887)—but the only funeral service was held at the interment in the borough cemetery, Hastings, on 15 December; Reynold Harwood, who had become an Anglican priest in 1859, was among the mourners.   R. K. WEBB

Sources A. M. Hill, 'The successors of the remnant: a bicentenary account of St. Mark's Unitarian Church, Edinburgh [pt 2]', *Transactions of the Unitarian Historical Society*, 16/4 (1978), 149–75 · *Saturday Review*, 64 (1887), 808 · *The Inquirer* (24 Dec 1887) · *Christian Life* (17 Dec 1887) · *Hastings and St Leonards Observer* (24 Dec 1887) · M. M. Bevington, *The Saturday Review, 1855–1868: representative educated opinion in Victorian England* (1941) · R. Garnett and E. Garnett, *The life of W. J. Fox, public teacher and social reformer, 1786–1864* (1910) · S. K. Ratcliffe, *The story of South Place* (1955) · H. C. Robinson, diaries, DWL, 20 Feb, 4 April, 21 June, 15 July 1841; 4 Jan, 14 Sept 1842 · S. S. Hennell, *A memoir of Charles Christian Hennell* (1899) · Alexander Gordon, notes for a history of St Mark's Church, Edinburgh, JRL · Bristol street directories, 1815–45, Bristol Central Library · U. Edin. L., special collections division • minute book, Finsbury Chapel, South Place, 1836–41, South Place Ethical Society, London • *Christian Pioneer*, 14 (1840), 555–7 • list of subscribers, Lewin's Mead Chapel, Bristol, 1831, DWL, MS, O.D.30 • marriage register, St Margaret's parish, Shrewsbury, 1802, PRO • Broadmead (Baptist) Chapel register, Bristol, PRO • nonconformist registers, DWL, vol. D of abstracts in PRO • *GM*, 2nd ser., 29 (1848), 449 [death notice of William Harwood] • d. cert. • m. cert. • A. Gordon, *The Irish book lover* (1910), 108–9

Archives JRL, Alexander Gordon papers, Unitarian College MSS

Wealth at death £7755 4*s*. 8*d*.: probate, 9 Jan 1888, *CGPLA Eng. & Wales*

Harwood, Thomas (1767–1842), Church of England clergyman and writer, was born on 18 May 1767 at Shepperton, Middlesex, of which parish his father and grandfather had been both patrons and rectors. His father was Thomas Harwood (1728/9–1796). The younger Thomas Harwood went to Eton College on 18 November 1773, when only six and a half years old, and in September 1775 he was admitted on the foundation. In 1784 he was matriculated at Oxford as a commoner of University College. In 1789 he was ordained deacon, and was admitted sizar of Emmanuel College, Cambridge. He was headmaster of the grammar school at Lichfield from October 1791 until 1813, but the school was effectively defunct and he had very few pupils. In 1813 he gave up his post to live in a house of his own in that city. He married, on 7 January 1793, Maria (*d*. 1830), eldest daughter of Charles Woodward, of Birmingham, and they had a family of ten children.

From 1800 to 1842 Harwood was perpetual curate of Hammerwich, near Lichfield. He graduated BD at Cambridge in 1811, and in 1814 was presented, on his own nomination, to the rectory of Stawley, Somerset, but after living there two years, he resigned the living in 1819, and returned to Lichfield, where he was a magistrate and president of the public library. He was created DD of Cambridge University in 1822, and for many years was a fellow of the Society of Antiquaries. He was presented in 1828 to the chapelry of Burntwood, which he served, together with Hammerwich, until his death. In politics Harwood was a follower of C. J. Fox and an upholder of civil liberties. He strenuously and consistently supported Roman Catholic emancipation. It is thought that these sentiments stood in the way of his professional preferment.

Harwood wrote on various topics. After trying his hand at drama with two verse plays (1787 and 1788), he went on to produce various theological works and sermons, works on classical antiquity, a biographical dictionary, and a manual of geography. In later life he turned to topography and published a *History and Antiquities of Lichfield* in 1806 and an edition of Sampson Erdeswicke's *Survey of Staffordshire* in 1820. Harwood died at Lichfield on 23 December 1842 and was buried in Hammerwich church in the same vault as his wife.

THOMPSON COOPER, *rev.* ELIZABETH BAIGENT

Sources *GM*, 2nd ser., 19 (1843), 203–4 • Venn, *Alum. Cant.* • R. A. Austen-Leigh, ed., *The Eton College register, 1753–1790* (1921) • Foster, *Alum. Oxon.*

Archives Bodl. Oxf.

Likenesses engraving, repro. in S. Erdeswicke, *Survey of Staffordshire*, ed. T. Harwood (1820)

Hary [Harry; *called* Blind Hary] (*b. c.*1440, *d.* in or after 1492), poet, was the author of *The Actis and Deidis of the Illuster and Vailzeand Campioun Schir William Wallace* (title as in a 1570 edition by Robert Lekpreuik), an epic poem in which Scottish patriotic sentiments are embodied in an elaborately presented, but historically much distorted, life story of William *Wallace. It is the only work which can be attributed with certainty to him. The earliest text of the poem is a manuscript by John Ramsay dated 1488 (NL Scot., Adv. MS 19.2.2), written, according to a colophon, for the vicar of Auchtermoonzie in Fife; this was part of the estate of Sir William Wallace of Craigie, who may have been Hary's patron.

Contemporary documentation of Hary's life is very sparse. His name appears five times in the Scottish treasurer's accounts in the years 1490–92, with reference to payments made to him 'at the Kingis command' (for what service is not specified), and in each instance the name is written as Blind(e) Hary. The same appellation is used by William Dunbar in his 'Lament for the Makaris', probably written in 1505, in which Hary is stated to be dead. Since this is the invariable form of his name in early sources, it may be taken as authentic. The practice of referring to him as Henry, which became customary after John Jamieson in his 1820 edition of *Wallace* styled its author Henry the Minstrel, is without historical warrant.

A reference by John Mair identifies Hary (Henricus) as the author of *Integrum librum Guillelmi Wallacei*. A vague clue to the date of the poem is furnished by Mair's statement that the book was written during his own childhood, which, as he was born in 1467, presumably implies the 1470s. This dating is confirmed by Hary's own mention of Sir William Wallace of Craigie as being alive at the time of the poem: Wallace was knighted in 1471–2 and killed at the siege of Dunbar in 1479. Mair also states that Hary was blind from birth, and that he earned food and clothing by telling tales to noble patrons (a detail which probably suggested to Jamieson his designation of minstrel). The internal evidence of the poem, however, by no means supports the claim that Hary was born blind. Topographic descriptions and references to conditions of natural light are frequent, and a quite striking visual intensity is noteworthy in many passages: a good example is Wallace's dream-vision, a pivotal episode in the poem, in which the symbolism of colours, metals, and precious stones is central to the interpretation of the passage.

Evidence for other details of Hary's life must be sought within the poem. Frequent references to families with seats in central and eastern Scotland—Perthshire, Stirlingshire, Linlithgow, and Fife—and a detailed knowledge of the topography of that area suggest that it was his place of origin. That he was a man of wide reading is evident from the breadth and variety of his literary influences, an aspect of his work which has only recently been fully recognized. The many scenes of conflict, ranging in scale from single combats to pitched battles, show a familiarity with the nature of warfare which could hardly have been acquired without firsthand experience—clearly a further argument against the poet's having been blind from birth. (Hary's most recent editor, Matthew P. McDiarmid, suggests that he may have fought in the wars between Louis XI of France and the duke of Burgundy, perhaps as a member of the former's Garde Écossaise). Manifest throughout the poem is not only an intense Scottish patriotism, but a bitter opposition to James III's policy of alliance with Edward IV, seen by Hary as a foolish and treacherous risking of the subjugation of Scotland to the traditional enemy. Since the king's pro-English policy was not unpopular with the merchants and bourgeoisie, it may be conjectured that both Hary and his patrons belonged to the landowning class.

The poem, written mostly in easy and fluent pentameter couplets, tells the story of William Wallace's career as a patriotic hero of Scotland's struggle against the occupying English forces of Edward I. The protagonist is shown growing to manhood in a Scotland suffering under English oppression, and increasing in stature from a young adventurer bent on taking vengeance for injuries to himself and his kinsfolk to the ruthless and dedicated leader of the national resistance movement, and finally to a divinely appointed martyr to the cause of Scottish independence. The pace is rapid, and sequences of exciting events are related with a high degree of narrative skill. Famous episodes include his single-handed victory over a party of five English troopers intent on stealing his catch of fish, his vengeance for the murder of his wife by the sheriff of Lanark, his burning of the garrison of Ayr in retribution for the treacherous hanging of a group of Scots nobles, his victory at the battle of Stirling Bridge, and his defiant bearing at his execution. Throughout Wallace is presented as ardently patriotic, indomitably brave, ferocious in combat, and merciless to his and his country's enemies, but personally loyal, courteous, and strong in his affections. Underpinning the entire poem is the author's passionate commitment to the justice of the Scottish cause: the English are shown as brutal, arrogant, and treacherous, and Wallace in his vision is charged by the Blessed Virgin herself with the task of liberating Scotland from English oppression. (It is possible that Hary's treatment of his hero was inspired to some extent by the story of Jeanne d'Arc.)

Despite its outstanding merits as a dramatic narrative and as a stirring manifestation of patriotic feeling, the poem has been much criticized for its lack of historical accuracy. Many episodes have no other surviving attestation, several are distorted, and some are obvious fabrications (such as a victory by which Wallace partially redeems his defeat at the battle of Falkirk and an invasion of England from which he desists at the pleading of the English queen). This has been explained as the result of Hary's uncritical use of doubtful sources: besides the early fifteenth-century chroniclers Walter Bower and Andrew Wyntoun, from whom part of his material is clearly derived, and an unidentified (and almost certainly fictitious) Latin book by Wallace's chaplain John Blair to which Hary himself refers, many episodes probably have

their origin in the gestes of Wallace which, according to Wyntoun, existed in great numbers. Recent critics, however, setting the patent inauthenticity of much of the narrative against the literary sophistication of the poem and its strongly emphasized political message, have attributed Hary's cavalier treatment of facts neither to naïvety nor to simple mendacity, but to a desire to reinforce the patriotic sentiments of the Scots of his own time, and their determination to maintain Scotland's integrity, by presenting Wallace's conflicts in the most dramatic and morally inspiring manner possible.

Despite the lack of contemporary evidence regarding Hary himself, his poem has proved to be one of the most enduringly popular and most influential in all Scottish literature. John Mair and Hector Boece used it in the sixteenth century as a historical source; Robert Burns remarked on how it had inflamed his patriotic feeling; Sir Walter Scott drew on it for his *Tales of a Grandfather*; and its influence is visible in the hugely popular film *Braveheart* (1995). The place held to this day by Wallace in the popular imagination is principally due to Hary's portrayal; and on a more general level, his contribution to the Scottish sense of national identity is fundamental, matched only by that of Scott. This has long been recognized, but recent critical reassessments of his poem have materially raised his accepted standing as a writer, demolishing the notion of an untutored 'minstrel' and revealing him as a poet of genius.

J. DERRICK McCLURE

Sources *Hary's Wallace*, ed. M. P. McDiarmid, 2 vols., STS, 4th ser., 4–5 (1968–9) · R. J. Goldstein, *The matter of Scotland: historical narrative in medieval Scotland* (1993) · E. Walsh, 'Hary's *Wallace*: the evolution of a hero', *Scottish Literary Journal*, 11/1 (1984), 5–19 · N. Macdougall, *James III: a political study* (1982) · A. Fisher, *William Wallace* (1986) · *The poems of William Dunbar*, ed. J. Small, 3 vols., STS, 2 (1893) · Hary, *The actis and deidis of the illuster and vailzeand campioun Schir William Wallace*, ed. R. Lekpreuik (1570) · Hary, *Wallace, or, The life and acts of Sir W. Wallace*, ed. J. Jamieson (1820)
Archives NL Scot., Advocates MS 19.2.2

Haryett [*married name* Trelawny], **Elizabeth Ann** [*known as* Lizzie Howard], **countess of Beauregard in the French nobility** (*bap.* 1823?, *d.* 1865), courtesan, was, like most of her kind, of obscure origins, but she has been tentatively identified with the Elizabeth Ann Haryett who was baptized at the church of St Nicholas, Brighton, on 13 August 1823, the daughter of Joseph Gawan Haryett and Elizabeth Alderton. After an early introduction to the life of a courtesan, she took the name Lizzie Howard and rapidly advanced in her profession; by 1840 she was among the most sought-after whores in London. She rapidly made a large fortune (one client was said to have paid £1000 for one night's entertainment).

Haryett was introduced to Prince Louis Napoleon, later Napoleon III, by the Count D'Orsay at Gore House in 1839, and apparently fell in love. Whether she part-financed his Boulogne expedition of 1840 as was often claimed is not now known, but over the next eleven years she certainly advanced him large sums of money. The son she bore in 1842, Martin Constantin Haryett, was widely regarded as Louis Napoleon's, although it is equally likely that he was not. She rebuffed a potential client, the historian A. W.

Elizabeth Ann Haryett [Lizzie Howard], **countess of Beauregard in the French nobility** (*bap.* 1823?, *d.* 1865), by Sir William Charles Ross

when in Paris flaunted herself before them, taking boxes at the opera opposite theirs and driving her carriage behind the empress's. In the early 1860s Trelawny took a shooting lodge in Scotland for two years, but they did not visit the neighbours; great was the consternation when it was discovered that the religious and moral society of Ross-shire had been harbouring so notorious a woman. After the divorce the countess returned to her château outside Paris, and to her amusement of pestering the imperial couple. She died unexpectedly on 19 August 1865 at the Château Beauregard. Rumours of foul play were probably unsubstantiated. Her entry in the death registers of La Celle St Cloud described her as 'Elizabeth Ann Haryett, called Miss Howard, Countess de Beauregard, born in England in 1823'.   K. D. REYNOLDS

Sources Le Petit Homme Rouge, *The court of the Tuileries* (1907) · C. Pearl, *The girl with the swansdown seat* (1955) · Lady St Helier [S. M. E. Jeune], *Memories of fifty years* (1909) · A. L. M. Lancastre Saldanha, Lady Cardigan, *My recollections* (1909) · *IGI*
Likenesses W. C. Ross, miniature, priv. coll. [*see illus.*]

Haschenperg, Stephen von (*fl.* 1535–1547), military engineer, was a native of Moravia, who probably followed Mary of Hungary to the Netherlands when she became regent there for her brother, the emperor Charles V, in 1531. He is first recorded in an English context in 1535, when he offered his services to Thomas Cromwell as 'armourer and architect' ('pro armamentario et architecto'; PRO, SP 1/100, 60), having first approached the duke of Suffolk. He was not then employed, but cannot have been entirely rebuffed, for on 12 April 1539 he wrote again to Cromwell, from Dol in Brittany, in terms suggesting both that he was an intelligence agent for the secretary, and also, since he claimed to be able to understand the speech of Polish sailors, that he knew eastern Europe and the Baltic.

The threat of foreign invasion in 1539, and perhaps also this reminder of his existence, now led to Haschenperg's finding employment in England, at first on the south-east coast. In 1539–40 he undertook works at Sandgate and Camber castles, devising fortifications of considerable, indeed unnecessary, complexity. With their concentric defences and use of bastions they were among the earliest English fortifications to show a knowledge of Italian innovations in military design, though Haschenperg, who seems to have been a land surveyor by training, may not in fact have fully understood the significance of the models he imitated. Hence, for instance, his repeated tendency to leave dead ground in front of his defences. His technical weaknesses were not appreciated at first, however, and he was granted an annuity of £60 in 1539, raised to £75 in July 1540. Then in November 1540 he was sent to Calais, to survey its defences and prepare a plan for their strengthening.

Having returned to England, Haschenperg went north shortly afterwards. At Berwick with the duke of Norfolk in January 1541, by June he was at Carlisle, where substantial works on the defences of both castle and city were in progress. Perhaps he was here executing works planned by others rather than a programme of his own devising, a

Kinglake, at about this time: he was unremittingly hostile to the French emperor. In 1846, when Louis Napoleon escaped from his captivity and returned to London, he set her up as his mistress in a house in Berkeley Street, where they remained until, following the revolution of 1848, he returned to France to contest the presidential elections. Miss Howard, who followed him across the channel, contributed largely to the presidential coffers (the sums have been estimated at anything between £13,000 and £320,000) and lived openly as his mistress. She evidently hoped to emulate the great mistresses of previous French kings, but in 1852, having declared himself emperor, Napoleon III decided to marry. Miss Howard was now surplus to requirements and, after some difficult scenes, was paid off. Accounts of the total amounts she received from the emperor vary as wildly as those of her gifts to him, but it is certain that she was created countess of Beauregard, and given the Château Beauregard and its 450 acre estate near Versailles, together with an annual pension estimated at £20,000. Her son was created count of Bechevet, which some have taken as an acknowledgement of his imperial parentage.

On 16 May 1854 the countess married Clarence Trelawny (*b.* 1826), a scion of the Salusbury–Trelawny family, who was at that time an officer in the Austrian army. It was an unhappy marriage and ended in divorce in February 1865. (No mention of it is made in the genealogies of *Burke's Peerage*.) Elizabeth long bore a grudge against the emperor, and especially against his wife, the Empress Eugénie, and possibility that could explain why he achieved more of lasting utility at Carlisle than elsewhere. Haschenperg was responsible for strengthening the castle so that it could carry more guns, for building an elaborate half-moon battery to protect its inner ward and bulwarks to act as outworks, and for at least beginning a citadel designed to command the city from its southern end. Nevertheless, he soon ran into difficulties, at least some of them apparently of his own making. He had begun his time at Carlisle with quarrels, with his colleague Thomas Gower, who was sent to Berwick, and with the captain of the castle, Sir Thomas Wentworth, who was ordered to 'use himself more temperately' (*LP Henry VIII*, vol. 16, no. 958). By the end of 1542 the progress of the works was giving rise to concern. The march warden and the bishop of Carlisle were ordered to inspect them, and in the following July Haschenperg was dismissed, on the grounds that he had 'behaved lewdly and spent great treasure to no purpose' (*LP Henry VIII*, vol. 18/1, no. 901). Perhaps his lack of qualifications had caught up with him, though he did not help his own cause by his disrespectful bearing towards the king's council.

Haschenperg left England in 1543, subsequently forfeiting property at West Ham, Essex, and went to the Baltic; on his return in 1544 he persuaded Mary of Hungary to write to Henry VIII on his behalf. He himself then approached Henry's agent in Brussels with offers of intelligence concerning Scots who were recruiting soldiers in Denmark, but received a cool reception, as one who 'will pretend more knowledge than he hath indeed' (*LP Henry VIII*, vol. 19/2, no. 132). On 4 August 1545 he wrote to Henry from Lübeck, lamenting his loss of favour and offering to put a number of useful inventions at the king's disposal, for instance a method of making saltpetre; he also referred to the evangelical princes of Germany in terms suggesting that he was himself of their religious persuasion. Later that year he returned to London, hoping to enlist the support of the duke of Suffolk, but his expedition was in vain—the duke died that year—and he returned to 'Oestlandt'. In January 1547 he was back in London, this time with his (unnamed) wife, trying to persuade the imperial ambassador to speak up for him. The latter was unenthusiastic, and seems to have been correct in believing that Haschenperg 'will only find a refusal here to his petition' (*CSP Spain*, 1547-9, 1), for he makes no further appearance in English records, and it is not known when or where he died. HENRY SUMMERSON

Sources PRO, state papers Henry VIII, general series, SP1/100 · *LP Henry VIII*, vols. 9-21/2 · *CSP Spain*, 1545-9 · B. H. St J. O'Neil, 'Stefan von Haschenperg, an engineer to King Henry VIII, and his work', *Archaeologia*, 91 (1945), 137-55 · H. M. Colvin and others, eds., *The history of the king's works*, 3-4 (1975-82) · M. McCarthy, H. Summerson, and R. Annis, *Carlisle Castle* (1990)

Haselbury, Wulfric of. *See* Wulfric of Haselbury (*c.*1090–1154/5).

Haselden, Thomas (*d.* 1740), mathematician, spent nearly twenty years as a schoolmaster in the navy, after which he established a school at Wapping Old Stairs. He was later 'head-master of the Royal Academy at Portsmouth'. In 1722 he published *Description and use of … that most excellent invention commonly call'd Mercator's chart, to which is added the description of a new scale whereby distances may be measured at one extent of a pair of compasses*. To this was prefixed a letter to Dr Halley concerning the 'globular chart', an invention of Henry Wilson, who claimed that it was superior to Mercator's chart and was all that was necessary to solve the problem of great circle sailing. Haselden's letter sparked a controversy between the two men which Haselden attempted to settle by enlisting Halley's support and provoking a debate in the Royal Society. Halley was non-committal but the argument subsided when Wilson's planned atlas was abandoned.

In 1722 Haselden called himself 'Teacher of Mathematics to his Majesty's Volunteers in the Royal Navy'. In 1730 he published *Mathematic lessons for students in the mathematics and natural philosophy, composed by the Abbot de Molières, done into English by T. H.* In 1761 a new edition of the *Seaman's Daily Assistant*, said to be by Haselden, appeared.

Haselden was elected to the Royal Society on 17 January 1740, but he may not have lived to attend as fellow. He died at Portsmouth in May of the same year.

R. E. ANDERSON, *rev.* H. K. HIGTON

Sources E. G. R. Taylor, *The mathematical practitioners of Hanoverian England, 1714-1840* (1966) · Engraved Brit. ports.
Likenesses J. Faber, mezzotint, 1740 (after T. Frye, 1735), BM; copy, RS

Haselden, William Kerridge (1872-1953), cartoonist and caricaturist, was born on 3 December 1872 in Seville, Spain, the second of the five children of Adolphe Henry Haselden (1834-1878), a civil engineer, and his wife, Susan Elizabeth, *née* Kerridge (*d.* 1929). His parents were both English but met in Seville where his father was director of the Seville gasworks. In 1874 the family moved from Seville to Linares. During a holiday in England in 1877 his father contracted pneumonia and died the following year. The remaining family stayed resident in England, settling in Hampstead, London, living off the profits from shares in the family business, and William was sent to private school in Carlton Hill, St John's Wood, in north-west London. His education was, however, cut short by his mother's increasingly desperate financial straits following the sale of the family mines, and he left school in 1888 at the age of sixteen. He received a little extra private tuition after this date but never received any formal artistic training.

Haselden obtained a post as an underwriter at Lloyd's in London through the patronage of a family friend. He remained there unhappily for thirteen years and his first step in the direction of following a career as a cartoonist did not come until 1902 when, indulging his recreation of sketching, he submitted to the periodical *The Sovereign* a caricature of one of the Lloyd's underwriters. It was published and he was invited to join the staff of the paper, drawing mainly political cartoons along with theatrical sketches. Temporarily unemployed after *The Sovereign* ceased publication in April 1903, he produced some freelance cartoons and sketches for *The Tatler* and *St James's*

Gazette, though he did not manage to obtain a full-time staff post until later in 1903 when he approached the offices of Alfred Harmsworth. He was referred to a colleague of Harmsworth's, Arkas Sapt, who hired him at a salary of £5 a week for a new journalistic venture, the *Daily Mirror*.

Originally starting with political work similar to that of *The Sovereign*, by 1906 Haselden had settled on the formula which remained intrinsic to his work in the *Daily Mirror* until his retirement in 1940. Social commentary replaced political satire in his daily cartoons, in which he reflected on the different fads, fashions, manners, and modes of the average middle-class householder in a single frame divided into a number of panels, a style which merits his position as the father of the British newspaper strip cartoon. Central to each cartoon was his own quintessential brand of gentle, conservative, subtle wit rather than the perfection of drawing which, even so, managed to capture the expressions and emotions of the characters he illustrated. Walter Sickert complimented his ability to 'draw everything, even ideas and expressions with complete mastery' (*A Free House!*, 247). Between 1906 and 1935 annual collections of these cartoons were gathered together in twenty-nine volumes of '*Daily Mirror' Reflections*. In 1907 he married Eleanor Charlotte Lane-Bayliff (1875–1944). They had two children, Celia Mary and John Kerridge.

Haselden made his mark most clearly in the popular memory during the First World War. The wartime series ridiculing Kaiser Wilhelm II and his son, the crown prince, in the guise of 'Big and Little Willie' remains his crowning achievement and his only genuinely sustained attempt at political caricature. The first six months' worth of the series was collected in the publication *The Sad Adventures of Big and Little Willie* (1915). It was claimed after the war that the crown prince deemed these cartoons 'damnably effective' (Cudlipp, 70), though this is unsubstantiated. Alongside these Haselden narrated a comic social history of the war with characters including Joy Flapperton, the young 'flapper', and Colonel Dugout, government administrator.

From 1906 Haselden also contributed to *Punch* as a theatrical caricaturist. His caricatures were praised by Max Beerbohm who complimented them for the portrayal of 'the figures and faces of even the people who, until one sees your drawings of them, seem to have no distinct appearance whatsoever' (*The Times*). As a result of increasing deafness Haselden was forced to retire from this role in September 1936. In the late 1990s a near complete collection of his work for the *Daily Mirror* and *Punch* was loaned to the Centre for the Study of Cartoons and Caricature at the University of Kent at Canterbury.

Haselden's work was greatly admired. Sickert declared that he would live 'like Aristophanes as the most important historian of our age' (*The Times*). Paul Nash similarly endorsed him as 'not only a valuable historian of our age but one of the best craftsmen of our times' (Nash, 71). He also found devotees in the fields of politics and society. Baldwin and McKenna both owned original artwork, and Margot Asquith declared that she only took the *Daily Mirror* for his cartoons. According to family tradition he was offered a knighthood by Baldwin in 1923 but turned it down, not wanting 'all the fuss'.

Haselden was conservative in personality and appearance, having the mien of 'a tall, elegant insurance clerk' (Cudlipp, 70) with raven black hair and a serious, almost melancholic air. Resident at 1 Pelham Place in south-west London for most of his career, from the mid-1930s he spent more and more time at the family's holiday home, Dudley Dene, Lee Road, Aldeburgh, Suffolk, where he eventually retired and spent the rest of his life. He died of natural causes at Dudley Dene on Christmas day 1953 and was cremated at Ipswich crematorium on 31 December.

DAVID JAMES LITTLE

Sources private information (2004) · *The Times* (29 Dec 1953) · E. Keown, *Punch*, 226 (1954), 78 · W. K. Haselden, 'How I began as an artist', *T. P.'s Weekly* (29 May 1914) · H. Cudlipp, *Publish and be damned! The astonishing story of the 'Daily Mirror'* (1953) · *A free house! or, Artist as craftsman; being the writings of Walter Richard Sickert*, ed. O. Sitwell (1947) · P. Nash, 'English humorous draughtsmen', *The Week-end Review* (18 July 1931) · 'The satire of W. K. Haselden', *Strand Magazine*, 36 (1908), 521–7 · D. J. Little, 'Images of Germany as portrayed in the cartoons of W. K. Haselden, 1905–1918', MA diss., University of Kent, 1996

Archives University of Kent, Canterbury, Centre for the Study of Cartoons and Caricature, Templeman Library, cartoons

Likenesses E. O. Hoppe, photograph, repro. in *The sad adventures of Big and Little Willie* (1915)

Wealth at death £41,087 8s. 1d.: probate, 7 April 1954, *CGPLA Eng. & Wales*

Haseley, William of (*d.* in or before **1283**), monastic writer, was sub-prior and novice-master of Westminster Abbey. His name, if a toponym, points to an origin in Oxfordshire, Warwickshire, or Wiltshire. Haseley was the actual compiler of the customary, or directory relating to liturgical and other matters, which became known as Ware's customary from the circumstance that Richard of Ware was abbot of Westminster at the time (1258–83). It was in four parts, of which only the final part survives, in a fifteenth-century copy (BL, Cotton MS Otho C.xi). The colophon records that Haseley began his work in 1266. Given the derivative character of much of the contents, it may have been finished quickly, although ordinances of Abbot Ware published in chapter in, respectively, 1270 and 1275 were interpolated later. The extensive, though unattributed, quotations from the monastic constitutions of Lanfranc of Canterbury were doubtless present in Haseley's exemplar: this was probably the customary of the Anglo-Norman abbey, hitherto unrevised. Ware's customary provided the main source for the new customary compiled for their own use by the monks of St Augustine's Abbey, Canterbury, in the early fourteenth century. Two books which, according to their inscriptions, Haseley procured, and which were added to the library of Westminster Abbey after his death, may have been part of a larger collection of which he was allowed the use during his lifetime. On 5 November 1283, perhaps soon after Haseley's death, Hugh of Balsham, bishop of Ely, granted twenty days' remission of enjoined penance to those who should attend divine service at the abbey and pray at his tomb—an indulgence suggesting that Haseley had a connection with Ely diocese or with Balsham in person. The customary was published in 1904 in an edition by Edward Maude Thompson.   BARBARA F. HARVEY

Sources BL, Cotton MS Otho C.xi · E. M. Thompson, ed., *Customary of the Benedictine monasteries of Saint Augustine, Canterbury, and Saint Peter, Westminster*, 2, HBS, 28 (1904) · N. R. Ker, ed., *Medieval libraries of Great Britain: a list of surviving books*, 2nd edn, Royal Historical Society Guides and Handbooks, 3 (1964), 314 · E. H. Pearce, *The monks of Westminster* (1916) · J. Flete, *The history of Westminster Abbey*, ed. J. A. Robinson (1909)

Hasell, Elizabeth Julia (1830–1887), writer, was born on 17 January 1830, the second daughter of Edward Williams Hasell (1796–1872) of Dalemain, near Penrith, Cumberland, where he was an extensive landowner, and his wife, Dorothea, daughter of Edward King of Hungerhill, Yorkshire. She was carefully educated at home, at the same time teaching herself, with little or no assistance, Latin, Greek, Italian, German, Spanish, and Portuguese.

From 1859 until her death Hasell wrote a large number of essays and reviews including over thirty for *Blackwood's Magazine*. Her contributions show a wide knowledge of European literature from Homer to recently published works by English poets: her reviews in *Blackwood's* include Lord Derby's translation of the *Iliad* (April 1865), Tennyson's *Idylls of the King* (November 1859), *Enoch Arden* (November 1864), and *Becket* (July 1885), and William Morris's *Poems* (July 1869). Some of her essays compare the treatment of Greek myths by dramatists of various periods; she also wrote extensively on Spanish and Portuguese authors. She compiled two volumes in the series of Foreign Classics for English Readers on Calderon (1879) and Tasso (1882). She also reviewed occasionally in *The Athenaeum*.

Besides pursuing her studies Hasell gave a large portion of her time to promoting education and the general welfare of the district in which she lived, walking long distances across the hills to teach in village schools or deliver extempore addresses, in which she showed an unusual facility. Her philanthropic exertions probably hastened her death, as in her desire to do good to a scattered population she made light of fatigue and exposure to rain and cold. A deeply religious woman, she was well read in theology, and published several devotional works. She died, unmarried, at Dalemain on 14 November 1887.

NORMAN MOORE, *rev.* RICHARD SMAIL

Sources Boase, *Mod. Eng. biog.* · *Wellesley index* · Walford, *County families* · private information (1891) · *CGPLA Eng. & Wales* (1888)
Archives NL Scot., letters to Blackwoods
Wealth at death £4069 14s. 5d.: probate, 11 Feb 1888, *CGPLA Eng. & Wales*

Hasell, (Frances Hatton) Eva (1886–1974), traveller and missionary, was born on 13 December 1886 at Dalemain, Dacre, Penrith, Cumberland, the younger of two daughters of John Edward Hasell JP DL (1839–1910), a substantial landowner in Cumberland and Westmorland, and his wife, Frances Maud Flood (*d.* 1911). She grew up in Cumberland where she did voluntary work for the Church of England in the diocese of Carlisle. In 1910 she became a collector for the fund launched jointly by the archbishops of Canterbury and York to provide for clergy in the isolated parts of western Canada. The diocese of Carlisle raised £3000 for the Western Canada Fund, and Hasell's involvement marked the beginning of a lifelong commitment to this cause.

In 1914, after becoming diocesan Sunday school organizer for Carlisle, Hasell was sent to St Christopher's College, Blackheath, for specialized training in religious education and religious social work. While there she met Aylmer Bosanquet, an Anglican missionary who later went to work in the diocese of Qu'Appelle, Saskatchewan, an area about twice the size of England without a single Sunday school. Bosanquet feared for the future of the Anglican church in the vastness of the prairies, and believed that the teaching of children was essential to its survival there. In letters home she inspired Hasell with her vision of a small army of itinerant women Sunday school teachers, travelling in pairs by caravan to remote regions during the short summers, and conducting the Sunday schools by post from the larger towns in the rest of the year.

Bosanquet proposed horse-drawn caravans for this work but Hasell, who learned to drive while carrying out her diocesan work in Carlisle, knew that only motorized transport would be practicable. During the First World War she drove for the Red Cross and took a course in car mechanics, gaining practical experience for the caravan work that she planned for after the war. She used her contacts in the Victoria League, the women's imperial movement, to make the necessary preparations, and with the help of a 'daughter of the empire' in Winnipeg purchased a Ford caravan. In February 1920 she left Liverpool with her companion, Miss Winifred Ticehurst, a fellow graduate of St Christopher's. They spent two months giving lectures in Regina, Saskatchewan, before setting out on 21 May equipped with all the necessities for survival. Their caravan bore an unfortunate resemblance to a Black Maria, but its light body and high chassis made it ideal for the rough roads and dirt tracks of the prairie, where they expected to achieve an average speed of only 10 m.p.h. In three months they covered over 3000 miles, visiting ten existing Sunday schools, beginning four new ones, and enrolling sixty children in the Sunday school by post. They also held religious services, spoke to schoolteachers, and generally 'did a lot of visiting' (Hasell, *Across the Prairie*, 98). They met with great hospitality and enthusiasm wherever they went, but witnessed too the extreme poverty in which many settlers lived. And they experienced considerable hardship themselves, negotiating dangerous roads, forest fires, bears, swarms of mosquitoes, and extremes of temperature. Occasionally they encountered the unwanted attentions of lonely farmers, whose help might be sought in pulling the caravan out of mud, and who invariably asked the question, 'Are you married?' and its inevitable sequel, 'Why not?' (ibid., 69).

The success of the caravan mission in 1920 laid the foundation for future ventures, and before leaving Regina in September Hasell reported to senior Anglicans there. She had found the prairie settlers 'in an intensely receptive state', but was aware also of their sense of desertion by the church, which appeared unwilling to send clergy to areas where they could not be guaranteed a stipend. It was a serious problem, to which the church must respond: 'The worship of the almighty dollar may easily take the place of true religion unless this present hunger for spiritual things is satisfied' (Hasell, *Across the Prairie*, 104, 105). On her return to England she began raising money for future caravan missions and later established the Western Canada Sunday School Caravan Fund, of which she became honorary secretary and treasurer. The expedition of 1920 had cost £1000, excluding personal expenses which she had met herself. Future funding came from the church, as well as from groups such as the Mothers' Union, to whom Hasell lectured about her experiences. She returned to Canada in the spring of 1922, spent that summer in the diocese of Calgary, and returned to England in the autumn. It was a pattern repeated in the years ahead when, always with a woman companion, she pioneered missionary trails. The caravans were welcomed with enthusiasm by the bishops of the 'frontier' dioceses who struggled to cope with increasing numbers of settlers, and in November 1926 the bishop of Kootenay praised Hasell's initiative as 'the greatest work being done for the Church or Empire in Western Canada' (Hasell, *Canyons*, 113). By 1935 there were seventeen caravans operating in nine western dioceses, run by thirty-four women workers. The work reached its peak in the early 1950s when there were thirty-two vans in action.

Hasell worked in loose association with the women's branch of the Anglican Church Missionary Society for Canada, the 'women's auxiliary', and also with the Fellowship of the Maple Leaf, a teaching organization that aimed to inculcate values of empire, Englishness, and Anglicanism among settlers. She saw the diversity of nationalities and religions in western Canada as a potential threat to the moral development of the children there and she feared in particular the rise of militant atheism. There were 1700 'Bolshevist Sunday schools' in western Canada, she informed a meeting of the Society for Promoting Christian Knowledge in London, in March 1930, warning that the Bolsheviks were better organized than the Christians. Believing that poverty was a key factor in the spread of Bolshevism, she argued that the mother country must do more to support Canadian farmers. She told a London audience in February 1931:

> It is no wonder that feeling sometimes runs high that Britain should buy her wheat from Russia and Germany, instead of from her dominions; these settlers had been persuaded to leave England for Canada only to be left to starve. (*The Times*, 13 Feb 1931)

Her religious work was inextricably bound up with the advance of empire, in which she believed Canada would play an important part: 'This nation in the making may be a great power, for good or evil, when the Mother Country is on the wane' (Hasell, *Through Western Canada*, 252).

In the 1950s Hasell reluctantly gave up her missionary work and retired to her Lake District home, Dacre Lodge, Dacre, in Penrith. She had been created MBE in 1935. In 1965 she became the first woman awarded the degree of doctor of divinity by the College of St Emmanuel and St Chad, Saskatoon, and in 1969 she was invested as an officer of the order of Canada. Hasell, who wrote three books about her caravan experiences, died, unmarried, at Penrith Hospital, Penrith, on 3 May 1974.

MARK POTTLE

Sources *The Times* (8 March 1930), 17g; (13 Feb 1931), 16b; (6 May 1974); (11 May 1974), 16d · E. Hasell, *Across the prairie: a 3000 miles tour by two Englishwomen on behalf of religious education* (1922) · J. Robinson, ed., *Wayward women: a guide to women travellers* (1990) · M. Hessell Tiltman, *Women in modern adventure* (1935) · E. Hasell, *Through western Canada in a caravan* (1925) · E. Hasell, *Canyons, cans and caravans* (1930) · Burke, *Gen. GB* (1914) [Hasell of Dalemain] · b. cert. · d. cert.
Likenesses photograph, repro. in Hasell, *Through western Canada*, facing p. 72
Wealth at death £155,524: probate, 19 July 1974, *CGPLA Eng. & Wales*

Hasilwode [Haselwood], **Thomas** (*fl.* 1321), chronicler and Augustinian canon, of Leeds Priory, Kent, is said by John Bale to have acted as a schoolmaster at the priory, teaching the young in 1321 (Bale, *Cat.*, 1.398). He is also said to have devoted himself to the reading of history, and to have compiled a *Chronicon compendiarum* as well as other works; Bale had not seen this chronicle (or he would have stated its opening words), and he appears to have relied on a statement by William Worcester, whose collectanea he cites; however, this cannot now be verified.

John Weever, in his *Ancient Funerall Monuments* (1631), quotes a short eulogistic account of Edward, the Black Prince, from the 'compendious chronicle' of Canterbury in the Cotton Library, which he says was written by Hasilwode, but his quotation is merely from the *Chronica bona et compendiosa de regibus Angliae* or *Abbreviationes chronicorum*, which comes down to 1377 (or sometimes 1399). This survives in many copies, including five in the Cotton collection in the British Library, and there is no other ground for attributing its authorship to Hasilwode; it has sometimes been ascribed to Ranulf Higden.

NIGEL RAMSAY

Sources Bale, *Cat.*, 1.398 · Bale, *Index*, 440 · J. Weever, *Ancient funerall monuments* (1631), 206 · J. Taylor, *The 'Universal Chronicle' of Ranulf Higden* (1966), 184
Archives BL, Cotton MS Nero D.vi, fols. 76–81 · BL, Cotton MS Vitellius C.iv, fols. 119–128v · BL, Cotton MS Claudius D.x, fols. 1–8 · BL, Cotton MS Tiberius E.viii, fols. 7v–15v, 220–25 [copies] · BL, Stowe MS 140, fols. 125–35

Haskell, Arnold Lionel David (1903–1980), ballet critic, was born on 19 July 1903 in London, the only child of Jacob Silas Haskell, banker, of Queen's Gate, London, and his wife, Emmy Mesritz. He was educated at Westminster School and at Trinity Hall, Cambridge, where he studied law, obtaining a second class (division two) in part one (1924). He received his BA with an *aegrotat* on account of

Arnold Lionel David Haskell (1903–1980), by Gordon Anthony, 1937

illness, and, after a brief and unsuccessful attempt at business, worked as a reader for William Heinemann Ltd from 1927 to 1932. He was a joint founder of the Camargo Society in 1930, from 1933 to 1934 worked as an administrative assistant to Colonel De Basil's Russian Ballet on its American tour, and in 1934 published a widely successful book, *Balletomania*, adding that word to the language. From 1935 to 1938 he was dance critic to the *Daily Telegraph* and again worked with the Russian Ballet on its Australian tour of 1938–9. During the Second World War he assisted air raid precautions and gave lecture tours for the forces and industry. In 1946 he was asked by Ninette de Valois to become director of the new Royal Ballet School, which became his main activity from 1946 to 1965.

Slight and small in build, Haskell had considerable charm and force of personality. He fell in love with ballet early in life, and, as a result of childhood friendship with Alicia Markova, had an immediate entrée to the dazzling world of the Diaghilev Ballet when Markova joined that company in 1925. His enthusiasm and attractive personality quickly gained friends among dancers and choreographers, and his wide interests as an avowed dilettante, particularly in sculpture and painting, but also literature and music, gave him the necessary intellectual background to make the most of the Diaghilev company, then reaching the height of its influence as the élitist avant-garde of Parisian culture.

Yet Haskell's real strength was as a popularizer, and in a stream of books and articles on ballet, all well written and compulsively readable, he helped to spread enthusiasm for ballet from a small if influential upper-class opera house audience to the average middle-class theatre-going public. During the 1930s De Basil's Russian Ballet, gathering popular success on the coat-tails of Diaghilev's status and largely depending on past achievement, captured Haskell's allegiance more than the struggling British Ballet, but by 1946 what was to become the Royal Ballet was firmly established, and, as director of its school for the first two crucial decades, Haskell established as an educator a style and an ambience that influenced succeeding generations of dancers. His urbane, civilized, and tolerant approach helped to counterbalance the fiercely competitive pressures inevitable in a specialized school where pupils were very much aware that only a few precious places would be available at the end of each year in the dance company itself.

Appropriately for a ballet critic Haskell was fascinated by sculpture, vigorously defending Jacob Epstein in *The Sculptor Speaks* (1931). After visiting Australia with the Russian Ballet in 1938 he wrote three books on Australia, *Waltzing Matilda* (1940), *Australia* (1941), and *The Australians* (1943). He also wrote two books of autobiography, *In his True Centre* (1951) and *Balletomane at Large* (1972), but his major achievement rests on over twenty books on the art of ballet. Closely in touch with dancers and choreographers, his judgement widened and assisted by his lifelong enthusiasms in so many arts, he approached new work with an open mind, was sympathetic to current trends, and had a rare gift for defending, explaining, and clarifying for his readers what ballet was attempting to achieve. His careful analysis invariably spotted what was wrong as well as what was right, and as a critic his kind but firm integrity shone through everything he wrote. The development of British ballet was fortunate to have such a persuasive and influential publicist to espouse its cause in its vital early years, and the subsequent popularity of the art owed something to Haskell's efforts as well as to the dancers, choreographers, composers, and designers he wrote about so attractively.

In 1927 Haskell married Vera Saitsova (*d.* 1968), daughter of Mark Saitzoff, a Russian émigré industrialist; they had two sons, one of whom, Francis James Herbert *Haskell (1928–2000), became professor of the history of art at Oxford University, and one daughter. In 1970 he married Vivienne Diana, third daughter of Arthur Tristman Marks, mining engineer, and sister of Alicia Markova. Haskell died at his home, 6A Cavendish Crescent, Bath, on 15 November 1980.

He became a chevalier of the Légion d'honneur (1950), was appointed CBE (1954), was awarded an honorary degree of DLitt by Bath (1974), became FRSL (1977), and won the Queen Elizabeth coronation award of the Royal Academy of Dancing (1979).

NICHOLAS DROMGOOLE, *rev.*

Sources A. Haskell, *In his true centre* (1951) · A. Haskell, *Balletomane at large* (1972) · personal knowledge (1986) · private information (1986) · *CGPLA Eng. & Wales* (1981)

Haskell, Francis James Herbert (1928–2000), art historian, was born on 7 April 1928 in London, the eldest of three children (two sons and one daughter) of Arnold Lionel David *Haskell (1903–1980), a ballet critic, and Vera Saitsova (*d.* 1968), a Russian émigrée. His parents' common language was French, which Francis spoke before he learned English. He was educated at the London Lycée and later at Eton College, where he was a scholar, specializing in science. His initial ambition was to study medicine. Immediately after the Second World War he visited Paris, where he attended some of the trials of the Vichy collaborators in order to experience a major historical event at first hand. After a period of military service in the education corps, in 1948 he went up to King's College, Cambridge, where he read history and then English. His tutors included the young Eric Hobsbawm, who remained a lifelong friend, and Dadie Rylands, who later eliminated hundreds of adjectives from his first book.

After taking his degree, Haskell was given a grant by his college to write a fellowship dissertation. The topic was suggested by Nikolaus Pevsner, then Slade professor of the history of art at Cambridge. Pevsner proposed that he should investigate the relationship between baroque art and the Jesuits. The notion that changes in artistic style closely mirrored wider intellectual developments was then widely accepted, and the idea that there was some link between the Jesuit mentality and the baroque was something of a commonplace. Pevsner probably expected that Haskell would explore this relationship by means of analogies, but instead his pupil chose to investigate what had actually happened. On his arrival in Rome in 1951 he had the good fortune to live briefly with a well-connected Catholic family, and was thus able to gain access to the Jesuit archives. He soon realized that in their early days the Jesuits were extremely poor and that they had little say in the crucial decisions about the decoration of their principal churches, which instead were taken by wealthy patrons with agendas of their own. The Jesuit style, in short, was a myth.

Haskell completed his dissertation while working as a clerk in the House of Commons library, and in 1954 he was awarded a fellowship at King's, which was to remain his home until 1967, and whose distinctive intellectual and social ambience he found extremely congenial. But instead of publishing a specialized study based directly on his research, he chose instead to attempt something much more ambitious, extending his studies to provide a survey of Italian patronage from the beginning of the seventeenth century to the end of the eighteenth. The result was *Patrons and painters: a study in the relations between Italian art and society in the age of the baroque* (1963), which remains his most famous and influential book. The topic was one on which the secondary literature was still very limited and the abundant primary sources scarcely explored. To survey this material was a prodigious achievement, based on exceptionally wide reading, on massive archival research, and on a familiarity with the works of art themselves which few scholars could then equal. Haskell himself later stated that the encouragement of the émigré scholars at the Warburg Institute and the resources of its unique library were decisive for the direction of his work. He was not the first to shift the focus away from the artists themselves to those who employed them, but he did so without ideological preconceptions and with notable insight into the motives and personalities of a huge range of characters.

In 1962, while completing his research in Venice, Haskell met Larissa Salmina, curator of Venetian drawings at the Hermitage, who was then acting as commissar at the Soviet pavilion at the Biennale. Three years later they were married in a Soviet palace of weddings in Leningrad. Given Haskell's apparent incapacity when confronted with any practical problem, as well as his deeply rooted pessimism and anxiety, the fact that he managed to obtain the consent of the Soviet authorities seems scarcely credible, and without the influential help of his father, whose status as an expert on ballet had gained him great prestige in the eyes of the Russians, it would never have happened. From the moment Larissa arrived in Cambridge six months later, she and Haskell were inseparable, and their marriage gave him a happiness and a security he had never expected to find.

In 1967 Haskell was appointed professor of the history of art in Oxford, a post which he held until his retirement in 1995, and which was associated with a fellowship at Trinity College. By this time he had decided to study an entirely new topic, one related to his teaching in Oxford, namely the process by which French academic art of the nineteenth century lost its prestige and ceased to be admired. His research, which paralleled a similar reappraisal undertaken by scholars in France, led to a series of important articles. It also encouraged him to turn his department in Oxford into a centre of international importance for the study of French art and attracted a series of highly gifted doctoral students.

Related to his research on French art was his second major book, *Rediscoveries in Art* (1976), based on his 1973 Wrightsman lectures at the Metropolitan Museum of Art in New York. Here he extended his work on French art to explore the dramatic changes in the canon of great artists in the late eighteenth and nineteenth centuries, showing how such developments were often prompted by accidents of history and the vagaries of the art market. His conclusions provided a powerful challenge to the prevailing idea of art as a repository of timeless values. A similar idea underlay *Taste and the Antique* (1981), written jointly with Nicholas Penny; this was concerned with the rise and fall of the taste for a number of ancient, principally Roman, statues, which for centuries were widely regarded as the supreme creations of Western art, before being almost entirely forgotten except by a small number of specialists.

In *History and its Images* (1993) Haskell returned to some of the issues that had preoccupied him in his early research on the Jesuits, namely the use, or more often mis-use, of art by historians, from the late middle ages until the early years of the twentieth century, and notably the idea that art provided a particularly sensitive indicator of wider social attitudes and ideals. The subject was too vast and too diffuse to permit a comprehensive treatment, and Haskell's conclusions were characteristically tentative and nuanced. The great value of the book lies in the range of topics that he examined and the issues that he raised, as well as in the characteristic scepticism of his conclusions. His last book, *The Ephemeral Museum* (2000), was again con-cerned with an unexplored but important topic, the growth of exhibitions of old master paintings, a phenom-enon about which he had ambivalent feelings.

Rather than concentrating on artists and their works, Haskell chose to study the circumstances which led to the production of art and the responses it aroused among con-temporaries and later generations. In doing so, he extended the frontiers of his subject more than any other scholar of his generation. Scornful of all talk of theory, he was an empirical historian of exceptional range and ori-ginality, with an unsurpassed gift for asking new ques-tions. He was also convinced of the need to understand as fully as possible the character, attitudes, and foibles of those he studied. His writing was informed by an encyclo-paedic knowledge of European art acquired through constant travel with Larissa, which was his greatest pleas-ure. In his later years, having overcome a fear of flying which had long confined him to Europe, he was also a regular visitor to the Getty Research Center in Los Angeles.

Haskell lectured with equal fluency in English, French, and Italian. His house at Walton Street in Oxford, presided over by Larissa, was the centre of a vast and international network of friends, which included many of the leading art historians of his day, as well as past and present stu-dents. Witty, gregarious, candid, and entirely without solemnity or self-importance, Haskell was wonderful and wonderfully indiscreet company. He was also a highly effective member of committees concerned with the sup-port of museums and of the study of art history. Elected a fellow of the British Academy in 1971, he was awarded their Serena medal for Italian studies in 1985. A chevalier of the Légion d'honneur, he was a corresponding or hon-orary member of ten foreign or learned societies and an honorary fellow of King's College, Cambridge, and Trinity College, Oxford. When he learned, late in 1999, that he had incurable liver cancer, he set to work to complete his last book, while continuing to receive a stream of friends from all over the world. He died at home in Oxford on 18 January 2000 and was cremated at Oxford crematorium on 25 January. CHARLES HOPE

Sources F. Haskell, *Maler und Auftraggeber: Kunst und Gesellschaft im italienischen Barock* (1996), preface · N. Penny, *Burlington Magazine*, 142 (2000), 307–8 · interview, 21 Oct 1999, *La Vanguardia* [Barcelona] [n.d.] · *The Times* (21 Jan 2000) · WW · *The Guardian* (21 Jan 2000) · *The Independent* (20 Jan 2000) · *Daily Telegraph* (21 Jan 2000) · personal knowledge (2004)

Archives King's AC Cam., letters and postcards to G. H. W. Rylands
Wealth at death £1,177,157: probate, 2001, *CGPLA Eng. & Wales*

Haslam, Sir Alfred Seale (1844–1927), engineer and polit-ician, was born on 27 October 1844 in Derby, the fourth of the five sons and the fourth of the eight children of Wil-liam Haslam, ironmaster of Derby, and his wife, Ann, daughter of Joseph Smith of Branstone, Staffordshire. He was educated privately in Derby and was taken into apprenticeship with the Midland Railway Company. Once qualified, he joined the firm of Sir William G. Armstrong in London as a hydraulic engineer. In 1868, in partnership with his father and financed by his uncle Joseph Smith, he purchased the old Union foundry in Derby.

He started the Haslam engineering works with a staff of twenty and by 1871 he was able to repay the loan from his uncle and later dissolve the partnership with his father, leaving himself in sole charge. By 1876 the firm had become a limited company. In 1875 he married Annie (*d.* 1924), the daughter of Thomas Tatam, farmer, of Little Eaton, Derbyshire. They had three sons, one of whom was killed in the First World War, and three daughters.

Haslam was a perceptive developer of the promising research of others, having that rare combination of com-mercial acumen and technical expertise, making him one of the great engineers. He could see that refrigeration would bring about a complete change in people's life-styles and in 1880 he took over the patents of the Bell–Coleman cold-air machine and developed what was known as the dry air refrigerator. The excellence of this machine eventually gave him a monopoly in refrigerated shipping. His equipment on board ship and on land enabled British people to enjoy meat, fruits, and other perishable products from countries overseas. On 5 Octo-ber 1881 the SS *Orient* docked at Plymouth with 150 tons of frozen Australian meat on board, an event described viv-idly by many newspapers (for example, *Daily News*, 5 October).

By 1900 the dry air refrigerator had lost its place to chemical machines using carbon dioxide or ammonia. Haslam produced equipment using these refrigerants for most purposes where cold was required, such as meat freezing stations, meat cargoes on board ship, cold stores of all kinds for perishable food, ice factories, chemical works, dye works, and works for the manufacture and storage of explosives and ammunition on land and on warships.

Haslam also played a busy role in public life. In 1879 he became a Derby town councillor and in 1886 was made a JP for the borough. In 1890 he was elected mayor of Derby and in 1891 became JP for the county. His biggest achieve-ment in his year of office was the replacement of the old William Strutt Infirmary. He invited Queen Victoria to lay the foundation stone for the new Derbyshire Royal Infirm-ary and at the end of her visit she knighted Haslam (1891).

Politically Haslam was prominent in the Liberal Union-ist cause. In 1892 he unsuccessfully contested Derby, but he entered parliament in 1900 as a representative of Newcastle under Lyme, retaining his seat until the election of 1906. He was a generous benefactor—for example, he presented bronze statues of Queen Victoria to Newcastle under Lyme, Derby, and London.

His fellowships and honours were numerous and included membership of the Iron and Steel Institute, the Institution of Mechanical Engineers, the Royal Institution, and the Institute of Refrigeration, of which he was president in 1914–15. He was a liveryman of the City of London and in 1905 was presented with the freedom of Newcastle under Lyme, having occupied the chair of mayor for three consecutive years (1901–4).

Haslam died at the St Pancras Hotel, London, on 13 January 1927 while on a business trip. He was buried in Morley churchyard, Derbyshire. Two sons and a daughter predeceased him. A. J. COOPER, rev.

Sources *British Journal of Commerce* (11 June 1892) · E. W. Webbe, *Oddfellows companion and guide to Derby* (1892) · *Derbyshire Advertiser* (14 Jan 1927) · private information (1993)
Wealth at death £1,064,393 17s. 7d.: probate, 22 March 1927, CGPLA Eng. & Wales

Haslam [née Fisher], **Anna Maria** (1829–1922), campaigner for women's rights, was born in Youghal, co. Cork, in April 1829, sixteenth of the seventeen children of Abraham Fisher (1783–1871), a corn miller, and his wife, Jane Moor (1789–1877), of Neath, Wales. She had eight sisters and eight brothers. She was educated at the Quaker school at Newtown, co. Waterford, from 1840 to 1842, and then, until 1845, at the Quaker school at Castlegate in York. Her parents were active in the anti-slavery, temperance, and international peace movements, and the family helped in a soup kitchen in Youghal during the great famine. Anna later linked her activism in women's rights to her upbringing, noting in an interview that she 'could not remember any time when she was not a believer in women's equality. It came to her naturally and was always taken for granted in her household' (*Irish Citizen*, 21 March 1914).

From 1847 Anna taught at Ackworth School, Yorkshire, where she met her future husband, a fellow teacher, **Thomas Joseph Haslam** (1825–1917). Born in Mountmellick, Queen's county, he had been educated at the Quaker provincial school in that town. In 1840 he became an apprentice teacher at the Friends' School, Lisburn. He became interested in the issue of women's suffrage from reading the works of Herbert Spencer. The couple returned to Ireland and married in Cork in 1854. They then moved to Dublin, where Thomas was employed as a clerk, but in 1866 his health broke down and Anna was left to support them both. This she did by opening a 'stationer's and fancy goods repository' at their home in Rathmines, Dublin; the business survived until 1906, when the assistance of friends made the enterprise unnecessary. The nature of Thomas's illness remains a mystery, and he continued to be an active scholar, a member of the Rathmines Public Library Committee, and a 'great figure' at the Dublin Friends Institute, where he regularly read papers. The marriage appears to have been a particularly happy one; there were no children. The suffragist Margaret Cousins, who met the Haslams in 1906, described them as 'a remarkable old pair, devoted to one another and dedicated to the cause of the advancement and enfranchisement of women … she a dynamo of energy, small and sturdy; he intellectual, tall, rather like a university don, a good speaker, very refined and kindly' (Cousins and Cousins, 129).

Anna Haslam's interests spanned a range of organizations and campaigns. In 1861 she helped establish the Irish Society for the Training and Employment of Educated Women in Dublin. She campaigned to have girls included in the Intermediate Education (Ireland) Act of 1878, and in 1882 was involved in setting up the Association of Schoolmistresses and Other Ladies Interested in Irish Education, which sought to protect rights won for girls' education and to fight for further changes. In 1870 she established a branch of the Ladies' National Association for the Repeal of the Contagious Diseases Acts in Dublin. She also served as an executive committee member of the National Association for the Repeal of the Contagious Diseases Acts. In 1886 she became secretary to the Women's Vigilance Committee, part of the social purity movement which developed from the Contagious Diseases Acts campaign. When the First World War broke out in 1914 she was instrumental in setting up 'women patrols' which aimed to keep young girls off the streets of Dublin for fear they would fall into prostitution.

Anna Haslam established the first suffrage society in Dublin in 1876. After many name changes, this organization was to become the Irish Women's Suffrage and Local Government Association (IWSLGA) in 1901. She was secretary to this association from 1876 until 1913, and was then elected life president. A pacifist throughout her life, she did not support the militant tactics of the Irish Women's Franchise League. In addition to campaigning for the national franchise, the IWSLGA also sought to win the right for women to become poor-law guardians and to vote in municipal elections, rights which were eventually won in 1896 and 1898 respectively. Anna Haslam, a leading figure in these campaigns, wrote a number of articles on these issues in the *Englishwoman's Review*.

Anna Haslam was a staunch unionist and opposed the introduction of home rule for Ireland, fearing that its passage would result in the loyalists of Ireland being 'politically extinguished'. She nevertheless welcomed women and men of all political persuasions and all religious denominations into her organizations. To the end of her life she was held in very real affection by feminists of widely differing political opinions.

In the 1918 election, the first in which women over thirty were allowed to vote, Anna Haslam was paraded to the polling booth by members of different suffrage groups, as a symbol of the long years of struggle to attain the franchise. Thomas Haslam, a significant feminist in his own right, did not live to see his wife cast her vote. Like his wife, he had devoted his energies to securing rights for women, and had been active in the IWSLGA. Interested in birth control, he published *The Marriage Problem* on the subject in 1868 under the pseudonym Oedipus. In 1870 he wrote a pamphlet, *A Few Words on Prostitution and the Contagious Diseases Acts*, as a contribution to the Irish campaign for the repeal of the acts. He published the first newspaper in Ireland to support women's suffrage, the *Women's Advocate*; but it ran to only three issues, in April, May, and July 1874. He wrote a number of pamphlets on women's suffrage, the last being published in 1916, a year before his death. He was buried in the Quaker burial-ground at Temple Hill, Blackrock, in co. Dublin. Anna Haslam died in Dublin on 28 November 1922 at the age of ninety-three, and was buried beside her husband in the Quaker burial-ground.   MARIA LUDDY

Sources M. Cullen, 'Anna Maria Haslam, 1829–1922', *Women, power and conciousness in nineteenth-century Ireland*, ed. M. Cullen and M. Luddy (1995) · C. Quinlan, *Genteel revolutionaries: Anna and Thomas Haslam and the Irish women's movement* (2002) · C. H. Oldfield, obituary of T. J. Haslam, Religious Society of Friends Historical Library, Swanbrook House, Dublin · *Irish Citizen* (21 March 1914) · J. H. Cousins and M. E. Cousins, *We two together* (1950)
Archives Irish Housewives Association Archive · U. Hull
Likenesses S. Purser, double portrait, 1904 (with Thomas Haslam), Hugh Lane Municipal Gallery of Modern Art, Dublin
Wealth at death £479 8s. 10d.: probate, 5 Jan 1923, *CGPLA Éire*

Haslam, John (*bap.* 1764, *d.* 1844), physician and specialist in insanity, was baptized at St John Zachary, London, on 12 February 1764, the son of John Haslam (1737–1829), and his wife, Mary. Little is known of Haslam's early life. After serving a period of apprenticeship he gained clinical experience as a student and subsequently as a house surgeon at St Bartholomew's Hospital, London, attending the lectures of George Fordyce (1736–1802) and serving as a pupil under David Pitcairn (1749–1809). Subsequently, during 1785–7, Haslam pursued his education at Edinburgh University, the leading centre for medical instruction at the time, attending lectures and becoming acquainted with Andrew Duncan sen. (1744–1828) and the young Thomas Beddoes (1760–1808). Haslam took an energetic role in student life, writing dissertations for the university's medical society, of which he was president in 1786, and defending student rights of admission to the Edinburgh Royal Infirmary. He proceeded to take further studies in Uppsala, Sweden, finally enrolling as a student at Pembroke College, Cambridge, but did not take the degree of MD. Lacking the qualification required to practise as a physician in London, Haslam qualified instead as a member of the Company of Surgeons.

Haslam was appointed as resident apothecary to Bethlem Hospital in July 1795. His starting salary of £100 per year, with additional supplements for necessaries and furniture, was ultimately raised to £335 as the hospital's governors grew more appreciative of the demands of the post. Although subordinate to the physician, Haslam's duties were the most exacting of any medical officer at Bethlem, requiring him to visit patients every morning at least, to supervise the keepers' management of them and to oversee the preparation and quality of all medicaments. Serving in that capacity until 1816 Haslam succeeded for almost two decades in building up a creditable reputation as an experienced and able specialist, in particular through a number of early and widely read publications on insanity. While at Bethlem, Haslam also received regular payments for recommending patients to Sir John Miles's Hoxton madhouse, and for his twice-weekly inspections of naval patients at Hoxton.

However, Haslam's record and reputation were seriously marred when he forfeited his office (along with the physician, Thomas Monro (1759–1833)) as a result of the 1815–16 House of Commons select committee enquiry into madhouses. Its report made trenchant and resounding criticisms of the conditions and treatment of patients at Bethlem, and also of the naval patients Haslam had been responsible for scrutinizing. Haslam's case was not helped by the way in which he and other Bethlem officers turned upon each other under cross-examination. To some extent Haslam was made a medical scapegoat by asylum reformers and Bethlem's own governors for the endemic failings of old Bedlam's management and an increasingly outmoded style of therapeutics. Certainly, he had only limited authority over the attendants with whom many of the abuses originated. Yet, as the medical officer most regularly in attendance (even if his day-to-day influence may have declined after 1803, when he was obliged to live outside of the hospital), Haslam was perhaps more responsible than any other officer for the abuses exposed by the reformers. His attempts to explain away the severity of mechanical restraint employed at Bethlem and the evidence of abuse and neglect of patients' health and comfort reveal how entrenched was the ineffective managerial and therapeutic mindset at the hospital. Haslam and Monro made spirited defences of their conduct in some observations addressed to the governors which they immediately published (in 1816), but to no avail. Having originally supported their medical officers the hospital's governors eventually caved in under the combined pressure of political and press influence and the weight of public opinion, as much as a result of the evidence thrust before them. In May 1816 they voted resoundingly not to re-elect Haslam and Monro to their posts, and cast Haslam off without a pension. Lacking a livelihood Haslam was forced within months of his dismissal to auction off his large library. Two years later he published a letter to the Bethlem governors confirming (while denying personal responsibility for) the failings of inferior officers and implicating the governors for their mismanagement of the institution over the previous twenty years.

Haslam was a prolific author on various aspects of mental diseases. His earliest and major work was *Observations on Insanity* (1798). The book, translated into German as early as 1800, was greatly enlarged and retitled for its second edition in 1809. Despite its somewhat exaggerated claims for uniqueness, it was widely read by fellow specialists, and incorporated one of the earliest statistical surveys of insanity. Haslam's commitment to detailed post-mortem investigation in order to understand the pathology of mental diseases won particular plaudits from other authors, including Francis Willis jun. and Thomas Mayo (1790–1871). Although occasional aspersions were cast on Haslam's intellectual rigour in some quarters of the English medical press, especially after his somewhat disgraceful exit from Bethlem, his writings on insanity generally received a great deal of praise, especially from conservative colleagues who shared Haslam's faith in experience as the key to success in mental science and his disdain for lay interference in asylums. His publications and their promotion of some of the tenets of moral management helped to ensure that Haslam's reputation as a specialist on mental diseases remained high, especially on the continent where his books were in great currency. Philippe Pinel (1745–1826) repeatedly made reference to Haslam's work in his *Treatise on Mental Alienation* (1801), Haslam returning the compliment in his own second edition. Haslam's stress on management via gentleness and kindness, and via the moral authority of the mad-doctor, chimed in particularly strongly with Pinel and a new generation of asylum practitioners beginning to espouse moral (more than medical) means of treating the insane. The English doyen of moral therapy, Samuel Tuke (1784–1857), likewise accorded Haslam repeated endorsements in his *Description of the [York] Retreat* (1813). Others among Haslam's contemporaries were more critical. Joseph Mason Cox (1762–1822), for example, sniped intermittently at his assertions, and criticized Haslam's somewhat bigoted attitude to Methodism and views on the role of religion in encouraging insanity. However, Cox himself had been piqued by Haslam's criticisms of his own first edition, and such critics were mostly in the minority.

Despite Haslam's advocacy of some of the tenets of the new moral therapy, the discoveries of the 1815–16 committee on madhouses had revealed the superficiality of his status as an especially progressive practitioner of moral management. Indeed, Haslam still remained wedded to techniques more redolent of older, 'terrific' forms of management. For example, he was renowned for his defence of mechanical restraint with chains as more practical and more humane than strait waistcoats. He was also distinguished for inventing and promoting an instrument for the more effectual force-feeding of patients, known as Haslam's key, which he claimed made damage to patients' teeth less liable to occur. Although a practical device in its time, by the 1850s it was being taken (somewhat out of context) as a symbol of dark age asylumdom.

Haslam has also been distinguished for being the first English practitioner to publish a book devoted to a single psychiatric case history. His *Illustrations of Madness* (1810) in which he presented the case of the Bethlem patient James Tilly Matthews has often been seen by modern psychiatrists and historians as one of the earliest and most complete presentations allowing for a confident retrospective diagnosis of schizophrenia. However, Haslam's approach to Matthews's case had a propensity to dismiss the testimony of the insane as meaningless, and his design of

merely illustrating madness, by presenting Matthews's words verbatim as self-evidently mad, and therefore not worth much deeper exploration, was not free of a tendency to ridicule his patient. Ironically, Matthews was to have his posthumous revenge: Matthews had passed on documents to the 1815–16 parliamentary committee which had helped to expose Haslam and other medical officers to charges of medical negligence and cruelty.

Aggrieved by what he saw as his unfair treatment at Bethlem, Haslam devoted more and more attention to his publications and to securing a path back to a respectable position within the medical establishment. Uncontrite and arrogant, if not indignant, towards his critics, he proceeded in ensuing publications to defend his record at Bethlem, and to go on the attack against the reformers and against his former employers. Firmly dissociating himself from the proponents of moral treatment, his tract on the subject (1817) assailed those who threatened to supplant medicine and medical officers with lay managers, and to dispense with mechanical restraint. In subsequent publications he censured those framing a bill to set up a central madhouses inspectorate for their inexperience and antipathy towards medical practitioners. His treatise *Medical Jurisprudence* (1817) sought further to assert the importance of medical expertise on insanity and his own claims to such. From early in his career Haslam had begun to establish his reputation and bolster his income as an expert witness in insanity trials. It was on this experience that he relied for his 1817 treatise, and his work on the subject was cited approvingly by a number of subsequent authors. Other publications, such as his book *Sound Mind* (1819) and a letter to the lord chancellor (1823) on the same subject with reference to Lord Portsmouth's case, attempted to define more clearly the criteria on which insanity should be defined.

Haslam continued to practise medicine privately after his ousting from Bethlem, including certifying patients for admission to private madhouses. He gained the degree of MD from Marischal College, Aberdeen, on 17 September 1816, but this did not permit him to practise in London. It was evidently with a view to complying with College of Physicians regulations for medical practice that Haslam enrolled at Pembroke College. He finally gained a licence to practise medicine in the metropolis from the Royal College of Physicians on 12 April 1824 but was never elected a fellow. A month later he paid the 50 guineas required to become a governor of St Bartholomew's Hospital, and also gained election as a governor of St Luke's. During 1826–8 Haslam delivered a course of public lectures before the London Medical Society, comprising one on the study of the human mind and a course of six on the intellectual composition of man; these were well received and were published in *The Lancet*. In such ways Haslam was clearly seeking to rebuild his reputation, an ambition he realized with qualified success. Notably, in 1827 he was elected president of the Medical Society, chairing its meetings until 1829. Haslam seems to have been on friendly terms with the famous anatomist John Hunter (1728–

1793), whom he had studied under at Edinburgh, but he was rather closer to Alexander Morison (1779–1866), physician to Bethlem from 1835 to 1853. His intimate friendship with Dr William Kitchiner (1775–1827) saw him become one of the founding members of the Committee of Taste, a small dining and conversational club. His relations with these men and others, such as William Jerdan (1782–1869), the editor of the *London Literary Gazette*, to which Haslam was a regular contributor, permitted him to widen his social circle, and to cement his links with sympathetic figures within and outside of the medical profession, while sniping in print at others he disagreed with.

In subsequent years Haslam persisted in his defence of traditional therapeutics against the claims of asylum reformers which he attacked in his writings as fashionable, pseudo-philanthropy. Following the report of the parliamentary select committee of 1827 and the ensuing legislation of 1828, which saw a metropolitan commission established to inspect madhouses in the city, Haslam published an impassioned and comprehensive attack on the commission and on the wider programme of the reformers. Allying himself with other critics within the profession and the college, who resented central and lay interference in medical matters, Haslam published a letter to the commissioners (1830), in particular condemning the involvement of 'ignorant' laymen in asylum visitation and administration as 'detrimental interference', and censuring the influence of religious evangelicals on the committee's composition and on the reform movement in general. In *On the Nature of Thought* (1835) he rehashed many of the propositions he had made in *Sound Mind*. Haslam was also one of the first to join and deliver a paper before the Society for Improving the Condition of the Insane (founded in 1842 by his friend Alexander Morison), attacking the non-restraint movement and endorsing the historical and continuing importance of restraint in the treatment of insanity. The last papers he gave, on the distinction between crime and insanity and on the causes of the increase of insanity, were delivered before the same society, the first asserting the need for expert psychiatric assessment before trials, and the latter complaining about the premature discharge of asylum patients.

Haslam and his wife (*d.* before 1825) had two children. His first born, also named John Haslam, was baptized in 1790 at St Leonard's Church, Shoreditch, became a naval surgeon, and occasionally substituted for his father at Bethlem. By the 1820s the family was living at 1 Hart Street, Bloomsbury. In 1830, relying on and inspired by the experience she had gained as a result of her father's long career in the asylum business, Haslam's widowed daughter, Henrietta Hunter, succeeded in securing the post of matron to Dundee Asylum, where she served until 1840. In that year she was appointed in the same capacity to Bethlem, until yet another official enquiry and scandalous revelations forced her own and the physician's resignation (for neglect of duty) in 1852.

By the 1840s Haslam had retired from active medical practice. He died of 'debility' at his house at 56 Lamb's Conduit Street, St George the Martyr, London, on 20 July 1844. JONATHAN ANDREWS

Sources A. Scull, C. MacKenzie, and N. Hervey, *Masters of Bedlam: the transformation of the mad-doctoring trade* (1996) · *DNB* · *The Lancet* (27 July 1844), 571 · Munk, *Roll*, 3.282 · *Literary Gazette* (27 July 1844), 484–5 · *GM*, 2nd ser., 22 (1844), 322–3 · D. Leigh, 'John Haslam, M.D., 1764–1844: apothecary to Bethlem', *Journal of the History of Medicine and Allied Sciences*, 10 (1955), 17–44 · D. Leigh, 'John Haslam, M.D.: a pioneer of forensic psychiatry', *Journal of Delinquency* (1954?) · R. Hunter and I. Macalpine, 'John Haslam: his will and his daughter', *Medical History*, 6 (1962), 22–6 · F. Schiller, 'Haslam of "Bedlam", Kitchiner of the "oracles": two doctors under mad King George III and their friendship', *Medical History*, 28 (1984), 189–201 · P. K. Carpenter, 'Descriptions of schizophrenia in the psychiatry of Georgian Britain: John Haslam and James Tilly Matthews', *Comprehensive Psychiatry*, 30 (1989), 332–8 · J. L. Waddington, 'Ventricular enlargement in schizophrenia and the historical studies of John Haslam', *American Journal of Psychiatry*, 141 (1984), 1640 · J. Haslam, *Observations on insanity, with practical remarks on the disease and an account of the morbid appearances on dissection* (1798) · J. Haslam, *Observations on madness and melancholy: including practical remarks on those diseases together with cases; and an account of the morbid appearances on dissection*, 2nd edn (1809) · J. Haslam, *Illustrations of madness: exhibiting a singular case of insanity and a no less remarkable difference in medical opinion … with a description of the tortures experienced by the patient, James Tilly Matthews, in hallucinations* (1810) · J. Haslam, *Illustrations of madness*, ed. R. Porter (1988) · J. Haslam, 'Observations of Mr. Haslam, the apothecary', in T. Monro, *Observations of Dr Monro (physician to Bethlem Hospital) upon the evidence taken before the committee of the hon. House of Commons for regulating mad-houses* (1816), 37–55 · *IGI* · R. Hunter and I. Macalpine, *Three hundred years of psychiatry, 1535–1860* (1963), 580, 632–9, 697, 700–02 · R. Porter, *Mind-forg'd manacles: a history of madness from the Restoration to the Regency* (1987), 124–5, 167, 209, 236–62 · R. Howard, 'James Tilly Matthews in London and Paris 1793: his first peace mission — in his own words', *History of Psychiatry*, 2 (1991), 53–69

Archives Bethlem Royal Hospital, Beckenham, Kent | U. Cam., Richard Hunter collection

Likenesses H. Dawe, mezzotint, pubd 1812 (after G. Dawe), BM, Department of Prints and Drawings

Wealth at death under £100: will, Hunter and Macalpine, 'John Haslam'

Haslam, Thomas Joseph (1825–1917). *See under* Haslam, Anna Maria (1829–1922).

Haslam, John (1808–1884), enamel painter, was born in Carrington, Cheshire, and baptized on 21 February 1808. He left home as a boy to live at Derby with his uncle, James Thomason, afterwards manager of the Derby china works. He entered the china works at the age of fourteen and he studied under George Hancock. He spent thirteen years there as a china painter, when he first devoted himself to flower painting, but subsequently took to figure painting, in which he was very successful. He painted *c.*1830 for the duke of Sussex a miniature of Lord Byron after the portrait by Thomas Phillips (1813; priv. coll., version at Newstead Abbey, Nottinghamshire) as a present for Otto, king of Greece, and at the duke's instigation went to London and studied under E. T. Parris. He copied many pictures in miniature on enamel, and was a frequent exhibitor at the Royal Academy from 1836 to 1865. In 1843 he obtained a silver medal from the Society of Arts for a portrait on china. He painted a small enamel portrait of Queen Victoria, and thenceforward obtained many commissions from the royal family and the nobility, especially for copies of ancestral portraits. He was also frequently employed by jewellers and art dealers, and on one occasion was employed to paint a set of enamels in imitation of miniatures by Jean Petitot, which were so successful that they appeared in the loan exhibition at South Kensington in 1862 and the exhibition of portrait miniatures held there in 1865, as the work of Petitot himself. In 1857 Haslem returned to reside with his uncle in Osmaston Road, Derby, where he died on 30 April 1884. He was apparently unmarried. In 1876 he published *The Old Derby China Factory: the Workmen and their Productions*.

L. H. CUST, rev. ANNETTE PEACH

Sources DNB · Graves, *RA exhibitors* · J. Haslem, *The old Derby china factory: the workmen and their productions* (1876) · A. Peach, 'Portraits of Byron', *Walpole Society*, 62 (2000), 1–144 · *CGPLA Eng. & Wales* (1884) · *IGI*
Archives Derby Local Studies Library, records of visits and paintings; letters
Wealth at death £15,040 6s. 6d.: probate, 16 July 1884, *CGPLA Eng. & Wales*

Hasler, Herbert George (1914–1987), inventor of sailing equipment and Royal Marines officer, was born in Dublin on 27 February 1914, the younger child and younger son of Lieutenant Arthur Thomas Hasler, quartermaster, of the Royal Army Medical Corps, and his wife, Annie Georgina Andrews. His father was drowned when the troopship *Transylvania* was torpedoed on 4 May 1917, leaving his mother to bring up the young boys on her own. She sent Herbert, with a bursary, to Wellington College, where he distinguished himself at cross-country running, rugby football, and as captain of swimming. He also boxed but, according to him, with rather less distinction.

Blondie Hasler, as he became known, except to his family, because of his (thinning) blond hair and fair moustache, combined remarkable powers of physical endurance with above average strength and fitness (he was about 6 feet tall). Yet, throughout his subsequent career, he was loath to take advantage of these attributes, although they stood him in good stead in war and peace, preferring a well-reasoned, calm, and quietly conducted discussion to make his case. He also hated punishing men under his command, believing that their failure was the result of his lack of leadership. He had a totally original mind.

Hasler was commissioned into the Royal Marines on 1 September 1932, and by 1935 had already achieved yachting distinction by sailing a 12 foot dinghy single-handed from Plymouth to Portsmouth and back again. It was then that he began expounding advanced nautical theories through illustrated articles in the international press—a hobby that he pursued until his death. After the Second World War broke out, as fleet landing officer in Scapa Flow in 1940, he was sent to Narvik in support of the French Foreign Legion. In just a few weeks he was appointed OBE, mentioned in dispatches, and awarded the Croix de Guerre.

On his return he wrote a paper suggesting the use of canoes and underwater swimmers to attack enemy shipping, but this was rejected by combined operations as being too radical and impracticable. However, in January 1942 Hasler was appointed to the combined operations development centre where, after the Italians had severely damaged HMS *Queen Elizabeth* and HMS *Valiant* in Alexandria harbour by the use of 'human torpedoes', his paper was immediately resurrected. He was ordered to form the Royal Marines boom patrol detachment (later to be dubbed the 'Cockleshell heroes'—an expression of which he disapproved). When the problem of blockade-runners operating out of Bordeaux was identified in September, Hasler had his solution ready the next day. The submarine HMS *Tuna* launched a raid on the night of 7 December 1942. Four men out of the original twelve reached the target in tiny two-man canoes, and only two, Hasler and Corporal Bill Sparks (1922–2002), returned, having made their way overland to Spain. Hasler was recommended for the VC, but was technically ineligible, having not been fired on. He was appointed DSO. The episode was turned into a film, *Cockleshell Heroes* (1955), which was only loosely based on fact; it starred José Ferrer and Trevor Howard.

Subsequently, Hasler experimented with different methods of attack, employing some of these ideas between 1944 and 1945 while serving as training and development officer with 385 Royal Marines detachment in the small operations group (Ceylon), planning submarine- and flying boat-launched raids into Burma.

In 1946 Hasler won the Royal Ocean Racing Club's class three championships in his unconventional yacht, the 30 square-metre *Tre Sang*. This was a remarkable achievement for a young officer. Hasler was invalided out of the Royal Marines in 1948 with the wartime rank of lieutenant-colonel. Retirement now allowed him time to concentrate on exploring, writing (in 1957 he wrote a play with Rosamund Pilcher, *The Tulip Major*, which was performed in Dundee), inventing, and developing a wide range of ideas, many of which are still in daily use. They included a floating breakwater and towed dracones (Hasler developed an earlier idea into a feasible design for transporting bulk oil).

In 1952 Hasler published *Harbours and Anchorages of the North Coast of Brittany* (rev. 1965), which set the standard for the genre, but his greatest civilian triumphs of invention—and quiet, gentlemanly persuasion—were yet to come. In 1953 he conceived and built *Jester*, based on a modified 26 foot Folkboat design, as a test bed for various sail plans (he eventually settled on the junk rig), and the internationally acclaimed, and first commercially successful, Hasler self-steering gear. *Jester* was a radical advance in British yacht design and she was not the last yacht to come from his drawing-board.

In 1957 Hasler proposed the idea of a quadrennial single-handed transatlantic race for yachts and after many setbacks this was sailed in 1960 by five yachts; Hasler came second in *Jester*. He followed this in 1962 with a search for the Loch Ness monster and in 1966 by the first quadrennial two-handed round-Britain and Ireland race, in which Hasler (again, the instigator) was crewed by his wife in the equally radical *Sumner*. These two races spawned almost all modern, short-handed racing worldwide, with Hasler acknowledged as the founding father: he received a number of international awards. In his later years he moved to the west of Scotland, where he farmed organically and wrote *Practical Junk Rig* with J. K. McLeod (1988). His most important invention had been the self-steering gear, which became standard equipment and revolutionized sailing.

Hasler was married in 1965, when in his early fifties, to Bridget Mary Lindsay Fisher, then in her mid-twenties, the daughter of Rear-Admiral Ralph Lindsay Fisher, and herself an experienced yachtswoman. Despite the age difference the marriage brought them immense happiness and a son and a daughter. Hasler died of a heart attack in Glasgow on 5 May 1987.   EWEN SOUTHBY-TAILYOUR, rev.

Sources U. Southampton, Hartley Library, Mountbatten MSS · C. E. L. Phillips, *Cockleshell heroes* (1956) · L. Foster, *OSTAR* (1989) · E. Southby-Tailyour, *Blondie Hasler: a biography* (1996) · personal knowledge (1996) · private information (1996) · J. Thompson, *The royal marines: from sea soldiers to a special force* (2000) · J. D. Ladd, *The royal marines, 1919–1980: an authorised history* (1980) · J. Thompson, *The Imperial War Museum book of war behind enemy lines* (1996) · CCI (1987)
Archives Royal Marines Museum, Eastney barracks, Southsea, Hampshire, archives | U. Southampton, Hartley Library, Mountbatten MSS | FILM BBC TV South-west
Wealth at death £48,613.39: confirmation, 1987, CCI

Hasleton, Richard (*fl.* **1577–1595**), captain in the merchant marine, was born in Braintree, Essex. He sailed from London in May 1582 on board the *Mary Marten*. He states himself to have been nearly five years before this a captain in the Algiers trade. Bound for Petrach, he and his crew successfully discharged their business there and were headed for home some twenty-eight days later when their troubles began. The ship survived being grounded off Lepanto, but was then attacked and sunk by Turkish galleys, and Hasleton was forced to serve as a galley slave on a Turkish ship for two years. He managed to escape only to become a galley slave on a Genoan vessel, from where he was taken to a prison in Majorca. Brought before an inquisitor he consistently refused to abandon his allegiance to the Church of England in favour of Rome. He survived interrogation and imprisonment underground in solitary confinement for a year before managing to escape. He was recaptured and returned to prison, where followed further interrogation and torture, which he describes graphically in his later account.

Having escaped again, Hasleton managed to reach the Barbary coast, where he met with the only kindness in his ten years of misery when an old man gave him food and shelter and helped him on his way. He was, however, recaptured, and there began a new phase of his troubles in which various parties tried to convert him to Islam, as unsuccessfully as the Inquisition had tried to win him for Rome. Escapes proved only temporary before finally he reached Algiers. His hopes of reaching home shortly afterwards were dashed when he was pressed into slavery again on a Genoan galley after the English consul in Algiers had refused help. His final enslavement lasted

three years before he finally managed to sail home on board the *Cherubim* of London, arriving home in February 1593. He describes his extraordinary adventures in *Strange and Wonderful Things* (1595), which is engagingly written and illustrated with woodcuts. Nothing further is known of Hasleton, other than that he was married and had children, but the details of his family are unknown.

ELIZABETH BAIGENT

Sources R. Hasleton, *Strange and wonderful things* (1595)

Haslett, Dame Caroline Harriet (**1895–1957**), electrical engineer and electricity industry administrator, was born at Worth, Sussex, on 17 August 1895, the second of the five children of Robert Haslett (*b. c.*1864, *d.* after 1957), a railway signal fitter and a pioneer of the co-operative movement, and his wife, Caroline Sarah, formerly Holmes (*d. c.*1939). She was educated at Haywards Heath high school (1906–13) and then took a post as secretary with the Cochran Boiler Company. Clerical work did not particularly attract her and she asked to be transferred to the works where she was given practical engineering training. For a period she was associated with Sir Charles Parsons, the inventor of the Parsons turbine, in the promotion of a journal devoted especially to women in the engineering industry.

Haslett was the first secretary of the Women's Engineering Society founded in 1919 by Lady Parsons, wife of Sir Charles, and she edited the society's journal, *Woman Engineer*, from 1919 to 1932. Haslett was never an ardent feminist but perceived the possibilities of engineering to raise the whole social status of women. She did valuable work in persuading engineering institutions to admit women to their examinations and not least in inducing employers to engage female labour. She founded the Electrical Association for Women in 1924 and became its first director. Through this organization she exercised a powerful influence on the development of the domestic use of electricity, encouraged by progressively minded people in the electrical industry. A strong personality, Haslett yet had the capacity for self-elimination at public functions, almost invariably preferring to delegate to other women such activities as would bring them into prominence. She aroused intense loyalty and enthusiasm among her colleagues. She resigned the directorship in 1956 owing to ill health, remaining as an honorary adviser. Appointed CBE in 1931 and DBE in 1947, Caroline Haslett was a justice of the peace for the county of London and in 1932 was made a companion member of the Institution of Electrical Engineers. She was president of the Women's Engineering Society from 1939 to 1941.

An ardent champion of the causes she advocated, Dame Caroline spoke and wrote frequently on the subjects which she had at heart, and the pages of the *Electrical Age*, the journal of the Electrical Association for Women, which she edited from 1926 to 1956, reflect her tireless energy in promoting the development of electricity for domestic purposes. In 1934 she edited the *Electrical Handbook for Women*, which went through six editions during her lifetime, and in 1949 she wrote *Problems Have No Sex*. At

Dame Caroline Harriet Haslett (1895–1957), by Sir Gerald Kelly, c.1949

the time of her withdrawal from active work the association had 14,000 members, most of them housewives, domestic science teachers, and educationists, organized in 160 branches. The association continued to flourish after her death but by the 1980s it was clear that it was no longer attracting new members and it was voluntarily dissolved in 1986. Dame Caroline's solicitude for the well-being of women in their homes was only rivalled by her enthusiasm for the development of electricity as an agent in reducing domestic chores. She early realized the need for ensuring the safety and efficient design of these devices and devoted much of her energy to promoting this.

Dame Caroline was the first and only woman to be appointed a member of the British Electricity Authority on its inception in 1947 and to serve on its successors until the time of her death. Her keen mind and refreshing zest were a valuable asset to the newly integrated industry. Her practical wisdom and lively sense of humour did much to lessen the stresses and tensions of the early years when organization and human problems of some complexity had to be resolved. A motor vessel of the authority's collier fleet was named *Dame Caroline Haslett*, and the association founded the Caroline Haslett Trust to provide scholarships and travelling fellowships and exhibitions for its members.

Dame Caroline served on numerous public bodies including the British Institute of Management, the Industrial Welfare Society, the National Industrial Alliance, the British Electrical Development Association, the Royal Society of Arts, Bedford College for Women, the London School of Economics, Queen Elizabeth College, the Administrative Staff College, King's College of Household

and Social Science, and the Crawley Development Corporation. She travelled widely, and on government missions, to the United States, Canada, Sweden, and Finland. She attended the World Power Conference several times as a British delegate and was the author of papers on home management to international scientific management congresses in Europe. In 1950 she became the president of the International Federation of Business and Professional Women. After the Second World War she took a leading part in conferences organized for women in Germany by the British and American authorities and at the invitation of the United States government visited the American zone of Germany to address conferences there.

Dame Caroline never swerved from her high purpose of raising the social status of women, and her flair for organization and administration, her integrity of mind, healthy common sense, and love of simple things endeared her to those who had the good fortune to work with her. She never married, although she maintained a close relationship with F. S. Button of the National Union of Railwaymen until his death in the 1940s.

When her health began to fail Dame Caroline left London to live with her widowed sister, Rosalind Messenger, at Worth Cottage, Bungay, Suffolk; she died there on 4 January 1957. In fulfilment of her wish to be cremated by electricity she was cremated at the City of London crematorium, Manor Park, and her ashes were scattered in its garden of remembrance. A memorial service was held on 25 January 1957 at St Martin-in-the-Fields, London.

CITRINE, rev. ELEANOR PUTNAM SYMONS

Sources R. Messenger, *The doors of opportunity* (1967) · Inst. EE, Dame Caroline Haslett papers · Inst. EE, Women's Engineering Society papers · Inst. EE, Electrical Association for Women papers · *The Times* (5 Jan 1957) · private information (2004) [John Messenger]
Archives Inst. EE, corresp. and papers; Electrical Association for Women MSS, NAEST 93; Women's Engineering Society MSS, NAEST 92 | U. Warwick Mod. RC, corresp. with A. P. Young, MSS 242/C/1/145–158, 242/C/3/44–5
Likenesses numerous photographs, 1930–50, Inst. EE · D. Vicaji, oils, 1934, Inst. EE · E. Gabain, lithograph, c.1949, IWM Art Gallery · G. Kelly, oils, c.1949, RSA [see illus.] · H. Coster, photographs, NPG · G. Kelly, oils, second version, NPG · D. Vicaji, oils, Electrical Association for Women, London
Wealth at death £26,521 6s. 6d.: probate, 4 March 1957, CGPLA Eng. & Wales

Haslewood, Joseph (1769–1833), bibliographer and antiquary, was born at the lying-in hospital, Brownlow Street, Covent Garden, Westminster, on 5 November 1769, and baptized on 9 November, the son of Richard Haslewood and his wife, Mary Dewberry. He was apprenticed to his mother's brother, a solicitor in Conduit Street, and became a partner in the firm before eventually succeeding his uncle. From an early age he took a keen interest in early English literature, and although never wealthy he began to collect books. This brought him into contact with other antiquaries and book collectors, who found his enthusiasm and vigour congenial. His first literary publication was a collection of dramatic anecdotes, *Green-Room Gossip, or, Gravity Gallinipt* (by 'Gridiron Gabble, Gent., godson to Mother Goose', 1809); his choice of a mock-ancient title was characteristic. He provided Sir Samuel Egerton Brydges with material for *Censura literaria* (1807–9) and *The British Bibliographer* (1810–14). Along with his friends Philip Bliss and Thomas Frognall Dibdin, Haslewood was a founder of the Roxburghe Club, which was started on 16 June 1812—the eve of the sale at record-breaking price of the Valdarfer Boccaccio (1471), part of the library of John, duke of Roxburghe.

By this time Haslewood had achieved some renown as an editor of early English literature; with Samuel Waller Singer, he became one of the most prolific publishers of sixteenth- and seventeenth-century texts. In 1810 he produced the first modern editions of Thomas Tusser's *Five Hundred Points of Good Husbandry* and of *The Book of St Albans*, then attributed to Juliana Berners. These were followed by Puttenham's *Arte of English Poesie* (1811), Painter's *The Palace of Pleasure* (1813), and *The Mirror of Magistrates* (1815); he was the first to draw attention to the importance of the last two as Shakespearian sources. His compilation *Antient Critical Essays upon English Poets and Poesy* (1811–15) and his edition of *Drunken Barnaby's Journal* (1817–18) have lasted better; the second edition of the latter (1820), a well-known picaresque travelogue of northern England, contained a long account of Richard Brathwaite which firmly established his claim to its authorship. Haslewood also wrote a series of articles on old London theatres for the *Gentleman's Magazine* (1813–14) under the pseudonym Eu. Hood, and also contributed a series entitled 'Fly leaves' (1822–5). His chief literary legacy is probably the series of books that he edited for the Roxburghe Club, among them the fine edition of Cutwoode's *Calthea poetarum* (1815); the production of such texts became an important and ongoing activity of the club. At the same time Haslewood enjoyed its tradition of informal fun (the Horatian 'dulce desipere in loco' tradition), which he recorded in his own mock-antique style in 'Roxburghe Revels', an account of the club's early activities (the original manuscript of which was presented to the club by the earl of Powis in 1932).

This light-hearted piece had an unfortunate impact on Haslewood's posthumous reputation. After his death on 21 September 1833, at Addison Road, Kensington, Middlesex, his book collection was sold on the following 16 December. The manuscript of 'Roxburghe Revels' was injudiciously included in the sale, and was bought by the bookseller Thomas Thorpe, who sold it on to the editor of *The Athenaeum*. Thence it passed directly or otherwise to the author (almost certainly James Silk Buckingham) of a violent attack on Haslewood and the Roxburghe Club, citing the manuscript in such a manner as to denigrate both. This appeared in *The Athenaeum* in January 1834, after which the Scottish antiquary James Maidment, a friend of Haslewood, reprinted the articles, with replies, as *Roxburghe Revels, and other Relative Papers* (1837). This also featured a memoir of Haslewood.

Haslewood is better remembered as a collector of ephemera and other material that stood in danger of being lost or forgotten, including the large collection of printed proclamations, now in the library of the duke of Buccleuch; nine volumes of cuttings, playbills, and dramatic prints in the British Library; and, most especially, the volumes of tracts that he assembled, often under alliterative titles of his own devising (one of these volumes, bought by Isaac D'Israeli, remains at Hughenden).

Some of Haslewood's own letters, which are written in a lively style, are held at the British Library—most notably those to Brydges, Bliss, and Dibdin; he remembered the last two in his will, which was proved on 9 November 1833.   ALAN BELL

Sources N. J. Barker, *The publications of the Roxburghe Club, 1814–1962* (1964) · Viscount Mersey [J. C. Bigham], *The Roxburghe Club, its history and its members, 1812–1927* (1929) · *GM*, 1st ser., 103/2 (1833), 467 · *DNB* · will, PRO, PROB 11/1823/697 · *IGI*
Archives BL, corresp. as editor of Barnabee's Itinerary by Richard Brathwaite, Add. MS 22308 · Yale U., Beinecke L., notebook relating to archery | BL, letters to Philip Bliss, Add. MSS 34567–34581, *passim* · BL, letters to Sir S. E. Brydges, Add. MS 25102 · BL, letters to T. F. Dibdin

Hasluck, Frederick William (1878–1920), archaeologist and ethnologist, was born at Eythan Lodge, Southgate, Middlesex, on 16 February 1878, the son of Percy Pedley Hasluck and his wife, Edith Louisa (*née* Battley). He was educated at the Leys School, Cambridge (May 1893–July 1897), where he won a prize for his original drawings of Cambridgeshire antiquities. He then went to King's College, Cambridge, with a foundation scholarship, gaining a first in the classical tripos part one and (with distinction) part two, and thereafter a fellowship. He spent the years from 1899 to 1916 mainly in Greece and Anatolia. He was noted for his gentleness, refinement, and gift for friendship. His witty letters, very much influenced by the allusive style of Edward Lear, charmed his friends. Extracts of his letters to Richard Dawkins were published by his widow in 1926 as *Letters on Religion and Folklore*. He was well known in the Levant as a traveller and latterly as a student of the Bektashi order of dervishes then to be found in Albania, Serbia, and northern Greece. He was widely believed to know more of their customs and history than they did themselves.

In 1901 Hasluck became a student of the British School of Archaeology at Athens and in 1905 its librarian for one year. From 1905 to 1910 and again from 1911 to 1915 he was assistant director and librarian of the British School, building up the library holdings in early travellers and in medieval and post-medieval Balkan culture and history. On 26 September 1912 he married Margaret Masson Hardie (1885–1948) [*see* Hasluck, Margaret Masson], who joined the British School in 1911, and who shared his interests in contemporary Balkan culture. They did not have children. In the same period he travelled widely in the Greek islands and in Anatolia with the school's director, Richard Dawkins. These travels resulted in more than fifty articles and three books, building on the fieldwork of Sir William Ramsay, with whom he often disagreed. Most of this work, dealing with medieval and modern Smyrna, the development of the monasteries of Athos, and Genoese and Venetian influences on the Aegean, remains of great value and some of it still the only work in the field.

His study of the city of Cyzicus and its environs (*Cyzicus*, 1910) was his only foray into classical archaeology and, for its time, a model of competent field archaeology. It is still a starting point for any research on that area. His other books were *Athos and its Monasteries*, published posthumously in 1924, and, with H. H. Jewel, *The Church of Our Lady of the Hundred Gates at Paros* which appeared in 1920: both works are still consulted. In the spring of 1913 Hasluck visited Konia and became interested in the interrelationship of Christianity and Islam. The fruit of his labours was the monumental *Christianity and Islam under the Sultans*, published posthumously in 1929. It is a fine example of interdisciplinary research and writing notable not just for its arcane material but for the sensitivity, acumen, and sheer knowledge of its author. This was Hasluck's most important work. As a reference work it may be read as much for pleasure as for instruction.

Hasluck's knowledge of the Levant was put to use in the summer of 1915 when he joined the intelligence department of the British legation in Athens, working among the refugees who came to the city. Something of his work in this role as well as insights into his character may be gleaned from Compton Mackenzie's *First Athenian Memories* (1931). It was work which Hasluck did not enjoy and it certainly led to the breakdown of his health. In 1916 tuberculosis forced him to retire to France and in 1917 to a sanatorium, Beau Réveil, Leysin, Switzerland, where he died on 22 February 1920, a few days after his forty-second birthday.

He was survived by his wife, Margaret. After his death she spent much time researching in Albania, living at Elbasan until April 1939, and editing Hasluck's manuscripts for publication, in addition to her own books. There is a wall monument in Hasluck's memory in the Penrose Library at the British School in Athens.

PETER W. LOCK

Sources F. W. Hasluck, *Letters on religion and folklore* (1926) · H. Waterhouse, *The British School at Athens* (1986) · *The Times* (24 Feb 1920) · J. Isnard, *The Fortnightly* (28 Feb 1920) · C. Mackenzie, *First Athenian memories* (1931) · b. cert. · m. cert. · *CGPLA Eng. & Wales* (1920) · M. Clark, 'Margaret Masson Hasluck', *Black lambs and grey falcons: women travellers in the Balkans*, ed. J. B. Allcock and A. Young (2000)

Archives British School of Archaeology, Athens, archives

Likenesses photograph, repro. in Hasluck, *Letters*, frontispiece · photograph, repro. in Waterhouse, *British School*, 21 · photographs, British School at Athens

Wealth at death £9242 14s. 6d.: probate, 6 July 1920, *CGPLA Eng. & Wales*

Hasluck [*née* Hardie], **Margaret Masson** (1885–1948), ethnographer, was born on 18 June 1885 at Chapelton, Drumblade, near Elgin, Scotland, the eldest of the nine children of John Hardie, a farmer, and his wife, Margaret Leslie. Brought up jointly by her grandparents, she was educated at Elgin Academy before taking first-class degrees in classics from Aberdeen and Cambridge universities. In 1910 she became the first woman nominated for a studentship at the British School at Athens. In the following summer she joined a dig in Anatolia under William Ramsay.

In Athens, Margaret met the distinguished archaeologist Frederick William *Hasluck (1878–1920), and they married at her home in Scotland on 26 September 1912. For the rest of her life she blamed herself for her husband's early death, convinced that the tuberculosis that slowly killed him had been contracted on a trip to Konia in 1913. The trip had been his wedding present to her; the destination had been her choice. After his death she spent many months assembling and editing his notes for posthumous publication.

Gradually Hasluck returned to her own work and interests. In 1921, having received a travelling fellowship from Aberdeen University, she began ethnographic fieldwork in Macedonia and Albania. From 1923 she lived in Albania, where her husband had studied the Bektashi. She became 'the first west European scholar, female or male, to do systematic, sustained, ethnographic work' in large parts of the country (Clark, 128). She travelled all over Albania, in all weathers and by all modes of transport, spending whole seasons in the mountains. Her extensive notes and data covered a wide variety of topics: from local dialects, coinage, and customs, to witches, blood feuds, and botany. She sent dozens of artefacts to the Marischal Museum in Aberdeen. Indeed, in methodology and commitment, Hasluck far surpassed her contemporary Edith Durham (1863–1944). Unlike Hasluck, Durham never learnt Albanian, for example, and she spent only a fraction of Hasluck's sixteen years in the country.

In 1935 Hasluck settled in the town of Elbasan, where in the following year she built a house. Elbasan was also the home of Lef Nosi, a distinguished Albanian patriot and a cabinet minister in Albania's first government. He shared her interests in archaeology and ethnography and the pair became very close, though the claim by Albanian communist writers that Hasluck was Nosi's mistress is impossible to substantiate. Whatever the relationship, it too ended in tragedy. In April 1939, on the eve of the Italian invasion of Albania and for reasons still unclear, King Zog demanded that Hasluck leave the country. She never returned to Albania or saw Nosi again. A member of a puppet government set up by the Germans in 1943, he was shot by Albania's communist regime in 1946.

In February 1942, while living in Cairo, Hasluck was recruited by the Special Operations Executive (SOE) and charged with exploring possibilities of encouraging resistance in occupied Albania. During the First World War both she and her husband had spent time working for British intelligence, as had many members of the British School at Athens. At that time her own work had been of little account, but she now assumed a significant role. From Istanbul she established lines into Albania and sought to recruit exiled Albanians for operations. By 1943 she was back in Cairo as head of SOE's Albanian section, briefing SOE operatives before they parachuted into Albania, teaching them the rudiments of the language, and providing and collating intelligence. Within SOE she became known affectionately as Fanny Hasluck, a reference to the many younger FANYs, women of the First Aid Nursing Yeomanry, who worked for SOE in administrative roles. For her tireless efforts she was appointed MBE in 1944.

To Hasluck's great dismay, however, SOE came to support Albania's communist-led partisans, the most committed and dynamic of the country's guerrilla bands. And as the partisans became stronger, threatening to tear apart the pre-war Albania she had known of relative peace and established order, she resigned, although it is likely her deteriorating health also played a part. Early in 1944 she was diagnosed with advanced leukaemia and given little time to live. SOE considered it possible that overwork had exacerbated her condition.

Margaret Hasluck was a tall, handsome woman whose height and bearing had, on occasion, caused her to be mistaken in Albania for a man. To the end, her life interspersed moments of distinction and achievement with others of terrible tragedy and loss, but any depression she may have nursed was disguised beneath enormous reserves of energy, enthusiasm, and kindness. Yet she could be obstinate and impatient, traits that could alienate her even from friends. And though she loved and was rigorous in fieldwork, self-doubt made her slow to publish. Had she published more and for a wider audience, she might have become as well known as Edith Durham.

After spells spent for health reasons in Switzerland and Cyprus, Hasluck moved to Dublin, where she died of leukaemia on 18 October 1948. She was buried beside her parents in the churchyard at Dallas, Scotland. Her most significant work, *The Unwritten Law in Albania* (1954), a comprehensive study of the Albanian custom of blood feud, was published after her death.   RODERICK BAILEY

Sources M. Clark, 'Margaret Masson Hasluck', *Black lambs and grey falcons: women travellers in the Balkans*, ed. J. B. Allcock and A. Young (2000) · *Folklore*, 60/2 (June 1949) · private information (2004) · b. cert. · m. cert.

Archives U. Oxf., Taylor Institution, papers | RGS, photographs

Hasluck, Sir Paul Meernaa Caedwalla (1905–1993), diplomatist and politician, was born on 1 April 1905 at Perth, Western Australia, the second child of English-born parents, E'thel M. C. Hasluck and his wife, Patience Eliza Wooler. Both parents were Salvation Army officers and moved at regular intervals around the state to wherever the army required them to work. Hasluck attended various state schools. The four years spent at Collie in the south-west of Western Australia from 1913 left 'a deeper imprint' on him than any other period of his life (Hasluck, *Mucking About*, 52). He took part in farm work, learned to ride and to love horses, and read avidly. He also became acquainted with several Aboriginal boys at the home, whom he greatly admired. In bush life Hasluck found a 'sense of peace' and 'intimacy with the whole of existence', which he would always 'search to recapture' (ibid., 54).

Hasluck won a scholarship to the Perth modern school, which he attended from 1918 to 1922. In January 1923 he began work as a cadet journalist on the *West Australian*. Journalism gave him a 'crash course of education in the ways of the world', and the chance 'to meet people of all kinds' (Hasluck, *Mucking About*, 120). He became an active

Sir Paul Meernaa Caedwalla Hasluck (1905–1993), by unknown photographer, 1969 [with his wife, Alexandra, Lady Hasluck]

member of the Australian Journalists' Association. Through the association he became friendly with a future prime minister, John Curtin. In 1928 and 1929 Hasluck won the Lovekin prize for journalism, and went on to complete a diploma of journalism course at the University of Western Australia. A founding member (1926) and office-bearer of the Royal Western Australian Historical Society, Hasluck was one of the 'earliest and most innovative practitioners of oral history' (G. Bolton, 'Oral historian', Stannage, Saunders, and Nile, 37). On 14 April 1932 he married Alexandra Margaret Martin Darker (d. 1993), a schoolteacher whom he had met at university. They had two sons. In 1934 he commenced an arts course at the University of Western Australia. He graduated BA in 1937 and later completed an MA.

From 1925 Hasluck read widely in Aboriginal anthropology. He found that 'being interested in Aboriginals was unusual in those days'. He was invited to accompany the 1934 Moseley royal commission into the social and economic condition of Western Australian Aborigines. He continued to write about the social problems of Aboriginal communities, and was highly critical of official incompetence and neglect. His MA thesis, on nineteenth-century native policy in Western Australia, was published in 1942 as *Black Australians*.

In 1939–40 Hasluck held a temporary appointment as lecturer in history at the University of Western Australia. Early in 1941 a chance encounter with John Curtin (by then federal opposition leader) resulted in Hasluck accepting an offer of appointment to the department of external affairs in Canberra. From 1942 he worked closely with his minister, Dr H. V. Evatt, as speechwriter and adviser. He was a delegate to the San Francisco conference of June 1945, where the United Nations charter was drawn up. He was then appointed to the executive committee of the United Nations preparatory commission, which met in London over several months in late 1945. He then became Australia's first permanent representative to the Security Council. The beginnings of the cold war saw constant conflict between the Soviet Union and other council members, and Hasluck performed admirably under testing circumstances. His task was not made easier by Evatt's capricious personality. Hasluck resigned his post in March 1947. He later accused Evatt of wishing to make the staff of external affairs 'his personal possession'.

Hasluck returned to the University of Western Australia as reader in history in March 1948. He worked half-time on the political and social volume of the official history of Australia's participation in the Second World War, having in 1943 accepted an invitation to contribute two volumes. The first volume was published, to considerable acclaim, in 1952. However, by this time Hasluck had left academic life and embarked on a career in politics (the second volume did not appear until 1970). In 1948 he was invited to contest the federal seat of Curtin for the Liberal Party. Hasluck had not sought a political career. His own approach to politics was humanitarian and non-ideological, emphasizing both individual respect and individual responsibility. He was pleased to hear himself described as a 'nineteenth-century liberal' (Hasluck, *Mucking About*, 282–3). He won the seat at the general election of December 1949, which saw the Liberals, led by Robert Menzies, returned to power. As Hasluck saw it, he did 'not have to clamber and contrive' to be elected to parliament. He 'was asked to do it and complied' (ibid., 286).

In May 1951, after only eighteen months on the back benches, Hasluck was appointed minister for territories, a post he was to retain for twelve years. The newly created portfolio, which gave him responsibility for both the Northern Territory and Papua New Guinea, presented formidable difficulties. Both territories required policies for the development of indigenous populations, were severely lacking in infrastructure and basic services, were heavily dependent on parsimonious Australian commonwealth funding, and were further handicapped by inadequate administrative structures. Both territories were also on a path of constitutional development that would, eventually, lead to self-government. In the case of Papua New Guinea there was the further need to create a sense of nationhood. Hasluck was criticized for proceeding too cautiously along the road to independence. Yet he set an 'often frenetic pace' to bring about change, securing significant funding increases for infrastructure, and for education and social welfare (Porter, 157). He succeeded in his broad goal of promoting truly national institutions. Central to his approach was his belief that the people of Papua New Guinea should make their own choice as to when independence should come and what form it would take.

Hasluck was a formidable administrator. He was 'remarkably successful in being able to move from bold policy principles to a methodical and painstakingly close scrutiny' of policy implementation (Porter, 154). 'Uncompromising in his readiness to monitor, inspect and scourge', he was, it was accurately said, determined to be both his own minister and departmental head (H. Nelson, 'Papua New Guinea', Stannage, Saunders, and Nile, 158). His exacting standards and impatience for results did not make him easy to work with. None the less, he retained the respect of his senior officers. His 'nation building' achievements on behalf of Papua New Guinea constituted an outstanding legacy.

The territories portfolio made Hasluck *de facto* minister for Aboriginal affairs, a position for which he was well suited. His first major speech in parliament had called for 'comprehensive national action' to improve the conditions of Aborigines (Porter, 194). In line with his belief in the primacy of local solutions, he proposed commonwealth–state co-operation, with the commonwealth of Australia offering new funding for state programmes rather than taking direct responsibility for Aboriginal affairs. Hasluck was disappointed and bewildered by the indifferent response from the states. He responded by working vigorously to increase provision for health, education, and welfare for Aborigines in the Northern Territory. He also sought to lead by example by abolishing racially based legislation, but the principal measure, the 1953 welfare ordinance, created new problems of racial categorization.

Hasluck's personal ethos placed great emphasis on individual responsibility. In *Black Australians* he had noted how, over the course of the nineteenth century, Aborigines had gradually lost their status as British citizens, and had been reduced to the condition of dependent beings in need of protection. Accordingly, while not the originator, he became the most prominent advocate of the policy of 'assimilation', which he saw as a process by which Aborigines would gradually regain full citizenship and, as he put it, come to 'live in the same manner as White Australians do' (Porter, 197). The cultural paternalism implicit in assimilation provided justification for the long-established practice of removal of half-caste children from their families. Hasluck was not an unqualified supporter of that practice, but neither did he condemn it. Although he respected Aboriginal cultural values, his historical perspective had convinced him that these values could not endure sustained contact with white society. He underestimated the resilience of Aboriginal culture, with its focus on the group rather the individual. In the context of the 1950s Hasluck's policies, based upon equality and social justice, were 'innovative and idealistic', raising expectations and bringing Aboriginal issues into the mainstream of political debate (Read, 285).

Hasluck served briefly as minister for defence during 1963–4. For the next five years he held the post of minister for external affairs under four prime ministers, Menzies, Holt, McEwen, and Gorton. Vietnam was the dominant foreign policy issue, and Hasluck maintained a firm line against what he saw as Chinese-inspired aggression by communist North Vietnam. In early 1968, in the aftermath of the death by drowning of the prime minister, Holt, Hasluck was the most obvious choice as Holt's successor. Hasluck 'adopted a Coriolanus-like attitude' and refused to lobby his party colleagues for their votes (A. Downer, quoted in H. S. Albinski, 'Vietnam', Stannage, Saunders, and Nile, 180). He was defeated narrowly by John Gorton. On 10 February 1969 his parliamentary career ended, concurrently with his appointment as GCMG and the announcement that he would be Australia's next governor-general. (He had already been sworn of the privy council in 1966, and was appointed GCVO in 1970.)

Hasluck's performance of his constitutional role was flawless. As governor-general he took seriously his right 'to be consulted, to encourage and to warn', and lucidly expounded the role and responsibilities of his office (Hasluck, 'Tangled in the harness', *Light that Time has Made*, 1995, 187). He was known to be discreet and could offer advice, based on years of political experience. Gough Whitlam's inexperienced ministry found Hasluck's 'interest and counsel very valuable' (G. Whitlam, *The Truth of the Matter*, 1979, 17). Whitlam offered him an extension of office, but in deference to his wife's wishes he relinquished the post at the end of his five-year term in July 1974. He was appointed KG in 1979.

Freed from the requirements of public office, Hasluck relished the opportunity to return to writing. In 1976 he published *A Time for Building*, a consideration of his stewardship of Papua New Guinea. An autobiography, *Mucking About*, appeared in 1977. *Diplomatic Witness* (1980) was an account of his time in external affairs, and an indictment of Evatt. *Shades of Darkness* (1988) reflected on Aboriginal affairs and administration. His *Collected Poems* had been published in 1969, but two more volumes now followed. There was a steady output of book reviews and journal articles. The posthumous *The Chance of Politics* (1997), drawn from notes written during his years in parliament, contained some scathing portraits of his political contemporaries.

Hasluck's character defies easy assessment. His was a long and active life, with a remarkable variety of significant achievements. Yet in his judgements of himself and of the value of his work, there is a recurrent sense of pessimism. In *Mucking About* he describes himself as a 'failure as a human being' (Hasluck, *Mucking About*, 28). He ended *Mucking About* at the point where he was about to enter politics, saying:

> From that point onward my life ceased to be my own. I was unable to do many things I would have liked to do and was required to do many things I had no personal interest in doing. Duty took charge … I kept assiduously to my political career, often feeling I was the wrong driver in the wrong truck. (ibid., 287)

Some of the sense of loss may have reflected family circumstances. He became estranged from his wife, although they remained under the one roof. In 1973 one of their sons, Rollo, died suddenly of viral myocarditis.

Hasluck's devotion to 'duty' meant the suppression of many youthful character traits. The gregarious young man, who was also capable of a mystical sense of communion with the bush and with animals, was not easily recognized in the prim and pedantic public man, who inspired respect rather than affection. Away from official tasks, youthful exuberance could return. In New York the minister for external affairs was once reported as having spent the early hours of the morning playing bongoes and snare drums at a party. Among friends he was regarded as excellent company, appreciative of good talk, wine, and food. He died in Perth on 9 January 1993. His son Nicholas, a novelist and judge, survived him, as did his wife, who died five months later. Dame Alexandra Hasluck was herself a distinguished social historian. Hasluck's state funeral was held at St George's Anglican Cathedral, Perth. At his wish, eulogies were replaced by trombonists playing 'When the saints go marching in'.

GEOFFREY BROWNE and D. J. MARKWELL

Sources P. Hasluck, *Mucking about: an autobiography* (1977) · R. Porter, *Paul Hasluck: a political biography* (1993) · T. Stannage, K. Saunders, and R. Nile, eds., *Paul Hasluck in Australian history: civic personality and public life* (1998) · P. Hasluck, *Diplomatic witness: Australian foreign affairs, 1941–1947* (1980) · A. Hasluck, *Portrait in a mirror: an autobiography* (1981) · P. Boyce, 'Great Australian leaves a legacy worthy of respect', *West Australian* (21 Jan 1993) · G. Woodard and J. Beaumont, 'Paul Hasluck as minister for external affairs: towards a reappraisal', *Australian Journal of International Affairs*, 52/1 (1998), 63–75 · C. D. Rowley, 'Hasluck and Papua New Guinea', *Historical Studies*, 18/70 (April 1978), 118–26 · G. Cowlishaw, *Rednecks, eggheads and blackfellas: a study of racial power and intimacy in Australia* (1999) · P. Read, 'Northern Territory', *Contested ground: Australian Aborigines under the British crown*, ed. A. McGrath (1995), 269–305 · G. Partington, *Hasluck versus Coombs: white politics and Australia's Aborigines* (Sydney, 1996) · P. Ryan, 'Hasluck: the private man', *Quadrant*, 37/3 (March 1993), 21–4 · *WWW, 1991–5*

Archives FILM BFI NFTVA, news footage

Likenesses double portrait, photograph, 1969, National Archives of Australia [*see illus.*] · R. Templeman [Morrow], oils, repro. in Porter, *Paul Hasluck*; priv. coll. · R. Templeman [Morrow], oils, Parliament House, Canberra, Historic Memorials collection

Hassall, Arthur Hill (1817–1894), physician and microscopist, was born at Teddington, Middlesex, on 13 December 1817, the son of Thomas Hassall (1771–1844), surgeon, and Ann Sherrock (1778x80–1817). After attending school at Richmond, Surrey, he was apprenticed in 1834 to his uncle Sir James Murray, who had a fashionable Dublin medical practice. In 1839 he became a member of the Royal College of Surgeons, in London, and in 1841 he was awarded the diploma of the Society of Apothecaries. Hassall's apprenticeship had included walking the wards of Jervis Street Hospital in Dublin, and the Mercers' Hospital. He had also taken the midwifery diploma in 1837 from Trinity College, Dublin, studied the nearby seashore and the coasts, and won a prize in botany. He presented his *Catalogue of Irish Zoophytes* to the Dublin Natural History Society on 6 November 1840. Hassall went on in 1848 to graduate MB from University College, London; in 1851 he proceeded MD and became a member of the Royal College of Physicians.

His return to Richmond, near the Royal Botanic Gardens

at Kew, enabled Hassall to study structural and physiological botany at Kew. Between 1840 and 1845 he published several articles and books on botanical topics, mostly on freshwater algae, though many of the papers suggested a rather haughty concern with claims to priority. His *History of the British Freshwater Algae* (1845) became something of a controversial classic in the field; most of his research for this work came from the region of Cheshunt, Hertfordshire, and the specimens he left are now largely in the possession of the Natural History Museum, London. Hassall's studies on fungal rot of fruits and potatoes by experimental inoculation of sound tissues were highly apposite given the subsequent potato famine in Ireland. On 26 May 1846 Hassall married Fanny Augusta, daughter of Alexander Du Corron.

Hassall came to public attention with his book *A microscopical examination of the water supplied to the inhabitants of London and the suburban districts* (1850), in which he reported on the state of the water supplied by each of the London water companies. Containing colour illustrations of the organisms found, this work helped to convince people of the revolting nature of having living organisms in their water and drew their attention to the 'carcasses of dead animals, rotting, festering, swarming with flies and maggots' on the banks of the Thames (Hamlin, 115). According to Christopher Hamlin, the book was 'one of the most effective appeals to sensibility in the history of public health', and that one of the most important things it did 'was to make microscopic life a new category of impurity' (ibid., 104). There was, however, a great deal of debate about what the presence of such organisms in the water signified. Hassall found that all waters contained microscopic life but 'was not able to recognise a distinct flora and fauna for each company as he had hoped to' (ibid., 111). He testified before the Board of Health in March or April of 1850 and in parliament Sir Benjamin Hall used Hassall's drawings to attack opponents of water reform. Organisms came to be seen as proof of impurity.

Over this same period, and despite ill health, Hassall began to study food adulteration. This brought him to the attention of Thomas Wakley, who between 1851 and 1854 published in *The Lancet* reports by Hassall concerning the virtually universal practice of adulteration. *The Lancet* reports led in 1855 to a parliamentary select committee (with Hassall as chief scientific witness) and later to the first general preventative (and other) Adulteration Acts (1860), as well as to the presentation on 4 May 1856 from both houses of parliament to Hassall, for public services, of an elegant silver statuette of Angel Ithuriel. Hassall established a reputation as Britain's leading food analyst and was employed as an analytical microscopist by the General Board of Health.

Hassall also became a physician at the Royal Free Hospital, London, which later named a ward after him. By 1866 he was suffering from severe lung problems. His recovery involved long periods confined to bed at his brother's house in Richmond, at Hastings, and at St Leonards, before he transferred to Ventnor, Isle of Wight, as winter approached. Hassall made his home there until at least mid-1877, though he was still able to undertake professional duties in London at least twice a week. During 1866 he was allotted a civil-list pension of £100 per year for public service. While at Ventnor, Hassall and his assistants continued to investigate food adulteration, using the laboratory he had built there.

Hassall decided that Ventnor would be an ideal place to establish a hospital for treating lung disease. The first block was completed in 1868 and the Ventnor Hospital inspired moves to establish similar institutions in Vienna and elsewhere. Hassall's concept was so successful that, by 1908, 23,000 or more patients had been treated there. This hospital finally closed on 15 April 1964, the remaining patients being transferred to the Hassall ward in St Mary's Hospital, Newport, Isle of Wight.

Hassall left Ventnor in 1877 and was presented with a silver service and 300 guineas. Aiming to rest in warmer climes, he spent over a year in Germany and one winter season in Cannes. Italy's ready acceptance of foreign medical qualifications led Hassall finally to settle in San Remo, with occasional stays in London over the summer. Hassall acquired permission to practise in Switzerland and thereafter worked in Lucerne in summer and San Remo in winter; at San Remo he attended Edward Lear. Hassall's time on the continent enabled him to establish a role in pioneering climatic cures for consumption. His *San Remo and the Western Riviera Climatically and Medically Considered* (1879) was a classic of its kind. Hassall died at his home, Casa Bosso, San Remo, on 9 April 1894 and was buried at All Saints' Church, San Remo. He was survived by his second wife, Alice Margaret, whom he had married some time between 1858 and 1866. JAMES H. PRICE

Sources E. A. Gray, *By candlelight: the life of Dr Arthur Hill Hassall, 1817–94* (1983) · J. N. Blau, 'Hassall—physician and microscopist', *BMJ* (8 June 1968), 617–19 · E. G. Clayton, *A memoir of the late Doctor Arthur Hill Hassall* (1908) · *Later letters of Edward Lear*, ed. Lady Strachey (1911) · A. H. Hassall, *The narrative of a busy life: an autobiography* (1893) · C. Hamlin, *A science of impurity: water analysis in nineteenth-century Britain* (1990) · T. Radford, 'Life in the time of cholera', *On Sunday*, 3/33 · *Buenos Aires Herald* (13 Aug 2000) · m. cert. · d. cert. · *CGPLA Eng. & Wales* (1894)

Archives NHM, algae herbarium, botany department, specimens of Hassall's freshwater algae collections | NHM, corresp. with John Ralfs (Penzance) · NHM, corresp. with Miles Joseph Berkeley · RBG, Kew, archives, corresp. with Sir William J. Hooker · corresp. with Edward Lear

Likenesses photograph, 1879, repro. in Gray, *By candlelight*, following p. 64 · L. Calkin, oils, 1894, St Mary's Hospital, Newport, Isle of Wight; repro. in Gray, *By candlelight*, facing p. 65 · I. Sabatini, oils, 1894, repro. in Clayton, *Memoir* · S. Marks, mezzotint (after photograph by Mayall, c.1862), repro. in Gray, *By candlelight*, facing p. 64

Wealth at death £55 2s. 4d.: probate, 6 June 1894, *CGPLA Eng. & Wales*

Hassall, Christopher Vernon (1912–1963), writer and librettist, was born in London on 24 March 1912, the son of John *Hassall (1868–1948), the painter and illustrator, and his second wife, Constance Maud Brooke Webb (c.1878–1950), daughter of the Revd Albert Brooke Webb, rector of Dallinghoe, Wickham Market, Suffolk. He was the younger brother of Joan *Hassall (1906–1988), the wood-

Christopher Vernon Hassall (1912–1963), by Howard Coster, 1955

engraver, who decorated many of the title-pages and jackets of his books. He was educated at Brighton College (for which he composed the school song), and Wadham College, Oxford, which, because of a family financial crisis, he left without taking finals. After leaving Oxford, where he played Romeo alongside Peggy Ashcroft, Edith Evans, and George Devine in the Oxford University Dramatic Society *Romeo and Juliet*, a notable production directed by John Gielgud, he spent some years as an actor. He toured with Ivor Novello in 1933, having a small part in his play *Proscenium*. In 1934 Novello asked him to write lyrics for his melodies and their first joint success was *Glamorous Night* (1935). Novello introduced Hassall to Edward Marsh, who acted as *advocatus diaboli* and critic for Hassall's early poetry, *Poems of Two Years* (1935). Convinced of his limited talent as an actor, he performed for the last time in his own play *Devil's Dyke* in 1937.

Hassall was adopted by Marsh as a protégé. Under his tutelage Hassall produced *Christ's Comet*, a poetic drama for which he composed the music, written for the 1938 Canterbury Cathedral festival, and *Penthesperon* (1938) which won the Hawthornden prize. In this year, on 28 December, he also married Evelyn Helen Lynett Hill (*b.* 1908/9), daughter of Eustace Chapman. They had a son and a daughter. In 1939 *Crisis*, a sonnet sequence, won the A. C. Benson medal. *S.O.S. ... 'Ludlow'* (1940) was published soon after he had joined the Royal Artillery as a gunner. In 1941 he was commissioned, and in 1942 he joined the army education corps, in which he attained the rank of major. After the war he published *The Timeless Quest* (1948), a biography of his friend the actor Stephen Haggard. *The Slow Night*, containing some of his most moving poetry, was published in 1949, and *The Red Leaf* in 1957. Poetry collections were interspersed with drama: *The Player King* was the Edinburgh festival play of 1952. *Out of the Whirlwind* (1953) was the first secular play to be staged in Westminster Abbey since the Reformation.

Novello's early patronage had enabled Hassall to concentrate on his own writing but he continued to compose original librettos for cantatas and operas, most notably *Tobias and the Angel* (1960) for Arthur Bliss, and *Song of Simeon* (1959) for Malcolm Arnold. His English versions of foreign works, notably Bartók's *Bluebeard's Castle*, placed him foremost among contemporary librettists. His libretto for Walton's *Troilus and Cressida* (1954) was described by Ernest Newman as 'the best poetic opera text since Hofmannsthal'.

Hassall also made his mark as a biographer. His major biography *Edward Marsh: Patron of the Arts* (1959, awarded the James Tait Black memorial prize) is a lasting contribution to the cultural and social history of the first half of the twentieth century, and was the result of his long friendship with Eddie. Hassall also contributed the notice of Marsh to the *Dictionary of National Biography*. *Ambrosia and Small Beer*, a record of their voluminous correspondence, appeared posthumously in 1964, as did also his biography of *Rupert Brooke* (1964), though he was able to complete and revise the text before his sudden death. He did not, however, live to see the publication of *Bell Harry and other Poems* (1963), which contained a sequence of forty sonnets in memory of his friend the poet Frances Crofts Cornford.

Hassall's lifetime covered a period of accelerating and often hectic change in the arts. Temperamentally he was not always in sympathy with the new developments and this was partly the legacy of Marsh, who had schooled him in Georgian aesthetics. Though his interest in the younger poets never flagged, his own work showed a concern to further and expand the traditional, rather than a desire to break with it. His poetry, sometimes lyrical and sometimes ruminative, almost conversational, was always direct in theme and statement. At its best it was distinguished by emotional depth and clarity, with a startling fluency of expression. He will also be remembered for his poetry recitals on behalf of the Apollo Society. He was a councillor and fellow of the Royal Society of Literature and a governor of the London Academy of Music and Dramatic Art.

During the last six years of his life Hassall lived at Tonford Manor, near Canterbury, a fortified house dating from the twelfth century which he carefully restored. He suffered a heart attack on a train and died at St Bartholomew's Hospital, Rochester, on 25 April 1963. The funeral service was in the crypt of Canterbury Cathedral, and he was buried on 2 May at the church of St Nicholas, near his home, where he had regularly worshipped. He was survived by his wife, Evelyn.

JOHN GUEST, *rev.* CLARE L. TAYLOR

Sources C. Hassall, ed., *Ambrosia and small beer: the record of a correspondence between Edward Marsh and Christopher Hassall* (1964) · m. cert. · d. cert. · *The Times* (27 April 1963) · personal knowledge (1981)

Archives CUL, papers | CUL, letters to Geoffrey Keynes · Royal Society of Literature, London, letters to Royal Society of Literature · U. Birm., letters to Jessica Brent Young

Likenesses oils, *c.*1930–1931, NPG · J. Hassall, oils, *c.*1931, priv. coll. · J. Hassall, pen and wash drawing, 1936, repro. in Hassall, ed., *Ambrosia and small beer* · H. Coster, photograph, 1955, NPG [*see illus.*] · J. Hassall, wood-engraving, repro. in C. Hassall, *Penthesperon* (1938)

Wealth at death £24,416 15s. 0d.: administration, 21 June 1963, *CGPLA Eng. & Wales*

Hassall, Edward. *See* Halsall, Edward (c.1627–1686).

Hassall, Joan (1906–1988), artist and wood-engraver, was born on 3 March 1906 at 88 Kensington Park Road, Notting Hill, London, the only daughter and elder child of John *Hassall (1868–1948), painter and illustrator, and his second wife, Constance Maud, daughter of the Revd Albert Brooke Webb, rector of Dallinghoe, Wickham Market, Suffolk. Her brother was the poet, biographer, and playwright Christopher *Hassall. She was educated at Parsons Mead School, Ashtead, Surrey, and though she wished to study music, trained instead as a schoolteacher at the Froebel Educational Institute, Roehampton. For two years (1925–7) she worked at her father's London School of Art, as its secretary and as a student, but on its closure went to the Royal Academy Schools from 1928 to 1933, winning the Landseer scholarship in 1931. She learned to engrave on wood in 1931, being taught by R. J. Beedham at the London County Council School of Photo-engraving and Lithography. At the time she felt she was remembering rather than learning how to handle the tools.

Joan Hassall's first substantial book illustration was for Francis Brett Young's *Portrait of a Village* (1937), which established her as an illustrator of consequence. She studied nineteenth-century women's costume for the engravings for the 1940 edition of Elizabeth Gaskell's *Cranford*, which were a pattern for much later work. During the war she taught printing and engraving at Edinburgh College of Art (1940–46), and between 1943 and 1951 designed and illustrated eleven chapbooks for the Saltire Society. The light-hearted designs for *A Child's Garden of Verses* by Robert Louis Stevenson (1947) had much of Thomas Bewick about them, as did the thirty vignettes for the National Book League's *Reader's Guides* (1947–51). Mary Russell Mitford's *Our Village* (1947) followed *Cranford* in its style, but with *The Strange World of Nature* (1950), by Bernard Gooch, she started a long series of engravings of wildlife, conveying with consummate skill the textures of hair and feathers. For *Fifty-one Poems* by Mary Webb (1946) and *Collected Poems by Andrew Young* (1950) she cut a great many small vignettes that give visual life to the poems they decorate.

Troubled with arthritis in the early 1950s, Joan Hassall turned to scraperboard, drawing about 150 small designs for *The Oxford Nursery Rhyme Book*, edited by Peter Opie and his wife, Iona (1955). She engraved some 120 blocks for the Folio Society, illustrating two collections of Anthony Trollope's stories in 1949 and 1951, and, during periods of remission from the arthritis, a complete Jane Austen in seven volumes (1957–63). The usual sobriety of her figures disappeared in the last of these, with a new excitement in their character, and this same vivacity was continued in the seventy-seven vignettes (two of them in colour) for *The Poems of Robert Burns* (1965). She added twenty-eight scraperboard drawings to a new edition of the Jane Austen, issued in 1975. In all she illustrated over eighty books.

Joan Hassall did a great deal of more ephemeral work, providing drawings and engravings for British Transport, the BBC, and various publishers and booksellers, as well as for a number of magazines including *Housewife*, *London Mystery Magazine*, and *The Masque*. She designed thirty-five bookplates, including twenty-four on wood, and was responsible for the £1 royal silver wedding stamp (1948) and the queen's invitation card to her guests for the coronation (1953). A fine artist, skilled as a watercolourist as well as at drawing, it was as an engraver that she excelled, cutting perhaps a thousand blocks, which she proofed with great skill on an Albion hand-press. Inspired by Bewick, she preferred small vignettes to full-page illustrations, and enjoyed engraving for ordinary people, ordinary readers, rather than moneyed collectors. She preferred descriptive work to mere decoration. No more than the outlines of her designs would be drawn on the surface to be engraved, the detail coming from the burin, whose movement had sometimes the careless ease of a pencil. She was a slow worker, a perfectionist who would recut a design that had failed in some way, without regard for any urgencies of publication. Financial help from her brother and Sir Edward Marsh enabled her to escape from home in 1937, but she always had to live very modestly. She lived in her father's house in Notting Hill after his death in 1948, then moved in 1976 to Priory Cottage in Malham, Yorkshire, which had been bequeathed to her by a friend. She was a friend of Sydney Cockerell and her letters to him from Italy and France in April–May 1950 were published in 1991 as *Dearest Sydney* (edited by Brian North Lee).

Joan Hassall was a plumpish woman, shy in her early years, but with a friendly disposition that made her many friends and admirers. She played the harpsichord, harp, viola da gamba, piano, and recorder, and in her retirement was organist at Kirkby Malham church. In 1938 she was elected an associate, and in 1948 a fellow of the Royal Society of Painter-Etchers and Engravers, and in 1947 a member of the Society of Wood Engravers. She was made a fellow of the Society of Industrial Artists and Designers (1948), and was one of the first three women members of the Art Workers' Guild (1964) and its first woman master in 1972. She was awarded the bronze medal of the Paris Salon (1973) and was appointed OBE in 1987. For many years suffering from arthritis, and latterly from failing sight, Joan Hassall died of bronchopneumonia and diabetes on 6 March 1988 in Airedale General Hospital, Keighley, Yorkshire. Her remains were cremated at Oakworth crematorium, Keighley, and her ashes were scattered in the grounds of the crematorium. She never married. She is commemorated by a memorial window by David Peace in Kirkby Malham church. DAVID CHAMBERS, *rev.*

Sources R. McLean, *Wood engravings of Joan Hassall* (1960) · B. Peppin and L. Micklethwaite, *Dictionary of British book illustrators: the twentieth century* (1983) · D. Chambers, *Joan Hassall: engravings and drawings* (1985) · personal knowledge (1996) · *CGPLA Eng. & Wales* (1988) · J. Hassall, 'My engraved work', *Private library*, 2nd ser., 7 (1974), 139–64 · B. North Lee, ed., *Dearest Joana: a selection of Joan Hassall's lifetime letters and art*, 2 vols. (2000) · *Daily Telegraph* (8 March 1988) · *The Guardian* (10 March 1988) · *The Independent* (9 March 1988) · *The Times* (9 March 1988)

Archives FM Cam., corresp., drawings, and papers | BL, corresp. with Sir Sydney Cockerell, Add. MSS 52719–52720 | FILM BFI NFTVA, *Celluloid love: the Hassalls*, BBC 2 television documentary, 16 Nov 1971
Likenesses Harrods, photograph, *c.*1932–1936, repro. in North Lee, ed., *Dearest Joana* · C. W. Foret, photograph, 1942, repro. in Chambers, *Joan Hassall* · photograph, *c.*1971, repro. in Chambers, *Joan Hassall* · photograph, repro. in B. North Lee, ed., *Dearest Sydney: Joan Hassall's letters to Sydney Cockerell* (1991)
Wealth at death £96,925: probate, 11 May 1988, CGPLA Eng. & Wales

Hassall, John (*bap.* 1571, *d.* 1654), dean of Norwich, was baptized in St Andrew's parish, Norwich, on 4 December 1571, the son of John Hassall. He was educated at St Paul's School, London, and from 1587 at Winchester College (where in 1588 in typical schoolboy fashion he carved his name on one of the piers of the south aisle in the cathedral) before matriculating at New College, Oxford, in 1593. He was a fellow there from 1594 to 1603, graduating BCL in 1600. In July 1601 he was made minister of Burton upon Trent, Staffordshire, by William Paget, to whom he was also chaplain. From July 1604 to about April 1606 he was prebendary of Eccleshall in Lichfield Cathedral. He was also preferred to two Norfolk rectories—Brancaster in 1603 and Great Bircham in 1608—and presented to the third prebend in Norwich Cathedral on 11 December 1615. Although he resigned his Burton cure in 1609 he remained close to Paget, cataloguing Paget's library in 1617 (BL, Harleian MS 3267).

For eight years, probably from 1617 to 1625, Hassall was preacher to Sir Horatio Vere's regiment in the Netherlands, and while at The Hague he secured both the reputation as a good preacher and the patronage of Elizabeth, queen of Bohemia. Having gained a DD in 1626, through her patronage he was in July 1628 made dean of Norwich, a post for which he had been angling since the end of 1624. At Burton he had been on good terms with his neighbour William Bradshaw, the puritan preacher in Stapenhill, Derbyshire, who described Hassall as 'a man of very rare parts for all kind of learning' (Clarke, 55). On his return from the Netherlands, however, Hassall changed with the times, gaining the approbation of the anti-puritan Samuel Harsnett, bishop of Norwich until 1628, and the grudging acceptance of William Laud. During Matthew Wren's episcopate at Norwich (1635–8), although he had made an unsuccessful bid for the bishopric himself, he co-operated fully in reforming cathedral and diocese along ceremonial and Laudian lines: in 1636 he was described by one of Wren's associates as 'very right to the Church gouernement' (MS Tanner 68, fol. 82*r*). Even while soliciting for the deanery of Norwich, Hassall had described it as a poor piece of preferment, but he was frustrated in his hopes of further advance, acquiring only the rectory of North Creake, Norfolk, in 1640. About 1647 he was twice saved from losing Brancaster by his fellow Norfolk minister Thomas Thorowgood. After the abolition of cathedral offices in 1649 he lived at North Creake where he died on 27 December 1654. So great was his poverty there, it was later alleged, that after his death one of his daughters was maintained by the parish. Hassall was also survived by his wife, Mary, *née* Harris, who as executrix gained probate of his will on 15 February 1655. He was buried at North Creake.
IAN ATHERTON

Sources Wood, *Ath. Oxon.: Fasti* (1815), 424–5 · Foster, *Alum. Oxon.* · S. Clarke, *The lives of two and twenty eminent divines* (1660), 55 · *CSP dom., 1623–35* · F. Blomefield and C. Parkin, *An essay towards a topographical history of the county of Norfolk*, [2nd edn], 11 vols. (1805–10), vol. 3, pp. 622–3 · Bishop Wren's MSS, Bodl. Oxf., MS Tanner 68, fols. 82*r*, 86–7, 167–8, 219–20 · J. Walker, *An attempt towards recovering an account of the numbers and sufferings of the clergy of the Church of England*, pt 2 (1714), 56 · BL, biographical notice of Hassall, Lansdowne MS 985 [fol. 103] · *Fasti Angl., 1541–1857*, [Ely] · *Fasti Angl.* (Hardy), 1.602 · J. Hassall, letters to Lord Paget, Staffs. RO, D603/K/1/11/52–4, D603/K/1/11/71 · B. Cozens-Hardy, 'A puritan moderate: Dr Thomas Thorowgood', *Norfolk Archaeology*, 22 (1924–6), 311–37, esp. 327 · parish register, Burton upon Trent, Staffs. RO, D4219/1/1 · BL, J. Hassall to mayor of Norwich, 22 Sept 1643, Add. MS 22619, fol. 121*r* · M. McDonnell, ed., *The registers of St Paul's School, 1509–1748* (privately printed, London, 1977), 86 · *Walker rev.*, 268 · IGI · will, PROB 11/247/214, fol. 37
Archives PRO, letters, SP 84/92, fols. 99A–99B; SP 84/93, fols. 46–7; SP 84/121, fols. 53–4, 85–6 | PRO, protest in the Netherlands, SP 84/106, fols. 143–4
Wealth at death presumed very little: Walker, *An attempt*

Hassall, John (1868–1948), poster designer, was born on 21 May 1868 at Walmer, Kent, the eldest son of Lieutenant Christopher Clark Hassall RN (1838–1876), of a Cheshire family of wine merchants, and his wife, Louisa Sparkes, daughter of the Revd Joseph Butterworth Owen, incumbent of St Jude's, Chelsea, London, and son of the architect Jacob Owen. Hassall's father, who had served in the fleet at the siege of Sevastopol during the Crimean War, was paralysed as the result of an accident on his ship and died at the age of thirty-eight. His mother remarried; her second husband was an officer in the Royal Marines at Chatham who later became General Sir William Purvis Wright. John Hassall, who was educated at Newton Abbot College, Devon, and Neuenheim College, Heidelberg, Germany, was intended by his stepfather for the army, but he twice failed to pass the examination for Sandhurst. Accordingly in 1888 he and his brother Owen were sent on a cattle boat to a ranch in Minnedosa, Manitoba, Canada, to study farming. The two years that he spent there were vital to the development of his imagination and personality. For a time he acted as pathfinder to a group of Sioux.

Hassall occupied his spare time with sketching, and his efforts were so much admired that he sent some pen drawings depicting a Manitoba 'surprise party' to the *Daily Graphic*, which published them on 26 February 1890. This decided him to make a living as a draughtsman. He returned home and was sent by his mother to the Koninklijke Academie voor Schone Kunsten in Antwerp, where he worked under Piet van Havermaet and his son Charles. He studied there for two years, spending six months in Paris at the Académie Julian. In 1893, while abroad he married a fellow student, Isabel Dingwall (*c.*1866–1900), with whom he had one son and two daughters.

Hassall returned to London, where he made his first appearance at the Royal Academy exhibition in 1894 with two large paintings which were hung 'on the line'. Meanwhile, his drawings were appearing in *The Sketch*, *Pick-Me-*

Up, and other papers. In 1895, in answer to a recruiting circular issued by David Allen & Sons, the printers, Hassall entered on a career which lasted for fifty years, earning the title of 'the poster king' and, in 1939, the grant of a civil-list pension for his services to poster art. When he began, poster advertising as an art was in its infancy and his designs were a cheerful addition to the street scene. His work was humorous, robust, and simple, with a direct advertising message which nevertheless attained a high standard of decorative art. He advertised many commodities and also designed the posters for many of the Drury Lane pantomimes.

In 1901 Hassall was elected a member of the Royal Institute of Painters in Water Colours, and in 1903 president of the London Sketch Club. Also in 1903—his first wife having died young in 1900—he married Constance Maud Brooke Webb (*b. c.*1878, *d.* 1950), daughter of the Revd Albert Brooke Webb, rector of Dallinghoe, Wickham Market, Suffolk; they had a son, the author Christopher Vernon *Hassall, and a daughter, the painter and engraver Joan *Hassall. In 1905 he opened an art school in London, whose students were to include the cartoonist H. M. Bateman.

Hassall was working at this time as an illustrator of children's books, which became the delight of generations of youngsters. He also helped Baden-Powell to design the uniform for the Boy Scouts. His *Jolly Fisherman* tourist poster dates from this period. The fat man in oilskins prancing along the sands, with the caption 'Skegness is so Bracing', was typical of his work. The poster was still in use after his death and remains an instantly recognizable image. During the First World War he was a special constable in London and frequently appeared at charity shows, where over 3000 of his drawings were auctioned. In later years he illustrated the works of several British poets, including Robert Burns, William Dunbar, John Donne, and William Wordsworth.

During his holidays at Walton on the Naze, Essex, Hassall accumulated one of the largest private collections of prehistoric flint implements, which substantially contributed to the archaeological history of East Anglia. He was a man of strong personality whose great friendliness and charm made him a much loved member of the Savage Club in London. John Hassall died at his home, 88 Kensington Park Road, Kensington, London, on 8 March 1948; he was survived by his second wife.

BERT THOMAS, *rev.* BEN WHITWORTH

Sources B. Peppin and L. Micklethwaite, *Dictionary of British book illustrators: the twentieth century* (1983) · M. Bryant and S. Heneage, eds., *Dictionary of British cartoonists and caricaturists, 1730–1980* (1994) · J. Johnson and A. Greutzner, *The dictionary of British artists, 1880–1940* (1976), vol. 5 of *Dictionary of British art* · WW (1938); (1947) · A. Jarman and others, eds., *Royal Academy exhibitors, 1905–1970: a dictionary of artists and their work in the summer exhibitions of the Royal Academy of Arts*, 3 (1978) · Graves, *RA exhibitors* · B. Dolman, ed., *A dictionary of contemporary British artists, 1929*, 2nd edn (1981) · F. Spalding, *20th century painters and sculptors* (1990), vol. 6 of *Dictionary of British art* · CGPLA Eng. & Wales (1948) · index to register of deaths, Family Record Centre · Naval service register, PRO, ADM 196/15, vol. 3 · personal knowledge (1959) · private information (1959) · A. E. Johnson, *John Hassall R.I.* (1907)

Archives Kensington Central Library, illustrated corresp. Art Course · University of Essex, Colchester, corresp., diaries, and papers | Richmond Local Studies Library, corresp. with Douglas Sladen
Likenesses K. van Havermaet, oils, 1891; Sothebys, Summers Place, 28 Jan 1997 · J. Hassall, self-portrait, pen, ink and wash, 1899, NPG · W. True, watercolour caricature, *c.*1904, repro. in *Studio*, 30 (1904), 35 · J. Gunn, oils, *c.*1936, Savage Club, London · Strickland, caricature, NPG; repro. in *VF* (21 Aug 1912)
Wealth at death £2844 16s. 2d.: probate, 24 April 1948, *CGPLA Eng. & Wales*

Hassan, Sir Joshua Abraham (1915–1997), chief minister of Gibraltar, was born in Gibraltar on 21 August 1915, the son of Abraham M. Hassan, a cloth merchant, from a distinguished merchant family of Moroccan Sephardi extraction that had first settled in Gibraltar in 1728. He was educated by the Christian brothers of Line Wall College, then studied law in London, and was called to the bar by the Middle Temple in 1939. For most of his life he managed to combine both law and politics.

Hassan's particular eminence derived from the exceptional circumstances in which Gibraltar found itself during and immediately after the Second World War. After the fall of France in 1940, the early successes of the axis powers in north Africa had an immense impact on the vulnerable but vital crown colony. While the colonial authorities were obliged to stay put, the safety and well-being of the women, children, and elderly could not be guaranteed in the desperate military situation, and they were evacuated. Hassan gained respect for his work on the Gibraltar evacuation committee and by his equally energetic efforts in 1944 to have the evacuees returned, despite severe transport restrictions. His active participation in Gibraltar's defence as a Bofors gunner enhanced his political credentials. Meanwhile, in 1941 he became deputy coroner, and in 1945 he was elected to the city council of Gibraltar. He served as mayor from 1945 to 1950 and from 1953 to 1969 (when the city council was merged with the legislative council to form the house of assembly). He married, in 1945, Daniela Salazar, of La Línea de la Concepción, Spain. They had two daughters.

The wartime privations on the Rock demonstrated to authorities and inhabitants alike the limitations of the chaotic multiple administrative systems that had developed in *ad hoc* fashion. By 1949 the administration of Gibraltar, with its total area of 1360 acres and population of 27,000 civilians and military, was divided among no fewer than five semi-autonomous authorities: the three military services plus the colonial and municipal institutions. Such complexity was 'neither intelligible, reasonable, or sensible', noted a Colonial Office report in 1949, but 'foolish, absurd, and extravagant' (PRO, CO 91/537–9). As a result a new legislative council was set up in 1950. The elections to the new council held that autumn brought in two conservative independents and three candidates (including Hassan) sponsored by the Association for the Advancement of Civil Rights (AACR). The AACR had been founded by Hassan during the war and was closely linked to the Gibraltar Confederation of Labour, which he had long championed. Two positions on the executive council

Sir Joshua Abraham Hassan (1915–1997), by unknown photographer, c.1950

could be nominated by the governor. The favourite from the shortlist proved unavailable, since the American consulate for which he worked would not release him, and a second, on account of a communist affiliation, was regarded as unsuitable. The Colonial Office wanted at least one position to go to an AACR member. Hassan, though a one-time radical activist, had all the right qualifications. He was a Gibraltarian, he was a lawyer, he was fiercely loyal to Britain, and he had strong links to Gibraltar's workers, whose votes would prove vital in upholding the colony's links with Britain.

Hassan's appointment to the executive council and as chief member of the legislative council marked the beginning of a career dedicated to making clear Gibraltar's rejection of Spanish claims while at the same time minimizing Whitehall's control as much as possible. In this, the international situation was to Hassan's advantage. Of all Britain's colonial possessions during this period of intense decolonization, the escalation of the cold war ensured that Gibraltar remained the most significant strategically and politically. Consequently the Gibraltar question was handled with exceptional tact and co-operation by the Colonial Office and Gibraltarians alike.

Hassan was knighted in 1963 (he had been made LVO in 1954 and CBE in 1957). In 1964, under a new constitution, he became the first chief minister of Gibraltar. He headed petitions in 1963, 1964, and 1966 before the United Nations Committee of Twenty-four, created in November 1961 to examine questions of independence. His aim, contrary to Spanish demands, was for Gibraltar not to relinquish ties with Britain but to have an administration similar to that of the Channel Islands or the Isle of Man. This had been suggested in a Colonial Office report of 1949, possibly at the instigation of Hassan himself. The United Nations was unimpressed by the arguments he and his colleague Peter Isola put forward. Nevertheless, a referendum of 10 September 1967 infuriated Spain but vindicated his approach, with a vote of 12,138 (95.8 per cent) in favour of remaining, as he put it, 'With Britain, but not under

Britain' (*The Independent*, 2 July 1997). In 1969 Hassan achieved his aim of a new constitution, which removed the anomaly of separate city and legislative councils, and in which Britain guaranteed that Gibraltar would never be ceded to another state against the wishes of its citizens. For Gibraltarians this proved something of a pyrrhic victory, however, with the closing in June 1969 of Spain's border with Gibraltar. Hassan's private life caused controversy the same year, when he introduced a private member's bill allowing him to divorce his wife, Daniela. Divorce was then otherwise impossible in predominantly Roman Catholic Gibraltar. Following the divorce Hassan married, the same year, Marcelle Bensimon. They, too, had two daughters.

In the election of 1969 Hassan's AACR was narrowly defeated by Robert Peliza's Integration with Britain party. He nevertheless returned as chief minister in 1972, an office he retained through subsequent elections until 1987. Although Spain's claims to Gibraltar and its closure of the border continued after General Franco's death in 1975, the situation could be approached with less tension. Prime Minister Margaret Thatcher found the new Spanish premier someone with whom she could converse, if not agree. Thatcher used the threat of a veto on Spanish entry into the EU and NATO to force the reopening of the border; the price, through the Brussels agreement of 1984, was discussion of sovereignty. Hassan's albeit reluctant endorsement of the agreement undermined his position with the people of Gibraltar. The closure of Gibraltar's airport for flights to anywhere but Britain, following the breakdown of a 1983 agreement with Spain, further weakened Hassan's support. He resigned as chief minister on 9 December 1987 and retired from politics at the election the following year. He was appointed KCMG in 1986 and GBE in 1988.

Throughout his years as chief member and chief minister, Hassan continued to work as a practising lawyer, the position of chief member/minister being only part-time. He represented Robert Maxwell, whose holding company was registered in Gibraltar, and following his retirement as chief minister he represented one of the witnesses at the inquest into the shooting by the SAS of three suspected IRA terrorists in Gibraltar in 1987. He was chairman of the Gibraltar bar council from 1992 to 1995.

Hassan was 'an open and accessible man, greeting people on the street of his colony, and claiming to know the names of most of them' (*The Independent*, 2 July 1997). He enjoyed wide popularity, being fondly known as Salvador—though also, less fondly, as El Pulpo, the octopus, whose tentacles reached into every aspect of Rock life. He died in Gibraltar on 1 July 1997, survived by his wife, Marcelle, their two daughters, and the two daughters of his first marriage.   JILL EDWARDS

Sources PRO, CO 91/517; CO 91/537–9; CO 5381/1 · *Negotiations on Gibraltar, a new Spanish red book*, Spanish Ministry for Foreign Affairs (Madrid, 1968) · M. Thatcher, *The Downing Street years* (1993) · J. Edwards, *Anglo-American relations and the Franco question, 1945–55* (1999) · *The Independent* (2 July 1997) · *The Times* (2 July 1997) · *Daily Telegraph* (3 July 1997) · *The Guardian* (2 July 1997) · WWW · Burke, *Peerage*

Archives PRO, CO 91, 5381
Likenesses photograph, *c.*1950, Hult. Arch. [*see illus.*] · photograph, 1984, repro. in *The Guardian* · photograph, 1987, repro. in *Daily Telegraph* · photograph, repro. in *The Independent* · photograph, repro. in *The Times*

Hassé, Christian Frederick (1771–1831), composer and organist, born at Sarepta, southern Russia, was educated at Barby, near Halle, in Prussia, and at Niesky in Silesia, under Gregor, a Moravian bishop and composer of hymns. After filling the post of classical master at Barby, Niesky, and Hennersdorf, near Herrnhut, Hassé taught music and foreign languages at Fulneck, the Moravian settlement near Leeds, and became organist to the church of the United Brethren there. He did much to improve musical taste and knowledge in that part of Yorkshire, by introducing foreign masterpieces and organizing orchestral meetings. He arranged the music for James Montgomery's *Polyhymnia, or, Select Airs by Celebrated Foreign Composers, Adapted to English Words* (1822) and also compiled *Sacred Music, Partly Original, Partly Selected*, which included his chorus, 'Blessed are they', his recitative and air 'The Mountains Shall Depart', and a bass solo and chorus entitled 'Amen, praise the Lord'. In addition he composed many hymns which have not been collected. Hassé died very suddenly at Fulneck on 1 May 1831; he was buried there. 　　　　L. M. MIDDLETON, *rev.* NILANJANA BANERJI

Sources *Leeds Intelligencer* (5 May 1831) · *Memoirs of the life and writings of James Montgomery*, ed. J. Holland and J. Everett, 7 vols. (1854–6), vol. 3, p. 302 · W. Cudworth, *Round about Bradford* (1876)

Hassel, Werner (*fl.* 1674–1710), portrait painter, lived in London but was probably a native of Germany, where he also worked; his first name is sometimes incorrectly given as William. He was a pupil of Sir Godfrey Kneller, who painted a portrait of him in 1700, which was engraved by P. Schenck. Hassel is known by a few portraits, some of which have been engraved, including two mezzotints by J. C. Smith of C. L. Fels (1690) and J. Witt (1707), a Frankfurt merchant, and a line engraving of an unidentified sitter by P. Vanderbank. He also painted miniatures in watercolour and enamel as well as full-size portraits in oil. Foskett noted that 'Hassel was a good artist whose works are scarce' (Foskett, 559). An enamel battle piece, signed 'Werner Hassel 1674 Decembris', is in the Bayrisches Nationalmuseum, Munich; a miniature on parchment of a lady, signed and dated 'WH 1687', is in the Victoria and Albert Museum, London. Although Vertue recorded that the painter George *Lambert 'learnt of … Hassel' (Vertue, *Note Books*, 3.6), whether Lambert was ever his pupil remains conjectural. 　　　　L. H. CUST, *rev.* ANNETTE PEACH

Sources D. Foskett, *Miniatures: dictionary and guide* (1987) · *DNB*
Likenesses G. Kneller, oils, 1700 · P. Schenck, engraving (after G. Kneller)

Hassell, Edward (*d.* 1852). *See under* Hassell, John (1767–1825).

Hassell, John (1767–1825), watercolour painter and engraver, was born in 1767 and was probably the individual of that name, son of John and Ann Hassell, who was

baptized in November 1767 at St Mary, Whitechapel, Stepney. He exhibited twenty paintings at the Royal Academy between 1789 and 1819, including many scenes of waterfalls, castles, and salmon leaps in Wales, and of houses and cities, including a view of the city of Bath (exh. 1796). He published many guidebooks, illustrated with engravings in aquatint from his own drawings, including *A Tour of the Isle of Wight* (1790), *A Picturesque Guide to Bath, Bristol Hot-Wells, the River Avon and the Adjacent Country* (1793), *Views of Noblemen's and Gentlemen's Seats … in the Counties Adjoining London* (1804), *Picturesque rides and walks, with excursions by water, thirty miles round the British metropolis* (1818), and *Excursions of Pleasure and Sports on the Thames* (1823). Working also as a drawing master, he wrote works on painting and drawing, including *The Speculum, or, Art of Drawing in Watercolours* (1809), *Calcographia, or, The Art of Multiplying Drawings* (1811), and *The Camera, or, Art of Drawing in Watercolours* (1823). A life of his friend, the painter George Morland, was published in 1806. Hassell died in 1825.

Edward Hassell (*d.* 1852), watercolour painter, the son of John Hassell, painted landscapes and the interiors of Gothic churches and buildings. He exhibited thirteen paintings at the Royal Academy between 1827 and 1840, and also showed frequently at the Society of British Artists from 1827 to 1852. Elected a member in 1841, he became secretary in 1846. Some of his paintings are in the National Gallery, Dublin, and *Barrow, Derwentwater* is held in the Victoria and Albert Museum. He died in Church Street, Lancaster, on 3 November 1852.

　　　　L. H. CUST, *rev.* ANNE PIMLOTT BAKER

Sources Mallalieu, *Watercolour artists* · J. Johnson, ed., *Works exhibited at the Royal Society of British Artists, 1824–1893, and the New English Art Club, 1888–1917*, 2 vols. (1975) · Graves, *RA exhibitors* · Wood, *Vic. painters*, 3rd edn · d. cert. [Edward Hassell]

Hasted, Edward (1732–1812), county historian, was born on 20 December 1732 at Dove Court, Lombard Street, London, the only son of Edward Hasted (1702–1740), landowner, of Hawley, in Sutton-at-Hone parish, and Anne Tyler, daughter and coheir of Joseph Tyler of London. His father was a member of Lincoln's Inn, but did not practise law, living instead as a country gentleman. He served as clerk to the Wax Chandlers' Company. The landed wealth of the family had been assembled by Hasted's grandfather Joseph Hasted, chief painter–stainer to the Royal Navy at Chatham Dockyard. Hasted's father died young, at the age of thirty-eight, in 1740, and the family, under financial constraints, moved to Rome House in Chatham. Hasted was educated privately at Darent (1737–40), at King's School, Rochester (1740–44), at Eton College (1744–8), and at a private school in Esher (1748–50). He became a student of Lincoln's Inn in 1750, but was not called to the bar.

Hasted first collected material on Kent as a pleasurable activity, to give him knowledge of the past. Only later was he persuaded by scholarly friends to collect more systematically and to contemplate publication. But the many volumes of his manuscript notes in the British Library show his original interest in collecting documents on a wider variety of subjects, including the sequestrations of royalist estates in the English Civil War, seizures by the

Edward Hasted (1732–1812), by unknown artist, 1801

commissioners for prizes taken during the Dutch War, and stores and ammunition sent to Ireland in the Commonwealth period.

Hasted inherited enough land and rents to live as an independent country gentleman. He married in 1755 Anne Dorman (d. 1803), third daughter of John Dorman of Sutton-at-Hone, described by him as 'a wife without any fortune'. After living for two years in Canterbury, the couple moved to a commandery of the knights of St John, at Sutton-at-Hone, a house which Hasted refurbished expensively; it now belongs to the National Trust. They lived there from 1757, then returned after nineteen years to Canterbury in 1776. Hasted served as a JP from 1757, was briefly chairman of quarter sessions, and also deputy lord lieutenant of the county. He made friendships with learned antiquaries, notably Dr Charles Lyttleton, bishop of Carlisle and president of the Society of Antiquaries, and Dr Andrew Coltee Ducarel, librarian at Lambeth Palace, and thus he was introduced to archives. Two months in 1763 spent at his mother's house in London consulting records in the Tower of London, the British Museum, and Lambeth Palace, were a decisive experience, and more purposefully thereafter Hasted's *History of Kent* took shape. He became a fellow of the Society of Antiquaries in 1763, and was elected a fellow of the Royal Society on 8 May 1766.

For his Kent history Hasted scoured sources everywhere. For documents in the Public Record Office he relied on calendars, or on lists found in other collections such as the Lansdowne Manuscripts. But he himself abstracted wills in the prerogative court of Canterbury,

worked extensively at the British Museum, the Tower of London, Lambeth Palace, in Canterbury Cathedral, using both archives and books, and among the private papers of the Dering family at Surrenden. He also perambulated parishes himself. A basic framework for his *History of Kent* was built from earlier histories of Kent and other printed sources, but he relied on a large number of local informants among gentry, lawyers, and parsons, to whom he sent questionnaires. His work occupied nearly forty years from about 1763 to 1799; it was prolonged by his care to incorporate corrections and the most up-to-date information, but was also complicated by a flight to France in 1790 to escape creditors, and a spell in the king's bench prison from 1795 to 1802, though in both places he continued to work.

The first edition of the *History of Kent*, in four folio volumes, appeared between 1778 and 1799. Debt obliged Hasted to sell his manuscripts in 1796, and a large number are now in public collections. While the fourth and last folio volume was in preparation, Mr Bristow of Canterbury undertook in 1796 to publish an octavo edition in twelve volumes, and dictated a different style. The new edition (1797–1801) was much revised by one, or more probably two, unknown editors, omitting many footnotes and much detail about families and their lands, especially about female descendants, but containing new and more complimentary descriptions of landscape, and giving prominence to charities, numbers of poor, and other lively, gossipy detail, thereby increasing its popular appeal. Hasted, impoverished and in prison, acquiesced. His other lesser publications included articles in the *Philosophical Transactions* and *Gentleman's Magazine*, *A Genealogical and Historical Table of the Families of Heron of Newark* (1797), and *A Canterbury Guide* (c.1805).

Hasted had loyal and long-suffering helpers with local knowledge, notably William Boteler, William Boys, John Lyon, and John Thorpe, who organized and digested much material before it reached him. Hasted is accused of many inaccuracies in his work, including serious errors on his maps, revised from the *Atlas of Kent* of 1769 by Andrews and Drury, which for east Kent was dubbed by Boteler 'shocking work'. Yet for its time it was a heroic achievement, since Kent is a county of innumerable small manors which, through the system of land tenure known as gavelkind, underwent subdivision and many changes of ownership. Hasted was indefatigable in his research.

Hasted and his wife had six sons and three daughters, of whom one son and one daughter failed to survive infancy. But in 1785 he deserted his wife to live with a young woman, Mary Jane Town: he moved with her into lodgings around Kent, then in London, then in France, and returned in 1793 to live in Cirencester, and finally London. There he was arrested for debt and imprisoned with her in 1795 in the king's bench prison. He parted from her in 1797, and was reconciled with his wife and family in 1798. He was discharged of his debts in 1802. His wife died in 1803.

Hasted owned land in seven or eight parishes round Rochester and Sittingbourne but lived above his means and in 1784 mortgaged some land, and in 1787 sold some. More secret sale negotiations followed before he fled to France. His failure to redeem the mortgages deprived him of his whole estate. His solicitor was subsequently charged with corrupt dealings, but Hasted's version of this story, told in his self-written obituary, proclaimed him as the triumphant plaintiff. This was untrue: he was the defendant who did not recover his estate, nor did his family; the final decree was dated 1822.

Hasted obtained his release from prison through an agreement with the two mortgagees who prosecuted the above lawsuit, to whom he assigned all interest in the outcome. He lived in straitened circumstances in London until the earl of Radnor presented him in 1807 to the mastership of Lady Hungerford's Hospital at Corsham, Wiltshire. He died at the master's house there on 14 January 1812, and was buried in an unmarked grave in Corsham.

Hasted was a tireless gatherer of facts, but his writing is dull and unimaginative, and his papers do not always reveal an agreeable or honest person. A contemporary, Sir Samuel Egerton Brydges (1762–1837), described him harshly in his autobiography as:

> a voluble and flighty talker … a little, mean-looking man, with a long face and a high nose; quick in his movements and sharp in his manner. He had no imagination or sentiment, nor any extraordinary quality of the mind, unless memory. (*The Autobiography, Times, Opinions and Contemporaries of Sir Egerton Brydges*, 1834, 1.50–51)

Nevertheless, as regards the *History* Brydges admitted that 'altogether it is a great work' (ibid.).　　　JOAN THIRSK

Sources 'Anecdotes of the Hasted family', *Archaeologia Cantiana*, 26 (1904), 267–94 · J. Boyle, *In quest of Hasted* (1984) · J. Boyle, 'Some discoveries about Edward Hasted and his *History of Kent*', *Archaeologia Cantiana*, 97 (1981), 235–59 · A. Everitt, introduction, in E. Hasted, *The history and topographical survey of the county of Kent*, 2nd edn, 1 (1972), v–xlix · J. Thirsk, 'Hasted as historian', *Archaeologia Cantiana*, 111 (1993), 1–15 · BL, Add. MSS 5479, 5483, 5490–5492, 5499, 5537 · Canterbury Cathedral archives, Hasted MSS · *GM*, 1st ser., 82/1 (1812), 189–90, 672 · *DNB*

Archives BL, notes, indexes to his *History of Kent*, Add. MSS 5491–5492, 5517–5519 · Bodl. Oxf., genealogical collection; letters · Canterbury Cathedral, archives, corresp. and working papers; volumes of transcripts of Canterbury documents with later notes and engravings · CKS, papers · priv. coll. · Rochester Museum | Bodl. Oxf., letters to Mark Noble · priv. coll., letters to second earl of Radnor

Likenesses pastel drawing, c.1790, Maidstone Museum, Kent; repro. in Boyle, *In quest of Hasted*, pl. 3 · drawing, 1801, Medway Archives and Local Studies Centre, Rochester, Kent [*see illus.*] · portrait, BL; repro. in Boyle, *In quest of Hasted*, pl. 2 · portrait (aged sixty-nine), Rochester Museum; repro. in Boyle, *In quest of Hasted*, pl. 4

Hasted, William Freke (1897–1977), army officer, was born on 28 September 1897, in Waltair, India, son of William Anderson Hasted (1864?–1928), an official of the Madras survey department of the Indian Civil Service (1884–1922), and his wife, Mabel Jessie. After attending Cheltenham College (c.1910–1915), Hasted was commissioned in the Royal Engineers (1915) and served in the First World War, receiving the MC. On 9 June 1920 he married

William Freke Hasted (1897–1977), by Walter Stoneman, 1948

Helen Elizabeth Mary, daughter of Lieutenant-Colonel Arthur Edward Cuming; they had no children. He represented England at hockey in 1923. Hasted was an instructor at the Royal Military Academy, Woolwich (1924–6) and at the Royal Military College of Canada (1926–30). After being posted to India in 1936 he served with the Bengal sappers–miners (Peshawar) before appointment to northern command headquarters (1937).

For his part in Waziristan operations Hasted was appointed DSO (1937). He was commander of the Royal Engineers in Waziristan (1938–41) and then deputy chief-engineer at headquarters of the Tenth Army (1941–2). As deputy engineer-in-chief for air at New Delhi general headquarters (1942–3), he was in charge of airfield construction. In Burma during 1944–5 he was chief engineer of the Fourteenth Army: Viscount Slim hailed him as 'one of the heroes of the campaign' (Slim, 397–8). Hasted reciprocated Slim's admiration. Among other contributions to military transport he built roads, in the absence of road-metal or road-making machinery, with overlapping strips of bitumen-soaked Hessian cloth ('bithess'). Hasted was afterwards chief engineer of allied land forces of southeast Asia command (1945–6). Some 200 airfields, depots, and stations costing £100 million were erected under his wartime directions. Hasted was gazetted major-general in 1946 and was last holder under the raj of the appointment of engineer-in-chief in India (1946–7) before going onto retired pay in 1948. He was appointed CBE (1941), CIE (1943) and CB (1946).

Hasted was controller of aerodromes under the Ministry of Civil Aviation (1947–8). As such he developed and administered state-owned airports in Britain and advised on those in the colonies. Next in 1951 he became president of Loughborough College, which specialized in engineering, but he did not remain long in higher education. In the early 1950s the sheikhdom of Kuwait (a British protectorate since 1899) was induced to begin spending some of its immense oil revenues on modernizing its institutions and infrastructure. After the formation of the Kuwait development board to supervise this expenditure (1952) Hasted accepted the position of controller of development. The board's first priorities were school-building, water distillation, power stations, and the design of a new port at Shuwaikh. Kuwait Airways had its inaugural services in 1954, the year of Hasted's retirement from the Persian Gulf.

As a military engineer Hasted was resourceful, determined, reliable, and taciturn. Shortly after his wife's death in Ireland on 4 January 1961 he married, on 4 April 1961, Catherine Levis (b. 1920), a widow with whom he was farming in Devon; she was the daughter of John Crowley, a farmer. They had two sons. Hasted died of prostate cancer on 29 October 1977, at Norfolk and Norwich Hospital, and was cremated on 3 November at Ipswich.

RICHARD DAVENPORT-HINES

Sources *The Times* (3 Nov 1977) · Viscount Slim [W. J. Slim], *Defeat into victory*, 2nd edn (1956) · R. Lewin, *Slim* (1976) · m. certs. · d. cert. · BL OIOC, N/2/83, fol. 130
Archives CAC Cam., business MSS on Kuwait | Ronald Lewin MSS, corresp. | SOUND IWM SA, oral history interview
Likenesses W. Stoneman, photograph, 1948, NPG [*see illus.*]

Hastie, James (1786–1825), British agent in Madagascar, was born to a Quaker family in Cork. He found his religious upbringing constraining and enlisted in the 56th foot, leaving for India where he served during the Second Anglo-Maratha War. In 1815 Hastie, now a sergeant, was quartered with his regiment at Port Louis, Mauritius, and attracted the notice of Governor Farquhar by his conduct during a fire. He was recommended for a commission, and in the meantime appointed preceptor to two Malagasy princes, with whom he returned to Madagascar. There he became assistant agent to Mr Pye, the civil agent of the British government at Tamatave.

Hastie reached the court of King Radama I, at the capital of Imerina, on 6 August 1817 and soon won the trust and friendship of the Hova monarch, with whom he was able to negotiate, in 1817 and 1820, treaties of friendship and commerce, and a treaty for the prevention of the export slave trade. From 1818 to 1825 Hastie acted as civil agent in Madagascar (including two years *per interim* at Mauritius), helping to reform the military, and accompanying King Radama throughout the campaigns which subjugated the eastern, northern, and western peoples of the great island. Hastie's journals, later deposited in the Public Record Office, London, gave the only geographical information which was then available of the interior of Imerina, Antaukay, and Iboina, and his observations on the manners and character of the inland Malagasy tribes were treated as authoritative throughout the nineteenth century. He died on 18 October 1825, at Tananarive, where he was buried in a vault prepared by King Radama who, largely through Hastie's help, had won recognition as the sole ruler of Madagascar. Hastie was survived by his one-year-old son.

S. P. OLIVER, *rev.* LYNN MILNE

Sources W. Ellis, *History of Madagascar, comprising also the progress of the Christian mission*, 2 vols. (1838), vol. 2 · S. P. Oliver, *Madagascar: an historical and descriptive account of the island and its former dependencies*, 2 vols. (1886), vol. 1 · J. E. Flint, ed., *The Cambridge history of Africa from c.1790 to c.1870* (1976), vol. 5 of *The Cambridge history of Africa*, ed. J. D. Fage and R. Oliver (1975–86) · *N&Q*, 173 (1937), 190
Archives PRO, journals and papers relating to slave trade

Hastie, William (1842–1903), Church of Scotland minister and theologian, third son and fourth child in the family of four sons and three daughters of James Hastie (d. 1873) and his wife, Catherine, *née* Weis (d. 1890), was born on 7 July 1842 at Wanlockhead, Dumfriesshire, where his father was a manager of lead mines. After education in the local school under John MacArthur he taught in the neighbourhood, and studied privately. Entering Edinburgh University in 1859, he distinguished himself in both his arts and his divinity courses, graduating MA with first-class honours in philosophy in 1867, and BD in 1869; he also won the Pitt theological scholarship. He supplemented his theological studies at Glasgow (1870–71), attending the class of Dr John Caird, professor of divinity. After becoming a licentiate of the Church of Scotland, he was for some years a wandering student among continental universities—in Germany, Holland, and Switzerland—mastering foreign languages and widening his theological knowledge. In the intervals passed at home he took occasional work as a university deputy, or as assistant to parish ministers, among them Paton James Gloag, at Galashiels.

In 1875 Hastie was fully licensed for the ministry of the Church of Scotland. He had developed wide intellectual and theological interests, but, with little inclination for the life of a parish minister, he was restless. At this time he published translations of works on Romanism by J. Froschammer. In 1878 he was appointed principal of the Church of Scotland College at Calcutta, where he arrived in January 1879. His acceptance of the post was perhaps rushed and unwise (his ambition was a chair in a Scottish university), but he proved a competent and energetic administrator, and he determined on a wider role for the Church of Scotland in India, identifying Govindpore as a suitable place for an evangelical mission centre. At the same time, though, he quarrelled with Free Church of Scotland missionaries and was censured. In 1881 he published the first part of *The Elements of Philosophy*, and in 1882 he issued *Protestant Missions to the Heathen*, an enlarged version of the work by Dr T. Christlieb. In 1883 his *Hindu Idolatry and English Enlightenment* (a reprint of six letters from the Calcutta *Statesman*) caused a furore among educated Hindus, whose reaction was exacerbated perhaps by the general political tension in India at that time. In January 1883 Hastie was attacked in his carriage. In addition, allegations of gross mismanagement of the orphanage run in

Calcutta by the Scottish Ladies' Association were forwarded to Edinburgh by Hastie, with his support. In response there arrived in Edinburgh in 1882 the orphanage's superintendent, Miss Pigot, seen by Hastie as his 'enemy' (Macmillan, 96). She sued him for libel in Calcutta in 1883: he was fined 1 anna and the costs were divided; in the trial, Hastie made a number of allegations against Miss Pigot. The case caused a sensation in Calcutta (Miss Pigot being of Indian and European parentage), and it led to his dismissal as principal in November 1883. Miss Pigot appealed and was vindicated by the second judge; Hastie was required to pay 3000 rupees and all costs, and his witnesses received especial condemnation. His appeal to the general assembly in Edinburgh against his dismissal was rejected on 29 May 1884 by 193 votes to 90; he unsuccessfully sued the assembly and other parties. Somewhat provocatively, he then returned to Calcutta knowing that his failure to pay the libel damages and costs would lead to imprisonment, as it did on 13 February 1885.

Hastie declared himself bankrupt and was released, leaving India in April 1885 and retiring to Wanlockhead to write. He earned a living by translating, notably *Philosophy of Art* (1886), a translation of *Vorlesungen über die Ästhetik* by Hegel, and works by other German authors including Kant, Schliermaster, and Pünjer. His introductions to these did much to encourage educated interest in German theology and philosophy. Opinion began to swing Hastie's way, and the Church of Scotland repented of its treatment of him. He became examiner in theology, and in 1892 he was Croall lecturer at Edinburgh. On 13 April 1894 he received the honorary degree of DD from Edinburgh University, and in 1895 he succeeded William Purdie Dickson as professor of divinity at Glasgow, having previously failed in a number of similar applications. There he was popular with his students, whom he impressed with his attainments and method. He began a libel action against a Dutch professor but was persuaded to abandon it. He published *Theology as Science* (1899), and was an important contributor to the broad church movement in Scotland. His course of philosophical lectures, published posthumously at Edinburgh in 1904 as *The Theology of the Reformed Church in its Fundamental Principles*, proved valuable. He also published poetry. Hastie suffered from depression after 1883, and was in poor health in the 1890s; it may be the case that he was mentally unstable from an earlier date. He died suddenly and intestate at Edinburgh on 31 August 1903, and was interred on 4 September in the family burying-ground at Wanlockhead. He was unmarried; Macmillan mentions his 'gallantry to ladies' (Macmillan, 185). A memorial Hastie lecture was established in Glasgow University and his friends founded the Hastie Club.

H. C. G. MATTHEW

Sources DNB · D. Macmillan, *The life of Professor Hastie* (1926) · G. White, 'William Hastie: professor from Calcutta gaol', *College Courant: Journal of the Glasgow University Graduates Association*, 72 (March 1984), 26–9 · DSCHT · *The Scotsman* (1 Sept 1903) · *Glasgow Herald* (1 Sept 1903)

Likenesses photograph, repro. in Macmillan, *Life of Professor Hastie*

Wealth at death £5709 3s. 3d.: confirmation, 6 June 1904, CCI

Hastings. For this title name *see* individual entries under Hastings; *see also* Rawdon, Elizabeth, *suo jure* Baroness Botreaux, *suo jure* Baroness Hungerford, *suo jure* Baroness Moleyns, *suo jure* Baroness Hastings, and countess of Moira (1731–1808).

Hastings family (*per. c.*1300–*c.*1450), gentry, had established themselves in Allerston in the North Riding of Yorkshire in the early thirteenth century, but enhanced their wealth and social status during the fourteenth century through military talent and magnate service. Although **Sir Nicholas Hastings** (*d.* before 1316) inherited from his father, Hugh, lands at Wistowe, Leicestershire, and Gissing, Norfolk, the prospects of advancement offered by the wars in Scotland led him to concentrate his activities around the family's most northerly manor at Allerston. Summoned to serve against the Scots in 1300 and 1301, he entered the service of Sir Ralph Fitzwilliam of Hinderskelfe, Lord Greystoke, in May 1311, taking a rent of £8 per annum as his retaining fee, and subsequently served in the English garrisons at Berwick and Dundee.

It was the career of Sir Nicholas's son and heir, **Sir Ralph [i] Hastings** (*d.* 1346), that transformed the expectations of the family, however. By 1332 he had established himself in the service of Henry, third earl of Lancaster (*d.* 1345), acting as constable and steward of the earl's honour of Pickering and serving with the earl's eldest son, Henry of Grosmont (*d.* 1361), on a series of successful military campaigns—in Scotland (1336), Brittany (1342), and Aquitaine (1344, 1345–6). The substantial rewards of this service (a fee of £20 as steward of Pickering and an additional £40 retaining fee) enabled Sir Ralph to expand the Hastings family estates, both in the North Riding, where he purchased the manors of Slingsby, Howthorp, and Colton, and in Leicestershire, where he acquired estates at Newton Harcourt and Welford. A series of royal privileges, including free warren in all his lands (1329) and a licence to crenellate and impark his new residence at Slingsby (1344), underlined his increased status and prosperity, while the acquisition of the advowson of Sulby Abbey, Northamptonshire, in 1343 allowed the Hastings family to treat this Premonstratensian house as their mausoleum—both Sir Ralph and his eldest son requested burial there. Appointed a keeper of the peace in the North Riding in 1332, Sir Ralph served as sheriff of Yorkshire between March 1337 and October 1340 and was closely involved, during his tenure of the shrievalty, in implementing Edward III's schemes for the regulation and financial exploitation of the wool export. He died in November 1346, less than a month after he had led the rearguard of the army that defeated the invading Scots at Nevilles Cross.

Where his father had led, his son and heir, **Sir Ralph [ii] Hastings** (*c.*1322–1397), followed, confirming the Hastings' position among the most substantial Yorkshire gentry families and establishing himself as a figure of some national consequence. After early military experience at Nevilles Cross and in the sea-fight off Winchelsea (1350),

Sir Ralph [ii] made his reputation in the service of successive dukes of Lancaster. He was in Henry of Grosmont's company at Calais (1347) and on the Rheims campaign (1359–60), before serving with the duke's son-in-law, John of Gaunt, in Spain (1367)—where Hastings was captured and put to ransom—France (1369, 1373), Aquitaine (1370), Scotland (1385), and at sea (1372). As a brave and experienced soldier, who 'cared not two cherries for death' (Pope and Lodge, ll. 2729–30), Sir Ralph was a valued member of the Lancastrian affinity, retained by both Grosmont and Gaunt at a yearly fee of 40 marks, whose reputation brought him additional fees from regional magnates such as John, Lord Neville, and Thomas, Lord Ros. Such influential connections, and the substantial landed estate his father had assembled, gave Sir Ralph [ii] considerable local consequence in Yorkshire: he was chosen as sheriff of the county in October 1376 and October 1380, and was returned to parliament twice by the shire electors, in October 1378 and January 1380. He had already served as one of the MPs for Leicestershire in January 1365, soon after inheriting the estates of his mother, Margaret, daughter of Chief Justice Sir William Herle, at Braunston and Kirby Muxloe, Leicestershire. In addition, the close involvement of John of Gaunt, his principal patron, in the government of the realm meant that Sir Ralph was entrusted with some tasks of national significance: he was appointed a warden of the east march in October 1371, and continued to be involved in marcher business for several years thereafter, while in January 1380 he was chosen as one of the three knights on the parliamentary committee established to inquire into the conduct of the great officers of state and the expenses of the royal household.

Sir Ralph [ii] married twice: his first wife was Isabel, daughter and heir of Sir Robert *Sadyngton, and his second was Maud, widow of Sir John Meaux; he left a large, young family at his death in October 1397. His eldest son, **Ralph** [iii] **Hastings** (c.1379–1405), was still under age and the Hastings' local influence fell temporarily into abeyance; it was left to a cousin, Sir Edmund Hastings of Roxby, Yorkshire, to assume the place in Lancastrian service traditionally enjoyed by the head of the Slingsby branch of the family. Their social position was placed more permanently at risk when Ralph [iii] joined the Percy-influenced rising of north Yorkshire gentry against Henry IV in May 1405, for, following his trial and execution at Durham (20 July 1405), all Ralph's estates were forfeited to the crown. Seventy years of loyal Lancastrian service did not go unrecognized, however, and in 1410 Richard Hastings (c.1387–1436), Ralph's eldest surviving brother, was fully restored to the family lands. His career, and that of his brother Leonard (d. 1455), swiftly re-established the traditions of loyalty and reliability that had transformed the fortunes of the Hastings family.

SIMON WALKER

Sources PRO · *Chancery records* · W. Dugdale, *The baronage of England*, 2 vols. (1675–6) · A. Gooder, ed., *The parliamentary representation of the county of York, 1258–1832*, 1, Yorkshire Archaeological Society, 91 (1935) · *Report on the manuscripts of the late Reginald Rawdon Hastings*, 4 vols., HMC, 78 (1928–47) · [J. Raine], ed., *Testamenta Eboracensia*, 1, SurtS, 4 (1836), 19–20, 216–17 · V. H. Galbraith, ed., *The Anonimalle chronicle, 1333 to 1381* (1927) · Chandos herald, *Life of the Black Prince by the herald of Sir John Chandos*, ed. M. K. Pope and E. C. Lodge (1910) · M. Jones and S. Walker, eds., 'Private indentures for life service in peace and war, 1278–1476', *Camden miscellany, XXXII*, CS, 5th ser., 3 (1994), 1–190 · *VCH Yorkshire North Riding*, vol. 2

Archives Hunt. L., papers

Hastings family (*per.* 1759–1907), farmers, were tenant farmers from 1759 to 1907 on the Holkham estate belonging to the Coke family of Norfolk, who were created earls of Leicester in 1837. Their farming activities were representative of the progressive tenants of the large Norfolk farms which made the estate famous for its part in promoting agricultural improvements.

The first member of the family to lease land on the estate was Thomas Hastings (1729–1804), who took over Hall Farm, Longham, in 1759. In 1776 he was paying £225 per annum in rent for 'Hall Farm, Brakelands and sheep walk'. This entry in the Holkham audit book suggests that at this date part of the farm was still open heath and intermittently ploughed breck.

John Sutton Hastings (1790–1869), another member of the family, who was born at Longham on 4 December 1790, held the farm from 1816. An enclosure act for Longham parish had been passed in 1813, when the common was enclosed and the fields rearranged to form a compact farm of the large rectangular fields so typical of the Holkham estate. Although these improvements were initiated by the landlord, much of the work was done by the tenants, who were responsible for claying newly enclosed land, planting new hedges, and grubbing up and levelling old hedgerow banks.

A detailed investigation of the estate in 1816 included a brief vignette about Hall Farm. 'Much money has been expended upon the improvement of the farm with a *very* far distant prospect of a return', it reported; 'A very large sum is still required to complete the present improvements.' The rent of this 580 acre farm was £600, which the agent considered 'high'. Mr Hastings was described as 'a zealous and industrious tenant heart-broken by his present undertaking'. However, a note was added to this description by the agent, Francis Blaikie, saying, 'Mr Coke has promised to take him by the hand' (Blaikie, report, 1816, Holkham Hall). This probably involved financial assistance and in 1822 the rent was reduced to £400.

After the recession of the early 1820s, agricultural fortunes improved and John Sutton Hastings was at the forefront of progress. By 1845 he was a member of the Royal Agricultural Society of England and in 1843 he responded to a farming questionnaire circulated by R. N. Bacon of the *Norwich Mercury* in order to obtain information for his book on the agriculture of Norfolk. By this time the farm was farmed on a four-course rotation (although Hastings believed that there were some circumstances in which two grain crops could be grown in succession). Hastings fed half his turnips to the sheep in the field, but he also bought oil cake and malt dust as feed. He drilled his seeds rather than sowing or dibbling them by hand, and he altered the standard implements to suit his purposes. He did try new methods, 'but generally went back to the old' (Norfolk RO, Bacon MS). His belief in the scientific basis of the high-input, high-output system of 'high farming' was illustrated by his optimistic closing comment, so different from the sentiments expressed in 1816, that 'production will increase as knowledge itself increases' (ibid.).

Married by 1816, Hastings and his wife Barbara had one surviving daughter, Charlotte; she and their nephew, John, described as 'farm manager' in the 1851 census, were living at their home. During this period the farm continued to be well farmed and stocked. Large numbers of animals were kept and in 1864 the possibility of using modern fertilizers meant that John Sutton Hastings was given permission to depart from the terms of his lease and grow two crops of corn in succession (Holkham Hall, letter books).

Active in the community, John Sutton Hastings was instrumental in organizing the building of Longham School in 1859 and the restoration of the church in 1867, with much of the finance being provided by the Holkham estate. Hastings himself built 'a double cottage for two married couples or four widows not under the age of 60 years' (White, 403). His interest in parish affairs was recorded on his monument in Longham church, which stated that 'during more than half a century he was a steady friend and benefactor of this parish'. He died at Longham on 9 July 1869. **John Hastings** (1830/31–1884), his nephew, took over the farm on his uncle's death. He had married, by 1853, Mary Alice Hunt (b. 1828/9), of neighbouring Gressenhall parish. Hastings died at Hall Farm on 31 December 1884, and was survived by his wife.

The general decline in farming fortunes as cereal prices collapsed during the 1870s meant that, in spite of the large number of cattle kept on the farm, profits fell and the rent was unpaid in 1883. The previous year the estate had been informed that the family intended to quit. Following the death of his father, **John Hastings** (1853–1907) took over the farm, but was never able to make the levels of profit typical of the middle of the century. Rents were reduced from a peak of £1013 in the 1870s to £700 in 1885, £600 in 1887, and £477 in 1895. On four separate occasions between 1882 and 1895 John Hastings handed in notice that he intended to quit, and the family finally left the farm after he died at Longham on 10 May 1907. By this time the farm was running relatively smoothly as John had developed a business breeding horses for hackney carriages, which was more likely to remain profitable than conventional farming.

This mid-Norfolk family, renting the same farm from a famous estate for more than 150 years, illustrates the reaction of intelligent farmers of capital to the changes in agricultural practice and fortunes over the periods of the 'agricultural revolution', 'high farming', and the 'great depression'.   SUSANNA WADE MARTINS

Sources S. W. Martins, *A great estate at work* (1980), 119–26 • audit and letter books, estate surveys, Holkham Hall, Norfolk [by F. Blaikie, 1816 and William Keary, 1851] • replies to Bacon questionnaire, 1844, Norfolk RO, Bacon MS 4363 (MFRO 11–13) • d. cert. [John Sutton Hastings] • d. cert. [John Hastings, 1884] • d. cert. [John Hastings, 1907] • W. White, *Norfolk directory* (1883), 403 • CGPLA Eng. & Wales (1969) [John Sutton Hastings] • CGPLA Eng. & Wales (1885) [John Hastings] • CGPLA Eng. & Wales (1907) [John Hastings] • census returns for Longham, Norfolk, 1851
Archives Norfolk RO | Holkham Hall, Norfolk, Holkham estate papers
Likenesses pen-and-ink drawing (John Hastings), repro. in Martins, *Great estate*, 123; in possession of a relative in 1980
Wealth at death under £12,000—John Sutton Hastings: probate, 25 Aug 1869, CGPLA Eng. & Wales • £12,822 19s. 3d.—John Hastings: probate, 1885, CGPLA Eng. & Wales • £7643 10s. 6d.—John Hastings: probate, 10 June 1907, CGPLA Eng. & Wales

Hastings, Anthea Esther. *See* Joseph, Anthea Esther (1924–1981).

Hastings, Barbara Rawdon [*née* Barbara Yelverton], **marchioness of Hastings** and *suo jure* **Baroness Grey of Ruthin** (1810–1858), fossil collector and geological author, was born on 20 May 1810 at Brandon House in Warwickshire, the only child of Henry Edward Yelverton, Baron Grey of Ruthin (1780–1810), and his wife, Anna Maria Kelham (1792–1875). In 1811, following the death of her father, Barbara Yelverton became Baroness Grey of Ruthin. Little else is known of her early life or education. On 1 August 1831 she married George Augustus Francis Rawdon Hastings, second marquess of Hastings (1808–1844), with whom she had six children. On 9 April 1845 Barbara Rawdon Hastings married her second husband, Hastings Reginald Henry (1808–1878), a captain in the Royal Navy. (In 1849 her husband took, by royal licence, the surname Yelverton [*see* Yelverton, Hastings Reginald].) The couple settled at Efford House, near Lymington in Hampshire, and had a daughter.

Hastings's life was a mixture of social and scientific activity. During her first marriage she was nicknamed the jolly fast marchioness, and developed a taste for foreign travel and gambling. However, she was also a keen collector of fossil vertebrates, and during her second marriage established a private museum at Efford House for her specimens. The palaeontologist Richard Owen noted that among the thousands of fossils in the museum were some of the finest in the world (Owen, *Life*, 1.296).

Hastings's fossil collection was a valuable scientific resource. 'Most of the specimens', she told G. R. Waterhouse of the British Museum in 1854, 'are figured in the Palaeontological work' (Archives of the British Museum of Natural History, Correspondence, 1851–5, DF 100/7). However, Hastings did more than simply amass raw material for research; her detailed knowledge of local geology (particularly of the Eocene beds of Hordle cliff), together with her painstaking reconstruction of fossil remains, gave her an expertise that was valued by her contemporaries. She was, said geologist Edward Forbes, 'a "fossilist" and knows her work' (Wilson and Geikie, 423). Richard Owen named a fossil crocodile from Hordle cliff *Crocodilus hastingsiae* 'in honour of the accomplished lady by whom the singularly perfect example of the species had been recovered and restored' (Owen, 'Fossils', 66).

Nevertheless, despite her expertise, Hastings occupied an ambiguous place in Victorian geology. At a time when science was the preserve of gentlemen scholars she often took on the role of female drudge: 'I have been six hours mending bones, & feel tired & stupid', she wrote to Owen in 1847 (Archives of the British Museum of Natural History, Owen correspondence, vol.14 NH 14:400). High birth and independent wealth, however, secured her access to the world of her male contemporaries, able to pursue their chosen specialism at leisure. In 1847 Hastings became 'a fixed star' (Owen, *Life*, 1.296) of the Oxford meeting of the British Association when she exhibited two crocodile skulls and a turtle shell excavated from Hordle cliff. Genuine significance was attached to these specimens, as Owen explained when he addressed the meeting. Some of the reptilian remains, he suggested, indicated that there was 'a new genus of Pachyderm' (Owen, 'Fossils', 65), named Paloplotherium by Owen, between the Palaeotherium and Anoplotherium. Hastings also addressed the meeting and argued that the presence of crocodile remains on both the Hampshire coast and the Isle of Wight revealed that the space occupied by the Solent had once been occupied by a freshwater lake or river (see 'On the freshwater Eocene beds of Hordle cliff, Hampshire', *Report of the British Association for the Advancement of Science*, 1848).

Hastings continued her studies of local geology and published papers on the stratigraphy of Hordle cliff in 1852 and 1853. Having spent six years on very minute researches of the strata she was well placed to assess the impact of phenomena such as cliff falls and sea erosion which might have eluded the short-term observer (see 'On the Tertiary beds of Hordwell, Hampshire', *Philosophical Magazine*, 4th ser., 1853, 1). Hastings's were the first accurate stratigraphical accounts of Hordle cliff to be published, and contributed to knowledge of the Tertiary period.

In 1855 Hastings sold her collection of mammalian and reptilian fossils. Her gambling instincts seemed to come in to play for, after threatening to send the fossils to Paris (where 'they would be treated as immense treasures'), she secured £300 for the entire collection from the British Museum (Archives of the British Museum of Natural History, Correspondence, 1851–5, DF 100/7). The collection subsequently went to the palaeontology department of the Natural History Museum in London. Hastings died of apoplexy in Rome on 18 November 1858, and was buried in the English cemetery there a week later. She was survived by her second husband.   PORTIA DADLEY

Sources N. Edwards, 'The Hastings collection (fossil vertebrates): history of the additions made by the marchioness of Hastings between 1845–51 from the Upper Eocene beds at Hordle cliff, Hampshire', *Journal of the Society of the Bibliography of Natural History*, 5 (1968–71), 340–43 • *GM*, 3rd ser., 6 (1859), 92 • H. Blyth, *The pocket Venus: a Victorian scandal* (1966) • R. Owen, *The life of Richard Owen*, 1 (1894) • Owen correspondence, NHM, vol. 14, NH 14:400 • correspondence, 1851–5, NHM, archives, DF 100/7 • R. S. Owen, 'On the fossils obtained by the marchioness of Hastings from the freshwater Eocene beds of Hordle cliff', *Report of the British Association for the Advancement of Science* (1848), 65–6 • B. Hastings, 'On the freshwater Eocene beds of Hordle cliff, Hampshire', *Report of the British Association for the Advancement of Science* (1848), 63–4 • Marchioness of Hastings, 'On the Tertiary beds of Hordwell, Hampshire', *London, Edinburgh, and Dublin Philosophical Magazine*, 4th ser., 6 (1853), 1–

10 • G. Wilson and A. Geikie, *Memoir of Edward Forbes, F.R.S., late regius professor of natural history in the University of Edinburgh* (1861) • *CGPLA Eng. & Wales* (1859) • GEC, *Peerage*, new edn
Archives NHM, corresp., DF 100/7 | NHM, Owen correspondence, vol. 14
Wealth at death under £100: administration with will, 1859, *CGPLA Eng. & Wales*

Hastings, Beatrice. *See* Haigh, Emily Alice (1879–1943).

Hastings, Sir Charles (1794–1866), physician and founder of the British Medical Association, was born on 11 January 1794 at a lodging house in Ludlow, Shropshire, the ninth of the fifteen children of James Hastings (1755–1856), Church of England rector, and his wife, Elizabeth (*née* Paget). In 1795 the Hastings family moved from Bitterley in Shropshire to Martley, Worcestershire. Little is known of Hastings's early education except that he attended the grammar school in Martley. In 1806 his father suffered a riding accident which rendered him permanently unfit for work owing to physical and mental incapacity. Soon afterwards his clerical living was placed in chancery and the Hastings family, in reduced financial circumstances, moved to Worcester.

In September 1810, after toying with the possibility of a naval or military career, Hastings began a two-year medical apprenticeship with Richard Jukes and Kenrick Watson at their practice in Stourport-on-Severn. In 1812, following a few months of further study in London, Hastings was elected house surgeon at Worcester Infirmary. Three years later he entered Edinburgh University medical school; he graduated MD in August 1818 with a doctoral thesis on the blood vessels. It has been said that he alone of his Edinburgh student contemporaries made use of the microscope in his studies. For a short time Hastings was clerk to the Edinburgh Royal Infirmary but, though offered the post of extramural teacher of anatomy and physiology in his university, he returned to Worcester and in November 1818 was appointed junior physician at the infirmary. He spent the rest of his professional life in Worcestershire, retaining his infirmary post (as senior physician from 1858) until 1862.

On 20 May 1823 Hastings married Hannah (*d.* 1866), the eldest daughter of George Woodyatt, a prosperous Worcester medical practitioner; they had three children, Mary Anne Elizabeth, who was born on 8 May 1824, George Woodyatt *Hastings (1825–1917), and Elizabeth Frances (*bap.* 1827). In early 1824 his father-in-law died and Hastings moved into his house at 43 Foregate Street, Worcester, and took over a large part of his lucrative practice. Thereafter, with patients as far afield as north Wales, he became 'the best known physician in the West Midlands' (McMenemey, 55). As he gained financial security, so he was able to avoid becoming 'a mere receiver of fees' (*The Lancet*, 11 Aug 1866, 163). He continued to practise medicine, taking on the additional appointments of physician to Ledbury Infirmary in 1824, and visiting physician to Droitwich Asylum in 1828, but from the age of thirty he had the means to pursue his interests in medical science,

Sir Charles Hastings (1794–1866), by Samuel William Reynolds junior, pubd 1839 (after Benjamin Rawlinson Faulkner)

professorial fellowship, natural history, and public service.

In 1828, while recovering from a serious accident, Hastings conceived the idea for a quarterly medical journal entitled the *Midland Medical and Surgical Reporter and Statistical Journal* (*MMSR*). It is unclear whether it was the success of this publication, or the example of the British Association for the Advancement of Science, which provided the inspiration for the foundation of a provincial medical society, but the new society, entitled the Provincial Medical and Surgical Association (PMSA), was formally established at a meeting convened by Hastings and held in the boardroom of Worcester Infirmary on 19 July 1832. The PMSA was renamed the British Medical Association (BMA) in 1855, and two years later the PMSA's weekly publication, the *Provincial Medical and Surgical Journal* (*PMSJ*) (founded in 1840 and which had come into the PMSA's proprietorship in 1844), became known as the *British Medical Journal* (*BMJ*). Hastings's original idea was for a scientific and social society, the main object of which was 'the diffusion and increase of medical Knowledge in every department of science and practice' (*MMSR*, 1831–2, no. 3, 302–3). This object was to be achieved by members coming together at an annual meeting in a provincial town or city and by the publication of an annual volume of transactions.

Although 'maintenance of the honour and respectability of the profession' (*MMSR*, 1831–2, no. 3, 302–3) was one of the association's original objectives, Hastings at first had little interest in medical politics; by the late 1840s, however, he was at the centre of the PMSA's medical reform campaign which helped to bring about the Medical Act of 1858. Throughout his life he was the association's driving force and dominating personality, and there were few aspects of its affairs in which he was not closely involved. He was its joint secretary between 1832 and 1843; its treasurer from 1843 to 1866; its president of council for the same period; its president in 1849–50; and its permanent vice-president from 1851 until his death. However, though held in high esteem by most members, Hastings received criticism for his shortcomings as treasurer and his lack of enthusiasm for the *PMSJ*/*BMJ*; he was also reproached for his opposition to the association's democratic governance, its change of name, and its proposed relocation as a national body in London.

Aside from his involvement with the PMSA/BMA Hastings was throughout his life an enthusiastic participant in numerous learned societies and public bodies. While at Edinburgh he belonged to the Royal Medical Society and served as its president; on his return to Worcester he was active in the Worcester Medical and Surgical Society, over which he presided in 1819; in the early 1830s he became a member of the British Association for the Advancement of Science; and in 1833 he was prominent in the formation of the Worcester Natural History Society. He was elected an alderman for the city of Worcester in 1835 and regularly attended council meetings until pressure of work made this impossible. In 1839 he rejected the opportunity to become mayor. In 1857 Hastings was a member of the founding committee of the National Association for the Promotion of Social Science, of which his son was for many years the secretary. He read a paper on tobacco smoking and health at the association's 1860 annual meeting in Glasgow, and he delivered the presidential address to its public health section at the 1864 York meeting. In November 1858, following the passage of the Medical Act, Hastings was appointed to the newly created General Medical Council, on which he sat until his retirement in November 1862. He was also associated, in various capacities, with the Epidemiological Society, the Sydenham Society, and the New Equitable Assurance Company. In addition he was a corresponding member of the Massachusetts Medical Society, president of the Medical Officers of Asylums for the Insane, a charity commissioner for Worcestershire, and deputy lieutenant for the same county.

Hastings gained several honours, the foremost of which was the knighthood conferred upon him in July 1850 following political lobbying by senior members of the PMSA. He was also awarded the diploma of the Royal Medical Society in 1818 and an honorary DCL degree by Oxford University in 1852. He published many scientific papers and newspaper articles. His first book, *A Treatise on Inflammation of the Mucous Membrane of the Lungs* (1820), which was translated into German in 1822, confirmed him as an authority on chest diseases. His one other book, *Illustrations of the Natural History of Worcestershire* (1834), was an expanded version of his inaugural address to the Worcester Natural History Society.

Hastings possessed a genial personality but could also

be forthright and abrasive. On several occasions he clashed with colleagues over their conduct of business meetings and alleged professional 'poaching'. In his youth he was tall and strikingly handsome but a carriage accident he sustained in 1828 inflicted permanent hip damage which afterwards prevented him from standing upright or walking without a limp. Five of his siblings died before reaching adulthood, and while a student in Edinburgh a serious bronchial disorder compelled him to return to Worcester for many months. Thereafter he enjoyed good health until a few years before his death. Hastings died from cancer of the colon on 30 July 1866, at Barnard's Green House, Malvern, one of the several houses he possessed. His wife had died a few months earlier, on 21 March 1866. He was buried at Astwood cemetery in Worcester on 6 August 1866. His medical books were eventually deposited in the British Medical Association's library.

P. W. J. BARTRIP

Sources W. H. McMenemey, *The life and times of Sir Charles Hastings* (1959) · *The Lancet* (23 Aug 1851), 182–8 · *The Lancet* (11 Aug 1866), 162–4 · *BMJ* (4 Aug 1866), 128–9 · *Medical Times and Gazette* (4 Aug 1866), 122 · *Medical Press and Circular* (8 Aug 1866), 166–7 · *London and Provincial Medical Directory* (1867), 958 · *BMJ* (6 Jan 1906), 27–9 · V. Z. Cope, *Some famous general practitioners and other medical historical essays* (1961) · Ward, *Men of the reign* · E. O. Browne and J. R. Burton, eds., *Short biographies of the worthies of Worcestershire* (1916) · Boase, *Mod. Eng. biog.* · E. M. Little, *History of the British Medical Association, 1832–1932* [1932] [no date] · P. Bartrip, *Mirror of medicine: a history of the British Medical Journal* (1990)

Archives Bodl. Oxf. · British Medical Association · Worcester City Museum, family MSS | Bodl. Oxf., corresp. with Sir Thomas Phillipps

Likenesses B. R. Faulkner, oils, 1839, probably British Medical Association House, London · S. W. Reynolds junior, mezzotint, pubd 1839 (after B. R. Faulkner), BM, NPG, Wellcome L. [*see illus.*] · T. Brock, marble bust, 1882, Worcester Museum, Worcester · E. Edwards, photograph, Wellcome L. · drawing and wash, Worcester Museum, Worcester · pen-and-ink drawing, repro. in *The Lancet* (23 Aug 1851), 183 · photographs, British Medical Association, London

Wealth at death under £20,000: probate, 2 Oct 1866, *CGPLA Eng. & Wales*

Hastings, Edmund, Lord Hastings of Inchmahome (1263×9–1314), soldier and administrator, was the younger son of Henry *Hastings (1235?–1269) and his wife, Joanna de Cantilupe. The birth of his elder brother, John *Hastings, first Lord Hastings, in May 1262 and the death of his father before 5 March 1269 place his birth between 1263 and 1269. On 26 December 1295 Edward I restored his lands in Suffolk because he was a loyal Englishman who had not deserted to the Scots; and on 28 August 1296 he swore fealty to Edward as overlord of Scotland. Through Edward's favour, he had recently married Isabel, widow of William Comyn of Kirkintilloch and daughter and heir of Isabel, countess of Menteith in her own right, and of John Russell. In 1259 Countess Isabel had been deprived of the earldom of Menteith following accusations that she had poisoned her first husband. Menteith was then held by Walter Stewart, her brother-in-law, until he was compelled by judgment of the Scottish parliament in 1285 to partition it with the younger Isabel and Comyn; and half the earldom lands, without the title of earl, were duly

acquired by Hastings on his marriage *c.*1293. Shortly before it, on 5 January 1293, Edward I ordered King John Balliol to release Isabel from her oath not to marry without his consent, curtly reminding him that he had already promised her to Edmund Hastings when the Scots realm had been in his possession (1291–2). Although Edmund had difficulty controlling his wife's estates after the outbreak of the Scottish wars, his rights were specifically protected when on 22 May 1306 Edward I granted to his elder brother, John Hastings, the forfeited lands of Alan, earl of Menteith, Walter Stewart's grandson. Edmund also held or claimed property in Dundee and shares of the baronies of Inverbervie, Kincardineshire, and Longforgan, Perthshire, as part of the Hastings inheritance from David, earl of Huntingdon (*d.* 1219).

Hastings was summoned by the English crown for military service against the Scots (1298–1310) and to parliament (1299–1313). He supported Edward I in Annandale early in 1300, and was at the siege of Caerlaverock in July. Taking the title of Lord Hastings of Inchmahome, Perthshire, after the chief lordship of Menteith, he was one of many English nobles to join in the letter of 12 February 1301 protesting that the pope had no jurisdiction over Edward I's claims to Scotland. During the next few years he played a full role in upholding English rule in Scotland. He was appointed warden of Berwick in February 1302, keeper of Perth in July 1306, and one of Edward II's three military governors between the Forth and Orkney in June 1308. He occurs as constable of Dundee in 1310–11, and returned to Berwick as warden and sheriff in May 1312. According to the *Annales Londonienses*, a knowledgeable source, he was slain at the battle of Bannockburn (23–4 June 1314). He left no known children.

KEITH STRINGER

Sources *Scots peerage*, vol. 6 · GEC, *Peerage* · *CDS*, vols. 2, 5 · C. Moor, ed., *Knights of Edward I*, 2, Harleian Society, 81 (1929) · W. Stubbs, ed., 'Annales Londonienses', *Chronicles of the reigns of Edward I and Edward II*, 1, Rolls Series, 76 (1882), 1–251 · G. W. S. Barrow and others, eds., *Regesta regum Scottorum*, 5, ed. A. A. M. Duncan (1988) · W. Fraser, ed., *The Red Book of Menteith*, 2 vols. (1880)

Hastings, Sir Edward (1382–1438), soldier and litigant, was born on 21 May 1382 at Fenwick, Yorkshire, the second son of Sir Hugh Hastings (*d.* 1386/7) of Elsing, Norfolk, and great-grandson of Sir Hugh *Hastings (*c.*1310–1347). His father, a noted soldier, served on most of the principal campaigns of the 1370s and 1380s, and was a prominent retainer of John of Gaunt, duke of Lancaster: he died on Gaunt's expedition to Galicia in 1386–7. On the death in 1389 of John Hastings, earl of Pembroke, Edward's brother Hugh, and after Hugh's death at Calais in 1396 Edward himself, were the heirs of the half-blood, being descended from the earl's great-great-grandfather, John *Hastings, first Lord Hastings (*d.* 1313), and his second wife, Isabel Despenser, in an unbroken male line. Reynold, Lord Grey of Ruthin, however, claimed priority, as heir of the whole blood, being descended in the female line from John, Lord Hastings, and his first wife, Isabel de Valence. There were other descendants too, but most of the earl's lands passed eventually to Grey: Hugh and

Edward, being under age, were in the 1390s in a poor position to contest his claims.

In 1399, soon after Henry IV's accession, Edward Hastings was knighted: he is described as a 'king's knight' and was granted £40 p.a. to maintain his knighthood while his minority lasted. On Henry IV's expedition to Scotland in 1400 both Edward Hastings and Lord Grey appeared in the arms of Hastings of Pembroke, 'or a manche gules', and Grey challenged Edward's right to them. In the next year Grey petitioned the king to appoint a procurator for Sir Edward, who was still a minor, so that the case could be heard, and there were some proceedings before the constable; but full proceedings only began after the issue of a commission to hear the case, from John of Lancaster as constable of England, in May 1407. The hearings in the case, which became one of the *causes célèbres* of the middle ages, were lengthy (a full record is preserved in a seventeenth-century transcript in *Processus in curia marescalli*, London, College of Arms). Judgment was finally given in favour of Grey on 9 May 1410: Hastings was condemned in costs, but at once appealed against the judgment.

At the coronation of Henry V in 1413 Hastings made another claim as heir to Hastings of Pembroke, to the right to carry the royal spurs and the second sword, and to perform the office of naperer, which claim appears not to have been allowed. Later in the year he was imprisoned in the Tower of London, but in April 1414 he was set free. Commissions were appointed to hear his appeal, on 22 May and 22 November 1413, and again on 8 February 1415, but, probably owing to the French war, no hearings took place. In 1415–16 Hastings was in war service in the retinue of the earl of Dorset, at Harfleur. On 11 February 1417 Grey obtained an order for the taxation of costs of the original trial (which were assessed at £987 10s. 10d.) and when Hastings refused to pay, lest this should be construed as acknowledgement of Grey's rights, he was imprisoned in the Marshalsea, where he remained until some time after January 1434.

Though at times 'boundyn in fetters of iron liker a thef or traitour than lik a gentilman of berthe' (Young, xiv), Hastings steadfastly refused to purchase his release by abandoning his claims. In 1420 he made an offer that, if his son John should marry a daughter of Lord Grey, he would bestow on the pair 100 marks a year and the Hastings inheritance and arms, but this was refused. He was still in prison in January 1434 when he wrote from the Marshalsea an appeal to his peers: he was probably released soon after that.

Hastings seems finally to have paid off his costs; on 20 October 1436 his recognizance in the sum of £1000 to John, earl of Huntingdon, Reynold Grey, and his son John was cancelled, the earl and the Greys acknowledging themselves to be content. Hastings was twice married, first to Muriel (who died before 1420), daughter of Sir John Dinham, with whom he had a son John and other children; and second to Margery (d. 1456), daughter of Sir Robert Clifton of Bokenham, who after his death on 6 January 1438 married Sir John Wyndham. John Hastings never

prosecuted the family claim to the arms 'or a manche gules', nor did he use the title his father had claimed, Lord Hastings and Stuteville. He married Anne, daughter of John, Lord Morley, and died in 1471. He was buried in Elsing church (Blomefield 9.519). His descendants in the male line became extinct in 1542; the barony of Hastings fell into abeyance until 1841 when it was revived, in favour of Sir Jacob Astley, who was able to trace his descent (at several points through the female line) from John, Lord Hastings, via Sir Edward. M. H. KEEN

Sources C. G. Young, ed., *An account of the controversy between Reginald lord Grey of Ruthyn and Sir Edward Hastings in the reign of King Henry IV* (1841) · R. I. Jack, 'Entail and descent: the Hastings inheritance, 1370–1436', *BIHR*, 38 (1965), 1–19 · GEC, *Peerage* · 'Processus in curia marescalli', Coll. Arms · M. H. Keen, 'English military experience and the court of chivalry: the case of Grey and Hastings', *Guerre et société en France, en Angleterre et en Bourgogne, XIVe–XVe siècle*, ed. P. Contamine, M. H. Keen, and C. Giry Deloison (Lille, 1991), 123–42 · *Chronicon Adae de Usk*, ed. and trans. E. M. Thompson (1876) · *CClR, 1435–41* · *CPR, 1399–1401; 1413–16* · *RotP*, vol. 3 · F. Blomefield and C. Parkin, *An essay towards a topographical history of the county of Norfolk*, [2nd edn], 11 vols. (1805–10), vol. 5, p. 186; vol. 6, p. 414; vol. 8, pp.112, 201–3; vol. 9, pp. 470, 513–14, 519; vol. 10, p. 52 · R. Gough, *Sepulchral monuments in Great Britain*, 2 vols. (1786–96) · W. Dugdale, *The baronage of England*, 2 vols. (1675–6)

Hastings, Edward, Baron Hastings of Loughborough (1512x15?–1572), nobleman and soldier, was the third son of George *Hastings, third Baron Hastings of Hastings and first earl of Huntingdon (1486/7–1544), and Anne Stafford, sister of Edward Stafford, third duke of Buckingham. Anne had previously been the wife of Sir Walter Herbert, and married Hastings in December 1509. Edward was therefore probably born between 1512 and 1515. Nothing is known of his upbringing, but he was trained as a soldier, becoming a gentleman pensioner in 1540 and serving in the French campaign of 1544, and in the duke of Somerset's army against Scotland in 1547. According to William Patten he was knighted by the duke, along with fifty-one others, at the close of the campaign. He sat in the parliament of 1545 for the borough of Leicester, and in November 1547 was returned as a knight for Leicestershire, where the influence of his brother Francis *Hastings, since 1544 second earl of Huntingdon, was strong. He was clearly regarded as a competent officer, because in October 1549 he was designated for a responsible command in the sensitive garrison at Boulogne, although that intention was not fulfilled. In 1550 he served with his brother the earl on a commission to delimit the boundary of the Calais pale, and in 1551 was sheriff of Warwickshire and Leicestershire. During the Christmas season of 1552 he was present at Calais, where he fell out with Edward Underhill, a militant evangelical who was also controller of the ordnance there. According to Underhill they disputed on the nature of the real presence in the eucharist, Hastings taking the traditional or Catholic position on the mass (by that time illegal in England). A rather inarticulate religious conservatism does not seem to have impeded his career under the protestant government of Edward VI, and he again sat for Leicestershire in the parliament of March 1553.

Edward Hastings, Baron Hastings of Loughborough (1512x15?–1572), by unknown artist

After Edward's death on 6 July 1553 Hastings took a leading role in assembling supporters of Princess Mary in the Thames valley; their threat to London was an important factor in destroying support in the privy council for Lady Jane Grey. He then joined Mary at Framlingham where he was sworn of the privy council on 28 July. He quickly became one of her inner circle of trusted confidants, and was appointed master of the horse. During the disputes over the queen's marriage in the autumn of 1553 he was one of those councillors who sided with the lord chancellor, Stephen Gardiner, in opposing Philip's candidature, but like Gardiner he accepted her decision once reached. Later, after Gardiner's death on 12 November 1555, he became a supporter of Lord Paget. Hastings was regularly used for missions that required a high level of trust. On 28 January 1554 he was sent with Sir Thomas Cornwallis to negotiate with Sir Thomas Wyatt, then raising forces in Kent to oppose the queen's marriage. The mission achieved nothing positive, but it did serve to make Wyatt's hostile intentions clear. On 11 February Hastings accompanied Lord William Howard in the even more sensitive task of escorting Princess Elizabeth from Ashridge to London to face questioning about her role in the disturbances (a move of which he disapproved). In November 1554 he accompanied Lord Paget to Brussels to escort Cardinal Reginald Pole back to England, and in the spring of 1556 was one of those councillors selected for the tedious task of unravelling the so-called Dudley conspiracy. He held a number of minor but lucrative offices during the reign, and sat for Middlesex in the parliaments of 1554

and 1555, a clear indication of the trust in which he was held. In the latter parliament he was a strong supporter of anti-protestant bills, and nearly came to blows with Sir George Howard on the issue on the floor of the house. He also received substantial grants of land in Leicestershire and Somerset, and was elected to the Order of the Garter in 1555. During Philip's residence in England in 1554–5 Hastings served as a gentleman of his privy chamber, and he accompanied the king back to the Low Countries on his departure in August 1555, apparently remaining with him for several weeks. On 25 December 1557 he succeeded Sir John Gage as lord chamberlain after a vacancy of some eighteen months, and was created Baron Hastings of Loughborough on 19 January 1558.

Hastings remained personally close to the queen, and was among those chosen to be an executor of her will. His only military service during the reign was in the army that the earl of Pembroke led to support Philip at the siege of St Quentin in August 1557, but it is not known that he played an active role. As a councillor of irreproachable religious conservatism, Hastings was regularly involved in the policy of persecuting heretics, but he seems to have regarded this as an unavoidable duty rather than a virtue, and was not noted by John Foxe for particular zeal. Initially Elizabeth showed no disfavour to Hastings. Nevertheless, Mary's death spelt the end of his public career, as it did for most of her intimate councillors. He was not reappointed to the privy council, and was replaced as lord chamberlain by Lord Howard of Effingham. He performed minor services at court in November 1558 and September 1559, but there was nothing to attract him there, and he was completely out of sympathy with the new protestant ascendancy. In April 1561 he was arrested and sent to the Tower for hearing mass, it being the government's policy to make examples of a few prominent offenders. Hastings, however, was not made of the stuff of martyrs; he sued for pardon, took the oath of supremacy, and was released. It is very unlikely that he changed his opinions, but he was discreet and was not troubled further. In April 1563 he is known to have attended the Garter feast, when he stood as one of the sponsors for the election of the fourth duke of Norfolk. After 1558 he spent most of his time on his estates at Stoke Poges in Buckinghamshire; there he carried out various improvements, which included building a hospital and almshouses, and there he died on 5 March 1572.

Virtually nothing is known about Hastings's private life. He married about 1544 Joan, the daughter of John Harington of Bagworth, Leicestershire, and widow of George Villiers. She survived him, but they are not known to have had children. He made a will in May 1556, making no reference to her but mentioning an illegitimate son, Edward, then a minor, so they may have been estranged. He also made various traditional religious bequests, but when he died sixteen years later the will was not admitted to probate and his nephew the earl of Huntingdon was granted administration. The chill of royal disfavour had an adverse effect upon his fortunes after 1558, and he died owing the crown £1800.   DAVID LOADES

Sources J. Nichols, *The history and antiquities of the county of Leicester*, 3/2 (1804), 577–9 · GEC, *Peerage*, new edn, 6.384–5 · HoP, *Commons, 1509–58*, 2.315–17 · APC, 1547–54, 2–4 · CSP dom., 1547–58 · A. F. Pollard, ed., *Tudor tracts, 1532–1588* (1903) · N. H. Nicolas, ed., *Testamenta vetusta: being illustrations from wills*, 2 (1826), 740
Archives PRO, domestic state papers, SP1, SP10, SP11
Likenesses oils (aged twenty-eight), Montacute House, Somerset · oils, unknown collection; copyprint, NPG [*see illus.*] · stained-glass window, probably Stoke Poges church, Leicestershire
Wealth at death in debt: HoP, *Commons, 1509–58*, 2.315–17

Hastings, Lady Elizabeth [Betty] (1682–1739), benefactor, was born on 19 April 1682 at Great Charles Street, London, the eldest daughter of Theophilus *Hastings, seventh earl of Huntingdon (1650–1701), and his first wife, Elizabeth (1654–1688), eldest daughter and coheir of Sir John Lewis, bt, of Ledstone Hall in Yorkshire. Of eight children born to the earl and his first wife, only Lady Elizabeth and the second son, George (*d.* 1705), who succeeded his father as eighth earl, reached adulthood. Their mother died in childbirth in December 1688, and in May 1690 the earl married Frances, widow of Viscount Kilmorey, with whom he had a further two sons and five daughters. Following the seventh earl's death in May 1701, George inherited his maternal grandfather's estate at Ledstone. The eighth earl bestowed this on Lady Elizabeth on condition that she abandon any claim to their father's estate, a generous settlement which included a yearly income of £3000. Lady Betty (as she was known) was a beauty (as is evident in a portrait by Sir Godfrey Kneller), and had several suitors, but preferred to remain single. Her half-sisters, the ladies Anne, Frances, Catherine, and Margaret Hastings, lived with her at Ledstone for many years, and she supervised the education of her half-brother Theophilus, the ninth earl (1697–1746), and his brother Ferdinando.

Lady Betty became notable for her intelligence, her pious character, and her support of charitable causes. She was commemorated in no. 42 of *The Tatler* (16 July 1709) as 'Aspasia', a 'female philosopher', possibly by William Congreve, who was a friend of the family. In no. 49 Richard Steele stated that 'to behold her is an immediate check to loose Behaviour, and to love her is a liberal education' (Bond, 302, 349). Her household, where prayers were said four times a day, entertained a constant stream of visitors, including prominent theologians such as Richard Lucas, Thomas Wilson, bishop of Sodor and Man, John Sharp, archbishop of York, Robert Nelson, and William Law. As this list indicates, Lady Betty's religious sympathies inclined towards the high church, and she gave financial support to the Society for the Propagation of Christian Knowledge (SPCK) and the Society for the Propagation of the Gospel (SPG). Her political opinions are unknown, but her father was noted for his Jacobite views.

The objects of Lady Betty's charity included members of her family and indigent families in her neighbourhood, as well as several parish churches. She purchased several advowsons and gave money to charity schools both local and distant, with special attention to her own school for girls at Ledsham. In addition, she supported Mary Astell's school at Chelsea, subscribed to George Berkeley's missionary project, and was probably the unnamed benefactor of William Law's charity school for girls. She may have been the model for the pious and charitable Miranda in Law's *A Serious Call to a Devout and Holy Life* (1728). In 1716 Lady Betty and her banker, Henry Hoare (1677–1725), proposed to found a hospital in Bath for the sick poor, but she was not involved in the hospital's eventual organization. Lady Betty spent about half of her yearly income on charity, and lived comfortably at Ledstone on the remainder. Although known for her personal abstemiousness in clothing, food, and drink, she was a generous host. Her personality was, by all accounts, exceptionally warm, gracious, and courteous, and she was known as a conversationalist. She managed her estate with great skill and imagination, and hired the architect Charles Bridgeman to design the grounds, which included one of the first ha-has in England. Her attention to planting trees, irrigation, and fertilizing places her among the improving landlords of the era.

During the ninth earl's childhood, Lady Betty acted as the head of the family, and negotiated the marriage of Lady Catherine Hastings to Grenville Wheler in 1725 and that of the earl himself to Selina Shirley, daughter of Earl Ferrers, in 1728. Despite her own and her family's commitment to high Anglicanism, Lady Betty also undertook a period of theological investigation during which she met John Wesley in 1730. While remaining quite orthodox, she was clearly sympathetic to Methodism. Via the SPG she contributed to Wesley's missionary career and that of George Whitefield, one of her scholars at Queen's College, Oxford. Their companion Benjamin Ingham later married Lady Betty's half-sister Margaret. Her family's turn towards Methodism was inspired in part by Lady Betty's fortitude in her final illness. A cancer was discovered in her right breast early in 1738, and despite a mastectomy—a harrowing operation without anaesthesia—Lady Betty continued to decline. Her piety only increased during her final illness, and she continued her charitable dispositions up to the moment of her death, unmarried, at Ledstone Hall, on 21 December 1739, aged fifty-seven. She was buried on 7 January 1740 at Ledsham church, where, against her wishes, a monument was erected with a portrait drawn from Kneller's portrait.

Hastings's lengthy will, signed on 23 February 1739, indicates both the extent of her charities and her meticulous attention to detail. While the bulk of her estate went to her nephew Francis, Lord Hastings, son of the ninth earl, she made many individual bequests to churches, hospitals, charity schools, and relatives. A codicil to the will, dated 24 April 1739, bequeathed the manor of Wheldale to Queen's College, Oxford, for the maintenance of five poor scholars from twelve specified schools in the north of England. The Hastings Trust still supports scholarships and exhibitions at Queen's College, open to students from thirty schools with a focus on institutions in Cumberland and Westmorland; in addition, senior scholarships are awarded to graduates of the universities of Leeds, Sheffield, Hull, York, and Bradford.

Lady Betty's life, and especially her fortitude and piety at her death, inspired a number of eighteenth-century pamphlets, most of them drawing liberally from Thomas Barnard's 1742 biography, *An historical character relating to the holy and exemplary life of ... Lady Elizabeth Hastings*. She exercised considerable influence by her philanthropy and by the example of her life.   ANITA GUERRINI

Sources *DNB* · C. E. Medhurst, *The life and work of Lady Elizabeth Hastings* (1914) · T. Barnard, *An historical character relating to the holy and exemplary life of the right honourable the Lady Elizabeth Hastings* (1742) · E. Welch, *Spiritual pilgrim: a reassessment of the life of the countess of Huntingdon* (1995) · G. H. Wheler, ed., *Hastings Wheler family letters, 1704–1739*, 2 vols. (1929–35) · R. Perry, *The celebrated Mary Astell* (1986) · A. Guerrini, *Obesity and depression in the enlightenment: the life and times of George Cheyne* (2000) · D. F. Bond, ed., *The Tatler*, 3 vols. (1987)

Archives Hunt. L., family and personal MSS · Leics. RO | NL Ire., letters to Jane Bonnell · W. Yorks. AS, Leeds, papers relating to charities and livings

Likenesses I. Naylor, line engraving, pubd 1777, BM, NPG · G. Kneller, portrait, priv. coll. · monument, Ledsham church

Wealth at death estate of Ledstone; £3000 p.a.; considerable number of bequests indicating substantial wealth: will, copy at University of York

Hastings, Lady Flora Elizabeth (1806–1839), courtier, was born on 11 February 1806, the eldest of the four daughters and two sons of Francis Rawdon *Hastings, first marquess of Hastings, and his wife, Flora Mure-Campbell (1780–1840), in her own right countess of Loudoun. Brought up at Loudoun Castle, Ayrshire, she was beloved by her sisters, despite her reserved temperament, and was noted for her piety. Early in 1834 she was appointed lady of the bedchamber to the duchess of Kent, the widowed mother of the future Queen Victoria, with the express aim of providing companionship for the princess, and the veiled intention of detaching her from her governess, Lehzen. The duchess's household was dominated by Sir John Conroy, and Lady Flora was immediately aligned with the faction which supported his ambitions, earning in consequence the dislike of the young Victoria, who described her as 'an amazing *spy*, who would repeat everything she heard' (Woodham-Smith, 162).

The tory politics of the Hastings family were in strong opposition to the whig ministry, and the royal household formed by Lord Melbourne (as prime minister) on Victoria's accession was almost exclusively whig; politics were to add a significant dimension to the crisis which broke in the relationship between Lady Flora and the queen early in 1839, and which was not fully played out until the establishment of Peel's ministry in 1841. After spending the Christmas of 1838 in Scotland, Lady Flora returned to London in a post-chaise which she shared with Sir John Conroy, and immediately upon her resumption of her waiting at Buckingham Palace, she consulted one of the royal physicians, Sir James Clark, about pains and a swelling in her stomach, for which he prescribed a mild remedy. The change in Lady Flora's figure rapidly aroused the suspicions of the court; the queen, willing to believe all evil of her mother's household, confided in her diary that Lady Flora was '*with child!!*', attributing the fatherhood to 'the Monster and demon Incarnate', Sir John Conroy

Lady Flora Elizabeth Hastings (1806–1839), by W. & E. Finden, pubd 1840 (after E. Hawkins)

(Longford, 121). The whig ladies of the queen's household were outraged and sent one of their number, Lady Tavistock (the sister-in-law of Lord John Russell), to Melbourne to demand action. The prime minister consulted Clark, who was unable to deny the unfavourable appearance of the case: in exoneration of his gross misdiagnosis, Lady Flora had declined physical examination. No action was taken until Lady Portman came into waiting and required Clark to inform Lady Flora of the suspicions of the household. The duchess of Kent resolutely supported Lady Flora, and Lady Flora herself determined upon a medical examination to prove that her condition was not pregnancy. The examination entirely vindicated Lady Flora by establishing her virginity. Victoria sought a reconciliation, despite being encouraged by the doctors to believe that, the evidence notwithstanding, pregnancy was still a possibility.

By March, gossip about the affair was beginning to circulate widely outside the palace. Lady Flora had, naturally, communicated with her family the details of the case, and, incensed, they demanded to know who had originated the slander. Accusations and counter-accusations flew about, coloured by the opposing political views of the participants; the whigs' precarious hold on office and the queen's well-known horror of an incoming tory ministry formed the background to the heightened atmosphere of the spring of 1839. The affair took on renewed energy when members of the Hastings family went to the press with their story, publishing correspondence which showed Victoria, her ladies, and her prime minister in a most unfavourable light. On 7 May, Melbourne's ministry resigned; the subsequent 'bedchamber' crisis, in which Victoria refused to part with any of the ladies of her household to accommodate Peel's wishes and which resulted in Melbourne's return to office, was a continuation of the Lady Flora Hastings affair. Removal of any of the whig ladies who had been involved in the scandal would be interpreted as an admission of Victoria's errors in the affair, and a triumph for the tory Hastings faction. Lady Flora herself continued to appear in public to counter the rumours of her pregnancy, despite her worsening condition. By early June, she had taken to her bed at Buckingham Palace, the swelling in her stomach having returned with renewed force. On 26 June Victoria finally visited her, finding her 'stretched on a couch looking as thin as anybody can be who is still alive' (Woodham-Smith, 179). Lady Flora lingered for a few more days, dying at two o'clock in the morning of Friday 5 July 1839. The post-mortem, which Lady Flora herself had requested, showed that she had been suffering from a tumour on the liver for several months. She was buried at Loudoun, Ayrshire, on 15 July.

The affair did not end with Lady Flora's death, which the press greeted with fresh excoriation of the queen and the court: one pamphlet, Lady Flora Hastings: her Life and Death, ran through twenty-five editions in the six months after her death. However, when her brother, the marquess of Hastings, published further documents on the case in September, public interest was waning, although the Hastings family maintained their feud with the court for years. Lady Flora's Poems (1841) was edited by her sister Sophia, marchioness of Bute.   K. D. REYNOLDS

Sources C. Woodham-Smith, Queen Victoria: her life and times, 1: 1819–1861 (1972) · E. Longford, Victoria RI (1964) · Burke, Peerage · GM, 2nd ser., 12 (1839), 321 · M. Charlot, Victoria: the young queen (1991) · R. F. Spall, 'The bedchamber crisis and the Hastings scandal: morals, politics and the press at the beginning of Victoria's reign', Canadian Journal of History, 22 (April 1987), 19–39
Archives BL OIOC, papers relating to slander against her and publication of her poems · Hunt. L., corresp. and verses · Mount Stuart Trust, Isle of Bute, corresp. and papers
Likenesses W. & E. Finden, engraving, pubd 1840 (after E. Hawkins), NPG [see illus.] · W. & E. Finden, engravings (after E. Hawkins), BM, NPG · Pearce, silhouette, Royal Collection · lithograph, NPG · portrait, repro. in Woodham-Smith, Queen Victoria

Hastings, Francis, second earl of Huntingdon (1513/14–1560),

magnate, was the eldest of the five sons of George *Hastings, first earl of Huntingdon (1486/7–1544), and his wife, Anne, daughter of Henry Stafford, second duke of Buckingham. When his father, a personal friend of Henry VIII, was made an earl on 8 December 1529, Francis, though still a very young man, was himself summoned to parliament as a baron. In the autumn of 1530 he obtained a reversionary stewardship of the lands of Coventry Priory and stewardships of the lands of Launde Abbey and of the college of the Newarke in Leicester. In 1531 his father entered into negotiations with the countess of Salisbury and Henry, Lord Montague, for Francis's marriage to Katherine Pole, Lord Montague's daughter and coheir, which took place in the summer of the following year. In 1533 Lord Hastings attended the coronation of Anne Boleyn, at

which he became a knight of the Bath; in 1537 he participated at both the baptism of Prince Edward and the funeral of Jane Seymour, and through Cromwell's agency early in 1538 procured a grant of the lands of Burton upon Trent Priory. Despite his close connections with the Pole family he avoided involvement in the alleged plot against the Tudor dynasty for which Lord Montague was executed late in 1538 and the countess of Salisbury in 1541, and in 1539 served in the reception party for Anne of Cleves. He also began taking part in Leicestershire administration, viewing the musters at Shepshed in the spring of 1539, and in the summer of 1541 bore the sword before the king on his visit to Lincoln. He succeeded to the earldom on the death of his father on 24 March 1544, when he was said to be thirty years old.

For the remainder of Henry VIII's reign Huntingdon alternated between local government in Leicestershire and attendance at court where his eldest son, Henry *Hastings, was being educated alongside the young Prince Edward. Soon after the latter's accession Lord Grey of Wilton in the summer of 1548 asked Somerset to dispatch Huntingdon or some other young gentleman to Berwick to aid him in campaigns against the Scots, and the following year the government employed him to quell enclosure riots in Leicestershire. An ally of the earl of Warwick, in the coup d'état of October 1549 he helped conduct Protector Somerset to the Tower and in the same month was admitted a knight of the Garter.

From this time onwards Huntingdon gained rapid promotion. In November 1549 the king made him, 'a brave and hardy man, but not over experienced in war' (CSP Spain, 1547–9, 477), lieutenant-general over the army sent to relieve Boulogne and he spent four ultimately fruitless months in France until given leave to return to England in April 1550. Created lord lieutenant of Leicestershire and Rutland in May 1550, on 4 September that year he was sworn of the privy council, which he then regularly attended for the last two and a half years of the reign. He appeared at the reception for the regent of Scotland on her visit to London in 1551, and accompanied Edward VI on his progress in May 1552. On the disgrace in that year of John Beaumont, master of the rolls, the duke of Northumberland (as Warwick now was) procured for Huntingdon the custody of Beaumont's Leicestershire lands. In May 1553, days after the marriage of Lady Jane Grey to Guildford Dudley, Huntingdon bound himself yet further to Northumberland with the marriage of his own eldest son to Katherine Dudley, the duke's youngest daughter.

When Edward VI died Huntingdon lent Northumberland his full support in his attempt to secure the crown for Lady Jane Grey, with his son joining the forces which set out from London to capture Mary Tudor. When the duke capitulated at Cambridge on 24 July 1553 Huntingdon and his son were sent to the Tower. Their imprisonment, however, proved to be relatively brief; Huntingdon was allowed the liberty of the Tower garden in August and released to house arrest on 12 October, and a month later Mary granted him and Lord Hastings a full pardon. The good offices of his wife and his brother, Sir Edward *Hastings, Mary's master of the horse, did much to accelerate the earl's rehabilitation. Eager to demonstrate his new allegiance as lord lieutenant of Leicestershire, Warwickshire, and Rutland at the time of Wyatt's rebellion in late January 1554, Huntingdon routed the rebels in the midlands and seized the duke of Suffolk on 2 February. In this instance public and private interest coincided and Leicestershire, long divided between the Grey and Hastings families, from this date became a Hastings preserve.

In response to a parliamentary petition in 1554 Mary restored the countess of Huntingdon and her sister Winifred, who had married Thomas Hastings, to the blood and estates of Henry Pole, Lord Montague. Even before the return to England of her uncle, Cardinal Pole, the countess began corresponding with him, among other things inviting him to become godfather to her youngest son, Walter. Huntingdon attended the joint session of parliament at which the cardinal presided over the reconciliation of the nation to the Roman obedience, and in August 1555 he helped escort King Philip to Brussels. In 1556 he received from the queen a confirmation of various Leicestershire offices and in the same year gained an apparently advantageous discharge of debts of almost £2500 to the crown, but he never recovered the political influence he had exercised in the previous reign.

On Mary's death Huntingdon had no difficulty in transferring his loyalty to the new queen, attending with his son some of the debates in the first parliament of the reign. In May 1559 the queen appointed him lord lieutenant of Leicestershire, with permission for his son to deputize for him during his sickness, and in June of the same year master of the hart hounds. Elizabeth's accession meant the restoration of the Dudleys to favour, and in particular Robert Dudley. Adroit as ever at utilizing his connections in high places, Huntingdon in October 1559 began making overtures to the new favourite, who was also Henry Hastings's brother-in-law.

Huntingdon died at Ashby-de-la-Zouch on 20 June 1560 (the date on his monument is a year out), leaving five sons and five daughters, most of them still under age. In addition to the marriage of his eldest son, he had also contracted the alliance of his eldest daughter, Katherine, to Lord Clinton's heir, and that of his second son, George, to a Derbyshire heiress, Dorothy Porte. Moreover, in his will he bequeathed to each of his other sons estates of £60 a year for life, and to his four other daughters £1000 apiece as a dowry. One of them, Frances, subsequently wed the eldest son of the earl of Northampton, and another, Elizabeth, the heir of the earl of Somerset; but despite the Russian ambassador's attempt to obtain Mary Hastings as a bride for his master, Ivan the Terrible, the other daughters Anne and Mary both died unmarried. His fifth son, Sir Francis *Hastings, became a politician and author. The third earl of Huntingdon erected an elaborately carved monument in the chancel of St Helen's Church at Ashby-de-la-Zouch, with life-size figures of his father and mother; the latter survived her husband by sixteen years.

CLAIRE CROSS

Sources PRO, SP10, state papers domestic, Edward VI; SP11, state papers domestic, Mary I; SP12, state papers domestic, Elizabeth I; SP 50, state papers Scotland series I, Edward VI; C54, chancery, close rolls; E150, exchequer, king's remembrancer, inquisitions post mortem series II · BL, Cotton MS Vespasian F.xiii, fol. 117b · BL, Harley MS 3881, fols. 36, 40–42, 44–8 · BL, Egerton MS 2986, fols. 9, 11, 12, 14, 15 · Hunt. L., Hastings papers, HA 10332, 10333, 10336–10341; manorial box various counties and France [for 1545 rental] · Bodl. Oxf., MS Carte 78, fols. 137, 239, 241, 243, 247, 249, 251 · Belvoir Castle, letters, II, 266 · Longleat House, Wiltshire, Dudley MSS 1/86, 1/135 · *LP Henry VIII*, vols. 5–21 · *CSP Spain, 1547–58* · *CSP for., 1547–53; 1559–60* · *CSP Venice, 1534–56* · *CPR, 1547–60* · *APC, 1547–58* · *Report on the manuscripts of the late Reginald Rawdon Hastings*, 4 vols., HMC, 78 (1928–47), vol. 2 · *The manuscripts of his grace the duke of Rutland*, 4 vols., HMC, 24 (1888–1905), vols. 1, 4 · *Calendar of the manuscripts of the most hon. the marquis of Salisbury*, 1, HMC, 9 (1883) · E. Lodge, *Illustrations of British history, biography, and manners*, 1 (1791), 163 · *The diary of Henry Machyn, citizen and merchant-taylor of London, from AD 1550 to AD 1563*, ed. J. G. Nichols, CS, 42 (1848) · W. Turner, *A new booke of spirituall physik for dyverse diseases of the nobilitie and gentlemen of England* (1555) · G. W. Barnard, *The power of the early Tudor nobility* (1985) · H. N. Bell, *The Huntingdon peerage* (1820) · C. Cross, *The puritan earl: the life of Henry Hastings, third earl of Huntingdon* (1966) · D. M. Loades, *Two Tudor conspiracies* (1965) · D. M. Loades, *The reign of Mary Tudor: politics, government and religion in England, 1553–58* (1979) · D. Loades, *John Dudley, duke of Northumberland, 1504–1553* (1996) · E. A. Bond, ed., *Russia at the close of the sixteenth century*, Hakluyt Society, 20 (1856)

Archives Hunt. L. | Belvoir Castle, letters, II, 266 · BL, Cotton MS Vespasian F.xiii, fol. 117b · BL, Egerton MS 2986, fols. 9, 11, 12, 14, 15 · BL, Harley MS 3881, 36, 40, 41, 42, 44, 45, 46, 47, 48 · BL, Lansdowne MS II, 78 · Bodl. Oxf., MS Carte 78, fol. 137 · Longleat House, Wiltshire, Dudley MSS, 1/86, 1/135 · PRO, C 54/499 m. 32 · PRO, E 150/1158/12 · PRO, SP 10/VII/31 · PRO, SP 11/VII/14 · PRO, SP 11/XIII · PRO, SP 11/XIV/2 · PRO, SP 12/XI/33 · PRO, SP 50/IV/33

Likenesses alabaster effigy, St Helen's Church, Ashby-de-la-Zouch, Leicestershire; repro. in Cross, *Puritan earl*, facing p. 14

Wealth at death see estates valued, PRO, E 150/1158/12

Hastings, Sir Francis (*c*.1546–1610), politician and author, fifth son of Francis *Hastings, second earl of Huntingdon (1513/14–1560), military commander, and Katherine Pole (*d*. 1576), daughter of Henry *Pole, Baron Montagu (1492–1539), was still a minor on the death of his father in June 1560. He owed his education to his revered eldest brother, Henry *Hastings, third earl of Huntingdon, who arranged for him to study under Lawrence Humphrey at Magdalen College, Oxford, thereby reinforcing his lifelong commitment to protestantism. He also attended Gray's Inn. When he came of age, Huntingdon granted him the manor of Market Bosworth in Leicestershire and may well have had a hand in his marriage in 1567 to Magdalen (*d*. 1596), widow of Sir George Vernon and daughter and coheiress of Sir Ralph Langford. In Leicestershire he associated himself closely with Anthony Gilby, Huntingdon's preacher at Ashby-de-la-Zouch, and Thomas Sampson, for whom the third earl had found a refuge at Wyggeston's Hospital in Leicester.

On Huntingdon's appointment as president of the council in the north late in 1572 Francis Hastings deputized for him in Leicestershire, combating recusancy and fostering the cause of protestantism generally. A justice of the peace from about 1573, he first represented Leicestershire as a knight of the shire in the parliament of 1571 and thereafter actively participated in every session of every parliament, apart from that of 1572, until his death, attempting in season and out of season to promote the further reformation of the church.

In financial difficulties from the moment he succeeded to the title, Huntingdon found it impossible to supervise his far-flung estates from York, and in 1583 gratefully accepted Hastings's offer to move to Dorset, initially for three years, to act as his representative in the west country. This marked the beginning of Hastings's permanent residence in the south-west. In 1586, in exchange for Market Bosworth, Huntingdon granted his brother manors and lands in the vicinity of North Cadbury, where Hastings rebuilt the manor house. He at once gained a place for himself in Somerset local government, sitting for the county in the parliaments of 1589 and 1593. He was knighted in 1592. The death of Huntingdon in December 1595, followed by that of Lady Hastings on 14 June 1596, robbed his life of much of its purpose; his brother George, the new earl of Huntingdon, had no need of his services, and he could not bear to continue living in Somerset without his wife. So he sold the North Cadbury house and returned for a time to Leicestershire, sharing one of the two county seats with his brother Sir Edward Hastings in the parliament of 1597.

Hastings did not, however, remain long in Leicestershire. His clerical friends begged him to return to Somerset, and a judicious second marriage, to the recently widowed Mary Hannam, daughter of Richard Watkins, brought him by 1598 to Holwell, where he took charge of his new wife's children and their portions. Perhaps because of his temporary absence from the south-west he had to content himself with the borough seat of Bridgwater in the 1601 parliament.

In 1587 Hastings had submitted a 'Christian treatise' to a supportive Thomas Cartwright, and in 1596 circulated in manuscript a long eulogy of the third earl of Huntingdon and Magdalen Hastings; but he did not venture into print until 1598, when, impelled by his detestation of popery, he published *A Watch-Word to All Religious, and True Hearted English-Men*. This provoked the next year *A Temperate Ward-Word* from the Jesuit Robert Parsons. In 1600 Sir Francis retaliated with *An Apologie or Defence of the Watch-Word*, the choleric exchange reaching an impasse in 1602 with Parsons's *The Warn-Word to Sir Francis Hastinges Wast-Word*.

Almost as a matter of course Hastings took his seat as one of the knights for Somerset in parliament in the spring of 1604. Like many forward protestants disappointed by the failure of the Hampton Court conference to countenance substantial further reform of the church and dismayed by the ensuing eviction of nonconforming clergy, at the prompting of some midlands friends, who included Sir Edward Montague and Sir Richard and Sir Valentine Knightley, Hastings composed an appeal on behalf of the dispossessed ministers of Northamptonshire. The petition, signed by forty-five local gentlemen, came before the king in early 1605. James regarded it as a veiled incitement to rebellion and commanded Hastings, Montague, and the Knightleys to appear before the privy council. Hastings readily acknowledged his fault in intruding in

the religious affairs of a county not his own, but stood by the ministers, who he maintained had refused to observe the ceremonies for conscience's sake and not for factious reasons. His resistance did nothing to assuage the king's anger and, some individual sympathizers notwithstanding, the privy council corporately had little choice but to strip him of all his local offices and order his retirement to his house in the country.

Hastings felt his disgrace acutely, but despite numerous appeals to Salisbury, never regained royal favour nor restoration to the commission of the peace, and spent the last five years of his life as a mere private gentleman. Only his seat in parliament remained to him, and there he played as active a part as ever in the sessions of 1606, 1607, and in the first part of that of 1610, still advocating measures to curb recusancy and advance reform in the church. Troubled by debts in his final years, he died intestate at Holwell and was buried alongside his first wife in North Cadbury church on 22 September 1610. He had no children by either of his marriages.   CLAIRE CROSS

Sources *The letters of Sir Francis Hastings, 1574–1609*, ed. C. Cross, Somerset RS, 69 (1969) · M. Bateson and others, eds., *Records of the borough of Leicester*, 3: 1509–1603 (1905) · S. D'Ewes, ed., *A compleat journal of the votes, speeches and debates … throughout the whole reign of Queen Elizabeth*, 2nd edn (1693) · H. Townshend, *Four last parliaments of Queen Elizabeth* (1680) · *APC* · F. Hastings, *A watch-word to all religious, and true hearted English-men* (1598) · R. Parsons, *A temperate ward-word, to the turbulent and seditious wach-word of Sir F. Hastinges* (1599) · F. Hastings, *An apologie or defence of the watch-word against the ward-word* (1600) · R. Parsons, *The warn-word to Sir Francis Hastinges wast-word: conteyning the issue of three former treateses* (1602) · HoP, *Commons, 1558–1603* · C. Cross, *The puritan earl: the life of Henry Hastings, third earl of Huntingdon* (1966) · J. Foster, *The register of admissions to Gray's Inn, 1521–1889, together with the register of marriages in Gray's Inn chapel, 1695–1754* (privately printed, London, 1889) · *JHC*, 1 (1547–1628) · *Notes and Queries for Somerset and Dorset*, 2 (1890–91), 184 · *Report on the manuscripts of the late Reginald Rawdon Hastings*, 4 vols., HMC, 78 (1928–47), vol. 2 · *The parliamentary diary of Robert Bowyer, 1606–1607*, ed. D. H. Willson (1931); repr. (1971) · Bodl. Oxf., MS Carte 78, fol. 177 · *DNB* · inquisition post mortem, PRO, C142/183/58

Archives Alnwick Castle, Northumberland, no. 100 23/2 · Belvoir Castle, Lincolnshire, MS letters 5.95, 134; 9.189; 13.53, 80 · Bodl. Oxf., French Church, Soho Deacons' Account Book 1572–3, fol. 30v · Hunt. L., corresp. and family papers incl. criticism of Marprelate tracts · Hunt. L., MSS, HA 1265, 2380, 4624, 5079, 5086, 5087, 5090, 5091, 5092, 5093, 5096, 5097, 5099, 5101, 5102, 5103, 5719, 6722, 10347, 10356, 13766, 13878, 1546; Leicestershire Box 1 (unindexed); religious MSS box 1 (unindexed); religious MSS box 2 (unindexed); misc. box of letters and other MSS (unindexed); family MSS box 1600–1609; family MSS box 1691–1699 | BL, Harl. MS 3881,fol. 53; Harl. MS 6998, fol. 198; Harl. MS 7188, fol. 94; Egerton MS 2644, fol. 172; Add. MS 33594, fol. 10; Add. MS 5752, fol. 107; Add. MS 8978 fols. 109, 116 · Bodl. Oxf., MS Carte 78, fol. 177; MS Carte 289, fol. 53 · Hatfield House, Cecil MSS, 59/25; 59/26; 68/14; 82/17; 82/87; 85/66, 85/93; 86/69; 89/135; 97/56; 105/102/2; 106/2; 107/142; 110/76; 113/22; 114/37; 125/67; 125/37; 191/140; 203/108; petitions 1938 · Leics. RO, portfolio of letters II 5. 18; Hall MSS III. 150; B R II/5/97/7 · Longleat, Dudley MSS, 1/248; II/191 · PRO, SP 12/106/21; SP 12/117/19; SP 12/118/34; SP 12/150/6; SP 12/229/6; SP 14/216/72; SP 14/216/94; SP 14/12/69; SP 14/12/74; SP 14/49/52; SP 15/32/141; C 82/1363; C 3/289/63; C 66/1430; C 66/1450; C 66/1464; C 66/1495; C 368/471 m. 139; STAC 8/1/40 · Som. ARS, Phelips MS, DD/PH p. 5

Wealth at death £350 9s. 4d.: inventory, PRO STAC 8/1/40

Hastings, Francis John Clarence Westenra Plantagenet, sixteenth earl of Huntingdon [*known as* Jack Huntingdon] (1901–1990), artist and politician, was born on 30 January 1901 in Manchester Square, London, the only son and youngest of three children of Warner Francis John Plantagenet Hastings, fifteenth earl of Huntingdon (*b.* 1868; whom he succeeded in 1939), and his wife, (Maud) Margaret (*d.* 1953), daughter of Sir Samuel Wilson, MP for Portsmouth. He was educated at Eton College and at Christ Church, Oxford, where he played in the university polo team and obtained a third class in modern history in 1923. Descended from George, duke of Clarence, brother of Edward IV, he was the senior legitimate male Plantagenet. But the undoubted hereditary claim of his ancestor Henry Hastings, third earl of Huntingdon, to succeed Elizabeth I did not pass to him, being diverted through a female line. Huntingdon was more interested in an alleged but impossible descent from Robin Hood, described in folklore as the earl of Huntingdon.

In 1925 Jack Huntingdon, who painted under the name John Hastings, married (Maria) Cristina (*d.* 1953), daughter of the wealthy Marchese Casati, head of one of the families which had ruled Milan for centuries. They travelled extensively in Australia and the Pacific, living for a while on the island of Moorea, after which they named their only child, a daughter. In San Francisco the couple met Diego Rivera, the celebrated Mexican communist mural painter. Huntingdon, who had studied at the Slade School of Art after leaving Oxford, became a pupil of Rivera's and learned the technique of fresco. He became Rivera's assistant, branching out into mural painting on his own account. In 1933 he painted a mural depicting dentistry in the Hall of Science at the Chicago World Fair, to accompany a display of George Washington's teeth. Already inclined to be left-wing at Oxford, he was further influenced by Rivera's ideology, and involved himself in the Spanish Civil War, taking medical assistance to republicans. His parents' anger at his marriage to a Roman Catholic foreigner, who shared their son's political outlook and eventually became a communist, was not assuaged by her high aristocratic lineage and there was a long breach during which the couple had little money other than a legacy from his grandmother.

On return to England, Huntingdon in 1935 painted a remarkable 10 feet by 20 feet fresco on a wall in the Marx Memorial Library, Clerkenwell Green, London, entitled *Worker of the Future Upsetting the Economic Chaos of the Present*. Though slightly wooden in the Soviet realist manner, it had distinctive original and pleasing touches. For his friend Lord Faringdon, the eccentric and rich socialist, he painted murals at Buscot Park depicting local Labour Party activities. Despite his far-left phase, he was a second lieutenant (Territorial Army) in the Royal Horse Guards. He was deputy controller of civil defence for Andover from 1941 to July 1945, when he joined Attlee's government as parliamentary secretary at the Ministry of Agriculture and Fisheries. He stayed there until November 1950, when he left politics for the painting he preferred.

As Huntingdon's faith in socialism declined, his paintings abandoned ideology for almost surrealist shapes and writhings of serpents in bright colours, expressing cheerful distaste for conventional restraints, whatever their provenance. He was chairman of the Society of Mural Painters in 1951–8 and his works were widely exhibited. Among his murals are those at Birmingham University (1965), the Women's Press Club in London (1950), and the Casa dello Strozzato, Tuscany (early 1970s). He taught fresco at the Camberwell and Central schools of art in London.

Huntingdon's marriage to the strong-willed Cristina, whose southern temperament did not easily fit with his gentler, more placid English ways, ended with divorce in 1943 and she married Wogan Phillips (previously married to Rosamond Lehmann) who, as the second Baron Milford, was the first communist to take his seat in the House of Lords.

Tall, athletic, and an expert yachtsman, Huntingdon strongly resembled the portrait he owned of the Elizabethan third earl in the reddish colour of his hair and finely delineated features. He played a number of musical instruments well and was a wine connoisseur with impeccable taste. He was the quintessence of a cultured, civilized man and in addition to his talents as a painter he was the author of two intelligently written books, *Commonsense about India* (1942) and *The Golden Octopus* (1928), a book of legends of the south seas. A delightful, convivial companion with a lively, intelligent wit, full of kindness and amusing stories and quick to laugh at himself, he was vague, gentle, courteous, and charming, with exquisite manners sometimes taken for weakness, but he was politely resolute in avoiding inconvenience to himself. When his second wife, the author Margaret *Lane (1907–1994), whom he married in 1944, proposed that her father should live with them, he said nothing but quietly packed his bags ready to move out. She was formerly the wife of Bryan Wallace and daughter of Harry George Lane, newspaper editor, of Vernham Dean, Andover. This second marriage ran less excitingly and more smoothly than the first. From it there were two daughters, of whom one, Lady Selina Hastings, wrote a number of successful biographies. Huntingdon died on 24 August 1990 in a nursing home in Beaulieu, Hampshire. He was succeeded in the earldom by a first cousin once removed, William Edward Robin Hood Hastings Bass (*b.* 1948).

WOODROW WYATT, *rev.*

Sources personal knowledge (1996) · private information (1996) · *The Independent* (10 Sept 1990) · *CGPLA Eng. & Wales* (1990)
Wealth at death £646,334: probate, 20 Dec 1990, *CGPLA Eng. & Wales*

Hastings, Francis Rawdon, first marquess of Hastings and second earl of Moira (1754–1826), army officer and politician, was born in Dublin on 7 December 1754, the eldest of the six sons and the second of the ten children of Sir John Rawdon (1720–1793), fourth baronet, of Rawdon Hall, Yorkshire, and Moira House, co. Down, created Baron Rawdon in the Irish peerage (1750), and his third wife and kinswoman, Lady Elizabeth Hastings (1731–

April 1781 his success in the battle of Hobkirk's Hill against General Greene's superior numbers earned him Cornwallis's admiration. He afterwards retreated to Charlestown. That summer severe illness caused him to leave America, and the vessel in which he sailed was captured by a French cruiser and taken to Brest. A prisoners' exchange enabled his release, from Paris, in December 1781, despite an American bid to extradite and hang him for ordering the execution of the turncoat Isaac Hayne.

When in Ireland, where he obtained the freedom of Dublin and became a volunteer, Rawdon was arraigned on 4 February 1782 by the duke of Richmond in the British House of Lords for hanging Isaac Hayne at Charlestown. Challenging Richmond, he obtained a public apology. His friend Thomas William Coke recalled that he dissuaded him from also challenging Charles Fox, to whom Coke introduced him. On 20 November, ranked colonel (having been lieutenant-colonel commandant of the 105th foot since 1781), he was appointed an aide-de-camp to George III.

Political development From 1781 to 1783 Rawdon was an MP in the Irish parliament, returned in absentia by John O'Neill for Randalstown, but he had little chance to sit and apparently never voted. On 5 March 1783, at Shelburne's instigation, he became Baron Rawdon of Rawdon in the British peerage, and took his seat in the House of Lords on 25 March. His maiden speech opposing Fox's India Bill, on 17 December 1783, adumbrated his leaning towards Pitt, at least until 1787 (the year he became FRS). Malice attributed his defection from Pitt to failure to obtain office to match his ambition.

On 22 May 1787 Rawdon advocated relief of imprisoned debtors; the ensuing bill was lost in 1788. On 20 February 1788 he pleaded for naval officers denied promotion, and on 12 March he objected to infringing East India Company control. A member of the Northern Irish Whig Club, but also of the 'armed neutrality' at Westminster, he championed the prince of Wales's sole regency bid in December 1788. Persisting, he was rebuked by the lord chancellor for his desertion of the government. Rawdon nevertheless objected on 18 February 1789 to the queen's sole control of the royal household. This conduct attached him for life to the prince. He also cultivated the younger royal princes and defended their interests in parliament. In May 1789 he was the duke of York's second in his duel with the duke of Richmond's nephew. That July he was Sir Joshua Reynolds's last portrait sitter. In November 1789 he claimed that he would take office only at the prince's wish. On 10 February 1790, by royal licence, he added Hastings to his surname, having succeeded, with £3000 a year, to most of the estates of his maternal uncle, Francis Hastings, tenth earl of Huntingdon, whose earldom temporarily lapsed, his baronies passing to Rawdon's mother. He was acting grand master, under the prince, for English freemasons (1790–1813). From 1790 to 1792 Rawdon opposed ministerial policy on three fronts. He twice advocated Catholic relief, particularly for Ireland, whose Catholic delegates he welcomed to London; deprecated the bank loan (a published speech) and multiplication of paper money; and

Francis Rawdon Hastings, first marquess of Hastings and second earl of Moira (1754–1826), by George Chinnery

1808), the daughter of Theophilus Hastings, ninth earl of Huntingdon. Styled Lord Rawdon from 1762, when his father became earl of Moira, he was at Harrow School by 1770, and in October 1771 entered University College, Oxford, though he never graduated. Tall and statuesque, in August 1771 he was commissioned ensign in the 15th foot. He attended a Hoxton academy for aspirants to East India Company service, and toured the continent, particularly Italy, with his uncle and mentor Lord Huntingdon.

Army career Having been promoted lieutenant in the 5th foot in 1773, the following year Rawdon went to North America. He was commended for fearlessness in 1775 at Bunker Hill, where two bullets passed through his hat, and obtained a company in the 63rd foot. After seeing further action during the New York, New Jersey, and Philadelphia campaigns as aide-de-camp and adjutant to Sir Henry Clinton, he was promoted lieutenant-colonel in 1778 and appointed adjutant-general to the British forces. In August 1779 he resigned, having fallen out with Clinton by his championing of regular officers against rankers assigned to the provincial corps. His raising of a provincial corps, the volunteers of Ireland, at Philadelphia involved him in further action. He checked the South Carolina rebels until Cornwallis arrived, and was a divisional commander in the battle of Camden on 16 August 1780. On 25 supported immediate abolition of the slave trade. He attempted to exonerate the Society of the Friends of the People from unconstitutional intentions, and he criticized preparations for war against revolutionary France.

Further military and political career Following his father's death in June 1793, Rawdon succeeded as earl of Moira, with an income estimated at £18,000. No longer a royal aide-de-camp, he resumed active service, having been promoted major-general on 12 October 1793. Cornwallis had recommended him for an expeditionary force to Brittany to assist the royalist rebels. Waiting unavailingly for artillery and stores, he embarked in December, but arrived too late; he returned, his force lingering in Cowes until June 1794, when he led a reinforced army of 7000 men to Flanders to assist the duke of York. Again too late, he fought his way across the French lines to join the duke, but returned home, frustrated, in December: his military journal was published (1796). He was again prepared for a Breton expedition, with French émigré cavalry, in July 1795, but following the loss of Quiberon resigned the command beforehand. He continued to associate with, and succour, leading French émigrés. Pitt proposed a British earldom, but he demurred. His debts and expeditionary expenses provoked the sale of his Meath inheritance.

In the House of Lords Moira criticized Earl Fitzwilliam's recall from Ireland (8 May 1795) and the allegedly inadequate financial provision offered the prince (24 June). He tried in 1796 to reconcile the prince with his bride, Princess Caroline, and with the king. On 9 December he criticized the bill against seditious meetings, and on 27 February 1797 he voted against the Austrian subsidy. In March he feared imminent French invasion of Ireland, urging the remedying of Irish discontent—to which he had alerted Chief Secretary Pelham—in order to forestall it. He supported a motion of 27 March to dismiss Pitt's ministry, playing figurehead until June in a neutral party bid to take power, procure peace and retrenchment, and alleviate Irish grievances. He wanted Charles James Fox as premier, but the king objected, pushing the prince, who had offered to go to Ireland as viceroy—probably with Moira as commander-in-chief—into opposition. Lady Holland wrote of Moira:

> he is a conceited, solemn coxcomb, with as much ambition as the coldness of his disposition allows. Since the unpopularity of the Prince of Wales he has been the only man of distinction … who has supported him. He is his adviser and certainly looks forward to being at the head of affairs in this country after the King's death if not before … He is a man of veracity, a quality strictly necessary to him … His politics he conducts so that he may be in power with either side. (*Journal*, 1.165–6)

Moira's concern for Ireland, caricatured by Gillray ('Lord Longbow the alarmist'), inspired speeches at Westminster of 30 May and 22 November 1797 (published), and a motion defeated on 19 February 1798 in Dublin, published alongside the reply, among others, of Lord Clare. Continuing his criticism of the Irish government, he accused the Irish army of illegal methods of repression. On 26 March 1798 he clashed in debate with the marquess of Downshire over the application of military force to disarm the

United Irishmen; in the 1790s he frequently entertained Wolfe Tone and others at his mother's Dublin house. The Ards rebels' last stand was on Moira's estate at Montalto, co. Down (while Moira was in London). He and his mother helped Lord Edward FitzGerald (who had served under him in America), and, fearing reprisals by government forces, he moved his family and library to England. He attempted to have Lord Lieutenant Camden recalled. Although he had recently been promoted lieutenant-general, Moira disclaimed any wish for a military command. On 19 March 1799 he claimed that Anglo-Irish union was worthless without forsaking coercion and reforming the Irish parliament through Catholic relief. Having voted by proxy against union in Dublin, he changed his mind at Westminster on 30 April 1800, hoping it would meet his objectives. He immediately opposed Addington's ministry in 1801. If the king's illness produced a regency, he was expected to be a councillor, if not the framer of a new administration. He had rallied the opposition to his town house to concert measures. He then modified his stance by approving peace preliminaries with France in November 1801, when he was thought, with Charles Grey, to be coming to terms with Addington. Moira approved, as a courtier, the redress of civil-list arrears on 29 March 1802. He opposed renewed restriction of cash payments by the bank (17 and 22 February 1803), but advocated home defence against invasion (9 March), publishing his views. He was then reported to have refused office, singly. French encroachments on the continent seemed to him a far better cause for ending the peace of Amiens and resuming hostilities than Malta. His reputation was such that on 23 October 1803 John Freeman-Mitford, first Baron Redesdale, the lord chancellor of Ireland, described him as 'that wild, wrong-headed man, with a considerable show of talent and much earnestness of manner' (Johnston-Liik, 6.148).

In Scotland In September 1803 Moira was appointed commander-in-chief in Scotland, and in October he was promoted general. He found this laborious, and wrote that, but for the prince, he would readily give up public life. The following May he became colonel of the 27th Inniskilling foot. He was narrowly defeated in the election for Glasgow University in December 1803. In 1804, summoned by the prince, he joined the combined opposition to Addington, expecting a cabinet place in a comprehensive ministry, and snubbing Addington's competitive offer. Pitt's exclusive return to office thwarted his scheme to detach Lord Melville's party in Scotland, assiduously cultivated by him. He opposed Pitt's Additional Forces Bill on 25 May, advocating more regulars, although he praised Scotland's volunteers. On 12 July 1804 he married Flora Mure-Campbell (1780–1840), countess of Loudoun in her own right, the only child of James Mure-Campbell, fifth earl of Loudoun. They had two sons, the elder of whom died in infancy, and four daughters, among them Lady Flora Elizabeth *Hastings. A few months later Moira was reportedly offered Dublin Castle or the Foreign Office if Pitt succeeded, with his help, in reconciling the king and prince over Princess Charlotte's education. This exasperating process required frequent mediation, but he declined office, as well as the governorship of Stirling Castle, in December 1804. The prince, in April 1805, desired him to resign the Scottish command, but the king's contrary wish detained him, though he returned to the Lords to advocate Irish Catholic relief.

In political office In Lord Grenville's January 1806 'ministry of all the talents' Moira was expected to become Irish viceroy, but the prince, to keep him near, approved on 8 February his becoming master-general of the ordnance, with a cabinet seat and privy councillorship. On 12 February the constableship and lord lieutenancy of the Tower of London were added. His colleague William Windham expected Moira to assume the home command in case of invasion. He failed, however, to become ministerial manager for Scotland, where his military command ceased, though he acted as masonic grand master from 1806 to 1808. Lord Holland, believing Moira's pretensions in Scotland had sunk those of Lauderdale, recalled that patronage was lavished on him and the prince to the government's detriment. Moira found little to do at the ordnance, but defended Windham's military reforms, particularly substitution of limited for life service on 13 June 1806. For the prince he investigated Princess Caroline's alleged indiscretions, of which the cabinet acquitted her. On Fox's death he declined the Foreign Office. In cabinet on 7 January 1807 he shocked Grenville by advocating revolution in South America. Lady Holland thought his wish to assume Fox's mantle distanced him from Grenville. He supported the abolition of the slave trade. The ministry fell in March 1807, and Moira resigned from the ordnance office.

Out of office Moira assured Lord Holland that he would shortly have resigned, even if ministers had retained office; he wished to give up both the military and party politics. Royal opposition to Catholic relief vexed him, although in cabinet he had favoured procrastination in order to stay in office, and he argued in debate on 26 March that ministers were justified in refusing to forswear a measure conciliating Irish loyalty in wartime. He defended the Irish Catholics' right to press their claims on 13 April. Although Moira informed Holland on 27 April 1807 that he adhered only to the prince, he was a critic of the Portland ministry, particularly of the imprudent—if well-conducted—Copenhagen expedition, their military organization, and their failure to defend reversionary appointment to office. His mother's death in April 1808 brought him English baronies vested in the Hastings family. He therefore took his seat as Baron Hastings on 19 January 1809, when he blamed ministers' faulty planning for the convention of Cintra, although he had agreed in a court of inquiry against prosecuting the conduct of the British generals. Privately he was critical, particularly of Sir Arthur Wellesley, and condemned Sir Harry Burrard's omission from the vote of thanks on Vimeiro. On 25 January he described Corunna as the extinction of British

hopes in Spain. He supported a censure motion on 7 February, and on 21 April deplored the lack of co-ordination with patriotic Spaniards. Rumours of his obtaining a command arose when the duke of York faced forfeiture of the command-in-chief because of the scandal of his mistress Mary Anne Clarke (whom Moira had allegedly tried to buy off) receiving bribes for supposedly influencing military promotions. He understood the unlikelihood of his obtaining a foreign expedition unless as York's accomplice. He joined Grenville on 23 January 1810 in condemning the stagnant war effort in a speech he thought ill-reported, and spoke again on 22 February and 8 June.

After allowing time, ostensibly as the prince's spokesman, though without consultation, for the ailing king's recovery (15 November 1810), Moira advocated a regency (29 November and 27 December). In January 1811 he defended the regent's interests, opposing restrictions. He had drafted much of the prince's reply to the regency offer, and it was expected that if this produced a fresh administration he would go to Ireland as viceroy. He was ready for this, regardless of the ministry's composition, urging the regent to appoint him and Lord Wellesley to office. The regent, refusing Wellesley, offered to make Moira a secretary of state, but he declined. By August 1811, when the regent was happy to send him to Dublin, he refused that too if Spenser Perceval remained premier— though Perceval was ready to appoint him. Moira had, on 18 February, opposed suppression of Irish public meetings. While the regent avoided him and any change, Moira distanced himself from the opposition leaders. In debate he welcomed the victory of Albuera and resumed his championship of imprisoned debtors, which he had previously undertaken in 1793, 1797, 1801, 1806, 1808, and 1809 (he finally obtained some success in 1812), and as doggedly supported the compensation claims of John Palmer, the Post Office reformer.

In January 1812 Moira tried to reconcile the regent and the opposition leaders: a dukedom for this was rumoured, but the regent merely sought his mediation. On 28 February he refused the Garter, hinting at political betrayal by the prince: they were estranged until May. Lord Wellesley, who had joined, but resolved to quit, the ministry, thought Moira should head a new administration. He had insisted on Irish Catholic relief in debate on 31 January, having backed their appeal to the regent. On 5 March he advocated a new ministry to propitiate discontent, and on 19 March he supported a motion calling for change, deploring ministerial contempt for Catholic aspirations at a time when Ireland furnished half the country's forces. Following Perceval's assassination (11 May 1812) and parliamentary pressure for a stronger administration, he wrote to Wellesley on 23 May defining his objectives as Irish Catholic relief and support of Spanish patriots against Bonaparte. Wellesley, then the regent's first choice for premier, conveyed this information to the prince and consulted Moira, but found the opposition leaders unamenable.

The regent, having composedly received Moira four days before at Wellesley's instigation, turned to him in tears on 26 May. According to Creevey, Moira described the plight of the country, of which the regent admitted ignorance. After another meeting with him, Moira met Grenville and Grey at Wellesley's house, negotiating three days running. Moira still did not look beyond a cabinet seat under Wellesley, who now withdrew. Moira deplored this in the Lords on 3 June, and on the 5th added that the regent was not responsible for the animosities of which Wellesley complained. However, prodded by Grenville, Moira refused to elaborate in Wellesley's absence, a move calculated to encourage renewed negotiation. After a speech from Grey he pointed to his own support of opposition for seven years, without explaining that the regent had commissioned him to form a ministry. Knowing that Wellesley, though supportive, would not take second place to him, he tried to conciliate Grenville and Grey. After ascertaining his credentials they required, on 6 June, changes in the regent's household to remove the Hertford clan. Moira demurred, and turned desperately to Lord Melville and Canning, and more amenable oppositionists. On 8 June he admitted failure, and the regent reverted to Liverpool, who had refused Moira's overture from doubts about Catholic relief. Samuel Whitbread reported that Moira's programme had embraced revocation of orders in council, reconciliation with America, and retrenchment, possibly parliamentary reform. It was at once supposed that the regent had intended the outcome, Moira being his dupe. In debate Moira denied this, but offered conditional support to Liverpool. He published the negotiations, with the regent's consent. He accepted the Garter on 12 June 1812 and confirmed the truth of the publication, maintaining that he disliked ejecting office-holders from non-political departments. To his cousin Charles Hastings, Moira wrote that the need to vote the allies' subsidy had curtailed negotiations, but he also escaped admitting that there was inadequate support for Catholic relief and giving offence to the regent and the Hertfords. He nevertheless believed that the opposition would eventually succeed.

A journey to India On 1 July 1812 Moira supported Wellesley's narrowly defeated motion for Catholic relief, warning that ministerial policies limped fifty years behind the times. But by now he knew that not even the premiership would solve his financial problems, and on 31 August he confided that he could not afford to be Irish viceroy. In September he was reported to be going to India as governor-general, and on 18 October his appointment, instigated by the regent, was confirmed. Lady Charlotte Bury alleged that this 'honourable banishment' arose from the regent's inability to 'bear to have him near his person', having for years accepted unstinted financial assistance from him, unrepaid. 'Vanity and ambition were his only flaws, but his attachment to the Regent was sincere, chivalrous, and of a romantic kind' (*Diary of a Lady-in-Waiting*, 1.55). Nevertheless his bankruptcy was also political. In approving the vote of thanks to his predecessor in India, he had stated on 10 January 1812 that he disliked adding colonies to the empire while the enemy remained undefeated in Europe. Although he was appointed both

commander-in-chief and governor-general, he was unaware that Sir George Nugent, commander in Bengal, would remain in place, which he did until December 1814. Before leaving, Moira presented a Galway Catholic relief petition on 4 March 1813, and on the 22nd denied Whitbread's allegations that he had secretly concocted evidence damaging the princess of Wales and published anonymous statements against her. He was entangled too in another royal imbroglio, having, to the queen's annoyance, procured a member of her household as governess to Princess Charlotte.

Moira took leave of the regent by letter on 22 April 1813, having sailed for India with his family in the man-of-war *Stirling Castle* two days before. He blamed Lord Melville for his protracted voyage as part of a trade convoy, for he reached Calcutta only on 4 October. Once there he restored etiquette, in Dublin Castle style, to the viceregal household, changed by his predecessor's informalities. He expected no trouble, except on the borders. On 6 December he wrote to the regent fearing that they would never meet again, but discounted subsequent reports that the regent was maligning him. Following Gurkha encroachments on Oudh, on 1 November 1814 he declared war on Nepal. Sir David Ochterlony defeated the Gurkhas at Mukwanpoor (February 1816), and they made peace in March 1816. Moira received parliamentary thanks on 6 February 1817, and on the 13th was created Viscount Loudoun, earl of Rawdon, and marquess of Hastings. He had meanwhile persuaded the India Board of Control under Canning that the Pindaris, encroaching on Hyderabad, should be checked, as well as their Maratha backers. The East India Company's directors hesitated, but further Pindari aggression provoked the Calcutta council into approving military action. In late 1817, with Indian allies, Hastings advanced to Cawnpore, commanding the central division himself. The peshwa at Poona, after making peace in 1816, resumed hostilities in November 1817; but following his defeat, and that of the raja of Nagpur and the army of Indore by Hastings's commanders, the governor-general was able to offer the East India Company both Poona and its choice of other territories. This was beyond his remit, but the success of the Third Anglo-Maratha War effectively extended British dominion in India. Hastings was awarded the GCB on 14 October 1818, then the GCH, and in 1819 was thanked by the company and by parliament. The company awarded him £60,000 to purchase an estate administered for his family by trustees. In 1819 he supported Raffles's securing of Singapore for the British.

Despite the cost of his campaigns, Hastings boasted that the company's revenues had multiplied threefold and could easily cover the outlay. He had, however, in 1816 suspended a statutory prohibition of loans to Indian princes by British subjects in order to accommodate William Palmer & Co. and the nizam of Hyderabad. When a new loan, with large interest, was made in 1820, the company directors ordered an end to it. Hastings was implicated because a ward of his was married to Palmer's partner, Sir William

Rumbold. Always touchy about aspersions on his integrity, he resigned in 1821. Writing to George IV's secretary in advance, on 11 November 1820, he blamed Canning's intrigues for company hostility to him. This letter was to be handed over by a trusted emissary, at his discretion. Canning's removal from the India board did not affect Hastings's resolve, but in June 1821 he switched his retirement motive to domestic considerations. When Doyle eventually proffered the letter in November, the king treated it as stale news, but neither he nor Liverpool warmed to Doyle's verbal suggestion that Hastings should become a duke, though Liverpool approved his becoming ambassador to Austria and receiving parliamentary thanks for his services. The king suggested the Paris embassy. Canning was appointed his successor in India in March 1822, but delayed his departure until he could exonerate himself personally to Hastings, and so never went. Hastings received the company's thanks in May 1822, and left India on 1 January 1823. His debts soon drove him to the continent, but he was mollified by appointment as governor and commander-in-chief of Malta on 22 March 1824. He delayed departure, hoping for financial redemption. Douglas Kinnaird appealed to the company, but the general court of proprietors called for papers relating to the Hyderabad loan, which were not printed until 1825, whereupon, in March, the court voted them a blot on Hastings's reputation. He was by then in Malta, where he published his refutation. He returned home and on 17 June 1825 introduced a bill to regulate the interest rate on loans in India, then well above the 12 per cent ceiling previously fixed in 1773, but inapplicable to British residents under native princes. The bill lost, he returned to Malta a broken man, having made his will. A riding accident exacerbated his hernia weeks before his death, on 28 November 1826, aboard HMS *Revenge* in Baia Bay, Naples. He was buried in Malta, his right hand cut off, at his request, to be placed in his widow's coffin.

Financial problems and reputation Hastings was habitually extravagant, generous, and hospitable, and spent beyond his large income. In the late eighteenth century he sold some of his Irish landholdings, and by 1807 the Moira estate was no longer his, unbeknown to his wife; an arrangement was afoot to pay debts of £270,000 and secure him an adequate allowance, which he hoped to enlarge. In 1811, still insolvent, he borrowed from bankers and brokers. The following year he was reported to be about to abscond to Germany, and in 1813 his London house was sold. In 1817 he reduced his expenditure in India. His wife, returning to England in 1816, when even Princess Charlotte felt sorry for her, lingered there until 1819. His requirements allegedly provoked, inadvertently, a financial scandal and the ruin of Sir Gerard Noel's bank. Hastings was honourable and offered interest on unpaid bills, had his life insured repeatedly as a security, and disclaimed the departing Nugent's commander's salary in Bengal. Nevertheless his extravagance was, effectively, his worst characteristic. More engaging were his hallmark courtesy and his ready assistance in redeeming others humiliated by their misfortunes or vices. However, his

championship of imprisoned debtors served to highlight his own parliamentary immunity from arrest. Overconfident of his nurtured abilities, he encountered a series of fiascos, military and political, and thwarted ambitions. He was therefore jealous of the professional triumphs of Cornwallis and Wellington, and was outmatched by the political nerve of Pitt, Grenville, Grey, and Canning. In 1858 his daughter Lady Bute published a journal he kept in India until 1818 for family edification: it simplified public affairs, but showed a certain affection for India, where Hastings had interested himself in improving administration, justice, education, and freedom of the press: he valued publicity. His marquessate became extinct on the death of his grandson, the fourth marquess, in November 1868.

ROLAND THORNE

Sources *Report on the manuscripts of the late Reginald Rawdon Hastings*, 4 vols., HMC, 78 (1928–47), vol. 3 (1934), pp. 154–310 · *GM*, 1st ser., 97/1 (1827), 85 · *DNB* · J. Ross of Bladenburg, *The marquis of Hastings* (1893) · E. M. Johnston-Liik, *History of the Irish parliament, 1692–1800*, 6 vols. (2002), 146–8 · *The correspondence of George, prince of Wales, 1770–1812*, ed. A. Aspinall, 8 vols. (1963–71) · *The later correspondence of George III*, ed. A. Aspinall, 5 vols. (1962–70), vol. 1, pp. 434, 548; vol. 2, pp. 963, 975, 1175, 1266, 1277, 1293, 1296, 1406, 1565; vol. 3, p. 1688; vol. 4, pp. 2914, 2991, 2994 · *The letters of King George IV, 1812–1830*, ed. A. Aspinall, 3 vols. (1938) · *The correspondence of King George the Third from 1760 to December 1783*, ed. J. Fortescue, 6 vols. (1927–8), vol. 4, p. 2892; vol. 5, p. 3523; vol. 6, p. 4151 · Cobbett, *Parl. hist.*, vols. 24–36 · *Hansard 1* (1803–13), vols. 2–25 · *Hansard 2* (1825), vol. 13 · *The manuscripts of J. B. Fortescue*, 10 vols., HMC, 30 (1892–1927), vols. 1, 3, 6–10 · Farington, *Diary*, 3.927; 8.2884, 3175; 9.3466, 3489; 11.4073, 4085; 12.4221, 4365; 13.4617; 14.5090 · *The Creevey papers*, ed. H. Maxwell, 1 (1903), vol. 1, pp. 113, 146, 149, 157–61, 164, 165 · *The journal and correspondence of William, Lord Auckland*, ed. [G. Hogge], 4 vols. (1861–2), vol. 1, p. 327; vol. 2, pp. 259, 264; vol. 4, pp. 245, 370, 372, 378 · Walpole, *Corr.*, 12.66, 72, 84, 156; 35.388, 466 · *The journal of Elizabeth, Lady Holland, 1791–1811*, ed. earl of Ilchester [G. S. Holland Fox-Strangways], 2 vols. (1908), vol. 1, pp. 165–6; vol. 2, pp. 137, 195–6, 222, 268, 269 · H. R. Vassall, Lord Holland, *Memoirs of the whig party during my time*, ed. H. E. Vassall, Lord Holland, 2 vols. (1852–4), vol. 1, pp. 227–230 · H. R. V. Fox, third Lord Holland, *Further memoirs of the whig party, 1807–1821*, ed. Lord Stavordale (1905), 139–49 · *The diary of a lady-in-waiting*, ed. A. Stewart, 2 vols. (1908), vol. 1, p. 55 · *The diary and correspondence of Charles Abbot, Lord Colchester*, ed. Charles, Lord Colchester, 3 vols. (1861), vol. 1, pp. 499, 531; vol. 2, pp. 249, 255, 259, 370, 384, 424, 601; vol. 3, pp. 29–32, 240, 316, 332 · A. Stirling, ed., *Coke of Norfolk and his friends* (1912), 19, 253–4, 492 · *The last journals of Horace Walpole*, ed. Dr Doran, rev. A. F. Steuart, 2 vols. (1910), 364, 377, 491 · *The private journal of the marquess of Hastings*, ed. marchioness of Bute, 2 vols. (1858) · *The diaries of Sylvester Douglas, Lord Glenbervie*, ed. F. Bickley (1928), vol. 1, pp. 27, 184; vol. 3, pp. 12, 119, 121 · *Lord Granville Leveson Gower: private correspondence, 1781–1821*, ed. Castalia, Countess Granville [C. R. Leveson-Gower], 2nd edn, 2 vols. (1916), vol. 1, pp. 286, 484, 497; vol. 2, pp. 42, 173, 177 · M. Roberts, *The whig party, 1807–1812* (1939), 391–3 · *The manuscripts of the earl of Carlisle*, HMC, 42 (1897), 546, 550, 585, 591 · *Report on manuscripts in various collections*, 8 vols., HMC, 55 (1901–14), vol. 6, pp. 203, 205 [Knox] · *Report on the manuscripts of Earl Bathurst, preserved at Cirencester Park*, HMC, 76 (1923), 166, 348, 363, 393, 409, 411, 420, 439, 468–79, 586, 612 · *The journal of Henry Edward Fox*, ed. earl of Chichester (1923), 206, 334 · *The diary of Henry Hobhouse, 1820–1827*, ed. A. Aspinall (1947), 79, 86 · *The manuscripts of his grace the duke of Rutland*, HMC, 24 (1888–1905), vol. 3, pp. 6, 400 · *The correspondence of Edmund Burke*, ed. T. W. Copeland and others, 10 vols. (1958–78), vol. 7, pp. 498, 518; vol. 8, pp. 238, 269; vol. 9, p. 292 · *The Glenbervie journals*, ed. W. Sichel (1910), 92 · A. P. W. Malcomson, ed., *18th century Irish* official papers on Great Britain, private collections, 2 (1990), 293, 384, 390 · W. Leeky, History of Ireland in the 18th century (1913), vol. 3, pp. 438, 483, 487; vol. 4, pp. 44, 204; vol. 5, pp. 284, 409 · R. McDowell, Ireland in the age of imperialism and revolution, 1760–1800 (1979), 535, 587, 596–7, 641 · J. A. Froude, The English in Ireland in the eighteenth century, 3 vols. (1872–4), vol. 3 · M. George, ed., Catalogue of political and personal satires in the British Library, 7 (1942), 9184 · W. B. Willcox, Portrait of a general: Sir Henry Clinton in the war of independence (1964), 284–8 · N. Penny, ed., Reynolds (1986), 327 [exhibition catalogue, Royal College of Art, 1986]

Archives BL OIOC, corresp. and papers relating to India, Home misc. series · BL OIOC, corresp. and papers relating to India, MS Eur. F 206 · BL OIOC, letters on British embassy to China, MS Eur. F 140 · Cleveland Public Library, corresp. and papers relating to India · Duke U., Perkins L., journal · Hunt. L., corresp. and papers · JRL, corresp. relating to Pindari War · Mount Stuart Trust, Isle of Bute, corresp. and papers · NRA priv. coll., corresp. · priv. coll., letters from India [copies] · PRO, corresp., PRO 30/55 · Royal Arch. | BL, letters to Lord Bathurst, loan 57 · BL, corresp. with Sir Rufane Donkin, Add. MS 23759 · BL, corresp. with Lord Grenville, Add. MS 58962 · BL, corresp. with Warren Hastings, Add. MSS 29187–29191, 29233–29234 · BL, corresp. with Lord Holland, Add. MS 51533 · BL, corresp. with earls of Liverpool, Add. MSS 38213–38309, 38410, 38578, passim · BL, letters to earls of Liverpool, loan 72 · BL, corresp. with Sir Hudson Lowe, Add. MSS 20118–20150, passim · BL, letters to Sir Thomas Munro, Eur. F 151 · BL, letters to Lord Spencer · BL, corresp. with Lord Wellesley, Add. MSS 37296–37297 · BL, corresp. with William Windham, Add. MSS 37874–37875, 37888 · BL, letters to J. Young, Add. MS 38517 · BL OIOC, corresp. with Elphinstone family, MS Eur. F 87–89 · BL OIOC, letters to Sir Thomas Munro, MS Eur. F 151 · BL OIOC, letters to Sir George Robinson, MS Eur. F 142 · Castle Forbes, co. Longford, Granard MSS · Duke U., Perkins L., letters to Sir John Macra · Dysart House, Rosslyn MSS · Leics. RO, letters to J. W. Dalby · Morgan L., letters to Sir James Murray-Pulteney · NA Scot., letters to Sir Alexander Hope · NL Ire., letters to T. Kemmis · NRA priv. coll., letters to William Adam · NRA priv. coll., letters to Sir John Sinclair · PRO, corresp. with Lord Cornwallis, PRO 30/11 · PRO, corresp. with George Napier and Sarah Napier, PRO 30/64 · U. Durham L., corresp. with second Earl Grey · Elphinstone MSS

Likenesses T. Gainsborough, oils, c.1784, São Paulo Library, Brazil · J. Reynolds, oils, 1784, Royal Collection · J. Jones, mezzotint, pubd 1792 (after oil painting by J. Reynolds, c.1789–1790), NG Ire. · J. Collyer, stipple, pubd 1794 (after E. C. Stuart), NG Ire. · J. Hoppner, oils, 1794, Royal Collection · J. Hoppner, oils, 1795, Lady Lever Art Gallery, Port Sunlight, Merseyside · J. Gillray, stipple and line with watercolour, pubd 1801 (The Union Club), NG Ire. · attrib. H. D. Hamilton, oils, c.1801, NPG · J. Nollekens, marble bust, 1802, Holkham Hall, Norfolk · J. S. Harvie, watercolour miniature, 1804, Scot. NPG · H. Landseer, stipple, pubd 1804 (after J. Hoppner), NG Ire. · M. A. Shee, oils, 1804, Royal Military Academy, Sandhurst · G. Clint, mezzotint, pubd 1805 (after M. A. Shee), NG Ire. · J. Nollekens, marble bust, 1810, Royal Collection · H. Raeburn, oils, c.1813, NAM · J. Jones, stipple, pubd 1815 (after oil painting by J. Reynolds, c.1789), NG Ire. · J. Atkinson, pen-and-ink drawing, 1820, NPG · H. Raeburn, oils, c.1823, NAM · G. Chinnery, oils, Raj Bhavan, Calcutta, Government of West Bengal · G. Chinnery, portrait, HSBC Group Archives, London, Midland Bank archives [see illus.] · J. Heath, stipple (after oil painting by H. D. Hamilton, exh. 1804), NG Ire.; repro. in J. Barrington, Historic anecdotes and secret memoirs (1809–15) · J. Lough, marble statue (posthumous), Malta · P. Maguire, stipple (after oil painting by J. Reynolds, c.1790), NG Ire.; repro. in Universal Magazine (1791) · T. Mitchell, miniature (after M. A. Shee), NPG · S. Percy, wax, NG Ire. · W. Ridley, stipple, NG Ire.; repro. in European Magazine (1811) · M. A. Shee, oils, NG Ire. · R. Staines, stipple (after J. Reynolds), NG Ire.; repro. in European Magazine (1791) · stipple, NG Ire.; repro. in Dublin Magazine (1813) · watercolour, Scot. NPG

Hastings, Frank Abney (1794–1828), naval officer in the Greek service, was the younger son of Lieutenant-General Sir Charles Hastings, baronet, an illegitimate son of Francis Hastings, earl of Huntingdon. He entered the navy when about eleven years old, and was present at Trafalgar on board the Neptune. During his fifteen years of service he visited every quarter of the globe, and was finally sent to the West Indies, in command of the Kangaroo, for surveying. Entering Port Royal harbour, Jamaica, he reportedly brought his ship to anchor in an unseamanlike way. The flag captain of the admiral's ship consequently so insulted him that (once on half pay) Hastings challenged him to a duel. The admiral reported this, and Hastings was dismissed from the service in 1820. He resolved to take service under a foreign power. After living in France to learn the language he sailed from Marseilles on 12 March 1822 to join the Greeks. He reached Hydra on 3 April, and was welcomed by the brothers Jakomaki and Manoli Tombazes, then commanding the Greek fleet. On 3 May 1822 this fleet, which was poorly manned, sailed from Hydra with Hastings on the Themistocles as volunteer. The value of his services was soon evident, and he built a furnace on board for heating shot. He first became popular among the Greek sailors by saving the Tombazes' corvette off Cape Baba, north of Mitylene, which had accidentally got within range of Turkish guns. When the naval campaign ended, Hastings joined the siege of Nauplia, and assisted in the defence of the little Greek-held port of Burdzi. He raised a company of fifty men, armed and equipped at his own expense. During part of 1823 he served in Crete as commander of the artillery, but left the island in the autumn because of a violent fever.

Hastings recommended the construction of armed steam vessels to give the Greeks command of the sea, and in the latter part of 1824 he went to England to purchase steamers which were to be armed under his direction. In May 1826 the Karteria departed for Greece and was put under his command. This steamer, the first seen in Greece, was armed with 68-pound guns, firing shells and red-hot shot. Her crew consisted of Englishmen, Swedes, and Greeks. After a troubled passage she arrived in September. In February 1827 Hastings co-operated with Thomas Gordon (1788–1841), and attempted to relieve Athens, then besieged by the Turkish commander Reshid, by steaming into Piraeus and shelling the enemy's camp. His attack was successful, but the city was forced to capitulate to the Turks on 5 June. Hastings interrupted Turkish communications between Volo and Oropus, and captured several vessels. At Tricheri he destroyed a Turkish man-of-war, but the Karteria suffered severely, and was obliged to go to Poros for repairs. On 29 September 1827 Hastings destroyed Turkish ships, in the Bay of Salona. Ibrahim Pasha, who was at Navarino, prepared to attack him, but the allied fleets closely blockaded his fleet and on 20 October 1827 annihilated it at the battle of Navarino.

On 29 December 1827 Hastings took Vasiladi, the key to the fortifications of Missolonghi. He released the prisoners he captured, together with the Turkish governor.

Capodistrias arrived in Greece as president, and Hastings, disgusted with the negligent conduct of the war, proposed to resign. In 1828 Hastings's pamphlet *Memoir on the Use of Shells, Hot-Shot and Carcass Shells from Ships' Artillery* was published in London. In May 1828 he resumed active operations in command of a small squadron in western Greece. On the 25th he was wounded in an attack on Anatolikon, and amputation of his left arm was believed necessary. He sailed for Zante in search of a competent surgeon, but tetanus set in and, on 1 June 1828 he died on board the *Karteria* in Zante harbour. Hastings's service in the Greek cause demonstrated both technical expertise and strategic vision. George Finlay, his friend and the historian of the war, described him as the best foreign officer who embarked in the Greek cause, and the only foreigner in whose character and deeds there were the elements of true greatness.

W. R. MORFILL, *rev.* ANDREW LAMBERT

Sources W. St Clair, *That Greece might still be free* (1972) · G. Finlay, *History of the Greek revolution*, 2 vols. (1861) · D. Dakin, *British and American philhellenes during the War of Greek Independence, 1821–1833* (1955) · D. K. Brown, *Before the ironclad* (1990) · C. M. Woodhouse, *The battle of Navarino* (1965) · G. Finlay, 'Biographical sketch of Frank Abney Hastings', *Blackwood*, 58 (1845), 496–520
Archives BL, letters to J. C. Hobhouse, Add. MSS 36461–36464 · British School at Athens, corresp., journals, and papers · NA Scot., letters to Thomas Cochrane, tenth earl of Dundonald
Likenesses engraving, repro. in St Clair, *That Greece might still be free*, p. 295

George Hastings, first earl of Huntingdon (1486/7–1544), by Ambrosius Benson

Hastings, George, first earl of Huntingdon (1486/7–1544), magnate, was the son of Edward, second Baron Hastings (*c.*1465–1506), and Mary, Baroness Hungerford (*d. c.*1530), granddaughter of Robert, third Baron Hungerford. Born four years after the execution of his grandfather, William, Lord Hastings, the principal councillor of Edward IV, he was created a knight of the Bath at the wedding of Prince Arthur to Katherine of Aragon in November 1501, suggesting close court connections from an early age. Five years later, still a minor, he succeeded as third Baron Hastings on the death of his father on 9 November 1506, being summoned to parliament in October of the following year. In June 1507 he was said to be twenty years old. In December 1509 he married Anne Stafford, daughter of Henry, second duke of Buckingham, and from this date if not earlier actively participated in many court celebrations. He served in the vanguard of the royal army when Henry VIII invaded France in 1513, and in 1516 had to answer in Star Chamber for displaying too many of his servants in livery at a meeting with the Scottish queen dowager. In 1520 he accompanied the king to the Field of Cloth of Gold, was present in 1522 at the signing of the treaty of Windsor between the king and the emperor, and a year later took part in Suffolk's expedition to France.

In addition to stewardships of the lands of local monasteries his developing friendship with the king brought Hastings a number of grants from the crown which included the manors of Enderby (1510) and Evington (1527). Both were in Leicestershire, which his grandfather,

with his castle at Ashby-de-la-Zouch and fortified manor house at Kirby Muxloe, had made the main power base of the family. However, George Hastings seems to have preferred his mother's estate at Stoke Poges, Buckinghamshire, because of its greater proximity to the court. When on 8 December 1529 he was elevated to the earldom of Huntingdon his family at last attained a title commensurate with its standing. In 1531 Huntingdon set in train negotiations with the countess of Salisbury and Henry, Lord Montague, for the marriage of Lord Montague's eldest daughter and coheir, Katherine Pole, to his eldest son, Francis *Hastings, later obtaining Lord Montague's other daughter, Winifred, as a wife for one of his younger sons, Thomas Hastings; early in 1538 the earl's debts caused him to seek an alteration in the terms of the settlement. In 1536, moreover, he procured the marriage of his daughter Dorothy to Richard Devereux, son of Lord Ferrars.

During Cromwell's supremacy Huntingdon frequently sought his favour, particularly over legal suits concerning the inheritance of his mother. In 1537 he sold some of his Oxfordshire lands to Cromwell, and when in residence in Leicestershire reported to the king's minister on possible instances of sedition in the county. As a peer of the realm he took part in the trials of Lord Dacre in June 1534, of Sir Thomas More in July of the following year, and of Anne Boleyn in May 1536. The Pilgrimage of Grace provided him with the opportunity of making his most signal demonstration of loyalty to the monarchy. At Ashby-de-la-Zouch in early October 1536, when news came of the risings in the north, he was swift to indicate his readiness to raise troops against the king's rebellious subjects, and together with the earls of Shrewsbury and Rutland joined the forces headed by the duke of Norfolk, remaining in Yorkshire until the dissemination of the royal pardon in December.

Despite Sir Geoffrey Pole's attempt to implicate him in the alleged plot against the crown which resulted in the execution of Lord Montague late in 1538 and the countess of Salisbury three years later, Huntingdon survived the crisis unscathed, retaining his office as a servant of Prince Edward and his wife that of a servant of Princess Mary. About this time a Spanish observer dismissed him as a courtier 'of great power, little discretion and less experience' (*LP Henry VIII*, 13/2 no. 732).

Huntingdon was appointed to levy the subsidy in Leicestershire in 1543, and early in 1544 he and his son Francis were commissioned to raise troops for the invasion of France, but by this date the earl had become too infirm to face further military service. He died on 24 March 1544 with debts approaching £10,000 (apparently caused by the expense of court life and the need to provide for a large family), and was buried in the church of his manor of Stoke Poges. He was survived by his wife.

CLAIRE CROSS

Sources HA deeds, Hunt. L., Hastings papers · exchequer, inquisitions post mortem series II, PRO, E 150/1146/5 · chancery, inquisitions post mortem series II, C 142/70/1 · BL, Harley MSS 3881, fols. 29–37, 40; 4774, fol. 102; Cotton MS, Vespasian, F.xiii, fol. 91v · Bodl. Oxf., MS Carte 78, fols. 180, 182 · *LP Henry VIII* · *CPR, 1495–1509* · *Report on the manuscripts of the late Reginald Rawdon Hastings*, 4 vols., HMC, 78 (1928–47), vols. 1–2 · *Sixth report*, HMC, 5 (1877–8) · H. N. Bell, *The Huntingdon peerage*, 2nd edn (1821) · G. W. Bernard, *The power of the early Tudor nobility: a study of the fourth and fifth earls of Shrewsbury* (1985) · C. Cross, *The puritan earl: the life of Henry Hastings, third earl of Huntingdon* (1966) · W. A. Shaw, *The knights of England*, 1 (1906), 145
Archives Hunt. L., MSS, HA deeds
Likenesses A. Benson, oils, Musées Royaux des Beaux-Arts de Belgique, Brussels [*see illus.*]
Wealth at death £9466 in debt: PRO, E 150/1146/5

Hastings, George Fowler (1814–1876), naval officer, second son of Hans Francis *Hastings, twelfth earl of Huntingdon (1779–1828), and his first wife, Frances (1780/81–1820), daughter of the Revd Richard Chaloner Cobbe, rector of Great Marlow, Buckinghamshire, was born on 28 November 1814. He entered the navy in September 1824, and on 7 January 1833 was promoted lieutenant. He was then appointed to the gunnery training ship *Excellent* at Portsmouth; in May 1834 to the *Revenge* (74 guns) in the Mediterranean; and in September 1837 to the steamer *Rhadamanthus*, also in the Mediterranean. On 30 June 1838 he was made commander; in the following January was appointed to the coastguard, and then, in August 1841, to the *Harlequin* (16 guns), in which he went out to China, arriving in time to take part in the closing operations of the war, after which he was employed in the suppression of piracy on the coast of Sumatra.

On paying off the *Harlequin*, Hastings was advanced to post rank, on 31 January 1845. From September 1848 to February 1851 he commanded the steam frigate *Cyclops* on the west coast of Africa; and from August 1852 to May 1857 the *Curaçao* in the Mediterranean and Black Sea during the

operations of the Crimean War. This latter service was acknowledged by a CB (2 January 1857), and the Mejidiye (third class). In January 1858 he was appointed superintendent of Haslar Hospital and the Royal Clarence victualling yard, in which post he continued until he gained his flag on 27 April 1863. On 14 September 1864 he married Mathilde Alice (d. 6 July 1916), only daughter of W. H. Hitchcock (later Degacher); they had three sons and one daughter. In November 1866 Hastings was made commander-in-chief in the Pacific, with his flag in the *Zealous*, one of the earlier wooden-built ironclads; he became vice-admiral on 10 September 1869, shortly before the end of his service in the Pacific in November. In February 1873 he was appointed commander-in-chief at the Nore, which office he held for the usual term of three years, ending on 14 February 1876. He died suddenly at his residence, 41 Stanhope Gardens, South Kensington, London, on 21 March 1876.

J. K. LAUGHTON, *rev.* ROGER MORRISS

Sources O'Byrne, *Naval biog. dict.* · *Annual Register* (1876) · *Navy List* · E. Holt, *The opium wars in China* (1964) · G. S. Graham, *The China station: war and diplomacy, 1830–1860* (1978) · A. D. Lambert, *The Crimean War: British grand strategy, 1853–56* (1990) · Boase, *Mod. Eng. biog.* · GEC, *Peerage* · *CGPLA Eng. & Wales* (1876) · Burke, *Peerage*
Wealth at death under £800: resworn administration, Feb 1879, *CGPLA Eng. & Wales*

Hastings, George Woodyatt (1825–1917), social reformer and politician, was born on 28 September 1825 at 43 Foregate Street, Worcester, the second of three children, and the only son, of Sir Charles *Hastings (1794–1866), physician and founder of the British Medical Association (BMA), and his wife, Hannah (d. 1866), eldest daughter of George Woodyatt MD, physician to the Worcester Infirmary. He was educated at Bromsgrove grammar school and at Christ's College, Cambridge (1844–50), where he took a first class in civil law; he was admitted to the Middle Temple in November 1846 and called to the bar in May 1850. He practised as a barrister for the next twenty-one years. From his father, a Liberal in politics who not only helped organize the medical profession but was active in several causes, including anti-slavery and the improvement of public health, he inherited a taste for public service. He assisted his father and the BMA in drafting, and lobbying for, versions of the bill which became the 1858 Medical Act and established the modern medical profession in Britain. In the 1850s he was secretary of the Society for Promoting the Amendment of the Law, a London-based pressure group seeking to rationalize and improve aspects of English law, and of the National Reformatory Union, concerned with the care and moral redemption of young offenders. Lord Brougham, who provided patronage for Hastings, was president of both organizations. In the period from 1855 to 1857 Hastings was instrumental in joining together these two groups with a third constituency—those women who had come together as the Langham Place circle to publish the *English Woman's Journal*—to form the National Association for the Promotion of Social

Science, which held the first of its annual congresses in 1857 and which disbanded in 1886.

The Social Science Association, so-called, was modelled on the British Association for the Advancement of Science, and became an important forum for the promotion of institutional and legislative reform in mid-Victorian Britain. It was Hastings's role at the heart of the organization, first as secretary and then, from 1868, in succession to Brougham, as president, which brought him a place in public life. He was known to the whole political and administrative class of the age as an expert on social questions. His interests were broad, including not only legal and penal reform but also the promotion of women's causes. Among other projects, he assisted the foundation of Girton College, Cambridge.

Hastings was married first, on 10 August 1858, to Catherine Anna, daughter of the Revd Samuel Mence, rector of Ulcombe, Kent. She died without children in 1871. His second wife, Frances Anna (d. 1915), whom he married in 1877, was the only child of the Revd W. H. Pillans, rector of Himley, Staffordshire. They had three children.

From 1854 Hastings was unsuccessful in several attempts to secure the Liberal nomination as a candidate for various seats in parliament. Adopted for West Worcestershire, he failed to win election in 1874 but was elected Liberal MP for Worcestershire East in 1880, which he represented until 1892, sitting after 1886 as a Liberal Unionist. He served in many capacities in Worcestershire, including chairman of the quarter sessions and of the new county council. Hastings was representative of a new type of figure who entered politics through campaigns and movements for social reform. But Victorian Britain had not yet developed professional structures and organizations for this kind of public service, which remained voluntary and unpaid. He was expelled from the House of Commons on 21 March 1892 following his conviction for fraudulent conversion. As sole trustee of a substantial fund for the education of a deceased friend's children, he had used the capital for his own purposes, could not repay it, and was sentenced to five years' penal servitude. He had many outstanding debts in addition: his finances had never been adequate for the life he led as a public figure, and he had speculated without success. On his expulsion, the prime minister, Gladstone, paid tribute to his 'special services to the House'.

On his release Hastings lived quietly in his native county. In 1909 he published *A Vindication of Warren Hastings*, his famous ancestor, and two years later, *The Story of the Malverns*. He died on 21 October 1917, and was buried in the churchyard of Guarlford, near Malvern.

LAWRENCE GOLDMAN

Sources W. H. McMenemey, *The life and times of Sir Charles Hastings* (1959) · *Worcester Herald* (20 Feb 1892) · *Worcester Herald* (27 Feb 1892) · *Worcester Herald* (12 March 1892) · *Worcester Herald* (26 March 1892) · *Transactions of the National Association for the Promotion of Social Science* (1857–84) · *Hansard 4* (1892), 2.1339–42 · L. Goldman, *Science, reform, and politics in Victorian Britain: the Social Science Association, 1857–1886* (2002) · J. D. Schooling, 'The county fathers: a history of Worcestershire county council, 1889–1974', 1983, 13–16 [unpubd MS, Worcester] · B. Stephen, *Girton College, 1869–1932* (1933) · private information (2004) · Venn, *Alum. Cant.*

Archives priv. coll. · Worcs. RO, papers concerning trial and bankruptcy | UCL, Brougham MSS

Likenesses photograph, repro. in J. L. Clifford-Smith, *National Association for the Promotion of Social Science: a manual for the congress with a narrative of past labours and results* (1882), 40

Hastings, Gilbert of (d. 1166?), bishop of Lisbon, acquired that office after the conquest of Lisbon by Afonso Henriques, first king of an independent Portugal, with the aid of seaborne forces, among whom Gilbert had served, drawn from England, Flanders, and the Rhineland. Apart from his presumed origins in Sussex, nothing is known of Gilbert's antecedents. His appointment to the see of Lisbon is mentioned by the English author, designated only by his initial R., of the *De expugnatione Lyxbonensi*, who had participated in the events that he so vividly described. R.'s testimony appears to date Gilbert's appointment to the week between the sack of the city on 24 October 1147 and the consecration of the principal mosque to be its Christian cathedral on All Saints' day, 1 November—a speed of decision that suggests that Gilbert had already made his mark as a man of episcopal potential. His consecration cannot be dated, but its circumstances gave rise to controversy. Gilbert was consecrated by João, archbishop of Braga, to whom he made written profession of obedience, despite the well-founded claims of the archbishop of Santiago de Compostela that Lisbon lay within his province. The metropolitical loyalties of the see of Lisbon were to be a matter of contention for some years to come.

Little is known of Gilbert's episcopate at Lisbon. He received endowments from the king, organized a cathedral chapter, and started to build a new cathedral. His subscriptions to royal diplomas indicate regular attendance at the king's court. In a frontier zone where jurisdictional boundaries were still fluid Gilbert reached accommodations, invariably not without difficulty, with neighbouring ecclesiastical corporations such as the Augustinian canons of Santa Cruz de Coimbra, the Cistercian monks of Alcobaça, and the knights templar. It was in order to resolve conflict with the latter order concerning jurisdiction over the town and territory of Santarém that Gilbert travelled to the papal curia in 1153, probably visiting the court of the Emperor Alfonso VII of León–Castile on his return journey. In 1150–51 Gilbert went to England to preach and recruit for a military campaign to be directed against Seville. The source of information on this point, John of Hexham, may have been a little hazy about Iberian geography: it has been suggested that English troops participated in King Afonso's unsuccessful assault, not on Seville, but on Alcácer do Sal to the south-east of Lisbon, in 1151 or 1152. It appears that on this or other occasions Gilbert also recruited clerical personnel in the north. The dignitaries and canons of the Lisbon Cathedral chapter, their names known from episcopal *acta* dating from 1150, 1156, and 1159, included Walter of Hastings and Walter of Flanders, and several others bearing names then common in England or Flanders but rare in Portugal, such as Robert, the dean, Durand, the precentor, Bartholomew and Matthew, the archdeacons, and canons named Arnulf, Nicholas, and Rainald. Episcopal encouragement may be suspected, but remains unproven, in the settlement of lay colonies in and near Lisbon: for example, a certain Gilbert de Chent (Kent or Ghent), apparently a layman, subscribed the deed of 1150. The importation of some English liturgical uses to the bishopric of Lisbon has also been attributed to Gilbert. Gilbert was described by a near contemporary Portuguese author, in wholly conventional phraseology, as learned and pious. The meagre documentation relating to his episcopate at Lisbon suggests that he was energetic and forceful too. Gilbert's death was dated 27 April 1166 by Lisbon's seventeenth-century historian Da Cunha. If this date, which might have been drawn from a now lost cathedral necrology, is accurate, Gilbert must have resigned his see a little earlier. He makes no certain appearance in surviving documents after March 1162 and his successor, Alvaro, was in place as bishop of Lisbon by October 1164.

RICHARD FLETCHER

Sources C. W. David, ed. and trans., *De expugnatione Lyxbonensi | The conquest of Lisbon* (1936); repr. with foreword and bibliography by J. Phillips (2001) · *Documentos régios* (1958), vol. 1 of *Documentos medievais Portugueses*, ed. R. P. de Azevedo · A. de J. da Costa, ed., *Liber fidei Sanctae Bracarensis ecclesiae*, 1 (1965) · John of Hexham, 'Historia regum continuata', Symeon of Durham, *Opera*, vol. 2 · *Portugalliae monumenta historica, scriptores* (1856) · R. Da Cunha, *Historia ecclesiastica da igreja de Lisboa*, ed. M. d'Escobar (Lisbon, 1642) · A. Herculano, *História de Portugal*, 9th edn (1910) · R. de Azevedo, 'A carta ou memória do cruzado Inglês R. para Osberto de Bawdsey sobre a conquista de Lisboa em 1147', *Revista Portuguesa de História*, 7 (1957), 343–70 · Braga, Arquivo distrital, Gaveta dos arcebispos, MS no. 4

Hastings, Hans Francis, twelfth earl of Huntingdon (1779–1828), naval officer, fourth and only surviving son of George Hastings (*b.* 1734/5, *d.* 6 Feb 1802), lieutenant-colonel, 3rd regiment of foot, and his wife, Sarah, daughter of Sir Richard Fowler, second baronet, of Harnage Grange, Shropshire, was born in London on 14 August 1779. He was educated at Repton School, Derbyshire, from 1787 to 1790 and at John Bettesworth's academy at Chelsea, London, from 1790 to 1793. Early in 1793 he began his naval career under Sir John Borlase Warren, then captain of the *Flora*. He took part in the action off Cancale Bay, Brittany, in April 1794, and in the following year was wounded in the battle of Quiberon Bay. After having served six years with Warren, he was appointed acting lieutenant in the brig *Sylph*, and subsequently received his commission as second lieutenant of the *Racoon*. Early in 1800 he was appointed first lieutenant of the *Thisbe*, in which he accompanied the expedition to Egypt. He was afterwards appointed second lieutenant of the *Aigle*. He married, on 12 May 1803, at St Anne's, Soho, London, Frances (*b.* 1780/81, *d.* 31 March 1820), third daughter of the Revd Richard Chaloner Cobbe, rector of Great Marlow, Buckinghamshire; they had ten children, including George Fowler *Hastings.

At the outbreak of war in 1803 Hastings was sent to Weymouth Roads to impress seamen. His party was attacked by protesters, and seventeen of his men were wounded and three of their assailants killed. Upon landing at Weymouth he was seized, and committed by the mayor, on the charge of murder, to Dorchester gaol. After six weeks in prison, he was removed by habeas corpus to Westminster, when he was bailed out by his relative, Lord Moira, and was subsequently acquitted at the Dorchester summer assizes. From the *Aigle* Hastings joined the *Diamond*, and afterwards served as second lieutenant on the *Audacious*, and as flag lieutenant on the *Hibernia*. On his refusal to go out to the West Indies, where two of his brothers had died, he was appointed acting ordnance barrackmaster in the Isle of Wight, and in 1808 was promoted to the post of ordnance storekeeper in Enniskillen, where he lived for more than nine years.

When Francis, tenth earl of Huntingdon, died in October 1789, the earldom of Huntingdon became dormant, while the ancient baronies of Hastings devolved upon his elder sister, Lady Elizabeth Hastings, third wife of John Rawdon, first earl of Moira. Although Theophilus Henry Hastings, the eccentric rector of East and West Leake, Nottinghamshire, and uncle of Hans Francis Hastings, assumed the title of earl of Huntingdon, to which he was entitled by his descent from Francis, the second earl, he never took any steps to prove his right. Upon the death of his uncle in April 1804, Hastings made some attempt to investigate his claim to the earldom, but was soon compelled to abandon it for want of money. In July 1817 his friend Henry Nugent Bell took up the case, and it was mainly owing to his exertions that the attorney-general, Sir Samuel Shepherd, reported on 29 October 1818 that Hastings had 'sufficiently proved his right to the title of Earl of Huntingdon'. On 14 January 1819 he took his seat in the House of Lords, where, as a tory, he does not appear to have taken any part in the debates. Though successful in his claim to the earldom, he failed to recover the Leicestershire estates, which formerly went with the title. On 28 September 1820 he married his second wife, Eliza Mary Thistlethwayte, *née* Bettesworth (*d.* 9 Nov 1846), eldest daughter of Joseph Bettesworth of Ryde, Isle of Wight, and widow of Alexander Thistlethwayte of Hampshire; they had no children.

On 7 March 1821 Huntingdon obtained the rank of commander and the command of the *Chanticleer*. While cruising in the Mediterranean he was appointed governor of Dominica, in the West Indies, on 13 December 1821, and took the oaths of office on 28 March 1822. In 1824, because of a misunderstanding with the other authorities on the island, he resigned and returned home. He was promoted post captain on 29 May 1824, and on 14 August was appointed to command the *Valorous*. Illness compelled him to relinquish his command in the West Indies. He returned to England in May 1828 and died at Green Park, Youghal, co. Cork, Ireland, on 9 December of that year, aged forty-nine. He was succeeded in the earldom by his eldest son, Francis Theophilus Henry Hastings. On 26 April 1838 his widow married her third husband, Colonel Sir Thomas Noel Harris KH; she died at Boulogne.

Hastings's career revealed the limits of patronage: Warren, his early patron, had many protégés, and Hastings, lacking other support, and his own means, was condemned to fall behind his contemporaries after receiving his first commission. Only a lack of money could explain his failure to press the claim to his family title. His career was dogged throughout by ill fortune and ill health.

G. F. R. BARKER, rev. ANDREW LAMBERT

Sources GEC, *Peerage*, new edn · Burke, *Peerage* (1959) · *GM*, 1st ser., 99/1 (1829), 269–72 · *Navy List* · H. N. Bell, *The Huntingdon peerage*, 2nd edn (1821) · *GM*, 2nd ser., 27 (1847), 110
Archives BL, corresp. with second earl of Liverpool, Add. MSS 38276–38284
Likenesses C. Warren, line engraving, pubd 1820 (after W. S. Lethbridge), NPG · portrait, repro. in Bell, *Huntingdon peerage*

Hastings [*née* Daunais], **Hazel Mary** (1897–1993), teacher and Roman Catholic laywoman, was born on 8 November 1897 on a farm at Eagle Hills, near Battleford, Saskatchewan, Canada, the daughter of Charles Michel Daunais (*d.* 1901), a farmer, and his wife, Mabel Grant Hutchison (1873–1961). Of old French Canadian stock, her father hailed from a village near Montreal while her mother had emigrated from Devon and become a Roman Catholic at the Peigan Reserve mission. Before she was three Hazel's showpiece was to sing 'Vive la Canadienne', and she always retained her Canadian citizenship.

In May 1901 her father died and her mother returned with her to England; a little later her mother became a Benedictine nun, with the name of Paula, at Stanbrook Abbey, Worcestershire. In consequence of this extraordinary decision, something she never afterwards criticized, Hazel, at little more than five, found her home to be the tiny school of no more than twelve girls, a relic of former ages, inside the monastic enclosure. It was a strangely medieval education. The girls wore a black habit and a veil for much of the time, shared in the liturgy and became expert in plainsong, Latin, calligraphy, heraldry, and astronomy, but not much else. Holidays were spent with her grandmother or in the homes of fellow pupils, such as the Eystons at East Hendred, descendants of Thomas More, for whom Hazel developed a lifelong passion. In 1911 she was sent for two years to the English convent at Bruges to perfect her French and, incidentally, become a natural European through the international mix of the Bruges girls and the Belgian homes where she stayed during the holidays.

With the First World War came work, first in a bank—Cox & Co.—and then in the machine-gun corps pay office in South Kensington. In her shared room in the Queensberry Club, opened by Baroness von Hügel for Catholic girls, Dorothy Howell lay on her stomach on the floor putting in the orchestral score to her symphonic poem 'Lamia'. When Sir Henry Wood conducted it at the Queen's Hall with Howell at the piano Hazel was there to applaud. Soon afterwards she married Major William George Warren Hastings (1881–1952), just demobilized, a lawyer who had already arranged to join a firm in Malaya. They first met in September 1919; they were married on 13 October and he had left within a month. The 1920s she spent mostly in Malaya, where she gave birth to five of her six children, and threw herself into the activities with Malay and Chinese girls as deputy commissioner for the Girl Guides. At one fund-raising concert for them she appeared as a bearded conjuror, the mysterious Professor Zog. She was, however, never happy with the conventions and racial barriers of formal colonial life. From 1930 she settled back in England with her children in St Werstan's, a ten-bedroomed Malvern house, while her husband continued his legal practice in Malaya. Here her combination of Catholic devotion, liberal attitudes, and open hospitality flourished. When Baldwin retired to the House of Lords in 1937, producing a Worcestershire by-election, she raised the Liberal flag in the forlorn hope of overturning a huge tory majority. Her father-in-law, George Woodyatt Hastings, had been a Liberal MP for Worcestershire fifty years before.

In 1938, endeavouring to economize, she moved the family to a north Oxford flat, tiny in comparison with the house she had left, but the atmosphere of Oxford was far more congenial and she welcomed into it numerous central European refugees like the historians Willie and Hans Schenk, as also Dominicans from Blackfriars, German prisoners-of-war, and innumerable friends of her children studying at the university. They all became her friends too, as did, very particularly, Penelope Betjeman. Never keen on the chores of regular housekeeping (though she did them without complaining), she excelled in making fancy dress, icing fantastic birthday cakes, and laying treasure hunts. On one memorable occasion the clues were scattered up and down the banks of the Cherwell and the groups of participants were all in punts.

After her husband died in 1952 Hazel Hastings sold their retirement home at Childrey, near Wantage, and resolved to start a new life, teaching English, something which had long excited her. Three of her children were working in Uganda in the late 1950s and she went there too, offering to live at the Generalate of the Bannabikira, at Bwanda, a large congregation of African nuns whose English needed improving. Later, in her mid-sixties, she taught English at Bukalasa seminary very successfully up to the A level Shakespeare paper.

After leaving Uganda, and spending a while at Mindolo Ecumenical Foundation, Zambia, Hazel Hastings set off again, this time for the continent of Europe, teaching English first in Lisbon and then at Tor Lupara, Rome, and finally, from 1973, now over seventy-five, at Offenburg in the Black Forest, becoming the resident expert on English in another large convent school but—to her great regret—unable to learn German. In her eightieth year she moved to Aberdeen, to housekeep for her university lecturer son. Her last years were spent with her daughter Barbara back in Oxford, where she died, at 186 Iffley Road, on 27 January 1993. She was buried beside her husband in the graveyard of the Roman Catholic church at East Hendred three days later.

Hazel Hastings was short, sturdy, and extremely strong. She had a huge capacity for friendship and letter-writing; she loved music, travel, especially long sea voyages, fine handwriting, and language precision. Always a deeply committed Catholic, she grew ever more liberal and ecumenical in both religion and politics but, above all, she excelled in generosity. She left no will. There was no need, because she had already given almost everything away.

ADRIAN HASTINGS

Sources H. M. Hastings, 'A mingled yarn', unpublished autobiography, priv. coll. · personal knowledge (2004) · private information (2004) [family]

Hastings, Sir Henry (1235?–1269), nobleman and baronial leader, was the son of Henry Hastings (d. 1250) and Ada, third daughter of *David, earl of Huntingdon, brother of William the Lion, and Maud, daughter and coheir of Hugh, earl of Chester. His grandfather William Hastings (d. 1226) took part with the barons against King John, and in 1216 his lands were forfeited; he was taken prisoner at Lincoln in 1217, and was one of William of Aumale's supporters at Bytham in 1221. Henry Hastings the elder, in contrast, was loyal to Henry III; he fought for the king on the Breton campaign in 1230 and in Poitou in 1242, and was taken prisoner at Saintes; he served in Scotland in 1244. His lands were much enriched by his wife's being a coheir to John the Scot, earl of Chester (d. 1237): in the subsequent settlement they received manors 'in tenancy' from the king, allegedly in lieu of one-third of the value of the earldom. In 1250 he was one of the nobles who took the cross, but died in July of the same year. Matthew Paris called him 'a distinguished knight and wealthy baron' (Paris, 5.174). His estates, in fact, extended over eleven counties, the core being in the north and west midlands.

Henry Hastings the younger was about fifteen at his father's death, worth more than £600 per annum, and early in 1251 the king divided the wardship of the huge estate between no fewer than eight grantees, the lion's share going to Guy and Geoffrey de Lusignan and Guy de Rochford. Hastings's marriage was granted to Guy de Lusignan, but about a year later Lusignan sold it, along with the marriages of his sisters, to Hastings's near neighbour, William (III) de *Cantilupe. Hastings himself remained a ward in the queen's care, with a yearly pension of £10, along with the Lord Edward and other young nobles. He married between 1252 and 1261 Joanna de Cantilupe, the daughter of William de Cantilupe, niece of the prominent Montfortian St Thomas of Hereford, and sister and coheir of George de Cantilupe, lord of Abergavenny. She received in 1269 dower extended at £230 p.a., but died about July 1271. They had three daughters and two sons, John *Hastings, first Lord Hastings, born on 6 May 1262 at Allesley, Warwickshire (d. 1313), and Edmund *Hastings, Lord Hastings of Inchmahome.

In 1255 Hastings accompanied the king to Scotland, losing a horse in the process. He came of age on 10 May 1256 and in August 1260 received his first military summons from the king. By 1261, however, he was in rebellion against Henry III. It is possible that he was drawn to support Simon de Montfort through their common sphere of interest in the west midlands, or their mutual close ties with the Cantilupes and Segraves, links strengthened by Hastings's father's interest in crusading. The Hastings family, in turn, may well have felt cheated by the king out of their full share of the earldom of Chester. Hastings himself certainly resented Henry III's Lusignan half-brothers: there is evidence that they had despoiled his estates while in their wardship, and they demanded over £200 in entry fines from him when he came of age. While in the queen's custody Hastings also built up friendships with other rich wards of similar age, especially Geoffrey de Lucy, later his executor, who had similarly received rough handling from the Lusignans. This group, among whom, besides Hastings and Lucy, William de Munchensi and Nicholas of Segrave were most prominent, can be seen in action even in July 1260 when they stood bail for Geoffrey de Lucy in a hunting offence. In the winter of 1261 Hastings and the same young friends lay at the core of the opposition to the king's overthrow of the provisions of Oxford; they were required by him to send their seals to be affixed to the treaty of Kingston if they wished to be pardoned. They seem to have remained unreconciled, for it was Hastings and his friends who were noted by the chronicler Thomas Wykes as the young nobles who, at the parliament held in May 1263, supported Simon de Montfort in his complaint of non-observance of the provisions of Oxford. In May the king attempted to summon them to fight against the Welsh and to take up knighthood from him, but they refused. Hastings sided with the baronial opposition in the war of 1263 and was one of those excommunicated by Archbishop Boniface. On 13 December 1263 Hastings also joined in signing the instrument which bound the barons to abide by the award of Louis IX. In April 1264 he was in Kent with Gilbert de Clare and took part in the siege of Rochester. Hastings put pressure on David of Ashby, and no doubt others, to support Montfort. He marched with Earl Simon to Lewes and was knighted by him, either on the morning before the battle on 14 May 1264 (according to Gervase of Canterbury) or at London on 4 May (according to the Dover chronicle in BL, Cotton MS Julius D.ii). In the battle of Lewes Hastings, along with (depending on various accounts) Geoffrey de Lucy, Hervey of Boreham, or Humphrey (V) de Bohun, commanded the Londoners, and took part in their flight from Edward. Afterwards Montfort made him constable of the castles at Scarborough, Kirtling in Cambridgeshire, and Winchester; he was summoned to Montfort's Model Parliament on 14 December 1264. In June 1264 Hastings was one of the judges assisting Simon de Montfort the younger in his arbitrary vendetta against William de Braose of Sussex, whereby the latter was fined 10,000 marks, and he was one of those who were to take part in the abortive tournament at Dunstable in February 1265.

Hastings was wounded and taken prisoner by Thomas de Clare at Evesham on 4 August 1265. Half his retinue of four knights was slain in the battle. The king afterwards granted Hastings's wife £100 p.a. from his estates but the residue was divided among no fewer than eight royalists. Hastings obtained his release after February 1266 and joined Robert de Ferrers, earl of Derby, at Chesterfield in the following May, and only escaped capture with him because he was out hunting. He then went to Kenilworth, and, joining with John de la Ware, Montfort's old retainer, and others, ravaged the surrounding country, and held the castle against the king from June to December 1266. Hastings, as leader of the Kenilworth garrison which had cut off the hand of a royal messenger, was specially excepted from the dictum of Kenilworth, and sentenced to pay a fine of seven years' value of his estates. But on his release he broke his oath not to take up arms again; he joined the disinherited in the Isle of Ely and became their leader. He was, however, forced to submit to Edward in return for the dictum of Kenilworth in July 1267. He seems to have settled most of his ransom without difficulty, being in the end probably only charged a fine at a five-year rate.

Hastings died, aged about thirty-four, before 5 March 1269, perhaps from wounds obtained during the war. On his death his estates once again became valuable royal patronage, the wardship of his heir, John, being granted to the king's brother and nephew, Richard and Edmund of Cornwall; in 1269 John was contracted to marry one of the daughters of the Lusignan, William de Valence, and it is interesting that in 1275 it was alleged before the pope that this marriage was intended to settle the enmity between the Hastings family, Henry III, and Edward I. Hastings and his wife were buried in the chapel of the Friars Minor at Coventry. Wykes, who was a royalist, spoke of his inordinate pride and violence, and called him 'malefactorum maleficus gubernator' (*Ann. mon.*, 4.203).

C. L. KINGSFORD, rev. H. W. RIDGEWAY

Sources Chancery records · *CIPM*, 1, no. 719 · Paris, *Chron.*, vols. 4–5 · *Ann. mon.*, vols. 2–4 · *The historical works of Gervase of Canterbury*, ed. W. Stubbs, 2: *The minor works comprising the Gesta regum with its continuation, the Actus pontificum and the Mappa mundi*, Rolls Series, 73 (1880) · 'Robert of Gloucester's chronicle', *The church historians of England*, ed. and trans. J. Stevenson, 5 (1858), 349–81 · W. Dugdale, *The antiquities of Warwickshire illustrated*, rev. W. Thomas, 2nd edn, 1 (1730), 183 · [W. Rishanger], *The chronicle of William de Rishanger, of the barons' wars*, ed. J. O. Halliwell, CS, 15 (1840) · *CEPR letters* · J. R. Maddicott, *Simon de Montfort* (1994) · W. Stubbs, ed., 'Annales Londonienses', *Chronicles of the reigns of Edward I and Edward II*, 1, Rolls Series, 76 (1882), 1–251 · *Chancery records* (RC) · *CDS*, vols. 2–3 · [Walter of Exeter?], *The siege of Carlaverock ... with a translation, a history of the castle and memoirs of the personages commemorated by the poet*, ed. and trans. N. H. Nicolas (1828) · J. R. S. Phillips, *Aymer de Valence, earl of Pembroke, 1307–1324: baronial politics in the reign of Edward II* (1972)

Hastings, Henry, third earl of Huntingdon (1536?–1595), nobleman, was the eldest son of Francis *Hastings, second earl of Huntingdon (1513/14–1560), and his wife, Katherine Pole (d. 1576). His grandfather George *Hastings, first earl of Huntingdon, a personal friend of Henry VIII, introduced him to the court at a very early age. A year or so senior to Edward VI, Lord Hastings joined the young prince at his studies at the king's invitation. Francis Hastings became second earl of Huntingdon in 1544, and three years later Lord Hastings was knighted at the coronation of Edward VI. In 1548 he spent a brief period at Queens' College, Cambridge, profoundly influenced by the evangelical protestantism he encountered at court and at the university. During the reign of Edward VI the second earl

Henry Hastings, third earl of Huntingdon (1536?–1595), by unknown artist, 1588

of Huntingdon threw in his lot with the duke of Northumberland, sealing the alliance with the marriage of his eldest son to Katherine Dudley [see Hastings, Katherine, countess of Huntingdon], the duke's youngest daughter, in May 1553. Both Huntingdon and Lord Hastings backed Northumberland in his attempt to divert the succession in favour of Lady Jane Grey in July 1553, and on Mary Tudor's triumph they found themselves imprisoned for a time in the Tower.

In the Marian period the countess of Huntingdon used her family connections to rehabilitate her husband and son. Having granted a free pardon to Lord Hastings in November 1553, the following year, out of devotion to her godmother, the countess of Salisbury, Mary restored the lands of Henry *Pole, Lord Montagu, to his coheirs Katherine and Winifred Pole. In his turn, Reginald, Cardinal Pole, responded with great eagerness to the overtures of his nearest surviving relative, and soon after his arrival in England he congratulated his niece on the accomplishments God had disposed upon her eldest son. In 1555 he took Lord Hastings with him briefly to Calais and later encouraged him to translate Osorius's *De nobilitate*. Hastings was also a member of King Philip's English household.

The deaths of both Mary and Pole in November 1558 brought a further change in the family fortunes. Together with the second earl, Lord Hastings received a summons to the Lords in the first parliament of Elizabeth, and attended assiduously, being present (among much else) at the passage of the Acts of Supremacy and Uniformity in the spring of 1559. The second earl of Huntingdon, who had been unwell for some years, died prematurely in June 1560, and Hastings acceded to the title at the age of twenty-four. He thus assumed responsibility for his widowed mother and his ten brothers and sisters, only two of whom, his eldest brother, George, and his eldest sister, Katherine, had gained their inheritance in their father's lifetime.

With his humanist education, experience of court life, and a brother-in-law, Robert *Dudley, high in the new queen's favour, Huntingdon might well have expected early advancement. However, he soon discovered that his Yorkist ancestry barred his way. When Elizabeth fell ill with the smallpox in October 1562, the protestant group put him forward as a potential successor and, though he subsequently did all in his power to convince her of his loyalty, the queen proved very slow thereafter to employ him outside his native county of Leicestershire.

On the eclipse of the Grey family in the second half of the sixteenth century, Leicestershire became a Hastings fiefdom governed by Huntingdon from Ashby-de-la-Zouch. He was assisted by his four brothers, Sir George at Loughborough and then Castle Donington, Sir Edward at Leicester Abbey, Sir Francis *Hastings at Market Bosworth, and Walter at Kirby Muxloe. From the first, Huntingdon gave priority to the religious complexion of the county. Within months of his father's death he brought the Genevan exile Anthony Gilby to be his chaplain at Ashby-de-la-Zouch, and helped finance the ministry of William Whittingham and other itinerant preachers in the county. Subsequently he provided Thomas Sampson with the mastership of Wyggeston's Hospital after his deprivation in 1565 from the deanery of Christ Church, Oxford, for his nonconformity at the time of the vestiarian controversy. Huntingdon engineered the appointment of a civic lecturer at Leicester as early as 1562, and established or re-established protestant grammar schools at both Ashby and Leicester. He always retained this interest in education, settling his four best livings in Leicestershire and Somerset upon Emmanuel College, Cambridge, soon after its foundation in 1584. It was also during this period that he began the patronage of protestant writers which he continued for the remainder of his life.

The flight of Mary Stuart to England in the spring of 1568 caused Elizabeth to see Huntingdon's birth in a somewhat different light. On the disclosure of plans for Mary's marriage to the duke of Norfolk, the queen, considering the earl of Shrewsbury too lenient a gaoler, to Mary's great indignation named Huntingdon as her joint custodian. For three months during the northern uprising in the autumn of 1569, Shrewsbury and Huntingdon shared the guardianship of the Scottish queen, first at Tutbury and then at Coventry, until, the crisis over, Elizabeth restored Mary to Shrewsbury's sole care in January 1570. Throughout this period Huntingdon corresponded with Cecil almost daily, and in the process secured an important new advocate at court. Elizabeth formally recognized

his service by creating him a knight of the Garter in April 1570 and from this time seems to have regarded him as a suitable recipient for high office.

The rebellion of the earls had demonstrated the ineffectiveness of Sussex as president of the council in the north, and in a deliberate attempt to strengthen the control of the central government over the region, in the autumn of 1572 the queen appointed Huntingdon as Sussex's replacement. With jurisdiction in civil matters over Yorkshire, co. Durham, Northumberland, Westmorland, and Cumberland, and in ecclesiastical affairs throughout the northern province which extended additionally to Lancashire, Cheshire, and Nottinghamshire, the promotion at a stroke transformed Huntingdon into the most powerful royal official in the whole of northern England. At the start his fellow councillors considered him to be very inexperienced, but within a short time Grindal was commenting upon the way in which his office had 'made manifest to many those excellent virtues and good gifts which afore were in a manner hid in him' (Nicholson, 355). Since Northumberland's execution had taken place in York only three months previously, Huntingdon's first priority was the restoration of good government in the region. With the earls of Northumberland, Westmorland, and Cumberland broken or confined to the south, he worked incessantly to fill the power vacuum with loyal northern gentlemen. As cases of land rights had contributed to the restiveness of the commons earlier in the century, Huntingdon now used the conciliatory services of the council in the north to resolve conflicts between landlords and tenants and to arbitrate in trading disputes among rival northern towns.

Throughout the period the north of England stood as a buffer zone against Scotland, still in a highly volatile state after Mary's flight. As soon as he arrived in York, Huntingdon added his weight in support of the protestant regent, Morton, subsequently acting as the chief government negotiator when border raids threatened to disrupt the peace. When, after Morton's fall, the young James VI began to take power into his own hands, Huntingdon did his best to maintain the previously good relations between the two countries. With the office of lord lieutenant permanently annexed to his presidency from 1580, as fears of a Spanish invasion were intensifying in July 1586 he obtained with Lord Eure a defence pact with Scotland. Assigned supreme control over all the forces in the north at the time of the Armada, Huntingdon moved to Newcastle in the autumn of 1588 to secure the border in the event of invasion. Even after the threat from Spain had diminished, and James had become a pensioner of the English crown, he continued building up northern resources to withstand any fresh onslaughts from Spain.

As an administrator, diplomat, and military commander Huntingdon considered himself an instrument of central government. He was at times almost obsessively anxious to fulfil to the letter the commands of the queen and the privy council, but in the sphere of religion he never felt any hesitation about seizing the initiative. After the papal excommunication of Elizabeth in 1570 he, like

Cecil, equated Catholicism with disloyalty to the state. From the beginning of his presidency he launched a campaign to bring the north to religious conformity. During his first decade in office he used the northern high commission to try to overawe conservative gentry and townspeople, and after the passing of the penal laws from 1581 preferred the more stringent penalties obtainable in the secular courts. Over and above those seminary priests dispatched for trial in the south, between 1582 and 1595 thirty priests and eight lay people were sentenced to death at York; most of them had previously appeared for a preliminary examination before the president and council in the north.

Alongside Huntingdon's unrelenting attack on Catholicism went his self-imposed mission to promote protestantism. Sir Francis Hastings maintained with little exaggeration that his brother 'never sett a straying foote in anye place where hee did not labor at the leaste to settle the preachinge of the word to the people' (Cross, *Letters*, 59). In 1575 he sided with William Whittingham, then dean of Durham, when Archbishop Sandys was questioning the validity of his ordination in a protestant church abroad; in 1579 he began pressing for the appointment of a civic lecturer in York, with which the corporation reluctantly complied in 1582; and he encouraged the town of Newcastle to invite John Udall to serve as town preacher after his silencing at Kingston upon Thames. He furthered preaching exercises throughout the north and, though he owned no direct patronage in the region, still contrived to place evangelical protestants in strategic town livings such as Leeds, Guiseley, Hull, and Halifax and used his best efforts to encourage 'the well plantinge of the gospell in Manchester' (CUL, Add. MS 17, fol. 38v).

This absorption with the government of the north exacted a heavy price. Almost as soon as he succeeded to the title, Huntingdon began making inroads into his inheritance, perhaps raising as much as £100,000 from land sales by the time of his death. His obligations towards his mother and his brothers and sisters accounted for his indebtedness in his early years, and an unwise investment in copperas mines at Canford in Dorset and ensuing lawsuits subsequently made his situation worse; but there seems little doubt that royal service in the last instance caused the financial chaos from which the family never fully recovered. Huntingdon himself claimed in 1587 that since he had become president he had spent 'more than her majesty's allowance above 20,000 li.' (*Salisbury MSS*, 3.275). Despite commissioning Sir Francis Hastings from 1583 to supervise his estates in the south-west, he succeeded only in stalling these debts.

Having gone north to Newcastle to oversee the musters in the autumn of 1595, Huntingdon planned to join his wife at court for Christmas and to use the opportunity to reorder his finances. On his return to York in late November, however, he fell ill with a fever and died there, much mourned, on 14 December 1595. As he had tried to set an example of protestant commitment all his adult life, so at the end he strove to achieve a Calvinist death. At court Elizabeth went out of her way to comfort his distraught

widow, though she did little to mitigate the debts. Childless, Huntingdon had educated Francis Hastings, the eldest son of his brother Sir George Hastings, as his heir, sending him for a time to Geneva. Francis's ten-year-old son Henry was being brought up in his great-uncle's household at York in 1595. Since his brother had died intestate, George, fourth earl of Huntingdon, tried to avoid taking up the administration of his estate, but the queen insisted upon Huntingdon's being given a funeral commensurate with his rank, and he was buried with his nephew, Francis, who had outlived him by three days, at St Helen's Church, Ashby-de-la-Zouch, on 26 April 1596. A portrait of Huntingdon in armour dated 1588 now hangs in the Tower.

CLAIRE CROSS

Sources Hunt. L., Hastings papers • PRO, chancery proceedings C 2 and C 3 • chancery close rolls, PRO, C 54 • patent rolls, PRO, C 66 • PRO, state papers SP 10, 11, 12, 15, 19, 38, 39, 52, 59 • PRO, STAC 5 • PRO, E 150/1158/12 • BL, Add. MSS • BL, Cotton MSS, Caligula • BL, Cotton MSS, Titus • BL, Egerton MSS • BL, Harleian MSS • BL, Lansdowne MSS • Coll. Arms, Talbot MSS, vols. E–I, P • Bodl. Oxf., MSS Carte 78, 105, 234, 235, 289 • CUL, Baker MSS, Mm.1.43 • Emmanuel College library, Cambridge, boxes A, C, D, 3A, 9, 29 • Hull RO, bench book 4 • portfolio of letters, Leicestershire Archives Office, 20 D 52 • Leicestershire Archives Office, Hall books 1 and 2 • Leicestershire Archives Office, Hall MSS, vols. 1–3 • chamberlains' accounts, 1555–96, Leicestershire Archives Office • York City Archives, housebooks B 25–31 • Borth. Inst., high commission act books 1–12 • W. Nicholson, ed., *The remains of Edmund Grindal*, Parker Society, 9 (1843) • *The letters of Sir Francis Hastings, 1574–1609*, ed. C. Cross, Somerset RS, 69 (1969) • C. Cross, 'The third earl of Huntingdon's death-bed: a Calvinist example of the *ars moriendi*', *Northern History*, 21 (1985), 80–107 • M. Bateson and others, eds., *Records of the borough of Leicester*, 3: *1509–1603* (1905) • *CSP dom., 1547–97; addenda, 1566–79; addenda, 1580–1625* • J. Bain, ed., *The border papers: calendar of letters and papers relating to the affairs of the borders of England and Scotland*, 2 vols. (1894–6) • *CSP for., 1547–8* • *CSP Scot., 1547–69* • *CSP Spain, 1558–1608* • H. Sydney and others, *Letters and memorials of state*, ed. A. Collins, 2 vols. (1746) • *Calendar of the manuscripts of the most hon. the marquis of Salisbury*, 24 vols., HMC, 9 (1883–1976) • *The manuscripts of his grace the duke of Rutland*, 4 vols., HMC, 24 (1888–1905) • *Report on the manuscripts of Lord De L'Isle and Dudley*, 6 vols., HMC, 77 (1925–66) • E. Lodge, *Illustrations of British history, biography, and manners*, 2nd edn, 3 vols. (1838) • H. E. Malden, ed., 'Devereux papers, with Richard Broughton's memoranda, 1575–1601', *Camden miscellany, XIII*, CS, 3rd ser., 34 (1924) • *Diary of Lady Margaret Hoby*, ed. D. M. Meads (1930) • J. Morris, ed., *The troubles of our Catholic forefathers related by themselves*, 3 vols. (1872–7) • *Literary remains of King Edward the Sixth*, ed. J. G. Nichols, 2 vols., Roxburghe Club, 75 (1857) • F. Peck, ed., *Desiderata curiosa*, new edn, 2 vols. in 1 (1779) • H. N. Bell, *The Huntingdon peerage*, 2nd edn (1821) • C. Cross, *The puritan earl: the life of Henry Hastings, third earl of Huntingdon* (1966) • J. Nichols, *The history and antiquities of the county of Leicester*, 4 vols. (1795–1815) • R. R. Reid, *The king's council in the north* (1921) • parish register, Ashby-de-la-Zouch

Archives BL, corresp. and MSS, Add. MSS 5458, 5752, 6113, 6167, 6672, 12507, 19188, 21432, 27632, 29546, 33207, 33594, 34218, 34889, 38113, 38141, 39117, 41178, 45866, 48099, 66575 • Hatfield House, Hertfordshire, corresp. and MSS • Hunt. L., letter-book and MSS • PRO, MSS, Chancery proceedings C 2 and C 3 • PRO, MSS, close rolls C 54 • PRO, MSS, patent rolls C 66 • PRO, MSS, state papers SP 10, 11, 12, 15, 19, 38, 39, 52, 59 | BL, Cotton MSS, Caligula C 1, 2, 3, 4, 5, 7, 8, D 2; Nero B 6; Vespasian F 12, 13; Titus B 3 8, F 3 13 • BL, Egerton MSS 1694, 2642, 2644, 2790, 2986, 3052 • BL, Harley MSS 36, 254, 260, 289, 304, 416, 433, 465, 787, 807, 851, 1074, 1088, 1155, 1160, 1196, 1393, 1394, 1529, 1576, 1951, 1985, 3881, 4199, 4698, 4774, 4849, 4990, 6124, 6991, 6992, 6994–6999, 7031, 7033, 7035, 7042, 7177 • BL, Lansdowne MSS 2, 7, 16–19, 20, 22,

24, 27, 30–33, 38, 40, 42–44, 46, 49, 52, 53, 57, 63, 67, 68, 73, 76–79, 82–87, 99, 101, 102, 107–109, 155, 156, 162, 229, 256, 260, 775, 860, 863, 978
Likenesses oils, 1588, royal armouries, Tower of London [*see illus.*] · M. Gheeraerts senior, group portrait, etching (*Procession of Garter Knights, 1576*), BM · oils, NPG · portrait (posthumous), Leicester Guildhall
Wealth at death many thousands of pounds in debt: Cross, *Puritan earl*, 306–4

Hastings, Henry (*bap.* 1562, *d.* 1650), landowner and eccentric, was the second son of George Hastings (*d.* 1604), who in 1595 became fourth earl of Huntingdon, and his wife, Dorothy Port (*d.* 1607). His epitaph states that he died on 5 October 1650, aged ninety-nine, so indicating that he was born in 1550 or 1551, but this exaggerates his age. His parents were married in 1557, his elder brother was born in 1560, and Henry himself was baptized on 20 June 1562 at Lubbesthorpe, a family manor in Leicestershire where he was presumably born. His uncle Henry, the third earl, took an active interest in his nephews, and in 1587 arranged Henry's marriage to Dorothy, second daughter of Sir Francis Willoughby of Wollaton Hall, Nottingham, who gave the couple the estate of Woodlands, near Horton in Dorset, which the Willoughby family had inherited. Hastings was later to acquire other properties in Dorset and Hampshire, where he was appointed one of the keepers of the New Forest, but Woodlands remained his principal home. In 1645 the estate, which had been valued at £300 in 1641, was sequestered owing to his royalist sympathies, but he compounded for it with a payment of £500.

At Woodlands, Hastings led a life almost entirely devoted to hunting, hawking, and fishing, and still rode well in his old age. He kept all sorts of hounds; dogs and cats and their litters had the freedom of the house, so that he kept a short stick on his table to defend his meals from them. The hall was full of hawks on their perches, hunting equipment, and trophies of the chase, and the floor was strewn with marrowbones from his hospitable table, for he entertained widely though not extravagantly; he was unusually moderate in his drinking. In the parlour a Bible, Foxe's book of martyrs, old hats containing pheasants' eggs, dice, cards, and used tobacco pipes lay close together. The pulpit of the disused chapel held such dishes as a venison pasty, a cold joint of beef, or a large apple pie. In person Hastings was short and sturdy, and always dressed in green. He was popular locally, and it was said that there was not a woman in the neighbourhood 'under the age of forty, but it was extremely her fault if he was not intimately acquainted with her' ('Character of Mr Hastings', 160). The principal source of all these details is an account written by his godson and neighbour Sir Anthony Ashley Cooper, later first earl of Shaftesbury, which has been copied several times, notably by the *Gentleman's Magazine* in 1754 and later in Hutchins's *Dorset* and Nichols's *Leicestershire*. Shaftesbury and Hastings can have had little in common and supported opposing sides during the civil war, which may explain the satirical tone of the description of Hastings, especially in the allusion to

Henry Hastings (*bap.* 1562, *d.* 1650), by unknown artist

his attentions to the local women, with an insinuation that he had illegitimate children. Shaftesbury had a portrait of his godfather in his mansion at Wimborne St Giles; an engraving of it by James Bretherton (1782) is reproduced by both Hutchins and Nichols.

Dorothy Hastings died on 5 December 1638. According to some writers Hastings subsequently married Jane Langton, who had already borne him a son, but no record of such a marriage appears to have been traced. It is possible, however, that the Henry Hastings, son of Henry Hastings of Woodlands, Dorset, who is recorded as having matriculated at St Edmund Hall, Oxford, on 2 April 1641, aged fifteen, was the child of this union. Hastings died on 5 October 1650, aged eighty-eight, and was buried at St Wolfrida's Church, Horton on 8 October. With his wife, Dorothy, he had five sons and one daughter. His eldest son, George (1588–1651), was knighted by James I in 1619. In 1818, during investigations to determine the succession to the earldom of Huntingdon, it was established that the male line of descendants from Henry Hastings had become extinct in 1755.   T. Y. COCKS

Sources J. Hutchins, *The history and antiquities of the county of Dorset* (1861–74), vol. 2, p. 165; vol. 3, pp. 154–5, 157–8 [repr. 1973] · J. Nichols, *The history and antiquities of the county of Leicester*, 3/2 (1804); repr. (1971), 592–3 · H. Nugent Bell, *The Huntingdon peerage* (1820) · 'A character of Mr Hastings of Woodlands ... by Anthony Ashley Cooper', *GM*, 1st ser., 24 (1754), 160–61 · GEC, *Peerage*, 6.657–8 · C. Cross, *The puritan earl: the life of Henry Hastings, third earl of Huntingdon* (1966) · parish register, Aylestone, Leicester, St Andrews [baptism] · parish register, Horton, Dorset, St Wolfrida's [burial] · Foster, *Alum. Oxon.*, 1500–1714, 2.671 · memorial, St Wolfrida's Church, Horton, Dorset
Likenesses J. Bretherton, etching, BM, NPG; repro. in Hutchins, *History and antiquities* · oils, priv. coll. [*see illus.*]

Hastings, Henry, fifth earl of Huntingdon (1586–1643), nobleman and landowner, was born on 24 April 1586 at Exton, Rutland, the eldest son of Francis Hastings, Lord Hastings (1560–1595), heir apparent to the earldom of Huntingdon, and Sarah, daughter of Sir James Harrington, of Exton. As a boy he was described as 'low in stature, but of comely countenance and lively wit' (*CSP dom.*, 1595–7, 164). He was educated under the direction of his great-uncle, the third earl, by a 'learned and godly schoolmaster', probably Nathaniel Gilby, the earl's chaplain. His Latin exercises suggest a curriculum parallel to that established by the third earl for Leicester grammar school. Later he was entered at Gray's Inn and at Queens' College, Cambridge, matriculating in 1601. This education endowed the fifth earl with sense of his lineage, the importance of honour, and a deep-seated religious conviction. Although his uncle the puritan Sir Francis Hastings congratulated the new earl for 'resolving religiously' on 'the godly government' (*Letters*, 98) of his household, and although religiosity shapes his patronage (he continued to support Arthur Hildersham into the 1620s), Huntingdon's own religious attitudes were moderately protestant.

From 1595 to 1604 Hastings was styled Lord Hastings, inheriting the earldom from his grandfather George Hastings, fourth earl of Huntingdon, in 1604. As a minor he succeeded to some local family offices such as keeper of the royal forest of Leicester, but not to the lord lieutenancy of Leicestershire which he regained in 1607, retaining the office until his death; he was lord lieutenant of Rutland from 1614 to 1642. He married Lady Elizabeth *Stanley (*bap.* 1587, *d.* 1633), one of the coheirs of Ferdinando *Stanley, fifth earl of Derby, on 15 January 1601 at Stoneleigh, Warwickshire. The couple had four children: Alice (*b.* 1606), Ferdinando (*b.* 1608), Henry *Hastings, Baron Loughborough (1610–1667), and Elizabeth (*b.* 1612).

Huntingdon inherited an impoverished estate which curtailed his activities and he lamented how 'without meanes honour look[s] as naked as Trees that are cropped' (Hunt. L., Hastings papers, HAP 15/8). Even with his wife's £4000 dowry he faced catastrophe. It was estimated that the third earl had sold lands worth £90,000 and the fourth earl alienated further lands, reducing his annual income in 1604 to just over £37. The estate, encumbered with two dowagers, was so bereft of cash that no money existed in 1604 to cover immediate expenses and creditors, including the exchequer, threatened land seizures. Further land sales commenced and the countess's jointure was renegotiated. By 1622 the deficit had fallen to £11,662 and Huntingdon's income stabilized at about £2032 although after his costs and repayments the remaining £900 failed to match his annual expenditure of about £1400. Vigorous measures such as the collection of arrears, deforestation, coalmining, personal borrowing, the dowry from his future daughter-in-law, and even payments from lawsuits (he gained £2506 from the Fawnt case in 1639) barely kept the earl afloat.

Impoverishment appears to have limited Huntingdon's participation in national politics, although he was associated with the earls of Southampton and Pembroke and supported the Bohemian war as part of the pro war patriot faction on his occasional parliamentary appearances. A portrait even existed of him holding the petition of right. Interestingly, he did remain involved with the Virginia Company, and was elected to its council for his efforts in finding settlers, although he was perhaps motivated by the hope of riches as his letters to his agent, Captain Martiau, illustrate. His most distinctive contribution lay in local governance and as lord lieutenant and *custos rotulorum* Huntingdon used his expanded powers to dominate the local élite and, in general, even ensured the collection of extra-parliamentary levies. Much of this local power was directed towards sustaining his familial position and the continued feud with the Greys of Groby. His two famous lawsuits, against Shirley and Fawnt, are both products of this feud, although in the late 1630s Huntingdon found himself employed by central government, perhaps precisely because of his 'quasi-feudal paternalism' and rigorous county governance. Thus, although of little significance in national politics, Huntingdon's career has been studied for the detailed information it provides about aristocratic attitudes and the interaction of local politics and central government in the 1620s and 1630s. Huntingdon wrote extensively, including 'The directions' (a compendium of his views for his son Ferdinando), household ordinances, directions on the etiquette of gift-giving, travel journals, and numerous notes on honour, his family history, religion, and aristocratic precedent and privilege. It is precisely the lack of originality of these works that renders them a valuable source.

Within his financial limits Huntingdon patronized the arts, and was interested in gardening and architecture. His most singular act of literary patronage was the performance of John Marston's *Entertainment at Ashby* (August 1607, with additions by Sir William Skipwith), celebrating the arrival of his mother-in-law, the dowager countess of Derby, and Huntingdon's own coming of age. During his lifetime eight books were dedicated to him, largely by authors associated with his family estates, or recipients of his family's educational and clerical patronage, although he also amassed a substantial library. Significantly, these books from Leicestershire authors were often printed by Samuel Macham, a printer from Ashby who worked from the Bull's Head (the Huntingdon device) in St Paul's Churchyard and who acted as Huntingdon's agent in London.

Faced with a limited material patrimony and an extensive spiritual and aristocratic lineage, Huntingdon fostered his local roots in order to sustain his dignity. He relied on the rigorous exercise of local and hereditary offices, extensive hospitality, the cultivation of county and familial networks, and the judicious use of ecclesiastical, educational, and other notably cost-effective means of patronage to represent his status and views. Until the 1630s he cultivated a deliberately non-court oriented position and an ascetic protestantism that translated poverty into virtue. Indeed, Huntingdon is summed up by his motto *Honorantes me honorabo* which, according to his grandson, showed his 'true sense of religion', the motto 'intimating that those only should be esteemed by him who did faithfully honour God' (Bodl. Oxf., MS Carte 78, fol. 410). He died at Ashby-de-la-Zouch on 14 November 1643 and was buried there on 16 December. Ferdinando succeeded to the title as sixth earl of Huntingdon.

JAMES KNOWLES

Sources Hasting papers, Hunt. L. · Bodl. Oxf., MSS Carte 77, 78, 79 · schedule of Hastings debts, 1622, Leics. RO, DG30/25 · *CSP dom.*, 1595–7 · *The letters of Sir Francis Hastings, 1574–1609*, ed. C. Cross, Somerset RS, 69 (1969) · C. Cross, 'The third earl of Huntingdon's death-bed: a Calvinist example of the *ars moriendi*', *Northern History*, 21 (1985), 80–107 · R. Cust, 'Honor, rhetoric and political culture: the earl of Huntingdon and his enemies', *Political culture and cultural politics in early modern Europe*, ed. S. Amssen and M. Kishlansky (1985), 84–111 · T. Cogswell, *Home divisions: aristocracy, the state and provincial conflict* (1998) · J. D. Knowles, 'John Marston's "Entertainment" and its makers', contexts and location', DPhil diss., U. Oxf., 1993 · C. Brown, *John Milton's aristocratic entertainments* (1985) · S. Kingsbury, *Records of the Virginia Company of London, 1619–1626*, 4 vols. (Washington, 1906–35)
Archives Bodl. Oxf., private papers · Folger, parliamentary journal · Hunt. L., corresp. and papers
Likenesses portrait, Queens' College, Cambridge

Hastings, Henry, Baron Loughborough (1610–1667), army officer, was born on 28 September 1610, the second son of Henry *Hastings, fifth earl of Huntingdon (1586–1643), and Lady Elizabeth *Stanley (*bap.* 1587, *d.* 1633), daughter of Ferdinando *Stanley, fifth earl of Derby. As Lord Henry Hastings he was admitted to Queens' College, Cambridge, on 30 June 1627 and later in that decade he was apparently at court, where his father thought he was wasting his time. Although the family's financial difficulties meant that his landed inheritance was small and probably explains why he never married, its local pre-eminence established him as a notable figure in 1630s Leicestershire: about 1638 he served as a deputy lieutenant during the joint lord lieutenancy of his father and his elder brother Ferdinando Hastings, Lord Hastings (1609–1656), and he was a captain of the Leicestershire trained bands during the bishops' wars.

As civil war became imminent in the early summer of 1642 Henry, in contrast to his brother, emerged as one of the king's earliest supporters. Having joined Charles at York he returned to Leicestershire with royal authority to raise a commission of array and to take command of the resulting regiment. However, it was Henry Grey, earl of Stamford, an old rival of his family's, who armed with a parliamentary militia ordinance won over the trained bands in a confrontation beginning at Leicester on 4 June. The king responded by making Hastings high sheriff of the county, but initially his efforts at securing stores of weapons and powder gained him only parliamentary impeachment. By August he managed to raise a regiment of horse with which he joined Prince Rupert in a devastating raid on Stamford's home. He finally controlled most of the militia's munitions, but at the cost of significantly escalating violence in the locality. Having fought with the king's field army during the autumn at Powick Bridge and Edgehill, he was dispatched from royalist headquarters at Oxford at the end of November to raise forces and establish bases in the midlands. In January 1643 concerted but fruitless efforts were made to dislodge him from his father's fortified manor house at Ashby-de-la-Zouch. On 25 February Hastings was appointed colonel-general (under the command of William Cavendish, earl of Newcastle) of Derbyshire, Leicestershire, Nottinghamshire, Staffordshire, Rutland, and Lincolnshire. The last two counties were soon regrouped under another of Newcastle's subordinates, but Hastings retained authority over the rest for the next three years.

Over the spring and summer of 1643 Hastings gradually established a degree of control over the region. Three county towns had already fallen into parliamentarian hands—Derby to John Gell in October 1642, Nottingham to John Hutchinson in November, and Leicester to Thomas Grey, Lord Grey of Groby, in January 1643; a fourth, Stafford, fell to Sir William Brereton in May, though this proved less significant. In February Hastings had fended off attacks by Sir Thomas Ballard on Newark, and in late April with Prince Rupert's help he recaptured Lichfield, held for the previous two months by Gell. In June he and Sir Charles Cavendish, commander of the Lincolnshire forces, joined Queen Henrietta Maria on her march from York to Oxford. Using their combined forces, Hastings attacked Nottingham, where they made little headway, and then on 2 July successfully stormed Burton upon Trent. Interventions by the earl of Newcastle in Nottinghamshire and Lincolnshire in the following months enabled Hastings to improve his position, and by the end of the year his midland counties were controlled by at least sixteen minor and eight major garrisons, with forces numbering about 5000 men, sufficient to hold in check the small parliamentarian garrisons at Nottingham, Leicester, Stafford, and Derby. His success was acknowledged in October, when he was created by the king Baron Loughborough; he was also appointed lieutenant-general.

However, though in 1644 he attended the House of Lords in the Oxford parliament, Loughborough had reached the limit of his power and influence. His very success led the king to make use of his resources from early 1644. Some of his forces were assigned to Sir Charles Lucas and sent north in an attempt to stem the invasion by the Scottish covenanting army. Resulting military weakness was compounded by internal dissension. Hastings's authority was challenged by several of his commanders. Two Staffordshire colonels, Thomas Leveson and Richard Bagot, had a series of territorial disputes in which they refused to recognize Hastings's arbitration. After the battle of Marston Moor, Colonel Gervaise Lucas, governor of Belvoir Castle, refused to acknowledge Hastings's command and would not attend councils of war, claiming that as the earl of Newcastle had gone into exile, Hastings's authority was at an end. When parliamentarian forces besieged Newark from late March 1644 Hastings had to request support from Prince Rupert. On 21 March Hastings and Rupert executed a lightning march from Ashby-de-la-Zouch and surprised Sir John Meldrum's army east of

Newark. This strengthened Hastings's position temporarily, but, unfairly, he was accused of failing to aid the Yorkshire royalists in April when they were defeated at Selby. Hastings had sent Major-General George Porter into Yorkshire, but Porter returned south and obtained Prince Rupert's permission to stay in Nottinghamshire. When three of Hastings's Derbyshire colonels and two of his Staffordshire colonels joined Prince Rupert's march to the relief of York, Derbyshire parliamentarians took the opportunity to attack minor county garrisons, while the south Staffordshire garrison at Dudley was attacked by the earl of Denbigh. The defeat of the earl of Newcastle and Prince Rupert at Marston Moor had dire consequences for Hastings. The eastern association army, having marched unhindered from York, occupied northern Derbyshire and Nottinghamshire, and local parliamentarians began to capture outlying garrisons across Hastings's territory. On 30 October 1644 Hastings's army and forces from Newark were defeated at Denton near Belvoir Castle.

Following rumours early in 1645 that Hastings was disgruntled with the cause, George Digby urged Prince Rupert to solve Hastings's problems: being still of 'great importance' he was not to be 'sent home discontented, as here he appears to be highly' (Warburton, 3, 65–7). Hastings was involved, during the spring of 1645, in Rupert and Maurice's attempts to secure the northern Welsh marches. Sections of his army were later involved in the Naseby campaign and, after the capture of Leicester, Hastings was appointed governor with Sir Matthew Appleyard as his deputy. Sir George Lisle was appointed to serve as Hastings's lieutenant-general in Leicestershire, suggesting that Hastings may have received promotion at this time or earlier in the spring. However, the defeat of the royalists at the battle of Naseby on 14 June ended the renaissance of the royalist forces in the midlands and Hastings's territorial hold declined steadily during the next nine months. At the end of February 1646 through his brother, now the sixth earl of Huntingdon, Hastings arranged to surrender Ashby-de-la-Zouch on advantageous terms. Hastings eventually compounded with parliament for a mere £87 10s. in 1653.

In 1648 Hastings participated in the Essex rebellion and served as commissary-general in the garrison at Colchester. On its surrender to Sir Thomas Fairfax, Hastings was sent to Windsor Castle, becoming termed one of the seven 'great delinquents'. Probably destined for trial by the high court of justice, he escaped from Windsor on the eve of the king's execution and went to the Netherlands, where he joined Charles Stuart in March 1649. In the winter of 1650–51 it was hoped that Hastings should lead a rising in the midlands, but this never materialized. During the 1650s Hastings was a founder member of the Sealed Knot, on several occasions returning to England under assumed names. He was summoned before the council of state in 1652. He was also involved in plotting which led to the mistimed Penruddock's rising in 1655. It would appear that his brother supported him with financial aid during this period, though his exploits had occasioned first the installation of a parliamentary garrison at Ashby, and then, to the family's despair, its demolition.

After the Restoration Hastings was appointed lord lieutenant of Leicestershire. However, he set up home in London at Loughborough House in Lambeth. In 1664 he was granted the right to make navigable the river from Brixton Causeway to the Thames. He was given a concession on the export of cattle to Ireland, which was later commuted to a pension of £500 a year, in an effort to settle his outstanding debts from the war, estimated at £10,000 at the time of his death, at Lambeth, on 10 January 1667. He was buried at St George's Chapel, Windsor, near his great-uncle Edward Hastings, Baron Hastings of Loughborough, as he had requested in his will, signed on 1 August 1665. His executors, Francis Colles, his agent in Ireland, and Francis Eaton, his servant at Baty Lodge, Sussex, were to administer the profits of the manor of Okethorpe, Derbyshire, on behalf of his sister, Lady Alice Clifton, who was to receive a £200 annuity, and his nephew, Theophilus Hastings, earl of Huntingdon.   MARTYN BENNETT

Sources M. Bennett, 'The royalist war effort in the north midlands', PhD diss., Loughborough, 1986 · H. N. Bell, *Memoirs of the house of Hastings* (1820) · GEC, *Peerage*, new edn, vol. 8 · P. R. Newman, *Royalist officers in England and Wales, 1642–1660: a biographical dictionary* (1981) · E. Warburton, *Memoirs of Prince Rupert and the cavaliers* (1849) · Venn, *Alum. Cant.* · *Report on the manuscripts of the late Reginald Rawdon Hastings*, 4 vols., HMC, 78 (1928–47) · M. Bennett, 'Henry Hastings and the flying army of Ashby de la Zouch', *Transactions of the Leicestershire Archaeological and Historical Society*, 126 (1980), 62–70 [1980 for 1982] · *Diary of the marches of the royal army during the great civil war, kept by Richard Symonds*, ed. C. E. Long, CS, old ser., 74 (1859) · *CSP dom.*, 1663–4 · T. Cogswell, *Home divisions: aristocracy, the state and provincial conflict* (1998) · will, PRO, PROB 11/324, sig. 62
Archives Hunt. L., personal, official, and family corresp. and papers · William Salt Library, Stafford, Salt MS 550 | Bodl. Oxf., letters to Sir Robert Clayton · Bodl. Oxf., Dugdale MS 19 · Northants. RO, Finch-Hatton MS 133
Likenesses oils, *c.*1650, priv. coll. · oils, *c.*1650, NPG

Hastings, Henry Weysford Charles Plantagenet Rawdon, fourth marquess of Hastings (1842–1868), rake, was born on 22 July 1842, at 6 Cavendish Square, Marylebone, Middlesex, second son of George Augustus Francis Rawdon Hastings, second marquess of Hastings (1808–1844), and his wife, Barbara Yelverton, *suo jure* Baroness Grey of Ruthin (1810–1858) [see Hastings, Barbara Rawdon, marchioness of Hastings], only child of Henry Edward Yelverton, the nineteenth Baron Grey of Ruthin, who had initiated his country neighbour the poet Byron in homosexuality. In 1851 Hastings succeeded his brother in the marquessate, three earldoms, a viscountcy, and nine baronies; he inherited his mother's barony in 1858. Together with the dukes of Abercorn, the marquesses of Lansdowne, and the earls of Verulam, the marquesses of Hastings were the only peers who enjoyed distinct peerages in the three kingdoms of England, Scotland, and Ireland. He was educated at Eton College (1854–5) and at Christ Church, Oxford (1860–61), but left both institutions abruptly for unknown reasons.

Having already owned racehorses under the alias of Mr Weysford, Hastings was elected as a member of the Jockey

Club on his twenty-first birthday. He was not wildly extravagant at horse sales—his two best runners, the Duke and the Earl, cost him 500 and 450 guineas respectively—but his craving for the odds became excessive. This feeble, runtish, orphaned *enfant gâté* revelled in the deference of the betting ring and the admiration which accompanied his huge wagers. Initially his betting coups were so brilliant that he believed in his power to break the ring. Although for Hastings the excitement of gambling was more intense and enduring than sex, he attracted Lady Florence Cecilia Paget (1842–1907), youngest daughter of the second marquess of Anglesey. On 16 July 1864, shortly before her intended marriage to a rich squire, Henry Chaplin, afterwards first Viscount Chaplin, she went to Marshall and Snelgrove's drapery store in Oxford Street, entering by one door and swiftly leaving by another for the nearby church of St George, Hanover Square. There she married Hastings. This elopement raised a great stir in society. The marriage proved anxious, discontented, and childless.

In 1866 Hastings became master of the Quorn hounds, but never cared much for hunting and knew little about the sport. Dissolute living was ruining his judgement and health: mackerel poached in gin, with caviare on devilled toast, washed down by claret cup was his favourite breakfast; an eternal cigarette in his mouth maintained his famous pose of nonchalance. He lost heavily at Crockford's gaming club as well as on the turf. His estate at Donington, Leicestershire, was neglected; he sold Scottish land to the third marquess of Bute for £300,000. By the winter of 1867–8 he had gravely damaged his kidneys. It is difficult to say whether, knowing that he was doomed by illness, he became wilder in his betting, or whether his losses drove him deeper into desperate, self-destructive courses. Despite the magnanimity of Chaplin after the theft of his fiancée, Hastings developed a spiteful and immature obsession against him. This came to focus on his rival's colt Hermit, and he lost £120,000 in wagers against the horse when it won the Derby by a neck at 66 to 1 (22 May 1867). Much of that money was lost to Hermit's owner. 'Every one will be glad that [Chaplin] has this sweet revenge for Lord H.'s shabby conduct about Lady F. P.', noted John Wodehouse, afterwards first earl of Kimberley (*Journal*, 203). Rather than retrench after this fiasco, Hastings persisted in a reckless gambling campaign which only more tightly ensnared him in the moneylenders' traps. 'For the sake of the peerage wh. he disgraces the sooner he disappears from public view, the better', Wodehouse wrote in May 1868 of 'that miserable man Lord Hastings' (ibid., 220).

Hounded by creditors, Hastings resigned from the Jockey Club, and broken in fortune, nerves, and health succumbed to Bright's disease on 10 November 1868, at 34 Grosvenor Square, Mayfair. Reportedly his last words were, 'Hermit's Derby broke my heart; but I did not show it, did I?' (Blyth, 266). On 14 November he was buried at Kensal Green cemetery. E. H. Stanley, afterwards fifteenth earl of Derby, noted in his diary on 16 November:

Much writing in the papers about the death of Lord Hastings, aged 26: in five years he had destroyed a fine fortune, ruined his health, and by associating with low characters, on the turf and elsewhere, considerably damaged his reputation. To the peerage his death is a clear gain: and as his titles (except a Scotch earldom) die with him, the ruin of his family matters less. His sister has saved the family place.

RICHARD DAVENPORT-HINES

Sources *The Times* (11–12 Nov 1868) • H. Blyth, *The pocket Venus: a Victorian scandal* (1966) • Thormanby [W. W. Dixon], *Kings of the turf: memoirs and anecdotes* (1898) • 'The marquis of Hastings', *Baily's Magazine*, 12 (1866), 279–81 • Fifteenth earl of Derby, diary, 16 Nov 1868, Lpool RO • *The journal of John Wodehouse, first earl of Kimberley, for 1862–1902*, ed. A. Hawkins and J. Powell, CS, 5th ser., 9 (1997), 141, 203, 220 • GEC, *Peerage* • *Debrett's Peerage* • *The Post Office London directory* • Marquis of Huntly [C. Gordon], *Milestones* (1926?), 55–6
Likenesses photograph, 1864?, V&A; repro. in Blyth, *Pocket Venus*, facing p. 192 • Tilt, watercolour, *c*.1865, repro. in Blyth, *Pocket Venus* (1966), facing p. 80 • J. Freeman, photograph, *c*.1866, repro. in Blyth, *Pocket Venus* (1966), following p. 256 • caricature, 1868 (*Home from the Derby!*), BL; repro. in Blyth, *Pocket Venus*, following p. 256 • Mayall and Brown, engraving, repro. in 'The marquis of Hastings', *Baily's Magazine*, facing p. 279
Wealth at death under £90,000: probate, 20 Nov 1868, CGPLA Eng. & Wales

Hastings, Hubert de Cronin (1902–1986), editor, was born on 18 July 1902 at Spring House, Kingston Road, Merton, Surrey, the third son of Percy Hastings, proprietor of the Architectural Press and founder in 1896 of the *Architectural Review*, and Lilian Julie Bass. He was educated at Berkhamsted School, Hertfordshire, but circumstances prevented him from going to university, and in 1918 he joined the Architectural Press. He was eventually allowed time off to study architecture at London University's Bartlett School of Architecture, under Professor Albert Richardson. However, he disliked the school's emphasis on *beaux arts* discipline, and in an act of revolt he threw his T-square across the studio, and walked out and into the Slade School of Fine Art, next door. There he was influenced by cubism and by Clive Bell's hypothesis of 'significant form'. He also developed a skill for caricature (with architects largely his target); a small book of them was published in the 1930s.

On 23 July 1927 Hastings married Hazel Rickman (*b*. 1902/3), a daughter of Charles Frederick Garrard, with whom he had a son, John, and a daughter, Priscilla, both of whom eventually worked with him on occasion. Also in that year Hastings was appointed joint editor, with Christian Berman, of both the weekly *Architects' Journal* and the prestigious monthly *Architectural Review*. Their first acts were to define policies for both magazines and to raise standards. The weekly was to be concerned with the practice of architecture and building techniques, and the monthly with the arts in general, giving emphasis to architecture. The journal was promptly given a new look by adopting the new type faces, Baskerville and Plantin, and, over time, colophons heading different sections, drawn by Edward Bawden. Eric Gill was commissioned to do two wood engravings—an Inigo Jones medallion and an emblem of a boy architect—both of which appeared in the magazines and signalled a departure from tradition.

Hastings commissioned contributions from a rising

generation of new writers: Robert Byron, Evelyn Waugh, Cyril Connolly, Sacheverell Sitwell, and P. Morton Shand. He was an innovator in graphic design and page layouts, and the review broke new ground, to the discomfort of traditionalists. He had basic rules: details large, general views small, and—most important of all—every page a surprise. By 1929 he was starting to bleed photographs over the generously-sized pages of the review. In 1930 John Betjeman joined the review, bringing an irreverence that may have stimulated H. de C. (as he came to be called) into being more experimental with Victorian typefaces and into employing type to emphasize different literary moods. Sheets of special coloured papers were inserted, even a William Morris wallpaper. Also accelerating change was the contributor P. Morton Shand, who was convinced of the logic of the new modern movement in architecture and the irrelevance of historical styles. Hastings saw the logic of this as a bright new future for society and also as a highly desirable editorial campaign for both magazines. His journalistic campaigning streak never left him, and within a few years he was campaigning for a 'new monumentalism' and a 'new empiricism'. He also believed in the *genius loci* and in the picturesque (of the eighteenth-century English landscape tradition) to combat the heavy-handed discipline of axial planning.

Hastings was an idealist and a perfectionist. He dressed well and ensured that his staff were well accommodated in Queen Anne's Gate, a distinguished publishing house and not just an office. He had immense charm but a certain diffidence; on the only occasion that he gave a talk—at the Architectural Association—he turned his back on the audience. In 1973 he was the first editor awarded the royal gold medal by the Royal Institute of British Architects (RIBA). At a meeting with the RIBA, during which the president, Peter Shepheard, started describing the constituents of a town, Hastings suddenly shouted that, at the risk of losing his medal, he had never heard such bloody nonsense. This irascibility tormented his editorial board of Nikolaus Pevsner, Hugh Casson, Osbert Lancaster, James Richards, and others.

After the war, partly with his own hands Hastings created the facsimile bars of a public house in the basement of Queen Anne's Gate (dismantled); he also organized an architectural competition for the design of a modern pub and had the designs exhibited at the Victoria and Albert Museum. Hastings saw the potential that existed in the near derelict canal system after the war, and with the brilliant photographs of Eric de Maré, who had explored those canals still open, published a special issue of the *Architectural Review* that launched a national campaign to preserve them if not for commerce, as Hastings hoped, then at least for tourism.

One of Hastings's most important achievements was to popularize the idea of townscape. In this he was helped by exceptional draughtsmen: Donald Dewar Mills, Kenneth Browne, and—greatest of all—Gordon Cullen. This led to other-scapes: roofscape, floorscape, wirescape—all the aspects of semi-civilized life of which engineers, surveyors, town planners, and even architects, he believed, were

either unaware or ignorant. This climaxed in a special issue of *Architectural Review*, entitled 'Outrage', produced by Ian Nairn. It sought to expose the consequences of the lack of visual education in Britain—poor design and poor planning, which Nairn stigmatized as 'Subtopia'. It was an 'outrage' that stirred politicians and led Duncan Sandys to create the Civic Trust.

Hastings did not himself contribute many articles to the *Architectural Review*; when he did it was always under a pseudonym, usually Ivor de Wolfe (Wofle was a printer's error that was allowed to stand). He published two books on town design: *The Italian Townscape* (1963) followed two years of studying and photographing many Italian cities, and *Civilia: the End of sub-Urban Man* (1971) was a passionate attempt to create, with photo-montage, the ideal city. A third book, *The Alternative Society*, which addressed sociological issues, was published in 1980. Hastings died on 4 December 1986 at Bedham Farm, Fittleworth, Sussex. Following cremation his ashes were removed to Bedham.

D. A. C. A. BOYNE

Sources *The Times* (6 Dec 1986) · *Daily Telegraph* (8 Dec 1986) · *WWW* · personal knowledge (2004) · private information (2004) · **Wealth at death** £812,171—net: *The Times* (12 May 1987)

Hastings, Sir Hugh (*c*.1310–1347), administrator and soldier, was the second son of John *Hastings, first Lord Hastings (1262–1313), and his second wife, Isabel, daughter of Hugh *Despenser the elder, earl of Winchester (*d*. 1326). He married, before 18 May 1330, Margery Foliot (*c*.1312–1349), who had been his mother's ward since 1325. Margery was the elder sister and coheir of Richard Foliot, and it was in her right that Hastings acquired the manors of Elsing and Weasenham, Norfolk, and property in Nottinghamshire and Yorkshire. Following his mother's death in December 1334 Hastings inherited the manor of Monewdon, Suffolk, and a moiety of the manor of Sutton Scotney, Hampshire; he obtained livery on 28 March 1335.

Hastings pursued an administrative and military career befitting his social position. On 8 November 1338 he was appointed justice of the peace in the West Riding of Yorkshire. Thereafter, when not on campaign, he was employed on commissions of oyer and terminer and in various other administrative capacities with great regularity. He never served as sheriff or knight of the shire, but was one of 106 lay magnates summoned to the council that met at Westminster on 29 April 1342. He was also Queen Philippa's steward in the mid-1340s. Hastings was no less active as a soldier. It is not known when he first bore arms, but he certainly campaigned each year in Scotland from 1335 to 1338. He accompanied Edward III's army to the Low Countries in July 1338 and again two years later, when he fought at the battle of Sluys (24 June 1340). Much of this military service was performed in the retinue of Henry of Grosmont, earl of Derby, later duke of Lancaster (*d*. 1361), from whom Hastings held several manors; but for the expedition to Brittany in 1342–3 he served in the *comitiva* of his half-nephew, Laurence Hastings, earl of Pembroke (*d*. 1348), from whom he had acquired a life interest in the manor of Oswardbek, Nottinghamshire, shortly before. It was also under Pembroke's banner that

Sir Hugh Hastings
(*c*.1310–1347),
memorial brass

was never to take up this post, however, for having drawn up his will at Old Ford, Middlesex, on 22 July 1347, he died a week later, perhaps as a result of sickness contracted in the siege-camp outside Calais. He was buried in the chancel of the church that he had built at Elsing, Norfolk.

Here Hastings's life as a man of action is admirably commemorated by one of the most celebrated of all English brasses, in which his armoured image is flanked by smaller figures bearing the arms of some of the great men with whom he had been associated during his military career, including the king and the earls of Lancaster, Warwick, and Pembroke. Investigation of the contents of Hastings's tomb in September 1978 revealed a man about 5 feet 10 inches tall, who had been buried wearing a cowhair wig or hat. The cause of death was not revealed, but various injuries, including damaged incisor teeth, apparently the result of a severe blow to the mouth, and the presence of osteoarthritis in shoulder and elbow joints, suggest that Hastings's military career had taken its toll. His widow, Margery, died on 8 August 1349, leaving two sons, John (*c*.1328–1393) and Hugh (*d*. 1369), and a daughter, Maud.   ANDREW AYTON

Sources GEC, *Peerage*, new edn · records, PRO · *Chancery records* · Rymer, *Foedera*, new edn · A. Hartshorne and W. H. St J. Hope, 'On the brass of Sir Hugh Hastings in Elsing church, Norfolk', *Archaeologia*, 60 (1906–7), 25–42 · A. R. Wagner and J. G. Mann, 'A fifteenth-century description of the brass of Sir Hugh Hastings at Elsing, Norfolk', *Antiquaries Journal*, 19 (1939), 421–8 · B. Hooper, S. Rickett, A. Rogerson, and S. Yaxley, 'The grave of Sir Hugh de Hastings, Elsing', *Norfolk Archaeology*, 39 (1984–7), 88–99 · [J. Raine], ed., *Testamenta Eboracensia*, 1, SurtS, 4 (1836), 38–9 · G. Wrottesley, *Crécy and Calais* (1897); repr. (1898) · *Œuvres*, ed. K. de Lettenhove and A. Scheler, 28 vols. (Brussels, 1867–77) · *Chronique de Jean le Bel*, ed. J. Viard and E. Déprez, 2 (Paris, 1905), 343–4 · J. Sumption, *The Hundred Years War*, 1 (1990) · J. Coales, ed., *The earliest English brasses: patronage, style and workshops, 1270–1350* (1987) · L. Dennison and N. Rogers, 'The Elsing brass and its East Anglian connections', *Fourteenth century England*, ed. N. Saul, 1 (2000), 167–93 · *CIPM*, 7, no. 646; 9, no. 47
Likenesses memorial brass, Elsing church, Norfolk [*see illus.*]
Wealth at death manorial holdings: *CIPM*, 9

Hastings took part in the earl of Derby's successful campaign in Aquitaine in 1345. Since Pembroke arrived on the field too late to take part in Derby's triumph over the French at Auberoche (21 October 1345), Froissart was probably wrong to place Hastings at that battle. Nor is it likely that Hastings was involved in the defence of Aiguillon (April–August 1346), for he seems already to have returned to England.

The climax of Hastings's career, and the clearest indication of the high regard in which he was held by Edward III, was his appointment to the post of king's captain and lieutenant in Flanders on 20 June 1346. While the king landed in Normandy with the main English army, Hastings mounted a diversion on the northern frontier of France. With a personal retinue of about 250 men, mainly archers, Hastings recruited a large but undisciplined army from the Flemish towns and laid siege to Béthune. This proved unsuccessful, and the Flemish army dispersed before the end of August. Although probably not present at the battle of Crécy (26 August 1346), Hastings did serve at the siege of Calais with a company of men-at-arms and archers. Towards the end of the siege, in early May 1347, Hastings was appointed seneschal of Gascony, with a personal retinue of fifty men-at-arms and eighty archers. He

Hastings, James (1852–1922), United Free Church minister and journal editor, was born on 26 March 1852 at Huntly, Aberdeenshire, the second son and fifth child of James Hastings, miller, of the mill of Huntly, and his wife, Hope Ross. He was educated at Huntly School, then at Aberdeen grammar school (*c*.1864–1871), before matriculating at the University of Aberdeen. He graduated MA in 1876, and then proceeded to study divinity at Christ's College, the Free Church college in Aberdeen. He later received two honorary doctorates, the first from Aberdeen in 1897, followed in 1920 by one from Queen's University, Halifax, Nova Scotia.

After serving as assistant minister in Broughty Ferry, Dundee, Hastings was ordained and inducted in 1884 to the charge of Kinneff Free Church, Kincardineshire, with a stipend of £160. In that same year, he married Ann Wilson, daughter of Alexander Forsyth of Elgin. They had one son and one daughter.

In 1897, Hastings accepted a call to Willison church, Dundee. But he found the demands of a city charge were too great and four years later, he was translated back to rural Kincardineshire, and to the United Free church in St Cyrus. He remained in this position until he retired from the ministry in 1911, after which he returned to Aberdeen.

James Hastings had a lively Christian faith, which was coupled with a love of learning. He was a notable preacher, simple and direct, and an eager supporter of social welfare. But over and above all these concerns, his real achievement lies in his commitment to promoting knowledge of the Christian faith, but especially of the Bible. He is particularly remembered for his works of reference. These include his two-volume *Dictionary of Christ and the Gospels* (1906–7), his *Dictionary of the Bible* (1898–1902), and his *Dictionary of the Apostolic Church* (1915–18); but these pale into insignificance when compared to his thirteen-volume work, the *Encyclopaedia of Religion and Ethics* (1908–21). These works bore witness to Hastings's conviction that modern biblical criticism, far from undermining Christian belief, would serve to reinforce the fundamental tenets of his faith.

Hastings was a man of many interests and had a most impressive library; several scholars travelled from England just to view his collection. But he also loved games and would regularly go to England to watch cricket matches. For his own exercise, he would take long walks, often late at night. In 1913, he was awarded the Dyke Acland medal, which was awarded biennially to a distinguished scholar whose work is especially directed to making knowledge of the Bible more accessible to all.

Hastings died unexpectedly at his home, 11 King's Gate, Aberdeen, on 15 October 1922. The *Expository Times*, which Hastings had founded in 1899, continued to be published after his death under the joint editorship of his two children.   MICHAEL D. McMULLEN

Sources DNB · *Aberdeen Press and Journal* (16 Oct 1922), 7–9 · J. A. H. Dempster, 'Hastings, James', *DSCHT* · W. Ewing, ed., *Annals of the Free Church of Scotland, 1843–1900*, 1 (1914), 182 · J. A. Lamb, ed., *The fasti of the United Free Church of Scotland, 1900–1929* (1956), 390–409 · '"Incomparable encyclopaedist": the life and work of Dr James Hastings', *Expository Times*, 100 (1988–9), 4–8
Likenesses photograph, 1922, repro. in *Aberdeen Daily Journal*
Wealth at death £11,202 16s. 7d.: confirmation, 18 Dec 1922, CCI

Hastings, John, first Lord Hastings (1262–1313), soldier and landowner, was born on 6 May 1262 at Allesley, Warwickshire, the eldest son and heir of Sir Henry *Hastings (1235?–1269) and Joanna, sister and heir of Sir George de *Cantilupe (d. 1273). He was given possession of his mother's family's castle and barony of Abergavenny on 12 July 1283, having reached the age of twenty-one. During the next few years he undertook a number of missions for Edward I, to Scotland, Ireland, Wales, and Gascony. In 1285 his sister Ada married Rhys ap Maredudd and Hastings granted the couple all his lands in St Clare, Angoy, and Pemmlick. Two years later Rhys rebelled against the English and captured Emelyn Castle, where Hastings was ordered to attack him. The uprising was put down and Hastings was permitted to receive the fines, which were

not to be severe, from his own Welsh tenants who had supported Rhys.

In 1291, as grandson of Ada, youngest of the three daughters of David, earl of Huntingdon (d. 1219), and thus great-great-great-grandson of David I of Scotland, Hastings put forward a claim to the vacant throne of Scotland. He had little chance of becoming king since, unlike John Balliol, he was not descended from the eldest daughter of Earl David, nor, unlike Robert (V) de Brus, was he nearer by degree. Instead he asserted that Scotland, as an English fief, was not a kingdom and that the royal lands therein should be treated like any other landed estate and divided between the descendants of the three coheirs. The auditors, eighty of whom represented Balliol and Brus, rejected this argument, but when it became clear that John Balliol was likely to win, Robert de Brus was suddenly persuaded by Hastings's reasoning, to no avail. Brus had previously sought to deprive both Balliol and Hastings of their share of Earl David's lordship of the Garioch.

Present among the magnates in the parliament of 1290, and regularly summoned to parliament from 1295, Hastings is consequently regarded as having become Lord Hastings. In 1296 he played an active part in the campaign which brought Scotland directly under King Edward's control. However, war broke out again a year later and Hastings regularly served in royal armies in the north. The war also affected his financial arrangements, since Joan de Clare, the dowager countess of Fife, who owed him 960 marks sterling, was forced to repay him by granting him a number of her manors in Scotland and England because her lands and property had been plundered by a 'rebel' Scot, Sir Herbert Morham. She was re-enfeoffed in these lands three years later. In 1300 Hastings, who had also been formally knighted, was present at the siege of Caerlaverock Castle in Dumfriesshire and consequently featured in a poem composed for the occasion. It was noted that he conducted the banner of his close friend Antony (I) Bek, bishop of Durham (d. 1311); Hastings was described as a man who 'was known by all to be in deeds of arms daring and reckless, but in the hostel mild and gracious, nor was there ever a judge in eyre more willing to judge rightly' (Moor, 2.194).

Hastings's standing with and usefulness to the crown is attested by his appointment as seneschal of Gascony in December 1302. He returned to English, and Scottish, affairs in 1306, after the uprising of Robert Bruce, now king as Robert I. Hastings remained in Scotland for the next few years and was rewarded for his commitment to the English cause by a grant of the earldom of Menteith, forfeited by the late Earl Alexander for supporting Bruce. His most important function was to maintain a naval blockade up and down the west coast of Scotland from a base at Ayr. He was subsequently ordered to continue these activities as commander of Brodick Castle on Arran. He was not entirely effective in this, however, since in February 1307 a group of Bruce's followers, led by James Douglas and Robert Boyd, managed to land on Arran from Kintyre and seize arms and equipment from a contingent on its way to reinforce Brodick. This was a precursor to the successful Bruce landing in Carrick.

Hastings seems to have gone back to England about the time of the accession of Edward II, whose coronation he attended on 25 February 1308. He returned to Gascony on the new king's behalf in October 1309 and became seneschal of Guyenne a month later. He was dead by 28 February 1313 and was buried in the Hastings chapel in the church of the Friars Minor at Coventry. He married first Isabel (d. 1305), daughter of William de *Valence, earl of Pembroke (d. 1296), and they had a son, John. His second wife was another Isabel (d. 1334), daughter of Hugh *Despenser (d. 1326); she married Ralph de Monthermer five years after Hastings's death.

John Hastings, second Lord Hastings (1287–1325), was twenty-six when he succeeded his father in 1313. He attended Edward I's queen, Margaret, when she came to Scotland in 1306 and was a regular participant in the Scottish wars between 1311 and 1319. Especially as a leading retainer of his uncle Aymer de Valence, earl of Pembroke (d. 1324), he also played a role in English politics. He attested the treaty of Leake of 9 August 1318, which sought to reconcile Edward II and his opponents, led by the earl of Lancaster, at the price of substantial constitutional concessions on the part of the king. In the same year Hastings was acknowledged as coheir of the earl of Pembroke, along with David Strathbogie, titular earl of Atholl (d. 1326), whose wife, Joan, was the sister of Hastings's mother. In 1320, when Lancaster again challenged Edward, Hastings at first sided with the rebel lords, but he later joined the king at Cirencester. He evidently found it easy to make his peace with Edward and was sent to take control of Glamorgan, while in 1323 he became governor of Kenilworth Castle. He fell foul of the younger Hugh Despenser, however, to whom he was obliged to make a recognizance of £4000 in August 1324. At some point before his death in 1325 Hastings arranged that the French monks of Abergavenny Priory should be replaced with Englishmen. The supplanted Frenchmen brought an action against him, but the case was still not settled when he died. He married Juliana *Leybourne (1303/4–1367), granddaughter and heir of William Leybourne. Their son, Laurence *Hastings, became earl of Pembroke through his descent from his grandmother Isabel de Valence.

FIONA WATSON

Sources C. Moor, ed., *Knights of Edward I*, 2, Harleian Society, 81 (1929) • G. W. S. Barrow, *Robert Bruce and the community of the realm of Scotland*, 3rd edn (1988), 39–43, 169 • *Willelmi Rishanger … chronica et annales*, ed. H. T. Riley, pt 2 of *Chronica monasterii S. Albani*, Rolls Series, 28 (1865), 257, 309–42 • *CDS*, vols. 2, 5 • *RotS*, vol. 1 • J. Stevenson, ed., *Documents illustrative of the history of Scotland*, 2 vols. (1870) • *Chancery records* • J. R. S. Phillips, *Aymer de Valence, earl of Pembroke, 1307–1324: baronial politics in the reign of Edward II* (1972) • W. Dugdale, *The baronage of England*, 2 vols. (1675–6)

Hastings, John, second Lord Hastings (1287–1325). *See under* Hastings, John, first Lord Hastings (1262–1313).

Hastings, John, thirteenth earl of Pembroke (1347–1375), magnate and soldier, was the only child of Laurence *Hastings, twelfth earl of Pembroke (1320–1348), lord of Abergavenny in Monmouthshire, Pembroke Castle, the Irish lordship of Wexford, and substantial English estates, and of Agnes (d. 1368), a daughter of Roger (V) *Mortimer, first earl of March. In 1328 Laurence Hastings had been married as a child of eight to Agnes Mortimer, in the presence of King Edward III. In 1330 Agnes's father was executed. When Laurence was old enough, the marriage was consummated and John, their only child, was born on 29 August 1347 at Sutton Valence, a Hastings manor in Kent. Exactly one year later Laurence died and John spent his early years in his mother's care. Agnes quickly remarried, but her new husband, John Hakluyt, was dead by 1357. The wardship of the Pembroke land had been distributed among a number of royal nominees including Agnes and her husband, John's grandmother, now countess of Huntingdon, and Sir John Grey of Ruthin, whose nephew inherited the Hastings lands after 1389. In the 1360s John Hastings gradually gained control over his estates and on 12 September 1368 he finally proved his age.

In May 1359, at the age of eleven, John Hastings had been married to Margaret (b. 1347), the twelve-year-old daughter of *Edward III, but she died late in 1361. Now in 1368, a man of twenty-one, the earl married Anne (b. 1355), daughter and sole heir of the legendary soldier, Sir Walter *Mauny. Anne was only thirteen in 1368 and her husband left her in England while he pursued a military career overseas.

In January 1369 Pembroke accompanied the king's son Edmund of Langley, then earl of Cambridge, to Aquitaine with 400 men-at-arms and 400 archers, to reinforce the position of Edward, the Black Prince, after his disastrous intervention in the Spanish Civil War. Pembroke and Cambridge landed at St Malo in Brittany and marched south to join the prince in Angoulême. A *chevauchée* into Perigord culminated in a successful eleven-week siege of the castle of Bourdeilles, the earl's knighting, and his triumphant return to Aquitaine.

Pembroke, Cambridge, and John Chandos, along with Sir James Audley, then besieged La Roche-sur-Yon in the Vendée in July and August 1369. The fortress fell to the English through the treachery of the French captain, but aristocratic arrogance had made Pembroke unwilling to serve under Chandos, despite Chandos's appointment as seneschal of Poitou to replace Audley. In October Pembroke campaigned alone in Anjou but was ambushed and had to be rescued by Chandos. This did nothing to abate the ill feeling between the two leaders: it damaged the English cause and contributed to Chandos's failure to recapture the abbey of St Savin in the Vienne from the French late in November: this in turn led directly to the death of Chandos on 1 January 1370. This was a serious blow to Edward III's attempts to stabilize Aquitaine, and neither Pembroke nor Cambridge could command the respect that Chandos had earned as a soldier and as a knight. None the less Pembroke was nominated by the king to the Garter stall vacated by the death of Thomas Beauchamp, earl of Warwick, on 13 November 1369. Still in Aquitaine early in 1370 Pembroke, in company with Cambridge, relieved the French siege of Belle-Perche in

Anjou and then both earls rejoined the Black Prince. Despite severe ill health, the prince embarked on a major campaign, supported by another brother, John of Gaunt, duke of Lancaster, and by the two earls. This culminated in September and October 1370 in the major siege of the episcopal city of Limoges. Pembroke participated in the severe treatment meted out to the citizens of Limoges for allowing the French to occupy the city too easily late in August, although the deaths among civilians seem to have been greatly exaggerated.

When the Black Prince returned to England in January 1371, Pembroke stayed behind with Cambridge under the overall command in Aquitaine of John of Gaunt. Pembroke soon returned to England, however. He attended the parliament of February–March 1371, where he seems to have led the successful Lancastrian attack on Edward III's clerical ministers. On 12 March his Garter robes were ordered for him in the expectation that he would attend the order's annual feast in April. He was still in England early in 1372, when his wife, now aged sixteen, conceived a child, but on 20 April 1372 he was appointed lieutenant of the English forces in Aquitaine, in succession to Gaunt. In June 1372 Pembroke sailed for the Bay of Biscay: he did not see England again and never saw his child.

Pembroke's orders were to recruit a substantial army in Aquitaine itself and he took with him £12,000 in treasure to meet the wages of this army. He himself travelled with a retinue of only 160 men, horses, and supplies, in a fleet of little more than a dozen small vessels protected by three larger ships with towers requisitioned from Dartmouth. Off La Rochelle, still held by the English, his fleet was intercepted by a much more impressive contingent of some twelve Castilian galleys. This was the first naval result of the Franco-Castilian treaty of 1368 and was disastrous for Pembroke. Early on the second day of the engagement, on 23 June 1372, after Pembroke had been obliged to lie offshore while the galleys commanded the approaches to La Rochelle, the entire English fleet was either burnt or captured. Many of Pembroke's troops were killed; some two dozen others, including Pembroke, were captured and taken to Castile before being ransomed. At the coastal town of Santander the knightly captives, including the earl, were kept in irons, and the *Chronique des quatre premiers Valois* describes how the less important prisoners were 'encouples comme chiens en lesse en une corde' (Luce, 235). Later in 1372 the Castilian king, Enrique da Trastamara, sold the right to ransom Pembroke to the constable of France, Bertrand du Guesclin, in return for Soria and Molina, which had been part of du Guesclin's territorial gains in Spain.

Du Guesclin then negotiated with England, offering to free Pembroke for 120,000 francs, a proportion to be paid before the earl was released from captivity. Despite Pembroke's royal connections, no movement towards paying any part of the ransom was made until early 1375, when moneys were deposited in Bruges, to be paid when Pembroke embarked for England. But as du Guesclin was taking his prisoner from Paris to Calais, the earl died on 16 April 1375. Walsingham recounts a rumour that he had been poisoned by the Castilians, but ill treatment and poor conditions in the earlier part of his captivity seem more likely causes. While his political reputation rests on a single important intervention in government, there are signs of his immaturity in his relations with Chandos. But no particular failure of leadership is discernible in the disaster off La Rochelle. Pembroke was luckless and arrogant, but not necessarily incompetent.

While Pembroke was in chains in Santander, his only child, another John, had been born in England. Dugdale observed that after Aymer de *Valence concurred in the death sentence on Thomas of Lancaster 'none of the succeeding Earls of *Pembroke* ever Saw his Father, nor any Father of them took delight in seeing his Child' (Dugdale, 1.578). In 1375 the two-year-old John Hastings succeeded to the earldom and the family's ill luck persisted. The third Hastings earl was accidentally eviscerated at a tournament in December 1389, the earldom became extinct, and the barony of Hastings, together with many of the family's estates, was successfully claimed by Reynold *Grey, third Baron Grey of Ruthin.   R. IAN JACK

Sources GEC, *Peerage* · *DNB* · J. W. Sherborne, 'The battle of La Rochelle and the war at sea, 1372–5', *BIHR*, 42 (1969), 17–29 · R. I. Jack, 'Entail and descent: the Hastings inheritance, 1370–1436', *BIHR*, 38 (1965), 1–19 · R. Delachenal, *Histoire de Charles V*, 4 (Paris, 1928) · R. Barber, *Edward, prince of Wales and Aquitaine: a biography of the Black Prince* (1978) · *Chroniques de J. Froissart*, ed. S. Luce and others, 8 (Paris, 1870) · *Thomae Walsingham, quondam monachi S. Albani, historia Anglicana*, ed. H. T. Riley, 2 vols., pt 1 of *Chronica monasterii S. Albani*, Rolls Series, 28 (1863–4) · A. Leroux, 'Le sac de la cité de Limoges et son relèvement, 1370–1464', *Bulletin de la Société Archéologique et Historique de Limoges*, 56, 155–233 · Chancery records · S. Luce, ed., *Chronique des quatre premiers Valois, 1327–1393* (Paris, 1862) · P. Lopez de Ayala, *Crónicas de los reyes de Castilla*, ed. C. Rosell, 3 vols. (Madrid, 1875–8); repr. (1953) · W. Dugdale, *The baronage of England*, 2 vols. (1675–6) · G. F. Beltz, *Memorials of the most noble order of the Garter* (1841) · PRO, DL 43/14/3

Wealth at death over £1000 p.a.; incl. seventeen estates valued at approx. £400: PRO, DL 43/14/3

Hastings, John (1830/31–1884). *See under* Hastings family (*per.* 1759–1907).

Hastings, John (1853–1907). *See under* Hastings family (*per.* 1759–1907).

Hastings, John Sutton (1790–1869). *See under* Hastings family (*per.* 1759–1907).

Hastings [née Dudley], **Katherine, countess of Huntingdon** (c.1538–1620), noblewoman, was one of the youngest of the thirteen children of John *Dudley, duke of Northumberland (1504–1553), and his wife, Jane (c.1509–1555), daughter of Sir Edward Guildford. On 25 May 1553, four days after the marriage of Guildford Dudley to Lady Jane Grey, Northumberland celebrated Katherine's wedding to Henry *Hastings (1536?–1595), the eldest son of Francis *Hastings, second earl of Huntingdon. Within a year the bride saw her father executed and her husband imprisoned in the Tower for their involvement in the attempt to divert the succession in favour of Lady Jane Grey, though Mary quickly pardoned Lord Hastings, great-nephew of her archbishop of Canterbury, Cardinal Pole. Elizabeth's promotion of Robert Dudley immediately after her accession further reinforced the young couple's connections with the court.

The premature death of the second earl of Huntingdon in June 1560 placed upon the new earl responsibility for the education and settlement of his nine brothers and sisters, while the countess increasingly concerned herself over her husband's financial difficulties. Both having been introduced to protestantism at an early age, as soon as they came into their inheritance they set about creating a godly household at Ashby-de-la-Zouch in Leicestershire under the guidance of the former Genevan exile Anthony Gilby. In 1570 Gilby published for the use of their family his translation of Calvin as *Commentaries … upon the Prophet Daniell*, following it in 1580 with another translation from Beza, *The Psalmes of David Truely Opened and Explaned*, intended specifically for Lady Katherine.

When Elizabeth fell ill with smallpox in November 1562, the protestant party looked to Huntingdon as her successor, on which account his wife received a 'privy nippe' from the queen the following spring (BL, Harley MS 787, fol. 16). Handicapped by his birth, Huntingdon obtained no major public office until 1569, when the queen employed him to guard Mary, queen of Scots. Then, late in 1572, she appointed him president of the council in the north and the countess, while still frequently attending court, assumed charge of the viceregal household at the King's Manor in York. Although she had no children of her own (she may have suffered a miscarriage in early 1566), she showed a particular interest in the training of young people. As he lay dying in Dublin in 1576, the first earl of Essex entrusted his two daughters and younger son to the earl and his wife at York, where they also welcomed the countess's favourite nephew, Thomas Sidney, after his father's death in 1586. The household established at Hackness in Yorkshire at the turn of the century by Margaret Hoby with its round of public and private religious observances almost certainly mirrors the practices she learned from her mistress the countess of Huntingdon, who at this time received the dedications of Nathaniel Gilby's translation of G. Sohn as *A Briefe and Learned Treatise … of the Antichrist* (1592), John Stockwood's translation of L. Daneau entitled *A Fruitfull Commentarie upon the Twelve Small Prophets* (1594), and Francis Bunny's *A Comparison betweene the Auncient Fayth of the Romans, and the New Romish Religion* (1595).

The earl of Huntingdon was planning to join his wife at court when he died unexpectedly at York on 14 December 1595. Despite the great care the queen took over breaking the news, the countess was devastated by grief. Refusing to accept the administration of her husband's much encumbered estate, she settled in Chelsea and remained very close to Elizabeth until the queen's death. In her widowhood she devoted herself to advancing the career of Sir Robert Sidney, delighting in having his young children

in her care during his embassies abroad. Theological writers also continued to seek her patronage, and books dedicated to her in her latter years included Henry Holland, *The Workes … of M. Richard Greenham* (1599), Thomas Savile, *The Raising of them that are Fallen* (1606), and Thomas Collins, *The Penitent Publican* (1610). Approaching eighty in 1618, she still prided herself on her ability 'to breed and govern yong gentlewomen' (*Rutland MSS*, 1.99). She died at Chelsea, and was buried in her mother's tomb in Chelsea Old Church on 14 August 1620.   CLAIRE CROSS

Sources PRO, SP 15/XIII/7, SP 15/XVII/31, C 54/1664 · BL, Lansdowne MSS 82, fols. 2, 5, 18; 156, fols. 82, 332; 162, fol. 132 · BL, Harley MS 787, fols. 16 · Hunt. L., Hastings papers, HA 13057, 1021, 12667, 5720 · Longleat House, Wiltshire, Dudley MSS 1/4, 1/183 · York City Archives, C 7 2; C 8 2; C 8 3; C 5, fol. 69; C 6, fols. 64, 66, 68, 72; C 8, fol. 57 · *Report on the manuscripts of the late Reginald Rawdon Hastings*, 4 vols., HMC, 78 (1928–47), vols. 1–2 · *Report on the manuscripts of Lord De L'Isle and Dudley*, 2, HMC, 77 (1933) · *Calendar of the manuscripts of the most hon. the marquis of Salisbury*, 7, HMC, 9 (1899) · *Seventh report*, HMC, 6 (1879) [W. More-Molyneux (Loseley MSS)] · *The manuscripts of his grace the duke of Rutland*, 4 vols., HMC, 24 (1888–1905), vol. 1 · H. Sydney and others, *Letters and memorials of state*, ed. A. Collins, 2 vols. (1746) · H. E. Malden, ed., 'Devereux papers, with Richard Broughton's memoranda, 1575–1601', *Camden miscellany, XIII*, CS, 3rd ser., 34 (1924) · C. Cross, 'The third earl of Huntingdon's death-bed: a Calvinist example of the *ars moriendi*', *Northern History*, 21 (1985), 80–107 · *Diary of Lady Margaret Hoby*, ed. D. M. Meads (1930) · C. Cross, *The puritan earl: the life of Henry Hastings, third earl of Huntingdon* (1966) · D. Loades, *John Dudley, duke of Northumberland, 1504–1553* (1996) · D. Wilson, *Sweet Robin: a biography of Robert Dudley, earl of Leicester, 1533–1588* (1981) · GEC, *Peerage*
Archives Hunt. L., MSS, HA 13057, 1021, 12667, 5720 · PRO, SP 15/XIII/7, SP 15/XVII/31, C 54/1664 | BL, Harley MS 787, fol. 16 · BL, Lansdowne MSS 82, fols. 2, 5, 18; 156, fols. 82, 332; 162, fol. 132 · Longleat, Wiltshire, Dudley MSS, 1/4; 1/183

Hastings, Laurence, twelfth earl of Pembroke (1320–1348), soldier, was the son of John *Hastings, second Lord Hastings (1287–1325) [*see under* Hastings, John, first Lord Hastings], and Juliana *Leybourne (d. 1367). He was born at Allesley, Warwickshire, on 20 March 1320. He was, therefore, not yet five years old when his father died early in 1325 and his inheritance passed into wardship. Custody of his lands was held, successively, by Hugh Despenser the younger, Edward III, and William Clinton, earl of Huntingdon, Laurence's stepfather. Shortly after Trinity Sunday (29 May) 1328 Hastings was married at Hereford to Agnes (d. 1368), third daughter of Roger (V) *Mortimer, first earl of March. Hastings is recorded as an esquire in Queen Philippa's household at the baptism of her daughter Isabella in July 1332. Having received financial assistance from the king—a gift of 100 marks in April 1338 and an annuity of 200 marks in September—Hastings served with Edward III in Flanders from July 1338 until the end of October 1339, accompanied by a retinue of three men-at-arms. Although Laurence was still a minor, on 4 February 1339 the king ordered that he should have livery of his inheritance, excepting the lands in the custody of Henry of Grosmont, earl of Derby. In the autumn of the same year Hastings participated in the king's *chevauchée* in the Cambrésis, Vermandois, and Thiérache, during which, at the nunnery of Mont-St Martin on, or a day or two after, 9 October, he was created earl of Pembroke, as grandson of

Isabella, eldest sister of Aymer de *Valence (d. 1324), with the prerogatives and honour of earl palatine in the lands inherited from Aymer. He accordingly bore the arms of Valence quartered with those of Hastings. His first summons to parliament was dated 16 November 1339 and for several years thereafter he was more involved in domestic affairs than military activity. There is no reliable evidence that he served at either the battle of Sluys or the siege of Tournai during the summer of 1340; nor, indeed, that he accompanied the king's army to Scotland during the winter of 1341–2. Pembroke was, however, summoned to all parliaments and councils held during 1340 and 1341; on 30 September 1340 he was appointed keeper of Ferns Castle, Wexford, with custody of the late earl of Atholl's land in Ireland during the minority of his heir; and he was present at the great tournament at Dunstable on 11 February 1342. He was also at this time gaining control of the entirety of his inheritance (he proved his age in May 1341) and attracting men into his service: four who received grants of land from Pembroke can later be seen in his military retinue. One of these was his half-nephew, Sir Hugh *Hastings (d. 1347), whose fine brass at Elsing, Norfolk, included a depiction of Pembroke (now lost, but shown in late eighteenth-century rubbings) as one of eight side figures.

During the last weeks of 1342 Pembroke resumed his military career, serving with Edward III in Brittany until early in the following year. According to the payroll, his retinue had a peak strength of 64 men-at-arms and 100 mounted archers. Adam Murimuth relates that Pembroke was one of the knights of the Round Table in January 1344; he was not, however, included in the regular foundation of the Order of the Garter. Pembroke was actively involved in the intense military activity in France during the mid-1340s. Contracted to provide a retinue of 80 men-at-arms and 80 mounted archers, he accompanied Henry of Grosmont to Aquitaine in early August 1345 and for a year took a prominent part in Henry's campaigns there. He was present at the capture of Bergerac on 24 August 1345, but missed the battle of Auberoche on the following 21 October, arriving on the battlefield a day after the action. According to Froissart, he was much hurt that Henry had not awaited his coming, and plainly expressed his feelings. He was one of the principal captains of the English garrison at Aiguillon, which was unsuccessfully besieged by John, duke of Normandy, from late March until early August 1346. Pembroke returned to England in December; Henry Knighton relates that the sea journey was made hazardous by a severe storm. Within a few months Pembroke was involved in the siege of Calais. In June 1347 he was appointed with the earl of Northampton to command a fleet that was to prevent the introduction of provisions into the town; on the 25th they won a complete victory, and dispersed the French near Le Crotoy. This was Pembroke's last exploit, for, having made a will on 24 August 1348, he died a few days later at his principal residence, Abergavenny, and was buried there in the priory church of St Mary. He was succeeded by a one-year-old

son, John *Hastings, who became thirteenth earl of Pembroke (1347–1375). His widow, Agnes, married John Hakluyt.   ANDREW AYTON

Sources GEC, *Peerage* · PRO · *Chancery records* · BL, Cotton MS, Galba, E.111, fol. 186v · *Report of the Lords committees … for all matters touching the dignity of a peer of the realm*, 4 (1829) · Rymer, *Foedera*, new edn · G. Wrottesley, *Crécy and Calais* (1897); repr. (1898) · *The wardrobe book of William de Norwell*, ed. M. Lyon and others (1983) · *Œuvres*, ed. K. de Lettenhove and A. Scheler, 28 vols. (Brussels, 1867–77) · *Adae Murimuth continuatio chronicarum. Robertus de Avesbury de gestis mirabilibus regis Edwardi tertii*, ed. E. M. Thompson, Rolls Series, 93 (1889) · *Knighton's chronicle, 1337–1396*, ed. and trans. G. H. Martin, OMT (1995) [Lat. orig., *Chronica de eventibus Angliae a tempore regis Edgari usque mortem regis Ricardi Secundi*, with parallel Eng. text] · K. Fowler, *The king's lieutenant: Henry of Grosmont, first duke of Lancaster, 1310–1361* (1969) · A. R. Wagner and J. G. Mann, 'A fifteenth-century description of the brass of Sir Hugh Hastings at Elsing, Norfolk', *Antiquaries Journal*, 19 (1939), 421–8 · CIPM, 9, no. 118

Likenesses church brass, repro. in Wagner, 'A fifteenth-century description of the brass of Sir Hugh Hastings' · effigy on monument, priory church of St Mary, Abergavenny

Wealth at death manorial holdings: CIPM, 9, no. 118

Hastings [*née* Davies], **Lucy, countess of Huntingdon** (1613–1679), noblewoman, born on 20 January 1613 in Dublin, was the daughter of Sir John *Davies (*bap.* 1569, *d.* 1626), attorney-general of Ireland, and his wife, Eleanor *Davies (1590–1652), daughter of George Touchet, Baron Audley. At the age of five Lucy moved to England when Davies sought to further his career at court. Educated at home, she learned Latin, French, Spanish, Greek, and Hebrew, and inherited her mother's interest in religion. Basua Makin, who taught her, paid tribute to her sagacity: she was 'an ornament of our sex' (*Hastings MSS*, 4.348).

In 1623, first without licence at the house of the dowager countess of Derby, and again on 7 August at Englefield parish church, Berkshire, Lucy married Ferdinando, Lord Hastings (1609–1656), the eldest son of Henry Hastings, fifth earl of Huntingdon. Her dowry was £6500. Letters between Lucy and her husband during this period demonstrate affection and friendship. However, tensions existed between the two families, in particular between Lucy's mother and mother-in-law. After the death of her father in 1626 a legal battle commenced between her mother and the Hastings family for the manor of Englefield. Lucy's mother, Eleanor Davies, was imprisoned from 1633 to 1635 and from 1637 to 1640 due to her prophetic activities. Lucy petitioned the king in 1633 on her mother's behalf and in 1640 secured her release from the Tower.

Ferdinando Hastings succeeded as sixth earl of Huntingdon on 14 November 1643. During the 1640s his brother, Lord Loughborough, a royalist soldier, garrisoned the family castle of Ashby-de-la-Zouch, Leicestershire, which was besieged by parliamentary forces and surrendered on 28 February 1646. Due to the damage suffered by the castle the Huntingdons made Donington Park their main residence. They also had a house at Highgate, near London.

Huntingdon's estates were eventually sequestrated and after successfully compounding his income was reduced

Lucy Hastings, countess of Huntingdon (1613–1679), by John Hoskins, 1649

from £1808 to only £900. He had to sell some land to pay his debts and obtained an act of parliament in 1653 to break the entail. He and his wife also petitioned the committee on articles of war to secure their Irish estates which were threatened with seizure.

Of the Huntingdons' ten children, at least three of their six daughters—Elizabeth [see Langham, Lady Elizabeth], Mary, and Christiana—and only their youngest son, Theophilus *Hastings (1650–1701), survived to adulthood. Their eldest son, Henry, born in 1630, died of smallpox in 1649; Lady Huntingdon may be the author of a manuscript poem in the Huntington Library copy of *Lachrymae musarum* (1650), a collection of commemorative verse on the young man. Possibly also a contributor to *The New Proclamation, in Answer to a Letter* (1649), a defence of, and usually attributed to, Lady Davies, she was certainly actively exercising her intellectual skills on her children's behalf, educating her daughter Elizabeth in Latin, French, and Italian as well as instructing her in the Bible.

When Lady Huntingdon's husband died 'of an asthma' (*Hastings MSS*, 4.351) on 13 February 1656, Theophilus succeeded him as earl aged only five, and the full burden of his upbringing and of contending with a debt-burdened estate fell on Lady Huntingdon's shoulders. She, or perhaps someone acting on her behalf, tried in 1656 and 1657 to get a private bill through parliament to confirm the sale of land her husband had made to pay his debts and also to confirm the sale of other land for payment of the remaining debts. At this time she was also involved in a dispute with her brother-in-law, Lord Loughborough, over her jointure estates. In addition to estates in England she had

charge of land in Ireland for which she received rents, dealt with tenants, and instructed solicitors and stewards.

Despite financial difficulties and other distractions, Lady Huntingdon, in common with other aristocratic women in similarly taxing circumstances, was instrumental in safeguarding her family's interests through the interregnum and beyond. She continued to campaign to restore her mother's reputation, enlisting the help of first her friend Katherine Stanley, marchioness of Dorchester, and later her son Theophilus in protesting against the portrayal of Lady Davies in the 1660 *Continuation* of Richard Baker's *Chronicle*; offending passages were eventually removed. She also successfully arranged marriages for her children—Elizabeth to Sir James Langham in 1662, Theophilus to Elizabeth Lewis in 1672, and Mary to Sir William Jolliffe in 1674. Although sale of her Irish estates in 1673 helped fund portions for her daughters, these dowries were not large, and they were considered to have married beneath them. In particular, Jolliffe was not considered good enough for the daughter of an earl. However, in spite of such criticism, Theophilus was supportive of his sisters and encouraged their marriages. Lady Huntingdon died on 14 November 1679 and was buried at Ashby.

TANIA CLAIRE JEFFRIES

Sources correspondence, Hunt. L., Hastings papers · *Report on the manuscripts of the late Reginald Rawdon Hastings*, 4 vols., HMC, 78 (1928–47), vol. 4 · E. S. Cope, *Handmaid of the Holy Spirit: Dame Eleanor Davies, never soe mad a ladie* (1992) · CSP dom., 1633–4; 1649–50; 1656–7 · M. A. E. Green, ed., *Calendar of the proceedings of the committee for compounding … 1643–1660*, 5 vols., PRO (1889–92) · *Diary of Thomas Burton*, ed. J. T. Rutt, 4 vols. (1828); repr. (1974), vol. 1 · JHC, 7 (1651–9) · VCH Warwickshire · GEC, *Peerage*, new edn, vol. 6 · GEC, *Peerage*, new edn, vol. 2 · M. Bell, G. Parfitt, and S. Shepherd, *A biographical dictionary of English women writers, 1580–1720* (1990), 97 · Greaves & Zaller, BDBR, 216–17 · A. Fraser, *The weaker vessel: women's lot in seventeenth-century England* (1984), 136, 282
Archives Hunt. L.
Likenesses M. Gheeraerts junior, oils on panel, 1623, priv. coll. · J. Hoskins, miniature, 1649, priv. coll. [see illus.] · studio of A. Van Dyck, double portrait (with Katherine Stanhope), Yale U. CBA, Paul Mellon collection; see illus. in Stanhope, Katherine, *suo jure* countess of Chesterfield, and Lady Stanhope (*bap.* 1609, *d.* 1667)

Hastings, Marian [*née* Anna Maria Apollonia Chapuset; *other married name* Marian von Imhoff, Baroness von Imhoff] (**1747–1837**), wife of Warren Hastings, was, on the evidence of the act granting her British nationality in 1796, born in Nuremberg. No date is stated, but a secondary source indicates 2 February 1747. Her grandfather was Charles Chapuset de St Valentin, protestant officer in the household troops of the king of France, who was obliged to go into exile following the revocation of the edict of Nantes in 1685. He went to Berlin as a teacher of languages and of dancing but finally settled at Altdorf, near Nuremberg, where, as a widower, he married Katharina Maria Müller, a clergyman's daughter, in 1693. They had two sons. Another son was born from a third marriage. This last son, Johann Jakob, married Caroline Friederike Grundgeiger or Krongeiger (*b.* 1720) at Karlsruhe. He is said to have died in 1758, leaving a widow and two children, Anna Maria Apollonia, the future Mrs Hastings, and Johann Paul Thomas (b. 1749).

Nothing is known of Anna Maria Chapuset's childhood and adolescence, and the place and date of her marriage to Baron Christoph Carl Adam von Imhoff (c.1734–c.1802) are uncertain. Nuremberg, Stuttgart, and Strelitz have all been advanced as hypothetical venues and the years from 1765 to 1768 as likely dates. Imhoff was an officer in the Württemberg army left unemployed by the end of the Seven Years' War. Some sources maintain that he met his future wife in Nuremberg; others argue for Strelitz, where she was said to be a maid of honour at the court of the duke of Mecklenburg-Strelitz. The Imhoffs and their two sons, Charles and Julius, moved to England in 1768 through the good offices of Elizabeth Schwellenberg, Queen Charlotte's mistress of the robes. Imhoff soon obtained a cadetship in the East India Company's Madras army but, as an accomplished miniature portraitist, he no doubt also saw a market for his artistic skills in India. Early in 1769, accompanied by his wife and elder child, he embarked for Madras in the *Duke of Grafton*. Among the passengers was Warren *Hastings (1732–1818), then a widower of thirty-seven, returning to India. The baroness took Hastings under her care when he fell ill and a shipboard romance blossomed. Imhoff lived in Madras with his wife until the latter part of 1770, when, having resigned his army commission, he moved to Calcutta in search of a wider clientele for his portraits. His wife remained in Madras, for part of the time at least, a resident in Hastings's house. She joined her husband in Calcutta in October 1771. Hastings followed in February 1772 on taking up his new appointment as governor of Bengal. In a company general letter to Madras dated 25 March 1772

Imhoff was ordered to return to Europe for declining military service. He arrived back in September 1773 and, presumably, started divorce proceedings.

Many questions remain unanswered regarding the course of events that led up to the marriage of Warren Hastings and the former Baroness von Imhoff in Calcutta on 8 August 1777. It is supposed that she lived in Hastings's house at Alipore or one nearby. Suggestions by Macaulay and Wraxall that Hastings simply paid Imhoff a large sum of money to divorce his wife oversimplify more sophisticated transactions. Hastings undertook to adopt the Imhoffs' two boys and almost certainly made funds available for legal and other expenses which probably erred on the side of generosity. However Hastings and the baroness may have lived before their marriage, discretion prevailed. Philip Francis, Hastings's severest political foe, mocked the liaison but never seriously traduced it. In fact he wrote of Marian Hastings as 'accomplished' and deserving of 'every mark of respect' (Parkes and Merivale, 2.96). Relations between Imhoff, his former wife, and Hastings remained amicable during and after the divorce proceedings.

A decree of divorce, dated Weimar, 1 June 1776, was granted by the duke of Saxony on Imhoff's petition that he considered himself 'an abandoned conjugal mate' (BL, Add. MS 39903, fol. 65). It did not reach Calcutta until July 1777, where its validity was confirmed by an English missionary. The baroness reverted to her maiden name, and a marriage licence was issued on 5 August 1777 in which she was described as a 'singlewoman' (BL, Add. MS 39904A). The wedding took place three days later. The marriage brought enduring happiness to both parties, but also regrets that there were no children. Marian Hastings, as she became known, sailed to England for her health in

Marian Hastings (1747–1837), by Johan Zoffany, 1784–7 [with her husband, Warren Hastings, and an Indian servant]

1784. Hastings left India in 1785, and they eventually settled at Daylesford in Worcestershire, where Hastings built a new house on his ancestral estate. Marian continued to live there after her husband's death in 1818.

Hastings took his wife into his confidence over political affairs, but Wraxall exaggerated when he wrote that Marian 'invariably maintained her ascendancy over his [Hastings's] mind as well as his affections' (*Historical and Posthumous Memoirs*, 4.17–18). Certainly Hastings indulged her and she had influence, but ultimately he kept his mind his own. In their personal financial affairs Marian's prudence contrasted with Hastings's extravagance. In a statement to the East India Company in 1795 Hastings declared his wife's fortune to be £40,000, her marriage settlement accounting for the greater part of the total. However, it has since been estimated that 'at the time she actually possessed at least £107,725' (Marshall, 252). Marian's financial affairs in India remain an enigma and she appears to have concealed her wealth from her husband. She palpably suffered a substantial loss in 1797 when one of her bankers stopped payments.

Marian's jewel-bedecked figure dazzled society in London and Calcutta. It was a gift to caricaturists and satirists, and a general source of amusement or concern. 'Our weather remains unparagoned', wrote Horace Walpole. 'Mrs. Hastings is not more brilliant' (Walpole to Mary Berry, 7 Nov 1793, Walpole, *Corr.*, 12.55). Fanny Burney complained that she made everyone else look underdressed and thought that 'a modest & quiet appearance & demeanour' would be more becoming during Hastings's trial (*The Journals and Letters of Fanny Burney (Madame D'Arblay)*, ed. J. Hemlow, 1, 1972, 25 May 1792, 165–6). In spite of this, Burney thought well of Marian Hastings. She was indeed an agreeable and handsome woman with especially beautiful hair, which she wore loose and unpowdered. Her imperfect command of English, in speech and in writing, perhaps added to her distinctly exotic air. She died at Daylesford House on 29 March 1837 and was buried in the churchyard close to her husband on 7 April 1837.

T. H. Bowyer

Sources BL, Warren Hastings MSS, Add. MSS 28973–29236, 39871–39904, 41606–41611 • *The letters of Warren Hastings to his wife*, ed. S. C. Grier [H. C. Gregg] (1905) • S. C. Grier [H. C. Gregg], 'Some fresh light on the second Mrs. Hastings and her family', *Bengal Past and Present*, 5 (1910), 333–8 • S. C. Grier [H. C. Gregg], 'The first marriage of Mrs. Hastings', *Bengal Past and Present*, 24 (1922), 47–8 • W. Foster, 'The Hastings–Imhoff romance', *Bengal Past and Present*, 33 (1927), 106–12 • J. J. Cotton, 'The second Mrs Hastings and her sons', *Bengal Past and Present*, 30 (1925), 9–17 • K. Feiling, *Warren Hastings* (1954) • H. E. Busteed, *Echoes from old Calcutta*, 4th edn (1908) • P. J. Marshall, 'The private fortune of Marian Hastings', *BIHR*, 37 (1964), 245–53 • [Lord Macaulay], *EdinR*, 74 (1841–2), 160–255 • *The historical and the posthumous memoirs of Sir Nathaniel William Wraxall, 1772–1784*, ed. H. B. Wheatley, 5 vols. (1884), vol. 4, pp. 16–19 • C. A. Lawson, *The private life of Warren Hastings* (1905) • J. Parkes and H. Merivale, *Memoirs of Sir Philip Francis*, 2 vols. (1867) • *Memoirs of the life of the Right Hon. Warren Hastings, first governor-general of Bengal*, ed. G. R. Gleig, 3 vols. (1841) • parish register (baptism), London, St Giles • *GM*, 2nd ser., 7 (1837), 557 • parish register, Worcestershire, Daylesford [burial]

Archives BL, Warren Hastings MSS, Add. MSS 28973–29236; 39871–39904; 41606–41611 • Bodl. Oxf., MS Dep. c.185

Likenesses W. Dickinson, mezzotint, 1769 (Baroness Imhoff and her son Charles; after R. E. Pine), BM, NPG; repro. in Grier, ed., *Letters of Warren Hastings to his wife*, 98 • J. Zoffany, oils, *c.*1783, Victoria Memorial Hall, Calcutta; repro. in *Bengal Past & Present*, 30 (1925), 42 • J. Zoffany, group portrait, oils, 1784–7, Victoria Memorial Hall, Calcutta [*see illus.*] • Gillray, repro. in M. D. George, *Catalogue of political and personal satires in … BM*, 6, 7324, 7330 • W. Greatbach, engraving (after O. Humphry), BM, NPG; repro. in Gleig, *Memoirs* • Schlotterbeck, portrait, repro. in *Bengal Past & Present*, 30 (1925), 9, 13

Hastings, Sir Nicholas (*d.* before 1316). *See under* Hastings family (*per. c.*1300–*c.*1450).

Hastings, Sir Patrick Gardiner (1880–1952), lawyer, was born in London on 17 March, St Patrick's day, 1880 and was consequently given the name of Ireland's patron saint, there being Irish blood on both sides of the family. He was the younger son of Alfred Gardiner Hastings and his wife, Kate Comyns Carr, a Pre-Raphaelite painter who exhibited in the London galleries and elsewhere. The elder Hastings, although originally a solicitor, can hardly have been long in practice and seems to have been an unreliable parent. His son's early memories were of alternating penury and affluence. 'Bankruptcy in my family', he wrote, 'was not a misfortune, it was a habit' (Patrick Hastings, 5). His recollections of childhood included hours spent in his mother's studio where he was allowed to play with the paints on her palette, and of late nights spent in company with his father and his father's 'business friends', which frequently ended with himself falling asleep across the table. At ten he was sent to a preparatory boarding-school which he hated, and the two years spent at Charterhouse School were no improvement. He resented both the discipline and the classical regimen which taught him, he claimed, none of the practical things he required to know. He left Charterhouse at sixteen, undistinguished in work or games and a victim of chronic asthma.

Family fortunes at this time were at a low ebb. After eighteen months of precarious living in Corsica, France, and Belgium with his mother and elder brother, Hastings took a subordinate post as a mining engineer in north Wales. The mine proved unproductive and with his brother he joined the Suffolk imperial yeomanry and saw two years of active service in the Second South African War. On his return he found his parents in no position to help him towards a career. From quite early years, however, he had wanted to be a barrister and with scarcely a penny in his pocket he was admitted as a student to the Middle Temple. He did all his reading there since he could not afford to buy books. From Putney he walked to work each day, went without lunch, but treated himself to dinner at a Soho restaurant for the price of 1s. 6d. He earned a few pounds weekly by writing theatre reviews and gossip for several newspapers. With no dress clothes for attending the theatre, he wore a greatcoat tactically fastened over a white shirt and white tie. By such expedients he saved the £100 to pay for his call in 1904.

Hastings contrived almost immediately to obtain some devilling work from Charles Gill, a busy lawyer with a large criminal practice; some two years later he found a

Sir Patrick Gardiner Hastings (1880–1952), by Dudley Glanfield

seat in the chambers of Horace Avory. When Avory went to the bench Hastings boldly took on the chambers. He always declared that his debt to Avory was enormous. From him he learned never to make notes but to read a brief thoroughly and commit it to memory; then, as soon as the case was over, dismiss the whole thing from his mind.

In 1906 Hastings married Mary Ellenore, the third daughter of Lieutenant-Colonel Frederick Leigh Grundy; they had two sons and three daughters. At the time of his marriage he and his wife possessed no more than £20 between them; but this did not last for long, for during the next few years he became one of the busiest juniors at the common-law bar. When in 1919 he took silk, having been rejected during the war as medically unfit for service, his reputation as an advocate was firmly established. He was no less successful as a silk, and at forty found himself with 'all the cases that I wanted and perhaps more than I could do' (Patrick Hastings, 147).

Politically Hastings was always to the left and he was adopted as the Liberal candidate at Ilford in 1918. But he was soon disillusioned by the feud between Asquith and Lloyd George, as well as by the 'coupon' election itself, and he quit both the party and the campaign. In 1921 he was adopted as Labour candidate for Wallsend, in Northumberland, an industrial seat which, at the general election in 1922, he won against the odds. The move to Labour cost Hastings friendships as well as clients, but he was driven by a genuine desire to improve the living conditions of the poorest. Parliament, however, proved 'a bitter disappointment' to him (Patrick Hastings, 229). He was frustrated by its slow working, and shocked at the hostility of Conservative members towards their Labour counterparts. He nevertheless attended the house regularly, and Ramsay MacDonald valued his presence there. When the first Labour government was formed in January 1924 he became attorney-general, with the customary knighthood.

Hastings later wrote that he never worked harder than during the short period of this administration, in whose downfall he played a central part. Much of his time was taken up with the Irish boundary commission, but in July, in an apparently routine matter, he authorized the prosecution under the Incitement to Mutiny Act (1797) of John Campbell, acting editor of the communist *Workers' Weekly*, over an article that urged soldiers not to fire on striking workers. The indignation with which this action was met in Labour circles took Hastings by surprise, and after a cabinet meeting on 6 August, in which ministers voiced fears that a trial would only advertise the communist cause, he withdrew the prosecution. But this opened the government to the charge that it had subverted the law on grounds of political expediency, and in October it fell on a censure motion over its handling of the 'Campbell case'. Hastings defended himself adroitly in parliament in the face of severe criticism, which was echoed in two *Times* leaders, but he was deeply disillusioned by the lack of loyalty shown him by Ramsay MacDonald, and perhaps even more by the cynical opportunism of erstwhile legal friends on the opposition benches. Although he held Wallsend at the ensuing general election, his political career was effectively over; in 1926, in poor health, he resigned his seat. According to MacDonald's biographer 'Hastings was a brilliant advocate, but a novice in Labour politics' (Marquand, 365).

From this date began Hastings's rapid climb to leadership of the common-law bar, an eminence which he shared for many years with his friend and frequent opponent Norman Birkett. Spectacular cases, such as the actions between Marie Stopes and Halliday Sutherland, and the Savidge tribunal, brought him much publicity. In 1936, in the case widely known as the 'Talking Mongoose', he successfully represented Richard Lambert, the editor of *The Listener*, in a slander action against Sir Cecil Levita. The latter had, among other things, alleged that Lambert had given credence to the claims of an Isle of Man farmer, supported by a psychical researcher, to have seen a remarkable mongoose which possessed the power of speech in several languages. But most of what became a very large income inevitably derived from less exciting commercial work. Hastings had a great gift for simplification and could make a commercial case so easy to follow that what might otherwise have taken weeks was completed in a few days. Although he often appeared in the criminal courts, he had a deep dislike of murder cases.

In the Second World War Hastings served for a time as an intelligence officer at Fighter Command headquarters, but his health proved unequal to the strain, and he returned to a law practice in which most cases were heard without a jury and the importance of an advocate's role had greatly diminished. The death in action of his younger son, David, hit him hard. His last great success, in 1946, the defence against an action for libel brought by H. J. Laski, took a heavy toll on him; in 1948 he decided to retire. He occupied himself by writing, and achieved considerable success with his *Autobiography* (1948), *Cases in Court* (1949), and *Famous and Infamous Cases* (1950). The theatrical sense was very strong in him and he tried his hand at half a dozen plays, of which only *The River* (1925), *Scotch Mist* (1926), and *The Blind Goddess* (1947) achieved any real success; the latter, a play about the law courts, was also made into a film.

Hastings was not an intellectual by temperament and his reading was largely confined to law reports and thrillers such as those of his friend Edgar Wallace. A devoted husband and father, he enjoyed nothing better than an open-air country life spent with his family and intimate friends. He was a good horseman, a first-class shot, and a passionately keen fisherman. Tall, thin, dark-haired, with blue eyes and a very straight carriage, he had a forceful and somewhat intolerant personality; he was a master of simple, unadorned language. Above all, he was a man of tremendous enthusiasms and great courage.

Hastings's stature as an advocate was the result primarily of his brilliance in cross-examination. He learned from one of his early mentors, Sir Edward Carson, the art of brevity and of getting under a witness's skin with the first question. Once he had done this he pursued his case ruthlessly and relentlessly, firing questions 'in such quick succession that he sometimes laid himself open to the charge of bullying' (Hyde, *Norman Birkett*, 221). He was a dangerous, but always an honourable opponent, at his best when speaking directly to a jury. For the thundering emotional appeals which used to be the fashion he substituted an incisive appeal to intelligence. He is said by his family to have been incapable of dissimulation, but Birkett watching him in court was fascinated by the play of expressions on his face—'anger, surprise, incredulity, disdain … They were meant for the jury and were indeed more eloquent than words' (Hyde, *Sir Patrick Hastings*, xiv–xv).

In 1950 Hastings visited his son Nicholas who was farming in Kenya; there he suffered a slight stroke from which he never fully recovered. He died at his London home, 9 Dorchester Court, Sloane Street, Belgravia, on 26 February 1952.   ANTHONY LEJEUNE, rev. MARK POTTLE

Sources P. Hastings, *The autobiography of Sir Patrick Hastings* (1948) · H. M. Hyde, *Sir Patrick Hastings: his life and cases* (1960) · Patricia Hastings, *The life of Patrick Hastings* (1959) · *The Times* (1 Oct 1924), 8b–c, 15d; (9 Oct 1924), 15b–c; (27 Feb 1952), 6e · *Law Journal* (7 March 1952) · D. Marquand, *Ramsay MacDonald* (1977) · T. Jones, *Whitehall diary*, vol. 1: *1916–1925* (1969) · J. Rozenberg, *The case for the crown: the inside story of the director of public prosecutions* (1987) · H. M. Hyde, *Norman Birkett: the life of Lord Birkett of Ulverston* (1964) · J. Johnson and A. Greutzner, *The dictionary of British artists, 1880–1940* (1976), vol. 5 of *Dictionary of British art* · private information (1971)

Likenesses N. C. Bentley, ink and pencil caricature, 1948, NPG · D. Glanfield, photograph, NPG [*see illus.*] · photographs, repro. in Hastings, *Autobiography* · photographs, repro. in Hyde, *Sir Patrick Hastings*

Wealth at death £14,532 8*s.*: probate, 29 April 1952, *CGPLA Eng. & Wales*

Hastings, Sir Ralph (*d.* 1346). *See under* Hastings family (*per. c.*1300–*c.*1450).

Hastings, Sir Ralph (*c.*1322–1397). *See under* Hastings family (*per. c.*1300–*c.*1450).

Hastings, Ralph (*c.*1379–1405). *See under* Hastings family (*per. c.*1300–*c.*1450).

Hastings [*née* Shirley], **Selina, countess of Huntingdon** (1707–1791), founder of the Countess of Huntingdon's Connexion, was born on 13 August 1707, probably at Astwell House, Northamptonshire, the second of three daughters of Washington Shirley, second Earl Ferrers (1677–1729), and Mary (*d.* 1740), daughter of Sir Richard Levinge of co. Westmeath, Ireland, and his wife, Mary. Nothing is known of Liny's early life, some of it probably spent in Ireland. The child of a broken marriage, she sided with her father and rejected her mother.

Marriage and conversion, 1728–1746 Lady Selina married, on 3 June 1728, Theophilus Hastings, ninth earl of Huntingdon (1696–1746), and they lived at his Leicestershire seat at Donington Park. Her father's death the following year created extensive conflict, especially with her mother, over his estate. All seven of the countess's children were born during the first decade of her marriage, and early on she developed gynaecological complications. In 1731 she and her husband leased a summer house outside London, The Grove, at Enfield Chase, Middlesex; other seasons were spent at additional rented houses, first at 2 Savile Row, later in Downing Street and in Chelsea. In January 1739 the countess attended the prince of Wales's birthday party, dressed the 'most extraordinary' of all, in a costume 'much properer for a stucco staircase than the apparel of a lady' (Llanover, 2.28). Six weeks later she joined a cadre of a dozen aristocratic ladies who vehemently opposed the ministry's pacifying position regarding Spain, and who noisily disrupted a sitting of the House of Lords by barracking speakers with whom they disagreed.

During the first decade of her marriage, Lady Huntingdon supervised many of the practical details on her husband's estates, supported the religious enterprises connected with them, and engaged in various charitable activities. What led her to accept Methodism in 1739 was a combination of increasing religious, emotional, health, family, and financial anxieties, when she was telling others that she had lived a 'disagreeable' life (Hastings MS 13035). That summer she received visits from several men of Methodist inclination. Yet her noted sister-in-law, Lady Betty *Hastings, rejected Methodism, and upon her death late that year deprived the Huntingdons of an expected inheritance. Soon after, the countess was described as having a 'very choleric and violent temper' (Benham, 68).

In 1741 Lady Huntingdon initiated a relationship with John and Charles Wesley. Hoping they 'might think on me as you would do on no one else!' (Huntingdon to J. Wesley, 24 Oct 1741, *Works of John Wesley*, 26.67), she adopted John Wesley's belief in Christian perfection and when in London attended his West Street Chapel. For a brief period

Selina Hastings, countess of Huntingdon (1707–1791), by unknown engraver, pubd 1773 (after John Russell, 1773)

Donington provided Wesley with a base in the midlands. The countess read religious works to her servants and attempted to convert society ladies at Bath. Continuing clashes with various family members over financial settlements, together with the deaths of two of her four sons, increased her anxiety. 'No soul can conceive the darkness perplexity misery I have constantly surrounds me … O! the distress of my soul' (Methodist archives, black folio, 13, 85). Finding no comfort in Wesley's notion of perfection, by 1744 she shifted towards Calvinistic predestination, especially as proclaimed by George Whitefield, with whom she began a correspondence. In 1743 she had met the Welsh Calvinistic exhorter Howel Harris, who by the following year was frequently preaching to small groups of her friends in London. Under his influence she attended the Tabernacle Chapel in London, yet was still attracted to the mystical writings of William Law, who had often visited her. The earl and countess were fatefully caught up in the turmoil of the Jacobite rising of 1745, both secret supporters. Its defeat drove him to despondency and fears that his estates might be confiscated. Totally careless of his health, he died in London on 13 October 1746; she erected an elaborate memorial to him in Ashby-de-la-Zouch parish church, Leicestershire.

Emergence as a Methodist leader A widow at thirty-nine, Lady Huntingdon assumed responsibility for her four surviving children, her husband's dying intestate adding further burdens. Still religiously insecure, she sought direct mystical union with God, yet contact with Harris and

other Calvinists led her to appoint Whitefield her personal chaplain. He immediately proclaimed her divine calling to pursue England's redemption: 'This honour hath been put upon your Ladyship by the great head of the church' (*Works of the Reverend George Whitefield*, 2.294). She always expected deference from her followers, and Whitefield proved the most adept at offering it. The countess's relationship with him put further distance between her and John Wesley, to whom Calvinism was abhorrent. To her Chelsea salon services she invited the titled and wealthy to hear Whitefield and other fervent preachers, hoping to foster England's religious rebirth from the top. Although unsuccessful in 'converting' these worthies, all ardent political supporters of Frederick, prince of Wales, she sought to induce the prince to secure protection for the Methodist movement. Through personal contact with various Church of England bishops, she attempted to soften their opposition and to persuade them to ordain evangelical clergymen. In this she met with some limited success.

Frederick's death in 1751, soon followed by Whitefield's departure for America, threw Lady Huntingdon back into spiritual turmoil and a serious dabbling in mysticism and millenarianism. To one religious friend, 'what she talks appears to me a Hotch Potch of Opinions glean'd from every where without direction' (Methodist archives, DD Pr 1.6.75). She found consolation in contact with Charles Wesley during the mid-1750s but in the process drove a serious wedge between him and his brother John. Taking a house in the Clifton area of Bristol, she formed a small group of women to counter Moravian activities. Though she struggled to inculcate her beliefs into her children, none responded. Her elder daughter found life with her mother 'void of every thing agreeable' (Hastings MS 6294). Viewing the countess as 'righteous over-much' (J. Wesley to Lady Rawdon [E. Hastings], 18 March 1760, *Letters of … John Wesley*, 4.88), she married Lord Rawdon and moved to Ireland, saying that escaping her mother was her sole inducement. Following the death of her other remaining daughter, Lady Huntingdon's hope rested with her firstborn, Francis, who at his father's death had assumed the earldom. Yet he died in 1789, also immune to her religious entreaties.

Trevecca and Georgia During the 1760s the countess established chapels at major watering places of the noble and wealthy. In 1761 she appointed William Romaine and Martin Madan chaplains and opened her first chapel—in the grounds of her Brighton residence. The Bath chapel, opened in 1765, was to prove the jewel in her crown outside London. A chapel at Tunbridge Wells was established in 1769. In 1768 she became drawn into the controversy surrounding the parish living of Aldwincle, Northamptonshire. Madan and another cleric, Thomas Haweis, stood accused of simony regarding its ownership, and Lady Huntingdon was required to purchase the living in an attempt to remove the scandal.

At the same time the countess secretly supported evangelical students at St Edmund Hall, Oxford. When six were expelled from the university, it fitted a long-held plan to establish her own college. Apparently locked out of the universities and spurning the existing academies of the dissenters (whom she always rejected, apart from Philip Doddridge), she could expand evangelical preaching by providing the training of ministers, for whom she sought episcopal ordination. With Howell Harris's assistance, a Brecknockshire farmhouse was renovated and opened as Trevecca College on 24 August 1768. Fascinated with overseas missions, she sent two students to the East Indies. Though the venture proved a disaster, Whitefield's death in America in 1770 opened prospects for a mission to Georgia, where he had bequeathed her the Bethesda orphanage. She sent a small group of Trevecca students to use it as a base from which to 'convert the poor people in America' (Granard MS T3765/M/2/21) and seriously considered accompanying them. In the event, they were led by an evangelical cleric, William Piercy, whose overbearing leadership they unanimously rejected. He also so infuriated the Georgians that Bethesda was burnt to the ground; this and his squandering her open purse in the end cost Lady Huntingdon well over £6000. Part of this was to purchase slaves, and the countess proved immune to rising calls against the ownership of slaves, even instructing her Georgia managers to purchase a slave to 'be called SELINA, after me' (Seymour, 2.266).

Relations with Wesley The catastrophic failure in America hardened Lady Huntingdon's belief that only her personal control could ensure productive religious fruit. She was drawn into Augustus Toplady's rigidly Calvinistic camp. Matters had come to a head with Wesley's 1770 conference minutes, which claimed continuing good works a condition of a Christian's salvation. This notion she frantically countered, stating that she abhorred Wesley more than any other person in the world, denouncing him as 'a papist unmasked, a heretic, an apostate' (Tyerman, 195). She mounted a vigorous campaign, sponsoring Toplady's anti-Wesley *Gospel Magazine*. Egged on by the countess and Wesley, the preachers they sent out actively attacked one another, a combat in the field lasting many years. Her relationship with the Wesleys was never re-established. Towards the end of her life, when she learned that one of her former ministers was to preach in John Wesley's chapels, she wrote that this was intended 'as an imposition & an affront to our People & *first* to me' (Methodist archives, black folio, 129). Demanding that Trevecca be cleansed of any Wesleyan sentiments, Lady Huntingdon lost the services of its overseer, John Fletcher, and tutor, Joseph Benson. She exerted total control over the institution, which became her home for at least six months each year, and where she was, according to one student, 'a stern disciplinarian' (Aveling, 17), supervising all aspects of her students' education. More importantly to her, she assumed full control of the places and times they preached, and they referred to her as their 'commanding officer' (Cheshunt Foundation MS F1/1290).

Lady Huntingdon's wondrous energy and increasingly aggressive activities exposed her to the satirical pen. Her sanity had frequently been questioned by those about her. Now, as Lady Sherwood, she was depicted as 'labouring under a hypochondriacal distemper' (Graves, 204). Another publication fixed on her the charge of antinomianism, which would long cling to her and her followers. At her death, an engraving portrayed her seated in a Gothic church, wearing nun's robes, with clasped hands and upturned eyes, while beside her rested a skull. This correctly conveyed her taste for the Gothic and Romantic, in which she frequently indulged with the architecture and fittings of her chapels. Another distinctive feature was her insistence on the use of the Book of Common Prayer at main services of worship. She rejected for herself and other women the role of preacher and never published her own religious views. The only exceptions were a brief introduction and conclusion to a work attacking Wesley's 1770 conference minutes; a preface to a 1789 reprinting of the sermons of the seventeenth-century Calvinist cleric William Bridge; and a pious letter to her students.

By the late 1770s the extent of her enterprises meant that the countess was seriously financially embarrassed. She continued a bitter struggle with the Ferrers family over her father's unresolved estate, not settled until well after her death. She occasionally sold valuables to raise cash and regularly let her houses at Tunbridge Wells and Brighton to members of the nobility, using these funds to support her ministers. She now rejected giving to normal charitable enterprises: providing preaching was the 'greatest of all charitys I know on earth' (22 July 1785, Countess of Huntingdon Connexion MSS). She famously refused appeals that she intercede for William Dodd, condemned to death for forgery.

Secession, 1777–1787 By 1777 it was observed that 'the Countess of Huntingdon's people are peculiarly obnoxious to the bishops in general' (Aveling, 33). Although she had consistently professed loyalty to the Church of England, her activities—especially dispatching disruptive itinerant preachers and building chapels—appeared tangible evidence to the contrary. A determination in the late 1770s to establish her work in London set the stage for the final break. When a former amusement house in Clerkenwell was converted into a chapel, the bishop of London's consistorial court ordered its closure. She immediately took over and altered the chapel. Hard against the building stood a private dwelling, where she took up residence and had a door knocked through to the chapel, an arrangement similar to earlier chapels; she maintained that they were merely extensions to her private residences. She appointed Thomas Haweis one of her chaplains and claimed that, in spite of seating over 2000, what she christened Spa Fields was her private chapel. The following year, 1780, the consistorial court forbade Haweis to preach there. In a despondent rage, Lady Huntingdon seceded from the Church of England, and Spa Fields formally became a dissenting chapel on 12 January 1782. Those Anglican clerics who had assisted her, refusing now to be tarred with a dissenting brush, fled from her service, and she denounced them all as 'plausible pleaders for Satan only' (Cheshunt Foundation MS E4/10/19). In the process she lost all four of her chaplains, and in the end only two clerics followed her into secession. In 1783 the rigidly Calvinistic Countess of Huntingdon's Connexion was born when several Trevecca students were ordained at Spa Fields.

The secession crisis led the countess to believe that she was being comprehensively persecuted. Curiously, her attention was diverted from Trevecca, and a lack of funds meant that by 1788 its ten students were virtually in rags. Ever refusing to allow any of her preachers to settle, to the end of her life she frequently devoted six or seven hours a day to writing letters, attempting to exercise a meticulous control over their movements, together with all aspects of her chapels' affairs.

Final years, 1787–1791 After American independence, Lady Huntingdon projected plans to resuscitate Bethesda and to develop other enterprises, all under her direct control. A suspicious new America rejected these schemes, and her Georgia property was finally confiscated by the state. In 1787 she planned her first step outside Great Britain, having been informed that a large chapel in Brussels had been 'taken for me' (Cheshunt Foundation MS B4/3). The project was aborted when she was assured that it was part of a papal plot to orchestrate her assassination. In highly charged circumstances during the spring of 1789 she expelled the two clerics who had joined her secession and, desperate for assistance, induced Thomas Haweis to return. From then until her death two years later he manoeuvred himself into a commanding position, and he and his wife were two of the four trustees to whom Lady Huntingdon left control of her connexion, together with the ownership of much of its property. In her final year, cynical about her work in England, her hopes were fixed on mounting a missionary crusade to the south seas, where she could 'get some precious souls out of the Devils fingers' (Leete collection, countess of Huntingdon MS 129). She died at Spa Fields from respiratory complications on 17 June 1791 and ten days later was buried next to her husband in Ashby-de-la-Zouch parish church. Her personal annual income of £1200 ceased at her death, and she left overall debts of £3000, with no bequests for her chapels or college.

Although she was personally brave and frequently self-giving, the countess of Huntingdon's enterprises were hindered by her highly impulsive cyclothymic temperament. Always sincere, she was too often sour. The arbitrary nature of her leadership played a significant part in religious conflict and kept her contribution to English evangelicalism from proving more than a mixed blessing.

Despite her importance to the Hanoverian Methodist movement, the countess of Huntingdon was subsequently dwarfed by the historical reputation of her associates and rivals, Whitefield and the Wesleys. The serious defects of a voluminous biography, *The Life and Times of Selina, Countess of Huntingdon*, published in 1839, have since been redressed by Edwin Welch's *Spiritual Pilgrim* and by the present author's *Queen of the Methodists* (1997).

At her death more than sixty chapels were formally associated with the countess, though only a handful as a result of her financial assistance. During the nineteenth century, without her leadership and owing to significant internal conflict, the denomination experienced serious atrophy, with large numbers of ministers and congregations leaving to join the Independents. At the beginning of the twenty-first century the connexion had twenty-three chapels, all in England, supervised by the evangelical Christian denomination, the Countess of Huntingdon's Connexion. In 1792 her college at Trevecca was relocated to Cheshunt, Hertfordshire, and in 1906 to Cambridge. The Cheshunt College Foundation maintains the countess's reputation as a benefactor, providing funds for the training of ministers in England and, since the 1970s, in Sierra Leone, through the connexion's Sierra Leone mission.

BOYD STANLEY SCHLENTHER

Sources B. S. Schlenther, *Queen of the Methodists: the countess of Huntingdon and the eighteenth-century crisis of faith and society* (1997) · E. Welch, *Spiritual pilgrim: a reassessment of the life of the countess of Huntingdon* (1995) · Westminster College, Cambridge, Cheshunt Foundation MSS, series B, C, D, E, and F1 · black folio of letters, JRL, Methodist Archives and Research Centre · Hunt. L., Hastings papers · Southern Methodist University, Dallas, Texas, Bridwell Library, Leete collection, countess of Huntingdon MSS · A. Harding, 'The countess of Huntingdon and her connexion in the eighteenth century', DPhil diss., U. Oxf., 1992 · D. Brown, 'Evangelicals and education in eighteenth-century Britain: a study of Trevecca College, 1768–1792', PhD diss., University of Wisconsin, Madison, 1992 · JRL, Methodist Archives and Research Centre, DD Pr 1 · T. Aveling, *Memorials of the Clayton family* (1867) · *The works of the Reverend George Whitefield*, 6 vols. (1771–2) · PRO NIre., Granard MS, T3765 · Countess of Huntingdon Connexion Archives, Rayleigh · *The works of John Wesley*, [another edn], 26, ed. F. Baker and others (1982) · D. Benham, *Memoirs of James Hutton* (1856) · [A. C. H. Seymour], *The life and times of Selina, countess of Huntingdon*, 2 vols. (1839) · *The autobiography and correspondence of Mary Granville, Mrs Delany*, ed. Lady Llanover, 1st ser., 3 vols. (1861) · L. Tyerman, *Wesley's designated successor: the life, letters, and literary labours of the Rev. John William Fletcher* (1882) · R. Graves, *The spiritual Quixote*, ed. C. Whibley (1926) · GEC, *Peerage* · E. P. Shirley, ed., *Stemmata Shirleiana, or, The annals of the Shirley family*, 2nd edn (1873) · G. Baker, *The history and antiquities of the county of Northampton*, 2 vols. (1822–41) · *The letters of the Rev. John Wesley*, ed. J. Telford, 8 vols. (1931)

Archives Drew University, Madison, New Jersey, letters, mainly to her husband · DWL, Congregational Library, letters · Hunt. L., corresp. and family papers · JRL, Methodist Archives and Research Centre, letters, papers · Leics. RO, corresp. · Southern Methodist University, Dallas, Texas, Bridwell Library, letters · Westminster College, Cambridge, Cheshunt Foundation, papers · Rayleigh, Essex, Countess of Huntingdon MSS, letters | Duke U., Wesley family MSS · NL Wales, letters to Howel Harris

Likenesses oils, *c.*1728, Walters Art Gallery, Baltimore · P. Soldi, oils, 1740–44, Westminster College, Cambridge · J. Rysbrack, marble effigy on monument, 1746, Ashby-de-la-Zouch parish church · J. Russell, oils, 1773, Bethesda orphanage, Georgia · mezzotint, pubd 1773 (after J. Russell, 1773), BM, NPG [*see illus.*] · engraving, *c.*1780, repro. in Seymour, *Life and times of Selina*, vol. 1, frontispiece · J. Cross, stipple, pubd 1824 (after F. Hurlstone), BM, NPG · attrib. J. Highmore, oils, Worcester Art Gallery, Massachusetts · J. Russell, oils, Westminster College, Cambridge · oils, Woburn Abbey · oils, NPG

Wealth at death £1200 p.a. from husband's estate; debts of £3000: Cheshunt Foundation archives, C4/1, p. 79; Hunt. L., HAP 31 (7)

Hastings, Somerville (1878–1967), surgeon and politician, was born on 4 March 1878 in Boreham Road, Warminster, Wiltshire, the son of Henry George Hastings (1850?–1905), Congregationalist minister, and his wife, Ellen (née Ward). He was educated at Wycliffe College, and, on a medical scholarship, at University College and the Middlesex Hospital, London, during which he received a number of prizes, including medals in botany, an enduring interest. Hastings's academic and professional qualifications were MB, MRCS, and LRCP (1902); BS (1903); FRCS (1904); and MS (1908). Alongside his lucrative private practice, Hastings had a lifetime association with the Middlesex Hospital, specializing in ear, nose, and throat medicine. On 19 October 1911 he married Bessie Tuke (1881/2–1958), daughter of William Tuke, architect; they had two children.

Hastings was active in labour and medical reform politics before 1914, and by the 1920s he had formulated what were to remain his core beliefs. Hastings's socialized health service was to have a full-time, salaried medical personnel, and hence no private practice; and an integrated hospital system. Free and comprehensive services were to be organized around health centres, with an accompanying shift from curative to preventive medicine. Control was to be by democratically elected local authorities, centrally co-ordinated by the Ministry of Health.

After the First World War Hastings emerged as an important figure on the medical left. He became a leading member of the Labour Party's public health advisory committee; and, in 1923–4 and again in 1929–31, the Labour member of parliament for Reading. In 1930 Hastings helped form the organization with which he is most closely associated, the Socialist Medical Association, which affiliated to the Labour Party in 1931. Hastings was its founding president and he retained the presidency until 1951. He expended considerable energy, particularly in the association's crucial pre-war and wartime period, on socialist medical politics. He was often the association's delegate to the Labour Party conference, and was instrumental in having the party commit itself by 1934 to a national health service. He wrote and lectured extensively on his vision of a socialized medical service, and travelled abroad to study foreign medical systems and meet other socialist doctors. Most significant of all was his election in 1932 to the London county council as member for Mile End. Hastings held this seat until 1946, during which time he served (in 1944–5) as council chairman. Thereafter he was, from 1946 to 1964, an alderman, and he continued to serve on various committees. He was also a member of the London Labour Party's executive committee from 1934 to 1950. Membership of the London county council was Hastings's most successful and important venture into politics. After Labour took control in 1934 he was chairman of its hospital and medical services committee for ten years. As London was the largest provider of hospital beds in the country, this was a great responsibility. His council experience confirmed Hastings's view that

Somerville Hastings (1878–1967), by Rodrigo Moynihan, exh. RA 1946

medical services should be provided by democratic local bodies.

During the Second World War the influence of Hastings and the Socialist Medical Association increased. He was one of the three original association representatives on the British Medical Association's medical planning commission; and he was chairman of Labour's revived advisory committee on public health, a body charged with formulating proposals for a national health service. It seemed possible that Hastings's vision of a socialized medical service would be realized, given his own and his organization's heightened influence in labour and medical politics.

Hastings was elected member of parliament for Barking at the 1945 general election, a seat he held until his retirement in 1959. He claimed publicly that the post-war Labour government's National Health Service was in large part attributable to the work of the Socialist Medical Association. However, not all that Hastings desired was achieved. The minister of health, Aneurin Bevan, would have little to do with Hastings or the association. Bevan created a centrally controlled system and made concessions to the medical profession over issues such as private practice. Although a commitment was made to develop health centres, this did not happen. Hastings therefore welcomed and defended the National Health Service, but only as a first, imperfect, step towards a socialized medical service. He continued to agitate for his ideal of socialized medicine; to work as an active constituency member of parliament; and to serve on numerous boards and committees. He died at the Royal Berkshire Hospital, Reading, on 7 July 1967.

Hastings deserves acknowledgement as a pioneer of socialized medicine. But while it is easy to obtain a picture of the public figure, it is harder to see beyond this to the private individual. Hastings was a lifelong Christian (this being central to his political beliefs) and a teetotaller, and seems to have led an unpretentious, possibly somewhat austere, life. Some contemporaries have described him as rather cold, even aloof, with colleagues and patients. He was, however, regarded by others with considerable respect. He was described, on occasions, as shy; but also as enthusiastic in his passions, generous to his friends, and without pomposity. Hastings typifies the professional, altruistic, middle-class Christian socialist of his time.

JOHN STEWART

Sources J. Stewart, 'Socialist proposals for health reform in interwar Britain: the case of Somerville Hastings', *Medical History*, 39 (1995), 338–57 · F. Honigsbaum, *The division in British medicine* (1979) · J. Stewart, '"For a healthy London": the Socialist Medical Association and the London county council in the 1930s', *Medical History*, 41 (1997), 417–36 · *Medical World* (1953), 305–9 · *Socialism and Health* (Nov 1970), 3 · D. S. Murray, *Why a national health service?* (1971) · C. Brook, *Making medical history* (1946) · J. P. Ross and W. R. Le Fanu, *Lives of the fellows of the Royal College of Surgeons of England, 1965–1973* (1981) · *The Lancet* (15 July 1967) · *BMJ* (15 July 1967), 182 · *The Times* (8 July 1967) · *Socialism and Health* (Sept–Oct 1967) · m. cert. · b. cert.

Archives U. Hull, Brynmor Jones L., biographical material, corresp., notes | U. Hull, Brynmor Jones L., Socialist Medical Association archive

Likenesses R. Moynihan, portrait, exh. RA 1946, Guildhall Art Gallery [*see illus.*] · photograph, repro. in *Paragon Review*, 4 (Nov 1995), 15 · photographs, LMA · photographs, U. Hull

Wealth at death £41,905: probate, 9 Oct 1967, *CGPLA Eng. & Wales*

Hastings, Theophilus, seventh earl of Huntingdon

(1650–1701), politician, was born on 10 December 1650 at Donington Park, Leicestershire, the fourth, but only surviving, son of Ferdinando Hastings, sixth earl of Huntingdon (1609–1656), and Lucy *Hastings née Davies (1613–1679), his wife, daughter of Sir John *Davies of Englefield, Berkshire, and his wife, the prophetess Lady Eleanor *Davies. He was born to his parents in the twenty-seventh year of their marriage, after they 'despaired of a son'; Lady Elizabeth *Langham was one of his six sisters. His grandmother Davies, 'one not a little Enthusiastical', conferred the name Theophilus on him (MS Carte 77, fol. 201). He succeeded to the earldom upon his father's death on 13 February 1656. At his mother's direction, his education was 'wholly domestic' (*Hastings MSS*, 4.353). Living principally at the family's Leicestershire estates of Donington Park and Ashby-de-la-Zouch during his early years, he married on 19 February 1672, by his mother's choice, Elizabeth Lewis (1654–1688), eldest daughter and coheir of Sir John Lewis, bt, of Ledstone Hall, Yorkshire, and his wife, Sarah. They had eight children, of whom six died as minors. Their eldest daughter, Lady Elizabeth (Betty) *Hastings, became a notable benefactor.

Huntingdon was called to the House of Lords in 1672, but took his seat by proxy (the duke of York) on 15 February 1673. He became *custos rotulorum* of Warwickshire in 1675 and high steward of the honour of Leicester in 1677. In 1677 he moved to London, where he became heavily involved in the factional politics of the day, initially allying himself with Anthony Ashley Cooper, first earl of Shaftesbury. In December 1678 he chaired the Lords' committee on the Children of Recusants Bill, while in May 1679 he joined the lords protesting the bill to banish popish recusants from London, because it adversely affected dissenters. While attending a lord mayor's dinner with other whig lords in December 1679, he proposed the health of the duke of Monmouth and 'confusion to Popery', precipitating a pointed exchange with Chief Justice Scroggs (Thompson, 208–9). He later protested against Scroggs's freedom from commitment while under impeachment for treason (7 January 1681), and he protested the Lords' vote against impeaching Edward Fitzharris. In 1680 he was left off the commissions of the peace for Leicestershire and Derbyshire. By October 1681, however, he had experienced a political change of heart, kissing the king's hand at Whitehall on 21 October. Thereafter, he remained a staunch supporter of Stuart monarchy, enjoying the favour of Charles II and James II. He became captain of the king's band of gentleman pensioners in February 1682 (paying £4500 for the privilege) and was sworn of the privy council on 28 February 1683. His elevation at court raised his profile in provincial politics; he promoted candidates in parliamentary elections and helped suppress dissenting conventicles in the midlands. He also orchestrated the surrender and regrant of the town of Leicester's charter in 1684, being named recorder of the corporation in the new charter (10 December 1684). The earl was present in the bedchamber at King Charles's demise and was among the lords who proclaimed James II. At James's coronation, he served as cupbearer to the king (*Hastings MSS*, 4.353). During Monmouth's rebellion he raised a regiment of foot, holding the rank of colonel until November 1688.

Although he remained a lifelong member of the Church of England, Huntingdon was greatly in grace with King James. He held the offices of chief justice in eyre of the royal forests south of Trent (16 January 1686 – 23 December 1688); commissioner for ecclesiastical causes (12 January 1687 – 5 October 1688); lord lieutenant of Leicestershire (4 August 1687 – 23 December 1688) and Derbyshire (2 December 1687 – 23 December 1688); and groom of the stole and gentleman of the bedchamber to Prince George of Denmark (December 1687 – December 1688). He claimed he was present in the queen's bedchamber at the birth of the prince of Wales in June 1688 (*Hastings MSS*, 4.353). Huntingdon dutifully enforced James's policies, making inquiries of Leicestershire and Derbyshire JPs concerning the Test Act and supporting the purge of the corporation of Leicester in 1688. He also signed the warrant for commitment of the seven bishops to the Tower of London. At the news in November of the arrival of the Dutch fleet under William, the earl headed to Plymouth with his regiment, hoping to hold the citadel for King

James. Instead, Huntingdon was imprisoned in late November by the Williamite earl of Bath, governor of Plymouth, whom, it was rumoured, Huntingdon 'and the papists' tried to poison (Luttrell, 1.480). Huntingdon was released on 26 December, upon the news that his wife had died in childbirth two days earlier.

Huntingdon retired from public life and forfeited all of his offices for his adherence to James's cause. He was among those few excepted from the Act of Indemnity in July 1689. On 8 April 1690 he joined the Lords' protest against affirming the acts of the Convention. On 8 May 1690 he took as his second wife Frances (d. 27 Dec 1723), daughter and sole heir of Sir Francis Levison Fowler of Harnage Grange, Shropshire, and widow of Thomas Needham, Viscount Kilmorey. The couple had two sons and five daughters. Huntingdon remained loyal to James to the end of his life. In 1692, upon rumours of a Jacobite invasion, the earl was suspected in the plot; he received a letter purportedly from James and his stables were found full of horses. He was sent to the Tower in May 1692 and bailed in August. In March 1696 he refused to sign the association in favour of William III, and in 1701 protested against the Act of Settlement. Towards the end of his life he fell out with his son and heir, George, over the estates of his first wife in Yorkshire, but George ultimately succeeded him to the title. He died on 30 May 1701 in Charles Street, St James's, London, and was buried in the family chapel in the parish church at Ashby-de-la-Zouch.

CATHERINE F. PATTERSON

Sources *Report on the manuscripts of the late Reginald Rawdon Hastings*, 4 vols., HMC, 78 (1928–47), vol. 4 · Bodl. Oxf., MS Carte 77 · Hastings correspondence, Hunt. L. · GEC, *Peerage*, new edn, 5.659–60 · J. E. T. Rogers, ed., *A complete collection of the protests of the Lords*, 1 (1875), 61, 64, 65, 97 · N. Luttrell, *A brief historical relation of state affairs from September 1678 to April 1714*, 1 (1857), 138, 251, 425, 480, 554; 2 (1857), 441, 443, 543; 4 (1857), 34 · E. M. Thompson, ed., *Correspondence of the family of Hatton*, 1, CS, new ser., 22 (1878), 208–10 · H. N. Bell, *The Huntingdon peerage*, 2nd edn (1821), 138–41 · J. E. Doyle, *The official baronage of England*, 2 (1886), 238–40 · *Bishop Burnet's History of his own time*, ed. G. Burnet and T. Burnet, 2 (1734), 271 · *The manuscripts of the House of Lords*, 4 vols., HMC, 17 (1887–94), vol. 1, pp. 112, 177; vol. 2, pp. 17n., 32, 302

Archives Bodl. Oxf., corresp. and papers · Hunt. L., corresp. and family MSS · Leics. RO, corresp. | Bodl. Oxf., corresp. with Thomas Smith

Likenesses R. Williams, mezzotint (after G. Kneller, 1687), BM, NPG

Hastings, Thomas (*bap.* 1741, *d.* 1801), pamphleteer, was baptized on 24 May 1741 in Sunderland, Durham, the son of William and Eleanor Hastings. He was apprenticed to an uncle who helped to build Lord Lyttelton's mansion at Hagley, Worcestershire. After rambling over England, Hastings worked for a while as a carpenter on the new buildings in Marylebone, Middlesex. He supported Charles James Fox in the Westminster election of 1784, with *The book of the wars of Westminster, from the fall of the Fox at the close of 1783, to the 20th day of the 3rd month of 1784, an oriental prophecy by Archy Macsarcomica* (1784), which was followed by other pamphlets in the style of oriental apologues, such as *The regal rambler, or, The eccentrical adventures of the devil in London, with the manoeuvres of his ministers*

towards the close of the 18th century, translated from the Syriac MS. of Rabbi Solomon (1793). These productions were hawked by the writer about the town. For some years he published in the newspapers on 12 August an 'ode' on the birthday of the prince of Wales, for which he received a small annual present from Carlton House. He was a regular attendant at the popular Sunday lectures; he dressed as a clergyman, and became known as Dr Green. He died in New Court, Moor Lane, Cripplegate, London, on 12 August 1801.   H. R. TEDDER, *rev.* REBECCA MILLS

Sources *IGI* · *GM*, 1st ser., 71 (1801), 859 · S. Halkett and J. Laing, *A dictionary of the anonymous and pseudonymous literature of Great Britain*, 4 vols. (1882–8) · Watt, *Bibl. Brit.* · Nichols, *Lit. anecdotes*, 3.726

Hastings, Sir Thomas (1790–1870), naval officer, eldest son of the Revd James Hastings, rector of Martley, Worcestershire, and a distant cousin of Warren Hastings, was born on 3 July 1790. He entered the navy in September 1803, served on the channel, West Indies, and home stations, commanded a gunboat in the Walcheren expedition in 1809, and in January 1810 was promoted lieutenant of the *Badger* in the North Sea. From 1811 to 1813 he served in the *Hyacinth*, and from 1813 to 1815 in the *Undaunted*, on the Mediterranean coasts of France and Spain, where he was frequently engaged in boat expeditions. He was first lieutenant of the *Undaunted* when she took Napoleon to Elba in 1814. He continued on active service, principally in the Mediterranean, until promoted commander in May 1825. He married, on 12 May 1827, Louisa Elizabeth, daughter of Thomas Humphrey Lowe of Bromsgrove, Worcestershire, and his wife, Lucy, *née* Hill.

In November 1828 Hastings was appointed to the sloop *Ferret*, again in the Mediterranean, and was posted from her in July 1830. He was a favourite of William IV. In April 1832 he was selected as captain of the *Excellent*, the new gunnery training ship at Portsmouth. He held this important post for thirteen years, during the last six of which he was also superintendent of the Royal Naval College at Portsmouth. He played the major role in establishing professional gunnery training and scientific education in the navy. He taught the seamen gunners by example and created the traditions that made the *Excellent* the pride of the navy. For fifteen years he was directly involved in the design of new artillery, being an early proponent of shell-firing guns, and he advised the government to adopt screw steam warships in 1844. His services were rewarded by a knighthood in July 1839; and in August 1845, when he retired from the *Excellent*, he was appointed storekeeper to the ordnance, where he continued his work on improved heavy artillery design. In November 1850 he was made a CB civil division; and in September 1855, on reaching his flag by seniority, he was placed on the retired list. He was made a KCB civil division in March 1859, and became in due course vice-admiral in October 1862 and admiral in April 1866. He died at his residence, 7 Seymour Street, Marylebone, London, on 3 January 1870; his wife survived him.   J. K. LAUGHTON, *rev.* ANDREW LAMBERT

Sources J. G. Wells, *Whaley: the story of HMS Excellent, 1830 to 1980* (1980) · A. D. Lambert, *The last sailing battlefleet: maintaining naval mastery, 1815–1850* (1991) · C. J. Bartlett, *Great Britain and sea power,*

1815–1853 (1963) • O'Byrne, *Naval biog. dict.* • *CGPLA Eng. & Wales* (1870) • *The Times* (13 Jan 1870) • *Army and Navy Gazette* (8 Jan 1870) • *Colburn's United Service Magazine*, 1 (1870), 290 **Archives** NMM, Minto MSS **Wealth at death** under £5000: probate, 15 March 1870, *CGPLA Eng. & Wales*

Hastings, Thomas (*fl.* 1803–1837), customs officer and artist, whose origins are unknown, had been, according to his own statement of 1813, a captain and assistant quartermaster-general in the army. This position frequently required drawing skills for surveying duties, but Hastings has not been traced in either the British or the East India Company forces. His earliest surviving sketches (now in BL OIOC) were made in India in 1803 and on his voyage to England, in that year or the next, via the Cape of Good Hope and St Helena. These probably formed the basis for his now untraced paintings *Junction of the Rivers Malpoorba and Kistnah in the Interior of India* and *Painted from a Sketch Taken during a Storm off the Cape of Good Hope*, shown at the Royal Academy in 1821.

Hastings publicly exhibited in 1812–14 at the Liverpool Academy, first with *Ruins of St Pancras, in the Entrance to Canterbury* (1812). The picturesque decay of early nineteenth-century Canterbury and its cathedral caught his imagination and in 1813 he published *Vestiges of Antiquity, or, A Series of Etchings of Canterbury*. He later supplied drawings and worked up H. S. Storer's sketches for engraving by W. Woolnoth in that artist's *Canterbury Cathedral* (1816). He exhibited at the Royal Academy in 1813 and 1821, and at the British Institution in 1823, always giving London addresses. Surviving paintings, in particular *Woodbury Tower, Devon* (signed and dated 1813) and *One of the Great Ponds between Hampstead and Highgate* (signed and dated 1831; both formerly priv. coll.), are influenced by the landscape painter Richard Wilson. Between 1820 and 1824 Hastings made forty etchings of paintings by this artist (two owned by himself and thirty-eight either in, or previously in, the celebrated collection formed by Benjamin Booth and inherited by Lady Ford). These were published by subscription as *Etchings from the Works of Richard Wilson* (1825). Drawings connected with the project are in the National Museums and Galleries of Wales, which also formerly held an oil copy made by Hastings of Wilson's *The Tiber: Rome in the Distance*, when owned by Lady Ford.

Hastings was sworn in the customs service on 3 March 1819 and eventually rose to be collector at Cowes, on a salary of £400, in 1834. Between 1827 and 1833 he paid rates as a resident of Whippingham, East Cowes, in respect of a house and land. He founded in 1829 the Carisbrooke Archery Society. To celebrate archers of the past and to promote the fashionable contemporary sport, he wrote and illustrated *The British Archer, or, Tracts on Archery* (1831). After his departure from the island he was, in 1837, made an honorary member of the society. On boxing day 1834 he drew, much in the manner of Joseph Farington, *Lees Water* (now Thirlmere; Abbot Hall, Kendal), the latest dated work to be traced. Nothing is known of his final years.

TIMOTHY STEVENS

Sources T. Hastings, *Vestiges of antiquity, or, A series of etchings of Canterbury* (1813) • John Murray, London, archives • W. G. Constable, *Richard Wilson* (1953) • *GM*, 1st ser., 99/1 (1829), 553 • M. Archer, *British drawings in the India office library* (1969) • Isle of Wight RO, Newport • PRO, CUST 39/1 • PRO, CUST 39/175 **Archives** Abbot Hall Art Gallery, Kendal • BL OIOC • John Murray, London, archives • NMG Wales

Hastings, Warren (1732–1818), governor-general of Bengal, was born at the rectory at Churchill in Oxfordshire on 6 December 1732. Hastings proudly traced his descent from a family that had been settled at Daylesford in Worcestershire since the twelfth century. By the eighteenth century, however, the family was in reduced circumstances. The Daylesford lands had been sold, although Hastings's grandfather, Penyston Hastings (*d.* 1752), and his father, also called Penyston (*d.* 1743), both in holy orders, continued to live nearby. Hastings's mother, Hester, *née* Warren (1705–1732), died shortly after giving birth to him. He and his elder sister, Anne, were left as virtual orphans when, within nine months of Warren's birth, their father abandoned them, remarried, and moved to Barbados, where he lived out the rest of his life. Hastings was brought up first in the Cotswolds by his grandfather and then by his uncle Howard Hastings, who took him to London in 1740.

Schooling and first years in India Howard Hastings sent his nephew to school at Newington Butts and then in 1743 to Westminster School, where he became king's scholar and captain of the school in 1747, leaving prematurely on his uncle's death in 1749, to the dismay of the headmaster, John Nicoll. In later life Hastings was inclined to portray himself as a person who had been cut off from formal education at an early age and thus been forced to equip himself for the great responsibilities that came to him by native wit and practical experience. His time at Westminster seems, however, to have been a good preparation. It left him with a capacity to write cogently and elegantly, with a facility to learn languages, with a cultivated taste for literature, and above all with a quick, inquiring intelligence that absorbed new knowledge very readily.

With the death of his uncle Hastings had to fend for himself. His new guardian, Joseph Creswicke, used his influence to get him an appointment as a writer in the East India Company's Bengal service. After the obligatory brief course in merchant's accounts he sailed for India in January 1750, arriving at Calcutta in September.

Calcutta in 1750 was already a rich commercial city. It was the centre for the huge trade conducted by the East India Company in what had become a virtually autonomous province under the rule of governors, or nawabs, who owed only a nominal allegiance to the Mughal emperor at Delhi. From Calcutta and a series of subordinate commercial 'factories' in other parts of Bengal the East India Company procured its cargoes for London, consisting largely of cotton cloth and silk. The employees of the company, private British merchants, and many Indian ones who worked with the British also traded on a large scale. Commercial expansion was, however, creating political tensions. On the south-east or Coromandel coast

Jane Austen, was in fact Hastings's child rather than that of his business partner, Tysoe Saul Hancock, cannot be substantiated.

The 'Plassey revolution', 1757–1765 Hastings's brief first marriage spanned the years of what contemporaries came to call the 'Plassey revolution'. In 1757 an expedition from Madras under Robert Clive, with which Hastings served as a volunteer, forced the nawab out of Calcutta and recovered it for the company. Clive's army then became the force that brought about the overthrow of Siraj ud-Daula at the battle of Plassey on 23 June 1757 and his replacement by a new nawab. In theory, the new nawab, Mir Jafar, was the independent ally of the company. In practice, the company maintained a large army that assumed the responsibility for the defence of Bengal and insisted on payments from the nawab for its services, thus quickly eroding his autonomy. The appointment of a British resident at Murshidabad to exert pressure on the nawab was a clear sign of his altered status. From 1758 Hastings served as resident. He was still at Murshidabad in 1760, when a coup engineered by the British brought down Mir Jafar and replaced him with another nawab, Mir Kasim.

Shortly afterwards Hastings went to Calcutta and succeeded to the council that managed the company's affairs under a new governor, Henry Vansittart. Hastings formed a close friendship with Vansittart, who was a man of intellectual tastes similar to his own. He allied with the governor in disputes that split the council. Contention raged around the extent to which the nawab should be permitted to regulate the private trade of British merchants. Mir Kasim tried to impose controls, which Vansittart and Hastings, although they themselves traded on a large scale, accepted that he had a right to do. On two missions to the nawab in 1762–3, once on his own and once with Vansittart, Hastings attempted to reach agreements with him. The treaty drawn up during the second mission was, however, rejected by a majority on the council, in spite of a spirited defence of it by Hastings. Tensions then erupted into armed conflict. Mir Kasim was driven out of Bengal and he and his allies were defeated in 1764 at the battle of Buxar. The violence with which Mir Kasim took revenge on the British whom he captured and on Indians who had allied with them seemed wholly to discredit Vansittart's and Hastings's policy of conciliation. Vansittart resigned his governorship and returned to Britain. In January 1765 Hastings followed him.

Early assessments and return to England, 1765–1769 Hastings's first fifteen years in India had ended in failure. His family had been wiped out. He had vainly sought to achieve a settlement with Mir Kasim and had created many enemies in doing so. One of them wrote of him, 'never was a worse Politician, credulous and to the highest degree; alarm'd by every idle report, wholly diffident in himself' (J. Carnac to R. Clive, 2 Nov 1760, BL OIOC, MS Eur. G 37/28, fol. 120). He had by no means made his fortune. Vansittart had accepted large presents from Mir Kasim, and it was strongly rumoured that Hastings had also taken

Warren Hastings (1732–1818), by Sir Joshua Reynolds, 1766–8

Anglo-French rivalry had already led to open warfare in which Indian contenders for power participated. In 1750 the Bengal nawabs were still able to maintain control, but within a few years Bengal too was to be thrown into turmoil and a political revolution was to ensue that would transform Hastings's career.

In 1750 Hastings's prospects were those of company servants of previous generations. He had to learn how to order textiles and check their quality. Were he to survive the high mortality from disease, he could expect to rise in the service and would try to accumulate a fortune from his personal trade. Hastings's first appointment was at Cossimbazar, a major centre for procuring silk, near the nawab's capital at Murshidabad. He was at Cossimbazar in 1756 when relations between a new nawab, called Siraj ud-Daula, and the East India Company broke down catastrophically. The nawab was provoked to attack and storm Calcutta, rounding up the British at Cossimbazar in the process. Hastings's release was secured by Dutch merchants and he went to Falta, where refugees from Calcutta had gathered. At Falta in 1756 he married Mary, *née* Elliott, widow of Captain John Buchanan, who had been killed at Calcutta. Neither the first Mrs Hastings nor the two children that she bore her husband were to live long. Her daughter, Elizabeth, was dead within a month of her birth. Mary Hastings died on 11 July 1759. The son, George, was sent to England in 1761, where he too died in 1764. Rumours that Elizabeth, daughter of Philadelphia Hancock, born in December 1761 and cousin of the novelist money. These rumours were never substantiated and, if it is likely that money was promised, nothing significant seems to have been handed over. He had traded extensively, but he had not realized his assets, and his friends warned him that little could be recovered.

Nevertheless, Hastings lived in some style in Britain, where he sought to influence future Indian policy and to secure his return with a prestigious position. A striking portrait depicting him holding documents in Persian script, which he commissioned from Joshua Reynolds, seems to be a clear statement of his ambitions. He drew up a proposal for a 'Professorship of the Persian Language' at Oxford, which he sent to Samuel Johnson, among others. In the proposal he used arguments that he was to develop in the future. Knowledge of Asian languages was not simply a tool for ruling in Asia; it created awareness of rich cultures of which British people were ignorant and inclined to be contemptuous. Such awareness would be, he was later to write, the means of a 'reconciliation' of 'the people of England to the natives of Hindostan' (Marshall, 'Hastings as patron and scholar', 256). On 31 March 1767 he gave evidence to the first parliamentary inquiry into Indian affairs. Neither the Mughal emperor nor the nawabs of Bengal, he told the committee, now had any effective authority. 'Possession of the country is in the English' and 'we have it in our power to make Bengal the most beneficial spot to this country' (BL, Add. MS 18469, fols. 20–30). In 1768 he was given the chance to go back to India when he was appointed second in the council of the settlement at Fort St George, Madras.

Return to India, 1769–1772 Hastings sailed for Madras on 26 March 1769. Also on the ship was the person who eventually became his second wife. She was Anna Maria Apollonia Chapuset, always Marian to Hastings [see Hastings, Marian (1747–1837)], born at Nuremberg of a Huguenot family. Then aged twenty-two, she was married to Baron Carl von Imhoff, who was going to India as a cadet in the Madras army and also to paint miniatures. Hastings evidently fell in love with Anna Maria during the voyage. When Imhoff moved on from Madras to Bengal, she apparently lived in Hastings's house before she followed her husband. The Imhoffs continued to live together in Calcutta when Hastings arrived there in 1772, but in February 1773 the baron went back to Europe leaving his wife in India. Imhoff applied for a divorce in a German court on grounds of desertion. This was granted in 1776. A year later, on 8 August 1777, when news of the divorce had reached India, Hastings and Marian were married. They had no children, but Hastings seems to have become attached to his wife's two sons by her former marriage, Charles and Julius Imhoff. The marriage was a source of great happiness to him for the rest of his life.

Hastings spent two successful years at Madras. His management of the company's commercial concerns was particularly commended. In 1771 the directors of the East India Company, looking for a new governor of Bengal, where recent administration was regarded as seriously flawed, chose Hastings. He returned to Calcutta on 17 February 1772.

Governor: Bengal in 1772 In his evidence to the House of Commons in 1767 Hastings had stated bluntly that Bengal was now effectively a British province. By 1772 this proposition was irrefutable. Mughal authority in Bengal was extinct, while British interference and a series of coups had left the nawabs powerless. In 1765 by the treaty of Allahabad the *diwani*—that is, the right to collect a territorial revenue, usually assessed at the equivalent of around £2 million—had been surrendered to the East India Company. What remained to the nawabs was responsibility for the defence of the province, the maintenance of law and order, and the enforcement of criminal justice. Inroads had, however, been made here too. The nawabs' army had been disbanded, and they had no power to implement any decision that was not acceptable to the company.

Hastings saw himself in 1772 as governor of what was now fully part of the British empire. He dismissed as harmful fictions formal acknowledgements of Mughal authority. Since 1765 the company had delegated a great part of its new responsibilities to what was styled a deputy nawab, called Muhammad Reza Khan. Hastings had orders to dismiss the khan and to assert the company's direct authority. He complied with alacrity and expressed the hope that no similar appointment would ever be made. He had no qualms about making further incursions into areas of government allocated to the nawabs. He believed that sovereignty, a concept that he frequently invoked, was vested in the 'British nation' (Jones, 191) and that there must be no equivocation about that. The East India Company might for the present be the duly constituted agent of the British nation, but it must be guided by national purposes, and in due time he anticipated that the company would surrender its powers over Indian government to the state, a prospect that he welcomed.

Hastings's view of his task From the outset of his government Hastings saw himself as bound to impress on British opinion the importance of what Britain had acquired in Bengal. Its 'extent … and its possible resources, are equal to those of most states in Europe' (Gleig, 1.368). Its population was usually estimated at some 20 million people, its public revenue amounted to about one quarter of that of Britain itself, it maintained a British army of approximately 25,000 men, it had its own foreign policy with other Indian states, and the value of its exports to Britain was rising towards £1 million a year. Hastings pointed out that the management of the complex affairs of this great possession was a task of the highest responsibility. In the past he had been accused of timidity and self-mistrust, but now he had no inhibitions in proclaiming his ambition to discharge these responsibilities with éclat. 'I have catched the desire for applause in public life' (ibid., 1.375). 'I own I possess a more than ordinary degree of ambition to act in an elevated sphere under the auspices of my sovereign' (ibid., 1.472). Previous governors of Bengal had, he believed, regarded their tenure of office as an opportunity to round off their careers by adding to their fortunes before making a quick retreat to Europe. He would serve for a long period and honourable recognition would be his chief reward. He was in fact to stay in Bengal for thirteen years.

Hastings shared the view, universal among contemporary Europeans, that Bengal was a naturally rich province with a highly productive agriculture and skilled manufacturers that had suffered from misgovernment under its later Indian rulers and during the British takeover. It had been afflicted in 1770 by a very severe famine. The new regime's task was to enable recovery to take place. In the years after 1772 Hastings developed a distinctive point of view on how this should be done. He believed that Bengal must be governed in ways to which its people were presumed to be accustomed. Indian methods of government and Indian law must be preserved. The British should aim 'to rule this people with ease and moderation according to their own ideas, manners, and prejudices' (Gleig, 1.404). He considered that Hinduism and Hindu and Islamic law were in certain respects admirable in themselves as well as being suited to the needs of the population who had come under British rule. He encouraged British officials to learn languages, make studies, and translate texts. While he believed that there could be no limitations on the company's sovereignty and that no Indian authority could be allowed to compete with it, he felt that the exercise of the powers of government under British direction should for the most part be left in Indian hands. He had no high opinion of the capacity or the disinterestedness of the great bulk of the company's British servants.

The revenue issue Revenue was the central issue of early British government in India. The huge sums levied in taxation made Indian provinces colonial possessions of unique value. Hastings always felt himself to be under irresistible pressures to maximize the revenue yield on which the company's army, its capacity to make war, and the volume of its trade depended. On the other hand, he also believed that moderate rather than rapacious management of the revenue would generate long-term prosperity that would ultimately enrich Bengal and therefore make it an even more valuable asset for Britain. Attempts to devise policies that would meet these potentially contradictory aims were gravely handicapped by ignorance. The British were uncertain both as to how much they could extract from the province without inflicting damage on it and from whom they should receive their revenue. The revenue originated in a tax that was in theory a proportion of the value of the crops grown by millions of cultivators. It was extracted from them by a complex system of intermediaries who paid a quota assessed by the government. The commonest term for these intermediaries was *zamindar*, literally landholder. The status of a Bengal *zamindar* was the subject of much debate. To some British people, they were the equivalent of European landlords, who owned the land from which they collected revenue from a mass of tenants. To Hastings, they were government-appointed tax collectors who had acquired a hereditary right to their offices.

In 1772 Hastings decided that the best way of finding out what Bengal could afford to pay was to invite competition for the right to collect revenue for a period of five years. Where the *zamindars* did not make adequate offers, higher bids would be accepted. This so-called 'farming' system was adjudged even by Hastings to have been a failure. Bids for lands were often unrealistically high and the farmers failed to pay their quotas, in spite, it was often alleged, of oppressively rigorous exactions from the cultivators. In 1776 Hastings ordered an inquiry into local revenue accounts in order to give the government some indications of what had been collected in the past. This failed to provide an effective basis for an assessment, and for the rest of Hastings's administration the company negotiated revenue assessments year by year, usually with the *zamindars*.

The role that Europeans should play in the management of the revenue was also contentious. Hastings inherited a system in which British company servants had been appointed to districts to supervise the assessment and the collection. He had no liking for this. He thought that most of the British 'collectors' were ignorant and corrupt, and he had much more confidence in experienced Indian revenue administrators. In 1781 he withdrew nearly all Europeans from the districts.

By the time he left India in 1785, Hastings's revenue administration was generally regarded as a failure. There seemed to be no evidence of improvement or growing prosperity in the countryside; the yield of Bengal's revenue to the company, in spite of higher assessments, had hardly increased and Hastings had been forced to augment the company's finances by indirect taxes, such as the monopolies created over the sale of salt and opium. British opinion began to turn against what seemed to be a policy of experiments in favour of certainty. *Zamindars* were declared to have property rights to their lands, the level of tax they paid was fixed for ever, and British collectors were reappointed to manage districts. In old age Hastings may have derived some satisfaction from knowing that it was becoming clear that these measures, embodied in the so-called 'permanent settlement' of 1793, were not proving markedly more successful in stimulating rural prosperity.

The administration of justice As *diwans* of Bengal after 1765 the company acquired responsibility for administering civil justice, cases of property and inheritance being closely involved with the payment of revenue. Criminal justice was the concern of the nawab's courts, which enforced the Islamic criminal law. Europeans had a hearty contempt for Bengal courts, dismissing them as incurably corrupt, but no effective intervention was attempted before Hastings's governorship. He believed that the British must intervene to restore a decayed system of indigenous justice. He created new hierarchies of courts, both civil and criminal. Local civil courts were to be supervised by British revenue officials. There were to be new criminal courts, which would remain under the nawab's law officers until the appointment of British magistrates in 1781. Appeals were to be heard by new British appeal courts in

Calcutta. The law administered by the courts was to be the law of Hindus and Muslims. Hastings set about obtaining translations that would make the law accessible to those Europeans who had to administer it. He launched projects for the translation of commentaries on Muslim law and of a code of Hindu law done for him in Sanskrit by a group of pandit scholars. The extent to which Hastings was able by these means to bring about the restoration of indigenous justice that he intended is highly debatable. It was impossible for European judges, with their preconceptions, such as a commitment to equality before the law, to behave like Indian judges. The translations made under Hastings's patronage were remarkable works of scholarship, but translations of classical texts were a somewhat unreal guide to current usage in evolving legal traditions. Rather than guaranteeing legal continuity, as he intended, Hastings's judicial reforms began the process, accelerated by subsequent reforms and new codifications, of producing the hybrid Anglo-Indian law that survives in contemporary India.

Diplomacy in India As governor of Bengal, Hastings not only had to direct the internal administration of a huge province, but he had to conduct a complex diplomacy with Indian states and on occasions with other European powers trading in India. By the 1770s it was impossible for the British in Bengal or indeed in their other settlements at Madras and Bombay to isolate themselves from the new order of states that was replacing the Mughal empire. Bengal was relatively invulnerable to attack, except on its western frontier. Along the Ganges valley the British province of Bihar bordered on the territory of the wazir of Oudh. Since 1765 the wazirs had been linked in a close alliance with the British and had British troops stationed with them for their defence. On the south-western frontier of Bengal were the lands of one of the chieftains of the Maratha confederacy that extended to the west coast, where the Marathas hemmed in Bombay. In the late eighteenth century the Marathas were pressing northwards. They had raided into Bengal in the past and for most of the period the Mughal emperor at Delhi was under their patronage. In the south the British at Madras had turned the neighbouring Carnatic territory into their satellite. This brought them into close contact with two powerful rulers, the nizam of Hyderabad and Haidar Ali, who had seized control of Mysore.

The armies which the British had deployed in the wars of the mid-eighteenth century had made them a formidable force in India, but they certainly could not as yet aspire to supremacy. Indian rulers were imitating European methods of equipping and training troops. Wars would not necessarily produce decisive results and would be certain to cost a great deal. Attempts to expand British territory by conquest were therefore almost universally rejected as an option for the company: great gains had come through war, but these must now be consolidated in peace. Debate focused on the extent to which the British should seek influence beyond their boundaries. Some argued for policies of strict non-intervention. Hastings had no ambition to make new conquests, but he was strongly in favour of seeking influence by alliances. In his most elaborate statement of his aims he wrote of

> a general system … to extend the influence of the British nation to every part of India not too remote from their possessions, without enlarging the circle of their defence or involving them in hazardous or indefinite engagements and to accept the allegiance of such of our neighbours as shall sue to be enlisted among the friends and allies of the King of Great Britain.

British agents were to be posted as residents at Indian courts, Indian rulers should sign treaties, preferably directly with the British crown, and they should accept garrisons of British troops, for which they would pay subsidies (Weitzman, 87–8).

Hastings's ideal of peaceful influence over allies bore little relation to the way events unfolded. Alliances tended quickly to become subordination, as the pattern played out in Bengal after 1757 repeated itself elsewhere and rulers who entered into connections with the British faced escalating demands on their resources. Moreover, the company was to be repeatedly drawn into war, as events very early in Hastings's administration demonstrated. In order to strengthen the company's major ally in northern India, the wazir of Oudh, Hastings was willing to sanction his ambitions to absorb the territory dominated by the Rohilla people of Afghan origin. Company troops would be used against the Rohillas and be paid for their services, while the wazir would gain a secure boundary against Maratha incursions. The Rohillas were duly expelled in a short campaign in 1774. This was the first of many wars that were to mark Hastings's governorship and to prove extremely damaging to his reputation.

The business of administration The company's government was one of record. Business was transacted in consultations on which councillors entered minutes. Dispatches were sent to the directors, and men in power in India kept their friends at home well briefed. In minutes and letters Hastings was extremely adept at presenting persuasive rationalizations for his policies and in outlining ambitious future plans. To one friendly critic, he was rather too fluent on paper. 'I like Hastings's private Character exceedingly', wrote a Scottish company servant. 'I also think he would make a damnd good Governor if he was not so clever, that is, he has *too much Sail and no Ballast*. He deceives people by his writings and he is a great Schemer' (C. Alexander to D. Anderson, 13 Nov 1784, BL, Add. MS 45424, fol. 144).

Hastings's minutes and dispatches were often little more than a façade. Much of the essential business of government was transacted not on paper but in face-to-face contact between the governor and a group of Europeans and Indians upon whom he relied. When he was not actually quarrelling with his fellow councillors, he was still ill at ease with them and had no taste for collective government or shared responsibility. He dealt instead with younger company servants, often well-educated Scots, such as David Anderson, George Bogle, and Alexander Elliot, brother of the future governor-general, the earl of Minto. Such men were sent as envoys to Indian rulers or given key posts in the revenue administration. He saw them as his own appointments, personally giving them their orders and receiving their reports rather than using official channels.

Hastings also dealt directly with Indians in a way that would have been inconceivable for his successors. He seems to have been a good linguist. The sketch for a painting by Johan Zoffany in 1784 shows him speaking, presumably in Urdu, to a Mughal prince without an interpreter. He could also conduct diplomatic and revenue negotiations in Urdu on his own. Indian rulers and great Bengal *zamindars* had to maintain personal relations with him. They corresponded directly with him and appointed Calcutta agents who paid court to him. Hastings made it abundantly clear that he expected their loyalty to be to him personally as well as to the company. He was unforgiving to those whom he supposed to be cultivating his opponents. Hastings considered that few Europeans had as yet mastered revenue and judicial administration to any great depth. The company had, in his view, to depend on learned pandits to expound the law, like Radhakanta Tarkavagisa, on Muslims brought up in the Mughal tradition of state service, and on revenue administrators, like Ganga Govind Singh, described as Hastings's 'prime minister' and as 'looked upon by the natives as the second person in the government, if not the first'. Finally, like all prominent Europeans, Hastings had a banyan, or personal agent, to manage his household and private business affairs, in this case the redoubtable Krishna Kanta Nandy (Cantoo Babu), who was a highly successful businessman in his own right and held lucrative revenue contracts.

The confident programmes of reform which he sent back to Britain did not necessarily bear much relation to the intractable realities facing Hastings: a limited direct British engagement with the great mass of their new subjects and relations with other Indian states upon which it was beyond his capacity to impose his will. Even with a high level of Indian assistance, the British could not form an accurate assessment of the revenue resources of Bengal. Nor could they re-create and apply authentic Indian jurisprudence in their courts, which in any case had a very restricted jurisdiction outside certain towns. Hastings certainly could not slot the states of post-Mughal India into a system of dependent alliances. Indian rulers could be as adept at manipulating the British for their own purposes as the British were at manipulating them. Even if he had enjoyed uncontested authority over the government of Bengal and had been able to avoid major wars, Hastings's governorship would still have been a struggle from one expedient to another. In the event, Hastings was to enjoy neither uncontested authority nor peace for most of his administration.

Structure of government and disputed authority From his arrival in Bengal in 1772 Hastings had complained about the form of government that he had to operate, inherited from the practice of a trading company and, in his view, unsuited to ruling a great political concern. As governor, he was merely one of a large council chosen by seniority and subject to orders from directors elected by a body of shareholders in Britain. In 1773 the national government intervened to impose reforms on the company. By what was called the East India Regulating Act of that year authority in Bengal was concentrated in a governor-general and a new supreme council of five. A supreme court, staffed by royal judges, was to be established in Calcutta. The members of the supreme council were named in the act and were thus the nominees of the national government. Hastings was chosen as the first governor-general, apparently without serious opposition, evidence of the good reputation he had won for his work in Bengal since 1772. Three men were sent out to join the council from Britain, General John Clavering, George Monson, and Philip Francis, to whom Richard Barwell, who was already in India, was added.

Whatever expectations Hastings may have had from the honour done to him and from the powers added to his office were quickly dashed by the unremitting opposition to all his policies shown by the three new councillors from Britain immediately after their arrival in Calcutta on 19 October 1774. Acting together, they constituted a majority against him and Barwell. The motives for the virulence of their opposition have been much debated. They quickly professed to find corruption behind every policy of the old government and to believe that, far from having begun the regeneration of a great national asset, Hastings was allowing the resources of Bengal to be plundered and wasted. They were fed inflammatory material by British company servants and Indians who were disaffected to Hastings, and there is no reason to doubt, particularly in the case of the soldiers, Clavering and Monson, that they believed what they heard and that their sense of outrage was genuine. Francis was a more complex case. An intellectual of a calibre to match Hastings, he had held minor government offices and was well versed in political intrigue, which he practised unremittingly in India. Within a few years the main aim of his life came to be to force Hastings out and to succeed him. Yet Francis too was an idealist who believed much of what he wrote. He too was appalled by what he interpreted as corruption and, from material largely supplied to him from the dismissed deputy nawab, Muhammad Reza Khan, he formulated a version of an idealized Mughal constitution which he accused Hastings of violating.

The new councillors began by denouncing the war against the Rohillas and demanding an investigation into the motives behind it. Hastings's revenue policy was also denounced as destructive of the province by displacing its natural gentry in favour of extortionate adventurers. Within a few months accusations of personal corruption were levelled against Hastings himself.

Accusations of corruption The accusations were brought in March 1775 by Nandakumar, a man who had been active in the administration of the nawabs and who, like others in his position, had sought to secure a role for himself in the new order of the East India Company. In the faction-ridden company government of the 1760s this had meant allying with certain Europeans against others. Hastings had been his enemy in the past and, although there had been a limited reconciliation since 1772, Nandakumar evidently calculated that he stood to gain ample rewards were the new councillors to displace Hastings. To help them bring Hastings down, he accused him of having accepted presents from the court of the nawabs worth some £40,000, and other allegations were added. Hastings refused to answer these charges at the time. Much later he admitted that over £15,000 had been paid to him as the customary allowances given to the governor visiting the nawab. If the rest of Nandakumar's charges cannot be substantiated and his crude allegations of selling offices are most implausible, Hastings probably had accepted other customary emoluments. He frequently declared his lack of interest in making money, but he considered that the governor should live in a manner appropriate to his office and he was determined to send money home which would enable him to rebuild the shattered fortunes of his family. His personal accounts reveal that he sent more than £120,000 to Britain in the first four years of his government, a sum which comfortably exceeded all his official emoluments. Hastings was therefore vulnerable, if not in his own eyes, to such accusations.

Those who brought accusations against the governor-general were even more vulnerable, as Nandakumar was soon to discover. Charges of forgery were brought against him in the new supreme court. He was found guilty, sentenced to death, and executed on 5 August 1775. 'With the life of Nundcomar has ended the prevalent spirit of informants and of the litigious; the Blacks know not which way to look' (Marshall, *Impeachment*, 141), wrote an exultant British observer. The case of Nandakumar has attracted much controversy. Critics of Hastings from his own time onwards have drawn the not unreasonable inference that he promoted the prosecution and may have influenced the verdict. He stoutly denied such accusations and he has found a succession of defenders who have tried to substantiate his denials. The independence of the judges, whatever the merits of their verdict, seems in retrospect to be beyond question. It seems also clear that the prosecution against Nandakumar was promoted by his Indian enemies. There are no indications that they communicated directly with Hastings, but evidence has come to light to show that one of his closest friends was well aware of what they were doing and encouraged them.

In sentencing Nandakumar and refusing a reprieve or stay of execution, Sir Elijah Impey, the chief justice of the supreme court, an old friend of Hastings since school, and the other royal judges had acted in a way that was highly advantageous to Hastings. In other respects, however, the court proved to be another unwelcome consequence for him of the 1773 Regulating Act. Its jurisdiction was ill defined, and its attempts to extend this, and with it the use of English law in conflict with the Indian courts set up by the company, provoked bitter disputes, which required a further act of parliament of 1781 to resolve.

Even if he had no direct hand in it, the destruction of Nandakumar was an important success for Hastings in halting the flow of accusations. Whether he survived the onslaught of his opponents now largely depended on the reactions of the authorities at home, both in the company and in the national government, to the material from the rivals in Bengal with which they were being bombarded. The government tried to dismiss Hastings in 1776, but the company rejected this. Even so, Hastings's friends in Britain thought it wise to negotiate an honourable resignation on his behalf. Before this could take effect, events in India went his way. One of his opponents, Monson, died in September 1776, and by use of the governor-general's casting vote in council Hastings regained control of the government. When news of his resignation reached India, Hastings repudiated it and defeated an attempt by Clavering to assume the governor-generalship in June 1777. Two months later Clavering died. Francis alone remained to carry on the opposition against Hastings, which he did until a truce was patched up in 1780. It broke down over conflicting interpretations of its terms. Hastings accused Francis of being 'void of truth and honour' in his public and private conduct. Francis called him out, and in a duel on 17 August Francis was slightly wounded. Francis left India in December 1780. By then the national government had become reconciled to keeping Hastings in India as the least bad alternative in difficult times.

Wars: saving the empire in India? War was the main source of difficulty. From early in Hastings's administration the British at Bombay had been involved in the politics of the Maratha states seeking small territorial gains on the west coast. In 1778 fresh opportunities for intervention presented themselves when a claimant to the authority of the peshwa, or titular leader of the Marathas, sought Bombay's support. Hastings backed intervention, believing that it would enable the British to establish a dominant influence over the Marathas. Bengal troops were assembled to cross northern India in support of Bombay's efforts. Questions of influence over Indian states seemed to Hastings to become urgent with the entry of France into the American War of Independence in 1778. French diplomats were believed to be already active, and in January 1781 the first French expeditionary force arrived in India.

Unhappily for Hastings, projects for limited operations to assert British influence were engulfed in a series of wars that threatened the stability of British India. Bombay's intervention in Maratha affairs ended in the defeat of their army. In spite of Hastings's efforts to win over some of the Maratha powers, they combined against the British and in 1780 extended the alliance to include other states normally hostile to one another, Hyderabad and Mysore. Mysore was by far the most dangerous enemy. In 1780 its troops routed British armies outside Madras and the French were able to land forces to co-operate with Mysore.

Hastings took some credit for the diplomacy that broke up the formidable Indian coalition opposing him, for directing operations by the Bengal army that forced the Maratha states into a peace concluded in 1783, and for sending money, supplies, and troops on a very large scale from Bengal to Madras, thus enabling the Mysore forces to be pushed back and the French to be contained. With some justification, Hastings saw himself as the saviour of the British empire in India, in sharp contrast with those who had lost an empire in America.

Nevertheless, the scale of the wars did Hastings great damage. Massive military exertions put a huge strain on the resources of Bengal. Its government went heavily into deficit. Virtually no funds were available for trade for some years, while some Indian costs were passed back to Britain, causing an acute financial crisis for the East India Company, which eventually had to call for aid from the state. Instead of being an asset for Britain, India was becoming a liability. Hastings was blamed for this. He was accused of being a warmonger with a lust for conquest. While he certainly had no ambitions for conquest, he was vulnerable to accusations that his intervention in Maratha affairs had been reckless and provocative.

Benares and Oudh, 1781 The needs of the war affected Hastings's dealings with the company's dependants and allies in northern India. These too damaged his reputation. During the eighteenth century the rulers of Benares had carved out a domain for themselves which came under British authority in 1775 by an arrangement carried by Hastings's opponents against him. Chet Singh, the raja of Benares, was required to pay a subsidy which, in line with the company's increasing needs, Hastings forced him to augment. On the pretext that he was evading legitimate demands, Hastings proposed to exact a large fine from him on a personal visit in 1781. The raja's retainers resisted the demand and forced Hastings to flee from the city. With considerable coolness he organized military measures to crush the uprising and eventually imposed a settlement that fully incorporated Benares into British territory. The episode left, however, a strong impression that Hastings had acted tyrannically as well as subjecting himself to needless risks.

At Benares in 1781 Hastings also tried to settle the company's relations with Oudh, its major ally in northern India. Since 1765 the wazirs of Oudh had been obliged to maintain British troops in their territory and to pay subsidies for them. The number of troops increased, as did the size of the subsidy required from Oudh. The wazir proved to be extremely adept at preventing the British from getting access to his resources and thus fell heavily into arrears with his subsidy. In 1781 Hastings tried to clear off these arrears, which were urgently needed for the war effort, by forcing the wazir to resume alienations of land revenue and by confiscating a large hoard of treasure in the possession of his mother and grandmother, the begums of Oudh. British troops stormed the begums' palaces in a largely ineffectual search for treasure. Again, Hastings appeared to have acted with a ruthless high-handedness.

Hastings in private life and as a patron As governor-general, Hastings lived either in a house to which his offices were attached, rented for him in Calcutta, or in the 'garden house' that he had built for himself at Alipore, just outside the city. Those who visited the Alipore house described it

as 'most superbly fitted up with all that unbounded affluence can display' (Grier, 30). If he and his wife spent lavishly, he had little taste for public display. A slight figure, 5 feet 6 inches high and weighing 8 stone 10 pounds in his fifties, he dressed without ostentation and was abstemious in food and drink. He seemed shy and reserved in public. 'I neither drink, game, nor give my vacant hours to music, and but a small portion of them to other relaxations of society', Hastings wrote towards the end of his governorship. He then went on to describe his main relaxations as literary, encouraging accomplished British linguists to make translations from Indian texts (letter to J. Scott, 24 Nov 1784, BL, Add. MS 29129, fol. 270). Hastings rightly regarded the translation of the *Bhagavad Gita* by Charles Wilkins, for which he wrote a memorable preface ('Letter to Nathaniel Smith', *The Bhagvat-geeta, or Dialogues of Kreeshna and Arjoon*, 1785), as the crowning achievement of his patronage. In spite of his disclaimer, Hastings was also a patron of Indian music. He employed Indian musicians and was said himself to sing what were called 'Hindostannie airs' 'perfectly well' (Woodfield, 196). He collected Indian paintings and was extremely generous to European painters: William Hodges travelled in India under his patronage and Zoffany received several rich commissions from him. He sent young employees of the East India Company on missions to territories largely unknown to Europeans, such as Bhutan, Tibet, or Vietnam, not only in search of commercial opportunities, but to gather and disseminate information about their peoples. Hastings's role as patron of the arts and learning, which laid the foundations for the Asiatic Society of Bengal of 1784, is evidence not only of the sophistication of his taste but also of his sense of what was appropriate to the holder of what he regarded as now one of the most important offices in the British empire.

Resignation, 1785 By 1785 Hastings had seen war give way to peace for all parts of British India. His standing at home had, however, deteriorated. He was widely held to be responsible for the extent of the wars. Since 1781 Philip Francis had been doing his utmost to discredit him and to propagate alternative views about the governance of India. Francis gained success with politicians who were in opposition to the government that had been giving Hastings support for the last few years. Most portentously for the future, Francis's arguments about what had been happening in Bengal and what should be done in future made a favourable impression on Edmund Burke, who was giving increasing attention to India. Committees of the House of Commons, dominated by Burke and by Henry Dundas, another formidable politician who was beginning to take a serious interest in India, produced reports generally hostile to Hastings. Burke frequently denounced Hastings in extravagant terms in parliamentary speeches. When the old government fell in 1782, it was common ground for the administrations that succeeded it that there was a crisis in the government of India. Peace, reform, and retrenchment must be imposed on the company, and Hastings must be removed. Hastings's support in the company meant that he could defy orders for his recall, but his willingness to continue serving was evaporating. In January 1784 illness had forced his wife to leave India, a separation that he found very taxing. A year later, in failing health and convinced that he had little to hope for from the new administration of William Pitt the younger, he resigned and sailed from Bengal on 7 February 1785.

Retirement Hastings landed at Plymouth on 13 June 1785, after an absence from Britain of over sixteen years. He immediately set about trying to realize the objective that he had long set himself, the recovery of the Daylesford estate for the Hastings family. After three years of negotiations he was successful, acquiring 550 acres and a ruined house. He commissioned a new house, designed for him by Samuel Pepys Cockerell, and he laid out gardens and pleasure grounds. On 29 June 1791 he moved into his new house. By then, however, he had spent some £60,000. This was greatly in excess of what he could realistically afford. He had made a considerable fortune in India, sending more than £220,000 to Britain during the period of his governorship, most of it probably acquired by perquisites of office and by private trade in the first years of his return to Bengal. Even before he reached Britain, he had, however, with characteristic generosity and lack of financial prudence permitted most of this to be spent on gifts to his family and others, and in payments to his agents, who were trying to frustrate efforts to remove him. Even in favourable circumstances, it is hard to see how he could afford to live in Daylesford.

It soon became apparent that circumstances would be far from favourable. Hastings had not unreasonable expectations of acclaim and honours on his return. He was in fact to meet attacks which culminated with his being put on trial. The trial began in 1788 and lasted until he was acquitted in 1795.

Impeachment and trial, 1787–1795 Unfortunately for Hastings, Edmund Burke, whose passionate concern for what he saw as gross misgovernment in British India had focused on Hastings, was not prepared to let him go. Burke believed that the East India Company was laying India waste by rapacious policies within its own provinces, by the exploitation of its allies, and by its wars. He held Hastings to be responsible for all this. Whatever may be thought about his judgement, there can be no question of Burke's sincerity or of his lack of ulterior motive. He stood to gain neither personally nor politically by what seemed to be a forlorn attempt to make an example of the former governor-general. Burke was now in opposition to the Pitt ministry, and Indian policies for which he had previously been responsible were held to have done much to ensure Pitt's victory. So forlorn did Burke's attempt seem that Hastings appears seriously to have underestimated the danger that he was in when in 1786 Burke produced charges for an impeachment to be voted by the House of Commons and then to be heard by the House of Lords. On 1 and 2 May Hastings delivered a hastily compiled defence. Characteristically, he refused to admit that there was a case to answer or to plead his great services in mitigation of any faults. The first charge, which related to the Rohilla War, was thrown out by the Commons, but the second, on Hastings's dealings with the raja of Benares, was passed, as were others introduced in the 1787 session of parliament. On 10 May 1787 Hastings was formally impeached.

Burke's wholly unexpected success seems to have been largely due to the attitude towards Hastings of Pitt and most members of his administration. Although Hastings had some fervent admirers, notably George III, ministers did not wish to be identified with him, and they waited for expressions of opinion by ordinary members of parliament. In 1786 and 1787 the House of Commons and a wider public was very inclined to take a high line on moral issues such as the evils of the slave trade. Burke was able to present Hastings's record in India as such an issue. Uncommitted members together with Pitt and his colleagues clearly thought that there was a case to answer and voted for the impeachment.

The case was presented in Westminster Hall in orations taking several days by Burke himself, by Richard Brinsley Sheridan, and by Charles Fox and other opposition politicians. The orations were followed by the examination of witnesses and documentary evidence. Huge crowds attended the early sessions of the trial, which was regarded as a great public spectacle. For Hastings, who could never concede that he deserved other than the gratitude of his country, the ordeal must have been unendurable. He cultivated a resigned stoicism, seeing himself, as he had so often done in the past, as a heroic lone individual battling against malignant adversity. 'You may rest assured', he told one of his friends in India, 'that the worst shall affect me no more than the spray of the wave, or the Beating of the Tempest, can injure the Plumage of an Albatross in the wide Ocean' (letter to G. Thompson, 10 April 1788, BL OIOC, MS Eur. D 1083).

By 30 May 1791, when the prosecution closed their case, only four articles of charge had been heard, that relating to the raja of Benares, a charge of oppressive treatment of the begums of Oudh, allegations of personal corruption in accepting presents, and of political corruption in distributing contracts to perform services for the company on prodigal terms to favoured individuals. By the time the prosecution case ended, few could doubt that the tide was running in Hastings's favour. His lawyers effectively emasculated allegations about presents by objections to the most important evidence. Effective press campaigns were mounted in his favour, extolling his virtues and ridiculing the prosecution. In the new climate of opinion of a more assertive nationalism in reaction to the French Revolution, empire came increasingly to be seen as part of Britain's greatness rather than as a cause of shame. Hastings's claims to have been the saviour of empire were therefore viewed increasingly sympathetically. In 1791 Hastings delivered a relatively brief statement on his own behalf, and his counsel then took two more years to reply to the prosecution's case. The 1794 session of the trial was taken up by more prosecution speeches, including a nine-day concluding speech by Burke. In 1795 the Lords gave judgment. Twenty-nine peers delivered verdicts. In every case a large majority voted 'not guilty', the largest number voting against him on any count being six.

Assessment of Hastings's career The stark legal alternatives of 'guilty' or 'not guilty' are an inappropriate basis for any assessment of a career as complex as Hastings's. It is impossible to endorse Burke's extravagantly vituperative depiction of him in terms such as 'the captain-general of iniquity'. Few would now believe that he deserved impeachment, let alone being found guilty. Those likely to be hostile to him because of their dislike of British imperialism in India still find it difficult to see how he could be convicted on a prosecution that assumed the continuation of empire; for them he is being made a scapegoat for a rotten system. On the other hand, equally unsustainable is the tendency in much writing until quite recently which identifies Hastings's cause with the cause of empire in India against its liberal and later against its Indian nationalist critics and denies that he had any significant case to answer, beyond some minor blemishes committed in a good cause. Strictly within the terms argued out in the impeachment, Hastings was vulnerable to accusations of high-handedness in Benares and Oudh, he had accumulated a fortune by methods that the new official morality of the late eighteenth century did not sanction, and he had undoubtedly used contracts as a form of patronage.

Any assessment of him in terms that go beyond those of the impeachment must recognize Hastings's exceptional qualities of mind. He brought a creative intelligence of a very high order to Indian government. He also showed an appreciation of Indian culture and a regard for individual Indian people most unusual in any British official in high office at any time. This closeness to Indians had its harsh as well as its benevolent sides, epitomized in his dealings with the city of Benares, whose raja he drove out in 1781 but the greatest of whose Hindu temples he endowed with a 'music-house'. Partly in reaction to him, British administration in India would be more closely bound by rules and more distant from Indians.

Hastings's government can in general be seen as a mixture of benevolence and harshness writ large. He professed his desire 'to rule this people with ease and moderation' (Gleig, 1.404), but he fully recognized the difficulty of reconciling his government's 'primary exigencies with those which in all States ought to take place of every other concern, the interests of the people who are subjected to its authority' (ibid., 2.149). His primary exigency was to raise money, through revenue assessments, duties on monopolized commodities, and subsidies paid by the company's allies. In reality he lacked the knowledge and the means to extract as much as he felt that British needs required, but the pressure to extract what he could left its mark on his administration, especially in its later years, when he faced the demands of ever more expensive wars.

After the acquittal The impeachment left Hastings with bills of over £70,000, which he had no means of paying unless he sold Daylesford. The East India Company gave him an annuity backdated to 1785—that is, to when he had left India—and an interest-free loan. This did not clear his accumulated debts, nor provide him with what he regarded as an adequate income. He continued to live beyond his means and to contract new debts, in spite of further help from the East India Company, for the rest of his life.

After his acquittal in 1795 Hastings lived for another twenty-three years. Most of that time was spent at Daylesford, where he lived the life of a country gentleman, engaged in local affairs and farming that part of the estate that he kept in his own hands. He continued to read extensively and, as he had done for much of his life, to write verse. Visits were made to London and to the houses of friends, nearly always connections from India. Friends were received at Daylesford in return. Hastings frequently confessed to being content with domesticity and with rural life. No doubt he was, but frustration sometimes broke through. He then confessed that he found his life 'inconceivably dull' and that, were a return to public life possible, he would not 'cast a reflective thought on my wheat, turnips or sheep' (letters to D. Anderson, 6, 8 June 1800, BL, Add. MS 45418, fols. 98, 100).

Public employment never came again, but at least in the last years of his life Hastings received some public recognition. In 1813 he was asked to give evidence to the House of Commons on the renewal of the East India Company's charter. When he finished, 'all the members by one simultaneous impulse rose with their heads uncovered, and stood in silence, till I passed the door of their chamber' (Gleig, 3.460). He received an honorary doctorate from Oxford University and was made a privy counsellor. Had he known, he would no doubt have derived further comfort from the apprehension of those preparing for publication the impeachment speeches of the long-dead Edmund Burke that public opinion had swung strongly to Hastings's side. In the summer of 1818 Hastings complained of swelling in his throat, which eventually prevented him from swallowing anything except water. Emaciated and in much pain, he died in the evening of 22 August in his eighty-sixth year. He was buried in Daylesford churchyard, probably on 9 September. A monument to him was placed inside the church. His wife inherited Daylesford. Showing, as she had always done, much greater financial acumen than her late husband, she continued to live there until her own death in 1837.

P. J. MARSHALL

Sources G. R. Gleig, *Memoirs of the Rt. Hon Warren Hastings*, 3 vols. (1841) · K. Feiling, *Warren Hastings* (1954) · P. J. Marshall, *The impeachment of Warren Hastings* (1965) · P. J. Marshall, 'The personal fortune of Warren Hastings', *Trade and conquest: studies on the rise of British dominance in India* (1993) · P. J. Marshall, 'The personal fortune of Warren Hastings: Hastings in retirement', *Trade and conquest: studies on the rise of British dominance in India* (1993) · P. J. Marshall, 'Warren Hastings as patron and scholar', *Statesmen, scholars and merchants: essays in eighteenth-century history presented to Dame Lucy Sutherland*, ed. A. Whiteman and others (1973) · *The letters of Warren Hastings to his wife*, ed. S. C. Grier [H. C. Gregg] (1905) · M. E. M. Jones, *Warren Hastings in Bengal, 1772–4* (1918) · P. Moon, *Warren Hastings* *and British India* (1947) · L. S. Sutherland, *The East India Company in eighteenth century politics* (1952) · S. Weitzman, *Warren Hastings and Philip Francis* (1929) · I. Woodfield, '"The Hindostannie air": English attempts to understand Indian music in the late eighteenth century', *Journal of the Royal Musical Association*, 119 (1994), 189–211 · G. Larken, 'The unknown cousin: Warren Hastings and Barbara Gardiner', *Wiltshire Archaeological Magazine*, 72–3 (1977–8), 107–18 · P. J. Marshall, *The British discovery of Hinduism in the eighteenth century* (1970) · P. J. Marshall, *Bengal—the British bridgehead: eastern India, 1740–1828* (1987), 2/2 of The new Cambridge history of India, ed. G. Johnson and others · R. B. Barnett, *North India between empires: Awadh, the Mughals and the British, 1720–1801* (1980) · M. Archer, *India and British portraiture, 1770–1825* (1979) · A. M. Khan, *The transition in Bengal, 1756–1775: a study of Saiyid Muhammad Reza Khan* (1969) · BL, Warren Hastings MSS, Add. MSS 28973–29236, 39871, 41606–41611 · BL, David Anderson MSS, Add. MSS 45417–45440 · BL OIOC, George N. Thompson MSS, MS Eur. D 1083 · BL, Add. MS 18469, fols. 20–30

Archives BL, corresp. and MSS relating to trial, Add. MSS 17061–17062, 16261–16267 · BL, corresp. and papers, Add. MSS 28973–29236, 39871–39904 · BL, corresp., Add. MSS 63090, 63104 · BL, estate, family, literary corresp. and MSS, Add. MSS 41606–41611, 39073, 39076, 39873 · BL OIOC, corresp. and papers, home misc. series · BL OIOC, papers, Eur MS D 1190 · Glos. RO, letters and MSS relating to estates · HLRO, shorthand notebooks of his trial; additional shorthand notebook for his trial · Lincoln's Inn, London, MSS on trial · NAM, MSS · National Archives of India, New Delhi, official papers · NL Scot., journal of tour of Scotland · University of Minnesota, Minneapolis, James Ford Bell Library, solicitor's briefs for trial | BL, corresp. with David Anderson, Add. MSS 45417–45420, 45433 · BL, corresp. with earls of Liverpool, loan 72 · BL, letters to Lord North, Add. MS 61685 · BL, letters to Laurence Sulivan, Stephen Sulivan, and Lord North, RP 360 [copies] · BL, letters to George Vansittart, Add. MS 48370 · BL OIOC, corresp. with George Bogle, Eur MS E 226 · BL OIOC, letters to William Harwood, Eur MS D 566 · BL OIOC, corresp. with Randolph Marriott and Elizabeth Marriott, Eur MS C 133 · Bodl. Oxf., corresp. with Lord Macartney · Bodl. Oxf., corresp. with Laurence Sulivan · Bodl. Oxf., his wife's legal MSS · CKS, letters to William Pitt · Hunt. L., letters to Sir Charles Hastings · JRL, corresp. with Richard Johnson · Mitchell L., Glas., corresp. with George Bogle · Mount Stuart Trust Archives, Isle of Bute, letters to Lord Hastings · priv. coll., letters to Lord Lansdowne · Yale U., Farmington, Lewis Walpole Library, account book of R. Shawe, solicitor for the defence in his trial

Likenesses J. Reynolds, oils, 1766–8, NPG [*see illus.*] · T. Kettle, oils, 1772, Victoria Memorial Hall, Calcutta · T. Kettle, oils, 1774–5, Asiatic Society of Bengal, Calcutta · T. Kettle, oils, 1774–5, NPG · gouache, 1782, BL · J. Seton, mezzotint, 1784, BL OIOC · J. Seton, oils, 1784, Victoria Memorial Hall, Calcutta · J. Zoffany, oils, 1784 (with Prince Jawon Bakht), Victoria Memorial Hall, Calcutta · A. Devis, oils, 1784–5, Rashtrapati Bhavan, Delhi · attrib. A. W. Devis, oils, *c.*1784–1785, Government House, Calcutta · J. Zoffany, oils, 1784–7 (with Mrs Hastings), Victoria Memorial Hall, Calcutta; *see illus. in* Hastings, Marian (1747–1837) · T. Lawrence, pastel drawing, 1786, NPG · R. Cosway, ivory miniature, 1787, NPG · O. Humphry, ivory miniature, 1789, V&A · T. Banks, bust, 1790, BL OIOC · G. Stubbs, oils, 1791, Victoria Memorial Hall, Calcutta · G. Romney, oils, *c.*1795, BL OIOC · L. F. Abbott, oils, *c.*1796, NPG · W. Beechey, oils, 1806 · J. J. Masquerier, oils, 1806, Oriental Club, London · P. Rouw, wax medallion, 1806, NPG · T. Lawrence, oils, exh. RA 1811, NPG · J. Flaxman, marble statue, 1823, India Office, London · J. Bacon jun., marble bust, Westminster Abbey, London · group portrait, oils (with the nawab of Murshidabad), Victoria Memorial Hall, Calcutta

Wealth at death none; technically insolvent: Marshall, 'Personal fortunes' · mortgaged Daylesford estate for £24,000 to wife; had other debts; lived on annuity from the East India Company that ended on death

Hastings, William, first Baron Hastings (*c.*1430–1483), courtier and administrator, was the eldest son and heir of Sir Leonard Hastings of Kirby, Leicestershire, and Alice, daughter of Thomas, Lord Camoys.

Yorkist attachment and ennoblement William Hastings was aged twenty-four and more at his father's death in October 1455. Leonard had been a retainer of Richard, duke of York, since at least 1435, and William turned to the duke for lordship in his turn. He succeeded his father as ranger of York's chase of Wyre, Shropshire, and in the following year was granted an annuity of £10 by the duke. He was pricked as sheriff of Warwick and Leicester just one month after his father's death, during the period of York's ascendancy following the first battle of St Albans. He was with the Yorkist forces when they confronted Henry VI at Ludlow in 1459 but did not accompany the leaders into exile, and managed to secure a pardon. He may have sought to keep a low profile during the events of the following year. He was not with York at Wakefield and the next firm reference to him is in the company of York's heir, Edward, after the battle of Mortimer's Cross in 1461. He was present at the battle of Towton on 29 March 1461 and was knighted on the field.

From that point Hastings's rise was extremely rapid. In May he was made receiver of the duchy of Cornwall. By July 1461 his closeness to the king had been recognized by his appointment as chamberlain of the royal household. In the previous month he had received a personal summons to Edward IV's first parliament as Lord Hastings of Hastings. A grant of the lordship, barony, and rape of Hastings followed in November. More land to support his new status was granted to him in the following February, including Ashby-de-la-Zouch in Leicestershire, which had been forfeited by the earl of Wiltshire, and land forfeited by Viscount Beaumont and Thomas, Baron Ros. In October 1464 the grant was backdated to the beginning of Edward IV's reign, and Hastings was granted in addition more Beaumont and Ros land, including Belvoir, Nottinghamshire, during the lifetime of Katherine Neville, dowager duchess of Norfolk. In the following month he was granted the honours of Peverel, Boulogne, and Hagenet, late of John Hastings, earl of Pembroke (*d.* 1389).

Alongside these landed gains Hastings received extensive office within the duchy of Lancaster, complementing his inherited interests in Warwickshire and Leicestershire. In July 1461 he was made steward of the duchy lands in those counties and in Northamptonshire and Huntingdonshire, including the lordships of Leicester, Castle Donington, and Higham Ferrers. In April 1469 he was made steward and surveyor of the king's own lordship of Fotheringhay and master of the game there.

Relations with Edward IV and Warwick, 1461–1471 Early in the reign Hastings was involved in the Yorkist military efforts in the north of England, where he took part in the sieges of Alnwick and Dunstanburgh. The trust Edward IV placed in him is reflected in the grant to him, in June 1462, of full power to receive persons into the king's grace at his discretion. In the same year he was made a knight of the

Garter. In 1465–6 Hastings became active in Edward's diplomacy, being commissioned to treat with Burgundy, Brittany, and France. In 1467 he played a leading role in negotiating the marriage of Edward's sister Margaret to Charles, count of Charolais, the heir to the duchy of Burgundy.

In the embassies of 1465–6 Hastings acted with his brother-in-law Richard Neville, earl of Warwick. The earl subsequently became increasingly distanced from Edward's court, but apparently remained on good terms with Hastings, and in 1468 made him steward of all his lands in Leicestershire, Rutland, and Northamptonshire. After Warwick's rebellion of the following year, which culminated in the king's imprisonment at Middleham, Hastings was granted the chamberlainship of north Wales—which he had initially been granted by the king in July 1461 but which he had subsequently surrendered to William Herbert, one of the victims of Warwick's coup. The grant suggests that Warwick saw Hastings as the acceptable face of Edward IV's court circle, but is certainly not evidence that Hastings had supported the earl. His loyalties remained with Edward, and after Warwick and Clarence had fled into exile in the spring of 1470 he was rewarded with the earl's office of chief steward of the duchy of Lancaster. When, later that year, Warwick and Clarence returned with French backing and drove Edward from his kingdom, Hastings accompanied the king into exile in the Low Countries. He played a leading role in the efforts to broker an agreement between Clarence and his brother the king—efforts that bore fruit when Edward returned to England, with Burgundian backing, in 1471. According to the author of *The Historie of the Arrivall of Edward IV in England* (10–11) Hastings was also largely responsible for raising the 3000 men who joined the king at Leicester and provided his first significant body of recruits.

The Hastings affinity In the redistribution of power that followed Edward's restoration, Hastings was not initially given major new responsibilities within England. The chief stewardship of the duchy of Lancaster, which he had been granted in May 1470, was now shared instead between the duke of Gloucester and the earl of Essex, although Hastings retained the lesser office of steward of Pickering, which he had been granted at the same time, and was also made constable of Nottingham and steward of Sherwood Forest, which extended his existing midland power base northwards. The new role envisaged for Hastings lay instead in Calais, where Warwick had been influential and where the garrison urgently needed to be brought securely under Yorkist control. Hastings was made lieutenant on 17 July 1471, replacing Anthony Woodville, Earl Rivers, and shortly afterwards crossed to Calais with his deputy, John, Lord Howard, and reduced the garrison to submission. Hastings was to hold the lieutenancy for the rest of his life, although he spent relatively little time in Calais, relying on his brother Ralph to watch his interests there.

It was not until the territorial reorganization of 1474 that Hastings was given a significantly enlarged regional role in England, after Edward's resumption of the duchy of Lancaster estates in the north midlands held by his brother Clarence. Hastings was not given the lands themselves, but was awarded all the key offices within them, including those of steward and constable of Tutbury and the High Peak, and steward of Newcastle and Ashbourne. Hastings was also granted (on 31 July 1474) the wardship and marriage of George, son and heir of John Talbot, earl of Shrewsbury, who had died earlier that year, along with the castle and manor of Sheffield. The eclipse of the Talbots contributed to Hastings's new importance in the region, but that importance rested essentially upon his ability to call upon the loyalty of the duchy of Lancaster affinity: a loyalty primarily owed to Hastings as steward rather than in his own right. Analysis of Hastings's retaining in the area shows how narrowly it was restricted to the areas of duchy influence. He did not, for instance, build up links with the Staffordshire gentry outside the honour of Tutbury.

Hastings was formally granted the Tutbury offices on 30 March 1474 (the High Peak appointments followed in August) and began retaining extensively in the region in April. Significantly, he did not generally offer a fee—a reflection of the value attached to his lordship within the duchy. In the course of 1474 he retained thirteen local men, and the same number in the following year. Hastings continued to build up his retinue throughout the rest of Edward's reign, and it has been calculated that members of Hastings's retinue were sheriffs of Staffordshire eight times, of Nottinghamshire and Derbyshire eight times, and of Warwickshire and Leicestershire five times (Rowney, 'Hastings affinity', 37). He evidently used the region as a recruiting ground for the Calais garrisons, which still contained a perceptible north midlands element in the early years of Henry VII. Hastings also extended his influence beyond the duchy of Lancaster, into north Warwickshire and Leicestershire, through followers such as Catesby and Ferrers of Tamworth.

Influence and its rewards, 1471–1483 Hastings's power derived from his closeness to the king. His influence was already apparent to a Paston correspondent in May 1461 and in 1472 a Paston servant commented: 'what my seyd lord Chamberleyn may do wyth the Kyng and wyth all the lordys of Inglond I trowe it be not unknowyn to yow, most of eny on man alyve' (*Paston Letters*, 1.581). Awareness of that influence made Hastings's fortune. *Ad hoc* gifts for his goodwill are generally invisible, but temporal and spiritual lords as well as religious houses created a more permanent bond by making him their steward or granting him an annuity, the fees ranging from the £3 6s. 8d. offered by Welbeck, Nottinghamshire, to the £26 13s. 4d. paid by Richard, Earl Rivers, and his wife. In March 1472 Clarence made Hastings his chief steward and master of game in Tutbury and steward of High Peak, with combined fees of £40. Foreign rulers read his importance as well. In May 1471 Charles, duke of Burgundy, rewarded him with an annuity of 1000 écus for his services to the king of England in his recovery of his realm, and in 1475 Louis XI granted him a pension of 2000 crowns. Putting a total value on such gains is impossible, but some measure of his wealth comes from his ability to buy land and his planned building works at Ashby-de-la-Zouch, Bagworth, Thornton, and Kirby Muxlowe, Leicestershire, and at Slingsby, Yorkshire. Only work at Ashby and Kirby survives, but the outlay was clearly enormous, even after the cannibalization of other properties. He is said to have stripped the lead off Belvoir to roof Ashby, for instance.

Unusually for a royal favourite, Hastings seems to have been not only successful, but well liked too. There seems no reason to quarrel with the later verdict of Thomas More: '[an] honourable man, a good knight and a gentle … a loving man, and passing well beloved' (More, 52). He was not criticized by the rebels in 1469–70 or by Richard III in 1484, when he was distancing himself from his brother's regime. There are, however, some suggestions of friction between Hastings and other members of the royal circle in the 1470s. There seems to have been confusion, if not tension, between Hastings and the queen over the division of the lands of the earldom of Shrewsbury; and More believed that the queen's brother Rivers was jealous of Hastings's command at Calais and sought to undermine him. Mancini gives an account of the queen's personal dislike for Hastings, and of tension between him and the marquess of Dorset (the queen's son by her first marriage), but his reading of events, like More's, may have been shaped by the desire to explain what happened in 1483.

Relations with Gloucester and execution Edward IV's death on 9 April 1483, leaving an under-age heir, gave any existing tensions a new significance. Chronicle accounts of what followed are inevitably coloured by hindsight, but there seems general agreement that Hastings feared that the queen's family would seize an undue share of power. He apparently spoke out strongly against Rivers putting himself at the head of a large force to escort the new king from Ludlow to London, and argued for a formal minority, with the appointment of the duke of Gloucester as protector, rather than the immediate coronation of the young king, which seems to have been Edward IV's own preferred solution. Gloucester and Hastings had been on good terms in the previous reign: Gloucester's role as chief steward of the duchy of Lancaster in the north had meant that their spheres of interest in the north midlands had overlapped and they had apparently worked harmoniously together. But there is no contemporary suggestion that they had formed a 'faction' opposed to the queen's family. Indeed, there is no evidence that Gloucester was perceived as a rival by the Woodvilles before his seizure of Edward V at the end of April.

That action pre-empted discussion about the form the minority government should take, and Gloucester was recognized as protector from his arrival in London with the young king at the beginning of May. Hastings presumably welcomed this turn of events and the Crowland chronicler's description of him as 'bursting with joy over this new world' (*Crowland Chronicle Continuations*, 159), although deliberately overdrawn, seems more plausible than Polydore Vergil's claim that the seizure of Edward V triggered Hastings's anxieties about Gloucester's ultimate intentions. The two men apparently remained on good terms throughout May and early June, although Hastings was inevitably less close to the protector than he had been to Edward IV. But on 13 June 1483 Gloucester had Hastings summarily executed in the Tower of London for conspiring against him. The chroniclers who mention the conspiracy are clear that the accusation had no substance and that Hastings's real fault lay in his unwillingness to countenance the deposition of Edward V, although a few later historians have argued that there was a genuine conspiracy involving Hastings and the Woodvilles and that Richard was panicked into seizing the crown.

Hastings's royal grants were seized, with the duke of Buckingham the chief beneficiary in the north midlands. This transfer of authority was evidently anticipated, and on 21 June Simon Stallworth could already report 'All þe lord Chamberleyne mene be come my lordys of Bokynghame menne' (*Stonor Letters and Papers*, 2.161). But Hastings's family escaped further penalties. His widow was allowed the custody of his land and heir, and was also confirmed in possession of the Shrewsbury wardship. Hastings's executors were able to prove his will, and shortly after his execution he was buried, as he had wished, near Edward IV in St George's Chapel, Windsor, and a chantry was founded for him there in 1503. He was also commemorated in Leicester, by the dean and chapter of the collegiate church, and in Northampton, where he and his brother Ralph had been chosen founders by the fraternity of the Holy Rood in the Wall in the church of St Gregory.

Succession and reputation Hastings had married, by February 1462, Katherine (d. 1503/4), the daughter of Richard Neville, earl of Salisbury, and Alice Montagu. Katherine was the widow of William Bonville, Lord Harrington (d. 1460), with whom she had a daughter, Cecily, who married Thomas Grey, marquess of Dorset, in 1474. Hastings's heir with Katherine was Edward, born in 1466. In 1472 Hastings was already negotiating for Edward to marry Mary, the heir of Thomas Hungerford, whose marriage he had acquired from the king. If Edward were to die, or Mary refused him, his place was to be taken by his younger brothers Richard and George in turn, but this eventuality did not materialize. Letters of dispensation were granted in 1479 and the couple had married by 1481. By this date Edward's brother George was probably dead, for Hastings's will of June 1481 names his sons as Edward, Richard, and William. He also had a daughter, Anne, whom he married to his ward George Talbot, earl of Shrewsbury.

As chamberlain, Hastings naturally took a leading role in court festivities and ceremonial. He was an active tourneyer, at least in the 1460s, leading one of the teams at the Eltham tournament of 1467. He was prominent in the celebrations surrounding the visit of Lord Gruthuyse in 1472. He shared Edward IV's enthusiasm for remodelling the household and court along Burgundian lines in the 1470s, and wrote in 1474 to Olivier de la Marche for a copy of his *État de la maison du duc Charles*. His own artistic tastes were influenced by Burgundy and he evidently favoured the style of the Master of Mary of Burgundy. Appropriately, it was another contemporary admirer of Burgundy, Philippe de Commines, who summed up Hastings as 'a man of great sense, virtue and authority' (Commynes, 2.241).   ROSEMARY HORROX

Sources *Chancery records* · GEC, *Peerage* · *Report on the manuscripts of the late Reginald Rawdon Hastings*, 4 vols., HMC, 78 (1928–47), vol. 1 · W. Dugdale, *The baronage of England*, 2 vols. (1675–6) · C. Ross, *Edward IV* (1974) · R. Horrox, *Richard III, a study of service*, Cambridge Studies in Medieval Life and Thought, 4th ser., 11 (1989) · W. H. Dunham, 'Lord Hastings' indentured retainers, 1461–83', *Transactions of the Connecticut Academy of Arts and Sciences*, 39 (1955) · R. Somerville, *History of the duchy of Lancaster, 1265–1603* (1953) · I. Rowney, 'The Hastings affinity in Staffordshire and the honour of Tutbury', *BIHR*, 57 (1984), 35–45 · I. Rowney, 'Resources and retaining in Yorkist England: William, Lord Hastings and the honour of Tutbury', *Property and politics: essays in later medieval English history*, ed. T. Pollard (1984), 139–55 · P. A. Johnson, *Duke Richard of York, 1411–1460* (1988) · C. A. J. Armstrong, 'L'Échange culturel entre les cours d'Angleterre et de Bourgogne à l'époque de Charles le Téméraire', in C. A. J. Armstrong, *England, France and Burgundy in the fifteenth century* (1983), 403–17 · N. Davis, ed., *Paston letters and papers of the fifteenth century*, 2 vols. (1971–6) · *The usurpation of Richard the third: Dominicus Mancinus ad Angelum Catonem de occupatione regni Anglie per Ricardum tercium libellus*, ed. and trans. C. A. J. Armstrong, 2nd edn (1969) [Lat. orig., 1483, with parallel Eng. trans.] · N. Pronay and J. Cox, eds., *The Crowland chronicle continuations, 1459–1486* (1986) · J. Bruce, ed., *Historie of the arrivall of Edward IV in England, and the finall recoverye of his kingdomes from Henry VI*, CS, 1 (1838) · St Thomas More, *The history of King Richard III*, ed. R. S. Sylvester (1963), vol. 2 of *The Yale edition of the complete works of St Thomas More* · C. L. Kingsford, ed., *The Stonor letters and papers, 1290–1483*, 2 vols., CS, 3rd ser., 29, 30 (1919) · P. de Commynes, *Mémoires*, ed. J. Calmette and G. Durville, 3 vols. (Paris, 1924–5)
Archives Hunt. L.

Haston, Duncan Curdy McSporran

Haston, Duncan Curdy McSporran [Dougal] **(1940–1977)**, mountaineer, was born on 19 April 1940 at 21 Dolphin Road, Currie, Midlothian, Scotland, the second of two children of Robert Bremner Haston (1900–1972), journeyman baker, and his wife, Margaret Curdy McSporran (1900–1967). He was educated at state schools in Currie and, an early beneficiary of British educational reforms easing working-class access to higher education, attended Edinburgh University in 1959 to read philosophy, but did not complete his degree.

Youthful adventures on the Currie Railway walls were followed by Haston's first visits to the highlands while at West Calder high school. By the late 1950s he had become a serious climber on rock and snow and ice. He was part of the small group of Edinburgh climbers who helped to regenerate Scottish climbing at this time, and he made a number of important first ascents. Haston also began climbing in the Alps, and came to prominence with the second British ascent of the north face of the Eiger in 1963.

At Easter 1965 Haston was involved in an automobile accident that resulted in the death of a hiker in Glencoe. He was charged with causing death by careless driving and served a sixty-day prison sentence. His friends disagree about the chastening effect of the incident, but he never drove again. Subsequently, Haston decided to devote himself to alpinism and began to spend the majority of his time outside the UK.

Duncan Curdy McSporran [Dougal] **Haston (1940–1977)**, by Doug Scott

Haston joined John Harlin at the International School of Mountaineering (ISM) at Leysin, Switzerland, where they planned a direct ascent of the north face of the Eiger. The successful ascent in winter 1966, on which he teamed up with a rival German group, made Haston famous, but Harlin fell and was killed when a rope broke during the climb (Gillman and Haston; Haston, *The Eiger*).

Haston took over from Harlin as director of the ISM in 1967, and carried out a series of major ascents (including first ascents and first winter ascents) in the Alps, and a notable early attempt on Cerro Torre (Patagonia, 1968), during the next three years. He met Anne Jennifer (Annie) Farris, an English registered nurse, at Leysin; they married on 8 October 1969. The marriage is given one line in his autobiography (*In High Places*, 1972) which, characteristic of the terse style of writing he developed at university (cf. 'Nightshift in Zero', *Edinburgh University Mountaineering Club Journal*, 1962), contains very few details of his private life. The élite French Groupe de Haute Montagne invited him to join in 1969, and Annie notes that he was 'inordinately proud' of being one of the first foreigners admitted.

In 1970 Haston and Don Whillans (1933–1985) reached the summit of Annapurna via the south face—the first major face route in the Himalayas. Midlothian county council presented him with an address on 19 May 1971, in honour of his mountaineering achievements; and he was also awarded the Royal Scottish Geographical Society medal. In 1975, during the south-west face expedition, Haston and Doug Scott became the first British climbers to reach the summit of Everest. This was the sixth attempt on the difficult high-altitude route (Haston had been on three of the previous attempts), and the best publicized, adding to Haston's fame. His other important ascents with Scott include Changabang (Himalayas, 1974), and the south face of McKinley (Alaska, 1976).

Scott notes that Haston 'was very much like a Sherpa—reticent, self-contained, economical in word and deed'; he 'never wasted a step'. Other views of Haston characterize him on the one hand as anti-social, critical, icy, and aloof, and on the other as a hard-drinking risk taker who, according to Jimmy Marshall, 'set out to test every transgression, every canon prevailing in climbing society'. His appearance also left a strong impression. Jim Gilchrist likened him to a rock star, and Dennis Gray to a Pre-Raphaelite poet. Robin Campbell recalled Dougal's 'long loping stride, narrow hips, wide shoulders, a lipless grin and bright blue bivouacked eyes' (Campbell).

Dougal Haston died in an avalanche while skiing alone below the Col de Luisset, near Leysin, on 17 January 1977. The accident was foreshadowed in his novel *Calculated Risk* (1979), which his girlfriend, Ariane Giobellina, typed up and sent to a publisher after his death. The title captures Haston's driving, single-minded, and self-reliant approach to climbing. He was buried in Leysin cemetery and is memorialized by a stone plinth outside the post office in Currie.   PETER DONNELLY

Sources D. Haston, *In high places* (1972) · *Mountain*, 53 (1977), 43 · D. Scott, 'Introduction', in D. Haston, *In high places*, 2nd edn (1997), vii–x · J. Gilchrist, 'Rock legend', *The Scotsman Weekend* (6 Sept 1997), 8–10 · J. Marshall, J. Bonington, and D. Scott, *Alpine Journal*, 82 (1977) · R. Campbell, 'Dougal Haston: Cumha Dughall', *Scottish Mountaineering Club Journal* (1977) [repr. in K. Wilson, ed., *The games climbers play* (1978), 538–9] · P. Gillman and D. Haston, *Eiger direct* (1966) · D. Haston, 'Eiger: projections and reflections', *Mountain*, 10 (1970), 14–21 · D. Haston, *The Eiger* (1974) · D. Haston, *Calculated risk* (1979) · D. Haston, 'Nightshift in zero', *Edinburgh University Mountaineering Club Journal* (1962) [repr. in J. Perrin. ed., *Mirrors in the cliffs* (1983), 51–4] · C. McNeish and R. Else, *The edge: one hundred years of Scottish mountaineering* (1994) · C. Bonington, *Annapurna south face* (1971) · C. Bonington, *Everest south west face* (1973) · C. Bonington, *Everest the hard way* (1976) · C. Bonington and others, *Changabang* (1976) · W. Unsworth, *Encyclopaedia of mountaineering*, 2nd edn (1992) · private information (2004) [J. Connor]
Likenesses D. Scott, photograph, Alpine Club, London [*see illus.*]

Hatch, Edwin (1835–1889), theologian, was born at Derby on 4 September 1835 into a nonconformist family; Samuel Hatch was his father. In 1844 his family moved to Birmingham, and he entered King Edward's School, at that time under Dr Prince Lee. Hatch began on the modern side, but his promise was discovered, and he was transferred to the classical department, where he rapidly rose until he left with an exhibition for Pembroke College, Oxford, in 1853. Shortly before this he had joined the Church of England, through the influence of Dr J. C. Miller. At Oxford he moved in a stimulating society, of which the artist Edward Burne-Jones, an old schoolfellow, and the poets William Morris and Algernon Swinburne were prominent members. Hatch was already contributing to magazines and reviews when he took his degree, with second-class honours in *literae humaniores* at the end of 1857. Ordained deacon in 1858, he worked in an East End parish in London and was ordained priest in 1859. That year he was appointed professor of classics at Trinity College, Toronto. He held this post until 1862, when he accepted the rectorship of the high school of Quebec. Here he married. His work at Quebec left a lasting impression; but in 1867 he returned to Oxford to become vice-principal of St Mary Hall, an office which he resigned under pressure of other duties in 1885. Along with his teaching at St Mary Hall he took private pupils, and actively shared in the practical

work of the university. It was through him that the university *Gazette* was started in 1870, and he was its first editor. Not much later he compiled the first edition of *The Student's Handbook to the University*, and in 1879 edited Aristotle's *Ethics* in a new translation begun by his brother the Revd W. M. Hatch (*d.* 1879). In 1884 he was appointed secretary to the boards of faculties. Meanwhile he was collecting materials for the work which he had planned in theology. The first fruits of these labours appeared in a series of important articles ('Holy orders', 'Ordination', 'Priest') in the second volume of the *Dictionary of Christian Antiquities* (1880). In the same year he delivered the Bampton lectures on 'The organisation of the early Christian churches', published the following year. The bold and original views put forward in these lectures aroused considerable controversy, in which Hatch himself took little part. In Scotland and Germany the recognition that the lectures received was even greater than in England. In 1883 the University of Edinburgh conferred on the author the distinction of an honorary DD, while the eminent theologian Adolph Harnack himself translated the lectures into German. In 1887 Hatch brought out a little volume, *The Growth of Church Institutions*, intended to be the pioneer of a larger work, continuing the Bampton lectures, and dealing comprehensively with the whole subject.

From 1882 to 1884 Hatch was Grinfield lecturer on the Septuagint, another branch of study to which he had devoted himself. The substance of the lectures was published in *Essays in Biblical Greek* (1889). His long-planned concordance to the Septuagint was published posthumously, completed by H. A. Redpath (1892).

In 1883 Hatch was appointed to the living of Purleigh in Essex, and in 1884 he was made university reader in ecclesiastical history, lecturing on 'Early liturgies', the 'Growth of canon law', and the 'Carlovingian reformation'. In 1888 his philosophical interests found expression in his Hibbert lectures on the Greek influence on Christianity, published in 1890 under the editorship of A. M. Fairbairn.

Hatch had difficulty maintaining his momentum on all these projects. His restless curiosity was based in a 'strictly inductive method' (*DNB*), but he aimed also—partly as a response to the polemical antiquarianism of the authors of the Tracts for the Times—at the rather un-English objective of the compilation of something approaching a systematic theology. In the latter he was unsuccessful, but his breadth of reading and writing was unusual for an English theologian of his time, and his contribution was and remains undervalued. By the 1880s he was seen as something of a relict of the theological liberalism of the 1860s. Though sceptical about certain aspects of belief, he was not at all a sceptic. His private difficulties with aspects of Christian belief—he had ceased to believe in miracles—are recorded in his poems *Towards Fields of Light* (1890) and in his privately printed *Between Doubt and Prayer* (1878). His still popular hymn 'Breathe on me, breath of God' exemplified his theology. His optimistic chapter on liberal theology in *The Reign of Queen Victoria* (ed. T. H. Ward, 1887) claimed a success for broad-church views which was, ironically, perhaps truer in the secular than in the ecclesiastical sphere. Overburdened with work, Hatch died from pleurisy and heart disease at his house, Marchfield, Canterbury Road, Oxford, on 10 November 1889 and was buried in Holywell cemetery, Oxford, where his wife, Bessie, was also buried.   H. C. G. MATTHEW

Sources *DNB* · S. C. Hatch, ed., *Memorials of Edwin Hatch* (1890) · B. M. G. Reardon, *From Coleridge to Gore: a century of religious thought in Britain* (1971) · I. Ellis, *Seven against Christ: a study of 'Essays and reviews'* (1980) · O. Chadwick, *The Victorian church*, 2 (1970) · Pembroke College, Oxford

Archives LPL, corresp. · Oriel College, Oxford, corresp. and papers · Pembroke College, Oxford, engagement diaries
Likenesses photograph, repro. in Hatch, ed., *Memorials*
Wealth at death £1712 19s. 9d.: administration, 9 Jan 1890, CGPLA Eng. & Wales

Hatch, Frederick Henry (1864–1932), geologist and mining engineer, was born on 7 March 1864 at 7 Westbourne Park Place, Bayswater, London, eldest son in the London family of five sons and two daughters born illegitimately to Henry Hatch (1817–1885) of Oxford, boot- and shoemaker (later merchant, draper, Liberal councillor, and lessee of the Theatre Royal, Oxford) and his common-law wife, Elizabeth Ann (*bap.* 1832) of Witney, Oxfordshire, daughter of William Collier, weaver, and his wife, Elizabeth. (In 1838, Henry Hatch had married Eliza, daughter of John Thomas Dobney, superintendent registrar of births, deaths and marriages for the district of Oxford, and his wife, Ann; their four sons and two daughters were born between 1840 and 1847.)

Hatch was educated at private schools in London and Paris. By 1879 he was studying general science, both privately and at University College, London. Passing the intermediate science exam in 1883, he was second in the first division with honours in chemistry, his 'obtained number of marks qualifying [him] for Scholarship, Exhibition or prize' (private information). His subsequent claim to have 'gained a gold medal and the Tuffnell scholarship for proficiency in analytical chemistry' (Hatch, 'Vita') appeared widely in contemporary biographical notices. However, University of London records do not show him receiving such an award, nor taking a London degree. Nevertheless, in 1883 he began study at the University of Bonn, and from April 1885 also worked as assistant to A. von Lasaulx in the museum of the Institute of Mineralogy. He completed his dissertation 'Ueber die Gesteine der Vulcan-Gruppe von Arequipa' ('On the volcanic rocks of Arequipa' [Peru]) in December 1885 and was awarded his PhD in 1886.

Having returned to London, Hatch joined the Geological Survey of Great Britain as a temporary assistant geologist (petrologist for England and Wales), undertaking studies of rocks from Britain and Ireland. He translated K. H. F. Rosenbusch's *Hilfstabellen zur Mikroskopischen Mineralbestimmung in Gesteinen* in 1889 and published his own *Introduction to the Study of Petrology* (1891) and *Mineralogy* (1892). He was also instructor in geology at the Royal Geographical Society and lectured aspiring explorers in the subject.

On 13 September 1890 Hatch married Mary Elizabeth (1866–1921), eldest daughter of William Henry Randall, merchant and one-time American consul in Madeira, and his wife, Mary Ann de Villiers. She was an intrepid, high-spirited woman of feminist views who felt that 'a career in the civil service however distinguished did not offer the prospects commensurate with the talents she believed her good-looking husband possessed' (private information). She persuaded him, in 1892, to go to Johannesburg as a mining engineer. Hatch joined the South African Trust and Finance Company, and soon demonstrated that the apparently separate gold-bearing 'reefs' being worked in several mines were all down-faulted parts of the same main reef leader, thus providing an important guide for future exploration.

In 1893, Hatch became assistant to the American mining engineer John Hays Hammond (1855–1936) who had recently joined the De Beers Consolidated Mines company. Early in the following year Hammond was invited by Cecil Rhodes to become chief consulting engineer to Consolidated Gold Fields of South Africa, and Hatch moved with him. He subsequently accompanied Hammond and Rhodes on a two-month expedition to evaluate the gold-mining potential of Matabeleland and Mashonaland. By 1895, Rhodes was encouraging Dr Leander Jameson and Hammond (by then a ringleader of the reform movement) to engineer a general uprising against the Boers. Hatch wisely returned with his family to England that summer. The subsequent failure of the Jameson raid on the fort at Johannesburg at the turn of the year 1896 resulted in the imprisonment by the Boers of Hammond and other leading reformers.

After some months of work on copper mines in Huelva, Spain, Hatch returned to South Africa where, under difficult conditions, he mapped 8000 square miles of the southern Transvaal, greatly assisting subsequent exploration for the main reef. A steadily worsening political situation led Hatch to return to England in October 1897. Subsequently, as a consultant, he studied gold, copper, and nickel mines in Canada, Spain, India, and Eritrea. He returned to Johannesburg as a mining engineer following the end of the Second South African War in 1902. His subsequent proof that gold-bearing reefs similar to those of the Central Rand were also present at depth in the East Rand was another important aid to future gold exploration. He also served as president of the Geological Society of South Africa for 1905–6.

Hatch returned to England in March 1906, and again set up as a consultant mining engineer, travelling to the Orenburg goldfields in Siberia (1906) and undertaking a survey of the mines and mineral resources of Natal and Zululand, South Africa (1909). From 1910 to 1913 he was a member of Christ's College, Cambridge, and he lectured in economic geology. He gave the James Forrest lecture to the Institution of Civil Engineers (1911) and was a member of the advisory board of the Royal School of Mines, London (1912–14).

The First World War began shortly before Hatch became president of the Institution of Mining and Metallurgy (IMM) for the 1914–15 session. As the war progressed, stocks of imported iron and manganese ores, vital to production of the steel used in munitions and ship construction, became increasingly critical. Hatch was appointed to the Imperial Institute advisory committee on mineral resources in 1916 (a move which soured his relationship with the IMM) and in March 1917, he moved to the iron and steel production department of the Ministry of Munitions with responsibility for ensuring a sufficient home-production of ferrous ores. Following the armistice, he was appointed director of the mineral resources development branch of the Board of Trade (1919–20). He became a technical adviser to the mines department (1920–32) and was on the governing boards of the Imperial Mineral Resources Bureau (1919–25) and Imperial Institute (1927–32).

Hatch's publications include *The Gold Mines of the Rand* (with J. A. Chalmers, 1895); *The Geology of South Africa* (with G. S. Corstorphine, 1905); *An Introduction to the Study of Ore Deposits* (1929); and the two volumes of *The Textbook of Petrology—Igneous Rocks* (1914; 8th edn, with A. K. Wells, 1926; 10th edn, with A. K. and M. K. Wells, 1949) and *Sedimentary Rocks* (with R. H. Rastall and T. Crook, 1913; 3rd edn, with M. Black, 1928)—which became standard university texts, in addition to over one hundred scientific papers and discussions.

Photographs show Hatch to have been an imposing moustached figure. His contemporaries knew him as 'a painstaking, studious, highly-cultured scientist' who 'always retained a scholar's intellectual integrity and … intolerance of sham' (private information); as president of the IMM he had 'by example, and by precept, cultivated the habit of studiously short speeches' (Trewartha-James). Correspondence and anecdotal evidence suggest that, at least in later life, he may have had a somewhat irascible nature. He was a keen golfer and a member of the Bath Club and the Athenaeum. He was appointed OBE in 1920, principally for his work on ore-supplies during the First World War. The rare sulphide mineral hatchite is named after him.

Hatch's wife accompanied him to the Transvaal and on fieldwork in the Indian jungle. They had four sons, the two youngest of whom were killed in action in 1915 and 1916, and one daughter. Following his wife's death from influenza in 1921, he married Amie (*b.* 1873) (daughter of William Henry Poole, and the divorced wife of Henry Farquharson Kerr, president of the Kerr Steamship Company of Kingston, Jamaica) in 1923, but they appear to have lived apart in 1925–7 and finally separated in 1928. Hatch died of bronchopneumonia on 22 September 1932, at his home, D3 The Albany, Albany Square, Piccadilly, London, following an operation, and was buried in Gap Road cemetery, Wimbledon, the next day, adjacent to his first wife's grave.   RICHARD J. HOWARTH

Sources H. Hatch, will, proved, London, 12 Oct 1932 · U. Lond., archives · F. H. Hatch, 'Vita', 5 March 1891, Archives of the Institution of Mining and Metallurgy, London · Archiv der Rheinischen Friedrich-Wilhelms-Universität, Bonn · J. S. Flett, *The first hundred years of the geological survey of Great Britain* (1937) · private information (2004) · F. H. Hatch, 'The geology of the Far East Rand and the Heidelberg District, Southern Transvaal: a retrospect', *Geological Magazine*, 59 (1922), 249–56 · J. H. Hammond, *The autobiography of John Hays Hammond*, 2 vols. (1935) · M. J. Jones, 'From the archives', *Minerals Industry International*, 1013 (July 1993), 34–50 · W. H. Trewartha-James, 'Vote of thanks to Dr. Hatch', *Transactions of the Institution of Mining and Metallurgy, London*, 24 (1915), xxviii–xxix, xxxiii–xxiv · D. J. L. Visser, 'Hatch, Frederick Henry', *DSAB* · A. W. Rogers, 'The pioneers in South African geology and their work', *Transactions of the Geological Society of South Africa*, 39 Annexure (1937), 128–9 · m. cert. [Mary Elizabeth Randall] · m. cert. [Amie Kerr] · d. cert.

Likenesses photographs, priv. coll. · portrait, Geological Society of South Africa · portrait photograph, BGSL

Wealth at death £32,691 0s. 3d.: probate, 12 Oct 1932, *CGPLA Eng. & Wales*

Hatch, John Charles, Baron Hatch of Lusby (1917–1992), author and politician, was born in Stockport, Cheshire, on 1 November 1917, the son of John James Hatch (1864–1939), temperance advocate, and his wife, Mary, *née* White (1886–1980), headmistress. Although Lancashire-born he was brought up in Yorkshire, and his early education was at Keighley Boys' Grammar School. He graduated from Sidney Sussex College, Cambridge, in 1942 and, rejecting military service, became a tutor with the National Council of Labour Colleges. From 1944 to 1948 he was national organizer of the Independent Labour Party and a lecturer at Glasgow University. On 1 November 1941 he married Laura Alberta Brown (*b.* 1915), a nurse, and daughter of Jonathan Brown, an engine driver. There were two sons of the marriage, which ended in divorce.

In 1954 Hatch was appointed head of the Commonwealth department of the Labour Party, and in 1961 he became director of the extra-mural department of the University of Sierra Leone. From 1964 to 1970 he was the founder director of the African studies programme at Houston, Texas, and from 1980 to 1982 director of the department of human relations at Zambia University. Later he became honorary lecturer in the school of development studies at the University of East Anglia. He knew most of the African leaders before they were leaders, and he became political adviser to men he had taught as students, including Julius Nyerere and Kenneth Kaunda. He recognized the quality of Nelson Mandela and was tireless in demands for his release from prison long before the true stature of the man was generally accepted. Later Mandela invited him to the first post-banning meeting of the African National Congress, where he was greeted as an honoured guest. He had, of course, been banned from South Africa during the years of apartheid. On this last visit to Africa he also stayed with Kenneth Kaunda, accompanied by his second wife, Evangelia (Eva) Grant (*b.* 1924), a divorced lecturer and guide and daughter of Theodore Copellos, a stage manager, whom Hatch had married on 29 May 1991. Hatch was Commonwealth correspondent of the *New Statesman* from 1950 to 1970, and his books included *The Dilemma of South Africa* (1953), *A History of Post-War Africa* (1964), *The History of Britain in Africa* (1966), *Tanzania* (1969), *Nigeria* (1971), *Africa Emergent* (1974), and *Two African Statesmen* (1976).

Hatch's life, however, was not confined to political endeavour. He was keen on sport, particularly cricket and

John Charles Hatch, Baron Hatch of Lusby (1917–1992), by unknown photographer

rugby football, and was a referee for rugby union at senior level. Needless to say, when a tour of the Springboks from South Africa was arranged Hatch made it publicly clear that he would not be available. Some of his fellow members of the county championship panel thought he was being immodest in supposing himself to be on the short-list of referees for the tour, but others agreed with him that in avoiding a possible choice and refusal scene he was simply being sensible. Certainly there were few people less interested in personal publicity.

The shape of Hatch's career precluded parliamentary candidature for the Commons, but he was delighted when in 1978 he was created Baron Hatch of Lusby and thus enabled to further, at the place of government, causes dear to his heart while still in full possession of his considerable, indeed exceptional, abilities. He was a formidable presence in the Lords, calm and burly, but not fat. When he spoke in his deep voice from his place high on the top back bench, noteless and unhurried, the house listened. Even those irritated by his explicit exposure of cherished beliefs as questionable if not fallacious could only put their heads in their hands, for experience showed that Hatch would seize on interruption to argue his case at even greater length. He would not sit down until he was good and ready, even when his own front bench was showing signs of becoming restive. On one occasion his fellow peers were forced to use a little-known device, 'that the Noble Lord be heard no longer'. We had adjacent desks in a room with eight others, which was said to contain the

nearest thing to a left wing the Lords was likely to experience. There John explained to me that in a time-limited debate he would always take slightly less than his allotted five minutes, or whatever it was, but if he took part in an unrestricted discussion he alone would determine the extent of his contribution. As he did his homework and seldom strayed outside the range of his own expertise that seemed reasonable, even if it sometimes strained the patience of the less tolerant or more percipient.

Hatch remained active until his death from heart failure on 11 October 1992 in a London hospital. He donated his body to London University for medical research, and his remains were subsequently cremated. He was survived by his second wife, and by Stuart and Barrie, the two sons of his first marriage. Although personally agnostic, Hatch respected and enjoyed the friendship of many believers, and a memorial service was conducted by the Revd Lord Soper at St Mary Undercroft in the Palace of Westminster, on 19 January 1993. Among those who spoke were the Most Revd Trevor Huddleston, the Zambia high commissioner, lords Pitt and Judd, the dean of the school of development studies at the University of East Anglia, and Hatch's fellow agnostic, the present writer. Hatch will be remembered as a man of total integrity, a true internationalist of proud commitment to his socialist conviction.   JENKINS OF PUTNEY

Sources *The Times* (14 Oct 1992) · *The Independent* (13 Oct 1992) · *WWW* · Burke, *Peerage* · personal knowledge (2004) · private information (2004) [Lady Hatch] · m. certs.
Archives SOUND BL NSA, performance recording
Likenesses photograph, repro. in *The Independent* · photograph, News International Syndication, London [*see illus.*]
Wealth at death under £125,000: probate, 23 Dec 1992, *CGPLA Eng. & Wales*

Hatchard, John (1768–1849), publisher and bookseller, was born on 17 October 1768. He is thought to have been the youngest among the three sons of Thomas Hatchard and Sarah Clarke, of St Margaret's, Westminster. Educated at Grey Coat Hospital, on 7 January 1782 Hatchard went on trial to the printer Thomas Bensley, of Swan Yard, Strand. Not liking it there, he left before the end of the month and in June went to Mr Ginger, printer and bookseller, of Great College Street, Westminster. He was bound as an apprentice—in reality, an errand-boy—on 18 September of that year. Ginger had connections with Westminster School and the Royal Society, and Hatchard made acquaintances that were important to his later career. He celebrated the completion of his apprenticeship in October 1789 with friends, enjoying at his father's expense 'a good supper and flowing bowl of punch, with some good songs, toasts, and sentiments' (Humphreys, 5). According to his biographer, Arthur L. Humphreys, it was one of the few occasions when Hatchard 'gave way to right merry jollity. He was too industrious ever to give much time to amusements' (ibid., 9).

After completing his apprenticeship Hatchard became shopman to the leading London bookseller Thomas Payne, starting on 26 October 1789. He married on 11 July

John Hatchard
(1768–1849), by
unknown artist

1790 Elizabeth Lambert, daughter of Thomas and Elizabeth Lambert; they had two sons and two daughters. The elder son, the Revd John Hatchard, became vicar of St Andrew's, Plymouth, and the younger, Thomas [*see below*], succeeded his father in running the family business. Hatchard learned from Thomas Payne respect for the book trade and the importance of 'fair dealing'. Payne's shop in Mews Gate, Castle Street, St Martins, was the first to be known as a 'Literary Coffee House and Bookseller's combined', and Hatchard met there 'the best book-buyers in a great book-collecting period' (Humphreys, 11). The experience was of inestimable value to him and on 30 June 1797 he left Payne's employment and opened business on his own account. Although confident of his future he was unable to pay the modest rental on premises at 173 Piccadilly and relied on the help of friends. He later recalled: 'When I commenced business I had of my own a property less than five pounds, but God blessed my industry, and good men encouraged it' (ibid., 6).

Hatchard's new premises were on the unfashionable side of 'the most magnificent street in London' (Humphreys, 27). He was a shrewd and determined businessman and not unduly worried by competition, realizing that the principal West End thoroughfare could sustain a healthy book trade. Nearby Albany in particular brought him many wealthy patrons. As a bookseller and publisher Hatchard favoured works that reflected his own tory and evangelical beliefs, and in both 'he was speculating on a rising market' (Laver, 11). By the mid-1790s the conservative reaction against the revolution in France was in full swing. Within a year of setting up in business Hatchard published the ultra-respectable admonitory tract *Reform or Ruin: Take your Choice* (1797), by John Bowdler. This sold in phenomenal numbers and laid the foundation for Hatchard's future success. He stocked a wide assortment of anti-revolutionary tracts, posters, and songs, and among the early works to issue from 173 Piccadilly were *The Anti-Jacobin* and pamphlets by Edmund Burke. Hatchard also sold the halfpenny tract *Prospect* which foretold the consequences of a Napoleonic invasion: 'Universal Pillage. Men

of all Parties Slaughtered. Women of all Ranks Violated. Children Murdered. ... The remaining Inhabitants carried away by Ship-loads to Foreign Lands' (ibid.).

Hatchard was the early publisher and bookseller of Hannah More, and issued the reports of the Society for Bettering the Condition of the Poor, founded in 1796 by William Wilberforce, Sir Thomas Bernard, and E. J. Eliot, the brother-in-law of William Pitt. Such was his standing that he was made bookseller to Queen Charlotte, from 1800 to 1809. About June 1801 he moved to larger premises at 190 Piccadilly and in the next year gained an important commission when he was appointed publisher of the *Christian Observer*. This famous periodical circulated among members of the Clapham Sect, including Wilberforce, Granville Sharp, and Zachary Macaulay. Members of the group regarded Hatchards 'as a kind of club' and according to Sydney Smith, a tory but not an evangelical, those who gathered there were 'well in with the people in power, delighted with every existing institution and almost with every existing circumstance' (Laver, 13). It was at Hatchards, too, that the inaugural meeting of the Royal Horticultural Society took place on 7 March 1804.

According to a voluminous 3 shilling catalogue the general stock at 190 Piccadilly comprised some 7000 items, ranging from Hogarth to Hooker, Juvenal to Josephus, Southey to Scott. There was considerable emphasis on 'improving' literature, with Paley well represented, and an extensive collection of classical authors. The list of works published by Hatchard ran to fifty pages and began with *The Anti-Jacobin* and *Antidote to Infidelity*:

> Here in a nutshell (the mere chance-bracketing of an index) is that Grand Alliance of tory and Evangelical which did so much to determine the course of English history ... and upon which ... the fortunes of the House of Hatchard were built. (Laver, 17)

In addition to a wide variety of books Hatchards was famous for pamphlets, which were specially important in the days before the proliferation of newspapers and magazines, and 'an avalanche of instruction and exhortation' fell from the shelves (ibid., 18). Hatchard also published plays and poetry, notably the poems of George Crabbe in 1807, but works of literature were outnumbered by singly issued sermons.

In February 1817 Hatchard was found guilty of libel after publishing an uncorrected error in an official report. Although technically guilty he was, as many publishers found themselves in such cases, 'the scapegoat for the delinquencies of others'. Reflecting on the outcome of the trial William Wilberforce wrote: 'We, of course, shall prevent his suffering' (Humphreys, 47–8). Hatchard was not damaged by the verdict and in 1823 moved premises for the last time, settling at 187 Piccadilly. There he continued the tradition of the literary coffee house. In the centre of the room was a table with newspapers and old-fashioned chairs, where readers could sit and talk and, not infrequently, fall asleep by the fireside. Outside the shop was a bench for the coachmen to sit. Hatchard, the epitome of the 'conversible' bookseller, had risen from an errand-boy to the front rank of the London book trade. Long-standing patrons and friends included George Canning, the dukes of Wellington, Richmond, and Leeds, Earl Bathurst, Robert Peel, and lords Palmerston and Derby. Nearly all Canning's publications bore the Hatchard name, which appeared, such was the firm's reputation as a 'church house', on *Defence of the Church* (1838) by W. E. Gladstone, then 'the rising hope of stern and unbending Tories' (ibid., 58). In the 1830s Gladstone was a regular visitor to Hatchards, where, eschewing company and the comfort of an armchair, he would busy himself with a list of pamphlets for purchase, 'even then demanding ten per cent. or threatening to go elsewhere' (ibid., 67).

Hatchard was held in high esteem by a large circle, not least for 'his strict piety and goodness of heart, his extensive benevolence and upright character' (*Annual Register*, 1849, 249). Though a warmly attached member of the Anglican faith, he respected those who differed from him but who acted with Christian charity towards others. He was empowered by members of the Clapham Sect to receive subscriptions for charitable causes, and helped to find situations as governesses for young ladies whose parents had given them an education but little or no money to live on. He was forced by ill health to retire in 1845 and died after a short illness on 21 June 1849, at his home on Clapham Common, London. He left legacies to over thirty-seven charitable institutions in his will. In appearance he was 'the very acme of respectability' (Humphreys, 63), habitually wearing semi-clerical dress with a black frock coat in the style of a bishop's. He always had a word for the errand-boys bearing their loads of books into his shop, 'encouraging them to be industrious, and never afraid of work' (ibid., 64).

Thomas Hatchard (1794–1858), publisher and bookseller, was born on 24 April 1794, the second son of John Hatchard and his wife, Elizabeth, *née* Lambert. He was baptized at St Martin-in-the-Fields in Westminster on 25 May 1795. He married on 23 May 1815, Elizabeth Goodwin; they had one son and three daughters. Thomas Hatchard became a partner in Hatchards in 1819 and after taking over the firm in 1845 ran it along the same lines as his father. Although 'cast in a smaller mould', he had his father's reputation for generosity, philanthropy, and probity (Laver, 28). He was, though, 'a little more flighty in appearance', commonly wearing 'a blue dress coat with velvet collar, gilt buttons, white cravat, yellow waistcoat, and brown nankeen trousers' (Humphreys, 73). Thomas Hatchard died on 13 November 1858 at Chichester Terrace, Brighton. The family connection in the firm continued after his death, and although Hatchards faded as a publishing house it continued to thrive as a bookseller, notably under the management of Edwin A. M. Shepherd and Arthur L. Humphreys from 1891.   Mark Pottle

Sources J. Laver, *Hatchard's of Piccadilly, 1797–1947: one hundred and fifty years of bookselling* (1947) · A. L. Humphreys, *Piccadilly bookmen: memorials of the house of Hatchard* (1893) · *DNB* · *GM*, 2nd ser., 32 (1849), 210–11 · *Annual Register* (1849), appx 249 · D. M. Lewis, ed., *The Blackwell dictionary of evangelical biography, 1730–1860*, 2 vols. (1995), vol. 1 · I. Maxted, *The London book trades, 1775–1800* (1982) · Nichols, *Illustrations*, 8.520–24

Likenesses portrait, repro. in Humphreys, *Piccadilly bookmen* [see illus.]

Wealth at death under £50,000—Thomas Hatchard: probate, 1858, *CGPLA Eng. & Wales*

Hatchard, Thomas (1794–1858). *See under* Hatchard, John (1768–1849).

Hatchard, Thomas Goodwin (1818–1870), bishop of Mauritius, was the son of Thomas *Hatchard (1794–1858), the publisher [see under Hatchard, John]. He was born at 11 Sloane Street, Chelsea, on 18 September 1818, and educated at King's College, London. He matriculated at Brasenose College, Oxford, on 11 April 1837, where he was inscribed as Thomas Goodwyn Hatchard. He graduated BA in 1841, MA in 1845, and DD on 4 February 1869. After being ordained by the bishop of Winchester in 1840, he served as curate of Windlesham, Surrey, from 1842 to 1844; as domestic chaplain to Marquess Conyngham from 1845 to 1869; as rector of Havant, Hampshire, from 1846 to 1856; and as rector and rural dean of St Nicholas, Guildford, Surrey, from 1856 to 1869.

On 19 February 1846 Hatchard married Fanny Vincent Steele (d. 7 Dec 1880), the second daughter of the Right Revd Michael Solomon Alexander, bishop of Jerusalem. They had at least one daughter, called Adelaide Charlotte, who died young, and a son. Hatchard was consecrated bishop of Mauritius in Westminster Abbey on 24 February 1869. He was a moderate evangelical in his religious outlook and was a conscientious parochial clergyman. He published four sermons as pamphlets between 1847 and 1862, and also *The German Tree: a Moral for the Young* in 1851 and a brief memoir of his daughter, entitled *The Floweret Gathered*, in 1858.

Hatchard died of cholera in Mauritius on 28 February 1870. His widow published a number of works about motherhood, including *Eight Years' Experience of Mothers' Meetings* (1871), *Mothers' Meetings and How to Organize Them* (1875), and *Mothers of Scripture* (1875). His son, Alexander, joined the family publishers.

    G. C. Boase, *rev.* Lynn Milne

Sources *ILN* (16 April 1870), 411 · *The Times* (31 March 1870), 9 · *The Guardian* (30 March 1870), 367 · *The Guardian* (6 April 1870), 399

Wealth at death under £12,000: probate, 30 June 1870, *CGPLA Eng. & Wales*

Hatcher, Henry (1777–1846), antiquary, was born at Kemble, near Cirencester, on 14 May 1777, the son of a farmer. His parents moved to Salisbury about 1790. Educated by a schoolmaster named West, Hatcher excelled in classics and mathematics. At the age of fourteen he became junior assistant in the school, and during the next three years filled similar posts elsewhere. He left an affectionate memoir of another Salisbury mathematics teacher, a Mr Moon.

About 1795 Hatcher was engaged as assistant to the historian and archaeologist the Revd William Coxe. He was a fine linguist, versed in Latin, Greek, French, German, Italian, Spanish, Portuguese, and Dutch; in his *Memoirs of the Kings of Spain of the House of Bourbon* (1813), Coxe acknowledged Hatcher's assistance in the translation of Spanish and Portuguese. Coxe later left Hatcher a legacy of £220. Both men helped Sir Richard Colt Hoare with his edition of Gerald of Wales's *Itinerary* (1806); this induced Hatcher to undertake a translation of the *Speculum historiale* of Richard of Cirencester. In 1814 he supplied the letterpress for *An Historical Account of the Episcopal See, and Cathedral Church, of Sarum* (1814), published under the name of William Dodsworth; in 1834 he wrote *An Historical and Descriptive Account of Old and New Sarum*. He assisted Hoare with his *Classical Tour through Italy and Sicily* (1813) and his *Recollections Abroad* (1817), and John Britton with the third volume of his *Beauties of Wiltshire* (1801) and the Salisbury part of his *Picturesque Antiquities of English Cities* (1830).

On 22 May 1817 Hatcher married Anne (*d.* 1846), daughter of Richard Amor of Durrington. In the same year, he became postmaster in Salisbury, but continued to assist Coxe. At Christmas 1822 he resigned his post, and started a private school at Fisherton Anger, near Salisbury, moving to Endless Street in Salisbury two years later. In 1835 he published *A Supplement to the Grammar, Containing Rhetorical and Logical Definitions and Rules*, for the use of his pupils.

About 1835 Hoare renewed an offer that Hatcher should compile the Salisbury part of *The History of Modern Wiltshire* (1822–44), and he was given the materials which Richard Benson, the recorder of Salisbury, had earlier collected. Benson proposed that his name should appear on the title-page as joint author; although Hatcher objected, Benson's influence with Hoare was the greater and the two parts of the publication appeared in 1843 with both names, and a preface by Benson. The dispute was never resolved, and it embittered Hatcher's last years. Hatcher died suddenly at home in Endless Street, on 14 December 1846, and was buried five days later at St Edmund's, Salisbury. Among the manuscripts which he left behind him were an Anglo-Saxon glossary and grammar, a treatise on the art of fortification, and a dissertation on military and physical geography. A monument by William Osmond, a local sculptor, was placed by public subscription in Salisbury Cathedral.

W. P. COURTNEY, *rev.* PENELOPE RUNDLE

Sources J. Britton, *Memoir of the life, writings and character of Henry Hatcher* (1847) · *GM*, 2nd ser., 22 (1844), 323–5 · *GM*, 2nd ser., 25 (1846), 445 · *GM*, 2nd ser., 27 (1847), 437–40 · *GM*, 2nd ser., 28 (1847), 656–7 · Nichols, *Illustrations*, 6.438–9, 449 · J. Britton, *The autobiography of John Britton*, 1 (privately printed, London, 1850), 18–19, 454; 2 (1850), 2, 34–6 · R. Benson and H. Hatcher, *The history of modern Wiltshire*, ed. R. C. Hoare, 6 (1843), 546–7 [note], appx, 88 · parish register, 1817, Durrington, Wiltshire [marriage] · parish register, 1846, St Edmund, Salisbury, Wiltshire [burial] · *Salisbury and Winchester Journal* (1846)

Likenesses W. Gray, oils, 1834, Guildhall, Salisbury · W. Osmond, effigy on monument, 1847, Salisbury Cathedral · G. F. Storm, stipple (after W. Gray), BM, NPG; repro. in *The autobiography of John Britton*

Hatcher, Thomas (*d.* 1583), antiquary, was born at Cambridge, probably in St Edward's parish, the son and heir of John Hatcher MD (*d.* 1587), fellow of St John's College, regius professor of physic (*c.*1554), and vice-chancellor of the university (1579–80). His mother was Alice, daughter of Edward Green of London. Hatcher was educated at Eton College, where he was elected in 1555 to King's College,

Cambridge. He proceeded BA in 1559–60, MA in 1563, and was a fellow of the college from 1558 to 1566. Hatcher studied law at Gray's Inn, where he was admitted in 1565, and subsequently studied medicine, but there is no evidence that he practised either profession. In 1565 Hatcher and other fellows of King's College wrote a letter of complaint against the provost, Phillip Baker, accusing him of Catholic tendencies.

Hatcher married Catharine, daughter and heir of Thomas Rede, son of Richard Rede of Wisbech. They had three sons, John (1566–1640), who was elected from Eton to King's College, Cambridge, in 1584, succeeded to his grandfather's estates, and was knighted; Henry, of St John's College, Cambridge; and William. In addition Hatcher was survived by three daughters, Alice, wife of Nicholas Gunter, mayor of Reading, Elizabeth, and Anne.

Hatcher's friends included John Caius, who in 1570 inscribed to him 'De Libris suis propriis', and John Stow. Hatcher wrote to Stow on 15 January 1581 returning borrowed books, raising questions about authors cited in Stow's chronicles, and asking him to speak with William Camden about publishing the history of Tobit, from the biblical Apocrypha, in Latin verse. In 1565 he wrote to Sir William Cecil requesting his patronage for publication of the collected writings of the ecclesiastical lawyer Walter Haddon, who was also famous for his Latin verses.

Hatcher duly edited Haddon's *Lucubrationes et poemata* (1567, STC 12596, 12597), and also *De scriptorum Britannicorum paucitate* (1576, STC 4686) by Nicholas Carr (formerly regius professor of Greek at Cambridge). Among his own manuscript works, the most notable is a catalogue of the fellows and scholars of his college, 'Catalogue praepositorum, sociorum, et scholarium Collegii Regalis Cantabrigiae, a tempore fundationis ad annum 1572' (Gonville and Caius College Library, Cambridge, MS 173/94, fols. 119–203; BL, Harleian MS 614, Add. MSS 5954 and 5955). In this chronological list, with biographical details attached, Hatcher was responsible for the first 869 names, from 1441 down to the end of 1562, after which the work was continued by other hands until 1646. His continuators clearly added to Hatcher's entries; for example the notice of Richard Cox, who entered the college in 1519, concludes with his death in 1581, nineteen years after Hatcher ceased to be responsible for the catalogue. Such additions make it hard to tell exactly what Hatcher's work consisted of, or what sources he employed, but he seems to have consulted college and university records, to have scrutinized the plate and contents of the library at King's, and to have been alert to the value of inscriptions in stone and glass. He also records college traditions and gossip: thus the young Nicholas West, later bishop of Ely, is said as a young man to have been a trouble-maker who 'set fire on the provosts lodgings & stole away silver spoones', and Robert Bygs was 'always a peacemaker of such controversies as hapned in the Colledge' (BL, Add. MS 5955, fols. 9v, 13v). The entry on Hatcher himself in the catalogue also records him as the author of '2 bookes according to the Centuries of Baleus of excellent men that had bene of this universitie since the foundation of our Colledge & a

Chronographie of Cambr. Antiquities' (BL, Add. MS 5954, fol. 25*v*); these works do not appear to have survived. His catalogue with its continuations was subsequently incorporated in William Cole's 'History of King's College, Cambridge' (BL, Add. MSS 5814–5817). Manuscript writings in Latin verse also survive. In 1567 he gave a Greek text of the gospels, probably dating from the twelfth century, to the library of Gonville and Caius College.

During his later years Hatcher lived on his father's manor at Careby, near Stamford, Lincolnshire, where he was buried on 14 November 1583. In his will (PRO, PROB 11/66, fols. 218*v*–219*r*), dated 10 November, Hatcher said, 'I have hetherto lyved and have bene maintayned cheiflye by [my father's] paynes and travell'. After committing his soul 'to our heavenly Christ in whome and by whome all externall fantasies sett asyde I hope assuredly to be saved', he divided his goods and chattels among his wife and children. His eldest son was to have the use of his books of logic and philosophy while he was at university. He bequeathed to his 'loving' wife horses and sheep as well as the residue of his estate. Money was provided for the three daughters payable on the day of their marriage or at age eighteen. At the end of the will Hatcher begged his father to assist his wife and children, and to permit them to remain at Careby, where they had lived together with 'some comforte'. The will leaves little doubt that Hatcher's father provided the means that allowed him to pursue a life of scholarship.　　　　　　　　　　　BARRETT L. BEER

Sources Venn, *Alum. Cant.*, 1/2 · Cooper, *Ath. Cantab.*, vol. 1 · *DNB* · will, PRO, PROB 11/66, sig. 28 · T. Hatcher to J. Stow, BL, Harleian MS 374, fol. 14 · *CSP dom.*, 1547–80 · H. C. Porter, *Reformation and reaction in Tudor Cambridge* (1958) · M. H. Curtis, *Oxford and Cambridge in transition, 1558–1642* (1959) · J. Stow, *A survay of London*, rev. edn (1603); repr. with introduction by C. L. Kingsford as *A survey of London*, 2 vols. (1908), vol. 1 · J. Caius, *The annals of Gonville and Caius College*, ed. J. Venn (1904) · V. Nutton, *John Caius and the manuscripts of Galen* (1987) · C. D. O'Malley, *English medical humanists: Thomas Linacre and John Caius* (1965) · BL, Add. MSS 5954–5955

Archives BL, catalogue of provosts, fellows etc. of King's College; letter to John Stow · Bodl. Oxf., catalogue of Eton scholars going to Cambridge

Wealth at death see will, PRO, PROB 11/66, sig. 28

Hatcher, Thomas (*c.*1589–1677), parliamentarian army officer, was the first son of Sir John Hatcher (*d.* 1640) of Careby, Lincolnshire, and his first wife, Anne Crewes (*d.* 1595), daughter of James Crewes of Fotheringhay, Northamptonshire. He was admitted to Emmanuel College, Cambridge, on 18 June 1603 (there is no record of his graduation), and to Lincoln's Inn on 9 May 1607. On 14 October 1617 he married Katherine Ayscough (*d.* 1651), daughter of William Ayscough of South Kelsey, Lincolnshire, with whom he had two children. Although the Hatchers were a prominent Lincolnshire family, Thomas was the first of his line to enter parliament. He was returned for Lincoln in 1624; and for Grantham in 1628. He probably owed these electoral successes to his family's intimacy with Lincolnshire's influential puritan knights Sir William Armyne, Sir Edward Ayscough, and Sir Thomas Grantham. Although largely inactive at Westminster, Hatcher became a close friend of Sir John Eliot,

who numbered him among the 'honest sons of Lincolnshire' (Forster, 2.650).

Hatcher was returned MP for Stamford (near Careby) in March 1640, and again in October. In the early months of the Long Parliament he was named to numerous committees for reforming the 'abuses' of the personal rule of Charles I, suppressing popery, and abolishing Laudian innovations. In the spring of 1642 he was named to several parliamentary commissions for securing Lincolnshire and for assisting Sir John Hotham at Hull. In June Lord Willoughby of Parham appointed him a deputy lieutenant and militia captain for Lincolnshire, and on 1 September he was commissioned a captain in the earl of Essex's army. In October 1642 Hatcher and Sir Christopher Wray led their troops into Yorkshire, where they joined the forces under Ferdinando, Lord Fairfax and Captain John Hotham fighting the earl of Newcastle's army.

By summer 1643 Hatcher was closely identified with John Pym's policy of seeking Scottish military support, and he was one of the Commons' commissioners who negotiated the solemn league and covenant at Edinburgh in August and September. He played a leading role in parliament's efforts to meet its political and logistical commitments under the covenant, and, having entered England with the Scottish army in January 1644, did not return to Westminster until after the battle of Marston Moor. In August the earl of Manchester appointed him governor of Lincoln in place of the quarrelsome Colonel Edward King. Hatcher's spell as governor (which was terminated by the self-denying ordinance) was marked by 'sweet harmony' between the county committee and local commanders (*CSP dom.*, 1644–5, 473). In April 1645 the Commons appointed him a commissioner to persuade the Scots to bring their army south to cover for the fledgeling New Model Army. During the course of 1645 Hatcher seems to have gravitated towards the anti-Scottish 'Independent' faction. In July the Commons appointed him a commissioner to negotiate with the Scots for the surrender of the English towns they held, and in December he was appointed to yet another parliamentary commission—this time to supply and police the ill-disciplined Scottish army at Newark in order to prevent any 'plundering, robbing or spoiling' (*JHC*, 1644–6, 4.374).

Hatcher was largely inactive in the Commons after 1645, though his tellership with the radical MP Herbert Morley on 29 March 1647 suggests his continuing alignment with the political Independents. He retained his seat at Pride's Purge, but withdrew from the house completely, and on 14 June 1649 was issued with a pass to go to France 'for recovery of his health' (*JHC*, 1648–51, 6.228). He had returned to England by July 1653, and in 1654 was elected for Lincolnshire to the first protectorate parliament. Of the ten successful candidates who stood for Lincolnshire in 1656 he apparently received the second-largest number of votes, and was deemed by Major-General Edward Whalley to be conformable to the protectorate. Hatcher was returned for his county a third time in January 1659. He did not sit in the restored Rump, and was omitted from the July 1659 militia commission. His son John was one of the Lincolnshire gentlemen who presented the county's petition for a 'free, full Parliament' to General Monck (*A Letter from Divers of the Gentry of the County of Lincolne … to General Monck*, 18 Feb 1660, BL, MS 669, fols. 23/51). Hatcher stood for Lincolnshire with Colonel Edward Rosseter in April 1660, but following his defeat by George, Viscount Castleton, was returned for Boston with the help of Sir Anthony Irby. At the Restoration Hatcher retained his place on the Kesteven bench and was appointed a Lincolnshire deputy lieutenant. He died in 1677 and was buried at Careby church on 11 July. DAVID SCOTT

Sources HoP, *Commons, 1690–1715* [draft] • *JHC*, 2–7 (1640–59) • *JHL*, 4–10 (1628–48) • Lincs. Arch., Holywell papers, H/93 • *CSP dom., 1635–60* • C. H. Firth and R. S. Rait, eds., *Acts and ordinances of the interregnum, 1642–1660*, 3 vols. (1911) • HoP, *Commons, 1660–90* • J. Forster, *Sir John Eliot: a biography*, 2 vols. (1864) • *The manuscripts of his grace the duke of Portland*, 10 vols., HMC, 29 (1891–1931), vol. 1 • G. W. Johnson and R. Bell, eds., *The Fairfax correspondence*, 4 vols. (1848–9) • T. Blore, *The history and antiquities of Rutland* (1811), vol. 1, pt 2 • hall book 1, Stamford Town Hall, fols. 400v, 402r, 404v, 428r, 443v • crown office entry books of commissioners, 1606–73, PRO, C181/2–7 • crown office docket books, 1615–29, 1644–60, PRO, C231/4, 6 • Lincs. Arch., MM6/10/6–10 • Bodl. Oxf., MSS Nalson II, III, XIX • Bodl. Oxf., MS Tanner 59
Archives Lincs. Arch., Holywell MSS

Hatchett, Charles (1765–1847), chemist, was born in Long Acre, London, on 2 January 1765, the son of John Hatchett, a successful coach-builder, and his wife, Elizabeth. Hatchett attended Fountayne's, a fashionable private school in Marylebone Park, Middlesex; he was self-taught in chemistry and mineralogy. He entered his father's business and in 1786 married Elizabeth Collick (1765–1837), daughter of a London wig maker. On a business journey to Russia (where he delivered a coach to Catherine II), Poland, and Germany in 1790–91 he met many prominent figures in politics, commerce, and science.

On his return Hatchett equipped a private chemical laboratory at his home in Hammersmith. An analysis of lead molybdate in 1796 established his reputation as a mineral chemist and in the same year he toured England and Scotland visiting mines, factories, and geological sites. He was elected FRS on 9 March 1797. About 1800 he employed the young William Thomas Brande in his laboratory, teaching him chemistry and mineralogy. Brande, who later succeeded Humphry Davy as professor of chemistry at the Royal Institution, married Hatchett's second daughter, Anna Frederica. In 1801 Hatchett discovered a new metal in a mineral from North America. He named this metal 'columbium' but could not isolate it. He also analysed animal substances such as bones, shells, dental enamel, and other natural materials including an artificial tannin extracted from charcoal. He observed the formation of bitumen from vegetable matter and examined Bovey coal. Between 1796 and 1806 he published at least nineteen important scientific papers, mainly in *Nicholson's Journal* and the *Philosophical Transactions of the Royal Society*. After his father's death in 1806 necessary attention to business caused a decline in his scientific work, but in 1808 he was a founder member and president of the Animal Chemistry Club, a special-interest group within the Royal Society.

Hatchett had wide cultural interests apart from science. He was a good organist and owned a large collection of rare books, musical scores, pictures, and curios. In 1810 he moved to Bellevue House, Chelsea, built by his father in 1771. There is a brief description of the house and its contents in Thomas Faulkner's 1829 history of Chelsea. Hatchett was wealthy, and his distinguished appearance, good humour, and lively conversation made him a popular member of London society. On 21 February 1809 he was elected to the Literary Club, established in 1764 by Dr Johnson and Sir Joshua Reynolds. In 1814 Hatchett became its treasurer and he wrote an account of the club, with a complete list of its members, for Croker's edition of Boswell's *Life of Johnson* (1832). He was a long-standing member of the Royal Society Club and was frequently asked to serve on public committees, especially when scientific issues were involved. Hatchett's last publication was a small brochure *On the Spikenard of the Ancients* (1836). He died of 'water on the chest' (pleurisy) at Bellevue House on 10 February 1847, aged eighty-two, and was buried at Upton, Buckinghamshire, near his parents and wife.

N. G. COLEY

Sources J. Barrow, 'Charles Hatchett esq.', *Sketches of the Royal Society and Royal Society Club* (1849); repr. (1971) • M. E. Weeks, 'The chemical contributions of Charles Hatchett', *Journal of Chemical Education*, 15 (1938), 153–8 • M. E. Weeks and H. M. Leicester, 'Niobium (columbium), tantalum, vanadium', *Discovery of the elements*, 7th edn (1968), 323–44 • E. L. Scott, 'Hatchett, Charles', *DSB* • T. Faulkner, *An historical and topographical description of Chelsea and its environs*, [new edn], 1 (1829), 89–92 • W. Walker, *Memoirs of the distinguished men of science of Great Britain living in the years 1807–08* (1862), 83–5 • *The Hatchett diary: a tour through the countries of England and Scotland in 1796 visiting their mines and manufactories*, ed. A. Raistrick (1967) • *GM*, 2nd ser., 28 (1847), 214–15 • N. G. Coley, 'The Animal Chemistry Club: assistant society to the Royal Society', *Notes and Records of the Royal Society*, 22 (1967), 173–85 • J. R. Partington, *A history of chemistry*, 3 (1962), 705–6 • T. Thomson, *History of chemistry*, 2 (1831), 231
Archives RS, papers • U. Wales, Swansea, corresp. and papers | Dorset RO, letters to Thomas Rackett
Likenesses F. Chantrey, pencil drawing, 1820, NPG • W. Drummond, lithograph, pubd 1836 (after T. Phillips), BM, NPG; repro. in *Athenaeum Portraits*, no. 15 • J. Gilbert, pencil and wash, 1855–8, NPG • F. Chantrey, busts, AM Oxf., Linn. Soc. • F. C. Lewis, engraving (after T. Phillips), repro. in Faulkner, *An historical and topographical description*, vol. 1, facing p. 89 • F. C. Lewis, engraving (after T. Phillips), RS • portrait, University of Pennsylvania, Philadelphia, Edgar Fahs Smith Memorial Coll.
Wealth at death £80,000–£90,000: administration

Hatfield, John (c.1758–1803), impostor and forger, was born at Mottram in Longdendale, Cheshire, one of the many children of a poor estate woodsman. His mother, the daughter of a schoolteacher, taught him to read and write but he received no formal education. After the imprisonment of his father and the death of his mother he was apprenticed to a Chester linen draper. At the age of fifteen he married a natural daughter of Lord Robert Manners, who gave him £1500 as her dowry. Hatfield took his bride to London, where they rented a house in Mayfair and lived in luxurious style. Trading on his Manners connection, Hatfield ran up heavy debts which Lord Robert settled on condition he left the capital. The Hatfields emigrated to the American colonies but, after his wife had given birth to three daughters, John deserted his family and returned alone to England. The first Mrs Hatfield was said to have died broken-hearted and destitute.

In 1782 Hatfield reappeared in London where more debts landed him in the king's bench prison. Again he was bailed out by Lord Robert. Still exploiting the Manners name, he followed the duke of Rutland to Dublin in 1784, when the duke was appointed lord lieutenant. Another unpaid bill put him in the Dublin Marshalsea until rescued by the duke and escorted to the packet boat bound for Holyhead. For a time he frequented the resorts of southern England before making his way north to Scarborough. There, still claiming falsely that he had Rutland's favour, he presented himself to the corporation as Major Hatfield, prospective parliamentary candidate for the borough. Failure to meet the New Inn's bill led to his arrest, and from 1792 until 1800 he languished in the local debtors' gaol. During his incarceration he somehow succeeded in publishing anonymously *A New Scarborough Guide* (1797), dedicated to John, duke of Rutland, who failed to respond with the necessary release money. However, across the street from the prison were rooms occupied by a Devon woman, Michelli Nation, and almost every day for more than six years John and Michelli gazed at each other until finally she secured his freedom by satisfying all his creditors. The next morning, 14 September 1800, they were married by special licence in St Mary's parish church. Soon afterwards the couple left Scarborough to live in Tiverton, but within eighteen months Hatfield had abandoned his pregnant wife and daughter without a penny and resumed his life of deception and extravagance in London. To circumvent the demands of a growing number of creditors he tried and failed to get himself elected MP for Queenborough.

In July 1802, now posing as the Hon. Colonel Alexander Augustus Hope, brother of the earl of Hopetoun and MP for Linlithgow, Hatfield arrived at Keswick in a handsome carriage. He carried off his new role with such skill that all the neighbourhood accepted it without question. At Grasmere he duped John Crump, a wealthy Liverpool merchant, into advancing him money, but his scheme to marry a rich heiress was frustrated by her guardian's insistence on proof of identity. Nevertheless, Joseph Robinson, landlord of The Fish inn at Buttermere, was delighted to agree to the marriage of his only daughter **Mary Robinson** (1778–1837), shepherdess and social celebrity, to 'Colonel Hope' on 2 October 1802 in Lorton parish church. Mary was already famed as 'the Maid of Buttermere' and the wedding of a supposed earl's brother to a shepherdess aroused widespread public interest. Under the heading 'The romantic marriage', Samuel Taylor Coleridge's report of the event was soon printed in the London *Morning Post*. George Hardinge, senior justice of Brecon and an old friend of Colonel Hope, sought out the bridegroom at Keswick. Confronted by Hardinge, Hatfield said he was Charles, not Alexander, Hope, MP for Dumfries, but his lies were exposed when the real Charles Hope denounced him as an impostor in a letter to the

Morning Post. None the less Hatfield eluded arrest by taking a 'fishing trip' on the lake which turned into a successful flight. Letters he left behind at Buttermere revealed him as a forger as well as a bigamist and a police notice was circulated describing his appearance in detail and offering £50 for information regarding his whereabouts.

Hatfield was finally caught in south Wales, questioned before Bow Street magistrates, and sent for trial at Carlisle assizes. Though neither Michelli Nation nor Mary Robinson would condemn him, he was found guilty on two out of three indictments for forgery, and was hanged at Carlisle on 3 September 1803. His corpse was buried in the town's St Mary's churchyard in a place reserved for criminals. Hatfield's 'widow', Mary Robinson, won the sympathy and admiration of poets, dramatists, journalists, and biographers. Public subscriptions were raised for her benefit. Four years later she married Richard Harrison, a prosperous farmer of nearby Caldbeck in Cumberland; they had four children. The death of 'the Beauty of Buttermere' was considered sufficiently noteworthy to be published in the *Annual Register*.

Hatfield was a professional liar constantly on the run from law officers, creditors, and victims of his deceits. It is therefore impossible to be sure of his exploits and movements. His 'extraordinary career' is 'veiled in mystery and will, most likely, remain so' (*Annual Register*, 1803, 422).

JACK BINNS

Sources DNB · *Annual Register* (1802) · *Annual Register* (1803) · *Annual Register* (1837) · W. Boyne, *The Yorkshire library* (1869) · C. Medley, *Memorials of Scarborough* (1890) · *The life of John Hatfield* (1846)
Archives priv. coll., corresp. and MSS
Likenesses J. Chapman, stipple, pubd 1803, NPG · stipple, pubd 1810, BM · line engraving (aged forty-six), BM, NPG; repro. in R. S. Kirby, *The Wonderful and scientific museum*, 1 (1803)

Hatfield [*married name* Nesbit], **Martha** (*b.* 1640), prophet, was born on 27 September 1640, the third child and second daughter of Anthony Hatfield (1598–1666) of Laughton-en-le-Morthen, West Riding of Yorkshire, and his second wife, Faith (*d.* 1659), daughter of Thomas Westby of Gilthwaite in the same county. The family in which she grew up was a godly one and had many links with prominent parliamentarians in Yorkshire. Her father's brother, John, was an officer in the parliamentarian cavalry, and another uncle, James Fisher, had become vicar of Sheffield by 1646.

Martha was assiduous in prayer and read pious books to her sick mother. Whether as a result of a physical condition or for emotional and spiritual reasons, the young girl 'was observed to be of a sad spirit, oft retiring into corners, and weeping'. This was followed by physical ailments such as vomiting and convulsions, which were attributed to 'Spleen-wind' (Fisher, 2), and in April 1652 her family became convinced that she was on the point of death. Instead she fell into convulsions, which were followed by two seventeen-day periods divided by a brief interval of illness in which she lay stiff, silent, and trance-like, taking no food and just having her mouth washed out with small beer or water. However, on 19 May, just as her mother came into the room where she was lying, she began to speak, and up to 21 June 1652 she uttered a succession of pious sayings. Thereafter her pronouncements became less frequent, and after she was examined by a physician on 8 September, her mouth became closed fast and her teeth clenched until December (though on occasions she still managed to testify). During this interval she took no food except what milk and other sustenance could be poured into her mouth through a gap where she had lost a tooth. Despite this prodigious abstinence she remained healthy and actually gained weight. Early in December the family began a prolonged period of prayer and fasting, petitioning God to restore her to health, and after some days her jaw relaxed; on 8 December she became aware of her family and the following day was restored to health and was once again playing with her toys. By the day of thanksgiving on 28 December she was able once again to walk.

Hatfield's long affliction attracted a good deal of attention; she was attended not only by medical practitioners and members of her extended family but also by other interested parties including Quakers, possibly from Tickhill nearby, and by Lady Lambert, wife of General John Lambert. As with other notable contemporary cases of prolonged abstinence and religious pronouncements or prophecy, such as Sarah Wight or Anna Trapnel, Hatfield's condition was open to a range of possible interpretations ranging from demonic possession or divine inspiration to physical disease.

The interest which Hatfield had aroused, along with the desire to provide a record of these events and to place them within a providential framework, led her uncle James Fisher to publish a long account of them. Fisher, who was to be deprived in 1662, was not only vicar but also pastor of an Independent congregation in the town. In his account he demonstrated a familiarity with learned commentaries on spirits such as Ludwig Lavater's *De spectris*, (Fisher, 17), but was careful to note the scriptural passages to which Martha seemed to be referring. He further noted that he doubted whether she:

> ever had in her thoughts, or ever read many of those Scripture-phrases which she uttered, but God did specially help and guide her in her expressions, to the praise of his glorious grace; in a poor weak unlikely instrument. (ibid., 19)

His publication clearly sought to co-opt her testimony to sectarian ends, for he noted the way in which Martha testified against Quakers—refusing at one point during her recovery to wear shoes made by a Quaker cobbler.

Materially Martha Hatfield seems to have gained little from her experiences, except by being sent to writing school. She certainly played no part in the publication of her experiences, and Fisher notes that she wept after the book came out, fearing that she would be seen as a hypocrite and that God would withdraw from her. However, the five editions of the book between 1653 and 1664 kept alive the memory of her experiences and her testimony, particularly among nonconformists. In November 1666 the dissenting minister Oliver Heywood noted visiting the Hatfields at Laughton and recorded in his diary that he

had met there both Fisher and 'that precious gentlewoman Mtris Martha Hatfield, concerning whom so many strange things are recorded in a book concerning her' (*Autobiography*, 1.233). Just over eight years later, in 1675, Martha married Thomas Nesbit of York, clerk; no further record of her appears to survive. The memory of Martha's experiences and testimony seems to have faded from public consciousness—satirical references to 'Hatfield's vision' or the 'Hatfield Maid' during the exclusion crisis refer not to Martha Hatfield but to the visions of Elizabeth Freeman of Bishop's Hatfield, Hertfordshire, which were published in *A True and Perfect Relation of Elizabeth Freeman of Bishops-Hatfield* (1680).   MARK S. R. JENNER

Sources J. Fisher, *The wise virgin, or, A wonderfull narration of the hand of God* (1653); [2nd edn] (1654); 3rd edn, enl., as *The wise virgin, or, A wonderfull narration of the various dispensations of God* (1656); 4th edn (1558); 5th edn (1664) · *Dugdale's visitation of Yorkshire, with additions*, ed. J. W. Clay, 3 vols. (1899–1917) · W. T. Freemantle, *A bibliography of Sheffield and vicinity* (1911) · *The Rev. Oliver Heywood … his autobiography, diaries, anecdote and event books*, ed. J. H. Turner, 4 vols. (1881–5) · C. W. Hatfield, *Historical notes of Doncaster*, 3rd ser. (1870), 176–208 · B. Dale, *Yorkshire puritanism and early nonconformity*, ed. T. G. Crippen [n.d., c.1909] · *Calamy rev.* · J. Hunter, *Hallamshire: the history and topography of the parish of Sheffield*, rev. A. Getty (1869) · N. Smith, 'A child prophet: Martha Hatfield as "the wise virgin"', *Children and their books*, ed. G. Avery and J. Briggs (1989), 79–93 · G. Nuttall, *James Nayler: a fresh approach* (1954) · S. Shaffer, 'Piety, physic and prodigious abstinence', *Religio Medici: medicine and religion in seventeenth-century England*, ed. O. P. Grell and A. Cunningham (1996) · [R. Wilkinson], *A true and perfect relation of Elizabeth Freeman of Bishops-Hatfield* (1680)

Likenesses line engraving, 1664, BM; repro. in Fisher, *The wise virgin* (1664), frontispiece · line engraving, NPG

Hatfield, Thomas (c.1310–1381), administrator and bishop of Durham, was probably born about 1310—this is suggested by the fact that in 1337 he received a royal presentation to his first benefice, Stanford-on-Avon, Northamptonshire, and on his election to the episcopate in 1345 was termed *iuvenis*. The nineteenth-century antiquarian George Poulson claimed him as a son of Walter Hatfield of Holderness, but two separate chantry ordinances name his parents John and Margery, his brother William (a knight), and his sisters Joan and Margaret. He himself claimed that he had been brought up under Edward III's protection, and he also enjoyed the favour of Queen Philippa. There is no evidence of his attending university.

On his promotion to the bishopric of London in 1338 Richard Bintworth was ordered to provide Hatfield with a benefice. As receiver of the chamber (1338–44), an internal promotion, Hatfield was engaged in raising money for the French war, but for part of that time was with the king in the Netherlands. His goods and chattels were confiscated during the purge of officials in the Stratford crisis of 1340–41. Soon restored to favour, in 1341–2 he was contracted to go abroad in the king's service with a substantial military retinue. He resigned his office in 1344, to become king's secretary by 12 October.

As a royal clerk Hatfield received generous advancement: canonries and prebends at Lincoln, Salisbury, Wells, and St Paul's; he secured another at York by exchange. When the see of Durham fell vacant on 14 April

1345, he was Edward III's candidate. Hatfield was elected on 8 May; the temporalities were restored on the 24th, and he received Archbishop William Zouche's confirmation on 1 June. But the see had been reserved. According to the St Albans chronicler the cardinals considered him to be *levis et laicus*, to which Clement VI (r. 1342–52) allegedly replied that had the king petitioned on behalf of an ass he would have been accommodated on that occasion. Adam Murimuth, a cynical contemporary critic of episcopal appointments, declares Hatfield's elevation to have been the outcome of significant lobbying. None the less, a papal bull of provision was issued on 10 June, but his consecration has been variously dated 1 June, 10 or 11 July, and 7 August. Both 10 July and 7 August fell on a Sunday, as appropriate. A papal licence permitting consecration *alibi*—saving the rights of the archbishop of York—is dated 20 June 1345. Murimuth writes that Hatfield was consecrated by Archbishop John Stratford at Otford on 7 August and he may well be correct, since the royal chancery addressed him as 'elect and confirmed' until 5 August but as bishop of Durham on the 10th. He was enthroned on Christmas day.

Thanks to the survival of Hatfield's register—although there are gaps between 1345 and 1350 and between 1355 and 1359—much is known about his episcopate. It is largely made up of the 'registers' of his chancellors, masters John Grey (1352) and John Maundour (1375), and is supplemented by the various *acta* surviving either as originals (enumerated in the *Repertorium magnum*) or as copies in the calendars, registers, and cartularies that constitute the unusually coherent medieval archive at Durham. His continued service with the king meant that he was often absent on that account or for business concerning his diocese. He was therefore obliged to appoint vicars-general: masters William Legat in 1351, John Appleby in 1353 and 1360, and Alan Shutlington in 1374. The intervals between these commissions and other evidence suggest that for the greater part of his episcopate Hatfield was occupied with northern affairs, both ecclesiastical and secular. None the less, he was reluctant to carry out ordinations in person. Out of some 103 recorded ordinations (Durham, Register Hatfield, fols. 92r–113r) he conducted a mere handful himself, only two of them—the eve of Trinity 1368 and Saturday in Embertide after the eve of the Exaltation 1370—in his cathedral church. The remainder were celebrated by four suffragans: the last of these, Bishop Philip 'Lechlinensis', was initially appointed by an indenture of January 1372 for a year at a salary of £10.

The relationship between bishop and chapter had been regulated by *Le convenit*, a mutual agreement sealed in 1229. Hatfield confirmed this in 1354 with an exemplification covering doubtful points. In 1346 he ratified the right of the sub-prior and monks to have complete charge of the priory during vacancies in the priorate. Visitation was subject to the canonical regulation *Debent*. Three personal visitations of the cathedral priory were undertaken, in February 1347, July 1354, and May 1371 respectively. In each instance the chapter appointed a monk 'assessor'.

Following the 1354 visitation the brethren were summoned to respond to *comperta*. Hatfield subsequently issued injunctions, but offered to indemnify the monks if his visitation had contravened *Debent*. Evidence for visitation of the diocese itself is fragmentary, but between visitations the diocesan official was under obligation to hold general inquisitions for the reform of behaviour and the punishment of offences.

Hatfield's relationship with the archbishops of York, William Zouche (r. 1342–52), John Thoresby (r. 1352–73), and Alexander Neville (r. 1374–88) was not harmonious. He was suspected of being behind a 'disgusting disturbance' of 1349 in York Minster caused by two members of his clerical *familia*, William Legat and John Grey. In 1358, following an inquiry, the king issued an official denial of Hatfield's complicity in an armed attack on Thoresby's suffragan, the bishop of Chrysopolis. In the York convocation of February 1360 Hatfield caused his chancellor, Grey, to publish a protest declaring his complete exemption from obedience or subjection to the archbishop (Durham, Register Hatfield, fol. 39v). When Neville attempted as metropolitan to visit Durham diocese in 1376–7, the king prohibited such action as being likely to promote disturbance.

On 30 July 1345 Edward III, who was in Flanders, appointed Hatfield a councillor for his son Lionel, then regent. Hatfield was abroad with Edward in 1346 and at the battle of Crécy came to the aid of Edward, the Black Prince. Afterwards he conducted the funeral of John, the blind king of Bohemia, and accompanied King Edward to Calais. Prior John Fossur warned him about danger from the Scots and then sent details of the victory of Nevilles Cross (17 October 1346). To enable him to attend the Westminster parliament of 1354 he was provided with three ships. In October–November 1355 he went with Edward III to France with a hundred men-at-arms, and crossed to Calais in 1360 for the ratification of the treaty previously arranged at Brétigny. In 1356 he was one of those charged with the defence of the northern border and was present at the negotiations that culminated in October 1357 with arrangements for David II's release. After David's death in 1371 he was instructed in 1372 and 1377 to guard against Scottish incursions.

The chronicler William Chambre wrote appreciatively of Hatfield's attitude towards the monastery. While approving his bounty he was critical of his acquisitiveness. He was, says Chambre, a formidable figure, who strove to be foremost among the magnates, was tenacious of the rights of his see, open-handed to the poor, and conscious of his own importance. On the south side of the choir he had built a remarkable structure ('curiosum opus construxit') incorporating his episcopal seat with ingenious carvings. Below was a place for his tomb, where he was subsequently buried. He also provided an altar where a monk was to pray for his soul. The surviving structure, occupying a bay between two Norman pillars, is highly ornamented. There is no inscription, and the once elaborate paintings have disappeared. The episcopal throne flanked by two seats on each side—a symbol of ecclesiastical and secular authority—is surmounted by an ornate tabernacled canopy. The throne rests on a gallery reached by steps. Beneath is a mutilated alabaster effigy placed upon an elaborately panelled altar tomb.

At Durham Castle, Chambre claims, Hatfield restored and enlarged the bishop's hall; likewise the constable's hall, to which he is thought to have added a high-pitched timber roof as well as inserting the west window; and also other buildings. He added a tower to the city's defences. This, Hamilton Thompson suggested, was a (possibly loftier) polygonal shell-keep (destroyed in 1840), which replaced the Norman keep on the castle mound. Hatfield joined the prior and convent in forwarding a project of earlier bishops by endowing a college of eight monks and eight secular scholars at Oxford. He bequeathed £3000 to the project and his executors were charged with its completion. But it was not until the early fifteenth century that Durham College was firmly established. Subsequently it was incorporated in Trinity College.

In London, Hatfield built an episcopal residence, Aldeford (Old Ford), with a chapel and rooms on a sumptuous scale, south of the Strand, off Ivy Lane. It was later known as Durham House. At Northallerton, Yorkshire, he gave land to the Carmelites and was accounted one of the founders of their house there. In 1349 he drew up a 'foundation' document for the twelfth-century leper hospital at Sherburn (Durham, Register 2, fol. 322v). To support his chantry in the cathedral he granted lands to the priory at 'Henknoll' by Auckland, and in 1378 pensions from Simonburn, Benton, and Ovingham churches.

Hatfield became a *confrater* of St Albans Abbey, and to mark the occasion presented a covered cup later called Wesheyl; in the St Albans book of benefactors he is painted as a stout figure holding the cup. On his deathbed he gave 100 marks to the monks. At the Augustinian abbey of Lesness, Kent, in gratitude for his gifts, a chantry was founded (1381) for the souls of Edward III and Queen Philippa and for those of Bishop Hatfield and his family. Another was established at the Cistercian abbey of Stratford Langthorne, Essex, but here the consideration is unknown. In return for building two cells at the London Charterhouse, their occupants were to say masses for the bishop and his family, and for property in Bow Lane a daily mass was to be said for his soul at the hospital of St Katharine by the Tower. Yet another chantry was being supported by St Albans Abbey at Aldeford in the 1380s.

Despite his largesse Hatfield remained a wealthy man. During his episcopate a survey of his lands was undertaken, though probably not completed until after his death. He lent 2000 marks to Edward III and in his will assigned a debt of 1000 marks to his godson, the king's youngest son, Thomas of Woodstock, and to his nephew, John Popham. This sum was owed by William Windsor, knight, on account of his wife, Alice Perrers, the king's mistress. To Thomas he also left an embroidered bed.

In December of 1379 or 1380 Hatfield requested the prayers of his cathedral monks for the amendment of his life and his soul's salvation. He made his will at his London house on 28 March 1381 and died there on 8 May. His body was conveyed to Durham on a funeral chariot. The exequies were marred by a dispute between his executors and the monks with respect to the latter's perquisites. His will was proved on 6 June 1381 before the archbishop of York at Beverley. It provided 100 marks for the poor on the day of committal and until the eighth day thereafter. Fifty poor men with wax torches were to act as mourners. Among his executors were Bishop John Gilbert of Hereford, the Dominican Thomas Stubbs, believed to have been the biographer of the archbishops of York, William Walworth, the celebrated mayor of London, and John Popham.   ROY MARTIN HAINES

Sources *Repertorium magnum, Repertorium parvum, Registers I–II, Cartularies Durham, Register of Thomas Hatfield (fragmentary); and Durham, register 2,* U. Durham L., department of palaeography and diplomatic [holograph notes of Hamilton Thompson] · *Registrum parvum,* BL, Cotton MS Faustina A.vi · Book of St Albans' benefactors, BL, Cotton MS Nero D.vii · Lesnes/Lesness Abbey chantry, Westminster Abbey, Muniment no. 5116 · PRO, Special collections ancient correspondence, Anc. Corr. S.C.1 · repertorium of Durham material, Bodl. Oxf., MS Carte 177 · R. Donaldson, 'Patronage and the Church: a study in the social structure of the secular clergy in the diocese of Durham (1311–1540)', PhD diss., Edinburgh, 1953 · *Historiae Dunelmensis scriptores tres: Gaufridus de Coldingham, Robertus de Graystanes, et Willielmus de Chambre,* ed. J. Raine, SurtS, 9 (1839) · *Bishop Hatfield's survey,* ed. W. Greenwell, SurtS, 32 (1857) · [J. Raine], ed., *Wills and inventories,* 1, SurtS, 2 (1835) · J. Raine, ed., *Historical papers and letters from the northern registers,* Rolls Series, 61 (1873) · 'Registrum palatinum Dunelmense': the register of Richard de Kellawe, lord palatine and bishop of Durham, ed. T. D. Hardy, 4 vols., Rolls Series, 62 (1873–8), vol. 4 · *Richard d'Aungerville, of Bury: fragments of his register and other documents,* ed. [G. W. Kitchin], SurtS, 119 (1910) · [J. Raine], ed., *Testamenta Eboracensia,* 1, SurtS, 4 (1836) · Tout, *Admin. hist.,* vols. 3–6. · *Chancery records* · *Adae Murimuth continuatio chronicarum. Robertus de Avesbury de gestis mirabilibus regis Edwardi tertii,* ed. E. M. Thompson, Rolls Series, 93 (1889) · [T. Walsingham], *Chronicon Angliae, ab anno Domini 1328 usque ad annum 1388,* ed. E. M. Thompson, Rolls Series, 64 (1874) · B. Harbottle, 'Bishop Hatfield's visitation of Durham Priory in 1354', *Archaeologia Aeliana,* 4th ser., 36 (1958), 81–100 · J. R. L. Highfield, 'The English hierarchy in the reign of Edward III', *TRHS,* 5th ser., 6 (1956), 115–38 · G. H. Cook, *Mediaeval chantry chapels* (1947) · A. H. Thompson, *Military architecture in England during the Middle Ages* (1912) · *Fasti Angl., 1300–1541,* [Lincoln; Salisbury; St. Paul's, London; Bath and Wells; Introduction]

Archives BL, Cotton MS Faustina A.vi · Bodl. Oxf., MS Carte 177 · U. Durham L., dept. of palaeography and diplomatic, registers

Wealth at death wealthy: Raine, ed., *Testamenta Eboracensia,* 121–2

Hathaway, Richard (*fl.* 1696–1702), alleged victim of witchcraft, details of whose parents and upbringing are unknown, moved to Southwark about 1696 to be apprenticed to Thomas Welling, blacksmith. According to the testimony of a neighbour, Hathaway had suffered from convulsive fits before moving into the house of Welling and his wife, Elizabeth; he subsequently received medical treatment for his condition. In 1700 Hathaway began to talk of witchcraft. Early that year he publicly declared that Sarah Moredike, wife of Edward Moredike, a waterman of Southwark, had bewitched him. As a consequence he had, he claimed, been unable to eat, drink, or open his eyes for ten weeks. If this was not bad enough, he also vomited crooked pins and nails, a distressing affliction he apparently demonstrated several times before witnesses.

It was suggested that the only cure for Hathaway's condition was to draw blood from Moredike. Accordingly, on 11 February 1700 she was forcibly taken to Welling's house, where Elizabeth Welling scratched her face, while her husband kicked her in the belly and stamped on her. Hathaway claimed to feel much better after the assault, thus confirming Moredike's guilt. It was not long, however, before his debilitating fits returned and another scratching of Moredike was called for.

These events caused a sensation in the neighbourhood, and the local minister, Dr Martin, decided to investigate Hathaway's claims. He found him in an apparently semiconscious state, struck deaf, dumb, and blind. Martin brought with him Sarah Moredike, her brother James Hearne, and a woman named Johnson. To test Hathaway's condition Martin asked Sarah to speak to the stricken young man while silently requesting Johnson to present her arm for the invalid to scratch. Blood having been drawn, Hathaway experienced an instant and miraculous recovery, but his sense of well-being was short-lived as the trick played upon him was revealed. Martin upbraided him for his imposture in front of the Wellings and other neighbours who had gathered in their house. It later emerged that the Wellings were manipulating Hathaway and orchestrating the campaign against Sarah Moredike. When she fled to London, they even sought out her new lodgings and whipped up a mob to surround it. An alderman was called but instead of taking action against Hathaway's supporters, he had Moredike searched for teats and allowed Hathaway to scratch her again. He then had her committed for trial.

Moredike's case was heard at the Guildford assizes on 28 July 1701. She was acquitted, and Hathaway was arrested for imposture three days later and taken to the Marshalsea prison. The constable assigned to watch over him reported that he slept, drank, and ate well during that time. He was then taken to the house of a surgeon named Kensey who wished to examine his extraordinary symptoms. Kensey made a hole in the wall of Hathaway's bedchamber secretly to monitor his behaviour. Although the young man continued to maintain that he was under Moredike's spell, and so was unable to eat or drink, Kinsey saw him eating and drinking everything that was left for him. On one occasion, having been offered an extra allowance of spirits, a tipsy Hathaway was even seen dancing before the fire while playing a tune with the tongs.

All this evidence was heard during Hathaway's trial at the Surrey spring assizes, presided over by Judge John Holt. He was indicted not only for imposture but also for riot and assault along with Thomas and Elizabeth Welling. Found guilty on all charges, Hathaway was fined, ordered to stand in the pillory at Southwark, Cornhill, and Temple Bar, and sentenced to a flogging and six months' hard labour.   OWEN DAVIES

Sources *The tryal of Richard Hathaway upon an information for being a cheat and imposter* (1702) · C. L'Estrange Ewen, *Witch hunting and witch trials: the indictments for witchcraft from the records of 1373 assizes held for the home circuit, A.D.1559–1736* (1929)

Hathaway [*née* Collings], Dame **Sibyl Mary** (1884–1974), dame of Sark, was born on 13 January 1884 in Guernsey at the house once owned by her privateer great-great-grandfather, John Allaire, whose business dealings led to the seigniory of Sark passing into her family. The elder daughter (there were no sons) of William Frederick Collings, twenty-first seigneur of Sark, and his Canadian wife, Sophia Wallace (daughter of George Moffat of Montreal), she grew up on Sark to become a lively, intelligent, and headstrong young woman, encouraged by her eccentric father to ignore her congenital lameness and follow many physically demanding pursuits. With the rest of the household she also had to contend with his uncertain temper and even wilder moments during occasional drinking bouts. Few of her governesses stayed for long and, with the exception of two terms at a French convent near Tours, she had little formal education.

She met Dudley John Beaumont, son of Captain William Spencer Beaumont, of the 14th King's hussars, in the spring of 1899 when he visited Sark and painted her portrait. Two years later, following a fierce argument with her father, she fled to England and married Beaumont in London. The marriage produced four sons and three daughters, the youngest of whom was born seven months after her husband's death at the age of forty-one in the influenza epidemic of 1918.

From 1921 to 1923 Sibyl Beaumont lived with her family in Cologne, helped run YMCA canteens, and learned the German which twenty years later was to prove so useful to her. On her father's death in June 1927 she succeeded to the seigniory and became dame of Sark, determined from the outset to bring improvements to the island without sacrificing its unusual charms. After a brief engagement to a man later convicted for bigamy and fraud, in 1929 she married American-born Robert Woodward Hathaway (second of three sons of Charles Hathaway, a Wall Street banker). According to Sark law, by her marriage her estate, including the seigniory, passed to her husband, but she had no intention of relinquishing her hold on island affairs and, although he then became the official seigneur, she sat beside him at meetings of the chief pleas (Sark's governing body), prompting his actions and continuing, albeit illegally, to give voice to her own opinions.

It was during the Second World War that Sibyl Hathaway faced her greatest challenge, when Sark, with the other Channel Islands, was occupied by the Germans in July 1940. She managed throughout the following years to maintain a front of firmness and dignity, earning the respect of the Germans and at the same time extracting the best terms she could for Sark and its people, with whom she shared the hunger and other privations of occupation, the anxieties engendered by two unsuccessful British commando raids, and the pain of separation when many islanders, including her husband, were deported to German prison camps. Liberation finally came on 10 May 1945.

Dame Sibyl Mary Hathaway (1884–1974), by Pamela Chandler, 1961

When Robert Hathaway died in December 1954 she regained her full status as dame of Sark and, despite many stormy passages with her islanders, continued to be treated by the majority with the greatest respect, if not always with affection. Through her travels and writings (which included a novel, *Maid of Sark*, in 1939 and an autobiography, *Dame of Sark*, 1961) and television, radio, and press interviews, her island became known worldwide and its subsequent prosperity owed much to her determination to retain its unique laws and peaceful atmosphere, unpolluted by cars or aeroplanes. She was appointed OBE (1949) and DBE (1965). She died on 14 July 1974 on Sark, having outlived five of her children. Her eldest son was killed in an air raid on Liverpool in 1941, the second died in Australia in 1973, the third (aged nine months) in 1909, and two of her daughters in 1948 and 1967 respectively. Her grandson (John) Michael Beaumont succeeded her to the seigniory. BARBARA STONEY, *rev.*

Sources B. Stoney, *Sibyl, dame of Sark* (1978) · S. Hathaway, *Dame of Sark* (1961) · private information (1993)
Archives FILM BFI NFTVA, *About Britain*, Channel TV, 27 June 1986 | SOUND BL NSA, news recordings · BL NSA, performance recordings
Likenesses P. Chandler, photograph, 1961, NPG [*see illus.*] · W. Bird, photograph, 1965, NPG

Hatherley. For this title name *see* Wood, William Page, Baron Hatherley (1801–1881).

Hatherton. For this title name *see* Littleton, Edward John, first Baron Hatherton (1791–1863).

Hathway, Richard (*fl.* 1598–1603), playwright, made his living by writing for two acting companies that were contemporary with Shakespeare's. Despite previous speculation, Hathway was not related to the Shottery family of Shakespeare's wife, Anne Hathaway, or to her father, Richard Hathaway. Nor is there any evidence that he wrote for the playing companies with which Shakespeare was involved (the Chamberlain's Men and the King's Men), and he was not the Richard Hathway who was awarded his BA at Oxford in 1592 (this Hathway was later vicar of Frocester, Gloucestershire, 1610–40). However, Richard Hathway probably was the 'poett' whose son Edmund was baptized on 28 March 1601 at St Giles Cripplegate, London, the parish associated with the Fortune Playhouse and the Admiral's Men, the company for whom Hathway wrote most of his plays (McManaway, 561–2). Moreover, he might also have been the 'Poet' who, the next year, baptized a son at St Botolph, Aldgate (Eccles, 65).

Hathway can be associated with seventeen plays during the five years that define his brief heyday. Many were multipart dramas; most seem to have been histories or comedies. He composed 'King Arthur' ('Life of Arthur, King of England') alone, for which he received a payment from Philip Henslowe, the financier of the Admiral's Men, on 12 April 1598 (*Henslowe's Diary*, 1961, 89). In collaboration with Anthony Munday he wrote 'Valentine and Orson' (19 July 1598; ibid., 93), but during the next eighteen months Hathway was involved only in parts 1 and 2 of *Sir John Oldcastle* (ibid., 125–6).

Within the next three years, fourteen plays by Hathway followed in rapid succession. All were written in collaboration with different professional playwrights, including Anthony Munday, Michael Drayton, Robert Wilson, Thomas Dekker, William Rankins, William Haughton, Wentworth Smith, and John Day. In 1600 he composed 'Owen Tudor' and '1, 2 Fair Constance of Rome'. During the next year he completed five plays: 'Hannibal and Scipio', 'Scogan and Skelton', 'The Conquest of Spain by John of Gaunt', and parts 1 and 2 of 'Six Clothiers'. In 1602 Hathway worked on two plays, 'Too Good to be True' and 'As Merry as May Be', also for the Admiral's Men; however, soon thereafter he began to write for Worcester's Men, who were then performing at Henslowe's Rose Playhouse. The reason for this change is unclear, although Henslowe was clearly financing both companies. In the period from November 1602 to February 1603 Hathway collaborated on parts 1 and 2 of 'Black Dog of Newgate' and 'The Unfortunate General'. Yet there was no apparent animosity between Hathway and the Admiral's Men. He wrote his final play for them in 1603 ('The Boss of Billingsgate'), collaborating with John Day and other 'felowe poetes' (Chambers, 3.333–4).

Greg concluded that Hathway's periods of frantic activity, in combination with what appear to be long intervals of professional silence, suggest that he probably wrote for other playing companies for which there are no extant records (*Henslowe's Diary*, 1908, 2.270). The letter from the actor–playwright Samuel Rowley to Philip Henslowe

(April 1601?) would suggest that this is indeed plausible. In it Rowley asks that Hathway be allowed to take back his 'papers' of 'John of Gaunt', presumably because Hathway wished to withdraw the play from the Admiral's Men and sell it to another company (*Henslowe Papers*, 56). This might also have been the case with *Sir John Oldcastle*, which was originally contracted by Henslowe to be written in two sections, but there is no evidence that the second part was ever completed for, or delivered to, the Admiral's Men. Consequently, *Sir John Oldcastle* has for some time attracted great attention, not only because it is the sole extant play in which Hathway had a hand, but because it has become part of the Shakespeare apocrypha. Theatre historians commonly agree that *Oldcastle* influenced Shakespeare's *Henry IV*, parts 1 and 2, and *Henry V* (Corbin and Sedge, 9–12). Moreover, there are two recorded court performances of *Oldcastle* by the King's Men, the playing company in which Shakespeare was earlier an actor and shareholder. These were preserved in the office book kept by the master of the revels, Sir Henry Herbert, in entries for 6 January 1631 and 29 May 1638 (Bentley, 1.96, 99).

Possibly it was William Rankins, with whom Hathway wrote two plays in 1601, who fostered Hathway's poetic career. Both Hathway and Rankins contributed verses to John Bodenham's *Belvedére, the Garden of the Muses* (1600), a collection of poems by distinguished contemporary poets. (Another poet whose verses preface the volume, identified only as A. M., could well have been Anthony Munday, the dramatist–collaborator involved with Hathway and his plays.) Although Bodenham states in his preface that some of the verses were taken from 'Maskes, Shewes, and devises perfourmed in prograce [progress]' (*Bodenham's Belvedére*, sig. A4r) before the queen, it would seem that Hathway's ten-line poem 'Of the Booke' was written specifically in praise of Bodenham's collection. Here Hathway characterizes the book as a 'Guide to the soule, and ruler of the sense', likening the individual poems to 'beames proceeding from the Sunne'. Nevertheless, Hathway's literary reputation seems to have depended primarily on his talents as a playwright. Francis Meres referred to him as 'the best for comedy' in 1598 (Chambers, 3.332).

A play entitled *Hannibal and Scipio* was performed by Queen Henrietta's Men at the Phoenix, or Cockpit, in Drury Lane (1635). It was subsequently entered into the Stationers' register (6 August 1636) and published the following year as written by Thomas Nabbes. Some historians have assumed that Nabbes was borrowing or revising the earlier play by Hathway and Rankins; however, there is no evidence by which the later play can be identified with the earlier play of the same name. It is not known when Hathway died.　　　　　　　　S. P. CERASANO

Sources E. K. Chambers, *The Elizabethan stage*, 4 vols. (1923) · *Henslowe's diary*, ed. R. A. Foakes and R. T. Rickert (1961) · *Henslowe's diary*, ed. W. W. Greg, 2 vols. (1904–8) · W. W. Greg, *Henslowe papers: being documents supplementary to Henslowe's diary* (1907) · M. R. McManaway, 'Poets in the parish of St. Giles, Cripplegate', *Shakespeare Quarterly*, 9 (1958), 561–2 · P. Corbin and D. Sedge, eds., *The Oldcastle controversy* (1991) · M. Eccles, 'Richard Hathaway', *Studies in Philology*, 79 (1982), 64–5 · *Bodenham's Belvedére, or The garden of the muses* (1600) · G. E. Bentley, *The Jacobean and Caroline stage*, 7 vols. (1941–68) · *DNB*

Hatry, Clarence Charles (1888–1965), company promoter, was born on 16 December 1888 at 48 Belsize Park, London, the eldest of four sons of Julius Hatry (1856/7–1907), silk merchant, and his wife, Henriette Ellen Katzenstein (1861/2–1943). In childhood he felt lonely, browbeaten, and disheartened by a severe father and a mother whom he thought snobbish and neglectful; he was a dreamy, inward, and dissatisfied child. After attending St Paul's School (1903–5) he studied French and German on the continent before marrying in 1909 Violet Marguerite ('Dolly') (1892–1980), daughter of Charles Ferguson. They had at least one son and at least one daughter. In March 1910 Hatry took over the family silk business, which had been conducted by his mother since his father's death; shortly afterwards he was stricken with rheumatic fever, and the business failed in October, with Hatry bankrupt for personal guarantees of £8000 and his mother following him into bankruptcy. Despite this set-back, he paid off all the debts in less than two years.

About 1911 Hatry became an insurance broker. After acquiring control of City Equitable Fire Insurance for £60,000 in 1914, he reorganized it before selling it for £250,000 in 1915. This success encouraged his taste for making deals. In 1916 he took over the Commercial Bank of London, which he renamed in 1921 the Commercial Corporation of London to reflect its interest in the provision of finance rather than banking services. In the false boom at the end of the war Hatry proved a keen and successful speculator. In 1919 he bought Leyland Motors for a reputed £350,000 and immediately resold it for double that figure. He professed a belief in strength through consolidation. Jute Industries, which he formed in 1920, had some success, but there was little strategic logic or managerial vigour in such creations as British Glass Industries (formed in 1919) and Amalgamated Industrials (also in 1919), a hodgepodge of cotton spinning, shipbuilding, and pig farming. Hatry made a quick fortune, which he began spending ostentatiously, but the Commercial Corporation collapsed in 1923 with a deficit approaching £3 million.

In 1925 Hatry organized a private company called the Aylesbury Trust to take over his liabilities to earlier creditors and to act as a finance house. Later that year he bought department stores in London and the provinces for combination in the Drapery and General Investment Trust, which he sold at a handsome profit to Debenhams in 1926. In the same year Hatry formed Corporation and General Securities, which operated in the money market and vied with the stockbroking firm of Robert Nivison, Lord Glendyne, in providing funds for municipal corporations. In 1927 Hatry registered the Austen Friars Trust and embarked on an energetic campaign of amalgamations and promotions. His methods were complex, involving voluntary liquidations, reconstructions, name changes, and intra-group share dealings. Sir Gilbert Garnsey, the accountant who was eventually appointed liquidator of Hatry's interests, believed that the Austen Friars Trust was insolvent from its inception. In 1928 Hatry, who had a life-long weakness for gadgetry, became obsessed with promoting a system for securing photographic impressions electronically; his company Photomaton became a severe drain on his resources, and was mistrusted by those in the City whose goodwill he needed.

His successful promotion early in 1929 of Allied Ironfounders, a combine of light castings manufacturers, led Hatry to attempt the rationalization of the steel industry. In April 1929 he acquired control of the United Steel companies. The election of a Labour government in May depressed stock exchange values, and Hatry's plans were ruthlessly opposed by Montagu Norman, governor of the Bank of England. To surmount his difficulty in raising money for the United Steel stock, Hatry borrowed £789,000 from banks on the security of forged Corporation and General scrip certificates ascribed to the municipalities of Gloucester, Wakefield, and Swindon. £822,000 was withheld from these three corporations and another £700,000 was raised by duplicating shares in other companies he had promoted. As rumours about the Hatry companies circulated in the City, he spent large sums vainly trying to support their share values. On 20 September Hatry voluntarily confessed his frauds to Sir Archibald Bodkin, director of public prosecutions, inaccurately taking all blame.

Hatry and three colleagues appeared at the Old Bailey before Sir Horace Avory on 20 January 1930. After the attorney-general Sir William Jowitt had closed the prosecution case, the defendants changed their pleas to guilty (on 25 January). Hatry was sentenced to the maximum term of fourteen years' penal servitude. A campaign for clemency, organized by his son Cecil and supported by his counsel, Norman Birkett, enlisted the parliamentary support of Harold Nicolson and J. T. C. Moore-Brabazon, and he was released in 1939.

Private investors in Hatry's companies lost about £15 million. The 'first impressions of Hatry' of the marquess of Winchester, who was the guinea-pig chairman of Corporation and General:

> were that he was an example of the alert business brain having an unusually quick perception of any proposition, a marvellous gift for shifting the intricacies of a Balance Sheet, a power of putting his case with a clarity of expression rarely found apart from legal training, coupled with an apparent frankness which amounted to a charm of manner.

After the crash, in which Winchester lost money and reputation, he decided that Hatry had:

> the supreme quality of dangerous optimism coupled with inordinate conceit … his brain was honeycombed with crevasses into which unpleasant facts were allowed to slip and there he permitted them to remain in the hope that the glacier would never reveal its secrets. (Winchester, 250, 268, 274)

After Hatry's release he published *Light out of Darkness* (1939), advocating mass migration to solve global economic and political tensions: black Americans were to be relocated in equatorial Africa, and Ukrainians, Czechs, and Jews were to be given new homelands to prevent them cramping Germany. He owned the Piccadilly bookshop of Hatchard's in the early 1950s and London coffee bars in the late 1950s, and he maintained other business interests until his death of heart failure on 10 June 1965, at Westminster Hospital, Horseferry Road, Westminster, London. After a funeral service at St Paul's Church, Onslow Square, Knightsbridge, he was cremated on 16 June. He was survived by his wife. Dame Ngaio Marsh's novel *Death at the Bar* (1939) contains a fictionalized version of Hatry's crimes. RICHARD DAVENPORT-HINES

Sources *The Times* (12 June 1965) · *The Times* (15 June 1965), 16 · Marquess of Winchester, *Statesmen, financiers and felons* (1934), 249–75 · C. A. Hatry, *The Hatry case: eight current misconceptions* (1938) · A. Vallance, *Very private enterprise* (1955), 134–45 · H. M. Hyde, *Norman Birkett* (1964), 275–87 · G. Lang, *Mr Justice Avory* (1935), 273–91 · W. H. Hunt, ed., *The registers of St Paul's Church, Covent Garden, London*, 1–4, Harleian Society, register section, 33–6 (1906–8) · probate · b. cert. · d. cert. · D. Fanning, 'Hatry, Clarence Charles', *DBB* · calendar indices, Family Record Centre · *Debrett's Peerage* (1995), 241

Wealth at death £828: probate, 18 Aug 1965, *CGPLA Eng. & Wales*

Hatsell, Henry (d. 1667), naval official and politician, was probably born in Plymouth of a commercial family. He married at Barnstaple on 6 February 1637 Margaret Dawe, with whom he had at least one son, Sir Henry *Hatsell (*bap.* 1641, *d.* 1714), later baron of the exchequer. He became a freeman of Plymouth in 1641, and after the outbreak of civil war was commissioned as an army officer on the side of parliament. By April 1645 he was a captain in the Plymouth garrison, and lent the committee of safety £50 to help sustain the defence against the besieging royalists. After the victories of Sir Thomas Fairfax in the south-west in 1646 Hatsell was able to act on a wider stage for the parliamentary cause, beginning work for the navy in a variety of locations. He was imprisoned by the royalists in Jersey and the Isles of Scilly in 1649, and on his release became pressmaster at Minehead. After moving to Plymouth he first made a significant impression in April 1651 when his promptness and efficiency in assembling men and boats helped General Robert Blake embark nine companies of foot for a successful campaign in the Isles of Scilly against the desperate royalists. Hatsell gave a personal account of the campaign to the House of Commons, which he delivered on 13 June.

In 1652 Hatsell was appointed naval agent at Plymouth, a position he held with that of check of customs there. This gave him an unrivalled authority in maritime affairs in the south-west, with a degree of initiative more appropriate to the post of navy commissioner. His routine problems of recruiting for the navy over far-flung territory and providing it with *matériel*, often from unsympathetic or self-interested suppliers, were punctuated by consultations with the generals-at-sea, who evidently valued his expertise and godly commitment to the republic. He nominated men for naval captaincies, often with comments on their godly qualities. After the dismissal of the Rump Parliament, Hatsell retained his post and his importance was enhanced with a place on the bench of magistrates in Devon. He survived the transition to the protectorate, and in 1654 became a commissioner for ejecting 'scandalous' ministers.

Fierce hostility to the drink trade and other vested interests in Plymouth made Hatsell a natural ally of John Disbrowe in his tour of duty as major-general for the south-western counties in 1655–6. Hatsell was appointed commissioner under him, given command of a militia troop, and helped manage the trials of the Penruddock rebels. He was responsible for arranging the transportation to Barbados of a number of people implicated in these disturbances. His religious outlook accorded with that of the regime, although his antipathy to Quakers, including James Nayler, indicates that his tolerance was not unlimited.

From 1651 Hatsell sought to recover sums he had laid out in the service of parliament by acquiring the properties of sequestered royalists and, when available, crown estates. The most important of these was Saltram House, Plympton St Mary, home of the royalist Bagge family, which Hatsell occupied by 1656. With his new estate went status of another kind: he was elected to sit for Devon in the 1654 parliament and in 1658 for Plympton and Tavistock, choosing the former. In the House of Commons he was named to a wide range of committees, with matters of trade, revenue, and religious provision in the south-west being dominant among them. In March 1657 he was among those attending Lord Protector Oliver Cromwell on the details of 'The humble petition and advice'. He spoke frequently, took an interest in procedural matters, and resisted moves to allow the 'other house' to resume the title and privileges of the House of Lords lest it allowed the king to return. Hatsell was active in resisting moves towards monarchy in 1659, and ordered part of the western squadron to Chester Water to prevent help reaching Sir George Booth by sea. When the Restoration did come, he was slow to recognize the implications for his career. He lost all local government office, but stayed for the time as navy agent. Imprisoned at Exeter early in 1661, he returned to his post in February until he was dismissed in September. He may have married, on 17 June 1661, Susanna Evanse. Throughout the 1660s until his death he was identified by the government as one who might cause trouble, but in fact he retired to Saltram. He died there in 1667 and was buried at Plympton St Mary on 19 March. The family lost Saltram at his death.

STEPHEN K. ROBERTS

Sources CSP dom., 1649–50; 1661–2 · B. Capp, Cromwell's navy: the fleet and the English revolution, 1648–1660 (1989) · S. K. Roberts, Recovery and restoration in an English county: Devon local administration, 1646–1670 (1985) · JHC, 7 (1651–9), 368a–772a · Diary of Thomas Burton, ed. J. T. Rutt, 4 vols. (1828) · J. R. Powell, Robert Blake: general-at-sea (1972) · black book, Plymouth and West Devon Record Office, Plymouth, Plymouth city archives, fol. 317 · Plymouth and West Devon Record Office, Plymouth, Plymouth city archives, MS W73A · PRO, E 372/500 · J. D. Davies, 'Devon and the navy in the civil war and the Dutch wars', The new maritime history of Devon, ed. M. Duffy and others, 1 (1992) · J. D. Davies, 'The naval agents at Plymouth, 1652–88', The new maritime history of Devon, ed. M. Duffy and others, 1 (1992) · PRO, PROB 11/324, fol. 52 · parish register (marriage), Barnstaple, Devon, 6 Feb 1637 · parish register (marriage), London, St Leonard Eastcheap, 17 June 1661 · parish register, Plymouth and West Devon Record Office, Plymouth, accession 414/1
Archives PRO, corresp. with navy commissioners, SP 18
Wealth at death Saltram House, Plympton, Devon: will, PRO, PROB 11/324, fol. 52

Hatsell, Sir Henry (*bap.* **1641**, *d.* **1714**), judge, was the eldest son of Henry *Hatsell (*d.* 1667) of Saltram in Plympton St Mary, Devon, and Margaret Dawe. Hatsell's father had been an active Cromwellian, serving as soldier, customs official, navy commissioner, godly magistrate, and MP. At the Restoration he retired to Saltram, which he had bought from the Royalist delinquent Sir James Bagg. Hatsell was baptized at Barnstaple, Devon, on 7 March 1641. He matriculated at Exeter College, Oxford, on 15 June 1657, graduating BA on 4 February 1660. Almost immediately he entered the Middle Temple (3 March 1660), and was duly called to the bar on 17 May 1667, shortly after the death of his father. He presumably continued quietly in practice and was made a serjeant-at-law in May 1689.

Before 1698, when a daughter was baptized, Hatsell married Judith (*bap.* 1662, *d.* 1729), daughter of Josiah Bateman, a London merchant, and the widow of Sir Robert Shirley, second baronet, of Preston, Sussex, who died in 1692. Political conditions were ripe for Hatsell's further advancement, and on 25 November 1697 he was appointed a baron of the exchequer and was knighted on 12 December. His most notable case as a judge was to preside over the trial at Surrey assizes of Spencer Cowper for the murder of Sarah Stout in 1699. On 8 June 1702, in the changed political climate after the accession of Queen Anne, his patent was revoked. Hatsell lived on in retirement and on 20 June 1713, 'very weak in limbs', he made a will in which he expressed the wish that his two sons study the common law or become merchants. He was buried in the Temple Church on 10 April 1714.

STUART HANDLEY

Sources Sainty, Judges, 127 · Baker, Serjeants, 450, 516 · private information (2004) [Dr S. K. Roberts] · S. K. Roberts, Recovery and restoration in an English county: Devon local administration, 1646–1670 (1985), 50–55, 148–54 · IGI · will, PRO, PROB 11/539, sig. 71 · Foss, Judges, 8.385–6 · Foster, Alum. Oxon. · H. A. C. Sturgess, ed., Register of admissions to the Honourable Society of the Middle Temple, from the fifteenth century to the year 1944, 1 (1949), 163 · Register of burials at the Temple Church, 1628–1853 (1905), 34 [with introduction by H. G. Woods]
Archives CUL, legal opinion
Likenesses J. Gisborne, mezzotint (after G. Kneller), BM, NPG

Hatsell, John (**1733–1820**), clerk of the House of Commons, was born on 22 December 1733, the eldest son of Henry Hatsell, lawyer, and Penelope, daughter of Sir James Robinson of Cranford Hall, Kettering. He was admitted to the Middle Temple in 1750, and made senior bencher in 1789 and treasurer in 1802. In 1778 he married Mrs Barton (*d.* 1804), widow of Major Newton Barton of Irthlingborough.

Hatsell's reputation derived from his unrivalled knowledge of parliamentary procedure. In 1760 he was appointed clerk assistant to the Commons, and succeeded as clerk in 1768. His friends included the speakers Henry Addington and Charles Abbot. The latter, who was himself an expert in procedure, acknowledged Hatsell as the foremost authority. Hatsell published *A Collection of Cases of Privilege of Parliament* (1776) and *Rules and Standing Orders of the House of Commons* (1809), but is best known for *Precedents of Proceedings in the House of Commons* (4 vols., 1776–96), which provides a thorough and systematic analysis of practice and procedure. Further improvements were made by the inclusion of Abbot's marginalia in 1818, together with a new index compiled by John Rickman. It remains a standard work.

On 11 July 1797 Hatsell retired in favour of John Ley, who became deputy clerk. Although Ley conducted day-to-day business, Hatsell retained his official title and house, together with substantial emoluments. He continued to influence clerical appointments, clashing with Ley in an acrimonious dispute from 1811 to 1814, in which Hatsell sided with Abbot in resisting the growing hegemony of the Ley family. Hatsell died, from an apoplectic stroke, on 15 October 1820 at his house at Marden Park, near Godstone, Surrey, and was buried in the Temple Church, in London. THOMPSON COOPER, *rev.* CLARE WILKINSON

Sources C. Wilkinson, 'The practice and procedure of the House of Commons, *c*.1784–1832', PhD diss., U. Wales, Aberystwyth, 1998 • O. C. Williams, *The clerical organization of the House of Commons, 1661–1850* (1954) • *The diary and correspondence of Charles Abbot, Lord Colchester*, ed. Charles, Lord Colchester, 3 vols. (1861) • *GM*, 1st ser., 90/2 (1820), 372–3

Archives BL, corresp. with Lord Auckland, Add. MSS 34415–34460 • Devon RO, corresp. with J. Ley, incl. description of a visit to Voltaire, 63/2/75 • Devon RO, corresp. with first Viscount Sidmouth, 152M • HLRO, Ley papers, corresp. and MSS, 138/300 • PRO, Colchester MSS, PRO 30/9

Likenesses J. Sayers, caricature, etching, pubd 1785, NPG • C. Picart, stipple, pubd 1806 (after J. Northcote), BM, NPG • K. A. Hickel, group portrait, oils (*The House of Commons, 1793*), NPG

Hatteclyffe, William (*d.* 1480), physician and diplomat, was admitted as a fellow of Peterhouse, Cambridge, in June 1437. He was a foundation fellow of King's College in 1441/2. In January 1446, as an MA of the diocese of Lincoln, he was studying medicine at Padua, where he was admitted MD on 5 March 1447. He returned to King's College, where he was bursar in 1447/8. He was one of Henry VI's physicians by November 1452, when he was granted £40 p.a., and on 15 March 1454 he was one of the doctors commissioned to attend the king during his illness. By March 1457 he was also acting as physician to Queen Margaret, but by the beginning of 1461 he had apparently joined the Yorkists. After the Lancastrian victory at St Albans in that year he tried to flee to Ireland, but his vessel was captured by the French. Edward IV contributed to his ransom, and in January 1462 he was granted his fee as the king's physician, backdated to the first day of the reign.

Hatteclyffe began to be employed on diplomatic missions in September 1464, when he was sent to treat with François, duke of Brittany, and by January 1466 he had become one of the king's secretaries—an unusual change of career that may owe something to his acquaintance with Henry Sharpe, the king's protonotary. Over the next decade he was extensively employed on diplomatic missions without entirely giving up his medical interests. He appears to have specialized in negotiations with Burgundy and the Hanse, but also had dealings with Denmark and Scotland. During the readeption of Henry VI, Hatteclyffe was imprisoned and was thought to be in some danger of being put to death, but on Edward's return he was restored to his former position and was also made master of requests and a royal councillor. He had links with the queen's circle, and in 1473 was acting with the queen on behalf of her kinswoman Anne Haute. He attended Edward IV to France in 1475, and his last diplomatic assignment was in 1476, after which the king's French secretary, Oliver King, appears to have taken over his diplomatic responsibilities. In June 1480 King was made his coadjutor as secretary and granted the reversion of the office. Hatteclyffe died later the same year and was buried in the lady chapel of Westminster Abbey. His wife Elizabeth survived him. They had moved to a house in Westminster in 1478, after living in London. Hatteclyffe also owned property on the south bank of the Thames, and in East Greenwich, Deptford, and Rotherhithe.

Hatteclyffe was a member of an extensive bureaucratic and clerical dynasty and several namesakes exist. One, who witnessed his will, was an administrator in the stable of the Yorkist kings and Henry VII; he died in 1510. Another **William Hatteclyffe** (*d.* 1519) was the clerk of accounts of Henry VII's household and was appointed under-treasurer of Ireland on 26 April 1495. In 1497–8 he was appointed to levy fines from Perkin Warbeck's adherents in the western counties. Under Henry VIII he combined the office of clerk of the green cloth with *ad hoc* responsibilities such as victualling the royal army. His home was at Lewisham, where he was visited in 1518 by Cardinal Campeggi. He died in late 1518 or early 1519 and was buried in St Mary-at-Hill, London, where his kinsman and namesake Dr William Hatteclyffe was rector. He married, probably as his second wife, Isabel, widow of John Legh of Addington and stepdaughter of John Paston (*d.* 1503). ROSEMARY HORROX

Sources Chancery records • Rymer, *Foedera* • Emden, *Cam.* • G. Zonta and J. Brotto, eds., *Acta graduum academicorum gymnasii Patavini, 1406–1450*, 2 (1970) • J. Otway-Ruthven, *The king's secretary and the signet office in the XV century* (1939) • C. L. Scofield, *The life and reign of Edward the Fourth*, 2 vols. (1923) • *Registrum Thomae Bourgchier ... 1454–1486*, ed. F. R. H. Du Boulay, CYS, 54 (1957) • G. Rosser, *Medieval Westminster, 1200–1540* (1989) • D. A. L. Morgan, 'The house of policy: the political role of the late Plantagenet household, 1422–85', *The English court: from the Wars of the Roses to the civil war*, ed. D. R. Starkey and others (1987), 25–70 • N. Davis, ed., *Paston letters and papers of the fifteenth century*, 2 vols. (1971–6) • C. H. Talbot and E. A. Hammond, *The medical practitioners in medieval England: a biographical register* (1965), 398–9 • PRO, Prob. 11/7, fols. 8v–9 • PRO, PROB. 11/19 [William Hatteclyffe], fol. 122–*v* • *LP Henry VIII*, vol. 8 • J. Gairdner, ed., *Letters and papers illustrative of the reigns of Richard III and Henry VII*, 2, Rolls Series, 24 (1863) • V. J. B. Torr, 'Campeggio's progress through Kent in 1518', *Archaeologia Cantiana*, 43 (1931), 255–65 [William Hatteclyffe] • R. Griffin and M. Stephenson, *A list of monumental brasses remaining in the county of Kent in 1922* [n.d., *c*.1923]

Wealth at death William Hatteclyffe: will, PRO, PROB 11/7, fols. 8v–9

Hatteclyffe, William (*d.* 1519). *See under* Hatteclyffe, William (*d.* 1480).

Hattersley, Richard Longden (1820–1900), manufacturer of textile machinery, was born on 1 December 1820 at Keighley, the eldest of seven sons of George Hattersley, textile machine maker, and his first wife, Elizabeth, *née* Mitchell. He had a limited education at a private school in Keighley, and at Mr Turley's West House, Yeadon, near Leeds, before starting work, at the age of fifteen, as an apprentice in his father's business of textile machine manufacture and repair.

Richard Hattersley was born at the time when his father was trying to rebuild the family business, founded by his grandfather in 1789. Its main activity had been the manufacture and repair of rollers, spindles, and flyers: precision parts for textile machinery. The grandfather died in 1829, just as the business was beginning to experiment with the manufacture of power-looms for the wool textile industry, for which it was to become world famous in later decades. It passed to Richard Longden Hattersley's father, and two of his father's brothers, but there was personal friction, and after the bankruptcy of the firm in 1832 the brothers separated, George being the only one to stay in Keighley. He took over the premises and trade of the old firm, and struggled to rebuild the business by concentrating on the manufacture of power-looms. At this stage, the business was very small and later accounts suggest that Richard Hattersley received a grounding in all branches of the business, as George had done under his father. On 22 December 1846 Hattersley married Ann Smith (1819–1905), second daughter of James Smith, grocer, of Keighley. They had seven daughters.

As an apprentice, Little Dick—as he was familiarly known throughout his life—appears to have developed technical skills that were to contribute to the subsequent engineering success of the business, but his more significant role was through his commercial acumen, and his active search for business and technical opportunities. It was reported that he was ever on the look-out for patents and sought to employ men with inventive capacity to work out and experiment with new technical ideas. He encouraged his workforce to suggest contrivances or improvements. By 1882 he had filed thirteen patents, including those for a revolving box-loom, and looms for weaving fancy goods.

From 1846 Hattersley began to travel widely. He kept detailed notebooks of his summer excursions to the continent, recording itineraries and sales. At first he drew on contacts through the Leeds machine makers that the firm had supplied with components, but soon developed his own, gathering information, establishing a reputation, and encouraging sales. His regular European tours were interspersed with visits further afield. And at a time when British industrialists were being criticized for their laxity in adapting to the languages, weights, measures, and customs of their foreign customers, and for their complacency, Hattersley was producing sales material in several languages and dispatching his expert staff worldwide. In the year of his death, 1900, the firm manufactured over 3500 looms, about half of which were exported.

In 1860 Hattersley was taken into partnership in the business by his father, along with his brother, Edwin Greaves Hattersley. Other brothers joined the firm, but did not enjoy the advantages and risks of partnership. George retired in 1863, ceding control to Richard, who then took the opportunity to expand rapidly the loom-making activities of the business at North Brook Works, Keighley. Edwin ran the firm's subsidiary worsted-spinning interests in the nearby Worth valley, and at Bradford. George died in 1869. The firm was incorporated in 1888, with a share capital of £100,000 in Hattersley, Sons & Co. Ltd, the textile branch, and £90,000 in George Hattersley & Sons Ltd, the machine makers. By this time the firm had become an internationally famous loom manufacturer, establishing a reputation that was to survive to the middle of the twentieth century.

It is difficult to judge the relative importance of Hattersley's technical and commercial contributions to the firm. On the technical side his skill may primarily have been identifying, recruiting, and encouraging highly competent technical staff. On the commercial side, his role was undoubtedly strong. Besides his market-opening foreign travels, he was active at the Bradford and Manchester exchanges, and at the Keighley chamber of commerce. He went out to the market, rather than waiting for the market to come to him.

Hattersley took a benevolent interest in the well-being of his workers, but expected strong loyalty from them and opposed trade union membership. His personality was described as outwardly haughty, cold, and self-contained, but inwardly warm-hearted and kindly. He was a man of few words, and rather brusque to strangers. An obituarist said he never stooped to flattery, evasion, expediency, or opportunism. He was described as having great vitality, and physical endurance. A commitment to Wesleyanism, which involved Sunday school teaching for a while, and a belief in the Liberal cause underlay his personal attitudes. He was an active member of his local Liberal Party until 1894, when he transferred his affiliation to the Unionist cause.

As a major employer in Keighley, Hattersley played a significant role in the affairs of the town. He held a variety of civic offices between 1869 and 1894, including being elected as mayor in 1883. He applied his energies to such varied tasks as the improvement of local gas supply, the running of the mechanics' institute, serving as a governor of several local schools, and acting as a chief magistrate. He was a director of the Craven Banking Company. His interests were primarily local. Hattersley died at his town residence, Burrage House, York Place, Harrogate, on 3 August 1900. He was buried four days later in Keighley cemetery. His personal worth had been extended by the earlier death, childless, of his brother Edwin. Before his own death, he had given £100,000 to each of his seven daughters.

D. T. JENKINS and GILLIAN COOKSON

Sources *Keighley News* (4 Aug 1900) · *Keighley News* (11 Aug 1900) · *Keighley Year Book* (1901) · C. Simmons and H. Clay, 'Hattersley, Richard Longden', *DBB* · *Industries of Yorkshire* (1888) · *Leeds Mercury* (25 Feb 1832) · *Leeds Mercury* (8 Sept 1832) · *Bradford Weekly Telegraph* (18 Nov 1882) · J. Hodgson, *Textile manufacture, and other industries, in Keighley* (1879) · m. cert. · d. cert. · *CGPLA Eng. & Wales* (1900)
Archives W. Yorks. AS, Bradford, business records
Likenesses W. Yorks. AS, Bradford
Wealth at death £350,673 1s. 8d.: probate, 18 Sept 1900, *CGPLA Eng. & Wales*

Hatton [*née* Kemble; *other married name* Curtis], **Ann Julia** (1764–1838), writer and actress, was born on 29 April 1764 in Worcester, the daughter of Roger *Kemble (1722–1802), owner of a travelling theatre company, and his wife, Sarah Ward (1735–1807). Her siblings included Sarah *Siddons (1755–1831), John Philip *Kemble (1757–1823), Charles *Kemble (1775–1854), and Stephen George *Kemble (1758–1822). Congenitally lame and scarred by smallpox, she claimed that she was neglected by both parents, and although nicknamed the Genius by other members of the family, received little schooling. She was apprenticed to a mantua maker before going on the stage. Her marriage to an actor, C. Curtis (*d.* 1817), proved bigamous but it was as Ann Curtis that she published *Poems on Miscellaneous Subjects* (1783). Accusing her family of failing to help her, a newspaper advertisement of 1783 solicited donations from the public to relieve her financial distress; she lectured at James Graham's notorious 'Temple of Health', and later attempted to poison herself in Westminster Abbey. A press report of 1789 indicates that she was working in a bagnio when she was accidentally shot in the eye.

On 30 January 1792, Ann Julia married William Hatton (*d.* 1806), and a year later went to America where she addressed an ode to the Democratic Society of New York and wrote the libretto for an opera, *Tammany, or, The Indian Chief*, first performed in 1794. Yellow fever drove the Hattons to Nova Scotia but by 1799 they had returned to Britain and settled in Swansea where William Hatton took out a lease on the bathing house, providing bathing machines, an assembly room, and lodgings for visitors to the 'Brighton of Wales'. After her husband died in 1806 Ann Julia kept a dancing school in Kidwelly; she returned to Swansea in 1809 and made her home there for the rest of her life. For many years she received an allowance from her relatives on condition (so it was said) that she lived at least a hundred miles from London.

For some years Ann Julia Hatton was connected with the Swansea Theatre. In 1803 J. T. Barber described her as lame and grossly overweight, but in reciting 'Alexander's Feast', 'the lady did not fail to exhibit a vivid tincture of the family genius' (Ross, 83). In 1810 she wrote *Zaffine* for Edmund Kean and the following year adapted a novel by Madame de Genlis. At Neath in 1815 her performance of Lady Randolph in *Douglas* was so well received that it was announced in *The Cambrian* that she intended playing Calista in *The Fair Penitent*, 'expressly after the manner of Mrs Siddons' (Price, 120). According to J. Jones, however, the 'Old rancarous hag' [*sic*] had become 'The scoff of grinning Neath' (Jones, 'To Mrs Hatton').

Ann Julia Hatton's first prose work was possibly 'The Unknown, or, The Knight of the Blood-Red Plume' (Haining, 1.200–26), a story which appeared anonymously in *Welsh Legends* (1802). In 1810 *Cambrian Pictures*, the first of her fourteen novels, was published under the pen-name Ann of Swansea. At her best, she was capable of writing fluent narrative and lively dialogue, but the novels are immensely long and for the most part undeniably tedious. As she confesses in the preface to *Lovers and Friends* (1821), 'an author finds his inventive faculties spun as thin as a cobweb in supplying the requisite number of pages for his story'. The novels, all but one published by the Minerva Press, have some generic interest in reflecting the literary fashions of the time—*Sicilian Mysteries* (1812) is a pale imitation of Ann Radcliffe's Gothic tales while both *Secret Avengers* (1815) and *Cesario Rosalba* (1819) feature Byronic antiheroes. *Cambrian Pictures*, *Secrets in every Mansion* (1818), and *Gerald Fitzgerald* (1831) utilize motifs familiar in contemporary fictions of Wales, Scotland, and Ireland. *Gonzalo de Baldivia* (1817), dedicated to William Wilberforce, includes the story of an African family brutally transported to the Peruvian silver mines, annotated with a personal statement by the author deploring slavery. *Conviction* (1814) is notable for a self-portrait: Mrs Mortimer, author of *Welsh Likenesses*, a 'coarse, large, ill-shaped creature', who squints abominably and is pitted with the smallpox (3.204), vigorously denies that she is about to bring out a novel containing 'scandalous anecdotes of this most immaculate town' (3.238). Ann Julia Hatton herself, however, did not scruple to reveal in *Chronicles of an Illustrious House* (1816) that 'your little town of Gooselake abounds with all the vices of the metropolis' (2.120). The novel caused a furore in Swansea.

Ann Julia Hatton was a prolific writer of verse. *Poetic Trifles* (1811) includes the celebrated 'Swansea Bay'. In 1832 she was seeking subscriptions for *Fifty-Two Poetic Cumaean Leaves. Predicting the Destiny of Ladies and Gentlemen*. In 1834 she approached the publisher Richard Bentley with *The Raconteur*, and presented a scrapbook of verse to the young Swansea physician, Dr Douglas Cohen, fulfilling a promise that she would write him a poem every day for a year. Although 'A Resident of Swansea' described her at seventy as 'still a splendid woman' (Highfill, Burnim & Langhans, *BDA*, 7.175), her autobiographical verses are a poignant expression of her sense of desolation in old age, as well as conveying her bitterness towards her family.

Ann Julia Hatton wrote 'Farewell Lines' to Dr Cohen on 28 September 1838 and dictated her last letter to him on 21 December, 'when in *articula mortis*' (D. Cohen to J. D. Francis). She died on 26 December 1838 at 15 Park Street, and was buried in St John's churchyard on 31 December. Brought up a protestant like her mother, it is said that she died a Catholic like her father. The bulk of her estate was left to Mary Johns, her servant.   MOIRA DEARNLEY

Sources I. J. Bromham, '"Ann of Swansea" (Ann Julia Hatton: 1764–1838)', *Glamorgan Historian*, 7 (1971), 173–86 · Highfill, Burnim & Langhans, *BDA*, 7.171–5, 8.387–94 · P. Fitzgerald, *The Kembles: an account of the Kemble family*, 2 vols. (1871) · C. J. L. Price, *The English theatre in Wales in the eighteenth and early nineteenth centuries* (1948) · D. Boorman, *The Brighton of Wales: Swansea as a fashionable seaside resort, c.1780– c.1830* (1986) · J. E. Ross, ed., *Letters from Swansea* (1969),

79–84 • J. Jones, 'To Mrs Hatton', Swansea Museum, 112/1 [poem, copy in hand of Ann Julia Hatton, endorsed 8 March 1815] • P. Haining, ed., *Great British tales of terror: Gothic stories of horror and romance, 1765–1840* (1972), 1.200–26 • D. Cohen to J. D. Francis, 24 Aug 1886, typescript copy, Swansea Museum, 112/1 • M. Dearnley, 'Condem'd to wither on a foreign strand', *New Welsh Review*, 11/1 (1998), 56–9 • *IGI*

Archives Swansea Museum, MSS, incl. album and scrapbook | Folger, corresp. with R. Bentley, Douglas Cohen, and J. P. Collier **Likenesses** H. Watkeys, oils, 1834, Glynn Vivian Art Gallery, Swansea • H. A. Chapman, photograph (after H. Watkeys), Swansea Museum • painting on copper, Swansea Museum **Wealth at death** less than £100: Bromham, 'Ann of Swansea' • bequests of personal effects, books, and the portrait by Watkeys to Dr Douglas Cohen; effects to her stepdaughter; a small ring to Revd William Boyd; remainder of estate to executor, Mary Johns: will, Highfill, Burnim & Langhans, *BDA*

Hatton, Sir Christopher (*c*.1540–1591), courtier and politician, was the second son of William Hatton (*d.* 1547) of Holdenby, Northamptonshire, and Alice, daughter of Lawrence Saunders. The family were lesser gentry with modest resources. Hatton entered St Mary Hall, Oxford, *c*.1556–7, probably as a gentleman commoner, where William Allen (afterwards cardinal) was president. On 26 May 1560 he was enrolled in the Inner Temple. He may have been a barrister, but was never reader or bencher.

Early career In the new year festivities of 1562 at the Inner Temple, members presented the play *Gorboduc* to an audience that included the queen; Robert Dudley participated in the performance of a masque in which Hatton probably figured. It was here or on a similar occasion that he attracted Elizabeth's attention. He became a gentleman pensioner some time between 25 March and 30 June 1564 when a royal warrant commanded the issue of a suit of armour for Hatton's use. In September of that year the queen sent him to welcome Sir James Melville, ambassador from Scotland, and to escort him to the royal presence. In 1566 he was a member of Bedford's suite when the earl was sent to Edinburgh to attend the baptism of Prince James.

Hatton continued his association with the Inner Temple and was one of four joint authors of *Gismond of Salem*, played before the queen in 1566 or 1567. He was active in the social life of the court, a participant in the tilts celebrating the earl of Warwick's marriage in 1565 and again on two occasions in 1571 where the other participants were the earls of Leicester and Oxford, and other court notables. Tangible rewards for his service at court soon began to appear. In 1568 he exchanged his hereditary manor of Holdenby for the site of Sulby Abbey and then received Holdenby back on a forty-year lease. In the same year he became keeper of the parks of Eltham (Kent) and Horne (Surrey); in 1569 he had the farm of a Pembrokeshire chapel. In 1571 there followed the reversion of the office of queen's remembrancer in the exchequer, a London inn, lands in Yorkshire and Dorset, monastic lands in Leicestershire, and the keepership of Wellingborough, Northamptonshire. From 1572 he joined in the customary exchange of gifts between courtiers and queen. The queen's gift to him singled him out since he received 400

Sir Christopher Hatton (*c*.1540–1591), by Nicholas Hilliard, *c*.1588–91

oz of silver plate, twice the amount awarded to ranking dignitaries and eight times the usual gift of 50 oz.

The courtier In July 1572 Hatton was appointed a gentleman of the privy chamber and captain of the yeomen of the guard. In 1569 he appears in a list of Northamptonshire JPs and in 1571 he sat in parliament for Higham Ferrers; in the following year he represented his native county. His seat in parliament was the first step in his transformation from courtier to politician. The flow of gifts from a sovereign usually so sparing in her benefactions was an effect of Elizabeth's fascination with Hatton's personal qualities. Tradition, not of contemporary date, ascribed his appeal to his skill as a dancer. Camden wrote of the attractions of a man 'young and of comely tallness of body' and 'modest sweetness of condition' (Camden, 2.43).

Whatever the circumstances, Hatton had established a personal relationship with Elizabeth which would last a lifetime. It was more private than that with Leicester, whose ambitions were straightforwardly public: success in politics and—he hoped—as a soldier. Failing the royal marriage, the earl quickly emerged on the public stage where he took the initiative as a promoter of causes and patron of an extensive following. Hatton was content for the first decade of his court career to enjoy a wholly private relationship with Elizabeth.

Beyond his personal charms Hatton was a consummate player of a game which Elizabeth adored, that of courtly love. His role was that of the perpetual suitor, who forever worships an earthly goddess with unwavering devotion—

a devotion that cannot be fulfilled but never wanes. Hatton was a master of the extravagant rhetoric in which the play was acted out. In 1573, forced by illness to seek relief, he travelled to Spa. His letters to Elizabeth survive: 'This the twelfth day since I saw the brightness of the sun that giveth light unto my sense and soul, I wax an amazed creature' (Nicolas, 27). He describes himself her 'most happy bondman', Lyddes, who with 'pure love and diligent faith may everlastingly serve you' (ibid., 29). The queen gave him, as with other intimates, special names— her 'lids' or her 'sheep'—and he used the special symbol of three parallel triangles in writing to her. In later years when a new favourite, Walter Ralegh, appeared on the scene, Hatton sent her a token, a silver bucket, symbol of wa[l]ter. Water, he wrote, an unstable element, would breed confusion. She responded that her *pecora campi* were so dear that she had bounded the banks so that no water should overthrow him. She sent him a symbol, a dove, the biblical herald of receding flood.

Behind all this play-acting there stood a stable relationship. Sealed by their constant companionship, Hatton's offices at court kept him in close contact. He not only stood closer to her than any other man, but his loyalty was undivided. Unmarried, he had no family ambitions. Given the special nature of his relationship with Elizabeth, he could not, like Dudley, risk marriage, even had he wished it. The only public cause for which he spoke was the conservative churchmanship of Whitgift in which his sympathies chimed with those of his mistress. Yet this does not explain the metamorphosis from courtier-in-chief to senior councillor of state.

Parliamentary manager One clue lies in Hatton's first open participation in business of state. In the parliament of 1572 (his second) he was a member of the committee dealing with the case of the queen of Scots. At a crucial moment in the debate it was he who whispered in the speaker's ear a royal message ordering him to shorten discussion. After parliament went into recess Hatton complained that he was being blamed for the failure of a bill concerning Mary Stewart and the duke of Norfolk as well as bills on religion. There is no parliamentary evidence, but he may well have been employed in relaying royal interference in the business of the house.

In the parliament of 1576 Hatton, sitting again for Northamptonshire (as he would until his lord chancellorship), played a much expanded role. He sat on no fewer than fourteen committees, including those of the subsidy and the queen's marriage. The session had opened with Peter Wentworth's motion on liberty of speech, for which he was sent to the Tower of London. Hatton sat with the privy councillors in the house as one of Wentworth's examiners, and subsequently announced to the house Elizabeth's order for his release. Later in the session he became involved in the complicated case of Arthur Hall over the issue of parliamentary privilege. The privy councillors in the Commons intervened to bring about a settlement. Their collaborator was again Hatton who took an active role in pressing, unsuccessfully, Hall's case. Hatton's association with the privy councillors was a token of his coming promotion to their ranks, which occurred in November 1577. At the same time he was made vice-chamberlain of the household and knighted.

When parliament reassembled in 1581 Hatton in his new dignities was even more to the fore. At the opening of the session the motion proposed by the indefatigable Peter Wentworth for a public fast was given approval, sparking off the indignant intervention of the queen. Hatton delivered a message from Elizabeth, condescendingly forgiving the house but warning them that on religious matters they should await direction from the crown. Hatton was charged by the house to carry to the queen their humble submission and the next day reported Elizabeth's gracious acceptance. He was settling into a permanent role as spokesman for the queen, the regular channel of communication between sovereign and parliament.

The first piece of crown legislation in 1581 was a bill imposing harsh penalties on recusants. Passage was deflected when Hatton proposed a conference with the Lords where a similar bill was pending. Presumably he acted on royal command. Certainly the resulting statute reflected the queen's leniency towards recusants rather than the Commons' harsh proposals. A second measure, sponsored by the government, was entitled 'an act against seditious words and rumours uttered against the Queen's Most Excellent Majesty' which provided extreme penalties and added a new crime, prophesying how long Elizabeth would live or who would succeed her. The religious left wing, scenting dangers to their spokesmen, sought to amend the bill, softening the extreme penalties and adding a specifically anti-Catholic clause, punishing anyone who asserted the Church of England to be heretical or schismatic. The Lords rejected the amendments. The council then put Hatton forward. In an emollient speech, which blamed the Lords, he persuaded the house to adopt a new bill in which the crucial amendment was omitted.

Even before his promotions Hatton had attained a semi-official status, both in Commons and in state business. When in 1576 Champagny, the special ambassador of the Spanish government in Brussels, went to London, Hatton was called upon to entertain him officially. In the course of the affair Hatton took aside Philip's agent in London to assure him of Elizabeth's desire to act as mediator in the Low Countries dispute. He was again acting as a royal messenger, this time to the Spanish king.

Privy councillor With his appointment to the council Hatton was quickly inaugurated into its business. His attendance record equalled that of Lord Burghley and Francis Walsingham, the two principal executive officers. In 1578 the urgent business before the council was the troubled situation in the Low Countries where all was in confusion following the collapse of Spanish authority and where French intervention threatened. Secretary Walsingham and Lord Cobham had been dispatched to Brussels in June as prospective mediators. Correspondence with them was handled by a small committee, Burghley, Leicester, the earl of Sussex, Sir James Croft, and Hatton. They also received the ambassador of the states general in March. Walsingham was already looking to Hatton as a mediator with the queen, who was angry at the secretary's handling of negotiations; the vice-chamberlain was able to soften the royal displeasure. Walsingham's trust in Hatton was further revealed in their correspondence, where he freely expressed his criticism of royal policy towards both the Low Countries and Scotland. In the meantime news of French encroachments in the Low Countries led the worried queen into consultation with Burghley, Leicester, and Hatton and a month later, when the duc d'Anjou sent an agent with proposals for renewing his courtship, it was the same trio who, with the queen, saw the envoy and composed an answer to the duke.

Hatton had entered the council just as the Anjou marriage project, which would focus its attention for the next three years, emerged. After various exchanges, Simier, Anjou's representative, arrived in January 1579 to open serious discussion. It fell to Hatton to entertain him. According to the Spanish ambassador, Leicester and Hatton had now become allies in forwarding the match and also in promoting Thomas Bromley as chancellor, in which they succeeded. The ambassador's accuracy may be questioned, although they may have temporized in the early stages of negotiation.

Debate continued through the summer while the council waited to see what direction matters would follow. In August the duke himself arrived for a ten-day visit. In the early autumn the queen signalled her willingness to marry and sought the council's advice. By then there had been a strong public reaction, most forcibly expressed in Stubbs's *Gaping Gulf*. Whatever their earlier views, Hatton and Leicester now joined with the rest of the council in a sullen acquiescence, offering to support the match if it pleased her. Any affirmative commitment lacking, a tearful queen vented her wrath on the offenders. According to the Spanish ambassador it was in the wake of this episode that Hatton and the queen quarrelled and she banned him from her presence for a week.

Elizabeth was still unwilling to break off the Anjou suit altogether and in November she appointed a commission of seven, including Hatton, Burghley, and Walsingham, but not Leicester, to negotiate with Simier on articles for a marriage treaty. But by new year 1580 the queen had admitted to Anjou that public opinion made their marriage impossible.

When Anjou seemed about to become commander of the states army, Burghley, Hatton, Sussex, and Walsingham pressed the queen to succour the prince of Orange if he rejected Anjou. Failing that, they renewed the possibility of alliance. Finally Anjou himself reappeared in England in November 1581. The queen, to their dismay, gave the duke a ring as a token of her acceptance of his wooing. Then, again according to the Spanish ambassador, Hatton spoke forthrightly to Elizabeth warning her of the dangers of a marriage being popularly rejected. He was backed by Leicester. Whatever the exact circumstances, the queen saw Anjou and retracted her promise. In 1581, when Burghley proposed overtures for a treaty with France, Leicester, Hatton, and Walsingham opposed him. Negotiations were in fact begun but soon failed. The queen, compelled to become Anjou's paymaster in the Low Countries, could only look on as his folly alienated the Dutch.

How should Hatton's part in this prolonged episode be interpreted? He entered high politics reputedly pro-Spanish, in other words favouring some kind of negotiated settlement. This may well have represented his earlier views, but once on the political stage he attached himself to Leicester. Their alliance continued through 1581. Thereafter the record is blank as to Hatton's views on foreign policy. Rumour reached the Spanish ambassador that during a revival of the Leicester–Sussex rivalry in 1582 Hatton supported Sussex.

The only clue to Hatton's position in these years is a letter of 1580 in his own hand to Walsingham. He sings a familiar litany. Philip II, now master of Portugal, will be free to assist the pope in his designs. England must foresee the dangers of his ancient and crooked malice and prepare to resist it. He then recounts the besetting dangers that surround England—French influence in Scotland, the risk that James may be taken to France, French alliance with Spain, the broken state of Ireland, the weakness of the French protestants. Why does the queen delay, if she intends to marry? All this chimes in with Walsingham's grim view of England's prospects.

From the sparse and scattered sources available it would appear that Hatton regularly sided with Leicester and Walsingham in the struggle over the Anjou match. The Spanish ambassador, Mendoza, regarded him as an outright enemy of his master, alleging that Leicester and he sought his expulsion. What this reveals is a political figure who took no initiative of his own but did follow a consistent line of action. His support was highly valuable since his unique relationship with Elizabeth enabled him to report her views in these matters and, on occasion, to sway them. It secured him an essential place in the inner circle where decisions were made. His relations with his fellow councillors seem to have been smooth.

Hatton's personal ambitions did not clash with those of others while his special status enabled him to avoid the petty rivalries of less privileged courtiers. He made little effort to build up a clientele. Aside from his ecclesiastical connections he had few protégés. Sir Henry Unton, the diplomat, was one such. In 1587–8 he made some effort to protect Thomas Wilkes, the clerk of the council, against Leicester's wrath. The unlucky William Davison seems also to have looked to him for backing and his fellow councillor, Sir Thomas Heneage, spoke of him as the man he best loved in court. He was, of course, the recipient of countless petitions from office-seekers or others hoping for some benefit from the crown, but his help was also sought by those who, for one reason or another, suffered from the queen's personal disapproval. Archbishop Grindal, for instance, turned to Hatton in hopes of softening the royal displeasure, an instance quite surprising given Hatton's own religious allegiance. Lady Sussex, after her husband's death, sought his help in recovering the queen's good graces.

When in 1585 Elizabeth finally agreed to an alliance

with the states general, Hatton was a member of the committee to deal with their delegation in drawing up the terms. Later, when Leicester went off on his Low Countries venture, it was Hatton's aid that he sought after having invoked Elizabeth's anger by accepting the governorship. Both he and Burghley acted as buffers between the earl and the queen. With Burghley and Walsingham he was immersed in the business of the war. Letters to the queen from the Netherlands were sent to Hatton for him to pass them on to her.

While Philip was assembling his Armada, a feeler was put out from Brussels through a Flemish merchant in London. Burghley, responsive to this opportunity, obtained the queen's consent and opened the matter to a small group of fellow councillors; Comptroller Croft, a longtime friend of Spain, was the leading figure. The only others included Hatton, Cobham, and Sir Walter Mildmay. Leicester and Walsingham were carefully excluded. The negotiations continued up to the arrival of the Armada; nothing further of Hatton's role is known, but clearly Burghley thought him sympathetic to this negotiation with Spain.

Lord chancellor Hatton's attentions were now suddenly wrested in a wholly new direction. Lord Chancellor Bromley died on 12 April 1587. The vacant office was offered to the earl of Rutland, whose death followed almost immediately. The queen then turned to Hatton, signing his patent on 24 April, and in early May he rode in state to his inauguration, accompanied by Leicester on one side and Burghley on the other.

The legal profession was much affronted by this appointment. Apart from his youthful days at the Inner Temple, Hatton had no formal legal experience, although as a councillor he had sat in Star Chamber. Camden reported that Hatton's appointment was the work of his rivals, who hoped his necessary absence from court would diminish his attendance with the queen. Leicester, writing to Walsingham just after Bromley's death, expressed his satisfaction that Elizabeth was willing to hear of Hatton's appointment to the great seal, declaring he would surely be fittest for it.

Of Hatton's four years as chancellor little record remains (for only one case is there a report). He sensibly turned to skilled assistants, particularly Richard Swale, a fellow of Caius College, a man who had been accused of papist leanings and had been refused the proctorship by Burghley as chancellor of Cambridge. However, he had been elected president of Caius and in May 1587 was appointed a master in chancery. He and a team of four assistants provided their services in aid of Hatton. Camden's judgement on Hatton's legal career was that what he lacked in legal knowledge he sought to supply by equity. In 1588 the queen augmented his honours by the Garter, and Oxford University chose him as chancellor in succession to Leicester.

Hatton was employed in a semi-legal role in the two conspiracies against Elizabeth's life in the 1580s, the Parry plot and the Babington plot. In the former the accused was both an MP and a former secret agent employed by the government. Hatton, as a trial commissioner, took special pains to establish Parry's guilt and to discredit any suggestion he was acting as an *agent provocateur*. Hatton intervened again at the conclusion of the trial to ensure maximum publicity was given to Parry's confession. In the Babington case Hatton was again a major player, sitting on the trial commission. Here he took the lead in pressing the prisoners to full confession of their intent. He made no further recorded intervention in the trial, but it fell on him to make the condemnation a public and a national act. Among the conspirators three were connected with Hatton. One, Captain Jacque (Jacomo di Francisci), was a shady character whom Hatton had employed in Ireland, for what purpose is unclear. He had returned with a letter of commendation from Archbishop Loftus. He was then put to work spying on Ballard, an exiled priest and zealous plotter. When the trials of the conspirators took place, the government was careful to avoid placing him on the witness stand. A nominal sentence of a year in the Fleet prison was deemed sufficient. This man afterward defected to the Spanish in Flanders. The other two, Henry Donne and Chidiock Tichborne, were part of the cluster of young Catholic gentry moving in court circles. Donne was named by the Spanish ambassador as Hatton's 'secretary'. Clearly these two were commonly regarded as moving in Hatton's circle, but there is no evidence of formal service. Hatton singled each of them out, loading them with reproach.

Hatton was also a commissioner for the trial of the queen of Scots. When in the opening session she pleaded that as a queen she could not be tried by a foreign court, he persuaded her to lay aside her dignity so that she might prove in court her innocence. Further proceedings were in Burghley's hands.

Hatton's parliamentary appearances in these great causes reflected the continuing role he had in that body's business. That role embraced two functions. On the one hand he continued to shepherd bills proposed by the ministers through the process of enactment to statute. Beyond this he continued in his special task of mediating between sovereign and Commons. This task increased with the growing restiveness of a small but determined minority who pushed for discussion of the sensitive question of religion, seeking to unsettle the settlement of 1559. Hatton's function was to check these manifestations. Often a peremptory command sufficed, but on other occasions subtler means were used and it was here that Hatton held the stage.

In 1584 the puritan party in the house put forward a bill and a book which aimed at nothing less than the replacement of the Book of Common Prayer and establishment of a presbyterian polity. Hatton rose to urge the house not to read the bill but to trust the queen to reform the grievances alleged. The house agreed and nothing more was heard of the bill. In 1586–7 the reformers did succeed in getting the bill read and debated; the queen ordered the speaker to give her the bill while the ringleaders in the house went to the Tower. When a member proposed a petition for their release, Hatton rose to reply, embarking on a reasoned defence of the royal policy. After defending the superiority of a formal liturgy, which the common people could learn by often hearing so that it became a common inheritance, over extempore prayers, he went to the core of the matter. Presbyterian government of the church would deprive the queen of her rightful and necessary power and open the door to rebellion as preached by Buchanan and Beza. In an address opening the parliament of 1589 Hatton dwelt on the same theme, going on to rank the puritans as much enemies of the crown as the papists. He then straightforwardly charged the Commons not to meddle in matters religious except to bridle the activities of the queen's enemies, papist and puritan alike.

Hatton's parliamentary functions went beyond the negative tasks of checking incursions on the royal prerogative to the positive promotion of patriotic response to encompassing danger. From the early 1580s onwards England faced compelling decisions in its foreign relations with the looming threat of war in the background. These threats would incur heavy costs; the people of England must be prepared to bear them. In 1584–5 Hatton, speaking on measures to protect the queen's safety, took the opportunity to review Anglo-Spanish relations since 1558, recounting the expulsion of the English ambassador in 1566 and successive events down to the Throckmorton plot and the consequent dismissal of Mendoza. A member of the Commons expressed his amazement at the confidence in the house displayed in his speech: 'They were *magnalia regni*' (Neale, 2.28). Hatton shared with Burghley the need to involve public opinion in support of crown policy.

In the parliament of 1586–7 Hatton followed up by telling the house it was the royal pleasure that he disclose to them the dangers threatening their country from the Catholic crusade now preparing. Philip had assembled a great fleet, composed of Spanish and Italian ships, and an army of similar composition. Aid to the Low Countries was imperative, given the long-standing commercial and diplomatic ties as well as the overriding strategic consideration. 'It must not be suffered that a neighbour should grow too strong' (Neale, 2.167). In a later session he expanded this theme. Spain in control of the narrow seas could check England's commerce, choking the cloth trade; defending the Low Countries was defending England's commercial survival. He went on to hint that all this would cost more than the routine single subsidy. The house responded by offering a benevolence, accompanied by a petition that Elizabeth accept the sovereignty of the Low Countries. She thanked them and declined the benevolence. How far this whole episode was an effort of Leicester and Walsingham to press the queen to accept the government of the Low Countries remains a speculation.

In 1589 Hatton, now chancellor, gave the opening oration, in which he surveyed the post-Armada state of the nation. Burghley had provided him with a brief on the matters to be included. In a historical survey going back to Henry VIII he traced the history of papal hostility, of the measures taken by the present pope ('that wolfish blood-sucker') and his champion the king of Spain ('that insatiable tyrant') (Neale, 2.197). He then listed and excoriated English traitors from Cardinal Pole to Cardinal Allen. It was an appeal designed to rouse both patriotic and ideological responses.

Another great parliamentary occasion in which Hatton had a major part was the case of Mary Stewart. She had already been tried and condemned, but the government wanted an expression of public support. Hatton opened debate by a speech condemning the Scottish queen's whole course of action since 1559. As the Catholic candidate for the throne she constituted a deadly menace to the queen. He ended with a ringing declaration, 'Ne pereat Israel pereat Absalom' ('Let Absalom perish that Israel perish not'; Neale, 2.107). The result was a petition to the queen to approve the execution, which Hatton duly presented to Elizabeth. She thanked them but gave no answer. Hatton then engineered a joint petition of both houses only to produce another burst of cloudy royal rhetoric. At last, at adjournment, Hatton could tell the members that the sentence against Mary would be proclaimed, a step towards execution of judgment. In the storm that followed the execution Hatton was the first to feel Elizabeth's wrath, but it was Burghley who suffered the longest expulsion from the court.

Hatton had, of course, continuing routine responsibilities in the dispatch of parliamentary business—promoting, with Mildmay, an unpopular bill on wardship or, unsuccessfully, pushing renewal of Cecil's Wednesday fast. In the bill formalizing the oath of association Hatton intervened to protect the rights of James of Scotland. His membership on countless committees enabled him to promote government-sponsored legislation while watching over other bills, intervening where crown interest obtained. He did not apparently follow Burghley's example in promoting measures of his own.

It fell to Hatton to carry the queen's prohibitions or rebukes to the house. He felt the need to sweeten such episodes by countervailing exchanges of mutual goodwill. One such occasion offered at Christmas 1584. The house had just finished giving the oath of association statutory form. The queen, considerate of her subjects' pleasures, adjourned parliament so that members could enjoy the festival at home. The house returned its thanks for the favour. Elizabeth responded, through Hatton, with her gracious acceptance, ascribing the successes of her reign to the virtues of her subjects. Hatton then capped this effusion of mutual regard by moving that the Commons join in a prayer for their sovereign for the continuance of the blessings poured on them. All fell on their knees to recite a prayer, opportunely provided by him for the occasion.

Religion and private affairs If Hatton took few initiatives of his own in foreign policy and made little attempt to form a political clientele, there was one area in which he did take a positive, clearly directed position—that of religion. Throughout his career there had been recurrent rumours of his Catholic sympathies. He had been at Oxford in

Mary's time when William Allen (afterwards cardinal) was head of his college. The latter wrote of him years later, presuming him to be a fellow believer. In 1573 a fanatic attacked Sir John Hawkins under the mistaken impression that he was Hatton, whom he considered to be a papist. These allegations, which continued through his career, are not borne out by contemporary evidence. Camden wrote of him as someone whom Catholics thought inclined to their side and opposed to fire and sword in matters of religion. Whatever his private views, in public life he denounced the pope in ringing terms and condemned Allen as a savage priest.

However, within the framework of the Elizabethan settlement, Hatton was a consistent and active opponent of the puritans. It was shown above how skilfully he deflected the first attempt to bring forward the book and bill measure and how in the parliament of 1586–7, in a speech drafted by Bancroft, he brought his heaviest artillery to bear in denunciation of its sponsors. In 1589 Bancroft, his chaplain, preached at Paul's Cross a sermon pushing the divine right of episcopacy. It was published at the direction of Hatton and, somewhat surprisingly, Burghley. At the same time, he pushed for a new set of articles, incorporating Bancroft's views; the queen refused it her backing.

It is plain that from the early 1580s on Hatton was zealous in promoting the programme of an ally—John Whitgift. For instance, when a group of Kentish gentry appealed to the council for the release of some imprisoned non-signers of the articles required by the primate, Hatton sent the text of their petition to Whitgift to enable him to anticipate their argument. He was, of course, an invaluable ally for the archbishop in winning royal approval for his programme. In all probability this was an easy task, given the royal predisposition. In this activism he parted company with Burghley, who shared the royal objections to the radicals but declined to punish recalcitrant clergy. Hatton's death was a loss to Whitgift, but his cause was firmly established.

Hatton's rise from courtier to statesman had been paralleled by the rise of his private fortune. In 1575, at a time when he complained of his debts of £10,000, he received a £400 annuity and in 1578 the receivership of first fruits and tenths. In 1576 the queen gave him the Isle of Purbeck with Corfe Castle. At some time he had the farm of sweet wines, although for one term only. He shared in the spoils of Ireland with a grant from the confiscated Geraldine lands of some 10,000 acres in extent.

All these benefactions, however, failed to match his expenditure. Determined to surpass his colleagues' seats, such as Burghley's Theobalds, in grandeur, Hatton set out to erect on his ancestral Northamptonshire manor of Holdenby a palace that would fulfil his ambition. First, however, in 1576 he purchased the newly built Kirby Hall, not far from Holdenby. The erection of his own house began shortly thereafter. He himself, tied as he was to the royal presence, rarely saw either property. In 1580 he declared he would not visit Holdenby until his holy saint, to whom it was dedicated (namely Queen Elizabeth), came to sit in

it. That vow was not kept literally nor did the 'saint' ever visit the shrine. Many of Hatton's associates did, among them Burghley and Mildmay in 1579, but in his absence. On one festive occasion he did inhabit his house, when in June 1589 his nephew and heir was married there and the chancellor shed his gown to join the dance. The house, of which one wing still survives, was built on the same general plan as Theobalds; there were two great courts— one 128 feet by 104 feet, the second 140 feet by 110 feet, covering 2 acres, about the same size as Hampton Court— a chapel, and a characteristic long gallery, 146 feet by 22 feet. This enormous structure, built between 1578 and 1583, effectively bankrupted its owner. His too generous estimate of his fee as receiver of first fruits and tenths occasioned a rebuke from Burghley. On his death, Hatton owed the queen £18,071 in arrears.

Given Hatton's situation a London residence was also a necessity. Here he set his sights high: nothing less than the palatial residence of the bishops of Ely, England's fourth wealthiest see. At Hatton's request the queen pressed the reluctant Bishop Cox to yield, first in 1576 a short-term and then a perpetual lease at a nominal rent. Hatton spent £1900 in repairs to an establishment some 7 acres in extent with a hall, garden, and chapel.

Another aspect of Hatton's courtly career was his patronage of men of learning. Both Burghley and Camden attested to his reputation as a lover of learned men. There are over a dozen dedications by authors to Hatton. Three of these authors had a traceable connection with the favourite and seem to have enjoyed material benefits given by him. Thomas Churchyard was a correspondent for some years and probably received some financial assistance. Barnaby Rich completed *Riche his Farewell to Military Profession* while enjoying the hospitality of Holdenby. The Elizabethan magus Dr John Dee was in regular contact up until his departure for Poland. None of the other authors who dedicated work to Hatton seems to have enjoyed personal contact.

Hatton, always in need of money, was an eager investor in overseas enterprises. He joined Leicester and Walsingham in supporting—and investing in—Drake's circumnavigation voyage of 1577–80. Two of his nominees, one a ship's captain, the other Drake's trumpeter, served in the expedition. On entering the Strait of Magellan, Drake renamed the *Pelican*, his own ship, the *Golden Hind* in Hatton's honour. His investment is not known, but his profit was a substantial £2300. When on Drake's return Burghley persuaded the queen to seize the treasure, holding it for restitution to Spain, Leicester, Hatton, and Walsingham refused to sign the council order. The money in fact ultimately came to the investors.

Hatton's interest in overseas expeditions continued. He invested in Frobisher's three north-west passage voyages, sending a nominee, George Best, in one of them. Best published an account of the voyage, dedicated to Hatton. He ventured again in Fenton's East India voyage, a sum of £250. He shared in the intended Moluccas voyage (which became the Indies voyage of 1584) to the extent of £1000 and another £1000 went into the Portugal expedition of 1589.

At home Hatton had various interests. In the 1570s, when he acquired Corfe Castle with the office of vice-admiral of the Isle of Purbeck, he added the keepership of Branksea Castle in Poole harbour. This gave him admiralty jurisdiction over a stretch of Dorset coast with various privileges. Private jurisdiction of this kind offered cover for pirates and their booty. On at least one occasion Hatton fell under suspicion as a protector of such gentry. In 1577 Burghley rebuked Hatton for his relations with a notorious pirate, Callis. Presumably he had sought Corfe because of the large opportunities that the office opened for increasing his always inadequate income.

Hatton's active life continued to the end. In October 1591 he was writing to Essex in Normandy; he died at Ely Place on 20 November, having been visited by the queen who, according to some accounts, brought him broth. He was buried on 16 December 1591 in St Paul's Cathedral, where an elaborate monument was erected by his nephew and heir, Sir William Hatton.

WALLACE T. MACCAFFREY

Sources N. H. Nicolas, *Memoirs of the life and times of Sir Christopher Hatton* (1847) · J. Neale, *Elizabeth I and her parliaments, 1584–1601* (1957) · P. Collinson, *The Elizabethan puritan movement* (1967) · W. Camden, *The history of the most renowned and victorious Princess Elizabeth*, rev. edn (1675) · *Calendar of the manuscripts of the most hon. the marquis of Salisbury*, 24 vols., HMC, 9 (1883–1976), vols. 2–4 · *CSP Spain, 1568–1603* · *CSP for., 1575–91* · *CSP dom., 1547–94* · *CPR, 1558–82* · *HoP, Commons, 1558–1603*, 2.276–9 · E. St J. Brooks, *Sir Christopher Hatton* (1946)
Archives BL, Harley MSS, corresp. and papers · Hatfield House, Hertfordshire, letters and papers · Holkham Hall, Wells-next-the-Sea, Norfolk, evidence book · Inner Temple, London, papers · Northants. RO, estate, legal, and personal papers with historical and other collections | Hunt. L., letters to Lord Chancellor Ellesmere · Staffs. RO, letters to Lord Paget
Likenesses oils, *c.*1580, City of Northampton Central Museum and Art Gallery · oils, *c.*1585, Inner Temple, London; version, NPG · N. Hilliard, miniature, *c.*1588–1591, V&A [*see illus.*] · oils, *c.*1588–1591, NPG

Hatton, Christopher, first Baron Hatton (*bap.* **1605**, *d.* **1670**), politician, was baptized on 11 July 1605 at Barking, Essex, the eldest surviving son of Sir Christopher Hatton (*d.* 1619) and his wife, Alice (*fl.* 1570–1630), daughter of Thomas Fanshawe of Ware Park, Hertfordshire. As the cousin and heir male of Sir Christopher Hatton, the Elizabethan lord chancellor, he inherited a substantial estate, including the ostentatious Kirby Hall in Gretton, Northamptonshire, described by John Evelyn in 1651 as 'a very noble house' (Evelyn, 3.133). He succeeded his father in September 1619 and was admitted to Jesus College, Cambridge, and Gray's Inn in 1620. Created MA of Cambridge in 1622 he returned afterwards to take his place as one of Northamptonshire's principal gentlemen.

Hatton was elected MP for Peterborough in 1625 and for Clitheroe in 1626, and was created KB at Charles I's coronation in February 1626. He strengthened his Northamptonshire ties through his marriage, on 8 May 1630, to Elizabeth (*c.*1610–1672), daughter of Sir Charles Montagu of

Boughton. In 1631 the king named him to Northamptonshire's commission for knighthood fines and in 1636 he became high steward of Higham Ferrers as well as of several other Northamptonshire manors. In 1640 Higham Ferrers returned Hatton as a member of the Long Parliament. Active for the king as a commissioner of array in Northamptonshire by August 1642, Hatton did not resume his seat at Westminster, and joined the king at Oxford. The university bestowed an honorary doctorate upon him, and the king took him into his service. Charles appointed him comptroller of the household, named him to the privy council, and in July 1643 raised him to the peerage as Baron Hatton of Kirkby. Clarendon pronounced him a 'person of great reputation at that time' (Clarendon, *Hist. rebellion*, 7.396) and in December 1646 he served as one of the king's negotiators at Uxbridge. But the end of the first civil war and the possible loss of his estates forced Hatton to reconsider his royalist commitments. He left his post as comptroller, and in December 1646 asked leave to compound for his property. In March 1647 parliament fined him £4156, a sum later reduced to £3226.

Fundamentally a royalist, however, Hatton left England for France in 1648. Throughout the interregnum he struggled to stave off the loss of his property while remaining loyal to the king. This careful balancing act earned him the enmity of some in the exiled court, including Clarendon. In the spring of 1651 he was in London, apparently in an attempt to reverse the government's seizure of his property, ordered in May 1650. Unsuccessful, he returned to Paris, where he distanced himself from the royalist exiles. In November an English government spy reported: 'Hatton, to save his own estate in England, never comes at [Charles II] by his own consent' (*CSP dom., 1651–2*, 3). At the same time, however, Hatton claimed to be working hard in the king's behalf in a letter to the royalist Lord Inchiquin. In February 1654 Lady Hatton, in England, petitioned the committee for compounding for the return of the family property, asserting that her husband's exile was not political, but rather 'to lead a quiet life and pay his great debts' (Green, *Compounding*, 1579–80). An investigation of Lady Hatton's claims reported that her husband had ended his contact with the royalists. Angry at being excluded from the privy council, he had refused an offer to serve as ambassador to Sweden. He was, the report said, 'not countenanced by the English Court' (Green, *Compounding*, 1580). As a result, in May 1654 the government discharged Hatton's estate.

The committee's report notwithstanding Hatton did maintain some connections with the Stuarts. In December 1654 he played host to the duke of Gloucester, then quarrelling with his mother the queen, and was said to be angling for the duke's guardianship. It is also clear that he lent the king money which, given his circumstances, he could ill afford. He returned to England in late 1656 and spent the rest of the interregnum recouping his fortunes. One of his projects during this period was the development of his London property at Hatton Garden, which was subdivided and built upon.

Given Hatton's ambivalence during the interregnum

and Clarendon's enmity, it is perhaps unsurprising that rewards for his services were slow in coming. He was named to the privy council in January 1662, but soon after dispatched to Guernsey as governor. While in Guernsey he provoked several furious disputes with his deputy, who in 1664 accused him of pocketing money meant for the garrison, as well as of favouring dissenters. Hatton denied the former charge, though he admitted that he sometimes dealt with nonconformists in secular matters. In December 1664 the king ordered him home for consultations—an order that had to be repeated twice, to Charles's great annoyance. While he did not lose his office Hatton never returned to Guernsey. In any event he preferred life in London, where he was prominent in the fledgeling Royal Society, of which he was an original member. A collector of books and antiquities, he patronized Gregory King and William Dugdale and carried on an extensive correspondence on scientific and philosophical matters. He died on 4 July 1670 at Kirby Hall, and was buried the following month at Westminster Abbey. He was succeeded by his son Christopher *Hatton, first Viscount Hatton.

VICTOR STATER

Sources GEC, *Peerage* · M. A. E. Green, ed., *Calendar of the proceedings of the committee for compounding ... 1643–1660*, 1, PRO (1889) · M. A. E. Green, ed., *Calendar of the proceedings of the committee for advance of money, 1642–1656*, 3 vols., PRO (1888) · *CSP dom.*, *1631–3; 1641–3; 1651–2; 1660–61; 1663–4; 1668–9; 1670; addenda, 1660–70* · Clarendon, *Hist. rebellion*, 7.396; 8.211 · Evelyn, *Diary*, 3.38, 133, 191, 231 · *Calendar of the manuscripts of the marquess of Ormonde*, new ser., 8 vols., HMC, 36 (1902–20), vol. 1, pp. 168, 245, 311 · *The manuscripts of his grace the duke of Portland*, 10 vols., HMC, 29 (1891–1931), vol. 1, p. 60 · *Report on the manuscripts of his grace the duke of Buccleuch and Queensberry ... preserved at Montagu House*, 3 vols. in 4, HMC, 45 (1899–1926), vol. 3, pp. 357–8 · Venn, *Alum. Cant.*

Archives Bodl. Oxf., MSS relating to library, MS Bodley 878 · Northants. RO, corresp., family MSS, and MSS | BL, letters to Sir Edward Nicholas, Egerton MSS 2533–2535

Hatton, Christopher, first Viscount Hatton (*bap.* **1632**, *d.* **1706**), politician, was baptized on 6 November 1632 at St Bartholomew-the-Great, London, the eldest of the two sons and three daughters of Christopher *Hatton, first Baron Hatton (*bap.* 1605, *d.* 1670), and Elizabeth (*d.* 1672), daughter and coheir of Charles Montagu of Boughton, Northamptonshire.

Hatton, who was educated at home, followed his father's politics. In 1654 he was involved in cavalier plotting and was the principal agent in bringing his cousin Edward Montagu, later the earl of Sandwich, over to the Stuarts. He subsequently joined his father in exile in Paris. At the Restoration he became steward of Higham Ferrers, Northamptonshire, a gentleman of the privy chamber in 1662, and a justice of the peace in Northamptonshire in 1663. In 1664 he became a captain of foot (Guernsey) and made a report to Colonel William Legge on the state of the island of which his father was governor. The following year he deputized for his father in his absence. In 1663 he was elected to parliament for Northampton, a seat he held until his father's death elevated him to the House of Lords. He was not an active MP and was noted as a court dependent.

On 12 February 1667 Hatton married Lady Cicely (1648–1672), daughter of John Tufton, second earl of Thanet. They had three daughters. Her £5000 portion helped to save the family from the financial disasters wrought by the civil war and his father's subsequent extravagances. In 1667 he was made a captain in the Earl of Manchester's Foot and in March 1670 became a deputy lieutenant in Northamptonshire. On his father's death, on 4 July 1670, he succeeded as second Baron Hatton and governor of Guernsey, and was granted a pension of £1000 per annum. Roger North credited his 'unparalleled prudence and application' at this time with restoring his family's estate, setting his brother and sisters at ease, and comforting the last years of his mother's life (R. North, *The Lives of ... Francis North ... Dudley North ... John North*, new edn, 1826, 2.293). As part of this financial prudence he sold 112 medieval manuscripts accumulated by his father to the Bodleian Library. His Northamptonshire estate was valued at £1370 per annum.

On the night of 29–30 December 1672 the powder magazine at Cornet Castle, Guernsey, exploded following a lightning strike while Lord Hatton and his family were in residence. His wife and mother were killed, although he and two of his children escaped serious injury. Despite the tragedy he spent a further eight years on the island. In 1675, by 27 December, he married Frances, only daughter of Sir Henry Yelverton, second baronet, of Easton Maudit, Northamptonshire. They had several children, although only one daughter survived beyond infancy. In 1680 he compiled a report on the state of Guernsey for Charles II (BL, King's MS 48); in the same year he returned to the family estate at Kirby, Northamptonshire, and exercised his governorship thereafter by deputy. On his return he became *custos rotulorum* for Northamptonshire. Having shown his loyalty to the Stuarts by voting against the second Exclusion Bill in 1680, on 17 January 1683 he was created Viscount Hatton of Gretton, the warrant reciting that a warrant had been signed at St Germain-en-Laye in 1649 for conferring that rank on his father.

After the death of Frances, on 15 May 1684, Hatton married, in August 1685, Elizabeth (*d.* 1733), the daughter and coheir of Sir William Haslewood of Maidwell, Northamptonshire, a rich heiress. They had three sons and three daughters. In 1687 he became captain of grenadiers in the Earl of Huntingdon's Foot. Although he had supported Charles II in his struggle with Shaftesbury and the exclusionists, in 1687 Hatton was listed as one of the opponents of James II. A naturally cautious man he avoided providing active support to either side in 1688 by excusing himself on the grounds of illness. In 1696 he was sent for by the House of Lords to explain his non-attendance and was one of the last peers to sign the 1696 Association proclaiming William III's right to the throne and abjuring James II. Thereafter he lived with his growing family predominantly at Kirby, where he developed a fine garden. Throughout his life he displayed a reluctance to live in London and many of the Hatton papers deposited in the British Library were letters written to him either on Guernsey or at Kirby. In 1697 he was removed from the stewardship of Higham

Ferrers by the earl of Stamford, chancellor of the duchy of Lancaster, but was restored in 1702. In 1704 he was again sent for by the House of Lords.

Hatton died in September 1706 and was succeeded by his son William (1690–1760), who died unmarried and was in turn succeeded by his brother Henry Charles (1693–1762). As Henry Charles also died unmarried the title expired and the estate passed to their sister Elizabeth. On her death she bequeathed it to the youngest son of her half-sister Anne, Hatton's daughter by his first wife, and Daniel Finch, earl of Nottingham, on condition that he took the name Finch-Hatton.   JAN BROADWAY

Sources E. R. Edwards, 'Hatton, Hon. Christopher', HoP, *Commons, 1660–90*, 2.512 · H. Turner, 'Charles Hatton: a younger son', *Northamptonshire Past and Present*, 3 (1960–66), 255–61 · E. M. Thompson, ed., *Correspondence of the family of Hatton*, 2 vols., CS, new ser., 22–3 (1878) · I. Philip, *The Bodleian Library in the seventeenth and eighteenth centuries* (1983) · G. H. Chettle, *Kirby Hall*, 3rd edn (1980) [Department of the Environment official handbook] · *IGI*
Archives BL, corresp. and papers, Add. MSS 29548–29587, 29594–29596 · Northants. RO, corresp. and papers
Likenesses C. Johnson, oils, 1641, Gov. Art Coll.
Wealth at death value of estate £1370 p.a. in 1660s

Hatton, Denys George Finch- (1887–1931), settler in Kenya and lover of Karen Blixen, was born on 24 April 1887 at 22 Prince of Wales Terrace, Kensington, London, son of Henry Stormont Finch-Hatton, thirteenth earl of Winchilsea (1852–1927) and Annie Jane (*d.* 1924), eldest daughter of Sir Henry John *Codrington KCB (1808–1877), admiral of the fleet, and his first wife, Helen Jane Smith. His father's brother was Harold Heneage Finch-Hatton. With his parents, elder sister, and younger brother he lived in a dower house on the Haverholme estate, near Sleaford, Lincolnshire. At Eton College (1900–06) he gained a reputation for charm and easy success in sport and music, but he failed to gain the scholarship to Balliol which he expected, and went up instead to Brasenose, from where he graduated BA in 1910 with a fourth-class degree in modern history and a golf blue.

In the same year Finch-Hatton sailed for British East Africa, reaching Nairobi in 1911. With uncertain finances and no experience of business or farming his aims were unclear, but he was immediately fascinated by the country and its people. He bought farmland at Sosiani (later Eldoret) and Naivasha and traded on a small scale, but his plans, such as they were, were disrupted by the First World War. He joined the East Africa Protectorate forces in 1914 as a temporary captain and saw action in the guerrilla war against General von Lettow-Vorbeck's troops with the force raised by his close friend Berkeley Cole known as Cole's Scouts. He served with distinction, being mentioned in dispatches and awarded the Military Cross. He was later ordered to Mesopotamia where in 1918 he joined the Royal Flying Corps and qualified as a pilot before returning to Kenya after the end of the war.

In 1918 Finch-Hatton first met Karen *Blixen (1885–1962), then the wife of Baron Bror von Blixen-Finecke and a struggling coffee farmer; later she became a famous writer under various names including Isak Dinesen. They

Denys George Finch-Hatton (1887–1931), by unknown photographer

quite openly became lovers before the Blixens formally separated: indeed at one point the two men used the same bedroom in the Blixen house between safaris. After her husband's departure Finch-Hatton moved his possessions into her house, which he regarded as his home. Suggestions that theirs was a companionate relationship, fostered by Blixen's great discretion in her writings, are refuted by Blixen's manuscripts, which show that she twice thought herself pregnant by Finch-Hatton (Thurman, 174, 208). To her disappointment, but not his, her expectations ended in miscarriage or the realization that she had been mistaken, and both died childless. Many of their circle expected them to marry after Blixen's divorce was finalized in 1925, but the marriage never took place. From about 1924 Finch-Hatton increasingly turned to leading safaris for a living. His talents for meticulous organization and hunting itself were widely admired, and in 1928 and 1930 he led the prince of Wales on highly successful safaris. His success as a guide enhanced his own reputation, but strained his relationship with Blixen as it prolonged his absences from her farm and cut her off from his life, particularly when, as with the prince of Wales's safaris, he worked with her former husband and his new wife, or when he led parties interested principally in photography. She shared his enthusiasm for hunting, but not photography. Their affair ended in a bitter quarrel in 1931 shortly before his death and her departure for Denmark.

Though a friend of Lord Delamere (they shared a bungalow after the war) Finch-Hatton took little part in the debate surrounding east Africa's destiny as a white settler or an African colony. His own rather desultory efforts at farming suggest he was little moved by the notion of a settler colony. He was more concerned with the great expansion of hunting. He condemned the indiscriminate slaughter practised by many hunters (for example in an article in *The Times* of 21 January 1928), but it was the excess, not the killing *per se* which he disliked. He advocated shooting with the camera as a means of combining the excitement of hunting while conserving game stocks, though such photographic hunts still involved considerable slaughter.

In 1930 Finch-Hatton took out from England a Gipsy Moth aircraft, partly for the sheer enjoyment, but also to locate animals for his safaris, a practice employed by Beryl *Markham (1902–1986), the pioneer aviator with whom some, notably Markham herself, suggest he had had an affair. He and his passenger, his African servant, died when his aircraft crashed at Voi on 14 May 1931 shortly after taking off. He was buried later that month high in the Ngong hills, a place chosen earlier by him and Blixen as their graves. Finch-Hatton's brother later erected an obelisk on the spot. A stone bridge designed by Lutyens was erected in his memory by his school contemporaries at Eton.

Finch-Hatton is best known through Karen Blixen's *Out of Africa* (1st edn 1937) and *Shadows on the Grass* (1960) and especially in the film version of the former (1985, script Kurt Luedtke, direction Sydney Pollack), in which Robert Redford played Finch-Hatton to Meryl Streep's Blixen. In her book Blixen portrays their relationship as one of equals: he shares her home and hospitality, and in return reveals the landscape to her on safari and from the air. They share equally in the triumphs of hunting and simultaneously appreciate the pleasures of European civilization and empathize with Africa and its people. He teaches her Latin and to read the Bible and the Greek poets, and she describes how he knew great parts of the Old Testament by heart and how he had the Bible with him on all his journeys. He reveals to her pleasure in music and fine wine: she provides stories, and fine china, food, and glass. The film script and Errol Trzebinski's *Silence will Speak*, on which it is based, are less sympathetic. Finch-Hatton dictates the nature of their relationship, appearing when it suits him, but rejecting the more permanent ties she seeks after her estrangement from her husband. Blixen is a social climber whose jealousy ultimately drives away Finch-Hatton. Subsequent archival research has revealed how far her farm, to which she clung desperately, depended on his financial support. He was universally thought captivating, both physically (he was tall, slim, and handsome, though his blond hair fell out prematurely, leading him to adopt a characteristic blue bowler hat to hide his baldness) and in personality (his taste and cultivation set him apart from most of his contemporaries). Blixen describes him and his companion Berkeley Cole as outcasts:

It was not a society that had thrown them out, and not any place in the world either, but time had done it, they did not belong to their century. No other nation than the English could have produced them, but they were examples of atavism, and theirs was an earlier England, a world which no longer existed. In the present epoch they had no home, but had got to wander here and there … He did cut a figure … but it did not quite fit in anywhere.   (Blixen, 184, 186)

She captures the contradictions of a man who continues to arouse sympathetic curiosity, despite having left few marks.   ELIZABETH BAIGENT

Sources E. Trzebinski, *Silence will speak: a study of the life of Denys Finch Hatton and his relationship with Karen Blixen* (1977) · K. Blixen, *Out of Africa* (1937); repr. (1986) · b. cert. · *The Eton register*, 7 (privately printed, Eton, 1922) · Burke, *Peerage* (1959) · J. Thurman, *Isak Dinesen: the life of Karen Blixen* (1982) · I. Dinesen [K. Blixen], *Shadows on the grass* (1960) · J. Walker, ed., *Halliwell's film and video guide*, 14th edn (1999) · V. Harlow, E. M. Chilver, and A. Smith, eds., *History of East Africa*, 2 (1965)
Archives Northants. RO, diary · Rungstedlund, Sjaelland, Denmark, MSS
Likenesses photograph, repro. in Trzebinski, *Silence will speak* · photograph, Kongelige Bibliotek, Copenhagen [see illus.]
Wealth at death £1526 6s. 8d.: probate, 9 June 1931, CGPLA Eng. & Wales

Hatton, Edward [*name in religion* Anthony; *pseud.* Constantius Archaeophilus] (**1701–1783**), Dominican friar, was probably the son of Edward Hatton, yeoman, of Great Crosby, Lancashire. He was educated in the English Dominican College at Bornhem, near Antwerp, and on being professed in 1722 took the name in religion of Anthony. After teaching for some years he was ordained priest, and sent to the English mission in 1730. He officiated as chaplain to several gentlemen in Yorkshire, and in 1739–40 served as chaplain to Bishop Williams, vicar apostolic of the northern district. In 1749 he went to assist Father Thomas Worthington at Middleton Lodge, near Leeds. That mission he subsequently moved to Stourton Lodge, a few miles distant. In 1754 and again in 1770 he was elected provincial of his order. In 1776 he started the mission at Hunslet, near Leeds, but died at Stourton Lodge on 23 October 1783.

Hatton was the author of *Moral and Controversial Lectures upon the Christian Doctrines and Christian Practice* (not dated); and he also compiled (under the name Constantius Archaeophilus) *Memoirs of the Reformation of England*, in two parts (1826 and 1841), which contained relevant acts of parliament and extracts from protestant historians.

THOMPSON COOPER, *rev.* ROBERT BROWN

Sources Gillow, *Lit. biog. hist.* · G. Oliver, *Collections illustrating the history of the Catholic religion in the counties of Cornwall, Devon, Dorset, Somerset, Wilts, and Gloucester* (1857) · C. F. R. Palmer, *Obituary notices of the friary preachers, or Dominicans, of the English province, from …* 1650 (1884)

Hatton, Edward Finch- (**1697?–1771**), diplomatist, was born Edward Finch, the fifth son of Daniel *Finch, seventh earl of Winchilsea and second earl of Nottingham (1647–1730), politician, and Anne Hatton (1668–1743). After attending Mr Ellis's school in Isleworth, Middlesex, he was admitted fellow-commoner of Trinity College,

Cambridge, in 1713 and he proceeded MA in 1718. He went on the grand tour to France, Italy, and Hanover from 1720 to 1723 and his hopes of a diplomatic career were met with his appointment as envoy-extraordinary to the imperial diet of Regensburg (September 1724–February 1725). He served in succession as envoy to the Polish court from 1725 to 1727, to the Swedish court from 1728 to 1739, and to the Russian court from 1740 to 1742.

In 1727 Finch was elected MP for Cambridge University, which he represented until 1768. A fellow of Christ's College, Cambridge (1728–46), he and his fellow MP Thomas Townshend instituted the members' prizes in the university for essays in Latin prose. On his return from abroad in 1742 he declared his support for Lord Carteret and was appointed groom of the royal bedchamber; in spite of the subsequent changes in government, the king ensured that Finch remained in post until 1756. On 6 September 1746 he married Elizabeth Palmer, daughter of Sir Thomas Palmer, fourth baronet, of Wingham, Kent; they had three daughters and two sons. He assumed in 1764 the additional name of Hatton, under the terms of the will of his great-aunt, Anne Hatton, daughter of Christopher, Viscount Hatton. He was appointed master of the robes in June 1757 and surveyor of the king's private roads in November 1760; he retired from the Commons before the general election of 1768. Finch-Hatton died on 16 May 1771.   [ANON.], *rev.* R. D. E. EAGLES

Sources A. B. I'Anson, *The history of the Finch family* (1933) · D. B. Horn, ed., *British diplomatic representatives, 1689–1789*, CS, 3rd ser., 46 (1932) · J. F. Chance, *The alliance of Hanover* (1923) · R. R. Sedgwick, 'Finch, Hon. Edward', HoP, *Commons* · A. N. Newman, 'Finch, Hon. Edward', HoP, *Commons* · Burke, *Peerage* (1980) · A. Collins, *The peerage of England: containing a genealogical and historical account of all the peers of England* · Venn, *Alum. Cant.* · GEC, *Peerage* · J. Ingamells, ed., *A dictionary of British and Irish travellers in Italy, 1701–1800* (1997), 355 **Archives** BL, letters to duke of Newcastle, Add. MSS 32414, 32419, 32694–33067, *passim* · BL, letters to Thomas Robinson, Add. MSS 23780–23810, *passim* · BL, corresp. with Walter Titley, Egerton MSS 2684–2689

Hatton, Elizabeth [*née* Lady Elizabeth Cecil], **Lady Hatton** [*other married name* Elizabeth Coke, Lady Coke] (**1578–1646**), courtier, was the fourth daughter of Thomas *Cecil, first earl of Exeter (1542–1623), and Dorothy Latimer (1548–1609). In the early 1590s she married Sir William Hatton, who died in 1597, bequeathing her Corfe Castle, the Isle of Purbeck, Hatton House in Holborn, and the care of her stepdaughter, Frances Hatton. On 6 November 1598 she married Sir Edward *Coke (1552–1634), a lawyer, who had ten children by his previous marriage, and they had two daughters, Frances and Elizabeth. She was popular at court, performing with the queen as one of the goddesses in the masque *The Vision of Twelve Goddesses* (1604), and was well known for her lavish and lively entertainments at Hatton House. Jonson's masque *The Hue and Cry after Cupid* (1608) commended her as one of the loveliest court ladies. In 1621 she was one of the select members of the audience directly addressed by one of the Gypsies in Jonson's *The Gypsies Metamorphosed* (1640):

Others' fortunes may be showne
You are the builder of your owne
(p. 71)

exemplifying her reputation as an independent, forceful, and powerful woman. She corresponded with Elizabeth of Bohemia and visited her in exile at The Hague in 1627.

Elizabeth's marriage to Edward Coke was difficult. She initiated several legal actions against his appropriation of lands and revenue inherited from her first husband, in 1617 and after Coke's death in 1634. The 1634 text of her petition to the privy council outlines their financial disagreements, claiming Coke refused her maintenance and used profits from her lands to advance the children of his first marriage. Lady Hatton's resistance to the view that a husband owned his wife's property displays her strong, intelligent, and independent temperament, exemplifying how powerful married women conceived of their property, and the fight they faced to retain it. In 1600 she left him for at least a year, using her connections with influential men to force Coke to grant her an annual allowance. She refused to take his name, continuing to use 'Lady Hatton', and for most of their marriage they lived apart. In 1617 she petitioned the council for her assets, condemning his appropriation of land, revenue, and a mortgage. Chamberlain described her performance before the council: 'divers said Burbage could not have acted better' (*CSP dom.*, 1611–18, vol. xcii, no.42). The dispute was settled by negotiation.

Coke treated his wife's daughters as he did her property. In 1605 he forced the marriage of her stepdaughter Frances Hatton to Sir Robert Rich. The marriage of Coke's and Hatton's own daughter, Frances Coke, to Sir John Villiers, George Villiers's brother, is renowned. Coke negotiated the details, to which neither mother nor daughter were party, in 1617. Lady Hatton removed her daughter, but Coke obtained a warrant, forcing entry to obtain her. Francis Bacon, then lord keeper, was petitioned by Lady Hatton, who described herself as 'like a cow that has lost a calf' (Spedding, 4.225). He ruled that both parents' consent was needed (given Frances was heir to her mother's estates), ordering Coke to return Frances to her mother. Lady Hatton agreed to the marriage on terms ensuring her daughter an income, but Frances's life with Villiers was unhappy and she was arraigned for adultery in 1627. Lady Hatton provided equivocal support for her daughter, but did leave her estate to her son.

Hatton was actively involved in the financial management of her estates: there are records of disputes about leases for Hatton House and about access over her land. Her will gives precise details of the disposal and care of her properties and large bequests for poor relief in Holborn and Stoke Poges. During the civil war she supported parliament. She died on 3 January 1646 and was buried in St Andrew's parish church in Holborn. There is no monument, despite a request in her will that one be erected to her there; the exigencies of the civil war may explain its absence.   KATE AUGHTERSON

Sources L. Norsworthy, *The lady of Bleeding Heart Yard: Elizabeth Hatton* (1935) · A. Fraser, *The weaker vessel: women's lot in seventeenth-*

century England (1984); repr. (1993), 13–17, 192–3 • E. M. Thompson, ed., *Correspondence of the family of Hatton*, 2, CS, new ser., 23 (1878) • L. Pollock, *A lasting relationship: parents and children over three centuries* (1987), 27, 64, 81 • *The letters of John Chamberlain*, ed. N. E. McClure, 2 vols. (1939) • *CSP dom.*, 1611–18 • *The letters and life of Francis Bacon*, ed. J. Spedding, 7 vols. (1861–74) • 'Coke, Sir Edward', *DNB* • 'Cecil, Thomas, first earl of Exeter', *DNB* • Lady Hatton's petition to privy council, 1634

Archives BL, Hatton-Finch MSS, Add. MSS 29550 ff. • Northants. RO, MSS FH

Wealth at death properties and bequests: Norsworthy, *The Lady of Bleeding Heart Yard*

Frank Hatton (1861–1883), by unknown engraver, pubd 1883

Hatton, Frank (1861–1883), explorer, only son and second child of Joseph *Hatton (1841–1907), journalist, and his wife, Louisa Johnson (1840/41–1901), was born at Berkeley Road, Horfield, Bristol, on 31 August 1861. Soon after his birth his family moved to Durham, then Worcester, before settling in London. Hatton was educated from 1874 at Marcq, near Lille, and in 1877–8 at King's College School, London. He then studied geology and chemistry at the Royal School of Mines, South Kensington, where he obtained the Frankland prize of the Institute of Chemistry, entitling him to associateship of the institute at the age of twenty. He had considerable laboratory and field experience when he was appointed mineral explorer to the British North Borneo Company. He left England in August 1881, and arrived at Labuan in October, and on 19 November at Abai, Keppel province. After a two months' expedition to the interior, he had to recover his health at Singapore. From March to June 1882 he made further explorations, but found few traces of minerals. From July to October he explored the Kinoram district. After another rest at Singapore he started on 19 December for Sandakan, and journeyed up and down the Kinabatangan River until near the end of February, when he reached the Segamah River. On 1 March 1883, while returning from pursuing an elephant, he was killed by the accidental discharge of his rifle, which caught in the thick jungle. His body was carried by canoe for several days along the Kinabatangan River, to the principal settlement, Elopura. A European jury recorded a verdict of accidental death and he was buried at Sandakan cemetery.

Hatton's work, so far as it had gone, and his diaries give evidence of high promise as a scientific explorer. He had learned the Malay and Duson dialects, which contributed to his success in dealing with the local tribesmen, and had the true explorer's temperament, power of command, fertility of resource in the presence of danger, cool courage, and self-control, and was a bright and engaging companion. He contributed to popular and learned journals, and was a skilful pianist and a keen sportsman.

G. T. BETTANY, *rev.* ANITA McCONNELL

Sources *Nature*, 27 (1882–3), 515–16 • J. Hatton, 'Frank Hatton in N. Borneo', *Century Magazine*, 30 (1885), 437–46 • SOAS, British North Borneo MSS, MS 283792 (15) • b. cert.

Archives SOAS, album relating to his life and death

Likenesses engraving (after photograph by Van der Weyde), repro. in Hatton, 'Frank Hatton in N. Borneo', 441 • woodengraving, NPG; repro. in *ILN* (12 May 1883) [*see illus.*]

Hatton, George William Finch-, tenth earl of Winchilsea and fifth earl of Nottingham (1791–1858), politician,

was born at Kirby, Northamptonshire, on 22 May 1791. He was a grandson of Edward Finch-*Hatton, and son of George Finch-Hatton (1747–1823) of Eastwell Park, near Ashford, Kent, MP for Rochester in 1772–84, and his wife (whom he married in 1785), Elizabeth Mary (d. 1825), eldest daughter of David Murray, second earl of Mansfield. George William, who had one younger brother and three sisters, was educated at Westminster School and at Christ's College, Cambridge (BA, 1812). In 1809 he became a captain in the Ashford regiment of the Kentish local militia; in 1819 began acting as a lieutenant of the Northamptonshire regiment of yeomanry; and in 1820 was named a deputy lieutenant for the county of Kent. On 2 August 1826, on the death (without legitimate issue) of his cousin, George Finch, ninth earl of Winchilsea, and fourth earl of Nottingham, he succeeded to these peerages.

Winchilsea was tall, well-built, and black-haired, and in his prime was an imposing figure and an inspiring orator. His integrity and sincerity impressed his contemporaries. He presided at a very large and influential meeting held on Penenden heath, Kent, on 10 October 1828, when strongly worded resolutions in favour of protestant principles were carried. In his place in the House of Lords he was a very frequent speaker and vigorously defended the protestant tory cause. He was particularly noted as being almost the only English nobleman who was willing to identify himself with the Orange party in Ireland, and he was accustomed to denounce in forceful terms Daniel O'Connell and Maynooth College and its system of education. Occasionally he took the chair at May meetings at Exeter Hall, but his protestantism was more political than spiritual and he did not become a leader of evangelicalism.

The Catholic Relief Bill of 1829 aroused Winchilsea's most vehement hostility, and led him to fight a duel with the duke of Wellington. In a published letter he wrote that the duke, 'under the cloak of some outward show of zeal for the Protestant religion', had carried on 'insidious designs for the infringement of our liberties, and the introduction of Popery into every department of the State'. The duke asked for an apology, and, when this was not forthcoming, demanded satisfaction. The meeting took place in Battersea Fields on 21 March 1829, the duke being attended by Sir Henry Hardinge, and his opponent by Edward Boscawen, Viscount Falmouth. The duke fired and missed, whereupon Winchilsea fired in the air and then apologized for the language of his letter (*Annual Register*, 1829, 58–63).

In November 1830 Winchilsea was a leading figure in the ultra-tory rebellion which led to the downfall of the Wellington government. At this time he professed himself favourable to moderate reform, but in June 1831 he withdrew his support from Earl Grey's administration (*Hansard 3*, 4.107–11) and subsequently strenuously opposed the Reform Bill and other whig measures. He was gazetted lieutenant-colonel commandant of the East Kent regiment of yeomanry in 1830, named a deputy lieutenant for the county of Lincoln in 1831, and created a DCL of Oxford on the occasion of Wellington's installation as chancellor of the university in 1834. His protestant convictions continued undimmed in later life, and in 1851, in a letter to *The Times*, he denounced the new Roman Catholic hierarchy and the Russell administration's half-hearted response to it.

Winchilsea was married three times: first, on 26 July 1814, to Lady Georgiana Charlotte, eldest daughter of James Graham, third duke of Montrose. An 'earnest disciple of the Evangelical school of her day' (GEC, *Peerage*), she died, leaving a son and a daughter, at Haverholme Priory on 13 February 1835. His second wife, whom he married on 15 February 1837, was Emily Georgiana, second daughter of Sir Charles Bagot GCB; she died childless at Haverholme Priory on 10 July 1848. His third marriage was on 17 October 1849, to Fanny Margaretta (d. 26 April 1909), eldest daughter of Edward Royd Rice of Dane Court, Kent. There were three sons, including the politician Harold Heneage Finch-*Hatton, and a daughter from this marriage. Winchilsea died at Haverholme Priory, near Sleaford, Lincolnshire, on 8 January 1858.

G. C. BOASE, rev. JOHN WOLFFE

Sources *The Times* (13 Jan 1858) · J. Wolffe, *The protestant crusade in Great Britain, 1829–1860* (1991) · Burke, *Peerage* · *Random recollections of Exeter Hall in 1834–1837, by one of the protestant party* (1838) · Venn, *Alum. Cant.* · GEC, *Peerage*
Archives Northants. RO, corresp. and papers | BL, corresp. with W. E. Gladstone, Add. MSS 44352–44362, *passim* · BL, Peel MSS · CKS, letters to W. M. Smith · U. Nott. L., letters to fourth duke of Newcastle · W. Sussex RO, letters to fifth duke of Richmond
Likenesses T. Phillips, portrait, repro. in J. E. Doyle, *The official baronage of England*, 3 vols. (1886)
Wealth at death under £40,000: probate, 20 March 1858, *CGPLA Eng. & Wales*

Hatton, Harold Heneage Finch- (1856–1904), politician, born at Eastwell Park, Kent, on 23 August 1856, was fourth son of George William Finch-*Hatton, tenth earl of Winchilsea (1791–1858), and his third wife, Fanny Margaretta (d. 1909), daughter of Edward Royd Rice, of Dane Court, Kent. His brother, Murray Edward Gordon Finch-Hatton, twelfth earl of Winchilsea (1851–1898), MP for South Lincolnshire (1884–5) and the Spalding division (1885–7), was well known as a leading agriculturist. Finch-Hatton was educated at Eton College, and he matriculated at Balliol College, Oxford, on 20 October 1874, but did not graduate.

In 1876 Finch-Hatton joined his brother Henry in Queensland, remaining in the colony until 1883. For some time he was engaged in cattle-farming at a settlement later named Mount Spencer, but subsequently went prospecting for gold in the Nebo goldfields, some 40 miles further inland. Gold was found at Mount Britten and shares were bought in other claims; but he made a return of only about £10,000 in an outlay of £16,000 (*AusDB*). After some eighteen months the Finch-Hatton brothers disposed of their rights to a Melbourne syndicate, retaining only a fourth share in the concern. Finch-Hatton always preserved his interest in Queensland, and as permanent delegate and chairman of the London committee of the North Queensland Separation League (of which he was for a time the sole member) rendered energetic service to the colony. In 1885 he published a readable record of his Australian experiences in a book entitled *Advance, Australia!* containing a sympathetic account of the Aborigines, founded on his personal contacts with them. He favoured cheap coolie labour for the sugar industry. The final chapter on imperial federation condemned the action of Lord Derby as colonial secretary in dealing with the New Guinea question.

On his return to England Finch-Hatton occupied himself in financial work. But his chief interest was in imperial politics. He was one of the founders of the Imperial Federation League, and for some time acted as its secretary; he was also secretary to the Pacific Telegraph Company, formed for the promotion of cable communication between Vancouver and Australia. When, in the autumn of 1885, he contested East Nottingham as a Conservative he strongly advocated imperial federation as a prelude to free trade within the empire. He was defeated by a majority of 991; he was also defeated there in July 1886 and July 1892. In 1895 he was returned unopposed for Newark. His political career, however, was brief. He made an able but highly conservative maiden speech (28 April 1896) on agricultural rating but before long fell victim to bad health. Falling out of sympathy with his party, he resigned his seat rather suddenly in May 1898 (*The Times*, 13 May 1898). He regarded Lord Salisbury as insufficiently imperial, and he disapproved of the Irish Land Act of 1896 and of what he saw as excessive concessions to the Liberal Unionist wing of the Unionist coalition.

When not in London Finch-Hatton henceforth lived at Harlech, and in 1903 was high sheriff of Merioneth. Highly skilled in field sports, a good rifle shot and keen huntsman, he excelled at golf, often competing for the amateur championship. He was also a skilled thrower of the boomerang.

He died, unmarried, from heart failure, on his own doorstep at 110 Piccadilly, London, on 16 May 1904, 'after having completed the last of his morning runs round the park'. He was buried in Ewerby churchyard, near Sleaford, Lincolnshire.

G. LE G. NORGATE, rev. H. C. G. MATTHEW

Sources The Times (18 May 1904) · Sleaford Gazette (21 May 1904) · Sleaford Gazette (28 May 1904) · R. Nevill and C. E. Jerningham, Piccadilly to Pall Mall (1908) · AusDB · The Australasian (16 April 1887)

Hatton, John Liptrot (1809–1886), composer and conductor, born in Concert Street, Liverpool, on 12 October 1809, was the son and grandson of professional violinists. With the exception of some musical tuition received at the academy of a Mr Molyneux, he was virtually self-taught; yet by the time he was sixteen years old he was already organist at Woolton and Childwall churches, Lancashire, and at the Roman Catholic church in Liverpool, for the last of which he wrote a mass, which remained in manuscript. He was later organist at the Old Church (St Nicholas) in Chapel Street, Liverpool. It is characteristic of the irrepressible animal spirits which in after years made him universally popular that he should have ventured to play 'All round my hat' (a street song of the time), of course carefully disguised, when competing for one of these appointments. In his youth he also acquired some experience as an actor, successfully playing the part of Blueskin in Jack Sheppard at the Little Liver Theatre in Church Street. In 1832 he moved to London, and made his first public appearance there as an actor. A playbill was preserved by him, containing his name as playing Marco [sic] in Othello with W. C. Macready and Charles Kean at Drury Lane on 20 December 1832. In the following year he wrote some piano pieces, among them six impromptus which attained considerable success.

At Drury Lane Theatre Hatton obtained his first important musical engagement when he directed the choruses in the season of English operas given from 1 October 1842 to 3 April 1843. On 25 February in the latter year his own operetta The Queen of the Thames (words by Edward Fitzball) was given successfully six times. It contains some pretty numbers, and the madrigal 'The Merry Bridal Bells' shows his technical skill and familiarity with seventeenth-century models. Among the company engaged for the operatic performances was Joseph Staudigl, who encouraged Hatton to write another opera, Pascal Bruno, to a libretto by Fitzball. This was translated, mainly by Staudigl himself, into German, and was brought out at Vienna on 2 March 1844 for the benefit of the singer, who performed the principal role. The only part of the opera to be published was a song, 'Revenge', sung by Staudigl, which became very popular in England. While staying in Vienna to supervise the production of the opera, Hatton was the guest of Staudigl, who introduced him to the Concordia Society. His piano playing, more especially of Bach's fugues, which he performed from memory, attracted much attention. Meanwhile he took advantage of the opportunities for advanced study of music, and received counterpoint lessons from Simon Sechter. On his return to England Hatton published several vocal trios and a set of eighteen songs to words by T. Oliphant. They were furnished with German translations, and published under the pseudonym 'Czapek', the genitive plural of a Hungarian word for 'hat'. These and some other songs published about the same time were considered by some critics to be on a level with those of Schubert. They were obviously influenced by German models, and one song, 'To Anthea', was felt to reveal particular beauty and sincerity of expression.

The popularity of Hatton's songs (numbering some three hundred in all) resulted partly from his practical experience as both a singer and a pianist. At the Hereford festival of 1846 he appeared as a vocalist and played a concerto by Mozart. In the same year he began a series of tours with Camillo Sivori, Henry Vieuxtemps, and other celebrated performers. In August 1848 he paid his first visit to America, remaining there until the spring of 1850, when he returned in order to accompany Sims Reeves on a tour; he went again to America in the following September. His playing and singing were both admired, and he introduced some of Mendelssohn's music to the Boston public. Frequently, it was unclear whether the position assigned him in the programme would be filled by a Bach fugue or instead by a comic song he had written himself. It is said that his hearers were delighted with a song called 'The Sleigh Ride', in the course of which he produced 'realistic' effects by means of bells tied to his leg. Soon after his return to England at the end of 1850 he became conductor of the Glee and Madrigal Union, a post which he retained for some years. He was for a time (probably 1853–9) conductor and arranger of the music for Charles Kean's management at the Princess's Theatre, but it is difficult to disentangle his own compositions from those of other composers arranged by him during this period for theatrical purposes. The music to Henry VIII, Richard II, Sardanapalus, and The Winter's Tale is undoubtedly by him; the first and third sets of compositions were published, and contain some vigorous and effective numbers. It is probable that few of the plays produced by Kean were altogether without original work by Hatton. In many of the Shakespearian performances he skilfully adapted old English airs.

Meanwhile the concert tours continued. In the course of one of these journeys Hatton's once popular song 'Good-bye, sweetheart, good-bye' was composed for Giovanni Matteo Mario. On 26 August 1856 his cantata Robin Hood, to words by George Linley, was delivered at the Bradford music festival, with more success than attended most of his longer works. The last of his operas, Rose, or, Love's Ransom, set to words by H. Sutherland Edwards, was produced at Covent Garden by the English Opera Association on 26 November 1864; the libretto was based on Halévy's Val d'Andorre. In 1866 Hatton contributed several songs to Watts Phillips's play The Huguenot Soldier, and in the same year he went again to America. The 'ballad concerts' at St James's Hall, London, were begun in this year, and for the first nine seasons Hatton held the post of accompanist and conductor. In October 1875 he went to Stuttgart, which he frequently revisited afterwards. There he wrote an oratorio entitled Hezekiah, which, when given at the Crystal Palace on 15 December 1877, failed to please. Though much of the choral writing was censured on account of its imitations of Handel and Mendelssohn, traces of Hatton's old taste for counterpoint and the severer forms of music could still be detected. Among his later compositions were a cantata to words by Milton (manuscript), a trio for piano and strings, published in Germany, and a chorus, 'The earth is fair'. His Aldeburgh Te Deum (published) commemorates his fondness for the Suffolk village in which some part of his later years was spent. He edited many song albums, collections of old English songs, ballad operas, and other works for Boosey & Co.

Hatton married Emma, the second daughter of William Freelove March, of Southampton, and the widow of R. F. Poussett, consul at Buenos Aires; they had two daughters. He was a freemason and a member of the Goldsmiths' Company, and belonged also to the Royal Yacht Club. He died at 31 Marine Terrace, Margate, where he had chiefly lived since 1877, on 20 September 1886, and was buried at Kensal Green cemetery on 25 September.

Hatton's musical reputation has not endured; contemporaries admired his natural gifts, but deplored his lack of artistic earnestness. His part-songs, such as 'When evening's twilight', remained popular for some years, as did a number of his songs; his humorous song 'Simon the Cellarer' was recorded by Sir Charles Santley in 1913. Hatton was popular wherever he went, having the reputation of a bon vivant, though a temperate one.

J. A. F. MAITLAND, rev. CLIVE BROWN

Sources MT, 27 (1886), 607 · W. Spark, 'John Liphot [sic] Hatton', Musical memories, 2nd edn (1888), 309ff. · D. Baptie, Sketches of the English glee composers: historical, biographical and critical (from about 1735–1866) [1896], 139ff. · M. B. Foster, Anthems and anthem composers (1901), 174f. · H. Simpson, A century of ballads, 1810–1910 (1910) · N. Temperley, 'Hatton, John Liptrot', New Grove · CGPLA Eng. & Wales (1886)
Likenesses Kniehuber, lithograph, c.1844, NPG · R. T., wood-engraving, NPG; repro. in ILN (2 Oct 1886) · H. Watkins, carte-de-visite, NPG · lithograph (after photograph), repro. in Tonic Sol-Fa Reporter (Dec 1886)
Wealth at death £90: administration, 28 Oct 1886, CGPLA Eng. & Wales

Hatton, Joseph Paul Christopher (1841–1907), novelist and journalist, was born at Andover, Hampshire, on 3 February 1841 (although there appears to be no official record of this date), the son of Francis Augustus Hatton, a printer and bookseller at Chesterfield who in 1854 founded the Derbyshire Times. He was educated at Bowker's School, Chesterfield, and was intended for the law, entering the office of the town clerk at Chesterfield, William Waller. However, on 5 April 1858 he married Louisa (1840/41–1901), the daughter of Robert Johnson, a stud groom. From this time he engaged in journalism and in 1861 published Provincial Papers, a collection of tales and sketches. In 1863 he was appointed editor of the Bristol Mirror, holding that and other provincial posts until he moved to London in 1868. Pushing and energetic, he was entrusted by Messrs Grant & Co., newspaper and magazine proprietors, with the editorship of the Gentleman's Magazine, the School Board Chronicle, and the Illustrated Midland News. Mark Lemon, editor of Punch, was among Hatton's early London acquaintances and in 1871 Hatton published a volume of reminiscences of Lemon, With a Show in the North, based on articles originally published in the Gentleman's Magazine. A further series of articles, entitled 'The True Story of

Punch', appeared in London Society. In 1874 Hatton retired from his editorship of Grant's periodicals and acted as London correspondent for the New York Times, the Sydney Morning Herald, and the Berlin Kreuz-Zeitung, besides editing for a time the Sunday Times and making his name as a novelist. In 1881 The Standard sent him to the United States to establish on its behalf an independent telegraph service. He described his activities in Journalistic London, being a Series of Sketches of Famous Pens and Papers of the Day in 1882, a volume derived from articles published in Harper's Magazine. He also recorded his impressions of the United States in Today in America: Studies for the Old World and the New (2 vols., 1881). It was during his American visit that President Garfield was shot and Hatton cabled the news to The Standard in London with what was then the longest recorded telegraphic message, having held the line for 3 hours (The People, 4 Aug 1907). A member of the Garrick Club, he was an intimate of Sir Henry Irving and J. L. Toole, accompanying the former on his visit to the United States in 1883 and describing the visit in Henry Irving's Impressions of America, Narrated … by Joseph Hatton (2 vols., 1884). In 1889 he 'chronicled' J. L. Toole's reminiscences (2 vols.). In 1892 Hatton became editor of The People, a Conservative Sunday newspaper, and contributed to that paper (and also to a syndicate of provincial papers) his 'Cigarette papers for after-dinner smoking', a weekly medley of reminiscences, stories, and interviews (issued in book form in 1892). He was latterly a close friend of the sculptor Alfred Gilbert and published, as the 1903 Easter art annual, a pioneer study of Gilbert's life and work.

In addition to his journalistic work, Hatton's literary industry was considerable. His novels include Bitter Sweets: a Love Story (1865), Christopher Henrick: his Life and Adventures (1869), Clytie: a Novel of Modern Life (1874), The Gay World (1877), Cruel London (1878), The Park Lane Mystery: a Story of Love and Magic (1887), By Order of the Czar: the Tragic Story of Anna Klostock (1890), The Banishment of Jessop Blythe (1895), The Dagger and the Cross (1897), When Rogues Fall Out: a Romance of Old London (1899), and In Male Attire: a Romance of the Day (1900). He also worked steadily for the stage. Birds of a Feather: a Serio-Comic Play, his adaptation of his story 'Kites and Pigeons', was published in 1871, and he later adapted Clytie, Cruel London, and By Order of the Czar for the stage, the first being produced at the Amphitheatre, Liverpool, on 29 November 1875 before transferring to the Olympic, London, on 10 January 1876. A dramatic version of Hawthorne's The Scarlet Letter proved popular in the United States. His other works include Old Lamps and New: an After-Dinner Chat (1889) and Club-Land, London and Provincial (1890).

Hatton's only son, Frank *Hatton (1861–1883), an explorer, also influenced his writing and in 1882 he published 'The New Ceylon': being a Sketch of British North Borneo, or Sabah. In 1886 he issued a biographical sketch of his son, who had been killed while travelling in North Borneo (North Borneo Explorations … with a Biographical Sketch and Notes). His novel Captured by Cannibals: some Incidents in the Life of Horace Durand (1888), aimed at the juvenile market, also bears on this incident.

Joseph Hatton died at his London home, 15 Elm Tree Road, St John's Wood, on 31 July 1907 and was buried in St Marylebone cemetery, East Finchley, Middlesex. He was survived by his two daughters: Ellen Howard Hatton, wife of the artist William Henry Margetson, and Bessie Lyle Hatton, a novelist. ANDREW SANDERS

Sources *The Times* (1 Aug 1907) · *The Standard* (1 Aug 1907) · *The People* (4 Aug 1907) · *WWW* · J. Hatton, *Old lamps and new* (1889) · J. Hatton, *Journalistic London* (1882) · W. Tinsley, *Random recollections of an old publisher*, 2 vols. (1900) · M. H. Spielmann, *The history of 'Punch'* (1895) · R. Dorment, *Alfred Gilbert* (1985) · J. Sutherland, *The Longman companion to Victorian fiction* (1988) · d. cert. · m. cert. · *DNB* · *CGPLA Eng. & Wales* (1907) · d. cert. [Elizabeth Sonntag]
Archives SOAS, papers | Bodl. Oxf., letters to W. Tinsley · ICL, corresp. with T. Huxley · U. Leeds, Brotherton L., letters to Bram Stoker
Likenesses P. Naumann & R. Taylor & Co, wood-engraving, BM, NPG; repro. in *ILN* (14 May 1892) · wood-engraving (after photograph by Van der Weyde), NPG; repro. in *Harper's Magazine* (1888)
Wealth at death £7689 14s. 4d.: probate, 3 Sept 1907, *CGPLA Eng. & Wales*

Hatton, Sir Ronald George (1886–1965), horticulturist, was born in Hampstead, London, on 6 July 1886, the youngest child of Ernest Hatton, barrister, and his wife, Amy, daughter of William Pearson KC, the brother of Karl Pearson, the biometrician. Hatton was educated at Brighton College and Exeter School and was an exhibitioner at Balliol College, Oxford, from 1906 to 1910. He obtained a fourth class in modern history in 1910, graduating BA in 1912 and MA in 1913. He worked as a labourer on a farm near Bristol and wrote *Folk of the Furrow*, published in 1913 under the pen-name of Christopher Holdenby. In 1912 he went to study agriculture at Wye College in Kent. In 1914 Hatton married Hannah Rachel, daughter of Henry Rigden, of Ashford, Kent; they had one son. The Wye College Fruit Experimental Station became the East Malling Research Station in 1914 with Hatton as acting director after its first director had left on military duties.

Hatton was appointed director of East Malling in 1918, and spent the next thirty years of his life developing it into the leading fruit research institute in the world, enlarging its area from 22 to 360 acres and its staff to more than eighty. His enthusiasm and financial acumen enabled him to raise funds for this expansion from fruit growers, the Empire Marketing Board, and the Treasury. His best-known contribution to research was the study of the effect of rootstock on scion growth and fruiting of apples, pears, and plums. In the course of this work he classified and standardized fruit tree rootstocks, including those which were ultimately known as the Malling series which became widely used. His influence and that of his co-workers transformed horticulture, and fruit growing especially, from folklore to science. He emphasized field experimentation, keen observation, and work on control measures against pests and diseases.

Hatton initiated productive collaborations with the John Innes Horticultural Institute, which resulted in the production of the Malling–Merton apple rootstocks, one of which proved the most successful stock for Cox's orange pippin, and with the Institute of Plant Physiology of the Imperial College of Science, London, which laid the basis of fruit tree physiology.

Many graduate students came to East Malling to study for higher degrees after 1932 when the University of London recognized the station as suitable for this purpose. Hatton's influence thus reached the many countries from which these students came, and he visited and advised on fruit growing in Australia, Canada, Ceylon, Java, New Zealand, South Africa, and the United States of America.

Hatton published many papers on fruit culture. He was instrumental in starting, in 1919, the *Journal of Pomology* (after 1948 the *Journal of Horticultural Science*) and was its joint editor from 1924 until 1947. He was the first director of the Imperial (later Commonwealth) Bureau of Horticulture and Plantation Crops when it was established at East Malling in 1929. Its journal, *Horticultural Abstracts*, begun in 1931, became the standard source for information on fruit and other tree crops. Hatton also played a leading role in the Royal Horticultural Society, which awarded him its Victoria medal in 1930 and elected him vice-president in 1952. He was appointed CBE in 1934, knighted in 1949, and elected to fellowship of the Royal Society in 1944.

After his retirement in 1949 Hatton continued as an enthusiastic grower of fruit and flowers. He died at his home, Sleightholme, Benenden, Kent, on 11 November 1965 and, by his request, was buried in the East Malling churchyard adjoining the land of the research station.

A. F. POSNETTE, *rev.*

Sources T. N. Hoblyn, 'R. G. Hatton', *East Malling Report* (1948) · W. S. Rogers, 'Sir Ronald Hatton', *East Malling Report* (1965) · E. J. Salisbury, *Memoirs FRS*, 12 (1966), 251–8 · I. Elliott, ed., *The Balliol college register, 1900–1950*, 3rd edn (privately printed, Oxford, 1953) · *WWW*
Likenesses W. Stoneman, photograph, 1945, NPG · R. Lewis, portrait, East Malling Research Station, Kent
Wealth at death £28,183: probate, 1 March 1966, *CGPLA Eng. & Wales*

Haughton, Sir Graves Chamney (1788–1849), orientalist, was the second son of John Haughton, a Dublin physician, and his wife, the daughter of Edward Archer of Mount John, co. Wicklow. He was educated principally in England, and, having obtained a military cadetship on the Bengal establishment of the East India Company in 1808, went to India. He gained his first commission on 13 March 1810. At the cadet institution of Barasat, near Calcutta, he distinguished himself by his progress in Hindustani and won the highest honour of the institution, a sword and a handsome pecuniary reward. After serving some time with his regiment, Haughton was among the first who responded to the permission, granted in 1812 by the government of Bengal to young officers, to study oriental languages in the college of Fort William at Calcutta, and he there received seven medals, three degrees of honour, and various financial awards for proficiency in Arabic, Persian, Hindustani, Sanskrit, and Bengali. On 16 December 1814 he was promoted to a lieutenancy. Ill health, caused by his application to study, obliged him to return on leave to England at the end of 1815. In 1817 he was appointed assistant oriental professor in the East India College at

Haileybury. When Alexander Hamilton retired in 1819 Haughton succeeded to the professorship of Sanskrit and Bengali at Haileybury, and he held it until 1827. During this period he published a number of pedagogical works, including *Rudiments of Bengáli Grammar* (1821), *Bengáli Selections, with Translations and a Vocabulary* (1822), and *A Glossary, Bengáli and English* (1825), in which he was assisted by John Panton Gubbins, then a student at the college. He also issued an edition, admirable for its time, of the Sanskrit text of the *Institutes of Menu* (2 vols., 1825), with a revision of Sir William Jones's translation and additional notes. Further editions were published in Madras (1863) and London (1869). Ill health prevented Haughton from adding a third volume, which was to have contained either the whole or a selection of the commentary of Kulluka Bhatta.

Haughton resigned his commission on 12 February 1819, and was created an honorary MA at Oxford on 23 June of that year. He was elected FRS on 15 November 1821, a foreign member of the Asiatic Society of Paris in 1822, a corresponding member of the Royal Society of Berlin in 1837, and a member of the Asiatic Society of Bengal in 1838. In May 1832 he was elected a member of the Royal Irish Academy, and he was also a foreign member of the Institute of France. He took a warm interest in the formation of the Royal Asiatic Society in London, of which he was an original member. He acted as its honorary secretary from November 1831 to May 1832, when the labour of bringing out his *Dictionary, Bengáli and Sanskrit, Explained in English* (1833) compelled him to resign. Among his contributions to the society's *Transactions* was a brief note in vindication of Henry Colebrooke's views of the Vedanta philosophy against the remarks of Colonel Vans Kennedy. The latter replied angrily, and Haughton ably retorted in the monthly *Asiatic Journal* for November 1835. This communication, with some additions, was printed separately in the following December. In 1832 he printed for private circulation *A short inquiry into the nature of language, with a view to ascertain the original meanings of Sanskrit prepositions; elucidated by comparisons with the Greek and Latin*, of which another edition appeared in 1834. The essay was also printed as part of the introduction to the Bengali and Sanskrit dictionary (1833). Early in 1832 he was a candidate, with the support of some of the leading scholars of that time, for the new Boden professorship of Sanskrit at Oxford, but he withdrew in favour of his old fellow student Horace Hayman Wilson. On this occasion he received a complimentary address from two hundred professors, fellows, and graduates, including seven heads of houses. On 18 July 1833 he was made a knight of the Royal Guelphic Order. A metaphysical paper, published in the *Asiatic Journal* for March 1836, on the Hindu and European notions of cause and effect, was followed in 1839 by his *Prodromus, or, An inquiry into the first principles of reasoning; including an analysis of the human mind*, intended as a prelude to a larger work upon the 'necessary connection, relation, and dependence of physics, metaphysics, and morals', entitled *The Chain of Causes*, of which only the first volume appeared (1842). He printed a tabular view of his system

on a single folio sheet in 1835, exhibiting the 'development of minds and morals from their original divine source'. In 1833 he published an *Inquiry into the Nature of Cholera, and the Means of Cure*; in 1840 a *Letter to the Right Hon. C. W. Williams Wynn on the danger to which the constitution is exposed from the encroachments of the courts of law*; and in 1847 were printed his experiments to prove the common nature of magnetism, cohesion, adhesion, and viscosity, in Brewster's *Philosophical Magazine*. He also corresponded with the *Literary Magazine* on the related subject of electricity. Haughton spent much of his later life in Paris. After a prolonged period of ill health he died of cholera at St Cloud on 28 August 1849 and was buried in the east cemetery, Paris, on 30 August. A funeral address was delivered by the president of the Institut de France, who spoke of the affection and respect Haughton had enjoyed, though illness had in his final years limited both his energy and his social contact with friends and colleagues. Upon the death of Sir Charles Wilkins in May 1836 he had written a memoir in the *Asiatic Journal*. He was intimately acquainted with Dr F. A. Rosen, and liberally helped to raise an appropriate monument to his memory. Among his papers preserved in the Bodleian Library, Oxford, is a file of correspondence of over twenty years with his friend Dr Julius Mohl, the French Persian scholar. Mohl was named as one of the executors of his will. Haughton did not marry, but in his will he bequeathed in trust all his property to two daughters, whom he acknowledged and named as Sophia and Eliza Haughton. Their mother was Fanny, probably Chaseman, later Mills. The girls were baptized on 25 February 1828 at Clerkenwell.

GORDON GOODWIN, *rev.* J. B. KATZ

Sources 'Annual report of the Royal Asiatic Society', *Journal of the Royal Asiatic Society of Great Britain and Ireland*, 13, ii–v [May 1850] • *Wilson's Dublin directory* (1790), 121 • testimonials and additional testimonials submitted to the University of Oxford in support of Haughton's candidature for the Boden professorship, Feb–March 1832, Bodl. Oxf. • testimonials and additional testimonials submitted to the University of Oxford in support of Haughton's candidature for the Boden professorship, Feb–March 1832, BL OIOC • *GM*, 1st ser., 103/2 (1833), 76 • Dodwell [E. Dodwell] and Miles [J. S. Miles], eds., *Alphabetical list of the officers of the Indian army: with the dates of their respective promotion, retirement, resignation, or death … from the year 1760 to the year … 1837* (1838), 138–9 • *Royal Kalendar* (1818), 293 • Foster, *Alum. Oxon.* • A. Farrington, *The records of the East India College: Haileybury and other institutions* (1976) • Bodl. Oxf., Haughton MSS • will, PRO, PROB 11/2107

Archives BL OIOC, testimonials etc., MS Eur. D 930 • Bodl. Oxf., corresp. and papers | BL OIOC, records of the East India College, Haileybury, letters, petitions, etc.

Haughton, James (1795–1873), social reformer and temperance activist, son of Samuel Pearson Haughton (1748–1828) and Mary, daughter of James Pim of Rushin, Queen's county, Ireland, was born in Carlow on 5 May 1795. He was educated at Ballitore, co. Kildare, from 1807 to 1810, under James White, a Quaker. After holding several situations to learn business, in 1817 he settled in Dublin, where he became a corn and flour factor, in partnership with his brother William. He retired in 1850.

Although educated as a Friend, Haughton joined the

Unitarians in 1834, and remained throughout his life a strong believer in their tenets. He supported the anti-slavery movement from an early period and in 1838 and 1840 he attended the World Anti-Slavery Conventions in London as a delegate of the Hibernian Anti-Slavery Society.

Haughton was also one of the earliest and most devoted disciples of the leading Irish temperance reformer, Father Mathew (1790–1856). For many years he gave most of his time and energies to promoting total abstinence and to advocating legislative restrictions on the sale of intoxicating drinks. In December 1844 he was the chief promoter of a fund which was raised to pay some of the debts of Father Mathew and release him from prison. He was a vice-president of the United Kingdom Alliance, an auxiliary society of which was formed in Dublin in January 1854.

In 1838 Haughton began a series of letters in the public press which made his name widely known. He wrote on temperance, slavery, British India, peace, capital punishment, sanitary reform, and education. His first letters were signed 'The Son of a Water Drinker', but he soon began using his own name and continued to write until 1872. He took a leading part in a series of weekly meetings which were held in Dublin in 1840, when so numerous were the social questions discussed that a newspaper editor called the speakers the 'anti-everythingarians'. In association with Daniel O'Connell, of whose character Haughton had a very high opinion, he advocated various plans for improving the condition of Ireland and for the repeal of the union, but was always opposed to physical force.

Haughton became a vegetarian in 1846, both on moral and sanitary grounds: for two or three years before his death he was president of the Vegetarian Society of the United Kingdom. He was one of the first members of the Statistical Society of Dublin (1847), a founder of the Dublin Mechanics' Institute (1849), and a member of the committee of the Dublin Peace Society. He aided in abolishing Donnybrook fair (1855), which had long been a target of temperance reformers owing to the alleged high incidence of drunkenness at the popular Dublin event, and took a chief part in 1861 in opening the botanic gardens at Glasnevin on Sundays. He was the author of *Slavery Immoral* (1847), *A Memoir of Thomas Clarkson* (1847), and *A Plea for Teetotalism and the Maine Liquor Law* (1855).

Haughton died at his home, 35 Eccles Street, Dublin, on 20 February 1873, and was buried in Mount Jerome cemetery on 24 February in the presence of a large crowd. He had married, but his wife died after only a few years. He was survived by one son and one daughter.

G. C. BOASE, *rev.* MARK CLEMENT

Sources S. Haughton, *Memoir of James Haughton* (1877) • A. J. Webb, *A compendium of Irish biography* (1878) • C. Kerrigan, *Father Mathew and the Irish temperance movement, 1838–49* (1992) • B. Harrison, *Drink and the Victorians: the temperance question in England, 1815–1872*, 2nd edn (1994) • *Freeman's Journal* [Dublin] (21 Feb 1873)

Archives Boston PL, letters and papers

Likenesses portrait, repro. in Haughton, *Memoir*

Wealth at death under £2000 (in England): probate, 11 March 1873, *CGPLA Ire.*

Haughton, John Colpoys (1817–1887), army officer, was born in Dublin on 25 November 1817, the son of Richard H. Haughton, professor of oriental languages at Addiscombe College, and his wife, Susanna. Sir Graves Champney Haughton was his uncle; his grandfather, Dr John Haughton, was an eminent Dublin physician.

Haughton was educated at Shrewsbury, and on 30 March 1830 was entered on the books of HMS *Magnificent*, receiving ship at Jamaica, as a first-class volunteer. His relative, Admiral Edward Griffiths Colpoys, was then commanding on the West India, North American, and Newfoundland station. On 11 May 1832 he was appointed midshipman to the *Fly*, and on 8 December 1834 to the *Belvidera*, both on the above station, but on 12 January 1835 he was invalided from the Royal Navy.

On 15 February 1837 Haughton obtained a Bengal cadetship, and on 9 December 1837 was appointed ensign in the 31st Bengal native infantry. He served in the First Afghan War of 1839–42 as adjutant of the 4th Gurkha regiment, in the service of Shah Shuja, commanded by Captain Christopher Codrington of the 49th Bengal native infantry. In April 1841 the 4th Gurkhas was sent to occupy Charikar, about 40 miles north of Kabul. Major Eldred Pottinger, who had shortly before become famous by his defence of Herat, was stationed at Laghman, 3 miles off, as political agent. On 2 November 1841, the day on which Sir Alexander Burnes was killed at Kabul, an attack was made on Laghman. After a gallant defence Pottinger took refuge in Charikar. Charikar was besieged by the insurgents, and gallantly defended from 5 to 14 November, despite being in the worst condition for defence. The insurgents amounted for some days to more than 20,000 men, and had control of the water supply. Pottinger was present only in a political capacity, and confined to his bed by a wound. Codrington was killed on 6 November, and the command then devolved on Haughton. On 14 November a mutiny occurred among some of the shah's gunners, in which Haughton was cut down and seriously wounded in the neck, shoulder, and arm. The same night the Gurkhas evacuated Charikar. Pottinger and Haughton, with his right hand freshly amputated, with his head hanging on his breast from the severing of his neck muscles, and held in his saddle by a faithful Gurkha orderly, got separated from their following, and eventually succeeded in reaching Kabul on 16 November, where they were received as men risen from the dead. Haughton published an account, *Char-ee-kar*, in 1867, and a revised edition in 1879.

When Elphinstone withdrew from Kabul at the end of December 1841, Haughton was unable to move, and stayed with a friendly chief until after the second advance of the British under General Sir George Pollock in September 1842. He then collected the remains of his late regiment, and returned with Pollock to India. On 15 December 1842 he was appointed lieutenant in the late 54th Bengal native infantry, his army rank dating from 16 July previous. On 8 January 1844 he was appointed second in command of the Bundelkhand police battalion.

On 16 June 1845, at Calcutta, Haughton married Jessie Eleanor, daughter of Colonel Presgrove, with whom he had four children, of whom two sons and a daughter survived him. On 23 February 1847 he was made first-class assistant to the governor-general's agent on the south-west frontier, and principal assistant on 24 December 1851. Awarded a brevet captaincy on 15 February 1852, he was appointed magistrate at Moulmein in Burma on 5 September 1853 and promoted captain on 15 November 1853. From 19 July 1859 he served as superintendent at Fort Blair and the Andaman Islands (promoted major on 18 February 1861), and from 17 March 1862 was deputy commissioner first class at Sibsagar. While acting commissioner he accompanied the expedition to the Khasi and Jaintia hills in 1862–3, and the Bhutan expedition of 1864–5. He was made brevet lieutenant-colonel on 15 February 1863, and full lieutenant-colonel three days later. From 16 May 1865 he served as commissioner at Cooch Behar, and also managed the large estates of the infant maharaja, who had been made his ward. He was made CSI in 1866 and brevet colonel on 15 February 1868, and accompanied the expedition to the Garo hills in 1872–3.

Haughton retired in 1873, returning to England to live in Gerrards Cross. In January 1874, his first wife having died, he married Barbara Emma, daughter of the Revd Canon Pleydell Bouverie; they had no children and she survived him. He was promoted major-general on 18 December 1880 and lieutenant-general on 1 April 1882. Haughton was over 6 feet in height, with a spare wiry frame capable of great physical endurance, aquiline features, and a kindly, resolute face. He died at 4 Sion Hill, Ramsgate, on 17 September 1887. H. M. CHICHESTER, *rev.* ALEX MAY

Sources Army List · Indian Army List · private information (1891) · J. C. Haughton, *Char-ee-kar, and service there with the Fourth Goorkha regiment*, 2nd edn (1879) · V. Eyre, *The military operations at Cabul, which ended in the retreat and destruction of the British army, January 1842* (1843) · T. A. Heathcote, *The Afghan wars, 1839–1919* (1980) · J. A. Norris, *The First Afghan War, 1838–1842* (1967) · J. W. Kaye, *History of the war in Afghanistan*, rev. edn, 3 vols. (1857–8) · *Friend of India* (10 July 1865) · CGPLA Eng. & Wales (1887)

Archives BL, corresp., letter-books, and papers, MSS Eur. B 135–136, D 490, 529–530

Likenesses lithograph, NPG

Wealth at death £3377 16s.: probate, 19 Nov 1887, CGPLA Eng. & Wales

Haughton, Matthew (*bap.* 1766, *d.* 1821). *See under* Haughton, Moses, the younger (1773–1849).

Haughton, Moses, the elder (*bap.* 1735, *d.* 1804). *See under* Haughton, Moses, the younger (1773–1849).

Haughton, Moses, the younger (1773–1849), miniature painter and engraver, the son of William Haughton (1737–1769), a gun locksmith, and his wife, Elizabeth, was born on 7 July 1773 in Wednesbury, Staffordshire, where he returned as an adult to be rebaptized, on 20 October 1807. About 1790 he went to Liverpool and was befriended by William Roscoe, whose portrait he painted; later he engraved the frontispieces for Roscoe's *Leo X* (1805). Haughton was reputedly a pupil of George Stubbs. He entered the Royal Academy Schools on 31 July 1795 as a student of engraving, although in January 1801 he had to

request reinstatement, perhaps because of his absence in Liverpool from 1798 to 1800.

Haughton's first engraving after Fuseli was the proposed frontispiece (not used) to Roscoe's *Nurse* (1798). Fuseli complained that Haughton had 'travestied' his figures but later praised his qualifications (*English Letters*, 187). In 1803 Haughton became Fuseli's resident engraver, and he paid the latter 100 guineas per annum to cover rent. In 1805, when Fuseli became keeper of the Royal Academy, Haughton accompanied him to Somerset House. Haughton engraved a total of fourteen large plates in stipple and aquatint after Fuseli, culminating with the grandiose *Vision of the Lazar House* (1813); nine of these were published as 'from the Royal Academy'. Haughton also engraved Fuseli's four illustrations to Erasmus Darwin's *Temple of Nature* (1803) and four to Joel Barlow's *Columbiad* (which were not used).

Although best known as Fuseli's engraver, Haughton was a successful miniaturist, who charged 5 to 8 guineas a head. He exhibited more than eighty portraits at the Royal Academy between 1804 and 1848, three paintings at the British Institution in 1840–41, and fourteen at the Liverpool Academy between 1810 and 1838. His portraits of Fuseli, Roscoe, and John McCreery were engraved. Haughton's designs for the booksellers included 105 for Edward Moor's *The Hindu Pantheon* (1810) and at least four drawings and two 'large miniature pictures' for the *British Gallery of Contemporary Portraits* (1813). In May 1819 he left Somerset House and moved to 86 Newman Street, thence to 38 Great Marlborough Street. By 1838 he was at 4 Percy Street, and from 1844 at 5 Percy Street. He married Elizabeth Sarah Blackburn on 2 August 1827 at St James's, Westminster; their son Moses Cartwright was baptized on 12 December 1828. The child's godmother was Fuseli's widow, Sophia, who resided from about 1825 in the Haughton household. Haughton died at his home in Percy Street on 26 June 1849.

His uncle, **Moses Haughton the elder** (*bap.* 1735, *d.* 1804), portrait and still-life painter, the second of the three sons of Moses Horton and Mary Tibbetts, was born at Wednesbury and baptized there on 27 March 1735. He was trained by an uncle, Hyla Holden, in his Wednesbury factory as a painter on enamel and in 1761 moved to Birmingham to work for John Baskerville and Henry Clay, manufacturers of superior enamelled, japanned, and papier-mâché ware. Typical articles decorated by Haughton were 'tripod salt-cellars and mustard pots with small landscapes in panels on pink, green or dark blue backgrounds' (Cope, 130).

The elder Haughton also executed numerous portraits, but his strength was as a painter of still life, most famously his *Dead Game* and *Kingfisher*. He executed twenty-six designs and sixteen drawings after biblical paintings (engraved by Robert Hancock) for Pearson and Rollason's *Holy Bible* (1788). Between 1788 and 1803 he exhibited six paintings at the Royal Academy (Graves has conflated the contributions of uncle and nephew). Three of his paintings formed part of Matthew Boulton's series of 'mechanical paintings' (*Burlington Magazine*, 112, 1970, 505, 507). On

10 January 1765 he married Elisabeth Austin (*b.* 1749) at St Martin's, Birmingham. He died on 24 December 1804 in Ashted, Birmingham, but was interred in St Bartholomew's Church, Wednesbury. There is a high-relief portrait of him in profile in St Phillip's Cathedral, Birmingham.

His only son, **Matthew Haughton** (*bap.* 1766, *d.* 1821), painter and engraver, was born in Birmingham and baptized there at St Martin's Church on 10 October 1766. He entered the Royal Academy Schools on 19 November 1790 as a student of engraving. In the mid-1790s he settled in Liverpool and became a protégé of William Roscoe, for whom he executed (1795) a miniature and engraved fourteen vignettes for the *Life of Lorenzo de' Medici* (1796). He also executed (1794) 'an ambitious watercolour, *L'Allegro*, somewhat in Samuel Shelley's allegorical manner' (Williams, 148). He died on 24 March 1821 at West Bromwich, bequeathing his cousin Moses '1 shilling and a volume of Dr. Young's *Night Thoughts*'.   D. H. WEINGLASS

Sources *The collected English letters of Henry Fuseli*, ed. D. H. Weinglass (1982), 187, 189–90, 250, 256, 263–6, 270–71, 279, 291, 294, 295–6, 300, 307, 313, 324–5, 345–6, 376–7, 384, 386–91, 398, 400, 406, 412–13, 417, 419, 446, 515–16, 521, 534, 543, 558–9 · D. H. Weinglass, *Prints and engraved illustrations by and after Henry Fuseli* (1994), xxx–xxxii; nos. 150, 173–6, 178–9, 188, 226, 256–60, 263–6, 284–6, 288, 293 · Graves, *RA exhibitors* · Graves, *Brit. Inst.* · S. Wildman, *The Birmingham school* (1990), 33–4 · D. Foskett, *A dictionary of British miniature painters*, 2 vols. (1972) · T. Cope, *Bilston enamels of the 18th century* [1980], 120–30, 139 · *GM*, 1st ser., 74 (1804), 1250 · Farington, *Diary*, 6.2255; 10.3513; 12.4371; 14.4961 · Bénézit, *Dict.* · Bryan, *Painters* · Thieme & Becker, *Allgemeines Lexikon* · Getty Provenance Index, vol. 3/1, 472 · S. Morris and K. Morris, *A catalogue of Birmingham and west midland painters of the nineteenth century* (1974) · *The life of William Hutton* (1816); repr. (1998), 137 · I. O. Williams, *Early English watercolours and some cognate drawings by artists born not later than 1785* (1952); repr. (1970), 147–8 · d. cert. · *IGI* · E. Morris and E. Roberts, *The Liverpool Academy and other exhibitions of contemporary art in Liverpool, 1774–1867* (1998)

Archives Lpool RO, Roscoe papers, papers to W. Roscoe · Yale U., receipts to Cadell & Davies

Likenesses G. Shepheard, pen-and-ink drawing, 1796, Birmingham Museums and Art Gallery · M. Haughton the elder, self-portrait, oils, exh. RA 1800 · M. Haughton the younger, self-portrait

Haughton, Samuel (1821–1897), geologist and physiologist, was born on 21 December 1821 in Carlow, Ireland, the second of three sons of Samuel Haughton (1786–1874), merchant, and his wife, Sarah (*d.* 1861), who was the daughter of John Hancock, a linen merchant from Lisburn. The Haughtons were descended from a Quaker family established in Ireland during the Cromwellian settlements. Samuel was brought up within the Church of Ireland, as his father had withdrawn from active membership of the Society of Friends at the time of his marriage, but his upbringing undoubtedly reflected the Quaker tradition to which so many of his relatives and close family friends adhered. Growing up in the Carlow countryside, in the fertile and attractive valley of the River Barrow, stimulated his interest in natural history and the environment: this interest was further encouraged by the local rector, whose school in Carlow the boy attended.

Samuel Haughton (1821–1897), by Sarah Purser, 1883

Haughton entered Trinity College, Dublin, in 1838. He studied mathematics, obtaining a gold medal in 1843, and was elected to fellowship the following year. The fellowship examination was a formidable one and it was quite unusual to succeed, as Haughton did when he was only twenty-two, at the first attempt. His early scientific work was in mathematical physics. A paper entitled 'On the laws of equilibrium and motion of solid and fluid bodies', published in the *Cambridge and Dublin Mathematical Journal* in 1846, won him the Cunningham medal of the Royal Irish Academy and he published various other papers on fluid dynamics and wave propagation. From his teacher and colleague James MacCullagh he had also acquired an interest in the refraction of light within crystalline media. This led him to a wider interest in mineralogy and it was presumably on the basis of this that he was deemed eligible for appointment to the chair of geology which became vacant in 1851. He was professor for thirty years until he was required to resign on becoming a senior fellow in 1881. Throughout that time he was diligent in promoting and developing his subject.

Haughton's geological work encompassed a wide span including aspects of regional geology, stratigraphy, palaeontology, mineralogy, petrology, and structural geology. He calculated the age of the earth on the basis of sedimentary thicknesses and estimated rates of deposition. His first results suggested about 2000 million years but he subsequently revised this result, reducing it by a factor of ten. Climatic change was another of his interests; in this context he calculated the effect of geological changes on the direction of the earth's axis, carried out detailed calculations of solar radiation, and also examined the effect of ocean currents on climate. He examined the distortion of fossils, drawing conclusions from this about rock development, and carried out chemical rock analyses. He established the Trinity Mining Company, which in 1854 opened a copper mine at Ardtully in co. Kerry, but this venture was not a commercial success. He was an expert on tides, correlating and analysing observational data from Irish coastal stations and producing detailed tables. Later he carried out similar analyses of data from the Arctic seas. He used his tidal calculations to throw light on the sequence of events at the battle of Clontarf in 1014 and to examine the evidence at a murder trial which had taken place ten years previously.

Fellows of Trinity College were normally required to take holy orders and Haughton was ordained a priest in the Church of Ireland in 1847. Although not obliged to undertake any particular pastoral function, he took his orders seriously and preached regularly throughout his life. Many of his sermons were published: these display his robust and confident religious faith. His view of the world, profoundly shaped by his firmly held, biblically founded religious beliefs, was one with which Darwin's evolutionary theories did not appear to be reconcilable.

In 1859 Haughton, although by that time well established as a professor and a scientist of recognized standing, chose to become a medical student and, while still retaining his fellowship and his chair, pursued the Trinity medical course for three years, graduating MB in 1862. It is said that as a boy he had the idea that he might one day work as a medical missionary in China; this may have been a factor in drawing him towards his medical studies, but it is likely that his primary motivation was scientific. Studies of animal fossils had stimulated an interest in the anatomy and physiology of vertebrates and Haughton used his training in anatomy to pursue this through an ongoing investigative programme of detailed dissection. His investigations were not limited to human subjects. Drawing on material available from the Dublin Zoo, of which he had become a council member in 1860, he compiled data from over a hundred dissections of large animals. One account describes how, when a hippopotamus died, he rushed to the zoo armed with saws and butcher's knives and spent forty-eight hours dissecting the huge beast.

Haughton's particular interest in these comparative anatomical studies was to understand the detailed basis of muscular action. He became convinced that the very different modes of organization of limbs and muscles in the wide range of animal species which he had examined could all be explained in terms of the principle of least action, which he took from mathematical physics and reformulated in the following terms: that the muscular action is organized in such a way that the work done in performing a particular limb movement is less than would be the case for any alternative form of muscular arrangement. These conclusions, and the detailed basis for them, were set out in his book *Animal Mechanics*, published in 1873. One conclusion which he drew from this

work was that, as far as bones, muscles, and joints are concerned, the permanence and stability of each species is absolutely secured. He was quite satisfied that his studies lent no support to the Darwinian postulate that the similarities found to exist in the bones, muscles, and joints of animals may be explained by common descent from a supposed common ancestor. It was clear to him that each limb and its mode of action had been planned by a foreseeing mind.

One application of Haughton's physiological studies which gained him some notoriety was his investigation of the practice of execution by hanging. In a paper published in 1866 in the *Philosophical Magazine* he put the case on humane grounds for a significantly longer drop than was normally used, so as to ensure instantaneous death. He derived a formula for the length of drop as a function of the weight of the unfortunate 'patient' (as the doomed individual is described in the paper). The scientific interest in the vertebrates went hand in hand with a genuine affection for animals. Haughton's dog, shown with him in Sarah Purser's portrait, was a constant companion. The zoo, which he served as secretary and later as president, was a special interest. The building known as the Haughton House was erected after his death by public subscription in recognition of his outstanding services.

Although Haughton never engaged in clinical practice, he none the less exercised a major influence on Irish medicine. In 1863 the Trinity board appointed him registrar of the medical school, a post he held for fifteen years during which time he introduced substantial reforms despite a sometimes strained relationship with the clinical professors. He also represented the university on the General Medical Council. He served on the board of Sir Patrick Dun's Hospital for thirty-four years, becoming its dominant figure. It was his initiative that led to the extension of the hospital from a purely medical one to include surgical as well as obstetric and gynaecological services. To encourage students in their clinical work he endowed clinical prizes and medals in both medicine and surgery, leaving the residue of his estate for that purpose.

The fact that Trinity graduates were particularly successful in obtaining coveted positions in the Indian Civil Service was significantly due to Haughton and his colleague J. A. Galbraith, who introduced courses to prepare candidates for the Indian Civil Service competitive examination. Haughton and Galbraith also collaborated in writing a series of elementary manuals on various topics in mathematics and physics, and at Haughton's initiative the college established a lectureship in pathology in 1895, and erected a building to house that activity. He was deeply interested in education at both school and university level. He contributed to the public debate in the 1860s on the future of the Irish universities: he maintained that Trinity College should continue to be linked with the Church of Ireland, but was not averse to the setting up of a college for Catholics and dissenters should a genuine demand for this become evident. Haughton was also an active member of the Royal Irish Academy, to which he had been elected in 1845, and was its president from 1886 to 1891. He was elected to the Royal Society in 1858, and received various other honours including honorary degrees from Bologna, Cambridge, Edinburgh, and Oxford.

Haughton's wife, Louisa (1828–1888), *née* Haughton, was a half-first cousin—her father and his were half-brothers. They had four sons and two daughters, one of whom died in infancy. Louisa died in 1888 and Haughton died at his home at 12 Northbrook Road East in Dublin on 31 October 1897. Following a funeral service in the college chapel his remains were buried in the family plot at Killeshin church, just outside Carlow, on 3 November.

T. D. SPEARMAN

Sources W. J. E. Jessop, 'Samuel Haughton', *Hermathena*, 116 (1973), 5–26 · N. D. McMillan, 'Revd. Samuel Haughton and the age of the earth controversy', *Science in Ireland, 1800–1930: tradition and reform*, ed. J. Nudds, N. McMillan, D. Weaire, and S. M. Lawlor (1988), 151–62 · D. Spearman, 'Samuel Haughton', *More people and places in Irish science and technology*, ed. C. Mollan, W. Davis, and B. Finucane (1990), 36–7 · P. W. Jackson, ed., *In marble halls: geology in Trinity College Dublin* (1994) · R. B. McDowell and D. A. Webb, *Trinity College, Dublin, 1592–1952: an academic history* (1982) · T. Ó Raifeartaigh, *The Royal Irish Academy: a bicentennial history, 1785–1985* (1985) · D. Coakley, *Irish masters of medicine* (1992) · T. G. Moorhead, *A short history of Sir Patrick Dun's Hospital* (1942) · *DNB* · D. J. C., *PRS*, 62 (1897–8), xxix–xxxvii · *The Times* (1 Nov 1897) · *The Times* (4 Nov 1897) · *Irish Times* (1 Nov 1897) · *Irish Times* (4 Nov 1897) · Burke, *Gen. Ire.* (1976) · private information (2004)
Archives Meteorological Office, Bracknell, Berkshire, National Meteorological Library and Archive, meteorological journal relating to Ennistimon and Ballyaughan · priv. coll. · TCD, papers | CUL, letters to Sir George Stokes
Likenesses S. Purser, oils, 1883, TCD [*see illus.*] · S. Purser, oils
Wealth at death £5422 7s. 5d.: probate, 25 Jan 1898, *CGPLA Ire.*

Haughton, William (d. 1605), playwright, was probably born in the mid-1570s, since Philip Henslowe called him 'yonge horton' in November 1597 (*Henslowe's Diary*, 72). Cooper's assertion that he was incorporated MA at Cambridge in 1604 is based upon a misreading of the name 'Langton', but Baugh suggests that he may have had some connection with Oxford because of his favourable comments about that institution. An apparent reference in Philip Henslowe's diary to 'will hamton sadler' led Chambers to suggest that Haughton was related to William Houghton, saddler, who held a house in Turnmill Street in 1577, but Foakes and Rickert read the reference as 'will hauton fidler' (*Henslowe's Diary*, 295). Haughton was living in London by 1594, when he married Alice Agar on 22 March at St Mary Abchurch.

Haughton wrote his first known play, *Englishmen for my Money, or, A Woman will Have her Will*, for the Lord Admiral's Men at Henslowe's Rose Theatre in early 1598. The plot concerns a Portuguese usurer living in London, Pisaro, who wants to marry his three daughters against their wills to a Dutchman, a Frenchman, and an Italian. The daughters instead love three witty young Englishmen who have become indebted to Pisaro after being swindled by him. After much amusing trickery, the three English youths outwit Pisaro to marry his daughters and cancel their debts. Many elements of this plot were familiar to Elizabethan audiences, but Haughton was the first to combine them in a contemporary London setting, making *Englishmen for my Money* the first of the immensely popular genre of London city comedies. The play was entered in the Stationers' register in 1601, but the earliest surviving edition is from 1616, with further editions in 1626 and 1631.

Between August 1599 and May 1600 Haughton wrote a dozen plays for Henslowe's Admiral's Men, many in collaboration with other playwrights. Eight of these are now completely lost: 'Beech's Tragedy' (with John Day), 'The Arcadian Virgin' (with Henry Chettle), 'The Seven Wise Masters' (with Day, Chettle, and Thomas Dekker), 'Strange News out of Poland' (with 'Mr. Pett'), and 'The Poor Man's Paradise', 'Ferrex and Porrex', 'The English Fugitives', and 'Judas' (alone). Another collaboration with Day, 'Cox of Collumpton', survives only in a description in the diary of astrologer Simon Forman, who saw it at the Rose on 9 March 1600. This bloody domestic tragedy told the story of Cox, who slays his uncle for his land but is himself slain seven years later to the day. Two of his sons subsequently kill their brother and later commit suicide. These various deaths occur, as Forman notes, 'all on St Markes dai' (Cerasano, 158).

Two of Haughton's collaborations from this period do survive. The first of these is the moral comedy *Patient Grissil*, written with Dekker and Chettle in early 1600 and printed in 1603. It elaborates a familiar story, previously told by Chaucer and Boccaccio, in which the nobleman Gwalther cruelly tests his humbly born wife, Grissil, before ultimately proclaiming his true love. Haughton is probably responsible for two sub-plots, in which a Welsh knight woos and wins the widow Gwenthyan (much as in Shakespeare's *Taming of the Shrew*) and Gwalther's sister Julia entertains and rejects three foreign suitors (much as in *Englishmen for my Money*).

Haughton also collaborated with Dekker and Day in early 1600 on a play called 'The Spanish Moor's Tragedy', now generally identified with *Lust's Dominion*, printed in 1657 with a dubious attribution to Christopher Marlowe. This revenge tragedy about the evil Spanish Moor Eleazar is strongly influenced by Marlowe and by Shakespeare's *Titus Andronicus*, but it also shows clear signs of Dekker's hand. Haughton's contribution was small, perhaps limited to scenes involving the friars Crab and Cole. Hoy suggests that the 1600 version was a revision of an older play, with John Marston also contributing to the revision.

Haughton's final surviving play is the comedy *Grim the Collier of Croydon, or, The Devil and his Dame*, written in 1600 but not published until 1662. Although the printed version is attributed to 'I. T.' (perhaps a reviser), Henslowe paid Haughton in May 1600 for 'a Boocke wch he wold calle the devell & his dame' (*Henslowe's Diary*, 134), and Baillie and Sykes summarize the strong internal evidence for Haughton's authorship. The main plot centres around Belphegor, a devil sent from hell disguised as a Spaniard to test the shrewishness of earthly women. He marries the sharp-tongued shrew Mariana, who cuckolds him with three different lovers before poisoning him, sending him back to hell in disgrace. Haughton skilfully weaved his plot from various sources, primarily Machiavelli's *Marriage of Belfagor* and the pamphlet *Tell-Trothes New-Yeares Gift* (1593), but this play was the first to have a devil as such a central character, and it inspired numerous other devil plays.

After a seven-month absence, Haughton wrote or co-wrote nine plays, all now lost, for Henslowe's companies between December 1600 and November 1601. These included 'Robin Hood's Pen'orths' (by himself), '2 and 3 The Blind Beggar of Bednal Green', 'The Six Yeomen of the West', '2 Tom Dough', and 'Friar Rush and the Proud Woman of Antwerp' (with John Day), 'The Conquest of the West Indies' (with Day and Wentworth Smith), and '1 and 2 The Six Clothiers' (with Smith and Richard Hathway). After one final play for the Admiral's Men in September 1602 called 'William Cartwright' (also lost), Haughton disappears from the theatrical record. However, he may be the author of the anonymous plays *Wit of a Woman* (1604) and *Wily Beguiled* (1606).

Because the name is relatively common, Haughton's non-theatrical activities are difficult to trace. Henslowe lent 10s. to have Haughton released from the Clink prison on 10 March 1600, and directly lent Haughton 4s. the following June, suggesting that the playwright's finances were precarious. Baugh suggests plausibly that he was the William Haughton who was taxed on £3 of goods in October 1599 in St Botolph, Aldgate, London. On 6 June 1605 Haughton made his nuncupative will in neighbouring All Hallows Staining, with his fellow playwright Wentworth Smith as a witness. He gave all his goods, valued at £19 1s., to his wife, Alice, toward the raising of their children. He probably died within a day or two.   DAVID KATHMAN

Sources A. C. Baugh, introduction, *William Haughton's 'Englishmen for my money, or, A woman will have her will'* (1917), 7–92 · *Henslowe's diary*, ed. R. A. Foakes and R. T. Rickert (1961) · E. K. Chambers, *The Elizabethan stage*, 4 vols. (1923), vol. 3, pp. 334–6 · W. M. Baillie, 'Grim the collier of Croydon: introduction', *A choice ternary of English plays* (1984), 171–200 · H. D. Sykes, 'The authorship of *Grim, the collier of Croydon*', *Modern Language Review*, 14 (1919), 245–53 · Cooper, *Ath. Cantab.*, vol. 2 · C. Hoy, *Introductions, notes, and commentaries to texts in 'The dramatic works of Thomas Dekker'*, edited by Fredson Bowers, 4 vols. (1980), 1.129–47; 4.56–73 · M. B. Rose, 'Where are the mothers in Shakespeare? Options for gender representation in the English Renaissance', *Shakespeare Quarterly*, 42 (1991), 291–314 · E. A. J. Honigmann and S. Brock, eds., *Playhouse wills, 1558–1642: an edition of wills by Shakespeare and his contemporaries in the London theatre* (1993), 75–6 · S. P. Cerasano, 'Philip Henslowe, Simon Forman, and the theatrical community of the 1590s', *Shakespeare Quarterly*, 44 (1993), 145–58 · IGI [parish register of St Mary Abchurch, London]

Archives Dulwich College, London, signature and other handwriting, Henslowe's diary, MS VII

Wealth at death £19 1s.: probate act book, GL, MS 9168/16, fol. 10v, as cited by Honigmann and Brock, *Playhouse wills*, 76

Hauksbee, Francis (*bap.* **1660**, *d.* **1713**), natural philosopher and scientific instrument maker, was baptized on 27 May 1660 in the parish of St Mary-at-the-Walls, Colchester, the fifth of five sons born to Richard Hauksbee (*b.* 1621), a draper and common councillor of Colchester, and his wife, Mary. Hauksbee entered Colchester grammar school in 1673, and from 1678 to 1685 was apprenticed as a draper in the City of London, initially to his eldest brother, John. He was married to Mary (*d.* after 1730) by May 1687, when a daughter was born. Five out of eight children survived infancy: Ann, Mary, Francis, Richard, and Calvin; Francis graduated BA from the Queen's College, Oxford, in 1722. Hauksbee took the freedom of Colchester (by patrimony) in 1710 and was free of the Drapers' Company in 1712.

Nothing is known of Hauksbee's move from drapery into the emerging and fashionable business of mathematical and scientific instrument making. He was praised in John Harris's *Lexicon technicum* (1704) as one of six 'Ingenious and Industrious Artificers' (Preface). He made air-pumps and pneumatic engines from premises in the City's Giltspur Street, near the pioneering mathematical school of Christ's Hospital, where he had lived since at least March 1701. Isaac Newton certainly knew of his reputation: Hauksbee was admitted at the first meeting of the Royal Society under Newton's presidency on 15 December 1703. He demonstrated a new air-pump and the intriguing, unstable phenomenon of 'mercurial phosphorus' (actually an electrostatic discharge), showing that his ability was already rare. Thereafter he experimented regularly before the society; the work made his name.

In 1704 Hauksbee expanded into the more genteel and 'philosophical' business of public lecturing, and engaged the experienced James Hodgson to teach a course in experimental philosophy. Hauksbee's performances in 1704 rehearsed his staple pneumatic experiments, but from April 1705, when Newton was revising his *Opticks*, he returned to the mercurial phosphorus. He became FRS on 30 November 1705, his status the lowest among the gentry elected hitherto. He offered an important and dramatic experiment at the next meeting, when a 'fine *purple* Light, and *vivid*' was produced by a glass sphere rotated rapidly against woollen cloth. The light diminished when air was let in, suggesting that it depended neither upon mercury nor air.

Hauksbee's success at the society stemmed from his usefulness to Newton. The new president revived the tradition of weekly experiments, specifically to further his research into light, magnetism, and other phenomena suggesting the existence of active principles or attractive effluvia. Besides the wide-ranging nature of his experiments, Hauksbee's particular skill was the development of apparatus that rendered 'Effluvia more remarkably conspicuous and … pleasing to the eye of a Spectator' (*Physico-Mechanical Experiments*, 52)—and thereby more investigable. From Newton's acknowledgements and Hauksbee's use of Newtonian discourse, one infers that Newton was Hauksbee's philosophical master. In return, Hauksbee made many highly novel and significant experimental discoveries, especially in the field of electricity. Indeed, the society left experimenting to Hauksbee and filled its *Philosophical Transactions* with his accounts, which he collated in his *Physico-Mechanical Experiments on Various Subjects* (1709); a posthumous second edition, including later work, appeared in 1719.

In accordance with Newton's speculation that light was

an emitted effluvium, Hauksbee pursued in 1706 the effects of friction upon large evacuated glass tubes. When he found that air-filled tubes emitted no light, but crackling sounds, he recognized the similarity to well-known 'electric' effects. His improved apparatus, of sturdy glass tubes and small pieces of leaf brass, enabled him to observe attraction, repulsion, the effect later known as 'electric wind', and the screening effect of muslin. It quickly became standard equipment.

Hauksbee then developed the first continuous generator of static electricity, using a glass globe rapidly rotated by a geared handle and rubbed, and a primitive electroscope, a semicircle of wire from which dangled woollen threads. Placed around the globe, the threads straightened as if they were attracted to the centre of the globe, suggesting that electricity was a centripetal force like gravity, but caused by the emission of effluvia. Placed inside the globe, threads were repelled from the centre. Despite his Newtonian distaste for 'Vain Hypotheses', Hauksbee philosophized that the globes had 'some little Resemblances of the Grand Phenomena of the Universe' (*Physico-Mechanical Experiments*, 57). Such highly visual experiments changed Newton's theory of forces from one of action at a distance to one of 'subtle effluvia' modelled on electricity.

Hauksbee's second ground-breaking experimental series, on 'the ascent of liquors', was equally Newtonian. In 1708 came the first methodical work on capillarity, showing that it varied with the internal diameter of the tube, but not the thickness. To prove that the attractive forces were possibly universal, Hauksbee demonstrated the rise of liquids between plates not only of glass but also of marble and brass, and showed the attraction also to operate in a vacuum. Later he produced 'a very Curious Experiment', which Newton related to the 'Congruity or Agreement of the Parts of Matter' (Royal Society, *Journal Book*, 24, 31 Jan 1712). This developed into a series in which drops of liquid were trapped between a horizontal glass base plate and another plate on top, angled down from the top of the drop to the base. Surface tension sucked the drop into the angle, and Hauksbee found a relationship between the angle and the force required to move the drop. In his last work, concluding on 29 January 1713, he confirmed Brook Taylor's conjecture that the meniscus between two plates of glass, inclined at a slight angle to each other, resembled a hyperbola.

In at least ninety experimental performances Hauksbee also investigated prisms, gunpowder, thermometers, and various engines. He carried out more sustained work on the refractive indices of liquids, combustion and respiration, and attempts at a law of magnetic attraction. He also read numerous papers, and was on hand to impress the society's visitors with his striking experiments.

By 1709 Hauksbee had relocated to Wine Office Court, and by 1712 to Hind Court, both off Fleet Street and near to the Royal Society's house at Crane Court. After the publication in 1709 of his internationally acclaimed *Physico-Mechanical Experiments* he appears to have given lectures himself, and was sought out as a natural philosopher by visiting foreigners such as Abraham Vater and Zaccharius von Uffenbach.

By January 1712 the science business was more competitive. Francis *Hauksbee junior, son of his brother John, established a rival instrument shop in Crane Court itself, and advertised the educated Humphry Ditton as his lecturer. Hauksbee immediately counter-advertised a course of experiments, based on his Royal Society work, and stressed that he was 'the only Person to whom the late Improvements are owing' (*Daily Courant*, 14 Jan 1712). In the summer he engaged the renowned but theologically disgraced William Whiston, who went on to lecture for Francis junior from March 1713. After Hauksbee's death the rising star Jean Theophilus Desaguliers briefly lectured for his widow. Although the venture failed, it was Desaguliers, not the ambitious Francis junior, who filled Hauksbee's position at the Royal Society.

Hauksbee's *Physico-Mechanical Experiments* was translated into Italian (1716), Dutch (1735), and French (1754), and was widely read throughout the eighteenth century; it established his international reputation. The French introduction eulogized his experiments as the first exemplification of the systematic spirit in science and Hauksbee himself as possessing the four 'qualités dont la reunion forme le Physicien' ('qualities that together make up the natural philosopher'; Desmarest, xliii). The opinions of outsiders were not shared by his London colleagues, nor perhaps by Hauksbee. Presenting himself as 'undeserving' with a 'want of a learned Education' he merely proffered 'surprizing observations' to 'the Intelligent *Philosophical Reader*' (*Physio-Mechanical Experiments*, dedicatory letter). For Desaguliers, Hauksbee's experiments were not true philosophy because they followed no mathematical order.

Other fellows of the Royal Society did not treat Hauksbee as a natural philosopher. Although its curator of experiments *de facto*, he was never curator by office as had been Robert Hooke, his predecessor. He was treated as a servant, employed part-time, ordered to experiment, occasionally chastised, and given no fixed salary. The society's council remunerated him retrospectively 'as he deserves'. His deserts ranged from £15 to a maximum in 1707 of £40 'for his last years waiting upon the Society and shewing and trying their experiments' (Royal Society, council minutes, 2 July 1707). Hauksbee died in Hind Court, intestate, aged fifty-two, and was buried on 29 April 1713 in the churchyard of St Dunstan-in-the-West. The society acknowledged his death only by granting his widow £20 outstanding remuneration. In 1714 Mary was granted administration of a surely meagre estate. She moved to a Tower Hill almshouse, returned to drapery (taking three apprentices, including her son Calvin), and was given charity by the Drapers' Company in 1716 and, grudgingly, by the Royal Society in 1731.

STEPHEN PUMFREY

Sources journal book, 1703–13, RS · council minutes, 1703–13, RS · L. R. Stewart, *The rise of public science: rhetoric, technology, and natural philosophy in Newtonian Britain, 1660–1750* (1992) · S. Pumfrey,

'Who did the work? Experimental philosophers and public demonstrators in Augustan England', *British Journal for the History of Science*, 28 (1995), 131–56 · *Daily Courant* (1710–13) · N. Desmarest, 'Discours historique et raisonné sur les expériences de M. Hauksbee', in F. Hauksbee, *Expériences physico-mécaniques sur différents sujets*, trans. M. de Brémond, 2 vols. (1754) · J. Harris, *Lexicon technicum, or, An universal English dictionary of arts and sciences*, 1–2 (1704–10) · H. Guerlac, 'Francis Hauksbee: expérimentateur au profit de Newton', *Archives Internationales d'Histoire des Sciences*, 16 (1963), 113–28 · P. Boyd, 'Register of the apprentices and freemen of the Drapers' Company of London', Drapers' Company, London · freedom book, Drapers' Company, London, FA4 · quarterage book, Drapers' Company, London, QB10 · J. H. Round, ed., *Register of the scholars admitted to Colchester School, 1637–1740* (1897) · Colchester Borough Monday Court books, Essex RO, D/B 5 Cb1/25, fol. 97r · parish register, London, Holy Sepulchre without Newgate, GL, MS 7219/2–3 · parish register, St Mary-at-the-Walls, Colchester, 27 May 1660, Essex RO, D/P 245/1/2, 246/1/2 [baptism] · parish register, Earls Colne, Essex, Essex RO, D/P 209/1/2 · parish register, London, St Dunstan-in-the-West, 29 April 1713, GL, MS 10350 [burial] · bishop's commissary court act books, GL, MS 9168/32, fol. 8r · *London in 1710: from the travels of Zacharias Conrad von Uffenbach*, ed. and trans. W. H. Quarrell and M. Mare (1934)

Archives RS, classified letters and papers

Hauksbee, Francis

Hauksbee, Francis (1688–1763), instrument maker and lecturer on science, was born in April 1688 in London, the son of John Hauksbee of the Drapers' Company and his wife, Mary. He was the nephew of the instrument maker Francis *Hauksbee the elder (d. 1713). Hauksbee was apprenticed in 1703 to John Marshall, a noted optical instrument maker. In 1710, the German traveller Conrad Zacharias von Uffenbach met him at the elder Hauksbee's house in Wine Office Court, Fetter Lane, London. By 1712 uncle and nephew were in competition, the younger Hauksbee having set up as a rival instrument maker and experimental lecturer in Crane Court, near Fetter Lane, close to the new premises of the Royal Society. Thus began a career among the public scientific lecturers that emerged in the reign of Queen Anne. Here the younger Hauksbee forged links with the mathematician Humphry Ditton and with the controversial natural philosopher and theologian William Whiston.

With the death of his uncle in 1713, Hauksbee had the opportunity to assume many of the activities in which the elder Hauksbee had been concerned. He soon engaged with Whiston in a series of lectures that were to take place at the house in Crane Court. The nearby Royal Society from time to time called him in to demonstrate, especially before their foreign visitors, such as the duc d'Aumont. He did not however replace his uncle as permanent demonstrator, which post went to the rival lecturer and Newtonian experimentalist John Theophilus Desaguliers. Hauksbee soon advertised the production of scientific instruments like hydrostatic balances, reflecting telescopes, and air-pumps for which his uncle had been renowned. Hauksbee got into a dispute with Richard Bridger, a former apprentice to the elder Hauksbee, over the nephew's advertising of improvements to the air-pump.

Hauksbee was undeterred and became very active in the lecturing world, advertising courses given with Whiston at Crane Court. His co-operation with Whiston, who like Hauksbee failed to obtain the distinction of FRS, continued for many years. In 1715 Hauksbee took in subscriptions for Whiston, who was then proposing a new and highly ridiculed method for discovering longitude, which Whiston projected as a means for mapping the coasts of Britain. Whiston had long been interested in the problem of longitude and had hoped to plot coastal positions by means of the difference in time between the flash of an explosion and the time taken for the sound to travel. At least until 1727 Hauksbee was still giving 'A Course of Mechanical and Experimental Philosophy' with Whiston, in which Newton's improvements to the reflecting telescope were demonstrated, along with magnetical experiments and entertainments.

In 1723, ten years on from his first involvement with the Royal Society, in competition with many applicants who were better educated, Hauksbee was appointed to a secure post, not as demonstrator, but as housekeeper and clerk to the society. This position precluded the possibility of his election as fellow, and he was required to provide the then considerable but customary surety of £400–500. To what extent his family connections to the society were significant is unclear. During his tenure his widowed aunt, Mary Hauksbee, while carrying on her own trade as a draper, continued her late husband's instrument business for a short time, and also petitioned the society for a pension to assist in supporting the large family with which she had been left. Moreover, though he was not a fellow, Hauksbee appears to have frequented the Royal Society dining club at The Sun in St Paul's Churchyard, where the discussion frequently dealt with theological and natural philosophical issues.

Overshadowed by the reputation of his more famous uncle, whom the Royal Society had at least taken seriously as an experimentalist, the younger Hauksbee had to compete in the world of lecturers and inventors that developed in Hanoverian London. Hauksbee performed experiments while Whiston provided the explanations to subscribing audiences, which included the anatomist Alexander Monro *primus*, but they also published and sold printed versions of their courses with plates, which may have served to advertise Hauksbee's instruments. Hauksbee's connection with John Hadley, inventor of the optical sextant, led him to try manufacturing a reflecting telescope.

Hauksbee also forged an alliance with the chemist and physician Peter Shaw in the provision of lectures on chemistry. By 1731 they were marketing a portable laboratory for 'the improvement of Philosophy, Arts, Sciences, Trade and Commerce'. Hauksbee, perhaps because of his trade background, was alert to such commercial possibilities, and like many others at the time was involved with inventors who were eager to secure patents for their inventions. He collaborated with Benjamin Robinson, who in 1728 obtained a patent for a concoction that would allegedly preserve wood. There were many such claims at the time, especially in the almost desperate need to protect wooden pipes and ships' bottoms. In the same year

Hauksbee was similarly involved with the mining promoter Benjamin Lund in his patent for the manufacture of copper, brass, and silver. Hauksbee was an entrepreneur and about 1742 he entered into a partnership with the apothecary J. Watson, probably of the Strand, to market an alternative therapy for the treatment of venereal disease. In 1753 he was still advertising his cure in the daily press.

The identity of Hauksbee's wife is unknown; she probably predeceased him, for his six children were cared for by a widow, Mary Powell, at his house in St Paul's Churchyard. In his will Hauksbee left instructions that his clocks, his instruments and apparatus, his artificial jewels, the stocks of materials ready to be made up into the anti-venereal medicine, as well as his personal valuables, should be sold and the proceeds shared among his dependants. He died in London on 11 January 1763.

LARRY STEWART

Sources L. R. Stewart, The rise of public science: rhetoric, technology, and natural philosophy in Newtonian Britain, 1660–1750 (1992) · S. Pumfrey, 'Who did the work? Experimental philosophers and public demonstrators in Augustan England', British Journal for the History of Science, 28 (1995), 131–56 · S. D. Snobelen, Experimental lecture course advertisements in the Daily Courant, 1704–1728 (1995), vol. 1 of Archive of early eighteenth-century science advertisements · S. D. Snobelen, 'Selling experiment: public experimental lecturing in London, 1705–1728', master's diss., University of Victoria, 1995 · London in 1710: from the travels of Zacharias Conrad von Uffenbach, ed. and trans. W. H. Quarrell and M. Mare (1934) · W. Whiston and F. Hauksbee, An experimental course of astronomy [n.d., c.1714] · F. Hauksbee, Proposals for making a large reflecting telescope (1730?) · P. Shaw and F. Hauksbee, An essay for introducing a portable laboratory: by means whereof all the chemical operations are commodiously perform'd, for the purposes of philosophy, medicine, metallurgy, and a family (1731) · P. Shaw and F. Hauksbee, Proposals for a course of chemical experiments (1731) · J. Watson, An account of the effects of Mr Hauksbee's alternative medicine ... in the cure of venereal diseases, etc. (1742) · J. Watson, A further account of the effects of Mr Hauksbee's alternative medicine (1743) · E. G. R. Taylor, The mathematical practitioners of Tudor and Stuart England (1954) · G. Clifton, Directory of British scientific instrument makers, 1550–1851, ed. G. L'E. Turner (1995), 128 · M. B. Hall, The library and archives of the Royal Society, 1630–1990 (1992), 7–10, 60 · DSB, vol. 6
Archives RS | BL, letters to T. Birch, Add. MSS 4309–4443

Hausted, Peter (c.1605–1644), playwright and Church of England clergyman, was born in Oundle, Northamptonshire. His parentage is uncertain but William Hawsted, a yeoman of Oundle who testified at an inquest at Peterborough in 1603, may have been the poet's father. Hausted was probably educated at the free Oundle School before he matriculated as a sizar at Queens' College, Cambridge, in Easter term 1620. He proceeded BA in 1624 and MA in 1627 but remained at Cambridge for seven more years, studying divinity.

In 1623, while still an undergraduate, Hausted became involved in academic drama, playing the minor role Hirsutus in Robert Ward's anti-puritan allegorical satire Fucus histriomastix. Before 1630 he wrote 'Verses Made by Mr. Hausted in Amputationem comae suae' (BL, Add. MS 15227, fol. 83b), in which he seems to express reservations about acting. To this period may also belong Hymnus tabaci,

his translation of Raphael Thorius's poem, published posthumously in 1651.

In 1632 Hausted became embroiled in controversy when his comedy The Rival Friends was acted before the king and queen on 19 March with Hausted himself acting the leading role of Anteros. In Jonsonian fashion this play satirizes the abuse of poorer clergy by impropriation of parish churches, a practice opposed by King Charles. Despite the king's presence Hausted's play was ridiculed and cried down, in contrast to Thomas Randolph's play The Jealous Lovers, which was received much more favourably three days later. Hausted rushed his play into print with a long, defensive 'Preface to the reader' and commendatory verses by two of the actors in the play, Edward Kemp and John Rogers. Randolph, in turn, ridiculed Hausted in his Latin speech Oratio praevaricatoria in July, and more subtly in the printed version of The Jealous Lovers later the same year.

Hausted responded by having his Latin play Senile odium printed the following year, 1633, with commendatory poems by Edward King (Milton's Lycidas), Kemp, and Rogers, all praising and defending Hausted. The play itself had been written before The Rival Friends (a manuscript version survives in the marquess of Bath's collection at Longleat, G. drawer 9); it is a skilled comedy which shows deep knowledge of classical drama, especially that of Terence and Plautus, and also satirizes euphuism and alchemy. Another Latin play existing only in a manuscript dated 1635, Senile amor, has been attributed to Hausted but the attribution is rejected by Mills. The rivalry between Hausted and Randolph was ended by the latter's premature death in 1635, after which Hausted wrote the epitaph for Randolph's grave at the request of Sir Christopher Hatton.

In 1634 Hausted was appointed curate at Uppingham, Rutland, by Dr Edward Martin. On 2 November of that year he was preaching at Great St Mary's in Cambridge when his pointed criticisms of lax religious practices at the university caused him to be arrested on the spot, hauled through the streets, and suspended by a de facto tribunal. Martin, who described the event as 'the greatest uproare and concourse of people that ever I saw at any arraignment' (Mills, Peter Hausted, 39), upbraided his curate the next day but apparently forgave him. Two years later, in 1636, Hausted published Ten Sermons, with a dedication to Sir Christopher Hatton, and in 1638 he left Uppingham. Wood says that he became rector of Hadham, Hertfordshire, but there is no trace of him in the records there (Wood, Ath. Oxon., 2.29; Mills, Peter Hausted, 49).

Hausted became vicar of Gretton, Northamptonshire, on 13 March 1640 but upon the outbreak of civil war in 1642 he joined the royalist cause as chaplain with the earl of Northampton's forces. He may have written the royalist Satyre Against Separatists (1642) and almost certainly wrote Ad populem (1644); he also wrote a manuscript elegy on Colonel Robert Arden, who died in August 1643 (Bodl. Oxf., MS Ashmole 36–37, fol. 125). On 26 February 1643 he was appointed rector of Wold, Northamptonshire, through the influence of Hatton but he apparently never lived there. He died on 20 July 1644, on the second day of the siege at Banbury Castle, Oxfordshire, and was probably buried there.   DAVID KATHMAN

Sources L. J. Mills, *Peter Hausted: playwright, poet, and preacher* (1944) · M. P. Steppat, 'Peter Hausted', *'Senile odium', 'Senilis amor', 'Alphonsus'*, ed. M. P. Steppat and G. Schmitz, facs. edn (1991), 1–15 · Wood, *Ath. Oxon.*, 2nd edn, 2.29–30 · G. E. Bentley, *The Jacobean and Caroline stage*, 7 vols. (1941–68), vol. 4, pp. 532–7 · P. Elmen, 'The death of Peter Hausted', *N&Q*, 195 (1950), 16–17 · [P. Hausted], *Senilis amor*, ed. and trans. L. J. Mills (1952), 1–9 · L. J. Mills, 'The rival friends: a critical essay', *Peter Hausted's 'The rival friends'* (1951), xi–xvi · L. J. Mills, *Peter Hausted's 'Senile odium'* (1949), 8–9

Haute family (*per. c.*1350–1530), gentry, was active in Kent and Sussex from at least the early thirteenth century. Bishopsbourne, between Canterbury and Dover, was their principal residence from the end of the fourteenth century, and they acquired Ightham Mote, near Sevenoaks, through the marriage of **Sir Nicholas Haute** (1358–1416) and Alice, daughter of Sir Thomas Cawne, probably in 1389. Sir Nicholas was a Kentish MP and sheriff during the 1390s, and for the 1412 subsidy he was assessed at £122 6s. 8d., putting him among the wealthiest in the county. His eldest son, **William** [i] **Haute** (*c.*1390–1462), enjoyed the reputation of a capable soldier: he served in the duke of Gloucester's retinue for the Agincourt campaign in 1415, and he was appointed to his first two commissions of array in 1419 and 1420. He was also elected MP in 1419, and was appointed to the county bench in 1424, as well as serving a term as sheriff in 1420–21.

William [i] Haute's first marriage, to Margaret Berwyk, brought property in Berkshire, Somerset, and Buckinghamshire, but it was his second marriage, to Joan, daughter of Richard Woodville of Maidstone, in 1429, which laid the foundations for the family's significance in a wider sphere, by allying his family with that of a future queen of England. Woodville, who was captain of Calais, where William was serving when the marriage was contracted, was father of Richard *Woodville, first Earl Rivers, and grandfather of Queen *Elizabeth (*née* Elizabeth Woodville). The settlement suggests that William was very eager for this alliance with an up-and-coming family, even going so far as to disinherit his daughter from his first marriage. Later the same year he was again elected to parliament for Kent. He served with his father-in-law in France from 1434, and was among Woodville's executors in 1441. Simultaneously, he maintained links with members of Humphrey of Gloucester's circle, men like Geoffrey Louther, Gloucester's lieutenant as warden of the Cinque Ports, with whom he sat as MP in 1432. In April 1450 he was a Kentish commissioner of array, and was among those pardoned in July, in the immediate aftermath of the Cade rising, but he is unlikely to have sided with the rebels. In 1460 Haute was commissioned to resist the Yorkist earls, but he joined them after their landing in Kent. Although he was appointed to a Yorkist commission of array in January 1461, he was by then too old to play a significant part in the new regime. His will is notable for its mention of a number of religious relics, including the stone on which the archangel Gabriel stood during the annunciation. Haute was buried in the Austin Friary at Canterbury, next to his wives.

William [i] Haute's eldest son, **Sir William** [ii] **Haute** (*d.* 1497), was knighted at the coronation of his cousin Elizabeth Woodville as queen of England in 1465, and thereafter he was a mainstay of Kentish administration. Appointed sheriff in 1465, 1474, and 1482, JP from 1467, and a frequent commissioner, his only periods of rest from county service were enforced: the first during the readeption of Henry VI, the second during the reign of Richard III. He joined his Woodville cousins in their uprising against King Richard in October 1483, and after its failure he was among those for whose capture a reward was offered. He returned to favour under Henry VII. In his leisure time he composed music (including carols and polyphonic settings of the Benedicamus domino) and patronized musicians. His are the only known English amateur compositions before the reign of Henry VIII. He died on 2 July 1497, leaving Kentish property of an annual rental value of over £62.

The existence of two contemporary Richard Hautes with parallel careers complicates the family's later fifteenth-century history. The list of offices held by one or other of these two Richards is long: sheriff of Kent in 1477–8; JP from 1479 to 1481 for Kent, and for Essex, Gloucestershire, Hereford, Shropshire, and Worcestershire in the 1470s; MP for Canterbury in 1478, and on numerous Kentish commissions under Edward IV; carver to Queen Elizabeth Woodville from 1466 to 1469, and nominated by the queen as a justice in her forest eyre in 1477; among those who accompanied Margaret of Anjou to France in 1475; steward of Gower and constable of Swansea Castle from 1481 to 1483. But it can at least be said that the elder **Richard Haute** (*d.* 1487) was the son of William [i] and Joan, and that in 1469 or 1470 he married Elizabeth (*d.* after 1487), the daughter of Sir Thomas Tyrell and widow of Sir Robert Darcy of Danbury in Essex (which manor she brought to Richard). This Richard was probably lieutenant of the Tower from 1471 to 1473. He too rose in 1483, for which he was attainted and suffered forfeiture. This was reversed by Henry VII, under whom he served as a Kentish JP and justice of gaol delivery.

The mother of the younger Richard, **Sir Richard Haute** (*d.* 1492), was named Margery, and he may have been the son or grandson of Nicholas Haute (*b. c.*1395), William [i]'s younger brother. It was probably this Richard who was appointed to the household of the prince of Wales at Ludlow in 1473, although both Richards were active in south Wales and the marches. He was knighted in 1482, during Richard of Gloucester's Scottish campaign. Less than a year later he was among those members of the Woodville circle taken at Stony Stratford during Gloucester's *coup d'état*; but unlike Rivers, Grey, and Vaughan his life was spared, and he lived out Richard III's reign in quiet obscurity. After Bosworth, however, he made a successful return to court life: he was one of the bearers of Elizabeth of York's canopy at her coronation, a royal carver by 1488, and knight of the body three years later. He also served in a military capacity: he was part of the royal bodyguard during Henry VII's northern progress of Easter 1486, he fought at Stoke in 1487, and in 1488 he was at sea defending the channel. His final mission was to meet the French ambassadors come to sue for peace after the siege of Boulogne in 1492. He died in the December of that year, possibly while returning from France. He held property in Kent, Berkshire, Essex, and London. This Richard married first, in 1474, Eleanor, daughter of Sir Robert Roos of Northamptonshire; she died about 1486, and between then and 1489 he married Katherine Boston (*d.* 1493), the widow of Walter Wryttel and of John Green. Katherine was the heir to four of Wryttel's Essex manors. Richard seems to have had literary interests: he may have owned an English version of Christine de Pisan's *Livre du corps de policie*, perhaps translated by his friend, Anthony Woodville, while Eleanor was bequeathed a volume of French grail romances by her uncle, the poet and translator Sir Richard Roos, which she signed, 'thys boke ys myne dame Alyanor Haute' (BL, Royal MS 14 E. iii).

The Haute family's Woodville connections increased its members' value on the marriage market. In 1468 or 1469 Anne Haute, probably William [i]'s daughter, was betrothed to Sir John Paston of Norfolk. This relationship persuaded the Woodvilles to promote Sir John's interests at court, but did not lead to marriage, and the Pastons had to procure an expensive papal dispensation to annul it.

The Woodville connection brought other Hautes into the court circle, among them Edmund (*d.* 1488?), who may have been a son of Nicholas, the younger brother of William [i], and who became Queen Elizabeth's carver, and **Martin Haute** (*fl.* 1466–1483), possibly his brother. Martin was a yeoman of the king's household and receiver of the queen's Northamptonshire properties from 1466 (and remained receiver until the end of Edward IV's reign), and ten years later he was described as a servitor and usher of the chamber to Queen Elizabeth. His son, James [i] Haute, followed his father into royal service, and in September 1485 he was granted the stewardship of Hanslope, Northamptonshire. He was one of three contemporaneous James or Jakes Hautes in the Yorkist and early Tudor period, whose separate identities and careers are impossible to disentangle. **James** [ii] **Haute** (*d.* 1505x8) was the son of William [i] Haute, and father, by his marriage to a woman named Katherine, of Edward (*d.* 1537?), of Alan (*fl.* 1518–1529), and of Henry Haute [*see below*]. This James was pardoned in 1483, when he was described as of London, late of Bishopsbourne, Kent, and late of Harpenden, Hertfordshire, where he had held the manors of Annables and Kingsbourne Hall since at least 1473. He was probably a member of Elizabeth of York's household from at least 1502, and it may have been this James who organized court festivities from 1494 to 1501. James [iii] Haute was probably dead by 1496. One of these three was a member of the royal household by 1469, and in 1482 one was granted the reversion of the keepership of the exchange and mint at the Tower, to be held for life. More surprisingly, one James did not join the rest of his family in opposing Richard III, and in March 1484 was rewarded for his good service against the rebels with the grant of the elder Richard Haute's confiscated Kentish properties, including Ightham Mote, to the annual value of over £28 (this property was returned to Richard by Henry VII in November 1485). This was probably the James who seems to have died by 1496: the ready acceptance of the others into the Tudor court may argue against Ricardian sympathies on their part.

Henry Haute (1474–1508), the son of James and Katherine Haute, was an apostolic protonotary at the age of twelve in 1486, and four years later he went up to Oxford with a letter of recommendation from his cousin, Elizabeth of York. From 1495 he was rector of Great Hallingbury in Essex and Hothfield in Kent, and in 1498 he became a canon of Salisbury. Hothfield was a royal advowson, and in 1500 he was a chaplain in Henry VII's entourage at his meeting with Archduke Philip at St Pierre, near Calais. He may have been a member of the household of William Blount, Lord Mountjoy, who had humanist interests, and he was working on 'Les petites oeuvres contemplatives' (BL, Royal MS 16 E. xiv), a French translation of works by Erasmus and Pico della Mirandola, when he died in January 1508.

Edward Haute (1476–1530), the son and heir of Richard Haute and Elizabeth Tyrell, established himself as a London mercer (he also imported wine and woad), in which trade he was associated with his cousins Alan and Henry, the sons of James and Katherine. Edward did not have a head for business. In 1514 his property in Wrotham, Ightham, and Dover was confiscated to pay his debts. To satisfy his creditors he also sold his manor of Bearsted in Wrotham in 1518, and the Newark-on-Trent property of his wife, Elizabeth, daughter of Thomas Frognal, in 1528. In July 1518 he mortgaged Ightham Mote for £360; in December he sold his remaining share, and the house passed out of the family: in 1521 it was bought by Sir Richard Clement. After a spell in Ludgate prison for debt Edward died in Ireland in 1530, whither he had presumably fled from his many creditors. His wife was still alive in 1544.

PETER FLEMING

Sources P. Fleming, 'The Hautes and their "circle": culture and the English gentry', *England in the fifteenth century*, ed. D. Williams (1987) · C. Meale, 'The manuscripts and early audience of the Middle English prose Merlin', *The changing face of Arthurian romance*, ed. A. Adams, A. Diverres, and others (1986), 92–111 · *Chancery records* · *A descriptive catalogue of ancient deeds in the Public Record Office*, 6 vols. (1890–1915) · *LP Henry VIII*, vol. 1/1 · *CIPM, Henry VII*, 1, nos. 373–895; 2, no. 145 · J. C. Wedgwood and A. D. Holt, *History of parliament*, 1: *Biographies of the members of the Commons house, 1439–1509* (1936), 435–7 · W. G. Davis, *The ancestry of Mary Isaac, c.1549–1613* (Portland, Maine, 1955), 102–54 · P. Fleming, 'The character and private concerns of the gentry of Kent, 1422–1509', PhD diss., U. Wales, 1985
Archives BL, Add. MS 5665 · BL, Royal MS 16 E. xiv [Henry Haute] · Magd. Cam., MS Pepys 1236, fols.124v–125 | BL, charters, Harley MSS · BL, Royal MS 14 E.iii [Eleanor Haute] · PRO, early chancery proceedings, C1
Wealth at death at least £62 annual rents—Sir William [ii] Haute: *CIPM, Henry VII*, 2, no. 145 · at least £16 annual rent—Richard Haute (*d.* 1487: *CIPM, Henry VII*, 1, no. 373

Haute, Edward (1476–1530). *See under* Haute family (*per. c.*1350–1530).

Haute, Henry (1474–1508). *See under* Haute family (*per.* c.1350–1530).

Haute, James (d. 1505×8). *See under* Haute family (*per.* c.1350–1530).

Haute, Martin (*fl.* 1466–1483). *See under* Haute family (*per.* c.1350–1530).

Haute, Sir Nicholas (1358–1416). *See under* Haute family (*per.* c.1350–1530).

Haute, Richard (d. 1487). *See under* Haute family (*per.* c.1350–1530).

Haute, Sir Richard (d. 1492). *See under* Haute family (*per.* c.1350–1530).

Haute, William (c.1390–1462). *See under* Haute family (*per.* c.1350–1530).

Haute, Sir William (d. 1497). *See under* Haute family (*per.* c.1350–1530).

Hauville, Jean de [John de Hauteville] (d. 1200?), poet, was probably Norman by birth, rather than English as was once believed. Hauville, near Rouen, has been suggested as a possible birthplace. Little is known about his life, but the fact that he was still young in 1184, when he composed his only known work, the Latin satirical poem *Architrenius*, makes a date c.1150 (or perhaps even slightly later) likely for his date of birth. The name Magister Johannes de Hauvilla appears on Rouen Cathedral witness lists of 1199, suggesting that by then he had become a master at the cathedral school. It was most likely at Rouen that Jean taught the noted grammarian, Gervase of Melkley, who refers to the *Architrenius* and his former tutor in his prose *Ars poetica* (1216). There is, however, no reason to believe that Jean de Hauville was a monk of St Albans, as claimed by the Benedictine Hugh Legat in his fifteenth-century commentary on *Architrenius*. Legat's work was also the source of Bale's assertion that Hauville had connections with Oxford, another claim now considered to be false. It is thought that Jean died in 1200.

Jean de Hauville's only known work, the nine-book hexameter epic *Architrenius*, was dedicated to Walter de Coutances at the time of the latter's translation from the bishopric of Lincoln to the archbishopric of Rouen in 1184. The title *Architrenius* means 'Arch-mourner'; the poem relates how the narrator, lamenting humanity's natural tendency towards vice, seeks out Nature for an explanation. On his journey, the arch-mourner travels through the various institutions of medieval life and the familiar subjects of twelfth-century satire: the church, the court, the schools. In all of these places he discovers nothing but greed, pride, arrogance, and ambition. The narrator eventually encounters the ancient philosophers, who lecture him on the vices and the need for self-discipline. At the end of his journey he finds Nature; she reveals to the arch-mourner that moral philosophy is the solution to the problems of the world, and presents him with the maiden Moderation as a bride.

Although modern scholarship has deprived Jean de Hauville of all his personal English connections, his *Architrenius* nevertheless made a significant contribution to medieval England's intellectual formation. It was known, for instance, to Walter of Wimborne in the thirteenth century and Thomas Walsingham in the fourteenth, and copies of it survive in several manuscripts in English collections. In 1872 Thomas Wright published it in his Rolls Series compilation, *The Anglo-Latin Satirical Poets and Epigrammatists of the Twelfth Century*. Late twentieth-century editions and translations by Schmidt (1974) and Wetherbee (1994) have made Hauville's work accessible to a modern readership. VICTORIA CHRISTINE APPEL

Sources Johannes de Hauvilla, *Architrenius*, ed. and trans. W. Wetherbee (1994) · Johannes de Hauville, *Architrenius*, ed. P. G. Schmidt (Munich, 1974) · A. G. Rigg, *A history of Anglo-Latin literature, 1066–1422* (1992) · A. G. Rigg, 'Satire', *Medieval Latin: an introduction and bibliographical guide*, ed. F. A. C. Mantello and A. G. Rigg (1996) · Emden, *Oxf.*, 2.886 · R. Sharpe, *A handlist of the Latin writers of Great Britain and Ireland before 1540* (1997) · T. Wright, *The Anglo-Latin satirical poets and epigrammatists of the twelfth century*, 1; Rolls Series, 59 (1872) · *DNB* · Gervase of Melkley, *Ars poetica*, ed. H.-J. Gräbener (1965)

Havard [Harvard, Haverd], **William** (1710–1778), actor and playwright, was born on 12 July 1710 in Dublin, the son of a vintner. He was briefly apprenticed to a surgeon before he moved to London in 1730. His first noteworthy acting appearance was as Fenton in *The Merry Wives of Windsor* for Henry Giffard's company at Goodman's Fields Theatre on 10 December 1730; this inaugurated a career on the London stage, confined almost exclusively to supporting roles, which was to last for nearly four decades. He remained at Goodman's Fields, playing a wide range of minor parts, until 1736, when he moved with Giffard to the Lincoln's Inn Fields Theatre; when this closed a year later he joined Charles Fleetwood's company at Drury Lane. Apart from brief spells at Covent Garden, in Bristol and Dublin, and on tour in the north of England between 1740 and 1747, Havard remained at Drury Lane for the rest of his working life. On 22 May 1745 he married the actress Elizabeth Kilby, who acted periodically at Drury Lane as Mrs Havard, and the pair took up residence in Hanover Street, Longacre.

From 1747, when David Garrick took over the management of the theatre, to his retirement in 1769, Havard was a stalwart of the Drury Lane company, 'the graceful, reliable wheelhorse for excellency in supporting roles' (Stone and Kahrl, 25). Although he occasionally aspired to major roles (Prospero in *The Tempest*, Ford in *The Merry Wives of Windsor*, Plume in Farquhar's *The Recruiting Officer*) he was generally cast as middle-ranking courtiers, ministers, and citizens. His competent approach to his craft was regarded with polite appreciation and affection rather than admiration. Contemporary accounts refer to his solid dependability and amiability, but also to his predictability and lack of range; his supporters usually preferred to stress his personal virtues—his amiability, intelligence, and sound moral character—rather than make great claims for his histrionic prowess. Havard's solid diligence was not immune to satirical attack: in *The Rosciad* (1761) the

William Havard (1710–1778), by Edward Fisher, 1773 (after Thomas Worlidge)

Revd Charles Churchill wrote of 'poor Billy Havard' whose 'easy vacant face proclaimed a heart, Which could not feel emotions, nor impart'. Even Garrick, who maintained an enduring friendship with Havard, could not resist a slightly barbed comment in the epitaph he composed for his gravestone:

> Howe'er defective in the mimic art,
> In real life he justly played his part!
> The noblest character he acted well,
> And heaven applauded—when the curtain fell.

Havard enjoyed some modest success as a playwright and poet. His *Scanderbeg*, which appeared in 1733, was played twice: it was not well received, and provoked the accusation that Havard had plagiarized its plot from a play by Thomas Whincop then in Giffard's possession. Both Havard and Giffard denied the charge. His tragedy *Regulus* was more successful, and was first performed with Garrick in the title role in 1744. Havard's most durable and highly regarded play, however, was *King Charles I*, billed as 'an historical play' written 'in imitation of Shakespear', which played to large audiences at Lincoln's Inn Fields over three months in 1737, and which ran to ten editions between 1737 and 1810. According to Tate Wilkinson, a performance of the play in Hull in 1777 or 1778 was also the occasion of 'a melancholy accident', where a young female member of the audience 'in almost a second after the play finished … dropped down dead'. While the part played by Havard's play in her untimely demise is unclear, it is a measure of the sensitivity of its subject matter and of the volatility of opinion over the theatre at the time that the incident provoked some debate: 'some urged that

the melancholy of the tragedy had affected her senses: the enemies of the theatre were certain it was Divine judgement, as a punishment for her being in so profane a place as the devil's house' (Wilkinson, 2.7–8). Havard also wrote occasional verses, on subjects ranging from the death of a friend's dog to the duke of Cumberland's return from the battle of Culloden. His 'Ode to the Memory of Shakespeare' was set to music by William Boyce and performed at Drury Lane in 1756; reprinted in the *London Chronicle* of 7 April 1757, it was, characteristically, attended by the kind of faint praise that greeted its author's stage appearances: 'lofty jargon Mr Harvard [*sic*] has not aspired to, but has modestly contented himself with uniting both sentiment and suitable diction' (Vickers, 289). In 1769 Havard wrote to Garrick offering the ode as a contribution to the latter's Stratford jubilee: although the offer was declined, Garrick's own ode for the occasion not only had a number of echoes of Havard's but also appropriated a number of its lines.

If Havard's talents were widely perceived by his contemporaries as limited in scope, he was none the less a popular actor, and a gregarious, well-liked, and respected individual. He retired from the stage for reasons of ill health in 1769 and settled in Tavistock Street (his wife, Elizabeth, had died five years previously, on 27 April 1764). He remained there until his death on 20 February 1778, and was buried on 26 February in the churchyard of St Paul's, Covent Garden. ROBERT SHAUGHNESSY

Sources Highfill, Burnim & Langhans, *BDA* • *The private correspondence of David Garrick*, ed. J. Boaden, 2 vols. (1831–2) • T. Wilkinson, *The wandering patentee, or, A history of the Yorkshire theatres from 1770 to the present time*, 4 vols. (1795) • P. Fitzgerald, *The life of David Garrick* (1899) • B. Vickers, ed., *Shakespeare: the critical heritage*, 4: *1753–1765* (1976) • G. W. Stone and G. M. Kahrl, *David Garrick: a critical biography* (1979)
Archives Folger, manuscript book and MSS
Likenesses E. Fisher, mezzotint, 1773 (after T. Worlidge), BM, NPG, Harvard TC [*see illus.*]

Havell family (*per. c.*1775–1934), artists and publishers, came to prominence with **Luke Havell** (*d.* 1810) and **Daniel Havell** (*d.* 1825/6). The exact relationship of these two men, who represent the two branches of the Havell family, remains unclear but it is thought that they were either brothers or cousins. They came from an ancient but impoverished Reading family and it was not until the artistic talents of the farmhand Luke Havell were brought to the attention of the local squire that he was apprenticed to a local signwriter named Cole. Soon afterwards he was appointed drawing-master at Reading School and set up a modest print shop, also in Reading. In 1778 he married Charlotte Phillips (*d.* 1825) and they had fourteen children including Edmund Havell senior (1785–1864) who took over his father's business and succeeded to his post at Reading School. With his wife, Maria Binfield, Edmund had three sons: Edmund Havell junior (1819–1894), Charles Richard Havell (1827–1892), and George Havell (*d.* 1840), who all became practising artists and printmakers specializing in landscape and topography. Of these three, Edmund set his sights much wider than his siblings and after training under Benjamin Robert Haydon, he regularly exhibited paintings in London and also visited the USA, where he exhibited work in Philadelphia. Among their grandfather Luke's other artistic offspring were Frederick James Havell (1801–1840/41), who worked in line engraving and mezzotint, and his much more successful older brother William *Havell (1782–1857), the genre and landscape painter, who was born in Reading on 9 February 1782. William Havell earned a reputation for his sensitive lakeside views in the manner of J. M. W. Turner. The best known of these were, undoubtedly, his designs for *Twelve Picturesque Views of the River Thames* (1812), a series of coloured aquatint plates engraved and published by his uncle Daniel and his cousin **Robert Havell senior** (1769–1832), who was born in Reading on 29 December 1769. This was the first collaborative work between the two branches of the Havell family.

Although born in Reading, Daniel Havell moved to London, where he worked for publishers such as Rudolph Ackermann who specialized in aquatint. His first commercial venture with his son Robert Havell senior was on Henry Salt's *Twenty Four Views Taken in St. Helena* (1809–10); however, this partnership was short-lived and in 1816 Daniel was working independently at 5 Charles Street, Covent Garden. His last series of aquatints were commissioned for Edward Wedlake Brayley's *Historical and Descriptive Accounts of the Theatres of London* (1827), which appeared after he died in 1825 or 1826.

After severing business relations with his father Daniel, Robert Havell senior set up at 79 Newman Street in Fitzrovia, London. With his wife, Lydia Miller Phillips, he had a son, **Robert Havell junior** (1793–1878), a printmaker and painter, who was born in Reading on 25 November 1793. The firm of R. Havell & Son produced lavish suites of aquatints; the first was *A Series of Picturesque Views of Noblemen's & Gentlemen's Seats* (1814–23), followed by a variety of projects such as a *Series of Views of the Public Buildings & Bridges in London* (1821–2) or *Views in the Himala Mountains* (1820), after the designs of the traveller J. B. Fraser. The Havells' most famous enterprise commenced in 1827 when, following a failed relationship with William Lizars of Edinburgh, the celebrated American ornithologist John James Audubon commissioned a series of plates to illustrate his *Birds of America* (4 vols., 1827–39). Such was the magnitude of this project that the Havells had to employ fifty new staff and move to larger premises at 77 Oxford Street which they proudly named the Zoological Galleries, as a reference to their new-found artistic speciality. On 21 November 1832, the year after this expansion, Robert Havell senior died and was buried at St Pancras, London. From this time Robert junior was completely responsible for the production of Audubon's 435 ornithological plates, which are noted for their skill, accuracy, and subtle colour tones.

During this period Robert Havell junior established a firm friendship with Audubon and, following the untimely deaths of his two young sons in 1829 and 1838, Robert and his wife Amelia Jane Edington (d. 1878), whom he had married in 1824, decided to emigrate to America. On their arrival in 1839 they stayed with Audubon in New York and Havell's first American publication was a *Panoramic View of New York* (1840). Although he continued as an aquatint engraver, during the following few years Havell began to focus on oil painting and after moving to Tarrytown, in upstate New York, in 1857 he became a leading member of the Hudson River school, exhibiting over seventy-five canvases of American landscapes. He died on 11 November 1878 and it is fitting that he was buried in Sleepy Hollow cemetery, overlooking the Hudson which he loved so much.

The last member of the Havell family to come to prominence in the art world was Ernest Binfield *Havell (1861–1934), teacher of art and specialist in Indian art who was born in Reading and was a great-nephew of William Havell. After training at the South Kensington School of Art and studying in Italy and Paris in the early 1880s, he left Europe to teach art in India. In 1884 he was appointed superintendent of the Madras School of Industrial Arts and in 1896 moved to the Calcutta School of Art. During the next forty years he published sixteen polemical studies on the history and state of Indian art and craft and was an ardent supporter of the first Indian nationalist art movement. He died in Oxford on 30 December 1934, when the Havell family's prominence in the art world came to an end. LUCY PELTZ

Sources J. R. Abbey, *Scenery of Great Britain and Ireland in aquatint and lithography, 1770–1860* (1952); repr. (1972) • Redgrave, *Artists* • R. Hyde, 'Robert Havell junior: artist and acquatinter', *Maps and prints: aspects of the English book trade*, ed. R. Myers and M. Harris (1984), 81–108 • *DAB* • F. Owen, 'The life and work of William Havell', in F. Owen, *William Havell, 1782–1857: paintings, watercolours, drawings and prints* (1981), esp. 7–18 [exhibition catalogue, London, Reading, and Kendal, 24 Nov 1981 – 10 April 1982] • E. J. Stanford, *Nineteenth century painters and engravers: the Havell family* (1973) [exhibition catalogue, Reading Museum and Art Gallery, 10 Feb – 17 Mar 1973] • E. Stanford, *William Havell, 1782–1857* (1970) [exhibition catalogue, Reading Museum and Art Gallery, 20 Feb – 21 Mar 1970] • J. Turner, ed., *The dictionary of art*, 34 vols. (1996) • G. A. Williams, 'Robert Havell, engraver of Audubon's *The birds of America*', *Print Collectors' Quarterly*, 6 (1916), 227–57 • Graves, *RA exhibitors* • Graves, *Soc. Artists* • Bénézit, *Dict.*, 3rd edn • Thieme & Becker, *Allgemeines Lexikon* • E. B. Havell, *The basis for artistic and industrial revival in India* (1912); repr. (New Delhi, 1986) • *The Times* (7 Nov 1883), 6 • *The Times* (31 Oct 1904), 4 • *The Times* (1 Jan 1935) • P. Mitter, *Much maligned monsters: history of European reactions to Indian art* (1977)

Archives Reading Museum Service, 'A reminiscence of Sobury Farm on the banks of the Thames' (1857) MS in sketchbook [William Havell]

Likenesses W. Havell, self-portrait, oils, 1830, V&A • A. J. Havell, watercolour, c.1845 (Robert Havell junior) • Rockwood, photograph, 1851 (Robert Havell junior) • C. L. Elliot, oils (Robert Havell junior), Pennsylvania Academy of Fine Arts, Philadelphia

Havell, Daniel (d. 1825/6). See under Havell family (per. c.1775–1934).

Havell, Ernest Binfield (1861–1934), artist and art teacher, was born on 16 September 1861 at 1 Jesse Terrace, Reading, the second son and third child in the family of three sons and two daughters of Charles Richard Havell, professional artist, and his wife, Charlotte Amelia Lord. The *Havell family had been leading artists and publishers since the late eighteenth century. He was educated at Reading

School, and trained at the Royal College of Art, at Paris studios, and in Italy. Havell joined the Madras School of Industrial Arts as principal in 1884, a post he held until 1892, when he returned to England. He won early recognition with his report on Indian industrial arts, thus laying the foundations of his later influential doctrine on the Indian arts. The revival of traditional handloom weaving initiated by him was later to win the support of M. K. Gandhi.

Appointed principal of the Calcutta School of Art and keeper of the Government Art Gallery in 1896, a post he held until 1906, Havell was responsible for momentous changes in the art school curriculum which led to the first Indian nationalist art movement, the Bengal school of painting, under the artist Abanindranath Tagore. Although a believer in raj paternalism, Havell's aesthetically radical, anti-Renaissance, arts and crafts tenets, and his synthetic vision of architecture as unifying all the different traditional arts of India, helped undermine the primacy of salon art in India, hitherto identified as one of the triumphs of the raj westernization of the subcontinent.

Even though his period in Calcutta was extremely brief—for he was forced to retire in 1906 after a breakdown—Havell became celebrated in the West and in India for advocating the greatness of Indian art with a fervour that bordered on fanaticism. He was largely responsible for its recognition in the West: by his pioneering studies in ancient Indian art, such as *Indian Sculpture and Painting* (1908) and *The Ideals of Indian Art* (1911); by encouraging the fledgeling Bengal School with sustained writings on its behalf; and finally by helping to found the India Society with William Rothenstein, for many years the bastion of Indian culture in Europe. The society was set up in 1910 in the aftermath of the controversy surrounding the disparaging remarks of Sir George Birdwood about Indian art.

Although Havell was away from Britain between 1916 and 1923 as a member of the British legation in Copenhagen, 'India was his first and remained his only love.' He plunged headlong into the controversy over the architectural style for New Delhi, urging the imperial government to adopt the Mughal style for its new capital as a gesture of goodwill towards their Indian subjects. The appointment of Sir Edwin Lutyens as the city's architect put an end to Havell's dream. None the less the pronounced Indian elements in the otherwise classical design of New Delhi were a tribute to Havell's persistence.

Havell married Lili, daughter of Admiral George Jacobson, of the Danish royal navy, in 1894; they had one daughter. He died on 30 December 1934 at the Acland Nursing Home, Oxford, and was survived by his wife.

PARTHA MITTER, rev.

Sources *The Times* (1 Jan 1935) · P. Mitter, *Much maligned monsters: history of European reactions to Indian art* (1977) · private information (1993) [S. Wilson, B. Vibart] · *WWW*, 1929–40 · O. Tamal, 'E. B. Havell: the art and politics of Indianness', *Third Text* 1997, 39 (summer 1997), 3–19 · b. cert. · d. cert. · *CGPLA Eng. & Wales* (1935)
Archives BL OIOC, corresp. and papers, MS Eur. D 736
Wealth at death £8854 8s. 3d.: probate, 2 March 1935, *CGPLA Eng. & Wales*

Havell, Luke (d. 1810). *See under* Havell family (*per. c.*1775–1934).

Havell, Robert, senior (1769–1832). *See under* Havell family (*per. c.*1775–1934).

Havell, Robert, junior (1793–1878). *See under* Havell family (*per. c.*1775–1934).

Havell, William (1782–1857), landscape painter, was born in Reading on 9 February 1782, the son of Luke *Havell (d. 1810) [*see under* Havell family (*per. c.*1775–1934)], a drawing-master and printseller, and his wife, Charlotte Phillips. The third of fourteen children, William Havell is now considered as the most talented of his artistic family. Despite his natural talent it is said that his father did not want him to become an artist and so he was given a classical education, between 1794 and 1797, at Reading grammar school, where his father was drawing-master. Nevertheless, the determined and adventurous spirit that characterized Havell's career was quickly evident; through practice and observation he taught himself to paint in watercolours and adopted a style much influenced by the work of J. M. W. Turner. In 1802 he made his first tour of Wales during which he amassed an extensive number of *plein air* sketches; during this trip he also met up with other young artists such as watercolourists Cornelius Varley (1781–1873) and Joshua Cristall (1768–1847).

In 1804 Havell moved from Reading to London and quickly joined a number of London-based sketching societies where he gained a reputation as an acute observer of nature. In the following year he was invited to become one of the founder members of the new Society of Painters in Water Colours and remained an active member and exhibitor until 1816, specializing in lakeside and Thames subjects. During this time he also regularly exhibited oil paintings, many of which were worked up from his watercolour sketches, at the Royal Academy and the British Institution. He also produced commissioned designs for a number of topographical publications including John Britton's *Architectural Antiquities of Great Britain* (1814) and for *Twelve Picturesque Views of the River Thames* (1812), a series of coloured aquatint plates engraved and published by his uncle Daniel Havell and his cousin Robert Havell senior. He also made a number of sketching tours, for example to Hastings in 1812, and continued to exhibit his landscapes at the Society of Painters in Water Colours, the Royal Academy, and the British Institution.

Havell's alleged desire for acclaim and his impetuous nature are evident in the events surrounding his oil painting of *Walnut Gathering at Petersham* (1815), which was rejected by the British Institution and failed to attract a buyer. After complaining vociferously to the British Institution, and being ridiculed in the press for doing so, Havell took on a commission to accompany William Pitt, Earl Amherst of Arracan, on an embassy to China which departed in February 1816. After landing in August that year, Lord Amherst was abruptly dismissed for refusing to *kowtow*, in the Chinese court. Thus Havell was left in China without purpose or protector. He quickly obtained a passage to India and was established in Madras by 1820, where he supported himself by painting portraits; he also turned his hand to sketching landscapes and scenes of local life. After ten years abroad, during which he suffered cholera and yellow fever, he left India on 14 January 1826 on the *Alfred* bound for Liverpool.

Once back in England, Havell began again to exhibit with the revived Society of Painters in Oil and Water Colours, many of his subjects being drawn from his Chinese and Indian experiences. Dogged by ill health and enjoying only limited success, Havell journeyed to Italy to join the painter Thomas Uwins (1782–1857) who noted in a letter to his brother David Uwins from Naples, 1 July 1828, 'Havell is now with me' (Uwins, 2.109), and in October that year he wrote to his other brother, Zechariah, that 'Havell and I have taken a house at the foot of Vesuvius' (ibid., 2.132). There he hoped not only to improve his health but also to tailor his style to the Neapolitan subjects which were popular among British patrons. This was not to be the case and after his return in 1829 Havell concentrated on oil painting, again with only limited success. He also developed an interest in early photography and read a paper to the Chalon Society in 1839. After the failure of an Indian bank resulting in the loss of all his savings, Havell eventually became a recipient of the Royal Academy's Turner Fund for the relief of poor artists in 1856. His final years were impoverished and lonely and he died, unmarried, in Kensington, on 16 December 1857 and was buried at Kensal Green cemetery.   LUCY PELTZ

Sources J. R. Abbey, *Life in England in aquatint and lithography, 1770–1860* (privately printed, London, 1953); repr. (1972) · J. R. Abbey, *Scenery of Great Britain and Ireland in aquatint and lithography, 1770–1860* (1952); repr. (1972) · J. R. Abbey, *Travel in aquatint and lithography, 1770–1860*, 2 vols. (1956–7); repr. (1972) · Bryan, *Painters* (1903–5) · A. Bury, 'William Havell', *Old Water-Colour Society's Club*, 26 (1948), 1–18 · W. Foster, 'British artists in India, 1760–1820', *Walpole Society*, 19 (1930–31), 1–88 · Graves, *RA exhibitors* · Graves, *Soc. Artists* · Graves, *Brit. Inst.* · F. Owen, 'The life and work of William Havell', in F. Owen, *William Havell, 1782–1857: paintings, watercolours, drawings and prints* (1981), 7–18 [exhibition catalogue, London, Reading, and Kendal, 24 Nov 1981 – 10 April 1982] · Mallalieu, *Watercolour artists* · J. L. Roget, *A history of the 'Old Water-Colour' Society*, 2 vols. (1891) · E. Stanford, *William Havell, 1782–1857* (1970) [exhibition catalogue, Reading Museum and Art Gallery, 20 Feb – 21 Mar 1970] · S. Uwins, *A memoir of Thomas Uwins*, 2 vols. (1858)
Archives Reading Museum Service, MS in sketchbook, 'A reminiscence of Sowbury Farm on the banks of the Thames'
Likenesses W. Havell, self-portrait, oils, V&A; repro. in Owen, *Life and work*

Havelock, Sir Arthur Elibank (1844–1908), colonial governor, born at Bath on 7 May 1844, was the fifth surviving son in a family of six sons and seven daughters of Lieutenant-Colonel William *Havelock (1793–1848) and his wife, Caroline Elizabeth (d. 1866), the eldest daughter of Major Acton Chaplin of Aylesbury. He was a nephew of Sir Henry Havelock. In 1846 the family went to India, where his father commanded the 14th light dragoons at Ambala. After his father's death, during the battle of Ramnagar on 22 November 1848, the Havelocks went back to England, but returned to India in August 1850 and settled at Ootacamund in the Nilgiri hills. Havelock attended Mr Nash's school there, but completed his education in England at a private school at Lee, near Blackheath, London (1859–60).

In 1860 Havelock entered the Royal Military College, Sandhurst, and on 14 January 1862 was gazetted ensign in the 32nd Cornwall light infantry. Having been promoted lieutenant on 10 April 1866, he was stationed at Gibraltar (1866–7), at Mauritius (1867–8), and at the Cape (1868–72). He married, on 15 August 1871, Anne Grace (d. 6 Jan 1908), the daughter of Sir William Norris; they had one daughter. In August 1872 Havelock returned to Mauritius, where he acted as paymaster; he was promoted captain on 1 February 1873, and served as aide-de-camp successively to the acting governor, and then to Sir Arthur Gordon (afterwards Lord Stanmore), the governor. From February 1874 to 1875 he was chief civil commissioner in the Seychelles, and from 1875 to 1876 colonial secretary and receiver-general in Fiji. After returning to England in 1876 he joined the colonial civil service, and he retired from the army with the rank of captain in March 1877. In the same year he went to the West Indies as president of Nevis, and in August 1878 was transferred to St Lucia as administrator. In 1879 he returned to the Seychelles as chief civil commissioner, and in 1880 was made CMG.

In February 1881 Havelock became governor of Sierra Leone and the west African settlements. Before assuming office he acted as British commissioner at a conference in Paris for the provisional demarcation of boundaries between Sierra Leone and French Guinea. During his administration he was actively engaged in a frontier dispute with the republic of Liberia: on 20 March 1882, by order of the Colonial Office, he went to Monrovia with four gunboats and demanded from the Liberian government the immediate extension of the British protectorate to the River Mafa and an indemnity of £8500 for British merchants. A treaty was signed to this effect, stipulating that Havelock should intercede with the British government to fix the River Mano as the frontier, and that Liberia should be repaid all the sums she had spent in acquiring territories west of the Mano. The Liberian senate refused to ratify the treaty and Havelock returned to Monrovia with the gunboats on 7 September 1882. His diplomacy averted hostilities, but the senate would not give way, and in March 1883 Havelock quietly occupied the territories claimed by the British government between the rivers Sherbro and Mano. The boundary between Sierra Leone and Liberia was eventually defined in 1903 by a mixed commission.

In 1884 Havelock was created KCMG, and the following year he served as governor of Trinidad. In 1886 he became governor of Natal. The colony was in a financial depression, and administrative difficulties were increased by the annexation of Zululand in May 1887 and Dinizulu's unsuccessful rebellion in 1888. Havelock returned to England in 1889 and served on the international anti-slavery commission at Brussels. In 1890 he was appointed governor of

Ceylon, where he carried out the railway extension to Kurunegala and Bandarawela, and abolished the obnoxious 'paddy' tax, or levy on rice cultivation.

Havelock was nominated governor of Madras in 1895, and became a vigorous champion of its interests. He defied orders from the Calcutta government to allow the Mecca pilgrim ships to touch at Madras. His action was later justified by the comparative immunity of the Madras presidency from the plague of 1899 and 1900. He was made GCMG in 1895, GCIE in 1896, and GCSI in 1901, when he left Madras. In poor health, in 1901 he refused the governorships of the Straits Settlements and of Victoria, but later accepted the more congenial governorship of Tasmania. He resigned in 1904 and retired to Bishopstone, Torquay. He died at Bath on 25 June 1908, less than six months after his wife. Competent and painstaking, Havelock was a humane and sympathetic administrator.

G. S. WOODS, *rev.* LYNN MILNE

Sources B. J. T. Leverton, 'Havelock, Sir Arthur Elibank', *DSAB* · G. B. Cartland, 'Havelock, Sir Arthur Elibank', *AusDB*, vol. 9 · *The Times* (26 June 1908) · *WWW* · *Madras Weekly Mail* (2 July 1908) · private information (1912) · *CGPLA Eng. & Wales* (1908)

Archives BL OIOC | BL, Hamilton-Gordon MSS · BL OIOC, Hamilton MSS · Bodl. Oxf., Wodehouse MSS · Bodl. RH, corresp. with Francis Ernest Colenso · CKS, Stanhope MSS

Likenesses photograph, Natal Archives, Pietermaritzburg

Wealth at death £23,776: administration with will, 8 Aug 1908, *CGPLA Eng. & Wales*

Havelock, Sir Henry (1795–1857), army officer, was born on Easter day, 5 April 1795, at Ford Hall, Bishopwearmouth, near Sunderland, second son of William Havelock (1757–1837), shipbuilder and shipowner, and Jane, daughter of John Carter, solicitor, of Stockton-on-Tees. She gave her children a strict religious upbringing and her premature death in 1810 came as a grievous shock to young Henry. While he was still a child the family moved to Ingres Park, Dartford, Kent, and Henry was sent with his elder brother William to the Charterhouse in London. Intended for the law, he was a student at the Middle Temple in 1813–14. Unfortunately his father lost his money, through solicitors' fraud and the loss of uninsured ships, and the failure in 1820 of the London firm of Howard and Gibbs, through which he had been speculating in mortgages and annuities. He had to move to Clifton, and later to Teignmouth. Henry was thrown on his own resources in 1814, having quarrelled with his father, but with his brother William's help, and against his father's wishes, he joined the army. William had already done so and had distinguished himself at Waterloo.

Havelock joined the 95th foot (Rifle brigade) and was commissioned second lieutenant on 30 July 1815, spending the next eight years at home on garrison duties. He was fortunate to serve under Captain (later Major-General Sir) Harry Smith, a truly professional soldier, who encouraged Havelock to study his profession. He decided to try his fortunes in India (where his brothers William and Charles Frederick were already serving), but not before he had made intensive studies in Hindustani and Persian at the Oriental Institute; he then exchanged into the 13th foot (Somerset light infantry) which was under orders for

Sir Henry Havelock (1795–1857), by Frederick Goodall, c.1857

India. He was now a lieutenant but dependent solely on his pay in an army ruled by purchase of promotion. He sailed for India on 3 January 1823, in the contingent of his regiment commanded by Major Robert Sale, who was to play an important part in Havelock's career. An even more important part was that played by a fellow subaltern, James Gardner, who rekindled Havelock's deep religious faith, an evangelical theology which became the guiding principle of his life.

The regiment was bound for Calcutta, and there, soon after his arrival, Havelock met Bishop Heber. He also became a regular visitor to the Baptist mission station based in the Danish enclave at Serampore, where he met doctors Carey and Joshua *Marshman, whose daughter Hannah he later married. Less than a year after their arrival in India the 13th embarked for Rangoon for the First Anglo-Burmese War (1823–6), under General Campbell. It was a war of ambushes and stockades fought in thick jungle, and casualties from tropical diseases far exceeded those from battle. Havelock distinguished himself, and was also noted for his conduct of religious services, on one occasion at least in a Buddhist temple. In the soldiers' argot he was known as a 'Bible-puncher', and those who followed him were nicknamed 'Havelock's saints'. On the occasion of a night attack these men were called for by the general to take the place of men unfit for duty owing to drink, the 'saints' always being sober and dependable in an emergency. Eventually Havelock fell victim to the climate and spent a year in India convalescing with his brother William at Poona. After his return to Burma he again distinguished himself in numerous actions, and as the war dragged to a close Havelock was made a member of the British delegation appointed to negotiate a peace treaty with the Burmese.

Havelock published an account of the Burma campaign after his return to India, while at the same time preparing for his marriage. He often resorted to his pen to add to what was a miserable stipend, but his first book did not arouse much interest. He had probably been inspired to write it by his brother-in-law John Marshman, one of the most prominent civilians in India, and the founder and editor of *The Friend of India*, printed in Serampore. On 9 February 1829 Havelock married Hannah (1809–1882), youngest daughter of the Revd Dr Joshua Marshman (1768–1837): they had four sons and four daughters. Previously Anglican, Havelock had earlier that year been baptized into the Baptist community. He continued his religious and philanthropic activities among the troops, forming a regimental temperance society and himself taking the pledge. In 1836 Havelock was still a subaltern but adjutant of the 13th at Karnal. He had sent Hannah and the children—two boys and a baby girl—to the hills at Landour to escape the hot weather. In the last week in October he learned that the bungalow had burnt down, and that Hannah and the baby were dying of their burns. The two boys had escaped. Hannah, though badly burnt, survived, but both the baby and her ayah died. The Havelocks lost almost all their possessions. When the family returned to Karnal in mid-January 1837 they were met by a deputation from the regiment who offered to help them replace their losses by each man contributing a month's pay. Naturally the offer was refused but it demonstrated Havelock's personal standing in his regiment.

On 5 June 1838 Havelock was promoted captain without purchase in a vacancy caused by the death of 'a dear friend'. Havelock was then forty-three years old, and had twenty-three years' service. Well might he grumble that without the means to purchase, promotion proceeded at the pace of a glacier. However, the First Anglo-Afghan War was about to begin. He was appointed aide-de-camp to Major-General Sir Willoughby Cotton who commanded the Bengal division of the 'army of the Indus'. Havelock spent the next year in Afghanistan, and was present at the storming of Ghazni and the triumphal entry into Kabul. Cotton was keen to retain his services, but Havelock wanted to publish an account of the war and returned to Serampore for the writing. It is a remarkably clear and impartial narrative, in two volumes, but it did not turn out to be a best-seller. Disappointed with his lack of success with his pen, he again took up his sword and set off for Afghanistan with reinforcements for the Kabul garrison. On the journey he fell in with Major-General William Elphinstone, who was on his way to succeed Cotton in Kabul. Elphinstone was impressed by Havelock and took him on his staff as Persian interpreter. It was fortunate that Havelock had left his family in India since matters in Afghanistan went from bad to worse. Before long it became clear that communications with India were likely to be cut off by the tribes. Brigadier-General Sir Robert Sale was sent with the 13th foot and the 35th native infantry to clear the passes as far as Jalalabad. This involved hard fighting in which Havelock, who had obtained a few days' leave to accompany Sale, was much to the fore. When Jalalabad was eventually reached on 13 November 1841 there followed orders for the return of the force to Kabul. Sale, whose wife and daughter were in Kabul, was inclined to agree but was dissuaded from returning by George Broadfoot, his engineer officer, strongly supported by Havelock. Instead they worked hard to put Jalalabad in a state of defence. On 13 January 1842 a lone horseman, Dr William Brydon, brought news of the annihilation of the Kabul garrison while they were withdrawing through the passes. (Havelock was to meet Brydon again at the relief of Lucknow, where Brydon survived the siege.) A month later, on 19 February, an earthquake levelled the laboriously constructed defences. Broadfoot and Havelock set to work to restore them, and Havelock found time to conduct church services and prayer meetings.

On 7 April 1842 the garrison sallied out in three columns, one commanded by Havelock, and totally defeated the Afghans under Akbar Khan. Havelock called this battle his 'Crowning Mercy'. On 16 April the relief force under General Pollock marched into Jalalabad, and its siege was over. Havelock accompanied Pollock in his advance to Kabul which was re-occupied on 15 September 1842. Thereafter he accompanied Sir Richmond Shakespear in the rescue of the prisoners held as hostages, and was responsible for planning the successful attack on Istalif on 29 September. When Havelock was told that, had he been present, Kabul would never have fallen to the Afghans, he replied: 'I will not undertake to say that I could have saved Kabul, but I feel confident George Broadfoot could have done it' (Pollock, 97). The reward for his Afghanistan service was being made a CB and receiving a brevet majority. Back he went to commanding a company and complaining that none of the generals he had served remembered him afterwards. He even quarrelled with Sale. None the less the *London Gazette* of 30 June 1843, which he did not see until late August, announced he had been given a regimental majority without purchase. A week later he was appointed Persian interpreter to Sir Hugh Gough, the newly arrived commander-in-chief, in time to take part in the Gwalior campaign. He was present at the battle of Maharajpur, for which he received the medal and a brevet lieutenant-colonelcy.

At the close of 1845 the First Anglo-Sikh War began. Havelock was present at the battles of Mudki and Ferozeshahr; in the former he had two horses shot under him, and in the latter lost two old friends, Broadfoot and Sale. He was later present at Sobraon. By then he had exchanged into the 39th, from which he later exchanged into the 53rd. He was not permitted to serve in the Second Anglo-Sikh War, in which his brother William was killed leading the 14th light dragoons in their charge at Ramnagar (22 November 1848). Havelock wrote a memoir of his brother which was published in Dr Buist's *Annals of the Year*. He then went home on furlough after some twenty-six years' continuous service in India.

On 20 June 1854 Havelock obtained his regimental lieutenant-colonelcy and brevet colonelcy. He had left his family in Bonn when he returned to India at the end of 1851. War with Persia was declared on 1 November 1856, and early in 1857 Havelock was given a brigade in a force commanded by Brigadier-General Sir James Outram, an officer of the East India Company. Havelock drew up the plan for the successful attack on Muhammarah, but the war petered out when a peace treaty was signed in Paris on 4 March 1857. Havelock then returned to India, arriving back in Bombay on 20 May to find that the Bengal native army had broken out into mutiny. Travel overland being unsafe, he took the first available ship for Calcutta but was wrecked off Ceylon. He eventually reached Calcutta via Madras on 17 June. He was at once given command of a column to be sent up-country to relieve Cawnpore where the garrison was besieged in makeshift entrenchments. Thereafter he was to support Sir Henry Lawrence who was under siege in the residency compound in Lucknow. Havelock's appointment was not universally approved in Calcutta, but as Lady Canning, wife of the governor-general, was to comment:

> General Havelock is not in fashion, but all the same we believe he will do well. No doubt he is fussy and tiresome, but his little, old, stiff figure looks as active and fit for use as if he were made of steel.   (Pollock, 153)

Havelock's force consisted of the 64th foot (North Staffords), four companies of the 78th highlanders (Seaforths), two companies of the 84th (York and Lancaster) regiment, and a detachment of the 1st Madras European fusiliers (an East India Company regiment), the balance of which was in Allahabad under Lieutenant-Colonel J. G. Neill. There was a scratch collection of gunners to serve the six guns, twenty assorted officers and civilians to form the few cavalry, and some native irregulars. In total the force amounted to fewer than 2000 all ranks. There was also a huge train of transport to be gathered: elephants, camels, horses, bullocks, carts, and Indian followers. Havelock reached Allahabad, 120 miles from Cawnpore, on 29 June. It was the hottest season of the year, with frequent torrential rainstorms which reduced the low-lying fields to a bog. The news from Cawnpore, such as it was, was grim. They did not hear of the capitulation and massacre of the garrison until 3 July. Leaving Neill and some of his Madras fusiliers to hold Allahabad, Havelock on 7 July marched out for Cawnpore. The sun soon proved to be far more deadly than sepoy bullets, many men dropping out from the heat. The rainstorms made movement off the road difficult, particularly for the gun teams and supply carts, but Havelock pressed on remorselessly. He defeated the rebels at Fatehpur on 12 July, and again at Unao on 15 July. At the Pandu Nadi, a broad stream in flood, the only bridge was seized by the Madras fusiliers with the bayonet, and a full-scale battle followed. For a moment it seemed that the 64th, exhausted by the marching, had had enough, but they were rallied by Havelock's eldest

son and deputy assistant adjutant-general, Henry (Harry) Marshman Havelock (1830–1897) [*see* Allan, Sir Henry Marshman Havelock-], who displayed great bravery. Meanwhile his father, dismounted after having two horses shot under him, placed himself at the head of the 78th and led their final bayonet charge as darkness fell. When it was all over after three hours of fighting, the highland officers gathered round Havelock who told them:

> I have never seen anyone behave so well as the 78th Highlanders this day. I am proud of you, and if ever I have the good luck to be made a major-general the first thing I will do will be to go to the Duke of Cambridge and request that when my time comes for the colonelcy of a regiment, I may have the 78th.   (Pollock, 185)

The relief column entered Cawnpore on 17 July, too late to save the hard-pressed garrison or the women and children who had been butchered on the orders of the treacherous Nana Sahib. Lucknow must be the next objective, and on 25 July they crossed the flooded Ganges and set foot in Oudh. Havelock left Neill to safeguard Cawnpore. The two men were not on good terms, Neill disloyally corresponding with Calcutta behind Havelock's back. The cholera had arrived to add to Havelock's burdens and the ranks were thinning rapidly. After several hard fought actions which brought them within sight of Lucknow, Havelock decided he lacked the strength to fight his way into the city. He ordered a withdrawal to Cawnpore to await the reinforcements he believed to be on the way. This resulted in a furious letter from Neill that provoked a thunderous reply. He was lucky to avoid arrest. None the less it required great moral courage to turn about with Lucknow on the horizon. Even Harry Havelock found it hard to understand, and so did most of the soldiers. Once Cawnpore was regained, however, it did provide the opportunity to march on Bithur, Nana Sahib's palace, and give him and his followers a good drubbing.

In Cawnpore, Havelock found awaiting him a copy of the *Gazette* announcing the appointment of Sir James Outram as commissioner of Oudh, and to supersede Havelock as commander of the troops. This was a bitter disappointment, and not surprisingly it was attributed by many to Havelock's failure to relieve Lucknow. However, Outram set the record straight when he arrived on 15 September with some reinforcements. He paid great tribute to Havelock and announced that he intended to waive his rank and leave to Havelock the honour of relieving Lucknow. Outram would accompany the force in his purely civilian capacity, only taking over the command after Lucknow had been relieved. This has been described as 'one of the most memorable acts of self-abnegation in military history' (*DNB*). Havelock was duly grateful. He and Outram were old friends and respected each other. Generously meant, and generously accepted, it could never work: there cannot be two commanders of the same military force at any one time. Outram continually interfered with Havelock's plans, and both men became exasperated. It is clear that towards the end Outram regretted his generous impulse, ascribing it to allowing sentiment to obscure duty. The relieving force had to fight hard to reach the residency, which it did before it grew dark on 25 September. Outram had been wounded, though not seriously, and Neill was killed.

Harry Havelock distinguished himself, but his left arm was broken. He was lucky to escape when the sepoys set about killing the convoy of wounded. He was to return later. Outram was put to bed in the residency, assuming the command the next day, and Havelock was taken to dinner by Mrs Inglis, wife of Colonel John Inglis who had commanded the beleaguered garrison after the death of Sir Henry Lawrence. Havelock had believed the garrison was running short of supplies and was surprised to sit down to a dinner of beef cutlets, with mock turtle soup and champagne. Lucknow had been relieved at a cost of 535 men killed and wounded. Carts for the evacuation of women, children, and wounded were impossible to obtain. It was clear that a retreat to Cawnpore would be a difficult, if not impossible, operation. Outram, with Havelock's agreement, decided to remain in the residency and reinforce its garrison. They knew that the newly arrived commander-in-chief, Sir Colin Campbell, was gathering together a substantial force for Lucknow's relief. It was a wise decision.

Campbell finally arrived on 16 November after hard fighting. Outram and Havelock went to meet him and were greeted as 'Sir James' and 'Sir Henry', the first time Havelock learned that he had been made a KCB. There was also a letter from the duke of Cambridge telling Havelock he had been promoted major-general. This was wonderful news, but Havelock was daily growing weaker as a result of dysentery, added to the effects of six months' campaigning in a difficult climate. Nursed by Harry, one arm in a sling, and his faithful aide-de-camp Hargood, Havelock was quietly slipping away. At 9.30 a.m. on Monday, 24 November 1857, he finally did so, in the arms of his son, to whom his last words supposedly were, 'Harry, see how a Christian can die' (Pollock, 252). Campbell had already decided to evacuate the residency, leaving a substantial force under Outram at the Alambagh as a base for a future attack. By the day of Havelock's death the evacuation was virtually complete. They buried him in the garden of the Alambagh, under a mango tree on which Harry carved the letter 'H', and took careful measurements of the grave before smoothing it down. It is there to this day.

The British public seem to find a strange attraction in religious generals, and Havelock's death was a great shock. Before news of his death reached Britain, letters patent were directed, on 26 November, to create him a baronet. His widow was given the rank of a baronet's widow, a pension for life of £1000 a year, and a grace-and-favour residence. She died on 25 August 1882. A bronze statue (1861) of Havelock, by William Behnes, was erected by public subscription in Trafalgar Square. (In October 2000 this was the subject of public controversy when Ken Livingstone, mayor of London, demanded its removal as he 'hasn't a clue' who Havelock was: this caused strong protest from Scots and others in defence of the statue.) Harry Havelock was created a baronet in January 1858 and

given an annuity of £1000 a year for life. He was awarded the VC in 1858, and continued in the army until 1873 when he retired as a lieutenant-general. He was a Liberal Unionist MP (1874–81, 1885–92, 1895–7), and in 1880 he inherited from a distant cousin the estate and fortune of the Allans of Blackwell in co. Durham, taking by royal licence the additional surname and arms of Allan. On 30 December 1897, when accompanying a parliamentary commission to the north-west frontier of India, he was shot by an Afridi and bled to death.

His father, Henry Havelock, was one of the best British generals of his time, a clever tactician with a good eye for ground. Cool in action, he won the confidence of his troops, who admired his courage. Something of a martinet, his deep religious feeling kept him somewhat apart. A lion in action, he could be pernickety in barracks. His religion was crucial, and he died a national hero, perceived particularly as a Christian hero. He was a supreme exemplar and symbol of what historians later called Christian militarism, and his reputation—partly the result of his brother-in-law J. C. Marshman's influential and much reprinted biography, *Memoirs of Major-General Sir Henry Havelock* (1860)—was indicated by the popularity of Havelock as a Victorian Christian name and by something of a Havelock cult in Victorian Britain.

JAMES LUNT

Sources J. C. Pollock, *Way to glory: the life of Havelock of Lucknow* (1957) [incl. bibliography] · J. C. Marshman, *Memoirs of Major-General Sir Henry Havelock* (1860) · J. W. Kaye, *History of the war in Afghanistan*, 3rd edn, 3 vols. (1874) · J. W. Kaye and G. B. Malleson, *Kaye's and Malleson's History of the Indian mutiny of 1857–8*, 6 vols. (1888–9) · H. Havelock, *Memoir of the three campaigns of Major-General Sir Archibald Campbell's army in Ava* (1828) · H. Havelock, *Narrative of the war in Affghanistan in 1838–39*, 2 vols. (1840) · W. Broadfoot, *The career of Major George Broadfoot … in Afghanistan and the Punjab* (1888) · G. R. Gleig, *Sale's brigade in Afghanistan: with an account of the seisure and defence of Jellalabad* (1846) · H. Everett, *The history of the Somerset light infantry* (1934) · O. Anderson, 'The growth of Christian militarism in mid-Victorian Britain', *EngHR*, 86 (1971), 46–72 · Burke, *Peerage* (1999) · *WWBMP*, vol. 2 · *DNB*

Archives BL OIOC, papers relating to the Indian mutiny, MS Eur. F 84 · Durham RO, corresp. and papers · N. Yorks. CRO, corresp. and papers

Likenesses M. Mannin, watercolour drawing, 1851, N. Yorks. CRO · F. Goodall, pencil and wash drawing, c.1857, NPG [*see illus.*] · G. G. Adams, plaster bust, 1858, NPG · W. Behnes, bust, 1858, Guildhall Museum, London · C. G. Lewis, engraving, 1860 (after T. J. Barker), NPG · W. Behnes, bronze statue, c.1861, Trafalgar Square · M. Noble, marble relief, 1866, Westminster Abbey · T. J. Barker, group portrait, oils (*The relief of Lucknow, 1857*; after sketches by E. Lundgren), Corporation of Glasgow, NPG · photograph, N. Yorks. CRO · portrait (*Henry Havelock in 1851*), priv. coll. · print (*General Havelock*), priv. coll.

Havelock, Sir Thomas Henry (1877–1968), mathematician, was born in Newcastle upon Tyne on 24 June 1877, the son of Michael Havelock, marine engineer, of Newcastle, and his wife, Elizabeth Burn Bell. Four of their six children (two boys and two girls) survived to maturity, but only the eldest girl married. For most of his life Thomas Havelock lived with his younger sister and his brother, who became a director of the Moor Line, and he shared the family love of ships. At first Thomas hoped to become a draughtsman in the Neptune Works of Swan, Hunter, and Wigham Richardson on Tyneside, but while waiting for an apprenticeship to fall vacant he entered Durham College of Physical Science in Newcastle upon Tyne, and a natural gift for mathematics and physics soon became apparent. Having completed a BSc course in 1895 at the age of eighteen, he stayed for a further two years of postgraduate studies in the college before entering St John's College, Cambridge, in 1897, first as a pensioner and the following year as a scholar. Nevertheless, all his life he retained his love of ships.

In 1898 Havelock suffered serious injury when some railings, which he had climbed in order to get a better view of Lord Kitchener, who had come to receive an honorary degree, gave way outside the Senate House at Cambridge; as a result his health was impaired for the rest of his life.

Despite the consequent interruption of his studies Havelock was placed in the second division of class one in part one of the mathematical tripos in 1901, with J. E. Wright alone above him in the first division. In 1902 he shared the Smith's prize with Wright, and was awarded an Isaac Newton studentship. He was elected to a six-year Gregson fellowship in his college in 1903, but in 1906 returned to Armstrong College (as the Durham College of Science had become in 1904) as a special lecturer in applied mathematics. He received a DSc there (by examination) in 1907. He was elected to fellowship of the Royal Society in 1914, and the following year Armstrong College created a second chair of (applied) mathematics especially for him. His damaged health ruled out active service in the First World War.

Havelock's scientific work lay in two main areas: the passage of light through materials and naval hydrodynamics. Although he wrote some twenty papers on the first of these, they did not attract lasting attention, and Havelock himself appears to have lost interest in optics by 1930. He did, however, do pioneering work on the wave resistance of ships and related problems, topics which interested him into his eighties. His most significant contributions started in 1923 after he had discovered a much neglected, but fundamental, paper by J. H. Michell (1898). In following years he applied and generalized its methods with conspicuous success. He discovered much about the way a ship's resistance to motion depends on the form of its hull. Later in his life he answered sophisticated questions about the trim and the heaving and pitching of a ship. He constantly compared his theory with experiment, and sought to improve the extent of the agreement between the two.

Havelock's impact on this branch of naval architecture was strong and fully recognized in his lifetime. He was made an honorary member of the Institution of Naval Architects in 1943, and awarded its first William Froude gold medal in 1956. Durham University conferred an honorary DCL in 1958, and Hamburg an honorary DSc in 1960; he became an honorary fellow of St John's in 1945. The French Académie des Sciences made him a corresponding member in 1947. He was the featured guest of the United

States Society of Naval Architecture and Marine Engineers in 1950, and in 1963 the United States office of naval research paid him the unusual compliment of collecting together and publishing sixty of his papers on hydrodynamics. He was knighted in 1951.

In 1928 Havelock became head of both the pure and the applied mathematics departments in Armstrong College. He maintained strong links with the department of naval architecture, of which he became honorary acting head for three years from 1941, when Sir Westcott Abell retired. He was vice-principal of Armstrong College from 1933 to 1937, and took a leading part in the negotiations which brought it and the College of Medicine together to form King's College of the federal University of Durham at Newcastle upon Tyne. He was sub-rector of King's College from 1937 to 1942, and retired from his chair in 1945. His work for the university was marked in 1968 by the opening of Havelock Hall for student residence.

Havelock owed much of his success, and perhaps also his longevity, to the devoted care of his sister, Alice, who survived his death, at their home, 8 Westfield Drive, Gosforth, on 1 August 1968, by only a few weeks.

P. H. ROBERTS, *rev.*

Sources *Cambridge Express* (26 Nov 1898) · *Cambridge Weekly News* (25 Nov 1898) · J. H. Michell, *Philosophical Magazine*, 5th ser., 45 (1898) · P. H. Roberts, *Bulletin of the London Mathematical Society*, 2 (1970) · A. M. Binnie and P. H. Roberts, *Memoirs FRS*, 17 (1971), 327–77 · *The collected papers of Sir Thomas Havelock on hydrodynamics*, ed. W. C. S. Wigley, US Office of Naval Research, ACR-103 (1963) · *CGPLA Eng. & Wales* (1968)
Archives U. Newcastle, Robinson L., papers
Wealth at death £114,063: probate, 30 Aug 1968, *CGPLA Eng. & Wales*

Havelock, William (1793–1848), army officer, was born on 23 January 1793, the eldest son of William Havelock (1757–1837) of Ingress Park, Kent, a Sunderland shipbuilder, and his wife, Jane (*d.* 1811), daughter of John Carter of Stockton-on-Tees. He was the brother of Sir Henry *Havelock and of Major-General Charles Havelock (*d.* 1868), of the 16th lancers, who commanded a brigade of Turkish irregulars in the Crimean War. He was educated at Charterhouse School and by a private tutor.

On 12 July 1810 Havelock was appointed ensign in the 43rd (Monmouthshire) light infantry, in which he became lieutenant on 12 May 1812. He immediately saw active service in the Peninsula. He carried one of the colours of the 43rd at the passage of the Coa in 1810, and was present in all the subsequent actions in which the Peninsula light division was engaged to the end of the war, latterly as aide-de-camp to Count Alten. Havelock displayed conspicuous bravery at the engagement at Vera in October 1813, when a Spanish force was held in check by a formidable abattis defended by two French regiments. Havelock, who had been sent to ascertain their progress, called on the Spaniards to follow him, and, putting spurs to his horse cleared the abattis in one bound and charged headlong among the enemy. Then the Spaniards, cheering for 'el chico blanco' (the fair boy), for he was very young, and had very light hair, followed Havelock and broke through the French lines. Havelock continued to serve as Alten's aide-de-camp at Waterloo, where he was wounded at Quatre Bras, and during the occupation of Paris. On 19 February 1818 Havelock was promoted captain in the 32nd foot, and served with that regiment in Corfu. On 19 July 1821 he exchanged to the 4th (Queen's Own) light dragoons, with which he went to India. In 1824 he married Caroline Elizabeth (d. 1866), daughter of Major Acton Chaplin of Aylesbury; they had thirteen children, including the colonial governor Sir Arthur Elibank *Havelock.

Havelock was for some time aide-de-camp to Sir Charles Colville when commander-in-chief at Bombay, and was military secretary to Lord Elphinstone while governor of Madras. He was promoted major in the 4th light dragoons on 31 December 1830 and exchanged into the 14th (King's) light dragoons, becoming lieutenant-colonel of that regiment on 30 April 1841. He commanded it in the field under Sir Charles Napier, and with the Bombay troops sent to reinforce Lord Gough's army during the Second Anglo-Sikh War of 1848–9. He fell mortally wounded at the head of his regiment in a desperate charge under artillery fire on the Sikhs at Ramnagar, on the banks of the River Chenab, on 22 November 1848. His sword arm disabled, his left arm and leg nearly cut off, after eleven of his troopers had been killed beside him, he was left for dead on the field.　　　　　　　　　H. M. CHICHESTER, rev. ALEX MAY

Sources Army List · R. G. A. Levinge, Historical records of the forty-third regiment, Monmouthshire light infantry (1868) · H. B. Hamilton, Historical records of the 14th (king's) hussars (1901) · J. C. Pollock, Way to glory: the life of Havelock of Lucknow (1957) · E. J. Thackwell, Narrative of the Second Seikh War, in 1848–49 (1851) · H. C. B. Cook, The Sikh wars: the British army in the Punjab, 1845–1849 (1975) · W. F. P. Napier, History of the war in the Peninsula and in the south of France, rev. edn, 6 vols. (1876) · C. W. C. Oman, A history of the Peninsular War, 7 vols. (1902–30) · GM, 2nd ser., 31 (1849), 318–19
Likenesses portrait, repro. in Hamilton, Historical records

Haverfield [née Scarlett], **Evelina** (1867–1920), suffragette and aid worker, was born at Inverlochy Castle, Kingussie, on 9 August 1867, the third daughter of William Frederick Scarlett, third Baron Abinger (1826–1892), landowner and army officer, and his wife, Helen (c.1840–1915), daughter of Commodore George Allan Magruder of the US navy. She was educated at home by governesses and in 1880 attended a school in Dusseldorf, becoming fluent in German. Spending much of the year on the family's Scottish estate, she was a keen sportswoman, especially adept at riding astride. On 10 February 1887 in the parish church of St Stephen's, Kensington, she married Henry Wykeham Brook Tunstall Haverfield (c.1847–1895), a major in the Royal Artillery; the couple moved to Dorset, and had two sons (John, who was killed in 1915, and Brook, who emigrated to Canada). Widowed in 1895, on 8 July 1899 in the parish church at Caundle Marsh, Dorset, she married John Henry Balguy (1859–1933), another Royal Artillery major. Within a month of the marriage she enacted a document by which she reverted to the name Haverfield. She spent two years with her husband in South Africa during the

Second South African War, and while there formed a retirement camp for horses left to die on the veldt. Evelina Haverfield returned to an active country life in Dorset and, although she had never previously evinced any interest in politics, at some point joined the Sherborne branch of the National Union of Women's Suffrage Societies. As the campaign for women's enfranchisement gathered momentum, she transferred her allegiance to the militant section of the movement in March 1908, and after attending a large rally in the Albert Hall, joined the Women's Social and Political Union (WSPU). In June 1909 she was arrested after taking part in a WSPU deputation to the House of Commons. With that of Mrs Pankhurst, hers was treated as a test case, Sir Robert Cecil defending her on the grounds that she had been wrongfully arrested while exercising a constitutional right. She was found guilty, however, and fined; the case went to appeal, and the fine was upheld. Although she was determined to go to prison, the fine was paid without her consent. She was arrested again in November 1910, charged with assaulting a policeman after taking part in a WSPU demonstration in Parliament Square. She denied neither the charge nor the suggestion that she had said that the next time she would bring a revolver. She was sentenced to a fine or a month's imprisonment, but again the fine was paid without her consent. Imprisonment for the suffrage cause was at length achieved in November 1911, after she had attempted to break a police cordon by leading police horses out of their ranks; she spent two weeks in Holloway. Sylvia Pankhurst noted of Mrs Haverfield that:

> When she first joined the Suffragette movement her expression was cold and proud … I was repelled when she told me she felt no affection for her children. During her years in the Suffrage movement her sympathies so broadened that she seemed to have undergone a rebirth. (Pankhurst, 345)

On the outbreak of the First World War in August 1914 Evelina Haverfield founded the Women's Emergency Corps and in late 1914 served briefly as commander-in-chief of the Women's Reserve Ambulance (Green Cross Corps), which was a founding unit of the future Women's Army Auxiliary Corps. In May 1915 she joined Elsie Inglis and the Scottish Women's Hospital unit in Serbia, working there until forced out in February 1916 by the German advance. Undeterred, in August Mrs Haverfield sailed for Russia, in charge of the unit's transport column, which comprised seventy-five women noted for their smart uniforms and shorn locks. She herself is invariably described as being small, neat, and aristocratic, able to command devotion from her troops, although some of her peers, not so enamoured, were scathing of her ability. By March 1917 the harshness of the weather, combined with the disrepair of the vehicles and internal feuding, led Mrs Haverfield to return to Britain where, for the remainder of the war, she campaigned for the Serbian cause. After the armistice Mrs Haverfield founded an orphanage in Serbia and was working there when she contracted pneumonia and died on 21 March 1920 at Bajna Bashta, where she was buried. A plaque in her orphanage building, later a co-operative health centre, commemorates her work for the Serbian people.   ELIZABETH CRAWFORD

Sources V. Holme, MS biography, Museum of London, Suffragette Fellowship Collection · B. Gaddes, *Evelina: outward bound from Inverlochy* (1995) · L. Leneman, *In the service of life: the story of Elsie Inglis and the Scottish women's hospitals* (1994) · M. Krippner, *The quality of mercy: women at war, Serbia, 1915–18* (1980) · E. S. Pankhurst, *The suffragette movement: an intimate account of persons and ideals* (1931); repr. (1977) · Burke, *Peerage* (1939) · b. cert. · m. certs. · *CGPLA Eng. & Wales* (1921)

Archives FILM BFI NFTVA, news footage

Likenesses photograph, Women's Library, London · photographs, repro. in Gaddes, *Evelina*

Wealth at death £2612 8s. 1d.: administration, 13 June 1921, *CGPLA Eng. & Wales*

Haverfield, Francis John (1860–1919), historian and archaeologist, was born at Shipston-on-Stour, Worcestershire, on 8 November 1860, the only son of the Revd William Robert Haverfield (d. 1882) and his wife, Emily, sister of John Fielder Mackarness, bishop of Oxford. He was a great-grandson of the miniature painter Jeremiah Meyer. Haverfield's mother died when he was still in early childhood, and soon afterwards his father fell into a hopeless and prolonged decline. Growing up without experience of a normal home life, Haverfield was seriously handicapped. He developed a certain abruptness of manner, which, superimposed upon a character of marked strength and individuality, often prevented the recognition of what he really was—a simple, kind, and unselfish man.

From a preparatory school at Clifton, Bristol, Haverfield entered Winchester College as senior scholar in 1873. Six years later he went up to New College, Oxford, once more as scholar. He obtained a first class in moderations with no great difficulty. A second class in Greats was the penalty of paying less attention to Greek philosophy than to Latin lexicography. In 1884, a year after taking his degree, he went as sixth-form master to Lancing College, Sussex, where his somewhat unconventional methods proved highly successful. During this time he pursued various lines of original research, but finally concentrated on Roman epigraphy and Roman Britain, mainly under the influence of Mommsen, for whose work he had a profound admiration and whose personal acquaintance he had made during one of his frequent visits to the continent. This contact resulted in Mommsen's invitation to him to undertake the corrections of the seventh volume of the *Corpus inscriptionum Latinarum*.

In 1892, as a result of his growing reputation, Haverfield was invited to return to Oxford, where he resided at Christ Church as a senior student and tutor. This period allowed him to consolidate the contacts he had made. Practically every important classical book that appeared was reviewed by him in *The Guardian* or elsewhere; and he edited Henry Nettleship's *Essays* and re-edited Conington's *Eclogues* and *Georgics* (1895). Among his various interests, Roman Britain became more and more his

chief concern. During his vacations he travelled around the country, visiting museums and excavations, guiding and advising local antiquaries.

In 1907 Henry Pelham Francis died, and Haverfield was chosen to succeed him as Camden professor of ancient history at Oxford, the appointment carrying with it an official fellowship at Brasenose College. In April 1907, a month before his election, he had married Winifred E. Breakwell (d. 1920). This was his happiest and most fruitful period. Freed from college routine, he was able to concentrate on his research interests. At home his influence grew and abroad he commanded a respect such as few British scholars of the time enjoyed. The outbreak of war in 1914 was thus a stunning blow, bringing the loss of many friends and students of his work. At the end of 1915 the continuous strain and anxiety induced a stroke. Despite a partial recovery he never regained full vigour. The end came quite suddenly, on 1 October 1919, at Winshields, the house that he had had built for himself and his wife on Headington Hill, Oxford. The couple had no children.

Haverfield redefined the study of Roman archaeology as it was then understood in Britain. His work was prompted by Mommsen's development of the study of ancient history and in particular by his use of archaeological evidence. When Haverfield first approached it, the subject of Roman Britain was, to use his own phrase, 'the playground of the amateur'. Before his death he could claim that 'our scientific knowledge of the island, however liable to future correction and addition, stands by itself among the studies of the Roman Empire'. He might truthfully have added that this was his own achievement. And it was accomplished almost single-handed; such good work as was done by others was done largely through his inspiration and example. Although never a significant figure in the academic politics of his own university, Haverfield played a crucial part in the establishment of Romano-British studies as part of the nationwide university curriculum. Much of this was accomplished by his own teaching, and by co-ordinating a series of major excavations. His ability to obtain appointments for some of his former students in universities and elsewhere facilitated the wider recognition of the discipline. Through his membership of numerous regional archaeological and antiquarian societies, he was able to direct research into the areas that he considered most important. This aspect of his work culminated in 1910 in the creation of the Society for the Promotion of Roman Studies, which remains the pre-eminent body in Britain for Roman studies. His European connections combined with his knowledge of the archaeology of the continent created an important counter-balance to the largely parochial nature of Roman history and archaeology in Britain at this time.

Although Haverfield did not live to produce the systematic treatise which he contemplated, the bibliography of his writings, containing some 500 entries, is singularly impressive. His principal publications were the two sets of *Additamenta* (1892, 1913) to the Berlin *Corpus inscriptionum*

Latinarum, his *Romanization of Roman Britain* (1905; 4th edn 1923), and the numerous chapters that he contributed to the Victoria History of the Counties of England. His Ford lectures, published posthumously in 1924 as *The Roman Occupation of Britain*, provide the most convenient conspectus of his results. The decades since his death have not seen a diminution of his reputation or influence. Although advances in methods and in intellectual perspectives have rendered many of his conclusions doubtful, if not redundant, and there is now available a range of evidence that he could never have imagined, his significance remains in the way that he defined Romano-British archaeology. What he thought important continues to be debated.

GEORGE MACDONALD, *rev.* P. W. M. FREEMAN

Sources AM Oxf., Haverfield Archive · J. G. C. Anderson, *Classical Review*, 33 (1919), 165–6 · R. C. Bosanquet, 'Francis John Haverfield', *Archaeologia Aeliana*, 3rd ser., 17 (1920), 137–43 · H. H. E. Craster, 'Francis Haverfield', *EngHR*, 35 (1920), 63–70 · G. Macdonald, 'A bibliography', *Journal of Roman Studies*, 8 (1918), 184–8 · G. Macdonald, 'F. Haverfield, 1860–1919', *PBA*, [9] (1919–20), 475–91 · G. Macdonald, 'Biographical note: F. Haverfield', *The Roman occupation of Britain*, ed. G. Macdonald, rev. edn (1924), 15–38 · G. Macdonald, 'A bibliography: F. Haverfield', *The Roman occupation of Britain*, ed. G. Macdonald, rev. edn (1924), 38–57 · M. V. Taylor, 'F. J. Haverfield', *Journal of the Chester and North Wales Archaeological and Historic Society*, new ser., 23 (1920), 64–71 · [W. G. Collingwood], 'In memoriam', *Transactions of the Cumberland and Westmorland Antiquarian and Archaeological Society*, new ser., 20 (1919–20), 255–7 · private information (1927) · personal knowledge (1927) · private information (2004)

Archives AM Oxf., archive, archaeological notes and papers | Man. CL, letters to Charles Roeder · Staatsbibliothek, Berlin, collection of corresp. with Mommsen

Likenesses photograph, repro. in G. Macdonald, ed., *Roman occupation of Britain* · photograph, repro. in *Journal of the Chester and North Wales Archaeological and Historical Society*

Wealth at death £12,330 6s. 3d.: probate, 16 Dec 1919, CGPLA Eng. & Wales

Havergal, (Grace) Beatrix Helen (1901–1980), horticulturist and teacher, was born on 7 July 1901 at Roydon Manor House near Bressingham, Norfolk, the second of three children of the Revd Clement Havergal (1858–1941), vicar of Bressingham, and his wife, Eveline Mary Barrett (1869–1931). The children had a happy life despite friction between their father, an eccentric and repressive character, and their artistic and romantic mother. In 1902 the family moved to Inkberrow, near Redditch, after which they moved to Paris, where the Revd Havergal was assistant chaplain to the British embassy for two years. After a short stay in Bagthorpe about 1905, he became rector of Brent Eleigh, in Norfolk. At first the children were educated at home by a governess but in 1912 Trix, as she was called, and her elder sister, Frances, went to St Katherine's, a boarding-school at Walmer in Kent. In 1914, after a legal separation, Mrs Havergal took the children to live at 13 Sidney Road, Bedford, and they then attended Bedford high school.

Trix left school in 1916 and took on local gardening jobs under the auspices of the Women's War Agricultural Committee. Clement Havergal rejoined the family and

(Grace) Beatrix Helen Havergal (1901–1980), by Valerie Finnis, 1960s

fortunes improved sufficiently for his daughter to consider some training; she had to choose between an outdoor life and a musical career. She had a strong and beautiful contralto voice and played the cello with a skill that matched the family traditions. Both her paternal grandfather and great-grandfather had been talented musicians and her great-aunt, Frances Ridley Havergal, was a well-known composer of Anglican hymns.

Trix chose horticulture and went as a student to Thatcham Fruit and Flower Farm near Newbury, Berkshire, where women were trained in the art and craft of gardening. She spent three years there and in 1920 she obtained the Royal Horticultural Society's certificate with honours. Her first challenge was to design and make a garden at Cold Ash, near Newbury. Here chance played a part, for her excellent work was noticed by Miss Willis, the founder and headmistress of nearby Downe House boarding-school, who asked her to become the head gardener and to make six grass tennis courts, later known as the Havergal courts.

Inspired by Miss Willis's gift for making learning exciting, Beatrix Havergal longed to teach as well as to do. This strong desire and her outstanding ability to illustrate how each job should be done led to the idea of starting her own school. At Downe House she met Avice Sanders, the school's housekeeper, who was to become her lifelong partner and who made the creation of their school of horticulture possible. Music was not forgotten, however: Beatrix continued to play the cello and to sing with the Newbury choral society and later with the Bach Choir in Oxford. She also joined the Thatcham special police rifle club and became a skilled shot.

In 1927, with the help and encouragement of Miss Willis

and with less than £250 capital, Beatrix Havergal and Avice Sanders moved to a cottage at Pusey near Faringdon, rented some land, and took their first students. Money was very short, so cash crops were grown for sale in Swindon market. The partners and students worked together, the course aiming to combine theory and practical expertise with high standards of efficiency and speed. This unique training endowed the students with a good reputation. Beatrix Havergal studied in her spare time and in 1932 obtained the Royal Horticultural Society's national diploma of horticulture (later master of horticulture).

By 1932 larger premises were needed and Havergal and Sanders moved to Waterperry House, near Wheatley, Oxfordshire, a small manor house which they rented from Magdalen College. At the outbreak of war the school was well established, offering a two-year course for fifteen to twenty students; these came from every type of background, from all over the British Isles and abroad. At first all paid their own fees but after 1958, when the school was inspected and officially recognized by the Department of Education, scholarships were granted by some county councils. The syllabus covered all aspects of gardening. The working day began at 7 a.m. and tasks were arranged so that each student became proficient at every job. Crops were sold in Oxford market, where students soon learned if their produce was not up to standard. Each had charge of a section of glasshouse and took turns to stoke the boilers before the introduction of an oil-fired system. Towards the end of their two years students took the Royal Horticultural Society general examination and the Waterperry diploma, which was examined externally and became an accepted qualification. Beatrix fought to have her women's qualifications recognized on an equal footing with those of men, particularly in the public parks department. The Waterperry diploma was accepted by the Institute of Parks Administration in 1960 as one equivalent to the Kew and Edinburgh diplomas for exemption purposes, and in 1962 as an appropriate qualification for associate membership of that institute.

Students and staff at Waterperry worked side by side, shared accommodation, and often spent free time together, boating, fishing, playing tennis, rehearsing plays, or going into Oxford to the cinema or theatre. Although the principals were strict, even stern at times, they were deeply interested in and concerned for their students' welfare and happiness. 'Miss H.', as she was known, was always the life and soul of any gathering—even a cinema queue! She held prayers for students and staff each morning in the village church, where she was also church warden and played the harmonium for regular services.

Waterperry Gardens were gradually developed to establish a series of teaching units: fruit, flowers, and vegetables were grown, and new glasshouses were built. Growing fruit was Beatrix's particular joy but she also loved the herbaceous border and took great pride in its design. During the war the two-year course was suspended in favour of short courses for women in the land army, and a further 30 acres were cultivated for food production as part of the war effort; Beatrix herself chaired the horticultural sub-committee of the Oxfordshire agricultural committee. The two partners also wanted to reach a wider audience and from 1943 onwards gardening demonstrations were held for the general public in aid of the Queen's Institute of Nursing. The estate had nearly been sold to the John Innes Institute in 1940 but the sale had fallen through at the last moment and in 1948 Havergal and Sanders were finally able to buy the estate with the help of an anonymous benefactor. In 1963 a further gift allowed day classes to be started.

Beatrix Havergal was appointed MBE in 1960, and was awarded the Royal Horticultural Society Veitch memorial medal and Victoria medal of honour in 1966; she was also president of the Horticultural Education Association. She published little, though she took part in various radio programmes, and she took films of the work in the gardens from which a short video was made. She was liked and admired throughout the horticultural world and was well known to a wider public for her exhibits of strawberries at the Chelsea flower show, where she received fifteen gold medals.

Beatrix Havergal was a well-built, handsome woman, nearly 6 feet tall, and a commanding figure in her uniform of green breeches, green overalls, and felt hat. She had a warm personality and infected others with her tremendous zest for life and work. Her generous spirit and obvious enthusiasm created a loyalty in her staff which was vital in developing and maintaining the high standards of workmanship and attention to detail which she demanded, but she did not delegate easily. However, though she was strict and had high moral standards, she was also great fun with a keen sense of humour and a flair for, and constant flow of, anecdotes. Her partner was shy and retiring, but of vital support behind the scenes, running the domestic side of the school with great skill and efficiency. Avice Sanders died in 1970 and was buried at Waterperry.

In 1971, in failing health, Beatrix Havergal sold the estate and retired to live in one of the cottages in the grounds. She died on 8 April 1980 at Tower House, Woolton Hill, near Newbury, when visiting her brother. She was buried in Waterperry churchyard on 14 April 1980.

MARY SPILLER

Sources U. Maddy, *Waterperry: a dream fulfilled* (1990) · personal knowledge (2004) · Oxon. RO · private information (2004)
Archives Oxon. RO, Oxfordshire Archives | FILM priv. coll., films of Waterperry by B. Havergal
Likenesses V. Finnis, photograph, 1960–69, Royal Horticultural Society, Lindley Library [*see illus.*] · C. Hardaker, oils (after a photograph; posthumous), Waterperry Gardens Ltd, Wheatley, Oxford · photographs, Oxfordshire Archives, County Hall, Oxford · photographs, repro. in Maddy, *Waterperry* (1990)
Wealth at death £31,046: probate, 1 July 1980, *CGPLA Eng. & Wales*

Havergal, Frances Ridley [*pseuds.* Sabrina, Zoide] (1836–1879), poet and hymn writer, the youngest of the six children of William Henry *Havergal (1793–1870), Church of England clergyman and composer, and his first wife, Jane Head (*d.* 1848), was born on 14 December 1836 at her father's rectory at Astley, Worcestershire. She was an intelligent child and an eager student, attending Belmont School at Campden Hill, London (1850), and Powick Court at Worcester (1851), but a severe attack of erysipelas brought an end to her formal education. In 1852 she accompanied her father and his second wife, Caroline Ann Cooke, to Germany, where she studied first for over a year at the Louisenschule at Düsseldorf, coming first in the final examination, and then with a German pastor's family at Oberkassel near Düsseldorf, returning to England in December 1853. She wrote fluent verses from the age of seven and her poems were published in *Good Words* and other religious periodicals and pocket books, under the pseudonyms Sabrina and Zoide. In 1865–6 Havergal revisited Germany; while there she sought Professor Ferdinand Hiller's opinion of her musical talent. Hiller believed that she had the skill to become a professional musician; however, she never followed his advice, which was to study with a good teacher. Her father died suddenly in 1870, and she prepared for the press a new edition of his *Psalmody*. With Reverend C. B. Snepp she edited *Songs of Grace and Glory* (1872). After her stepmother's death in 1878, she moved from Leamington Spa in Warwickshire to Caswall Bay in south Wales, near Swansea and The Mumbles. She died of hepatitis and acute peritonitis at Park Villa, Newton Oystermouth, Glamorgan, on 3 June 1879 and was buried at the church in Astley on 9 June.

Havergal energetically committed her life to religious and philanthropic work, contributing most of her author's earnings to good causes. In fact, her religious devotion was such that she refused several offers of marriage. Collections of her poems and hymns were published in many separate volumes. Among them were *The Ministry of Song*, which first appeared in 1869 and ran into five editions; *Under the Surface* (1874); *Loyal Responses* (1878); *Life Chords* (1880); *Life Echoes* (1883); and *Coming to the King* (1886). Her poems and hymns were also collected by her sister, Maria Vernon Graham Havergal, in two volumes of *Poetical Works* (1884). Havergal also wrote many short devotional tracts and prose narratives, some designed for children. Her introspective nature is reflected in her writing, which emphasizes piety and dedication. Her religious poetry became popular in evangelical circles, and her hymns are still to be found in many collections. Her autobiography was published in *Memorials of Frances Ridley Havergal, by her Sister, M. V. G. Havergal* (1880), and in the last decades of the nineteenth century it achieved the extensive popularity which her poems had enjoyed. It presents an account of single-minded and committed spiritual life.　　　　　　RONALD BAYNE, *rev.* ROSEMARY SCOTT

Sources J. Grierson, *Frances Ridley Havergal: Worcestershire hymnwriter* (1979) · *Letters by the late Frances Ridley Havergal*, ed. M. V. G. H. [M. V. G. Havergal] (1885) · M. V. G. H. [M. V. G. Havergal], *Memorials of Frances Ridley Havergal* [1880] · C. Bullock, 'Near the throne': Frances Ridley Havergal—the sweet singer and royal writer, new edn (1902) · Blain, Clements & Grundy, *Feminist comp.* · T. H. Darlow, *Frances Ridley Havergal: a saint of God* (1927) · d. cert. · *CGPLA Eng. & Wales* (1879)
Archives Worcs. RO, corresp. and papers | U. Birm. L., special collections department, notebook of poems and corresp.

Likenesses Elliott & Fry, photograph, *c.*1878, priv. coll.
Wealth at death under £7000: administration with will, 20 Aug 1879, *CGPLA Eng. & Wales*

Havergal, Francis Tebbs (1829–1890). *See under* Havergal, William Henry (1793–1870).

Havergal, Henry East (1820–1875), Church of England clergyman and organist, was born on 22 July 1820 at Coaley, Gloucestershire, the second child and eldest son in the family of six children of William Henry *Havergal (1793–1870), curate of Coaley and later rector of St Nicholas, Worcester, and his first wife, Jane, the daughter of William Head of East Grinstead, Sussex. His mother died in 1848 and his father remarried in 1851. His sister, Frances Ridley *Havergal (1836–1879), became well known as a writer of religious poetry. He was a chorister at New College, Oxford, from 1828 to 1834, and was Bible clerk there from 1839. He matriculated from Magdalen Hall on 18 May 1839, and graduated BA 1843 and MA 1846. In 1843 he became chaplain of Christ Church, and from 1844 to 1847 he was chaplain of New College. On 16 September 1847 he married Frances Mary, the eldest daughter of George J. A. Walker.

From 1847 until his death Havergal was vicar of Cople, Bedfordshire. He built an organ himself for the church there, on which he carried out many experiments. He also acted as organist. He constructed a chiming apparatus, and often chimed the bells himself before service. For some years he was the conductor of a music society at Bedford. He had a natural alto voice, and in a run-through of William Crotch's oratorio *Palestine* he played the double bass and sang the alto part in the choruses at the same time. He also played the trumpet.

Havergal's many musical publications included *A Selection from the Hymns and Songs of the Church by George Wither* (1846), *Tunes, Chants, and Responses* (1865), and *Forty-Two Chants* (1870). He died at Cople vicarage on 12 January 1875.　　　　　G. C. BOASE, *rev.* ANNE PIMLOTT BAKER

Sources Grove, *Dict. mus.* · Boase, *Mod. Eng. biog.* · Foster, *Alum. Oxon.* · *CGPLA Eng. & Wales* (1875) · *Record* (18 Jan 1875), 3 · *Record* (20 Jan 1875), 2 · *The Choir* (23 Jan 1875), 50
Wealth at death under £1500: probate, 9 March 1875, *CGPLA Eng. & Wales*

Havergal, William Henry (1793–1870), composer, the only son of William Havergal (*d.* 1854) and his wife, Mary, the daughter of Thomas Hopkins, was born at Chipping Wycombe, Buckinghamshire, on 18 January 1793. After beginning his education at Princes Risborough in 1801, he entered Merchant Taylors' School in July 1806. From the age of fourteen he often played the organ in his parish church. He was originally intended for the medical profession, but eventually went to Oxford, and matriculated from St Edmund Hall on 10 July 1812. He graduated BA in 1816 and MA in 1819, and was ordained on 24 March 1816 to an assistant curacy under Thomas Tregenna Biddulph at the churches of St James, Bristol, and Creech Heathfield. On 2 May of that year he married Jane, the fifth daughter of William Head of East Grinstead, with whom he had several children; she died on 5 July 1848.

In June 1820 Havergal became curate in charge of Coaley, Gloucestershire, and lecturer of Dursley, and took pupils. On 25 June 1822 he became curate of Astley, Worcestershire. He visited Cornwall and Yorkshire in 1826 and the two following years in connection with the Church Missionary Society. On 14 June 1829 he was thrown out of a carriage and suffered concussion, which appears to have had long-term consequences; in 1832 he virtually went blind, and his sight was never fully restored. Despite his accident he was presented to the rectory of Astley on 13 November 1829. At about that time he began seriously to devote himself to music.

Havergal's first published composition was an anthem-like setting of Reginald Heber's 'From Greenland's icy mountains', the proceeds of which (£180) he devoted to the Church Missionary Society. In 1836 he published his op. 36, *An Evening Service in E♭ and One Hundred Antiphonal Chants*. One of these, a 'recte et retro' chant in C, sometimes called Worcester chant, became very widely known. In the same year Havergal was awarded the Gresham prize medal for an evening service in A, op. 37. In 1841 he gained a second medal for the anthem 'Give thanks', op. 40. He became well known for his exertions for the restoration of metrical psalmody to its original purity. In 1844 he published a reprint of Ravenscroft's *Whole Booke of Psalmes*, and in 1847 he brought out his *Old Church Psalmody*, op. 43, which made a significant contribution to the development of the Victorian hymn tune. *A Hundred Psalm and Hymn Tunes*, op. 48, entirely his own composition, was published in 1859. Handel and Corelli were his models, and his aim was to preserve purity of style. He also wrote songs, rounds, and catches for the young, besides carols, hymns, and sacred songs, for which he composed both words and music. Many of the sacred songs and carols appeared in the earlier volumes of *Our Own Fireside*, and were republished under the title *Fireside Music*. His sacred song 'Summer tide is coming' and his psalm tune 'Evan' became widely known.

In June 1845 Havergal moved to St Nicholas rectory, Worcester, and was soon appointed an honorary canon of Worcester Cathedral. In the early 1850s he was involved in a dispute with his curate, Joseph Hesselgrave Thompson, which became a matter of public notice. Three years after the death of his first wife he married Caroline Ann, the daughter of John Cooke of Gloucester, on 29 July 1851. She outlived him by several years, and died on 26 May 1878. Because of declining health Havergal resigned St Nicholas in March 1860 and was presented to the country vicarage of Shareshill, near Wolverhampton. In 1867 increasing infirmity forced him to give up all regular parish work and move to Leamington Spa, where, with the exception of visits to the continent, he continued to reside. He died at his home, Pyrmont Villa, Binswood Terrace, Leamington Spa, on 19 April 1870, and was buried at Astley on 23 April.

Havergal published a number of books and pamphlets on religious, moral, musical, and other subjects, including several volumes of sermons, an essay on the biblical doctrines relating to the use of the death penalty for murder (1849), *A History of the Old Hundredth Psalm Tune* (1854), in which he attempted to prove that it was by William Franc, and an account of the curative properties of the waters at Pyrmont, which was posthumously published by his second wife.

Havergal's children Henry East *Havergal and Frances Ridley *Havergal are separately noticed. Another daughter, Maria Vernon Graham Havergal, who died on 22 June 1887, wrote several books, including an autobiography. This was edited by her sister Jane Miriam Havergal, who married, in October 1842, Henry Crane. Mrs Crane also published records of her father's life.

Havergal's youngest son, **Francis Tebbs Havergal** (1829–1890), author and editor, born on 27 August 1829, was a Bible clerk of New College, Oxford (BA 1852, MA 1857). He served as vicar-choral in Hereford Cathedral (1853–74), vicar of Pipe with Lyde (1861–74) and of Upton Bishop (1874–90), and prebendary of Hereford (1877–90). He died at Upton on 27 July 1890. He wrote a number of books on Hereford Cathedral and on other matters connected with Herefordshire, as well as *Memorials of the Rev Sir Frederick Arthur Gore Ousley, Baronet* (1889).

G. C. BOASE, rev. CLIVE BROWN

Sources A. J. Symington, 'Biographical sketch', in C. Bullock, *The pastor remembered, and the brethren entreated: a memorial of the Rev. W. H. Havergal* (1870), 43–54 · J. M. Crane, *Records of the life of the Rev Wm Havergal* (1882) · C. Bullock, *The crown of the road* (1884) · J. Miller, *Singers and songs of the church* (1869), 429–30 · *The Record* (25 April 1870), 3 · *The Guardian* (27 April 1870), 483 · M. Frost, ed., *Historical companion to 'Hymns ancient and modern'* (1962), 117, 674 · CGPLA Eng. & Wales (1890) [Francis Tebbs Havergal]
Archives U. Birm. L., papers
Likenesses two portraits, repro. in Crane, *Records of the life of the Rev Wm Havergal* · two portraits, repro. in Bullock, *Crown of the road*
Wealth at death £15,673 7s. 1d.—Francis Tebbs Havergal: resworn probate, March 1892, CGPLA Eng. & Wales (1890)

Havers [*married name* Morgan], **Alice Mary** (1850–1890), genre and landscape painter, was born at Thelton Hall, Norfolk, the third daughter of Thomas Havers (d. 1870), colonial governor, and his wife, Ellen, daughter of the numismatist Rogers Ruding (1751–1820). The writer Dorothy Henrietta *Boulger (Theo Gift) (1847–1923) was her sister. Alice Havers's childhood was spent in the Falkland Islands where her father was governor (1854–61) and in Montevideo, Uruguay (1861–70). On her father's death in 1870, the family returned to England and she enrolled as a pupil at the South Kensington art schools, having been granted a free studentship during her first year.

On 13 April 1872 Alice Havers married the artist Frederick Morgan (1847/8–1927) and lived at various London addresses before settling at 1 Cathcart Road, Redcliffe Gardens (1875–82) and subsequently at 11 Marlborough Road, St John's Wood (1884–90). She exhibited widely (and always under her maiden name) at the Society of British Artists (1872/3–1881/2), the Royal Academy (1873–89), the Liverpool autumn exhibitions (1874–89), the Royal Glasgow Institute (1875–88), the Dudley Gallery (1878–9), the Royal Manchester Institution (1879–90), the Grosvenor

Gallery (1881–7), the Society of Lady Artists (1883–90)—of which she became an honorary member in 1885—the Royal Hibernian Academy (1883), the Institute of Painters in Oil Colours (1883–4), and the Paris Salon (1889). She quickly gained a reputation: 'Ought and Carry One' (exh. RA, 1874) was bought by Queen Victoria and engraved, while *A Montevidean Carnival* (exh. RA, 1875) was commissioned by Henry Blackburn. According to Harry Furniss she achieved popularity as a result of German reproductions of her pictures showing subjects in semi-classical costume. The majority of her exhibited paintings were genre scenes depicting rural life and work, often featuring women and children: examples include 'They Homeward Wend their Weary Way' (exh. RA, 1876; National Museum and Gallery of Wales, Cardiff), *Blanchisseuses: 'What, No Soap!'* (exh. RA, 1880; Walker Art Gallery, Liverpool), *Rush-Cutters* (exh. RA, 1880; Mappin Art Gallery, Sheffield), and *The Belle of the Village* (exh. RA, 1885; Atkinson Art Gallery, Southport). Several of her most ambitious paintings involved social comment on the condition of the poor: *The End of her Journey* (exh. RA, 1877; Rochdale Art Gallery) represents a woman who has collapsed by the roadside with her child, while *Trouble* (exh. RA, 1882) portrayed 'a cottage family in time of want and sickness' (*Art Journal*, 44, 1882, 238). Both these works were priced at £200 when exhibited at the Glasgow Institute of the Fine Arts in 1878 and 1884 respectively. *'Tis a Very Good World we Live in* (exh. Liverpool autumn exhibition, 1874; ex M. Newman, 4–21 May 1966) which contrasts the lot of rich and poor and *The Rights of the Poor* (exh. Institute of Painters in Oil Colours, 1883/4) further exemplify this theme in her work.

Two other paintings by Alice Havers are noteworthy: 'But Mary kept all these things and pondered them in her heart' (exh. RA, 1888; Castle Museum, Norwich), which received an honourable mention when exhibited at the Paris Salon in 1889, and 'The Moon is up and yet it is not night' (exh. RA, 1878), a hayfield scene which was offered at £250 during its exhibition at the Glasgow Institute of the Fine Arts in 1880. Between 1875 and 1890 Havers was also a successful illustrator of stories—including many by her sister, Theo Gift—and in the years following her death several collections of poetry contained illustrations by the artist: *A Book of Modern Ballads*, *A Book of Old Ballads*, *Some Old Love Songs* (all 1892), and Lewis Morris's *Odatis* (1892) and *Love and Sleep* (1893).

By 1888 Alice Havers had separated from her husband because of what a contemporary described as 'incompatibility' (Fox, 225); the couple later divorced. After the separation she took her two children, Lilian and Reginald, to Paris where she studied under the artist Filippo Colarossi. After what Furniss described as a sad life, Alice Havers committed suicide on 26 August 1890 at 11 Marlborough Road, St John's Wood, London.

CHARLOTTE YELDHAM

Sources ILN (6 Sept 1890), 295 · H. Furniss, *Some Victorian women: good, bad and indifferent* (1923) · Graves, *RA exhibitors* · J. Johnson, ed., *Works exhibited at the Royal Society of British Artists, 1824–1893, and the New English Art Club, 1888–1917*, 2 vols. (1975) · J. Soden and C. Baile de Laperrière, eds., *The Society of Women Artists exhibitors, 1855–1996*, 4 vols. (1996) · E. Morris and E. Roberts, *The Liverpool Academy and other exhibitions of contemporary art in Liverpool, 1774–1867* (1998) · H. Blackburn, *Academy notes* (1875–8) · R. Billcliffe, ed., *The Royal Glasgow Institute of the Fine Arts, 1861–1989: a dictionary of exhibitors at the annual exhibitions*, 4 vols. (1990–92) · S. Fox, *An art student's reminiscences of Paris in the 1880s* (1909) · WWW, 1929–40 · exhibition catalogues [Dudley Gallery, 1878–9; Grosvenor Gallery 1881, 1885–7; Royal Hibernian Academy, 1883; Institute of Painters in Oil Colours, 1883–4; Paris Salon, 1889; Royal Manchester Institution, 1879–90] · m. cert. · d. cert.

Likenesses wood-engraving (after photograph by H. S. Mendelssohn), NPG; repro. in *ILN*, 97 (6 Sept 1890), 295

Wealth at death £2066 0s. 6d.: probate, 29 Sept 1890, CGPLA Eng. & Wales

Havers, Clopton (1657–1702), physician and anatomist, was one of at least three sons of the Revd Henry Havers (1620–1705×13), rector of Stambourne, Essex, who was ejected in 1662 for his Presbyterian convictions. Clopton Havers entered St Catharine's College, Cambridge, as a pensioner on 6 May 1668, but did not complete any degree. He was admitted an extra-licentiate of the Royal College of Physicians on 28 July 1684. On 3 July 1685 he graduated MD at Utrecht, where his dissertation, *De respiratione*, was published in 1685 in quarto. He then settled in London, where he was elected a fellow of the Royal Society on 17 November 1686. He became a licentiate of the College of Physicians on 22 December 1687, probably practising in Fenchurch Street. On 9 January 1692 a licence was issued for the marriage of Havers, and Dorcas Fuller (1668/9–1743), daughter of the Revd Thomas Fuller (d. 1701), rector of Willingale, Essex, and nephew of Archbishop Thomas Fuller (1593–1667).

Havers provided the first European account of the minute structure of bone. Communicated to the Royal Society in sections that were published as *Osteologia nova, or, Some New Observations of the Bones and the Parts Belonging to them* (1691), it described what subsequently became known as 'Haversian canals', the tiny channels of bone through which blood vessels course. The text, which was well received on the continent, was published in two Latin editions (Frankfurt, 1692; Amsterdam, 1731). Havers also oversaw publication of the English version of Johann Remmelin's *Catoptrium microcosme*, which he titled *A Survey of the Microcosme, or, The Anatomy of the Bodies of Man and Woman* (1695). It used superimposed slips of dissected anatomical plates to show the relations of parts of the body with descriptions. Two of his articles were published in *Philosophical Transactions* during the 1690s: 'An account of an extraordinary haemorrhage at the glandula lacrymalis', which described a case involving the shedding of bloody tears, and 'Discourse of the concoction of the food'. Havers died of a malignant fever on 15 April 1702 and was buried at Willingale Doe, Essex, leaving a widow and children. His daughter Mary was buried at the same church in May that year. Lilly Butler, minister of St Mary Aldermanbury, London, preached his funeral sermon, which was printed in 1702. In it Butler described Havers as:

a most respectful, dutiful son to his aged Father … Having engag'd himself in an honourable and useful Calling, he faithfully perused the designs of it, as one who remembered the account he must give to the Maker of those Bodies he had undertaken the care of, and truly *Watched for their Lives* … His countenance was grave and serious, without any Lines of Sowreness or Affectation; his speech was soft and obliging, without any Air of Conceit or Flattery; his behaviour gentile and Courteous, without any Appearance or Art or Design. (Dobson, 704–5)

ROBERT L. MARTENSEN

Sources DNB • Venn, *Alum. Cant.* • Munk, *Roll* • J. Dobson, 'Clopton Havers', *Journal of Bone and Joint Surgery*, 34B (1952), 702–7 • *Calamy rev.* [Henry Havers] • private information (2004) • *The record of the Royal Society of London*, 4th edn (1940) • A. Kippis and others, eds., *Biographia Britannica, or, The lives of the most eminent persons who have flourished in Great Britain and Ireland*, 2nd edn, 5 vols. (1778–93)

Havers, (Robert) Michael Oldfield, Baron Havers (1923–1992),

lawyer and politician, was born on 10 March 1923 at 126 Mortlake Road, North Sheen, Surrey, the second of three sons and third of four children of Sir Cecil Robert Havers (1889–1977), barrister and High Court judge, and his wife, Enid Flo (d. 1956), daughter of William Oldfield Snelling. His sister Dame (Ann) Elizabeth Oldfield Butler-Sloss (b. 1933) also practised at the bar, and became president of the Family Division of the High Court.

(Robert) Michael Oldfield Havers, Baron Havers (1923–1992), by unknown photographer

Education, war service, and early legal practice Educated at Westminster School, Havers joined the Royal Navy in October 1941. While he was serving as a cadet, the converted Belgian cross-channel ship in which he was serving received a direct hit. Fortunately he was uninjured. This was the first of three occasions on which he 'came to' in the water, after the ships in which he was serving were destroyed. He was appointed midshipman in October 1942 and commissioned a lieutenant in the Royal Naval Volunteer Reserve in 1943. He served in the Mediterranean, Normandy, and the Far East. The first of these gave him, he claimed, unrivalled knowledge of the brothels of Alexandria—not on his own account but from having to extricate his sailors and return them to his ship. The final posting gave him his first experience of advocacy, defending in courts martial.

In 1946 Havers left the navy to attend Corpus Christi College, Cambridge, for two years, where he read law. He was called to the bar in 1948 and joined the chambers of Fred Lawton as pupil to Gerald Howard, who became an MP shortly thereafter. On 3 September 1949 he married Carol Elizabeth (b. 1928/9), daughter of Stuart Lay, company director. They had two sons.

Havers's attractive and vigorous style as an advocate enabled him to build up a substantial civil and criminal practice on the south-eastern circuit, primarily in East Anglia. There, in successive summers, he prosecuted a number of heavy frauds, including the Suffolk lime fraud trials, which ended with the Court of Appeal laying down guidelines as to the number of counts to be included in an indictment. His most famous client was probably Mick Jagger, whose sentence of three months' imprisonment for a minor drugs offence, promptly set aside by the Court of Appeal, produced a public outcry. Havers was appointed QC in 1963. From 1962 to 1968 he was recorder of Dover, and then until 1971 recorder of Norwich. He was chairman of the west Suffolk quarter sessions from 1965

to 1971, having been vice-chairman for the previous four years. He also served as chancellor of the dioceses of St Edmundsbury and Ipswich from 1965 to 1973 and of Ely from 1969 to 1973.

Member of parliament Havers entered politics comparatively late, when he was elected for the then safe Conservative seat of Wimbledon in succession to Sir Cyril Black, with a majority of 13,000 in June 1970, a seat he held until his appointment in 1987 as lord chancellor. He was elected a bencher of the Inner Temple in 1971. In November 1972 he was appointed solicitor-general by Edward Heath, succeeding Sir Geoffrey Howe, who had moved to the cabinet, and he worked closely with Sir Peter Rawlinson, the attorney-general, until the fall of the Conservative government in February 1974. He was knighted on assuming office in 1972.

Following the Conservatives' defeat, Havers was appointed shadow attorney-general and continued to serve in that capacity and as legal adviser to the shadow cabinet throughout the period of Conservative opposition in 1974–9. Nineteen seventy-four saw his first and, in his own memory, his greatest parliamentary occasion, in the attack on the Labour attorney-general, Sam Silkin, over the Housing Finance (Special Provisions) Bill. This granted retrospective immunity to the Clay Cross councillors who faced surcharges and disqualification from office for having refused to increase council rents under the Housing Finance Act of 1972. The roar of support from the Conservative benches behind him as he laid into the attorney-general for advocating this legislation in the teeth, as was known from a leaked letter, of even his own advice, was something he never forgot.

Attorney-general On taking office on 4 May 1979, Margaret Thatcher immediately appointed Havers attorney-general. That office had, in the words of Professor J. Ll. J. Edwards, been 'no sinecure throughout its long history' and frequently the subject of stormy controversy (Edwards, 57). This was equally true of Havers's period in office. Those eight years from 1979 to 1987 were the longest unbroken tenure of the office since the eighteenth century, and included the Falklands War, where he was a member of the small inner 'war cabinet', the miners' strike of 1983, and the Westland crisis.

The first significant controversy of Havers's long period of office came in the autumn of 1979. The Rhodesia sanctions affair, in which his stout endorsement of the decision of the director of public prosecutions not to prosecute anyone for breaching sanctions occasioned some criticism. It related, however, to events involving ministers and senior officials of both major parties in the late 1960s and early 1970s, in circumstances where witnesses were very unlikely to be available, although there were strong grounds for suspecting that at least some in high places both in government and in the oil industry must have known very well what was going on. No one, however, suggested that there had been any political involvement in the decision. Havers was always scrupulous to prevent any attempt at such interference. He believed firmly in the constitutional convention that has applied ever since the Campbell case which brought down the first Labour government in 1924, that the attorney-general, though of cabinet rank, should not be a member of the cabinet, and that the independence of his legal advice and of prosecution decisions should be beyond question.

Two major issues, which were to arise continually during Havers's term of office, were the need to prosecute on several occasions under the Official Secrets Act of 1911, and the growing difficulty of effectively prosecuting cases of serious financial fraud. The latter was a problem highlighted in particular by the Lloyds cases of Peter Cameron-Webb, and the so-called 'Gang of Four' case involving Kenneth Grobb, Ian Posgate, and others, which took some seven years from initiation by the Department of Trade until conclusion of the unsuccessful prosecution. It was Havers's initiative in setting up and encouraging the fraud investigation group concept, whereby for the first time hand-picked teams of lawyers, accountants, and police officers worked together as dedicated teams on such cases, which began to turn the tide, and led, following the report of Lord Roskill's commission in 1986, to the subsequent establishment of the Serious Fraud Office.

On those difficult issues, particularly those involving prosecution under the Official Secrets Act, which required his express authorization, Havers demonstrated not only his personal skills as an advocate but also his pre-eminent recognition that his duty as her majesty's attorney-general was owed not to the government of which he was a member but to the crown and to the upholding and impartial administration of the law. He was centrally involved in Thatcher's decision to expose in the House of Commons the government's knowledge of Anthony Blunt's treacherous links with the Soviet Union. His forensic skills were engaged in the prosecution of the traitors Geoffrey Prime and Michael Bettany and, most dramatically, in 1982 when his cross-examination of Professor Hugh Hambleton, a Canadian economist, culminated in Hambleton's confessing in court to having passed NATO secrets to the Soviet Union. He was also closely involved in the prosecution of Sarah Tisdall, a Foreign Office clerk. She had leaked details of cruise missiles arriving at Greenham Common and, despite her plea of guilty, was sentenced by the lord chief justice to nine months' immediate imprisonment. He was likewise closely involved in the unsuccessful prosecution of Clive Ponting for disclosing secret information concerning the sinking of the *General Belgrano*.

Meanwhile the danger of his involvement in high-profile terrorist cases, both as attorney-general and as former prosecutor of the Birmingham six and Guildford four, had been vividly brought home to Havers when his flat in Wimbledon was bombed by the IRA, fortunately at a time when he and his wife were on holiday in Spain. He reacted publicly with insouciance, being reported as saying to his wife, 'Darling, we seem to have had a slight accident at home' (*The Times*, 3 April 1992). But the narrowness of his escape was not lost on him. He described how he went to his clothes cupboard to find his row of suits hanging apparently untouched, until he felt one and the material simply lifted away in his fingers like cotton wool. He kept his small steel safe from the flat, the one he used to store secret documents, in his room at the law courts. It was crushed like a beer can and he kept it on a high desk like a memento, a St Jerome's skull. Thereafter he had to put up with the burdens of round-the-clock protection.

Echoing an earlier tradition in which the attorney-general would prosecute personally in major criminal cases, Havers led for the crown in the case of the Yorkshire Ripper, where he found himself embarrassed by the refusal of Mr Justice Boreham to countenance the crown's acceptance of the defendant's plea of diminished responsibility. However, he proceeded calmly to cross-examine all four psychiatrists who propounded that defence, including the two called by the prosecution, to the effect that a conviction for murder was obtained. The net result was the same, detention for life, but justice was at least seen to be done. However, such tactics would not have been open to him had the option of capital punishment still been available.

The episode which Havers regarded as the most fascinating of his career was his involvement as a member of the small inner cabinet appointed by Thatcher to supervise the conduct of the Falklands War. His experience was engaged in particular in relation to the deployment of and rules of engagement for the nuclear-powered submarine HMS *Conqueror* in relation to the 26,000 ton Argentine cruiser the *General Belgrano*. Thatcher valued not only his legal expertise, especially in relation to international law and the actions available to Britain under article 51 of the United Nations charter, but also because he was the only member of the inner cabinet with firsthand naval experience.

It was a significant disappointment to Havers when, following the general election of June 1983, Lord Hailsham continued as lord chancellor and the promotion for which he had hoped was not forthcoming. His second parliament as attorney-general, from 1983 to 1987, saw the groundwork for the major change in the prosecution system nationally which came with the advent of the crown prosecution service, though the detailed preparation for this major change fell, on account of Havers's illness, on the solicitor-general, Sir Patrick Mayhew.

In the autumn of 1985 Havers was taken ill while out shooting and was obliged to undergo major heart surgery to correct aortic stenosis. The operation was performed on the National Health Service at St George's Hospital, Tooting. It was during that illness that the Westland helicopter crisis, in which his courage and independence were put to their sternest test, took place. The protagonists were Leon Brittan as secretary of state for trade and industry, backed by the prime minister, and Michael Heseltine, the secretary of state for defence. In the course of the dispute it had fallen to Havers's deputy, Sir Patrick Mayhew, to write to Heseltine with advice on legal aspects of the problem, and passages from this confidential letter, harmful to Heseltine's political case, were published in the media. There was little doubt that the leak, by a civil servant to the Press Association, must have been authorized at a high level and that it had taken place after exchanges between Leon Brittan's department and 10 Downing Street. Havers returned to work, contrary to medical advice, at the heart of this crisis. He was quite clear that to breach the confidentiality of the letter of a law officer of the crown was a gross impropriety, and secondly that the leak had to be treated as an offence under the Official Secrets Act, just as much as the one which had sent Sarah Tisdall to prison. When the suggestion was made that he was taking an unduly legalistic approach, he replied that unless the leak were taken seriously, he would order the police to enter Downing Street the next morning and conduct a criminal investigation. After this it became almost inevitable that heads would roll, and Leon Brittan accepted ministerial responsibility and resigned.

The last of the famous cases with which Havers had to deal as attorney-general was the attempt to suppress the book *Spycatcher* (1987), written by the former MI5 agent Peter Wright, or at least to prevent his profiting from it. Havers not only accepted responsibility for the overall conduct of this difficult case but, despite criticism, pursued the matter with determination. It led at one point to a contretemps with the cabinet secretary, Sir Robert Armstrong, who in giving evidence in the Australian court had indicated that Havers had been party to an earlier decision not to prosecute the author of another book on the security services, a point which Havers insisted be retracted.

Following the general election of 1987 Thatcher showed her loyalty to Havers by promoting him to be lord chancellor. Sadly his health was not good enough to enable him to continue and in October 1987 he resigned. His heart surgery had never really succeeded and he suffered far more pain than he ever made known to any but his closest family and confidants.

Character and interests Key features of Havers's character were his ebullience and his determination to live life to the full. About 5 feet 10 inches tall, with a distinguished head of grey hair, he was friendly, gregarious, and a noted bon viveur with a considerable appetite for fine wines and good cigars. His favourite clubs were the Garrick and Les Ambassadeurs. At the Garrick he enjoyed the company not only of many lawyers and actors but also of several members from Fleet Street, and it is from his conversations there that a number of the indiscretions for which he became celebrated, and some of which got him into hot water, were said to have come.

Havers loved the theatre and was interested also in literature. He co-authored, with different writers, three books on famous trials, which included *The Poisoned Life of Mrs Maybrick* (1977), about the Liverpool poisoner, and *Tragedy in Three Voices: the Rattenbury Murder* (1980), about Alma Rattenbury, who was acquitted for the murder of her husband. His book *The Royal Baccarat Scandal* (1977) was turned into a successful West End play by Royce Ryton. In 1987 he was a judge on the panel for the Whitbread literary awards.

Following his retirement from the woolsack Havers became chairman of RHM Outhwaite, the Lloyds underwriters, the Solicitors' Law Stationery Society, and the Playhouse Theatre, London. He died of heart failure on 1 April 1992, at St Bartholomew's Hospital, Smithfield, London. He was survived by his wife, Carol, and their two sons, Philip (*b.* 1950), a barrister, and Nigel (*b.* 1951), an actor. A memorial service was held on 8 June 1992 at the Temple Church, London.   NICHOLAS LYELL

Sources *The Times* (2–3 April 1992) · *The Independent* (2 April 1992) · J. Ll. J. Edwards, *The attorney general, politics, and the public interest* (1984) · WWW · personal knowledge (2004) · private information (2004) · b. cert. · m. cert. · d. cert.
Likenesses photograph, 1987, repro. in *The Independent* · photograph, repro. in *The Times* (2 April 1992) · photograph, News International Syndication, London [see illus.]
Wealth at death under £125,000: probate, 22 June 1992, *CGPLA Eng. & Wales*

Haversham. For this title name *see* Thompson, John, first Baron Haversham (1648–1710); Hayter, Arthur Divett, Baron Haversham (1835–1917) [*see under* Hayter, Sir William Goodenough, first baronet (1792–1878)].

Haverty, Joseph Patrick (1794–1864), painter, was born in Galway city, but spent most of his life in Dublin. He also resided in Limerick and, sometimes for considerable intervals, in London. It is not known where he received his artistic training, but in 1814, he sent for exhibition four portraits to the Hibernian Society of Artists in Dublin, followed by a picture entitled *Cupid and Psyche* in 1815. With his wife, Maria (*d.* 1852), whom he married in 1816, Haverty had several children. His second son, Thomas (*b.* 1825), was also a painter, exhibiting pictures at the Royal Academy in 1847–58.

Haverty must have become well established over the following few years, as in 1823, on the foundation of the Royal Hibernian Academy, he was elected an associate. He exhibited at their first exhibition in 1826, and remained a regular contributor until 1861. He also exhibited at the

Royal Academy between 1835 and 1838, and with the Society of British Artists in Suffolk Street. During his career, Haverty enjoyed considerable celebrity as a portrait painter, but also produced a large number of historical and religious works. Perhaps his best-known history painting, *The Monster Meeting* (National Gallery of Ireland, Dublin), referred to by a reviewer in the *Freeman's Journal* as 'the most valuable monument of Irish history, Irish enthusiasm and Irish genius' (30 July 1864), was painted over several years. At the centre stands Daniel O'Connell, whose likeness was acclaimed by some at the time as the best ever painted. Around him are grouped some of the leading political figures of the day. Despite its artistic merits and positive reception by press and public alike, the painting remained unsold. Haverty painted other works of political significance, including *The Embarkation of George IV from Kingston, September 3, 1821*. His portraits included the Reilly family of Scarvagh (1823; priv. coll.); Father Theobald Mathew (*c*.1838; National Gallery of Ireland, Dublin); the Manders sisters of Breckdenstown (priv. coll.); Captain Wickham (priv. coll.); Richard Robert Madden (National Gallery of Ireland, Dublin); the Dunalley family (priv. coll.); and the children of John J. Blake (1844; priv. coll.). Among his religious works were a series of paintings the *Seven Sacraments*, a large *Disrobing of the Saviour*, of which he wrote a lengthy description for the *Freeman's Journal* (25 March 1837), and a rather unusual picture entitled *First Confession* (National Gallery of Ireland, Dublin). Numerous churches throughout Ireland were believed to have purchased altar pieces or other pictures by the artist, including the chapel of St Joseph's Asylum in Limerick, which held a copy of Murillo's *Immaculate Conception* by him. Haverty received considerable patronage in that city, and while living there executed such works as his well-known *Limerick Piper* (exh. British Institution 1844; version, National Gallery of Ireland, Dublin), and a portrait of O'Connell and a picture of the Irish Jacobite commander Patrick Sarsfield for the town hall. Yet another portrait of O'Connell was painted for the Catholic Association, and later acquired by the Reform Club in London.

Haverty's ambition seems to have offset a lack of self-confidence; he was prolific, and in spite of a lengthy illness, continued painting up to within a fortnight of his death. He died of dropsy on 27 July 1864, at his home at 44 Rathmines Road, Dublin, and was buried on 30 July at Glasnevin cemetery. The journalist and antiquary Martin *Haverty was his brother.   BRENDAN ROONEY

Sources W. G. Strickland, *A dictionary of Irish artists*, 2 vols. (1913) · 'Death of J. P. Haverty', *Freeman's Journal* [Dublin] (30 July 1864) · A. J. Webb, *A compendium of Irish biography* (1878) · A. Crookshank and the Knight of Glin [D. Fitzgerald], *The painters of Ireland, c.1660–1920* (1978) · J. P. Haverty, 'Description of a picture, The disrobing of the Saviour, in a letter to a friend', *Freeman's Journal* [Dublin] (25 March 1837) · C. Wood, *Victorian panorama* (1976), 95, pl. 96 · *The Times* (1 Aug 1864) · A. Stewart, *Fifty Irish portraits* (1984) · A. M. Stewart and C. de Courcy, *Royal Hibernian Academy of Arts: index of exhibitors and their works, 1826–1979*, 3 vols. (1985–7) · A. M. Stewart, ed., *Irish art loan exhibitions, 1765–1927*, 1 (1990)
Wealth at death £800: probate, 20 Sept 1864, *CGPLA Ire.*

Haverty, Martin (1809–1887), journalist and antiquary, born in co. Mayo on 1 December 1809, was educated at the Irish College at Paris, and went to Dublin in 1836. In the following year he joined the staff of the *Freeman's Journal*, with which he was closely connected until 1850. In 1851 he made an extended tour through Europe, which he described in a long series of dispatches. On his return to Dublin he was made sub-librarian at the King's Inns, where he remained for nearly a quarter of a century, devoting himself principally to the preparation of a general index to the library.

Haverty's *Wanderings in Spain in 1843* (2 vols., 1844) gives a balanced and informed account of the political scene, and evinces a thorough acquaintance with Spanish literature and art. His major work, *The history of Ireland, ancient and modern, derived from our native annals … with copious topographical and general notes* (1860), is remarkable for its impartial tone and original research, largely conducted in foreign archives; an edition for schools was published in the same year as the original work. His report on the excursion of the ethnological section of the British Association to the Aran Islands in 1857, published in 1859, gives a vivid and entertaining account of that memorable expedition, led by Sir William Wilde and attended by the leading Irish scholars of the day.

Haverty died at his home, 40 Alphonsus Road, Drumcondra, co. Dublin, on 18 January 1887, and was buried in Glasnevin cemetery. The painter Joseph Patrick *Haverty was his brother.

W. A. J. ARCHBOLD, *rev.* G. MARTIN MURPHY

Sources *Irish Law Times and Solicitors' Journal* (1887), 49, 110 · *Freeman's Journal* [Dublin] (19 Jan 1887) · J. S. Crone, *A concise dictionary of Irish biography*, rev. edn (1937) · Allibone, *Dict.* · *CGPLA Ire.* (1887)
Wealth at death £233 3s. 2d.: probate, 25 Feb 1887, *CGPLA Ire.*

Haviland, John (1785–1851), physician, son of John Haviland, a Bridgwater surgeon, and his wife, Mary Glover, was born at Bridgwater on 2 February 1785. He was educated at Winchester College, matriculated in 1803 at Gonville and Caius College, Cambridge, and migrated to St John's College, where he graduated BA as twelfth wrangler in 1807; he subsequently became a fellow of his college. He proceeded MA in 1810, ML in 1812, and MD in 1817. He studied medicine at Edinburgh for two sessions, and for three years at St Bartholomew's Hospital, London. He was elected a fellow of the Royal College of Physicians in 1818 and delivered the Harveian oration there in 1837.

Haviland was elected professor of anatomy at Cambridge in 1814 on the death of Sir Busick Harwood. He delivered an annual course of lectures on human anatomy, which Harwood had not done for some twenty years. On Sir Isaac Pennington's death in 1817, Haviland was appointed regius professor of physic, resigning the anatomical chair. In the same year he was elected physician to Addenbrooke's Hospital, Cambridge, a position he held until 1839, when he retired from practice after an attack of typhus fever followed by a slight paralysis. On 31 March 1819 he married Louisa, youngest daughter of the Revd G. Pollen. They had five sons, one of whom, Henry James

Haviland, was physician to Addenbrooke's Hospital from 1861 to 1863.

Haviland's contribution to the history of the Cambridge medical school was largely forgotten until his reputation was justly restored by Sir Humphry Rolleston in his book *The Cambridge Medical School: a Biographical History* (1932). In 1819 Haviland began a systematic course of lectures on general pathology and the principles of medicine. In the same year he instituted a private written examination for the MB, conducted in English, which tested candidates' knowledge of anatomy, botany, chemistry, pharmacy, and therapeutics. He taught clinical medicine at the bedside in Addenbrooke's Hospital. Attendance at his lectures was made mandatory for candidates for the MB degree. Haviland lectured, ensured his students attended, and examined them on what they had learnt: it was, by the standards of his predecessors, startling behaviour. These changes, ratified by the university in 1829 and 1834, bore fruit as the number of students studying medicine at Cambridge increased through the 1820s, but Haviland's efforts were dashed by a combination of the 1832 Anatomy Act (which, in stark contrast to its major contributions to medical education in London, effectively stopped the supply of bodies for dissection in Cambridge) and the reform of the Royal College of Physicians in London, which opened its fellowship to physicians not educated at Oxford or Cambridge.

Haviland published little, but was active in the early affairs of the Cambridge Philosophical Society, serving as its president from 1823 to 1825. He presided over the committee of anatomy and physiology of the 1833 meeting of the British Association for the Advancement of Science, held in Cambridge. He spent much of his time in the 1830s and 1840s defending the medical faculty from its many critics; he gave evidence to the select committee on medical education in 1834, to the select committee on medical registration in 1848, and to the Cambridge University commissioners in 1850. In his time he built up a programme of elementary teaching in clinical medicine and surgery which served to deflect criticism that the university had no interest in the professional aspects of medical education, and therefore could not survive as a medical school. Haviland himself was an inspirational role model for his students, whom he advised to study surgery as thoroughly as medicine; he was remembered as an excellent practical physician of high character and good judgement. He died of apoplexy on 8 January 1851 at Trumpington Street, Cambridge. He was buried at Fen Ditton.

MARK W. WEATHERALL

Sources H. D. Rolleston, *The Cambridge medical school: a biographical history* (1932) · *GM*, 2nd ser., 35 (1851), 205 · Munk, *Roll* · A. Rook, M. Carlton, and W. G. Cannon, *The history of Addenbrooke's Hospital, Cambridge* (1991) · d. cert. · *DNB*
Likenesses engraving, repro. in Rolleston, *The Cambridge medical school*

Haviland, William (1718–1784), army officer, was born in Ireland, the only son of a scion of an old English gentry family, Peter Haviland (1691–1775), a long-serving (1714–44) subaltern and captain in the 31st foot, and his wife,

Lucy. Having acquired his first commission, a lieutenancy in Spotswood's regiment of foot dated 26 December 1739, he accompanied Colonel William Blakeney to North America early in 1740, when that officer went on ahead of the Cartagena expedition to assist in raising Spotswood's (later Gooch's), an American corps. Haviland sailed with Gooch's for Jamaica late in 1740, and served throughout the expedition's ill-fated West Indian operations, including the 1741 assault on Cartagena. On 7 September 1742 he was promoted to a death vacancy as captain in Blakeney's 27th foot, in which he was to serve for the next eighteen years; shortly thereafter he went home with the expedition's survivors, the 27th disembarking in England in December 1742. Haviland and the 27th were still in England late in 1745 when the Jacobite rising broke out, and he acted as aide-de-camp to Blakeney in the 1745–6 operations. After Culloden he rejoined his regiment, which remained in Scotland during 1746–8 as part of the 'pacification' of the highlands. He returned to Ireland early in 1749 when, with the post-war redistribution of the forces, the 27th embarked for Belfast, and remained there until 1757.

On 5 July 1748 Haviland married Caroline, the daughter of Colonel Francis and Lady Elizabeth Lee and the granddaughter of the first earl of Lichfield; when she died, childless, in 1751, he married secondly Salusbury (d. 1807), the daughter of Thomas Aston of Beaulieu, co. Louth, with whom he had a son, Thomas (b. 1757, entered the army in 1773), and a daughter, Mary (b. 1756).

Haviland continued as a regimental officer in Ireland during the inter-war years. He was promoted major on 24 May 1751 and lieutenant-colonel on 16 December 1752, in both cases by purchase. With the new war he embarked with his regiment at Cork in May 1757 and reached Halifax, Nova Scotia, early in July for Loudoun's abortive attempt on Louisbourg; from there he and the 27th were sent on to the upper New York theatre and wintered at Fort Edward, where he commanded. He was promoted to the local rank of colonel on 9 January 1758 and, having been appointed brigadier, took part in Abercromby's disastrous attack that July on Montcalm's lines before Fort Carillon. He commanded again at Fort Edward during the ensuing winter, led the advance down lakes George and Champlain under Amherst in 1759, and commanded at Crown Point over the winter of 1759–60. In 1760 Amherst chose Haviland to lead the 3400-man force of regulars and provincials that advanced down Lake Champlain and the Richelieu, mopping up the French works at Ile-aux-Noix, St Jean, and Chambly, the central command of the three-pronged operation that saw Amherst, Haviland, and Murray converge on and take Montreal (and with it French Canada) in August and September. For this success he was rewarded on 9 December 1760 with the colonel-commandantcy of the 3rd battalion of the 60th foot. Once Canada was taken, Haviland sailed from New York in November 1761 with Monckton's expedition to the West Indies, and was second-in-command at the capture of Martinique in January and February 1762. That May he sailed with Albemarle's Cuban expedition, once again in command of a brigade, and landed before Havana in July; the town was captured in August. He had been promoted major-general on 10 July 1762. The advance on Montreal and the capture of Havana were the high points of Haviland's career, during which he earned the confidence of Abercromby and the friendship of Amherst.

With the peace of 1763 Haviland and his 3/60th were reduced to half pay, but on 1 June 1767 he was rewarded for his services with the colonelcy of the 45th foot, which he retained until his death. To the regiment 'he was a kind of father, and to the younger officers of it his house was literally a home' (*GM*, 1st ser., 54, 1784, 718–19). He was promoted lieutenant-general on 25 May 1772. During the years 1768–77 he was occasionally on the staff in England as a reviewing officer. When the French entered the War of American Independence he joined Amherst's staff, and from 1779 commanded the western district from Plymouth; he commanded encampments of regulars and militia in the vicinity during the annual troop concentrations of 1779 through 1782, sometimes carrying on advanced manoeuvres in his camps. He was promoted full general on 17 February 1783. Haviland died at his seat of Penn, in Burnham parish, Buckinghamshire, on 16 September 1784, 'of a constitution harrassed and broken, not least from the variety than from the length of his services'. His liberality meant that he left his family 'in very narrow circumstances' (*GM*, 1st ser., 54, 1784, 718–19). Edmund Burke, whose niece Haviland's son married, was his neighbour and friend.   J. A. HOULDING

Sources *The royal Inniskilling fusiliers: being the history of the regiment from December 1688 to July 1914*, ed. Regimental Historical Records Committee (1928) · army lists, PRO, WO. 64/9. fol. 84; 64/10, fol. 108; 64/11, fol. 98 · *Army List* (1754–84) · Fortescue, *Brit. army*, vol. 2 · *The journal of Jeffery Amherst*, ed. J. C. Webster (1931) · D. Syrett, ed., *The siege and capture of Havana, 1762*, Navy RS, 114 (1970) · J. Knox, *An historical journal of the campaigns in North America, for the years 1757, 1758, 1759, and 1760*, ed. A. G. Doughty, 3 vols. (1914–16) · J. R. Cuneo, *Robert Rogers of the rangers* (1959) · *GM*, 1st ser., 54 (1784), 718–19 · J. D. Krugler, 'Haviland, William', *DCB*, vol. 4 · marching orders, PRO, WO 5/61–64 · Burke, *Gen. GB* (1871) · N. B. Leslie, *The succession of colonels of the British army from 1660 to the present day* (1974) · *DNB*

Archives Hunt. L., Abercromby MSS · Hunt. L., Loudoun MSS · PRO, Amherst MSS, WO. 34 · U. Mich., Clements L., American Ser., Thomas Gage MSS

Likenesses half-tone engraving, repro. in L. Butler, *The annals of the King's Royal Rifle Corps*, 1: *The royal Americans* (1913)

Havilland, Sir Geoffrey de (1882–1965), aircraft and aero-engine designer and manufacturer, was born at Magdala House, Terriers Wycombe, Buckinghamshire, on 27 July 1882, second of three sons of the Revd Charles de Havilland (1854–1920) and his first wife, Alice Jeannette (1854–1911), daughter of Jason Saunders, of Medley Manor, Oxfordshire. His early life was tense and miserable, with an irascible, improvident father and a harassed, tearful mother, who eventually suffered a depressive decline. Originally destined for the church, de Havilland was educated at Nuneaton grammar school, St Edward's School, Oxford, and the Crystal Palace School of Engineering (1900–03). He then served an apprenticeship at Rugby with Willans and Robinson, engine manufacturers. In

Sir Geoffrey de Havilland (1882–1965), by Sir Oswald Birley, 1940

1905 he became a draughtsman at 30s. a week with the Wolseley Tool and Motor Car Company in Birmingham, but, disliking the dull work and harsh management, he resigned after a year. He then worked for two years in the design office of an omnibus company in Walthamstow.

Inspired by the aeronautical flights of Wilbur Wright, de Havilland in 1908 borrowed between £500 and £1000 from his maternal grandfather (an Oxford businessman) and designed his own aeroplane and engine. During 1910 he taught himself to fly in a second prototype. His first employee was Frank Trounson Hearle, who in 1914 married de Havilland's fiery socialist sister, Ione (1885–1953). De Havilland himself married, in 1909, Louise (1881–1949), daughter of Richard Thomas, engineer, of Chepstow; his wife had formerly been companion to his mother and governess to his two sisters. She made the fabric coverings of the first De Havilland aircraft on a hand-turned Singer sewing machine which she continued to use until her death. They had three sons.

In 1912, flying one of his own machines, de Havilland established a new British altitude record of 10,500 feet. During the following two years he evolved an important range of generic aeroplanes before his appointment in January 1914 as an inspector of aircraft in the aeronautical inspection directorate. He felt miserable and wasted at leaving design work, and in May 1914 became chief designer for the Aircraft Manufacturing Company (Airco) of George Holt Thomas at an annual salary of £600 plus commission on aircraft sold. After the outbreak of war he joined the Royal Flying Corps but continued working at

Airco. In the next four years he designed and flew eight military aeroplanes, five types going into war service in large production. He was an original but never outlandish designer who had an unerring instinct about his work. The number of 'DH' aeroplanes built in Britain and the USA amounted to about 30 per cent of the total output of those two allies.

Following the closure of Airco in 1920, de Havilland raised £20,000 and founded the De Havilland Aircraft Company with a staff of fifty. He was neither chairman nor managing director of his company, begrudging all time lost to technical work and feeling exasperated by financial responsibilities. He preferred instead in the 1920s to devote himself to the possibilities of civil aviation. In 1925 he pioneered the light aeroplane movement with the Moth. This famous model, originally selling at £650, had a simple, practical design and sturdy construction. Over 7000 Moths of different marks were built in Britain in the next seven years, and there were many overseas sales. Thousands of civilians learned to fly in Moths, inaugurating the era of popular civil aviation and winning financial security for De Havillands. The Tiger Moth trainer (first sold in 1931) became the standard Royal Air Force trainer in the Second World War, 8300 being built.

As a result of design work begun in the 1920s, the De Havilland Aircraft Company manufactured 862 airliners in Britain during the 1930s, of the Dragon, Express, and Dragon Rapide types. All were equipped with De Havilland engines. In 1934 the De Havilland Comet Racer (of which only five were built) won a race from London to Melbourne in under seventy-one hours. During the following year de Havilland pioneered the British manufacture of American controllable pitch propellers, which subsequently were crucial in winning the battle of Britain.

De Havilland's prime contribution in the Second World War was the Mosquito, perhaps the most versatile warplane ever built, and for most of the war, the fastest aircraft. His company also operated the government's 'shadow' factories of the second aircraft group and the northern propeller division. Group personnel (including shadow factories) rose from 5191 in 1937 to 38,311 in 1944, and aircraft production from 200 in 1937 to 2327 in 1941. Turnover rose from £1.4 million in 1936 to £25 million in 1945.

After the war De Havillands returned to civil markets with the Dove and Heron types, and built the jet-powered Vampire fighter. Rocket engines followed in 1947 and guided weapons in 1951. The company's engine division had produced the first British jet propulsion engine in 1942, and its Comet airliner, which first flew in 1949, pioneered the civilian jet airliner. Twenty-one Comets were built in Britain up to 1954, when production was suspended after metal fatigue caused two machines to crash with heavy loss of life. De Havilland was distressed by these accidents, and although manufacture of an improved prototype was resumed in 1958, memories of the catastrophe were never erased.

De Havilland was not involved in design work after 1945, and he retired from active involvement in his company in 1955, thereafter remaining as president. His eldest son, Geoffrey de *Havilland, who first flew at the age of eight weeks, was killed while flying an experimental DH fighter near the speed of sound; his youngest son, John (1918–1943), died in an air collision. His wife suffered a nervous breakdown after these deaths and died in 1949. In 1951 de Havilland married Joan Mary (1900–1974), daughter of Edward Philip Frith, chartered accountant, and the divorced wife of Godfrey Mordaunt (d. 1951).

De Havilland was a keen natural historian and photographer, whose attractive personality shines from his memoirs, *Sky Fever*, published in 1961. Imaginative, sensitive, enthusiastic, and tenacious, he was tactful, friendly, and disarming in manner. As the leader of a design team he was deeply admired by his assistants. His modesty and dislike of fuss were such that for two decades he limited his entries in reference books to three or four lines. He was a brave pilot, who won the king's cup air race in 1933 and continued flying until his seventieth year. He was probably unique among the pioneer designers in flying his own creations. He was made OBE in 1918 and CBE in 1934, received the Air Force Cross in 1919, was knighted in 1944, and appointed to the Order of Merit in 1962. He received numerous national and international gold and silver medals and honorary fellowships of learned and engineering societies. De Havilland died of a cerebral haemorrhage on 21 May 1965 at Watford Peace Memorial Hospital, Stanmore, Middlesex.

RICHARD DAVENPORT-HINES

Sources G. de Havilland, *Sky fever: the autobiography of Sir Geoffrey de Havilland* (1961) · C. M. Sharp, *D. H.: an outline of de Havilland history* (1960) · R. M. Clarkson, 'The first de Havilland memorial lecture: Geoffrey de Havilland, 1882–1965', *Journal of the Royal Aeronautical Society*, 71 (1967), 67–92 · *The Times* (22 May 1965) · *Flight* · d. cert. · b. cert.
Archives Royal Air Force Museum, Hendon, corresp. and papers | PRO, Air Ministry MSS
Likenesses O. Birley, oils, 1940, BAE Systems [*see illus.*] · W. Stoneman, photograph, 1944, NPG · Y. Karsh, photographs, 1950–60, BAE Systems · photograph, *c.*1952, repro. in *ILN* (29 May 1965), 19 · F. Eastman, oils, 1953, British Airport Authority · H. Coster, photographs, NPG · M. Wrightson, photograph, NPG
Wealth at death £63,959: probate, 6 Aug 1965, CGPLA Eng. & Wales

Havilland, Geoffrey Raoul de (1910–1946), aviator, was born on 18 February 1910 at Crux Easton, Hampshire, the son of Sir Geoffrey de *Havilland (1882–1965) and his wife, Louise (1881–1949), daughter of Richard Thomas, of Chepstow. His father in 1920 founded the De Havilland Aircraft Company Ltd, which became a worldwide enterprise under his technical leadership.

The eldest of three sons, Geoffrey Raoul was born near to the site of his father's first flying experiments, which attained the success of full controlled flight in the summer of 1910. It was about this time that he experienced his first flight, carried in his mother's arms in a plane piloted by his father. When he and his brothers later went to school—Geoffrey was educated at Stowe School (1924–7)—their parents would visit them by Gipsy Moth, landing in a field in the school grounds for a picnic lunch. All three boys grew up with the sound of aeroplane engines a constant presence in their lives.

In 1928 Geoffrey entered the De Havilland company at Stag Lane, Edgware, as an apprentice. While serving his three years in the engineering departments, he learned to fly at the Royal Air Force Reserve School on Stag Lane aerodrome, and then spent about a year in South Africa, where he gained useful flying experience. After returning to England in 1932 he became a flying instructor at the De Havilland Aeronautical Technical School and later at the London Aeroplane Club, which had by then moved to the company's new aerodrome at Hatfield, Hertfordshire. From the first he had shown exceptional ability as a pilot, and a desire to follow this calling in its most exacting branch led him to turn, at the age of twenty-five, from flying instructor to test pilot on the staff of the parent De Havilland company.

The first aircraft which de Havilland tested was an economical twin-engined transport called the Dragon, which was being manufactured for world use. Aircraft of this class, including Dragonflies, Dragon Rapides, and four-engined DH 86s, occupied him for a couple of years until the company produced a clean, high-performance twenty-two-passenger monoplane airliner, the Albatross, for Imperial Airways. The later development trials of this were conducted by Geoffrey de Havilland when he became chief test pilot in succession to Robert John Waight, who was killed in a flying accident on 1 October 1937.

Taking Waight's place was a considerable step for one who had not up to that time flown a wide variety of aircraft. Fifteen months later de Havilland undertook the first flight of a twin-engined metal transport aircraft, the Flamingo, and conducted its whole flight development. For the next seven years he made the first flight, and did the tests, of every De Havilland prototype. They were the years of the war when the De Havilland company entered wholesale the field of military aviation, and the aircraft concerned were high-performance combat machines, the fastest in their categories. Notable among them were the Mosquito twin-engined two-seat multi-purpose aircraft, first flown on 25 November 1940; the Vampire jet fighter with De Havilland Goblin engine, 20 September 1943; and the Hornet long-range twin-propeller fighter, 28 July 1944. He visited Canada in 1942 to test the Canadian-built Mosquito and to demonstrate it in Canada and the United States. In recognition of his services he was appointed OBE in 1945.

De Havilland was a keen sporting pilot and took part in a great many races and contests. He shone in the low turns of pylon racing and was one of the finest exhibition pilots British aviation has known. His favourite personal racer was a clean little monoplane, the TK 2, designed and built by students of the De Havilland Aeronautical Technical School. With a love of the sport he combined a serious attitude to his work. His upbringing helped him to become a practical and analytical test pilot of the calibre most valuable to the aerodynamicist and the designer. In 1933 de Havilland married Gwendoline Maud Alexander. The marriage was dissolved in 1942 and he married in 1943 Pipette

Marion Scott Bruford. There were no children of either marriage.

Geoffrey de Havilland met his death above the Thames estuary on 27 September 1946, when testing an experimental tailless high-speed jet aircraft, the DH 108, in preparation for an attempt on the world speed record. It is probable that he exceeded this during his last flight. The wreckage of his plane was found the next day, scattered over the mudflats of Egypt Bay, near Sheerness, and his body was discovered at West Beach, Whitstable, over a week later. The precise cause of the crash was never established. Geoffrey's youngest brother, John, had been killed while testing a Mosquito on 23 August 1943, and their father later recalled how he had discussed with both of them the dangers of test flying, but that neither had taken these talks 'very seriously':

> They started a strange habit of refusing to call aeroplanes by their proper name. Geoffrey usually referred to them as 'boilers'. 'If I take a boiler up and it blows up,' he used to say, 'it's just bad luck. But nothing's going to stop me.' (de Havilland, 197)

They were buried in Tewin churchyard, near Hatfield, where their mother was also laid to rest, not long after her eldest son's death. MARTIN SHARP, *rev.* MARK POTTLE

Sources G. de Havilland, *Sky fever: the autobiography of Sir Geoffrey de Havilland* (1961); repr. (c.1979) · *The Times* (20 Sept 1946) · *The Times* (28 Sept 1946) · *The Times* (3 Oct 1946) · *The Times* (8 Oct 1946) · *The Times* (11 Oct 1946) · *The Times* (29 Oct 1946) · P. J. Birtles, *Mosquito* (1998) · CGPLA Eng. & Wales (1946)
Archives Royal Air Force Museum, Hendon, corresp. and MSS | FILM BFI NFTVA, documentary footage · BFI NFTVA, news footage · IWM FVA, actuality footage | SOUND IWM SA, documentary recordings · IWM SA, oral history interview
Likenesses O. Birley, portrait, priv. coll. · E. Kennington, bronze bas-relief, De Havilland Company headquarters, Hatfield · photographs, Hult. Arch.
Wealth at death £2486 11s. 11d.: administration, 16 Dec 1946, CGPLA Eng. & Wales

Havilland, Thomas Fiott de (1775–1866), army officer in the East India Company, was born in April 1775 at Havilland Hall, Havilland, Guernsey, the eldest son of Sir Peter de Havilland (d. 1821), knight, of Havilland Hall and his wife, Cartaretta, daughter and heir of the Revd Thomas Fiott. In 1793 he obtained a Madras cadetship, and on 3 May 1793 was appointed ensign in the Madras engineers (Pioneers). He served at the siege of Pondicherry in 1793, and in the campaign in Ceylon in 1795–6; he was promoted lieutenant on 8 January 1796. He marched with Colonel Browne's force from Trichinopoly to assist in the operations against Tipu Sultan in 1799, and accompanied Sir David Baird's troops to Egypt in 1801. On his return he was captured by a French cruiser, but was speedily released. He was made brevet captain on 12 August 1802, and captain on 1 January 1806.

In 1808 Havilland married Elizabeth, daughter of Thomas Saumarez. They had two daughters and two sons, Thomas, an army officer, and Charles, a clergyman, both of whom died before their father. Meanwhile, Havilland served with his corps until 1812, when he returned home on furlough, and was commissioned to build the Jeybourg barracks, Guernsey. He was made brevet major on 4 June 1813.

In 1814 Havilland was appointed civil engineer and architect for the Madras presidency. He proved an officer of much zeal, ability, and originality. When stationed at Seringapatam, he proposed to bridge the Cauvery with five brick arches of 110 feet span and only 11 feet rise. The authorities scouted the idea, and to prove its feasibility Havilland erected a similar arch in his garden. He attempted to determine the mean sea level at Madras from daily observations extending over six months, and a datum line, known as De Havilland's benchmark, was inscribed on the wall of Fort St George. He constructed the Mount Road, the bulwark or old sea wall of Madras, the cathedral, and St Andrew's Presbyterian Church, Madras. He recommended the survey of the Panjam passage for the improvement of the port, a work carried out by one of his subalterns, Sir Arthur Thomas Cotton.

After his retirement, which took place on 20 April 1825, Havilland devoted himself to the affairs of Guernsey, where he was a justice and member of the legislature. He died at Beauvoir, Guernsey, on 23 February 1866, aged ninety.   H. M. CHICHESTER, *rev.* ALEX MAY

Sources *Indian Army List* · Burke, *Gen. GB* · T. Vibart, *History of the Madras sappers and miners* (1882) · Boase, *Mod. Eng. biog.* · *GM*, 4th ser., 1 (1866), 603
Archives NAM

Haward, Charles (*fl.* 1668–1689), musical instrument maker, was part of a family of harpsichord, spinet, and virginal makers living and working in the City of London. Nothing is known of his parents, or of his early life, but his earliest surviving instrument, a single-manual harpsichord, is signed and dated 'Carolus Haward 1683', while the latest is a wing spinet signed 'Carolus Haward fecit 1689'. The one harpsichord noted above plus seven wing spinets have survived, and a further four surviving spinets are probably from his workshop. He lived in Aldgate Street, London, as is evidenced by a well-known excerpt from the diary of Samuel Pepys for 4 April 1668:

> Up betimes, and by coach to White-hall, took Aldgate street in my way, and there called upon one Hayward that makes virginalls, and did there like of a little Espinette and will have him finish them for me: for I had a mind to a small Harpsicon, but this takes up less room and will do my business as to finding out of Chords—and I am very well pleased that I have found it.

It seems that Pepys called again on Haward on 13 July 1668, and on 15 July he took delivery of the spinet: the cost was £5. In 1672 Haward was referred to by Thomas Salmon in his *Vindication of an Essay to the Advancement of Music* (1672) in the statement: 'A curious pair of Phanatical Harpsichords made by that Arch Heretick Charles Haward' (p. 68). The exact meaning of a pair of 'Phanatical Harpsichords' is unclear, as is the reason for Salmon's description of Haward as an 'Arch Heretick'.

However, the esteem in which Haward's work was held can be judged from the fact that Queen Anne was said to have highly prized a virginal by him—but the loose way in which the terms 'spinet' and 'virginal' were applied to the

smaller domestic instruments in the seventeenth century makes it unclear whether the instrument was a wing-shaped spinet as bought by Pepys, or the rectangular coffer-shaped instrument built in England in the period 1641–84, of which only nineteen survive.

A transcript from the lord chamberlain's accounts relating to music and musicians records a payment in 1674 of £6 10*s*. 'for mending the harpsichords and pedalls in the Great Hall in the Privy Lodgings and for the private musick, for 2 whole years', and in the next year £2 was paid to 'Mr. Haward, the virginall-maker, for mending the harpsichords' (Lafontaine). The mention of 'pedalls' may indicate that it is John Haward (*fl.* 1649–1667) to whom the payment was made, for Thomas Mace, *Musick's Monument* (1676) has a long and interesting section (pages 235–6) on 'the Pedal' (for changing the registration of a harpsichord) 'contriv'd … by one Mr. *John Hayward* of London'. So far as is known, Charles Haward did not make such pedals. This John Haward was almost certainly a relative of Charles Haward, as was also probably a third member of the family, Thomas Haward (*fl.* 1656–1663).

CHARLES MOULD

Sources Pepys, *Diary* · H. C. de Lafontaine, ed., *The king's musick: a transcript of records relating to music and musicians, 1460–1700* [1909] · D. H. Boalch, *Makers of the harpsichord and clavichord, 1440–1840*, ed. C. Mould, 3rd edn (1995)

Haward, Francis (1759–1797), engraver, was born on 19 April 1759 of unknown parentage. He was apprenticed to the engraver Thomas Watson in 1774 for a £75 premium. In 1776 he became a student of the Royal Academy Schools and in the same year engraved a portrait of the astronomer James Ferguson after James Northcote. He scraped only *Master Bunbury* (1781) after Sir Joshua Reynolds and *Euphrasia* (1782) after William Hamilton before abandoning the process to work in techniques based on stipple. In an attempt to imitate Reynolds's style in particular, Haward developed idiosyncratic methods combining the use of various roulettes and other tools to produce a richly textured surface which Sir Joshua evidently admired. He was elected an associate engraver of the academy in 1783. *The Infant Academy* (1783) was a first attempt, but his interpretation of *Mrs Siddons as the Tragic Muse* (1787) saw the fruition of his efforts. The painting was exhibited by Reynolds in 1784 and Valentine Green sought permission to publish it from the painting's owner, Siddons's manager, Sheridan. But Sarah Siddons wrote to Reynolds asking that the painting be given to the engraver of the *Infant Academy*, which she admired. So her portrait went to Haward, who shared publication with James Birchall, publisher of most of his earlier plates. Green was so annoyed that he never produced another engraving after Reynolds. Haward exhibited the print at the Royal Academy in 1787, dedicated it to George III, and presented it to him in January 1788. Other prints exhibited at the academy included *A Cupid* (1783), a portrait of the transsexual fencer and spy Madam D'Éon (1788), and in 1792 an unfinished engraving, followed the next year by the finished plate of *The Prince of Wales* after Reynolds. On the strength of this last, Haward was appointed engraver to the prince of Wales. For many years Haward and his wife Mary lived at 29 Marsh Street, Lambeth, London, and there he died in June 1797, shortly after completing a last plate after Reynolds, *Cymon and Iphigenia*. He was buried on 30 June at St Mary Lambeth. Mary Haward received a pension of £20 from the Royal Academy until her own death in 1839.

TIMOTHY CLAYTON and ANITA McCONNELL

Sources 'Francis Haward', BL, Dodd's history of English engravers, Add. MS 33401 • Redgrave, *Artists* • W. Sandby, *The history of the Royal Academy of Arts*, 2 vols. (1862); facs. edn (1970) • will, PRO, PROB 11/1294, sig. 501 • D. Alexander and R. Godfrey, *Painters and engraving: the reproductive print from Hogarth to Wilkie* (1980) [exhibition catalogue, Yale Center for British Art, New Haven, CT] • T. Clifford, A. Griffiths, and M. Royalton-Kisch, *Gainsborough and Reynolds in the British Museum* (1978) [exhibition catalogue, BM] • N. Penny, ed., *Reynolds* (1986) [exhibition catalogue, RA, 16 Jan – 31 March 1986] • I. Maxted, ed., *The London book trades, 1710–1777: index of the masters and apprentices recorded in the inland revenue registers at the Public Record Office* (privately printed, Exeter, 1983) • E. Hamilton, *Catalogue raisonné of the engraved works of Sir Joshua Reynolds* (1874) • parish register, Lambeth, St Mary, LMA [burial]
Likenesses O. Humphrey, chalk drawing, NPG

Haward, Nicholas (*fl.* 1564–1569), author, was born in Norfolk of unknown parents, and described himself as a student of Thavies Inn. He produced a translation of Flavius Eutropius, published by Thomas Marshe in 1564 as *A briefe chronicle, where in are described shortlye the originall, and the successive estate of the Romaine weale publique*. The text was dedicated to the old Oxonian Master Henry Compton, praised by Haward as a man of great learning and gentleness. The prefatory letter contains a defence of history, and answers to the charge that translation of the classics into English contributes to the decay of knowledge. In 1569 the same printer published Haward's *The line of liberalitie dulie directing the wel bestowing of benefites and reprehending the comonly used vice of ingratitude*, written in praise of generosity, and dedicated to Sir Christopher Heydon, dubbed by Haward the 'most courteouse Creditour of many his bounties and benefites'.

CATHY SHRANK

Sources W. T. Lowndes, *The bibliographer's manual of English literature*, ed. H. G. Bohn, [new edn], 2 (1864) • W. C. Hazlitt, *Collections and notes, 1867–1876* (1876) • E. Brydges, *The British bibliographer*, 4 vols. (1810–14), vol. 2 • *DNB*

Haward, Sir William (*c.*1617–1704), courtier and antiquary, was the third son of John Haward (*c.*1571–1631) of Tandridge Hall, Surrey, and his first with his second wife, Elizabeth, daughter of William Angell, gentleman pensioner to James I. In November 1635 Haward—his own preferred spelling of the name—was granted special admission to the Inner Temple as the son of a bencher. Soon afterwards he purchased Tandridge Hall and two Surrey manors worth £600 per annum from his older half-brother John. From 1641 to 1646 he served as gentleman of the privy chamber to Charles I, who knighted him on 9 September 1643 at Sudeley Castle. Five days earlier, in the garrison at Oxford, he had married Martha (*d.* 1689), youngest daughter of John Acton, a London goldsmith. She brought with her a dowry of £1250, and in due course they had six daughters and four sons. In the autumn of 1645 Haward retired to Tandridge, claiming in his petition to compound of the following April that he had never borne arms. His fine, fixed in January 1647 at the rate of one sixth of his estate, totalled £437.

Although Evelyn dismissed Haward as 'a greate pretender to English antiquities &c' (*Diary*, 6 Dec 1671), Aubrey pronounced him 'a learned Gentleman and great *Antiquary*' (Aubrey, 3.36). Dugdale too thought him 'well accomplisht with learning especially in points of Honour and Armes' (*Life … of Sir William Dugdale*, 32). By 1663, when he was elected fellow of the Royal Society, he had already begun to collect or make copies of monastic and genealogical records. His transcripts are executed in a bold and regular script well suited to the large folio format in which he preferred to work. Examples range from a volume of genealogical, heraldic, and historical material that includes a copy of a Glastonbury chartulary (BL, Add. MS 58216), by way of Becher's account of the amours of Henri IV of France (BL, Sloane MS 841), to an important 700-page miscellany that mingles Restoration verse, scandal, and politics with history, commerce, and much else (Bodl. Oxf., MS Don. b. 8). Peter Le Neve, who in 1695 bought an even larger antiquarian compilation (BL, Harleian MS 3875), along with two original chartularies (BL, Harleian MSS 391, 4809), drew up a list of twenty-seven Haward manuscripts purchased by Lord Chancellor Somers in 1697 (Bodl. Oxf., MS Rawl. D. 888, fol. 41*v*). Several of these later found their way to the earls of Oxford and are now BL, Harleian MSS 4785, 4786, 6016, 6025, 6166, 6193, 6266, and 6829. A catalogue of Haward's library belonged to Richard Rawlinson (sale catalogue, Barnard, 4 March 1733/4, lot 387).

At the Restoration Haward resumed his post in the household, retaining it under each successive sovereign until 1702. From 1661 to 1678 he sat in the Cavalier Parliament for his father's old seat of Bletchingley and was moderately active for the court party, serving on some seventy committees. In 1672 he gave money towards rebuilding the College of Heralds, though he failed five years later in his bid to become Garter. Three years after the dissolution of parliament he sold his Surrey estate and bought an interest in the Broken Wharf waterworks, while continuing to occupy his official lodging in old Scotland Yard. In the following decade he was constrained to sell his collection of manuscripts. His wife was buried in Westminster Abbey cloisters on 24 March 1689. In May 1704, when aged almost ninety, he petitioned Queen Anne for relief but did not long enjoy it, being buried on 28 July in St James's, Piccadilly.

W. H. KELLIHER

Sources W. P. Baildon, *The Hawardes of Tandridge* (1894) • J. Aubrey, *The natural history and antiquities of the county of Surrey*, 5 vols. (1718–19) • Evelyn, *Diary* • *The life, diary, and correspondence of Sir William Dugdale*, ed. W. Hamper (1827) • H. Love, *Scribal publication in seventeenth-century England* (1993) • M. A. E. Green, ed., *Calendar of the proceedings of the committee for compounding … 1643–1660*, 2, PRO (1890) • W. A. Shaw, ed., *Calendar of treasury books*, 19, PRO (1938) • W. B. Bannerman, ed., *The visitations of the county of Surrey … 1530 … 1572 … 1623*, Harleian Society, 43 (1899) • G. J. Armytage, ed., *A visitation of the county of Surrey, begun … 1662, finished … 1668*, Harleian

Society, 60 (1910) • F. A. Inderwick and R. A. Roberts, eds., *A calendar of the Inner Temple records*, 5 vols. (1896–1936) • HoP, *Commons, 1660–90* • C. E. Wright, *Fontes Harleiani* (1972)

Archives BL, Add. MS 58216 • BL, Harley MSS 391, 3875, 4785, 4786, 4809, 6016, 6025, 6166, 6193, 6266, 6829 • BL, Sloane MS 841 • Bodl. Oxf., MS Don. b. 8

Hawarde, John (*c*.1571–1631), barrister, was the third and surviving son, and the heir, of Henry Hawarde (*d*. 1610), citizen and fishmonger of London, and his second wife, Agnes Castell, daughter and heir of a London merchant. Henry had acquired considerable property around Tandridge, Surrey, including the seat which his son John inherited in 1610. By 1586 Hawarde had married Agnes Wilkinson, whose mother was Henry Hawarde's third wife. His second wife, whom he married about 1600, was Elizabeth Angell, whose father was fishmonger to James I. He had two sons and one daughter with Agnes and two sons and eight daughters with Elizabeth.

Hawarde was admitted to the Inner Temple from Clifford's Inn in 1588, and was called in November 1598. His dilatoriness in taking a decade to complete the exercises for the bar might be explained by his diligence in court-watching, particularly in the Star Chamber. Such was a large part of the education of students at the inns, and it also provided entertainment. Even after call, possibly because his practice began modestly and with his father still seated at Tandridge he preferred town to country, Hawarde was a frequent attender in the court. The fruit of his assiduity was a manuscript volume of reports, entitled 'Les reportes del cases in camera stellata', between January 1594 and February 1609. In its 364 pages a total of 224 Star Chamber cases are reported, most of them of trials with judgments (there are only a few interlocutory matters noted), covering in considerable detail a period for which otherwise reports are thin. A privately printed transcription of the volume by William Paley Baildon published in 1894 has given considerable prominence to Hawarde's reports for want of much else in print. A comparison of Baildon's work with the original (now in the Carl H. Pforzheimer Library, New York) indicates some few but not disfiguring errors and inspires confidence in its accuracy.

Hawarde's reports include a few cases at Surrey assizes, Newgate, king's bench, chancery, and wards, along with *Calvin's Case* (1608)—much truncated by Baildon—the trial of the Gunpowder Plot conspirators (1606), and the dispute between Sir Christopher Yelverton and Thomas Cecil, second Lord Burghley, heard before the privy council in 1602. There is incidental material, including charges of the lord chancellor to the judges of assize, accounts of Garter ceremonies, the death of Elizabeth, and the accession of James. There is only one reference, dating from before he was called, in which Hawarde indicates having spoken in Star Chamber, though he clearly was involved in some of the cases in the other courts. In fact, he seems to have had a very slight practice in Star Chamber: he signed pleadings in only three cases there between 1603 and 1625, and two were from Surrey. He was one of those

county-based counsel who had a mixed practice with occasional appearances in Star Chamber. His clientele was substantial but local, such neighbouring gentry as Sir Nicholas Carew and Sir Thomas Gresham prominent among them. Indeed, Hawarde was almost as much litigant as counsel in the court, bringing a bill in 1597 for a riotous assault and battery sustained by him in Maidstone and himself being charged with subornation of perjury in a London case involving bigamy in 1613. He was prominent enough to be made a bencher of the Inner Temple in 1613. He held no office in the inn, though in the late 1620s he was an auditor of the steward's accounts. In 1615 he was the Lent reader. There is no indication of the subject of his reading, and he does not appear to have written anything else.

After he took up residence at Tandridge Hall in 1610, Hawarde's ties to London became increasingly tenuous. He was a Surrey justice of the peace (of the quorum) and coroner for the county. He sat in the parliaments of 1621 and 1624 for the nearby borough of Bletchingley. He did not distinguish himself in debate, though his disputed election in 1624 provided some excitement in the early days of the session. He was a careful steward of his extensive estates in Surrey, which he fully settled before his death. He found portions for three married daughters and provision for the remaining surviving spinsters. He cut out his eldest son entirely, deeming him 'undutifull and unthriftie' (will), but looked to the education in both the law and the church of his other sons. His churchmanship was decidedly puritan. He died in January 1631 at Tandridge, and was buried there.   THOMAS G. BARNES

Sources J. Hawarde, 'Les reportes del cases in camera stellata', Carl H. Pforzheimer Library, New York • will, PRO, PROB 11/159, fol. 94 • star chamber proceedings, PRO, Elizabeth, STAC5; James I, STAC8 • Libri pacis, PRO, C193/12/2, C193/13/1, E163/18/12 • *Les reportes del cases in camera stellata, 1593 to 1609, from the original ms. of John Hawarde*, ed. W. P. Baildon (privately printed, London, 1894) [introduction provides biographical detail] • F. A. Inderwick and R. A. Roberts, eds., *A calendar of the Inner Temple records*, 2 (1898) • T. G. Barnes, 'Star chamber litigants and their counsel, 1596–1641', *Legal records and the historian*, ed. J. H. Baker (1978), 7–28 • W. R. Prest, *The rise of the barristers: a social history of the English bar, 1590–1640* (1986) • W. Notestein, F. H. Relf, and H. Simpson, eds., *Commons debates, 1621*, 7 vols. (1935) • R. E. Ruigh, *The parliament of 1624: politics and foreign policy* (1971)

Archives Carl H. Pforzheimer Library, New York, 'Les reportes del cases in camera stellata' • Wilts. & Swindon RO, parliamentary diaries

Wealth at death sizeable estate, virtually all settled before death: will, PRO, PROB 11/159, fol. 94

Hawarden. For this title name *see* Maude, Clementina, Viscountess Hawarden (1822–1865).

Hawarden, Edward (1662–1735), Roman Catholic priest, probably the son of Thomas Hawarden of Croxteth, Lancashire, and Jane Tarleton of Aigburth, Lancashire, was born on 9 April 1662, had entered the English College at Douai by 1676, and was ordained priest on 7 June 1686. He had been previously engaged as tutor of classics in the college, and after ordination was appointed professor of philosophy. He took the degree of BD at the University of Douai, and was immediately afterwards placed at the head of a group of priests sent in September 1688 from Douai to Oxford. When James II had determined to make Magdalen College a seat of Catholic education, Hawarden was intended for the tutorship of philosophy there. The expected revolution forced him to leave Oxford on 16 November and return to Douai, where he was installed as professor of divinity, an office he held for seventeen years. He took the degree of DD at Douai University soon after his return, and was appointed vice-president of the college in 1702 to Edward Paston. In the same year he was an unsuccessful candidate for one of the royal chairs of divinity in Douai University. A little later, having seemingly made himself some enemies in the concursus for the catechetical chair at the university, he was groundlessly and unjustly accused of Jansenism.

Hawarden left Douai in September 1707, and at first resided with the Dalton family at Thurnham in Lancashire. Then for a few years, from about 1709 to 1711, he conducted the mission at Gilesgate in Durham. On the death of his friend Bishop Smith in 1711 he returned to another Dalton house, Aldcliffe Hall, near Lancaster, where he is reported as celebrating midnight mass at Christmas 1713. He probably left in 1715, on the seizure of the hall by the commissioners for forfeited estates. Appointed to the chapter, and to the position of 'catholic controversy writer', by 1719 he was settled in London, a more convenient location for publishing his many books in defence of the Catholic faith. He published an important work, entitled *The True Church of Christ*, containing treatises on supremacy, transubstantiation, and the invocation of the saints. On the publication of the second edition of Samuel Clarke's *Scripture Doctrine of the Trinity*, which came out in 1719, a conference was arranged by the desire of Queen Caroline between Hawarden and Clarke for the express purpose of discussing the trinitarian doctrine. The meeting took place in the presence of the queen, and Hawarden was thought to have the best of the dispute. He returned to the subject some years later in his *Answer to Dr. Clarke and Mr. Whiston*, which was first published in 1729. His many other works caused him to be eulogized by Bishop Milner as 'one of the most profound theologians and able controversialist of his age' (*DNB*). He died on 23 April 1735 in London.   C. W. SUTTON, rev. G. BRADLEY

Sources G. Anstruther, *The seminary priests*, 3 (1976), 94–5 · J. Kirk, *Biographies of English Catholics in the eighteenth century*, ed. J. H. Pollen and E. Burton (1909), 113–16 · D. A. Bellenger, ed., *English and Welsh priests, 1558–1800* (1984), 69 · E. Duffy, ed., *Challoner and his church: a Catholic bishop in Georgian England* (1981), 117 · E. Duffy, 'A rubb-up for old soares; Jesuits, Jansenists, and the English secular clergy, 1705–1715', *Journal of Ecclesiastical History*, 28 (1977), 291–317 · F. Blom and others, *English Catholic books, 1701–1800: a bibliography* (1996), 1362–82 · Gillow, *Lit. biog. hist.*, 3.167–82 · W. V. Smith, 'Was Dr Edward Hawarden a missioner in Durham?', *Biographical Studies*, 1 (1951–2), 40–44 · F. O. Blundell, *Old Catholic Lancashire*, 3 (1941), 14–15 · P. Guilday, *The English Catholic refugees on the continent, 1558–1795* (1914)
Archives Ushaw College, Durham, Ushaw MSS, dictates of Douai lectures
Likenesses C. Turner, engraving, pubd 1816, Douai Abbey, Woolhampton, Berkshire · C. Turner, mezzotint, pubd 1816, BM, NPG · portrait, repro. in Blundell, *Old Catholic Lancashire*

Haweis, Hugh Reginald (1838–1901), author and Church of England clergyman, born on 3 April 1838, at Egham, Surrey, was grandson of Thomas *Haweis, the friend and trustee of Lady Huntingdon, and was son of John Oliver Willyams Haweis (1809–1891), Church of England clergyman, and his wife, Mary. His father matriculated in 1823 at Queen's College, Oxford, graduating BA in 1828 and proceeding MA in 1831. From 1846 he was morning preacher at the Magdalen Hospital in London, and from 1874 to 1886 rector of Slaugham, Sussex. In 1883 he was made Heathfield prebendary of Chichester Cathedral. He was the author in 1844 of *Sketches of the Reformation*.

Hugh Reginald, the eldest son in a family of four children, showed great musical sensibility and aptitude for violin playing from early years, but poor health prevented systematic education. He suffered from hip disease, and when he was twelve Sir Benjamin Brodie, the surgeon and anatomist who had written on the hip, pronounced his case hopeless. He was taken to his grandmother's house at 54 Brunswick Square, Brighton, and recovered, although his growth had been badly stunted (he was scarcely 5 feet tall) and he was left with a club foot and continued to suffer periodically from pain in his hip. At Brighton he practised the violin assiduously, receiving instruction from several masters including Antonio Oury, the distinguished violinist and professor at the Royal Academy of Music. He also gained orchestral experience and wrote for the Brighton papers.

By the age of sixteen Haweis was so much stronger that he was sent to a tutor to prepare for matriculation at Cambridge. In 1856 he matriculated at Trinity College, Cambridge, his paternal grandfather's college, and quickly became a notoriety. He was the principal violinist of the Cambridge Musical Society, formed a quartet society, read German poetry and philosophy, started a short-lived magazine called *The Lion*, and wrote voluminously for several newspapers. He made the acquaintance of a French violinist, J. G. R. R. Venua, who interested him in violinmaking, a subject upon which he began researches. After graduating BA in 1860 (he proceeded MA in 1864) he travelled for his health. His father had wished him to avoid Italy, but he fell in with Signor Li Calsi, a professional musician whom he knew at Brighton, and the pair went to Genoa, and thence to join Garibaldi at Capua. Haweis survived the war unscathed. He met King Victor Emmanuel and was present at the peace celebrations in Milan. He described his part in the war of independence in *The Argosy* in 1870.

Before leaving Italy Haweis decided to seek orders in the English church, and in 1861 he passed the Cambridge examination in theology and was ordained deacon in London that year, becoming priest in 1862. He was curate of St Peter, Bethnal Green (1861–3). In east London he threw himself enthusiastically into parish work. He was a close friend of John Richard Green, who was in sole charge of Holy Trinity, Hoxton, and Green greatly influenced his views on social questions. From 1864 to 1866 he was curate to St James-the-Less, Westminster, and then to St Peter, Stepney. In 1866 he was appointed perpetual curate of St

Hugh Reginald Haweis (1838–1901), by Barraud, pubd 1888

James, Westmoreland Street, Marylebone. He found the church nearly empty and in need of immediate repair. By his energy, ability, and somewhat sensational methods he quickly filled his church, and kept it full and fashionable for thirty-five years until his death.

Haweis was a powerful preacher. His theatrical manner and vanity (he always preached in a black gown) frequently exposed him to charges of charlatanry and obscured his genuine spiritual gifts: but he was sincere and untiring in his efforts. He organized in his church 'Sunday evenings for the people', at which orchestral music, oratorio performances, and even exhibitions of sacred pictures were made 'to form portions of the ordinary church services'. His aim was to provide edifying entertainment and simultaneously keep his followers from the entertainments of the public house. His success encouraged him to use St James's Hall, Regent Street, for Sunday morning services of a similarly unconventional character, and he received numerous invitations to preach elsewhere. Haweis's theology was controversial as well as his style. He explicitly and repeatedly repudiated the doctrine of eternal damnation and was an outspoken advocate of the compatibility of spiritualism and Christianity. He attended séances and was a member of the Society for Psychical Research. His unconventional style filled his churches and lecture halls, although it stood in the way of church preferment.

An energetic advocate of the provision of wholesome recreations for townspeople, he was an early promoter of the Sunday opening of museums and picture galleries. He interested himself in the provision of open spaces in London and in the laying out as gardens of disused churchyards.

Haweis continued to write prolifically, not least because he needed money. His lecturing fees often failed to cover his expenses, and invitations to fashionable social gatherings involved him in considerable expense. He wrote much for magazines, *The Times*, the *Pall Mall Gazette*, and *The Echo*. His musical books included *Music and Morals* (1871), *My Musical Life* (1884), and *Old Violins* (1898). As musical critic to *Truth* and the *Pall Mall Gazette* Haweis helped to introduce Wagner's works to English audiences. His best work was on music, although his theological writings were more numerous. They included works which reflected on current debates, such as *Thoughts for the Times* (1872) and a historical survey of the origins of Christianity, which he published in 1886–7 in five volumes as *Christ and Christianity*. He also published many sermons, edited the work of others, and wrote books on popular themes.

Haweis's chief success was achieved as a popular lecturer in England and the colonies, as well as in America, on musical and religious themes. In 1885 he gave the Lowell lectures in Boston, USA. During the Chicago Exposition in 1893 he was an Anglican delegate to the Parliament of Religions, and in the following year he visited the Pacific coast, preaching to crowded congregations in Trinity Church, San Francisco. Thence he toured through Canada, the south sea islands, Australia, and New Zealand, lecturing and preaching. He described his American and colonial experiences in *Travel and Talk* (2 vols., 1896).

Haweis was short, with olive skin and hazel eyes, and long black hair. Described by his future wife in her journal as vivacious and with a reputation for lack of ceremony extending to flirtatiousness, he retained to old age his capacity to attract and inspire.

In 1867 Haweis married Mary Eliza (1848–1898), elder daughter of Thomas Musgrave *Joy (1812–1866), portrait painter, and his wife, Eliza. As Mary *Haweis she became a distinguished artist and book illustrator. They were at first a devoted couple in their private life, and each helped the other in their writing and publishing, he with his experience of editors and publishers, she with her talent for illustration. Their first child died in infancy but they had three surviving children, a girl and two boys. After D. G. Rossetti's death in 1882 the Haweis family occupied the poet's house, the Tudor House, renamed the Queen's House, in Cheyne Walk, Chelsea. Haweis died suddenly of heart seizure on 29 January 1901 at 15 Bulstrode Street. His body was cremated at Woking, and the remains interred beside his wife in the churchyard of St Peter's Church, Boughton Monchelsea, Kent, her family graveyard.

Haweis's public reputation survived unchallenged until the publication in 1967 of a biography of his wife by Bea Howe. Written with the help of the brothers Stephen and Lionel Haweis, to the former of whom it is dedicated, and relying extensively on Mary Haweis's letters and journals, the book portrays the dark side of Haweis. His and Mary Haweis's once happy and mutually supportive marriage began to break down in the 1880s. Haweis, who had always been attractive to women, began to take an interest in a parishioner, Miss Emmeline Souter, which made his wife unhappy and which exposed him to gossip. Mary Haweis, who had been unable to understand why her husband was so short of money and why the household depended so heavily on her own earnings, discovered the answer when her husband's mistress and their six-year-old illegitimate child arrived at the family home in 1894 when her husband was away on a preaching tour. His erratic, deceitful, and unreasonable behaviour had already forced a rift between Mary Haweis and her daughter Hugolin, though his efforts to embitter her relations with her sons failed. He was aided by his sisters, 'those interfering and rude women' as Mary Haweis called them in a letter to Lionel of 31 March 1897 (Howe, 261). He grew increasingly jealous of her popularity as a writer and particularly her involvement in social movements, such as women's suffrage, in which he played no part. Such jealousies were especially apparent as his own popularity grew uneven and it became clear to him that preferment in the church would elude him. Despite her increasingly frenetic writing and journalism, his imprudent spending obliged them in 1897 to move from Queen's House, in Chelsea, which Mary loved, to the dingy house in Devonshire Street which she loathed. Exhausted, Mary Haweis finally died on 24 November 1898. Her husband spent her last days trying unsuccessfully to persuade her to alter the terms of her will, under which she left everything to her son Stephen rather than to him. Legal wrangling surrounding the will continued until his death in 1901, by which time he had managed to deprive Stephen, a minor in his legal guardianship, of much of his inheritance. He destroyed many of his wife's letters and journals, which she had expressly left to Stephen, not least because they showed him in an unflattering light. Howe attributes Haweis's behaviour less to malice than to mental instability, and perhaps most of all to an unlimited capacity for self-deception. Certainly he regarded himself as the aggrieved party in the marriage and insisted until the end on his affection for his wife. He seems to have died a lonely, frustrated, and sad figure, having at his best put unstinting effort into his music, preaching, and family life. ELIZABETH BAIGENT

Sources B. Howe, *Arbiter of elegance* (1967) · *DNB* · *WWW* · Venn, *Alum. Cant.* · Foster, *Alum. Oxon.* · J. Oppenheim, *The other world: spiritualism and psychical research in England, 1850–1914* (1985) · *The Times* (30 Jan 1901)

Archives Boston PL, corresp. · University of British Columbia, corresp. and MSS | Hove Central Library, letters to Lord Wolseley and Lady Wolseley · LPL, corresp. with A.C. Tait

Likenesses F. H. Lewis, oils, 1913, NPG · Ape [C. Pellegrini], watercolour caricature, NPG; repro. in *VF* (22 Sept 1888) · Barraud, print, NPG; repro. in *Men and Women of the Day*, 1 (1888) [*see illus.*] · W. & D. Downey, photograph, woodburytype, NPG; repro. in W. Downey and D. Downey, *The cabinet portrait gallery*, 4 (1893) · F. Moscheles, oils · G. J. Stoddart, stipple, BM · etching, repro. in Howe, *Arbiter of elegance*, facing p. 249 · woodcut (after photograph by Mayall), NPG; repro. in *Harper's Magazine* (1888)

Wealth at death £1302: resworn probate, Sept 1901, *CGPLA Eng. & Wales*

Haweis [*née* Joy], **Mary Eliza** (1848–1898), writer and illustrator, was born on 21 February 1848 in London, the elder daughter of Thomas Musgrave *Joy (1812–1866), genre and portrait painter, and Eliza Rohde Joy, *née* Spratt. Mary Eliza herself had considerable artistic talent: at eighteen she exhibited at the Royal Academy and also undertook some portrait commissions. In later life she illustrated both her own books and those of her husband, Hugh Reginald *Haweis (1838–1901), whom she married on 30 November 1867 at St Mary's Church, Kilburn. Hugh Reginald Haweis was an author and popular preacher, and incumbent at St James, Westmoreland Street, Marylebone. Their first-born son, Reginald Joy, died in infancy in 1869, but three further children survived to adulthood: Lionel (*b.* 1870), Hugolin Olive (*b.* 1873), and Stephen Hugh Wyllyams (*b.* 1878). Mary accompanied her husband on preaching tours of the continent and North America, and adopted many philanthropic causes, including women's suffrage.

Haweis's knowledge of art and literature can be seen in the range of her published books. The first, *Chaucer for Children: a Golden Key* (1st edn 1877, 2nd edn 1882), skilfully combined both interests; aiming at a historically accurate representation of medieval costume and furniture, it was meticulously illustrated with woodcuts and colour plates whose details were drawn from medieval manuscripts. Her knowledge of the history of fashion clearly informed her series of publications on domestic décor: *The Art of Beauty* (1878), *The Art of Dress* (1879), and *The Art of Decoration* (1881), and these books also provided a forum for the expression of her wholesome views on the dangers fashion posed to health, and on the necessity that decoration should be both useful and in harmony with natural proportion.

Haweis economically recycled material between publications. Essays on certain well-known artistic houses were first published in the journal *Queen* during 1880–81 and were then reprinted in *Beautiful Houses* (1882). Her somewhat more advanced edition of Chaucer's poetry, *Chaucer for Schools* (1881; 2nd edn 1899), reused material from *Chaucer for Children*, though not the illustrations. Her comparatively scholarly approach led her to provide her own modernized translations of Chaucer's verse, an extended introduction and critical apparatus; she checked her text against F. J. Furnivall's six-text edition. Haweis believed that Chaucer's lines could be enjoyed by anyone who had 'moderate intelligence and an ear for musical rhythm' (M. Haweis, *Chaucer for Schools*, 1881, xi). Further attempts to popularize Chaucer may be seen in two more ephemeral publications: *Chaucer's Beads: a Birthday Book, Diary and Concordance of Chaucer's Proverbs or soothsaws* (1884), a collection of Chaucer's pithy sayings with glosses and suggested modern equivalents, for every day of the year; and *Tales from Chaucer* (1887), a small-format volume in the Routledge's World Library series edited by her husband, which included paraphrases of ten of the *Canterbury Tales*, mostly composed by herself, with selections of original verse. At the same time she continued to publish material relating to home management, producing *Rus in urbe, or, Flowers that Thrive in London Gardens and Smoky Towns* (1886), and *The Art of Housekeeping: a Bridal Garland* (1889). The latter was intended as a practical guide for newly married women and offered advice on economical budgeting, equipping a home, managing servants, and dealing with infestations of beetles; Haweis practised such economies in her own household, where money was always in short supply. Her last publication, the novel *A Flame of Fire* (1897), reflects her strong support for the women's franchise movement.

Mary Haweis died at Lansdown Grove House, Bath, on 24 November 1898 from kidney disease and heart failure; she was cremated at Woking on 26 November, and her ashes were interred in the Joy family vault at St Peter's, Boughton Monchelsea, Kent.   MARGARET CONNOLLY

Sources B. Howe, *Arbiter of elegance* (1967) · D. Matthews, 'Infantilizing the father: Chaucer translations and moral regulation', *Studies in the Age of Chaucer*, 22 (2000), 93–114 · *CGPLA Eng. & Wales* (1899) · *DNB* · d. cert.
Archives University of British Columbia Library, corresp. and papers
Likenesses portraits, repro. in Howe, *Arbiter of elegance*
Wealth at death £2920 17s.: probate, 17 April 1899, *CGPLA Eng. & Wales*

Haweis, Thomas (1734?–1820), Church of England clergyman, was probably born at Truro, Cornwall, on 1 January 1734, but was baptized in Redruth on 20 February. His father, Thomas Haweis, was a Redruth solicitor, and his mother was Bridgeman Willyams of Mawgan in Pydar, Cornwall, through whom he was eventually to inherit considerable property. His father, however, died leaving little fortune, and his mother took her young son to live in her family home. Haweis was sent to Truro grammar school, where the master, George Conon, and the curate, Samuel Walker, were at the centre of a religious revival. After leaving school Haweis was apprenticed to a local surgeon and apothecary (for which training he eventually received a Scottish MD). After completing his apprenticeship he decided that he had a call to the ministry. His relatives raised sufficient money to send him to Oxford, where he matriculated at Christ Church in 1755, but subsequently moved to Magdalen Hall in 1757. He does not appear to have graduated at Oxford, but after moving to Northamptonshire he became a fellow-commoner at Christ's College, Cambridge, in 1772 and was given an LLB. His attempt to obtain an LLD in 1776 was unsuccessful despite the support of his diocesan bishop, who was also master of Trinity College. His account of his life at Oxford concentrates on his efforts to obtain ordination. Despite Bishop Lavington's opposition, the bishop of Oxford finally ordained him deacon on 9 October 1757 and priest on 19 February 1758 on the title of St Mary Magdalen. His Methodist sermons attracted the attention of the university, and its students were already causing disturbances in his church by December 1761. Eventually the refusal of the bishop formally to license him to his curacy caused him to leave Oxford for London in 1762.

In London Haweis became assistant to the Revd Martin Madan at the Lock Hospital. Here on 17 February 1764 John

Thomas Haweis (1734?–1820), by Ridley, pubd 1796 (after Henry Edridge)

Kimpton, a member of the Revd Samuel Brewer's Independent congregation, came to consult Madan. Kimpton had married one of the three daughters of Miles Fleetwood, a descendant of Cromwell's general. Their only dowry was shares in the advowson of Aldwincle All Saints, and Kimpton had concocted a plan to buy out his sisters-in-law and sell the advowson for a profit since the present incumbent was very old. Unfortunately the incumbent died before the transaction was completed, which meant that the sale could not proceed until a new incumbent was inducted. Kimpton had considerable difficult in finding a clergyman who would resign when requested, and came to Madan, probably at Brewer's suggestion, because he had trained as a lawyer. Madan merely read him the oath against simony and took him to Haweis. The meeting ended with Kimpton convinced that Haweis had made a verbal promise to resign when requested, and with Haweis believing that Kimpton wanted an evangelical minister for the parish. On 25 February 1764 Haweis was instituted by the bishop of Peterborough after a searching enquiry into the arrangements. As a result the scene was set for a national scandal involving Brewer, his friend the Revd John Newton, and the Madan and Cowper families.

Kimpton soon began to ask Haweis when he was ready to resign and after several indignant refusals, resorted in 1766 to a pamphlet stating his grievances. Replies and replies to replies followed, including an attack on Kimpton's treatment of his mother-in-law, all of which gave the opponents of Methodism ammunition for their attacks. Haweis was even to be ridiculed on the stage.

Kimpton was now in a debtors' prison, having defaulted on the loan of £700 with which he had paid his sisters-in-law. Attempts by the Olney Methodists, the London tabernacle, Selina, countess of Huntingdon, and others to achieve a compromise had failed, so the countess decided in March 1768 to pay the £1000 owing to Kimpton's creditors in exchange for the advowson. This was successfully accomplished by George Whitefield and John Thornton, both of whom considered Kimpton a villain. Martin Madan objected to this as impugning his character, and others thought it savoured of simony. The animus against Haweis continued for many years, but with a rich benefice, a small parish (Aldwincle was divided between All Saints' and St Peter's), and a private income from mines in Cornwall and south Wales, Haweis was in a strong position.

Haweis did not quarrel with Lady Huntingdon and soon received invitations to preach for her. He had successfully converted most of his parish—one of his congregation attended her college and became a minister in her connexion—and the surrounding area, so he was free to travel. This continued until March 1779, when she appointed him one of her chaplains and invited him to preach at her new chapel, Spa Fields in Clerkenwell, London. Haweis thus became one of the ministers cited to appear in the London consistory court by the incumbent for preaching in his parish without his permission. Fortunately proceedings against him were dropped at an early stage. This, together with Lady Huntingdon's decision to ordain her students, led Haweis to cease preaching for her, since as a beneficed clergyman he had the most to lose. In this he chose discretion over valour, because he had no personal objection to her actions. He appears to have kept on good terms with his diocesans, the bishops of Peterborough, and especially Spencer Madan (1794–1813), who was the brother of Martin. In 1808, after he had resumed preaching for Lady Huntingdon, he wrote to Spencer assuring him that he took no part in connexion ordinations—a letter more important for its omissions than its content. From as early as 1810, and probably much earlier, he was able to obtain licences of non-residence from the bishops, on the grounds of the illness of either his wife or himself. He then spent much of his time at Bath, leaving All Saints' to a succession of underpaid curates. After his move to Bath he was not only able to take charge of the connexion's chapel, but also to attend meetings in London and widen his circle of acquaintances. In 1794 he was an original member of the London Missionary Society—a successor to attempts by Lady Huntingdon and Haweis to send missionaries to the Pacific. This was also the year when he preached at the Brighton chapel, and rescued a party of French Catholic clergymen who had fled from persecution. When the society's first mission was ready to sail in August 1796, Haweis attended the ceremony of 'setting apart' the missionaries, helped with the outfitting in the Thames, and followed their ship, the *Duff*, to Portsmouth to ensure that all went smoothly. While there he launched a short-lived campaign to convert the local Jews. He continued to help the London Missionary Society until old age and illness prevented him.

On Lady Huntingdon's death in 1791 Haweis found himself among a list of friends to whom she had bequeathed the chapels which she owned; however, he always refused to act as the principal agent, and he may have insisted on the chapels being put in trust in 1807—a vital step to avoid their being seized by the next of kin under the Mortmain Act. He had little to do with the countess's college at Trefeca (Talgarth, Brecon), which the Apostolic Society moved to Cheshunt after her death. The Apostolic Society consisted of a group of London merchants and tradesmen who worshipped at connexion chapels. They rigidly excluded clergymen from their deliberations, and Haweis merely paid an annual subscription of 1 guinea to the society. His energies turned instead more to writing. From a large history of the church, to pamphlets addressed to soldiers, sailors, and householders, Haweis produced more than forty books.

Haweis married three times. His first wife was Mrs Judith Wordsworth, sister of the Revd Joseph Townsend of Pewsey. Her first husband, John Wordsworth, was a drunken, very unpleasant man, from whom she had fled to her brother and the consolations of Methodism. As soon as her first husband was dead, Haweis married her in London on 3 January 1771. At her death in August 1786 he was devastated, but in 1788 he followed her advice to remarry. His second wife was Janet Payne Orton, one of Lady Huntingdon's companions. She died on 15 February 1799, and his third wife, whom he married in 1802, was Elizabeth McDowall (*d.* 1855) of Bath, who had nursed him through a dangerous illness. Together they had his only child, John Oliver Willyams Haweis, rector of Slaugham, Sussex, and author of *Sketches of the Reformation* (1844), whose family inherited Thomas Haweis's extensive archives. Haweis died on 11 February 1820 at Beaufort Buildings, Bath, and was buried in Bath Abbey church.

EDWIN WELCH

Sources A. S. Wood, *Thomas Haweis, 1734–1820* (1957) · T. Haweis, autobiography, Mitchell L., NSW, MS · E. Welch, *Spiritual pilgrim: a reassessment of the life of the countess of Huntingdon* (1995) · Westminster College, Cambridge, Cheshunt Archives, E2 · H. Mawdsley, *Woodforde at Oxford, 1759–76* (1969) · A. J. Shirren, *The chronicles of Fleetwood House* (1951) · Foster, *Alum. Oxon.* · DNB

Archives Mitchell L., NSW, autobiography and other volumes · NL Aus., corresp. relating to London Missionary Society · SOAS, Council for World Mission Archives · Southern Methodist University, Dallas, Center for Methodist Studies, corresp. | Sutro Library, San Francisco, Joseph Banks's MSS · Westminster College, Cambridge, Cheshunt archives, corresp. incl. letters to Selina, countess of Huntingdon, E2

Likenesses Ridley, stipple, pubd 1796 (after H. Edridge), BM, NPG; repro. in *Evangelical Magazine* (1796) [*see illus.*] · engraving, repro. in Wood, *Thomas Haweis*, frontispiece · oils, Christ's College, Cambridge

Hawes, Sir Benjamin (1797–1862), politician, was the son of Benjamin Hawes, a wealthy Lambeth soap-boiler, and his wife, Ann, *née* Feltham. The soapworks stood opposite the Temple and was a prominent London landmark. Hawes was educated at a private school in Putney run by the Revd William Carmalt. In 1820 he married Sophia Macnamara, daughter of Marc Isambard Brunel, and supported the various engineering projects of his brother-in-law Isambard Kingdom Brunel. He first lived at New Barge House, Lambeth, moving by 1846 to Queen Square (now Queen Anne's Gate), Westminster. Hawes entered the family business in 1818 and later championed the industry in parliament, once complaining that the president of the Board of Trade, C. P. Thomson, 'betrayed a very singular want of acquaintance' with soap-boiling (*Hansard* 3, 32, 15 March 1836, cols. 373–4). Although he probably soon withdrew from active involvement in this declining trade, he was always tagged as 'Hawes the Soap-Boiler'. He became a Surrey magistrate in 1828, and 'acquired a little county fame' (*The Times*, 21 May 1862, 5) before his election as MP for the new constituency of Lambeth in 1832, after the withdrawal of Lord Palmerston. Physically short, Hawes was mocked for wearing evening dress and kid gloves in the house. Detractors felt that he 'took a more active part in the public business than either his position or his experience appeared to warrant' and his trade 'was an additional enormity' in the eyes of gentlemen (Francis, 345). Monckton Milnes described him as 'the type of the respectable and intelligent bourgeois' (Reid, 1.380). During a visit to the zoo in 1833, Sophy Horsley, a family friend, was very relieved when Hawes chose to inspect the elephant because it was 'a decent animal'. It would have been 'most indelicate' to look at monkeys in male company (Gotch, 48).

As an MP Hawes backed standard radical causes; he campaigned for reform of parliamentary procedure, such as the publication of division lists, and for the introduction of the penny post. He was an early supporter of the electric telegraph. In the planning of new buildings after fire destroyed the old Palace of Westminster in 1834, he wished to encourage 'young and aspiring artists' (*Hansard* 3, 30, col. 620). His motion in 1841 for a select committee to consider 'the promotion of the fine arts of this country' led to the establishment in 1841 of the (Royal) Fine Arts Commission, of which he was an initial member (*Hansard* 3, 67, 30 April 1841, col. 1289). He chaired the committee that recommended the installation of the unsuccessful ventilation system designed by David Boswell Reid.

After 1841 Hawes emerged as a leading opposition speaker for free trade. But he was not a member of the Anti-Corn Law League and hinted that he would accept a low fixed duty. A supporter of the New Zealand Company, in 1845 he delivered an uncharacteristically vitriolic attack on the Colonial Office. Samuel Wilberforce feared that Hawes would become the first middle-class cabinet minister in 1846, but Lord John Russell made him under-secretary for colonies, believing that this would be acceptable to Earl Grey, the incoming secretary of state. In fact, Grey would have preferred Charles Buller, and Hawes immediately offered to resign. The senior civil servant, the aloof James Stephen, described Hawes as 'an under-bred man in manner, something of a shopkeeper with no great promise of capacity' (J. Stephen, diary, 12 July 1846, CUL, ADS MS 7511). Despite this unpromising reception,

Hawes quickly made his mark as an administrator. When Stephen retired in 1847, Russell considered appointing Hawes as his successor.

Hawes paid the price for taking junior office in a ministry whose policy he could not determine. In 1847 he was defeated at Lambeth after a raucous campaign, thanks to the defection of nonconformist supporters who objected to Russell's education policy and the creation of the Manchester bishopric. After a vacancy failed to materialize at Wolverhampton, Hawes retreated in March 1848 to the corrupt Irish borough of Kinsale, where he was elected by just three votes. Critics said he had 'put on the Whig livery' as Russell's 'parliamentary lacquey' (*Weekly Dispatch*, 249) and that he should 'lend Lord Grey a little of his own excessive humility' (*The Spectator*, 199). In April 1851 his vote for the Ecclesiastical Titles Bill led to angry repudiation of him by Catholic voters in Kinsale.

In November 1851 Hawes became deputy secretary at the war department and left parliament in the following February. Thanks to the Crimean War, the new post did not prove to be a 'quiet haven' (H. G. Ward to Hawes, 11 Nov 1851, NL Scot., Gleig MS 3871, fols. 11–12). Although Hawes favoured integration of the various military departments, his opposition to root-and-branch reorganization in wartime made an enemy of Florence Nightingale who denounced him as 'a dictator, an autocrat irresponsible to Parliament, quite unassailable from any quarter' (Woodham Smith, 308). Hawes commissioned Brunel to design a prefabricated hospital for Scutari, and in February 1856 was created KCB for war services. Although his retirement had been rumoured in 1861, his death at his home, 9 Queen Square, Westminster, on 15 May 1862 was unexpected. An obituary in *The Times* praised his ability 'to reconcile the zeal of a reformer with the routine of office', adding that 'he had a clear head which could take in a new idea, and he had a practical talent which could give it effect' (*The Times*, 5). He was buried in Highgate cemetery and survived by his wife.

GED MARTIN

Sources *Hansard* 3 (1832–52) · PRO, Lord John Russell MSS · G. Hill, *Electoral history of Lambeth* (1879) · *The Times* (21 May 1862) · G. H. Francis, *Orators of the age* (1847) · *Mendelssohn and his friends in Kensington: letters from Fanny and Sophy Horsley, written 1833–36*, ed. R. B. Gotch (1934) · L. T. C. Rolt, *Isambard Kingdom Brunel* (1957); repr. (1980) · C. Woodham-Smith, *Florence Nightingale, 1820–1910* (1950); repr. (1952) · *The Spectator* (3 March 1849) · *Weekly Dispatch* (6 May 1849) · J. Sweetman, *War and administration* (1984) · T. W. Reid, *The life, letters, and friendships of Richard Monckton Milnes, first Lord Houghton*, 2 vols. (1890) · *DNB* · *CGPLA Eng. & Wales* (1862)

Archives BL, corresp. with Charles Babbage, Add. MSS 37187–37200 *passim* · BL, corresp. with Lord Carnarvon, Add. MS 60785 · BL, corresp. with Sir Robert Peel, Add. MSS 40416–40602 *passim* · NA Scot., letters to Lord Panmure · National Museums and Galleries on Merseyside, Liverpool, letters to J. T. Danson · PRO, corresp. with Lord John Russell, PRO 30/22 · U. Durham L., letters to third Earl Grey · W. Sussex RO, letters to duke of Richmond · Wilts. & Swindon RO, corresp. with Sidney Herbert

Likenesses J. Partridge, group portrait (*The fine arts commissioners, 1846*), NPG · photograph (in later life), repro. in Hill, *Electoral history*, facing p. 84

Wealth at death under £8000: probate, 12 June 1862, *CGPLA Eng. & Wales*

Hawes, Edward (*b.* **1589/90**), poet, was the son of Christopher Hawes (*b. c.*1562), a Lincolnshire cleric who had spent two terms at Magdalene College, Cambridge. Edward Hawes was author of *Trayterous Percyes and Catesbyes Prosopopeia* (1606). According to the title-page Hawes was, at the time of writing, 'Scholler at Westminster, a Youth of sixteene yeers old'. On 23 June 1606 Hawes was admitted as a pensioner at St John's College, Cambridge, and on 9 June 1607 he migrated to Gonville and Caius College. The *Prosopopeia* is dedicated to Tobias Matthew, bishop of Durham and later archbishop of York.

RONALD BAYNE, *rev.* ELIZABETH GOLDRING

Sources W. T. Lowndes, *The bibliographer's manual of English literature*, ed. H. G. Bohn, [new edn], 6 vols. (1869) · Venn, *Alum. Cant.*

Hawes, Maria Dowding Billington (1816–1886). *See under* Hawes, William (1785–1846).

Hawes, Richard (**1603/4–1668**), clergyman and ejected minister, was born in East Anglia to unknown parents. His father was 'a religious man, dying when he was very young', and his mother married 'soon after … a man wholly carnal … utterly negligent about instilling the principles of religion into his family' (*Nonconformist's Memorial*, 2.290). When he was about nine Hawes was sent to school in Ipswich, where he heard the lecturer Samuel Ward, and repeating the lectures to his stepfather's mother, with whom he was lodging, effected her conversion. Admitted a pensioner to Corpus Christi College, Cambridge, on 16 June 1620 (as 'of Suffolk'), he graduated BA in 1624 and proceeded MA in 1627.

According to Edmund Calamy, Hawes was then disowned by his stepfather, having declined the latter's offer of a valuable living which he claimed to have in his gift. Hawes accepted instead from the rival claimant, Lord Keeper Sir Thomas Coventry, the alternative offer of the rectory of Humber, Herefordshire, on 1 September 1627. On 9 December that year he was also inducted as vicar of Ilketshall St John, Suffolk. From 23 March 1638 he was rector of Kenderchurch, Herefordshire. Having lost at university the faith of his childhood, 'for many years after he entered into the ministry, he continued much addicted to vain company, and was sometimes guilty of excessive drinking' (*Nonconformist's Memorial*, 291). At some date he married, but his wife's name is unknown.

When Hereford was garrisoned by the royalists during the civil war, Hawes was imprisoned and 'a council of war ordered to try him for his life', but once the governor, 'a man of violent temper', was replaced, the prosecution was discovered to have been malicious, and he was 'courteously' freed. After this experience Hawes's behaviour visibly altered: he gained the respect of the godly and 'became a plain, earnest and useful preacher' (*Nonconformist's Memorial*, 291). He did not, however, escape abuse and plunder by the soldiers. In 1651 he was ministering in Llangua, Monmouthshire, and having had little success in Kenderchurch, 'a Paganish and brutish place', was about 1659 induced by Sir Edward Harley to accept the rectory of Lantwardine, Herefordshire.

Shortly after the Restoration Hawes was again imprisoned 'upon the noise of plots' (*Nonconformist's Memorial*, 291) at the instance of Sir Henry Lingen, but released when Lingen died. As a moderate, he was expected to conform in 1662, but when he refused, was ejected, although Bishop Herbert Croft allowed him a month's grace in preaching. Thereafter he lived with a daughter, probably Grace (*d.* 1701), and her husband, Nicholas Billingsley (1633–1709), from 1657 vicar of Weobley, Herefordshire; they lived first at Weobley, then at Abergavenny, where Billingsley was schoolmaster from February 1664, and finally at Awre, Gloucestershire. Both Bishop Hugh Lloyd of Llandaff and Bishop Nicholson of Gloucester permitted Hawes to preach without subscribing, and he occasionally made use of their licence. After an illness 'occasioned by a journey to Kidderminster, for Mr Hieron', during which Calamy visited him and he expressed 'in his last hours, great satisfaction with his Nonconformity', Hawes died at Awre in December 1668 'in his 65th year' (*Nonconformist's Memorial*, 291). VIVIENNE LARMINIE

Sources *The nonconformist's memorial … originally written by … Edmund Calamy*, ed. S. Palmer, [3rd edn], 2 (1802), 290–93 · Venn, *Alum. Cant.* · *Calamy rev.*, 54–5, 253

Hawes, Robert (**1664/5–1731**), lawyer and topographer, was the eldest of the five children of Henry Hawes (1634–1718), a yeoman farmer of Brandeston, Suffolk, and Mary, his wife (*c.*1640–1718), daughter and coheir of John Smith of Pyshalls in Dennington, also in Suffolk. His father was the second son of Robert Hawes (1601–1679), who had served as chief constable of Loes hundred through two reigns and the interregnum. Hawes, who was well educated and a competent Latinist, probably acquired a taste for heraldry under Zaccheus Leverland, first master of Sir Robert Hitcham's Free School in Framlingham. He could have trained for the law under Richard Porter, steward of the lordships and manors of Framlingham and Saxstead and of other manors in Loes hundred, left in 1636 to the masters and fellows of Pembroke College, Cambridge under Hitcham's will. He married Sarah Sterling (*c.*1668–1731), youngest daughter of George Sterling of Charsfield, at Framlingham on 11 August 1686. They had no children.

When in 1703 Porter died, Hawes collected the working documents for the next steward, on whose death in 1712 Hawes succeeded with the unanimous consent of the college. He was intensely proud of his appointment, and was ready to address his manuscript 'History, or, Memoirs of Framlingham and Loes-hundred in Suffolk' to the master and fellows, enthusing that his 'only design at first, was to reduce … your Lordships or Manors … out of the confusions wherein I found them, to a better order and method' (BL, Add. MS 33247, fol. 4*r*). 'Time and opportunity' (ibid.), for he finished in 1724, encouraged him to gather information about the whole hundred, particularly its chief town, the church, and castle. Richard Attwood, fellow and college antiquary, helped him bring Matthew Wren's earlier account of the masters and fellows up to date; he also acknowledged the help of Thomas Tanner, then chancellor of Norwich diocese. Hawes made four complete copies on paper, each of over 700 folio pages, legibly written in his own hand: one for the college, for which he was rewarded with an engraved silver-covered cup costing the estate £14 3s., and two others which are now lost. It is his own copy, with additions made up to the year of his death, now in the British Library, which has had the most use. Hand-coloured arms and pasted-in portrait prints of monarchs and others associated with the lordship fill the margins. Most usefully, he drew head-on elevations of all the churches and the more important houses, and a few monuments, all tolerably accurate and having a peculiar charm. The master set of the larger drawings are in Craven Ord's Suffolk collections, also in the British Library. For his friend John Revett (1691–1756), of Brandeston Hall, collaborator in collecting materials, he produced the Brandeston and Cretingham sections in duodecimo in 1725, but Revett also inherited Hawes's personal copy. It was John Revett the grandson who in 1806 allowed David Elisha Davy and Henry Jermyn to copy both Hawes manuscripts into their Suffolk collections.

When in 1729 the town was 'at great charge' to build 'a large worke house' (Framlingham MS N5, Cambridge, Pembroke College) inside the castle walls, extending the one provided by the college a century earlier, the chief parishioners received only a lofty letter of thanks from the Pembroke president. This led Hawes to pen a critical history of the management of Hitcham's estate, showing that the fellows had where possible evaded their responsibilities. By then his firm script was shaky, but he drew as well as ever. He died in Framlingham on 26 August 1731 and was buried three days later in St Michael's, Framlingham; his wife survived him by only six weeks and died on 11 October 1731. Both lie under a modestly inscribed grey stone in the south aisle near Hitcham's fine tomb.

Always looking for promising material, Robert Loder (1749–1811), the Woodbridge bookseller and printer, borrowed the Hawes–Revett copy and prepared the Framlingham and Saxstead sections for publication in 1798. Loder added much additional material from Ord and Ashby, an extensive list of local flora by George Crabbe, the poet-parson of Great Glemham, and ten engravings after drawings by Isaac Johnson. The edition was said to be limited to 250 copies, but the volume is commoner than that figure would indicate. Hawes's useful observations in the other parishes of the hundred have been largely overlooked.

J. M. BLATCHLY

Sources R. Hawes, *The history of Framlingham*, ed. R. Loder (1798) · *DNB* · *The East Anglian, or, Notes and Queries on Subjects Connected with the Counties of Suffolk, Cambridge, Essex and Norfolk*, new ser., 8 (1899–1900), 373–4 [transcript of BL Add. MS 19172] · parish register (marriage), Framlingham, 11 Aug 1686 · parish register (burial), Framlingham, 1731 · parish register (burial), Brandeston, 1718 · memorial inscription, Brandeston parish church · Pembroke Cam., Framlingham estate MSS
Archives BL, MS history of Framlingham and Loes hundred, Add. MS 33247 · Bodl. Oxf., Loes hundred collections · CUL, extracts from MS history of Framlingham and Loes hundred · Suffolk RO, Ipswich, MS Epitome of Heraldry, incl. arms of Suffolk nobility and gentry | Pembroke Cam., Framlingham estate MSS

Hawes, Stephen (*b. c.*1474, *d.* before 1529), poet, was possibly born in East Anglia, where the surname was fairly common in the later middle ages. He may have attended Magdalen College, Oxford, in 1493. Bale asserts that he studied in Scotland and France as well as England but corroboration is lacking (Bale, *Cat.*, 632). He first appears in official records as groom of the chamber to Henry VII in 1503: this title appears in the first printings of all his poems. Bale reports that Henry 'called him to his court, to his inner chamber and to his private counsels, on the sole recommendation of his virtue' (Bale, *Cat.*, 632). In 1506 he is recorded in the king's book of payments as receiving 10s. for 'a ballet that he gave to the kings grace in reward' (Gluck and Morgan, xi). He was certainly dead before 1529 when a poem by Thomas Feylde includes a prayer for his soul.

Hawes's earliest recorded poem was *The Example of Virtue*, first published in 1509 but, according to the colophon, composed in 1503/1504 and presented to Henry VII. Set in the form of a dream vision it comprises 2129 lines, almost entirely in rhyme royal. The dreamer is taken by a beautiful guide, Discretion, on a voyage to an island where Nature, Fortune, Hardiness, and Wisdom all debate before Justice which is the most profitable to man. The dreamer then sets out to seek a lady, subsequently called Cleanness. On his journey, accompanied by Discretion, he meets various temptations, before arriving at her dwelling. There he kills a three-headed dragon and marries Cleanness. The final part of the poem deals with the death of the protagonist. The poem ends with prayers to Henry VII, his mother, Margaret Beaufort, and his son, Prince Henry.

The visionary and allegorical form of this poem is elaborated in Hawes's most famous work, *The Pastime of Pleasure*, first published in 1509, but composed in 1505/1506. This comprises 5816 lines, in rhyme royal and couplets. It traces the career of Graunde Amour as he pursues the active life in his quest for the lady, La Belle Pucelle. To prepare him for this quest he receives instruction at the tower of doctrine in the seven liberal arts, before undergoing a series of battles, after which he wins La Belle Pucelle. The educational and chivalric aspects of the poem are counter-balanced by two lengthy passages in couplets in which a dwarf, Godfrey Gobelive, recounts anti-feminist anecdotes and is subsequently punished for telling them. After their marriage and Graunde Amour's death, the poem concludes with visions of the seven deadly sins, time, the nine worthies, and eternity. The poem contains acknowledgements to Hawes's 'masters', the medieval triumvirate of Chaucer, Gower, and Lydgate. Lydgate has often been held to be an important influence on Hawes's writings, but his role seems largely limited to offering the latter a model of highly aureate lexis on which he occasionally drew.

Hawes's other poems are briefer. His *Conversion of Swearers*, which was written in a mixture of rhyme royal and tail rhyme, attacks those who take Christ's name in vain. He also wrote a poem in praise of the coronation of Henry VIII. Both these were also first printed in 1509.

Hawes's last poem, *The Comfort of Lovers*, is the only one not to be first printed in 1509. The title-page of the only surviving edition, published *c.*1515, reports that it was composed in 1510/1511. It comprises 938 lines in rhyme royal. Composed after Henry VIII's accession, the narrative seems to suggest that Hawes had fallen into disfavour in courtly circles. It is again set in the form of a dream vision in which the dreamer laments his lost love. In his dream he (Amour) encounters Pucell (his love). A lengthy dialogue ensues which concludes with Pucell establishing that their love must be resolved by Venus and Fortune. The dreamer then awakes. The cryptically allusive texture of the poem suggests that its allegorical mode may conceal some autobiographical element. It has been speculated, on insubstantial grounds, that the poem refers to Hawes's relationship with the future queen Mary Tudor (Gluck and Morgan, 154).

The publication of Hawes's verse is unusual in some respects. It was all first published by one contemporary printer, Wynkyn De Worde. The relationship between printer and poet seems to have been unusual in its exclusivity and in De Worde's attention to the production of Hawes's poems. He seems to have executed woodcuts specifically for his editions of *The Example of Virtue* and *The Pastime of Pleasure* and to have sought a degree of careful integration of text and image that on occasions incorporates passages from Hawes's verse into the woodcuts.

Hawes's poems enjoyed some popularity in the sixteenth century. *The Pastime of Pleasure* was reprinted in 1517, 1554, and 1555, the *Example of Virtue* c.1520 and 1530, and *The Conversion of Swearers* in 1510, 1530, and 1551. The *Pastime* was probably an influence on Spenser's *Faerie Queene* and earned the approval of Thomas Warton, who praised Hawes as 'the restorer of invention' to English poetry (Warton, *Observations*, 2.105–6) and included a lengthy appreciation in his *History of English Poetry* (Warton, *History*, 3.43–71).   A. S. G. EDWARDS

Sources A. S. G. Edwards, *Stephen Hawes* (1983) · S. Hawes, *The pastime of pleasure*, ed. W. E. Mead, EETS, 173 (1928) · F. W. Gluck and A. B. Morgan, introduction, in *Stephen Hawes: the minor poems*, ed. F. W. Gluck and A. B. Morgan, EETS, original ser., 271 (1974) · Emden, *Oxf.*, 2.888–9 · Bale, *Cat.* · T. Warton, *The history of English poetry*, rev. edn, ed. R. Price, 4 vols. (1824) · T. Warton, *Observations on the Fairy queen of Spenser* (1754), 2.105–6

Hawes, William (1736–1808), philanthropist and physician, was born on 28 November 1736 at the Thatched House tavern, midway between Astey's Row and Cross Street, Islington, the son of the landlord, Thomas Hawes. Educated first at John Shield's academy, Islington, he became a scholar at St Paul's School on 4 November 1748. After apprenticeship to Robert Carsan, a medical practitioner near Vauxhall, he assisted Mr Dicks in the Strand, shortly taking over his practice as apothecary and surgeon. In May 1759 he married Sarah Fox (1740–1814); their children were Harriot (*bap.* 1760), Sophia (*bap.* 1762), Thomas (*bap.* 1765), Sarah (*bap.* 1772), Sarah (*b.* 1773), William (*b.* 1774), Mary Ann (*b.* 1781), Mary Ann (*b.* 1782), and Benjamin (1770–1861). Benjamin, soap-boiler and philanthropist, married Ann Feltham in 1796; their sons, Benjamin *Hawes (1797–1862) and William (1805–1885), continued the family tradition of public service.

In 1773 Hawes attracted attention by his interest in

William Hawes (1736–1808), by Pierre François Bertonnier (after A. Lefèvre)

resuscitating victims of apparent drowning and other causes of asphyxia. This project had been encouraged by a sporadic campaign in the *Gentleman's Magazine* since 1745, and was the subject of two pamphlets by Thomas Cogan and by Alexander Johnson (1716–1799), published in 1773, both of which recommended the establishment of institutions similar to the Amsterdam society for the resuscitation of the drowned, founded in 1767. At first, Hawes encountered much opposition and some ridicule from those who doubted the practicability of resuscitation. He put matters to the test by offering financial incentives to anyone who recovered persons from the water between Westminster and London bridges, within a reasonable time after immersion, and who then brought them to an appointed place where treatment could be provided, and let him know immediately. The response was enthusiastic: Hawes and other medical men were credited with saving many lives which would otherwise have been lost.

After a year Cogan warned Hawes that he was incurring excessive expense, and suggested they should form a public charity. Each man agreed to bring fifteen friends to an inaugural meeting. A setback threatened when Hawes's friend, Oliver Goldsmith, the most celebrated potential founder, died on 4 April 1774; his death was allegedly hastened by taking Dr James's powders, a proprietary remedy whose principal active ingredient was antimony. Acting as Goldsmith's apothecary, Hawes had supplied some of the powders himself, though he strongly advised against their use. He defended his conduct, and exposed the dangers of rash self-medication, in *An Account of the Late Dr Goldsmith's Illness* (1774). The proposed meeting eventually took place at the Chapter Coffee House on 18 April 1774, and 'The Institution for affording immediate relief to persons apparently dead from drowning' was founded; this became the Humane Society in 1776, acquiring the prefix 'Royal' in 1787. It promoted research into the causes and treatment of asphyxia, disseminated information about resuscitation techniques, rewarded people who attempted rescues and resuscitations, recruited physicians and surgeons to act as unpaid medical assistants, and appointed receiving houses, including the Thatched House, which was conveniently situated near the New River.

Hawes became registrar in 1778, and treasurer in 1796, preparing reports from 1780 until his death as well as pocket-cards for emergency use, and organizing the annual festivals. An indefatigable publicist, he rose at five every morning to write numerous lengthy letters. He slipped pocket-cards into letters on unrelated matters, and frequently introduced the topic of resuscitation into private conversations. In numerous publications, including pseudonymous magazine articles, he applied the society's principles to every eventuality from still birth to premature burial, and appealed powerfully, though unsuccessfully, for government support. His *magnum opus* was *The Transactions of the Royal Humane Society* (1795), a rich source of information on resuscitative practice, which, however, contained no reference to Alexander Johnson; instead, he made the untenable claim that Cogan 'opened the door to the practice of resuscitation' in England. Hawes became a revered public figure, senior physician of the Surrey and London dispensaries, vice-president of the London Electrical Dispensary, and honorary member of humane societies from Bath, Manchester, and Edinburgh to Massachusetts.

Resuscitation was not, however, Hawes's only interest. His *Examination of the Rev. John Wesley's 'Primitive Physic'* (1776) condemned Wesley for dangerously misleading his readers, ridiculed his remedies, and cast doubt on his religious and personal probity. Resident in Palsgrave Place by 1778, Hawes received the degree of MD from Marischal College, Aberdeen, in 1779, and began to practise as a physician. In 1780 he republished some early works, announcing in the preface that 'I have made Quacks of all denominations my enemies: but what Medical Man of honour and reputation, would wish to be upon tolerable terms with the Murderers of the Human Race' (Hawes, *An Account*). In 1782 he moved to Great Eastcheap. Elected physician to the London Dispensary in 1785, he moved to Bury Street in 1786. In 1791 he moved to Spital Square; appalled by the poverty of local unemployed silk-weavers in 1793, he organized a campaign which saved 1200 families from destitution.

Hawes was an elder in Abraham Rees's Presbyterian church at St Thomas's, Southwark, but maintained Anglican affiliations. He fell ill and died at Spital Square on 5 December 1808 and was buried on 13 December in the cemetery near St Mary's Church, Islington. Those who knew him admired his undeviating friendship, cheerful society, and rational conviviality. Although his features were rugged and unsymmetrical, his expression was considered habitually benevolent. Contemporary assessments of Hawes as a guileless innocent who never made an enemy were excessively bland. He was, however, an energetic philanthropist, whose personal generosity equalled his institutional zeal.

CAROLYN D. WILLIAMS

Sources European Magazine and London Review, 41 (1802), 427–31 · GM, 1st ser., 78 (1808), 1121–4 · Nichols, *Lit. anecdotes*, 9.180–83nn., 627n. · P. J. Wallis and R. V. Wallis, *Eighteenth century medics*, 2nd edn (1988) · P. J. Bishop, *A short history of the Royal Humane Society* (1974) · R. H. Marten, *The substance of an address to the Rt. Hon. Charles Flower, lord mayor of London* (1812) · Marriage licences in London: parish church of St Clement Danes in the county of Middlesex, 25 May 1759, GL [microfilm] · parish register, St Clement Danes, 1760–72 [baptisms] · Alphabetical register of births, Index to London, 1759–1812, DWL · 'Rees, Abraham', *DNB* · 'Hawes, Sir Benjamin', *DNB* · R. B. Gardiner, ed., *The admission registers of St Paul's School, from 1748 to 1876* (1884) · Boase, *Mod. Eng. biog.* · W. Hawes, *An account of the late Dr Goldsmith's illness*, 4th edn (1780)

Likenesses R. Pollard, engraving, 1787 (*The young man restored to life*; after watercolour by R. Smirke), repro. in Bishop, *Short history* · J. Owen, engraving, 1801, repro. in *Public characters of 1800–1801* (1807), frontispiece · aquatint silhouette, 1801, Wellcome L. · W. Ridley, stipple, 1802, BM, NPG, Wellcome L.; repro. in *European Magazine* (1802) · L. Gahagan, marble bust, 1809, NG Ire. · J. Basire, engraving (after tablet, St Mary's Church, Islington, now destroyed), repro. in GM, 81 (1811) · P. F. Bertonnier, line engraving (after A. Lefèvre), AM Oxf., NPG, Wellcome L. [see illus.] · W. Ridley, engraving (after miniature by A. Lefèvre?), repro. in Bishop, *Short history* · R. Smirke, oils, Gov. Art Coll. · R. Smirke, watercolours (*A man recuperating in bed after a resuscitation*), Wellcome L.; repro. in J. P. Griffith, 'A tale of two paintings and the London medical scene of the late eighteenth century', *Journal of the Royal Society of Medicine*, 83 (1990), 520–23 · stipple silhouette, BM

Hawes, William (1785–1846), composer, born in London on 21 June 1785, was a pupil of Reginald Spofforth. He was a chorister of the Chapel Royal from 1795 to 1801, and a gentleman of the same chapel from 1805. In the interim he played the violin in the Covent Garden orchestra and also taught singing, and in 1803 served as deputy lay vicar at Westminster Abbey. He sang at Gloucester shortly after the festival of 1811. He was appointed master of the choristers at St Paul's Cathedral in 1812, and was one of the original associates of the Philharmonic Society on its foundation in 1813. On the death of Samuel Webbe in 1816, he competed (unsuccessfully) for the prize offered for the best setting of a memorial ode by William Linley. On 1 July 1817 Hawes was appointed master of the children of the Chapel Royal, in which post he became known as a harsh disciplinarian; in the same year he became lay vicar of Westminster, a position he retained until 1820. In 1818 he edited in score the great collection of English madrigals known as *The Triumphs of Oriana*, first published in 1601, prefixing an introduction and short biographies of the composers (see *Quarterly Musical Review*, 500–15).

Hawes later became associated with the Royal Harmonic Institution in the Argyll Rooms, Regent Street, which operated as a kind of publishing company, but which ultimately failed, leaving Hawes and one other as the only representatives of the original promoters of the scheme. Hawes declared himself bankrupt and afterwards set up as a publisher in the Strand. In 1822 he tried to establish exclusive rights to one of twelve Scottish songs which he had edited and published, but the suit he brought against the proprietors of the *Gazette of Fashion* with this action was dismissed by the lord chancellor.

From 1804 Hawes had been increasingly involved with the theatre and adapted a number of continental operas, to which, according to the fashion of the day, he added his own musical interpolations. He gave much assistance to his intimate friend Samuel Arnold during the latter's management of the English Opera House at the Lyceum Theatre; in 1824 he was appointed musical director there, and the theatre became the venue for the staging of many of his adaptations. It is said that the production of Weber's *Der Freischütz* in July 1824 was mainly Hawes's doing, and he certainly wrote several songs which were interpolated in Weber's score. Other works arranged by him included Salieri's *Tarare* (1825), Weber's *Preciosa* (1825), Peter Winter's *Das unterbrochene Opferfest* (1826), Ferdinando Paer's *I fuorusciti* (1827), Mozart's *Così fan tutte* (1828) and *Don Giovanni* (1830), Ferdinand Ries's *Die Räuberbraut*, H. A. Marschner's *Der Vampyr* (1829), and Hérold's *Le pré aux clercs* (1833). Hawes also wrote several original operettas and songs for plays, a Requiem, and a monody on the death of Princess Charlotte (1817), and published some collections of glees, madrigals, and church music. His glee 'The bee, the golden daughter of the spring' won the prize at the Glee Club in 1836. In 1825 he directed a series of Lenten oratorios at Covent Garden, and in 1830 engaged in similar ventures at both the patent theatres. In 1828 he managed a festival in Brighton (29–31 October). He was for many years conductor of the Madrigal Society and organist of the Lutheran chapel of the Savoy. Hawes died at his home in Adelphi Terrace, London, on 18 February 1846.

His second daughter, **Maria Dowding Billington Hawes** (1816–1886), to whom Elizabeth Billington stood godmother, was a distinguished contralto, for whom Mendelssohn wrote the aria 'O rest in the Lord'. She was the principal contralto in the first performances of that composer's *Lobgesang* (23 September 1840) and *Elijah* (26 August 1846). She died at Ryde, Isle of Wight, on 24 April 1886; her husband, J. D. Merest, had predeceased her.

J. A. F. MAITLAND, *rev.* DAVID J. GOLBY

Sources review, *Quarterly Musical Magazine and Review*, 1 (1818), 500–15 · *Quarterly Musical Magazine and Review*, 4 (1822), 102–4 · 'Sketch of the state of music in London', *Quarterly Musical Magazine and Review*, 7 (1825), 186–211, esp. 195–7 · 'Grand musical festivals', *Quarterly Musical Magazine and Review*, 10 (1828), 135–82, esp. 168–9 · W. H. Husk and B. Rainbow, 'Hawes, William', *New Grove* · Boase, *Mod. Eng. biog.* · *Musical Standard* (24 April 1886), 406–7
Wealth at death £875 14s. 10d.—Maria Hawes: probate, 12 June 1886, CGPLA Eng. & Wales

Hawford, Edward (*d.* 1582), college head, was the son of Thomas Hawford and Margaret Wade of Clipston, Northamptonshire. He was educated at Cambridge, graduating BA from Jesus College in 1542/3 and MA from Christ's in 1545. A fellow of the college from 1559 to 1582, Hawford was awarded his bachelor of theology degree in 1554 and his doctorate in 1564. He was appointed a university proctor in 1552/3 and served as vice-chancellor in the year 1563/4. He was rector of Glemsford, Suffolk, between 1553 and 1574. On 12 June 1554 he was instituted to two-thirds of the rectory of Clipston, and was reinstituted, possibly to the last third, on 8 February 1561; he also held the advowson of this living, which he bequeathed to Christ's College. In 1560 he acquired another rectory, that of Kegworth, Leicestershire, which he also held for life. In his will he provided for a preacher to give sermons at these three parishes. On 14 February 1560, on the death of William Collingwood, he was collated to the fifth prebend of Chester Cathedral, probably holding it until his death.

Hawford is chiefly remembered, however, for his university career, and especially for his mastership of Christ's College, Cambridge, between 1559 and 1582. He had been one of those members of the college who on 26 July 1555 signed the Catholic articles of subscription, to which was appended a 'detestation' of all heretics. However, Hawford was a mere fellow, and less compromised than many in the university hierarchy. On the accession of Elizabeth his business acumen and moderate church views found influential supporters, including Dr John Pory, who had the ear of William Cecil. Despite heavy government hints, the then master of Christ's, William Taylor, clung on for several months before decamping at the end of June 1559. On the recommendation of Cecil the fellows elected Hawford, one of their own number, as Taylor's successor and he was admitted as master on the following 23 July.

Hawford was not an enthusiast of the old religion, but a competent administrator, conservative in his general outlook, distrustful of religious enthusiasm in general. Probably his instincts were not far removed from those of the queen herself. In the summer of 1564 Elizabeth paid a royal visit to Cambridge, and it was to Hawford that Cecil wrote, on 12 July and 1 August 1564, committing the arrangements to his charge. Hawford was one of the four doctors who bore the canopy under which the queen entered the chapel of King's College on Saturday 5 August, and it was he who made the presentation to her of the traditional pair of gloves on the ninth. It seems, however, that Elizabeth tired of the elaborate efforts in her honour, and she left somewhat abruptly early the following morning.

From the first Hawford's commitment to the protestant cause was regarded with deep suspicion. In November 1570 Edward Dering wrote to Burghley that Hawford 'could not be brought to take away popish books nor garments without great importunity, and in the end all the best and richest he hath conveyed the fellows know not whither' (Strype, *Parker*, 2.175). It is likely that Hawford's motives were financial rather than religious: an early end to the Elizabethan settlement might restore the value of college treasures sold cheaply in haste. As the new establishment took root, however, the fellows increased their pressure to jettison the relics of the old religion. Thus, in 1568:

> three chalices were sold to Mr Ringstede for £17 14, also certain 'chapel stuff'. In 1570 there was received £15 for copes, vestments, tunicles, and altar cloths; and 'Malton 71 Bell' with two great candlesticks and a cross, went for £4 19 9d. (Peile, *Christ's*, 72)

During Hawford's tenure Christ's became famous as the centre of Cambridge puritanism and a large proportion of fellows elected were eager for further reformation in religion. Hawford himself was strongly opposed to the puritan tendency. He was active against Thomas Cartwright in summer 1570 and was one of the nine heads who in December formally deprived him of his Lady Margaret professorship. The case was a catalyst for the redrafting by Whitgift of the university statutes in September. In this he enjoyed the active support of Hawford, who had just succeeded him as deputy vice-chancellor, and other college heads who favoured the 'bridling of the untamed affections of young regents' by curbing their powers of election (Peile, *Christ's*, 78). The new rules strengthened the powers of college masters, but were opposed by many of a puritan disposition, including Edward Dering. In a letter to Burghley he attacked the college heads who supported Whitgift as 'either enemies to God's gospel or so faint professors that they do little good in the church' (Strype, *Parker*, 2.175).

In 1579 Hawford was involved in a battle with another famous puritan, Hugh Broughton, who had been elected to a fellowship granted by Edward VI. Formally the case turned on the conflict between the terms of that grant and a statute of Christ's College. The statute, invoked by Hawford in order to exclude Broughton, proscribed the simultaneous tenure of college fellowships by more than one man of any given county. The grant of Edward VI provided otherwise for its own foundation. Broughton was able to point to a precedent case in support of the contention that this scholarship had been treated as exceptional. Despite his departure for the north-east, Broughton's cause aroused extraordinary rancour. The fellows split along party lines, the conservatively minded minority of four supporting Hawford, the puritan majority of eight siding with Broughton. Several appeals on his behalf were addressed to Lord Burghley, who made clear his sympathy with the disbarred fellow, but Hawford would not relent. In 1581 the case was remitted to Vice-Chancellor Perne and two college heads, who judged that the county restriction did not apply to the Edwardian fellowship. Hawford was told that, accordingly, Broughton should be readmitted, but this appears not to have happened.

Hawford's long tenure at Christ's and his good relationship with Cecil contributed to his prominence in university affairs. In the college the growing strength of puritan radicalism contributed to the growth of a party atmosphere which his policy in some cases exacerbated. Edward Hawford died on 14 February 1582, leaving £700 in the college treasury. His business skill helped restore the finances of Christ's, but it is not clear whether the growth in the number of its fellows is to be attributed to his administration or to the ideals and ideas of his puritan opponents. STEPHEN WRIGHT

Sources J. Peile, *Biographical register of Christ's College, 1505–1905, and of the earlier foundation, God's House, 1448–1505*, ed. [J. A. Venn], 1 (1910) · J. Peile, *Christ's College* (1900) · H. C. Porter, *Reformation and reaction in Tudor Cambridge* (1958) · Venn, *Alum. Cant.* · Cooper, *Ath. Cantab.* · J. Strype, *Annals of the Reformation and establishment of religion … during Queen Elizabeth's happy reign*, new edn, 4 vols. (1824) · J. Strype, *The life and acts of Matthew Parker*, new edn, 3 vols. (1821) · *Fasti Angl., 1541–1857*, [Canterbury] · J. Nichols, *The progresses and public processions of Queen Elizabeth*, new edn, 3 vols. (1823) · J. W. Clay, ed., *The visitation of Cambridge … 1575 … 1619*, Harleian Society, 41 (1897)

Haw-Haw, Lord. *See* Joyce, William Brooke (1906–1946).

Hawisa, *suo jure* **countess of Aumale, and countess of Essex** (d. 1213/14), noblewoman, was the child of *William le Gros, count of Aumale and sometime earl of York (c.1110–1179), and of Cecily de Rumilly (d. 1188×90?), daughter and coheir of William fitz Duncan and Alice de Rumilly. Her father's title was derived from Aumale, on the north-east border of Normandy; William also held the honour of Holderness in east Yorkshire, with lands in Lincolnshire and elsewhere. Although Hawisa had an illegitimate brother, Geoffrey, and may possibly have had a sister, Amice, she inherited all her father's lands, and also her mother's baronies of Skipton in Yorkshire and Copeland in Cumberland. Nothing is known of her birth and early years: she was unmarried at her father's death, and became a royal ward. Her marriage to William de *Mandeville, third earl of Essex, took place at the earl's castle of Pleshey in Essex on 14 January 1180. He occasionally used the title of count of Aumale until his death on 14 November 1189; the marriage was childless.

After the earl's death Richard I arranged for Hawisa to marry his Poitevin naval commander, William de Forz. The countess refused the match, and her goods were distrained until she capitulated. Before Michaelmas 1190 Hawisa travelled with Queen Eleanor in the royal galley to Normandy, and possibly to Sicily. It seems likely she married Forz at the end of 1190, as he was responsible for scutage from her lands at Michaelmas 1190. Forz died in 1195, leaving at least one son from this marriage, William de *Forz (d. 1241).

Hawisa's third husband was the household knight Baldwin de Béthune, an aristocrat of Flemish origin. One of the men captured with King Richard in 1192, he played a significant role in obtaining the release of the king, for whom he was a hostage. He married Hawisa at Sées in 1195. The only recorded child of this marriage, Alice, married William (II) *Marshal in 1214. Béthune died in the autumn of 1212, and was buried at Meaux Abbey.

After Béthune's death Hawisa made fine with King John, offering 5000 marks for her inheritance and dowers, and for not being forced to marry again. The large sum is easily explained, for she was one of the great Anglo-Norman landowners of the early thirteenth century, with castles at Aumale, Skipsea, Castle Bytham, and Skipton, and an important manor house at Burstwick in Holderness. The constant warfare around Aumale seems to have resulted in her living mainly in England. That Richard of Devizes should have described her as 'a woman who was almost a man, lacking nothing virile except virility' (*Chronicon*, ed. Appleby, 10), underlines the impression conveyed by other sources of her independence and reluctance to marry. A lost story lies behind an entry on the pipe roll of 1209, that the bishop of Winchester owed a tun of good wine, because he did not remind the king to give a belt to the countess of Aumale. Recipients of her charters include her chief officer, Fulk de Oyry, her chamberlain, and her nurse: unusually, on two occasions she used women as witnesses.

Hawisa died in either 1213 or 1214, and probably before 8 March 1214, when it was ordered that the profits of her lands should be kept in the Temple, London. Her seal was vesica-shaped, and shows a woman (presumably Hawisa herself) in a long, pleated robe with a cloak. Her right hand is on her hip, and she carries a hawk with jesses on her left wrist. Four impressions of her seal survive, which suffice to show that, although she is styled countess of Aumale in all her surviving charters, until the end of her life she continued to use the seal of her first marriage, which carried the legend '† SIGILLUM.HAWIS.DE ALBEMARLA.COMITISSE.Essexe'.   BARBARA ENGLISH

Sources W. Farrer and others, eds., *Early Yorkshire charters*, 12 vols. (1914–65), vols. 3, 7 · B. English, *The lords of Holderness, 1086–1260: a study in feudal society* (1979) · Pipe rolls · Chancery records (RC) · *Radulfi de Diceto … opera historica*, ed. W. Stubbs, 2 vols., Rolls Series, 68 (1876) · *Chronicon Richardi Divisensis / The Chronicle of Richard of Devizes*, ed. J. T. Appleby (1963) · *Chronica monasterii de Melsa, a fundatione usque ad annum 1396, auctore Thoma de Burton*, ed. E. A. Bond, 3 vols., Rolls Series, 43 (1866–8) · *Sir Christopher Hatton's Book of seals*, ed. L. C. Loyd and D. M. Stenton, Northamptonshire RS, 15 (1950) · B. English, 'The counts of Aumale and Holderness, 1086–1260', PhD diss., U. St Andr., 1977 · A. Beanlands, 'The claim of John de Eston', *Miscellanea*, Thoresby Society, 24 (1919), 227–44
Archives BL · Bodl. Oxf. · East Yorkshire RO, DDCC | Bodl. Oxf., Dodsworth MSS
Likenesses drawing, repro. in Loyd and Stenton, eds., *Sir Christopher Hatton's book of seals* · seal (after a drawing), Belvoir Castle, Leicestershire; repro. in English, *Lords of Holderness*, p1. 8 · seal, BL · seal, Archives de France, Paris

Hawke, Sir (John) Anthony (1869–1941), judge, was born on 7 June 1869 at Tolgulla, near Redruth, Cornwall, the second son of Edward Henry Hawke, merchant, and his wife, Emily Catherine, daughter of Captain Henry Wooldridge RN. He was educated at Merchant Taylors' School and at St John's College, Oxford, of which he was a scholar and from 1931 an honorary fellow. He gained a first in jurisprudence in 1891, and was called to the bar by the Middle Temple in 1892. In 1894 he married Winifred Edith Laura, daughter of Nicholas Henry Stevens, surgeon, of London; they had a son and a daughter.

Both in London and on the western circuit, where he was marked as a future judge and became a keen and deservedly popular figure, Hawke showed himself a vigorous and forceful advocate who, although a doughty opponent, never violated the good traditions of his profession. He took silk in 1913. Although his all-round practice did not involve him in many *causes célèbres*—perhaps the most notable was that inquiry in which he defended the cause of Miss Violet Douglas-Pennant in 1919—it was with universal approbation, both from the bar and from his fellow Cornishmen, that he was appointed a justice of the King's Bench Division by Lord Chancellor Cave, with a knighthood, in 1928.

Before this the closeness of Hawke's ties to his native county had appeared in his appointment as recorder of Plymouth in 1912, and in 1923 as attorney-general to the prince of Wales. That his affection for Cornwall was reciprocated was proved by his being returned twice to parliament: in 1922 and, after a defeat in 1923, in 1924 as a Conservative member for the traditionally Liberal constituency of St Ives. Although he addressed the house only occasionally, he appealed to his fellow Cornishmen not only by his frank and candid approach to local and national problems, but also by his diligence in serving the constituency to which he devoted all his vacations. He was president of the London Cornish Association for many years, and he saw the association grow from a comparatively small body to one of the largest and most active of the county associations.

On the bench Hawke showed himself industrious, conscientious, and essentially kindly, and he invariably maintained its dignity. In criminal trials he never overstrained the case against the prisoner, and his sentences were tempered with understanding and mercy. In the case of *Fender* v. *Mildmay* (1935), he was called on to decide whether a promise of marriage made between the decree *nisi* and absolute was void; he decided that it was. The decision was upheld in the Court of Appeal, but was reversed by three to two in the Lords. On more than one occasion, however, after reversal in the Court of Appeal, his judgments were restored by the House of Lords. He was elected treasurer of the Middle Temple in 1937. On 30 October 1941 Hawke was found dead in his bed at the judges' lodgings at Chelmsford. He was survived by his wife. His son, Sir (Edward) Anthony *Hawke, became recorder of London.

J. D. CASSWELL, *rev.* ALEC SAMUELS

Sources *The Times* (31 Oct 1941) · personal knowledge (1959) · private information (1959)
Likenesses R. E. Eves, oils, *c*.1910, Middle Temple, London · W. Stoneman, photograph, 1920, NPG · R. G. Eves, priv. coll.
Wealth at death £5348 16s. 10d.: resworn probate, 9 Jan 1942, CGPLA Eng. & Wales

Hawke, Sir (Edward) Anthony (1895–1964), judge, was born in London on 26 July 1895, the son of Sir (John) Anthony *Hawke (1869–1941), judge, and his wife, Winifred Edith Laura, daughter of Nicholas Henry Stevens, surgeon. He had one sister. He was educated at Charterhouse School and in 1914 went to Magdalen College, Oxford. His undergraduate career was interrupted by the outbreak of the First World War, after which he did not return to Oxford. Instead he studied law and was called to the bar by the Middle Temple in 1920.

Hawke joined the western circuit and the Devon sessions. On 1 January 1931 he married Evelyn Audrey Lee Davies (1905/6–1977), a widow and the daughter of Major John Norman Meares; they had one daughter. As the years passed his practice became more confined to the central criminal court, where he was junior prosecuting counsel in 1932, third senior prosecuting counsel in 1937, second senior prosecuting counsel in 1942, and senior prosecuting counsel from 1945 to 1950. Among the trials in which he prosecuted were those of the murderers Neville Heath and Daniel Raven and of the two men found guilty of the chalk-pit murder, one of whom was a former minister of justice in the government of New South Wales.

Hawke began to occupy official positions, holding the recordership of Bath from 1939 to 1950 and the deputy chairmanship of Hertfordshire quarter sessions from 1940 to 1950. He became a bencher of his inn in 1942 and in 1950 was appointed chairman of the county of London quarter sessions. In 1954 he was knighted and made common sergeant of the City of London. Held in high esteem, he could look forward to prospects of further promotion and indeed succeeded Sir Gerald Dodson as recorder of London in 1959, in which year also he became a member of the standing committee on criminal law revisions.

With such a background and experience of the criminal law Hawke was a successful and highly respected recorder whose gaiety, handsome and debonair appearance, and keen sense of humour made him a popular friend throughout and beyond the legal profession. One of the last cases to come before him at the Old Bailey (in December 1963) was that in which Christine Keeler was convicted of perjury. He showed himself, especially in the sentence that he imposed, to be possessed of a superb judicial temperament which enabled him to conduct the trial free from any consideration of events (concerning the accused) which caused considerable public and political concern for the security of the state—events which had occurred before the perjury and had led up to it.

In 1962 Hawke became treasurer of his inn. When in this capacity he exercised his right to nominate honorary benchers, he showed his interest in cricket by nominating Sir Learie Constantine, who thus became a valued and popular colleague of the other benchers of that inn. Hawke was also a keen golfer. As a master of the bench his qualities of kindness, wisdom, and humour endeared him to his fellows. He also added the weight of his authority, as editor, to the fifteenth edition of Roscoe's *Criminal Evidence*. Hawke died in Italy on 25 September 1964 while on holiday at Menaggio, Lake Como.

FRED E. PRITCHARD, *rev.*

Sources *The Times* (26 Sept 1964) · personal knowledge (1981) · *CGPLA Eng. & Wales* (1965) · m. cert.

Wealth at death £21,466: probate, 1 Jan 1965, *CGPLA Eng. & Wales*

Hawke, Edward, first Baron Hawke (1705–1781), naval officer, was born in London, the only son of Edward Hawke (*d.* 1718), barrister of Lincoln's Inn, whose family was for many generations settled at Treriven in Cornwall. His mother was Elizabeth, daughter of Nathaniel Bladen of Hemsworth in Yorkshire, granddaughter of Sir William *Fairfax of Steenton, and sister of Colonel Martin *Bladen. It was on his uncle, Colonel Bladen, who was a commissioner of trade and plantations from 1717 to 1746,

Edward Hawke, first Baron Hawke (1705–1781), by Francis Cotes, *c.*1767–70

that Hawke depended for his early naval patronage. On his father's death in 1718 Hawke became his uncle's ward. He joined the navy on 10 February 1720, having been appointed by warrant a volunteer in the frigate *Seahorse* (20 guns; Captain Thomas Durell).

Early career A superfluity of officers from the War of the Spanish Succession, together with a lack of very powerful connections, permitted Hawke's career to advance at only a modest pace. Having served as a midshipman, he passed for lieutenant in Galleons Reach on 2 June 1725. From that date onwards he was in the *Kinsale* (40 guns) on the west African coast as well as in the West Indies, where he had been in the *Seahorse*. He was apparently unemployed from 12 July 1727 until he was at last commissioned on 11 April 1729 as third lieutenant of the *Portland* (50 guns). Of special interest is the month that he then spent, from 25 November 1729, in the *Leopard* (50 guns) commanded by Captain Peter Warren who would rise by 1747 to command the western squadron and recommend Hawke as his relief. After a spell on half pay from January 1730 to May 1731, Hawke was in the *Edinburgh* (64 guns) with Admiral Wager's fleet which suffered severe storm damage in the Bay of Biscay during November and December 1731. From January 1732 he was again with Captain Durell on the North American station. Then comes a crucial sequence, plausibly attributed to Colonel Bladen's influence. Hawke was sent to Jamaica to be first lieutenant of the *Kingston* (60 guns), the flagship of Commodore Sir Chaloner Ogle. The fearsome toll of disease on the station enabled Hawke's new patron to promote him master and commander of the *Wolf* (10 guns) on 13 April 1733 and, on 20 March 1734, to post him captain of the frigate *Flamborough* (24 guns). She paid off in England in September 1735. Hawke then remained on half pay until war with Spain opportunely threatened in 1739.

On 3 October 1737 Hawke, aged thirty-two, had married Colonel Bladen's seventeen-year-old niece, Catharine Brooke (1719/20–1756). The marriage proved a happy one and Hawke was an affectionate father to their three sons and one daughter; three other children died in infancy. On 30 July 1739 Hawke commissioned the *Portland* (50 guns) and was sent again to protect trade in the West Indies. On this occasion his wife went out to be with him when he was in Barbados. As ever, the main problems were health aboard ship and seasonally tempestuous weather—excellent, if stressful, preparation for future campaigns in the Bay of Biscay. Hawke's own constitution proved strong. On 17 March 1743 the storm-damaged *Portland* paid off at Longreach in the Thames.

Colonel Bladen's friendship with Admiral Cavendish, a lord commissioner, underlay Hawke's appointment to a new ship, the *Berwick* (70 guns). Taking command at Deptford on 14 June 1743, he had difficulty in manning her. He told the Admiralty that he had had to take 'very little, weakly, puny fellows' who had 'never been at sea, and can be of little or no service' (Mackay, *Admiral Hawke*, 20). The Admiralty waxed impatient but it was not until 24 September that Hawke could sail to join Admiral Thomas Mathews's fleet in the Mediterranean. Not only did his men need much training; they also fell sick in numbers. Nearly half of the complement of about 500 was sent ashore to the hospital at Mahon. On 11 January Hawke finally joined Mathews off Toulon.

The battle of Toulon, 1744 When, on 9 February 1744, a Franco-Spanish fleet slowly emerged from Toulon, Mathews knew that France had now joined Spain as a belligerent power. He had an apparent equality of force and it was his duty to attack. What ensued on 11 February was a notorious fiasco, due partly to Mathews's poor relations with his second-in-command, Richard Lestock, and especially to his own tactical error in the matter of signals. He had the initiative, being to windward of the allies as they sailed slowly southwards with a light breeze at east-north-east, but found that his line of battle lagged behind that of the allies. It is evident that, when bearing down to attack, Mathews should have struck his signal for the line at the moment when he hoisted that to engage. Although Mathews and his seconds became quite closely engaged, most of his fleet did not, on account of the enemy's evasive tactics. Hawke, however, saw from his station in the van division that enemy ships were edging away from the fire of the British centre. He boldly decided on his own initiative, much as Nelson later did at Cape St Vincent, to leave the line and attack the Spanish *Poder* (60 guns) which was escaping from Mathews's aligned group. Not only did Hawke manage to get to leeward of the *Poder*; he fought her for over an hour, closing to pistol shot (a range of less than 50 yards). After suffering heavy casualties, the *Poder* struck to the *Berwick*. The rate of fire achieved by Hawke with so unpromising a ship's company is shown by the

Poder's having about 200 dead or wounded against only six wounded in the *Berwick*, even allowing for some Spanish losses before Hawke's intervention. Hawke's moral courage and good tactical judgement were fully appreciated later by Lord St Vincent.

No prize money was forthcoming from this feat of arms because the *Poder* was recaptured by the French and finally burnt by a British pursuer, much to Hawke's understandable annoyance. However, during the subsequent eighteen months Hawke gained valuable experience in the Mediterranean through being detached as commodore in command of squadrons consisting respectively of seven, eight, and six ships. Having finally shifted into the *Neptune*, he brought a convoy into Plymouth on 20 September 1745. He was then kept available to testify at the successive courts martial which dissected the British performance at the battle of Toulon. Meanwhile the death of Colonel Bladen in 1746 removed his sole political backer. However, although Hawke testified only at the trial of Robert Pett, the evidence relating to his own conduct much impressed George II. The king's support now proved timely in ensuring the survival of Hawke's naval career. Under an important new 'yellow admiral' scheme devised by Vice-Admiral George Anson, the Admiralty was keen to force Hawke's retirement and to promote to rear-admiral three senior captains of stronger political background. However, the king refused to allow Hawke to be 'yellowed' (retired with the rank of rear-admiral). Having already on 30 March 1747 been appointed to command the *Mars* (64 guns) at Plymouth, Hawke was promoted on 15 July to rear-admiral of the white and was ordered on 17 July to take command of the port.

The second battle of Cape Finisterre, 14 October 1747 Hawke's career as an admiral was much influenced by Anson's victory over the French at the first battle of Cape Finisterre in May 1747. This featured effective, if somewhat cautious, use of a general chase to defeat the much inferior, though important, escort of an outward-bound French convoy. Anson, who had strong political connections, was made a baron. He was also enriched by the exceptional resulting prize money. Hawke was soon to benefit from Anson's work, dating from August 1746, in raising the efficiency of the western squadron.

On 3 August 1747 Vice-Admiral Peter Warren (Hawke's commander in 1729), who had succeeded Anson in the chief seagoing command, came unexpectedly into Plymouth in the *Yarmouth*, suffering from scurvy. Warren's recommendation that Hawke should relieve him prevailed, despite concerns raised by Anson at the Admiralty about Hawke's junior status as an admiral. As Warren's second-in-command, Hawke was ordered to report to him, presumably at Portsmouth—an arrangement that eventually proved unworkable. Warren supplied Hawke with all the instructions which he had received from Anson, including a set of Anson's additional fighting instructions. These, annexed to the general printed fighting instructions, were duly distributed over Hawke's name to all his ships, but he was not, as sometimes supposed, their originator.

On 9 August Hawke hoisted his flag at Plymouth in the *Windsor* (60 guns). By 12 August he was off Ushant where he found four ships of the line. His instructions were to cruise between the latitudes of Belle Île and Ushant, keeping about 100 miles west of Ushant. Although he could, and did, go down to Cape Finisterre, the only connection between that Cape and Hawke's forthcoming battle, fought about 200 miles west of Ushant, is that it took place almost in Cape Finisterre's meridian.

Hawke's squadron was progressively reinforced until it consisted of fourteen of the line. Accumulated intelligence indicated that a large convoy would soon come out from La Rochelle, and Hawke prepared for battle. On 27 September he shifted his flag to his most powerful ship, the *Devonshire* (66 guns). Dignified but affable, he made himself accessible to his captains. From their performance on 14 October, it may be inferred that he effectively communicated his basic principle—already exemplified by his own conduct off Toulon—that every captain should aim to engage at pistol shot. Otherwise, as in 1759, he was ready to signal for a general chase in order to close quickly, make maximum use of daylight, and achieve a concentration on the enemy's rear.

At 7 a.m. on 14 October enemy ships were sighted. Hawke immediately signalled a general chase. He was to leeward of the French and it took over four hours to catch up with them. At 10 a.m., to concentrate his force, Hawke signalled for a line of battle ahead. Captain Thomas Fox signalled that the French had twelve large ships. The breeze was moderate at south-east by south and the French convoy of about 150 vessels was seen crowding away westwards, covered by its escort which formed a close-hauled line of battle standing south-west. Contrasting somewhat with Anson's more cautious approach on 3 May, Hawke, at 11 a.m., hauled down the line signal and substituted that for a general chase. This he left flying until the end of the day. The enemy turned out to have only eight ships of the line, but five of them carried more guns and had larger complements than the *Devonshire*.

Hawke's insistence on very close action can be traced in the records. At 11.30 a.m. he deemed his leading ships to be 'within a proper distance' and signalled to engage (Mackay, *Hawke Papers*, 51). Almost immediately Captain Charles Watson 'got within pistol shot of the enemy's sternmost ship of 70 guns' and *then* opened fire. 'The Monmouth', Watson continued, 'came up and seconded me with great bravery, and as I found the rest of our ships were coming up, I stretched ahead to engage the other ships' (captain's log, *Princess Louisa*, 14 Oct 1747). Henry Harrison of the weatherly *Monmouth* (like Watson, John Bentley, and Philip Saumarez) had not been able to engage during Anson's battle. On 14 October Harrison got to windward of the French and gave good measure. Meanwhile George Rodney in his turn engaged the *Neptune* at 'pistol shot' (Mackay, *Hawke Papers*, 73). None of Hawke's ships was as powerful as the *Monarque* (74 guns), the *Terrible* (74 guns), or the *Neptune* (70 guns), yet all three were battered into submission. The mighty *Tonnant* (80 guns), together with the *Intrépide* (74 guns) finally escaped the

pursuit, well after dark, of Saumarez (who was killed) and Charles Saunders. After fighting various ships the *Terrible*, the *Trident* (64 guns), and the *Severn* (50 guns) all finally struck to the *Devonshire*. The *Fougueux* (64 guns) was also taken.

On 29 October the six severely damaged prizes were triumphantly carried under jury masts into Portsmouth harbour. The French navy had lost some 4000 seamen—a crippling blow. Hawke's conclusive victory was marked by the admirable conduct of his captains. Pointedly several of them complained that Captain Fox had not engaged closely enough and he had to face a court martial. As for Hawke, he became a knight of the Bath and an MP for Portsmouth, also receiving a share of prize money. Suddenly he was a person of some consequence, though still quite weak politically.

In 1748, from April to July, Hawke cruised under Warren's command in the Spanish approaches, being promoted in May vice-admiral of the blue. Enemy shipping, whether French or Spanish, was notably absent. After peace was concluded in October Hawke commanded at Portsmouth until 1752 when he went on half pay. In February 1755 he was recalled to the Portsmouth command. Having seen two squadrons fitted, he himself cruised in the Bay of Biscay before France formally declared war on Britain in May 1756. The Seven Years' War had begun.

Minorca, Rochefort, and the Basque Roads, 1756–1758 After a month's leave Hawke, now a vice-admiral of the white, was recalled to make good the impending loss of Minorca. With Rear-Admiral Charles Saunders he was sent, as the wits said, to hearten the Mediterranean Fleet with a 'little cargo of courage'. On 2 July Hawke arrived at Gibraltar and superseded Admiral John Byng who was sent home under arrest to be tried for his conduct off Minorca. Hawke hoisted his flag in the *Ramillies* (90 guns) and hurried to sea. Despite his own best endeavours, however, he could do nothing to recover the island from the French invaders to whom the British garrison had surrendered on 27 June. Augustus Hervey, a spirited captain attached to Byng, served with Hawke for some months. In his entertaining, if tendentious, *Journal* he points accurately to a certain naïveté in Hawke's character in his acquisition, dating from 1747, of one John Hay: 'a damned interested Scotch secretary with whom Sir Edward was ever cursed', who 'had the impudence to show his ascendancy over the Admiral to the whole fleet' (*Hervey's Journal*, 217, 220). Until 1762 Hay (formerly a purser) remained an abiding, if usually minor, nuisance in Hawke's flagships. Meanwhile a great personal misfortune had befallen the admiral with the death of his wife, Catharine, at Lymington on 29 October 1756.

On arriving back at Portsmouth on 14 January 1757, Hawke applied for leave to re-establish his health. 'Since my embarking', he wrote, 'I have never slept one night out of the ship, or scarce ever set my foot on shore' (Mackay, *Hawke Papers*, 145). Hawke soon went to The Grange in Swaythling, near Southampton, where he had settled his family.

From July to October 1757 Hawke commanded the naval

side of the expedition intended to capture Rochefort. Writing after 1766 (when hoping to see Hawke dislodged from the Admiralty) Hervey noted that he had, in 1757, anticipated the 'miscarriage' as he 'had much experience' of Hawke's 'not having a head to conduct an expedition, however much he certainly had a heart to gain an engagement' (*Hervey's Journal*, 262). Even if William Pitt, the originator of the expedition, was also inclined to mete out to Hawke a share of blame for the failure, the facts of the case do not support such criticism. The question is whether, having conducted fifty transports safely to the Basque Roads under cover of sixteen of the line and other warships, Hawke was to blame when the soldiers, commanded by Sir John Mordaunt, despite every assistance from the navy, refused to land. On arriving in the Basque Roads Hawke (now an admiral of the blue) agreed with Mordaunt that the first step must be to capture the fortified island of Aix. On 23 September this was accomplished, on Hawke's orders to Vice-Admiral Charles Knowles, by Captain Richard Howe of the *Magnanime* (74 guns). As Hawke afterwards reported, Howe intrepidly 'brought up within less than forty yards of the fort, where he kept up an incessant fire for about thirty-five minutes … About three-quarters after one … the garrison … surrendered' (Mackay, *Hawke Papers*, 177). But nothing that the navy could do, or Hawke could reasonably propose, sufficed on 29 September, with all preparations made, to persuade Mordaunt to go ahead and land his troops.

On 8 October the fleet returned to Portsmouth and a derisive welcome. At court the king gave an appropriately good reception to Hawke and an indifferent one to Mordaunt, who soon had to face a court martial. On 22 October Hawke sailed again with Vice-Admiral Edward Boscawen, then a lord of the Admiralty, as his second-in-command, but boisterous weather prevented him from intercepting a French squadron returning from Louisbourg. However, he had, on 21 October, issued to his squadron copies of the general printed fighting instructions containing a remarkable amendment whereby he ordered his captains 'on no account to fire until they shall be within pistol shot' (Mackay, *Admiral Hawke*, 181). This highly aggressive order applied to any form of engagement.

March 1758 found Hawke sailing with a sense of grievance. Lacking frigates, fireships, or bomb vessels, he was nevertheless ordered, with six ships of the line, to attack a convoy assembling in the Basque Roads for the relief of Louisbourg. The French evaded destruction by precipitate lightening of warships and beaching of merchant ships. However, their plan was completely disrupted and Louisbourg duly fell to Boscawen. Two months later, influenced by his secretary, the execrable Hay, Hawke unfortunately took it as an affront when the Admiralty ordered him at Portsmouth to equip Commodore Richard Howe, apparently for an attack on Rochefort, a place about which Hawke remained sensitive. In fact, the undisclosed target was St Malo. On 10 May, believing that his honour was at stake, Hawke committed a serious act of indiscipline by striking his flag at Portsmouth. The situation was regularized by Anson's (then first lord) taking over the command

in chief and sailing with Hawke as his second-in-command.

The blockade of Brest, 1759 In the spring of 1759 it seemed that the French fleet at Brest was preparing to escort an invasion force to the British Isles. It is a measure of Hawke's indispensability that he was now restored to the chief seagoing command. At Spithead on 14 May he again issued his order (dating from 21 October 1757) that ships were not to fire until within pistol shot. On 20 May, with his flag again in the *Ramillies*, he sailed from Torbay with twenty-five ships of the line, four 50-gun cruisers, nine frigates, and a fireship. The Admiralty envisaged the possibility of a prolonged blockade. Hawke was to station his battle fleet near Ushant and detach some of his smaller ships to intercept seaborne supplies bound for Brest or Rochefort. During the next six months the blockade of Brest was the key to British grand strategy and to the future of Canada and India.

By 24 May Hawke was off Ushant and by 27 May he had stationed Captain Robert Duff to keep a continuous inshore watch on Brest. When, early in June, westerly gales drove Hawke back to Torbay, he left Duff's light squadron to find shelter near Brest and report the course and number of any French ships emerging on a change of wind. The Admiralty, recognizing that so large a fleet could more easily shelter in Torbay than in Plymouth, made great efforts to replenish the fleet there. Likewise the subsequent victualling of the fleet at sea was a notable achievement. Having got back to sea, Hawke had barely reached the Lizard when a violent storm drove him back into Torbay with many damaged ships. He finally sailed on 19 June and was much relieved on 21 June to find Duff on watch and the French still in port. During the following four months Hawke settled down to a systematic close blockade. This entailed the constant readiness of the battle fleet to move in and support the inshore squadron if any large French warships stirred. Meanwhile, before leaving Torbay, Hawke had informed Augustus Hervey that he intended to put him in command of a strengthened inshore squadron, and this he did on 3 July. Hawke's selection of Hervey for this important role, like his earlier choice of Duff, proved well founded. Until forced in early November, by the state both of his ship, the *Monmouth*, and of his health, to go into port, Hervey showed great imagination, courage, and enterprise.

Besides avoiding the danger presented by a rocky lee shore, Hawke's main concerns were the health and morale of his men, the exercising of the fleet and regular gunnery drills, the victualling of the fleet, and the system whereby his ships were relieved and cleaned in port. As originally intimated by the Admiralty, he had to detach most of his lighter ships, either singly or in groups, to collect intelligence (largely from neutral vessels), to blockade such subsidiary ports as Lorient and Port Louis, and to seal off the narrow channels whereby coastal craft might slip into Brest. Duff was at first employed on this last-mentioned task, but in September Hawke sent him to take command of the light squadron in Quiberon Bay, in the northerly recesses of which the French transports had collected, ready to embark an army of invasion. The army was quartered at Auray and Vannes; the transports lay within the entrance to the Auray estuary and the Gulf of Morbihan. From Duff's ships in Quiberon Bay hundreds of masts could be seen.

In September the news of Boscawen's victory off Lagos relieved Hawke from the possibility of French warships coming round from Toulon. By mid-October, however, the weather finally began to loosen Hawke's blockade; yet his fleet was ready for the crisis to come. As the naval physician James Lind observed, Hawke's ships were enjoying 'a most perfect and unparalleled state of health'. That 14,000 men could, in cramped conditions, be kept for six months in better fettle than 'on the most healthful spot of ground in the world' was indeed an extraordinary and crucial achievement (Lloyd, 121).

The battle of Quiberon Bay, 20 November 1759 In mid-October Hawke in the *Ramillies* was again, with most of the fleet, forced by westerly gales to seek refuge—this time in Plymouth. After hasty replenishment he was relieved on 19 October to find Hervey's three ships still on station. The French fleet at Brest had not stirred. Hervey, however, was now suffering from gout in both feet and, with the *Monmouth* leaking badly, he soon had to be sent into port. On 5 November Hawke was informed that the French admiral, Hubert de Brienne, comte de Conflans, had been ordered to sail at the first opportunity, but a great westerly gale arose and by 9 November Hawke had to bear up for Torbay. Even the inshore squadron had to follow him in. The *Ramillies*, Hawke's flagship since July 1756, had become unseaworthy. He therefore on 14 November shifted his flag to the *Royal George* (100 guns), commanded by Captain John Campbell, without fuss or discernible loss of efficiency.

Meanwhile on 7 November Conflans had received a welcome reinforcement of experienced seamen from Bompart's squadron which, returning from the West Indies, was blown into Brest. On 14 November Conflans sailed for Quiberon Bay with twenty-one of the line. He was 200 miles ahead of Hawke, with only 120 miles to go. However, for the next five days the winds, often strong, proved contrary and Hawke's fleet derived critical advantage from its superior seamanship, perfected by the rigours of the long blockade. Moreover, the morale and health of the fleet exceeded reasonable expectation. Having been, on 15 November only about 30 miles from Belle Île, Conflans was even closer to it by dawn on 20 November—unaware that Hawke, with twenty-three of the line, was nearby to the north-west. With the wind now westerly, Hawke brought to before 7 a.m., calculating that he would find the French near Belle Île at first light. At 8.30 a.m. one of Hawke's frigates sighted ships to the east. Conflans meanwhile began chasing Duff's frigates which had, thanks to a warning, escaped from Quiberon Bay.

At 9.45 a.m. Howe's *Magnanime* confirmed that it was an enemy fleet that was coming into view ahead. Hawke soon afterwards hoisted the signal for a general chase. This, despite the mounting dangers, he resolutely kept flying throughout the day. A strengthening north-westerly gale,

soon reaching about 40 knots, was combining with unfamiliar rocks and shoals to produce a setting for a battle unique in the days of sail. By firing three guns Hawke implemented an article of Anson's additional fighting instructions whereby the seven leading ships formed a line ahead as they chased. As on 14 October 1747, the leaders would attack the enemy's rear ships and then stretch ahead as other ships came up.

Despite the gales, Hawke's ships carried a great crowd of sail—even topgallant sails were set by the *Royal George* and the *Magnanime*. Meanwhile Conflans, surprised by sightings of Hawke's fleet, stopped chasing Duff's ships, but he lost precious time in forming a single line with his flagship, the *Soleil Royal* (90 guns), at its head. It was not until he had rather slowly, by 2 p.m., got round the Cardinals Rocks into Quiberon Bay that he appreciated the speed and astonishing purpose of Hawke's pursuit, namely to follow him in. With hard gales blowing from west-north-west and all sails set, the estimated speed of the *Royal George* was 8 knots. Meanwhile the French in the bay steered close-hauled in a disorderly line to the north-east. At 2.45 p.m., on seeing his headmost ships coming into action, Hawke hoisted the red flag to confirm an engagement. A heavy northerly squall was experienced at 3.17 p.m., after which the gales blew from north-west. Conflans feared that tacking up towards the Morbihan might now prove impractical.

By 3.55 p.m. Hawke himself had got round the Cardinals and he soon knew that the *Formidable* (80 guns), the flagship of the French rear division, had surrendered. The closeness and persistence of the British fire had left her 'pierced like a cullender' (Marcus, 152). As his ships progressed up the disordered French line Hawke gathered that the *Thésée* (74 guns), while returning the fire of Augustus Keppel's *Torbay* (74 guns), had foundered. Despite the dangerous conditions, Keppel's boats rescued twenty-nine survivors.

Frustrated by the northerly veering of the gales Conflans, with a dozen following ships, could be seen heading back towards the entrance. Tradition has it that Hawke commended the flagship's master for reminding him of the hidden dangers, and then reiterated 'Lay me alongside the French admiral!' (Mackay, *Admiral Hawke*, 247). Effectively the French were acting as trustworthy pilots.

Hawke swiftly converged on the *Superbe* (70 guns) and fired two broadsides whereupon, at 4.41 p.m., she abruptly sank—a remarkable testimony to the closeness and ferocity of his onslaught. He then tried to rake the *Soleil Royal*. The *Intrépide* bravely intervened but Conflans was forced far to leeward. By 5 p.m. it was dusk and Conflans could no longer weather the Four Shoal and escape from the bay. Hawke and most of the fleet anchored for the night between Dumet Island and the Cardinals. Meanwhile some French ships had weathered the Shoal and run out to sea. Eight of the line reached Rochefort. Otherwise Conflans's fleet was annihilated. The *Soleil Royal* and the *Héros* were burnt next day on the rocks near Croisic. The *Juste* was wrecked near the mouth of the Loire and the *Inflexible* foundered on the bar of the Vilaine, within which six ships of the line were imprisoned. Altogether seven, as mentioned, had been destroyed or captured. Meanwhile two of Hawke's ships were lost on the Four Shoal. He afterwards commented: 'Had we but two hours more daylight, the whole had been totally destroyed or taken' (Mackay, *Hawke Papers*, 347). As it was, he had ensured unchallenged British maritime predominance over France until the war ended in 1763.

Hawke henceforth based his blockade of the Biscay ports on a sheltered anchorage in Quiberon Bay. In miserable weather and with supplies curtailed, he himself remained there until 11 January. As the sailors' doggerel ran: 'Ere Hawke did bang Mounseer Conflans, You sent us beef and beer. Now Mounseer's beat, We've nought to eat, Since you have nought to fear' (*DNB*).

On 21 January 1760 Hawke was given a flattering reception by the king and, on 28 January, the thanks of the House of Commons. He was granted a pension of £2000 a year for two lives but, on account of his continuing political isolation, no peerage. In February Hawke was shocked by news that the *Ramillies*, manned by many who had served with him, had been wrecked on Bolt Head. More than 700 lives were lost. He promptly acted very much in character by entreating the Admiralty to provide for the widows of four warrant officers 'left destitute of everything' and for the widow of his former flag-captain, Witteronge Taylor (Mackay, *Admiral Hawke*, 265).

Hawke again commanded in chief in Quiberon Bay from August 1760 to March 1761. He investigated the defences of Belle Île (subsequently captured in the summer of 1761). On board the *Royal George* during 1760 and 1761 was Lieutenant William Locker (later Nelson's mentor) who noted the admiral's 'manly decision' and civilizing influence. 'He was a strict but temperate disciplinarian—affable rather than familiar with his officers' (Mackay, *Admiral Hawke*, 278). During a final cruise between April and September 1762 Hawke derived benefit from the capture of some valuable Spanish prizes.

Hawke's tactical contribution Hawke's use of a general chase in October 1747 and November 1759 has tended to categorize him as a tactician. Under sail no other tactical approach brought on an engagement more expeditiously. Moreover if, as usual, the enemy formed a single line of battle, the chase would probably ensure a concentration of power against the enemy's rear ships. Hawke clearly assumed superior British seamanship and gunnery. His reliance on very few signals limited the likelihood of confusion.

Less noticed has been his doctrine, demonstrated in action on 14 October 1747 and explicitly formulated in his amendment of 21 October 1757, which was reissued on 14 May 1759, that his captains were 'on no account to fire until they shall be within pistol shot'. This handwritten amendment (applicable to line or chase engagements) radically transformed the unaggressive tendency of article 13 of the general printed fighting instructions (copies of which were supplied unaltered—though open to amendment—during most of the eighteenth century to

commanders-in-chief when asked for). At Quiberon Bay the weather prevented some captains from achieving this maximum of aggression, but the *Formidable*, *Superbe*, and other French ships certainly experienced it. No other admiral seems to have emulated Hawke's explicit order but its essence was certainly transmitted to his successors, culminating with Nelson. Captain William Locker was brought up in the Seven Years' War as a young officer by Hawke and (as already indicated) much admired him. After the battle of the Nile Nelson wrote on 9 February 1799 to Locker: 'I have been your scholar … It is you who always said "Lay a Frenchman close and you will beat him"' (*DNB*). Hawke finally, on 16 July 1759, issued an emphatic additional instruction to ensure close engagement by every ship if he had to fight in a line of battle. But his preference for the chase, whenever circumstances permitted, is clearly demonstrated in his two great, yet contrasting, victories.

First lord of the Admiralty When Anson returned to the Admiralty in 1757 he wished to have Hawke as a member of his board, but Hawke's lack of political weight counted against him. For the same reason, when it was rumoured on Anson's death in 1762 that Hawke would succeed him as first lord, he failed to do so. It was only in 1766 that Lord Chatham, faced with politically motivated resignations from the Admiralty, turned belatedly to Hawke. On 11 December 1766 he became first lord. Nicholas Rodger's researches have reinforced much that was supposed about Hawke's tenure at the Admiralty. On the one hand, as a naval officer, he was, like Anson, better placed than a career politician to resist political encroachment on naval patronage; and it is also clear that he sustained a rate of shipbuilding which compares well with that achieved by Lord Sandwich, who succeeded him in 1771. On the other hand, by the late 1760s Hawke lacked the comparative youth and vigour offered by Sandwich, together with Sandwich's proven talent for initiating and effecting administrative reform.

On 15 January 1768 Hawke succeeded Sir William Rowley as the one and only admiral of the fleet. Meanwhile he attended conscientiously at the board, presiding at 118 out of 131 meetings in 1767, 126 out of 144 in 1768, 118 out of 146 in 1769, and 156 out of 186 in 1770, despite worsening health. In general his record of health while at sea had been very good, but from 1763 he had suffered increasingly from a painful urinary complaint, common among seamen, called the gravel.

While Hawke's board transacted its business with humanity and good sense, being always open to suggestions of technical improvement, the war scare of 1770 over the Falkland Islands revealed the unreadiness of several guardships. These had been rotting internally as they lay in the navy's contingency reserve, partly due to their having been hastily built of unseasoned timber during the Seven Years' War. After Hawke's retirement through ill health in January 1771, Sandwich managed to tighten the Admiralty's administrative control and improve the navy's readiness for war, as Hawke was, in 1778, generous enough to intimate to George III.

Later years After retiring in 1762 from seagoing service, Hawke lived comfortably at Sunbury, while from 1770 his eldest son and heir, Martin Bladen Hawke (1744–1805), lived in a house owned by the admiral in Bloomsbury Square. Hawke's own household continued, somewhat as in his wife's time, to be run by one Sally Birt. In 1770 Martin (a qualified barrister) married Cassandra, youngest daughter of Sir Edward Turner, and they soon had a daughter, followed by a son and heir, much to Hawke's pleasure and satisfaction. In 1773 his second son, Edward, a lieutenant-colonel aged twenty-seven, was, to Hawke's great distress, killed in a hunting accident.

On 20 May 1776 the admiral was at last elevated to the peerage as Baron Hawke of Towton in Yorkshire, where he had inherited property from his wife. Meanwhile Hawke's daughter Catharine lived at home, apparently often unwell. In 1777 his third son Chaloner, a wild young man and a spendthrift, was killed while riding recklessly. Hawke himself died at Sunbury on 17 October 1781 and was buried near his wife in the church of St Nicolas at North Stoneham, near Swaythling, on 31 October. His surviving son, Martin, succeeded him as second Baron Hawke.

Tall, dignified, unostentatious, affable, Hawke was a committed Christian and a civilizing influence on the navy. Inspiring through example and timely word, he was a firm but humane disciplinarian, consistently concerned for the welfare of his officers, men, and their families. Like many contemporaries, he was sensitive on points of honour. His simplicity, straightforwardness, and common sense served him well at sea, but less well as first lord.

Hawke's resolute, but finely judged, acceptance of risks, especially at Quiberon Bay, left a deep impression on his naval successors. His proto-Nelsonic stature as the winner of two conclusive victories has been recognized by British and French historians (especially Georges Lacour-Gayet). However, though a fair amount has been published about Hawke since Montagu Burrows's original biography of 1883, he has not been well remembered by the general public. His undemonstrative character and unsensational private life have not endowed him with universal appeal.

RUDDOCK MACKAY

Sources DNB · R. F. Mackay, *Admiral Hawke* (1965) · *The Hawke papers: a selection, 1743–1771*, ed. R. F. Mackay, Navy RS, 129 (1990) · G. J. Marcus, *Quiberon Bay* [1960] · R. F. Mackay, 'Edward Hawke', *The great admirals*, ed. J. Sweetman (1997) · N. A. M. Rodger, *The wooden world: an anatomy of the Georgian navy* (1986) · N. A. M. Rodger, *The insatiable earl: a life of John Montagu, fourth earl of Sandwich* (1993) · B. Tunstall, *Naval warfare in the age of sail: the evolution of fighting tactics, 1650–1815*, ed. N. Tracy (1990) · J. S. Corbett, ed., *Fighting instructions, 1630–1816*, Navy RS, 29 (1905) · *The Barrington papers*, ed. D. Bonner-Smith, 1, Navy RS, 77 (1937) · *The health of seamen: selections from the works of Dr. James Lind, Sir Gilbert Blane and Dr. Thomas Trotter*, ed. C. Lloyd, Navy RS, 107 (1965) · captain's log, *Princess Louisa*, PRO, Adm 51/739(5), 14 Oct 1747 · [earl of Bristol], *Augustus Hervey's journal*, ed. D. Erskine (1953) · J. Creswell, *British admirals of the eighteenth century: tactics in battle* (1972) · G. Lacour-Gayet, *La marine militaire de la France sous le règne de Louis XV* (1910) · M. Burrows, *Life of*

Edward, Lord Hawke (1883) · C. Wilkinson, 'The earl of Egremont and the navy, 1763–6', *Mariner's Mirror*, 84 (1998), 418–33

Archives Birr Castle archives, Offaly, corresp. and papers · NMM, letters and order books · priv. coll., MSS | BL, Anson MSS, Add. MSS 15955–15957 · BL, Hardwicke MSS and Newcastle MSS · BL, corresp. B. Keene, Add. MS 43431 · BL, corresp. with Sir B. Keene, Add. MS 43439 · NMM, Duff MSS and M. Clements MSS · PRO, Admiralty records

Likenesses portrait, *c.*1748 (as a vice-admiral of the blue; after mezzotint by J. MacArdell; after G. Knapton), NMM · C. Spooner, mezzotint, pubd 1762, BM · F. Cotes, oils, *c.*1767–1770, NMM [*see illus.*] · J. Macardell, mezzotint (after G. Knapton), BM, NPG · group portrait, Shugborough, Staffordshire

Wealth at death £2000 p.a. pension since 1760; considerable accumulated prize money; house in Bloomsbury Square; property in Yorkshire

Hawke, Martin Bladen, seventh Baron Hawke (1860–1938), cricketer, was born at the rectory, Willingham, Lincolnshire, on 16 August 1860, the second and eldest surviving son of Edward Henry Julius Hawke (1815–1887) and his wife, Jane (*d.* 1915), third daughter of Henry Dowker of Laysthorpe, Yorkshire. His father, who was rector of Willingham from 1854 to 1875, succeeded as sixth Baron Hawke in 1870. His great-great-grandfather was Edward Hawke, first Baron Hawke, the celebrated admiral.

Hawke's first school was at Newark, where the headmaster, the Revd Herbert Plater, forbade him to bat left-handed. Thereafter, Hawke, who was naturally left-handed as a child, would bat right-handed. In later life he played billiards left-handed and put his gun to his left shoulder. When he was ten Hawke was sent to St Michael's, Aldin House, Slough, then a preparatory school for Eton College, which he attended from 1874 to 1879. Hawke was tall and strong for his age, and although a moderate scholar he became a superb all-round athlete at Eton. In the winter he concentrated on running, sprints up to the quarter-mile, and the field game, the Eton version of football. In the summer he played cricket. An erratic, hard-hitting batsman with a disregard for personal injury, he gained his cricket colours in 1878, playing against Harrow that season, and again in 1879.

After Eton Hawke's father sent him to a private tutor for two years. This decision, made on both scholastic and financial grounds, in no small measure changed the course of his life. During his time at Eton, Hawke and his father were frequent companions. The enforced interregnum enabled Hawke to throw himself into country pursuits. He also regularly turned out for the Yorkshire gentlemen's cricket club, bringing him to the attention of the committee of the Yorkshire County Cricket Club. In the late summer of 1881 he was invited to make his début for the county club, in two matches at the Scarborough festival. Both matches were lost but he had begun a lifelong connection with the Yorkshire club with which his name will always be associated.

Hawke went up to Magdalene College, Cambridge, in the autumn of 1881 and entered swiftly into the university cricket eleven; he won blues in 1882, 1883, and 1885. At Cambridge he was planning a military career, and in 1884 his militia duties impinged upon his cricket to the extent

Martin Bladen Hawke, seventh Baron Hawke (1860–1938), by Elliott & Fry, pubd 1904

that they cost him his place in the side against Oxford. The following year he returned to captain the Cambridge side to victory.

Hawke might have captained Yorkshire in 1882, but wisely he declined the opportunity, preferring to extend his apprenticeship by another year. While the county club boasted several of the finest professional cricketers of the age, the eleven lacked collective discipline and had never fulfilled their potential. The problem was partly on the field, partly in a committee room entirely dominated by the unrepresentative Sheffield districts. The club lacked a sense of common purpose, a leader behind which it could unite. When in 1883 Hawke accepted the captaincy, he had no illusions as to the task ahead. The early years were not plain sailing and there were times when his commitment to the county club wavered, but gradually he rebuilt the county eleven and instilled a philosophy of attacking cricket into his players. His was a pragmatic root-and-branch reform and modernization of the whole club, a

model of changes he would see adopted throughout the English game in later years.

As captain of Yorkshire until 1910 and president of the club from 1898 until his death, Lord Hawke (he succeeded to his father's title in 1887) came to control almost every aspect of the county's affairs. In matters of discipline he could be harsh. Several players were summarily dismissed for transgressing Hawke's law, most notably Robert (Bobby) Peel in 1897 for drunkenness. But these incidents apart, no man of his era did more for the welfare of the professional cricketer than Hawke. Moreover, his concern for his players went far beyond the cricket field. He introduced winter pay for his professionals and ensured that moneys they received from benefit matches were wisely invested.

In 1893 the Yorkshire eleven, now leavened with amateurs—including F. S. Jackson, arguably the finest all-round amateur cricketer of the day—won the championship under Lord Hawke's command for the first time. It was a feat to be repeated in 1896, 1898, 1900, 1901, 1902, 1905, and 1908. The achievements of the Yorkshire sides Hawke captained have tended to obscure his own playing contribution. He was a useful batsman, a dangerous, tenacious hitter rather than a master of his craft, as his career first-class average of 20.15 indicates. However, he often made runs when his side was in trouble, when the competition was hottest. His highest score, 166 against Warwickshire in 1896, was made in a partnership of 292 that was still in 1998 the English record for the eighth wicket.

If Hawke the batsman is overshadowed by his incomparable Yorkshire elevens of the 1890s and 1900s, his place in cricket history is assured for his work spreading the gospel of cricket. He was responsible for organizing and leading cricket tours from England to the farthest corners of what was then the empire, and to other parts of the world. His first tour was to Australia in 1887. Owing to his father's death in December that year he was obliged to return home, but later he took teams to India (in 1889 and 1892), the United States of America and Canada (in 1891 and 1894), South Africa (in 1895 and 1898), the West Indies (in 1896), and Argentina (in 1911). He lived to see South Africa, India, and the West Indies admitted to full test-match status. If, in the history of cricket, the immortal W. G. Grace was the ultimate exponent of the game and George Harris, fourth Lord Harris, its foremost administrator, Hawke was its great exporter.

Although the ancestral Hawke estate at Towton had long been lost to the family, Hawke's father, the sixth baron, had enjoyed the friendship of the millionaire Andrew Montague, who furnished him with a fifty-year lease on Wighill Park, near Tadcaster, and enabled him to become in later years, something of a 'City man'. Hawke inherited from him extensive estates in the West Riding of Yorkshire. He also held a number of company directorships, income from which allowed him to devote much of his life to the game he loved. On 1 June 1916, he married Marjory Nelson Richie (*d.* 1936), third daughter of William Peacock Edwards JP, of Edinburgh, and widow of Arthur J. Graham Cross. There were no children of the marriage.

When his playing career ended Hawke found it hard to avoid controversy. His friends wondered how the tactful, hard-working, kindly man they knew could behave so ineptly in public. Hawke's impulsiveness and his willingness to speak his mind were his downfall in the public arena. His infamous off-the-cuff remark at the Yorkshire annual general meeting in 1925 that 'Pray God, no professional shall ever captain England', made in defence of A. E. R. Gilligan's much criticized captaincy of England in Australia, drew a torrent of criticism. Later, he explained that what he had meant to say was that it would be a bad day for England if there was no amateur good enough to play for his country, but by then the damage had been done. He was god-fearing, having found Christianity as a child, and decent to the core. He could be very naive, but knew his limitations. Although he regularly attended the House of Lords, he never made his maiden speech, recognizing that he was a poor public speaker. In the 1920s and 1930s he travelled widely. At home grouse moors and golf links became safe havens from his critics in the press.

For many years Hawke served the MCC as a member of various committees, including that charged with selecting the England team between 1899 and 1911. He was elected president of the club in 1914, normally an annual appointment, which owing to the exigencies of war he held until 1918; on the death of Lord Harris in 1932 he became treasurer.

Lord Hawke died on 10 October 1938 at 12 Randolph Crescent, Edinburgh, a few days after collapsing at North Berwick. He was succeeded as eighth baron by his brother Edward Julian (1873–1939). Hawke's portrait hangs in the Long Room at Lord's, looking down on the comings and goings of the modern players of the game that in his life he did so much to promote. JAMES P. COLDHAM

Sources J. P. Coldham, *Lord Hawke: a cricketing biography* (1990) [incl. comprehensive bibliography] · Lord Hawke [M. B. Hawke], *Recollections and reminiscences* (1924) · *Wisden* (1939) · *CGPLA Eng. & Wales* (1938)

Archives Marylebone Cricket Club, Lord's, London · Yorkshire County Cricket Club | FILM BBC WAC · BFI NFTVA · BFI NFTVA, news footage

Likenesses Elliott & Fry, photogravure, pubd 1904, NPG [see illus.] · W. Stoneman, photograph, 1920, NPG · W. Allingham, stipple and line engraving (after photograph by Dickinson & Foster, 1894), NPG · black and white photographs, Marylebone Cricket Club, Lord's, London · black and white photographs, Yorkshire County Cricket Club · oils, Marylebone Cricket Club, Lord's, London · oils, Yorkshire County Cricket Club

Wealth at death £59,043 16s. 11d.: probate, 5 Dec 1938, *CGPLA Eng. & Wales*

Hawker, Edward (1782–1860), naval officer, son of Captain James *Hawker (*b.* in or before 1730, *d.* 1786), had his name placed by Prince William Henry on the books of the frigate *Pegasus* in 1786, but he first went to sea in 1793 on the *Pegasus*, and afterwards in the *Swiftsure*, with his brother-in-law Captain Charles Boyles. In July 1796 he was promoted lieutenant of the *Raisonnable*, also with Boyles. In 1799–1800 he was in the sloop *Spitfire* with his brother-in-law Commander Michael Seymour (1768–1834), and from

1801 to 1803 in the frigate *Thames* with Captain Aiskew Paffard Hollis, at Gibraltar and on the coast of Egypt. He afterwards commanded the cutter *Swift* in the West Indies, and in August 1803 was promoted to the command of the brig *Port Mahon*.

In June 1804 Hawker was advanced to post rank, and in the following month was appointed to the *Theseus* (74 guns), flagship of Rear-Admiral Dacres, on the West Indian station. He afterwards commanded there the *Tartar* (32 guns) and the *Melampus* (36 guns) until 1812, continually and successfully cruising against privateers. From 1813 to 1815, first in the *Bellerophon* (74 guns) and afterwards in the *Salisbury* (58 guns), he was flag captain to Sir Richard Goodwin Keats, commander-in-chief at Newfoundland, and from 1827 to 1830 was flag captain to the earl of Northesk at Plymouth.

Hawker had no further service afloat, but became in due course rear-admiral in 1837, vice-admiral in 1847, and admiral in 1853. During his later years he was a frequent correspondent of *The Times*, writing as 'A Flag Officer'. He was also well known in low-church religious and philanthropic circles. He was married and had children, including Edward James Hawker, of Ashford Lodge, near Petersfield, Hampshire. He died at Brighton, Sussex, on 8 June 1860. J. K. LAUGHTON, *rev.* ROGER MORRISS

Sources O'Byrne, *Naval biog. dict.* · *The Record* (18 June 1860) · private information (1891) · A. B. Rodger, *The war of the second coalition: 1798–1801, a strategic commentary* (1964) · R. Muir, *Britain and the defeat of Napoleon, 1807–1815* (1996) · *GM*, 3rd ser., 9 (1860), 105–6 · Boase, *Mod. Eng. biog.* · *CGPLA Eng. & Wales* (1860)

Archives NMM, logbooks and order books

Wealth at death under £6000: probate, 12 July 1860, *CGPLA Eng. & Wales*

Hawker, Sir Frank Cyril (1900–1991), banker, was born on 21 July 1900 at Walthamstow, Essex, to Frank Charles Hawker, civil servant, and his wife, Bertha Mary Bastow. Educated at the City of London School, Hawker was briefly at the stock exchange and at a firm of solicitors before joining the Bank of England in 1920. He remained there for forty-two years and left only to become chairman of Standard Bank. In 1931 he married Marjorie Anne, daughter of Thomas Henry Pearce and his wife, Amelia Harriet; they had three daughters.

Hawker rose rapidly through the Bank of England's ranks. He served as deputy to George Bolton, when the latter was made head of the bank's new foreign department in 1934. Then he became, successively, deputy chief cashier (1944), chief accountant (1948), adviser to the governor (1953), and executive director (1954).

In 1953 the then governor of the bank asked Hawker to contact various industrialists as part of a crusade to make the bank less isolated. Hawker did so, first in the UK and then in the Commonwealth. For this he was knighted in 1958. He also acquired an extensive knowledge of the banking industry of the Commonwealth and especially of South Africa, which was going through the difficult period that culminated in its withdrawal from the Commonwealth.

In 1962 Hawker was appointed chairman of Standard

Bank, whose core business had traditionally been in South Africa. He was one of the few strategic thinkers of his day in the banking profession, and in his new position he tried to restructure and reorganize British overseas banking to meet the needs and pressures of the modern world.

By the 1960s the future of British overseas banking looked bleak. The end of the British empire meant that London was no longer automatically the centre of trade finance. Banks faced a future in which business would have to be fought for, against strong foreign, especially American, competition. Moreover, the advent of new independent governments meant that banks had to confront tough political constraints in areas where traditionally they had had a free hand. Logic therefore dictated that there should be fewer and larger banks, based in London, rather than many localized overseas banks.

Within Standard this idea was known as the 'grand design', and Hawker was its chief proponent. Given the particular political circumstances of South Africa and of emergent Africa, he looked to amalgamation for geographical diversification. While the negotiations were necessarily complex, there were three main strands to this design: a link with a British domestic bank, a link with an American bank, and mergers with other overseas banks. None of these strands was altogether successful, but each set of negotiations resulted in moves which changed the face of British overseas banking. Standard succeeded in consolidating its trans-African persona and in 1969 it amalgamated with the Chartered Bank, which traditionally banked in the East. The merger, creating the Standard Chartered Bank Ltd, was a triumph, though Hawker's considerable management skills were required to combine two very different banking cultures.

As well as being the first chairman of the Standard and Chartered group, Hawker was chairman of the Bank of West Africa (taken over by Standard in 1965) from 1965 to 1973, and of the Union Zairoise de Banques from 1969 to 1974. He was also deputy chairman of Midland and International Banks, and of two industrial companies: Head Wrightson and the Davy Corporation.

Despite his highly successful career Hawker's first love, arguably, was cricket; he was a talented batsman and captained several club sides. He was also a keen footballer and sportsman generally. In later life he became chairman of the Amateur Football Alliance and the Minor Counties Cricket Association; he was the finance committee chairman for the National Playing Fields Association, and then the association's honorary vice-president; and he was vice-chairman of the Football Association. The summit of his sporting career came in 1970–71, when he was made president of the MCC, though his South African connection led to adverse press exposure in a year when the South African touring team visited England.

Hawker died on 22 February 1991 at his home Hadlow Lodge, Burgh Hill, Etchingham, Sussex, aged ninety, and was survived by his wife and daughters.

FRANCES BOSTOCK

Sources G. Jones, *British multinational banking, 1830–1990: a history* (1993) • R. Fry, *Bankers in west Africa* (1976) • archive, GL, Standard Bank and Standard Chartered MSS • *The Times* (26 Feb 1991) • *WW* • b. cert. • m. cert. • d. cert.
Archives GL, Standard Chartered archive, Standard Bank and Standard Chartered MSS
Likenesses photograph, repro. in *The Times*
Wealth at death under £115,000: probate, 29 Aug 1991, *CGPLA Eng. & Wales*

Hawker, James (*b.* in or before **1730**, *d.* **1786**), naval officer, was the son of a Plymouth wine merchant and his wife, daughter of an alderman of Plymouth. He entered the navy on 1 July 1743 in the *Shrewsbury* (Captain Solomon Gideon) as servant to the first lieutenant, Lucius O'Bryen, and moved with him when he was made commander of the *Portsmouth* storeship. Subsequently he was in the *Sheerness* with George Brydges Rodney in the North Sea, and then the *Colchester*, *Unicorn* and the *Peggy* sloop, again with O'Bryen. After nearly eleven years' service he passed for lieutenant on 4 June 1755, when he was stated 'as more than 24 years of age'.

On 31 December 1755 Hawker was appointed as lieutenant to the *Colchester* at the request of Captain O'Bryen. Sir George Pocock, as MP for Plymouth, obtained for him on 6 August 1761 the command of the *Barbados* sloop, though he did not join her until November, and he served at the capture of Martinique and later at Havana, until moved to the *Sardoine* in April 1763 for the North American station. He did not, however, attain post rank until 26 May 1768, and was then appointed to the *Aldborough* from 1770 to March 1773 for the Newfoundland station, followed by the *Mermaid* in North America from 8 April 1776 until she was chased ashore in the Delaware River on 8 July 1778 by d'Estaing's squadron. On return home he commissioned the *Iris*, again for North America, where on 6 June 1780 he fought a well-conducted action against the French frigate *Hermione*, in which both ships were much damaged and were obliged to return to their respective bases. Some angry correspondence ensued, apparently to determine who ran away from whom. Soon after, Hawker was moved to the *Renown* and took a convoy home. He was then appointed on 10 November to the *Hero*, which formed one of Commodore George Johnstone's squadron, which fought the action at Porto Praya on 16 April 1781. Hawker soon after resigned his command at St Helena on grounds of ill health, and returned home in the *Jason*. He had no further service.

Hawker married Dorothea O'Bryen, sister of his captain, with whom he had at least three sons; John and James entered in the *Mermaid* as captain's servants, but eventually went into the army, while the youngest son, Edward *Hawker, became an admiral. Three of his five daughters married naval officers, namely Charles Boyles, E. Oliver Osborne, and Sir Michael Seymour, bt. A fourth daughter married Sir William Knighton, private secretary and keeper of the privy purse to George IV. A Captain Thomas Hawker may have been a relative, as he was an able seaman in the *Peggy* sloop from 1750, and moved, as did James, to the *Colchester* when Captain O'Bryen was appointed to that ship. James Hawker died in early 1786, probably at Plymouth, where he held property at Mount

Gould and in Caskin Street with a lease on a timber yard at Britton Side, possibly inherited from his father and left to his eldest son, John. His wife survived him.

J. K. LAUGHTON, rev. A. W. H. PEARSALL

Sources C. Gill, 'Some diaries and memoirs of Plymouth in the French Revolutionary and Napoleonic wars', *Report and Transactions of the Devonshire Association*, 115 (1983), 7 · R. Beatson, *Naval and military memoirs of Great Britain*, 3 vols. (1790) · letters; passing certificate; muster books, PRO, Adm.1/1906–7; Adm.107/4 p.310; Adm.36/3720 *Shrewsbury*, 4448 *Unicorn*, 5082, 5083 *Barbadoes*, 5690 *Granado*, 6311 *Peggy*, 7556 *Aldborough*, 7675 *Sardoine*, 7761 *Mermaid* · N. A. M. Rodger, *The wooden world: an anatomy of the Georgian navy* (1986) · will, PRO, PROB 11/1141, fols. 123v–5r
Wealth at death property in Plymouth; left small bequests and an annuity: will, PRO, PROB 11/1141, fols. 123v–5r

Hawker [alias Collis], **James** (1836–1921), poacher and autobiographer, was born in Daventry, Northamptonshire, and baptized there in the Wesleyan Methodist Chapel on 29 August 1836. He was the first of the eight children of Charles Hawker and his wife, Charlotte Parbery (bap. 1816).

Hawker's early life is scarcely documented, other than in his own recollections. It is clear that his early years were spent in poverty, as his father failed first as a tailor and later as a second-hand clothes dealer. Hawker must have received some education, though he later denied it, writing a clear, sloping hand in later life, but by the age of eight was in full-time employment as a bird scarer. In 1848 he was apprenticed to a bootmaker and from 1850 supplemented his family's income further by poaching.

In 1852 Hawker enlisted in the Northamptonshire militia. Though he later claimed this was solely to gain the 10s. bounty and thereby buy a gun for poaching, the military life clearly suited him. On disbandment Hawker received a further £1, which was spent on a better, percussion-cap, firearm. In 1854 the militia was again embodied and Hawker, promoted to corporal, served in Dublin.

In 1857 Hawker fled Daventry following a confrontation with the head gamekeeper at Badby. By his own account Hawker worked in Leicester until spring 1858 under the assumed name of James Collis. He enlisted in the Leicestershire militia and is recorded in the muster roll as corporal of the light company. He enlisted in and deserted from the regular army, and by July 1858 was established once again as a bootmaker, with lodgings in Town Hall Lane, Leicester.

On 10 November 1861 Hawker's first child, Albert, was baptized at Oadby, Leicestershire, under the mother's surname, Norman. On 31 May 1863 Sarah Norman became Mrs James Collis at St John's Church, Leicester. Six months later, on 8 November 1863, Charlotte Ann, their daughter, was baptized at Oadby, followed by James on 4 August 1867. The following year Hawker fled again to avoid a fine of £8 for poaching, his family settling first at New Duston, Northamptonshire, and then at Northampton.

The Hawkers remained in Northampton until 1880. From 1875 Hawker developed a passion for bicycling, forming with friends the Rovers Bicycle Club. The attempts by the atheist and radical Charles Bradlaugh to gain and keep a Northampton seat in parliament also gave

rise to a more conventional interest in radical politics. His political views having been formed by bitter experience of poverty and harsh treatment, Hawker had hitherto regarded poaching as his personal attempt at a fairer redistribution of wealth. He also strengthened his stand against drink, though he had little sympathy for the more violently outspoken temperance campaigners: 'a man Has as much Right to Drink has we Have to abstain' (*Hawker's Journal*, 40).

In 1890, after ten years in Leicester, Hawker moved to Oadby. He continued to poach but had achieved some respectability. In 1893 he was elected, with the support of the Working Men's Club, to the Oadby school board, and in December 1894 joined the new Oadby parish council. His eldest son, Albert, had gained considerable fame as a racing bicyclist and the younger, James Hawker junior, prospered as a boot and shoe manufacturer.

In 1909, on the death of his wife, Hawker moved in with his daughter, Charlotte, who had married James Barker, at 13 Sandhurst Street, Oadby. He became a village character, still poaching, until his death from a heart attack in Stoughton Road, Oadby, on 7 August 1921.

Hawker wrote his memoirs, seemingly in several versions, in 1904–5. They are a mixture of autobiography, poacher's handbook, and radical philosophy. The illegality of much that is described, coupled with the memory of an old man, make them suspect as the only source for much of Hawker's life. 'If i Had been Born an idiot and unfit to Carry a Gun but with Plenty of Cash they would Call me a Grand Sportsman but for being Born Poor i are Called Poacher' (*Hawker's Journal*, 151). Hawker's celebrity was secured in 1961 when Oxford University Press published his memoirs as *A Victorian Poacher*, edited by Garth Christian. In 1980 the Emma Theatre Company produced a play by Andrew Marley and Lloyd Johnston, *The Poacher*, based on Hawker's life. A public collection at the first performance funded a headstone for Hawker's grave in Oadby cemetery. In addition to his name and dates, it bears his motto: 'I will Poach till I die'.

ROBIN P. JENKINS

Sources J. Hawker, autobiography, Leics. RO, DE 2403 · *James Hawker's journal: a Victorian poacher*, ed. G. Christian (1961) · D. Sneath and B. Lount, *The life of a Victorian poacher: James Hawker* (1982) · census returns · parish register, Oadby, Leics. RO, DE 1136/4 [baptism] · parish register, Leicester, St John's, 31 May 1863, Leics. RO, DE 1544/6 [marriage] · Leics. RO, Leicestershire militia muster roll, LM4/4 · Leicestershire directories, 1890, 1895, 1901 · IGI · gravestone, Oadby cemetery, Leicestershire
Archives Leics. RO, memoirs, autobiography, diary, and scrapbook, DE 2403

Hawker, Mary Elizabeth [pseud. Lanoe Falconer] (1848–1908), writer, was born on 29 January 1848 at Inverurie, Aberdeenshire, the elder daughter of Major Peter William Lanoe Hawker (1812–1857), of the 74th highlanders, and his wife Elizabeth, née Fraser (d. 1901). The family home, to which they returned in 1854, was Longparish House, near Whitchurch, in Hampshire. Hawker's grandfather, Lieutenant-Colonel Peter *Hawker (1786–1853), was the author of *Instructions to Young Sportsmen* (1814).

Although Hawker's formal education could be characterized as desultory, she read widely and was an accomplished pianist. Her father died in 1857, and after her mother's second marriage, to Herbert Fennell, with whom Hawker did not have a good relationship, the family lived from 1863 until 1868 in France and Germany, and Hawker became proficient in both French and German. She began to write early in life for family publications and private theatricals, producing a few stories and essays that appeared in magazines and newspapers. Her first real success came in 1890 with the publication of *Mademoiselle Ixe* under the pseudonym Lanoe Falconer. Having been rejected by many publishers this short mystery novel formed the initial volume in the Pseudonym Library, a new series of shorter fiction published by T. Fisher Unwin and designed to compete with John Lane's Keynotes series. The heroine of *Mademoiselle Ixe* is a governess in an English country house who is connected with Russian nihilists and becomes involved in an assassination attempt. Hawker was not familiar with Russian people, but her political sympathies, already liberal, were evidently inspired by the 'anguish' and 'torment' of a Russian musical air (Phillips, 'Lanoe Falconer', 232–3). *Mademoiselle Ixe* also contains some pointed satire on the narrow English view of foreigners. Circulation of Hawker's book was forbidden in Russia; Hawker gave a portion of her royalties to help Russian exiles. Hippolyte Adolphe Taine and Gladstone admired the book, and the English edition sold over 40,000 copies. An American edition was printed, as were translations in French, German, Dutch, and Italian.

Hawker's subsequent works of fiction include *Cecilia de Noël* (1891), a 'morbid psychic romance' (Sutherland, 285), and *The Hôtel d'Angleterre* (1891), a collection of character sketches and other short atmospheric pieces. Hawker also contributed an essay, 'The short story' to *On the Art of Writing Fiction* (1894), which foreshadowed the importance of her preferred fictional form to the modernist writers of the early twentieth century. Hawker believed that 'the length of a work is no measure of its importance or effect' (Phillips, *Lanoe Falconer*, 206).

Hawker's health declined from 1894, interrupting her work. She was unable to take up an offer of £250 for a short story to be published in a series with Rudyard Kipling and J. M. Barrie. Hawker, who did not marry, cared for her mother before she died in the spring of 1901 and for her stepfather in his final illness in 1902. Family commitments occupied her time, although she was able to travel to Switzerland with her sister's family in 1904. She died from rapid consumption on 16 June 1908 at what may have been her sister's house, Broxwood Court, Pembridge, Herefordshire, and was buried at Lyonshall, Herefordshire.

ELIZABETH LEE, rev. MEGAN A. STEPHAN

Sources Blain, Clements & Grundy, *Feminist comp.*, 354 · E. M. Phillips, *Lanoe Falconer* (1915) · E. M. Phillips, 'Lanoe Falconer', *Cornhill* (Feb 1912), 231–44 · *WWW*, 1897–1915 · J. Sutherland, 'Hawker, Mary Elizabeth [Morwenna Pauline]', *The Longman companion to Victorian fiction* (1988), 285 · L. Falconer, *Mademoiselle Ixe* (1891), [1890] · The *Times* (20 June 1908), 1 · '"Lanoe Falconer", Mary Elizabeth Hawker', *The Cambridge bibliography of English literature*, ed. J. Shattock, 3rd edn, 4: 1800–1900 (1999), 1522 · S. J. Kunitz and H. Haycraft, eds., *British authors of the nineteenth century* (1936), 281 · IGI
Likenesses portrait, repro. in Phillips, *Lanoe Falconer*, frontispiece
Wealth at death £12,452 10s. 6d.: probate, 27 Aug 1908, CGPLA Eng. & Wales

Hawker, Peter (1786–1853), army officer and writer, born on 24 December 1786, was the son of Colonel Peter Ryves Hawker (d. 6 Feb 1790) of Longparish, Hampshire, and his wife, Mary Wilson Yonge, who was of an Irish family. He was born in London and educated at Eton College. Like his father and many of his ancestors Hawker entered the army, his commission as cornet in the 1st (Royal) Dragoons dating from 1801. In 1803 he joined the 14th light dragoons, in which regiment he became captain the following year and served with it in the Peninsular War. Being badly wounded at Talavera, he retired from active service in 1813, but by the recommendation of the duke of Clarence he was made major (1815) and then lieutenant-colonel (1821) of the North Hampshire militia.

Hawker, a man of wide interests, was a good musician as well as a keen shot and active sportsman. In 1818 he studied harmony and composition at the London academy of J. B. Logier, and in 1821 was a piano student of H. J. Bertini in Paris. He composed much music, and in 1820 patented his invention of hand moulds to facilitate pianoforte playing. At the Great Exhibition of 1851 some improvements in firearms manufacture which Hawker devised attracted attention, and he hoped in vain that they would be adopted by the War Office.

Hawker was twice married, and with his first wife, Julia, daughter of Hooker Bartellot, whom he married in 1811, he had two daughters and a son, Peter William Lanoe Hawker, who served as a lieutenant in the 74th Highland regiment.

Hawker's publications included *Journal of a Regimental Officer during the Recent Campaign in Portugal and Spain* (1810) and *Instructions to Young Sportsmen in All that Relates to Guns and Shooting* (1814). This work, by which Hawker became widely known, passed through many editions. Hawker died at 2 Dorset Place, Dorset Square, London, on 7 August 1853.　　　　　W. A. J. ARCHBOLD, rev. JAMES FALKNER

Sources Army List · GM, 2nd ser., 40 (1853), 313 · P. Hawker, *Journal of a regimental officer during the recent campaign in Portugal and Spain under Lord Viscount Wellington: with a correct plan of the battle of Talavera* (1810) · Colburn's United Service Magazine, 3 (1849), 141 · Boase, *Mod. Eng. biog.* · New Grove
Likenesses M. Gauci, lithograph, 1830 (after A. E. Chalon), BM · H. Robinson, stipple (after bust by W. Behnes), NPG; repro. in P. Hawker, *Instructions to young sportsmen in all that relates to guns and shooting*, 11th edn (1814) · portrait, repro. in ILN (1853), 138 · wood-engraving (after daguerreotype by Claudet), NPG; repro. in ILN (1851)

Hawker, Robert (1753–1827), Church of England clergyman, born at Exeter on 13 April 1753 and baptized at St Mary Steps, Exeter, on 14 May, was the son of Jacob Hawker (d. 1754), surgeon, and Sarah Smith (d. 1801). After the early death of his father, he was raised by his mother and two aunts. He was educated at the grammar school,

Exeter, before becoming a pupil of Mr White, surgeon, of Plymouth. He married at the parish church of Charles, Plymouth, on 6 January 1772, Anne Rains (d. 3 April 1817), daughter of Lieutenant Rains RN; they had four sons and four daughters. Three of their sons entered the Anglican ministry, one of whom, the Revd John Hawker, seceded to protestant dissent, while another, the Revd Jacob Hawker, was father of the Revd Robert Stephen Hawker, poet and vicar of Morwenston, Cornwall.

During his surgical training Hawker attended lectures at various London hospitals. On returning to Devon he obtained an appointment as assistant surgeon in the Royal Marines. After about three years, however, and for reasons which are not entirely clear, he abandoned surgery for the church; he matriculated on 27 May 1778 at Magdalen Hall, Oxford, but left before taking a degree. He was ordained deacon on 20 September 1778 by John Ross, bishop of Exeter, and priest on 30 May 1779, and was presented to the curacy of St Martin's, Looe, Cornwall; three months later he became curate of the parish of Charles, Plymouth, under the Revd John Bedford. On the death of Bedford in 1784 Hawker became vicar of Charles, where he remained for the next forty-three years. His *Sermons on the Divinity of Christ* (1792) procured for him the diploma of DD from the University of Edinburgh.

Hawker carried on a varied and energetic ministry, which touched the lives of many in Plymouth and further afield. In 1797 he became deputy chaplain of the local garrison. He also founded, or became involved in, a number of voluntary societies, including the Religious Tract Society (1799–1808), the Great Western Society for Dispersing Tracts among the Poor (1802–27), the London Missionary Society (1802–8), the Corpus Christi Society (1813–27), and the Gospel Tract Society (1824–7), which competed with its moderate rival, the Religious Tract Society, provoking a bitter, albeit short-lived, public controversy. Hawker was also interested in community issues, promoting Sunday schools as a remedy for social problems and encouraging penal reform; at his urging, a penitentiary for women was established at Plymouth in 1808.

Hawker exercised an important, albeit sometimes controversial, influence in evangelical circles. His voice was powerful, yet harmonious, and as a pulpit orator he was impressive and fascinating. For many years he paid an annual visit to London, preaching to large congregations. Doctrinally he was reckoned an ultra-Calvinist, and his parish of Charles was notorious for its high predestinarian doctrine. Having rejected 'growth in grace', Hawker was denounced by one critic as 'the great patron and apostle of antinomianism' (J. Cottle, *Strictures on the Plymouth Antinomians*, 2nd edn, 1841, 4, 11). William Wilberforce prohibited his children from attending services at London's Locke Hospital when Hawker was preaching, lest they drink in his 'poison' (R. I. Wilberforce and S. Wilberforce, *The Life of William Wilberforce*, 1838, 3.473). His impact, however, both direct and indirect, can be clearly traced on the spread of extreme forms of 'serious religion' in the west of England, for the Western Schism (c.1815–17), the Oxford

evangelical secessions (c.1831–5), and the (Plymouth) Brethren (c.1830s) were all influenced by his teachings.

Hawker was the author of a large corpus of religious writings, his *Works* (1831) filling ten quarto volumes. He was also a frequent contributor to various religious journals, especially (from 1798) *Zion's Trumpet*. He died at Plymouth on 6 April 1827, aged seventy-four, and was buried in the church at Charles, where a tablet, surmounted by a marble bust, was erected to his memory. Although his church was almost entirely destroyed by aerial bombardment during the Second World War, its outer walls have been preserved as a memorial.   GRAYSON CARTER

Sources *The works of the Rev. Robert Hawker … with a memoir of his life*, ed. J. Williams, 10 vols. (1831) · H. Dowling, *The riches of God's grace displayed in the life, ministry, and death of R. Hawker, D.D.*, 2nd edn (c.1827) · J. Dixon, *The autobiography of a minister of the Gospel* (1866) · J. Darling, *Cyclopaedia bibliographica: a library manual of theological and general literature*, 2 vols. (1854–9) · *GM*, 1st ser., 97/2 (1827), 87 · R. H. Martin, *Evangelicals united* (1983) · Boase & Courtney, *Bibl. Corn.* · G. Carter, 'Evangelical seceders from the Church of England, c.1800–1850', DPhil diss., U. Oxf., 1990 · parish register (baptism), 14 May 1753, Exeter, St Mary Steps · *DNB* · *IGI*

Archives Plymouth and West Devon RO, church wardens' accounts; parish registers of church; rate books; vestry minute books

Likenesses W. Blake, line engraving (after J. Ponsford), BM, NPG · M. R. Cooper, stipple (after J. S. Wetherall), BM, NPG · A. Smith, line engraving (after Williams), BM, NPG · R. Woodman, engraving (after painting by G. Patten), repro. in Williams, ed., *Works of the Rev. Robert Hawker*, vol. 1, preface · marble bust, Charles parish church, Plymouth; destroyed in Second World War

Hawker, Robert Stephen [*pseud.* Reuben] (1803–1875), poet and Church of England clergyman, was born on 3 December 1803 at Charles Church vicarage, 6 Norley Street, Plymouth, the eldest of the nine children of Jacob Stephen Hawker (c.1775–c.1845), doctor, and his wife, Jane Elizabeth Drewitt. The vicarage belonged to his grandfather Dr Robert *Hawker (1753–1827) who was famous in the west country as a charitable and eloquent Calvinist divine. The younger Robert was baptized on 29 December by Dr Hawker's eldest son, John, at Stoke Damerel church, near Plymouth. A few years after his son's birth Jacob Hawker took holy orders, serving as curate (later vicar) of Stratton, near Bude in north Cornwall, and leaving Robert to be brought up by Dr Hawker.

Robert Hawker was a high-spirited youth who reacted against the evangelical discipline of his family. He sought adventure among books discovered in a pawnbroker's warehouse and revelled in the beauties of sea and woods, subjects of his early verse. He ran away from several preparatory schools and played practical jokes on the inhabitants of Plymouth and Stratton. The most celebrated of these was his impersonation of a mermaid, singing dirges and combing his seaweed hair, on Bude breakwater. At sixteen he left Liskeard grammar school, Cornwall, to train as a solicitor. But he soon decided to become a clergyman and his aunt Mary paid for him to attend Cheltenham grammar school. By 1823 he had published (under the pseudonym Reuben) his first volume of poetry, *Tendrils*, and gained a place at Pembroke College, Oxford.

After his first term Hawker, aged only nineteen, married

Charlotte I'ans (1781/2–1863), a 41-year-old gentlewoman with an income of £200 a year. Their marriage in 1823 was a love match, though it is true that her money helped him to complete his education. In 1824 he transferred to Magdalen Hall, and continued to write poetry. *The Song of the Western Men*, the most familiar of his works, was published in 1825, attracting favourable attention from Scott, Macaulay, and Dickens. Two years later he won the Newdigate prize for a poem on Pompeii, which smacked of plagiarism. During his five years at university Hawker assimilated some ideas of the embryonic Oxford Movement but he never became an acknowledged high-churchman. After graduating in 1828 he prepared for holy orders and was ordained in 1831. His curacy was spent at North Tamerton, Cornwall. In 1834 Bishop Phillpotts appointed him to the remote living of Morwenstow on the north Cornish coast, where he remained until his death.

Hawker became well known not only as a romantic poet but as an eccentric vicar. He dressed flamboyantly, wearing a brown cassock, scarlet gauntlets, and a hat like a fez, or a claret-coloured coat, fisherman's jersey, and sea boots. He talked to birds, and his congregation often included his nine cats and many dogs, which he preferred to the uncharitable farmers, over whom he once 'read the Exorcistic Service' (Byles, 227). He cultivated his reputation as a local character, which attracted many visitors, including Tennyson. Behind his showmanship, however, there lay a genuine concern for his parishioners. He built a new bridge, a vicarage, and a school. He instituted church collections for the poor—a controversial move to counteract the effects of the new poor law, movingly evoked in his poem *The Poor Man and his Parish Church* (1840), which haunted John Keble. Hawker also gave generously from his own pocket to help the labourers of Morwenstow, including dissenters. He restored his beautifully situated church, in which he performed services twice daily even if no one was present except his wife, whom he would address as 'Dearly Beloved Charlotte' (Brendon, 101). He tried to attract more parishioners to the services, improving carol singing and reviving harvest festivals.

A task which Hawker found most disturbing was the burial of corpses of shipwrecked sailors (or putrefying parts of them) which were frequently washed up on the rugged shore of his parish. This gruesome duty, combined with the struggle to prevent local people from stripping the wrecks, contributed to his mounting mental instability. From the timbers of the ships he built a hut on the clifftop, where he watched for wrecks and heard 'in every gust of the gale a dying sailor's cry' (Byles, 532). Here he also saw devils, mermaids, and mystical visions, wrote poetry, succumbed to persecution mania, and fell into depression. Increasingly he took refuge in opium.

Hawker's mental distress became acute in 1862 during Charlotte's final illness—he nursed her until she died, on 2 February 1863. In that year there was also a fire at the vicarage and two shipwrecks so harrowing that he felt a 'terrible dread of losing power over my own mind' (Byles, 487). Yet this burly, flaxen-haired, blue-eyed, ruddy-faced priest never lost his power to charm and, after a brief courtship, he married a young governess, Pauline Anne Kuczynski (1844–1892), on 21 December 1864. His second marriage was also a happy one, and the couple had three children: Morwenna, Rosalind, and Juliot, born respectively in 1865, 1867, and 1869. Hawker delighted in his daughters (though he had yearned for a son) but agonized about his ability to provide for them. He begged shamelessly and even sold Charlotte's family silver.

Throughout these troubles Hawker continued to write prose and poetry, published in such journals as *Notes and Queries* and Dickens's *Household Words*. In fact it was during the wretched year of 1863 that he wrote *The Quest of the Sangraal*, praised by Longfellow and Tennyson and still considered one of the most successful nineteenth-century renditions of the Arthurian legend. In 1869 he published a collection of his poems under the title *Cornish Ballads*. Although it received a 'long and kindly notice' in *Fraser's Magazine* (Byles, 579), the book brought him little profit. Nevertheless these ringing ballads memorably sealed his association with the north Cornish coast,

> Where rock and ridge the bulwark keep,
> The giant-warders of the deep.
> ('The Storm')

He wrote little poetry after 1869 but published his collected prose sketches, *Footprints of Former Men in Far Cornwall*, in 1870. They have modest literary merit but are full of antiquarian interest.

Latterly Hawker found himself increasingly at odds with the secular and religious temper of his day. His letters suggest that he was turning from protestantism, which amounted to nothing more than 'a gigantic sneer of religious negation' (Brendon, 228), towards the positive dogmas of the Roman Catholic church. Nevertheless it was a shock to almost everyone except his wife when the vicar of Morwenstow was baptized a Roman Catholic on his deathbed. Pauline wrote afterwards that her husband had been 'at heart a Catholic' ever since she had known him (Lee, 2).

Hawker died on 15 August 1875 at 17 Lockyer Street, Plymouth, and was buried three days later in Plymouth cemetery. Within a few months the Revd Sabine Baring-Gould had published his confessedly 'gossiping' biography (Baring-Gould, 63), which exaggerated Hawker's eccentricities. Despite subsequent corrections and several further biographies, notably the authoritative *Life and Letters* compiled by Hawker's son-in-law C. E. Byles in 1905, Baring-Gould's myth still lingers on. When, in 1880, Pauline Hawker received a civil-list pension of £80 a year, W. E. Gladstone assured her that it had been 'awarded on the ground of true poetical merit' (Byles, 651). Although a minor poet, Hawker did pen some 'magnificent images and lines, unsurpassed in Victorian blank verse' (Brendon, 20). Nevertheless he is best remembered for his strange, lonely ministry beside the 'Severn Sea'.

PIERS BRENDON

Sources C. E. Byles, *The life and letters of R. S. Hawker* (1905) • P. Brendon, *Hawker of Morwenstow* (1975) • J. G. Godwin, ed., *The poetical works of Robert Stephen Hawker* (1879) • S. Baring-Gould, *The vicar of*

Morwenstow, 12th edn (1949) • F. G. Lee, *Memorials of the Rev. R. S. Hawker* (1876) • *CGPLA Eng. & Wales* (1875)

Archives BL, 'The book of wrecks at Bude' • BL, notebook, Add. MS 41090 • Bodl. Oxf., corresp. and papers • Exeter Central Library, letters • Westcountry Studies Library, Exeter, articles, short story, and miscellany | BL, Maskell MSS • Bodl. Oxf., letters to Frederick G. Lee • Bodl. Oxf., Nicholas Ross collection • Cornwall RO, letters to J. T. Blight • Pembroke College, Oxford, corresp. with W. D. Anderson and articles collected by Steve Goard • Ransom HRC, letters to Mrs Watson [microfilm in Bodl. Oxf.] • Tonacombe Manor, Morwenstow, letters to William Waddon-Martyn • parish registers of Morwenstow Church

Likenesses W. Wright, pencil and watercolour drawing, 1825, Pembroke College, Oxford • drawing, 1825, repro. in Brendon, *Hawker of Morwenstow*, 64 • R. Budd, photograph, 1864, repro. in Byles, *Life and letters*, 482 • S. Thorn of Bude, photograph, June 1870, repro. in Byles, *Life and letters*, 588 • G. Howard, sketch, 1873, repro. in Byles, *Life and letters*, frontispiece • T. R. Way, lithograph (after photograph by S. Thorn), repro. in Byles, *Life and letters*, 84 • stipple, NPG

Wealth at death under £3000: probate, 15 Nov 1875, *CGPLA Eng. & Wales*

Hawker, Thomas (*b.* before 1641?, *d.* in or after 1721?), portrait painter, was of obscure origins. Waterhouse noted that Hawker was 'pretty certainly the same as the painter called by Walpole (after Vertue) "Edward" Hawker' (Waterhouse, 117). According to Vertue, Hawker came to live in Sir Peter Lely's house after Lely's death, in the hope of benefiting by the famous associations of the house. This hope was not realized; he defaulted on the lease. He was still in Covent Garden in 1700. He is known by a full-length portrait of the duke of Grafton (*c.*1680/1681), engraved in mezzotint by Isaac Beckett, a portrait of Titus Oates, engraved in mezzotint and published by R. Tompson, and a head of Sir Dudley North. Described by Waterhouse as 'a close but pedestrian follower of Lely', Hawker charged £15 for a work 50 inches by 40 in 1683 (ibid.). One Hawker (called by Vertue, perhaps in error, Edward Hawker) is stated to have been admitted a poor knight of Windsor, and to have been living in 1721, over eighty years of age.   L. H. CUST, *rev.* ANNETTE PEACH

Sources E. K. Waterhouse, *The dictionary of British 16th and 17th century painters* (1988) • E. Waterhouse, *Painting in Britain, 1530–1790*, 4th edn (1978); repr. (1994) • J. Kerslake, *National Portrait Gallery: early Georgian portraits*, 2 vols. (1977), 37

Hawkes, (Charles Francis) Christopher (1905–1992), archaeologist, was born on 5 June 1905 at 35 De Vere Gardens, Kensington, London, the elder child and only son of Charles Pascoe Hawkes (1877–1956), a lawyer, soldier, and author, and his wife, Eleanor Victoria (1874–1966), daughter of Charles Davison Cobb, a wine shipper, and his Spanish wife, Victoria. Christopher was a precociously clever child, and after preparatory school in Surrey he went to Winchester College in 1918. He flourished as a classical scholar, also showing a talent for music and drawing. His father's military service included postings in the north-east of England and on Salisbury Plain, and Hawkes became familiar with monuments such as Hadrian's Wall, the monastery church at Jarrow, and Stonehenge. At Winchester he wrote to O. G. S. Crawford, the newly appointed archaeology officer of the Ordnance Survey, whose encouragement to him to explore the field monuments of the district led to his first published work.

In 1924 Hawkes went up to New College, Oxford. He became increasingly interested in ancient history and archaeology, studying Roman Britain with R. G. Collingwood and acquiring his basic training in excavation with Mortimer Wheeler at Brecon in 1925 and with Donald Atkinson at Wroxeter in 1926. In 1925–6, with Nowell Myres and Charles Stevens, he began to excavate the medieval chapel on St Catherine's Hill, Winchester; in 1927–8 this work was extended to the Iron Age hill fort there.

After taking a first-class degree in 1928 Hawkes moved to the department of British and medieval antiquities at the British Museum, as (successively) assistant, assistant keeper (second class), and assistant keeper (first class). He was responsible for compiling the accessions register, and though this was often behind schedule his scholarship and talent for drawing made the registers of this period a mine of information. His intellectual ambition spread far beyond the museum, however, and he continued busily writing, researching, and excavating. His excavation in 1930–32 with Rex Hull at Colchester was the first serious attempt to understand the complexities of a late Iron Age town. From 1935 to 1939 he excavated three more Iron Age hill forts in Hampshire.

Hawkes's work launched a new phase of Iron Age studies. His article on hill forts (*Antiquity*, 5, 1931, 60–97) reviewed the evidence for this type of site, and introduced a new chronological and cultural scheme for the Iron Age, linked to a theory of cultural change by migration, which dominated the subject for the next forty years. Another article, written with Gerald Dunning, on the Belgae (*Archaeological Journal*, 87, 1930, 150–335), provided detailed documentation of the continental background to the final period of the Iron Age in Britain. With Thomas Kendrick he produced *Archaeology in England and Wales, 1914–1931* (1932), a major synthesis of recent archaeological work which offered a new formulation of later prehistory.

At Colchester Hawkes had met (Jessie) Jacquetta Hopkins (1910–1996) [*see* Hawkes, (Jessie) Jacquetta]. They were married on 7 October 1933, and collaborated fruitfully in several subsequent projects. Their only child, Nicolas, was born in 1937, but the marriage ended in June 1953. Strained by his intellectual ambition, his heavy workload, and his lifelong inability to start the day promptly, Hawkes's relationship with his departmental keeper, Reginald Smith, became increasingly sour. Matters improved after Smith's retirement in 1937, but it was clear that Hawkes's future lay elsewhere. Further progress was stalled by the Second World War, when he was seconded to the Ministry of Aircraft Production. He returned to the museum in 1946, but was soon appointed to the new chair of European archaeology at Oxford. He took up the post on 1 October 1946, and held it until his retirement in 1972. On 30 January 1959 he married the archaeologist Sonia Elizabeth Chadwick [*see below*]. After a brief period living at Dorchester-on-Thames, they settled at 19 Walton Street,

Oxford, which with the later inclusion of no. 20 remained their home until his death.

Hawkes did not have an easy ride at Oxford. His informative and entertaining memorandum submitted in 1965 to the Franks commission on the plight of new subjects at Oxford (Franks commission, written evidence, part 11, 55–64) was tartly reminiscent of Cornford's *Microcosmographia academica*. With mock puzzlement it described the ingenuity of Oxford's devices for politely blocking change, and boldly sought a remedy in 'a period of directorial government' (ibid., 61). Beneath the humour lay Hawkes's deep frustration at the complex structures and short-sighted priorities which caused Oxford to lag behind other universities in its research and teaching. The frustration born of long years spent in trying to advance his subject also stood out in Hawkes's oral evidence to the committee. In the time spent writing memoranda during his eighteen years at Oxford he said, 'I could have written at least one archaeological book'. When asked if there had been rows, he replied: 'A good many … some of them exceedingly fierce, of which I have been the centre' (Franks commission, oral evidence, O. 33, p. 12).

Hawkes made Oxford a centre for postgraduate teaching and research in archaeology. His interest in the later prehistoric and early historic periods were complemented in 1956 by the appointment of Ian Richmond to a chair in the archaeology of the Roman empire. These developments culminated in the establishment of the Institute of Archaeology in 1961. Hawkes was an inspiring teacher; though there were never many students the proportion who went on to prominent positions in archaeology was remarkable. He quickly appreciated the potential contribution of the natural sciences to knowledge of the past, and responded enthusiastically to Lord Cherwell's suggestion that Oxford should found a research laboratory for archaeology; it came into being in 1955. He was also instrumental in founding its journal *Archaeometry* (a word he claimed to have invented).

Hawkes continued to publish well into his eighties. He declined to revise his one major work of synthesis, *The Prehistoric Foundations of Europe* (1940), because his interests were now firmly in the first millennium BC, but a stream of articles on Bronze Age and Iron Age Europe confirmed his position as Britain's leading authority on these periods. He did not accept a divide between prehistory and history, and believed firmly in the value of the written sources. His work was characterized by a detailed familiarity with the textual and material evidence and by a firm commitment to understanding the past on a pan-European scale. From the 1930s he was a regular visitor to Europe, and he was greatly respected by his continental contemporaries. Though some of his ideas, especially the explanation of culture change by a series of migrations, became unfashionable, the rapid progress made in Iron Age studies would have been impossible without his pioneering efforts.

Hawkes was a striking figure, despite his spare build and his increasingly severe limp. He had penetrating pale eyes behind his thick glasses, and a shock of dark hair, which later turned to silver. He was a good listener, but also an intimidatingly well-informed, though always witty, talker. His distinctive handwriting was matched by an idiosyncratic English style, which, though always accurate, could be highly compressed. He died in Oxford on 29 March 1992. His funeral took place on 3 April 1992 at St Cross Church, Oxford.

Hawkes's second wife, **Sonia Elizabeth Hawkes** [née Chadwick] (1933–1999), archaeologist, was born on 5 November 1933 at Barnes Cray Nursing Home, Crayford, near Dartford, Kent, the only child of Albert Andrew Chadwick, engineer, and his wife, Doris, née Benger. She was educated at school in Dartford, and read English at Bedford College, London, before becoming an archaeologist and expert on the artefacts of the fifth to seventh centuries AD. From 1958 to 1959 she was curator of the Scunthorpe Museum. After her marriage to Hawkes in 1959 she was research assistant (1959–73) at the Oxford Institute of Archaeology. There she began her most significant research, on Anglo-Saxon graves and grave goods, focusing on the Kent cemeteries and especially Finglesham. Elected FSA in 1961 she was university lecturer in European archaeology from 1973 to 1994. She suffered from stage nerves and disliked lecturing, but was an effective supervisor of graduate students and created a notable seminar series which resulted in *Weapons and Warfare in Anglo-Saxon England* (1989). In 1979 she was a founding editor of *Anglo-Saxon Studies in Archaeology and History*. She nursed her husband in his declining years, took early retirement in 1994, and married Svetislav Petkovic (b. 1923/4), a retired factory inspector, on 13 May 1995. Following a long illness she died of cancer on 29 May 1999 at Sobell House, Oxford, and was cremated on 8 June at Oxford crematorium. She was survived by her second husband.

T. C. CHAMPION

Sources D. W. Harding, 'Charles Francis Christopher Hawkes', *PBA*, 84 (1994), 322–44 · C. F. C. Hawkes, 'Archaeological retrospect 3', *Antiquity*, 56 (1982), 93–101 · D. B. Webster, *Hawkseye: the early life of Christopher Hawkes* (1991) · *The Times* (31 March 1992) · *The Independent* (1 April 1992) · personal knowledge (2004) · *The Independent* (4 June 1999) · *The Independent* (24 June 1999) · *The Times* (15 June 1999) · *WWW* · b. cert. [Sonia Chadwick] · m. cert. [Sonia Hawkes and Svetislav Petkovic] · d. cert. [Sonia Petkovic]

Archives Bodl. Oxf., corresp. and papers · English Heritage National Monuments Record, Swindon, notes for unpublished volume on Roman Wiltshire · S. Antiquaries, Lond., corresp. and papers relating to Corpus of Ancient Brooches | Bodl. Oxf., letters to O. G. S. Crawford · Bodl. Oxf., corresp. with J. L. Myres · S. Antiquaries, Lond., letters to W. F. Grimes · U. Cam., faculty of archaeology and anthropology, corresp. with C. F. Fox

Likenesses photograph, 1928, repro. in Webster, *Hawkseye* · W. Bird, photograph, c.1970, repro. in Harding, 'Charles Francis Christopher Hawkes' · D. B. Webster, pencil drawing, 1987, repro. in Webster, *Hawkseye*

Hawkes [née Hopkins; *other married name* Priestley], **(Jessie) Jacquetta** (1910–1996), archaeologist and writer, was born on 5 August 1910 in Cambridge, the younger daughter and third and youngest child of Sir Frederick Gowland *Hopkins (1861–1947), biochemist and Nobel prize winner, and his wife, Jessie Ann (1869–1956), daughter of Edward William Stevens, ship's fitter, of Ramsgate. Her

(Jessie) Jacquetta Hawkes (1910–1996), by Jorge Lewinski, 1968

eminent father was a distant cousin of the poet Gerard Manley Hopkins. In her imaginative writing style she was to embrace both academic exactness and poetic form, producing work that was ahead of its time in its lyrical synthesis of science and art; she would argue that the two were inseparable. In the range of her published work—poetry, plays, journalism, fiction, biography, popular guide books, and academic papers—she communicated, at all levels, her passion for archaeology, and the response of people, and places, to change over time. In a childhood essay she declared that passion. She was already inspired by visits to museums with her mother, and the discovery that her own home, at 71 Grange Road, Cambridge, was built where a Roman road overlapped an Anglo-Saxon cemetery. She attended the Perse School for Girls (1921–8) and then went to Newnham College, Cambridge, in 1929, the first woman to read archaeology and anthropology for the new undergraduate degree. In her second year she took part in her first proper excavation, a Roman site near Colchester, and met (Charles Francis) Christopher *Hawkes (1905–1992), a young and already brilliant archaeologist, whose proposal of marriage she preferred over several others.

Privately surprised at gaining a first, Jacquetta went on to excavate at Mount Carmel in Palestine with Dorothy Garrod. Her work there, unearthing a Neanderthal skeleton, moved her to poetry. On 7 October 1933 she married Hawkes in the chapel of Trinity College, Cambridge, her father's college. It appeared a blissful union of mutual interests, but some fifty years later, recalling the Majorcan honeymoon in her partly autobiographical A Quest of Love (1980), Jacquetta wrote simply and revealingly: 'We

enjoyed the sun and visiting antiquities—and were not unhappy' (Hawkes, Quest of Love, 212). Her only child, Nicolas, was born in 1937, and from a marriage at that time 'admirably well-balanced and free' (ibid.), the pair also produced a book together, Prehistoric Britain (1943), largely written by her. They set up home in London, most notably at 39 Fitzroy Road, Primrose Hill, the back garden of which featured in Jacquetta Hawkes's most acclaimed work, A Land (1951). This fusion of geology, archaeology, literature, and art, illustrated by her friend Henry Moore, was hailed for its Donne-ish lyricism. It was a considerable departure from her other solo publications, the second volume of the Archaeology of the Channel Islands (1938), on Jersey, and Early Britain (1945), and its unique appreciation of the past, and the problems of the dawning nuclear age, set its author apart as an archaeologist not shy of offering up a new perspective. Her literary interests also found a place in her private life, in an affair with the Australian poet Walter *Turner. Jacquetta Hawkes's only volume of poetry, Symbols and Speculations (1949), was a response to Turner's early and sudden death in 1946. During the war she had also become involved in an affair with a woman which, although platonic, left her emotionally confused.

Christopher Hawkes's work for the British Museum was successful but all-demanding, and the couple's increasingly separate lifestyles and interests were exacerbated by his wartime employment as a principal in the Ministry of Aircraft Production. Finding her niche as a consummate communicator, Jacquetta also joined the civil service in 1941, working on post-war reconstruction, and for the Ministry of Education from 1943. In her role as editor-in-chief of its film unit she produced The Beginning of History, which was a novel attempt at presenting prehistory, then thought unfilmable, in a new format, with an Iron Age site reconstructed at Pinewood Studios. In 1943 she was also made principal and secretary of the UK national commission for UNESCO, and protested vigorously against the inclusion of the playwright and author, John Boynton *Priestley (1894–1984), on the grounds that he was not of sufficiently high literary calibre. She only admitted later that she had not read his books. Her objection was overruled, Priestley and Jacquetta met, and at a conference in Mexico City in 1947 began an affair which she held to be the great love of her life and which ultimately led to two much publicized divorces. In July 1953 the couple were married. They lived at the Albany in London, and at Brook Hill on the Isle of Wight, and moved to Kissing Tree House at Alveston, near Stratford upon Avon, in 1960.

Jacquetta Hawkes gave up the civil service in 1949 to concentrate on writing. As well as producing archaeology books she collaborated with Priestley on two plays, one of which, A Dragon's Mouth (1952), was experimental but well received, as was Journey Down a Rainbow (1955), a series of letters based on their travels in south-west America, dedicated to Carl Jung, to whose works Priestley introduced Jacquetta. Marriage with Priestley was deeply and mutually satisfying, as Jacquetta often pronounced, but she did not neglect her other passion. Her post-war role as archaeology adviser to the Festival of Britain gave her a stage for her own sweeping view of the history of Britain, and in 1952 she was made an OBE. In subsequent years she travelled widely as a correspondent for *The Observer* and the *Sunday Times*, and maintained a high profile. She wrestled with the hugely ambitious UNESCO project *The History of Mankind*, as co-editor of the prehistory volume, and provoked debate with her 1971 John Danz lecture, delivered in Seattle, in which she urged that science should be complemented by intuition. This was published as *Nothing But or Something More*. In 1950 she became a governor of the British Film Institute and was instrumental, with Priestley and their great friends Canon John Collins and his wife, Diana, in the founding of the Campaign for Nuclear Disarmament—being distinguished at the front of the Aldermaston march by her stature and large hat. In 1971 she was made vice-president of the Council for British Archaeology, and in 1982 produced a biography of her close friend and fellow archaeologist Sir Mortimer Wheeler. Her last publication was the *Shell Guide to British Archaeology*, published in 1986.

After Priestley's death in 1984, Jacquetta Hawkes, who firmly believed that death was the end, moved to Littlecote in the Cotswold town of Chipping Campden, Gloucestershire. She remained a trustee of the Shakespeare Birthplace Trust, and continued her interests in church architecture and ornithology, as well as in such issues as homosexual law reform and education; she was a governor of two grammar schools. She died in Cheltenham on 18 March 1996, and was cremated on 25 March at Warwickshire crematorium, near Chipping Campden. Her ashes were interred near the resting place of J. B. Priestley at Hubberholme, Yorkshire.

Her death left archaeology bereft of one of its most enigmatic personalities, whose personal life overshadowed her response to a rapidly evolving discipline, as it oscillated between science and humanities. Her life presented a veritable Minoan labyrinth of apparently contradictory paths: she championed Robert Graves's 'mother goddess' theories, but spoke against the champions of women's liberation; she demanded respect as an academic, but courted disaster by the sexual frankness of *A Quest of Love*. Some never forgave her for breaking up Christopher Hawkes's family life (as noted by Vincent Brome, *The Guardian*, 20 March 1996). Jacquetta Hawkes strove to achieve the Jungian balance; she was a unique woman who, if often haughty and aloof, was also, to those who knew her well, both compassionate and passionate—'a mixture of Athena and Aphrodite', as Diana Collins contended (*The Independent*, 20 March 1996). As Priestley famously remarked on first meeting her: 'What a woman! Ice without, fire within!' (ibid.).　　　CHRISTINE FINN

Sources priv. coll., Hawkes MSS · D. Collins, *Time and the Priestleys: the story of a friendship* (1994) · J. Hawkes, *A quest of love* (1980) · J. Hawkes, *A land* (1951) · *The Independent* (20 March 1996) · *The Times* (20 March 1996) · *The Guardian* (20 March 1996) · *Daily Telegraph* (21 March 1996) · J. Hawkes, *Symbols and speculations* (1949) · C. Finn, '"Ways of telling": Jacquetta Hawkes as film-maker', *Antiquity*, 74 (2000) · *WWW* [forthcoming] · private information (2004) [N. Hawkes; family] · m. cert. [parents]

Archives priv. coll., MSS · Shakespeare Birthplace Museum, Stratford upon Avon | Bodl. Oxf., letters to O. G. S. Crawford · Rice University, Houston, Texas, Woodson Research Center, corresp. with Sir Julian S. Huxley | FILM BFI NFTVA, interview with Mavis Nicolson in later life · BFI NFTVA, 'The beginning of history' | SOUND BL NSA, Bow dialogues, 30 March 1971, C812/31 C1 · BL NSA, Bow dialogues, 21 June 1977, C812/57 C5 · BL NSA, *Desert Island Discs* · BL NSA, oral history interview · BL NSA, performance footage

Likenesses photograph, 1953, Hult. Arch.; repro. in *The Independent* · J. Lewinski, photograph, 1968, NPG [*see illus.*] · J. Bown, double portrait, photograph (with J. B. Priestley), repro. in *The Guardian* · photograph, repro. in *The Times* · photograph, repro. in *Daily Telegraph* · photographs, priv. coll.

Hawkes, Sonia Elizabeth (1933–1999). *See under* Hawkes, (Charles Francis) Christopher (1905–1992).

Hawkesworth, John (*bap.* 1720, *d.* 1773), writer, was born in Tottenham Court, London, and baptized on 28 October 1720 at St Pancras, the second of three children of John Hawkesworth (*d.* 1752), a watch engraver, and his wife, Ann, *née* Cornford. His father, who was a dissenter, probably presbyterian, had some knowledge of Latin and Greek and was fluent in French. Partly because of the collapse of the South Sea Bubble, partly because of ill health, he failed in trade and became a French teacher.

Hawkesworth received an elementary education in writing, arithmetic, and 'knowledge of his own language, chiefly from the Bible, from which text his parents diligently inculcated religious principles on his mind' (Abbott, 5). The mastery of French displayed in his translation of Fénelon, *The Adventures of Telemachus* (1768), was presumably acquired from his father. Through wide reading he later became knowledgeable on many subjects, but in the eyes of contemporaries his lack of a classical education remained a deficiency. Sir John Hawkins called him 'a man of fine parts, but no learning' (Hawkins, 252). At sixteen he was apprenticed to an attorney in the City. The dullness of this work was relieved by literary conversations with John *Ryland, a young merchant, who married Hawkesworth's sister Honor in 1742. By then Hawkesworth had found employment as writing-master at a girls' boarding-school in Kent run by Mary Brown (*d.* 1796), daughter of a Bromley butcher. On 11 May 1744 Hawkesworth married Mary, and the couple moved into Thornhill Mansion, Bromley, a handsome Tudor building which also housed the school. Hawkesworth became governor of the school, and the couple remained in Bromley throughout their evidently happy and prosperous married life. Mary Hawkesworth was described by friends as intelligent, capable, and 'a very well-bred, obliging, & sweet tempered Woman' (*Early Journals and Letters*, 1.241).

Hawkesworth's first known composition, a poem of impassioned sentiment, was written in 1738. It was never published, but his verse fable, 'The Fop, Cock and Diamond', written in 1740, was printed in the *Gentleman's Magazine* in June 1741. The publication of more of his fables in the magazine in 1741–2 provided Hawkesworth with an entry into the literary world, for it was in the offices of Edward Cave, founder of the *Gentleman's Magazine*, that he first met Samuel Johnson. Johnson was already writing and editing for Cave, and Johnson and Hawkesworth became close friends. From 1743 onwards Hawkesworth gradually assumed Johnson's responsibilities on the magazine: writing up parliamentary debates, editing the poetry section, and contributing his own essays, reviews, and poems, finally becoming literary editor in 1756. His work 'gave him great opportunities of improvement by an extensive correspondence with men of all professions' (Hawkins, 252), and he remained until his death a dominant force on this influential periodical.

In 1749 Hawkesworth joined Johnson's literary group the Ivy Lane club, where he was valued as an 'instructive and entertaining companion' on account of his eclectic knowledge and 'good share of wit' (Hawkins, 252). Encouraged by fellow members, he became editor and principal writer for a new journal, *The Adventurer* (7 November 1752–9 March 1754), successor to Johnson's *Rambler*. As he explained retrospectively, his aim was to provide moral guidance for the young, but by indirect means: 'I knew it would be necessary to amuse the imagination while I was approaching the heart' (*The Adventurer*, no. 140, 2.356). Of about seventy papers written by Hawkesworth himself, the majority were in narrative form: stories of middle-class English life, or oriental tales, a genre in which he was particularly adept; his formula, blending moral sentiment with exotic trappings, magic, and melodrama, proved a popular one. As an essay writer, too, he was considered a rival of Addison and Johnson. His achievements on *The Adventurer* were rewarded in 1756 by grant of the Lambeth degree of doctor of laws from the archbishop of Canterbury. This honour gratified Hawkesworth but failed to impress his Ivy Lane friends and caused a rupture in his friendship with Johnson, who felt that 'Hawkesworth—who had set out as a modest, humble man—was one of the many whom success in the world had spoiled' (Prior, 441). This judgement was endorsed by the testimony of other acquaintances.

Hawkesworth's next successful venture was an edition of *The Works of Jonathan Swift* (6 vols., 1755), which for a long period supplanted Faulkner's Dublin edition (1735) as the authoritative text of Swift. Modern scholarship has exposed its editorial deficiencies, but Hawkesworth's critical notes retain some historical interest. The life of Swift prefixed to the first volume was a milestone in literary biography, being the first attempt at a balanced and judicious assessment of an author's character. From 1756 Hawkesworth was involved in theatrical activities, through his long-standing friendship with David Garrick. He supported Garrick in his theatrical quarrels, supplied him with versions of Dryden's *Amphitryon* (1756) and Southerne's *Oroonoko* (1759), and wrote oratorios and dramas of his own. His *Edgar and Emmeline: a Fairy Tale* (1761), a combination of romance, farce, and comedy of manners, embellished with music by Michael Arne, played to packed houses at the Theatre Royal, Drury Lane, and was enthusiastically reviewed by Arthur Murphy.

Hawkesworth's most popular literary work, *Almoran and Hamet: an Oriental Tale* (1761), was also written initially in dramatic form, but recast as narrative when Garrick took

fright at the potential costs of staging it. Hawkesworth had a political motive in rewriting it after the accession of George III, to whom it was dedicated: Mary Hawkesworth recalled that he 'thought the sentiments peculiarly adapted for the use of a young monarch' (Abbott, 113). Although *Almoran and Hamet* may have been influenced by Johnson's *Rasselas* (1759) in its ethical framework, it has a more fantastic plot, involving a genie and magic spells. Comparing the two, Thomas Percy thought Johnson superior 'in style, and in having confined his narrative within the Limits of possibility', but Hawkesworth 'contrived to interest his readers more, by introducing a very pleasing Love-Story' (*Correspondence of … Percy and … Shenstone*, 7.102).

Hawkesworth was busy in other spheres at the same time. Through his interest in scientific subjects and his friendship with Benjamin Franklin he was elected to the Society for the Encouragement of Arts, Manufactures, and Commerce in 1761, and his experience as a political writer led to a close association with the Irish baronet Sir James Caldwell whom he served from 1759 for several years as literary and personal adviser. By this connection Hawkesworth made aristocratic friendships of which he was naïvely vain. A much older friendship with Charles Burney, however, led to Hawkesworth's most lucrative and prestigious commission. On the recommendation of Burney, supported by Garrick, he was appointed by Lord Sandwich, first lord of the Admiralty, to compile the official account of the voyages to the south Pacific in 1764–71, based on the journals kept by Captain James Cook and others. Hawkesworth sold the copyright to the publishers Strahan and Cadell for the then colossal sum of £6000, a deal which led to a breach with Garrick, who thought Thomas Becket should have had the option to publish and accused Hawkesworth of putting financial gain before friendship. Hawkesworth was also involved in litigation in 1773 to prevent publication of a rival account of Cook's voyages. In both affairs he acted within his legal rights, but his reputation as a high-minded moralist was tarnished. In April 1773 Hawkesworth was elected to the board of the East India Company, a position for which he had been angling since 1771, and in June *An account of the voyages undertaken by … Commodore Byron, Captain Wallis, Captain Carteret, and Captain Cook* (3 vols., 1773) was published. Although it became a best-seller, it proved disastrous for Hawkesworth. He was publicly attacked on three different counts: by the captains for tampering with the texts of their journals, by prudish readers for reprinting descriptions of the sexual freedoms of the South Sea islanders, and by devout churchmen for impiety in the general introduction to the work, in which Hawkesworth had rashly challenged the doctrine of providential intervention. He was devastated by this critical barrage, and it was thought to be the main cause of his death. The rumour recorded by Malone that he killed himself with an overdose of opium is uncorroborated, but Fanny Burney's conviction that his health was destroyed by the vilification he suffered seems well founded. He died at Lime Street, London, of 'a slow Fever' on 17 November 1773; 'his

6000 l. was dearly purchased, at the price of his Character & peace' (*Early Journals and Letters*, 1.324–5). He was buried in the churchyard of St Peter and St Paul, Bromley, on 22 November.

Ironically, the lasting popularity of 'Hawkesworth's *Voyages*', as they soon came to be known, kept his name alive among general readers more successfully than anything else he wrote. But as a man of versatile talents who was widely read and a leading figure in the cultural life of eighteenth-century London, his virtual eclipse in the twentieth century seems curious.

KARINA WILLIAMSON

Sources J. L. Abbott, *John Hawkesworth: eighteenth-century man of letters* (1982) · 'Memoirs of the life of Dr John Hawkesworth', *Universal Magazine of Knowledge and Pleasure*, 111 (1802), 233–9 · J. Hawkins, *The life of Samuel Johnson, LL.D.* (1787) · *The early journals and letters of Fanny Burney*, ed. L. E. Troide, 1: 1768–1773 (1988) · *The early journals and letters of Fanny Burney*, ed. L. E. Troide, 2: 1774–1777 (1990) · J. Hawkesworth and others, *The adventurer*, new edn, 3 vols. (1794) · J. Prior, 'Maloniana', *Life of Edmond Malone, editor of Shakespeare* (1860), 441–2 · *GM*, 1st ser., 11 (1741), 327 · *GM*, 1st ser., 43 (1773), 582, 614 · *GM*, 1st ser., 44 (1774), 231–2 · *The correspondence of Thomas Percy and William Shenstone*, ed. C. Brooks (1977), vol. 7 of *The Percy letters*, ed. C. Brooks, D. N. Smith, and A. F. Falconer (1944–88) · H. Wallis, 'John Hawkesworth and the English circumnavigators', *Commonwealth Journal*, 6 (Aug 1963), 167–71 · W. H. Pearson, 'Hawkesworth's alterations', *Journal of Pacific History*, 7 (1972), 45–72
Archives JRL, letters | Four Oaks Farm, near Somerville, New Jersey, Hyde collection · JRL, letters to Sir James Caldwell and Lady Caldwell · NL NZ, Turnbull L., letters to Mrs Currey · Yale U., James Marshall and Marie-Louise Osborn collection
Likenesses J. Watson, mezzotint, pubd 1773 (after portrait by J. Reynolds), BM
Wealth at death see widow's will discussed in Abbott, *John Hawkesworth*

Hawkesworth, Walter

Hawkesworth, Walter (*c.*1573–1606), playwright, was probably the son of John Hawkesworth, an attorney in the exchequer of pleas at Westminster, a member of the Hawkesworth family of Hawkesworth, in the parish of Otley, West Riding of Yorkshire. He has been confused with his nephew of the same name. Walter matriculated as a pensioner of Trinity College, Cambridge, on 30 March 1588, was elected scholar in 1590 (graduating BA in 1592 and MA in 1595), and was admitted minor fellow in October 1593 and major fellow two years later.

Hawkesworth's long and successful university career is now remembered for his contribution, as actor and author, to his college's theatrical activities. His *Labyrinthus*, erroneously attributed to Thomas Goffe, an adaptation in Latin of Giambattista della Porta's *La cintia* with a subplot borrowed from the anonymous Spanish novel *La vida de Lazarillo de Tormes*, was performed at Trinity College in March 1603 and supposedly before James I in December 1624. *Labyrinthus* was published in 1636, and may have been the play of the same name dismissed by Pepys on 2 May 1664 as 'the poorest play methinks that ever I saw' (Pepys, *Diary*, 5.139). Hawkesworth was also the likely author of *Leander*, sometimes attributed to William Johnson, the author of another Cambridge Latin play, *Valetudinarium*. *Leander*, based on Sforza degli Oddi's *Erofilomachia*, was performed at Trinity in 1598 and again in 1603, the day after *Labyrinthus*. Cast lists in contemporary manuscripts of the plays name Hawkesworth as the eponymous hero in both performances of *Leander* and as the old hedonist Tiberius in *Labyrinthus*. The popularity of these comedies of sexual intrigue and infidelity is attested by the survival of seven manuscript copies of *Labyrinthus* and eight of *Leander*. Claims for Hawkesworth's contributions to revisions of the play *Pedantius* published in 1631 and to a collection of verses on the death of Sir Edward Lewkenor and his wife in 1606 are unsupported by contemporary evidence. Hawkesworth's importance lies in introducing to England the Italian *commedie erudite* as source material and being the first adapter of the work of Giambattista della Porta, establishing a precedent for the use by popular dramatists of the plays of Italy as well as its novels.

Hawkesworth resigned his university fellowship at or before Michaelmas 1605, when he became secretary to Sir Charles Cornwallis, also a Trinity man, appointed earlier that year as James I's ambassador in Madrid. Hawkesworth's family, like many in Yorkshire, had Catholic sympathies, and it has been suggested that Hawkesworth himself was 'not an unprejudiced party' (Speight, 272) in the affairs of the embassy, which were extremely delicate in the months following the Gunpowder Plot in November 1605. He may have been among the seven recusants on Cornwallis's staff who, according to contemporary gossip, were reclaimed for the church.

Hawkesworth's diplomatic career was brief, but he was entrusted with confidential and important matters of state before his death, of the plague, in Madrid between 25 and 30 September 1606, when Cornwallis wrote to the earl of Salisbury: 'For myne own particular I am yet continuing in my infected House, where sythence my last Letters advertizeing the Death of Hawkesworth and four more; … there are lately fallen downe of the same Disseaze three more' (Sawyer, 2.261). Hawkesworth was unmarried and without children. His will, dated 5 October 1606 NS (25 September 1606 OS), names as his sole heir and executor Edward Goldingham, 'my boy', who played the role of Hawkesworth's servant on stage in *Labyrinthus* and, it seems, in real life.

SUSAN BROCK

Sources W. Hawkesworth, *Leander, Labyrinthus*, ed. S. Brock (1987) · Cooper, *Ath. Cantab.*, 2.441–2 · J. Hunter, *Familiae minorum gentium*, ed. J. W. Clay, 3, Harleian Society, 39 (1895), 971–3 · H. Speight, 'Hawksworth Hall and its associations', *Bradford Antiquary*, new ser., 2 (1901–5), 246–96 · *Memorials of affairs of state in the reigns of Q. Elizabeth and K. James I, collected (chiefly) from the original papers of … Sir Ralph Winwood*, ed. E. Sawyer, 3 vols. (1725), vol. 2, pp. 151, 164–7, 168–9, 223, 261 · J. Foster, ed., *The visitation of Yorkshire made in the years 1584/5 … to which is added the subsequent visitation made in 1612* (privately printed, London, 1875), 299 · Venn, *Alum. Cant.* · will (register copy), 5 Oct 1606, PRO, PROB 11/108, fol. 233
Archives CUL, MS Ee.v.16 · Emmanuel College, Cambridge, MS I.2.30 · LPL, MS 838 · St John Cam., MS J.8 · Trinity Cam., MS R.3.9 | BL, Sloane MS 1762 · Bodl. Oxf., Douce MS 315 · Bodl. Oxf., Rawl. MS D341 · Warks. CRO, Newdigate MS, CR136/B761 · Yale U., Vault MS
Wealth at death legacies of £45 and gifts valued at 16 angels (Spanish): will, 5 Oct 1606, PRO, PROB 11/108, fol. 233

Hawkey, John

Hawkey, John (1702/3–1759), classical scholar, the son of John Hawkey, gaoler, may have been born in Cove, Devon.

He may have been educated at Mr Spare's school in Liskeard before he entered Trinity College, Dublin, in 1720, aged seventeen. He won a foundation scholarship in 1723 and graduated in 1725. Little is known of him, except for his translation of Xenophon's *Anabasis*, before the publication in 1745 of his elegant and accurate editions of Virgil and Horace. In the same year he dedicated an edition of *P. Terentii Afri comoediae* to the earl of Chesterfield. By 1746 he had established a school in Dublin, but continued his scholarly publications with editions of the satires of Juvenal and Persius (1746), dedicated to Bishop Mordecai Cary, and of Sallust in 1747. Hawkey projected an edition of Cicero in twenty volumes, which, however, was not printed. The year 1747 also saw the publication of Hawkey's edition of Milton's *Paradise Lost*, fated to be overshadowed two years later by Bishop Newton's compendious variorum edition. His aim was to present a clean text, 'freed from all blunders and absurdities', by careful collation with the earliest editions. He included only a very few of the 'bold corrections of Dr. Bentley' in his endnotes; he rather followed Zachary Pearce in affirming both Milton's authority and his peculiarities. An edition of *Paradise Regained* followed in 1752. Hawkey died in Dublin in 1759.

J. T. GILBERT, *rev.* PATRICK BULLARD

Sources Burtchaell & Sadleir, *Alum. Dubl.*, 2nd edn · A. Oras, *Milton's editors and commentators from Patrick Hume to Henry John Todd, 1695–1801* (1931) · W. B. S. Taylor, *History of the University of Dublin* (1845) · E. Harwood, *A view of the various editions of the Greek and Roman classics*, 4th edn (1790) · T. F. Dibdin, *Introduction to the knowledge of … the Greek and Latin classics*, 4th edn, 2 vols. (1827)

Hawkins, Sir Anthony Hope [*pseud.* Anthony Hope] (1863–1933), novelist, was born on 9 February 1863 at Clapton House, Clapton, London, the third and youngest child of the Revd Edwards Comerford Hawkins (*d.* 1906), headmaster of St John's Foundation School for the Sons of Poor Clergy, and Jane Isabella Grahame, daughter of Archibald Grahame of Brighton and aunt of the author Kenneth *Grahame (1859–1932). His mother also claimed descent from Robert the Bruce. Hawkins was educated at his father's school in Clapton, at Leatherhead when the school moved there, and at Marlborough College, where he excelled at athletics and edited *The Marlburian*. He proceeded to Balliol College, Oxford, with an exhibition (which in his first term was raised to a scholarship) in 1881. He was a member of the college rugby team, obtained a first class in classical moderations (1882) and in *literae humaniores* (1885), and became president of the Oxford Union (1886). He was called to the bar by the Middle Temple in 1887 but had already started writing short stories. He privately published *A Man of Mark* in 1890; it was his first experiment with the romance form by which he would make his name, and a 'skit on democracy' in South America.

Hawkins made his home for the next seventeen years with his widowed father who had been presented to St Bride's Church, Fleet Street, and was juggling careers in law, authorship, and politics (a staunch Liberal, he stood without success but without disgrace for a Conservative constituency, South Buckinghamshire in 1892). At this time his appearance combined elements of the dandy and the staid barrister. After six years at the bar he was finally holding important briefs from the Great Western Railway. But by June 1893 he had published five novels: *Father Stafford* (1891), a story of a moral and religious quandary; *Mr Witt's Widow* (1892), which gave him his first taste of success; *Sport Royal* (1893), an early romance fantasy using a favourite trope of mistaken identity; *A Change of Air* (1893) and *Half-a-Hero* (1893), both political novels.

On 28 November 1893 Hawkins's career choice was made for him when he was struck by the sight of two men of very similar appearance on his walk back to the Temple. *The Prisoner of Zenda*, set in the fictional kingdom of Ruritania, and a story of court intrigue and romance, unrolled itself before him and he began it the next morning and finished it rapidly. It was published in April 1894 and enjoyed almost immediate success and popularity. Andrew Lang acclaimed it at the Royal Academy banquet; R. L. Stevenson sent congratulations from Samoa; while Hawkins ascribed its success to the combination of 'royalty and red hair' (Mallet, 76). The novel insinuated itself into the collective consciousness giving rise to the romanticizing of middle Europe and to a new term, 'Ruritania', to describe 'the novelist's and dramatist's locale for court romances in a modern setting' (*Oxford English Dictionary*). According to his biographer, Sir Charles Mallet, the novel has been abridged as a 'primer for young Indians', serialized in a Japanese newspaper, and given the name Zenda to a town in Canada. It has been filmed on six occasions; the most acclaimed was the 1937 adaptation starring Ronald Coleman, Douglas Fairbanks junior, and Madeleine Carroll.

Summer 1894 saw the publication of *The Dolly Dialogues*, a serial which had originally appeared in the *Westminster Gazette* dramatizing the flirtation between Dolly Foster, later Lady Mickleham, and Samuel Carter. It is a witty if poignant evocation of *fin de siècle* society which spawned numerous imitations and parodies in *Punch*. This book enhanced the fame and profits gained by *The Prisoner of Zenda*, which in its turn had increased demand for the author's previous novels, and on 4 July Hawkins left the bar and established himself in rooms off the Strand to devote the next twenty years to writing.

From now on Hawkins would alternate between romances and more 'serious' fiction. *The Indiscretion of the Duchess* (1894) was a return to adventure, while *The God in the Car* (1894) was a study of power and politics with parallels with empire-builder Cecil Rhodes. *The Chronicles of Count Antonio* was marred by archaisms and had a lukewarm reception, while the Ruritanian *The Heart of the Princess Osra* (1896) and *Phroso* (1897) were favourably reviewed. Hawkins embarked on a three-month lecture tour of America from October 1897. In 1898 *Simon Dale* was not a completely satisfactory experiment with the historical novel but the *Zenda* sequel *Rupert of Hentzau* (1898) restored him to public affection. *The King's Mirror* followed in 1899; it was well received and was considered by many, including J. M. Barrie and Hawkins himself, to be his best book along with *Double Harness* (1904). The political adventure

Quisanté (1900) kept him in the public eye, and in January 1900 he was elected chairman of the committee of the Society of Authors on which he served for twelve years, for four years as its chairman; he was founder of its pension scheme. *A Servant of the Public* (1905) revealed his life-long love of acting. During this period he also turned playwright. *The Adventure of Lady Ursula* was produced in October 1898, with Evelyn Millard and Herbert Waring, and was followed in 1900 by *English Nell*, a version of *Simon Dale*, with Marie Tempest as Nell Gwyn. Both were profitable, but *Pilkerton's Peerage* (1903), a satire on the distribution of honours, also added to his reputation.

On the return journey from his second tour of America Hawkins met Elizabeth Somerville (1885/6–1946), daughter of Charles Henry Sheldon, of New York. They were married soon after, on 1 July 1903, and had two sons and a daughter. They lived thereafter at 41 Bedford Square, London, but, warned by ill health, Hawkins rented and subsequently bought Heath Farm, Walton on the Hill, Surrey, exchanging the big London house for a smaller one in Gower Street.

After mixed reviews and poor sales for *Sophy of Kravonia* (1906), *Second String* (1910), and *Mrs Maxon Protests* (1911), Hawkins's reputation was in decline and he relied on film rights and reprints for income. He enjoyed a period of activity and fulfilment during the war working for the editorial and public branch department (later the Ministry of Information) as part of a government initiative to counteract German propaganda under the direction of Charles Frederick Gurney Masterman at Wellington House. Among other tracts he wrote *The New (German) Testament* (1914), which argued against German militarism, and he was knighted for his services in 1918. After the war, however, Hawkins found literary composition increasingly arduous and was plagued by depression. He continued to publish, but only *Beaumaroy Home from the Wars* (1919) was applauded. *Memories and Notes*, a partial and modest autobiography, was published in 1927. Hawkins had suffered from a heart condition since 1900 and he died at his home at Heath Farm on 8 July 1933 of cancer of the throat. He was buried at Leatherhead.

Considered old-fashioned by the next generation of writers, Hawkins deplored the way more philosophical fiction was superseding the novel of character and manners. To his great distress Hawkins recognized this fact and believed that he had not achieved greatness. He never recaptured the freshness of *The Prisoner of Zenda*; although it can be argued that some of his other fiction deserves reassessment, including *Sophy of Kravonia*, which it is said inspired Graham Greene to take up travel (Henderson). *The Prisoner of Zenda* will, however, ultimately secure his reputation as one of the pre-eminent romance writers. As Tony Watkins observes, this novel 'set the style of romantic adventure novels for at least thirty years after publication' (Watkins, xxi).

CLARE L. TAYLOR

Sources C. Mallet, *Anthony Hope and his books, being the authorized life of Sir Anthony Hope Hawkins* (1935) • A. Hope, *Memories and notes* [n.d., *c*.1927] • G. M. Johnson, ed., *Late-Victorian and Edwardian British novelists: first series*, DLitB, 153 (1995) • L. Henderson, ed., *Twentieth-century romance and historical writers*, 2nd edn (1990) • W. F. Nauffuts, ed., *British short-fiction writers, 1880–1914: the romantic tradition*, DLitB, 156 (1996) • T. Watkins, introduction, in A. Hope, *The prisoner of Zenda* (1994) • P. C. Carr, 'The four Anthony Hopes', *The Listener* (18 Aug 1949) • V. T. Neuburg, *The Batsford companion to popular literature* (1982) • *DNB* • personal knowledge (1949) [*DNB*] • private information (1949) • b. cert. • d. cert.

Archives NRA, corresp. | BL, corresp. with Society of Authors, Add. MSS 56722, 63261 • BL, corresp. with Marie Stopes, Add. MS 58498 • Bodl. Oxf., letters to Kenneth Grahame and Elspeth Grahame • CAC Cam., letters to J. H. Roskill • Richmond Local Studies Library, London, corresp. with Douglas Sladen • U. Leeds, Brotherton L., letters to C. K. Shorter

Likenesses H. de T. Glazebrook, oils, *c*.1904, Garr. Club; repro. in Mallet, *Anthony Hope* • A. A. Wolmark, oils, 1908, NPG • H. Furniss, pen-and-ink caricature, *c*.1910, NPG • J. Russell & Sons, photograph, *c*.1915, NPG; repro. in *National Photographic Record*, vol. 1 • W. Stoneman, photograph, 1924, NPG • G. C. Beresford, three photographs, NPG • Lenare, photograph, repro. in Hope, *Memories and notes* • D. Low, pencil caricature, NPG • E. K. Mills, photograph (in middle age), repro. in Mallet, *Anthony Hope* • Piccini, drawing, repro. in Mallet, *Anthony Hope*

Hawkins, Benjamin Waterhouse (1807–1889?), natural history artist and sculptor, was born on 8 February 1807 in Devonshire Street, London, of unknown parents. Educated at St Aloysius College, he studied sculpture under William Behnes. He specialized in natural history subjects and displayed a number of paintings of animals at the Royal Academy, the British Institution, and elsewhere from 1832 to 1849. He illustrated numerous works, including contributing forty-nine plates, illustrating fish and reptiles, to Charles Darwin's *The Zoology of the Voyage of HMS Beagle* (pts 4 and 5, 1838–43). In 1842–7 he produced a series of studies of living animals from the menagerie of the earl of Derby at Knowsley. Other early works included animal sculptures for the gardens of Biddulph Grange, Staffordshire. Elected a member of the Society of Arts in 1846, a fellow of the Linnean Society in 1847, and a fellow of the Geological Society in 1854, he was an assistant superintendent and exhibitor at the 1851 Great Exhibition.

In September 1852 Hawkins was appointed director of the fossil department of the Crystal Palace, under reconstruction at Sydenham, south London, and in collaboration with Richard Owen began to construct the first major public display of the progression of life on earth, comprising life-sized iron and stone models of fourteen genera of extinct animals, together with reconstructions of fossil plants and geological strata. He held a dinner party on 31 December 1853 in the mould of the largest model, of the dinosaur *Iguanodon*. The Crystal Palace work was terminated in the summer of 1855, with the display incomplete, but it made a significant contribution to popular understanding of the nature of the development of life on earth and now provides an important insight into palaeontological knowledge in the mid-1850s.

Hawkins travelled to the United States in 1868 and was commissioned to create a similar display of models of extinct animals in Central Park, New York. By early 1871 he had completed numerous moulds and some finished models. The project was abandoned, however, following the destruction of the work on the orders of a new, corrupt, New York administration. He continued to work in the United States, producing a number of casts of fossil skeletons of hadrosaur dinosaurs (including the first mounted dinosaur fossil in the US). In 1875 he began a series of paintings of prehistoric scenes at Princeton University, New Jersey. His subsequent fate is obscure. He may have returned to England to spend his remaining years at his house, Fossil Villa, near the Crystal Palace, the scene of his greatest work. His death is not recorded in the UK, however, and he may have remained in the United States. One report suggests that he died in New York in 1889.

STEVE MCCARTHY

Sources S. McCarthy and M. Gilbert, *The Crystal Palace dinosaurs: the story of the world's first prehistoric sculptures* (1994) · *Men of the time* (1887) · R. Owen, *Geology and inhabitants of the ancient world* (1854) · B. W. Hawkins, 'On visual education as applied to geology', *Journal of the Society of Arts*, 2 (1853–4)
Archives Library of the Academy of Natural Sciences, Philadelphia, album, collection 803 · NHM
Likenesses photograph, 1870, Library of the Academy of Natural Sciences, Philadelphia, Pennsylvania, Waterhouse Hawkins album · photograph, 1875?, Library of the Academy of Natural Sciences, Philadelphia, Pennsylvania, Waterhouse Hawkins album

Hawkins, Sir Caesar, first baronet (1711–1786), surgeon, son of Caesar Hawkins (1688–1750), surgeon practising in Shropshire, and his wife, Ann Bright (d. 1725), was born at Kelston, Somerset, on 10 January 1711, and studied with his father and with John Ranby for seven years. On 1 July 1735 he was admitted to the Company of Barber–Surgeons, and on 19 August 1736 was made a member of the livery and chosen demonstrator of anatomy. This latter office he resigned in the next year on being appointed surgeon to the prince of Wales and to one of the troops of guards. In 1735 he was elected surgeon to St George's Hospital, and held this office until 1774. He was made sergeant-surgeon to George II on 7 September 1747, and occupied the same post in the next reign. On 3 September 1778 he was created a baronet. He married Sarah (1718/19–1801), daughter of John Coxe, and left a family; one of his sons, Charles, was also sergeant-surgeon, and another, the Revd Edward Hawkins, was the father of Edward Hawkins, provost of Oriel College, Oxford, of Francis Hawkins, and of the surgeon Caesar Henry Hawkins (1798–1884). The post of sergeant-surgeon was also held by Pennell Hawkins, a brother of Sir Caesar, and by George, son of Pennell, being thus occupied by four members of the same family in three generations.

Hawkins's professional success was mainly due to patronage. His baronetcy 'clearly rewarded his royal practice, not his intellectual or scholarly attainments' (Lawrence, 221). He is said to have made £1000 a year by phlebotomy alone. He was the inventor of an instrument called the cutting gorget, but published nothing. Hawkins died at Kelston on 13 February 1786 and was buried there. A monument to him and his wife was erected against the south wall of the south aisle of Kelston church.

J. F. PAYNE, rev. MICHAEL BEVAN

Sources R. R. James, 'Two celebrated Salopian surgeons', *Transactions of the Shropshire Archaeological and Natural History Society*, 4th

Sir Caesar Hawkins, first baronet (1711–1786), by William Hogarth, c.1740

ser., 6 (1916–17), 107–22 · *IGI* · S. C. Lawrence, *Charitable knowledge: hospital pupils and practitioners in eighteenth-century London* (1996)
Archives BL, letters to duke of Newcastle, Add. MSS 32734–33067, *passim*
Likenesses W. Hogarth, oils, c.1740, RCS Eng. [*see illus.*]
Wealth at death property at Kelston; freehold messuage in Pall Mall, London; leaseholds in Pall Mall, Pall Mall Court, and Jermyn Street, London: James, 'Two celebrated Salopian surgeons'; will, PRO, PROB 11/1140, sig. 159

Hawkins, Caesar Henry (1798–1884), surgeon, was born on 19 September 1798 at Bisley, Gloucestershire, one of the ten children of the Revd Edward Hawkins (d. 1805) and his wife, Margaret, née Howes (d. 1859). His grandfather Sir Caesar Hawkins, baronet, was surgeon to St George's Hospital, London, and sergeant-surgeon to both George II and George III. Edward *Hawkins (1789–1882) and Francis *Hawkins (1794–1877) were his elder brothers. Hawkins received his early education at Christ's Hospital, London, but was withdrawn from the school in 1813 when it became apparent that he was not destined for either Oxford or Cambridge. After serving as pupil to a Mr Sheppard, of Hampton Court, he entered St George's Hospital in London under Sir Everard Home and Benjamin Brodie in 1818. He became a member of the Royal College of Surgeons in 1821, and he taught anatomy with Sir Charles Bell in the Hunterian School, Windmill Street, where he started a collection of specimens that was later to become part of St George's Hospital pathological museum. In 1823 he set up practice in Vere Street, off Oxford Street. In 1825 he moved to Half Moon Street, where he took house pupils. He was appointed surgeon to St George's Hospital in 1829, and held this office until 1861, when, on his resignation, he was appointed consulting surgeon. Hawkins was president of the Royal College of Surgeons in 1852 and again in 1861; he was examiner for many years, and delivered the Hunterian oration at the college in 1849. In 1862 he was appointed sergeant-surgeon to Queen Victoria, having previously been one of her majesty's surgeons. He was elected a trustee of the Hunterian Museum in 1871, and was also a fellow of the Royal Society.

Hawkins was an eminent and successful surgeon, though he never received a title in recognition for his work. His opinion was especially valued in difficult cases. While in comparative retirement as consulting surgeon he was often seen in the wards of St George's Hospital, where he gave his colleagues the benefit of his long experience. For a long time he was known as the only surgeon to have performed the operation of ovariotomy successfully in a London hospital, and he did much to popularize the operation of colotomy. But he always leaned towards conservative surgery, and it was said of him that 'he was always more anxious to teach his pupils how to save a limb than how to remove it'.

Hawkins contributed many memoirs and lectures to medical journals which were collected and printed for private circulation with the title *The Hunterian Oration, Presidential Addresses, and Pathological and Surgical Writings* (2 vols., 1874). Among the more important are 'The Hunterian oration for 1849'; 'On the relative claims of Sir Charles Bell and Magendie to the discovery of the functions of the spinal nerves'; 'Experiments on hydrophobia and the bites of serpents'; 'On excision of the ovarium'; 'On stricture of the colon treated by operation'; and 'Lectures on tumours'.

Hawkins was twice married: his first wife was a Miss Dolbel; his second wife, who survived him, was Ellen Rouse. There were no children of either marriage. Hawkins died on 20 July 1884 at 26 Grosvenor Street, London, where he had lived since 1842.

J. F. PAYNE, *rev.* ORNELLA MOSCUCCI

Sources *BMJ* (16 Aug 1884), 345–7 · *The Lancet* (26 July 1884), 172–3 · V. G. Plarr, *Plarr's Lives of the fellows of the Royal College of Surgeons of England*, rev. D'A. Power, 2 vols. (1930) · *The Times* (21 July 1884) · *Medico-Chirurgical Transactions*, 68 (1885), 16–20 · *IGI* · d. cert. · *CGPLA Eng. & Wales* (1884)
Likenesses Dickinson Bros., photograph, Wellcome L. · G. Halse, marble bust, RCS Eng.
Wealth at death £45,099 19s. 6d.: probate, 23 Sept 1884, *CGPLA Eng. & Wales*

Hawkins, Edward (1780–1867), museum curator and numismatist, was born on 5 May 1780 at Macclesfield, the eldest son of Edward Hawkins, banker, and his wife, Ellen, daughter of Brian Hodgson of Ashbourne, Derbyshire. He was educated at Macclesfield grammar school, and privately from 1797 to 1799 by George Ormerod, vicar of Kensington and father of George Ormerod, the Cheshire historian. He returned to Macclesfield about 1799 and received a commission in a local volunteer corps. He was employed under his father in the Macclesfield Bank until

1802, when the family moved to Court Herbert, Glamorgan. While there he was a partner with his father in a bank at Swansea, and they also superintended the copper works at Neath Abbey. He left Court Herbert in 1807 and lived in various places in north Wales and at Cadoxton, Glamorgan, before moving to Surrey in 1819, first to Nutfield and then to East Hill, Oxted. He married on 29 September 1806 Eliza, daughter of Major Rohde, with whom he had three sons and a daughter: Edward (*d.* 1867); the Revd Herbert Samuel, rector of Beyton, Suffolk; Major Rohde [*see below*]; and Mary Eliza, wife of John Robert Kenyon QC, and mother of Sir Frederic Kenyon.

In early life Hawkins was interested in botany, and in 1806 he was elected a fellow of the Linnean Society. Another field of interest at this time was the local history of Chester, on which he formed a large collection of books and prints. He was elected a fellow of the Royal Society in 1821 and of the Society of Antiquaries in 1826, and of both societies he subsequently served as a vice-president. He was a founder member and president (1839–41, 1849–51) of the Numismatic Society of London.

In May 1825, at the age of forty-five, Hawkins obtained a post as assistant keeper in the British Museum's department of antiquities, and the following year, on the unexpected death of Taylor Combe, he became keeper, a position he retained for some thirty-five years. This was very much a formative period both for the museum and for the development of archaeology. The department of antiquities then covered a vast field, encompassing most of the present departments of the British Museum after the separation of natural history and the British Library. Hawkins, a man with wide interests in antiquities, combined the talents of a meticulous scholar and a highly acquisitive curator. Under his care the collections grew dramatically and purposefully, two of the most notable achievements being the acquisition of Henry Layard's rich finds of Assyrian and Babylonian material from Nineveh and elsewhere and the establishment of a collection of prehistoric, Roman, and medieval artefacts from western Europe. The antiquities galleries also expanded enormously during his term as keeper, although shortage of space always remained a problem. These developments were achieved against a background of frequent disputes between the museum's trustees and its keeper staff, and latterly the ageing Hawkins ran his much enlarged department with little reference to the trustees. On his retirement antiquities was divided into three separate departments.

As a scholar, Hawkins's main contribution was in the field of numismatics. Besides a stream of articles in the *Antiquaries Journal* and the *Numismatic Chronicle*, including a remarkably detailed account of the 1840 Cuerdale hoard, he was the author of two major works. One was his *Silver Coins of England* (1841; 2nd and 3rd edns revised by his grandson R. Lloyd-Kenyon in 1877 and 1887), which remained the standard manual on English coinage for almost a century. The other was on English historical medals, of which he formed an outstanding personal collection that the British Museum bought on his retirement in 1860. His interest in medals dates from before his appointment to the museum, and in the 1830s he had sought, without success, government funding to publish a portfolio of engravings of British medals with an accompanying catalogue. He continued to pursue plans for a descriptive catalogue, based largely on his own and the museum's collections, and a volume, *Numismata Britannica*, to the end of William III's reign, was typeset in 1852, but the trustees refused to sanction its publication, mainly because it contained some paragraphs expressing strong anti-Catholic sentiments. It was subsequently revised and completed by A. W. Franks and H. A. Grueber and published as Hawkins's *Medallic Illustrations of the History of Great Britain and Ireland* (2 vols., 1885), with plates added in 1904–11. Over a century later it was still the standard work on British medals before 1760.

Hawkins, partially bald and with strong features, struck a handsome and vigorous profile even at the age of seventy, to judge from the wax portrait by R. C. Lucas in the Victoria and Albert Museum. He died at his house, 6 Lower Berkeley Street, London, on 23 May 1867.

Major Rohde Hawkins (1820–1884), architect and antiquary, the third son, was born on 4 February 1820 at Nutfield, Surrey. He studied architecture, and in 1841 was appointed travelling architect to the expedition sent out under Sir Charles Fellows to Caria and Lycia. The Harpy Tomb at the British Museum, and other antiquities, were reconstructed from his drawings and measurements. He subsequently worked as architect to the committee of the council on education. He died at Redlands, near Dorking, Surrey, on 19 October 1884.   M. A. S. BLACKBURN

Edward Hawkins (1789–1882), by Sir Francis Grant, 1854

Sources *DNB* · E. Miller, *That noble cabinet: a history of the British Museum* (1973) · *The Athenaeum* (15 June 1867), 791 · *Numismatic Chronicle*, new ser., 7 (1867), 11 · *Proceedings of the Society of Antiquaries of London*, 2nd ser., 4 (1867–70), 103–6 · preface, E. Hawkins, A. W. Franks, and H. A. Grueber, *Medallic illustrations of the history of Great Britain and Ireland to the death of George II*, 2 vols. (1885), v–viii, esp. vi–vii · *Men of the time* (1865), 401–2 · J. M. Crook, *The British Museum* (1972) · d. cert. · Boase, *Mod. Eng. biog.* [Major Rohde Hawkins] · *Hansard 3* (1854), 134.1055

Archives BL, corresp. and papers, Egerton MSS 3814–3818 · BL, Egerton charters 8853–8858 | BL, corresp. with Sir A. H. Layard, Add. MSS 38942–38943, 38978–38979 · Bodl. Oxf., corresp. with Sir Thomas Phillipps

Likenesses M. Gauci, lithograph, pubd 1833 (after E. U. Eddis), BM, NPG · W. Drummond, engraving, 1835 (after E. U. Eddis), NPG · R. C. Lucas, wax sculpture, 1850, V&A · H. Thornycroft, bust, 1891; in possession of H. S. Hawkins, 1891 · H. Courbould, lithograph, BM

Wealth at death under £35,000: probate, 8 July 1867, *CGPLA Eng. & Wales* · £24,773 11s.—Major Rohde Hawkins: resworn probate, Sept 1885, *CGPLA Eng. & Wales* (1884)

Hawkins, Edward (1789–1882), college head, was born at Bath on 27 February 1789, the eldest child of Edward Hawkins (d. 1805), successively vicar of Bisley in Gloucestershire and rector of Kelston in Somerset, and his wife, Margaret (d. 1859), daughter of Thomas Howes of Morningthorpe, Norfolk. After about four years at a school at Elmore in Gloucestershire, he was sent to Merchant Taylors' School in February 1801. While he was a schoolboy he

was placed in a position of great responsibility by the death of his father, who left behind him a widow with ten children (who included Caesar Henry *Hawkins and Francis *Hawkins) and had appointed Edward one of his executors. In June 1807 he was elected to an Andrew exhibition at St John's College, Oxford, and in 1811 graduated BA with a double first class in classics and mathematics (MA 1814, BD and DD 1828). In 1812 he became tutor of his college, and in 1813 he was elected fellow of Oriel.

Oriel was at this time the most distinguished college in Oxford. Its system of 'open fellowships', that is, without restriction to a candidate's college or place of birth, as well as the insistence, introduced by the provost of the time, John Eveleigh, that election to a fellowship was to be on the basis of merit alone, attracted to the college some of the keenest minds in the university. When Hawkins was elected the college already had among its fellows leading figures in the university such as Edward Copleston, Richard Whately, and John Keble, and in the years after his election he was joined by Thomas Arnold (1815), John Henry Newman (1822), and E. B. Pusey (1823). Oriel was noted also for a group of its fellows led by Copleston and Whately and known as the Noetics, a school of freethinkers who subjected received traditions, institutions, and beliefs to Socratic-like debate and critique. Hawkins, at this stage of his life on the 'progressive' wing of thought, found in such new colleagues kindred spirits to his own and readily associated himself with them. Both Copleston and Whately were to remain his close friends throughout their lives.

Although Hawkins had at first considered a career at the

bar, his family responsibilities persuaded him that ordination offered a more secure source of income. Devoting himself to divinity, he was ordained in 1816. He made an early impact as a theological thinker, delivering what was perhaps his most remarkable sermon in the university church in May 1818, the substance of which was published in 1819 under the title *A Dissertation upon the Use and Importance of Unauthoritative Tradition*. Newman, who as an undergraduate heard it preached, later wrote in his *Apologia* of the profound effect it had upon him:

> It made a most serious impression upon me. … He lays down a proposition, self-evident as soon as stated, to those who have at all examined the structure of Scripture, viz, that the sacred text was never intended to teach doctrine, but only to prove it; and that if we would learn doctrine we must have recourse to the formularies of the church; for instance, to the Catechism and to the Creeds.   (Newman, 22)

Hawkins afterwards treated the same subject more fully in his Bampton lectures (1840). When Newman became a fellow of Oriel in 1822 he came under the more direct influence of Hawkins, who immediately befriended him and set about weaning him from his Calvinist upbringing. From 1823 to 1828 Hawkins was vicar of St Mary's, a college living and the university church, and he is believed to have introduced the Sunday afternoon sermon, which afterwards became so famous under his successor, Newman.

By the 1820s Hawkins, who had resided in college since his election, was one of its leading fellows, and when in 1827 Copleston, who succeeded Eveleigh as provost in 1814, was appointed bishop of Llandaff he was an obvious candidate for the provostship. The other candidate was Keble. Hawkins gained the strong backing of both Pusey and Newman, who considered him the more likely of the two to maintain discipline, which they regarded as having of late become lax, and to further the educational reputation of Oriel. For personal and family reasons Keble soon withdrew his candidature, and Hawkins was elected on 2 February 1828. Later that year, on 20 December, he married Mary Anne (d. 1892), daughter of Richard Buckle of Clifton. Annexed to the provostship were a canonry at Rochester and the living of Purleigh in Essex.

Hawkins's provostship of Oriel was however, disappointing, and when Dean Burgon gives him the title of 'the great provost' the epithet requires much qualification. His stern demeanour impaired his relationship with the undergraduates. In a letter, as distinct from his published memoir of Hawkins, Burgon wrote that as an undergraduate he 'hated to have anything to do with him: there was nothing genial in his manner to us, though I have no doubt that he felt a real responsibility for our well-being' (Burgon to Greenhill, 6 Jan 1890, Oriel letters, F1262), adding, however, what many others also recorded, that when he became a fellow Hawkins at a personal and private level always showed great kindness to him. He was over-jealous of his authority and became intolerably autocratic in his management of the college. Keble accused him of overrating his own importance at the expense of

the wishes of the fellows. He failed to take any constructive initiatives in the development of the college. Even his friend Whately warned him of the risk of failing to take a larger and comprehensive view of issues.

Burgon described Hawkins as provost, during the years of the Tractarian theological movement, as feeling 'like the Captain of a crew on the verge of mutiny' (Burgon to Greenhill, 6 Jan 1890, Oriel letters, F1262). His handling of a number of internal matters gradually alienated the fellows from him. In 1831 the three tutors, Newman, Froude, and Robert Wilberforce, wished to make some changes in the tutorial system, especially to establish a more intimate and pastoral relationship with their best pupils. The provost, fearing that this would lead to favouritism, refused his assent, assigned no more pupils to them, and the three tutors resigned. He made energetic efforts to supply their place by lecturing himself and engaging Renn Dickson Hampden, formerly a fellow of Oriel, to assist him, but the college never quite recovered from their loss. Ignoring wise advice he received on the matter from both Copleston and Keble, he also rejected a move to abandon the custom of admitting gentlemen commoners, whom Newman and others regarded as idle and the ruination of the college. In these and other matters the essential cordial co-operation necessary between the provost and the fellows was more and more eroded. Burgon, who became a fellow in 1845, later wrote of those years that 'Democratic rule was in the process of being substituted for a (rather unlimited) monarchy' (ibid.), while Oriel gradually lost the pre-eminence it had achieved under his two predecessors.

Hawkins was one of the most influential among the Oxford heads of colleges, taking the lead in their measures against the Oxford Movement. In 1835 he supported the unsuccessful move to replace subscription to the Thirty-Nine Articles by undergraduates at matriculation, which the Tractarians set out to uphold, with a declaration of conformity to the Church of England, and was subsequently a defender of R. D. Hampden against his Tractarian opponents. When in 1841 the university's hebdomadal board moved to condemn Tract 90, which Newman had composed, it was Hawkins who was commissioned to draw up the document. Dean Church later wrote that he was 'in Oxford, at least, the ablest and most hurtful opponent' of the Oxford Movement, a 'hard hitter' from whom 'it received its heaviest blows and suffered its greatest losses' (Church, *Occasional Papers*). While extolling Hawkins's virtues, Church also accused him of misunderstanding and intolerance towards the founders of the movement, and of resenting 'its taking out of his hands a province of theology which he and Whately had made their own, that relating to the church'. Unmentioned, however, are the many provocations of which Newman was guilty towards the episcopal and academic authorities of the time, and the fact that Hawkins was naturally exasperated by the Tractarians' doubtful claims to be the true heirs of Caroline Anglican theology. Hawkins's reputation as a theologian within the old high-church tradition was recognized by his election by his fellow heads in

1847 to the newly established chair of the exegesis of the holy scripture, the Dean Ireland professorship, which he held until 1861.

Winds of change began to blow across the university as a whole with the setting up of the royal commission of 1850. Hawkins was one of the heads of colleges who supplied no official information to the commissioners, and he drafted the heads' retort to the commissioners' report in 1853. After the government was informed that in several colleges—Oriel included—the heads had not consulted the fellows, Palmerston issued a direct enquiry to be sent to each college asking that it should be considered by the college as a whole. At Oriel counsel's opinion established that the college's response could not be limited to the provost and the senior fellows, as laid down in the original constitution. This ruling removed the provost's last defence against majority rule, and thereafter Hawkins frequently found himself in a minority, as low at times as two, in measures and changes voted upon by the fellows. Though he became an embattled figure in his own college, he enjoyed a wider reputation as a defender of the principle that government and teaching in the university should remain in the hands of members of the established church. He became a trusted friend of W. E. Gladstone, who stayed and dined with him frequently at Oriel, regarding him as an important point of reference in university affairs.

In 1874 the visitor (the crown) granted a petition from Hawkins that a vice-provost be appointed to manage the college, and he retired, at the age of eighty-five, to his house in the precincts of Rochester Cathedral, where he had almost always been a reformer among his fellow canons. He protested in vain in 1875 against the future severance of the canonry at Rochester from the provostship of Oriel, which removed the remaining obstacle to the laicization of the provostship, and in 1879 he petitioned Oxford University commissioners against the abolition at Oriel of the necessity for all fellows, except three, to be in holy orders. Hawkins died at his Rochester home, after a few days' illness, on 18 November 1882, and was buried on 24 November in the cathedral cemetery. On 20 December 1882 the fellows elected David Binning Monro, a layman who had been vice-provost since 1874, as provost.

Hawkins was 'of middle size, or rather under, slender, with pale, finely cut, and beautiful features' (DNB). He had two sons and three daughters, of whom two daughters and his eldest son died before him; the latter went out on the universities' mission to central Africa, and died in 1862.   E. W. NICHOLSON

Sources DNB · J. W. Burgon, 'The great provost', *Lives of twelve good men*, [new edn], 1 (1888), 374–465 · Oriel letters, Oriel College · K. C. Turpin, 'The ascendancy of Oriel', *Hist. U. Oxf. 6: 19th-cent. Oxf.*, 183–94 · R. W. Church, *The Oxford Movement: twelve years, 1833–1845* (1891) · R. W. Church, 'Retirement of the provost of Oriel', *Occasional papers, selected from the Guardian, the Times, and the Saturday Review, 1846–1890*, ed. M. C. Church, 2 (1897), 343–50 · J. H. Newman, *Apologia pro vita sua*, ed. M. J. Svaglic (1967) · P. B. Nockles, *The Oxford Movement in context: Anglican high churchmanship, 1760–1857* (1994) · Boase, *Mod. Eng. biog.* · Burke, *Peerage* · Gladstone, *Diaries*

Archives Oriel College, Oxford, corresp. and papers · Pusey Oxf. | Balliol Oxf., letters to Henry Jenkyns · Birmingham Oratory, letters to J. H. Newman relating to the Oriel tutorship · BL, corresp. with W. E. Gladstone, Add. MS 44206 · Bodl. Oxf., corresp. with Samuel Wilberforce · LPL, letters to Archbishop Tait · Trinity Cam., letters to W. Whewell
Likenesses F. Grant, oils, 1854, Oriel College, Oxford [*see illus.*]
Wealth at death £29,061 8s. 8d.: probate, 30 Dec 1882, *CGPLA Eng. & Wales*

Hawkins, Ernest (1802–1868), missionary society administrator, sixth son of Henry Hawkins of Lawrence End in the parish of Kimpton, Hertfordshire, and Anne, only child of John Gurney of Bedford, merchant, was born at Lawrence End on 25 January 1802; his father was a major in the East India Company's service. Hawkins was educated at Bedford and at Balliol College, Oxford, where he matriculated on 19 April 1820 and graduated BA in 1824, MA in 1827, and BD on 14 June 1839. On his ordination he became curate to the Revd Joseph Gould of Burwash, Sussex, and he subsequently travelled on the continent with a pupil. He returned to Oxford as a fellow of Exeter College on 26 December 1831, and then acted as an under-librarian of the Bodleian Library, and as curate at St Aldates in the city of Oxford. After leaving Oxford about 1835 he undertook the curacy of St George's, Bloomsbury, London.

In 1838 Hawkins was appointed under-secretary of the Society for the Propagation of the Gospel (SPG), and he succeeded the Revd Archibald Campbell in the secretaryship in 1843. It was during this period that he assisted Charles Blomfield, bishop of London, in launching the Colonial Bishoprics Council at a meeting in Willis's Rooms on 27 April 1841. They were supported in this by W. E. Gladstone, who was a member of the standing committee of the SPG and later a treasurer of the Colonial Bishoprics Fund, of which Hawkins himself was secretary until 1864. Hawkins's pamphlet *Documents Relating to the Erection of Bishoprics in the Colonies, 1841–1855* (1855) includes a lengthy historical preface in which he analyses the failure of the Anglican church to provide bishoprics for the colonies. The success of the fund is evident, for by his retirement the number of colonial bishoprics had increased from eight to forty-seven.

Hawkins was the first secretary of the SPG to travel overseas, making a private visit to the eastern parts of the USA and Canada in 1849. This was partly to study the differences between the American and Canadian churches, and partly to see for himself the conditions under which many SPG clergy were labouring. He was also concerned to help the Canadian church towards greater financial independence through an equitable settlement of the problem of the clergy reserves (lands from which the Anglican church in Canada derived most of its income). His close association with Bishop Strachan of Toronto over this vexed question led to a satisfactory outcome in 1855, after fifteen years of uncertainty. Also during this visit Hawkins had discussions with Lord Elgin, governor-general of Canada, about the creation of a new see at Montreal. It was proposed that Hawkins should be its first bishop, but with typical modesty he declined. From the journal he wrote during this visit it is clear that Canada was dear to his heart, and three of its bishops—Fulford, Medley, and Field—were among his closest friends.

One other important contact that Hawkins made during his Canadian visit was Captain Lefroy, later Sir John Lefroy, the scientist and colonial administrator. Hawkins married Lefroy's sister, Sophia Anna (1823–1897), on 29 July 1852. John and Sophia Lefroy were children of John Henry George Lefroy, rector of Ashe in Hampshire, who was distantly connected to the family of Jane Austen. The Hawkinses had no children.

Apart from some devotional works, an edition of St John's gospel, and various works on colonial church history, Hawkins's literary energies bore fruit, soon after he became secretary, in initiating the SPG periodicals *The Church in the Colonies* and *Missions to the Heathen*. These were followed in 1852 by *The Gospel Missionary*, designed for children, and in 1856 by *The Mission Field*, which became the society's most popular journal.

Hawkins seems to have been sympathetic to the Tractarians but was not doctrinaire. It is perhaps noteworthy that in the notorious controversy surrounding William George Ward, also of Balliol College, he voted against Ward's degradation at the meeting of the university convocation in Oxford on 13 February 1845. Known as a fairminded man, this seems not to have harmed his reputation.

The 150th anniversary of the founding of the SPG occurred in 1851, coinciding with the Great Exhibition and with the mid-point of Hawkins's twenty-six years of service to the society. The expansion of the SPG's work abroad owed much to Hawkins's energy and zeal, but perhaps more to his tact and patience, his gift for friendship, and his freedom from self-interest and narrow party feeling. By the time he retired in 1864 the SPG's income had risen from £16,557 to £91,703; missionaries from 180 to 493; and parishes supporting the society from 290 to 7270. Hawkins was not, however, to visit any other colonial territories despite serving as vice-president of Bishop's College, Cape Town, in 1859, and maintaining a cordial correspondence with the Revd Alfred Street, professor at Bishop's College, Calcutta.

Apart from his responsibilities in London at the SPG, Hawkins became assistant preacher at Lincoln's Inn in 1844, a prebendary of St Paul's Cathedral, and in 1850 minister of Curzon Chapel, Mayfair. On his retirement he was promoted by the crown on 7 November 1864 to a canonry at Westminster, vacated expressly for him by the voluntary resignation of William Henry Edward Bentinck, archdeacon of Westminster. Hawkins died in London at his home, 20 Dean's Yard, Westminster, on 5 October 1868, and was buried in the cloister of the abbey on 12 October.

CLARE BROWN

Sources H. P. Thompson, *Into all lands* (1951) · C. F. Pascoe, *Two hundred years of the SPG*, rev. edn, 2 vols. (1901) · T. R. Millman and J. L. H. Henderson, 'Hawkins, Ernest', *DCB*, vol. 9 · *The Guardian* (14 Oct 1868) · C. W. Boase, *Registrum Collegii Exoniensis*, 2 vols. (1879–94) · Gladstone, *Diaries* · O. Chadwick, *The Victorian church*, 3rd edn, 1 (1971) · *Men of the time* (1868) · J. L. Chester, ed., *The marriage, baptismal, and burial registers of the collegiate church or abbey of St Peter, Westminster*, Harleian Society, 10 (1876) · m. cert. · Burke, *Gen. GB* (1937)

Archives BL, corresp. with W. E. Gladstone, Add. MSS 44359–44406 · Bodl. RH, SPG MSS · LPL, corresp. with A. C. Tait and related papers

Likenesses photograph, Bodl. RH

Wealth at death under £10,000: probate, 17 Dec 1868, *CGPLA Eng. & Wales*

Hawkins, Francis (1628–1681), Jesuit, was born in London, the son of John *Hawkins (*c*.1587–*c*.1641), a physician and grammarian, and his wife, Frances Power of Bletchingdon, Oxfordshire. He was the nephew of both the poet Sir Thomas *Hawkins and the Jesuit Henry *Hawkins. During his youth Francis produced two translations: *An Alarum for Ladyes*, from a work by M. de La Serre, which appeared in 1638 with a dedication to Edward Sackville, fourth earl of Dorset; and *Youths Behaviour, or, Decency in Conversation amongst Men*, which was published, at John Hawkins's request, by the London bookseller William Lee in 1641. The latter work may have been circulating before 1638, as the preface to *An Alarum for Ladyes* noted that the 'first Treatise I presented the[e] with, was of good behaviour' (preface). *Youths Behaviour* ran to a further ten editions by 1672; the fourth edition of 1646 is the earliest that survives. A second part, *Youths Behaviour, or, Decency in Conversation amongst Women*, was added by the puritan Robert Codrington in 1664. As proof of the child's precocity the address to the reader in the 1646 edition of *Youths Behaviour* observes:

> Though here be wonder when 'tis knowne,
> A Child should make this worke his owne,
> (Since he that can translate and please,
> Must needs command two Languages).
> (sig. A4r)

Editions of both translations carry engraved portraits of the boy in their frontispieces although while *An Alarum for Ladyes* is inscribed 'Francis Hawkins tirant a l'aage des dix ans', the 1654 edition of *Youths Behaviour* claims the likeness was drawn 'a l'aage huict ans'.

On 8 October 1649 Hawkins entered the noviciate as a scholastic at the English Jesuit College at Watten and from 1650 to 1653 he studied theology at the English Jesuit house of studies in Liège. In 1654 he returned to the noviciate at Watten. Before being professed of the four vows on 14 May 1662 he moved between Watten, Ghent, and St Omer colleges and spent two years at the Holy Apostles and Blessed Aloysius colleges in England during 1657 and 1658. This was to be the pattern of his future career: in 1663 he became prefect of the church at St Omer before moving back to Watten, where he was socius to the master of novices; he returned to St Omer in 1667, taking the office of confessor to the Jesuits and students and acting as both admonitor and spiritual prefect. He was again moved to Watten, where he could be found in 1672–3 as assistant prefect, consultor, confessor, and again acting as assistant to the novice master. In 1673 he was sent again to Ghent becoming confessor and tertian master. In 1675 he moved to Liège where he remained until his death. During these

Francis Hawkins (1628–1681), by John Payne, pubd 1654

last few years of his life he was spiritual prefect and confessor to the Jesuits and in 1676 was professor of holy scripture. He died on 19 February 1681; the cause of death is unknown although his last recorded entry describes his health as 'firme' (transcripts of Jesuit catalogues, catalogi III).　　　　ROBERTA ANDERSON

Sources transcripts of Jesuit catalogues, Department of Archives and Historiography of the English Province of the Society of Jesus, London, catalogi I, III · H. Foley, ed., *Records of the English Province of the Society of Jesus*, 3 (1875), 492; 4 (1878), 700; 7 (1882–3), 346 · G. Oliver, *Collections towards illustrating the biography of the Scotch, English and Irish members, SJ* (1838), 99 · Gillow, *Lit. biog. hist.* · W. T. Lowndes, *The bibliographer's manual of English literature*, ed. H. G. Bohn, [new edn], 6 vols. (1890), 2000
Likenesses J. Payne, line engraving, BM, NPG; repro. in F. Hawkins, trans., *Youths behaviour, or, Decency in conversation amongst men*, 6th edn (1654) [*see illus.*] · engraving, repro. in J. Puget de la Serre, *An alarum for ladyes*, trans. F. Hawkins (1638)

Hawkins, Francis (1794–1877), physician, was born at Bisley, Gloucestershire, on 30 July 1794, the son of the Revd Edward Hawkins and his wife Margaret, daughter of the Revd Thomas Howes, of Morningthorpe, Norfolk, and sister of Francis *Howes. His grandfather was the eminent surgeon Sir Caesar *Hawkins; Caesar Henry *Hawkins and Edward *Hawkins were his brothers. He was educated

at Merchant Taylors' School, London (1805–12), and St John's College, Oxford, where he gained a fellowship. He won the Newdigate prize in 1813, and in 1816 took a double second-class degree in classics and mathematics. He graduated BA 1816, BCL 1819, MB 1820, and MD 16 April 1823. He was admitted as an inceptor candidate of the Royal College of Physicians on 16 April 1821, as a candidate on 30 September 1823, and as a fellow on 30 September 1824. He became physician to the Middlesex Hospital in 1824, and was elected the first professor of medicine at King's College, London, in 1831. He resigned the chair in 1836, and left his hospital appointment in 1858. He was physician to the royal households of William IV and Queen Victoria.

Hawkins was connected with the Royal College of Physicians for many years, and held various offices. He gave the Goulstonian (1826), Croonian (1827–9), and Lumleian (1832–4, 1840–41) lectures, as well as the Harveian oration (1848). However, his most important contribution to the college was through serving as registrar, an office he held for twenty-nine years from 30 September 1829. Hawkins only resigned this post to become registrar of the General Medical Council on its foundation in 1858, and remained in this office until 1876. He was highly regarded as an excellent and courteous administrator. In both cases a special vote of thanks, accompanied by a liberal honorarium, was presented to him when he resigned the office.

Hawkins was married twice. In 1831 he married Hester (d. 1847), third daughter of Sir John *Vaughan, baron of the exchequer, with whom he had three sons and one daughter. He married his second wife, Sarah Jane (d. 1890), daughter of G. Haywood, in July 1859.

Hawkins was an accomplished physician, whose genial temperament made him very popular in professional circles. His Harveian oration in 1848 was admired for its Latin style. He also wrote *Lectures on Rheumatism and some Diseases of the Heart and other Internal Organs* (1826). He died on 13 December 1877, at his address at 16 Ashley Place, Victoria Street, London.　　　J. F. PAYNE, *rev.* CLAIRE L. NUTT

Sources Munk, *Roll* · Foster, *Alum. Oxon.* · *The Lancet* (22 Dec 1877), 938 · Burke, *Peerage*
Archives Yale U., Beinecke L., Osborn collection
Likenesses portrait, Middlesex Hospital
Wealth at death under £1500: probate, 18 Jan 1878, *CGPLA Eng. & Wales*

Hawkins, George (1809–1852), lithographer, was the son of the landscape painter and engraver George Hawkins (*fl.* 1795–1820). He began as an architectural draughtsman and then became a successful lithographer. The *Art Journal* noted: 'his pencil was peculiarly correct and delicate, and his knowledge of effect enabled him to produce pictures out of the most unpromising materials' (*Art Journal*, 14, 1852, 375). He worked chiefly for the lithographic printers Messrs Day. Hawkins recorded contemporary as well as historical architecture, which included bridges, churches, railway viaducts, and marine views after his own designs and those of contemporaries; his views of the Great Exhibition were published by Ackerman & Co. in 1851. His *Bath from Beacon Hill* (a pair with *Bath from Beechey*

Hill, both after John Syer) is reproduced in Mackenzie's *British Prints* (1987). One of his most important undertakings was a series of plates in *The Monastic Ruins of Yorkshire*, from sketches made by W. Richardson, and with historical descriptions by E. Churton (2 vols., 1844–56). He was frequently employed by architects in colouring their designs, and many of these were exhibited at the Royal Academy between 1830 and 1848. Hawkins died at 116 Camden Road Villas, Camden Town, London, on 6 November 1852.   GORDON GOODWIN, *rev.* JOANNA DESMOND

Sources GM, 2nd ser., 38 (1852), 655 • *Art Journal*, 14 (1852), 375 • Graves, *RA exhibitors*, 4 (1906), 32 • Boase, *Mod. Eng. biog.* • catalogue [print room, V&A] • Mallalieu, *Watercolour artists*, 1.128 • I. Mackenzie, *British prints: dictionary and price guide* (1987)

Hawkins, Henry (*bap.* 1577, *d.* 1646), Jesuit, was born in London or Kent and baptized in Boughton under Blean, near Canterbury, on 8 October 1577, the second son of Sir Thomas Hawkins (1548/9–1617) of Nash Court, Boughton, and Ann (1552–1616), daughter of Cyriac Pettyt and his wife, Florence, also of Boughton. The Hawkins and the Petits were both recusant families. Henry's elder brother, Sir Thomas *Hawkins (*bap.* 1575, *d.* 1640?), was a translator of recusant books. Other surviving brothers were Daniel (*bap.* 1578); Richard (*bap.* 1581), who married Mary Langworth (daughter of church papist John Langworth DD); John *Hawkins, a physician and author; and Cyriac. His surviving sisters were Susanna (*bap.* 1580), who married the recusant John Finch of Grovehurst, Milton next Sittingbourne; Anne, who married William Hildesley of Oxfordshire; and Bennet (*bap.* 1586) and Benedicta (1588–1661), both nuns in Brussels. A monument in Boughton church to Hawkins's father, Sir Thomas, and his family was designed by Epiphanius Evesham with exquisite sensitivity. The monument shows a group of thirteen children. The tall bearded man, raising his hand in blessing, is considered to be Henry Hawkins.

As a boy Henry Hawkins would have received private tuition: the name of Mr Greene, a recusant schoolmaster in his father's house about 1587–9, appears in the Hussey manuscripts at Lambeth Palace (Lottes, 146). Following his brother Thomas, Henry matriculated from Gloucester Hall, Oxford, on 3 November 1592, aged fourteen. On 9 February 1604 he married Aphra (*b.* 1583/4), daughter of Thomas Norton, in Fordwich, Kent. She died on 16 January 1605, her brass in Fordwich church describing her as 'scarcely having arrived to 21 yeares of age yet fully attayned perfection'. Hawkins is believed to have studied humanities at the English College, St Omer, before entering the English College, Rome, under the alias Brooke, on 19 March 1609, being described as 'a man of mature age, intelligent in affairs of government, very learned in the English laws', and having 'left … office, and many … expectations' (Foley, 3.491–2). His choice of alias 'may have been inspired by Sir Basil Brook, a prominent recusant' (Lottes, 146). He was ordained priest on 25 March 1614 and entered the Society of Jesus in 1615. On coming to England he seems to have been captured and imprisoned, and in 1618 was sent into exile with eleven other Jesuits. He returned and worked principally in London for twenty-

five years. He is named among the 'veterani missionarii' in the list of Jesuits found among the papers seized in 1628 in Clerkenwell.

Seven of the eight works attributed to Hawkins appeared between 1630 and 1634. Most were translations, including saints' lives and devotional works, from Latin, French, and Italian. His *History of St. Elizabeth* (1632) was dedicated to the recusant Lady Mary Teynham of Lynsted Lodge, near Sittingbourne. He was responsible for producing two of the three extant recusant emblem books in English. He translated Stephen Luzvic's *The Devout Heart* (1634), the object of which was to combine the functions of an emblem book with those of a devotional manual. His own composition was the remarkable *Partheneia sacra* (1633), subtitled 'the mysterious and delicious garden of the sacred Parthenes'. In it the garden provided a framework for devotion. Twenty-four symbols associated with the Virgin Mary are all in the frontispiece and provide its framework and main themes. The book has been considered 'stylistically, in the mainstream of English prose of the seventeenth century' while his translations have been deemed 'significant contributions to vernacular prose literature' (Secker, 242, 250). He was said to be residing in London in 1641. 'In his old age Hawkins withdrew to the house of the English Tertian Fathers at Ghent, established in 1622 under the patronage of Lady Anne, countess of Arundel and Surrey' (Lottes, 146). He died there on 18 August 1646.   ANTONY CHARLES RYAN

Sources J. E. Secker, 'Henry Hawkins, SJ, 1577–1646: a recusant writer and translator of the early seventeenth century', *Recusant History*, 11 (1971–2), 237–52 • R. Freeman, *English emblem books* (1948), 173–248 • H. Foley, ed., *Records of the English province of the Society of Jesus*, 7 vols. in 8 (1875–83) • C. Buckingham, 'The Hawkins of Boughton-under-Blean', *London Recusant*, 2 (1972), 1–11 • G. Anstruther, *The seminary priests*, 2 (1975), 152 • G. Holt, *St Omers and Bruges colleges, 1593–1773: a biographical dictionary*, Catholic RS, 69 (1979) • W. Lottes, 'Henry Hawkins and "Partheneia sacra"', *Review of English Studies*, new ser., 26 (1975), 144–53, 271–86 • K. H. Jones, 'The Hawkins monument by Epiphanius Evesham at Boughton-under-Blean', *Archaeologia Cantiana*, 45 (1933), 205–8 • Stonyhurst MS, Angl., vol. 4, n. 41 [printed in Foley's *Records*] • parish register, Boughton under Blean, 8 Oct 1577 [baptism] • Foster, *Alum. Oxon.* • J. M. Cowper, ed., *Canterbury marriage licences*, 6 vols. (1892–1906), vol. 1 • W. Kelly, ed., *Liber ruber venerabilis collegii Anglorum de urbe*, 1, Catholic RS, 37 (1940) • T. M. McCoog, *English and Welsh Jesuits, 1555–1650*, 2 vols., Catholic RS, 74–5 (1994–5) • G. J. Armytage, ed., *A visitation of the county of Kent, begun … 1663, finished … 1668*, Harleian Society, 54 (1906) • C. E. Woodruff, *A history of the town and port of Fordwich* (1895)

Archives Stonyhurst College, Lancashire, Stonyhurst MS, Angl., vol. 4, n. 41

Likenesses E. Evesham, monument, Boughton under Blean church, Kent

Hawkins, Henry, Baron Brampton (1817–1907), judge, was born at Hitchin on 14 September 1817, the son of John Hawkins, a solicitor with a considerable 'family' practice, and his wife, Susanna, daughter of Theed Pearse, clerk of the peace of Bedfordshire. After attending Bedford School until 1835, Hawkins was employed in his father's office long enough to take a dislike to solicitors' work, and with his parents' reluctant consent on 16 April 1839 entered the Middle Temple, taking out a special pleader's licence in

Henry Hawkins, Baron Brampton (1817–1907), by Barraud, pubd 1889

1841. He was the pupil of Frederick Thompson, a special pleader, and of George Butt, later a QC. On 3 May 1843 Hawkins was called to the bar, joining the home circuit and the Hertfordshire sessions. Although his earlier progress was not exceptionally rapid, it was unbroken from his call until he took silk in 1858. For the next eighteen years Hawkins's lively intelligence in handling complicated factual issues, well-chosen language, attractive voice, histrionic ability, sense of humour, thoroughness of preparation, and mastery of the art of cross-examination made him exceedingly successful in winning the verdicts of juries. He equalled the ablest of his contemporaries, serjeants Ballantine and Parry, as a leader of the common-law and criminal bar, being engaged in many cases of great ephemeral importance.

In 1852 Hawkins was counsel for Simon Bernard, who was acquitted of complicity in the Orsini conspiracy against Napoleon III. As junior to Serjeant Byles he defended Sir John Dean Paul, who was convicted in 1855 of fraud. In 1862 he was led by William Bovill in *Roupell* v. *Waite*, in which Roupell confessed himself guilty of forgery. He also appeared for various defendants in the prosecutions instituted after the failure of Overend and Gurney's Bank in 1866, all of them being acquitted. Appearing for Miss Sugden, he was largely instrumental in securing the establishment by secondary evidence of the will and codicils of Lord St Leonards, and was able to hold his judgment on appeal (1875–6).

Hawkins was at the height of his powers when he appeared in all but the earliest stages of the litigation in which Arthur Orton, claiming to be Sir Roger Tichborne, was the principal figure (1867–74). When he was originally retained for the family in the civil action (1871–2), it was no doubt intended that he should cross-examine the 'claimant', but before the trial John Duke Coleridge, who had also been instructed, became solicitor-general, and as such the leader in the defence. This accident which deprived Hawkins of the right to cross-examine Orton was a bitter disappointment, though his cross-examination of several other important witnesses maintained his reputation as a master of that art. When the criminal trial for perjury followed the collapse of the 'claimant's' civil action, Hawkins led for the crown (23 April 1873). His opening speech and his reply, which lasted 8 and 10 days respectively, were masterpieces of concise exposition, compared with the prosecution, which lasted 188, and Lord Chief Justice Cockburn's summing-up, which lasted 20 (February 1874). Coleridge by contrast had spent 23 days in opening the case for the defence in the civil action. Hawkins's handling of this extraordinary prosecution was widely admired, though even at the time some thought that the relentless and not wholly scrupulous vigour with which he pursued the 'claimant', the ferocity of his cross-examinations (which sometimes elicited protests from the judges), and the ridicule he poured on the defendant and his witnesses were not altogether seemly in a prosecutor.

Hawkins was also continually, and lucratively, employed in compensation cases, before either juries or arbitrators, notably in those connected with the purchase of the site for the Royal Courts of Justice. He had too a considerable practice in election petitions when, after the general election of 1868, those disputes were first tried before judges. He himself stood unsuccessfully as one of two Liberal candidates for Barnstaple in 1865; he made no other effort to enter the House of Commons.

Hawkins declined the judgeship offered him on the conclusion of the Tichborne prosecution in 1874, but in November 1876 he was appointed a judge of the Queen's Bench Division, knighted, and almost immediately transferred to the Exchequer Division, where he remained until it was absorbed in the Queen's Bench Division in 1880. Like Chief Baron Kelly he resented the provision of the Judicature Acts by which every High Court judge was to be styled 'Mr Justice' and the old title of baron of the exchequer was dropped. He made vain efforts to secure the appellation of 'Baron Hawkins', and invariably called himself Sir Henry Hawkins, instead of Mr Justice Hawkins. Hawkins's conduct of his first major murder trial at the Old Bailey in September 1877 was much criticized, and earned him the undying enmity of Edward Clarke who, for more than forty years, repeatedly denounced Hawkins as a 'wicked judge'. Louis and Patrick Staunton, Patrick's wife, and a servant, Alice Rhodes, were jointly indicted for the murder, by ill treatment and intentional neglect, of Louis's wife, Harriet. Her death was certainly welcome to them, but it was less clear that they had intended to bring it about, and even less so that she had died of starvation rather than of tubercular meningitis, while the sufficiency of the evidence of complicity against Alice Rhodes was open to question (and had been questioned by Sir James Stephen when directing the grand jury). But Hawkins had not shaken off the habits of a prosecutor. He summed up for murder convictions against all four defendants, ignoring the conflicting medical evidence, and keeping the jury in court from before eleven in the morning until after ten at night, when he required them to consider their verdict. All four were convicted of murder and sentenced to death, but a petition signed by 700 doctors, headed by Sir William Jenner, led the home secretary to consult three senior judges. To Hawkins's displeasure, Rhodes received a free pardon and the sentence on the others was commuted to penal servitude for life.

The Stauntons' trial, together with a number of other murder cases coming before him which attracted public attention, together with the alliterative attractiveness of the nickname Hanging Hawkins, gave rise to the popular view that Hawkins was a judge of a peculiarly severe or even savage temper. To this his cruel practice of postponing sentence on all (except murderers) convicted at an assize until the last day, when he had them all brought up into the dock, often filling it, sentencing one after another 'in a grand *battue* of punishment' (Purcell), certainly contributed. Hawkins was none the less in many ways an admirable criminal judge. Extremely patient and thorough, he generally took care that both the case for the crown and that for the accused should be exhaustively stated and tested. His summings-up—in which in his later years it was his invariable practice never to open his notebook unless to read to the jury some fragment of the evidence in which the actual words used were important—were models of lucidity and completeness. His manner, while dignified, was (unless he was crossed) considerate to the point of being almost gentle. In the gravest cases he did not shrink from severity. But he supported the contemporary movement for greater leniency in sentencing, taking the view that recidivism did not justify significantly greater sentences than the offences committed warranted, and being strongly opposed to corporal punishment. He favoured the establishment of a sentencing commission, as a means of reducing the great disparities in sentencing that then prevailed. He thus stood in striking contrast to Sir James Stephen, his only judicial contemporary who was his equal as a criminal judge. Hawkins's foreword to the police code (1882) in several respects anticipated the judges' rules (1912–84) on the interrogation of suspects by the police.

As a civil judge, however, Hawkins failed to convey the impression that to do justice between the parties was his single aim. Innumerable stories were told—some of them with substantial foundation—of the ingenious devices whereby he contrived that cases should either be referred by consent to arbitration or not tried out to a clear determination on the merits. The principal motive for these mischievous devices, usually extremely adroit, was, no doubt, to avoid the reversal of his decisions on appeal. He admitted to 'a horror of adverse criticism, to which I am perhaps unduly sensitive'. He also took what those appearing before him saw as a malign pleasure in causing the greatest possible inconvenience to counsel, litigants, and witnesses. He even went to great lengths to exclude fresh air from his courtroom, keeping it as hot and stuffy as possible. On circuit, where his judicial brethren sought to avoid his company, he often sat for very long hours (he was once said to have passed sentence of death at 1 a.m.), although in London, he habitually rose quite punctually.

Hawkins's judicial behaviour presented other strange contrasts. When doing the work he liked—summing up important or complicated evidence in a criminal case—he had a command of excellent English, accurate, forcible, and dignified, which would have stood the test of absolutely literal reproduction in print. But in delivering a considered judgment he was verbose and tautological; he failed to grasp the principles of the law or to deduce from them the true effect of the facts before him, and he fell into contradictions. Two examples of such judgments are those in *Hicks* v. *Faulkner* on malicious prosecution, and in *R.* v. *Lillyman* (1896) on the admissibility of evidence of a complaint of a sexual offence. The latter judgment of the Court for Crown Cases Reserved was so unsatisfactory that for nine years it was invariably construed as meaning the contrary of what it said, until in *R.* v. *Osborne* (1905), in the same court, it was substantially overruled.

Hawkins resigned his judgeship at the end of 1898 after the legal press had begun complaining about his 'advanced age and crippled health rendering necessary neglect of his duty in order to recover in foreign climes', urging him to take his pension and give way to 'an efficient successor'. He asked for and was given a peerage (27 January 1899), becoming Baron Brampton; the prime minister (Salisbury) commented to the lord chancellor (Halsbury), 'Hawkins' letter is pathetic. I have had considerable prepossessions against him, but considering that he is 83 and childless I have put the said prepossessions in my pocket, and have sent in his name to the Queen' (Heuston, 58). Until August 1902 he sat occasionally in the House of Lords (as a peer who had held judicial office) or the privy council (of which he was sworn on 7 March 1899). His speeches in such famous cases as *Allen* v. *Flood*, the Taff Vale Railway case, and *Quinn* v. *Leatham* exhibited the same weaknesses as his judgments given when a puisne judge. In 1904 he caused or permitted to be published two volumes entitled *The Reminiscences of Sir Henry Hawkins, Baron Brampton, Edited by Richard Harris, KC*. This book, though written in the first person, was the work of Harris. It has no pretence of arrangement and is a miscellaneous collection of anecdotes wholly lacking in literary skill and in verisimilitude, many of them being demonstrably inaccurate and none of them in any degree trustworthy. It did nothing to increase the reminiscent's reputation.

Brampton was a small man of slender build, but his features were handsome and imposing and his aspect eminently judicial. He was extremely fond of horse-racing. He never ran horses himself, but he had been standing counsel to the Jockey Club, of which he was elected an honorary member in 1878, and an ordinary member in 1889. Brampton was twice married but had no children by either marriage. His first wife, Hannah Casey, who died in September 1886, was said to have been 'an illiterate person of the domestic servant class, who was bed-ridden for some years before her death' (GEC, *Peerage*). His second wife, whom he married on 17 August 1887, and who survived him by only six weeks, was Jane Louisa (*c*.1827–1907), daughter of Henry Francis Reynolds of Hulme, a former actress and a Roman Catholic. Hawkins, who had long been a friend of Cardinal Manning, was himself received into the Roman Catholic church in 1898, and in 1903 with his wife presented the chapel of Sts Augustine and Gregory to Westminster Cathedral. Originally envisaged as 'the Brampton chantry' (complete with tomb chest), it contains an opus sectile picture, *The Just Judge* (Solomon). But after his death at his house at 5 Tilney Street, Park Lane, London, on 6 October 1907, Brampton was buried at Kensal Green cemetery. The bulk of both his estate (£141,000) and that of his wife (£315,000) was left to the archbishop of Westminster and applied, as they had wished, to the Hospital of St John and St Elizabeth. Antony Hope (Hawkins), the novelist, was a relative.

HERBERT STEPHEN, *rev.* P. R. GLAZEBROOK

Sources GEC, *Peerage* · R. F. V. Heuston, *Lives of the lord chancellors, 1885–1940* (1964) · J. D. Woodruff, *The Tichborne claimant: a Victorian mystery* (1957) · J. B. Atlay, *The trial of the Stauntons* (1911) · E. Clarke, *The story of my life* (1918) · E. S. Purcell, *Forty years at the criminal bar* (1916) · W. de L'Hopital, *Westminster Cathedral and its architects*, 1 (1919) · E. Bowen-Rowlands, *In court and out of court: some personal recollections* (1925) · C. Biron, *Without prejudice: impressions of life and law* (1936) · T. Humphreys, *Criminal days* (1946) · *Times Law Reports* · *The Times* (7–12 Oct 1907) · d. cert. [Hannah Hawkins] · d. cert. [Jane Louisa Hawkins]

Likenesses J. Collier, oils, exh. RA 1878, NPG · Barraud, photograph, pubd 1889, NPG [*see illus.*] · R. Barnes, oils, 1891 (*Justice Hawkins sums up*) · H. Furniss, pen-and-ink caricature, NPG · J. A. Innes, crayon drawing; formerly in possession of family; sold after death of Lady Brampton · J. A. Innes, oils; formerly in possession of family; sold after death of Lady Brampton · Spy [L. Ward], caricature, repro. in *VF* (1893) · Spy [L. Ward], chromolithograph caricature, NPG; repro. in *VF* (21 June 1873) · J. W. Swynnerton, marble bust, Guildhall Art Gallery, London · bust, Old Bailey · photograph, repro. in Woodruff, *Tichborne claimant* · photographs, repro. in H. Hawkins, *Reminiscences of Sir Henry Hawkins, Baron Brampton* (1904)

Wealth at death £141,853 17s. 8d.: probate, 29 Oct 1907, CGPLA Eng. & Wales

Hawkins, Herbert Leader (1887–1968), geologist and palaeontologist, was born in Reading, Berkshire, on 1 June 1887, the only son of John Luther Hawkins and his wife, Mary Elizabeth Leader. His father was a master baker and the family were Quakers. Hawkins was educated at Reading School and afterwards at the grammar school at Kendal, Westmorland. He entered Manchester University with a classical scholarship in 1905 and transferred from classics to geology. He gained a first-class honours degree in that subject and the first Mark Stirrup palaeontological scholarship in 1908. A further two years of postgraduate

work resulted in his MSc in 1910. During this time he settled on what was to be his principal palaeontological research—the study of fossil echinoids. In 1909 he was appointed part-time lecturer at the University College of Reading (from 1926 the University of Reading), and even before completion of his studies at Manchester was given a full-time post, which enabled him to initiate and develop the department of geology in that institution. In 1912 Hawkins married Amy (*d*. 1953), daughter of Alexander Morrison Mitchell, a photographer. They had two sons and a daughter.

Hawkins was appointed professor of geology at Reading in 1920, the year in which Manchester University awarded him the degree of DSc. He was elected a fellow of the Royal Society in 1937, by which time he was recognized as the foremost specialist on fossil Echinoidea in the United Kingdom.

Between 1909 and 1965 Hawkins published 102 scientific communications, almost half of which report his fossil echinoid research, mainly on the morphology of the Holectypoida. Meticulous observation, new techniques, and laborious, patient dissection revealed new morphological features which Hawkins interpreted in terms of phylogeny. Particularly admirable papers were those on 'Morphological studies on the Echinoidea Holectypoida and their allies', in twelve parts between 1917 and 1922. The papers are illustrated with fine drawings made by himself.

Another aspect of Hawkins's writing concerned certain philosophical aspects of palaeontology, its contribution to evolution extrapolated into the future, and its implications for humankind. This phase culminated in *Humanity in Geological Perspective*, the Alexander Pedler lecture in 1938, which achieved international acclaim when it was republished the following year by the Smithsonian Institution. The lecture reveals Hawkins as an accomplished writer and an imaginative thinker, with a deep concern for humanity.

As a teacher Hawkins was unusual. He lectured without notes. He was concerned to fire the imagination and engender a devotion to the subject. His students found his lectures entertaining, enjoyable, and often inspired performances. Of the six of his students who proceeded to higher degrees, four eventually occupied chairs in British universities, while the other two attained high office in the national geological surveys.

Hawkins made significant contributions to British Tertiary stratigraphy, periglacial phenomena, and some aspects of economic geology. He was much in demand as lecturer and president of minor natural history societies, and in 1936 served as president of the geological section of the British Association for the Advancement of Science.

Hawkins was awarded the Lyell medal of the Geological Society (1940) and served as its president (1941–2). He took great interest in the Geologists' Association, serving as president (1938–40); he was elected honorary member in 1949. The *Proceedings of the Geologists' Association*, vol. 78, 1967, comprising papers by his students and associates, was issued as a Festschrift for his eightieth birthday. He was president of the Palaeontographical Society from 1943 to 1966.

Tall and spare, moustached, with brilliant blue eyes, Hawkins was gentle and entertaining, ever ready to talk about his subject at any level. He partly had and partly assumed a bewildered helplessness in the face of administrators, technologists, and rich benefactors, as a consequence of which a new building and cash endowments fell into his hands to form the nucleus of a department, in which he continued to take an interest after his retirement in 1952, and subsequent appointment as professor emeritus. In 1961 he was appointed consulting geologist to the Thames Valley Water Board.

Following the death of his first wife in 1953, Hawkins married in 1955 Sibyl Marion Hampton, his former research student, who survived him. Hawkins died in Reading on 29 December 1968.   F. HODSON, *rev.*

Sources P. Allen, *Memoirs FRS*, 16 (1970), 315–29 · *WWW* · personal knowledge (1981) · *CGPLA Eng. & Wales* (1969)
Archives U. Reading L., corresp. and MS maps
Likenesses photographs, repro. in *Memoirs FRS*
Wealth at death £14,589: probate, 28 April 1969, *CGPLA Eng. & Wales*

Hawkins, James (1662/3–1729), organist and composer, was apparently a chorister of St John's College, Cambridge, from which college he graduated MusB in 1719. In the same year he dedicated his anthem 'Behold, O God, our defender' (the manuscript of which is in the Royal College of Music) 'to the very Revnd Mr Tomkinson, and the rest of the Great, Good and Just Nonjurors of St John's College in Cambridge'. In 1682 he became organist of Ely Cathedral and master of the choristers, retaining the posts until his death. Hawkins's compositions (some seventeen services and seventy-five anthems survive at Ely Cathedral) have been deemed 'in no way significant' (*New Grove*), but the transcripts he made of manuscripts at Ely remain useful to scholars, and he assisted Thomas Tudway in the formation of the Harleian collection of musical manuscripts. He died on 18 October 1729 and was buried in the cathedral, where a memorial inscription (now obliterated) recorded his 'cheerfulness' and remarked that he was in his sixty-seventh year. His wife, Mary (d. 1732), 'the tender mother of ten children', was buried in the same place three years later. Their son **James Hawkins** (*bap.* 1688) was organist of Peterborough Cathedral from 1714 to 1750. One of his anthems, 'O praise the Lord', is in Tudway's collection.

                    L. M. MIDDLETON, *rev.* K. D. REYNOLDS

Sources *New Grove* · Grove, *Dict. mus.* (1927) · Venn, *Alum. Cant.* · *IGI*

Hawkins, James (*bap.* 1688). *See under* Hawkins, James (1662/3–1729).

Hawkins, Sir John (1532–1595), merchant and naval commander, was born in Plymouth, the second son of William *Hawkins (*b.* before 1490, *d.* 1554/5), merchant, sea captain, and shipowner, and his wife, Joan, only child of Roger Trelawny of Brighter, Cornwall.

Sir John Hawkins (1532–1595), attrib. Federico Zuccaro, 1591

Early years Hawkins was probably brought up in the family home in Kinterbury Street, Plymouth. Nothing is known of his education, though the script and orthography of his letters, and his technical memoranda as navy treasurer, suggest a cultivated man, schooled in mathematics and navigation. By the time he was twenty Hawkins had killed a man, a Plymouth barber named White; but the coroner adjudged White to have been the aggressor, and Hawkins's father, realizing the seriousness of the offence, shrewdly secured translation of the verdict into a royal pardon, inscribed on the patent roll. During the negotiations for the marriage of Queen Mary to Philip of Spain, Hawkins seems to have performed some useful service for Spanish emissaries passing through Plymouth. The later Spanish claim that Philip actually knighted him seems far-fetched; but Hawkins did persistently refer to the king of Spain as 'my old master', probably as a formula designed to lend some legitimacy to his commercial forays in the Caribbean.

In the 1550s Hawkins was a partner with his elder brother, William *Hawkins (*c.*1519–1589), in the family shipping business. He spent considerable time in France (1556), attempting in the law courts of Brest to retrieve one of the firm's ships, captured as a prize but later impounded by its original owners. It is unclear whether Hawkins was successful, but his diplomatic skill was evident in his enlisting both the French ambassador in England and the English envoy in France in support of his suit.

During the Anglo-French war (1557–8) Hawkins and his brother were successfully engaged in channel privateering. By the end of the decade he was a man of importance in Plymouth, where he had become a freeman (1556) and a common councillor (1558). But from c.1559 he began to denote himself as 'of London'. Hawkins bought a house in Deptford, and soon afterwards another in the city, in the parish of St Dunstan-in-the-East, which he retained for the remainder of his life. Until recently historians have believed that Hawkins's move to London coincided with his marriage to Katherine (d. 1591), daughter of Benjamin *Gonson [see under Gonson, William], treasurer of the navy. It now seems clear that the marriage, at St Dunstan-in-the-East, did not take place until 20 January 1567. This means that their only child, Sir Richard *Hawkins (c.1560–1622), may have been born to John and Katherine before they got married, only to be legitimated by their subsequent union. Since Richard later spoke affectionately of Katherine, this would seem more likely than the view that he was Hawkins's illegitimate son by a mistress or an unrecognized earlier Catholic marriage. It is unclear whether Richard is synonymous with the base-born son of Hawkins who allegedly captained a pinnace involved in Drake's 1587 Cadiz expedition. Hawkins's move from Plymouth resulted in the winding up of his formal partnership with his brother, from which he emerged with £10,000; but he kept his properties there, maintained many of his ships in the port, and he and his brother continued to invest in each other's undertakings.

By 1561 Hawkins had made several voyages to the Canary Islands. There he became known as an honest trader, and from the friends he made he heard about the possibilities of trading slaves, garnered on the coast of Guinea, with the Spanish Caribbean colonies. He received promises of help to enter this trade, not least from the influential Pedro de Ponte, a scion of one of the great Canarian families. Such ventures would require more powerful backing than Plymouth could provide: hence the move to London.

The first voyage, 1562–1563 Hawkins received support for a first, exploratory voyage from a syndicate that included his father-in-law, Gonson, Sir William Winter, surveyor of the navy and master of the ordnance, and two leading city merchants, Sir Lionel Ducket and Sir Thomas Lodge. These men had all been active in the Guinea gold trade, which lately had become less attractive; Hawkins's slaving voyage provided a tempting alternative for further profit.

Sailing in October 1562, in at least 3 small ships totalling 260 tons and with 100 men from Plymouth, Hawkins picked up an experienced Caribbean pilot at Tenerife, and by the end of the year reached the Guinea coast, which he followed as far south as Sierra Leone. The account in Hakluyt, provided by Hawkins a quarter of a century later, says that he captured at least 300 African slaves. Hakluyt ignores Portuguese allegations that Hawkins took 6 of their ships. These may in part have been reports by local factors afraid of punishment for trading with interlopers; but Hawkins certainly used the largest ship to help transport his slaves across the Atlantic. On reaching Hispaniola, where de Ponte had already confirmed he and his cargo would be welcome, he avoided the seat of government at San Domingo, and disposed of his English merchandise and slaves, without violence, at the small north coast ports of Isabella (25 April 1563), Puerto de Plata, and Monte Christi, which were poorly served by official shipping. Hawkins was careful to appear as a peaceful trader rather than a pirate: he paid the correct customs dues to collusively participating local officials, from whom he secured written permissions to trade and certificates of fair dealing. He combated the dearth of coined money in the Indies by exchanging his goods for bills drawn on Seville, or bartering them for small quantities of gold, ginger, sugar, pearls, and—the bulk of his homeward cargo—hides.

In addition to his own ships, Hawkins chartered a vessel locally and, possibly angling for an official *asiento* to supply slaves, sent it, with part of his new cargo, to Hugh Tipton, one of the most important English merchants at Seville, headquarters of the Spanish colonial administration. There the goods were confiscated as contraband, Tipton was arrested, and Spanish officials in the Caribbean were forbidden to trade with English interlopers. The Portuguese ship he also sent to Seville, under its Portuguese captain and crew; but it sailed to Lisbon, where its cargo was seized by the farmers of the Guinea trade. With the rest of his ships Hawkins reached England in August 1563 and, on hearing of the seizure at Seville, he went to London, and by 8 September had persuaded the government to take up his case. But although the queen wrote to Sir Thomas Chaloner, her ambassador in Spain, and to Philip II himself, Hawkins's cargo remained confiscated; he had no redress either on the Portuguese cargo. Although Hawkins claimed that the two seizures had cost him £20,000, the voyage still paid a handsome dividend.

Hawkins had travelled to and traded with the Spanish Caribbean colonies without the requisite licences, carrying goods not previously declared at Seville. He may have thought that the Anglo-Spanish commercial treaty of 1489 (which allowed English trade to the Canary Islands) would extend to territories 'beyond the line' discovered since that date; or that Philip would grant him privileged access to the Indies because of his past services, and as a potential aid against French, mainly Calvinist, freebooters who were sacking Spanish West Indian ports. But he had clearly contravened declared Spanish and Portuguese monopolies, and he should not have been too surprised at the confiscations, given a deteriorating Anglo-Spanish alliance and Spanish concern at Elizabeth's alleged patronage of a projected French colony in Florida. What he had done was to prove the possibility of extending the long-established English triangular trade via Guinea to Brazil—in which his father had taken a pioneering role thirty years earlier—to a new, and readily available commodity, namely African slaves, and to a new Caribbean destination, where Spanish colonists welcomed slaves as an important constituent element in their internal economy—a valuable, harder-working, and longer-living antidote to the chronic wastage of the aboriginal population, and furnished more cheaply than their own compatriots managed via Seville.

The second voyage, 1564–1565 By the time of Hawkins's second slaving voyage, a semi-official venture, Anglo-Spanish relations had further deteriorated. The investing syndicate was joined by three privy councillors: Robert Dudley (earl of Leicester from the summer of 1564), the earl of Pembroke, and Lord Clinton, the lord admiral. William Cecil did not invest in the voyage, but he had a clear supervisory role. Hawkins, possibly using his connections with the court through west-country gentry like the Carews, managed to get the queen's backing. He was allowed to charter one of the largest ships in her navy, the 700 ton *Jesus of Lubeck*, purchased from the Hanseatic port under Henry VIII (but now riddled with dry rot), and to sail under the royal standard. Williamson suggests that this voyage had a more overtly political motive: to examine the newly planted French colony in Florida, which clearly threatened Spanish Caribbean hegemony, and to rebuild the moribund Anglo-Spanish alliance by helping to defend their colonies against the French—a task seemingly beyond Spanish capacity—in return for privileged access to colonial trade, possibly even a slaving monopoly on the lines of Spanish arrangements with the Genoese. But Andrews denies that, once in the Caribbean, Hawkins made more than vague and insincere promises to aid Philip, and these merely to show goodwill to the colonists for trading purposes: 'There is no evidence that he meant to serve the king of Spain in any other way than by doing business with his subjects' (Andrews, *Trade, Plunder and Settlement*, 120). De Silva, the Spanish ambassador in London, clearly voiced his government's opposition to the voyage, but his protests were ignored.

In addition to the *Jesus*, Hawkins took 3 of his own, Plymouth-based, ships, totalling 220 tons. For a combined tonnage of 920, he used a crew of only 150. This use of only 1 sailor for 6 tons reduced overcrowding and meant that he lost no more than a dozen men from sickness on the whole voyage. Hawkins sailed from Plymouth on 18 October 1564. Off north-west Spain a head wind delayed him for five days, and there he issued his famous orders to the crews: 'Serve God daily, love one another, preserve your victuals, beware of fire and keep good company' (Williamson, 71)—the last an instruction to sail close together. Hawkins secured over 400 slaves on the coast of Sierra Leone, partly from the Portuguese, partly by direct seizure, but he lost 7 men while seeking gold at Bymba (27 December). Leaving the African coast on 29 January 1565, he reached Borburata in Venezuela (3 April) where, to marry the colonists' wish to trade and a trade ban imposed by the *audiencia* at San Domingo, he was induced into the charade of a threat of force to protect the governor, Bernaldez, which turned into a more serious incident, to achieve satisfactory trading terms. After lading a cargo of hides at Curaçao, which he left on 15 May, Hawkins traded profitably at Rio de la Hacha, after again using force to dictate slave prices. Here he offloaded 300 negroes, wine,

flour, biscuit, cloth, linen, and ready-made clothing. So successful was his stay, that he even took orders for slaves and other goods to be furnished on a subsequent voyage. Hawkins was paid in gold and silver nuggets, and worked precious metals, so that he had room for a further consignment of hides, which he hoped to acquire on Hispaniola. Unfortunately the Caribbean currents carried him west of Jamaica, and he failed to land at Havana; on reaching Florida (July) he found René de Laudonnière's French colony at Fort Caroline (established in June 1564) in the direst straits. His aid to the French sits uneasily with Williamson's view that he aimed to help Philip clear the Caribbean of French privateers. They refused his offer of a passage home, but he sold them his smallest ship, shoes, beans, and meal. Now low on victuals for the voyage home, Hawkins late in August caught and purchased cod off Newfoundland, and arrived back at Padstow, Cornwall, on 20 September, having lost only 20 men overall.

The voyage had clearly yielded a good profit: de Silva reported it to have been 60 per cent. Hawkins also brought back the sweet potato; tobacco, at first used as a fumigant and narcotic; and a detailed and encouraging report of Florida's potential value as a site for permanent self-sufficient settlement. In celebration the queen granted Hawkins a coat of arms: the crest, a demi-Moor proper bound in a cord, was a direct reference to his slaving activity. Over the next six months, in two meetings with de Silva, Hawkins seems to have discussed the possibility of aiding Philip II against the Turks in the Mediterranean with armed ships; the king did not take up the idea. Indeed Philip's intentions in the Caribbean were made perfectly clear. Only weeks after Hawkins's visit, the French colony in Florida was brutally destroyed (Hawkins had been fortunate to avoid the avenging Spanish fleet), and the governor of Borburata was sent back to Spain as a prisoner. At the ambassador's request, Hawkins signed a bond promising not to trade again in the Spanish West Indies.

The third voyage, 1567–1569 In summer and autumn 1566 four ships owned by the Hawkins brothers were fitted out at Plymouth for another slaving expedition to the Spanish main. After further charades with the privy council over their destination, to satisfy Spanish protests Hawkins was barred from going (31 October 1566). But from spring 1567 he was involved in preparing for his largest and most momentous voyage, which had more the appearance of a national undertaking, possibly a veiled threat by the queen to increasingly menacing Spanish pressure in north-west Europe. She was again a shareholder, supplying the still-rotten *Jesus*, and an even older 300 ton vessel, the *Minion*, built in 1536. No list of the new syndicate survives, but Winter and Clinton were involved and the whole scheme was again masterminded by Cecil. Using the fiction that the ships were bound merely for the African coast to exact reparation for previous injury, the promoters fooled de Silva by alleging they were also to investigate vague claims of the existence in Africa, unoccupied by Portugal, of a rich goldmine, surrounded by fertile, dye-wood producing land; these were being peddled in

England by two renegade Portuguese, Luis and Homem, who were supposed to sail with Hawkins. De Silva was given renewed assurances after he discovered that the ships being loaded at Chatham contained beans, the staple food for slaves on the middle passage, and fine cloths and linens, suitable for Spanish planters.

To the queen's ships were added 4 owned by Hawkins and his brother, together 333 tons; the crew totalled 408, 1 man to 3¼ tons, almost double the proportion of Hawkins's second voyage. By the end of July the ships had assembled in the deep anchorage of the Cattewater, at Plymouth. A month later an armed Spanish squadron under the Flemish admiral de Wathen, allegedly driven into the harbour by bad weather while waiting to escort Philip II to the Netherlands, but possibly also aiming to delay the expedition, refused to dip its flags—a clear sign of hostile intent. Hawkins opened fire to enforce the salute, an action for which he was publicly reproved by the government, after Spanish protests. On 16 September Luis and Homem disappeared from Plymouth, so demonstrating their imposture. Hawkins easily persuaded the government to approve conversion of the expedition into the slaving voyage he had probably always meant it to be.

Hawkins set sail on 2 October 1567. Despite a severe gale north of Finisterre, which scattered his ships and destroyed some of their boats, they were able to rendezvous at Santa Cruz, in Tenerife, where Hawkins was wounded above the eye in a fracas with Edmund Dudley, and managed to anticipate hostile Spanish fire from the guns of the fort. On the African coast he took an abandoned Portuguese caravel, bought another, and was joined by two French ships, which helped to replenish his stock of boats, needed to enter the various rivers for slaving. But Hawkins found slaves hard to come by, and the Portuguese factors unwilling to trade. Near Cape Verde he was wounded by a poisoned arrow when trying to surprise a native village; the antidote of a clove of garlic allegedly saved him. It took a joint attack, with the local king, on the town of Conga in Sierra Leone to bring his slave numbers up to over 500, though he had lost at least 17 men in their capture. Hawkins sailed west on 7 February 1568, and after a lengthy seven-week crossing spent nine days in friendly trading at Margarita, followed by two months at Borburata. But early in June, at Rio de la Hacha, the truculent governor, after Drake had shot up his house, forced Hawkins to take the town by direct assault before trading took place. After a further revictualling stop at Santa Marta (10 July) Hawkins did not attempt an attack on the heavily fortified Cartagena, and, reducing his ships to 8, turned for home (24 July) as the hurricane season set in. After the *William and John* became detached (and made her own way home), Hawkins was determined not to lose the *Jesus*, by now a floating, worm-eaten wreck, through whose gaping holes fish swam among the ballast.

Hawkins put in to San Juan d'Uloa, on the Mexican coast, for repairs (16 September), hoping to sail away before the Spanish plate fleet arrived to transport the year's silver output at the end of the month. The Spaniards, believing Hawkins's ships to be the plate fleet, made

no resistance, and he occupied a low, 240 yard island 500 yards off the shore as a safeguard during refitting. Unfortunately the plate fleet arrived the next day: it contained Don Martin Enriquez, the new viceroy of Mexico, who resented the presence of a heretic corsair on the threshold of his dominion. After being allowed to enter the harbour he took on board, by night, 120 soldiers acquired from Vera Cruz, and at 10 a.m. on 23 September began a six-hour battle. The Spanish soon captured the island, and although Hawkins sank 3 Spanish ships, only the *Minion* and the *Judith*, commanded by Francis Drake, escaped. Hawkins managed to transfer most of his treasure from the stricken *Jesus* to the *Minion* before fire-ships increased the English panic. Next morning the *Judith*, with most of the stores, had vanished; in Hawkins's words, it 'forsook us in our great misery' (Williamson, 145). It made its own way back to England, but to this day it is unclear why Drake deserted his commander.

Hawkins, having lost about 90 of his 320 surviving men at San Juan d'Uloa—about 30 of them being taken prisoner to Spain aboard the *flota*—was left with about 200 men on the badly leaking and unvictualled *Minion*, reduced to stewing oxhides and eating rats and parrots. After a fortnight battling against contrary winds, Hawkins landed 96 in the Gulf of Mexico, north of the area of Spanish settlement, giving each man cloth for barter. Most were captured by the Spaniards and later tried by the Mexican Inquisition: only 4 are known to have reached England. On 16 October Hawkins sailed for home. After a protracted Atlantic passage, on which many more died, he reached the port of Vigo on 31 December, there losing perhaps a further 45 crew through their devouring an excess of red meat. He reached Mount's Bay in Cornwall on 25 January 1569, with perhaps 15 survivors, and wrote to the queen, 'All is lost, save only honour' (Rowse, 381). His brother dispatched from Plymouth a fresh crew to bring the *Minion* home. Although the voyage had been a disaster, it was not a financial failure: admiralty court records confirm that nearly all the treasure—gold, silver, and pearls—arrived safely. The Spanish actions at San Juan d'Uloa were not forgotten for generations: English slaving voyages ceased, but were replaced by open attacks on Spanish cities and treasure ships.

1569–1577 Early in February 1569 Hawkins proceeded to London, where he published a brief pamphlet on his third voyage, and he and his syndicate opened proceedings against Spain in the admiralty court. The damage suffered in Mexico, allegedly over £25,000, was clearly outside the court's jurisdiction; what Hawkins wanted was leave to make reprisals—which he failed to get. He was probably the commander of a 60-strong fleet which between April and July went to land supplies and English volunteers at the French Huguenot stronghold of La Rochelle, and returned with a cargo of wine, prize goods, and church bells. From mid-1569 to February 1570 there is no evidence of Hawkins's presence in England: Spanish sources reported him to have been seen off Cape St Vincent and near Tenerife, supposedly on his way to rescue the men he had left behind in Mexico. In February 1570 he was certainly in England, since he received a commission to impress men for his *New Bark*—to be employed on an unspecified service to the queen. At the end of April he helped escort the Merchant Adventurers' fleet to Hamburg. He pressed Philip II's ambassador, de Spes, to intercede for the release of the survivors of his third voyage, who were languishing in dungeons at Seville. Hawkins was also meditating capture of Spain's homeward-bound plate fleets off the Azores (August 1570), employing a fighting squadron of 10–12 ships he had established at Plymouth, 'the first appearance of a western squadron in the plan of national defence' (Williamson, 174). But the government forbade Hawkins to leave the English coast: the papal bull excommunicating the queen had been issued in February, and in the summer Alva threateningly sailed from the Netherlands down the channel with a fleet of 90 ships. By the time he had left English waters it was too late to attack the plate fleets.

In March 1571, as part of the government's web of counter-espionage, Hawkins offered de Spes, obviously with Cecil's connivance, the services of his Plymouth fleet to further Spanish designs, especially the enthronement of Mary, queen of Scots (a captive in England since 1568), and the restoration of Catholicism. In return for the release of the English captives in Spain (which did occur) he was to take his fleet to the Netherlands, so leaving the west of England unprotected against assault, and help facilitate an invasion of England by Alva's troops. Using as an intermediary George Fitzwilliam, one of Hawkins's former shipmates imprisoned at Seville, but released earlier, probably because of his kinship to Jane Dormer, the English wife of the duke of Feria, Hawkins received the endorsement of Mary, queen of Scots, and details from Feria, in invisible ink, of the Ridolfi plot. Philip made Hawkins a Spanish noble, pardoned him for his Caribbean offences, and promised to pay for the upkeep of 16 ships and 1600 men for two months (September–October). Hawkins passed all his information on to Cecil, and after the duke of Norfolk, the main English conspirator, was put in the Tower (7 September), and Mary's ambassador, the bishop of Ross, confessed everything, there was no insurrection and Philip dropped his invasion plans. De Spes was expelled from England (January 1572), carrying with him a cipher from Hawkins, by which they could continue to communicate.

By spring 1572 England was growing closer to France, and Hawkins was involved in March in the pressure to clear out from the ports of south-east England the mainly Dutch privateers who damaged French trade. In the summer he was prepared to lead a contingent of English volunteers to aid William of Orange and Louis of Nassau in an invasion of the Netherlands to expel the Spanish—but he was stopped by the privy council. The massacre of St Bartholomew (August) caused the end of the invasion plans, and Hawkins and his brother helped instead to equip an English expedition which failed to relieve La Rochelle. Between 1569 and 1573 they were involved in various expeditions for trade and reprisal, financed and equipped in London, fitted out, manned, and managed from Plymouth, which the Hawkinses made 'an ocean port, a naval base, a privateers' mart, the western bastion of England's defences' (Williamson, 196). From 1571 to 1581 Hawkins was MP for Plymouth; in February 1576 he sat on a committee concerned with ports. On 11 October 1573 he narrowly avoided death in London. While riding near Temple Bar with Sir William Winter, he was stabbed by Peter Burchet, a puritan fanatic of unsound mind, who confused Hawkins with Sir Christopher Hatton, possibly because of the fine clothes Hawkins habitually wore. For some days his recovery was uncertain.

Throughout the 1570s details of merchantmen owned by Hawkins and his brother occasionally reveal themselves: in 1575 and 1576 two of their ships freighted currants to England from Zante and Cephalonia; in 1577 four were chartered to ship alum from Civitavecchia. On one occasion the underwriters challenged Hawkins's collusive activities with Huguenot privateers at Plymouth. In 1577 he invested £500 in Drake's voyage of circumnavigation, and he was vice-admiral of the squadron sent to patrol the Irish coast against the threatened invasion of Thomas Stucley.

Treasurer of the navy On 18 November 1577 Hawkins, having acquired the reversion some years previously, succeeded to the office of treasurer of the navy, at first jointly with his father-in-law, Gonson (who died ten days later). His appointment was clearly engineered by Burghley, who, as lord treasurer (from 1572), supervised naval administration. Hawkins's influence on the navy board, probably through Gonson, seems to have antedated his formal appointment, after which he became the dominant figure, presiding over its affairs. The old orthodoxy, led by Williamson, that Hawkins, disgusted with the performance of the high-castled *Jesus* in the Caribbean (but impressed with her devastating firepower), spearheaded a change in naval design to favour low-built warships, better for oceanic voyages, almost solidified into fact. But, although he may well have persuaded the admiralty to accept such designs, he did not invent the 'galleon': its design indeed derived from the galleasses of Henry VIII's reign. 'Accumulated experience rather than the inspiration of any one man tilted the balance of opinion within the naval hierarchy' (Quinn and Ryan, 66). The 300 ton *Foresight* had been built on the new lines as early as 1570, and the *Revenge*, prototype for later battleships, in 1575. Overall, much more credit should be given to Sir William Winter, who made the ships into floating gun platforms, gradually replacing the demi-cannon with the more accurate, longer-range culverin, and to the royal shipwrights, Peter Pett, Matthew Baker, and Richard Chapman. Hawkins, the only member of the navy board who had actually sailed outside Europe, did arguably produce the overall drive which ensured that by 1588 two-thirds of the queen's ships had been built or rebuilt to the new design, so making them more adept at operating on the high seas.

The majestic, but unwieldy, old carracks, with top-heavy castles at bow and stern, floating fortresses mainly useful in close fighting, and prone to unfortunate stresses and strains, were replaced by streamlined galleons, with proportion of beam to length on the water line of about 1:3½, and lower poop and forecastle. This, together with a more efficient sail plan, increased their speed and manoeuvrability, caused them to roll less in heavy weather, and, with their armament increased, greater use could be made of the gun-ports on the lower decks in fighting at long range. After his experiences in the tropics Hawkins introduced the double skin method of ship construction, with horsehair between the planking, to keep out woodboring beetles. In the ships' interior economy, he encouraged a ratio of 1 man to 2 tons rather than 1:1½, so reducing victual consumption, and prolonging the time a fleet could stay at sea to four, even six months. He also increased the basic pay for ordinary seamen by a third to 10s. a month, partly to improve the quality of recruits, and ensured that his sailors were properly clad. Williamson regards Hawkins as 'the only captain of his generation recorded to have shown any interest in hygiene' (Williamson, 85). On his own ships he kept live sheep and pigs, carried apples and pears, experimented with 'Brasill beds' (probably hammocks), and, on his final voyage, loaded macaroni and instruments for seventeen musicians.

A report by Hawkins—probably to Burghley, and probably dating from the first half of 1579—lambasted the rampant corruption present in the dockyards whereby over half the queen's naval expenditure and the best materials were finding their way into private hands, 'which proceeds of the wilful covetousness of one man, and to set forth his glory' (Williamson, 252). This was Winter, who appears to have dominated the navy board until Hawkins's arrival and, although he had been a partner in Hawkins's transatlantic voyages, was to be a thorn in the treasurer's side for some time. Hawkins's central proposal was an offer to reduce the combined ordinary charge and repair expenses to £4000 per annum from the £7000 he alleged they had recently been costing. By the so-called 'first bargain' with the crown of 29 September 1579, Hawkins agreed to maintain fleet moorings at Chatham for £1200 per annum. A similar crown agreement with the shipwrights Pett and Baker covered the regular grounding and caulking of ships. The bargain aimed to save the queen from peculators, so implicitly reducing the need for extraordinary warrants. To help protect Chatham, the navy's principal dockyard, from a sudden cross-channel raid, Hawkins reconstructed the fort at Sheerness and laid an iron chain boom across the river at Upnor Castle. At Dover a barrier with sluice gates prevented drifting shingle from choking the harbour entrance, so that even the largest royal ship could enter the port. From c.1582 Hawkins was a JP for Kent.

But Hawkins's activities did arouse opposition, especially from Winter, who had powerful allies on the privy council. Charges that Hawkins was corrupt and his ships unseaworthy peaked at the end of 1582, and were investigated (together with Hawkins's countercharges) by a privy council commission of 1583. Its original report is lost. A

version of 25 January 1584 has recently emerged—possibly a submission to it, or a summary of its findings—which plainly exonerates Hawkins; but since it seems Hawkins was the paper's author, it clearly did not fully resolve the dispute. Hawkins did reduce ordinary naval expenditure to about £4000 per annum, as he had promised in 1579; but only once, in 1583, did he reduce total annual spending on the navy significantly below £10,000, and he never fully avoided reliance on extraordinary warrants. Indeed, total naval expenditure increased from £17,903 in 1585 to £90,813 in 1588. Hawkins was criticized for a lower rate of repair, but he changed the emphasis to rebuilding a single ship annually. His ambitious rolling plan for such repairs (which extended up to 1599) was the basis of the 'second bargain' of June 1585, best viewed as a compromise between Hawkins and his opponents. Winter described it as 'nothing … but cunning and craft to maintain [Hawkins's] pride and ambition' (Quinn and Ryan, 67), but henceforth they seem to have collaborated amicably. Hawkins additionally took over, for a further £1714 per annum, the master shipwrights' responsibility for extraordinary ship-repairs, principally heavy repair activity in dry dock, including payment of wages and provision of the necessary materials and victuals. The second bargain was never effectively implemented, since war with Spain broke out soon after it was signed and Hawkins's orderly plans were overtaken by extensive new shipbuilding, which rendered a regular repair schedule impossible. Six brand-new ships were built (1586–7) and major reforms were made to 13 others, under extraordinary warrants. By December 1587 the queen had 25 fighting ships of 100 tons or above, and 18 ocean-going pinnaces, useful for inshore activity. By the end of 1587 the second bargain had become unworkable, and was terminated, at Hawkins's request; he wished to free himself for the role of commanding the western squadron, based at Plymouth.

The Armada, 1579–1588 As early as August 1579, in a memorandum on an opening naval campaign in the event of war, Hawkins suggested sending such a squadron to capture the *flota* and systematically raid the Spanish Indies to stem Spanish wealth. A more precise memorandum to Burghley of July 1584, as war loomed, suggested an agreement with the Portuguese pretender, Dom Antonio, for Englishmen to fight under his flag alongside Dutch and Huguenot raiders. The aim was to encourage revolt in the Portuguese colonies against Spain, destroy Spanish fishing by attacking the annual Basque fleets to the Newfoundland Banks, sack the Atlantic islands, and keep the coast of Spain under constant alarm, all the while accommodating the queen's aversion to a formal declaration of war, and fighting in a way that was largely self-financing and, for Hawkins, self-enriching (since booty taken would be disposed of in Plymouth). All this would avoid expensive military adventures. In 1586 Hawkins was given command of a squadron which may have been intended for some of these objectives. But the Babington plot, the presence of Guise troops in Normandy, and the realization that Philip's Armada was being constructed, led to the council limiting Hawkins's activities to plying up and down the channel. When, in late summer, he was allowed off the leash, he failed to intercept either the silver fleet or the Portuguese East Indian carracks; but, after cruising along the coasts of Spain and Portugal, he did return home in late October with four minor prizes. It had been a low-key venture, and its primary object may have been support for the Huguenots in La Rochelle rather than the disruption of Spanish commerce. But as Rodger notes, Hawkins had shown that English ships could remain at sea for three months, off an enemy coast, 600 miles from base—a rare feat.

During the wait for the Armada Drake had been put in command at Plymouth, while Hawkins remained at Chatham at the elbow of the lord admiral, Lord Howard of Effingham. In December 1587 Hawkins showed he could fully mobilize the fleet in little more than a fortnight; Howard confirmed to Burghley (21 February 1588) that the ships were in excellent condition. It was early in June 1588 before Hawkins finally joined the assembled fleet at Plymouth. He owned 3 of the ships that fought the Armada and, as rear-admiral and later vice-admiral, he commanded the 800 ton *Victory*, one of the ships he had rebuilt at Deptford. Ranking third in seniority after Howard and Drake, he was a member of the war council. When the fleet spread out towards Ushant, Hawkins commanded the inshore squadron towards the Isles of Scilly. He hotly engaged a group of Spanish ships off Eddystone (21 July), expended much powder and shot off Portland Bill (23rd), and, after commanding one of the four squadrons at the Isle of Wight (25th), he was knighted by the lord admiral on board the *Ark Royal* (26th). The English galleons completely outsailed and outmanoeuvred the clumsy Armada carracks, and decisively outgunned them at their chosen range. Not a single English ship withdrew from the fight through damage by the elements or the enemy, and Hawkins's effective victualling of the fleet allowed it to chase the Armada past the Firth of Forth.

The last years, 1589–1595 Once it was clear that Parma's invasion had been baulked, Hawkins began paying off the sailors and refitting the ships at Chatham. Delays through bad weather and shortage of money made Burghley angry, and he wrote a sharp letter to Hawkins, who complained to Sir Francis Walsingham:

> My pain and misery in this service is infinite … God, I trust, will deliver me of it ere … long, for there is no other hell. I devise to ease charge and shorten what I can … but my Lord Treasurer thinketh I do little.   (Read, *Lord Burghley*, 431)

From 1 January 1589 Hawkins was given a year's leave of absence from the office of navy treasurer to enable him to sort out the muddled accounts left by the Armada campaign. Later in that year he took on the additional navy board role of comptroller. In spring 1589, although he distrusted continental military operations, he and his brother helped to collect supplies for Drake's disorderly and abortive attempt to capture Lisbon.

Hawkins submitted to Burghley (July 1589) a scheme for a 'silver blockade', which he had suggested to Walsingham the previous year. This involved maintaining a continuous patrol of the area between Spain and the Azores, in relays of 6 large ships and 6 pinnaces, with 1800 men, victualled for four months, and partly financed by private adventurers. The aim was to stop the flow of East Indian and American wealth to Spain, so crippling her war machine, as well as assuring handsome profits by way of prizes, and opening the way for further English oceanic enterprises. This influenced Elizabethan strategic thinking, but it is unclear whether Hawkins was right, since the continuity essential to the plan was never realized, even for a single year, and such a commitment would have meant half the Royal Navy being unavailable for home defence. Early in 1590 Hawkins did fit out an expedition in two squadrons: 7 galleons under Sir Martin Frobisher were to sail to the Azores; Hawkins, victualled for six months, was to operate off the Spanish coast with a further 6 ships. The aim was to intercept the Spanish treasure fleet. But the queen, worried by reports of another Spanish armada massing at Corunna, and of Philip's intention to use Brittany as a base for the invasion of England, kept Hawkins in port until late June, when the treasure was safely home, transported in fast frigates (*gallizabras*). He captured some prizes off the Spanish coast, but abandoned his blockade to relieve Frobisher off the Azores, so allowing a Spanish fleet to sail unmolested and occupy Blavet in Brittany. As a result Hawkins was summoned home, and he returned to Plymouth in October. Even such an ineffective blockade certainly disrupted Spanish trade, and persuaded Philip to hold back the main *flota* in Havana that year. Indeed, during the period 1589–91, 236 English privateering vessels, working as individuals rather than a team, took 300 prizes, worth £400,000.

In 1590 Hawkins and Drake took the lead in founding the pioneer scheme of contributory social insurance known as the Chatham chest, a fund used to compensate injured and disabled sailors, pay pensions to the aged, and burial money for the dead—so-called because the 5 per cent deducted from the wages of all seamen on the royal ships was lodged in a large chest. Hawkins also built an almshouse at Chatham (1592) for 12 poor seamen and shipwrights (and their wives), known as Sir John Hawkins' Hospital; it survives today. Hawkins's wife died early in July 1591; soon after he married Margaret (d. 1619), daughter of Charles Vaughan, of Hergest Court, Herefordshire, and a lady of the bedchamber to the queen. They had no children. After Hawkins's death she behaved meanly to her stepson Richard, withholding money which would have ransomed him from Spanish captivity.

After Hawkins's expedition of 1590 the government made no attempt to launch a silver blockade. The fleet was kept at Chatham to prevent a Spanish army landing, while English troops were employed in costly military operations in France and the Netherlands. The fleet was increased by the construction (1590–96) of 16 more ships. In July 1592 and February 1594 Hawkins attempted to resign from the navy board, but was not allowed to do so.

On 12 February 1593 he was awarded £2400 from the plunder of the *Madre de Dios*. In 1594 his son Richard was captured by the Spaniards in Peru; he was not to return to England until 1602.

1595 saw Hawkins, with Drake, embarking on his final expedition, which aimed to follow up John Oxenham's abortive attempt of 1576–7 and land at Nombre de Dios, cross the isthmus, and capture Panama, thereby choking off supplies of Peruvian silver from Spain. It was clearly a mistake to give Hawkins and Drake equal command: they were temperamentally unsuited to co-operation. Hawkins worked with foresight and careful planning; Sir Thomas Gorges reported from Plymouth on 16 July that Hawkins 'sees all things done properly' (Harrison, 1.308). By contrast Drake disliked administration, rarely thought ahead, and was mercurial in his changes of plan. The choice of Hawkins may have represented the influence of the queen, to provide a moderating influence on the impetuous Drake; or it may have been a temporary alliance between competing privateering factions. The two commanders were each to take a third of any booty. The queen, who provided 6 ships, was to receive the rest. By the beginning of March, reports of the preparations had reached Spain; by early in May the ships were in Plymouth, ready to depart, with 2500 men on board (half of them soldiers). But a long delay, for which the queen personally blamed them, allowed a Spanish raid from Brittany (23 July) to burn three Cornish ports. Elizabeth, to the fury of her commanders, frequently changed her mind, ordering them to cruise off the Irish and Spanish coasts—to forestall a further Spanish armada, aimed at Ireland or England—then banned them from sailing at all.

When Hawkins and Drake finally departed, it was only on condition that they returned within six months, to counter the Spanish invasion envisaged in 1596. This was hardly enough time in which to capture Panama, and clearly reduced the expedition to a mere hit-and-run treasure hunt. Before the 27-strong fleet finally left Plymouth on 28 August, with Hawkins in the 660 ton *Garland*, built in 1590, they had learnt that the plate fleet was already in Spain, apart from its bullion-laden but crippled flagship, lying at San Juan, Puerto Rico; this Drake aimed to capture. Since Drake and Hawkins sailed on different ships, often out of communication for days on end, factional disputes were liable to occur. Hawkins agreed only reluctantly to a time-wasting and ultimately abortive diversion to Gran Canaria (27 September) for further victualling of Drake's ships. The delay allowed Philip to send ships to the Caribbean, which captured the *Francis* off Guadeloupe, so discovering the fleet's destination. They then moved to strengthen the defences at Puerto Rico. On 31 October 1595 Hawkins became ill; by 2 November he was unable to leave his bed, and at about 3 p.m. on the 12th he died. He was buried at sea off Puerto Rico.

The fleet returned with a fifth of the complement dead, including Drake, and a pitiful £5000 in booty. 'It represented the nadir of Elizabethan strategy' (Andrews, *Trade, Plunder and Settlement*, 241). Hawkins's will left funds for the poor of London, Deptford, and Plymouth; in a codicil

he left the queen £2000. There was no monument to Hawkins in Plymouth. But his will provided for one to be erected to his memory in the church of St Dunstan-in-the-East, in which parish he had lived for thirty years. This had a long Latin inscription; another, even longer, in English, appeared on a nearby mural tablet. Both perished, along with the church, in the fire of 1666.

Character and achievement The Victorians, judging sixteenth-century morals from the standpoint of Wilberforce, saw Hawkins as primarily the greedy and unscrupulous father of a lucrative English slave trade. Williamson's three, increasingly refined, volumes (1927–69) produced an exhaustive and very readable narrative that embraced Spanish sources and widened the picture to show Hawkins's role as a maritime strategist and naval reformer. But both he and Lewis (a Hawkins descendant), in a rather cloying work of familial piety, portrayed him in roseate hues, at times approaching idolatry. A further corrective has been spearheaded by Andrews, whose lucidly sharp yet temperate writings emphasize the immaturity of Elizabethan sea power and naval strategy, and view Hawkins as a more autocratic figure, whose hands were less clean and heart less pure than Williamson suggests. More recently specialist periodical articles have further clarified Hawkins's role as naval treasurer.

A product of his age, which accepted slaving with an easy mind, Hawkins was probably happier at sea than ashore, and showed a mastery of all aspects of ship-handling. As a commander he enforced strict discipline, but seems to have won affection as well as respect—praying with dying seamen, showing an interest in their families, and less prone to use corporal punishment on shipboard than many of his contemporaries. He was a first-class businessman, and his three slaving voyages demonstrated his robust and opportunistic eye for profit. His drive, method, and relative honesty in an age when public and private funds are difficult to disentangle, helped advance a revolution in English ship design, though his criticism of Winter is not substantiated elsewhere. As a naval strategist, his boldness and imagination paid insufficient attention to the needs of home defence. Hawkins took every chance of personally acquainting himself with politicians and courtiers. His courtesy, charm, and diplomatic finesse could gull Philip II and his ambassadors in England, and caused Castellanos, his adversary at Rio de la Hacha in 1565 and 1568, to be reported as saying, 'No-one talking to him hath any power to deny him anything that he doth request ... not through any villainy ... but because of his great nobility' (Lewis, 107). Once an orthodox Catholic, by degrees his letters developed a puritan ring, so that the queen, on reading his letter to Burghley of 31 October 1590, is alleged to have exclaimed, 'God's death! This fool went out a soldier and has come home a divine' (*DNB*). Overall, if Drake's maritime pyrotechnics have given him a higher historical profile, it was the steadying ballast provided by Hawkins that did more to stiffen the Elizabethan response to the challenge of Spain. Long after his death, when naval administration was ineffective and the condition of the royal ships had noticeably deteriorated, observers looked back at Hawkins's stewardship as a golden age of efficiency and probity. BASIL MORGAN

Sources J. A. Williamson, *Hawkins of Plymouth*, 2nd edn (1969) · K. R. Andrews, *Trade, plunder and settlement* (1984) · D. M. Loades, *The Tudor navy* (1992) · S. Adams, 'New light on the *Reformation* of John Hawkins: the Ellesmere naval survey of January 1584', *EngHR*, 105 (1990), 96–111 · D. B. Quinn and A. N. Ryan, *England's sea empire, 1550–1642* (1983) · N. A. M. Rodger, *The safeguard of the sea: a naval history of Britain*, 1: 660–1649 (1997) · G. Parker, 'The dreadnought revolution of Tudor England', *Mariner's Mirror*, 82 (1996), 269–300 · K. R. Andrews, ed., *The last voyage of Drake and Hawkins* (1972) · M. W. S. Hawkins, *Plymouth Armada heroes* (1888) · M. Lewis, *The Hawkins dynasty* (1969) · R. Unwin, *The defeat of John Hawkins* (1960) · D. W. Waters, 'The Elizabethan navy and the Armada campaign', *Mariner's Mirror*, 35 (1949), 90–138 · R. B. Wernham, 'Elizabethan war aims and strategy', *Elizabethan government and society*, ed. S. T. Bindoff, J. Hurstfield, and C. H. Williams (1961), 340–68 · W. N. Gunson, 'Who was Richard Hawkins?', *Mariner's Mirror*, 80 (1994) · G. Mattingly, *The defeat of the Spanish Armada* (1962) · K. R. Andrews, *Drake's voyages: a re-assessment of their place in Elizabethan maritime expansion* (1967); pbk edn (1970) · HoP, *Commons, 1558–1603* · A. L. Rowse, *Tudor Cornwall: portrait of a society* (1957) · E. Burton, *The Elizabethans at home* (1958); pbk edn (1973) · C. Martin and G. Parker, *The Spanish Armada* (1988) · G. B. Harrison, ed., *The Elizabethan journals*, 2 vols. (1965) · C. Read, *Mr Secretary Cecil and Queen Elizabeth* (1955); pbk edn (1965) · C. Read, *Lord Burghley and Queen Elizabeth* (1960); pbk edn (1965) · M. J. Rodriguez-Salgado and others, *Armada, 1588–1988* (1988) · D. Loades, *The mid-Tudor crisis, 1545–1565* (1992) · J. McDermott, *Martin Frobisher, Elizabethan privateer* (2001) · T. Glasgow, review of J. A. Williamson, *Hawkins of Plymouth*, *Mariner's Mirror*, 56 (1970), 122–3 · *DNB*
Archives Shrops. RRC, account of voyage to the West Indies
Likenesses oils, 1581, NMM · attrib. F. Zuccaro, oils, 1591, Plymouth City Museum and Art Gallery [*see illus.*] · R. Boissard, engraving, *c.*1603, repro. in Holland, *Baziliologia* (1618) · S. de Passe, line engraving, BM, NPG; repro. in Holland, *Herōologia* (1620) · W. and M. van de Passe, line engraving (after unknown artist), BM, NPG · photograph of bas-relief, repro. in Hawkins, *Plymouth Armada heroes*
Wealth at death see Hawkins, *Plymouth Armada heroes*, 72–5

Hawkins, John (*c.*1587–*c.*1641), grammarian and translator, belonged to the old Catholic family of Hawkins from Nash Court, Boughton under Blean, Kent. He was the son of Sir Thomas Hawkins (1548/9–1617), landowner, and his wife, Ann, *née* Pettyt (1551/2–1616). Two of his elder brothers, Sir Thomas *Hawkins and Henry *Hawkins, matriculated at Gloucester Hall, Oxford, in 1591 and 1592 respectively, but did not graduate. John's medical degree was probably obtained at Padua, a popular university with English Catholics; but he is not included in the roll of members of the Royal College of Physicians. He is recorded in the Kent visitation of 1619–21 as doctor in 'physick' in London, and in 1624 he was described by John Gee as 'a popish physition' resident there in Charterhouse Court. He married Frances Power of Bletchingdon, Oxfordshire, and they had a son, Francis *Hawkins, an infant prodigy as a translator, and a Jesuit in adult life.

Hawkins's most important publications were his grammatical writings, since in them he claimed to have introduced to English scholars the works of the great Spanish linguist Nebrissa, whose grammar of Castilian (1492) was the first grammar of any European vernacular to appear in print. Nebrissa also compiled a Latin grammar (1481), part of which was edited and translated by Hawkins as *A Brief Introduction to Syntax … Collected out of Nebrissa* (1631). A third linguistic work by Hawkins was a dictionary of Latin verbs with their derivatives (1634), in an arrangement which he claimed was entirely original. Finally, he composed a treatise on the use of Latin particles (1635).

Hawkins published only one original non-linguistic work, a Latin text on melancholia (*Discursus de melancholia hypochondriaca*, 1633), but he also produced several translations from Italian and Spanish. Their dedications show how greatly he was admired by influential (largely Roman Catholic) friends such as Kenelm Digby and the dramatist James Shirley. Hawkins probably died before being able to see through the press a translation made by his son from the French, *Youths Behaviour* (*c.*1641); he seems never to have been accorded the recognition which he deserved for his pioneering advocacy of Nebrissa.

VIVIAN SALMON

Sources J. A. Boodle, ed., 'Registers of Boughton under Blean', *The Parish Register Society*, 49 (1903) · H. Foley, ed., *Records of the English province of the Society of Jesus*, 4 (1878) · Gillow, *Lit. biog. hist.*, vol. 3 · A. Nebrissa, *A briefe introduction to syntax*, ed. and trans. J. Hawkins (1631) · F. Hawkins, *Youths behaviour* [n.d., *c.*1641] · J. J. Howard and G. J. Armytage, eds., 'The visitation of London in the year 1568', *Harleian Society Publications*, 1 (1869) · W. B. Bannerman, 'The visitations of Kent … in 1574 and 1592', *Harleian Society Publications*, 75/2 (1898) · R. Hovenden, ed., 'The visitation of Kent … 1619–1621', *Harleian Society Publications*, 42 (1898) · J. Gee, *The foot out of the snare* (1624) · Munk, *Roll*

Hawkins, Sir John (1719–1789), music scholar and lawyer, was born on 29 March 1719 at Green Dragon Court, Cow Lane, London, the only surviving son of John Hawkins (1691–1771) and his wife, Elizabeth (*bap.* 1686, *d.* 1760), daughter of Thomas Gwatkin of Fownhope, Herefordshire. Nothing further is known about his paternal relatives: though family tradition claimed descent from the English admiral Sir John Hawkins (*c.*1520–1595), no surviving evidence substantiates the claim. The memoirs of Laetitia-Matilda *Hawkins, only daughter of the present subject, further suggest that the family was upwardly mobile from her grandfather's time, but in fact it seems unlikely that the subject's father was anything more than a carpenter.

Hawkins originally studied architecture with Edward Hoppus, but in 1737 he exchanged this for the law on the advice of his cousin Thomas Gwatkin. Hawkins was successfully examined for an attorney in November 1742. He may have realized that legal studies alone would not fit him with the profile of a true gentleman that he apparently craved, so he also made time during his apprenticeship to study the arts. He began to write pieces for the *Gentleman's Magazine*, the first being published in March 1739. Edward Cave, the magazine's editor, knew Samuel Johnson, and it seems likely that he introduced the two men, initiating an acquaintance which lasted until Johnson's death. Thus Hawkins became one of only nine founder members of Johnson's Ivy Lane Club in 1749, and of his literary club in April 1764. He contributed notes to Johnson's edition of Shakespeare (1765), and with Sir Joshua Reynolds and William Scott he was an executor of

Johnson's will. His edition of Johnson's works and his *Life of Samuel Johnson*, the first substantial biography to appear, were published in 1787.

From the 1740s Hawkins was active in musical circles, numbering John Stanley, William Boyce, and even Handel among his acquaintances. Late in 1741 he sent a text, 'In vain Philander at my feet', to Boyce, who subsequently set it to music. In 1742 he collaborated with Stanley on six cantatas, contributing texts for five of them. Finding their work successful at the London pleasure gardens, the two men promptly produced a further six. In spite of his musical leanings there is no evidence that Hawkins himself composed music; and while he surely must have been able to play an instrument, no definitive data on this matter survive, Busby noting only (Busby, 1.157) that he played a 'variety of instruments' to a high level. At some time between 1743 and 1748 Hawkins became a member of the Academy of Ancient Music, in whose support he wrote a history in 1770; and in 1748 he was accepted for membership of the Madrigal Society, of which he remained a member until March 1765. Through the brewer Richard Hare he met the attorney Peter Storer, whose second daughter, Sidney (1726–1793), he married on 24 March 1753: this circumstance, unusual because it was conventionally the bride rather than the groom who was expected to marry to advantage, brought him a dowry of £10,000. This enabled him to move from lodgings to a house of his own in Austin Friars, near Broad Street, London. He hosted fortnightly concerts at this residence, attended by some distinguished musicians. A further upturn in his affairs occurred in August 1759, upon the death of his brother-in-law Peter Storer: Storer's legacy enabled Hawkins, his wife, and his son John Sidney to move to Twickenham House, Middlesex, which they used as a 'country' residence until 1771. The house apparently included a circular room that Hawkins used for concerts (R. S. Cobbett, *Memorials of Twickenham: Parochial and Topographical*, 1872, 347). For a town house they leased a property in Hatton Garden. Most importantly for Hawkins's later literary activities, his new wealth made it possible to abandon his solicitor's practice.

Three further opportunities now presented themselves. Hawkins's interest in fishing led to his publishing the first of several editions of Izaac Walton's *Compleat Angler* in summer 1760. Second, and according to Laetitia-Matilda at the suggestion of Horace Walpole (L.-M. Hawkins, *Anecdotes*, 101), he began thinking seriously about writing a history of music. And third, in 1761 he became a Middlesex magistrate, a position he improved upon in 1765 when elected chairman of the Middlesex quarter sessions, which office he occupied until February 1781. This promotion was probably partly due to two legal publications: his *Observations on the State of the Highways* (1763), subsequently made into law; and a plea for the inhabitants of Middlesex to be relieved of the financial burden of rebuilding Newgate prison. As magistrate he also had to deal with riots at Brentford in 1768 and with an uprising of weavers at Moorfields in 1769, partly in consequence of which he was knighted in October 1772. The first half of the 1770s was mostly spent writing and researching his music history, which he appears to have produced at the rate of one volume per year from 1771. The whole work, in five volumes, was available from November 1776 under the title *A General History of the Science and Practice of Music*, and was the first extended treatment of its subject to appear in English. For assistance with its compilation Hawkins twice visited the musical antiquarian William Gostling at Canterbury to collect musical reminiscences (upon Gostling's death Hawkins penned some appreciative verses, set to music by Boyce). In 1772 he visited several Oxford libraries, taking with him an engraver to make copies of portraits in the university's music school. Hawkins's history appeared several months after volume 1 of the *General History of Music* of Charles Burney, and although Burney's final (fourth) volume was not published until 1789, his history was preferred to that of Hawkins in its day. Hawkins was attacked on several fronts, the chief criticisms of his work being that he, not being a trained musician, was being presumptuous in writing a history of the subject; and that his writing style was pompous and its writer too readily inclined to digress at length on subjects not strictly relevant to his narrative. George Steevens, who after early good relations with Hawkins had transferred his allegiance to Burney, has been credited with trying to spike sales of Hawkins's book (Nichols, *Illustrations*, 5.428); while Davis (*A Proof of Eminence*, 134) suggests that Burney and the actor David Garrick may deliberately have tried to sabotage Hawkins's work by contributing several critical articles to London's *Morning Post* early in 1777. The nineteenth century regarded Hawkins more highly, probably because his work, while not perhaps as entertaining as Burney's (Hawkins was an antiquary who preferred the music of an earlier age, while Burney was at his best when commenting on his own century), is factually very accurate. As a consequence, when a decision came to be taken on a new edition, it was Hawkins's history, not Burney's, that was favoured, a second edition appearing in 1853, and a third in 1875.

Following three attempted burglaries at his Hatton Garden house in November 1777, Hawkins and his family moved to Westminster, where he spent the remainder of his life. His literary work now confined itself to antiquarian topics, and to occasional pieces such as the appreciation of Boyce provided as a preface to the 1788 edition of Boyce's anthology *Cathedral Music*. In November 1784 Hawkins took instructions from Johnson regarding his will. Several people criticized Hawkins's performance as an executor, Edmond Malone accusing him of stealing some of Johnson's property and others claiming that he was parsimonious over Johnson's funeral. Various accounts survive of how Hawkins subsequently came to be asked to write a biography of Johnson: Laetitia-Matilda (L.-M. Hawkins, *Memoirs*, 1.155) states that Johnson himself entrusted it to Hawkins, and that this was backed up by Hawkins being commissioned by a consortium of London booksellers. James Boswell, whose own life of Johnson appeared in 1791, and George Steevens (Hawkins's old enemy) attempted to discredit Hawkins's biography, Boswell suggesting that it was inaccurate, wordy, prone to digression, and of a 'dark uncharitable cast' (J. Boswell, *The Life of Samuel Johnson*, 1791, introduction). Even Laetitia-Matilda preferred Boswell's book, declaring it 'entertaining to a degree that makes my father's appear stiff, cold, and turgid' (L.-M. Hawkins, *Memoirs*, 1.230).

In May 1789, feeling unwell, Hawkins took the waters at Islington. On 14 May he was 'seized with a paralytic affliction' (probably meaning a stroke), and following a further attack he died at Broad Sanctuary, Westminster, about 2 a.m. on 21 May. He was buried in Westminster Abbey on 28 May under a stone that, on his own instructions, carried only his initials, date of birth, and age. He left three children: John Sidney *Hawkins and Laetitia-Matilda, already mentioned, and Henry. Two daughters, both named Charlotte, born in 1755 and 1763, died in infancy. His estate included several thousand pounds' worth of stocks, plus significant quantities of land in the London area.

Forming an accurate character sketch of Hawkins is difficult, because most surviving accounts are affected, in one way or another, by partiality. He himself left few autobiographical details, most of them in his history of music or *Life of Samuel Johnson*. His daughter, if occasionally mildly critical, tends in general to cast him favourably, though having been born when Hawkins was in his forties she would surely have been unable to make objective judgements of her parent until he was in his fifties. The account in the *New and General Biographical Dictionary* (1798), largely repeated in Chalmers's *New Biographical Dictionary* (1814), was compiled 'from information communicated by the family'; and the 'Life of Sir John Hawkins, compiled from original sources' that prefaces the second and third editions of Hawkins's musical history seems likewise to rely on the family. The 1853 life notes that:

> while few persons have been, both during life and after death, so rancorously attacked as Sir John Hawkins, none have come out of an ordeal so severe as that to which his reputation has been exposed, more thoroughly than he has done.

Madame D'Arblay (Fanny Burney) reported in her *Diary* (p. 66) Johnson's opinion that Hawkins 'was an honest man at bottom, but it must be owned that he had a degree of brutality and a tendency to savageness which cannot easily be defended', a blow followed up by Johnson's criticism that Hawkins was a most 'unclubbable' man. He seems to have been viewed by his Twickenham neighbours as a mixed blessing, his usefulness over Newgate prison and the state of English highways being overshadowed by a litigious nature that initiated petty disputes at those neighbours' expense. Walpole, a critic of Hawkins the lawyer, wrote that 'he grew hated by the lower class, and very troublesome to the gentry, with whom he went to law on both private and public causes' (H. Walpole, *Last Journals*, ed. A. F. Stuart, 1910, 2.399). His death went largely unremarked by the press. Twentieth-century commentators were more sympathetic, with historical research by Percy Scholes and especially by Bertram H. Davis removing much of the

misrepresentation, some of it surely politically motivated, that affected Hawkins during his lifetime. Davis views him as an over-proud man whose virtues outnumbered his vices (Davis, *A Proof of Eminence*, 373). Clarence Miller noted that 'There has been written into the [history] books an anthology of abuse of Sir John Hawkins such as no other man of his era has had to overcome in order to stand before the world with his accomplishments recognized', and that 'everybody, except his devoted daughter, has concentrated on his minor human weaknesses to the prejudice of his really good qualities' (Miller, 2).

The only portrait of Hawkins ever painted is now in the faculty of music of Oxford University. It is by James Roberts, and was probably presented to the university in 1788. According to Hawkins's daughter (L.-M. Hawkins, *Anecdotes*, 137) it was Dr Philip Hayes, at that time professor of music in the school of music, who persuaded him to have it painted, in 1786. She also reports that the family did not like the image. An engraved copy of the portrait appeared in the supplementary volume of portraits appended to the second and third editions of Hawkins's history of music.

JOHN WAGSTAFF

Sources B. H. Davis, *A proof of eminence: the life of Sir John Hawkins* (1973) · L.-M. Hawkins, *Anecdotes, biographical sketches, and memoirs* (1822) · L.-M. Hawkins, *Memoirs, anecdotes, facts and opinions*, 2 vols. (1824) · P. Scholes, *The life and activities of Sir John Hawkins* (1953) · 'Hawkins, Sir John', *A new and general biographical dictionary*, ed. W. Tooke (1798) · 'Life of Sir John Hawkins, compiled from original sources', J. Hawkins, *A general history of the science and practice of music*, new edn, 1 (1853), iii–xii · B. H. Davis, *Johnson before Boswell: a study of Sir John Hawkins's Life of Samuel Johnson* (1960) · J. Hawkins, *The life of Samuel Johnson, LL.D*, ed. B. H. Davis (New York, 1961) · C. A. Miller, *Sir John Hawkins, Dr Johnson's friend—attorney—executor—biographer: a reorientation of the knight, the lady and Boswell* (privately printed, Washington, DC, 1951) · *Diary and letters of Madame D'Arblay*, ed. [C. Barrett], 7 vols. (1842–6) · T. Busby, *Concert room and orchestra anecdotes of music and musicians, ancient and modern*, 3 vols. (1825) · J. Prior, *Life of Edmond Malone, editor of Shakespeare* (1860) · Nichols, *Illustrations* · E. B. V. Christian, *Leaves of the lower branch: the attorney in life and letters* (1909)

Archives Harvard U., Houghton L., notebook | BL, memoir of Diogenio Bigalia, Add. MS 15516

Likenesses silhouette, c.1781, NPG · J. Roberts, oils, 1786, U. Oxf., faculty of music

Wealth at death £3755 9s. 0d. in capital bonds; £1000 bank stock; land in London area: Davis, *Proof of eminence*

Hawkins, John (1761–1841), traveller and geologist, was born on 6 May 1761 at Trewithen, Probus, Cornwall, the fourth and youngest son of Thomas Hawkins (1724?–1766), MP for Grampound from 1747 to 1754, and his wife, Anne, daughter of James Heywood, of Austin Friars, London, a merchant. He was educated at Helston School, Winchester College (1775–7), and Trinity College, Cambridge, whence he matriculated in 1778 and graduated BA in 1782.

The family's Cornish estates included much mining property. Hawkins's first interests were in mineralogy and about 1780 he took lessons from Rudolf Eric Raspe (1737–1794), a German-born geologist whom he helped bring to Cornwall. Hawkins originally intended to follow family tradition and enter the law and he was admitted at

Lincoln's Inn in June 1782. But, being a man of considerable property, he instead decided to travel and went first to Germany, inspired by Raspe. In 1786 he became the first English student to attend the Freiberg Bergakademie under Abraham Werner, where he studied mining and became a Neptunian geologist. He then studied mineralogy in Berlin under Martin Heinrich Klaproth (1743–1817), who acknowledged Hawkins's help in providing mineral specimens and analyses for his *Observations Relative to the Mineralogical and Chemical History of the Fossils of Cornwall* (1787).

Throughout 1787 and 1788 Hawkins travelled in Austria, Hungary, Greece, Turkey, and Italy. At Constantinople towards the end of a journey from Vienna via the Hungarian mines through the Balkans, and after a first visit to Crete, he joined the botanist Dr John Sibthorp (1758–1796) and the army captain (and later Wernerian geologist) Ninian Imrie (*c*.1752–1820). Together they toured the Greek islands, inspired again by Raspe, who had described Thira after it was raised from the sea in 1707, Cyprus, and the coasts of Greece and Asia Minor. Hawkins reported to Sir Robert Murray Keith in February 1788 how 'few men have made a more complete tour of Greece' and that he had had to undergo a month's quarantine at Messina (26 Feb 1788, BL, Add. MS 35540).

On his return to England, Hawkins graduated MA from Cambridge in 1789 and in May 1791 was elected FRS, particularly for his mineralogical and metallurgical knowledge. He was now an enthusiast for revolutionary France and was soon travelling again. He was away from 1793 to 1798, collecting plants in Crete in 1794 and, again with Sibthorp, in Greece in 1795, and later exploring Greece and parts of Turkey. He wrote to his friend Davies Gilbert (1767–1839) on his return late in 1798, how 'there is scarcely any part of Greece which I have not examined … I have accomplished a regular Trigonometrical Survey of almost all Greece having drawn a chain of triangles from Salonica and Mount Athos to Cape Matapan' (Gilbert to Wedgwood, 5 Jan 1799, Wedgwood MS 1548-2, Keele University). Hawkins's geological survey of Thira was never published, but his essays on his travels in the area were published by the Revd Robert Walpole (1781–1856) in 1817–20, and he directed the posthumous publication of Sibthorp's *Flora Graeca* up to his death. In 1801 Hawkins advised Robert Brown (1773–1858) of HMS *Investigator* on gathering geological specimens in Australia.

On 17 August 1801 Hawkins married Mary Esther Sibthorp (1778–1861), daughter of Humphrey Sibthorp (1713?–1797), MP for Lincoln, and half-sister of his former botanical co-explorer. They had four daughters and two sons, John Heywood (1802–1877), who was MP for Newport, Isle of Wight, and inherited his Sussex estates, and Christopher (1820–1903), who inherited his Cornish estates. In 1806 Hawkins bought the estate of Bignor Park, near Petworth, Sussex, and henceforth divided his residence between Sussex and London. Between 1826 and 1830 he completely rebuilt his Sussex home in Grecian style, filling it with his fine artistic and scientific collections. He was an enthusiastic gardener, having been a founder member of the Horticultural Society in 1804. In 1808 he was elected an early honorary member of the Geological Society of London. He took a considerable interest in archaeology, particularly after the discovery in 1811 of the great Roman villa at Bignor, Sussex. In 1814 he became a founder member and early supporter of the Royal Geological Society of Cornwall and contributed a number of papers on Cornish mineral veins and mining technology to its journal from 1818, drawing particular attention in his earliest papers to the extraordinary submarine mining at Wherry mine near Penzance. In his last years Hawkins was active in disseminating and supporting geological work in Sussex and was an important correspondent of the geologist Gideon Mantell (1790–1852). In 1826 he served as sheriff of Sussex and he was also a magistrate in both Sussex and Cornwall. He died at Trewithen on 4 July 1841 and was buried there.

Hawkins had extraordinarily wide interests. Davies Gilbert noted how he was 'celebrated throughout Europe for his general knowledge on all subjects, his science, literature, and travels, especially through Greece, the most interesting portion of the ancient world' (*Parochial History of Cornwall*, 1, 1838, 358). But Hawkins failed to write up many of his researches and later historians have been hindered by the dispersal of his very fine mineral collection by public auctions in 1905 and the deliberate destruction of all his notebooks and manuscripts on mines and minerals just before this.   H. S. TORRENS

Sources A. Russell, 'John Hawkins (1761–1841): a distinguished Cornishman and early mining geologist', *Journal of the Royal Institution of Cornwall*, new ser., 2 (1954), 98–106 • F. W. Steer, *I am, my dear sir: a selection of letters written mainly to and by John Hawkins* (1959) [privately printed] • F. W. Steer, *The Hawkins papers: a catalogue* (1962) • F. W. Steer, *The letters of John Hawkins and Samuel and Daniel Lysons, 1812–1830* (1966) • GM, 2nd ser., 16 (1841), 322–3 • D. A. Crook, 'The origins of the Royal Geological Society of Cornwall', *Transactions of the Royal Geological Society of Cornwall*, 21 (1991), 216–46 • T. G. Vallance and D. T. Moore, 'Geological aspects of the voyage of H.M.S. Investigator … 1801–5', *Bulletin of the British Museum of Natural History, Historical Series*, 10 (1982), 1–43 • H. R. Fletcher, *The story of the Royal Horticultural Society 1804–1968* (1969) • R. E. Raspe, *An introduction to the natural history of the terrestrial sphere* (1970), xcviii–cx • P. G. Embrey and R. F. Symes, *Minerals of Cornwall and Devon* (1987) • R. Polwhele, *The language, literature and literary characters of Cornwall* (1806), 121–3 • *Memoir and correspondence of the late Sir James Edward Smith*, ed. Lady Smith, 2 vols. (1832) • R. J. Cleevely, 'A note on the archive of John Hawkins (1761–1841) and the Hawkins Archive', *Archives of Natural History*, 27/2 (2000), 261–8 • R. J. Clevely, 'The contributions of a trio of Cornish geologists to the development of eighteenth-century mineralogy', *Transactions of the Royal Geological Society of Cornwall*, 22 (2001), 89–120

Archives AM Oxf., notebook • Bodl. Oxf., letters • Cornwall RO, Truro • NHM, corresp. | Cornwall RO, corresp. with Samuel Lysons and Daniel Lysons • Linn. Soc., letters to James Smith • NL NZ, letters to Gideon Algernon Mantell

Likenesses R. Cosway, portrait, Trewithen, Cornwall; repro. in Steer, *I am, my dear sir*, frontispiece

Hawkins, John Edward [Jack] (**1910–1973**), actor, was born at Lyndhurst Road, Wood Green, Middlesex, on 14 September 1910, the son of master builder Thomas George Hawkins and his wife, Phoebe, *née* Goodman. The youngest of four children in a close-knit (though not at all theatrical) family, Jack joined his school choir (at Trinity

John Edward [Jack] **Hawkins** (1910–1973), by Anthony Buckley, 1968

county school, Middlesex) at the age of eight; two years later he sang in the local operatic society's *Patience* by Gilbert and Sullivan.

Enrolment with the Italia Conti School led to Hawkins's stage début in Clifford Mills and John Ramsey's *Where the Rainbow Ends* at the Holborn Empire on 26 December 1923. Soon after, his professional acting career began with Lewis Casson casting him as Dunois's page in the original production of Shaw's *Saint Joan* (1924). In the course of three years with the Casson-Thorndike company he played in *Macbeth*, *Henry VIII*, *Medea*, and Shelley's *The Cenci*. In the last play, critic James Agate singled him out as the most promising boy player he had ever seen. As a (by now) juvenile actor, Hawkins distinguished himself under Basil Dean's direction in John Van Druten's *Young Woodley* (1928). Under the same director he played opposite Laurence Olivier in *Beau Geste* (January 1929). He first appeared on the New York stage as Second Lieutenant Hibbert in R. C. Sherriff's *Journey's End* (22 March 1929).

During the 1930s Hawkins extended his range over a wide spectrum of classical roles such as Milton's Comus, and Shakespeare's Caliban, Orsino, Horatio, Leontes, Benedick, and Orlando; but he also performed in more lightweight plays such as those of Dodie Smith or the stage adaptation of Edgar Wallace's *The Frog* (1936). As early as 1933 the drama critic of the *Evening News* called him 'the most indubitable of matinée idols' (Hawkins, 71) and predicted that he might outstrip talented contemporaries such as Ralph Richardson and John Gielgud, and in the pre-war years Hawkins often worked with the latter.

The high point of this collaboration was Gielgud's staging, in the period of the phoney war, of *The Importance of Being Earnest* in which Hawkins scintillated in the role of Algernon Moncrieff.

After the fall of France in 1940, Hawkins volunteered for service with the Royal Welch Fusiliers. Posted to India with the 2nd British division, he was put in charge of troop entertainment; by July 1944 he was a colonel commanding the administration of the Entertainments National Service Association for India and South-East Asia. On demobilization in 1946 he returned to the London theatre. After his comeback as Magnus in Shaw's *The Apple Cart*, he played Othello in a British Council-sponsored tour of recently liberated continental countries. At this point his life was to see a change. No novice to film acting (though initially camera-shy), he had appeared in a good many prewar motion pictures from *Birds of Prey* (1930) onwards. But following the *Othello* tour he launched himself on a predominantly cinematic career; he signed a three-year film contract with Alexander Korda and later switched to Rank, ceasing to appear on the stage after 1951. When he played a group captain in a war film, *Angels One Five* (1952), the reception was such that he tended thereafter to be typecast as a senior British officer: his rugged features and resolute persona matched the public's ideal expectations of the type. Corvette commander Ericson in *The Cruel Sea* (1953), test pilot John Mitchell in *Man in the Sky* (1956), Major Warden in *The Bridge on the River Kwai* (1957), and General Allenby in *Lawrence of Arabia* (1962) all confirmed this stalwart image. As he put it himself: 'Every time an army, navy or air force part comes up they throw it at me. There is nothing left now but the women's services!' (Hawkins, 122). An amusing variation was Norman Hyde, a former army officer who collects a group of wartime comrades to plan and execute a bank robbery, in *The League of Gentlemen* (1960). Other authoritative screen characterizations included the headmaster of a school for deaf mute children in *Mandy* (1951), Quintus Arrius in the 1959 version of *Ben Hur*, and Inspector Gideon of Scotland Yard in *Gideon's Day* (1959). Opinion polls in 1953, 1954, and 1957 declared him to be the most popular British film actor—a standing confirmed by his appointment as CBE in 1958. He also performed in television drama from 1956 onwards, notably in the thirty-nine-episode series *Four Just Men* (1959–60).

Jack Hawkins was married twice: from 22 October 1932 until 1942 to the actress Jessica *Tandy (1909–1994), with whom he had a daughter, and from 31 October 1947 until his death to actress Doreen Lawrence (whose real name was Doreen Mary Atkinson, née Beadle), with whom he had a daughter and two sons.

A throat condition which had long troubled him worsened appreciably during the making of *The League of Gentlemen*; cobalt treatment afforded only temporary relief. It was—ironically enough—while working on the television play *The Trial and Torture of Sir John Rumpayne* (1965) that he was discovered to be suffering from throat cancer. After an operation which practically deprived him of his voice, he continued to act in films (either in near silent parts or having his voice dubbed over) with a fortitude equal to that of the wartime heroes he had so often portrayed. Following an unsuccessful operation to fit him with an artificial voice box, he died at St Stephen's Hospital, Fulham Road, London, on 18 July 1973, mourned by his fellow actors and the general public. GEORGE W. BRANDT

Sources J. Hawkins, *Anything for a quiet life* (1975) · *The Times* (19 July 1973), 20 · *WWW* · F. Gaye, ed., *Who's who in the theatre*, 14th edn (1967) · *The international dictionary of films and filmmakers*, 3: *Actors and actresses*, ed. J. Vinson (1986) · E. Katz and others, eds., *The Macmillan international film encyclopedia*, 3rd edn (1998) · A. Spicer, 'Male stars, masculinity and British cinema, 1945–1960', *The British cinema book*, ed. R. Murphy (1997), 144–53 · R. Durgnat, *A mirror for England: British movies from austerity to affluence* (1970) · J. Richards, 'Jack Hawkins: an officer and a gentleman', *Movie*, 45 (1980), 896–7 · D. J. Hall, 'Gentleman Jack', *Films and Filming* (Sept 1970) · L.-A. Bawden, ed., *The Oxford companion to film* (1976) · T. Vahimagi, ed., *British television: an illustrated guide*, 2nd edn (1996) · m. certs.
Archives FILM BFI NFTVA, *The British greats*, BBC 1, 13 Aug 1980 · BFI NFTVA, *Those British faces*, Channel 4, 11 July 1993 · BFI NFTVA, performance footage | SOUND BL NSA, documentary recordings
Likenesses photographs, 1934–73, Hult. Arch. · A. Buckley, photograph, 1968, NPG [*see illus.*] · stills, NFTVA
Wealth at death £13,019: probate, 12 Sept 1973, *CGPLA Eng. & Wales*

Hawkins, John Sidney (*bap.* 1758, *d.* 1842), antiquary, was baptized at St Peter-le-Poer, London, on 11 February 1758, the elder son of Sir John *Hawkins (1719–1789), author of *The General History of the Science and Practice of Music* (1776), and Sidney (*d.* 1793), youngest daughter of Peter Storer of Highgate. The author Laetitia-Matilda *Hawkins (*bap.* 1759, *d.* 1835) was his younger sister. His parents moved in 1777 from Hatton Street to Queen Square, Westminster, from where the young Hawkins often accompanied his father to the abbey to hear the music and study the architecture. In 1782–3 he contributed essays on some plates from subjects in Westminster Abbey to *Specimens of Ancient Sculpture and Painting* (1780–94) by the architect John Carter. On Dr Johnson's recommendation to John Nichols in 1784, Hawkins published in 1787 an edition of George Ruggle's Latin comedy *Ignoramus* (1630). From 1791 he contributed to Jacob Schnebbelie's newly founded *Antiquaries' Museum*, and in 1792 he edited a fifth edition of his father's edition of Izaac Walton's *Compleat Angler*, originally published in 1760. In 1802 he published *A Treatise on Painting*, a translation by John Francis Rigaud (1742–1810) of Leonardo da Vinci.

Hawkins undertook to write an account of the paintings discovered in 1800 on the walls of the House of Commons, to accompany drawings made by John Thomas Smith. A misunderstanding arose and Smith completed and published the work himself in 1807 as *Antiquities of Westminster*. Hawkins immediately published *A Correct Statement and Vindication* of his conduct, to which Smith issued *A Reply* (1808). The material originally intended for inclusion in Smith's *Antiquities* was published by Hawkins in 1813 as *An History of the Origin and Establishment of Gothic Architecture*. This elicited a highly critical review from John Carter, which precipitated a protracted dispute conducted through the pages of the *Gentleman's Magazine* during 1814

and billed by the editor as 'Hawkins v. Carter'. Hawkins thought Carter parochial; Carter, passionate but knowledgeable only about things English, considered Hawkins unqualified and disliked his partiality towards continental examples. Hawkins simultaneously engaged in a similar dispute in the same journal with Isaac D'Israeli in vindication of his father, after D'Israeli had accused Sir John, as Johnson's executor and editor, of 'ingenious malice', 'meanness', and being 'guilty of *Clipping*' (*GM*, 1st ser., 84/2, 1814, 664). Hawkins seems to have got the worst of it. In 1817 he published *An Inquiry into … Greek and Latin Poetry* and *An Inquiry into the Nature of … Thorough Bass on a New Plan*.

Hawkins married, probably in middle age, Emily, with whom he had a son, John Sidney Hawkins (*bap.* 13 Nov 1817), and a daughter, Emily Louisa Hawkins (*bap.* 4 March 1826). He died on 12 August 1842, aged eighty-four, at Lower Grove, Brompton, the family home for many years, and was survived by his wife. He was a fellow of the Society of Antiquaries, and an obituary described him as 'an antiquary of much learning, research, and industry, but his talents were overshadowed by a sour and jealous temper; and he had lived in such retirement that his existence was scarcely known to the present generation' (*GM*, 2nd ser., 18, 1842, 664). W. W. WROTH, *rev.* RICHARD RIDDELL

Sources *GM*, 1st ser., 58 (1788), 49–51 · *GM*, 1st ser., 77 (1807), 626–7 · *GM*, 1st ser., 83/2 (1813), 321–4 · *GM*, 1st ser., 84/1 (1814), 5–12, 133–5, 144, 242–5, 329–32, 348, 456, 551–3 · *GM*, 1st ser., 84/2 (1814), 12–13, 114–15, 313–16, 361, 664 · *GM*, 2nd ser., 18 (1842), 662–4 · Nichols, *Lit. anecdotes*, 9.35–7 · *IGI* · will, PRO, PROB 11/1972, sig. 824 · J. M. Crook, *John Carter and the mind of the Gothic revival*, Society of Antiquaries of London Occasional Papers, 17 (1995)

Hawkins, Laetitia-Matilda (*bap.* 1759, *d.* 1835), writer, was born in London and baptized on 8 August 1759, the second of three children and only daughter of Sir John *Hawkins (*d.* 1789), attorney, musicologist, and biographer whom Samuel Johnson famously called 'unclub[b]able' (Hill, 2.297–8), and his wife, Sidney Storer (*d.* 1793), whose inheritance (added to her original dowry) enabled the family in 1760 to acquire a fine house in Twickenham.

Hawkins's first novel was published before 1780 by Thomas Hookham after rejection by Thomas Cadell. Written to raise money for 'a whim of girlish patronage' (Hawkins, *Memories*, 2.156), it brought in twice as much as was needed. The work is now unidentified, as are 'many subsequent volumes' whose production she was too ashamed to mention.

After the deaths of her father and mother in 1789 and 1793 respectively, Hawkins remained at Twickenham, living with her scholarly brother Henry and a friend, Margaret Mitchell. In 1793 she replied to the politically radical *Letters from France* of Helen Maria Williams with *Letters on the Female Mind, its Powers and Pursuits*. After maintaining that with few exceptions 'the feminine intellect has less strength but more acuteness' (*Letters*, 1.2), she argued the Christian anti-revolutionary case.

Hitherto anonymous ('I chuse to be concealed'; Hawkins, *Letters*, 1.2), Hawkins set her name in 1806 to her translation from German of Johann Martin Miller's *Siegwart* and then, 'with the utmost repugnance', to *The Countess and Gertrude, or, Modes of Discipline* (1811, xxix). Hawkins is a busy authorial presence in this *Bildungsroman*, which she dedicated to Henrietta Maria Bowdler, not for her own writings but as friend and editor of the scholar Elizabeth Smith. The popularity of this novel has been linked to its didacticism; a second edition followed the next year. *Rosanne, or, A Father's Labour Lost* (1814), in which a daughter becomes her father's religious and moral salvation, and *Heraline, or, Opposite Proceedings* (1821) share many of its features: slightly heavy-handed authorial notes, careful attention to the influences which shape their heroines' moral and intellectual development, condemnation of various aspects of behaviour prescribed for women, and matter-of-fact presentation of libertinism in high life. Each is published by name and dedicated to a noblewoman. Jane Austen called *Rosaline* 'very good and clever, but tedious' (Austen, 289). The anonymous *Annaline, or, Motive-Hunting* (1824) is also ascribed to Hawkins.

Hawkins collaborated with her brother Henry on *Sermonets* (1814) 'Addressed to Those Who have not yet Acquired, or who may have lost, The Inclination to Apply the Power of Attention to Compositions of a Higher Kind'. Her topics include female dress, female education, and 'the female Character of the present Age', which begins with the fact that Christ chose to confide in women. She compiled *Devotional Exercises* (1823) from an earlier book by Bishop Simon Patrick, and left to Margaret Mitchell a manuscript diary of travels round much of England and Wales between 1824 and 1827. Her *Anecdotes, Biographical Sketches, and Memoirs* (1822) and the more personal and autobiographical *Memoirs, Anecdotes, Facts and Opinions* (1824) are her best-known works; they were abridged and adapted by Francis Henry Skrine (1926) and D. H. Simpson (1978). Laetitia-Matilda Hawkins died on 22 November 1835 in Twickenham. She was unmarried.

ISOBEL GRUNDY, *rev.*

Sources G. Paston [Emily Morse Symonds], 'A spinster's recollections', *Side-lights on the Georgian period* (1902) • P. A. Scholes, *The life and activities of Sir John Hawkins* (1953) • J. P. de Casto, 'Laetitia Hawkins and Boswell', *N&Q*, 193 (18 Dec 1948), 146–98 • B. H. Davis, *A proof of eminence: the life of Sir John Hawkins* (1973) • *Johnsonian miscellanies*, ed. G. B. Hill, 2 vols. (1897) • L.-M. Hawkins, *Memories, anecdotes, facts, and opinions*, 2 vols. (1824) • L.-M. Hawkins, *Letters on the female mind, its powers and pursuits*, 2 vols. (1793) • *Jane Austen's letters*, ed. D. Le Faye, 3rd edn (1995)

Hawkins, Major Rohde (1820–1884). *See under* Hawkins, Edward (1780–1867).

Hawkins, Nicholas (*c.*1495–1534), Catholic ecclesiastic and diplomat, was born at Putney, the nephew and godson of Nicholas West, bishop of Ely. He was educated at Eton College, where he was a king's scholar, and was admitted to King's College, Cambridge, in 1514. He graduated BA in 1519 and, apparently, proceeded MA in 1522. There is no record of his receiving a degree in law but he is said to have devoted himself to the study of civil and canon law, and was admitted as an advocate in 1528.

Thanks to his uncle, Hawkins was rector of Doddington, Cambridgeshire, from 1519, resigning when he was named archdeacon of Ely in 1527. He held the benefice of East Dereham, Norfolk, from 1520 and of Snailwell, Cambridgeshire, from 1526. He may also have been rector of Haddenham and of Wilburton, both in Cambridgeshire, but was certainly presented to the benefice of Fakenham, Norfolk, by the king on 30 January 1532, presumably as a reward for his services in obtaining convocation's recognition of the king as supreme head of the English church in the previous year. However, later in 1532 he petitioned the king to pass that benefice to one Croke out of pity for his circumstances.

Eustace Chapuys, in a letter to the emperor dated 1 October 1532, claimed that Hawkins was attracted to the teachings of Luther and was imprisoned for his heterodox opinions while a young man. After recantation, he was required to carry a faggot as penance by his uncle the bishop of Ely. Hawkins himself never refers to this incident, but he was friendly with Cranmer and appears to have made himself useful to the king in the first stages of the break with Rome. He is alleged by Chapuys to have written against the authority of the pope but, if so, these writings do not survive. By 1527 he was abroad, possibly serving the crown as a diplomat, but more likely studying law, and he appears to have been still abroad when he was collated by proxy to the archdeaconry of Ely on 9 November 1527. In 1529 he was back in England and attended the convocation as archdeacon.

By 1532 Hawkins had acquired enough of a reputation as an ecclesiastical lawyer and a diplomat to be appointed to succeed Thomas Cranmer as ambassador to the imperial court of Charles V. He was sent with letters of credence to the king of Hungary and various German princes. According to Chapuys, Hawkins was instructed to procure opinions concerning the king's proposed annulment of his marriage to Katherine of Aragon and had been provided with ample funds to do this. He was also given a commission, with Cranmer and others, to treat with the emperor for universal peace, in conjunction with the French ambassadors. Chapuys's intelligence was accurate and Hawkins was sending a book treating *De potestate papae* from Mantua in December 1532, while reporting back to the king by February 1533 that he had found a monk in Bologna with a favourable opinion of the king's position. He was also well provided for, being paid in advance 30*s.* a day (a total of £447 10*s.* for a year) for his maintenance. After landing at Calais on 5 October, he had arrived at Mantua by 16 November, when he received an audience with the emperor and was acknowledged as Cranmer's successor.

Some time before his dispatch to the imperial court, Hawkins had been commissioned to translate into Latin Henry VIII's treatise *The Glass of Truth*, on the unlawfulness of marriage with a deceased brother's wife. By 21 November 1532 he had half finished this work, although he seems to have felt that some of the passages might be politically too sensitive to be translated into Latin and thus made available to a wider audience. He had, however, completed his translation by Christmas eve, 1532, when he arrived at Bologna where Pope Clement VII and Charles V were in conference. In a letter to Cromwell written on the same day he complained that, unlike other ambassadors, he had no silver plate and had to eat off pewter or tin. He desired permission to 'turn unprofitable plate into profitable' (*LP Henry VIII*, 5, no. 661).

On 22 February 1533 Hawkins had an audience with the pope and discussed the question of the annulment. He found Clement cordial but noncommittal. In conjunction with Geronimo Ghinucci, bishop of Worcester, Edmund Bonner, and others, he participated in negotiations with the pope until April 1533. During this time he reported, with some frustration, on the delaying tactics of the pope and formed a low opinion of the papal strategy, writing that the pope acted only out of 'worldly motives'. He was, however, also able to pass on some useful information to the king regarding the state of Italian politics.

By 12 April 1533, Hawkins was reported to be travelling overland to the emperor at Barcelona, because he claimed to be a bad seaman. For part of the way he had been in the company of Augustine de Augustinus, who praised Hawkins's amiability and gravity. From 11 June he reported to the king on events at the imperial court. At the same time, he wrote to Cranmer claiming that he was short of funds and missing home. Cranmer's reply on 17 June must have taken Hawkins by surprise, because in addition to 400 ducats Cranmer also sent news of the annulment of the king's first marriage at Dunstable, and of Henry's secret marriage to Anne Boleyn. In July Hawkins received a packet of letters from the king instructing him to inform the emperor of events, and setting out how he was to justify them. Having received the instructions on 18 July, on the 27th he delivered the king's message verbally (in Italian because of the emperor's poor French), and subsequently in writing. The response that Hawkins received was hardly encouraging, and the rest of his time at the imperial court became an exercise in damage limitation. Reports that Katherine and Princess Mary were being mistreated in England had reached Spain and Hawkins was instructed to counter these rumours with urgency. However, Hawkins found the men in Spain 'immovable' and despite his efforts the rumours persisted.

On 17 June 1533 Hawkins was nominated bishop of Ely, but he was still in Spain on 20 December when Cranmer informed him of the birth of Elizabeth. Cranmer's reference to the appointment to Ely was ambiguous, but there can be little doubt that Hawkins began his journey home expecting to be elected. However, no formal election had taken place when news arrived in England of Hawkins's death. He died of dysentery in January 1534 at Balbase in Aragon and was buried there, according to provision made in his will. The emperor sent him medicine in his illness, an action that, as Chapuys later reported, prompted Anne Boleyn, with whom Hawkins was friendly, to suggest that he had been poisoned.

It is difficult to get a firm grasp on Hawkins's personality. On the one hand, there seems to have been a general opinion that he was a serious but amiable man, given to acts of charity and self-restraint. On the other, the man who emerges in letters to Cromwell and Cranmer is one who seems overly concerned that the outward trappings of his station be maintained, and who continually complains of a lack of money. However, taking into account the fact that the archdeaconry of Ely was worth £100, Dereham £49, and Snailwell £24 per annum, it is hard to see him as impoverished, especially given the ample provision made for him by the king during his ambassadorship. He was, however, a useful and diligent, if not acute, observer of the imperial court. Despite the awkward messages he had to present there, he seems to have earned himself the emperor's respect. D. G. NEWCOMBE

Sources LP Henry VIII, vols. 5–7 · Venn, *Alum. Cant.* · *Fasti Angl., 1300–1541*, [Monastic cathedrals] · J. Strype, *Memorials of the most reverend father in God Thomas Cranmer*, 3 vols. in 4 (1848–54) · *Miscellaneous writings and letters of Thomas Cranmer*, ed. J. E. Cox, Parker Society, [18] (1846) · W. Sterry, ed., *The Eton College register, 1441–1698* (1943) · J. Bentham, *The history and antiquities of the conventual and cathedral church of Ely* (1771)

Hawkins [Hawkyns], **Sir Richard** (*c.*1560–1622), naval officer, was born in Plymouth, the only son of Sir John *Hawkins (1532–1595) and his first wife, Katherine Gonson (*d.* 1591). He had the sea in his blood on both sides, because Katherine was the daughter of Benjamin *Gonson [see under Gonson, William], the treasurer of the navy whom John Hawkins succeeded in 1577. Where Richard received his education is not clear. He seems never to have attended a university or inn of court, but he had a respectable command of Latin and of the intellectual skills by that time expected of a gentleman. Consequently, although he is reputed to have been 'brought up among ships and seamen', he must have enjoyed some sustained period of schooling, probably in Plymouth. Much of what is known about his life and career is derived from his autobiographical *Observations of Sir Richard Hawkins, knight in his voyage into the southern sea, anno domini 1593*, which he wrote in the last years of his life and which was published shortly after his death. There is no reason to doubt either the substance of his story or the self-revelation of Hawkins's character, though details, where verifiable, do not always appear to be correct.

His first known voyage took place in 1582, when Hawkins sailed under the command of his uncle William Hawkins to the West Indies. Three years later he was given the command of the galliot *Duck* in Drake's raid on the West Indies and Florida, and was the first to bring back the news of the success of that expedition. At 20 tons, the *Duck* was not much more than a rowing boat, so its young captain must have possessed considerable skill. By 1588 he was well enough established and regarded to be entrusted with the 360 ton *Swallow* in the campaign against the Armada. He sailed in the squadron commanded by his father, and acquitted himself with credit, if no particular distinction. At this stage in his career he was very much in the shadow of his father, for whom he had the warmest admiration, but he seems to have been ambitious to establish his own individuality. In 1590 he again accompanied Sir John, first to the coast of Portugal, in command of the *Crane*, and later to the Azores, when he was vice-admiral and captain of the queen's ship *Nonpareil*. By this time his great project was already in the planning stages. Later, in 1622, he claimed that his intention had been to sail around the world 'to make a perfect discovery of all those parts where he should arrive'. However, the commission under which he sailed authorized him 'to attempt some enterprise against the king of Spain', and his subsequent actions appear to confirm that priority. Perhaps the two aims were not entirely incompatible, but in 1593 his expedition was an act of war.

Hawkins left Plymouth in the *Dainty* about the middle of June, accompanied by a pinnace and a victualler. By this time he had married, probably about the end of 1591, Judith Hele (*c*.1565–1629), the daughter of a west country merchant family similar to his own, and their first child, a daughter, was born in November 1592. The first part of the voyage was marked mainly by the routine hazards of storms and scurvy. Remarkably, he appears to have had on board some apparatus for distilling sea water, and even more remarkably gave up using it after a while. Perhaps it was not very effective, or too heavy on fuel, but the idea is extraordinary at that date. By early November he had reached the Santa Anna Islands to the north of Cape Frio, where they emptied out and burned the victualler, presumably in accordance with plan. Not in accordance with plan was the disappearance of the pinnace, which at this point deserted and made her way home. Between mid-December and the end of January (the height of summer), the *Dainty* made the hazardous passage of the Strait of Magellan, and revictualled at the island of Mocha in mid-April 1594. During May Hawkins attacked and plundered the town of Valparaiso, but the Pacific coast was no longer the soft touch that it had been sixteen years earlier, and on 19 June the *Dainty* was caught at San Mateo by two large and well armed Spanish galleons, which had been sent out specifically for that purpose. The reduced crew of the English ship now numbered no more than seventy-five fit men and, uncharacteristically, its guns were poorly serviced and maintained. Whether this was mainly the fault of the master gunner, whose responsibility they were, or of Hawkins himself, who had a misplaced confidence in his subordinate, is not clear, but the consequences were fatal. The *Dainty* held out for three days and then, with Hawkins severely wounded and the ship virtually knocked to pieces, surrendered.

The Spanish commander, Beltran de Castro, pledged that the prisoners of war would be spared and returned to their own country. The first part of his pledge he was able to honour without difficulty, and Hawkins recovered from his injuries. However, the Inquisition then attempted to claim them and, though Beltran managed to stall off the

Inquisition, release became virtually impossible. After being held at Lima for almost three years Hawkins was transferred in 1597 to a prison in Seville, to Beltran's indignation and chagrin. In September 1598 he attempted to escape, but was recaptured and confined more strictly. His *Observations* come to an end with his capture at San Mateo, but he wrote a separate account of his unsuccessful breakout, which he addressed to the earl of Essex and was able to smuggle out, probably in 1599. He was then confined to a close prison in Madrid, whence he wrote a number of letters to the queen, and to the English ambassador in Paris, begging for their good offices. Meanwhile his father had died in 1595, leaving in his will the large sum of £3000 towards his son's ransom, a sum which Sir John's second wife apparently attempted to withhold, although there is no clear evidence that it was ever called for. Beltran was still exercising what influence he had on Hawkins's behalf, and the war was becoming desultory on both sides. In June 1602 Richard addressed a plea to Sir Robert Cecil which was finally successful, and he was released after eight years in captivity.

Hawkins returned to Plymouth late in that year and picked up the threads of his disrupted life with surprising speed. In 1603–4 he was mayor of the town and on 23 July 1603 was knighted by the new king (who was generous with such honours). In 1604 he was elected to serve for the town in parliament and was appointed vice-admiral of Devon, effectively taking up the local responsibilities to which he was entitled as head of the Hawkins family. Neither his faculties nor his energy seem to have been impaired by imprisonment. In 1604 he wrote to the commissioners charged with the negotiation of peace with Spain, making extravagant claims for compensation from the Spanish government. These went back to losses allegedly incurred by his father at San Juan de Ulúa in 1568. It is unlikely that he expected these claims to be met and the real purpose of his petition was probably contained in the rider that if no 'clause of satisfaction' for him could be included in the peace terms 'that I may not be concluded by them, but left free to seek my remedy according as the law of God and nations alloweth'. In other words, he wanted to be permitted to wage his own private war until he chose to regard his claim as satisfied. Needless to say, no such permission was granted, and the king of Spain proved unforthcoming. Hawkins seems to have regarded this lack of satisfaction as sufficient pretext for extensive abuse of his office as vice-admiral. He 'had dealings with almost every pirate of note who set foot in the west country' (Senior, 131), using his office to enrich himself and pervert the course of justice. He took a share of the loot and in return issued them with discharges over his signature, sometimes blank. One John Payne is noted as having paid him £40 for such a discharge. He did not confine his patronage to those attacking Spanish ships. In 1605 the Venetian ambassador complained bitterly that valuables belonging to him, which had been looted out of a French ship from Toulon by English pirates, had ended up in the possession of Sir Richard Hawkins. At the same time he was unwise enough to quarrel with one of his successors as mayor of Plymouth, who also denounced him to the council.

This combination of local and international pressure forced the lord admiral, the earl of Nottingham, to send his secretary Humphrey Jobson to Plymouth with a commission to investigate. Hawkins did everything in his power to obstruct Jobson, and there was a furious quarrel. He was suspended from office, fined, and briefly imprisoned in August 1606 but had sufficient local influence, and enough friends at court, for this set-back to be only temporary. He was allowed to purge himself and in April 1607 restored to his post. The fact that he was not reappointed after 1610 may reflect the fact that his misdemeanours were well enough established, and that his friends had been mainly concerned to save his honour. He did not retire because of advancing age or ill health, being no more than fifty and active in other respects. In 1614, when the governors of the East India Company were planning to send an expedition through the Strait of Magellan into the Pacific, he was named as commander and was eager to accept the mission. However, the plan was aborted, possibly to avoid causing offence to Spain, with whom relations were at a delicate stage. In 1617 he was again considered for the command of a company fleet, but nothing came of the proposal.

During these years Hawkins seems to have been at sea for other reasons, and was not losing his sea legs ashore, but fleeting glimpses do not give any indication of what he was about. There were no further complaints against him and he seems to have become increasingly prosperous, so probably he had resumed the family business. In the later years of his life he left Plymouth, perhaps seeing no further advantage in involvement with the town's affairs, but more likely to build up his credentials as a country gentleman. He went to the manor of Slapton, 22 miles to the east, where he had a small estate, but this withdrawal does not seem to have impaired his active participation in business; Richard Hawkins was not of a retiring disposition. In 1620–21 he was appointed vice-admiral under Sir Robert Mansell of the fleet sent into the Mediterranean against the Algerian corsairs. He commanded the 600 ton *Vanguard*, probably the largest ship he had ever sailed in. At this point he was described as 'a very grave, religious and experienced gentleman', which may reflect no more than a normal progression from an adventurous youth and a somewhat lawless middle age. A serious but not obsessive puritanism seems to have characterized him throughout his life, as it had such kindred spirits as his father and Sir Francis Drake. The expedition against Algiers was prolonged, exhausting, and eventually a miserable failure, all of which factors were calculated to undermine the health of a man already over sixty. When he made his will on 16 April 1622 he was already sick, but not, it would seem, too sick to attend the privy council the following day on business. There, apparently in the council chamber itself, he died of a stroke. His wife, Judith, survived him until 1629. After an enforced interval she had presented him with three more daughters and two sons:

John, who went to sea with no very great success, and Richard, who remained quietly ashore and ensured the continuity of the Hawkins family in south Devon.

DAVID LOADES

Sources *DNB* · R. Hawkins, *Observations*, ed. J. A. Williamson (1933) · C. M. Senior, *A nation of pirates* (1976) · A. L. Rowse, 'Sir Richard Hawkins: last of a dynasty', *History Today*, 30/6 (1980), 24–7 · M. Lewis, *The Hawkins dynasty* (1969) · D. Hebb, *Piracy and the English government, 1616–1642* (1994)

Hawkins, Susanna (1787–1868), poet, was the daughter of John Hawkins, a blacksmith near Burnswark near Ecclefechan, Dumfriesshire. She was in early life a herd- and dairymaid at Gillesbie but later improved on her basic education to become an author in her middle age. The owner of the *Dumfries Courier* was charmed by her and printed her poems for free in little volumes with paper covers. She published her *Poetical Works* in nine volumes (1829–61), on local and occasional subjects. For half a century Hawkins was known as a wandering minstrel of the borders, selling her booklets from house to house and travelling as far as England in search of natives of Dumfries. A genial Manchester patron declared that there were two forces a Dumfriesian in England could not escape— death and Susy Hawkins (Boase, *Mod. Eng. biog.*). Sir F. W. Johnstone, bt, of Wester Hall, Dumfriesshire, granted her ground for a cottage at Relief, near her brother's home in the neighbourhood of Ecclefechan, where she died of a head injury sustained in a fall on 29 March 1868.

T. W. BAYNE, *rev.* SARAH COUPER

Sources Boase, *Mod. Eng. biog.*, 1.1390 · Irving, *Scots.* · *Dumfries Courier and Annan Observer* (7 April 1868), 3 · private information (1891) [Mr Cuthbertson of the *Annan Observer*, Mr Anderson, publisher, Dumfries, and Mr Fraser, publisher, Dalbeattie] · d. cert.

Hawkins, Sir Thomas (*bap.* 1575, *d.* 1640?), poet and translator, was baptized on 20 July 1575 at Boughton under Blean, Kent, the eldest son of Sir Thomas Hawkins (1548/9–1617) of Nash Court, Boughton, and his wife, Ann (1552–1616), daughter and heir of Cyriac Pettyt, esq., of Colkyns, Boughton. The Hawkins family had held land in the parish since the fourteenth century and by 1640 the family estates in Boughton, Faversham, Herne Hill, and Seasalter comprised some 110 acres. Hawkins was the eldest of six brothers, who included the Jesuit Henry *Hawkins (*bap.* 1577, *d.* 1646), and the physician and translator John Hawkins. Hawkins's parents' magnificent tomb at Boughton under Blean parish church, carved by Epiphanius Evesham, includes side panels of alabaster depicting Thomas and his siblings kneeling in prayer.

Between about 1587 and 1589 Mr Greene, a recusant schoolmaster, was living in the Hawkins household and presumably provided private tuition to the sons. On 15 October 1591 Hawkins matriculated at Gloucester Hall, Oxford (where his age is erroneously given as fifteen), but he evidently left before taking a degree. At an unknown date he married Elizabeth, daughter of George Smith of Ashby Folville, Leicestershire, probably the George Smith from Leicestershire who matriculated at Gloucester Hall two years before Hawkins but was almost exactly the same age. The Smith family were, like his own, noted

Catholics. The couple had two sons, John and Thomas. On the death of his father on 19 April 1617 Hawkins succeeded to the family estates, and in the following year, on 4 May, he was knighted by James I at Whitehall. However, his religious sympathies did not go unnoticed. In 1626 he and his wife were indicted for recusancy, and in December 1633 the privy council authorized a search of Nash Court, describing Hawkins as 'a great papist and harbourer of priests'; however, his wife refused entry to the officers on the ground that her husband had apparently received formal exemption under the great seal, and the matter seems to have been dropped (CSP dom., 1633–4, 319). None the less further local indictments against other members of his family were issued in 1636 and 1637.

In 1624 Hawkins was one of eighty-four nominees for Edmund Bolton's proposed Royal Academy. He was a friend and correspondent of the author and traveller James Howell, probably from at least 1621. In 1632 Howell wrote effusively to Hawkins thanking him for the 'choice Stanzas' he had sent:

> I find that you were thoroughly heated, that you were inspir'd with a true Enthusiasm when you compos'd them … your Muse soars up into the upper; and transcending that too, takes her flight among the Celestial Bodies to find a fancy.   (Howell, 413)

It is also clear that Hawkins was connected with the Jonson circle. In April 1636 a letter from Howell began by noting that Hawkins had been 'deeply remember'd' at a dinner with the poet (Howell, 403). Hawkins knew Jonson's patron, Sir Kenelm Digby—he was staying at the Digby household on the morning that Digby's wife was found dead in 1633—and Hawkins composed an elegy on Jonson for the commemorative collection Jonsonus virbius (1638). He also was a friend of Sir John Beaumont and wrote an elegy of him for Beaumont's Bosworth-Field (1629).

Wood described Hawkins as an 'ingenious man … as excellent in the fac[ulty] of music as in poetry' (Wood, Ath. Oxon., 3.524); however, it is as a translator that he is primarily known. In 1625 he published a translation of Horace, The Odes of Horace the Best of Lyrick Poets, which was republished in 1631, 1635, and 1638. Offering a slightly more chaste selection of poetry than John Ashmore's Horatian translations of 1621 Hawkins claimed that his work was 'a reflection, from that brighter body of his living Odes' that 'sought his Spirit, [rather] than Numbers' (sig. A1r–v). Plagiarized by Barton Holyday's Horace of 1652, Hawkins's translations were also included in a collection of Horatian translations published in 1666. Hawkins also translated works by Giovanni Botero (The Cause of the Greatnesse of Cities, 1635), Giovanni Battista Manzini (Political Observations upon the Fall of Sejanus, 1634) and three works by Pierre Matthieu (including another on Sejanus); the translation A Saxon Historie, of the Admirable Adventures of Clodaldus and his Three Children (1634) was also his work. In addition to this literary and historical work his translating skills were used extensively by the Jesuits, presumably through his brother Henry, to produce pious works aimed at the English market. Between 1626 and 1638 came Hawkins's translation, with the assistance of Sir Basil

Brooke, of the massive four-volume work, Holy Court, by the French Jesuit Nicholas Caussin. Published in France these volumes were dedicated to Queen Henrietta Maria, the earl of Dorset, the countess of Portland, and the duchess of Buckingham respectively. The work, which included biographies and portraits of Mary, queen of Scots, and Cardinal Pole, proved immensely popular among Catholics; at least three editions of the work were published in London between 1650 and 1678. Hawkins also translated Caussin's Christian Diurnal (Paris, 1632), dedicated to Viscountess Savage (this edition differs from the Cambridge edition of 1648 which was aimed at protestant readers), and Étienne Binet's The Lives and Singular Vertues of Saint Elzear (Rouen, 1638), dedicated to the earl and countess of Shrewsbury. Hawkins has also been plausibly identified as the translator of The Angel-Guardian's Clock (Rouen, 1630) by the Jesuit Jeremias Drexelius; Hawkins's brother Henry had already produced a translation of another of Drexelius's works.

Hawkins died at some point between the drawing up of his will on 29 October 1639 and its proving on 13 April 1641, probably towards the end of 1640. Although he asked to be buried in Boughton parish church as close to his parents as possible his burial is not recorded in the parish registers. Hawkins outlived both his sons (neither of whom married) and his wife. He left his estate to his brother and executor, Richard (bap. 1581), conditional on the payment of £300 to Hawkins's nephew, John Kirton, a physician. The will refers to a house in St Sepulchre, London, which Hawkins presumably used when attending court, and it is possible that he was buried in that parish (the relevant registers are lost). He left all his books 'in my studdy at London and at my house at Nash' to Richard's eldest son, John, except his music books which, with his viols, he bequeathed to John's brother Charles (PRO, PROB 11/185, sig. 41, fol. 317r). His Mercator atlas was left to his friend Thomas Chester.

The Hawkins family remained Catholic into the eighteenth century; during the Jacobite rising of 1715 the valuable library was destroyed by fire when a protestant mob attacked Nash Court.   ANTHONY R. J. S. ADOLPH

Sources H. Foley, ed., Records of the English province of the Society of Jesus, 7 vols. in 8 (1875–83), vol. 3, p. 491; vol. 4, p. 700 · Gillow, Lit. biog. hist. · C. T. Ramage, 'Hawkins family', N&Q, 3rd ser., 4 (1863), 506–7 · Wood, Ath. Oxon., new edn, 3.524 · K. H. Jones, 'The Hawkins monument by Epiphanius Evesham at Boughton-under-Blean', Archaeologia Cantiana, 45 (1933), 205–8 · C. Buckingham, 'The Hawkins of Boughton-under-Blean', London Recusant, 2 (1972), 1–11 · will, PRO, PROB 11/185, sig. 41 · J. S. Cockburn, ed., Calendar of assize records. Kent indictments: Charles II: 1660–1675 (1995), 21–2, 299, 310 · parish register of Boughton under Blean, Canterbury Cathedral Archives, Canterbury · W. C. Metcalfe, A book of knights banneret, knights of the bath and knights bachelor (1885) · J. M. Blom, 'The adventures of an angel-guardian in seventeenth-century England', Recusant History, 20 (1990), 48–57 · CSP dom., 1633–4 · J. Howell, Epistolae Ho-elianae, ed. J. Jacobs, 2 vols. (1890–92) · D. S. Carne-Ross and K. Haynes, Horace in English (1996) · Foster, Alum. Oxon.

Likenesses E. Evesham, carved effigy on tomb, c.1617, Boughton under Blean parish church, Kent

Wealth at death over £300

Hawkins, Thomas (1810–1889), palaeontological collector, was born on 25 July 1810 near Glastonbury, the son of John Hawkins (d. 1830), farmer and cattle dealer, and his wife, Edith (d. 1811). After his father's marriage in 1812, to Jane, his first wife's sister, Hawkins apparently lived for a time with his maternal grandmother. Details of his early education are unclear but he was at least tutored by William Seabrook, a dissenting minister of Glastonbury. He professed knowledge of the classics and of Hebrew. He was apprenticed to a Mr R. C. King of Saxmundham, probably a surgeon, and he entered Guy's Hospital as a surgeon's pupil in 1831. It is not known whether he completed the course. He claimed to have studied anatomy under Sir Astley Cooper.

From about 1832 to about 1845 Hawkins lived at Sharpham Park, near Glastonbury. A fellow of the Geological Society, he collected superb dolphin-like ichthyosaurs and long-necked plesiosaurs from Jurassic rocks, through quarriers at Street, Somerset, and through professional collectors such as (the younger) Mary Anning of Lyme Regis, Dorset. He sold two collections to the British Museum (1834 and 1840) for a massive £3110 5s., after intensive lobbying by the geological community. Together with Gideon Mantell's collection, these made the museum the pre-eminent collection of fossil reptiles. Hawkins also donated smaller collections to the universities of Cambridge (1856) and Oxford (1874). His collections contain some of the oldest known complete plesiosaurs and remain scientifically important.

Hawkins seems to have aspired to social success through science. He was respected as a collector and preparator, often supervising his specimens' excavation and carefully cleaning rock from the bones himself, though he was known for over-restoring missing parts with plaster or extraneous bones, and confusion over this marred one British Museum sale. Two huge books, *Memoirs on Ichthyosauri and Plesiosauri* (1834), and *The Great Sea Dragons* (1840), mixed anatomical description and fine illustration with autobiography, sacred history, eschatology, and grandiloquent visions of the 'Gedolim Taninim of Moses, extinct monsters of the Ancient Earth'. Such admixture was not then unusual in geologists' writing, but Hawkins's extreme lack of restraint was far more typical of the 'hyper-Miltonic' poets, whose style he later followed in his epic poetry, for example *The Wars of Jehovah in Heaven, Earth and Hell* (1844), illustrated by John and Alfred Martin. John Martin's frontispiece of battling sea-saurians in Hawkins's *Great Sea Dragons* is the classic expression of fossil saurians' impact on the Romantic imagination.

Hawkins's social failure was presumably due to his eccentricity. He mentions his own deafness and tinnitus but the underlying problem was evidently a serious personality disorder of unclear nature and onset. Manifestations include his delusion that he was the 'Rightful Earl of Kent' (as he described himself, for example, in the 1871 census), and crankish letters to the great and good, and to newspapers, as well as pamphlets about current affairs and real or imagined slights. His litigiousness led to court cases and a prosecution for perjury. He claimed involvement in progressive schemes such as the London improvements, and to have saved Robert Peel from assassination after he lost office (in Hawkins's mind because of his support for acquiring the 1840 fossil collection for the nation). Hawkins's desperate sycophancy drove him to offer collections directly to Cambridge University's vice-chancellor, Whewell, and Oxford's chancellor, the marquess of Salisbury, rather than the museums in question. To equals and inferiors, however, Hawkins was dangerously quarrelsome. Somerset people remembered him for feuds and provoking riots. Hawkins threatened Edward Charlesworth, editor of the *Annals and Magazine of Natural History*, with a criminal libel prosecution over dinner-table remarks about Hawkins's restoration practices. Charlesworth retorted that 'Mr Hawkins could adopt the language of cringing adulation, as well as that of the coarsest bullying, just as it chanced to suit his purpose'.

According to Somerset gossip Hawkins obtained his money by marrying two or three wealthy women. Only one marriage is, however, known. This took place on 30 June 1855, and his wife was Mary (bap. 1796, d. 1858), daughter of James Webb, of Northumberland Street, London. They had no children. By the end of 1856 they were apparently living apart. Hawkins appears to have received at least £800 from her will.

Hawkins's autobiography, *My Life and Works* (1887), like anything he wrote about himself, is unreliable, notably omitting his marriage to Mary Webb. After leaving Sharpham Park about 1845 he lived in a sequence of mostly rented houses, hotels, and lodgings in London, the Isle of Wight, Oxford, Chester, Somerset, and elsewhere, interspersed with continental visits. In the 1860s he formally adopted Charles F. Bonney (1851–1919), the son of a Southampton stationer and book-seller, presumably as a companion–attendant. He had no known profession or trade other than his sale of specimens to the British Museum (an attempted auction in 1844 was unsuccessful), and as far as is known he lived off this capital supplemented with inheritances and a marriage settlement. He died of intestinal blockage and haemorrhage at Schönberg Villa, St Boniface Road, Ventnor, Isle of Wight, on 15 October 1889, and was buried at Ventnor under a grandiloquent epitaph. He was described as 'of middle height, (with) light hair, and a foxy unpleasant face' (Clark).   M. A. TAYLOR

Sources J. Clark, 'Memoirs', 1920, C. and J. Clark Ltd, Street, Somerset, Clark archive · T. Hawkins, 'My life and works', *Prometheus*, 2nd edn, 1 (1887) · parish registers, Glastonbury, St John · Som. ARS, Bulleid MSS, DD/GSL · private information (2004) [J. Melluish] · wills of Mary Hawkins (Webb) and Thomas Hawkins · M. A. Taylor, 'Thomas Hawkins FGS, 22 July 1810 – 15 October 1889', *Geological Curator*, 5 (1988–94), 112–14 · A. Bulleid, 'Notes on the life and work of Thomas Hawkins, FGS', *Proceedings of the Somersetshire Archaeological and Natural History Society*, 89 (1943), 59–71 · E. Charlesworth, *Magazine of Natural History*, N.S. 4 (1840), appendix, 11–44 · T. Hawkins, *Statement relative to the British Museum* (1848) · 'Select committee on the … British Museum', *Parl. papers* (1835), vol. 7, no. 479; repr. in *Education: British Museum*, 1–2 (1968) · *A catalogue of the valuable Ichthyosaurian and Plesiosaurian remains,* *from Street in Somersetshire; and general collection of fossils … of Mr Hawkins* (1844) [sale catalogue, J. C. & S. Stevens, Covent Garden, London, 25 July 1844] · *The journal of Gideon Mantell, surgeon and geologist, covering the years 1818–1852*, ed. E. C. Curwen (1940) · *The Times* (31 Oct 1889), 10a · W. T. Blanford, *Proceedings of the Geological Society of London*, 46 (1889–90), 48 · d. cert. · R. O'Connor, 'Thomas Hawkins and geological spectacle', *Proceedings of the Geological Association*, 114 (2003) · C. McGowan, *The dragon seekers* (2001) · D. R. Dean, *Gideon Mantell and the discovery of dinosaurs* (1999)

Archives NHM · Oxf. U. Mus. NH · U. Cam., Cambridge, Sedgwick Museum of Earth Sciences | BL, letters to Sir Robert Peel, Add. MSS 40564–40597, *passim* · NHM, corresp. with Richard Owen and William Clift · Oxf. U. Mus. NH, Buckland and Phillips MSS

Likenesses photograph, before 1870, Som. ARS · photograph, 1873–80, Som. ARS; repro. in Bulleid, 'Notes on the life and work'; copy, Somerset County Museum

Wealth at death £2013 7s. 9d.: probate, 18 Nov 1889, *CGPLA Eng. & Wales*

Hawkins, William (b. before 1490, d. 1554/5), merchant and sea captain, was probably born in Tavistock, Devon, the eldest of three children of John Hawkins (d. in or before 1490), merchant, of Tavistock, and his wife, Joan, daughter of William and Margaret Amadas of Launceston, Cornwall. Hawkins may have been master of Henry VIII's 'great galley' during the Anglo-French war of 1512. By about 1518 he had married Joan, only child of Roger Trelawny of Brighter, Cornwall. They had two sons: William *Hawkins (c.1519–1589) and Sir John *Hawkins (1532–1595), respectively a merchant and sea captain and the treasurer of the Elizabethan navy.

By the early 1520s Hawkins was certainly based in Plymouth, and in 1523 he was one of the town's five richest men, worth £150 per annum. He was a collector of the subsidy in Devon in 1523 and 1524, and receiver for Plymouth (1524–5), when the town's revenue he handled was less than half his own. In 1527 Hawkins contributed to Plymouth's defences by selling to the town 196 lb of gunpowder and two brass guns, which helped repel a French raid. But the same year he and five others were hauled before the courts, accused of a serious assault; no decision is recorded. Hawkins was mayor of Plymouth in 1532–3 and 1538–9. The town's politics in the 1530s were robustly factional, with Hawkins and his allies, Horsewell and Elyot, involved in a prolonged dispute, which led to a summons before the privy council (1535). The case initially went against Hawkins, but the next year, Thomas Cromwell, sweetened by his discreet gifts of hake, a local delicacy, set up a commission of county magnates, which decided in his favour. The contest developed into one between Plymouth and Saltash for pre-eminence in the sound, and Hawkins brought the case to Star Chamber (1538). The record of the decision is missing, but it is clear that Hawkins triumphed; henceforth his position in Plymouth was unchallenged, he was in favour with the government, and Hakluyt suggests he could claim the unnerving privilege of being 'esteemed and beloved' (Blake, 299) by Henry VIII. In 1543–4 he was sent by the corporation to London to purchase arms after disposing of some former church plate. Hawkins was MP for Plymouth in 1539, 1547, and October 1553, when he was noted as a firm protestant. In Plymouth he lived in Kinterbury Street, he clearly owned quays and warehouses on Sutton Pool, and in 1544 he purchased the manor of Sutton Vautort for 1000 marks.

If factional triumph secured Hawkins's position in Plymouth, it was transatlantic commerce that gave him a national profile. In the 1520s he traded with France and Spain, himself visiting Andalusia. The surviving Plymouth customs ledgers (1539–41) show him exporting cloth and tin to western European ports, and importing salt, French and Iberian wine, sugar, pepper, soap, and fish from Newfoundland, probably bought from French middlemen. In the early 1530s he became the first Englishman to trade regularly across the Atlantic from Guinea to Brazil, possibly using French pilots. Details of three voyages (1530–32), made in the 250 ton *Paul*, were narrated to Hakluyt half a century later, from family tradition, by John Hawkins. In 1530 Hawkins collected ivory, and possibly pepper, in upper Guinea (now Liberia), then crossed to the coast of Brazil, probably south of Pernambuco, where he laded local produce, presumably including brazilwood, valuable in the dyeing of cloth, and largely re-exported to the Mediterranean. On a second voyage (1531) Hawkins's friendship with a Brazilian chief led to his coming to England and being exhibited before Henry VIII, for Hawkins a valuable contact with the crown. Unfortunately, the chief died on his return voyage (1532), but Hawkins allayed native suspicions sufficiently to secure the release of Martin Cockeram, who had been left in Brazil as a pledge for the chief's safety. From October 1533 to July 1536 Hawkins's whereabouts are unknown, but during that period at least one further Atlantic voyage was made, which 'miscarried' under another captain, as Hawkins indicated in a letter (1536) to Cromwell, when he requested, seemingly in vain, brass ordnance, powder, and a £2000 loan over seven years for further voyages. The *Paul*'s best-documented venture (25 February 1540), on which Hawkins himself did not sail, saw the export of hatchets, combs, knives, cloth, copper and lead (partly in the form of arm rings), and over 200 nightcaps. She returned with ivory and brazilwood, and showed a net profit of at least 1000 per cent.

During the Anglo-French hostility and invasion fears of the 1540s Hawkins abandoned transatlantic trading for privateering nearer home. In September 1544 he received letters of marque for up to eight ships to take prizes from the French. His lack of scruple sometimes led him into trouble. In 1545 one of his ships captured a Spanish vessel, whose cargo he correctly alleged was really French; the case reached the admiralty court, and when Hawkins arrogantly sold the goods before the case was settled, he was imprisoned for contempt, probably a gesture to appease Charles V. Hawkins was in trouble again when his frigate, the *Mary Figge*, illegally captured some Flemish goods, and he took a Breton ship just after peace with France was signed in 1546. But he was too valuable to be cold-shouldered, and appears to have acted as an unofficial crown agent in the west country: in 1549–50 he strengthened Plymouth's fortifications, supplied victuals for the navy, and was paid £50 under a privy seal writ for building the 200 ton *Jesus of Plymouth*. The final reference to Hawkins, a pardon dated 2 May 1554, shows him suspected of being involved in subversive activity in Plymouth against the possible landing of Philip II of Spain. On 8 February 1555 he was noted as recently dead.

Hawkins was clearly a troublesome, headstrong figure, bold in his approach, even to king or minister, contemptuous of officialdom, who saw the law as a weapon rather than a restraint. Self-reliant and a shrewd businessman, he was ready to take initiative and responsibility in serving town and country, without pay, but rewarded by power and place through his achievements as a merchant and pioneer of oceanic enterprise.   BASIL MORGAN

Sources J. A. Williamson, *Hawkins of Plymouth*, 2nd edn (1969) · HoP, *Commons, 1509–58*, vol. 2 · M. Lewis, *The Hawkins dynasty* (1969) · M. W. S. Hawkins, *Plymouth Armada heroes* (1888) · *LP Henry VIII* · J. W. Blake, ed., *Europeans in west Africa, 1450–1560*, 2 vols. (1942) · G. Connell-Smith, *Forerunners of Drake* (1954) · C. Gill, *Plymouth, a new history* (1966) · C. W. Bracken, *A history of Plymouth and her neighbours* (1931) · *DNB* · J. D. Alsop, 'William Hawkins and the construction of the *Jesus of Plymouth*', *Mariner's Mirror*, 65 (1979), 83–4

Hawkins, William (*c*.1519–1589), merchant and sea captain, was the elder of two sons of William *Hawkins (*b*. before 1490, *d*. 1554/5), merchant and MP, and his wife, Joan, only child of Roger Trelawny, of Brightor, Cornwall. Little is known of his youth, but he probably served on some of his father's voyages to Brazil. By the 1550s he was a Plymouth shipowner, in active partnership with his brother John *Hawkins. During the Anglo-French war (1557–8) they made successful privateering forays into the western channel, though Hawkins, like his father, occasionally fell foul of the admiralty court over seizure of neutral shipping and the sale of booty in anticipation of court decisions. He also shared his father's litigiousness: local records show him bringing a suit for debt (1555–6) and claiming 1000 marks in damages for slander (1557). In 1558 an act of parliament fixed Hawkins' quay as the sole legal place for landing goods in Plymouth.

The formal partnership with his brother seems to have ended in the early 1560s, possibly when John went to London, but each continued to invest in the other's concerns, and Hawkins was a major contributor to his brother's three voyages to Africa and the West Indies (1562–9). Yet Plymouth remained the centre of his activities: he lived in Woolster Street, and was mayor in 1567–8, 1578–9, and 1587–8. During his first term he took into custody Spanish treasure, destined for the duke of Alva's troops in the Netherlands. In January 1569, after Francis Drake, in Hawkins's own ship the *Judith*, brought news of his brother's disaster at San Juan d'Uloa, Hawkins wrote furiously to Cecil and the privy council, demanding sequestration of this treasure, or reprisals on Spanish shipping. He completed (1570), at his own expense, a new conduit to enhance Plymouth's water supply; in 1573 he and his brother provided the tide-powered town mills with a weigh-house and transport for the townspeople's grain; and in 1579 he procured the patent that gave Plymouth authority over St Nicholas (later Drake) Island, which lay across the entry to the port. By his first wife, whose identity is unknown, Hawkins had a son, William *Hawkins, and three daughters. His second wife was Mary, daughter of John Halse, of Efford, Devon, with whom he had four sons and three daughters; after his death she married Sir Warwick Hele, of Wembury, Devon.

In the 1560s Hawkins masterminded further privateering in the channel, largely on behalf of foreign protestants, using Plymouth as both supply base and emporium for the sale of spoil. In 1569 he held a Huguenot commission from the prince de Condé to attack Spanish shipping, and in April he produced eight ships for an expedition to aid La Rochelle. Spanish sources (1569–70) suggest that Hawkins was involved in a voyage to Brazil or the Caribbean, and compliment him on his treatment of Spanish prisoners, but there is no evidence of ships reaching either destination. Hawkins and Richard Grenville managed to avoid punishment in 1576 when one of their ships captured a vessel from St Malo. After the Spanish takeover of Portugal in 1580, Hawkins led an expedition of seven ships (1582–3), probably with a commission from Dom Antonio, pretender to the Portuguese throne, which went via the Cape Verde Islands to the Caribbean, visiting Margarita and Puerto Rico, and returning with a rich cargo of hides, sugar, pearls, and treasure. In November 1584 he invested £1000 in Drake's aborted Moluccas expedition. He led Plymouth's provision of seven ships against the Armada.

Hawkins died on 7 October 1589, probably at his brother's house, at Deptford, where he was buried in St Nicholas's Church; John Hawkins erected a monument and Latin eulogy to his memory, of which no trace remains. His will was proved on 20 October.

BASIL MORGAN

Sources J. A. Williamson, *Hawkins of Plymouth*, 2nd edn (1969) · M. Lewis, *The Hawkins dynasty* (1969) · M. W. S. Hawkins, *Plymouth Armada heroes* (1888) · *DNB* · *CSP dom.*, 1547–80 · K. R. Andrews, *Trade, plunder and settlement: maritime enterprise and the genesis of the British empire, 1480–1630* (1984) · A. L. Rowse, *Sir Richard Grenville of the Revenge* (1963) · J. Barber, 'New light on the Plymouth friaries', *Report and Transactions of the Devonshire Association*, 105 (1973), 59–73 · A. L. Rowse, *Tudor Cornwall: portrait of a society* (1941) · J. Sugden, *Sir Francis Drake* (1990)

Hawkins, William (*b*. *c*.1560), sea captain and merchant, was the eldest of the three children of William *Hawkins (*c*.1519–1589), sea captain, merchant, and shipowner, and his first (unknown) wife, and nephew of Sir John Hawkins (1532–1595). He served in Sir Francis Drake's circumnavigation of 1577–80, probably in the *Elizabeth* though possibly in the *Golden Hind* with Drake himself. On 17 June 1581 Hawkins had his horoscope calculated by Dr John Dee at Mortlake. He was nominated (October 1581), apparently at the request of his uncle, then treasurer of the navy, as lieutenant to Edward Fenton, appointed to replace Martin Frobisher in command of an expedition to the East Indies via the Cape. The voyage, promoted, among others, by Leicester, Burghley, Drake, and the Muscovy Company, was designed to follow up Drake's contact with the Moluccas by establishing an English factory there and a regular trade in spices. At an early stage of the planning Hawkins had been nominated to command the *Bark Francis*, though it was recommended that some other strong personality be joined with him. Clearly there was a body of mercantile opinion which felt that Hawkins, despite his relative youth, should have commanded the whole expedition. Henry Oughtred, previous owner of the *Galleon Leicester*, on which Hawkins and Fenton sailed, in a letter to Leicester (17 March 1582) called Hawkins '(the chief) hoope of the viyage, butt w^thall … made … an underlyng to one (Fenton) who ys (without) knowledge, which att the sea will make great dis(content)' (Taylor, 33–4). The diary of Richard Madox, a chaplain on the voyage, suggested that 'Fenton feareth lest William Hawkins should outmatch him' (ibid., 152). Fenton was clearly a fussy, stubborn, choleric soldier, with little understanding of the responsibilities of commanding such an expedition, and somewhat despised by his sailors; but he was Leicester's choice as 'general', and Leicester had provided the voyage's flagship. Fenton's powers were, however, on 9 April limited on all weighty matters by a ten-strong council of assistants which included Hawkins.

It was already late for the projected voyage round the Cape when the four ships on the expedition gathered at Calshot on 1 May; for twenty days unpropitious channel weather kept them idle around the Isle of Wight, while Hawkins liberally entertained the sailors. Relations with Fenton were not improved when he tried to leave Hawkins ashore while he was visiting Drake at Buckland (1 June); crew protests resulted in Hawkins being picked up the following day. Fenton and Hawkins were to remain at odds throughout the voyage, and Hawkins's 'Narrative', written on their return (6 July 1583)—and damaged by fire in the nineteenth century—says, 'I had not from that tyme till my comyng home any good countenaunce' (Taylor, 277). A two-month delay in Sierra Leone (August–October 1582) annoyed Hawkins, intensified antagonisms, caused morale to decline, and saw alternative courses being projected on the indecisive Fenton, who seems to have decided early in the voyage to avoid the hazardous journey to the Moluccas in favour of Atlantic plunder. Hawkins's diary alleges that when Fenton offered bribes to those who would support the plunder of returning Portuguese spice carracks at St Helena, he protested that the original instructions of the voyage should be adhered to, though clearly Hawkins was among those who favoured approaching the Moluccas via the Magellan Strait and Peru, rather than round the Cape—an idea probably bruited in England before departure, and clearly demanded by the pilots on board. When the ships reached the coast of Brazil Hawkins opposed abandonment of the voyage through the strait on the grounds that the spice islands presented the best 'hoape of a good releefe for our money' (ibid., 280); he also thought the ships leaked too much for the voyage back to England. When Hawkins refused to sign the agreement to stay at San Vicente on the Brazilian coast '(there) grew foule speeches betweene the Generall, and his lieutenant, after the olde custome'

(Donno, 33n.). Hawkins jeered at Fenton's failure to consult and his indecisive navigation: 'all knewe that he understoode not what he did' (Taylor, 282). The ships sailed separately back to England, and the *Galleon* arrived in Kinsale, Ireland, on 15 June 1583. Before it anchored in the Downs Hawkins was disarmed and clapped in irons by Fenton, allegedly because of his drunken and mutinous behaviour. There is no record of Hawkins's being punished once on shore, but no indication of his family's support for his actions. Indeed his uncle gave Fenton (they were brothers-in-law) a post on the navy board (1589).

Hawkins is next heard of (1583–4) bringing into Milford Haven for his father a prize taken in the West Indies the previous year, which had possibly been left in Ireland. It is likely that he was the William Hawkins who (1587) commanded the *Advice* on the Irish coast, and the *Griffin* against the Armada (1588). In his father's will he received a rather beggarly annuity of £40; his uncle Sir John Hawkins left him a share of the prospective profits of his ill-fated last voyage and an annuity of £10.

Hawkins then disappears from history. He may have been the man who, having spent some years in the Levant, spoke fluent Turkish and was familiar with the manners and customs of the orient, and, bearing a letter from James I to the Mughal emperor, Akbar, commanded the *Hector* on the third East India Company voyage, led by William Keeling, which left the Downs on 1 April 1607. But, if he was the same man, it is rather surprising that Hawkins's own knowledge of Sierra Leone is not mentioned as influencing Keeling's decision to call there, whereas the favourable reports of Drake and Cavendish are. The fleet reached the island of Socotra (April 1608) and, while Keeling sailed off for Bantam, Hawkins, in the *Hector*, reached India and rowed the 20 miles up to Surat, the Mughal empire's principal port, to investigate its trading potential. Within days Hawkins encountered Mukarrab Khan, the Mughal official in charge of the Gujarat ports, who impounded the company's goods and was in league with the Portuguese, who had great influence at the Mughal court and policed Indian trade from their base at Hormoz in the Persian Gulf. Despite the Anglo-Spanish peace signed in 1604, the Portuguese had no intention of letting the English intrude on their lucrative Indian trade. They captured two of the *Hector*'s boats and, after Hawkins challenged the local Portuguese commander to a duel, he sent his English prisoners off to Goa. The *Hector* then sailed away to Bantam, leaving only Hawkins and William Finch behind to seek recompense for their confiscated goods and attempt to get permission for a factory. While Finch remained at Surat, Hawkins, after surviving two Portuguese attempts on his life, set out on the 700 mile journey to the Mughal capital, Agra, in February 1609, guarded by a band of Pathans. Ten weeks later he arrived to find that Akbar had died in 1603 and had been succeeded by Jahangir. Despite his inability to offer the costly presents expected by the emperor, Hawkins soon developed a close relationship with Jahangir, who found him an exotic adornment to his court, and he achieved a position in the imperial entourage closer than any of his successors: the journal of this William Hawkins relates that he was asked to remain indefinitely and offered an annual salary of £3200, the rank of khan, and, initially, permission for a factory at Surat, which lay in a major textile-producing area. At Jahangir's bidding he married the daughter of an Armenian Christian who had been high in Akbar's favour; and he became the emperor's boon companion in his nightly, opium-enhanced, drinking binges and at his lion and elephant fights. But Hawkins's position was now undermined by a combination of circumstances: the return to imperial favour of Mukarrab Khan; Hawkins's obstinate refusal to accept his valuation of the confiscated East India Company goods; the arrival in Surat of drunken and abusive English sailors from the wrecked *Ascension*, and their appearance in Agra in January 1611 led by the factor, John Jourdain, who took an immediate dislike to Hawkins; and the continued jealousy of Jahangir's ministers. When the Portuguese, especially the Jesuits, annoyed at the increased English presence, outbid him for the emperor's favour, Hawkins, his allowance stopped, applied for leave to depart from Agra. He seems to have hoped to be detained with fair promises, but was dismissed without any final grant of a firman for an English factory. In November 1611 he left Agra with his wife and many of her relatives, aiming, with ready Portuguese assistance, to reach Goa and sail from there to Europe. But, changing his plans, he made for Surat, where he found Sir Henry Middleton's fleet, on board which he and his wife sailed to the Red Sea and Java, before finally transferring to the *Hector*, the ship he had commanded on his entry to India five years previously, for the voyage to England. She touched at the Cape in April 1613, but some time after 20 May (when his report to the East India Company directors ceases), together with most on the ship, Hawkins died. His remains were taken to Ireland and there buried. His wife was given a purse of 200 gold sovereigns by the East India Company the following February; the same year she married the Bantam factor (and commander of the *Hector*), Gabriel Towerson, and returned to India. In an interesting final sidelight on Hawkins's identity, after his death a Charles Hawkins, claiming to be his brother, was involved in dealings with the company, but the nephew of Sir John Hawkins seems to have had no such brother or half-brother.

There were at least four men called William Hawkins at sea during the period, so it is very difficult to disentangle their exploits. The Hawkins on Fenton's 1582–3 expedition was obviously a rather impetuous and volatile young firebrand, given in Madox's diary the nickname Glaucus, a naïve Homeric sea-god. Madox calls him (24 September 1582) 'stupid and indiscreet, very boastful, but open and honourable in his fashion'; and (21 December) 'now cruel, now compassionate … He behaves without reason, like a child … inconstant every way' (Donno, 196, 255). The Indian Hawkins was unsubtle, vigilant, stubborn, and pugnacious. Chroniclers of British India, comparing him to William Adams (*d.* 1620) in Japan in his willingness to play the oriental courtier, have censured Hawkins's

drunkenness and his failure to secure anything of substance. But, given his isolated position at the Mughal court, and the odds stacked against him, it is difficult to see what more he could have achieved.

BASIL MORGAN

Sources E. G. R. Taylor, ed., *The troublesome voyage of Captain Edward Fenton, 1582–1583*, Hakluyt Society, 2nd ser., 113 (1959) · *An Elizabethan in 1582: the diary of Richard Madox, fellow of All Souls*, ed. E. S. Donno, Hakluyt Society, 2nd ser., 147 (1976) · J. Keay, *The honourable company: a history of the English East India Company* (1991) · G. Milton, *Nathaniel's nutmeg* (1999) · M. Lewis, *The Hawkins dynasty* (1969), 221–42 · *DNB* · K. R. Andrews, *Trade, plunder and settlement: maritime enterprise and the genesis of the British empire, 1480–1630* (1984) · *CSP col.*, vol. 2 · J. A. Williamson, *Hawkins of Plymouth*, 2nd edn (1969) · C. R. Markham, ed., *Hawkins' voyages*, Hakluyt Society (1878) · A. Calder, *Revolutionary empire* (1981) · F. C. Danvers and W. Foster, eds., *Letters received by the East India Company from its servants in the east*, 6 vols. (1896–1902), vol. 6 · M. W. S. Hawkins, *Plymouth Armada heroes* (1888)

Archives BL, journal of voyage to Surat, Egerton MS 2100 · BL, narrative of the 1582–3 expedition, Cotton MS Otho E.VIII, fols. 224–8

Hawkins, William (*d.* 1637), schoolmaster and writer, matriculated as a sizar from Christ's College, Cambridge; he graduated BA in 1623 and MA in 1626. The date of his birth is unknown; and Rhoads's suggestion that his birthplace was Oakington or Long Stanton in Cambridgeshire remains merely a guess. He was ordained deacon and priest at Peterborough in 1625, and in the same year served as minister of Fen Drayton. In 1626 he became schoolmaster and by 1634 headmaster at Hadleigh, Suffolk. On 29 June 1637 the parish burial record describes him as curate to the rector, Thomas Goad.

Hawkins's Virgilian pastorals (collected as *Tres eclogae* in 1631) focus on the miseries of exile from Cambridge ('Pestifugium' and 'Postliminium'), or of schoolteaching ('Ludimagistrum'); the 'Corydon aufuga', designed to be recited by Hadleigh schoolboys before the visiting bishop of Rochester in 1632, looks like a bid for a benefice. These poems reappear in *Corolla varia* (1634) with more or less minor revisions of the versions earlier published. Printed along with them is the most ambitious of his Latin poems, 'Nisus verberans et vapulans', a rambling satire in two parts, developed from a shorter version published in 1632 under the title *En Priscianus verberans et vapulans*. It concerns the legal repercussions of his confessed assault on a delinquent pupil; Rhoads (17–27) summarizes it.

Better known is Hawkins's anonymously published English play, *Apollo Shroving*, written for classroom production at Hadleigh as an academic 'by-exercise' for the Shrove Tuesday of 1627 (6 February), and celebrating the rewards of good discipline. The list of players assigns major parts to Joseph Beaumont. Its publisher Robert Milbourn was subsequently involved in all of Hawkins's major publications. Hawkins also contributed complimentary verses to Alexander Gil the younger's *Parerga* (1632), whose poem on Gustavus Adolphus he translated into English in the same year. Beyond that he contributed verses to Cambridge collections on the king's return from Scotland (*Rex redux*, 1633) and the birthdays of the princesses Elizabeth (*Carmen natalitium*, 1635) and Anne

(*Synōdia*, 1637). The British Library's Add. MS 15227 contains, at folios 65–7, versions of 'Pestifugium' and 'Ludimagistrum', with the latter's Nisus (suggesting 'Hawk[ins]') replaced by Leucus ('White', perhaps the 'J. Leucus' who contributed complimentary verses to the *Corolla*); and, folios 63–4, two elegies from 1630 on the Hadleigh apothecary Edward Gale, and a piece of self-promotion imitated from Horace.

Hawkins died in 1637, perhaps of the plague, and was buried at Hadleigh on 29 June.   ROBERT CUMMINGS

Sources H. G. Rhoads, introduction, in *Wm Hawkins' Apollo shroving*, ed. H. G. Rhoads (Philadelphia, PA, 1936) · W. Hawkins, *Corolla varia* (1634) · BL, Add. MS 15227 · A. Gil, *Epinikion: a song of victorie … Englished and explaned by W. H.* (1632) · Venn, *Alum. Cant.* · J. Peile, *Biographical register of Christ's College, 1505–1905, and of the earlier foundation, God's House, 1448–1505*, ed. [J. A. Venn], 2 vols. (1910–13) · H. Pigot, *Hadleigh: the town, the church, and the great men* (1860) · G. E. Bentley, *The Jacobean and Caroline stage*, 7 vols. (1941–68) · *The complete poems of Dr Joseph Beaumont*, ed. A. B. Grosart (1880) · *The complete works of Richard Crashaw*, ed. A. B. Grosart, 2 vols. (1872–3) · *DNB*

Hawkins, William (1681/2–1750), serjeant-at-law, was one of at least four sons and one daughter of John Hawkins of London, barrister of the Inner Temple, and his wife, Mary, daughter of Edward Dewe of Islip, Oxfordshire. His father was said to be a descendant of Sir John Hawkins of Devon, the Tudor naval commander. He was sent to Pembroke College, Oxford, at the age of fourteen in 1696, migrated to Oriel College in 1698 (graduating BA in 1699), and was elected a fellow of Oriel in 1700 as of Milton, Oxfordshire. Some authorities have confused him with an older namesake of St John's College, Cambridge, who became a prebendary of St Paul's, and there was another contemporary of the same name in the Middle Temple. Hawkins married first Sarah Jenyns, with whom he had two sons who both became clergymen; and second a Miss Ram of Coleraine, and they had a daughter.

Hawkins was admitted to the Inner Temple on 10 February 1701 and called to the bar in 1707. In 1719 he served as deputy chief justice of the Brecon circuit in south Wales, in the absence of William Wright, and in April 1724 he was advanced to the degree of serjeant-at-law, his patrons being the archbishop of Canterbury and Lord George Parker. His career as a legal writer began as early as 1711 with an abridgement of *Coke upon Littleton*, which reached a fourth edition in 1822. He is best known in the legal profession for his *Pleas of the Crown* (1716–21), a copy of which he presented to Oriel. This treatise may indeed have been his principal qualification for the coif. It was the first substantial exposition of English criminal law to be printed since that by Sir Edward Coke (1552–1634), and it represented a distinct advance in terms of analysis and detail. The masterpiece by Sir Matthew Hale (1609–1676), the *Historia placitorum coronae*, was not published until 1736, and even then it did not supplant Hawkins, being an earlier composition. In the third edition of Hawkins, in 1739, references to Hale were inserted by G. L. Scott. Posthumous editions appeared in 1762, 1771 (by Thomas Leach), 1787, 1795,

and 1824 (by John Curwood), and a summary was published in 1728 (second edition 1770). Hawkins also produced a new edition of the *Statutes at Large* in 1734–35, which was soon superseded by the edition of John Cay and Owen Ruffhead. Hawkins settled at Hornchurch, Essex, where he died on 19 February 1750. The eldest son from his first marriage was William *Hawkins (1721–1801), a theologian and poet.   J. H. BAKER

Sources Baker, *Serjeants* · G. C. Richards and C. L. Shadwell, *The provosts and fellows of Oriel College, Oxford* (1922), 125 · Foster, *Alum. Oxon.* · Inner Temple, London · W. R. Williams, *The history of the great sessions in Wales, 1542–1830* (privately printed, Brecon, 1899) · Burke, *Gen. GB* (1837) · H. W. Woolrych, *Lives of eminent serjeants-at-law of the English bar*, 2 vols. (1869), 2.512–19 · will of W. Hawkins, PRO, PROB 11/777, fols. 256r–256v
Wealth at death approx. £756; plus land leased in London and Islip, Oxfordshire

Hawkins, William (1721–1801), writer and Church of England clergyman, was the eldest son of William Hawkins, serjeant-at-law, and his first wife, daughter of Sir Roger Jenyns and sister of Soame Jenyns. Through his grandmother he was descended from Thomas Tesdale, one of the founders of Pembroke College, Oxford, where Hawkins matriculated on 12 November 1737, aged sixteen. He graduated BA on 26 February 1742 and on 2 March was admitted a fellow on the Tesdale foundation. On 10 April 1744 he proceeded MA and in 1751 succeeded Lowth as professor of poetry, a position he held until 1756. Dr Johnson spoke fondly of Pembroke College as 'a nest of singing birds' and praised its reputation for eminent scholars, among whom he included 'Mr Hawkins the Poetry Professor' (Boswell, *Life*, 1.75). Hawkins had been ordained in the Church of England for some years before he was instituted on 27 August 1764 to the small rectory of Little Casterton, Rutland. In 1764 he also acquired the valuable rectory of Whitchurch Canonicorum, Dorset, which he retained until his death. From 7 March 1767 until his death he also held the prebendal stall of Combe (seventh) in Wells Cathedral. Hawkins was an engaged commentator on theological debate, including the Bangorian controversy. He was also one of the earliest Bampton lecturers.

Very early in life Hawkins contributed 'a few trifling pieces to the magazines' and in 1743, when he was only twenty-one, he published his first work, *The Thimble, an Heroi-Comical Poem in Four Cantos, by a Gentleman of Oxford*, which was revised in 1744 with the addition of a new first line ('What art divine the shining thimble found') and reissued in an expanded five-canto version, with notes of explanation by Scriblerus Secundus, in his *Works* of 1758. The poem, which is an obvious imitation of Pope's *Rape of the Lock* (1714), was dedicated to Miss Anna-Maria Woodford, 'the compleatest housewife in Europe'. Goldsmith classed the piece as a failed satire and as a work in which 'Humour once missed, most effectually turns the author ridiculous' and concluded that 'Mr Hawkins was not born a poet' (*Collected Works*, 1.204, 205). 'Female Empire, or, Winter Celebrated in London' (1746), a panegyric which praises the metropolis in typical eighteenth-century terms (the first line reads: 'Where proud Augusta, empire of the great'), has been attributed to Hawkins.

Hawkins's next venture was playwriting, which remained his passion for nearly twenty-five years. His first play, *Henry the Second, or, The Fall of Rosamond* (1749), nicely illustrates eighteenth-century notions of the Shakespearian manner, and Shakespeare remained the model for many of Hawkins's dramatic pieces. The play was published in London in 1749 and was at once pirated by the Dublin printers, but was not acted until 1 May 1773 at Covent Garden, when the tragedy was revised by Thomas Hull, who acknowledged that his play was based on a version by William Hawkins (Van Lennep and others, 8.1718). In the advertisement to the play text Hawkins attributed its failure to Garrick, who refused the play because he considered it 'rather a Poem, than a Play' (*Collected Works*, 1.204). Hawkins's *Cymbeline* was accepted by Rich, manager of Covent Garden theatre, in order to match Garrick's Shakespearian revival at Drury Lane. *Cymbeline* was first acted at Covent Garden on 15 February 1759 and again on 19 April (Van Lennep and others, 7.711, 721) but was unfavourably reviewed as being 'entirely ruined by his unpoetical additions and injudicious alterations' (*DNB*). His *Siege of Aleppo* (published in his *Works*, 1758), although refused by both houses, was considered by Goldsmith to be Hawkins's best play and a work that 'really deserves applause' (*Collected Works*, 1.204). The failure of *Siege of Aleppo* instigated heated correspondence between the author and Garrick. In defence of his play Hawkins cited the approval of Dr Johnson, Judge Blackstone, Mr Smart of Cambridge, and Thomas Warton. Garrick rejected the play as being 'wrong in the first concoction' and Hawkins rejoined that he would publish the play in order that 'the world will be a proper judge whether ... I have been candidly treated by you'. The tone of the exchange, as narrated in Boswell's *Life of Johnson*, may be more bluster than serious rupture, as the two continued to correspond in the 1770s, although Hawkins had no better luck with Garrick. In a letter of 1774 signed 'Your much dissatisfied humble servant' he claimed that he did not wish to 'come to an open rupture' with Garrick and offered him 'once more my friendship and my play' to no avail (Boswell, *Life*, 3.259, 1.75 n. 2). He had further dealings with Garrick concerning three more plays: *The Queen of Lombardy, or, The Ambitious Lover*, *Troilus and Cressida*, and *Alfred*. The author accounted for the rejection of these plays by alleging that he had given Garrick some offence in connection with his earlier play, *Henry and Rosamond*. In Garrick's defence, it might be noted that while Hawkins's works reveal a passion for dramatic poetry, in general his plays are studied and lack dramatic engagement.

A volume issued in 1754 under the pseudonym of Gyles Smith, entitled *Serious Reflections on the Dangerous Tendency of the Common Practice of Card-Playing*, has been attributed to Hawkins. In 1758 a collection of his writings in three volumes appeared (at 12 s.): volume 1 comprised his writings on divinity (*Tracts in Divinity*), volume 2 his poems, plays, and miscellaneous writings (*Dramatic and other Poems, Letters, Essays, &c.*); and volume 3 his lectures and

critical opinions (*Praelectiones poeticae in schola naturalis philosophae, Oxon, habitae*). Goldsmith reviewed the *Works* in the *Critical Review* (*Collected Works*, 1.198–205); although not wholly unfavourable, the review prompted Hawkins to respond with a maladroit defence signed Veridicus and entitled 'A review of the works of the Rev. W. Hawkins and of the remarks made on the same in the "Critical Review" for August and in the "Monthly Review" for September 1759'. Goldsmith then responded in the *Critical Review* (*The Works of Oliver Goldsmith*, ed. J. W. M. Gibbs, 4.399–403). Hawkins's translation of the first six books of the *Aeneid* appeared in 1764 but quickly became a scarce work (Conington, *Miscellaneous Writings*, 1.160). Although the translation of the rest of the books was ready for the press, the reception given to the first portion did not warrant the printing of the remainder. A collection, *Poems on Various Subjects* (1781), has been attributed to Hawkins. Throughout his career he was a prodigious writer of sermons. He died of a fit at Oxford on 13 October 1801, aged seventy-nine.

GAIL BAYLIS

Sources D. F. Foxon, ed., *English verse, 1701–1750: a catalogue of separately printed poems with notes on contemporary collected editions*, 2 vols. (1975) · W. Van Lennep and others, eds., *The London stage, 1660–1800*, 5 pts in 11 vols. (1960–68) · Boswell, *Life* · *Collected works of Oliver Goldsmith*, ed. A. Friedman, 5 vols. (1966) · *Boswell's Life of Johnson*, ed. H. Frowde, 2 vols. (1904) · *DNB* · *The letters of David Garrick*, ed. D. M. Little and G. M. Kahrl, 3 vols. (1963) · Foster, *Alum. Oxon.*
Archives V&A NAL, corresp. with David Garrick

Hawks family (*per. c.*1750–1863), iron manufacturers and engineers, formed one of the most notable industrial dynasties on Tyneside in the eighteenth and nineteenth centuries. Until its closure in 1889 the family's New Greenwich ironworks at Gateshead was the town's largest employer, and several members of the family firm were prominent in local politics.

The Hawks firm was established by **William** [i] **Hawks** (1708–1755), a foreman smith at the iron manufactory established by Sir Ambrose *Crowley (1658–1713) at Swalwell, 2 miles to the west of Newcastle upon Tyne. Hawks and his wife, Jane, had three sons, the eldest of whom, William [ii], was baptized at Gateshead on 29 June 1730. In the late 1740s Hawks decided to work on his own account and established a set of workshops on waste ground along the river foreshore at Gateshead. His scale of operations was modest when compared to the giant enterprise of the Crowleys and displayed little of the organizational and technological sophistication of that firm. Nevertheless, William [i] Hawks was able to exploit the availability of cheap scrap metal, which was carried up the Tyne as ballast by returning collier vessels. Scrap could be reprocessed into the nails, bolts, chains, shovels, and tools for which there was a brisk demand in the local coal industry and shipping trade. This was to be a lucrative niche, employing cheap materials, cheap energy, and simple technology (a hearth and a hammer), and allowing the accumulation of capital (albeit slowly) from a minimal initial outlay. However, the firm had not progressed much beyond this unspectacular beginning by the time its founder died intestate at the age of forty-six, for the administrators of his estate posted a bond of only £39. Hawks died at Gateshead on 23 February 1755, but his wife lived on until 28 February 1773. The works passed to the eldest son, **William** [ii] **Hawks** (*bap.* 1730, *d.* 1810); he and his first wife, Elizabeth Dixon (1735/6–1808), whom he married in 1759, are credited with the great expansion of the Hawks industrial empire.

During the 1760s and 1770s William [ii] Hawks featured in several partnerships with local ironmongers and edge tool makers. But it was the formation of a fresh partnership in the late 1770s, with **Thomas Longridge** (*bap.* 1751, *d.* 1803), a Sunderland merchant, that was the springboard for a sudden expansion of the Hawks enterprises: a plating forge was acquired at Beamish, co. Durham, in 1779, the first of four separate metalworking sites operated by Hawks and Longridge along Beamish Burn; additional smiths' shops were rented at Ouseburn on the north bank of the Tyne in 1780; a forge at Lumley, co. Durham, was occupied by the firm in the mid-1780s; and in the late 1780s slitting and rolling mills on the River Blyth in the modern county of Northumberland were taken on. By the 1790s the works at Gateshead comprised a substantial industrial complex, now producing steel, anchors, heavy chains, and steam-engine components, as well as a great diversity of smaller iron wares. The supply of ironware to the Navy Board became a speciality—as the title New Greenwich implied. The firm's products were shipped via Hawks's London partners, the Gordon and Stanley families. These families were involved in a series of partnerships with William [ii] Hawks and his successors, with whom the Stanleys intermarried. William [ii] married for a second time in 1809. His new wife, Elizabeth (*d.* 1831), was the widow of Joseph Atkinson. Both the Hawks and Stanley families, it may be presumed, could supply the merchant capital which William [ii] Hawks lacked, and both had links to the old ordnance industry of the Weald and the naval yards of the Thames and Medway.

These maritime and military markets were evidently profitable, for the estate of William [ii] Hawks was assessed at 'under £30,000' at his death at Gateshead on 4 December 1810, when the works in the north-east passed to his surviving sons: **George Hawks** (1766–1820) of Blackheath, who was born on 19 May 1766 in Gateshead, the firm's London agent, **Sir Robert Shafto Hawks** (1768–1840), born on 17 May 1768, and **John Hawks** (1770–1830), born on 19 February 1770. Increasingly, the firm's activities were focused on Gateshead, where the Hawks works covered 44 acres by the end of the 1830s, supporting a workforce of between 800 and 900. The Ouseburn workshops were relinquished before the eighteenth century was out, while Lumley forge was let to subtenants in the 1840s. The Bedlington works passed eventually to a cousin of the Hawkses, Michael Longridge (1785–1853), a pioneer of railway technology and an associate of Robert Stephenson, under whose superintendence the works became a training ground for a generation of celebrated engineers; some of the most distinguished, such as Sir Daniel Gooch, had links of kinship with the Longridges and the Hawkses. Meanwhile, the Hawkses' industrial eminence

in Gateshead was reflected in local political prominence. Robert Shafto Hawks was knighted in 1817 for his role in suppressing riots in the winter of that year and for presenting a loyal address to the prince regent. His nephew and successor as head of the firm, **George Hawks** (1801–1863), was a political notable in a more liberal vein. Born on 7 January 1801, he was a key local supporter of Sir William Hutt, Gateshead's free-trade MP after 1841, and he served as mayor of the borough in 1836, 1848, and 1849. His home at Redheugh Hall became one of the organizing centres of Liberalism in the north east. He married Elizabeth Clark Wright in 1827, and died on 15 October 1863. He was buried at Gateshead.

The firm reached its apogee in the early Victorian period, when its reputation for engineering and bridge building was worldwide, and to which the striking High Level Bridge across the Tyne, completed by the firm in 1849, stands as a fitting memorial. At its height the New Greenwich works could boast a workforce of more than 2000. However, the grip of the Hawks family upon the firm which bore its name was increasingly tenuous. Of the fourth generation, only George Hawks displayed the entrepreneurial ability of his forebears. Hannah, Lady Hawks (*d.* 1863), the widow of Sir Robert Shafto Hawks, and her two sons—the one blind, the other destined for the church—sold their shares in 1840 to George Crawshay (1794–1873), a member of the great iron-making family of south Wales, who had himself recently been bought out of his family's iron merchanting business in London by his brother William *Crawshay (1788–1867). The business developed by William [ii] Hawks had been divided between his three eldest surviving sons in 1810. George Crawshay had thus acquired one of these three blocks. When he was able to acquire the shares of Joseph Stanley Hawks (1790–1875), the only surviving son of George Hawks of Blackheath, he captured a second.

The dominant influence over the firm of Hawks, Crawshay & Sons in its last years was George *Crawshay (1821–1896), the son of George Crawshay and his wife, Louise (*née* Dufaud, of the family of French ironmasters). Like George Hawks, George Crawshay became a considerable political figure in the north-east. It may be that he devoted too much of his time to his political pursuits, however, for by the 1870s and 1880s the overcrowded Gateshead site, home to a great diversity of processes and product lines, compared unfavourably with the more streamlined and specialized engineering yards established along the Tyne by entrepreneurs such as Sir William Armstrong. Product diversity had once been the foundation of the Hawks family's success; it was increasingly a sign of technological senescence. A crisis was reached in 1889, when New Greenwich was suddenly closed. The circumstances surrounding the closure remain somewhat mysterious, for the firm's creditors were paid in full (and the company's archive destroyed). However, the dismantling of the works finally ended the association of the Hawks family with Gateshead.   CHRIS EVANS

Sources *Tyneside industries: Newcastle and district, an epitome of results and manual of commerce* (1889) · 'The Hawks family', *Monthly*

Chronicle (March 1887) · R. E. C. Waters, *Genealogical notes of the kindred families of Longridge, Fletcher and Hawks* (privately printed, [n.d.]) · F. W. D. Manders, *A history of Gateshead* (1973) · C. Evans, 'Manufacturing iron in the north east during the eighteenth century: the case of Bedlington', *Northern History*, 28 (1992), 178–96 · D. J. Rowe, 'Crawshay, George', *DBB* · W. Bourn, *Annals of the parish of Whickham* (1902), 64 [William [i] Hawks] · Burke, *Gen. GB* (1965) [George Crawshay]

Likenesses J. Craggs, statue (George Hawks), Windmill Hills, Gateshead · portrait (Robert Shafto Hawks), Shipley Art Gallery, Gateshead

Hawks, George (1766–1820). *See under* Hawks family (*per. c.*1750–1863).

Hawks, George (1801–1863). *See under* Hawks family (*per. c.*1750–1863).

Hawks, John (1770–1830). *See under* Hawks family (*per. c.*1750–1863).

Hawks, Sir Robert Shafto (1768–1840). *See under* Hawks family (*per. c.*1750–1863).

Hawks, William (1708–1755). *See under* Hawks family (*per. c.*1750–1863).

Hawks, William (*bap.* 1730, *d.* 1810). *See under* Hawks family (*per. c.*1750–1863).

Hawkshaw, Benjamin (1671/2–1738), Church of Ireland clergyman, was born in Dublin, the son of Richard Hawkshaw (*d.* 1687), of the same city, and his wife, Elinor Parry. He entered Trinity College, Dublin, in 1688, but left Ireland following the revolution of 1688 and entered St John's College, Cambridge, in 1689. He graduated BA there in 1691, and subsequently returned to Dublin, where he proceeded BA in 1693 and MA two years afterwards. He took orders, and from 1704 to 1730 was perpetual curate of St Nicholas-within-the-Walls at Dublin. He was married but the identity of his wife is unknown. He died in Dublin in June 1738, 'in a very poor and melancholy condition' (J. Hawkshaw to F. Price, 17 June 1738, NL Wales, MS 3585c). He published *Poems upon Several Occasions* in 1693. In the dedicatory letter to 'the Learned and Ingineous Dr. Willoughby' prefixed to the volume, the poet described his effusions as 'the essays but of a very young pen, a few by-thoughts in my vacancies from Irish studies'. He also published sermons in 1704, 1706, and 1712, and in 1709 *The reasonableness of constant communion with the Church of England represented to the dissenters*.

W. C. SYDNEY, *rev.* TOBY BARNARD

Sources J. B. Leslie, Dublin succession list, Representative Church Body Library, Dublin, MS 61/2/4/2 · genealogy of Hawkshaws *et al.*, NL Ire., department of manuscripts, GO MS 173, fol. 86 · J. Hawkshaw, letters, NL Wales, Puleston MSS, 3585C [esp. of 17 June 1738] · Burtchaell & Sadleir, *Alum. Dubl.*

Archives NL Ire.

Hawkshaw, Sir John (1811–1891), civil engineer, was born on 9 April 1811 at Leeds, one of three children of Henry Hawkshaw (1774–1813), publican of Briggate, Leeds, and

Sir John Hawkshaw (1811–1891), by Ernest Edwards, pubd 1865

his wife, Sarah Carrington. After attending Leeds grammar school Hawkshaw became a pupil of Charles Fowler, a local road surveyor, for about five years, working on turnpike schemes. In 1830 he became assistant to Alexander Nimmo (1783–1832) and helped survey a railway from Liverpool to the Humber via Leeds. The prospective railway company purchased the Manchester, Bolton, and Bury Canal, and obtained parliamentary approval for a railway along its route, but was unsuccessful with the rest of its scheme. Before this railway could be built Nimmo died, in 1832.

In July 1832 Hawkshaw became engineer to the Bolivar Mining Association in Venezuela, where he lived until mid-1834, when ill health forced him to return. He described his experiences in *Reminiscences of South America* (1838). This was the first example of a literary work of this type to be written by a civil engineer. Back in England, Hawkshaw worked initially for Jesse Hartley, and subsequently for James Walker. For Walker he surveyed the Leipzig–Dresden Railway, and the Hull and Selby Railway, giving parliamentary evidence for the first time on this line in March 1836.

While working for Walker, at Whixley on 20 March 1835 Hawkshaw married Ann Jackson (1812–1885), the daughter of the Revd James Jackson of Green Hammerton, Yorkshire. In the following year he was appointed engineer to the Manchester, Bury, and Bolton Canal and Railway, still not completed, and shortly afterwards moved to Manchester, where he lived until 1850. His eldest son John Clarke (*d.* 1921) was born there on 17 August 1841, and was to play an important part in his later career.

In 1838 Hawkshaw wrote his famous *Report to the Directors of the Great Western Railway*, which was critical of the broad gauge, particularly for the inconvenience of the break of gauge. This brought him to national prominence for the first time. He maintained his hostility to the break of gauge when giving evidence to the gauge commission in 1845. At that time he also advocated a light rail system, with frequent services, in preference to a network of trunk routes with infrequent express trains. Hawkshaw later opposed the introduction of a new gauge to India in 1872–3.

In the 1840s Hawkshaw was engineer to a series of railways in the Lancashire–Yorkshire area and in 1845 became the engineer to the Manchester and Leeds Railway, the nucleus of the Lancashire and Yorkshire Railway Company, with which he was to remain associated until his retirement. His experience of work in the Pennine valleys led to Hawkshaw's becoming a leading exponent of working steep gradients with locomotive power. The Pennine lines involved major heavy civil engineering works, numerous tunnels, and an impressive series of masonry viaducts of which the most famous was perhaps the Lockwood Viaduct near Huddersfield.

Hawkshaw was also responsible as railway engineer for a large number of iron bridges and viaducts. These included the Junction Railway in Salford, where he constructed a viaduct on iron columns above the street. Extensive tests were carried out in connection with this structure. Hawkshaw noted that the tight bolting-down of the iron plates designed to screen off the New Bailey prison helped counter the expansion and contraction of the metal. Following the 1847 Dee Bridge failure Hawkshaw gave evidence to the commissioners on the application of iron to railway structures in 1849. He was responsible for some of the earliest lattice girder bridges in Britain, such as those over the Leeds and Liverpool Canal in Liverpool (1849).

Hawkshaw thoroughly investigated all aspects of the railways for which he was responsible. In 1850 he produced his *Report on the Rolling Stock and Permanent Way* for the Lancashire and Yorkshire Railway, which dealt with the need for a reserve fund. In that year he moved to London, and set up as a consulting engineer at 33 Great George Street, where he remained for the rest of his career.

His practice, which had essentially been that of a railway engineer for the previous twenty years, was considerably broadened when in 1856 he became engineer for Holyhead harbour on the death of James Meadows Rendel. On completion of these works in 1873 Hawkshaw was knighted. The resident engineer at Holyhead was Harrison Hayter, and he joined Hawkshaw's staff, becoming his chief assistant. From the mid-1850s the practice undertook all kinds of civil engineering work. This included sewerage schemes at Dover, Torquay, Lowestoft, Norwich, and Ayr and the design of the Brighton intercepting sewer, 7 miles long. In 1862, following the failure of the St Germans sluice on the Middle Level Drainage, Hawkshaw advised the construction of thirteen large syphons. He became consultant to the drainage commissioners until his retirement. Land drainage and river works became an important part of his practice. He was consultant to the Witham drainage, and the Thames valley drainage commissioners. He reported on flood works at Lincoln and Norwich in 1877, and at Burton upon Trent in 1879. He recommended improvements to navigation channels on the Humber and Clyde and was consultant to the Weaver Navigation for many years.

Hawkshaw's practice was particularly noted for its dock and harbour works. One of his pupils was L. F. Vernon-Harcourt (1839–1907) who wrote a leading treatise, *Harbours and Docks* (1885). At Hull Hawkshaw was consultant from 1862 until his retirement. Other works were carried out at Bristol, Boston, Penarth, Fleetwood, Maryport, Dover, Belfast, Greenock, Folkestone, Aberdeen, Alderney, and Wick. In London he was engineer for the south dock of the East and West India Dock Company.

In addition to his responsibilities for the Lancashire and Yorkshire Railway Hawkshaw was engineer for the Charing Cross Railway, including its Cannon Street extension, and associated bridge and station works. These involved the demolition of I. K. Brunel's Hungerford suspension bridge. He re-used the chains and completed the Clifton suspension bridge as a tribute to Brunel, in partnership with W. H. Barlow. He was engineer for the South Eastern Railway from 1861–81, and also engineer for the Staines and Wokingham Railway, which involved a bridge across the Thames at Staines. He also designed Londonderry Bridge and South Bridge, Hull. Overseas, Hawkshaw was consultant to railways in Mauritius and Jamaica, and the Madras and East Bengal lines in India. His most important work in India was the Nerbudda Viaduct, nearly 1 mile long. He was also engineer for the West of India Portuguese Railway.

Hawkshaw's international reputation was not, however, reliant on colonial work. He was consultant on the Riga and Dünaberg, and Dünaberg and Vitebsk railways in Russia, and the Franz Josef Canal in Hungary. His name was associated with some of the most important engineering projects of the second half of the nineteenth century. He was invited in July 1862 by Sa'id Pasha, viceroy of Egypt, to report on the proposed Suez Canal, and spent nearly a month there. His favourable report induced Said to let the project proceed, and De Lesseps later acknowledged his debt to him. However, although Hawkshaw attended the international congress on the proposed Panama Canal in 1879, he was critical of De Lesseps's plans for the canal. Hawkshaw himself was engineer with J. Dirks for the Amsterdam Ship Canal (1862–78), 16 miles long, one of the largest ship canals to be built in the nineteenth century.

Hawkshaw's practice was so extensive from the 1860s onwards that it was only possible to manage it with the help of capable assistants. Aside from Hayter, the most important was his own son, John Clarke, who joined the practice after leaving Cambridge in 1865, and then worked on the Albert Docks, Hull, until their completion in July 1869. In 1870 he and Hayter became partners in the firm, whose prestige can best be gauged by the fact that all three became presidents of the Institution of Civil Engineers. They had many capable assistants including Henry Marc Brunel and Sir John Wolfe Barry. The most important was James Murray Dobson, who in 1885 went to supervise the dock works at Buenos Aires which took ten years to build; from 1890 he was resident partner there. Hawkshaw had himself visited Brazil in 1874 and reported on many of its harbours.

In the 1860s Hawkshaw became interested in the idea of a channel tunnel. By 1867, following investigations by the geologist Hartzinck Day in 1865, H. M. Brunel's marine survey in 1865–6, and deep borings into the chalk near Dover and Calais, paid for by the contractors Brassey and Wythes, Hawkshaw was convinced of the practicability of the scheme. From 1872 until 1886 he acted as joint engineer with James Brunlees to the Channel Tunnel Company.

Hawkshaw was responsible for other important tunnelling works including the completion of the Inner Circle Railway between Mansion House and Aldgate with Barry, and also for the East London Railway, which involved the conversion of Sir Marc Isambard Brunel's Thames Tunnel to railway traffic, and a new tunnel beneath London docks. The contractor on both these railways was Thomas A. Walker (1828–1889).

The Severn railway tunnel was arguably Hawkshaw's greatest engineering achievement. The tunnel was some 4⅓ miles long, with 2¼ miles beneath the Severn, and was the longest railway tunnel in the country at that time, and the longest subaqueous tunnel in the world. It was intended to improve the connection between the Great Western Railway system in south Wales and its main lines in England. The tunnel was originally designed by Charles Richardson, with Hawkshaw as consultant. The problems encountered particularly from underground springs were so great that he took charge in 1879. He felt that it was important to have a competent contractor, and Walker, who had tendered earlier, was appointed on his advice, and had his full confidence. The tunnel was completed in 1886 after thirteen years work.

Hawkshaw's approach to engineering was essentially a practical one, and this is reflected in his reports and professional papers. He was heavily involved in the activities of the Institution of Civil Engineers. He was president 1862–3, and was one of the most prolific contributors to its discussions. He encouraged his assistants and partners to give papers on the works of his practice. He was a member of other learned societies including the Royal Society (elected 1855), the Royal Society of Edinburgh, the Royal Geographical Society, and the Geological Society. His presidential address to the British Association in 1875 attracted considerable press attention.

Hawkshaw stood as an unsuccessful Liberal candidate at Andover in 1863, and intended to do the same at Lyme Regis in 1865, where he had bought an estate in 1864, but was prevented by his holding of government appointments. His son, standing in his stead, lost by nine votes.

Hawkshaw's standing resulted in his being continually consulted by the government. In 1860 he reported on the competing schemes for the Dublin water supply. In 1861 he designed the foundations of the Spithead forts for the War Office. In 1868 he was one of five commissioners selected to report on the country's fortifications. In the same year he was appointed arbitrator to decide on compensation to the shareholders affected by nationalization of the telegraph companies. In 1874 he became the royal commissioner responsible for investigating the pollution of the Clyde. In 1880 he was appointed to the Board of Trade committee on wind pressure on railways structures, established in the wake of the Tay Bridge failure.

Hawkshaw was in his seventies when the Severn Tunnel was completed. On 31 December 1888 he formally retired, his business being continued by John Clarke Hawkshaw, Harrison Hayter, James Murray Dobson, and latterly his grandson Oliver, down to 1920. Although his life was dominated by professional activities he owned a country house at Hollycombe in Sussex, which he purchased in 1865, and enjoyed shooting in Scotland. He died at his town house, Belgrave Mansions, Grosvenor Gardens, London, on 2 June 1891. His wife had predeceased him, dying there on 29 April 1885, at the age of seventy-two. She was the author of several volumes of poetry, including nursery rhymes published under the pseudonym of 'Aunt Effie'. They had two other sons, Oliver and Henry Paul, and a daughter, Editha.   MIKE CHRIMES

Sources PICE, 106 (1890–91), 321–35 · W. Humber, ed., *A record of the progress of modern engineering*, 1 (1863), i–ii [biographical sketch] · *Engineering* (5 June 1891), 679 · *The Times* (3 June 1891) · F. W. Steer and others, *Dictionary of land surveyors and local mapmakers of Great Britain and Ireland, 1530–1850*, ed. P. Eden, 2nd edn, ed. S. Bendall, 2 vols. (1997) · T. A. Walker, *The Severn Tunnel: its construction and difficulties, 1872–1887*, 3rd edn (1891) · d. cert. · DNB
Archives CUL, report on the Nile · GS Lond., notes on Albert Dock, Hull · PRO, papers relating to harbours; rail papers
Likenesses E. W. Wyon, model for bust, 1860; destroyed? · G. B. Black, lithograph, c.1862, Inst. CE · Cundall Downes & Co., photograph, c.1863, repro. in Humber, *Record of engineering* · J. Collins, oils, c.1865, Inst. CE · E. Edwards, photograph, pubd 1865, NPG [see illus.] · Lock & Whitfield, woodburytype photograph, 1877, NPG · Lock & Whitfield, photograph, c.1880, repro. in PICE · C. H. Mabey, marble bust, 1899 (after Wyon), Sci. Mus. · G. J. Stoddart, engraving (after photograph by Barraud), repro. in Walker, *The Severn Tunnel* · G. F. Watts, three oil paintings; formerly priv. coll. · Wontner, bust; formerly priv. coll. · wood-engraving, NPG; repro. in ILN (18 March 1865)
Wealth at death £220,074 19s. 4d.: resworn probate, Dec 1891, CGPLA Eng. & Wales

Hawksley, Bourchier Francis (1851–1915), lawyer and imperialist, was born on 4 April 1851 at Barlborough, near Chesterfield, Derbyshire, the son of John Hawksley, a Church of England priest who in 1874 was commissioner to the bishop of Saskatchewan and in 1883 became an honorary canon of Saskatchewan, and his wife, Henrietta Cordelia, *née* Jackson. Hawksley became a solicitor, after being articled in Bristol in 1866. He moved to London in

1872 and was married there, on 3 April 1873, to Clara Elizabeth, the daughter of Leonard Addison Duncan, gentleman. By 1881 they had a daughter and a son. It was through his appointment as solicitor for the British South Africa Company's London office that he came into contact with Cecil Rhodes and his imperial project. From 1889 until Rhodes's death in 1902 Hawksley was his trusted lawyer and confidant.

Hawksley never set foot in Africa himself, but in 1889 he was entrusted by Rhodes with concluding the legal formalities that turned a supposed grant of authority from Lobengula, paramount chief of the Ndebele (Matabele), into the British South Africa Company charter. The company proved to be Rhodes's vehicle for the conquest and administration of the lands that later became Zimbabwe, Zambia, and Malawi, as well as for ultimately unsuccessful assaults on Mozambique and Zaïre. Hawksley, an austere, combative man, was entirely committed to Rhodes's 'big idea', the quasi-Jesuitical dream of uniting all English-speaking lands into a commonwealth to improve and save the world. Rhodes's 'band of brothers' was the vehicle of mystical imperialism. What Hawksley eventually helped to develop was more practical and lasting. As the drafter of Rhodes's final four versions of his will Hawksley was able to refine what became the Rhodes scholarship scheme, and was almost certainly responsible for the final definition of the qualities to be sought in Rhodes scholars. As an executor of the will, he was an important interpreter of Rhodes's wishes to the committee which implemented the scholarship plan after Rhodes's death.

Hawksley was influential in the selection of the members of the House of Commons select committee of inquiry into the Jameson raid of 1895; he also inspired many of the favourable lines of questions put to Rhodes and his accomplices who testified during the summer of 1897. Under Rhodes's instructions, he refused to reveal a clutch of secret telegrams to the committee. The telegrams, which Hawksley wanted to produce, implicated Joseph Chamberlain (who could protect the company's charter) in the planning of the raid; Rhodes obfuscated, and Hawksley fumed privately. Hawksley also acted to extricate Rhodes from the clutches of Princess Catherine Radziwill, who had been forging his name and causing him financial embarrassment, and, in order to protect the British South Africa Company's share price, managed the news of Rhodes's long illness and death in 1902.

Hawksley was a member of the Liberal Party from the mid-1890s, stood unsuccessfully in 1895 for Holderness, campaigned for several colleagues in 1897, and always hoped that Rhodes would leave Africa for British politics. He died on 22 December 1915 at his home, 14 Hyde Park Gardens, London, and was survived by his wife and at least one daughter.   ROBERT I. ROTBERG

Sources J. E. Butler, *The liberal party and the Jameson raid* (1968) · R. I. Rotberg, *The founder: Cecil Rhodes and the pursuit of power* (1988) · J. G. Lockhart and C. M. Woodhouse, *Cecil Rhodes: the colossus of southern Africa* (New York, 1963) · b. cert. · m. cert. · d. cert. · *CGPLA Eng. & Wales* (1916) · census returns, 1881 · *The Times* (23 Dec 1915), 5
Archives BL, letters to Lord Gladstone and others · Bodl. RH, British South Africa Co. MSS · CAC Cam., letters to W. T. Stead · Derbys. RO, corresp. with P. L. Gell and others · U. Durham L., corresp. with Lord Grey, C. J. Rhodes, and others
Likenesses portrait, *c*.1905, Bodl. RH; repro. in Rotberg, *The founder*
Wealth at death under £5000: probate, 14 Jan 1916, *CGPLA Eng. & Wales*

Hawksley, Thomas (1807–1893), civil engineer, son of John Hawksley, a manufacturer, and his wife, Mary Whittle, was born at Arnold, near Nottingham, on 12 July 1807. He was educated at Nottingham grammar school under Dr Wood, then in 1822 articled to Edward Staveley, architect and surveyor, of Nottingham. He subsequently became a partner in this business, known as Staveley, Hawksley, and Jolland. After Staveley's death he continued in partnership with Jolland until 1850 and then continued in practice on his own in Nottingham until he left for London in 1852. While in Nottingham, in 1831 Hawksley married his first wife Phillis (*d*. 1854), daughter of Francis Wright. They had several children of whom two sons and one daughter were to survive him. One son, Charles Hawksley, became his partner in 1866, and was an eminent engineer in his own right. In 1855 Hawksley married Eliza Litt (*d*. 1893).

Hawksley's first important piece of engineering work was a scheme for additional water supply to Nottingham in 1830 for the Trent Waterworks Company. In 1845 he became engineer to the newly amalgamated Nottingham Waterworks Company, and continued in that position until 1880, when the company was bought out by the Nottingham municipal authorities.

Hawksley first rose to national prominence at the time of the health of towns inquiry in 1844. His advocacy of a constant supply of water to consumers brought him immediate acclaim. Edwin Chadwick adopted Hawksley as an ally and he was announced as engineer to Chadwick's Town Improvements Company. It was not long before the two fell out as Chadwick campaigned for a comprehensive solution to urban sanitary problems involving joint water supply and sewerage schemes, whereas Hawksley adopted a more pragmatic approach and was prepared to act for any undertaking.

About 1847 Hawksley invented, in collaboration with the north-eastern industrialist William George Armstrong, a self-acting valve designed to close the pipe automatically when the velocity of the water passing through it exceeds a certain limit, an invention adopted by many water companies.

There is scarcely a large city in the United Kingdom which did not make use of Hawksley's services at one time or another, but the three cities with which he had the closest connection were Liverpool, Sheffield, and Leicester. His connection with the water supply of Liverpool began in 1846, when he recommended the Rivington scheme, completed in 1857. The rapid growth of the city, however, made it necessary to find a further source for the supply of water, and in 1874 Hawksley and John Frederic La Trobe Bateman were asked to consider six potential sources. In the event none proved suitable, and in 1879 Hawksley was again brought in to act as joint engineer with George Frederick Deacon, the borough engineer, for the parliamentary plans for the Vyrnwy scheme. Following the passage of the act of parliament, in March 1881 he was appointed engineer-in-chief for the scheme by the corporation. Unfortunately at the same time Deacon was appointed joint engineer by the corporation in an incompatible contract. Initially, apparently, Hawksley was unaware of this but when concerns about rising costs were raised by the corporation in 1885 the ambiguity about his position was a factor in Hawksley's resignation. This was an unfortunate end to Hawksley's involvement with the project which Deacon saw through to completion. Apparently Hawksley first suggested the use of masonry for the scheme, and it was his office which prepared all the designs for what was a very large masonry dam across the valley of the Vyrnwy. The result was the creation of an artificial lake almost as large as any natural lake in the British Isles, and it was probably the most important scheme completed in Britain before Hawksley's death.

Hawksley's connection with Sheffield was brought about by the terrible disaster due to the failure of the rock-fill dam of the Dale Dike Reservoir on 11 March 1864. He was called in by the water company, with other engineers, to report on this accident and to prepare plans for other works for supplying the city. He remained engineer-in-chief of these works until his death.

At Leicester, where he was involved from 1845, Hawksley was responsible for and planned the Thornton Park Reservoir (1852–60) and the Bradgate Reservoir (1868). Hawksley was also responsible for an important group of dams in the Weardale district, at Waskerley, Smiddy Shaw, and Tunstall reservoirs. Waskerley (1868–72), with the possible exception of Hawksley's Lower Rivington Dam, probably exceeded in volume any other dam previously executed. While Tunstall (1879) was under construction it was discovered water was percolating through rock beyond the puddle clay cut-off. To deal with this cement grout was pumped into the rock, and Tunstall, along with Cowm Embankment (Rochdale, 1877), another Hawksley scheme, were the first two embankment dams in the world where grouting was used.

Hawksley was renowned for his skill as a parliamentary witness. The expertise which he showed in working out his estimates for the water supply of any district upon which he was consulted mainly depended upon the elaborate preliminary calculations he always made, based on rainfall and evaporation measurements taken throughout the district. He developed rules for reservoir yield, which, with modification by A. R. Binnie, remained the basic guidelines for engineers until the 1960s.

In addition to waterworks Hawksley was also responsible for numerous gas supply and sewage works. He was the first president of the Gas Managers' Association (subsequently the Institution of Gas Engineers) from 1864 to 1867; early in his career he was engineer for gasworks at Nottingham and became well known for the quality of his designs. He was consulted in 1857 about the London main drainage scheme: generally he advocated chemical treatment of sewage rather than adoption of sewage farms.

Elected a member of the Institution of Civil Engineers in 1840, Hawksley was elected to the council in 1853, and served as president in 1872–3. He was also president of the Institution of Mechanical Engineers in 1876–7, and became a fellow of the Royal Society in 1878. A good mathematician, he took a keen interest in questions of statistics. In 1876 he gave an address at St George's Hall, Liverpool, as president of the health section of the Association of Social Science, dealing with the application of statistics to various social problems.

For an engineer of his eminence surprisingly few of his reports were published. His writings are almost entirely confined to presidential addresses, although he was a prolific contributor of parliamentary evidence, and to debates at the Institution of Civil Engineers.

Hawksley designed a number of schemes abroad, including gasworks in Bombay and Denmark and waterworks in Stockholm, Altona, and Vienna. As a result of his overseas work, he was awarded several foreign honours. He was made commander of the order of Franz Josef of Austria, was a commander of the Rose of Brazil, and was a member of the Swedish order of the Polar Star, and knight of the Danebrog.

Hawksley was, with John Frederic La Trobe Bateman, the leading British water engineer of the nineteenth century and was personally responsible for upwards of 150 water-supply schemes, in the British Isles and overseas. Professionally active until the end of his life, he died on 23 September 1893 at his home, 14 Phillimore Gardens, Kensington, at the age of eighty-six. His second wife had predeceased him by a few months. He was buried on 27 September 1893 at Woking necropolis.

T. H. BEARE, rev. MIKE CHRIMES

Sources G. M. Binnie, *Early Victorian water engineers* (1981) · PICE, 117 (1893–4), 364–76 · *Engineering* (29 Sept 1893), 395–6 · *The Engineer* (29 Sept 1893), 311 · *The Times* (25 Sept 1893) · CGPLA Eng. & Wales (1894)
Archives Leics. RO · Lpool RO · Montgomery Watson Harza, High Wycombe · Notts. Arch. | UCL, corresp. with E. Chadwick
Likenesses H. von Herkomer, oils, 1887, NPG; copy, Inst. CE · T. Kell & Son, photogravure (after H. von Herkomer), repro. in *PICE*
Wealth at death £104,654 11s. 2d.: probate, 21 March 1894, CGPLA Eng. & Wales

Hawksmoor, Nicholas (1662?–1736), architect, was born probably early in 1662, the son of Nicholas Hawksmoor, a husbandman, of East Drayton, Nottinghamshire; his mother's name is unknown. The traditional birth date of 1661 rests on Hawksmoor's monumental inscription, which records his death in his seventy-fifth year (baptismal records for the 1660s are defective—according to a collateral descendant, papers and even gravestones were unaccountably but deliberately destroyed). A calculation among notes on the back of, but irrelevant to, a drawing of 1707 (now in the British Library) refers to the span of years since 1662, lending support to the belief that he was born in the first quarter of that year. The elder Nicholas, not

Nicholas Hawksmoor (1662?–1736), attrib. Sir Henry Cheere, c.1736

recorded after 1665, left a widow who subsequently married William Theaker; grandchildren of this second marriage ultimately inherited Hawksmoor properties near Drayton after the death of the architect's widow.

Early life and training From Hawksmoor's enduring fondness for Latin inscriptions and the proximity of a grammar school in the nearby village of Dunham, it may be inferred that he received schooling there. At some time he also acquired a working knowledge of applied mathematics, of French, and probably Italian. Youthful promise and enthusiasm rather than accomplishment must have induced Samuel Mellish, a Doncaster justice, to employ Hawksmoor as a clerk. Mellish owned property near East Drayton, and George Vertue implies that in Doncaster Hawksmoor met the celebrated decorative plasterer Edward Gouge, through whom he went to London at the age of eighteen. Here he met Sir Christopher Wren, by whom he was employed as a personal clerk. Little is known of Wren's personal life at this time, but he lived in his official residence (as surveyor of works) at Scotland Yard, Whitehall, and his second wife's death on 4 October 1680 left him with three young children. There is no reason to doubt that young Hawksmoor became part of the household at this time; later he inscribed it as his address in a copy of Claude Perrault's 1684 edition of Vitruvius. Hawksmoor gradually moved from Wren's personal service to a variety of junior posts in the office of works and other concerns under Wren's control, notably from 1687

to 1701 the office for rebuilding the London City churches after the great fire. By 1688 he was designing buildings, and by about 1690 executing them, both under Wren's continued direction and on independent commissions. There was no recognized tuition in architecture—Wren himself was self-taught—but Hawksmoor proved an able pupil, gradually learning not only the routines of an architect's office and a minor government department but also the practice of drawing and the theory of design and construction.

A little topographical sketchbook by Hawksmoor (RIBA BAL) includes his earliest known drawings—two dated 1680 and 1683, his initials, and a blot-impression of his full signature. The handwriting is immature but studied, and the draughtsmanship is naïve but renders vividly the atmosphere and details of buildings. In 1684 he witnessed signatures both at Winchester Palace (then under construction) and in the London City churches office. Specimens of his hand and signature from 1684 onwards show that the characteristic penmanship of his mature years developed slowly through the later 1680s in parallel with growing confidence and expressiveness in the use of drawing instruments. Wren evidently sent him wherever he could be most useful, but a surviving notebook (National Maritime Museum) shows that at Winchester and elsewhere he made his own notes of quantities and prices of materials and workmanship. From 1685 he was paid at Whitehall, and in 1687 he had charge of stationery at the churches office; having begun to write accounts, he was paid in 1693 for a complete transcript and summary of its building accounts. From 1691 (and for almost twenty years) he was the leading draughtsman at St Paul's.

Collaboration with Wren Hawksmoor took it as a reward for his service that in 1689 Wren procured for him the clerkship of works at Kensington House (later Palace), which he held until 1715. This post included an official house, although he was still using Wren's address in 1693. However, this did not immediately affect his collaboration with Wren, whose patronage had made him the best-trained English architect of his generation. A careful free-hand plan dated 1688 for a 'Villa Chetwiniana', a probably unsolicited proposal for Ingestre Hall, Staffordshire, the seat of Walter Chetwynd FRS, is remarkable for one so apparently unpractised. Based on a module of 10 feet, the plan sets out succinctly the essentials of a double-storey entrance hall, a grand staircase, a long gallery, and several state rooms. Even the plan reveals an exterior designed to impress, a sequence of interior spaces designed to captivate the visitor, and an ensemble as novel and as accomplished as anything in English domestic architecture of its date.

In 1690–93 Hawksmoor directed work at Broadfield Hall, Hertfordshire, for James Forester, brother-in-law of the London engraver Peter Vanderbank; the house was rebuilt about 1870 but most of Hawksmoor's brick stable block survives. In the 1690s he was still described as Sir Christopher Wren's 'man', or 'gentleman' (meaning assistant), the most important occasion being at Christ's Hospital, London, where he was paid for designing and overseeing the new writing school (1692–5, dem. 1902). Like his grander preliminary design, the completed building, of brick and strikingly plain, is a practical interpretation of Wren's theory of architecture as solid geometry made actual and demonstrated.

Soon afterwards Wren delegated to Hawksmoor the commission for Easton Neston, Northamptonshire. This building marked the end of Hawksmoor's apprenticeship and made him one of the leaders of the style known as English baroque. William Fermor, first Baron Leominster, had originally approached Wren as a kinsman. The origins of the house are obscure: both Wren and Hawksmoor were involved in the 1680s but neither designed the service wings built then. Hawksmoor later claimed the main house, finally begun about 1694, as one of his 'owne children' (Webb, 126). On a site limited by the wings he provided a building of exceptional grandeur and elegance, built in the fine local stone and encased in a giant order of Composite pilasters. Here the spatial flexibility and dramatic room sequences of the Ingestre plan were refined and realized; much of the state interior survives, as do the mezzanine suites of small rooms packed into the ends of the house and reached by independent staircases. The house was roofed in 1702, the date it bears, and the interior was fitted a few years later to display some of the Arundel collection of ancient marble sculpture which Leominster had bought in 1691. Hawksmoor's obituary stresses his wide knowledge of historical architecture, and Easton Neston displays not only an understanding of classical design and an intuitive feeling for space and mass, but also an eye for the niceties of detail and the latest trends in design, in particular the work of Hugh May and William Talman. It is only in the light of this independent work that Hawksmoor's creative relationship to the ageing Wren and the young John Vanbrugh can be understood. Although even in the late seventeenth century the head of an office was responsible for all its products, it is impossible even in a small practice for either supervision or invention to rest entirely with one person. It is perhaps not surprising that Wren, as well as delegating private or external commissions to his informal pupil, on occasion shared with him work that would be known publicly by his own name. In the 1920s the first critical historians of the period saw the hand of Sir John Vanbrugh in the larger unit scale and dramatic massing of some of Wren's work towards and beyond the turn of the century. Subsequent study both of original drawings and of written documents, however, has clarified the relationship between Wren and the two younger men. In the first place, Vanbrugh was in no position to influence Wren or Hawksmoor in those years. In the second place, in the 1690s Wren himself developed a more baroque, dramatic, and sculptural style. The question of Hawksmoor's contribution to Wren's work is more complicated: although he made some of the drawings, there is no evidence that he influenced the appearance of Hampton Court or, notwithstanding his industry in the drawing office, of Wren's final achievement at St Paul's, the dome and western towers.

Nor do Wren's unexecuted designs for rebuilding Whitehall Palace after the fire of 1698 show more than a very slight contribution from his pupil. On the other hand, the king's gallery forming the south front of the state rooms at Kensington Palace (1695–6) reveals Hawksmoor's idiosyncrasies, and, as resident assistant, specific payments for designs were not necessarily due to him.

In 1696 Hawksmoor again assisted Wren on preparatory work for the new Royal Naval Hospital at Greenwich, founded in 1694; his contribution here is clear to the eye. As Wren's personal clerk from 1696 to 1698 he was paid for drawings, and he was later reimbursed for the making of models; but otherwise he received no *ex gratia* rewards. But in the 1920s it was recognized that Wren, who gave his services for nothing, must have allowed his colleague initiative in parts of the hospital away from the central axis—much of King William court (1699–1707) and the back range of Queen Anne block (1700–03)—which reveal a quite different mind at work. Several ambitious designs for expansion also survive. The obvious candidate was once thought to be Vanbrugh, but Vanbrugh did not take up architecture until 1699, relying heavily on Hawksmoor, and his connections with the office of works and Greenwich began only in 1702, when work on the relevant buildings was well advanced. Surviving drawings as well as stylistic analysis confirm Hawksmoor's responsibility: the abrupt contrasts of scale and the arbitrary placing and shaping of windows to make interesting patterns, so evident in King William court, had already appeared at Easton Neston. Officially too, Hawksmoor's role at Greenwich increased: in 1698 he became clerk of works there; he retained this post until 1735, being also deputy surveyor from 1705 to 1729. Although there was little further creative opportunity after 1705, the worthy completion of Greenwich continued to exercise him for many years.

Hawksmoor and Vanbrugh Hawksmoor's relationship to Vanbrugh was on an altogether different footing from that to Wren. They met before the end of 1699 when Vanbrugh was 'newly turned', in Jonathan Swift's poetic phrase (*The History of Vanbrug's House*, 1706), to architecture. To Vanbrugh, Hawksmoor's skill and experience were indispensable in the design and execution of his first two great houses, Castle Howard (1700–12), where Hawksmoor was paid by the patron, Charles Howard, third earl of Carlisle, and Blenheim Palace (1705–16), where Hawksmoor was assistant surveyor.

It is not uncommon in a successful partnership for responsibility to be, or become, unassignable: such is to some extent the case with Castle Howard. Vanbrugh was without any doubt the architect, but from the start Hawksmoor was indispensable. When Lord Carlisle agreed on his remuneration he had already, with Carlisle's knowledge, been assisting Vanbrugh in practical matters. Moreover, the preliminary drawings for the house range from Vanbrugh's naïve sketches to Hawksmoor's painstaking professional draughtsmanship. Hawksmoor could readily specify, or calculate, the requisite number of masonry courses, the dimensions of an arch, the depth or the unique character of a moulding, the shape of a finial, the fit of tapestries to a room. On occasion he wrote, as a judicious deputy would, as if he knew Vanbrugh's mind. His obligations included an annual site visit, probably until 1712, when the great house was sufficiently advanced for Carlisle and his family to move in. Years later (in 1722) Hawksmoor compared his feeling for Blenheim, the second commission in which he assisted Vanbrugh, to that of 'the loving nurse, that almost thinks the child her own' (BL, MS 61353, fol. 239). These were not, as Easton Neston was, his 'owne children'.

Hawksmoor's role at Blenheim was defined with greater formality and is documented in greater detail: as a state gift to the victorious duke of Marlborough, Blenheim Palace was in the charge of a miniature version of the office of works. Vanbrugh as surveyor (architect) was the personal choice of the duke; Hawksmoor (again the principal draughtsman) was his official deputy from the start in 1705, and Hawksmoor's letters to the young Henry Joynes, resident clerk of works, with the latter's draft replies between 1705 and 1713, not only show the extent of Hawksmoor's executive directions for detailing and construction but also give some idea of the teaching he had in his turn received, mostly by word of mouth, from Wren. As at Castle Howard, Vanbrugh was unequivocally the architect, but some of Hawksmoor's contributions to the design can be identified. A preliminary design for embellishing the saloon with sculptures was discussed by a contemporary artist (Louis Silvestre) as their joint work— although the proposed statues are drawn by Grinling Gibbons, then chief carver at Blenheim—and other drawings show Hawksmoor suggesting alternative treatments for the entrance hall. The massive stone structures which give Blenheim its romantic roof-line (called by Hawksmoor 'the Eminencys') have a formal complexity and a baroque sculptural excitement unlike anything at Castle Howard but close in spirit and handling to the London church towers of Hawksmoor's later years. Vanbrugh's own expressed preference for the 'figure and proportions' of a building rather than the 'delicacy of the ornaments' is confirmed by comparison with his later independent work: on the whole he used existing formulas, be they the classical orders, the obelisks, or the house plans of Palladio, whereas Hawksmoor patently enjoyed breaking down and recombining the elements of architecture and devising novel and surprising formal and spatial effects.

These distinctions are illustrated in two dissimilar buildings of the first decade of the eighteenth century which involved both architects. At Kimbolton Castle, Huntingdon—the occasion of Vanbrugh's dismissive remark about ornament—Hawksmoor provided advice and drawings in 1707–10, but clearly no more than that. On the other hand, although the orangery at Kensington Palace (1704–5) was officially Wren's responsibility and Hawksmoor is not named in surviving documents, he was still resident architect, and this elegant brick building displays all his talent for external elaboration in windows, blind arches, niches, and roof-top abstractions, as well as his fastidious detailing in the three linked spaces of the interior. The circumstances that Vanbrugh, as comptroller of works, found irregularities in the contracting and that an alteration to the design was proposed by him and accepted by the Treasury are insufficient to overturn the visual evidence of Hawksmoor's authorship.

Work for the universities As he approached the age of fifty, Hawksmoor's creative genius received new stimulus from two quarters which were to occupy the rest of his life: the universities of Oxford and Cambridge and the London 'Queen Anne' churches. Accident has preserved more drawings in these two categories than in any others and, as with the Royal Naval Hospital at Greenwich, he proposed far more than he achieved; nevertheless his six churches and two university commissions are among the finest of his independent works.

The seventeenth and early eighteenth centuries saw considerable, although discontinuous, expansion at Oxford and Cambridge, and much of the designing was shared between the commissioning patrons—senior fellows with private means or fund-raising abilities, some with architectural pretensions—and the local families of stonemasons and other builders. Wren, who made significant contributions to the architecture of both universities in the 1660s and 1670s, was engaged as a distinguished colleague, or in one case as the nephew of the donor. Hawksmoor, coming from outside, depended on the recommendation of his mentor or another academic figure, and on his own demonstrable talent and industry. At King's College, Cambridge, he was approached through Wren by Dr John Adams, the new provost, in 1712. Hawksmoor's ambitious drawings for completing the college followed the general disposition of buildings laid down by its founder, Henry VI. He also made alternative designs for the fellows' building, which are recorded in two detailed wooden models, still in the college. But Adams failed to attract funds, and Hawksmoor's designs were not entirely acceptable; after Adams's death in 1719 James Gibbs was called in, and his fellows' building, completed in 1724, owes less to Hawksmoor's designs than to contemporary criticisms of them.

At Oxford Hawksmoor's success was more material, though not unqualified. His primary contact was with Dr George Clarke, fellow of All Souls, amateur architect and collector of architectural drawings, whom he had probably met in connection with the Royal Naval Hospital during Clarke's term as secretary to the Admiralty (1702–5). By 1708 he was submitting designs for expansion or rebuilding in Oxford. The proximity of Blenheim within an easy ride not only ensured Hawksmoor's passage through Oxford from time to time but also gradually made known there, to scholars and builders alike, the eloquent grandeur of the Hawksmoor–Vanbrugh style. Even so, this was not always to his advantage: in 1734 Sir Nathaniel Lloyd of All Souls complained that 'he designs [too] grandly, for a college' (Downes, *Hawksmoor*, 1979, 99), and it is clear that piecemeal addition was often not only economically more feasible but also more acceptable to conservative tastes.

The old college tradition attributing to Hawksmoor the

library of the Queen's College, built in the 1690s, cannot be sustained, and none of the several designs he sent in 1708–9 to Provost William Lancaster, perhaps introduced by Clarke, was adopted. They offered alternative proposals for a new front quadrangle including a monumental chapel, hall, and gatehouse. While Wadham College, an entirely new foundation built just a century earlier, had introduced to Oxford the idea of arranging hall and chapel symmetrically across the principal axis, Hawksmoor's towers, giant orders, and in some of the projects free-standing central chapels, would have brought to Oxford the monumental architecture of Blenheim and Greenwich. Indeed, his drawings bore indirect fruit in the front quadrangle actually begun in 1714. The closest known designs are by Clarke himself and the Oxford mason William Townesend, but Hawksmoor's influence can be felt in the concept, the overall symmetry, the grandeur of scale, and to some extent in the detailed vocabulary.

Although Clarke may have adjudicated, Provost Lancaster was vice-chancellor in 1710 when Hawksmoor won an informal competition for the design of the 'new printing-house' (now the old Clarendon building) at the end of Broad Street, adjoining the Bodleian Library and Wren's Sheldonian Theatre. The *architypographus* or university printer was responsible for two enterprises, one the lucrative licence to print the Authorized Version of the King James Bible and the Book of Common Prayer, the other a 'learned press' for scholarly works. Upon the opening of the Sheldonian Theatre in 1669 the presses were crammed into its basement and the rooms under its tiered seating. After the profitable publication, in 1703–4, of the first earl of Clarendon's *History of the Great Rebellion*, it was decided to build more suitable premises, constructed in 1712–13. From the common features of Hawksmoor's several proposals and two by other architects it appears that the brief was precise and detailed: the two presses were to be located on either side of a central passage flanked by a columnar portico, on the axis of the Bodleian Library quadrangle to the south.

Hawksmoor met the specification with a building of exceptional grandeur and gravity, using a giant Doric order for the free-standing portico on the north and a similar frontispiece applied to the south side facing the Bodleian. The giant order is not used in the rest of the elevations, only the entablature is carried all around the exterior, and much of the Clarendon building's character comes from other formal devices which Hawksmoor, never having travelled abroad, managed to interpret and re-create imaginatively from engravings of Italian mannerist and baroque architecture.

All Souls College, Oxford　Hawksmoor's major Oxford commission was the completion of All Souls College. Here he was consulted as early as 1709 by Clarke, who had outlined a proposal for building a hall, east of the chapel and mirroring it in plan, and, building on the fellows' garden and buying additional land to the north, to make a large new quadrangle the width of both buildings, closed on the

north by a range of fellows' lodgings. Clarke also considered the possibility of a complete and symmetrical rebuilding. Hawksmoor's several preliminary designs became obsolete with the death in 1710 of Christopher Codrington, who left £6000 to build a new library. Property purchase was not complete until 1715; meanwhile, by the beginning of 1714 it had been decided, probably at Hawksmoor's instance, to place the library on the north and the lodgings on the east.

Hawksmoor explored the choice not only between additions and complete renewal but also between classical and gothick buildings, or even a mixture of both. In a long 'Explanation' of his designs, dated 17 February 1715, he argued for 'the preservation of Antient durable Publick Buildings', meaning the old south quadrangle in particular. 'What ever is good in its kinde', he wrote, 'ought to be preserv'd … for destruction can be profitable to none but such as live by it' (Downes, *Hawksmoor*, 1979, 138, 241). His remarks have led to his being claimed as a pioneer of the conservation movement, but his enthusiasm for the old was strictly relative to his creative ambition. His submitted drawings included not only a scheme for rebuilding the old south quadrangle in a gothick style (engraved for fund-raising in 1721) but also one with a gothick hall matching the chapel, the rest of the new buildings being 'after the Antique'.

In fact Hawksmoor's fire was directed, as much as anywhere, at the poor general building and planning standards of the day, and the ignorance of artificers to whom, as he complained in another context, 'it is indifferent … whether they get Money by destroying or erecting Fabricks' (Bolton and Hendry, 6, 1929, 20). He must also have been sensitive to the fact that in Oxford during the course of the seventeenth century Gothic survival blended seamlessly into revival. He had learned from Wren the occasional need (in the latter's phrase) 'to deviate from a better style' (Downes, *The Architecture of Wren*, 89). In 1697 he had, in Wren's stead, advised on the reconstruction of St Mary's, Warwick, after a fire, although his design was not adopted. His last months in the City churches office saw the start of work on recasing the old tower of St Mary Aldermary, twenty years after the reconstruction of the church in a neo-Gothic style. Around the turn of the century his work is not easy to distinguish from that of William Dickinson, something of a gothick specialist who continued work in that office; nevertheless the outsize corner pinnacles of the Aldermary tower have much in common with Hawksmoor's self-acknowledged rebuilding of the tower of St Michael Cornhill for the Fifty New Churches Commission in 1718–24. He also advised on, and campaigned for, the repair of Beverley Minster about 1716–20. It was against this background that he produced definitive designs for the north quadrangle at All Souls, on which work began in 1716.

The exteriors are based on, but not overburdened by, the wide knowledge of sources for which Hawksmoor's obituarist praised him. His gift was to succeed in re-creating the fall of light and cast of shadow of Gothic originals, rather than the wealth of detail that characterizes most revivalist architecture; the twin towers flanking the common room on the east were a notable addition to Oxford's picturesque skyline—the only one, of those he proposed, to be realized. On the other hand, although Hawksmoor entertained the prospect of an entirely gothick library, all the interiors of library, hall, and common room are classical; indeed on the outside the windows of the common room and the large lights at either end of the library are barely disguised Venetian windows. In the library, then second in size only to Wren's at Trinity College, Cambridge, Hawksmoor abandoned tradition, keeping the whole floor clear of desks and book-stacks, and ranging all the books around the walls; placing the library not upstairs over a loggia but at ground level, and providing a formal central entrance from the quadrangle which, if used, admits the reader to face a large recess designed for a monumental statue, with the interior, 60 metres long, extending dramatically to left and right.

The foundation stone was laid on 30 June 1716, but construction, after a promising start, became fitful and dependent on further donations. The library was not fitted in Hawksmoor's lifetime, and the understated plaster ceiling executed in 1750 (by Thomas Roberts of Oxford) leaves the visitor with a vague sense of disorientation, which Hawksmoor's intended coffered ceiling would have turned to more positive effect. The most remarkable interiors are the hall, whose billowing plaster vault has a strange affinity with the baroque ceilings of central Europe, and the small but noble buttery, oval in plan with a coffered masonry dome. These were built in the early 1730s, and suggest that Hawksmoor's knowledge (in his obituarist's phrase) 'of all the famous Buildings, both Antient and Modern, in every Part of the World' extended to the most recent European architectural publications.

Hawksmoor closed the quadrangle on the west with a cloister walk, screened from the outside and opening in the middle to a domed and pinnacled gothick gateway for which the mason contracted in 1734. At the same time work was progressing on a similar, but classical, screened walk at the front of the Queen's College, whose gate is surmounted by a delicate circular temple sheltering a figure of Queen Caroline. Thus at Queen's Hawksmoor provided at least the finishing touches to the quadrangle he inspired but did not himself design; his authorship of the screen, recorded on completion in the *Daily Post* of 12 February 1736, is confirmed by surviving drawings indisputably from his office. Moreover, these two fronts must have been, in his mind, complementary. In 1713 he had made several large plans for rebuilding much of the area between the High Street, Broad Street, and New College, embracing All Souls, the Queen's, and Brasenose colleges, the new church of All Saints (on whose steeple he had some influence), and the Clarendon, Sheldonian, and old Ashmolean buildings, with a new university church (a huge peripteral temple) and campanile, and a Trajanic column and forum at Carfax.

The germ of this plan perhaps lay in the Clarendon building, with its portico facing nowhere in particular; a year earlier he had planned the 'reform' of Cambridge around his design for King's College. In both towns he envisaged a network of buildings and vistas that combined Roman and Greek prototypes with the urban planning of Pope Sixtus V and Domenico Fontana in late Renaissance Rome. But one other factor led to his creating not a new building but the setting for one: the Radcliffe Library. In 1712 Dr John Radcliffe decided to contribute to an addition to the Bodleian Library; after considerable discussion he settled on a building attached to the south side of the Bodleian quadrangle, on a site then occupied by small houses. Hawksmoor was soon making drawings, and the library features in his urban plans. Subsequently Radcliffe's executors consulted several architects; in 1734 Hawksmoor and James Gibbs submitted new plans, and a model (now in the Bodleian) was made of Hawksmoor's. Gibbs proposed a traditional long library, but Hawksmoor, scenting that Radcliffe was (in Thomas Hearne's words) 'very ambitious of Glory' (*Oxford Historical Society*, 42, 1901, 2), had looked from the start for prototypes, in the mausoleum and the martyr's shrine, for a circular domed building. The circular library finally begun by Gibbs in 1737 suggests a debt to Hawksmoor's drawings, and while it was Gibbs who made the building freestanding, the square surrounding it had been cleared on Hawksmoor's recommendation. Moreover, it was his principal reason for giving All Souls a gate in that direction.

The fifty new churches From 1711 Hawksmoor was also busy in London. The Fifty New Churches Act of that year sprang from a petition by the parish of Greenwich, whose church had been wrecked in a storm. It was carried on a wave of high-church and tory optimism: with the construction of St Paul's virtually complete, it was suggested that the London coal tax which had paid for it could, if renewed, provide churches in the expanding suburbs east of the City and north and west of the West End. On 10 October 1711 Hawksmoor and William Dickinson were appointed surveyors, initially to find and assess possible sites, and later to oversee every aspect of building on those chosen and approved. Hawksmoor held the post until the virtual winding up of the commission in 1733; Dickinson was soon succeeded by Gibbs and then by John James. The design of churches was not the surveyors' responsibility, and a number of architects submitted designs at various times. Nevertheless, Hawksmoor designed half of the dozen churches built: St Alfege, Greenwich (1712, consecrated 1718), three Stepney churches, begun in 1714—St Anne's, Limehouse (consecrated 1730), St George-in-the-East, Wapping, Stepney (interior destroyed 1941), and Christ Church, Spitalfields (both consecrated 1729)—and two others, begun in 1716: St George's, Bloomsbury (consecrated 1731), and the rebuilding of St Mary Woolnoth, a City church patched up after the great fire (finished 1727). He also adapted a chapel in Red Lion Fields as St George the Martyr, Queen Square (1717–23, extensively remodelled 1867). He produced jointly with James two late churches (1727–33), on which the commission, embarrassed by the excessive cost of earlier ones, imposed a rigid budget. These were St Luke's, Old Street, whose walls and fluted obelisk steeple remain, and St John Horselydown, Bermondsey (gutted 1940), whose tapering Ionic column steeple was dismantled in 1948. He also designed the rectories at Bermondsey and Spitalfields.

Initially the commission explored ideas of liturgical settings based on research into early Christian practice, and of building the churches to a more or less standard 'general design or forme'. Hawksmoor worked on both ideas before they ran out of momentum; while the second cannot have excited him, the first engaged his historical imagination and was a factor in the prominence of galleries in his designs. Although each is uniquely personal, they are far from uniform, and only the two late, economical, churches follow the traditional basilican plan of Wren's larger parish churches and many other eighteenth-century churches. Instead Hawksmoor's churches—as also the two designed by Thomas Archer—are planned like many European baroque ones, around two main axes at right angles; this applies even to the Spitalfields church, which superficially appears to be basilican. Spatially, nothing is as simple as it seems; this happens in other Hawksmoor interiors, but it may be appropriate to sacred architecture and particularly to the Anglican liturgy of the time, in which there was no single and sole focus of attention. Externally, Hawksmoor exploited the commission's preference for Portland stone and for porticoes and steeples. The tower he designed at Greenwich was not built, but the steeples of the Stepney churches and St Mary Woolnoth are lofty, impressive, and without obvious prototypes. At St George's, Bloomsbury, he finished the tower in a stepped pyramid based on the Mausoleum at Halicarnassus.

Other later work As a local resident Hawksmoor designed the Kensington charity school (1711–12, dem.). In 1715, following a Treasury reorganization of the office of works, he relinquished his Kensington clerkship for a similar one covering the palaces of Whitehall, Westminster, and St James's, together with the post of secretary to a new board of works, nominally under the direction of the aged Wren. In addition to office work he made minor improvements at St James's and Westminster, but in 1718 when—for political reasons—Wren was dismissed from the surveyorship, Hawksmoor also lost his Whitehall posts. Both his successor and Wren's soon proved incompetent, but it was not until 1726, after the death of Vanbrugh and with the help of Lord Carlisle, that he regained the secretaryship, which he then held until his death. From his letters to Lord Carlisle it is clear that he hoped for the surveyorship, or at least the second post of comptroller in place of Vanbrugh. He received neither, and found it increasingly irksome to be passed over in favour of younger and less able men.

Such a man—a cabinet-maker—had been engaged at Blenheim by the duchess of Marlborough for six years after the resignation of Vanbrugh in 1716 and the termination of state funding. When he proved inadequate, and

the duke's death in 1722 left her in sole charge, Hawksmoor returned for three years (1722–5) to the building he knew so well. He made a significant contribution in his own name, adding the Woodstock gate (based on an esoteric reconstruction of the arch of Titus in Rome), forming the gallery or long library on the west side into a dramatic sequence of connected spaces, and designing ceilings for state rooms. At Ockham Park, Surrey, he modernized a Jacobean house for Lord Chancellor Peter King (c.1723–9); the house was further altered in succeeding centuries, and the main building was burnt down in 1949. His hand can now be traced only in the brick stable block and in the small chapel added to the parish church in 1735 to contain King's monument. However, his most important late work is at Castle Howard and Westminster Abbey.

At Castle Howard Hawksmoor was, for the decade between Vanbrugh's death and his own, sole architect, supervising the building of Vanbrugh's Temple and designing the great mausoleum (1729–42) as well as other structures in the gardens and environs. These included the Pyramid and the medievalizing Carrmire gate. The design and construction of the mausoleum, in whose crypt Lord Carlisle and his successors are buried, are exceptionally documented by Hawksmoor's letters to a patron who, like him, found in later years the journey between London and Yorkshire increasingly tedious. Built of local stone and sited on a small hilltop a mile from the house, and usually seen against the sky, this large building is a domed cylinder rising through a Doric peristyle 19 metres in diameter, its columns severe and closely spaced; it is the most impressive and most evocative of eighteenth-century variations on this ancient Roman theme. The interior is at once luminous and claustrophobic, with none of the coldness that characterizes so many neo-classical funeral chapels. If any one building epitomizes Hawksmoor's art it is the mausoleum.

Hawksmoor's most public work, however, is familiar to millions ignorant of his name. In 1723 he succeeded Wren as surveyor to Westminster Abbey, where in 1725–8 he designed new stalls in Henry VII's chapel for the Order of the Bath, and a choir screen, part of which survives inside the present structure designed by Sir George Gilbert Scott. He made tentative designs for a central spire and for the west front, which for two centuries had risen no higher than the great window. But in 1734 his final design for the towers and gable-end was put in hand, being finished about ten years later. With hardly any Gothic detailing, his restrained completion of this famous building is exceptionally successful.

Conclusion: the man and his work Hawksmoor was, wrote his obituarist, both 'learned and ingenious', and was 'bred a Scholar' (Blackerby); however, his attitude to the past was more imaginative than scholarly, and his tendency to specify his historical sources reflected the need, as he expressed it, for 'some old father to stand by you' (Downes, *Hawksmoor*, 1979, 244) against the swelling tide of eighteenth-century architectural orthodoxy. A child of the Restoration, contemporary of Henry Purcell, and grandchild of the English Renaissance, he declared the basis of his art ('following the Rules of the Ancients') to lie less in rules and systems than in reason, imagination, experience, and experiment—in his own words, in 'strong reason and good fancy, joyn'd with experience and tryalls, so that we are assured of the good effect of it' (ibid.). His visual geometry was more often intuitive than calculated; rules were a means, not an end. His eclecticism had as much to do with rhetoric and surprise as with what might be appropriate or symbolic. In a culture which received the baroque architecture of Italy and France with increasing suspicion and its emulation in Britain with diminishing enthusiasm, Hawksmoor owed the relative success of his later years less to his creative genius, only adequately recognized during the twentieth century, than to the support and recommendation of Wren and later of Vanbrugh, and to the training, experience, skill, energy, and wisdom that earned the respect of all who engaged him, often in minor matters such as surveys and fire prevention. Even the duchess of Marlborough, notoriously disdainful of architects, commended in 1715 his modesty and honesty, adding that 'everybody that knows him will allow him to bee one of the most able in his profession' (ibid., 272).

The eighteenth and nineteenth centuries thought Hawksmoor industrious but odd; the generosity of the account of him in Horace Walpole's *Anecdotes of Painting* (1780) stemmed from his reading of Hawksmoor's obituary, from the transcript in George Vertue's notebooks. However, among later architects Sir John Soane and C. R. Cockerell studied Hawksmoor with profit, and William Wilkins's gothick additions to King's College, Cambridge, are patently indebted to All Souls.

With the early twentieth-century revival of general interest in the baroque, Hawksmoor's real talents were discerned, and it is hardly accidental that the peak of the Modern Movement in architecture coincided with the recognition of his art as essentially one of masses and spaces rather than of decorative detail. Architects have always worked from precedents; Hawksmoor sought them anywhere in the past or present, from the primitive to the increasingly fashionable neo-Palladianism of his maturity, extracting whatever could be used to move the beholder and eschewing the dogmatic and restrictive taste of Palladian orthodoxy which, for him, was 'but dress[ing] things in Masquerade' (Downes, *Hawksmoor*, 1979, 244). Similarly, Hawksmoor's attitude to his sources was a world away from the arbitrary stylistic eclecticism and mediocre detailing of later twentieth-century postmodernist architecture. His own style was too personal for imitation; Henry Joynes was his informal pupil but not his stylistic follower. His influence on the mostly anonymous buildings of the Board of Ordnance between 1715 and 1724 has been confirmed by the discovery of an autograph sketch for one of them, the barracks at Berwick upon Tweed.

Beyond the obituarist's glimpse of a sincere friend and companion we have no character sketch. But Hawksmoor's correspondence reveals, away from the drawing table, a modest man but one who knew his own mind and expressed it in a forthright and pithy style. This impression of an unassuming individual is suggested, too, by his only portrait, the informally dressed black-painted plaster bust in his buttery at All Souls, made by Sir Henry Cheere in his last years. (In 1961 the college commissioned bronze casts—one is in the National Portrait Gallery.) The draughtsmanship he learned in his twenties speaks equally directly, but the dreams it brings to life are as expansive as any architect's. He would submit designs by the handful, and he did not see a building in isolation. Besides his schemes for Oxford and Cambridge, he planned a precinct of buildings around St Paul's and a succession of grand schemes for the Royal Naval Hospital in Greenwich which occupied him for thirty years. Projects for a central chapel at Greenwich included one with a huge oval forecourt recalling St Peter's piazza in Rome. Still hopeful of proper public funding, he published in 1728 a pamphlet on the hospital, reviving some of his proposals. But in the following year his assistantship was abolished and Thomas Ripley appointed surveyor over his head. 'I once thought', he told Lord Carlisle in 1734, 'it wou'd have been a publick Building, but it will sink into a deformed Barrac' (Webb, 153). In 1735 even his clerkship, by then nominal, was withdrawn. Apart from the creation of Radcliffe Square, his only environmental successes were the obelisk forming the 'market cross' in Ripon (1702–3) and the dramatic little square that opens at the end of the main street of Woodstock to reveal his triumphal gateway to Blenheim.

Although he complained in a late letter (17 February 1736) that 'the world is determined to starve me for my good services' (Webb, 159), Hawksmoor left property in Millbank and James Street, in Lambeth, in Highgate, in Shenley, Ridge, and Aldenham, Hertfordshire, and at Great Drayton. He was fortunate, in an age without pension schemes, to continue working, in spite of over twenty-five years of chronic, and sometimes crippling, affliction by 'the Gout'. His last letter (2 March 1736) concerns his architectural and political efforts to get a bridge built at Westminster; his pamphlet on London Bridge— and some others—was written in support of this project. He died, of 'gout in his stomach' (*Grub Street Journal*, 25 March 1736), at the house in Millbank, where he had lived since 1715, on 25 March 1736 and was buried on 3 April in the churchyard at Shenley, Hertfordshire. The church is now secularized, but his large inscribed grave-slab survives. His widow, Hester Wells (whom he had married in 1696), outlived him by a year. Their daughter, Elizabeth, married first Nicholas Philpot, commissioner for hackney coaches, and second, in 1735, Nathaniel Blackerby, treasurer to the Fifty New Churches Commission, who wrote the informative obituary of Hawksmoor in *Read's Weekly Journal*.

In 1740 Hawksmoor's library was sold at auction, together with some 2000 drawings. Few of these can be identified with about 600 drawings now known, of which two in three reveal his own hand. The largest groups of letters are at Castle Howard and in the British Library.

KERRY DOWNES

Sources [N. Blackerby], *Read's Weekly Journal* (27 March 1736); repr. in K. Downes, *Hawksmoor* (1979) · K. Downes, *Hawksmoor*, 2nd edn (1979) · K. Downes, *Hawksmoor*, 3rd edn, The World of Art (1996) · G. F. Webb, 'The letters and drawings of Nicholas Hawksmoor relating to the building of the mausoleum at Castle Howard, 1726–1742', *Walpole Society*, 19 (1930–31), 111–64 · K. Downes, 'Hawksmoor's house at Easton Neston', *Architectural History*, 30 (1987), 50–77 · K. Downes, 'Hawksmoor's sale catalogue', *Burlington Magazine*, 95 (1953), 332–5 · A. N. L. Munby, ed., *Sale catalogues of libraries of eminent persons*, 4, ed. D. J. Watkin (1972), 45–105 · *Hawksmoor: an exhibition* (1977) [exhibition catalogue, Whitechapel Art Gallery, London] · R. Hewlings, 'Ripon's forum populi', *Architectural History*, 24 (1981), 39–52 · R. Hewlings, 'Hawksmoor's brave designs for the police', *English architecture public and private*, ed. J. Bold and E. Chaney (1993), 215–29 · K. Downes, *The architecture of Wren*, 2nd edn (1988) · P. du Prey, 'Hawksmoor's *Basilica after the primitive Christians*: architecture and theology', *Journal of the Society of Architectural Historians*, 48 (1989), 38–52 · H. M. Colvin, *Catalogue of architectural drawings of the 18th and 19th centuries in the library of Worcester College, Oxford* (1964) · H. M. Colvin and others, eds., *The history of the king's works*, 5 (1976) · E. G. W. Bill, ed., *The Queen Anne churches: a catalogue of the papers in Lambeth Palace Library of the Commission for Building Fifty New Churches* (1979) · A. T. Bolton and H. D. Hendry, eds., *The Wren Society*, 20 vols. (1924–43) · H. Walpole, *Anecdotes of painting in England*, ed. R. Wornum, new edn, 3 vols. (1849); repr. (1876), vol. 2 · *Genealogist's Magazine*, 12/12 (1957), 411–15
Archives LPL, corresp. and papers · NMM, notebook, MS ART/8 | BL, corresp. with Henry Joynes relating to Blenheim, Add. MS 19607 · Castle Howard, North Yorkshire, letters to earl of Carlisle
Likenesses attrib. H. Cheere, black plaster bust, *c.*1736, All Souls Oxf. [*see illus.*] · bronze bust, 1962 (after bust attrib. H. Cheere, *c.*1736), NPG

Hawkwood, Sir John (*d.* 1394), military commander, was the second son of Gilbert Hawkwood, a tanner and minor landowner at Sible Hedingham, Essex, where the family had held land since the beginning of the thirteenth century. The date of his birth is not recorded, but he was evidently in his early manhood by the time of his father's death in 1340, since, along with his elder brother, also called John, and the vicar of Gosfield, he was made one of the executors who secured legal possession and power of administration of the properties mentioned in Gilbert's will.

Military apprenticeship and early campaigns Little is known about Hawkwood's life before 1340, or his whereabouts during the next twenty years. The tradition that he was apprenticed to a London tailor has generally been dismissed, although his father had important connections with the London merchant community, and apprenticeship of sons of the gentry was not uncommon. The story may have arisen from a misreading of Matteo Villani's chronicle, but it is also recounted by the generally reliable Monk of Westminster, who believed the apprenticeship was to a hosier. That he was recruited for service in Edward III's wars in France is certain. This may have been as early as the campaigns in Brittany in 1342–5, and tradition has it that he fought at Crécy and Poitiers, on one of which occasions he may have won his spurs; but it is equally possible that he did not see service in France much before the great campaign of 1359–60. The appearance of his arms in an Anglo-Scottish roll of arms, which can be dated to the years 1357–61, is more likely to indicate his participation in a tournament at Smithfield on St George's

Sir John Hawkwood (*d.* 1394), by Paolo Uccello, 1436

day 1358, than his involvement in a crusade to Prussia during these years.

The first real evidence of Hawkwood's life as a soldier is from 1360, when, following the peace concluded at Brétigny in May, he was serving in one of the brigades (*routes*) of freebooters, the 'great companies' (*grandes compagnies*), sometimes known as 'latecomers' (*tard-venus*) because they had formed together from different bands following the conclusion of peace, and were in many cases raiding territories already plundered and devastated in previous raids. During the night of 28–29 December, in an abortive attempt to seize a part of the money collected for the ransom of Jean, king of France, a number of these companies occupied Pont-Saint-Esprit in the Rhône valley and blockaded Avignon, before being bought off by the pope. Some of them (as many as three-fifths of the total, according to Froissart; constituting some 3500 cavalry and 2000 infantry according to Matteo Villani) including Hawkwood, were recruited to serve the marquess of Montferrat in his war against the Visconti of Milan. When they first appeared in Italy, they were known as the great company of English and Germans (*magne societatis Anglicorum et Alamanorum*) and subsequently as the English White Company (*compagne bianca degli inghilesi*; *societatis albe Anglicorum*), and were commanded by a German mercenary called Albert Sterz, who had seen service in the French wars, and according to the Italian chronicler Piero Azario was 'so valiant in the field as to inspire others with courage' (Azario, col. 380), and who had the advantage that he could speak English. Before advancing into the Milanese, they created havoc in Piedmont, which at the time formed part of the territories of the count of Savoy, who was then allied to the Visconti, taking the count and some of his principal barons prisoner in a surprise attack on the town of Lanzo in the autumn of 1361, and ransoming them for 180,000 florins. Some contingents, Hawkwood apparently among them, may then have returned to France, where they joined forces with other *routes* of the great companies, together defeating a French army commanded by Jacques de Bourbon at Brignais (6 April 1362), before returning to Italy to rejoin Sterz, who remained in Montferrat's service until July 1363. Here, they devastated the countryside on either side of the River Po from Novaro to Pavia and Tortona, crossing the Ticino to proceed within 6 miles of Milan, before returning to Romagnano and defeating the Milanese forces commanded by another German mercenary, Konrad von Landau, at the bridge of Canturino on 22 April.

Following this victory, in July 1363 Sterz was appointed captain-general of the Pisan army for six months, the republic at that time being allied to Milan and at war with Florence; but on the expiry of his contract in December, Hawkwood replaced him as commanding officer, and the companies under his command were reformed. Sterz, an Englishman called Andrew Belmont, and later Haneken Bongard (another German mercenary hired by Montferrat), became Hawkwood's subordinate officers until they deserted Pisan service for that of Florence in the following summer. Thereafter Hawkwood never left Italy, and when he was not fighting on his own account he was successively employed by Bernabò Visconti of Milan (1368–72) principally in his wars with the Florentine league, by Pope Gregory XI in his attempts to restore papal authority in Italy (September 1372–April 1377), and subsequently in the service of the Florentine republic. He fought in the kingdom of Naples for both Charles of Durazzo (1382–3) and Queen Marguerite (1386 and 1388–9), and in the Veronese for Francesco Carrara, marquess of Padua (1386–7). But during the last fourteen years of his life, from the spring of 1380, his services were principally, although by no means exclusively, contracted to Florence, latterly as captain-general of the army of the republic.

Hawkwood was undoubtedly one of the ablest military commanders of his day, and acknowledged as such by his contemporaries; but he was not crowned with success immediately. He suffered several fairly serious set-backs in the 1360s, and fortune did not come his way until several years into the next decade. There was no real stability in the composition, nor continuity in the command, of the various English brigades serving in Italy before they were brought together under his command in the service of the church in 1372; but from that time onwards his reputation was in the ascendant, despite continuing evidence of insubordination in the English forces serving under him. When Sterz and Bongard deserted Pisan service in the summer of 1364, joining forces to form the Company of the Star, which headed south for the kingdom of Naples, the majority of the English contingents formerly serving with Hawkwood had joined a new Anglo-Hungarian White Company, of which Hugh Mortimer, lord of La Zouche, was captain-general, and Hawkwood was left with only 800 of his men in Pisan pay. The war with Florence went badly, and his forces suffered continual set-backs and a serious defeat at the hands of the Florentine army, which had an overwhelming numerical superiority. After a revolution in Pisa, in which he played no small part, the Pisans were obliged to make peace on humiliating terms.

Thereafter, although the Florentine republic twice sought Hawkwood's services (in July 1365 and the spring of 1367), he refused them, preferring to resume his old profession of free-lance in the Perugino, and still hankering after Pisan employ. Perhaps it was a mistake. Defeated with considerable losses in a pitched battle with Bongard on 25 July 1365, he joined his English forces for a while with those of Ambrogio, one of Bernabò Visconti's illegitimate sons, to form the Company of Saint George, but abandoned it in the spring of 1366. In June 1369 he was taken prisoner by two other German mercenaries, Johann Flach von Reischach and Johann von Riedheim, who were then in papal service. While in the service of the Visconti the fortunes of his brigade among predominantly German forces were mixed. Defeated by a Florentine army before Reggio in August 1370, Hawkwood subsequently surprised the forces of the Florentine league in an ambush near Mirandola, taking their commanders-in-chief prisoner. Then, on 2 June 1372, only a matter of months before quitting Milanese service, he defeated a considerably larger army under Lutz von Landau, which was coming to the aid of the marquess of Montferrat, who was once again at war with the Visconti. After switching from Milanese to papal service in the autumn of 1372, he pursued and virtually annihilated the Milanese forces on the Panaro between Modena and Bologna in the following January, but subsequently failed to effect a junction with the count of Savoy's forces when they crossed the Ticino in February, an essential part of the strategic plan of campaign in that year.

The English companies Hawkwood's military fortunes were in part determined by the composition of the forces serving under him. The mercenary companies employed by the different Italian states in the second half of the fourteenth century, placed under the command of one or more captains-general, were made up of a variable number of brigades, each under a captain or constable, depending on the number of units of which they were composed. Among the English contingents the essential unit was the lance, introduced to Italy by the White Company, with its distinctive three-man lance component (two men-at-arms and a page), and its combination with archers, equipped with longbows, some accompanied by a page. A lance thus normally constituted four or five men. The men-at-arms were mounted on war-horses or dextriers, the archers and their pages on lighter horses or rouncies. Hawkwood's personal brigade was almost always small in comparison to the total forces under his command or in which he served; but it was the essential nucleus, with a greater continuity in its personnel than in the companies under his command, where the number and personnel of the brigades fluctuated, often because of the recruitment policies of rival employers. The Visconti had been accustomed to employing German and Hungarian mercenaries, and it was alongside these contingents, always in the majority, that he had fought for Bernabò from 1368 to 1372. However, following his engagement in papal service in September 1372, the forces which were brought under his command, and which were styled the English Company (*compagnie seu societatis Anglicorum*), was an amalgam of the English brigades that had previously operated under different commanders, and of which he became captain-general following the conclusion of the offensive of 1373. A significant number of the constables serving with him came from Essex, some of the more notable among them from villages and manors in the neighbourhood of Sible Hedingham. The English brigades were also distinguished by their habit of dismounting to fight on foot, and being accustomed to riding at night and fighting deep into the winter.

These essential features of the forces at his disposal served Hawkwood well; but they were brought into play by his real talent as a military commander: in effecting long marches, creating diversions, and pulling victory out of failure. He also built up a well-organized intelligence service, and was adept in the use of disinformation, seeking safe conducts for routes he had no intention of taking, dispatching letters detailing sensitive troop movements which were intended to be leaked to the enemy, feigning a retreat while he placed his troops in ambush, or disguising another with a smokescreen of presence. He was well aware that careless words cost lives, and played his cards close to his chest. Even his closest councillors were frequently kept in the dark about his true intentions until the last minute, and there is ample evidence to show that outside informers were invariably perplexed as to what his next moves might be.

Hawkwood's military achievements These characteristics of Hawkwood's military genius were displayed on many occasions. Following his defeat by Giangaleazzo Visconti at Montechiaro on 8 May 1373, he rallied his forces, pursued the Milanese, routed them, and took their principal officers prisoner. In command of the Paduan forces in 1387, he was pursued by a much larger Veronese army which threatened to cut off his supply lines, and was forced to fall back to Castelbaldo on the northern bank of the Adige. Here he decided to make his stand at Castagnaro, on the south side of the river, where he was able to take up a battleground of his own choosing, with the river at his back, on firmer land with his flanks protected by marshy ground bisected by irrigation canals. Dismounting his cavalry, he drew them up in close array,

concealing archers, crossbowmen, and a few cannon on the flanks, pushed forward of the main position. The Veronese thus had to attack him across a difficult terrain, under heavy fire, and Hawkwood only gave orders for his men-at-arms to move in after the archers had done their work and gaps had begun to appear in the Veronese ranks. The Scaliger army collapsed under the onslaught, and the rout was complete. Almost half of the Veronese forces were taken prisoner, including nearly eighty captains and subordinate officers, and the number of killed and wounded was also high.

Four years later, when Florence finally decided to make a stand against Giangaleazzo Visconti, an essential part of the republic's strategy was to take the Milanese armies in a pincer movement in which Hawkwood would join up forces on the Po with a mercenary army recruited in France by the count of Armagnac. On this occasion Hawkwood led an army of 2000 lances and a large number of infantry to within 10 miles of Milan; but the plan for a simultaneous attack on two fronts was shattered by Armagnac's failure to keep to the prearranged timetable, which allowed the Milanese captain, Jacopo dal Verme, to concentrate his attention on Hawkwood's forces and pursue them as far as the Adige, where the enemy had broken the dykes, turning the country into a vast lake around Castagnaro. Hawkwood knew the terrain well, but his success in getting the greater part of his forces through the deep waters and across the river to safety at Castelbaldo was a stroke of military genius which the republic duly acknowledged in a letter to him of 27 July 1391, praising the forces under his command and his 'incomparable leadership', which would be proclaimed and commended throughout Italy; they recalled his 'inextinguishable glory', which they would extol in the future, granting him every favour (Florence, Archivio di Stato, Signori, Missive, 1 Cancelleria, reg. 22, fol. 148). In the following month, when dal Verme invaded Tuscany, Hawkwood impeded his advance by a succession of attacks, forcing him to retreat towards Lucca and driving him into Liguria during the course of September. There can be little doubt that his actions saved Florence from Milanese expansion at a critical juncture. In two further letters, dated 21 and 23 September, and penned, like that of 27 July, by Coluccio Salutati, the chancellor of the republic, the Signoria had encouraged him to achieve a glorious victory, for which they would 'magnanimously carry out that which we owe you, to throw light and glory on your eternal and inextinguishable fame', urging him to emulate Scipio Africanus, one of Rome's greatest generals, skilful alike in strategy and tactics, and with the faculty of inspiring his soldiers with confidence (Florence, Archivio di Stato, Signori, Missive, 1 Cancelleria, reg. 22, fols. 160v–161r). They did not have long to wait. During the night of 24 September, as the enemy continued to retreat up Monte Albano, Hawkwood forced dal Verme's rearguard to battle, and completely routed it at the entrance to the Val di Nievole to the west of Pistoia. The Signoria had already granted him substantial financial rewards for his services earlier in the campaign, and it seems that they were now thinking of some monument to commemorate his victories. It was Hawkwood's last major campaign, and it sealed his reputation.

The material rewards of service and Hawkwood's investments

There can be little doubt that Hawkwood amassed considerable wealth, not only from ransoms and booty, and in bribes extracted from different Italian communes to secure his departure from their *contados* or to ensure his goodwill, but also in lands and pensions. The extent of his takings in the first category is not easily computed. While in the course of his military career the forces under his command evidently acquired substantial booty and numerous prisoners, of which he had his share, the surviving evidence does not permit his gains to be quantified, or his own ransom payments to be balanced against those extracted from others. More precise calculations can be made of the moneys paid as bribes by the Italian communes, but even here there are difficulties, since the global sums negotiated with the communes had to be divided between him and his subordinate officers, and had frequently also to be shared with one or more fellow commanders. In 1375, for instance, Hawkwood extracted 30,500 florins from Siena; but a further 68,000 florins paid over a period of five years between 1379 and 1385 had to be shared with co-commanders. Moreover, there were often additional payments to the main sums that were paid out to individual captains and officers, and these were frequently substantial. When the companies were operating independently, some of these moneys were effectively in lieu of pay. It is thus easier to compute the cost of the mercenary activities to the communes than it is to calculate the profits of military captains. Nevertheless, the rewards were sometimes considerable. During the course of three months in 1375, the bribes paid by Florence, Pisa, Siena, Lucca, and Arezzo together amounted to more than 204,500 florins, that is, in excess of 723 kilograms of gold.

With regard to his lands and property, some of these were acquired by conquest, or came to him in lieu of pay, which was by no means negligible; others were granted by appreciative employers, or as bribes similar to those referred to above. In April 1391, during the course of the campaign against the Visconti, the annual pension of 1200 florins first awarded to him by the Florentine republic in 1375 to secure his goodwill was raised to 3200 florins, a jointure of 1000 florins per annum settled on his wife, and 2000 florins granted on the marriage of each of his three daughters. In addition he and his male heirs were granted Florentine citizenship, excepting the right to hold office. The lands and property he acquired were extensive and, like the campaigns he fought in, were geographically widely spread. From his service with the church he secured castles and lands in the Romagna and in the marches of Ancona, notably Castrocaro, Bagnacavallo, Cotignola, Conselice, and Montefortino, and a house in Bologna. While in Neapolitan service he acquired estates in Naples, Capua, and Aversa, and secured a number of strongholds in the Aretino (notably the castle of Montecchio and the strongholds of Badia al Pino and Migliari), possibly acquired while returning to central

Italy from that service in 1384. He had a house called Polverosa in the Florentine suburb of San Donato di Torre, an estate called La Rochetta in the Val d'Elsa near Poggibonsi, a property at Gazzuolo in the Cremonese (probably granted to him by Ludovico Gonzaga, either in appreciation or as a bribe), and a mansion with a cloister in Perugia, granted to him by the priors of that city in 1381. What explanation can therefore be given for Hawkwood's claim, in the summer of 1393 that, considering his innumerable daily expenses, his income was insufficient to support his family? It is probable that the administrative costs of his numerous estates were high, and there is little doubt that he had been scrupulous in paying and rewarding the men who had served him both in war and peace. He may also have been living beyond his means, or in modern parlance have been capital-rich but income-poor; but there was another factor which sheds much light on his ambitions and how he saw himself in the world.

The lure of the ancestral lands Hawkwood clearly had no desire to carve out a patrimony and establish a dynasty in Italy. From as early as 1375 he had sought and secured an assurance that the annual pension of 1200 florins then offered to him by Florence would be paid to him even if he left that country, and this was confirmed by the Signoria in July 1376. From this period in papal service he was sending some of his pay and subsequently other moneys back to England by way of Luccese merchants operating through Bruges, and these were used to buy property in London and Essex, and to advance some moneys to the English crown in aid of the war in France. Some time between June 1377 and February 1380, through his agents in England (including, perhaps significantly, John Cavendish and Robert Lyndeseye, a draper and tailor of London, respectively), he acquired the reversion of the Leadenhall in London from the widow of Sir John Neville, with whom he may have served in the expedition to Brittany under the earl of Northampton in 1345, and whose family seat was at Wethersfield in Essex, less than 5 miles from Sible Hedingham. However, the story was not altogether a happy one. Other moneys he advanced to the Luccese in 1382 were not passed on to his agents and were the subject of subsequent litigation, and some of the lands that he purchased, and which were enfeoffed to his use, were subsequently detained by his feoffees. Hawkwood's intention to return to England was thus evident, but there were hurdles to be overcome, some of them new, others dating from his past life in France. In the parliament held at Westminster in January 1377 he had sought, and in the following March secured, a royal pardon for his youthful misdemeanours 'in like manner to that granted to Sir Robert Knowles' (*RotP*, 2.372). The latter had embraced, among other things, 'all disobediences, takings of towns, castles and fortresses and prisoners surrendered without licence, breakings of truces and safe-conducts, sales of castles, cities and boroughs, towns, manors, lands, rents, services and prisoners to the king's enemies and others' (*CPR*, 1374–7, 435). In the fragmented political structure of fourteenth-century Italy, where the king of England had no claims and where the royal writ did not run, he had encountered no such obstacles. But two months after his pardon had been granted he married Donnina, one of Bernabò Visconti's illegitimate daughters, which brought him, in addition to handsome presents and the benefits of a sizeable dowry, powerful family connections, which included his fellow *condottiere*, Count Lutz von Landau, who was married to Donnina's sister, Elisabetta, on the same day, and doubtless for the same reasons. The unity of purpose between Florence and Milan at this juncture was also critical, for it allowed Hawkwood simultaneously to serve two masters, who were subsequently bitterly opposed, to take up his appointment as commander of the forces of the Florentine league, and to enjoy the benefits of the life annuity granted to him by the republic, now apparently backdated, on the conditions already noted.

In 1387, following the conclusion of his services with the Carrara of Padua, Hawkwood may once again have considered returning home. Later that year he disposed of his properties in the kingdom of Naples and was planning the sale of those at San Donato and La Rochetta; but it was not until five years later, on the conclusion of the war with Milan, and when he was doubtless aware that his days were numbered, that the die was cast. During the winter of 1392–3 he was making the necessary dispositions: providing husbands for his two eldest daughters by Donnina, who were of marriageable age, settling his debts, attempting to recover sums of money and other properties due to him and his wife in Milan and Bologna, and seeking the necessary safe conducts for his passage to England. Allowing for the possibility that he might die before his return, he made known to Thomas Coggeshall of Essex, by way of a nuncupative will, his wishes with regard to the disposal of his properties in England. These included the sale of the Leadenhall, and the foundation of chantries in the church at Sible Hedingham and in the priory of Castle Hedingham with some of the proceeds. In the event of Donnina's surviving him and coming to England, she was to be enfeoffed with his properties of Liston in Gosfield and Hostages in Sible Hedingham, to be held during her lifetime with reversion to their son John. Hawkwood's other properties in England were to be held by his feoffees until his son came of age, when they were to be surrendered to him.

A year later, in March 1394, 'weary by reason of his great age', and, as he himself asserted 'weighed down by infirmity' and wishing to return 'to his old country' (Florence, Archivio di Stato, Capitoli, reg. 1, fol. 164v), Hawkwood concluded an arrangement with the Florentine Signoria for the commutation of the pensions and other payments granted to himself and his family, and the disposal of his remaining possessions in the Aretino. It is clear that by this time Hawkwood was confined to his house at San Donato, and then to his bed. Five days later, during the night of 16–17 March, he died of a stroke. On the 20th the republic gave him a magnificent funeral, and his body was temporarily laid to rest in the choir of Santa Maria del Fiore (Florence Cathedral). It was left to Sir John's widow and his Florentine attorney to conclude the arrangements for the disposal of the patrimonial estate in Italy and the liquidation of the accounts between Hawkwood's heirs and the Signoria.

Two cenotaphs and two families Even before Hawkwood's death, in August 1393, the Signoria had determined that an elaborate marble tomb would be constructed in his honour, and early in 1395 they commissioned Taddeo Gaddi and Giuliano d'Arrigho to design and paint a monument in fresco on the north wall of the cathedral. In the event the tomb itself was never executed, following a request from Richard II that Hawkwood's body be returned to England, and on 3 June 1395 the Signoria acceded to this request. In 1436 the original fresco was replaced by another in *terra-verde* by Paolo Uccello, which represents Hawkwood mounted on an ambling charger, wearing a short doublet over his armour, a light cap or *berret* in place of the helmet worn in battle on his head, and carrying the baton of a captain of war in his right hand. In the early nineteenth century the painting was transferred to canvas and moved to the west wall of the church. As for Hawkwood's remains, there is no reason to doubt that they were returned to Sible Hedingham, and buried in the parish church of St Peter, where a noble cenotaph was constructed with the moneys raised by his feoffees. The tomb recess, and parts of the canopy with spandrels bearing carvings of a hawk and other animals in a wood, may still be seen; but the tomb chest itself has long since vanished. Unfortunately, there is no mention of the church in John Leland's account of his tour through England and Wales in 1535–43, and by the time John Weever published his *Ancient Funeral Monuments* (1631) the tomb had largely been destroyed. But both Weever and Philip Morant, in his *History and Antiquities of the County of Essex* (1768) were of the opinion that it had been paid for by the abundant money Hawkwood sent back to England, and Morant, who must have seen some old drawings, adds 'From the effigies on this monument it should seem that he had two wives' (Morant, 2.288).

Neither the date nor the fact of Hawkwood's first marriage has been established, but before his marriage to Donnina he had two sons, who may or may not have been legitimate, but who were only boys when they were held hostage in Bologna in 1376. He also had a daughter, Antiocha or Mary, who by March 1379 was married to Sir William Coggeshall, apparently the cousin of Sir Thomas, afterwards of Codham Hall, Essex, then in Hawkwood's service in Italy and residing in Milan. There may also have two other daughters: Fiorentina, who married a Milanese noble, Lancellotto del Mayno, and Beatrice, who married John Shelley, an ancestor of the poet. With Donnina Hawkwood had one son, John, and three daughters. The eldest daughter, Giannetta, was married on 7 September 1392 (aged fifteen) to Brezaglia, son of Count Lodovico di Porciglia, formerly captain of the Bolognese forces, subsequently *podestà* of Ferrara and, for a brief period after Hawkwood's death, captain of the Florentine forces. The second, Caterina, was married on 20 January 1393 (aged fourteen), to Konrad von Prassberg, a German captain who had served with Hawkwood. In March 1395 the

Signoria had envisaged that the son and the third daughter, Anna, who were both under age, would go to England with their mother, as Hawkwood and Donnina had clearly planned. However, it seems unlikely that mother and daughter ever made the journey, and Anna was subsequently married to Ambrogiuolo di Piero della Torre of Milan; but the son, John, went, and settled on the ancestral lands at Sible Hedingham. Naturalized in 1407, two years later he secured possession of the estates in Essex purchased by his father, which were then released by his principal feoffee, who in 1412 also obtained licence to found the two chantries his father had envisaged, where three priests were to incant the offices and pray for the souls of his father and two of his military companions, both from Essex, who had also died in Italy, namely John Oliver and Thomas Newenton. That no will has come to light in Italy is not surprising. Hawkwood had realized his estate there, and made settlements on those members of his family who were to remain behind when he left. Doubtless the greater part of the proceeds were sent to England, but too late to make the formal testamentary bequests, of which the essentials were conveyed orally to Thomas Coggeshall by way of one of Hawkwood's squires, John Sampson, in two of the earliest private letters in the English language to survive. The oral testament was drawn up in the form of an indenture on Sampson's arrival in England, which gave the necessary instructions to his feoffees, who had now become his executors.

Noblesse oblige? There can be no doubt that Hawkwood was one of the greatest military commanders of his day, but what distinguished him from other *condottieri* of his own generation, and others who came before him, was the loyalty that he showed to his principal employers, firstly Pisa and then, more notably, Florence. This was a quality also evident in his relations with the men serving under him, and with his compatriots from Essex. It gave a greater cohesion and *esprit de corps* to his own brigade than was common in other companies (including other English brigades) in the period. His failure to obey Bernabò Visconti's orders during the siege of Asti in 1372, and his desertion of Milanese service, may well have been connected with the position in which he then found himself, rather than a question of pay. For among the opposing forces attempting to relieve the town were other English contingents under his old comrade-in-arms, John Musard, an Englishman from Worcestershire who had risen to eminence and respectability in the service of Count Amadeus (VI) of Savoy, a founder member of the count's order of the Collar, and who had fought with him in France, notably at Pont-Saint-Esprit. Nor was money the reason for his switching from papal to Florentine service in April 1377. He may well have been disillusioned by the way the church leaders were conducting the war, especially after the massacres of significant numbers of the civilian population at Faenza and Cesena in March 1376 and February 1377 respectively, in which the forces under his command had played their part. He had in fact been courted by the Florentine republic for some time, and remained loyal to his employer; but the evidence suggests that the life pension promised to him, and the possibilities of a more permanent contract, if not a contract for life, were a tempting prospect, which held out new opportunities as well as greater stability and the chances of a family life. What he got, initially, was in effect a series of short-term contracts, of which some were a specie of *condotta in aspetto*, which allowed the republic to secure the first option of his services during periods in which he was free to serve elsewhere. It is against this background that his military career after 1377 must be interpreted.

Many questions remain to be answered about Hawkwood's life, not least why he should have wished to return to England when he had been so successful in Italy, was well married and powerfully connected, and probably prosperous enough, for all his protestations to the contrary; he was respected, even revered in governing circles in Florence, with whom he was on easy terms as he was also with some of her leading citizens. That he spoke reasonably fluent Italian seems certain, frequently attending meetings of the war council, the Ten of War, when he was in Florence, and arguing details of military policy with them. Was it some distant memories of youth that beckoned him to return to his native soil, and to Sible Hedingham in particular? For it was there that he early decided to extend the family patrimony, and that ambition never deserted him. KENNETH FOWLER

Sources *Chancery records* · A. H. Thomas and P. E. Jones, eds., *Calendar of plea and memoranda rolls preserved among the archives of the corporation of the City of London at the Guildhall*, 3 (1932) · M. Villani and F. Villani, *Istorie*, ed. L. A. Muratori, original edn, 28 vols., Rerum Italicarum Scriptores (1723–51), 14, cols. 9–770 · P. Azario, *Chronicon*, vol. 16 of L. A. Muratori, *Rerum Italicum scriptores*, 25 vols. in 28 (1723–51), cols. 297–424 [and other works in this edn and the new ser., from 1900, in progress] · *Chroniques de J. Froissart*, ed. S. Luce and others, 15 vols. (Paris, 1869–1975) · *Œuvres de Froissart: chroniques*, ed. K. de Lettenhove, 25 vols. (Brussels, 1867–77) · L. C. Hector and B. F. Harvey, eds. and trans., *The Westminster chronicle, 1381–1394*, OMT (1982) · J. Temple-Leader and G. Marcotti, *Sir John Hawkwood: story of a 'condottiere'* (1889) · K. A. Fowler, *Medieval mercenaries* [forthcoming], 1–2 (2001–) · K. A. Fowler, 'Sir John Hawkwood and the English *condottieri* in Trecento Italy', *Renaissance Studies*, 12 (1998), 131–48 · K. A. Fowler, 'Condotte e condottieri. Mercenaires anglais au service de Florence au XIVᵉ siècle', *Mélanges Contamine* [forthcoming] · F. Gaupp, 'The *condottiere* John Hawkwood', *History*, new ser., 23 (1938–9), 305–21 · D. M. B. de Mesquita, 'Some *condottieri* of the Trecento and their relations with political authority', *PBA*, 32 (1946), 219–41 · W. Caferro, *Mercenary companies and the decline of Siena* (1998) · M. Mallett, *Mercenaries and their masters: warfare in Renaissance Italy* (1974) · B. G. Kohl, *Padua under the Carrara, 1318–1405* (1998) · W. Paravicini, 'Heraldische Quellen zur Geschichte der Preußenreisen im 14. Jahrhundert', *Ordines Militares 4: Werkstatt des Historikers* (1987), 111–28 · A. H. Thomas, 'Notes on the history of Leadenhall, 1195–1488', *London Topographical Record*, 13 (1923), 1–22 · *An inventory of the historical monuments in Essex*, Royal Commission on Historical Monuments (England), 1 (1916) · J. Weever, *Ancient funerall monuments* (1631) · P. Morant, *The history and antiquities of the county of Essex*, 2 vols. (1768) · S. L. Thrupp, *The merchant class of medieval London, 1300–1500* (1948) · *RotP*, vol. 2 · Archivio di Stato, Florence, Capitoli, reg. 1 · Archivio di Stato, Florence, Signori, Missive, 1 Cancelleria, reg. 22

Likenesses P. Uccello, fresco transferred to canvas, 1436, Santa Maria del Fiore, Florence [*see illus.*]

Hawkyns, Henry (*c.*1553–1630), civil lawyer and diplomatic agent, was the son of John Hawkyns and his wife, Ann Yelverton. He was connected to the leading East Anglian protestant families through his mother, and was probably born at Wisbech on property which she had acquired through her first marriage to Thomas Rede. Hawkyns matriculated at Peterhouse, Cambridge, in 1568, and graduated BA in 1571 or 1572 and MA in 1575. He became a fellow of Peterhouse in 1575 and served as a university proctor in 1583–4. In March 1584 he entered Gray's Inn, where many of his relatives were members, being admitted on the same day as fellow puritans Sir Richard Knightley and Humphrey Davenport. In November 1585 Hawkyns was given leave from Peterhouse to join the staff of Sir Thomas Cecil, newly appointed as governor of Brill. It is unclear how long he served as legal adviser in the Low Countries, but he was nominated to accompany Edward, eleventh Lord Zouche, 'for conference in learning' during his European tour in July 1586 (Walker, 1.267). Hawkyns's name may have been suggested to Zouche by mutual contacts at Gray's Inn.

Zouche's party left England in March 1587 and spent the next few years travelling through Germany, Switzerland, and Italy. Hawkyns apparently left Zouche and returned to England by March 1591, when Archbishop Whitgift wrote to the University of Cambridge and requested that he be made doctor of laws on the basis of his study in European universities, especially Padua, where he had been unable to take his degree for religious reasons. Hawkyns received the degree, but had to perform the requisite exercises in Cambridge. He now began to be 'employed in publick matters of state' (Hammer, 362) and was resident in London, relying upon Whitgift to prevent the forfeiture of his fellowship at Peterhouse on grounds of absenteeism. In 1594 Hawkyns visited Scotland, probably as an aide to Lord Zouche, who served as Elizabeth's special ambassador to James VI during the early months of the year.

In mid-1595 Hawkyns was chosen for a quasi-diplomatic role as gatherer of intelligence and formal representative of the earl of Essex in Venice. Approved by the queen, this venture was intended to co-ordinate intelligence gathering by Italian contacts of Antonio Perez, the exiled former secretary of Philip II of Spain, to recruit new spies in Italy, and to establish an open, but deniable, diplomatic presence for England. More covertly, the agent at Venice was also expected to burnish the earl's international reputation. Hawkyns was chosen for this position in some haste, after the sudden death of the original choice, Peter Wroth. Essex and Elizabeth clearly approved Hawkyns's nomination at the urging of Anthony Bacon, who oversaw the Venice operation on the earl's behalf. Bacon was a distant relative of Hawkyns, a fellow member of Gray's Inn, and regular correspondent and former student of Whitgift. Bacon presumably judged that Hawkyns's expertise and travel, together with his continuing correspondence with foreign contacts such as Richard Willoughby of Padua, made him an ideal choice for Essex's work.

Hawkyns was based at Venice from December 1595 until about March 1598. After an uncomfortable start (which helped to spark a feud between Bacon and Henry Wotton, one of the earl's secretaries), he proved an adequate co-ordinator of intelligence from Venice (Ungerer, vol. 2), but his resolute puritanism made him a less than ideal diplomat in a Catholic country. A complaint by the tutor of Francis Davison, who travelled through Venice in 1596, criticized Hawkyns, perhaps unfairly, for being both petty and excessively proud of his quasi-ambassadorial status (BL, Harley MS 296, fol. 114*v*). Hawkyns visited Vienna and Paris on his journey home to England. He finally resigned from Peterhouse in January 1599. Unfortunately his hopes of further advancement, as promised by Essex and Bacon, were dashed by the earl's declining influence and subsequent collapse into political oblivion. As a well-known partisan of Essex, Hawkyns was arrested after the earl's London insurrection in February 1601 and briefly placed in the custody of Alderman Lee. Although Hawkyns was a commissioner for the admiralty court in Middlesex in 1603, his career apparently never recovered from the fall of Essex and the death soon afterwards of Anthony Bacon.

Hawkyns's will indicates that he spent his old age in the company of influential London puritans such as William Gouge, Richard Sibbs, and John Davenport. His legacies included money for the poor of the French church in London, distressed protestant ministers in England and Germany, and towards the purchase of impropriated livings. He also provided £300 to build almshouses for the godly poor of Wisbech, £100 'for the erecting of twoe new Bible clarks' at Peterhouse, and various bequests (including his books) to members of the Hatcher family of Careby, Lincolnshire, to whom he was related by the marriage of his half-sister, Katherine Rede, the child of his mother's first marriage. Hawkyns apparently never married; he died in London in early December 1630 and was buried on 15 December at St Andrew's, Holborn.

PAUL E. J. HAMMER

Sources LPL, MSS 652, 654–61 [papers of Anthony Bacon] · will, PRO, PROB 11/157, fols. 5*r*–6*r* · T. A. Walker, *A biographical register of Peterhouse men*, 2 vols. (1927–30) · BL, Harley MSS 286, 288, 295–6 · P. E. J. Hammer, 'Essex and Europe: evidence from confidential instructions by the earl of Essex, 1595–6', *EngHR*, 111 (1996), 357–81 · G. Ungerer, *A Spaniard in Elizabethan England: the correspondence of Antonio Pérez's exile*, 2 vols. (1974–6) · *Calendar of the manuscripts of the most hon. the marquis of Salisbury*, 24 vols., HMC, 9 (1883–1976) · A. R. Maddison, ed., *Lincolnshire pedigrees*, 4 vols., Harleian Society, 50–52, 55 (1902–6) · W. Rye, ed., *The visitacion of Norffolk … 1563 … 1613*, Harleian Society, 32 (1891) · J. Foster, *The register of admissions to Gray's Inn, 1521–1889, together with the register of marriages in Gray's Inn chapel, 1695–1754* (privately printed, London, 1889) · Venn, *Alum. Cant.*, 1/1–4 · B. P. Levack, *The civil lawyers in England, 1603–1641* (1973) · CUL, MS Mm.i.45 · LUL, MS 187 · Bodl. Oxf., MS Eng. hist. c. 121 · parish register, Holborn, St Andrew's, London, GL, 15 Dec 1630 [burial]
Archives Hatfield House, Hertfordshire | LPL, papers of Anthony Bacon, MSS 652, 654–661
Wealth at death £1780 in bequests; excl. value of his library: will, PRO, PROB 11/157, fols. 5*r*–6*r*

Hawles, Sir John (*bap.* 1645, *d.* 1716), lawyer and politician, was baptized on 18 March 1645, the second son of Thomas Hawles (*d.* 1678) of The Close, Salisbury, Wiltshire, and

Elizabeth (b. c.1608, d. in or after 1671), daughter and heir of Thomas Antrobus of Heath House, Petersfield, Hampshire. Hawles's father was active in the neutralist Clubmen movement in 1645. Not much is known about Hawles's early career, apart from his education. He attended Winchester College, matriculated at Queen's College, Oxford, on 15 May 1662, and entered Lincoln's Inn on 10 February 1664, being called to the bar on 10 February 1670. No doubt it was his learning which prompted John Aubrey to describe him as 'an exceeding ingenious young man' (Brief Lives, 305) and led Anthony Wood to see him as 'a person of note for his profession, but ill-natured, turbulent and inclining to a republic' (Wood, Ath. Oxon., 4.528–9). Hawles's concern with the liberty of the subject was first evinced in his The English-Man's Right: a Dialogue Between a Barrister at Law, and a Jury-Man (1680), which was republished frequently in the eighteenth century.

Hawles came to prominence on 25 March 1689 with his election to the convention for Old Sarum and the publication of his Remarks upon the Trials of Edward Fitzharris. He was very active in the House of Commons, both as a committee man and as a speaker. He made his first recorded speech on 8 May, and seems to have paid particular attention to events of the previous two reigns, such as the Popish Plot, the tribulations of Titus Oates, and the Indemnity Bill. He was critical of some of those employed by King William, noting that 'if King James II was to come in again, he could not make a better choice of some persons in employment' (HoP, Commons, 1660–90, 2.514). Professionally he prospered too, appearing eight times as counsel before the Lords during the Convention. However, Hawles could not find a seat at the 1690 election, losing at both St Ives and Banbury. In October 1691 he failed in his attempt to become recorder of London. In July 1694 Lord Keeper Somers, backed by the duke of Shrewsbury and the earl of Sunderland, recommended Hawles as a king's counsel specifically to engage him for the crown, should he be returned to parliament 'where he was much harkened to formerly' (CSP dom., 1694–5, 246). He was duly appointed a king's counsel on 16 August 1694 and was immediately employed in the prosecution of suspected Jacobite plotters in Lancashire and Cheshire. He was appointed solicitor-general on 12 July 1695, and in the general election of October he was returned for Wilton. The Commons elected him chairman of the committee of privileges and elections and he was knighted on 28 November 1695. As solicitor Hawles undertook the prosecution of Sir John Fenwick by parliamentary act of attainder in 1696, and according to James Vernon spoke very well. His opposition to the earl of Ailesbury's motion for bail saw Hawles 'as fierce as a bull dog' and earned him a rebuke from the lord chief justice as one 'that was in time past so great a stickler for liberty of the subject' (Memoirs of Thomas, Earl of Ailesbury, ed. W. E. Buckley, 1890, 2.426). In the 1698 election he was returned for both Mitchell and Bere Alston (and never chose between them). Hawles was clearly a whig in politics and was perceived as a follower of the whig junto; as the ministry came under increasing pressure in this parliament Hawles was often called upon to defend royal policies such as the standing army and the conduct of the whig ministers over such matters as the grant to Captain Kidd. In 1700 he was listed as an adherent of Charles Montagu. It was rumoured in 1700 that Hawles would be made a judge, possibly to make room for Simon Harcourt as solicitor-general, but any ambitions in this regard were probably blocked by another of the junto, Lord Chancellor Somers, who believed that Hawles 'was not orthodox in criminal law, and would never let him be a judge' (HoP, Commons, 1690–1715). In the next two parliaments he sat for Truro and St Ives respectively.

Following the accession of Queen Anne, Hawles lost his office as solicitor-general and was not reappointed a queen's counsel. However, he was returned again to the Commons in 1702, sitting for Wilton. In this parliament he played a prominent role in the Ashby v. White case and in opposition to the tack of the Occasional Conformity Bill to the Land Tax Bill. In the election of 1705 he was returned for Stockbridge, and was again an active speaker in debates in the Commons. Early in 1706 he acted as defence counsel for James Drake and entered into an exchange with the lord chief justice in which he offered the opinion that it was 'uncertain what Revolution principles are' because they 'are new and have as yet obtained no fixed and general construction' (Kenyon, 103). In 1708 he was again returned for Stockbridge, although he retained his connection with Wilton, serving as recorder from 1706 to his death.

Hawles's last prominent role was as a manager of the impeachment of Doctor Sacheverell. He was one of those named to manage the impeachment in December 1709, and took a prominent part in the trial before the Lords in February–March 1710. However, Hawles was significantly out of step with his fellow whig managers when he seemed almost to invite the Lords to impose a light sentence, and when he agreed with Sacheverell that there was a supreme power in the state—although his view that it was in the queen, Lords, and Commons might not accord with Sacheverell's opinion of where it was located. Hawles did not stand at the election of 1710. He died on 2 August 1716, leaving an illegitimate son, presumably the John Hawles Johnson who, in 1733, was living at Monkton up Wimborne, in Cranborne parish, Dorset.

STUART HANDLEY

Sources HoP, Commons, 1690–1715 [draft] · HoP, Commons, 1660–90, 2.514–15 · Sainty, King's counsel, 64, 90 · R. L. Antrobus, Antrobus pedigrees: the story of a Cheshire family (1929), 11 · N. Luttrell, A brief historical relation of state affairs from September 1678 to April 1714, 3 (1857), 381, 555 · will, PRO, PROB 11/358, sig. 141 [Thomas Hawles] · will, PRO, PROB 11/694, sig. 36 [Sir John Hawles] · G. Holmes, The trial of Doctor Sacheverell (1973), 97, 137, 140 · Letters illustrative of the reign of William III from 1696 to 1708 addressed to the duke of Shrewsbury by James Vernon, ed. G. P. R. James, 3 vols. (1841), vol. 1, pp. 63, 380; vol. 3, p. 79 · Cobbett, Parl. hist., 5.1011–67 passim · J. P. Kenyon, Revolution principles: the politics of party, 1689–1720 (1977), 103, 136 · The parliamentary diary of Sir Richard Cocks, 1698–1702, ed. D. W. Hayton (1996), 52, 73, 131, 149, 161, 164, 252 · W. A. Speck, ed., 'An anonymous parliamentary diary, 1705–6', Camden miscellany, XXIII, CS, 4th ser., 7 (1969), 29–84, 48–9, 55, 59, 64, 67, 80 · Brief lives, chiefly of contemporaries, set down by John Aubrey, between the years 1669 and 1696, ed. A. Clark, 1 (1898), 305 · Wood, Ath. Oxon., new edn, 4.528–9

Hawley, Frederick [*performing name* Frederick Haywell] (1827–1889), actor and librarian, was born at Portsea, Hampshire, on 10 January 1827, the only son and eldest of six children of Benjamin Buck Hawley (1785–1838), a soldier, and Mary Anne Wyke (d. 1850). Frederick studied law in London, settling, with his wife, Emma Cox (d. 1898), at 17 Shepperton Gardens, Islington, London. Of their children, Wyke and John died young, Frederick became a scenic artist at the Prince's Theatre, Manchester, and a daughter took the stage name Miss Ingram. Hawley was admitted as a solicitor on 10 June 1852. He became secretary of the newly established Great Eastern Steamship Company, founded to build Brunel's SS *Great Eastern*, and established his office in Chancery Lane.

Shortly after this Hawley's interest in theatre led him to take the stage name of Frederick Haywell and to appear at Marylebone Theatre on 5 March 1855 as Florizel in *The Winter's Tale*. He toured to Paris with J. W. Wallack, then joined Samuel Phelps at the Sadler's Wells later in 1855, where he remained until 1860. His roles began with small Shakespearian parts including Philostrate (*A Midsummer Night's Dream*) and Polixenes (*The Winter's Tale*), progressing to Sebastian (*Twelfth Night*), Duke Frederick (*As You Like It*), and Albany (*King Lear*). In 1856 his Hortensio in *The Taming of the Shrew* was 'nicely played' (Phelps and Forbes-Robertson, 157). On 30 November 1859 he was Escalus in *Romeo and Juliet* played before Queen Victoria at Windsor Castle. In the following few years he appeared in Birmingham, Bath, Nottingham, Bristol, and Dublin, but continued to be associated with the legal profession at Montague, Leverson and Hawley of 12 St Helen's Place, London. Between 1870 and 1875 he acted at the Prince's Theatre, Manchester, in Shakespearian parts including the Prince of Aragon (*The Merchant of Venice*), as well as in comic afterpieces as he had done in his early days for Phelps's company. He then became stage manager for John Knowles at Manchester's Theatre Royal. His acting also took him to play Ford (*The Merry Wives of Windsor*) at London's Gaiety Theatre where two of his own plays, *Agnes of Bavaria*, dedicated to Louis, king of Bavaria, and his society drama, *Found*, were also produced.

On 17 May 1886 Hawley was appointed librarian at the seven-year-old Shakespeare Memorial Theatre, Stratford upon Avon. The library was dependent on donations for its growing collections and, with the aid of theatre governor Sir Theodore Martin, Hawley organized a meeting on 16 April 1887 at the Lyceum Theatre, London, under the chairmanship of Henry Irving, to promote the library. Following this meeting the Memorial Library Committee attracted gifts including 285 volumes from Dr F. J. Furnivall and many from overseas, which established the theatre's library as a centre for Shakespearian research. Hawley worked on an extensive catalogue of Shakespeariana, based on the collections of Birmingham's Shakespeare Memorial Library, the library of Shakespeare's birthplace, and the Memorial Theatre's collections. Despite constant ill health Hawley fulfilled his role as a scholar–librarian and continued to give occasional lectures and recitals in aid of the Memorial Theatre, and in 1888 wrote an anonymous defence of J. O. Halliwell-Phillipps. He died at home, 46 West Street, Stratford upon Avon, of pneumonia, on 13 March 1889, and was buried five days later in the family grave at Highgate cemetery, Middlesex.

MARIAN J. PRINGLE

Sources Boase, *Mod. Eng. biog.* · C. E. Pascoe, ed., *The dramatic list*, 2nd edn (1880) · *Law List* (1853) · *Law List* (1859) · W. M. Phelps and J. Forbes-Robertson, *The life and work of Samuel Phelps* (1886), 157 · *Shakespeare Memorial Theatre minute book 1, 1875–1945*, Shakespeare Centre Library, Stratford upon Avon, MSS 71.2 (S.4601) · playbills and playtexts collections, Shakespeare Centre Library, Stratford upon Avon · playbills collection, Manchester Department of Libraries · *Morning Post* (24 Jan 1887) [reports of Lyceum Theatre meetings] · *Stratford-upon-Avon Herald* (28 Jan 1887) [reports of Lyceum Theatre meetings] · *Birmingham Daily Post* (16 April 1887) [reports of Lyceum Theatre meetings] · *Morning Advertiser* (23 April 1887) [reports of Lyceum Theatre meetings] · *Daily Telegraph* (23 April 1887) [reports of Lyceum Theatre meetings] · *Stratford-upon-Avon Herald* (29 April 1887) [reports of Lyceum Theatre meetings] · *Shakespeare Memorial Theatre records*, vol. 2, 1420, Shakespeare Centre Library, Stratford upon Avon, F.71.2 · F. Hawley, *Mr Halliwell-Phillips and the Stratford oligarchy*, 'by an onlooker', 1887, Shakespeare Centre Library, Stratford upon Avon, MSS 87.4 (409) · *The Era* (23 March 1889) · *The Times* (18 March 1889) · *Stratford-upon-Avon Herald* (15 March 1889) · *Stratford-upon-Avon Herald* (22 March 1889) · d. cert.

Archives Shakespeare Birthplace Trust RO, Stratford upon Avon, Royal Shakespeare Theatre collection

Likenesses watercolour on wood, 1875, Shakespeare Centre Library, Stratford upon Avon · H. Miles, photograph, c.1886, Shakespeare Centre Library, Stratford upon Avon · L. Fuidge, photograph, 1889, Shakespeare Centre Library, Stratford upon Avon

Wealth at death £33 10s.: probate, 1 April 1889, *CGPLA Eng. & Wales*

Hawley, Henry (bap. 1685, d. 1759), army officer, baptized at St Martin-in-the-Fields, Westminster, on 12 January 1685, was the eldest child of Captain (later Colonel) Francis Hawley (1653/4–1692) and his wife, Judith, née Hughes (1658/9–c.1735). Francis Hawley was later killed at Steenkerke and, dying intestate, left his widow practically penniless. She, however, through the good offices of her husband's half-brother Brigadier-General Thomas Erle was able to secure from King William III commissions in the army for her three sons and a pension for herself. Henry Hawley's commission, dated 10 January 1694, was for an ensigncy in Thomas Erle's own regiment, later the 19th foot; he first saw service in the Low Countries in 1697 as his uncle's aide-de-camp. With the peace of Ryswick, Hawley was put on half pay, and Prince George of Denmark, out of regard for Hawley's father, appointed him page to his son William, duke of Gloucester. Although Hawley was placed an ensign with Sir Richard Temple's newly raised regiment on 10 March 1702, Prince George retained him in his household and secured for him instead a cornetcy in the Royal Horse Guards (11 September 1704). Hawley then, on 27 May 1706, purchased a captaincy in the 4th dragoons, his father's old regiment, and went with it to Spain.

During the peninsular campaign of 1707 and at the battle of Almanza, Hawley served once more as aide-de-camp to his uncle Lieutenant-General Erle, and did so again in the expedition to Cherbourg the following year. In 1709, after service at Ostend, Hawley rejoined his regiment in

Henry Hawley (*bap.* 1685, *d.* 1759), by David Morier, *c.*1748

Scotland. Having been a brevet major since 1 November 1707, he endeavoured to impose on the 4th dragoons the kind of unyielding discipline which in later life earned him the sobriquet the Lord Chief Justice, but which for the present saw him challenged to a duel by a fellow officer, whom Hawley killed. He fled to Berwick and in due course heard that he had been pardoned by Queen Anne; this was largely because she was aware that Hawley had been a favourite of her late husband, Prince George of Denmark. The following year, on 27 January 1711, Hawley succeeded in purchasing his majority, whereupon the lieutenant-colonelcy of the 4th dragoons fell vacant. Although Hawley lacked the funds to purchase this further step in rank, Queen Anne gave him £1000 and on 4 April 1711 he achieved his promotion. A brevet as colonel followed on 16 October 1712.

Between 1713 and 1715 Hawley's regiment served in Ireland before returning to Scotland to combat the Jacobite rising. Hawley took part in the drawn battle of Sheriffmuir, was wounded, but came away with the conviction that the Scottish highlanders could not withstand cavalry: it was a misapprehension which would cost him dear thirty-one years later at Falkirk. On 19 March 1717 Hawley was given command of the 33rd foot and in 1719 he took his regiment on the expedition to Vigo. The colonelcy of the 13th dragoons was conferred upon him on 7 July 1730 and promotions to the rank of brigadier and of major-general followed in 1735 and 1739. On 12 May 1740 he received the colonelcy of the 1st (Royal) Dragoons, which he retained for the remainder of his life.

In 1741 Hawley declined command of the expedition to the West Indies but sailed to Flanders the following year to

serve with the pragmatic army. Promoted lieutenant-general on 30 March 1743, he voted in council of war for the advance across the Rhine and in June commanded the left of the second line of cavalry at the battle of Dettingen. He then served during the sterile Flanders campaign of 1744 and was present at the battle of Fontenoy in May 1745. He took command of the right wing of cavalry after Sir James Campbell was mortally wounded. Later that campaign, in October, Hawley successfully led a force to extricate the former British garrison of Ostend from Mons.

On 29 November 1745 Hawley left the Low Countries for England to join the army being assembled in the midlands to face Prince Charles Edward's highlanders. He was present at the skirmish at Clifton on 18 December, and two days later was appointed commander-in-chief in Scotland. An army numbering some 8000 men was subsequently assembled under his command at Edinburgh. Although Hawley considered his force to be over-marched and in poor condition, his disdain for the highlanders ruined his judgement. It never occurred to him, as his army advanced to raise the siege of Stirling Castle, that the highlanders would dare attack him; and when they did so at Falkirk on 17 January 1746 his surprise enabled the enemy to gain of him the advantage of both terrain and weather. Hawley's attempt to retrieve the situation by launching his three regiments of mounted dragoons in an unsupported attack against the highlanders was a disastrous failure. Over half his infantry, their cartridges drenched by the rain blowing in their faces, then proceeded to fly the field. Only the steadfastness of the troops on his right and confusion in the ranks of the highlanders saved Hawley's army from total defeat. In the days that followed Hawley had occasion to confirm his reputation as a fierce disciplinarian. The two sets of gibbets which he had erected in Edinburgh to punish Jacobite rebels were used instead to execute his own deserters. Not for nothing was he known as Hangman Hawley.

The government meanwhile took a generous view of Hawley's setback. When William, duke of Cumberland, arrived in Edinburgh on 30 January to take charge of the army it was impressed upon Hawley that he was not being superseded; indeed, he remained titular commander-in-chief in Scotland. As such he was at Culloden three months later when the Jacobite rising was finally crushed. Cumberland used the cavalry under Hawley's command first to outflank the highlanders and then to mount a bloody pursuit. Hawley was also prominent in the battle's brutal aftermath: 'if his Majesty would leave me the Foot here', he wrote,

> and the Parliament give the men a guinea and a pair of shoes for every rebell's head they brought in, I would still undertake to clear this country …. There's still so many more houses to burn and I hope still some more to be put to deathe.   (March, 511–12)

In July 1746, however, Hawley left Scotland and relinquished his command to William Anne Keppel, second earl of Albemarle; he served the campaigns of 1747 and 1748 in the Low Countries.

Hawley had long coveted the governorship of a fortress and in 1748 he was given that of Inverness; the same year he was appointed a general officer on the staff in Ireland. He became governor of Portsmouth in July 1752. With the French invasion alarm of 1755, Hawley took command of the troops in Kent. James Wolfe, who had been Hawley's aide-de-camp at Culloden, was unimpressed: 'They could not make choice of a more unsuitable person, for the troops dread his severity, hate the man, and hold his military knowledge in contempt' (Willson, 280). Yet on the evidence of the military writings among his papers, the traditional view that Hawley was simply an unthinking martinet cannot be sustained, and certainly the duke of Cumberland, who in 1748 considered that 'Hawley is the first I know of in the whole Aly'd army for leading a line of cavalry' (NAM, Hawley MSS, ARC7411-24-112-8), retained his high opinion of Hawley throughout.

Hawley died unmarried at his residence at West Green, near Hook, Hampshire, on 24 March 1759. In his will, which achieved wide publicity because of its objectionable tone ('I hate all priests of all professions', and so on), Hawley left £5000 to his sister Anne, a life interest in his many properties to the widowed Elizabeth Toovey 'for many years my friend and companion, and often my careful nurse', and the reversion to Captain William Toovey of the Royal Dragoons, her second son whom Hawley adopted as his heir and who was obliged by the terms of the will to take Hawley's name (*GM*, 29, 1759, 157–9); it has been speculated that Toovey was Hawley's natural son (Atkinson, 146). ALASTAIR W. MASSIE

Sources Royal Arch., Hawley papers [copies in NAM, ARC7411-24-100 to -143] · C. Dalton, *George the First's army, 1714–1727*, 2 vols. (1910–12) · *GM*, 1st ser., 29 (1759), 146, 157–9 [death notice and will] · P. Sumner, 'The battle of Almanza: an eye-witness account by General Hawley', *Journal of the Society for Army Historical Research*, 25 (1947), 27–31 · P. Sumner, 'General Hawley's scheme for light-dragoons', *Journal of the Society for Army Historical Research*, 25 (1947), 63–6 · C. T. Atkinson, 'More light on Almanza', *Journal of the Society for Army Historical Research*, 25 (1947), 144–61 · P. Sumner, 'General Hawley's "Chaos"', *Journal of the Society for Army Historical Research*, 26 (1948), 91–4 · [H. R. Duff], ed., *Culloden papers* (1815) · Walpole, *Corr.* · R. Forbes, *The lyon in mourning, or, A collection of speeches, letters, journals … relative to … Prince Charles Edward Stuart*, ed. H. Paton, 3 vols., Scottish History Society, 20–22 (1895–6) · Royal Arch., Cumberland papers · Earl of March, *A duke and his friends*, 2 vols. (1911) · G. Thomas, earl of Albemarle, *Fifty years of my life*, 2 vols. (1876) · *The life and letters of James Wolfe*, ed. H. B. Willson (1909) · parish register, St Martin-in-the-Fields, City Westm. AC [baptism] · J. L. Chester and J. Foster, eds., *London marriage licences, 1521–1869* (1887)
Archives NAM, papers · Royal Arch., MSS | NL Scot., corresp. with General Campbell · Royal Arch., Cumberland MSS
Likenesses D. Morier, oils, *c*.1748; Sothebys, 13 Nov 1991, lot 40 [*see illus.*]
Wealth at death houses in Hampshire, Middlesex, and Sussex; land in Hampshire; £7500 in bank annuities (1748): will, *GM*, 157–9

Hawley, Jack. *See* Pilkington, Lionel Scott (1830–1875), *under* Pilkington, William (1758–1848).

Hawley, John, the elder (*c*.1350–1408), pirate, merchant, and administrator, of Dartmouth, Devon, was the

John Hawley the elder (*c*.1350–1408), memorial brass

younger son of the first John Hawley who settled in Dartmouth some time before 1340. Hawley was elected mayor for the first time in 1374—the beginning of a career which would make him the richest and most important man in Dartmouth. He was in fact mayor a total of fourteen times between 1374 and 1401 and also an MP in the 1390s and in 1402. In the royal service he was involved in the collection of the customs, a job he did not finally relinquish until two years before his death, and escheator of Devon and Cornwall in 1390–91. The first of his two wives, Joan, may have been the daughter of Sir Robert Tresilian, the chief justice of the king's bench who suffered at the hands of the Merciless Parliament in 1388; certainly Hawley bought the forfeited Tresilian lands in Cornwall from the crown and also undertook the wardship of Elizabeth Tresilian, said to be an 'idiot'. It took a series of chancery actions against his tenants, however, and a royal order to the sheriff of Cornwall to secure Hawley's quiet possession of his lands.

Hawley's prominence comes largely from his activities at sea off the coasts of Devon and Cornwall and in the channel. He was not only a merchant and shipowner but has been described as at best a privateer and at worst a ruthless pirate. The king would at times commission him to 'keep the seas', and at other times summon him before the council to make restitution to the foreign merchants whose goods and ships he and his men were accused of seizing without any justification. No truce with France was in operation until 1389 and thus Hawley, with a relatively clear conscience, could send his ships to rove the channel as happened in, for example, 1379 and 1388. In 1395, on the other hand, two of his ships, the *Margret* and the *Petre* were in the fleet taking Richard II to Calais for his marriage with Isabella of France.

On the accession of Henry IV Hawley was briefly appointed lieutenant to the earl of Worcester, the admiral of England. The rolls, however, also record an increasing volume of furious complaints, largely by Spanish and Italian merchants, that Hawley's men had made off with their goods on the high seas and taken them into a west-country port. The value of these cargoes could be high; Richard Garner from Piedmont spent years trying to get compensation for the loss of a cargo of wine valued at £398 and one of olive oil valued at £210. The king, it is thought, was prepared to turn a blind eye to the losses of French and Breton merchants as a matter of policy but did not wish to cause unnecessary offence to Italians, Flemings, and Spaniards. Hawley, and even more his seamen, were not always as careful as they might have been about the ownership of the goods and ships they plundered. In late 1406 Hawley's habit of ignoring those royal orders that reached him in the west country caught up with him, and he was arrested and confined in the Tower of London for six weeks until February 1407. This was a severe punishment for an elderly man who, in 1404, had explained to the king that he could not come to London to sort out the ransoms of prisoners taken in an abortive Breton attack on Dartmouth because pains in his leg made riding impossible. He died on 30 December 1408 and was buried between his wives, Joan (d. 12 July 1394) and Alice (d. 7 Jan 1403), in the chancel of St Saviour's Church, Dartmouth, which he himself had founded.

This did not mean that the name of Hawley was no longer heard in the channel ports; his only son, **John Hawley the younger** (c.1384–1436), mariner and administrator, had served the king since 1400 and in many ways followed in his father's footsteps. He had a long career as an MP between 1410 and 1432, was escheator in Devon and Cornwall from 1402 until his death, and a JP for Cornwall from 1422 to 1431. All this did not prevent him from both taking part in royal expeditions to keep the seas and also seizing alien merchant ships when occasion offered. In 1419 and 1420 he was at sea with Sir Hugh Courtenay on royal business; the 1420 expedition is particularly notable as among the vessels engaged was Henry V's enormous *Gracedieu*. Hawley had earlier in 1416 presented the king with the balinger *Cracher* for his own fleet, perhaps to mollify him over the trouble caused when his men took the *Gracedieu* of Brittany only to find the cargo was the property of a Bristol merchant and covered by a safe conduct issued by Henry IV. The *Cracher* was sold in 1422 by the crown to John William of Kingswear, one of Hawley's shipmasters and also master of the great ship *Gracedieu* for the king, showing how narrow was the gap at this date between royal and private service. In 1427 Hawley came close to arrest by the council when he was involved in the

seizure of the goods and ship of a Scottish merchant, valued at £220; the resulting court case hinted at some readiness by Hawley to conspire against the law even if he was a JP. He died on 8 May 1436 leaving a son, Nicholas, and a daughter, Elizabeth.   SUSAN ROSE

Sources C. L. Kingsford, 'West country piracy: the school of English seamen', *Prejudice and promise in fifteenth century England* (1962), 78–106 · S. P. Pistono, 'Henry IV and John Hawley, privateer, 1399–1408', *Report and Transactions of the Devonshire Association*, 111 (1979), 145–63 · C. J. Ford, 'Piracy or policy: crisis in the channel, 1400–1403', *TRHS*, 5th ser., 29 (1979), 63–78 · F. C. Hingeston, ed., *Royal and historical letters during the reign of Henry the Fourth*, 1, Rolls Series, 18 (1860) · HoP, *Commons* · PRO, early chancery proceedings · CPR · CClR · *Report of the Deputy Keeper of the Public Records*, 44 (1883), appx 3, pp. 543–638 [French rolls] · memorial brass, St Saviour's Church, Dartmouth

Likenesses memorial brass, St Saviour's Church, Dartmouth [*see illus.*]

Wealth at death John Hawley the younger; estates valued at £69 10s. in Devon and £54 2s. 8½d. p.a. in Cornwall

Hawley, John, the younger (c.1384–1436). *See under* Hawley, John, the elder (c.1350–1408).

Hawley, Joseph (1723–1788), lawyer and revolutionary leader, was born on 8 October 1723 in Northampton, Massachusetts, the first of two sons of Lieutenant Joseph Hawley (1682–1735), a trader and cattle drover, and Rebecca Stoddard (1686–1766). After attending local schools and being tutored by his first cousin Jonathan Edwards, Hawley enrolled at Yale College in 1739 and graduated BA in 1742. The Great Awakening, a religious revival promoted by Edwards since the mid-1730s that had contributed to the suicide of Hawley's father in 1735, peaked during Hawley's college years and influenced his later life. Having left Yale he studied theology for several years before serving as chaplain to the 9th Massachusetts regiment, raised for the successful assault on the French fortress at Louisbourg in 1745. On returning to Massachusetts he began to study law. His choice of a secular occupation accompanied a turn towards Arminianism, the moderate theological position acknowledging the role of human moral agency in attaining salvation that Edwards condemned.

On completing his legal studies Hawley assumed leadership of the movement in Northampton that led to the expulsion of Edwards from his pulpit in 1750. Hawley subsequently apologized to Edwards for his role in the dismissal and in 1760 he wrote an agonized letter of contrition to a minister who had participated in the church council hearing the case. Whatever the price to his conscience the Edwards controversy launched Hawley's political career. Northampton elected him a selectman in 1747, a position he continued to occupy until the end of his life. In 1750 he was appointed justice of the peace, and in 1751 he served the first of many terms as the town's representative in the provincial legislature. During the Seven Years' War he was commissioned major in the Massachusetts militia and was active in organizing the military effort of that colony's western territories. In 1760 he was admitted to plead before the colony's superior court.

During the ensuing decade Hawley emerged as western

Massachusetts's foremost revolutionary leader, similar in stature to Samuel Adams in eastern Massachusetts. Doing so required neutralizing the political influence of the loyalist-inclined Williams family, to whom Hawley was related. His 1767 defence of Seth Warner, accused of riotous behaviour during 1765, established his revolutionary credentials in the west. Though the jury had been instructed by the judges to find Warner guilty Hawley managed to sway it in Warner's favour by arguing that the province had been reduced to a state of nature by the Stamp Act. The superior court temporarily disbarred Hawley for libelling it in his account of the case printed in the *Boston Evening-Post* (3 and 6 July 1767).

Hawley's growing prominence enhanced his stature in the provincial legislature, where he took the lead in ensuring that any measure to compensate victims of the Stamp Act riots be accompanied by a general indemnity. Subsequently the house of representatives appointed him to the committee that drafted the Massachusetts circular letter of 1768 initiating the first non-importation movement. During a house debate in 1769 Hawley was the first openly to question parliament's right to legislate for the colonies. In 1772 the house adopted Hawley's resolutions condemning, as a violation of the province's charter rights, the crown's payment of the governor's salary. And in 1773 he was a member of the committee that rebutted the constitutional plea of the governor of Massachusetts for parliamentary supremacy in America.

Parliament's Coercive Acts of 1774 led Hawley to espouse independence. Though he declined to represent Massachusetts in the continental congress he drafted a memorandum for the province's delegation, entitled 'Broken Hints' (1774), which argued that there was no alternative to war and outlined the steps congress needed to take in order to secure America's freedom. When royal authority collapsed in Massachusetts he helped to persuade the provincial congress to resume the charter of 1629. While his primary concern remained nurturing the revolutionary coalition in Massachusetts, he was an early champion of military operations against Quebec and recognized that independence would require the colonies to vest supreme authority in congress.

A crippling depression forced Hawley, in 1776, into prolonged retirement from all but local affairs. He re-emerged briefly to shape Northampton's response to the proposed Massachusetts constitution of 1780, urging that all adult males be eligible to vote for the governor and town representatives. Though he objected to other features of the constitution of 1780 he vigorously supported the government's authority in its western territories. He was active against the insurgency led by Samuel Ely in 1782 and would have exerted himself against Shays's rebellion in 1786, had health permitted. He died on 10 March 1788, survived only by his childless widow, Mercy Lyman (1729–1806), whom he had married on 30 November 1752, much against his mother's wishes, and one adopted child.   RICHARD BUEL JUN.

Sources E. Francis Brown, *Joseph Hawley: colonial radical* (1931) · S. E. Patterson, 'Hawley, Joseph', *ANB* · F. B. Dexter, *Biographical sketches of the graduates of Yale College*, 6 vols. (1885–1912), vol. 1, pp. 709–12 · J. R. Trumball, *History of Northampton, Massachusetts*, 2 (1902) · S. E. Dwight, *The life of Jonathan Edwards* (1830), 421–7 · D. Adair and J. A. Schutz, *Peter Oliver's origin and progress of the American revolution* (1961) · R. Taylor, *Western Massachusetts in the revolution* (1954) · L. N. Newcomer, *The embattled farmers* (1953) · IGI
Archives Forbes Library, Northampton, Massachusetts, MSS · Mass. Hist. Soc., MSS · NYPL, MSS | Forbes Library, Northampton, Massachusetts, Judd MSS, MSS
Wealth at death see will, registry of probate books, Connecticut Valley Historical Museum, Springfield, Massachusetts

Hawley, Sir Joseph Henry, third baronet (1813–1875), racehorse owner, was born in Harley Street, London, on 27 October 1813, the eldest son in the family of three sons and seven daughters of Sir Henry Hawley, second baronet (1776–1831), and his wife, Catherine Elizabeth (d. 1862), daughter of Sir John Gregory Shaw, bt. In 1832, following his succession to the baronetcy, he became a cornet in the 9th lancers and in the following year a lieutenant. After leaving the army in 1834, he sailed the Mediterranean, visiting Greece, Sicily, and Morocco in his yacht before taking up temporary residence in Florence. On 18 June 1839 he married Sarah Diana (d. 1881), third daughter of General Sir John Crosbie of Watergate, Sussex, with whom he had two daughters. While in Italy he took up racing, and on his return to England in 1844 he registered his famous cherry and black cap racing colours. He became a successful owner, winning eight classics—including four Derbys—with eight different horses. In 1851 he retired temporarily from the turf in pique at the hostility in racing circles following the Doncaster Cup, when many believed that he had infringed the rules of racing by running two horses in which he had a part share.

In 1870 Hawley turned his attention to turf reform. He advocated the idea that no two-year-old racing should occur before 1 September to reduce the risk of breakdown to these immature animals. However, the Jockey Club banned it only before 1 May and even this restriction was rescinded within four years because of special pleading by the Lincoln and Northampton spring meetings. Hawley found even less support for his suggestions to make the Jockey Club more representative of racing interests. This was partly because he lacked tact and patience in putting his case, but was also owing to the implacable opposition of Admiral Rous, doyen of the Jockey Club. Rous hated tobacco, heavy gambling, and most jockeys; Hawley smoked, on at least three occasions won over £70,000 in bets, and frequently gave large presents to his winning riders. He retired from the turf on 19 July 1873, selling his racing stud for 23,575 guineas.

Intelligent, well read, and a bibliophile, Hawley created a substantial library at Leybourne Grange, near Maidstone, the family estate from before the Norman conquest. He died at 34 Eaton Place, London, on 20 April 1875, and in the absence of a male heir his title and estate passed to his brother.   WRAY VAMPLEW

Sources R. Mortimer, R. Onslow, and P. Willett, *Biographical encyclopedia of British flat racing* (1978) · Thormanby [W. W. Dixon], *Famous racing men* (1882) · W. Vamplew, *The turf: a social and economic*

history of horse racing (1976) • G. Plumptre, *The fast set: the world of Edwardian racing* (1985) • J. Rice, *History of the British turf*, 2 vols. (1879)

Archives Lincs. Arch., family and estate papers

Likenesses J. Brown, stipple (after photograph by Southwell), BM, NPG; repro. in *Baily's Magazine* (1861) • A. Thompson, chromolithograph caricature, NPG; repro. in *VF* (21 May 1870) • portrait, repro. in *Baily's Magazine* (1861) • portrait, repro. in *Illustrated Sporting and Dramatic News* (1875) • portrait, repro. in Thormanby, *Famous racing men*

Wealth at death under £90,000: probate, 15 June 1875, *CGPLA Eng. & Wales*

Hawley, Susan [*name in religion* Mary of the Conception] (1622–1706), Sepulchrine prioress, was born in Brentford, Middlesex, to Thomas Hawley and his wife, Judith, *née* Hawkins. She decided aged nineteen that she wanted to found a religious house for Englishwomen in Flanders. She was clothed at the Convent of the Canonesses Regular of the Holy Sepulchre (Sepulchrines) at Tongres (Tongeren) in 1641 with the name in religion of Mary of the Conception. Shortly afterwards, with two other English nuns, she set out to establish an English house of that order at Liège. Gradually others joined them from England until after seven years there were twenty-two sisters in total. Susan Hawley was elected the first prioress in 1652. Disorders in the town of Liège led to concern about the privacy and safety of the nuns. They applied to the prince-bishop for new premises and were granted occupation of property in the faubourg d'Avroy previously inhabited by a long established local religious order which had fallen into decay; a transfer initially unpopular with local people. The sisters began thorough repairs and the construction of a new church, while increasing numbers led them to start building new accommodation funded by an unexpected legacy. Progress on the work was paid for by careful management of existing resources supervised by the prioress. Several items of donated silver were sold in London to raise cash for the building works and by 1660 the new building was complete. The sisters contributed to their own upkeep by selling items they had made or providing services locally. According to the account books they made surplices and pairs of woollen gloves, they washed, starched, and pleated church clothes, and sold barrels of beer and seeds from the garden.

At the same time as the work on practical construction continued Susan Hawley led her community in establishing a reputation for zeal in regular observance of divine office, which was the primary aim of the canonesses. They laid special emphasis on singing the glory of Christ's resurrection from the sepulchre; from this they derived their name, the Sepulchrines. In Susan Hawley's account of the order attention is drawn to a special category of nun which she said was unique to the canonesses: young gentlewomen who were chronically sick or disabled and thus unable to keep the rigours of daily office. They were not to have a voice in chapter, nor to be allowed to hold senior positions, but their situation could be reviewed should their health improve (Hawley, 51).

From early days the convent contained a girls' boarding-school since educational work was central to the existence of the canonesses. The first entries in the account books are for 1651 which noted the receipt from pensioners of 1409 florins for the year. Susan Hawley explicitly stated that the girls who entered the school were under no obligation to join the order. The curriculum aimed to provide the pupils with the skills and qualities appropriate for young gentlewomen including writing, reading, needlework, French, and music at a cost of £20 per annum.

As prioress for over forty years, Susan Hawley led her convent through the initial challenging period of the foundation and major building works, through the consolidation, continuing to attract new recruits from England, and through the difficult periods when financial concerns threatened to overwhelm the existence of the convent. She provided leadership both in the management skills needed to build the convent, securing the necessary permits, negotiating with builders, and supervising the financial arrangements, and at the same time providing spiritual and pastoral direction for the sisters under her care. The reputation of the house spread, helped partly by her book *A Brief Relation of the Order and Institute of the English Religious Women at Liège* (1652), published to encourage recruitment to the convent: some copies contained directions for travel from England to Liège. In 1663 Susan Hawley founded a confraternity of the Holy Sepulchre, erecting a chapel in Liège where prayers could be said. It became popular with local people and was thronged on feast days. As prioress she was a benefactor of the convent in her own right. In 1667 she provided 24 florins for a recreation to celebrate her silver jubilee, in 1669 she gave a silver basin and two cruets, followed by substantial sums of money in the 1680s, and in 1692 heavy silver candlesticks and a feast to mark her golden jubilee.

In January 1698 Susan Hawley petitioned for permission to retire on the grounds of age and ill health and her last years she spent quietly in continual prayer. The convent recorded that she made a good death in 1706. During her last illness her conversation was always on the happiness of her vocation and the great desire she had to die so that she could possess God. Susan Hawley had established the first English priory of the order which remained in Liège until driven out by the French Revolution and continued thereafter at New Hall in Chelmsford.

CAROLINE M. K. BOWDEN

Sources *History of the New Hall Community* (1899) • S. Hawley, *A brief relation of the order and institute of the English religious women at Liège* (1652) • P. Guilday, *The English Catholic refugees on the continent, 1558–1795* (1914) • R. Trappes-Lomax, ed., 'Records of the English canonesses of the Holy Sepulchre of Liège, now at New Hall, 1652–1793', *Miscellanea, X*, Catholic RS, 17 (1915), 1–247

Archives New Hall, Chelmsford, canonesses of the Holy Sepulchre

Hawley, Thomas (d. 1557), herald, was groom porter of the chamber to Queen Margaret of Scotland, daughter of Henry VII, from her marriage in 1503 until 1508. Although said to have been nominated Rose Blanche pursuivant in the reign of Henry VII, he is merely called 'messenger of the chamber' in Henry VIII's patent of 26 August 1509 appointing him Rouge Croix pursuivant. In the latter capacity he began his lifelong career as a diplomat, employed especially on Scottish affairs. He accompanied the earl of Surrey on the campaign of 1513 against James IV; he was detained prisoner when delivering the English challenge before the battle of Flodden but released before the fighting began and carried news of the victory to the English court. His good judgement is noticed in contemporary chronicles and in the ballad of 'Flodden Field'. On 1 November 1514 he was created Carlisle herald, and on 30 January 1515 the king granted him an annuity of 20 marks for his services at Flodden.

As Carlisle herald Hawley also performed the ceremonial and other duties of an officer of arms. On 16 June 1530 he was appointed deputy to Thomas Benolt, Clarenceux king of arms, and undertook a visitation on Benolt's behalf of London churches from 28 July to 3 September 1530 'to reforme all false armorye & Armes devysed without auctoritie' (Wagner, Heralds and Heraldry, 9). His record of the occasion is the earliest extant narrative of heraldic visitation. In 1531–2 he went on a series of diplomatic missions to Scotland. By patent dated 15 June 1534 he was made Norroy king of arms and principal herald in the northern part of England with a salary of £20 a year, but on 2 August 1534, he agreed to make over his power in the north to Sir Thomas Wriothesley, Garter king of arms, for half the profits. This arrangement did not prevent Hawley's subsequently engaging in a long-running dispute with Garter over the privileges of their respective offices. On 19 May 1536 Hawley was appointed Clarenceux king of arms and principal herald of the southern, eastern, and western parts of the kingdom, his patent expressly confirming Clarenceux's authority to grant arms.

At the time of the Pilgrimage of Grace, Hawley was employed by the duke of Norfolk in treating with the northern rebels; in December 1536 he proclaimed the king's pardon at Wakefield, Halifax, and other towns, and he was present in the following year at the execution of Robert Aske and fellow leaders. He also with colleagues gave evidence against Thomas Miller, Lancaster herald, who was hanged at York in August 1538 for supporting the rebellion. Miller's counter-accusations against Hawley—including the claim that his chief delight was gaming ('hassardey')—vividly demonstrate the strife prevailing within the College of Arms at this period. Hawley was successful in retaining his position under successive Tudor regimes, any harm done by his initial support for the cause of Lady Jane Grey being countered by his assistance in pacifying the rebellion of Sir Thomas Wyatt. Visitation commissions were issued to Hawley on 2 July 1541, 28 June 1552, and 19 March 1555, but the only evidence of his acting upon them is contained in a later heraldic visitation of Essex, Surrey, and Hampshire (BL, Add. MS 7098). This purports to include copies of entries made by Hawley during 1553, suggesting a visitation perhaps begun by him but not completed. Original grants of arms, several of them containing portrait initials (such as GL, MS 21734), survive in the British Library, the College of Arms, and the London Guildhall.

Hawley died at his house in the Barbican, London, on 22 August 1557 and was buried on the 24th with elaborate ceremony in the church of St Giles Cripplegate. He is not known to have married, and by his will, dated 21 and proved 25 August 1557, he appointed William Harvey, Norroy, his executor, and gave him all his books (presumably the substantial library he had inherited from his predecessor, Clarenceux Benolt). The will was subsequently contested and administration granted on 27 June 1558 to his kinsman John Skipwith.

ANN PAYNE

Sources DNB · W. H. Godfrey, A. Wagner, and H. Stanford London, The College of Arms, Queen Victoria Street (1963) · J. B. Paul, ed., Compota thesaurariorum regum Scotorum / Accounts of the lord high treasurer of Scotland, 2 (1900), 337; 3 (1901), xcix, 119, 123, 325, 373; 4 (1902), xxv, 98 · LP Henry VIII, vols. 1–16 · CSP dom., 1547–53 · CPR, 1548–9 · A. R. Wagner, The records and collections of the College of Arms (1952), 10, 14, 24n., 62, 68 · A. R. Wagner, Heralds and heraldry in the middle ages, 2nd edn (1956), 9–10, 98, 102, 118–19, 139–43, 150–75 · A. Wagner, Heralds of England: a history of the office and College of Arms (1967), 120–85 passim · L. Campbell and F. Steer, A catalogue of manuscripts in the College of Arms collections, 1 (1988), 5–7, 17–19, 484 · The diary of Henry Machyn, citizen and merchant-taylor of London, from AD 1550 to AD 1563, ed. J. G. Nichols, CS, 42 (1848), 149, 378 · Rymer, Foedera, 3rd edn, 6/3.172; 6/4.36, 39 · M. Noble, A history of the College of Arms (1805), 119, 122, 128, 130, 143, 151–3 · BL, Harley MS 897 · will, PRO, PROB 11/39, fol. 29 · PRO, PROB 11/40, fol. 31 [sentence on will and administration] · G. M. Bell, A handlist of British diplomatic representatives, 1509–1688, Royal Historical Society Guides and Handbooks, 16 (1990)

Archives BL, visitation entries for Essex, Surrey, and Hampshire, Add. MS 7098 · Coll. Arms, heraldic collections · GL, grants of arms · PRO, letters and papers, Henry VIII, passim

Likenesses illuminated portrait, initial, 1 Dec 1539, BL, Harley MS 7025, fol. 202 · illuminated portrait, initial, 20 Feb 1544, Coll. Arms, Box 13, no. 15; repro. in Heralds' commemorative exhibition, 1484–1934 (1936), pl. XXXVII [exhibition catalogue, College of Arms, London, 1934] · illuminated portrait, initial, 10 Dec 1547, BL, Add. MS 60514 · illuminated portrait, initial, 5 April 1556, BL, Add. MS 37687 · illuminated portrait, initial, 15 Oct 1556, GL, MS 21734 · engraving (after illuminated initial), repro. in J. Dallaway, Inquiries into the origin and progress of the science of heraldry in England, pl. 12

Wealth at death see will, 21 Aug 1557, proved, 25 Aug 1557 (PRO, PROB 11/39, fol. 29)

Haworth, Adrian Hardy (1768–1833), botanist and entomologist, was born on 19 May 1768 at Hull, a younger son of Benjamin Haworth (1728–1790), merchant and landowner, and his wife, Anne Booth (d. 1784). He belonged to a wealthy and well-established family who resided at Hullbank (or Haworth) Hall, near Hull. He was educated at Hull grammar school and was then articled to a solicitor, but renounced the legal profession on completion of his articles and settled at his family's dower house at Cottingham, near Hull, where he began to study natural history. He was probably inspired by the example of Gilbert White in recording his observations of the natural history and antiquities of Cottingham and its vicinity, but this work was never published. During his first period there he developed special abilities in the study of plants growing in the wild; the careful observation of live growing plants (as opposed to dried specimens) became his forte, and the reason for his lasting reputation.

After his father's death, Haworth's elder brother, Benjamin Blaydes Haworth (1763–1836), who inherited the family estates, settled a fixed income upon him sufficient to allow him to continue his studies in comfort. In 1792 Haworth married Eliza Sidney Cumbrey (1768/9–1803); they had four children. Following their marriage he moved to Little Chelsea, a favoured location of gardeners, horticulturists, and botanists, remaining there until 1812. He became a fellow of the Linnean Society in 1798, founded an aurelian society, which never reached twenty members, about 1802, and on its dissolution in 1806 took the lead in establishing the Entomological Society of London, which was afterwards merged in the zoological club of the Linnean Society.

Haworth's first significant publication was his botanical description of pubescent poison ivy, *Rhus toxicodendron*, included in J. Alderson's *An Essay on the Rhus toxicodendron* (1794). This was followed by one of his most important works, *Observations on the Genus Mesembryanthemum* (1794–5), in which he distinguished over 200 species, where previously only about 70 had been clearly described. For his work on *Mesembryanthemum* (as well as on other succulent plants) he made much use of the Royal Botanic Gardens, Kew, where a large number of specimens were newly available as a result of Francis Masson's plant hunts in South Africa. He was also assisted by a number of private nurseries around London.

During his stay at Chelsea, Haworth was also active in entomology, going on extended walking tours around England, alone and with friends, collecting specimens. This work resulted in his *Lepidoptera Britannica* (1803–28), which was the first comprehensive work on English butterflies and moths and remained the standard work on the subject for fifty years. He is, however, probably best known for his *Synopsis plantarum succulentarum* (1812, 2nd edn 1819), where his facility at the careful distinction of small differences in growing plants came out at its strongest, even if the validity of his taxonomic procedures was open to criticism. This work was still of interest to specialists long after his death, and his various works on succulent plants were reprinted in five volumes as Haworth's *Complete Works on Succulent Plants* in 1965.

Following his first wife's death in 1803 Haworth twice remarried, and had children from each marriage. In 1812 he moved back to Cottingham, but in 1817 returned to London where he went to live at 10 Salamanca Terrace, Church Street, Queen's Elm, Little Chelsea. There he established a private natural history museum and botanical garden; by 1833 his collection numbered 40,000 insects, 20,000 specimens in his herbarium, 1600 natural history books in the library, and 500 plants in the garden. He was remarkably amiable and easily approachable, and became something of a celebrity, consulted by the managers of provincial natural history museums and visited by foreign botanists. In 1833 he was struck by cholera; the symptoms appeared suddenly while he was working in his garden during the afternoon of 23 August and he died the following day, one of the last of the 22,000 victims of the epidemic that had begun spreading in Britain in 1829. His collections were sold after his death, part of his herbarium being incorporated in the Fielding herbarium at the University of Oxford.

G. S. Boulger, *rev.* Joseph Gross

Sources W. T. Stearn, 'Adrian Hardy Haworth, 1768–1833', in A. H. Haworth, *Complete works on succulent plants*, 5 vols. (1965), 1.9–57 [incl. bibliography] · *DSB*
Archives Hollandsche Maatschapij der Wetenschappen, Haarlem, The Netherlands, letters to M. van Marum · Linn. Soc., Swainson corresp. · Oxf. U. Mus. NH, letters to J. C. Dale · RBG Kew, letters to H. N. Ellacombe
Likenesses portrait, Hunt Botanical Library, Pittsburgh

Haworth, Sir (Walter) Norman (1883–1950), chemist, was born on 19 March 1883 at White Coppice, near Chorley, Lancashire. The second son and fourth child of Thomas and Hannah Haworth, he came from a family of distinguished business and professional men. After attending the local school until the age of fourteen, he entered the Rylands linoleum factory where his father was manager. There he gained a knowledge of the use of dyestuffs which in turn led to an interest in chemistry. Despite active discouragement from family and friends, he studied the subject under a private tutor in Preston, passed the entrance examination and entered Manchester University in 1903. There he took the honours course in chemistry, graduating with a first in 1906. He was a pupil of W. H. Perkin, under whom he began research on the synthesis of terpenes. After three years' work on this subject he was awarded an 1851 Exhibition scholarship, which he elected to hold at Göttingen, where he worked with Otto Wallach. After only one year of study he was awarded a PhD; for the second year of his scholarship he returned to Manchester as a research fellow to continue his work on the terpenes.

In 1911 Haworth was awarded the Manchester DSc degree and appointed senior demonstrator in the chemistry department of the Imperial College of Science and Technology. The following year, he moved to a lectureship in chemistry at the University of St Andrews. There he came into contact with a vigorous research school, headed by Thomas Purdie and James Colquhoun Irvine, which was engaged in investigating the structural chemistry of carbohydrates, especially sugars. Gradually Haworth abandoned terpenes to concentrate on carbohydrates—work interrupted by the First World War.

In 1920 Haworth was elected to the chair of organic chemistry at Armstrong College, Newcastle upon Tyne, in the University of Durham. The following year he became head of department. Despite limited resources he managed to sustain his own research and to attract an increasing number of postgraduate researchers to join him. In 1922 he married Violet Chilton Dobbie, the daughter of Sir James Johnston Dobbie. The couple had two sons, James and David.

In 1925 Haworth was selected to succeed Gilbert Morgan as Mason professor of chemistry at Birmingham University. He took with him from Newcastle a large nucleus of

Sir (Walter) Norman Haworth (1883–1950), by Walter Stoneman, 1943

research students and rapidly developed what was probably the most important school of carbohydrate chemistry in the world, attracting researchers from many other countries. Haworth established a reputation among his collaborators as an enthusiastic, efficient, and inspired leader, as well as sustaining a constant and rapid flow of papers throughout his tenure. In 1929 he published a classic text, *The Constitution of the Sugars*. Among the foremost achievements of his research school were the elucidation of the structures of simple and complex saccharides, work on the chain structure of cellulose, and research into the nature of biologically important bacterial polysaccharides. It was also responsible for the structural determination and synthesis of vitamin C. This was the first chemical synthesis of a vitamin, and it made large-scale production possible. This work, much of it carried out in collaboration with E. L. Hirst, and published in 1933, contributed to the award of the Nobel prize for Chemistry (shared with Paul Karrer) in 1937.

Although Haworth took on many responsibilities within the university—he was dean of the faculty of science (1943–6) and vice-principal (1947–8)—he maintained a range of extramural activities. He had close contacts with industry both directly and through the Society of Chemical Industry, which he joined in 1916 and whose jubilee memorial lecture he delivered in 1938. He played a

part in building up the Rubber Producers' Research Association and served on the Colonial Products Research Council from its foundation in 1943. During the Second World War he was a member of the MAUD Committee which oversaw the early stages of the British atomic bomb project, and directed research, in collaboration with ICI, into chemical problems associated with the project, in particular the preparation of highly purified uranium and the search for volatile compounds of the metal. After the war he joined the Atomic Scientists' Association and was a signatory to the memorandum on international control of atomic energy submitted to the United Nations. He chaired the Chemical Research Board of the Department of Scientific and Industrial Research from 1947.

Haworth's achievements were honoured around the world. Elected a fellow of the Royal Society in 1928, he was awarded the Longstaff medal of the Chemical Society (jointly with Irvine) in 1933, and the Davy (1934) and the royal (1942) medals of the Royal Society. At the meeting of the British Association in Norwich in 1935 he presided over the chemistry section. He received honorary degrees from Queen's University Belfast, Oslo, Zürich, Cambridge, and Manchester, and was an honorary member of the academies of science at Haarlem, Brussels, Munich, Vienna, Finland, and Dublin, and of the Swiss Chemical Society. He was president of the Chemical Society in 1944–6 and vice-president of the Royal Society in 1947, the year in which he was knighted.

After his retirement in 1948 Haworth represented the Royal Society at the seventh Pacific science congress, which was held in New Zealand in 1949. He took the opportunity to visit and lecture at a number of universities in Australia and New Zealand. Less than a year after his return he suffered a heart attack and died at his home, Thurcroft, in Barnt Green, Birmingham, on 19 March 1950. He was survived by his wife.

L. L. BIRCUMSHAW, rev. SALLY M. HORROCKS

Sources E. L. Hirst, *Obits. FRS*, 7 (1950–51), 373–404 • *The Times* (20 March 1950) • *The Times* (21 March 1950) • *Nature*, 165 (1950), 587 • *Chemistry and Industry* (25 March 1950) • *WWW* • *DSB* • E. Farber, *Nobel prize winners in chemistry, 1901–1961*, rev. edn (1963) • M. Gowing, *Britain and atomic energy, 1939–1945* (1964) • *CGPLA Eng. & Wales* (1950)

Archives Atomic Energy Research Establishment, Harwell, reports and corresp. relating to work on atomic energy • U. Nott., school of chemistry, notebooks and papers

Likenesses W. Stoneman, photograph, 1943, NPG [see illus.] • photograph, Hult. Arch.

Wealth at death £21,070 17s. 9d.: probate, 6 Sept 1950, *CGPLA Eng. & Wales*

Haworth, Samuel (b. 1659/60), empirical physician, was born probably in St Albans, Hertfordshire, the son of William Haworth (d. 1703), and his first wife, Mary (d. 1661). William Haworth, initially vicar of St Peter's in St Albans, was ejected from his living and became a Congregational minister; he wrote a series of pamphlets during a fierce dispute with Hertfordshire Quakers during the 1670s. On 24 April 1677 Samuel Haworth was admitted to Sidney Sussex College, Cambridge, as a sizar, at which time it was noted that he was seventeen years old; there is no record of his taking a degree.

In January 1680 Haworth was lodging in Sighs Lane, near Budge Row, London, and practising medicine. In October he was granted a licence to practise by the Royal College of Physicians, and during the same year he published (in Greek) *Anthropologia*, a discourse on anatomy which was full of pious sentiments and which demonstrated his wide reading in ancient and modern medical authorities but which betrayed little evidence of practical experience in dissection. It concluded by advertising for sale 'excellent and effectual Tablets' (1680, p. 212) to preserve health and an 'approved Tincture' (p. 215) against scurvy. The volume was dedicated to Sir John Hartopp (1637–1722), the dissenting whig and exclusionist MP who had acted as his father's patron; however, Hawarth soon began to move in court circles. He had begun treating patients suffering from consumption using a secret nostrum and this apparently attracted the interest of Charles II, who commanded that he should try his cure upon Kennedy O'Brian, one of the guards. Haworth was evidently successful and his practice prospered.

In 1682 Haworth spent time practising in Paris, but announcements in the *London Gazette* indicate that he was now usually resident in Brompton, near Kensington, to the west of London (*LondG*, 12–15 June 1682; 19–23 Oct 1682) The following year Haworth dedicated *A Description of the Duke's Bagnio* to the duke of York, thanking him for the favour which he had shown him. This pamphlet describes a recently opened Turkish bath and medicinal establishment in Covent Garden in which Haworth and Sir William Jennens (*fl.* 1661–1690) were involved. However, his practice, based as it was on secret remedies, was controversial. In his *True Method of Curing Consumptions* (1683) he complained of many attacks made upon him by rival practitioners. Haworth's name surfaced in debates within the Royal College of Physicians over empirical practice during the same year. In August 1683 he informed the college that he had been awarded the degrees of MD from Paris and MB from Cambridge. (His name does not appear in degree lists of the latter.) The following month the college ordered one of their fellows, Andrew Clench (*d.* 1692), to desist from associating with Haworth, and in September 1683 Richard Darnelly (*d.* 1733) accused Haworth of practising illegally. There is no record that the college took any action against him and no further trace can be found of Haworth's life.   MARK S. R. JENNER

Sources Venn, *Alum. Cant.* · S. Haworth, *The true method of curing consumptions* (1683) · S. Haworth, *A description of the duke's bagnio* (1683) · annals, RCP Lond. · *LondG* (12–15 June 1682) · *LondG* (19–23 Oct 1682) · parish register, St Albans, St Peter's Church, Herts. ALS, D/P 93 1/1 · W. Urwick, *Nonconformity in Hertfordshire* (1884) · *Calamy rev.* · Munk, *Roll* · F. H. W. Sheppard, ed., *Southern Kensington: Brompton*, Survey of London, 41 (1983)
Likenesses R. White, line engraving, BM, NPG; repro. in Haworth, *Description of the duke's bagnio*, frontispiece

Hawthorn, (John) Michael [Mike] (1929–1959), racing motorist,

was born in Mexborough, Yorkshire, on 10 April 1929, the only son of Leslie Hawthorn (*d.* 1954), motor

(**John**) **Michael** [Mike] **Hawthorn** (1929–1959), by Barham, 1955

engineer and racing motor cyclist, and his wife, Winifred Mary Symonds. Educated at Ardingly, he achieved no great success as a sportsman, being 'indolent by nature'. His parents moved to Farnham in Surrey when his father became involved in motor cycle racing at Brooklands, and when Mike left school in 1946 he was apprenticed to Dennis Brothers, the commercial vehicle builders, in Guildford. Following the wish to join his father in business and become an automobile engineer, he went on from his apprenticeship to Kingston Technical College and then the College of Automobile Engineering at Chelsea. The result of his efforts in this direction only made him certain that he would find his métier in the driving seat rather than at the drawing-board. Not unnaturally, his first interest as a young man was motor cycles and it was in motor cycle sport that the name of Mike Hawthorn first came to the public notice—it was always Mike, a diminutive which fitted his character absolutely; but despite his modest success as a motor cyclist, his parents were understandably anxious to get him on to four wheels, and as soon as was practicable his father provided him with a small car.

For a young man to break into motor racing—as a professional—has always been among the least easily satisfied of dreams, but Mike had a great ally in his father, who was not only keen to see him do it, but wealthy enough to help him toward this end. During 1951 he had his first racing season and achieved some success in a number of club races with a pre-war Riley. His first big chance came early in 1952, when an old friend of the family purchased one of the new Cooper-Bristols with a view to entering it in international races. He invited Hawthorn to be the driver.

Hawthorn's first appearance with this car was at Goodwood on Easter Monday 1952, when in the opening race he won the Lavant cup. He proceeded to win the Chichester cup, in which he beat a strong field that included the reigning world champion, Juan Fangio, and came a highly creditable second in the main race, the Richmond trophy. These three drives, in a single day's racing, changed his life: he became an overnight sensation and the subject of intense media interest, which afterwards never left him.

Hawthorn's continued success in that year was rewarded by an invitation from Enzo Ferrari to drive for him in the following season. It was during 1953, while he was still a comparatively new boy, that he won the French grand prix at Rheims from Fangio by a matter of seconds only. The sheer dash and courage he displayed on this occasion endeared him to everyone. For a part of this race the cars travelled three abreast along ordinary French roads, approaching speeds of 160 m.p.h., and Hawthorn later recalled that it was 'a bit frightening to see the nose of one of the other cars come alongside, then drop back again as the driver decided he could not make it before the next corner' (Hawthorn, *Challenge Me*, 76). He also acknowledged Fangio's sportsmanship during their tremendous battle:

> We would go screaming down the straight side-by-side absolutely flat out, grinning at each other, with me crouching down … trying to save every ounce of wind resistance. We were only inches apart and I could clearly see the rev counter in Fangio's cockpit.   (Hawthorn, *Challenge Me*, 77)

At the end of the year he found his successes had brought him the coveted gold star of the British Racing Drivers' Club.

The year 1954 was an ill-fated one for Hawthorn. In February the popular press picked up the story that he had not been called up for national service, after a question about him was raised in parliament. Hawthorn's father publicly blamed himself for a misunderstanding with the authorities concerned, but there is no doubt that his son, having established himself as a racing driver, was reluctant to serve. Once he turned twenty-six, in April 1955, he would no longer be eligible, and until then he clearly meant to stay abroad racing and return to Britain as seldom as possible. The *Daily Mirror* was prominent in the press campaign to have Hawthorn called up and devoted three editorials to the subject, one headlined 'Catch this dodger'. Then, on 22 March, he crashed in the Syracuse grand prix and was very badly burnt, and would probably have lost his legs but for the devoted nursing of some nuns in Sicily.

Hawthorn was moved to hospital in Rome, where he was to remain for some time. The lasting effect of these burns would eventually rule him out of national service, though Hawthorn proved determined to drive again as soon as possible, and it was while *en route* for the Le Mans twenty-four-hour race in early June that he learned of the death of his father in a motor accident. On his return to Britain for the funeral the *Daily Mirror* renewed its demand for his immediate call-up, and the attitude of officialdom can perhaps be gauged from the fact that a policeman served him with three summonses for minor motoring offences just hours before the service itself. He nevertheless bounced back to win the Spanish grand prix at the end of the year.

In 1955 Hawthorn drove briefly for Tony Vandervell, but the Vanwall team was then having difficulty with its cars and Hawthorn soon left, frustrated by their unreliability. In June he scored a victory for Jaguar at Le Mans, but this success was overshadowed by a tragedy for which many on the continent held Hawthorn responsible. During the race he had braked suddenly approaching his pit lane, causing the Austin-Healey of Lance Macklin behind him to swerve into the path of Pierre Levegh's oncoming Mercedes-Benz. The ensuing crash resulted in the death of Levegh and some eighty spectators. The Mercedes-Benz team pulled out of the race, virtually handing victory to Jaguar, who afterwards vigorously defended their driver. Most observers accepted that if Hawthorn was guilty of a driver error, as seemed likely, he could not be blamed for the disastrous train of consequences that followed.

Despite his normally happy disposition, Mike Hawthorn was unfortunately capable of reacting very badly to press comment, particularly when he felt it to be uninformed, and in such circumstances he was usually his own worst enemy. For a man who led so sophisticated a life he was in some ways quite naïve, and deeply hurt when he thought, to use his own words, that he was 'being got at'. Nevertheless, he brought to motor sport a sense of chivalry and good fun, and his close friendship with Peter Collins and their constant references to each other as 'mon ami, mate' gave even those outside the sport some insight into his ebullient nature.

Hawthorn had a reasonably successful season in 1956 and returned in 1957 to Ferrari, showing that he had lost none of his early ability and had gained much in experience and determination. In 1958 he again won the French grand prix and at Casablanca on 19 October he achieved his highest honour and became the first British driver to be world champion. He had produced a nerveless drive to finish second, one place behind Stirling Moss in the race, but one crucial point ahead in the championship. He was awarded the British Automobile Racing Club's gold medal in recognition.

Within a week of becoming world champion Hawthorn had decided to quit motor racing. He was put off by the intensity of media and public interest now surrounding him. He had also been affected by the death of Peter Collins, following an accident at the German grand prix at the Nürburgring the previous August, which he had witnessed. It was common knowledge that he now hoped to get married and settle down to build up the business he had taken over on his father's death, and also care for his mother in her declining years. He announced his retirement in mid-December. There was some surprise that he did not feature in the new year's honours list, when Stirling Moss, his great rival, was appointed OBE, but Hawthorn accepted his omission with resignation. Weeks later, on 22 January 1959, he was killed while driving his customized Jaguar at speed against a friend's Mercedes in wintry conditions on the Guildford by-pass in Surrey. Hawthorn was two months short of his thirtieth birthday; to the end his great love of life was matched only by his love of the race.

MICHAEL FROSTICK, *rev.* MARK POTTLE

Sources *The Times* (23 Jan 1959) · M. Hawthorn, *Challenge me the race* (1958) · M. Hawthorn, *Champion year* (1959) · personal knowledge (1971) · private information (1971) · C. Nixon, *Mon ami mate: the bright, brief lives of Mike Hawthorn and Peter Collins* (1991) · *CGPLA Eng. & Wales* (1959)
Archives FILM BFI NFTVA, documentary footage · BFI NFTVA, 'Mike Hawthorne honoured' 22 Jan 1959 · BFI NFTVA, sports footage
Likenesses Barham, photograph, 1955, NPG [*see illus.*] · photographs, repro. in Nixon, *Mon ami mate*
Wealth at death £68,604 16s. 8d.: probate, 28 May 1959, *CGPLA Eng. & Wales*

Hawtrey, Sir Charles Henry (1858–1923), actor and theatre manager, was born on 21 September 1858 at Keate's Lane, Eton, the fifth son and eighth of the ten children of the Revd John William Hawtrey (*d.* 1891) and his first wife, Frances Mary Anne, the daughter of Lieutenant-Colonel George Procter, historical writer and superintendent of studies at the Royal Military College, Sandhurst. The Hawtreys had long been numbered among the squirearchy of England, and continuously from the early seventeenth century they were represented at Eton College, whether as masters or boys. Charles Hawtrey's father was a first cousin once removed of Dr Edward Craven Hawtrey, headmaster of Eton from 1834 to 1852, and was a housemaster there when Charles was born. The boy, in his turn, entered the lower school of the college when he was eight years old. Three years later his father left Eton to found St Michael's School at Aldin House, Slough; and there Charles Hawtrey was educated until he returned to Eton in 1872. He moved to Rugby the following year, where he established himself as a sportsman of dash and endurance. Cricket, running, and football he loved, and in later years golf; but the obsession of his life from the age of fourteen, when he placed his first bet, was the turf. In his twenties he owned twelve racehorses, though with scant success. Much of his life was passed in a state of financial precariousness, irrespective of an often lucrative career, and belied by the unfailingly immaculate standard of his personal appearance.

Upon leaving Rugby in 1875 Hawtrey went to Dawson Clark's crammer in Gower Street, London, with a view to entering the army; but his attendance was irregular, especially during the principal race meetings, and the intention was soon abandoned. After working as a private tutor from 1876 to 1879 he secured a start on the stage—a false start, however, for he broke his collarbone while playing football before the opening night. In February 1881 he matriculated at Pembroke College, Oxford, but withdrew in October, having obtained a small part in F. C. Burnand's

Sir Charles Henry Hawtrey (1858–1923), by Bassano

The Colonel at the Prince of Wales's Theatre, Tottenham Street. Uncertain of success, he adopted the stage name Charles Bankes for that engagement only.

Early in 1883, with his actor brothers William and George, Hawtrey took a small touring company to towns in south-east England; but it was on 29 March 1884, again at the Prince of Wales's (known by then as the Prince's), that his managerial flair came into its own with his production of a German farce by Gustav von Moser, *Der Bibliothekar*, rewritten by Hawtrey in an English setting and retitled *The Private Secretary*. This was at first denounced by the critics and played to sparse audiences; but Hawtrey, in the biggest gamble of his life, raised money to transfer the production (now reduced from four acts to three) to the Globe Theatre on 19 May of the same year, when W. S. Penley succeeded Herbert Beerbohm Tree as the Revd Robert Spalding, and Hawtrey, henceforth acting under his own name, took over the part of Douglas Cattermole. He earned from the run at the Globe £123,000; but after that sum had passed through his lands, Hawtrey, the bookmaker's friend, was said to be £13,000 in debt.

As an actor Hawtrey strayed little from the line of smooth, moustached, deceitful men in which he made his mark. As a manager he took at various times eighteen London theatres—including the Globe until 1887 and the Comedy from then until 1893 and again from 1896 to 1898—and produced with great attention to detail about a hundred plays, in many of which he also appeared. Among the most successful were two more adaptations from von Moser, *The Pickpocket* by George Hawtrey and *The*

Arabian Nights by Sydney Grundy; *Jane* by Harry Nicholls and William Lestocq; *One Summer's Day* by H. V. Esmond; *Lord and Lady Algy* by R. C. Carton; *A Message from Mars* by Richard Ganthony; *The Man from Blankley's* by 'F. Anstey'; *Jack Straw* and *Home and Beauty*, both by W. Somerset Maugham; and *Ambrose Applejohn's Adventure* by Walter Hackett, in which Hawtrey played two parts. He produced his own play *Mr Martin* at the Comedy Theatre in 1896. At the Haymarket in the previous year he had been seen as Lord Goring in the first production of Oscar Wilde's *An Ideal Husband*; and it was to Hawtrey, who struggled vainly to raise the required sum, that Wilde first offered *The Importance of being Earnest*. Shortly after, Hawtrey was instrumental in obtaining witnesses to condemn Wilde in the famous libel case.

The knighthood Hawtrey received in 1922 was regarded as a tribute to the art of comedy in its consummate living exponent. Four times between 1906 and 1909 he gave performances for royalty by command. His acting style, derived from the Bancrofts, developed into something distinctive: he seldom raised his voice, gesticulated, or grimaced. Never before had such a level of naturalness been seen on the London stage. Portly, well groomed, and softly spoken, Hawtrey took the audience into his confidence, as if seeing in the people before him a reflection of his character's guilty conscience. He excelled in the portrayal of liars, particularly of erring husbands and incorrigible cads—'Hawtrey parts', as they were known—and his audience, delighting in them, wanted him ever to be the same, extricating himself from a dilemma by widening his expressive blue eyes with an implacable semblance of candour and uttering in tones of easy refinement a cool untruth. As a comic actor he held in unity three exceptional gifts: wonderful repose, deadpan perfection, and impeccable timing.

Hawtrey was twice married: first, on 3 June 1886, at St Peter's, Pimlico, to Madeline ('Mae') Harriet, daughter of Thomas Bowen Sheriffe, of Henstead Hall, Suffolk, who divorced him in 1893 and died in 1905; and second, on 10 November 1919, at the Roman Catholic church of Our Lady of the Assumption, in the London district of St Martin, to Katherine Elsie Emma, known as Elsie (*d.* 1930), the daughter of the Revd William Robinson Clark, and widow of the Hon. Albert Henry Petre, son of William Henry Francis Petre, eleventh Baron Petre. There were no children from either marriage; but with Olive Morris, an unmarried actress twenty-six years his junior and a niece of Dame Ellen Terry's, he had a son, Anthony, who was born in 1906 and himself became an actor and stage producer. The boy—who first bore his mother's surname, and then by deed poll his father's—was raised by his mother only.

After 1920 Hawtrey's health was predominantly poor, and, on 30 July 1923, suffering lobar pneumonia followed by heart failure, he died in a nursing home at 4 Dorset Square, Marylebone, London, a mile and a half from his residence at 37 Hertford Street, Mayfair.

Charles Hawtrey was a paradox. Though often seen in the guise of immorality and deceit, he read the Bible daily and steadfastly believed in the efficacy of prayer. Though stolidly built he was elegant. A *bon viveur*, he was hard up. Seemingly untheatrical, he taught Noël Coward and A. E. Matthews, both of whom he employed, everything they claimed to know about the theatre; others who asserted his influence included Ben Travers, Harley Granville Barker, and J. T. Grein. His easy-going, courtly manner masked an indefatigable worker. Between 1901 and 1912 he took his productions on five tours of the United States, where, for much of 1904, travelling and giving several shows a day, Hawtrey, the suave Old Etonian, became the first English actor to work in American vaudeville. The exertion was characteristic; even in the month of his death he opened in a new play. The man who looked so languid died from overwork. His impact upon English theatrical artistry outlives his name. MICHAEL READ

Sources *The truth at last from Charles Hawtrey*, ed. W. S. Maugham (1924) · *The Times* (31 July 1923), 13–14 · *Daily Telegraph* (31 July 1923), 11 · B. Travers, *A-sitting on a gate* (1978) · J. Gielgud, *Backward glances* (1989) · S. Morley, *A talent to amuse* (1969) · J. T. Grein, *Premières of the year* (1900) · C. B. Purdom, *Harley Granville Barker* (1955) · R. Ellmann, *Oscar Wilde* (1987) · M. Steen, *A pride of Terrys* (1962) · W. J. Macqueen-Pope, *Ghosts and greasepaint* (1951) · M. Beerbohm, *Around theatres*, new edn (1953) · *DNB* · m. certs. · d. cert.

Likenesses woodburytype photograph, *c.*1897, NPG · Bassano, photograph, NPG [*see illus.*] · M. Beerbohm, caricature, Harvard TC · Spy [L. Ward], chromolithograph caricature, NPG; repro. in *VF* (21 May 1892) · photographs, repro. in Hawtrey, *Truth at last* · prints, Harvard TC

Wealth at death £1180 12*s*. 2*d*.: probate, 24 Aug 1923, *CGPLA Eng. & Wales*

Hawtrey, Edward Craven (1789–1862), headmaster, was born at Burnham, 4 miles from Eton, on 7 May 1789. He was the only son of Edward Hawtrey, scholar of King's College, Cambridge, fellow of Eton College, and vicar of Burnham. His mother, Elizabeth Foster, was a sister of Dr John Foster, headmaster of Eton from 1765 to 1773. His father's family had been connected with Eton College for nearly 300 years and Hawtrey himself entered the school in 1799. In 1807 he was admitted scholar, and three years later fellow, of King's College, Cambridge. He graduated BA in 1812, MA in 1815, and DD in 1835. For a time he was private tutor to three sons of the earl of Shrewsbury, but in 1814 Dr Keate, the headmaster, appointed him to an assistant mastership at Eton.

Hawtrey proved to be an excellent schoolmaster, with a mind which ranged beyond the classics of the curriculum. He studied a number of modern languages, and published translations from German and Italian. His linguistic skills earned him a reputation as 'the English Mezzofanti'. Under his care an *Eton Atlas of Comparative Geography* was published. He encouraged his personal pupils and the boys he taught in class. He helped the young Winthrop Mackworth Praed not only to start a school library, to which he gave many books, but to publish one of the best of school ephemerals, *The Etonian* (1820–1).

When Dr Keate resigned in 1834, Hawtrey, by then the senior assistant, was chosen as headmaster. He had the good sense to consult Dr Kennedy of Shrewsbury, for he was well aware that Eton needed to reform its teaching;

Edward Craven Hawtrey (1789–1862), by unknown engraver, pubd 1862 (after John Jabez Edwin Mayall)

schoolmasters, for he was beyond his fellows candid, fearless, and bountiful; passionate in his indignation against cruelty, ardent in admiring all virtue and all show of genius. (Thackeray, 119–20)

Hawtrey became provost after Hodgson's death in December 1852. Sadly he had to sell part of his library below its worth to furnish the provost's lodge. He had held the King's College living of Ewhurst in Sussex since 1835, and in 1854 he exchanged this for the Eton College living of Mapledurham, where he was a popular figure. His eldest sister, Elizabeth, lived with him, though she became senile by the end of his life. During his rule as provost opposition to change, which has sometime affected those who have lived too long at Eton, gained on him. His last year in particular was distressed by the agitation for reform that preceded the appointment of the Clarendon commission on the public schools. It was perhaps a dispensation that he died on 27 January 1862. He died at the school, and was buried within Eton College chapel, where a substantial monument was erected to him.

TIM CARD

Sources F. St J. Thackeray, *Memoir of Edward Craven Hawtrey, D.D.* (1896) · H. C. Maxwell Lyte, *A history of Eton College, 1440–1910*, 4th edn (1911) · A. D. Coleridge, *Eton in the forties* (1896) · *Etoniana* · Venn, *Alum. Cant.* · *CGPLA Eng. & Wales* (1863)
Archives Eton | BL, corresp. with W. E. Gladstone, Add. MSS 44356–44397, *passim* · Trinity Cam., letters to William Whewell
Likenesses H. Feillet, oils, 1853, Eton · engraving, pubd 1862 (after J. J. E. Mayall), NPG [*see illus.*] · Nicholls, sculpture, 1878 (recumbent figure), Eton, chapel · C. Baugniet, lithograph, BM · F. Tarver, cartoons, repro. in Thackeray, *Memoir of Edward Craven Hawtrey*
Wealth at death under £18,000: administration with will, 11 July 1863, *CGPLA Eng. & Wales*

but he also knew that the provost and fellows, led by the obdurate conservative, Dr Goodall, would only accept minor reforms. He was able to subdivide the school further, in particular limiting his own teaching to the thirty-two top boys, which made his own task far more manageable. It was only, however, when Hodgson succeeded Goodall as provost that more serious changes could occur. In some, for example the improvement of the living conditions of the scholars and the abolition of 'montem' (the custom of collecting money from the public to support the captain of the school at Cambridge—a sort of prototype university rag day), Hodgson may have taken the lead. Mathematics was introduced to the regular curriculum. Modern languages could be taken by boys as extras, and Hawtrey certainly welcomed the language prizes established by the prince consort; he himself founded an English essay prize. A sanatorium was opened, for the building of which the headmaster made himself financially responsible; this was a real innovation. He was also able to secure the closing of the Christopher Inn, a coaching house in the very centre of Eton to which boys had ready access. He improved the lot of the younger Etonians by abolishing cricket fagging, and by the stern line he took against bullying (from which he had himself suffered as a boy). The school increased in size from under 450 to over 750 in the mid-1840s, before dropping back to 600—a measure of Hawtrey's success.

Hawtrey was singularly ugly and curiously dandified, and he lisped; thus he was an easy subject for caricature and mimicry. He was, however, popular with the boys. His generosity was exceptional: he would often reward boys with books, and he personally gave £300 to the captain of the school who would have benefited from the cancelled montem. William Johnson (later Cory) summed up his limitations and his merits:

> Not an accurate scholar, though versed in many tongues; not thoroughly well informed, though he had spent £30,000 on books; not able to estimate correctly the intellectual development of younger men, though he corresponded with the leaders of England and France; ... not one that could be said to organise well, for from first to last he dealt in makeshift and patchwork; yet for all that, a hero among

Hawtrey, Sir Ralph George (1879–1975), economist, was born on 22 November 1879 at Langley, near Slough, the only son and third and last child of George Procter Hawtrey (*b*. 1850), headmaster of St Michael's preparatory school, Slough, and his first wife, Eda Strahan. He was educated at Eton College (1893–8); and at Trinity College, Cambridge, where he read mathematics and graduated as nineteenth wrangler in 1901. At Cambridge he was elected to the Apostles and in that society met G. E. Moore, whose philosophy influenced him deeply for the rest of his life. Many of his Cambridge friends later formed part of the Bloomsbury group, and it was through his continued association with Bloomsbury that Hawtrey met (Hortense) Emilia Sophie d'Aranyi (*d*. 1953), the concert pianist, whom he married on 24 April 1915; they had no children. She was the daughter of Taksony d'Aranyi de Hunyadvar, chief of police of Budapest, and the sister of the violinists Jelly d'Aranyi and Adila Fachiri.

Hawtrey entered the home civil service in 1903, and after one year in the Admiralty moved to the Treasury. He was appointed its director of financial inquiries in 1919, and remained at the Treasury until 1947. In 1928–9 he was given leave of absence to take up a visiting professorship of economics at Harvard University, and from 1947 until 1952 he was Price professor of international economics at the Royal Institute of International Affairs, London.

Although Hawtrey spent his working life as an economic adviser at the Treasury and, under Sir John Bradbury, learnt his monetary economics largely from experience there, outside office hours he wrote and published more contributions to monetary theory than most of his academic contemporaries. The system of analysis that he developed continuously in his writings was based on one central idea: 'inflation; the cyclical alternations of activity and depression; financial crises, disturbances of the balance of payments and rates of exchange—all these were to be traced to changes in the wealth-value or purchasing power of the monetary unit' (R. G. Hawtrey, *Currency and Credit*, 4th edn, 1950, vii). In the first four decades of the twentieth century these 'cyclical alternations of activity and depression' were a main preoccupation of monetary theorists; by 1913 Hawtrey had reached his view that 'the trade cycle is a purely monetary phenomenon', due ultimately to changes in bank credit and short-term interest rates. In the 1920s Hawtrey's ideas and those of his friend J. M. Keynes, at first similar, diverged on this issue, Hawtrey holding that changes in bank rate operated through their effect on the cost to merchants of holding stocks, while Keynes argued that such changes, by altering long-term rates, influenced investment in fixed capital. After 1930 Keynes sought to move to a more general theory of relations between aggregate demand and supply, which was to become the starting point for modern macroeconomics and eclipse Hawtrey's doctrines. However, Hawtrey's very detailed and constructive criticisms of Keynes's *Treatise on Money* (1930), and especially the ideas that these contained about the effect of changes in expenditure on levels of output, were acknowledged by Keynes himself to be 'tremendously useful' in helping him to develop his *General Theory of Employment, Interest and Money* of 1936 (cf. Davis, 216–17 and 231).

The advice on policy that Hawtrey gave at the Treasury also developed consistently from his view that maintaining constancy in the wealth-value of the monetary unit must be the primary objective. In 1919 he therefore supported the policy of a return to the gold standard, but in the form of a gold exchange standard with international agreements on uncovered paper issues and credit control. An opportunity to have the implementation of something like this policy occurred when an international economic conference was convened at Genoa in 1922, and Hawtrey as one of the British delegates secured the incorporation of his proposals into the resolutions adopted by the conference. These were never put into effect, and when it became clear in 1925 that the return to gold involved continued deflation Hawtrey became a persistent critic of the conduct of British monetary policy. Nevertheless, he remained convinced that the economy could best be regulated by monetary methods alone, without the addition of fiscal policies such as public works as advocated by Keynes and the Liberals in 1929. In this connection he admitted in later years that he had assumed 'too readily that money saved would be invested and that money invested would be spent' (*Currency and Credit*, 4th edn, 1950, vi).

Since the 1930s witnessed a decline in the use of interest rate changes in monetary policy it is not surprising that Hawtrey's influence on policy also declined in these years. After the Second World War Hawtrey's doctrines made him critical of the Bretton Woods proposals, and in later years he constantly argued that the 1949 devaluation of sterling had been a policy error comparable in magnitude to the 1925 return to gold, and was the root cause of Britain's later inflationary problems.

Gentle in character and courteous in debate, Hawtrey was nevertheless a tenacious advocate of his ideas, whether or not they were fashionable. As he grew older this led to his being typecast by his critics as holding inflexibly to extreme positions and outdated ideas—a view which does less than justice to the subtlety of Hawtrey's thinking and the pains that he took to revise his work in the light of changes in both facts and theories. Recently the importance of his contributions to macroeconomics has come to be more fairly judged and recognized. His contributions to other areas of economics merit similar recognition but have yet to receive it. Among the best-known of his many books were: *Currency and Credit* (1919; 4th edn, 1950), *The Economic Problem* (1926), *The Art of Central Banking* (1932; 2nd edn, 1962), *Capital and Employment* (1937; 2nd edn, 1952), and *Economic Destiny* (1944).

Hawtrey was elected a fellow of the British Academy in 1935, received the honorary degree of DSc (Econ.) from London University in 1939, was president of the Royal Economic Society in 1946–8, and became an honorary fellow of Trinity College, Cambridge, in 1959. He was appointed CB in 1941 and knighted in 1956. He died at St Stephen's Hospital, London, on 21 March 1975, and was cremated at West London crematorium, Kensal Green, on 26 March.

R. D. COLLISON BLACK

Sources *The Times* (22 March 1975) • R. D. C. Black, 'Ralph George Hawtrey, 1879–1975', *PBA*, 63 (1977), 363–97 [incl. bibliography] • E. G. Davis, 'R. G. Hawtrey, 1879–1975', *Pioneers of modern economics in Britain*, ed. D. P. O'Brien and J. R. Presley (1981), 203–33 • P. Deutscher, *R. G. Hawtrey and the development of macroeconomics* (1990) • R. W. Dimand, 'Hawtrey and the multiplier', *History of Political Economy*, 29 (1997), 549–56 • D. E. Moggridge, *British monetary policy, 1924–31: the Norman conquest of $4.86* (1972); repr. (1992) • S. Howson, *British monetary policy, 1945–51* (1993) • S. Howson and D. Winch, *The economic advisory council, 1930–1939: a study in economic advice during depression and recovery* (1977) • P. Clarke, *The Keynesian revolution in the making, 1924–1936* (1988) • *WWW, 1971–80* • Venn, *Alum. Cant.*

Archives CAC Cam., corresp. and papers | BLPES, corresp. with the editors of the *Economic journal* • BLPES, corresp. with J. E. Meade • PRO, treasury papers; Bradbury papers, T. 170; Niemeyer papers, T. 176

Likenesses photograph, *c*.1935, British Academy, London • W. Stoneman, three photographs, 1939–58, NPG

Wealth at death £43,200: probate, 24 July 1975, *CGPLA Eng. & Wales*

Haxey, Thomas (*d.* 1425), ecclesiastic and administrator, probably came from Haxey, Isle of Axholme, Lincolnshire. Apparently of humble family, his early career and patrons are obscure; his two earliest benefices, Pulham, Norfolk (1384), and Somersham, Huntingdonshire (1388), were obtained at the presentation of Thomas Arundel (*d.* 1414), then bishop of Ely, but he was later associated with members of the Ravenser–Waltham family, which was influential in late fourteenth-century government. Haxey was described as a king's clerk from October 1382, but it is not known what position he held in crown service; however he acted under commissions from the crown in 1385 and 1386. In spring 1387 he was described as a clerk of John Waltham (*d.* 1395), keeper of the privy seal. On 18 July 1387 Haxey was appointed keeper of the rolls and writs of the court of common pleas and held this post until 8 February 1397. Though its precise duties are unclear, and its remuneration was modest, this office was prestigious; it was in the immediate gift of the crown, and it could afford the holder opportunities to increase his income by other means. In Haxey's case these were ecclesiastical preferment and moneylending. He held a number of benefices but mostly for brief periods. Presentations to the Nottinghamshire churches of Rampton (a prebend of Southwell) in 1388 (until death), and Laxton in 1393 (until 1408), marked a strengthening of ties with his home area. As moneylender and mainpernor he acquired contacts over a very wide area. In 1395 he was an executor of the will of John Waltham, now bishop of Salisbury. Haxey acted as a proctor for the abbot of Selby in the parliaments of 1386, 1391, 1393, 1394, 1395, January 1397, October 1404, and 1406. He was also a proctor for the bishop of Lincoln in 1393 and for the bishop of Lichfield in 1395, while Ramsey Abbey presented him to the rectory of Brington, Huntingdonshire, in 1396. In addition, Haxey acquired the prebends of Tervin (Lichfield) from 1388 to 1425, Beminster Secunda (Salisbury) from 1391 to 1419, and Scamblesby from 1395 to 1402, and Frandon-cum-Balderton from 1402 to 1425 (both Lincoln).

In the parliament of January 1397 the Commons presented to the Lords a four-point petition, which in its concluding section asked that the great cost of the king's household should be reduced and the number of bishops and ladies at court be decreased. The king ordered an inquiry to discover who had brought this bill before the Commons, and Haxey was named. Richard was furious, not least because this controversial proposal had originated with a long-standing royal servant, and the Lords then declared, retrospectively, that it was treasonable to call for reform of the king's household. Condemned as a traitor on 7 February Haxey was in a dangerous position, since benefit of clergy had been abolished for treason, but Thomas Arundel, now archbishop of Canterbury, swiftly claimed custody of him as a criminous clerk, and Haxey was pardoned on 27 May at the request of 'the bishops and multitude of ladies' in the king's household (*CPR, 1396–9,* 141). Meanwhile Haxey was confirmed as warden of Lazenby chapel, Yorkshire, on 25 February and as the holder of his six other benefices on 25 April, and received his back pay on 21 July. In Henry IV's reign he was again referred to several times as a king's clerk, the latest in 1412 when he was ordered to hold an inquiry in York. In July 1423 he was appointed warden and receiver of the profits of the York mint. The focus of his life apparently shifted

northwards after 1397: in 1399 he was resident at Rampton, and in 1419 he exchanged his Salisbury prebend for one at Ripon, which in turn was exchanged for a Beverley prebend in 1423.

The fifteenth century saw Haxey's talents turned to ecclesiastical administration and to the disposal of his considerable wealth. By 1408 he was a canon residentiary at York, where he had been prebendary of Barnby since 1405. In December 1418 he became treasurer of York, holding office until his death, and he was keeper of the spiritualities of the diocese *sede vacante* in 1423 and 1424. Haxey was an energetic builder, perhaps at Rampton, and certainly at Southwell, where he built a house for the chaplains of his chantry which stood until 1784, and at York, where, in addition to overseeing building works on the chapter's behalf, he paid for the lead roofing of the minster library, his generosity being rewarded by his arms (or, three buckles in fess, sable) being placed in a window of the room. He established chantries at York and at Southwell, where he drew up both his will and testament. He probably died in the earliest days of 1425 (perhaps 8 January); his will was proved on 23 January. He was buried in York Minster. Haxey left bequests to the poor parishioners of all the churches he had held, and made bequests of cash and clothing to eighteen individuals including relatives, household servants, and the prioress of Broadholme. A notable aspect of his considerable wealth was his collection of precious and jewelled plate; he had a fondness for aquamarines. Collectively the greatest value of his bequests went to the fabric and personnel of York Minster, so that even in 1858 it could be said that Haxey was 'still remembered in York for his piety and munificence' (Raine, 203). A. K. McHARDY

Sources A. K. McHardy, '*Haxey's case*, 1397: the petition and its presenter reconsidered', *The age of Richard II*, ed. J. L. Gillespie (1997), 93–114 · Chancery records · parliamentary proxies, PRO, special collections, SC10 · *RotP*, vol. 3 · J. Raine, ed., *The fabric rolls of York Minster*, SurtS, 35 (1859) · A. H. Thompson, ed., 'Documents relating to diocesan and provincial visitations from the registers of Henry Bowet, lord archbishop of York, 7 Oct 1407 – 20 Oct 1423', *Miscellanea*, 2, SurtS, 127 (1916), 131–302 · *Fasti Angl., 1300–1541,* [Lincoln] · *Fasti Angl., 1300–1541,* [Salisbury] · *Fasti Angl., 1300–1541,* [York] · *Fasti Angl., 1300–1541,* [Coventry] · M. Aston, *Thomas Arundel* (1967) · Tout, *Admin. hist.,* 4.17–20 · Chapter Acts, 1410–29, York Minster Library, York, H2/1 · J. H. Tillotson, *Monastery and society in the late middle ages: selected account rolls from Selby Abbey* (1988) · will, York Minster Library, York, L 2/4, Register of wills 1, fols. 219–220v
Wealth at death approx. £300 in bequests, plate, and textiles: will, York Minster Library, York, L 2/4, register of wills, 1, fols. 219–220v

Hay family (*per. c.*1295–*c.*1460), nobility, originated in the seigneurie of La Haye-Hue, by Soulles, south of St Lo in Normandy. It seems certain that the Hays came to Scotland through their connection with Ranulf de Soules, an Anglo-Norman in the service of David I, since one of the earliest recorded Hays in Scotland, William de la Hay, was Soules's nephew. From being knights in the service of Soules, the family became established in central and north-east Scotland, eventually rising sufficiently to hold the important household office of constable of Scotland, formerly the possession of the Comyns. The Hay family had held the barony of Erroll in the sheriffdom of Perth, by knight service, since the early years of William the Lion's reign, but the foundations of their rise to national prominence were laid by **Sir Gilbert Hay of Erroll** (d. 1333), who had succeeded his father by June 1306 and received remittance from Edward I (to whom he had sworn fealty at Aberdeen on 16 July 1296) for the relief due for his lands, severely ravaged during the wars of independence. However, Hay joined the cause of Robert Bruce in March 1306, and in consequence Aymer de Valence, earl of Pembroke, received orders from Edward I to burn and destroy Hay's lands, presumably in Perthshire. Nevertheless Hay continued to serve Robert I loyally and consistently, for which he received a charter of the lands of Slains in Aberdeenshire, together with the office of constable of Scotland, positive evidence for his rise in political importance.

Hay is described as constable in a letter from the nobles of Scotland to Philippe IV of France, dated 16 March 1309, although his tenure of the office was clearly provisional, as it was granted to David, earl of Strathbogie, in 1312. The latter's disgrace in 1314 led to the return and confirmation of the office to the Hays, but now in heredity, being given in a charter by Robert I, dated at Cambuskenneth on 12 November 1314, to Gilbert Hay and his heirs. The duties of the constable included presiding over the judicial court of the household and organizing the king's bodyguard and security wherever he happened to be residing, in addition to various ceremonial duties, some of which were apparently shared with the marischal. A safe conduct was issued to Hay by Edward II on 18 September 1314 as one of the Scottish ambassadors to go to England, and he was a signatory to the letter to Pope John XXII drawn up at Arbroath on 6 April 1320. He was named as one of the conservators of the truce in 1323, and he died in April 1333.

Nicolas Hay was the eldest son of Sir Gilbert, but he appears to have predeceased his father, and may have been the Hay, mistakenly named William, said by Hector Boece to have fallen at the battle of Dupplin in 1332. Sir David Hay of Erroll, who witnessed a charter by David II on 17 June 1341, and who may have been Nicolas's son, was killed at the battle of Nevilles Cross on 17 October 1346.

Sir Thomas Hay of Erroll (d. 1406) was the son of Sir David and his first wife, the daughter and heir of Sir John Keith of Innerpeffer. As constable of Scotland, Hay was one of the commissioners appointed to treat with the English for the release of David II in 1353, and was proposed as a hostage for the king's ransom in 1357. He does not appear to have served as such, possibly because of his official duties as constable. However, his primary loyalty was to the Stewarts rather than to the king, as is indicated by the fact that although he does not appear to have attended at court under David II, he was sufficiently in favour with the Stewarts to secure a royal bride, for he married Elizabeth, the third daughter of *Robert II and his first wife, Elizabeth Mure. He was present at the coronation of Robert II at Scone on 26 March 1371, where, as constable, he received the oaths of homage and fealty given to the king. On 4 April 1373 he swore to the maintenance of the Act of

Settlement entailing the crown on Robert II's male heirs, and his lands of Slains were erected into a free barony by royal charter dated at Dundee on 5 January 1377. But thereafter he seldom appears in official records until his death in July 1406.

Sir William Hay of Erroll (d. 1436), who succeeded his father, had on 19 March 1393 obtained an undertaking from Robert III not to ratify or approve any alienations made by his father, Thomas, without either William's consent or that of the king's council, indicating some tension within the family. Hay was one of the commissioners appointed to treat with the English for the release of James I in 1423, and was knighted at the coronation of the king in 1424, his son Gilbert (d. 1436) having been sent to England as a hostage for James I's ransom, serving thus until 1427. The king's reliance on Hay as one of his trusted northern councillors is indicated by his inclusion in James I's expedition to the north in 1428, and he followed the king's instructions to coerce a reluctant Coupar Angus Abbey, of which he was patron, into surrendering the church of Erroll near Perth, so that it might be added to the king's endowment of Perth Charterhouse. (In 1446 Hay's grandson, subsequently the first earl of Erroll, attempted to recover his rights in the church, claiming that the grant had been made under duress and through fear of the king.) In 1430 Hay, possibly because he held the office of constable rather than because he had any landed interest in the borders, was appointed one of the wardens of the marches. He was married to Margaret, daughter of Sir Patrick Gray, and he died in 1436, being succeeded by his grandson.

William Hay, first earl of Erroll (d. 1462), was the son of Gilbert Hay, who died in the same year as his father, and Alicia, daughter of Sir William Hay of Yester. In the June parliament of 1452 William Hay was raised from the peerage rank of lord of parliament, which he had held in official records at least since 1450, to the earldom of Erroll, resigning all his lands into the king's hands to be erected into the lordship of Erroll and regality of Slains, for which he received royal charters on 31 July 1452. Although the title derived from his estates, Hay's elevation, like that of William Keith, created Earl Marischal in 1458, followed from his hereditary office, reflecting the family's high status as constables of Scotland. It also contributed towards replenishing the then depleted ranks of the higher nobility with loyal supporters of the king, without requiring much expenditure of crown lands or revenue. James II may also have been moved by a desire to secure Hay's allegiance, undermining any ties of kinship the new earl may have had with the Black Douglases, to whom Hay was related through his marriage, before 17 March 1450, to Beatrix Douglas. She was the sister of the eighth earl of Douglas, whom James slew in 1452. The creation of the earldom of Erroll certainly survived the Douglas crisis and the king's act of revocation in 1455. Erroll is mentioned in a charter of 15 November 1461, but was dead by October 1462.   C. A. McGladdery

Sources Rymer, *Foedera*, new edn, vols. 3, 6, 10 • J. Robertson, ed., *Illustrations of the topography and antiquities of the shires of Aberdeen*

and Banff, 3, Spalding Club, 29 (1857) • J. Stuart, ed., 'The Errol papers', *The miscellany of the Spalding Club*, 2, Spalding Club, 6 (1842) • G. Burnett and others, eds., *The exchequer rolls of Scotland*, 23 vols. (1878–1908), vols. 1, 7 • *Scots peerage*, vol. 3 • W. Bower, *Scotichronicon*, ed. D. E. R. Watt and others, new edn, 9 vols. (1987–98), vol. 8, bks 15–16 • J. M. Thomson and others, eds., *Registrum magni sigilli regum Scotorum* / *The register of the great seal of Scotland*, 11 vols. (1882–1914), vol. 2 • G. W. S. Barrow, *The kingdom of the Scots: government, church and society from the eleventh to the fourteenth century* (1973), 325–6

Hay, Alexander, of Easter Kennet, Lord Easter Kennet

(d. 1594), administrator and judge, was a younger son of John Hay of Lochloy and Park, Moray, and grandson of a parish clerk of Fordyce, Banffshire. His official career began in 1564 when William Maitland of Lethington, secretary to Mary, queen of Scots, chose him as his deputy. He also became clerk of the privy council in 1564 and held that office until 1572. Hay accompanied Moray, the regent, and Lethington to York in 1568 to witness against Queen Mary at her first English trial. From 1567 to 1579, moreover, he was director of chancery and keeper of the quarter seal. In 1579 he reached his highest position, that of clerk register, the government officer responsible for the framing and custody of the principal series of public registers and records. Consequently he became a privy councillor, and was also made a judge in the court of session, the supreme civil court; his judicial title was Lord Easter Kennet. He held these three offices until his death. When James VI sailed to Norway in October 1589 to meet his bride, Anne of Denmark, Hay was one of the government officials left behind to run Scotland, being appointed interim secretary for the Scots language. Nothing is known of his formal education, but that he was not made king's secretary during the royal absence suggests that his education, his command of foreign languages, and perhaps his diplomatic skills were not of the very highest standards. Mary, queen of Scots, had earlier remarked that Hay was 'honest but not of the quickest wit' (*CSP Scot.*, 6.86) There are no sources which refute this biting assessment.

Crown service enabled Hay to enter the ranks of landed men. In 1582 he bought the lands of Easter Kennet in Clackmannanshire from Sir Robert Bruce, father of Edward Bruce, later Lord Kinloss, for £5000 Scots, and had a grant of adjoining lands from John Erskine, earl of Mar, his patron. Hay was granted very little property by James VI directly, but as some of his acquisitions were technically held from the crown, he became a top-level landowner, or laird, with the designation 'of Easter Kennet'. For 2500 merks (£1500 Scots) he bought a property in Edinburgh, the Carsehouse in Conns Close; he also had a property at the head of the Castle Wynd in Stirling, which was convenient during the minority of James VI (1567–78), when the king's guardians conducted much state business from nearby Stirling Castle. Hay, who was undoubtedly a skilled administrator, appears to have maintained his position at court through the support which James VI customarily gave to loyal and hard-working government servants. A protestant in religion, he became a commissioner of the kirk. For his services to Edinburgh he was

made a burgess of that town in September 1573. He died there on 16 September 1594 and was buried in Holyrood Abbey church. His estate was valued at £1424 Scots, £580 in cash and £844 in debts, the latter being due for rents from his lands, a pension from the earl of Angus, and his fee as a judge.

Hay married Marion Farquhar, probably before 1573. They had at least four sons, of whom the eldest, John (d. 1637), inherited the Easter Kennet estate and Edinburgh house, and became deputy clerk of the privy council. Little is recorded of Andrew and Daniel, but the third son, **Alexander Hay**, Lord Whitburgh (d. 1616), enjoyed a career which had much in common with that of the elder Alexander. His father procured a gift under the privy seal to support his tuition at Musselburgh Academy, and he eventually graduated MA at an unidentified university. Thanks to his brother John he became a clerk to the privy council, and he was a clerk to the court of session until 1608. Based in Edinburgh, Hay worked closely with the Scottish officials who remained in Scotland after 1603. He came into prominence in 1608, when he was appointed secretary of state for Scotland after the disgrace of Lord Balmerino. This office required him to travel often between Edinburgh and London. He was made an ordinary lord of the court of session on 3 February 1610 under the designation of Lord Newton, and later took the unusual step of changing his designation to Lord Whitburgh. He was also a royal commissioner to the general assembly in Glasgow in 1610. In 1612 he exchanged the office of secretary of state with Lord Binning for the office of clerk register. One source suggests that Hay was 'prevailed upon' to make the exchange, suggesting an adjustment of patronage on James VI's part. Clearly the office of clerk register was the lesser of the two offices in prominence and responsibility, and the work more sedentary; the trials of travel may have affected Hay's decision. He died in 1616. He was the author of 'Manuscript notes of transactions of King James VI', written for the use of Charles I.

R. R. ZULAGER

Sources G. Brunton and D. Haig, *An historical account of the senators of the college of justice, from its institution in MDXXXII* (1836), 175–6, 252 • NA Scot., Rose of Kilvarok MSS, GD/125 • R. Zulager, 'A study of the middle-rank administrators in the government of King James VI of Scotland, 1580–1603', PhD diss., U. Aberdeen, 1991, 272–8 • testaments, NA Scot., CC8/8/XXX/36–4 • *CSP Scot.*, 1586–9 • *Reg. PCS*, 1st ser., vols. 2–5 • J. M. Thomson and others, eds., *Registrum magni sigilli regum Scotorum* / *The register of the great seal of Scotland*, 11 vols. (1882–1914), vols. 5–6 • M. Livingstone, D. Hay Fleming, and others, eds., *Registrum secreti sigilli regum Scotorum* / *The register of the privy seal of Scotland*, 6–8 (1963–82)

Archives BL, state papers relating to Anglo-Scottish relations, Add. MS 33531 • U. Edin. L., David Laing MSS, notes of transactions of King James VI

Wealth at death £1424 Scots: testaments, NA Scot., CC8/8/XXX/36–4

Hay, Alexander, Lord Whitburgh (d. 1616).

See under Hay, Alexander, of Easter Kennet, Lord Easter Kennet (d. 1594).

Hay, Alexander

(d. 1639), army officer in the Swedish service, was born in Scotland of unknown parents. Although there are references to Hay's arriving in Sweden in 1600, nothing more is known of him there until 1632. There was also a Lieutenant Alexander Hay serving in the kingdom of Denmark–Norway before this time, who achieved the rank of captain and was paid off in 1628. This date coincides with Danish–Norwegian withdrawal from the Thirty Years' War, so it is probable that Hay then entered into Swedish service, as this was a common path for many other Scots in Danish service. Robert Monro mentions one Saunders Hay who became captain for Annan's company and initially remained in Scotland before entering Swedish service. This would fit with Hay's first listing on Swedish military muster rolls in 1632, serving as a major in Patrick Ruthven's regiment. The following year, while serving in Francis Ruthven's recruited regiment, he gained promotion to lieutenant-colonel. He also acted as the chief of a squadron of dragoons. At some point before 1631 Hay married Dorotea Plessen, and they had at least two sons.

Hay was stationed at Memel, a Polish town which had been taken by the Swedish king Gustav II Adolf in 1628 and subsequently handed over to Sweden for six years. While in the service of the governor there, Hay became involved in the Polish authorities' complaints against a certain Captain Thomas Hume who had plundered some Jews in 1633. Hay himself offered to compensate the Jews, but as Hume was already in gaol and could not repay Hay, he turned to Colonel Ruthven for help. Ruthven took great offence at this and made Hay's life so unpleasant that he wanted to leave the regiment. At this time a Polish nobleman, Crispin Kerstenstein, corresponded with Hay, and suggested that he enter Polish service. Hay then approached the Swedish authorities and requested the termination of his commission because of his problems with Colonel Ruthven. However, when the Swedish General Herman Wrangel heard of this Hay was summoned for an interview. Hay explained that he would have served in Polish forces on campaign only against the Russians, never against the Swedish crown, and that this only came about because of Colonel Ruthven's intolerable attitude towards him. General Wrangel did not believe Hay and had him incarcerated pending further investigation, and informed the Swedish chancellor, Axel Oxenstierna, of the matter. Shortly after this Hay was released from prison to attend his young son's funeral in Memel. At the end of November General Wrangel had Hay brought before a military tribunal to answer charges of corresponding with the enemy. The tribunal decided in favour of Hay for two reasons. The relations had been initiated by the enemy, relieving Hay of some of the charges, and Hay had been disadvantaged by his lack of fluency in German, which meant he was liable to have misunderstood the initial proposition. He was therefore not subject to 'the usual' punishment (the latter was not specified) and his verdict would be decided by Oxenstierna. Hay was also in the process of obtaining a copy of his response to the Pole, which he believed had been wrongly worded by his scribe.

There does not appear to be any further mention of Hay after this in Swedish sources so it must be presumed that the issue was settled. Hay died in 1639. There is a further reference to Alexander Hay in Denmark in 1643 where his wife and his brother were involved in litigation over his inheritance. This implies that his wife was Danish and had returned to Denmark after her husband's death. Hay's surviving son, Henrik, was born in Stockholm in 1631 and was ennobled in 1689. A. N. L. GROSJEAN

Sources military muster rolls, Krigsarkivet, Stockholm, MR 1629/14, 18–20; 1630/22–29; 1631/12, 15–21; 1632/10–21; 1633/11–22; 1634/12–23; 1635/20–26, 29–31; 1636/17, 18; 1637/15 · G. Elgenstierna, Den introducerade svenska adelns ättartavlor med tillägg och rättelser, 9 vols. (1925–36), vol. 3 · Rikskansleren Axel Oxenstiernas skrifter och brefvexling, 1/9 (Stockholm, 1946), 2 · R. Monro, Monro his expedition with the worthy Scots regiment (called Mac-Keyes regiment) levied in August 1626 (1637) · Rigsarkivet, Copenhagen, Danish state archives, Ra, TKUA Alm. del. 1 no 11: Latina 1632–51, fols. 270–71 · T. Riis, Should auld acquaintance be forgot … Scottish–Danish relations, c.1450–1707, 2 (1988) · H. Marryat, One year in Sweden: including a visit to the isle of Gotland, 2 vols. (1862), vol. 2 · J. Grant, Memories and adventures of Sir John Hepburn (1851) · O. Donner, A brief sketch of the Scottish families in Finland and Sweden (Helsingfors, 1884) · T. A. Fischer [E. L. Fischer], The Scots in Sweden (1907) · J. Mackay, 'Mackay's regiment', Transactions of the Gaelic Society of Inverness, 8 (1878–9), 128–89

Hay, Alexander (c.1735–1806), topographer, was a master of arts probably of a Scottish university, who was ordained in the Church of England. He settled at Chichester, Sussex, and served as curate of the nearby parish of Selsey from 1769 to 1784, and was chaplain of St Mary's Hospital, Chichester from c.1778 to c.1786. He was vicar, albeit non-resident, of Wisborough Green, Sussex, from 1785 to 1806. He kept a school at his house in Chapel Street, Chichester, from c.1780 to c.1805, although he complained in his History that he found it 'a very irksome and laborious employment' (Hay, xiii).

About 1784 Hay wrote the first Chichester Guide, which passed through several editions. Twenty years afterwards, at the age of nearly seventy, he transmuted it into a single volume of over 600 pages as The history of Chichester, interspersed with various notes and observations on the early and present state of the city … its vicinity and the county of Sussex in general: with an appendix containing the charters of the city (1804). The book is as prolix and idiosyncratic as its title suggests, with disproportionate space devoted to somewhat speculative Saxon history, but it is none the less the product of considerable reading and research. For the following century Hay's work provided the basic source for Chichester's history, and even then was not entirely superseded. Even its digressions into county history brought together material not otherwise available to the general reader.

Hay seems to have been a protégé of William Hayley, to whom he dedicated the History, and who commemorated him in his 'Epitaph book'. Hayley describes him as a 'humble yet animated Divine' whose career had suffered 'from having conscientiously opposed the electioneering ambition of the late domineering Duke of Richmond' (W. Sussex RO, Add. MS 2758, fol. 41).

Hay married first Mary (d. 1777), with whom he had a daughter and three sons, and second, on 3 February 1778,

Elizabeth Rolfe of Chichester, with whom he had two sons and four daughters. He died on 15 November 1806 and was buried at the subdeanery church, Chichester on the 19th.

PETER M. WILKINSON

Sources A. Hay, preface, *The history of Chichester* (1804) · H. Johnstone and F. W. Steer, *Alexander Hay, historian of Chichester*, Chichester Papers, no. 20 (1961) · J. Caffyn, *Sussex schools in the eighteenth century*, Sussex RS, 81 (1998) · W. Hayley, 'Epitaph book', W. Sussex RO, Add. MS 2758 fol. 41 · private information (2004) · bishop's transcripts, Selsey, Chichester, W. Sussex RO, Ep. I/24/101 · J. Marsh, diary, Hunt. L., MS HM 54457, vol. 26, p. 4 [microfilm copy at W. Sussex RO, MF 1169] · T. J. McCann, 'Poems, posters and poll books: eighteenth-century printing in Chichester', *Sussex Archaeological Collections*, 130 (1992), 189–99
Archives W. Sussex RO, Chichester diocese episcopal records | W. Sussex RO, Hayley MSS, Add. MS 2758

Hay, Alexander Leith (1758–1838). *See under* Hay, Sir Andrew Leith (1785–1862).

Hay, Andrew (*d.* 1593), Church of Scotland minister, was the son of William Hay, fourth laird of Talla, and his wife, Janet Spottiswood; George *Hay, minister of Eddleston and Rathven, was his brother. Andrew Hay was a university graduate, possibly of Glasgow, and also studied at Paris, where he learned Greek. In 1556 he was a canon of Glasgow Cathedral, holding the prebend of Renfrew—a vicar-pensioner served the parish. Two years later he was himself rector and parson there. In 1559 Hay conformed to the Reformation and then became parson and minister of Hamilton. From no later than 1564 he was also commissary of Hamilton and Dunserf. He was assisted by a reader, William Jackson, who may have been a chaplain in Glasgow Cathedral before 1555. Following the murder of David Riccio, Queen Mary's secretary, on 9 March 1566, Hay was accused of involvement in the crime, and in July he was warded within the burgh of Dunbar and 2 miles around. He was released on the queen's orders on 29 January 1567.

Hay became very active in the administration of the kirk. On the reconstitution of the chapter of Glasgow Cathedral in 1572 he was appointed dean, and early in that year was one of the commissioners who negotiated the convention of Leith, settling the administrative structure of the kirk. He attended almost every general assembly, served on a number of committees, and from 1578 to 1590 acted as one of the assessors to the moderator. He was himself moderator of the assemblies of March 1573 and August 1580. Between 1569 and 1587 Hay was often named to deputations appointed to present petitions from the assembly to, variously, the regent, the privy council, and the king, and from 1569 until 1588 successive assemblies appointed him the commissioner to visit kirks in Clydesdale, Renfrew, and Lennox. On 6 March 1589 the privy council made him a commissioner for the maintenance of the true religion in Clydesdale.

In 1569 Hay became rector of Glasgow University, then in a state of advanced decay; he held the position until 1586. In 1573 he was closely involved in the process whereby the town council of Glasgow not only conveyed former ecclesiastical revenues to the university, thereby stabilizing the latter's finances, but also substantially rewrote the university's constitution. A year later he encouraged Andrew Melville to come to Glasgow as principal of the university, to whose library he himself gave books. In 1580 he tried in vain to oppose Melville's departure from Glasgow for St Mary's College, St Andrews. In the meantime he collaborated with Melville in the production of the second Book of Discipline (1578). Closely involved throughout, he was one of the members of the assembly to whom the preparation of a draft text was entrusted, his responsibility being the section dealing with the kirk's ministry. Like Melville he favoured a presbyterian structure of church government; he was described as one 'wha lyked never those bischopries and wha specialie was the ernest suttar for Mr Andro Melvill' (Kirk, 55). Hay showed his hostility to bishops during the efforts made by successive governments between 1581 and 1585 to install Robert Montgomerie in the see of Glasgow. In 1582 Hay protested to the privy council in the name of the kirk, and so prominent was he in the opposition to the new bishop that in May 1584 he was denounced as a rebel and warded north of the Tay.

In 1586 Hay resigned as rector of Glasgow University. For the rest of his life he was seldom involved in church affairs beyond the bounds of his parish. He was censured in 1592 for shortcomings which included failing to execute discipline at Renfrew and not preaching on Sunday afternoons (which may have been due to old age). No later than 1566 he had married Janet Wallace of Craigie, almost certainly the daughter of the John Wallace who was prominent among the godly lairds of Ayrshire in 1559–60 and who married Margaret Cunningham, daughter of the staunchly protestant fourth earl of Glencairn. Three of their sons became ministers, John at Renfrew, succeeding his father, Theodore at Peebles, and Andrew at Erskine; another son, David, became commissary clerk of Glasgow. Andrew Hay died in 1593.

DUNCAN SHAW

Sources *Fasti Scot.*, 3.185 · C. H. Haws, *Scottish parish clergy at the Reformation, 1540–1574*, Scottish RS, new ser., 3 (1972), 102, 110, 204, 206 · D. Calderwood, *The history of the Kirk of Scotland*, ed. T. Thomson and D. Laing, 8 vols., Wodrow Society, 7 (1842–9), vols. 2–6 · T. Thomson, ed., *Acts and proceedings of the general assemblies of the Kirk of Scotland*, 3 pts, Bannatyne Club, 81 (1839–45) · J. Durkan and J. Kirk, *The University of Glasgow, 1451–1577* (1977) · J. Kirk, *The Second Book of Discipline* (1980) · A. R. Macdonald, *The Jacobean kirk, 1567–1625* (1998)

Hay, Andrew (1762–1814), army officer, son of George Hay of Mount Blairy and Carnousie House, Forglen, Banffshire, was appointed ensign in the 1st or Royal foot on 6 December 1779. He became a captain in the 88th in 1783, and subsequently returned to the 1st Royals. In September 1794, following his retirement on half pay, Hay was appointed major and attached to the 93rd foot, which was broken up in Demerara in 1796. Again on half pay, he raised the Banffshire or Duke of York's Own fencible infantry, and commanded it in Guernsey, Gibraltar and elsewhere between 1798 and 1802.

In 1803 Hay was appointed lieutenant-colonel of the 16th battalion of the army of reserve, and afterwards of a second battalion of the 72nd, formed out of men enrolled in the army of reserve in Scotland; this he commanded until 1807, when he was transferred to the 3rd battalion 1st Royals, which he led as part of Baird's reinforcements at Corunna. After commanding a brigade at Walcheren, he returned with his battalion to Spain. He took command of a brigade of the 5th division in the Peninsula on 1 June 1810, and participated in the battles of Busaco, Salamanca and Vitoria; the assault on San Sebastian, where his brigade took a leading part; the passage of the Bidassoa, and the succeeding operations on the Adour, during which he was in temporary charge of the 5th division; the battles on the Nive; and the siege of Bayonne.

Hay was appointed major-general on 4 June 1811. He was mortally wounded, when general officer of the day, commanding the outposts during the French sortie from Bayonne on 14 April 1814. The officers of the 3rd battalion, 1st Royals, erected a monument to Hay at St Étienne, Bayonne, and, as usual with general officers killed in action, a public monument was erected, a huge and tasteless composition by Humphrey Hopper, which was placed in St Paul's Cathedral, west of the north door.

Hay married, on 2 April 1784, Elizabeth Robinson of Banff, who, with two sons and four daughters, survived him. The older son, Captain George Hay, 1st Royals, was mortally wounded at the battle of Vitoria in 1813, when serving as his father's aide-de-camp. After selling Mount Blairy in 1801 Hay bought Packham House, Fordingbridge, Hampshire. His widow lived there for a time after his death, and placed a monument to him in Fordingbridge church. H. M. CHICHESTER, *rev.* DAVID GATES

Sources *GM*, 1st ser., 84/1 (1814), 517, 624 · R. Cannon, ed., *Historical record of the seventh regiment, or the royal fusiliers* (1847) · *The dispatches of … the duke of Wellington … from 1799 to 1818*, ed. J. Gurwood, 7: *Peninsula, 1790–1813* (1837), 454, 490 · *Supplementary despatches (correspondence) and memoranda of Field Marshal Arthur, duke of Wellington*, ed. A. R. Wellesley, second duke of Wellington, 15 vols. (1858–72), vol. 7; vol. 8, pp. 303, 309, 421–3 · D. Gates, *The Spanish ulcer: a history of the Peninsular War* (1986) · A. B. Rodger, *The war of the second coalition: 1798–1801, a strategic commentary* (1964)
Likenesses H. Raeburn, oils, North Carolina Museum of Art, Raleigh, North Carolina

Hay, Sir Andrew Leith (1785–1862), writer on architecture, was born in Aberdeen on 17 February 1785. His father, **Alexander Leith Hay** (1758–1838), army officer, was born in Aberdeen on 21 December 1758, the second son of John Leith (1731–1763) of Leith Hall, Aberdeenshire and his wife, Harriet (*d*. 1780), daughter and heir of Alexander Steuart of Auchluncart. Formerly Alexander Leith, he was appointed a lieutenant in the 7th dragoons immediately on his birth, captain in 1768, and colonel in the army in 1794. He succeeded his elder brother, John, in 1778, and inherited the estate of Rannes in 1789, when he assumed the additional surname and arms of Hay, being descended from that family through his paternal grandmother. On 1 October in the same year he was gazetted colonel of a regiment raised by himself and called by his name. In 1784 he married Mary Forbes (*d*. 1824), the daughter of Charles Forbes of Ballogie, with whom he had two sons and four

daughters. He was promoted to be major-general in 1796, lieutenant-general in 1803, and full general in 1838. He was deputy lieutenant and justice of the peace for the county of Aberdeenshire. He died in August 1838.

His eldest son, Andrew Leith Hay, entered the army as an ensign in the 72nd foot on 8 January 1806, went to the Peninsula in 1808 as aide-de-camp to his uncle General Sir James Leith, and served through the war until 1814. He was much employed in gaining intelligence, and was present at many of the actions from Corunna to the storming of San Sebastian. During this time he made many sketches, and in 1831 these were published in two volumes, entitled *A Narrative of the Peninsula War*. On General Leith's being appointed in 1816 to the governorship of Barbados, his nephew accompanied him, and discharged the duties of military secretary and also those of assistant quartermaster-general and adjutant-general. It was also in 1816 that he married Mary Margaret, (*d*. 1859) daughter of William Clark of Buckland House, Devon. Their eldest son, Colonel Leith Hay CB, of the 93rd highlanders, was well known by his service in the Crimea and India. As captain in the 2nd foot Andrew Leith Hay served from 21 November 1817 to 30 September 1819, when he was placed on half pay. He had previously been named a knight commander of the order of Charles III of Spain, and a member of the Légion d'honneur.

Having retired from the army, Hay turned his attention to politics, took an active part in the events preceding the passing of the Reform Bill, and on 29 December 1832 became member for the Elgin burghs. Shortly after entering parliament his readiness as a speaker and his acquaintance with military affairs attracted the notice of Lord Melbourne, who on 19 June 1834 conferred on him the lucrative appointment of clerk of the ordnance and in 1836 made him a KH. On 6 February 1838, on being appointed to the governorship of Bermuda, he resigned his seat in parliament. Circumstances, however, arose which prevented him from going to Bermuda: he inherited his father's estate that year, but poverty prevented him taking up residence in Leith Hall and he and his wife went to live in Belgium before returning to Scotland in 1840.

On 7 July 1841 Hay was again elected for the Elgin burghs and he continued to sit until 1847, when he lost his seat. He contested the city of Aberdeen on 10 July 1852, but was again unsuccessful. He paid much attention to county matters, especially to the affairs of the county of Aberdeen. In 1849 he published *The Castellated Architecture of Aberdeenshire*, which includes large lithographs of the principal baronial residences in the county, all from sketches by himself. Shortly before his death he was made convener of the county of Aberdeenshire. He died at home at Leith Hall on 13 October 1862.

G. C. BOASE, *rev.* KAYE BAGSHAW

Sources *Leith Hall* (1985) · *GM*, 2nd ser., 10 (1838), 321 · *GM*, 3rd ser., 14 (1863), 112–13 · R. B. Mosse, *The parliamentary guide* (1836) · NA Scot., SC 1/36/53, 594–7 · Boase, *Mod. Eng. biog.*
Archives NA Scot., corresp. and papers | W. Sussex RO, letters to duke of Richmond

Likenesses G. Hayter, group portrait, oils (*The House of Commons, 1833*), NPG · portrait, Leith Hall, Aberdeenshire · portrait (Alexander Leith Hay), Leith Hall, Aberdeenshire

Wealth at death £350 15s. 6d.: confirmation, 8 Jan 1864, NA Scot., SC 1/36/53, 594–7

Hay, Archibald (d. 1547), humanist scholar and writer on education, whose parents are not known, was a nephew of James *Beaton (archbishop of St Andrews, 1523–39), and a cousin of David *Beaton (cardinal and archbishop of St Andrews, 1539–46). Like many Scots of his generation he studied for much of his career in France. He matriculated at the University of Paris in the rectorial quarter following 16 December 1530, and graduated MA in the quarter following 15 December 1536. By 1538 he was at the Collège de Montaigu, formerly notorious for its austerity and its old-fashioned learning, but which by this stage counted several Scots humanists as members. By 1543 Hay had moved to the Collège du Plessis, from where he published an edition of Erasmus's translation of Euripides' *Hecuba*. At Paris Hay also published his two principal works, *Ad … D. Jacobum Betoun … pro collegii erectione … oratio* and *Ad … D. Davidem Betoun … de foelici accessione dignitatis cardinalitiae, gratulatorius panegyricus*.

In each of these books Hay urges the establishment of a new college of liberal arts in the University of St Andrews. Archbishop James Beaton had petitioned the pope over this project as early as 1525, and again, successfully, between 1537 and 1538. The formalities of its foundation were rushed through just before the archbishop's death on 14 February 1539. Cardinal David Beaton proved less dilatory than his predecessor, though progress remained slow. In 1545 Hay returned to St Andrews and was incorporated in the university, being given the unusual description of 'supreme lover of philosophy' in the matriculation register (Anderson, 252). In July 1546 he became principal of the new St Mary's College, on the resignation of the previous head of the college, the long-standing principal regent in arts. However, Hay's career was cut short by his early death, and on 27 September 1547 Hay's friend and colleague from Paris, John Douglas, was appointed to succeed him as principal. From the way in which the transfer of his church benefices is recorded in the registers of the privy seal of Scotland, it seems likely that Hay was one of those who lost their lives in the battle of Pinkie (10 September 1547) and its aftermath.

Hay's Latin prose and verse writings offer the best evidence for the adoption of a Renaissance humanist educational programme by a Scottish scholar in the 1530s. Although the *Oratio* is ostensibly about the founding of the new college, and the *Panegyricus* purports to congratulate David Beaton on his cardinalate, both these works are manifestos. They argue that modern education in the liberal arts is needed to produce a moral and responsible priesthood, and that a good prelate must use his resources to make this possible. They include the by now formulaic humanist denunciation of lazy, greedy, ignorant priests and old-fashioned scholars, and argue that linguistic and literary scholarship in Latin, Greek, and Hebrew should replace the traditional Latinate logic. Coincidentally they give powerful evidence of Hay's own command of rhetoric, poetry, and Renaissance humanist theology. However, Hay's rhetoric works on several levels. In the *Oratio* he quotes copiously, without acknowledgement, from Erasmus's *Praise of Folly*, in a way which implies coded mockery of his patron the archbishop, whose avarice and delay he later criticizes openly in the *Panegyricus*. At other points he shows familiarity with the rationalist attitude to the origins of religion associated with advanced Italian philosophers working at Paris at the time. Had Archibald Hay lived longer, Scottish academic life might have embraced Renaissance values more fully before the Reformation supervened.   EUAN CAMERON

Sources A. Hay, *Ad reverendissimum in Christo patrem D. Iacobum Betoun, S. Andreae archipraesulem, Scotiae primatem, ac legatum natum, pro collegii erectione Archibaldi Hayi, oratio* (Paris, 1538–47) [unique copy, York Minster Library collection, York UL, quire signatures] · A. Hay, *Ad illustrissimum tituli s. Stephani in monte Coelio cardinalem, d. Davidem Betoun, primatem Scotiae … de foelici accessione dignitatis cardinalitiae gratulatorius panegyricus Archibaldi Hayi* (Paris, 1540) · Spiritus Martinus, trans., *Procli insignis philosophi de motu disputatio* (1542), poem facing 1st p. of text: 'Alchibaldi Hayi Scoti carmen in Spiritum Martinum cuneatem, collegii Lombardorum primarium' · W. A. McNeill, 'Scottish entries in the *Acta rectoria universitatis Parisiensis*, 1519 to *c.*1633', *SHR*, 43 (1964), 66–86 · J. M. Anderson, ed., *Early records of the University of St Andrews*, Scottish History Society, 3rd ser., 8 (1926) · A. I. Dunlop, ed., *Acta facultatis artium universitatis Sanctiandree, 1413–1588*, 2 vols., Scottish History Society, 3rd ser., 54–5 (1964) · E. Cameron, 'Archibald Hay's "Elegantiae": writings of a Scots humanist at the Collège de Montaigu in the time of Budé and Beda', *Actes du iiiᵉ congrès d'études neo-latines, Tours, 1976* (1980), 277–301 · E. Cameron, 'Archibald Hay and the Paduan aristotelians at Paris, 1530–1545', *Acta Conventus Neo-Latini Bononiensis: proceedings of the fourth international congress of neo-Latin studies, Bologna, 26 August to 1 September 1979*, ed. R. J. Schoeck (1985), 8–17.7 · *University of St. Andrews* (1837), vol. 3 of *Evidence, oral and documentary, taken and received by the commissioners … for visiting the universities of Scotland* · J. Durkan, 'The beginnings of humanism in Scotland', *Innes Review*, 4 (1953), 5–24 · J. K. Cameron, 'A trilingual college for Scotland: the founding of St Mary's College', *In divers manners: a St Mary's miscellany to commemorate the 450th anniversary of the founding of St Mary's College, 7th March 1539*, ed. D. W. D. Shaw (1990), 29–42 · R. G. Cant, *The University of St Andrews: a short history*, rev. edn (1970)

Hay, Arthur, ninth marquess of Tweeddale (1824–1878), army officer and naturalist, was born at Yester, East Lothian, on 9 November 1824, the son of George *Hay, eighth marquess of Tweeddale (1787–1876), army officer and agriculturist, and his wife, Lady Susan (1797–1870), daughter of William *Montagu, fifth duke of Manchester (1771–1843). Hay studied at Leipzig, and afterwards at Geneva under D'Aubigné, the historian. He became ensign and lieutenant in the Grenadier Guards in 1841, and four years later he served with distinction in the Sutlej campaign of the First Anglo-Sikh War, acting as aide-de-camp to Sir Henry Hardinge, the governor-general. In 1846, he became lieutenant and captain. In the same year he made a tour in the further Himalayas before returning to his unit in England. In 1851 he travelled in Germany and Austria, and went on to Constantinople. In December 1854 he went to the Crimea as captain and lieutenant-colonel. He served the remainder of the war there, and was noted as never having been absent from duty for a day, except he did much good for his tenants and the neighbourhood, providing them with a medical officer at a fixed salary and founding a library and reading-room, besides giving aid to the schools.

Tweeddale died on 28 December 1878, at the age of fifty-four, at his home, Walden Cottage, Chislehurst, after five days' illness. He was buried on 2 January 1879 at St Nicholas's Church, Chislehurst, beside his first wife. He was survived by his second wife. The *Ornithological Works of Arthur, Ninth Marquis of Tweeddale* was published privately in 1881 in a single volume, edited by Captain Robert Gordon Wardlaw Ramsay (Tweeddale's nephew) and containing a memoir of the author by Sir William Howard Russell, the war correspondent. Tweeddale's contemporaries commented on his shrewdness of observation, diligence in study, and amiable disposition; he appeared shy and retiring to strangers, and was both unselfish and considerate.   H. G. KEENE, *rev.* YOLANDA FOOTE

Sources *The ornithological works of Arthur, ninth marquis of Tweeddale*, ed. R. G. Wardlaw Ramsay (1881) · R. B. Mosse, *The parliamentary guide* (1836) · GEC, *Peerage* · Irving, *Scots.* · Boase, *Mod. Eng. biog.* · Burke, *Peerage* (1879) · *Debrett's Peerage* (1868) · *Hart's Army List* (1854) · *The record of the Royal Society of London*, 4th edn (1940)
Archives NL Scot., corresp. and papers
Likenesses T. R. Williams, photograph, *c*.1860, NPG [*see illus.*] · wood-engraving (after Barraud & Jerrard), NPG; repro. in *ILN* (18 Jan 1879)
Wealth at death £84,395 8*s.* 8½*d.*: confirmation, 22 April 1879, *CCI*

Arthur Hay, ninth marquess of Tweeddale (1824–1878), by Thomas Richard Williams, *c*.1860

when attacked by cholera. He returned to England in 1856 by way of Greece, Italy, and Switzerland, and did not again go on active service.

On 18 February 1857 Hay married Hélène Eleanore Charlotte Augusta (1836–1871), daughter of Count Kielmansegge, Hanoverian minister in London; she was for some time lady of the bedchamber to the princess of Wales. Having obtained a colonelcy in 1860, Hay retired on half pay in 1863; three years later, shortly after being made lieutenant-colonel of the 17th lancers, he retired from half pay. Despite a military career rewarded by various medals (including the Sardinian medal of valour), he decided to devote his life to ornithology. His interest in the subject dated from before 1845, the year in which he contributed to a Madras journal some descriptions of rare birds from the Straits archipelago. Between 1844 and 1879 his ornithological works appeared in the *Madras Journal of Literature and Science*, the *Proceedings of the Zoological Society*, *The Ibis*, the *Annual and Magazine of Natural History*, and the *Journal of the Asiatic Society of Bengal*.

On the death of his elder brother George, earl of Gifford, in December 1862, Hay became heir to his father's title and estates. He did not assume the courtesy earldom, and was known as Viscount Walden. He settled at Chislehurst, in Kent, where he built a house and grew roses. He was made fellow of the Linnean Society (1865), president of the Zoological Society of London (1868), and fellow of the Royal Society (1871). Following the death of his first wife on 30 September 1871, he married Julia Charlotte Sophie (1846–1937), daughter of Keith William Stewart-Mackenzie of Seaforth, on 8 October 1873. He succeeded his father as ninth marquess on 10 October 1876. At Yester

Hay, Lord Charles, of Linplum (1700?–1760), army officer, was probably born in 1700, the third son of Charles Hay, third marquess of Tweeddale (1667–1715), and his wife, Susan (*d.* 1737), the widow of John Cochrane, second earl of Dundonald, and the third daughter of William Douglas and Anne Hamilton, duke and duchess of Hamilton. He entered the army as an ensign in the 2nd foot guards (the Coldstream Guards) in 1722. In 1727 he was made captain in the 33rd regiment of foot, and in 1729 he was promoted to a troop in the 9th dragoons. He was reported to have been present at the siege of Gibraltar in 1727 and to have served as a volunteer under Prince Eugene during the prince's campaign in 1734 on the Rhine, in the War of the Polish Succession. He was elected MP for Haddingtonshire in 1741, and upon the fall of Walpole supported the new government, in which his eldest brother, John Hay, fourth marquess of Tweeddale, was secretary of state for Scotland.

Hay transferred to the 1st foot guards (the Grenadier Guards) as captain (and lieutenant-colonel) on 7 March 1743. He served with the regiment at Dettingen and later, in December that year, was one of the officers who spoke in the House of Commons in defence of the Hanoverian troops against an opposition motion to disband those in English pay.

As captain of the king's company of the 1st battalion of the 1st foot guards he distinguished himself greatly at the battle of Fontenoy (11 May 1745). At 10 a.m., following the failure of initial flanking attacks by the Dutch forces to take the village of Fontenoy and of British and allied forces to overcome the d'Eu redoubt, William Augustus, duke of Cumberland, ordered the British and Hanoverian infantry in the centre, now under heavy French artillery fire, to advance. Just as Hay's company was coming up to the crest of a ridge, the French guards, hitherto unseen, came forward to protect their guns and there was a momentary stand-off. According to Hay:

> It was our regiment that attacked the French Guards: and when we came within twenty or thirty paces of them, I advanced before our Regiment; drank to them (the French) and told them that we were the English guards, and hoped that they would stand till we came quite up to them, and not swim the Scheld as they did the Mayn at Dettingen. Upon which I immediately turned about to our own regiment; speeched them, and made them huzzah … An officer, (d'Auteroche) came out of the ranks and tried to make his men huzzah; however there were not three or four in their brigade that did. (Carlyle, 6.44)

According to all the English accounts the French then opened fire and Hay was wounded in the arm, though he fought on until the close of the battle. His regiment (together with the rest of the guards brigade) replied with a deadly rolling volley and pushed the French guards back in disorder some 300 yards. The British guards continued their advance and repulsed a series of French cavalry charges with disciplined musket fire, but in the absence of support from their own cavalry were eventually forced to withdraw in the face of a withering artillery barrage from the French flanks. By noon Cumberland had restored the line, and a second advance was attempted, again with Hay's regiment in the van. Again the French infantry was broken, but once more the British were forced to withdraw (this time on account of the failure of the Dutch troops to come up in support), unpursued and in good order, in the face of heavy French artillery fire and fresh French infantry reserves (the Irish brigade). Shortly after the battle Hay was reported killed, but he recovered from his wounds. He was complimented on his conduct by both the officers and men of his regiment.

Shortly after the Jacobite rising of 1745 broke out he returned to London. It was reported that at a royal audience where he gave:

> some account of the state of affairs in Flanders, the King said how ungrateful his countrymen were to rise up in rebellion. Lord Hays answered that his majesty need only to order some magistrate to read the proclamation to them and he was sure they would disperse. After the battle of Preston, the King seeing Lord Hays at his levee, told him, 'Well, lord Hays, I think you had best go down and read the proclamation to the rebels'. (Hastings MSS, 3.53)

In November 1746 he was reported to be 'confined raving mad' and had been 'tied to his bed some time' (Polwarth MSS, 5.187), and as a result of this bout of insanity he did not seek re-election in 1747. In March 1749, presumably having recovered, he was made aide-de-camp to George II, and in 1751 he succeeded to the estate of his kinsman Sir Robert Hay, bt, of Linplum.

In 1752 Hay was made colonel of the 33rd regiment of foot, and in 1757 he was promoted major-general. He immediately received a high command in the force under

General Hopson sent to Halifax, Nova Scotia, to join the expedition which was gathering there, under John Campbell, fourth earl of Loudoun, to attack the French at Louisville. Loudoun's dilatoriness (he was later recalled from his command) provoked Hay into publicly criticizing his failure to attack Louisville, whereupon he was arrested and placed aboard ship at Halifax and sent home in late 1758. He demanded and was eventually granted a court martial, which sat from 12 February until 4 March 1760. The decision was not made public, and the case was referred to the king. When preparing his defence Hay requested that Samuel Johnson be introduced to him, and after several visits Johnson pronounced it 'a very good soldierly defence', but advised 'that it was in vain to contend with those who were in possession of power, if they would offer him the rank of Lieutenant-General, and a government, it would be better judged to desist from urging his complaints' (Boswell, The Life of Samuel Johnson, ed. R. W. Chapman and J. D. Fleeman, 1980, 1780). Hay died, unmarried, on 1 May 1760, before George II could make up his mind what course to take. Later, Johnson wrote that he suffered a great loss when Hay died: 'he was a mighty pleasing man in conversation, and a reading man' (ibid., 723). Horace Walpole wrote in a different vein: 'The third prisoner and second madman, Lord Charles Hay, is luckily dead, and has saved much trouble' (Walpole, Corr., 21.403).

JONATHAN SPAIN

Sources 'Tweeddale', GEC, Peerage, new edn · Scots peerage [Tweeddale] · F. W. Hamilton, The origin and history of the first or grenadier guards, 3 vols. (1874) · Fortescue, Brit. army · R. S. Lea, 'Hay, Lord Charles', HoP, Commons, 1715–54 · T. Carlyle, History of Friedrich II of Prussia, called Frederick the Great, new edn, 6 vols. (1858–65), vol. 4, pp. 118–120 · GM, 1st ser., 15 (1745), 291–6 · GM, 1st ser., 30 (1760), 100, 249 · Report on the manuscripts of Lord Polwarth, 5, HMC, 67 (1961), 187 · Report on the manuscripts of Earl Bathurst, preserved at Cirencester Park, HMC, 76 (1923), 356 · Manuscripts of the earl of Egmont: diary of Viscount Percival, afterwards first earl of Egmont, 3 vols., HMC, 63 (1920–23), vol. 3, p. 278 · Report on the manuscripts of the late Reginald Rawdon Hastings, 4 vols., HMC, 78 (1928–47), vol. 3, p. 53 · Walpole, Corr., 18.519, 540; 21.367, 385, 403; 37.190, 192, 502; 36.11–12; 38.49

Archives NL Scot., corresp. and papers, MSS 7081–7097, 14430–14433

Hay, David Ramsay (1798–1866), decorative painter and writer on art and design, was born in Edinburgh in March 1798. His mother, Rebecca Carmichael, a cultivated woman who in 1790 had published a volume of poems in Edinburgh, was left entirely destitute on the early death of her husband. David Ramsay, banker and proprietor of the Edinburgh Evening Courant, after whom the boy had been named, ensured that he received some education and placed him in a printing office as a 'reading boy'. Hay showed a talent for drawing which led to his apprenticeship, at the age of fourteen, to Gavin Beugo, a heraldic and decorative painter in Edinburgh. A fellow apprentice who became a lifelong friend was the painter David Roberts, of whose work Hay later owned a number of examples including The Cathedral of Seville during the Ceremony of Corpus Christi and two designs for the Scott monument (all three exh. Royal Scottish Academy, 1836). In his spare time Hay made some copies after works by Antoine Watteau and some animal paintings which remained in the possession of his family. The latter drew the attention of Sir Walter Scott for whom he painted a portrait of his favourite cat, and on seeking Scott's advice regarding his early wish to become an artist, was taken into the author's study where they conversed at length. Scott recommended that unless he felt such a 'glow of ambition that [he] would rather run a hundred chances of obscurity and penury than miss *one* of being a Wilkie … he should resolutely set himself to introducing something of a more elegant style of house-painting' (Lockhart, 7.201–2). Hay was 'modest and wise enough to accept the advice with thankfulness, and to act upon it. After a few years he had qualified himself to take charge of all this delicate limning and blazoning at Abbotsford' (ibid.). By 1820 Hay and his partner George Nicholson had set up a house decorating firm, and were assisted by Nicholson's brother William, who later became a successful portrait painter. By the late 1820s Hay was established at 89 and afterwards at 90 George Street, Edinburgh. Now considered to be an important example of early nineteenth-century interior design, Abbotsford forms one of a select group of houses described by Clive Wainwright in *The Romantic Interior* (1989). Hay's own account of his work for Scott, written many years after the poet's death, is there cited at length (Wainwright, 167). Hay noted that he began work on the dining room with eight assistants on 20 March 1820; in 1824 they began to decorate the library (ibid., 188, photograph, pl. 156) and then progressed to the hall and the armoury (ibid., 200). Scott continued to promote Hay's career and artistic education; in 1823 Hay wrote to Scott:

do me the honour of accepting the old cabinet which accompanies this as a trifling mark of the gratitude which I feel, for the kindness and liberality with which you encourage my early efforts in painting and especially for the trouble you had the goodness to take in getting me admitted to the Drawing Academy and by your valuable advice directing my future pursuits to that line of business in which by the aid of your support and recommendation I have been so successful. (Wainwright, 167)

Hay was hugely successful in this line of business, carrying out important commissions at Holyrood Palace and the National Gallery of Scotland, Edinburgh, and, about 1846, the hall of the Society of Arts, London. In the early 1840s he was appointed 'decorative painter to Her Majesty, Edinburgh'. In establishing Hay's contribution to the vogue for historicized interior design Wainwright included Hay's comment that in 1822 (when shops scarcely existed outside London):

there were no shops in Edinburgh, such as those where old carvings can now [1847] be so easily obtained—for I believe Sir Walter Scott's adoption of these articles as a decoration, gave the first impulse to that rage for them which has since existed, and which is now so well responded to by all who deal in other antiquities. (Wainwright, 180)

Several of the leading house decorators in Edinburgh

and Glasgow were Hay's pupils, and they founded in memory of their master the Ninety Club, named after the number of his place of business in George Street, a society which, in 1891 when his entry was published in the *Dictionary of National Biography*, continued to hold an annual dinner.

From the outset, Hay took an interest in the theoretical side of his work and in 1828 published a slim volume, the *Laws of Harmonious Colouring*. The work ran to six editions in nineteen years, each edition increasing in scope, and was essentially rewritten after the fourth edition. In a notice of 1843 in the *Edinburgh Review*, the eminent scientist David Brewster acclaimed Hay's work for bringing 'scientific truth' to the otherwise murky speculations abounding on the fine arts. (Hay and Brewster were both involved in the Aesthetical Club, a society with masonic leanings dedicated to founding a science of beauty on fixed mathematical principles, which also included among its members John Goodsir and possibly James Clerk Maxwell.) Heartened by his success, Hay gained confidence in his theoretical positions and proceeded to produce a series of involved works during the 1840s—mostly published in expensive editions by William Blackwood & Sons—on subjects including the harmony of form, the principles of colouring, and the role of symmetry and proportion in defining beauty. Among these works, the most successful was his *Nomenclature of Colours*, the first edition of which was published in 1845, and which earned him the acclaim of much of the British press, as well as the acceptance of scientific authorities as respected as James David Forbes and Clerk Maxwell, both of whom made use of Hay's system. He was subsequently elected a fellow of the Royal Society of Edinburgh and, under the burden of his growing fame, published a catalogue raisonné of his own works in 1849. In 1846 Hay received from the Royal Scottish Society of Arts a silver medal 'for his machine for drawing the perfect egg-oval or composite ellipses', and was a founder member of the Aesthetic Society, established in Edinburgh in 1851.

Subsequent volumes extended Hay's ideas on beauty and proportion to the human head, the human figure, and architecture, culminating in his treatise of 1856, *The Science of Beauty*, largely premised on Pythagorean notions of harmonic numbers and ratios. His theories reflect a curious admixture of influences, ranging from Scottish commonsense philosophy to phrenology, and demonstrating a close proximity to the ideas of George Field, probably the most widely read authority on colour in nineteenth-century Britain and author of the theory of chromatic equivalents, which established specific mathematical proportions for defining colours. Both Field's and Hay's theories were adopted in the 1850s by the Department of Science and Art at South Kensington, and continued to be taught in the British system of government-supported schools of art well into the 1880s, gaining currency through their incorporation into the works of art-educational authorities such as Richard Redgrave and Owen Jones. Despite his evident debt to Field, it would be wrong to dismiss Hay as a mere follower of the latter. Picking up on Field's ideas of quantitative analogies between music and colour, Hay developed this principle into a complex system of so-called 'harmonic ratios' which supposedly permeated all forms of natural and manmade beauty and which he expounded in great detail in his *Principles of Beauty in Colouring Systematized* (1845). Most of Hay's works were illustrated from his own designs. Although most of his ideas are completely discredited today and dismissed as pseudo-science, Hay's influence in his own time was extensive. Following his death at his home, 7 Jordan Bank, Edinburgh, on 10 September 1866, he was eulogized as nothing less than 'the modern Pythagoras' and described by his obituarist as 'a true philosopher' (*Art Journal*, 28, 363). Hay moved in the most cultivated Edinburgh society of his day, and accumulated a fine collection of pictures by contemporary Scottish painters and other art objects. In 1867 a large series of his 'educational diagrams, illustrative of his theory of the beautiful and its application to architecture, sculpture, and art production in general' was presented to the board of manufactures, Edinburgh, by his family and trustees. An extensive list of Hay's theoretical works is included in his entry in the *Dictionary of National Biography*.　　　　　R. C. DENIS

Sources D. R. Hay, *A catalogue raisonné of the works of D. R. Hay, with critical remarks by various authors* (1849) · W. Wallace Fyfe, 'David Ramsay Hay, the mathematician of taste', *Art Journal*, 28 (1866), 331 · *The anatomical memoirs of John Goodsir*, ed. W. Turner, 2 vols. (1868) · *DNB* · D. Brett, 'The aesthetical science: George Field and the "science of beauty"', *Art History*, 9 (1986), 336–50 · K. Montague, 'The aesthetics of hygiene: aesthetic dress, modernity, and the body as sign', *Journal of Design History*, 7 (1994), 91–112 · R. C. Denis, 'The educated eye and the industrial hand: art and design instruction for the working classes in mid-Victorian Britain', PhD diss., U. Lond., 1995, chap. 2 · C. Wainwright, *The romantic interior: the British collector at home, 1750–1850* (1989) · D. Brewster, 'Hay on harmonious colouring and form', *EdinR*, 78 (1843), 300–26 · W. D. McKay and F. Rinder, *The Royal Scottish Academy, 1826–1916* (1917) · J. G. Lockhart, *The life of Sir Walter Scott*, 7 (1902), 201–2
Archives U. Edin., corresp. | NL Scot., corresp. with John E. Ingpen · NL Scot., papers relating to the Parthenon · NL Scot., corresp. with David Roberts · V&A, letters to David Roberts
Likenesses G. Harvey, portrait, Royal Scot. Acad.
Wealth at death £21,064 19s. 0d.: confirmation, 30 Nov 1866, NA Scot., SC70/1/132/411–440

Hay, Edmund (*c*.1534–1591), Jesuit, was a younger son of Peter Hay of Megginch, bailie to the earl of Erroll, and Margaret Crichton of Ruthven, both of Perthshire. After attending St Salvator's College, St Andrews, he graduated bachelor of theology at Rome. In 1562 Hay, recently ordained, volunteered to accompany the Jesuit Nicolas de Gouda as a papal legate to Mary, queen of Scots. A highly secret interview took place at Holyrood in Edinburgh, with Hay acting as Latin interpreter. Based at Megginch, the legate made contact with the bishop of Dunkeld, who had just been condemned for celebrating Easter. After arranging the legate's escape from Scotland with William Crichton, a future Jesuit activist, Hay followed with four youths from Perthshire, who also became Jesuits. After Rome he went to Innsbruck, and then in 1564 he became rector of the new Collège de Clermont in Paris. In 1566 a

second papal legate was intended for Scotland but on Mary's insistence travelled no further than Paris. Hay went instead, along with William Chisholm, bishop of Dunblane, but they failed to convince her of the need for strong measures. After her enforced abdication Hay described Mary as 'that sinner' (Pollen, 508), but wrote supportively to her during her English captivity.

Hay's treatment of Thomas Smeaton when the latter, who had moved to France with the idea of becoming a Jesuit, but instead opted for protestantism, has been cited as an example of 'auld Parisiane kyndnes' among Scots abroad (Ross, 370). Though a foreigner, Hay was chosen as provincial superior of France (1571–4) before becoming rector of the new University of Pont-à-Mousson in Lorraine. He was in Scotland for four years from 1585 at a time when Robert Persons still regarded that country, through James VI, as 'our greatest hope' for the conversion of England (Law, 223). Working with James Gordon in the northeast, Hay is credited by a visiting Irish bishop, who confirmed them, with having made at least 10,000 converts in six months. His final appointment was as assistant to the Jesuit general in Rome.

Hay had early made clear his disapproval of Jesuits who confused religion with politics, and the fact that he held such positions of responsibility within the order has been taken to show that 'far from altering his views on so vital a point, he came in the course of years to hold it more strongly than ever' (Chadwick, 'Memoir', 69). Hay died on 4 November 1591 at the Vatican in Rome, and was buried there.　　　　　ALASDAIR ROBERTS

Sources J. H. Pollen, ed., *Papal negotiations with Mary queen of Scots during her reign in Scotland, 1561–1567*, Scottish History Society, 37 (1901) · H. Chadwick, 'A memoir of Fr Edmund Hay S. I.', *Archivum Historicum Societatis Iesu*, 8 (1939), 66–85 · W. Forbes-Leith, ed., *Narratives of Scottish Catholics under Mary Stuart and James VI* (1885) · H. Chadwick, 'Father William Creighton S. I., and a recently discovered letter (1569)', *Archivum Historicum Societatis Iesu*, 6 (1937), 259–86 · M. J. Yellowlees, 'Dunkeld and Nicholas de Gouda's mission to Scotland, 1562', *Innes Review*, 44 (1993), 48–57 · A. Ross, 'Reformation and repression', *Essays on the Scottish Reformation, 1513–1625*, ed. D. McRoberts (1962), 371–414 · T. G. Law, 'English Jesuits and Scottish intrigues, 1581–82', *Collected essays and reviews of Thomas Graves Law*, ed. P. H. Brown (1904), 217–43 · A. Bellesheim, *History of the Catholic Church in Scotland*, ed. and trans. D. O. H. Blair, 3 (1889)

Hay, Edward (*c*.1761–1826), historian and political activist, was born at Ballinkeele, co. Wexford, Ireland, the eldest son of Harvey Hay (*d.* 1796), landowner, and Catherine Fergus, who were Roman Catholics. He studied in France and Germany before returning to Ireland, where he took part in the public movements for effecting a relaxation of the penal laws against Catholics. In 1791 he was elected by the Wexford Catholics to the Catholic committee, whose exertions led to the Catholic Relief Act of 1793. Hay endeavoured at this time to suppress the disturbances in Wexford and to restore peace in the county, and was one of the delegates who, on behalf of the Irish Catholics, presented an address to Lord Fitzwilliam, and laid a petition before George III at London in 1795. Edmund Burke in a letter to Thomas Hussey in that year referred to him as a 'zealous, spirited, and active young man' (*Correspondence*,

264). Hay also devised a project for obtaining a statistical enumeration of the population of Ireland. His plan received the commendation of Lord Fitzwilliam and Burke, as well as of Bishop Milner. His census, which concentrated on his home parish of Ballinkeele, included denominational data in order to provide demographic arguments for Catholic emancipation. Hay was made a member of the Royal Irish Academy in 1795 for his census efforts.

During the disturbances in Wexford in 1798 Hay acted as a negotiator between the rebels and the government forces. His motives were political; however, he was arraigned on a charge of treason, and, although acquitted, he suffered protracted imprisonment until liberated through the intervention of Lord Cornwallis. In 1803 he published at Dublin *History of the insurrection of the county of Wexford, A.D. 1798, including an account of transactions preceding that event, with an appendix*; it was reprinted at Dublin in 1842, 1847, 1848, and 1898, and in New York in 1873. To it he appended statements in contravention of allegations made against him and his brother, John Hay, by Sir Richard Musgrave in his *Memoirs of Various Rebellions in Ireland* (1801). His *History* was written to vindicate and conceal his activities. Contrary to Musgrave's claim that the rebellion was a Catholic act of subversion designed to eliminate all protestants, Hay's book minimized the role of Catholic lay involvement in the rebellion, and he was clearly sympathetic towards the 'intrepid' rebels, though critical of sectarian violence. Hay actively marketed his book and claimed that 3000 copies were sold.

Hay subsequently acted as secretary for various associations for the emancipation of the Irish Catholics between 1807 and 1819. His tasks included routine paperwork, advertising meetings, keeping the public informed about Catholic activities, and circulating policy documents. His voluminous official correspondence suggests that he was relentless in canvassing support for the Catholic cause. Letters between Hay and English Catholics demonstrate his desire for a pan-Catholic league. He was somewhat unjustly superseded as secretary to the Catholic board in 1819, nominally for having without authority opened communication with a cabinet minister, George Canning. Daniel O'Connell left Hay responsible for the debts of the Catholic body when subscriptions dried up as a result of the split over the veto controversy in the 1810s. Hay was reduced to penury in his later years and was imprisoned for debt in 1822. He died of blood poisoning in very necessitous circumstances in Dublin on 13 October 1826 and was buried in St James's Church, Kilmainham, Dublin. He was survived by his wife.

Hay's career spanned the era from Wolfe Tone to O'Connell, from political exclusion to mass mobilization of the Irish Catholics. According to Henry Grattan he was a 'well-meaning person; very busy, always in a bustle, and extremely loquacious' (Grattan, 5.403), and O'Connell described him as the 'servant of eight million people' (Madden, 4.528).

J. T. GILBERT, *rev.* MARGARET Ó HÓGARTAIGH

Sources R. R. Madden, *The United Irishmen: their lives and times*, 2nd edn, 4th ser. (1860) · M. Whelan, 'Edward Hay "Styled Mr Secretary Hay": Catholic politics, 1792–1822', MA diss., University College, Galway, 1991 · NA Ire., Frazer MS · Dublin Diocesan Archives, Catholic Association MSS and Caulfield Troy correspondence · K. Whelan, *The tree of liberty: radicalism, Catholicism and the construction of Irish identity, 1760–1830* (1996) · *The correspondence of Daniel O'Connell*, ed. M. R. O'Connell, 8 vols., IMC (1972–80) · B. C. MacDermot, ed., *The Catholic question in Ireland and England, 1798–1822: the papers of Denys Scully* (1988) · H. Grattan, *Memoirs of the Right Honourable Henry Grattan*, 5 vols. (1849) · Fitzwilliam papers, Sheff. Arch., Wentworth Woodhouse muniments · J. Milner, *An inquiry into certain vulgar opinions concerning the Catholic inhabitants and antiquities of Ireland* (1808) · *The correspondence of Edmund Burke*, 8, ed. R. B. McDowell (1969) · F. O'Higgins, 'Catholic Association papers in the Dublin diocesan archives', *Archivium Hibernicum*, 39 (1984), 58–61 · G. P. Bushe, 'An essay towards ascertaining the population of Ireland', *Transactions of the Royal Irish Academy*, 3: Science (1789–90), 145–155 · *Dublin Evening Post* (5 June 1813) · minute book, 1795, Royal Irish Acad. · M. Ó hÓgartaigh, 'Edward Hay, historian of 1798', *Eighteenth-Century Ireland*, 13 (1998), 121–34

Archives NA Ire., Rebellion MSS, 620/11, 620/38–39, 620/46, 620/51, 620/56; 620/66 · NA Ire., state prisoners' petition no. 166, 10/10/1798 · NL Ire., Catholic committee minute books, MSS 4321–4322; 27530; 27564 · PRO NIre., Donoughmore MSS, corresp. with Lord Donoughmore, T.3459 · PRO NIre., Pelham MSS, T.755 (2) · Sheff. Arch., corresp. with Earl Fitzwilliam

Likenesses T. Kelly, sketch, 1808, NL Ire. · sketch, repro. in E. Hay, *History of the insurrection of the county of Wexford* (1803), inside cover

Wealth at death died in penury: *Dublin Evening Post* Oct 1826; *Freeman's Journal* Oct 1826

Hay, Francis, ninth earl of Erroll (*bap.* 1564, *d.* 1631), rebel, was baptized on 30 April 1564, the second of the four children of Andrew Hay, eighth earl (*d.* 1585) and his first wife, Lady Jean Hay (1540–1570), daughter of William Hay, sixth earl of Erroll. His elder brother Alexander, was set aside on account of physical defect, being deaf and dumb. Francis had a charter of the lands of Argath and Inchmichael, Perthshire, on 22 August 1582 and the lands of the barony of Erroll on 29 March 1584. By contracts dated between 22 April and 27 June that year he married Lady Margaret Stewart, daughter of the late James *Stewart, earl of Moray (1531/2–1570), regent of Scotland; they had no children. Following his father's death at Slains on 8 October 1585, he succeeded to the earldom, being still under age. His wife died before 3 August 1586, and by contract dated 17 to 28 January 1587 he married Lady Mary Stewart, daughter of John *Stewart, fourth earl of Atholl (*d.* 1579), but she too died childless in 1589. On 6 February 1588 Erroll had a charter of the Kirktown of Slains.

At an unknown date Erroll was converted to Roman Catholicism by his kinsman Father Edmund Hay (*c.*1534–1591). With George Gordon, sixth earl of Huntly, he became a leader of the pro-Spanish faction which openly desired the re-establishment of the old religion. Following the defeat of the Spanish Armada, in 1589 Erroll entered into a treasonable correspondence with Philip II of Spain hoping to induce the Spanish monarch to undertake a second expedition. A letter from Erroll to the duke of Parma asserting his loyalty to the king of Spain was intercepted in England, and on 17 February was sent by Elizabeth I to James VI.

On 29 February Erroll was ordered to appear before the

privy council on a charge of perverting the true religion, within eight days under pain of rebellion. On 13 March, the earls of Erroll and Huntly had a secret conference with James VI but the king refused to be drawn into the matter and warned them against entering into conspiracies. Erroll failed to appear before the council and was denounced a rebel on 21 March; he was put to the horn (declared an outlaw), his goods and lands were confiscated, and his person was to be pursued as a traitor. The next day, probably ignorant of this, he wrote to Robert Bruce, minister in Edinburgh, denying the accusations made by John Maitland, the chancellor.

On 7 April Erroll was charged to deliver the castles of Slains and Logiealmond but with the earls of Crawford, Huntly, and Bothwell, he responded by raising a rebellion in the north. James VI left Linlithgow on 10 April, and five days later arrived at Cowie, Aberdeenshire. By this time the earls had assembled at the Bridge of Dee with a force of 3000 men. While James aimed to 'wracke and ruine his papistes and disobedient subjectes, and keap his cowtrie from being a receptacle to forein forces' (*Reg. PCS*, 4.371), the rebels hoped to liberate a king they saw as sympathetic to their religion but the captive of pressures from the English, the kirk, and Scottish protestants. Erroll was ready to attempt this by force but Huntly surrendered while the king was still in the north, and once he was taken the others fled. One by one they were taken into custody, with Erroll, the most militantly Catholic, the last to surrender in July. Following a second interview with the king, on 4 August 1589 Erroll received his liberty and his goods and lands were declared extant by an act of council in Aberdeen. That month Huntly and Erroll made a bond to have each other as ally, defending the other against enemies, except the king ('Errol papers', 2.279).

Before 10 July 1590 Erroll married his third wife, Lady Elizabeth Douglas, youngest daughter of the protestant magnate William *Douglas, sixth earl of Morton (*c.*1540–1606); they had five sons and eight daughters. This new alliance notwithstanding, Erroll repeatedly committed treasonable acts. On 27 June 1592 he was with the king at Falkland Palace when the earl of Bothwell attempted to capture it. Suspected of involvement in the conspiracy, Erroll was imprisoned in Edinburgh Castle. He was recommitted on 31 July under suspicion of being a papist but after a very short time he was liberated, only to renew his treasonable correspondence with Spain. In December 1592 he was suspected of complicity in the famous conspiracy known as the Spanish blanks, allegedly a Spanish-backed plot to resurrect, first in Scotland and then in England, the enormous enterprise of the Great Armada, in order to restore the Catholic faith in the island. On 8 January 1593 he was summoned to surrender, and on 5 February was denounced a rebel for 'practizing and traffiquing with Jesuites, seminari preistis, and utheris excommunicat and trafficquing papistis, aganis the state of the trew religioun' (Pitcairn, 1.283). On 9 March the earl marischal was deputed to apprehend him, but on 16 March the king, with advice of his council, ordained letters 'to issue to relax the Earls of Angus, Huntly, Erroll,

Gordon of Aunchindoun' and others from the horn (*Reg. PCS*, 5.52n.) and summoned them to appear before parliament on 2 June. On 4 August the earl of Erroll 'submitted him selffe to his [the King's] marcy very humbly, and reprented muche, accusynge Huntley of many thinges that the King knew not before' (ibid., 5.131). He had to pay a fine of 2000 crowns and was briefly imprisoned.

After some confusion and petitioning of the king by the earls their trial was held on 26 November. The court decided that the three noblemen and their followers should be exempt from prosecution on condition of not repeating the offences and making a payment of £400 each. It was also decided that by 1 February they should submit to the church and renounce the errors of popery, or be removed from the kingdom. However, by 31 January it had become clear that the earls would not comply with the terms, and they were charged to return to specified prisons within ten days. When Erroll failed to appear at Edinburgh Castle, parliament declared him a traitor. This verdict was confirmed at the end of the trial on 8 June.

Meanwhile Erroll had joined the earl of Huntly in Aberdeenshire with a formidable army. When on 16 July 1594 the crew of a Spanish ship and some Jesuits, including Huntly's uncle James Gordon, were arrested both earls sought their release, threatening to attack and burn the towns of Glenlivet and Glenrinnes. On 3 October 1594 they defeated a royal army of 7000 men commanded by the earl of Argyll at Glenlivet, although Erroll was wounded by an arrow and sustained other severe injuries. When the king himself arrived in the north, the earls swayed by Huntly and against Erroll's more belligerent judgement, withdrew north and avoided further confrontation. Although the king ordered the demolition of Erroll's castle at Slains before he left the north on 9 November, no further reprisals were taken against the rebels. The duke of Lennox, left to secure the north as his lieutenant, obtained for the earls the king's permission to go into exile, in return for forswearing unauthorized return and further conspiracy against the established religion or the peace of the kingdom.

Erroll went to the Netherlands. His lands were given to Lennox 'by way of factorie', but his wife, Elizabeth, remained in the country as 'intrometter therewith' (Calderwood, 5.357). However, rumours of further conspiracy soon led the estates in the Low Countries to arrest Erroll and imprison him at Middelburg. Robert Dennistoun, James VI's conservator of privileges in those countries, was appointed as his keeper but let him escape. In September 1596 Erroll and others returned secretly to Scotland. On 22 November a council proclamation forbade his feudal tenants from making contact with him and ordered them to satisfy the kirk. On 30 November David Black, minister of St Andrews, was summoned for asserting that the rebels had returned with the king's consent. However, James VI desired reconciliation between them and the kirk. On condition of his abjuration of popery and his subscription to the confession of faith, the general assembly decided against excommunicating Erroll; absolution was given on 26 June. In August the earls were relaxed from the horn at the cross of Edinburgh, and on 16 December 1597 they were restored in their estates and dignities by an act of parliament.

Further signs of royal favour followed. On 10 August 1600 the earl and countess had a charter of the lordship of Erroll and other lands. On 30 October 1601 Erroll was appointed commissioner of justiciary for the king against a group of rebels, including Gordon of Gicht, and on 11 July 1604 he was a commissioner to treat the union with England. During those years, Erroll enjoyed the king's confidence. Although a long-running dispute between Erroll and the earl marischal with regard to the privileges of the high constable, a hereditary office in both families, surfaced in 1606, it does not seem to have had serious political repercussions at this time. Erroll received further charters of land, at Turnaluif on 29 July 1607 and the barony of Crimond on 7 June 1608.

However, the kirk still held Erroll in suspicion. In February 1608 he was summoned for not taking communion; the sentence was a penalty of £1000. In May of that year, the general assembly, meeting at Linlithgow, denounced him as one of the heads of the 'Catholic party' of Scotland and threatened him with excommunication. This became effective on 11 October following Erroll's refusal to conform to the Reformed religion. Subsequently he obeyed a privy council order to enter into ward, and was confined at Dumbarton and elsewhere, but this was not the end of the matter. On 11 March 1609 he lost his life-rent and was put to the horn by a decree of the council. In 1610, a review of his case on his own petition led to further detention in Edinburgh Castle until late May 1611. Six years later he was finally released from his excommunication 'upon some offers given in of him to some bishops convented at Perth' (Calderwood, 8.244).

In the 1610s Erroll was a frequent, but not a prominent attender at parliaments. On 28 March 1620 he was accused of sending his son to France with Patrick Con, a well-known papist. After a long period of sickness, Erroll obtained a royal warrant to go abroad for the benefit of his health, under caution of £10,000. Little is known of his last years. He died on 16 July 1631 at his house of Bownes, erected on the ruins of the ancient castle of Slains, and was buried in the parish church. There was no ceremony because he left instructions that the money which might have been spent on his funeral should be given to the poor. He claimed in his will, dated 9 June 1628, that he died, as he had lived, a true and sincere apostolic Roman Catholic. He was succeeded as tenth earl by his son William Hay (d. 1636), who had been educated as a protestant. CONCEPCION SAENZ

Sources Reg. PCS, 1st ser., vols. 5–8 • CSP Scot., 1547–1603 • CSP dom., 1603–25 • Scots peerage • D. Calderwood, The history of the Kirk of Scotland, ed. T. Thomson and D. Laing, 8 vols., Wodrow Society, 7 (1842–9) • The diary of Mr. James Melvill, 1556–1601, ed. G. R. Kinloch (1829) • J. Spalding, Memorialls of the trubles in Scotland and in England, AD 1624 – AD 1645, ed. J. Stuart, 2 vols., Spalding Club, [21, 23] (1850–51) • 'Errol papers', The miscellany of the Spalding Club, 2 (1842) • J. Colville, The historie and life of King James the Sext: being an account of the affairs of Scotland from … 1556 to … 1596, with a short continuation to … 1617 (1825) • D. Moysie, Memoirs of the affairs of Scotland, 1577–1603, ed. J. Dennistoun, Bannatyne Club, 39 (1830) • APS, 1567–1625 • 'Register of deeds', 1554–1649, NA Scot., RDI–5, vol. 2, vol. 31 • R. Pitcairn, Criminal trials in Scotland, from A.D. M.CCCC.LXXXVIII. to A.D. M.DC.XXIV., embracing the entire reigns of James IV. and V., Mary Queen of Scots and James VI (1833) • NA Scot., Slains Charters, GD175, RH1/6, NRAS925 • J. M. Thomson and others, eds., Registrum magni sigilli regum Scotorum / The register of the great seal of Scotland, 11 vols. (1882–1914) • GEC, Peerage

Archives NA Scot., Slains charters and register of deeds • Scottish Catholic Archives, Edinburgh, William Semple's papers

Hay, George (c.1530–1588), Church of Scotland minister, was the second son of William Hay, fourth laird of Talla and also of Linplum, Peeblesshire, and his wife, Janet Spottiswood. Andrew *Hay, rector of Glasgow University, was his brother. By papal dispensation he held the benefices of Eddleston, Peeblesshire, and Rathven, Aberdeenshire, where he was rector by 10 July 1558. At the Reformation he embraced protestantism and retained both livings, though he employed a reader to serve at Eddleston. At the home of Sir James MacGill, clerk register, in November 1561 he joined John Knox, John Row, and Robert Hamilton in arguing against Lord James Stewart and others that subjects had the right to prevent Queen Mary from having mass in her chapel. Commissioned by the general assembly, Hay preached 'with great fruit' throughout Carrick for a month in 1562 (Knox's History, 2.55); his efforts, along with those of John Willock and, in Kyle, of Knox, won numerous converts and resulted in the signing of a covenant at Ayr on 4 September 1562.

Hay also engaged in a disputation with Quintin Kennedy, abbot of Crossraguel, at Maybole, Ayrshire. The abbot was familiar with patristic and scholastic writings, causing Hay concern that he would mislead the uneducated, but he accused Kennedy of self-deception because of his ignorance of Greek. An account of the debate was published as The Confutation of the Abbote of Crosraguels Masse (1563), with an epistle to Lord James, now earl of Moray. The records of the general assembly refer to Hay in December 1563 as minister to the privy council, a status he probably attained through his association with Moray. In June 1564 Moray, the earls of Argyll and Morton, and their associates sent him to arrange a conference between them and superintendents and learned ministers at the general assembly. Morton and William Maitland of Lethington urged Hay to condemn Knox's views on the right of subjects to disobey magistrates who ordered them to contravene divine precepts, but he refused. In 1565 the general assembly commissioned him to visit churches, schools, and colleges in Aberdeen and Banff. His second publication, a lecture delivered at King's College, Aberdeen, on 2 July 1569, as part of a campaign to end its continued attachment to Catholicism, appeared in 1571 under the title M. G. Hayi oratio habita in gymnasio Aberdonensi.

In 1567 Hay was granted a third of the stipends of his livings at Rathven and Eddleston on condition that he supply the church he did not serve, and he also held the parishes of Bellie and Dundurcas in Moray from this time until his death. Although he was reprimanded in 1568 for not preaching or administering the sacraments at Eddleston, he continued to play a prominent role in church affairs, serving as moderator of the general assembly at Edinburgh in March 1571 and commissioner to consult with the regent and parliament the same year concerning the selection of qualified men for the superintendency. A committee of the general assembly was assigned to revise his response to the Jesuit James Tyrie's *The Refutation of ane Answer Made be Schir Johne Knox* (1573), but this was apparently not published. In March 1574 the general assembly named him one of the examiners of the chapter of Moray after it approved George Douglas as bishop without examining his qualifications, and the same assembly dispatched him as part of the delegation to confer with the regent and privy council regarding the church's jurisdiction.

Although Hay was charged with allowing the observance of patron and festival days and maintaining inadequate discipline in his province, in August 1575 the general assembly named him commissioner of Caithness. In the same assembly he was assigned, with John Row and David Lindsay, to argue against Andrew Melville and others that bishops as constituted in the Church of Scotland accorded with scripture, and he subsequently helped draft a statement for the regent explaining the church's position on episcopacy. With Melville and Alexander Arbuthnot he was to have represented the Scottish church at the Magdeburg conference on the Augsburg confession in 1577, but the government decided not to send them for financial reasons. At the behest of the general assembly Hay helped draft the second Book of Discipline (1578) and then took part in a conference with the earl of Morton and others to discuss it. On 25 July 1578 he was appointed a visitor of the University of Aberdeen. Although he was responsible for establishing presbyteries in Caithness, Ross, Sutherland, and Moray, the only progress he could report to the general assembly in April 1583 was a plan to constitute them in Moray. This 'man of learning and of modesty', as Knox once called him (*Knox's History*, 2.115–16), died at Rathven in 1588. With his wife, Marion Henderson, or Henryson (*d.* 1577), he had four children, George of Rannes, James of Rannes (*d. c.*1630), William, an Edinburgh tailor, and Janet.   RICHARD L. GREAVES

Sources Fasti Scot., new edn, 1.270–71; 6.294, 298, 339, 468; 7.438; 8.59, 478, 652 · J. Spottiswoode, *The history of the Church of Scotland* (1655) · D. Calderwood, *The true history of the Church of Scotland, from the beginning of the Reformation, unto the end of the reigne of King James VI* (1678) · J. Row, *The history of the Kirk of Scotland, from the year 1558 to August 1637*, ed. D. Laing, Wodrow Society, 4 (1842) · *John Knox's History of the Reformation in Scotland*, ed. W. C. Dickinson, 2 vols. (1949) · *The autobiography and diary of Mr James Melvill*, ed. R. Pitcairn, Wodrow Society (1842) · T. Thomson, ed., *Acts and proceedings of the general assemblies of the Kirk of Scotland*, 3 pts, Bannatyne Club, 81 (1839–45) · J. Kirk, *Patterns of reform: continuity and change in the Reformation kirk* (1989) · J. Kirk, *The Second Book of Discipline* (1980) · M. F. Graham, *The uses of reform: 'Godly discipline' and popular behavior in Scotland and beyond, 1560–1610* (1996) · *DNB* · G. R. Hewitt, *Scotland under Morton, 1572–80* (1982) · J. Durkan, 'Education: the laying of fresh foundations', *Humanism in Renaissance Scotland*, ed. J. MacQueen (1990), 123–60

Hay, George, **first earl of Kinnoull** (*bap.* 1570, *d.* 1634), politician and entrepreneur, was baptized on 4 December 1570, probably at Megginch, Perthshire, the second son of

George Hay, first earl of Kinnoull (*bap.* 1570, *d.* 1634), by Daniel Mytens, 1633

Peter Hay (*d.* 1596), laird of Megginch and bailie to his distant kin the earls of Erroll, and his wife, Margaret (*fl.* 1554–1572), daughter of Patrick Ogilvy of Inchmartin. From 1588 he received a Jesuit education at the Scots College, Pont-à-Mousson, Lorraine, where his uncle Edmund Hay (*c.*1534–1591) was rector, and took minor orders. Sir John Scot of Scotstarvet, who later worked resentfully under him, said that he 'had little or no learning' (Scot of Scotstarvet, 48), but this may be doubted.

Some time in the 1590s Hay went back to Scotland, where, outwardly at least, he conformed to protestantism. His return may have been prompted by the death of his father in 1596. He acquired the estate of Nether Liff from which he took his title for some years. After 1592 he married Margaret Haliburton (*d.* 1633), widow of Patrick Ogilvy the younger of Inchmartin. On 1 February 1599 he became commendator of the Charterhouse of Perth. Having some business with the neighbouring earl of Gowrie, he was present at Gowrie House when King James was allegedly attacked there on 5 August 1600.

Hay seems not to have frequented the Scottish court, but shortly after the accession of James I to the English throne he was introduced at court by his first cousin, the royal favourite James Hay, later earl of Carlisle. He became a gentleman pensioner, and then (by 1607) a gentleman of the privy chamber. He was knighted some time between May 1606 and July 1607.

Hay used his court connections to establish a business career in Scotland. In July 1605 he became a commissioner of justiciary to assist the syndicate attempting to colonize the Isle of Lewis. The syndicate's two expeditions to the island (1598–1601, 1605–6) were defeated by native resistance. On 18 October 1607 Hay became one of three members of a new syndicate, but their one expedition, in 1609, was also defeated, and the following year they sold out to a neighbouring chief, Kenneth Mackenzie of Kintail.

Hay then moved into the iron and glass businesses, possibly with English financial backing. In 1610 he leased the woods of Letterewe on Loch Maree, Wester Ross, from Mackenzie, in exchange for Hay's Lewis rights. By 1612 Hay and his associates and licensees had established a blast furnace there for iron manufacture, the first in Scotland. He established a glassworks at the same time, probably in the same place—again Scotland's first. He imported skilled English ironworkers and continental (probably Venetian or Dutch) glass-workers. Both industries were successful and Hay soon obtained a monopoly of glass manufacture in Scotland. The Scottish glass market was small but in 1620 he got the English market opened to him—a blow to the English monopolist Sir Robert Mansell. Hay had already trespassed on Mansell's territory in 1616, obtaining an English patent for making smalt (cobalt blue glass). In 1621 he consolidated his Scottish monopoly, with a ban on glass imports. Meanwhile, in May 1615 he and his servant Thomas Murray had received a nineteen-year monopoly of whaling. They sent out two ships in 1616, but it is not known whether the enterprise continued.

In 1616 Hay moved suddenly into Scottish politics. From this time he was frequently at court, and probably through the intercession of his patron, the marquess of Hamilton, obtained two posts that year. On 11 March he became clerk register, though he had never even been a privy councillor and took his seat on the council only on 26 March, and on 4 December he also acquired a more minor position as commissioner for the king's rents. Suspicion over his religion, raised in 1620 when an arrested Catholic messenger was alleged to have been carrying a letter to him, proved no bar to preferment. Further cultivation of Hamilton, the marquess of Buckingham, and their associate the Catholic earl of Nithsdale resulted in his obtaining on 3 July 1622 the chancellorship of Scotland; he retained it until his death.

As chancellor, Hay lacked the standing of his predecessor, and generally co-operated with his senior colleagues, the earls of Mar and Melrose, respectively treasurer and secretary. During the famine of 1623 he went to Perth to encourage his local JPs to take vigorous action on poor relief. In July 1624 he issued a ruling defining conventicles narrowly, impeding the prosecution of religious dissidents. On 22 August 1624 he received a feu of the lands of the forfeited earldom of Orkney, for an annual duty to the crown of 40,000 merks (about £2222 sterling). The previous tacksman (lessee) of Orkney, Sir John Buchanan, initially remained as manager of the rents, paying his tack duty of 45,000 merks to Hay. Hay took over Buchanan's tacks in March 1625.

Following the accession of Charles I, Hay had a difficult relationship with the king, who did not trust his father's councillors. He surrendered his Orkney rights in May 1625 for substantial compensation in cash. At a conference with the king in January 1626, he, Mar, and Melrose led the councillors' opposition to Charles's revocation, disputing hotly with the king and his supporters. Hay also protested against the use of informers by the new commission for grievances, and the king objected that he and Mar had opposed the royal desires at the recent convention of estates. Hay's standing with the king probably never recovered from this. In June he led those who 'crushte in peices' the king's proposals (promoted by Sir James Skene, lord president) to restructure the court of session (Balfour, 2.138). Nevertheless, he remained in post and continued his alliance with Melrose and Mar.

When Hay visited the court early in 1627, the Venetian ambassador reported that he had, 'in the course of a few weeks, allowed himself to be gained by the favourite [Buckingham], notwithstanding his having been hitherto considered a person of integrity and good character' (*CSP Venice*, 20.119–20). The reported price was a third of the 'contribution' of 600,000 merks (about £33,333 sterling) allegedly offered by the Scots in connection with the revocation. But since no such 'contribution' had been offered and since Hay was not a stranger to Buckingham before 1627, the basis for the story remains unclear. On 4 May 1627 he was created Viscount Dupplin; his patent, unusually, was sealed with the privy seal, since as chancellor he was keeper of the great seal.

On 25 May 1633, during Charles's visit to Scotland, Dupplin was further honoured, being created earl of Kinnoull. However, the next day he refused Charles's request to yield precedence to the archbishop of St Andrews in the coronation procession, protesting that 'never a ston'd [stoled?] preist in Scotland should sett a foote befor him so long as his blood wes hotte', whereupon the king referred to him as an 'olde canckered goottishe man' (Balfour, 2.141–2). However, in presiding over the subsequent parliament he was prompt in deflecting opposition calls for a second vote that might have led to defeat for some of the governmental programme.

Kinnoull was active in tax administration, and was said to have devised the innovative tax on annual rents of 1621, though the main author seems to have been Melrose. He took over as collector of the tax of 1625–30 in November 1627, and was from the outset the collector of the next tax (1630–34). As late as May–August 1634 he served on a major financial reform commission. Late in life he suffered from gout and gravel. He died of apoplexy in London on 16 December 1634, and was interred at Kinnoull on 19 August 1635.

JULIAN GOODARE

Sources M. Lee, *Government by pen: Scotland under James VI and I* (Urbana, Ill., 1980) · M. Lee, *The road to revolution: Scotland under*

Charles I, 1625–1637 (Urbana, Ill., 1985) • J. Turnbull, *The Scottish glass industry, 1610–1750*, Society of Antiquaries of Scotland (2001) • J. M. Thomson and others, eds., *Registrum magni sigilli regum Scotorum / The register of the great seal of Scotland*, 11 vols. (1882–1914); facs. repr. (1984) • *Reg. PCS*, 1st ser. • *Reg. PCS*, 2nd ser. • *CSP dom.*, 1603–34 • *CSP Venice*, 1626–8 • J. Scot, *The staggering state of Scottish statesmen from 1550 to 1650*, ed. C. Rogers (1872) • D. Calderwood, *The history of the Kirk of Scotland*, ed. T. Thomson and D. Laing, 8 vols., Wodrow Society, 7 (1842–9) • P. J. Anderson, ed., *Records of the Scots colleges at Douai, Rome, Madrid, Valladolid and Ratisbon*, New Spalding Club, 30 (1906) • *The historical works of Sir James Balfour*, ed. J. Haig, 4 vols. (1824–5) • *Scots peerage* • E. B. Fryde and others, eds., *Handbook of British chronology*, 3rd edn, Royal Historical Society Guides and Handbooks, 2 (1986)

Archives NA Scot., letters to the Campbells of Glenorchy

Likenesses D. Mytens, oils, 1633, Scot. NPG [*see illus.*] • D. Mytens, oils, 1633, Duff House, Banff; on loan from present earl of Kinnoull • marble funeral effigy, 1635, St Constantine's Church, Kinnoull

Hay, George, eighth earl of Kinnoull (1689–1758), politician and diplomatist, was born in Canongate, Edinburgh, on 23 June 1689, the eldest son of Thomas Hay, seventh earl of Kinnoull (*c*.1660–1719), landowner and politician, and Elizabeth Drummond (*d*. 1696), daughter of William, first viscount of Strathallan, and Elizabeth, *née* Johnston. On his father becoming earl in 1709, George took the title Viscount Dupplin. In September of the same year he married Abigail Harley (*d*. 1750), second daughter of the tory politician Robert Harley (later first earl of Oxford), and his first wife, Edith, *née* Foley; the couple, who endured a bitter relationship brought about by Dupplin's domineering presence, had four sons and six daughters.

A year later Dupplin himself entered politics as MP for Fowey in Cornwall. He briefly supported Harley's tory ministry in the lower house until, on 31 December 1711, he was made Baron Hay of Penwardine, Herefordshire, in the British peerage, one of twelve newly created peers born of Harley's need to defend the tory stance on the treaty of Utrecht. During the Jacobite rising of 1715 Dupplin, like his father, was detained in London on suspicion of support for the Stuart cause, being held until June 1717. His brother John *Hay of Cromlix (1691–1740) was a career Jacobite, but Dupplin was not. On his father's death in January 1719 he succeeded as the eighth earl of Kinnoull.

Kinnoull's Stuart sympathies again came under investigation when he was suspected of involvement in Christopher Layer's conspiracy to enlist noblemen for a Jacobite rising in 1722. After consideration no proceedings were taken by the House of Lords. Later that decade he inherited estates in Perthshire and Argyll formerly in the possession of his father and his cousin Viscount Strathallan.

Between 1729 and 1737 Kinnoull served as the British ambassador to Constantinople. To the job of diplomat the earl brought his own blend of tactlessness and a lingering whiff of Jacobitism. Writing in July 1735 Lord Harrington commented on the king's wish for Kinnoull's immediate recall, 'his conduct being certainly too suspicious to be borne any longer' (to Horace Walpole, *Eglinton MSS*, 257). Several months later Jonathan Swift, in a letter to Kinnoull's brother-in-law, Lord Oxford, wrote both of his dwindling respect for the earl—a man 'I exceedingly loved in the Queen's time. But ... my opinion of him for several years past hath been wholly changed'—and of his ongoing sympathy for his wife who suffered at the hands of her irascible husband (*Portland MSS*, 6.61). Kinnoull's poor family relations had also featured regularly in correspondence between Lord Oxford and his former tutor, William Stratford. Writing in October 1724 Stratford had predicted a downturn in the earl's professional fortunes. 'Should this be true', he concluded, 'whatever was done for his wife and children, I think he ought to be left to die in a ditch' (ibid., 7.386–7).

Two years after his return from Constantinople, Kinnoull was involved in a dispute with the general assembly of the Church of Scotland over his right to nominate his placeman, George Blaikie, to the parish of Madderty, Perthshire. The presbytery rejected Blaikie as unacceptable; the earl in turn refused to waive his right to presentation and attacked what he saw as this challenge to his standing as a patron. The dispute ended with Blaikie's departure for the American colonies.

Kinnoull died on 28 July 1758 at Ashford in Yorkshire where he was buried four days later. His long-suffering wife had predeceased him in July 1750. The eldest of his long-suffering children, Thomas *Hay, Lord Dupplin, now assumed the earldom and achieved celebrity as a politician and promoter of the moderate party within the Church of Scotland; his second son, Robert Hay *Drummond (1711–1776), later became archbishop of York.

PHILIP CARTER

Sources DNB • GEC, *Peerage* • *The manuscripts of his grace the duke of Portland*, 10 vols., HMC, 29 (1891–1931) • *Reports on the manuscripts of the earl of Eglinton*, HMC, 10 (1885) • *Scots peerage* • IGI

Archives BL, letters to Thomas Robinson, Add. MSS 23781–23797 • NA Scot., letters to Robert Craigie • priv. coll., letters to first Earl Waldegrave

Hay, Sir George (1715–1778), judge and politician, was born on 14 or 25 January 1715, probably in London, the son of John Hay, rector of St Stephen, Coleman Street, London, and his wife, Sarah. He was later described as Scottish, and may have been a kinsman of the earl of Kinnoull. He entered Merchant Taylors' School, London, in 1725 and was elected Sir Thomas White scholar and Merchant Taylors' fellow at St John's College, Oxford, in 1731, where he matriculated on 30 June. He graduated BCL on 29 April 1737 and DCL on 23 February 1742. On 23 October 1742 he was admitted a member of Doctors' Commons, and began to practise in the fields of ecclesiastical and Admiralty law. From early in his career he established a circle of friends that included the painter William Hogarth and the actor David Garrick, and became better known for his social life than his interest in the law. It was for him that Hogarth painted *The Savoyard Girl*, a satire on an unsuccessful sexual pursuit by William, duke of Cumberland, in 1749. In 1751 he was appointed chancellor of the diocese of Worcester, which may have been the news that Garrick found 'surprising' (*Letters*, 1.172).

Hay entered parliament in 1754 as member for Stockbridge, Hampshire, nominated by Sir Robert Henley. In

Sir George Hay (1715–1778), by Sir Joshua Reynolds, 1760–61

1755 he was appointed king's advocate-general and, after appealing to the duke of Newcastle, gained the more lucrative post of vicar-general to the archbishop of Canterbury as well. As king's advocate-general he gave two rulings on Admiralty law that shaped naval practice during and after the Seven Years' War: first, in July 1755, that it was possible to prosecute in a single action the entire crew of a merchant vessel who resisted impressment; and second, in July 1756, that only the officers and men on board ships actually present at the capture of an enemy vessel could share the prize.

Politically Hay detached himself from the war policies of the Newcastle administration in November and December 1755, when he spoke and voted against the subsidy treaties with Hesse and Russia, aligning himself with William Pitt; the two had a mutual friend in Henry Bilson Legge. The government was alarmed at losing a strong orator and did not dismiss Hay from the post of king's advocate-general until May 1756. Horace Walpole had thought Hay's speech on the treaties 'easy, but not striking' (Walpole, *Corr.*, 37.415) but later listed him as one of the twenty-eight best speakers in the Commons during the 1755–6 session. Hay was reinstated by the Devonshire administration, in which Pitt had a leading role, and was also appointed a lord of the Admiralty. He was required to offer himself again for election at Stockbridge but Henry Fox, who had acquired the patronage from Henley, refused to return him, and Hay remained outside the Commons. As a lord of the Admiralty he signed Admiral John Byng's death warrant on 16 February 1757; George II held Hay and his colleagues responsible for the public hostility directed at the king following Byng's execution and

refused the suggestion that Hay succeed Byng at Rochester. He lost his place at the Admiralty board in April, on the collapse of the Devonshire administration, but returned in July, when Pitt joined Newcastle's ministry, and was found a seat in the Commons at Calne, in Wiltshire. Hay's complicated search for a seat may have inspired Hogarth to dedicate to him the fourth print in his series *The Election*, published on 1 January 1758. Hogarth painted a portrait of Hay in 1757, now lost, of which John Hoadly wrote:

> if I were like, I would not have my picture drawn: I should not like to meet that figure alive in the fields going to Chelsey, for fear of dying that night in a ditch—With twenty gaping gashes in my crown. (Paulson, 295)

Hay became a prominent government speaker, particularly on naval and legal matters; during a debate on the Habeas Corpus Act in 1758 Alexander Carlyle thought that he spoke 'with a clearness, a force, and a brevity, which pleased us much' (*Autobiography*, ed. Burton, 352). He migrated to the Admiralty borough of Sandwich for the 1761–8 parliament. He was considered for the position of speaker of the House of Commons but Lord Hardwicke wrote to Newcastle that 'The chief objections are that he is too low, and a Scotchman, and … I doubt whether he would quit his profession for it' (Namier). In the new parliament he grew away from Pitt, whom he apparently disliked and had only supported out of regard to Legge, whose health was in decline. He retained his position as a lord of the Admiralty under the Bute ministry and in the Grenville administration. On 17 February 1764, during the debate on the validity of general warrants inspired by the arrest of John Wilkes in the previous year, Hay moved the government amendment to the opposition motion with the intention of making the motion too complex for debate, a tactic condemned by his former patron Pitt. He also had to excuse his hostility to his old friend Wilkes, arguing that Wilkes had been led astray by bad company. Despite his changes of political allegiance he applied through Newcastle for the positions of judge of the prerogative court of Canterbury, chancellor of the diocese of London, and dean of the arches when the last fell vacant in May 1764; Newcastle agreed to nominate him only after sustained persuasion from Hay's friend Charles Yorke. On appointment he ceased to be king's advocate-general and chancellor of the diocese of Worcester. He continued to speak for the Grenville government in the Commons. He contributed to another debate on general warrants on 29 January 1765, when his statement 'the law of government is superior to the law of the land' (Walpole, *Memoirs of the Reign of King George III*, 2.86)—also quoted by Nathaniel Ryder as 'there is a law superior even to the law of the land, the law of government by public safety' (Namier)— led to accusations that his background as a civil lawyer had led him to introduce notions of arbitrary power alien to English common law. The charges were repeated by Pitt during the debate on the repeal of the Stamp Act on 4 March 1766, although by this time Hay had left office.

Hay left the Admiralty in July 1765, at the fall of Grenville's ministry; Charles Yorke used the Rockingham ministry's refusal to reappoint Grenville as a reason not to accept its offer of a post. He voted against the repeal of the Stamp Act and mocked the government's American policy. His relations with the administration of Chatham (formerly Pitt) were cautious. The lord chancellor was Charles Pratt, Baron Camden, who was a personal friend—Garrick received an invitation from Camden, through Hay, to meet Camden at Doctors' Commons in June 1766—but Hay did not want to break faith with Charles Yorke and chose instead to 'take his chance' (Namier) and refuse nomination by a borough patron. At the 1768 election he hoped to be elected for Oxford University, but came bottom of the poll and was found a seat by Granville Leveson-Gower, second Earl Gower, at Newcastle under Lyme. He voted with the Grafton and North ministries but was less active in parliament and may have concentrated on his legal career, as in 1773 he was appointed a judge of the high court of Admiralty, retaining his positions as dean of the arches, judge of the prerogative court of Canterbury, and chancellor of the diocese of London. He was knighted on 11 November 1773.

Hay presided at the high court of Admiralty for over four and a half years. There he made a series of rulings that defined the limits of the court's jurisdiction and clarified points of Admiralty law. Among these were the case of *Meake* v. *Lord Holland* (1774), where he refused to decide a dispute between the part-owners of a ship before a suit concerning the ownership of some of the shares had been settled by the court of chancery. In *Fairless* v. *Thorsen* (1774) 'he held that the court had jurisdiction to try the question of whether one ship had damaged another in Greenwich reach' (Holdsworth, *Eng. law*, 12.673). He continued as member for Newcastle under Lyme in the 1774 parliament but made few appearances in the Commons. In December 1775 he spoke in favour of the bill prohibiting trade with the American colonies, and looked to the Admiralty courts in America to compel the Americans to return to their allegiance. When he had to apply what resulted—the Prohibitory Act of 1776, also known as the Intolerable Act—he sought a 'humane interpretation' (ibid., 12.674), attempting to distinguish between those carrying on trade who were loyalists and would probably move to Britain should the colonies become independent, and those who could or would not return. He tried to respect the rights of neutral powers but considered that 'I cannot judge politically, nor have I any discretionary power but on legal grounds' (ibid., 12.673), and where international law was concerned stated that it was for the privy council to interpret treaties and the crown to make rules for the Admiralty courts. He was present, as a judge of the prerogative court of Canterbury, during the trial of Elizabeth Chudleigh, duchess of Kingston and countess of Bristol, for bigamy, in April 1776; Edward Thurlow, attorney-general, said during the trial that 'The most loose and unconsidered notion escaping in any manner from that able and excellent judge, should be received with respect, and certainly will' (ibid.).

Hay remained close to David and Eva Garrick—'Kiss the blooming Wrinkles of my antient Love for my sake, and believe me Always Your's & Her's' (*Letters*, 3.1105), he wrote

to them in June 1776, while also chiding Garrick for his formality. He was still active in March 1778, when he was offered but 'positively refused' (*Last Journals of Horace Walpole*, 2.129) a place on the commission to negotiate with the American colonies, and also in that month planned to entertain Garrick, Thurlow, and Richard Rigby to dinner at his house. However, in May his mind became disturbed, and in August he was relieved of the duties of his offices. He died at Battersea on 6 October 1778. According to Horace Walpole:

> the day after his keepers left him, [he] walked deliberately into the Thames at noon in the sight of fifty persons, and when he had waded up to his chin, deliberately plunged his head down and was suffocated, before he was taken out. (Walpole, *Corr.*, 33.59)

Hay was unmarried. He left behind him a substantial library of books and manuscripts covering politics, history, classics, and literature in French and Italian, as well as legal authorities. The collection was sold in 1233 lots, many containing several volumes, by Hutchins in Covent Garden between 19 and 27 April 1779.

Charles Coote wrote that Hay was 'an eloquent, ingenious, and impressive advocate' but that 'if his application had been equal to his talents, he might have excelled all his contemporaries in professional learning' (Coote, 119). William Prideaux Courtney thought that Hay was 'lax in application to the duties of his profession' (*DNB*), but Sir William Holdsworth thought him 'a sounder lawyer' with 'a far more judicial temperament than his successor, Sir James Marriott' (Holdsworth, *Eng. law*, 12.674). He was certainly not single-minded in his devotion to the law, but by no means neglected it. Bishop John Butler, who knew Hay through Henry Bilson Legge, wrote in May 1778 that Hay had deliberately concealed his abilities and the reasons for his inconstant behaviour in politics:

> The true account of it was that he had no opinion of any cause, but considered them all as the pretences under which men carry on their selfish schemes; yet he was a friend to liberty, and did not think it in danger in any hands. (Namier)

Hay owned Hogarth's *The Bench*, which suggests that he did not have high expectations of his legal colleagues. He seems to have been happiest to be thought of as good company among a select circle of friends, and allowed his conviviality to overshadow his abilities as a debater in the House of Commons and as a responsible and influential judge.   MATTHEW KILBURN

Sources L. B. Namier, 'Hay, Sir George', HoP, *Commons, 1754–90* · Holdsworth, *Eng. law*, 12.673–4 · Walpole, *Corr.* · H. Walpole, *Memoirs of King George II*, ed. J. Brooke, 2 (1985) · H. Walpole, *Memoirs of the reign of King George III*, ed. D. Jarrett, 4 vols. (2000) · *The last journals of Horace Walpole*, ed. Dr Doran, rev. A. F. Steuart, 2 vols. (1910) · [C. Coote], *Sketches of the lives and characters of eminent English civilians, with an historical introduction relative to the College of Advocates* (1804) · R. Paulson, *Hogarth*, 3 (1993) · *The letters of David Garrick*, ed. D. M. Little and G. M. Kahrl, 3 vols. (1963) · W. Burrell, *Reports of cases determined by the high court of admiralty: and upon appeal therefrom, temp. Sir Thomas Salusbury and Sir George Hay, 1758–1774*, ed. R. G. Marsden (1885) · *The autobiography of Dr Alexander Carlyle of Inveresk, 1722–1805*, ed. J. H. Burton (1910); facs. edn with introduction by R. B. Sher (1990) · Mrs E. P. Hart, ed., *Merchant Taylors' School register, 1561–1934*, 2 vols. (1936) · *DNB* · *A catalogue of the genuine library of Sir*

George Hay, deceased (1779) · Foster, *Alum. Oxon.* · *London Chronicle*, 44 (1778), 340 · *IGI*

Likenesses Hogarth, portrait, 1757 · J. Reynolds, oils, 1760–61, Harvard U., law school [*see illus.*]

Hay, George (1729–1811), vicar apostolic of the lowland district, was born in Edinburgh on 24 August 1729, the second child and only son of James Hay (*d.* 1756×1759), writer to the signet, and his wife, Mary Morrison (*d.* 1756). His parents were Scottish Episcopalian, and his father a Jacobite who had been imprisoned for his part in the rising of 1715. After schooling in Edinburgh, George Hay was apprenticed to a surgeon named George Lauder, which led to his tending the wounded of the battle of Prestonpans (1745) and medically serving Prince Charles's army for four months. For this he was imprisoned in Edinburgh Castle and in London. After the Act of Indemnity of June 1747 he returned to Edinburgh where he was received into the Roman Catholic church by the Jesuit John Seton on 21 December 1748. On his return to Edinburgh he resumed his medical studies for two years under John Rutherford, but being unable to graduate on account of his new religious affiliation he kept a chemist's shop for a year. He next became a ship's surgeon, and when his ship stopped at London, John Gordon of Glencat introduced him to Bishop Richard Challoner of the London district who persuaded him to seek ordination to the priesthood. Consequently on 10 September 1751 Hay was received into the Scots College, Rome, where he began his lifelong friendship with John Geddes, a fellow student who later became his coadjutor bishop. Hay was ordained priest in Rome on 2 April 1758 and returned to Scotland in August of the following year in the company of two other priests, Geddes and William Guthrie. As they travelled without passports it was feared that they might be arrested at Leith and subjected to penal laws against priests. A contrary wind, however, forced their vessel to anchor at Buckhaven, where they jumped ship, and were treated civilly by the inhabitants who mistook them for smugglers.

Hay's first appointment as a priest was to Preshome, where he lived with Bishop James Grant, serving in that mission until appointed procurator in Edinburgh in August 1767. On 5 October 1768 he was nominated titular bishop of Daulis (hence an alias, Dauley) and coadjutor to Bishop Grant, and he was consecrated at Scalan on 21 May 1769. As coadjutor Bishop Hay was based in Edinburgh, caring for the mission there, although his position necessitated sojourns in various parts of Scotland and even a journey to Paris. Hay was deeply involved in all the wider developments of the Scottish mission, which included the appointment of a secular priest as rector of Douai after the expulsion of the Jesuits from France, the reclaiming of the Spanish seminary and its reopening at Valladolid with John Geddes as rector, and the procuration of two places for Scottish students in the Propaganda College at Rome. Hay had printed 10,000 copies of a catechism, assisted Catholic emigrants to America who were escaping from religious harassment in the highlands, and managed to obtain a private agreement with the army whereby Catholics were exempted from that part of the oath that

George Hay (1729–1811), by G. A. Periam (after George Watson)

demanded allegiance to the established religion. After the suppression of the Jesuits, Hay co-ordinated their incorporation into the secular clergy. Hay drew the plans for the building of a new chapel in Leith Wynd, Edinburgh, commenced in 1777, and had to expend much labour not only in raising funds, but also in managing property disputes with a neighbouring landlord. Yet he found time to write his two-volume book *The Scripture Doctrine of Miracles Displayed* (1775), arguably his best work on account of its thoroughness. The appendix on transubstantiation was attacked in print by the Scottish Episcopal clergyman William Abernethy, later the celebrated Bishop Abernethy Drummond, and in 1776 Hay published a reply entitled *Explanatory Remarks on the Dialogue between Philathes and Benevolus*.

When Bishop Grant died on 3 December 1778 Hay succeeded him as vicar apostolic of the lowland district. At this time there were still hopes of a Scottish Catholic relief bill being passed by parliament although considerable opposition to it had been voiced in Scotland in the previous few months. One attack came from the pen of William Abernethy Drummond, whose pamphlet *The Lawfulness of Breaking Faith with Heretius* (1778) was addressed to Hay and called forth his reply, *An Answer to Mr W. A. D.'s Letter to G. H.*. Protest reached a climax on 2 February 1779 when the new chapel and priests' dwelling house were completely destroyed by the Edinburgh mob. Hay, arriving back in Edinburgh in the midst of the riot, was forced to seek refuge in the castle. The Relief Bill had to be set aside, but thanks largely to Hay's efforts Catholics were awarded full compensation for the damage to their property, half being paid by the government, and half by the city of Edinburgh. At this juncture, Hay thought it expedient not to remain in Edinburgh, and took up residence in Aberdeen, where he remained until 1788. His close friend John Geddes, then rector of the Scots College, Valladolid, was appointed coadjutor, ordained bishop at Madrid on 30 November 1780, and returned to Scotland in the following spring. The year 1781 saw the publication of Hay's second major work, *The Sincere Christian*, an apologetic exposition of the Catholic faith, which went through several editions and was translated into foreign languages. *The Devout Christian*, a comprehensive survey of the law of God, followed in 1783. Though generally reckoned to be excessively dry, a characteristic of all Hay's works, it nevertheless proved to be a valuable reference work for clergy and catechists. A sequel entitled *The Pious Christian* (1786) was an ascetical work with instruction in exercises of piety, to which were added prayers and an examination of conscience. Like his previous works this had several editions and widespread influence.

One of Hay's major concerns was the education of future priests. The colleges abroad, which had been the chief source of supply, gave the bishop great anxiety. In 1781, under the alias of Signor Tommase Scotti, he journeyed to Rome with the main purpose of obtaining a Scottish rector for the Scots College, Rome, and, though he stayed for six months, he failed to achieve his purpose. On the road home he tried in vain while in Paris to retrieve for the Scots College, Douai, funds which had been suspended on the expulsion of the Jesuits from France. A long acrimonious dispute with Principal Gordon of the Scots College, Paris, hindered the achievement of that college, Hay even refusing to send more students after 1783. The colleges at both Douai and Paris collapsed at the time of the French Revolution, and a plan of Hay to turn the monastery at Regensburg into a Scottish seminary came to nothing. On the continent only the Scots College at Valladolid gave the bishop satisfaction. This necessitated the development of the tiny college in Scotland, situated at Scalan in Glenlivet. Hay took up residence there, acting as rector from 1788 until 1793. In 1799 he moved the Scottish seminary to Aquhorties in Aberdeenshire, and once again lived in the seminary, where he taught logic, metaphysics, natural theology, and the rudiments of grammar. The long awaited Catholic Relief Act was passed by parliament in 1793, and was favourably received by almost everyone in the land. This massive change in public opinion had been greatly furthered by the good graces and friendly social intercourse of Bishop Geddes. Hay, however, must be given credit for the appointment of Geddes as coadjutor, and for placing Geddes rather than himself in the capital city. Hay had also insisted on all his Catholic subjects maintaining goodwill towards the government, and it was Hay who, realizing the opportune moment in 1793, ordered Geddes to get his friends to apply for the act. When it became law Hay and Geddes went together to the office of the sheriff-substitute of Midlothian to subscribe the oath, adjuration, and declaration under the act of 33 George III for the relief of Catholics in Scotland.

Almost immediately after this epoch making event, on account of the failed health of his coadjutor, Hay decided to change stations with Geddes. Hay would live in Edinburgh for six years. Geddes lived until 11 February 1799, but was too ill for episcopal duties, and so, on 19 September 1797, Rome nominated a new coadjutor, Alexander Cameron, rector at Valladolid, who was consecrated at Madrid on 28 October 1798, but was unable to return to Scotland until August 1802. Consequently Hay had to undertake the pastoral oversight of the lowland district single-handedly for nine years. In 1796–7 Bishop Hay had new editions of the Bible printed for Catholics, personally subscribing £80. In 1799, after three years' negotiation, he obtained relief from the British government for his straitened Catholic clergy, a benefit which they enjoyed until May 1805.

It was in the period of Hay's residence at Aquhorties that he bought the site for a new church in Edinburgh and most prudently finalized investment arrangements with the Bank of Scotland for the benefit of the mission. His health declined, and his resignation, refused in December 1803, was accepted by Rome on 16 June 1805, and he handed over the reins of office to his coadjutor on 24 August 1805. During a visit to Edinburgh in the winter of 1807–8, he sat for a portrait by George Watson. It is preserved in Blairs College, Aberdeen, and shows the bishop in peaceful mood, with wrinkled brow, large aquiline nose, and pointed chin. He looks hunched or stooped, no doubt the effect of age. In the last two years of his life Hay's reason declined; he died at Aquhorties on 15 October 1811 and was buried in an old graveyard at Fetternear on 21 October.

Hay led the Roman Catholic church in Scotland during a crucial stage of its history, in its evolution from persecution and antipathy to freedom and respect. He won regard for his church by his patient endurance and untiring attention to duty, always urging his people to bear their trials with fortitude, and to be loyal to their country and government. Hay strenuously avoided giving offence to other denominations, perhaps sometimes overcautiously, as with his prohibition of music in Catholic chapels. He was, however, extremely strict with his priests, sometimes excessively, and when prejudiced, could be judgemental and even condemn without evidence. Fortunately, his coadjutor, Bishop Geddes, often succeeded as peacemaker. Hay has been fortunate that his chief biographer, James Augustine Stothert, was a strong admirer who usually defended Hay's side in disputes. Even he, however, had to admit that Hay was immoderately severe at times and generally opposed to schemes not initiated by himself. The Catholic archivist William Anderson was not always so sympathetic, believing, for example, that in the disputes with the Scots College, Paris, Hay was more to blame than the principal. A more human side of the bishop's character was seen when he played the fiddle, when he sang for schoolgirls in Miss Rankine's school in Aberdeen, and when he told the boys at Aquhorties and the children of Fetternear stories from the past, of his father's capture and escape in 1715, or his own adventures in Prince Charles's army. When boys were ill at

Aquhorties he nursed them with his own hands. His habit of chewing tobacco he himself described as disgusting, but claimed it was necessary for health reasons. Hay's achievement, however, was outstanding. His literary output, which included controversial pamphlets, letters to newspapers, pastoral letters, and many manuscript letters, as well as his four major works, met a long felt need in the Roman Catholic church, and had a widespread influence. During his tenure much church building was undertaken; new missions were founded in Glasgow and in Dundee; and the bishop made wise investments which were of benefit for many generations. The Roman Catholic church in Scotland was much better respected at the end of his long episcopate than it had been at the outset of his rule.

BRIAN M. HALLORAN

Sources J. A. Stothert, 'George Hay, 1729–1811', *Ecclesiastical chronicle for Scotland*, ed. J. F. S. Gordon, 4: *Journal and appendix to Scotichronicon and Monasticon* (1875), 15–53 · 'Biographical memoir of the Right Revd. George Hay', *Catholic Directory* (1842), 85–90 · A. Cameron, *A short account of Rt Rev George Hay DD, Valladolid* (1829) · W. M. Brady, *The episcopal succession in England, Scotland, and Ireland, AD 1400 to 1875*, 3 (1877), 461–2 · A. Dick, *Reasons for embracing the Catholic faith* (1855), 184–97 · G. St L. Mason, *Bishop Hay: a memoir* [n.d.] · W. Anderson, 'Unpublished remarks', Scottish Catholic Archives, CA 1/23/2, 1 · B. M. Halloran, *The Scots College, Paris, 1603–1792* (1997), 154, 166–73
Archives NL Scot., notebook · Scottish Catholic Archives, Edinburgh, corresp. and papers | Lancs. RO, letters to J. P. Coghlan
Likenesses portrait, 1781/2, Scots College, Rome · G. Watson, portrait, 1807–8, Blairs College, Aberdeen · G. A. Periam, line engraving (after G. Watson), NPG [*see illus.*]
Wealth at death fifty shares of the Bank of Scotland stock: Scottish Catholic Archives, Edinburgh, PL 5/70; W. Clapperton, 'Notes on Bishop Hay's bank shares'

Hay, George, eighth marquess of Tweeddale (1787–1876), army officer, was born at Bonnington on 1 February 1787, the son of George Hay, seventh marquess of Tweeddale (1753–1804), and his wife, Lady Hannah Charlotte (d. 1804), daughter of James Maitland, seventh earl of Lauderdale. He succeeded to the title and estates on the death of his father in August 1804, having entered the army as an ensign in the 1st foot guards the previous June. In 1806 he went to Sicily, on the staff, and soon after obtaining his company, in May 1807, he joined Wellington's army in the Peninsula. He was made aide-de-camp, and was wounded at the battle of Busaco on 27 September 1810. He subsequently became quartermaster-general, received his majority on 14 May 1812, and was again wounded, at Vitoria on 21 June 1813. He was at once promoted lieutenant-colonel, and went home invalided. As soon as his health was sufficiently restored he joined his regiment, then engaged in the Anglo-American War. He was once more wounded at the hard-fought battle of Niagara in 1813, when, on refusing to surrender, he was after a great struggle overpowered by the enemy. After his return in 1814 he saw no further active service, though he continued on the employed list, and rose through the higher ranks: colonel, 27 May 1825; major-general, 10 January 1837; lieutenant-general, 9 November 1846; general, 20 June 1854; and field marshal, 29 May 1875.

Tweeddale married, on 28 March 1816, Lady Susan Montagu (1797–1870), third daughter of William *Montagu, fifth duke of Manchester. They had seven sons and six daughters; the eldest son, George, earl of Gifford, died in 1862 and the second, Arthur *Hay, succeeded him. Tweeddale settled at Yester House, near Gifford, on his family estates in East Lothian, and in 1824 he was appointed lord lieutenant of the county, where he spent the next eighteen years in the improvement of his estates, acting as a conscientious landed proprietor and county magnate. In 1842 he was made governor of Madras, and also, by special arrangement of the duke of Wellington, commander-in-chief of the Madras army, then in need of reorganization. After a successful tenure of office Tweeddale retired in 1848, when he returned to Yester House and resumed his agricultural pursuits. He led the way in modern draining techniques, in deep ploughing, and in many bold and costly experiments for the benefit of his land. He also showed a keen interest in meteorology and mechanics, and invented machinery useful to farmers. His services were acknowledged by election as president (1869–73) of the Highland Agricultural Society.

Tweeddale was made a CB in 1815, a KT in 1820, KCB in 1862, and GCB in 1867. He was gold-stick in waiting, and was successively colonel of the 30th regiment (1846), 42nd (Royal Highland) regiment (1862), and 2nd Life Guards (1863). He was from 1818 until his death representative peer for Scotland, and was grand master of the freemasons, 1818–20. A man of conspicuous and healthy physique, he was known in the army as a horseman and sabreur. He was also an accomplished coachman, and is said to have once driven the mail coach from London to Haddington without a halt or relief. He died from the effects of an accident, on 10 October 1876, aged eighty-nine, at Yester House, and was buried in Yester on 16 October.

H. G. KEENE, *rev.* JAMES FALKNER

Sources *Army List* · *The Times* (11 Oct 1876) · J. Taylor, *Great families of Scotland* (1887) · Burke, *Peerage* · *Hart's Army List* · *Colburn's United Service Magazine*, 3 (1849), 141 · GEC, *Peerage*
Archives BL OIOC, corresp. and papers as governor of Madras · NL Scot., corresp. and papers; letters | BL, letters to J. C. Hobhouse, Add. MSS 36464–36467, 36478 · NA Scot., letters to Lord Dalhousie · PRO, corresp. with Lord Ellenborough, PRO 30/12 · W. Sussex RO, letters to duke of Richmond
Likenesses J. W. Gordon, oils, *c.*1843, United Service Club · F. Grant, oils, Scot. NPG · H. Raeburn, oils, Scot. NPG · engraving, repro. in *Household Brigade Journal* (1864)
Wealth at death £209,502 6s. 1d.: confirmation, 15 Dec 1876, *CCI*

Hay, George Campbell [Mac Iain Deòrsa] (1915–1984), poet, was born on 8 December 1915 at the manse, Elderslie, Renfrewshire, where his father was a minister. His father, John MacDougall *Hay (1879–1919), was born in Tarbert, Loch Fyne, and based his novel *Gillespie* there. George Campbell Hay regarded Tarbert and Kintyre as his home territory, frequently staying there, learning Gaelic in his teens, and sharing the life of the local fishermen. His mother, Catherine, *née* Campbell (b. 1883), had Islay connections, and had some knowledge of Gaelic. His father died in 1919 and the family lived in Edinburgh from 1925. In 1934 Hay won a major scholarship in classics and

George Campbell Hay (1915–1984), by Gordon Wright, 1975

took a degree at Corpus Christi College, Oxford, afterwards taking a teacher's training course at Edinburgh and teaching briefly at the Royal High School there.

On the outbreak of the Second World War in 1939 Hay refused conscription (apparently on Scottish nationalist grounds, like his contemporary Douglas Young), spent some time 'on the run' in the Argyll hills, and finally joined the Royal Army Ordnance Corps. During the war he served in north Africa, Italy, and Macedonia, where he learned modern Greek. He was suspected of acting as a communist agitator there, simply because of his friendship with Greek people, and suffered a violent attack. This led to his being invalided out of the army and to severe traumatization in later years, when he developed a drinking problem. He returned to Edinburgh, spending some time in hospitals, and working in the National Library of Scotland for some years.

A versatile linguist, Hay published poetry in Scots, English, and Gaelic, with occasional pieces in French and Norwegian, and he translated from modern Greek, Croatian, Arabic, Italian, Finnish, Icelandic, Irish, and Welsh. In his metrics he was deeply influenced by medieval and early modern Irish verse.

Hay's second book was *Wind on Loch Fyne* (1948), and it is here that he includes his wide-ranging translations, and also a good number of poems in Scots, whether on Loch Fyne and Kintyre subjects or on Edinburgh:

A windy toon o cloods an' sunny glints;
pinnacled, turreted, stey an' steep grey toon;
her soughin' gables sing their norlan' rants
tae sant an' caller blufferts on her croon.

Hay had published a Gaelic collection in the previous year: *Fuaran slèibh* ('Upland spring') (1947), and this has some evocative poems on Kintyre and the Argyll countryside, as well as a series of poems modelled on Irish courtly love poetry and deeply influenced by its metrics. There are humorous and philosophic poems here too, and the highly effective 'Tilleadh Uiliseis' ('The return of Ulysses'), a dramatic interpretation of the classical story.

Hay's next volume, *O na ceithir àirdean* ('From the Four Airts') appeared in 1952, and here his war experiences, especially in north Africa, and his reflections on the devastation war has caused throughout Europe, are powerfully deployed, producing some of his most memorable poems such as 'Truaighe na h-Eòrpa' ('Europe's wretchedness'), 'Atman', and 'Bisearta' ('Bizerta'). This collection also includes a large number of translations from Italian, Greek, Croatian, and Arabic verse.

Hay's reputation, especially as a Gaelic poet, became firmly established, but there was to be a long wait for another collection. He published spasmodically in periodicals, for example, in the *Akros* anthology of contemporary Gaelic verse (1976) and in *Gairm* over many years, latterly developing very effectively a series of poems/songs in the folk style, founded on surviving fragments. He also published Scots and English verse of a strongly nationalistic sort in the *Scots Independent*.

In the early 1980s it transpired that Hay had written a long poem or sequence in the latter part of the war and early post-war period (writing in Italy, Macedonia, and Tarbert), but had never completed it. He gave permission for this to be published in its unfinished state, and it appeared in 1982 under the title *Mochtàr is Dùghall* ('Mochtar and Dougall'). The original purpose may have been to compare and contrast these two civilizations that had attracted him so strongly: the Arabic and Gaelic ones. But it is only the Arabic section that was virtually completed, while only preliminary sections of the Gaelic one were composed. This Arabic section gives an extraordinarily vivid and colourful account of three generations of an Arab family in the African desert and elsewhere, and this can well be regarded as Hay's most powerful achievement. It is fortunate that it has survived the sad but buoyant chaos of this poet's life. Hay died alone in his house, 6 Maxwell Street, Edinburgh, a victim of alcoholism, on 25 March 1984. DERICK S. THOMSON

Sources C. J. Smith, *Historic South Edinburgh*, 4 (1988), 284–6 · A. Martin, 'George Campbell Hay; bard of Kintyre', *Kintyre, the hidden past* (1984), 48–71 · d. cert.
Archives NL Scot., corresp. and literary MSS | NL Scot., letters to Angus Martin
Likenesses G. Wright, photograph, 1975, Gordon Wright Photo Library [see illus.] · portrait, repro. in D. S. Thomson, *Companion to Gaelic Scotland* (1994)
Wealth at death £13,229.83: confirmation, 20 Sept 1984, NA Scot., SC 70/3/41; 70/1/3936–89

Hay, Sir Gilbert, of Erroll (d. 1333). *See under* Hay family (*per. c.*1295–*c.*1460).

Hay, Sir Gilbert (b. *c.*1397, d. after 1465), soldier and poet, has been identified with various Gilbert Hays who appear in the records of the period, and his family background remains elusive. Later to describe himself as master of arts and bachelor of canon law, he was probably a graduate of St Andrews University (a Gilbert Hay is recorded there in 1418 and 1419). Although he also called himself a priest, he seems to have abandoned a career in the church, embarking instead on military service in France. He was probably not the Gilbert Hay knighted at the siege of Liège (1408), and most likely arrived in France as part of the contingent led by John Stewart, earl of Buchan, in 1421. Active in fighting for the French against the English in the 1420s, he was present at the coronation of Charles VII in 1429; he was subsequently knighted by Charles and entered royal service as the French king's 'chaumerlayn'. An unknown scribe later stated that Hay had spent twenty-four years in France. This means that he returned to Scotland about 1445, a decision which may have been prompted by the death that year of Margaret of Scotland, who had married the dauphin in 1436. When she travelled to France for her wedding, she had been escorted by William Sinclair, earl of Orkney and Caithness, which probably explains how Hay later entered the earl's service.

By 1456 Hay was at Roslin, Edinburghshire, where he was remembered in the will of Sinclair's father-in-law, Alexander Sutherland of Dunbeath, Caithness, and also completed his Prose manuscript (NL Scot., Acc. 9253). Consisting of 'The buke of the law of armys', 'The buke of the ordre of knychthede', and 'The buke of the gouvernaunce of princis', this was a lively rendition—much more than a straightforward translation—of three popular treatises (known to him in French): Honoré Bonet's *L'arbre des batailles*, Ramon Lull's *L'ordre de chevalerie*, and the pseudo-Aristotelian *Secreta secretorum*. About 1460 he completed 'The buik of King Alexander the Conquerour', written for Thomas, Lord Erskine, and based on Latin and French versions of the popular Alexander romance; this survives in two manuscripts (BL, Add. MS 40732, and NA Scot., GD 112/71/9). Exactly when Hay died is, like so many details of his life, unclear, but it was probably some time after 1465, when a Gilbert Hay, possibly the poet, received a gift from the crown.

Although difficult to pin down, Hay's career is testimony to the close military, political, and cultural links which existed between Scotland and France, to the increased literary sophistication of the fifteenth-century Scottish nobility, and to the growing vitality of vernacular culture.   C. EDINGTON

Sources J. H. Stevenson, ed., *Gilbert of the Haye's prose manuscript* (AD 1456), 2 vols., STS, 44, 62 (1901–14) · J. Cartwright, 'Sir Gilbert Hay's "Buik of King Alexander the Conquerour": a critical edition of lines 1–4263', PhD diss., University of Toronto, 1974 · J. M. Anderson, ed., *Early records of the University of St Andrews*, Scottish History Society, 3rd ser., 8 (1926) · G. Burnett and others, eds., *The exchequer rolls of Scotland*, 23 vols. (1878–1908) · W. Forbes-Leith, *The Scots men-at-arms and life-guards in France*, 2 vols. (1882) · W. Bower, *Scotichronicon*, ed. D. E. R. Watt and others, new edn, 9 vols. (1987–98) · J. Robertson, ed., *Illustrations of the topography and antiquities of the shires of Aberdeen and Banff*, 2, 3, Spalding Club, 17, 29 (1847–57), vols. 2, 3 · 'The testament of Alexander Suthyrland of Dunbeath, at Roslin Castle, 15th November 1456', *The Bannatyne miscellany*, ed. D. Laing, 3, Bannatyne Club, 19b (1855) · *CEPR letters*, vol. 10

Archives BL, Add. MS 40732 · NA Scot., GD 112/71/9 · NL Scot., Acc. 9253

Hay, Sir Harley Hugh Dalrymple- (1861–1940), civil engineer, was born, probably at Rawalpindi, India, on 7 October 1861, the third son of Colonel George James Dalrymple-Hay, of the Bengal Staff Corps, and his wife, Amelia Emily, daughter of Colonel Henry Daniel Maitland, and grandson of Sir James Dalrymple-Hay, second baronet, of Park Place, Glenluce. Educated at a private school in Edinburgh, and by army tutors, he began his engineering career as a pupil of Edward Newcombe, civil engineer, on the south Wales line of the Midland Railway, and in 1882 joined the engineering staff of the London and South Western Railway (LSWR), working on a succession of railway projects in Hampshire. During this time he married, in 1891, Agnes Yelland Waters, daughter of Frederick Waters, a grocer. They had one child, a daughter.

In 1894 Dalrymple-Hay joined the staff of W. R. Galbraith, and became resident engineer on the Waterloo and City Railway. He devised a technique for driving the tunnel under compressed air, through waterbearing ground, whereby small pockets of ground were excavated by hand up to 2 feet ahead of the hooded cutting edge of the shield, and packed with clay; when the shield was advanced, the hood entered the clay pockets, and provided a seal behind the lining. This system, which he patented in 1896, and other improvements in the methods of constructing tube railways also originated by Dalrymple-Hay, were subsequently widely used, both in Britain, and in the United States of America. In 1902 he became civil engineer to the Underground Electric Railways Company of London. Following Galbraith's retirement in 1907, he began his own private practice as a consulting civil engineer in Westminster, remaining consultant to the Underground Electric Railways Company and its successors until his death.

Dalrymple-Hay's tube-railway works comprised over 60 miles of tunnels in London alone, including works on the Bakerloo, Hampstead (Northern), and Piccadilly lines; extensions from Golders Green to Edgware, from Finsbury Park to Cockfosters, and from Highgate to East Finchley; stations at Piccadilly Circus, Leicester Square, Waterloo (Bakerloo Line), King's Cross, Hyde Park Corner, Knightsbridge, Elephant and Castle, and many others; also numerous escalator schemes, among which was the first escalator on the underground system, that at Earls Court, which was completed in 1911. Throughout these works Dalrymple-Hay demonstrated an innovative approach including the application of the François cementation process of ground stabilization to tunnelling.

Dalrymple-Hay was asked in 1921 to report on a system of tube railways for Calcutta, and later designed a tunnel to carry electricity supply cables under the River Hooghly. This tunnel, completed in 1931, was the first shield-driven iron-lined tunnel under a great tidal river in Asia, and its construction was carried out under high air pressures, in difficult climatic conditions, and with the use of unskilled labour. Among other works outside London, for which he

Sir Harley Hugh Dalrymple-Hay (1861–1940), by Maull & Fox, in or before 1884

was responsible, were a system of culverts for Bristol corporation's generating station at Portishead, and tunnels for Edinburgh corporation under the Firth of Forth at Portobello.

Although Dalrymple-Hay's work was mostly concerned with the construction of tunnels and tube railways, a branch of civil engineering in which he was probably the greatest expert of his day, he also was concerned in other engineering projects. Possibly the most interesting of these was the widening of Richmond Bridge. The 150-year-old bridge was strengthened and widened by some 11 feet, without interruption to road or river traffic, and without any alteration to the architectural design; the existing façade stonework and parapet were dismantled, numbered, and later replaced on the widened bridge.

Dalrymple-Hay was consulting engineer for the construction of the Post Office (London) Railway, a system of great ingenuity, which was opened in 1928, and it was for the Post Office that he undertook his last major work. This was a secret system of deep-level tunnels beneath Whitehall designed to allow communication between government offices to continue, despite aerial bombardment.

Dalrymple-Hay was knighted in 1933, and served on the council of the Institution of Civil Engineers from then until his death. As a student of the institution he was awarded a Miller prize in 1885 for a paper on trigonometrical surveying, and in 1900 he won a Telford gold medal for his paper on 'The Waterloo and City Railway' (*Minutes of Proceedings of the Institution of Civil Engineers*, 139, 1899–1900, 25–55). A characteristic of Dalrymple-Hay was his

strong belief that practice was preferable to theory, and experience more valuable than scholarship. He had a great human touch, a quality which endeared him to men of all walks of life, who worked under him. A Conservative in politics, he was a member of the Junior Carlton Club. He died at Thorpemead, Chenies Road, Chorleywood, Hertfordshire on 17 December 1940.

A. Y. DALRYMPLE-HAY, *rev.* MIKE CHRIMES

Sources *The Engineer* (27 Dec 1940), 409 · *Engineering* (27 Dec 1940), 515 · *Journal of the Institution of Civil Engineers*, 15 (1940–41), 314 · M. E. Day, ed., *The engineers' who's who* (1939), 179 · *WWW* · H. J. B. Harding, *Tunnelling history and my own involvement* (1981) · W. C. Copperthwaite, *Tunnel shields and the use of compressed air in subaqueous works* (1906) · d. cert. · m. cert. · *The Times* (20 Dec 1940), 1a, 7e · *The Times* (3 Jan 1941)
Archives Inst. CE, membership records · London Transport Museum, London · PRO, Rail MSS | LMA, London Underground records · U. Glas. L., letters to D. S. MacColl
Likenesses Maull & Fox, photograph, in or before 1884, Inst. CE [*see illus.*] · photographs, 1930–39, Inst. CE · Elliott & Fry, photograph, repro. in *Engineering* · Swain, photograph, repro. in *The Engineer*
Wealth at death £87,787 5s. 10d.: probate, 18 April 1941, *CGPLA Eng. & Wales*

Hay [*née* Sheridan], **Helen Selina**, **countess of Gifford** [*other married name* Helen Selina Blackwood, Lady Dufferin and Claneboye] (**1807–1867**), author and song writer, was the eldest daughter of Thomas *Sheridan (1775–1817), colonial administrator (younger son of Richard Brinsley *Sheridan), and his wife, Caroline Henrietta Callander (1779–1851), novelist [*see* Sheridan, Caroline Henrietta]. She was taken by her parents in 1813 to the Cape of Good Hope, whence, after her father's death on 12 September 1817, she returned to England, where she grew up in an apartment in Hampton Court Palace. At seventeen she became engaged to Commander Price Blackwood (1794–1841), the youngest of three sons of Hans, Lord Dufferin, and Mehetabel Temple; owing to the deaths of his brothers, he was heir to the title and estate in Ireland of Baron Dufferin and Claneboye. His parents opposed the marriage, on financial grounds. Hence, after their wedding at St George's, Hanover Square, London, on 4 July 1825, the young couple went to Italy. They lived in Florence, where their only child, Frederick Temple Hamilton-Temple *Blackwood, subsequently marquess of Dufferin and Ava, was born on 21 June 1826.

After two years they returned to England, and lived in a cottage at Thames Ditton. When visiting her sisters, Mrs Caroline *Norton and Lady Seymour, in London, Helen Blackwood was introduced to the world of wit and fashion in which they moved, and there she made the acquaintance of the Misses Berry, Samuel Rogers, Henry Taylor, Brougham, Lockhart, Sydney Smith, and Benjamin Disraeli. Her husband succeeded his father as Baron Dufferin and Claneboye in the peerage of Ireland in November 1839, and he died on 21 July 1841, on board the *Reindeer*, off Belfast, aged forty-seven, from an overdose of morphia, taken inadvertently.

Lady Dufferin dedicated herself to her son, with whom

Helen Selina Hay, countess of Gifford (1807–1867), by Camille Silvy, c.1860

she enjoyed a particularly close relationship. A trip up the Nile in his company led to the publication, in 1863, of *Lispings from Low Latitudes, or, Extracts from the Journal of the Hon. Impulsia Gushington*, in which she made fun of the genre of travel writing. She also wrote a play called *Finesse, or, A Busy Day in Messina*, which was first performed at the Haymarket Theatre in 1863. The acting of John Baldwin Buckstone and Alfred Wigan contributed to a highly successful run. She neither acknowledged the authorship, nor attended any performance. Her songs and verses were published anonymously, the first dating from her girlhood. Her earliest publication was a collection of songs written with her sister Caroline, for which they were paid £100. She also published several volumes of songs and ballads, the most successful of which were 'The Irish Emigrant' (1845) and 'Terence's Farewell' (1840).

George Hay, earl of Gifford (1822–1862) and son and heir of the marquess of Tweeddale, had been a friend and suitor for some fifteen years when in 1862 he was seriously injured by holding back a stone which was falling on some of his workmen. They were married on 13 October 1862, at Dufferin Lodge, in London, and he died there on 22 December. Lady Dufferin explained her motives to Gifford's father: '[It] gives me the right to devote every hour and every day God spares him to his comfort and relief, and ... the right to mourn him openly' (Dufferin, memoir).

She died five years later from breast cancer, on 13 June 1867 at Dufferin Lodge, and was buried with her second husband at Friern Barnet, Middlesex.

W. F. RAE, *rev.* K. D. REYNOLDS

Sources GEC, *Peerage* · *Songs, poems and verses by Helen, Lady Dufferin*, ed. Marquess of Dufferin and Ava (1894) · C. J. Hamilton, *Notable Irishwomen* (1904) · Brown & Stratton, *Brit. mus.* · Boase, *Mod. Eng. biog.* · Burke, *Peerage* · H. Nicolson, *Helen's tower* (1937)
Archives PRO NIre., corresp., literary MSS, and papers, D1071 F/A | BL, letters to R. B. Sheridan and Lord Tweeddale, Add. MS 42768 · Bodl. Oxf., corresp. with Sir Robert Hay
Likenesses C. Silvy, photograph, c.1860, NPG [*see illus.*] · Swinton, crayon drawing, repro. in Helen, Lady Dufferin Hay, *Songs, poems and verses*

Hay, James, first earl of Carlisle (*c.*1580–1636), courtier and diplomat, was the son of Sir James Hay (*d.* 1610) of Fingask, comptroller of Scotland in 1608, who lived in Pitscottie, Fife, and was descended from the earls of Erroll; his mother was probably Sir James's first wife, Margaret Murray. At least two siblings survived until adulthood, Robert and Agnes, but they may have been the children of Sir James's second wife, a widow named Barclay. There is no record of Hay receiving a university degree, but at some point in his life he became fluent in French and Latin. Since his first patron was Charles Cauchon de Maupas, baron du Tour, it seems safe to assume that Hay spent time in France.

Rise to prominence Hay first attracted King James's attention in the wake of baron du Tour's special embassy to Scotland from Henri IV of France in the summer of 1602. In May 1603, at du Tour's request, the king made Hay a gentleman of the privy chamber. No record exists of what drew the king to make Hay one of his favourites. Contemporaries remark on Hay's charm, grace, and taste. As for his appearance, surviving portraits date from Hay's middle age. What they show is a man with a broad forehead and soft eyes. He had a thin-bridged nose, but with flaring nostrils. The general impression is of someone with a triangular shape to his face. In her letters the king's daughter, Elizabeth, addressed Hay as 'camel-face' and it is not difficult to see why.

Although as early as July 1603 Francis Bacon made a note to himself to cultivate Hay, the first mention of the young Scot in England does not occur until the following October. That month, at Queen Anne's request, the king elevated Hay to the bedchamber. In March 1604 James sent him on an extraordinary embassy to Henri IV with condolences on the death of the French king's sister. He became a Scottish knight before being naturalized as an Englishman on 14 May 1604, and was created Lord Hay on 21 June 1606, but without the right to sit in the English parliament. Although the king granted Hay lands in Yorkshire and Northamptonshire he was never active in county affairs and, indeed, throughout his career lived in leased or borrowed houses.

After some years of resistance on the part of his future father-in-law, on 6 January 1607 Hay married Honora Denny (*d.* 1614), daughter of Sir Edward *Denny, later earl of Norwich (1569–1637) [*see under* Denny, Sir Anthony

James Hay, first earl of Carlisle (c.1580–1636), by unknown artist, 1628

(1501–1549)] and granddaughter of Thomas Cecil, second Lord Burghley (later earl of Exeter). They had two children who survived to adulthood, James (b. c.1612) and Anne. Honora died in August 1614 after a miscarriage, and was buried at night on 16 August at Waltham Abbey.

Domestic career What contemporaries noted about Hay was the extravagance with which he lived. By all reports he followed his family motto, 'Spare naught', and his lavish banquets were the best-known indication.

In December 1605 he received his first appropriation as master of the robes, whose responsibility it was to provide the king with all the clothes he wore ranging from his boots and shoes to his beaver hats. The original annual budget for the post was £2500, but within three years Hay had overspent that appropriation by £7000. From 1608 the budget was adjusted upward to £4000 per annum. Whatever sums of money passed through Hay's hands as master of the robes a great deal more came his way from February 1613 when he became in addition master of the great wardrobe. Whereas his profits from the robes were probably counted in hundreds of pounds a year, running the wardrobe brought him upwards of £4000 per annum and the use of a house in the city of London. The wardrobe

was responsible for supplying everything from the liveries worn by royal servants to the carriages in which royalty rode. By the time Hay relinquished both his offices to Sir Lionel Cranfield in 1618 his debt was approximately £42,000. As late as 1641 the second earl of Carlisle found that he still owed between £2000 and £3000 of his father's debt.

Meanwhile Hay, who on 29 June 1615 had become an English baron as Baron Hay of Sawley, Yorkshire, played other useful roles at court. In May 1616 he negotiated a deal with the king's disgraced favourite Robert Carr, earl of Somerset, concerning what Carr could expect after his trial for the murder of Sir Thomas Overbury. Carr had begun his career in England as a page for Hay and specifically requested his former master act as a royal agent to negotiate this settlement.

Diplomatic career It was Hay's tact that was responsible for his frequent appointments as extraordinary ambassador. Perhaps because he was flexible enough to conform to changing orthodoxies in the church under James I and Charles I, Hay was one of the few staunch protestants at the royal court who could effectively negotiate with Roman Catholics from other countries. In March 1616 Hay was appointed extraordinary ambassador to the court of Louis XIII, with the mission of bringing an end to the lengthy marriage negotiations involving Prince Charles and Louis's sister, Christine. When Hay reached the French court in July he found that the dowager queen, Marie de' Medici, and her favourites, the Concinis, controlled the government in the name of the teenaged king. When a month later they arrested the duc de Condé, one of the nobles at the French court favoured by James I, the marriage negotiations collapsed. By October 1616 Hay had received instructions to return home. He did so with reluctance because he recognized that the alternative to a French bride for Prince Charles was a Spanish one, and Hay had too many ties with France to favour such a course of action.

Once back in England, Hay began marriage negotiations of his own. Initially he encountered the same problems as he had the first time. Despite imprisonment in the Tower of London in the wake of the Gunpowder Plot, his prospective father-in-law, Henry *Percy, ninth earl of Northumberland (1564–1632) did his best to prevent his daughter, Lady Lucy Percy (1599–1660) [see Hay, Lucy, countess of Carlisle], from marrying Hay. However, after less than a year's courtship, Northumberland relented and the couple married on 6 November 1617. There were no surviving children from this marriage. In the end Hay enjoyed a good relationship with both his fathers-in-law. While his charm undoubtedly played a role he saw to it that Northumberland and Denny received honours and favours from James I, in particular the release of the former from the Tower in 1621. Hay himself received a further mark of royal favour when on 5 July 1618 he was created Viscount Doncaster.

In 1619 Doncaster was again sent on a diplomatic mission, this time as part of James I's effort to mediate peace between the Spanish and Austrian Habsburgs on the one hand and the Dutch and the German princes on the other. As in France, however, the English embassy was overtaken by events—in this case the crisis precipitated by the acceptance of the throne of Bohemia by James's son-in-law Frederick, the elector palatine—and Doncaster's mission was a total failure. Similarly abortive was an embassy in summer 1621, when, to help in the eyes of a suspicious parliament, James sent Doncaster to France in an effort to mediate a cease-fire between Louis XIII and the Huguenots in their current conflict. Once again the chances of success seemed slight, but Doncaster was willing to undertake the mission regardless of the odds. As matters developed, by December 1621 when he was about to bring both sides together to negotiate a peace agreement, James I dissolved parliament, lost interest in France's difficulties, and recalled his ambassador. None the less, Doncaster's standing was unimpaired and on 30 September 1622 he was created earl of Carlisle.

It was not until 1624, in the aftermath of the collapse of the Spanish marriage negotiations, that Carlisle had his one and only overseas diplomatic success. Working in a joint embassy with his protégé Henry Rich, newly created earl of Holland, he finally arranged a French marriage for Prince Charles with Louis XIII's youngest sister, Henriette Marie (Henrietta Maria). The initial instructions for the embassy were drawn up in April 1624 while Holland was already in Paris, but Carlisle did not arrive until the middle of May. The marriage was part of a political alliance between England and France designed to limit imperial and Spanish power and restore Elector Frederick to his palatinate lands. Both sides knew that a key point of dispute would be the extent of religious toleration the English king would be willing to grant his Roman Catholic subjects. Thanks in large measure to Carlisle's diplomatic skills in late July it looked as if a satisfactory agreement had been reached. Unfortunately for him at that point the French government underwent a major change when Cardinal Richelieu became Louis XIII's chief minister. As this change was in process Carlisle advised James to approve the treaty quickly before the French could make any changes, but the advice went unheeded. At one point, in autumn 1624, Carlisle was so frustrated with Richelieu that he was ready to break off negotiations. The final agreement was not reached until the following year, after Charles I was the king. The marriage took place in May 1625, by which time Carlisle had become embittered toward French policy in general and Cardinal Richelieu in particular.

Over the next four years Carlisle became determined to punish the French government for its failure to support military efforts to reinstate Frederick in the Palatinate. He hoped to drive Cardinal Richelieu from power and have him replaced by someone who was more tolerant of the Huguenots and more willing to challenge the Habsburgs militarily. In 1628 Carlisle went on one last, fruitless diplomatic mission hoping to put together a diverse group of allies including the Dutch republic, Savoy, Venice, and the Huguenots. In the end he returned to England in early 1629 favouring a peace treaty with Spain before one with France.

Final years Carlisle had managed to remain in the good graces of Charles I both before and after his travels abroad. In the aftermath of the murder of the king's favourite, George Villiers, duke of Buckingham, Hay was generally acknowledged as one of the three most important men at the royal court. His appointment in February 1631 as groom of the stole made him first gentleman of the king's bedchamber and meant that he controlled access to Charles I. In terms of governmental policy there is no evidence that Carlisle was able to influence the king to become more militarily active in reinstating Frederick or Frederick's son in the Palatinate. Toward that end in 1633 he reversed his opinions again and finally decided Cardinal Richelieu was someone worth cultivating for this purpose and by March 1635 his relationship with the French was very much what it had been when he first appeared at the royal court.

If the continental European scene continued to be largely politically unproductive from Carlisle's point of view, he did have some financial success in Ireland and more spectacularly in the West Indies. As early as 1607 he claimed the profits from the Irish customs duties on imported wine. By 1615 he asserted the right to license the sale of wine and spirits. Given Carlisle's standard of living, neither venture was especially profitable over the extended time he controlled them. Potentially his most profitable Irish undertaking involved ownership and control of a portion of co. Wicklow, known as Byrnes Country. Carlisle spent the last ten years of his life trying to take possession of this property, but he never succeeded because various Irish government officials, including Lord Deputy Thomas Wentworth, had their own plans for the land. With respect to the Caribbean islands, despite early difficulties, they became his own highly valuable domain. He managed to outmanoeuvre the earls of Marlborough and Montgomery and take possession of all the islands from Barbados and St Kitts. By the time he died the customs revenue alone reached £9000 per annum and from all sources on the island closer to £12,000.

Carlisle had a stroke on 13 March 1636 and died at the Strand, Westminster, on 20 April. After an impressive funeral procession he was buried the next day in St Paul's. He was survived by his wife and his son, James, who became the second earl. James married, on 21 March 1632, Lady Margaret Russell, daughter of Francis Russell, fourth earl of Bedford, but he died childless on 30 October 1660.

Reputation Of all the Scots who came to England with James I, Carlisle was probably the most successful at blending into his new surroundings. He returned to his homeland only twice in over three decades and on both occasions it was because he was required to accompany his royal master on progress there. He was always very careful not to challenge the English power structure by either becoming too closely identified with one of the existing factions, as Robert Carr did with the Howards, or setting up a faction of his own, as many people pressured him to do after Buckingham's death in 1628. Therefore it is hardly surprising that he was not a major figure in the House of Lords and never had a group associated with him in the House of Commons. He relied on the king to provide him with protection and employment. Thanks to his skills in dealing with people in general and his royal masters in particular, that reliance was not ill-placed or unrewarded.

It is possible to argue that except for his part in the French marriage, Carlisle was a singularly ineffective diplomat. He certainly never was able to negotiate the return of the palatine family to its German territory. Yet he did the best he could under difficult circumstances. In order for diplomacy to succeed even the most skilful of ambassadors must have either military power or money to use in their bargaining. For a whole variety of reasons Carlisle seldom had either. Yet what he wanted most was to keep the French and the various Habsburg rulers from uniting against either James I or Charles I. In this respect he was certainly more successful.   ROY E. SCHREIBER

Sources R. E. Schreiber, *The first Carlisle: Sir James Hay, first earl of Carlisle as courtier, diplomat and entrepreneur, 1580–1636* (1984) · *Scots peerage*, vols. 4–5 · GEC, *Peerage*, vol. 3 · J. A. Williamson, *The Caribbee Islands under proprietary patents* (1926) · M. Prestwich, *Cranfield … politics and profit under the early Stuarts* (1966) · *The letters and life of Francis Bacon*, ed. J. Spedding, 7 vols. (1861–74), vol. 5 · *CSP Venice, 1621–3* · Clarendon, *Hist. rebellion* · *CSP dom., 1603–18* · PRO, IND 6744 · PRO, C3/408/45, C78/515 case 7, C206/60, C/115/N4 no. 8607 · BL, Stowe MS 176 · BL, Egerton MS 2594 · PRO, SP78/73 · PRO, PRO31/3/68 · PRO, SP16/121 · T. Raylor, *The Essex House masque of 1621* (2000)
Archives BL, corresp. and papers, Egerton MSS 2592, 2593, 2594, 2596, 2597 | BL, Harley MSS 1580–1581, 1583–1584 · BL, Stowe MS 176 · PRO, C3/408/45 · PRO, IND 6744–6748 · PRO, PRO 31/3: 50, 51, 54–58, 63, 64, 66–68 · PRO, PRO 31/4: 1–4 · PRO, SP 14: 9a, 14, 28, 40, 83, 94, 112, 149, 150, 162, 163, 167, 169, 171 · PRO, SP 16: 33, 72, 75, 101, 110, 116, 118, 121–123, 136, 145, 147, 153, 172, 203, 204 · PRO, SP 46: 90–93 · PRO, SP 63: 227, 246, 247, 252, 254 · PRO, SP 78: 51, 66, 69–74, 79, 83 · PRO, SP 84: 91, 92, 94, 98, 139, 143 · PRO, SP 92: 13–16
Likenesses oils, 1628, NPG [*see illus.*] · F. Aliamet, line engraving (after A. Van Dyck), BM, NPG · S. de Passe, line engraving, BM, NPG · A. Van Dyck, engraving, NPG
Wealth at death appointed trustees to pay down approx. £42,000 debt from West Indian holdings

Hay, Jane E. [*known as* Jane Benham Hay] (*b.* **1829**). See under Pre-Raphaelite women artists (*act.* 1848–1870s).

Hay, John, first Lord Hay of Yester (*c.*1450–1508), landowner, was the eldest son of Sir David Hay of Yester and Mary, daughter of George Douglas, first earl of Angus (*d.* 1403), and Mary, sister of James I. The Hays of Yester were an important baronial family in Edinburghshire, Haddingtonshire, and Tweeddale and ancestors of the earls of Hay. On 12 July 1470 John received Olivercastle in Peeblesshire (inherited by the Hays through marriage to the heiress of Simon Fraser of Olivercastle, executed by Edward I in 1306) from his father, whom he had succeeded by 1 March 1479, inheriting Yester, with its castle, various Haddingtonshire lands, and the sheriffship of Peebles, as well as some lands in Lanarkshire and Perthshire.

A regular attender of parliament in the 1480s, Hay

became a lord of parliament on 29 January 1488: James III probably looked to Hay (whose first wife belonged to the family of Lindsay of the Byres, which remained loyal to the king in 1488) to act as a counter in Peeblesshire and Haddingtonshire to the rebellious Hepburns, Humes, and Archibald Douglas, fifth earl of Angus (Hay's mother was an Angus Douglas). Loyal to James III in the civil war of 1488, Hay temporarily lost his family's sheriffship of Peebles and his Haddingtonshire barony of Locherworth: the former was held by the earl of Angus from 1488 to 1491 and the latter by Patrick Hepburn, earl of Bothwell, from 1488 to 20 September 1500. Between July 1501 and 27 January 1502, moreover, the lords of council decided that his (repeated) 'partial process' should again cost him his sheriffship; he was fined £10 for missing a justice ayre at Jedburgh in 1501.

Hay married first Mary (*d.* before 1468), daughter of John, first Lord Lindsay of the Byres (contract dated 1462); they had one son, Thomas, who predeceased him. His second marriage was to Elizabeth (*d.* after February 1509) daughter of Sir George Cunningham of Belton (contract dated 17 December 1468). They had four children: John, who was granted the barony of Snaid in 1505 by James IV, and succeeded his father as second Lord Yester; George, ancestor of the Hays of Menzion; Margaret, who married William *Borthwick, third Lord Borthwick [*see under* Borthwick family]; and Isabel, who married Robert Lauder of Bass. Hay died in late September 1508, possessed of lands worth at least £115 annually: in 1479—with Locherworth—they had been worth £175.

MICHAEL A. PENMAN

Sources J. M. Thomson and others, eds., *Registrum magni sigilli regum Scotorum / The register of the great seal of Scotland*, 11 vols. (1882–1914), vol. 2 · C. C. H. Harvey and L. MacLeod, eds., *Calendar of writs preserved at Yester House, 1166–1625*, Scottish RS, 55 (1930) · G. Burnett and others, eds., *The exchequer rolls of Scotland*, 9–12 (1886–9) · T. Dickson and J. B. Paul, eds., *Compota thesaurariorum regum Scotorum / Accounts of the lord high treasurer of Scotland*, 1–4 (1877–1902) · [T. Thomson] and others, eds., *The acts of the lords of council in civil causes, 1478–1503*, 3 vols. (1839–1993) · [T. Thomson], ed., *The acts of the lords auditors of causes and complaints, AD 1466–AD 1494*, RC, 40 (1839) · *APS, 1424–1567* · *Scots peerage* · N. Macdougall, *James IV* (1989)
Archives NA Scot., Yester writs, GD 28 · NL Scot., genealogical papers, MSS 7110, 7113, 14500, 14826
Wealth at death over £115 p.a. in land: Harvey and Macleod, eds., *Calendar of writs*

Hay, John (1547–1607), Jesuit, was born on 25 January 1547, a younger son of the Hay family of Delgaty, Aberdeenshire, where his eldest brother, William, was later to build Delgaty (Delgatie) Castle. At least one other brother lived in the north, and a sister married a Barclay of Towie. Another brother, Edmund, owner of a farm near Dundee and an Edinburgh lawyer, defended the earl of Bothwell after the murder of the queen's husband. The family was related to the earl of Erroll, hereditary constable of Scotland.

Hay went to Rome in 1566 with his cousin Edmund Hay, a Jesuit, and himself entered the Society of Jesus on his nineteenth birthday. Having been a novice for three months alongside Stanislas Kostka, his first posting was in

1572, to the college at Vilna in Lithuania. There he contributed three years of stability to the early teaching of philosophy. In 1576 he was sent to the new university of Pont-à-Mousson in Lorraine, where again he taught philosophy until an outbreak of plague caused the suspension of classes. In Strasbourg to consult a doctor, Hay then stepped into a debate on transubstantiation at the Lutheran university there, triumphing (as Hay reported the opinion of its president) over the renowned John Pappius. Uncertain about the status of his young opponent (in layman's clothes because not yet a priest) Pappius concluded that he was either the devil or a Jesuit. Shortly after this Hay received permission to return to Scotland for his health's sake, on the understanding that there would be no trouble or debating triumphs.

Hay sailed from Bordeaux on the wine route, landing on 20 January 1579 at the strongly protestant port of Dundee for what proved to be a dramatic nine months' stay in Scotland. Despite the protection of relations in Perthshire, Hay found himself the focus of controversy as rumours circulated about the new Jesuit menace. He withdrew to the greater security of Aberdeenshire. There he became an object of wonder in the midst of a religious revival which owed a good deal to the popular discontent which followed the closure of Deer Abbey. Despite his own poor health, Hay was assumed to be capable of effecting cures for invalids who also sought help on pilgrimages to holy wells. Turriff near Delgaty was a particular centre of devotion, with crowds 'clothed only in linen garments imploring the aid of God and the saints, and especially of the Blessed Virgin' (Forbes-Leith, *Narratives of Scottish Catholics*, 161). Rosaries were on sale at the market fair. Summoned to the royal court at Stirling, Hay was interrogated by senior clergy on behalf of the regent's privy council. He declined an invitation for private debate with professors of the University of Glasgow, while his request for a public one before the boy king, James VI, was refused. His last weeks in Scotland, granted by the privy council and guaranteed by Delgaty's £1000 Scots bond, were conditional on his doing 'nothing offensive to the trew and Christiane religion established' (*Reg. PCS, 1578–85*, 204), so that a sense of unfinished business motivated his polemical writing in France.

Hay's *Certain demandes concerning the Christian religion and discipline proposed to the ministers of the new pretended Kirk of Scotland* was published at Paris in 1580. The author described himself as a clerk of the Society of Jesus, although he was ordained priest later that year. 'Reminiscent of the method and style of [Ninian] Winzet' (Taylor, 271), the book was highly influential on the continent. Its 166 questions brought together many points of controversy in an accessible way. One may be quoted in relation to the former dependants of the monks of Deer: 'Quhether maa pure [more poor] was nurished daylie be almes of Abbay places? Or maa householders maid beggars this day be your preaching?' (Law, 64). The fact that no answer came back from kirk ministers (nor to John Hamilton's *Catholic and Facile Traictise*, 1581), helped to develop a counter-Reformation climate in north-east Scotland. In

Europe there were sharp responses to French and German translations of the *Demandes*, in particular from the University of Nîmes, to which Hay (as professor of theology and dean of arts at Tournon) published a reply in 1584. This was followed four years later by a response to Theodore Beza, who had mocked him as a monk.

Latterly Hay lived in several Jesuit houses in Flanders, translating mission reports from Japan and Peru into Latin from Italian, but in 1598 he wrote to James VI from Antwerp drawing a contrast with the state of Scotland as it had been forty years earlier, in his own grandfather's time. Placed as he was near the channel ports, Hay was described by William Crichton, in a letter of 2 August 1598, as desolated at not being trusted by his fellow Jesuits to go to Scotland because he was 'unable to keep silence on hearing heresy'. General Acquaviva, writing to James Gordon 'Huntly' on 24 December 1599, acknowledged Hay's 'well known excessive zeal'. Hay's short visit of 1601 was prolonged on account of the deaths of two of his brothers' heirs—a property matter which on 25 April that year prompted him to reassure the general that 'my hopes remain centred on God alone. I must also clearly acknowledge that my enthusiasm for disputations has weakened' (Jesuit Archives). Latterly Hay was appointed rector of the college at Pont-à-Mousson where he had formerly taught. He died there 'beloved and regretted' on 21 May 1607 and was buried locally, to be commemorated in the society's archives as 'a man of commanding abilities, primitive fervour, apostolic zeal, and infantine docility' (Gordon, 564).

ALASDAIR ROBERTS

Sources T. G. Law, *Catholic tractates of the sixteenth century, 1573–1600*, STS, 45 (1901) · W. Forbes-Leith, ed., *Narratives of Scottish Catholics under Mary Stuart and James VI* (1885) · A. Bellesheim, *History of the Catholic Church in Scotland*, ed. and trans. D. O. H. Blair, 3 (1889) · R. Darowski, 'John Hay, SJ, and the origins of philosophy in Lithuania', *Innes Review*, 31 (1980), 7–15 · W. Forbes-Leith, *Pre-Reformation scholars in the XVIth century* (1915) · M. Taylor, 'The conflicting doctrines of the Scottish Reformation', *Essays on the Scottish Reformation, 1513–1625*, ed. D. McRoberts (1962), 245–73 · J. F. S. Gordon, ed., *The Catholic church in Scotland* (1874) · William Crichton to George Duras, 2 Aug 1598, London, Jesuit archives · Claudio Acquaviva to James Gordon, 24 Dec 1599, London, Jesuit archives · Hay to Acquaviva, 25 April 1601, London, Jesuit archives

Hay, Sir John, Lord Barro (1578–1654), judge, was the son of William Hay (d. 1597), of Barro and Wyndon, Haddingtonshire, and Margaret, daughter of George Hay of Monkton, Haddingtonshire. He was educated at the College (University) of Edinburgh, graduating MA in August 1594. After working some six years in England, in March 1602 he was made clerk-depute of Edinburgh, rising to conjunct clerk in May 1618. Edinburgh commissioned him to prepare a Latin oration for James VI on his visit to the capital in 1617; the text was published in *Muses' Welcome*, printed by Andro Hart. His first marriage, in May 1602, was to Marion, daughter of John Johnston, merchant burgess of Edinburgh, with whom he had one daughter and four sons, including Sir Henry, commissary of Edinburgh. His second marriage, in 1622, was to Rebecca, daughter of Alexander Thomson of Duddingston, with whom he had four sons and two daughters. In 1612 he purchased lands in the barony of Kinderlock in Kirkcudbrightshire and in 1633, after Charles I's act of revocation saw him lose lands, he repurchased the family estate at Barro near Haddington.

For thirty years Hay represented the interests of Edinburgh and the royal burghs to successive absent kings. Much favoured by Charles I, preferment came quickly in the early 1630s. Knighted on 29 July 1632, on 12 December he was appointed lord clerk register in succession to Sir John Hamilton of Magdalens, joining the privy council and becoming an extraordinary lord of session. In January 1634 he became an ordinary lord of session as Lord Barro. His appointment to the court of high commission that year cemented what was by then his close relationship with episcopacy, and he was now used by Charles I to force Edinburgh to accept his religious policies. Plans to restructure St Giles as a cathedral in 1634 increased Hay's unpopularity in the city. Although he 'inveighed against the [Service] Booke as much as any' (*Letters and Journals of Robert Baillie*, 1.38), his royal nomination as provost of the burgh in October 1637 meant he had the hopeless task of defusing burgh opposition to the new liturgy. With the onset of the first bishops' war in 1639 he fled the country, and was later forced to resign his offices. Although compensated financially, on his return in August 1641, accompanying the king, he was tried inconclusively as an 'incendiary' by the covenanter regime, briefly imprisoned, and excluded from the Act of Oblivion. The king, however, declared Hay innocent on 24 September 1642, and his last act of defiance was to join Montrose at the battle of Philiphaugh (1645), at which he was captured; he was imprisoned in Dumbarton Castle. He was allowed to retire to Duddingston, near Edinburgh, where he died on 20 November 1654; he was buried on 24 November at Greyfriars churchyard, Edinburgh. His will and testament have not survived. A view of his character is not helped by presbyterian invective and political jealousy, but he was an effective servant of crown and burgh.

J. A. HAMILTON, rev. A. J. MANN

Sources J. Inglis, *Sir John Hay: the incendiary, 1578–1654* (1937) · Calendar of Yester writs (Tweeddale / Hay), NA Scot., GD.28.1434, GD.28.1033, GD.28.1201 · J. Bain, ed., *The border papers: calendar of letters and papers relating to the affairs of the borders of England and Scotland*, 2 vols. (1894–6), vol. 2, p. 680 · G. Brunton and D. Haig, *An historical account of the senators of the college of justice, from its institution in MDXXXII* (1832), 291–2 · *The letters and journals of Robert Baillie*, ed. D. Laing, 1 (1841), 38 · R. Hay, 'The Hayes of Tweeddale', NL Scot., fols. 40–43 · *The historical works of Sir James Balfour*, ed. J. Haig, 2 (1824), 193, 218, 378 · M. Wood, ed., *Extracts from the records of the burgh of Edinburgh, 1604–1626*, [7] (1931) · M. Wood, ed., *Extracts from the records of the burgh of Edinburgh, 1626–1641*, [8] (1936) · APS, 1625–41 · old parish registers (Canongate), NA Scot., OPR.685.1.43, May 1602 [marriage to Marion Johnston] · J. M. Thomson and others, eds., *Registrum magni sigilli regum Scotorum / The register of the great seal of Scotland*, 11 vols. (1882–1914), vols. 7–9 · D. Laing, ed., *A catalogue of the graduates … of the University of Edinburgh*, Bannatyne Club, 106 (1858), 21

Hay, John, first marquess of Tweeddale (1626–1697), politician, was the eldest son of John Hay, eighth Lord Hay of Yester and first earl of Tweeddale (c.1593–1654), and his

John Hay, first marquess of Tweeddale (1626–1697), by Sir Peter Lely

first wife, Lady Jean Seton (d. 1626/7), daughter of Alexander *Seton, first earl of Dunfermline (1556–1622). Styled the master of Yester until 1646, John Hay attended the University of Edinburgh. In 1640 he went to London with his uncle, Charles Seton, second earl of Dunfermline, who was one of the Scottish commissioners appointed to arrange peace with England. Yester returned to Scotland with Charles I in 1641 and he later joined the king at Nottingham in August 1642 at the outbreak of the English civil war. However, he became dissatisfied with the king's stance towards the covenanters and in 1643 he returned to Scotland. By a marriage contract dated 24 September 1644 he married Lady Jean Scott (1629–1688), second daughter of Walter Scott, first earl of Buccleuch (d. 1633), and granddaughter of Walter *Scott, first Lord Scott of Buccleuch (1565?–1611). The marriage produced seven sons and two daughters.

Yester had already been appointed colonel of the Linlithgow and Tweeddale foot in the army of the solemn league and covenant, which invaded England in 1644. He fought against the king at the battle of Marston Moor on 2 July 1644, but after the king's surrender to the covenanters on 5 May 1646 he waited on the king at Newcastle. Now known as Lord Hay of Yester, he aligned himself with the engagement and on 4 May 1648 he was appointed a colonel of the foot for Haddingtonshire; the regiment fought at the battle of Preston on 17 August 1648. In the aftermath of defeat, he fled back to Scotland where he reconciled himself with the radical regime of covenanters. He was present at the coronation of Charles II at Scone on 1 January 1651 and on 13 March he was added to the committee for grievances set up by the committee of estates of 23 December 1650. Yester remained with the king until the invasion of England in 1651. He retired to his house at Neidpath, which he garrisoned for the king; this was the last place that surrendered to the English south of the River Forth. He succeeded his father as earl of Tweeddale in 1654 and he also collaborated in the Cromwellian parliaments, being elected as a member of parliament for Haddingtonshire in 1656 and 1659. It is possible that he was in favour of Cromwell accepting the royal title.

Tweeddale attended the first session of the Restoration parliament in Scotland (1 January – 12 July 1661), and served on several financial and religious commissions. He was admitted as a member of the new privy council on 13 July, but on 13 September the council received instructions from Charles II for him to be imprisoned in Edinburgh Castle for speeches which he was supposed to have made relating to the trial and execution of James Guthry, the protester minister of Stirling, which were deemed prejudicial to the king's authority. Tweeddale wrote to Secretary Lauderdale that he was 'as thunder struke with the order for his commital' (*Lauderdale Papers*, 1.99) and on 17 September he petitioned the privy council to intercede with the king on his behalf and secure his release. After examining him on 2 October about his behaviour concerning the parliamentary vote of 12 April for Guthry's execution the council ordered Tweeddale's release, but he was instructed to remain within a 3 mile radius of his own home until the king's thoughts on the issue were further known, under the pain of 100,000 merks. It was not until 7 May 1662 that Tweeddale's confinement was removed.

Tweeddale attended the 1662 parliament which commenced the following day on 8 May, and the 1663 session commencing on 18 June. The same month he became president of the privy council, and he again served on financial and religious commissions. In January 1664 Tweeddale was appointed to the high commission for the execution of laws in church affairs and in early June he was made an extraordinary lord of session. In September that year, with Sir John Wauchope of Niddrie, he was required to provide thirty men for service in the English navy. In the winter of 1664–5 he was among those charged with taking action against Quakers, while on 3 May 1665 he became a privy council commissioner for Selkirkshire for the apprehension and trial of moss-troopers, robbers, and thieves in the borders (a commission later renewed). He attended the 1665 convention of estates and on 2 August he was included on the committee for inbringing of taxation.

From 1667 to 1674 Tweeddale was one of the leading figures in the administration of Scotland. He used his influence to limit the severity of the government towards the covenanters by pursuing a policy of compromise, embodied especially in the first indulgence of June 1669. He was active in the parliament of 1669–74. Appointed one of the lords of the articles on 19 October 1669, he was also a commissioner in the abortive union project with England in 1670, and for the plantation of kirks and valuation of teinds in 1672. Tweeddale again played an important role

on privy council committees reviewing religious policy, both towards Catholics and Quakers, and towards absentees from parish churches, clandestine marriages, and conventicles. On 6 May 1668 he was appointed as a colonel of foot for the militia in Haddingtonshire, and he was involved in discussion on militia policy in Dumfriesshire, Lanarkshire, Ayrshire, and Renfrewshire. His report for the king on the issue of settling the highlands was produced on 8 July 1669. He was involved in formulating privy council procedure and on 20 July 1671 and 7 March 1673 he was appointed as a commissioner for Haddingtonshire to enforce parliamentary legislation concerning highways.

In the early 1670s Tweeddale clashed politically with the influential John Maitland, from 1672 duke of Lauderdale. On 20 November 1673 Lauderdale informed the king that Tweeddale, 'at first an underhand contriver and counsellor' against the policy of the government (concerning the covenanters) had 'now shown himself openly' (*Lauderdale Papers*, 3.17). Through Lauderdale's influence Tweeddale was dismissed from office and deprived of his seat on the privy council. However, in January 1678 Tweeddale subscribed the bond for the peace as part of the presbytery of Kirkcaldy in Fife and on 22 March at Peebles he subscribed the bond by nobles and other men in Peeblesshire concerning conventicles. On 2 May he was reappointed as a commissioner for Haddingtonshire concerning highways and bridges and on 11 March 1679 he was ordered to suppress conventicles in the regality of Pittenweem Easter. With the downfall of Lauderdale in 1680 Tweeddale was appointed as commissioner of the Treasury, but in July, however, Sir George McKenzie of Rosehaugh, king's advocate, complained to the privy council that Tweeddale had failed to suppress the meeting of conventicles in his 'great teind barn', in the burgh of Inverkeithing (*Reg. PCS*, *1678–80*, 486–7). On showing that the 'barn held burgage of the town' (ibid.) Tweeddale was assoilzied and the legal process was continued against the magistrates of Inverkeithing. On 10 August the privy council appointed Tweeddale convener of the commissioners of the excise in Peeblesshire.

Tweeddale subscribed the declaration of 28 July 1681, issued on the opening day of parliament, stating that it was unlawful under all circumstances to take up arms against the king, and with other privy councillors subscribed the Test Act on 22 September. On 10 November he was instructed to receive subscriptions to the Test Act in Peeblesshire and the regality of Dunfermline and on 30 December he again subscribed the Test Act as sheriff principal of Peeblesshire and baillie of the regality of Dunfermline in the presence of Sir George Gordon of Haddo, lord president of the session. Following his reappointment to the privy council by the king Tweeddale formally took his seat on 15 May 1682 and in the same month he was appointed as a commissioner for trying the state of the coinage and mint. With the exposure of the Rye House plot in 1683 he was involved in the examination of Alexander Gordon of Earlston and the countess of Argyll. The following year he was again active in committee.

Tweeddale was one of the lords of the articles appointed

on 23 April 1685 at the opening of parliament. He again served on numerous committees and commissions, including those concerned with devising a reply to James VII's letter to parliament, supply for Haddingtonshire and Peeblesshire, trade, the plantation of kirks and valuation of teinds, and the regulation of inferior judicatories. He also attended the 1686 parliamentary session (29 April to 15 June) and later in September he was admitted as a Treasury commissioner. In September he was among privy councillors deputed to consider James VII's letter concerning the free private exercise of religion for Catholics in Scotland as well as the establishment of a chapel at Holyrood. In November 1686 Tweeddale was instructed to oversee the election of the burgh magistrates of Haddington. On 19 January 1687 he was admitted as a Treasury commissioner and on 10 March he was added to the commission for auditing the former treasurer's accounts.

As a supporter of the cause of William of Orange, Tweeddale was present in the 1689 convention which met from 14 March to 24 May. On 14 March he and the earl of Lothian were deputed by the estates to present the order to the duke of Gordon to surrender Edinburgh Castle within 24 hours. Tweeddale subscribed the act of 16 March declaring the meeting of the estates to be free and lawful and on the same day he was appointed to the committee for securing the peace. On 22 March an act was passed approving his conduct in authorizing William Drummond, deputy keeper of the magazine, for providing forty-one barrels of powder for the protestant defence of Londonderry in Ireland. Tweeddale also subscribed the convention's letter of 22 March replying to William as king of England and on 30 March he was named as an additional member on the committee for settling the government. He was included on committees to report on the public accounts (2 April) and to consider the supply of oats and fodder for the troops of horse and dragoons under the command of Major-General McKay (11 April), but on 12 April the convention gave Tweeddale a pass to go to England for health reasons. However, this would appear to be a cover to promote his own interests in England since, on 22 April, as an enthusiast for the project, he was named as one of the convention's commissioners to treat concerning a union between Scotland and England and he shortly afterwards became a commissioner of supply for Haddingtonshire and Edinburghshire.

Tweeddale was one of the privy councillors named in King William's commission from Hampton Court on 18 May 1689 and on 7 December orders from Holland House appointed Tweeddale as one of the Treasury commissioners. On 21 November he had also been appointed by the privy council as a JP for the shire of Edinburgh. He was also named as a privy councillor in 1690 and 1691, but for two and a half years he stayed in England, moving between Tunbridge Wells and London and courting political influence among a variety of episcopalian and presbyterian interests, all of which were opposed to Secretary of State George Melville. He had been promoting his own political advancement in 1689: on 16 July the earl of Crawford, president of parliament, wrote to Secretary of State

Melville (from 1690 earl of Melville) informing him that Tweeddale was making 'a strong partie' for Melville's position and that 'the Episcopall partie in our Parliament are strong agents for him' (Melville, 172).

Tweeddale was appointed lord high chancellor of Scotland on 5 June 1692, following a reconstruction of the Scottish administration. In this capacity he spoke in parliament on 18 April 1693 outlining the king's objectives for the forthcoming session. On 17 December 1694 he was created marquess of Tweeddale, earl of Gifford, viscount of Walden and Lord Hay of Yester. He was high commissioner to the 1695 parliamentary session which set up a special commission of enquiry into the controversial issue of the Glencoe massacre, and he played an important role in steering the report through parliament. However, the passing of the act for a Scottish company trading to Africa and the Indies on 26 June 1695, to which Tweeddale gave the royal assent, aroused the hostility of King William (and the English East India Company) and he fell from favour. He had acted 'almost certainly outside the intended limits' of his instructions as commissioner in a matter which, in the aftermath of the 1695 parliament, was 'the only topic to arouse William's anger' (Riley, 98). Tweeddale's political career ended with his dismissal as chancellor in 1696. He died at Edinburgh on 11 August 1697, and was buried at Yester. His wife had died in November 1688; he was succeeded as second marquess of Tweeddale by his son John *Hay (1645–1713).

JOHN R. YOUNG

Sources *Scots peerage*, vols. 2–3, 7 · *APS*, 1648–86, 1689–95 · *Reg. PCS*, 3rd ser. · W. H. L. Melville, ed., *Leven and Melville papers: letters and state papers chiefly addressed to George, earl of Melville … 1689–1691*, Bannatyne Club, 77 (1843) · R. Wodrow, *The history of the sufferings of the Church of Scotland from the Restoration to the revolution*, ed. R. Burns, 1 (1828) · *Bishop Burnet's History* · *Historical notices of Scotish affairs, selected from the manuscripts of Sir John Lauder of Fountainhall*, ed. D. Laing, 2 vols., Bannatyne Club, 87 (1848) · *The Lauderdale papers*, ed. O. Airy, 3 vols., CS, new ser., 34, 36, 38 (1884–5) · J. Nicoll, *A diary of public transactions and other occurrences, chiefly in Scotland, from January 1650 to June 1667*, ed. D. Laing, Bannatyne Club, 52 (1836) · C. Lindsay [earl of Balcarres], *Memoirs touching the revolution in Scotland*, ed. A. W. C. Lindsay [earl of Crawford and Balcarres], Bannatyne Club (1841) · *The diary of Mr John Lamont of Newton, 1649–1671*, ed. G. R. Kinloch, Maitland Club, 7 (1830) · C. S. Terry, ed., *The Cromwellian union: papers relating to the negotiations for an incorporating union between England and Scotland, 1651–1652*, Scottish History Society (1902) · E. M. Furgol, *A regimental history of the covenanting armies, 1639–1651* (1990) · *State papers and letters addressed to William Carstares*, ed. J. M'Cormick (1774) · 'Scotland's ruine': Lockhart of Carnwath's memoirs of the union, ed. D. Szechi, Association of Scottish Literary Studies, 25 (1995) · P. W. J. Riley, *King William and the Scottish politicians* (1979)
Archives NA Scot., letters · NL Scot., corresp. and papers · NL Scot., Yester papers | BL, letters to Lauderdale and Charles II, Add. MSS 23113–23135, 23243–23245 · Buckminster Park, Grantham, corresp. with duke of Lauderdale · NL Scot., corresp. with duke of Lauderdale
Likenesses attrib. G. Kneller, oils, 1678, Floors Castle, Borders region · G. Kneller, oils, c.1695, Tate collection · P. Lely, oils, Scot. NPG [*see illus.*] · J. Smith, two mezzotints (after G. Kneller), BM

Hay, John, second marquess of Tweeddale (1645–1713), politician, was the eldest son of John *Hay, first marquess of Tweeddale (1626–1697), and Lady Jean (1629–1688),

John Hay, second marquess of Tweeddale (1645–1713), by Gerard Soest, c.1670

daughter of Walter Scott, first earl of Buccleuch (d. 1633). From 1654 he was styled Lord Hay of Yester or Lord Yester. He was admitted a fellow of the Royal Society on 23 May 1666, and on 11 December that year he married Lady Mary (d. 1702), only daughter of John *Maitland, duke of Lauderdale (1616–1682), at Highgate, Middlesex. They had three sons and two daughters. Their second son was the distinguished army officer Lord John *Hay.

On 6 May 1668, with his father, Lord Yester was appointed a colonel of foot of the militia in Haddingtonshire, a position he held frequently throughout the late 1660s and early 1670s (1668, 1672, 1673, and 1674). Appointed a privy councillor on 25 July 1670, two years later Yester served on a commission for the suppression of crime on the borders. However, on 28 January 1675 George Seton, earl of Winton, replaced Yester and Tweeddale as colonel of the militia in Haddingtonshire, and their commissions were declared null and void. On 1 April 1678 Yester, like other Peeblesshire landowners, subscribed a privy council bond agreeing to abstain from attendance at conventicles. Through the late 1670s and early 1680s he continued on the privy council and sat on various commissions, including that of 1678 for supply in Haddingtonshire and Peeblesshire, for enforcement of legislation prohibiting the destruction of game and fish (1682), for government of the borders in general (1684), and specifically to deal with the 'disaffected and disorderly people in severall of the westerne and southerne shyres' who 'continue in rebellious convocationes, seditions, conventicles and other disorderly practises' (Reg. PCS, 9.155–156). Yester, along with one William Hay of Drumellzier, was appointed a commissioner for the shires of Roxburgh, Selkirk, Peebles,

and the Merse. An active member of a formal privy council committee anent fines about this time, he worked with James Douglas, earl of Drumlanrig, in considering the cases of several gentlemen and/or their wives in Teviotdale who had been fined. On 10 March 1685 he was a member of a privy council committee appointed to visit and examine prisoners in Leith tolbooth. On 9 April 1685 he was included on the new privy council.

As part of the security measures adopted to deal with the duke of Argyll's invasion of Scotland, Yester was appointed in May 1685 a colonel of the East Lothian regiment. Later that month he was appointed by the Scottish parliament as a commissioner of supply for Haddingtonshire and as a master of game for Peeblesshire. Yester played an important role on the privy council in the aftermath of Argyll's failed uprising. On 7 August Yester joined the important committee for public affairs, which was empowered to examine all prisoners and suspected persons and to sentence and banish prisoners to the plantations. From September he was involved in drawing up a letter to James VII providing details of the council's dealings with informers concerning the Argyll rebellion and he remained a council member in the controversial years of 1686 and 1687. Following anti-Catholic rioting in Edinburgh on 31 January and 1 February 1686, Yester was an official investigator, and in March he was a member of a privy council committee to report on shipping and navigation. In the summer of 1686 Yester and his father examined people who had attended a conventicle near Lauder and imprisoned one of the leading protagonists in Haddington prison.

Despite his previous record, after the revolution Yester became associated with the Williamite regime, even though he has been seen as 'sadly out of his depth at court and, for that matter, in most other places' (Riley, King William, 49). Yester's poor interpersonal skills hindered his political advancement and he appears to have been infuriating to his father who was trying to enhance the family's influence, although acting on his father's instructions, Yester presented at court a concocted address from Haddingtonshire which pressed the cause of union between England and Scotland. In the spring of 1689 he was appointed captain of the militia horse in Haddingtonshire, a commissioner for ordering the militia in that shire, and finally captain of a troop of horse for Berwickshire and Haddingtonshire. While his regiment was active in the north-east of Scotland, he had much to keep him in Edinburgh. A member of William's first privy council, he was also appointed sheriff of Haddington and in the early months of 1690 served on committees for peace and for supply in the area. Although not included in the new privy council appointed on 4 June 1690, five years later he made what seems to have been his first appearance in parliament, and did so as lord high treasurer, one of the great officers of state. On 20 June he was appointed as a commissioner of supply for Fife. While he did not attend the 1696 parliamentary session, following the death of his father on 11 August 1697, and his succession as second marquess of Tweeddale, he attended parliament regularly and he was present in the three parliamentary sessions between 1698 and 1701. He was a defender of the Darien project and he became associated with the parliamentary opposition against the court. On 14 January 1701 he voted in favour of a formal act being passed, as opposed to an address to the king, defending the rights and interests of the kingdom of Scotland in Darien, on 28 January he voted against the continuation of the armed forces until December 1702, and on 31 January he also voted against the continuation for four months of the number of troops over 3000 men.

Absent from the 1702 parliamentary session, Tweeddale was prominent in the parliament of 1703–7. On 19 May 1703 he presented an overture arguing that:

> before all other business the Parliament might proceed to make such conditions of government and regulations in the constitution of this Kingdom to take place after the decease of her Majestie and the heirs of her body as shall be required for the preservation of our religion and liberty. (*APS*, 11.41)

As a spokesman for the country party, Tweeddale was attempting to ensure that the bargaining position of supply was not given away prior to discussion of the succession and future constitutional reform. Nevertheless, he allowed himself to be diverted into presenting a protestation on 13 September against the act allowing the import of French wine and brandy, describing it as 'dishonourable to her Majestie, inconsistent with the grand alliance wherein she is engaged and prejudicial to the honour, safety, interest and trade of this Kingdom' (ibid., 11.217). Following the exposure of the Queensberry plot, James Johnston, King William's former secretary 'in concert with the Marquess of Tweedale and some others in Scotland' (*Bishop Burnet's History*, 4.77), proposed that Queen Anne should empower her commissioner in Scotland to consent to the revival of the 1641 constitutional settlement in Scotland in return for the securing of the Hanoverian succession in Scotland. Tweeddale was appointed as high commissioner to the 1704 parliamentary session which began on 6 July and on 5 August was named as a commissioner of supply for the shires of Edinburgh, Haddington, Berwick, and Fife. No progress was made on securing the succession and an act for the security of the kingdom, which received the royal assent on 5 August, led to increased tension in Anglo-Scottish relations, but when in September Tweeddale went to London, he was well received by Anne. From 17 October he replaced James Ogilvy, earl of Seafield, as lord high chancellor of Scotland, but was unseated on 9 March 1705 and lost his place as high commissioner in the parliamentary session of 28 June to 21 September 1705. However, he still attended and on 1 September he adhered to a protestation by John Murray, first duke of Atholl, against approving the act for a treaty with England.

Tweeddale was one of the leading figures in the *squadrone volante*, the political grouping whose votes were crucial for securing the passage of the treaty of union through the Scottish parliament in its final session from 3 October 1706 to 25 March 1707; Thomas Hay, Viscount Dupplin, dubbed it 'the Marques of Tweddals party' (Hume Brown, 173). He was a member of the important parliamentary committee established on 23 October for examining the calculation of the equivalent, the sum (eventually fixed at £400,000) to be advanced for the discharge of Scottish Treasury debts and to compensate shareholders in the Company of Scotland for the fiscal union. Tweeddale consistently voted in favour of the articles of the treaty of union from 4 November 1706 to 16 January 1707. At the time of the Union, Tweeddale was due arrears of salary of £2577 15s. 7d. Scots and he received £1000 sterling (£12,000 Scots) out of the £20,000 sterling (£240,000 Scots) sent north for distribution by the Scottish treasurer, David Boyle, first earl of Glasgow. On 13 February 1707 Tweeddale was chosen as one of the sixteen Scottish representative peers to sit in the House of Lords in the new British parliament. Tweeddale died suddenly in a fit of apoplexy on 20 April 1713 at Yester and he was privately buried there.

In writing of the 1704 parliamentary session, the Jacobite George Lockhart commented that Tweeddale was a 'well-meaning, but simple man … I may safely say he was the least ill-meaning man of his party, either through inclination or capacity' (*'Scotland's Ruine'*, 66). John Macky described him as a:

> great Encourager and Promoter of Trade, and the Welfare of his Country. He hath good Sense, is very modest, much a Man of Honour, and hot when picqued; is highly esteemed in his country, and may make a considerable Figure of it now. (*Memoirs of the Secret Services*, 186)

Although Tweeddale's reputation currently rests on his prominent role in the treaty of union in Scotland, it has been argued that he 'was, and to the end of his life remained, almost entirely devoid, not of ambition, but of the necessary drive and initiative for political success' (Riley, *King William*, 50).   JOHN R. YOUNG

Sources APS · *Reg. PCS*, 3rd ser., vols. 11–16 · *Scots peerage* · *Letters relating to Scotland in the reign of Queen Anne by James Ogilvy, first earl of Seafield and others*, ed. P. Hume Brown, Scottish History Society, 2nd ser., 11 (1915) · *Bishop Burnet's History of his own time*, ed. T. Burnet, 4 vols. (1815), vol. 4 · *A selection from the papers of the earls of Marchmont, 1685–1750* (1831) · *'Scotland's ruine': Lockhart of Cornwath's memoirs of the Union*, ed. D. Szechi (1995) · *Memoirs of the secret services of John Macky*, ed. A. R. (1733) · D. Haig and G. Brunton, *The senators of the college of justice* (1832) · G. Crawford, *The lives and characters of the officers of the crown and of the state in Scotland, from the beginning of King David 1st to the Union of the kingdoms* (1726) · P. W. J. Riley, *King William and the Scottish politicians* (1979) · P. W. J. Riley, *The Union of England and Scotland* (1978) · P. H. Scott, *Andrew Fletcher and the treaty of union* (1992) · *DNB*

Archives NL Scot., corresp. and papers | Buckminster Park, Grantham, corresp. with duke of Lauderdale and duchess of Lauderdale · CUL, letters to his father · NL Scot., letters to Queen Anne and earl of Godolphin

Likenesses G. Soest, oils, *c*.1670, Art Gallery and Museum, Glasgow [*see illus.*] · attrib. J. F. Voet, oils, Scot. NPG · attrib. J. F. Voet, portrait, repro. in Scott, *Andrew Fletcher*

Hay, Lord John (*d.* 1706), army officer, was the second son of John *Hay, second marquess of Tweeddale (1645–1713), and his wife, Lady Mary Maitland (*d.* 1702), only child of John Maitland, duke of Lauderdale. He entered the army in the Scots dragoons, became lieutenant-colonel of the regiment in 1694, and commanded it in the campaigns under Marlborough in 1702–3. He became colonel of the regiment by purchase in 1704, and was made a brigadier-general. Under his command the greys, the Royal Scottish dragoons, or Scots regiment of white horses, as they were sometimes called, greatly distinguished themselves in the succeeding campaigns, particularly at Schellenberg, where, dismounted, in hand-to-hand fighting they turned the battle. Later, remounted and in pursuit, the greys captured the enemy artillery and baggage train. At Ramillies in 1706 they took prisoner the famous French régiment du roi, and, according to tradition, won the distinction of wearing grenadiers' caps since enjoyed by the regiment. Hay married, first, Lady Mary Dalzell, only daughter of James, third earl of Carnwath, and Lady Mary Seton; secondly, Elizabeth, daughter of Sir Thomas Orby, bt, of Crowland, Lincolnshire; she survived him, and later married Major-General Robert Hunter. Hay died of a lingering fever at Courtrai on 25 August 1706. Marlborough wrote that his death was 'generally regretted through the whole army' (*Letters and Dispatches*, 3.105).

H. M. CHICHESTER, *rev.* TIMOTHY HARRISON PLACE

Sources Anderson, *Scot. nat.* · GEC, *Peerage* · GEC, *Baronetage*, 3.19–20 · *The letters and dispatches of John Churchill, first duke of Marlborough, from 1702 to 1712*, ed. G. Murray, 3 (1845), 105, 177 · M. Blacklock, *The royal Scots greys (the 2nd dragoons)* (1971) · E. Almack, *The history of the second dragoons, 'royal Scots greys'* (1908) · R. Cannon, ed., *Historical record of the royal regiment of Scots dragoons, now the second royal north British dragoons, commonly called the Scots greys* (1840) · P. Groves, *History of the 2nd dragoons—the royal Scots greys* (1893)
Archives NL Scot., corresp. with the first and second marquesses of Tweeddale

Hay, John, of Cromlix, Jacobite duke of Inverness (1691–1740), Jacobite courtier and army officer, was the third son of Thomas Hay, seventh earl of Kinnoull (*c*.1660–1719), and Elizabeth (1669–1696), only daughter of William *Drummond, first viscount of Strathallan. George *Hay, eighth earl of Kinnoull (*d*. 1758), was his elder brother. He inherited an estate at Cromlix, Perthshire, from his grandfather Lord Strathallan. The Hays of Kinnoull were sympathetic to the Jacobite cause, but they did not feel that their loyalty to the Stuarts was compromised by service to Queen Anne. They supported the Harley administration, and in 1714 Hay purchased a company in the foot guards. On 29 May 1715, at Aberdalgie, Perthshire, he married Marjorie Murray (*d*. in or after 1765), daughter of David Murray, fifth Viscount Stormont, and sister of James Murray, later Jacobite earl of Dunbar, and William *Murray (1705–1793), who prospered in the service of the Hanoverians and became lord chief justice of king's bench in England and first earl of Mansfield.

Hay's sister Margaret had died in 1707, but the family still had ties to her husband John *Erskine, twenty-second or sixth earl of Mar. Hay acted as political agent for Mar in Perth, an affiliation which earned him the enmity of John Murray, first duke of Atholl, and his faction. Although his presence was contested by Mar's personal servant, Hay may have accompanied Mar in disguise from Gravesend to Fife on a collier to raise the standard of rebellion in Scotland in summer 1715, and he was privy to his political plans. In Scotland, Hay was dispatched by Mar to offer command of the Jacobite army, under the overall command of James Fitzjames, duke of Berwick, who was to arrive from France, to Atholl, who refused. Instead, Hay was sent with 200 men to seize Perth, which he accomplished on 14 September 1715, after which Mar appointed him governor of the city. This appointment caused great resentment among the other Jacobites, since Hay had no actual military experience, despite his military rank. With Perth secured, Mar sent Hay to France to make contact with James Francis Edward Stuart, the Pretender, and secure more aid for the rebellion. Upon his return, Mar promoted Hay to major-general, and he was himself appointed master of the horse to the Pretender. When the 1715 rising collapsed, Hay did not flee Scotland with Mar and the Pretender, but retreated with John Sinclair, master of Sinclair, and the army to Caithness; from there he then made his way via the Orkney Islands to the Jacobite court at St Germain, France, where he was named groom of the bedchamber to the Pretender, and then with the court to Avignon. Hay was attainted by parliament in 1716, on account of his participation in the rising, and all his property was forfeited.

Joined by his wife, Hay then followed the Pretender and his swelling court of exiles from Avignon to Rome in 1717, where Hay, an episcopalian, was chagrined to have to kiss the slipper of Pope Clement XI when the Pretender visited the pope incognito. Hay was regarded highly by James, however, and on 5 October 1718 was created earl of Inverness, viscount of Innerpaphrie, and Lord Cromlex and Erne in the Jacobite Scots peerage. When a marriage was arranged between the Pretender and (Maria) Clementina Sobieska that year, Hay was dispatched to meet her at Ohlau, Silesia. Marjorie prepared to welcome the princess to Rome, only to learn that she had been imprisoned by the holy Roman emperor, Charles VI, at the request of George I. After returning to James, Hay accompanied him to Urbino and then to Spain while they waited for the princess to arrive in Italy. Hay and his wife were witnesses to the wedding at Montefiascone on 2 September 1719, and Marjorie was named one of Clementina's ladies, a post which placed the couple at the centre of the exiled Jacobite court. From this privileged position, Hay was able to express his long-standing distrust of and misgivings about Mar, who was serving as the Pretender's secretary of state and minister in Paris. In 1723 the Pretender sent Hay as his agent to Brussels, where he met with Francis Atterbury, former bishop of Rochester and architect of the unsuccessful Atterbury plot of 1721–2. While there, Hay and Atterbury, who had become convinced that Mar was a double agent, outlined a plan by which Atterbury would convince the Pretender of Mar's perfidy and Hay would take his place as secretary of state, while Atterbury would replace Mar as minister in Paris. Atterbury's letters succeeded in undermining the Pretender's confidence in Mar, and late in 1724 Hay was offered the position of secretary of state. New circumstances prevented him from accepting immediately. Early in 1723 Hay had stopped receiving money from his elder brother Kinnoull, who wished to build a career in the service of George I. Hay was anxious to secure further sources of revenue, and sent his wife to Britain to consult members of their families, but she was arrested on 3 / 14 September 1724 on landing at Dover, and imprisoned in Newgate for six months. This was a serious insult, as it placed her among common criminals; there she was interrogated several times by Charles, second Viscount Townshend, secretary of state to George I. Her brother William asked Hay's great-uncle James Johnston, who had been secretary of state in Scotland under William III, for advice, but Johnston only suggested capitulation to the government or a request for safe passage to the continent. In the end, Clementina, who was particularly attached to Marjorie and wanted her to attend the birth of her second child as she had the first, petitioned the British government for Marjorie's release, which was granted, and Marjorie returned in time to witness the delivery of Prince Henry Benedict. With Marjorie no longer a hostage, Hay accepted the position of secretary of state in March 1725, when he began to use the Jacobite earldom awarded in 1718.

Hay was a devoted and trusted servant to the Pretender, but his protestantism, as well as his elder brother's acceptance of a pension and service as a diplomat to George I, made him the object of suspicion among his rivals at the exiled court. Many Jacobites became convinced that during Marjorie's imprisonment the Hays had agreed to become agents for the British government. The rumour may have been originated by Cardinal Giulio Alberoni, who became close to Clementina at this time, and encouraged her deepening resentment of the Hays. He and Mrs Sheldon, the governess to Prince Charles Edward, became the focus of a 'queen's party' that exploited Clementina's depression and religious devotion to turn her against the Hays. Hay had been remarking on the deteriorating state of the Pretender's marriage in letters to Mar at Paris, and Mar had exploited Hay's naivety in confiding in him by circulating Hay's opinions in Paris. About this time Hay wrote to Clementina assuring her that his wife was not the Pretender's mistress as was alleged. Hay was associated with the appointment of his brother-in-law James Murray, a protestant, as governor to Prince Charles Edward in 1725, supplanting Mrs Sheldon, who protested to the Pretender and was ordered from Rome as a result; in response Clementina left James and took up residence in a convent, Mrs Sheldon taking refuge in another, and Hay's position as the Pretender's confidant was cited by Clementina as her grievance.

Meanwhile, Hay and Atterbury seized an opportunity for another try at retrieving the crown for their master. In 1725 the French government, needing to marry off Louis XV so that he could begin producing heirs and avoid a disputed succession, sent home the child Spanish infanta to whom the king had been engaged, outraging Spain, who then formed an alliance with Austria. In the hopes of using this to their advantage, Hay and Atterbury dispatched agents to Vienna and Madrid, and began talks with Russia to attempt to draw her into attacking Britain's allies in northern Europe. This was to be complemented by a rising in the highlands spearheaded by William Mackenzie, fifth earl of Seaforth. Instead of ending in triumph, the plan collapsed as Seaforth double-crossed the Jacobites by using his knowledge of the plot to buy a pardon and the restoration of his estates, and the diplomats of Europe smoothed out their differences before the international embarrassment of the return of the infanta could flare into actual war.

Following this disaster, Hay's influence at court steadily waned under the sniping of Clementina and her Catholic circle of courtiers. Hay's position was undermined further by the enmity of Pope Benedict XIII (who believed the enduring gossip that Marjorie was the Pretender's mistress and feared that Hay and Dunbar were bringing up the Pretender's sons as protestants) and by Clementina herself. With Alberoni's assistance, Clementina wrote to Louis XV, Queen Elisabeth of Spain, Atterbury, and others, describing the Hays as 'persons that have no religion, honour nor conscience' (Miller, 279) and declaring that she would not live under the same roof with them. The breach contributed towards the removal of the Jacobite court, including the Hays, from Rome to Bologna in October 1727. Sympathy at the courts of France and Spain was with Clementina, and Hay realized that his presence was hindering the progress of the Jacobite cause. He resigned as secretary of state on 3 April 1727, and was replaced by Sir John Graham, formerly his agent at Vienna. He was compensated with a Jacobite English peerage, as Baron Hay, and a promotion in the Jacobite Scottish peerage to duke of Inverness.

The Hays moved to Pisa, but the Pretender remained close to his friend, and wrote affectionate letters to him describing the progress of the two princes. In June 1727, upon learning of the death of George I, Hay accompanied the Pretender to Nancy in Lorraine, to discuss options for another rising, which never materialized. When the Pretender was reconciled to Clementina, Hay remained behind. In 1728 he was called to meet the Pretender in Parma and was offered restoration to the secretaryship, which he declined as he did not want to endanger the reconciliation between James and Clementina. The Hays moved in 1731 from Pisa to Avignon, where Hay converted to Catholicism that year. This was a pathetic attempt to win the queen's favour, paralleled by the conversion of Philip, duke of Wharton, in 1726, which had sought to gain support from the Spanish court. To the Catholic Jacobite courtiers, the conversion confirmed their opinion of Hay as a cynical favourite, and Clementina was unmoved. Protestant Jacobites felt the conversion seriously damaged their cause, and Atterbury was convinced that Hay was indeed an agent of the British government bent on destroying the movement's credibility. In April 1736, following the death of Clementina, Hay returned to Rome and rejoined the personal circle of the Pretender as one of the last remaining Jacobites of the Pretender's generation, although with no official position. He was welcomed by Roman society at large, but his enemies at court now said he had come to unseat James Murray, and rather than be the cause of further disputes he returned to Avignon in July. Suffering from gout, Hay died at Avignon on 24 September 1740 and was buried there, leaving behind no children. His widow was still alive on 25 December 1765, when James Boswell spent Christmas with her and the earl of Dunbar at Avignon—Boswell thought her 'a lively, clever, agreeable woman' (*Boswell on the Grand Tour*, 262). The forfeited Cromlix estate had been retrieved by the family for his nephew Robert Hay *Drummond (1711–1776). Although innocent of the charges of duplicity levelled at him by his rivals at the small and intrigue-ridden Jacobite court, Hay was only a devoted, not a talented, servant, and his lack of qualification and experience did little to advance the Pretender's cause.

MARGARET D. SANKEY

Sources H. Tayler, ed., *The Jacobite court at Rome in 1719* (1938) · J. Sinclair, *Memoirs of the insurrection in Scotland* (1858) · Royal Arch., Stuart papers · marquess of Ruvigny and Raineval, *The Jacobite peerage* (1904) · P. Miller, *James* (New York, 1971) · E. Gregg, 'The politics of paranoia', *The Jacobite challenge*, ed. E. Cruickshanks and J. Black (1988), 42–56 · F. McLynn, *Charles Edward Stuart* (1988) · GEC, *Peerage*, new edn, 7.68–9 · *Boswell on the grand tour: Italy, Corsica, and France, 1765–1766*, ed. F. Brady and F. A. Pottle (1955), vol. 5 of *The Yale editions of the private papers of James Boswell*, trade edn (1950–89)
Archives NRA, priv. coll., papers | BL, corresp. with F. Gualterio, Add. MSS 20295, fols. 380–406, 20303, 20316 · BL, letters to F. A. Gualterio, Add. MSS 31264–31266 · NA Scot., corresp. with T. Gordon · NL Scot., letters to Alexander Robertson [copies] · Royal Arch., Stuart MSS
Wealth at death estates forfeited; lived on pension which ceased at death

Hay, John, fourth marquess of Tweeddale (1695–1762), politician, was born in 1695, probably at Yester in Haddingtonshire, the eldest son of Charles Hay, third marquess (*c*.1666–1715), and his wife, Lady Susan Hamilton (*d*. 1737), third daughter of Anne *Hamilton, duchess of Hamilton in her own right, and William Douglas, duke of Hamilton [*see* Hamilton, William (1634–1694)]. He may have matriculated at Edinburgh University and may also have undergone some legal training. He succeeded his father as fourth marquess in 1715. Scottish politics at this time was marked by bitter rivalry between the squadrone and the Argathelians, followers of John Campbell, second duke of Argyll, and his brother, Archibald, earl of Ilay. Like his father and grandfather (the second marquess, who had formed the party), Tweeddale adhered to the squadrone. In 1721 he was appointed an extraordinary lord of session and as such repeatedly voted in favour of the nomination of Patrick Haldane, a squadrone supporter, to the bench against bitter Argathelian opposition. Haldane was eventually forced to give up. The government then passed an act in 1724 which provided that when the existing extraordinary lords died, no replacements were to be appointed. The post finally lapsed with Tweeddale's death in 1762.

In 1722 Tweeddale was elected on the squadrone interest as one of the sixteen representative peers to sit in the Lords for Scotland. He was re-elected in 1727. During the 1730s he was active in the opposition to Walpole and along with other squadrone peers unsuccessfully opposed the king's list, from which they had been excluded, at the representative peers election of 1734. For a time he deserted politics, concentrating on improving his estate at Yester, Haddingtonshire.

In opposition Tweeddale had become a friend and political ally of Carteret, who was appointed a secretary of state in the new ministry following the resignation of Walpole in February 1742. On the strength of his connections with Carteret, Tweeddale was appointed on 15 February principal secretary of state for Scotland and keeper of the signet. In April he returned to the Lords as a representative peer following the death of Charles Hope, first earl of Hopetoun. He also became governor of the Bank of Scotland, a post he held until his death. Carteret's intention was to bypass the entrenched position of the Argathelians in Scotland. Tweeddale, however, had little political influence in Scotland, even compared to other squadrone peers, most of whom resented his elevation and withdrew from politics during his secretaryship. Temperamentally he was unsuited to political management; he fussed but rarely took decisive action. His lack of a political power base in Scotland, coupled with the instability of the English ministry, was at the root of all the difficulties he faced in trying to control Scotland over the next four years. He also received little support from Carteret, who was preoccupied with foreign affairs and with safeguarding his own position within the ministry. As far as Scottish affairs were concerned, Carteret lacked the energy to support an overhaul of the administration and despite his earlier intentions was content with a Scotland that was kept out of political controversy. As a result, Tweeddale was able to make little headway and most Argathelian supporters remained in office.

Tweeddale, who went to Scotland only once—in 1742—during his time in office, sought to manage Scotland through a small group of advisers—Lord Advocate Robert Craigie, Robert Dundas, Lord Arniston, his son Solicitor-General Robert Dundas, and the deputy keeper of the signet, Thomas Hay—but they frequently quarrelled among themselves. Their position was further weakened by Tweeddale's obsession with secrecy and by his unwillingness to take his advisers fully into his confidence. His failure to make widespread changes and dismantle the influence which the Argathelians had built up within the administration quickly disillusioned his friends and potential supporters. The appointment of Charles Erskine, previously Argathelian lord advocate, to the bench in November 1744 and the resignation of Carteret later that month destroyed any remaining authority Tweeddale had both within the ministry and in Scotland, and effectively ended his administration. He clung to office for another year or so but it was clear to all that he had no real power or influence.

Thus during the first half of 1745 there was a lack of any real government in Scotland, and Tweeddale failed to take any precautionary measures against the Jacobite threat. When the uprising did break out, Tweeddale was not up to the crisis. At first he tried to minimize the threat and then, through a large part of the critical November when the

Jacobite army was marching south, he was unable to get to cabinet meetings because of gout. He was almost totally bypassed as far as official business was concerned and finally resigned on 4 January 1746. The office of secretary for Scotland was not revived until 1885, and not advanced to full secretary of state rank until 1926. Tweeddale's failure also saw the end of the squadrone as a coherent political group.

Tweeddale continued to be returned as a representative peer at the elections of 1747, 1754, and 1761 but played little further active part in politics. On 24 May 1748 he married Carteret's daughter Lady Frances Carteret (*bap.* 1718, *d.* 1758), and they had a family of two sons and four daughters. The marchioness died on 25 December 1758. In 1755 Tweeddale was appointed to the annexed estates commission. In June 1761 he was appointed lord justice general, on Ilay's death, but by this stage he was severely disabled and could barely stand. He died in London on 9 December 1762, and was privately buried at Yester.

RICHARD SCOTT

Sources J. Hay, fourth marquess of Tweeddale, correspondence, NL Scot., Yester MSS YP 7044–7119; SYP Acc. 7174 · R. Scott, 'The politics and administration of Scotland, 1725–48', PhD diss., U. Edin., 1982, esp. chap. 11 · microfilm of letterbooks kept in Arniston House, Midlothian, NA Scot., Arniston MSS, RH/4/15/2–4, vols. 2–5 · R. Douglas, *The peerage of Scotland*, 2nd edn, ed. J. P. Wood, 2 vols. (1813) · J. S. Shaw, *The management of Scottish society, 1707–1764: power, nobles, lawyers, Edinburgh agents and English influences* (1983) · R. Mitchison, 'The government and the highlands', *Scotland in the age of improvement*, ed. N. T. Phillipson and R. Mitchison (1970), 24–46 · *DNB* · GEC, *Peerage*, new edn

Archives NL Scot., corresp. and MSS | BL, corresp. with duke of Newcastle, Add. MSS 32699–32918 *passim* · NA Scot., Arniston MSS; letters to Robert Craigie; letters to Sir Andrew Mitchell · NL Scot., corresp. with Duncan Forbes

Likenesses W. Aikman, oils, *c.*1728, Scot. NPG

Hay, Lord John (1793–1851), naval officer and politician, third son of George Hay, seventh marquess of Tweeddale (1753–1804), and his wife, Hannah Charlotte Maitland (*d.* 8 May 1804), daughter of James Maitland, seventh earl of Lauderdale, was born in Scotland on 1 April 1793. In December 1804 he was nominally entered on the books of the *Monarch*, Lord Keith's flagship in the Downs, but it seems probable that he did not in fact enter the service until December 1806, when he joined the *Sea-horse* (42 guns), going to the Mediterranean. He remained in this ship until June 1811, and saw much active service, losing his left arm in a cutting-out expedition in Hyères Roads in 1807, and sharing in the capture of a Turkish ship of fifty-two guns on 5 July 1808. He was made lieutenant in April 1812 and in June was appointed to the *Pique*, going to the West Indies. In May 1814 he transferred to the *Venerable*, carrying the flag of Sir Philip Durham, and was promoted commander on 15 June. In November he was appointed to the *Bustard* at Lisbon, and in 1815 commissioned the *Opossum*, which he commanded on the channel and Halifax stations until August 1818. He was promoted captain on 7 December.

Hay was MP for Haddington burghs from 1826 to 1830, but as a whig had no employment afloat until September 1832, when he was appointed to the frigate *Castor*. In November 1836 he was transferred to the steamship *Phoenix*, and in March 1837 to the *North Star*, which he paid off in 1840. For a great part of this time he was employed as commander of a small squadron on the north coast of Spain during the First Carlist War, and was frequently landed in command of a naval and marine brigade. In acknowledgement of his services, especially at the siege of Bilbao, he received the CB in February 1837, and the grand cross of Charles III. From August 1841 to October 1843 he commanded the *Warspite* (50 guns) on the North America and West Indies station. He married, on 2 September 1846, Mary Anne (*d.* 30 Nov 1850), eldest daughter of Donald Cameron of Lochiel; they had no children. In 1846 Hay was briefly superintendent of Woolwich Dockyard, and in 1847 was returned to parliament as member for Windsor. From 1846 to 1850 he was a junior sea lord of the Admiralty.

An experienced steam and sail officer, Hay exploded the invasion scare of 1847–8 in an important memorandum (16 January 1848) for Lord Auckland. As a junior sea lord he chaired the committee of reference on designs that was used to engineer the retirement of the surveyor of navy, Sir William Symonds. However, when he tried to direct the development of the steam warship his ideas proved unsound, the committee was broken up, and the task was left to the new surveyor, Captain Sir Baldwin Walker. Hay was appointed commodore-superintendent of Devonport Dockyard on 9 February 1850, and his removal there reflected the desire of the first lord, Sir Francis Baring, to direct the policy of the board himself. Hay was still in this post at the time of his death, at Devonport Dockyard, on 9 September 1851, two days after he had hoisted his flag as rear-admiral on the *St George*.

As a well-connected Scottish whig Hay had the connections to succeed under the earl of Minto. He proved politically adept on the coast of Spain, but he was less influential under Lord Auckland and was removed from office by Baring. He delighted in power, but his outdated views on naval technology—notably the application of the screw propeller to the battle fleet—and his conduct at the board made him a liability.

J. K. LAUGHTON, *rev.* ANDREW LAMBERT

Sources A. D. Lambert, *The last sailing battlefleet: maintaining naval mastery, 1815–1850* (1991) · C. J. Bartlett, *Great Britain and sea power, 1815–1853* (1963) · 'Select committee on navy, army, and ordnance estimates', *Parl. papers* (1847–8), vol. 21/1, no. 555; vol. 21/2, no. 555-II · PRO, Admiralty MSS · O'Byrne, *Naval biog. dict.* · NMM, Minto MSS · GEC, *Peerage*, new edn · Burke, *Peerage* (1907)

Archives NL Scot., family corresp. | Bodl. Oxf., letters to fourth earl of Clarendon · NL Scot., letters to Lord Tweeddale · NMM, corresp. with Lord Minto · NRA, priv. coll., letters to Sir Charles Adams

Hay, Sir John (1816–1892), politician and pastoralist in Australia, was born on 23 June 1816 at Little Ythsie, Aberdeenshire, the eldest son of John Hay (*b. c.*1790), a farmer, and his wife, Jean Mair (*b. c.*1794). He was educated at King's College, University of Aberdeen (MA, 1834), and then studied law in Edinburgh, but did not enter the profession.

On 28 February 1838 Hay married Mary (*c.*1820–1892), the daughter of James Chalmers. They had no children.

That same year the couple emigrated to Australia and settled at Walaregang in the Upper Murray region of New South Wales, where they established a successful squatting run. Hay was elected, as a conservative, for the seat of Murrumbidgee in 1856, and held the seat until a redistribution in 1858, after which he represented Murray (1858–64) and then Central Cumberland (until 1867). Taking the role of 'the leading squatter in the house' (Hirst, 147), Hay immediately established himself as a political force. He carried a motion of no confidence in the new Cowper ministry on the basis of questions regarding the fitness of Cowper's chosen attorney-general, James Martin, to hold office. Hay became secretary for lands and public works in the subsequent ministry, which itself fell the following year.

In 1860 the issue of land reform was the central political question. The government's proposed bill, which allowed small free selection of land, was strongly opposed by Hay, again representing the squatter interest, on the basis that it 'would destroy the pastoral interest and injure the revenue by diminishing the value of pastoral property' (*Sydney Morning Herald*, 21 Jan 1892). The government was defeated on the bill and resigned, although it won the ensuing election easily.

Hay became speaker of the legislative assembly in October 1862, but resigned in 1865 on account of ill health. In 1867 he was appointed to the legislative council, where he was elected president in 1873. He was knighted in 1878. Although he was respected for his impartiality during his long tenure in the chair's role, Hay's 'artificial and affected' manner (Martin, 'Hay, Sir John') and his tendency to treat 'the locally born and educated with supercilious condescension' (Grainger, 85) were often noted. His politics had a very narrow, but non-party, focus. He had, said one commentator, 'a reverence for No. 1 exceedingly profound' (Martin, 'Hay, Sir John').

Hay died on 20 January 1892 at his home in Rose Bay, Sydney, and was buried two days later at Waverley cemetery, Sydney.   MARC BRODIE

Sources *Sydney Morning Herald* (21 Jan 1892), 8 · A. W. Martin, 'Hay, Sir John', *AusDB*, vol. 4 · J. B. Hirst, *The strange birth of colonial democracy: New South Wales, 1848–1884* (1988) · C. N. Connolly, *Biographical register of the New South Wales parliament, 1856–1901* (1983) · E. Grainger, *Martin of Martin Place: a biography of Sir James Martin* (1970) · *IGI* · A. W. Martin, *Henry Parkes: a biography* (1980) · *DNB*
Archives Mitchell L., NSW, letters | Mitchell L., NSW, Parkes MSS
Likenesses A. Simonetti, marble bust, 1879–89, Legislative Council, Sydney, New South Wales · E. Dalton, photograph, Mitchell L., NSW · W. Sargent, group portrait, photograph (*Magistrates of Sydney*), Mitchell L., NSW

Hay, Lord John (1827–1916), naval officer and politician, was the ninth child and fourth son of George Hay, eighth marquess of Tweeddale (1787–1876) and his wife, Lady Susan Montagu (1797–1870), daughter of the duke of Manchester. He was born in Geneva on 23 August 1827. His namesake uncle significantly furthered his early career. He joined the navy in 1839, and served in the *Vestal* on the China station from 1842 to 1847, including the final stages

of the First Anglo-Chinese War. He was promoted lieutenant on 19 December 1846, and came home in the following year with the steam sloop *Spiteful*. Between 1848 and 1851 he served in the *Powerful* (Captain Richard Dundas) in the Mediterranean, and on 28 August 1851 he was promoted commander. He returned to the Mediterranean as commander of the steam screw sloop *Wasp* in 1852 and remained in her during the Eastern crisis of 1853 and Black Sea campaign of 1854, playing a noteworthy part in the defence of Eupatoria in November.

Hay was made captain on 27 November 1854, by which time he and most of his crew were serving ashore with the naval brigade. He left the command of the *Wasp* in February 1855, and was wounded on 9 April while serving ashore. He then returned to Britain, and was made a CB on 5 July 1855. In December he was appointed to command the screw mortar frigate *Forte*, part of the 'great armament' assembled for an assault on Kronstadt in early 1856. After participating in the Spithead review of St George's day, which both celebrated the peace and issued a warning to rival powers, he continued in the ship until November that year. After he came ashore he took the parliamentary seat for Wick, but on the return to office of Palmerston in 1859 he was appointed to the paddle frigate *Odin* for the East Indies and China station. He commanded a division of gunboats during the second capture of the Taku (Dagu) forts in August 1860, and became commodore on the station in 1861, remaining there until 1863.

Having been elected MP for Ripon, a pocket borough controlled by Earl De Grey, in April 1866 Hay joined the Admiralty board, serving out the last three months of Russell's Liberal administration. Defeated at the polls in 1867, he returned to his Ripon seat in 1868 and rejoined the board. His tact and good sense helped to keep naval administration functioning during the turbulent period under Hugh Childers, when the Admiralty board was reduced to a cipher and the senior personnel were engaged in a bitter power struggle. In May 1871, shortly after the resignation of Childers, Hay resigned both his seats and took command of the ironclad *Hotspur* until his promotion to rear-admiral on 7 May 1872. From 1875 to 1876 he was second in command of the Channel Fleet. During this command he married Annie Christina, daughter of Norman Lambert MP, of Denham Court, Buckinghamshire.

Hay was appointed commander-in-chief of the Channel Fleet in November 1877, and was promoted vice-admiral on 21 December 1877. During the strategic redeployment caused by the Russo-Turkish War of 1877–8 and the Russian war scare of 1878 he took three battleships from his fleet to reinforce the Mediterranean Fleet. Under the Cyprus convention he took formal possession of the island from the Turkish authorities on 8 July 1879. In 1880 he returned to the Admiralty as second naval lord on Lord Northbrook's board. He resigned in February 1883 to become commander-in-chief in the Mediterranean, in the *Alexandra* (Captain Rawson), where his fleet supplied naval parties to survey the Nile and support the Gordon relief expedition. While in the Mediterranean, Hay tried to draw attention to the weakness of the navy, but was largely ignored until the 'truth about the navy' alarm generated by Admiral Sir Geoffrey Hornby and W. T. Stead in 1884. In February 1885 Hay served as commander of an international fleet blockading Crete, then a Turkish possession, against Greek intervention.

Hay left the Mediterranean command in March 1886, and that year was briefly first naval lord, under his old friend and patron the marquess of Ripon. Between May 1887 and December 1888 Hay served as commander-in-chief at Devonport, and on hauling down his flag he was promoted admiral of the fleet. He was placed on the retired list on 23 August 1897, and died at his home, Fulmer Place, Fulmer, Buckinghamshire, on 4 May 1916; his wife survived him. Hay was one of the last 'political' admirals: his family connections and Liberal politics played a vital part in his career, though his service in the Crimea and China justified his promotion. His Admiralty service always coincided with Liberal administrations, as did almost all his seagoing commands. An officer of solid talents, he had a career crowned with a rare distinction, even though he lacked the eminence of his near contemporary Geoffrey Hornby.   ANDREW LAMBERT

Sources WWW, 1929–40 · A. J. Marder, *The anatomy of British sea power*, American edn (1940) · W. L. Clowes, *The Royal Navy: a history from the earliest times to the present*, 7 vols. (1897–1903), vol. 7 · J. W. D. Dundas and C. Napier, *Russian war, 1854, Baltic and Black Sea: official correspondence*, ed. D. Bonner-Smith and A. C. Dewar, Navy RS, 83 (1943) · H. J. Hanham, *Elections and party management: politics in the time of Disraeli and Gladstone* (1959) · J. H. Briggs, *Naval administration, 1827 to 1892: the experience of 65 years*, ed. Lady Briggs (1897) · L. Wolf, *Life of Lord Ripon* (1921) · CGPLA Eng. & Wales (1916) · Burke, *Peerage* · J. F. Beeler, *British naval policy in the Gladstone–Disraeli era, 1866–1880* (1997)
Archives Bodl. Oxf., letters to fourth earl of Clarendon; corresp. with Lord Kimberley · NL Scot., letters to Sir Charles Adam; letters to Lord Tweeddale · NMM, corresp. with Lord Minto
Likenesses W. S. Cumming, watercolour, 1892, NPG
Wealth at death £8149 12s. 9d.: probate, 24 June 1916, CGPLA Eng. & Wales

Hay, Sir John Charles Dalrymple, third baronet (1821–1912), naval officer and politician, was born at 113 Princes Street, Edinburgh, on 11 February 1821, eldest surviving son of Sir James Dalrymple Hay, second baronet (1788–1861), and his wife, Elizabeth, *née* Maxwell (d. 1821). Hay's career was dominated by his close family ties and friendship with prominent Scottish naval officers, including the Cochranes and Sir Houston Stewart. In 1833 Hay entered Rugby School. In 1834 he joined the navy as a first-class volunteer aboard the frigate *Thalia*, flagship of Rear-Admiral Campbell on the Cape of Good Hope station. In 1835 and 1836 he served in the brig *Trinculo* on the west coast of Africa anti-slavery patrol, and was very nearly turned out of the navy by Sir Robert Peel's brief administration, which disapproved of his entry by the preceding Admiralty board. After his return to Britain in 1836 Hay was briefly appointed to the *Minden* (72 guns) in the channel squadron before he joined the frigate *Imogene* (Captain Henry Bruce) for the South America and Pacific station. On 25 January 1837 he became a midshipman. He returned to Britain in November 1839 and then joined the *Benbow*

(72 guns, Captain Houston Stewart) in the Mediterranean. During the Syrian campaign of 1840 he was noticed for his conduct during the boat attack on Tortosa on 26 August. Having been passed for lieutenant on 17 February 1841, he joined the steamer *Spiteful* (Captain William Maitland) for the China station in late 1842. Despite a severe illness Hay remained on the station, relying on his relative, the new commander-in-chief Admiral Sir Thomas Cochrane, for promotion. In October 1844 he was appointed by Cochrane his flag lieutenant aboard the *Agincourt*, where he served for a year before promotion to commander of the *Wolverine* on 28 August 1846. He returned home in 1847.

On 18 August 1847 Hay married the Hon. Eliza Napier, third daughter of William Napier, eighth Baron Napier. He was appointed to the brig *Columbine* in December, and joined her in Chinese waters. In 1849 he engaged and destroyed the fleet of the notorious pirate Shap'ngtzai. In the first action with a pirate squadron, on 28–9 September 1849, he was helped by the P. & O. steamer *Canton*. The main pirate fleet was pursued by Hay, with the steamers *Fury* and *Phlegethon*, and destroyed in the Tonkin River. There were no British casualties. For this service Hay was promoted post captain on 20 January 1850. He attended the Royal Naval College at Portsmouth in 1851, and saw no further service until 1853, when he was appointed captain of HMS *Victory*, flagship of Vice-Admiral Sir Thomas Cochrane at Portsmouth. Early in 1854 Vice-Admiral Sir Charles Napier applied for him as flag captain for the Baltic fleet, but Cochrane and Sir James Graham, the first lord, retained him at Portsmouth to supervise the manning of ships being fitted for service.

At the end of 1854 Hay took command of the steam screw battleship *Hannibal* (91 guns) in the Black Sea as flag captain to Rear-Admiral Houston Stewart. He took part in the capture of Kerch and Kinburn and the re-embarkation of the Crimean army. When the *Hannibal* paid off in October 1856 Hay followed Stewart, and in 1857, after an illness, took command of the sailing battleship *Indus* (70 guns), flagship on the North America and West Indies station. He left the *Indus* in September 1859 and came ashore for the last time. In October he served on the royal commission to investigate the Royal Naval Hospital, Greenwich, and the following year he chaired the committee to inquire into armour plate, which sat for nearly five years. This resulted in his election as a fellow of the Royal Society in 1864.

On 19 March 1861 he became third baronet, and in March 1862 Hay was elected Conservative MP for Wakefield and continued in parliament until July 1865. His main themes were the crowded state of the navy list, and the inadequacy of the navy. He secured the payment of the prize money for the capture of Kerch in 1862. In June 1864 he became chairman of the Millwall Shipbuilding Company and several other commercial concerns. On 6 April 1866 he was promoted rear-admiral, missing the offer of a ship. A month later he was elected for Stamford, a seat at the disposal of Lord Exeter, which he retained for the next fourteen years. In 1866 he was appointed junior naval lord in the Derby ministry, and by threatening to resign helped to secure four new battleships, which did not endear him to Disraeli, who, as chancellor, wanted to keep down the estimates. He directed the transport arrangements of the Abyssinia campaign.

On 1 March 1870 Hay, who had not served afloat as an admiral and was only forty-nine years old, was placed on the list of officers to be retired under the reform introduced by the Liberal first lord, Hugh Childers. When Hay protested in parliament, Childers offered him the East Indies command, but this was refused on the advice of Disraeli. Hay had applied for a command while at the board, but had been dissuaded by his political colleagues. He was offered the post of first or second naval lord in 1874 by Disraeli, but turned this down as he believed that retired officers should not be placed in authority over those still serving. Disraeli did not reappoint him to the active list—Hay's friend Henry Corry had promised to do so, but he had died in 1873. Hay remained on the retired list, serving as chairman of the explosive substances committee. In 1874 he published *Ashanti and the Gold Coast*, which dealt with an area he had visited in his youth (1834–5). During the 1878 Russian war scare, Hay advised Disraeli to reinforce the fleet by purchasing four ironclads that were being built in Britain for foreign powers. In 1880 Hay lost his seat at Stamford, but was returned for the Wigton burghs until he stepped down in 1886. He was made CB (1869), KCB (1885), and GCB (1902). He was one of the last admirals to believe that it was possible for a naval officer to be first lord. In 1898 he published his memoirs, *Lines from my Log-Books*. He died at his London home, 108 St George's Square, on 28 January 1912, leaving three sons and five daughters.

Hay entered the navy surrounded by relatives and close friends, and his marriage to a daughter of Lord Napier increased the family group to include almost every significant Scottish sea officer. An able, hard-working, and well-connected officer, Hay reached the rank of captain through the support of Sir Thomas Cochrane and his own exertions. He never commanded a private ship as a captain, and despite his talents and youth was denied the opportunity for a flag appointment. His later career was dominated by tory politics, and by the animus against him and the navy generally that was evident in Disraeli's conduct before 1878.   ANDREW LAMBERT

Sources J. C. D. Hay, *Lines from my log-books* (1898) • O'Byrne, *Naval biog. dict.* • W. L. Clowes, *The Royal Navy: a history from the earliest times to the present*, 7 vols. (1897–1903), vols. 6–7 • R. Blake, *Disraeli* (1966) • *CGPLA Eng. & Wales* (1912) • Burke, *Peerage* • J. F. Beeler, *British naval policy in the Gladstone–Disraeli era, 1866–1880* (1997)
Archives BL, corresp. with Lord Ripon, Add. MS 43636
Likenesses portrait, repro. in Hay, *Lines from my log-books*, frontispiece
Wealth at death £11,442 1s. 1d.: confirmation, 24 June 1912, CCI

Hay, Sir John George (1883–1964), East India merchant, was born on 1 February 1883 at 5 Craigholm Crescent, Burntisland, Fife, the seventh child in a family of ten children of Peter Hay, a village shopkeeper, and his wife, Jane Hedderwick Nisbet. He was privately educated. At the age of seventeen he went to work in a draper's shop. Later

he obtained an accountancy qualification at night school and moved on to work as a clerk at Aberdeen railway station. In 1904 he followed a friend to London and to the employ of Guthrie & Co. Ltd as an assistant cashier.

Guthries was a traditional agency house based in Singapore and London, and its chairman, Sir John Anderson, was emerging as leader in the development of Malaya's nascent rubber industry through the provision of a wide range of secretarial, accountancy, and other agency services to a large number of publicly quoted plantation companies. Such relationships gave the management of Guthries, a private company, great power, for in effect it controlled the policy, purchases, and sales of the public companies it served. By the time of the First World War, when Malaya's rubber industry was the world's largest, Guthries was reckoned the oldest and greatest mercantile firm in south-east Asia. Hay was to be its most important leader from the 1920s to the 1960s, and a key figure in the international rubber industry.

The early expansion of Malaya's rubber production required considerable capital, which was raised mostly through London stock exchange flotations. To facilitate this, in 1902 Guthries had established a companies department in London, to which Hay was appointed. In the decade before the First World War, when rubber prices and production boomed, he was absorbed in the process of converting privately owned plantations into public companies. His most important creation was the giant Sua Betong Rubber Estates Ltd in 1909, of which he was successively secretary, director, and chairman until his death. In 1910 Hay married his neighbour in London's Forest Hill, Constance Maye (d. 1959), daughter of Thomas Leveritt of Bath; they had one son and two daughters.

As the most influential if not the most senior figure in Guthries' London office, Hay dominated his department, where he never learnt to delegate. As his mettle showed through, he competed vigorously with Anderson, who had returned to London in 1912; their relationship ruptured entirely in 1924 when Anderson, from his deathbed, sacked Hay. Anderson, sole owner of the business, appointed his wife to succeed him as chairman but so strong was Hay's grip that within a year he was fully reinstated. He became general manager and acquired a sixth share of the business.

In the context of plummeting prices throughout much of the inter-war period, Hay came into his own as the first industry leader to view rubber production as a global rather than as a local issue. He was too junior to play a part in a discredited scheme in 1922 to control rubber prices through restricting international production, but he became its most vociferous critic, petitioning for its abolition. This was achieved in 1928. Working through the Rubber Growers' Association, in 1934 he brought the rubber producing nations together in the International Rubber Regulation Committee, which effectively controlled international production and prices; undoubtedly he was its most influential and effective member.

Hay foresaw the outbreak of war in 1939 and persuaded

the rubber committee to increase international production of what would be a critical and profitable wartime material. In 1940 and 1941, with plenipotentiary powers, he persuaded the Americans to purchase virtually the entire output of Malaya's rubber industry, thereby establishing a vital wartime stockpile in allied hands. Hay became chairman of very many of the 'managed' companies which comprised the so-called Guthrie group; by 1945 he sat on the boards of twenty-one commodity-producing companies and was chairman of fourteen. Confronted by the devastating fall in rubber prices from the 1920s, he ruthlessly drove down production costs and diversified the companies into new activities such as oil palm production. After the war, to head off competition from synthetic rubber producers, Hay again tackled production costs, pioneered the replacement of existing rubber trees with higher-yielding clones, and established in Malaya a research station and a cadet scheme to train Malay boys as assistants and managers.

In 1950 Hay sold back his sixth share in the business to the Anderson family and in the late 1950s he lobbied hard for a reorganization. This resulted in 1961 in nine of the companies managed by Guthries breaking away to form Guthrie Estates Agency Ltd, essentially a co-operative from which secretarial and agency services were purchased. Hay was chairman of many of these managed companies and was both chairman and managing director of the new business; notwithstanding his seventy-eight years he exercised total control. This produced in 1963 an acrimonious boardroom quarrel, which led to the resignation of almost the entire board. Hay refused to be coerced by such tactics, and he appointed his managers as successor directors and withstood calls in the press for his resignation. He was still chairman and in control when he died in 1964, but the very public dispute was not to his credit; he had stayed in the job for too long and had failed to find his own successor.

Although something of a dandy, the elegant appearance of this strong-willed Scot belied his ruthlessness and his extraordinary determination to have his way. Hay was sharp-tongued and outspoken and made exceptional demands on his colleagues, but no one doubted his ability nor questioned his position as the most important figure in the international rubber industry from the 1930s to the 1950s. He was knighted in 1939 and also received honours in the Netherlands and in Malaya. Hay died at his home, Hawthorn Dene, Westcott, Surrey, on 26 May 1964.

JOHN ORBELL

Sources S. Cunyngham-Brown, *The traders: a story of Britain's southeast Asian commercial adventure* (1971) · R. P. T. Davenport-Hines and G. Jones, eds., *British business in Asia since 1860* (1989) · *The Times* (27 May 1964) · *Financial Times* (27 May 1964) · *CGPLA Eng. & Wales* (1964) · b. cert. · *WWW*
Likenesses W. Hutchinson, portrait
Wealth at death £531,335: probate, 14 Aug 1964, *CGPLA Eng. & Wales*

Hay, Sir John Hay Drummond- (1816–1893), diplomatist, was the third son of Edward William Auriol Drummond-

Hay (d. 1845), and Louisa Margaret, daughter of John Thomason, deputy commissary-general; he was the nephew of Robert Auriol Hay, ninth earl of Kinnoull. Drummond-Hay was born on 1 June 1816 at Valenciennes, where his father was major on Lord Lynedoch's staff in the army of occupation in France. He was educated at Charterhouse School from 1827 to 1832, when he joined his father, then consul-general of Morocco, at Tangier. He entered the diplomatic service as a paid attaché under Ponsonby and, at the relatively early age of twenty-four, served as attaché under Stratford Canning at Constantinople, although he spent most of the year 1840 working in Egypt.

Drummond-Hay's achievements as a diplomatist were mainly identified with his term of over forty years in Morocco. After a visit to England, Stockholm, and Copenhagen, in 1844 he was sent to Morocco as assistant to the acting consul-general to help with communications with the court of Morocco at a time of tension with the French government. Although only a paid attaché, he became consul-general and agent in his own right on 22 March 1845. He subsequently served as chargé d'affaires (1847–60), minister resident (1860–72), and finally as minister-plenipotentiary (1872–86). During his long residence in the country he did much to improve Morocco's relations with European powers, believing this was best achieved by encouraging commerce and improving conditions for the Moors. Besides acting for Britain and working towards the consolidation of British interests in Morocco, he was also agent for Austria and Denmark. He was the first to break with the custom of envoys of presenting their credentials to the sultan on their knees. In 1844 he attempted, without success, to arrange terms between the French and the Moors before the bombardment of Mogador by the prince de Joinville on 15 August. In the same year he published *Western Barbary: its Wild Tribes and Savage Animals*, which reached a second English edition in 1861, was translated into French in 1844, and into Spanish in 1859. In 1845 Drummond-Hay married Annette, daughter of M. Cazytensen of Copenhagen, privy councillor to the king of Denmark. They had at least two daughters, who left a memoir of their father after his death.

In the same year as his marriage, Drummond-Hay mediated between Morocco and Denmark, Sweden, and Spain to negotiate conventions and also mediated between the sultan and the court of Modreal. On 9 December 1856 he successfully negotiated the treaty of friendship, trade, and navigation between Great Britain and Morocco. This treaty supported free trade, the opening of consulates, personal safety, and exemption from taxes with the exception of customs duties. Drummond-Hay reformed customs matters after peace had been established. He supported the sultan's sovereignty and territory throughout his time in Morocco.

In 1848 Drummond-Hay published his *Journal of an Expedition to the Court of Morocco*; the later *Memoir* (1896) also drew on journals kept during this time, which were said to offer, 'valuable insight into local politics and character', and to reflect the mind of 'a keen and careful student' (Meakin, 479). He was created KCB on 20 May 1862, GCMG on 4 December 1884, and was also KGC of the Danebrog. He retired on 1 July 1886, on a pension of £1333 6s. 8d., and in the same year was sworn of the privy council.

Drummond-Hay spoke Turkish, Italian, Spanish, French, and Arabic, was a keen sportsman, and travelled to Marrakesh, Fez, Meknès, and Rabat. His diplomatic skills, long residence, and intimate knowledge of Morocco made him a person of influence there. After retirement he divided his time between Ravenrock, a private house near Tangier, and Wedderburn Castle, Duns, Berwickshire, the family seat, where he died of influenza on 27 November 1893. J. M. RIGG, rev. LYNN MILNE

Sources J. D. Hay, *A memoir of Sir John Drummond Hay* (1896) • *The Times* (29 Nov 1893) • *Annual Register* (1893) • S. Lane-Poole, *The life of … Stratford Canning*, 2 vols. (1888) • B. Meakin, *The Moorish empire* (1899)
Archives Bodl. Oxf., corresp. and papers | Balliol Oxf., letters to Sir Robert Morier • BL, corresp. with Sir Austin Layard, Add. MSS 38939–39134, *passim* • BL, corresp. with Sir Charles Napier, Add. MS 40041 • Lpool RO, corresp. with fifteenth earl of Derby • NMM, letters to Sir Charles Napier • U. Nott. L., letters to Sir Andrew Buchanan
Likenesses Barraud, photogravure, NPG • photographs, repro. in Hay, *Memoir of Sir John Drummond Hay*
Wealth at death £11,187 8s. 9d.: probate, 27 Jan 1894, CGPLA Eng. & Wales

Hay, John MacDougall (1879–1919), Church of Scotland minister and novelist, was born on 23 October 1879 in Tarbert, Loch Fyne, son of Mary MacDougall and George Hay, a steamship agent. He was educated at Tarbert high school and at the University of Glasgow, where he studied natural and moral philosophy and English literature. He graduated in 1900, and became the headmaster of the Lionel public school, Ness, Lewis, later moving to teach in Ullapool. There, during a bout of rheumatic fever, he decided to enter the Church of Scotland ministry, returning to Glasgow to study divinity in 1905. He gained a first in church history and biblical criticism.

Hay was an intense individual, deeply exercised by the content of his studies. His relentless search for a solution to the problems of evil and suffering was conducted within a tortured Christian profession. Though subject to profound inner struggle, informed by a sharp intellect and a vibrant imagination, he was well liked by contemporaries, one of whom remembered him as 'quiet and reserved, almost shy, … a man gifted beyond the ordinary, and on the rare occasions when he did talk he never lacked eager listeners' (*Glasgow Herald*).

From his undergraduate days, and particularly during his theological training, Hay helped support himself by writing for newspapers and journals such as *Macmillan's Magazine*, *Chambers*, *The Spectator*, the *Glasgow Herald*, and the *Glasgow Evening News*, whose influential editor, Neil Munro, he later met. As natives of Argyll both men studied the mingling of highland Gaelic and lowland Scottish cultures in that area.

After finishing his divinity studies Hay became a student missionary at Morven and was licensed by the presbytery of Inveraray in 1908. He moved to an urban parish which had Argyll connections and became assistant minister at Govan old parish church. In 1909 he was ordained and moved to a charge in Elderslie, a similarly urban parish near Paisley, Renfrewshire, to which he did not feel wholly suited; he would have preferred a highland parish. On 28 October 1909 he married Catherine Campbell (b. 1882/3), daughter of Janet McMillan and Duncan Campbell, a minister. They had two children: Sheena (b. 1911) and George Campbell *Hay (1915–1984), who later became a distinguished Gaelic poet.

John MacDougall Hay's first novel, *Gillespie*, was published in 1914 and dedicated to Neil Munro. Though its impact was blunted by the onset of the First World War, *Gillespie* never entirely disappeared from view. The novel is set in the small fishing community of Brieston, based on Tarbert, Loch Fyne. This poor, hard-working, and gossip-ridden community is dominated by Gillespie Strang, an unscrupulous capitalist. *Gillespie*'s characterization and setting demonstrate that the seminal influence on Hay's work was George Douglas Brown's *The House with the Green Shutters*. Both works were regarded by contemporary literary critics as a welcome counterblast against the sentimental Scottish fiction of the kailyard school. Unlike Brown, however, Hay takes a religious stance. *Gillespie* grapples with problems of severe religious doubt expressed in the terrifying nightmares of Gillespie's son, Eoghan, who seeks some creed which will enable him to condemn his father but remain just. The Christ of the gospels seems to offer him this, but Christ's ethic, though deeply attractive, seems powerless against the suffering which Brieston endures in the tragedy of the plague and at the hands of Gillespie. In *Gillespie* a weak Christ cannot modify the overwhelming presence of fate, which is the strongest spiritual reality in the novel, deriving its potency from the superstitious highland background of Eoghan's grandmother.

After the publication of *Gillespie* Hay considered leaving the ministry to take up a career in writing, but did not carry the idea through. He published another novel, *Barnacles* (1916), set around Elderslie and Paisley. In it the struggle between good and evil in its religious dimension is more obvious. Barnacles is a holy fool whose innocence and goodness help save the heroine from the horrific abuse of an evil husband. The violence in the novel is disproportionate to the motivations of the characters and, although derangement accounts for the power of the scenes, it is not one of the novel's ostensible themes. Hay's writing was not always under his literary control.

Hay planned a third novel, *The Martyr*, and published a volume of free verse poetry entitled *Their Dead Sons* (1918). In 1919 'The Agony and after', his sermon commemorating the fallen, was published at the request of his congregation. In it Hay flounders between anguished descriptions and fine writing about the fallen and the meaningfulness of their deaths, 'They won their victories with their knees in the mud, but the sacrifice of their lives was the purest victory of the spirit' ('The Agony and after', 22). These works show Hay's continuing struggle with the problem of evil, particularly in the aftermath of the carnage of the First World War. However, Hay's affirmation of the doctor in *Gillespie* who cares for the poor and the plague victims demonstrates the move from a religious to a secular outlook which was to characterize the Scottish novel in the twentieth century.

A victim of poor health, Hay remained a parish minister until his death at the manse, Elderslie, from tuberculosis on 10 December 1919, aged forty. He was buried at the abbey cemetery, Elderslie, on 13 December. His early death, though not unexpected, was felt to be a literary loss and, taken together with George Douglas Brown's similarly early death in 1902, denied Scotland the mature vision of two of its most promising writers of the period.

B. DICKSON

Sources *Fasti Scot.*, new edn, 3.138 · *Glasgow Herald* (11 Dec 1919) · *Paisley and Renfrewshire Gazette* (13 Dec 1919) · *Paisley and Renfrewshire Gazette* (20 Dec 1919) · T. Scott, 'A note on J. MacDougall Hay', *Scotia Review*, 7 (1974), 35–9 · A. Bold, 'J. MacDougall Hay: Gourlay into *Gillespie*', *Modern Scottish literature* (1983), 117–23 · B. Tait and I. Murray, 'Introduction', in J. M. Hay, *Gillespie* (1979), vii–xvi · W. R. Aitken, ed., *Scottish literature in English and Scots: a guide to information sources* (1982) · *CCI* (1920)
Likenesses photograph, repro. in *Paisley and Renfrewshire Gazette* (20 Dec 1919)
Wealth at death £1124 6s. 3d.: confirmation, 1 May 1920, *CCI*

Hay, Josslyn Victor, twenty-second earl of Erroll (1901–1941), colonist in Kenya and philanderer, was born on 11 May 1901 at 17 Hertford Street, Mayfair, the elder son of Victor Alexander Sereld Hay (1876–1928), then styled Lord Kilmarnock, who succeeded as twenty-first earl of Erroll in 1927. His mother was (Mary) Lucy Victoria (1875–1957), only daughter of Sir Allan Mackenzie, second baronet. The hereditary office of lord high constable of Scotland had been conferred upon the Hays by Robert the Bruce in 1314 and was expressly reserved to them by the treaty of union. Its ancient prerogatives, including the command in the king's absence of all his armies in the field, had been reduced by the 1920s to bearing a silver baton in coronation processions. Successive earls of Erroll, however, remained the first subjects in Scotland after the blood royal with precedence before every other hereditary honour. The sale by the twentieth earl in 1916 of Slains Castle, with the family's last 4000 acres in Aberdeenshire, severed the Hays' territorial connection with Scotland; the old man moved to a small property at Ravenglass before settling in the terraced house near Paddington Station where he died.

Josslyn Hay, as the most handsome boy at Eton College, was followed down the street by half 'Pop'; perhaps in consequence of this effect on the older boys he was sacked from the school after two years, in 1916. His father, Kilmarnock, was a diplomat of charm and ability (he learnt Japanese when posted to Tokyo) who acted as chargé d'affaires at Berlin from the resumption of diplomatic relations with Germany until the arrival of the new ambassador, Viscount D'Abernon. On 12 January 1920 Josslyn Hay was appointed honorary attaché at Berlin under his father, who afterwards became British high commissioner on the inter-allied Rhineland commission with the local rank of ambassador (1921–8). Hay, however, remained under D'Abernon in Berlin, until his resignation

on 6 March 1922. He had at this time 'wonderful good looks', augmented by 'straight pale gold hair' and 'great sartorial elegance', but an 'impudent' manner and 'scornful way of looking at people—an oblique blue glance under half-closed lids' (Fielding, 93). Though he passed the Foreign Office examinations, the plan that he should follow his father into diplomacy was ruined by his infatuation with an older married woman. Lady (Myra) Idina Sackville (1893–1955), elder daughter of the eighth Earl De La Warr and divorced wife of the Conservative politician Euan Wallace, was then married to Charles Gordon, whom she swiftly divorced. Hay married her at the earliest opportunity, on 22 September 1923, in Kensington. Their only child, a daughter, later inherited Erroll's Scottish titles.

This *mésalliance* mortified Hay's parents and raised a society scandal. In 1924 the Hays settled in Kenya, initially occupying a bungalow which they called Slains, after the lost family castle in Aberdeenshire. The new Slains lay on the slopes of the Aberdare Mountains, where white settlers were establishing high altitude farms. In 1925 the Hays moved to a thatched mansion, Clouds, in a valley beneath the Aberdares, which became notorious as Happy Valley. The Happy Valley set (which also congregated in the Muthaiga country club) were displaced patricians seeking to re-establish their hegemony in a malleable, rural society clean of the taint of modern industrial democracy. 'Life out there was', said Baroness Blixen, 'rather like eighteenth-century England: one might often be hard up for cash, but life was still rich in many ways, with the lovely landscape, dozens of horses and dogs, and a multitude of servants' (*Writers at Work*, 10). Mentally undisciplined and physically restless, Erroll's set pursued a raffish life of adulteries, binge drinking, cocaine, card sharping, bilked tradesmen, spasmodic violence, and insanity. His debts accumulated as did his tally of adulteries. He was a sensualist with no sense of irony, whose conquests were an exercise of power over women and of humiliating dominance over their menfolk. 'To hell with husbands' was one of his favourite sayings. It amused him to borrow fivers from men he had recently cuckolded. His wife divorced him in 1929 because he was cheating her financially. With mercenary motives he swiftly married, at St Martin's register office, on 8 February 1930, another older woman, Edith Mildred Mary Agnes (1893–1939), daughter of Richard Watson Maude (1850–1921); her former husband, Cyril Ramsay-Hill, had cited Erroll in a turbulent divorce. Erroll encouraged his wife in the self-destructive combination of drink, morphine, and heroin. They lived in Oserian, a crenellated, white-washed, Moroccan-style house on the shores of Lake Naivasha.

After his father's death at Koblenz Hay had inherited the earldom, together with the lord high constableship (1928), and rose to prominence among what his friend Ewart Grogan called Kenya's 'large, virile and articulate European population' (Grogan, 83). Erroll joined Sir Oswald Mosley's British Union of Fascists (1934–5), but though his political instincts were both violent and reactionary, his extremism receded. Accordingly he was elected president of the Convention of Associations, known as the Settlers' Parliament (1935), and to the legislative council as member for Kiambu (1939). Commissioned as a captain in the Kenya regiment (1939), he was an exacting and efficient deputy director of manpower and military secretary to east Africa command from 1940. Though he had coarsened, and weighed 15 stone, Erroll continued to attract women. On 30 November 1940 at the Muthaiga club he met the young, newly married wife of Sir Delves Broughton; they were soon lovers. Broughton played the part of a complaisant husband, but was goaded by spiteful anonymous letters. On 21 January 1941 both men consulted lawyers about the Broughtons' divorce. After an evening which they spent together at the Muthaiga club, Erroll was ambushed and shot under the left ear on 24 January 1941, on the Nairobi–Ngong Road, while motoring in his Buick. He was buried at Nairobi on 25 January.

Sir (Henry John) Delves [Jock] **Broughton**, eleventh baronet (1883–1942), was accused of the murder. Born on 10 September 1883, he was the only surviving child of Sir Delves Louis Broughton, tenth baronet (1857–1914), and his first wife, Rosamond Broughton (1862–1885). A loveless childhood left him with a lifelong sense of deprivation, which did not diminish when he inherited the baronetcy with extensive estates in Cheshire and Staffordshire. He was educated at Eton College (1897–1900), where his father's meanness supposedly drove him to steal, and at a crammer before entrance to the Royal Military College, Sandhurst. Commissioned second lieutenant in the Irish Guards (10 December 1902), he was aide-de-camp to the lieutenant-governor of the United Provinces of Agra and Oudh (1908) and promoted major (15 July 1915) despite evading military action in the European war on the pretext of sunstroke. He retired from the army on 15 April 1919 and was excluded from the published *List of Etonians who Fought in the Great War*. Broughton was a proud, unintelligent man who was easily bored and had few distractions except extravagant living. He lost his fortune not only on racecourses but in foolish speculations in foreign exchange markets, commodity dealing, and mining shares. For a time he was chairman of Dalkeith (Ceylon) Rubber Estates and a director of Pindenioya Rubber and Tea Estates; he also bought coffee plantations in Kenya after 1923. He funded these business forays with characteristic deviousness by selling pictures, heirlooms, and over 30,000 acres in several tranches. These were not his possessions but belonged to family trusts. His son took legal action during 1939 to protect his interests, but Broughton was determined not to be bested, and arranged for a young Harrovian to steal heavily insured pearls from a car on the French riviera that summer, and then blackmailed his accomplice into stealing three heavily insured portraits from his Cheshire seat, Doddington (October 1939). Despite these frauds Broughton (a Cheshire magistrate since 1915) had so wasted his assets that he was obliged to shut Doddington and decamp to Africa.

Broughton had married, on 8 July 1913, at the guards' chapel, Wellington barracks, London, Vera Edyth (1894–1968), daughter of Boscawen Trevor Griffith-Boscawen of Trevalyn Hall, Trefalun, Denbighshire. They had one son and one daughter. Vera Broughton was a hard, pleasure-loving woman whose passion for big-game hunting first took them to Kenya in 1919–20. After affairs with the third earl of Wharncliffe and the first Baron Sherwood, she deserted Broughton in 1935 for Walter Guinness, first Baron Moyne. The aridity of Broughton's marriage increased his tendency to sourness, sulks, loneliness, and self-pity. From 1935 he pursued another cold, hard *femme fatale* of implacable chic, Diana (1913–1987), divorced wife of a society musician, Vernon Motion, daughter of Seymour Caldwell, gambler, and sister of the marchioness of Willingdon. She ran the Blue Goose cocktail club in Bruton Mews, Mayfair, and was a fashionable aviator. Broughton's wife began divorce proceedings in 1939 in expectation of marrying Moyne. Following the dissolution of the marriage, Broughton married Diana Caldwell (5 November 1940) in a register office at Durban, South Africa. Three weeks later his wife met Erroll, who was murdered within three months. Broughton was arrested (10 March 1941) and stood trial from 26 May. The prosecution's ballistic evidence was weak, there was no eyewitness connecting him with the crime, and his witness-box performance was effective. Despite his acquittal on 1 July, evidence of a confession published forty years later confirmed the probability of his guilt. After a miserable interval Broughton returned to England (November 1942) to find that he was the object of police investigations into the insurance frauds. Having injected himself fourteen times with a morphine derivative, he died on 5 December 1942 in an ambulance speeding from the Adelphi Hotel to Northern Hospital, Liverpool, and was interred on 10 December at Broughton church, Eccleshall, Staffordshire. The Erroll murder was depicted in Michael White's film *White Mischief* (1987). RICHARD DAVENPORT-HINES

Sources J. Fox, *White mischief* (1982) · R. Furneaux, *The murder of Lord Erroll* (1961) · C. Connolly, 'Christmas at Karen', *Sunday Times Magazine* (21 Dec 1969) · D. Fielding, *Mercury presides* (1954), 93 · E. Walter, 'Isak Dinesen', *Writers at work: the Paris interviews*, ed. G. Plimpton, 4 (1977), 1–19 · [E. S. Grogan], 'Kenya: the settlers' case', *Round Table*, 26 (1935), 82–97 · C. À Court Repington, *After the war* (1922) · E. Trzebinski, *The Kenya pioneers* (1985) · b. cert. · m. cert. (2nd marriage) · Burke, *Peerage* (1939) · *The Times* (24 Sept 1923), 15b · *Sunday Times* (21 Dec 1969) · *The old public school-boys' who's who: Eton* (1933), 103 · *Debrett's Peerage* · *The Times* (9 Dec 1942), 1a · Viscountess D' Abernon, *Red Cross and Berlin embassy, 1915–1926* (1946)

Likenesses oils, 1937 · T. Hill, paintings, 1970 (*The death of Lord Erroll*)

Wealth at death £8334 16s. 1d.—Sir Henry John Delves Broughton: probate, 16 Feb 1943, *CGPLA Eng. & Wales*

Hay [*née* Percy], **Lucy, countess of Carlisle** (1599–1660), courtier, was the daughter of Henry *Percy (1564–1632), the so-called 'wizard' ninth earl of Northumberland, and Dorothy (1563x5?–1619), widow of Sir Thomas Perrott and daughter of Walter *Devereux, first earl of Essex, and Lettice Knollys. Algernon *Percy (1602–1668) and Henry *Percy (c.1604–1659) were her brothers. According to Lucy's brother-in-law, the earl of Leicester, she was born about Michaelmas 1599 (*De L'Isle and Dudley MSS*, 6.623). It is unknown when she first attracted the attention of her

Lucy Hay, countess of Carlisle (1599–1660), by Sir Anthony Van Dyck

future husband, James *Hay (*c.*1580–1636). Rumours began as early as February 1617 that the countess of Bedford was acting as a marriage broker, and had brought both Lucy and her mother to favour the idea. The earl of Northumberland proved more difficult to convince. Initially he insisted that his daughter stay with him in the Tower of London, where he was imprisoned in the aftermath of the Gunpowder Plot. When she refused to remain there and went to live at one of Hay's London residences with a £2000 entertainment allowance, Northumberland reportedly offered his daughter £20,000 not to marry Hay. The earl finally gave his approval in October 1617 and the couple married in early November 1617, with James I, Prince Charles, and the new royal favourite, George Villiers, present at the ceremony. In November of the following year Lucy gave birth to a son, but he died in less than a month. Although Lucy was sick from what may have been a failed pregnancy that became a near fatal illness in 1622, after 1618 no one ever again reported her as pregnant. By the time she was twenty-six, stories started to circulate about the impact her beauty and personality had on members of the royal court.

In 1625, with the accession of Charles I and his marriage to Henrietta Maria, Lucy became increasingly influential at court. Initially, however, the new queen did not want Lucy, who became the countess of Carlisle in 1622, as one of her ladies-in-waiting, and if reports of that time are accurate, her objections are reasonable enough. By this time Lucy was having an affair with George Villiers, now duke of Buckingham, and both her husband and her lover intended her to use her talents to ensnare the king. When

this scheme failed, the Carlisles chose an alternate path to Charles I. Over the summer of 1627 the two of them spent much time with Henrietta Maria and managed to ingratiate themselves with her. At about this time their alliance with Buckingham collapsed. The earl of Carlisle had political differences with him over his policy of fighting France and Spain at the same time. Lucy's reasons were more personal. The duke was vainly pursuing an affair with the French queen, Anne. It is entirely possible that the story concerning the stolen diamond necklace, related by La Rochefoucauld and used by Dumas as the basis for *The Three Musketeers*, had some truth to it. The reputed thief was Lucy.

Following the political realignments that took place after Buckingham's assassination in August 1628, many letter writers noted that the queen made the countess of Carlisle one of her prime favourites. Yet as early as 1629 Lucy briefly lost favour. Over the next thirty years the relationship between Henrietta Maria and Lucy was anything but constant, because the two women had little in common. The countess admired wit and intelligence. She established a salon where politically influential members of court came to pay their respects and trade stories with her, and where poets and writers of widely varying talents paid her court. The French provided the model for these gatherings, and the duchesse de Chevreuse, a good friend of the countess, undoubtedly encouraged her during her periodic stays in England. Henrietta Maria's tastes centred on the visual arts and participating in masques rather than witty conversations and literature. She also shared her husband's aversion to flagrantly immoral persons.

The earl of Carlisle understood the advantages he could gain from Lucy's inclinations and reputation. In 1635, when he needed help securing the goodwill of Lord Deputy Wentworth for various projects in Ireland, he successfully used Lucy as an intermediary. After Carlisle's death in 1636, by the terms of his will his widow received all of his Irish holdings, consisting of both lands and monopolies. Lucy now had sound economic reasons to keep Wentworth's favourable opinion. She also tried to use his influence and the queen's to place the earl of Leicester as either secretary of state or preferably lord deputy of Ireland when the current holder retired. Leicester did receive the lord deputy's post, but the Irish rising and the civil wars limited his power, and left Lucy with no one to protect her Irish interests. By 1651 the monopolies had long since vanished and at least part of the landed estate was worthless.

After Wentworth's execution in 1641, Lucy did her best to cultivate members of the factions that opposed Charles I, especially John Pym. Numerous reports name her as one of the people who warned Pym that the king planned to arrest him and his associates in the House of Commons. Once the war began, Lucy primarily associated herself with a group of aristocrats and their near relatives, including the earls of Holland and Essex and Denzil Holles, who wanted to make peace with the king and who became increasingly alarmed at the growing influence of the independents and the army. She also maintained contacts with the members of the French government with the hope that they could mediate a peace; successive French ambassadors to England found her a useful contact. During March 1649, in the wake of Charles I's execution and the second civil war, the council of state imprisoned Lucy in the Tower. She remained there until September 1650, when she was released on bond. Her unrestricted freedom had to wait until March 1652.

None of these experiences lowered Lucy's status as one of the most admired women of her time or inhibited her political involvement. In 1653 young Dorothy Osborne felt that the countess of Carlisle's letters should act as models for wit and good breeding, 'only I am a litle scandalized I confess that she uses that word faithfull, she that never knew how to bee soe in her life' (*Letters of Dorothy Osborne*, 109). As for the politics, Lucy helped arrange mediation in a dispute between Denzil Holles and the earl of Salisbury, and supported Holles when he tried to convince Charles II to move to France before his restoration. Lucy died at Little Salisbury House, Hertfordshire, on 5 November 1660, as she planned a journey to meet with Henrietta Maria. She was buried that month at Petworth, Sussex.

In the course of her life the countess of Carlisle achieved a status in politics normally reserved for the queen. Confirmation of her eminence comes from a variety of sources, including Edward Hyde, earl of Clarendon, who was far from her friend. In his secret correspondence during the civil wars and interregnum, Lucy is one of the few women to whom he assigns her own cipher. She began as someone who fed her vanity through the personal devotion of a wide variety of prominent men to further her husband's political aims, and, after his death, to protect her own economic interests. Later, however, she developed a political agenda that was more than purely self-interested. She wanted to see the monarchy retained and risked her life to achieve that goal. Unlike many other women of that era, her motivation was not religious. She had no lasting association with those who valued religion as a driving force in politics. As late as 1647 the earl of Leicester related a story he claimed Lucy told him about the sexual escapades of the presbyterian minister Obadiah Sedgwick. In this and other ways the countess of Carlisle anticipates such women as Sarah Churchill, duchess of Marlborough, and Georgiana Cavendish, countess of Devonshire.   ROY E. SCHREIBER

Sources *Report on the manuscripts of Lord De L'Isle and Dudley*, 6, HMC, 77 (1966) · *The letters of John Chamberlain*, ed. N. E. McClure, 2 (1939) · R. Lockyer, *Buckingham: the life and political career of George Villiers, first duke of Buckingham, 1592–1628* (1981) · F. de La Rochefoucauld, *Mémoires de La Rochefoucauld* (Paris, 1836–9) · R. E. Schreiber, *The first Carlisle: Sir James Hay, first earl of Carlisle as courtier, diplomat and entrepreneur, 1580–1636* (1984) · *CSP Ire., 1647–60* · C. V. Wedgwood, *The king's war, 1641–1647* (1958) · P. Crawford, *Denzil Holles, 1598–1680: a study of his political career* (1979) · *CSP dom., 1652–3* · *The letters of Dorothy Osborne to William Temple*, ed. G. C. Moore Smith (1928) · *Calendar of the manuscripts of the most hon. the marquess of Salisbury*, 22, HMC, 9 (1971) · S. H. Mendelson and P. Crawford, *Women in early modern England, 1550–1720* (1998) · Clarendon, *Hist. rebellion* · PRO, 31/3/64 and 67 · PRO, SP 16/153, no. 77 · PRO, PROB 11/306, fols. 106–10 · 'Hay, James', *DNB* · 'Percy, Henry', *DNB* · *DNB*

Archives PRO, SP/16: 79, 118, 120, 123, 275, 280 · Sheffield Central Library, Wentworth–Woodhouse MSS, vols 8, 10, 10a, letterbook 3
Likenesses portrait, *c.*1630–1639?, Ham House, Richmond upon Thames · P. de Baillieu, line engraving (after A. Van Dyck), BM, NPG; repro. in A van Dyck, *Iconographie* · A. Van Dyck, double portrait, oils (with her sister, Dorothy); in possession of Lord Waldegrave, 1891 · A. Van Dyck, oils, Petworth House, West Sussex [*see illus.*] · A. Van Dyck, oils, Windsor · G. Vertue, line engraving (after A. Van Dyck), BM, NPG

Hay, Mary Cecil (1840/41–1886), novelist, born at Market Square, Shrewsbury, Shropshire, was the daughter of Thomas William Hay, watch- and clockmaker, of Market Square, Shrewsbury, and his wife, Cecilia. After her father's death she moved, with her mother and two sisters, to Chiswick, Middlesex. Throughout her life she was a frequent visitor to Cornwall, and she used it as the setting of many of her novels.

Hay's first work to appear in print was *Kate's Engagement*, serialized in *The Belgravia* magazine in 1873. Nearly all her novels were published serially at first, and throughout her career she produced many short stories for various magazines. Later in 1873 a second novel, *Hidden Perils*, was published in three volumes, and a second cheap one-volume edition was released two years later. In 1874 *Victor and Vanquished* appeared, running to a second edition in the following year, and in 1875 she wrote her best-seller, *Old Myddelton's Money*, which was constantly in print over the next forty years. This novel was published in a series of popular sixpenny novels as late as 1914.

Hay was a prolific writer, publishing fifteen novels and collections of short stories over thirteen years. She specialized in light romantic fiction, and, though popular in Britain, her novels had their strongest following in the United States and Australia. After the success of *Old Myddelton's Money* she published one novel a year until 1885, the most successful being *The Squire's Legacy* and *Nora's Love Test*, both of which appeared in 1876. By the early 1880s her health was beginning to fail, and she moved with her mother and sisters to East Preston, near Worthing, Sussex. Her later novels, perhaps reflecting her declining energies, failed to enjoy the popularity of her earlier works. She continued to write, however, and corrected, in the final months of her life, the proofs of a collection of fiction published posthumously as *A Wicked Girl, and other Tales* (1886).

Hay died on 24 July 1886, after a long and painful illness, aged forty-five, at the Bay Trees, East Preston. She was buried on 29 July in Highgate cemetery, Middlesex. *The Athenaeum* described her as 'an excellent and charitable woman, who worked exceedingly hard' (7 Aug 1886).   KATHERINE MULLIN

Sources Boase, *Mod. Eng. biog.* · Allibone, *Dict.* · *The Athenaeum* (7 Aug 1886), 176 · *DNB* · d. cert.

Hay, Matthew (1855–1932), physician and expert in forensic medicine and public health, was born at Hill Head, Denny, Stirlingshire, on 27 December 1855, the son of Matthew Hay, colliery owner, and his wife, Elizabeth (*née* Stirling). An outstanding scholar, educated at Dollar Academy, Hay studied the arts course for two years and the first year of medicine at Glasgow University. He then transferred to Edinburgh University and graduated MB, CM, with highest honours, in 1878; he also won the Ettles prize and the Goodsir fellowship. He became assistant to Richard Fraser, professor of materia medica, and during vacations he studied under Schmiedeberg at Strasbourg. In Berlin he reputedly shared rooms with William Osler, and in 1881 his MD thesis on saline cathartics won him the gold medal and the triennial Goodsir prize for physiological research.

Hay worked on the effects of sodium nitrite and nitroglycerine on angina pectoris and developed a test (which now bears his name) for bile acids. The period he spent as Fraser's assistant fostered his studies in toxicology, and these stood him in good stead when, aged twenty-seven, he successfully applied for the Aberdeen chair of forensic medicine vacated on Francis Ogston's retirement. Hay had barely settled into his teaching of forensic medicine when Dyce Davidson died; Hay then also taught his materia medica course until the university appointed a new professor.

In 1884 Hay was offered and accepted the prestigious chair of pharmacology and therapeutics at Johns Hopkins University medical school, Baltimore. He did not take up the position for what his obituarists have politely termed 'family reasons', but these may well have been connected to a wrangle between Hay and Johns Hopkins over Hay's desire to continue treating private patients. He became a director of the Hay family business, the Callendar ironworks. On 27 August 1884 Hay married Margaret Ferguson Crawford (1854/5–1926), daughter of John Crawford, a Grangemouth shipowner; they had four sons and two daughters.

Hay was appointed part-time medical officer of health at Aberdeen in 1888, following two short-term appointments for the post. His own appointment was bitterly contested within the town council, which was split by fears that a part-time medical officer could not give sufficient time to the city's health needs. Hay gave up private practice in exchange for a salary of £300 per annum. He had already introduced public health and hygiene lectures into his forensic medicine course at Aberdeen, thus conforming to the established Scottish pattern of undergraduate teaching of forensic medicine and public health in tandem. Following the example of Sir Douglas Maclagan at Edinburgh, in 1891 Hay instituted postgraduate public health teaching, for a diploma in public health; in addition he provided separate laboratory facilities for public health and forensic medicine.

As well as his medical teaching, by 1890 Hay was also carrying out part-time duties as crown medico-legal examiner, police surgeon, and medical officer of health for Aberdeen city—in positions similar to those held by Henry Duncan Littlejohn in Edinburgh. In 1893 Hay and Littlejohn gave medical and ballistic testimony for opposing counsels in the Monson murder trial at the Edinburgh High Court. As Aberdeen's medical officer of health, Hay brought scientific logic and organization into the realms of mother and child care, the treatment of tuberculosis

and venereal disease, medical statistics, and many other areas of public health. His analytical talents were employed not merely in health and sanitary matters, but included the more exotic tasks of ensuring the purity of water used in local whisky distilling and of analysing the city's gas supply. In Aberdeen Hay is remembered mostly for his farsighted plan to centralize the city's municipal and voluntary hospital provision together with university medical teaching, at the Foresterhill site; his plans were brought to fruition by his successor, John Parlane Kinloch.

Hay was a quiet, inventive man. At the age of twenty he planned the processes of the family's newly acquired ironworks. In later life he designed anthropological instruments for his own purposes which were considered valuable by experts. During his teaching career he played a major role in university affairs, which included the building of extensions to Marischal College and which cost more than £250,000. Hay represented Aberdeen University on the General Medical Council and was an original member of the Medical Research Council. As a member of the Carnegie Trust, he drafted the conditions for research fellowships and scholarships. In 1902, together with Leslie Mackenzie, the royal commission appointed him to enquire into the health of schoolchildren. The commission's 1903 recommendation on the medical inspection of schoolchildren was based on their report.

Ill health forced Hay to resign as medical officer of health in 1923 and to resign his chair in 1925. He died at his home, 14 Rubislaw Terrace, Aberdeen, on 30 July 1932. His funeral service on 2 August, held in Marischal College, was a notable Aberdeen town-and-gown occasion, after which his body was buried on the following day at Cameloan cemetery, Stirlingshire. BRENDA M. WHITE

Sources *The Lancet* (13 Aug 1932), 369–70 · *BMJ* (13 Aug 1932), 332–3 · *BMJ* (20 Aug 1932), 386–7 · *Aberdeen Press and Journal* (1 Aug 1932) · *Aberdeen Press and Journal* (3 Aug 1932) · *Aberdeen Press and Journal* (11 Aug 1932) · *Aberdeen Press and Journal* (22 May 1932) · *Aberdeen Press and Journal* (14 Jan 1925) · *Aberdeen Press and Journal* (15 Oct 1926) [death of Margaret Hay] · *Evening Express* (3 June 1967) · *George Walker's Journal*, no. 8 (22 March 1883), 1371 [local history department, Aberdeen Central Library] · I. McQueen, 'A hundred years of health workers in Aberdeen', typescript memoir by current medical officer of health, Aberdeen, 1962, Aberdeen Central Library, local history department · L. Wilson, 'Matthew Hay (1855–1932)', *Aberdeen Medico-Chirurgical Society, a bicentennial history, 1789–1989*, ed. G. Milne (1989) · D. Rorie, ed., *The book of Aberdeen* (1939) · C. Pennington, *The modernisation of medical teaching at Aberdeen in the nineteenth century* (1994) · M. A. Crowther and B. White, *On soul and conscience: the medical expert and crime* (1988) · b. cert. · m. cert. · d. cert. · B. M. White, 'Training medical policemen', *Legal medicine in history*, ed. M. Clark and C. Crawford (1994), 145–63 · B. White, 'The police surgeon as medical officer of health in Scotland, 1862–1897', *Police Surgeon*, no. 35 (May 1989) · *Medical Directory* (1902)
Archives U. Aberdeen · Wellcome L., papers
Likenesses C. Sims, oils, Marischal College, Aberdeen
Wealth at death £79,002 8s. 9d.: confirmation, 2 Dec 1932, CCI

Hay, Richard [*name in religion* Augustine] (1661–1736?), Augustinian canon and antiquary, born at Edinburgh on 16 August 1661, was second son of George Hay (*d. c.*1666), who was the youngest son of Sir John Hay of Barra, lord clerk register of Scotland. His mother was Jean Spottiswood, daughter of Sir Henry Spottiswood, high sheriff of Dublin. Baptized in the Tron Kirk, Edinburgh, Hay then was brought up with his cousins and attended school at various places in Fife, Lothian, and the Scottish borders. When he was about five his father died, and his mother soon afterwards married James Sinclair of Roslin. Thereafter a Roman Catholic, Richard was eventually sent to the Scots College, Paris, where he remained from March 1673 to August 1677, while attending the Collège de Navarre. His schooling was completed in an ancient abbey of canons regular near Chartres.

On 25 August 1678 Hay took the habit as a canon regular at St Genevieve's in Paris, assuming the religious name Augustine, and after the customary year's noviciate made his vows on 3 September 1679. His further training and studies for the priesthood were carried out in various religious houses, until he was ordained priest at Chartres on 22 September 1685.

A year later, with a commission from the abbot of St Genevieve to establish monasteries of canons regular in England and Scotland, Hay travelled to London and stayed some weeks at court before setting sail for Scotland. James VII and II had at that time established a Catholic chapel, school, and printing press in his palace of Holyrood, on the outskirts of Edinburgh. Hay was present at the opening of the chapel on St Andrew's day, 30 November 1686. This was no doubt the reason for his journey, as Holyrood Abbey had originally been an Augustinian foundation. In May and June 1687 he discussed with the lord chancellor, the earl of Perth, the project of establishing canons regular at Holyrood and he officiated there on occasion. Perth was sympathetic, but the flight of the king in December 1688 put an end to such plans.

Hay remained in Scotland some months longer and has left a valuable detailed record of the happenings following the change of government. Eventually, in May 1689, he sailed for France, made his way to Paris, and resumed life with the canons regular. He was given various placements with the title of sub-prior or prior and finally, in January 1695, was transferred as prior to St Pierremont in northern France. The dignities were apparently merely titular.

Thus far Hay's life was described in circumstantial detail by himself, but after 1700 information has to be gleaned piecemeal. He remained at St Pierremont until 1714, initially in favour with the bishop but later less so. During those years he began his six large compilations of Scottish historical sources, offered to supply documents to J. Mabillon, and planned to return to Scotland to compile a Scottish *Monasticon*. In February 1714 he was transferred to Bourges, again with the title of prior, but his role there is uncertain. In May 1714 it was testified that he had graduated in the faculty of arts and another priest took over his pastoral duties, then in August 1716 he was given leave to return to Scotland. He was, however, still in Bourges in May 1718 when he was given notice of a diocesan visitation.

By August 1719 Hay was resident in Edinburgh and soon after was planning to edit John of Fordun's *Scotichronicon* and its continuation by Walter Bower. Although Thomas Hearne, who was planning much the same, wrote in October 1721 assuring Hay that the two projects did not prejudice each other, Hearne's edition appeared in 1722 but Hay's never did.

In 1722 Hay published a short work entitled *Origine of the royal family of the Stewarts, in answer to Dr Kennedy's ... dissertation ... with an appendix of charters* (1722; repr. 1793). This Kennedy had asserted the royal family's Irish origin. A year later a longer work appeared: *Vindication of Elizabeth More from being a concubine, and her children from the tache of bastardy* (1723; repr. in R. Buchanan, ed., *Scotia rediviva*, 1826). It contained transcripts of about sixty documents aiming to show that Elizabeth Mure was the lawful wife of Robert II, as opponents of the Stuarts were claiming that this marriage was not legal and the Stuart dynasty was therefore illegitimate. The historian Thomas Innes had found in the Scots College in Paris and made public a document proving the legality of the marriage. Hay went further in showing that the marriage took place before the birth of the heir.

Hay is said to have been living in poverty in Edinburgh, and certainly in 1728–31 he sold some of his manuscript collections to the Advocates' Library. He died at Cowgate, Edinburgh, where he was living, before September 1736. At this time his reputation as an antiquary was high; his religious leanings are less clear, for he continued to call himself canon regular but almost certainly did not operate as a priest. Baptized a protestant in a strongly episcopalian family, he came at the age of five under the influence of his Roman Catholic stepfather, and his career in France and at Holyrood was with institutional Catholicism. His comments on Scottish priests and Scottish Catholicism, however, were almost always critical and acid.

Despite his plans to publish and his voluminous collections, Hay's printed work was meagre. He is chiefly known for the extracts from his compilations published long after his death: *Genealogie of the Hayes of Tweeddale ... Including Memoirs of his Own Times* and *Genealogie of the Sainteclaires of Rosslyn ... Including the Chartulary of Rosslyn* (both 1835). Nevertheless he deserves to be better known for his pioneering work as a records scholar, and many later writers have used his collections. MARK DILWORTH

Sources R. A. Hay, *Genealogie of the Hayes of Tweeddale* (1835), i–xvi, 40–83 · NL Scot., Acc. 5022, 2933 · H. Jadart, 'Correspondance de Richard de La Haye', *Revue de Champagne et de Brie* (1887), 321–34 · R. A. Hay, *Genealogie of the Sainteclaires of Rosslyn* (1835), 164–7 · B. M. Halloran, *The Scots College, Paris, 1603–1792* (1997)
Archives Bibliothèque Ste Geneviève, Paris, letters and compilations · NL Scot., collections and papers
Likenesses drawing, Scottish Catholic Archives; repro. in Halloran, *The Scots College*, illus. 8(b)

Hay, Robert (1799–1863), Egyptologist, was born on 6 January 1799 at Duns Castle, Berwickshire, Scotland, the fourth son and tenth child of Robert Hay (1731–1807) of Drumelzier and Whittingehame (a great-grandson of John Hay, first earl of Tweeddale) and his wife, Janet, daughter of James Erskine of Cardross. Hay's father was a servant of the East India Company in Sumatra. The son's promising naval career (February 1812–December 1819) was cut short when he inherited the Linplum estate in East Lothian on the death of his brother James. Fired by G. B. Belzoni's *Narrative*, which described recent discoveries and excavations in Egypt, Hay financed two recording expeditions to Egypt: 8 November 1824 to 25 March 1828 and 29 September 1829 to 19 March 1834. Hay's purpose was to preserve, with plaster casts and drawings, the monuments of ancient Egypt. He was accompanied by a team of artists and architects including Joseph Bonomi the younger, Frederick Catherwood, Francis Arundale, Charles Laver, and Owen Browne Carter. Their forty-nine volumes of drawings, plans, notes, elevations, copies, and maps, now in the British Museum Library, still await publication. Experts praise the material as an accurate and thorough record of monuments and decorations since damaged or destroyed.

Paradoxically, it is for *Illustrations of Cairo*, published in November 1840, that Hay is known. The thirty drawings, executed in 1829–30 by Carter, Laver, and Hay, and lithographed by J. C. Bourne, are the first accurate representations of Cairo's picturesque Islamic urbanism, predating the better-known images by David Roberts. The book failed financially, which discouraged Hay from further publishing ventures. In Egypt, Hay's circle of independent scholar enthusiasts included John Gardner Wilkinson and Edward W. Lane. Hay's contribution to Egyptology has received scant recognition partly because he had neither clear purpose for his portfolio nor application and financial sense.

On 9 May 1828 Hay married Kalitza Psaraki (1814–1885), daughter of the chief magistrate of Apodhulo in Crete, who had been captured by Turks in 1822 during the Greek War of Independence and rescued by Hay in 1824 from the slave market in Alexandria. They had two sons and two daughters. After his return to Scotland in 1834 Hay took pleasure in the life of a country squire, but he experienced financial problems in the management of his estates, and from 1850 to 1858 lived abroad with his family, in Florence and Dresden. Hay died of pneumonia at Amisfield, East Lothian, on 4 November 1863, and was buried in the Tweeddale family chapel at Yester House, Gifford. Of his extensive collection of Egyptian antiquities (about 10,000 objects in 200 cases), the British Museum purchased 529 in 1868 for £1000. The rest were purchased thereafter at auction for £1500, and donated by the Revd C. Granville Way, in 1872, to the newly formed Boston Museum of Fine Arts as the nucleus of its Egyptological collection. Hay's sons, Robert James and James William, in the 1870s married Italian women and lived in Italy. Nunraw, last of the family estates, was sold in 1880.   CAROLINE WILLIAMS

Sources S. Tillett, *Egypt itself: the career of Robert Hay* (1984) · J. Thompson, *Sir Gardner Wilkinson and his circle* (1992) · A. B. Edwards, *A thousand miles up the Nile* (1891); repr. (Los Angeles, 1983), 307–309 · BL, Add. MSS 29812–29860

Archives BL, corresp., diary and papers, Add. MSS 38095, 29812–29860, 31054 · NRA Scotland, priv. coll., accounts, letters, and papers · U. Oxf., Griffith Institute, journals [typescript copies] | Bodl. Oxf., corresp. with Caroline Norton and Helen Selina Sheridan · CUL, letters to Joseph Bonomi

Wealth at death £14,163 16s. 8d.: confirmation, 1864, Scotland

Hay, Robert Edwin [Roy] **(1910–1989)**, horticulturist, was born on 20 August 1910 at Hopetoun Gardens, Abercorn, Linlithgow, the only son of Thomas Hay (1874–1953), horticulturist, and his wife, Annie Buttars, *née* Methven. At the time of Hay's birth his father was head gardener at Hopetoun Gardens, but in the following year he moved to London, where he was superintendent, successively, of Greenwich Park (1911–19), Regent's Park (1919–23), and Royal Central Parks (1923–40), the latter including Hyde Park, St James's Park, and the gardens at Buckingham and Kensington palaces and Marlborough House. His father's profession ensured that Hay (known throughout his life as Roy) grew up in a home where horticulture was never far from the breakfast table and where distinguished horticulturists comprised many of the visitors. It was therefore almost inevitable that when he left Marylebone grammar school in 1928 he should find employment with a wholesale seed merchant. The work soon entailed travelling abroad to negotiate seed-buying contracts, and so he learned about the international horticultural business. This helped him in his subsequent career but, though a committed European, he was later saddened to see how far the British horticultural industry had declined and how heavily the country depended on imported plants and products.

Hay's distinguished career in journalism began in 1936, when he was appointed assistant editor of the leading publication for professional gardeners, the *Gardeners' Chronicle*. He returned to this later when from 1954 to 1964 he served as its editor, but in 1939 he moved to the Royal Horticultural Society, as editor of publications. Following the outbreak of the Second World War he moved again, to the Ministry of Agriculture, and there was responsible for leading the Dig for Victory campaign that so successfully encouraged the growing of produce in home gardens. In 1942 he was in Malta, organizing the growing of food for the island while it was under siege, and then, after the German surrender in 1945, he was controller of the horticulture and seeds division of the British zone of Germany, and was responsible for planning the growing of seed crops there.

For the rest of his life Hay was to be found wherever good gardening was spoken and written about. He was gardening correspondent of *The Times* for more than thirty years and set a standard there that many believed was not subsequently approached. He wrote a regular column in *Amateur Gardening*, and wrote and edited numerous books. He was also an early radio broadcaster, most notably on the BBC programme *Home Grown*, of which he was the compère and which was broadcast at 2.00 p.m. on Sundays, the slot later taken by *Gardeners' Question Time*. He was always an advocate of gardeners moving with the times and absorbing the latest advances and technology. But perhaps his most enduring achievement was Britain in Bloom, the floral competition between towns that he started following a family visit to France in 1963. He was impressed by the displays in towns and villages and discovered that President de Gaulle had given instructions to the French Tourist Authority to improve the nation's appearance. With the British Tourist Authority he found support and sponsors, and so Britain in Bloom was born in 1964, based on the Fleurissement de France campaign.

Hay was a big man in every sense, with a commanding presence and a deep, firm, though gentle voice. He stood out in a horticultural crowd because of his height, his neat moustache, and, in later life, his fine head of silver hair. He could be daunting in debate and sometimes impatient with those who did not grasp a line of thought or appreciate the significance of a fact as quickly as he did. He was almost universally liked and admired in his profession and honours inevitably came to him. The Royal Horticultural Society awarded him the Veitch medal in gold in 1957 and its highest honour, the Victoria medal of honour, in 1971. In between, in 1970, came the MBE—curiously, many thought, since though recognizing his work with Britain in Bloom it was for services to tourism rather than to horticulture. He received the award of officier du mérite agricole from Belgium in 1956 and from France in 1959.

On 17 November 1938 Hay married Mildred Diana (b. 1911/12), daughter of William Griffiths, a Kensington fishmonger, but the union was short-lived and they were later divorced. On 6 December 1946 he married Elizabeth Jessie (b. 1909/10), daughter of the Revd Howard Johnston Charter, Baptist missionary; they had two daughters, Susan and Alison. Elizabeth Hay died in 1976, and on 27 July of the following year Hay married his long-time colleague and fellow horticulturist Frances Mary *Perry (1907–1993), to the great delight of their many mutual friends. He died at his home, in Bulls Cross, Enfield, Middlesex, on 21 October 1989, and was survived by Frances Perry and by the two daughters of his second marriage.

STEFAN BUCZACKI

Sources *The Times* (23 Oct 1989) · personal knowledge (2004) · *WWW* · b. cert. · m. cert. [Mildred Diana Griffiths] · m. cert. [Elizabeth Jessica Charter] · m. cert. [Frances Mary Perry]
Likenesses photograph, repro. in *The Times*
Wealth at death £261,695: probate, 3 Jan 1990, *CGPLA Eng. & Wales*

Hay, Robert William (1786–1861), civil servant and dilettante, was born and baptized on 9 January 1786 in Brodsworth, Yorkshire, the eldest child of George William Auriol Hay-Drummond (1761–1807)—himself the youngest son of George Henry Hay, eighth earl of Kinnoull—author, poet, prebendary of York, and vicar of Doncaster and Brodsworth, and his first wife, Elizabeth Margaret (1767–1799), the daughter of Captain Sir Samuel Marshall RN, deputy comptroller of the navy, and his wife, Elizabeth Worsley. Robert Hay descended from an illustrious Scottish family. His paternal grandfather, Robert Hay *Drummond (1711–1776), was archbishop of York and preached at George III's coronation.

Hay was educated (like his father and paternal grandfather before him), probably at Westminster School, and at Christ Church, Oxford, where he was nominated to a studentship in December 1803 and graduated BA in 1807 and MA in 1809. His studentship, nominally for those studying medicine or law, required its holder be unmarried: he retained it until his death. During his formative years he befriended many young men, such as Robert Wilmot (later Sir Robert Wilmot-Horton), who went on to distinguished careers in public life.

After completing his education the impecunious Hay served briefly as a captain in the Perthshire militia. However, he eventually found more agreeable employment in London. 'An impeccable Tory' (Snelling and Barron, 147) and consummate political networker, he became in 1812 private secretary to Viscount Melville, first lord of the Admiralty and one of Scotland's most influential peers. Hay also became in 1821 a commissioner of the Royal Navy's victualling office. On 6 July 1825 Lord Liverpool's government appointed him to the important new post of permanent under-secretary of state for the colonies.

Hay's career as a senior bureaucrat proved lacklustre. Generally responsible for the eastern (Mediterranean and African) division of the Colonial Office, he had an impetuous nature, quite unsuited to an administrator and policy maker. Henry Taylor referred to his 'permanent chief' as 'the blindly bold' (Taylor, 1.100). Knaplund has written that Hay was:

> a civil servant of the old school—easygoing and ineffective. He loved gossip and carried on an extensive private correspondence with officials and other individuals in the colonies without paying much attention to the real business of the office entrusted to his care.   (Knaplund, *James Stephen*, 40)

However, during his tenure the department dealt with such major issues as the abolition of slavery in the British empire.

In January 1836, succumbing to pressure engineered by Viscount Howick (later Earl Grey) and James Stephen, Baron Glenelg, the whig colonial secretary, reluctantly replaced 'Mr. Hay, the intelligent, patriotic, and urbane under-secretary' (Martin, 4.xiin.). Hay's successor was his able and ambitious assistant Stephen, who immediately overhauled the onerous business of the office, bringing greater efficiency and order. Already in declining health at the age of fifty, Hay was not awarded an honour for his work in the Colonial Office, but he did obtain a dormant pension set up for him before his tory patrons had left office.

Hay was a man of many parts. A bon vivant with numerous interests and a wide circle of admiring, influential friends, he enjoyed society and became a founder member and later a secretary of Grillion's Club in London. While at the Colonial Office he built up a fine botanical collection from specimens sent to him by officials in distant parts of the empire. His expertise 'in various branches of Natural Knowledge' was cited on his certificate of election to FRS in March 1814. He was also an enthusiastic traveller who published two learned papers on New Zealand and Africa in the *Journal* of the Royal Geographical Society, of which he was elected fellow in 1830. His surviving manuscript journals describe his journeys to Scandinavia, Russia, Spain, Morocco, Italy, Egypt, and other Mediterranean countries, where he visited relatives scattered in imperial service. However, he never set foot in the township in Huron county, Upper Canada (later Ontario) named after him (c.1828) by John Galt's Canada Company.

During his final years Hay retired to Southampton, near where his mother's family had lived, and also maintained a residence in Rome. In these soothing climes he sought relief from chronic attacks of rheumatism ('Rheumatiory', according to his will). He continued to travel, draw, and correspond, and published his own English translations of selected poetical works by Horace. On 9 May 1861, while a guest of Lady Hamilton Chichester, he died on Malta, one of his old haunts, and was buried four days later in the British protestant (later Ta'Braxia) cemetery, near Valletta. In his will the 75-year-old bachelor left his estate of £2000 to his close relatives, friends, and servants.　　　　　　　　　　　　JOHN D. BLACKWELL

Sources D. M. Young, *The colonial office in the early nineteenth century* (1961) · J. Hunter, *South Yorkshire: the history and topography of the deanery of Doncaster*, 2 vols. (1828–31) · R. C. Snelling and T. J. Barron, 'The colonial office and its permanent officials, 1801–1914', *Studies in the growth of nineteenth-century government*, ed. G. Sutherland (1972), 139–66 · P. Knaplund, *James Stephen and the British colonial system, 1813–1847* (1953) · J. C. Beaglehole, 'The colonial office, 1782–1854', *Historical Studies: Australia and New Zealand*, 1 (1940–41), 170–89 · R. M. Martin, *History of the British colonies*, 5 vols. (1834–5) · J. C. Sainty, ed., *Colonial office officials: officials of the secretary of state for war, 1794–1801, of the secretary of state for war and colonies, 1801–54, and of the secretary of state for colonies, 1854–70* (1976) · [H. Taylor], *Autobiography of Henry Taylor*, 2 vols. (1885) · *Collins peerage of England: genealogical, biographical and historical*, ed. E. Brydges, 9 vols. (1812), vol. 7, p. 211 · *Hay township highlights: 150 years of diversified progress, 1846–1996* (1996) · W. L. Burn, *Emancipation and apprenticeship in the British West Indies* (1937) · J. Holland Rose and others, eds., *The growth of the new empire, 1783–1870* (1940), vol. 2 of *The Cambridge history of the British empire* (1929–59) · E. A. Benians, J. Butler, and C. E. Carrington, eds., *The empire-commonwealth, 1870–1919* (1959), vol. 3 of *The Cambridge history of the British empire* (1929–59) · P. Barberis, *The elite of the elite: permanent secretaries in the British higher civil service* (1996) · J. W. Cell, *British colonial administration in the mid-nineteenth century: the policy-making process* (1970) · Foster, *Alum. Oxon.* · J. Foster, *The peerage, baronetage, and knightage of the British empire for 1883*, 2 vols. [1883] · *Grillion's Club: a chronicle, 1812–1913* (1914) · H. L. Hall, *The colonial office: a history* (1937) · P. Knaplund, *The British empire, 1815–1939* (1941) · *Scots peerage · Members of Grillion's Club from 1813 to 1863* (1864) · E. T. Williams, 'The colonial office in the thirties', *Historical Studies: Australia and New Zealand*, 2 (1942–3), 141–60 · parish register (baptism), Brodsworth, Yorkshire, 9 Jan 1786 · *Malta Times* (16 May 1861)

Archives BL, letters to various correspondents · Bodl. Oxf., travel journals and journal-letters · PRO, Colonial Office MSS | BL, corresp. with Sir Robert Peel, Add. MSS 40232–40497, *passim* · Derbys. RO, corresp. with Sir R. J. Wilmot Horton · NA Scot., corresp. with Lord Dalhousie · NL Scot., letters to Sir Thomas Cochrane · U. Durham L., Grey of Howick MSS, journal of the third Earl Grey · U. Mich., Clements L., Melville MSS

Likenesses F. C. Lewis, engravings, stipple (after drawings by J. Slater, c.1813), NPG; repro. in *Portraits of members of Grillion's Club*

Wealth at death under £2000: resworn probate, Jan 1862, *CGPLA Eng. & Wales* (1861)

Hay, Sir Thomas, of Erroll (d. 1406). *See under* Hay family (*per. c.*1295–c.1460).

Hay, Thomas, ninth earl of Kinnoull (1710–1787), politician, was born on 4 June 1710 at Dupplin House, near Perth, the eldest son of George *Hay, eighth earl of Kinnoull (1689–1758), and his wife, Abigail (d. 1750), daughter of Robert Harley, first earl of Oxford. After an early childhood marred by parental disagreements, he was educated at Westminster School, which he entered in 1718, and at Christ Church, Oxford, where, as Viscount Dupplin, he matriculated on 13 June 1726. He attained some distinction as a classical scholar and may have been maintained as an undergraduate partly at the crown's expense, through the influence of Walpole. The correspondence of Dr William Stratford, canon of Christ Church, reveals a highly-strung young man—'poor Dupplin'—prone to tearfulness and often unhappy at Oxford (*Portland MSS*, 7.459).

On leaving the university in 1729, Dupplin accompanied his father on the latter's outward journey as ambassador to Constantinople: he was at Lisbon in January 1730. Already known in metropolitan literary circles, in 1735 he was satirized as Balbus in Pope's *Epistle to Dr John Arbuthnott*. Despite his father's erstwhile toryism and the suspicion of Jacobitism which surrounded the family, Dupplin from the outset inclined towards the whigs. In 1736 he was elected MP for Scarborough but was unseated on petition. On 12 June 1741 he married at Oxford Chapel, Marylebone, Middlesex, Constantia (d. 1753), only daughter and heir of John Kyrle-Ernlie of Whetham, Wiltshire. They had one son, born in London on 12 August 1742, who died on 14 October 1743. Lady Dupplin died on 29 June 1753 and was buried at Calne, Wiltshire.

In 1741 Dupplin had also become MP for Cambridge and was appointed commissioner of the revenues in Ireland. Noted for his accommodating nature and possessing a firm grasp of detail, Dupplin was to become a fixture in the administrations of Walpole, Pelham, and Newcastle. His competence in fiscal affairs was legendary, and he was often involved in the negotiation of government money matters in the City of London. Commissioner of trade in 1746, and from 1747 chairman of the parliamentary committee on privileges and elections, he became a lord of the Treasury in 1754, joint paymaster of the forces in 1755, and both chancellor of the duchy of Lancaster and a privy councillor in 1758. Horace Walpole, whose letters contain many references to Dupplin, reckoned him among the thirty ablest men in the Commons. Under Newcastle he was simply 'one of the pivots of his political system' (Namier, 130).

In 1758, on the death of his father, Dupplin succeeded to the earldom as ninth earl of Kinnoull. In 1759 he was again in Lisbon, charged with negotiating a settlement following the breach of Portuguese neutrality during Admiral Boscawen's naval victory over the French at Lagos. He also provided tactical advice to the prime minister on the conduct of the general election of 1760. Following Bute's triumph, Kinnoull retired to his Perthshire estate. Despite Newcastle's heartfelt imprecations, he departed political life in 1762, aggrieved at the dismissal of his friend the duke of Devonshire. At Dupplin House he devoted himself

Thomas Hay, ninth earl of Kinnoull (1710–1787), by William Hoare

to improving the commercial management of his property, including the granting of secure tenancies and the planting of 80,000 trees 'besides Scotch firs' in the single year of 1768 (Pennant, 74).

Resident in Scotland, Kinnoull also committed himself to public works, such as Smeaton's Bridge across the Tay at Perth, to whose completion, in 1772, Kinnoull contributed both £500 of his own funds and energetic advocacy of the scheme. From 1765 he was chancellor of the University of St Andrews, whose muniments contain many records of his tenure. He was also in 1768 elected president of the Society in Scotland for the Propagation of Christian Knowledge (SSPCK). When in England he had regularly attended Anglican services (his brother Robert Hay *Drummond became archbishop of York in 1761), and in Scotland Kinnoull 'conformed to the usages of the Church of Scotland' (Kemp, 4.290). Both at St Andrews, where he ensured the appointment of theological liberals such as Robert Watson and Joseph McCormick, and in his work with the SSPCK, which endeavoured to spread an enlightened Presbyterian message throughout the Scottish highlands, he was in sympathy with the dominant moderate interest in the contemporary church, and was a dependable supporter of that party's leaders, William Robertson and Hugh Blair.

In old age the stately, heavy-jowled figure portrayed by his compatriot David Martin, Kinnoull was a convivial man, on intimate terms with the literary and political élite of his day. Known to Gay, Pope and Secker, he was also acquainted with lords Mansfield, Portland, Leeds,

Rockingham, Seafield, Hopetoun, and the Hardwickes (to each of whom letters are extant). However, his love of minutiae, which made him such a competent manager of the government finances, combined strangely with his diffuse knowledge and interests to make his conversation somewhat wearing and unimaginative. A letter from the Marchioness Grey mocks the 'incessant small talk of my good Lord Duplin, that flows and flows as smoothly as ever, and as uninterrupted in its course' (GEC, *Peerage*, 7.323–4). He was also given to hypochondria, as well as genuine ill-health, throughout his life.

Kinnoull died at Dupplin on 27 December 1787, and was buried the next day at the parish church in Aberdalgie, near Dupplin. A valedictory sermon composed and published for the SSPCK exists. He was succeeded as earl by his nephew Robert Auriol Hay Drummond, eldest son of the English primate.   DAVID ALLAN

Sources *Scots peerage*, vol. 5 · GEC, *Peerage*, new edn, 7.323–4 · A. Valentine, *The British establishment, 1760–1784: an eighteenth-century biographical dictionary*, 2 vols. (1970) · J. Kemp, 'The character of the right honourable Thomas late earl of Kinnoull', *The Scotch preacher* (1789), 4.287–306 · *The manuscripts of his grace the duke of Portland*, 10 vols., HMC, 29 (1891–1931) · W. Anderson, *The Scottish nation*, 2 (1869), 610 · L. B. Namier, *England in the age of the American revolution* (1930) · Walpole, *Corr.* · T. Pennant, *A tour in Scotland, 1769*, 3rd edn (1774) · R. B. Sher, *Church and university in the Scottish Enlightenment: the moderate literati of Edinburgh* (1985) · Foster, *Alum. Oxon.* · Burke, *Peerage* (1939) · A. McInnes, *Robert Harley, puritan politician* (1970)

Archives BL, dispatches and papers as ambassador at Lisbon, Add. MSS 32903–32913, 34412, 40760 · Condies Solicitors, 2 Tay Street, Perth, Scotland, Kinnoull family MSS | BL, letters to first and second earls of Hardwicke, Add. MSS 35447–35693, *passim* · BL, corresp. with duke of Newcastle, T. Hundis, and others, Add. MSS 32695–33072 · NA Scot., letters to H. Dundas · NA Scot., letters to Lord Seafield · NL Scot., letters to Robert Liston · NRA Scotland, priv. coll., letters to Lord Hopetown · Sheff. Arch., letters to marquess of Rockingham · U. Nott. L., letters, incl. letters to Lord Lincoln · U. Nott. L., letters to third duke of Portland · U. St Andr. L., university muniments, incl. letters and other materials as chancellor · V&A NAL, letters to David Garrick

Likenesses D. Martin, oils, *c.*1780–1789, U. St Andr. · W. Hoare, portrait; Christies, 10 Dec 1985, lot 34 [see illus.] · D. Martin, oils, Scot. NPG

Hay, Sir William, of Erroll (d. 1436). *See under* Hay family (*per. c.*1295–*c.*1460).

Hay, William, first earl of Erroll (d. 1462). *See under* Hay family (*per. c.*1295–*c.*1460).

Hay, William, fifth Lord Hay of Yester (1537/8–1586), landowner, was the son of John Hay, fourth Lord Hay of Yester (*c.*1510–1555/6), and his wife, Margaret, daughter of William Livingstone, fourth Lord Livingstone. He succeeded his father between 30 September 1555 and 30 January 1556, and was served heir to him either in 1559 or 1560. In June 1559 Nicholas Throckmorton, the English ambassador to the French court, requested a passport for Hay to travel from Paris via England to Scotland; he had arrived there by November. A contract dated 28 October 1559 arranged his marriage to Margaret, daughter of Sir John Kerr of Ferniehirst; they were married before 12 September 1560. They had eight children: two sons and six daughters.

The Hays of Yester were hereditary sheriffs of Peebles. The provostry of the burgh of Peebles had been secured by the fourth lord, following whose death William obtained the grant of it from Mary of Guise. The burgesses challenged the appointment, but on 30 January 1556 the town agreed to accept Hay as provost when he came of age. This agreement took effect in October 1562.

Hay ratified the treaty of Berwick in May 1560 and sat in the Reformation Parliament in August that year. He supported the proposal for the marriage of the third earl of Arran and Queen Elizabeth, and subscribed the Book of discipline.

Throughout the reign of Queen Mary and the ensuing civil war, Hay vacillated in his allegiance to the queen's and king's parties. Having initially supported the congregation, he came round to approve the Darnley marriage and to lead Mary's army, with Darnley, in the chaseabout raid. Hay was with Mary at Carberry in June 1567 but attended Moray's privy council meeting in December. Following the queen's escape from Lochleven he signed the bonds of 1568 pledging to support her, but then abandoned Mary at Langside when he saw that her defeat was imminent.

Hay's support for Queen Mary caused him to be forfeited by parliament, though this was later suspended at the request of Queen Elizabeth. Hay was with the regent Moray on the borders in 1569 but returned to the queen's party after the former's murder. He can be identified as one of the queen's men in 1570–71, but he shifted his allegiance back to the king and attended Lennox's parliament in 1571. Hay signed the bond of allegiance to the king and Regent Morton in 1576, and then in 1582 acquiesced in the Ruthven raid.

Hay was intermittently a member of the privy council throughout the 1570s, but in his later years he seems to have been involved in numerous feuds and lawsuits. In 1585 he was accused of using his position as sheriff and provost of Peebles to support his son's feud with the Stewarts of Traquair. He was warded in Edinburgh Castle, from which he escaped, only to be warded again.

Hay died in August 1586, and his eldest son, William, was served his heir the following October. His wife was still alive in March 1594.   MARY BLACK VERSCHUUR

Sources M. Livingstone, D. Hay Fleming, and others, eds., *Registrum secreti sigilli regum Scotorum / The register of the privy seal of Scotland*, 4–6 (1952–63) · *Reg. PCS*, 1st ser. · J. M. Thomson and others, eds., *Registrum magni sigilli regum Scotorum / The register of the great seal of Scotland*, 11 vols. (1882–1914), vols. 4–5 · J. W. Buchan, *A history of Peeblesshire*, 3 vols., 2 (1925) · W. Chambers, ed., *Charters and documents relating to Peebles*, Scottish Burgh Records Society, 10 (1872) · G. Donaldson, *All the queen's men* (1983) · *Scots peerage*, 8.436–42 · *CSP for.*, 1558–9 · J. K. Cameron, ed., *The first book of discipline* (1972) · R. Bannatyne, *Journal of the transactions in Scotland, during the contest between the adherents of Queen Mary, and those of her son*, ed. J. G. Dalyell (1806) · *John Knox's History of the Reformation in Scotland*, ed. W. C. Dickinson, 2 vols. (1949) · GEC, *Peerage*, 6.424–5

Hay, William (1695–1755), politician and writer, was born on 21 August 1695 at Glyndebourne, Sussex, the second son of William Hay (1669–1697) and his wife, Barbara (*bap.* 1661, *d.* 1700), youngest daughter of Sir John Stapley, bt,

and his wife, Mary. His early life was unsettled. After the death of his parents he was brought up first by his maternal grandparents and then by an aunt, Mary Dobell. In 1705 he was sent to school in the village of Newick, in Sussex, and then to the grammar school at Lewes. Thence he went to Oxford, matriculating at Christ Church on 20 March 1712. However, he left in 1715 without taking a degree. In 1714 he was admitted to Lincoln's Inn and then in 1715 to the Middle Temple. According to Tutté his legal studies were cut short by an attack of smallpox which damaged his eyesight. But, while there is no evidence that he ever worked as a lawyer, he kept rooms at the Middle Temple until his death.

In his twenties Hay travelled widely in Britain and on the continent and he also undertook extensive work on the gardens at Glyndebourne. In 1728 he embarked on a career as a minor 'man of letters', publishing anonymously his *Essay on Civil Government*, a vigorous defence of the revolution settlement of 1688–9 and of whig principles. Two years later there followed his only original poetic composition, *Mount Caburn*, dedicated to the duchess of Newcastle, the wife of the secretary of state. The link with the powerful Newcastle connection at which this dedication hinted was confirmed on 3 May 1731 by Hay's marriage to Elizabeth Pelham (1709–1793), the second daughter of Thomas Pelham of Catsfield Place, Sussex, and a cousin of the duke. By this time Hay was emerging as an influential whig in east Sussex. He had become a JP in 1727 and was appointed chairman of the eastern division of Sussex in 1733. It was hardly surprising, therefore, that he was returned to parliament on Newcastle's interest as MP for Seaford in January 1734, or that he acted as the duke's election agent in the bitterly contested Lewes election later that year.

In parliament Hay quickly emerged as a loyal supporter of the administration of Walpole and then of the Pelhams. On his death in 1755 Newcastle lamented the loss of 'a very faithful, and useful Servant in the House of Commons; Who, in Two and Twenty Years Attendance there, was scarce ever absent at one single Question; and never gave a wrong Vote, to the best of my Remembrance' (BL, Add. MS 32856, fols. 167–8). As both a placeman and a pensioner Hay was undoubtedly a committed ministerial whig, but Newcastle's elogium should not be allowed to obscure the fact that he was capable of demonstrating a certain independence. Even Walpole was not beyond reproach, and Hay condemned the grants which he obtained just before his resignation in 1742 as 'an Abuse of the Kings favour' (Taylor and Jones, 176). Hay was also a dedicated parliamentarian, a fact which emerges clearly from his parliamentary journal, which is one of the best surviving sources for debates in the Commons in the 1730s. The issue to which he devoted most attention was the reform of the poor law, a subject of recurrent debate during his twenty years as an MP. Perhaps drawing on his experience as a JP, he published a major pamphlet on the subject in 1735. *Remarks on the Laws Relating to the Poor*, which was reprinted in 1751, advocated an ambitious reform on the basis of the 'union' of parishes. Thereafter he was the driving force behind a number of parliamentary initiatives aimed at poor law reform. Almost all of these failed, but despite this Hay, more than any other person, helped to determine the framework of the debate, both in parliament and in the press, in the middle years of the eighteenth century.

To his contemporaries, however, Hay was probably best known as an author. Alexander Pope liked his early poems (*Correspondence of Alexander Pope*, ed. G. W. Sherburn, 1956, 3.173), but his fame rested primarily on works published in the last years of his life. *Religio philosophi*, a discussion of the principles of religion and morality which revealed a strident anti-clericalism, appeared in 1753. This was followed by a translation of Isaac Hawkins Browne's *De animi immortalitate* in 1754 and a selection of the epigrams of Martial in 1755. His most popular, and possibly his most interesting, work, however, was *Deformity: an Essay* (1754), a discussion of his own physical disabilities—he had been born a hunchback dwarf. It attracted some critical acclaim, one contemporary describing it as 'a masterpiece of humour, wit, ingenuity, elegant style, fancy, and good sense. But, above all, it has the simplicity of Montaigne without his vanity' (Nichols, 8.520).

Following an 'apoplectic fit', Hay died at Glyndebourne on 22 June 1755 leaving four children; a son, Henry, and a daughter, Elizabeth, had predeceased him (Tutté). His eldest son, Thomas, followed his father into parliament, serving as MP for Lewes between 1768 and 1780, while his second son, William, became a member of the supreme council at Calcutta and was murdered at Patna in 1763. However, none of the children produced any heirs and, after the deaths in 1794 and 1803 of his daughters, Henrietta and Frances, Glyndebourne passed to his nephew, the Revd Francis Tutté, who composed the memoir which prefaces Hay's collected works. Hay was buried at Glynde, Sussex, on 26 June 1755. STEPHEN TAYLOR

Sources *Tory and whig: the parliamentary papers of Edward Harley, third earl of Oxford, and William Hay, MP for Seaford, 1716–1753*, ed. S. Taylor and C. Jones (1998) · F. Tutté, 'Introductory preface', *The works of William Hay*, 2 vols. (1794) · Nichols, *Lit. anecdotes*, vol. 8 · Newcastle to Holdernesse, 24 June 1755, BL, Add. MS 32856, fols. 167–8 · will of William Hay (d. 1755), PRO, PROB 11/817, sig. 192 · L. F. Salzman, ed., *The parish register of Glynde, Sussex, 1558–1812*, Sussex RS, 30 (1924) · will of William Hay (d. 1697), PRO, PROB 11/441, sig. 233 · PRO, *Morrice v. Langham* MSS, C109/15–18 · register, St Margaret's, Westminster, City Westm. AC · parish register, Lewes, St Michael, E. Sussex RO, PAR 414 1/1/2 · marriage register of Holy Trinity Minories, GL, MS 9243, 154 · will, E. Sussex RO, SM/D3 [Barbara Jenkins], 167 · W. P. Baildon, ed., *The records of the Honorable Society of Lincoln's Inn: admissions*, 2 vols. (1896) · H. A. C. Sturgess, ed., *Register of admissions to the Honourable Society of the Middle Temple, from the fifteenth century to the year 1944*, 3 vols. (1949) · *GM*, 1st ser., 25 (1755), 284 · W. Hay, *Remarks on the laws relating to the poor* (1735) · W. Hay, *Remarks on the laws relating to the poor*, 2nd edn (1751) · W. Hay, *Deformity: an essay* (1754) · IGI

Archives Northants. RO, parliamentary notebooks | BL, letters to duke of Newcastle, Add. MSS 32687–32992, *passim* · E. Sussex RO, Glyndebourne MSS, GBN · PRO, *Morrice v. Langham* chancery papers, C109/15–18

Likenesses engraving, repro. in W. Hay, *The works of William Hay* (1794) · portraits, Glyndebourne

Hay, William Thomson [Will] (1888–1949), comedian and actor, was born on 6 December 1888 in Stockton-on-Tees, the second of the three sons and third of the six children of William Robert Hay (d. 1919), engineer, of Invernessshire, and his wife, Elizabeth Ebden (d. 1910), the daughter of a Barnsley fish merchant. He was educated at local authority schools in Lowestoft, Hemel Hempstead, and London, and in evening classes in Manchester. While working as a commercial correspondent in Manchester he married, on 7 October 1907, Gladys, the eighteen-year-old daughter of Thomas Perkins, postmaster of Broughton, Salford. They had three children: Will junior and Gladys (both of whom went on the stage), and Joan. The marriage broke down in 1934, but the couple never divorced; Hay subsequently formed a relationship with Randi Kopstadt, a Norwegian showgirl.

Soon after his marriage Will Hay embarked on a music-hall and concert-party career (he tried several times to enlist for active service in the First World War but was rejected on medical grounds; he served instead with the voluntary training corps, a forerunner of the Home Guard). His initial sketch, 'Bend Down', was based on the anecdotes of his schoolteacher sister, Elspeth. After obtaining valuable experience with the Fred Karno troupes during the war he concentrated on developing his character of the Schoolmaster Comedian. From about 1920 he performed his main sketch, 'The Fourth Form at St Michael's', which soon became something of a national institution and was featured in the royal command variety performance of 1925 (he also appeared at the royal command shows in 1928, 1938, and 1945). After years of apprenticeship, Hay's triumph came suddenly and comprehensively. His first overseas tours, to Australia and New Zealand in 1923–4 and to the USA (where British comedians usually failed) in 1927, were successes, and by the early 1930s 'The Fourth Form at St Michael's' was featured on radio, on record, and in the children's comic *Radio Fun*.

Cautious with money, and often intimidatingly caustic as a theatrical overseer, Hay was more respected than loved by his fellow professionals. His private life was conservative, austere—even niggardly—with little of show-biz glitter about it. He was largely self-educated, with a particular interest in astronomy. He was a fellow of the Royal Astronomical Society; he built his own observatory, and in 1933 discovered a white spot on the surface of Saturn. He published *Through my Telescope* in 1935. Having entertained the troops in the First World War with Fred Karno, he was more likely to have been found in the Second World War offering them lectures on astronomy.

Such private endeavours were far removed from the seedy, blustering, and ineffectual teacher of Hay's stage creation, and the potency of his prototype was so vivid that for decades his name remained a byword for hapless teaching. With a small company of three or four 'boys', he topped variety bills across the country for many years. The verbal character of much of his comedy promoted its transfer to radio; he became a noted broadcaster, among

William Thomson Hay (1888–1949), by John Gilroy, *c*.1945

whose other characters was the failing academic Dr Muffin.

Hay transferred his mastery of comic timing and expression to film more successfully than many other British comedians. Most famously in concert with Graham 'Albert' Moffatt (1919–1965) as the impertinent fat boy, and Moore 'Harbottle' Marriott (1885–1949) as the resilient ancient, he made some seventeen films between 1934 and 1944, many of them directed by Marcel Varnel. Nine were made by Gainsborough Pictures. Hay was adept at ringing the changes on his characterization of grudging, evasive, and inadequate authority, playing, *inter alia*, a prison governor, a fire chief, a civil servant, a sea captain, a disbarred solicitor, and a police sergeant, as well as a schoolmaster. *Oh, Mr Porter!* (1937), with Hay as the troubled stationmaster of Buggleskelly, is regarded as both the popular and critical pick of the genre, and, together with *Good Morning, Boys* (1937), *Ask a Policeman* (1939), *The Ghost of St Michael's* (1941), and *My Learned Friend* (1944), this, his best work, has

been favourably compared with the screen antics of the Marx brothers.

Hay played his pathetic, seedy characters with a firm sense of their background and personal histories. This made for three-dimensional portrayals, which, temporizing between guile and befuddlement, led his audiences to feel sympathy as well as disdain. The tilted mortarboard, the crumpled gown, the wispy hair, the devious countenance, the slightly husky voice, the deprecating cough, the disapproving sniff, and above all the pinched eyeglasses which provided a focus for a wide range of facial reactions, from foxiness via smugness and irascibility to dismay, were the physical keynotes of his performance. Like the American comedian Jack Benny he was the master of the slow and silent double take, a skill which was to stand him in glorious stead on film. His fictitious school, Narkover, was adopted from Beachcomber's log of its adventures in the *Daily Express*. It is an interesting cultural reflection that vast audiences, most of whom had no experience of minor private boarding-schools, comprehended every last nuance of Hay's presentation, a tribute to the lengthy popular appeal of the Billy Bunter school of popular literature. Will Hay suffered a stroke in 1946 from which he only partially recovered; another stroke led within hours to his death in the early hours of Easter Monday, 18 April 1949, at his London flat, 16 Chelsea Embankment. He was buried in the garden of remembrance, Streatham.   ERIC MIDWINTER

Sources R. Seaton and R. Makin, *Good morning boys: Will Hay, master of comedy* (1978) · E. C. Midwinter, *Make 'em laugh: famous comedians and their worlds* (1979) · J. Fisher, *Funny way to be a hero* (1973) · R. Busby, *British music hall: an illustrated who's who from 1850 to the present day* (1976) · b. cert. · m. cert.

Archives BFI, corresp. and papers incl. typescript notes for memoirs | FILM BFI NFTVA, *Those British faces*, Channel 4, 18 April 1997 · BFI NFTVA, news footage · BFI NFTVA, performance footage | SOUND BBC WAC · BL NSA, 'Will Hay: master of comedy', BBC Radio 4, 2 June 1976, NP2746 WTR1 · BL NSA, documentary recording · BL NSA, performance recordings

Likenesses photographs, 1926–48, Hult. Arch. · J. Gilroy, oils, *c*.1945, NPG [*see illus.*] · photographs, Theatre Museum, London · photographs, Mitchensen and Mander Museum

Wealth at death £27,155 9*s.* 8*d.*: probate, 11 June 1949, *CGPLA Eng. & Wales*

PICTURE CREDITS

Hanbury, Daniel (1825–1875)—© National Portrait Gallery, London

Hanbury, William (1725–1778)—© National Portrait Gallery, London

Hancock, Anthony John [Tony] (1924–1968)—© Bob Collins; collection National Portrait Gallery, London

Hancock, Dame Florence May (1893–1974)—© National Portrait Gallery, London

Hancock, John (1737–1793)—Copyright 2004 Museum of Fine Arts, Boston; Deposited by the City of Boston

Hancock, Sir (William) Keith (1898–1988)—photograph reproduced by courtesy of The British Academy

Hancock, Thomas (1786–1865)—Science & Society Picture Library

Hancock, Walter (1799–1852)—© National Portrait Gallery, London

Handel, George Frideric (1685–1759)—private collection

Handl, Irene (1901–1987)—© reserved; British Film Institute

Handley, Thomas Reginald [Tommy] (1892–1949)—© National Portrait Gallery, London

Hanger, George, fourth Baron Coleraine (1751–1824)—photograph by courtesy Sotheby's Picture Library, London

Hankey, Maurice Pascal Alers, first Baron Hankey (1877–1963)—© National Portrait Gallery, London

Hanmer, Sir Thomas, fourth baronet (1677–1746)—private collection. Photograph: Photographic Survey, Courtauld Institute of Art, London

Hanna, William (1808–1882)—© National Portrait Gallery, London

Hanneman, Adriaen (c.1604–1671)—© Rijksmuseum, Amsterdam

Hannington, James (1847–1885)—© National Portrait Gallery, London

Hansard, Luke (1752–1828)—Palace of Westminster Collection

Hanway, Jonas (bap. 1712, d. 1786)—private collection. Photograph: Photographic Survey, Courtauld Institute of Art, London

Hapgood, Edris Albert [Eddie] (1908–1973)—© Estate of Frederick William Daniels; collection National Portrait Gallery, London

Harbutt, William (1844–1921)—courtesy of the Harbutt Family

Harcourt, Augustus George Vernon (1834–1919)—reproduced courtesy of the Library and Information Centre, Royal Society of Chemistry

Harcourt, Edward (1757–1847)—Sudbury Hall, The Vernon Collection (The National Trust). Photograph: Photographic Survey, Courtauld Institute of Art, London

Harcourt, Lewis Vernon, first Viscount Harcourt (1863–1922)—© National Portrait Gallery, London

Harcourt, Simon, first Viscount Harcourt (1661?–1727)—private collection. Photograph: Photographic Survey, Courtauld Institute of Art, London

Harcourt, Simon, first Earl Harcourt (1714–1777)—private collection. Photograph: Photographic Survey, Courtauld Institute of Art, London

Harcourt, William Edward, second Viscount Harcourt (1908–1979)—© National Portrait Gallery, London

Harcourt, Sir William George Granville Venables Vernon (1827–1904)—© National Portrait Gallery, London

Harcourt, William Venables Vernon (1789–1871)—© National Portrait Gallery, London

Hardcastle, William (1918–1975)—© National Portrait Gallery, London

Hardie, (James) Keir (1856–1915)—© National Portrait Gallery, London

Hardie, Martin (1875–1952)—by kind permission of the family of James and Marguerite McBey; Aberdeen Art Gallery and Museums Collections

Harding, Gilbert Charles (1907–1960)—© Cornel Lucas; collection National Portrait Gallery, London

Harding, John, first Baron Harding of Petherton (1896–1989)—© National Portrait Gallery, London

Hardinge, Charles, first Baron Hardinge of Penshurst (1858–1944)—© National Portrait Gallery, London

Hardinge (1743–1816)—reproduced by kind permission of His Grace the Archbishop of Canterbury and the Church Commissioners. Photograph: Photographic Survey, Courtauld Institute of Art, London

Hardinge, Henry, first Viscount Hardinge of Lahore (1785–1856)—© National Portrait Gallery, London

Hardy, Sir Alister Clavering (1896–1985)—© National Portrait Gallery, London

Hardy, Sir Charles, the younger (bap. 1717, d. 1780)—© National Maritime Museum, London, Greenwich Hospital Collection

Hardy, Gathorne Gathorne-, first earl of Cranbrook (1814–1906)—© National Portrait Gallery, London

Hardy, Godfrey Harold (1877–1947)—© The Royal Society

Hardy, Herbert Hardy Cozens-, first Baron Cozens-Hardy (1838–1920)—Estate of the Artist / The Honourable Society of Lincoln's Inn. Photograph: Photographic Survey, Courtauld Institute of Art, London

Hardy, Theodore Bayley (1863–1918)—The Imperial War Museum, London

Hardy, Sir Thomas (1666–1732)—© National Portrait Gallery, London

Hardy, Thomas (1748–1798)—© National Portrait Gallery, London

Hardy, Thomas (1752–1832)—© National Portrait Gallery, London

Hardy, Thomas (1840–1928)—© National Portrait Gallery, London

Hardy, Sir Thomas Masterman, baronet (1769–1839)—© National Maritime Museum, London, Greenwich Hospital Collection

Hardyng, John (b. 1377/8, d. in or after 1464)—© The Bodleian Library, University of Oxford

Hare, Henry, second Baron Coleraine (bap. 1636, d. 1708)—© National Portrait Gallery, London

Hare, Henry, third Baron Coleraine (1693–1749)—© Copyright The British Museum

Hare, James (bap. 1747, d. 1804)—© National Portrait Gallery, London

Hare, Sir John (1844–1921)—Garrick Club / the art archive

Hare, Julius Charles (1795–1855)—© National Portrait Gallery, London

Hare, Thomas (1806–1891)—© National Portrait Gallery, London

Hargrave, Francis (1740/41–1821)—The Honourable Society of Lincoln's Inn. Photograph: Photographic Survey, Courtauld Institute of Art, London

Hargreaves [Liddell], Alice Pleasance (1852–1934)—© National Portrait Gallery, London

Harington, John, first Baron Harington of Exton (1539/40–1613)—Parham House and Gardens

Harkness, Edward Stephen (1874–1940)—private collection

Harley, Sir Edward (1624–1700)—private collection

Harley, Edward, second earl of Oxford and Mortimer (1689–1741)—© Copyright The British Museum

Harley, Henrietta Cavendish, countess of Oxford and Mortimer (1694–1755)—private collection

Harley, Robert, first earl of Oxford and Mortimer (1661–1724)—© National Portrait Gallery, London

Harlow, George Henry (1787–1819)—© reserved

Harlowe, Sarah (1765–1852)—The Royal Collection © 2004 HM Queen Elizabeth II

Harman, Sir John (d. 1673)—© National Maritime Museum, London, Greenwich Hospital Collection

Harmsworth, Alfred Charles William, Viscount Northcliffe (1865–1922)—The de László Foundation / Witt Library, Courtauld Institute of Art, London

Harmsworth, Harold Sidney, first Viscount Rothermere (1868–1940)—The de László Foundation; Witt Library, Courtauld Institute of Art, London

Harmsworth, Vere Harold Esmond, third Viscount Rothermere (1925–1998)—Nils Jorgensen / Rex Features

Harney, (George) Julian (1817–1897)—© National Portrait Gallery, London

Harold I (d. 1040)—© Copyright The British Museum

Harold II (1022/3?–1066)—by special permission of the City of Bayeux

Harriman, Pamela Beryl (1920–1997)—Getty Images – Diana H. Walker

Harrington, James (1611–1677)—© National Portrait Gallery, London

Harrington, Timothy Charles (1851–1910)—© National Portrait Gallery, London

Harriott, (Arthurlin) Joseph (1928–1973)—photograph © Val Wilmer

Harris, Sir Arthur Travers, first baronet (1892–1984)—© National Portrait Gallery, London

Harris, Sir Augustus Henry Glossop (1852–1896)—© National Portrait Gallery, London

Harris, Sir Charles Herbert Stuart- (1909–1996)—© reserved; News International Syndication; photograph National Portrait Gallery, London

Harris, George Robert Canning, fourth Baron Harris (1851–1932)—Marylebone Cricket Club, London / Bridgeman Art Library

Harris, Henry (1633/4–1704)—The President and Fellows of Magdalen College Oxford

Harris, James (1709–1780)—© National Portrait Gallery, London

Harris, James, first earl of Malmesbury (1746–1820)—private collection. Photograph: Photographic Survey, Courtauld Institute of Art, London

Harris, James Howard, third earl of Malmesbury (1807–1889)—© National Portrait Gallery, London

Harris, James Thomas [Frank] (1856?–1931)—© National Portrait Gallery, London

Harris, John (c.1666–1719)—Yale Center for British Art, Paul Mellon Collection

Harris, Moses (1730–c.1788)—Ashmolean Museum, Oxford

Harris, Sir Percy Alfred, first baronet (1876–1952)—© reserved; photograph National Portrait Gallery, London

Harris, Sir Percy Wyn- (1903–1979)—© National Portrait Gallery, London

Harris, Reginald Hargreaves (1920–1992)—Getty Images – Bert Hardy

Harris, Sir William Snow (1791–1867)—© The Royal Society

Harrison, Benjamin (c.1726–1791)—The Virginia Historical Society, Richmond, Virginia

Harrison, Charles (1835–1897)—© National Portrait Gallery, London

Harrison, Frederic (1831–1923)—© National Portrait Gallery, London

Harrison, George Bagshawe (1894–1991)—© National Portrait Gallery, London

Harrison, Jane Ellen (1850–1928)—Newnham College, Cambridge; photographer James Austin

Harrison, John (bap. 1693, d. 1776)—Science & Society Picture Library

Harrison, Sir Reginald Carey [Rex] (1908–1990)—© Kenneth Hughes / National Portrait Gallery, London

Harrison, Ruth (1920–2000)—© News International Newspapers Ltd

Harrod, Charles Digby (1841–1905)—Company Archive, Harrods Limited, London

Harrod, Charles Henry (1799–1885)—Company Archive, Harrods Limited, London

Harrod, Sir (Henry) Roy Forbes (1900–1978)—© National Portrait Gallery, London

Hart, Aaron (1670–1756)—© National Portrait Gallery, London

Hart, Sir Basil Henry Liddell (1895–1970)—© National Portrait Gallery, London

Hart, Edith Tudor (1908–1973)—© Wolfgang Suschitzky

Hart, Ernest Abraham (1835–1898)—© National Portrait Gallery, London

Hart, Herbert Lionel Adolphus (1907–1992)—© Steve Pyke; collection National Portrait Gallery, London

Hart, Judith, Baroness Hart of South Lanark (1924–1991)—Getty Images – Hulton Archive

Hart, Sir Robert, first baronet (1835–1911)—© National Portrait Gallery, London

Hart, Solomon Alexander (1806–1881)—Exeter City Museums & Art Gallery

Harte, (Francis) Bret (1836–1902)—V&A Images, The Victoria and Albert Museum

Harthacnut (c.1018–1042)—© Copyright The British Museum

Hartley, David (bap. 1705, d. 1757)—© National Portrait Gallery, London

Hartley, Elizabeth (1750/51–1824)—© Tate, London, 2004

Hartley, Sir Harold Brewer (1878–1972)—© National Portrait Gallery, London

Hartley, Leslie Poles (1895–1972)—© Mark Gerson; collection National Portrait Gallery, London

Hartnell, Sir Norman Bishop (1901–1979)—Snowdon / Camera Press

Hartnell, William Henry (1908–1975)—Getty Images – Hulton Archive

Hartshorn, Vernon (1872–1931)—© National Portrait Gallery, London

Harty, Sir (Herbert) Hamilton (1879–1941)—© reserved / Photograph courtesy the National Gallery of Ireland

Harvey, Gideon (1636/7–1702)—© National Portrait Gallery, London

Harvey, John (1740–1794)—© National Maritime Museum, London

Harvey, Oliver Charles, first Baron Harvey of Tasburgh (1893–1968)—© National Portrait Gallery, London

Harvey, William (1578–1657)—© National Portrait Gallery, London

Harwood, Sir Henry Harwood (1888–1950)—© National Portrait Gallery, London

Haryett, Elizabeth Ann [Lizzie Howard], countess of Beauregard in the French nobility (bap. 1823?, d. 1865)—unknown collection / Christie's; photograph National Portrait Gallery, London

Haskell, Arnold Lionel David (1903–1980)—V&A Images, The Victoria and Albert Museum

Haslett, Dame Caroline Harriet (1895–1957)—© reserved; by courtesy of the Royal Society of Arts / National Portrait Gallery, London

Hasluck, Sir Paul Meernaa Caedwalla (1905–1993)—from the collection of the National Archives of Australia: A1200, L81524

Hassall, Christopher Vernon (1912–1963)—© National Portrait Gallery, London

Hassan, Sir Joshua Abraham (1915–1997)—Getty Images – Hulton Archive

Hasted, Edward (1732–1812)—Medway Archives and Local Studies Centre, Education and Leisure Directorate, Medway Council

Hasted, William Freke (1897–1977)—© National Portrait Gallery, London

Hastings, Sir Charles (1794–1866)—© National Portrait Gallery, London

Hastings, Edward, Baron Hastings of Loughborough (1512x15?–1572)—© National Portrait Gallery, London

Hastings, Lady Flora Elizabeth (1806–1839)—© National Portrait Gallery, London

Hastings, Francis Rawdon, first marquess of Hastings and second earl of Moira (1754–1826)—HSBC Holdings plc

Hastings, George, first earl of Huntingdon (1486/7–1544)—© Royal Museums of Fine Arts, Brussels, Belgium

Hastings, Henry, third earl of Huntingdon (1536?–1595)—© Board of Trustees of The Armouries (accession no. I.46)

Hastings, Henry (bap. 1562, d. 1650)—private collection. Photograph: Photographic Survey, Courtauld Institute of Art, London

Hastings, Sir Hugh (c.1310–1347)—reproduced by courtesy of H. M. Stutchfield, F.S.A., Hon. Secretary of the Monumental Brass Society

Hastings, Lucy, countess of Huntingdon (1613–1679)—unknown collection; photograph A. C. Cooper

Hastings, Marian (1747–1837)—© reserved

Hastings, Sir Patrick Gardiner (1880–1952)—© National Portrait Gallery, London

Hastings, Selina, countess of Huntingdon (1707–1791)—© National Portrait Gallery, London

Hastings, Somerville (1878–1967)—© reserved; Guildhall Art Gallery, Corporation of London

Hastings, Warren (1732–1818)—© National Portrait Gallery, London

Haston, Duncan Curdy McSporran [Dougal] (1940–1977)—Alpine Club Photo Library, London

Hatch, John Charles, Baron Hatch of Lusby (1917–1992)—© News International Newspapers Ltd

Hatchard, John (1768–1849)—© National Portrait Gallery, London

Hathaway, Dame Sibyl Mary (1884–1974)—© Estate of Pamela Chandler / National Portrait Gallery, London

Hatton, Sir Christopher (c.1540–1591)—V&A Images, The Victoria and Albert Museum

Hatton, Denys George Finch- (1887–1931)—The Royal Library, Copenhagen

Hatton, Frank (1861–1883)—© National Portrait Gallery, London

Haughton, Samuel (1821–1897)—© Estate of Sarah Henrietta Purser; by kind permission of the Board of Trinity College Dublin

Havard, William (1710–1778)—© National Portrait Gallery, London

Havelock, Sir Henry (1795–1857)—© National Portrait Gallery, London

Havergal, (Grace) Beatrix Helen (1901–1980)—© Valerie Finnis; collection Royal Horticultural Society, Lindley Library

Havers, (Robert) Michael Oldfield, Baron Havers (1923–1992)—© News International Newspapers Ltd

Havilland, Sir Geoffrey de (1882–1965)—reproduced with permission of BAE Systems plc

Haweis, Hugh Reginald (1838–1901)—© National Portrait Gallery, London

Haweis, Thomas (1734?–1820)—© National Portrait Gallery, London

Hawes, William (1736–1808)—Ashmolean Museum, Oxford

Hawke, Edward, first Baron Hawke (1705–1781)—© National Maritime Museum, London, Greenwich Hospital Collection

Hawke, Martin Bladen, seventh Baron Hawke (1860–1938)—© National Portrait Gallery, London

Hawkes, (Jessie) Jacquetta (1910–1996)—© Jorge Lewinski; collection National Portrait Gallery, London

Hawkins, Sir Caesar, first baronet (1711–1786)—reproduced by kind permission of the President and Council of the Royal College of Surgeons of England. Photograph: Photographic Survey, Courtauld Institute of Art, London

Hawkins, Edward (1789–1882)—courtesy of the Provost and Fellows of Oriel College, Oxford

Hawkins, Francis (1628–1681)—© National Portrait Gallery, London

Hawkins, Henry, Baron Brampton (1817–1907)—© National Portrait Gallery, London

Hawkins, Sir John (1532–1595)—Plymouth City Art Gallery; photograph National Portrait Gallery, London

Hawkins, John Edward [Jack] (1910–1973)—© Kenneth Hughes / National Portrait Gallery, London

Hawkshaw, Sir John (1811–1891)—© National Portrait Gallery, London

Hawksmoor, Nicholas (1662?–1736)—All Souls College, Oxford

Hawkwood, Sir John (d. 1394)—photograph: AKG London

Hawley, Henry (bap. 1685, d. 1759)—photograph by courtesy Sotheby's Picture Library, London

Hawley, John, the elder (c.1350–1408)—by kind permission of Becky Wright Photos; St Saviour's Church, Dartmouth

Haworth, Sir (Walter) Norman (1883–1950)—© National Portrait Gallery, London

Hawthorn, (John) Michael [Mike] (1929–1959)—© Science & Society Picture Library; photograph National Portrait Gallery, London

Hawtrey, Sir Charles Henry (1858–1923)—© National Portrait Gallery, London

Hawtrey, Edward Craven (1789–1862)—© National Portrait Gallery, London

Hay, Arthur, ninth marquess of Tweeddale (1824–1878)—© National Portrait Gallery, London

Hay, George, first earl of Kinnoull (bap. 1570, d. 1634)—Scottish National Portrait Gallery

Hay, Sir George (1715–1778)—Collection Harvard University Law School, Cambridge, Massachusetts; © reserved in the photograph

Hay, George (1729–1811)—© National Portrait Gallery, London

Hay, George Campbell (1915–1984)—photograph: Gordon Wright Photo Library

Hay, Sir Harley Hugh Dalrymple- (1861–1940)—courtesy of the Institution of Civil Engineers Archives

Hay, Helen Selina, countess of Gifford (1807–1867)—© National Portrait Gallery, London

Hay, James, first earl of Carlisle (c.1580–1636)—© National Portrait Gallery, London

Hay, John, first marquess of Tweeddale (1626–1697)—Scottish National Portrait Gallery

Hay, John, second marquess of Tweeddale (1645–1713)—© Glasgow Museums

Hay, Lucy, countess of Carlisle (1599–1660)—Lord Egremont; photograph: The Paul Mellon Centre for Studies in British Art

Hay, Thomas, ninth earl of Kinnoull (1710–1787)—unknown collection / Christie's; photograph National Portrait Gallery, London

Hay, William Thomson (1888–1949)—© Estate of John Gilroy; collection National Portrait Gallery, London